ਪੰਜਾਬੀ-ਅੰਗਰੇਜ਼ੀ : ਅੰਗਰੇਜ਼ੀ-ਪੰਜਾਬੀ ਕੋਸ਼

PUNJABI-ENGLISH
ENGLISH-PUNJABI
DICTIONARY

ਪੰਜਾਬੀ-ਅੰਗਰੇਜ਼ੀ : ਅੰਗਰੇਜ਼ੀ-ਪੰਜਾਬੀ ਕੋਸ਼

PUNJABI-ENGLISH
ENGLISH-PUNJABI
DICTIONARY

Compiled by
Dr. K.K. Goswami

Hippocrene Books, Inc.
New York

Hippocrene Books, Inc.
171 Madison Avenue
New York, NY 10016

Compilation & Arrangement
Copyright © Dr. K.K. Goswami

First Published 2000

Published in arrangement with :

UBS Publishers' Distributors Ltd.
5 Ansari Road, New Delhi-110 002 (India)

All rights reserved. No part of this publication may be reproduced or transmitted in any form or by any means, electronic or mechanical, including photocopying, recording, or any information storage or retrieval system, without prior permission in writing from the publisher.

Printed in India.

Dedicated to
The Punjabi Speakers
as well as
the lovers of
Punjabi Language and Culture
in
India and abroad.

PREFACE

Punjabi is one of the national languages of multilingual India. It has a long tradition and cultural identity. The vital characteristic of language needs constant change and modification in its vocabulary repository. Therefore, dictionary work is necessary for the development of the language. The present Punjabi-English and English-Punjabi dictionary has been developed on this point of view.

This is a dictionary with a difference in that it makes a truly linguistic approach to Punjabi lexicography. This is a medium sized dictionary having two parts — one from Punjabi to English and second from English to Punjabi. It comprises well over 25,000 entries (round about 11,000 entries from Punjabi and 14,000 entries from English), which one comes across most frequently during contact with people or in literature today. These are explained firstly in main meaning and then in various nuances and their modern renderings are set out in all accuracy. Efforts have also been made to add idioms or idiomatic usages. Meanings of a word have been arranged on the basis of their frequencies. Some words have quite a large number of meanings but some have given exhaustive signification.

This dictionary is meant for a foreign learner but will it also be of immense use to the general reader as well as the students who are called upon to translate in both languages; i.e., English and Punjabi. Hence, this dictionary has a special purpose, that it teaches both Punjabi and English. Rather, it teaches Punjabi to English speakers and English to Punjabi speakers.

There is a lack of standardization in the Punjabi writing system; therefore, we do not find homogeneity in Punjabi spellings. However, the pronunciation of English words has been transcribed in Gurmukhi letters of Punjabi in the common script, not in the International Phonetic Alphabets System because this dictionary is mainly meant for the common reader and not for the linguists or the language experts and scholars.

The transliteration system adopted for indicating the pronunciation of Punjabi words in the dictionary is based on principles which are, by an large, accepted by modern scholars and Orientalists. Even then, efforts have been made to standardize the spellings and meanings of Punjabi words as prevalent in the standard books. The significant feature of the sound patterns of Punjabi is the existence of the tone. Therefore, Punjabi is also called as a tonal language. The tones are phonetic realizations of pitch and duration which roughly correspond to the gh, jh, ḍh, dh, bh (the aspirated voiced sounds) series of consonants of Hindu and other North Indian languages.

It gives me great pleasure to acknowledge the assistance I have received from a number of Punjabi scholars and speakers. I owe a debt of gratitude to my friends Dr. Thakur Dass and Dr. R.C. Garg who gave fruitful suggestions for this work. I express my love and affections to my children Namrata, Gaurav and Mudita who are always prepared to help me a lot in my academic works.

I express my sincere thanks to Sardar Jaswant Singh 'Ajit' who has not only read the proofs efficiently but has also given valuable suggestions in the finalization of the dictionary.

I am also thankful to M/s Rachna Enterprises, especially Smt. Manorama Aggarwal, who took lot of pain to ensure the correct composing of the dictionary.

Every effort has been made to make the dictionary useful to the learners and translators of Punjabi and English languages.

Dr. K.K. Goswami

Points to be Noted on Transcription of English and Punjabi Pronunciation

1. All main or primary entries have the phonetic transcription but the derived words begining with swing dash (~) are not transcribed because of the economy.

2. Nasalized vowel has mostly been taken as Gurmukhi ਟਿੱਪੀ /ੰ/ and ਬਿੰਦੀ /ਂ/, as ਚੰਗਾ, ਨੀਂਦਰ. English word 'fund' and 'banned' have been transcribed as ਫੰਡ and ਬੈਂਡ respectively.

3. The addak /ੱ/ sign has been used in the germinated or over stressed syllables e.g. ਸੱਚ, ਪੱਕਾ.

4. English words ending with 'r' in spelling but pronounced when followed by a vowel sound have been represented as /ਅ*/ e.g. brother /ਬਰਅਦਾਅ*/, here /ਹਿਅ*/. In the middle of the word, 'r' is mostly represented as /:/ e.g. pierce /ਪਿਅ:ਸ/.

5. When a consonant occurs initially in the second syllable as 'mea**s**ure', it is transcribed as /ਮੈਯ਼ਅ*/ whereas in 'ye**s**', it is transcribed as /ਯੈਸ/. Here, in mea**s**ure, ਯ਼ is fricative and in **y**es, ਯ is semivowel.

6. In the word 'Singh' /ਸਿਙ/, **ng** word final combination has been represented by Gurmukhi velar nasal consonant /ਙ/.

7. When an entry is used on different parts of speech with differing pronunciations, the transcriptions are provided after the entry in the order of parts of speech as shown after the transcription, such as Conflict /ਕੋਨਫਲਿਕਟ, ਕਅਨ'ਫ਼ਲਿਕਟ/. Here /ਕੋਨਫਲਿਕਟ/ is noun and /ਕਅਨ'ਫ਼ਲਿਕਟ/ is a verb.

8. If a given sound in the transcription is put in the bracket, this sound is often omitted in pronunciation, such as maladjustment /'ਮੈਲਅ'ਜਅੱਸ(ਟ)ਮਅੰਟ/.

9. English distinguishes between the initial consonantal sounds in

the pair 'vent' and 'went' which are transcribed as ਵ਼ and ਵ. A dot under ਵ has been put to make the sound of English fricative V effective possibly.

10. The **tone** bearing **consonants of Punjabi** have been transcribed in the traditional style with a diacritic mark upon them, such as gh́, jh́, ḍh́, dh́, bh́ for the common reader, although these can be transcribed as k+tone, ch+tone, ṭ+tone, t+tone and p+tone sounds (such as kóra, chágg, ṭól, táan and páajjee respectively) for the linguists, language experts and language teachers. In the final position, they indicate high tone on the preceding vowels and aspiration form is not given, such as ਮਾਘ (maag), ਦੁਧ (dud), ਲਾਭ (laab).

11. Subscript of ਰ /r/ in the clusters of sounds has been used by adding to the bottom of the letters, such as /ਪ੍ਰ/ in ਪ੍ਰੇਮ (**prem**).

12. Similarly, subscript of ਹ /h/ is added to the letters ਨ੍ਹ, ਲ੍ਹ, ੜ੍ਹ to denote the high tone, such as ਚਿੰਨ੍ਹ (chinnh) sign, ਕਿਲ੍ਹਾ (kilhaa) fort, ਦਿੜ੍ਹਤਾ (driṛhtaa) determination.

13. Subscript of ਵ (w) has also been added to the letter ਸ in some of the Sanskrit borrowings to denote the semivowel's sound, such as ਸ੍ਵਰ, ਸ੍ਵਦੇਸ਼ੀ.

14. The variations found in the vocabulary of Punjabi has also been given in one entry e.g. ਉਸਤਾਦਰਗੀ~ਉਸਤਾਦੀ, ਦੇਸ਼ੀ~ਦੇਖੀ, ਨਾਲਸ਼~ਨਾਲਿਸ਼.

15. The grammatical categories have also been provided after the transcribed phonetic form. But the derived forms have not been provided with the grammatical categories as a measure of economy.

ਸੰਖੇਪ (ਪੰਜਾਬੀ ਵਿਚ)
Abbreviations in Punjabi

ਅਪ੍ਰ	ਅਪ੍ਰਚਲਤ
ਇਤਿ	ਇਤਿਹਾਸਕ
ਸਿਖਿ	ਸਿਖਿਆ-ਸ਼ਾਸਤਰ
ਸੰਗੀ	ਸੰਗੀਤ
ਕਾ	ਕਾਨੂੰਨ
ਕਾਵਿ	ਕਾਵਿਕ, ਕਾਵਿ-ਸ਼ਾਸਤਰ
ਗਣਿ	ਗਣਿਤ
ਚਿਕਿ	ਚਿਕਿਤਸਾ
ਜੀਵ	ਜੀਵ-ਵਿਗਿਆਨ
ਜੋ	ਜੋਤਸ਼
ਤਰਕ	ਤਰਕ-ਸ਼ਾਸਤਰ
ਦਰਸ਼	ਦਰਸ਼ਨ-ਸ਼ਾਸਤਰ
ਧੁਨੀ	ਧੁਨੀ-ਵਿਗਿਆਨ
ਬਹੁ	ਬਹੁਵਚਨ
ਪ੍ਰਾ	ਪ੍ਰਾਚੀਨ
ਬਾਈ	ਬਾਈਬਲ
ਬੋਲ	ਬੋਲ-ਚਾਲ
ਭਾਸ਼ਾ	ਭਾਸ਼ਾ-ਵਿਗਿਆਨ
ਭੂ	ਭੂਗੋਲ
ਭੌ	ਭੌਤਕ-ਵਿਗਿਆਨ
ਮਨੋ	ਮਨੋ-ਵਿਗਿਆਨ
ਰਸਾ	ਰਸਾਇਨ-ਵਿਗਿਆਨ
ਲਾਖ	ਲਾਖਣਕ
ਵਿਆ	ਵਿਆਕਰਨ

Abbreviations in English
(Parts of speech)

a	adjective	F	French
adv	adverb	L	Latin
conj	conjunction	pl.	plural
interj	interjection	pred.	predicate
n	noun	pref.	prefix
v	verb	pron.	pronoun
aux	auxiliary	usu	usually

symbols

~ represents the first part of the entry/word.

* represents the pronunciation of 'ra'.

: represents the pronunciation of 'r'.

Phonetic Transliteration of English words in Gurmukhi Script

Effort has been made to follow the standard English pronunciation of both vowels and consonants. However, some of the exceptions and additional symbols are to be followed :

Vowel

(Initial and combined with a consonant)

ਅੰ	*a* in **a**genda; *u* in b**u**t; *o* in c**o**me;	ਅਜੰਡਾ, ਬੰਟ, ਕੰਮ
	er in mak**er**; *e* in brok**e**n	ਮੇਕਅੰ, ਬ੍ਰੋਕਨ
ਅ*	*ear* in **ear**th; *ir* in b**ir**d; *ere* in wh**ere**	ਅ*ਥ, ਬ*ਡ, ਵੇਅ*
	or in w**or**d; *ur* in t**ur**n	ਵ*ਡ, ਟ*ਨ
ਆ	*ar* in c**ar**	ਕਾ*
ਔ	*o* in **o**ffice, **o**n, n**o**t	ਔਫਿਸ, ਔਨ, ਨੌਟ
	aw in l**aw**.	ਲਔ
ਆਇ	*i* in **i**dea, l**i**ne	ਆਇਡਅ, ਲਾਇਨ
ਅਉ	*o* in h**o**me, *oa* in b**oa**t, *ou* in m**ou**ld	ਹਅਉਮ, ਬਅਉਟ, ਮਅਉਲਡ
ਆਉ	*ou* in h**ou**se	ਹਾਉਸ
ਐ	*e* in **e**gg, m**e**mory	ਐਗ, ਮੈਂਮਅਰਿ
	a in **a**ct, m**a**n, **a**bject	ਐਕਟ, ਮੈਨ, ਐਬਜੈਕਟ
ਏਇ	*a* in **a**ge	ਏਇਜ

Consonant

ਟ and ਡ	the English *t* and *d* are neither dental nor cerebal; *t* is alveolar, *d* is a dental fricative.	
	th in **th**eory, fil**th**	ਥਿਅਰਿ; ਫਿਲਥ
	th in fa**th**er, **th**is	ਫ*ਦ, ਦਿਸ
	ng in maki**ng**, ki**ng**dom	ਮੇਕਿਙ, ਕਿਙਡਮ
Si and Su	*si* in occa**si**on,	ਅ'ਕੇਇਯ਼ਨ
	su in plea**su**re	ਪਲੈਯ਼ੁਅ*

Phonetic Transcription of Punjabi words in Roman Script

Vowel (ਸਵਰ)

Punjabi shape	English sign	Matra	Word	
ਅ	a	∅	ਅਮੀਰ (ameer)	ਰਸ (ras)
ਆ	aa	ਾ	ਆਸ (aas)	ਰਾਸ (raas)
ਇ	i	ਿ	ਇਕ (ik)	ਸਿਰ (sir)
ਈ	ee	ੀ	ਈਸਾ (eesaa)	ਰੀਸ (rees)
ਏ	e	ੇ	ਏਲਚੀ (elchee)	ਕੇਸ (kes)
ਐ	ae	ੈ	ਐਸ਼ (aesh)	ਖ਼ੈਰ (khair)
ਉ	u	ੁ	ਉਮਰ (umar)	ਸੁਰ (sur)
ਊ	oo	ੂ	ਊਤ (oot)	ਸੂਮ (soom)
ਓ	o	ੋ	ਓਸ (os)	ਮੋਰ (mor)
ਔ	au	ੌ	ਔਖ (aukh)	ਖ਼ੌਫ਼ (khauf)

Consonant (ਵਿਅੰਜਨ)

Punjabi shape	English sign	Word	
ਸ	s	ਸਸ	(sas)
ਹ	h	ਹਰਮ	(haram)
ਕ	k	ਕਾਰ	(kaar)
ਖ	kh	ਖੀਰ	(kheer)
ਗ	g	ਗਰਮ	(garam)
ਘ	gh'	ਘਰ	(gh'ar)
ਙ	–		–
ਚ	ch	ਚਾਬੀ	(chaabee)
ਛ	chh	ਛੇਤੀ	(chhetee)
ਜ	j	ਜਾਪ	(jaap)
ਝ	jh'	ਝੂਠ	(jh'ooṭ)
ਞ	nj		–

ਟ	ṭ	ਟਮਾਟਰ	(ṭmaaṭar)
ਠ	ṭh	ਠਾਠ	(ṭhaaṭ)
ਡ	ḍ	ਡਾਕ	(ḍaak)
ਢ	ḍh'	ਢਾਬਾ	(ḍh'aabaa)
ਣ	ṇ	ਲੂਣ	(looṇ)
ਤ	t	ਤੀਰ	(teer)
ਥ	th	ਥਣ	(thaṇ)
ਦ	d	ਦੂਰ	(door)
ਧ	dh'	ਧਰਮ	(dh'aram)
ਨ	n	ਨਰਮ	(naram)
ਪ	p	ਪੁੱਲ	(pull)
ਫ	ph	ਫਾਟਕ	(phaaṭak)
ਬ	b	ਬੀਬਾ	(beebaa)
ਭ	bh'	ਭੋਗ	(bh'og)
ਮ	m	ਮਸ	(mas)
ਯ	y	ਯਾਰੀ	(yaaree)
ਰ	r	ਰਸਮ	(rasam)
ਲ	l	ਲਾਲਾ	(laalaa)
ਵ	v (w)	ਵੈਰ	(vair)
ੜ	ṛ	ਮਾੜਾ	(maaṛaa)

ਪੰਜਾਬੀ-ਅੰਗਰੇਜ਼ੀ ਕੋਸ਼

ੳ

ੳ First letter of Gurmukhi alphabets, pronounced as 'uṛa'; a vowel.

ਉਸਤਤ, ਉਸਤਤਿ, ਉਸਤਤੀ (ustat, ustati, ustatee) *n f* Praise, appreciation, eulogy; **~ਗੀਤ** Psalm.

ਉਸਤਰਾ (ustra) *n m* Razor, blade; **~ਫ਼ੇਰਨਾ** To shave, to swindle.

ਉਸਤਾਦ (ustaad) *n a* Teacher, instructor, tutor, master; Expert; Clever, cunning, tricky.

ਉਸਤਾਦਗੀ (ustaadgee) *n f* Teachership, tutorship, guidance, mastery, artfulness; Tact, cleverness, prudence. Also **ਉਸਤਾਦੀ**

ਉਸ਼ਨਾਕ (ushnaak) *a* Wise, intelligent, sharp, witty, active, clever, prudent.

ਉਸ਼ਨਾਕੀ (ushnaakee) *n f* Wisdom, intelligence, cleverness, prudence.

ਉਸਰਨ (usaran) *n f* Growth, growing.

ਉਸਰਨਾ (usarnaa) *v* To grow, to develop, to be built up.

ਉਸ਼ਾ (ushaa) *n f* Dawn.

ਉਸਾਸ (usaas) *n* Breath, expiration; Sigh.

ਉਸਾਰਨਾ (usaarnaa) *v* To construct, to build.

ਉਸਾਰਾ (usaaraa) *n m* Porch, vestibule, room built on top floor.

ਉਸਾਰੀ (usaaree) *n* Construction, structure, act of building.

ਉਹ (oh) *pron* He, she, it, they.

ਉਹ-ਹੋ (o'ho) *interj.* Oh!

ਉਹਨਾਂ (o'nā) *pron* They.

ਉਹਲਾ (ohlaa) *n* Aside, secret, curtain.

ਉਹਲੇ (ohle) *n* Out of side, aside, concealed, behind the scene.

ਉਹੀ, ਓਹੀ (uhi, ohi) *a* The same, ibid. Also **ਉਹੋ**

ਉਕਸਣਾ (ukasṇaa) *v* To be excited, to be agitated, to be kindled.

ਉਕਸਾਉਣਾ (udksaauṇaa) *v* To instigate, to stimulate, to excite, to kindle.

ਉਕਸਾਹਟ (uksaahaṭ) *n f* Excitement, instigation, stimulation, temptation.

ਉਕਤਾਉਣਾ (uktaauṇaa) *v* To bore, to feel melancholy, to be dejected, to be tired of, to be weary.

ਉਕਤੀ (uktee) *n f* Maxim, aphorism; Speech.

ਉੱਕਰ (ukkar) *adv* Similar, like the same, in the same way;

Engrave, inscribe.

ਉਕਰਨਾ (ukarnaa) *v* To engrave, to inscribe, to etch, to pendown.

ਉਕਰਾਈ (ukraaee) *n f* Carving, inscription or embossing, act of engraving; Wages for carving.

ਉਕੜ-ਦੁਕੜ (ukaṛ-dukaṛ) *a adv* Haphazard; Haphazardly.

ਉਕੜੂ (ukaṛoo) *a* Posture of sitting on hams with soles of feet on the ground, bent or tilted forward. Also **ਉਕੜ**

ਉੱਕਾ (ukkaa) *a* Wholly, Quite, at all; ~ਹੀ Out and out; ~ਪੁਕਾ The whole, complete, the only, in lumpsum.

ਉਕਾਉਣਾ (ukkaunaa) *v* To cause, to miss, to omit.

ਉਕਾਈ (ukaaee) *n f* Error, mistake, default, blunder, lapse, omission.

ਉਖੱਲ (ukkhal) *n m* Lubber, large wooden morter for pounding grains.

ਉਖਲੀ (ukhalee) *n f* Small wooden or stone mortar for pounding grains.

ਉਖੜਨਾ (ukharnaa) *v* To be uprooted, to be dislocated, to be dislodged, to be unhinged.

ਉਖਾੜਨਾ (ukhaaṛnaa) *v* To uproot, to dislocate, to disjoin, to tear up.

ਉੱਗਣਾ (uggṇaa) *v* To grow, to crop up, to germinate.

ਉਗਰ (ugar) *a* Austere; Fierce, wrathful; Intense; ~ਤਾ Fierceness, intensity, tersocity, terror, wrathfulness; ~ਵਾਦ Terrorism; ~ਵਾਦੀ Militant, terrorist, extremist.

ਉਗਰਾਹੀ (ugraahee) *n f* Collection (of donation or subscription), realization.

ਉਗਰਾਹੁਣਾ (ugraauṇaa) *v* To collect, to realize, to encash.

ਉੱਗਲਨਾ (uggalnaa) *v* To disclose, to reveal (a secret or misappropriated property).

ਉਗਲੱਛਣਾ (uglacchṇaa) *v* To vomit, disgorge, throw out; To disclose, to reveal (secret or misappropriated property).

ਉੱਂਗਲ (ungal) *n f* Finger; ~ਕਰਨੀ To hint, to blot, to defame.

ਉਂੱਗਲੀ (unglee) *n f* Finger; ~ਕਰਨੀ To hint, to point out, to censure; ~ਧਰਨੀ To select, to choose; ~ਫੜਨੀ To give or receive support or helping hand; ~ਮੂੰਹ ਵਿਚ ਪਾਉਣੀ To wonder, to be astonished, to be amazed.

ਉਗਾਉਣਾ (ugaauṇaa) *v* To grow, to cause, to raise.

ਉਗਾਹ (ugaah) *n m* Witness. Also **ਗਵਾਹ**

ਉਗਾਲ (ugaal) *n* Vomit, spit; ~ਦਾਨ Spittoon, cuspidor.

ਉਗਾਲਣਾ (ugaalṇaa) *v* To chew the cud.

ਉਗਾਲੀ (ugaaḷee) *n f* Cud; Cud-chewing, ruminating, mastication.

ਉਘਰਨਾ (ugharnaa) *v* To intimidate, to bully by showing a fist, to blow a fist in anger.

ਉਘਲਾਉਣਾ (ughlaauṇaa) *v* To doze, to slumber.

ਉਘਲਨਾ (ughalnaa) *v* To become clear, to be exposed, to be uncovered, to be disclosed, to be revealed.

ਉੱਘਾ (unghaa) *a* Famous, reputed, well-known, eminent, prominent, popular.

ਉਘਾੜ (ughaaṛ) *n m* Disclosure, exposure, divulgence, manifestation. Also ਉਘਾੜਾ

ਉਘਾੜਨਾ (Ughaarṇaa) *v* To disclose, to expose, to lay bear, to uncover, to divulge (secret).

ਉਘੇੜਨਾ (ugheṛnaa) *v* To open (eyes or door), to uncover (deceit, conspiracy); To separate maize from cob.

ਉੱਚ (uchch) *a* Exalted, high, superior, grand; ~ਨਿਕ Up and down, rise and fall.

ਉਚਕਣਾ (uchakṇaa) *v* To jump, to bounce, to startle.

ਉਚੱਕਾ (uchakkaa) *n m* Robber, thief, pickpocket.

ਉਚਕਾਉਣਾ (uchkaauṇaa) *v* To cause, to startle.

ਉਚਟਣਾ (uchatṇaa) *v* To be displeased, to grow tired, to be fed up.

ਉਚਤਮ (uchatam) *a* Superb, supreme, highest, maximum, super, excellent.

ਉੱਚਤਾ (uchchtaa) *n f* Superiority, transcendence, transcedency; ~ਭਾਵ Superiority complex.

ਉੱਚਰ (uchchar) *v* To Speak out, to utter, to spell-out.

ਉਚਰਨਾ (ucharnaa) *v* To say, to speak, to utter, to pronounce, to sermonize.

ਉਚੜਨਾ (uchaṛnaa) *v* To be separated, to be bruised.

ਉਚੜਵਾਂ (Ucharvaan) *a* Movable; Portable.

ਉੱਚਾ (uchchaa) *a* Tall, high, lofty, noble, loud, elevated, eminent; ~ਸੁਣਨਾ To be hard of hearing, ~ਹਥ ਹੋਣਾ To have an upper hand, to be winning; ~ਚੜ੍ਹਨਾ To rise, to climb, ~ਨੀਵਾਂ Uneven;

~ਹੋਣਾ To pick up a quarrel, **~ਬੋਲ** Tall talk. Also **ਉੱਚੀ**

ਉਚਾਈ (uchaaee) *n f* Height, altitude, rise, elevation, loudness.

ਉਚਾਟ (uchaat) *n m* Indifference, dejection, restlessness; **~ਹੋਣਾ** To lose interest, to be indifferent, to grow tired.

ਉਚਾਰ (uchaar) *n m* Speech, utterance.

ਉਚਾਰਨ (uchaaran) *n m* Pronunciation, articulation.

ਉਚਾਲਾ (uchaalaa) *n m* Instigation.

ਉਚਾਵਾਂ (uchaavaan) *a* Portable; **~ਚੁੱਲਾ** Portable oven, fickle minded.

ਉਚਾਵੀਂ (uchaaveen) *a* Movable.

ਉਚਿਤ (uchit) *a* Reasonable, proper, appropriate, fit, legitimate; **~ਤਾ** Legitimacy, appropriateness, justification.

ਉਚੇਚ (uchech) *n m* Formality.

ਉਚੇਚਾ (uchechaa) *a adv* Special, particular, exclusive; Specially, particularly.

ਉਚੇੜਨਾ (Uchernaa) *v* To separate forcibly, to strip off, to pluck, to disunite.

ਉਛਲਣਾ (uchhalnaa) *v* To jump, to leap, to hop, to spring up.

ਉਛਾਹ (uchhaah) *n m* Enthusiasm, zeal, zest. Also **ਉਤਸਾਹ**

ਉਛਾਲ (Uchhaal) *n f* Buoyancy, upthrust.

ਉਛਾਲਨਾ (Uchhaalnaa) *v* To throw up, to toss up, to hurl; **ਪਗੜੀ~** To disgrace, to defame.

ਉਛਾਲਾ (uchhaalaa) *n m* Jump, upward, thrust.

ਉਛਾੜ (uchhaar) *n m* Cover, casing, covering, covor (for a pillow or quilt).

ਉੱਜਡ (Ujjad) *a* Rustic, unrefined, foolish, rash, clownish, inconsiderate.

ਉਜ਼ਰ (Uzar) *n f* Objection, excuse, plea; **~ਦਾਰੀ** Objection filed in court.

ਉਜਰਤ (Ujarat) *n f* Remuneration, wages, emoluments, pay, fee.

ਉਜਰਤੀ (Ujaratee) *a* Paid, on wages, remunerative.

ਉਜਲ (Ujal) *a* Clear, sparking, shining, bright, radiant, brilliant, elegant; **~ਦੀਦਾਰ** Good-looking, handsome, well-dressed, smart; **~ਤਾ** Elegance, serenity, purity.

ਉਜਲਾ (Ujlaa) *a* Pure, clean, shining, bright, luminous, radiant.

ਉਜੜਨਾ (Ujarnaa) *v* To be destroyed or ruined, to perish, to be laid waste.

ਉਜੜ-ਪੁਜੜ (Ujar-Pujar) *n m* Vandalism.

ਉਜੜਿਆ (Ujariaa) *a* Destroyed, laid

ਉਜਾਗਰ / ਉਡਕੇ ਲਿਆਉਣਾ

waste, uprooted; ~ਉਜੜਿਆ ਨਗਰ Ghost town.

ਉਜਾਗਰ (Ujaagar) *a* Famous, popular, well-known, renowned, bright.

ਉਜਾਲਾ (Ujaalaa) *n m* Light, daybreak, dawn, splendour; ~ਹੋਣਾ To dawn.

ਉਜਾੜ (Ujaaṛ) *n f a* Desert, lonely place, solitude; Desolate, ruined, deserted.

ਉਜਾੜਨਾ (Ujaaṛnaa) *v* To ruin, to wreck, to destroy, to ravage, to devastate.

ਉਜਾੜਾ (ujaaṛaa) *n m* Destruction, ruination, devastation; ~ਕਰਨਾ To destroy, to lay waste, to ruin.

ਉਜਾੜੂ (ujaaṛoo) *a* Wastrel, spendthrift, extravagant, squanderer.

ਉਜੇਬਾ (Ujebaa) *a* Like that, such as, that, similar. Also ਉੱਵੇਂ

ਉਂਝ (Unjh) *adv* Otherwise.

ਉਟੇਕਣਾ (Uṭeknaa) *v* To quarrel, to strike, to hit query, question.

ਉਤਕਣਾ (Utaknaa) *v* To go astray

ਉਠ (Uth) *v* Rise, stand up; ~ਖੜੋਣਾ/ਖਲੋਣਾ To stand up, to rise, to get up, to wake up, to become alert; ~ਜਾਣਾ To go away, to run away, to die; ~ਬੈਠਣਾ To wake up, to sit up in bed, to be well.

ਉਠਕ-ਬੈਠਕ (Uṭhak-baeṭhak) *n* Company, close acquaintance.

ਉਠਣਾ (Uṭhaṇaa) *v* To rise, to get up, to wake up, to stand up, to grow.

ਉਠਵਾਉਣਾ (Uṭhwaauṇaa) *v* To help or cause, to carry.

ਉਠਵਾਈ (Uṭhwaaee) *n f* Wages for carrying.

ਉਠਾ (Uṭhhaa) *n m* Swelling, sore, boil, rise. Also ਉਠਾਅ

ਉਠਾਉਣਾ (Uṭhaauṇaa) *v* To awaken, to carry, to remove, to suffer, to bear, to loft, to raise, to elevate. Also ਉਠਾਣਾ

ਉਠਾਉ (Uṭhaau) *n v* Move from the spot; Take it away.

ਉਠਾਈਗੀਰ (Uṭhaaeegeer) *n m* Petty thief. Also ਉਠਾਈਗੀਰਾ

ਉਡਣਾ (udnaa) *v a* To fly, to soar, to disappear, to vanish, to explode, to volatilize, to difuse in air, flying fast.

ਉਡਦੀ ਖਬਰ (Uḍdee khabar) *n f* Hearsay, rumour, uncertified report, doubtful news.

ਉਡਦੇ ਫਿਰਨਾ (Uḍde phirnaa) *v* To roam about in delight, to reel lost in delight.

ਉਡਕੇ ਲਿਆਉਣਾ (Uḍke liaauṇaa) *v* To

ਉੱਡਰ (uddar) *n m* Otter.

ਉਡਵਾਉਣਾ (udvaauṇaa) *v* To let fly, to cause to fly, to waste, to squander, to dissipate, to diffuse in air, to entice, to blow up, to destroy; ਗੁੱਡੀ ~ To fly the kite. Also ਉਡਾਉਣਾ

do or bring instantly or enthusiastically.

ਉਡਾਊ (udaaoo) *a* Spendthrift, lavish; Squanderer, extravagant.

ਉਡਾਣ (udaan) *n f* Flight.

ਉਡਾਰ (udaar) *a* Capable for flying.

ਉਡਾਰੀ (udaree) *n f* Flight, act of flying, sortie; ~ਮਾਰਨੀ To fly away, to take to flight, to disappear, to vanish.

ਉਡਾਰੂ (udaaroo) *n a* Flier, pilot, aeronaut, aviator, airman; Wilful; ~ਹੋ ਜਾਣਾ To slip away, to disappear.

ਉਡੀਕ (udeek) *n f* Wait, waiting expectation.

ਉਡੀਕਣਾ (Udeekṇaa) *v* To wait, to say, to expect.

ਉਣ (uṇ) *v* Weave, knit.

ਉਣੰਜੁਵਾਂ (uṇajva) *a m* Forty-nine.

ਉਣੰਜਾ (uṇaja) *a* Forty-nine.

ਉਣਤਾਲੀ (uṇtalee) *a* Thrity-nine.

ਉਣਤਾਲੀਵਾਂ (uṇtaliva) *a* Thrity-ninth.

ਉਣਤੀ (uṇtee) *n f* Process, design or pattern of knitting, texture.

ਉਣੱਤੀ (uṇattee) *a* Twenty-nine.

ਉਣਨਾ (uṇnaa) *v* To knit, to weave.

ਉਣਵਾਈ (uṇavaaee) *n f* Knitting, weaving, wages for knitting or weaving. Also ਉਣਾਈ

ਉਣਾਸੀ (uṇaasee) *a* Seventy-nine.

ਉਣਾਠ (uṇaaṭh) *a* Fifty-nine.

ਉਣਾਨਵੇਂ (uṇaanve) *a* Eighty-nine.

ਉਤਸਵ (uttasav) *n m* Festival, function, festivity, fete, rejoicing; Occasion, opportunity.

ਉਤਸਾਹ (utsaah) *n m* Zeal, zest, incentive, enthusiasm, eagerness; ~ਜਨਕ Encouraging, inspiring, inspirational; ~ਦੇਣਾ/ਵਧਾਉਣਾ To inspire, to enthuse, to encourage; ~ਭੰਗ Discouraging, demoralising, demoralisation.

ਉਤਸੁਕ (utasuk) *a* Keen, eager, curious.

ਉਤਸੁਕਤਾ (utasuktaa) *n f* Curiosity, eagerness, yearning, keeness.

ਉਤਕੰਠਾ (utakanthaa) *n f* Longing, craving, passion, solitude.

ਉਤਪਤੀ (utpatee) *n f* Birth, production, reproduction, origin, growth, derivation.

ਉਤਪੰਨ (utpann) *a* Created, born, produced; ~ਹੋਣਾ To grow, to comeforth, to take berth.

ਉਤਪਾਤ (utpaat) *n m* Cicisbeo.

ਉਤਪਾਦਕ (utpaadak) *n a m* Producer;

Productive, generative.

ਉਤਪਾਦਨ (utpaadan) *n m* Production, output.

ਉੱਤਮ (uttam) *a* Good, of good quality, best, highest, top, perfect, supreme, superior, excellent, superb; ~ਪੁਰਖ (gr.) First person.

ਉੱਤਰ (uttar) *v m n* Get down; Answer, reply; ਜੋੜਵੇਂ~ Replication, retort.

ਉੱਤਰ (uttar) *n m* North.

ਉੱਤਰ-ਅਧਿਕਾਰੀ (uttar-adhikaree) *n m* Descendant, successor, inheritor.

ਉੱਤਰਦਾਇਕ (uttardaayik) *a* Answerable, accountable, responsible. Also **ਉੱਤਰਦਾਈ**

ਉਤਰਨਾ (utarnaa) *v* To descend, to dismount, to disembark, to come down, to diminish, to decrease, to fall in value, to decay, to fade, to be copied, to subside.

ਉੱਤਰਵਰਤੀ (utarvartee) *a* Subsequent, latter; successor.

ਉਤਰਵਾਈ (utarvaaee) *n f* Wages or act of bringing down or unloading, unloading.

ਉਤਰਾਉ (utraau) *n f* Inclination, slope, descent.

ਉਤਰਾਅ-ਚੜ੍ਹਾਅ (utraa-charaa) *n m* Fluctuation, rise and fall.

ਉਤਰਾਈ (utraaee) *n f* Decline, declination, regress, descent, slope.

ਉਤਰਾਧਿਕਾਰ (utraadhikaar) *n m* Inheritence.

ਉਤਰਾਧਿਕਾਰੀ (utraadhikaaree) *n m* Successor.

ਉਤਰਾਧੀ (utraadhee) *a* Belonging to the north.

ਉਤਰਾਰਧ (utraaradh) *a m* Latter-half.

ਉਤਰੀ (utree) *a* Northern, northly.

ਉੱਤਰੋਤਰ (utrottar) *a adv* Successive, successively.

ਉਤਲਾ (utlaa) *a* Upper, over and above the income, additional; External, outward; ~ਦਿਲੋਂ Superficially, insincerely, in a light manner. Also **ਉਤਲੇ**

ਉਤਾਣਾ (utaanaa) *v* To lie facing downward or upside down.

ਉਤਾਰ (utaar) *n m* Fall, slope, decline, descent, decrease, reduction; ~ਚੜ੍ਹਾਓ Ups and downs, ascent and descent, rise and fall.

ਉਤਾਰਨਾ (utaarnaa) *v* To copy, to help in descending, to cast off, to take off, to degrade, to lower, to bring down, to unload, to dismount, to dethrone, to remove, to dislocate, to cause, to disembark.

ਉਤਾਰਾ (utaaraa) *n m a* Copy, halting place, stage (Journey), a bent upon, determined, intent, dead set, ready for; ~करना To stay, to sojourn, to prepare a copy; ~कराउना To lodge, to accommodate, to get a copy made.

ਉਤਾਰੂ (utaroo) *n a* Hurry, haste, hastiness, impatience; Impatient, anxious, rash, speedy, quick, hasty, swift, one who can do things quickly.

ਉਤਾੜ (utaaṛ) *n m* Upstream, upland, highland, elevated region.

ਉੱਤੇ (utte) *prep* Upon, on, over, above, upward, on the top.

ਉਤੇਜਕ (utejak) *a* Stimulant, stimulating, exciting, provocating, provocative, inspiring.

ਉਤੇਜਨਾ (utejnaa) *n f* Excitement, provocation, stimulation, inspiration.

ਉਤੇੜਨਾ (uteṛnaa) *v* To dilate.

ਉੱਤੋਂ (utton) *prep* From above.

ਉਥਲ-ਪੁਥਲ (uthal-puthal) *n f* Upheaval, turmoil.

ਉਥਲਣਾ (uthalṇaa) *v* To turn over.

ਉਥਾਈਂ (uthaaeen) *a* Exactly there, there, at that very place.

ਉਥਾਨ (uthaan) *n m* Pitch, rise; ~ਪਤਨ Fluctuation, rise and fall.

ਉਥਾਨਕਾ (uthaankaa) *n m* Preface, foreword, introduction, prelude.

ਉਥਾਪਣ (uthaapaṇ) *n m* Dissolution.

ਉਥਾਪਣਾ (uthaapaṇaa) *v* To transplant.

ਉਥੇ (uthe) *adv* At that place, there, over there.

ਉਥੋਂ (uthon) *adv* From there, from that place.

ਉਦਕ (udak) *n m* Water.

ਉਦਕਰਥ (udkarath) *n* Creation.

ਉਦਗਮ (udgam) *n m* Origin, rising, upcoming.

ਉਦਗਾਰ (udgaar) *n m* Inner feelings, sentiments.

ਉਦਘਾਟਨ (udghaaṭan) *n m* Inauguration, opening, ceremony; ~ਕਰਤਾ Inaugurator, release, uncovering; ~ਕਰਨਾ To inaugurate, to declare open, to expose, to exhibit, to bring to view.

ਉੱਦਘਾਟਨੀ (udghaaṭanee) *a* Inauguratory, inaugural; ~ਭਾਸ਼ਨ Inaugural speech.

ਉਦਮ (udam) *n m* Effort, exertion, endeavour, industry, diligence.

ਉਦਮੀ (udamee) *a* Industrious, enterprising, diligent.

ਉਦਯੋਗ (udyog) *n m* Industry, enterprise.

ਉਦਯੋਗਿਕ (udyogik) *a* Industrial.

ਉਦਯੋਗੀ (udyogee) *n m* Industrialist.

ਉਦਰ (udar) *n m* Abdomen, belly, womb, stomach, livelihood.

ਉਦਰੇਵਾਂ (udarevaan) *n m* Homesickness; Longing, yearning.

ਉਦਾਸ (udaas) *a* Sad, dejected, sorrowful, disconsolate, sullen, dull, rueful.

ਉਦਾਸੀ (udaasee) *n f* Sadness, cheerlessness, sorrow, depression, dejection, melancholy.

ਉਦਾਸੀਨ (udaaseen) *a* Neutral, apathetic.

ਉਦਾਸੀਨਤਾ (udaaseentaa) *n f* Apathy, depression, dejection etc.

ਉਦਾਹਰਣ (udaaharaṇ) *n m* Example, illustration, instance.

ਉਦਾਤ (udaat) *a n* Sublime.

ਉਦਾਤੀਕਰਣ (udaateekaraṇ) *n m* Sublimation; ~**ਕਰਨਾ** To sublimate.

ਉਦਾਰ (udaar) *a* Liberal, generous, large hearted, open minded, bounteous, bountiful, benevolent, humane; ~**ਤਾ** Magnaminity, catholicity, liberality, bounty; ~**ਵਾਦ** Liberalism; ~**ਵਾਦੀ** Liberal, Liberalist.

ਉਦਾਲਾ (udaalaa) *n m* Environment, neighbourhood, surroundings.

ਉਦਿਆਨ (udiyaan) *n m* Garden, orchard, forest; Solitude, deserted place.

ਉਦੇ (ude) *n m* Rising, dawn; ~**ਹੋਣਾ** To rise.

ਉਦੇਸ਼ (udesh) *n m* Aim, purpose.

ਉਦੇਸ਼ਾਤਮਕ (udeshaatmak) *a* Purposive, purfroseful, teteological.

ਉਦੋਂ (udon) *adv* Then, at that time; ~**ਕਣ** Since then, from that time.

ਉੱਧਰ (udhar) *adv* There, on that side, in that direction, yonder; ~**ਤੋਂ** From that side.

ਉਧਰਣ (udharaṇ) *n m* Deliverance, redemption, salvation.

ਉਧਰਨਾ (udharnaa) *v* To be redeemed, to be rescued, to attain salvation, to be liberated.

ਉਧਰਿਤ (udharit) *a* Based, on the basis of.

ਉਧਰੋਂ (udhron) *adv* From that side, from there.

ਉਧਲਣਾ (udhalṇaa) *v* To run away with some one to elope.

ਉਧੜਨਾ (udharnaa) *v* To be unsewn, to be encorded, to be unstitched, to be unravelled, to be unstrung, to be ripped.

ਉਧੜਵਾਉਣਾ (udharvaauṇaa) *v* To get unstitched, to get uncorded.

ਉਧੜਾਈ (udharaaee) *n f* Wages for

unstitching or uncording, act of unstitching or uncording.

ਉਧਾਰ (udhaar) *n a m* Loan, credit; ~**ਦੇਣਾ** To give on credit; To loan; ~**ਲੈਣਾ** To take on credit, to borrow; ~**ਪੱਟਾ** Debenture.

ਉਧਾਰਾ (udhaaraa) *a* On loan, borrowed.

ਉੱਧਾਰ (uddhaar) *n m* Salvation, redemption, deliverance; Reformation, uplift; ~**ਕਰਨਾ** To redeem, to uplift; ~**ਨਾ** To liberate, to redeem, to discharge, to save.

ਉਧਾਲਣਾ (udhaalṇaa) *v* To abduct, to kidnap, to seduce.

ਉਧਾਲਾ (udhaalaa) *n m* Elopement, abduction, act of running away with someone.

ਉਧੇੜਬੁਣ (udherbuṇ) *n m* Indecision, planning indecisively, perplexity.

ਉਧੇੜਨਾ (udherṇaa) *v* To unsew, to remove the seams, to unravel, to rip, to unweave, to undo.

ਉੱਨ (un) *n f* Wool; ~**ਵਰਗਾ** Woolly.

ਉਨਸ (unas) *n f* Attachment, love, sociability.

ਉਨਸਰੀ (unasaree) *n f* A fruit of blackberry, *Rubus flavus*; A fruit of yellow berry, *Rubus fructicosa*.

ਉੱਨਤ (unnat) *a* Developed, thriving, ameliorated, improved, advanced.

ਉਨਤੀ (unati) *n m* Uplift, progress, advancement, evolution, improvement, development, amelioration; ~**ਸ਼ੀਲ** Progressive, growing, developing; ~**ਕਰਨੀ** To progress, to improve, to develop, to rise, to thrive, to advance.

ਉਨੱਤੀ (unattee) *a* Twenty-nine.

ਉਨਮੱਤ (unmatt) *a* Intoxicated, frenzied, insane.

ਉਨਮਨਾ (unmanaa) *a* Absent-minded, agitated; ~**ਅਵਸਥਾ** A stage of mind (according to yoga).

ਉਨਮਾਦ (unmaad) *n m* Insanity, frenzy intoxication.

ਉਨਾਬੀ (unnabi) *a* Maroon.

ਉੱਨੀ (unni) *a* Nineteen.

ਉਨੀਂਦਾ (uneendaa) *n m* Sleeplessness, insomnia.

ਉਨੀਵਾਂ (univān) *a* Nineteenth. Also **ਉਨੀਆਂ**

ਉਨ੍ਹਾਂ (unaan) *pr* Them, those.

ਉਨ੍ਹਾਲਾ (unhaalaa) *n m* Summer, hot weather.

ਉਪ (upa) *a* (*Prefix for*) Deputy, Vice, Sub-, *Pre*; ~**ਅੰਗ** Appendage; ~**ਸਰਗ** Prefix; ~**ਕਲਪਣਾ** Hypothesis.

ਉਪਸੰਹਾਰ (upsanhaar) *n m* Denouement, end.

ਉਪਸਥਿਤ (upasthit) *a* Present.

ਉਪਸਥਿਤ (upasthiti) *n f* Presence, attendance.

ਉਪਹਾਸ (uphaas) *n m* Joke, jest, ridicule, satire.

ਉਪਹਾਸੀ (uphaasee) *a* Satirical, ridiculous, jovial.

ਉਪਹਾਰ (uphaar) *n m* Present, gift.

ਉਪਕਰਣ (upkaran) *n m* Instrument, apparatus.

ਉਪਕਾਰ (upkaar) *a* Beneficence, kindness, help, assistance; Benefactor, philanthrope, benevolent.

ਉਪਖੇਤਰ (upkhetar) *n m* Sub-area.

ਉਪਗ੍ਰਹਿ (upgreh) *n m* Satellite, moon.

ਉਪਚਾਰ (upchaar) *n m* Treatment remedy.

ਉਪਚਾਰੀ (upchaaree) *a n* Remedial; Fellow who treats or administers treatment.

ਉਪਚੇਤਨ (upchetan) *a* Subconscious.

ਉਪਜ (upaj) *n f* Produce, crop, yield, result, product, out-turn, out-put, growth, original idea.

ਉਪਜਣਾ (upajṇaa) *v* To grow, to be born, to shoot forth, to originate.

ਉਪਜਾਊਣਾ (upjaauṇaa) *v* To produce, to cultivate.

ਉਪਜਾਊ (upjaaoo) *a* Fertile, rich, productive, vegetative, fecund; ~ਪਣ Producer, cultivator.

ਉਪਜੀਵਕਾ (upjeevakaa) *n f* Vocation, profession, livelihood, subsistence.

ਉਪੱਦਰ (upaddar) *n m* Tyranny, oppression, turbulence, crime, persecution, outrage, rowdyism.

ਉਪੱਦਰੀ (upaddaree) *a n* Rowdy, mischievous; Rioter.

ਉਪਦੇਸ਼ (updesh) *n m* Precept, teaching, preaching, advice, counsel, lecture, sermon; ਦੇਣਾ To sermonise, to teach, to lecture, to preach, to advise; ~ਵਾਦ Didacticism; ~ਕ Lecturer, sermonizer, preceptor, preacher; ~ਣ (fem) Lecturer.

ਉਪਧਾਰਾ (updhaaraa) *n* Sub-clause.

ਉਪਨਗਰ (upnagar) *n m* Suburb; suburban.

ਉਪਨਾਮ (upnaam) *n m* Nick name, alias, surname.

ਉਪਨਿਆਸ (Upaniyaas) *n m* Novel, fiction; ~ਕਾਰ Novelist, fiction writer; ~ਕਾਰੀ Fiction-writing.

ਉਪਨਿਯਮ (upniyam) *n m* Subrule.

ਉਪਨਿਵੇਸ਼ (upnivesh) *n m* Colony; ~ਵਾਦ Colonialism.

ਉਪਭੋਗ (upbhog) *n m* Consumption; ~ਕਰਨਾ To consume; ~ਤਾ Consumer.

ਉਪਮਾ (upmaa) *n f* Comparison,

simile, analogy; Praise, eulogy.

ਉਪਮਾਉਣਾ (upmaaunaa) *v* To compare; To praise, to eulogize.

ਉਪਮਾਨ (upmaan) *n m* (poetics) That with which comparison is made.

ਉਪਯੋਗ (upyog) *n m* Use, utilisation.

ਉਪਯੋਗਤਾ (upyogtaa) *n f* Utility service, usefulness; ~**ਵਾਦ** Utilitarianism; ~**ਵਾਦੀ** Utilitarian.

ਉਪਯੋਗੀ (upyogee) *adv* Useful, serviceable.

ਉਪਰ (upar) *adv* Above, up, upon, on, over, on the top; ~**ਸੁੱਟਣਾ** To toss, to throw up; ~**ਚੜ੍ਹਨਾ** To climb, to ascend, to rise; ~**ਤੋਂ** From above; Successively, continuously, one after the other; ~**ਥਲੇ ਕਰਨਾ** To scatter things, to disarrange; ~**ਵਲ** Upwards.

ਉਪਰੰਤ (uprant) *adv* After, next, since, afterwards.

ਉਪਰਲਾ (uparlaa) *a* Upper, extra; External, superficial, outward; ~**ਖਰਚਾ** Overhead cost or expenses. Also **ਉਪਰਲੀ**

ਉਪਰੀ ਆਮਦਨ (upree aamdan) *n f* Tips, income through unfair means, income in addition to salary.

ਉਪਰਲੇ (uparle) *a* Extra, overhead (charges), seniors.

ਉਪਰਾਉ (Upraau) *n m* Aloofness, estrangement.

ਉਪਰਾਉਣਾ (upraaunaa) *v* To estrange, to make oneself appear, a stranger, to stand aloof.

ਉਪਰਾਮ (upraam) *a* Despondent, sick, disgusted, dejected, disconsolate; ~**ਹੋਣਾ** To become sad, to be distracted, to turn one's mind from the material objects; ~**ਤਾ** Sadness, despondency, distraction, act of turning one's mind from the world despair.

ਉਪਰਾਲਾ (upraalaa) *n m* Effort; Suggestion, means, method.

ਉਪਰੋਂ (upron) *adv* From above; ~**ਉਪਰੋਂ** Formally, as a formality; ~**ਲੰਘ ਜਾਣਾ** To run over; To supersede.

ਉਪਲਾ (uplaa) *n m* Dried cake of cow-dung. Also **ਪਾਥੀ**

ਉਪੜਨਾ (uparnaa) *v* To reach, to arrive.

ਉਪਾਉ (upaau) *n m* Remedy; Step; Means, measures, contrivance, plan.

ਉਪਾਸ਼ਕ (upaashak) *n m* Worshipper, adorer, devotee.

ਉਪਾਸ਼ਨਾ (upaashnaa) *n f* Worship, devotion, adoration.

ਉਪਖਿਆਨ (upakhiaan) *n m* Legend, anecdote, episode.

ਉਪਾਧ (upaadh) *n* Trouble, riots, upheaval.

ਉਪਾਧਿਆਇ (upaadhiai) *n m* Spiritual, preceptor, teacher.

ਉਪਾਧੀ (upaadhee) *n f* Degree, epithet, nick-name, title, designation; ~ਦਾ Root of the trouble, basis of the upheaval.

ਉਪਾਰਜਿਤ (upaarjit) *a* Acquired.

ਉਪਾਰਨਾ (upaarnaa) *v* To break (fast).

ਉਪਾਵਣਹਾਰ (upaavanhaar) *n* Creator, maker.

ਉਪੇਖਿਆ (upekhiaa) *n f* Neglect, negligence, ingoring, disregard.

ਉਫ਼ (uf) *int* oh! alas!

ਉਫਰਾਉ (ufraau) *a* Swellings, rising.

ਉਫਲਣਾ (ufalnaa) *v* To rebound, to spring.

ਉਬਸਣਾ (ubasnaa) *v* To putrefy, to become mouldy

ਉਬਸਾਉਣਾ (ubasaaunaa) *v* To cause to putrefy.

ਉਬਕ (ubak) *n m* Vomit.

ਉਬਾਕੀ (ubaakee) *n f* Vomit, vomiting.

ਉਬਕਾਈ (ubkaaee) *n f* Retching, nausea.

ਉਬਲਣਾ (ubalnaa) *n a* To boil, to be boiled, to simmer, to bubble, to be enraged.

ਉਬਲਦਾ (ubaldaa) *a v* Ebullient, boiling, very hot; To cause to boil.

ਉਬਾਸੀ (ubaasee) *n f* Yawn, gape.

ਉਬਾਕ (ubaak) *n f a* Retching, vomitting sensation; Spasm; Nausea.

ਉਬਾਕਣਾ (ubaakanaa) *v* To retch; To vomit, to regurgitate.

ਉਬਾਰ (ubaar) *v m* Deliverance, liberation, upward projection.

ਉਬਾਰਨਾ (ubaarnaa) *v* To deliver, to liberate, to lift or project upward, to salvage, to redeem.

ਉਬਾਲ (ubaal) *n m* Ebullition, boiling simmering, spurt, Passion; ~ਉਠਣਾ/ਆਉਣਾ To boil, rising of passions or sentiments.

ਉਬਾਲਣਾ (ubaalnaa) To boil, boiling.

ਉਭਰਨਾ (ubh'arnaa) *v* To swell, to rase; To boil over; To excite; To bounce; To bulge; To heave, to protrude; To make prominent.

ਉਭਰਵਾਂ (ubharvaā) *a* Protruding, bulging, swollen, embossed

ਉਭਰਿਆ (ubhariaa) *v a* Risen, protructed, boiled over; ~ਪੈਂਦਾ Flanged bottom.

ਉਭੜਵਾਹੇ (ubharvaahe) *adv* With a start; Spontaneously.

ਉਭਾ (ubhaa) *n a* East, short (breath); ~ਸਾਹ Groan, sigh.

ਉਭਾਸਰਨਾ (ubhaasarnaa) *v* To speak out, to speak up, to spell out ones trouble moaringly.

ਉਭਾਨ (ubhaan) *n* Tree *Populus eupharatica*.

ਉਭਾਰ (ubhaar) *n m* Prominence, swelling, profuberance, bulge, rise, boil; Bossing.

ਉਭਾਰਨਾ (ubhaarnaa) *v* To excite, to swell, to raise, to arouse, to rouse, to incite, to instigate.

ਉਮਸ (umas) *n f* Sultriness, mugginess.

ਉਮੰਗ (umang) *n f* Ambition, hope, passion, longing, desire, exultation.

ਉਮੜਨਾ (umaḍnaa) *v* To overflow, to overwhelm, to swell, to gush out, to gather quickly.

ਉਮਤ (umat) *n m* Followers, people of the same belief, off spring, pupils.

ਉਮਦਾ (umdaa) *a* Better, good, nice.

ਉਮਰ (umar) *n f* Age, lifetime, life; ~ਢਲਣੀ To age; ~ਕੈਦ Life sentence; ~ਕੈਦੀ Life convict; ~ਪਟਾ Lease for life; ~ਭਰ (ਸਾਰੀ ਉਮਰ) For life, through out life.

ਉਮਰਾ (ਉਮਰਾਉ) (umraa) *n* Courtiers, nobes.

ਉੱਮੁਲਣਾ (ummalṇaa) *v* To gush out, to spring forth.

ਉਮਾਹ (umaah) *n m* Ambition, excessive joy, exuberance.

ਉਮੀ (umee) *a* Illiterate, uneducated.

ਉਮੀਆ (umeeaa) *n m* Wheat or barley roasted in the ear.

ਉਮੀਦ (umeed) *n f* Hope, confidence, expectation, reliance; ~(ਉਮੀਦਾਂ) ਤੇ ਪਾਣੀ ਫਿਰਨਾ All hopes to be dashed to the ground. Also ਉਮੈਦ

ਉਮੀਦਵਾਰ (Umeedvaar) *n m* Candidate, applicant, expectant, hopeful.

ਉਮੀਦਵਾਰੀ (Umeedvaaree) *n f* Hopefulness, pregnancy, expectancy.

ਉਰ (ur) *n m* Heart, breast, bosom.

ਉਰਸਾ (ursaa) *n m* A stone on which a brahmin grinds sandalwood.

ਉਰਲ-ਪਰਲ (ural-paral) *n m* (articles) Superfluous, meaningless, additional; ~ਕੰਮ Superfluous work.

ਉਰਲਾ (urlaa) *a* Belonging to this side, on the nearer side. Also ਉਰਲੀ

ਉਰਵਾਰ (urvaar) *prep* On this side; ~ਪਾਰ Through to the other side, across.

ਉਰੁੰ (uraan) *a* On this side, here, higher, nearer.

ਉਰੇ (ure) *adv* Here, near, on this side; ~ਪਰੇ Out of the way, hidden; ~ਪਰੇ ਹੋਣਾ To elope, to be somewhere nearby, to go or be out of sight, to hide, to go underground.

ਉਰਾਰ (uraar) *n m* On this bank or nearer side of a river or canal or pitch or tank etc.

ਉਰਿਓਂ (uriōn) *adv* From a nearer place.

ਉਰੇਰੇ (urere) *adv* A little on this side, a little nearer.

ਉਲਕਾ (ulkaa) *n* Meteor. Also ਉਲਕਾਪਾਤ

ਉਲੰਘਨਾ (ulanghnaa) *n f* Violation, contravention; Transgression, intringement, contravention; ~ਕਰਨੀ To violate, to transgress, to intringe, to contravene.

ਉਲਝਨ (uljhan) *n f* Tangle, complication, confusion, fix, intricacy, entanglement, dilemma, perplexity.

ਉਲਝਣਾ (uljhnaa) *v* To be involved or entangled, to be confused or puzzled, to dispute, to enter into a dispute.

ਉਲਝਾਉ (uljhaau) *n m* Entanglement, involvement, involution, confusion, perplexity.

ਉਲਝਾਉਣਾ (uljhaaunaa) *v* To entangle to complicate, to involve, to confuse, to perplex.

ਉਲਟ (ulat) *n a m* Inverse, reverse, change inversion, Opposite, reversed, contrary; ~ਜਾਣਾ To be turned over, to capsize; ~ਤੋਂ ਤੇ Conversely; ~ਪੁਲਟ Upside down, topsy turvy, in disorderly manner; ~ਪੈਠੀ ਪਰਤ To return without a pause; ~(ਉਲਟੇ) ਬਾਂਸ ਬਰੇਲੀ ਨੂੰ To carry coal to new castle.

ਉਲਟਣਾ (ulatnaa) *v* To upset, to invert, to reverse, to turn upside down, to be upset, to be inverted.

ਉਲਟਵਾਂ (ulatvaan) *a* Inversive. Also ਉਲਟਵੀਂ

ਉਲਟਾ (ultaa) *a adv* Opposite, converse reversed, overturned, inverse, inverted; On the contrary; ~ਸਮਝਣਾ To misunderstand; ~ਚਲਾਉਣਾ To drive backward; ~ਚੋਰ ਕੋਤਵਾਲ ਨੂੰ ਡਾਂਟੇ The case of thief threatening a policeman; ~ਜ਼ਮਾਨਾ Preposterous times; ~ਤਵਾ Jet black, coal black.

ਉਲਟਾਉ (ultaau) *n m* Inversion, overturning.

ਉਲਟਾਉਣਾ (ultaaunaa) *v* To reverse, to invert, to upset, to overturn, to interchange; ~ਪੁਲਟਾਉਣੀ Topsy turvy, disconnected.

ਉਲਟੀ (ultee) *n f a* Vomit; Contrary, capsized, overturned, inverted upside down, inverse, inside out; ~ਕਰਨੀ To vomit; ~ਪੱਟੀ ਪੜ੍ਹਾਉਣੀ To mislead, to misguide, to poison the mind; ~ਮਾਲਾ ਫੇਰਨੀ To invoke a curse; ~ਉਲਟੀ ਸਮਝ Perverted mind, perversion; ~ਸਿੱਧੀ Absurd, irrelevant; ~ ਸੁਣਾਉਣਾ To insult, to scold, to revile.

ਉਲਥਾ (ulthaa) *n m* Translation, rendering version; ~ਕਰਨਾ To translate, to interpret, to render; ~ਕਾਰ Translator.

ਉਲੱਦਣਾ (uladdṇaa) *v* To pour, to invert, to overturn, to reveal (the secrets).

ਉਲਫ਼ਤ (ulfat) *n f* Love.

ਉਲਰਨਾ (ularnaa) *a* To tilt, to sway, to lurch, to lean, to be off-balance, to bound.

ਉਲਰਵਾਂ (ularvaan) *a* Tipped, off-balance.

ਉਲਰਿਆ (ulariaa) *a* Tilted, off-balance.

ਉਲਾਹਮਾ (ulahmaa) *n m* Reproof, complaint, blame. Also ਉਲਾਂਭਾ

ਉਲਾਹੁਣਾ (ulaahuṇaa) *v* To mourn for the dead.

ਉਲਾਂਘ (ulaangh) *n f* Jump. pace, stride, long step.

ਉਲਾਰ (ulaar) *a n m* unbalanced, off balance, tilted, depressed by weight on oneside, lopsided, raised in a threatening manner; Tilt, inclination.

ਉਲਾਰਨਾ (ulaarnaa) *v* To tilt, to sway.

ਉੱਲੀ (ullee) *n f* Fungus, mould, mildew.

ਉਲੀਕਣਾ (uleekṇaa) *v* To draw, to outline, to sketch, to trace, to portray.

ਉੱਲੂ (ulloo) *n m* Owl; Foolish, simpleton; ~ਸਿੱਜਾ ਕਰਨਾ To grind one's own axe, to take some work; ~ਦਾ ਪੱਠਾ Idiot, dullard, an arrant fool, silly fellow, fool; ~ਬਣਨਾ To be fooled; ~ਬੋਲਣੇ To be deserted (place).

ਉਲੇਹਰਣਾ (uleharnaa) *v* To hem.

ਉਵੇਂ (ooven) *adv* Likewise, so, similarly, by the way, in that way.

ਉੜਦ (uṛad) *n f* Horse bean.

ਉੜਾਕ (oṛaak) *a* Haughty, insolent, disrespectful.

ਊਸ਼ਾ (ushaa) *n f* Early morning, redness of dawn.

ਊਗਲ (ugal) *n f* Buckwheat.

ਊਂਘ (oongh) *n f* Doze, slumber.

ਊਂਘਣਾ (oonghṇaa) *v* To doze, to feel sleepy, to slumber.

ਊਜ (ooj) *n f* Imputation, blame, aspersion, allegation.

ਊਜਣ (oojaṇ) *n f* Grain, *Hordeum caeleste*.

ਊਟ-ਪਟਾਂਗ (ooṭ-paṭaang) *n* Nonsense, irrelevant or absurd talk.

ਊਠ (ooṭh) *n m* Camel; ~ਦੇ ਮੂੰਹ ਜੀਰਾ A drop in the ocean; ~ਕਿਸ ਕਰਵਟ

ਬੈਠਦਾ ਹੈ Wait and see how things turn out.

ਉਠਕ-ਬੈਠਕ (oothak-baethak) *n f* Sitting and standing, sit-ups.

ਉਠਨੀ (oothnee) *n f* Dromedary, she camel.

ਉਣ (oon) *n f* Deficiency, shortage.

ਉਣਤਾਈ (oontaaee) *n f* Flaw, defect, shortcoming lack.

ਉਣਾ (oonaa) *a* Deficient, defective, incomplete.

ਉਤ (oot) *a* Foolish, stupid, rude, childless; ~ਜਾਣਾ To die issueless; ~ਪੁਣਾ Foolishness, stupidity.

ਉਦ (ood) *n f* Aloe, Eaglewood.

ਉਦ-ਬਲਾਉ (ood-balaau) *n m* Otter, an aquatic cat.

ਉਦਾ (ooda) *a* Violet, of the colour of a brinjal.

ਉਧਮ (oodham) *n m* Uproar, agitation, noise, revolt, rebellion, disturbance, furore, riot, pandemonium, turmoil; ~ਮਚਾਉਣਾ To create disturbance, to make noise, to agitate.

ਉਂਧਾ (oondhaa) *a* Overturned, upside down.

ਉਰਜਾ (oorjaa) *n f* Energy, power.

ਉਰਾ (ooraa) *a n m* Incomplete, uneducated; Reel, bobbin, winder, windlass. Also **ਉੜੀ**

ਉਲ-ਜਲੂਲ (ool-jalool) *a* Senseless (talk), nonsense, absurd.

ਉੜਾ-ਐੜਾ (oora-aera) *n m* Alphabets; ~ਨਾ ਜਾਣਨਾ To be illiterate, to be unlettered, to be ignorant.

ਓਅੰਕਾਰ (ounkaar) *n m* God, Saviour of all.

ਓਹਦਾ (ōda) *pron* Same as **ਓਸਦਾ**

ਓਹਲਾ (ōla) *n m* cover, veil, screen, protection, support, refuge; Privacy, secrecy.

ਓਹਲਾ (ohlaa) *n m* Cover, secret, refuge, protection; ~ਕਰਨਾ To conceal, to keep secret; ~ਦੇਣਾ To give refuge, to keep secret.

ਓਹੜ-ਪੋਹੜ (ohar-pohar) *n m* First aid.

ਓਹੋ (oho) *pron* The same, the very fellow.

ਓਕ (ok) *n f* Cuplike shape of a hand to drink water.

ਓਕੜਾ (okṛaa) *a* Strong, headstrong.

ਓਗਰਾ (ograa) *n m* A type of coarse grain; Rice-water.

ਓਛਾ (ochhaa) *a* Mean, narrow-minded, undignified, shallow.

ਓਝਰੀ (ojhree) *n f* Stomach, intenstine.

ਓਝਲ (ojhal) *a* Behind the scene, out of sight, concealed; Retirement; ~ਹੋਣਾ To disappear, to be out of sight; ~ਕਰਨਾ To conceal.

ਓਝਾ (ojhaa) *n m* Occultist, necromanner, witch doctor.

ਓਟ (ot) *n f* Protection, shelter, refuge, shadow, screen, partition.

ਓਟਣਾ (otnaa) *v* To shelter, to give refuge; To confess (to a crime), to accept responsibility (for a crime).

ਓਥੇ (othe) *adv* There, at the place.

ਓਥੋਂ (otheōn) *adv* From there.

ਓਦਣ (odan) *adv* On that day.

ਓਦਰਨਾ (odarnaa) *v* To become sad in separation, to become eager, to meet, to long for, to yearn.

ਉਦਰੇਵਾਂ (udervaan) *n m* Longing for meeting depression as a result of separation from a dear relation, homesickness.

ਓਦਾਂ (odaan) *adv* Like that, in that way; otherwise.

ਓਦੋਂ (oden) *adv* Then, at that time.

ਓਪਰਲਾ (oparlaa) *adv* Belonging to the other side.

ਓਪਰਾ (opraa) *a* Stranger, unfamiliar, outsider, alien; ~**ਪਣ** Otherness strangeness, unfamiliarity, alienation.

ਓਭੜ (ōbhar) *a* Unknown, stranger.

ਓਲਾ (ola) *n m* Hail-stone.

ਓੜਨੀ (ornee) *n f* Cover, headgear, veil, wrapper.

ਅ

ਅ Vowel, second letter of Gurmukhi letter pronounced as airaa.

ਅਉਸਰ (ausar) *n m* Opportunity occasion, time.

ਅਉਗੁਣ (augun) *n m* Vice, fault, defect, shortcoming.

ਅਉਤ (aut) *a* Issueless, rude.

ਅਉਧ (audh) *n f* Term, tenure, age, life span.

ਅਇਆਣਾ (aiaanaa) *a m* Infant, child, ignorant, innocent.

ਅਇਆਲੀ (aiaalee) *n m* Shepherd.

ਅੰਸ਼ (ansh) *n m* Part, constituent, degree, numerator.

ਅੰਸ (ans) *n f* Progeny, lineal descendant, offspring, progeny.

ਅਸ਼ਕ (ashak) *n m* Tear.

ਅੰਸ਼ਕਾਲੀ (anshkaalee) *a* Part time.

ਅਸੰਖ (asankh) *a* Countless, infinite, innumerable.

ਅਸੰਗਤ (asangat) *a* Irrelevant, inconsistant, incoherant.

ਅਸ਼ੱਗਨ (ashaggan) *n m* Ill omen, inauspicious omen.

ਅਸਚਰਜ (ascharaj) *n a m* Wonder, astonishment; Wonderful, astonishing; ~ਜਨਕ Surprising, astonishing, marvellous.

ਅਸ਼ਟਾਮ (ashtaam) *n m* Stamp paper, stamp, bond.

ਅਸਤਬਲ (astabal) *n m* Stable.

ਅਸਤਬਾਜ਼ੀ (astabaazee) *n f* Fireworks.

ਅਸਤਰ (astar) *n m* Missile, weapon; Inner coating, lining of a garment.

ਅਸਤੀਫ਼ਾ (asteefaa) *n m* Resignation; ~ਦੇਣਾ To Resign.

ਅਸੰਤੁਸ਼ਟ (asantusht) *a* Dissatisfied, displeased, discontented.

ਅਸੰਤੋਖ (asantokh) *n m* Dissatisfaction, discontentment.

ਅਸਥਾਈ (asathai) *a* Temporary, impermanent, transitory.

ਅਸਥਾਨ (asthaan) *n m* Place, position room, residence, space.

ਅਸਥਾਪਤ (asthaapat) *a* Installed, established, appointed.

ਅਸਥਾਪਨ (asathapan) *n m* Installation.

ਅਸਥਾਪਨਾ (asathapana) *n f* Establishment, instalment.

ਅਸਪਸ਼ਟ (aspasht) *a* Ambigious, vague, obscure, dubious imperceptible, illegible, not clear; ~ਤਾ Lack of clarity, obscureness, vagueness, ambiguity.

ਅਸਪਾਤ (aspaat) *n m* Steel.

ਅਸਬਾਬ (asbaab) *n m* Luggage, baggage, reasons, causes.

ਅਸੰਭਵ (asambhav) *a* Impossible, impracticable, improbable.

ਅਸਮਤ (asmat) *n f* Modesty, chastity.

ਅਸਮਤਾ (asamtaa) *n f* Inequality, dissimilarity.

ਅਸਮਰਥ/ਅਸਮਰਥਕ (asmarath/asmarathak) *a* Incapable, unable, incompetent, weak, Impotent.

ਅਸਮਾਨ (asmaan) *n m* Sky, heaven; ~ਸਿਰ ਤੇ ਚੁਕਣਾ To create havoc, to make exclusive noise; ~ਟੁੱਟ ਪੈਣਾ To be struck by calamity; ~ਤੇ ਉਡਣਾ To be proud; ~ਤੇ ਚੜ੍ਹਨਾ To be too proud, to be too vain; ~ਤੋਂ ਡਿਗਣਾ To fall from a great height; ~ਨੂੰ ਟਾਕੀ ਲਾਉਣੀ To be crafty.

ਅਸਮਾਨੀ (asmaanee) *a* Sky blue, azure, heavenly.

ਅਸਰ (asar) *n m* Effect, influence, impression; Result, consequence; ~ਦਾਇਕ Effective, impressive, forceful, influential.

ਅਸਲ (asal) *a* Real, true, pure de facto, capital, amount.

ਅਸਲਾ (aslaa) *n* (1) Arms, military weapons; (2) Root, source, origin.

ਅਸਲੀ (aslee) *a* Original, real, true, pure, unadulterated.

ਅਸਲੀਅਤ (asliyat) *n f* Reality, fact, actuality.

ਅਸ਼ਲੀਲ (ashleel) *a* Obscene, vulgar, indecent; ~ਲਿਖਤ Pornography.

ਅਸਵਾਰ (aswaar) *n m* Rider.

ਅਸ਼ਾਂਤੀ (ashaantee) *n f* Disorder, disquiet, dissatisfaction.

ਅਸਾਧ (asaadh) *a* Incurable, Incorrigible, desperate.

ਅਸਾਧਾਰਨ (asaadhaaran) *a* Uncommon, extraordinary, unusual, abnormal, a typical.

ਅਸਾਨ (asaan) *a* Easy, facile.

ਅਸਾਰ (asaar) *n a* (1) Traces, signs, characteristics; (2) Width; Meaningless, unreal.

ਅਸਾਵਧਾਨ (asaawdhaan) *a* Careless, inadvertent.

ਅਸਾਵਧਾਨੀ (asavdani) *n f* Inattention, inattentiveness, heedlessness, carelessness, inadvertence, inadvertency.

ਅਸਿੱਖ (asikkh) *a* Unteachable, untutored; Not sikh-like.

ਅਸੀਂ (aseen) *pron* We.

ਅੱਸੀ (assee) *a* eighty.

ਅਸੀਸ (asees) *n m* Blessing, benediction.

ਅਸ਼ੁਧ (ashudh) *a* Impure, adulterated; Wrong, incorrect.

ਅਸ਼ੁਧੀ (ashudhee) *n f* Mistake, error, inaccuracy, misprint; ~**ਪਤਰ** Errata, erratum.

ਅਸੁਰ (asur) *n m* Demon, devil, satan.

ਅਸੂਝ (asoojh) *n* Indirection.

ਅਸੂਲ (asool) *n m* Principal, rule, law, theory, doctrine, canon; ~**ਨ** On principle, in principle.

ਅਸੂਲੀ (asuli) *a* Principled, morally correct or vaild, righteous.

ਅਹੰਕਾਰ (ahāankaar) *n m* Same as **ਅਹੰ**; Pride, arrogance, conceit.

ਅਹੰਕਾਰੀ (ahāankaari) *a* Proud, arrogant, conceited.

ਅਹਿਦ (ahed) *n m* Resolve, vow, determination, promise.

ਅਹਿਮ (ahem) *a* Important, essential, significant, momentous.

ਅਹਿੰਸਾ (ahinsaa) *n f* Non-violence.

ਅਹਿਮਕ (ahemak) *n m* Fool, stupid; ~**ਪੁਣਾ** Foolishness stupidity.

ਅਹਿਮੀਅਤ (ahimeeyat) *n f* Importance, significance.

ਅਹਿੱਲ (ahill) *a* Immovable, employee, agent, public servant, petty official.

ਅਹਿਲਕਾਰ (ahilkaar) *n m* Official, clerk in a court of law.

ਅਹੁਦਾ (auhdaa) *n m* Rank, post.

ਅਹੂਤੀ (ahootee) *n f* Oblation, burnt offering, immolation.

ਅੰਕ (ank) *n m* (1) Numeral, number, mark, figure; (2) Letter of the alphabet; (3) Act (of a drama); (4) Issue (of a newspaper or magazine).

ਅਕਸ (aks) *n m* Reflection, reflected image.

ਅਕਸਰ (aksar) *adv* Often, frequently, mostly.

ਅਕਸਰੀਅਤ (aksareeat) *n f* Majority.

ਅੱਕਣਾ (akkanaa) *v* To be fed up, to be bored, tired (of), irritated.

ਅਕਦ/ਅਗਦ (akad/agad) *n* Marriage.

ਅਕਲ (akal) *n f* Wisdom, intelligence, sense, head, reason; ~**ਟਿਕਾਣੇ ਲਾਉਣੀ** To set right, to bring sense, to cut to size; ~**ਮੰਦ** Wise, sensible; ~**ਤੇ ਪਥਰ ਪੈਣੇ** To be out of one's head, to be bereft of all intellect; ~**ਤੇ ਪੜਦਾ ਪੈਣਾ** To be stupid; ~**ਦਾ ਅੰਨ੍ਹਾ** Fool, block head, stupid; ~**ਦਾ ਦੁਸ਼ਮਨ** Silly, stupid; ~**ਦਾ ਪੂਰਾ** Foolish (sarcastically); ~**ਦੁੜਾਉਣੀ** To think, to reason.

ਅਕਾ (akaa) *n* Boredom, tedium, iksomeness, wearisomeness, nuisance, annoyance, exasperation.

ਅਕਾਉਣਾ (akaaunaa) *a* Boring, monotonous, tedious, dreary.

ਅਕਾਉ (akaaoo) *a* Boring, dreary.

ਅਕਾਰਥ (akaarath) *a* Useless, fruitless, unprofitable; ~ਜਾਣਾ To go waste, to be wasted.

ਅਕਾਰਨ (akaaran) *a adv* Without cause, unprovoked, needless, groundless, unnecessary, unwarranted; Needlessly, unnecessarily.

ਅਕਾਲ (akaal) *a n m* Untimely, before time, immortal, timeless, god; ~ਪੁਰਖ God, not affected by death or time; ~ਚਲਾਣਾ ਕਰਨਾ To pass away, to die, to breathe one's last away.

ਅਕਾਲੀ (akaalee) *a m* Divine, a sect of the sikhs.

ਅਕੀਦਾ (akeedaa) *n* Faith, belief, doctrine, principle.

ਅਕੇਵਾਂ (akevaan) *n* Boredom, tendium, weariness, exasperation.

ਅੱਖ (akkh) *n f* Eye; ~ਆਉਣੀ To have sore eye; ~ਨਾ ਚੁਕਣੀ To be ashamed, not to look up; ~ਬਚਾਉਣੀ To avoid notice, to slip away, to blink; ~ਮਚੋਲੀ Hide and seek; ~ਲੜਨੀ To fall in love.

ਅਖੰਡ (akhand) *a* Indivisible, undivided; continuous, whole entire, uninterrupted; ~ਪਾਠ Uninterrupted recitation, non-stop recital of Sikh or Hindu scripture.

ਅਖਤਿਆਰ (akhtiyaar) *n m* Authority, competency, right, discretion.

ਅਖ਼ਬਾਰ (akhbaar) *n m* Newspaper.

ਅੱਖਰ (akkhar) *n m* Letter, character (of alphabet); Syllable; ~ਕ੍ਰਮ Alphabetical order.

ਅੱਖਰੀ (akkharee) *a* Pertainning to letters, literal.

ਅੱਖਰੋਟ (akhrot) *n m* Walnut.

ਅਖਵਾਉਣਾ (akhvaaunaa) *v* Get communicated or recommended; To be called, to cause to say.

ਅਖੜ (akhar) *a* Rude, haughty, quarrelsome, obstinate, wild, impolite, rough, uncivilized; ~ਪੁਣਾ Brusqness, stubborness, arrogance.

ਅਖਾਣ (akhaan) *n m* Proverb, saying, aphorism, adage.

ਅਖਾੜਾ (akhaaraa) *n m* Arena, wrestling place, plaestra, amphitheatre.

ਅਖੀਰ (akheer) *n adv f* End, extreme; Limit; Atlast.

ਅਖੁੱਟ (akhutt) *a* Boundless, inexhaustible.

ਅੱਗ (agg) *n a f* Fire, heat, flame, jealousy, passion; Burning, very hot; ~ਤੇ ਤੇਲ ਪਾਉਣਾ To add fuel to the fire; ~ਤੇ ਪਾਣੀ ਪਾਉਣਾ To pacify, to calm down; ~ਤੇ ਲੇਟਣਾ To be uneasy, to be restless; ~ਦੇਣੀ To light the pyre, to perform funeral rites; ਪਾਣੀ ਦਾ ਵੈਰ Innate mutual hostility; ~ਬਗੋਲਾ ਹੋਣਾ To fly into rage; ~ਭੜਕਾਉਣੀ To excite.

ਅੰਗ (ang) *n m* Limb, part, portion, fraction, division; Member.

ਅਗਰ (agar) *n conj f* Front; If, in case; ~ਗਾਮੀ Forerunner, progressive, foremost, precedent.

ਅੰਗਰੇਜ਼ (angrez) *n m* Englishman, The English, Britisher.

ਅੰਗਰੇਜ਼ੀ (angrezee) *a n m* English, British; English language.

ਅਗਵਾ (agwaa) *n m* Abduction; ~ਕਰਨਾ To abduct, to hijack.

ਅਗਵਾਈ (agwaaee) *n f* Guidance, leadership; ~ਕਰਨਾ To lead, to guide, to provide leadership.

ਅਗਵਾਨੀ (agvaanee) *n f* Welcome, reception; ~ਕਰਨੀ To welcome, to receive, to usher.

ਅਗਵਾੜਾ (agvaaraa) *n m* Front side, front portion, foreground, front, facade.

ਅਗੜ-ਪਿਛੜ (aggar-picchar) *adv* One after the other, one behind the other, successively, in quick succession.

ਅਗੜਮ-ਬਗੜਮ (agaram-bagram) *a* Worthless, absurd, irrelevant.

ਅੰਗੜਾਈ (angraaee) *n f* Stretching of the limbs.

ਅਗਾਂਹ (agaanha) *a m* Forword, onward, future, more; ~ਚਲਣਾ To march forward.

ਅਗਾੜੀ (agaaree) *n f* Front position, forepart, future; Rope with which horse is tied; ~ ਪਿਛਾੜੀ One behind the other, forward and backward.

ਅੰਗੀ (angee) *n f* Brassiere, bodice.

ਅੰਗੀਠੀ (angeethee) *n f* Furnace, fire pot, stove, heater.

ਅੰਗੂਠਾ (angoothaa) *n m* Thumb, the great toe; ~ਵਿਖਾਉਣਾ To defy, to challenge.

ਅੰਗੂਠੀ (angoothee) *n m* Finger ring, ring.

ਅੰਗੂਰ (angoor) *n m* Grapes, vines, scale.

ਅਗੇ (agge) *adv* Before, in front, onward; ~ਅਗੇ Ahead, forward, a course of time; ~ਕਰਨਾ To present, to put forward, to push forward; ~ਦੌੜ ਪਿਛੇ ਚੋੜ Haste makes waste; ~ਨਿਕਲਣਾ To surpass, to cross, to advance, to overtake; ~**ਵਧਣਾ** To progress, to proceed, to improve.

ਅਗੇਤਰ (agetar) *n* Prefix, affix.

ਅੰਗੋਛਾ (angochhaa) *n m* Towel, any piece of cloth for wiping.

ਅਚੰਭਾ (achambhaa) *n m* Wonder, ashtonishment, amazement, marvel.

ਅਗੇਤ (aget) *n m* Early time, earliness, advance (in relation to sowing operation); Prefix.

ਅਗੇਰੇ (agere) *adv* Forward, further on, more forward, more to the front.

ਅਗੋਂ (aggon) *adv f* From the front, from the opposite direction; Next, hereafter, henceforth; ~**ਪਿੱਛੋਂ** sooner or later; From anyside.

ਅਚਨਚੇਤ (achanchet) *adv* Suddenly, all of a sudden, without warning, abruptly, unexpectedly, precipitately.

ਅਚਰਜ (acharaj) *a* Wondeful, ashtonishing, strange, amazing, marvellous.

ਅਚਰ (achar) *a* Inanimate; ~**ਚਰ** Animate and inanimate.

ਅਚਲ (achal) *a* Immovable, static, stationary, constant, invariable, fixed, motionless, Invariant, constant.

ਅਚਾਨਕ (achaanak) *a* Suddenly, by chance, unexpectedly, all of a sudden.

ਅਚਾਰ (achaar) *n m* Pickles.

ਅਚੇਤ (achet) *a* Senseless, unconscious, inattentive; ~**ਅਵਸਥਾ** Trance.

ਅੱਛਾ (achhaa) *a* Good, nice, pleasant, fine; Well, alright; ~**ਹੋਣਾ** To recover, to be healed; ~**ਕਰਨਾ** To cure, to heal.

ਅਛੂਤ (achhoot) *a* Untouchable.

ਅੱਜ (ajj) *adv* Today, This day, now; ~**ਕਲ** Now a days, in a few days.

ਅਜਨਬੀ (ajanabee) *n m* Stranger, unfamiliar, alien.

ਅਜਪਾ (ajapaa) *a* Unrecited, unpronounced, unutterable.

ਅਜਬ (ajab) *a* Curious, rare, strange, wonderfull.

ਅਜਮਤ (azamat) *n f* Honour, dignity, greatness.

ਅਜਮਾਇਸ਼ੀ (azmayishee) *a* Probationary, on probation.

ਅਜਲਾਸ (ajlaas) *n m* Session.

ਅਜ਼ਾਦੀ (azaadee) *n f* Freedom, independence, liberty. Also **ਆਜ਼ਾਦੀ**

ਅਜ਼ਾਬ (azaab) *n m* Torture, torment, suffering, pain.

ਅੰਜਾਮ (anjaam) *n m* Consequence,

end, result, outcome.

ਅਜ਼ੀਜ਼ (azeez) *a* Dear, son.

ਅਜੀਬ (ajeeb) *a* Strange, wonderful, peculiar.

ਅਜੀਮ (azeem) *a* Great, grand, huge, stupendous.

ਅਜੁੜਵਾਂ (ajuṛvaan) *a* Incompatible; Not matching; Different; Disjointed, disconnected, separate.

ਅਜੇ (aje) *adv* Yet, still, as yet.

ਅਜੋਕਾ (ajokaa) *a* Upto date, of present date, modern.

ਅਟਕ (aṭak) *n* Hindrance, obstacle, impediment, bar, hitch, hurdle.

ਅਟਕਲ (aṭakal) *n f* Guess, conjecture, rough estimate; Rough and ready solution, trial and error method.

ਅਟਕਣਾ (aṭakaṇaa) *v* To stop, to halt, to stay, to stick, to be hindered.

ਅਟਕਾ (aṭka) *n m* Stoppage, obstruction, delay, interruption, impediment, hinderance.

ਅਟਕਾਉਣਾ (aṭkaauṇaa) *v* To stop, obstruct, impede, retard, delay, interrupt.

ਅਟਾ-ਸਟਾ (aṭṭaa-saṭṭaa) *adv* Rough estimate.

ਅਟਾਰੀ (aṭaaree) *n f* Mansion, loft.

ਅਟੇਰਨਾ (aṭernaa) *v* To bring under control, to influence.

ਅੱਠ (aṭṭh) *a* eight.

ਅੱਠਤਰ (aṭhattar) *v* seventy-eight.

ਅਠਵੰਞਾ (aṭhvanjaa) *a* fifty-eight.

ਅਠਾਈ (aṭhaaee) *a* twenty-eight.

ਅਠਿਆਨੀ (aṭhiaanee) *n f* Eight anna coin, half rupee, fifty paisa coin.

ਅਡਣਾ (adṇaa) *v* To spread, to open.

ਅੰਡਾ (anḍaa) *n m* Egg.

ਅੱਡਾ (aḍḍaa) *n m* Stand, station, base, rendezvous; ~ਜਮਾਉਣਾ To settle down, to set up a base.

ਅੱਡਾਣਾ (aḍaaṇaa) *n m* Obstruction.

ਅੱਡੀ (aḍḍee) *n f* Heel, spur; ~ਨਾ ਲਾਉਣਾ To take no rest, not to pause.

ਅਡੋਲ (adol) *a* Steady, unshaken, immovable.

ਅਣਹੋਣੀ (aṇhonee) *a* Impossible, unfamiliar, improbable.

ਅਣਖ (aṇakkh) *n* Self-respect, self honour.

ਅਣਗਿਣਤ (aṇgiṇat) *a* Innumberable, countless.

ਅਣਚਾਹਿਆ (aṇchahiyaa) *a* Undesired, unwanted.

ਅਣਛਪਿਆ (aṇchhapiyaa) *a* Unpublished, unprinted.

ਅਣਡਿਠ (aṇḍiṭh) *a* Unseen.

ਅਣਬਣ (aṇbaṇ) *n f* Discord, quarrel.

ਅਣਮੋਲ (aṇmol) *a* Precious invaluable, priceless.

ਅਨ-ਵਿਆਹਿਆ (anviaahiaa) *n a m* Bachelor; Unmarried.

ਅਣੂ (anoo) *n m* Molecule, smallest particle.

ਅੱਤ (att) *a* Too much, very, excess.

ਅੰਤਮ (antam) *a* Last.

ਅੰਤਰ (antar) *n a Prep m* Difference, Spacing, contrast; Internal, inner; Between, amongst; ~ਸੂਝ Intuition; ~ਧਿਆਨ Lost in meditation, invisible; ~ਬੋਧ Inner knowledge, self realisation, intuition.

ਅੰਤਰਜਾਮੀ (antarjaamee) *n m* The supreme spirit; Omniscient.

ਅਤਰ (attar) *n m* Scent, perfume, essence, otto; ~ਦਾਨੀ Perfumebox.

ਅੰਤਰਰਾਸ਼ਟਰੀ (antarraashtree) *a* International.

ਅੰਤਰਾ (antraa) *n* Part of a song or hymn.

ਅਤਾ-ਪਤਾ (ataa-pataa) *n m* Whereabouts, information.

ਅਤਿਵਾਦ (ativaad) *n m* Terrorism.

ਅਤੇ (ate) *Prop* And, as well as.

ਅੱਥਰੂ (atthroo) *n m* Tear.

ਅਦਨਾ (adnaa) *a* Small, poor, inferior.

ਅਦਬ (adab) *n m* (1) Respect, civility; (2) Literature.

ਅਦਬੀ (adbee) *a* Literary.

ਅਦਰਕ (adarak) *n f* Ginger.

ਅੰਦਰ (andar) *n adv m* Inside, interior room, in, inside, within; ~ਅੰਦਰ Internally, mentally; ~ਖਾਤੇ Secretly, confidentially; ~ਖਾਨੇ/ਗਤੀ Surreptitously, clandestinely, under the table.

ਅੰਦਰੋ-ਅੰਦਰ (andro-andar) *adv* Secretly, internally.

ਅੰਦਰਲਾ (andarlaa) *a n m* Internal, interior, inner, intrinsic; Mind.

ਅਦਲ (adal) *n* Justice, equity; ~ਬਦਲ Exchange, alteration.

ਅਦਾ (adaa) *n f* Grace, beauty; Coquetry, gesture, expression; ~ਕਾਰ Actor, performer; ~ਕਾਰੀ Acting, performance.

ਅੰਦਾਜ਼ (andaaz) *n m* Style, manners, mode.

ਅੰਦਾਜ਼ਨ (andaazan) *adv* Approximately, nearly, roughly.

ਅੰਦਾਜ਼ਾ (andaazaa) *n m* Guess, estimate.

ਅਦਾਰਾ (adaaraa) *n m* Institution.

ਅਦਾਲਤ (adaalat) *n f* Court, tribunal.

ਅਦਾਲਤੀ (adaaltee) *a* Judicial, pertaining to court.

ਅਦਾਵਤ (adaavat) *n* Enmity, hostility.

ਅੰਦੇਸ਼ਾ (andeshaa) *n m* Apprehension, fear, scare.

ਅੱਧ (addh) *prop* Half; ~ਪਕਾ Half

baked, semi-ripe; ~ਰੰਗ Paralysis, hemiplegia.

ਅੰਧਰਾਤਾ (andhrata) Night blindness.

ਅੱਧਾ (addhaa) *a* Half.

ਅਧਾਨ (adhaan) *n* Pregnancy, conception.

ਅੰਧਾ (andhaa) *a* Blind, rash; ~ਧੁੰਦ Blindly, rashly, excessively, unwittingly. Also ਅੰਨ੍ਹਾ

ਅੰਧਾਰ (andhaar) *n m* Gloom, anarchy.

ਅਧਿਅਕਸ਼ (adhiyaksh) *n m* Head, president, chairman.

ਅਧਿਆਇ (adhiyae) *n m* Chapter, portion.

ਅਧਿਆਪਕ (adhiyaapak) *n m* Teacher, tutor, instructor, professor, educator, pedagogue, percepter.

ਅਧਿਆਪਨ (adhiyaapan) *n m* Teaching.

ਅੰਧਿਆਰਾ (andhıyaraa) *n m* Darkness, obscurity.

ਅਧਿਐਨ (adhiyan) *n m* Study, learning, perusal.

ਅਧਿਕਾਰ (adhikaar) *n m* Right, authority, privilege, title, power, claim.

ਅਧਿਕਾਰੀ (adhikaaree) *n m* Officer, authority, entitled.

ਅਧੀਨ (adheen) *a n f* Dependent; Slave, servant, ~ਗੀ Subordination, submission, humility, meekness.

ਅਧੀਰਾਜ (adheeraj) *n m* Emperor, ruler, sovereign.

ਅਧੂਰਾ (adhooraa) *a* Incomplete, unfinished, half-done; ~ਪਣ Incompletion.

ਅੱਧੋ-ਅੱਧ (addho-addh) *n m* Half and half, fifty-fifty.

ਅੰਨ (ann) *n m* Grain, corn, food; ~ਦਾਤਾ God, farmer.

ਅਨਸਰ (ansar) *n m* Element.

ਅਨਹੋਣਾ (anhoṇaa) *a* Impossible, improbable, unpromising.

ਅਨਘੜ (anaghaṛ) *a* Crude, rough, uncivilised, primitive, unchiselled.

ਅਨਜਾਣ (Anajaaṇ) *a n m* Innocent, unknown, unacquainted, ignorant; Stranger.

ਅਨੰਦ (anand) *n m* Pleasure, joy, happiness, delight, tranquility, comfort, ~ਕਾਰਜ Marriage ceremony.

ਅਨਪੜ੍ਹ (anapaḍh) *a* Uneducated, illiterate; ~ਤਾ Illiteracy.

ਅਨਾਜ (anaaj) *n m* Grain, corn.

ਅਨਾਥ (anaath) *a* Orphan, destitute, desolate, poor, unprotected.

ਅਨਾਦ/ਅਨਾਦੀ (anaad/anaadee) *a* Eternal, uncreated, ever existant; God.

ਅਨਾਦਰ (anaadar) *n m* Insult, disrespect, irreverence.

ਅਨਾਨਾਸ (anaanaas) *n m* Pine apple.

ਅਨਾਰ (anaar) *n m* Pomegranate.

ਅਨਾੜੀ (Anaaree) *a n m* Inexpert, clumsy, unskilled, artless; Simpleton, novice.

ਅਨੁਸ਼ਾਸਨ (anushaasan) *n m* Discipline.

ਅਨੁਸੂਚੀ (anusoochee) *n f* Schedule.

ਅਨੁਦਾਨ (anudaan) *n m* Grant, subsidy.

ਅਨੁਪਾਤ (Anupaat) *n m* Ratio, proportion.

ਅਨੁਪੂਰਕ (Anupoorak) *a* Suplementary.

ਅਨੁਭਵ (anubhav) *n m* Feeling, perception, sensation, experience, cognition.

ਅਨੁਯਾਈ (anuyaaee) *n m* Follower, disciple, adherent.

ਅਨੁਵਾਦ (anuvaad) *n m* Translation, interpretation, adaptation.

ਅਨੁਵਾਦਕ (anuvaadak) *n m* Translator, interpreter.

ਅੰਨ੍ਹਾ (annaa) *n m a* Blindman; Blind; ਅਕਲ ਦਾ~ Fool; ~ਦੀਵਾ Dimlight; (ਅੰਨ੍ਹਾ)~ਧੁੰਦ Recklessly, indiscreatly, at random, indiscriminately.

ਅੰਨ੍ਹੇਰ (anner) *n m* Injustice, tyranny, darkness; ~ਗਰਦੀ Anarchy, lawlessness, mismanagement.

ਅੰਨ੍ਹੇਵਾਹ (annevaah) *adv* Blindly, rashly recklessly, slapdash.

ਅਪੰਗ (apang) *a* Crippled, disabled, handicapped.

ਅਪਜਸ (apjas) *n m* Infame, notoriety, ignominy, ill fame, ill repute, defamation, slander, calumny.

ਅਪਣੱਤ (apaṇatt) *n* Intimacy, familiarity, affection, attachment.

ਅਪਣਾ (apṇaa) *a* Own. Also **ਆਪਣਾ**

ਅਪਣਾਉਣਾ (apṇaauṇaa) *v* To own, to declare or claim as one's own, to acknowledge, to adopt, to espouse.

ਅਪਮਾਨ (apmaan) *n m* Insult, dishonour, disrespect, slur; ~ਕਰਨਾ To insult, to disgrace, to stigmatise.

ਅਪ੍ਰਵਾਨ (apravaan) *a* Unapproved, unacceptable.

ਅਪਰਾਧ (apraadh) *n m* Crime, offence, sin, transgression, fault.

ਅਪਰਾਧੀ (apraadhee) *a m* Criminal, offender, guilty, delinquent.

ਅਪਵਾਦ (apvaad) *n m* Exception, reproach.

ਅਪਵਿਤਰ (apvitar) *a* Impure, unholy, defiled.

ਅੱਪੜ (appaṛ) *a n v* Fallow; Uncultivated land; Reach

(Imperative).

ਅਪੜਨਾ (aparnaa) *v* To arrive, to reach, to approach.

ਅਪੁੱਠਾ (aputthaa) *a* Perverse, backwards, upside down.

ਅਫਸਰ (afsar) *n m* Officer, boss.

ਅਫਸਾਨਾ (afsaanaa) *n m* Fiction, story, tale; ~ਨਵੀਸ Fiction writer.

ਅਫਸੋਸ (afsos) *n m* Sorrow, regret; ~ਨਾਕ Deplorable.

ਅਫਰਾ (aphraa) *n m* Flatulence, bloat, bloating. Also ਅਫਾਰਾ

ਅਫਰਾ-ਤਫਰੀ (afraa-tafree) *n f* Stampede.

ਅਫਲਾਤੂਨ (aflatoon) *n m* Plato (the philospher); A clever person.

ਅਫਲਾਤੂਨੀ (aflatoonee) *a* Platonic; clever, smart.

ਅਫਵਾਹ (afvaah) *n f* Rumour, hearsay, unverified statement.

ਅਫੀਮ (afeem) *n f* Opium.

ਅਫੀਮੀ (afeemee) *a n* Opium eater or addict; Lazy or whimsical person.

ਅੰਬ (amb) *n m* Mango.

ਅੰਬਰ (ambar) *n m* Cloud, sky.

ਅੰਬੜੀ (ambaree) *n f* Mamma, mother.

ਅੰਬਣਾ (ambnaa) *v* To get tried, fatigued, exhausted; (for a limb or muscle) To get numb.

ਅੱਬਾ (abbaa) *n m* Father.

ਅਬਾਦੀ (abbadee) *n f* Population, habitation, census.

ਅੰਬਾਰ (ambaar) *n m* Heap, stock, multitude, lump.

ਅਬੁਝ (aboojh) *a* Subtle, unintelligible, unwise.

ਅਭੰਗ (abhang) *a* Indivisible, unbroken, unimpaired.

ਅਭਾਗਾ (abhaagaa) *a* Unlucky, unfortunate, miserable.

ਅਭਿਆਸ (abhiyaas) *n m* Practice, exercise, training, rehearsal.

ਅਭਿੰਨ (abhinn) *a* Integral, indistinguishable, similar.

ਅਭਿਨੇਤਾ (abhinetaa) *n m* Actor.

ਅਭਿਨੇਤਰੀ (abinetree) *n f* Actress.

ਅਭਿਮਾਨ (abhimaan) *n m* Pride, arrogance, haughtiness, vanity, ego.

ਅਭਿਲਾਖਾ (abhilaakhaa) *n f* Desire, wish, craving.

ਅਮਨ (aman) *n m* Peace, tranquility.

ਅਮਰ (amar) *a* Eternal, immortal, undying.

ਅਮਲ (amal) *n m* Action, conduct, habit; ~ਕਰਨਾ To act upon, to carry out, to execute, to follow; ~ਵਿਚ ਲਿਆਉਣਾ To implement; To put into practice.

ਅਮਲਾ (amlaa) *n m* Subordinate staff,

personal staff.

ਅੰਮਾ (ammaa) *n f* Mother; ~ਜਾਏ Brothers.

ਅਮਾਨਤ (amaanat) *n m* Trust, deposit, faith; ~ਦਾਰ Trustee; Trust worthy ~ਵਿਚ ਖ਼ਿਆਨਤ Breach of trust; ~ਨਾਮਾ Trust deed.

ਅਮਾਨਤੀ (amaantee) *a* Keeper of safe deposits, trustee.

ਅਮਾਮ (amaam) *n m* Priest, spiritual guide, successor of prophet mohammad.

ਅਮੀਰ (ameer) *n a m* Chief, nobleman; Rich.

ਅਮੋਲ (amol) *a* Precious, invaluable.

ਅੰਮ੍ਰਿਤ (ammrit) *n m* Nectar, ambrosia, panacea, holywater, water of life baptism or initiation ceremony; ~ਛਕਣਾ To undergo initiation ceremony of the Khalsa; ~ਧਾਰੀ duly baptised (Sikh).

ਅੱਯਾਸ਼ (ayyaash) *n a* Voluptuary, debauch, lewd.

ਅੱਯਾਸ਼ੀ (ayyaashee) *n a f* Profigacy, dissipation, pleasure-seeking, love of pleasure, voluptuousness, voluptuosity, dissoluteness.

ਅਰਸ਼ (arash) *n m* Sky, heaven; God's abode.

ਅਰਸਾ (arsaa) *n m* Duration, period, span of time, time-span.

ਅਰਕ (arak) *n* Distilled product, distillated, extract; ~ਕਢਣਾ To distil; To cause to perspire, to tire out; ~ਦਾਨੀ Fancy container for ~ਅਰਕ for perfumes.

ਅਰਜ਼ (araz) *n f* request, supplication, solicitation, petition, appeal, entreaty; ~ਕਰਨੀ To make a request, to request, to supplicate, to petition, to appeal, to entreat; Petitioner, supplicant.

ਅਰਜ਼ੀ (arzee) *n f* Written request, application; Petition, representation.

ਅਰਜ਼ੀਨਵੀਸ (arzeenavees) *n m* Petition writer, writer of petitions and other legal documents or private accounts, scribe.

ਅਰਜ਼ੀਨਵੀਸੀ (arzeenaveesee) *n f* Profession or art of writing petitions.

ਅਰਥ (arath) *n m* Meaning, purpose, intention, interpretation; Finance; ~ਵਿਗਿਆਨ Semantics; ~ਸ਼ਾਸਤਰ Economics.

ਅਰਥੀ (arthee) *n f* Bier, hearse.

ਅਰਦਲੀ (ardlee) *n m* Orderly, attendant, peon.

ਅਰਦਾਸ (ardaas) *n f* Prayer, request, supplication, offering to a deity.

ਅਰਬ (arab) *a n* A thousand million;

ਅਰਮਾਨ (armaan) *n m* Desire, longing, aspiration; Sorrow.

ਅਰੜਾਉਣਾ (arṛaauṇaa) *v* To cry hoarsely or at the highest pitch, to blubber; (of cattle) To low, to moo.

ਅਰਾਧਨਾ (araadhnaa) *n f* Worship, prayer.

ਅਰਾਮ (araam) *n m* Rest, comfort, ease; ~ਤਲਬ or ਪਰਸਤ Lazy, ease lovings, idolent; ~ਪਰਸਤੀ Indolence, sloth, laziness.

ਅਲਸਾਉਣਾ (alsaauṇaa) *v* To dose, to relax, to laze.

ਅਲੜ (allaṛ) *a* Immature, childish, foolish, young.

ਅਲਖ (alakh) *n f* Invocation.

ਅਲਜ਼ਾਮ (alzaam) *n m* Blame, censure, accusation.

ਅਲਬੇਲਾ (albelaa) *a* Carefree, jaunty, bonny.

ਅਲਮਸਤ (almast) *adv* Carefree.

ਅਲਮ-ਗਲਮ (alam-glam) *n m* Knickknack, miscellaneous articles.

ਅਲਮਾਰੀ (almaaree) *n f* Almirah, bookshelf.

ਅੱਲਾ (allaa) *n m* God.

ਅਲਾਉਣਾ (alaauṇaa) *v* To say, to speak out.

ਅਲਾਪ (alaap) *n m* Talk, dialogue, conversation, song.

ਅਲਾਪਣਾ (alaapṇaa) *v* To speak out, to say, to sing.

ਅਲਾਮਤ (alaamat) *n f* Sign, indication, symptom, characteristic.

ਅਲਾਲਤ (alaalat) *n f* Disease, ailment, indisposition, sickness.

ਅਲੂੰਆ (alloonaa) *a* (lit hairless), young, unfledged, tender, adolescent, immature.

ਅਲੂਣਾ (alloonaa) *a* Without salt, unsalted, tasteless.

ਅਲੋਚਕ (alochak) *n m* Critic, reviewer.

ਅਲੋਚਨਾ (alochnaa) *n f* Criticism, review, critique.

ਅਵਤਾਰ (avtaar) *n m* Incarmation.

ਅਵਤਾਰੀ (avtaaree) *n m* Incarnated, superhuman.

ਅੱਵਲ (avval) *a* First, topmost, foremost, principal.

ਅਵਾਈ (avaaee) *n f* Rumour, hearsay

ਅਵਾਜ਼ (avaaz) *n f* Sound, voice.

ਅਵਾਮ (avaam) *n m* People, masses.

ਅਵਾਰਗੀ (avaargee) *n f* vagrancy, vagabondage, wandering.

ਅਵਾਰਾ (avaaraa) *a* Vagrant, vegabond, loafer, errant; ~ਪਨ Vagabondage. Also ਆਵਾਰਾ

ਅਵੇਰ (aver) *n f* Delay, lateness.

ਅੜ (aṛ) *n f* Stubbornness,

obstinacy, obdurateness.

ਅੜੰਗਾ (aṛangaa) *n m* Obstacle, entanglement; Difficult or problematic situation; **~ਪਾਉਣਾ** To make things difficult, to create problems, to oppose; **~ਪੈਣਾ** Difficult situation arisen or be created.

ਅੜਚਨ (aṛachan) *n f* Difficulty, obstruction, problem.

ਅੜਨਾ (aṛnaa) *v* To stop, to resist, to baulk on.

ਅੜੀਅਲ (aṛiyal) *a* Stubborn, inflexible, mulish.

ਆਂ (aan) *n m* Mucus.

ਆਇਆ (aaiyaa) *n* Maid servant.

ਆਸ (aas) *n f* Hope, trust, faith, expectation, longing, reliance.

ਆਸ਼ਕ (aashak) *n m* Lover, sweet heart, paramour.

ਆਸਣ (aasaṇ) *n m* Seat, place, yogic posture; **~ਉਖੜਨਾ** To be thrown out of gear, to be dislodged; **~ਡੋਲਣਾ** Seat or throne to be shaky, to get panicky.

ਆਸਤੀਨ (aasteen) *n f* Sleeve; **~ਚੜ੍ਹਾਉਣੀ** To threaten, to get ready (to fight); **~ਦਾ ਸੱਪ** Serpent in the bosom, a foe in the guise of a friend.

ਆਸ਼ਨਾ (aashnaa) *n f* Friend, lover, acquaintance.

ਆਸ਼ਨਾਈ (aashnaaee) *n f* Love affairs, courtship, friendship.

ਆਸਰਾ (aasraa) *n m* Protection, Dependence, backing, hope.

ਆਸਾਨ (aasaan) *a* Easy, convenient, light.

ਆਸਾਰ (aasaar) *n m* Sign, traces, symptoms, indications, effects.

ਆਸ਼ਿਆਨਾ (aashiaanaa) *n m* Nest, resting place.

ਆਹ (aah) *n f* Sigh.

ਆਹਰ (aahar) *n m* Impulse, enthusiasm, zeal, occupation, activity.

ਆਹਲਕ (aahlak) *n m* Laziness, sloth, sluggishness, indolence.

ਆਹੜਤ (aaharat) *n f* Commission, brokerage.

ਆਹੜਤੀ (aaharatee) *n m* Commision agent, broker.

ਆਹੋ (aaho) *adv* Yes.

ਆਕੜ (aakaṛ) *n f* Haughtiness, arrogance, stiffness, pride, coquetry.

ਆਕੜਨਾ (aakaṛnaa) *v* To stiffen, to become starchy or stiff; To be proud, arrogant, supercilious, overbearing, haughty; To behave in a haughty manner, to take airs.

ਆਕਾ (aakaa) *n m* master, employer.

ਆਕੀ (aakee) *a* Rebel, defiant, disobedient, recalcitrant.

ਆਖਣਾ (aakhnaa) *v* To say, to tell, to ask; ਰੋਟੀ~ To invite to lunch or dinner.

ਆਖਰ (aakhar) *n adv* The end, limit; In or at the end, at last, ultimately.

ਆਖਰੀ (aakhree) *a* Last, ultimate, final, decisive.

ਆਂਗਣ (aangan) *n m* Compound, courtyard.

ਆਗਤ (aagat) *n f* Arrival, income, proceeds.

ਆਗਿਆ (aagiaa) *n f* Permission, order, command, instruction; ~ਕਰਨੀ To order, to command; ~ਦੇਣੀ To permit, to sanction, to approve; ~ਵਿਚ ਰਹਿਣਾ To be loyal, obedient, subservient.

ਆਗੂ (aagoo) *n m* Leader, guide, captain, forerunner.

ਆਚਰਨ (aacharan) *n m* Conduct, character, behaviour, demeanour, practice, custom.

ਆਚਾਰੀਆ (aachaariyaa) *n* Professor; A religious orator.

ਆਜਜ਼ (aajaz) *a* Helpless, humble, incapable.

ਆਟਾ (aataa) *n m* Flour.

ਆਡ (aad) *a* Channel, water-channel.

ਆਂਢ (aandh) *n* Knot; Joint, relation, connection.

ਆਂਢ-ਗੁਆਂਢ (aandh-guaandh) *n m* Neighbourhood, surrounding, vicnity, environment.

ਆਤਸ਼ (aatash) *n* Fire, flame; ~ਬਾਜ਼ੀ Firework, pyrotechmy; ~ਮਜ਼ਾਜ Hot tempered.

ਆਤੰਕ (aatank) *n m* Terror; ~ਵਾਦ Terrorism.

ਆਤਮ (aatam) *n* Self, life; ~ਸੰਘਰਸ਼ Self struggle; ~ਹਤਿਆ/ਘਾਤ Suicide; ~ਕਥਾ Autobiography.

ਆਤਮਾ (aatmaa) *n f* The soul, spirit.

ਆਦਤ (aadat) *n f* Habit, nature, characteristic.

ਆਦਮ (aadam) *n m* Adam, man, mankind, the first man; ~ਖੋਰ Maneater, connibal.

ਆਦਮੀ (aadmee) *n m* Man, Person.

ਆਦਮੀਅਤ (aadmeeyat) *n f* Humanity, civility, good breeding.

ਆਂਦਰ (aandar) *n f* Intestine.

ਆਦਰ (aadar) *n m* Respect, honour.

ਆਦਰਸ਼ (aadarsh) *n m* Ideal, model, standard, goal, aim.

ਆਦਲ (addal) *a* Accustomed habituated.

ਆਦੀ (aadee) *a* Accustomed, habituated.

ਆਨ (aan) *n f* Honour, grace, dignity; ~ਸ਼ਾਨ Glory, splendour, grandeur, pomp, lustre; ~ਬਾਨ Grandeur, pomp and show.

ਆਨਾ (aanaa) *n m* Eyeball; Anna (a coin) sixteenth part of a rupee.

ਆਨਾ-ਕਾਨੀ (aanaa-kaanee) *n f* Deliberate delay, neglact or refusal, procrastination, finding, excuses, avoidance.

ਆਪੱਤੀ (aappatee) *n f* Objection, catastrophe; ~ਜਨਕ Objectionable.

ਆਪਾ (aapaa) *n m* Selfhood, one's own existence, one's own self; ~ਖੋਣਾ To lose consciousness of one's self, to become abnormal; ~ਧਾਪੀ Race for promotion, personal anxiety or interest.

ਆਪੇ (aape) *adv* Automatically; ~ਤੋਂ ਬਾਹਰ ਹੋਣਾ To be in fury, to lose senses, to lose self control.

ਆਫ਼ਤ (aafat) *n f* Calamity, misfortune, disaster, misery.

ਆਫਰਨਾ (aapharnaa) *v* To swell out, to boast, to be gorged, to swagger.

ਆਬ (aab) *n* Water, lustre.

ਆਬਸ਼ਾਰ (aabshaar) *n* Waterfall, cascade.

ਆਬਕਾਰੀ (aabkaaree) *n f* Excise, distillery.

ਆਬਰੂ (aabroo) *n f* Honour, character.

ਆਬੋਹਵਾ (aabo-hawaa) *n f* Climate.

ਆਮ (aam) *a* Common, general, ordinary, undistinguished; Plenty, abundant, plentiful, easily available, frequent.

ਆਮਦ (aamad) *n f* Arrival.

ਆਮਦਨ (aamdan) *n f* Income; Profit. Also ਆਮਦਨੀ.

ਆਯਾਤ (aayaat) *n m* Imports.

ਆਰਸੀ (aarsee) *n m* Looking glass, mirror set in a ring.

ਆਰਜ਼ੀ (aarzee) *a* Temporary, provisional.

ਆਰਜ਼ੂ (aarzoo) *n f* Desire, wish, expectation, hope, longing, yearning, aspiration.

ਆਰਾ (aaraa) *n m* Pit-saw, lumberman's saw, sawing machine, sawmill, lumber mill.

ਆਰੀ (aaree) *n f* Small hand saw.

ਆਲਸੀ (aalsee) *a* Idle, lazy, sluggish, lethargic.

ਆਲ੍ਹਣਾ (aalhṇaa) *n m* Nest.

ਆਲਮ (aalam) *n m* State, condition, universe, world; A learned scholar.

ਆਲਾ (aalaa) *n* Asylum, abode.

ਆਲੀਸ਼ਾਨ (aaleeshaan) *a* Splendid, magnificent.

ਆਲੂ (aaloo) *n m* Potato.

ਆਵਾ (aavaa) *n m* Kiln, brick kiln.

ਆਵਾ-ਜਾਈ (aavaa jaaee) *n f* Traffic, frequenting transport and communication.

ਆੜ (aar) *n f* Shelter, curtain, hindrance, wall, screen.

ਆੜ੍ਹਤ (aarhat) *n f* Brokerage, agency, commission.

ਆੜੀ (aaree) *n m* Friend, companion teammate.

ਐਸ਼ (aesh) *n f* Pleasure, luxury, delight; ~ ਪਰਸਤ, ~ਪੱਠਾ Enjoyment, loving, pleasure, voluptuous, prifilgate.

ਐਂਠ (aenth) *n f* Uppishness, arrogance, presumptuousness.

ਐਤਵਾਰ (aetwaar) *n m* Sunday.

ਐਥੇ (aethe) *adv* Here, at this place.

ਐਥੋਂ (aethon) *adv* From here.

ਐਨਾ (aenaa) *a adv* This much, so much.

ਐਬ (aeb) *n m* Defect, vice, fault drawback.

ਐਰਾ-ਗੈਰਾ (aeraa-gaeraa) *n m* Stranger, alien.

ਐਲਾਨ (aelaan) *n m* Announcement, proclamation.

ਐਵੇਂ (aiven) *a* Gratis, by the way; Free of cost.

ਔਸਤ (ausat) *n f* Average, mean; ~ਨ On the average.

ਔਸਰ (ausar) *n m* Opportunity, occasion, time.

ਔਕੜ (aukar) *n* Difficulty, dilemma.

ਔਂਕੜ (aunkar) *n* Short vowel or maatra indicated by (ੁ) and wirtten below a letter in Gurmukhi script.

ਔਖ (aukh) *n f* Difficulty, trouble, discomfort.

ਔਖਾ (aukhaa) *a* Difficult, arduous, uncomfortable.

ਔਘਟ (aughat) *n a* Crisis; Difficult, rugged, uneven, inaccessible.

ਔਜ਼ਾਰ (auzaar) *n m* Tool, instrument, implement.

ਔਤ (aut) *a* Issueless, childless. Also ਔਤਰਾ

ਔਥੇ (authe) *adv* There, at that place (pointing out); Also ਉਥੇ and ਓਥੇ

ਔਰਤ (aurat) *n f* Women, lady, female, wife.

ਔਲਾਦ (aulaad) *n f* Children, offspring, progeny generation.

ਔੜ (aur) *n f* Drought, scarcity, dearth, dire need.

ਔੜਾ (auraa) *n m* Obstacle, hitch.

ੲ

ੲ Third letter of Gurmukhi alphabets pronounced as eeṛee.

ਇਆਣਾ (iaaṇaa) *n m* Child, infant.

ਇਆਲੀ (iyaalee) *n m* Shepherd, goat herd.

ਇਸ਼ਕ (ishak) *n m* Love, passion, amour; **~ਮਿਜ਼ਾਜੀ** Carnal love, lust.

ਇਸ਼ਤਿਹਾਰ (ishitihaar) *n m* Poster, notice, advertisement, bill.

ਇਸਤਿਕਬਾਲ (istikbaal) *n m* Welcome.

ਇਸਤ੍ਰੀ (istree) *n f* Women, female, wife; Smoothing iron.

ਇਸਥਿਰ (isthir) *a* Still, motionless, unmoving.

ਇਸਰਾਰ (israar) *n m* Insistance.

ਇਸ਼ਾਰਾ (ishaaraa) *n m* Sign, hint, mark; **~ਕਰਨਾ** To point out, to indicate.

ਇਹਸਾਨ (ehesaan) *n m* Favour, obligation, courtesy, kindness; **~ਮੰਦ** Grateful, thankful, obliged.

ਇਹਤਿਆਤ (ehetiaat) *n m* Precaution, care; **~ਨ** As a precaution, cautiously.

ਇਹਾਤਾ (ihaataa) *n m* Compound, campus.

ਇੱਕ (ik) *a pref adv* One, a, an, united; Signifying unity, uniformity or continuity; Uniformly, constantly, continuously, consistently; **~ਸਾਰ** Continuously, uninterruptedly, in the same breath; **~ਸਾਰ** Uniform, similar, throughout constant, continuous; **~ਸੁਰ** In unison, harmonious, consonant; Of the same opinion, unanimous, united; **~ਕਰਨਾ** To unite, unify, bring together; To combine, to mix, to amalgamate, to integrate; **~ਜੁਟ** United; **~ਤਰਫ਼ਾ** One-sided, partial; Ex parte; **~ਦਮ** One breath; At once, immediately, instantly, forthwith; Suddenly, all at once; **~ਮਿੱਕ** Completely united, closely mixed, indistinguishable.

ਇੱਕਠ (ikaṭh) *n m* Unity, harmony, harmoniousness; Assembly, assemblage, gathering, meeting; Funeral feast and congregation *usually* held after the death of old heads of families.

ਇਕੱਠਾ (ikaṭhaa) *a adv* Collected,

united, amass, collectively.

ਇਕਤੰਤਰ (ikatantar) *n m* Monocracy.

ਇਕਬਾਲ (ikbaal) *n m* Greatness, eminence, dignity; Confession.

ਇਕਰਾਰ (ikraar) *n m* Agreement, assurance, undertaking, commitment; Promise; ~**ਨਾਮਾ** Agreement, contract.

ਇਕਲਾ (ikalaa) *a* Alone, single, one only, single-handed, unaided or unaccompanied, all by oneself.

ਇਕਲੌਤਾ (iklautaa) *a* Only, lonely, solitary.

ਇਕਾਸੀ (ikaasee) *a* Eighty-one.

ਇਕਾ-ਦੁਕਾ (ikaa-dukaa) *a* A few, rare, sporadic.

ਇਕਾਨਵਾਂ (ikaanvaan) *a* Ninety-first.

ਇਕੀ (ikee) *a* Twenty-one.

ਇੱਕੋ (ikko) *a* Only one; ~**ਇੱਕ** The only, the only one; ~**ਜਿਹਾ** Similar, identical, alike.

ਇਖ਼ਤਿਆਰ (ikhtiaar) *n m* Authority discretion, choice, right.

ਇਖ਼ਲਾਕ (ikhlaak) *n m* Manners, morality, ethics.

ਇਜ਼ਤ (izat) *n f* Honour, dignity, glory, grandeur, respect, esteem; ~**ਦਾਰ** Respectable, honourable.

ਇਜਾਜ਼ਤ (ijaazat) *n f* Permission.

ਇਜਾਰਾ (ijaaraa) *n m* Lease, monopoly.

ਇੱਟ (itt) *n f* Brick; ~**ਘੜੇ ਦਾ ਵੈਰ** Arch enmity; ~**ਨਾਲ ਇੱਟ ਵਜਾਉਣੀ** To raze to the ground, to bring ruination.

ਇਤਹਾਦ (ithaad) *n m* Unity, alliance.

ਇੰਤਕਾਮ (intkaam) *n m* Revenge.

ਇੰਤਕਾਲ (intkaal) *n m* Death.

ਇੰਤਖ਼ਾਬ (intkhaab) *n m* Selection.

ਇੰਤਜ਼ਾਮ (intzaam) *n m* Arrangement, management, order.

ਇੰਤਜ਼ਾਮੀਆ (intzaamia) *a* Executive, administrative, managerial; Executive committee, management, managing committee.

ਇੰਤਜ਼ਾਰ (intzaar) *n f* Waiting, expectation, looking for.

ਇਤਫ਼ਾਕੀਆ (itfaakiaa) *a* Accidentical, by chance, casual.

ਇਤਬਾਰ (itbaar) *n m* Reliance, trust, confidence.

ਇਤਮੀਨਾਨ (itminaan) *n m* Satisfaction.

ਇਤਰਾਜ਼ (itraaz) *n m* Objection, point of order.

ਇਤਲਾਹ (itlaah) *n f* Information, intimation, report; ~**ਕਰਨੀ/ਦੇਣੀ** To intimate to inform; ~**ਨਾਮਾ** Written information.

ਇਤਿਹਾਸ (itihaas) *n m* History, chronicle, annals, tradition; ~**ਕਾਰ** Historian; Chronicler.

ਇਤਹਾਦ (itihaad) *n m* Unity, union, alliance, coalition, concord, association.

ਇਤਹਾਦੀ (itahaadee) *n m a* Ally, confederate; Allied.

ਇੰਦਰੀ (indree) *n f* Generative organ.

ਇਨਸਾਨ (insaan) *n m* Man, mankind, humanbeing, mankind; A virtuous or cuetureo person.

ਇਨਸਾਨੀਅਤ (insaaniat) *n f* Humanness, humanity, human nature; Virtuousness, right conduct, propriety; Mankind.

ਇਨਸਾਫ਼ (insaaf) *n m* Justice, fairness, fairplay, impartiality; ~**ਪਸੰਦ** Impartial, lover of justice.

ਇਨਕਲਾਬ (inklaab) *n m* Revolution, change.

ਇਨਕਾਰ (inkaar) *n m* Refusal, denial, dissention, objection; ~**ਕਰਨਾ** To refuse, to deny, to disobey.

ਇੰਨਾ (innaa) *adv* So much, this much that.

ਇਨਾਇਤ (inaayit) *n f* Benevolence, generosity, grace.

ਇਨਾਮ (inaam) *n m* Prize, gift, reward.

ਇਬਾਦਤ (ibaadat) *n f* Prayer, worship, devotion.

ਇਮਤਿਹਾਨ (imtihaan) *n m* Examination, test, investigation, trial.

ਇਮਦਾਦ (imdaad) *n f* Help, assistance, aid, succour, support.

ਇਮਾਨ (imaan) *n m* Faith, belief. Also **ਈਮਾਨ**

ਇਮਾਰਤ (imaarat) *n f* Building.

ਇਰਾਦਾ (iraadaa) *n m* Intention, idea, purpose, mind.

ਇੱਲ (ill) *n f* Kite (a bird).

ਇਲਹਾਮ (ilhaam) *n m* Prophecy, revelation.

ਇਲਜ਼ਾਮ (ilzaam) *n m* Allegation, blame, charge.

ਇੱਲਤ (illat) *n f* Bad habit, mischief; ~**ਕਰਨੀ** To make mischief, to frolic; ~**ਪੈਣੀ** To develop a bad habit.

ਇਲਮ (ilam) *n m* Knowledge, education, learning, science; ~**ਹੋਣਾ** To have knowledge, to have information, to be aware of.

ਇਲਾਹੀ (ilhaahee) *a* Celestial, divine.

ਇਲਾਕਾ (ilaakaa) *n m* Area, territory, jurisdiction, ward; ~**ਈ** Territorial, regional.

ਇਲਾਜ (ilaaj) *n m* Treatment, remedy, cure.

ਇਲਾਨ (ilan) *n m* declaration, proclamation, announcement, promulgation; ~**ਕਰਨਾ** To declare, proclaim, announce, promulgate.

ਇਲਾਨੀਆ (ilaaniaa) *adv* Openly, publicly, by proclamation.

ਇਲਾਵਾ (ilava) *adv* Besides, in addition to, over and above.

ਇਵਜ (evaz) *n m* Return, exchange, replacement; ~**ਵਿੱਚ** In return for, in exchange, in place of, as a substitute.

ਇਵਜ਼ਾਨਾ (ivazana) *n m* compensation, recompense, reparation.

ਈਰਖਾ (eerkhaa) *n f* Jealousy, envy, malice, malevolence.

ਏਕਣ (aekaṇ) *adv* Like this.

ਏਕਮ (ekam) *n f* One, first (data).

ਏਕਾ (aekaa) *n m* Unity, one.

ਏਡਾ (eḍaa) *adv* So much, this much.

ਏਦੂੰ (edoon) *adv* Compared to this, from this.

ਏਲਚੀ (elchee) *n m* Ambassador, messenger of some empire or a country.

ਸ

ਸ Fourth letter of Gurmukhi alphabets, pronounced as sassa.
ਸ਼ਊਰ (shaoor) *n m* Etiquette.
ਸੱਸ (sass) *n f* Mother-in-law.
ਸੰਸਕ੍ਰਿਤੀ (sanskriti) *n f* Culture.
ਸੰਸਕਾਰ (sanskaar) *n m* Sacrament, rite, ceremony, (last rite); Refinement; Mental impression; There are sixteen Hindu ceremonies.
ਸਸਕਾਰ (saskaar) *n m* Cremation.
ਸ਼ਸਤਰ (shastar) *n m* Weapon, arms, instrument.
ਸਸਤਾ (sastaa) *a* Cheap, trivial, easy.
ਸੰਸਥਾ (sansthaa) *n f* Institution, organisation, concern.
ਸੰਸਥਾਨ (sansthaan) *n m* Institute, Institution.
ਸੰਸਦ (sansad) *n f* Parliament.
ਸੰਸਾ (sansaa) *n m* Doubt, fear, suspicion, uncertainty.
ਸੰਸਾਰ (sansaar) *n m* Universe, world.
ਸੰਸਾਰਿਕ (sansaarik) *a* Worldly, mundane, physical, temporal, pertaining to mundane existence.
ਸੰਸਾਰੀ (sansaaree) *a* Of this world, worldly, mortal (usually for person).

ਸ਼ਸ਼ੋਪੰਜ (shashopanj) *n m* Hesitation, indecision, perplexity, hesitancy.
ਸਹਾਇਤਾ (sahaayitaa) *n f* Assistance, help, aid, succour; **~ਕਰਨੀ** or **ਦੇਣੀ** To assist, to help, to support, to succour.
ਸ਼ਹਾਦਤ (shahaadat) *n f* Martyrdom; testimony, evidence.
ਸਹਾਈ (sahaaee) *a* (one) who provides help, assistance or support; conducive; **~ਹੋਣਾ** To go to one's help, to come to one's resuce, to be conducive to.
ਸਹਾਰਨਾ (sahaarnaa) *v* To endure, to bear, to suffer; To support, to hold, to sustain.
ਸਹਾਰਾ (sahaaraa) *n m* Support, assistance, help, shoulder, succour, aid.
ਸ਼ਹਿ (sheh) *n* Instigation, incitement.
ਸਹਿਆ (sahiaa) *n m* Rabbit, hare.
ਸਹਿਹੋਂਦ (saihond) *n* Coexistence, symbiosis.
ਸਹਿਕਣਾ (saihkaṇaa) *v* To long for, to wish to have.
ਸਹਿਕਰਮੀ (saihkarmee) *n m* Colleague, officemate.
ਸਹਿਕਾਰ (saihkaar) *n m* Cooperation,

collaboration. Also ਸਹਿਕਾਰਿਤਾ

ਸਹਿਕਾਲੀ (saihkaalee) *a* Contemporary, coeval.

ਸਹਿਗਾਣ (saihgaaṇ) *n* Chorus.

ਸਹਿਚਾਰਤਾ (saihchartaa) *n f* Association.

ਸਹਿਜ (Saihj) *a* Natural, native, cognate, easy.

ਸਹਿਣਾ (saihṇaa) *v* To bear, to endure, to suffer, to sustain.

ਸਹਿਣਸ਼ੀਲ (saihnsheel) *a* Tolerable, forbearing, endurable, moderate.

ਸਹਿਮਣਾ (saihmṇaa) *v* To be afraid, overawed; To wince, to finch to recoil.

ਸਹੀ (sahee) *n a m* Signature, attestation; Correct, accurate, right.

ਸ਼ਹੀਦ (shaheed) *n* Martyr.

ਸੰਹੁ (sanhu) *n f* Oath, vow, pledge, affirmation.

ਸਹੁਰ (sauhr) *n m* Husband.

ਸਹੁਰਾ (sauhraa) *n m* Father-in-law.

ਸਹੂਲਤ (sahoolat) *n f* Facility, ease.

ਸਹੇਲੀ (sahelee) *n f* Female friend of a lady or girl. Also ਸਹੇਲੜੀ

ਸਹੇੜਨਾ (saherṇaa) *v* To contract, to enter into relationship with; To acquire, to own, to adopt.

ਸੱਕ (sakk) *n m* Bark, peel, sliver, splinter, spill; Bark of a particular plant used, usually by women to clean teeth and mouth and as a cosmetic for colouring lips and gums.

ਸੰਕਟ (sankaṭ) *n m* Distress, crisis, agony, calamity, danger; ~ਕਾਲ Emergency; ~ਮਈ Dangerous, hazardous.

ਸਕੱਤਰ (sakatar) *n m* Secretary.

ਸੱਕਤਰੇਤ (sakatteret) *n m* Secretarial job or duties.

ਸ਼ਕਤੀ (shaktee) *n f* Power, strength, vigour, might, capacity, energy, potency, calibre, force.

ਸੰਕਰ (sankar) *a* Hybrid, integrade, crossbreed.

ਸ਼ੱਕਰ (shakkar) *n f* Sugar, rawsugar.

ਸ਼ਕਲ (shakal) *n f* Figure, shape, form face, appearance.

ਸੰਕਲਨ (sankalan) *n m* Compilation, collection, consolidation.

ਸ਼ੰਕਾ (shankaa) *n f* Doubt, suspicion, disbelief, suspense.

ਸਕਾਰਥ (sakaarath) *a* Purposeful, meaningful.

ਸਕਾਰਨਾ (sakaarna) *v* To accept, to approve, to endorse.

ਸਕਾਰਾ (sakaaraa) *n m* Commission (for encashment).

ਸ਼ੱਕੀ (shakkee) *a* Doubtful, sceptic.

ਸੰਕੀਰਨ (sankeeran) *a* Narrow, Parochial, complex; ~ਤਾ Narrowness, pettiness, meaness, complexity.

ਸਕੂਨ (sakoon) *n m* Peace; ~ਮਿਲਣਾ To have peace; To feel relieved.

ਸੰਕੇਤ (sanket) *n m* Sign, symbol, code, hint, suggestion; ~ਕਰਨਾ To point out, to hint, to allude.

ਸ਼ਖਸ (shakhs) *n m* Person, individual.

ਸੱਖਣਾ (sakhnaa) *a* Hollow, vacant, empty.

ਸਖਤ (sakhat) *a* Hard, harsh, stiff, rigid, cruel.

ਸਖਾਵਤ (sakhaawat) *n f* Generasity, munificance, charity.

ਸੰਖਿਆ (sankhiaa) *n f* Number, sum, calculation.

ਸਖੀ (sakhee) *a* Generous, liberal, bountiful.

ਸੰਖੇਪ (sankhep) *n a m* Abridgement, brevity, precis, resume, synopsis, abstract; brief, short, concise, extract.

ਸੰਗ (sang) *n m* Association, company, friendship.

ਸੰਗਤ (sangat) *n f* Company, association; Religious congregation; (math) Correspondence.

ਸੰਗਤਰਾ (sangtaraa) *n m* Orange, *Citrus aurantium, Citrus sinesis*.

ਸੰਗਠਨ (sangaṭhan) *n m* Organisation.

ਸੰਗਣਾ (sangnaa) *v* To feel shy, to hesitate, to be bashfull.

ਸੰਗਦਿਲ (sangdil) *a* Cruel.

ਸਗਨ (sagan) *n m* Presage, augury, portent; Gift in cash made to bride or bridegroom on the occasion of betrothal or marriage, or to a child on its birth; ~ਪਾਉਣਾ To give a monetary gift on an auspicious occassion.

ਸੰਗਮ (sangam) *n m* Junction, union, juncture, confluence.

ਸੰਗਲ (sangal) *n f* Chain, signal.

ਸਗਾਈ (sagaaee) *n f* Betrothal, engagement.

ਸ਼ਗਿਰਦ (shagird) *n m* Pupil, student.

ਸੰਗੀਤ (sangeet) *n m* Music.

ਸੰਗੀਨ (Sangeen) *a* Severe, serious, intense, heavy.

ਸੰਗ੍ਰਹਿ (sangreh) *n m* Collection, compilation.

ਸਗੋਂ (sagon) *adv conj* But, rather, on the contrary.

ਸੰਘ (sangh) *n m* (1) Throat, gullet; (2) Association, organisation, guild.

ਸੰਘਾਰ (sanghaar) *n m* Massacre, annihilation.

ਸੱਚ (Sachch) *n a m* Truth; Right; True.

ਸੱਚਾਈ (sachaaee) *n f* Truth, fact, sincerity, veracity. Also ਸਚਿਆਈ

ਸੰਚਾਰ (sanchaar) *n m* Communication, propagation, penetration.

ਸੰਚਾਲਕ (sanchaalak) *n m* Director, conductor.

ਸੱਜਣ (sajjaṇ) *n m* Virtuous man; Respectable person; Well wisher friend; Lover.

ਸੰਜਮ (sanjam) *n m* Restraint, discipline, soberness, brevity.

ਸੱਜਾ (Sajja) *a n f* Right; Decoration.

ਸਜ਼ਾ (sazaa) *n f* Punishment, penalty.

ਸਜਾਉਣਾ (sajaauṇaa) *v* To decorate, to adorn, to beautify, to embellish, to grace, to equip.

ਸਜਾਵਟ (sajaawaṭ) *n f* Decoration, Adornment, display, embellishment.

ਸੰਜੀਦਗੀ (sanjeedgee) *n f* Seriousness.

ਸੰਜੀਦਾ (sanjeedaa) *a* Serious, soleman.

ਸਜੀਲਾ (sajeelaa) *a* Handsome, beautiful, graceful, well-shaped.

ਸੱਜੂ (sajoo) *a* Right handed; Rightist.

ਸੰਜੋਗ (sanjog) *n m* Chance, opportunity, luck; Coherence, cohesion, event; Association.

ਸੰਝ (sanjh) *n f* Evening, sunset.

ਸੱਟ (saṭṭ) *n f* Stroke, hit, injury; ~ਮਾਰਨੀ or ਲਾਉਣੀ To strike, to whack, to blow.

ਸੱਟਾ (saṭṭaa) *n m* Speculation, business at stock exchange, forward dealing; Wild guess, bluff; Gambling; ~ਬਜ਼ਾਰ Stock exchange.

ਸੱਟੇਬਾਜ਼ (saṭṭebaaz) *n m* Speculator; bluff, bluffer.

ਸੱਟੇਬਾਜ਼ੀ (saṭṭebaazee) *n f* Speculation; Bluffing.

ਸੱਠ (saṭṭh) *a* sixty.

ਸੰਢਾ (sandhaa) *a* Stout, strong, robust; Bull.

ਸਤ (sat) *n m* Essence, juice, sap.

ਸੱਤ (satt) *a n* seven.

ਸੰਤ (sant) *n m* Saint, holy man, a pious or deeply religious person; An ascetic, mendicant; ~ਬਾਣੀ Utterances esp hymns of saints.

ਸਤਕਾਰ (satkaar) *n m* Respect, honour, reverence, hospitality, veneration, treatment.

ਸਤੱਰ (satarr) *n m* Standard, level, degree of excellence.

ਸਤਵੰਤ (satwant) *a* Virtuous.

ਸਤਾਉਣਾ (Sataauṇaa) *v* To tease, to torture, to harass, to oppress, to torment, to vex.

ਸਤਾਈ (sataee) *a* twenty-seven.

ਸੰਤਾਨ (santaan) *n m* Children, issue, offspring, progeny.

ਸ਼ਤਾਨ (shataan) *n m* Satan, devil.

ਸੰਤਾਪ (santaap) *n m* Distress, agony, sorrow, repentance, woe.

ਸ਼ਤਾਬੀ (shataabee) *adv* Quickly, hastily.

ਸਤਿਆ (satiaa) *a* Teased, vexed.

ਸੱਤਿਆ (sattiaa) *n m* Strength, power, truth, virtue.

ਸਤਿਆਨਾਸ (satiaanaas) *n m* Ruin, destruction.

ਸ਼ਤੀਰ (shateer) *n m* Beam, log, sleeper.

ਸੰਤੁਸ਼ਟੀ (santushṭee) *n m* Satisfaction, satiation.

ਸੰਤੋਖ (ਸੰਤੋਸ਼) (santokh/santosh) *n m* Satisfaction, contentment, patience, complacence, gratification, comfort.

ਸਥਾਪਨਾ (sthaapnaa) *n m* Installing, foundation, establishing.

ਸਦਕਾ (Sadkaa) *n m adv* Alm, secrifice; Due to, for the sake of, because of.

ਸੱਦਣਾ (sadnaa) *n m* To call, to invite.

ਸਦਮਾ (sadmaa) *n m* Shock, blow, trauma; Sorrow, grief, bereavement; ~ਪਹੁੰਚਣਾ To suffer shock or trauma; ~ਪਹੁੰਚਾਉਣਾ To cause, to shock.

ਸਦਰ (sadar) *n m* President, chairman, chairperson.

ਸਦਾ (sadaa) *adv* Always, perpetually, constantly.

ਸੱਦਾ (saddaa) *n m* Invitation, call.

ਸਦਾਕਤ (sadaakat) *n m* Truth.

ਸਦਾਰਤ (sdaarat) *n f* Presidentship, chairmanship, headship.

ਸਦਾਚਾਰ (sadaachaar) *n m* Virtue, morality, etiquette, conduct.

ਸੰਦੂਕੜੀ (sandookaṛee) *n f* Small box. Also ਸੰਦੂਕ

ਸੰਧੂਰ (sandoor) *n m* Vermillion, red lead; ~ਦਾਨੀ Casket for containing vermilion.

ਸਨਕ (sanak) *n f* Mania, fad, sneering.

ਸਨਕੀ (sankee) *a* Whimisical, capricious, eccentric, idiosyncratic, cranky; Daft, crazy; Cynic, cynical.

ਸਨਤ (sanat) *n m* Industry; ~ਕਾਰ industrialist.

ਸਨਤੀ (sanatee) *a* Industrial; ~ਕਰਨ industrialisation.

ਸਨਦ (sanad) *n m* Certificate, testimonial.

ਸਨਮ (sanam) *n m* Sweet heart, beloved; Statue.

ਸਨਮਾਨ (sanmaan) *n m* Honour,

respect.

ਸਨਮੁਖ (sanmukh) *adv* Before, in front of, facing.

ਸ਼ਨਾਖਤ (shanaakht) *n f* Indentification.

ਸੰਨਾਟਾ (sannaataa) *n m* Absolute silence, stillness, quiet.

ਸਨਾਤਨ (Sanaatan) *a* Ancient, eternal, classical, premedieval, traditional.

ਸੰਨਿਆਸ (sanniyaas) *n m* Asceticism, renunciation, monasticism.

ਸਨੇਹਾ (sanehaa) *n m* Message esp. oral communication, information; ~ਘੱਲਣਾ To send a message; ~ਦੇਣਾ To give or deliver a message.

ਸੱਪ (sapp) *n m* Snake, serpent, viper; ~ਸੁੰਘਣਾ To be rendered still.

ਸਪਰੇਟਾ (sapretaa) *n m* Skimmed milk.

ਸ਼ਪਾਸ਼ਪ (shapaashap) *adv* Quickly, hurriedly.

ਸੰਪਾਦਕ (sampaadak) *n m* Editor.

ਸੰਪਾਦਕੀ (Sampaadkee) *n f* Editorial.

ਸਪੋਲੀਆ (sapoliyaa) *n a m* Small snake, untrustworthy, dangerous.

ਸਫਰ (safar) *n m* Journey, travel.

ਸਫਾ (safaa) *n m* Page, leaf.

ਸਫਾਈਆ (saffaaiaa) *n m* Elimination, extinction, annihiliation, eradication.

ਸਫਾਈ (safaaee) *n f* Cleanliness, cleanness, hygiene, sanitation; Evidence or statement in defence esp. During a court case, defence, exculpation, vindication.

ਸਫਾਰਸ਼ (safaarash) *n f* Recommendation.

ਸਫਾਰਤ (safaarat) *n* Embassy, diplomatic mission; ~ਖ਼ਾਨਾ Embassy (building of office).

ਸਫੀਰ (safeer) *n m* Ambassador, envoy.

ਸਫੇਦ (safaid) *a* White, blank; ~ਝੂਠ Blatant lie, white lie.

ਸਫੇਦਾ (safaedaa) *n m* Eucalyptus, white paint in paste form, putty, white lead; Zinc oxide; Whitish variety of mango or of muskmelon.

ਸਫੇਦੀ (safaedee) *n f* Whiteness; White wash; White of egg.

ਸਬਕ (sabak) *n m* Lesson, lecture, moral.

ਸਬਜ਼ (sabaz) *a* Green fresh, verdant, unripe.

ਸ਼ਬਜ਼ੀ (saubzee) *n f* Vegetable, greenery, herbage.

ਸ਼ਬਦ (sabad) *n m* Sound, voice, religious hymn, word; ~ਜੋੜ

Spelling; ~ਕੋਸ਼ Dictionary.

ਸਬੱਬ (sabab) *n m* Reason, cause, excuse, ground, basis.

ਸਬਰ (sabar) *n m* Patience, contentment.

ਸ਼ਬਾਬ (shabaab) *n m* Youth.

ਸਬੀਲ (sabeel) *n m* plan, scheme.

ਸਬੂਤ (saboot) *n m* Evidence, proof.

ਸੰਭਲਣਾ (sambhalna) *v* To be alert, to be cautious.

ਸਭਾ (sabhaa) *n f* Association, assembly, society, convention, board, meeting.

ਸੰਭਾਲ (sambhaal) *n f* Care, control, upkeep, supervision.

ਸੰਭਾਲਣਾ (sambhaalnaa) *v* To protect, to nourish, to support, to retain, to sustain, to prop.

ਸਭਿਅਤਾ (sabhiyataa) *n f* Civilization, decency, politeness, etiquette.

ਸ਼ਮਸ਼ਾਨ (shamshaan) *n m* Cemetry, cremation ground.

ਸਮੱਸਿਆ (samasiyaa) *n f* Problem, dilemma.

ਸ਼ਮਸ਼ੀਰ (shamsheer) *n f* Sword.

ਸਮਝ (samajh) *n f* Understanding, comprehension, sense, knowledge; ~ਦਾਰ Intelligent, wise.

ਸਮਝਣਾ (samajhnaa) *v* To understand, to comprehend, to think, to suppose, to deem, to taken for.

ਸਮਝਾਉਣਾ (samjhaaunaa) *v* To explain, to instruct, to advise, to inculcate, to cause to understand.

ਸਮਝੌਤਾ (samjhautaa) *n m* Agreement, treaty, negotiation, compromise, concilliation, understanding.

ਸਮਰਥ (samrath) *a* Capable, fit.

ਸਮਰਥਨ (samarathan) *n m* Support, backing, agreement.

ਸਮਰਥਾ (samarthaa) *n f* Ability, power, competence, capacity, strength, vitality, vigour, might...

ਸਮਰਪਣ (samarpan) *n m* Dedication, surrender.

ਸਮਰੂਪਤਾ (samrooptaa) *n f* Similarity, homomorphism.

ਸਮਾ (samaa) *n m* Time, moment, period, season.

ਸਮਾਗਮ (samaagam) *n m* Assembly, meeting, conference, celebration.

ਸਮਾਚਾਰ (samaachaar) *n m* News, message, information, report; ~ਪਤਰ Newspaper.

ਸਮਾਜ (samaaj) *n m* Society, community institution, assembly.

ਸਮਾਧਾਨ (samdhaan) *n m* Solution.

ਸਮਾਪਨ (samaapan) *n m* Completion,

ਸਮਾਪਤੀ (smaaptee) *n f* Completion, end, expiry, termination; conclusion, termination, valedictory.

ਸਮਾਯੋਜਨ (smaayojan) *n m* Adjustment.

ਸਮਾਰਕ (smaarak) *n m* Memorial.

ਸਮਾਲੋਚਨਾ (samaalochnaa) *n* Criticism, commentry.

ਸ਼ਮੀਜ (shameez) *n f* Bodice, brassiere, feminine underwear.

ਸਮੁੰਦਰ (samunder) *n m* Sea, ocean.

ਸਮੇਟਣਾ (sametnaa) *v* To collect, to gather, to amass, to fold up, to finish.

ਸਰ (sar) *n m* Tank, pond.

ਸਰਸਰਾਉਣਾ (sarsraaunaa) *v* To rustle.

ਸਰਸਰੀ (sarsaree) *a n f* Cursory, superficial, hurried; Summary (trial) haste, hurry.

ਸਰਹੱਦ (sarhadd) *n f* Boundary, frontier, limit.

ਸਰਹਾਣਾ (sarhaanaa) *n m* Pillow.

ਸਰਕਣਾ (sarknaa) *v* To move, to slide, to crawl, to slip, to creep.

ਸਰਕਾਉਣਾ (sarkaaunaa) *v* To shift, to displace, to push ahead.

ਸਮਗਰੀ (samaggree) *n f* Material, ingredients, stuff, equipment, tools, appliances, provisions (collectively).

ਸਮਾਉਣਾ (samaunaa) *v* To be adjusted or accommodated, to be absorbed, assimilated, imbibed; To combine; To be contained, held; To permeate, pervade.

ਸਮਾਗਮ (samaagam) *n m* Function, celebration; Gathering, reunion.

ਸਮਾਧ (samaadh) *n* Tomb, sepulchre, shrine raised over the ashes of a deceased person.

ਸਮਾਧੀ (samadāi) *n f* Deep meditation, contemplation, concentration as a mystic exercise or experience, trance; Sitting posture for meditation; Shrine raised over the ashes of a deceared great man, tomb.

ਸਮੀਖਿਆ (sameekhiaa) *n f* Review, careful, detiailed or critical study, critique, commentary, analysis; ~ਸ਼ਾਸਤਰ Criticism, art of criticism; ~ਕਰਨੀ To review, criticise, comment upon, to conduct a thorough study (of or about)

ਸਮੋਸਾ (samosaa) *n m* A kind of roasted sandwich, a snack.

ਸਮੋਣਾ (samonaa) *v* To absorb, subsume, assimilate, incorporate.

ਸੱਯਾਹ (sayyaa) *n m* Traveller, tourist, explorer.

ਸੱਯਾਦ (sayyaad) *n m* Bird-catcher, fowler, hunter.

ਸਰਕਾਰ (sarkaar) *n f* Government, administrator, master.

ਸਰਕਾਰੀ (sarkaaree) *a* Of pertaining to government, governmental, official, public, state.

ਸਰਗਨਾ (sarganaa) *n m* leader, head, chief, (usually of a group of criminals of rebels).

ਸਰਗਰਮ (sargaram) *a* Active, actively engaged, zealously busy; enthusiastic, intent, energetic, dilligent.

ਸਰਗਰਮੀ (sargarmee) *n f* Zeal, passion, activity.

ਸ਼ਰਨ (sharaṇ) *n f* Shelter, refuge, protection.

ਸ਼ਰਤ (sharat) *n f* Condition, bet, stipulation.

ਸਰਦਾਰ (sardaar) *n m* Chief, leader, eminent person, foreman.

ਸਰਦੀ (sardee) *n f* Winter, coldness, cold, chilliness.

ਸ਼ਰਧਾ (shardhaa) *n f* Faith, trust, belief, reliance.

ਸਰਪ੍ਰਸਤ (sarprast) *n m* Guardian, patron.

ਸਰਫ਼ (saraf) *n m* Expenditure, expense.

ਸਰਫ਼ਾ (sarfaa) *n m* Saving, economy.

ਸ਼ਰਬਤ (sharbat) *n m* Syrup, sweet drink.

ਸਰਬੱਤ (sarbatt) *adv* All & sundary, all.

ਸ਼ਰਮ (sharam) *n f* Shame, modesty, bashfulness; ~ਨਾਕ Shameful, disgraceful.

ਸ਼ਰਮਾਕਲ (sharmaakal) *a* Shy, modest, bashful.

ਸ਼ਰਮੀਲਾ (sharmeelaa) *a* Shy, bashful.

ਸਰਲ (saral) *a* Plain, straight, easy, upright, simple, honest; ~ਤਾ Simplicity.

ਸਰਾਂ (saraan) *n f* Inn, tavern.

ਸਰਾਹੁਣਾ (sraahuṇaa) *v* To praise, to admire, to applaud, to appreciate, to laud, to eulogize. Also ਸਲਾਹੁਣਾ

ਸਰਾਪ (sraap) *n m* Curse.

ਸ਼ਰਾਫ਼ਤ (shraafat) *n f* Nobility, gentlemanliness, politeness.

ਸ਼ਰਾਬ (shraab) *n f* Liqour, wine, alcohal.

ਸ਼ਰਾਰਤ (shraarat) *n f* Mischief, vice, villainy, wickedness.

ਸ਼ਰਾਰਤੀ (shraartee) *n m* Mischievous, wicked.

ਸ਼ਰੀਕ (shreek) *n m* Partner, relative, friend; Included.

ਸ਼ਰੀਕਾ (shreekaa) *n m* Relationship, companionship.

ਸ਼ਰੀਫ਼ (shreef) *a n* Noble, gentle, holy; Nobleman.

ਸਰੀਰ (sreer) *n m* Body, physique person; ~ਤਿਆਗਣਾ to pass away, to die.

ਸ਼ਰੀਰ (shreer) *a* Mischievous, vicious, wicked.

ਸਰੋਕਾਰ (sarokaar) *n m* Concern, relation, interest.

ਸਰੋਪਾ (saropaa) *n m* Robe of honour.

ਸਰੋਵਰ (sarovar) *n m* Tank, lake, a large pond.

ਸਲਾਹ (slaah) *n m* Advice, counsel; Consulation; Opinion; ~ਕਾਰ adviser, consultant, counseller.

ਸਲਾਖ਼ (salaakh) *n f* Rod, bar. Also ਸਰੀਆ

ਸਲਾਨਾ (slaanaa) *a* Annual, yearly.

ਸਲਾਮ (slaam) *n m* Salutation, compliments, adieu, goodbye.

ਸਲਾਮਤ (slaamat) *a* Safe, sound.

ਸਲੀਕਾ (sleekaa) *n m* Etiquette, decorum.

ਸਲੂਕ (salook) *n m* Behaviour, conduct, treatment, mode.

ਸਲੂਣਾ (saloonaa) *n m* Cooked vegetable dish; Saltish, saline; Tasty, savoury; ~ਪਣ Saltishness, salinity; Saltish taste.

ਸਲੋਨਾ (Saloonaa) *a* Charming.

ਸਵਰਗ (Sawarag) *n m* Heaven, paradise; Happiness; ~ਵਾਸ Death, demise, heavenly abode.

ਸਵਾਇਆ (swaaiaa) *a* One and a quarter times, informal, a little, in a small quantity.

ਸਵਾਸ (swaas) *n f* Breath, respiration.

ਸਵਾਹ (swaah) *n m* Ash, dust.

ਸਵਾਂਗ (swaang) *n m* Imitation, mimicry, drama, mockery, disguise, burlesque, mosquerade, folk play, fancy dress. Also ਸਾਂਗ

ਸੰਵਾਦ (sanwaad) *n m* Dialogue, conversation, correspondence, intelligence, information; ~ਦਾਤਾ Correspondent, pressmen.

ਸਵਾਦ (swaad) *n m* Taste, flavour; Relish pleasure, savour, delight.

ਸਵਾਦੀ (swaadee) *a* Tasteful, delicious, amorous.

ਸਵਾਰਥ (swaarath) *n m* Self-interest, selfishness, desire.

ਸਵਾਰਥੀ (swaarthee) *a* Selfish, selfseeking.

ਸੰਵਿਧਾਨ (sanvidhaan) *n m* Constitution.

ਸਵੀਕਾਰ (saweekar) *n m a* Assent, acceptance, agreement, promise; Accepted.

ਸਵੀਕਾਰਨਾ (sweekaarnaa) *v* To accept, to consent, to agree.

ਸੜਕ (sarak) *n f* Road, path, highway.

ਸੜਨਾ (sarnaa) *v* To rot, to decay, to perish, to burn.

ਸੜਾਂਹਦ (sraanhd) *n f* Stench, purtrid smell, putrefaction, disagreeable. Also **ਸੜਿਆਂਦ**

ਸਾਇਤ (saait) *n f* Time, moment (auspicious).

ਸਾਹ (saah) *n m* Breath, respite, rest, relaxation; ~**ਆਉਣਾ** To regain breath; To breathe easily or freely, to feel respite, to relax; ~**ਸੁੱਕਣਾ** To be frightened; ~**ਘੁਟਣਾ** To feel suffocation; ~**ਚੜ੍ਹਨਾ** To breathe heavily; To be out of breath; ~**ਫੁਲਣਾ** To breathe hard, heavily or rapidly, to feel difficulty in breathing, to be out of breath, with slight exertion; ~**ਲੈਣਾ** To breathe; To have respite to take rest, to relax after exertion, to take a breather; To wait; ~**ਵਿਚ ਸਾਹ ਆਉਣਾ** To breathe easily (after tension), to feel relief (following despair).

ਸ਼ਾਹ (shah) *n m* Money lender, banker, merchant, richman, king, gentleman, shopkeeper.

ਸ਼ਾਹਾਨਾ (shaahaanaa) *a* Regal, royal, majestic, princely.

ਸਾਹਿਤ (saahit) *n m* Literature; ~**ਕਾਰ** Literateur, writer, man of letters.

ਸਾਹਿਲ (saahil) *n m* Sea coast, sea shore.

ਸ਼ਾਹੂਕਾਰ (shaahookaar) *n m* Richman, wealthy, person, banker, moneylender.

ਸ਼ਾਹੂਕਾਰਾ (shaahookaaraa) *n m* Money lending, business, banking profession.

ਸਾਖ (saakh) *n f* Credibility, trust.

ਸਾਖ (shaakh) *n f* Branch, bough, sect, offshoot.

ਸਾਖਰ (saakhar) *a* Literate; ~**ਤਾ** literacy.

ਸਾਖਿਆਤ (sakhiaat) *a* Present, visible, manifest, in person, in conrete form.

ਸਾਖੀ (saakhee) *n f* Story, anecdote *usu.* Connected with a holy person; Evidence, testimony; Witness, deponent, testifier.

ਸਾਗ (saag) *n m* Green leafy vegetable; A dish of vegetables.

ਸ਼ਾਗਿਰਦ (shaagird) *n m* Disciple, pupil, follower, student.

ਸਾਜ਼ਸ਼ (saazash) *n f* Conspiracy, intrigue, plot, complot collusion; ~**ਕਰਨੀ** To conspire, to plot, to complot, to collude, to intrigue.

ਸਾਜ਼ਬਾਜ਼ (saazbaaz) *n f* Illegal or secret contacts, collusion, conspiracy.

ਸਾਂਝ (saanjh) *n* Partnership, share, association.

ਸਾਂਝਾ (saanjhaa) *a* Common.

ਸ਼ਾਂਤੀ (shaantee) *n f* Peace, tranquility.

ਸਾਥੀ (saathee) *n m* Companion, comrade, associate, partisan.

ਸਾਦਗੀ (saadgee) *n f* Simplicity, plainness, homliness.

ਸਾਧਣਾ (saadhnaa) *v* To achieve, to resolve, to settle, to gain.

ਸਾਧਨ (saadhan) *n m* Channel, means, resource, equipment, accomplishment, device, medium.

ਸਾਧੂ (saadhoo) *n a m* Saint, hermit, sage, monk, ascetic, mendicant; Pious, holy, virtuous.

ਸ਼ਾਨ (shaan) *n f* Glory, grandeur, splendour, majesty, elegance, magnificence, dignity, lustre, embellishment.

ਸਾਨੀ (saanee) *a* Equal; Identical.

ਸਾਫ਼ (saaf) *a* Clean, clear, neat, distinct, vivid; Legible, intelligible; Unobstructed, smooth, frank, straightforward; Blatant, obvious; Cloudless; ~ਸਾਫ਼ Quite clear, categorical, frank, frankly, flatly; Lucidly, clearly; ~ਸੁਥਰਾ Clean, neat and clean, tidy; ~ਕਰਨਾ To clean, to wash, to cleanse, to rub, to scrub, to wipe, to mop; To clear, to clarify, to purify, to depurate, to refine; To spruce up, tidy up; To dress (meal); ~ਦਿਲ Honest, uprightness, guilelessness, candour.

ਸਾਫ਼ਗੋ (saafgo) *a* Truthful, frank; Upright, candid; ~ਈ Truthfulness, frankness, candour, uprightness, rectitude.

ਸਾਫ਼ਾ (saafaa) *n m* Turban, washcloth.

ਸਾਬਕ (saabak) *a* Former, ex-.

ਸਾਬਣ (saaban) *n m* Soap.

ਸਾਬਤ (saabat) *a* Complete, whole, full, compact.

ਸਾਂਭ (saambh) *n m* care, caretaking, maintenance, upkeep, Protection, custody, looking after; Preservation, conservation; ~ਕੇ ਰੱਖਣਾ To preserve, keep in good condition or safely.

ਸਾਂਭਣਾ (sambhnaa) *v* To secure, to keep safely; To occupy forcibly.

ਸਾਮੰਤ (saamant) *n m f* Feudal lord, mandarin, satrap, noble.

ਸਾਮੂਟਾ (saamanaa) *n m* Encounter,

confrontation, front, opposition; ~ਕਰਨਾ To face, to oppose, to fight, to stand upto.

ਸਾਮੁਣੇ (saamaṇe) *adv* In front of, opposite, before, face to face, in the presence of; ~ਹੋਣਾ To be in front, to be present.

ਸ਼ਾਮਤ (shaamat) *n f* Misfortune, illluck, misadventure, adversity, disaster, affliction.

ਸਾਮਾਨ (samaan) *n m* Goods, stock, material, apparatus.

ਸਾਰਨਾ (saarnaa) *v* To avail, to accomplish, to complete, to arrange.

ਸਾਰਨੀ (saarnee) *n f* Table, list.

ਸਾਲਣ (saalaṇ) *n m* Meat, fish or vegetable curry.

ਸਾਲਮ (saalam) *a* Complete, uncut, undivided, full, whole.

ਸਾਲਾ (saalaa) *n m* Brother-in-law, wife's brother.

ਸਾਲਾਨਾ (saalaanaa) *a* Annual, yearly.

ਸਾਵਧਾਨੀ (saavdhaanee) *n* Vigilance, alertness, consciousness.

ਸਾਂਵਲਾ (saanwlaa) *a* Dark complexioned, tawny.

ਸਾੜਨਾ (saaṛnaa) *v* To burn, to char, to cremate, to rot.

ਸਿਆਸਤ (siaasat) *n f* Politics; ~ਦਾਨ Politician.

ਸਿਆਹੀ (siaahee) *n f* Ink; Darkness.

ਸਿਆਣਨਾ (siaaṇnaa) *v* To recognise, to identify.

ਸਿਆਣਪ (siaaṇap) *n m* Wisdom, intelligence, dexterity, cleverness.

ਸਿਆਣਾ (siaaṇaa) *a* Wise, intelligent, sagacious, prudent, circumspect, sensible; Physician; Old person.

ਸਿਆਪਾ (siaapaa) *n m* Mourning, wailing; ~ਪਾਉਣਾ To creat problem; ~ਪੈਣਾ To be in trouble

ਸਿਆਲ (siaal) *n m* Winter, cold season.

ਸਿਸਕਣਾ (sisakṇaa) *v* To sob, to flutter, on the death bed.

ਸਿਸਕਾਰਨਾ (siskaarṇaa) *v* To hiss, to produce a hissing sound.

ਸਿਸਕੀ (siskee) *n f* Sobbing, sighing.

ਸਿਹਤ (sihat) *n f* Health; Physical fitness.

ਸਿਹਾਰੀ (sihaaree) *n f* Vowel sign ਇ in Gurmukhi script.

ਸਹੇੜਨਾ (saheṛnaa) *v* To adopt, to acquire, to take responsibility of.

ਸਿੱਕ (sikk) *n f* Longing, yearning, love, desire.

ਸ਼ਿਕਸਤ (shikast) *n f* Defeat, failure.

ਸ਼ਿਕੰਜਵੀ (shikanjavee) *n f* Lemon juice.

ਸ਼ਿਕੰਜਾ (shikanjaa) *n m* Clamp, press,

ਸਿਕਟਾ rack, torture.

ਸਿਕਣਾ (siknaa) *v* To yearn, to be fond of.

ਸਿੱਕਣਾ (sikknaa) *v* To long, to yearn, to desire, to hope.

ਸਿਕਰੀ (sikree) *n f* Dandruff, scurf.

ਸਿਕਵਾਉਣਾ (sikvaaunaa) *v* To get some thing warmed, heated or baked. Also ਸਿਕਾਉਣਾ

ਸਿੱਕਾ (sikkaa) *n m* Coin.

ਸ਼ਿਕਾਇਤ (shikaayit) *n f* Complaint, grievance, ailment, accusation.

ਸ਼ਿਕਾਰ (shikaar) *n m* Prey, victim, chase, quarry.

ਸਿੱਖ (sikh) *n f* Sikh (Community), pupil; Advice, instruction.

ਸਿਖਣਾ (sikhnaa) *v* To learn, to acquire knowledge or skill, to receive training.

ਸਿਖਲਾਈ (sikhlaaee) *n f* Instruction, training, teaching, schooling.

ਸਿੱਖਿਆ (sikhiaa) *n f* Education, schooling, tutuion, instruction, training, advice, teaching, precept: ~ਸਿਖਾਇਆ Already trained; Under instigation; ~ਸ਼ਾਸਤਰ Pedagogy, paedantics, theory and art of teaching; ~ਦੇਣਾ To advise, to instruct, to educate, to train.

ਸਿਖਾਉਣਾ (sikhaaunaa) *v* To teach, to instruct, to train, to educate.

ਸਿਟਣਾ (sitnaa) *v* To throw, to drop.

ਸਿਤਮ (sitam) *n m* Tyranny, oppression.

ਸਿਥਲ (sithal) *a* Inactive, ineffective, dormant, feeble, weak, weary, sickly; ~ਤਾ Inactiveness, infirmity, laxity, inertia, weariness, dormancy, sickliness.

ਸਿਧੱੜ (siddhar) *a* Simple, simlpleton.

ਸਿੱਧਾ (siddhaa) *a* Straight, direct, plain, simple, erect, innocent.

ਸਿਧਾਉਣਾ (sidhaaunaa) *v* To tame, to domesticate.

ਸਿਧਾਂਤ (sidhaant) *n m* Theory, principle, doctrine, axiom, thesis.

ਸਿਧਾਰਨਾ (sidhaarnaa) *v* To depart, to proceed; ਪਰਲੋਕ~ To die, to breathe one's last.

ਸਿਪਾਹਸਲਾਰ (sipaahslaar) *n m* Commander, general, commander-in-chief

ਸਿਪਾਹੀ (sipaahee) *n m* Soldier, constable.

ਸਿਫ਼ਤ (sifat) *n f* Glorification, Praise, attribution, appreciation.

ਸਿਫ਼ਰ (sifar) *n f* Zero, nil, naught, cypher.

ਸਿਮਟਣਾ (simatnaa) *v* To contract, to shrink, to shrivel.

ਸਿਮਰਨ (simaran) *n m*

ਸਿਮਰਨਾ (simaranaa) Rememberance, recollection, memory.

ਸਿਮਰਨਾ (simaranaa) v To remember, to recollect, to meditate.

ਸਿਰ (sir) *n m* Head, top, apex; ~**ਉੱਚਾ ਕਰਨਾ** To stand up with honour; ~**ਅੱਖਾਂ ਤੇ** With pleasure, most cordially, most cheerfully; ~**ਸਿਹਰਾ** Credit; ~**ਸਾਅਹ** To damn; ~**ਖਪਾਈ** Wearisome labour, irritation, idle talk, drudgery; ~**ਖਾਣਾ** To bore, to vex, to tease, to bother; ~**ਖੇਹ ਪੈਣੀ** To be insulted, to be disgraced; ~**ਘੁਮਣਾ** To feel giddy; ~**ਚੁਕਣਾ** To rebel, to rise against; ~**ਚੜ੍ਹਨਾ** To be impudent, to become arrogant; ~**ਤੇ ਬਣਨੀ** To be in trouble; ~**ਤੇ ਭੂਤ ਸਵਾਰ ਹੋਣਾ** To be crazy, to be under obsession; ~**ਨਿਵਾਉਣਾ** To salute, to bow in abeisance; ~**ਨੀਵਾਂ ਹੋਣਾ** To be disgraced, to be ashamed, to lose face; ~**ਪਿਟਣਾ** To lament; ~**ਪੈਰ ਨਾ ਹੋਣਾ** Not in order; ~**ਫਿਰਨਾ** To go mad, to run amuck; ~**ਭਾਰੀ ਹੋਣਾ** to have, an headache; ~**ਮਾਰਨਾ** To workhard, to make diligent search.

ਸਿਰੜੀ (sirṛee) a Obstinate, stubborn; Hardworking.

ਸਿਰਾ (siraa) *n m* Side, end, apex, edge, margin, point.

ਸਿਲ (sil) *n f* Stone slab, flat piece of rock; ~**ਵੱਟਾ** Stone and pestle, grinding stone.

ਸਿਲਸਿਲਾ (silsilaa) *n m* Series, sequence, concatenation; Serial order, arrangement, der, system.

ਸਿਲਸਿਲੇਵਾਰ (silsilevaar) *a adv* Serial, serially arranged, concatenate, consecutive, successive; In a row, serially, consecutively, successively; ~**ਕਰਨਾ** To serialise, to arrange serially or in a particular order.

ਸਿਲਮਾ (silmaa) *n m* Fine gold, silver or copper wire or thread used in embroidery or filigree; ~**ਸਿਤਾਰਾ** Ornamentation, embellishment.

ਸਿਲਾ (silaa) *n m* Consequence; Reward, recompense, requital; ~**ਦੇਣਾ** To reward, to recompense or repay, to requite.

ਸਿਆ (sia) *n m* Mild, pleasant warmth (provided by sunshine during winter), sun.

ਸ਼ੀਸ਼ਾ (sheeshaa) *n m* Mirror, looking glass, glass, pane.

ਸ਼ੀਸ਼ੀ (sheeshee) *n f* Small bottle.

ਸੀਟੀ (seetee) *n f* Whistle, buzzer

ਸੀਨਾ (seenaa) *n m* Chest, bosom,

breast; ~ਜੋਰ Aggressor.

ਸੀਮਾ (seemaa) *n f* Border, demarcation, limit, precinct, landmark.

ਸੀਖ (seekh) *n f* (1) Advice, instruction (2) Metallic rod or bar skewer; (3) Match stick; ~ਕਬਾਬ Minced meat roasted on a skewer, seekh kebab, shashlick.

ਸੀਮਿਤ (seemit) *a* Limited, finite.

ਸੀਰਤ (seerat) *n f* Temperament.

ਸੀਰਾ (seera) *n m* a Semi-solid or liquid dish of roasted wheat flour mixed with boiled, sweetened water; Syrup; Treacle; Molasses.

ਸੁਆਹ (suaah) *n m* Ash, ashes, cinder.

ਸੁਆਉਣਾ (suaaunaa) *v* (1) To assist (an animal) to clave or foal; (2) To lull or make (one) to sleep; (3) To get (a garment) stitched.

ਸੁਆਗਤ (suaagat) *n* Welcome, reception, acceptance. Also ਸਵਾਗਤ

ਸਵਾਗਤੀ (suaagatee) *n m* Receptionist.

ਸੁਆਦ (suaad) *n m* Taste, relish, pleasure, delight.

ਸੁਆਰਨਾ (suaarnaa) *v* To improve, refine, reform, repair; To accomplish or help in accomplishing; To clean, brush up, spruce, to adorn, to decorate; To repair, to set right, to remove fault or defect.

ਸੁਆਲ (suaal) *n m* Question, problem, sum, querry, interrogation, demand; ~ਜੁਆਬ Question-answer, controversy, interlocution, discussion, wrangling, querrel, dispute; ~ਪਾਉਂਣਾ To put a quootion, to request, to demand, to set a problem. Also ਸਵਾਲ

ਸੁਆਲੀ (suaalee) *n m* Beggar.

ਸੁਸਤੀ (sustee) *n f* Laziness, slowness, lethargy, idleness, indolence, dullness, negligence.

ਸੁਹੰਢਣਾ (suhandhṇaa) *a* Durable, long lasting.

ਸੁਹੰਪ (suhaṇṇap) *n m* Beauty, prettiness, comeliness, handsomensss, physical charm, attractiveness, grace

ਸੁਹਣਾ (suhnaa) *a* Charming, beautiful, handsome, graceful.

ਸੁਹਬਤ (sobat) *n f* Company, society, association.

ਸੁਹਰਤ (suharat) *n f* Fame, reputation, celebrity.

ਸੁਹਾਗ (suhaag) *n m* Married state of a woman while her husband is

ਸੁਹਾਗਣ — alive, bliss of married life; Ornaments worn by women only while their husbands are alive; Nuptial song; ~ਉਜੜਨਾ To become a widow; ~ਗੀਤ Nuptial song; ~ਭਾਗ good fortune, bliss of married women; ~ਰਾਤ The first night of the newly weds sharing a bed.

ਸੁਹਾਗਣ (suhaagan̩) n f Married or fortunate women, a woman whose hasband is alive.

ਸੁਹਾਗਾ (suhaagaa) n m Borax, tincal orrispowder.

ਸੁਹੇਲਾ (suhelaa) a m Easy; Comfortable, soothing.

ਸੁਕਣਾ (sukn̩aa) v To wither, to dry, to evaporate, to be lean and thin, to emaciate.

ਸ਼ੁਕਰੀਆ (shukriyaa) n m Thanks.

ਸੁਕੜਨਾ (Sukar̩naa) v To shrink, to contract.

ਸੁਕਾ (sukaa) a Dry, withered, anhydrous, arid, blank.

ਸੁਕਾਉਣਾ (sukaaun̩aa) v To dry, to air, to dehydrate, to evaporate, desicate, to cause, to wither.

ਸੁਕੇੜਨਾ (suker̩naa) v To compress, to deflate, to shrink; To collect.

ਸੁਖ (sukh) n m Comfort, amenity, ease, pleasure, delight, good health; ~ਦਾਈ Comfortable, soothing; ~ਦੁਖ Ups and downs.

ਸੁਖਾਉਣਾ (sukhaaun̩aa) v To agree, to suit, to soothe, to relieve pain.

ਸੁਗੰਦ (sugand) n f Oath, conjuration.

ਸੁਗੰਧ (sugandh) n f Fragrance, incense, odour, smell, perfume, aroma.

ਸੁਗਮ (sugam) a Facile, easy, exoteric, feasible.

ਸ਼ੁਗਲ (shugal) n m Hobby, avocation, amusement, recreation, pastime.

ਸੁੰਗੜਨਾ (sungar̩naa) v To shrink, contract, to shrivel, to pucker.

ਸੁੰਗੜਾ (sungr̩aa) n m Shrinkage, contraction (extent of).

ਸੁਗਾਤ (sugaat) n f Gift, present, curio, speciality.

ਸੁੰਘਣਾ (sunghn̩aa) v To smell, to sniff, to nose, to scent.

ਸੁਘੜ (sughar̩) a Elegant, sensible, competent, skillful, accomplished, decorous, virtuous; ~ਤਾ Accomplishment, intelligence, adroitness; Competence; ~ਸੁਜਾਨ Intelligent; Virtuous.

ਸੁੱਚਾ (suchchaa) a Pure, chaste, genuine, clean, unpolluted.

ਸੁਚੇਤ (suchet) a Cautious, alert, mindful, attentive, awake, aware, conscious, careful, watchful, wakeful, vigilant.

ਸੁੰਜ (sunj) *n f* Inhabitation, desolation, emptiness.

ਸੁਜਣਾ (sujnaa) *v* To swell, to be puffed, to be angry.

ਸੁੱਜਾ (sujjaa) *a* Swollen, inflamed, tumid, turgid, turgent.

ਸੁਝਨਾ (sujhnaa) *v* To Strike, to occur suddenly, to come to mind, at once.

ਸੁੰਞ (sunñ) *n f* Vaccum, vacuity, void, emptiness, vacant place, desolation, vacancy, nothingness; Lonelinesss, lonesomeness.

ਸੁੰਞਾ (suñaa) *a* Vacant, solitary, lone, deserted, naked.

ਸੁਟਣਾ (sutnaa) *v* To throw, to discard, to fling.

ਸੁੰਡ (sund) *n f* Trunk of an elephant.

ਸੁੰਢ (sundh) *n f* Dry ginger.

ਸੁਣਕਣਾ (sunaknaa) *v* To blow the nose.

ਸੁਣਨਾ (sunnaa) *v* To hear, to listen, to attend, to heed.

ਸੁਣਵਾਈ (sunvaaee) *n f* Hearing *esp* of petition in law suit.

ਸੁਣਾਉਨਾ (sunaaunaa) *v* To tell, to repeat, to read out, to say, to relate, to narrate.

ਸੁਤੰਤਰ (sutantar) *a* Independent, free, self-governing, unrestrained, uncontrolled; ~ਤਾ Independence, freedom, liberty.

ਸੁੱਥਣ (sutthan) *n f* Trousers usually worn by females. (Also called ਸਲਵਾਰ)

ਸੁਥਰਾ (suthraa) *a* Neat, clean, pure, orderly, chaste; ~ਪਣ Neatness, cleanliness, tidiness.

ਸੁੰਦਰ (sundar) *a* Beautiful, handsome, elegant, grand, pretty, fair, fine, bonny; ~ਤਾ Beauty, handsomeness, grace, prettiness.

ਸੁਦਰਸ਼ਨ (sudarshan) *a* Elegant, beautiful, good-looking; ~ਚੱਕਰ Mythical ring-shaped weapon wielded by Lord Krishana.

ਸੁਦਾਈ (shudaaee) *a* Eccentric insane, crazy, loony, mad.

ਸੁਦਾਗਰ (sudaagar) *n m* Merchant, trader

ਸੁੱਧ (suddh) *n f* Intelligence, sensation, attention, care, consciousness, feeling; ਬੁੱਧ~ Commonsense, sensibility, persence of mind; ~ਲੈਣੀ To remember to enquire after; ਬੇ~ Senseless.

ਸੁਧ (shudh) *a* Pure, uncorrupt, unpolluted, chaste, sanctified, pure; ~ਕਰਨਾ To purify, to chestena, to modify. Also ਸੁਧ

ਸੁੰਧਕ (sundhak) *n f* Information, clue, trace, hint, intelligence; ~ਲੈਣੀ To gather information, to try, to findout, to spy.

ਸੁਧਰਨਾ (sudharnaa) *v* To be improved, reformed, rectified or mended, to improve, to get better.

ਸੁਧਾਰ (sudhaar) *n f* Reforms, improvement, correction, reformation.

ਸੁਧਾਣਾ (sudhaaṇaa) *v* To tame, to train.

ਸੁਧਾਰਨਾ (sudhaarnaa) *v* To amend, to reform, to correct, to improve, to rectify, to renovate, to refine

ਸੁੱਧੀ (suddhee) *n f* Purification, purity, ablution, santification.

ਸੁੰਨ (sunn) *a* (1) Void, emptiness, absolute silence, (2) Benumbed, insane deed; ~ਹੋਣਾ To be benumed, to be stunned.

ਸੁਨਸਾਨ (sunsaan) *a* Desolate, barren, dreary, lonely.

ਸੁਨੇਹਾ (sunehaa) *n m* Message.

ਸੁਪਨਾ (supnaa) *n m* Dream, vision.

ਸੁਪਾਰੀ (supaari) *n f* Betel nut, arecanut; Betel-palm, *Areca catechu*.

ਸੁਬਕ (subak) *a* Thin, slender, slim, lean, delicate; Fast, swift-footed, agile.

ਸੁਬ੍ਹਾ (shubbaa) *n m* Doubt, distrust suspicion.

ਸੁਬੜਾ (subraa) *n m* A skin disease of chickenpox type.

ਸੁਭਾਉ (subhaau) *n m* Habit, nature, temperament, disposition, habitual behaviour, habitude; Character, mentality. Also ਸੁਭਾਅ

ਸੁਭਾਗ (subhaag) *n m* Good luck, good fortune, felicity; Lucky, fortunate.

ਸੁਯੋਗ (suyog) *a* Worthy, befitting, deserving; Acuminous.

ਸੁਰ (sur) *n m* (1) Angel, god; (2) Tune, melody, note; Cadence, tone, pitch; Musical sound or voice; ~ਸੰਗਮ Symphony; ~ਤਾਲ Musical rhythm, cadence; ~ਮਿਲਾਉਣਾ To harmonise, attune; *fig* To agree to, to chime in.

ਸੁਰਕੀ (surkee) *n f* Sip; Sound produced by sipping a liquid too hot for gulping; Slurp.

ਸੁਰਖ (surakh) *a* Red, scarlet.

ਸੁਰਖ਼ਾਬ (surkhaab) *n m* Ruddy sheldrake; ~ਦਾ ਪਰ ਲਗਣਾ To assume a novel or special position.

ਸੁਰਖ਼ੀ (surkhee) *n f* Redness, red

colour, pink-coloured face powder, reddle, ruddle; Headline, heading, title, caption, rubric.

ਸੁਰਗ (surag) *n f* Paradise, heaven, Elysium, Olympus, abode of God or gods, the next world.

ਸੁਰੰਗ (surang) *n f* Tunnel, mine, subterraneous.

ਸੁਰਜੀਤ (surjeet) *a* Alive.

ਸੁਰਤ (surat) *n f* Awareness, attention, awakening, presence of mind, reflection, sense.

ਸੁਰਮਾ (surma) *n m* Antimony or collyrium powder; Graphite, plumbago rod in a lead pencil, lead of a pencil.

ਸੁਰਾਹੀ (suraahee) *n f* Flagon, flask.

ਸੁਰਾਖ (suraakh) *n m* Hole, perforation, orifice, aperture, cavity, bore; ~ਕਰਨਾ/ ~ਕੱਢਣਾ To make, dig or pierce a hole to perforate, to bore; ~ਦਾਰ Perforated.

ਸੁਰਾਗ (suraag) *n m* Clue, trace, hint, sign, lead, leading intelligence; ~ਕੱਢਣਾ To trace, to spy.

ਸੁਰੀਲਾ (sureelaa) *a* Melodious, musical, harmonious, sonorous, sweet.

ਸੁਲਾਹ (sulaah) *n f* Agreement, rapprochment, peace; ~ਕਰਨੀ To make peace, to come, to terms, to compromise, to settle (dispute), to conclude peace treaty. Also ਸੁਲ੍ਹਾ

ਸੁਲੱਖਣਾ (sulakhnaa) *a* Fortunate, happy, gentle.

ਸੁਲਗਾਉਣਾ (sulgaaunaa) *v* To inflame, to kindle, to light, to fan.

ਸੁਲਛਣਾ (sulachhnaa) *a* Good natured, good mannered.

ਸੁਲਝਣਾ (sulajhnaa) *v* To be settled, to be unravelled.

ਸੁਲਝਾਉਣਾ (suljhaaunaa) *v* To disentangle, to unravel, to straighten, to solve.

ਸੁਲਤਾਨ (sultaan) *n m* King, emperor, ruler, sultan.

ਸੁਲਫਾ (sulfaa) *n A* small ball of crude tobacco or charas, an intoxicating drug.

ਸੁਵੰਨਾ (suannaa) *a m* Of good colour, pleasing to the eye.

ਸੁਵੱਲਾ (suvallaa) *a m* Cheap, lowpriced, inexpensive.

ਸੁਵਾਸ (suvaas) *n m* Fragrance, aroma, perfume, scent.

ਸੁੜਕਣਾ (suṛaknaa) *v* To slurp, to drink noisily.

ਸੂਆ (sooaa) *n m* Packing needle; Injection; Poker; Watercourse, canal distributory.

ਸੂਈ (sooee) *n f* Needle, pin, pointer.

ਸੂਹ (sooh) *n m* Clue, trace, inkling; Information, tip-off, news, intelligence; Acquaintance; ~**ਕੱਢਣੀ** To trace out, to find a clue, to detect, to spy, to find out; ~**ਮਿਲਣੀ/** ~**ਲੱਗਣੀ** To get an inkling of; ~**ਲੈਣੀ** To snoop, to sneak, to try, to find-out.

ਸੂਖਮ (sukham) *a* Fine, slender, delicate, light, subtle, imperceptible, abstract, tenuous, mysterious; ~**ਤਾ** Fineness, delicacy, lightness, subtletly, abstractness, mysteriousness, perspicacity.

ਸੂਚਨਾ (soochnaa) *n f* Information, notice, announcement, warning, notification, report, intimation.

ਸੂਚੀ (soochee) *n f* List, schedule, table, inventory, catalogue; ~**ਕਾਰ** Tabulator; ~**ਬੱਧ** Tabulated, catalogued.

ਸੂਜੀ (soojee) *n f* Coarsly ground flour of wheat.

ਸੂਝ (soojh) *n f* Sensibility, insight, perception, intelligence, discretion acumen; ~**ਵਾਨ** Intelligent, shrewd.

ਸੂਣਾ (soonaa) *v* (for cattle) To clave, (for horse) to foal, to give birth, reproduce, multiply.

ਸੂਤ (soot) *n m adv* Yarn esp cotton yarn; Cord or line used by carpenters and masons; Unit of measurement, 1/8th of an inch; Correct, proper; manageable, properly aligned or adjusted, in working order, slighty, a little distance.

ਸੂਤਕ (sootak) *n m* Child birth, impurity or uncleanliness associated by Hindu custom with birth in a house.

ਸੂਤਰ (sootar) *n m* Formula, maxim, brief precept, aphorism; ~**ਧਾਰ** Stage manager, director, controller, wirepuller (in a puppet show), puppeteer; Moderator.

ਸੂਤਰੀ (sootree) *a* Pronged, point (formula, policy or programme), starand; ~**ਕਰਨ** Formulation.

ਸੂਤਲੀ (sootlee) *n f* Twine string, pack thread.

ਸੂਤੀ (sootee) *a* Cotton, made of cotton.

ਸੂਦ (sood) *n m* Interest, profit on cash loan, rate of interest, name of a Khatri subcaste; ~**ਖੋਰ** Usurer, moneylender; ~**ਖੋਰੀ** Usury, moneylending.

ਸੂਫੀ (soofee) *a* Holy, pious, sober;

~ਆਨਾ Pertaining to Sufis or Sufism; Sober, simple.

ਸੂਬਾ (soobaa) *n m* Province; ~(ਸੂਬੇ)ਦਾਰ Governor.

ਸੂਮ (soom) *n m* Miser, niggard, stingy, hunks.

ਸੂਰਜ (sooraj) *n m* The sun.

ਸੂਰਤ (soorat) *n f* Form, figure; Face, visage, countenance, appearance; Situation, circumstance; Instance, case; Means, method, wayout.

ਸੂਰਮਾ (soormaa) *a* Brave, bold, hero, warrior.

ਸੂਲ (sool) *n m* Thorn, spike.

ਸੂਲੀ (soolee) *n f* The cross, crucifix, any cross; *fig* Torturous situation or life, torture; ~ਚੜ੍ਹਾਉਣਾ To crucify; ~ਤੇ ਟੰਗਣਾ To troture.

ਸੇਕਣਾ (seknaa) *v* To warm, to bask, to foment.

ਸੇਕਾ (sekaa) *n m* Heat, warmth.

ਸ਼ੇਖੀ (shekhee) *n f* Boast, brag, bravado, vaunt.

ਸੇਜ (sej) *n f* Bed *esp* a soft or decorated one, particularly one laid for a couple to lie on or in.

ਸੇਣਾ (senaa) *v* To foster, to brood.

ਸੇਧਣਾ (sedhnaa) *v* To aim at; To straighten, to align.

ਸ਼ੇਰ (sher) *n* Lion, tiger; ~ਨ· Lioness tigress.

ਸੇਵਾ (sevaa) *n f* Service, attendance, duty, worship; ~ਦਾਰ Servant, worker (paid or free). Same as ਸੇਵਕ

ਸੈ (shai) *n f* Thing, object, article.

ਸੈਂਕੜਾ (sainkraa) *n m a* Hundred, century (of runs); Percent.

ਸ਼ੈਤਾਨ (shaitan) *n m* Satan, devil.

ਸ਼ੈਦਾਈ (shaidaaee) *n m* Lover, love crazy.

ਸੈਨਾ (sainaa) *n f* Army, military, force, regiment, troop; ~ਪਤੀ Commander-in-chief, supreme commander.

ਸੈਨਿਕ (sainik) *n m* Soldier militaryman.

ਸੈਰ (sair) *n f* Walk, excursion, stroll, outing, promenade; ~ਗਾਹ A place for excursion or walk, park, tourist resort.

ਸੈਲਾਨੀ (sailaanee) *a* Jovial, rambler, traveller, tourist, vagrant, fond of excursion.

ਸੈਲਾਬ (sailaab) *n m* Flood.

ਸੋਹਣਾ (sohnaa) *a m* Beautiful, handsome, good-looking, comely, shapely, lovely, charming, pretty, cute; Grand, graceful, elegant, attractive, pleasing.

ਸ਼ੋਹਦਾ (shohdaa) *a* Innocent, poor fellow.

ਸ਼ੋਕ (shok) *n m* Grief, sorrow.

ਸ਼ੋਖ (shokh) *a* Brilliant, sancy, mercurial, audacious, cheeky, sportive.

ਸੋਗ (sog) *n m* Lamentation, mourning, sadness, sorrow, grief, woe; ~**ਮਈ** Sorrowful, grievous, melancholy.

ਸੋਚ (soch) *n f* Thought, anxiety, consideration, apprehension, reason, thinking, contemplation; ~**ਸਮਝ** Understanding, prudence, carefulness; ~**ਵਿਚਾਰ** Consideration, consultation, circumspection.

ਸੋਚਣਾ (sochnaa) *v* To think, to contemplate, to imagine, to suppose, to consider, to conceive.

ਸੋਜ (soj) *n f* Swelling, tumidity; ~**ਚੜ੍ਹਨੀ** To swell.

ਸੋਜ਼ਸ਼ (sozash) *n f* Inflammation, burning sensation.

ਸੋਟਾ (sotaa) *n m* Club, batton, stick; Staff, bludgeon.

ਸੋਤਾ (sotaa) *n m* Source, spring.

ਸੋਧਣਾ (sodhnaa) *v* To revise, to rectify, to correct, to amend, to purify, to purge.

ਸੋਨਾ (sonaa) *n m* Gold, riches.

ਸ਼ੋਰ (shor) *n m* Noise, clamor, cry, blatancy.

ਸ਼ੌਕ (shauk) *n m* Liking, fondness, zest, inclination, interest.

ਸੌਖਾ (saukhaa) *a* Easy, convenient.

ਸੌਗਾਤ (saugaat) *n f* Present, gift.

ਸੌਣਾ (saunaa) *v* To Sleep, to down.

ਸੌਦਾ (saudaa) *n m* Merchandise, bargain, business, transaction; ~**ਗਰ** Trader, merchant.

ਸੌਦਾਈ (saudaaee) *n m* Mad, crazy.

ਸੌਪਣਾ (saupnaa) *v* To entrust, to handover, to consign, to concede, to give charge.

ਸੌੜ (saur) *n f* Pinch, tightness.

ਸੌੜਾ (sauraa) *a* Close, narrow, tight, cramped; ~**ਪਨ** Closeness, narrowness.

ਹ

ਹ Fifth letter of Gurmukhi alphabets, pronounced as hahaa.

ਹਉਕਾ (haukaa) *n m* Sigh, moan, suspiration; **~ਭਰਨਾ** To heave a sigh, to moan, to groan, to suspire.

ਹਉਆ (hauaa) *n m* Object of fear or terror, bugbear, betenoire.

ਹੰਸ (hans) *n m* Swan, goose; Religious soul.

ਹੱਸਣਾ (hassnaa) *v n a* To laugh, to smile, to cut a joke, to make fun of; One who is always laughing, cheerful, jolly, jovial.

ਹਸਤਾਖਰ (hastaakhar) *n m* Signature, autograph.

ਹਸਤੀ (hastee) *n f* Position, personality, dignity; Life, existence.

ਹਸਦ (hasad) *n f* Envy, jealousy; **~ਕਰਨਾ** Envy, to be jealous.

ਹਸਪਤਾਲ (haspataal) *n m* Hospital, dispensary, infiremary.

ਹਸਮੁਖ (hasmukh) *a* Cheerful, blithesome, jolly, jovial, gay, jocose jocular, vivacious, risible.

ਹਸ਼ਰ (hashar) *n m* Result, end, doomsday.

ਹਸਰਤ (hasrat) *n f* Regret, sorrow, grief; Desire.

ਹਸਾਉਣਾ (hasaaunaa) *v* To make one laugh, to cause laughter, to amuse, tickle; Comic, comical, funny, amusing, humorous, witty, laughable, ludicrous.

ਹਸਾਣ (hasaan) *n m* Act or process of laughing.

ਹੱਕ (hakk) *n m a* Right, claim; adjust, true, proper; **~ਦਬਾਉਣਾ** To usurp a right; **~ਦਾਰ** Entitled, claimant, deserving; **~ਦਾਰੀ** Entitlement, title, claim.

ਹੱਕਣਾ (hakknaa) *v* To drive, to urge on, to push, to goad. Also **ਹਿਕਣਾ**

ਹਕਲਾ (haklaa) *n m* Stammer.

ਹਕਲਾਉਣਾ (haklaaunaa) *v* To stammer.

ਹੱਕਾ-ਬੱਕਾ (hakkaa-bakkaa) *a* Stunned, perplexed, bewildered, confused, stupefied.

ਹੰਕਾਰ (hankaar) *n m* Pride, egoism, haughtiness, arrogance.

ਹੰਕਾਰੀ (hankaaree) *a* Proud, vain, arrogant, haughty, conceited, pompous, egoistic.

ਹਕਾਰਤ (hakaarat) *n f* Contempt, hatred disdain.

ਹਕੀਕਤ (hakeekat) *n f* Reality, fact, truth.

ਹਕੀਕੀ (hakeekee) *a* Real, actual, true; Veritable; Own.

ਹਕੀਮ (hakeem) *n m* Physician, medico, doctor; ~ਨੀਮ Quack, charlatan.

ਹਕੂਮਤ (hakoomat) *n f* Government, administration, rule, authority.

ਹਗਣਾ (hagnaa) *v* To exrcete, to ease oneself.

ਹੰਗਾਮਾ (hangaarnaa) *n m* Disturbance, uproar, tumult.

ਹੰਘਾਲਣਾ (hanghalnaa) *v* To cleanse, to rinse, to swill.

ਹਚਕੋਲਾ (hachkaulaa) *n m* Swing, push, jolt.

ਹੰਜ (hanj) *n m* Tears. Also ਹੰਝੂ

ਹੱਜ (hajj) *n m* Purpose, use; Pilgrimage to mecca.

ਹਜ਼ਮ (hazam) *a* Digested, usurped.

ਹਜ਼ਰਤ (hazrat) *n m* a Majesty, dignity, highness; Clever, cunning (metaphorically).

ਹਜਾਮ (hajaam) *n m* Barber, hair dresser.

ਹਜਾਮਤ (hajaamat) *n f* Shaving, Hair cutting.

ਹਜੂਮ (hajoom) *n m* Crowd, multitude.

ਹਟਕਣਾ (hatáknaa) *v* To check, to restrain, to dissuade.

ਹਟਣਾ (hatnaa) *v* To go back, to withdraw, to return, to shift, to recede, to give way, to deviate.

ਹੱਟਾ (hattaa) *n m* Big shop, emporium.

ਹੱਟਾ-ਕੱਟਾ (hattaa-kattaa) *a* Strong, stout, robust, vigorous.

ਹਟਾਉਣਾ (hataaunaa) *v* To remove, to repulse, to drive away, to push back, to sack.

ਹੱਟੀ (hattee) *n f* Shop.

ਹੱਠ (haatth) *n m* Obstinacy, insistence, tenacity, stubbornness, disobedience.

ਹੱਠੀ (hatthee) *a* Obstinate stubborn, dogmatist, disobedient.

ਹੱਡ (hadd) *n m* Bone; Skeleton of animal; ~ਸੇਕਣੇ To beat, to give a thrashing; ~ਭੰਨਣੇ To work hard, toil, to drudge; ~ਭੰਨਵਾਂ Toilsome, arduous, strenuous, laborious, bone-breaking.

ਹੱਡੀ (Haddee) *n f* Bone; ~ਉਤਰਨੀ For bone or joint to be dislocated.

ਹੰਡੋਲਾ (handolaa) *n m* Cradle, swing, storm.

ਹੰਢਾਉਣਾ (handhaaunaa) *v a* To wear out, to use till it is worn out.

ਹੱਤਕ (hattak) *n f* Insult, disrespect, disgrace, dishonour.

ਹੱਤਿਆ (hattiaa) *n f* Murder

ਹਤਿਆਰਾ assasination, killing, slaughter, homicide; ~**ਕਰਨੀ** To commit, to kill, butcher, assassinate, slaughter; ~**ਕਾਂਡ** Murder story, massacre, carnage.

ਹਤਿਆਰਾ (hatiaaraa) *n m a* Murderer, assassin, murderous, ferocious, bloody.

ਹੱਥ (Hatth) *n m* Hand, arm; ~**ਉੱਚਾ ਹੋਣਾ** To have an upper hand; ~**ਸਾਫ਼ ਕਰਨਾ** To steal, to swindle, to misappropriate; ~**ਕਟ ਜਾਣੇ** To be rendered helpless; ~**ਖਿਚਣਾ** To avoid, to desist, to withdraw; ~**ਖੁਲ੍ਹਾ ਹੋਣਾ** To be bounteous, to have enough money; ~**ਗਰਮ ਕਰਨਾ** To bribe; ~**ਚੁਕਣਾ** To assault, to strike, to beat; ~**ਜੋੜਨਾ** To pray, to beg pardon; ~**ਆਉਣਾ** To come under the control of; ~**ਜੋੜਨੇ** To fold one's hand in respect, prayer or supplication, to beg, to entreat, to pray; To beg; To be excused, to express inabilite; ~**ਤੰਗ ਹੋਣਾ** To be tight financially, to be short of money, to be penniless; ~**ਦਾ ਸੁੱਚਾ** Honest, in dealing; ~**ਦੀ ਮੈਲ** Wealth, money; ~**ਪਾਉਣਾ** To interfere; ~**ਪੀਲੇ ਕਰਨਾ** To marry (daughter or Sister); ~ **ਫੇਰਨਾ** To rob; ~**ਮਲਣਾ** To repent, to be sorry; ~**ਲੰਮੇ ਹੋਣੇ** To have a long reach; ~**ਕੰਡੇ** Secret contrivances.

ਹਥਕੜੀ (hathkaṛee) *n f* Handcuff, manacies.

ਹੱਥਨੀ (hatthṇee) *n f* Female elephant.

ਹੱਥਾ (hatthaa) *n m* Handle; ~**ਪਾਈ** Fight, scuffle, violence.

ਹਥਿਆਉਣਾ (hathiaauṇaa) *v* To grab, to seize.

ਹਥਿਆਰ (hathiaar) *n m* Weapon, arms, tools, instruments; ~**ਸੁੱਟਣੇ** To surrender, capitulate, to accept defeat, to surrender arms, to throw down arms; ~**ਬੰਦ** Armed.

ਹੱਥੀ (hatthee) *n f* Handle, grip.

ਹਥੇਲੀ (hathelee) *n f* Palm, metacarpus.

ਹਥੌੜਾ (hathauṛaa) *n m* Hammer.

ਹੱਦ (hadd) *n f* Limit, border, limitations, boundary; ~**ਕਰਨੀ/~ਕਰ ਦੇਣੀ** To do something unusual, amazing, wonderful, laudable, or improper; ~**ਬੰਦੀ** Demarcation, delimitation.

ਹਦਵਾਣਾ (hadwaaṇaa) *n m* Watermelon.

ਹੰਦਾ (handaa) *n m* Cooked food collected daily by priests.

ਹਦਾਇਤ (hadaait) *n f* Instruction, guidance, direction. Also **ਹਦੇਤ**

ਹਨੇਰ (haner) *n* Darkness, misrule, tyranny, calamity, lawlessness; Injustice; ~ਖਾਤਾ Mismanagement, confusion; ~ਗਾਰਦੀ Anarchy, lawlessness.

ਹਨੇਰਾ (haneraa) *a* Dark, gloom, foggy, obscure; ~ਘੁੱਪ Blinding darkness.

ਹਨੇਰੀ (haneree) *n f* Dust-storm, wind-storm, tornado, hurricane; ~ਕੋਠੀ Dark cell, dungeon.

ਹਨੇਰੇ (Hanere) *a* Dark; ~ਸਵੇਰੇ At odd hours; ~ਵਿਚ ਤੀਰ ਚਲਾਉਣਾ To strike without taking aim; ~ਵਿਚ ਰਖਣਾ To keep in the dark, to keep ignorant, to keep uninformed.

ਹਪਣਾ (hapnaa) *v* To gulp, to swallow whole.

ਹਫਣਾ (haphnaa) *v* To be out of breath, to breathe heavily, to pant.

ਹਫਤਾ (Haftaa) *n m* Week; ~ਵਾਰ weekly. Also ਹਫ਼ਤੇਵਾਰ

ਹਫੜਾ-ਦਫੜੀ (haphra-daphree) *n f* Confusion, commotion, panic, bustle, stampede, hurry, haste, furmoil, flurry.

ਹਫ਼ੀਮ (Hafeem) *n f* Opium.

ਹਬਸ਼ੀ (habshee) *n m* Negro, negroid, an African, Abyssinian or Ethiopean.

ਹਬਕਾ (habkaa) *n m* Jerk; Sudden attack of sorrow, shock.

ਹੰਬਣਾ (hambanaa) *n m* Spring, jump, determined effort *esp*. after tiredness, sheer will.

ਹੰਭਾਉਣਾ (hambaaunaa) *v* To tire out, to exhaust.

ਹਮਸ਼ਕਲ (hamshakal) *a* Similar, resembling.

ਹਮਸਾਇਆ (hamsaaiyaa) *n m* Neighbour.

ਹਮਜੋਲੀ (hamjolee) *n m* Chum, nearest friend.

ਹਮਦਰਦੀ (hamdardee) *n f* Sympathy.

ਹਮਰਾਜ਼ (hamraaz) *n m* Confidant, confident.

ਹਮਲ (hamal) *n m* Pregnancy; ~ਗਿਰਨਾ Abortion, miscarriage.

ਹਮਲਾ (hamlaa) *n m* Attack, invasion, assault; ~ਕਰਨਾ To attack, to invade.

ਹਮਵਤਨ (hamwatan) *n m a* Countryman *or* country woman, compatriot, fellow citizen.

ਹਮਾਇਤ (hamayit) *n f* Support, protection, patronage, abetment; Sympathy.

ਹਮਾਕਤ (hamaakat) *n f* Stupidity, folly, foolishness.

ਹਮਾਮ (hamaam) *n m* Hot or turkish bath, a metallic drum with a tap.

ਹਮਾਮ-ਦਸਤਾ (hamaam-dastaa) *n m*

Pestle and mortar.

ਹਮੇਸ਼ਾ (hameshaa) *adv* Always, ever, perpetually

ਹਯਾ (hayaa) *n f* Modesty, coyness, sense of shameness; **ਬੇ~** Shameless, immodest.

ਹਰ (har) *a pref* Each, every, any; **~ਇਕ** Each one, everyone, all and sundry; **~ਹੀਲੇ** By all or any means; **~ਕੋਈ** Everyone, any Tom, Dick or Harry; **~ਜਾਈ** Fickle, inconstant (male lover); **~ਥਾਂ** Everywhere; **~ਦਮ** Always; **~ਦਿਲ ਅਜ਼ੀਜ਼** Popular, likeable, favourite of one and all; **~ਵਾਰੀ** Each or every time.

ਹਰਕਤ (harkat) *n f* Movement, motion, gesture, action.

ਹਰਕਾਰਾ (harkaaraa) *n m* Courier, postman, messenger, carrier.

ਹਰਜ (haraj) *n m* Loss, waste (of time, money or effort); **~ਕਰਨਾ** To waste.

ਹਰਜਾਈ (harjaae) *n m* Omnipresent.

ਹਰਜਾਨਾ (harjaanaa) *n m* Damage, compensation, indemnity.

ਹਰਣ (haran) *n m* Kidnapping, abduction, removal.

ਹਰਨ (haran) *n m* Deer, antelope; **~ਹੋ ਜਾਣਾ** To run away. Also **ਹਿਰਨ**

ਹਰਨਾ (harnaa) *v* To abduct, to kidnap.

ਹਰਫ (haraf) *n m* Alphabetical letter, particle, word.

ਹਰਫਨ ਮੌਲਾ (harfan maulaa) *a m* Master or jack of all trades, versatile.

ਹਰਮ (haram) *n m* Harem, seragilo, inner apartments of a house.

ਹਰਵਾਉਣਾ (harvaaunaa) *v* To cause defeat, to defeat through someone else; Also **ਹਰਾਉਣਾ**

ਹਰਾ (haraa) *a* Green, fresh, verdant.

ਹਰਾਉਣਾ (haraaunaa) *v* To defeat.

ਹਰਾਸਤ (haraasat) *n f* Custody, arrest, care. Also **ਹਿਰਸਤ**

ਹਰਾਮ (haraam) *a* Improper, unlawful, sinful, prohibited; **~ਖੋਰ** Corrupt person; **~ਜ਼ਾਦਾ** Illegitimate, bastard, rascal, scoundral.

ਹਰਾਮੀ (haraamee) *n m a* Rascal; *a* Illegal, illegitimate, bastard.

ਹਰਾਰਤ (haraarat) *n f* Heat, light, fever, feverishness, temperature.

ਹੱਲ (hall) *n m* Solution; Plough.

ਹਲਕ (halak) *n m* Throat.

ਹਲਕਣਾ (halknaa) *v* To go mad.

ਹਲਕਾ (halkaa) *a* Light, easy, soft, cheap.

ਹਲਚਲ (halchal) *n m* Commotion, tumult, agitation, disorder.

ਹਲਦੀ (haldee) *n f* Turmeric, *Curcuma longa*.

ਹਲਫ (halaf) *n m* Oath, vow; **~ਨਾਮਾ**

ਹਲਫ਼ੀਆ ਬਿਆਨ (halfiaa biaan) *n m* statement on oath, affidavit, deposition; ~ਬਿਆਨ ਦੇਣ ਵਾਲਾ Deponent; ~ਬਿਆਨ ਦੇਣਾ To depose.

ਹਲਵਾ (halwa) *n m* Pudding, Sweetmeat.

ਹਲਵਾਈ (halwaaee) *n m* Confectioner, sweet seller.

ਹੱਲਾ (hallaa) *n m* Assault, attack, noise, uproar, tumult.

ਹਲਾ (halaa) *n pron* All right, agreed; ~ਸ਼ੇਰੀ Encouragement, abetment, incitement, instigation; ~ਸ਼ੇਰੀ ਦੇਣੀ To encourage, to abet, to incite, to instigate.

ਹੱਲਾ (halla) *n m* Attack, assault, charge; noise, uproar; ~ਕਰਨਾ To make noise; same as ਹੱਲਾ ਬੋਲਣਾ; ~ਗੁੱਲਾ Noise, din, uproar, merrymaking, revel, mirth.

ਹਲਾਉਣਾ (halaaunaa) *v* To Shake, to mix, to move.

ਹਲਾਲ (halaal) *a* Legal, lawful, legitimate; Slaughtered.

ਹਲੂਣਨਾ (haloonnaa) *v* To shake, to give a jolt.

ਹਲੂਣਾ (haloonaa) *n m* Jerk, joilt, shaking up; Swaying motion, swing; ~ਦੇਣਾ To shake, sway, swing.

ਹਵਸ (hawas) *n f* Lust, longing, yearning, overambition.

ਹਵਾ (hawaa) *n* Air, wind, atmosphere; Reputation; ~ਕੱਢਣਾ To deflate; ~ਕਰਨਾ To fan; ~ਖਾਣੀ To go for a walk; ~ਪਾਣੀ Climate.

ਹੱਵਾ (havaa) *n f* Eve, the first woman

ਹਵਾਈ (hawaaee) *a* Airy, aerial; Flase; ~ਅੱਡਾ Aerodrome; ~ਕਿਲਾ Fertile ambition; ~ਜਹਾਜ਼ Aeroplane.

ਹਵਾਲ (hawaal) *n m* News; Condition; ~ਦਾਰ Sergeant, lower police officer.

ਹਵਾਲਾ (hawaalaa) *n m* Reference, mention, example; ~ਦੇਣਾ To refer, to mention, to quote.

ਹਵਾਲਾਤ (hawaalaat) *n m* Lock up, jail.

ਹਵਾਲੇ (havaale) *a* In custody (of); ~ਕਰਨਾ To hand over, deliver, give, entrust.

ਹਵਾੜ (havaar) *n m* Steam, visible evaporation, vapours or particles; hot breath; *fig* Suppressed or latent feeling esp. Anger; ~ਕੱਢਣੀ to let out steam; To give vent to anger or hurt feelings to leak out a secret, to have catharsis; ~ਲੈਣੀ To inhale steam, to have steam fomentation; *fig* To pry or spy.

ਹਵੇਲੀ (havelee) *n f* Large walled house, mansion.

ਹੜਤਾਲ (haṛtaal) *n m* Strike.

ਹੜਪਣਾ (haṛapṇaa) *v* To gulp, to usurp.

ਹੜਬੜੀ (haṛbaṛee) *n f* Confusion, melee, pell-mell; consternation.

ਹੜ੍ਹ (haṛ) *n m* Flood, deluge, inundation; **~ਆਉਣਾ** To be flooded; **~ਮਾਰ** Damage or destruction caused by flood.

ਹਾਏ (haae) *interj* An expression of pain, pleasure, grief or anxiety depending on intonation; Oh, ah, alack, alas; *n f* Cry of pain.

ਹਾਏਂ (haaen) *interj* Interrogative expression, what? is it?

ਹਾਸਾ (haasaa) *n m* Laughter, fun, joke, giggle, mockery, amusement.

ਹਾਸ਼ੀਆ (haashiyaa) *n m* Margin, edging, side, border, commentary.

ਹਾਹਾਕਾਰ (haahaakaar) *n m* Lamentation.

ਹਾਕਮ (haakam) *n m* Ruler, governor, officer, magistrate, administrator; Welider of authority to give command or order.

ਹਾਜਤ (haajat) *n f* (1) Need, necessity, want, requirement; (2) Call of nature; **~ਹੋਣੀ** To need, want, require to feel need; To feel call of nature.

ਹਾਜਮਾ (haajmaa) *n m* Digestion, digestive power, assimilation. Also **ਹਾਜ਼ਮਾ**

ਹਾਜਰ (haajar) *a* Present, in attendance, ready, readily available; **~ਹੋਣਾ** To be present, to present oneself, to attend, to appear; **~ਕਰਨਾ** To present, to produce, to supply, to make available; **~ਜਵਾਬ** Ready or nimble-witted; **~ਜਵਾਬੀ** Ready or nimble wit, wittiness; Repartee; **~ਨਾਜ਼ਰ** present, manifest, immanent, omnipresent. Also **ਹਾਜ਼ਰ**

ਹਾਜਰੀ (haajree) *n f* (1) Presence, attendance; rollcall; (2) *informal* breakfast, light meal; **~ਪੁਕਾਰਨੀ** To take roll-call, to call the roll; **~ਭਰਨੀ** To be in attendance, to be at someone's beck and call; to go and meet; to record attendance **~ਲਾਉਣੀ** To call and to mark attendance. Also **ਹਾਜ਼ਰੀ**

ਹਾਜਰੀਨ (haajreen) *n pl m* Audience, assembly of listeners or spectators viewers. Also **ਹਾਜ਼ਰੀਨ**

ਹਾਣ (haaṇ) *n m* Equality or near equality in age, coetaneousness.

ਹਾਣੀ (haaṇee) *n m* One's equal in

age; companion, pal, mate; lover.

ਹਾਨਣ (haanaṇ) *n f* Lady equal in age, lady mate of a lady.

ਹਾਥੀ (haathee) *n m* Elephant.

ਹਾਦਸਾ (haadsaa) *n m* Accident, casualty.

ਹਾਨੀ (haanee) *n f* Loss, harm, disadvantage, damage; **~ਕਾਰਕ** harmful, disadvantageous, adverse, detrimental.

ਹਾਮਲਾ (haamlaa) *a* Pregnant.

ਹਾਮੀ (haamee) *n f* Consent, assent, acceptance, support; **~ਭਰਨਾ** To support, to second, to back up, to advocate.

ਹਾਰ (haar) *n* (1) Defeat, loss, frustration, rout; (2) Necklace, wreath; **~ਸਿੰਗਾਰ** Ornamentation, adornment, make-up, cosmetics; **~ਪਾਉਣਾ** To garland; **~ਖਾਣੀ** To be defeated, to lose, to be overpowered.

ਹਾਰਨਾ (haarnaa) *v* To lose, to fail, to abandon.

ਹਾਲ (haal) *n m a* Condition, state, Situation; News; Hall; Recent, current, present.

ਹਾਲਤ (haalat) *n f* Condition, state, situation, position, circumstances, stage.

ਹਾਵੀ (haavee) *a* dominant, predominant, overbearing, overwhelming; **~ਹੋਣਾ** To dominate, predominate, to overbear, to overwhelm; To excel; To defeat.

ਹਾੜਨਾ (haarnaa) *v* To estimate, to guess at, to measure.

ਹਾੜ (haar) *n m* Fourth month of Bikrami calendar (mid-June to mid-July); Summer.

ਹਿੱਸਾ (hissa) *n m* share, part, portion, quota, contribution.

ਹਿਸਾਬ (hisaab) *n m* Account, Calculation, mathematics, arithmatics, computation; **~ਕਿਤਾਬ** Account, Book keeping, reckoning; **~ਚੁਕਾਉਣਾ** To clear, liquidate or settle account; **~ਦੇਣਾ** To render account; **~ਲਾਉਣਾ** To Calculate, to reckon, to estimate.

ਹਿੱਕ (hikk) *n f* Breast, bosom, chest.

ਹਿਕਣਾ (hikṇaa) *v* To drive (animal), to goad, to urge on. Also **ਹੱਕਣਾ**

ਹਿੰਗ (hing) *n f* Asafoetida; **~ਲਗੇ ਨਾ ਫਟਕੜੀ** *ph* Without cost or trouble.

ਹਿਚਕ (hichak) *n f* Hestiation, reluctance; Wavering, uacillation, uncertainty.

ਹਿਕਮਤ (hikmat) *n f* Wisdom

philosophy, physic, art of healing.

ਹਿਚਕਿਚਾਉਣਾ (hichkichaaunaa) *v* To hesitate, to waver, to vacillate, to falter. Also **ਹਿਚਕਿਚਾਣਾ**

ਹਿਚਕੀ (hichkee) *n f* Hiccough, sobbing, convulsion.

ਹਿਚਕੋਲਾ (hichkaulaa) *n m* Jolt, jerk, shock.

ਹਿਜਾ (hijjaa) *n m* Spelling.

ਹਿਣਹਿਣਾਉਣਾ (hinhinaaunaa) *v* To neigh (of horse).

ਹਿਤ (hitt) *n m Prep* Interest, affection, sincerity, gain; For.

ਹਿਤੂ (hittoo) *n m* Sincere, well-wisher, benefactor.

ਹਿੰਦਸਾ (hindsaa) *n m* Figure, digit.

ਹਿੰਦੁਸਤਾਨ (hindustaan) *n m* India.

ਹਿਫ਼ਾਜ਼ਤ (hifaazat) *n m* Safety, protection; **~ਕਰਨੀ** To protect, to guard, to keep in safe custody; **~ਵਿਚ ਲੈਣਾ** To take into custody, to provide protection.

ਹਿੰਮਤ (himmat) *n f* Courage, bravery, enterprise.

ਹਿਮਾਇਤ (himayit) *n m* Support, backing, help, aid, partisanship.

ਹਿਰਸ (hiras) *n f* Ambition, yearning, acquisitiveness, lust, desire, greed, avarice.

ਹਿਰਸੀ (hirsee) *a* Greedy, ambitious, covetous, avaricious.

ਹਿਰਖ (hirakh) *n m* Anger, irritation, displeasure, rage, complaint, grumble. Also **ਹਰਖ**

ਹਿਲਣਾ (hilnaa) *v* To move, to shake, to swing, to be dislocate.

ਹਿਲਾਉਣਾ (hillaunaa) *v* To shake, to toss to nod; To tame, to domesticate.

ਹੀਆ (heeaa) *n m* Heart, spirit; boldness, courage, guts.

ਹੀਂਗਣਾ (heengnaa) *v* To bray, to cry.

ਹੀਜੜਾ (heejraa) *n m* Eunuch.

ਹੀਣਤਾ (heentaa) *n f* Inferiority, abjectness, lowness.

ਹੀਣਾ (heenaa) *a* Low, poor, menial craven.

ਹੀਰਾ (heeraa) *n m a* Diamond, gem, pearl, jewel; Precious, costly, unique.

ਹੀਲ-ਹੁਜਤ (heel-hujat) *n f* Pretext, evasion, quirk, pretence.

ਹੀਲਾ (heelaa) *n f* Pretext, pretence, contrivance, way, effort, attempt.

ਹੁੱਸੜ (husar) *n m* Sultriness, stuffiness, stuffy weather; tiredness, tedium, boredom, impatience.

ਹੁਸੜਨਾ (husarnaa) *v* To long for, to feel uneasy.

ਹੁਸ਼ਿਆਰ (hushiaar) *a* Intelligent,

smart, competent; clever, shrewd, cunning; sensible, vigilant, cautious.

ਹੁਕਮ (hukam) *n m* Order, command, mandate, sanction; ~ਅਦੂਲੀ disobedience, defiance; ~ਨਾਮਾ Warrent, decree; ~ਰਾਨ Ruler, king, emperor.

ਹੁੱਕਾ (hukkaa) *n m* Smoking pipe, hookah; hubble-bubble; ~ਪਾਣੀ Social relations; ~ਪਾਣੀ ਬੰਦ ਕਰਨਾ To ostracise; ~ਪੀਣਾ To smoke hubble, bubble.

ਹੁੰਗਾਰਾ (hungaaraa) *n m* Monosyllabic response indicating assent or listener's attention, response or reaction, mostly in positive concurrence; ~ਭਰਨਾ To respond, to express support or concurrence.

ਹੁੱਜਤ (hujjat) *n m* Argument, controversy, disputation, excuse; joke, sarcasm; ~ਬਾਜ਼ੀ Pointless agrumentation; Jocularity, waggishness.

ਹਜੂਮ (hajoom) *n m* Crowd.

ਹੁੱਟਣਾ (hutnaa) *v* To feel tired, to be fatigued, to be weary.

ਹੁਣ (hun) *adv* Now, at present.

ਹੁਣੇ (hune) *adv* Just now, this very moment, presently; ~ਹੁਣੇ Just now, a little while ago.

ਹੁਨਰ (hunar) *n m* Accomplishment, craft, art, skill, talent; ~ਮੰਦ Skilful, meritorious.

ਹੁਨਾਲ (hunaal) *n m* Summer. Also ਹੁਨਾਲਾ

ਹੁਬਕਣਾ (hubaknaa) *v* To sob, to blubber, to snivel.

ਹੁਮਹੁਮਾਉਣਾ (humhumaaunaa) *v* To gather eagerly in large number.

ਹੁਲਸਾਉਣਾ (hulsaaunaa) *v* To be pleased, to be elated, to please.

ਹੁਲਣਾ (hulnaa) *v* To spread.

ਹੁਲੜ (hular) *n m* Tumult, uproar, disturbance, commotion, riot; ~ਬਾਜ਼ Disturbance maker, rioter

ਹੁਲਾਸ (hulaas) *n m* Joy, elation, cheerfulness, buoyancy, incentive.

ਹੁਲੀਆ (huliaa) *n m* Appearance, shape, features, description, descriptive roll.

ਹੁੜਕ (hurak) *n f* Longing, wish *esp* unfulfilled persistent expectation.

ਹੂਕਣਾ (hooknaa) *v* To raise, to utter cry fo pain.

ਹੂੰਝਣਾ (hoonjnaa) *v* To flush out, to scavenge, to sweep, to broom.

ਹੂਣਾ (hoonaa) *n m* Swing.

ਹੂਬਹੂ (hoobahoo) *adv* Exactly, actual, similar, graphic.

ਹੂਰ (hoor) *n f* Nymph, fairy of

ਹੇਕੜੀ (hekree) *n f* Arrogance, show of strength.

ਹੇਠ (heth) *adv* Below, under, beneath.

ਹੇਠਲਾ (Hethlaa) *adv* Bottom, lower, subordinate.

ਹੇਰਨਾ (hernaa) *v* To look, to search; To blockade

ਹੇਰ-ਫ਼ੇਰ (her-pher) *n* Exchange, reciprocation, shuffle, disorder, quirk.

ਹੇਰਾ-ਫੇਰੀ (heraa-pheree) *n f* Embezziement; deceit; trickery, pettifoggery, chicanery, gimmick, gimmickry; ~**ਕਰਨੀ** To embezzle; to deceive, to trick, to cheat, to pettifog.

ਹੈਸੀਅਤ (heseeat) *n f* Position, status, capacity.

ਹੈਰਤ (hairat) *n f* Ashtonishment, surprise, wonder.

ਹੈਰਾਨ (hairaan) *a* Surprised, perplexed, perturbed, worried.

ਹੈਰਾਨੀ (hairaanee) *n f* Surprise.

ਹੈਵਾਨ (haivaan) *n m* Rute, rustic, beast.

ਹੈਵਾਨੀਅਤ (haivaaniyat) *n f* Animal nature, animality, brutishness, beastliness.

ਹੋਕਾ (haukaa) *n m* Announcement, public proclamation.

ਹੋਰ (hor) *adv* More, other, additional.

ਹੋਸ਼ (hosh) *n m* Consciousness, sense, awakening; ~**ਉਡਣੇ** To be surprised, baffled, afraid or frightened; ~**ਹਵਾਸ** Consciousness, awareness, understanding, mental faculties, senses; ~**ਠਿਕਾਣੇ ਕਰਨੇ** To teach one a lesson, to bring one to one's senses.

ਹੋਛਾ (hochhaa) *a* Blunt, brusque, frivolous, flippant, uncivil, ill-mannered, undignified, mean.

ਹੋਣੀ (honee) *n f* Fate, destiny, predestination, the inevitable, appointed lot.

ਹੋੜ (hor) *n f* Competition.

ਹੌਂਸਲਾ (haunslaa) *n m* Courage, moral, spirit.

ਹੌਂਕਣਾ (haunknaa) *v* To breath quickly, to gast, to puff, to pant.

ਹੌਂਕਾ (haukaa) *n m* Sigh.

ਹੌਲ (haul) *n m* Fear, dread, terror, panic; ~**ਪੈਣਾ** To be terror-stricken.

ਹੌਲਣਾ (haulnaa) *v* To be frightened, to be horrified.

ਹੌਲਾ (haulaa) *a m* Light, undignified, easy, soft, sad, cheap; ~**ਪਣ** Lightness, pettiness, cheapness.

ਹੌਲੀ (haulee) *a f* Slow, mild, gradual.

ਕ

ਕ Sixth letter of Gurmukhi alphabets, pronounced as 'Kakkaa'.

ਕਉਲ (kaul) *n m* Promise; Brass bowl.

ਕਉਆ (kauaa) *n n* Crow.

ਕਸ਼ (kash) *n m* Puff, inhalation of tobacco, smoke; ~ਲਾਉਣਾ To smoke.

ਕਸ਼ਸ਼ (kashash) *n f* Attraction, tension. Also; ਕਿਸ਼ਸ਼

ਕਸਕ (kasak) *n f* Pang, twinge, spasm; Heartache, heartburning, anguish; grudge, enmity, jealousy; ~ਕੱਢਣੀ To Avenge, to retaliate.

ਕਸ਼ਟ (kasht) *n m* Hardship, agony, toil, tribulation.

ਕੱਸਣਾ (kassnaa) *v* To tighten, to clamp, to band, to clinch.

ਕਸਬਣ (kasban) *n f* Whore, prostitute.

ਕਸਬਾ (kasbaa) *n m* Town, townlet.

ਕਸਮ (kasam) *n f* Oath; ~ਖਾਣੀ To swear; ~ਦੁਆਉਣੀ To administer an oath.

ਕਸ਼ਮਕਸ਼ (kashmakash) *n f* Struggle, tension, dilemma; ~ਵਿੱਚ ਪੈਣਾ To be double minded.

ਕਸਰ (kasar) *n f* Default, deficiency, dearth, fraction, indisposition; ~ਕੱਢਣੀ To make up the loss; ~ਪੂਰੀ ਕਰਨੀ To make up the deficit; ~ਲਗਣੀ To incur a loss.

ਕਸਰਤ (kasrat) *n f* Exercise, sport, athletics, practice; ~ਕਰਨੀ To take exercise.

ਕਸਵਾਉਣਾ (kasvaaunaa) *v* To get tightened.

ਕੱਸਾ (kassaa) *a m* Deficient, less, short.

ਕਸਾਈ (kasaaee) *n m a* (1) Butcher; (2) Tightening, act of drawing out; (3) Cruel, merciless; ~ਪੁਣਾ Butcher's trade; Cruelty, mercilessness, pitiless nature, stone-heartedness.

ਕਸੀਦਾ (kaseedaa) *n m* Embroidery, needlework, broche.

ਕਸੈਲਾ (kasailaa) *a* Bitter, pungent, astringent; ~ਪਣ Bitterness, pungentness.

ਕਸੌਟੀ (kasautee) *n f* Criterion, norm, touch stone, proof, test.

ਕਹਾਉਣਾ (kahaaunaa) *v* To get some thing communicated, to cause or get someone say something, to be called, to be named. Also **ਅਖਵਾਉਣਾ**

ਕਹਾਣੀ (kahaanee) *n f* Story, tale, episode, fable; **~ਕਾਰ** Storywriter.

ਕਹਾਵਤ (kahaavat) *n f* Proverb, saying, maxim, dictum.

ਕਹਿਕਸ਼ਾਂ (kahekashaan) *n f* Rainbow.

ਕਹਿਕਹਾ (kahekahaa) *n m* Loud laughter.

ਕਹਿਣਾ (kahenaa) *v* To say, to speak, to tell, to utter, to address, to relate; **~ਸੁਣਨਾ** To counsel, to chat.

ਕਹਿਰ (kaehr) *n m* Wrath, anger, rage, ire; oppression; calamity, (divine) chastisement.

ਕਹਿਲਾਵਾ (kahelaavaa) *n m* Invitation, summon.

ਕਕੱਰ (kakkar) *n m* Frost, rime, glazedice.

ਕੰਕਰ (kankar) *n m* Small piece of stone, pebble, gravel, shingle.

ਕੰਕਰੀ (kankree) *n f* Pebble, small gravel.

ਕਕਰੀਲਾ (kakreelaa) *a m* Frosty, icycold, covered with frost.

ਕੱਕਾ (kakkh) *n m* Browm haired, golden (hair), auburn, blonde; The letter **ਕ**

ਕਕਾਰ (kakkar) *n m* The five symbols of Sikh faith, all with **ਕ** (k) in initial position-*Kachhaa*, underwear; *Karaa*, steel bangle; *Kirpaan*, sword or dagger; *Kes*, untrimmed hair; and *Kanghaa*, comb.

ਕਕੋਰੀਆ (kakoriaa) *a* Blue eyed.

ਕੱਖ (kakkh) *n m* Straw, piece of chaff dry stalk of grass.

ਕੰਗਣ (kangan) *n m* Bracelet, bangle, ornament for wrist.

ਕੰਗਲਾ (kanglaa) *a* Poor, beggerly.

ਕੰਗਾਲ (kangaal) *a n* Poor, penniloss, beggarly; Bankrupt.

ਕੰਘਾ (kanghaa) *n m* Comb.

ਕੰਘੀ (kanghee) *n f* Comb; **~ਪੱਟੀ** Hairdressing, make-up.

ਕੱਚ (kachch) *n m* Glass, sound of crushing or piercing, crudity, rawness, unripeness, inexperience; **~ਪੱਕ** Uncertainity.

ਕਚਹਿਰੀ (kachheree) *n f* Court, assembly, public office.

ਕਚਕਚ (kachkach) *n f* Excessive talk, foolish talk.

ਕਚਪਕਾ (kachpakka) *a m* Not fully ripe; half-baked.

ਕਚਰਾ (kachraa) *n m* Debris, rubbish, embryo.

ਕੱਚਾ (kachchaa) *a* Unripe, raw, unbaked, inexperienced, undeveloped, green, weak; **~ਕਾਗਜ਼** Provisional document;

~ਚਿੱਠਾ Inside story, naked truth, real tale; ~ਪੱਕਾ Undecided, undetermined, uncertain.

ਕਚਿਆਉਣਾ (kachiaaunaa) *v* To feel embarrassed, to feel ashamed.

ਕਚਾਵਾ (kachaavaa) *n m* Saddle (for came); pack-frame (for donkey), packsaddle.

ਕਚੂਮਰ (kachoomar) *n m* Anything cut into small pieces or crushed badly.

ਕੱਛਾ (kachhaa) *n m* Underwear, shorts.

ਕੱਛਣਾ (kachhnaa) *v* To measure (land).

ਕਛਾਉਣਾ (kachhaunaa) *v* to get measured.

ਕਛਾਰ (kachhaar) *n f* Marshy land.

ਕਛੀ (kachhee) *n f* Underwear of a child.

ਕੰਜ (kanj) *n f* A small girl; ~ਕੁਆਰੀ Innocent virgin; Barren.

ਕੰਜਕ (kanjak) *n f* Innocent virgin girl.

ਕੰਜਣਾ (kanjnaa) *v* To cover, to veil, to enshroud.

ਕੰਜਰ (kanjar) *n m* A man dealing with prostitutes, man with no respect, shameless man; ~ਖਾਨਾ Brothel, bawdy house, house of ill fame; ~ਪੁਣਾ Prostitution; shamelessness, utter lack of selfrespect.

ਕੰਜਰੀ (kanjree) *n f* Prostitute.

ਕੰਜੂਸ (kanjoos) *n m a* Miser, miserly, stingy, hunks.

ਕੰਜੂਸੀ (kanjoosee) *n f* Miserliness, niggardliness, stinginess, skimpiness,

ਕਟਣਾ (katnaa) *v* To cut, to bite, to chop, to intersect, to deduct, to strike out.

ਕਟਵਾਈ (katvaaee) *n* Cutting, mowing, reaping.

ਕੱਟੜ (katar) *a* Staunch, dogmatic, orthodox, bigot, fanatic, intolerant, fundamentalist; ~ਤਾ Dogmatism, fundamentalism; ~ਪੰਥੀ Orthodox, fanatic, fundamentalist (person) ਕੱਟੜ

ਕਟਾਰ (kataar) *n* Dagger, dirk, poniard.

ਕਟਾਰੀ (kataaree) *n* Dagger, dirk, poniard.

ਕਟੋਰਾ (katauraa) *n m* Bowl, cup,

ਕਟੋਰੀ (katauree) *n f* Small bowl, goblet of metal.

ਕਟੌਤੀ (katautee) *n f* Discount, commission, deduction.

ਕੰਠ (kanth) *n m a* Throat, committed to memory; ~ਮਾਲਾ Necklace; ~ਲਾਉਣਾ To embrace.

ਕਠਪੁਤਲੀ (kathputlee) *n f* Puppet; *fig*

a subservient, obsequious person, stooge, underling, accomplice.

ਕੰਠੀ (kanthee) *n f* Pearl necklace, an ornament for the neck..

ਕਠੋਰ (kathor) *a* Hard, harsh, rough, severe, rigid, stern, unbending; ~**ਤਾ** Hardness, rigidity, harshness

ਕੰਡ (kand) *n f* Back; behind, rear; ~**ਕਰਨਾ** To desert, To withdraw support; ~**ਪਿਛੇ** Behind the back; ~**ਲਗਣੀ** To be defeated; ~**ਵਿਖਾਉਣੀ** To flee, to show one's back.

ਕੰਡਾ (kandaa) *n m* (1) Thorn, fork, hindrance, impediment; (2) Big scale or balance, weighing machine.

ਕੰਡੀ (kandee) *n f* Small weighing scale.

ਕੱਢਣਾ (kadhnaa) *v* To draw forth, to oust, to turn out, to expel, to solve a question; To embroider.

ਕੰਢਾ (kandhaa) *n m* Shore, coast; Edge, verge, margin.

ਕਢਾਉਣਾ (kadhaaunaa) *v* To get embroided.

ਕਢਾਈ (kadhaaee) *n f* Embroidary.

ਕਣ (kan) *n f* Particle, seed, grain.

ਕਣਕ (kanak) *n f* Wheat.

ਕਣੀ (kanee) *n f* Rain drop; Broken rice.

ਕੱਤਣਾ (kattnaa) *v* To spin.

ਕਤਰਨਾ (katarnaa) *v* To cut, to trim, to chop, to strip.

ਕਤਰਨੀ (katarnee) *n f* Scissors.

ਕਤਰਾ (katraa) *n m* Drop.

ਕਤਰਾਉਣਾ (katraaunaa) *v* (1) To avoid, to shirk, to fudge, to dodge; (2) To get something cut, clipped.

ਕਤਲ (katal) *n m* Murder, slaughter; ~**ਕਰਨਾ** To murdor, to assassinate, to kill, to slay.

ਕਤਾਰ (kataar) *n f* Row, line, series, order.

ਕਤੂਰਾ (katooraa) *n m* Pup, cur, whelp.

ਕਥਾ (kathaa) *n f* Sermon, tale, anecdote, narrative.

ਕੱਦ (kadd) *n m* Height, stature, size, magnitude; ~**ਆਹਰ** tall

ਕਦਮ (kadam) *n f* Step, foot.

ਕਦਰ (kadar) *n f* Respect, value, worth, merit, deference; ~**ਕਰਨੀ** To respect, to honour, to appreciate; ~**ਦਾਨ** Patron, connoisseur.

ਕਦਾਚਾਰ (kadaachaar) *n m* Misconduct, delinquency, bad behaviour.

ਕਦਾਵਰ (kadaavar) *a* Stalwart, hefty, tall.

ਕਦੀ (kadee) *adv* Sometimes, seldom, ever, on some occasion.

ਕਦੀਮ (kadeem) *a* Ancient, old.

ਕਦੂ (kaddoo) *n m a* Gourd, pumkin, cucurbit; Dull, simpleton, foolish; ~ਕਸ਼ Grater.

ਕੰਧ (kandh) *n f* Wall.

ਕੰਧਾ (kandhaa) *n m* Shoulder.

ਕੰਧੀ (kandhee) *n f* Bank (of a river), border, margin.

ਕੰਧੂਈ (kandhooee) *n f* Darning needle

ਕੰਨ (kann) *n m* Ear; ~ਹੋ ਜਾਣੇ To be alert, to learn a lesson, to know; ~ਕੱਟਣਾ To excel in cunning or cleverness; ~ਕਰਨੇ To warn; To be attentive; ~ਖੜੇ ਹੋਣੇ To be alarmed; ~ਖਾਣਾ To make much noise, to vex; ~ਧਰਨਾ to listen attentively; ~ਨਾ ਧਰਨਾ To pay deaf ears to; ~ਪੈਣਾ To hear a rumour.

ਕਨਪੇੜਾ (kanperaa) *n m* Swelling behind the ears, mumps.

ਕਨਾਤ (kanaat) *n f* Canopy, canvas wall.

ਕੰਨੂਨ (kanoon) *n m* Law, statute, regulation, legislation, rule; ~ਛਾਂਟਣਾ To argue unnecessarily; ~ਦਾਨ Jurist, lawyer, legal expert; ~ਨ According to or as per law; ~ਬਣਾਉਣਾ To legistate, to make law Also ਕਾਨੂੰਨ

ਕਨੂੰਨੀ (kanoonee) *a* legal, lawful, legitimate, dejure; pettifogger.

ਕਪਟ (kapat) *n m* Fraud, deceit, trick, cajolery, malice, guile; ~ਤਾ Deceitfulness.

ਕਪਣਾ (kapnaa) *v* To cut, to chop

ਕਪਤਾਨ (kaptaan) *n m* Captain.

ਕੰਪਨ (kampan) *n m* Shivering, trembling, vibration.

ਕਪੜਾ (kapraa) *n m* Clothing, cloth, dress, fabric, apparel.

ਕਪਾਹ (kapaah) *n f* Cotton.

ਕਪਾਲ (kapaal) *n m* Skull, head; fate, destiny.

ਕਪੂਰ (kapoor) *n m* Camphor.

ਕਪੂਰਾ (kapooraa) *n m* Testicle or kidney of male goat.

ਕਫ਼ਨ (kafan) *n m* Coffin, shroud, pall.

ਕਫ਼ਾਇਤ (kafaait) *n f* Thrift, economy, sufficiency; ~ਕਰਨੀ To economise.

ਕੰਬਖ਼ਤ (kambhakhat) *a* Unfortunate, unlucky.

ਕੰਬਖ਼ਤੀ (kambhakhtee) *n f* Misfortune, wretchedness, adversity.

ਕਬਜ਼ (kabaz) *n f* Constipation, catching, seizure; ~ਕੁਸ਼ Laxative, purgative, digestive.

ਕਬਜ਼ਾ (kabzaa) *n m* (1) Seizure, hold, occupancy, possession,

(2) Handle, grip; Hinge; ~ਕਰਨਾ To occupy, to possess, to seize, to conquer.

ਕਬਜ਼ੀ (Kabzee) *n f* Constipation.

ਕੰਬਣਾ (kambṇaa) *v* To tremble, to shiver, to shake, to shudder.

ਕੰਬਣੀ (kambaṇee) *n f* Trembling motion, tremble, shiver, vibration, shudder, tremor. Also **ਕਾਂਬਾ**

ਕਬਰ (kabar) *n f* Tomb, grave; ~ਸਤਾਨ Graveyard, cemetry.

ਕੰਬਲ (kambal) *n f* Blanket, wollen sheet.

ਕਬਾਇਲੀ (kabaailee) *a* Tribal; Tribesman; The tribals.

ਕਬਾਬ (kabaab) *n m* Roasted meat, roast.

ਕਬਾਲਾ (kabaalaa) *n m* Transfer, sale deed.

ਕਬਾੜ (kabaaṛ) *n m* Junk, Useless broken material; ~ਖਾਨਾ Junk store.

ਕਬਾੜਾ (kabaaṛaa) *n m* Turmoil, Ruination.

ਕਬਾੜੀ (kabaaṛee) *n m* Junkman, dealer in second hand & useless material.

ਕਬਿੱਤ (kabitt) *n m* Poetry, verse.

ਕਬੀਲਾ (kabeelaa) *n m* Tribe, clan.

ਕਬੂਤਰ (Kabootar) *n m* Pigeon; ~ਖਾਨਾ Pigeon house, loft.

ਕਬੂਲ (kabool) *a* Accepted, confessed; ~ਕਰਨਾ To confess, to admit, to accept.

ਕਬੂਲਣਾ (kaboolṇaa) *v* To confess, to accept.

ਕਮ (kam) *a* Less, little; ~ਉਮਰ Adolescent; ~ਅਕਲ Stupid, feeble minded.

ਕੰਮ (kamm) *n m* Work, business, task, act, action, service, deed, occupation, purpose; ~ਆਉਣਾ To be use, to be helpful; ~ਕੱਢਣਾ To have one's purpose served; ~ਕਰਨਾ To work, to serve, To labour, to be busy.

ਕਮਜ਼ਾਤ (kamzaat) *a* Of low birth or caste, mean, base, ignoble.

ਕਮਜ਼ੋਰ (kamzor) *a* Weak, insecure, feeble; Impotent.

ਕਮਜ਼ੋਰੀ (kamzoree) *n f* Weakness, feebleness, infirmity, debility, fragility, Impotence, *Hyposthenia*.

ਕਮਰ (kamar) *n f* Waist, loins; ~ਸਿੱਧੀ ਕਰਨਾ To relax; ~ਕਸਨੀ To get ready, to gird up one's loins; ~ਟੁਟਣੀ To be discouraged, to lose support.

ਕਮਰਾ (kamraa) *n m* Room, chamber, closet.

ਕਮਲ (kamal) *n m* Lotus.

ਕਮਲਾ (kamlaa) *n f a* Beautiful lady,

the goddess lakshmi; Insane mad, crazy.

ਕਮਾਉਣਾ (kamaaunaa) *v* To earn, to acquire, to gain.

ਕਮਾਉ (kamaau) *a* Earning, earner, bread-winner, hard-working, industrious.

ਕਮਾਈ (kamaaee) *n f* Earning, wages, gain.

ਕਮਾਦ (kamaad) *n m* Sugarcane.

ਕਮਾਨੀ (kamaanee) *n f* Spring.

ਕਮਾਲ (kamaal) *n m* Miracle, accomplishment, excellence, perfection.

ਕਮੀ (kamee) *n f* Want, dearthy, paucity, shortfall, decrease.

ਕਮੀਜ਼ (kameez) *n f* Shirt.

ਕਮੀਨਾ (kameenaa) *a* Mean, base, low; ~**ਪਨ** Meanness.

ਕਮੇਰਾ (kameraa) *n m* Worker, labourer.

ਕਰਜ਼ (karaz) *n m* Debit, loan, credit; ~**ਦਾਰ** Debitor, indebted. Also **ਕਰਜ਼ਾ**

ਕਰਜ਼ਾਈ (karzaaee) *n m* Borrower, indebtor.

ਕਰਨੀ (karnee) *n f* Deed, doing, performance.

ਕਰਤਬ (kartab) *n m* Skill, trick, action, jugglery, performance.

ਕਰਤਾਰ (kartaar) *n m* God, the creator.

ਕਰਤੂਤ (kartoot) *n f* Misconduct, misdeed, action.

ਕਰਨਹਾਰ (karnanhaar) *a n m* Doer, creator; God.

ਕਰਨਾ (karnaa) *v* To do, to act, perform; To practice (as in **ਪੀਆ ਕਰਦਾ** used to drink or usually drank).

ਕਰਨੀ (karnee) *n f* Deeds, actions, conduct, practice.

ਕਰਨੈਲ (karnail) *n m* colonel.

ਕ੍ਰਮ (kram) *n m* Grade, Sequence, series; ~**ਸੰਖਿਆ** Serial number.

ਕਰਮ (karam) *n* (1) Action, deed, performance, (2) destiny, fate; (3) Object (gr) ; ~**ਸ਼ਾਲਾ** Workshop; ~**ਚਾਰੀ** Official, servant, worker.

ਕਰਵਟ (karvaṭ) *n f* Side, back.

ਕਰੜਾ (karraa) *a* Hard, strong, harsh, stiff, strict, tough, inflexible, difficult; ~**ਈ** Toughness, stiffness, hardness, strictness.

ਕਰਾਉਣਾ (kaaraaunaa) *v* To get or have (something) done; to assist in doing something. Also **ਕਰਵਾਉਣਾ**

ਕਰਾਏਦਾਰ (karaaedaar) *n m* Tenant, hirer, lodger.

ਕਰਾਹੁਣਾ (krahunaa) *v* To groan, to cry in pain, to moan.

ਕਰਾਮਾਤ (kraamaat) *n f* Miracle,

wonder, magic.

ਕਰਾਮਾਤੀ (karaamaatee) *a* Miraculous, thaumaturgic miracle-maker, thaumaturge.

ਕਰਾਰ (karaar) *n m* Promise, undertaking, word of honour; stability, satisfaction, mental calm.

ਕਰਾਰਾ (kraaraa) *a* Crisp, spicy, piquant, Strong.

ਕਰਾੜ (kraar̲) *a* Miser, thrifty; Money-lender; Petty shopkeeper, small businessman.

ਕਰਿਆਨਾ (kariyaanaa) *n* Grocery, provision.

ਕਰੀਚਣਾ (kareechnaa) *v* To grind, to gnash, grit (teeth).

ਕਰੀਬ (kareeb) *adv* Near, near about, close to, not far; About, nearly, approximately.

ਕਰੀਬਨ (kareeban) *adv* Nearly, approximately, roughly, almost.

ਕਰੀਬੀ (kareebee) *a* Near, close, (relation or place); nearness, closeness.

ਕਰੀਮ (kareem) *a* Kind, benign, benevolent, compassionate, bounteous, bountiful, clement; An attribute of God.

ਕਰੀੜਨਾ (kreer̲naa) *v* To grind (teeth), to gnash.

ਕਰੇਡਣਾ (karer̲naa) *v* To scrape.

ਕਰੋਸ਼ੀਆ (karoshiaa) *n m* Crochet, crochet-needle.

ਕਰੋਧ (krodh) *n m* Anger, wrath, rage, fury, resentment.

ਕਰੋੜ (karor) *a* Crore, ten million; **~ਪਤਿ** Multi-millionaire, a very rich person.

ਕੱਲ (kall) *n m* Tomorrow, yesterday.

ਕਲਹ (kalah) *n f* Clash, quarrel, scrimmage.

ਕਲੰਕ (kalank) *n m* Blemish, stigma, moral stain, blot, smudge, splodge smirch, smear; taint; ignominy disgrace.

ਕਲਤਰ (kalatar) *n f* Wife.

ਕਲਪਣਾ (kalapnaa) *v* To lament, to grieve.

ਕਲਪਾਉਣਾ (kalpaaunaa) *v* To cause grief or annoyance, to vex, to annoy, to irritate, to torment.

ਕਲਫ (kalaf) *n f* Starch, farina; hairdye.

ਕਲਬੂਤ (kalboot) *n m* Frame, body, mould; last, shoe-stretcher.

ਕਲਮ (kalam) *n f* Pen; Reed; Cutting, graft; Wedge; Unshaved tuft of hair near the temples; **~ਕਰਨਾ** To cut, to sever; **~ਬਣਨੀ** To sharpen reed-pen; **~ਚਲਾਉਣੀ** To exercise authority, to issue order or judgement; **~ਫੇਰਨੀ** To delete, erase, to cancel, to strike out, to bring to nothing, to destory; ~ਲਾਉਣੀ To plant a cutting; to graft; ~ਦਾਨ Ink-stand, inkpot stand.

ਕਲਮਾ (kalmaa) *n m* Muhammadan's sacred formula; speech, utterance, sentence.

ਕਲਮੀ (kalmee) *a* Written; grafted, (fruit) bone by a grafted tree; crystalline.

ਕਲਪਨਾ (kalpnaa) *n f* Imagination, assumption, notion, hypothesis, supposition, fancy, dream.

ਕਲਮੂੰਹਾ (kalmoonhaa) *a* Swart, swarthy.

ਕੱਲ੍ਹ (kallh) *n m* Yesterday, tomorrow; ~ਕੱਲ੍ਹ ਕਰਨਾ To go on postponing, delaying; ~ਪਰਸੋਂ A few day back.

ਕਲ੍ਹਾ (kalhaa) *n f* Quarrel, tussle, conflict, discord, trouble.

ਕਲਾ (kalaa) *n f* Art, skill, craft, fine, art, machine; Supernatural, power; Phase of moon; ~ਬਾਜ Acrobat, gymnast; ~ਬਾਜ਼ੀ Acrobatic feat, somersault; volteface; Acrobatics, gymnastics.

ਕੱਲਾ (kallaa) *a* Alone, lonely, single, solitary, lone. Also ਇਕੱਲਾ

ਕਲਾਮ (kalaam) *n m* Utterance, speech; sacred text; poem, verse, poetic work.

ਕਲਾਵਾ (kalaavaa) *n m* Armful; grip with both arms extended, encirclement with arm; Hug embrace.

ਕਲਿਆਣ (kaliyaan) *n m* Welfare, benediction, success; ~ਕਾਰੀ Auspicious, blissful, benedictory.

ਕਲੂਟਾ (kalootaa) *a* Dark, complexioned.

ਕਲੇਸ਼ (kalesh) *n m* Anguish, distress, trouble, agony, affliction, torment.

ਕਲੇਜਾ (kalejaa) *n m* Liver, bosom, heart, courage; ~ਸਾੜਨਾ To give pain, to torment, to cause jealousy.

ਕਲੇਜੀ (kalejee) *n f* Liver of slaughtered bird or animal.

ਕਵਾਰਾ (kawaaraa) *n m* Bachelor, unmarried youth.

ਕਵਿਤਾ (kavitaa) *n f* Poetry, poem, verse.

ਕੜਕ (karak) *n m* Crash, Cracking sound, sound of breaking up.

ਕੜਕਣਾ (karaknaa) *a* To crackle, to thunder, to chuck.

ਕੜਛਾ (karchhaa) *n m* Large cooking spoon, ladle.

ਕੜਛੀ (karchhee) *n f* Cooking or serving, spoon, ladle.

ਕੜਨਾ (karnaa) *a* To tie, to fasten or bind tightly.

ਕੜ੍ਹਨਾ (karhnaa) *v* To boil, to rise

ਕੜਾ (karaa) *n m* A metallic, metal ring, wrislet; Hard; Stout.

ਕੜਾਹ (karaah) *n m* Pudding of flour, sugar and butter.

ਕੜਾਹਾ (karaahaa) *n m* Cauldron, large frying pan.

ਕੜਾਹੀ (karaahee) *n f* Frying pan, stewpan.

ਕੜਾਕਾ (karakaa) *n m* Cracking sound; Intenseness; ~ਦਾਰ Crisp.

ਕਾਂ (kaan) *n* Crow. Also **ਕਾਉਂ**

ਕਾਇਦਾ (kaaidaa) *n m* (1) Custom, base, rule, law, practice, good manner, (2) Primer, elementary text book.

ਕਾਇਲ (kaail) *a* Convinced, subdued; ~ਹੋਣਾ To be convinced, the impressed, to believe.

ਕਾਈ (kaaee) *n f* Moss, fungus.

ਕਾਸਦ (kaasad) *n m* Messenger, ambassador. Also **ਕਾਸਿਦ**

ਕਾਸ਼ਤ (kaashat) *n f* Cultivation, sowing, tilage, tilth; ~ਕਰਨਾ To cultivate, grow, produce; to till, to plough; ~ਕਾਰ Cultivatior, farmer, agriculturist; ~ਕਾਰੀ Farming, agriculture, cultivation.

ਕਾਸਬੀ (kaasbee) *n m* Weaver.

ਕਾਹਲ (kaahal) *a* Lazy, lethargic, slothful, indolent.

ਕਾਹਲੀ (kaahlee) *a* Hurriedly, hastly, quickly, fast.

ਕਾਹਨੂੰ (kaahnoo) *adv* Why, what for.

ਕਾਹਲਾ (kaahlaa) *a* Hasty, impetuous.

ਕਾਹਵਾ (kahwaa) *n m* Tea without milk, coffee.

ਕਾਕੜਾ (kaakraa) *n m* Measles.

ਕਾਗਜ਼ (kaagaz) *n m* Paper, Written document.

ਕਾਂਗੜੀ (kanngree) *n f* Warming pan.

ਕਾਟ (kaat) *n* Cut, dissection, cutting, wound, deduction.

ਕਾਠ (kaath) *n m* Wood, timber.

ਕਾਠੀ (kaathee) *n f* (1) Saddle; (2) Frame, appearance, body, shape.

ਕਾਣ (kaan) *n m* Defect, blemish, crookedness.

ਕਾਣਾ (kaanaa) *a* One eyed.

ਕਾਤਲ (kaatal) *n m* Murderer, assassin, killer.

ਕਾਤੀ (kaatee) *n f* Scissors, dagger, Shears.

ਕਾਦਰ (kaadar) *a* Almighty, potent, all powerful; creator or lord of creation; God. Also **ਕੁਦਰਤ**

ਕਾਨਾਫੂਸੀ (kanaaphoosee) *n* Whisper,

Secret talk in a low tone.

ਕਾਫ਼ਰ (kaafar) *n m* Atheist, infidel, heretic, agnostic, non-believer in God or in Islamic; Renegade, apostate.

ਕਾਫ਼ਲਾ (kaaflaa) *n m* Caravan.

ਕਾਫ਼ੀ (kafee) *a n m* Sufficient, enough, adequate; Coffee.

ਕਾਬਜ਼ (kaabaz) *a* In possession, possessing, holding, in occupation, occupant.

ਕਾਬਲ (kabal) *n m* Able, capable, competent, qualified, worthy, deserving, fit, intelligent, learned, meritorious.

ਕਾਬਲੀਅਤ (kableeyat) *n f* Ability, worthiness, capacity.

ਕਾਬੂ (kaboo) *n m* Control, hold, command, power.

ਕਾਮਯਾਬ (Kaamyaab) *a* Successful; ~ਹੋਣਾ To be successful, to succeed.

ਕਾਮਰੀ (kaamree) *n m* Blanket.

ਕਾਮਲ (kaamal) *a* Perfect, complete, expert, accomplished.

ਕਾਰਸਤਾਨੀ (kaarastaanee) *n f* Mischief, doing, conspiracy.

ਕਾਰਕੁਨ (kaarkun) *n m* Worker, member, agent, clerk.

ਕਾਰਖਾਨਾ (kaarkhaanaa) *n m* Mill, factory.

ਕਾਰਗਰ (kaargar) *a* Effective, beneficial.

ਕਾਰਗੁਜ਼ਾਰ (kaarguzaar) *n m* Performer, worker.

ਕਾਰਗੁਜ਼ਾਰੀ (kaarguzaaree) *n f* Performance, work, achievement.

ਕਾਰਜ (kaaraj) *n m* Action, work, business, transaction, task; ~ਸਾਧਕ Useful, instrumental, officiating, executive; ~ਭਾਰ Work load, responsibility; ~ਵਾਹਕ Acting, officiating, temporary, adhoc.

ਕਾਰਨ (kaaran) *n m* Cause, reason, motive, ground; purpose; factor responsible for; Because of, due to, owing to, by reason of, by virtue of.

ਕਾਰਨਾਮਾ (kaarnaamaa) *n m* Achievement, adventure, feat, laudable deed.

ਕਾਰਵਾਈ (kaarvaaee) *n f* Proceedings; action, activity.

ਕਾਰਿੰਦਾ (kaarindaa) *n m* Agent, worker.

ਕਾਰੀਗਰ (kaareegar) *n m* Workman, artisan, mechanic, craftsman.

ਕਾਰੀਗਰੀ (kaareegaree) *n f* Skill, workmanship, mastery, proficiency, adroitness, dexterity.

ਕਾਰੋਬਾਰ (kaarobaar) *n m* Occupation, business.

ਕਾਲ (kaal) *n* (1) Time, period, era; (2) Death, famine; (3) Tense(gr); ~ਕੋਠੜੀ Dungeon, dark cell.

ਕਾਲਖ (kaalakh) *n f* Soot, smudge, blot, stain.

ਕਾਲਾ (kaalaa) *a m* Black, dark; ~ਸੱਪ Adder; ~ਚੋਰ Notorious thief; ~ਨੀਲਾ unfair, ugly; ~ਮੋਤੀਆ Glaucoma.

ਕਾਲੀ (kaalee) *a f* Black, dusky, dark; ~ਮਿਰਚ Black pepper.

ਕਾਵਿ (kaavi) *n m* Poetry, poesy, poetic literature, poetic composition or work; ~ਸ਼ਾਸਤਰ Poetics, prosody, treatise on versification; ~ਕਲਾ Art of poetry, poetic art; ~ਚੋਰੀ Plagiarism; ~ਰਚਨਾ Versification, poetic work or composition.

ਕਾੜ੍ਹਨਾ (kaarhnaa) *v* To boil thoroughly, to boil on low heat for a long time, to decoct.

ਕਾੜ੍ਹ (kaarhaa) *n m* Decoction, herbs or drugs decocted in water; Intensily hot; Sultry weather.

ਕਿਆਰਾ (kiara) *n m* Plot, subdivison of a field.

ਕਿਆਮਤ (kiyaamat) *n f* Calamity, oppression, doom, annihilation.

ਕਿਸ਼ਤ (kisht) *n f* Instalment.

ਕਿਸ਼ਤੀ (kishtee) *n f* Boat dinghy, canoe.

ਕਿਸਮ (kisam) *n f* Type, variety, kind, class.

ਕਿਸਮਤ (kismat) *n f* Fate, fortune, luck.

ਕਿੱਸਾ (kissaa) *n m* Story; ~ਤਮਾਮ ਕਰਨਾ To put on end to, to wind up.

ਕਿਸਾਨ (kisaan) *n* Farmer, peasant, agriculturist, cultivator.

ਕਿਹੜਾ (kehraa) *pron* Which, what, who?

ਕਿਕਣ (kikan) *adv* How?

ਕਿਕਲੀ (kiklee) *n f* A kind of folk dance performed by females; a peal of laughter.

ਕਿਚਕਿਚਾਉਣਾ (kichkichaaunaa) *v* To grind or gnash teeth in anger.

ਕਿਣਕਾ (kinkaa) *n m* Particle, speck, granule, broken piece of grain; Atom.

ਕਿਤਾਬ (kitaab) *n f* Book, publication; ~ਚਾ Booklet, pamphlet.

ਕਿਤਾਬੀ (kitaabee) *a* Bookish.

ਕਿਥੇ (kithe) *adv* Where?

ਕਿੱਦਣ (kiddan) *adv* When, on what day or date.

ਕਿਧਰੇ (kidhre) *adv* Perchance, possibly.

ਕਿਧਰੋਂ (kindron) *adv* Wherefrom, from

which side or direction, from where?

ਕਿਨਵਾਂ (kinvaan) *a* Which one, where (in a series or sequence).

ਕਿਨ੍ਹੇ (kinne) *pron* Who, which one (in subjective case).

ਕਿਨਾਰਾ (kinaaraa) *n m* Bank, shore coast; Border, side hem. Also **ਕੰਢਾ**

ਕਿਨਾਰਾਕਸ਼ੀ (kinaaraakashee) *n m* Standing apart, dissociation.

ਕਿਨਾਰੀ (kinaaree) *n f* Hem, edging, lace, fringe, tatting.

ਕਿਰਕਿਰਾ (kirkiraa) *a* Spoiled, gritty, sandy.

ਕਿਰੱਤਗ (kirtagg) *a* Obliged, grateful; ~ਤਾ Gratitude, obligation. Also **ਕ੍ਰਿਤਗਤਾ**

ਕਿਰਤਘਣ (kiratghaṇ) *a* Ungrateful, unthankful. Also **ਕ੍ਰਿਤਘਣ**

ਕਿਰਤਾਰਥ (kirataarath) *a* Obliged, grateful, gratified.

ਕਿਰਪਾ (kirpaa) *n f* Kindness, benignity, compassion; favour, benevolence, beneficence, benefaction; mercy, grace, graciousness; ~ਕਰ ਕੇ Kindly, please; ~ਕਰਨੀ To be kind, benign; to favour, oblige, bestow benefaction or benefit, to do a good turn, to do favour.

ਕਿਰਦਾਰ (kirdaar) *n m* Role, character.

ਕਿਰਪਾਨ (kirpaan) *n f* Sword.

ਕਿਰਪਾਲਤਾ (kirpaaltaa) *n f* Graciousness, beneficence.

ਕਿਰਲਾ (kirlaa) *n m* Big lizzard.

ਕਿਰਲੀ (kirlee) *n f* Lizzard.

ਕਿਰਾਇਆ (kiraayiaa) *n m* Rent, fare, hiring or Conveyance charges. Also **ਕਰਾਇਆ**

ਕਿੱਲ (kill) *n f* Iron nail, pin, tack.

ਕਿਲਾ (killaa) *n m* Fort, garrison, castle, citadel.

ਕਿਲਕਾਰੀ (kilkaaree) *n f* Outcry, joyful shriek.

ਕਿਲੱਤ (killat) *n f* Deficiency, scarcity, want, shortage, paucity, dearth.

ਕਿੱਲੀ (killee) *n f* Peg, trenail.

ਕਿਵਾੜ (kivaaṛ) *n m* Door, gate.

ਕਿੜਕਿੜ (kiṛkiṛ) *n f* Cracking sound.

ਕੀ (kee) *pron* What, whether. Also **ਕੀਹ**

ਕੀਕਣ (keekan) *adv* How, in what way. Also **ਕੀਕੂੰ**

ਕੀਨਾ (keenaa) *n m* Malice, spite, rancour, vindictiveness, vindictive feeling; ~ਰੱਖਣਾ To harbour Malice To be vindictive, rancorous

ਕੀਮਖ਼ਾਬ (keemkhaab) *n m* Costly silken cloth, brocade.

ਕੀਮਾ (keemaa) *n m* Minced meat.

ਕੀਰਤ (keerat) *n m* Reputation.

ਕੀਰਤਨ (kirtan) *n m* Hymn singing, devotional singing in praise of deity; ~ਕਰਨਾ To Perform hymn.

ਕੀਰਤੀ (keertee) *n f* Glory, fame, reputation, praise.

ਕੀੜਾ (Keeraa) *n m* Insect, worm, vermin.

ਕੁਸਕਣਾ (kusaknaa) *v* To speak meekly, to utter a word.

ਕੁਸੰਗਤ (kusangat) *n f* Bad company.

ਕੁਸ਼ਤੀ (kushtee) *n f* Wrestling, duel.

ਕੁਹਾੜਾ (kuhaaraa) *n m* Large axe.

ਕੁਹਾੜੀ (kuhaaree) *n f* Small axe, chopper, hatchet.

ਕੁੱਕੜ (kukkar) *n m* Cock; ~ਖਾਨਾ Poultry farm.

ਕੁੱਕੜੀ (kukkree) *n f* Hen; bobbin.

ਕੁੱਖ (kukkh) *n f* Womb, cavity; ~ਹਰੀ ਹੋਣੀ To be pregnant, to bear a child.

ਕੁਚੱਜਾ (kuchajjaa) *n m* Awkwardness, clumsiness, lack of proper manner or method; tactlessness.

ਕੁੱਚਲਣਾ (kuchalnaa) *v* To crush, to squash, to run over, to tread.

ਕੁੱਛੜ (kuchchhar) *n f* Lap, bosom, haunch.

ਕੁੰਜੀ (kunjee) *n f* Key, note, annotation of a book.

ਕੁੱਝ (kujh) *a* Some, a little, something.

ਕੁਟਣਾ (kutnaa) *v* To beat, to thrash, to pound, to cudgel.

ਕੁਟਾਈ (kutaaee) *n f* Beating, thrashing.

ਕੁੰਡਲ (kundal) *n m* Curl lock (of hair), ringlet; coil, spiral; noose of rope; large heavy ear-ring; curlicue curlycue; ~ਦਾਰ Curly, coiled, spiralled.

ਕੁੰਡਲੀ (kundlee) *n f* Small coil or ring, Horoscope.

ਕੁੰਡਾ (kundaa) *n m* Bolt, hook, chain, hatchet.

ਕੁੰਡੀ (Kundee) *n f* Bolt, hook, chain, staple.

ਕੁਤਪੁਣਾ (kutpunaa) *n m* Wrangling, querrel, meanness, doglike behaviour.

ਕੁਤਰਨਾ (kutarnaa) *v* To gnaw, to cut into small pieces.

ਕੁੱਤਾ (kuttaa) *n m* Dog, a low and mean person.

ਕੁਤਾਹੀ (kutaahee) *n f* Carelessness, deficiency, want, decrease.

ਕੁੱਤੀ (kuttee) *n f* Bitch.

ਕੁਦਣਾ (kudnaa) *v* To jump, to leap, to dance, to hop.

ਕੁੰਦਨ (kundan) *n m* Pure gold; Pure, good, honest; in perfect health.

ਕੁਦਰਤ (kudarat) *n f* Nature, divinity, power; ~ਨ Naturally, by chance, coincidently.

ਕੁਦਰਤੀ (kudartee) *a* Natural, divine; innate; unexpected; By chance, naturally.

ਕੁਨਬਾ (kunbaa) *n m* Family, kinsfolk.

ਕੁੱਪਤ (kupatt) *n m* Quarrel, altercation, wrangle, brawl, squabble; dishonourable or disorderly behaviour.

ਕੁੱਪਤਾ (kupattaa) *a* Quarrelsome, wrangler, squabbler; spoilsport.

ਕੁੱਪਾ (kuppaa) *n m* Large vessel made from raw hide (for holding and carrying oil); Any large container, canister; Fat, corpulent, bulky.

ਕੁੱਪੀ (kuppee) *n f* Lubricating can, Oil container, oil-can.

ਕੁਫ਼ਰ (kufar) *n m* Atheism, disbelief, unbelief in the existence of God, blasphemy

ਕੁੱਬ (kubb) *n f* Bend, curve, curvature; bend or crook in body, hump, hunch; ~ਕੱਢਣਾ To remove bending, to straighten.

ਕੁਮਲਾਉਣਾ (kumlaaunaa) *v* To fade, to wither, to shrivel, to lose luster.

ਕੁਰਸੀ (kursee) *n f* Chair, seat; authority.

ਕੁਰਕੀ (kurkee) *n f* Attachment, seizure.

ਕੁਰਬਾਨ (kurbaan) *a* Sacrificed, martyred; ~ਹੋਣਾ To die for, to become a martyr, to give one's life for.

ਕੁਰਬਾਨੀ (kurbaanee) *n f* Sacrifice.

ਕੁਰਲਾਉਣਾ (kurlaaunaa) *v* To moon, to groan, to cry.

ਕੁਰੇਦਨਾ (kurednaa) *v* To scrape, to scratch.

ਕੁੱਲ (kull) *n m* Dynasty, ancestry, family, lineage caste, race.

ਕੁਲਛਣਾ (kulachhnaa) *a* Ill mannered, ill-bred.

ਕੁਲਟਾ (kultaa) *n f* Prostitute, bad women.

ਕੁਲਾਂਚ (kulaanch) *n f* Jump, hop, bound.

ਕੁੜੱਕੀ (kurkkee) *n f* Trap, net.

ਕੁੜਮ (kuram) *n m* Father-in-law of one's son or daughter.

ਕੁੜਮਾਈ (kurmaaee) *n f* Betrothal, engagement.

ਕੁੜਨਾ (kurnaa) *v* To pine, to grieve, to feel displeased.

ਕੁੜੀ (kuree) *n f* Girl, daughter virgin.

ਕੁਹਣੀ (kuhnee) *n* Elbow, ancon.

ਕੂਕ (kook) *n f* Whistle, shout, complaint, woes.

ਕੂਕਣਾ (kooknaa) *v* To Scream, to cry, to sob, to shout.

ਕੂਕਾਂ (kookaan) *n f* Screams, cries.

ਕੂਚਣਾ (koochnaa) v To cleanse thoroughly by scrubbing.

ਕੂਚੀ (koochee) n f Brush, swab.

ਕੂਤਣਾ (kootnaa) v To evaluate, to estimate.

ਕੂੜ (koor) n m Lie, falsehood.

ਕੂੜਾ (kooraa) n m a Waste, rubbish, trash, sweepings, Liar; False, lying.

ਕੇਸ (kes) n m Hair.

ਕੇਸਰ (kesar) n m Saffron, *Crocus stivus*.

ਕੇਂਦਰ (kendar) n m Centre, core, nucleus; centroid; focus; head quarters; the central government; ~ਮੁਖੀ Centripetal.

ਕੇਂਦਰੀ (kendree) a Central, centric, core, main, nuclear.

ਕੈਦੀ (kaidee) n m Prisoner, detainee, captive; convict.

ਕੈਫ਼ੀਅਤ (kaifiat) n f State condition, well-being; remarks, detail, statement.

ਕੇਰਨਾ (kernaa) v To pour, to scatter, to spread, to drop.

ਕੈ (kai) n f Vomitting.

ਕੈਂਚੀ (kainchee) n f Scissors.

ਕੈਦ (kaid) n m Imprisonment, restraint, confinement; ~ਖ਼ਾਨਾ Prison, jail, gaol.

ਕੋਇਲ (koil) n f Cuckoo, nightingale.

ਕੋਇਲਾ (koilaa) n m Charcoal, coal.

ਕੋਸ਼ (kosh) n m Dictionary, lexicon, Treasure.

ਕੋਸਣਾ (kosnaa) v To curse, to damn, to execrate, to imprecate.

ਕੋਸਾ (kosaa) a Luke warm, tepid.

ਕੋਸ਼ਿਸ਼ (koshish) n f Attempt, endeavour.

ਕੋਹ (kōh) n m Mountain; A unit of distance approximately equal to 24 kilometres; ~ਸਤਾਨ Mountainous country, hilly tract, mountain range.

ਕੋਹਣਾ (kohnaa) v To torture, to slay, to kill.

ਕੋਹਰਾ (kohraa) n m frost.

ਕੋਹਲੂ (kohloo) n m Oil press.

ਕੋਹੜਾ (kohraa) n m Leper.

ਕੋਕਾ (kokaa) n m Small nil, nosepin.

ਕੋਝਾ (kojhaa) a Ugly, unseemly, awkward.

ਕੋਠੜੀ (kothree) n f Room, cabin, cell, closet.

ਕੋਠਾ (kothaa) n m House, terrace, upper storey.

ਕੋਠੀ (kothee) n f Banglow, mansion, masonary house.

ਕੋਠੇਲਾ (kothelaa) n m Young camel (Two year old).

ਕੋਣ (kon) n m Angle.

ਕੋਤਵਾਲ (kotwaal) n m Chief Police

Officer, Police Inspector.

ਕੋਤਵਾਲੀ (kotwaalee) *n f* Police station.

ਕੋਤਾਹੀ (kotaahee) *n f* Negligance, default.

ਕੋਫ਼ਤ (koft) *n f* Botheration, hardship, trouble.

ਕੋਰਮਾ (kormaa) *n m* Curry, cooked meat.

ਕੋਰਾ (koraa) *a* Fresh, new, unused, unwashed, foolish, stupid; ~ਜਵਾਬ Flat refusal, blank reply.

ਕੌਡੀ (kaudee) *n f* Small sea shell, cowrie.

ਕੌਮ (kaum) *n f* Nation, creed, tribe, clan, sect, caste.

ਕੌਮੀ (kaumee) *a* National; ~ਅਤ Nationality.

ਕੌਲ (kaul) *n m* Promise, word, consent, agreement.

ਕੌੜਾ (kauṛaa) *a* Bitter, acrimonious, pungent; ~ਪਣ Bitterness.

ਕੌੜੀ (kauṛee) *n m* Score; Cowrie.

ਖ

ਖ Seventh letter of Gurmukhi alphabets pronounced as khakhaa.

ਖਉ (khau) *n m* Destruction, annihilation, hardship, decay, decline, danger. Also ਖੈ

ਖਸਖਸ (khas khas) *n f* Poppy seed. Also ਖਸਖਾਸ

ਖਸਣਾ (khasnaa) *v* To Snatch, to deprive, to seize.

ਖਸਤਾ (khastaa) *a* Crisp, broken, dilapidated, poor, miserable; ~ਹਾਲ Miserable, wretched, pitiable.

ਖਸਮ (khasam) *n m* Husband, owner, master, lord; ~ਕਰਨਾ To marry, to remarry; ~ਖਾਣੀ Widow, devourer of husband.

ਖਸਮਾਨਾ (khasmaanaa) *n m* Husbandhood; Protection, patronage, refuge.

ਖਸਰਨਾ (khasarnaa) *v* To rub, to wipe, to scour.

ਖਸਰਾ (khasraa) *n m* Measles.

ਖੱਸੀ (khassee) *a* Sterilized, castrated, impotent, stoneless; ~ਕਰਨਾ To castrate, to sterilise, emasculate.

ਖਸੂਸੀਅਤ (khasoosiat) *n* Special quality, characersitic or trait, properly, peculiarity.

ਖਹਿਣਾ (khaihnaa) *v* To rub, to push with body, to jostle, to provoke or start a quarrel, to pick up quarrel, to bicker, to wrangle.

ਖਹਿਬੜਨਾ (khaibarnaa) *v* To altercate, to quarrel, to squabble, to wrangle.

ਖਹਿੜਾ (khairaa) *n m* Urging, impulsion, insistence, persistent entreaty; ~ਛੁਡਾਉਣਾ To disentangle, to disengage, oneself from, to get rid of.

ਖਹੁਰਾ (khauraa) *a* Hard, rough, coarse; hot-tempered, harsh, menacing.

ਖੱਖਰ (khakkhar) *n f* Hives of wasps.

ਖੰਗਾਲਣਾ (khangaalnaa) *v* To rinse, to cleanse.

ਖੰਘ (khang) *n f* Cough, coughing.

ਖੰਘਣਾ (khangh'naa) *v* To cough.

ਖੰਘਾਰ (khangh'aar) *n m* Sputum, phlegm.

ਖੰਘਾਰਨਾ (khangh'aarnaa) *v* To cough, to discharge phlegm.

ਖੱਚ (khachch) *n f* Noise, trouble,

vexation.

ਖਚਰ (khachar) *n m* Mule; ~ਪੁਣਾ Cleverness, williness; Wickedness.

ਖਚਰਾ (khachraa) *a* Mulish, deceitful, perverse.

ਖੰਜਰ (khanjar) *n m* Dagger.

ਖੱਜਲ (khajjal) *a* Ruined, wretched, forlorn, distressed.

ਖਜ਼ਾਨਚੀ (khazaanchee) *n m* Treasurer, cashier, bursar.

ਖ਼ਜ਼ਾਨਾ (khazaanaa) *n m* Treasury, repository, store, magazine.

ਖ਼ਜ਼ਾਬ (khazaab) *n m* Dye, hairdye.

ਖੱਜੀ (khajjee) *n f* Date, palm.

ਖਜੂਰ (khajoor) *n m* Date, Phoenix dactylifera.

ਖਟਕਣਾ (khataknaa) *v* To prick, to be terrified, to be offended.

ਖਟਕਾ (khatkaa) *n m* Apprehension, suspicion, anxiety, doubt, fear.

ਖਟਕਾਉਣਾ (khatkaaunaa) *v* To knock, to strike.

ਖਟਖਟਾਉਣਾ (khatkhataaunaa) *v* To knock, to thump, to rap

ਖਟਣਾ (khatnaa) *v* To gain, to benefit, to earn.

ਖਟਪਟ (khatpat) *n f* Estrangement, alienation, quarrel, conflict, disagreement, strained relations.

ਖਟਮਲ (khatmal) *n m* Bug, bedbug, *Cimex lectularius*.

ਖਟਵਾਉਣਾ (khatvaaunaa) *v* To cause to earn.

ਖੱਟੜਾ (khattraa) *n m* Plain bed.

ਖੱਟਾ (khattaa) *a n m* Sour, acidic, sharp; Ferment, curd (yoghurt); A little curd added to milk to curdle or coagulate it.

ਖਟਾਈ (khtaaaee) *n f* Sourness, acidity.

ਖਟਾਸ (khataas) *n f* Sourness, acidity.

ਖਟਿਆ (khatiaa) *a* Earned

ਖੱਟੀ (khatee) *n f* Earning, income, gain, emoluments.

ਖਟੀਕ (khateek) *n m* Tanner.

ਖੰਡ (khand) *n f* (1) Sugar; (2) Portion, part, region, piece, segment.

ਖੱਡ (khadd) *n m* Pit, ditch, ravine.

ਖੰਡਾ (khandaa) *n m* Broad sword.

ਖੱਡਾ (khaddaa) *n m* Pit, ditch, dugout; cavity, concavity. Also **ਖੱਢਾ**

ਖੱਡੀ (khaddee) *n f* Loom, Weaver's pit.

ਖ਼ਤ (khat) *n m* (1) Letter, a note; Handwriting; (2) line; shave.

ਖ਼ਤਮ (khatam) *a* Ended, finished, concluded, complete; ~ਹੋਣਾ To be completed, to be finished; to come to an end, to exhaust, to expire; ~**ਕਰ ਦੇਣਾ** To kill, to murder; ~**ਕਰਨਾ** To finish, to exhaust, to come to an end, to kill.

ਖਤਰਨਾਕ (khatarnaak) *a* Dangerous, risky, critical, alarming, serious.

ਖਤਰਾ (khatraa) *n m* Danger, jeopardy, peril, risk.

ਖਤੂੰਗੜਾ (khatoongṛaa) *n m* Young donkey.

ਖੰਦਕ (khandak) *n f* Deep ditch, trench.

ਖੱਦਰ (khaddar) *n m* Coarse cotton cloth.

ਖਦੇੜਨਾ (khadeṛnaa) *v* To cast out, to rout.

ਖੰਨੀ (khannee) *a* Half, quarter (loaf)

ਖੱਪ (khapp) *n f* Noise, fuss; ~**ਖਾਨਾ** Pointless, talk, noisy scene.

ਖਪਣਾ (khapṇaa) *v* To worry, to be spent, to be destroyed.

ਖਪਤ (khapat) *n f* Sale, consumption, expenditure; ~**ਕਾਰ** Consumer.

ਖਪਤੀ (khaptee) *a* Crack, insane, crazy, obsessed.

ਖਪਰੈਲ (khaprail) *n m* Tiled hut.

ਖਪਾਉਣਾ (khapaauṇaa) *v* (1) To tease, to vex; (2) To finish, to consume; To employ; (3) To destroy.

ਖੱਪੀ (khappee) *a* Noisy, bothersome, quarrelsome, prone to raise noise.

ਖਫਾ (khaffaa) *a* Angry, annoyed, unhappy, displeased; Estranged.

ਖੱਬਚੂ (khabchoo) *a n* Left handed.

ਖਬਰ (khabar) *n f* News, report, information; **ਉਡਦੀ**~ Hearsay, rumour, doubtful news uncertified report; ~**ਦਾਰ** Alert, vigilant, watchful, cautious; Beware.

ਖਬਰੇ (khabre) *adv* Perhaps, may be, could be, possibly.

ਖੱਬਾ (khabbaa) *a* Left, left handed.

ਖ਼ਬੀਸ (khabbees) *a m* Miser; Wicked, vile.

ਖੰਭ (khamb) *n m* Wing, feather.

ਖੰਭਾ (khambhaa) *n m* Pillar, post.

ਖਮਿਆਜ਼ਾ (khamiaazaa) *n m* Consequence, compensatory.

ਖਮੀਰ (khameer) *n m* Leaven, yeast, barm; Fermentation, bacterization.

ਖਮੀਰਾ (khameeraa) *a* Fermented, leavended.

ਖਮੋਸ਼ੀ (khamosi) *n m* Silence, quiet, quietude, muteness, speechlessness, dumbness.

ਖ਼ਰ (khar) *n m f* Ass, donkey; foolish, stupid.

ਖਰਚਾ (kharchaa) *n m* Expenditure,

charges, cost, overhead expenses; costs (in law suit); subsistence money paid to separated spouse, alimony. Also **ਖਰਚ**

ਖਰਬ (kharab) *a* One hundred thousand million; 100,000,000,00.

ਖਰਾ (kharaa) *a* Pure, genuine, real, sincere, true, unadulterated, plainspeaking; ~**ਪਨ** purity, geniuneness.

ਖਰਾਇਤ (kharaait) *n f* Charity, alms. Also **ਖਰੈਤ**

ਖਰਾਇਤੀ (kharaaitee) *a* Charitable

ਖਰਾਸ਼ (kharaash) *n f* Abrasion, bruise scratch.

ਖਰਾਂਟ (kharaanṭ) *a* Cunning, crafty, clever, smart, mischievous, deceitful; ~**ਪੁਣਾ** Cunningness, craftiness, cleverness, mischievousness, deceitfulness.

ਖਰਾਬ (kharaab) *a* Bad, defective, spoiled, nasty, sinful, wicked.

ਖਰੀਦ (khareed) *n f* Purchase, buying, shopping; ~**ਦਾਰ** Customer, buyer; ~**ਦਾਰੀ** Purchase, buying.

ਖਰੀਦਣਾ (khareednaa) *v* To buy, to purchase.

ਖਰੂੰਡ (kharoond) *n f* Scratch, caused by finger nails or paws or claws.

ਖਰੋਚਣਾ (kharochnaa) *v* To Scratch, to scrape.

ਖਲ (khal) *n f* Oil cake.

ਖੱਲ (khall) *n f* Skin, hide, bellows; ~**ਲਾਹੁਣੀ** To skin, to flay, to peel off skin; To beat, to thrash ruthlessly.

ਖਲਕ (khalak) *n f* Creation, creatures, created.

ਖਲਕਤ (khalkat) *n f* People, crowd, world.

ਖਲਬਲੀ (khalbalee) *n f* Disturbance, commotion, agitation, outrage.

ਖਲਲ (khalal) *n m* Obstruction, interruption, disturbance, confusion.

ਖਲੜ (khallar) *n m* Large or thick hide.

ਖਲੜੀ (khalree) *n f* Skin.

ਖੱਲਾ (khallaa) *n m* Shoe.

ਖਲ੍ਹਾਰਨਾ (khalihaarnaa) *v* To make one stay, to cause to stop, to halt.

ਖਲੋਣਾ (khalonaa) *v* To stand; To halt, to stop or wait, to be or stay erect without support; To be stable.

ਖਲੋਤਾ (khalotaa) *a* Stagnant, standing; ~**ਪਾਣੀ** Staganant water

ਖੜਕਣਾ (kharaknaa) *v* To rattle, to clank, to clink, to jingle, to ring, to tinkle; To clatter; To be knocked, thumped, tapped; To talk in a rage; To cross swords.

ਖੜਕਾ (kharkaa) *n m* Rattling, clattering sound, noise (as of bang, knock, etc); ~**ਦੜਕਾ** Threatening noise, show of force to create fear or awe; Brave posture; public disturbance, disorder.

ਖੜਕਾਉਣਾ (kharkaaunaa) *v* To knock, to rap, to tap; To ring, rattle; To thump; To shake, To beat producing ratting or clanking noise; To thrash, to chastise.

ਖੜਗ (kharag) *n f* sword.

ਖੜਨਾ (kharnaa) *v* To take away, to carry away.

ਖੜਾਉਣਾ (kharaaunaa) *v* To lose, to be deprived of.

ਖੜਾਵਾਂ (kharaawaan) *n f* Wooden sandles, wooden shoes.

ਖਾਈ (khaaee) *n f* Ditch, trench, pit, groove.

ਖਾਸ (khaas) *a* Special, particular, specific, peculiar, proper, Chief. Also ਖਸੂਸੀ

ਖਾਂਸੀ (khaansee) *n f* Cough; **ਕਾਲੀ** ~Whooping Cough.

ਖਾਸੀਅਤ (khaasiyat) *n f* Quality, peculiarity, natural disposition.

ਖਾਹਮਖਾਹ (khaamkhaa) *adv* Uncalled for, without reason or justification or provocation, unjustly, unjustifiably; Also ਖਾਹਮਖਾਹ

ਖਾਹਿਸ਼ (khaahish) *n f* Passion, desire, wish, longing, will aspiration; ~**ਮੰਦ** Willing, desirous.

ਖਾਕ (khaak) *n f* Ashes, earth, nothing; ~**ਛਾਨਣੀ** To labour in vain; ~**ਵਿਚ ਰਲਣਾ** To die, to perish; ~**ਵਿਚ ਰੁਲਣਾ** To be miserable, to live in misery.

ਖਾਕਾ (khaakaa) *n m* Sketch, outline map; Plan, rough plan; Also ਖ਼ਾਕਾ

ਖਾਕੀ (khaakee) *a* Of the dust colour, dusty, greyish brown; Made of earth, material (as against **ਨੂਰੀ**-Spiritual); Also ਖ਼ਾਕੀ

ਖਾਣ (khaan) *n f* Mine, mineral deposits or source; Abundant stock, store, treasure.

ਖਾਣਾ (khaanaa) *v n m* To eat, to dine, to take, to consume, to ingest; To suffer, endure (defeat, beating, deceit); To embezzle, to misappropriate; To take (oath); To corrode, to erode; Meal, dinner, feast, fare, food, diet, grub, repast.

ਖਾਤਮਾ (khaatmaa) *n m* End, death, annihitation.

ਖਾਤਰ (khaatar) *n f* Hospitality, Service; ~ਤਵਾਜ਼ਾ Hospitality; ~ਦਾਰੀ Hospitality, servitude, warm reception.

ਖਾਤਾ (khaataa) *n f* Account, Account book; ~ਵਹੀ Ledger.

ਖਾਤੀ (khaatee) *n m* Carpenter, woodcutter, carver, engraver.

ਖਾਦ (khaad) *n f* Manure, fertilizer, waste, dung.

ਖਾਦਮ (khaadam) *n m* Servant, attendant.

ਖਾਨਸਾਮਾ (khaansaamaa) *n m* Butler, steward.

ਖਾਨਦਾਨ (khaandaan) *n m* Family, race, dynasty.

ਖਾਨਦਾਨੀ (khaandaanee) *a* Hereditary, ancestral, of good birth, blue blooded; ~ਆਦਮੀ Noble man;~ ਵੈਰ vendetta.

ਖ਼ਾਨਾ (khanaa) *n m* House, chamber compartment, column, cell receptacle; ~ਖ਼ਰਾਬੀ Ruin, destruction; ~ਪੂਰੀ Filling in the blanks; ~ਬਦੋਸ਼ Nomad, nomadic; Vagaboned.

ਖ਼ਾਬ (khaab) *n m* Dream.

ਖਾਮੀ (khaamee) *n f* Defect, drawback, flaw.

ਖ਼ਾਮੋਸ਼ੀ (khaamoshee) *n f* Silence, reticence.

ਖਾਰਸ਼ (khaarash) *n f* itch, scabbies; Also ਖ਼ਾਰਸ਼

ਖ਼ਾਰਜ (khaaraj) *a* Discharged, dismissed, expelled; ~ਕਰਨਾ To discharge, to expel, to rusticate.

ਖ਼ਾਰਾ (khaaraa) *a n m* Saltish; Alkaline, saline, hardstone.

ਖਾਲਸਾ (khaalsaa) *n m* Pure; Sikh.

ਖਾਲਿਸ (khaalis) *a* Pure, genuine, real, undulterated. Also ਖਾਲਸ

ਖਾਲੀ (khaalee) *a* Empty, vacant, blank, void; ~ਕਰਨਾ To vacate, to clear.

ਖਾਵੰਦ (khaawand) *n m* Husband, lord, master.

ਖਾੜਕੂ (khaaṛkoo) *a* Courageous, bold, brave; dreaded, feared, dominating, terrorist, militant.

ਖਾੜੀ (khaaree) *n f* Gulf, bay, creek, oceanic channel.

ਖਿਆਨਤ (khiaanat) *n f* Dishonesty, misappropriation, breach of trust, embezzlement.

ਖਿਆਲ (khiyaal) *n m* Idea, belief, imagination, opinion, conception, impression, thought; ~ਨਾ ਕਰਨਾ To ignore, to overlook, to be careless; ~ਨਾ ਰਹਿਣਾ To forget; ~ਰਖਣਾ To take care of, to bear in mind.

ਖਿਆਲੀ (khiyaalee) *a* Imaginary, Idle,

visionary, dreamy.

ਖਿਸਕਣਾ (khisaknaa) *v* To slip, to steal away.

ਖਿਸਕਾਉਣਾ (khiskaaunaa) *v* To remove, to move, to draw back.

ਖਿਸਕੂ (khiskoo) *a* Truant, shirker, malingere; inconsistent, fickle, inconstant.

ਖਿੱਚ (khichch) *n f* Fascination, attraction, lure, affinity; Tension, strain.

ਖਿਚਣਾ (khichnaa) *v* To draw, to pull, to drag, to attract, to suck up.

ਖਿਚੜੀ (khichree) *n f* Dish of rice & pulse, a mixed heap, hotch-potch.

ਖਿਚਾਈ (khichaaee) *n f* Haulage.

ਖਿਜ਼ਾਬ (khizaab) *n m* Hair-dye.

ਖਿੱਝ (khijjh) *n f* Irritation, annoyance, vexation.

ਖਿੱਝਣਾ (khijjhnaa) *v* To be irritated, to be angry, to be annoyed, to be vexed.

ਖਿੰਡਣਾ (khindnaa) *v* To Scatter, to disperse, to diffuse, to adjourn.

ਖਿੰਡਾਉਣਾ (khindaaunaa) *v* To spread, to scatter, to break, to disperse.

ਖਿਡਾਰ (khidaar) *n m* Player.

ਖਿਡੌਣਾ (khidaunaa) *n m* Toy, plaything.

ਖ਼ਿਤਾਬ (khitaab) *n m* Title, surname, address.

ਖਿਦਮਤ (khidmat) *n f* Service, duty, appointment.

ਖਿਦੇੜਨਾ (khidernaa) *v* To push back.

ਖਿਨ (khin) *n m* Moment, instant.

ਖਿਮਾ (khimaa) *n f* Excuse, apology, pardon, forgiveness.

ਖਿਲੰਦੜਾ (khilandraa) *a* Playful, gamester, frolicsome.

ਖਿਲਾਫ਼ (khilaaf) *a* Contrary, opposite, against, adverse.

ਖਿਲਾਰ (khilaar) *n m* Spread, dissémination, expansion, dispersal.

ਖਿੱਲੀ (khillee) *n f* Jest, laughter, mockery, humour, fun, joke, ridicule.

ਖਿਲੇਰਨਾ (khilearnaa) *v* To scatter, to disperse.

ਖਿੜਕੀ (khirkee) *n f* Window, venthole.

ਖਿੜਖਿੜਾਉਣਾ (khirkhiraaunaa) *v* To laugh, to bloom, to delight.

ਖਿੜਨਾ (khirnaa) *v* To blossom, to be cheerful, to be delighted.

ਖੀਸਾ (kheesaa) *n m* Pocket, bag.

ਖੀਰ (kheer) *n f* Rice pudding, rice cooked in sweetened milk; Milk.

ਖੁਆਉਣਾ (khuaaunaa) *v* To feed, to cause to eat.

ਖੁਆਰ (khuaar) *a* Disgraced, dishonoured, inconvenienced.

ਖੁਆਰੀ (khuaaree) *n f* Disgrace, dishonour, humiliation, wretchedness.

ਖੁਸ਼ (khush) *a* Glad, happy, pleased, cheerful, gay, delighted, humorous; ~ਹਾਲ Fortune, Prosperous, happy; ~ਗਵਾਰ Pleasant, soothing, healthy.

ਖੁਸ਼ੀ (khushee) *n f* Joy, happiness, pleasure, cheerfulness, gaiety.

ਖੁਸ਼ਕ (khushak) *a* Dry, withered, arid.

ਖੁਸ਼ਕੀ (khushkee) *n f* Dryness, dryland, drought.

ਖੁਸ਼ਖਤ (khushkhat) *n m* Fine writing.

ਖੁਸਣਾ (khusnaa) *v* To be snatched, To be taken away by force, to be seized, plundered, robbed, lost.

ਖੁਸ਼ਬੂ (khushboo) *n m* Fragrance, odour, scent, flavour, perfume.

ਖੁਸਰਾ (khusraa) *n m* Eunuch, hermaphrodite.

ਖੁਸ਼ਾਮਦ (khushaamad) *n f* Flattery, sycophancy.

ਖੁਜਲਾਉਣਾ (khujlaaunaa) *v* To scratch, to itch.

ਖੁਟਕਣਾ (khutakanaa) *v* To strike, to apprehend, to be in doubt.

ਖੁਟਣਾ (khutnaa) *v* To be finished, to end, to be fully consumed.

ਖੁੱਡ (khudd) *n* Hole, pit, narrow cave.

ਖੁਣਸ (khunas) *n f* Animosity, rancour, malice, enmity, ill will.

ਖੁਣਨਾ (khunnaa) *v* To dig, to engrave, to sink.

ਖੁਤਖੁਤੀ (khutkhutee) *n f* Hesitation, fear.

ਖ਼ੁਦਕੁਸ਼ੀ (khudkushee) *n f* Suicide.

ਖ਼ੁਦਗਰਜ਼ (khudgarz) *a* Selfish.

ਖ਼ੁਦਗਰਜ਼ੀ (khudgarzee) *n f* Selfishness.

ਖ਼ੁਦਦਾਰ (khuddaar) *a* Self-respecting.

ਖ਼ੁਦਦਾਰੀ (khudaaree) *n f* Self-respect, self-esteem, sense of honour.

ਖ਼ੁਦ-ਬਖ਼ੁਦ (khudbakhud) *adv* Automatically, of or by oneself, of one's own volition, in voluntarily, by itself; Also ਖ਼ੁਦਬਖ਼ੁਦ

ਖ਼ੁਦਾ (khudaa) *n m* God, almighty, lord; ~ਵੰਦ God, lord, master.

ਖ਼ੁਦਾਈ (khudaaee) *n f* Excavation, digging, engraving.

ਖੁੰਧਕ (khundhak) *n f* Provocation, irritation.

ਖੁਨਕ (khunak) *a* Cold, chilled.

ਖੁਫ਼ੀਆ (khufiaa) *a* Disguised, secret, Confidential, hidden.

ਖੁੰਬ (khumb) *n f* Mushroom, agaricus.

ਖੁਭਣਾ (khubhṇaa) *v* To thrust, to push, press (into); To penetrate, pierce, enter, prick.

ਖੁਭੋਣਾ (khubhoṇaa) *v* To thrust, to push, press (into); To penertrate, to pierce, enter prick.

ਖੁਮਾਰੀ (khumaaree) *n f* Intoxication, drowsiness, hangover.

ਖੁਰ (khur) *n m* Hoof, cloven.

ਖੁਰਕ (khurak) *n f* Itch, ccabies.

ਖੁਰਕਣਾ (khurakṇaa) *v* To itch, to scratch.

ਖੁਰਚਣਾ (khurachṇaa) *v* To erase, to raze, to scrape.

ਖੁਰਦਬੀਨ (khuradbeen) *n m* Microscope.

ਖੁਰਦਰਾ (khurdaraa) *a* Rough, uneven, not smooth, coarse, not soft, crude; ~ਪਣ Roughness, coarseness.

ਖੁਰਪਾ (khurpaa) *n m* Weeding Knife, hoeing implement.

ਖੁਰਪੀ (khurpee) *n f* Small weeding tonife.

ਖੁਰਾ (khura) *n m* Footprint, footmark, trace, track.

ਖੁਰਾਕ (khuraak) *n f* Diet, food, Sustenance, victuals, dose.

ਖੁਰਾਂਟ (khuraanṭ) *a* Experienced, old, snob.

ਖੁਲਣਾ (khulṇaa) *v* To open, to get loose, to be untied, to be exposed.

ਖੁਲਾਸਾ (khulaasaa) *n m* Abstract, summary, gist, substance, essence, outline, inference.

ਖੂਸਟ (khoosaṭ) *a* Decrepit, haggard.

ਖੂਹ (khooh) *n m* Well.

ਖੂਹੀ (khooee) *n f* Narrow well.

ਖੂਨ (khoon) *n m* Blood, murder; ~ਸਫੇਦ ਹੋਣਾ To become inhumane, to loose natural affection; ~ਕਰਨਾ To murder; ~ਪਸੀਨਾ ਇਕ ਕਰਨਾ To work hard, to toil; ~ਪਸੀਨੇ ਦੀ ਕਮਾਈ Hard-earned money; ~ਪੀਣਾ To harass continually, to suck blood

ਖੂਨੀ (khoonee) *n m* Murderer, assassin.

ਖੂਬੀ (khoobee) *n f* Virtue, grace, beauty, quality, merit.

ਖੇਹ (kheh) *n f* Dust, ash; ~ਖਾਣਾ Adulterous, immoral person. ~ਛਾਣਨੀ To wander fruitlessly.

ਖੇਚਲ (khechal) *n f* Inconvenience, pains, trouble; ~ਕਰਨੀ To take Trouble, to bother.

ਖੇਡ (kheḍ) *n f* Play, game, fun, sport, pastime, show.

ਖੇਡਣਾ (kheḍṇaa) *v* To play, to act.

ਖੇਤ (khet) *n m* Farm, cultivated land, battle field.

ਖੇਤਰ (khetar) *n m* Region, sphere,

realm, field, land; ~ਫਲ Area.

ਖੇਤੀ (khetee) *n m* Farming, agriculture, crop; ~ਬਾੜੀ Agriculture.

ਖੇਪ (khep) *n* A load carried in one trip; Merchandise.

ਖੈਰ (khair) *n f* Well-being, welfare, health and happiness; Catechu (tree) *Accacia catechu*.

ਖੈਰਾਤ (khairaat) *n f* Alms, Charity.

ਖੋਖਲਾ (khokhlaa) *a* Hollow, empty, excavated.

ਖੋਖਾ (khokhaa) *n m* Empty cartridge or shell, fired case; Wooden packing case; Cabin, hut.

ਖੋਜ (khoj) *n f* Search, enquiry, discovery, investigation, a hunt.

ਖੋਜਣਾ (khojnaa) *v* To search, to trace, to discover to investigate, to seek.

ਖੋਟ (khot) *n m* Impurity, defect, adulteration, flaw, deception, blemish.

ਖੋਟਾ (khotaa) *a* Impure, defective, false, malicious, adulterated.

ਖੋਤਾ (khotaa) *n m* Ass, donkey.

ਖੋਦਣਾ (khodnaa) *v* To dig, to engrave.

ਖੋਪੜੀ (khopree) *n f* Skull, scalp, pate, cranium. Also ਖੋਪਰੀ

ਖੋਪਾ (khopaa) *n m* Coconut, copra.

ਖੋਭਣਾ (khobhnaa) *v* To thrust, to push in, to drive in, to stab, prick, pierce.

ਖੋਲਣਾ (kholnaa) *v* To open, to loose, to untie, to detach, to reveal, to unravel

ਖੌਫ (khauf) *n m* Fear, terror, dread, apprehension, misgiving, dismay, alarm; ~ਨਾਕ Fearsome, dreadful, terrible, terrifying.

ਖੌਲਣਾ (khaulnaa) *v* To boil, to bubble, to be excited, to be agitated.

ਗ

ਗ Eighth letter of Gurmukhi alphabets, pronounced as 'gaggaa'

ਗਉਂ (gaun) *n m* Act of going, Expedience, self-interest, selfishness; ~ਕੱਢਣਾ To achieve one's own objectives, to watch self interest.

ਗਊ (gau) *n f* Cow; Gentle, meek; ~ਸ਼ਾਲਾ Charitable home for old uncared for cows; ~ਮਾਸ Beef.

ਗਸ਼ (gush) *n m* Fainting, swoon, stupor.

ਗਸ਼ਤ (gasht) *n f* Patrolling walk, stroll, circuit; ~ਕਰਨੀ To patrol, to wander, to go round; ~ਚਿੱਠੀ Circular letter, circular.

ਗਸ਼ਤੀ (gashtee) *a* Mobile, circular.

ਗਹਿਣੇ (gahene) *n* Ornaments, jewellery; ~ਰਖਣਾ To pawn, to mortgage.

ਗੰਧਲਣਾਂ (ganghalnaa) *v* (For water) To become turbid, muddy, dirty, roily.

ਗੰਧਲਿਆ (ganghaliaa) *a* Turbid, muddy, dirty.

ਗੱਚਣਾ (gachchnaa) *v* To dig up (plant) alongwith earth covering its roots.

ਗੰਜ (ganj) *n f* Baldness; Grain market, small colony.

ਗਜ਼ (gaz) *n m* Yard, spike.

ਗਜਣਾ (gajnaa) *v* To thunder, to roar, to howl.

ਗ਼ਜ਼ਬ (qazab) *n m* Outrage, violence; Injustice; Something strange.

ਗਜਰਾ (gajraa) *n m* Armlet, bangles, chaplet, necklace.

ਗ਼ਜ਼ਲ (gazal) *n f* Ode, sonnet, lyric, poem.

ਗੰਜਾ (ganjaa) *a* Bold, scalp head.

ਗਟਕਣਾ (gataknaa) *v* To gulp, to swallow.

ਗੱਟਾ (gatta) *n m* Stopper, cork, plug; sprag.

ਗਠ (gath) *n f* Knot, node.

ਗਠਣਾ (gathnaa) *v* To tie, to join, to sew, to organize.

ਗੱਠਾ (gatthaa) *n* Package; Onion.

ਗੱਠੜ (gathar) *n m* A big packet, a large bundle, bale.

ਗਠੜੀ (gathree) *n f* Bundle

ਗਠੀਲਾ (gatheelaa) *a* Muscular, compact, well-built.

ਗਡਣਾ (gadnaa) *v* To bury, to fix, to plant, to entomb.

ਗਡਰੀਆ (gadariyaa) *n m* Shepherd, grazier.

ਗੱਡਾ (gadda) *n m* Bullock-cart.

ਗੰਡਾਸਾ (gandaasaa) *n m* Sickle, axe for chopping fodder, hatchet.

ਗੱਡੀ (gaddee) *n f* Cart, carriage, train, car, wagon.

ਗੰਢ (gandh) *n f* Bundle, pack, parcel, bale, knot.

ਗੰਢਣਾ (gandhnaa) *v* To patch, to mend, to cobble, to repair.

ਗੰਢਵਾਉਣਾ (gandhvaaunaa) *v* To get something repaired, mended, bobbled. Also ਗੰਢਾਉਣਾ

ਗੰਢਵਾਈ (gandhwaaee) *n f* Wages for repairing. Also ਗੰਢਾਈ

ਗੰਢਾ (gandhaa) *n m* Onion.

ਗਿਣਨਾ (gannna) *n f* Counting, enumeration, calculation.

ਗਣਿਤ (ganit) *n m* Arithmetic, calculation.

ਗਤ (gat) *n f* Condition, state, plight.

ਗੱਤਾ (gattaa) *n m* Card, cardboard.

ਗਤਕਾ (gatka) *n m* Sword play, sword practice with wooden swords or sticks; fencing, swordsmanship.

ਗਤੀ (gatee) *n f* Movement, motion, speed, velocity; ~ਸ਼ੀਲ Dynamic, kinetic; ~ਹੀਨ Static, motionless.

ਗੰਦ (gand) *n m* Impurity, refuse, dirt, filth, foulness; ~ਗੀ Dirt, filth, foulness.

ਗੱਦ (gadd) *n m* Prose; ~ਕਾਰ Prose-writer.

ਗਦਗਦ (gadgad) *a* Joyful, delighted, very happy.

ਗੰਦਮ (gandam) *n f* Wheat, Triticum stivum.

ਗ਼ਦਰ (gandar) *n m* Mutiny, revolt, rebellion; ~ਮਚਣਾ To occur chaos, to mutiny.

ਗੰਦਲ (gandal) *n f* Tender stem, stalk or shoot.

ਗੱਦਾ (gadda) *n m* Cushion, padded seat or mattress, pallet.

ਗੰਦਾ (gandaa) *a* Dirty, filthy, nasty, contaminated, impure.

ਗੱਦਾਰ (gaddaar) *a n m* Threacherous, turncoat; Traitor, disloyal.

ਗੱਦਾਰੀ (gaddaaree) *n f* Treachery, disloyalty, treason.

ਗੱਦੀ (gaddee) *n f* Pad, cushion, seat; Throne; Seat of temporal or spiritual authority.

ਗਦੇਲਾ (gadelaa) *n m* Cushion, quilt.

ਗੰਧ (gandh) *n f* Smell, odour.

ਗੰਧਕ (gandhak) *n f* Sulphur, brimstone; ~ਦਾ ਤੇਜ਼ਾਬ Sulphuric acid.

ਗੰਧਲਾ (gandhlaa) *a* Fragrant, sweet-smelling.

ਗਧਾ (gadhaa) *n m* Ass, donkey; Fool, stupid fellow.

ਗੰਨਾ (ganna) *n m* Sugarcane.

ਗਨੀਮਤ (ganeemat) *n f* Plunder, boon, blessing; Satisfaction.

ਗਨੇਰੀ (ganeree) *n f* Small bit of sugarcane.

ਗੱਪ (gapp) *n f* Gossip, chat, false report, rumour.

ਗੱਪੀ (gappee) *a m* Gossipy, boaster.

ਗਪੌੜ (gapour) *n m* Rumour, boastful gossip.

ਗਫ਼ਲਤ (gafalat) *n f* Carelessness, indifference, negligence.

ਗੱਫਾ (gapphaa) *n m* A lion's share, a big morsel.

ਗ਼ਬਨ (gaban) *n m* Embezzlement, misappropriation, fraud.

ਗੱਭਣ (gabbhan) *a* Pregnant mostly for cattles.

ਗਭਰੂ (gabhroo) *n m* Youngman, husband.

ਗੰਭੀਰ (gambheer) *a* Serious, sober, reserve, contemplative.

ਗਮ (gam) *n m* Grief, sorrow, woe, anxiety.

ਗਮਲਾ (gamlaa) *n* Flowerpot, vase.

ਗ੍ਰਹਿ (greh) *n m* Planet.

ਗ੍ਰਹਿਣ (grehn) *n m* Eclipse.

ਗਰਕ (garak) *a* Immersed, sunk.

ਗਰਕਣਾ (garaknaa) *v* To perish, to sink.

ਗਰਜ (garaj) *n f* Thunder, roar, gnarl, bellow.

ਗ਼ਰਜ਼ (garaz) *n f* Need, object, interest, selfishness, concern; **~ਮੰਦ** Self interested, needy, destitute. Also ਗਰਜ

ਗਰਜਣਾ (garajnaa) *v* To thunder, to howl, to gnarl.

ਗ਼ਰਜ਼ੀ (garzee) *a* Needy, selfish.

ਗ੍ਰੰਥ (granth) *n m* Book, scripture of the sikhs.

ਗ੍ਰੰਥੀ (granthee) *n m* Priest (in Sikh religion).

ਗ਼ਰਦਨ (gardan) *n f* Neck; **~ਉਡਾਉਣੀ** To behead, to chop off head.

ਗਰਦਾਨਣਾ (gardaannaa) *v* To involve, to implicate.

ਗਰਭ (garabh) *n m* Preganancy, conception, womb, gestation; **~ਪਾਤ** Miscarriage, abortion, feticide, aborticide.

ਗਰਮ (garam) *a* Hot, warm; **~ਜੋਸ਼ੀ** enthusiasm, warmth, warmheartedness, cordiality; **~ਮਿਜ਼ਾਜ** Short tempered, hot headed, short-tempered, touchy, irritable.

ਗਰਮਾਗਰਮੀ (garmaagarmee) *n f* Excitement, heated exchange.

ਗਰਮੀ (garmee) *n f* Heat, warmth, passion, summer.

ਗਰਾਰਾ (garara) *n m* (1) Loose-fitting trousers; (2) Gargle.

ਗਰਾਰੀ (graaree) *n f* Pinion, pulley, gear.

ਗ੍ਰਿਫ਼ਤਾਰ (griftaar) *a* Arrested, captured. Also **ਗਿਰਫ਼ਤਾਰ**

ਗ੍ਰਿਫ਼ਤਾਰੀ (griftaaree) *n m* Arrest, capture. Also **ਗਿਰਫ਼ਤਾਰੀ**

ਗ਼ਰੀਬ (gareeb) *a* Poor, needy, helpless; Meek.

ਗਰੂਰ (garoor) *n m* Pride, vanity.

ਗ੍ਰੋਹ (groh) *n m* Company, group, gang. Also **ਗਰੋਹ**

ਗੱਲ (gall) *n f* Talk, dialogue, affair.

ਗਲ (gal) *n m* Throat, larynx, neck.

ਗਲਣਾ (galṇaa) *v* To rot, to compose, to decay, to dissolve.

ਗ਼ਲਤ (galat) *a* Wrong, mistaken, faulty, incorrect, erroneous; **~ਸਮਝਣਾ** To misunderstand, misapprehend, misjudge; **~ਸਲਤ** Confused, jumbled, disordered, involved; **~ਧਾਰਨਾ** misconception; **~ਫ਼ਹਮੀ** Misunderstanding, misapprehension; disagreement, dissension; smugness.

ਗ਼ਲਤੀ (galti) *n f* Mistake, error, inaccuracy, misconception, misunderstanding, misjudgement; wrong-doing, blunder; Lapse, omission; **~ਦਾ ਪੁਤਲਾ** Fallible, liable to err.

ਗੱਲਾਂ (gallaan) *n f* Idle talk.

ਗਲਾ (galaa) *n m* Throat.

ਗ਼ੱਲਾ (gallaa) *n m* Corn, grain harvest.

ਗੱਲਾ (gallaa) *n m* Money, box, safe, a chest for money.

ਗਲਾਉਣਾ (galaaunaa) *v* To melt, to fuse.

ਗਲਾਸ (glaas) *n m* Tumbler, glass.

ਗਲਾਸੀ (glaasee) *n f* Small tumbler.

ਗਲਿਆਰਾ (galiaaraa) *n m* Corridor, gallery.

ਗਲੀ (galee) *n f* Street, lane, passage.

ਗ਼ਲੀਚਾ (galeechaa) *n m* Carpet.

ਗ਼ਲੀਜ਼ (galeez) *a* Dirty, filthy.

ਗਵੱਈਆ (gavvaiyaa) *n m* Singer, vocalist, musician.

ਗਵਾਹ (gawaah) *n m* Witness, deponent.

ਗਵਾਹੀ (gawahee) *n m* Testimony, deposition, evidence.

ਗਵਾਚਣਾ (gwaachṇaa) *v* To be lost.

ਗਵਾਂਢ (gawaanḍh) *n m* Neighbourhood.

ਗਵਾਂਢੀ (gawaandhee) *n m*

Neighbour.

ਗੰਵਾਰ (ganwaar) *a* Rustic, uncivilized, crude, vulgar; ~ਪੁਣਾ Vulgarity, rusticity.

ਗੜਕਣਾ (garaknaa) *v* To roar, to boil.

ਗੜਪਣਾ (garapnaa) *v* To swallow.

ਗੜਬੜੀ (garbaree) *n f* Confusion, disorder.

ਗੜਵਾ (garvaa) *n m* Medium-size pitcher like metal vessel.

ਗੜਵੀ (garvee) *n f* A small pitcher like metal vessel.

ਗਾਂ (gaan) *n f a* Cow; Meak, poor; ~ਦਾ ਮਾਸ Beef.

ਗਾਉਣਾ (gaaunaa) *v* To sing, to chant.

ਗਾਇਬ (gaaib) *a* Vanished, invisible.

ਗਾਹਕ (gaak) *n m* Customer, buyer, client.

ਗਾਹਕੀ (gaahkee) *n f* Purchase, sale, demand.

ਗਾਗਰ (gaagar) *n f* Metalic pitcher, water utensil; ~ਵਿਚ ਸਾਗਰ Too much in a few words.

ਗਾਚਣੀ (gaachnee) *n f* Yellow clay; fuller's earth.

ਗਾਚੀ (gaachee) *n f* Cake, sapling with earth round the roots.

ਗਾਜਰ (gaajar) *n f* Carrot.

ਗਾਟਾ (gaataa) *n m* Neck.

ਗਾਣਾ (gaanaa) *n* Song, singing, tune.

ਗਾਥਾ (gaathaa) *n m* Tale, narrative, a story.

ਗਾਦ (gaad) *n f* Silt, sediments, lees.

ਗਾਬ (gaab) *n f* Silt, mud, mire.

ਗਾਰ (gaar) *n f* Cave, hollow.

ਗਾਰਦ (gaarad) *n f* Guard, group of soldiers or police men deployed for protection.

ਗਾਰਾ (gaaraa) *n m* Morter of mud used as building material.

ਗਾਲੜ (gaallar) *n m* Squirrel.

ਗਾਲੀ (gaalee) *n f* Abuse.

ਗਾਲਣਾ (gaalnaa) *v* To melt, to decompose, to dissolve.

ਗਾਲੜੀ (gaalree) *a* Talkative.

ਗਾੜਾ (gaaraa) *a* Dense, thick intense, stiff, concentrated.

ਗਿਆਨ (giyaan) *n m* Knowledge; ~ਧਿਆਨ Meditation, spiritual pursuit.

ਗਿਆਨੀ (giyaanee) *n m a* Scholar philosopher, sage; Learned, intelligent.

ਗਿੱਚੀ (gichchee) *n f* Neck, nape.

ਗਿਜ਼ਾ (gizaa) *n f* Diet, food.

ਗਿੱਝਣਾ (gijjhnaa) *v* To be accustomed to, to get used to.

ਗਿਟਕ (gitak) *n f* Stone of fruit, endocarp.

ਗਿਟਮਿਟ (giṭmiṭ) *n f* Talk, conversation in an unfamiliar language English; Unintelligible talk.

ਗਿੱਟਾ (giṭṭaa) *n m* Ankle.

ਗਿੱਠ (giṭṭh) *n* Span, measure of length equal to stretched hand, about 9 inches; Fully stretched hand or palm.

ਗਿੱਠਾ (giṭṭha) *a* Dwarfish, dwarf, pigmy, midget, shorty, Tom Thumb. Also **ਗਿਠਮੁਠੀਆ**

ਗਿਣਤੀ (giṇtee) *n f* Number, count, calculation, roll call.

ਗਿਣਨਾ (giṇnaa) *v* To Count, to compute, to enumerate.

ਗਿਦੜ (gidaṛ) *n m a* Jackal; Coward.

ਗਿੱਧ (giddh) *n m* Vulture.

ਗਿਰਗਟ (girgaṭ) *n f* Chameleon.

ਗਿਰਨਾ (girnaa) *v* To fall, to drop, to stumble, to collapse.

ਗਿਰਾਂ (giraan) *n m* Village.

ਗਿੱਲਾ (gillaa) *a* Wet, damp.

ਗਿਲਾ (gilaa) *n m* Reproach, complaint, grievance; **~ਸ਼ਿਕਵਾ** Informal complaint.

ਗਿਲਾਫ਼ (gilaaf) *n m* Cover, covering.

ਗਿੜਗੜਾਉਣਾ (girgraaunaa) *v* To beseech earnestly, to grovel, to request very humbly.

ਗਿੜਨਾ (girnaa) *v* To revolve, to rotate, to turn.

ਗੀਗਾ (geegaa) *n m* Beloved child infant, innocent.

ਗੀਂਢਾ (geeṇdhaa) *a* Short (person); Shorty, short and stout.

ਗੁਆਉਣਾ (guaaunaa) *v* To lose, to waste, to miss, to forfeit.

ਗੁਆਂਢ (guaandh) *n m* Neighbourhood, Vicinage.

ਗੁਆਂਢੀ (guaandhee) *n m* Neighbour.

ਗੁਸਤਾਖ਼ (gustaakh) *a* Arrogant, impolite, rude, haughty, impudent; **~ਗੁਸਤਾਖ਼ੀ** (gustaakhee) Arrogance, impoliteness, rudeness.

ਗੁਸਲ (gusal) *n m* Bath, purification; **~ਖ਼ਾਨਾ** Bathroom.

ਗੁੱਸਾ (gussaa) *n m* Anger, rage, wrath, fury.

ਗੁਸੈਲ (gusail) *a* Wrathful, passionate, irritable.

ਗੁੰਗਾ (gungaa) *a* Dumb, mute, speechless.

ਗੁੱਗਾ (guggaa) *n m* Snake.

ਗੁੱਛਾ (gucchaa) *n m* Bunch, cluster, bouquet.

ਗੁਜ਼ਰ (guzar) *n m* Livelihood.

ਗੁਜ਼ਰਨਾ (guzarnaa) *v* To pass, To expire, to die, to pass away.

ਗੁਜ਼ਰਾਨ (guzraan) *n f* Living, livelihood.

ਗੁੰਜਾਇਸ਼ (gunjaaish) *n f* Capacity,

ਗੁਜ਼ਾਰਸ਼ (guzzarash) *n f* Request, petition, representation.

ਗੁਜ਼ਾਰਾ (guzaaraa) *n m* Living, maintenance, livelihood, Sustenance, adjustment; ~ਕਰਨਾ To subsist, to reconcile, to manage, to adjust.

ਗੁੰਝਲ (gunjhal) *n f* Entangled knot, snarl, entanglement; complication, knotty problem; intricacy, puzzlement, perplexity; enigma, puzzle; ~ਦਾਰ Entangled, snarled, tangled, complicated, knotty; intricate, puzzling, perplexing.

ਗੁੰਝਲਣਾ (gunjhalnaa) *v* To become snarled; To get entangled, involved, jumbled, enmeshed, to become problematic; to be confused, confounded, perplexed.

ਗੁੰਝਾ (gujjhaa) *a* Hidden, secret, invisible, surreptitious, covert, concealed; obscure, mysterious.

ਗੁਟ (gut) *n m* Group, faction, clique, coterie, combine, gang, bloc.

ਗੁਟਕਾ (gutkaa) *n m* Manual, handbook, Small piece (of wood).

ਗੁੱਡਾ (guddaa) *n m* Doll, kite.

ਗੁੰਡਾ (gundaa) *n m a* Scoundrel, rogue, hooligan, rascal; Wicked, knavish.

ਗੁੱਡੀ (guddee) *n f* Doll, kite, child's puppet.

ਗੁਣ (gun) *n m* Virtue, quality, excellence, merit, worth.

ਗੁਣਗੁਣਾ (gungunaa) *a* Luke warm.

ਗੁਣਗੁਣਾਉਣਾ (gungunaaunaa) *v* To murmur, to mutter, to hum, to buzz, to Snuffle.

ਗੁੱਤ (gutt) *n f* Plait, braid.

ਗੁੱਥਲੀ (gutthlee) *n f* Bag, money bag.

ਗੁੱਥੀ (gutthee) *n f* A riddle, knot, enigma.

ਗੁੰਦਣਾ (gundnaa) *v* To weave, to plait, to braid, to interlace.

ਗੁਦਾਮ (gudaam) *n m* Godown, Store, warehouse, depot, granary.

ਗੁਨਾਹ (gunaah) *n m* Fault, guilt, offence, crime.

ਗੁਪਤ (gupat) *a* Secret, concealed, hidden, private, mysterious, covert, latent.

ਗੁਫ਼ਤਗੂ (guftagoo) *n f* Dialogue, conversation, chat.

ਗੁਫ਼ਾ (gufaa) *n f* Cave, den, cavern.

ਗੁੰਬਦ (gumbad) *n m* Dome, vault.

ਗੁਬਾਰ (gubaar) *n m* Dust, dirt; Perplexity, suppressed, anger.

ਗੁਬਾਰਾ (gubaaraa) *n m* Balloon.

ਗੁੰਮਨਾਮ (gummnaam) *a* Anonymous, unknown, obscure, unimportant.

ਗੁਮਰ (gumar) *n m* Pride, vanity, envy, wish to wreck vengeance.

ਗੁਮਰਾਹ (gumraah) *a* Astray, stranded, following wrong or evil path, misled, erring, wandering, aberrant.

ਗੁਮਾਉਣਾ (gumaaunaa) *v* To lose, to misplace.

ਗੁਮਾਸ਼ਤਾ (gumaashtaa) *n m* Agent, manager, representative.

ਗੁਮਾਨ (gumaan) *n m* Pride, haughtiness, imagination, guess.

ਗੁਰ (gur) *n m* Formula, tip, method.

ਗੁਰਗਾਬੀ (gurgabi) *n f* Pumps; lowcut shoes without fastening; pump shoes.

ਗੁਰਦਾ (gurdaa) *n m* Kideny; courage, pluck, fearlessness; forbearance, patience, endurance.

ਗਰਮੁਖ (gurmukh) *a* Guru-oriented, pious, religious, devout, virtuous; A good, model or ideal Sikh, a noble person.

ਗੁੱਰਾਉਣਾ (gurraaunaa) *v* To roar, to growl, to howl.

ਗੁਰੂ (guroo) *n m* Spiritual guide, teacher, tutor, instructor; (planet) Jupiter; ~ਘੰਟਾਲ Perfect, rascal, reprobate.

ਗੁਲਸ਼ਨ (gulshan) *n m* Flower garden.

ਗੁਲਜ਼ਾਰ (gulzaar) *n m* Garden.

ਗੁਲਦਸਤਾ (guldastaa) *n m* Bunch of flowers, bouquet, nosegay.

ਗੁਲਦਾਨ (guldaan) *n m* Glowervase, flowerpot, snuff dish.

ਗੁਲਫਾਮ (gulpham) *a* Handsome, beautiful.

ਗੁਲਾਬ (gulaab) *n m* Rose.

ਗੁਲਾਮ (gulaam) *n m* Slave, bondman, servant.

ਗੁਲਿਸਤਾਨ (gulistaan) *n m* Garden.

ਗੁੱਲੀ ਡੰਡਾ (gullee dandaa) *n m* Tipcat.

ਗੁਲਬੰਦ (gulband) *n m* Muffler, scarf, necktie, neckcloth.

ਗੁਲੇਲ (gulel) *n f* Pelletbow, catapult; ~ਚੀ Person using or adept in the use of pellet bow or gulel.

ਗੁੜ (gur) *n m* Rawsugar, molasses, lumped brown sugar, jaggery.

ਗੁੜਕਣਾ (guraknaa) *v* To cackle, to chuckle.

ਗੁੜਨਾ (gurhnaa) *v* To digest, to realise.

ਗੂੰਹ (goonh) *n m* Exereta, faces.

ਗੂੰਜ (goonj) *n f* Echo, resonance, resounding.

ਗੂੰਜਣਾ (goonjnaa) *v* To resound, to echo.

ਗੂੰਦ (goond) *n f* Gum, glue.

ਗੂੜ੍ਹ (goorh) *n m* Close intimacy, fastness or deepness (colour), profundity.

ਗੂੜ੍ਹਾ (goorhaa) *a* Deep, fast, dark (colour); intense (love, friendship); profound.

ਗੇਂਦ (Gend) *n* Ball; ~ਬੱਲਾ Cricket (game).

ਗੇੜਾ (geraa) *n m* Turn, rotation, circuit; chance, opportunity, vicissistude.

ਗੇਂਦਾ (gendaa) *n m* Marigold flower.

ਗੈਂਡਾ (gaindaa) *n m* Rhinoceros.

ਗ਼ੈਰ (gair) *a* Stranger, alien, foreign, other, non, lack; ~ਅਬਾਦ Barren, unpopulated; ~ਸਰਕਾਰੀ Non-Government, private; ~ਹਾਜ਼ਰ Absent; ~ਕਾਨੂੰਨੀ Illegal, unlawful; ~ਜ਼ਿੰਮੇਵਾਰ Irresponsible; ~ਮਾਮੂਲੀ Extrordinary, excellent, strange.

ਗ਼ੈਰਤ (gairat) *n f* Shame, modesty, honour.

ਗੋਸ਼ਟੀ (goshtee) *n f* Seminar, symposium; conversation, discussion.

ਗੋਸ਼ਤ (gosht) *n m* Meat, flesh.

ਗੋਸ਼ਾ (goshaa) *n m* Corner, angle, a private place.

ਗੋਹਾ (gohaa) *n m* Cowdung, Ordure.

ਗੋਗੜ (gogar) *n f* Pot belly, paunch.

ਗੋਗਾ (gogaa) *n m* Rumour.

ਗੋਡਾ (godaa) *n m* knee.

ਗੋਤਾ (gotaa) *n m* Dip, drive immersion; ~ਖੋਰ diver.

ਗੋਦੀ (godee) *n f* Lap; ~ਪਾਉਣਾ To give away for adoption; Dock; ~ਮਜ਼ਦੂਰ Docker; ~ਵਾੜਾ Dockyard.

ਗੋਰਾ (gora) *a n m* White, fair, skinned, beautiful; Whiteman, Europeon.

ਗੋਲ (gol) *a n m* Round, circular, globular; Goal (in hockey); ~ਕਰਨਾ To score a goal, to embezzle, to evade, to avoid, not to implement; ~ਮਾਲ Confusion, mess, something fishy; ~ਮੋਲ Round, global; Vague, ambiguous, fat.

ਗੋਲਕ (golak) *n f* Moneybox, charitybox, cashchest.

ਗੋਲਾਬਾਰੀ (golaabaaree) *n f* Bombardment, shelling.

ਗੋਲਾਬਾਰੂਦ (golaabaarood) *n m* Ammunition.

ਗੌਣ (gaun) *n m a* Song, secondary auxiliary, minor.

ਗੌਰ (gaur) *n m* Consideration, close attention.

ਗੌਰਵ (gaurav) *n m* Glory, dignity.

ਘ

ਘ Ninth letter of Gurmukhi alphabets, pronounced as ghaghaa.

ਘਉਣਾ (ghauṇaa) *v* To grind, to pestle.

ਘਉ-ਘਪ (ghaoon-ghapp) *a* Disappeared, stolen, embezzled; ~ਕਰਨਾ To embezzle, steal, misappropriate, spend, waste, fritter away.

ਘਸਣਾ (ghasṇaa) *v* To rub, to wear out, to impair.

ਘੱਸਾ (ghassaa) *n m* Push with hip, powerful hard rub, jostle, jerk.

ਘਸਰ (ghasar) *n f* Abrasion, bruise, scratch, rub; ~ਮਸਰ Dallying, dilly-dallying, delaying; ~ਮਸਰ ਕਰਨਾ To dilly-dally, to delay, procrastinate, to try to avoid doing something.

ਘਸਾਈ (ghasaaee) *n m a* Work of rubbing, friction; Hard labour, depreciation.

ਘਸਿਆਰਾ (ghasiaaraa) *n m a* Grass cutter, Mean, lower person (proverbial).

ਘਸੀਟਣਾ (ghaseeṭṇaa) *v* To pull, to drag, to scribble.

ਘਸੁੰਨ (ghasunn) *n* Clenched fist, blow with clenched fist, box, punch, buffet, jab, fisticuff; ~ਜੜਨਾ/ ~ਫੇਰਨਾ/ ~ਮਾਰਨਾ To box punch, jab, buffet, pummel, fisticuff.

ਘਸੋੜਨਾ (ghsorṇaa) *v* To thrust, to penetrate.

ਘਰਾਰਾ (ghraaraa) *n* Petticoat.

ਘੱਗਾ (ghaggaa) *a* Hoarse.

ਘਗਿਆਉਣਾ (ghagiaauṇaa) *v* To implore.

ਘਚੋਰ (ghachor) *n m* Dark, narrow nock

ਘਚੋਲਣਾ (ghacholṇaa) *v* To foul, to mix, to make turbid.

ਘਚੋਲਾ (ghacholaa) *n m* Confusion, disorder, bungling.

ਘਟਣਾ (ghaṭṇaa) *v* To decrease, to fall, to lessen, to shorten; To happen, to take place.

ਘਟਨਾ (ghaṭnaa) *n f* Incident, occurrence, happening, event, accident, chance, occasion.

ਘੰਟਾ (ghanṭaa) *n m* Bell, hour, gong.

ਘੱਟਾ (ghaṭṭaa) *n f* Cloudiness, dust.

ਘਟਾ (ghaṭaa) *n f* Shortness, deficiency; decline (as of age or day); contraction, shrinkage.

ਘਟਾਉਣਾ (ghaṭaauṇaa) *v* To deduct,

to diminish, to reduce, to subtract, to decrease.

ਘਟਾਟੋਪ (ghataatop) *n m* Gathering of dark clouds in the sky; A covering for a palanquin or carriage.

ਘੰਟੀ (ghantee) *n f* Bell tinkle, call bell, telephone bee; Sound of bell ringing, tintunnabulation; instructional period.

ਘਟੀਆ (ghatiyaa) *a* Inferior, cheap, worthless, inexpensive.

ਘੰਡ (ghand) *n m a* Rascal, wicked, villainous, rough, reprobate; ~ਪੁਣਾ Wickedness, villainousness.

ਘੰਡੀ (ghandee) *n f* Adam's apple, larynx, uvula, sound box.

ਘੰਡੂਈ (ghandooee) *n f* Big needle.

ਘਨਚਕਰ (ghanchakar) *a m* Blockhead.

ਘਪਲਾ (ghaplaa) *n m* Bungling, mess, confusion.

ਘਬਰਾਉਣਾ (ghabraaunaa) *v* To be bewildered, to be baffled, to be confused, to be disturbed, to be puzzled, to be perturbed.

ਘਮੰਡ (ghamand) *n m* Pride, haughtiness, arrogance, conceit, elation.

ਘਮੰਡੀ (ghamandee) *a* Proud, haughty, arrogant, lofty, conceited.

ਘਰ (ghar) *n m* Home, house, dwelling, residence, family; ~ਆਬਾਦ ਕਰਨਾ To marry, to build a family; ~ਸਿਰ ਤੇ ਚੁਕਣਾ To create too much noise; ~ਜਵਾਈ Resident son-in-law; ਡਾਕ~ Post office; ~ਭਰਨਾ to amass wealth; ~ਦੀ ਖੇਤੀ Easy to procure, handy; ~ਦੀ ਗਲ Family affair, easy job, mutual affair; ~ਪੂਰਾ ਹੋਣਾ To be satisfied; To be compensated; ~ਵਾਲਾ Husband, owner, master of the house; ~ਵਾਲੀ wife, mistress of the house.

ਘਰੂਟਣਾ (gharootnaa) *v* To scratch (with nail).

ਘਰੋੜਨਾ (gharornaa) *v* to scrub, to scrape, to rasp.

ਘਲਣਾ (ghalnaa) *v* To send, to despatch, to forward, to remit, to transmit.

ਘੱਲੂਘਾਰਾ (ghalooghaaraa) *n m* Holocaust, massacre, great destruction, deluge, genocide, slaughter.

ਘੜਨਾ (gharnaa) *v* To mould, to fabricate, to coin, to frame, to fashion, to construct.

ਘੜਮੱਸ (gharmass) *n f* Milling crowd, stampede, confusion, tumult;

~ਪੈਣੀ Stampede to occur or be caused.

ਘੜਵੰਜੀ (gharvanjee) *n f* Pitcher-stand.

ਘੜਵਾਉਣਾ (gharvaaunaa) *v* To get something manufactured by cutting, etc.

ਘੜਾ (ghraa) *n m* Pitcher, waterpot.

ਘੜਿਆਲ (ghrriyaal) *n m* (1) Big bell, big gong; (2) Crocodile, alligator.

ਘੜੀ (gharee) *n f* Watch, clock; Small pitcher or water pot; Moment, 24 minute (measure of time); **ਔਖੀ~** Time of crisis; **~ਘੜੀ** Time and again; **~ਮੁੜੀ** Again and again, time and again.

ਘਾਈ (ghaaee) *n f* loincloth.

ਘਾਹ (ghaah) *n f* Grass, fodder, straw; **~ਖੋਦਣਾ** To idle away time, to undertake a petty job; **~ਵਢਣਾ** To do a job in hurried manner.

ਘਾਘ (ghaagh) *a* Shrewd, cunning, experienced

ਘਾਟ (ghaat) *n (m)* Quay, jetty, bathing place on the bank of river; *(f)* Shortage, want, deficiency, dearth, decrease, scarcity. **~ਘਰ** Dwelling; **~ਘਾਟ ਦਾ ਪਾਣੀ ਪੀਣਾ** To get varied experience, to wander from place to place.

ਘਾਟਾ (ghaataa) *n m* Loss, deficiency, deficit, decline, falling, inadequacy.

ਘਾਟੀ (ghaatee) *n f* Valley, dale, pass, gorge.

ਘਾਣੀ (ghaanee) *n f* Oil mill, oilpress.

ਘਾਬਰਨਾ (ghaabarnaa) *v* To feel perplexed, to be confused, to be anxious.

ਘਾਮੜ (ghaamar) *n m a* Blockhead, idiot, dull, idiotic, dullard.

ਘਾਲ (ghaal) *n* Toil, hard task, painful service, effort, labour.

ਘਿਓ (ghio) *n m* Butter oil, clarified butter; **~ਸ਼ਕਰ ਹੋਣਾ** To have intimate association.

ਘਿਸਣਾ (ghisnaa) *v* To be warn out, to wear out.

ਘਿੱਗੀ (ghigee) *n* Hiccup caused by crying and sobbing; **~ਬੰਝ ਜਾਣੀ** To cry hoarse, to cry one's heart out.

ਘਿਚ-ਪਿਚ (ghich-pich) *n* Illegible scribble, careless scrawl; **~ਕਰਨੀ/~ਮਾਰਨੀ** To write badly, illegibly. Also **ਘਿਚ-ਮਿਚ**

ਘਿਰਨਾ (ghirnaa) *n f* Hatred, contempt, scorn, abhorrence.

ਘਿਰਨਾ (ghirnaa) *v* To be surrounded, cornered, brought to bay, encircled.

ਘਿਰਨੀ (ghirnee) *n f* Pulley, wheel.

ਘੀਸੀ (gheesee) *n f* Rubbing of buttocks on the ground.

ਘੁਸਣਾ (ghusnaa) *v* To enter, to pentrate, to go in forcibly or without permission, to transgress, to interfere, to meddle.

ਘੁੱਸਣਾ (ghussnaa) *v* To err, to make a mistake; to miscalcuate; to miss (the right way); to be lost or stranded.

ਘੁਸਬੈਠ (ghusbaeth) *n f* Intrusion, infitration.

ਘੁਸਬੈਠੀਆ (ghusbaethiaa) *n* infiltratior, intruder.

ਘੁਸਮੁਸਾ (ghusmusaa) *n m a* Semidark, semi-darkness (as at dawn, or dusk); Dim, foggy or shadowy light, dusky, somewhat dark; Twilight, crepuscular.

ਘੁਸੜਨਾ (ghusarnaa) *v* To insert, to thrust, to pierce, to penetrate.

ਘੁਸਾਉਣਾ (ghusaaunaa) *v* To cause to enter, to shirk, to mislead, to miss.

ਘੁੰਗਰੂ (ghungroo) *n m* Small bells; An ornament worn round the ankle; The ratling sound of a dying person.

ਘੁਗੂ (ghugoo) *n m* Owl.

ਘੁੱਟ (ghutt) *n f* One sip, drought.

ਘੁੱਟਣ (ghuttan) *n f* Tightness, suffocation, stifle.

ਘੁਟਣਾ (ghutnaa) *v* To press, to copmress, to squeeze, to tighten.

ਘੁੰਡ (ghund) *n m* Veil.

ਘੁੰਡੀ (ghundee) *n f* Knot, button; Trick, problem, complication.

ਘੁਣ (ghun) *n m* Worm that infest wood; Decaying disease, diminishing process.

ਘੁਤਰ (ghutar) *n f* Any point of criticism, fault, blemish, shortcoming, defect, weakness; ~ਕੱਢਣੀ To find fault, to criticise.

ਘੁੰਨਾ (ghunnaa) *a* Deceitful, cunning.

ਘੁਪ (ghup) *a* Dark, dense.

ਘੁੰਮਕੜ (ghummakar) *n m* Wanderer, rover, traveller.

ਘੁੰਮਣਾ (ghummnaa) *v* To circulate, to revolve, to rotate, to spin, to roam.

ਘੁੰਮਰ (ghummar) *n m* Circular dance; Whirlpool spin, twirl.

ਘੁਮਾਉਣਾ (ghumaaunaa) *v* To rotate, to revolve, to spin, to whisk.

ਘੁਮੇਰ (ghumer) *n m* Dizziness, giddiness, vertigo.

ਘੁਰਕਣਾ (ghuraknaa) *v* To chide, to scold, to reprimand, to threaten.

ਘੁਰਨਾ (ghurnaa) *n m* Den, lair, hiding place, dugout, pit made by animals with their paws.

ਘੁਰਾੜੇ (ghuraare) *n m* Snorings.

ਘੁਲਣਾ (ghulnaa) *v* To dissolve, to wrestle, to combat.

ਘੁੜਸਵਾਰ (ghurswaar) *n m* Horseman, horse rider, cavalier.

ਘੁੜਸਾਲ (ghursaal) *n f* Horse stable.

ਘੂਸ (ghoos) *n f* Bribe, illegal gratification.

ਘੂਕਣਾ (ghooknaa) *v* To spin, to rotate, to produce whirling sound or buzzing sound. Also ਘੂਰਕਣਾ

ਘੂਰਨਾ (ghoornaa) *v* To stare, to frown; To look lustfully; To scorn, to rebuke.

ਘੇਰਨਾ (ghernaa) *v* To circumference, to surround, to fence, to blockade, to round up, to close.

ਘੇਰਾ (gheraa) *n m* Circumference, circuit, gamut, ambit, circle, periphery, closing.

ਘੋਸ਼ਣਾ (ghoshnaa) *v̸ n f* Announcement, proclamation; ~ਪੱਤਰ Manifesto.

ਘੋਗਾ (ghogaa) *n m* Sea-shell; Oyster, whelk, snail.

ਘੋਟਣਾ (ghotnaa) *v n m* To choke, to cram, to learn by rote, to repeat; To pound, to rub, to grind, to bruise, to polish; A short round club with which spice or Bhangs is ground.

ਘੋਟਾ (ghotaa) *n m* Cramming, learn by heart.

ਘੋਪਣਾ (ghopnaa) *v* To stab, to thrust into.

ਘੋਲ (ghol) *n m* Duel, wrestling, struggle, conflict, combat, solution.

ਘੋਲੀ (gholee) *n m* Wrestler.

ਘੋਲਣਾ (gholnaa) To dissolve.

ਘੋੜਾ (ghroaa) *n m* Horse; Steed chess knight; Trigger, gun-lock

ਘੋੜੀ (ghoree) *n* Mare; female horse A marriage song; Crutch Hammer of a gun; Portable wooden platform, stand for wood ~ਚੜ੍ਹਨਾ A marriage ceremony in which the bridegroom ride a mare while going to bride's place.

ਘੌਲ (ghaul) *n f* Laziness, negligence Carelessness, indifference, dilly dally, indolence; ~ਕਰਨੀ To delay through laziness, to dilly-dally, to neglect.

ਘੌਲੀ (ghaulee) *a* Lazy, indolent negligent, sluggard, careless indifferent.

ਙ

ਙ Tenth letter of Gurmukhi alphabet pronounced as 'ngaa'.

ਚ

ਚ Eleventh letter of Gurmukhi alphabets, pronounced as 'chachchaa'.

ਚਸਕਾ (chaskaa) *n m* Relish, taste; Habit, addiction; Pleasure, ardent desire; **~ਬਾਜ਼** Voluptuous, sensual.

ਚਸਕੇਖੋਰ (chaskekhor) *a* Greedy, having weakness for or easily tempted by something, such as spicy, juicy, eatables.

ਚਸਕੇਦਾਰ (chaskedaar) *a* Spicy, delicious, tempting; appetizing.

ਚਸ਼ਮਦੀਦ (chashamdeed) *a* Seen, witnessed; **~ਗਵਾਹ** Eye-witness

ਚਸ਼ਮਾ (chashmaa) *n m* (1) Spring; (2) Spectacles, goggles, glasses.

ਚਹਿਕਣਾ (chaheknaa) *v* To chirp, to warble. Also **ਚਹਿਚਹਾਉਣਾ**

ਚਹੇਤਾ (chahetaa) *a* Favourite

ਚਕਣਾ (chaknaa) *v* To lift, to raise; To incite, to instigate.

ਚਕਨਾਚੂਰ (chaknaachoor) *n m* splintered, broken to pieces; Dead tired.

ਚਕਮਾ (chakmaa) *n m* Trick, deception, temptation.

ਚੱਕਰ (chakkar) *n m* Circle, whirlwind, circular path, wheel, rotation, spin; **~ਆਉਣੇ** To feel giddy; **~ਖਾਣਾ** To be perplexed, to be confounded, to whirl; To rotate; **~ਚਲਾਉਣਾ** To launch a tricky move; **~ਮਾਰਨੇ** To come again and again; **~ਵਿਚ ਪੈਣਾ** To suffer harrassment, to be taken into; **~ਦਾਰ** Spirally, circuitous; **~ਵਰਤੀ** Emperor, universal monarch.

ਚਕਰਾਉਣਾ (chakraaunaa) *v* To be bewildered, to be confused.

ਚਕਲਾ (chaklaa) *n m* (1) An open space, a brothel, bagino; (2) flat round disc used for flattening bread.

ਚਕਲੀ (chaklee) *n f* A disc, pulley.

ਚੱਕ (chakk) *n m* (1) A bite or cut made with teeth; (2) Potter's wheel; (3) Village in canal colony; A compact piece of agriculture land; **~ਮਾਰਨਾ** To bite, to take a bite; **~ਬੰਦੀ** Demarcation of agricultural land; Divison of land into compact portions.

ਚਕਾਚੌਂਧ (chakaachaundh) *n m* Dazzle, brilliance.

ਚੱਕੀ (chakkee) *n f* A grinding mill,

handmill; Cake.

ਚਖਣਾ (chakhnaa) *v* To taste, to relish, to eat.

ਚੰਗਾ (changaa) *a* Good, nice, fine salutary; **~ਭਲਾ** Healthy, hale & hearty.

ਚੰਗਿਆਈ (changiaaee) *n f* Goodness.

ਚੰਗੇਰ (changer) *n f* A broad shallow, basket woven of bamboos etc.

ਚੰਗੇਰਾ (changeraa) *a* Better, superior, preferable.

ਚੰਘਿਆੜਨਾ (changhiaarnaa) *v* To roar, to trumpet.

ਚੰਚਲ (chanchal) *a* Unsteady, agile, inconstant, volatile, restless, energetic, playful, fickle.

ਚੱਜ (chajj) *n m* Dexterity, conduct, good behaviour, rules of etiquette.

ਚਟਣਾ (chatnaa) *v* To lick, to lap; To fondle, to embezzle.

ਚਟਕ (chatak) *n m* Smack, crash; **~ਮਟਕ** Brilliance, lustre, brightness, glitter.

ਚਟਕਣਾ (chataknaa) *v* To snap, to crack, to be split, to burst.

ਚਟਕਾਰਨਾ (chatkaarnaa) *v* To produce sound by snapping the tongue.

ਚਟਕੀਲਾ (chatakeelaa) *a* Relishing, pungent, flavoury, appetising.

ਚਟਣੀ (chatnee) *n f* Sauce, condiment.

ਚਟ ਪੁੰਜੀਆ (chatpunjiyaa) *a* Mean, Poor.

ਚਟਪਟਾ (chatpataa) *a* Spicy, saucy, pungent, delicious.

ਚਟਵਾਈ (chatwaaee) *n f* Act of licking.

ਚਟਾਈ (chataaee) *n f* Mat.

ਚਟਾਕ (chataak) *n m* Crack of sudden sharp noise as of a slap or whip; scar, patch, a healed wound.

ਚਟਾਕਾ (chataakaa) *n m* A Smack, crack, explosion.

ਚਟਾਨ (chataan) *n f* Rock.

ਚੱਟੀ (chattee) *n f* Fine, loss, Surcharge, expenditure; Punishment, penalty.

ਚੱਠ (chatth) *n m* Inauguration, house warming function.

ਚੰਡਾਲ (chandaal) *n m* Merciless, a wretch; Untouchable, a low born, an inferior caste; **~ਚੌਕੜੀ** Bunch of rascals or bad characters; **~ਪੁਣਾ** Meaness mercilessness.

ਚੰਡੂ (chandoo) *n* Smoking Opium; **~ਖਾਨਾ** Place for opium smokers, rumour manufacturing centre; **~ਬਾਜ਼** Opium addict; rumour monger.

ਚਤਰ (chatar) *a* Intelligent, shrewd, wise, sagacious, smart, ingeneous; Clever, cunning, sky, crafty, skillful, deft, adept.

ਚਤਰਾ (chatraa) *a* Cleaver, cunning, smart.

ਚੰਦਨ (chandan) *n m* Sandalwood.

ਚੰਦਰ (chandar) *n m* Moon.

ਚੱਦਰ (chaddar) *n f* A bed sheet, wrap.

ਚੰਦਰਾ (chandraa) *a* (1) Ill omened; evil, bad; (2) Hailstone, painful inflammation.

ਚੰਦਾ (chandaa) *n m* Contribution collection, subscription.

ਚੰਨ (chann) *a n m* Beautiful, pleasure giving; Moon

ਚਪਟਾ (chaptaa) *a* Flat, level, even, horizontal, plane.

ਚੰਪਤ (champat) *a* Disappeared, hidden, vanished, out of sight.

ਚਪਲ (chapal) *a* Playful, volatile, tricky, quick, brisk.

ਚੱਪਲ (chappal) *n f* A footwear, chappal.

ਚਪੜ-ਚਪੜ (chapar-chapar) *n f* Sound of lapping or eating; nonsensical talk, chatter, jabber; ~ਕਰਨੀ To lap or eat noisily; to chatter, jabber.

ਚਪੜਾਸ (chapṛaas) *n f* Post or function of a peon, peonage.

ਚਪੜਾਸੀ (chapṛaasee) *n m* Peon, official attendant or messenger.

ਚੱਪਾ (chappa) *a* One fourth, fourth part; Paddle, oar; ~ਚੱਪਾ Every little space; ~ਚੱਪਾ ਛਾਣ ਮਾਰਨਾ To make a thorough search.

ਚਪਾਤੀ (chapaatee) *n f* Bread; a thin cake.

ਚੱਪੂ (chappoo) *n m* An oar, a paddle.

ਚਪੇੜ (chaper) *n m* A slap, smack, blow; Risk, loss.

ਚੱਬਣਾ (chabbṇaa) *v* To chew, to munch, to masticate.

ਚੰਬੜ (chambaṛ) *n m* Clinging, clasping, adhesion.

ਚੰਬੜਨਾ (chambaṛnaa) *v* To stick, to cling, to hold fast, to adhere.

ਚਬੂਤਰਾ (chabootraa) *n m* Platform, dais, stage, terrace, stand.

ਚੰਭਲਾਉਣਾ (chambhlaaunaa) *v* To instigate, to excite, to spoil.

ਚੱਮ (chamm) *n m* Leather, skin, hide, felt; ~ਉਧੇੜਨਾ To thrash, to flog, to beat mercilessly.

ਚਮਕ (chamak) *n f* Brilliance, lustre, shine, illumination, gleam, flash; ~ਦਮਕ Splendour, brightness; ~ਦਾਰ Bright, shining, luminous.

ਚਮਕਣਾ (chamaknaa) *v* To sparkle,

to flash, to shine, to glow, to twinkle.

ਚਮਗਾਦੜ (chamgaadaṛ) *n m* Bat, a vampire.

ਚਮਚ (chamach) *n m* Spoon.

ਚਮਚਾ (chamchaa) *n m* Spoon; Scoop; Tout, protege; ~**ਗੀਰੀ** Sycophancy, obsequiousness.

ਚਮਨ (chaman) *n m* Small garden, a lawn.

ਚਮੜਾ (chamṛaa) *n* Leather.

ਚਮੜੀ (chamṛee) *n f* Skin.

ਚਰਸ (charas) *n f* Intoxicating drug of hemp.

ਚਰਕਣਾ (charaknaa) *v* To creak.

ਚਰਖੜੀ (charkhṛee) *n f* Pulley.

ਚਰਖਾ (charkhaa) *n m* Spinning wheel.

ਚਰਖੀ (charkhee) *n f* Pulley, spindle, a small spinning wheel.

ਚਰਚਾ (charchaa) *n f* Talk, discussion, report, remark, mention, rumour

ਚਰਨਾ (charnaa) *v* To graze, to pasture, to feed.

ਚਰਬੀ (charbee) *n f* Fat, grease, tallow.

ਚਰਵਾਹਾ (charwaahaa) *n m* Herdman, grazier.

ਚਰਾਉਣਾ (charaaunaa) *v* To graze, to pasture.

ਚਰਿੱਤਰ (charittar) *n m* Character, conduct, behaviour, nature, habit, act, deed, custom.

ਚਰੋਕਣਾ (charoknaa) *a* Pretty old.

ਚਲਣ (chalaṇ) *n m* Motion, conduct, method, habit, custom; ~**ਸਾਰ** Durable.

ਚਲਣਾ (chalnaa) *v* To walk, to move, to proceed, to go, to flow, to be in vogue.

ਚਲਦਾ (chaldaa) *a* Moving, in motion, on the move; Serviceable, in working order; Continuing, continued, ongoing, current; ~**ਪੁਰਜਾ** Component in motion or in working order; Clever, smart, resourceful, cunning; ~**ਫਿਰਦਾ** Mobile; Paddler; Active.

ਚਲਾਕ (chalaak) *a* Clever, cunning, nimble, artful, tricky.

ਚਲਾਣਾ (chalaaṇaa) *n m* Departure, exodus, passing away; ~**ਕਰ ਜਾਣਾ** To die, to pass away.

ਚੱਲਿਤਰ (chalitar) *n m* Trick, artifice, guile, pretence, coquetry; ~**ਕਰਨਾ** To beguile, to trick.

ਚੜਨਾ (charnaa) *v* To ascend, to rise, to go up, to climb, to mount, to ride (horse); **ਦਿਨ~** Day break.

ਚੜ੍ਹਾਈ (charhaaee) *n f* Ascent, rise, invasion, attack, push.

ਚੜ੍ਹਾਵਾ (charaawaa) *n m* Offering to

a god; Exaltation, oblation.

ਚਾ (chaa) *n f* (1) Eagerness, ambition, zest, enthusiasm; (2) Tea.

ਚਾਹ (chaah) *n f* Desire, aspiration, will, longing.

ਚਾਹਤ (chaahat) *n f* Fondness, desire longing.

ਚਾਹੁਣਾ (chaahunaa) *v* To desire, to like, to crave, to need, to require, to ask for.

ਚਾਕਰੀ (chaakree) *n f* Service, menialship, attendance.

ਚਾਕੂ (chaakoo) *n m* Knife.

ਚਾਚਾ (chaachaa) *n m* Uncle, father's younger brother.

ਚਾਟ (chaat) *n f* A kind of pungent, sour delicacy; Taste, liking, addiction, (bad) habit, weakness (for) allurement, temptation; ~ਲੱਗਣੀ/ਚਾਟ ਲੱਗਣਾ To be addicted to, to fall for, to be allured or tempted to a bad habit.

ਚਾਂਟਾ (chaantaa) *n m* Slap.

ਚਾਦਰ (chaadar) *n f* Bed sheet, bedspread, coverlet; ~ਪਾਉਣੀ To marry (a widow) Through a ceremony; ~ਵੇਖ ਕੇ ਪੈਰ ਪਸਾਰਨਾ To cut coat according to one's cloth.

ਚਾਂਦਨੀ (chaandnee) *n f* Moonlight; canopy, bed sheet.

ਚਾਂਦੀ (chandee) *n f* Silver.

ਚਾਨਣ (chaanan) *n m* Light, sunshine, brightness.

ਚਾਪਲੂਸ (chaaploos) *n m* Flatterer, servile, wheedler.

ਚਾਬਕ (chaabak) *n f* Lash, whip, a thrash.

ਚਾਬੀ (chaabee) *n f* Key; ~ਘੁਮਾਉਣੀ To tutor; to turn the key.

ਚਾਰਪਾਈ (chaarpaaee) *n f* Cot.

ਚਾਰਾ (chaaraa) *n m* Fodder, pasture; Lure; Remedy.

ਚਾਲ (chaal) *n f* Motion, movement walk, gait; Habit, procedure; Tradition, custom, manner; ~ਢਾਲ Gait, fashion, manner; ~ਬਾਜ਼ Deceitful, cunning, tricker.

ਚਾਲੂ (chaaloo) *n m* In vogue, current, prevalent; ~ਕਰਨਾ To promote, to promulgate.

ਚਾਵਲ (chaawal) *n m* Rice. Also ਚੌਲ

ਚਾੜ੍ਹਨਾ (chaarnaa) *v* To lift, to raise, to offer, to ascend; To cook.

ਚਾੜ੍ਹੀ (chaaree) *n f* Bribe; Flatter.

ਚਿੱਕ (chikk) *n f* Curtain or screen made of split bamboo sticks; Thin mortar of mud, mire.

ਚਿਕਣਾ (chiknaa) *a* Greasy, oily, smooth.

ਚਿਕਨਾਈ (chiknaaee) *n f* Fatness, greasiness, lubricant.

ਚਿੱਕੜ (chikkar) *n f* Filth, mire, mud, clay, marsh, morass.

ਚਿਕਿਤਸਾ (chikitsaa) *n f* Medical science, treatment.

ਚਿਖਾ (chikhaa) *n f* A funeral pyre.

ਚਿੰਗਾਰੀ (chingaaree) *n f* Spark.

ਚਿਘਾਉਣਾ (chighaaunaa) *v* To jeer, to huff, to mock.

ਚਿੰਘਾੜ (chinghaar) *n f* Shrill cry, a scream, the trumppeting of an elephant.

ਚਿੰਘਾੜਨਾ (chingaarnaa) *v* To trumpet, to scream.

ਚਿਚਲਾਉਣਾ (chichlaaunaa) *v* To cry out, to squeal, to hoot, to howl, to yell, to shriek.

ਚਿਚੜ (chichar) *n m* A louse or tick which sticks to the body of cattle.

ਚਿਟਕਣਾ (chitaknaa) *v* To crack.

ਚਿਟਕਨੀ (chitkanee) *n f* Bolt, catch-bar.

ਚਿਟਕਾ (chitkaa) *n m* Glare of the sun.

ਚਿੱਟਾ (chittaa) *a* White, fair, milky; ~**ਪਣ** Whiteness.

ਚਿੱਠਾ (chitthaa) *n m* Memorandum of accounts, balance sheet, account book, cheap pamphlet, invoice.

ਚਿੱਠੀ (chitthee) *n m* Letter, a written note, document, circular; ~**ਚਪੱਠੀ** Correspondence, letter writing; ~**ਰਸਾਨ** Postman.

ਚਿਨਣਾ (chinnaa) *v* To decorate, to arrange in an orderly manner; To lay (bricks).

ਚਿਨਾਈ (chinaaee) *n f* Masonary assortment, building work.

ਚਿਤ (chit) *n* Mind, attention; ~**ਲਾਉਣਾ** to concertrate, to pay heed to; ~**ਵਿਚ ਬਿਠਾਉਣਾ** To love; ~**ਕਬਰਾ** Dappled, speckled, spotted

ਚਿੰਤਨ (chintan) *n m* Contemplation, thinking, reflection.

ਚਿੱਤਰ (chittar) *n m* A picture, illustration, painting, diagram; ~**ਕਾਰ** Artist, painter; ~**ਪਟ** Screen. Also **ਚਿਤ੍ਰ**

ਚਿਤਰਾ (chitraa) *n m* Leopard, panther.

ਚਿਤਰੀ ਵਾਲਾ (chitree waalaa) *n* Spotted, speckled (banana).

ਚਿਤੜ (chitar) *n m* Buttock, posterior, bottom.

ਚਿੰਤਾ (chintaa) *n f* Worry, pensiveness, anxiety, doubt, thought.

ਚਿਤਾਉਣਾ (chitaaunaa) *v* To remind, to prompt.

ਚਿਤਾਰਨਾ (chitaarnaa) *v* To remember, to recollect, to entertain, to suppose.

ਚਿਤੇਰਾ (chiteraa) *n m* Painter.

ਚਿੱਥਣਾ (chitthnaa) *v* To munch, to crush with teeth, to masticate, to chew.

ਚਿੰਦੀ (chindee) *n f* Rag, small piece of cloth.

ਚਿੰਨ੍ਹ (chinnh) *n m* Sign, symbol, token, emblem, badge.

ਚਿਪਕਣਾ (chipaknaa) *v* To stick, to adhere.

ਚਿਪਚਿਪਾ (chipchipaa) *a* Greasy, waxy, adhesive, gummy, viscid.

ਚਿੰਬੜਨਾ (chimbarnaa) *v* To cling, to adhere, to embrace.

ਚਿਰਕ (chirak) *n f* Delay.

ਚਿਰਨਾ (chirnaa) *v* To be torn, to be sawn, to be split.

ਚਿਰਾਗ (chiraag) *n m* Lamp.

ਚਿਰੋਕਣਾ (chiroknaa) *adv* Since, long, of old.

ਚਿਲਕਣਾ (chilaknaa) *v* To shine, to glitter, to glow, to brighten.

ਚਿਲਮ (chilam) *n f* An earthen pipe where fire & tobacco are placed for smoking.

ਚਿਲਮਚੀ (chilamchee) *n f* A wash basin.

ਚਿਲਮਨ (chilman) *n f* Bamboo curtain.

ਚਿੜ (chir) *n f* Irritation, vexation, detestation, fretfulness; ~ਚਿੜਾ Irritable ill-tempered, peevish, short tempered; ~ਚਿੜਾਹਟ Peevishness, irritability, sourness, fretfulness.

ਚਿੜਨਾ (chirnaa) *v* To be irritated, to be chafed.

ਚਿੜਾਉਣਾ (chiraaunaa) *v* To vex, to chafe, to irritate, to provoke, to jeer at, to tease.

ਚਿੜੀ (chiree) *n f* Female sparrow; The shuttle cock; To club suit in playing cards; ~ਛਿੱਕਾ Badminton.

ਚੀਕ (cheek) *n f* Scream, shriek, yell, shrill cry.

ਚੀਕਣਾ (cheeknaa) *v a* To scream, to yell, to shout, to cry; Soapy, oily, slippery.

ਚੀਚੀ (cheechee) *n m* Smallest finger of hand.

ਚੀਜ਼ (cheez) *n* A thing, article, a commodity, a substance.

ਚੀਥੜਾ (cheethraa) *n m* Rag, a tatterred garment.

ਚੀਨੀ (cheenee) *n f* Sugar; Chinese national; ~ਮਿਟੀ China clay.

ਚੀਪੜ (cheepar) *a* Miser.

ਚੀਰਨਾ (cheernaa) *v* To saw, to tear, to rip, to rive.

ਚੀਰਾ (cheeraa) *n m* A cut, an incision, operation.

ਚੀਲ (cheel) *n f* A kite.

ਚੀੜ੍ਹਾ (chirhaa) *a* Hard, rigid, stiff;

gummy, gluey, glutinous; Fussy, difficult to deal with, hard bargainer; Firm, tough, resolute; Stingy, miser.

ਚੁਆਉਣਾ (chuaaunaa) *v* To get (A milk animal) milked; to drip something (on to).

ਚੁਆਤੀ (chuaatee) *n f* Spark, ember, small smouldring piece of wood; fire brand; inciter.

ਚੁਸਕੀ (chooskee) *n* Sip.

ਚੁਸਤੀ (chustee) *n f* Activity, alertness, readiness, promptness.

ਚੁਹਲ (chuhal) *n f* Merriment, festivity, sportiveness, blandishment; ~**ਬਾਜ਼** Sportive.

ਚੁੱਕ (chukk) *n f* Stiffening of or pain in back muscles or backbone; spinal disorder or dislocation; ~**ਕੱਢਣੀ** To treat or heal spinal disorder; ~**ਪੈਣਾ** To suffer from spinal dislocation; ~**ਦੇਣਾ** To lift, to raise; ~**ਲੈਣਾ** To lift, pick up, take up; to steal; to carry.

ਚੁੱਕਣਾ (chukknaa) *v* To lift, to arouse, to carry, to excite.

ਚੁਕੰਨਾ (chukannaa) *a* Alert, active, vigilant, cautions.

ਚੁਕਵਾਈ (chukwaaee) *n f* Act of lifting, porterage.

ਚੁੰਗ (chung) *n f* Retail; customer; Something given to a customer gratis as bonus on purchases; A handful, a pinch, a bit.

ਚੁਗਣਾ (chugnaa) *v* To peck, to pick food with beak.

ਚੁਗਲ (chugal) *n m* Tell-tale backbiting; Block head, owl, fool; ~**ਖੋਰ** Backbiter, sycophant.

ਚੁਗਲੀ (chuglee) *n f* An instance of backbiting, false and malicious report; ~**ਕਰਨੀ** To backbite.

ਚੁਗਿਰਦਾ (chugirdaa) *n m* Boundary, ambit, surrounding perimeter.

ਚੁੰਗੀ (chungee) *n f* Toll, octroi, cess, excise duty.

ਚੁੰਝ (chunjh) *n f* Beak; Nib, corner; Pointed end.

ਚੁਟਕਾਰਨਾ (chutkaarnaa) *v* To flick

ਚੁਟਕੀ (chutkee) *n f* A pinch, fillip, a snapping with finger.

ਚੁਣਨਾ (chunnaa) *v* To select, to pick, to sort, to choose, to arrange.

ਚੁਤ (chut) *n f* Vagina.

ਚੁਤੜ (chutar) *n m* Buttocks, rumps, hips.

ਚੁਧਰੱਮਾ (chudharmmaa) *n m* Leadership.

ਚੁੰਧਲਾਉਣਾ (chundhlaaunaa) *v* To dazzle.

ਚੁੰਨ੍ਹਾ (chunnhaa) *a* Bleary eyed, purblind, having Small eyes.

ਚੁੰਨੀ (chunnee) *n m* A head cloth for women.

ਚੁੱਪ (chupp) *a* Silent, mute, mum, speechless; ~**ਚਾਪ** In silence; ~**ਚੁਪੀਤਾ** Without uttering a single word.

ਚੁਪਾਲ (chupaal) *n m* Meeting place for village elders or assembly.

ਚੁਫੇਰੇ (chuphere) *adv* Around, all around. Also ਚੁਗਿਰਦੇ

ਚੰਬਕ (chumbak) *n m* Magnet, loadstone.

ਚੁਬਾਰਾ (chubaaraa) *n m* An attic, upper storey, summer house, upper open room.

ਚੁਬੁਰਜੀ (chuburjee) *n* Pavillion.

ਚੁਭਣਾ (chubhnaa) *v* To pierce, to sting.

ਚੁਭਨ (chubhan) *n f* Pricking, lingering pain, irritation.

ਚੁਮਣਾ (chumnaa) *v* To kiss, to suckle, to osculate, to lip.

ਚੁੰਮੀ (chummee) *n m* Kiss, osculation.

ਚੁਰਸਤਾ (churastaa) *n m* A crossing.

ਚੁਰਕਣਾ (churaknaa) *v* To be dysenteric.

ਚੁਰਾਉਣਾ (churaaunaa) *v* To steal, to pilfer, to thieve.

ਚੁਰੇੜਾ (chureraa) *a* Broader, wider.

ਚੁਲਬੁਲਾ (chulbulaa) *a* Vivacious, agile, mercurial, restless.

ਚੁਲਬੁਲਾਉਣਾ (chulbulaaunaa) *v* To be playful, to be fidgety, to be restless.

ਚੁਲੀ (chulee) *n f* A mouthful of liquid, oblation.

ਚੁੜਨਾ (churnaa) *v* To be an invalid, to linger a painful life.

ਚੁੜੈਲ (churail) *n f* Witch, hag, hobgoblin, female giant.

ਚੁਸਣਾ (choosnaa) *v* To suck, to suckle, to sip.

ਚੂਹਾ (choohaa) *n m* Mouse, rat.

ਚੂਕ (chook) *n f* Error, blunder, mistake, fault.

ਚੂਕਣਾ (chooknaa) *v* To err, to blunder, to fail, to miss.

ਚੂਚਾ (choochaa) *n m* Chicken, squeaker.

ਚੂੰਢੀ (choondhee) *n f* Pinch, clothes-pin, paper clip.

ਚੂਨਾ (choonaa) *n m* Lime, mortar.

ਚੂਰਨ (chooran) *n m* A powder (especially of medicine).

ਚੂਰਾ (chooraa) *n m* Sawdust, powder.

ਚੂਰੀ (chooree) *n m* Crushed bread mixed with ghee and sugar.

ਚੂੜੀ (chooree) *n f* Bangle, bracelet, spire, pitch.

ਚੇਹਰਾ (chehraa) *n m* Face, appearance.

ਚੇਚਕ (chechak) *n f* Small pox.

ਚੇਤਨਾ (chetnaa) *v* To recollect, to remember, to be alert.

ਚੇਤਨ (chetan) *n m a* Conscious soul, a living being; Conscious, alert, cautious, observant.

ਚੇਤਨਾ (chetnaa) *n f* Consciousness, awareness, sentiency, understanding.

ਚੇਪਣਾ (chepṇaa) *v* To paste, to stick, to glue.

ਚੇਪੀ (chepee) *n f* Sticker, patch, a piece of cloth or paper.

ਚੇਲਾ (chelaa) *n m* A pupil, follower, disciple.

ਚੈਨ (chain) *n m* Rest, tranquility, ease, relief, repose, piece.

ਚੋਖਾ (chokhaa) *a* Sufficient, enough, ample, tolerable.

ਚੋਗਾ (choga) *n m* Birdfeed, bait.

ਚੋਟ (choṭ) *n f* Wound, hurt, blow, bruise, percussion; Ironical remark; **ਡੰਕੇ ਦੀ~** Openly, challengingly.

ਚੋਟਾ (choṭaa) *n m* Thief, pilferer, rascal.

ਚੋਟੀ (choṭee) *n f* Top knot, a plait, pig tail; Summit, top, peak, vertex crest; A female thief.

ਚੋਣ (choṇ) *n m* Choice, selection, election, option, pick; **ਉਪ~** Bye election; **~ਹਲਕਾ** Constituency, electorate.

ਚੋਣਵਾਂ (choṇwaan) *a* Selected, chosen, selective.

ਚੋਪੜਨਾ (choparnaa) To butter, to besmear, to anoint.

ਚੋਰ (Chor) *n m* Thief, burglar, pilferer, swindler; **~ਬਜ਼ਾਰ** Black market; **~ਦਰਵਾਜ਼ਾ** Backdoor.

ਚੋਰੀ (choree) *n m* Theft, burglary; **~ਚੋਰੀ** Seretly, privately; **~ਛਿਪੇ** Stealthly.

ਚੋਲਾ (cholaa) *n m* A long robe worn by saints; Shirts; Human body; **~ਛਡਣਾ** To die; **~ਬਦਲਣਾ** To be reborn; To change physical frame.

ਚੋਲੀ (cholee) *n f* Bodice, blouse, vest, corset.

ਚੌਸਰ (chausar) *n m* Chess, chess board.

ਚੌਕ (chauk) *n m* Public square, cross road, road junction, crossing, plaza.

ਚੌਕਸ (chaukas) *a* Alert, careful, watchful, vigilant.

ਚੌਕਸੀ (chauksee) *n f* Alertness, carefulness, watchfulness, vigilance, wariness, precaution, circumspection.

ਚੌਂਕਣਾ (chaunkṇaa) *v* To stratle, to be astonished.

ਚੌਕੰਨਾ (chaukannaa) *a* Cautious, alert.

ਚੌਕੜੀ (chaukaṛee) *n f* Posture of sitting cross-legged.

ਚੌਕਾ (chaukaa) *n m* Kitchen, clean place for cooking.

ਚੌਕੀ (chaukee) *n f* Stool, a small wooden chair with no arm; **~ਦਾਰ** Watchman.

ਚੌਧਰੀ (chaudharee) *n m* Chieftain, headman, leader.

ਚੌਪੜ (chaupaṛ) *n m* Dice, chess.

ਚੌਪਾਲ (chaupaal) *n m* Rural meeting place.

ਚੌਰਸ (chauras) *a* Flat, plane, square, smooth, oblong.

ਚੌਲ (chaul) *n m* Rice. Also **ਚਾਵਲ**

ਚੌੜ (chauṛ) *n m a* Spoiling, destruction, ruin; Wasted, spoiled; **~ਕਰਨਾ** To spoil, to damage, to waste.

ਚੌੜਾ (chauṛaa) *a* Broad, wide, open, flat.

ਚੌੜਾਈ (chauṛaaee) *n f* Width, breadth, span, extension.

ਛ

ਛ Twelfth letter of Gurmukhi alphabets, pronounced as 'chhachhaa'.

ਛਕਣਾ (chhaknaa) *v* To eat satisfactorily, to be gratified; To deceive, to cheet.

ਛਕੜਾ (chhakṛaa) *n m* Cart, van, truck, wagon.

ਛੱਕਾ (chhakkaa) *n m* A group of six, Sixer, sixth at cards.

ਛਕਾਉਣਾ (chhakaaunaa) *v* To satiate, to serve; To deceive.

ਛੰਗਵਾਉਣਾ (chhangvaaunaa) *v* To get trimmed, to get pruned.

ਛਛੂੰਦਰ (chhachhoondar) *n m* Muskrat, mole.

ਛਛੋਹਰਾ (chhachhohraa) *a m* Sordid, trifling, shallow, childish, light headed.

ਛੱਜ (chhajj) *n m* Winnowing basket, winnower; ~**ਛੱਜ ਰੋਣਾ** To weep bitterly.

ਛਜਲੀ (chhajlee) *n f* Hood (of a Snake).

ਛੱਜਾ (chhajjaa) *n m* Balcony, gallery-shelf, penthouse, brim.

ਛਟਣਾ (chhatnaa) *v* To remove dust from the grain, to slander, to husk, to thresh.

ਛੰਡਣ (chhaddan) *n m* Quittance.

ਛੰਡਣਾ (chhandnaa) *v* To dust, to toss, to reprimand.

ਛਡਣਾ (chhadnaa) *v* To leave, to relinquish, to remit, to renounce, to quit, to release, to vacate, to forgo.

ਛਣਕ (chhanak) *n f* Clang, clink, jingle, sound produced by clattering of metal or coin.

ਛਣਕਣਾ (chhanaknaa) *v* To clatter, to clink, to babble.

ਛਣਨਾ (channaa) *v* To be sieved, strained; (for cloth, garment) to get worn out, thinned.

ਛੱਤ (chhatt) *n f* Roof, ceiling, storey.

ਛਤਰੀ (chhatree) *n f* Umbrella, parachute, dome.

ਛਤਰੇ (chhatre) *n m* Locks of hair.

ਛੱਤਾ (chhattaa) *n m* Beehive, honey comb.

ਛੰਨ (chhann) *n f* Small hut, thatched roof.

ਛੰਨਾ (chhannaa) *n m* Bowl, cup.

ਛੱਪਰ (chhappar) *n m* Thatched roof or shed, booth.

ਛੱਪਰੀ (chhappree) *n f* Cottage, hut,

shed, hovel.

ਛਪਵਾਉਣਾ (chhapvaaunaa) *v* To cause to be printed or embossed or stamped.

ਛਪਵਾਈ (chhapvaaee) *n f* Printing.

ਛੱਪੜ (chhappar) *n m* Pool, Pond.

ਛਪੜੀ (chhapree) *n f* Small, pond, puddle, cesspool.

ਛਪਾਕੀ (chhapaakee) *n f* White gum, erysipelas.

ਛਬੀਲ (chhabeel) *n f* Place where water is distributed gratuitously.

ਛਬੀਲਾ (chhabeelaa) *a* Elegant, handsome, beautiful, graceful.

ਛਮਕ (chhamak) *n f* Stick, cane; ~ਛੱਲੋ A passionate woman, a beautiful girl.

ਛਲ (chhal) *n m* Deception, dodge, trap, trick, fraud.

ਛਲਕਣਾ (chhalaknaa) *v* To spill, to overflow, to wobble, to shake.

ਛੱਲਾ (chhallaa) *n m* Plain ring worn on fingers, annulus.

ਛੱਲੀ (chhallee) *n f* Corncob of maize; spool; Enlarged spleen; Stiffened muscle.

ਛਲਾਵਾ (chhalaawaa) *n m* Illusion, hallucination, dodge.

ਛਲੀਆ (chhaliyaa) *a* Artful, crafty, fraudulent, cunning, tricky, deceitful, cheat.

ਛੜ (chhar) *n f* Bale, pole, staff (of a flag); Shaft (of spear).

ਛੜਾ (chharaa) *n m a* Bachelor, unmarried; Single, lone; ~ਛਾਂਟ All alone.

ਛੜੀ (chharee) *n f* A rod, cane, good, stick.

ਛਾਂ (chhaan) *n f* Shade. Also ਛਾਂਓਂ

ਛਾਉਣੀ (chhaaunee) *n* Cantonment, Permanant military camp or barrack; Encampment. Also ਛੌਣੀ

ਛਾਈ (chhaaee) *n f* Dark, spot, pimples; Ashes.

ਛਾਹ (chhaah) *n f* Butter milk, whey.

ਛਾਂਟਣਾ (chhaatnaa) *v* To select, to pick, to retrench, to clip, to choose, to sort out (mail).

ਛਾਣ (chaan) *v* Residue, refuse after sieving; bran; ~ਮਾਰਨਾ To search, explore, look for thoroughly.

ਛਾਣਨਾ (chhaannaa) *v* To filter, to percolate, To screen, to sieve, to sift.

ਛਾਣਨੀ (chhaannee) *n f* Sieve, bolter.

ਛਾਣਬੀਣ (chhaanbeen) *n f* Probe, scrutiny, sifting.

ਛਾਤੀ (chhaatee) *n f* Chest, breast, bosom, heart, bust; ~ਤਾਣਨਾ To stretch out one's chest; To offer a brave front, to face boldly.

ਛਾਪਣਾ (chhaapnaa) *v* To print, to

publish.

ਛਾਪਾ (chhaapaa) *n m* Sudden attack, surprise attack, surprise visit; ~ਮਾਰਨਾ To raid; to attack suddenly; To surprise.

ਛਾਬੜੀ (chhaabṛee) *n f* Small basket; ~ਵਾਲਾ Hawker, pedlar.

ਛਾਬਾ (chhaabaa) *n m* Small basket; A pan of weighing scale.

ਛਾਰ (chhaar) *n f* Alkali; Ashes, dirt.

ਛਾਲ (chhaal) *n f* Bark, peel; Jump, plunge; ~ਮਾਰਨਾ To jump, to leap, to skip.

ਛਾਲਾ (chhaalaa) *n m* Boil, burn, pock, skin-blister.

ਛਿਆਸੀ (chhiaasee) *a* Eighty-six.

ਛਿਆਲੀ (chiaalee) *a* Forty-six. Also ਛਤਾਲੀ

ਛਿੱਕਣਾ (chhiknaa) *v* To seneeze.

ਛਿੱਕਾ (chikkaa) *n m* Cup-shaped network with strings for fasterning over animal's mouth against its damaging crops or for hanging eatables to protect them against cats, mice or ants; Tennis or badminton racket.

ਛਿਜਣਾ (chhijṇaa) *v* To decrease, to lessen, to waste away.

ਛਿੱਟ (chhitt) *n f* Drop, splash.

ਛਿਟਣਾ (chhitṇaa) *v* To spatter.

ਛਿੱਟਾ (chhittaa) *n m* Water splash, spray, shower.

ਛਿਣਕਣਾ (chhiṇakṇaa) *v* To sprinkle.

ਛਿੱਤਰ (chhittar) *n m* Used foot wear, worn out shoes; ~ਮਾਰਨਾ To beat with shoes.

ਛਿੱਥਾ (chhitthaa) *a* Annoyed, angry, abashed, peevish.

ਛਿਦਣਾ (chhidṇaa) *v* To be perforated, to be piered with holes, to be wounded.

ਛਿੱਦਰ (chhiddar) *n m* Mistake, omission; Hole, slot.

ਛਿਨ (chhin) *n m* A moment.

ਛਿੰਨ-ਭਿੰਨ (chhinn-bhinn) *a* Decomposed, scattered, cut.

ਛਿਨਾਲ (chhinaal) *n f* A Strumpet, harolt, prostitute.

ਛਿਪਾਉਣਾ (chhipaaunaa) *v* To hide, to conceal, to cover.

ਛਿੱਲ (chhil) *n f* Skin, bark, peel, shell, husk, rind. Also ਛਿਲਕਾ

ਛਿਲਣਾ (chhilṇaa) *v* To peel, to raze, to rind, to pare, to chisel, to shell.

ਛਿੱਲੜ (chhillar) *n m* Rind, skin, crust, husk.

ਛਿੜ (chhir) *n f* Start; ~ਜਾਣਾ To straggle, to disperse, to dissolve, to break out (war).

ਛਿੜਕਣਾ (chhiṛakṇaa) *v* To sprinkle, to scatter, to spray.

ਛਿੜਨਾ (chhiṛnaa) *v* Beginning, to

continue, to start, to go for a grazing.

ਛੁਹਰ (chuhar) *n m* A lad, boy, youngster.

ਛੁਹਾਉਣਾ (chhuhaaunaa) *v* To touch.

ਛੁਹਾਰਾ (chhuhaaraa) *n m* Dried date, palm.

ਛੁਟਕਣਾ (chhutaknaa) *v* To slip, to break loose, to abscise.

ਛੁਟਕਾਰਾ (chhutkaaraa) *n m* Rescue, escape, release, exemption, discharge, acquittal.

ਛੁਟਣਾ (chhutnaa) *v* To get rid of, to be discharged, to escape, to slip away, to break loose.

ਛੁੱਟੜ (chhutar) *a* Divorced, derelict, woman abandoned by the husband.

ਛੁੱਟੀ (chhuttee) *n f* Leave, vacation, holiday, intermission.

ਛੁਡਾਉਣਾ (chhudaaunaa) *v* To save, to liberate, to get discharged, to get removed, to disentangle.

ਛੁਪਣਾ (chhupnaa) *v* To hide, to disappear, to be concealed.

ਛੁਰਾ (chhuraa) *n m* A long knife, chopper, dagger.

ਛੁਰੀ (chhuree) *n f* A knife.

ਛੁੱਛਾ (chhuchhaa) *a* Empty, unfilled or partly filled (vessel); Vain (person), hollow, mean.

ਛੂਤ (chhoot) *n f* Infection, contagion, contamination; ~ਛਾਤ Untouchability, (now legally banned in India).

ਛੇਕ (chhek) *n m* Hole, gap, loophole, flaw, puncture, cut.

ਛੇਕਣਾ (chheknaa) *v* To ostracise, excommunicate, to boycott; To ignore, to disown.

ਛੇਕੜ (chhekar) *adv* At last, ultimately, in the long run.

ਛੇਤੀ (chhetee) *n a* Expeditiousness briskness, promptness, haste, soon, shortly; ~ਕਰਨਾ To make haste, to expedite, to speed up; ~ਨਾਲ Swiftly, quickly.

ਛੇੜਨਾ (chhernaa) *v* To tease, to chaff, to harass, to irritate.

ਛੈਣੀ (chhainee) *n* Chisel, graver.

ਛੋਕਰਾ (chhokraa) *n* Boy, lad, youngster.

ਛੋਟਾ (chhotaa) *a* Small, little, short, junior, subordinate, tiny.

ਛੋਲਾ (chholaa) *n m* Gram, chickpea.

ਛੋਲੀਆ (chholiaa) *n m* Green gram.

ਛੋੜਨਾ (chhornaa) *v* To release, to leave, to relinquish, to renounce, to forego.

ਛੌਂਕਣਾ (chhaunknaa) *v* To fry and season with spices.

ਜ

ਜ Thirteenth letter of Gurmukhi alphabets, pronounced as 'jajjaa'.

ਜਈ (jaee) *n f* Oat.

ਜਸ (jas) *n m* Fame, reputation, praise, glory, splendour.

ਜਸ਼ਨ (jashan) *n m* Feast, celebration, merriment.

ਜਸੂਸ (jasoos) *n m* Spy, informer, detective. Also ਜਾਸੂਸ

ਜਸੂਸੀ (jasoosee) *a n f* Detective, detecting; Espionage, spying.

ਜਹੰਨਮ (jahannam) *n m* Hell, inferno.

ਜਹਾਜ (jahaaj) *n m* Ship, steamer, vessel, launch, liner; Aeroplane, aircraft; ~ਅਸਲਾ Air crew; (ਜਹਾਜੀ) ~ਬੇੜਾ Fleet; Navy; Armada; ~ਰਾਨ Sailor; Flier; ~ਰਾਨੀ Shipping, naval, nautical.

ਜਹਾਂ (jahaan) *n m* World; ~ਗੀਰ World conquerer. Also ਜਹਾਨ

ਜਹਾਦ (jahaad) *n m* Holywar, crusade.

ਜਹਾਲਤ (jahaalat) *n f* Stupidity, ignorance.

ਜ਼ਹਿਮਤ (zhemat) *n f* Botheration, affliction, perplexity, difficulty, calamity.

ਜ਼ਹਿਰ (zaher) *n m* Poison, venom.

ਜ਼ਹੀਨ (zaheen) *a* Intelligent, sagacious.

ਜਹੂਰ (Jahoor) *n* Manifestation, presence, appearance. Also ਜ਼ਹੂਰ

ਜਕ (jak) *n f* Shyness, hesitation, disgrace, disilusion.

ਜਕੜ (jakaṛ) *n f* Grip, hold.

ਜਕੜਨਾ (jakaṛnaa) *v* To grip, to tie up, to fasten tightly.

ਜ਼ਕਾਤ (zakaat) *n f* Alms, charity, tax, customs duty.

ਜੱਕੋ-ਤੱਕਾ (jakko-takkaa) *n m* Hesitation, reluctance, double mindedness, indecision, quandary, irresoluteness, ambivalence, dilemma; ~ਕਰਨਾ To hesitate, dither, procrastinate, to be double minded, irresolute, ambivalent.

ਜੱਖਣਾ (jakkhaṇaa) *n f* Existence; Essence.

ਜ਼ਖ਼ਮ (zakham) *n m* Wound, cut.

ਜ਼ਖ਼ਮੀ (zakhmee) *a* Wounded, hurt.

ਜ਼ਖੀਰਾ (zakheeraa) *n m* Store house, reservoir, hoard, repository, stock.

ਜਗ (jag) *n m* (1) World, universe,

cosmos; (2) Jug; ~ਹਸਾਈ Public disgrace, derision, contempt, infamy.

ਜੰਗ (jang) *n f* Battle, war, fight, compaign; ~ਕਰਨੀ To fight, to wage war; ~ਛੇੜਨੀ To declare war (against), To go to the war (with); ~ਬੰਦੀ Ceasefire, trace.

ਜਗ੍ਹਾ (jaggaah) *n f adv* Place, locality, location, space, station, post; Instead of. Also ਜਗਾਹ

ਜੰਗਜੂ (jangajoo) *n m* Warrior, fighter.

ਜਗਣਾ (jagnaa) *v* To burn, to light.

ਜਗਤ (jagat) *n m* World, universe.

ਜਗਮਗ (jagmag) *a* Shining, gleaming, glimmering.

ਜਗਮਗਾਉਣਾ (jagmagaaunaa) *v* To shine, to gleam, to glitter, to sparkle.

ਜਗਰਾਤਾ (jagraataa) *n m* Sleeplessness, nightly vigil, keeping awake throughout the night singing hymns.

ਜੰਗਲ (jangal) *n m* Forest, woods, wilderness.

ਜੰਗਲਾ (janglaa) *n m* Railing, fencing, palisade.

ਜੰਗਲੀ (janglee) *a* Wild, savage, barbarion.

ਜਗਾਉਣਾ (jagaaunaa) *v* To awaken, to raise, to wake up, to burn, to light, to illuminate.

ਜੰਗਾਲ (jangaal) *n m* Rust, verdigris, corrosion.

ਜੰਗੀ (jangee) *a* Martial, gigantic, brave, warlike.

ਜਗੀਰ (jageer) *n f* Manor, estate, rent, free land, grant, feud; ~ਦਾਰ Landlord, grantee. Also ਜਾਗੀਰ

ਜੰਘ (jangh) *n f* Leg, thigh.

ਜਚਗੀ (jachgee) *n f* Maternity, childbirth, Period of confinement for delivery and convalescence thereafter.

ਜਚਣਾ (jachnaa) *v* To suit, to match, to befit.

ਜੱਚਾ (zachchaa) *n f* Woman who has just delivered a child; ~ਖਾਨਾ Maternity home.

ਜੰਜ (janj) *n f* Marriage party; ~ਚੜ੍ਹਨੀ To depart for marriage; ~ਘਰ Place where marriage party is stayed.

ਜਜ਼ਬਾ (jazbaa) *n m* Feeling, emotion, sentiment.

ਜਜਮਾਨ (jajmaan) *n m* Host.

ਜੰਜਾਲ (janjaal) *n m* Trouble, difficulty, perflexity, fix.

ਜੱਜੀ (jajjee) *n f* Office, post; Function of Judge.

ਜਜ਼ੀਆ (jaziaa) *n m* Toll tax, capitation tax.

ਜ਼ੰਜੀਰ (zanjeer) *n f* Chain, Zipper.

ਜਜ਼ੀਰਾ (jazeera) *n m* Island.

ਜੰਞੂ (janjoo) *n m* The sacred thread worn by Hindus.

ਜੰਞ (janj) *n m* Marriage party, marriage procession led by the bridegroom.

ਜੰਞੂ (janju) *n* Sacred thread (worn by Hindus as mark of initiation).

ਜੱਟ (jaṭṭ) *n m* Name of an agricultural class of northwestern India; A member of this class; Farmer, agriculturist, peasant.

ਜਟਾ (jaṭaa) *n f* Strand of matted hair, elf-lock.

ਜਣਨਾ (Jaṇnaa) *v* To give birth to, to procreate, to bear, to bring forth, to breed.

ਜਣਨੀ (jaṇnee) *n f* Mother, projentrix.

ਜਣਾ (jaṇaa) *n* Man, individual, chap, husband.

ਜਤਨ (jatan) *n a m* Effort, attempt, diligence, endeavour, exertion; ~ਸ਼ੀਲ Endeavouring, attempting, trying on the job; Industrious.

ਜੰਤਰ (jantar) *n m* Instrument, implement, apparatus, machine.

ਜੰਤ੍ਰਿਕ (jantric) *a* Mechanical.

ਜੰਤਰੀ (jantree) *n f* Calendar, almanac.

ਜਤਾਉਣਾ (jataauṇaa) *v* To remind, to inform, to evince, to caution.

ਜਤੀ (jatee) *n m* Ascetic, chaste.

ਜੰਤੂ (jantoo) *n m* Animal, creature.

ਜਥਾ (Jathaa) *n m* Group, squad, corps, company, batch.

ਜਥੇਦਾਰ (jathedaar) *n m* Leader of a group.

ਜਥੇਬੰਦ (jatheband) *a* Organised, grouped, united, embodied as a working group.

ਜਥੇਬੰਦੀ (jathebandee) *n f* Organisation, union, grouping.

ਜੰਦਰਾ (jandraa) *n m* Lock, machine.

ਜੱਦੀ (jaddee) *a* Ancestral, hereditary, patrimonial.

ਜਦੀਦ (jadeed) *a* Fresh, new, recent, modern.

ਜਦੋਂ (jadon) *adv* When; ~ਕਦੀ/ ~ਕਦੇ/ ~ਜਦੋਂ Whenever, as and when; ~ਤਾਈਂ/ ~ਤੀਕ Until, till, as long as, till such time as; ~ਵੀ Whenever.

ਜ਼ਨ (zan) *n f* Woman, wife; ~ਮੁਰੀਦ Henpecked husband, cuckold.

ਜਨ (jan) *n m* A person, individual, mankind; ~ਸੰਖਿਆ Population; ~ਗਣਨਾ Census; ~ਤੰਤਰ Democracy.

ਜੰਨਤ (jannat) *n f* Paradise, heaven.

ਜਨਮ (Janam) *n m* Birth, origin; ~ਕੁੰਡਲੀ Horoscope, birth chart; ~ਜਾਤ Inborn, inherent; ~ਦਾਤਾ

Creator, father, god.

ਜਨਾਹ (janaah) *n m* Adulterer, fornicatior. Also ਜ਼ਨਾਹ

ਜਨਾਜ਼ਾ (janaazaa) *n m* Hearse, coffin, bier, funeral procession.

ਜਨਾਨਾ (zanaanaa) *a* Feminine, female.

ਜ਼ਨਾਨੀ (zanaanee) *n f* wife, women.

ਜਨੂੰਨ (jannoon) *n m* Mania, lunacy.

ਜਪ (jap) *n m* Meditate, repeat; Recitation or silent repetition of God's name, mystical formula or prayer; ~ਮਾਲਾ Rosary.

ਜਪਣਾ (japṇaa) *v* To repeat god's name mentally or orally in low tone; To tell one's beads.

ਜੱਫਾ (japphaa) *n m* Holding tightly by waist, a tight embrace.

ਜ਼ਬਤ (zabat) *n m* Forfeiture, control, self-command.

ਜਬਰ (jabar) *n m* Compulsion, coercion, opression, tyranny; ~ਕਰਨਾ To coerce, to oppress, to tyrannize; ~ਦਸਤ Strong, powerful, vigorous; ~ਨ By force, forcibly, illegally.

ਜਬਰੀ (jabree) *adv* Forcibly, coercive, repressive, compulsorily.

ਜ਼ਬਾਨ (zabaan) *n f* Tongue, dialect, language, speech, promise; ~ਖੋਲ੍ਹਣੀ To speak out; ~ਤੇ ਚੜ੍ਹਨਾ To be the subject of talk; ~ਦਰਾਜ਼ੀ Loquaciousness, rudeness, impertinence; ~ਦਾ ਕੋੜਾ Bitter tongued; ~ਦੇਣੀ To promise; ~ਲੜਾਉਣੀ To argue, to confort.

ਜ਼ਬਾਨੀ (jabaanee) *adv* Orally, verbally; Mentally; By word of mouth.

ਜਮ (jam) *n m* Messenger of death; God of death, yama. Also ਜਮਕਾਲ

ਜੰਮ (jamm) *a* Native (of), born (in).

ਜਮ੍ਹਾ (jamaa) *n m a* Accumulation, sum total; Accumulated, collected; ~ਹੋਣਾ To assemble, to collect; ~ਕਰਾਉਣਾ To deposit; ~ਖੋਰੀ Hoarding.

ਜਮਹੂਰੀ (janahooree) *a* Democratic; ~ਅਤ Democracy.

ਜਮਘਟਾ (jamghaṭṭaa) *n m* Crowd, throng, multitude, large assemblage.

ਜਮਣਾ (jammṇaa) *v* (1) To take birth, to be born, To take root, to sprout, to germinate; To give birth, to bear, to beget; To procreate; (2) To freeze, to condense; To congeal, to coalgulate, to curdle; To set, to settle.

ਜਮਦੂਤ (jamdoot) *n m* Angel of death.

ਜਮਾਉਣਾ (jamaauṇaa) *v* To beget, to

produce, to create, to breed, to grow.

ਜਮਾਤ (jamaat) *n f* Class, party, group, society.

ਜਮਾਤੀ (jamaatee) *n m* Classfellow, classmate.

ਜਮਾਂਦਰੂ (jamaandroo) *a* Congential, innate, inbred, inborn, since birth; Natural.

ਜਮਾਦਾਰ (jamaadaar) *n m* (1) A junior commissioned military rank (now ਨਾਇਬ ਸੂਬੇਦਾਰ in India); (2) Mate, supervisor of labour gang or squad; (3) Scavenger, sweeper.

ਜਮਾਦਾਰਨੀ (jamaadarnee) *n f* A female scavenger, sweeper.

ਜਮਾਦਾਰੀ (jamadari) *n f* Rank, post, job of junior military, commissioned officer, supervisory etc.

ਜ਼ਮਾਨਤ (zamaanat) *n f* Bond, security, guarantee, bail; ~ਨਾਮਾ Security bond.

ਜ਼ਮਾਨਾ (zamaanaa) *n m* Times, age, period, present day world; ~ਸਾਜ਼ Worldly wise, time server, prudent, clever, cunning. Also ਜਮਾਨੇਸਾਜ਼

ਜਮਾਲ (jamaal) *n m* Beauty, splendour, grandeur, elegance.

ਜ਼ਮੀਨ (zameen) *n f* Earth, land.

ਜ਼ਮੀਰ (zameer) *n f* Conscience.

ਜ਼ਰ (zar) *n m* Gold, wealth. Also ਜਰ

ਜ਼ਰਖੇਜ਼ (zarkhez) *a* Productive, fertile.

ਜ਼ਰਦ (zarad) *a* Pale, yellow.

ਜ਼ਰਦਾ (jardaa) *n m* Powdered tobacco.

ਜ਼ਰਾ (zaraa) *a adv* Little, a little, somewhat.

ਜ਼ਰਾਇਤ (zarraait) *n f* Agriculture, farming.

ਜੱਰਾਹ (jarrah) *n m* Surgeon.

ਜ਼ਰੀਆ (zariaa) *n m* Means.

ਜ਼ਰੂਰ (zaroor) *adv* Certainly, surely, doubtless, necessarily, essentially.

ਜ਼ਰੂਰਤ (zaroorat) *a* Need, necessity, want, requirement.

ਜ਼ਰੂਰੀ (zarooree) *a* Necessary, essential, requisite.

ਜਲ (jal) *n m* Water, aqua; ~ਘਰ Waterworks; ~ਥਲ Inundation, flood; ~ਧਾਰਾ Water current; ~ਨਿਕਾਸ Sewerage, dewatering; ~ਵਾਯੂ Climate.

ਜਲਸਾ (jalsaa) *n m* Gathering, conference, a meeting, a sitting, festivity.

ਜਲਜ਼ਲਾ (jalzalaa) *n m* Earthquake.

ਜਲਣਾ (jalṇaa) *v* To burn; To inflame, to be enkindled; To be jealous.

ਜਲਦਬਾਂਜ਼ (jaldbaz) *a* Prone to hasty

ਜਲਦੀ decision or action; Reckless, brash, impetuous, rash. Also ਜਲਦਬਾਜ਼

ਜਲਦੀ (jaldee) *n f* Hurry, quickness, speediness, haste.

ਜਲਵਾ (jalva) *n m* Splendour, glitter, resplendence, glow; Grace, pleasing glimpse or sight.

ਜਲਾਪਾ (jalaapaa) *n m* Heart burning; Jealousy. Also ਸਾੜਾ

ਜਲਾਲ (jalaal) *n m* Splendour, glory, diginty, majesty.

ਜਲਾਲਤ (zalaalat) *n f* Meanness, disgrace, wretchedness.

ਜ਼ਲੀਲ (zaleel) *a* Mean; Disgraced, humiliated; ~ਕਰਨਾ To humiliate, to dishonour, to mortify.

ਜਲੂਸ (jaloos) *n m* Procession, pageant.

ਜਲੇਪਾ (jalepaa) *n m* Jealousy.

ਜਵਾਈ (jawaaee) *n m* Son-in-law.

ਜਵਾਹਰ (jawahhar) *n m* Jewel, gem, precious stone.

ਜਵਾਨ (jawaan) *a n m* Young, youthful; Youth, youngman.

ਜਵਾਨੀ (jawaanee) *n f* Stage of life between boyhood and middle age, youth, youthfulness, manhood, prime, full bloom, maturity; Adolescence, puberty; ਚੜ੍ਹਦੀ~ Early youth, early manhood, adolescence; ਢਲਦੀ~ Middle age; ~ਚੜ੍ਹਨਾ To become youth to come of prime age.

ਜਵਾਬ (Jawaab) *n m* Answer, reply; Defense, refusal; ~ਸਵਾਲ Discussion, altercation; ~ਮਿਲਣਾ To get a refusal, to be dismissed; ~ਦੇ ਜਾਣਾ To break down, to collapse; ~ਤਲਬੀ Explanation; ~ਦੇਹ Accountable, answerable.

ਜਵਾਬੀ (jawaabee) *a* Reply paid, reciprocal, counter, corresponding.

ਜਵਾਂਮਰਦ (jawaanmarad) *a* Manly, brave person.

ਜਵਾਂਮਰਦੀ (jawaanmardee) *n f* Manliness, courage, bravery, virility, vigour.

ਜਵਾਰ (javar) *n f* a kind of Indian millet sorghum; ~ਭਾਟਾ Tide, tidal waves, ebb and flow, rise and fall of coas; Spring or neap tides.

ਜਵਾਲ (jawaal) *n f* Downfall, decline.

ਜਵਾਲਾ (jawaalaa) *n f* Flame, fire, blaze; ~ਮੁਖੀ A volcano.

ਜੜ (jar) *n a* Foundation, basis, root, source, origin, root cause; Senseless, numb, dumb, inert, inanimate, irrational; ~ਤਾ Inanimate state, inertia.

ਜੜਤ (jaṛat) *n f* Inlaying, insetting,

embedding, fixing; Inlay or inset work.

ਜੜਨਾ (jarnaa) *v* To fit, to strike, to set (jewels), to join.

ਜੜੀ (jaree) *n f* Herb medicainal herb. Also **ਜੜੀ ਬੂਟੀ**

ਜਾਇਆ (jaaiyaa) *n m* Born, son, offspring.

ਜ਼ਾਇਆ (zaaiyaa) *a* Waste, wasted in vain; ~**ਹੋਣਾ** To go waste, to be in vain.

ਜ਼ਾਇਕਾ (zaaikaa) *n m* Taste.

ਜਾਇਦਾਦ (jaaidaad) *n f* Property, estate, assets.

ਜਾਸਤੀ (jastee) *n f* High handedness, excess, oppression, injustice.

ਜਾਹਲ (jaahal) *a* Vulgar, unrefined, uncultured, untutored, lacking sophistication, uneducated, illiterate, ignorant, backward, stupid, rustic, boorish, uncivilized.

ਜਾਗਣਾ (jaagnaa) *v* To get up from the bed, to awake, to rise.

ਜਾਂਗਲੀ (jaanglee) *a* Wild, bestial, aboriginal, sylvan.

ਜਾਂਘੀਆ (jaanghiaa) *n m* Shorts, underwear, napkin (for child).

ਜਾਂਚ (jaanch) *n f* Trial, audit, inspection, investigation, scrutiny, assessment.

ਜਾਂਚਣਾ (jaanchnaa) *v* To examine, to calculate, to scrutinize, to inspect, to ascertain, to question.

ਜਾਚਨਾ (jaachnaa) *n f* Prayer.

ਜਾਣਕਾਰ (jaankaar) *a* Who knows, knower, knowing, knowledgeable, well-informed, familiar, conversant, acquainted; Cognisant.

ਜਾਣਕਾਰੀ (jaankaaree) *n f* Knowledge, information, familiarity, conversance, acquaintance, exeprience, understanding.

ਜਾਣਨਾ (jaannaa) *v* To know, to see, to consider, to comprehend.

ਜਾਣਾ (jaanaa) *v* To go, to depart, to continue.

ਜਾਤਕ (jaatak) *n m* Child, new born babe.

ਜਾਤਰੀ (jaatree) *n m* Traveller, pilgrim.

ਜ਼ਾਤੀ (zaatee) *a* Personal, self, individual, specific.

ਜਾਦੂ (jaadoo) *n m* Magic, charm, spell, black art, enchantment; ~**ਗਰ** Magician, wizard; ~**ਟੂਣਾ** Sorcery, black art.

ਜਾਨ (jaan) *n f* Life, essence, vital force, spirit, strength; ~**ਉਤੇ ਖੇਡਣਾ** To be ready, to stake one's life; ~**ਸੁਕਣੀ** To be much afraid or worried; ~**ਕਢਣੀ** To put too much trouble, to kill; ~ਧਾਉਣੀ To work very hard; ~ਦੇਣੀ To die, to scrifice one's life; ~ਪੈਣੀ To come to life, to get relief; ~ਸ਼ੀਨ Successor'e heir; ~ਦਾਰ Organic, living; ~ਬਾਜ਼ Brave, courageous; ~ਮਾਰੀ Hard work.

ਜਾਨਵਰ (jaanwar) *n m* Animal, beast.

ਜਾਨੀ (jaanee) *a* Dear, love, beloved, sweet heart; ~ਦੁਸ਼ਮਣ Deadly foe; ~ਦੋਸਤ Fast friend, bosom triend.

ਜਾਪਣਾ (jaapnaa) *v* To feel, to appear, to seem.

ਜ਼ਾਫ਼ਰਾਨ (zaafraan) *n* Saffron.

ਜ਼ਾਬਤਾ (zaabtaa) *n m* Control, code, procedure, discipline.

ਜ਼ਾਬਰ (jaabar) *a* Oppressor, tyrant.

ਜਾਮ (jaam) *n* (1) Wine glass, bowl; (2) Fruit jam; (3) Traffic jam.

ਜਾਮਾ (jaamaa) *n m* Garment, robe, gown, vestment.

ਜਾਰੀ (jaaree) *a* Continued, in force, running, current; ~ਕਰਨਾ To issue, to commence, to enforce; ~ਰਖਣਾ To continue, to carry on, to sustain.

ਜਾਲ (jaal) *n m* Net, web, trap, mesh, network.

ਜਾਲ੍ਹ (jaalh) *n m* Forgery, deception; ~ਸਾਜ Forger; ~ਸਾਜ਼ੀ Forgery.

ਜਾਲਣਾ (jaalnaa) *v* To burn, to ignite, to light; To vex, to irritate; To endure, to suffer.

ਜ਼ਾਲਮ (zaalam) *a* Tyrannical, barbarous, cruel, oppressive, brutal.

ਜਾਲਾ (jaalaa) *n m* Cobweb, net moss, spider's web; ਅਖਾਂ ਦਾ~ Cataract.

ਜਾਲੀ (jaalee) *n f* Network, snood, gauze, lattice; ~ਦਾਰ Gauzy, neted, latticed.

ਜਾਲ੍ਹੀ (jaalhee) *a* Forged, fake, fobricate, spurious. Also ਜਾਅਲੀ

ਜਾੜਾ (jaaraa) *n m* Winter, cold weather.

ਜਿਉਣਾ (jiunaa) *v* To live, to exist, to be alive.

ਜਿਸ (jis) *pron* Who, which, that; Whom, where, what (other than interrogative); ~ਕਰਕ/ ~ਕਾਰਨ Wherefor; ~ਤੇ Whereon, whereupon, where at; ~ਥਾਂ Where; ~ਦਮ When; ~ਨਾਲ Whereby, wherewith, with which or whom; ~ਨੂੰ Whom; ~ਵੇਲੇ When, at the time when.

ਜਿਸਮ (jisam) *n m* Body; ~ਮਾਨੀ Corporol.

ਜਿਹੜਾ (jera) *pron* Who, which, that, what; ~ਕਿਹੜਾ Anyone, anybody; Any Tom, Dick or Harry.

ਜਿਹਾ (jihaa) *adv* Like, similar, as;

~ਕਿਹਾ Howsoever.

ਜ਼ਿਕਰ (zikar) *n m* Mention, cursory remarks.

ਜਿਕਣ (jikaṇ) *adv* According as, as if, for instance, for example.

ਜਿਗਰ (jigar) *n m* Liver, bile; ~ਦਾ ਟੁਕੜਾ Son, life.

ਜਿਗਰਾ (jigraa) *n m* Courage, bravery, patience, perseverance.

ਜਿਗਰੀ (jigree) *a* Intimate, friendly.

ਜਿੱਚ (jichch) *a* Vexed, annoyed, irritated, sullen, peeved, peevish. Also ਜ਼ਿੱਚ

ਜਿੱਜੀ (jijjee) *n f* Thick or dried nasal mucus.

ਜਿਠਾਣੀ (jiṭhaaṇee) *n* Wife of husband's elder brother, sister-in-law.

ਜਿਠੇਰਾ (jiṭheraa) *a* Elder.

ਜਿਤਣਾ (jitṇaa) *v* To win, to conquer, to vanquish.

ਜਿੱਥੇ (jitthe) *adv* Where; ~ਕਿੱਥੇ Wherever; ~ਵੀ Wheresoever.

ਜਿੱਥੋਂ (jithon) *adv* From where, whence.

ਜ਼ਿਦ (zid) *n f* Obstinancy, persistance, stubbornness; ~ਲ Obstinate, bull headed.

ਜਿੰਦਣ (jiddaṇ) *adv* On the day when (ਜਿਸ+ਦਿਨ) on (a specified or appointed) day.

ਜ਼ਿੰਦਗੀ (zindagee) *n* Life, age, lifetime; ~ਹਰਾਮ ਹੋਣੀ To be miserable; ~ਦੇ ਦਿਨ ਕੱਟਣੇ To simply exist, to carry on somehow.

ਜ਼ਿੰਦਾ (zindaa) *a* Living, animate; ~ਦਿਲ Lively, vivacious, gay, buoyant; ~ਦਿਲੀ Vivacity, liveliness, gaiety, blithness; ~ਬਾਦ Long live, may....live long. Also ਜ਼ਿੰਦਾ

ਜ਼ਿੱਦੀ (ziddee) *a* Obstinate, pertinacious, stiff, stubborn.

ਜਿੰਨ (jinn) *n m* Ghost, devil, demon.

ਜ਼ਿਬਾਹ (zibbaah) *n m* Act of killing or slaughtering.

ਜ਼ਿੰਮਾ (zimaa) *n m* Responsibility, undertaking, trust, charge, accountability, liability, onus; ~ਵਾਰ Responsible liable.

ਜ਼ਿਮੀਂਦਾਰ (zimeendaar) *n m* Landlord, landholder.

ਜ਼ਿਮੀਂਦਾਰਾ (zimeendaaraa) *a n m* Pertaining to agriculture or farming.

ਜ਼ਿਮੀਂਦਾਰੀ (zimeendaaree) *n f* Landlordism, landed estate; Agriculture, farming.

ਜ਼ਿੰਮੇ (zime) *adv* Under responsibility, incharge; ~ਵਾਰ Responsible, liable.

ਜ਼ਿੱਲਤ (zillat) *n f* Insult, disgrace,

dishonour.

ਜਿਲਦ (jilad) *n f* Binding (of book), cover, ligament; **~ਸਾਜ਼** Bookbinder.

ਜ਼ਿਲ੍ਹਾ (zillaa) *n m* District, commune.

ਜਿੱਲ੍ਹਾ (jillaa) *a* Lazy, lethargic, sluggish.

ਜਿਵੇਂ (jiven) *adv* As, in the manner of; As if, as though, so to say, for example, for instance; **~ਕਿ** As it were; For example, for instance; **~ਕਿਵੇਂ** Somehow, somehow or the other, by any means, by hook or crook, by means fair or foul, howsoever.

ਜੀ (Jee) *n m v* Mind, heart, soul, live; Intial term 'yes', 'sir' etc; **~ਆਉਣਾ** To fall in love with; **~ਸੜ ਜਾਣਾ** To be grieved; **~ਕੱਢਣਾ** To take courage; **~ਕਰਨਾ** To desire; **~ਖੱਟਾ ਹੋਣਾ** To feel disgusted; **~ਖੋਲ੍ਹ ਕੇ** Freely, heartly; **~ਚੁਰਾਉਣਾ** To shirk, to desist from work; **~ਤਰਸਣਾ** To long, to yearn; **~ਫਿਕਾ ਹੋਣਾ** To be disenchanted; **~ਭਰ ਆਉਣਾ** To be moved to tears; **~ਭਰਨਾ** To be fully satisfied; **~ਰਖਣਾ** To gratify, to appeas; **~ਲਾਉਣਾ** To pay attention to.

ਜੀਭ (jeebh) *n f* Tongue; **~ਚਲਣੀ** To have a fluent tongue; **~ਚਲਾਉਣੀ** To talk too much; **~ਪਕੜਨੀ** To silent, to stop speaking.

ਜੀਵ (jeev) *n m* Creature, animal, mortal, soul.

ਜੀਵਨ (jeevan) *n m* Life, existence; **~ਸਾਥੀ** Life partner, husband.

ਜੀਵਨੀ (jeevnee) *n f* Biograply.

ਜ਼ੁਕਾਮ (zookaam) *n m* Cold, coryza.

ਜੁਗਤ (jugat) *n f* Method, manner, way, skill, skillfulness, knack; Tool; Device, contrivance; Plan, scheme, expedient.

ਜੁਗਨੀ (jugnee) *n f* A mode of Punjabi folk song; A heart shaped ornament for the neck.

ਜੁਗਨੂੰ (jugnoon) *n m* Glow-worm, firefly, glowfly, lightning bug.

ਜੁਗਾਲਣਾ (jugaalṇaa) *v* To chew.

ਜੁਗਾਲੀ (jugaalee) *n f* The chewing of the cud, rumination.

ਜੁਗਾੜ (jugaaṛ) *n m* Manoeuvre, contrivance, arrangement.

ਜੁਝਾਰੂ (juhjaaru) *a n m* Fighter, valiant; Heroic, militant, aggressive, vigorously combative; Intreped, fearless.

ਜੁਟਣਾ (juṭṇaa) *v* To unite, to be assembled; To entangled, to cohabit; To be ivolved in something with determination and vigour, to work seriously.

ਜੁਤਣਾ (jutṇaa) *v* To be yoked, to be engaged in a work.

ਜੁੱਤੀ (juttee) *n f* Shoe, boot, slipper.

ਜੁਦਾ (judaa) *a* Seperate, distinct, different, apart.

ਜੁਦਾਈ (judaaee) *n f* Separation from a dear one.

ਜੁੱਧ (juddh) *n m* Battle, fighting, war, skirmish, hostilities, armed encounter, warfare, combat action or engagement; ~ਕਰਨਾ To fight, to fight a war; ~ਛਿੜਨਾ For war to break out or commence; ~ਦਾ ਮੈਦਾਨ Battlefield.

ਜੁੰਬਸ਼ (jumbash) *n f* Movement; Motion.

ਜੁਰਮ (juram) *n m* Crime, offence, charge, fault, guilt.

ਜੁਰਮਾਨਾ (jurmaanaa) *n m* Fine, penalty.

ਜੁਰਾਬ (juraab) *n f* One of a pair of socks or stockings; Usually **ਜੁਰਾਬਾਂ**

ਜ਼ੁਲਫ (zulaf) *n f* Curl, lock of hair, ringlet, tress.

ਜ਼ੁਲਮ (zulam) *a* Tyranny, cruelty, oppression, brutality, outrage.

ਜ਼ੁਲਮੀ (zulamee) *n m* Tyrannical, oppressive.

ਜੁਲਾਹਾ (julaahaa) *n m a* Weaver; Timid, fool.

ਜੁੜਨਾ (juṛnaa) *v* To be joined, to be united, to collect, to associate, to get together.

ਜੁੜਵਾਂ (juṛvaan) *a* Twin, conjoint, synthetic, cohesive.

ਜੂੰ (joon) *n f* A louse, pediculus.

ਜੂਆ (juaa) *n m* Gambling, dice, any game of chance played with stakes; Grave risk; ~ਖਾਨਾ Gambling house, gamblers'den.

ਜੂਝਨਾ (joojhṇaa) *v* To fight, to struggle.

ਜੂਠ (jooṭh) *n f* Garbage, refuse, leavings, ort, offal, leftover.

ਜੂਠਾ (jooṭhaa) *a* Polluted, contaminated by taste or touch, partially eaten or drunk.

ਜੂੜਨਾ (jooṛnaa) *v* To bind, to yoke, to tie.

ਜੂੜਾ (jooṛaa) *n m* Tuft, knot of braided hair, top knot.

ਜੇਠ (jeṭh) *n m* Elder brother of husband, brother-in-law.

ਜੇਠਾ (jeṭhaa) *a* First born, senior.

ਜੇਬ (jeb) *n m* Pocket, pouch.

ਜੇਵਰ (zevar) *n m* Ornaments, jewellary.

ਜੋਸ਼ (josh) *n m* Zeal, enthusiasm, passion, emotion, fervency excitement, upsurge.

ਜੋਖਣਾ (jokhṇaa) *v* To estimate, to

weigh, to appraise, to span.

ਜੋਗੀ (jogee) *n m* Ascetic, saint, devotee.

ਜੋਟਾ (jotaa) *n m* Twosome, duo, couple, pair.

ਜੋਣਾ (jonaa) *v* To yoke, harness, to press into work, to engage, to force.

ਜੋਤਸ਼ (jotash) *n m* Astrology, astronomy.

ਜੋਤਸ਼ੀ (jotshee) *n m* Astrologer, fortune teller.

ਜੋਤਣਾ (jotnaa) To yoke, to harness. Also **ਜੋਣਾ** and **ਵਾਹੁਣਾ**

ਜੋਬਨ (joban) *n m* Lustre, bloom of youth, brilliance, puberty.

ਜ਼ੋਰ (zor) *n m* Strength, force, power, effort, influence, vigour, vitality, momentum, pressure, impetus; ~**ਚਲਣਾ** To have sway; ~**ਜ਼ੋਰ ਦਾ** Bitterly, intense; ~**ਦੇਣਾ** To emphasize; ~**ਮਾਰਨਾ** To try level best, to compel, to make frantic efforts; ~**ਅਜ਼ਮਾਈ** Trial of strength; ~**ਸ਼ੋਰ** Zest, enthusiasm; ~**ਜ਼ਬਰ** Oppression; ~**ਜ਼ਬਰਦਸਤੀ** Duress, coercion; ~**ਦਾਰ** Vigorous, energetic, powerful.

ਜ਼ੋਰਾਵਰ (joraavar) *a* (For persons) strong, powerful, mighty; Bully.

ਜੋਰੂ (joroo) *n f* Wife, life partner.

ਜੋੜ (jor) *n m* Joint, sum, addition, tally, connection, total, match, relevancy, bond, fellow; ~**ਦਾਰ** Having joints, not of one piece, seamy.

ਜੋੜਨਾ (jornaa) *v* To join, to sum up, to link, to collect, to cement, to gather, to set, to connect, to paste, to attach, to unite.

ਜੋੜਾ (joraa) *n m* Couple, pair, twin.

ਜੌਹਰ (jauhar) *n m* Excellence, talent, essence.

ਜੌਹਰੀ (jauhree) *n m* Jeweller.

ਝ

ਝ The fourteenth letter of Gurmukhi alphabets, pronouned as 'Jhájháa'.

ਝਉਣਾ (jháuṇaa) *v* To wither, to sage, to lose heart.

ਝਉਲਾ (jháulaa) *n m* Glimpse, glance.

ਝਈ (jháee) *n f* Sudden, furious attack, charge; Gritting teeth in anger; Crouching; **~ਲੈ ਕੇ ਪੈਣਾ** To attack suddenly or furiously.

ਝੱਸਣਾ (jhásṇaa) *v* To rub, to massage, (with oil, etc.).

ਝਕ (jhák) *n f* Shyness, hesitation, timidity. Also **ਝਿਝਕ**

ਝਕਝੋਰਨਾ (jhákjhornaa) *v* To jerk, to shake violently.

ਝਕਣਾ (jhákṇaa) *v* To hesitate, to feel shy, to blench, to quail.

ਝਕਾਉਣਾ (jhákaauṇaa) *v* To tease, to tentalize, to dodge.

ਝੰਕਾਰ (jhánkaar) *n f* Jingling sound, tinkling sound.

ਝੱਕੀ (jhákkee) *a* Hesitant, shy, reluctant, diffident.

ਝਕੋਲਣਾ (jhákolṇaa) *v* To Shake, to stir.

ਝਖ (jhákh) *n m* Nonsensical talk; **~ਮਾਰਨਾ** To waste time for nothing.

ਝਖਮਾਰ (jhákhmaar) *a* To shake, to rock, swing; To muddle, to rinse. Also **ਘਚੋਲ਼ਨਾ**

ਝਖਣਾ (jhákhṇaa) *v* To rave.

ਝੱਖੜ (jhákhaṛ) *n m a* Storm, strong wind, tempest, gust, hurricane, gust; Crazy, cranky, whimsical.

ਝੰਖਾਰ (jhánkhaar) *n f* Interwined branches, of bushes.

ਝੱਗ (jhágg) *n m* Foam, scum, lather, spume; **~ਦਾਰ** Foamy, frothy; Lathery.

ਝਗੜਨਾ (jhágaṛnaa) *v* To quarrel, to wrangle, to altercate, to squabble, to dispute.

ਝਗੜਾ (jhágṛaa) *n m* Conflict, quarrel, tussel, dispute, altercation, wrangling; **~ਲੂ** Contentious, rowdy, quarrelsome, bellicose.

ਝੱਗਾ (jhággaa) *n m* Frock, a loose garment for babies, shirt.

ਝੰਜਟ (jhánjat) *n m* Botheration, encumberance, perplexity, difficulty.

ਝੱਜਰ (jhájjar) *n m* Small porous earthen pitcher with a long neck.

Also **ਝੰਜਰੀ**

ਝੰਜੋੜਨਾ (jhanjoṛnaa) *v* To jog, to twitch, to shake, a thing with a voilent jerk.

ਝਟ (jhatṭ) *n adv* Moment; Immediately, quickly, atonce.

ਝਟਕਣਾ (jhataknaa) *v* To give a jerk, to toss violently.

ਝਟਕਾ (jhatkaa) *n m* Push, jerk, shock; Mode of beheading animal with one stroke.

ਝਟਕਾਉਣਾ (jhatkaaunaa) *v* To butcher.

ਝੰਡਾ (jhandaa) *n m* Flag, banner, ensign.

ਝੰਡੀ (jhandee) *n f* A small flag, bunting.

ਝਪਟਣਾ (jhapatnaa) *v* To pounce upon, to rush, to grab.

ਝਪੀੜ (jhapeeṛ) *n f* A tight squeeze, occlusion, constriction of muscles *especially* of anal region.

ਝਪੀੜਨਾ (jhapeeṛnaa) *v* To occlude or constrict anal passage; To squeeze, stringe muscles; To bear patiently.

ਝੰਬਣਾ (jhambnaa) *v* To flog, to thrash, to beat.

ਝਮਕ (jhamak) *n m* Splendour, glitter, twinkle.

ਝਮਕਣਾ (jhamaknaa) *v* To twinkle, to wink.

ਝਮਾਕਾ (jhamaakaa) *n* Glimpse, sight; Glance, blink.

ਝਮੇਲਾ (jhamelaa) *n m* Botheration, turmoil, disturbance, mess, complication, row.

ਝਰਨਾ (jharnaa) *n m* Fall, waterfall, spring, brook, cataract.

ਝਰੀਟ (jhareet) *n f* Scratch, abrasion, bruise, slight wound.

ਝਰੀਟਨਾ (jhareetnaa) *v* To scratch, to scribble.

ਝਰੋਖਾ (jharokhaa) *n m* Window, a small aperture, casement, loophole.

ਝੱਲ (jhall) *n m* Frenzy, craze, insanity, lunancy, madness, passion; Heat.

ਝਲਕ (jhalak) *n f* Glimpse, glance, reflection, blink, glimmer; Tinge, hint.

ਝਲਕਣਾ (jhalaknaa) *v* To sparkle, to glare, to shine, to glimmer.

ਝਲਕਾਰਾ (jhalkaaraa) *n m* Glimpse, sight reflection, flash, twinkle.

ਝੱਲਣਾ (jhallnaa) *v* To bear, to endure, to sustain.

ਝੱਲਾ (jhallaa) *a* Stupid, foolish, mad, lunatic, crazy.

ਝੜ (jhaṛ) *n f* Cloudy weather.

ਝੜਨਾ (jharnaa) *v* To drop, to fall off, to wither.

ਝੜਪ (jharap) *n f* Contention, quarrel, skirmish, scuffle.

ਝੜੀ (jharee) *n* Downpour, incessant rain.

ਝਾਂਸਣਾ (jhansnaa) *v* To deceive, to pilfer.

ਝਾਂਸਾ (jhaansaa) *n m* Deception, dodge, fraud, bluff; **~ਦੇਣਾ** To deceive, to dodge, to cheat, to mislead.

ਝਾਂਕਣਾ (jhanknaa) *v* To peep, to glance, to look, to pry.

ਝਾਕਾ (jhaakaa) *n m* Hesitation, shyness, diffidence, reluctance.

ਝਾਗਣਾ (jhaagnaa) *v* To suffer, to undergo, to endure, to bear.

ਝਾਂਜਰ (jhaanjar) *n f* An ornament for the ankles, jingling anklet.

ਝਾਂਜਾ (jhaanjaa) *n m* Storm, squall, tornado accompanied by rain.

ਝਾਂਟ (jhaant) *n f* Publis, public hair.

ਝਾਲਰ (jhaalar) *n m* Fringe, frill, hem, suffle, tatting, garnish, trimming, festoon, festooned edging or border; **~ਦਾਰ** Festooned, frilled, fringed.

ਝਾੜ (jhaar) *n f* Shrub, bosk, underwood, clump, coppice, censure, admonition, scolding, snubbing, reprimand, rebuke.

ਝਾੜਨ (jhaaran) *n m* Duster.

ਝਾੜਨਾ (jhaarnaa) *v* To brush, to sweep, to flick, to dust, to clean, to remove, to broom, to chide, to reprehend, to reprove.

ਝਾੜਾ (jhaaraa) *n m* Stools, excreta, faeces.

ਝਾੜੀ (jhaaree) *n f* Thicket, shrub, hedge, bush; **~ਦਾਰ** Bushy, shrubby, fruticose.

ਝਾੜੂ (jhaaroo) *n m* Broom, swab.

ਝਿਜਕ (jhijak) *n f* Hesitation, reluctance, shyness, chariness.

ਝਿਰਝਿਰਾ (jhirjhiraa) *a* Very thin, gauzy, flimsy.

ਝਿਲਮਿਲ (jhilmil) *v* Sparkling, glittering, gleaming, flickering (of light).

ਝਿਲਮਿਲਾਉਣਾ (jhilmilaaunaa) *v* To sparkle, to glitter, to flicker.

ਝਿੜਕ (jhirak) *n f* Rebuke, chiding, scolding, snub, reprimand. Also **ਝਿੜਕੀ**

ਝਿੜਕਣਾ (jhiraknaa) *v* To scold, to snub, to admonish, to reprimand.

ਝੀਖਣਾ (jheekhnaa) *v n m* To lament, to repent, to grieve; Grief, repentence, lamentation.

ਝੀਂਗਰ (jheengar) *n m* Grassshopper,

cricket, long mounted beetle.

ਝੀਲ (jheel) *n f* Lake.

ਝੁਕਣਾ (jhuknaa) *v* To droop, to bend, to sway, to tilt, to lean, to decline.

ਝੁੱਗਾ (jhuggaa) *n m* House, family, residential place.

ਝੁੱਗੀ (jhuggee) *n f* Cottage, hut, hovel.

ਝੁੰਜਲਾਉਣਾ (jhunjlaaunaa) *v* To be irritated, to be fretful, to be peevish.

ਝੁਠਲਾਉਣਾ (jhuthlaaunaa) *v* To falsify, to pretend, to be false.

ਝੁੰਡ (jhund) *n m* Flock, herd, crowd, group, troop.

ਝੁੱਡੂ (jhudoo) *n m* Dullard, a fool, dunce, henpecked husband.

ਝੁੰਮਰ (jhummer) *n m* Round dance, gathering, reel.

ਝੁਰਮਟ (jhurmat) *n m* A cluster of shrubs, array, hive.

ਝੁਲਸਣਾ (jhulasnaa) *v* To scorch, to char, to parch, to scald, to burn.

ਝੁਲਾਉਣਾ (jhulaaunaa) *v* To fan, to dangle, to vibrate, to rock.

ਝੁੰਗਾ (jhungaa) *n m* Tret, something given for bargaining.

ਝੂਟਣਾ (jhootnaa) *v* To swing, to oscillate, to dangle.

ਝੂਠ (jhooth) *n m* Lie, falsehood.

ਝੂਠਾ (jhoothaa) *a* Liar, false, artificial, bogus.

ਝੂਮਣਾ (jhoomnaa) *v* To swing, to reel, to rock.

ਝੂਲਣਾ (jhoolnaa) *v* To wave, to swing, to vibrate, to oscillate.

ਝੂਲਾ (jhoolaa) *n m* Swing, whirligig, merry go round.

ਝੇਪ (jhep) *n f* Abashment, shyness.

ਝੇਪਣਾ (jhepnaa) *v* To blush, to be shy.

ਝੇਲਣਾ (jhelnaa) *v* To endure, to bear.

ਝੋਕਣਾ (jhoknaa) *v* To throw, to stroke, to push violently.

ਝੋਂਕਾ (jhonkaa) *n m* Gust, whiff, puff.

ਝੋਟਾ (jhotaa) *n m a* Male buffalo, bull; Stout, fat, sturdy.

ਝੌਂਪੜਾ (jhaunpraa) *n m* Hut, a big cottage.

ਞ

ਞ The fifiteenth letter of Gurmukhi alphabets, pronounced as jhanja.

ਟ

ਟ Sixteenth letter of Gurmukhi alphabets, pronounced as 'ṭainkaa'.

ਟੱਸ (ṭass) *n f* Glamour, decoration, impressive personal appearance; ~ਕੱਢਣੀ To dress impressively, to be smarter, to decorate.

ਟਸੂਏ (ṭasooe) *n m* Tears.

ਟਹਿਕਣਾ (ṭaheknaa) *v* To bloom, to blossom, to be happy.

ਟਹਿਣੀ (ṭaheṇi) *n f* Branch (of tree).

ਟਹਿਲਣਾ (ṭahelnaa) *v* To roam, to walk, to stroll, to lounge.

ਟਕ (ṭak) *n f* Cut, notch; Gaze, stare.

ਟਕਸਾਲ (ṭaksaal) *n f* Mint; ~ਣ Standardization; ~ਣਾ To standardize.

ਟੱਕਰ (ṭakkar) *n f* Collision, smash, clash, knock, quarrel, conflict, contention encounter, skirmish.

ਟਕਰਨਾ (ṭakarnaa) *v* To collide, to come across, to meet, to fight.

ਟਕਰਾਉਣਾ (ṭakaraunaa) *v* To clash, to collide, to bump, to knock together, the heads of two persons.

ਟੰਕਾਰ (ṭankaar) *n f* Twang.

ਟੰਕੀ (ṭankee) *n f* Cistern, tank.

ਟਕੋਰ (ṭakor) *n f* Fomentation, a mild stroke, hit.

ਟਕੋਰਨਾ (ṭakornaa) *v* To thump gently, to tap, to jog, to dun.

ਟੰਗ (ṭang) *n f* Leg; ~ਅੜਾਉਣੀ To interfere, to obstruct; ~ਹੇਠੋਂ ਕੱਢਣਾ To defeat, to humiliate.

ਟੰਗਣਾ (ṭangnaa) *v n m* To hang, to suspend, to put to gallows; Hanger.

ਟੰਗੜੀ (ṭangree) *n f* Small leg, leg.

ਟਟਹਿਣਾ (ṭataheṇaa) *n m* Glowworm, firefly, glowfly, lightining bug.

ਟਟਪੂੰਜੀਆ (ṭatpoonjiaa) *n* Very poor man, a man of small means.

ਟੰਟਾ (ṭanṭaa) *n m* Wrangling, contest, quarrel, squabble, altercation.

ਟਟਾ (ṭaṭṭaa) *n m* Testicle.

ਟਟਿਆਉਣਾ (ṭaṭiaaunaa) *v* To cry, to raise hue and cry.

ਟੱਟੀ (ṭaṭṭee) *n f* Stools, faeces excreta, lavatory, latrine, toilet; A reed screen.

ਟੱਟੂ (ṭaṭṭoo) *n m* Pony; ~ਭਾੜੇ ਦਾ A mercenary, hack.

ਟਟੋਲਣਾ (ṭaṭolnaa) *v* To finger, to search, to fumble, to explore.

ਟੱਡਣਾ (ṭaḍḍnaa) *v* To open, to spread.

ਟਲਕਣਾ (ṭanknaa) *v* To clang.

ਟੱਪ (ṭapp) *n m* Tub, cistern; ~ਟੱਪ Sound of dripping water.

ਟਪਕਾ (ṭapakaa) *n m* Dripping, dribble. Also ਟਪਕ

ਟਪਕਣਾ (ṭapaknaa) *v* To drop, to drip, to dribble, to ooze.

ਟੱਪਣਾ (ṭapnaa) *v a* To jump, jump over, to cross, to leap, to skip, to hop, spring, gambol, frisk; Frisky, playful.

ਟਪਰੀ (ṭapree) *n f* Hut, thatched house, cottage.

ਟਪਲਾ (ṭaplaa) *n m* Doubt, suspicion, deception, misunderstanding, error. Also ਭੁਲੇਖਾ

ਟੱਪਾ (ṭappaa) *n m* A line of a song.

ਟਪਾਰ (ṭapaar) *n m* Gossip, yarn, bluff, exaggeration.

ਟੱਬਰ (ṭabbar) *n m* Family, clan, house hold; ~ਟੀਰ Family.

ਟਮਕ (ṭamak) *n m* Kettledrum.

ਟਮਕਾਉਣਾ (tamkaaunaa) *v* To twinkle, to wink; To light (a small lamp) with low, uncertain flame.

ਟਮਾਟਰ (ṭamaaṭar) *n m* Tomato.

ਟਰੰਕ (ṭarank) *n m* Trunk, metal box, suitcase.

ਟਰਕਣਾ (ṭaraknaa) *v* To be buffled, to abscond, to disappear.

ਟਰਕਾਉਣਾ (ṭarkaaunaa) *v* To evade, to bluff, to postpone, to remove.

ਟਰਟਰਾਉਣਾ (ṭarṭraaunaa) *v* To creak.

ਟੱਲ (ṭall) *n m* Bigbell, gong.

ਟਲਣਾ (ṭalnaa) To flinch, to slip, to vanish, to be averted.

ਟੱਲੀ (tallee) *n f* Small bell.

ਟਾਹਣ (ṭaahaṇ) *n m* Bough, large branch of tree.

ਟਾਹਣੀ (ṭaahṇee) *n f* Small branch of tree, twig.

ਟਾਂਕਣ (ṭaanknaa) *v* To stitch, to tag, to append, to solder.

ਟਾਕਰਾ (ṭaakraa) *n m* Collation, conflict, opposition, encounter, rivalry, competition.

ਟਾਂਕਾ (ṭaankaa) *n m* Stitching, solder, joint.

ਟਾਕੀ (takkee) *n f* Piece of cloth, patch; Talkie, motion picture, small cinema hall.

ਟਾਟ (ṭaaṭ) *n m* Convas, sack, matting, cloth.

ਟਾਪੂ (ṭaapoo) *n m* Island, isle.

ਟਾਲ (ṭaal) *n m* Heap, pile, stock, fire woodship, shop for buying wood.

ਟਾਲਣਾ (ṭaalnaa) *v* To avert, to put aside, to postpone, to shift, to avoid, to evade.

ਟਿਕਟਿੱਕੀ (ṭikṭikkee) *n f* Store, gaze.

ਟਿਕਣਾ (tiknaa) *v* To stay, to stop, to rest, to lodge.

ਟਿੱਕਾ (tikkaa) *n m* Sandal paste or vermillion mark on the forehead; An ornament worn on the forehead.

ਟਿਕਾਉਣਾ (tikaaunaa) *v* To lodge, to house, to station.

ਟਿਕਾਊ (tikkau) *a* Stable, lasting, permanent steady.

ਟਿਕਾਣਾ (tikaanaa) *n m* Dwelling, place, haltage, residence, station, destination.

ਟਿੱਕੀ (tikkee) *n f* Small loaf of bread, tablet cake (of soap etc).

ਟਿਟਿਆਉਣਾ (titiaaunaa) *v* To shriek.

ਟਿੰਡ (tind) *n f* Clean shaven head, baldness.

ਟਿੱਡਾ (tiddaa) *n* Grass hopper, cricket.

ਟਿੱਡੀ (tiddee) *n f* Locust.

ਟਿਪਸ (tipas) *n f* Arrangement manipulation, manoeuvering.

ਟਿੱਪਣ (tippan) *n m* Note, commentary, annotation.

ਟਿੱਬਾ (tibbaa) *n m* Sandy place, high mound small ridge, hillock, butt.

ਟਿਮਕਣਾ (timaknaa) *v* To glimner, to twinkle, to glitter.

ਟਿਮਟਿਮਾਉਣਾ (timtimaaunaa) *v* To twinkle, to ficker, to glimmer.

ਟਿਮਟਿਮਾਹਟ (timtimaahat) *n f* Flicker.

ਟਿੱਲ (till) *n m* Effort, attempt, force, might.

ਟਿੱਲਾ (tillaa) *n m* Mound, ridge, hillock.

ਟੀਕਰੀ (teekree) *n f* Mare.

ਟੀਕਾ (teekaa) *n f* Annotation, commentry, remarks; Inoculation, injection; ~ਕਾਰ Translator, exegete; ~ਟਿੱਪਣੀ Criticism, comment, remarks, observations.

ਟੀਰਾ (teeraa) *a* Croos-eyed, squint, squinty, strabismic.

ਟੁੱਕ (tukk) *a* Small, trivial, insignificant.

ਟੁਕਣਾ (tuknaa) *v* To cut, to chop, to bite.

ਟੁਕਰ (tukar) *n m* Indian loaf, bread; ~ਤੋੜ Parasite.

ਟੁਕੜ (Tukar) *n m* Piece, crumb.

ਟੁਕੜਾ (tukraa) *n m* A piece, a part, a portion, a fragment, morsel.

ਟੁਕੜੀ (tukree) *n f* Small piece, Inset work; Contingent; Posse, small body (of troops).

ਟੁੰਗਣਾ (tungnaa) *v* To tuck up, to tag.

ਟੁੱਟ (tutt) *n f* Break, fracture, rupture; ~ਕੇ ਪੈਣਾ To attack furiously, to sweep; ~ਭਜ Dilapidation, breakage.

ਟੁਟਣਾ (tutnaa) v To break, to burst, to rupture, to wreck.

ਟੁੱਟਾ (tuttaa) a Broken, cracked.

ਟੁੰਡਾ (tundaa) a Armless, a person with an amputated limb; ~ਕਰਨਾ To maim.

ਟੁਣਕਣਾ (tunaknaa) v To chime, to clink.

ਟੁੰਬਣਾ (tumbnaa) v To excite, to inspire, to stimulate, to prompt.

ਟੁੱਬੀ (tubbee) n f Dip, dive.

ਟੁਰਨਾ (turnaa) v To walk, to go. Also ਤੁਰਨਾ

ਟੁੱਲ (tull) n m Hit, blow; ~ ਲਗ ਜਾਣਾ To be successful by chance, to come true of guess; ~ਲਾਉਣਾ To hit (a ball), to make a wild guess. Also ਟੁੱਲਾ

ਟੂਟੀ (tootee) n f Tap, nozzle, pupa, stopcock.

ਟੂਣਾ (toona) n m Witchcraft, incantation, enchantment, hex.

ਟੇਕ (tek) n f Support, reliance, resort, stay, backing.

ਟੇਕਣਾ (teknaa) v To Support, to rest, to prop.

ਟੇਕਰੀ (tekree) n f Small hill, hillock, mound, knoll, underfearture, hummock.

ਟੇਟੂਆ (tetooaa) n m Trachea, windpipe.

ਟੇਢਾ (tedhaa) a Oblique, aslant, a slope, crooked, cross, lateral; Insincere, cunning (person); ~ਪਣ Crookedness, curve, slant.

ਟੇਵਾ (tewaa) n m Horoscope, calculation of nativity.

ਟੈਣਾ (tainaa) a Dwarf.

ਟੋਆ (toaa) n m A pit, a ditch.

ਟੋਹ (toh) n f Hint, clue, search, secret.

ਟੋਹਣਾ (tohnaa) v To gropo, to fathom, to search.

ਟੋਕਣਾ (toknaa) v To obstruct, to interrupt, to hinder, to check.

ਟੋਕਰਾ (tokraa) n m Basket, punnet.

ਟੋਕਰੀ (tokree) n f Small basket.

ਟੋਕਾ (tokaa) n m Grasscutter, chopper; ~ਟਾਕੀ Criticism, censoriousness.

ਟੋਟਕਾ (totkaa) n m Spell, charm, aphorism.

ਟੋਟਣ (totan) n f Bald or cleanshaven head, scalp, pate.

ਟੋਟਾ (totaa) n m Piece, fragment, deficiency, loss.

ਟੋਡਾ (todaa) n m Young one of camel; young camel.

ਟੋਡੀ (todee) a Toady, sycophant, lickspittle, fawning flatterer, yesman.

ਟੋਪ (top) n m Hat, cover, high cap.

ਟੋਪਾ (ṭopaa) *n m* A large cap to cover the ears also.

ਟੋਪੀ (ṭopee) *n f* Cap, hat.

ਟੋਰਨਾ (ṭornaa) *v* To cause, to walk, to send, to see off.

ਟੋਲਣਾ (ṭolṇaa) *v* To search for, to find out.

ਟੋਲਾ (ṭolaa) *n m* Group, crowd.

ਟੋਲੀ (ṭolee) *n f* Group, crew, company, batch, troop, bunch.

ਟੌਰ੍ਹ (ṭaurh) *n* Pomp, elegance, embellishment; gaudiness, foppery; ~ਕੱਢਣਾ To decorate, to dress up elegantly.

ਠ

ਠ Seventeenth letter of Gurmukhi alphabets, pronounced as 'thatthaa'.

ਠਹਾਕਾ (thahaakkaa) *n m* Loud laugh, peal of laughter; bang, resounding blow; ~ਮਾਰਨਾ To guffaw, to laugh loudly, to give out a full-throated laugh.

ਠਹਿਕਣਾ (thaheknaa) *v* To stumble, to be knocked or struck (as of metalic vessels); to colide, to clash.

ਠਹਿਰਨਾ (thahernaa) *v* To stop, to halt, to rest, to wait, to stay.

ਠਕਠਕਾਉਣਾ (thakthakaunaa) *v* To knock, to tap.

ਠੱਕਾ (thakkaa) *n m* Cold wind, thunder storm.

ਠਕੋਰਨਾ (thakornaa) *v* To rap, to knock or hammer gently.

ਠੱਗ (thagg) *n m* Cheat, trickester, robber, imposter, deceiver.

ਠੱਗਣਾ (thaggnaa) *v* To cheat, to rob, to swindle, to deceive.

ਠੱਗੀ (thaggee) *n f* Trickery, act of cheating, fraud, imposure.

ਠੱਟਾ (thattaa) *n m* Small village, hamlet.

ਠੱਠ (thatth) *n m* A throng, crowd, gathering.

ਠਠਣਾ (thathnaa) *v* To stay, to settle.

ਠਠੰਬਰਨਾ (thathambarnaa) *v* To tremble, to shudder with fear, to wince, shrink, cower.

ਠੱਠਾ (thatthaa) *n m* Joke, Jest, fun, witticism, derision.

ਠਠਿਆਰ (thathiaar) *n m* A brazier, brass worker, coppersmith.

ਠੱਠੀ (thatthee) *n* Inhabitation, settlement.

ਠੱਠੇਬਾਜ਼ (thatthebaaz) *n m* Jester, joker.

ਠਠੇਰਾ (thatheraa) *n m* Brass maker, tinker.

ਠਠੋਲੀ (thatholee) *n f* Waggery.

ਠੰਡ (thand) *n f* Cold, coolness, chilliness; Also ਠੰਢ

ਠੰਡਾ (thandaa) *a* Cold, chilly, cool; Dead, passionless; ~ਸਾਹ Mournful sigh; ~ਹੋਣਾ To die, to be pacified; ~ਕਰਨਾ To pacify, to cool, to lull; Also ਠੰਢਾ

ਠਣਕਣਾ (thanknaa) *v* To jingle, to resound.

ਠਪਣਾ (thapnaa) *v* To close down, to pat, to shut, to fold.

ੱਪਾ (thappaa) *n m* Stamp, impression, seal, label.

ਠਪਾਈ (thapaaee) *n f* Embossing, printing, price of stamping.

ਠਰ੍ਹਾ (tharhaa) *n m* Hooch, country made, inferior liquid.

ਠਰਕ (tharak) *n f* Infatuation, amorousness, craze, false desire.

ਠਰਕੀ (tharkee) *a* Amorous, crazy sexy; peeping tom.

ਠਰਨਾ (tharnaa) *v* To cool, to freeze, to be chilled.

ਠਲ੍ਹ ਣਾ (thalnaa) *v* To hold, to stop.

ਠਾਕਣਾ (Thaaknaa) *v* To prevent, to deter, to hinder.

ਠਾਕਾ (thaakaa) *n m* Engagement ceremony, preliminary to formal betrothal.

ਠਾਠ (thaath) *n m* Pomp, splendour, show, elegance, luxury; ~**ਬਾਠ** Luxiousness, splendour, grandeur, magnificence, pomp and show.

ਠਾਠਾਂ (thaathaan) *n f* Waves, breakers, billows.

ਠਾਠਾ (thaathaa) *n m* Turban band.

ਠਾਨਣਾ (thaannaa) *v* To intend, to determine, to resolve.

ਠਾਣਾ (thaanaa) *n m* Police station.

ਠਿੰਗਣਾ (thingnaa) *a* Short, dwarfish, pygmy. Also **ਠਿਗਣਾ**

ਠਿੱਠ (thitth) *a* Shamefaced, humiliated; ~**ਹੋਣਾ** To feel small, to blush; ~**ਕਰਨਾ** To humiliate, to put to shame.

ਠਿਠਰਨਾ (thitharnaa) *v* To shiver with cold.

ਠਿੱਪਰ (thippar) *n m* Turnip. Also **ਗੋਂਗਲੂ**

ਠੀਹਾ (theehaa) *n m* Dwelling, abode, smithy, shop.

ਠੀਕ (theek) *a* Correct, accurate, strict, precise, exact, proper; ~**ਆਉਣਾ** To fit, to set; ~**ਠਾਕ** Alright, hale & hearty; ~**ਠਾਕ ਕਰਨਾ** To renovate, to recondition; ~**ਵਕਤ ਤੇ** Punctually, on time.

ਠੀਕਰ (theekar) *n m* A broken piece of earthern ware, shard, potsherd, Also **ਠੀਕਰਾ** or **ਠੀਕਰੀ**

ਠੁਸਣਾ (thusnaa) *v* To cram, to stuff.

ਠੁਕ (thuk) *n m* Respect, pride, aptness; ~**ਠੁਕ ਕਰਨਾ** To knock.

ਠੁਕਣਾ (thuknaa) *v* To be beaten.

ਠੁਕਰਾਉਣਾ (thukraaunaa) *v* To kick, to spurn, to refuse.

ਠੁਕਾਉਣਾ (thukaaunaa) *v* To get inserted, to get hammered.

ਠੁਕਾਈ (thukaaee) *n f* Whack, thrashing, leathering.

ਠੁੰਗਣਾ (thungnaa) *v* To peck, to dig.

ਠੂਠ (ṭhuṭṭh) *n m* Thumb; Nothing; refusal. Also **ਠੀਂਗਾ**

ਠੁੱਡਾ (ṭhunḍḍaa) *n m* Kick, stumbling.

ਠੁਣਕਣਾ (ṭhuṇakṇaa) *v* To sob, to weep slowly, to whimper.

ਠੁਮਕ (ṭhumak) *n f* Jerky movement, rhythmic foot work in dancing; ~**ਠੁਮਕ** (To walk) gracefully coquettishly.

ਠੁਮਕਣਾ (ṭhumakṇaa) *v* To strut, to walk with grace.

ਠੁਲ੍ਹ (ṭhullh) *n m* Fatness.

ਠੁਲ੍ਹਾ (ṭhullhaa) *a* Coarse, crude, rough, rude, fat.

ਠੂੰਗਾ (ṭhoongaa) *n m* Pecking stroke, a tap with knuckles of forefinger; ~**ਮਾਰਨਾ** To peck at, to strike with forefinger.

ਠੂਠਾ (ṭhoothaa) *n m* A begging bowl, a clay pot.

ਠੂਠੀ (ṭhoothee) *n f* Small earthern pot, half of a coconut.

ਠੇਸ (ṭhes) *n f* Shock knock, percussion, hurt, injured feeling.

ਠੇਕਣਾ (ṭhekṇaa) *v* To imprint, to stamp.

ਠੇਕਾ (ṭhekaa) *n m* Contract, leasehold; Wineshop.

ਠੇਕੇਦਾਰ (ṭhekedaar) *n m* Contractor.

ਠੇਠ (ṭheṭh) *a* Pure, unpolluted, chaste, proper, plain.

ਠੇਲ੍ਹਣਾ (ṭhellhṇaa) *v* To shove, to push, to dislocate, to relegate.

ਠੇਲ੍ਹਾ (ṭhellaah) *n m* Trolley, wheel barrow, push.

ਠੋਸ (ṭhos) *a* Dense, solid, hard.

ਠੋਕਣਾ (ṭhokṇaa) *v* To strike, to blow, to insert, to hammer; to hit, to thrash.

ਠੋਕਰ (ṭhokar) *n f* Stroke, thump, kick, quay, bumper, blow.

ਠੋਕਾ (ṭhokaa) *n m* Rammer, carpenter.

ਠੋਡੀ (ṭhodee) *n f* Chin.

ਠੌਰ (ṭhaur) *n f* Place, room, residence, locality, situatuion; refuge, asylum.

ਡ

ਡ Eighteenth letter of Gurmukhi alphabets, pronounced as 'ḍaḍḍaa'.

ਡਸਣਾ (ḍasnaa) *v* To bite.

ਡਹਿਕ (ḍahik) *n f* Pain in eyes; Temptation, avarice, bait.

ਡਹਿਕਣਾ (ḍaheknaa) *v* To be tempted.

ਡਹਿਣਾ (ḍahenaa) *v* To be engaged, to engage.

ਡੰਕ (ḍank) *n m* Sting; Penholder.

ਡੱਕ (ḍakk) *n m* Wooden block, stopper, obstacle, hindrance, barrier.

ਡੱਕਣਾ (ḍakknaa) *v* To shut, to block the way, to stop, to detain.

ਡਕਰਾ (ḍakraa) *n m* Piece, slice.

ਡੰਕਾ (ḍankaa) *n m* A big drum.

ਡੱਕਾ (ḍakkaa) *n m* Clog, hindrance, block, twig.

ਡਕਾਰ (ḍakaar) *n m* Belch, eructation, bellowing; ~ਜਾਣਾ To devour; ~ਮਾਰਨਾ To belch; ~ਲੈਣਾ To embezzle, to swallow.

ਡਕਾਰਨਾ (ḍakaarnaa) *v* To bellow, to swallow up, to embezzle, to digest.

ਡਕੈਤ (ḍakaet) *n m* Decoit, robber.

ਡਕੈਤੀ (ḍaketee) *n f* Robbery dacoity, Piracy.

ਡੰਗ (ḍang) *n m* (1) Bite, sting, aculeus (2) Meal time.

ਡੰਗਣਾ (ḍangnaa) *v* To bite, to sting.

ਡੰਗਰ (ḍangar) *n m* Beast, animal, cattle; Foolish, stupid; ~ਪੁਣਾ Beastliness, stupidity.

ਡੰਗਾ (Dangaa) *n* Stitch, chain stitch, support.

ਡੱਗਾ (ḍaggaa) *n* Drum stick, tuck; ~ਮਾਰਨਾ To beat the drum.

ਡੰਝ (ḍanjh) *n f* Thirst, quest, inquisitiveness.

ਡਟਣਾ (ḍatnaa) *v* To stand firm, to face squarely.

ਡੱਟਾ (ḍattaa) *n m* Plug, cork, stopper.

ਡੰਠਲ (ḍanthal) *n m* Stem, a small shoot of a plant; Also **ਡੰਡਲ**

ਡੰਡ (ḍanḍ) *n m* (1) Ransom, penalty, punishment, Noise; (2) An exercise, push ups; ~ਕੱਢਣੇ To take exercise; ~ਪਾਉਣੀ To make noise, to create disturbance; ~ਪੇਲਣੇ To exercise continuously, to do push ups; ~ਬੈਠਕਾਂ Strenuous physical exercises sit and stand exercises; ~ਦੇਣਾ To punish, to chastise.

ਡੰਡਾ (ḍandaa) *n m* Rod, stick, club, cudgel, shaft, baton, a bar; ~ਮਾਰਨਾ To cudgel; ~ਵਿਖਾਉਣਾ To terrorise.

ਡੜਿਆਉਣਾ (ḍaḍiaaunaa) *v* To scream, to cry out of fear.

ਡੰਡੀ (ḍandee) *n f* A thin stick, butt, shaft, beam; ~ਮਾਰਨੀ To cheat in weighing, to weigh short.

ਡੱਡੂ (ḍaḍḍoo) *n m* Frog, toad.

ਡੰਡੌਤ (ḍandaut) *n* Salutation, prostration.

ਡੰਨ (ḍann) *n m* Fine, penality, punishment; ~ਲਾਉਣਾ To impose fine, to penalise.

ਡੰਨਣਾ (ḍannṇa) *n* Salutation, pros.

ਡਾਪਟਣਾ (ḍapatṇaa) *v* To rebuke, to shout at.

ਡਫਣਾ (ḍaphṇaa) *v* To swill, to devour, to eat too much (in bad sense).

ਡਫਲੀ (ḍaflee) *n f* A Small drum, timbrel, tabor.

ਡੱਬ (ḍabb) *n m* Spot, mark, blur, blot, stain, smear.

ਡੱਬਾ (ḍabbaa) *n m* Tin box, casket, can, compartment, bogie, coach, wagon.

ਡੱਬੀ (ḍabbee) *n f* Small box, case.

ਡਮਰੂ (ḍamroo) *n m* Tabor.

ਡਰ (ḍar) *n m* Fear, awe, terror, dread; ~ਹੋਣਾ To apprehend; ~ਜਾਣਾ To be freightened.

ਡਰਨਾ (ḍarnaa) *v* To fear, to be freightened.

ਡਰਪੋਕ (ḍarpok) *a* Timid, coward, sheepish, pigeon hearted, chicken hearted.

ਡਰਾਉਣਾ (ḍaraaunaa) *v a* To freighten, to alarm, to horrify, to terrify, to intimidater, to threaten, to cow, Appalling, dreadful, horrible, ghastly, formidable.

ਡਰਾਵਾ (ḍraavaa) *n m* Threat, scare.

ਡਲ੍ਹਕ (ḍalhak) *n f* Reflection, shine, brilliancy, glitter, flash.

ਡਲਾ (ḍalaa) *n m* Large piece, fragment, clod.

ਡਲੀ (ḍolee) *n f* Small piece, gobbet; ingot; Nugget.

ਡਾਹਣਾ (ḍaahṇaa) *v* To spread, to place, to engage.

ਡਾਕ (ḍaak) *n f* Post, mail, dock; ~ਬੰਗਾਲਾ Dak bangalow, rest house.

ਡਾਕਣਾ (ḍaaknaa) *v* To vomit.

ਡਾਕਾ (ḍaakaa) *n m* Robbery, dacoity.

ਡਾਕੀਆ (ḍaakiaa) *n m* Postman.

ਡਾਕੂ (ḍaakoo) *n m* Dacoit, bandit, robber, highwayman.

ਡਾਂਗ (ḍaang) *n f* Big thick rod, staff.

ਡਾਂਗਰ (ḍaangar) *n m* Grained wheat.

ਡਾਂਗਰੀ (ḍaangree) *n m* Cowherd, cattle grazer.

ਡਾਚੀ (ḍaachee) *n f* Dromedary, female camel yet to deliver for the first time.

ਡਾਂਟ (ḍaanṭ) *n f* Intimidation, chiding, rebuke, subjugation; ~ਡਪਟ Reprimand, curse, rebuke.

ਡਾਂਟਣਾ (ḍaanṭṇaa) *v* To chide, to rebuke, to take to task, to reprimand.

ਡਾਡ (ḍaaḍ) *n f* Wailing, cry, shriek.

ਡਾਢ (ḍaaḍh) *n f* Hardness; Firmness, rigidity, imflexibility, oppression; High handness, violence.

ਡਾਢਾ (ḍaaḍhaa) *a* Strong, mighty, powerful, vigorous, overwhelming.

ਡਾਢੀ (ḍaaḍhee) *a* Nasty, shocking, poignant; Strong; ~ਲੋੜ Crying need.

ਡਾਲ (ḍaal) *n f* Branch, bough, offshoot, offspring. Also ਡਾਲੀ

ਡਾਲਾ (ḍaalaa) *n m* A Small basket (of fruits, sweets, cold drinks etc.).

ਡਿਓੜੀ (ḍioṛee) *n f* Gateway, porch, portico, vestibule, antechamber.

ਡਿਗਣਾ (ḍignaa) *v* To fall, to stumble, to drop.

ਡਿੰਗਾ (ḍingaa) *a* Curved, bent, crooked, uneven.

ਡਿੰਘ (ḍingh) *n f* Pace, step, long stride.

ਡਿੰਭ (ḍimbh) *n f* Ovurn.

ਡੀਕ (ḍeek) *n f* Gulp, long sip, pull.

ਡੀਂਗ (ḍeeng) *n f* Boasting, Pretension, tall talk, braggadocio.

ਡੁਸਕਣਾ (ḍusakṇaa) *v* To sob, to weep, to blubber.

ਡੁਸਕਾਰਾ (ḍuskaaraa) *n m* Sob; ~ਭਰਨਾ To sob.

ਡੁਗਡੁਗੀ (ḍugḍugee) *n f* Small two-sided drum with lashes attached for drubbing the sides.

ਡੁਗਰੀਲਾ (ḍugreelaa) *a* Hilly.

ਡੁੱਡਾ (ḍuḍḍaa) *a* Lame, bandylegged.

ਡੁੰਨ (ḍunn) *a.* Foolish, dune; idiot, stupid, dull-witted, dolt, blockhead; ~ਵੱਟਾ Sullen, silent, sulking (person).

ਡੁਬਕੀ (ḍubkee) *n f* A dip, a plunge.

ਡੁਬਣਾ (ḍubnaa) *v* To sink, to drown, to dip, to plunge.

ਡੁਲ੍ਹਣਾ (ḍulhnaa) *v* To spill, to flow, to be split, to be passionate, to be enamoured, to be generous.

ਡੂੰਘਾ (ḍoongaa) *a* Deep, intense, below; ~ਕਰਨਾ To deepen; ~ਮਿੱਤਰ

Chum, intimate-friend.

ਡੂਮ (doom) *n m* Bard, village singer.

ਡੇਹਮੂ (dehmoo) *n m a* Wasp, yellow hornet, yellow insect; Short tempered.

ਡੇਗਣਾ (degnaa) *v* To topple, to drop, to bowl over, to debunk.

ਡੇਰਾ (deraa) *n m* Dwelling, camp, lodging, quarter, residence.

ਡੇਲਾ (delaa) *n m* An eye ball.

ਡੈਣ (dain) *n m* Witch, sorceress.

ਡੋਂਗਾ (dongaa) *n m* A large canoe, boat without sail.

ਡੋਂਗੀ (dongee) *n f* A small boat.

ਡੋਡਾ (dodaa) *n m* Pod of a poppy plant, boll.

ਡੋਡੀ (dodee) *n f* Bud, pod, boll (of cotton).

ਡੋਬਣਾ (dobnaa) *v* To submerge, to cause, to sink, to engulf, to drown, to dip, to immerse.

ਡੋਬਾ (dobaa) *n m* Dip, immersion.

ਡੋਰ (dor) *n f* String, cord, thread.

ਡੋਰਾ (doraa) *a n m* Deaf, String.

ਡੋਰੀ (doree) *n f* String, cord, jess; Strand, lace.

ਡੋਲ (dol) *n m* Bucket, pail.

ਡੋਲ੍ਹਣਾ (dolahnaa) *v* To spill, to overflow, to effuse.

ਡੋਲਚੀ (dolchee) *n f* Small bucket.

ਡੋਲਣ (dolan) *n m* Fluctuation, oscillation

ਡੋਲਣਾ (dolnaa) *v n m* To move, to swing, to fluctuate to sway; To shake; A pot used in milking.

ਡੋਲਾ (dolaa) *n m* A closed litter.

ਡੋਲੀ (dolee) *n f* Palanquin (in which bride is carried to her in-laws's house).

ਡੌਂਗਾ (daungaa) *n m* Serving bowl.

ਡੌਲ (daul) *n m* Manner, form, shape, mode.

ਡੌਲਣਾ (daulnaa) *v* To shape, to form, to sketch, to design.

ਡੌਲਾ (daullaa) *n m* Biceps, muscles of the upper arm.

ਢ

ਢ Ninteenth letter of Gurmukhi alphabets, pronounced as 'ḍhaḍḍhaa' (a tone marker).

ਢਹਿਣਾ (ḍhahenaa) *v* To fall down, to be defeated.

ਢਹੇ (ḍhahe) *adv* Under the influence.

ਢੱਕਣ (ḍhakkan) *n m* Lid, cover, shutter; ~ਦਾਰ Provided with a lid.

ਢੱਕਣਾ (ḍhakknaa) *v* To cover, to enshroud, to cloud, to hide.

ਢੱਕੀ (ḍhakkee) *n f* Brae, hillock, foothill.

ਢਕੋਸਲਾ (ḍhakoslaa) *n m* Myth, superstition, stunt, sham, delusion, deception.

ਢੰਗ (ḍhang) *n m* Manner, system, style, procedure, design, device, form.

ਢੱਗਾ (ḍhaggaa) *n m adv* Bull, ox; Poor, weak, small.

ਢੰਗੀ (ḍhangee) *a* Intelligent, clever, cunning, witty, manipulator, skilful.

ਢੱਗੀ (ḍhaggee) *n f* Cow.

ਢੱਟਾ (ḍhattaa) *n m a* Bull, buffalo bull; Astout, sturdy.

ਢੰਡੋਰਚੀ (ḍhandorchee) *n m* Announcer, annunciator.

ਢੰਡੋਰਾ (ḍhandoraa) *n m* Announcement proclamation by beating drum.

ਢੰਡੋਲਣਾ (ḍhandolnaa) *v* To search.

ਢੰਨ (ḍhann) *n m* Lake, pool, pond.

ਢੱਬ (ḍhabb) *n m* Mode, style, manner, position, form.

ਢਲਕਣਾ (ḍhalaknaa) *v* To be slackened, to be untied, to slip down.

ਢਲਣਾ (ḍhalnaa) *v* To decline, to flow, to thaw, to set, to be moulded into shape.

ਢਲਵਾਂ (ḍhalwaan) *a* Steepy, declining, slanting.

ਢਲਵਾਨ (ḍhalwaan) *n m a* Slope, tilt, slant; Slanting, tilted, steep.

ਢਲਾਈ (ḍhalaaee) *n f* Casting, moulding.

ਢਵਾਉਣਾ (ḍhawaaunaa) *v* To cause, to demolish, to dismantle.

ਢਾਇਆ (ḍhaaiaa) *a* Two and half times, multiplication table for this.

ਢਾਈ (ḍhaaee) *a* Two and half.

ਢਾਹ (ḍhaa) *n f* Ruin, erosion, landslide.

ਢਾਹੁਣਾ (ḍhaahunaa) *v* To pull down, to demolish, to raze, to overturn, to destroy, to depress (heart).

ਢਾਹੂ (dhaau) *a* Destructive, ruinous, damaging; subversive.

ਢਾਂਚਾ (dhaanchaa) *n m* Frame, format, framework, sketch, outline, skeleton, design, model.

ਢਾਠ (dhaath) *n* Ruined or demolished state, remains (of buildings), wreckage, ruins.

ਢਾਠਾ (dhaathaa) *n f* Turban band.

ਢਾਡੀ (dhaadee) *n m* bard, ballad singer, minstrel, musician. Also **ਢਾਢੀ**

ਢਾਬ (dhaab) *n f* Small lake, large pond.

ਢਾਂਦੀ (dhaandee) *a* A foolish woman.

ਢਾਬਾ (dhaabaa) *n m* A small hotel, wayside restaururants serving fast food.

ਢਾਰਸ (dhaaras) *n m* Consolation, solace, appeasment, confidence.

ਢਾਰਾ (dhaaraa) *n m* Thatched shed, tenement.

ਢਾਲ (dhaal) *n f* Slope, steepness, inclination, slant, manner, mode.

ਢਾਲਣਾ (dhaalnaa) *v* To mould, to shape, to cast, to form.

ਢਿੱਗ (dhigg) *n f* Landslide, large mass of rock or earth.

ਢਿੱਡ (dhidd) *n m* Abdomen, belly, stomach, tummy, womb, pregnancy; **~ਹੋਣਾ** To be in family way; **~ਤੇ ਲਤ ਮਾਰਨੀ** To deprive one of the means of livelihood; **~ਭਰਨਾ** To feed; **~ਵਿਚ ਚੂਹੇ ਦੌੜਨੇ** To feel very hungry; **~ਵਿਚ ਰਖਣਾ** To keep to oneself.

ਢਿੱਡਲ (dhiddal) *a* Abdominous, fat, potbelly.

ਢਿਬਰੀ (dhibree) *n f* Nut (for a bolt).

ਢਿੱਬੀ (dhibbee) *n* Rocky knoll, hillock.

ਢਿੱਲ (dhill) *n f* Slackness, sluggishness, looseness, tardiness, lag, delay; **~ਪੁਣਾ** Looseness; **~ਲਾਉਣੀ** To delay, to prolong, to hang fire; **~ੜ** Slacker, slow, tardy, laggard.

ਢਿਲਕਣਾ (dhilaknaa) *v* To roll, to slacken, to slide, to sag, to loosen.

ਢਿੱਲੜ (dhillar) *a* Tardy, slow-moving, sluggish, lazy; **~ਹੋਣਾ** To become loose, to be unwell; **~ਕਰਨਾ** To loosen, to slacken; to mollify, to calm down; **~ਪਣ** Looseness, slackness, sluggishness.

ਢਿੱਲਾ (dhillaa) *a* Slow, inert, inactive, tardy, sluggish, slack, lazy.

ਢੀਠ (dheeth) *a* Obstinate, ircorrigible, audacious, daring.

ਢੁਆਈ (dhuaaee) *n f* Cartage, porterage, transporation charges, haulage.

ਢੁਕਣਾ (dhuknaa) *v* To go, to approach, to go to bride's place for marriage; To comport with, to fit, to suit, to match.

ਢੁਕਾਅ (dhukaa) *n m* Approach, arrival of marriage party at the bride's house; Ceremony accompanying this.

ਢੁੱਚਰ (dhuchchar) *n f* Excuse, pretext, hindrance; ~ਬਾਜ Shirker; peevish, argumentative.

ਢੂਈ (dhooee) *n f* Back, rear part or back surface of human body, posterior, rump; Buttocks; Anus.

ਢੂੰਗਾ (dhoongaa) *n m* Rump, buttock, posterior, bum.

ਢੂੰਡ (dhoond) *n f* Search, investigation, hunt, quest; ~ਵਿਚ ਲਗਣਾ To pursue.

ਢੂੰਡਣਾ (dhoondnaa) *v* To search, to explore, to investigate, to trace, to look for, to hunt out, to seek, to strike.

ਢੇਕਾ (dhekaa) *n m* Born of illicit intercourse, wicked, lascivious.

ਢੇਰ (dher) *n m* Heap, pile, mass, collection; ~ਸਾਰੇ Plenty; ~ਲਾਉਣਾ To mass, to heap, to dump.

ਢੇਰੀ (dheree) *n f* Heap, collection; ~ਹੋ ਜਾਂਣਾ To collapse; ~ਕਰ ਦੇਣਾ To demolish.

ਢੇਲਾ (dhelaa) *n m* A piece of brick, or stone, or of earth.

ਢੋ (dho) *n m* Occasion, opportunity, chance, coincidence. Also ਢੋਅ

ਢੋਆ (dhoaa) *n f* Gift, offer, present.

ਢੋਈ (dhoee) *n f* Refuge; ~ਦੇਣੀ To give shelter.

ਢੋਕ (dhok) *n f* Detached village, hamlet, outlying homestead.

ਢੋਡਾ (dhodaa) *n m* Thick cake of bread (made of millet).

ਢੋਣ (dhon) *n f* Freight, transit, carriage, of goods.

ਢੋਣਾ (dhonaa) *v* To transport, to carry, to convey.

ਢੋਲ (dhol) *n m* Large drum, barrel, bin; ~ਚੀ Drummer. Also ਢੋਲਕ

ਢੋਲਣ (dholan) *n f* Sweetheart, beloved, paramour, love.

ਢੋਲਣਾ (dholnaa) *n m* An ornament.

ਢੋਲਾ (dholaa) *n m* Lover, sweetheart.

ਢੌਂਗ (dhaung) *n m* Fraud, trick, stunt, imposture, deceit.

ਢੌਂਗੀ (dhaungee) *n m a* Imposter, fraud; Deceitful.

ਣ

ਣ Twentieth letter of Gurmukhi alphabets, pronounced as 'naanaa'.

ਤ

ਤ Twenty first letter of Gurmukhi alphabets pronouncing as 'tattaa'

ਤਅੱਸਬ (tayassab) *n m* Religious bias, bigotry, fanaticism, fundamentalism.

ਤਅੱਸਬੀ (tayassbee) *a n m* Fanatic, bigoted, biased (in religion); Bigot, fanatic, fundamentalist.

ਤਅੱਜਬ (tajjab) *n m* Astonishment, amazement.

ਤਅੱਲਕ (tallak) *n m* Connection, concern, relation.

ਤਆਰਫ਼ (taaraf) *n m* Introduction, presentation (of one person to another); **~ਕਰਾਉਣਾ** To Introduce.

ਤਆਵਨ (t-aavan) *n m* Co-operation, mutual assistance; **~ਕਰਨਾ** To co-operate.

ਤਸਕਰ (taskar) *n m* Smuggler, thief.

ਤਸਕਰੀ (taskaree) *n f* Theft, pilferage.

ਤਸਕੀਨ (taskeen) *n f* Satisfaction, consolation, solace.

ਤਸ਼ਖੀਸ਼ (tashkheesh) *n f* Determination; Diagnosis, assessment.

ਤਸ਼ਤਰੀ (tashtree) *n f* Small plate, dish, saucer, tray.

ਤਸ਼ੱਦਦ (tashaddad) *n m* Violence, atrocity, oppression.

ਤਸਦੀਕ (tasdeek) *n f* Attestation, affirmation, verification, confirmation.

ਤਸਮਾ (tasmaa) *n m* Leather strap, brace, thong, shoe lace.

ਤਸ਼ਰੀਹ (tashree) *n f* Explanation, exegesis, elucidation, elaboration; **~ਕਰਨਾ** To elaborate, to illustrate, to clarify.

ਤਸ਼ਰੀਫ਼ (tashreef) *n f* Honouring, paying visit, presence.

ਤਸਲਾ (taslaa) *n* Basin, shallow pan.

ਤਸੱਲੀ (tasallee) *n f* Satisfaction, complacency, consolation; **~ਕਰਨੀ** To satisfy, to assure; **~ਦੇਣੀ** To console, to reassure.

ਤਸੱਵਰ (tasavvar) *n m* Assumption, supposition, imagination.

ਤਸ਼ਵੀਸ਼ (tashveesh) *n f* Anxiety, concern, apprehension, confusion; **~ਨਾਕ** Worrisome.

ਤਸਵੀਰ (tasveer) *n f* Picture, photo, portrait, image, sketch.

ਤਸੀਹੇ (taseehe) *n m* Torture, torment, persecution, agony.

ਤਹੱਈਆ (tahaiaa) *n m* Determination, resolve; **~ਕਰਨਾ** To determine, resolve, to make up one's mind, to make a resolve.

ਤਹਿ (tahe) *n f* Layer, surface, base, bed, bottom; **~ਕਰਨਾ** To fold, to pack; **~ਤਕ ਪੁਜਣਾ** To fathom.

ਤਹਿਕੀਕ (tahekeek) *n f* Investigation, enquiry.

ਤਹਿਕੀਕਾਤ (Tahekeekaat) *n f* Enquiry, inquest, investigation.

ਤਹਿਖਾਨਾ (tahekhaanaa) *n* Basement cellar, underground place.

ਤਹਿਜ਼ੀਬ (tahezeeb) *n f* Culture, civilization, refined behaviour; **~ਯਾਫ਼ਤਾ** Cultured, civilized, refined, gentlemantly.

ਤਹਿਤ (tahet) *n m* Domination, predominance, supremacy, control; Under, dominated by, headed by.

ਤਹਿਮਤ (tahmat) *n f* Sheet used as garment for the lower body.

ਤਹਿਲਕਾ (tahelkaa) *n m* Turmoil, commotion, disturbance, tumult, agitation; **~ਮਚਾਉਣਾ** To create commotion.

ਤਕ (tak) *prep n f* To, up to; courage boldness; **~ਧੈਣੀ** To dare.

ਤੱਕ (takk) *n f* Glance, look, sight, hope, expectation, wait; **~ਰਖਣੀ** To expect, to hope.

ਤਕਸੀਮ (takseem) *n f* Division, partition, distribution.

ਤਕਸੀਰ (takseer) *n f* Fault, error, offence, guilt, crime.

ਤੱਕਣਾ (takknaa) *v* To look at, to gaze at, to stare at, to watch, to observe.

ਤਕਦੀਰ (takdeer) *n f* Destiny, fate, luck.

ਤਕਨਾਲੋਜੀ (taknlojee) *n f* Technology.

ਤਕਨੀਕ (takneek) *n m* Technique.

ਤਕਨੀਕੀ (takneekee) *a* Technical, technological.

ਤਕਬੱਰ (takabbar) *n m* Pride vanity, arrogance.

ਤਕਰਾਰ (takraar) *n m* Controversy, dispute, contention, quarrel, wrangling.

ਤਕਰੀਬ (takreeb) *n f* Function; festivity.

ਤਕਰੀਬਨ (takreeban) *adv* Approximately, nearly, roughly.

ਤਕਰੀਰ (takreer) *n f* Speech, lecture, discourse, talk, address; **~ਕਰਨੀ** To deliver lecture, to address, to speak.

ਤਕਲੱਫ਼ (takalaf) *n f* Formality, etiquette, conventionality.

ਤਕਲਾ (taklaa) *n m* Ringworm, rain worm; Spindle, distaff.

ਤਕਲੀ (taklee) *n f* Bobbin for cotton thread, small spindle.

ਤਕਲੀਫ਼ (takleef) *n f* Inconvenience, difficulty, hardship, distress, trouble; **~ਉਠਾਉਣੀ** To suffer hardship; **~ਕਰਨੀ** To take trouble; **~ਦੇਣੀ** To cause trouble, to bother.

ਤਕਵਾ (takvaa) *n m* Faith, trust (in God), religious conviction.

ਤਕੜਾ (takṛaa) *a* Strong, tough, stout, healthy, sound, muscular. Also **ਤਗੜਾ**

ਤੱਕੜੀ (takkṛee) *n f* Balance, scale, ample (amount).

ਤਕਾਜ਼ਾ (takaazaa) *n f* Claim, insistence on demand, importunity.

ਤਕੀਆ (takiyaa) *n m* Pillow, cushion.

ਤਖ਼ਤ (takhat) *n m* Throne, royal seat; **~ਛੱਡਣਾ** To abdicate; **~ਤੋਂ ਉਤਾਰਨਾ** To dethrone.

ਤਖ਼ਤਾ (takhtaa) *n m* Wooden plank, perterre.

ਤਖ਼ਤੀ (takhtee) *n* Wooden tablet (for writing practice), writing tablet; Also **ਤਖ਼ਤੀ**

ਤਖ਼ਮੀਨਾ (takhmeenaa) *n m* Estimate, appraisal.

ਤਖ਼ੱਲਸ (takhallas) *n m* Nickname, poetic name, Nom-de-plume.

ਤੰਗ (tang) *a* Vexed, straitened, stringent, troubled, close, narrow; **~ਹਾਲ** Poor, destitute, distressed; **~ਹਾਲੀ** Poverty, destitution; **~ਕਰਨਾ** To trouble, to irk, to irritate, to oppress; **~ਦਿਲ** Narrowminded, intolerant.

ਤੱਗਣਾ (taggṇaa) *v* To last, to endure, to hold on, to hold out.

ਤਗਮਾ (tagmaa) *n m* Medal, decoration.

ਤਗਾਦਾ (tagaadaa) *n m* Demand, dunning, dispute. Also **ਤਕਾਜ਼ਾ**

ਤੰਗੀ (tangee) *n f* Paucity, tightness, difficulty, deficiency, penury.

ਤਜਣਾ (tajṇaa) *v* To abandon, to desert, to leave, to renounce.

ਤਜਰਬਾ (tajarbaa) *n m* Experience, experiment, trial; **~ਕਾਰ** Experienced, veteran, old bird.

ਤਜਵੀਜ਼ (tajveez) *n f* Scheme, plan, proposal, view, proposition; **~ਕਰਨੀ** To propose, to put forth a plan.

ਤਜਾਰਤ (tajaarat) *n f* Commerce, trade.

ਤਜੋਰੀ (tajoree) *n f* Cash box, safe.

ਤੱਟ (taṭṭ) *n m* Coast, bank, shore.

ਤਟਸਥ (taṭasth) *a* Neutral, impartial; **~ਤਾ** Impartiality, neutrality.

ਤਣਨਾ (taṇnaa) *v* To tighten, to stretch, to tauten.

ਤਣਵਾਉਣਾ (taṇvaauṇaa) *v* To get or cause to be stretched, to be tightened, to spread; To assist in the process.

ਤਣਾ (taṇaa) *n m* Trunk (of a tree), main stem.

ਤਣੀ (taṇee) *n f* String, cord; Strand.

ਤੱਤ (tatt) *n m* Essence, gist, element, substance, kernel; ~ਕੱਢਣਾ To extract essence, to sum up, to analyse.

ਤਤਕਰਾ (tatkaraa) *n m* Table of contents.

ਤਤਕਾਲ (tatkaal) *adv* Immediately, instantly, at that very moment.

ਤਤਪਰ (tatpar) *a* Ready alert; ~ਤਾ Readiness, preparedness.

ਤੱਤਾ (tattaa) *a* Warm, hot, annoyed.

ਤੱਥ (tatth) *n m* Fact, reality, basis; ~ਹੀਣ Pointless, inane.

ਤਦਬੀਰ (tadbeer) *n f* Plan, scheme, proposal, method.

ਤੰਦ (tand) *n m* Thread, strand, fibre; tendril; String (of musical instrument).

ਤੰਦਰੁਸਤ (tandrust) *a* Healthy, hale & hearty.

ਤੰਦੂਰ (tandoor) *n m* Oven.

ਤਨ (tan) *n m* Body, physique.

ਤਨਹਾ (tanhaa) *a* Alone, lone, single, solitary; Lonely, lonesome, all by oneself.

ਤਨਹਾਈ (tanhaaee) *n f* Loneliness, lonesomeness, sloitariness; seclusion, solitude.

ਤਨਕੀਦ (tankeed) *n f* Criticism.

ਤਨਖਾਹ (tankhaah) *n f* Salary, wages, pay.

ਤਪਸ਼ (tapash) *n f* Heat, warmth.

ਤਪਣਾ (tapṇaa) *v* To be heated, to glow, to burn with grief or pain.

ਤਪਦਿਕ (tapdik) *n f* Tuberculosis.

ਤੱਪੜ (tappaṛ) *n f* Matting, sack cloth.

ਤਪਾਉਣਾ (tapaauṇaa) *v* To heat, to warm, to trouble, to vex.

ਤਪੀ (tapee) *n m* Ascetic, hermit, devotee.

ਤਫਸੀਲ (tafseel) *n* Detail, elaboration, detailed description.

ਤਫਤੀਸ਼ (tafteesh) *n f* Investigation inquest.

ਤਫਰਕਾ (tafarakaa) *n m* Difference disagreement (in opinion) estrangement, distance in relations; discrimination. Also ਤਫ਼ਰਕਾ

ਤਫਰੀਹ (tafreeh) *n m* Past time recess.

ਤਬਕਾ (tabkaa) *n m* Sect, class stratum.

ਤਬਦੀਲ (tabdeel) *a* Change exchanged, bratered; altered transformed; transferred; ~ਕਰ

To change, alter, transform; to exchange, barter, swap, trade; to transfer.

ਤਬਦੀਲੀ (tabdeelee) *n f* Change, transfer, alteration, transition, variation, transformation.

ਤਬਲਾ (tablaa) *n f* Tambourine beater.

ਤਬਾਹ (tabaa) *a* Destroyed, ruined, totally damaged or spoiled; desolated, devastated, ravaged.

ਤਬਾਹੀ (tabaahee) *n f* Ruin, destruction, havoc, ravage, dilapidation, wreck, devastation, annihilation, downfall.

ਤਬਾਦਲਾ (tabaadlaa) *n m* Transfer, migration, change.

ਤੰਬੀ (tambee) *n f* A type of trousers.

ਤਬੀਅਤ (tabeeyat) *n f* Disposition, state of health, mood, temperament; ~**ਲਗਣੀ** To take interest.

ਤੰਬੀਹ (tambeeh) *n* Reprimand, warning, censure, reproof, rebuke; ~**ਕਰਨੀ** To reprimand, warn, censure, reprove, rebuke.

ਤਬੀਬ (tabeeb) *n m* Physician, doctor.

ਤੰਬੂ (tamboo) *n m* Tent, camp.

ਤੰਬੂਰਾ (tambooraa) *n m* Musical, tambourine, a musical instrument.

ਤਬੇਲਾ (tabelaa) *n m* Horse-stable, mews.

ਤਮਕਣਾ (tamaknaa) *v* To be redden, to be angry, to be instigated.

ਤਮੰਚਾ (tamanchaa) *n m* Pistol, revolver.

ਤਮੰਨਾ (tamannaa) *n* Desire, longing, wish.

ਤਮ੍ਹਾ (tammaa) *n m* Covetousness, temptation, avarice, bait.

ਤਮਾਸ਼ਬੀਨ (tamashbeen) *n m* On looker, sightseer, spectator, an epicure.

ਤਮਾਸ਼ਾ (tamaashaa) *n m* Show, fun, spectacle, performance, play; ~**ਈ** By stander, spectator.

ਤਮਾਕੂ (tamaakoo) *n m* Tabacco, weed; Also **ਤੰਬਾਕੂ**

ਤਮੀਜ਼ (tameez) *n f* Differentiation, distinction, good manners, decorum, sense.

ਤਰਸਣਾ (tarasnaa) *v* To long for, to yearn, to desire earnestly, to wish.

ਤਰਸਾਉਣਾ (tarsaaunaa) *v* To set agog, to tantalize, to torment with false hope.

ਤਰਸੇਵਾਂ (tarsevaan) *n m* Longing, yearning, desire, want.

ਤਰਕ (tarak) *n m* Rationale, reasoning argument; ~**ਸ਼ਾਸਤਰ** Logic; ~**ਵਾਦ** Rationalism, rationality.

ਤਰਕਸ਼ (tarakash) *n m* Quiver, arrow case.

ਤਰੱਕਣਾ (tarakknaa) *v* To rot, to stink, to putrefy, to decay, to ferment; Also **ਤੁਰਕਣਾ**

ਤਰਕਾਉਣਾ (tarkaaunaa) *v* To cause putrefaction, rot or decay, to putrefy, to decompose.

ਤੁਕਲਾ (traklaa) *n m* Spindle, iron pin (for spinning, the thread).

ਤਰਕਾ (tarkaa) *n m* Inheritance, legacy, share in inherited property, property, wealth.

ਤਰਕਾਰੀ (tarkaaree) *n f* Cooked or green vegetable.

ਤਰਕਾਲਾਂ (tarkaalaan) *n f* Evening, dusk nightfull. Also **ਤਕਾਲਾਂ**

ਤੁਕਿਆ (trakiyaa) *a* Rotten, putrefied, putrid.

ਤਰੱਕੀ (tarakkee) *n f* Promotion, progress, growth, improvement, development, increment; Also **ਤੁੱਕੀ**

ਤਰਕੀਬ (tarkeeb) *n f* Plan, device, arrangement, contrivance.

ਤਰਖਾਣ (tarkhaan) *n m* Carpenter.

ਤਰਖਾਣਾ (tarkhaanaa) *n m* Carpentary, joinery.

ਤਰੰਗ (tarang) *n m* Wave, ripple; Impulse, passion whim, fantacy, emotion.

ਤਰਜ਼ (taraz) *n f* Mode, tune, form, design, fashion, manner.

ਤਰਜਮਾ (tarjmaa) *n m* Translation, version, rendering.

ਤਰਜਮਾਨ (tarajmaan) *n m* Spokesman, representative.

ਤਰਜੀਹ (tarjeeh) *n f* Preference.

ਤਰਜੀਹੀ (tarjeehee) *a* Preferential.

ਤਰੱਟੀ (tarattee) *n f* Demotion, loss, destruction; Also **ਤੁੱਟੀ**

ਤਰਤੀਬ (tarteeb) *n f* Arrangement, plan, order, sequence, system; **~ਦਾਰ** Serially, systematically.

ਤਰੱਥਲੀ (tarthallee) *n f* Disorder, disturbance, disarray, uproar, tumult, turmoil.

ਤਰੱਦਦ (taraddad) *n m* Endavour, effort, exertion; discomfort, botheration, anxiety, worry; **~ਕਰਨਾ** To make effort, to exert oneself, to bother, worry.

ਤਰਦੀਦ (tardeed) *n f* Refultation denial, desavowal, repudiation, cancellation, contradiction.

ਤਰੰਨਮ (tarannam) *n m* Melody.

ਤਰੱਪਣਾ (tarappnaa) *v* To leap, to jump.

ਤਰਪਾਲ (tarpaal) *n m* tarpaulin.

ਤਰਫ਼ (taraf) *n f adv* Side, direction Towards, with; **~ਦਾਰ** Partial biased, accomplice; **~ਦਾ** Partiality, favouritism.

ਤਰਬੂਜ਼ (tarbooz) *n m* Watermelon.

ਤਰਮੀਮ (tarmeem) *n f* Amendment, modification.

ਤਰਲ (taral) *a* Liquid, unsteady; ~ਤਾ Liquidity, fluidity, fickleness.

ਤਰਲਾ (tarlaa) *n m* Entreaty, supplication; ~ਕਰਨਾ To beseech, to beg, to entreat.

ਤਰਵੰਜਾ (tarvanjaa) *a* Fifity-three.

ਤਰਾਉਣਾ (taraaunaa) *v* To float.

ਤਰਾਈ (taraaee) *n f* Foothill, low land, meadow, marsh; Watering the new construction.

ਤਰਾਸ਼ਣਾ (traashnaa) *v* To trim, to prune, to shape, to cut.

ਤਰਾਸਦੀ (taraasdee) *n f* tragedy.

ਤਰਾਕ (taraak) *a n m* Swimmer.

ਤਰਾਕੀ (taraakee) *n f* Swimming, aquatics.

ਤਰਾਜ਼ੂ (taraazoo) *n m* Scales, balance.

ਤਰਾਟ (traat) *n f* Shooting pain.

ਤਰਾਨਾ (traanaa) *n m* A kind of song, melody, harmony, anthem.

ਤਰਾਰਾ (traaraa) *n* Quickness, expedition.

ਤਰਾਵਟ (traavat) *n f* Freshness, moisture, verdure.

ਤ੍ਰਿਆ (tariaa) *n f* Woman, female, wife; Also ਤ੍ਰੀਆ or ਤਰੀਜਾ

ਤਰੀਕ (tareek) *n f* Date; Also ਤ੍ਰੀਕ or ਤਾਰੀਖ

ਤਰੀਕਾ (tareekaa) *n m* Manner, way, mode, method.

ਤਰੀਫ਼ (tareef) *n f* Praise, eulogy, description.

ਤ੍ਰੀਮਤ (treemat) *n f* Women, wife. Also ਤਰੀਮਤ

ਤਰੁੱਟੀ (trutee) *n f* Defect, flaw, short coming; Also ਤੁਟੀ

ਤਰੁਪਣਾ (trupnaa) *v* To stitch, to sew, to be stitched.

ਤਰੇਹ (treh) *n f* Thirst, longing.

ਤ੍ਰੇਲ (Trel) *n f* Dew.

ਤ੍ਰੇੜ (trer) *n f* Crack, fissure, fracture. Also ਤਰੇੜ

ਤ੍ਰੇੜਨਾ (trernaa) *v* to chap.

ਤ੍ਰੈਕੋਣ (trikon) *n m* Triangle. Also ਤਿਕੋਣ

ਤ੍ਰੌਂਕਣਾ (traunknaa) *v* To sprinkle, to spray. Also ਤਰੌਂਕਣਾ

ਤ੍ਰੌਂਕਾ (traunkaa) *n m* Sprinkling, spray. Also ਤਰੌਂਕਾ

ਤਲ (tal) *n m* Bottom, surface, depth.

ਤਲਖ (talakh) *a* Bitter, pungent, acrid, hot, acerb, acerbate; ~ਜ਼ਬਾਨ With a bitting tongue, impolite, acrimonious; ~ਮਿਜ਼ਾਜ Hot or harsh temperament; hot tempered, choleric, irascible.

ਤਲਖੀ (talkhee) *n f* Bitterness, acridity.

ਤਲਣਾ (talnaa) *v* To fry.

ਤਲਬ (talab) *n f* Desire, longing, craving, demand; Pay, salary; ~ਹੋਣੀ To have want, to desire, to need.

ਤਲਬੀ (talbee) *n f* Summon, call, requisition.

ਤਲਮਲਾਉਣਾ (talmalaaunaa) *v* To fidget, to writhe.

ਤਲਮਲਾਹਟ (talmalaahaṭ) *n f* Writhing, restlessness, distress.

ਤਲਵਾ (talvaa) *n m* Sole, bottom.

ਤਲਵਾਰ (talwaar) *n f* Sword, sabre, bilbo.

ਤਲਾ (talaa) *n m* Sole, bottom, base, the neither side; (sea) Bed.

ਤਲਾਅ (talaa) *n m* Tank, pond, water reservoir. Also **ਤਲਾਉ**

ਤਲਾਸ਼ (talaash) *n f* Search, investigation.

ਤਲਾਸ਼ੀ (talaashee) *n f* Search, rummage; ~ਲੈਣੀ To carry out search, to frisk.

ਤਲਾਕ (talaak) *n m* Divorce; ~ਸ਼ੁਦਾ Divorced; ~ਦੇਣਾ To divorce; ~ਨਾਮਾ Decree or document of divorce.

ਤਲਾਂਜਲੀ (talaanjalee) *n f* Abjuration, rununciation. Also **ਤਿਲਾਂਜਲੀ**

ਤਲਾਫ਼ੀ (talaafee) *n f* Amends, recompense, redress, remedy; ~ਕਰਨਾ To recumpensate, to make good. to make up.

ਤਲਾਬ (talaab) *n m* Tank, water, pool.

ਤਲਿੱਸਮ (talissam) *n m* Magic, charm, talisman.

ਤਲਿੱਸਮੀ (talissmee) *a* Magical.

ਤਲੀ (talee) *n f* Hand palm, sole; ~ਭਰ In small quantitiy, just a little, palmful.

ਤਲੂਨੀ (taloonee) *n f* Oilcan.

ਤਵੱਕੋ (tawakkoo) *n f* Expectation, hope.

ਤਵੱਜਾ (tawajjaa) *n f* Attention, favour, compliments, kindness.

ਤਵਾ (tawaa) *n m* Round iron plate for baking bread.

ਤਵਾਜ਼ਨ (twaazan) *n m* Balance, equilibrium.

ਤੜੱਕ (taṛrakk) *n f* Cracking or breaking sound, snapping.

ਤੜਕਣਾ (taraknaa) *v* To fry.

ਤੜਕਾ (taṛkaa) *n m* Day break, early morning.

ਤੜਤੜਾਹਟ (tartraahaṭ) *n f* Cracking or pattering, sound.

ਤੜਪ (taṛap) *n f* Writhing, palpitation, violent passion, keen desire.

ਤੜਪਣਾ (taṛapnaa) *v* To throb, to be dying for, to writhe, to be in agony, to pine, to flutter.

ਤੜਫੜਾਉਣਾ (taṛpharaaunaa) *v* To flutter, to palpitate.

ਤੜਫਾਉਣਾ (taṛphaaunaa) *v* To cause

to palpitate, or flutter, to put into a state of agitation.

ਤੜਫਾਟ (tarphaat) *n m* Widespread pain, wailing, suffering, misery.

ਤੜਾਕ (taraak) *n f* Cracking sound, crashing sound.

ਤੜਾਗ (taraag) *n m* Belt, zone, circle.

ਤੜਾਤੜ (taraatar) *adv* Quickly, continuously, one after the other.

ਤੜਿੰਗ (taring) *a* Angry, displeased, surly, sulky.

ਤੜੀ (taree) *n f* Drubbing, false pride reproof.

ਤਾਅ (taa) *n m* Heat, warmth, rage, temperature.

ਤਾਇਆ (taaiyaa) *n m* Elder paternal uncle (elder brother of father).

ਤਾਇਨਾਤ (taainaat) *a* Posted, appointed.

ਤਾਇਨਾਤੀ (taainaatee) *n f* Posting, appointment.

ਤਾਈਂ (taaeen) *adv* Upto, till.

ਤਾਈ (taaee) *n f* Elder paternal aunt.

ਤਾਈਦ (taaeed) *n f* Confirmation, seconding, ratification, support.

ਤਾਸ਼ (taash) *n f* Playing cards.

ਤਾਸੀਰ (taaseer) *n f* Effect, influence, impression.

ਤਾਹਨਾ (taahnaa) *n m* Taunt, sarcasm, quip; ~ਮਾਰਨਾ To taunt. to deride. Also ਤਾਨ੍ਹਾ

ਤਾਕ (taak) *n f a* Doorflap; Expectation, longing; Odd, fixed gaze; adept, skilled.

ਤਾਕਤ (taakat) *n f* Strength, force, might, power, vigour; ~ਵਰ Strong, powerful.

ਤਾਕੀ (taakee) *n f* window, arch.

ਤਾਕੀਦ (taakeed) *n f* Injunction, order or request with emphasis; ~ ਕਰਨੀ To emphasise, to stress; ~ਨ Repeatedly, emphatically.

ਤਾਗਾ (taagaa) *n m* Thread.

ਤਾਂਗਾ (taangaa) *n m* Horse driven carriage. Also ਟਾਂਗਾ

ਤਾਂਘ (taangh) *n f* Anxiety, expectation, desire, yearning, craving.

ਤਾਂਘਣਾ (taanghnaa) *v* To expect, to desire, to yearn.

ਤਾਂਘੜਨਾ (taangharnaa) *v* To behave rudely, arrogantly, defiantly.

ਤਾਜ (taaj) *n m* Crown, diadem; ~ਪੋਸ਼ੀ Coronation.

ਤਾਜ਼ਗੀ (taazgee) *n f* Freshness, greenness, health, pleasure.

ਤਾਜਰ (taajar) *n m* Trader, merchant, dealer, businessman.

ਤਾਜ਼ਾ (taazaa) *a* Fresh, recent.

ਤਾਣਨਾ (taannaa) *v* To stretch, to brace, to spread, to expand.

ਤਾਂਤਾ (taantaa) *n m* Series, long line.

ਤਾਦਾਦ (taadaad) *n f* Number,

quantity.

ਤਾਨ (taan) *n f* Tune, tone, trill; ~ਪੂਰਾ A stringed musical instrument.

ਤਾਨਾਸ਼ਾਹ (taanaashah) *n m* Autocrat, dictator.

ਤਾਨਾਸ਼ਾਹੀ (taanaashaahee) *n f* Dictatorship, autocracy, absolute rule.

ਤਾਪ (taap) *n m* Heat, warmth, fever; ~ਮਾਨ Temperature.

ਤਾਬ (taab) *n f* Luster, Splendour, endurance, power.

ਤਾਬੜ-ਤੋੜ (taabar-tor) *adv* Continually, successively, swiftly, promptly.

ਤਾਂਬਾ (taambaa) *n m* Copper.

ਤਾਬਿਆ (taabiaa) *a adv* Dependent, obedient, subordinate; Under command.

ਤਾਬੂਤ (taaboot) *n m* Coffin, effigy.

ਤਾਬੇਦਾਰ (taabedaar) *a* Loyal, dutiful, obedient, submissive.

ਤਾਬੇਦਾਰੀ (taabedaaree) *n f* Loyalty, obedience, submissiveness, allegiance.

ਤਾਮੀਰ (taameer) *n f* Construction, structure.

ਤਾਮੀਲ (taameel) *n f* Execution, compliance, obeyance; ~ਕਰਨੀ To implement, to carryout, to obey.

ਤਾਰ (taar) *n f* Wire, string, filament, thread, line; Telegram, wire; ਕੰਡਿਆਲੀ~ Barbed wire; ~ਕਰਨਾ To make thread bare, to untwist a thread; ~ਕੋਲ Coal tar; ~ਤੋੜਨੀ To disconnect, to dislocate; ~ਘਰ Telegraph office; ~ਜਵਾਬੀ Reply paid telegram; ~ਛਾਪਾ Teleprinter; ~ਦੇਣਾ To wire, to telegraph.

ਤਾਰਕ (taarak) *n m a* Saviour, redeemer, deliverer.

ਤਾਰਨ ਸ਼ਕਤੀ (Taaran-Shaktee) *n f* Buoyancy; ~ਹਾਰ Saviour, liberator.

ਤਾਰਨਾ (taarnaa) *v* To cause to swim, to float; To grant remission of sins, to exempt from future, transmigration, to emancipate, to save.

ਤਾਰਾ (taaraa) *n* Star, planet; ਅੱਖਾਂ ਦਾ~ Beloved, apple of eyes; ~ਚਿੰਨ੍ਹ Asterik.

ਤਾਰੀਖ਼ (taareekh) *n f* Date, fixed date, history; ~ਦਾਨ Historian; ~ਵਾਰ Datewise, chronologically.

ਤਾਰੀਫ਼ (taareef) *n f* Praise, eulogy, commendation.

ਤਾਲ (taal) *n f* (1) Musical tune, rhythm; (2) Tank, swimming pool; ~ਮੇਲ Coordination.

ਤਾਲਾ (taalaa) *n m* Lock padlock; ~ਬੰਦੀ Lockout.

ਤਾਲੀ (taalee) *n f* Key, small lock;

ਤਾੜੀ Clapping of hands; ~ਵਜਾਉਣੀ To clap, to applaud. Also ਤਾੜੀ

ਤਾਲੀਮ (taleem) *n f* Education, study, tuition; ~ਦੇਣਾ To teach, to educate, to instruct.

ਤਾਵਾਨ (taawaan) *n m* Penalty, damages, ransom.

ਤਾੜ (taar) *n m* (1) Palm tree caryota urens; (2) Watch, observation, look out; ~ਜਾਣਾ To spot, to espy, to guess; ~ਰਖਣੀ To be on the watch; ~ਲੈਣਾ To detect, to scent; ~ਵਿਚ In ambush; Under a watch.

ਤਾੜਨਾ (taarnaa) *v* (1) To conceive, to comperhend, to understand, to guess; (2) To chide, to rebuke, to admonish, to censure, to scold, to reprimand.

ਤਾੜੀ (taaree) *n f* (1) Toddy; (2) intent, gaze, stare; (3) Clapping.

ਤਿਉੜੀ (tiooree) *n f* Frown, scowl, angry look, wrinkle in brow.

ਤਿਓਹਾਰ (tiohaar) *n m* Festival.

ਤਿਆਗ (tiaag) *n m* Relinquishment, abandonment, abnegation, sacrifice, resignation, renunciation.

ਤਿਆਗਣਾ (tiaagnaa) *v* To abandon, to abdicate, to secede, to relinquish, to forgo, to abnegate, to renounce, to sacrifice.

ਤਿਆਗੀ (tiaagee) *a n m* Renouncer; recluse, hermit, ascetic.

ਤਿਆਰ (tiaar) *a* Ready, prompt, prepared, complete; ~ਕਪੜੇ Readymade clothes; ~ਕਰਨਾ To get ready.

ਤਿਆਰੀ (tiaaree) *n f* Readiness, preparation; completion; physical fitness; willingness; ~ਕਰਨੀ To be ready, to prepare, to make arrangements or preparations (ful).

ਤਿਹੱਤਰ (tihattar) *a* Seventy-three.

ਤਿਹਾਈ (tihaaee) *n f* One third, third part.

ਤਿਕੜੀ (tikaree) *n f* Group of three, trio, triad.

ਤਿੱਖਲ (tikkhal) *a* (son) born after three daughters or (daughter) born after three sons.

ਤਿੱਖਾ (tikkhaa) *a* Sharp, pungent, fast, smart, swift; ~ਮੋੜ Sharp turn.

ਤਿਜਾਰਤ (tijaarat) *n f* Business, trade.

ਤਿਜ਼ਾਬ (tizaab) *n m* Acid. Also ਤੇਜ਼ਾਬ

ਤਿਜੋਰੀ (tijoree) *n f* Safe, cash box.

ਤਿੱਤਰ (tittar) *n m* Partridge, pheasant; ~ਹੋ ਜਾਣਾ To run away; ~ਬਿਤਰ ਹੋਣਾ To disperse, to scatter, to vanish.

ਤਿਤਰਾ (titraa) *a* Dotted, pied, multicoloured.

ਤਿੱਤਲੀ (tittlee) *n f* Butterfly, ladybird.

ਤਿਨਕਾ (tinkaa) *n m* Straw, sedge, particle.

ਤਿਭਾਸ਼ੀ (tibaashee) *a* Trilingual, triglot.

ਤਿਮੰਜਲਾ (timanjalaa) *a m* Three-storeyed; A three-storey building.

ਤਿਮਾਹਾ (timaahaa) *a* Quarterly.

ਤਿਮਾਹੀ (timaahee) *n f* Quarter, three months.

ਤਿਰਸੂਲ (tirshool) *n m* Trident.

ਤਿਰਛਾ (tirchhaa) *a* Slanting, oblique, crooked, transvers.

ਤਿਲ (til) *n m* Mole, black spot on the body; Sesame seed; ~ਭਰ An iota, a little quantity; ~ਦਾ ਤਾੜ ਬਣਾਉਣਾ To make a mountain of a mole hill.

ਤਿਲ੍ਹਕਣ (tilhkaṇ) *a* Slippery (Place) *n* Slipping

ਤਿਲ੍ਹਕਣਾ (tillknaa) *v* To slip, to slide, to lose hold.

ਤਿਲਕ (tilak) *n m* Coronation, coloured, mark on the forehead.

ਤਿੱਲਾ (tillaa) *n m* Gold lace, gold thread.

ਤਿੱਲੀ (tillee) *n f* Spleen.

ਤਿੜ (tiṛ) *n f* Pride, arrogance, egotism; ~ਤਿੜ Crackling sound

ਤਿੜਕ (tiṛak) *n* Crack.

ਤਿੜਕਣਾ (tiṛaknaa) *v* To crack, to crackle.

ਤੀਹ (tee) *a* Thirty.

ਤੀਕ (teek) *prep* To, upto, till, until.

ਤੀਖਣ (teekhaṇ) *a* Acrid, pungent, acute, intense, vehement.

ਤੀਬਰ (teebar) *a* Intense, Sharp, severe, fierce, ardent; ~ਤਾ Intensity, vehemence, sharpness, ardency, fierceness, severity.

ਤੀਰ (Teer) *n m* Arrow, dart, spoke; waterside, bank; crest; ~ਹੋ ਜਾਣਾ To run away, to flee; ~ਤੁਕਾ Wild guess.

ਤੀਰਥ (teerath) *n* A sacred place, holy spot, shrine, pilgrimage centre; ~ਯਾਤਰਾ Pilgrimage; ~ਯਾਤਰੀ Pilgrim.

ਤੀਲੀ (teelee) *n f* Match stick; (pl) spokes of a bicycle; ~ਲਾਉਣੀ To set fire to.

ਤੀਵੀਂ (teeveen) *n f* Women, wife, fair sex; ~ਜਾਤ Eve, women folk; Also ਤੀਮੀ

ਤੁਹਮਤ (tohmat) *n f* Calumny, false accusation, allegation, blame, aspersion, slander, slur; ~ਲਾਉਣੀ To cast aspersion on, to slur, to accuse.

ਤੁਹਾਥੋਂ (tuhaathon) *a* From you.

ਤੁਹਾਨੂੰ (tuhaanoon) *adv* To you.

ਤੁਕ (tuk) *n f* Part of a song, a line of poetry, a verse; ~ਜੋੜਨੀ To rhyme; ~ਬੰਦੀ Versification, rhyming; ~ਬੇਤੁਕੀ At random, irrelevant, unconnected.

ਤੁਕਲ (tukal) *n f* Kite.

ਤੁੱਕਾ (tukka) *n m* Corn-comb; ~ਲਾਉਣਾ (ਮਾਰਨਾ) To guess, to concoct.

ਤੁਖਮ (tukham) *n m* seed, semen; egg; ~ਹਰਾਮ ਦਾ Illegal, illegitimate.

ਤੁੱਛ (tuchchh) *a* Small, poor, worthless, mean, absurd, insignificant, trifling, pitiful.

ਤੁਣਕਾ (tunkaa) *n m* Sudden pull, jerk.

ਤੁਤਲਾਉਣਾ (tutalaaunaa) *v* to lisp, to prattle.

ਤੁਤਲਾਹਟ (tutlaahat) *n f* Lisp, prattle.

ਤੁੰਦ (tund) *a* Fierce, ferocious, violent.

ਤੁਨਕ-ਮਿਜ਼ਾਜ (tunak mizaaj) *a* Mumpish.

ਤੁੰਨਣਾ (tunnaa) *v* To pack, to ram, to stuff, to thrust, to the full.

ਤੁਪਣਾ (tupnaa) *v* To be sewn or stitched.

ਤੁਫ਼ਾਨ (tufaan) *n m* Tempest, turmoil, gale, typhoon, hurricane, disaster; ~ਮਚਾਉਣਾ To create turmoil, to become boisterous.

ਤੁਫ਼ਾਨੀ (tufaanee) *a* Stromy, tempestuous, violent; ~ਹਮਲਾ Blitz; ~ਝਖੜ Blizzard; ~ਦਲ Flying squad; ~ਦੌਰਾ Flying visit.

ਤੁਫ਼ੀਕ (tufeek) *n f* Capacity, capability.

ਤੁਰਸ਼ (turash) *a* Bitter, pungent, acid, acidic, sour; ~ਮਿਜ਼ਾਜ Ill tempered, of irritable disposition.

ਤੁਰਤ (turat) *adv* Quickly, immediately, hastily, promptly, rapidly, swiftly, speedily, hurriedly. Also ਤੁਰੰਤ

ਤੁਰਨਾ (turnaa) *v* To walk, to proceed.

ਤੁੱਰਾ (turraa) *n m* Red breasted fly catcher, flying end of turban.

ਤੁਲਣਾ (tulnaa) *v* To be weighed, in a balance.

ਤੁਲਨਾ (tulnaa) *n f* Comparison, simile; ~ਕਰਨਾ To compare.

ਤੁਲਾਈ (tulaaee) *n f* Padded matteress, light quilt; Wages for weighing.

ਤੁੜਾਉਣਾ (turaaunaa) *v* To cause to be broken, to oncash, to exchange small coins for a higher valued note.

ਤੂਤੀ (tootee) *n f* Trumpet, horn. Also ਤੂਤਨੀ

ਤੂੜੀ (tooree) *n f* Wheat chaff.

ਤੇਈ (te-ee) *a* Twenty-three.

ਤੇਈਆ (teiaa) *n m* Malaria.

ਤੇਸਾ (tesaa) *n m* Adze.

ਤੇਹਾ (tehaa) *adv* Like that, so.

ਤੇਗ (teg) *n f* Sword, sabre.

ਤੇਜ (tej) *n m a adv* Splendour, glory, lustre, magnificence; Fast, speedy, swift, quick; sharp, piercing shrewd, clever; Intelligent; Hot, pungent, strong; Swiftly; ~ਕਰਨਾ To sharpen; To speed up; ~ਜ਼ਬਾਨ Talkative; Rude; ~ਤਰਾਰ Clever, smart; ~ਵੰਤ Glorious, splendid, luminous.

ਤੇਜ਼ਾਬ (tezaab) *n m* Acid.

ਤੇਜ਼ੀ (tezee) *n f* Sharpness, quickness, rapidity, speed, swiftness, readiness, fastness, poignancy.

ਤੇਤੀ (tetee) *a* Thrity-three.

ਤੇਥੋਂ (tethon) *adv* From you, by you.

ਤੇਲ (tel) *n m* Oil; ~ਦੇਣਾ To oil, to lubricate.

ਤੇਲੀ (tellee) *n m* Oilman.

ਤੈਸ਼ (taish) *n m* Wrath, anger, rage, strong emotion.

ਤੈਰਨਾ (tairnaa) *v* To swim, to float.

ਤੈਰਾਕ (tairaak) *n m* Swimmer.

ਤੋਸ਼ਾ (toshaa) *n m* Sugar coated cereals, eatable thing; Supplies, provision, store; ~ਖਾਨਾ Store room, a place for keeping precious articles.

ਤੋੱਟਾ (tottaa) *n m* Loss; deficiency; lack, scarcity.

ਤੋਡਾ (todaa) *n m* Camel's young.

ਤੋਤਲਾ (totlaa) *a* Lisping, stultering, stammering.

ਤੋਤਾ (totaa) *n m* Parrot; ਬੁੱਢਾ~ Too old to learn.

ਤੋਂਦ (tond) *n m* Pot belly, stomach, paunch.

ਤੋਦਾ (todaa) *n m* Heap, large accumulated mass; ਬਰਫ ਦਾ~ Iceberg.

ਤੋਪ (top) *n f* Gun, cannon; ~ਦਾ ਗੋਲਾ Cannon ball; ~ਖਾਨਾ Artillery battery; ~ਦਾਰ Gunner; ~ਚੀ Gunner, conductor of artillery.

ਤੋਪਾ (topaa) *n m* Stitch.

ਤੋਰਨਾ (tornaa) *v* To despatch, to cause to depart, to dismiss.

ਤੋਲਣਾ (tolṇaa) *v* To weigh, to estimate, to balance.

ਤੋਲਾ (tolaa) *n m* Weight of 11.664 gms (12 mashas); Weighman.

ਤੋੜ (toṛ) *n m a* Beach, break, Crack; Climax, extent, the utmost of beginning; ~ਦੇਣਾ To break down, to disband, to smash; ~ਚੜ੍ਹਨਾ To reach completion, to end; ~ਫੋੜ Sabotage, breakage, rupture.

ਤੋੜਨਾ (toṛnaa) *v* To break, to pluck, to cut, to snap, to crash.

ਤੌਹੀਨ (tauheen) *n f* Insult, disgrace, defamation.

ਤੌਬਾ (taubaa) *n f* Penitence, repentence, determination never to do again bad some things; **~ਕਰਨੀ** To forswear, to repent, to vow never to repeat; **~ਤੋਬਾ** An expression of horror. Also **ਤੋਬਾ**

ਤੌਰ (taur) *n m* Method, mode, manner, fashion, way; **~ਤਰੀਕਾ** Behaviour, conduct.

ਤੌਲੀਆ (tauliaa) *n m* Towel.

ਤੌਲੇ (taule) *adv* Hastily, quickly, hurriedly.

ਤੌੜਾ (tauṛaa) *n m* Earthern cooking pot.

ਥ

ਥ Twenty second letter of Gurmukhi alphabets, pronounced as 'thathaa'.

ਥਹੀ (thaee) *n f* Pile; Wad; Small heap or stack.

ਥਹੁ (Thaho) *n m* Inkling, clue, trace, location, information; Recollection, memory; method; ~**ਪਤਾ** Address, location; ~**ਟਿਕਾਣਾ** Whereabout, place; ~**ਲਾਉਣਾ** To Trace, to locate, to discover.

ਥਕਣਾ (thaknaa) *v* To be tired, to be weary, to be fatigued.

ਥਕਾਉ (thakaaoo) *a* Tiring, wearing, wearying, gruelling, wearisome, fatiguing, tiresome; Exasperating, irksome, tedious.

ਥਕਾਉਣਾ (thakaaunaa) *v* To tire, to weary, to fatigue.

ਥਕਾਵਟ (thakaavat) *n f* Weariness, fatigue, exhaustion, tiresomeness; ~**ਲਗਣਾ** To get tired, to get exhausted.

ਥਣ (than) *n m* Teat, udder, breast.

ਥੱਥਲਾ (thathlaa) *n m* Stammerer; Also ਥੱਥਾ

ਥਥਲਾਉਣਾ (thathlaaunaa) *v* To stammer, to lisp.

ਥੱਥਾ (thathaa) *a* Stammerer, stutterer.

ਥਪਕਣਾ (thapaknaa) *v* To pat, to soothe, to solace, to tap.

ਥਪਕੀ (thapkee) *n f* Pat, stroke.

ਥਪਣਾ (thapnaa) *v* To dab, to be smear, to impose, to apportion.

ਥੱਪੜ (thappar) *n m* Slap, spank, flap.

ਥਪੇੜਾ (thaperaa) *n m* Forceful slap; Also ਥਪੇੜ

ਥੱਬਾ (thabbaa) *n m* Heap, pile (grass or vegetable or papers), united bundle.

ਥੱਬੀ (thabbee) *n m* A smaller bundle or pile.

ਥੰਮ (thamm) *n m* Pillar, Support, post.

ਥੰਮ੍ਹਣਾ (thammnaa) *v* To stop, to cease, to support, to restrain.

ਥਰਕਣਾ (tharaknaa) *v* To tremble, to shake, to quake, to waver.

ਥਰਥਰਾਉਣਾ (tharthraaunaa) *v* To tremble, to quiver, to shiver, to shake, to trill, to vibrate.

ਥਲ (thal) *n m* Place, dryland, sandy region; ~**ਸੈਨਾ** Army, land forces

ਥਲਕਾ (thalkaa) *n m* Sensation; ~**ਮਾਰ**

ਦੇਣਾ To create sensation.

ਥਲਾ (thallaa) *n m* Base, basement, plinth, ground, footing, bottom, lower part.

ਥੱਲੇ (thalle) *adv* Under, beneath, below.

ਥੜਾ (tharraa) *n m* Platform, dais, stage, rostrum.

ਥਾਂ (thaan) *n f* Place, locality, site, spot, situation, venue, room; ~ਦੇਣੀ To accommodate, to house, to make room; ~ਬਦਲੀ Transfer, replacement, displacement; ~ਮੱਲਣੀ To occupy, to supplant.

ਥਾਊਂ (thaaun) *adv* Instead of, in place of, for.

ਥਾਹ (thaah) *n f* Bottom, depth, limit; ~ਪਾਉਣੀ To understand, to fathom; ~ਲੜਨੀ To seek refuge.

ਥਾਣਾ (thaanaa) *n m* Police station.

ਥਾਣੇਦਾਰ (thaanedaar) *n m* Police inspector office incharge of a police station.

ਥਾਨ (thaan) *n m* Roll of cloth (20 to 40 metres); Place, spot, site.

ਥਾਪਣਾ (thaapnaa) *v* To appoint, to fix, to engage, to install, to set.

ਥਾਲੀ (thaalee) *n f* Metal plate, small dish; ~ਦਾ ਬੈਗੰਨ Fickel person.

ਥਿਤ (thit) *n f* Date.

ਥਿੰਦ (thind) *n f* Grease, Wax. Also ਥਿੰਧ

ਥਿੰਦਾ (thindaa) *a* Greasy, oily.

ਥਿੰਦਿਆਈ (thindiaaee) *n f* Greasiness, oilness, lubricity.

ਥਿੜਕਣ (thirkaṇ) *n f* Deviation, slipping, aberration.

ਥਿੜਕਨਾ (thiraknaa) *v* To err, to be unsettled, to stagger, to slip, to stumble.

ਥਿੜਕਵਾਂ (thirkvaan) *a* Stumbling, staggering, unstable; uneven, rough slippery (ground or path).

ਥੁਕ (thuk) *n f* Spit, saliva, sputum; ~ਕੇ ਚਟਣਾ To break one's promise; ~ਦੇਣਾ To spit, to leave, to give up; ~ਲਾਉਣੀ To deceive, to dupe, to cheat.

ਥੁਕਣਾ (thuknaa) *v* To spit, to spittle, to curse.

ਥੁਥਨੀ (thuthnee) *n f* Animal's mouth; snout, muzzle. Also ਥੁਥਨੀ

ਥੁੰਨ (thunn) *n m* snout; ~ਮੁੰਨ Silent, sullen, illhumoured.

ਥੁੜ (thur) *n f* Want, scarcity, paucity, dearth, inadequacy, need, rarity, shortage.

ਥੁੜਨਾ (thurnaa) *v* To be in want, to feel hard up.

ਥੈਲਾ (thailaa) *n m* Sack, large bag.

ਥੈਲੀ (thailee) *n f* Small bag, pouch, purse, follicle, alary.

ਥੋਕ (thok) *a* Wholesale, bulk.

ਥੋਥਾ (thothaa) *a* Hollow, empty, worthless; **~ਪਣ** Hollowness, emptiness, vacuousness.

ਥੋਥੜਾ (thothṛaa) *n m* Snout of beast, puffed face.

ਥੋਪਣਾ (thopṇaa) *v* To foist upon, to impose upon.

ਥੋੜਾ (thoṛaa) *a* Small, inadequate, little, insufficient, meagre; **~ਥੋੜਾ** By & by, in small amounts; **~ਬਹੁਤਾ** More or less about.

ਥੌਹ (thau) *n m* Memory, recollection; estimate, measure; **~ਟਿਕਾਣਾ** Whereabouts; address; **~ਲਾਉਣਾ** Estimate, assess, to have or get a measure of.

ਦ

ਦ Twenty third letter of Gurmukhi alphabets, pronounced as 'daddaa'.

ਦਇਆ (daiaa) *n f* Pity, compassion, mercy, clemency, kindness, sympathy; ~ਲੂ/~ਵਾਨ Merciful, kind, compassionate, gracious.

ਦਸਖਤ (daskhat) *n m* Signature, handwriting. Also **ਦਸਤਖਤ**

ਦੱਸਣਾ (dassnaa) *v* To tell, to direct, to imply, to inform, to intimate, to acquaint.

ਦਸਤ (dast) *n m* (1) Hand; (2) Loose motion, dysentry, diarrhoea; ~ਕਾਰ Handicraftman, artisan; ~ਕਾਰੀ Handicraft, handwork; ~ਗੀਰ Helper, supporter, succourer; ~ਲਗਣੇ To suffer from diarrhoea.

ਦਸਤਕ (dastak) *n f* Knock, knocking.

ਦਸਤਰਖ਼ਾਨ (dastarkhaan) *n m* Dining table; Table cloth of a dining table.

ਦਸਤਾ (dastaa) *n m* Quire (of paper); Grip, helve, shank, handle of an instrument; Pounder, pestle; Troop, corps, squad.

ਦਸਤਾਨਾ (dastanaa) *n m* Glove, guantlet.

ਦਸਤਾਰ (dastaar) *n f* Turban; ~ਬੰਦੀ Turban ceremony; Consecration.

ਦਸਤਾਵੇਜ਼ (dastavez) *n m* Document, deed, bond; ~ਖ਼ਾਨਾ Archives.

ਦਸਤੀ (dastee) *a adv* Manual, hand made, through hand; Per bearer.

ਦਸਤੂਰ (dastoor) *n m* Custom, fashion, mode, method, manner, convention.

ਦਸਤੂਰੀ (dasturee) *n f* Customary, legal; Customary commission, perquisite.

ਦਸ਼ਮਲਵ (dashamlav) *n m* Decimal, decimal point.

ਦਸ਼ਮਿਕ (dashmik) *a* Decimal.

ਦਸ਼ਾ (dashaa) *n f* Condition, state, circumstance, position.

ਦਸਾਉਰੀ (dasauree) *a* Imported, foreign Also **ਦਸੌਰੀ**

ਦਸ਼ਾਬਦੀ (dashabdee) *n f* Decade.

ਦਸੋਰ (dasor) *n m* Foreign country, alien land.

ਦਹਾਈ (dahaaee) *n f* Place and value of tens digit in a number.

ਦਹਾਕਾ (dahaakaa) *n m* Tens, decade.

ਦਹਾੜਨਾ (dahaarnaa) *v* To roar.

ਦਹਿਸ਼ਤ (daheshat) *n f* Terror, panic, awe, dread, fear; ~ਗਰਦ Terrorist; ~ਗਰਦੀ Terrorism; ~ਗੋਜ਼ Horrible; ~ਨਾਕ Fearful, Terrible, dreadful.

ਦਹਿਲਣਾ (dahelnaa) *v* To tremble with fear, to be terrified, to dread, to get freightened.

ਦਹਿਲੀਜ਼ (dahileez) *n f* Doorsill, threshold. Also **ਦਲੀਜ਼**

ਦਹੀ (dahee) *n n* Curd, youghurt, coagulated milk; ~ਜਮਾਉਣਾ To curdle.

ਦਹੇਜ (dahej) *n* Dowry. Also **ਦਹੇਜ**

ਦਕਿਆਨੂਸ (dakiaanoos) *n m a* Stereotyped natured man, hackneyed viewed man.

ਦਕਿਆਨੂਸੀ (dakiaanoosee) *a* Stereotyped or hackneyed; outdated, obsolete, conservative.

ਦਖਣ (dakhan) *n m* The south, Deccan.

ਦਖਣਾ (dakhnaa) *n f* Donation, charity, alms. Also **ਦੱਛਣਾ**

ਦਖਲ (dakhal) *n m* Interference, intervention, intrusion, intermission, occupancy, possesion; ~ਅੰਦਾਜੀ Interference, intervention, meddling; ~ਦੇਣਾ To interfere, to invene, to interpose, to meddle.

ਦੰਗ (dang) *a* Astonished, amazed, wonder-struck; ~ਕਰਨਾ To astonish, to surprise.

ਦੰਗਾਈ (dangaee) *n m* Riotous person or mob, one causing or taking part in hooligan, rioter.

ਦਗਣਾ (dagnaa) *v* To be fired, to sparkle, to be kindled.

ਦੰਗਲ (dangal) *n m* Arena, wrestling tournament.

ਦੰਗਲੀ (danglee) *a* Qurrelsome.

ਦਗਾ (dagaa) *n m* Betrayel, deceit, disloyalty, cheating; ~ਬਾਜ਼ Betrayer, deceiver, disloyal, treacherous.

ਦੰਗਾ (dangaa) *n m* Riot, turbulance, disturbance, hub-hub; ~ਫਸਾਦ Riot, rowdyism, turbulance.

ਦੰਡ (dand) *n m* Punishment, penalty, sentence, fine. Also **ਡੰਨ**

ਦੰਤ (dant) *a* Mammoth.

ਦੰਦ (dand) *n m* Tooth; ਹਾਥੀ ਦੇ~Tusk; ~ਕਢਣੇ To extract teeth, to smirk, to laugh, teething; ~ਸਾਜ਼ Dentist; ~ਕਥਾ Hearsay; ~ਖਟੇ ਕਰਨੇ To discourage, to defeat ~ਨਿਕਲਣੇ To teethe.

ਦਦਿਅਹੁਰਾ (dadiahura) *n m* Husband's grand father.

ਦਦੇਹਸ (dadehas) *n f* Grandmother-in-law; mother of father-in-law.

ਦੰਦੇਹਾਰ (dandehaar) *a* Dented, dentale, denticulate, toothed, serrated.

ਦਨਾ (danaa) *n m* Wise, intelligent, knowledgeable; wiseacre.

ਦਨਾਈ (danaaee) *n f* Wisdom; intelligence.

ਦਫ਼ਤਰ (daftar) *n m* Office, bureau; ~ਸ਼ਾਹੀ Bureaucracy.

ਦਫ਼ਤਰੀ (daftaree) *a n m* Official, ministerial, record keeper; Book-binder.

ਦਫ਼ਨ (dafan) *a* Buried, entombed.

ਦਫ਼ਨਾਉਣਾ (dafnaaunaa) *v* To bury, to entomb.

ਦਫ਼ਾ (dafaa) *n f a* (1) Clause, section of law; (2) A Single term, One time, one turn; ~ਖ਼ਉਣੀ To frame a charge; Out of the way; ~ਕਰਨਾ To remove, to repel, to bundle off.

ਦਫ਼ੇਦਾਰ (dafedaar) *n m* Corporal.

ਦਬਕਣਾ (dabaknaa) *v* To hide (in fear), to lurk, to crouch.

ਦਬਕਾ (dabkaa) *n m* Verbal threat, chiding, snub; Cellar, vault.

ਦਬਕਾਉਣਾ (dabkaaunaa) *v* To threaten, to intimidate, to snub, to bully.

ਦਬਣਾ (dabnaa) *v* To bury, to entomb; To press, to supress, to crush, to succumb; To conceal.

ਦਬਦਬਾ (dabdabaa) *n m* Sway, grandeur.

ਦਬਾਉਣਾ (dabaaunaa) *v* To press, to overpower, to compel, to bury, to crush. Also ਦਬਾਣਾ

ਦਬੀਰ (dabeer) *n m* Scribe, writer, clerk.

ਦਬੂ (daboo) *a* Recessive, servile.

ਦਬੇਲ (dabel) *a* Servile, timid, depressed, under dog; ~ਕਰਨਾ To tame.

ਦਬੋਚਣਾ (dabochnaa) *v* To catch hold of, to suppress.

ਦੰਭ (damb) *n m* Hypocrisy, dissimulation, fraud.

ਦੰਭੀ (dambee) *a* Hypocrite, coxcomb, ostentations.

ਦਮ (dam) *n m* Breath, endurance; ~ਤੋੜਨਾ To die, to breathe one's last; ~ਭਰ ਲਈ for a while, for a short duration Instant, moment; ~ਮਾਰਨਾ To boast; ~ਖ਼ਉਣਾ To smoke; ~ਲੈਣਾ To take rest.

ਦਮਕ (damak) *n f* Lustre, brilliance.

ਦਮਕਣਾ (damaknaa) *v* To shine, to glitter.

ਦਮਦਮਾ (damdamaa) *n m* Mound, battery, raised platform; Temporary resting place.

ਦਮਨ (daman) *n m* Repression, subjugation; ~ਕਰਨਾ To suppress, to crush, to subjugate; to quell.

ਦਮੜਾ (damraa) *n m* Rupee, wealth.

ਦਮਾ (damaa) *n m* Asthma.

ਦਮਾਮਾ (damaamaa) *n m* Large kettle drum, pomp and show.

ਦਰ (dar) *n* (1) Door, gate; (2) Rate, price.

ਦਰਸ਼ਕ (darshak) *n m* Spectator, on looker, visitor, sightseer.

ਦਰਸ਼ਨ (darshan) *n m* (1) Philosophy; (2) Face, view, sight, appearance, glimpse, holy presence; ~ਸ਼ਾਸਤਰ Philosophy.

ਦਰਸ਼ਨੀ (darshanee) *a* Worthseeing, good looking, handsome, beautiful.

ਦਰਕ (darak) *n m* Fear; Loose motion caused by intense fear; Crack, fissure.

ਦਰਕਣਾ (darknaa) *v* To be cracked, to be split, to be freigtened.

ਦਰਕਾਰ (darkaar) *n m a* Need, necessity; A needed, necessary, required.

ਦਰਕਿਨਾਰ (darkinaar) *adv* Apart from, not to speak of, besides.

ਦਰੱਖਤ (darakkhat) *n m* Tree.

ਦਰਖਾਸਤ (darkhaast) *n f* Application, appeal, petition, request; ~ਕਰਤਾ Applicant, appellant.

ਦਰਗੜੀ (daragdee) *a* Half backed.

ਦਰਗਾਹ (dargaah) *n f* Tomb of a saint, shrine, mosque, threshold, court of law.

ਦਰਜ (daraj) *a* Entered, registered.

ਦਰਜਨ (darjan) *n f* Dozen, twelve in number.

ਦਰਜਾ (darjaa) *n m* Class, degree, rank, category, standard, grade, division.

ਦਰਜ਼ੀ (darjee) *n m* Tailor; ~ਗੀਰੀ Tailoring.

ਦਰਜੇਦਾਰ (darjedaar) *a* Graduated, marked with degrees.

ਦਰਜੇਵਾਰ (darjewaar) *adv a* Gradually, gradual.

ਦਰਦ (darad) *n m* Pain, ache, pathos, agony, pity, mercy, sympathy; ਬੇ~ Hard hearted, pitiless; ~ਨਾਕ painful, dreadful, pitiable; ~ਵੰਡਾਉਣਾ To sympathize.

ਦਰਦੀ (dardee) *a* Sympathiser.

ਦਰਪਣ (darpaṇ) *n m* Mirror, looking glass.

ਦਰਬ (darb) *n m* Wealth, riches, property.

ਦਰਬਾਨ (darbaan) *n m* Gatekeeper;

watchman, gateman, janitor.
ਦਰਬਾਰ (darbaar) *n m* Royal court, hall of audience.
ਦਰਬਾਰੀ (darbaaree) *n m a* Courtier, related to court.
ਦਰਮਿਆਨ (darmiaan) *n m adv* Centre, middle; Amid, between, in the course of, amongst, amidst.
ਦਰਮਿਆਨਾ (darmiaanaa) *a* Average, moderate, middle.
ਦ੍ਰਵ (drav) *n m* Liquid, fluid; ~ਸੀਲ Fusible.
ਦਰਵਾਜ਼ਾ (darwaazaa) *n m* Door, gate, entrance. Also **ਦਰ-ਦਵਾਰ**
ਦਰਵੇਸ਼ (darvesh) *n m* Hermit, a muslim saint, mendicant, recluse, beggar.
ਦਰੜ (darar) *a* Coarsely ground, crushed; crushed grain (used as cattle feed); ~ਫਰੜ Crushed partly or superficially; (something) done haphazardly, half-baked.
ਦਰੜਨਾ (dararnaa) *v* To crush, grind; to destroy, annihilate.
ਦੱਰਾ (darraa) *n m* Mountain pass, pass.
ਦਰਾਣੀ (daraanee) *n f* Sister-in-law, wife of husband's younger brother.

ਦਰਾੜ (daraar) *n f* Fissure, crevice, cleft, crack, slit, opening; rift, chink; Distance or break (in relations).
ਦਰਿਆ (dariaa) *n m* River, stream; ~ਦਿਲ Large-hearted, generous, benevolent, charitable; ~ਦਿਲੀ Large-heartedness, generosity, benevolence, charitableness.
ਦਰਿਆਈ (dariaaee) *a* Riverine, fluvial, riparian.
ਦਰਿੰਦਾ (darindaa) *n m* Carnivorous animal, carnivore, any dangerous or ferocious animal, beast.
ਦਰੀ (daree) *n f* Cotton mat or carpet, durrie.
ਦਰੁਸਤ (darust) *a* Correct, right, accurate, true, proper, fit, precise; ~ਕਰਨਾ To correct, to amend; to rectify, to adjust, to repair, to set or put right, to improve; to chasten.
ਦਰੋਗਾ (darogaa) *n m* Superintendent; jailor, inspector; Sub-inspector of police, station house officer.
ਦਲ (dal) *n m* Party, organised band, group or team; Armed force, fighting force, army, troop; Swarm, multitude.

ਦਲਣਾ (dalṇaa) *a* To grind coarsely, to bruise with millstones, to crush, to pulverise; To annihilate, destroy.

ਦਲਦਲ (daldal) *n f* Marsh, swamp, bog, marshland; Quagmire, quag.

ਦੱਲਾ (dallaa) *n m* Pimp, procurer, pander, panderer, go-between, tout procuress.

ਦਲਾਲ (dalaal) *n m* Broker, middleman, commission-agent.

ਦਲਾਲੀ (dalaalee) *n f* Profession of **ਦਲਾਲ** Brokerage, commission.

ਦਲਾਵਰ (dalaavar) *a* Brave. Also **ਦਲੇਰ**

ਦਲਿੰਦਰ (dalidar) *n m* Sloth, lethargy, laziness, idleness, indolence, sluggishness.

ਦਲਿੰਦਰੀ (daliddaree) *a* Wretched, poor, lethargic, lazy.

ਦਲੀਲ (daleel) *n f* Argument, plea, reason, consideration.

ਦਲੇਰ (daler) *a* Brave, bold, courageous, daring, valiant, dashing; **~ਨਾ** Courageous, undaunting.

ਦਲੇਰੀ (daleree) *n f* Valour, courage, boldness, bravery, generosity.

ਦਵਾ (davaa) *n f* Cure, remedy, drug, medicine; **~ਖ਼ਾਨਾ** Dispensary, pharmacy; **~ਦਾਰੂ** Medication, treatment.

ਦਵਾਈ (dawaee) *n f* Medicine, drug; **~ਕਰਨਾ** To treat, to medicate.

ਦਵਾਤ (dwaat) *n f* Inkpot, Inkstand.

ਦਵਾਰ (dwaar) *n m* Gate, door, passage; **~ਪਾਲ** Gatekeeper. Also **ਦੁਆਰ** and **ਦਰਵਾਜ਼ਾ**

ਦੜਕਾਉਣਾ (darkaauṇaa) *v* To snub, to awe.

ਦੜਨਾ (darnaa) *v* To hide, to remain inactive, to keep silent.

ਦੜਬਾ (darbaa) *n m* Hen house, hen-coop, roost, loft.

ਦੜਾ (daraa) *n m* Mixed grain, fruit, etc; any impure, mixed, adulterated or sub-standard stuff. Also called **ਦੜੇ ਦਾ ਮਾਲ** A kind of gambling. Also called **ਸੱਟਾ**

ਦਾਅ (daa) *n m* (1) Opportunity, manoevre, trick (in wrestling also), (2) strategem; (3) Turn, bet, stake, wager; **~ਮਾਰਨਾ** To make use of a trick. Also **ਦਾਉ**

ਦਾਅਵਾ (daawaa) *n m* claim, law suit, case, demand; **~ਕਰਨਾ** To sue, to claim. Also **ਦਾਹਵਾ** and **ਦਾਵਾ**

ਦਾਇਰਾ (daairaa) *n m* Circle, sphere, ring, circuit, society, club.

ਦਾਈ (daaee) *n f* Nurse, midwife.

ਦਾਸ (daas) *n m* Slave, servant, bondsman; ~ਤਾ Slavery, bondage, servitude.

ਦਾਸਤਾਨ (daastaan) *n f* Tale, story, incident.

ਦਾਹ (daah) *n m* Cremation, burning; ~ਸੰਸਕਾਰ Funeral ceremony.

ਦਾਹਵਤ (dahwat) *n f* Invitation, party; ~ਦੇਣਾ To give a feast/party.

ਦਾਖ (daakh) *n f* Dry grape, currant.

ਦਾਖਲ (daakhal) *a* Entered, inserted, admitted; ~ਹੋਣਾ To enter, to introduce; ~ਕਰਨਾ To admit, to enrol.

ਦਾਖਲਾ (dakhlaa) *n m* Admission, entry, entrance, enrolment.

ਦਾਗ (daag) *n m* Stain, spot, blemish, stigma, scar, blot, mark, burn.

ਦਾਗਣਾ (daagnaa) *v* To burn, to fire, to stain, to stigmatize.

ਦਾਜ (daaj) *n m* Dowry, bride's portion.

ਦਾਣਾ (daanaa) *n m* Grain, seed, granule; pellet, shot; bird or cattle-feed, provender; A unit, single (fruit etc.); Pimple, sore, eruption (as in chickenpox); ~ਪਾਣੀ Victuals; Livelihood; Fate; ~ਮੰਡੀ Grain market.

ਦਾਤਣ (daatan) *n f* Twing or walnut bark used for cleansing teeth.

ਦਾਤਰ (daatar) *n m* A falciform kitchen implement for cutting vegetables.

ਦਾਤਰੀ (daatree) *n f* Sickle, scythe, reaping hook.

ਦਾਤਾਰ (dataar) *n m* Giver, an attribution to God.

ਦਾਂਦ (daand) *n m* Ox, bull.

ਦਾਦ (daad) *n f* (1) Ringworm; (2) Praise, appreciation; ~ਦੇਣੀ To appreciate, to backup, to applause; ~ਫ਼ਰਿਆਦ Petition, complaint.

ਦਾਦਕਾ (daadkaa) *a* Paternal.

ਦਾਦਕੇ (daadke) *n m* Paternal home or village; Paternal ancestors

ਦਾਦਰ (daadar) *n m* Frog

ਦਾਦਾ (daadaa) *n m* Paternal grand father.

ਦਾਨ (daan) *n m* Donation, alms, charity, benefaction, gift.

ਦਾਨਸ਼ਮੰਦ (daanashmand) *a n* Wise, intelligent, prudent, a wise person, intellectual.

ਦਾਨਸ਼ੀਲ (daansheel) *a* Charitable, liberal, bountiful, munificent, generous, benevolent.

ਦਾਨਵ (daanav) *n m* Devil, demon,

evil spirit, ghost, giant.

ਦਾਨਾਹ (daanaah) *a* Wise, learned, sensible; ~ਈ Wisdom, sagacity, prudence. Also **ਦਾਨਾ**

ਦਾਬ (daab) *n f* Impression, pressure, suppression; Layer.

ਦਾਬਾ (daabaa) *n m* Coercion, imposition; Warning, threat; ~ਪਾਉਣਾ To dominate, to impose.

ਦਾਮ (daam) *n m* Price, value, rate.

ਦਾਮਨ (daaman) *n m* Skirt of garment, foot-hill; ~ਛੁਡਾਉਣਾ To get rid of.

ਦਾਰੂ (daaroo) *n f* Medicine, drug; Alcohal, wine, liquour.

ਦਾਰੋਮਦਾਰ (daaromadaar) *n m* Dependence, reliance.

ਦਾਲ (daal) *n f* Pulse, split grain; ~ਨਾ ਗਲਣਾ To be unsuccessful.

ਦਾਵਾ (daawaa) *n m* Claim, suit, legal, action. Also **ਦਾਅਵਾ**

ਦਾਵੇਦਾਰ (daavedaar) *n m* Claimant, plaintiff.

ਦਾੜ੍ਹ (daarh) *n f* Grinder tooth, cheek tooth, tricuspid.

ਦਾੜ੍ਹਨਾ (darhnaa) *v* To chew, to devour.

ਦਾੜ੍ਹੀ (daarhee) *n f* Beard; ~ਹੱਥ ਲਾਉਣੀ To beg, to appeal abjectly; ~ਖੋਹਣੀ To insult, to disgrace.

ਦਿਓਰ (dior) *n m* Husband's younger brother; brother-in-law.

ਦਿਆਨਤ (diaanat) *n f* Honesty, truthfulness; ~ਦਾਰ Honest, truthful; ~ਦਾਰੀ Honesty, moral integrity.

ਦਿਆਲ (diaal) *a* Merciful, kind, gracious, benign; ~ਤਾ Kindness, compassion, mercy. Also **ਦਿਆਲੂ**

ਦਿਸਣਾ (disnaa) *v* To be seen, to appear.

ਦਿੱਸ (diss) *n f* Appearance, looks, aspect, visual impression.

ਦਿਸ਼ਾ (dishaa) *n f* Direction, side, region.

ਦਿਹਾਤ (dihaat) *n m* Village, country side.

ਦਿਹਾਤੀ (dihaatee) *n m a* Villager; Rural, rustic.

ਦਿਹਾੜੀ (dihaaree) *n f* Daily wages, day's labour.

ਦਿੱਕ (dikk) *n m a* Tuber culosis, hectic fever; Vexed, annoyed, teased, bothered; ~ਤਪ Tuberculosis.

ਦਿੱਕਤ (dikkat) *n f* Difficulty, trouble.

ਦਿਖਾਉਣਾ (dikhaaunaa) *v* To show, to display, to exhibit, to expose.

ਦਿਖਾਵਾ (dikhaavaa) *n m* Show, display, ostentation hypocrisy, exhibition.

ਦਿਦਾਰ (didaar) *n m* Look, sight. Also ਦੀਦਾਰ

ਦਿਨ (din) *n m* Day, suitable occasion, luck; ~ਕਟਣਾ To pass time in misery; ~ਗੁਜ਼ਾਰਨਾ To idle, to waste time; ~ਚੜ੍ਹਨਾ Rising of sun; ~ਫਿਰਨੇ To begin, to prosper; ~ਰਾਤ At all time, day & night, always; ~ਦਿਹਾੜੇ In broad day light.

ਦਿਮਾਗ (dimaag) *n m* Brain, head, mind, intellect, arrogance; ~ਹੋਣਾ To be proud, to be arrogant; ~ਲੜਾਉਣਾ To cudgel one's brain, to think on a subject carefully.

ਦਿਮਾਗ਼ੀ (dimaagee) *a* Mental, intellectual, cerebral, brilliant.

ਦਿਲ (dil) *n m* Heart, mind, will, courage; ~ਉਚਾਟ ਹੋਣਾ To be disgusted; ~ਸਾਫ਼ ਹੋਣਾ To have no reservation; ~ਹਾਰਨਾ To lose heart; ~ਹੌਲਾ ਹੋਣਾ To feel easy; ~ਕਰਨਾ To aspire, to wish; ~ਖੱਟਾ ਹੋਣਾ To sicken; ~ਛੋਟਾ ਕਰਨਾ To be dejected, to feel disheartened; ~ਟੁੱਟਣਾ To lose courage, to be distracted; ~ਢਾਹੁਣਾ To sadden, to deject; ~ਤੋਂ ਦੂਰ ਹੋਣਾ To forget; ~ਦੇਣਾ To fall in love with; ~ਰਖਣਾ To oblige, to comply with one's wishes; ~ਲਗਣਾ To be attached to, to be fond of; ~ਵਿਚ ਰਖਣਾ To keep secret, not to divulge; ~ਬਰ Sweetheart, beloved, paramour; ~ਲਗੀ Joke, amusement.

ਦਿਲਾਸਾ (dilaasaa) *n m* Consolation, solace, encouragement.

ਦਿਲਾਵਰ (dilaavar) *a* Brave, courageous. Also ਦਲਾਵਰ

ਦਿਵਾਰ (divaar) *n f* Wall. Also ਦੀਵਾਲ

ਦਿਲੀ (dilee) *a* Hearty, sincere, cordial warm-hearted.

ਦਿਲੋਂ (dilon) *adv* Heartily, sincerely, earnestly, whole-heartedly; From the bottom of one's heart.

ਦਿਵਾਉਣਾ (divaaunaa) *v* To cause to give, to assist in getting, to get one something from someone else, to procure for.

ਦਿਵਾਲਾ (divaalaa) *n m* Bankruptcy, insolvency, liquidation.

ਦਿਵਾਲੀ (divaalee) *n f* Festival of lamps; Feast; ~ਆ Bankrupt, Insolvent. Also ਦੀਵਾਲੀ

ਦੀਆ (deeaa) *n m* Earthern lamp; ~ਬਾਲਣਾ To light a lamp; ~ਸਲਾਈ Match stick Also ਜੀਵ

ਦੀਗਰ (deegar) *a* Other, another, more.

ਦੀਦ (deed) *n f* Sight, glance, show; consideration, modesty.

ਦੀਦਾ (deedaa) *n m* Eye, orb.

ਦੀਨ (deen) *n m* Poor, needy, meek, humble; Religion, faith; ~ਈਮਾਨ Virtue religion; ~ਤਾ Humility, modesty; ~ਬੰਧੁ God, friend of the poor.

ਦੀਮਕ (deemak) *n f* White ant.

ਦੀਵਟ (deevat) *n f* Lamp stand.

ਦੀਵਾਨ (deewan) *n m* Minister, royal court; Congregation; ~ਖਾਨਾ Court chamber, audience hall. Also ਦਿਵਾਨ

ਦੀਵਾਨਗੀ (deevaangee) *n f* Madness, lunacy, insanity. Also ਦਿਵਾਨਗੀ

ਦੀਵਾਨਾ (deevaanaa) *n m* Insane, lunatic, mad. Also ਦਿਵਾਨਾ

ਦੁਆ (duaa) *n f* Prayer; Supplication, blessing; ~ਦੇਣਾ To bless; ~ਸਲਾਮ Greetings, salutation, compliments.

ਦੁਸ਼ਟ (dusht) *n m* Rascal, villain, scoundral; ~ਤਾ Meanness, wickedness, rascality, villainy.

ਦੁਸ਼ਮਣ (dushman) *n m* Enemy, foe.

ਦੁਸ਼ਮਣੀ (dushmanee) *n f* Enmity, animosity; ਖਾਨਦਾਨੀ ~Vendetta.

ਦੁਸ਼ਵਾਰ (dushwaar) *a* Difficult.

ਦੁਸ਼ਵਾਰੀ (dushwaaree) *n f* Difficulty.

ਦੁਸ਼ਾਲਾ (dushaalaa) *n m* Shawl, embroidered wrapper.

ਦੁਹਣਾ (duhnaa) *v* To milk. Also ਦੋਹਣਾ

ਦੁਹਰਾ (duhraa) *a* Double, duplicate, two fold.

ਦੁਹਰਾਉ (duhraau) *n m* Repetition, revision, iteration, tautology.

ਦੁਹਰਾਉਣਾ (duhraaunaa) *v* To repeat, to revise, to recapitulate, to reiterate, to go over, to echo. Also ਦੋਹਰਾਉਣਾ

ਦੁਹਾਈ (duhaaee) *n f* Cry for help, appeal, invocation, clamour; ~ਦੇਣੀ To call upon, to make an appeal.

ਦੁਹਾਜੂ (duhaaju) *n m* One who is married a second time.

ਦੁਕਾਨ (dukaan) *n f* Shop, warehouse; - ਚਲਾਉਣਾ To run a shop; ~ਵਧਾਉਣਾ to close a shop; ~ਦਾਰ Shopkeeper; ~ਦਾਰੀ Business, Shopkeeping.

ਦੁਖ (dukh) *n m* Suffering, grief, distress, misery, hardship, tribulation, pain, trouble, agony; ~ਉਠਾਉਣਾ To suffer; ~ਦੇਣਾ To torment, to harass.

ਦੁਖਣਾ (dukhnaa) *v* To ache, to pain, to hurt.

ਦੁਖੜਾ (dukhraa) *n m* Tale of sufferings, grievance, trouble.

ਦੁਖਾਉਣਾ (dukhaaunaa) *v* To inflict pain, to hurt, to torment.

ਦੁਖਾਂਤ (dukhaaant) *n m* Tragic end,

tragedy; tragic play.

ਦੁਖੀਆ (dukhiaa) *a* Unfortunate, troubled, grieved, sorrowful, miserable, sufferer. Also **ਦੁਖੀ**

ਦੁਚਿੱਤਾ (duchittaa) *a* In two minds, double-minded, diffident, hesitant.

ਦੁੱਛਤਾ (duchhattaa) *a* Double-storey (building).

ਦੁਤਰਫ਼ਾ (dutarfaa) *a* Mutual, reciprocal.

ਦੁੱਧ (duddh) *n m* Milk, sap, juice of some plants & trees; ~**ਉਤਰਨਾ** Lactation; ~**ਪਿਆਉਣਾ** To suckle; ~**ਵਾਲ਼ਾ** Milkman.

ਦੁਧਾਰਾ (dudhaaraa) *a* Double-edged (weapon).

ਦੁੱਧਲ (duddhal) *a* High-yielding (milch cattle).

ਦੁਨੀਆ (duniaa) *n f* The world, cosmos, people; ~**ਦਾਰ** Worldlywise; ~**ਦਾਰੀ** Worldliness.

ਦੁਪਹਿਰ (dupehr) *n f* Noon, midday

ਦੁਪੱਟਾ (dupaṭṭaa) *n m* Veil, wrapper.

ਦੁਫ਼ਾੜ (duphaaṛ) *n m* Two fragments, thing cut into two.

ਦੁਬਲਾ (dublaa) *a* Thin, lean, slim, slender; ~**ਪਤਲਾ** Slender, scrawny.

ਦੁੰਬਾ (dumbaa) *n m* Fat-tailed ram.

ਦੁਬਾਰਾ (dubaaraa) *a* Again, for the second time.

ਦੁਭਾਸ਼ੀਆ (dubhaashiyaa) *n m* Interpreter.

ਦੁਮ (dum) *n f* Tail, end; ~**ਕਟਾ** Bob tailed; ~**ਦਾਰ** Tailed, with tail.

ਦੁਮੰਜ਼ਲਾ (dummanzalaa) *a* Double storeyed.

ਦੁਰਕਾਰਨਾ (durkaarnaa) *v* To condemn, to repulse, to spurn.

ਦੁਰਗਤ (durgat) *n f* Dishonour, disgrace, insult, humiliation.

ਦੁਰਗੰਧ (durgandh) *n f* Bad smell, stench, fetid odour.

ਦੁਰਜਨ (durjan) *n m* Rascal, scounderal, mischief maker.

ਦੁਰਬਲ (durbal) *a* Weak, frail, slender, invalid, lean, thin, poor; ~**ਤਾ** Infirmity, feebleness, weakness; debility.

ਦੁਰਮਤ (durmat) *n f* Evilmindedness, wickedness.

ਦੁਰਲਭ (durlabh) *a* Rare, scare, unattainable.

ਦੁਰਾਚਾਰ (duraachaar) *n m* Malpractice, corruption, misconduct.

ਦੁਲਹਨ (dulhan) *n f* Bride, newly married woman.

ਦੁਲਾਰ (dulaar) *n m* love, affection, fonding.

ਦੁੜਾਉਣਾ (duṛaaunaa) v To make or get one run; To chase, drive away.

ਦੂਸ਼ਣ (dooshaṇ) n m Flaw, defect, blot, stigma; blame, accusation, calumny, slander; Pollution, contamination, defilement.

ਦੂਜ (dooj) n f Second date, second day of lunar for night; Second turn (in game).

ਦੂਜਾ (doojaa) a Second, next, another.

ਦੂਣਾ (dooṇaa) a Double, two times, twofold, twice in size or quantity.

ਦੂਤ (doot) n m Envoy, consul, messenger, courtier, ambassador; ਰਾਜ~ Ambassador, royal envoy ਦੇਵ~ Angel of God; ਜਮ~ Angel of death.

ਦੂਧੀਆ (doodhiaa) a Milky, white.

ਦੂਰ (door) n a Distance; Discount, far; Away; ~ਹੁੰਦੇ ਜਾਣਾ To recede; ~ਹੋਣਾ To be away; ~ਕਰਨਾ To remove, to repel; ~ਰਹਿਣਾ To stand off, to avoid; ~ਅੰਦੇਸ਼ Farsighted; ~ਦੂਰ Widely apart.

ਦੂਰਬੀਨ (doorbeen) n f Telesccope.

ਦੂਰੀ (dooree) n f Distance, farness, expanse, remoteness; estrangement.

ਦੂਲ੍ਹਾ (dulhaa) n m Bridegroom.

ਦੇਸ (des) n m Country, motherland, fatherland, territory, region; ~ਨਿਕਾਲਾ Deportation, exile, externment; ~ਵਾਸੀ Native, countrymen. Also ਦੇਸ਼

ਦੇਸੀ (desee) a Native, home made, local, indigenous; ~ਸ਼ਕਰ Jaggery; ~ਖੰਡ Brown sugar; ~ਬੋਲੀ Vernacular.

ਦੇਹਾਂਤ (dehaant) n m Death, demise.

ਦੇਖਣਾ (dekhnaa) v To see, to look to, to observe, to seek, to find, to take care, to examine.

ਦੇਖ-ਰੇਖ (dekh-rekh) n f .Care, supervision; ~ਕਰਨਾ To look after, to supervise.

ਦੇਖ-ਭਾਲ (dekh-bhaal) n f Supervision, Inspection, observation, reconnaissance.

ਦੇਖਿਆ-ਭਾਲਿਆ (dekhiaa-bhaaliaa) a Familiar, tried, tested.

ਦੇਗ (deg) n f Kettle, large narrow-mouthed cooking vessel, offering; ~ਚੀ Small cooking pot, kettle. Also ਦੇਗਚਾ

ਦੇਣ (deṇ) n m Debt, liability, due, contribution; ~ਵਾਲਾ Payer, debtor, bestower; ~ਹਾਰ Giver, worth giving; ~ਦਾਰ Debtor, indebted, liable; ~ਦਾਰੀ Debt, accountability.

ਦੇਣਾ (denaa) *v* To give, to pay, to offer, to grant, to allow, to bestow, to entrust, to hand over, to impart, to accord; **ਸੰਹੁ~** To administer an oath.

ਦੇਰ (der) *n f* Delay, lateness; **~ਬਾਦ** Later on. Also **ਦੇਰੀ**

ਦੇਵ (dev) *n m* God, Holy spirit, deity; **~ਅਸਥਾਨ** Temple; **~ਤਾ** God, deity, divinity, angel; **~ਦਰਸ਼ਨ** Visitation; **~ਦੂਤ** Mercury; **~ਲ** Temple.

ਦੇਵਰ (devar) *n m* Brother-in-law, younger brother of husband; Also **ਦਿਉਰ**

ਦੇਵੀ (devee) *n m* Goddess, pious lady.

ਦੈਵੀ (daivee) *a* Angelic, celestial, heavenly, divine, superhuman.

ਦੋਸ਼ (dosh) *n m* Fault, flaw, defect, offence, sin; **~ਸਿੱਧੀ** Conviction; **~ਲਾਉਣਾ** To blame, to accuse. Also **ਦੋਖ**

ਦੋਸਤ (dost) *n m* Friend, lover; **~ਨਾ** Friendly; **~ਤੀ** Friendship.

ਦੋਸ਼ੀ (doshee) *a n m* Accused, culpable, delinquent; Criminal, culprit. Also **ਦੋਖੀ**

ਦੋਗਲਾ (doglaa) *n m a* Bastard; illegitimate, half-bred, mongrel; **~ਪਣ** Hybridness, illegitimacy, double dealing.

ਦੌਰ (daur) *n m* Era, period; Phase, stage; Course, bout, circuit.

ਦੌਰਾ (dauraa) *n m* (1) Fit, paroxysm, spasm; (2) Tour, translocation; **~ਕਰਨਾ** To go round, to tour; **~ਪੈਣਾ** To suffer fits.

ਦੌਰਾਨ (dauraan) *n m adv* Duration, During, meantime.

ਦੌਲਤ (daulat) *n f* Wealth, property, money; **~ਖਾਨਾ** Residence, house; **~ਮੰਦ** Rich, wealthy.

ਦੌਲਾ ਮੌਲਾ (daulaa-maulaa) *n m* Simp-leton, goose.

ਦੌੜ (daur) *n f* Run, race, gallop; **~ਜਾਣਾ** To run away; **~ਦਾ ਘੋੜਾ** Race horse.

ਦੌੜਨਾ (daurnaa) *v* To run, to gallop, to speed up, to race.

ਦੌੜੀਆ (dauriaa) *n m* Runner, racer, sprintor.

ਧ

ਧ Twenty fourth letter of Gurmukhi alphabets, pronounced as 'dhaddhaa' (a tone marker).

ਧਸਣਾ (dhasnaa) *v* To thrust in, to enter, to penetrate, to sink, to go deep into.

ਧਸਾਉਣਾ (dhasaaunaa) *v* To pierce, to thrust, to penetrate.

ਧਸੋੜਨਾ (dhasornaa) *v* To penetrate, pierce, thrust, push or force into.

ਧਕਣਾ (dhaknaa) *v* To push, to oust, to thrust.

ਧਕ-ਧਕ (dhak-dhak) *n f* Palpitation, heart beat, fear, anxiety.

ਧਕਮ ਧਕਾ (dhakkam-dhakkaa) *n m* Hustle, Pushing and jostling, great rush.

ਧੱਕੜ (dhakkar) *a* Aggressive, violent, domineering, usurper; **~ਰੱਵਈਆ** Aggressive attitude, unreasonable attitude.

ਧੱਕਾ (dhakkaa) *n m* Jerk, push, jolt, shock, concussion, coercion, aggression, impulse, stroke; **~ਦੇਣਾ** To push, to jerk.

ਧੱਕੇਸ਼ਾਹੀ (dhake shaahee) *n f* High handedness, despotism.

ਧੱਕੇਬਾਜ਼ੀ (dhake-baazee) *n f* Force, violence, oppression.

ਧੱਕੇਲਣਾ (dhakelnaa) *v* To push, to shave, to thrust.

ਧੱਖ (dhakkh) *n f* Louse egg, young louse.

ਧਗੜਾ (dhagraa) *n m* Paramour.

ਧਣਨਾ (dhannaa) *v* To fertilize, to impregnate, to inseminate.

ਧੱਦਰ (dhaddar) *n f* Shingles, herpes, zoster; Ringworm, tinea.

ਧੰਦਾ (dhandaa) *n m* Profession, occupation, avocation, business. Also **ਧੰਧਾ**

ਧੰਨ (dhann) *n a* God bless you! Well done! Bravo!; **~ਧੰਨ** Applause, accolade; **~ਭਾਗ** Fortunately **~ਵਾਦ** Thanks.

ਧਨ (dhan) *n m a* Wealth, property, money, capital, riches; Plus, positive; **~ਨੀਤੀ** Fiscal policy; **~ਵਾਨ** Rich, wealthy, affluent.

ਧਨੁਸ਼ (dhanush) *n m* Bow; **ਇੰਦਰ~** Rainbow; **~ਧਾਰੀ** Archer. Also **ਧਨੁ**

ਧੱਪੜ (dhapphar) *n m* Nettle rash swelling due to biting of an insect.

ਧੱਬਾ (dhabbaa) *n m* Spot, stain, blot.

ਧੱਮ (dhamm) *n f* Thud, dull sound.

ਧਮਕਣਾ (dhamaknaa) To thump, to arrive suddenly; ਆ~ To appear unexpectantly or surprisingly.

ਧਮਕਾਉਣਾ (dhamkaaunaa) *v* To threaten, to chide, to intimidate.

ਧਮਕਾਊ (dhamkaau) *a* Threatening, frightening, intimidating, daunting.

ਧਮਕੀ (dhamkee) *n f* Threat, menace, bullying, intimidation.

ਧਮਾਕਾ (dhamaakaa) *n m* Explosion, thunder, thump, bump, crash.

ਧਰਤੀ (dhartee) *n f* Earth, land, soil, ground; ~ਮਾਤਾ Mother land.

ਧਰਨਾ (dharnaa) *n m v* Picket; To keep, to put, to place, to lay.

ਧਰਮ (dharam) *n m* Religion, duty, righteousness, sect, faith, belief; ~ਅਸਥਾਨ Holy place, religious place; ~ਸ਼ਾਸਤਰ Scriptures; ~ਸ਼ਾਲਾ Inn, pilgrims house; ~ਨਿਰਪੇਖਤਾ Secularism; ~ਪਤਨੀ Wife; ~ਬਦਲੀ Conversion.

ਧਰਮਾਤਮਾ (dharmaatmaa) *a* Pious, holy, virtuous, godly, religious.

ਧਰਵਾਉਣਾ (dharvaaunaa) *v* To get placed, to have something put down.

ਧਰਾਤਲ (dharaatal) *n m* Land surface, area.

ਧਰੀਕਣਾ (dhareeknaa) *n* To drag, to pull along a surface.

ਧੜ (dhar) *n m* Trunk of body, body.

ਧੜਕਣ (dharkan) *n f* Beating of the heart, palpitation, pulsation.

ਧੜਕਣਾ (dharaknaa) *v* To palpitate, to throb, to beat, to pulsate, to be terrified.

ਧੜਕਾ (dharkaa) *n m* Fear, palpitation, suspense, apprehension.

ਧੜੰਮ (dhrumm) *n* Thud, Thump. Also ਧੜਾਮ

ਧੱਲੇਦਾਰ (dharalledaar) *a* Forceful, vehement impressive.

ਧੜਾ (dharaa) *n m* Group, party, side; counterpoise, counter balance; ~ਧੜ Quickly, incessantly, continuously.

ਧੜਾਕਾ (dharaakaa) *n m* Thump, crash, explosion, out bust.

ਧੜੇਬਾਜ਼ (dharebaaz) *a f* Partisan, factious, cliquish.

ਧੜੇਬਾਜ਼ੀ (dharebaazee) *n f* Partisanship, factionalism, party spirit.

ਧਾਉਣਾ (dhaaunaa) *v* To run, to hasten, to hurry.

ਧਾਕ (dhaak) *n f* Awe, fear, terror, grandeur, fame, credit.

ਧਾਗਾ (dhaagaa) *n m* Thread, cord; **~ਪੋਣਾ** To needle, to thread.

ਧਾਂਤ (dhaant) *n f* Semen. Also **ਧਾਤ**

ਧਾਤ (dhaat) *n f* Metal, mineral; Semen; **ਕਚੀ~** Ore; **ਖੁਲ੍ਹੀ~** Bullion; **ਮਿਸ਼ਰਤ~** Alloy.

ਧਾਤੂ (dhaatoo) *n m* Root of a word, stem, element, constituent.

ਧਾਂਦਲੀ (dhaandlee) *n f* Anarchy, disorder, disturbance; **~ਮਚਾਉਣੀ** To create disturbance.

ਧਾਨ (dhaan) *n m* Paddy, husky rice, rice plant.

ਧਾਰ (dhaar) *n* (1) Edge, sharpness, line; (2) Limit, trend, current, stream; **~ਲਾਉਣੀ** To sharpen; **~ਕਢਣੀ** To milk; **ਤੇਜ਼~** Torent, strong current; **~ਮਾਰਨੀ** To urinate, to damn care.

ਧਾਰਨਾ (dhaarnaa) *n f* Conception, notion, assumption.

ਧਾਰਨਾ (dharnaa) *v* To determine, to resolve, to assume, to imagine.

ਧਾਰਾਵਾਹਿਕ (dhaaraavaahik) *a* Serial, serialised, continued.

ਧਾਰੀ (dhaaree) *n f* Suff stripe, line, streaker; Meaning wielder or bearer such as **ਪਗੜਧਾਰੀ, ਜਟਾਧਾਰੀ**; **~ਦਾਰ** Striped, streaked, striated.

ਧਾਵਾ (dhaavaa) *n m* Raid, attack, assault, invasion, incursion.

ਧਾੜਵੀ (dhaarvee) *n m* Robber, raider, dacoit, plunderer, marauder, mugger.

ਧਾੜਾ (dhaaraa) *n m* Raid, robbery, dacoity loot, spoil, plunder, extortion, exploitation.

ਧਿਆਉਣਾ (dhiaaunaa) *v* To meditate (upon), to contemplate, to reflect, to remember, to repeat (the name of Diety).

ਧਿਆਨ (dhiaan) *n m* Attention, meditation, absorption; **~ਕਰਨਾ** To pay attention to, to take care; **~ਦੇਣਾ** To pay heed, to attend; **~ਮੋੜਨਾ** To divert attention; **~ਯੋਗ** Note worthy, remarkable.

ਧਿਕਾਰ (dhikaar) *n f* Curse, seproach scorn, rebuke, phew! fie!

ਧਿਕਾਰਨਾ (dhikaarnaa) *v* To reproach, to curse, to anthematize.

ਧਿੰਗਾਣਾ (dhingaanaa) *n m* Use of force, wrong injustice oppression.

ਧਿੰਗਾਣੇ (dhingaane) *adv* By force forcibly, unjustly, wrongfully.

ਧਿਜਾਉਣ (dhijaaun) *v* To comfor console; To win or build u confidence, to reassure; T coax, to inveigle.

ਧੀ (dhee) *n f* Daughter.

ਧੀਮਾ (dheemaa) *a* Slow, mild, gentle, tardy, dim, feeble, faint.

ਧੀਰ (dheer) *n m* Patience, consolation, endurance, forbearance, solace. Also ਧੀਰਜ

ਧੀਰੇ (dheere) *adv* Slowly, lightly, gently, gradually, carefully; ~ਧੀਰੇ Little by little, step by step.

ਧੁਆਂਖ (dhuaankh) *n f* Soot, smoke-deposit, smut.

ਧੁੱਸਾ (dhussaa) *n m* Rough, coarse woolen blanket.

ਧੁਖਣਾ (dhukhnaa) *v* To ignite, to smoulder, to burn without flame, to take fire.

ਧੁਤਕਾਰਨਾ (dhutkaarnaa) *v* To rebuke, to chide, to rebuff.

ਧੁੰਦ (dhund) *n f* Mist, fog, haziness.

ਧੁੰਦਲਕਾ (dhundalkaa) *n m f* Dusk, haziness, fogginess, semi darkness.

ਧੁੰਦਲਾ (dhundlaa) *a* Foggy, dim, dull, blurred, shabby, doubtful, pale, smoky; ~ਪਣ Fogginess, mistiness, vagueness.

ਧੁਨ (dhun) *n f* Single mindedness, zeal, passion, abosorption in thought or action.

ਧੁਨਣਾ (dhunnaa) *v* To muzzle.

ਧੁਨੀ (dhunee) *n f* Tune, musical mode, musical sound, tone, melody, sound, speech-sound; ~ਵਿਗਿਆਨ Musicology, phonology, phonemics, phonetics.

ਧੁੰਨੀ (dhunnee) *n f* Navel, umbilicus.

ਧੁੱਪ (dhupp) *n f* Sunshine, sunlight, sun.

ਧੁੰਮ (dhumm) *n f* Frame, reputation, show, bustle.

ਧੁਰ (dhur) *n f adv* Extremity; Right from or upto; ਅਗਲਾ~ Foremost.

ਧੁਰਾ (dhuraa) *n f* Axle, shaft, hub, pivot.

ਧੂੰਆਂ (dhooaan) *n m* Smoke, fume; ~ਧਾਰ Full of smoke; High flown (speech), heavy (rain). Also ਧੂੰ

ਧੂਪ (dhoop) *n f* Incense, perfume, olibanum.

ਧੂਹ (dhoo) *n f* Pull; attraction, pang, pain; Spasm.

ਧੂਹਣਾ (dhoonaa) *v* To pull, to drag, to haul, to pull up, haul up, admonish, reprove; To manhandle; To snatch.

ਧੂਣੀ (dhoonee) *n f* Open fire, with straw; Fire kept going by ascetics practising austerities; Incense burning; ~ਬਾਲ਼ਣੀ To make an open fire; ~ਰਮਾਉਣੀ To make and maintain fire burning (by ascetics), to become an ascetic, to practise austerities.

ਧੂਮ (dhoom) *n f* Comet; Reputation, fame; ~ਧਾਮ Pomp and show, boom, tumplt.

ਧੂੜ (dhoor) *n f* Dust, grit; fine powder; ~ਉੱਡਣੀ For dust to blow or rise.

ਧੇਤੇ (dhete) *n m pl.* Members of daugher-in-law's family collectively. see ਪੁਤੇਤੇ

ਧੋਖਾ (dhokhaa) *n m* Deception, deceit, fraud, delusion, hoax, dupe.

ਧੋਣਾ (dhonaa) *v* To wash, to cleanse, to flush, to launder.

ਧੋਤੀ (dhotee) *n* Cloth worn round the waiste.

ਧੋਬੀ (dhobee) *n m* Washerman, launderer.

ਧੌਂਸ (dhauns) *n f* Bullying, awe, threat, bluster, swagger.

ਧੌਣ (dhaun) *n f* Neck; ~ਸੁਟਣੀ To lose heart, to be depressed; ~ਧੱਪਾ scuffle, row.

ਧੌਲਾ (dhaulaa) *a* Grey, white, hoary.

ਨ

ਨ Twenty fifth letter of the Gurmukhi alphabets, pronounced as 'nannaa'.

ਨਸ (nas) *n f* Vein, nerve, sinew.

ਨਸ਼ਈ (nashai) *a* Drunk, intoxicated, inebriate, under influence of drink; alcoholic, drunkard; drug-addict.

ਨਸ਼ਟ (nasht) *a* Lost, ruined, destroyed, smashed, demolished.

ਨੱਸਣਾ (nassnaa) *v* To run, to flee, to decamp.

ਨਸਬੰਦੀ (nasbandee) *n f* vasectomy.

ਨਸਲ (nasal) *n f* Race, breed, clan, genealogy, species, generation.

ਨਸਲੀ (naslee) *a* Racial.

ਨਸ਼ਾ (nashaa) *n m* Intoxication, stimulation, booze; ~ਬੰਦੀ prohibition.

ਨਸਾਉਣਾ (nasaaunaa) *v* To make run, to make one give up.

ਨਸੀਹਤ (naseehat) *n f* Advice, counsel, instruction.

ਨਸੀਬ (naseeb) *n* Destiny, fortune, fate, luck, lot. Also ਨਸੀਬਾ

ਨਸ਼ੀਲਾ (nasheelaa) *a* Intoxicating, inebriant.

ਨਹਕ (nahakk) *a* unjustly, without justification, undeservedly, unjustifiably, wrongly.

ਨਹਾਉਣਾ (nhaaunaa) *v* To bathe, to take bath; Also ਨੁਹਾਉਣਾ

ਨਹਿਰ (naher) *n f* Stream, canal, water way.

ਨਹੀਂ (naheen) *a* No, not, nay, refusal.

ਨਹੁੰ (nahun) *n m* Finger nail, nail.

ਨਹੂਸਤ (nahoosat) *n f* Inauspiciousness, bad luck.

ਨਹੂਸਤੀ (nahoostee) *n* Inauspicious, ill omened.

ਨੱਕ (nakk) *n m* Noise, organ; ~ਹੇਠਾਂ under the very nose of, in the presence of; ~ਰੱਖ ਲੈਣਾ To keep up one's prestige; ~ਰਗੜਨਾ To beseech humbly, to eat humble pie; ~ਵਢਣਾ To inflict humiliation, to dishonour; ~ਵਢਿਆ ਜਾਣਾ To be insulted, to be disgraced; ~ਵਾਲਾ Honourable, having prestige, ~ਵਿਚ ਦਮ ਕਰਨਾ To harass, to tease incessantly.

ਨਕਸ਼ (naksh) *n m* Impression, sign, features, appreance.

ਨਕਸ਼ਾ (nakshaa) *n m* Map, chart, layout plan, sketch, model, design, contour; ~ਕਸ਼ Cartographer; ~ਨਵੀਸ Tracer, draftsman; ~ਪੁਸਤਕ

Atlas

ਨਕਸੀਰ (nakseer) *n f* Bleeding from nose.

ਨਕਚੁੰਢੀ (nakchoondee) *n f* Clamp, clip, paper clip; Pincers.

ਨਕਦ (nakad) *n m adv* Cash; In cash; Ready money; ~**ਨਰੈਣ** Hardcash; Mammon, god of riches. Also **ਨਗਦ**

ਨਕਲ (nakal) *n f* Copy, duplicate, transcription, mimicry, parody; ~**ਕਰਨਾ** To copy, to imitate, to mimic; ~**ਚੀ** Imitator, mimic, buffon; ~**ਨਵੀਸ** Copyist.

ਨਕਲੀ (naklee) *a* False, fictitous, artificial, rake, imitative.

ਨਕਾਸ਼ੀ (nakaashee) *n f* Painting, drawing, engraving.

ਨਕਾਬ (nakaab) *n m* Veil, mask; ~**ਪੋਸ਼** Masked.

ਨਕਾਰਨਾ (nkaarnaa) *v* To reject, to dishonour.

ਨਕਾਰਾ (nakaaraa) *a* useless, valueless, unfit, good for nothing, of no use, rotter; ~**ਪਣ** Disability, indolence, handicap.

ਨਕੇਲ (nakel) *n f* Cavesson, camel's nose band; ~**ਪਾਉਣੀ** To put nosebar; to check, to restrain.

ਨਕੋੜਾ (nakauṛaa) *n m* Large or fat nose; noseband.

ਨਖੱਟੂ (nakhattoo) *a* Non-earning, worthless.

ਨਖ਼ਰਾ (nakhraa) *n m* Coquetry, pretence, trick.

ਨਖ਼ਲਿਸਤਾਨ (nakhlistaan) *n m* Oasis.

ਨਖਿੱਧ (nakhiddh) *a* Worthless, unworthy, inferior, wretched.

ਨਖੇੜਨਾ (nakheṛnaa) *v* To disunite, to disjoin, to separate, to individualize, to detach, to sunder, to divorce.

ਨੱਗ (nagg) *n m* Item, package, piece.

ਨਗ (nag) *n m* Precious stone.

ਨੰਗ (nang) *n m* Nudity, nakedness; Poverty, destitution; ~**ਧੜੰਗ** Absolute make, starked nude.

ਨਗ਼ਮਾ (nagmaa) *n m* Song, melody.

ਨਗਰ (nagar) *n m* City, town, borough; ~**ਨਿਗਮ** Municipal corporation; ~**ਪਤੀ** Mayor; ~**ਪਾਲਕਾ** Municipal committee.

ਨੰਗਾ (nangaa) *a* Naked, bare, nude, unclad, unclothed, undressed, shameless; **ਕਰਨਾ**~ To denude, to unclothe, to strip, to undress, to expose; **ਭੁੱਖਾ**~ Poor, destitute.

ਨਗਾਰਾ (nagaaraa) *n m* Kettle drum.

ਨਗੀਨਾ (nageenaa) *n m* Gem, precious stone set in ring.

ਨੱਚਣਾ (nachchnaa) *v* To dance, to fre

ਨਚੋੜ (nachoṛ) *n m* Gist, sum, substance, summary, digest; ~**ਕਢਣਾ** To condense,

ਨਚੋੜਨਾ (nachornaa) v To compress, to rinse, to squeeze, to wring.

ਨਛੱਤਰ (nachhattar) n m Star, planet; zodiac sign; Position of moon in lunar orbit.

ਨਜ਼ਦੀਕ (nazdeek) a Near, adjacent, close, in vicinity. Also **ਨਜ਼ੀਕ**

ਨਜ਼ਮ (nazam) n f Verse, poetry, poem.

ਨਜ਼ਰ (nazar) n f Present, gift, cosecration, dedication; Sight, vision, look, glance, attension, evil eye; ~ਕਰਨਾ To present, to offer, to devote; ~ਆਉਣਾ To come in sight, to be seen, to appear; ~ਅੰਦਾਜ਼ ਕਰਨਾ To ignore, to take no notice of; ~ਚੜ੍ਹਨਾ To be in one's good books; ~ਮਾਰਨੀ To glance, to go through, to survey; ~ਰਖਣਾ To watch, to care; ~ਬਟੂ To avert the evil eye; ~ਬੰਦੀ Detention, confinement.

ਨਜ਼ਰਾਨਾ (nazraanaa) n m Present, gift.

ਨਜ਼ਰੀਆ (nazariaa) n m Approach, point of view, attitude.

ਨਜ਼ਲਾ (nazlaa) n m Bad cold, catarrh, flu.

ਨਜ਼ਾਕਤ (nazaakat) n f Delicacy, elegance, coquetry.

ਨਜਾਤ (najaat) n f Release, salvation, freedom, emancipation, rid.

ਨਜ਼ਾਰਾ (nazaaraa) n m Sight, view, scene, glance, vista.

ਨਜਿੱਠਣਾ (najitthnaa) v To fulfil, to perform, to endure, to tackle, to settle, to conclude, to dispose of.

ਨਜੂਮ (najoom) n m Astronomy, astrology; Fortune-telling, foretelling, predictor.

ਨਜੂਮੀ (najoomee) n m Astrologer, fortune teller, star gazer, augur.

ਨਠਣਾ (nathnaa) v To flee, to run.

ਨਢਰੀ (nadharee) n f Girl, damsel, lass, young woman.

ਨੱਢਾ (naddhaa) n m Boy, youth, youngman.

ਨੱਢੀ (naddhee) n f Youngwoman, damsel.

ਨਤੀਜਾ (nateejaa) n m Result, consequence, conclusion, inference.

ਨੱਥ (natth) n f Nose ring.

ਨੱਥਣਾ (natthnaa) v To have the nose pierced, to bring under control, to ring (the nose).

ਨਥਨਾ (nathnaa) n m Nostril; ~ਫਲਣਾ To get angry.

ਨੱਥੀ (natthee) a Attached, appended, enclosed.

ਨੱਥੂ-ਖੈਰਾ (natthoo-khaeraa) n m Any Tom, Dick or Harry.

ਨਦਾਨ (nadaan) *a* Ignorant, innocent, foolish.

ਨਦਾਨੀ (nadaanee) *n f* Innocence, ignorance, foolishness.

ਨਦੀ (nadee) *n f* River, rivulet, small stream; ~ਤਲ River bed.

ਨਨਾਣ (nanaaṇ) *n f* Husband's sister, sister in law. Also ਨਣਾਣ

ਨਪਣਾ (napṇaa) *v* To catch, to nip, to press, to cover; To be measured.

ਨਪੀੜਨਾ (napeeṛnaa) *v* To squeeze, to compress, to press.

ਨਪੂਤਾ (napootaa) *a* Issueless, having no son.

ਨਫ਼ਰਤ (nafrat) *n f* Hatred, scorn, contempt, aversion, disgust.

ਨਫ਼ਾ (nafaa) *n m* Profit, gain, benefit, advantage; ~ਖ਼ੋਰ Profiteer; ~ਖ਼ੋਰੀ Profiteering.

ਨਫ਼ਾਸਤ (nafaasat) *n f* Decency, etiquette, nicety.

ਨਫ਼ੀ (nafee) *a n f* Negative, minus, subtracted; Subtration, reduction.

ਨਫ਼ੀਸ (nafees) *a* Nice, decent, delicate.

ਨਬਜ਼ (nabaz) *n f* Pulse (of the hand); ~ਦੇਖਣੀ To feel the pulse.

ਨੰਬਰ (nambar) *n m* Number, marks, score; ~ਦੇਣੇ To evaluate, to award marks; ~ਫੇਰਨਾ To dial; ~ਦਾਰ Village headman.

ਨੰਬਰੀ (numbree) *a* Regular, established, numbered.

ਨਬਾਲਗ਼ (nabaalag) *a* Minor, ward.

ਨਬੇੜਨਾ (baberṇaa) *v* To settle, to finish, to end, to conclude.

ਨਮਕ (namak) *n m* Salt; ~ਹਰਾਮ Disloyal, unfaithful; ~ਹਲਾਲ Loyal, faithful; ~ਛਿੜਕਣਾ To add insult to injury.

ਨਮਕੀਨ (namkeen) *a* Saltish, saline, beautiful, handsome.

ਨਮੀ (namee) *n f* Moisture, dampness, humidity.

ਨਮੂਨਾ (namoonaa) *n m* Model, sample, specimen, pattern, design, type, example.

ਨਰਕ (narak) *n m* Hell, inferno, very dirty place.

ਨਰਮ (naram) *a* Soft, gentle, mild, tender, delicate; ~ਦਿਲ Kind hearted.

ਨਰਾਜ਼ (naraaz) *a* Displeased, estranged, angry, offended, annoyed, unhappy; ~ਕਰਨਾ To displease, to offend, to annoy, to rub one up the wrong way. Also ਨਾਰਾਜ਼

ਨਰਾਜ਼ਗੀ (naraazgee) *n f* Displeasure, estrangement, anger, unhappiness. Also ਨਾਰਾਜ਼ਗੀ

ਨਰੇਲ (narel) *n m* Coconut, coconut

palm. Also ਨਾਰੀਅਲ

ਨਲਕਾ (nalkaa) *n m* Water tap, hand pump.

ਨਲੀ (nalee) *n f* Snot; Tube, pipe.

ਨਲੈਕ (nalaik) *a* Duffer, incompetent, inefficient, unworthy.

ਨਵਾਂ (nawaan) *a* New, fresh, recent, novel, modern; ~ਨਕੋਰ Brand new, unused, fresh.

ਨਵਾਬ (nawaab) *n m* Baron, nawab.

ਨਵਾਬੀ (nawaabee) *n f* Nawabship.

ਨਵੇਕਲਾ (naveklaa) *a* Isolated, separate, sole, solitary, exclusive, alone; ~ਪਣ Exculsiveness, isolation.

ਨੜੋਆ (naroaa) *n m* Funeral, bier, hearse.

ਨਾਂ (naan) *n m* Name, fame, reputation; ~ਹੋਣਾ To win credit, to be famous; ~ਦੇਣਾ To label, to name; Also ਨਾਉਂ and ਨਾਮ

ਨਾ (naa) *a adv n* No; Not, nay; Refusal, denial. Also ਨਾਂਹ

ਨਾਉ (naao) *n f* Boat, sailing, vessel. Also ਨਾਵ

ਨਾਅਰਾ (naaraa) *n m* Slogan, war cry.

ਨਾਇਬ (naaib) *a* Assistant, deputy.

ਨਾਈ (naaee) *n m* Barber, hair dresser.

ਨਾਸ (naas) *n m* Destruction, annihilation, ruin, waste. Also ਨਾਸ਼

ਨਾਸਤਕ (naastak) *n m* Infidel, atheist, unbeliever, heretic, sceptic

ਨਾਸ਼ਤਾ (naashtaa) *n m* Breakfast, light refreshment.

ਨਾਸੂਰ (naasoor) *n m* Ulcer, cancer.

ਨਾਹਕ (naahak) adv *a* Invain; Undeserved.

ਨਾਕਾ (naakaa) *n* Barrier, block, barricade; ~ਬੰਦੀ Blockade.

ਨਾਕਾਮ (naakaam) *a* Unsuccessful; ~ਯਾਬੀ Defeat, fallure.

ਨਾਖੁਨ (naakhun) *n m* Nail.

ਨਾਗ (naag) *n m* Snake, serpent; A cruel personal.

ਨਾਗਰਿਕ (naagrik) *n m* Citizen, city dweller; ~ਤਾ Citizenship.

ਨਾਗਾ (naagaa) *a n m* Vacant, blank; Omission, absence, suspension; Fast, starvation.

ਨਾਚ (naach) *n m* Dance, ballet; ~ਘਰ Ball room.

ਨਾਜ਼ (naaz) *n m* Dolicacy, gracefulness, fonding, blandishment; ~ਨੀਨ Delicate woman, beautiful damsel.

ਨਾਜਾਇਜ਼ (naajaaiz) *a* Improper, illigitimate, unbecoming, illicit.

ਨਾਟਕ (naaṭak) *n m* Drama, play; ~ਕਾਰ Dramatist, playwright.

ਨਾਤਾ (naataa) *n m* Relationship, alliance.

ਨਾਦਮ (naadam) *a* Ashamed.

ਨਾਦਰ (naadar) *a* Rare, uncommon.

ਨਾਨਕਾ (naankaa) *a* Belonging to maternal grandfather's family or village.

ਨਾਨਾ (naanaa) *n m* Maternal grandfather.

ਨਾਨੀ (naanee) *n f* Maternal grandmother; ~**ਯਾਦ ਆਉਣੀ** To be at one's wit's ends, to be in great trouble; ~**ਯਾਦ ਕਰਾਉਣੀ** To teach one a lesson.

ਨਾਪ (naap) *n m* Measurement, scale.

ਨਾਪਣਾ (naapṇaa) *a* To measure; to weigh.

ਨਾਪਾਕ (naapaak) *a* Polluted, unholy, unclean.

ਨਾਫ਼ਰਮਾਨ (naafarmaan) *a* Disobedience, insubordination.

ਨਾਫ਼ਰਮਾਨੀ (naafarmaanee) *n f* Disobedience, insubordination.

ਨਾਬਾਲਗ (naabaalag) *a* Under age; Minor.

ਨਾਬੀਨਾ (naabeenaa) *a* Blind.

ਨਾਭ (naabh) *n f* Navel, hilum, nucleus. Also **ਨਾਭੀ**

ਨਾਮ (naam) *n m* Name, designation, Fame; Reality, godi; ~**ਕਮਾਉਣਾ** To earn name and fame; ~**ਲੇਵਾ** Descendant, follower.

ਨਾਮਜ਼ਦ (naamzad) *a n* Nominated, designated; Nominee; ~**ਕਰਨਾ** To nominate, to designate, to appoint; ~**ਗੀ** Nomination.

ਨਾਮਣਾ (namṇaa) *n m v* Renown, fame, honour; To designate.

ਨਾਮਰਦ (naamarad) *a* Impotent, cowardly, eunuch.

ਨਾਮਵਰ (naamvar) *a* Renowned, famous.

ਨਾਮਾ (naamaa) *n* Letter, epistle; Cash; *As suffix* meaning letter, document or book such as **ਹੁਕਮਨਾਮਾ, ਸ਼ਾਹਨਾਮਾ**

ਨਾਮਾਕੂਲ (naamaakool) *a* unreasonable, stupid, foolish.

ਨਾਮਾਨਿਗਾਰ (naamaanigaar) *n m* Correspondent, Press Reporter.

ਨਾਮਾਵਲੀ (naamaavalee) *n f* List of names, schedule, catalogue, nominal roll.

ਨਾਮੀ (naamee) *a* Famous, reputed, renowned, notorious; ~**ਗਰਾਮੀ** Famous, well-known.

ਨਾਮੁਰਾਦ (naamuraad) *a* Issueless, childless, unlucky, ill-omened.

ਨਾਯਾਬ (naayaab) *a* Rare, scarce.

ਨਾਰ (naar) *n f* Woman, wife.

ਨਾਰਾਜ਼ਗੀ (naaraazgee) *n f* Anger, displeasure, resentment.

ਨਾਰੀ (naaree) *n f* Women, female, eve.

ਨਾਰੀਅਲ (naarial) *n m* Coconut; *Cocos*

nucifera. Also **ਨਰੇਲ**

ਨਾਲ (naal) *n f adv prep* Barrel, pipe, tube; Alongwith, accompanying; By the side of; ~**ਹੋਣਾ** To accompany, to side; ~**ਦਾ** Adjacent, near, immediate; ~**ਨਾਲ** Along, neck to neck; ~**ਨਾਲ ਰਹਿਣਾ** To live together, to shadow; ~**ਲਗਣਾ** To touch, to cohere, to conjoin; ~**ਲਾਉਣਾ** To attach.

ਨਾਲਸ਼ (naalash) *n f* Law suit, complaint. Also **ਨਾਲਿਸ਼**

ਨਾਲ (naall) *n f* Horse shoe, hoof.

ਨਾਲਾ (naalaah) *n m* Big drain, watercourse, sewer, gutter, channel, canal, rivulet; Trouser string.

ਨਾਲਾਇਕ (naalaaik) *a* Unitelligent, dull, obtuse, stupid; Intefficient; incapable.

ਨਾਲਾਇਕੀ (naalaiki) *a* Dullness, obtuseness, stupidity; Ineffciency.

ਨਾਲੀ (naalee) *n f* Drain, sewer, gutter, pipe, tube, channel; **ਬੰਦੂਕ ਦੀ**~ Barrel (of gun).

ਨਾਲੇ (naale) *adv* With, therewith; too, also, besides, at the same time.

ਨਾਂਵ (naanv) *n gr.* Noun, name; ~**ਰੂਪ** Declension.

ਨਾਵਾਂ (naavaan) *n m* Money; Entry, name.

ਨਾਵਿਕ (naavik) *a* Nautical, naval.

ਨਾੜ (naar) *n f* Pulse, vein.

ਨਾੜਾ (naaraa) *n m* Trouser string, Drawer string; Bamboo pole.

ਨਾੜੀ (naaree) *n f* Blood vessel, vein, pulse, nerve.

ਨਿਉਣਾ (nuinaa) *v* To bow, to stop, to bend.

ਨਿਉਲਾ (niolaa) *n m* Mongoose.

ਨਿਆਂ (niaan) *n m* Justice, logic, equity; ~**ਅਧੀਨ** Sub-judice; ~**ਕਾਰ** Judge; Justice. Also **ਨਿਆਉ**, **ਨਿਆਇ**

ਨਿਆਸ (niaas) *n m* Deposit; something entrusted for statekeeping; Pledge, investment.

ਨਿਆਂਸ਼ੀਲ (niaansheel) *a* Just, judicious, equitable; ~**ਤਾ** Justness, judiciousness.

ਨਿਆਂਹੀਣ (niaanheen) *a* Unjust, unfair inequitable; ~**ਤਾ** Unjustness; unfairness, inequity, inequitableness.

ਨਿਆਜ਼ (niaaz) *n m* Offering, prayer, dedication, devotion, petition.

ਨਿਆਣਾ (niaanaa) *a n m* Young, underage; Baby, infant, child.

ਨਿਆਮਤ (niaamat) *n f* Gift, present, blessing.

ਨਿਆਰਾ (niaaraa) *a* Uncommon, distinct, seperate; ~**ਪਣ** Uncommonness peculiarity, distinctness.

ਨਿਸੰਗ (nishang) *adv a* Certainly, without doubt; Shameless, impudent, outspoken, unhesitating, bold.

ਨਿਸ਼ਚਾ (nishchaa) *n m* Faith, certainty belief, determination.

ਨਿਸਚਿਤ (nishchit) *a* Definite, settled, resolved, sure, decided, determined, specific, certain.

ਨਿਸ਼ਠਾ (nishṭhaa) *n f* Allegiance, faith; ~**ਪੂਰਵਕ** Loyally, faithfully; ~**ਵਾਨ** Faithful, religious (person).

ਨਿਸਤਾਰਨਾ (nistaarnaa) *v* To liberate, to save, to redeem.

ਨਿਸਤਾਰਾ (nistaaraa) *n m* Salvation, liberation, emancipation, release, redemption, reclamation.

ਨਿਸਫਲ (nisphal) *a* Fruitless, useless, abortive, infructuous.

ਨਿਸਬਤ (nisbat) *n* Relation, proportion, comparison, connection; ~**ਨ** Comparatively, proportionately, relatively.

ਨਿਸਰਣ (nisaran) *n m* Growth.

ਨਿਸਰਨਾ (nisarnaa) *v* To come up, to spring up, to blossom, to grow.

ਨਿਸ਼ਾਨ (nishaan) *n f* Flag, banner, emblem, symbol, sign, mark, stamp, impression, standard; ~**ਚੀ** Marksman sriper; ~**ਦੇਹੀ** Demarcation.

ਨਿਸ਼ਾਨਾ (nishaanaa) *n m* Aim, mark, target, goal; ~**ਮਾਰਨਾ** To hit, to aim, to direct.

ਨਿਸ਼ਾਨੀ (nishaanee) *n f* Token, sign, symptom, indication, momento.

ਨਿਹੰਗ (nihang) *n m a* A sect of baptised Sikh, without taint, pure.

ਨਿਹਥਾ (nihathaa) *a* Unarmed, without means, empty handed; ~**ਕਰਨ** To disarm.

ਨਿਹਾਲ (nihaal) *a* Happy, delighted, exalted, satisfied. Also **ਨਿਹਾਲ਼ਾ**

ਨਿਹੋਰਾ (nihoraa) *n m* Complaint, reproach.

ਨਿਕਦਰੀ (nikadree) *n f* Degradation, devaluation.

ਨਿਕੰਮਾ (nikammaa) *a* Useless, idle, adject, worthless, valueless, ineffective.

ਨਿੱਕਰ (nikkar) *n f* Shorts, knicker.

ਨਿਕਲਣ (nikalaṇ) *n f* Emergence, exit.

ਨਿਕਲਣਾ (nikalṇaa) *v* To come out, to go out, to evolve, to germinate, to emanate, to derive, to issue, to be published.

ਨਿਕੜਾ (nikṛaa) *a* Small in stature, diminutive.

ਨਿੱਕਾ (nikkaa) *a* Small, little, petty, short.

ਨਿਕਾਸ (nikaas) *n m* Outlet, exit,

emergence, opening, emanation, evacuation, derivation.

ਨਿਕਾਸੀ (nikaasee) *n m* Out-turn, clearance, vacated.

ਨਿਕਾਹ (nikaah) *n m* Nuptial, muslim marriage.

ਨਿਖੱਟੂ (nikhattoo) *a* Worthless, unemployed, idle.

ਨਿਖਰਨਾ (nikharnaa) *v* To brighten up, to be clear, to be cleansed.

ਨਿਖੜਨਾ (nikharnaa) *v* To be separated, to come apart, to diverge.

ਨਿਖਾਰ (nikhaar) *n m* Whiteness, brightness, lustre, elegance.

ਨਿਖਾਰਨਾ (nikhaarnaa) *v* To cleanse, to brighten, to bleach, to purify.

ਨਿਖੇੜਨਾ (nikhernaa) *v* To separate, to differentiate, to select.

ਨਿਖੇੜਾ (nikheraa) *n m* Distinction, differentiation, separation.

ਨਿਗਮ (nigam) *n m* Corporation, corporate body.

ਨਿੱਗਰ (niggar) *a* Solid, hard, heavy, massy, sound, concrete, tangible, strong; ~**ਤਾ** Solidness, compactness, hardness.

ਨਿਗਰਾਨ (nigraan) *n m a* Supervisor, controller manager, caretaker, watch; Invigilator, surveillan.

ਨਿਗਰਾਨੀ (nigraanee) *n f* Observation, supervision, invigilation, watch, surveiliace, custody, upkeep; ~**ਕਰਨਾ** To watch, to look after; ~**ਵਿਚ ਰਖਣਾ** To keep under surveillance.

ਨਿਗਲਣਾ (nigalnaa) *v* To swallow, to gulp, to eat, to embezzle.

ਨਿਗਹਬਾਨ (nigahbaan) *n m* Protector, guardian.

ਨਿਗਹਬਾਨੀ (nigahbaanee) *n* Protection, guard, supervision.

ਨਿਗਾਹ (nigaah) *n f* Sight, vision.

ਨਿਗੂਣੀ (nigoonee) *a* Paltry, of little value.

ਨਿਘਰਨਾ (nigharnaa) *v* To be destroyed, to be immesed, to be swallowed, to be overwhelmed.

ਨਿਘਰਾ (nighraa) *a* Homeless, waif.

ਨਿੱਘਾ (nigghaa) *a* Moderately, warm, magnanimous, patient, self-controlling.

ਨਿਘਾਸ (nighaas) *n m* Warmth; Profit.

ਨਿਘਾਰਨਾ (nigaarnaa) *v* To cause to sink, submerge.

ਨਿਚਲਾ (nichlaa) *a* Lower, under.

ਨਿਚੁੜਨਾ (nichurnaa) *v* To drip, to be squeezed dry. Also **ਨਿਚੜਨਾ**

ਨਿਚੋੜ (nichor) *n m* Gist, essence, resume, quiteessence, summary.

ਨਿਚੋੜਨਾ (nichornaa) *v* To squeeze, to wring, to press, to pour out.

ਨਿੱਛ (nichchh) *n f* Sneeze; ~**ਮਾਰਨੀ** To

sneeze.

ਨਿਛਾਵਰ (nichhaawar) *n m* Sacrifice, offering.

ਨਿਜਾਤ (nijaat) *n f* Salvation, freedom. Also **ਨਜਾਤ**

ਨਿਜ਼ਾਮ (nizaam) *n m* Ruler, management, rule.

ਨਿਜੀ (nijee) *a* Personal, private, own, self.

ਨਿਝਕ (nijhak) *a* unhesitating, unabashed, forward, bold, fearless, reckless; Frank.

ਨਿਡਰ (niḍar) *a* Fearless, dauntless, undaunted, intrepid; ~ਤਾ Fearlessness, temerity, interpidity.

ਨਿਢਾਲ (niḍhaal) *a* Exhausted, depressed, weak, helpless, invalid.

ਨਿਤ (nit) *adv* Always, ever; ~ਨੇਮ Daily, routine.

ਨਿਤਰਨਾ (nitarnaa) *v* To be clarified, to be seprated, To be decanted.

ਨਿਤਾਣਾ (nitaaṇaa) *a* Weak, faint, powerless, feeble, sinewless, infirm.

ਨਿਤਾਰਨਾ (nitaarnaa) *v* To clarify, to decant, to winnow, to refine.

ਨਿੰਦਕ (nindak) *n m* Caluminator, defamer, slanderer, censorious, vilifier, backbiter.

ਨਿੰਦਣਾ (nindṇaa) *v* To defame, to vilify, to blaspheme, to censure, to condemn, to slander, to dispraise.

ਨਿੰਦਰਾਉਣਾ (nidaraunaa) *v* To feel sleepy; to make sleepy, to cause sleep.

ਨਿੰਦਰਾਇਆ (ninderaaiaa) *a* Sleepy, drowsy, slumberous, somnolent.

ਨਿੰਦਾ (nindaa) *n f* Censure, blasphemy, reproach, slander, backbiting; ~ਕਰਨਾ To condemn.

ਨਿੰਦਿਤ (nindit) *a* Criticised, condemned, malgned, columniated, defamed.

ਨਿਧੜਕ (nidharak) *a* Fearless, bold, dauntless, outspoken; ~ਤਾ Fearlessness, audaciousness.

ਨਿਪਟਣਾ (nipaṭṇaa) *v* To settle, to tackle, to decide.

ਨਿਪਟਾਰਾ (nipṭaaraa) *n m* Disposal, settlement; ~ਕਰਨਾ To settle, to dispose of, to finish, to decide.

ਨਿਪੁੱਤਾ (niputtaa) *a* Sonless, without male issue.

ਨਿਪੁੰਨ (nipuṇṇ) *a* Adept, proficient, skilful, expert; ~ਤਾ Efficiency, mastery.

ਨਿਬੰਧ (nibandh) *n m* Essay, treatise, article, thesis; ~ਕਾਰ Essayist, essay writer.

ਨਿਬੜਨਾ (nibaṛnaa) *v* To be settled,

to be brought to an issue, to be decided, to be finished.

ਨਿੰਬੂ (nimboo) *n m* Lime, lemon.

ਨਿਬੇੜਨਾ (bibernaa) *v* To finish, to end, to settle, to execute, to perform, to dispose of.

ਨਿਬੇੜਾ (biberaa) *n m* End, finish, settlement, conclusion; Speed or pace of executing a task.

ਨਿਭਣਾ (nibhṇaa) *v* To pull on, to carry on, to finish.

ਨਿਭਾਣਾ (nibhaaṇaa) *v* To perform, to accomplish, to conduct, to keep one's faith. Also **ਨਿਭਾਉਣਾ**

ਨਿੰਮ (nimm) *n f* Margosa tree; *Azadirachta indica*.

ਨਿੰਮਾ (nimmaa) *a* Dim, low, abscure, dubious.

ਨਿਮੰਤਰਨ (nimantaran) *n m* Invitation; ~ਪੱਤਰ Invitation card.

ਨਿਮਰਤਾ (nimartaa) *n f* Modesty, courtesy, humbleness, meekness.

ਨਿੰਮਲ (nimmal) *a* Cloudless, clear, fair. Also **ਨਿੰਬਲ**

ਨਿਮਾਣਾ (nimaaṇaa) *a* Humble, simple, meek, poor, devoid of pride.

ਨਿਯਤ (niyat) *a* Fixed, settled, prescribed, appointed; ~ਕੰਮ Assignment, allotted task.

ਨਿਯੰਤਰਣ (niyantraṇ) *n m* Control,
Management, restrain.

ਨਿਯਮ (niyam) *n m* Rule(s), norm, principle, canon.

ਨਿਯਮਿਤ (niyamat) *a* Regular, lawful, methodical.

ਨਿਯੁਕਤ (niyukta) *a* Appointed; ~ਕਰਨਾ To appoint.

ਨਿਯੁਕਤੀ (niyukti) *n f* Appointment, nomination.

ਨਿਰੰਕਾਰ (nirankaar) *a* Formless; The Formless One, God.

ਨਿਰਖ (nirakh) *n m* Rate, price, cost, current market rate.

ਨਿਰਖਣਾ (nirakhṇaa) *v* To see, to look, to appreciate, to ascertain.

ਨਿਰੱਖਰ (nirakkhar) *a* Illiterate, unlettered; ~ਤਾ Illiteracy.

ਨਿਰਗੁਣ (nirguṇ) *a* Absolute, virtueless, formless, transcendent, without qualities, unskilled.

ਨਿਰਛਲ (nirchhal) *a* Candid, frank, naive, sincere, guileless, unsophisticated.

ਨਿਰੰਜਣ (niranjaṇ) *a* Formless; The formless one, God.

ਨਿਰਜਨ (nirjan) *a* Unpopulated, desolate, uninhabited.

ਨਿਰਣਾ (nirṇaa) *n m* Decision, verdict, judgement, conclusion. Also **ਨਿਰਨਾ**

ਨਿਰੰਤਰ (nirantar) *a adv* Continous,

incessant, ceaseless, perpetual, constant, consecutive, uninterrupted; Ceaselessly; ~ਤਾ Continuity, continuum, uninterruptedness.

ਨਿਰਦਈ (nirdaee) *a* Cruel, merciless, callous, ruthless, brutal, stern.

ਨਿਰਦੇਸ਼ (nirdesh) *n m* Direction, reference; ~ਕ Director, supervisor.

ਨਿਰਦੋਸ਼ (nirdosh) *a* Faultless, innocent, inculpable, guiltless, correct.

ਨਿਰਧਨ (nirdhan) *a* Poor, penniless; ~ਤਾ Poverty, pauperism.

ਨਿਰਨਾ (nirnaa) *a* Empty stomach, taking no food. Also **ਨਿਰਣਾ**

ਨਿਰਨਾਇਕ (nirnaaik) *a* Decisive, affirmative.

ਨਿਰਪੱਖ (nirpakkh) *a* Impartial, unbiased, unprejudiced, neutral; ~ਤਾ Neutrality.

ਨਿਰਪੇਖ (nirpekh) *a* Absolute, neutral, independent.

ਨਿਰਬਲ (nirbal) *a* Weak, powerless, frail, decrepit; ~ਤਾ Weakness, fraility.

ਨਿਰਭੈ (nirbhai) *a* Fearless, dauntless, bold, intrepid; ~ਤਾ Fearlessness, dauntlessness, intrepidity, boldness, indomitability.

ਨਿਰਮਲ (nirmal) *a* Clear, transparent, pure, spotless, unpolluted, clean, lucid, crystalline; ~ਤਾ Cleanliness, purity, transparency.

ਨਿਰਮਾਣ (nirmaan) *n m* Construction, manufacture, production.

ਨਿਰਮੂਲ (nirmool) *a* Baseless, groundless.

ਨਿਰਮੋਹੀ (nirmohee) *a* Indifferent, without love and affection.

ਨਿਰਲੇਪ (nirlep) *a* Neutral, disinterested; ਗੁਟ~ Non-aligned.

ਨਿਰਵਾਸੀ (nirvaasee) *a* Non-resident.

ਨਿਰਵਾਚਨ (nirvaachan) *n m* Election.

ਨਿਰਵਾਣ (nirvaan) *n m* Emancipation salvation, denouement, freedom from worldly concern. Also **ਨਿਰਵਾਨ**

ਨਿਰਵੈਰ (nirvair) *a* Without malice without hatred, free from animosity.

ਨਿਰਾ (niraa) *a adv* More, simple unalloyed, only, sheer; Entirely merely, simply.

ਨਿਰਾਸ (niraas) *a* Disappointed Despaired, disconsolate; ~ਤ Despair, frustration, dejection Also **ਨਿਰਾਸ਼ਾ**

ਨਿਰਾਹਾਰ (niraahaar) *a* Fasting without meals.

ਨਿਰਾਕਾਰ (niraakaar) *a* Incorporeal, formless.

ਨਿਰਾਦਰ (niraadar) *n m* Insult, dishonour, disrespect.

ਨਿਰਾਦਰੀ (niraadaree) *n f* Disgrace, disrespect, insult, abasement, blasphemy.

ਨਿਰਾਲਾ (niraalaa) *a* Peculiar, extraordinary, excellent, odd strange, rare, distinct; ~ਪਣ Strangeness, unusualness, peculiarity.

ਨਿਰੀਖਕ (nireekhak) *n m* Inspector, supervisor, invigilator, observer.

ਨਿਰੀਖਣ (nireekhan) *n m* Observation, inspection, invigilation.

ਨਿਰੋਧ (nirodh) *n m* Restriction, obstruction, repression; Condom.

ਨਿਰੋਲ (nirol) *a* Unadurated, unmixed, clear, pure.

ਨਿਲੱਜ (nillaj) *a* Shameless, devoid of a sense of honour, immodest, brazen faced impudent.

ਨਿਲੰਬਨ (nilamban) *n m* Suspension.

ਨਿਲਾਮੀ (nillaamee) *n f* Auction.

ਨਿਵਾਉਣਾ (nivaaunaa) *v* To cause, to bend, to humble, to bring under descipline.

ਨਿਵਾਸ (nivass) *n m* Residence, house, dwelling quarter, habitation, domicile. Also ਨਿਵਾਸਾ

ਨਿਵਾਸੀ (nivaasee) *n m* Resident, inhabitant, dweller, citizen.

ਨਿਵਾਜਣਾ (nivaajnaa) *v* To honour, to dignify, to crown.

ਨਿਵਾਣ (nivaan) *n f* Slope, drop, downward, lowness, valley, depression.

ਨਿਵਾਰਨ (nivaaran) *n m* Healing, prevention, hindering or removing, eradication.

ਨਿਵਾਰਨਾ (nivaarnaa) *v* To heal, to prevent, to remove, to eradicate.

ਨਿਵਾਲਾ (nivaalaa) *n m* Morsel, mouthful.

ਨਿਵੇਦਨ (nivedan) *n m* Request, appeal, petition, representation; ~ਪੱਤਰ Application.

ਨੀਅਤ (neeyat) *n f* Intention, motive, desire, aim, purpose. Also ਨੀਤ, ਨੀਯਤ

ਨੀਂਹ (neenh) *n f* Foundation, base, basemen, bottom.

ਨੀਂਗਰ (neengar) *n m* Boy, child, infant, toddler.

ਨੀਚ (neech) *a* Mean, vile, low, humble, inferior, slavish, sordid, disgraceful; ~ਤਾ Meaness, degeneracy, vulgarity.

ਨੀਝ (neejh) *n f* Sharp look, close inspection; ~ਸ਼ਾਲਾ Observatory.

ਨੀਤੀ (neetee) *n f* Policy, diplomacy,

prudence, counsel, politics; ~**ਵਾਨ** Poltician, statesman, moralist.

ਨੀਂਦ (neend) *n f* Sleep, slumber; **ਡੂੰਘੀ~** Coma.

ਨੀਮ (neem) *a prep* Half, middle; Quasi, semi, demi; ~**ਗਰਮ** Lukewarm; ~**ਪਾਗਲ** Half mad.

ਨੀਲ (neel) *n m a* Bruise, blue; Indigo; Ten billion, 10,000,000,000,000 ~**ਕੰਠ** Blue Jay.

ਨੀਲਮ (neelam) *n m* Gem, sapphire.

ਨੀਲਾ (neelaa) *a* Blue, bluish, azure; **ਅਸਮਾਨੀ~** Sky blue.

ਨੀਵਾਂ (neevaan) *a* Low, lower; ~**ਕਰਨਾ** To lower, to demean.

ਨੁਸਖਾ (nuskhaa) *n m* Prescription, recipe, treatise.

ਨੁਸ਼ਾਦਰ (nushaadar) *n m* Ammonium chloride.

ਨੁਹਾਰ (nuhaar) *n f* Appearance, features, countenance, outline, face, similitude.

ਨੁਕਸ (nukas) *n m* Defect, fault, flaw, snag, lacuna, weakness, blemish; ~**ਕੱਢਣਾ** To find fault, to pick holes, to carp; ~**ਦਾਰ** Defective, faulty.

ਨੁਕਸਾਨ (nuksaan) *n m* Loss, harm, damage, deficiency.

ਨੁਕਤਾ (nuktaa) *n m* Point, dot; ~**ਚੀਨ** Critic, faultfinder; ~**ਚੀਨੀ** Criticism, fault finding.

ਨੁੱਕਰ (nukkar) *n m* Corner, extremity, nook, apex of an angel.

ਨੁਕੀਲਾ (nukeelaa) *a* Pointed, sharp, barbed, angular.

ਨੁਮਾਇੰਦਗੀ (numaindagee) *n* Representation; representativeness; ~**ਕਰਨਾ** To represent.

ਨੁਮਾਇੰਦਾ (numaindaa) *n m* Representative, deputy, agent.

ਨੁਚੜਨਾ (nucharnaa) *v* To exude.

ਨੁਮਾਇਸ਼ (numaaish) *n f* Show, exhibition, display, demonstration.

ਨੂੰਹ (noonh) *n f* Daughter-in-law, Son's wife.

ਨੂਰ (noor) *n m* Light, splendour, brilliance.

ਨੂਰੀ (nooree) *a* Bright, lustrous.

ਨੇਸਤੀ (nestee) *n f* Laziness, lethargy, langour; Non-existence, nothingness.

ਨੇਸਤੋਨਾਬੂਦ (nestonaabood) *a* Fully destroyed, utterly devastated.

ਨੇਹੁੰ (nehun) *n m* Love, affection.

ਨੇਕ (nek) *a* Good, kind, virtuous; ~**ਦਿਲ** Sincere, honest; ~**ਨਾਮ** Renowned, famous; ~**ਨਾਮੀ** Fame, good reputation; ~**ਨੀਅਤੀ** Honesty, integrity, rectitude.

ਨੇਕੀ (nekee) *n f* Goodness, virtue

kindness.

ਨੇਜ਼ਾ (nezaa) *n m* Long spear, lance.

ਨੇਤਰ (netar) *n m* Eye.

ਨੇਤਾ (netaa) *n m* Leader, chief, directing head; Demogogue; Torchbearer; ~ਗੀਰੀ Leadership, demogogy.

ਨੇਂਦਰਾ (nendraa) *n m* Contribution to a wedding feast. Also ਨਿਉਂਦਾ

ਨੇਮਾਵਲੀ (nemaavalee) *n f* Code, directory.

ਨੇੜੇ (nere) *adv* Near, close by, beside, at hand.

ਨੋਕ (nok) *n f* Point, end, tip, angle; ~ਝੋਕ Mutual repartee, pleasantry; ~ਦਾਰ Pointed, angular, sharp, conical, barbed.

ਨੋਚਣਾ (nochnaa) *v* To pinch, to tear, to scratch, to pluck.

ਨੋਟ (not) *n m* Note, noting, minutes; Currency note; ~ਕਰਨਾ To note, to note down, to take notes, to write; To take notice, to be warned.

ਨੌਕਰ (haukar) *n m* Servant, attendant, domestic employees; ~ਸ਼ਾਹੀ Bureaucracy.

ਨੌਕਰੀ (naukree) *n f* Service, employment, job, post.

ਨੌਕਾ (naukaa) *n f* Boat.

ਨੌਗਾ (naugaa) *n m* Portion, share, lot; Allotment, quota.

ਨੌਜਵਾਨ (naujawaan) *n m a* Youth, youngman; Youthful.

ਨੌਬਤ (naubat) *n f* Turn time, opportunity, state, condition.

ਨੌਲਖਾ (naulakhaa) *a* Very valuable, costing nine lakhs currency, priceless.

ਨੌਲੀ (naulee) *n f* Nose, turned up nose.

ਨੌਲਨਾ (naulnaa) *v* To abuse, to rebuke, to scold, to reprove, to revile at.

ਪ

ਪ Twenty sixth letter of Gurmukhi alphabets, pronounced as 'pappaa'.

ਪਉਂਚਾ (paunchaa) *n m* Talon, opening of trousers. Also **ਪੌਂਚਾ**

ਪਉਲਾ (paulaa) *n m* Shoe, footwear.

ਪਉੜੀ (pauṛee) *n f* Stanza.

ਪਸ਼ਚਾਤਾਪ (pashchaataap) *n m* Repetence, remorse, penitence, expiation.

ਪਸਤੌਲ (pastaul) *n f* Pistol, revolver.

ਪਸੰਦ (pasand) *n m* Choice, liking, approval, selection; **ਆਰਾਮ~** Easy going; **ਮਨ~** Favourite.

ਪਸੰਦੀਦਾ (pasandeedaa) *a* Liked, favourite, chosen.

ਪਸਪਾ (paspaa) *a* Stepping backward, running away, fleeing; **~ਕਰਨਾ** To make one run away, to defeat, to rout.

ਪਸ਼ਮ (pasham) *n f* Soft wool, fur; **~ਦਾਰ** wooly.

ਪਸ਼ਮੀਨਾ (pashmeenaa) *n m* Soft fine wool, fur.

ਪਸਰਨਾ (pasarnaa) *v* To Spread out, to expand, to be stretched out.

ਪਸਲੀ (paslee) *n f* Rib.

ਪਸ਼ਾਬ (pashaab) *n m* Urine; **~ਕਰਨਾ** To make water, to urinate; **~ਖ਼ਾਨਾ** Urinal. Also **ਪਿਸ਼ਾਬ**

ਪਸਾਰਨਾ (pasaarnaa) *v* To spread, to extend, to stretch, to diffuse.

ਪੰਸਾਰੀ (pansaaree) *n m* Grocer, druggist, spice seller, apothecary. Also **ਪੰਸਾਰੀ** or **ਪਨਸਾਰੀ**

ਪਸੀਜਣਾ (paseejṇaa) *v* To deliquesce, to be compassionate, to relent, to prespire.

ਪਸੀਨਾ (paseenaa) *n m* Sweat, prespiration; **~ਆਉਣਾ** To sweat, prespire.

ਪਸ਼ੂ (pashoo) *n m* Animal, beast, brute, cattle, quadruped; **~ਪਾਲਣ** Animal husbandry, cattle, breeding.

ਪਸ਼ੇਮਾਨ (pashemaan) *a* Sorry, ashamed, penitent, regretful, remorseful repentent.

ਪਹਾੜ (pahaaṛ) *n m* Mountain; **~ਟੁੱਟ ਪੈਣਾ** Advent of calamity.

ਪਹਾੜਾ (pahaaṛaa) *n m* Multiplication table.

ਪਹਾੜੀ (pahaaṛee) *n m a* Hill, hillock; Hilly, alpine, mountainous; **~ਦੱਰਾ** Revine, mountain pass.

ਪਹਿਨਣਾ (pahinṇaa) *v* To wear, to

put on, to dress.

ਪਹਿਰਾ (paheraa) *n m* Watch, escort, guard, patrol; ~ਦੇਣਾ To keep watch, to guard.

ਪਹਿਰਾਵਾ (paheraawaa) *n m* Dress, fashion, costume, attire.

ਪਹਿਲ (pahel) *n f* Priority, preference, precedence; ~ਕਰਨਾ To lead, to forestall.

ਪਹਿਲਵਾਨ (pahelwaan) *n m* Wrestler, champion, athlete.

ਪਹਿਲਾਂ (pahelaan) *adv* At first, formerly, previously, before; ~ਆਉਣਾ To precede, to come early.

ਪਹਿਲਾ (pahelaa) *a* First, primary, maiden, former, previous; ~ਭਾਸ਼ਣ Maiden speech.

ਪਹੀਆ (pahiyaa) *n m* Wheel, cart track.

ਪਹੁੰਚ (pahunch) *n f* Arrival, access, acknowledgement, approach, receipt.

ਪਹੁੰਚਾ (paunchaa) *n m* Claw, paw; Hand, wrist; Lower opening of trousers or shorts.

ਪਹੁੰਚਣਾ (pahunchnaa) *v* To reach, to arrive at, to attain.

ਪਹੇਲੀ (pahelee) *n f* Riddle, quiz.

ਪਕਣਾ (paknaa) *v* To ripen, to be cooked, to bake.

ਪਕਵਾਨ (pakwaan) *n m* Cooked delicacies, bakemeats, pastry, fried cakes, sweatmeats.

ਪਕੜ (pakar) *n f* Hold, seizure, catch, bout, clasp, clamp, influence; ~ਲੈਣਾ To catch, to arrest, to clutch, to hold, to grasp; ~ਵਿਚ ਆਣਾ Come in one's hold.

ਪਕੜਨਾ (pakarnaa) *v* To catch, to arrest, to hold, to seize, to grip.

ਪੱਕਾ (pakkaa) *a* Cooked, ripe, strong, perfect, firm, established, tight, permanent, certain, sure, resolute, stable, hard, solid; ~ਕਰਨਾ To confirm, to harden, to affirm, to stabilize; ~ਖਾਣਾ Fried cooked food; ~ਦੋਸਤ Fast friend; ~ਰੰਗ Fast colour; ~ਮਾਲ Finished goods.

ਪਕਾਉਣਾ (pakaaunaa) *v* To cook, to bake, to fry, to ripen, to make firm.

ਪਕਿਆਈ (pakiaaee) *n f* Hardness firmness, strength; Steadfastness.

ਪਖੰਡ (pakhand) *n m* Hypocrisy, humbug, deceit, prudery, pretence.

ਪਖੰਡੀ (pakhandee) *a* Imposter, cheat, hypocrite; Imposter, deceitful, dissembler. Also ਪਖੰਡਣ (*f*)

ਪਖਪਾਤ (pakkhpaat) *n m* Partiality, favour, bias, partisanship,

ਪਖਵਾੜਾ (pakhwaaraa) *n m* Fortnight, lunar fortnight.

ਪੱਖਾ (pakkhaa) *n m* Fan, propeller.

ਪਖਾਵਜ (pakhaavaj) *n m* A kind of drum.

ਪੱਖੀ (pakkhee) *a n m f* Partial, biased; Supporter, co-party man; Partisan; Bird; Hand fan.

ਪੰਖੇਰੂ (pankheroo) *n m* Bird, winged animal; Spirit.

ਪੱਗ (pagg) *n f* Turban; ~ਲਾਹੁਣੀ To insult; ~ਵਟਾਉਣੀ To make friends with.

ਪੰਗਤ (pangat) *n f* Line, row, column.

ਪਗੜੀ (pagree) *n f* Turban, imprest; ~ਉਛਾਲਣੀ To ridicule; ~ਪੈਰਾਂ ਤੇ ਰਖਣਾ To submit, to beg mercy; ~ਲਾਹੁਣੀ To disgrace, to insult. Also ਪੱਗ

ਪੰਗਾ (pangaa) *n m* Briar, thorn, splinter, prickle.

ਪੰਗੇਬਾਜ਼ (Pangebaaz) *n m* Problematist, quarrelsome.

ਪੰਘਰਨਾ (pangharnaa) *v* To melt, to fuse, to liquefy, to smell.

ਪੰਘੂੜਾ (panghooraa) *n m* Cradle, crib.

ਪਚਨਾ (pachnaa) *v* To be digested, to be consumed.

ਪੰਚਮ (pancham) *a* Fifth (note in music) high pitched, sharp.

ਪੰਚਰ (panchar) *n m* Puncture in rubber tube or bladder punctured; ~ਲਾਉਣਾ To mend, to repair, to puncture.

ਪਚਾਉਣਾ (pachaaunaa) *v* To digest, to assimilate; ਪੈਸਾ~ To embezzle money.

ਪੱਛਣਾ (pachchhnaa) *v* To scarify, to make incision, to incise.

ਪਛਤਾਉਣਾ (pachhtaaunaa) *v* To repent, to grieve, to regret.

ਪਛਤਾਵਾ (pachhtaavaa) *n* Repentence, regret, remorse, grief, penetence, ruefulness.

ਪੱਛਮੀ (pachhmee) *a* Western.

ਪਛੜਨਾ (pachharnaa) *v* To lag behind, to fall behind.

ਪਛਾਣ (pachaan) *n f* Recognition, acquaintance, identification.

ਪਛਾਣਨਾ (pachaannaa) *v* To identify, to recognise, to distinguish, to perceive, to make out.

ਪਛਾੜਨਾ (pachhaarnaa) *v* To over power, to prostrate, to defeat, to overthrow.

ਪੰਛੀ (panchhee) *n m* Bird; ~ਵਿਗਿਆਨ Ornithology.

ਪੱਛੀ (pachchhee) *n f* Small basket, sugarcane rind.

ਪੱਜ (pajj) *n m* Excuse, pretence, pretext.

ਪੰਜਾ (panjaa) *n m* Paw, claw, grip; The figure 5.

ਪਜਾਮਾ (pajaamaa) *n m* Trousers.

ਪੰਜੇਬ (panjeb) *n f* Anklet, tinkling silver ornament.

ਪਟਕਣਾ (pataknaa) *v* To knock down, to overthrow, to dash against.

ਪਟਕਾ (patkaa) *n m* A waist cloth, turban, sash, belt, girdle.

ਪਟੜਾ (patraa) *n m* Wooden plank, wash board.

ਪਟੜੀ (patree) *n f* Way, pavement, footpath; Silver ornament; **~ਬੈਠਣਾ** To have harmonious relations.

ਪਟਾ (pataa) *n m* Strap, badge, dog-coller; Lease deed.

ਪਟਾਕ (pataak) *n m* Crash, explosion, thump.

ਪਟਾਕਾ (pataakaa) *n m* cracker.

ਪਟਾਕਣਾ (pataaknaa) *v* To talk incessantly.

ਪੱਟੀ (pattee) *n f* Bandage, cloth or metal strip; **ਹਵਾਈ~** Air strep; **~ਪੜ੍ਹਾਉਣਾ** To tutor; **ਉਲਟੀ-ਪੜ੍ਹਾਉਣਾ** To misguide.

ਪੱਠਾ (patthaa) *n m* Muscles, tendon, sinew; A robust youngman; Young wrestler; A fodder plant or grass.

ਪਠਾਰ (pathaar) *n m* Plateau.

ਪਠੋਰਾ (pathoraa) *n m* Young goat; Kid.

ਪੰਡ (pand) *n f* Bundle, package, bale burden.

ਪੰਡਾਲ (pandaal) *n m* Sitting place for marriage or public meeting.

ਪਤ (pat) *n f* Honour, respect; **~ਲਾਹੁਣੀ** To dishonour, to disgrace.

ਪੱਤ (patt) *n m* Leaf. Also **ਪੱਤਾ**

ਪਤੰਗ (patang) *n f* Kite.

ਪਤੰਗਾ (patangaa) *n m* Worm, moth, spark, live coal.

ਪੱਤਰ (pattar) *n m* Letter, foliage, document, deed, leaf, paper, newspaper, periodical.

ਪਤਲਾ (patlaa) *a* Thin, lean, slim, weak, diluted, watery; **~ਪਣ** Thinness, leanness.

ਪਤਲੂਣ (patloon) *n f* Pantaloons.

ਪਤਾ (pataa) *n m* Address, knowledge, information, trace; **~ਲਗਣਾ** To know.

ਪੱਤਾ (pattaa) *n m* Card, leaf.

ਪਤਾਸਾ (pataasaa) *n m* A kind of sweet meat prepared by sugar only.

ਪਤਾਲ (pataal) *n m* Hell, lower world, infernal regions, nadir, hader.

ਪੰਤਾਲੀ (pantaalee) *a* Forty-five. Also **ਪੰਜਤਾਲੀ**

ਪਤਾਲੂ (pataaloo) *n m* Testes, testicles.

ਪਤਿਆਉਣਾ (patiaaunaa) *v* To confide in, to trust, to belive, to depend on, to appease, to soothe.

ਪਤੀ (patee) *n m* Husband, master; **ਸੈਨਾ~** Commander; **ਰਾਸ਼ਟ੍ਰ~** President; **~ਬ੍ਰਤਾ** Chaste woman; A woman faithful to her husband.

ਪੱਤੀ (pattee) *n f* Portion, share, division.

ਪਤੀਜਣਾ (pateejanaa) *v* To be reassured, satisfied or trustful, to be persuaded.

ਪਤੀਲਾ (pateelaa) *n m* Cooking pot, cooking vessel.

ਪੱਤੇਬਾਜ਼ (pattebaaz) *a* Tricksy, trickster, cheat, deceiver, swindler.

ਪੱਤੇਬਾਜ਼ੀ (pattebaazee) *n f* Trickery, cheating, swindling.

ਪੰਥ (panth) *n m* Religious sect, way, path, custom.

ਪੱਥਣਾ (patthnaa) *v* To make or mould with strokes of hand (bricks, cowdung cakes, etc.)

ਪੱਥਰ (patthar) *n m a* Stone, gem; Hard, heavy; **~ਤੇ ਲੀਕ** Certainly; **~ਦਾ ਕੋਲਾ** Hard coke; **~ਦਾ ਫ਼ਰਸ਼** Pavement; **~ਦਿਲ** Hard hearted; **~ਮਾਰਨਾ** To stone, to pelt.

ਪਥਰਾਉਣਾ (pathraaunaa) *v* To become hard, to be dead, to calcify, to fossilize, to become insipid.

ਪੱਥਰੀ (patthree) *n f* Flint, small stone, gallstone, stone in kidney.

ਪਥਰੀਲਾ (pathreelaa) *a* Strony, full of stones.

ਪੱਥਲਣਾ (pathallanaa) *v* To turn over, to cause to turn, to overturn.

ਪਥੇਰਾ (patheraa) *n m* Brick-maker.

ਪਦ (pad) *n* (1) Foot; Foot step; (2) Couplet, stanza, verse; Expression, word form; (3) Post, rank, degree, status; **~ਉਨਤੀ** Promotion; **~ਅਧਿਕਾਰੀ** Officer, official.

ਪੱਦ (padd) *n m* Fart, passing wind noisily through anus; **~ਮਾਰਨਾ** To fart, to pass wind.

ਪੱਦਣਾ (paddnaa) *v* To pass wind; To show fear or cowardice, to behave cowardly.

ਪੰਦਰਾਂ (pandraan) *a* Fifteenth.

ਪਦਵੀ (padvee) *n f* Position, rank, degree, status, designation.

ਪਦਾਉਣਾ (padaaunaa) *v* To weary out, to reduce, to frighten, to cause to pass the wind.

ਪਦਾਰਥ (padaarath) *n m* Thing, stuff, object, substance, matter, material, food; **~ਵਾਦ** Matrialism.

ਪੰਧ (pandh) *n m* Journey, route,

distance, passage, path, way; ~ਕਰਨਾ To travel.

ਪੱਧਤੀ (paddhatee) *n f* System, method; Custom; Ritual.

ਪੱਧਰ (paddhar) *n f* Level, plane, evenness; Standard, measure, norm, stratum.

ਪਧਰਾ (padhraa) *a* Smooth, even, easy, level, plain, flat, simple.

ਪੰਨਾ (pannaa) *n m* Leaf, page, foil; Emerald.

ਪਨਾਹ (panaah) *n f* Refuge, asylum, protection, shelter; ~ਦੇਣੀ To give refuge, to shelter; ਬੇ~ Unlimited, infinite, too much.

ਪਨੀਰ (paneer) *n m* Cheese.

ਪਪੜੀ (papree) *n f* Crust.

ਪੱਪੀ (pappee) *n f* Kiss.

ਪਪੀਹਾ (papeehaa) *n m* Rain bird.

ਪਪੀਤਾ (papeetaa) *n m* Papaya, papaw.

ਪੱਬ (pabb) *n m* Foot, fore part of the foot, toe; Water-lily.

ਪਰ (par) *n m conj Prep adv* Feather, wing; But, however; On, at; Last, bygone; ~ਉਪਕਾਰ Benevolence, philanthropy; Beneficence; ~ਅਧੀਨ (ਪਰਾਧੀਨ) Dependent, slave.

ਪ੍ਰਸੰਸਾ (prasansaa) *n f* Praise, applause, eulogy, admiration, appreciation. Also ਪਰਸੰਸਾ

ਪ੍ਰਸੰਗ (prasang) *n m* Context, theme, topic, incident, anecdote. Also ਪਰਸੰਗ

ਪਰਸਣਾ (parasnaa) *v* To touch, to feel.

ਪ੍ਰਸਤਾਵ (prastaav) *n m* Proposal, motion, proposition, resolution, essay; ~ਕ Mover, proposer; ~ਨਾ Prologue, preface, foreward, introduction.

ਪ੍ਰਸੰਨ (prasann) *a* Glad, happy, delighted; ~ਤਾ Happiness, joy, merriment.

ਪ੍ਰਸ਼ਨ (prashan) *n m* Question, enquiry, problem; ~ਪੱਤਰ Question paper.

ਪਰਸਪਰ (parsapar) *a* Mutual, reciprocal, respective.

ਪ੍ਰਸ਼ਾਸਨ (prashaasan) *n m* Administration. Also ਪਰਸ਼ਾਸਨ

ਪ੍ਰਸਾਦ (prasaad) *n m* Kindness, favour, boon, blessing, food offered to god, communion food. Also ਪਰਸਾਦ

ਪ੍ਰਸਾਰ (prasaar) *n m* Extension, transmission, propagation.

ਪ੍ਰਸਾਰਣ (prasaaran) *n m* Broadcast, transmission, propagation. Also ਪਰਸਾਰਣ

ਪ੍ਰਸਿੱਧ (prasiddh) *a* Famous, eminent, known, renowned, reputed, distinguished, popular. Also ਪਰਸਿੱਧ

ਪ੍ਰਸੂਤ (prasoot) *n m* Maternity, childbirth. Also ਪਰਸੂਤ

ਪਰਸੋਂ (parsoon) *a* Day after tomorrow, day before yesterday.

ਪਰਾਂ (praan) *adv* Beyond, farther, ahead, at a distance.

ਪਰਹੇਜ਼ (parhez) *n m* Forbearance, abstinence, prevention, avoidance.

ਪ੍ਰਕਾਸ਼ (prakaash) *n m* Light, day light.

ਪਰਕੋਟਾ (parkotaa) *n m* Parapet, rampart.

ਪਰਖ (parakh) *n f* Trial, examination, criticism, probation.

ਪਰਖਣਾ (parakhnaa) *v* To test, to examine, to evaluate, to review, to assess genuineness.

ਪਰਗਟ (pargat) *a* Apparent, clear, disclosed, overt, known, obvious, visible; ~ਕਰਨਾ To disclose, to express, to manifest, to unveil, to expose, to reveal. Also ਪ੍ਰਗਟ

ਪ੍ਰਗਤੀ (pragatee) *n f* Progress, growth.

ਪਰਚਨਾ (parchnaa) *v* To be amused, to be satisfied, to be entertained, to be diverted, to be engaged.

ਪਰਚੱਲਤ (parchallat) *a* Current, prevailing, in vogue.

ਪਰਚਾ (parchaa) *n m* Examination paper; Newspaper, tabloid; Bill, invoice.

ਪਰਚਾਉਣਾ (parchaaunaa) *v* To amuse, to entertain, to divert, assuage, console satisfy.

ਪਰਚਾਰ (parchaar) *n m* Propgation, publicity, preaching, promulgation, spreading. Also ਪ੍ਰਚਾਰ

ਪਰਚੂਨ (parchoon) *n f a* Grocery; In retail.

ਪਰਛੱਤੀ (parchhattee) *n f* Loft.

ਪਰਛਾਵਾਂ (parcchavaan) *n m* Shadow, shade, rejection.

ਪਰਜਾ (parjaa) *n f* Public, people, subjects, tenants, dependents, followers; ~ਤੰਤਰ Republic, democracy.

ਪਰਤ (parat) *n f* Fold, layer, stratum, crust; Copy, transcript; ~ਦਾਰ Stratified, laminated.

ਪਰਤੱਖ (partakkh) *a* Direct, obvious, evident, clear, overt, visible, red; ~ਹੋਣਾ To materialize; ~ਕਰਨਾ To actualize, to invoke.

ਪਰਤਣਾ (partanaa) *v* To turn, to return, to revert, to recede, to get back.

ਪਰਤੰਤਰ (partantar) *a* Dependent, subdued; ~ਤਾ Dependence,

reliance.

ਪਰਤਾਉਣਾ (partaaunaa) *v* To return, to turn over, to refund, to test, to experiment.

ਪਰਤਾਪ (partaap) *n m* Splendour, brilliance, glory, warmth.

ਪਰਤਾਵਾ (partaavaa) *n m* Trial, experiment, examination, test.

ਪ੍ਰਤਿਨਿਧ (pratinidh) *n m* Representative.

ਪ੍ਰਤਿਪੂਰਕ (pratipoorak) *a* Compensatory.

ਪ੍ਰਤਿਯੋਗਤਾ (pratiyogtaa) *n m* Competition.

ਪ੍ਰਤਿਵਾਦ (prativaad) *n m* Refutation, argument, protest.

ਪ੍ਰਤੀਕ (prateek) *n m* Symbol, sign, emblem; ~ਸ਼ਾਸਤਰ Symbolics; ~ਵਾਦ Symbolism.

ਪ੍ਰਤੀਖਿਆ (prateekhiyaa) *n f* Wait, expectation.

ਪਰਦਖਣਾ (pardakhṇaa) *n m* Circumambulation, perambulation.

ਪਰਦਾ (pardaa) *n m* Curtain, screen, mask, veil, fold, partition wall, privacy, concealment, disguise; ~ਉਠਣਾ Curtain to be raised; To be uncovered, to be disclosed; ~ਉਠਾਉਣਾ To raise curtain, to reveal; ~ਕਰਨਾ To draw a curtain or veil, to conceal, to hide from view.

ਪਰਦੇਸ (pardes) *n m* Foreign country.

ਪਰਧਾਨ (pardhaan) *n m* President, chairman, chief. Also ਪ੍ਰਧਾਨ

ਪਰਨਾਲਾ (parnaalaa) *n m* Gutter, spout, drain for leaving off water from roof.

ਪਰਪੰਚ (parpanch) *n m* Deceit, falsehood, treachery; The world.

ਪਰੰਪਰਾ (paramparaa) *n f* Tradition, convention, aeon.

ਪਰਫੁੱਲਤ (parphullat) *a* Glad, happy, pleased, flourishing.

ਪ੍ਰਬੰਧ (prabandh) *n m* Management, organisation, administration, arrangement, system.

ਪ੍ਰਬਲ (prabal) *a* Strong, mighty, powerful, violent, dominant.

ਪਰਭਾਤ (prabhaat) *n f* Dawn, early morning. Also ਪ੍ਰਭਾਤ

ਪਰਭਾਵ (parbhaav) *n m* Influence, effect, impression, sway; ~ਸ਼ਾਲੀ Effective, impressive, influential, inspiring; ~ਹੀਣ Ineffective; ਵਾਦ Impressionism. Also ਪ੍ਰਭਾਵ

ਪਰਮਾਣ (parmaaṇ) *n m* Proof, example, authority, illustration; ~ਪੱਤਰ Certificate.

ਪਰਮਾਣੂ (parmaaṇoo) *n m* Atom; ~ਸ਼ਕਤੀ Atomic energy.

ਪਰਮਾਤਮਾ (parmaatmaa) *n m* God, the supreme being.

ਪਰਮਾਰਥ (parmaarath) *n m* Virtue, the subtle truth, salvation, the first object, the best end.

ਪ੍ਰਯਤਨ (prayatan) *n m* Effort, endeavour, attempt, struggle.

ਪ੍ਰਯੋਗ (prayog) *n m* Experiment, usage.

ਪਰਲੋ (parlo) *n f* Doomsday, the day of last judgement, final destruction or end of the universe; Great widespread calamity.

ਪਰਲੋਕ (parlok) *n m* The other or the next world, the hereafter; ~ਸਿਧਾਰਨਾ To die, pass away, to breathe one's last, to expire, decease; ~ਗਮਨ Death, decease.

ਪਰਵਰ (parvar) *a* Patron, nourisher; ~ਦਗਾਰ Providence, God.

ਪਰਵਰਿਸ਼ (parvarish) *n m* Nourishment, fostering, patronising, support.

ਪਰਵਾਸ (parvaas) *n m* Migration.

ਪਰਵਾਸੀ (parvaasee) *a* Migrant, emigrant, resident in foreign country.

ਪਰਵਾਹ (parvaah) *n f* Care, concern, attention, anxiety, regard; ~ਕਰਨੀ To heed, to be care (about), to pay attention; ਬੇ~ Careless, indifferent, unmindful, unreflecting.

ਪਰਵਾਨ (parvaan) *a* Accepted, acknowledged, true, just; ਗੀ~ Approval, accepetence, sanction, recognition; ~ਚੜ੍ਹਨਾ To grow up, to be accepted.

ਪਰਵਾਨਾ (parvaanaa) *n* Moth, butterfly, lover; Note, warrant, written order.

ਪਰਵਾਰ (parvaar) *n m* Family, household, relation; ~ਨਿਯੋਜਨ Family planning. Also **ਪਰਿਵਾਰ**

ਪਰਾਂ (paraan) *adv* Away, beyond, further on, off, far, apart.

ਪਰਾਇਆ (praaiaa) *a* Stranger, foreign, alien.

ਪ੍ਰਾਸਚਿਤ (praaschit) *n m* Repentence, atonement, expiation.

ਪ੍ਰਾਹੁਣਾ (praahunaa) *n m* Guest, visitor.

ਪ੍ਰਾਣ (praan) *n m* Breath, life, soul courage, energy; ~ਦੇਣਾ To give up life; ~ਲੈਣਾ To kill.

ਪ੍ਰਾਣੀ (praanee) *n m a* Animal, living creature, man or woman; Living, alive, animate.

ਪ੍ਰਾਂਤ (praant) *n m* Province.

ਪ੍ਰਾਤ (praat) *n f* Large brass dish, kneeding pan.

ਪਰਾਂਦਾ (praandaa) *n m* Bandeau, braid, coloured yarn for tying up hair. Also **ਪਰਾਂਦੀ**

ਪਰਾਰ (paraar) *n adv* Year before last.

ਪ੍ਰਾਰਥਨਾ (praarthnaa) *n f* Prayer, request, entreaty, submission.

ਪ੍ਰਾਲਬਧ (praalabdh) *n m* Fortune, fate.

ਪਰਿਣਾਮ (parinaam) *n m* Conclusion, consequence, result.

ਪਰਿੰਦਾ (parindaa) *n m* Bird.

ਪਰਿਭਾਸ਼ਾ (paribhaashaa) *n f* Definition.

ਪਰੀ (paree) *n f* Fairy, nymph, elf, sprite; Very beautiful or graceful woman.

ਪਰੀਖਿਆ (pareekhiaa) *n f* Examination test, enquiry, investigation.

ਪ੍ਰੀਤ (preet) *n f* Love, affection, attachment.

ਪ੍ਰੀਤਮ (preetam) *a m n* Dearest, dear; Lover, paramour, beloved, husband.

ਪਰੇ (pare) *adv* Beyond, younger, at a distance.

ਪਰੇਸ਼ਾਨ (pareshaan) *a* Perplexed, confused, troubled, distressed.

ਪਰੇਸ਼ਾਨੀ (pareshaanee) *n f* Confusion, perplexity, distraction, trouble, harassment, vexation, distress.

ਪ੍ਰੇਤ (pret) *n m* Ghost, evil spirit, fiend, deceased. Also **ਪਰੇਤ**

ਪ੍ਰੇਮ (prem) *n m* Love, affection. Also **ਪਰੇਮ**

ਪ੍ਰੇਰਨਾ (prernaa) *n f* Inspiration, incentive, motivation.

ਪ੍ਰੇਰਿਤ (prerit) *a* Induced, motivated; ~**ਕਰਨਾ** To inspire.

ਪੋਸਣਾ (prosanaa) *v* To serve meal, to set at the dining table.

ਪਰੋਖ (parokh) *a* Indirect, not visible.

ਪੋਣਾ (pronaa) *v* To thread, to string, to needle. Also **ਪਰੰਣ**

ਪਰੌਠਾ (paraunthaa) *n m* Indian loaf inlaid with butter and then fried.

ਪਲ (pal) *n m* Moment, second, twinkling of an eye.

ਪਲਸੇਟਾ (palsetaa) *n m* Turning from side to side when lying, tripping (as wrestlers); ~**ਮਾਰਨਾ** To take a sideways roll or turn.

ਪਲਕ (palak) *n f* Eye lid, eye lash, moment, twinkling of an eye; ~**ਝਪਕਣੀ** To wink, to blink, ~**ਲਾਉਣੀ** To sleep.

ਪਲੰਘ (palangh) *n m* Sleeping couch, bed.

ਪਲਟਣ (paltan) *n f* Battalion, infantry, regiment, corps, brigade, platoon. Also **ਪਲਟਨ**

ਪਲਟਣਾ (paltnaa) *v* To overturn, to return, to upset, to convert, to retreat, to turnover, to reverse.

ਪਲਟਾ (paltaa) *n m* Turn, change, retaliation, alteration, conversion.

ਪਲਟਾਉਣਾ (paltaaunaa) *v* To alter, to change, to reverse, to retract, to retrace, to turn.

ਪਲਨਾ (palnaa) *v* To be nourished, to be reared, to grow, to develop.

ਪਲੰਦਾ (palandaa) *n m* Parcel, bundle, pad, wad.

ਪਲੜਾ (palraa) *n m* Pan (of a scale or balance). Also **ਪਲਾ**

ਪੱਲਾ (palla) *n m* Border of a cloth, lap, skirting; ~**ਛਡਣਾ** To let one go; ~**ਛੁਡਾਉਣਾ** To get rid of; ~**ਫੜਨਾ** To catch or hold; To shelter.

ਪਲਾਂਘ (palaangh) *n f* Long step, leap, jump, bounce.

ਪਲਾਲ (palaal) *n m* Vain talking, bragging, idle or random speech.

ਪਲੀਤ (paleet) *a* Impure, unclean, polluted, filthy.

ਪਲੀਤਾ (paleetaa) *n m* Torch, gun cotton; ~**ਲਾਉਣਾ** To ignite, to incite.

ਪੱਲੂ (palloo) *n m* Border of a garment, hem of cloth, sail, bunt, lappet.

ਪਲੇਠ (paleth) *a* First born. Also **ਪਲੇਠੀ ਦਾ, ਪਲੇਠਾ**

ਪਲੇਥਣ (palethan) *n* Dry flour dusted at the time of rolling bread, powder, dredge.

ਪਵਿਤਰ (pavitar) *a* Pure, sacred, holy, spotless, solemn, sanctified; ~**ਅਸਥਾਨ** Shrine; ~**ਆਤਮਾ** Holy spirit; ~**ਯਾਦਗਾਰਾਂ** Relics.

ਪੜਸਾਂਗ (parsaang) *n* Ladder.

ਪੜਚੋਲ (parchol) *n f* Investigation, inquiry; Criticism, verification; ~**ਕਰਨੀ** To inquire into, to investigate, to comment, to verify.

ਪੜਚੋਲੀਆ (parcholiaa) *n m* Investigator, researcher.

ਪੜਛੱਤੀ (parcchattee) *n f* Shelf made under the roof, attic, loft.

ਪੜਤਾ (partaa) *n m* Cost price; ~**ਖਾਣਾ** To gain a suitable profit.

ਪੜਤਾਲ (partaal) *n f* Enquiry, checking, scrutiny, verification, investigation, search, audit; **ਅਦਾਲਤੀ**~ Inquisition.

ਪੜਤਾਲਣਾ (partaalnaa) *v* To check, to verify, to audit. Also **ਪੜਤਾਲ ਕਰਨਾ**

ਪੜ੍ਹੰਦੜ (parhandar) *adv* Readable; ~**ਨਾਟਕ** Closet play.

ਪੜਦਾਦਾ (pardaadaa) *n* Great-grand father, father's grandfather.

ਪੜ੍ਹਨਾ (parhnaa) *v* To read, to learn, to study, to go through, to recite.

ਪੜਨਾਨਾ (parnaanaa) *n m* Great-grand father, mother's grand

ਪੜਪੋਤਾ (parpotaa) *n m* Great-grandson, son's grandson, grand son's son.

ਪੜ੍ਹਨਾ (paṛhnaa) *v* To read, study, learn, to recite.

ਪੜ੍ਹਾਉਣਾ (paṛhaaunaa) *v* To teach, educate, to tutor; To instruct, train in reading and writing; To have someone educated.

ਪੜ੍ਹਾਈ (paṛhaaee) *n* Education, study, learning; Teaching, tution.

ਪੜ੍ਹਾਕੂ (paṛhaakoo) *a n m* Studious; student.

ਪੜੋਸ (paṛos) *n m* Neighbourhood, vicinity.

ਪਾਂ (paan) *n f* Itch, scabies, pus; ~ਮਾਰਿਆ Scabious.

ਪਾਉਣਾ (paaunaa) *v* To find, to get, to obtain, to add, to pour, to mix, to put on (clothes).

ਪਾਉਲੀ (paaulee) *n m* Weaver; 25 paise coin. Also ਪੋਲੀ

ਪਾਏਦਾਨ (paaedaan) *n m* Footboard, footrest, doormat.

ਪਾਏਦਾਰ (paaedaar) *a* Durable, lasting, strong.

ਪਾਸਾ (paasaa) *n m* Side, direction, face, quarter, aspect, dimension; ~ਪਲਟਣਾ To change sides; ~ਬਦਲਣਾ To turn round.

ਪਾਗਲ (paagal) *a n m* Insane, mad, crazy, loony, lunatic, fool; Madman, lunatic; ~ਖ਼ਾਨਾ Lunatic asylum, mental hospital, bedlam; ~ਪਣ Madness, lunancy.

ਪਾਚਨ (paachan) *a n m* Digestive; Digestion, assimilation.

ਪਾਜੀ (paajee) *a* Mean, wicked, rascal, vile.

ਪਾਟਣਾ (paatṇaa) *v* To be torn, to split, to burst, to cleave, to be broken.

ਪਾਟਾ (paataa) *v* Torn, rent, split; ~ਪੁਰਾਣਾ Worn-out, old (garment) rag, tatters.

ਪਾਠ (paath) *n m* Lesson, text, chapter of a book, religious study; ~ਸ਼ਾਲਾ School; ~ਕ Reader, scholar; ~ਕ੍ਰਮ Syllabus; ~ਪੁਸਤਕ Text book.

ਪਾਣੀ (paanee) *n m* Water, Adam's scale Adam's ale; ~ਚੜ੍ਹਾਉਣਾ To glid, to polish; ~ਫਿਰਨਾ To be undone, to be destroyed; ~ਫੇਰਨਾ To spoil, to shatter, to submerg; ~ਭਰਨਾ To serve, to draw water; ~ਵਾਂਗ ਰੋੜ੍ਹਨਾ (ਪੈਸਾ) To spend lavishly.

ਪਾਤਸ਼ਾਹ (paatshaah) *n m* King, emperor, sovereign, monarch; ~ਤ Empire, government.

ਪਾਤਸ਼ਾਹੀ (paatshaahee) *n f* Kingship,

kingdom, dominion, empire, rule government; Kingly, imperial, regal, royal.

ਪਾਦਰੀ (paadree) *n m* Priest, clergyman, chaplain, bishop, pastor, padre; **~ਸੰਸਥਾ** Holy orders.

ਪਾਂਧੀ (paandhee) *n m* Traveller.

ਪਾਪ (paap) *n m* Sin, vice, evil, guilt, crime, fault, impiety; **~ਕਰਨਾ** To commit a sin.

ਪਾਪੜ (paapar) *n m* Thin crisp cake made of pulse.

ਪਾਪੀ (paapee) *n m a* Sinner, criminal, wretched; Sinful, immoral, vicious, impious.

ਪਾਬੰਦੀ (paabandee) *n* Restriction, check, ban, abidance, limitation, punctuality.

ਪਾਮਰ (paamar) *a* Mean, base, low, wicked, vile.

ਪਾਮਾਲ (paamaal) *a* Trampled; ravaged, destroyed, ruined, devastated, laid, waste; **~ਕਰਨਾ** To damage, to destroy, trample, ruin, devastate, crush, to lay waste, to ravage.

ਪਾਰ (paar) *n m* The opposite bank, far side; Limit, bound; Across, over, beyond, on the far side; **~ਉਤਾਰਾ** Salvation, liberation; Success; **~ਕਰਨਾ** To cross, to take across, to kill.

ਪਾਰਸ (paaras) *n m* Touchstone; **~ਪੱਥਰ** Philosopher's stone (which converts any metal into gold on touching).

ਪਾਰਖੂ (paarkhoo) *n m* Evaluator, assayer, critic, connoisseur.

ਪਾਰਾ (paaraa) *n m* Mercury, quick silver, hydrargyrum.

ਪਾਰਾਵਾਰ (paaraawaar) *n m* Farthest limit, expanse, vastness.

ਪਾਲਣ (paalan) *n m* Nourishing, bringing up, upbringing, nurture; Observing, obeying, execution, carrying out; **~ਹਾਰ** Nourisher, breeder, nurturer, sustainer, protector, God. Also **ਪਾਲਨ**

ਪਾਲਣਾ (paalnaa) *v* To nourish, to nurse, to bring up, to nurture, to breed, to tame, to feed, to foster, to rear.

ਪਾਲਤੂ (paaltoo) *a* Domesticated, tame, pet.

ਪਾਲਾ (paalaa) *n m* Frost, cold, chilly weather; **~ਮਾਰਨਾ** To feel afraid.

ਪਾਵਲੀ (paavlee) *n m* Weaver.

ਪਾਵਾ (paavaa) *n m* Leg of a piece of furniture.

ਪਾੜ (paar) *n m* Breach, gap, opening, hole, fissure; Split charm, rent, cut, gash, slash.

ਪਾੜਨਾ (paarnaa) *v* To tear, to split, to rip, to rend, to divide.

ਪਾੜਾ (paaraa) *n m* Gap, difference, distance; Furrows.

ਪਿਓ (pio) *n m* Father, sire, male parent.

ਪਿਆਉਣਾ (piaaunaa) *v* To serve (water or other liquid); To water to get or cause one to drink, to serve drinks.

ਪਿਆਉ (piaao) *n m* Stall for serving water free to the needy.

ਪਿਆਜ (piaaj) *n m* Onion, *Allium cepa*.

ਪਿਆਦਾ (piaadaa) *n m* Foot soldier, footman, court mesenger or attendent; (in chess) pawn.

ਪਿਆਸਾ (piaasaa) *n m* Thirsty, desirous of.

ਪਿਆਰ (piaar) *n m* Affection, love, regard.

ਪਿਆਲਾ (piaalaa) *n m* Cupbowl, goblet, chalice, powder-pan.

ਪਿਸਣਾ (pisnaa) *v* To be ground, to be pulverised.

ਪਿਸਾਈ (pisaae) *n f* Act of grinding, wages of grinding.

ਪਿਸ਼ਾਬ (pishaab) *n m* Urine, piss; ~ਖਾਨਾ Urinal.

ਪੱਸੂ (pissoo) *n m* Flea, gnat.

ਪਿਘਲਣਾ (pighalnaa) *v* To melt, to dissolve, to be moved.

ਪਿਚਕਣਾ (pichaknaa) *v* To be squeezed, to shrival.

ਪਿਚਕਾਉਣਾ (pichkaaunaa) *v* To squeeze, compress, constrict, press, to cause to shrink, shrivel, contract.

ਪਿੱਛਲਗ (pichchhlag) *n m* Henchman, appendent, follower, satellite.

ਪਿੱਛਲਾ (pichhlaa) *a* Last, back, past, late, previous, subsequent, former.

ਪਿਛਵਾੜਾ (pichhwaaraa) *n m* Rear, back.

ਪਿਛਾ (pichhaa) *a* The back part, rear, chase, following, posterior, buttocks.

ਪਿਛੇ (pichchhe) *adv* Behind, afterwards, on the backside; ~ਪਿਛੇ At one's heels, in the wake of.

ਪਿਛੋਂ (pichchhon) *adv* Afterwards, subsequently, at the back, from behind.

ਪਿਛੋਕਾ (pichhokaa) *n m* Antecedents, ancestors.

ਪਿੰਜਰ (pinjar) *n f* Rib, skelton, carcass, anatomy.

ਪਿੰਜਰਾ (pinjraa) *n m* Cage, trap.

ਪਿੰਜਵਾਉਣਾ (pinjwaaunaa) *v* To get the cotton carded for spinning.

ਪਿਟਣਾ (piṭnaa) *v n m* To lament by beating breast; Trouble, agony, mourning, lamentation.

ਪਿਟਵਾਉਣਾ (piṭvaaunaa) *v* To get someone beaten up.

ਪਿੱਠ (piṭṭh) *n f* Back, behind; ~ਠੋਕਣੀ To encourage, to praise, to pat on the back, to bolster up; ~ਤੇ ਹੋਣਾ To support, to assist; ~ਦੇਣੀ To leave, to depart, to run away, to desert; ~ਪਿੱਛੇ Behind one's back; ~ਪਿੱਛੇ ਕਹਿਣਾ To back bite; ~ਲਾਉਣੀ To defeat, to floor; ~ਵਿਖਾਉਣੀ To turn tail, to flee from the battle field.

ਪਿੱਠੂ (piṭṭhoo) *n m* Basket, pannier, pack carrier; Comrade, assistant.

ਪਿੰਡ (pind) *n m* Village; Heap, lump, cake or ball of meal.

ਪਿੰਡਾ (pindaa) *n m* Body; ~ਛੁੜਾਣਾ To get rid of.

ਪਿੱਤ (pitt) *n f* Prickly heat.

ਪਿੱਤਰ (pittar) *n m* Ancestors, forefathers.

ਪਿੱਤਲ (pittal) *n m* Brass.

ਪਿਤਾ (pitaa) *n m* Father, dad, daddy.

ਪਿਦਣਾ (pidnaa) *v* To run hither or thither in game.

ਪਿਦਾਉਣਾ (pidaaunaa) *v* To weary, to vex, to defeat in game.

ਪਿੱਦੀ (piddee) *a* Tomtit.

ਪਿੰਨਣਾ (pinnanaa) *a* To beg, to ask for alms.

ਪਿੰਨਾ (pinnaa) *n m* Ball, thread ball.

ਪਿਲਪਿਲਾ (pilpilaa) *a* Soft, flabby, flaccid, plump, pulpy, lymphetic; ~ਪਣ Flabbiness, softness.

ਪੀਸਣਾ (peesnaa) *v* To grind, to reduce, to powder, to mill, to gnash (teeth). Also ਪੀਹਣਾ

ਪੀਂਘ (peengh) *n f* Swing, trapeze; Rainbow.

ਪੀਂਘਾ (peenghaa) *n m* Hammock.

ਪੀਚਣਾ (peechnaa) *v* To absorb, to soak, to moistened, to be hard and tight.

ਪੀਡਾ (peedaa) *a* Firm, solid; ~ਪਣ Toughness, hardness.

ਪੀਣਾ (peenaa) *v* To drink, to absorb; to suppress (an emotion); ਸਿਗਰਟ~ To smoke.

ਪੀਪ (peep) *n f* Pus.

ਪੀਪਾ (peepaa) *n m* Cask, tin, car butt, barrel.

ਪੀਲਾ (peelaa) *a* Yellow, pale, bleak; ~ਪਣ Paleness, yellowness.

ਪੀਲੀਆ (peeliya) *n m* Jaundice, xanthosis.

ਪੀੜ (peer) *n f* Pain, ache, anguish, affliction, ailment.

ਪੀੜ੍ਹੀ (peerhee) *n f* Generation, race

descent; A wooden or iron stool, small square.

ਪੀੜਾਂ (peeraan) *n f* Pain, labour throes.

ਪੁਆੜਾ (poaaraa) *n m* Dispute, quarrel, wrangle, discord, trouble, inconvenience; ~**ਪਾਉਣਾ** To create or cause dispute.

ਪੁਸ਼ਟ (pusht) *a* Nourishing; Strong, muscular, stout, virile.

ਪੁਸ਼ਟੀ (pushtee) *n f* Support, ratification, aid, affirmation; ~**ਕਰਨੀ** To confirm, to corroborate.

ਪੁਸ਼ਤ (pusht) *n f* Generation, ancestry; ~**ਦਰ ਪੁਸ਼ਤ** Generation to generation.

ਪੁਸਤਕ (pustak) *n f* Book, volume.

ਪੁਸ਼ਾਕ (pushaak) *n f* Dress, costume, garment, clothes, array. Also **ਪੋਸ਼ਾਕ**

ਪੁਕਾਰਨਾ (pukaarnaa) *v* To shout, to call out, to exclaim, to evoke.

ਪੁਗਣਾ (pugnaa) *v* To arrive, to mature, to end, to reach destination.

ਪੁਗਾਉਣਾ (pugaaunaa) *v* To terminate, to make one succeed.

ਪੁਚਕਾਰਨਾ (puchkaarnaa) *v* To pat, to caress, to fondle, to blandish, to produce a hissing sound from lips.

ਪੁਚਾਉਣਾ (puchaaunaa) *v* To convey, to transmit, to extend, to carry, to cause to reach.

ਪੁਛ (puchh) *n f* Enquiry, investigation question, querry, question; ~**ਹੋਣੀ** To be sought after, to be in demand, to be important enough; ~**ਗਿਛ** Investigation, interrogation.

ਪੁਛਣਾ (puchhnaa) *v* To enquire, to ask, to question.

ਪੁੰਜ (punj) *n m* Heap, mass, aggregate, embodiment.

ਪੁਜਣਾ (pujnaa) *v* To reach, to get at, to arrive, to come.

ਪੁਟਣਾ (putnaa) *v* To dig, to pull out, to uproot, to excavate.

ਪੁੱਠ (putth) *n f* Hip, buttock; Backside, reverse side.

ਪੁੱਠਾ (putthaa) *a* Reversed, contrary, upside down, indirect.

ਪੁਣਨਾ (punnaa) *v* To filter, to strain, to abuse.

ਪੁੱਤਰ (puttar) *n m* Son.

ਪੁਤਰੇਲਾ (putrelaa) *n m* Adopted son, adoptee.

ਪੁਤਲਾ (putlaa) *n m* Idol, image, effigy, personification, incarnation.

ਪੁਤਲੀ (putlee) *n f* Doll, puppet; Pupil of the eye.

ਪੁੰਨ (punn) *n m* Charity, alms, virtuous deed, dole, benefiction.

ਪੁਨਿਆਂ (puniaan) *n f* Full moon night.

ਪੁਰਖ (purakh) *n m* Man, male, person, individual, mankind.

ਪੁਰਨੂਰ (purnoor) *a* Full of light, radiant, brilliant, resplendent.

ਪੁਰਵਾਉਣਾ (purvauṇaa) *v* To get (pit, ditch, form etc.) filled up.

ਪੁਰਾਣਾ (puraaṇaa) *a* Old, aged, ancient, antique, chronic.

ਪੁਲ (pul) *n m* Bridge, pons; ਤਰੀਫ਼ ਦੇ~ਬੰਨ੍ਹਣਾ To praise too much.

ਪੁਲੰਦਾ (pulandaa) *n m* Bundle, wad, sheaf.

ਪੁਲਾੜ (pulaaṛ) *n m* Space, cosmos.

ਪੁੜਾ (puṛaa) *n m* Large packet.

ਪੁੜੀ (puṛee) *n f* Small parcel, wrapper of paper, dose of medicine.

ਪੂਛ (poochh) *n f* Tail, hanger-on; Importance; ~ਲ Tail; Parasite.

ਪੂਜਣਾ (poojṇaa) *a* To worship, to rever, to adore, to respect.

ਪੂਜਾ (poojaa) *n f* Worship, adoration, veneration, respect, devotion; ~ਭੇਟ Offering.

ਪੂੰਜੀ (poonjee) *n f* Capital, wealth, principal assets, stock; ~ਵਾਦ Capitalism.

ਪੂੰਝਣਾ (poonjhṇaa) *v* To wipe, to clean, to scrub, to efface.

ਪੂਰਨ (pooran) *a* Full, entire, complete, perfect, complementary.

ਪੂਰਨਾ (poornaa) *v* To fill, to blow, to fulfil, to finish, to complete.

ਪੂਰਾ (pooraa) *a* Full, complete, total, whole, entire, thorough, all, perfect, adequate; ~ਸੂਰਾ Self-contained, just enough; ~ਪੂਰਾ Out and out, exhaustive, all out, adequate.

ਪੇਸ਼ਕਸ਼ (peshkash) *n f* Offer, present.

ਪੇਸ਼ਗੀ (peshgee) *n f* Advance, earnest money.

ਪੇਸ਼ਤਰ (peshtar) *adv* Before, earlier than, ahead of.

ਪੇਸ਼ਬੰਦੀ (peshbandee) *n* Forestalling, anticipation, precaution.

ਪੇਸ਼ਾ (peshaa) *n m* Profession, trade, occupation, vocation, pursuit; Prostitution, harlotry; ~ਵਰ Professional career.

ਪੇਸ਼ੀ (peshee) *n f* Presence, trial, hearing of law suit; ~ਆਂ Muscles; ~ਨ ਗੋਈ Prediction.

ਪੇਕਾ (pekaa) *n m a* Parent's house; Paternal.

ਪੇਚ (pech) *n m* Screw; ~ਕਸ Screw driver; ~ਦਾਰ Zigzag, complex, twisted.

ਪੇਚਸ (pechas) *n f* Dysentery.

ਪੇਚਾ (pechaa) *n m* Tangle

entanglement, involvement, convolution, complication; ~ਪਾਉਣਾ To entangle, complicate.

ਪੇਚੀਦਗੀ (pecheedgee) n f Complexity, intricacy, complication.

ਪੇਚੀਦਾ (pecheedaa) a Complex, complicated.

ਪੇਟ (pet) n m Stomach, abdomen, belly, womb, capacity; ~ਹੋ ਜਾਣਾ To conceive, to get pregnant; ~ਕਟਣਾ To starve one self; ~ਖਾਲੀ ਕਰਨਾ To relieve nature; ~ਪੂਜਾ ਕਰਨਾ To eat.

ਪੇਟੀ (petee) n f Belt, gridle; Box, chest, big trunk.

ਪੇਟੂ (petoo) a n m Glottonous, ravenous, rapacious, vocacious; Glutton, epicure.

ਪੇਂਡੂ (pendoo) n m a Village, peasant; Rustic, rural, agrestic; ~ਕਾਵਿ Pastoral poetry; ~ਬੋਲੀ Patois; ~ਲਹਿਜਾ Brogue.

ਪੈਸਾ (paesaa) n m Pice, money, wealth, paisa; ~ਉਡਾਉਣਾ To spend money lavishly; ~ਖਾ ਜਾਣਾ To misappropriate money; ~ਖੁਆਉਣਾ To bribe; ~ਬਣਾਉਣਾ To mint money; ~ਲਾਉਣਾ To invest money.

ਪੈਗੰਬਰ (paegambar) n m Prophet, apostle, messenger of God.

ਪੈਗਾਮ (paegaam) n m Message, embassy.

ਪੈਜ (paej) n f Honour, fair name; Vow, promise.

ਪੈਂਠ (paenth) a n Dominating influence; Reputation, awe, strong impression or effect; Sixty five.

ਪੈਂਡਾ (paendaa) n m Distance, trek, passage, journey.

ਪੈਂਤੜਾ (paentraa) n Strategy, position, posture, attitude.

ਪੈਦਲ (paedal) adv a Marching, foot(man); Onfoot, afoot.

ਪੈਦਾ (paedaa) a Born, produced, begotton; ~ਇਸ਼ Birth, creation, production; ~ਹੋਣਾ To be produced, to grow, to be born; ~ਕਰਨਾ To produce, to earn, to father, to breed; ~ਵਾਰ Produce, yield, crop, output, product, production.

ਪੈਮਾਇਸ਼ (paemaaish) n f Measurement, survey.

ਪੈਮਾਨਾ (paemaanaa) n m Scale, measure, instrument for measuring.

ਪੈਰ (paer) n m Foot, footprint, step, traces; ~ਉਖੜਨੇ To be uprooted; ~ਚਟਣੇ To fawn; ~ਚੁਮਣੇ To worship, to show reverence; ~ਜੰਮਣੇ To be well-settled, to be firmly lodged;

~ਪਸਾਰ ਕੇ ਸੋਣਾ To enjoy a carefree sleep; ~ਭਾਰੀ ਹੋਣੇ To be pregnant.

ਪੈਰਵੀ (paervee) *n f* Pursuit, follow up, prosecution, following, conduct.

ਪੋਸਣਾ (posnaa) *v* To nourish, to rear, to develop, to tame.

ਪੋਸਤੀ (postee) *n m a* Lazy person; One addicted to poppy pods.

ਪੋਹਣਾ (pohnaa) *v* To cause sensation, feeling or pain, to affect; To be felt.

ਪੋਟਲੀ (potlee) *n f* Small bundle or package tied in cloth piece; Cavity, gland, follicute.

ਪੋਣਾ (ponaa) *n m* (1) Straining cloth, dish cloth, kitchen napkin; perforated stone screen; (2) enclosure in a bathing tank meant exclusively for ladies.

ਪੋਚਣਾ (pochnaa) *v* To smear, to daub, to coat, to besmear.

ਪੋਚਾ (pochaa) *n m* Daub, dab, coating plaster; ~ਪਾਚੀ Camouflage.

ਪੋਤਰਾ (potraa) *n m* Grand son.

ਪੋਤੜਾ (potṛaa) *n m* Babycloth, napkin, diapers, nappies.

ਪੋਥਾ (pothaa) *n m* Big book, voluminous book, tome.

ਪੋਥੀ (pothee) *n f* Book, tract.

ਪੋਪਲਾ (poplaa) *a* Toothless, shrivelled.

ਪੋਲ (pol) *n m* Hollow, space; Pole, vacuity, vacuousness.

ਪੋਲਾ (polaa) *a* Soft, hollow, porous, placid, vacuous; ~ਪਣ Hollowness, weakness, flaccidness.

ਪੌਣ (paun) *n f* Air, wind, breeze.

ਪੌਦ (paud) *n f* Saplings, vegetation, plantation.

ਪੌਦਾ (paudaa) *n* Plant, sapling, young tree.

ਪੌਰਾਣਿਕ (pauraanik) *a* Mythological, legendary.

ਪੌਲਾ (paulaa) *n m* One foot of shoe.

ਪੌੜੀ (pauṛee) *n f* Ladder; Progression; ~ਦਾਰ Terraced.

ਫ

ਫ Twenty seventh letter of Gurmukhi alphabets, pronounced as 'phaphaa'.

ਫਸਣਾ (phasṇaa) *v* To be entrapped, to be ensnared, to be caught, to get into a difficulty, to be entangled, to be involved.

ਫਸਤਾ (fastaa) *n m* Dispute, quarrel; ~ਮੁਕਾਉਣਾ To finish, to put an end, to kill.

ਫਸਲ (fasal) *n f* Harvest, crop, produce, season.

ਫਸਲੀ (faslee) *a* Seasonal, pertaining to a crop.

ਫਸਾਉਣਾ (phasaauṇaa) *v* To implicate, to ensnare, to trap, to entangle. Also **ਫਾਹਉਣਾ**

ਫਸਾਹਤ (fasaahat) *n f* Sweet talk.

ਫਸਾਦ (fasaad) *n m* Dispute, quarrel, disturbance, faction, riot, agitation; ~ਛੇੜਨਾ To create disturbance; ~ਦੀ ਜੜ੍ਹ Root cause and trouble.

ਫਸਾਨਾ (fasaanaa) *n m* Story, narrative, fiction.

ਫਸੀਲ (faseel) *n m* Rampart, boundary.

ਫਹਾ (phahaa) *n m* Sticking, a flock of cotton or cloth impregnated with medicine to paste on a wound. Also **ਫਹਿਆ**

ਫਹਿਰਿਸਤ (faherisht) *n f* List, catalogue.

ਫੱਕ (phakk) *n f* Fine chaff of rice or barley.

ਫੱਕ (fakk) *a* Discoloured.

ਫੱਕਣਾ (phakṇaa) *v* To put something powdered into mouth from the palm, to waste.

ਫਕਤ (fakat) *adv* Only, merely.

ਫੱਕਰ (phakkar) *n m* Abuse, foul language, meaningless or useless or useless chatter. Also **ਫੱਕੜ**

ਫੱਕੜ (phakkaṛ) *n m* Carefree, poor, mendicant, hermit; ~ਪੁਣਾ Carelessness, carefreeness.

ਫੱਕੀ (phakkee) *n f* Medicinal powder.

ਫਕੀਰ (fakeer) *n m* Hermit, mendicant, sadhu, recluse, beggar.

ਫਕੀਰੀ (fakeeree) *a* Life of a fakir, reclusion, anchoritism, mendicancy.

ਫਖਰ (fakhar) *n m* Pride, justified, righteous. Also **ਫ਼ਖ਼ਰ**

ਫੱਗ (phagg) *n m* Feather.

ਫ਼ਜ਼ਲ (fazal) *n m* Favour, kindness, grace, bounty.

ਫ਼ਜ਼ਾ (fazaa) *n f* Atmosphere, climate, weather; Situation.

ਫ਼ਜ਼ੀਹਤ (fazeehat) *n f* Discomfiture, insult, disgrace.

ਫ਼ਜ਼ੀਲਤ (fazeelat) *n f* Importance, greatness, dignity.

ਫ਼ਜ਼ੂਲ (fazool) *a* Surplus, excess, useless, worthless; ~ਖ਼ਰਚ Extravagant; ~ਖਰਚੀ Extravagance.

ਫਟ (phat) *n m adv* Wound, cut, crack; Quickly, instantly, hastily.

ਫਟਕਣ (phaṭkaṇ) *n m* Flutter; Chaff separated from grain in winnowing.

ਫਟਕਣਾ (phaṭaknaa) *v* To winnow, to shake, to flutter; To throb.

ਫਟਣਾ (phaṭnaa) *v* To be torn, to burst, to explode, to be cut, to turn sour; ਛਾਤੀ ਦਾ~ To have unbearable sorrow.

ਫੱਟਾ (phaṭṭaa) *n m* A plank, wooden board, board, sign board.

ਫੱਟੀ (phaṭṭee) *n f* Small plank, school boy's board to write on.

ਫਟੀਕ (phaṭeek) *n f* Fatigue.

ਫੰਡਣਾ (phandṇaa) *v* To beat, to scold, to winnow, to dust.

ਫਣ (phaṇ) *n m* Expanded hood of snake. Also ਫਨ

ਫਣੀਅਰ (phaṇeear) *n m* Hooded snake, cobra.

ਫ਼ਤਿਹ (phate) *n f* Victory, success, triumph; Sikh salutation or greeting.

ਫਤੂਹੀ (fatoohee) *n f* A waist coat, a sleeveless coat.

ਫ਼ਤੂਰ (fatoor) *n m* Infirmity, disturbance, defect, interruption.

ਫੱਦ (phadd) *n m* Toothless gum.

ਫੰਦਣਾ (phandṇaa) *v* To trap, to ensnare. Also ਫੰਦਣਾ

ਫੱਦਡ਼ (phaddaṛ) *a* Very fat and ugly, worthless.

ਫੰਦਾ (phandaa) *n m* A snare, a loop, a knot, trap.

ਫ਼ਨ (fan) *n m* Skill, art; ~ਕਾਰ Artisan, artist, craftman, expert.

ਫ਼ਨਾਹ (fanaah) *n m* Destruction, ruin, devastation.

ਫਫੜਾ (phaphṛaa) *n m* Deceit, fraud; Flattery, sycophancy, hypocrisy.

ਫਫੇਕੁੱਟ (phaphekuṭ) *a* Deceitful, wily, cunning, hypocrite.

ਫਫੇਕੁਟਣੀ (phaphekuṭnee) *n f* Old talkative and cunning woman. Also ਫਫੇਕੁਟਣਾ

ਫਫੋਲਾ (phapholaa) *n m* Blister, scald, boiled, an eruption.

ਫਬਣਾ (phabṇaa) *v* To look well, to suit, to benefit, to appear beautiful.

ਫਰ (phar) *n m* Fur, soft wool on the body of sheep etc.

ਫਰਸ਼ (farash) *n m* Floor, pavement.

ਫਰਸਾ (pharsaa) *n m* Battle axe.

ਫਰਹੰਗ (farhang) *n m* Lexicon, key note, commentary.

ਫ਼ਰਕ (farak) *n m* Difference, deficiency, discrepancy, variance, disparity, destinction; ~ਪੈਣਾ To differ, to be displeased,

ਫਰਕਣਾ (pharaknaa) *v* To tremble, to vibrate, to quiver, to throb, to flutter, to beat, to wink.

ਫਰੰਗੀ (farangee) *n m* A foreigner, an English man.

ਫ਼ਰਜ਼ (faraz) *n m* Duty, moral duty, responsibility, obligation; ~ਕਰਨਾ To assume, to suppose.

ਫ਼ਰਜ਼ੰਦ (farzand) *n m* Son.

ਫ਼ਰਜ਼ੀ (farzee) *a* Fictitious, hypothetical, assumed, supposed.

ਫ਼ਰੰਟ (farant) *a* Opponent, one who opposes; Warfront; Disobedient; ~ਹੋਣਾ To stand against, to revolt, to oppose.

ਫ਼ਰਦ (farad) *n f* A list, a catalogue, document, sheet of wool or paper.

ਫ਼ਰਮਾ (farmaa) *n m* Frame, format.

ਫ਼ਰਮਾਉਣਾ (farmaauṇaa) *v* To order, to command, speak. Also ਫ਼ਰਮਾਣਾ

ਫ਼ਰਮਾਇਸ਼ (farmaaish) *n f* Command, order, recommendation, royal edict; ~ਕਰਨੀ To ask for, to request, to order.

ਫ਼ਰਮਾਨ (farmaan) *n f* A royal command, order. Also ਫ਼ਰਮਾਣ

ਫ਼ਰਮਾਂਬਰਦਾਰ (farmaanbardaar) *a* Obedient, dutiful, loyal.

ਫ਼ਰਮਾਂਬਰਦਾਰੀ (farmaabardaaree) *n* Obedience, dutifulness, compliance, docility; Loyalty.

ਫ਼ਰਲੋ (farlo) *n f* Absence without leave, furlough.

ਫੱਰਾ (pharraa) *n m* Banner, penant, any loose paper.

ਫ਼ਰਾਸ਼ (faraash) *n m* Personal attendant, a servant who spreads carpets or fixes tents etc ; Floorer.

ਫ਼ਰਾਖ (faraakh) *a* Open, spacious, commodious; ~ਦਿਲ Open-hearted, large hearted, generous, liberal; ~ਦਿਲੀ Open or large-heartedness, generosity, generousness, liberality.

ਫ਼ਰਾਟਾ (faraataa) *n m* Rush, puff, sound of anything rushing or fluttering.

ਫ਼ਰਾਰ (faraar) *a* Absconding, at large, fugitive.

ਫ਼ਰਿਆਦ (fariyaad) *n f* A request, a complaint; A petition, exclaiming for help.

ਫ਼ਰਿਆਦੀ (fariyaadee) *a* Suppliant, petitioner, appellant.

ਫ਼ਰਿਸ਼ਤ (ferisht) *n f* List, catalogue. Also ਫ਼ਹਿਰਿਸ਼ਤ

ਫ਼ਰਿਸ਼ਤਾ (farishtaa) *n m* An angel, a messenger of God.

ਫ਼ਰੇਬ (fareb) *n m* Fraud, deception, trick, treachery.

ਫ਼ਰੇਬੀ (farebee) *a* Fraudulant, deceptive cunning, artful.

ਫਰੋਲਣਾ (pharolnaa) *v* To search, to probe.

ਫਲ (phal) *n m* (1) Fruit; (2) Consequence, reward, yield, profit, produce; (3) Blade of instrument or weapon, a plough share, a point of piercing instrument; ਖੇਤਰ~ Area; ਗੁਣਨ ~Product; ~ਦੇਣਾ To yield fruit; ~ਦਾਰ Fruitful, productive, profitable.

ਫਲਸਫਾ (phalasaphaa) *n m* Philosophy. Also ਫ਼ਲਸਫ਼ਾ

ਫਲਸਫ਼ਾਨਾ (phalasphaanaa) *a* Philosophical.

ਫਲਸਫੀ (phalasphee) *n m* philosopher.

ਫਲਕ (phalak) *n m* Sky, heaven; Facet, plane.

ਫਲਣਾ (phalnaa) *v* to be fruitful, to bear fruit.

ਫਲਾਂਘ (phalaangh) *n f* Leap, jump.

ਫ਼ਲਾਣਾ (falaanaa) *n m* Such a one, so and so; ~ਢੀਂਗਣਾ Such and such, any Tom, dick or harry. Also ਫ਼ਲਾਂ

ਫਲੀ (phalee) *n f* Pod, seed pod, bean, silique.

ਫ਼ਲੂਸ (faloos) *n m* Balloon.

ਫੜ੍ਹ (pharh) *n f* Boast, false pomp, a bet; ~ਬਾਜ਼ Boastful, vaunta braggart; ~ਬਾਜ਼ੀ Bragging, boasting, vaunting; ~ਮਾਰਨੀ To boast, to talk tall.

ਫੜਕ (pharak) *n m* Writhing, flutter; ~ਉਠਣਾ To be thrilled, to be aroused emotionally.

ਫੜਕਣ (pharkan) *n f* Flutter, flap, throb, pulsation, palpitation, quiver, tremor.

ਫੜਕਣਾ (pharaknaa) *v* To pulsate, to throb, to flutter, to writhe.

ਫੜਨਾ (pharnaa) *v* To catch hold of, to seize, to grapple, to arrest, to catch, to hold.

ਫੜਫੜਾਉਣਾ (pharpharaaunaa) *v* To flutter, to flap, to flicker, to throb.

ਫ਼ਾਇਦਾ (faaidaa) *n m* Profit, gain, benefit, dividend, advantage.

ਫਾਸਣਾ (phaasṇaa) *v* To entrap.

ਫ਼ਾਸਲਾ (faaslaa) *n m* Distance, space, gap, interval.

ਫਾਂਸੀ (phaansee) *n f* Execution, gallows, death by hanging; ~**ਲੱਗਣਾ** To be hanged till death; ~**ਲਾਉਣਾ** To hang, to execute death sentence.

ਫਾਹ (phaah) *n m* Snarling, hanging; ~**ਦੇਣਾ** To strangle. Also ਫਾਹਾ

ਫਾਕਾ (phaakaa) *n m* Fast, going without food; ~**ਕਸ਼ੀ** Starvation, hunger; fasting; ~**ਕਰਨਾ** To fast, to go without food, to observe fast, to miss a meal.

ਫ਼ਾਜ਼ਿਲ (faazil) *a* Proficient, learned, scholar.

ਫਾਂਟ (phaanṭ) *n f* Beating, division, slice, scrap, chip.

ਫਾਟਕ (phaaṭak) *n m* Door, gate, drive way, postern; Barrier (at rail/road crossing).

ਫਾਂਟਣਾ (phaanṭṇaa) *v* To beat, to punish.

ਫਾਡੀ (phaaḍee) *a* Lazy, slack, sluggish, lethargic.

ਫ਼ਾਨੀ (faanee) a Mortal, temporal, perishable, destructible.

ਫ਼ਾਨੂਸ (faanoos) *n m* Chandelier; Any light with translucent glass housing.

ਫ਼ਾਰਗ (faarag) *a* Free. Also ਫ਼ਾਰਿਗ

ਫਾਲਜ (phaalaj) *n m* Paralysis, hemiplegia.

ਫਾਲਤੂ (faaltoo) *a* Extra, spare, excess, useless, worhtless.

ਫਾੜ (phaaṛ) *n m* A fragment, a piece, dissection.

ਫਾੜਨਾ (phaaṛnaa) *v* To tear, to chop (wood), to cut, to burst open, to cleave, to split, to saw.

ਫਾੜੀ (phaaṛee) *n f* Fragment, segment, natural section (as of certain fruits like orange); Slice, splinter, piece.

ਫਿਸਣਾ (phisṇaa) *v* To be shrivlled, to be crushed, to discharge matter.

ਫਿਸਲਣਾ (phisalṇaa) *v* To slip, to glide, to incline, to be degraded.

ਫ਼ਿਕਰ (fikar) *n f* Care, worry, concern, anxiety, consideration; ~**ਮੰਦ** Anxious, worried, pensive.

ਫ਼ਿਕਰਾ (fikraa) *n m* Sentence, a string of words.

ਫਿੱਕਾ (phikkaa) *a* Tasteless, insipid, dim, pale, light, vapid, unkind, devoid of radiance; ~**ਪਣ** Tastelessness, paleness, dimness, indifference.

ਫਿਟਕਾਰ (phitkaar) *n f* Disdain, chiding, scolding, censure, curse, reproof, rebuking.

ਫਿਟਕਾਰਨਾ (phitkaarnaa) *v* To rebuke, to chide, to scold, to censure, to repudiate, to insult.

ਫਿੱਟਣਾ (phitnaa) *v* To be overfed, to become bulky or hefty; To become proud or overbearing; To turn sour, to curdle or split.

ਫਿਟਾਉਣਾ (phitaaunaa) *v* To split (milk) into curd and whey, to cause (milk) to be split, to curdle (milk); To make fat or proud.

ਫਿਟਿਆ (phitiaa) *a* Spoilt, egoistic, haughty, turned sour, curdled, precipitated.

ਫਿੱਡਾ (phiddaa) *a* Deformed, clubfooted, snub-nosed.

ਫਿਤਰਤ (fitarat) *n f* Nature, disposition.

ਫਿਦਾ (fidaa) *a* Infatuated, devoted.

ਫਿਰਕਨੀ (phirkanee) *n f* Any rotating disc of a machine, fly-wheel.

ਫਿਰਕਾ (firkaa) *n m* Sect, tribe, clan; ~ਪ੍ਰਸਤੀ Communalism, sectarianism.

ਫਿਰਕੀ (phirkee) *n f* Bobbin, spool, reel; pulley; A paper toy stuck at the end of a stick so that it rotates as the child holding it runs.

ਫਿਰਨਾ (phirnaa) *v* To whirl, to go round, to be rotated, to roam, to be circulated, to walk about, to travel; ਉਡਦੇ~ To roam about in delight, to feel lost in delight; ਦਿਨ~ To take a favourable turn.

ਫਿਰਾਉਣਾ (phiraaunaa) *v* To rotate, to roll, to shift; ਅੱਖਾਂ~ To turn away one's eyes.

ਫ਼ਿਰੌਤੀ (firautee) *n f* Ransom.

ਫਿਲਹਾਲ (philhaal) *adv* For the time being, for the present.

ਫਿਲਫ਼ੌਰ (filfaur) *adv* Immediately.

ਫੀਤਾ (pheetaa) *n m* Measuring tape, ribbon, lace, strip of cloth.

ਫੀਲ (feel) *n m* Elephant; ~ਖਾਨਾ Stable for elephants.

ਫੁਸਕਣਾ (phusaknaa) *v* To wail, to weep, to cry in low tone.

ਫੁਸਲਾਉਣਾ (phuslaaunaa) *v* To lure, to fondle, to allure, to coax. Also ਫੁਸਲਾਨਾ or ਫਾਹੁਨਾ

ਫੁਸਲਾਹਟ (phuslaahat) *n f* Inducement, cajolery, temptation, seduction, allurement.

ਫੁਹਸ਼ (fuhash) *a* Indecent, immodest, obscene, vulgar. Also ਫੁਹਸ

ਫੁਹਾਰ (phuhaar) *n f* Drizzle; spray.

ਫੁਹਾਰਾ (phuhaaraa) *n m* Fountain; watering pot, sprinkler; Jet, discharge of liquid in fine spray or gush.

ਫੁਕਣਾ (phuknaa) *v* To be burnt, to burn, to be reduced to ashes, to be destroyed, to be wasted.

ਫੁੰਕਾਰ (phunkaar) *n f* Hissing sound (of snake), loud and strong breathing.

ਫੁੰਕਾਰਨਾ (phunkaarnaa) *v* To give out a hissing sound, to hiss.

ਫੁੰਕਾਰਾ (phunkaaraa) *n m* Hissing or hissing sound as of snake, Snort.

ਫੁਟ (phut) *n f* Discord, disunion, disagreement; **~ਪੈਣੀ** To be disunited, to be divided in opinion.

ਫੁਟਕਲ (phutkal) *a* Miscellaneous, retail, separate, not enmass.

ਫੁੱਟਣਾ (phutnaa) *v* To sprout, to burgeon, to ratoon; To go away; To run away, to flee, to disappear. Also **ਟੁਟਣਾ**

ਫੁੱਟਾ (phuttaa) *n m* Foot ruler.

ਫੁੰਡਣਾ (phundnaa) *v* To strike, to shoot.

ਫੁਦਕਣਾ (phudaknaa) *v* To leap, to hop, to jump.

ਫੁੱਫੜ (phupphar) *n m* Husband of father's sister; Uncle.

ਫੁੰਮਣ (phumman) *n m* Tassel, cockade (satirically, lovingly used for young man).

ਫੁਰਸਤ (fursat) *n f* Spare time, vacant hour, leisure.

ਫੁਰਤੀ (phurtee) *n f* Promptness, smartness, quickness, nimbleness; **~ਨਾਲ** Smartly, quickly; **~ਲਾ** Smart, prompt, active, nimble.

ਫੁੱਲ (phull) *n m* Flower, blossom; Light, Residual bones of a person after cremation; **~ਵਾੜੀ** Flower bed.

ਫੁਲਕਾ (phulkaa) *n m* Light Indian bread, loaf, same as **ਚਪਾਤੀ**

ਫੁਲਝੜੀ (phuljharee) *n f* A kind of firework emitting bright sparks; Slang. beautiful woman, sparkling beauty.

ਫੁਲਣਾ (phulnaa) *v* To swell, to be puffed, to bloom, to flower, to be happy.

ਫੁਲਾਉਣਾ (phulaaunaa) *v* To inflate, to puff up.

ਫੁਲਾਦ (phulaad) *n m* Steel.

ਫੁਲਾਦੀ (phulaadee) *a* Of or like steel, steely; Strong, tough.

ਫੁਲੇ (phule) *n m* Pop corn.

ਫੁੜਕਣਾ (phuraknaa) *v* To fall insensitive or unconscious, to flutter or writhe, to death, to die.

ਫੂਹੜ (phoohar) *n m* Crude matress.

ਫੂਕ (phook) *n f* Air blown with mouth or inflator; Puff, whiff, blow; **~ਕੱਢਣੀ**

To deflate, to demoralise, to bewilder, to frighten; **~ਦੇਣੀ** To flatter, to elate, to incite; **~ਨਿਕਲਣੀ** To be deflated; **~ਫੂਕ ਕੇ ਪੈਰ ਰੱਖਣਾ** To be very careful or cautious; **~ਭਰਨੀ/~ਦੇਣੀ** To inflate, to fill with air, to pump air (into); **~ਮਾਰਨੀ** To blow (in order to make fire or to warm up (skin), to puff; To blow off (as flame or candle) to puff, to whiff.

ਫੂਕਣਾ (phooknaa) *v* To blow, to whiff, to burn, to waste, to reduce to ashes.

ਫੇਹਣਾ (phehnaa) *v* To crush, to crack, to squeeze, to trample.

ਫੇਫੜਾ (phephraa) *n m* Lung.

ਫੇਰ (pher) *n m adv* Turn, rotation; Change, vicissitude; Later, in future, afterwards; Then, thereafter; Once again; Once more.

ਫੇਰਨਾ (phernaa) *v* To revolve, to rotate, to circulate, to return; **ਪਾਣੀ~** To undo.

ਫੇਰੀ (pheree) *n f* Circuit, hawking, going round; **~ਵਾਲਾ** Pedlar, hawker.

ਫੇਰੇ (phere) *n m pl* Rounds, circumambulation; **~ਲੈਣੇ** To marry.

ਫੇੜਨਾ (phernaa) *v* To harm, to spoil, to do an evil turn.

ਫੈਸਲਾ (faislaa) *n* Decision, judgement, settlement, arbitration, agreement; **~ਕਰਨਾ** To settle, to decide; **~ਹੋਣਾ** To come to a mutual agreement.

ਫੈਂਟਣਾ (phaintnaa) *v* To shuffle (cards), to beat.

ਫੈਲਣਾ (phailnaa) *v* To be stread, to expand, to be propagated.

ਫੈਲਾਉ (phaelaau) *v* To spread, extend, expand, dilate, open out; To scatter disperse; To diffuse, radiate; To become widely known (as news), to be disseminated, propagated, publicised; To be unfolded and stretched.

ਫੋਸ (phos) *n m* Fresh dung, excreta of an animal. Also **ਫੋਸੀ**

ਫੋਸੜ (phosar) *a* Worthless, lazy, sluggish, lethargic.

ਫੋਕਟ (phokat) *a* Useless, of no value.

ਫੋਕਾ (phokaa) *a* Hollow, tasteless, insipid.

ਫੋਗ (phog) *n f* Dregs, residual remains after extracting juice or essence. Also **ਫੋਕ**

ਫੋਤਾ (fotaa) *n m* Testicle.

ਫੋਲਣਾ (pholnaa) *v* To search, to expose, to find out, to scatter.

ਝਨਾ (phoṛnaa) *v* To break, to shatter, to split, to burst.

ੜਾ (phoṛaa) *n m* Ulcer, boil, abscess, sore, pustule.

ਜ (fauj) *n f* Military; Army, defence forces; **~ਦਾਰ** Commander; **~ਦਾਰੀ** criminal.

ਜੀ (phaujee) *n m* Solider, militiaman; Pertaining to Military.

ਫੋਰੀ (phauree) *a* Immediate, instant, instantaneous.

ਫੌਰਨ (fauran) *adv* Immediately, at once, quickly, instantaneously.

ਫੌਲਾਦ (faulaad) *n m* Steel.

ਫੰੜ੍ਹ (phauṛh) *n m* Boasting, falsehood, deceit.

ਬ

ਬ Twenty eighth letter of Gurmukhi alphabets, pronounced as 'babbaa'.

ਬੰਸ (bans) *n m* Dynasty, descent, tribe, descendant, family.

ਬੱਸ (bass) *n a f intj* Bus; Enough, sufficient, stop, no more; ~ਕਰਨਾ To stop, to finish; ਬੇ~ Helpless, powerless.

ਬਸੰਤ (basant) *n m* Spring (season).

ਬਸਤਰ (bastar) *n m* Clothing, dress, garments, robes; ~ਹੀਣ Nude, naked.

ਬਸਤਾ (bastaa) *n m* Satchel, bundle; ~ਬੰਨ੍ਹਣਾ To tie satchel or school bag; To be ready to go away; To be dismissed.

ਬਸਤੀ (bastee) *n f* Village, inhabitation, dwelling.

ਬਸੰਤੀ (basantee) *a* Light-yellow, xanthic.

ਬੰਸਰੀ (bansree) *n f* Flute, pipe, fife.

ਬਸਾਤ (basaat) *n f* Capital, stock, means, pecuniary power.

ਬਸਾਤੀ (basaatee) *n m* General merchant, grocer, haberdasher.

ਬਸੇਰਾ (baseraa) *n m* Resting place, bird's perch, haunt, roost; ~ਕਰਨਾ To settle, to dwell, to stay, to rest for the night; ~ਰੈਣ Night's lodging, temporary living place.

ਬਹੱਤਰ (bahattar) *a* Seventy two.

ਬਹਾਉਣਾ (bahaaunaa) *v* To set to flow, to spill, to throw away, to spend uselessly, to squander. Also ਬਹਾਨਾ

ਬਹਾਦਰ (bahaadar) *a* Valiant, brave, bold, courageous, fearless.

ਬਹਾਦਰਾਨਾ (bahaadraanaa) *a* Brave, bold, courageous (act or step).

ਬਹਾਦਰੀ (bahaadree) *n* Bravery, doughtiness, intrepidity, courage, daring, boldness, fearlessness, dauntlessness, Guts, spunk.

ਬਹਾਨਾ (bahaanaa) *n m* Excuse, pretence, pretext, veil, guise.

ਬਹਾਨੇਬਾਜ਼ (bahaanebaaz) *a* Habitual, malingerer, shammer, veader, or pretender.

ਬਹਾਨੇਬਾਜ਼ੀ (bahaanebaazee) *n* Habit of making of excuses, pretending, shamming, malingering, evading or avoiding work.

ਬਹਾਰ (Bahaar) *n f* Spring (season),

bloom, elegance, beauty, merriment, joviality.

ਬਹਾਲ (bahaal) *a* Reinstated, restored.

ਬਹਾਲੀ (bahaalee) *n f* Reinstatement.

ਬਹਿਸ (bahes) *n f* Discussion, debate, argumentation, pleading, wrangling.

ਬਹਿਸ਼ਤ (bahisht) *n f* Heaven, paradise, garden of Eden.

ਬਹਿਸ਼ਤੀ (bahishtee) *n m* Waterman, a person who carries water in a large leather bag.

ਬਹਿਕਣਾ (baheknaa) *v* To go astray, to be lead astray, to be mislead, to be deceived, to go out of one's control.

ਬਹਿਕਾਉਣਾ (bahekaaunaa) *v* To mislead, misguide, lead astray; To deceive, inveilge; To seduce, to intoxicate.

ਬਹਿਣਾ (bahenaa) *v* To sit, to flux, to flow, to float. Also **ਵਹਿਣਾ**

ਬਹਿਰਾ (baheraa) *a* Deaf, hard of hearing.

ਬਹਿਲਣਾ (bahelnaa) *v* To be mollified, to be amused.

ਬਹੀ (bahee) *n f a* Account book, ledger; Stale, not fresh, quince.

ਬਹੁ (bahu) *a* Many, several, multi;

~ਗੁਣਾ Many fold; ~ਤਾ Enough, plentiful; ~ਤੇਰ Plentiful, abundance, sufficient; ~ਭਾਸ਼ੀ Multilingual; ~ਮਤ Majority; ~ਮੁੱਲਾ Costly, precious, invaluable; ~ਰੂਪੀ Multiform; ~ਵਚਨ Plural.

ਬਹੁਤ (bahut) *a* Very, too much, sufficient, plenty, numerous.

ਬਹੁਤਾਤ (bautaat) *n* excess, abundance, excessiveness, copiousness, planteousness, profusion, superabundance.

ਬਹੁਮੁੱਲਾ (bahumullaa) *a* Costly, precious, dear, high-priced, valuable.

ਬਹੁੜਨਾ (bahurnaa) *v* To reach, to come back, to return.

ਬਕਸ (bakas) *n m* Box, case, chest. Also ਬਕਸਾ

ਬਕਸੂਆ (baksooaa) *n m* Safety pin, buckle.

ਬਕਣਾ (baknaa) *v* To chatter, to talk nonsense, to prattle, to jabber.

ਬਕਰਾ (bakraa) *n m* He goat.

ਬਕਰੀ (bakree) *n f* She goat.

ਬਕਵਾਸ (bakvaas) *n m* Prattle, gossip, chatter, talkativeness; ~ਕਰਨਾ To gossip, to cackle, to talk irreleventy.

ਬਕਾਇਆ (bakaaiyaa) *n m a* Balance, arrears, outstanding;

Residual, payable.

ਬਕਾਰ (bakaar) *a* Needful, needed.

ਬਕਾਲ (bakaal) *n m* Grocer. Also ਬਾਣੀਆ

ਬਖ਼ਸ਼ਣਾ (bakhashṇaa) *v* To bestow, to excuse, to pardon, to forgive.

ਬਖ਼ਸ਼ਿਸ਼ (bakhshish) *n f* Grant, donation, forgiveness, gratuity, tip. Also ਬਖ਼ਸ਼ੀਸ਼

ਬਖ਼ਤ (bakhat) *n m* Fate, fortune, luck, time.

ਬਖ਼ਤਾਵਰ (bakhtaavar) *a* Lucky, fortunate; prosperous, wealthy.

ਬਖਾਣ (bakhaaṇ) *n m* Exposition, description, praise.

ਬਖਾਧ (bakhaadh) *n m* Envy, hatred, quarrel, ill talk. Also ਬਿਖਾਧ

ਬਖੀਲ (bakheel) *a* Miser, niggard, backbiter.

ਬਖੀਲੀ (bakheelee) *n f* Miserliness, niggardliness, stinginess, parsimony, backbiting.

ਬਖੇਰਨਾ (bakhernaa) *v* To scatter.

ਬਖੇੜਾ (bakheṛaa) *n m* Joke, jest; Taunt, sarcasm. Also ਝਗੜਾ

ਬਗਲ (bagal) *n m* Armpit, side, neighbourhood; ~ਵਿਚ ਦਬਾਉਣਾ To have in possession, to conceal in the armpit; ~ਗੀਰ One who embraces.

ਬਗਲਾ (baglaa) *n m* Indian pond Heron; ~ਭਗਤ Hypocrite, deceitful.

ਬਗਲੋਲ (baglol) *a n m* Foolish (person), a fool, stupid.

ਬੱਗਾ (baggaa) *a* White, grey, colourless.

ਬਗ਼ਾਵਤ (bagaawat) *n f* Mutiny, revolt, rebellion.

ਬਗ਼ੀਚਾ (bageechaa) *n m* Garden, plantation. Also ਬਗੀਚੀ

ਬਗੈਰ (bagaer) *prep* Without, except, save, but, sans, but for.

ਬਗੋਣਾ (bagoṇaa) *v* To backbite, talk ill of, to slander; To harm, to damage, ruin.

ਬਗੋਲਾ (bagolaa) *n m* Whirlwind.

ਬਘਾਰਨਾ (baghaarnaa) *v* To talk ostentatiously; To season food with condiments; ~ਸ਼ੇਖੀ To boast.

ਬਘਿਆੜ (baghiaaṛ) *n m* Wolf.

ਬੱਘੀ (bagghee) *n f* Horse-driven fourwheeled carriage.

ਬਘੇਲਾ (baghelaa) *n* Whelp, young one of tiger; Tiger cub.

ਬਚਗਾਨਾ (bachgaanaa) *a* Childish.

ਬਚਨਾ (bachnaa) *v* To escape, to survive, to avoid, to get aside.

ਬਚਤ (bachat) *n f* Saving, gain, profit, surplus.

ਬਚਨ (bachan) *n m* Promise, speech, utterance; ~ਦੇਣਾ To

promise, to pledge; ~**ਪਾਲਣਾ** To keep one's words; ~**ਬੱਧ** Committed; ~**ਲੈਣਾ** To get a promise.

ਬਚਪਨ (bachpaṇ) *n m* Childhood.

ਬਚਪਨਾ (bachpanaa) *n m* Childishness, puerility.

ਬਚੜਾ (bachṛaa) *n m* Infant, child, an address term of endearment. Also **ਬਚੜੀ**

ਬੱਚਾ (bachchaa) *n m* Child, baby, boy, offspring.

ਬਚਾਉ (bachaau) *n m* Protection, defence, security, escape. Also **ਬਚਾਅ**

ਬਚਾਉਣਾ (bachaauṇaa) *v* To defend, to save, to spare, to protect.

ਬੱਚੂ (bachchoo) *n m* Diminutive and endearment term for 'bachchaa' child.

ਬਚੂੰਗੜਾ (bachoongaṛaa) *n m* A little one, tiny tot, kid.

ਬਚੇਦਾਨੀ (bachedaanee) *n f* Uterus, womb.

ਬਛੜਾ (bachhṛaa) *n m* Calf.

ਬੱਜ (bajj) *n f* Stigma, blemish, slur, defect; ~**ਲਗਦੀ** To be tarnished, to be blemished.

ਬੰਜਰ (banjar) *a* Barren, unproductive.

ਬਜਰ (bajar) *a* Heavy, strong, stout.

ਬਜਰੀ (bajree) *n f* Shingle, gravel, small stones used in concrete, calcareous nodules.

ਬਜਾਜੀ (bajaajee) *n f* Cloth for sale, textile, fabrics drapery.

ਬਜਾਉਣਾ (bajaauṇaa) *v* To obey, to accomplish. Also **ਵਜਾਉਣਾ** (**ਹੁਕਮ**)

ਬਜਾਜ (bajaaj) *n m* Cloth merchant, draper.

ਬਜ਼ਾਰ (bazaar) *n m* Bazar, market; ~**ਗਰਮ ਹੋਣਾ** To have a good sale.

ਬਜ਼ੁਰਗ (bazurg) *a n m* Elderly, order person.

ਬੱਝਣਾ (bajjhṇaa) *v* To be bound, to be entangled, to be arrested.

ਬਟਵਾਰਾ (baṭwaaraa) *n m* Partition, distribution, allotment.

ਬੰਟਾ (banṭaa) *n m* Glass crystle, glass ball.

ਬਟੂਆ (baṭooaa) *n m* Purse, wallet, small money bag.

ਬਟੋਰਨਾ (baṭornaa) *n* To gather, to accumulate.

ਬੱਠਲ (baṭṭhal) *n m* Earthen bowl or trough; Shallow person; Simpleton.

ਬਠਾਉਣਾ (baṭhaauṇaa) *v* To make one be seated, to seat, to usher one to a seat; to cause one withdraw (as from elections or competition); to set, to fix or mount properly. Also ਬਠਾਲਣਾ

ਬੰਡੀ (bandee) *n f* Jacket, waistcoat.

ਬਣਨਾ (bannaa) *v* To be made, to be prepared, to be cooked, to be constructed, to rise, to be befooled; ~**ਠਨਨਾ** To be decked, to try to appear beautiful.

ਬਣਾਉਟੀ (banaautee) *a* Artificial, fake, spurious, bogus, counterfeit, not genuine or real, sham; Mock, feigned, simulated.

ਬਣਾਉਣਾ (banaaunaa) *v* To build, to construct, to manufacture, to shape, to prepare, to form.

ਬੱਤੀ (battee) *n a f* Lamp, wick, lantern, electric light, stick; Thirty two; ਮੋਮ~ Candle.

ਬਤੀਸੀ (bateesee) *n f* Dentures, set of thirty two teeth in the jaws.

ਬਤੋਰ (bataur) *a* By way of, as in the position or capacity of, as a substitute for.

ਬੰਦ (band) *a n m* Closed, shut, locked, confined, stopped; Ties; Dam, bandage; ~**ਕਰਨਾ** To close, to shut, to stop, to imprison, to seal.

ਬਦ (bad) *a* Bad, knavish, vicious, mean, vile; ~**ਅਸੀਸ** curse; ~**ਅਮਨੀ** Disturbance, breach of peace, disorder, chaos; ~**ਸ਼ਕਲ** ugly; ~**ਹਜ਼ਮੀ** Indigestion; ~**ਕਾਰ** Wicked, vile, prostitute; ~**ਕਿਸਮਤ** Unfortunate, unlucky; ~**ਗੁਮਾਨ** Suspicious, distrustful, estranged; ~**ਜਾਤ** Mean, depraved; ~**ਤਮੀਜ਼** Discourteous, illmannered, rude, impolite, uncivil; ~**ਦਿਮਾਗ** Arrogant; ~**ਦੁਆ** Curse, malediction; ~**ਨਸੀਬ** Unfortunate, ill-fated; ~**ਨਾਮ** Ill-reputed, notorious; ~**ਨੀਤ** Intentioned, false, deceitful; ~**ਬਖ਼ਤ** Unfortunate; ~**ਮਿਜ਼ਾਜ਼** ill or short tempered, irritated or touchy, surly; ~**ਲਗਾਮ** Out of control, outspoken.

ਬੰਦਸ਼ (bandash) *n f* Restriction, restraint.

ਬਦਸਤੂਰ (badsatoor) *adv* As usual.

ਬਦਹਵਾਸ (badhavaas) *a* Out of one's senses or wits, confused, non-plussed, extremely perplexed, agitated or afraid, consternated.

ਬਦਹਵਾਸੀ (badhavaasee) *n f* State of being Confusion, perplexity, nonplus, consternation, dread.

ਬੰਦਗੀ (bandgee) *n f* Worship, prayer, salvation, service.

ਬਦਨ (badan) *n m* Body.

ਬਦਬੂ (badboo) *n f* Foul smell, stench, stink, bad odour.

ਬਦਮਾਸ਼ (badmaash) *a n m* Mischievous, wicked, immoral; Hooligan, rogue, debauch, villian, bad character person.

ਬਦਮਾਸ਼ੀ (badmaashee) *n f* A wicked, villanious act; villainy, rowdyism, rascality, rouguery, hooliganism.

ਬੰਦਰ (bandar) *n m* Monkey, ape. Also ਬਾਂਦਰ

ਬਦਰੰਗ (badrang) *a* Discoloured, faded; (cards) of a suit different from the one played. Also ਬਰੰਗ

ਬੰਦਰਗਾਹ (bandargaa) *n m* Port-harbour, haven, seaport, riverport.

ਬੱਦਲ (baddal) *n m* Cloud. Also ਬਦਲੀ

ਬਦਲਣਾ (badalnaa) *v* To change, to be transferred, to convert, to shift, to exchange, to barter; ਭੇਸ~ To disguise.

ਬਦਲਾ (badlaa) *n m* Revenge, vengeance, recompense; ~ਲੈਣਾ To avenge, to retalite.

ਬਦਲੀ (badlee) *n f* Change, exchange, replacement, substitute; transfer; Alteration; transmutation; ~ਕਰਨਾ To change, exchange, replace, substitute, alter, convert, transform; to transfer; ~ਕਰਾਉਣੀ To get one or oneself transferred.

ਬਦਲਾਉਣਾ (badlaaunaa) *v* To substitute, to change, to transfer.

ਬੰਦਾ (bandaa) *n m* Humanbeing, man; Servant, slave.

ਬਦਾਮ (badaam) *n m* Almond.

ਬੰਦੀ (bandee) *n f* Prisoner; Maid, woman slave; ~ਖਾਨਾ Prison, Jail, lockup.

ਬੰਦੂਕ (bandook) *n f* Gun, musket, carbine; ~ਚਲਾਉਣਾ To fire; ~ਚੀ Rifleman, gunman, musketeer; ~ਦੀ ਨਾਲੀ Barrel.

ਬੰਦੋਬਸਤ (bandobast) *n m* Arrangement, administration.

ਬਦੋਬਦੀ (badobadee) *adv* Forcibly, contentiously, unwillingly.

ਬਦੌਲਤ (badolat) *int* By virtue of, by means of, due to, through.

ਬੰਧ (bandh) *n m* Closure, strike.

ਬੰਧਕ (bandhak) *a* Binding, binder.

ਬੰਧਨ (bandhan) *n m* Restraint, check, attachment, restriction, hindrance; ~ਖੋਲ੍ਹਣਾ To untie.

ਬੰਧੂਆ (bandhuaa) *n m* Bonded labour, slave, prisoner. Also ਮਜ਼ਦੂਰ

ਬੰਧੇਜ (bandhej) *n m* Restriction, restrain, prohibition, taboo, fixed, customary wages, allowances or share.

ਬੰਨ੍ਹ (bannh) *n m* Dam, barrage, embankment; Hindrance, obstruction. Also **ਬਾਂਧ**

ਬਨਵਾਉਣਾ (banvaahunaa) *v* To get something to be tied, fastened, bound, packed, dammed, imprisoned; To assist in fastening.

ਬੰਨ੍ਹਣਾ (banhnaa) *v* To arrest, to bind, to commit, to clasp, to fasten, to tie, to chain.

ਬਨਬਾਸ (banbaas) *n m* Exile.

ਬਨੜਾ (banraa) *n* Bridegroom. Also **ਬੰਨਾ**

ਬਨੜੀ (banree) *n f* Bride. Also **ਬੰਨੀ**

ਬਨਾਤ (banaat) *n f* Wollen broad cloth, baize.

ਬਨਾਵਟ (banaawat) *n f* Construction, structure, formation.

ਬਨਿਆਨ (baniaan) *n f* Undergarment, vest. Also **ਬਨੈਨ**

ਬੰਨੇ (banne) *n m* Side, direction.

ਬਨੇਰਾ (baneraa) *n m* Roof boundry, parapet, coping.

ਬਫਾ (bafaa) *n f* Dandruff.

ਬੰਬ (bamb) *n m* Bomb, shell; Shaft of a carriage. Also **ਬਮ**

ਬੰਬਾ (bambaa) *n m* Water tap, water pipe; Engine, jet.

ਬੰਬਾਰੀ (bambaaree) *n* Bombardment, bombing shelling.

ਬੰਬੀ (bambee) *n f* Tube-well.

ਬਰਸਣਾ (barsnaa) *v* To rain, to pounce.

ਬਰਸਾਤ (barsaat) *n f* Rainy season, rains.

ਬਰਸਾਤੀ (barsaatee) *n f* Rain coat, Portico.

ਬਰਸੀ (barsee) *n f* Death anniversary.

ਬਰਕਤ (barkat) *n f* Blessing, prosperity, auspiciousness, gain.

ਬਰਕਰਾਰ (barkaraar) *a* Unchanged, same as before, continued, as formerly established, status quo.

ਬਰਖਾ (barkhaa) *n f* Rain.

ਬਰਖ਼ਾਸਤ (barkhaast) *a* Dismissed, discharged, adjourned (meeting).

ਬਰਖਾਸਤਗੀ (barkhaastagee) *n* Dismissal, discharge, termination; Dissolution, ending.

ਬਰਖ਼ਿਲਾਫ਼ (barkhilaaf) *a* Against, in opposition, on the contrary.

ਬਰਖੁਰਦਾਰ (barkhurdaar) *a* Obedient, faithful.

ਬਰਛਾ (barchhaa) *n m* Lance, dart.

ਬਰਤ (barat) *n m* Fast. Also **ਵਰਤ**

ਬ੍ਰਤ (brat) *n m* Pledge.

ਬਰਤਨ (bartan) *n m* Utensil, pot.

ਬਰਤਰਫ਼ (bartaraf) *a* Removed, dismissed, discharged, (from position); ~ਕਰਨਾ To remove, to dismiss, to discharge, to terminate services of.

ਬਰਤਰਫ਼ੀ (bartarfee) *n f* Removal, dismissal, discharge, termination of service.

ਬਰਤਾਂਤ (bartaant) *n m* Narration, narrative, tale, story, account, description, report, tidings or news (of any incident or occurance).

ਬਰਤਾਨੀਆ (bartaaniaa) *n m* Britain.

ਬਰਦਾਸ਼ਤ (bardaasht) *n f* Endurance, perseverance, toleration.

ਬਰਫ਼ (baraf) *n f* Ice, snow.

ਬਰਫ਼ਾਨੀ (barfaanee) *a* Snow-clad, Snowy.

ਬਰਫ਼ੀਲਾ (berfeelaa) *a* Icy, ice cold.

ਬਰਫ਼ੀ (barfee) *n f* A sweetmeat prepared by condensing milk.

ਬਰਬਰੀਅਤ (barbareeyat) *n f* Barbarity, barbarism.

ਬਰਬਾਦ (barbaad) *a* Ruined, destroyed; ~ਕਰਨਾ To ruin, to destroy.

ਬਰਬਾਦੀ (barbaadee) *n f* Ruin, destruction, ruination; Wastage, dissipation, havoc.

ਬਰੜਾਉਣਾ (barṛaaunaa) *v* To prate, to talk incohersantly in one's sleep, to mumble.

ਬਰਾਏ (baraae) *adv* For the sake of, with the object or purpose of, meant for.

ਬਰਾਸਤਾ (baraastaa) *int* En route, via.

ਬਰਾਂਡਾ (baraandaa) *n m* Balcony, terrace, corridor, verandah.

ਬਰਾਂਡੀ (baraandee) *n f* Brandy.

ਬਰਾਤ (baraat) *n f* Marriage party.

ਬਰਾਦਰ (barradar) *n m* Brother.

ਬਰਾਦਰਾਨਾ (baradaraana) *a* Brotherly.

ਬਰਾਦਰੀ (barradree) *n f* Community, relative, brotherhood, same clan or caste.

ਬਰਾਬਰ (baraabar) *a adv* Equal, plain, uniform, alike; Incessantly, continually, ever, always; ~ਕਰਨਾ To equalize, to make equal, to level.

ਬਰਾਬਰੀ (baraabaree) *n f* Equality, exactness.

ਬਰੀ (baree) *a* Relinquished, acquitted, released; ~ਕਰਨਾ To release, to set free, to acquit.

ਬਰੀਕ (bareek) *a* Thin, subtle,

ਬਰੀਕੀ (bareekee) *n f* Thinness, fineness, slenderness, minuteness, subtleness, bubtlety, finer or deeper meaning.

ਬਰੂਦ (barood) *n m* Gun powder.

ਬਰੂਦੀ (baroodee) *a* Explosive.

ਬਰੇਠਣ (barethan) *n f* Washerwoman, wife of a washerman.

ਬਰੇਠਾ (barethaa) *n m* Washerman.

ਬਲ (bal) *n m* Strength, powder, vigour, force, support; ~ਪੂਰਬਕ Forcibly, emphatically; ~ਹੀਨ Impotent, weak; ~ਵਾਨ Powerful, stout, vigorous, very strong.

ਬਲਗਮ (balgam) *n m* Phlegm.

ਬਲਣਾ (balnaa) *v* To burn, to smoulder, to be enkindled, to be jealous; ~ਸੜਨਾ To be jealous.

ਬਲਵੰਤ (balwant) *a* Strong, powerful, potent, vigorous.

ਬਲਵਾ (balwaa) *n m* Riot, tumult, insurrection; ~ਈ Rebel, rioter.

ਬਲਾ (balaa) *n f* Calamity, trouble, demon, witch, ghost.

ਬੱਲਾ (ballaa) *n m* Bat, racket, stump.

ਬਲਿਹਾਰ (balihaar) *a intj* Excellent, fine, very good; Bravo.

ਬਲਿਹਾਰੀ (balihaaree) *n f* sacrifice.

ਬਲੀ (balee) *n f* Sacrifice, immolation; Strong, powerful.

ਬੱਲੀ (ballee) *n f* Beam, rafter, support.

ਬਲੀਦਾਨ (baleedaan) *n m* Sacrifice, martyrdom.

ਬਲੂੰਗੜਾ (baloongraa) *n m a* Kitten; Very small baby.

ਬਲੈਕੀਆ (balaekiaa) *n m* Black-marketeer, smuggler.

ਬਵਾਸੀਰ (bawaaseer) *n m* Piles, haemorrhoid.

ਬੜਬੜਾਹਟ (barbraahat) *n f* Muttering, chattering, vain talk.

ਬੜਬੋਲਾ (barbolaa) *n m* Prattler, boaster, babbler.

ਬੜੋਤਰੀ (barautree) *n f* Increase, expansion, progress, rise.

ਬੜ੍ਹਕਣਾ (barhaknaa) *v* To thunder, to roar, to speak in gruff.

ਬਾਉਲਾ (baaulaa) *a n m* Insane, crazy, mad, rabid; Madman, mad person. Also ਬਾਉਰਾ

ਬਾਂਸ (baans) *n m* Bamboo, a rod; ~ਤੇ ਚੜ੍ਹਾਉਣਾ To defame.

ਬਾਸ (baas) *n* Residence, habitation, abode; Smell; Boss. Also ਵਾਸ;

ਬਾਸਿੰਦਾ (bashindaa) *n m* Resident, inhabitant.

ਬਾਸੀ (baasee) *a* Stale, not fresh.

ਬਾਂਹ (baanh) *n f* Arm, support,

associate; ~ਫ਼ਜ਼ਨੀ To support, to help.

ਬਾਹਰ (baahar) *adv* Outside, out of station, beyond; ~ਲਾ Outer, external, outsider, foreign.

ਬਾਹਰੀ (baahree) *a* External, outer, outward, extrinsic.

ਬਾਂਕਾ (baankaa) *a n m* Foppish, coquette, curved, crooked; Fop, dandy.

ਬਾਕਾਇਦਾ (baakaaidaa) *a adv* According to rules, formal, regular, regularly, formally, systematic, systematically, punctually.

ਬਾਕੀ (baakee) *a n f* Remaining, residuary, in arrears, due; Arrears, Remainder, balance.

ਬਾਂਗ (baang) *n f* Crowing of a cock or rooster, Muslim's call for prayer; ~ਦੇਣੀ To crow; To give the call for prayer.

ਬਾਗ਼ (baag) *n m* Garden, orchard; ~ਬਾਨ Grandener; ~ਬਾਨੀ Grandening, horticulture.

ਬਾਣਡੋਰ (baangdor) *n f* Control.

ਬਾਗੀ (baagee) *n m a* Rebel, mutineer, insurgent, insurrectionsist; Rebellious, disobedient, wayward, recusant, refractory, revolutionary. Also ਬਾਗ਼ੀ

ਬਾਜ (baaj) *n m* Hawk, falcon. Also ਬਾਜ਼

ਬਾਜੀ (baazee) *n f* Stake, turn, in a game or play; ~ਹਾਰਨੀ To lose a stake or game ~ਮਾਰਨੀ To win, to excel; ~ਗਰ Acrobat, one who performs athletic feats of agility and dexterity.

ਬਾਜੂ (baajoo) *n m* Arm, wing, side, helper; ~ਬੰਦ Armlet, an ornament for arm.

ਬਾਂਝ (baajh) *n f a* Barren woman; Barren, sterile, unproductive, unprolific.

ਬਾਢੀ (baḍhee) *n m* Carpenter. Also ਤਰਖਾਣ

ਬਾਣ (baaṇ) *n m* Arrow, shaft.

ਬਾਣਾ (baaṇaa) *n m* Dress, habit, apparel, garb.

ਬਾਣੀ (baaṇee) *n f* Speech, sacred hymn; Resolve, writings, in Guru Granth (a sacred book of Sikhism).

ਬਾਣੀਆ (baaṇiaa) *n m a* Trader, merchant, businessman, shopkeeper; Shrewd, calculating.

ਬਾਤ (baat) *n f* Talk, discourse, conversation, essence, matter; ~ਚੀਤ Conversation, dialogue.

ਬਾਤੂਨੀ (baatoonee) *a* Talkative, garrulous.

ਬਾਦਸ਼ਾਹ (baadshaah) *n m* King, ruler.

ਬਾਦਸ਼ਾਹਤ (baadshaahat) *n f* Kingship, empire, rule, kingdom domain.

ਬਾਦਸ਼ਾਹੀ (Baadshaaee) *n f a* Kingly, royal, regal, imperial.

ਬਾਂਦੀ (baandee) *n f* Maid servant.

ਬਾਦੀ (baadee) *n f* Flatulence.

ਬੰਧ (baand) *n m* Dam, Barrage. Also ਬੰਨ੍ਹ

ਬਾਨਵੇ (baanave) *a* Ninety-two.

ਬਾਬ (baab) *n m* Chapter; State, condition, mode, manner; ~ਕਰਨੀ To reprimand, to take to task.

ਬਾਬਤ (baabat) *n f* Prep Connection, affair, matter; In connection with, regarding, in relation to.

ਬਾਰੀ (baaree) *n f* Window; Turn; ~ਬਾਰੀ Turn by turn. Also ਵਾਰੀ

ਬਾਲ (baal) *n m a* Child; Younger, immature; Hair; ~ਵਾੜੀ Nursery, kindergarten; ~ਬਾਲ ਬਚਣਾ To have a hair breadth escape.

ਬਾਲਕ (baalak) *n m* Child, lad, infant, disciple, pupil.

ਬਾਲਗ (baalag) *n m* Adult, major.

ਬਾਲਟੀ (baaltee) *n f* Bucket, pail.

ਬਾਲਣ (baalan) *n m* Fuel, firewood.

ਬਾਲਣਾ (baalnaa) *v* To Kindle, to burn, to light, to ignite.

ਬਾਲਮ (baalam) *n m* Lover, paramour, husband.

ਬਾਲੜੀ (baalree) *n f* Innocent girl, infant.

ਬਾਲਾ (baalaa) *n f a* Teenage girl; Ear ring; High, above.

ਬਾੜ੍ਹ (baarh) *n f* Flood, spate, volley.

ਬਿਆਸੀ (biaasee) *a* Eighty-two.

ਬਿਆਨ (biaan) *n m* Statement, narration, explanation.

ਬਿਆਨਾ (biaanaa) *n m* Advance money.

ਬਿਸਤਰਾ (bistaraa) *n m* Bed, bedding, bed-clothes.

ਬਿਸਮਾਉਣਾ (bismaaunaa) *v* To extinguish, to put out.

ਬਿਸਰਨਾ (bisarnaa) *v* To forget. Also ਵਿਸਰਨਾ

ਬਿਖਮ (bikham) *a* Difficult, hard ardous; complex intricate, knotty, odd, unequal, incongruous; ~ਤਾ Difficulty, arduousness, complexity, intricacy, oddness, oddity, incongruity.

ਬਿਖਰਾਉਣਾ (bikhraaunaa) *v* To scatter, to disperse.

ਬਿਗਾਨਾ (bigaanaa) *a* Unrelated,

stranger, unacquainted, alien, another's; ~ਪਣ Otherness, alienage.

ਬਿਜਲੀ (bijlee) *n f* Electricity; ~ਘਰ Power house; ~ਬੁਝਾਉਣਾ To switch off the light.

ਬਿਠਾਉਣਾ (bithaaunaa) *v* To seat, to cause to sit or withdraw. Also ਬਿਠਾਣਾ

ਬਿਤਾਉਣਾ (bitaaunaa) *v* To spend.

ਬਿਦਾਰ (bidaar) *a* Awake, alert, conscious. Also ਬੇਦਾਰ

ਬਿੰਦੀ (bindee) *n f* Dot, point, zero, cypher, round mark on the forehead.

ਬਿੰਦੂ (bindoo) *n m* Drop, dot.

ਬਿਨਸਣਾ (binasanaa) *v* To be destroyed, to be ruined, to die, to perish.

ਬਿਪਤਾ (biptaa) *n f* Trouble, difficulty, adversity, distress, misfortune.

ਬਿਫਰਨਾ (bipharnaa) *v* To be furious, to rage.

ਬਿਬੇਕ (bibek) *n m* Discretion, discrimination, intelligence, reasoning.

ਬਿਭੂਤੀ (bibhootee) *n f* (1) Ashes; (2) Excellence.

ਬਿਮਾਰ (bimaar) *n m a* Ill, sick, indisposed. Also ਬੀਮਾਰ

ਬਿਮਾਰੀ (bimaaree) *n f* Disease, sickness, illness, indisposition; Pathology; Murrain. Also ਬੀਮਾਰੀ

ਬਿਰਕਣਾ (biraknaa) *v* To speak out, to confess (out of fear or under duress).

ਬਿਰਥਾ (birthaa) *a adv* Useless, vain, worthless; Worthlessly, uselessly, invain.

ਬਿਲਟੀ (biltee) *n f* Freight receipt, Invoice, R/R.

ਬਿੱਲਾ (billaa) *n m* Badge, medal; Tom cat.

ਬਿੱਲੀ (billee) *n f* Cat, puss.

ਬਿਲੋਣਾ (bilonaa) *v* To churn, to stir.

ਬੀਆਬਾਨ (beeaabaan) *n m* Deserted place, devastated place.

ਬੀਜ (beej) *n m* Seed, grain, source, origin, semen.

ਬੀਜਣਾ (beejnaa) *v* To sow, to cultivate.

ਬੀਤਣਾ (beetnaa) *v* To pass, elapse, expire; (For time or opportunity); To pass away; To expire; To die; To decease (for person).

ਬੀਨ (been) *n f* Harp, lyre, flute.

ਬੀਨਾਈ (beenaaee) *n f* Eye sight.

ਬੀਬਾ (beebaa) *a* Lovely, docile, amiable. Also ਬੀਬੀ

ਬੀਬੀ (beebee) *n f* Lady, dame, mistress.

ਬੀਮਾ (beemaa) *n m* Insurance.

ਬੀਵੀ (beewee) *n f* Wife, better half.

ਬੀੜਨਾ (beerṇaa) *v* To make a row, to bind, to arrange.

ਬੀੜਾ (beeṛaa) *n m* Betel; ~ਚੁੱਕਣਾ To accept a challenge; To undertake a challenging task.

ਬੀੜੀ (beeṛee) *n f* Crude form of Cigratte; a button supporting the spindle in a spinning wheel.

ਬੁਸਕਣਾ (busakṇaa) *v* To sob, to weep slowly.

ਬੁਸਣਾ (busṇaa) *v* To go stale, to stench, to give out foul smell.

ਬੁਸਬੁਸਾ (busbusaa) *a* Rotton, stinking.

ਬੁੱਸਾ (bussaa) *a* Rotton, stinking, sad, empty.

ਬੁਹਾਰਨਾ (buhaarnaa) *v* To Sweap, to clean.

ਬੁਹਾਰੀ (buhaaree) *n f* Broomstick, broom, a besom.

ਬੁੱਕ (bukk) *n f* Both hands joined with palms up and joined together to form a bowl or cup; Double palmful.

ਬੁਕਣਾ (bukṇaa) *v* To thunder, to roar, to speak loudly.

ਬੁਖਾਰ (bukhaar) *n m* Fever, vapour.

ਬੁੱਗ (bugg) *a* Stupid, brainless, blockhead.

ਬੁੰਗਾ (bungaa) *n m* House, living place, residence, dwelling place.

ਬੁੱਘੀ (bugee) *n f* Light bullock-cart.

ਬੁਜ਼ਦਿਲ (buzdil) *a* Coward, timid chicken-hearted.

ਬੁਜ਼ਦਿਲੀ (buzdilee) *n f* Timidity, timidness, cowardice, cowardness, chickenheartedness.

ਬੁਝਣਾ (bujhṇaa) *v* To be extinguished, to be quenched, to be off.

ਬੁੱਝਣਾ (bujjhṇaa) *v* To guess, to understand, to solve (riddle).

ਬੁਝਾਉਣਾ (bujjhaauṇaa) *v* To make one understand; To put out, to extinguish, to switch off light, to quench thirst. Also ਬੁਝਾਣਾ

ਬੁਝਾਰਤ (bujhaarat) *n f* Riddle.

ਬੁੰਡਰ (bunḍar) *n m* Buttock, anus. Also ਬੁੰਡਰੀ

ਬੁੱਢਾ (buḍḍhaa) *n m* Old man, aged person; Also ਬੁਢੜਾ

ਬੁੱਢੀ (buḍḍhee) *n f* Old or aged woman. Also ਬੁਢੜੀ

ਬੁਢੇਪਾ (budhepaa) *n m* Old age.

ਬੁਣਨਾ (buṇnaa) *v* To weave, to knit, to intertwine. Also ਬੁਨਣਾ

ਬੁਣਾਈ (buṇaaee) *n f* Act of weaving or knitting, wages for weaving or knitting. Also ਬੁਣਵਾਈ

ਬੁੱਤ (butt) *n m* a Idol, statue, image; Lifeless, motionless; ~ਖਾਨਾ Temple of idol worship.

ਬੁਥਾੜ (buthaar) *n m* Big face, face of an animal. Also ਬੂਥਾ

ਬੁੱਧੀ (buddhee) *n f* Mind, intelligence, knowledge, thought; ~ਜੀਵੀ Intellectual; ~ਮਾਨ Wise, intelligent.

ਬੁੱਧੂ (budhoo) *a n m* Foolish, stupid, silly; Idiot; ~ਪੁਣਾ Foolishness.

ਬੁਨਿਆਦ (buniaad) *n f* Foundation, base, origin, source, root; ਬੇ~ Baseless, imaginary, without any foundation.

ਬੁਨਿਆਦੀ (buniaadee) *a* Fundamental, basic, foundational, foundationary.

ਬੁਰਸ਼ (burash) *n m* Brush.

ਬੁਰਕਣਾ (buraknaa) *v* To sprinkle (powder).

ਬੁਰਕਾ (burkaa) *n m* Veil, mantle.

ਬੁਰਜ (buraj) *n m* Tower, dome, pinnacle.

ਬੁਰਾ (buraa) *a* Bad, faulty, worthless, wicked, undesirable; ~ਪਰਬੰਧ Mismanagement, maladministration; ~ਸ਼ਗਨ ill omen; ~ਭਲਾ ਆਖਣਾ To rebuke, to abuse; ~ਮੰਨਣਾ To take ill; ~ਲਗਣਾ To dislike.

ਬੁਰਾਈ (buraaee) *n f* Badness, evil, vice, viciousness, wickedness, depravity; faultiness, defect, harm, harmfulness

ਬੁਰਾਦਾ (buraadaa) *n m* Sawdust.

ਬੁਲਬੁਲ (bulbul) *n m* Nightingale.

ਬੁਲਬੁਲਾ (bulbulaa) *n m* Bubble; transient like bubble.

ਬੁਲਾਉਣਾ (bulaaunaa) *v* To call, to send for, to invite, to summon.

ਬੁਲਾਣਾ (bulaanaa) *n m* Invitaion, call, summon.

ਬੁੜਬੁੜਾਉਣਾ (burburaaunaa) *v* To mutter, to mumble, to murmur.

ਬੂਹਾ (booaa) *n m* Door.

ਬੂਝੜ (boojhar) *a* Ignorant, uncultured, rustic, foolish, stupid; Stump of sugracane or millet plant. Also ਬੂੜਾ

ਬੂਟਾ (bootaa) *n m* Herb, medicinal plant; Design or pattern worked on cloth. Also ਬੂਟੀ

ਬੂੰਦ (boond) *n f* drop.

ਬੂੰਦਾ-ਬੂੰਦੀ (boondaa-boondee) *n f* Drizzle, intermittent light rain.

ਬੇ-ਉਮੀਦ (be-umeed) *a* Without hope, hopeless.

ਬੇ-ਉਲਾਦ (be-ulaad) *a* Childless.

ਬੇ-ਅਕਲ (be-akal) *a* Foolish, stupid, unintelligent.

ਬੇ-ਅੰਤ (be-ant) *a* Limitless,

Unlimited, unending, infinite, innumerable, everlasting.

ਬੇ-ਅਦਬ (be-adab) *a* Impudent, unmannerly, rude.

ਬੇ-ਅੰਦਾਜ਼ (be-andaaz) *a* Boundless, limitless, countless, inestimable.

ਬੇ-ਅਵਾਜ਼ (be-awaaz) *a* Soundless, quiet.

ਬੇ-ਆਰਾਮ (be-aaraam) *a* Restless, without rest.

ਬੇਇਜ਼ਤ (be-izat) *a* Insulted, dishonoured, disgraced, notorious.

ਬੇਇਜ਼ਤੀ (be-iztee) *n m* Disgrace, insult, humiliation.

ਬੇ-ਇਤਬਾਰ (be-itbaar) *a* Undependable.

ਬੇ-ਇਨਸਾਫ (beinsaaf) *a* Unjust, invidious, biased, partial.

ਬੇ-ਇਲਾਜ (be-ilaaj) *a* Irremediable, incurable, without treatment.

ਬੇਈਮਾਨ (be-eemaan) *a n m* Dishonest, treacherous, cheat, unreliable; Cheater.

ਬੇਸ਼ਊਰ (be-shaur) *n m* Unmannered, nonsense, one having no decency.

ਬੇਸਹਾਰਾ (be-sahaaraa) *a* Helpless, unaided, unsupported, unbacked, having no support.

ਬੇਸ਼ੱਕ (beshakk) *adv* Of course, certainly, doubtlessly, undoubtingly.

ਬੇਸੰਕੋਚ (be-sankoch) *adv* Unhesitatingly, without hesitation.

ਬੇਸਬਰ (besabar) *adv* Impatient, restive. Also **ਬੇਸਬਰਾ**

ਬੇਸਮਝ (besamajh) *a* Fool, foolish, ignorant.

ਬੇਸ਼ਰਮ (besharam) *a* Shameless, unabashed.

ਬੇਸੁਆਦ (besuaad) *a* Tastless, unsavory, distasteful upleasant. Also **ਬੇਸਵਾਦ**

ਬੇਸੁਧ (besudh) *a* Senseless, unconscious, swooned.

ਬੇਸ਼ੁਮਾਰ (beshumaar) *a* Innumberable, numerous, countless, many.

ਬੇਹਦ (behad) *a* Too much, unlimited, unbounded, undue, inordinate (delay).

ਬੇਹਯਾ (behayaa) *a* Shameless, unashamed; ~ਈ Shamelessness.

ਬੇਹੂਦਗੀ (behoodgee) *n f* Nonsense, silliness, absurdity, absurdness.

ਬੇਹੂਦਾ (behoodaa) *a* Worthless, of no value, useless.

ਬੇਹੋਸ਼ (behosh) *a* Senseless, unconcious, delirious; ~ਹੋਣਾ To faint.

ਬੇਹੋਸ਼ੀ (behoshee) *n f* Unconsciousness swoon.

ਬੇਕਸੂਰ (bekasoor) *a* Innocent, faultless.

ਬੇਕਰਾਰ (bekaraar) *a* Impatient, restless.

ਬੇਕਾਇਦਾ (bekaidaa) *a* Irregular, unregulated, illegal.

ਬੇਕਾਬੂ (bekaaboo) *a* Out of control, uncontrolled; Runaway, uncontrollabel.

ਬੇਕਾਰ (bekaar) *a* Idle, unoccupied, unemployed, unserviceable, useless; ~ਬੈਠਣਾ To sit idle; ~ਹੋਣਾ To go waste; Unemployment.

ਬੇਖਬਰ (bekhabar) *a* Uninformed, unaware, ignorant. Also ਬੇਖਬਰ

ਬੇਗੁਨਾਹ (begunaah) *a* Innocent, guiltless.

ਬੇਗੁਨਾਹੀ (begunaahee) *n f* Sinlessness, innocence, guiltlessness, inculpability, blamelessness.

ਬੇਗੈਰਤ (begairat) *a* Shameless, devoid of self respect.

ਬੇਚੈਨ (bechain) *a* Restless, uneasy.

ਬੇਚੈਨੀ (bechainee) *n f* Restlessness.

ਬੇਜ਼ਬਾਨ (bozabaan) *a* Muto, dumb.

ਬੇਜਾਨ (bejaan) *a* Lifeless, dead, inaminate.

ਬੇਜੋੜ (bejor) *a* Matchless, unique, unparalleled, unrivalled.

ਬੇਟਾ (betaa) *n m* son.

ਬੇਟੀ (betee) *n f* Daughter, girl.

ਬੇਡੋਲ (bedol) *a* Ugly, mis-shapen, disproportionate.

ਬੇਤਅੱਲਕ (betallak) *a* Unconnected; Unconcerned; Disinterested.

ਬੇਤਹਾਸ਼ਾ (betahaashaa) *adv* Recklessly, without caution, at break neck speed.

ਬੇਤਕਲਫ (betakalaf) *a* No standing on formalities, intimate close.

ਬੇਤਰਤੀਬ (betarteeb) *a* Irregular, disorderly, unarranged, unadjusted.

ਬੇਤਾਜ (betaaj) *a* Uncrowned, without crown.

ਬੇਤਾਰ (betaar) *a* Wireless.

ਬੇਤਾਬ (betaab) *a* Eager; Ardent, anxious, impatient, vehement.

ਬੇਤਾਬੀ (betaabee) *n f* Eagerness, impatience.

ਬੇਤੁੱਕਾ (betukkaa) *a* Incongrous absurd, irrelevant.

ਬੇਦਸਤੂਰ (bedastoor) *a* Unprincipled.

ਬੇਦਖ਼ਲ (bedakhal) *a* Ejected, ousted, dispossessed.

ਬੇਦਰਦ (bedarad) *a* Cruel, hard hearted, unmerciful, unsympethetic.

ਬੇਦਾਗ਼ (bedaag) *a* Spotless, immaculate, unblemished.

ਬੇਦਾਰ (bedaar) *a* Awake, alert, conscious, active, wakeful, vigilant.

ਬੇਦਿਮਾਗ਼ (bedimaag) *a* Brainless, dunce, stupid.

ਬੇਦਿਲ (bedil) *a* Unwilling, heartless.

ਬੇਧੜਕ (bedharak) *a adv* Undaunted, unhesitating, dauntless; Fearlessly.

ਬੇਨਜ਼ੀਰ (benazeer) *a* Matchless, peerless, unprecedented, unequalled, unmatched.

ਬੇਨੂਰ (benoor) *a* Lightless, blind, dull, pale, pallied or wan (face).

ਬੇਮਿਸਾਲ (bemisaal) *a* Unexampled, unparalelled, matchless, peerless, unrivalled, unequalled, incomparable unique, rare.

ਬੇਮੁਰੱਵਤ (bemuravvat) *a* Inconsiderate, unneighbourly.

ਬੇਮੇਲ (bemail) *a* Discordant, misfit, incompatible.

ਬੇਰੁਖੀ (berukhee) *n f* Antipathy, unconcern.

ਬੇਰੁਜ਼ਗਾਰ (beruzgaar) *a* Unemployed.

ਬੇਰੁਜ਼ਗਾਰੀ (beruzgaaree) *n f* Unemployment.

ਬੇਰੋਕ (berok) *a adv* Unobstructed, unhindered, uninterrupted, without check or hinderance, freely.

ਬੇਲੱਜ (belajj) *a* Shameless.

ਬੇਲਾਗ (belaag) *a* Impartial, unconcerned, disinterested.

ਬੇ-ਲਿਹਾਜ਼ (be-lihaaz) *a* Unprejudiced, unobliging, unkind, rigid, strict, unaccomodating.

ਬੇਲੀ (belee) *n m* Associate, friend, chum.

ਬੇਵਫ਼ਾ (bewafaa) *a* Unfaithful, infidel.

ਬੇਵਾ (bevaa) *n f* Widow.

ਬੇੜਾ (beraa) *n m* Raft, float, navy.

ਬੇੜੀ (beree) *n f* Boat; Shackless, fetters for the legs; ~ਪੈਣੀ To be arrested, to be married.

ਬੈਠਕ (baithak) *n f* Sitting, meeting, drawing room; Act of sitting.

ਬੈਠਣਾ (baithnaa) *v* To sit, to occupy a seat; To withdraw; To be without work; ਗਦੀ ਤੇ~ To be enthroned; ਗਲਾ (ਸੰਘ)~ To have a hoarse throat; ਘੋੜੇ ਤੇ~ To ride; ਦਿਲ~ Sinking of heart. Also ਬਹਿਣਾ

ਬੈਰਾ (bairaa) *n m* Bearer.

ਬੈਲ (bael) *n m* Bull, ox, bullock.

ਬੋਹਣੀ (bohnee) *n f* First sale of the day.

ਬੋਝ (bojh) *n m* Burden, load, weight, heaviness; ~ਲ Heavy, burdensome, worrying.

ਬੋਝਾ (bojhaa) *n m* Pocket.

ਬੋਟੀ (botee) *n f* A piece or slice of flesh; ~ਬੋਟੀ ਕਰਨਾ To mince, to cut into small pieces.

ਬੋਣਾ (bonaa) *v* To sow.

ਬੋਤਲ (botal) *n f* Bottle; ~ਪੀਣਾ To drink.

ਬੋਤਾ (botaa) *n m* Camel, young camel for riding.

ਬੋਦਾ (bodaa) *a* Foolish, fragile, decayed.

ਬੋਦੀ (bodee) *a* Tuft of hair left unshorn on top of head (as a religious symbol of caste Hindus).

ਬੋਰਾ (boraa) *n m* Sack, big bag.

ਬੋਰੀ (boree) *n f* Small bag, sack; ~ਬਿਸਤਰਾ Bag and baggage, household goods.

ਬੋਲਣਾ (bolnaa) *v* To speak, to converse, to utter, to say, to tell.

ਬੋਲਾ (bolaa) *a* Deaf, hard of hearing.

ਬੋਲੀ (bolee) *n f* Dialect, language, tongue, taunt; Buffalo (having a spot of white hair on forehead); ~ਮਾਰਨਾ To jeer, to taunt.

ਬੌਣਾ (baunaa) *n m a* Dwarf; Dwarfish.

ਬੌਲ (baul) *n m* Urine.

ਬੌਲਦ (baulad) *n m* Bull, ox, bullock.

ਬੌਲਾ (baulaa) *a* Mad.

ਭ

ਭ Twenty ninth letter of Gurmukhi alphabets, pronounced as 'bhabhaa' (a tone marker)

ਭਉ (bhau) *n m* Fear, fright, alarm; Dizziness, vertigo.

ਭਸਮ (bhasam) *n f a* Ash, calx; Burnt to ashes; Cinereous; ~ਕਰਨਾ To consume, to reduce to ashes.

ਭਸੂੜੀ (bhasooree) *n f* Undue haste or confusion; Disputation, trouble, quarrel.

ਭਖਣਾ (bhakhnaa) *v* To burn, to burst into flame, to get hot.

ਭੱਖਣਾ (bhakkhanaa) *v* To eat devour, to consume. Also ਭੱਡਣਾ

ਭੰਗ (bhang) *n f a* Intoxicating hemp; Broken, dissolved; ~ੜ Hemp addict; ~ਪੀਣੀ To be intoxicated; ~ਕਰਨਾ To break, to dissolve.

ਭੰਗਣ (bhangan) *n f* Female sweeper, wife of scavenger.

ਭਗਤ (bhagat) *n m* Devotee, worshipper, votary; Holyman, pious person, lover of deity.

ਭਗਤੀ (bhagtee) *n f* Devotion, worship devotional love of deity; Meditation, religious observances.

ਭਗੰਦਰ (bhagandar) *n m* Fistula.

ਭੱਬਟ (bhambat) *n m* Moth.

ਭਗਦੜ (bhagdar) *n f* Stampede.

ਭਗਵਾ (bhagwaa) *a* Saffron coloured.

ਭਗਵਾਨ (bhagwaan) *n m* Supreme being, God.

ਭੰਗੜਾ (bhangraa) *n m* A folk dance of Punjab.

ਭੰਗੀ (bhangee) *n m a* Sweeper, scavenger; Addicted to ; Bhang.

ਭਗੋੜਾ (bhagoraa) *a* Absconder, fugitive, truant, deserter, runaway.

ਭਚੀੜਨਾ (bhacheernaa) *v* To squeeze.

ਭਜਣਾ (bhajnaa) *v* To run, to run away, to flee, to abscond, to escape; To break. Also ਭਜ ਜਾਣਾ

ਭਜਨ (bhajan) *n m* Devotional song, hymn, carol, orison; remembrance or repetition of God's name; religious devotion; ~ਮੰਡਲੀ Choir.

ਭਜਨੀਕ (bhajneek) *a* Regular in prayers, devotee, worshipper.

ਭਟਕਣਾ (bhataknaa) *v* To go astray, to wander, to lurk, to deviate.

ਭਟਕਾਉਣਾ (bhatkaaunaa) *v* To mislead, to bewilder, to cause to

ਭੱਠਾ (bhatthaa) *n m* Brick Kiln; a large oven or furnace.

ਭੱਠੀ (bhatthee) *n f* Furnace, small kiln, distillery, parcher's oven.

ਭੰਡਣਾ (bhandnaa) *v* To defame, to slander.

ਭੰਡਾਰ (bhandaar) *n m* Store house, repository, store. Also **ਭੰਡਾਰਾ**

ਭੰਡਾਰਾ (bhandaaraa) *n m* Feast (mostly for religious people); ~ਕਰਨਾ To organise a general feast.

ਭੰਡਾਰੀ (bhandaaree) *n m* Store-keeper, storeholder; Treasurer; Cook at a religious establishment; Built in tool box of a bullock-cart.

ਭੰਡੀ (bhandee) *a n m* Slanderer Defamation, slandering, noise.

ਭਣਵਈਆ (bhanvayiaa) *n* husband of sister, brother-in-law.

ਭਣੇਵਾ (bhanewaa) *n m* Sister's son.

ਭਣੇਵੀ (bhanewee) *n f* Sister's daughter.

ਭੱਤ (bhatt) *n m* Boiled rice mash with sugar.

ਭਤਣੀਆ (bhatneeyaa) *n m* Nephew, brother's son. Also **ਭਤੀਜਾ**

ਭੱਤਾ (bhattaa) *n m* Allowance, additional salary for some purpose.

ਭਤਾਰ (bhataar) *n m* Husband.

ਭਤੀਜੀ (bhateejee) *n f* Niece, brother's daughter.

ਭੱਦਰ (bhaddar) *a* Good, gentle, virtuous, worthy.

ਭੱਦਾ (bhaddaa) *a* Clumsy, ugly, Vulgar, awkward, ridiculous; ~ਪਣ Ugliness, awkwardness, bawdiness.

ਭਨਕਟ (bhankat) *n m* Change, small coins or notes of lower denomination.

ਭੰਨਣਾ (bhannaa) *v* To break, to smash, to bend, to fold.

ਭੱਪੀ (bhappee) *n f* Kiss. Also **ਭੱਪਾ**

ਭਬਕ (bhabak) *n f* (1) Roar; Thunderous or threatening speech; Threat; (2) Sudden, bursting into flame, combustion, explosion.

ਭਬਕਣਾ (bhabaknaa) *v* To speak in angry tone, to roar; To burst into flames.

ਭਬਕੀ (bhabkee) *n f* Threat; ~ਦੇਣੀ To frighten, to threaten, to bully.

ਭੰਬਟ (bhambat) *n m* moth.

ਭੰਬੀਰੀ (bhambeeree) *n f* Rotating toy.

ਭਬੂਕਾ (bhabookaa) *n m* Flame, blaze.

ਭਰਜਾਈ (bharjaaee) *n f* Brother's wife, sister-in-law. Also **ਭਾਬੀ**

ਭਰਤੀ (bhartee) *n f* Recruiting, recruitment, enlistment; ~ਹੋਣਾ To enrol or enlist (in armed forces); To be recruited, to be admitted (in hospital); ~ਕਰਨਾ To recruit, to enrol, to enlist; to admit (as a patient in hospital).

ਭਰਨਾ (bharnaa) *v* To fill, to gorge, to impregnate, to refill, to complete, to load, to pay (dues, fee etc.); ਹਾਮੀ~ To support; ਕੰਨ~ To instigate, to poison the mind.

ਭਰਨੀ (bharnee) *n f* Result of one's deeds.

ਭਰਪੂਰ (bharpoor) *a adv* Quite, full, comprehensive; Completely, quite.

ਭਰਮ (bharam) *n m* Suspicion, illusion, doubt, apprehension, confusion; Fallacy, fantasy.

ਭਰਮਣਾ (bharmanaa) *v* To be deluded, to be perplexed, to be induced to be misconceived, to be misled, to misapprehend.

ਭਰਮਾਉਣਾ (bharmaaunaa) *v* To misguide, to decieve, to be perplexed, to be induced.

ਭਰਮਾਰ (bharmaar) *n f* Sufficiency, plenty, abundance.

ਭਰਾ (bharaa) *n m* Brother.

ਭਰਿਸ਼ਟਣਾ (bharishtnaa) *v* To be polluted, to be defiled.

ਭਰਿਸ਼ਟਾਚਾਰ (bharishtachaar) *v* Corruption.

ਭਰੋਸਾ (bharosaa) *n m* Confidence, reliance, trust, faith, hope.

ਭਲਕੇ (bhalke) *adv* Tomorrow, on the morrow.

ਭਲਮਨਸਊ (bhalmansaoo) *n f* Godness, gentlemanliness, nobility. Also ਭਲਮਾਨਸੀ

ਭਲਾ (bhalaa) *intj a n m* Well, good; Good, gentle, noble; Godness, welfare, gain; ~ਕਰਨਾ To help, to assist, to do a good, turn; ~ਚੰਗਾ Hale and hearty, in good health; ~ਬੁਰਾ Virtue and vice, pros and cons, good and bad.

ਭਲਾਈ (bhalaaee) *n f* Wellbeing, goodness, welfare, virtue.

ਭੰਵਰ (bhanwar) *n m* Whirlpool, swivel.

ਭੰਵਰਾ (bhanwraa) *n m* Large black bee.

ਭਵਾਂ (bhawaan) *n f* Eyebrow.

ਭਵਾਉਣਾ (bhawaaunaa) *v* To revolve, to circumlocute.

ਭਵਾਟਣੀ (bhawaatnee) *n f* Circumlocution, somersault, acrobatics.

ਭਵਿੱਖ (bhavikkh) *a* Future, prospects; ~ਬਾਣੀ Prophecy, forecast, prediction. Also ਭਵਿਸ਼

ਭੜ (bhaṛ) *n m* Pomp and show, importance, dignity.

ਭੜਕ (bhaṛak) *n f* Ostentation, show, splendour, blaze; ~ਦਾਰ Splendid, shinning, glittering.

ਭੜਕਣ (bhaṛkaṇ) *n f* Blaze, flare-up.

ਭੜਕਣਾ (bhaṛknaa) *v* To burst into flames, to be furious, to be angry.

ਭੜਕਾਉਣਾ (bhaṛkaauṇaa) *v* To Inflame, to excite, to instigate, to provoke. Also ਭੜਕਾਣਾ or ਭੜਾਣਾ

ਭੜਕੀਲਾ (bhaṛkeelaa) *a* (1) Exciting, provocative, infuriating, inflammatory; (2) Pompous, showy, flasy, ostentatious.

ਭੜਭੂੰਜਾ (bhaṛbhoonjaa) *n m* Grain roaster, grain pracher. Also ਭਠਿਆਰਾ

ਭੜਾਸ (bhaṛaas) *n f* Pent up feelings, hot vapours; ~ਕਢਣਾ To give vent, to pent up feelings.

ਭੜਾਕਾ (bhaṛaakaa) *n m* Explosion.

ਭੜੂਆ (bhaṛooaa) *a n m* Shameless; Procurer, cuckold, person living on the prostitute's earning.

ਭਾ (bhaa) *n m* Rate, market price; Also ਭਾਉ, ਭਾਅ

ਭਾਉਣਾ (bhaauṇaa) *v* To like, to love, to agree, to satisfy.

ਭਾਈ (bhaaee) *n m* Elder brother, (Sikh) Priest; ~ਚਾਰਾ Fraternity, brotherhood; ~ਬੰਦ Brethern, kin, relations; ~ਵਾਲ Partner, co-sharer; ~ਵਾਲੀ Partnership.

ਭਾਈਆ (bhaaiyaa) *n m* Sister's husband brother-in-law; Elder brother, father; Old man.

ਭਾਸ਼ਣ (bhaashaṇ) *n m* Speech, talk, discourse; ~ਕਲਾ Elocution.

ਭਾਸ਼ਾ (bhaashaa) *n f* Language, speech. Also ਭਾਖਾ

ਭਾਗ (bhaag) *n m* Part, share, portion, division, fraction, segment; Luck, fortune, fate, destiny; ~ਹੀਣ Unfortunate.

ਭਾਜੀ (bhaajee) *n f* Gruel, vegetable.

ਭਾਂਡਾ (bhaandaa) *n m* Utensil, pot.

ਭਾਣਜੀ (bhaṇjee) *n f* Sister's daughter.

ਭਾਣ (bhaaṇ) *n f* Fatigue, weariness, tiredness, aching of muscles, body ache due to exertion; fold, crease.

ਭਾਣਾ (bhaaṇaa) *n m v* God's will, destiny, thought; To agree, to suit, to fit.

ਭਾਂਤ (bhaant) *n f* Kind, sort, class, manner, method; ~ਭਾਂਤ Miscellaneous, multifarious.

ਭਾਨ (bhaan) *n m* Sun; Change, smaller coins; ~ਮਤੀ Juggler, jugglery.

ਭਾਂਪਣਾ (bhaanmpṇaa) *v* To comprehend, to guess.

ਭਾਪਾ (bhaapaa) *n m* Elder brother; daddy, papa.

ਭਾਫ਼ (bhaaph) *n f* Steam; **~ਲੈਣੀ** To inhale the fumes.

ਭਾਂਬੜ (bhaambar) *n m* Big fire; Conflagration, high leaping flames, bonfire; Tumult, turbulence, outbreak, war; **~ਮਚਾਉਣਾ** To raise, to cause conflagration.

ਭਾਬੀ (bhaabee) *n f* Brother's wife; Mother.

ਭਾਰ (bhaar) *n m adv* Burden, load, responsibility, obligation; Support, leaning on; **~ਚੜ੍ਹਨਾ** To be under obligation.

ਭਾਰਾ (bhaaraa) *a* Heavey, weighty; Massive; Difficult to bear; Indigestible; Great, big, largely attended (function); overwhelming; **~ਪਣ** Heaviness, massiveness, mass.

ਭਾਲਣਾ (bhaalnaa) *a* To find, to search, to hunt.

ਭਾਲਾ (bhaalaa) *n m* Spear, lance, dart; Javelin.

ਭਾਵ (bhaav) *n m* Intention, meaning, effect, sentiment, emotion; **~ਹੀਣਤਾ** Inferiority complex; **~ਨਾ** Desire, feeling, Intensive emotion; **~ਵਾਚਕ** Abstract (Noun); **~ਤਮਕ** Emotional.

ਭਾਵੀ (bhaavee) *a n f* Predestined, future, expected, futuristic; Fortune; Destiny, fate, luck

ਭਾਵੁਕ (bhaavuk) *a* Sentimental, emotional; **~ਤਾ** Sentimentalism, sentimentality.

ਭਾਵੇਂ (bhaaven) *adv* Even if, eventhough, although, either, or albeit, though; Possibly, just possible, may be.

ਭਾੜਾ (bhaaṛaa) *n m* Fare, wages, rent, hire, freight, conveyance.

ਭਿਉਣਾ (bhiuṇaa) *v* To wet, to moisten, to drench, to soak.

ਭਿਆਣਾ (bhiaaṇaa) *a* Terrified, freightened, afraid.

ਭਿਆਨਕ (bhiaanak) *a* Terrible, horrible, dreadful, fearful; **~ਤਾ** Horribleness, dreadfulness, fearfulness.

ਭਿਸਤ (bhist) *n m* Heaven.

ਭਿਸ਼ਤੀ (bhishtee) *n m* Water-carrier.

ਭਿੱਖ (bhikkh) *n f* Alms, charity, begging; **~ਮੰਗਾ** Beggar, mendicant.

ਭਿਖਾਰੀ (bhikhaaree) *n m* Beggar, pauper.

ਭਿਖਿਆ (bhikhiyaa) *n f* Alms.

ਭਿਜਣਾ (bhijnaa) v To become wet, to be drenched.

ਭਿੱਟ (bhitt) n f Defilement, impurity, contamination.

ਭਿੱਟਣਾ (bhittnaa) v To be defiled, to be contaminated, to be soiled.

ਭਿਣਕ (bhinak) n f Clue, rumours, unconfirmed news.

ਭਿਣਕਣਾ (bhinaknaa) v To buzz, to hum.

ਭਿੜਨਾ (bhirnaa) v To collide, to quarrel, to fight.

ਭੀਤ (bheet) n m Wall. Also ਭਿੱਤ

ਭੀਤਰ (bheetar) adv Inside.

ਭੀੜ (bheer) n f Crowd, throng mob; Trouble, misfortune, hard time; ~ਭਾੜ Over crowding.

ਭੀੜਨਾ (bheernaa) v To close, to shut.

ਭੀੜਾ (bheeraa) a Narrow.

ਭੁਆਉਣਾ (bhuaaunaa) v To rotate, to revolve, to turn about.

ਭੁਇ (bhui) n f adv Land, earth, ground, field, soil on the ground. Also ਭੂਮੀ or ਭੂ

ਭੁਸ (bhus) n m Habit, addiction; ~ਭੁਸ ਕਰਨਾ To mumble, to grumble.

ਭੁੱਸਾ (bhussaa) a Anaemia, pale, pallid, wane, ashen.

ਭੁੱਖ (bhukh) n f Hunger, appetite, poverty; ~ਮਰੀ Starvation; ~ੜ Hung, gluttonous, starved.

ਭੁੱਖਾ (bhukkhaa) a Hungry, needy; ~ਭਾਣਾ Hungary, starving; ~ਨੰਗਾ Poor, pauper.

ਭੁਗਤਣਾ (bhugatnaa) v To suffer, to be finished, to be settled.

ਭੁਗਤਾਨ (bhugtaan) n m Payment, delivery, settlement.

ਭੁਚੱਕਾ (bhuchakkaa) a Startled, dumb founded, aghast.

ਭੁੱਚਰ (bhuchchar) a Foolish, fat, flabby. Also ਭੁੱਚੜ

ਭੁਚਾਲ (bhuchaal) n m Earthquake, upheaval.

ਭੁਜਣਾ (bhujnaa) v To be parched, to be annoyed.

ਭੁੰਨਣਾ (bhunnaa) v To parch, to roast.

ਭੁਰਨਾ (bhurnaa) v To crumble, to moulder.

ਭੁਰਭੁਰਾ (bhurbhuraa) a Brittle, frail, fragile.

ਭੁੱਲ (bhull) n f Mistake, slip, error, omission, oversight; ~ਚੁਕ Error and omissions; ~ਕੜ Forgetful, blunderhead; ਤਰਨੇ Rarely, once in a blue moon.

ਭੁਲਣਾ (bhulnaa) v To forget, to err, to lose.

ਭੁਲਾਉਣਾ (bhulaaunaa) v To forget, to neglect.

ਭੁਲਾਵਾ (bhulaavaa) *n m* Delusion, misconception, deception, illusion.

ਭੁਲੇਖਾ (bhulekhaa) *n m* Misunderstanding, oversight, omission, fallacy, wrong notion.

ਭੁੜਕਣਾ (bhurakṇaa) *v* To jump, to skip, to be happy.

ਭੂਆ (bhuaa) *n f* Father's sitster, aunt.

ਭੂਸਾ (bhoosaa) *n m* Straw, chaff, husk.

ਭੂਕਣਾ (bhooknaa) *n m* A hollow piece of bamboo; ~ਭੂਕਰੇ ਲਗਾਣੇ To suffer from acute dysentery.

ਭੂੰਡ (bhoond) *n m* Wasp, yellow insect, black bee; Slang, irascible person.

ਭੂਤ (bhoot) *n m a* Ghost, evil spirit, fiend; Past, gone; ~ਕਾਲ Past tense.

ਭੂਮਿਕਾ (bhoomikaa) *n f* Introduction, preface.

ਭੂਮੀ (bhoomee) *n f* Land, ground, fields, landed property, soil, earth; The Earth, its land surface.

ਭੂਰਾ (bhooraa) *a* Brown, grey, tan.

ਭੇਜਣਾ (bhejṇaa) *v* To send, to confine, to transmit.

ਭੇਜਾ (bhejaa) *n m* Brain.

ਭੇਟ (bhet) *n m* Meeting; offering, present, gift, donation. Also ਭੇਟਾ

ਭੇਡ (bhed) *n f* Sheep, Coward; ~ਚਾਲ Mob mentality.

ਭੇਤ (bhet) *n m* Secret, mystery; ~ਦੇਣਾ To divulge a secret; ~ਲੈਣਾ To find out the secret, to spy.

ਭੇਤੀ (bhetee) *n m* Spy, emissary.

ਭੇਦ (bhed) *n m* Difference, contrast; ਮਤ~ Difference of opinion; ~ਭਾਵ Discrimination.

ਭੇੜਨਾ (bhernaa) *v* To shut, to close.

ਭੈ (bhai) *n m* Fear, dread, awe, alarm, peril, fright. Also ਭੌ

ਭੈਂਸ (bhains) *n f* Female buffalo.

ਭੈਂਗਾ (bhaingaa) *a* Squinter, cock-eyed, squint eyed.

ਭੈਣ (bhain) *n f* Sister.

ਭੈੜਾ (bhairaa) *a* Bad, worthless, wicked, evil.

ਭੋਗਣਾ (bhognaa) *v* To endure, to suffer, to undergo.

ਭੋਜ (bhoj) *n m* Feast, entertainment, festivity.

ਭੋਜਨ (bhojan) *n m* Food, diet, victuals.

ਭੋਂਡਾ (bhondaa) *a* Deformed, ugly.

ਭੋਡਾ (bhodaa) *a* Hornless.

ਭੋਰਨਾ (bhornaa) *v* To break into small pieces.

ਭੋਰਾ (bhoraa) *n m* Underground apartment.

ਭੋਲਾ (bholaa) *a* Simple, innocent, artless, simpleton; ~ਪਨ Simplicity, innocence, naivete, guilelessness.

ਭੌ (bhau) *n m* (1) Fear, fright, dread, terror, scare, jitters, trepidation, panic; Awe.

ਭੌਂ (bhaun) *n m* Whirl, spin, pirouette, rotation, revolution, circulation; Vertigo, dizziness, giddiness, real; ~ਆਉਣੇ To reel, to feel dizziness, to suffer from vertigo.

ਭੌਂਕਣਾ (bhaunknaa) *v* To bark.

ਭੌਣਾ (bhaunaa) *v* To rotate, to revolve, to circumlocate, to loiter.

ਭੌਂਦੂ (bhaundoo) *a* Wanderer, vagobond.

ਮ

ਮ The thirtieth letter of Gurmukhi alphabets, pronounced as 'mammaa'.

ਮੱਸ (mass) *n f* Ink; First appearance of moustaches and beard.

ਮਸਹਿਰੀ (maseheree) *n f* Mosquito net.

ਮਸ਼ਹੂਰ (mashoor) *a* Famous, eminent, well-known, reputed.

ਮਸ਼ਹੂਰੀ (mashooree) *n f* Fame, renown, eminence, prominence, illustrious ness; Advertisement.

ਮਸ਼ਕ (mashak) *n f* (1) Leathern water bag; (2) Practice, exercise; **~ਕਰਨਾ** To practice.

ਮਸਕੀਨ (maskeen) *a* Wretched, poor, simple, humble.

ਮਸ਼ਕੂਕ (mashkook) *a* Doubtful.

ਮਸ਼ਕੂਰ (mashkoor) *a* Thankful, grateful, obliged.

ਮਸਖਰਾ (maskharaa) *n m* Jester, joker, buffoon; **~ਪਣ** Buffoonery.

ਮਸਜਦ (masjad) *n f* Mosque. Also **ਮਸੀਤ**

ਮਸਤ (mast) *a* Carefree, careless, lustful, intoxicated, drunk; **~ਮਲੰਗ** Carefree, lively.

ਮਸਤਾਉਣਾ (mastaaunaa) *v* To cause to be mischievous.

ਮਸਤਾਨਾ (mastaanaa) *a* Careless, mendicant, intoxicated, drunk.

ਮਸਤੀ (mastee) *n f* Intoxication, lust, wantonness, ardent passion; **~ਕਢਣੀ** To punish.

ਮਸਤੂਲ (mastool) *n m* Mast.

ਮਸਨਦ (masnad) *n m* Big pillow, bolster.

ਮਸਲਣਾ (masalnaa) *v* To crush, to press hard, to rub.

ਮਸਨੂਈ (masnooee) *a* Article, imitation, not real or genuine, simulated, counterfeit, fake, sham.

ਮਸਰੂਫ਼ (mashroof) *a* Busy, occupied or engaged (in work), preoccupied.

ਮਸਰੂਰ (masroor) *a* Happy, pleased, delighted, glad, cheerful; intoxicated.

ਮਸਲਣਾ (masalnaa) *v* To crush by rubbing, to crush, to trample.

ਮਸਲਤ (maslat) *n* Counsel, advice, consultation. Also **ਮਸਲਹਤ**

ਮਸਲਨ (maslan) *adv* For example, for instance; i.e.

ਮਸਲਾ (maslaa) *n m* Problem; **~ਹਲ**

ਕਰਨਾ To solve the problem.

ਮਸ਼ਵਰਾ (mashawaraa) *n m* Advice, consultation.

ਮਸਵਾਣੀ (masvaanee) *n f* Inkpot.

ਮੱਸਾ (massaa) *n m* Mole, wart, papilla.

ਮਸਾਂ (masaan) *adv* With great difficulty, hardy. Also ਮਸੀਂ

ਮਸਾਣ (masaan) *n m* Cemetry, creamation ground, burial ground.

ਮਸਾਨਾ (masaanaa) *n m* Urinary bladder, vesicle.

ਮਸ਼ਾਲ (mashaal) *n f* Torch; ~ਚੀ Torch bearer.

ਮਸਾਲਾ (masaalaa) *n m* Spices, condiment.

ਮਸਾਲੇ (masaale) *n m* Spices; ~ਦਾਰ Spicy, tasty; ~ਦਾਨੀ Spice case.

ਮੱਸਿਆ (massiaa) *n f* Moonless night, no moon.

ਮਸੀਹ (maseeh) *n m* Jesus Christ.

ਮਸੀਹਾ (maseehaa) *n m* Healer, saviour.

ਮਸ਼ੂਕ (mashook) *n f* Beloved, darling.

ਮਸੂਮ (masoom) *a* Innocent, child like.

ਮਸੂਮੀਅਤ (massomiat) *n m* Innocence, simlessness, guilthlessness.

ਮਸੂਲ (masool) *n m* Tax, toll, duty, cess, custom; ~ਚੁੰਗੀ Octroi.

ਮਸੂੜਾ (masooṛaa) *n m* Gum (of teeth).

ਮਸੋਸਣਾ (masosnaa) *v* To grieve, to regret, to squeeze, to wring.

ਮਸੌਦਾ (masodaa) *n m* Draft, manuscript.

ਮਹੰਤ (mahant) *n m* Monk, abbot.

ਮਹੱਤਵ (mahattav) *n m* Importance, superbness; ~ਪੂਰਨ Important. Also ਮਹੱਤ and ਮਹੱਤਾ

ਮਹੱਤਮ (mahattam) *n m* (maths) highest common factor (H.C.F.), greatest common measure (G.C.M.), greatest common factor (G.C.F.).

ਮਹੱਲ (maihall) *n f* Palace, stately mansion.

ਮਹੱਲਾ (mahallaa) *n* (1) Locality, ward (of town), street; (2) A term followed by numeral indicating guru-authors of hymms in Guru Granth Sahib.

ਮਹਾਜਨ (mahaajan) *n m* Money-lender, banker, capitalist.

ਮਹਾਜਨੀ (mahajnee) *n f* Banking business.

ਮਹਾਤਮ (mahaatam) *n m* Significance of a good deed; Grandeur, good return of a deed.

ਮਹਾਤਮਾ (mahaatmaa) *n m a* Saint, sage; Magnanimous, noble.

ਮਹਾਨ (mahaan) *a* Great; **~ਤਾ** Greatness, elegance.

ਮਹਾਮਾਰੀ (mahaamaaree) *n f* Epidemic, pestilence, plague.

ਮਹਾਰਤ (mahaarat) *n* Expertise, expertness, practice, skill, adroitness, experience.

ਮਹਾਰਾਜ (mahaaraaj) *n m* Emperor, king, your majesty, your highness; Holyman; A term of respect or reverence (such as yours, his) Excellency, majesty, highness, holiness.

ਮਹਾਰਾਜਾ (mahaaraajaa) *n m* King, emperor, monarch, sovereign.

ਮਹਿਕ (mahek) *n f* Odour, fragrance, scent.

ਮਹਿਕਣਾ (maheknaa) *n* To give out fragrance or smell.

ਮਹਿਕਮਾ (mahekmaa) *n m* Department.

ਮਹਿਕਾਉਣਾ (mahekaaunaa) *v* To perfume, to flavour.

ਮਹਿੰਗਾ (mahngaa) *a* Costly, highpriced, dear, expensive.

ਮਹਿੰਗਾਈ (maihngaaee) *n* Dearness, price rise, escalation of cost or price, costliness, expensiveness, inflation. Also **ਗਿਰਾਨੀ**

ਮਹਿਜ਼ (mahez) *a* Only, just.

ਮਹਿੰਦੀ (mahendee) *n f* Myrtle, henna; Lawsonia inermis.

ਮਹਿਫ਼ਲ (mahefal) *n f* Recreational assembly, social or cultural congregation.

ਮਹਿਬੂਬ (mahiboob) *a* Beloved, dear, darling. Also **ਮਹਿਬੂਬਾ**

ਮਹਿਮਾ (mahemaa) *n f* Praise, dignity, greatness, exaltation, grandeur.

ਮਹਿਮਾਨ (mahemaan) *n m* Guest; **~ਨਵਾਜ਼** Hospitable; **~ਨਵਾਜ਼ੀ** Hospitality.

ਮਹਿਰੀ (maehree) *n f* Utensil cleaner, waterwoman, water carrier. Also **ਮਹਿਰਾ**

ਮਹਿਰੂਮ (maihroom) *a* Deprived, dispossessed, bereft; Lacking, without; Bereaved.

ਮਹੀ (mahee) *n f* Earth.

ਮਹੀਨ (maheen) *a* Thin, fine, delicate.

ਮਹੀਨਾ (maheenaa) *n m* Month.

ਮਹੁਰਾ (mauhraa) *n m* Poison; hemlock or any other deadly drug or drink.

ਮਹੂਰਤ (mahoorat) *n m* Auspicious moment.

ਮਕਸਦ (maksad) *n m* Intention, aim, objective, motive, desire.

ਮਕਸੂਦ (maksood) *a* Aimed at, intended.

ਮਕਬਰਾ (makbaraa) *n m* Mausoleum, canotaph, tomb.

ਮਕਬੂਲ (makbool) *a* Popular, widely liked and accepted, favourite.

ਮਕਬੂਲੀਅਤ (makbooliat) *n f* Popularity, acceptance.

ਮਕਰ (makar) *n* (1) Pretence, feigning, shamming, malingering, dissemblance; dissimulation; deception, trickery, deceit; (2) The tenth sign of the zodiac, capricorn, capricornus, the Bikrami month of Magh (when the sun is in the Zodiac mansion).

ਮਕਰਾ (makraa) *a* Cunning, crafty, imposter.

ਮਕੜੀ (makṛee) *n f* Spider locust, grass hopper. Also ਮਕੜਾ

ਮਕਾਨ (makaan) *n m* House, residence, dwelling place.

ਮਕਾਮ (makaam) *n m* Place, stay, stoppage. Also ਮੁਕਾਮ and ਸਥਾਨ

ਮੱਕਾਰ (makkaar) *a* Imposter, cheat, cunning, deceitful, crafty.

ਮਕਾਰੀ (makaaree) *n f* Deception, deceit, craftness.

ਮੱਕੀ (makkee) *n f* Maize, *Zea mays*.

ਮਕੋੜਾ (makoṛaa) *n m* Large black ant, beetle.

ਮੱਖ (makkh) *n m* Large fly.

ਮੱਖਣ (makkhaṇ) *n m* Butter.

ਮਖਮਲ (makhmal) *n f* Velvet.

ਮੱਖੀ (makkhee) *n f* Fly; ਸ਼ਹਿਦ ਦੀ~ Bee; ~ਚੂਸ Miser, skinflint.

ਮਖੋਟਾ (makhoṭaa) *n m* Mask.

ਮਖੌਲ (makhaul) *n m* Joke, jest, mockery, buffonery; ~ਉਡਾਉਣਾ To mock, to deride; ~ਕਰਨਾ To joke, to jet.

ਮਗਜ਼ (magaz) *n m* Brain, marrow, kernel, pith; ~ਖਾਣਾ To tease, to bother, to tax, to harass; ~ਮਾਰਨਾ To think too much, to do too much brainwork.

ਮੰਗਣਾ (mangṇaa) *v* To demand, to seek, to request, to ask, to beg.

ਮੰਗਤਾ (mangtaa) *n m* Beggar.

ਮਗਨ (magan) *a* Absorbed, engrossed, happly and deeply engaged; ~ਤਾ Absorption, single mindedness.

ਮਗਰ (magar) *adv n f* Except, but; Back, behind; ~ਪੈਣਾ To follow, to force, to become hostile; ~ਮੱਛ Crocodile, alligator.

ਮਗਰਲਾ (magarlaa) *a* Subsequent, latter, last

ਮਗਰੂਰ (magroor) *a* Proud, haughty, arrogant.

ਮਗਰੂਰੀ (magrooree) *n f* Arrogance, haughtiness, Pride.

ਮਗਰੋਂ (magron) *adv* Later,

afterwards, after; **~ਲਾਹੁਣਾ** To get rid of; To disengage, to break contact.

ਮੰਗਲ (mangal) *n m* Rejoicing, prosperity, bliss; Planet Mars; **~ਵਾਰ** Tuesday.

ਮੰਗਾਉਣਾ (mangaaunaa) *v* To send for, to cause to be brought.

ਮੰਗੇਤਰ (mangetar) *a n m f* Betrothed; fiance, fiancee.

ਮੱਘਾ (maggaa) *n m* Earthen pitcher of medium size.

ਮਚਲਣਾ (machalnaa) *v* To persist, to insist, to be perverse, to be refractory.

ਮਚਲਾ (machlaa) *a* Stubborn, perverse, insisting, refrectory; In attentive, one who beigns ignorance.

ਮਚਾਉਣਾ (machaaunaa) *v* To excite, to produce, to light.

ਮਚਾਨ (machaan) *n m* Raised plateform, scaffold. Also **ਮਚਾਨ**

ਮੱਛ (machchh) *n m* Big fish, male fish, milter.

ਮੱਛਰ (machchhar) *n m* Mosquito; **~ਦਾਨੀ** Mosquito net.

ਮਛਰਨਾ (machharnaa) *v* To be excited, to be stubborn, to insist, to be mischievous.

ਮਛਲੀ (machhlee) *n f* Fish, bicep. Also **ਮੱਛੀ**

ਮਛੂਆ (machhooaa) *n m* Fisherman, fisher, piscator.

ਮਜ਼ਦੂਰ (mazdoor) *n m* Labourer, workman.

ਮਜ਼ਦੂਰੀ (mazdooree) *n f* Labour, wage.

ਮੰਜਨ (manjan) *n m* Tooth powder.

ਮਜ਼ਬੂਤ (mazboot) *a* Strong, stout, firm, sturdy, durable.

ਮਜ਼ਬੂਤੀ (mazbootee) *n f* Strength, firmness, durability.

ਮਜਬੂਰ (majboor) *a* Helpless, forced, compelled, obliged; **~ਨ** Perforce, under compulsion.

ਮਜ਼ਮੂਨ (mazmoon) *n m* Subject, topic, composition, article, essay.

ਮੰਜ਼ਲ (manzal) *n f* Destination, stage, target, goal; Journey; Storey; **~ਕਟਣਾ** To reach the goal.

ਮਜਲਸ (majlas) *n f* Convention, meeting, assembly, social or cultural gathering. Also **ਮਹਿਫਲ**

ਮਜ਼ਲੂਮ (mazloom) *a* Oppressed, persecuted, wronged; Victim of atrocity, tyranny or injustice.

ਮੰਜਵਾਉਣਾ (manjvaaunaa) *v* To get (utensils etc.) cleaned by rubbing and scrubbing; To assist in cleaning. Also **ਮੰਜਾਉਣਾ**

ਮਜ਼ਹਬ (mazhab) *n m* Religion, sect.

ਮਜ਼੍ਹਬੀ (mazhabee) *a* Religious; ~ਲੜਾਈ Crusade.

ਮੰਜਾ (manjaa) *n m* Cot, four poster.

ਮਜ਼ਾ (mazaa) *n m* Taste, fun, pleasure, deliciousness; ~ਚਖਾਉਣਾ To teach a lesson, to punish.

ਮਜ਼ਾਕ (mazaak) *n m* Joke, jest, witticism.

ਮਜ਼ਾਕੀਆ (mazaakiaa) *a* Witty, jovial, jolly, humorous, joker.

ਮਜ਼ਾਜ (mazaaj) *n m* Nature, pride, haughtness, health.

ਮਜ਼ਾਰ (mazaar) *n f* Tomb, grave, shrine.

ਮਜਾਲ (majaal) *n f* Strength, power, ability, daring.

ਮਜੀਠਾ (majeethaa) *a* Red, deep red.

ਮਜ਼ੀਦ (mazeed) *a* Additional, supplementary.

ਮਜ਼ੇਦਾਰ (mazedaar) *a* Delicious, tasty, tasteful, relishing, enjoyable, pleasant, delightful, scrumptious.

ਮੱਝ (majj) *n m* Adult female buffalo.

ਮੱਟ (matt) *n m* Large earthern pot, pitcher. Also ਮਟਕਾ

ਮਟਕਣਾ (matakṇaa) *v* To flirt, to walk sprightly.

ਮਟਕਾਉਣਾ (matkaauṇaa) *v* To wink, to coquette. Also ਮਟਕਾਣਾ

ਮਟਕੀ (matkee) *n f* Pitcher.

ਮੱਠ (matth) *n m* Monastery, convent, abbey, hermitage.

ਮੱਠਾ (matthaa) *n m a* Churned curd, butter milk; Slow, lazy.

ਮੱਠੀ (mathee) *n f* Small-sized crisp, round, flat, fried bread.

ਮੰਡਣਾ (manḍṇaa) *v* To fill in, to affirm, to thrust, to crush, to starch cloth.

ਮੰਡਪ (manḍap) *n m* Canopy, pavillion, temple, dome.

ਮੰਡਲ (manḍal) *n m* Board, Division, association, sphere, circle, circumference.

ਮੰਡਲਾਉਣਾ (manḍlaauṇaa) *v* To hover, to move about, to flutter about. Also ਮੰਡਲਾਣਾ

ਮੰਡਲੀ (manḍlee) *n f* Group, gang, band coterie, clique; Choir; Trupe.

ਮੱਡੀ (maḍḍee) *n f* Household luggage.

ਮੰਡੀ (manḍee) *n f* Market, mart, trading centre; Cattle fair.

ਮਣਕਾ (maṇkaa) *n m* Bead, perforated jewl, stone, etc.

ਮਣੀ (maṇee) *n f* Semen; Jewel, gem, precious stone.

ਮਤ (mat) *n m* Belief, dogma, theory, view, doctrine, faith, religion.

ਮੱਤ (matt) *n f* Advice, opinion, thought, sense, understanding; ~ਦੇਣੀ To advise; ~ਭੇਦ Differences, dissent; ~ਦਾਤਾ Voter, elector ~ਦਾਨ Poll.

ਮਾਤਹਿਤ (maateht) *a* Subordinate. Also ਮਤਹਿਤ

ਮੰਤਰ (mantar) *n m* Incantaton, spell, counsel, vedic text or hymn.

ਮੰਤਰੀ (mantree) *n m* Minister, adviser, counsellor.

ਮਤਰੇਆ (matreaa) *a* Step brother, sister, etc. Also ਮਤੇਆ

ਮਤਲਬ (matlab) *n m* Meaning, purpose, idea, object, motive, intention; ~ਦਾ ਯਾਰ Fair weather friend; ~ਪ੍ਰਸਤੀ Selfishness; ਬੇ~ Unmeaningly.

ਮਤਲਬੀ (matlabee) *a* Selfish, self-seeking, self-interested

ਮਤਵਾਤਰ (matvaatar) *adv* Constantly, without break, incessantly, continually, continuously, uninterruptedly.

ਮਤਵਾਲਾ (matwaalaa) *a* Intoxicated, tipsy, Insane; Carefree; ~ਪਣ Insanity.

ਮਤਾ (mataa) *n m* Resolution, motion, source of thought.

ਮਥਣਾ (mathnaa) *v* To churn. Also ਰਿੜਕਣਾ

ਮਥਾ (matthaa) *n m* Forehead, top, front; ~ਟੇਕਣਾ To pay respect; ~ਪਿਟਣਾ To lament, to wail; ~ਮਾਰਨਾ To try to convince, to argu, to ta one's head off.

ਮੰਦ (mand) *a* Slow, mild, dull; ~ਹਾਲ Bad days, hard time, pover distitution.

ਮਦ (mad) *n m* Intoxication, wine madness; Ecstacy; ~ਹੋ Intoxicated, drunk, unconsciou in ecstacy.

ਮਦਤ (madat) *n f* Help, assistance aid, support; ~ਗਾਰ Helpe supporter. Also ਮਦਦ

ਮੰਦਾ (mandaa) *a* Dull, feeble, slow bad, ill.

ਮਦਾਨ (maadaan) *n m* Plain; Ope ground of field, (play) ground (battle) field; Arena.

ਮਧਰਾ (madhraa) *a* Short statured dwarf; ~ਪਣ Short stature, lov height.

ਮਧਾਣੀ (madhaanee) *n f* Chrun churning stick or staff.

ਮਧੁਰ (madhur) *a* Mellodious, swee pleasant, soft; ~ਤਾ Euphony sweetness, mellifluence, softness

ਮਧੁ (madhoo) *n f* Honey; ~ਮੱਖੀ Bee

ਮਧੋਲਣਾ (madholnaa) *v* To crumple to crush in hands or under feet to spoil, to use carelessly (cloth or paper).

ਮਨ (man) *n m* Mind, soul, hear

intention, desire, wish, purpose, intellect; ~ਫੇਰਨਾ To turn one's mind from; ~ਭਰ ਜਾਣਾ To be fed up, wearied, satiated; ~ਮਾਰਨਾ To control one's mind or passion; to be patient, diligent.

ਮਨਸਬ (mansab) *n m* Office, rank, post; ~ਦਾਰ Official; Magistrate.

ਮਨਸ਼ਾ (manshaa) *n f* Wish, desire, will, purpose, motive, intention.

ਮਨਸੂਖ (mansookh) *a* Rescinded, annulled, cancelled; ~ਕਰਨਾ To cancel, to annual, to rescind.

ਮਨਸੂਖੀ (mansookhee) *n f* Cancellation, annulment, abrogation, revocation, invalidation.

ਮਨਸੂਬਾ (mansoobaa) *n m* Plan, intention.

ਮਨਹੂਸ (manhoos) *a* Inauspicious, illomened, unlucky, boding ill.

ਮਨੱਕਾ (mankkaa) *a* Dried grape, raisin or currant.

ਮਨਹੂਸੀਅਤ (manhoosiat) *n f* Inauspiciousness.

ਮਨਚਲਾ (manchalaa) *a* Fearless, assiduos, bold.

ਮਨਜ਼ੂਰ (manzoor) *a* Accepted, agreeable.

ਮਨਜ਼ੂਰੀ (manzooree) *n f* Acceptance, sanction, consent, approval.

ਮੰਨਣਾ (mannnaa) *v* To agree, to profess, to accept, to assent, to acknowledge, to accede.

ਮੰਨਤ (mannat) *n f* Vow, promise, decision to offer something to a deity after fulfilment of desire.

ਮਨਨ (manan) *n m* Thought, reflection, contemplation, internalization, thinking process; Deliberation.

ਮੰਨਵਾਉਣਾ (manvaaunaa) *v* To make one to agree, to persuade one to accept.

ਮਨ੍ਹਾਂ (manhaan) *a* Forbidden, prohibited; ~ਕਰਨਾ To forbid.

ਮਨਾਉਣਾ (manaaunaa) *v* To persuade, to appease, to reconcile.

ਮਨਾਹੀ (manaahee) *n f* Restraint, ban, prohibition.

ਮਨੁੱਖ (manukkh) *n m* Man, person, human being; ~ਤਾ Humanity, manhood, civility.

ਮਨੋਹਰ (manohar) *a* Alluring, beautiful, elegant, lovely, pleasing, fascinating, attractive.

ਮਨੋਰੰਜਨ (manoranjan) *n m* Recreation.

ਮਨੋਰਥ (manorath) *n m* Wish, hope, desire, purpose, aim.

ਮਨੌਤੀ (manautee) *n f* Postulate,

axiom something assumed without proof; promise, vow. Also ਸੁੱਖਣਾ or ਮੰਨਤ

ਮਫ਼ਰੂਰ (mafroor) *a* Absconder, underground.

ਮਮਟੀ (mamtee) *n f* A small room built above the first storey, loft.

ਮੰਮਾ (mammaa) *n m* Breast, teat.

ਮਮਿਆਉਣਾ (mamiaaunaa) *v* (for goats) To bleat.

ਮਰਹੂਮ (marhoom) *a* Late, dead, expired.

ਮਰਕਜ਼ (markaz) *n m* Centre, axis.

ਮਰਕਜ਼ੀ (markazee) *a* Central.

ਮਰਘਟ (marghaṭ) *n m* Cemetary, grave yard.

ਮਰਜ਼ (maraz) *n f* Disease, ailment, illness.

ਮਰਜ਼ੀ (marzee) *n f* Willingness, desire, inclination.

ਮਰਜੀਵੜਾ (marjeevaṛaa) *n m a* Parsimonious, living poorly, stingy, miser; (One) ready to lay down one's life for a cause.

ਮਰਤਬਾ (martabaa) *n m* Turn, post, position, status.

ਮਰਦ (marad) *n m* Man, a brave person, husband.

ਮਰਦਾਨਾ (mardaanaa) *a* Male, masculine, manlike, manly. Also ਮਰਦਾਵਾਂ

ਮਰਦਮਸ਼ੁਮਾਰੀ (mardamshumaaree) *n f* Census.

ਮਰਦੂਦ (mardood) *a* Damned, contemptible, despised, wicked.

ਮਰਨ (maran) *n m* Death; ~ਹਾਰ, ~ਕਿਨਾਰੇ Death bed, dying.

ਮਰਨਾ (marnaa) *v* To die, to succumb, to pass away, to expire, to fade.

ਮਰਮਰ (marmar) *n m* Marble.

ਮਰਮਰੀ (marmaree) *a* Marble, white, snow-white; Soft, tender; Made of marble.

ਮਰਯਾਦਾ (maryaadaa) *n f* Decorum, custom, tradition, propriety of conduct, practice; ~ਹੀਣ Wanton, unconventional. Also ਮਰਿਆਦਾ

ਮਰਲਾ (marlaa) *n m* A unit of area measuring 1/160th of an acre; 5 yards square or 25 square yards.

ਮਰੀਅਲ (mariyal) *a* Sickly, feeble, weak.

ਮਰੀਜ਼ (mareez) *n m* Patient, sick, ill, diseased (person).

ਮਰੁੰਡਣਾ (marunḍnaa) *v* To yank, to pluck, to rip, to tweak (top of plants or flowers)

ਮਰੋੜ (maroṛ) *n m* Twist, tortion, contortion, tweak; Stufy, oppressive, hot and windless weather; Loose motions preceded by contortion and pain in stomach; Tenesmus; Dysentery.

ਮਰੋੜਨਾ (marornaa) v To twist, to wring, to contrast.

ਮਰੋੜਾ (maroraa) n m Twist, dysentery.

ਮਲਕ (malak) n m King, chieftain, noble; Angel; Name of a Khatri subcaste.

ਮਲਕਾ (malkaa) n f Queen, empress.

ਮਲਕੀਅਤ (malkiat) n f Possesion, ownership; Property.

ਮਲੰਗ (malang) n m Fakir, Muslim mendicant; Carefree, indifferent to life; ~ਪੁਣਾ Mendicancy, mendicity; Carefreeness, indifference or indifferent attitude towards life.

ਮਲਣਾ (malnaa) v To rub, to massage, to anoint, to pound; To clean (untensils); To wring (hands); ਹੱਥ~ To regret, to chafe. Also ਮਲਨਾ

ਮੱਲਣਾ (mallnaa) v To occupy (seat, land etc.), to posses illegally.

ਮਲਬਾ (malbaa) n m Refuse, debris, rubbish.

ਮਲੁੱਪ (malapp) n m Stomach worm, round worm nematode, ascarid, *Ascaris lumbricoides*.

ਮਲ੍ਹਮ (malham) n f Ointment, salve, unguent; ~ਪੱਟੀ Dressing.

ਮਲਮਲ (malmal) n f Muslin, linen.

ਮਲਾਈ (malaaee) n f Cream (of milk), essence.

ਮਲਾਹ (malaah) n m Boatman, sailor, oarsman, rower; ~ਗੀਰੀ Boatmanship.

ਮਲਾਮਤ (malaamat) n f Reproach, rebuke, accusation, censure, scolding, chiding.

ਮਲਾਲ (malaal) n m Remorse, dejection, sorrow, regret, compunction.

ਮਲੀਆਮੇਟ (maliaamet) a Totally or completely destroyed, devastated, exterminated, ruined; ~ਕਰਨਾ To destroy completely, to raze to ground.

ਮਲੀਦਾ (maleedaa) a n m Crushed, mashed, reduced to pulp; Eatable thing.

ਮਲੂਕ (malook) a Tender, slender, delicate, unfit for hand work.

ਮਲੇਛ (malechh) a n m Wicked, of low caste; Barbarian, outcaste, sinful person.

ਮਵਾਦ (mavaad) n m Pus, purulent matter. Also ਮੁਆਦ

ਮਵੇਸ਼ੀ (maveshee) n m Cattle, beast.

ਮੜ੍ਹਨਾ (marhnaa) *v* To wrap, to surround with a layer, to entrust.

ਮੜ੍ਹੀ (marhee) *n f* Funeral pyre; memorial built at site of cremation.

ਮਾਂ (maan) *n f* Mother; ~ਜਾਇਆ Brother; ~ਜਾਈ Sister; ~ਪਿਉ Parents.

ਮਾਉਂ (maaun) *a n f* Coward, timid; simpleton, foolish; Mum, silent, cat, cat's mew.

ਮਾਅਨਾ (maaynaa) *n m* Meaning.

ਮਾਇਆ (maaiaa) *n f* Money, illusion, magical power of deity; ~ਵਾਦ Illusionism. Also ਮਾਯਾ

ਮਾਈ (maaee) *n f* Mother, old woman.

ਮਾਸ (maas) *n m* Flesh, meat; Month; ~ਖੋਰ Carnivorous.

ਮਾਸਟਰ (maastar) *n m* Teacher, master.

ਮਾਸਟਰੀ (mastree) *n f* Teaching profession, mastership.

ਮਾਸਾਹਾਰੀ (maasaahaaree) *a* Non-vegetarian.

ਮਾਸਿਕ (maasik) *a* Monthly, per month.

ਮਾਹ (maah) *n m* Month; ~ਵਾਰ Monthly; ~ਵਾਰੀ Menses, monthly.

ਮਾਹੀ (maahee) *n m* (1) Fish; Boatman. Also ਮਾਸ਼ਕੀ (2) Lover beloved, husband. Also ਮਾਹੀਆ; ~ਗੀਰ Fisherman. Also ਮਾਛੀ

ਮਾਹੌਲ (maahol) *n m* Environment, atmosphere.

ਮਾਕੂਲ (maakool) *a* Reasonable, proper, befitting, correct.

ਮਾਚਸ (maachas) *n f* Match-box, match stick, lucifer match.

ਮਾਂਜਣਾ (maanjnaa) *v* To scrub, to cleanse, to scour.

ਮਾਜਰਾ (maajraa) *n m* Happening, occurence, incident, matter, news.

ਮਾਂਝੀ (maanjhee) *n m* Boatsman, ferryman, steersman.

ਮਾਠਣਾ (mathnaa) *v* To acquire by stratagem or deceit, to swindle to wangle; To buy very cheap.

ਮਾਣ (man) *n m* Respect, regard honour, esteem; Self-respect, Pride, arrogance, conceit; ~ਹਾਨੀ Loss of self-respect, humilliation disgrace, insult; ~ਕਰਨਾ To be proud, to be proud of; to respect, to honour.

ਮਾਤਮ (maatam) *n m* Death bereavement; ~ਕਰਨਾ To mourn to lament; ~ਪੁਰਸੀ Consolence.

ਮਾਤਾ (maataa) *n f* Mother; Small pox; ~ਨਿਕਲਣੀ To have attack of small pox.

ਮਾਨਤਾ (maantaa) *n f* Recognition.

ਮਾਪ (maap) *n m* Measurement, size, dimensions.

ਮਾਪਣਾ (maapṇaa) *v* To measurer, to take measurement.

ਮਾਫ਼ (maaf) *a* Pardoned, excused; ~ਕਰਨਾ To pardon, to condone, to remit, to excuse.

ਮਾਫ਼ਕ (maafak) *a* Suitable, agreeable, fit, favourable, like.

ਮਾਫ਼ੀ (maafee) *n f* Pardon, remission; ~ਨਾਮਾ Written apology, request for pardon.

ਮਾਮਲਾ (maamlaa) *n m* Affair, matter, problem, business. Also ਮੁਆਮਲਾ

ਮਾਮੂਲ (maamool) *n m* Routine.

ਮਾਮੂਲੀ (maamoolee) *a* Ordinary, common, petty, insignificant, trivial, customary.

ਮਾਯੂਸ (maayoos) *a* Disappointed, frustrated.

ਮਾਯੂਸੀ (maayoosee) *n f* Disappointment, frustration.

ਮਾਰ (maar) *n f* Beating, blow, range; ~ਸੁਟਣਾ To kill, to put to death; ~ਕਾਟ Riot, flight; ~ਧਾੜ Robbery, spoilation; ~ਲੈਣਾ To conquer, to embezzle.

ਮਾਰਕਾ (maarkaa) *n m* Mark, sign, trade mark.

ਮਾਰਗ (maarag) *n m* Path, way, road, passage, channel.

ਮਾਰਨਾ (maarnaa) *v* To kill, to beat, to hit, to conquer, to embezzle.

ਮਾਰਫ਼ਤ (maarfat) *prep* Through, by, care of, via.

ਮਾਲ (maal) *n m* Public revenue, luggage, goods, commodity, money, wares; ~ਅਸਬਾਬ Luggage; ~ਅਫ਼ਸਰ Revenue officer; ~ਖ਼ਜ਼ਾਨਾ Treasury; ~ਖ਼ਾਨਾ Ware house, store house; ~ਗੱਡੀ Goods train; ~ਦਾਰ Wealthy; ~ਮਤਾ Wealth, effects; ~ਗੁਦਾਮ Godown.

ਮਾਲਸ਼ (maalash) *n f* Rubbing of oil on body, massage.

ਮਾਲਸ਼ੀਆ (malshiaa) *a n m* Masseur.

ਮਾਲਕ (maalak) *n m* Owner, master, lord, proprieter, husband; ~ਣ Matron; Housewife; Land lady.

ਮਾਲਕੀ (maalkee) *n f* Ownership.

ਮਾਲਾ (maalaa) *n f* Garland, rosary; ~ਮਾਲ Very rich, very wealthy.

ਮਾਲੀ (maalee) *n m a* Gardner; Recuniary, fiscal.

ਮਾੜਾ (maaṛaa) *a* Weak, poor, bad, very little; ~ਮੋਟਾ Ordinary, cheap, to some extent.

ਮਾੜੀ (maaṛee) *n f* Mansion, attic, a small room on the roof of house.

ਮਿਆਦ (miaad) *n f* Duration, time, term, tenure, period; Durability.

ਮਿਆਦੀ (miyaadee) *a* Periodical, for

ਮਿਆਨ a fixed period; **~ਬੁਖਾਰ** Typhoid.

ਮਿਆਨ (miyaan) *n f* Sheath, scabbard.

ਮਿਆਰ (miyaar) *n m* Standard.

ਮਿਆਰੀਕਰਨ (miaareekaran) *n m* Standardization.

ਮਿਸਤਰੀ (mistree) *n m* Craftman, artisan; **ਰਾਜ~** Mason.

ਮਿਸਰੀ (misree) *n f* Sugar candy.

ਮਿਸਲ (misal) *n f* File of office or court.

ਮਿਸਾਲ (misaal) *n f* Example, instance; **ਬੇ~** Unparalled, unmatched, unique, unexample.

ਮਿੱਸੀ (missee) *a* Mixed; **~ਰੋਟੀ** Bread by mixing wheat flour and gram flour.

ਮਿਹਣਾ (mehnaa) *v* To reproach, to chide, to upraide.

ਮਿਹਤਰ (mehatar) *n m* Sweeper, scavenger.

ਮਿਹਤਰਾਣੀ (mehtaraanee) *n* Female sweeper.

ਮਿਹਨਤ (mehnat) *n f* Labour, hard work, toil, effort.

ਮਿਹਨਤਾਨਾ (mehnatanaa) *n m* Wages, remuneration.

ਮਿਹਨਤੀ (mehnatee) *a* Labourious, industrious, hardworking.

ਮਿਹਮਾਨ (mehmaan) *n m* Guest; **~ਦਾਰੀ** Hospitality, feast, treat; Being a guest. Also **ਮਹਿਮਾਨ**

ਮਿਹਮਾਨੀ (mehmaanee) *n* Hospitality, care and service of quests.

ਮਿਹਰ (mehar) *n f* Kindness, mercy compassion; **~ਬਾਨ** Kind, merciful, compassionate; **~ਬਾਨੀ** kindness benevolence.

ਮਿਕਦਾਰ (mikdaar) *n f* Quantity amount, proportion.

ਮਿਜ਼ਾਜ (mizaaj) *n m* Temprament mood; Disposition, nature.

ਮਿੱਝ (mijj) *n f* Marrow, pitch, pulp ~**ਕੱਢਣੀ** To crush, squeze, press hard, to beat severely, to whop ~**ਨਿਕਲਣੀ** To be reduced, to pulp to be throughly beaten o defeated, to be crushed unde heavy weight or excessive work

ਮਿੰਟ (minṭ) *n m* Minute.

ਮਿਟਣਾ (miṭnaa) *v* To be erased, to be wiped out, to be effaced.

ਮਿਟਾਉਣਾ (miṭaauṇaa) *v* To erase, to wipe out, to efface, to annihilate to blot out, to destroy, to expunge.

ਮਿਟਿਆਲਾ (miṭiaalaa) *a* Grey, dusty dust coloured.

ਮਿੱਟੀ (miṭṭee) *n f* Clay, dust, earth dust, soil, ashes; **~ਖਰਾਬ ਹੋਣੀ** To be humiliated; **~ਦਾ ਤੇਲ** Kerosene oil; **~ਦਾ ਮਾਪੋ** Dunce, Simpleton, nitwit fool; **~ਦੇ ਮੁੱਲ** Damn cheap; **~ਪਾਉਣੀ** To hush up; **~ਵਿਚ ਮਿਲਾਉਣਾ** To ruin, to raze to the ground.

ਮਿੱਠਾ (miṭṭhaa) *a* Sweet, delicious; **~ਸ** Sweetness.

ਮਿਠਿਆਈ (miṭhiaaee) *n f* Sweetmeat, confectionary, candy.

ਮਿੱਡਾ (middaa) *a* Snub-nosed, snubby.

ਮਿੱਤਰ (mittar) *n m* Friend, comrade, companion; **~ਘਾਤ** Cheating a friend; **~ਤਾ** Friendship.

ਮਿਤੀ (mitee) *n f* Date.

ਮਿਥਣਾ (mithṇaa) *v* To decide, to arrange, to allot, to allocate, to imagine.

ਮਿਥਿਆ (mithiaa) *a n f* Untrue, false; Lie, delusion, falsehood.

ਮਿਧਣਾ (midhṇaa) *v* To crush (under feet), to trample, to pound.

ਮਿੰਨਤ (minnat) *n m* Request, entreaty, supplication.

ਮਿਮਿਆਉਣਾ (mimiaauṇaa) *v* To bleat, to supplicate.

ਮਿਰਗ (mirag) *n m* Deer, antelope. Also **ਮਿਗ**

ਮਿਰਗੀ (mirgee) *n f* Epilpsy, apoplexy.

ਮਿਰਚ (mirach) *n f* Chilli; **ਕਾਲੀ~** Pepper; **ਲਾਲ~** Capsicum.

ਮਿਰਤਕ (mirtak) *n a* Dead person, corpse; Deceased, lifeless.

ਮਿਰਤੂ (mritoo) *n f* Death, mortality, thanatos; **~ਦੰਡ** Death sentence, capital punishment, death penalty.

ਮਿਲਣ (milaṇ) *n m* Meeting, union, mixing, contact; **~ਸਾਰ** Sociable, qourteous.

ਮਿਲਣਾ (milṇaa) *v* To meet, to come across, to mix, to merge, to tally, to assemble, to mingle; **~ਜੁਲਣਾ** To meet cordially.

ਮਿਲਣੀ (milṇee) *n f* Formal or ceremonial meeting and embracing by relations of bride and bridegroom.

ਮਿਲਾਉਣਾ (millaauṇaa) *v* To mix, to blend, to affiliate, to adjust, to associate, to compare, to incorporate; **ਅੱਖ~** To see face to face. Also **ਮਿਲਾਣਾ**

ਮਿਲਾਪ (milaap) *n m* Union, concord, meeting, social intercourse; **~ੜਾ** Sociable, amiabie, courteous.

ਮਿਲਾਵਟ (milaavaṭ) *n f* Adulteration, blend, additive; **~ਕਰਨਾ** To adulterate.

ਮਿਲਾਵਟੀ (milaavaṭee) *a* Adulterated.

ਮਿਲੀ-ਭਗਤ (milee-bhagat) *n f* Collusion, conspiracy, secret

ਮੀਸਣਾ (meesṇaa) *a* Perverse, taciturn, not disposed to answer, understanding.

ਮੀਂਹ (meenh) *n* Rain.

ਮੀਚਣਾ (meechṇaa) *v* To close, to shut (eyes).

ਮੀਟਣਾ (meeṭṇaa) *v* To shut or close (as eye, palm, book, etc).

ਮੀਨਾ (meenaa) *n m* A type of precious stone of blue colour used in inset work; ~ਕਾਰ Artist or craftsman skilled in inset work in metal, stone or stucco; a painter of intricate designs; ~ਕਾਰੀ Inset work in stone, stucco or metal; painting or any other visual art in intricate designs.

ਮੀਨਾਰ (meenaar) *n f* Tower, minaret.

ਮੁਅੱਤਲ (muattal) *a* Suspended.

ਮੁਅੱਤਲੀ (muattalee) *n m* Suspension.

ਮੁਆਇਨਾ (muaainaa) *n m* Inspection, visitation, visit.

ਮੁਆਫ਼ਕ (muaafak) *a* Agreeable, likeable, favourable; Suitable; Effective.

ਮੁਆਵਜ਼ਾ (muaavazaa) *n m* Compensation; ~ਦੇਣਾ To, compensate, to indemnify.

ਮੁਸ਼ਕ (mushak) *n f* Smell, odour, fragrance; Stink, reek, stench, malodour.

ਮੁਸ਼ਕਣਾ (mushakṇaa) *v* To give out offensive odour, to come in heat (animals).

ਮੁਸ਼ੱਕਤ (mushakat) *n f* Hard work, labour, toil.

ਮੁਸਕਰਾਹਟ (muskaraahaṭ) *n f* Smile.

ਮੁਸ਼ਕਲ (mushkal) *a n f* Difficult, intricate; Hard, Difficulty, trouble, hardship.

ਮੁਸ਼ਟੰਡਾ (mushṭanḍaa) *a* Stout, robust, wicked, strong & powerful (not in good sense).

ਮੁਸਣਾ (musṇaa) *v* To be deprived of, to be cheated, to be pilfered, to be stolen.

ਮੁਸੱਦੀ (musaddee) *n m* Learned man, head man in King's household, chief writer.

ਮੁਸੱਰਤ (musarrat) *n f* Happiness, gladness, delight.

ਮੁਸੱਨਫ਼ (musannaf) *n m* Author, writer.

ਮੁਸਲਮਾਨ (musalmaan) *n m* Mohammedan, muslim.

ਮੁਸਾਫ਼ਰ (musaafar) *n m* Traveller, passenger, wayfarer; ~ਖਾਨਾ Waiting room, inn, serai; The transient world.

ਮੁਸਾਫ਼ਰੀ (musaafaree) *n f* Travel, traveling, journeying.

ਮੁਸੀਬਤ (museebat) *n f* Trouble,

ਮੁਹਤਾਜ misfortune, calamity, adversity; ~ਕਟਨੀ To suffer or undergo adversity; ~ਦਾ ਮਾਰਿਆ Afflicted by misfortune; ~ਦੇ ਦਿਨ Calamitous days.

ਮੁਹਤਾਜ (muhtaaj) *a* Needy, dependent, poor.

ਮੁਹੱਬਤ (muhabbat) *n f* Love, affection.

ਮੁਹੱਬਤੀ (muhabbatee) *a* Close, affectionate, friendly.

ਮੁਹਰ (muhar) *n f* Seal, stamp, gold coin; ~ਬੰਦ Sealed. Also ਮੋਹਰ

ਮੁਹਲਤ (muhalat) *n f* Reprieve, duration, limit of, leisure.

ਮੁਹੱਲਾ (muhalla) *n m* Particular portion of town, mohallaa.

ਮੁਹਾਸਾ (muhaasaa) *n m* Acne.

ਮੁਹਾਣਾ (muhaanaa) *n m* Mouth of river. Also ਮੁਹਾਨਾ

ਮੁਹਾਂਦਰਾ (muhaandraa) *n m* Feature (facial), appearance, face, visage, form.

ਮੁਹਾਰਤ (muhaarat) *n f* Expertise, expertness. Also ਮਹਾਰਤ

ਮੁਹਾਲ (muhaal) *a* Difficult, absurd.

ਮੁਹਾਵਰਾ (muhaavraa) *n m* Idiom, usage.

ਮੁਹਿੰਮ (muhimm) *n f* Compaign, attack, arduous task, expedition.

ਮੁਕਟ (mukat) *n m* Crown, crest, diadem.

ਮੁਕਣਾ (muknaa) *v* To end, to come to an end, to be finished.

ਮੁਕਤ (mukat) *a n m* Free, freed, released; Liberated, emancipated, redeemed; Liberated person.

ਮੁਕਤੀ (muktee) *n f* Liberation, release, redemption, salvation, riddance; ~ਦਾਤਾ Redeemer, liberator, saviour.

ਮੁਕਦਮਾ (mukadmaa) *n m* Law suit, a case; ~ਕਰਨਾ; To sue, to file a case; ~(ਮੇ) ਬਾਜ਼ੀ Litigation.

ਮੁਕੱਦਰ (mukaddar) *n m* Fortune, destiny, fate.

ਮੁਕੰਮਲ (mukammal) *a* Complete, completed, finished, finalised; entire, whole.

ਮੁਕਰਨਾ (mukarnaa) *v* To go back upon, to back out, to retreat.

ਮੁਕੱਰਰ (mukarrar) *a* Appointed, assigned, nominated, detailed; fixed, settled; Once again, once more, repeat, say again; ~ਕਰਨਾ To appoint, nominate, to assign, to fix, to determine, to set.

ਮੁੱਕਾ (mukkaa) *n m* Fist, blow with a fist; ~(ਬੇ) ਬਾਜ਼ Boxer; ~ਬਾਜ਼ੀ Boxing.

ਮੁਕਾਉਣਾ (mukaaunaa) *v* To bring to

an end, to complete, to finish, to spend, to consume.

ਮੁਕਾਣ (mukaaṇ) *n f* Consoling, condolence. Also ਮੁਕਾਣੇ

ਮੁਕਾਬਲਾ (mukaabalaa) *n* Competition, encounter, comparison, opposition.

ਮੁਕਾਮ (mukaam) *n m* Place, locale, site, halting place.

ਮੁਕਾਲਾ (mukaalaa) *n m* Disgrace, dishonour; Stigma.

ਮੁਖ (mukkh) *a* Main, chief, principal, premier, first, topmost, head, leading; ~ਮੰਤਰੀ Chief minister.

ਮੁਖਤਸਰ (mukhatsar) *a* Brief, short, abridged, condensed.

ਮੁਖਤਾਰ (mukhtaar) *n m* Attorney, agent.

ਮੁਖਤਾਰੀ (mukhtaaree) *n f* Independent control, absolute authority; ~ਨਾਮਾ Power of attorney; Also ਮੁਖਤਿਆਰ

ਮੁਖਬਰ (mukhbar) *n m* Spy, reporter, informer.

ਮੁਖਬਰੀ (mukhbaree) *n f* Tattle, tattling, telling on.

ਮੁਖੜਾ (mukhṛaa) *n m* Mouth, face.

ਮੁਖਾਲਫ਼ (mukhaalaf) *a n m* Opposite, antagonistic; Opponent; Adversary; ~ਤ Opposition.

ਮੁਖੀ (mukhee) *a* Head, chief; ~ਆ Head, leader, chief.

ਮੁਖੋਟਾ (mukhoṭaa) *n m* Mask.

ਮੁਗਾਲਤਾ (mugaaltaa) *n m* Misunderstanding. Also ਭੁਲੇਖਾ

ਮੁਚਣਾ (muchṇaa) *v* To sprain.

ਮੁੱਚਲਕਾ (muchchalkaa) *n m* Bond, agreement, binding.

ਮੁੱਛ (muchchh) *n f* Moustaches, whiskers; ~ਉਖੇੜਨੀ To humiliate; ~ਢਿਲੀ ਹੋਣੀ To be dishonoured; ~ਣਾ To cut, to secure by fraud; ~ਲ Person having long or thick moustaches.

ਮੁਜਰਮ (mujaram) *n m* Criminal, offender.

ਮੁਜਰਮਾਨਾ (mujarmaanaa) *a* Criminal.

ਮੁਜਰਾ (mujraa) *n m* Professional singing and dancing by prostitutes.

ਮੁਜਾਹਿਦ (mujaahid) *n m* Crusader.

ਮੁਜ਼ਾਹਿਰਾ (muzaahiraa) *n m* Demonstration.

ਮੁੰਜੀ (munjee) *n f* Rice, paddy.

ਮੁਟਾਪਾ (muṭaapaa) *n m* Fatness, corpulence.

ਮੁਟਿਆਰ (muṭiaar) *n f* Damsel, maiden, a young woman.

ਮੁੱਠ (muṭṭh) *n f a* Clutch, grip, fist; Handful; ~ਭੇੜ Tussle, encounter, clash, skirmish. Also ਮੁੱਠੀ

ਮੁੱਠਾ (muṭṭhaa) *n m* Handle of

instrument, haft, bundle.

ਮੁੱਠੀ (mutthee) *n* Grip, fist; ~ਭਰ Very few, a little.

ਮੁੰਡਨ (mundan) *n m* Tonsure; ~ਕਰਨਾ To tonsure.

ਮੁੰਡਾ (mundaa) *n m* Boy, lad, urchin; Lame; ~ਖੁੰਡਾ Boy irresponsible fellow.

ਮੁੰਡੀ (mundee) *n f* Head and neck.

ਮੁੱਢ (muddh) *n f* Root, origin, begining; ~ਲਾ Elementary, initial, primary, preliminary, original.

ਮੁਤਲਕ (mutalak) *adv* About, concerning, regarding, in connection with.

ਮੁਤਵਾਤਰ (mutvaatar) *adv* Constantly, continuously, continually, in cessantly, without break.

ਮੁਤਾਸਰ (mutaasar) *a* Affected, influenced; impressed, moved.

ਮੁਤਾਬਕ (mutaabak) *a* Corrresponding, suitable, coinciding, resembling, conforming, similar; according to, in accordance with, as per, as stated (by); On or under the authority of.

ਮੁਤਾਲਬਾ (mutaalbaa) *n m* Demand.

ਮੁਥਾਜ (muthaaj) *a* Needy, in want, poor, indigent, destitute, dependent.

ਮੁਥਾਜਗੀ/ਮੁਥਾਜੀ (muthaajgee/muthaajee) *n f* Need, want, poverty, indigence, distitution.

ਮੁੱਦਈ (muddaee) *n m* Plaintiff, prosecutor, complainant.

ਮੁੱਦਤ (muddat) *n f* Time, duration, space of time.

ਮੁੰਦਰੀ (mundaree) *n f* Ring, finger ring.

ਮੁਧਾਉਣਾ (mudhaaunaa) *v* To invert, to turn upside down.

ਮੁੰਨਣਾ (munnnaa) *v* To shave; to cheat.

ਮੁਨਾਦੀ (munaadee) *n f* Proclamation by beat of drum.

ਮੁਨਾਫ਼ਾ (munaafaa) *n m* Profit, gain; ~ਖੋਰ Profiteer.

ਮੁਨਿਆਰੀ (muniaaree) *n f* General stores, general merchandise, grocery.

ਮੁੱਨੀ (munnee) *n f* A small girl, a small support. Also ਮੁੱਨਾ

ਮੁਨੀ (munee) *n m* Ascetic, hermit, saint.

ਮੁਨੀਮ (muneem) *n* Accountant.

ਮੁਨੀਮੀ (muneemee) *n f* Accountancy, Book keeping.

ਮੁਫ਼ਤ (mufat) *a* Free, gratis.

ਮੁਫ਼ੀਦ (mufeed) *a* Beneficial, useful.

ਮੁਬਾਰਕ (mubaarak) *n f a* Congratulation, welcome, felicitation; Blessed, auspicious, happy.

ਮੁਮਕਿਨ (mumkin) *a* Possible, feasible.

ਮੁਯੱਸਰ (muyassar) *a* Available, obtainable, accessible; ~ਕਰਨਾ To provide, to make available.

ਮੁਰਸ਼ਦ (murshad) *n m* Spiritual teacher, preceptor.

ਮੁਰਕਣਾ (muraknaa) *v a* To be twisted, to writhe, to snap; Crisp.

ਮੁਰਗਾ (murgaa) *n m* Cock, rooster, broiler, male chicken.

ਮੁਰਗੀ (murgee) *n f* Hen, female chicken; ~ਪਾਲਣ Poultry farming; ~ਖਾਨਾ Poultry shed, poultry farm.

ਮੁਰਝਾਉਣਾ (murjhaaunaa) *v* To wither, to fade, to droop, to become dejected.

ਮੁਰਦਨੀ (murdanee) *n f* Gloomy countenance, gloom, lifelessness, listlessness.

ਮੁਰਦਾ (murdaa) *n m a* Corpse, dead body, carcass; Lifeless, deceased; ~ਘਰ Mortuary; ~ਰ Lifeless, dead.

ਮੁਰੱਬਾ (murabbaa) *n m* (1) Jam marmalade; (2) Square.

ਮੁਰੱਮਤ (murammat) *n m* Repair; Beating.

ਮੁਰਮੁਰਾ (murmuraa) *n m a* Parched millet or maize; Crisp.

ਮੁਰਲੀ (murlee) *n f* Flute, pipe.

ਮੁਰੱਵਤ (muravvat) *n f* Goodness, compassion, benevolence, accommodativeness, obliging nature.

ਮੁਰਾਦ (muraad) *n f* Wish, desire; ~ਮੰਗਣੀ To pray for boon.

ਮੁਰੀਦ (mureed) *n m* Follower, pupil, devotee, disciple.

ਮੁੱਲ (mull) *n m* Cost, rate, price, value, worth; ~ਘਟਾਉਣਾ To devalue; ~ਚੁਕਾਉਣਾ To settle the price.

ਮੁਲਕ (mulak) *n m* Country, realm, domain; region. Also ਮੁਲਖ

ਮੁਲਜ਼ਮ (mulzam) *n m* Accused.

ਮੁਲਤਵੀ (multavee) *a* Adjourned, postponed; ~ਕਰਨਾ To adjourn.

ਮੁਲੰਮਾ (mulammaa) *n m* Gilding, plating; False, outward show; Speciousness.

ਮੁਲਾਇਮ (mulaaim) *a* Tender, soft, gentle; ~ਕਰਨਾ To soften.

ਮੁਲਾਹਜਾ (mulaahjaa) *n m* Consideration, kindness, concession, regard.

ਮੁਲਾਹਜ਼ਾ (mulaahzaa) *n* Inspection; ~ਕਰਨਾ To inspect.

ਮੁਲਾਂਕਾਤ (mulaakaat) *n f* Visit, meeting, interview.

ਮੁਲਾਕਾਤੀ (mulaakaatee) *n m* Visitor, acquaintance.

ਮੁਲਾਜ਼ਮ (mulaazam) *n m* Servant.

ਮੁੜ (muṛ) *adv* Again; ~ਮੁੜ Repeatedly, again and again.

ਮੁੜਨਾ (muṛnaa) *v* To come back, to

ਮੁੰਡਾ (Munḍaa) *n m* Boy, son; bridegroom.

ਮੂੰਹ (moonh) *n m* Mouth, face, countenance; ~ਸਿਉਣਾ To make silent; ~ਸੁਕਣਾ To become thinner, to feel thirsty; ~ਸੁਜਾਉਣਾ To get displeased; ~ਕਾਲਾ ਕਰਨਾ To have illegitimate sex relations; ~ਚਟਣਾ To lick, to fondle; ~ਜ਼ਬਾਨੀ Oral; ~ਤਕਣਾ To graze, to scare in astonishment; ~ਫਟ Blunt, insolent, abusive; ~ਫੇਰ ਲੈਣਾ To shun, to abstain from; ~ਮੋੜਨਾ To desert, to refrain from; ~ਲੁਕਾਉਣਾ To hide, to avoid.

ਮੂਤ (moot) *n m* Urine. Also ਮੂਤਰ

ਮੂਰਖ (moorakh) *a* Foolish, stupid, silly, idiotic, dunce; ~ਤਾ Stupidity, foolishness.

ਮੂਰਛਾ (moorchhaa) *n* Fainting, coma, unconsciousness, insensibility, swoon.

ਮੂਰਤ (moorat) *n f* Portrait, form, picture.

ਮੂਰਤੀ (murtee) *n f* Idol, effigy, statue; ~ਕਾਰ Iconographer; ~ਪੂਜਾ Idol worship, idolatory.

ਮੂਲ (mool) *n m a* Root, source, base, original, principal; Substantive; ~ਅਧਿਕਾਰ Fundamental right; ~ਧਨ Capital; ~ਲਾਗਤ Basic cost.

ਮੂਲੀ (moolee) *n f* Radish, *Raphanus sativs.*

ਮੂੜ੍ਹ (moorh) *n m a* Simpleton, fool, nincompoop; Foolish, stupid, demented.

ਮੇਸਣਾ (mesnaa) *v* To rub off, to erase, to blot out.

ਮੇਹਰੂ (mehroo) *n f* Buffaloes.

ਮੇਖ (mekh) *n f* Nail, hob nail, pegcotter, brad.

ਮੇਚ (mech) *n m* Measurement, size; fit, fitting, matching; ~ਲੈਣਾ To take measurement (for garments, shoes etc.)

ਮੇਚਣਾ (mechnaa) *v* To measure, to take a measurement.

ਮੇਜ਼ (mez) *n f* Table; ~ਪੋਸ਼ Table cloth; ~ਬਾਨ Host.

ਮੇਟਣਾ (metṇaa) *v* To rub off, to erase, to delete, to wipe, to anihilate.

ਮੇਮਣਾ (memṇaa) *n m* Lamb.

ਮੇਲ (mel) *n m* Association intimacy; Connection, harmony; Correspondence, match; Guests collected as marriage or other family function.

ਮੇਲਣਾ (melṇaa) *v* To gather, to sweep, to mix; To cause to meet, to match.

ਮੇਲਾ (melaa) *n m* Fair, assembliage; ~ਠੇਲਾ Fanfare, hustle and bustle.

ਮੇਲਾਨ (melaan) *n m* Comparison, tally.

ਮੇਵਾ (mewaa) *n m* Dry fruit.

ਮੈਕਾ (maikaa) *n m* Wife's paternal house.

ਮੈਦਾਨ (maidaan) *n m* Open field, ground; ~ਮਾਰਨਾ To win, to go to answer the call of nature.

ਮੈਦਾਨੀ (maidaanee) *a* Plain, pertaining to plain.

ਮੈਲ (mail) *n f* Dirt, mud, filth, rust; ~ਖੋਰਾ Dust coloured, gray, colour that would not look dirty soon.

ਮੈਲਾ (mailaa) *a* Dirty, muddy, unclean; Feaces, filth; ~ਕੁਚੈਲਾ Dingy, dirty, polluted.

ਮੋਹ (moh) *n m* Attachment, attraction, infatuation, fondness, affection, love.

ਮੋਹਣਾ (mohṇaa) *v a* To attract, infatuate, to fascinate, to enchant, to charm, to enamour; Attractive, fascinating, charming, handsome, beautiful.

ਮੋਹਰਲਾ (moharlaa) *adv* Earlier, first, foremost, front, leading.

ਮੋਹਰੀ (mohṛee) *n f* Small wooden pillar.

ਮੋਹਿਤ (mohit) *a* Enchanted, allured fascinated.

ਮੋਂਗਾ (mongaa) *n m* Coral.

ਮੋਚ (moch) *n f* Sprain, twist.

ਮੋਚਨਾ (mochnaa) *v* To pull out.

ਮੋਚੀ (mochee) *n m* Shoemaker, Cobbler.

ਮੋਟੜ (moṭaṛ) *n m* Fat person.

ਮੋਟਾ (moṭaa) *a m* Fat, corpulent, heavy, coarse, fleshy; ~ਝੋਟਾ Rough, coarse; ~ਤਾਜ਼ਾ Plump, robust.

ਮੋਟੀ (moṭee) *a* fat; ~ਅਕਲ Poor intelligence, dim wittedness, dullness, obtuseness; ~ਸਾਮੀ Rich wealthy, affluent, opulent person.

ਮੋਢਾ (moḍhaa) *n m* Shoulder.

ਮੋਤੀ (motee) *n m* Pearl; ~ਆ Light yellow; Jasmine ~ਆ ਬਿੰਦ Cataract.

ਮੋਦੀ (modee) *n m* Storekeeper, grain dealer, steward.

ਮੋਨਾ (monaa) *n m* Clean shaven, (one) with cropped hair.

ਮੋਮ (mom) *n f* Wax, tallow; ~ਜਾਮਾ Oil cloth, waterproof cloth; ~ਹੋ ਜਾਣਾ To be softened, to melt; ~ਦਿਲ Soft hearted, kind, merciful; ~ਬਤੀ Candle.

ਮੋਮੀ (momee) *a* Waxy, waxen.

ਮੋਰ (moṛ) *n m* Peacock.

ਮੋਰਚਾ (morchaa) *n m* Trench, defence post; ~ਬੰਦੀ Entrenchment; ~ਮਾਰਨਾ To win, to be successful.

ਮੋਰੀ (moree) *n f* Hole, sewer.

ਮੋੜ (moṛ) *n m* Bend, turn of road, twist; ~ਤੋੜ Distortion; ~ਦਾਰ Zigzag.

ਮੁੜਨਾ (mornaa) *v* To return, to bend, to twist.

ਮੌਸਮ (mausam) *n m* Weather, season.

ਮੌਕਾ (maukaa) *n m* Opportunity, chance, occasion, situation; ~ਪ੍ਰਸਤ Opportunist.

ਮੌਜ (mauj) *n f* Enjoyment, pleasure, delight, emotion, wave.

ਮੌਜੀ (maujee) *a* Gayful, mirthful, jovial, Carefree (fellow).

ਮੌਜ਼ਾ (mauzaa) *n m* Sock, stocking. Also ਮੌਜਾ

ਮੌਜੂਦ (maujood) *a* Present, existing, at hand.

ਮੌਜੂਦਗੀ (maujoodgee) *n f* Presence.

ਮੌਜੂਦਾ (maujooda) *a* Present, current, modern, existing.

ਮੌਤ (maut) *n f* Death, demise, calamity, mortality.

ਯ

ਯ Thirty first letter of Gurmukhi alphabets, pronounced as 'yayyaa', semivowel.

ਯਹੂਦੀ (yahoodee) *n m* Jew.

ਯਕ (yak) *a* One, uni.

ਯਕਸਾਂ (yaksaan) *a adv* Similar, uniform, equal; ~ਕਰਨਾ To equalize, to level.

ਯਕਸਾਰਤਾ (yaksaartaa) *n f* Uniformity, similarity.

ਯਕਸਮਾਨ (yaksamaan) *a* Homogeneous.

ਯਕਜ਼ਬਾਨ (yakazabaan) *a adv* With singular voice.

ਯਕਤਰਫ਼ਾ (yaktarfaa) *a* Unilateral, one sided.

ਯਕਦਮ (yakdam) *a* Immediately.

ਯਕਮੁਸ਼ਤ (yakmusht) *adv* In one instalment, as a whole.

ਯਕਲਖ਼ਤ (yaklakht) *adv* All of a sudden, suddenly.

ਯਕੜ (yakaṛ) *n m* Meaningless or nonsensical, talk; gossip; ~ਬਾਜ਼ Chatterer, chatterbox, gossiper, tale-teller; ~ਮਾਰਨਾ To talk uselessly.

ਯੱਕਾ (yakkaa) *n m* Tonga, ace; ~ਯਕ All of a sudden.

ਯਕੀਨ (yakeen) *n m* Confidence assurance, faith, certainty; ~ਕਰਨ To believe, to have faith; ~ਨ Surely, certainly, definitely.

ਯੱਖ (yakkh) *n m a* Ice, snow; Ice cold.

ਯੱਗ (yagg) *n m* Oblation, religious sacrifice.

ਯਤਨ (yatan) *n m* Effort, attempt endeavour.

ਯੰਤਰ (yantar) *n m* Instrument implement, machine.

ਯੰਤਰੀਕਰਨ (yantreekaran) *n n* Mechanisation.

ਯਤੀਮ (yateem) *n m* Orphan, fatherless child; ~ਖ਼ਾਨਾ Orphanage.

ਯਥਾ ਸਥਿਤੀ (yathaa sthitee) *n* Status quo.

ਯਥਾਰਥ (yathaarath) *n m a* Reality fact; Real, accurate, actual; ~ਤ Reality; ~ਵਾਦ Realism.

ਯੱਭ (yabbh) *n m* Trouble, difficulty problem, nuisance, contention wrangling; ~ਲ Stupid, foolish.

ਯਮਲਾ (yamlaa) *a* Fool, stupid unintelligent; clever bu pretending to be a simpleton.

ਯਰਕਣਾ (yarkaṇaa) *v* To cower, to

shy away, to be bullied.

ਝਰਕਾਉਣਾ (yarkaaunaa) *v* To bully, to cow down.

ਝਰਕਾਨ (yarkaan) *n m* Jaundice.

ਝਰਕੂ (yarkoo) *a* Timid, coward, cowardly.

ਯਰਾਨਾ (yaraanaa) *n m* Friendship, love, association, illegal love affairs. Also ਯਾਰੀ

ਯਾਚਨਾ (yaachnaa) *n f* Appeal, petition, request.

ਯਾਤਰਾ (yaatraa) *n f* Journey, pilgrimage, travel; ~ਡਾਯ਼ਣ Travelogue.

ਯਾਤਰੀ (yaatree) *n m* Pilgrim, traveller.

ਯਾਦ (yaad) *n f* Memory, recollection, remembrance; ~ਆਉਣਾ To remember; ~ਕਰਨਾ To call; ~ਦਿਲਾਉਣਾ To remind; ~ਰਖਣਾ To bear in mind, to remember; ~ਗਾਰ Memorial, commemoration.

ਯਾਦਾਸ਼ਤ (yaadaasht) *n f* Memory.

ਯਾਨੀ (yaanee) *adv* Namely, that is, that is to say, meaning therby, I mean.

ਯਾਰ (yaar) *n m* Lover, friend, companion, paramour.

ਯੁਕਤ (yukat) *a* Combined, united, fitted with.

ਯੁਗ (yug) *n m* Epoch, era, period, age.

ਯੁੱਧ (yuddh) *n m* War, battle, combat, hostilities; ~ਵਿਰਾਮ Truce; ~ਖੇਤਰ Warfield; ~ਬੰਦੀ Truce; ~ਭੂਮੀ Battle field.

ਯੋਗ (yog) *a* Suitable, qualified, capable; Yoga; ~ਦਾਨ Contribution.

ਯੋਜਨਾ (yojnaa) *n f* Plan, scheme; ~ਬੱਧ Planned.

ਯੋਨੀ (yonee) *n f* Vegina, Source.

ਰ

ਰ Thirty second letter of Gurmukhi alphabets, pronounced as 'raaraa'.

ਰਈਸ (raees) *n m* Nobleman, rich person; **~ਜ਼ਾਦਾ** Son of a rich person.

ਰਈਸੀ (raeesee) *n f* Richness, nobility.

ਰਸ (ras) *n m* Juice, taste, essence, pleasure, enjoyment; **~ਹੀਣ** Tasteless; **~ਦਾਰ** Juicy, full of juice.

ਰਸ਼ਕ (rashak) *n m* Envy, emulation.

ਰਸਣਾ (rasṇaa) *v* To be absorbed or throughly mixed, to mix well socially, to be come intimate, to be reconciled; to become smooth-running (for machines or parts).

ਰਸਤਾ (rastaa) *n m* Road, street, way, path, route.

ਰਸਦ (rasad) *n f* Provision, supplies, ration, store.

ਰਸਨਾ (rasnaa) *n f* Tongue.

ਰਸਮ (rasam) *n f* Custom, practice, ritual, ceremony, rite.

ਰਸਮੀ (rasmee) *a* Customary, ceremonial.

ਰੱਸਾ (rassaa) *n m* Rope; **~ਕਸ਼ੀ** Tug of war; **~ਪਾਉਣਾ** To tie with a rope; to control.

ਰਸਾਤਲ (rasaatal) *n m* Under world, hell, lowest layer.

ਰਸਾਲਾ (rasaalaa) *n m* (1) Cavalry, battalion; (2) Journal, magazine.

ਰਸਿਕ (rasik) *n m* Admirer, lover, amorist, gallant; Amorous; Lover of beauty, music, dance, etc., pleasure-loving, libertine; **~ਤਾ** Amorousness, taste for good things of life, love for life, arts or pleasure, libertinism.

ਰੱਸੀ (rasee) *n f* Cord, string, twine.

ਰਸੀਦ (raseed) *n f* Receipt, acknowledgement, a note.

ਰਸੀਲਾ (raseelaa) *a* Amorous, delicious, tasty, sweet, attractive. Also **ਰਸੀਲੀ**

ਰਸੂਖ (rasookh) *n m* Influnce, access, friendship.

ਰਸੂਲ (rasool) *n m* Prophet, messenger of god.

ਰਸੋਈ (rasoee) *n f* Kitchen; **~ਆ** Cook.

ਰਹੱਸ (raihass) *n m* Secret, mystery, enigma; **~ਮਈ** Mysterious, mystical; **~ਵਾਦ** Mysticism.

ਰਹਿਣਾ (raihṇaa) *v* To stay, to reside, to remain, to live, to dwell.

ਰਹਿਨ (raihn) *a* Mortgaged; **~ਕਰਨਾ** To

ਰਹਿਨੁਮਾ (raihnumaa) *n m* Guide; ~ਈ Guidance.

ਰਹਿਬਰ (raihbar) *n m* Leader.

ਰਹਿਬਰੀ (raihbaree) *n f* Guidance, lead.

ਰਹਿਮ (raihm) *n m* Pity, mercy, kindness, compassion, sympathy; ~ਤ Mercy, pity, compassion.

ਰਕਸ (rakas) *n m* dance.

ਰਕਤ (rakat) *n m* Blood; ~ਦਾਨ Blood donation.

ਰਕਬਾ (rakbaa) *n m* Area.

ਰਕਮ (rakam) *n f* Sum, money.

ਰਕਾਬ (rakaab) *n f* Stirrup; ~ਤੇ ਪੈਰ ਰਖਣਾ To mount a horse.

ਰਕਾਬੀ (rakaabee) *n f* Plate, saucer, platter.

ਰਖਸ਼ਕ (rakshak) *n m* Protector, saviour.

ਰਖਣਾ (rakhnaa) *v* To keep, to put, to place, to lay, to insert, to hold, to possess, to have, to contain, to engage.

ਰਖਵਾਲਾ (rakhwaalaa) *n m* Guard, guardian, keeper, protector.

ਰਖਿਆ (rakhiyaa) *n f* Safety, patronage, protection; ~ਕਰਨੀ To preserve.

ਰਖੇਲ (rakhel) *n f* Keep, Concubine, mistress.

mortgage.

ਰਗ (rag) *n f* Vein, nerve, artery, streak; ~ਫੜਨੀ To understand trait or nature of.

ਰੰਗ (rang) *n m* Colour, complexion, paint, dye; Merriment; ~ਉਡਨਾ To fade, to lose lustre, to turn pale with fear; ~ਚੜ੍ਹਾਉਣਾ Colour, coloured stale; ~ਦਾਰ Coloured; ~ਨਿਕਲਣਾ To have a clear glossy complexion; ~ਸ਼ਾਲਾ Theatre; ~ਸਾਜ਼ Painter, Dyer; ~ਬਰੰਗਾ Variegated, colourful, multicoloured; ~ਭੂਮੀ Stage, theatre; ~ਵਾਈ Act of dyeing; ~ਮੰਚ Stage; ~ਰੰਗੀਲਾ Colourful, pleasure seeking, attractive; ~ਰਲੀਆਂ Merriment, mirth; ~ਰੂਪ Beauty, appearance, mode; ~ਰੇਜ਼ Dyer.

ਰੰਗਣਾ (rangnaa) *v* To dye, to colour, to paint, to stain.

ਰੰਗਰੂਟ (rangroot) *n m* Novice, recruit, newly recruited soldier.

ਰਗੜ (ragar) *n f* Friction, abrasion, concussion, bruise.

ਰਗੜਨਾ (ragarnaa) *v* To rub, to scrub, to grate, to grind, to wear out

ਰਗੜਾ (ragraa) *n m* Quarrel, rubbing, wrangling; ~ਮਾਰਨਾ To bruise, to scrap, to hit.

ਰੰਗੀਨ (rangeen) *a* Coloured, dyed, painted, mirthful.

ਰੰਗੀਨੀ (rangeenee) *n f* Colour, bright colouring, florid style; Merriment, colourfulness.

ਰੰਗੀਲਾ (rangeelaa) *a* Colourful, jovial, loving, merry, showy; ~ਪਨ Colourfulness, merriment, joviality.

ਰਚਣਾ (rachnaa) *v* To create, to make, to form, to permeate, to write (a book, poem etc).

ਰਚਨਾ (rachnaa) *n f* Creation, workmanship, literary composition; ~ਕਾਰ Creator, writer, workman; ~ਤਮਕ Constructive, compositional, creative; ~ਵਲੀ Writings.

ਰਛਕ (rachhak) *n* Preserver, defender, nourisher, helper. Also ਰਛਪਾਲ

ਰੱਛਾ (rachhaa) *n* Protection. Also ਰਛਿਆ or ਰਖਿਆ

ਰੰਜ (ranj) *n m* Grief, sorrow, pain, sadness, displeasure.

ਰੰਜਸ਼ (ranjash) *n f* Ill feeling, animus, estragement.

ਰੰਜਕ (ranjak) *a* Gladdening, delighting, recreative.

ਰੱਜਣਾ (rajjnaa) *v* To eat to the fill, to be satisfied, to be satiated.

ਰਜਮੰਟ (rajmant) *n m* Regiment.

ਰਜ਼ਾ (razaa) *n f* Will, God's pleasure, assent, consent, premission; ~ਕਾਰ Volunteer; ~ਮੰਦ Willing, consenting; ~ਮੰਦੀ Willingness; Agreement.

ਰਜਾਉਣਾ (rajaaunaa) *v* To fill, to satisfy, to satiate, to feed to the full.

ਰਜ਼ਾਈ (razaaee) *n f a* Quilt; Satisfied, happy.

ਰਜੂਹ (rajooh) *n m* Intension, inclination, aptitude, interest.

ਰਟਣਾ (ratnaa) *v* To learn by rote, to repeat, to cram, to mug up.

ਰੱਟਾ (rattaa) *n m* (1) Cramming, learning by rote; (2) Quarrel, trouble.

ਰੰਡਾ (randaa) *n m* Widower.

ਰੰਡੀ (randee) *n f* (1) Widow, (2) Prostitute; ~ਬਾਜ਼ੀ Adultery, prostitution; ~ਰੋਣਾ Constant whimpering, crying, complaining or nagging.

ਰੰਡੇਪਾ (randepaa) *n m* Widowhood.

ਰਣ (ran) *n m* Battle, war, combat; ~ਜੋਧਾ Warrior; ~ਭੂਮੀ Battle field; ~ਨੀਤੀ Strategy.

ਰਣਵਾਸ (ranvaas) *n m* Harem, seraglio, inner part of palace.

ਰਤ (rat) *a* Occupied, engaged, busy, absorbed; *Used as suffix also as* ਕਾਰਜ~ engaged in work.

ਰੱਤ (ratt) *n f* Blood; ~ਹੀਣ Bloodless, pale; ~ਪੀਣਾ Blood sucker, cruel, brutal.

ਰਤਨ (ratan) *n m* Gem, jewel, ruby.

ਰਤਨਾਕਰ (ratanaakar) *n m* Ocean, mine or jewels.

ਰਥ (rath) *n m* Chariot; Carriage car; ~ਵਾਨ Charioteer.

ਰੱਦ (radd) *a* Cancelled, refuted, null and void, rejected, repealed; ~ਕਰਨਾ To annul, to reject, to cancel, to set aside, to nullify.

ਰੰਦਣਾ (randṇaa) *v* To Smooth, to plane.

ਰੰਦਾ (randaa) *n m* Carpenter's plane, jack plane, router place.

ਰੱਦੀ (raddee) *a n f* Waste, useless, worthless, rejected; Waste paper, refuse.

ਰੰਨ (rann) *n f* Woman, lady, wife.

ਰਨ (ran) *n m* Run (cricket).

ਰਪਟੀਆ (rapteeiaa) *n m* Reporter; Informer.

ਰਪਟ (rapaṭ) *n f* Report, information.

ਰਫਤਾਰ (raftaar) *n f* Speed.

ਰਫੜ (raphaṛ) *n m* Quarrel. Also ਰਫੜਾ

ਰਫੀਕ (rafeek) *n m* Companion.

ਰਫੂ (rafoo) *n m* Darning, patching; ~ਕਰਨਾ To darn; ~ਗਰ Darner; ~ਚਕਰ Runaway, absconding; ~ਹੋਣਾ To run away, to disappear, to escape, to show a clean pair of heels.

ਰੱਬ (rabb) *n m* God; Lord, divinity, providence; ~ਰਜ਼ਾ Will of God; ~ਰਾਖਾ May God be with you.

ਰੱਬੀ (rabbee) *a* Divine, godly, providential.

ਰੰਭਣਾ (rambhṇaa) *v* To bellow.

ਰਮਣਾ (ramṇaa) *v* To wander, to rove about, to go away, to depart, to be absorbed.

ਰਮਣੀਕ (ramṇeek) *a* Beautiful, captivating, pleasing, pleasurable, pleasant, enjoyable, delightful (tor place, landscape).

ਰਮਤਾ (ramtaa) *a* Wandering, wanderer, roving, rover.

ਰਲਣਾ (ralṇaa) *v* To mix, to be intermixed, to resemble.

ਰਲਾਉਣਾ (ralaauṇaa) *v* To mix, to adulterate, to blend.

ਰਵਈਆ (ravaiyaa) *n m* Attitude, behaviour, trend.

ਰਵਾ (ravaa) *n m a* Pedigree, lineage, ancestry, breed; Granulated form of wheat flour, semolina; Proper justifiable, lawful.

ਰਵਾਂ (ravaan) *a* Flowing, running, moving; (for machinery or equipment) moving or working smoothly.

ਰਵਾਇਤ (ravaait) *n f* Tradition, legend, history.

ਰਵਾਦਾਰ (ravaadaar) *a* Just, liberal,

ਰਵਾਦਾਰੀ responsible, considerate.

ਰਵਾਦਾਰੀ (ravaadaaree) *n f* Justness, liberality, liberalism, broadmindedness, considerateness, catholicity.

ਰਵਾਨਗੀ (ravaangee) *n f* Departure, setting out, going.

ਰੜਕ (raṛak) *n f* Irritation, rankle, pain animosity; Deficiency, shortage, shortcoming; **~ਕੱਢਣੀ** To act with rancour, to give expression to enmity, to retaliate; To treat irritation or pain; **~ਰੱਖਣੀ** To harbour rancour, animosity or rankle or pain.

ਰਵਾਨਾ (ravaanaa) *a* Departed, proceeding to; **~ਹੋਣਾ** To start, to depart, to flow; **~ਕਰਨਾ** To despatch, to send, to remit.

ਰਵਾਨੀ (ravaanee) *n f* Fluency, flow, course, going.

ਰੜਕਣਾ (raṛakṇaa) *v* To munch, to eat with noise, to torment.

ਰੜਕਾ (raṛkaa) *n m* Broom.

ਰੜਕਾਉਣਾ (raṛkaauṇaa) *v* To be fried, to be thoroughly baked, parched or cooked; To be slightly overcooked or overbaked.

ਰੜ੍ਹਨਾ (raṛhnaa) *v* To be fried, to be thoroughly baked, parched or cooked; To be slightly overcooked or overbaked.

ਰੜਾ (raṛaa) *a* Plain, bare ground clear, clean.

ਰਾਉ (raao) *n m* King, prince, chieftain

ਰਾਇਜ (raaij) *a* Current, in vogue, in fashion, in practice, prevalent **~ਕਰਨਾ** To put or bring into vogue in fashion or in practice; To introduce, to enforce.

ਰਾਈ (raaee) *n f* Mustard, charlock *Brassica arvensis.*

ਰਾਏ (raae) *n f* Opinion, view, advice counsel; **~ਦੇਣੀ** To advise.

ਰਾਸ਼ਟਰ (raashṭar) *n m* Nation territory; Country; **~ਗਾਨ** National anthem; **~ਪਣ** Nationhood; **~ਪਤੀ** President; **~ਵਾਦ** Nationalism.

ਰਾਸ਼ਟਰੀ (raashtree) *a* National.

ਰਾਸ਼ਟਰੀਕਰਨ (raashtreekaran) *n m* Nationalization.

ਰਾਹ (raah) *n f* Path, way, road Custom, manner, method; **~ਕੱਢਣ** To find a way out; **~ਤੇ ਆਉਣਾ** To be reformed; **~ਦਸਣਾ** To guide, to lead; **~ਵੇਖਣਾ** To wait for, to expect **~ਗੀਰ** Traveller, pedestrian wayfarer; **~ਜ਼ਨ** Robber, highwayman; **~ਦਾਰੀ** Toll-tax, transit duties

ਰਾਹਤ (raahat) *n f* Relief, compensation, aid to victims of calamities

ਰਾਹੀ (raahee) *n m* Traveller, wayfarer

ਰਾਹੁਣਾ (raahuṇaa) *v* To sow, to

cultivate.

ਰਾਖ (raakh) *n f* Ashes; ~**ਕਰਨਾ** To reduce to ashes.

ਰਾਖਸ਼ (raakhash) *n m* Demon; A giant; A monster, wicked person.

ਰਾਖਵਾਂ (raakhwaan) *a* Reserved. Also **ਰਾਖਵੀਂ**

ਰਾਖਾ (raakhaa) *n m* Guard, protector, keeper, watchman.

ਰਾਗ (raag) *n m* Music, melody, singing; ~**ਅਲਾਪਣਾ** To relate one's own account; ~**ਰੰਗ** Merriment, dance and music; Fun and frolic; ~**ਨੀ** Musical mode.

ਰਾਗੀ (raagee) *n m* Singer, musician.

ਰਾਜ (raaj) *n* (1) Kingdom, goverment, rule, regiment; (2) Mason, brick layer; ~**ਸੀ** Political; ~**ਸੂਚਨਾ** Communique; ~**ਕਾਜ** Goverment; ~**ਕੁਮਾਰ** Prince; ~**ਕੁਮਾਰੀ** Princess; ~**ਕੋਸ਼** Exchequer, treasury; ~**ਗੱਦੀ** Throne; ~**ਗਰਦੀ** Anarchy, misrule, revolution; ~**ਗੀਰੀ** Mansory; ~**ਤੰਤਰ** Monarchy; ~**ਤਿਲਕ** Coronation; ~**ਦਰਬਾਰ** Royal court; ~**ਦਰਬਾਰੀ** Courtier; ~**ਦੂਤ** Ambassador; ~**ਦੂਤਵਾਸ** Embassy; ~**ਦ੍ਰੋਹ** Sedition, rebellion, conspiracy; ~**ਧਾਨੀ** Capital; ~**ਨੀਤਕ** Politician; ~**ਨੀਤਿਕ** Political; ~**ਨੀਤੀ** Politics, state policy; ~**ਪੱਤਰ** Gazette; ~**ਪੱਥ** Highway; ~**ਪਾਟ**

Dominion, kingdom; ~**ਪਾਲ** Governor; ~**ਵੰਸ਼** Imperial dynasty.

ਰਾਜ਼ (raaz) *n m* Secret, mystery; ~**ਕਾਰ** Confident; One who knows secret.

ਰਾਜਾ (raajaa) *n m* King, ruler, sovereign, rajah, monarch; Barber.

ਰਾਜ਼ੀ (raazee) *a* Willing, agreed, reconciliated, complacent, satisfied, contented; ~**ਹੋਣਾ** To agree, to consent, to be pleased; ~**ਖ਼ੁਸ਼ੀ** Hale and hearty, safe and sound; ~**ਨਾਮਾ** Deed of compromise, writ filed in court.

ਰਾਂਝਾ (raanjhaa) *n m* Title of a lover of heer, beloved.

ਰਾਤ (raat) *n f* Night; ~**ਦਿਨ** Day and night; Always; **ਰਾਤੋਂ**~ During night.

ਰਾੜ (raarr) *n f* Quarrel, wrangle, dispute.

ਰਾੜ੍ਹਨਾ (raarhnaa) *v* To roast.

ਰੜੀਆ (raariaa) *n m a* Quarrelsome person, disputant.

ਰਿਆ (riaa) concession, partiality.

ਰਿਆਇਆ (riaaiyaa) *n f* The public, subject.

ਰਿਆਇਤ (riyaait) *n f* Concession, relaxation, favour, partiality; ~**ਕਰਨੀ** To remit, to relax, to show favour.

ਰਿਆਇਤੀ (riyaaitee) *a* Concessional.

ਰਿਆਸਤ (riyaasat) *n f* Estate,

ਰਿਆਸਤੀ (riyaasatee) *a* Dominational, territorial.

ਰਿਆਕਾਰ (riaakaar) *a* cheat.

ਰਿਆਕਾਰੀ (riaakaaree) *a* Fraud, hypocrisy, decuitfulness.

ਰਿਆਜ਼ (riaaz) *n m* Regular practice.

ਰਿਸਣਾ (risṇaa) *v* To ooze, to leak, to drip, to exude.

ਰਿਸ਼ਤਾ (rishtaa) *n m* Relationship, connection, betrotheral, engagement; ~(ਤੇ)ਦਾਰ Relative, kith and kin, a relation; ~(ਤੇ)ਦਾਰੀ Relationship.

ਰਿਸ਼ਵਤ (rishwat) *n f* Bribe, illegal gratification; ~ਖੋਰੀ Bribery, corruption.

ਰਿਸਾਲਾ (risaalaa) *n m* (1) Cavalry, a cavalry regiment; (2) Magazine, journal, periodical.

ਰਿਸ਼ੀ (rishee) *n m* Saint, religious person. Also ਰਿਖੀ

ਰਿਹਾ (rihaa) *a* Released, discharged; ~ਕਰਨਾ To liberate, to release, to free; ~ਈ Release, acquittal, deliverance.

ਰਿਹਾਇਸ਼ (rihaaish) *n f* Residence, stay, dwelling; ~ਗਾਹ Place of residence, lodging, inn. Also ਰਹਾਇਸ਼

ਰਿਹਾਇਸ਼ੀ (rihaaishee) *a* Residential. Also ਰਹਾਇਸ਼ੀ deminion, territory.

ਰਿਕਤ (rikt) *a* vacant, unfilled, empty, blank; ~ਅਸਥਾਨ Vacancy, gap; ~ਅਸਾਮੀ Vacancy, vacant post.

ਰਿੱਛ (richchh) *n m* Bear.

ਰਿਜ਼ਕ (rizak) *n m* Food, provision, daily bread, subsistence.

ਰਿੱਝਣਾ (rijhṇaa) *v* To boil, to be boiled, or throughly cooked, to simmer; To rage to simmer with anger, to be angry or sullen, to sulk.

ਰਿਝਾਉਣਾ (rijhaauṇaa) *v* To allure, to captivate, to please, to charm, to bewitch.

ਰਿਣ (riṇ) *n m* Debt, obligation; ~ਪਤਰ Debenture.

ਰਿਣਾਤਮਕ (riṇaatmak) *a* Negative.

ਰਿਣੀ (riṇee) *n m a* Debtor; Indebted, obliged.

ਰਿਤੁ (ritoo) *n f* Season, weather; Blood, menses.

ਰਿੰਦ (rind) *n m* Quarrelsome, rascal, infidel, scoundre, drunkard.

ਰਿਵਾਜ (rivaaj) *n m* Custom, fashion, pratice, usage.

ਰਿਵਾਜੀ (rivaajee) *a* customary, ritualistic.

ਰਿੜ੍ਹਨਾ (riṛhnaa) *v* To slide, to slip, to glide, to roll.

ਰਿੜ੍ਹਵਾਂ (riṛhvaan) *a* Slopy, inclined.

ਰਿੜਕਣਾ (riṛaknaa) *v n* To churn; Churning, process churn.

ਰਿੜ੍ਹਨਾ (rirhnaa) *v* To roll, to slide, to slipdown or forward; To crawl; To roller-skate; To creep.

ਰੀਸ (rees) *n f* Emulation, habit of copying, following a precept; ~ਕਰਨੀ To vie with, to copy, to imitate.

ਰੀਂਗਣਾ (reengnaa) *v* To creep, to crawl.

ਰੀਝ (reejh) *n f* Ardent desire, fondness or wish, longing, craving.

ਰੀਝਣਾ (reejhnaa) *v* To be pleased, to be captivated, to be gratified, to be satisfied.

ਰੀਤ (reet) *n f* Custom, ceremony, rite, ritual, mode, manner.

ਰੀਤੀ (reetee) *n f* Custom, style; ~ਰਿਵਾਜ customs, traditions.

ਰੀਲ (reel) *n f* Reel, spool, cassette.

ਰੀੜ੍ਹ (reerh) *n* Back bone, spinal column, spine.

ਰੁਸਣਾ (rusnaa) *v* To be displeased, to be angry. Also ਰੁਸ ਜਾਣਾ

ਰੁਸ਼ਨਾਈ (rushnaaee) *n* (1) Light, brightness, glow, illumination, refulgence, radiance; (2) Ink, black ink.

ਰੁਸਵਾ (ruswaa) *a* Disgraced, ignominious, dishonoured, humiliated, infamous; ~ਈ Infamy, disgrace, ignominy, humiliation.

ਰੁਸੇਵਾਂ (rusevaan) *n m* Annoyance, vexation, anger, rage, displeasure.

ਰੁਹਬ (ruhb) *n m* Influence, dignity, state; ~ਦਾਰ Dignified, influential, impressive. Also ਰੋਹਬ, ਰੋਹਬਦਾਰ

ਰੁਹਾਨੀ (ruhaanee) *a* Spiritual; ~ਅਤ Spirituality. Also ਰੂਹਾਨੀ

ਰੁਕਣਾ (ruknaa) *v* To stop, to halt, to stay, to refrain.

ਰੁੱਕਾ (rukkaa) *n m* Note, scrap, letter, a piece of paper on which message in written.

ਰੁਕਾਵਟ (rukaawat) *n f* Check, restriction, resistance, obstruction, obstacle, hindrance, blockade, barrier; ~ਪਾਉਣੀ To obstruct, to hinder, to block.

ਰੁੱਖ (rukkh) *n m* Tree.

ਰੁਖ (rukh) *n m* Face, side, aptitude, direction, countenance; ~ਕਰਨਾ To proceed toward.

ਰੁਖਸਤ (rukhsat) *n f* Departure, leave, furlough; ~ਹੋਣਾ To depart, to take leave; ~ਕਰਨਾ To see off, to send away, to discharge.

ਰੁਖੜਾ (rukhraa) *a n m* Weak dry, tasteless, rude, impolite, rough; Tree.

ਰੁੱਖਾ (rukkhaa) *a* Harsh, rough, austere, inhospitable, rude, dry rugged; ~ਈ Harshness, roughness, dryness, indifference.

ਰੁਚੀ (ruchee) *n f* Interest, inclination, taste, liking, tendency, aptitude.

ਰੁਜ਼ਗਾਰ (ruzgaar) *n m* Service, occupation, trade, profession, empolyment, job. Also **ਰੋਜ਼ਗਾਰ**

ਰੁਜ਼ਾਨਾ (ruzaanaa) *a* Daily, everyday. Also **ਰੋਜ਼ਾਨਾ**

ਰੁਝਣਾ (rujhnaa) *v* To get busy, to be engaged.

ਰੁਝਾਉਣਾ (rujhaaunaa) *v* To engage, to engross, to make one busy.

ਰੁਝਾਨ (rujhaan) *n m* Aptitude.

ਰੁੱਠਣਾ (rutthnaa) *v* To be displeased, to get angry, to be annoyed.

ਰੁੱਠਾ (rutthaa) *a* Displeased, angry, annoyed. Also **ਰੁਠੜਾ**

ਰੁੰਡ-ਮੁੰਡ (runḍ-munḍ) *a* Truncated, doddered.

ਰੁਣ-ਝੁਣ (run-jhun) *n* Jingling, tinkling sound, singing, soft humming; ~**ਕਰਨਾ** To jingle, to sing soft.

ਰੁਤ (rut) *n f* Season.

ਰੁਤਬਾ (rutbaa) *n m* Status, rank, dignity, degree.

ਰੁੰਦਣਾ (rundnaa) *v* To be trampled, to be trodden.

ਰੁਦਨ (rudan) *n m* Wailing, weeping, lamentation, shedding tears.

ਰੁੱਧਣਾ (ruddhnaa) *v* To be engaged, to be occupied, to be in use.

ਰੁੱਧਾ (ruddhaa) *a* Busy, engaged, occupied.

ਰੁਬਾਈ (rubaaee) *n f* Stanza of four lines, a form of poetry.

ਰੁਮਕਣਾ (rumaknaa) *v* To blow slowly or elegantly.

ਰੁਮਕਾ (rumkaa) *n m* Puff of breeze, gust.

ਰੁਮਾਂਸ (rumaans) *n m* Romance.

ਰੁਮਾਂਚ (rumaanch) *n m* Thrill, rapture; ~**ਕ/ਕਾਰੀ** Horrifying, terrifying.

ਰੁਮਾਲ (rumaal) *n m* Handkercheif, searf.

ਰੁਮਾਲਾ (rumaalaa) *n m* Piece of cloth, to cover holy book, Guru Granth sahib.

ਰੁਲਣਾ (rulnaa) *v* To be trampled, to be uncared, to rot.

ਰੁਲਦਾ-ਖੁਲਦਾ (ruldaa-khuldaa) *v* In the state of neglect, uncared for.

ਰੁਲਾਉਣਾ (rulaaunaa) *v* To neglect, to desolate, to leave uncared, to winnow, to be wasted.

ਰੁੜ੍ਹਨਾ (rurhnaa) *v* To flow, to float, to glide, to be washed away, to flux.

ਰੂੰ (roon) *n m* Cleaned cotton; ~**ਕਤਰਨਾ** To spin.

ਰੂ (roo) *n f* Face; ~**ਬਰੂ** in front of, in the presence of before.

ਰੂਆਂ (rooaan) *n m* Small body hair,

ਰੂਸੀ (roosee) *n f* (1) Dandruff; (2) Russian language, people of Russia.

ਰੂਹ (rooh) *n m* Soul, spirit, life.

ਰੂਪ (roop) *n m* Form, countenance, beauty; ~ਹੀਣ Formless; ~ਰੰਗ Appearance, look, features; ~ਰੇਖ Outlines, synopsis, blue print; ~ਵਾਦ Formalism; ~ਵਾਨ Handsome, good looking, beautiful; ~ਵਿਗਿਆਨ Morphology.

ਰੂਪਾਤਮਕ (roopaatmak) *a* Formal.

ਰੂਪਕ (roopak) *n m* Allegory, metaphor; ~ਰੇਡਿਓ Radio drama or play.

ਰੂਪਾਂਤਰ (roopaantar) *n m* Adaptation allotropic form; (gr) inflexion; ~ਨ Metamorphism, modification, version, adaptation.

ਰੂਪੋਸ਼ (rooposh) *a* Disappeared, absconding, hiding, underground, fugitive, runaway; With face covered.

ਰੂੜੀ (roorhee) *n m* Convention, motif, tradition; ~ਗਤ Conventional traditional, stereotype; ~ਮੁਕਤ Unconventional; ~ਵਾਦ Conservatism; ~ਵਾਦੀ Conservative.

ਰੇਸ਼ਮ (resham) *n m* Silk.

ਰੇਸ਼ਮੀ (reshmee) *a* Silken.

ਰੇਸ਼ਾ (rashaa) *n m* Fibre, filament; Cold, bad cold, catarrh.

ਰੇਹੜ (rehar) *n m* Course of stream, flow of water, torrent.

ਰੇਹੜਾ (rehraa) *n m* Cart. Also ਰੇੜ੍ਹਾ

ਰੇਹੜੀ (rehree) *n f* Small cart, hand cart. Also ਰੇੜ੍ਹੀ

ਰੇਖਾ (rekhaa) *n f* Line; Fate, destiny; ~ਚਿੱਤਰ Diagram, pen portrait.

ਰੇਖਾਤਮਕ (rekhaatmak) *a* Linear.

ਰੇਗ (reg) *n f* Sand, silt; ~ਮਾਰ Sand paper.

ਰੇਗਿਸਤਾਨ (registaan) *n m* Desert, sandy place.

ਰੇਗਿਸਤਾਨੀ (registaanee) *a* Desert.

ਰੇਚਕ (rechak) *a* Purgative.

ਰੇਤ (ret) *n f* Sand. Also ਰੇਤਾ

ਰੇਤਣਾ (retnaa) *v* To rasp, to file.

ਰੇਤਲਾ (retlaa) *a* Sandy; Silty; ~ਪੱਥਰ Sandstone.

ਰੇਤੀ (retee) *n f* File, rasp, file.

ਰੇਲ (rel) *n f* Railway train; ~ਪਟੜੀ Railway track, railway line. Also ਰੇਲ ਗੱਡੀ

ਰੇਲਣਾ (relnaa) *v* To heap up, to shove together.

ਰੇਲ-ਪੇਲ (rel-pel) *n f* Crowd, rush, abudance, overcrowding, hustle and bustle.

ਰੇਲਾ (relaa) *n m* Flood, torrent, rush, push.

ਰੇੜ੍ਹ (rerh) *n m* Incline, flow.

ਰੇੜ੍ਹਨਾ (rerhnaa) *v* To roll, to move someting forward.

ਰੇੜਕਾ (rerkaa) *n m* Contention, quarrel, causeless dispute.

ਰੈਣ (rain) *n m* Night; ~**ਬਸੇਰਾ** Night's stay; Temporary stay.

ਰੈਤਾ (raitaa) *n m* Curd salad, vegetable etc. picked and spiced in curd.

ਰੋਸ਼ਨ (roshan) *a* Lighted, illuminated, bright, conspicuous.

ਰੋਸ਼ਨੀ (roshnee) *n f* Light, brightness, eyesight, lamp.

ਰੋਹ (roh) *n m* Anger, rage, fury.

ਰੋਹੇ (rohe) *n m* Trachoma.

ਰੋਕ (rok) *n f* (1) Cash, money; (2) Hindrance, restraint, barrier, interception; ~**ਟੋਕ** restriction, destruction, resistance.

ਰੋਕਣਾ (roknaa) *v* To stop, to check, to hinder, to restrict, to obstruct, to ban.

ਰੋਕੜ (rokar) *n f* Ready money, cash, fund; ~**ਖ਼ਾਤਾ** cash book, cash account.

ਰੋਗ (rog) *n m* Disease, sickness, illness, ailment, disorder, defect; ~**ਗ੍ਰਸਤ** Ill, morbid; ~**ਨ** Ailing woman, patient; Sick.

ਰੋਗਨ (rogan) *n m* Varnish, polish, oil paint.

ਰੋਚਕ (rochak) Interesting, sweet, piquant, I appetising; ~**ਤਾ** liveliness.

ਰੋਜ਼ (roz) *n ad* Day; Everyday, daily; ~**ਨਾਮਚਾ** Daily dairy, logbook; ~**ਬਰੋਜ਼** Daily, day by day.

ਰੋਜ਼ਾ (rozaa) *n m* Fast, fasting day; ~**ਰਖਣਾ** To observe a fast.

ਰੋਜ਼ੀ (rozee) *n f* Occupation, daily food, means of sustenance.

ਰੋਟ (rot) *n m* Thick loaf, thick bread.

ਰੋਟੀ (rotee) *n f* Bread, roasted cake, loaf, livelihood; ~**ਦਾਲ ਚਲਾਉਣੀ** To subsist.

ਰੋਡਾ (rodaa) *n m* Shaven head, bald with shaven head.

ਰੋਣ (ron) *n m* Weeping, crying, wailing, blubber, lamentation; tears; ~**ਧੋਣ** Wailing, lamentation, intense grief, unrestrained crying, mourning.

ਰੋਣਾ (ronaa) *v* To weep, to wail, to cry, to lament, to grieve.

ਰੋਂਦੂ (rondoo) *a* Weepy, weeper, foul player, player who cheats.

ਰੋਪਣਾ (ropnaa) *v* To plant, to transplant, to sow.

ਰੋਲਣਾ (rolnaa) *v* To pick over, to overcome, to subdue.

ਰੋੜਾ (roraa) *n m* Pebble, gravel,

brickbat, fragments of stone; ~ਅਟਕਾਉਣਾ To blockade, to put obstacles. Also ਰੋੜ

ਰੋੜ੍ਹਨਾ (rorhnaa) *v* To sweep away, to wash away.

ਰੌਣਕ (raunak) *n f* Splendour, elegance, mirth, embellishment.

ਰੌਣਕੀ (raunkee) *a* Gay, jovil, jolly, joyous, cheerful, humorous, witty.

ਰੌਂਦਣਾ (raudnaa) *v* To trample crush under feet; to spoil, to destroy.

ਰੌਲਾ (raulaa) *n m* Clamour, tumlut, uproar; ~ਗੌਲਾ Fuse, noise, confusion.

ਲ

ਲ Thirty third letter of Gurmukhi alphabets, pronounced as 'lallaa'.

ਲਈ (laee) *Prep* For, to, for the sake of, in order to, for the purpose of.

ਲਸੰਸ (lasans) *n m* Licence; ~**ਦਾਰ** Licensee, licence holder.

ਲਸ਼ਕਰ (lashkar) *n m* Army, artillery men, host.

ਲਸਲਸਾ (laslasaa) *a* Sticky, viscid.

ਲੱਸੀ (lassee) *n f* Buttermilk, whey, Drink by churning curd with water.

ਲਹਾਉਣਾ (lahaaunaa) *v* To help in bringing down, unloading.

ਲਹਾਈ (lahaaee) *n f* Descent, recession, unloading, bringing down; Insult, disgrace.

ਲਹਿਕਣਾ (laheknaa) *v* To wave, to quiver, to glitter.

ਲੰਹਿਗਾ (lahengaa) *n m* Skirt, petticoat.

ਲਹਿਜਾ (lahejaa) *n m* Accent, tone. Also **ਲਹਿਜ਼ਾ**

ਲਹਿਣਾ (lahenaa) *n m v* Luck, an outstanding debt; To get down, to come down, to descend.

ਲਹਿੰਦੀ (lahindee) *n m* A language spoken in West Punjab (now in Pakistan).

ਲਹਿਰ (laher) *n f* Wave, surge, surf, whim, rapture; Movement; ~**ਕਾਰ** Wavy, undulating.

ਲਹਿਰਾਉਣਾ (laheraaunaa) *v* To wave, to flutter, to ripple, to fluctuate.

ਲਹਿਰੀ (laehree) *a* Jovil, merry, gay, carefree, playful; Eccentric, whimsical; Unconventional.

ਲਹੁੜਾ (lahuraa) *a* Younger, junior.

ਲਹੂ (lahoo) *n m* Blood; ~**ਦੀ ਹੋਲੀ** Carnival of bloodshed; ~**ਦੇ ਘੁਟ ਪੀਣੇ** To suppress anger; ~ **ਠੰਡਾ ਹੋਣਾ** To be bereft of passion, to lose sense of respect; ~**ਲਹਾਨ** steeped in blood, covered with blood.

ਲੱਕ (lakk) *n m* Waist, girdle; ~**ਸਿੱਧਾ ਕਰਨਾ** To rest, to lie down; ~**ਟੁਟਣਾ** To be disappointed; ~**ਬੰਨ੍ਹਣਾ** Gird up to loins, to get ready.

ਲਕਸ਼ (lakash) *n m* Aim, object, objective target.

ਲਕਣਾ (laknaa) *v* To lap, To lick up.

ਲਕਵਾ (lakwaa) *n m* Paralysis, palsy; ~**ਮਾਰਨਾ** To be paralysed.

ਲਕੜ (lakar) *n f* Wood, log, timber, firewood; ~**ਹਾਰਾ** Woodcutter; ~**ਮੰਡੀ** Timber market. Also **ਲਕੜੀ**

ਲਕੜਬੱਘਾ (lakar bagghaa) *n m* Hyaena, jaguar.

ਲੰਕਾ (lankaa) *n m* Ceylon, Srilanka country.

ਲਕੀਰ (lakeer) *n f* Line, stripe, furrow; ~ਕਾਰ Lined streaked, striped; ~ਦਾ ਫ਼ਕੀਰ Traditionalist, slave of tradition or custom.

ਲੱਖ (lakkh) *a* Lac, one hundred thousand ~ਪਤੀ Millionaire, rich.

ਲਖਣਾ (lakhnaa) *v* To understand, to comperhend.

ਲਖਾਉਣਾ (lakhaaunaa) *v* To cause to understand; To explain.

ਲੰਗ (lang) *n m* Lameness, limp. Also ਲੰਙ

ਲੰਗੜਾ (langraa) *a n m* Crippled; Lame, cripple; ~ਉਣਾ To limp.

ਲੱਗਣਾ (laggnaa) *v* To pinch, to have painful sensation, to cause irritation.

ਲਗਣਾ (lagnaa) *v* To be applied, to be attached, to touch, to cast; ਅੱਖ~ To sleep; ਅੱਗ~ To catch fire, ਆਖੇ~ To obey; ਪਾਲਾ~ To feel cold; ਰੁਪਿਆ~ Spending of much money.

ਲਗਨ (lagan) *n f* Attachment, affection, devotion; Auspicious time. Also ਲਗਨ

ਲਗਭਗ (lagbhag) *adv* Approximately, almost, nearly, about.

ਲੰਗਰ (langar) *n m* (1) Anchor; Kedge, (2) Public kitchen; Free community kitchen.

ਲਗਵਾਉਣਾ (lagvaaunaa) *v* To get planted, to get engaged, to get posted.

ਲੰਗੜਾਉਣਾ (langraaunaa) *v* To limp, to cripple. Also ਲੰਙਾਉਣਾ

ਲਗਾਉਣਾ (lagaaunaa) *v* To employ, to fix, to appoint, to engage, to apply.

ਲਗਾਤਾਰ (lagaatar) *adv* Continuously, incessantly, consecutively.

ਲਗਾਨ (lagaan) *n m* Revenue, rent.

ਲਗਾਮ (lagaam) *n f* Bridle, hit and reins; ਬੇ~ ਹੋਣਾ To be out of control.

ਲੰਗੂਰ (langoor) *n m* Ape, monkey, gorilla.

ਲੰਗੋਟ (langot) *n m* Loin cloth; ਸੁੱਚਾ~ Sexually rightness; ~ਦਾ ਕੱਚਾ lustful having sex weakness. Also ਲੰਗੋਟਾ

ਲੰਗੋਟੀ (langotee) *n f* Loin cloth; ~ਵਿਚ ਮਸਤ Carefree in adversity; ~ਆ (ਯਾਰ) Intimate (friend), chum, bosom or fast (friend).

ਲੰਘਣਾ (langhnaa) *v* To pass, to cross, to transgress.

ਲੰਘਾਉਣਾ (langhaaunaa) *v* To pass through, to help in passing.

ਲੰਘਾਈ (langhaaee) *n f* Toll tax; Charges of getting some one to across through; Process of getting some one to pass through.

ਲਘੂ (laghoo) *a* Small, short, trivial.

ਲਚਕ (lachak) *n f* Elasticity, resilence, softness; ~ਦਾਰ Elastic, flexible.

ਲਚਕਣਾ (lachaknaa) *v* To bend, to spring.

ਲਚਕਾ (lachkaa) *n m* Jolt, flirtation.

ਲਚਕੀਲਾ (lackkeelaa) *a* Elastic, flexible, resilient, spring. Also ਲਚੀਲਾ

ਲਚਰ (lachar) *a* Lewd, obscene, foolish; ~ਪੁਣਾ Lewdness, obscenity, foolishness.

ਲੱਛਣ (lachchhan) *n m* Traits, qualities, character, sign, attribute; Features. Also ਲੱਖਣ

ਲੱਛਾ (lachchhaa) *n m* Bundle, coil, bunch.

ਲਛੇਦਾਰ (lachchhedaar) *a* With fine shreds, pleasant to hear, verbose.

ਲੱਜਾ (lajjaa) *n f* Shyness, modesty, shame, pudency, coyness. Also ਲੱਜ or ਲਜਿਆ

ਲੱਜ਼ਤ (lazzat) *n f* Taste; Flavour; Pleasure; ~ਦਾਰ Tasty, delicious, tasteful.

ਲਜਿਆਉਣਾ (lajiaaunaa) *v* To feel shy, to be abashed, to be ashamed.

ਲਜ਼ੀਜ਼ (lazeez) *a* Tasty, delicious, flavoursome.

ਲਜੀਲਾ (lajeelaa) *a* Coy, shy.

ਲਟ (lat) *n f* (1) Lock (of hair), ringlet; (2) Flame; ~ਲਟ In full swing, shining brightly.

ਲਟਕ (latak) *n f* Coquetry, love, affected gait.

ਲਟਕਣ (latkan) *n f* Pendulum, pendent, locket, embellishment.

ਲਟਕਣਾ (lataknaa) *v* To hang, to be postponed, to swing, to be kept waiting.

ਲਟਕਾਉਣਾ (latkaaunaa) *v* To hang, to suspend, to dangle, to put off.

ਲੱਟਰ (lattar) *a* Vagabond, loafer.

ਲਟਾਪਟਾ (lataapataa) *v* Miscellaneous items, odds and ends, paraphernalia.

ਲੱਟੂ (lattoo) *n m* Top, (child's) plummet. Also ਲਾਟੂ

ਲੱਠ (latth) *n m* Wooden axle, cudgel, club, stick; ~ਬਾਜ਼ Cudgel fighter. Also (ਲਠੈਠ); ~ਮਾਰ Oppressive, violent, uncouth.

ਲੰਡ (land) *n m* Penis.

ਲੰਡੇ (lande) *n f* Trader's script, script of Lahanda language.

ਲਤ (lat) *n f* Leg; ~ਅੜਾਉਣੀ To interfere; ~ਖਾਣੀ To be kicked; ~ਮਾਰਨੀ To kick, to put hindrance.

ਲੱਤਾ (lattaa) *n m* Tatter, rag.

ਲਤਾਫ਼ਤ (lataafat) *n f* Delicacy, grace.

ਲਤਾੜ (lataar) *n f* Scolding.

ਲਤਾੜਨਾ (lataarnaa) *v* To scold, to insult, to trample under foot.

ਲਤੀਫ਼ਾ (lateefaa) *n m* Witty remark,

joke, jest, tit bit; ~(ਡ਼ੇ) ਬਾਜ਼ Witticist, humorist.

ਲੱਥਪੱਥ (lathpath) *a* Besmeared, soaked, steeped. Also **ਲਤਪਤ**

ਲਦਣਾ (ladṇaa) *v* To load, to burden, to feight, to be laden.

ਲਦਵਾਉਣਾ (ladvaauṇaa) *v* To cause or help loading. Also **ਲਦਾਉਣਾ**

ਲਦਾਨ (ladaan) *n m* Loading.

ਲਪਕ (lapak) *n f* Flash, swiftness

ਲਪਕਣਾ (lapakṇaa) *v* To rush forth, to flash, to walk fast.

ਲੰਪਟ (lampaṭ) *a* Sexual, lustful, dissolute, wanton.

ਲਪਟ (lapaṭ) *n f* Blast of wind, odour, a swift form of fire.

ਲੱਪੜ (lappaṛ) *n m* Slap, smack; ~**ਲਪੜ** Non sensical talk, chatter.

ਲਪੇਟ (lapet) *n f* Envelopment, engulfment, fold, entanglement, convolution.

ਲਪੇਟਣਾ (lapetṇaa) *v* To wrap, to roll up, to coil, to pack, to embosom, to envelop.

ਲਫੰਗਾ (lafangaa) *n m* Vagabond, loafer, having loose character.

ਲਫ਼ਜ਼ (lafaz) *n m* Word, term, phrase; Saying; ~**ਬ ਲਫ਼ਜ਼** Word by word, verbatum.

ਲਫ਼ਟੈਨ (laftain) *n m* Lieutenant. Also **ਲਫ਼ਟੰਟ**

ਲਫ਼ਾਫ਼ਾ (lafaafaa) *n m* Envelope, paperbag; Outward show.

ਲੰਬ (lamb) *n m* Perpendicular; ~**ਕਾਰ** Perpendicular, vertical, longitudinal.

ਲਬ (lab) *n m* Lib, saliva, edge.

ਲੰਬੜ (lambaṛ) *n m* Leader, chief; ~**ਦਾਰ** village headman.

ਲੰਬਾ (lambaa) *a* Tall, long; ~**ਚੌੜਾ** Huge, vast; ~**ਈ** Length, tallness. Also **ਲੰਮਾ**

ਲਬਾਦਾ (labaadaa) *n m* Clock, greatcoat, pelisee; Disguise.

ਲਬਾਲਬ (labaalab) *a adv* Brimful, upto the brim or top.

ਲੰਬੂ (lamboo) *n m* A very tall man; Big fire, conflagration.

ਲੰਬੂਤਰਾ (lambootraa) *a* Oblong, elongated, long.

ਲਬੇੜਨਾ (labernaa) *v* To soak, to drench, to smear.

ਲਭਣਾ (labhṇaa) *v* To search, to find out, to get, to be discovered.

ਲਮ੍ਹਾ (lamhaa) *n m* Moment, instant.

ਲਮਕਣਾ (lamakṇaa) *v* To hang, to swing, to be suspended.

ਲਮਕਾਉਣਾ (lamkaauṇaa) *v* To hang, to suspend, to delay, to prolong.

ਲਮਢੀਂਗ (lamdheeng) *a* Awkwardly tall.

ਲਮੂਤਰਾ (lamootraa) *a* Tallish, longish.

ਲਰਜ਼ਣਾ (laraznaa) *v* To tremble, to vibrate, to throb.

ਲਲਕ (lalhak) *n f* Longing, intense desire, yearning, craving.

ਲਲਕਾਰ (lalkaar) *n f* Challenge, call, bawl, threat.

ਲਲਕਾਰਨਾ (lalkaarnaa) *v* To challenge, to threaten, to bawl.

ਲਲਕਾਰਾ (lalkaaraa) *n m* Shout, whoop, bawl, threatening or challenging cry.

ਲਲਚਾਉਣਾ (lalchaaunaa) *v* To tempt, to allure, to long for, to covet.

ਲਲੂ (laloo) *a* Ordinary, simpleton; ~**ਪੰਜੂ** Tom dick and Harry.

ਲਲੋ-ਪੱਤੋ (lalo patto) *n f* Flattery, wheeding.

ਲਵਾਉਣਾ (lavaaunaa) *v* To get sharpened, to get affixed, to get registered.

ਲੜ (lar) *n m* End or corner (of a cloth or garment); ~**ਫੜਨਾ** To take refuge.

ਲੜਕਪਨ (larakpan) *n m* Childhood, boyhood, frivolity.

ਲੜਕਾ (larkaa) *n m* Boy, son, child; Bridegroom.

ਲੜਕੀ (larkee) *n f* Girl, daughter.

ਲੜਖੜਾਉਣਾ (larkharaaunaa) *v* To stagger, to falter, to reel.

ਲੜਨਾ (larnaa) *v* To quarrel, to fight, to bite, to sting, to struggle.

ਲੜਾਈ (laraaee) *n f* Battle, fight, quarrel, clash, encounter; ~**ਝਗੜਾ** Quarrel, dispute, bickering, altercation.

ਲੜਾਕਾ (laraakaa) *a* Quarrelsome, belligerent, militant, pugnacious, fighter; ~**ਪਣ** Quarrelsomeness, pugnacity, militancy. Also **ਲੜਾਕੂ**

ਲੜਾਕੀ (laraakee) *a n f* Quarrelsome (woman), shrewish; Virago.

ਲੜੀ (laree) *n f* Chain, series, row, a string or pearls, link.

ਲਾਉਣਾ (laaunaa) *v* To fix, to appoint, to assign, to plant.

ਲਾਇਕ (laaik) *a* Able, capable, fit, intelligent.

ਲਾਇਕੀ (laaikee) *n f* worthiness, worth, suitability, fitness.

ਲਾਇਲਾਜ (laailaaj) *a* Incurable, irremediable, hopeless.

ਲਾਈਨ (laain) *n f* Line; **ਗੱਡੀ ਦੀ**~ Railway track; ~**ਦਾਰ** Striped, ruled.

ਲਾਸ਼ (laash) *n f* Deadbody, carcass.

ਲਾਸਾਨੀ (laasaanee) *a* Unequalled, unparalleled, unmatched.

ਲਾਹਨਤ (laahnat) *n f* Scolding, reproof, reproach, condemnation curse; ~**ਦਾ ਮਾਰਿਆ** Damned ~**ਮੁਲਾਮਤ** Censure, scolding reproach, rebuke. Also **ਲਾਨ੍ਹਤ**

ਲਾਖ (laakh) *n f* Shellac, sealing wax; Lac, hundred thousand.

ਲਾਗਤ (laagat) *n f* Cost, outlay, investment, expenditure.

ਲਾਗਤਬਾਜ਼ੀ (laagatbaazee) *n f* Enmity, grudge.

ਲਾਂਗਰੀ (laangree) *n m* Cook.

ਲਾਗਾ (laagaa) *n m* Nearness, closeness, vicinity, proximity; ~ਬੰਨਾ Relation, connection; surroundings, vicinity.

ਲਾਗੂ (laagoo) *a* Applicable, relevant; In force, enforced.

ਲਾਗੇ (laage) *adv* Near, near by, close by.

ਲਾਂਘਾ (lavanghaa) *n m* Thorough fare, passage, vestibule.

ਲਾਚਾਰ (laachaar) *a* Helpless, compelled, destitute, forlorn.

ਲਾਚਾਰੀ (laachaaree) *n f* Helplessness, handicap.

ਲਾਜ (laaj) *n f* Modesty, shyness, shame, pudicity bashfulness; ~ਰਖਣੀ To protect one's honour.

ਲਾਜ਼ਮ (laazam) *a* Necessary, essential, compulsory.

ਲਾਜ਼ਮੀ (laazmee) *a* Compulsory, mandatory, obligatory.

ਲਾਟ (laat) *n m* (1) Governor, lord; (2) Flame, blaze.

ਲਾਟਰੀ (laatree) *n f* Lottery.

ਲਾਠੀ (laathee) *n f* Stick, club, cudgel.

ਲਾਡ (lead) *n m* Love, fonding; caressing, endearment; ~ਕਰਨਾ To fondle, to caress; ~ਲਾ Dear, darling, pet.

ਲਾਪਤਾ (laapataa) *a* Disappeared, unknown, absconding.

ਲਾਪਰਵਾਹ (laaparwaah) *a* Careless, negligent, headless, reckless.

ਲਾਪਰਵਾਹੀ (laaparwaahee) *n f* Carelessness, inattentiveness.

ਲਾਭ (laabh) *n m* Advantage, profit, gain, dividend, use, benefit; ~ਦਾਇਕ (ਕਾਰੀ) Useful, fruitful, beneficial, advantageous, profitable.

ਲਾਂਭੇ (laambhe) *adv* Aside, away.

ਲਾਮ (laam) *n f* Army, crowd, brigade; War; Host; ~ਬੰਦੀ Mobilization, *levy en masse*.

ਲਾਰ (laar) *n f* Saliva.

ਲਾਰਾ (laaraa) *n* False promise, false hope, an excuse.

ਲਾਲ (laal) *a n m* Red, angry; Darling, son, boy; Ruby; ~ਬੁਝੱਕੜ A wiseacre; A conceited fool; ~ਮਿਰਚ Chilly.

ਲਾਲਸਾ (laalsaa) *n f* Longing, craving, ardent desire, ambition, yearning

ਲਾਲਚ (laalach) *n m* Greed, temptation, avarice.

ਲਾਲਚੀ (lalchee) *a* Greedy, priggish,

ਲਾਲਟੈਣ (laaltain) *n f* Lantern.

ਲਾਲਾ (laalaa) *n m* Address term for shopkeeper, businessman, oldman, father etc.

ਲਾਲੀ (laalee) *n f* Redness, crimson hue; A kind of myna.

ਲਾਵਾ (laavaa) *n m* Lava.

ਲਾਵਾਂ (laavaan) *n pl f* Circum ambulations in marriage ceremony; ~ਲੈਆਂ To marry. Also ਲਾਂ or ਲਾਂਵ

ਲਾਵਾਰਸ (laavaaras) *a* Heirless, orphan, unclaimed.

ਲਾੜਾ (laaraa) *n m* Bridegroom.

ਲਾੜੀ (laaree) *n f* Bride.

ਲਿਆਉਣਾ (liaaunaa) *v* To bring, to fetch, to carry over.

ਲਿਆਕਤ (liaakat) *n f* Ability, calibre, worth, proficiency, capability, skill.

ਲਿਸ਼ਕ (lishak) *n f* Shine, sheen, glitter, lustre; ~ਦਾਰ Shinning, glossy.

ਲਿਸ਼ਕਾਰ (lishkaar) *n f* Flash, reflection, bright reflecting light. Also ਲਿਸ਼ਕਾਰਾ

ਲਿਸ਼ਕਣਾ (lishaknaa) *v* To shine, to glitter, to sparkle.

ਲਿੱਸਾ (lissaa) *a* weak, pale, feeble; ~ਪਣ Thinness, weakness. Also ਲਿੱਸੜ

ਲਿਹਾਜ਼ (lihaaz) *n m* Consideration, deference, favour, indulgence.

ਲਿਹਾਜ਼ਾ (lihaazaa) *conj adv* Accordingly, therefore.

ਲਿਖਣਾ (likhnaa) *v* To write, to inscribe, to take down, to note down; ~ਪੜ੍ਹਨਾ Study, reading and writing.

ਲਿਖਵਾਉਣਾ (likhvaaunaa) *v* To get written, to dictate. Also ਲਿਖਾਉਣਾ

ਲਿਖਾਈ (likhaaee) *n f* Writing, art of writing, wages for writing.

ਲਿਖਾਪੜ੍ਹੀ (likhaaparhee) *n f* Correspondence, written negotiation.

ਲਿੰਗ (ling) *n m* Sex, gender, the male organ.

ਲਿੰਗੀ (lingee) *a* Sexual.

ਲਿਟ (lit) *n f* Lock, wisp or strand of hair.

ਲਿਟਣਾ (litnaa) *v* To lie down.

ਲਿਟਾਉਣਾ (litaaunaa) *v* To lay down, to cause to lie down.

ਲਿੱਤਰ (littar) *n m* Old and nearly worn out shoes. Also ਛਿਤਰ

ਲਿਤਾੜਨਾ (litaarnaa) *v* To trample under feet, to scold.

ਲਿੱਦ (lidd) *n f* Horse-turd, dung of ass or elephant; ~ਕਰਨਾ To act tamely.

ਲਿਪਟਣਾ (lipatnaa) *v* To cling, to embrace, to be coiled round.

ਲਿਫਣਾ (liphanaa) *v* To bend, to stoop; To yield, submit; To relent.

ਲਿਫ਼ਾਫ਼ਾ (lifaafaa) *n m* Envelope, wrapper.

ਲਿੰਬਣਾ (limbnaa) *v* To plaster.

ਲਿਬੜਨਾ (limbarnaa) *v* To smear.

ਲਿਬਾਸ (libaas) *n m* Dress, apparel, raiment, clothing, garb, vestment, attire.

ਲਿਬੇੜਨਾ (libernaa) *v* To besmear, to daub, to soil. Also ਲਬੇੜਨਾ

ਲਿਲ੍ਹਕ (lilhak) *n f* Cry, lament, scream; humble or abject entaty or appeal.

ਲਿਲਾਟ (lilaat) *n m* Forehead, destiny. Also ਲਲਾਟ

ਲੀਕ (leek) *n f* Line, mark, trace.

ਲੀਕਣਾ (leeknaa) *v* To rule, to draw lines, to spoil.

ਲੀਖ (leekh) *n f* Egg of a louse, nit.

ਲੀਚੜ (leechar) *a* Niggardly, mean, bad paymaster.

ਲੀਰ (leer) *n f* Rag, shred; ~ਲੀਰ ਹੋਣਾ To be torn into rags

ਲੀੜਾ (leeraa) *n m* Torn out, cloth, garment.

ਲੁਹਾਉਣਾ (luhaaunaa) *v* To get unloaded, to help in unloading.

ਲੁਹਾਰ (luhaar) *n m* Blacksmith, ironsmith. Also ਲੋਹਾਰ

ਲੁਹਾਰਾ (luhaaraa) *n m* Job of blacksmith.

ਲੁਕਣਾ (luknaa) *v* To be concealed, to hide.

ਲੁਕਾਉਣਾ (lukaaunaa) *v* To hide, to conceal, to cover.

ਲੁਗਾਤ (lugat) *n f* Dictionary, lexicon, glossary.

ਲੁੱਗਾ (luggaa) *a* Deserted, vacated, empty, bare (house), unoccupied and unguarded.

ਲੁਗਾਈ (lugaaee) *n f* Wife, woman.

ਲੁੰਗੀ (lungee) *n f* Striped, chequered or embroidered sheet for use as garment for lower body.

ਲੁੱਚਾ (luchchaa) *a* Wicked, shameless, knave, corrupt; Vagabond, scamp.

ਲੁੰਜਾ (lunjaa) *a* Crippled, having an arm or leg crippled, disabled.

ਲੁੱਝਣਾ (lujjnaa) *v* To quarrel, to fight, to provoke.

ਲੁਟਣਾ (lutnaa) *v* To plunder, to rob, to ravage, to ransack, to loot, to devastate.

ਲੁਟੇਰਾ (luteraa) *n m* Robber, plunderer, highwayman.

ਲੁਡਾਉਣਾ (ludaaunaa) *v* To swing, to oscillate.

ਲੁਤਫ਼ (lutaf) *n m* Enjoyment, pleasure, grace, taste.

ਲੁਪਤ (lupt) *a* Concealed, hidden, disguised, missing.

ਲੁਭਾਉਣਾ (lubhaaunaa) *v* To allure, to

entice, to captivate, to be charmed. Also ਲੁਭਾਣਾ

ਲੁੜ੍ਹਕਣਾ (lurhaknaa) *v* To roll, to be upset.

ਲੁੜੀਂਦਾ (iureendaa) *a* Wanted, required, needed, necessary, needful, desired.

ਲੂੰ (loon) *n m* Short hair on the body.

ਲੂਸਣਾ (loosanaa) *v* To be scorched; to feel burning sensation; to sulk, to be sulky, to smoulder with envy or jealousy.

ਲੂਣ (loon) *n m* Salt, sodium chloride; ~ਤੇਲ Articles of bare subsistence, bread and butter; ~ਮਿਰਚ ਲਾਉਣੀ To season or smear with salt and pepper; To state or report (an incident) in exaggerated or interesting manner, to exaggerate.

ਲੂੰਬੜ (loombar) *n m* Fox.

ਲੂਲ੍ਹਾ (loolhaa) *a n m* Maimed, crippled; Cripple.

ਲੇਸ (les) *n f* Sticking fluid, adhesiveness; ~ਦਾਰ sticky, gummy.

ਲੇਖ (lekh) *n f* Composition, essay, article, writing; Destiny, fate; ~ਕ Writer; ~ਨੀ Pen, style.

ਲੇਖਾ (lekhaa) *n m* An account, calculation; ~ਕਾਰ Accountant; ~ਜੋਖਾ Assessment.

ਲੇਟਣਾ (letnaa) *v* To lie down, to roll; to rest or relax lying down; to sleep, to wallow.

ਲੇਪ (lep) *n m* Layer, coat, spread (of plaster, ointment, etc); ~ਕਰਨਾ To spread or daub with; ~ਲਾਉਣਾ To flatter; To cheat.

ਲੇਪਣਾ(lepnaa) *v* To be smear, to embalm, to paint, to plaster.

ਲੇਫ਼ (lef) *n m* Quilt.

ਲੇਲਾ (lelaa) *n m* Lamb.

ਲੈਣ-ਦੇਣ (lain-den) *n m* Trade, commerce, give and take, transaction, exchange, barter; Business, relations, dealings; ~ਕਰਨਾ To transact business, to have commercial relations; To compromise, to give and take.

ਲੈਣਾ (lainaa) *v* To get, to receive, to take, to hold, to acquire.

ਲੋਈ (loee) *n f* A thin blanket or wrapper; People, public.

ਲੋਹਾ (lohaa) *n m* Iron; ~ਲੈਣਾ To wage a war.

ਲੋਕ (lok) *n m* People, mankind, public, folk, world; ~ਸਭਾ House of people; ~ਸੇਵਕ Public servant; ~ਹਿੱਤ Public interest; ~ਕਥਾ Folk tale; ~ਗਾਥਾ Ballad; ~ਰਾਜ Democracy.

ਲੋਕਾਚਾਰ (lokaachaar) *n m* Fashion, custom, convention, ethos; Public

ਲੋਚ (loch) *n f* Flexibility, elasticity, tenderness; ~ਦਾਰ Tender, flexible, soft, elastic. Also ਲਚਕ

ਲੋਟਣਾ (loṭnaa) *v* To roll, to somersault.

ਲੋਟਾ (loṭaa) *n m* Small metal pot.

ਲੋਥ (loth) *n f* Corpse, dead body, carcass; ~ੜਾ Lump of flesh.

ਲੋਭ (lobh) *n m* Greed, temptation, allurement.

opinion.

ਲੋਭੀ (lobhee) *a* Greedy, voracious.

ਲੋੜ (loṛ) *n f* Need, want, necessity.

ਲੋੜਨਾ (loṛnaa) *v* To search, to need, to expect.

ਲੋੜਾ (loṛhaa) *n m* Tragedy, calamity; Atrocity, oppression; Storm; Deluge.

ਲੌਂਡਾ (laundaa) *n m* Boy, lad, slave.

ਲੌਂਡੀ (laundee) *n f* Slave girl, bond maid.

ਵ

ਵ Thirty fourth letter of Gurmukhi alphabets, pronounced as 'vaavaa'.

ਵੱਸ (vass) *n m v* Power, control, will; To over power, to bring under control, to tame.

ਵੱਸਣਾ (vassnaa) *v* To dwell, to reside, to lodge; To rain.

ਵਸਲ (vasal) *n m* Union, meeting, copulation.

ਵਸਵਸਾ (vasvasaa) *n m* Apprehension, misgiving, anxiety, doubt, trepidation.

ਵਸਾਉਣਾ (vasaaunaa) *v* To populate, to colonise, to shower.

ਵਸਾਹ (vasaah) *n m* Trust, credit, reliance; **~ਖਾਣਾ** To trust, to rely, to have faith.

ਵਸਾਲ (vasaal) *n m* Union, meeting, cohabitation.

ਵਸੀਅਤ (vaseeat) *n f* Will, legacy, bequest; **~ਕਰਨੀ** To bequeath; **~ਨਾਮਾ** Will testament.

ਵਸੀਕਾ (vaseekaa) *n m* Bond, written agreement; **~ਨਵੀਸ** Deed writer.

ਵਸੀਕਾਰ (vaseekaar) *n m* Control, authority.

ਵਸੀਲਾ (vaseelaa) *n m* Support, means.

ਵਸੂਲ (vasool) *a* Obtained, collected, received, realised; **~ਕਰਨਾ** To collect, to realise, to fetch.

ਵਸੂਲੀ (vasoolee) *n f* Realisation of dues, recovery, collection of dues.

ਵਸੇਬਾ (vasebaa) *n m* Living, life with peace and honour, peaceful and honourable living.

ਵਹਾਉਣਾ (vahaaunaa) *v* To cause or make to flow, to float, to pour, to spill; to waste, to squander.

ਵਹਿਸ਼ਤ (vaheshat) *n f* Savagery, madness, rudeness, wildness.

ਵਹਿਸ਼ੀ (vaheshee) *a n m* Savage, rude, uncivilized; Barbarian, savage, brute.

ਵਹਿਣਾ (vehnaa) *v* To float, to flow.

ਵਹਿਣੀ (vaojnee) *n f* Drain, gutter, sewer, duct.

ਵਹਿਮ (vahem) *n m* False notion, whim, fallacy, misunderstanding, apprehension, doubt.

ਵਹਿਮੀ (vahemee) *a* Whimsical, suspecious.

ਵਹਿੜ (vaher) *n f* Young cow; **~ਕਾ** Calf, young ox.

ਵਹੀ (vahee) *n f* Accountbook, recordbook, record of debts and debtors; ~**ਖਾਤਾ** Cashbook, cash account, ledger of transactions.

ਵਹੁਟੀ (vahutee) *n f* Wife, bride.

ਵਕਤ (vakat) *n m* Time, season, opportunity, circumstances; ~**ਕਟਣਾ** To pass the time; ~**ਸਿਰ** In all time, timely; ~**ਬੇਵਕਤ** At all times, at odd hours. Also **ਵਖਤ**

ਵਕਤਾ (vaktaa) *n m* Speaker, orator.

ਵਕਤੀ (vaktee) *a* Occassional, timely, momentary, temporary, transient, impermanent.

ਵਕਫ (wakaf) *a n m* Reserved, allocated; Charitable, endowment, trust, ~**ਨਾਮਾ** Deed of reservation.

ਵਕਫ਼ਾ (wakfaa) *n m* Interval, recess, intermission, period.

ਵੱਕਾਰ (vakkaar) *n m* Prestige, honour, dignity

ਵਕਾਲਤ (vakaalat) *n m* Advocacy, pleadership, lawyer profession; ~**ਨਾਮਾ** Power of attorney given by client to advocate.

ਵਕੀਲ (vakeel) *n m* Lawyer, pleader, advocate, counsel.

ਵਖਰਾ (vakhraa) *a* Separate, distinctive, isolated; ~**ਪਣ** Distinctness, separateness.

ਵਖਾਣ (vakhaaṇ) *n m* Description, explanation.

ਵਖਾਨਣਾ (vakhaaṇnaa) *v* To describe, to relate, to explain.

ਵੱਖੀ (vakkhee) *n f* Side.

ਵੰਗ (vang) *n f* Glass bangle.

ਵਗਣਾ (vagṇaa) *v* To flow, to blow.

ਵਗਾਰ (vagaar) *n f* Forced or unpaid labour, bonded labour.

ਵੰਗਾਰ (vangaar) *n f* Challenge; ~**ਮੰਨਣੀ** To accept a challenge.

ਵੰਗਾਰਨਾ (vangaarnaa) *v* To challenge

ਵਚਨ (vachan) *n* (gr) (1) Number; singular number; **ਬਹੁ**~ plural number; (2) Speech, word, utterance, talk, promise; ~**ਬੱਧ** Committed.

ਵੰਚਿਤ (vanchit) *a* Deprived; ~**ਕਰਨਾ** To deprive.

ਵੱਛਾ (vachchaa) *n m* Calf.

ਵੰਜਣਾ (vanjṇaa) *v* To go, to part.

ਵਜਣਾ (vahṇaa) *v* To chime, to produce sound, to ring, to be struck; **ਨਾਂ** ~To be famous.

ਵਜਨ (vazan) *n m* Weight, burden, measure; ~**ਦਾਰ** Heavy, weighty.

ਵੰਜਾਉਣਾ (vanjaauṇaa) *v* To lose, to waste, to destroy.

ਵਜਾਉਣਾ (vajaauṇaa) *v* To play on a musical instrument; **ਢੋਲ**~ To beat a drum; **ਹੁਕਮ**~ To execute an order.

ਵਜ਼ਾਹਤ (vazaahat) *n f* Explanation,

elaboration, clarification; ~ਕਰਨਾ To elaborate, to explicate, to clarify.

ਵਜ਼ਾਰਤ (vazaarat) *n f* Ministry, cabinet; Ministership.

ਵਜ਼ੀਫ਼ਾ (vazeefaa) *n m* Scholarship, stipend.

ਵਜ਼ੀਰ (vazeer) *n m* Minister.

ਵਜ਼ੀਰੀ (vazeeree) *n m* Ministership.

ਵਜ਼ੀਰੇ-ਆਲ੍ਹਾ (vazeeree-aalhaa) *n m* Chief minister.

ਵਜ਼ੀਰੇ-ਆਜ਼ਮ (vazeere-aazam) *n m* Prime minister.

ਵਜੂਦ (vajood) *n m* Existence, body.

ਵੱਟਕ (vattak) *n f* Sale proceeds, takings.

ਵਟਣਾ (vatnaa) *v* To twist, to interwine, to be exchanged.

ਵੱਟਾ (vattaa) *n m* Stone, weight, measure, brickbat, discount; ~ਸੱਟਾ Exchange in trade, barter; ~ਖਾਤਾ Bad debt account, dead loss.

ਵਟਾਂਦਰਾ (vataandraa) *n m* Exchange, barter, replacement.

ਵੰਡਣਾ (vandnaa) *v* To divide, to distribute, to split, to allocate.

ਵੱਡਾ (vaddaa) *a n* Elder, great, senior, major; Share; ~ਦਿਨ Christmas day.

ਵੰਡਾਉਣਾ (vandaaunaa) *v* To divide, to distribute, to cause to be divided.

ਵਡਿਆਉਣਾ (vadiaaunaa) *v* To praise, to applaud, to puff up.

ਵਡਿਆਈ (vadiaaee) *n f* Praise, eulogy, greatness, excellence.

ਵੰਡੀਜਣਾ (vandeejnaa) *v* To be split.

ਵੱਡੀ ਮਾਤਾ (vaddee maataa) *n f* Small pox.

ਵਡੇਰਾ (vaderaa) *n m a* Ancestor, forefather; Larger, greater.

ਵੱਢਣਾ (vaddhnaa) *v* To cut, to amputate, to abscind.

ਵੱਢੀ (vaddhee) *n f* Bribe, hush money, illegal gratification; ~ਖ਼ੋਰੀ Bribery; ~ਦੇਣੀ To bribe.

ਵਣ (van) *n m* Wood, jungle, forest.

ਵਣਗੀ (vangee) *n f* Sample, specimen.

ਵਣਜ (vanaj) *n m* Business, trade, commerce.

ਵਤਨ (vatan) *n m* Motherland, fatherland, native country, one's own country, homeland.

ਵਤਨੀ (vatnee) *n m* Countryman, fellow countryman, compatriot, fellow citizen.

ਵਤੀਰਾ (vateeraa) *n m* Behaviour, treatment, attitude.

ਵਧਣਾ (vadhnaa) *v* To increase, to grow, to enlarge, to lengthen, to approach; ~ਫੁਲਣਾ To grow, to multiply.

ਵਧਾਉਣਾ (vandhaaunaa) *v* To extend,

ਵਧਾਈ (vadhaaee) *n f* Congratulation, felicitation.

ਵਧੀਆ (vadhiaa) *a* Fine, nice, excellent, superior; **~ਪਣ** Excellence, superiosity.

ਵਧੀਕ (vadheek) *adv* More, extra, in excess.

ਵਧੀਕੀ (vadheekee) *n f* Outrage, oppression.

ਵੰਨ ਸੁਵੰਨਾ (vann suvannaa) *adv* Of different shapes, of various kinds, variegated.

ਵੰਨਗੀ (vangee) *n f* Sample.

ਵਪਾਰ (vapaar) *n m* Business, trade; **~ਕ** Commercial, mercantile.

ਵਪਾਰੀ (vapaaree) *n m* Trader, businessman.

ਵਫ਼ਦ (vafad) *n f* Delegation.

ਵਫ਼ਾ (vafaa) *n f* Sincerity, fidelity, fulfilment of promise, **~ਦਾਰ** Faithful, loyal; **~ਦਾਰੀ** Loyalty, allegiance, faithfulness.

ਵਫ਼ਾਤ (vafaat) *n f* Death, demise.

ਵਰ (var) *n m* (1) Bridegroom, husband; (2) Boon, blessing, favour, solicitation.

ਵਰਸਣਾ (varasnaa) *v* To rain.

ਵਰਛਾ (varchaa) *n f* Rain. Also **ਵਰਖਾ**

ਵਰਸਾਉਣਾ (varsaaunaa) *v* To shower boons, benefaction or blessings. Also **ਵਰ ਦੇਣਾ**

ਵਰਕ (varak) *n m* Leaf (of gold, silver or tin).

ਵਰਕਾ (varkaa) *n m* Leaf (of book, etc.) folio; Piece of paper.

ਵਰਗ (varag) *n m* Square, a class, group, genus; **~ਸੰਘਰਸ਼** Class struggle; **~ਹੀਣ** Classless; **~ਭੇਦ** Class distinction, discrimination.

ਵਰਗਲਾਉਣਾ (varglaaunaa) *v* To seduce, to instigate, to coax.

ਵਰਗਾ (vargaa) *a* Similar, resembling, like.

ਵਰਜ਼ਸ਼ (varzash) *n f* Physical exercise, gymnastics (athletic).

ਵਰਜਣਾ (varjanaa) *v* To check, to forbid, to prohibit, to debar.

ਵਰਜਿਤ (varjit) *a* Forbidden, prohibited, banned, taboo, proscribed.

ਵਰਨ (varan) *n m* (1) Colour, caste; (2) Speech sound, a letter of alphabet; **~ਸੰਕਰ** Hybrid; **~ਹੀਨ** Casteless.

ਵਰਨਣ (varnan) *n m* Description, account, narration; **~ਕਰਨਾ** To describe, to narrate, to relate.

ਵਰਤ (varat) *n m* Fast; **~ਰਖਣਾ** To keep fast; **~ਲੈਣਾ** To take a fast.

ਵਰਤਨ (vartan) *n m* Treatment, dealings, use, business.

ਵਰਤਨਾ (vartanaa) *v* To use, to treat.

ਵਰਤਾਉਣਾ (vartaaunaa) To distribute.

ਵਰਦੀ (vardee) *n f* Uniform, dress.

ਵਰਧਨ (vardhan) *n m* Enhancement, increase, propagation.

ਵਰਯਾਮ (varlyaam) *n m* Brave person, hero.

ਵਰ੍ਹਾ (varhaa) *n m* Year.

ਵਰੀ (varee) *n f* Dresses, ornaments presented to bride by her in-laws.

ਵਲ (val) *a n m* Hale and hearty; Method, tact; Twist, coil, turn; ~ਹੋ ਜਾਣਾ To recoup, to recover health; ~ਪਾਉਣਾ To spiral, to make a loop.

ਵੱਲ (vall) *adv* On the side of, in The direction of, towards, against.

ਵਲਵਲਾ (valvalaa) *n m* Excitement, passion, sentimentality.

ਵਲਾਉਣਾ (valaaunaa) *v* To coil, to wrap round, to twist, to coax.

ਵਲਾਇਤ (valaait) *n f* Foreign country, alien country.

ਵਲਾਇਤੀ (vallaitee) *a* Foreign, European, Englishman. Also **ਵਲੈਤੀ**

ਵਲੀ (valee) *n m* Hermit, saint.

ਵਲੂੰਧਰ (valoondhar) *n m* Scratch.

ਵਲੂੰਧਰਨਾ (valoondharnaa) *v* To scratch, to claw.

ਵਲ੍ਹੇਟਨਾ (valhetnaa) *v* To fold, to wrap, to gird.

ਵੱਲੋਂ (valon) *adv* From, on behalf of, from the side of.

ਵੜਨਾ (varnaa) *v* To enter, to pierce, to step, to penetrate.

ਵਾਇਦਾ (vaaidaa) *n m* Promise; ~ਸ਼ਿਕਨ Promise breaker; ~ਖਿਲਾਫ਼ੀ Violation of commitment.

ਵਾਈ (vaaee) *n f* Flatulence.

ਵਾਸਕਟ (waaskat) *n m* Waist coat.

ਵਾਸਤਾ (vaastaa) *n m* Concern, relation, connection.

ਵਾਸਨਾ (vaasnaa) *n f* Lust, sensuality, desire, smell; ~ਮਈ Sensual, lusty.

ਵਾਹਿਗੁਰੁ (vaheguru) *n m* God, Almighty.

ਵਾਹਿਯਾਤ (vahiyaat) *a* Absurd, worthless.

ਵਾਹੁਣਾ (vaahunaa) *v* To plough, to till, to drive, (car, tonga etc), to discharge.

ਵਾਕਫ਼ (vaakaf) *n m a* Acquaintance; Conversant, knowing, aware of; ਨਾ~ Ignorant, unknown.

ਵਾਕਫ਼ੀਅਤ (vaafiat) *n f* Acquaintance, knowledge. Also **ਵਾਕਫ਼ੀ**

ਵਾਕਿਆ (vaakiaa) *n m* Event, incident, happening, news.

ਵਾਗ (vaag) *n f* Rein; ~ਗੁੰਦਣੀ To braid.

ਵਾਚਨਾ (vaachnaa) *v* To read, recite, study.

ਵਾਛੜ (vaachhar) *n f* Shower, rain.

ਵਾਜਬ (vaajab) *a* Reasonable, proper, fit, suitable.

ਵਾਜਬੀ (vaajbee) *a* Reasonable.

ਵਾਜਾ (vaajaa) *n m* Harmonium, musical instrument, band.

ਵਾਂਜਾ (vaanjaa) *a* Without, devoid of, lacking.

ਵਾਜ਼ਿਆ (vaaziaa) *a* Evident, clear, manfest, lucid; Explained, described, elucidated.

ਵਾਂਝਾ (vaanjhaa) *a* Bereft, divested, without.

ਵਾਢਾ (vaadhaa) *n m* Cut, mark of cutting.

ਵਾਣ (vaaṇ) *n m* Coarse twine for cot.

ਵਾਤਾਵਰਨ (vaataavaraṇ) *n m* Atmosphere, surroundings, climate.

ਵਾਦੀ (vaadee) *n f* Valley, vale.

ਵਾਧਾ (vaadhaa) *n m* Increase, extension, promotion, increment.

ਵਾਧੂ (vaadhoo) *a* Superfluous, not needed, in excels.

ਵਾਪਸ (vaapas) *a* Returned, given back; ~ਆਉਣਾ To come back, to return; ~ਦੇਣਾ To take back, to withdraw.

ਵਾਪਸੀ (vaapsee) *n f* Return, reversion.

ਵਾਪਰਨਾ (vaaparnaa) *v* To happen, occur, to come to pass, to take place, to befall.

ਵਾਬਸਤਾ (vaabastaa) *a* Connected, attached, linked, conjoint, conjunct, associated.

ਵਾਯੂ (vayoo) *n f* Air, wind.

ਵਾਰ (vaar) *n m* (1) Blow, attack, stroke; (2) Day; (3) Turn; Layer; (4) Sacrificing; Ballad.

ਵਾਰਸ (vaaras) *n m* Heir, successor; ~ਹੋਣਾ To succeed, to inherit.

ਵਾਰਸੀ (vaarsee) *n f* Inheriance, succession.

ਵਾਰਸ਼ਿਕ (vaarshik) *a* Yearly, annual.

ਵਾਰਤਾ (vaartaa) *n f* Negotiation, narrative, news, report; ~ਲਾਪ Dialogue, conversation, discourse.

ਵਾਰਦਾਤ (vaardaat) *n f* Incident, happening, affray, skirmish.

ਵਾਰਨਾ (vaarnaa) *v* To sacrifice, to devote, to offer something to deity.

ਵਾਲ (vaal) *n m* Hair; ~ਸੰਵਾਰਨ To comb the hair; ~ਵਾਲ ਬਚਨਾ To have a narrow escape.

ਵਾਲੀ (vaalee) *n m* Master, owner, lord, ruler, protector, guardian.

ਵਾਵੇਲਾ (vaavelaa) *n m* Hue and cry, outcry, clamour, lamentation.

ਵਾੜਨਾ (vaarnaa) *v* To thrust into, to stuff, to penetrate.

ਵਿਅਕਤਿਤਵ (viyaktitv) *n m* Personality.

ਵਿਅਕਤੀ (viyaktee) *n m* Person, individual; ~ਕਰਨ Individualisation; ~ਗਤ Personal, individual.

ਵਿਅੰਗ (viang) *n m* Irony, sarcasm, joke.

ਵਿਅਰਥ (viyarth) *a adv* Useless, fruitless, null; In vain, to no effect.

ਵਿਆਹ (viaah) *n m* Marriage, wedding, matrimony; ~ਕਰਨਾ To marry.

ਵਿਆਂਹਦੜ (viaanhdar) *n m* Bride, bridegroom, About to be married.

ਵਿਆਹੁਣਾ (viaahunaa) *v* To marry, to wed.

ਵਿਆਕਰਨ (viaakaaran) *n m* Grammar, Science of language.

ਵਿਆਕੁਲ (viaakul) *a* Confounded, distempered, impatient, agitated.

ਵਿਆਖਿਆ (viaakhiyaa) *n f* Elucidation, description, explanation; ~ਕਰਨੀ To elucidate, to expound, to interpret, to describe; ~ਪਰਕ Interpretative; ~ਤਮਕ Explanatory, elucidatory; ~ਨ Speech, ration, discourse.

ਵਿਆਜ (viaaj) *n m* Interest; ~ਖੋਰੀ Usury.

ਵਿਆਪਤ (viaapat) *a* Diffused, pervading, spread.

ਵਿਸਤਾਰ (vistaar) *n m* Extersion, expansion, elaboration, detail; ~ਕ Amplifying, amplifier; ~ਪੂਰਬਕ Indetail; ~ਵਾਦ Expansionism.

ਵਿ ਸਥਾਪਿਤ (visthaapit) *a* Displaced.

ਵਿਸਫੋਟ (visphot) *n m* Explosion, violent out burst.

ਵਿਸਰਜਨ (visarjan) *n m* Adjournment.

ਵਿਸਰਣ (visaran) *n m* Forgetfulness, forgetting.

ਵਿਸਰਨਾ (visarnaa) *v* To forget, to be forgotten.

ਵਿਸ਼ਰਾਮ (vishraam) *n m* Rest, repose, relaxation, stop; ~ਚਿੰਨ੍ਹ Punctuation.

ਵਿਸ਼ਵ (vishw) *n m* World, universe, cosmos; ~ਕੋਸ਼ Encyclopaedia; ~ਵਿਦਿਆਲਾ University.

ਵਿਸ਼ਵਾਸ (vishwass) *n m* Faith, belief, trust, reliance; ~ਕਰਨਾ To believe, to trust, to rely, to accredit; ~ਘਾਤ Betrayal, treason, deception, violation of trust; ~ਪਤਰ Credentials; ~ਪਾਤਰ Faithfully. Also ਵਿਸਾਹ

ਵਿਸਾਰਨਾ (visaarnaa) *v* To forget.

ਵਿਸੈਲਾ (vishailaa) *a* Poisonous, virose, toxic.

ਵਿਹਲੜ (vehlar) *a* Idle, unoccupied, unemployed, indolent, lazy, slothful.

ਵਿਹਲਾ (vehlaa) *a* Leisured, unoccupied, idle, unemployed, unengaged, not busy, relaxing.

ਵਿਕਣਾ (viknaa) *v* To be sold, to sell.

ਵਿੱਕਰੀ (vikkree) *n f* Sale, quantity sold, sale proceeds.

ਵਿਕਲਪ (vikalap) *n m* Alternation; alternate.

ਵਿਕਾਸ (vikaas) *n m* Development, evolution; ~ਸ਼ੀਲ Developing; evolving; ~ਵਾਦ Evolution.

ਵਿਖਾਉਣਾ (vikhaaunaa) *v* To show.

ਵਿਖਾਈ (vikjaaee) *n f* Showing, unveiling.

ਵਿਗੜਨਾ (vigarnaa) *v* To be spoiled, to be damaged, to be deteriorate.

ਵਿੰਗਾ (vingaa) *a* crooked, bent, not straight; ~ਤੜਿੰਗਾ Curved, wavy, uneven.

ਵਿਗਾੜ (vigaar) *n m* Breach, discord rupture, damage, disorder, deformity, impairment.

ਵਿਗਾੜਨਾ (vigaarnaa) *v* To spoil, to demage, to destory, to bungle.

ਵਿਗਿਆਨ (vigiaan) *n m* Science; ਅਰਥ~ Economics; ਸਮਾਜ~ Sociology; ਭਾਸ਼ਾ~ Lingiustics; ਪ੍ਰਾਣੀ~ Zoology; ਮਨੋ~ Psychology; ਰਸਾਇਣ~ Chemistry.

ਵਿਗਿਆਨਿਕ (vigiaanik) *a* Scientific.

ਵਿਗਿਆਨੀ (vigiaanee) *n m* Scientist.

ਵਿਗਿਆਪਨ (vigiaapan) *n m* Advertisement.

ਵਿਘਟਨ (vighatan) *n m* Disintegration, disorganisation, dissociation.

ਵਿਘਨ (vighan) *n m* Hitch, interruption, obtacle, hindrance.

ਵਿਚ (vich) Prep Inside, in, into; ~ਕਾਰ Among, during, in between, intermediate.

ਵਿਚਰਨਾ (vicharnaa) *v* To wander, to stroll about, to go.

ਵਿਚਾਰ (vichaar) *n m* Notion, idea, feeling, consideration, opinion, view, judgement; ~ਸ਼ੀਲ Deliberative; ~ਕਰਨਾ To consider, to ponder, to calculate; ~ਮੂਲਕ Ideational; ~ਵਾਨ Thinker, philosopher.

ਵਿਚਾਰਾ (vichaaraa) *a* Helpless, poor, wretched.

ਵਿਚਾਰਲਾ (vichaarlaa) *a* Middle, intermediate. Also ਵਿਚਾਲਾ

ਵਿਚੋਲਾ (vicholaa) *n m* Mediator, middleman.

ਵਿਛਣਾ (vichhnaa) *v* To be spread, to be stretched.

ਵਿਛੜਨਾ (vichharnaa) *v* To be separate, to part.

ਵਿਛਾਉਣਾ (vichhaaunaa) *v n m* To spread; Bedding.

ਵਿਛੋੜਾ (vichhoraa) *n m* Separation, parting, detachment.

ਵਿਜੈ (vijai) *n f* Conquest, victory.

ਵਿਜੋਗ (vijog) *n m* Separation, disunion, absence.

ਵਿੱਤ (vitt) *n m* Finance.

ਵਿਥ (vitth) *n f* Distance, difference, space.

ਵਿਦਰੋਹੀ (vidrohee) *a* Rebellious.

ਵਿਦਵਾਨ (vidwaan) *n m* Scholar, learned person.

ਵਿਦਾ (vidaa) *n f* Farewell, adieu, departure; ~**ਈ** Parting, departure, send off.

ਵਿਦਿਆ (vidiyaa) *n f* Education, instruction, learning, knowledge, study; ~**ਰਥੀ** Student, pupil; ~**ਲਾ** School, educational institution.

ਵਿਦੂਸ਼ਕ (vidooshak) *n m* Buffoon, clown.

ਵਿਦੇਸ਼ (videsh) *n m* Foreign country.

ਵਿਦੇਸ਼ੀ (videshee) *n m a* Foreigner; Foreign, aline.

ਵਿਧਾਤਾ (vidhaataa) *n m* Maker, God, providence.

ਵਿਧਾਨ (vidhaan) *n m* Legislation, constitution.

ਵਿਧੀ (vidhee) *n f* Method, manner.

ਵਿਨ੍ਹਣਾ (vinnhṇaa) *v* To pierce, to perforate.

ਵਿਨਾਸ਼ (vinaash) *n m* Destruction, ruin, annihilation, disaster.

ਵਿਪਖ (vipakh) *n m* Opposition.

ਵਿੱਪਖੀ (vipakhee) *a* Opponent, antagonist, antagonistic; Hostile, opposing.

ਵਿਫਲ (viphal) *a* Unsuccessful, fruitless, vain; ~**ਤਾ** Failure, uselessness.

ਵਿਭਚਾਰ (vibhchaar) *n m* Adultery, fornication, prostitution.

ਵਿਭਾਗ (vibhaag) *n m* Department.

ਵਿਭਾਗੀ (vibhaagee) *a* Departmental.

ਵਿਭਾਜਨ (vibhaajan) *n m* Division.

ਵਿਮਾਨ (vimaan) *n m* Aeroplane; ~**ਚਾਲਣ** Aerial navigation; ~**ਚਾਲਕ** Pilot.

ਵਿਮੋਚਨ (vimochan) *n m* Release, acquittal.

ਵਿਰਲਾ (virlaa) *a* Rare.

ਵਿਰਾਸਤ (viraasat) *n f* Inheritance, heredity, legacy.

ਵਿਰਾਨਾ (viraanaa) *n m* Ruins, deserted place.

ਵਿਰਾਮ (viraam) *n m* Stoppage, respite, cessation, prorogation.

ਵਿਰੇਚਨ (virechan) *n m* Purgation.

ਵਿਰੋਧ (virodh) *n m* Hostility, resistance, discord, opposition, discrepancy contradiction, constrast.

ਵਿਰੋਧੀ (virodhee) *a n m* Opposing, antagonistic; Hostile.

ਵਿਲਕਣਾ (vilakṇaa) *v* To sob, to weep, to lament, to cry.

ਵਿਵਹਾਰ (vivhaar) *n m* Behaviour; Conduct

ਵਿਵਾਦ (vivaad) *n m* Controversy, dispute; ~**ਗ੍ਰਸਤ** disputed, controversial.

ਵਿਵੇਕ (vivek) *n m* Discretion, reason; ~**ਸ਼ੀਲ** Rational; ~**ਹੀਨ** Irrational, unreasonable.

ਵਿਵੇਕੀ (vivekee) *a* Discretionary.

ਵੀ (vee) *adv* As well as, even.

ਵੀਹ (veeh) *a* Twenty.

ਵੀਟਣਾ (veetnaa) *v* To spill, to throw away.

ਵੀਰ (veer) *n m a* Brother; Brave, gallant, valiant.

ਵੀਰਾਨ (veeraan) *a* Deserted, desolate, uninhabited; ~**ਕਰਨਾ** To lay waste, to devastate.

ਵੇਸਣ (vesan) *n m* Gramflour.

ਵੇਖਣਾ (vekhnaa) *v* To see, to look, to observe, to view.

ਵੇਚਣਾ (vechnaa) *v* To sell, to dispose of, to vend.

ਵੇਦੀ (vedee) *n f* Altar.

ਵੇਰਵਾ (vervaa) *n m* Detail, particulars, description.

ਵੇਲਾ (velaa) *n m* Time, hour, occasion; **ਵੱਡਾ**~ Morning.

ਵੇਲ੍ਹਣਾ (vernaa) *v* To encircle, to enclose, to collect (scattered animals), to hem in fold.

ਵੇੜ੍ਹਾ (verhaa) *n m* Compound, courtyard; Patio.

ਵੈਣ (vain) *n m* Dirge, funeral song, threnody.

ਵੈਰ (vair) *n m* Enmity, ill will, hostility; **ਜੱਦੀ**~ Vendetta; ~**ਕਢਣਾ** To take revenge, to retaliate; ~**ਮੁੱਲ ਲੈਣਾ** To create bad bood.

ਵੈਰੀ (vairee) *n m* Enemy, foe, hostile person.

ਵੈਰਾਗ (vairaag) *n m* Renunciation, alienation, dejection, disconsolation.

ੜ

ੜ Thirtyfifth letter of Gurmukhi alphabets, pronounced as 'raaraa'.

ੜਾੜ (raar) *n f* Quarrel, dispute, wrangle, fight.

ENGLISH-PUNJABI DICTIONARY

A

A, a (ਏਇ) *n* ਰੋਮਨ ਵਰਨਮਾਲਾ ਦਾ ਪਹਿਲਾ ਅੱਖਰ, ਪਹਿਲੀ ਗੱਲ

a, an (ਅ, ਅਨ) *a* ਇਕ, ਕੋਈ ਇਕ, ਕੋਈ; ਫ਼ੀ, ਪ੍ਰਤੀ

A 1, A one (ਏਇ'ਵਅੱਨ) *a* ਉੱਤਮ, ਸ੍ਰੇਸ਼ਠ

aback (ਅ'ਬੈਕ) adv ਪਿੱਛੇ, ਪਿਛਲੇ ਪਾਸੇ, ਪਿਠ, ਵੱਲ, ਹਟਦਾ, ਪਿਛਾਂਹ ਨੂੰ; taken~ ਹੈਰਾਨ, ਡੌਰ-ਭੌਰ, ਚਕਿਤ

abandon (ਅ'ਬੈਂ ਡਅਨ) *v n* ਛੱਡਣਾ, ਛੱਡ ਦੇਣਾ; ਤਜਣਾ, ਤਿਆਗਣਾ, (ਦੇ) ਹਵਾਲੇ ਕਰਨਾ, ਖਹਿੜਾ ਛੱਡ ਦੇਣਾ, ਕਿਸੇ ਜਜ਼ਬੇ ਜਾਂ ਵਾਸਨਾ ਅਧੀਨ ਹੋਣਾ, ਸਾਥ ਛੱਡਣਾ; ਤਿਆਗ; ~ed ਛੱਡਿਆ, ਤਿਆਗਿਆ, ਵੀਰਾਨ, ਤੱਜਿਆ, ਲੁੱਚ-ਲਫ਼ੰਗਾ; ~ment ਤਿਆਗ, ਛੱਡ-ਛੜ੍ਹ; ਬੇਪਰਵਾਹੀ

abase (ਅ'ਬੇਇਸ) *v* ਨਿਰਾਦਰੀ ਕਰਨੀ, ਬੇਕਦਰੀ ਕਰਨੀ; ~ment ਨਿਰਾਦਰੀ, ਅਨਾਦਰ, ਬੇਕਦਰੀ

abask (ਅ'ਬਾਸਕ) *adv* ਧੁੱਪੇ

abate (ਅ'ਬੇਇਟ) *v* ਘਟਾਉਣਾ, ਘਟਣਾ, ਮੱਧਮ ਕਰਨਾ, ਮੱਧਮ ਹੋਣਾ, ਮੱਠਾ ਕਰਨਾ, ਮੱਠਾ ਪੈਣਾ, (ਰੋਗ ਦਾ) ਘੱਟ ਹੋਣਾ, ਮੰਦਾ ਪੈਣਾ; ਕਟੌਤੀ ਕਰਨੀ; ~ment ਕਮੀ

abbe (ਐਬੇਇ) *n* ਮਹੰਤ

abbey (ਐਬਿ) *n* ਮੱਠ

abbot (ਐਬਅਟ) *n* ਮਹੰਤ, ਮੱਠ ਦਾ ਸੁਆਮੀ

abbreviate (ਅ'ਬਰੀਵਿਏਇਟ) *v a* ਸੰਖੇਪ ਕਰਨਾ, ਛੋਟਾ ਰੂਪ ਦੇਣਾ; ਸਾਰ ਕੱਢਣਾ; ਸੰਖਿਪਤ, ਸੰਖੇਪ; ~d ਸੰਖਿਪਤ, ਸੰਖੇਪ, ਕੱਟਿਆ-ਵੱਢਿਆ

abbreviation (ਅਬਰੀਵਿਏਇਸ਼ਨ) *n* ਛੋਟਾ ਰੂਪ, ਸੰਖੇਪ, ਸੰਖਿਪਤ ਰੂਪ

ABC (ਏਇ ਬੀ ਸੀ) *n* ਵਰਨਮਾਲਾ, ਊੜਾ-ਐੜਾ; ਵਿਸ਼ੇ ਸਬੰਧੀ ਮੁੱਢਲੀਆ ਗੱਲਾਂ, ਆਰੰਭਕ ਜਾਣਕਾਰੀ

abdicate ('ਐਬਡਿਕੇਇਟ) *v* ਪਦ ਜਾਂ ਅਧਿਕਾਰ ਦਾ ਤਿਆਗਣਾ, ਰਾਜ-ਕਾਜ ਤਿਆਗਣਾ

abdication ('ਐਬਡਿ'ਕੇਇਸ਼ਨ) *n* ਪਦ-ਤਿਆਗ, ਰਾਜ-ਤਿਆਗ

abdomen ('ਐਬਡਅਮਅਨ) *n* ਢਿੱਡ, ਉਦਰ; ਕੀੜਿਆਂ ਆਦਿ ਦਾ ਢਿੱਡ

abdominal ('ਐਬ'ਡੌਮਿਨਲ) *a* ਢਿੱਡ ਦਾ, ਢਿੱਡ ਨਾਲ ਸਬੰਧਤ

abdominous (ਐਬ'ਡੌਮਿਨਅਸ) *a* ਢਿੱਡਲ, ਵੱਡੇ ਢਿੱਡ ਵਾਲਾ

abduct (ਅਬਡਅੱਕਟ) *v* ਅਗਵਾ ਕਰਨਾ, ਅਪਹਰਨ ਕਰਨਾ, ਉਧਾਲਣਾ; ~ion ਉਧਾਲਾ, ਅਗਵਾ, ਅਪਹਰਨ; ਸਰੀਰਕ ਅੰਗ ਦੇ ਟਿਕਾਣੇ ਤੋਂ ਹਟਣ ਦੀ ਕਿਰਿਆ; (ਤਰਕ) ਸੰਦੇਹਜਨਕ ਅਨੁਮਾਨ; ~or ਉਧਾਲੂ, ਅਗਵਾ ਕਰਤਾ, ਭਜਾ ਲੈ ਜਾਣ ਵਾਲਾ; ਉੱਤਰਿਆ ਅੰਗ

abeyance (ਅ'ਬੇਇਅੰਸ) *n* ਮੁਲਤਵੀ ਕਰਨਾ, ਅੱਗੇ ਪਾਉਣ, ਆਰਜ਼ੀ ਰੋਕ, ਅਟਕਾਉ

abhor (ਅਬ'ਹੋ*) *v* ਘਿਰਨਾ ਕਰਨੀ, ਨਫ਼ਰਤ ਕਰਨੀ; ~rence ਸਖ਼ਤ ਨਫ਼ਰਤ, ਘਿਰਨਾ; ~rent ਘਿਨਾਉਣਾ, ਘਿਰਨਾਜਨਕ, ਭ੍ਰਿਸ਼ਟ, ਤਿਰਸਕਾਰਯੋਗ; ਅਸੰਗਤ, ਬੇਮੇਲ, ਅਢੁੱਕਵਾਂ

abide (ਅ'ਬਾਇਡ) *v* ਟਿਕੇ ਰਹਿਣਾ, ਸਥਿਰ ਰਹਿਣਾ, ਕਾਇਮ ਰਹਿਣਾ ਜਾਂ ਰੱਖਣਾ; ਸਹਿਣਾ,

ਝੱਲਣਾ, ਪਾਬੰਦ ਰਹਿਣਾ, ਪੱਕੇ ਰਹਿਣਾ, ਪਾਲਣਾ ਕਰਨੀ

abiding (ਅ'ਬਾਇਡਿਙ) *a* ਪੱਕਾ, ਸਥਿਰ, ਟਿਕਵਾਂ, ਚਿਰਸਥਾਈ, ਕਾਇਮ ਰਹਿਣ ਵਾਲਾ

ability (ਅ'ਬਿਲਅਟਿ) *n* ਯੋਗਤਾ, ਕਾਬਲੀਅਤ, ਲਿਆਕਤ, ਕੁਸ਼ਲਤਾ, ਪ੍ਰਵੀਣਤਾ, ਸਮਰੱਥਾ, ਬਲ, ਹੈਸਿਅਤ; ਪ੍ਰਤਿਭਾ

abject (ਐਬਜੈਕਟ) *a v n* ਨੀਚ, ਕਮੀਨਾ, ਮੰਦਾ, ਹੀਣ, ਘਟੀਆ, ਮਾੜਾ, ਕਮੀਨਾ ਆਦਮੀ; **~ion** ਘਟੀਆਪਨ, ਖ਼ੁਆਰੀ; **~ness** ਨੀਚਤਾ, ਹੀਣਤਾ

abjure (ਅਬ'ਜੁਅ*) *v* (ਤੋਂ) ਤੋਬਾ ਕਰਨੀ, (ਦੀ) ਸਹੁੰ ਪਾਉਣੀ

ablative (ਐਬਲਅਟਿਵ਼) *a n* (ਵਿਆ) ਅਪਾਦਾਨ ਕਾਰਕ, ਸੰਸਕ੍ਰਿਤ ਵਿਆਕਰਣ ਵਿਚ ਪੰਜਵੀਂ ਵਿਭਕਤੀ

ablaze (ਅਬਲੇਇਜ਼) *a adv pred* ਮੱਚਦਾ, ਭੜਕਦਾ, ਉਤੇਜਤ

able ('ਏਇਬਲ) *a* ਯੋਗ, ਸਮਰੱਥ, ਪ੍ਰਵੀਣ, ਲਾਇਕ, ਕਾਬਲ, ਕੁਸ਼ਲ, ਗੁਣੀ; ਹੱਢਿਆ; **~bodied** ਤਕੜਾ, ਰਿਸ਼ਟ-ਪੁਸ਼ਟ, ਬਲਵਾਨ

ablution (ਅ'ਬਲੂਸ਼ਨ) *n* (ਆਮ ਤੌਰ ਤੇ ਬਹੁ ਵਚਨ) ਪੰਜ-ਇਸ਼ਨਾਨਾ, ਨਹਾਉਣ-ਧੋਣ, ਵਜ਼ੂ, ਸੁੱਧੀ

abnegate ('ਐਬਨਿਗੇਇਟ) *v* ਮਨ ਮਾਰਨਾ, ਪਰਹੇਜ਼ ਕਰਨਾ, ਛੱਡ ਦੇਣਾ, (ਅਧਿਕਾਰ ਆਦਿ ਨੂੰ) ਤਿਆਗਣਾ

abnegation (ਐਬਨਗੇਸ਼ਨ) *n* ਸੰਜਮ, ਪਰਹੇਜ਼, ਤਿਆਗ

abnormal (ਐਬ'ਨੋਰਮਲ) *a* ਅਸਾਧਾਰਨ , ਵਿਲੱਖਣ, ਵਚਿੱਤਰ, ਅਸੁਭਾਵਕ, ਅਸਚਰਜ, ਨਿਯਮ ਵਿਰੁੱਧ, ਕਸੂਤਾ, ਕੁਢੱਬਾ; **~ity**
ਅਸਧਾਰਨਤਾ, ਵਿਲੱਖਣਤਾ, ਵਿਚਿੱਤਰਤਾ, ਅਸੁਭਾਵਕਤਾ, ਬੇਕਾਇਦਗੀ, ਅਸਚਰਜਤਾ, ਵੱਖਰਾਪਣ

aboard (ਅ'ਬੋ:ਡ) *adv prep* (ਜਹਾਜ਼ ਜਾਂ ਗੱਡੀ) ਵਿਚ; (ਇਕ ਜਹਾਜ਼ ਦਾ ਦੂਜੇ ਜਹਾਜ਼ ਦੇ) ਨੇੜੇ (ਹੋਣਾ), ਨਾਲ ਨਾਲ

abode (ਅ'ਬਅਉਡ) *n* ਘਰ, ਨਿਵਾਸ-ਸਥਾਨ , ਮਕਾਨ ; ਟਿਕਾਣਾ, ਰਹਿਣ ਦੀ ਥਾਂ, ਰਿਹਾਇਸ਼

abolish (ਅ'ਬੋਲਿਸ਼) *v* ਅੰਤ ਕਰਨਾ, ਮਨਸੂਖ਼ ਕਰਨਾ, ਬੰਦ ਕਰਨਾ, ਹਟਾਉਣਾ, ਰੱਦਣਾ (ਰਿਵਾਜ ਆਦਿ ਨੂੰ) ਤੋੜਨਾ; **~ ment** ਅੰਤ, ਖ਼ਾਤਮਾ, ਮਨਸੂਖ਼ੀ, ਮੌਕੂਫ਼ੀ; (ਗ਼ੁਲਾਮੀ ਦੀ ਪ੍ਰਥਾ ਦਾ) ਕਾਨੂੰਨ ਰਾਹੀਂ ਅੰਤ

abominable (ਅ'ਬੋਮਿਨਅਬਲ) *a* ਘਿਰਣਾਜਨਕ, ਗੰਦਾ, ਕਰੂਜਾ, ਨਿੰਦਾਯੋਗ, ਭੈੜਾ ; ਕੁਲੱਛਣਾ

abomination (ਅ'ਬੋਮਿ'ਨੇਇਸ਼ਨ) *n* ਘਿਰਣਾ, ਨਫ਼ਰਤ, ਕਰਹਿਤ; ਘਿਰਣਾਯੋਗ ਕੰਮ ਜਾਂ ਆਦਤ

aboriginal ('ਐਬਅ'ਰਿਜਅਨਲ) *n a* ਆਦਿਵਾਸੀ, ਮੁਢਲੀ ਵਸਤੂ ਜਾਂ ਚੀਜ਼, ਪ੍ਰਾਚੀਨ, ਜਾਂਗਲੀ; **~ity** ਆਦਿਕਾਲੀਨਤਾ; **~s** ਆਦਿਵਾਸੀ, ਕਿਸੇ ਦੇਸ਼ ਦੇ ਮੂਲ ਵਸਨੀਕ

aborigines ('ਐਬਅ'ਰਿਜਅਨੀਜ਼) *n pl* ਆਦਿਵਾਸੀ, ਪੁਰਾਣੇ ਜਾਂਗਲੀ ਲੋਕ

abort (ਅ'ਬੋਟ) *v* (ਪਸ਼ੂਆਂ ਦਾ) ਤੂਣਾ, ਗਰਭਪਾਤ ਹੋਣਾ; ਮੁਰਝਾ ਜਾਣਾ; (ਯੋਜਨਾ ਆਦਿ) ਤਿਰਛੇ ਫਿਸ ਹੋਣਾ, ਠੱਪ ਹੋਣਾ; **~ion** ਪਸ਼ੂਆਂ ਦੇ ਤੂਣ ਦੀ ਕਿਰਿਆ, ਗਰਭਪਾਤ

abound (ਅ'ਬਾਉਂਡ) *v* ਭਰਪੂਰ ਹੋਣਾ, ਬਹੁਤਾਤ ਹੋਣੀ, ਕਾਫ਼ੀ ਹੋਣਾ, ਰੱਜੇ-ਪੁੱਜੇ ਹੋਣਾ, ਕਿਸੇ ਸਥਾਨ ਦਾ ਤਰੀਕਾ ਹੋਣਾ, ਛਲਕਣਾ

about (ਅ'ਬਾਉਟ) *adv prep* ਸਬੰਧ ਵਿਚ,

ਬਾਰੇ, ਵਿਸ਼ੇ ਵਿਚ, ਬਾਬਤ; ਧ੍ਰੰਮ ਕੇ, ਲਗਭਗ, ਤੇ, ਲਾਗੇ, ਕੋਲ, ਦੁਆਲੇ, ਚੁਫੇਰੇ, ਇੱਧਰ-ਉੱਧਰ, ਨੇੜੇ-ਤੇੜੇ; be~ ਕਰਨ ਲੱਗਣਾ, ਆਹਰ ਵਿਚ ਹੋਣਾ; bring~ ਕਰਾਉਣਾ, ਕਰਵਾ ਲੈਣਾ, ਹੋਂਦ ਵਿਚ ਲਿਆਉਣਾ; go~ ਕਰਨ ਲੱਗਣਾ, ਕਰਨ ਦੇ ਆਹਰ ਵਿਚ ਲੱਗਣਾ

above (ਅ'ਬਅੱਵ) *adv prep* ਉੱਤੇ, ਉੱਪਰ, ਉਤਾਂਹ, ਉੱਪਰ ਲਿਖਤ, ਉੱਪਰੋਕਤ, ਉਕਤ, ਸਿਰ ਉੱਤੇ, ਕੋਠੇ ਉੱਤੇ, ਉਤਲੇ ਪਾਸਿਓਂ ਆਉਂਦਾ (ਪਾਣੀ, ਨਦੀ, ਸੜਕ), ਆਕਾਸ਼ ਵਿਚ; ਪਰਲੋਕ ਵਿਚ; ~all ਸਭ ਤੋਂ ਵੱਧ ਇਹ ਕਿ; ~board ਖੁੱਲ੍ਹਮ-ਖੁੱਲ੍ਹਾ, ਸਪਸ਼ਟ ਰੂਪ ਵਿਚ, ਪਰਗਟ ਰੂਪ ਵਿਚ, ਖ਼ਰਾ, ਈਮਾਨਦਾਰ; ~ground ਜੀਉਂਦਾ-ਜਾਗਦਾ, ਜਾਨਦਾਰ; ~mentioned ਉੱਤੇ ਦੱਸਿਆ ਜਾਂ ਦਿੱਤਾ, ਉਪਰੋਕਤ, ਉਕਤ, ਉਪਰਲਿਖਤ; ~measure ਅਣਮਿਣਵਾਂ, ਬੇਹਿਸਾਬ, ਬੇਹੱਦ; ~par ਅੰਕਤ ਮੁੱਲ ਤੋਂ ਵੱਧ, ਸਧਾਰਨ ਤੋਂ ਵਧੇਰੇ, ਵਧ ਕੇ; over and~ ਇਸ ਤੋਂ ਇਲਾਵਾ, ਇਸ ਤੋਂ ਛੁੱਟ, ਅਤੇ ਨਾਲ ਹੀ

abrasion (ਅਬਰੇਇਯਨ) *n* ਰਗੜ, ਘਸਰ, ਘਿਸਾਈ, ਖੁਰਚ; ਖੁਰਚਣ ਨਾਲ ਪਿਆ ਜ਼ਖਮ

abrasive (ਅਬਰੇਇਸਿਵ) *a n* ਘਸਵਾਂ; ਰਗੜਨ ਵਾਲੀ ਵਸਤੂ

abreast (ਅਬਰੇਸਟ) *adv* ਨਾਲ-ਨਾਲ, ਬਰਾਬਰ ਤੇ; ਸਮੇਂ ਦੇ ਨਾਲ ਜਾਂ ਅਨੁਸਾਰ

abridge (ਅ'ਬਰਿਜ) *v* ਸੰਖੇਪ ਕਰਨਾ, ਛੋਟਾ ਕਰਨਾ, ਘਟਾਉਣਾ, ਖੁਲਾਸਾ ਕਰਨਾ; (ਅਧਿਕਾਰ ਜਾਂ ਵਸਤੂ) ਵਾਂਝਿਆ ਕਰਨਾ; ~d ਸੰਖਿਪਤ, ਛੋਟਾ; ~ment ਸੰਖੇਪ, ਖੁਲਾਸਾ, ਨਿਚੋੜ, ਸਾਰ; ਸੰਖੇਪੀਕਰਨ

abroad (ਅ'ਬਰੋਡ) *adv n* ਬਾਹਰ, ਪਰਦੇਸ, ਦੂਰ-ਦੁਰਾਡੀ ਥਾਂ

abrogate ('ਐਬਰਅ(ਉ)'ਗੇਇਸਟ) *v* ਰੱਦ ਕਰਨਾ, ਮਨਸੂਖ ਕਰਨਾ, ਨਿਰਕਰਨ ਕਰਨਾ, (ਕਾਨੂੰਨ ਆਦਿ ਰਿਵਾਜ ਨੂੰ) ਹਟਾ ਦੇਣਾ, ਭੰਗ ਕਰਨਾ, ਬੰਦ ਕਰਨਾ; ~d ਰੱਦਿਆ, ਹਟਾਇਆ

abrogation ('ਐਬਰਅ(ਉ)'ਗੇਇਸ਼ਨ) *n* ਖੰਡਨ, ਮਨਸੂਖੀ, ਨਿਰਕਰਨ, ਅੰਤ

abrupt (ਅ'ਬਰਅੱਪਟ) *a n* ਅਚਨਚੇਤ, ਅਚਾਨਕ; ਅਸੰਗਤ; ਬੇਢੰਗਾ, ਬੇਜੋੜ; (ਚੜ੍ਹਾਈ) ਸੁਖੜ, (ਬਣ) ਰੁੰਡ, (ਧਰਤੀ ਵਿਚੋਂ) ਅਚਨਚੇਤ ਫੁੱਟਿਆ ਹੋਇਆ

abruption (ਅ'ਬਰਅੱਪਸ਼ਨ) *n* ਨਿਖੇਤਰ, ਕਿਸੇ ਅੰਗ ਦੇ ਝੜਨ ਦੀ ਕਿਰਿਆ

abruptly (ਅ'ਬਰਅੱਪਟਲਿ) *adv* ਅਚਾਨਕ, ਝਟਪਟ

abscond (ਅ'ਬਸਕੌਂਡ) *v* ਫ਼ਰਾਰ ਹੋ ਜਾਣਾ, ਭਗੌੜਾ ਹੋਣਾ, ਨਠ ਜਾਣਾ, ਚੋਰੀ ਛਿੱਪੀ ਭੱਜ ਜਾਣਾ, ਕਾਨੂੰਨ ਦੀ ਮਾਰ ਤੋਂ ਬਚਣ ਲਈ ਕਿਧਰੇ ਲੁਕ-ਛਿਪ ਜਾਣਾ; ~ence ਫ਼ਰਾਰੀ, ਭਗੌੜਾਪਣ; ~er ਭਗੌੜਾ, ਫ਼ਰਾਰ, ਕਾਨੂੰਨ ਦੀ ਮਾਰ ਤੋਂ ਬਚਣ ਲਈ ਛਿਪਿਆ

absence (ਐਬਸੰਸ) *n* ਗ਼ੈਰਹਾਜ਼ਰੀ, ਅਣਉਪਸਥਿਤੀ; ਅਣਹੋਂਦ, ਘਾਟ; ਅਭਾਵ ਬੇਇਮਾਨੀ, ਬੇਖ਼ਿਆਲੀ

absent (ਅਬ'ਸੈਂਟ) *v a* ਗ਼ੈਰਹਾਜ਼ਰ ਹੋਣਾ, ਗਾਇਬ ਹੋਣਾ, ਲੁਕ ਜਾਣਾ; ਗ਼ੈਰਹਾਜ਼ਰ, ਅਣਉਪਸਥਿਤ, ਅਚੇਤ, ਬੇਧਿਆਨ; ~ee ਗ਼ੈਰਹਾਜ਼ਰ ਵਿਅਕਤੀ; ~minded ਬੇਧਿਆਨਾ, ਅਚੇਤ, ਅਵੇਸਲਾ, ਭਰਾਂਤ ਚਿੱਤ, ਭੁੱਲਿਆ-ਭੁੱਲਿਆ; ~mindedness ਬੇਧਿਆਨੀ, ਭਰਾਂਤੀ, ਅਚੇਤਤਾ, ਅਵੇਸਲਾਪਣ

absolute ('ਐਬਸਅਲੂਟ) *a* ਪੂਰਾ, ਨਿਰਾ, ਉੱਕਾ

ਕੇਵਲ; ਨਿਰਪੇਖ, ਪੂਰਨ, ਸੰਪੂਰਨ; ਸਰਬ ਅਧਿਕਾਰੀ; **~ly** ਪੂਰਨਬਾਂਤ, ਪੂਰੀ ਤਰ੍ਹਾਂ, ਪਰਮ, ਆਪਣੇ ਆਪ, ਬਿਲਕੁਲ, ਸੁਤੰਤਰਤਾ ਨਾਲ ਬਿਨਾ ਕਿਸੇ ਸ਼ਰਤ ਤੋਂ, ਮੂਲੋਂ, ਉੱਕਾ ਹੀ; **~ness** ਨਿਰਪੇਖਤਾ, ਅਸੀਮਤਾ, ਨਿਰੰਕੁਸ਼ਤਾ, ਖ਼ੁਦਮੁਖਤਾਰੀ, ਪੂਰਨ ਅਧਿਕਾਰ

absorb (ਐਬ'ਸੋਬ) *v* ਹਜ਼ਮ ਕਰਨਾ, ਰਚਾ ਲੈਣਾ, ਆਤਮਸਾਤ ਕਰਨਾ, ਲੀਨ ਕਰਨਾ, ਸਮਾ ਲੈਣਾ, ਖਪਾ ਲੈਣਾ, ਤਦਰੂਪ ਕਰਨਾ; **~ed** ਚੂਸਿਆ, ਇਕਮਿਕ ਕੀਤਾ; ਰਚਿਆ; ਰਚਾਇਆ, ਲੀਨ, ਮਸਤ, ਮਗਨ; (ਜਿਵੇਂ ਸਿਆਹੀ-ਚੂਸ); **~ing** ਮਨਮੋਹਕ, ਆਕਰਸ਼ਕ, ਮਨਮੋਹਣਾ, ਰੋਚਕ, ਦਿਲ-ਖਿੱਚਵਾਂ, ਦਿਲਚਸਪ

absorption (ਅਬ'ਸੋਃਪਸ਼ਨ) *n* ਚੂਸਣ, ਸ਼ੋਖਣ ਜਾਂ ਹਜ਼ਮ ਕਰਨ, ਜਜ਼ਬ ਹੋਣਾ

abstain (ਅਬ'ਸਟੇਇਨ) *v* ਪਰਹੇਜ਼, ਕਰਨਾ, ਦੂਰ ਰਹਿਣਾ, ਅਲੱਗ, ਪਰੇ ਰਹਿਣਾ, ਬਚਣਾ, ਲਾਂਭੇ ਰਹਿਣਾ, ਪਾਸੇ ਰਹਿਣਾ, ਗੁਰੇਜ਼ ਕਰਨਾ

abstract ('ਐਬਸਟਰੈਕਟ, ਐਬ'ਸਟਰੈਕਟ) *a n v* ਭਾਵਵਾਚੀ, ਭਾਵ-ਮਈ, ਸੂਖਮ, ਅਮੂਰਤ, ਅਡੋਲਕ, ਅਵਿਅਕਤ, ਨਿਰਪੇਖ, ਸੰਖਿਪਤ, ਤੱਤ, ਸਾਰ, ਖੁਲਾਸਾ, ਸਾਰਾਂਸ਼, ਸੰਖੇਪ; ਅਸਪਸ਼ਟ, ਸਾਰ-ਸੂਚੀ; ਸਾਰ ਕੱਢਣਾ; **~ed** ਮਗਨ, ਲੀਨ ਅਮੂਰਤੀਕ੍ਰਿਤ; ਸੰਖੇਪੀਕ੍ਰਿਤ; ਅਲੱਗ ਕੀਤਾ, ਘਟਾਇਆ; **~ion** ਕਲਪਨਾ, ਅਮੂਰਤਤਾ, ਬੇਖ਼ਬਰੀ, ਬੇਖ਼ਿਆਲੀ, ਕਢਾਅ

absurd (ਅਬ'ਸਅ:ਡ) *a* ਹਾਸੋਹੀਣਾ, ਬੇਢੰਗਾ, ਬੇਤੁਕਾ, ਬੇਢੱਬਾ, ਉਟ-ਪਟਾਂਗ, ਬੇਹੂਦਾ, ਲੱਚਰ, ਫਜ਼ੂਲ; **~ity** ਵਿਅਰਥਤਾ, ਵਿਵੇਕਹੀਨਤਾ

abundance (ਅਬਅੰਡਅੰਸ) *n* ਬਹੁਲਤਾ, ਬਹੁਤਾਤ, ਭਰਮਾਰ; ਸਮਰਿਧੀ

abundant (ਅਬਅੰਡਅੰਟ) *a* ਭਰਪੂਰ, ਬਹੁਤ, ਘਣਾ, ਮਾਲਾਮਾਲ, ਵਾਫ਼ਰ, ਅਤੀਅਧਿਕ, (ਨਾਲ) ਪਰਿਪੂਰਨ

abuse (ਅ'ਬਯੂਸ) *n v* ਗਾਲ੍ਹ, ਬਦਜ਼ਬਾਨੀ, ਦੁਰਵਿਹਾਰ, ਦੁਰਵਰਤੋਂ, ਦੁਰਪ੍ਰਯੋਗ; ਦੁਰਵਰਤੋਂ ਕਰਨੀ, ਅਯੋਗ ਵਰਤੋਂ ਕਰਨੀ; ਬੁਰਾ ਭਲਾ ਆਖਣਾ, ਗਾਲ੍ਹ ਕੱਢਣੀ

abusive (ਅਬਯੂਸਿਵ੍) *a* ਅਸ਼ਲੀਲ, ਬਦਜ਼ਬਾਨ ਅਪਮਾਨਜਨਕ, ਨਿੰਦਾਪੂਰਨ; **~ness** ਅਸ਼ਲੀਲਤਾ, ਅਪਮਾਨ, ਬਦਜ਼ਬਾਨੀ

abyss (ਅ'ਬਿਸ) *n* ਡੂੰਮ, ਰਸਾਤਲ, ਨਰਕ; ਖਾਈ

academic (ਐਕਅ'ਡੈਮਿਕ) *a n* ਵਿੱਦਿਅਕ, ਇਲਮੀ, ਸਿਧਾਂਤਕ, ਸ਼ਾਸਤਰੀ, ਅਕਾਦਮਿਕ; ਅਫ਼ਲਾਤੂਨ ਦੀ ਅਕਾਦਮੀ ਦਾ ਮੈਂਬਰ; **~council** ਵਿੱਦਿਆ-ਪਰਿਸ਼ਦ; **~year** ਵਿੱਦਿਅਕ-ਸਾਲ

academy (ਅ'ਕੈਡਅਮਿ) *n* ਅਕਾਦਮੀ; ਪਲੇਟੋਵਾਦ, ਪਲੇਟੋਵਾਦੀ; ਸਿੱਖਿਆ-ਸੰਸਥਾ, ਵਿਸ਼ੇਸ਼ ਪ੍ਰਕਾਰ ਦੇ ਹੁਨਰ ਦੀ ਸਿੱਖਿਆ ਦੇਣ ਦੀ ਥਾਂ

accede (ਐਕ'ਸੀਡ) *v* ਸਵੀਕਾਰ ਕਰਨਾ, ਮਨਜ਼ੂਰ ਕਰਨਾ, ਕਬੂਲ ਕਰਨਾ, ਸੰਮਿਲਤ ਹੋਣਾ, ਸਹਿਮਤ ਹੋਣਾ, ਮੰਨਣਾ, ਰਾਜ਼ੀ ਹੋਣਾ, ਮੰਨ ਲੈਣਾ, ਗ੍ਰਹਿਣ ਕਰਨਾ

accelerate (ਅਕ'ਸੈੱਲਅਰੇਇਟ) *v* ਚਾਲ ਵਧਾਉਣੀ, ਗਤੀ ਤੇਜ਼ ਕਰਨੀ, ਵੇਗਮਈ ਹੋਣਾ, ਜਲਦੀ ਕਰਨਾ; **~d** ਤੀਬਰ, ਵੇਗਮਈ, ਤੇਜ਼, ਤੀਖਣ

acceleration (ਅਕ'ਸੈੱਲਅਰੇਇਸ਼ਨ) *n* ਗਤੀ ਵਿਚ ਵਾਧਾ, ਗਤੀ-ਵਰਧਣ, ਵੇਗ-ਵ੍ਰਿਧੀ

accelerator (ਅਕ'ਸੈੱਲਅਰੇਇਟਅ*) *n* ਗਤੀ ਵਰਧਕ, ਵੇਗ-ਵਰਧਕ, ਐਕਸਲਰੇਟਰ

accent ('ਐਕ'ਸੈਂਟ/ਐਕ'ਸੈਂਟ) *n v* ਸਵਰ, ਸੁਰ; ਸੁਰਾਘਾਤ, ਧੁਨੀ-ਚਿੰਨ੍ਹ, ਸਵਰ-ਚਿੰਨ੍ਹ; ਲਹਿਜ਼ਾ, ਸਵਰ-ਉਚਾਰਨਾ

accept (ਅਕ'ਸੈਪਟ) *v* ਸਵੀਕਾਰ ਕਰਨਾ, ਅੰਗੀਕਾਰ ਕਰਨਾ, ਪਰਵਾਨ ਕਰਨਾ, ਮੰਨਣਾ, ਮਨਜ਼ੂਰ ਕਰਨਾ, ਲੈਣਾ, ਗ੍ਰਹਿਣ ਕਰਨਾ; **~able** ਸਵੀਕਾਰ ਕਰਨਯੋਗ, ਮੰਨਣਯੋਗ, ਪਰਵਾਨ ਕਰਨਯੋਗ; **~ance** ਸਵੀਕ੍ਰਿਤੀ, ਮਨਜ਼ੂਰੀ, ਪਰਵਾਨਗੀ, ਰਜ਼ਾਮੰਦੀ, ਮਾਨਤਾ, ਹੁੰਡੀ ਦੀ ਸਵੀਕ੍ਰਿਤੀ; **~ed** ਸਵੀਕ੍ਰਿਤ, ਮਨਜ਼ੂਰ, ਪਰਵਾਨਤ, ਮੰਨਿਆ ਹੋਇਆ

access (ਐਕਸੈੱਸ) *n* ਪਹੁੰਚ, ਰਸਾਈ, ਪ੍ਰਵੇਸ਼, ਸਬੀਲ, ਉਪਾਉ; **~aibility** ਸੁਲੱਭਤਾ, ਪ੍ਰਵੇਸ਼-ਯੋਗਤਾ, ਪਹੁੰਚ-ਯੋਗਤਾ, ਸੁਗਮਤਾ

accessible (ਅਕਸੈੱਸਅਬਲ) *a* ਸੁਲੱਭ, ਪ੍ਰਵੇਸ਼ਯੋਗ, ਸੁਗਮ

accessory (ਅਕ'ਸੈੱਸਅਰਿ) *n a* ਉਪਸਾਧਨ; ਗੌਣ, ਸਹਾਇਕ, ਪੂਰਕ

accident ('ਐਕਸਿਡਅੰਟ) *n* ਦੁਰਘਟਨਾ, ਹਾਦਸਾ, ਘਟਨਾ, ਇਤਫ਼ਾਕ, ਵਾਕਿਆ; ਬੇਤਰਤੀਬੀ, ਕ੍ਰਮਹੀਨਤਾ; **~al** ਇਤਫ਼ਾਕੀਆ, ਰੱਬ-ਸਬੱਬੀ, ਅਕਾਰਨ, ਅਟਾਵੱਧਾਯ,

acclaim (ਅ'ਕਲੇਇਮ) *n v* ਜੈਕਾਰ, ਧੰਨ ਧੰਨ, ਜੈ-ਧੁਨੀ, ਸ਼ਲਾਘਾ, ਵਾਹ-ਵਾਹ ਕਰਨੀ, ਉਸਤਤ ਕਰਨੀ, ਸਲਾਹੁਣਾ; **~ation** ਸਮਰਥਨ, ਜੈ-ਧੁਨੀ, ਵਿਸ਼ੇ-ਘੋਸ਼ਣਾ, ਉਸਤਤ, ਸ਼ਲਾਘਾ, ਸਲਾਹੁਤਾ, ਜੈ ਜੈ ਕਾਰ

accommodate (ਅ'ਕੌਮਅਡੇਇਟ) *v* (ਦੀ) ਵਿਵਸਥਾ ਕਰਨਾ, ਮੁਆਫ਼ਕ ਕਰਨਾ, ਥਾਂ ਦੇਣੀ, ਸਮਾਈ ਕਰਨਾ, (ਹਾਲਾਤ ਆਦਿ ਨਾਲ) ਸਮਝੌਤਾ ਕਰਵਾਉਣਾ, ਅਨੁਕੂਲ ਕਰਨਾ

accommodating (ਅ'ਕੌਮਅਡੇਇਟਿਙ) *a* ਲਿਹਾਜ਼ ਪਾਲਣ ਵਾਲਾ, ਨਰਮ ਸੁਭਾਅ ਵਾਲਾ, ਲਚਕੀਲਾ, ਉਦਾਰ, ਮਿਹਰਬਾਨ, ਝੱਲਣ ਵਾਲਾ, ਮਿਲਾਪੜਾ, ਕੰਮ ਆਉਣ ਵਾਲਾ

accomodation (ਅ'ਕੌਮਅ'ਡੇਇਸ਼ਨ) *n* ਰਿਹਾਇਸ਼, ਨਿਵਾਸ, ਠਾਹਰ; (ਹਾਲਾਤ ਆਦਿ ਨਾਲ) ਸਮਝੌਤਾ, ਅਨੁਕੂਲਤਾ

accompany (ਅ'ਕਅੰਮਪਅਨਿ) *v* ਸਾਥ ਹੋਣਾ, ਸੰਗ ਕਰਨਾ, ਸਾਥ ਦੇਣਾ, (ਕਿਸੇ ਦੇ) ਨਾਲ ਜਾਣਾ, ਸ਼ਾਮਲ ਹੋਣਾ

accomplish (ਅ'ਕਅੰਮਪਲਿਸ਼) *v* ਸਿਰੇ ਚਾੜ੍ਹਨਾ, ਪੂਰਾ ਕਰਨਾ, ਸੰਪੂਰਨ ਕਰਨਾ, ਸੰਪੰਨ ਕਰਨਾ, ਸਮਾਪਤ ਕਰਨਾ, ਨਿਭੇਣਨਾ; **~ed** ਨਿਪੁੰਨ, ਸੁੱਘੜ, ਸੁਰੱਜਾ, ਗੁਣਵਾਨ, ਸ਼ਾਇਸਤਾ, ਸ਼ਿਸ਼ਟ; **~ment** ਪੂਰਤੀ, ਸਿੱਧੀ; ਗੁਣ ਪ੍ਰਾਪਤੀ, ਕਮਾਲ

accord (ਅ'ਕੋਡ) *v* ਸਵੀਕ੍ਰਿਤੀ ਦੇਣੀ, ਪਰਵਾਨਗੀ ਦੇਣੀ, ਇਕ ਮੱਤ ਹੋਣਾ, ਮੇਲ ਖਾਣਾ; ਮੁਤਾਬਕ ਹੋਣਾ; ਅਨੁਕੂਲ ਹੋਣਾ, ਇਕ ਰੂਪ ਹੋਣਾ, ਇਕ ਸੁਰ ਹੋਣਾ; ਮਰਜ਼ੀ, ਸਵੀਕ੍ਰਿਤੀ, ਪਰਵਾਨਗੀ; ਮਿਲਾਪ, ਸੰਧੀ, ਇਕਰਾਰਨਾਮਾ; **~ance** ਇਕ ਰਾਇ, ਇਕ ਮੱਤ; ਮੇਲ-ਮਿਲਾਪ, ਪਰਵਾਨਤਾ, ਰਾਜ਼ੀਨਾਮਾ, ਮੁਤਾਬਕ, ਅਨੁਸਾਰ; **In ~ance with** ਦੇ ਅਨੁਸਾਰ, ਦੇ ਅਨੁਰੂਪ, ਦੇ ਮੁਤਾਬਕ

according (ਅ'ਕੋਡਿਙ) *adv* ਅਨੁਸਾਰ, ਮੁਤਾਬਕ, ਜਿਹਾ ਕਿ, ਵਾਂਗ, ਜਿਵੇਂ ਕਿ; **~as** ਜਿਵੇਂ ਕਿ, ਜਿਸ ਤਰ੍ਹਾਂ, ਮਨੋਂ; **~to** ਦੇ ਅਨੁਸਾਰ, ਦੇ ਮੁਤਾਬਕ; **~ly** ਇਸ ਲਈ, ਇਸ ਅਨੁਸਾਰ, ਸੋ; ਤਦਨੁਕੂਲ, ਤਦਨੁਰੂਪ

account (ਅ'ਕਾਉਂਟ) *n v* ਹਿਸਾਬ-ਕਿਤਾਬ, ਲੇਖਾ, ਚਿੱਠਾ, ਜਮ੍ਹਾਂ-ਖਰਚ, ਖਾਤਾ, ਕੈਫ਼ੀਅਤ, ਤਫ਼ਸੀਲ, ਬਿਰਤਾਂਤ, ਵਿਵਰਣ; ਗਿਣਤੀ ਕਰਨੀ, ਗਿਣਨਾ;

ਕਾਰਨ, ਨਿਮਿਤ; ਲੇਖਾਜੋਖਾ ਵੇਖਣਾ, ਵਿਚਾਰ ਕਰਨਾ; give ~ of ਸਪੱਸ਼ਟ ਕਰਨਾ, ਕਾਰਨ ਦੱਸਣਾ; keep ~s ਹਿਸਾਬ ਕਿਤਾਬ ਕਰਨਾ; on ~ of ਦੇ ਕਾਰਨ, ਫਲਸਰੂਪ; on no~ ਕਦੀ ਨਹੀਂ; ਕਿਸੇ ਤਰ੍ਹਾਂ ਵੀ ਨਹੀਂ; take into~ ਵਿਚਾਰਨਾ, ਧਿਆਨ ਵਿਚ ਰੱਖਣਾ; ~able ਉੱਤਰਦਾਈ, ਜ਼ੁੰਮੇਵਾਰ, ਜਵਾਬਦੇਹ; ~ancy ਲੇਖਾਕਾਰੀ, ਹਿਸਾਬ-ਕਿਤਾਬ, ਮੁਨੀਮੀ, ਲੇਖਾ ਸ਼ਾਸਤਰ, ਗਿਣਤੀ-ਵਿਗਿਆਨ; ~ant ਲੇਖਾਕਾਰ, ਮੁਨੀਮ, ਮੁਨਸ਼ੀ, ਹਿਸਾਬ-ਕਿਤਾਬ ਰੱਖਣ ਵਾਲਾ

accredit (ਅ'ਕਰੈਡਿਟ) v ਮਨਜ਼ੂਰ ਕਰਨਾ, ਸਵੀਕਾਰ ਕਰਨਾ, ਅਧਿਕਾਰ ਦੇਣਾ, ਸਬੰਧ ਜੋੜਨਾ, ਮਾਨਤਾ ਦੁਆਉਣਾ, ਮਾਨ ਦੇਣਾ; ~ed ਮਕਬੂਲ, ਪਰਵਾਨਤ, ਅਧਿਕਾਰ-ਪ੍ਰਾਪਤ, ਪ੍ਰਤਿਸ਼ਠਾਵਾਨ; ਕਬੂਲ

accrete (ਅ'ਕਰੀਟ) adv v ਇਕੱਤਰ ਕਰਨਾ, ਜੋੜਨਾ, ਜੁੜਵਾਂ, ਸੰਯੁਕਤ, ਵਧਵਾਂ

accretion (ਐ'ਕਰੀਸ਼ਨ) n ਵਿਕਾਸ, ਵ੍ਰਿਧੀ, ਸਹਿਵਰਧਨ, ਫੈਲਾਉ; ਪੌਦਿਆਂ ਦਾ ਉੱਗ ਕੇ ਗੁੱਛਾ-ਮੁੱਛਾ ਹੋ ਜਾਣ ਦੀ ਕ੍ਰਿਆ; ਮਿਲਾਪ, ਇਕਮਿਕਤਾ

accumulate (ਅ'ਕਯੂਮਯੁਲੇਇਟ) v ਜੋੜਨਾ, ਜਮ੍ਹਾਂ ਕਰਨਾ, ਸੰਗ੍ਰਹ ਕਰਨਾ ਜਾਂ ਹੋਣਾ, ਸੰਚਤ ਕਰਨਾ, ਸਮੇਟਣਾ, ਢੇਰ ਲਾਉਣਾ, ਸੰਕਲਤ ਕਰਨਾ, ਵਧਦੇ ਜਾਣਾ

accumulation (ਅ'ਕਯੂਮਯੁ'ਲੇਇਸ਼ਨ) n ਸਮੂਹ, ਪੂੰਜ, ਇਕੱਠ, ਢੇਰ, ਅੰਬਾਰ, ਸੰਗ੍ਰਹ

accumulative (ਅ'ਕਯੂਮਯੁ'ਲਅਟਿਵ) a ਇਕੱਠਣ, ਸੰਚਤ

accuracy ('ਐਕਯੁਰਅਸਿ) ਦਰੁਸਤੀ, ਸ਼ੁੱਧਤਾ, ਸਚਾਈ, ਸੁਨਿਸਚਿਤਤਾ

accurate ('ਐਕਯੁਰਅਟ) a ਸ਼ੁੱਧ, ਠੀਕ, ਸਹੀ, ਦਰੁਸਤ; ਸਚੇਤ, ਸਾਵਧਾਨ

accusation ('ਐਕਯੁ'ਜ਼ੇਇਸ਼ਨ) n ਦੋਸ਼-ਆਰੋਪਣ, ਇਲਜ਼ਾਮ, ਦੂਸ਼ਣ, ਤੁਹਮਤ

accuse (ਐ'ਕਯੂਜ਼) v ਉੱਜ ਲਾਉਣੀ, ਦੋਸ਼ ਲਾਉਣਾ, ਤੁਹਮਤ ਲਾਉਣੀ, ਇਲਜ਼ਾਮ ਲਾਉਣਾ, ਮੱਥੇ ਮੜ੍ਹਨਾ; ~d ਦੋਸ਼ੀ, ਅਪਰਾਧੀ, ਮੁਲਜ਼ਮ

accustom (ਅ'ਕੱਸਟਅਮ) v ਆਦੀ ਕਰਨਾ, ਆਦਤ ਪਾਉਣੀ, ਰੀਝਾਉਣਾ, ਸੁਭਾਅ ਪਾਉਣਾ; ~ed ਆਦੀ, ਗਿੱਝਿਆ

ace (ਏਇਸ) n ਇਕ, ਇਕਾਈ; ਤਾਸ਼ ਦੀ ਯੱਕਾ

ache (ਏਇਕ) n v ਦਰਦ, ਪੀੜ, ਵੇਦਨਾ, ਕਸਕ, ਹੂਕ, ਦੁਖਣਾ, ਦਰਦ ਹੋਣਾ, ਪੀੜ ਹੋਣੀ, ਸੂਲ ਉੱਠਣੀ, ਚੀਸ ਪੈਣੀ

achieve (ਅ'ਚੀਵ਼) v ਪ੍ਰਾਪਤ ਕਰਨਾ, ਪਾਉਣਾ, ਸਿਰੇ ਚਾੜ੍ਹਨਾ, ਨਿਬੇੜਤਾ, ਮਨੋਰਥ ਪ੍ਰਾਪਤ ਕਰਨਾ; ~ment ਪ੍ਰਾਪਤੀ, ਸਿੱਧੀ, ਪੂਰਤੀ, ਪੂਰਨਤਾ, ਕਾਮਯਾਬੀ, ਸਫਲਤਾ

acid ('ਐਸਿਡ) n a ਤੇਜ਼ਾਬ, ਖੱਟਾ ਪਦਾਰਥ, ਤੁਰਸ਼, ਸਿਰਕਈ, ਤੇਜ਼ਾਬੀ; ਵਿਅੰਗਮਈ, ਚੁੱਭਵਾਂ(ਬੋਲ); ~ify ਤੇਜ਼ਾਬੀ ਬਣਨਾ ਜਾਂ ਬਣਾਉਣਾ; ~ity ਤੇਜ਼ਾਬੀਅਤ; ਅਮਲਤਾ, ਖਟਾਸ, ਤੁਰਸ਼ੀ

acknowledge (ਅ'ਕਨੌਲਿਜ) v ਸਵੀਕਾਰ ਕਰਨਾ; ਪ੍ਰਸੰਸਾ ਕਰਨਾ, ਪਰਵਾਨ ਕਰਨਾ; ਪਹੁੰਚ ਦੇਣਾ, ਰਸੀਦ ਦੇਣਾ; ਮਾਨਤਾ ਦੇਣੀ, ਕਦਰ ਕਰਨਾ, ਹਾਮੀ ਭਰਨਾ; ~d ਸਵੀਕ੍ਰਿਤ, ਪਰਵਾਨਤ ਮੰਨਿਆ, ਜਾਣਿਆ; ~ment ਸਨਜ਼ੂਰੀ, ਹਾਮੀ, ਰਸੀਦ, ਆਧਾਰ; ਕਦਰ; ਪਹੁੰਚ, ਪ੍ਰਾਪਤੀ-ਸੂਚਨਾ

acoustic/-al (ਅ'ਕੂਸਟਿਕ/ਅ'ਕੂਸਟਿਕਲ) a ਸੁਣਨ ਸਬੰਧੀ, ਕੰਨਾਂ ਸਬੰਧੀ, ਧੁਨੀ ਸਬੰਧੀ, ਸ੍ਵਰਵੇਦੀ; ~s ਸ੍ਵਵਣ ਵਿਗਿਆਨ; (ਕਮਰੇ ਦਾ) ਧੁਨੀ-ਗੁਣ

acquaint (ਅ'ਕਵੇਇੰਟ) v ਵਾਕਫ਼ੀ ਕਰਾਉਣੀ, ਖ਼ਬਰ ਦੇਣੀ, ਪਰਿਚੈ ਦੇਣਾ, ਪਰਿਚਿਤ ਕਰਨਾ; ਜਾਣਕਾਰੀ ਪ੍ਰਾਪਤ ਕਰਨੀ ਜਾਂ ਕਰਾਉਣੀ, ਸੂਚਨਾ ਦੇਣੀ, ਸੂਚਤ ਕਰਨਾ ਜਾਂ ਹੋਣਾ, ਜਤਲਾਉਣਾ, ਜਾਣੂ ਕਰਨਾ, ਵਾਕਫ਼ੀ ਕਰਾਉਣੀ, ਖ਼ਬਰ ਦੇਣੀ; **~ance** ਜਾਣ-ਪਛਾਣ, ਜਾਣਕਾਰੀ, ਵਾਕਫ਼ੀਅਤ, ਪਰਿਚਯ; ਜਾਣਕਾਰ, ਵਾਰਫ਼; ਜਾਣੂ; ਪਰਿਚਿਤ, ਗਿਆਤ, ਸੂਚਤ; **~ed** ਪਰਿਚਿਤ, ਗਿਆਤ, ਸੂਚਤ

acquire (ਅ'ਕਵਾਇਅ*) v ਲੈਣਾ, ਹਾਸਲ ਕਰਨਾ, ਗ੍ਰਹਿਣ ਕਰਨਾ, ਪ੍ਰਾਪਤ ਕਰਨਾ, ਪਾਉਣਾ, ਮਾਲਕ ਬਣਨਾ, ਕਬਜ਼ਾ ਲੈਣਾ; **~d** ਪ੍ਰਾਪਤ, ਅਰਜਤ, ਗ੍ਰਹਿਤ, ਕਮਾਇਆ

aquisition ('ਐਕਵਿ'ਜ਼ਿਸ਼ਨ) n ਪ੍ਰਾਪਤੀ, ਗ੍ਰਹਿਣ, ਉਪਲਬਧੀ, ਲੱਭਤ, ਕਮਾਈ

acquit (ਅ'ਕਵਿਟ) v ਬਰੀ ਕਰਨਾ, ਰਿਹਾ ਕਰਨਾ, ਛੱਡਣਾ, ਦੋਸ਼-ਮੁਕਤ ਕਰਨਾ, ਕਰਤੱਵ ਪੂਰਾ ਕਰਨਾ, (ਫ਼ਰਜ਼) ਅਦਾ ਕਰਨਾ, ਨਿਬਾਹੁਣਾ; **~tal** ਰਿਹਾਈ, ਛੁਟਕਾਰਾ, ਮੁਕਤੀ, ਅਪਰਾਧ-ਮੁਕਤੀ, ਖ਼ਲਾਸੀ, ਨਿਸਤਾਰ; **~tance** ਰਿਹਾਈ, ਨਿਸਤਾਰਾ, ਅਪਰਾਧ-ਮੁਕਤੀ; ਅਦਾਇਗੀ, (ਕਰਜ਼ੇ ਤੋਂ) ਛੁਟਕਾਰਾ, ਚੁਕੌਤੀ, ਬੇਬਾਕੀ, **~ted** ਛੁਟਿਆ, ਬਰੀ, ਰਿਹਾ, ਵਿਮੁਕਤ

acre ('ਏਇਕਅ*) n ਏਕੜ, 4840 ਵਰਗ ਗਜ਼; **~age** (ਏਕੜਾਂ ਵਿਚ) ਖੇਤਰਫਲ; ਮਾਮਲਾ ਫ਼ੀ ਏਕੜ

acrid ('ਐਕਰਿਡ) a ਕੌੜਾ, ਤਲਖ਼ ਮਿਜ਼ਾਜ, ਉਤੇਜਕ, ਤਿੱਖਾ, ਤੇਜ਼-ਤਬੀਅਤ, ਚਿੜਚੜਾ; **~ity** ਤੀਖਣਤਾ, ਤਿੱਖਾਪਣ, ਤੇਜ਼ੀ, ਖਟਿਆਈ, ਖਰੂਵਾਪਣ

acrimonious (ਐਕਰਿ'ਮਅਉਨਯਅਸ) a ਤੇਜ਼, ਕੌੜਾ, ਕਾਵੜ, ਤਲਖ਼, ਖਰੂਵਾ, ਤੀਖਣ, ਚਿੜਚੜਾ

acrimony (ਐਕਰਿਮਅਨਿ) n (ਸੁਭਾਅ ਦੀ) ਤਲਖ਼ੀ, ਕੁੜੱਤਣ, ਕਟੁਤਾ

across (ਅ'ਕਰੌਸ) adv prep a ਪਾਰ, ਆਰ-ਪਾਰ, ਸਨਮੁਖ, ਸਾਮ੍ਹਣੇ, ਦੂਜੇ ਪਾਸੇ; ਆੜਾ, ਤਿਰਛਾ

act (ਐਕਟ) n v (1) ਅਧਿਨਿਯਮ; (2) ਨਾਟਕ ਦਾ ਅੰਕ; (3) ਕੰਮ, ਕਾਰਜ, ਕਾਜ, ਕਿਰਿਆ, ਕਰਤੱਵ, ਕਾਰਵਾਈ; ਵਿਹਾਰ ਕਰਨਾ, ਕਰਤੱਵ ਪਾਲਣਾ; ਅਭਿਨੇ ਕਰਨਾ; **~able** ਕਰਨ ਯੋਗ, ਕਰਤੱਵ ਯੋਗ, ਵਿਹਾਰ ਯੋਗ, ਅਭਿਨੇ ਯੋਗ; **~ing** ਅਦਾਕਾਰੀ, ਨਟਬਾਜ਼ੀ, ਅਭਿਨੈ, ਦਿਖਾਵਾ; ਕਾਰਜ; ਕਿਰਿਆਸ਼ੀਲਤਾ; **~or** ਕਰਤਾ, ਨਟ, ਅਦਾਕਾਰ, ਅਭਿਨੇਤਾ, ਨਾਟਕ ਦਾ ਪਾਤਰ, ਐਕਟਰ

action (ਐਕਸ਼ਨ) n v ਅਮਲ, ਕੰਮ, ਕਾਰਜ; ਕਿਰਿਆ, ਕਾਰਵਾਈ; ਵਿਹਾਰ; ਢੰਗ, ਹਰਕਤ; ਮੁਕੱਦਮਾ; ਪ੍ਰਭਾਵ; ਯੁੱਧ; ਦਾਅਵਾ ਕਰਨਾ, ਕਿਸੇ ਦੇ ਵਿਰੁੱਧ ਕਾਨੂੰਨੀ ਮੁਕੱਦਮਾ ਕਰਨਾ

active (ਐਕਟਿਵ) a ਕਿਰਿਆਸ਼ੀਲ, ਫੁਰਤੀਲਾ, ਉੱਦਮੀ, ਚੁਸਤ, ਜਾਗਰੂਕ, ਪ੍ਰਭਾਵਸ਼ਾਲੀ, ਸਾਹਸੀ **~voice** ਕਰਤਰੀਵਾਚ; **~ity** ਸਰਗਰਮੀ, ਚੁਸਤੀ, ਫੁਰਤੀ, ਰੁਝੇਵਾਂ, ਵਿਵਸਾਏ; ਮਿਹਨਤ

actual ('ਐਕਚੁਅਲ) a ਵਾਸਤਵਿਕ, ਯਥਾਰਥ, ਸੱਚਾ, ਸਹੀ, ਠੀਕ, ਅਸਲੀ, ਪ੍ਰਚਲਤ, ਚਾਲੂ; **~ity** ਯਥਾਰਥਕਤਾ, ਸੱਤਤਾ, ਵਾਸਤਵਿਕਤਾ, ਅਸਲੀਅਤ, ਸੱਚਾਈ, ਮੌਜੂਦਾ ਹਾਲਾਤ; **~ly** ਸਚਮੁੱਚ, ਅਸਲ ਵਿਚ, ਦਰਅਸਲ, ਵਾਸਤਵਿਕ ਤੌਰ ਤੇ

acute ('ਐਕਯੂਟ) a ਤਿੱਖਾ, ਤੇਜ਼, ਚਤਰ, ਤੀਬਰ, ਸਖ਼ਤ, ਪ੍ਰਚੰਡ, ਸੰਵੇਦਨਸ਼ੀਲ, ਅਤੀ ਅਵੱਸ਼ਕ; **~ness** ਤੀਬਰਤਾ, ਤੀਖਣਤਾ, ਤਿੱਖਾਪਣ, ਤੇਜ਼ੀ

A.D. ('ਏਇ'ਡੀ) (L) Anno Domini ਦਾ

ਸੰਖੇਪ, (ਭਗਵਾਨ ਈਸਾ ਦੇ ਵਰ੍ਹੇ ਵਿਚ) ਸੰਨ ਈਸਵੀ

adam ('ਐਡਅਮ) *n* ਬਾਬਾ ਆਦਮ, ਆਦਿ ਪੁਰਸ਼

adamant ('ਐਡਅਸਅੰਟ) *a n* ਦ੍ਰਿੜ੍ਹ, ਅਟਲ; ਕਰੜੀ ਵਸਤੁ; ਚੁੰਬਕ ਪੱਥਰ

Adam's apple (,'ਐਡਅਮਜ਼'ਐਪਲ) ਘੰਡੀ

adapt (ਅ'ਡੈਪਟ) *v* ਅਨੁਕੂਲ ਕਰਨਾ, ਮੁਆਫ਼ਕ ਬਣਾਉਣਾ, ਰੂਪ ਦੇ ਅਨੁਸਾਰ ਕਰਨਾ, ਇਕ ਤਰ੍ਹਾਂ ਦਾ ਬਣਾਉਣਾ, ਮੇਲਣਾ, ਢਾਲਣਾ; **~ability** ਢਲ ਜਾਣ ਦਾ ਗੁਣ, ਅਨੁਕੂਲਤਾ, ਅਨੁਕੂਲਣ ਯੋਗਤਾ; **~ation** ਅਨੁਕੂਲਣ, ਕਿਸੇ ਸ਼ਕਲ ਦਾ ਰੂਪਾਂਤਰ, ਰੂਪ ਅਨੁਕੂਲਣ, ਮੇਲ

add (ਐਡ) *v* ਜੋੜਨਾ, ਵਧਾਉਣਾ, ਮਿਲਾਣਾ, ਜਮ੍ਹਾਂ ਕਰਨਾ, ਸੰਮਿਲਤ ਕਰਨਾ, ਮਿਲਾਉਣਾ; **~endum** ਜੋੜ, ਵਾਧਾ, ਜੋਗ, ਅੰਤਕਾ; **~er** ਰਕਮਾਂ ਜੋੜਨ ਵਾਲਾ ਆਦਮੀ; ਇਕ ਤਰ੍ਹਾਂ ਦਾ ਜ਼ਹਿਰੀਲਾ ਸੱਪ

addict (ਅ'ਡਿਕਟ, 'ਐਡਿਕਟ) *v n* ਆਪਣੇ ਆਪ ਨੂੰ ਆਦਤ ਪਾਉਣੀ, ਗਿੱਝਣਾ, ਆਦੀ ਹੋਣਾ; ਅਮਲੀ, ਨਸ਼ੱਈ; **~ed** ਆਦੀ, ਅਮਲੀ, ਨਸ਼ੱਈ, ਵਿਸ਼ੇਰਗ੍ਰਸਤ, ਲਿਪਤ; **~ion** ਝੱਸ, ਵਾਦੀ

addition (ਅ'ਡਿਸ਼ਨ) *n* ਸੰਕਲਨ, ਜੋੜ, ਜਮ੍ਹਾਂ, ਵਾਧਾ, ਅਧਿਕਤਾ, ਯੋਗ, ਜੋੜਨ ਦਾ ਕੰਮ, ਜੁੜਾਈ; **~al** ਵਾਧੂ, ਵਧੀਕ, ਅਧਿਕਤਰ; (ਪਹਿਲਾਂ ਵਾਲੀ ਚੀਜ਼ ਆਦਿ ਤੋਂ) ਇਲਾਵਾ, ਅਤਿਰਿਕਤ, ਅਨੁਪੂਰਕ

address (ਅ'ਡਰੈੱਸ) *n v* (1) ਸਿਰਨਾਵਾਂ ਪਤਾ; (2) ਵਿਆਖਿਆਨ, ਸੰਬੋਧਨ; (3) ਅਭਿਨੰਦਨ-ਪੱਤਰ; (4) ਮੁਹਾਰਤ, ਸਲੀਕਾ; ਸੰਬੋਧਤ ਕਰਨਾ, ਪਤਾ ਲਿਖਣਾ, ਵਿਆਖਿਆਨ ਦੇਣਾ, ਭਾਸ਼ਣ ਦੇਣਾ; ਮੁਖਾਤਬ ਹੋਣਾ; **~ee** ਸਿਰਨਾਵਾਂਦਾਰ, (ਮਨੀ ਆਰਡਰ ਜਾਂ ਚਿੱਠੀ) ਪ੍ਰਾਪਤ ਕਰਨ ਵਾਲਾ, ਪ੍ਰਾਪਤ ਕਰਤਾ; **~er** ਪੱਤਰ ਭੇਜਣ ਵਾਲਾ, ਬੇਨਤੀ ਕਰਨ ਵਾਲਾ, ਸੰਬੋਧਨ ਕਰਤਾ, ਮੁਖ਼ਾਤਬ ਕਰਨ ਵਾਲਾ

adept ('ਐਡੈੱਪਟ) *a n* ਨਿਪੁੰਨ, ਕਾਰੀਗਰ, ਪ੍ਰਵੀਨ, ਉਸਤਾਦ, ਤਾਕ, ਮਾਹਰ ਕੀਮਿਆਗਾਰ

adequacy (ਐਡਿਕਵਅਸਿ) *n* ਯੋਗਤਾ, ਸਮਰਥਾ, ਢੁੱਕਵਾਂਪਨ, ਚੋਖਾਪਨ

adequate ('ਐਡਿਕਵਅਟ) *a* ਕਾਫ਼ੀ, ਪੂਰਾ, ਲੋੜ-ਅਨੁਸਾਰ, ਉਪਯੁਕਤ, ਚੋਖਾ, ਢੁੱਕਵਾਂ, ਮੁਨਾਸਬ; **~ly** ਪੂਰਾ-ਪੂਰਾ, ਕਾਫ਼ੀ, ਪੂਰੇ ਤੌਰ ਤੇ

adhere (ਅਡ'ਹਿਅ*) *v* ਡਟੇ ਰਹਿਣਾ, ਜੰਮੇ ਰਹਿਣਾ, ਚਿੰਬੜਨਾ, ਜੁੜ ਜਾਣਾ, ਦ੍ਰਿੜ੍ਹ ਰਹਿਣਾ; ਪਾਲਣ ਕਰਨਾ, ਅਨੁਸਰਨ ਕਰਨਾ, ਸਾਥ ਦਿੰਦੇ ਰਹਿਣਾ; **~nce** ਹਿਮਾਇਤ, ਲਗਾਉ, ਦ੍ਰਿੜ੍ਹਤਾ, ਸਮਰਥਨ, ਚਿਪਕਾਉ; ਪਾਲਣ; ਨਿਸ਼ਠਾ; **~nt** ਪੈਰੋਕਾਰ, ਹਿਮਾਇਤੀ, ਸਹਾਇਕ, ਸਮਰਥਕ, ਅਨੁਗਾਮੀ; ਸਬੰਧਤ

adhesive (ਅਡ'ਹਿਸਿਵ) *a* ਚਿਪਕੀਲਾ, ਗੂੰਦ ਵਾਲਾ ਚਿਪਕਵਾਂ, ਚਿਪਚਿਪਾ, ਚੇਪਨਦਾਰ; **~ness** ਚਿਪਚਿਪਾਹਟ

ad hoc ('ਐਡ'ਹੌਕ) (*L*) *a* ਉਚੇਚਾ, ਖ਼ਾਸ ਮਤਲਬ ਲਈ, ਤਦ-ਅਰਥੀ

adieu (ਅ'ਡਯੂ) *n* ਅਲਵਿਦਾ, ਰੱਬ ਰਾਖਾ, ਅੱਲਾ ਬੇਲੀ

ad infinitum ('ਐਡ'ਇਨਫ਼ਿ'ਨਾਇਟਅਮ) (*L*) *adv* ਹਮੇਸ਼ਾ ਲਈ, ਸਦੀਵੀ; ਅਨੰਤ ਤਕ

ad interim ('ਐਡ'ਇਨਟਅਰਿਮ) (*L*) *adv* ਵਿਚਕਾਰਲੇ ਸਮੇਂ ਲਈ, ਅਲਪਕਾਲੀਨ, ਅਸਥਾਈ

adjacent (ਅ'ਜੋਇਸਅੰਟ) *n* ਲਾਗਲਾ, ਜੁੜਵਾਂ, ਸਮੀਪਵਰਤੀ, ਨੇੜਲਾ, ਨਾਲ, ਲੱਗਵਾਂ

adject (ਅ'ਜੈੱਕਟ) *v* ਜੋੜਨ, ਮਿਲਾਉਣਾ **~ival** ਵਿਸ਼ੇਸ਼ਣੀ, ਵਿਸ਼ੇਸ਼ਣ ਸਬੰਧੀ, ਗੁਣਵਾਚਕ; **~ive**

ਵਿਸ਼ੇਸ਼ਣ, ਗੁਣਵਾਚਕ ਸ਼ਬਦ

adjoin (ਅ'ਜੋਇਨ) v ਮਿਲਿਆ ਹੋਣਾ, ਜੁੜਿਆ ਹੋਣਾ, ਮਿਲਾਉਣਾ, ਸੰਯੁਕਤ ਕਰਨਾ, ਪਾਸ ਲਿਆਉਣਾ, ਮੇਲ ਕਰਨਾ, ਜੋੜਨਾ, ਨੱਥੀ ਕਰਨਾ; ~ing ਕੋਲ ਦਾ, ਕੋਲ ਵਾਲਾ, ਨਾਲ ਲਗਦਾ, ਨਾਲ ਦਾ, ਨਾਲ ਵਾਲਾ, ਜੁੜਿਆ

adjourn (ਅ'ਜਅ:ਨ) v ਮੁਲਤਵੀ ਕਰਨਾ, ਸਥਗਤ ਕਰਨਾ, ਅੱਗੇ ਪਾਉਣਾ; ~ment ਅੱਗੇ ਪਾ ਦੇਣ, ਮੁਲਤਵੀ ਕਰਨ, ਕਾਰਜ-ਸਥਗਨ

adjudge (ਅ'ਜਅੱਜ) v ਨਿਆਂ-ਨਿਰਣਾ ਕਰਨਾ, ਫ਼ੈਸਲਾ ਕਰਨਾ, ਦੰਡ ਦਾ ਹੁਕਮ ਦੇਣਾ, ਤਜਵੀਜ਼ ਕਰਨਾ, ਰਾਇ ਦੇਣੀ; ~ment ਨਿਆਂ-ਨਿਰਣਾ, ਫ਼ੈਸਲਾ, ਹੁਕਮ

adjudicate (ਅ'ਜੁਡ੍ਰਿਕੇਇਟ) v ਫ਼ੈਸਲਾ ਕਰਨਾ, ਨਿਰਣਾ ਦੇਣਾ, ਨਿਬੇੜਨਾ, ਨਿਪਟਾਰਾ ਕਰਨਾ

adjudication (ਅ'ਜੁਡਿ'ਕੇਇਸ਼ਨ) n ਫ਼ੈਸਲਾ, ਨਿਆਂ ਨਿਰਣਾ, ਅਦਾਲਤੀ ਹੁਕਮ

adjunct (ਅ'ਜਅੰਕਟ) n ਸਹਾਇਕ; ਅਧੀਨ ਵਸਤੂ, ਜੋੜ, ਸੰਯੁਕਤ ਪਦਾਰਥ

adjust (ਅ'ਜਅੱਸਟ) v ਤਰਤੀਬ ਦੇਣੀ, ਇਕਸਾਰ ਕਰਨਾ, ਠੀਕ ਕਰਨਾ ਅਨੁਕੂਲ ਕਰਨਾ, ਮਿਲਾਉਣਾ, ਸਮਾਯੋਜਨ ਕਰਨਾ, ਵਿਵਸਥਿਤ ਕਰਨਾ; ~ment ਤਰਕੀਬ, ਅਨੁਕੂਲਤਾ, ਸਮਾਯੋਜਨ, ਸਮਾਧਾਨ, ਸਮਝੌਤਾ

administer (ਅਡ'ਮਿਨਿਸਟਾ*) v ਪ੍ਰਬੰਧ ਕਰਨਾ, ਇੰਤਜ਼ਾਮ ਕਰਨਾ, ਬੰਦੋਬਸਤ ਕਰਨਾ, ਵਿਵਸਥਾ ਕਰਨੀ, (ਕਸਮ) ਚੁਕਾਉਣੀ; ਪ੍ਰਦਾਨ ਕਰਨਾ, (ਦਵਾਈ) ਦੇਣੀ ਜਾਂ ਖਵਾਉਣੀ

administration (ਅਡ'ਮਿਨਿ'ਸਟਰੇਇਸ਼ਨ) n ਪ੍ਰਸ਼ਾਸਨ, ਸੰਚਾਲਨ, ਪ੍ਰਬੰਧ, ਇੰਤਜ਼ਾਮ, ਸਰਕਾਰ

administrative (ਅਡ'ਮਿਨਿ'ਸਟਰਅਟਿਵ) a ਪ੍ਰਸ਼ਾਸਕੀ, ਪ੍ਰਸ਼ਾਸਨ-ਸਬੰਧੀ; ਪ੍ਰਬੰਧਕੀ, ਇੰਤਜ਼ਾਮੀਆ

administrator (ਅਡ'ਮਿਨਿਸਟਰੇਇਟਅ*) n ਪ੍ਰਸ਼ਾਸਕ, ਪ੍ਰਬੰਧਕ, ਪ੍ਰਬੰਧ-ਕਰਤਾ, ਨਾਜ਼ਮ, ਸਰਬਰਾਹ, ਮੁੰਤਜ਼ਿਮ, ਵਿਵਸਥਾਪਕ

admirable ('ਐਡਮ(ਅ)ਰਅਬਲ) a ਪ੍ਰਸੰਸਾਯੋਗ, ਪ੍ਰਸੰਸਨੀ, ਅਦਭੁਤ, ਅਸਚਰਜ-ਜਨਕ, ਅਪੂਰਵ, ਸ਼ਲਾਘਾਯੋਗ, ਸਲਾਹੁਣਯੋਗ, ਅਤੀ ਉੱਤਮ, ਸ੍ਰੇਸ਼ਠ, ਵਧੀਆ

admiral ('ਐਡਮ(ਅ)ਰ(ਅ)ਲ) n ਨੌ-ਸੈਨਾਪਤੀ, ਜੰਗੀ ਬੇੜੇ ਦਾ ਸਰਦਾਰ

admiration (ਐਡਮਅ'ਰੇਇਸ਼ਨ) n ਸ਼ਲਾਘਾ, ਤਾਰੀਫ਼, ਪ੍ਰਸੰਸਾ; ਅਚੰਭਾ

admire (ਅਡ'ਮਾਇਅ*) v ਪ੍ਰਸੰਸਾ ਕਰਨਾ; ਸਲਾਹੁਣਾ, ਸ਼ਲਾਘਾ ਕਰਨੀ, ਸਿਫ਼ਤਿ ਕਰਨੀ, ਗੁਣ ਗਾਉਣਾ; ~r ਪ੍ਰਸੰਸਕ, ਆਸ਼ਕ

admissibility (ਅਡ'ਮਿਸਅ'ਬਿਲਅਟਿ) n ਯੋਗਤਾ, ਮੰਨਣ-ਯੋਗਤਾ, ਮਾਨਤਾ, ਪ੍ਰਮਾਣਕਤਾ

admissible (ਅਡ'ਮਿਸਅਬਲ) a ਦਾਖ਼ਲੇ ਯੋਗ, ਮੰਨਣ ਯੋਗ, ਜਾਇਜ਼, ਗ੍ਰਹਿਣ ਕਰਨ ਯੋਗ, ਸਵੀਕਾਰ ਕਰਨ ਯੋਗ

admission (ਅਡ'ਮਿਸ਼ਨ) n ਦਾਖ਼ਲਾ, ਪ੍ਰਵੇਸ਼, ਪਹੁੰਚ, ਪਰਵਾਨਗੀ, ਸਵੀਕ੍ਰਿਤੀ, ਅਨੁਮਤੀ; ਇਕਬਾਲ; ਪ੍ਰਵੇਸ਼-ਸੁਲਕ, ਭਰਤੀ

admit (ਅਡ'ਮਿਟ) v ਦਾਖ਼ਲ ਕਰਨਾ, ਪ੍ਰਵੇਸ਼ ਕਰਨਾ ਜਾਂ ਕਰਾਉਣਾ, ਆਉਣ ਦੇਣਾ, ਪ੍ਰਵੇਸ਼ ਦੇਣਾ ਆਗਿਆ ਦੇਣੀ, ਮੰਨਣਾ, ਸਵੀਕਾਰ ਕਰਨਾ, ਇਕਬਾਲ ਕਰਨਾ, ਭਰਤੀ ਕਰਨਾ; ~tance ਪ੍ਰਵੇਸ਼, ਦਾਖ਼ਲਾ, ਪ੍ਰਵੇਸ਼ ਦੀ ਅਨੁਮਤੀ, ਅੰਗੀਕਰਨ

admix ('ਐਡਮਿਕਸ) v ਮਿਲਣਾ, ਮਿਲਾਉਣਾ, ਰਲਣਾ, ਰਲਾਉਣਾ, ਮਿਸ਼ਰਣ ਕਰਨਾ, ਮਿਸ਼ਰਤ

ਹੋਣਾ, ਘੋਲ ਦੇਣਾ, ਘੁਲ ਜਾਣਾ, ਰਲ ਮਿਲ ਜਾਣਾ; ~ture ਮਿਲਾਵਟ, ਮਿਸ਼ਰਨ, ਰਲਾ

admonish (ਅਡ'ਮੌਨਿਸ਼) v ਤਾੜਨਾ ਕਰਨੀ, ਤੰਬੀਹ ਕਰਨੀ, ਝਾੜ ਪਾਉਣੀ, ਚੇਤਾਵਨੀ ਦੇਣੀ, ਚੁਕੰਨਾ ਕਰਨਾ, ਜਤਾਉਣਾ, ਸੁਚੇਤ ਕਰਨਾ, ਧਿਆਨ ਦਿਵਾਉਣਾ; ~ment ਝਿੜਕ, ਡਾਂਟ-ਡਪਟ, ਚੇਤਾਵਨੀ, ਤੰਬੀਹ, ਤਾੜਨਾ

admonition (ਐਡਮਆ(ਉ)'ਨਿਸ਼ਨ) n ਚਿਤਾਵਨੀ, ਤੰਬੀਰ, ਤਾੜਨਾ

ado (ਅ'ਡੂ) n ਝਮੇਲਾ, ਬਖੇੜਾ, ਪੁਆੜਾ, ਕਲਹ

adolescence (ਐਡਆ(ਉ)'ਲੈੱਸੰਸ) n ਅੱਲ੍ਹੜਪਨ, ਗਭਰੇਟ-ਉਮਰ, ਮੁਟਿਆਰ-ਅਵਸਥਾ, ਜੋਬਨ, ਕਿਸ਼ੋਰਅਵਸਥਾ

adolesent (ਐਡਆ(ਉ)'ਲੈਸੰਟ) a n ਕਿਸ਼ੋਰ, ਅਲੂਝ (ਵਿਅਕਤੀ), ਨਵ-ਯੁਵਤੀ, ਨਵ-ਯੁਵਕ

adopt (ਅ'ਡੌਪਟ) v ਅਪਣਾਉਣਾ, ਧਾਰਨ, ਗ੍ਰਹਿਣ ਕਰਨਾ, ਲੈਣਾ, ਪ੍ਰਾਪਤ ਕਰਨਾ, ਗੋਦੀ ਲੈਣਾ, ਮੁਤਬੰਨਾ ਬਣਾਉਣਾ; ~ion ਗੋਦੀ ਲੈਣ; ਅੰਗੀਕਰਨ, ਗ੍ਰਹਿਣ, ਚੋਣ

adorn (ਅ'ਡੋਨ) v (ਗਹਿਣਿਆਂ ਨਾਲ) ਸਜਾਉਣਾ, ਸੰਵਾਰਨਾ, ਸ਼ਿੰਗਾਰਨਾ, ਅਲੰਕਰਤ ਕਰਨਾ, ਸੁਸ਼ੋਭਤ ਕਰਨਾ; ~ment ਸ਼ਿੰਗਾਰ, ਸਜਾਵਟ, ਅਲੰਕਰਣ

adrift (ਅ'ਡਰਿਫ਼ਟ) adv a ਡਾਵਾਂਡੋਲ, ਨਿਥਾਂਵਾਂ, ਅਸਥਿਰ, ਭਟਕਦਾ, ਵਹਿੰਦਾ ਹੋਇਆ

adroit (ਅ'ਡਰੋਇਟ) a ਹੁਸ਼ਿਆਰ, ਚਲਾਕ, ਚੰਟ, ਲਿਫ਼ਤਾ, ਚਤਰ, ਚੁਸਤ, ਫੁਰਤੀਲਾ

adult (ਅ'ਡੱਲਟ) a n ਬਾਲਗ਼, ਪ੍ਰੌੜ, ਸਿਆਣਾ, ਗੱਭਰੂ

adulterant (ਅ'ਡਅੱਲਟਅਰਅਨਟ) a n ਮਿਲਾਵਟ ਵਾਲਾ, ਖੋਟਾ, ਰਲੇ ਵਾਲਾ, ਮਿਲਾਵਟ, ਖੋਟ

adulterate (ਅ'ਡਅੱਲਟਰੇਇਟ) v a ਮਿਲਾਵਟ ਕਰਨਾ, ਖੋਟ ਰਲਾਉਣਾ, ਰਲਾਵਟ ਕਰਨੀ; ਅਸ਼ੁਧ, ਭ੍ਰਿਸ਼ਟ, ਖੋਟਾ, ਨਕਲੀ, ਬਣਾਉਟੀ, ਹਰਾਮੀ, ਵਿਭਚਾਰੀ

adulteration (ਅ'ਡਅੱਲਟਰਇਸ਼ਨ) n ਮਿਲਾਵਟ, ਖੋਟ, ਰਲਾ

adulterer (ਅ'ਡਅੱਲਟਅਰਅ*) n ਵਿਭਚਾਰੀ, ਝਨਕਾਰ, ਦੁਰਾਚਾਰੀ, ਪਰ-ਇਸਤਰੀਗਾਮੀ

adulteress (ਅ'ਡਅੱਲਟਅਰਿਸ) a ਯਾਰਨੀ, ਵਿਭਚਾਰਨ, ਦੁਰਾਚਾਰਨ, ਬਦਕਾਰ, ਪਰ-ਪੁਰਸ਼ਗਾਮਨ (ਇਸਤਰੀ)

adultery (ਅ'ਡਅੱਲਟਅਰਿ) n ਬਦਕਾਰੀ, ਹਰਾਮਕਾਰੀ, ਵਿਭਚਾਰੀ, ਪਰ-ਗਮਨ

advance (ਅਡ'ਵਾਂਸ) v n ਅੱਗੇ ਵਧਣਾ, ਧਾਵਾ ਬੋਲਣਾ; ਤਰੱਕੀ ਕਰਨੀ, ਉੱਨਤੀ ਕਰਨੀ, ਵਿਕਾਸ ਕਰਨਾ; ਪੇਸ਼ਗੀ ਦੇਣੀ, ਸਾਈ ਦੇਣੀ; ਪ੍ਰਸਤੁਤ ਕਰਨਾ, ਉਧਾਰ ਦੇਣਾ; ਪਹਿਲ, ਪੇਸ਼ਗੀ, ਸਾਈ; ~d ਉੱਨਤ, ਵਿਕਸਤ, ਵਧਿਆ, ਉੱਚ; ~ment ਉੱਨਤੀ, ਤਰੱਕੀ, ਵਾਧਾ, ਪੇਸ਼ਗੀ

advantage (ਐਡ'ਵਾਂਟਿਜ) n v ਲਾਭ, ਨਫ਼ਾ, ਫ਼ਾਇਦਾ, ਬਿਹਤਰੀ, ਮਹੱਤ, ਭਲਾਈ, ਲਾਭ ਪਹੁੰਚਾਉਣਾ, ਲਾਭਕਾਰੀ ਹੋਣਾ, ਹਿਤਕਾਰੀ ਹੋਣਾ; ~ous ਲਾਭਕਾਰੀ, ਫ਼ਾਇਦੇਮੰਦ, ਲਾਹੇਵੰਦ, ਉਪਯੋਗੀ, ਅਨੁਕੂਲ; ~ously ਲਾਭਦਾਇਕ ਢੰਗ ਨਾਲ, ਉਪਯੋਗੀ ਤੋਰ ਤੇ

adventure (ਅਡ'ਵੈਂਚਅ*) n v ਸਾਹਸ, ਜਾਂਬਾਜ਼ੀ, ਖਤਰੇ ਵਾਲਾ ਕੰਮ, ਔਖਾ ਕੰਮ; ਖ਼ਤਰਾ ਸਹੇੜਨਾ, ਸੰਕਟ ਵਿਚ ਪੈ ਜਾਣਾ, ਹਿੰਮਤ ਕਰਨਾ, ਬੀੜਾ ਚੁੱਕਣ ਜਾਂ ਉਠਾਉਣਾ; ~r (ਆਦਮੀ) ਸਾਹਸੀ, ਜਾਂਬਾਜ਼ ਹਿੰਮਤੀ, ਸਿਰਲੱਥ, ਸੱਟੇਬਾਜ਼ (ਵਿਅਕਤੀ) ਤਿਕੜਮਬਾਜ਼

adventurours (ਅਡ'ਵੈਂਚਰਅਸ) *a* ਸੂਰਮਾ, ਬੀਰ, ਸਾਹਸੀ, ਹਿੰਮਤੀ, ਦਲੇਰ, ਜਾਂਬਾਜ਼, ਪਰਾਕਰਮੀ

adverb (ਐਡਵਅਬ) *n* ਕਿਰਿਆ-ਵਿਸ਼ੇਸ਼ਣ

adversary (ਐਡਵਸਰ(ਅ)ਰਿ) *n* ਵਿਰੋਧੀ, ਪ੍ਰਤੀਪੱਖੀ, ਵੈਰੀ, ਹਰੀਫ਼

adverse (ਐਡਵਅਸ) *a* ਉਲਟ, ਹਾਨੀਕਾਰਕ, ਵਿਰੋਧ, ਵਿਪਰੀਤ, ਪ੍ਰਤੀਕੂਲ; ਅਣ-ਸੁਖਾਵਾਂ; **~ly** ਪ੍ਰਤੀਕੂਲ ਰੂਪ ਵਿਚ, ਵਿਰੋਧੀ ਤੋਰ ਤੇ, ਮੰਦੇ (ਭਾਗਾਂ) ਨਾਲ

adversity (ਐਡ'ਵਅਃਸਅਟਿ) *n* ਬਿਪਤਾ, ਪ੍ਰਤੀਕੂਲਤਾ, ਸੰਕਟ, ਆਫ਼ਤ, ਦੁਰਭਾਗ, ਬੁਰੇ ਦਿਨ, ਮੁਸੀਬਤ, ਮੰਦਹਾਲੀ

advertise (ਐਡਵਅਟਾਇਜ਼) *v* ਇਸ਼ਤਿਹਾਰ ਦੇਣਾ, ਪ੍ਰਚਾਰ ਕਰਨਾ, ਫੈਲਾਉਣਾ, ਮਸ਼ਹੂਰ ਕਰਨਾ, ਖ਼ਬਰ ਦੇਣੀ, ਸੂਚਤ ਕਰਨਾ, ਇਤਲਾਹ ਦੇਣੀ, ਵਿਗਿਆਪਨ ਕਰਨਾ ਜਾਂ ਦੇਣਾ; **~ment** ਇਸ਼ਤਿਹਾਰ, ਵਿਗਿਆਪਨ, ਆਮ ਇਤਲਾਹ, ਸੂਚਨਾ, ਐਲਾਨ

advice (ਅਡ'ਵਾਇਸ) *n* ਸਲਾਹ, ਰਾਇ, ਮਸ਼ਵਰਾ, ਨਸੀਹਤ; ਸੰਮਤੀ ਉਪਦੇਸ਼; ਸੂਚਨਾ, ਸਮਾਚਾਰ; **~s** ਚਿੱਠੀਆਂ, ਮਾਲ ਭੇਜਣ ਦੀਆਂ ਰਸੀਦਾਂ; ਵਿਚਾਰਕ ਸੂਚਨਾਵਾਂ

advisable (ਅਡ'ਵਾਇਜ਼ਅਬਲ) *a* ਯੋਗ, ਮੁਨਾਸਬ, ਉਚਿਤ, ਢੁੱਕਵਾਂ; ਉਪਯੁਕਤ

advise (ਅਡ'ਵਾਇਜ਼) *v* ਸਲਾਹ ਦੇਣੀ, ਮਸ਼ਵਰਾ ਦੇਣਾ, ਨਸੀਹਤ ਦੇਣੀ; ਸਿਫ਼ਾਰਸ਼ ਕਰਨੀ; ਉਪਯੁਕਤ ਦੱਸਣਾ; ਸੂਚਨਾ ਦੇਣੀ, ਸੂਚਤ ਕਰਨਾ; **~r** ਸਲਾਹਕਾਰ, ਮੰਤਰੀ, ਮਸ਼ੀਰ, ਪਰਾਮਰਸ਼ ਕਰਤਾ

advocate (ਐਡਵਅਕਅਟ) *n v* ਵਕੀਲ, ਐਡਵੋਕੇਟ; ਸਮਰਥਕ, ਪ੍ਰਤਿਨਿਧ, ਬਸੀਠ; ਵਕਾਲਤ ਕਰਨਾ, ਹਿਮਾਇਤ ਕਰਨਾ

aegis ('ਈਜਿਸ) *n* ਸਰਪਰਸਤੀ; ਰੱਖਿਆ; ਆਸਰਾ, ਯੂਨਾਨੀ ਦੇਵਤਿਆਂ ਦੀ ਢਾਲ

aerial (ਏਅਰਿਅਲ) *a n* ਹਵਾਈ, ਹਵਾ-ਸਬੰਧੀ, ਹਵਾ ਵਾਂਗ ਸੂਖਮ, ਖਿਆਲੀ, ਕਾਲਪਨਕ; ਆਕਾਸ਼ੀ, ਵਾਯੂਮੰਡਲੀ; ਏਰੀਅਲ (ਰੇਡੀਓ ਦਾ), ਲਹਿਰਾਂ ਨੂੰ ਇਕੱਠਾ ਕਰਨ ਵਾਲੀ ਤਾਰ

aerobus (ਏਅਰੋਬਅਸ) *n* ਵਾਯੂਯਾਨ, ਹਵਾਈ-ਗੱਡੀ

aerodrome (ਏਅਰੋਡਰਅਉਮ) *n* ਹਵਾਈ-ਅੱਡਾ, ਹਵਾਈ-ਜਹਾਜ਼ਾਂ ਦਾ ਅੱਡਾ

aerogram (ਏਅਰੋਗਰੈਮ) *n* ਹਵਾਈ-ਪੱਤਰ, ਹਵਾਈ ਤਾਕ, ਵਾਇਰਲੈਸ ਨਾਲ ਭੇਜੀ ਤਾਕ

aeroplane (ਏਅਰੋਪਲੇਇਨ) *n* ਹਵਾਈ-ਜਹਾਜ਼, ਵਿਮਾਨ, ਉਡਣ ਖਟੋਲਾ,

aesthetic (ਈਸ'ਥੈਟਿਕ) *n* ਸੁਜਵਾਦੀ, ਸੁਹਜਾਤਮਕ, ਸੁਹਜ ਭਰਿਆ, ਸੁੰਦਰਤਮਈ

afar (ਅ'ਫ਼ਾ*) *adv* ਦੂਰ, ਦੂਰ ਤੀਕ; **~from** ਦੂਰ ਤੋਂ, ਦੂਰੋਂ

affair (ਅ'ਫ਼ੇਅ*) *n* ਕਾਰ-ਵਿਹਾਰ, ਮਾਮਲਾ, ਸਮੱਸਿਆ, ਕਾਰਜ, ਕੰਮ, ਕਾਰੋਬਾਰ, ਸਮਾਰੋਹ, ਆਸ਼ਕੀ, ਪ੍ਰੇਮ ਸਬੰਧ, ਯਾਰੀ

affect (ਅ'ਫ਼ੈਕਟ) *v* ਅਸਰ ਕਰਨਾ, ਪ੍ਰਭਾਵ ਪਾਉਣਾ, ਮਨ ਵਿਚ ਬੈਠਣਾ; ਪ੍ਰਹਣਾ, ਵਰਤੋਂ ਕਰਨਾ, (ਬੀਮਾਰੀ ਦਾ) ਲੱਗਣਾ, ਚੁੱਕਣਾ; ਵਰਤਣਾ, ਵਿਹਾਰ ਕਰਨਾ; ਕੰਮ ਵਿਚ ਲਿਆਉਣਾ, ਵਿਖਾਵਾ ਕਰਨਾ; **~ation** ਆਡੰਬਰ, ਦੰਭ, ਖੇਖਣ, ਬਨਾਵਟ, ਦਿਖਾਵਾ, ਨਖ਼ਰਾ, ਛਲ, ਕਪਟ, ਬਹਾਨਾ; **~ed** ਭਾਵਾਤਮਕ ਢੋਂਗੀ, ਪਖੰਡੀ, ਕਪਟੀ, ਆਡੰਬਰੀ, ਆਡੰਬਰਪੂਰਨ, ਬਨਾਉਟੀ, ਕਲਪਤ, ਦਿਖਾਵੇ ਦਾ; ਪ੍ਰਭਾਵਤ, ਗ੍ਰਸਤ; ਪ੍ਰਭਾਵੀ; **~ive** ਪ੍ਰਭਾਵੀ, ਭਾਵਾਤਮਕ

affection (ਅ'ਫ਼ੈਕੱਸ਼ਨ) *n* ਸਨੇਹ, ਪਰੇਮ, ਮੋਹ, ਪਰੀਤ, ਲਾਡ, ਸਦਭਾਵਨਾ; **~ate** ਸਨੇਹੀ, ਪਰੇਮੀ, ਪਰੀਤਵਾਨ, ਲਾਡਲਾ, ਚਾਹੁਣਵਾਲਾ, ਸਨੇਹਪੂਰਨ; **~ately** ਪਿਆਰ ਨਾਲ, ਸਨੇਹ ਨਾਲ, ਪਰੇਮ ਨਾਲ, ਚਾਹ ਕੇ, ਮੋਹਤ ਹੋ ਕੇ

affidavit ('ਐਫ਼ਿ'ਡੇਇਵਿਟ) *n* ਹਲਫ਼, ਹਲਫ਼ਨਾਮਾ, ਹਲਫ਼ਲੀਆ ਬਿਆਨ

affilate (ਅ'ਫ਼ਿਲਿਏਇਟ) *v* ਮਿਲਾਉਣਾ, ਨਾਲ ਜੋੜਨਾ, ਸ਼ਾਮਲ ਕਰਨਾ, ਜੋੜ ਦੇਣਾ, ਸਬੰਧ ਜੋੜਨਾ

affiliation (ਅ'ਫ਼ਿਲਿ'ਏਇਸ਼ਨ) *n* ਮੇਲ, ਲਗਾਉ, ਸਬੰਧ; ਸਬੰਧਨਾ, ਸਬੰਧੀ-ਕਰਨ; ਮੁਤਬੰਨਾ ਬਣਾਉਣਾ

affinity (ਅ'ਫ਼ਿਨਅਟਿ) *n* ਨੇੜਨਾ, ਲਗਾਉ, ਸਾਂਝ, ਨਾਤਾ, ਵਿਵਾਹ-ਸਬੰਧ, ਨੇੜੇ ਦਾ ਸਬੰਧ, ਆਕਰਸ਼ਣ, ਸੁਭਾਅ ਜਾਂ ਆਚਾਰ-ਵਿਚਾਰ ਦੀ ਇਕਰੂਪਤਾ; ਸਮਰੂਪਤਾ

affirm (ਅ'ਫ਼ਅ:ਮ) *v* ਪੱਕ ਕਰਨਾ, ਪ੍ਰਸ਼ਟੀ ਕਰਨੀ, ਤਸਦੀਕ ਕਰਨੀ, ਦ੍ਰਿੜ ਹੋਣਾ, ਹਾਮੀ ਭਰਨੀ, ਸਮਰਥਨ ਕਰਨਾ

affix (ਅ'ਫ਼ਿਕਸ, 'ਐਫ਼ਿਕਸ) *v n* ਜੋੜਨਾ, ਬੰਨ੍ਹਣਾ, ਨੱਥੀ ਕਰਨਾ, ਚਿਪਕਾਉਣਾ, ਲਾਉਣਾ; ਜੋੜ, ਜੋਗ, ਅਗੇਤਰ-ਪਿਛੇਤਰ

affluence ('ਅ'ਫ਼ਲੂਅੰਸ) *a* ਬਹੁਲਤਾ, ਇਫ਼ਰਾਤ, ਸੰਪੰਨਤਾ, ਸਮਰਿਧੀ, ਧਨ, ਦੌਲਤਮੰਦੀ, ਖ਼ੁਸ਼ਹਾਲੀ, ਅਮੀਰੀ

afford (ਅ'ਫ਼ੋ*ਡ) *v* ਕਰ ਸਕਣਾ, ਸਾਰ ਸਕਣਾ, ਸਮਰੱਥਾ ਰੱਖਣਾ, ਸਮਰੱਥ ਹੋਣਾ, ਪ੍ਰਦਾਨ ਕਰਨਾ, ਪੁਗਾਉਣਾ, ਵਾਰਾ ਖਾਣਾ, ਪੂਗ ਸਕਣਾ, ਸਾਧਨ ਇਕੱਠੇ ਕਰਨੇ

afforest (ਐ'ਫ਼ੋਰਿਸਟ) *v* ਬਿਰਛ ਲਾਉਣਾ, ਜੰਗਲ ਉਗਾਉਣਾ; **~ation** ਰੁੱਖ ਜਾਂ ਬਿਰਛ ਲਾਉਣ ਦਾ ਕੰਮ, ਜੰਗਲਾਉਣ

affront (ਅ'ਫ਼ਰਅੰਟ) *v n* ਮੁਕਾਬਲਾ ਕਰਨਾ, ਨਿਰਾਦਰ ਕਰਨਾ, ਅਪਮਾਨਤ ਕਰਨਾ, ਪੱਤ ਲਾਹੁਣੀ; ਅਪਮਾਨ, ਤਿਰਸਕਾਰ, ਅਵੱਗਿਆ

afloat (ਅ'ਫ਼ਲਅਉਟ) *adv a* ਤਰਦਾ, ਵਗਦਾ, ਪਰਵਾਹਤ; ਜਹਾਜ਼ ਵਿਚ, ਪ੍ਰਚਲਤ, ਵਹਿੰਦਾ ਹੋਇਆ

afoot (ਅ'ਫ਼ੁਟ) *n a* ਪੈਦਲ, ਪਿਆਦਾ; ਚਲਦਾ ਹੋਇਆ, ਚਲਿਤ

afore (ਅਫ਼ੋ*) *adv* ਪਹਿਲਾ, ਸਾਮ੍ਹਣੇ, ਅਗੇ, ਮੁਹਰੇ; ਪੂਰਵ ਕਾਲ ਵਿਚ; **~said** ਉਕਤ, ਪੂਰਵ ਕਥਿਤ

afraid (ਅ'ਫ਼ਰੇਇਡ) *a* ਡਰਿਆ, ਭੈਭੀਤ ਸਹਿਮਿਆ, ਠਠੰਬਰਿਆ, ਤ੍ਰਹਿਆ, ਤ੍ਰਸਤ, ਛਿਆ

afresh (ਅ'ਫ਼ਰੈਸ਼) *adv* ਨਵੇਂ ਸਿਰਿਓਂ, ਨਵੇਂ ਸਿਰੇ ਤੋਂ, ਪੁਨਰ, ਦੁਬਾਰਾ, ਮੁੜੋਂ

after ('ਆਫ਼ਟਆ*) *a adv prep con* ਮਗਰਲਾ, ਮਗਰੋਂ ਦਾ, ਪਿੱਛੇ ਦਾ, ਪਰਵਰਤੀ ਬਾਅਦ, ਪਿੱਛੋਂ, ਉਪਰੰਤ, ਪਿੱਛੇ, ਬਾਅਦ ਵਿਚ ਪਿੱਛੇ ਪਿੱਛੇ, ਫਿਰ ਵੀ, ਇੰਨਾ ਕੁਝ ਹੋਣ ਤੇ ਵੀ ਜਦ; **~math** ਸਿੱਟਾ, ਨਤੀਜਾ, ਪਰਿਣਾਮ **~noon** ਲੌਂਢਾ ਵੇਲਾ, ਤੀਜਾ ਪਹਿਰ, ਦੁਪਹਿਰ ਪਿੱਛੋਂ ਦਾ ਸਮਾਂ

again (ਅ'ਗੈੱਨੇ) *adv* ਫਿਰ, ਦੁਬਾਰਾ, ਮੁੜ ਕੇ ਨਵੇਂ ਸਿਰਿਓਂ, ਪੁਨਰ

against (ਅ'ਗੈਨਸਟ) *prep conj* ਵਿਰੁੱਧ ਵਿਪਰੀਤ, ਖ਼ਿਲਾਫ਼, ਉਲਟ, ਪ੍ਰਤੀਕੂਲ, ਮੁਕਾਬ ਵਿਚ, ਟਾਕਰੇ ਵਿਚ, ਬਦਲੇ

age (ਏਇਜ) *n v* ਉਮਰ, ਆਯੂ, ਅਵਸਥਾ, ਜੀਵਨ ਕਾਲ; ਕਾਲ, ਯੁੱਗ, ਪੀੜ੍ਹੀ, ਸਮਾਂ, ਜ਼ਮਾਨਾ; ਬੁਢੇਪਾ **~d** ਬੁੱਢਾ, ਬਿਰਧ, ਪੁਰਾਣਾ; **~less** ਨਿੱਤ ਨਵ ਸਦਾ ਜਵਾਨ, ਸਦਾ ਨਵੀਨ; **~old** ਪੁਰਾਤ

ਪ੍ਰਾਚੀਨ, ਪੁਰਾਣੀ

agency (ਏਜੇਂਸਿ) *n* ਸ਼ਾਖ਼; ਆੜ੍ਹਤ; ਸਾਧਨ, ਸਬੱਬ, ਏਜੰਸੀ

agenda (ਅ'ਜੈਨਡਅ) *n* ਕਾਰਜ-ਸੂਚੀ, ਕਾਰਜਕ੍ਰਮ, ਏਜੰਡਾ

agent ('ਏਇਜਅੰਟ) *n* ਪ੍ਰਤੀਨਿਧ, ਆੜ੍ਹਤੀ, ਦਲਾਲ, ਮੁਖ਼ਤਾਰ, ਕਾਰਿੰਦਾ, ਕਾਰਜ-ਕਰਤਾ

aggravate ('ਐਗਰਅਵ੍ਰੇਇਟ) *v* ਵਧਾਉਣਾ, ਵਧੇਰੇ ਵਿਗਾੜਨਾ; ਗੰਭੀਰ ਹੋਣਾ ਜਾਂ ਬਣਾਉਣਾ, ਚਿੜਾਉਣਾ, ਤੰਗ ਕਰਨਾ

agravating ('ਐਗਰਅਵ੍ਰੇਇਟਿਙ) *a* ਤੰਗ ਕਰਨ ਵਾਲਾ, ਸਤਾਊ

aggravation ('ਐਗਰਅਵ੍ਰੇਇਸ਼ਨ) *n* ਵਿਗਾੜ, ਗੰਭੀਰਤਾ

aggregate ('ਐਗਰਿਗਅਟ, 'ਐਗਰਿਗੇਇਟ) *a n v* ਕੁੱਲ ਜੋੜ; ਸਮੂਹ, ਭੀੜ, ਸਮੁਦਾਇ; ਕੁੱਲ, ਇਕੱਠਾ, ਸੰਕਲਤ, ਏਕੀਕ੍ਰਿਤ; ਸਮੂਹੀਕ੍ਰਿਤ ਹੋਣਾ, ਇਕੱਠੇ ਹੋਣਾ, ਜਮ੍ਹਾਂ ਹੋਣਾ ਜਾਂ ਕਰਨਾ ਢੇਰ ਲਗਾਉਣਾ

aggress (ਅ'ਗਰੈਸ) *v* ਹਮਲਾ ਕਰਨਾ, (ਛੇੜ-ਛਾੜ ਵਿਚ) ਪਹਿਲ ਕਰਨੀ; ~ion ਹੱਲਾ, ਹਮਲਾ, **ਚੜ੍ਹਾਈ**, ਪ੍ਵਾਂ, ਆਕ੍ਰਮਣ; ਵਧਾੀਕੀ, ਵਾਪ, ਧੱਕਾ; ~ive ਹੱਲੇ ਲਈ ਤਿਆਰ ਰਹਿਣ ਵਾਲਾ, ਹਮਲੇ-ਸਬੰਧੀ, ਹੱਲੇ ਬਾਰੇ, ਆਕ੍ਰਮਣ-ਸ਼ੀਲ, ਉੱਦਮਸ਼ੀਲ; ~or ਹਮਲਾਵਰ, ਵਿਰੋਧੀ, ਲੜਾਕਾ, ਵਧੀਕੀ ਕਰਨ ਵਾਲਾ

aggrieve (ਅ'ਗਰੀਵ੍) *v* ਦੁਖਾਉਣਾ, ਦੁੱਖ ਦੇਣਾ, ਕਸ਼ਟ ਦੇਣਾ, ਦੁਖੀ ਕਰਨਾ, ਤੰਗ ਕਰਨਾ

aghast (ਅ'ਗਾਸਟ) *a* ਚੱਕਾ-ਬੱਕਾ, ਹੈਰਾਨ, ਵਿਸਮਤ, ਡੌਰ-ਡੌਰ, ਬੌਦਲਿਆ

agile ('ਐਜਾਇਲ) *a* ਚੁਸਤ, ਫੁਰਤੀਲਾ

agility (ਅ'ਜਿਲਅਟਿ) *n* ਚੁਸਤੀ, ਚਲਾਕੀ, ਫੁਰਤੀ, ਤੀਬਰਤਾ

agitate ('ਐਜਿਟੇਇਟ) *v* ਭੜਕਾਉਣਾ, ਉਕਸਾਉਣਾ, ਭਖਾਉਣਾ, ਉਤੇਜਤ ਕਰਨਾ; ਅੰਦੋਲਨ ਕਰਨਾ, ਹਲਚਲ ਕਰਨਾ; ਸੰਘਰਸ਼ ਕਰਨਾ; ~d ਉਤੇਜਤ, ਭੜਕਿਆ, ਸਤਾਇਆ, ਦੁਖੀ

agitation ('ਐਜਿ'ਟੇਇਸ਼ਨ) *n* ਅੰਦੋਲਨ, ਗੜਬੜ, ਵਿਆਕੁਲਤਾ, ਉਕਸਾਹਟ, ਹਲਚਲ, ਕਲਹ, ਉਤੇਜਨਾ

agitator ('ਐਜਿਟੇਇਟਅ*) *n* ਅੰਦੋਲਨ-ਕਰਤਾ, ਅੰਦੋਲਕ; ਹਲਚਲ ਪੈਦਾ ਕਰਨ ਵਾਲਾ, ਅੰਦੋਲਨਕਾਰੀ, ਉਪਦਰਵੀ

agony ('ਐਗਅਨਿ) *n* ਮਾਨਸਕ ਪੀੜ, ਵੇਦਨਾ, ਸੰਤਾਪ, ਚਿੰਤਾ, ਤਸੀਹਾ, ਸਰੀਰਕ ਕਸ਼ਟ; ਸੰਘਰਸ਼

agree (ਅ'ਗਰੀ) *v* ਮੰਨਣਾ, ਰਜ਼ਾਮੰਦ ਹੋਣਾ, ਹਾਮੀ ਭਰਨਾ, ਸਹਿਮਤ ਹੋਣਾ, ਰਾਜ਼ੀ ਹੋਣਾ, ਸਹਿਮਤੀ ਦੇਣਾ; ਤੈ ਕਰਨਾ; ~able ਅਨੁਕੂਲ; ਅਨੁਸਾਰ, ਅਨੁਰੂਪ, ਰਾਜ਼ੀ, ਸਹਿਮਤ, ਸੁਖਾਵਾਂ, ਰਮਣੀਕ, ਮਨੋਹਰ; ~ment ਗਠਿਮਤੀ, ਰਜ਼ਾਮੰਦੀ; ਮੇਲ; ਅਨੁਰੂਪਤਾ; ਸਮਝੌਤਾ, ਰਾਜ਼ੀਨਾਮਾ, ਇਕਰਾਰਨਾਮਾ

agricultural ('ਐਗਰਿ'ਕਲਚ(ਅ)ਰਲ) *a* ਵਾਹੀ ਦਾ, ਬੋਂ ਦਾ, ਖੇਤੀਬਾੜੀ ਦਾ, ਕਿਰਸਾਨੀ ਦਾ; ~ist ਵਾਹਕ, ਕਿਸਾਨ, ਜ਼ਿਮੀਂਦਾਰ

agriculture ('ਐਗਰਿਅੱਲਚਅ*) *n* ਖੇਤੀਬਾੜੀ, ਵਾਹੀ, ਕਾਸ਼ਤਕਾਰੀ, ਖੇਤੀ, ਕਿਰਸਾਨੀ, ਕ੍ਰਿਸ਼ੀ

agriculturist ('ਐਗਰਿ'ਕਅੱਚਅਰਿਸਟ) *n* ਕਿਰਸਾਨ, ਕਿਸਾਨ, ਜ਼ਮੀਨ ਵਾਹੁਣ ਜੀ ਬੀਜਣ ਵਾਲਾ, ਕਾਸ਼ਤਕਾਰ, ਖੇਤੀਬਾੜੀ ਕਰਨ ਵਾਲਾ

ahead (ਅ'ਹੈੱਡ) *adv pred a* ਅੱਗੇ, ਅਗਾੜੀ, ਸਾਮ੍ਹਣੇ, ਅਗਾਂਹ, ਅੱਗੇ, ਵੱਲ; ਤੇਜ਼ ਕਦਮਾਂ ਨਾਲ, ਤੀਬਰ ਗਤੀ ਨਾਲ, ਵਧਦੇ ਹੋਏ

aid (ਏਇਡ) *v n* ਸਹਾਇਤਾ ਕਰਨੀ, ਮਦਦ ਕਰਨੀ, ਉਪਕਾਰ ਕਰਨਾ; ਸਹਾਇਤਾ, ਮਦਦ

aide-de-camp ('ਏਇਡਡਅ'ਕੈਂਪ) *n* ਸੈਨਾਪਤੀ ਦਾ ਸਹਾਇਕ ਅਧਿਕਾਰੀ, ਏਡੀਕਾਂਗ, ਅੰਗ-ਸੇਵਕ

ail (ਏਇਲ) *v* ਕਸ਼ਟ ਦੇਣਾ, ਪੀੜਤ ਹੋਣਾ, ਦੁੱਖ ਦੇਣਾ ਜਾਂ ਹੋਣਾ, ਰੋਗੀ ਹੋਣਾ; ~**ing** ਬੀਮਾਰ, ਦੁਖੀ, ਰੋਗੀ, ਪੀੜਤ; ~**ment** ਤਬੀਅਤ ਦੀ ਖ਼ਰਾਬੀ

aim (ਏਇਮ) *n v* ਨਿਸ਼ਾਨਾ, ਟੀਚਾ, ਉਦੇਸ਼ ਮਨਸ਼ਾ; ਨਿਸ਼ਾਨਾ ਬਨਣਾ, ਵਾਰ ਕਰਨਾ, ਚੇਸ਼ਟਾ ਕਰਨੀ; ~**less** ਮਨੋਰਥਹੀਣ, ਨਿਰਉਦੇਸ਼, ~**lessness** ਅਟਕਣ, ਉਦੇਸ਼ਹੀਣਤਾ

air (ਏਅ) *a n* ਹਵਾ, ਵਾਯੂ; ਵਾਤਾਵਰਣ, ਵਾਯੂ-ਮੰਡਲ; ਰੰਗ ਢੰਗ, ਨਖ਼ਰਾ, ਹਵਾ ਵਿਚ ਰਖਣਾ, ਹਵਾ ਲੁਆਉਣਾ, ਹਵਾ ਖਾਣਾ, ਪਰਗਟਾਉਣਾ; in the~ ਅਫਵਾਹ, ਅਵਾਈ; on the~ ਰੇਡੀਓ ਤੋਂ ਬੋਲਦੇ ਹੋਏ; open~ ਖੁੱਲ੍ਹ-ਬਹਾਰਾ, ਖੁੱਲ੍ਹੀ ਥਾਂ; ~**base** ਹਵਾਈ ਅੱਡਾ; ~**conditioned** ਵਾਯੂ-ਅਨੁਕੂਲਤ; ~**craft** ਹਵਾਈ ਜਹਾਜ਼, ਵਿਮਾਨ; ~**field** ਹਵਾਈ-ਅੱਡਾ; ~**force** ਹਵਾਈ ਸੈਨਾ, ਵਾਯੂ ਸੈਨਾ; ~**line** ਹਵਾਈ ਕੰਪਨੀ, ਵਾਯੂ-ਮਾਰਗ ~**mail** ਹਵਾਈ ਡਾਕ; ~**port** ਹਵਾਈ ਅੱਡਾ; ~**way** ਹਵਾ ਦੇ ਆਉਣ-ਜਾਣ ਦਾ ਰਾਹ; ਵਾਯੂਮਾਰਗ, ਖਾਣਾਂ ਵਿਚ ਹਵਾ ਆਉਣ ਜਾਣ ਲਈ ਬਣਿਆ ਰਸਤਾ; ~**iness** ਹੋਛਾਪਨ; ਦਿਖਾਵਾ; ~**less** ਹਵਾ ਰਹਿਤ, ਦਮ ਘੋਟੂ; ~**y** ਹਲਕਾ, ਹੌਲਾ, ਹਵਾਈ, ਖੁੱਲ੍ਹਾ, ਹਵਾਦਾਰ, ਪ੍ਰਸੰਨਚਿੱਤ, ਬੁਲੰਦ, ਉੱਚਾ; ਬਾਰੀਕ, ਪਤਲਾ, ਨਿਰਰਥਕ; ਜ਼ਿੰਦਾਦਿਲ, ਰੰਗੀਲਾ

alarm (ਅ'ਲਾਮ) *n v* ਚੇਤਾਵਨੀ, ਖ਼ਤਰੇ ਦਾ ਘੁੱਗੂ, ਬਿਗਲ, ਅਲਾਰਮ, ਖ਼ਬਰਦਾਰ ਕਰਨਾ, ਚੇਤਾਵਨੀ ਦੇਣਾ, ਡਰਾ ਦੇਣਾ, ਝਟਕਾ ਦੇਣਾ, ਹਾਲ ਦੁਹਾਈ ਪਾਉਣੀ, ਟਟਟਟਾਉਣਾ, ਅਲਾਰਮ ਬੋਲਣਾ; ਵਿਆਕੁਲ ਕਰਨਾ, ਉਤੇਜਤ ਕਰਨਾ; ~**clock** ਅਲਾਰਮ-ਘੜੀ; ~**ed** ਡਰਿਆ, ਭੈ-ਭੀਤ, ਘਬਰਾਇਆ, ਸਹਿਮਿਆ; ~**ing** ਖ਼ਤਰਨਾਕ, ਚਿੰਤਾਜਨਕ, ਡਰਾਉਣਾ, ਧੁਹ ਕੱਢ ਦੇਣ ਵਾਲਾ

alas (ਅ'ਲੈਸ) *interj* ਉਹੋ, ਅਫ਼ਸੋਸ! ਹਾਏ! ਹਾਏ-ਹਾਏ!

ablum ('ਐਲਬਅਮ) *n* ਐਲਬਮ, ਚਿਤਰਾਵਲੀ, ਚਿਤਰ-ਪੁਸਤਕ

alcohol (ਐਲਕਅਹੌਲ) *n* ਮਦਸਾਰ; ਸਪਿਰਿਟ; ਅਲਕੋਹਲ

alert (ਅ'ਲਅ:ਟ) *a n v* ਚੌਕੰਨਾ, ਖ਼ਬਰਦਾਰ, ਚੌਕਸ ਚੇਤਾਵਨੀ, ਸੰਕਟ ਸਮੇਂ ਦੀ ਸੂਚਨਾ; ਸਾਵਧਾਨ ਕਰਨਾ, ਸਚੇਤ ਕਰਨਾ; ~**ness** ਸਾਵਧਾਨੀ, ਚੇਤਨਤਾ, ਖ਼ਬਰਦਾਰੀ, ਤਕੜਾਈ, ਤਿਆਰੀ

algebra ('ਐਲਜਿਬਰਅ) *n* ਬੀਜ ਗਣਿਤ, ਅਲਜਬਰਾ

alias ('ਏਇਲਿਅਸ) *n* ਉਪਨਾਮ, ਅੱਲ, ਉਰਫ਼, ਅਸਲੀ ਨਾਂ ਤੋਂ ਬਿਨਾਂ ਕੋਈ ਦੂਜਾ ਨਾਂ

alien ('ਏਇਲਯਅਨ) *a n* ਬਾਹਰਲਾ ਵਿਦੇਸ਼ੀ, ਓਪਰਾ, ਪਰਾਇਆ, ਬੇਗਾਨਾ, ਨਾਵਾਕਫ਼ ਅਸੰਗਤ, ਬਾਹਰੀ ਵਿਅਕਤੀ

alike (ਅ'ਲਾਇਕ) *a adv* ਤੁੱਲ, ਵਰਗਾ, ਮਿਲਦਾ-ਜੁਲਦਾ, ਸਮਾਨ, ਉਹੋ ਜਿਹਾ, ਉਵੇਂ ਹੀ, ਉਸੇ ਤਰ੍ਹਾਂ

alive (ਅ'ਲਾਇਵ਼) *a* ਜੀਉਂਦਾ, ਜੀਉਂਦਾ-ਜਾਗਦਾ ਜੀਵਤ; ਫੁਰਤੀਲਾ, ਸਜੀਵ; ਵਰਤਮਾਨ ਸਾਵਧਾਨ, ਸੋਝੀਵਾਨ, ਚੇਤਨ; ਛੋਹਲਾ, ਭਰਪੂਰ

all (ਔਲ) *a n adv* ਸਾਰਾ, ਸਾਰੇ ਦਾ ਸਾਰਾ, ਪੂਰਾ ਸਮੁੱਚਾ, ਸਰਬ, ਕੁੱਲ, ਬਿਲਕੁਲ, ਸਭ ਕੁਝ

ਪੂਰੀ ਤਰ੍ਹਾਂ

allay (ਅ'ਲੇਇ) *v* ਮੱਠਾ ਕਰਨਾ, (ਪੀੜ ਆਦਿ ਦਾ) ਘਟਾਉਣਾ, (ਤੇਹ ਦਾ) ਹਟਾਉਣਾ, ਦੂਰ ਕਰਨਾ, (ਦੰਗੇ ਫ਼ਸਾਦ ਨੂੰ) ਦਬਾ ਦੇਣਾ

allegation ('ਐਲ਼ਿ'ਗੇਇਸ਼ਨ) *n* ਦੋਸ਼, ਇਲਜ਼ਾਮ, ਦਾਵਾ; ਦੂਸ਼ਨ, ਉਜ

allegiance (ਅ'ਲੀਜੀਅਨਸ) *n* ਤਾਬੇਦਾਰੀ, ਵਫ਼ਾਦਾਰੀ, ਨਿਮਕ ਹਲਾਲੀ, ਰਾਜ-ਭਗਤੀ, ਸੁਆਮੀ-ਭਗਤੀ; **oath of~** ਵਫ਼ਾਦਾਰੀ ਦੀ ਸੌਗੰਧ, ਹਲਫ਼ੇ-ਵਫ਼ਾਦਾਰੀ

allegory ('ਐਲਿਗਾਇਰਿ) *n* ਰੂਪਕ, ਦੁਅਰਥੀ ਗੱਲ ਜਾਂ ਬਿਆਨ, ਦੂਹਰੇ ਭਾਵ ਵਾਲੀ ਕਵਿਤਾ; ਦਿਸ਼ਟਾਂਤ, ਪ੍ਰਤੀਕ

allergy ('ਐਲਅ*ਜਿ) *n* ਜਿਸਮ ਉੱਤੇ ਪਿਆ ਬਾਹਰਲਾ ਅਸਰ ਜੋ ਕਿਸੇ ਬੀਮਾਰੀ ਦਾ ਕਾਰਨ ਬਣੇ, ਅਤੀ ਸੰਵੇਦਨਸ਼ੀਲਤਾ, ਐਲਰਜੀ

alley (ਐਲਿ) *n* ਗਲੀ, ਭੀੜੀ ਗਲੀ, ਪਟੜੀ, ਤੰਗ ਰਸਤਾ, ਲਾਂਘਾ, ਪਗਡੰਡੀ; **blind~** ਬੰਦ ਗਲੀ

alliance (ਅ'ਲਾਇਅੰਸ) *n* ਗੱਠਜੋੜ, ਸੰਧੀ, ਮਿੱਤਰਤਾ, ਭਾਈ-ਵਾਲੀ, ਸਾਕਾਦਾਰੀ, ਨਾਤਾ, ਰਿਸ਼ਤਾ

allied (ਅ'ਲਾਇਡ) *a* ਸਸੰਘਾਤ, ਨਾਲ ਦਾ ਗਾਢਿਆ, ਜੁੜਿਆ ਹੋਇਆ, ਸਮਾਨ

alliteration (ਅ'ਲਿਟਅ'ਰੇਇਸ਼ਨ) *n* ਅਨੁਪ੍ਰਾਸ, ਵਰਣਾਵ੍ਰਿਤੀ

allocate ('ਐਲਅ(ਉ)ਕੇਇਟ) *v* ਵੰਡ ਦੇਣਾ, ਵੰਡੀ ਪਾਉਣੀ, ਟਿਕਣਾ, ਸਿੰਬਣਾ; ਨਿਸ਼ਚਤ ਕਰਨਾ, ਨਿਰਧਾਰਤ ਕਰਨਾ, ਹਿੱਸਾ ਕੱਢਣਾ, ਹਿੱਸੇ ਵੰਡਣੇ; ਸਥਾਨ ਨਿਯੁਕਤ ਕਰਨਾ

allocation ('ਐਲਅ(ਉ)'ਕੇਇਸ਼ਨ) *n* ਵੰਡਾਰਾ, ਬਟਵਾਰਾ, ਹਿੱਸੇ-ਵੰਡ, ਵੰਡ

allot (ਅ'ਲੋਟ) *v* ਹਿੱਸੇ-ਪਾਉਣਾ, ਵੰਡ ਕੇ ਦੇਣਾ, ਗੁਣੇ ਪਾਉਣਾ, ਟਿਕਣਾ, ਸਿੰਬਣਾ; ਵੰਡਣਾ, ਮੁਕੱਰਰ ਕਰਨਾ, ਅਲਾਟ ਕਰਨਾ; **~ment** ਹਿੱਸੇ-ਵੰਡ, ਵੰਡਾਰਾ, ਵਿਭਾਜਨ; ਨਿਰਧਾਰਤ; ਹਿੱਸਾ, ਨਿਰਧਾਰਤ ਭਾਗ; ਪ੍ਰਾਲਬਧ, ਭਾਗ, ਕਿਸਮਤ, ਨਸੀਬ; **~tee** ਵੰਡ-ਪਾਤਰ, ਜਿਸ ਨੂੰ ਚੀਜ਼ ਦਾ ਹਿੱਸਾ ਵੰਡ ਕੇ ਦਿੱਤਾ ਜਾਵੇ, ਅਲਾਟੀ

allow (ਅ'ਲਾਉ) *v* ਆਗਿਆ ਦੇਣੀ, ਇਜਾਜ਼ਤ ਦੇਣੀ, ਮੰਨਣਾ, ਯੋਗ ਮੰਨਣਾ; ਸਹਾਰਨਾ, ਝੱਲਣਾ; ਘਟਾਉਣਾ, ਕਾਟ ਕੱਟਣੀ, ਪ੍ਰਬੰਧ ਕਰਨਾ

alloy (ਅ'ਲੋਇ) *n v* ਮਿਸ਼ਰਤ ਧਾਤ, ਧਾਤ-ਮਿਸ਼ਰਨ, ਖੋਟ, ਮਿਲਾਵਟ, ਰਲਾ; ਮਿਸ਼ਰਣ ਕਰਨਾ; ਖੋਟ ਮਿਲਾਉਣੀ, ਖੋਟ ਮਿਲਾਉਣੀ, ਮਿਲਾਵਟ ਕਰਨੀ; ਖੋਟਾ ਬਣਾਉਣਾ; ਮੁੱਲ ਘਟਾਉਣਾ

allure (ਅ'ਲਯੁਅ*) *v n* ਭਰਮਾਉਣਾ, ਲਾਲਚ ਦੇਣਾ, ਵਰਗਲਾਉਣਾ, ਛਲਣਾ, ਮੋਹ ਲੈਣਾ, ਆਕਰਸ਼ਤ ਕਰਨਾ, ਰੀਝਾਉਣਾ, ਲਾਲਚ, ਲੋੜ, ਛਲ, ਆਕਰਸ਼ਣ, ਖਿੱਚ; **-ment** ਲੋੜ, ਲਾਲਚ, ਲਲਚਾਉ, ਖਿਚਾਉ, ਰੀਝ, ਰੀਝਾਉ, ਆਕਰਸ਼ਣ; ਮੋਹ

alluring (ਅ'ਲਯੁਅਰਿੰਡ) *a* ਮਹਕ, ਆਕਰਸ਼ਕ

allusion (ਅ'ਲੂਯ਼ਨ) *n* ਸੰਕੇਤ, ਰਮਜ਼, ਹਵਾਲਾ, ਗੁੱਝਾ ਇਸ਼ਾਰਾ, ਨਿਰਦੇਸ਼ ਸੰਦਰਭ, ਇਸ਼ਾਰੇ ਦੀ ਗੱਲ, ਗੁੱਝੀ ਗੱਲ

alma mater ('ਐਲਮਾ'ਮਾਟਅ*) *n* ਮਾਤਰੀ ਸੰਸਥਾ, ਆਪਣਾ ਕਾਲਜ ਜਾਂ ਵਿਦਿਆਲਾ, ਯੂਨੀਵਰਸਿਟੀਆਂ ਅਤੇ ਕਾਲਜਾਂ ਲਈ ਵਰਤਿਆ ਜਾਂਦਾ ਆਦਰਸੂਚਕ ਸ਼ਬਦ

almighty (ਅਲ'ਮਾਇਟਿ) *a adv* ਸਰਬਸ਼ਕਤੀਮਾਨ; (ਅਪ) ਮਹਾਂ

almirah ('ਐਲਮਿਰਅ) *n* ਅਲਮਾਰੀ

almond ('ਆਮਅਨਡ) *n* ਬਦਾਮ, ਬਦਾਮ ਵਰਗੀ ਚੀਜ਼; ~**oil** ਬਦਾਮ-ਰੋਗਨ

almost ('ਔਲਮਅਉਸਟ) *adv* ਲਗਭਗ, ਕਰੀਬ ਕਰੀਬ, ਤਕਰੀਬਨ

alms (ਆਮ) *n* ਭਿੱਖਿਆ, ਖ਼ੈਰਾਤ, ਖ਼ੈਰ, ਦਾਨ

aloft (ਅ'ਲੌਫ਼ਟ) *adv* ਉਤਾਂਹ, ਉੱਚਾ, ਉੱਚੇ ਦਾਅ, ਉੱਪਰ ਨੂੰ (ਜਾਂ ਵੱਲ), ਆਕਾਸ਼ ਵਿਚ, ਹਵਾ ਵਿਚ

alone (ਅ'ਲਅਉਨ) *adv a* ਇਕੱਲਾ, ਇਕੋ ਹੀ, ਇਕਾਕੀ, ਕੱਲਾ-ਸੁਕੱਲਾ, ਇਕੋ-ਇਕ, ਛੜਾ, ਨਿਰਾ; ਸਿਰਫ਼; ਅਦੁੱਤੀ, ਲਾਸਾਨੀ, ਬੇਜੋੜ; **leave~** ਇਕੱਲੇ ਛੱਡਣਾ

along (ਅ'ਲੌਙ) *a adv prep* ਨਾਲ, ਨਾਲ-ਨਾਲ, ਲਾਗੇ-ਲਾਗੇ, ਕੰਢੇ; ਇਕ ਸਿਰੇ ਤੋਂ ਦੂਜੇ ਸਿਰੇ ਤਕ, ਪੂਰੀ ਲੰਬਾਈ ਵਿਚ ਜਾਂ ਲੰਬਾਈ ਦੇ ਕੁਝ ਭਾਗ ਵਿਚ, ਅਗਾਂਹ, ਅਗਾਂਹ ਵੱਲ (ਨੂੰ), ਸਿੰਧਾ; **all~** ਹਰ ਵੇਲੇ, ਹਰ ਮੌਕੇ, ਪੂਰੇ ਸਮੇਂ ਲਈ, ਅੰਤ ਤਕ, ਤੋੜ ਤਕ; ~**side** ਬਗਲ ਵਿਚ, ਨੇੜੇ, ਨਿਕਟ, ਕੋਲ, ਪਾਸ, ਬਰਾਬਰ-ਬਰਾਬਰ; ~**with** ਨਾਲ-ਨਾਲ, ਸੰਗ-ਸੰਗ, ਨਾਲ ਹੀ

aloof (ਅ'ਲੂਫ਼) *adv* ਅਲੱਗ, ਅੱਡ, ਵੱਖ, ਪਰਾਂ, ਦੂਰ; ਨਿਆਰਾ, ਅਲਹਿਦਾ, ਨਿਵੇਕਲਾ; ਲਾਂਭੇ

aloud (ਅ'ਲਾਉਡ) *adv* ਉੱਚੀ ਅਵਾਜ਼ ਵਿਚ, ਉੱਚਾ ਬੋਲ ਕੇ, ਸਪਸ਼ਟ ਰੂਪ ਵਿਚ, ਖੁੱਲ੍ਹਮ-ਖੁੱਲ੍ਹਾ, ਪਰਗਟ ਰੂਪ ਵਿਚ

alphabet ('ਐਲਫ਼ਅਬੇਟ) *n* ਵਰਣਮਾਲਾ, ਊੜਾ-ਐੜਾ; ਪੈਂਤੀ, ਮੁੱਢਲੇ ਸਿਧਾਂਤ, ਮੁੱਢ; ~**tical** ਵਰਨ-ਕ੍ਰਮ-ਸਬੰਧੀ, ਵਰਣਮਾਲਾ ਦਾ, ਵਰਣਾਤਮਕ

already (ਅਲ'ਰੈੱਡੀ) *adv* ਪਹਿਲਾਂ ਹੀ, ਪਹਿਲਾਂ ਤੋਂ ਹੀ, ਅੱਗੇ ਹੀ, ਹੁਣੇ, ਹੁਣ ਤੀਕ, ਹੁਣ ਤਾਈਂ

also ('ਅਲਸਅਉ) *adv* ਵੀ, ਨਾਲੇ, ਨਾਲ ਹੀ, ਅਤੇ, (ਇਸ ਤੋਂ) ਇਲਾਵਾ

altar ('ਅਲਟਅ*) *n* ਵੇਦੀ, ਕੁਰਬਾਨਗਾਹ, ਉਹ ਥਾਂ ਜਿੱਥੇ ਕੁਰਬਾਨੀ ਦਿੱਤੀ ਜਾਵੇ

alter ('ਅਲਟਅ*) *v* ਬਦਲਉਣਾ, ਬਦਲ ਦੇਣਾ, ਰੁਪਾਂਤਰ ਕਰਨਾ, ਪਰਿਵਰਤਨ ਕਰਨਾ; ~**ation** ਤਬਦੀਲੀ, ਪਰਿਵਰਤਨ, ਪਲਟਾ, ਰੁਪਾਂਤਰ; ~**nate** ਬਦਲਵਾਂ, ਪਰਤਵਾਂ, ਇਕ ਦੂਜੇ ਦੇ ਪਿੱਛੋਂ ਆਉਣਾ, ਵਾਰੀ ਵਾਰੀ ਆਉਣਾ ਜਾਂ ਰੱਖਣਾ, ਬਦਲ ਬਦਲ ਕੇ ਆਉਣਾ; ਫੇਰਵਾਂ, ਇਕਾਂਤਰ, ਹਰ ਦੂਜਾ, ਵਟਾਵਾਂ, ਇਵਜ਼ੀ; ~**nately** ਵਾਰੀ ਵਾਰੀ, ਬਦਲ ਕੇ, ਇਕ ਪਿੱਛੋਂ ਦੂਜਾ; ~**native** ਫੇਰਵਾਂ, ਬਦਲਵਾਂ ਬਦਲੇ ਦਾ ਵਟਾਵਾਂ, ਦੂਜੀ ਸੂਰਤ, ਆਖ਼ਰੀ ਤਰੀਕਾ, ਦੋਹਾਂ ਵਿੱਚੋਂ ਇਕ, ਇਹ ਜਾਂ ਉਹ, ਬਦਲ

although (ਅਲ'ਦਅਉ) *conj* ਭਾਵੇਂ, ਹਾਲਾਂਕਿ, ਜਦੋਂ ਕਿ, ਤਾਂ ਵੀ, ਚਾਹੇ

altitude ('ਐਲਟਿਟਯੂਡ) *n* ਉਚਾਨ, ਉਚਾਈ ਉੱਚੀ ਥਾਂ, ਮਹੱਤਾ, ਸ਼੍ਰੇਸ਼ਟਤਾ; (ਗਣਿ) ਖੜ੍ਹੀ ਲੰਬਾਈ, ਅਵਲੰਬ, ਉਚਾਈ, ਸਾਗਰ ਤਟ ਤੋਂ ਉਚਾਈ

altogether (ਔਲਟਅ'ਗੈਦਅ*) *adv* ਸਾਰੇ ਦਾ ਸਾਰਾ, ਉੱਕਾ-ਪੁੱਕਾ, ਸਭ ਮਿਲਾ ਕੇ, ਪੂਰੀ ਤਰ੍ਹਾਂ, ਨਿਰਾ, ਬਿਲਕੁਲ

always ('ਔਲਵਿਜ਼) *adv* ਸਦਾ, ਨਿੱਤ, ਹਮੇਸ਼ਾ, ਹਰ ਸਮੇਂ, ਹਰ ਦਮ, ਹਰ ਵੇਲੇ, ਨਿਰੰਤਰ

a.m. (ਏਇ'ਐੱਮ) (*L*) ਪੂਰਬ-ਦੁਪਹਿਰ

amalgam (ਅ'ਮੈਲਗਅਮ) *n* ਮਿਲਾਵਟ, ਰਲਾ, ਮਿਸ਼ਰਣ; ਕਿਸੇ ਧਾਤ ਦਾ ਪਾਰੇ ਨਾਲ ਮਿਸ਼ਰਣ; ~**ate** ਰਲਾਉਣਾ, ਮਿਲਾਉਣਾ, ਰਲਣਾ, ਮਿਲਣਾ, ਸਾਂਝ ਪਾਉਣੀ, ਕਿਸੇ ਧਾਤ ਨੂੰ ਪਾਰੇ ਨਾਲ ਮਿਲਾਉਣਾ, ਮਿਸ਼ਰਤ ਕਰਨਾ ਜਾਂ ਹੋਣਾ; ~**ated** ਮਿਲਿਆ-ਜੁਲਿਆ, ਮਿਸ਼ਰਤ, ਇਕੱਠ, ਸੰਯੋਜਤ,

~ation ਮਿਲਾਵਟ, ਰਲਾ, ਮਿਸ਼ਰਣ, ਇਕੱਠ, ਸਾਂਝ, ਸੰਯੋਜਨ, ਯੋਗ, ਜਾਤੀ-ਮਿਸ਼ਰਣ, ਧਾਤੂ-ਮਿਸ਼ਰਣ

amass (ਅ'ਮੈਸ) *v* ਜੋੜਨਾ, ਸਮੇਟਣਾ, ਇਕੱਠਾ ਕਰਨਾ, ਸੰਚਤ ਕਰਨਾ, ਇਕੱਤਰ ਕਰਨਾ, ਸੰਗ੍ਰਹ ਕਰਨਾ, ਢੇਰ ਲਾਉਣਾ

amateur ('ਐਮਅਟਅ*) *n* ਗੈਰ-ਪੇਸ਼ਾਵਰ, ਸ਼ੁਕੀਨ, ਕਲਾ-ਪਰੇਮੀ

amaze (ਅ'ਮੇਇਜ਼) *n* ਹੈਰਾਨ ਕਰਨਾ, ਅਚੰਭਾ ਪੈਦਾ ਕਰਨਾ, ਵਿਸਮਤ ਕਰਨਾ, ਹੱਕਾ ਬੱਕਾ ਕਰਨਾ, ਚਕਰਾਉਣਾ; **~d** ਭੌਰ-ਭੌਰ, ਤੇਹੱਕਾ, ਹੱਕਾ-ਬੱਕਾ, ਅਚੰਭਤ, ਵਿਸਮਤ; **~ment** ਵਿਸਮੈ, ਹੈਰਾਨੀ, ਅਚੰਭਾ, ਅਸਚਰਜਤਾ, ਚਮਤਕਾਰ

amazing (ਐ'ਮੇਇਜ਼ਿਙ) *a* ਅਸਚਰਜ, ਵਿਸਮੈਕਾਰ, ਵਿਸਮਾਦੀ, ਅਜੀਬ, ਹੈਰਾਨਕੁਨ

ambassador (ਐਮ'ਬੈਸਅਡਅ*) *n* ਸਫ਼ੀਰ, ਰਾਜਦੂਤ, ਏਲਚੀ, ਦੂਤ

ambiguity ('ਐਮਬਿ'ਗਯੂਅਟਿ) *n* ਸੰਦੇਹ, ਸ਼ੱਕ, ਦੁਅਰਥਤਾ, ਅਸਪਸ਼ਟਤਾ, ਗੋਲ-ਮੋਲ ਗੱਲ, ਵਕਰੋਕਤੀ

ambiguous (ਐਂ'ਬਿਗਯੁਅਸ) *a* ਦੁਅਰਥੀ, ਸੰਦੇਹ-ਯੁਕਤ, ਅਸਪਸ਼ਟ, ਦੂਹਰੇ ਮਤਲਬ ਵਾਲਾ, ਅਨਿਸ਼ਚਤ, ਸ਼ੱਕ ਵਾਲਾ, ਮਸ਼ਕੂਕ

ambit (ਐਂਬਿਟ) *n* ਦਾਇਰਾ, ਘੇਰਾ, ਆਲਾ-ਦੁਆਲਾ

ambition (ਐਂ'ਬਿਸ਼ਨ) *n* ਅਭਿਲਾਸ਼ਾ, ਆਕਾਂਖਿਆ; ਤਾਂਘ, ਇੱਛਾ, ਚਾਹ, ਲਾਲਸਾ, ਦਾਇਆ, ਟੀਚਾ, ਨਿਸ਼ਾਨਾ

ambitious (ਐਂ'ਬਿਸ਼ਸ) *a* ਅਭਿਲਾਸ਼ੀ, ਚਾਹਵਾਨ, ਤਾਂਘੀ, ਆਕਾਂਖਿਆਵਾਨ; ਜੋਸ਼ ਭਰਿਆ, ਉਤਸ਼ਾਹਪੂਰਣ; ਸ਼ਾਨਦਾਰ

ambulance ('ਐਂਬਯੁਲਅਨਸ) *n* ਹਸਪਤਾਲੀ-ਗੱਡੀ, ਐਂਬੂਲੈਂਸ

ambush ('ਐਂਬੁਸ਼) *v n* ਘਾਤ ਲਾਉਣੀ, ਛਹਿ ਕੇ ਬੈਠਣਾ, ਘਾਤ ਵਿਚ ਬੈਠਣਾ, ਤਾੜ, ਛਹਿ, ਘਾਤ, ਦਾਅ, ਘਾਤਸਥਾਨ, ਘਾਤ ਲਾਉਣ ਵਾਲੀ ਸੈਨਕ ਟੁਕੜੀ

amend (ਅ'ਮੈਂਡ) *v* ਸੋਧਣਾ, ਸੁਧਾਰਨਾ, ਸੰਸ਼ੋਧਨ ਕਰਨਾ, ਤਰਮੀਮ ਕਰਨਾ, ਸੁਧਾਰਨਾ, ਸਉਰਨਾ; **~able** ਸੁਧਾਰਨਯੋਗ, ਸੋਧਣਯੋਗ; **~ed** ਸੋਧਿਆ, ਸੰਸ਼ੋਧਿਆ, ਸੁਧਰਿਆ; **~ment** ਸੰਸ਼ੋਧਨ, ਤਰਮੀਮ, ਸ਼ੋਧ, ਸੁਧਾਰ

amiable ('ਏਇਮਯਅਬਲ) *a* ਮਿਲਾਪੜਾ, ਖ਼ੁਸ਼ਮਿਜ਼ਾਜ, ਮਿਲਣਸਾਰ

amicability ('ਐਮਿਕਅ'ਬਿਲਅਟਿ) *n* ਮਿੱਤਰਤਾ, ਸੁਹਿਰਦਤਾ, ਮੇਲ-ਮਿਲਾਪ, ਸੱਜਣਤਾ

amicable ('ਐਮਿਕਅਬਲ) ਸਨੇਹਪੂਰਨ, ਮੈਤਰੀਪੂਰਨ, ਦੋਸਤਾਨਾ, ਸੁਹਿਰਦਤਾਪੂਰਨ, ਮੇਲ-ਮਿਲਾਪ ਵਾਲਾ, ਅਪਣੱਤ ਵਾਲਾ

amicably ('ਐਮਿਕਅਬਲਿ) *adv* ਸੁਹਿਰਦਤਾ ਨਾਲ, ਦੋਸਤਾਨਾ ਤੌਰ ਤੇ

amid, -st (ਅਮਿਡ, ਅ'ਮਿਡਅਸਟ/ *prep* ਵਿਚ, ਵਿਚਕਾਰ, ਦਰਮਿਆਨ, ਅੰਦਰ

amiss (ਅ'ਮਿਮ) *adv* ਨਾਕਸ, ਬੇਰੁਖਾ, ਕਸੂਤਾ, ਬੇਮੌਕਾ, ਬੇਤੁਕਾ, ਘਾਟੇਵੰਦਾ, ਭੁੱਲ-ਭੁਲੇਖੇ, ਗ਼ਲਤੀ ਨਾਲ, ਵਿਰੋਧੀ ਭਾਵ ਨਾਲ

amity ('ਐਮਅਟਿ) *n* ਮਿੱਤਰਤਾ, ਸੱਜਣਤਾ, ਸਹਿਰਦਤਾ, ਦੋਸਤੀ, ਮੇਲ-ਮਿਲਾਪ, ਗਨੇਹ ਭਾਵ

ammunition ('ਐਮਯੁ'ਨਿਸ਼ਨ) *n* ਬਾਰੂਦ, ਗੋਲੀ-ਸਿੱਕਾ, ਗੋਲਾ-ਬਾਰੂਦ, ਜੰਗੀ ਸਾਮਾਨ

among, -st (ਅ'ਮਅੱਙ, ਅ'ਮਅੱਙਅਸਟ) *prep* ਵਿਚ, ਵਿਚਾਲੇ, ਸਭ ਵਿਚ, ਗਿਣਤੀ ਵਿਚ, ਤੁਲਨਾ ਵਿਚ, ਮਿਲਾ ਕੇ, ਆਪਸ ਵਿਚ, ਪਰਸਪਰ

amount (ਅ'ਮਾਉਂਟ) *n v* ਧਨ-ਰਾਸ਼ੀ, ਰਕਮ, ਪੂੰਜੀ, ਕੁੱਲ ਧਨ, ਕੁੱਲ ਜੋੜ; ਮਾਤਰਾ; ਜੋੜ ਬਣਨਾ, ਜੋੜ ਹੋਣਾ; ਬਣਨਾ, ਭਾਵ ਅਰਥ ਹੋਣੇ; ਬਰਾਬਰ ਹੋਣਾ, ਕੁੱਲ ਜੋੜ ਹੋਣਾ

ample ('ਐਂਪਲ) *a* ਚੋਖਾ, ਬਹੁਤ, ਕਾਫ਼ੀ, ਖੁੱਲ੍ਹਾ, ਵੱਡਾ, ਮੋਕਲਾ, ਵਿਸਤਰਤ

amplification ('ਐਂਪਲਿਫ਼ਿ'ਕੇਇਸ਼ਨ) *n* ਵਾਧਾ, ਵਿਸਤਾਰ, ਫੈਲਾਵਟ; ਫੈਲਾਉ

amplifier ('ਐਂਪਲਿਫ਼ਾਇਅ*) *n* ਧੁਨੀਵਰਧਕ ਜੰਤਰ, ਐਂਪਲੀਫ਼ਾਇਰ

amplify ('ਐਂਪਲਿਫ਼ਾਇ) *v* ਵਧਾਉਣਾ, ਵਿਸਤਾਰ ਦੇਣਾ, ਖੁੱਲ੍ਹਾ ਕਰਨਾ, ਖੋਲ੍ਹ ਕੇ ਦੱਸਣਾ, ਵਿਸਤਾਰ-ਪੂਰਵਕ ਵਰਨਣ ਕਰਨਾ; ਧੁਨੀ ਵਿਸਤਾਰ ਕਰਨਾ

amply ('ਐਂਪਲਿ) *a* ਕਾਫ਼ੀ, ਬਹੁਤਾ, ਵਿਸਤਾਰ ਨਾਲ

amputate ('ਐਂਪਯੁਟੇਇਟ) *v* ਸਰੀਰ ਦੇ ਕਿਸੇ ਅੰਗ ਨੂੰ ਵੱਢਣਾ

amputation ('ਐਂਪਯੁ'ਟੇਇਸ਼ਨ) *n* ਅੰਗਛੇਦ, ਅੰਗ ਕਟਣ ਦੀ ਕਿਰਿਆ

amputator ('ਐਂਪਯੁਟੇਇਟਾ*) *n* ਅੰਗ-ਵੱਢਣ ਵਾਲਾ, ਅੰਗ-ਕਟਾਈ ਕਰਨ ਵਾਲਾ, ਅੰਗ ਛੇਦਕ

amuck (ਅ'ਮਅੱਕ) *adv* ਪਾਗਲਾਂ ਵਾਂਗ, ਪਾਗਲ ਹੋ ਕੇ, ਅੰਨ੍ਹੇਵਾਹ

amuse (ਅ'ਮਯੂਜ਼) *v* ਪਰਚਾਉਣਾ, ਖ਼ੁਸ਼ ਕਰਨਾ, ਮਨੋਰੰਜਨ ਕਰਨਾ, ਵਿਚਾਰਾਂ ਜਾਂ ਵਾਸਨਾਵਾਂ ਨੂੰ ਜਗਾਉਣਾ; ~**ment** ਦਿਲਪਰਚਾਵਾ, ਮਨੋਰੰਜਨ, ਖੇਡ-ਤਮਾਸ਼ਾ, ਹਾਸਾ-ਮਖ਼ੌਲ, ਦਿਲਲਗੀ

amusing (ਅ'ਮਯੂਜ਼ਿਙ) *a* ਵਿਨੋਦਕ, ਮਨਹਰ, ਖ਼ੁਸ਼ ਕਰਨ ਵਾਲਾ, ਸੰਤੋਖਜਨਕ

anaemia (ਅ'ਨੀਮਯਾ) *n* ਸਰੀਰ ਵਿਚ ਲਹੂ ਦਾ ਘਾਟਾ, ਭੁੱਸ, ਰਕਤਹੀਣਤਾ

analogy (ਅ'ਨੈਲਅਜਿ) *n* ਸਦ੍ਰਿਸ਼ਤਾ; ਦ੍ਰਿਸ਼ਟਾਂਤ, ਉਪਮਾ, ਸਮਾਨਤਾ, ਇਕਰੂਪਤਾ, ਸਮਰੂਪਤਾ, ਦਲੀਲਬਾਜ਼ੀ ਦਾ ਢੰਗ, ਅਨੁਪਾਤ, ਨਿਸਬਤ

analyse ('ਐਨਅਲਾਇਜ਼) *v* ਨਿਖੇੜਨਾ, ਨਿਖੇੜ ਕਰਨਾ, ਵਿਸ਼ਲੇਸ਼ਣ ਕਰਨਾ, ਪੜਤਾਲ ਕਰਨਾ, ਪਰਖਣਾ, ਛਾਣਬੀਣ ਕਰਨੀ, (ਵਿਆਕਰਣ) ਵਾਕ-ਵੰਡ ਕਰਨੀ, ਤੱਤ-ਨਿਖੇੜਨਾ

analysis (ਅ'ਨੈਲਅਸਿਸ) *n* ਵਿਸ਼ਲੇਸ਼ਣ, ਨਿਖੇੜ, ਛਾਣਬੀਣ, ਅੰਗ-ਨਿਖੇੜ, ਵਾਕ-ਵੰਡ, ਤੱਤ ਦਾ ਨਿਖੇੜ

analyst ('ਐਨਅਲਿਸਟ) *n* ਵੰਡਕਾਰ, ਵਿਸ਼ਲੇਸ਼ਕ

analytical ('ਐਨਅ'ਲਿਟਅਕਲ) *a* ਨਿਖੇੜਵਾਂ, ਵਿਸ਼ਲੇਸ਼ਣੀ, ਵਿੱਛੇਦਾਤਮਕ, ਵਿਸ਼ਲੇਸ਼ਣਪੂਰਨ, ਵਿਯੋਗਾਤਮਕ

anarch ('ਐਨਾਕ) *n* ਅਰਾਜਕ, ਬਾਗ਼ੀ, ਵਿਦਰੋਹ ਦਾ ਨੇਤਾ; ~**ist** ਅਰਾਜਕਤਾਵਾਦੀ, ਵਿਦਰੋਹਵਾਦੀ; ~**y** ਅਰਾਜਕਤਾ, ਰਾਜਹੀਣਤਾ, ਰਾਜ-ਰੌਲਾ, ਰਾਜਗਰਦੀ, ਸ਼ਾਸਨਹੀਣਤਾ, ਹਨੇਰਗਰਦੀ

ancestor ('ਐਨਸੈਸਟਾ*) *n* ਪੂਰਵਜ, ਵਡੇਰਾ, ਵੱਡ-ਵਡੇਰਾ, ਪਿਤਰ, ਬਜ਼ੁਰਗ, ਪਿਓ-ਦਾਦਾ

anchor (ਐਙਕਅ*) *n v* ਲੰਗਰ, ਆਸਰਾ, ਸਹਾਰਾ, ਭਰੋਸਾ; ਜਹਾਜ਼ ਦਾ ਲੰਗਰ ਸੁੱਟਣਾ, ਠਹਿਰਨਾ, ਜੁੜਨਾ, ਬੰਨ੍ਹ ਦੇਣਾ, ਰੋਕ ਦੇਣਾ

ancient ('ਏਇਨਸ਼ਅੰਟ) *a* ਪ੍ਰਾਚੀਨ, ਪੁਰਾਤਨ, ਕਦੀਮੀ, ਬੜਾ ਪੁਰਾਣਾ, ਘੁੱਥਾ; ਪੁਰਾਣੇ ਵਿਚਾਰ ਵਾਲਾ

ancillary (ਐਨ'ਸਿਲਅਰਿ) *a* ਸਹਾਇਕ, ਅਨੁਸੰਗੀ, ਅਧੀਨ

anecdote ('ਐਨਿਕ'ਡਅਉਟ) *n* ਵਿਕਾਇਤ, ਚੁਟਕਲਾ

anew (ਅ'ਨਯੂ) *adv* ਨਵੇਂ ਸਿਰਿਓਂ; ਮੁੜ ਕੇ, ਦੂਜੀ ਵਾਰ, ਫੇਰ, ਮੁੱਢੋਂ

angel ('ਏਂਜਿੱਜਲ) *n* ਦੇਵਤਾ, ਫਰਿਸ਼ਤਾ, ਨਬੀ, ਰਸੂਲ, ਦੇਵਦੂਤ; ਪੈਗੰਬਰ; ਸੁੰਦਰ ਤੇ ਮਾਸੂਮ ਮਨੁੱਖ; ~of death ਜਮਦੂਤ, ਅਜ਼ਰਾਈਲ ਫ਼ਰਿਸ਼ਤਾ; ~ic ਅਲੌਕਿਕ

anger ('ਐਂਗਰਾ*) *n v* ਗੁੱਸਾ, ਰੋਹ, ਕਰੋਧ, ਨਰਾਜ਼ਗੀ; ਗੁੱਸੇ ਕਰਨਾ, ਨਰਾਜ਼ ਕਰਨਾ, ਰੁਸਾ ਦੇਣਾ

angle ('ਐਂਗਲ) *n v* (1) ਕੋਣ, ਜ਼ਾਵੀਆ, ਨੁੱਕਰ, ਖੂੰਜ, ਗੁੱਠ, ਕੋਨਾ, ਦ੍ਰਿਸ਼ਟੀਕੋਣ; (2) ਮੱਛੀਆਂ ਫੜਨ ਵਾਲੀ ਕੁੰਡੀ; **obtuse~** ਅਧਿਕ ਕੋਣ, ਚੌੜਾ ਕੋਣ; **right~** ਸਮਕੋਣ, ਰਾਮ ਕੋਣ

Anglican ('ਐਂਗਲਿਕਅਨ) *a n* ਇੰਗਲਿਸਤਾਨ ਦੇ ਪ੍ਰੋਟੈਸਟੈਂਟ ਮੱਤ ਨੂੰ ਮੰਨਣ ਵਾਲਾ, ਅੰਗਲੀਕੀ

angry ('ਐਂਗਰਿ) *a* ਗੁੱਸੇ, ਖਫ਼ਾ; ਨਰਾਜ਼, ਅਪ੍ਰਸੰਨ; ਕਰੋਧਿਆ, ਗੁਸੈਲਾ, ਚਿੜਚੜਾ; ਸੜਿਆ-ਭੁੱਜਿਆ

angular ('ਐਂਗਯੁਲਅ*) *a* ਨੁੱਕਰਦਾਰ, ਨੁਕਰੀਲਾ, ਕੋਣੀ, ਕੋਣਕ; ਨੁੱਕਰ ਤੇ ਸਥਿਤ, ਤਿੱਖੇ ਮੋੜ ਵਾਲਾ; ਕੋਣ ਨਾਲ ਨਾਪਿਆ; ਪਤਲਾ, ਮਾੜਾ, ਕਰੜਾ

animal ('ਐਨਿਮਲ) *n a* ਜਾਨਵਰ, ਪਸ਼ੂ, ਡੰਗਰ, ਪ੍ਰਾਣੀ, ਜੀਵ, ਜੀਵ-ਜੰਤ, ਹੈਵਾਨ, ਜਾਨਵਰਾਂ ਵਰਗਾ, ਪਸ਼ੂ ਬਿਰਤੀ ਵਾਲਾ, ਕਾਮੀ, ਜੰਗਲੀ ਗਰੁੱਪ

animate ('ਐਨਿਮਅਟ,'ਐਨਿਮੇਇਟ) *a v* ਸਜੀਵ, ਸਚੇਤ, ਚੇਤਨ, ਜੀਵਤ, ਜਾਨਦਾਰ, ਚੁਸਤ, ਉਤਸ਼ਾਹੀ; ਜਿਵਾਲਣਾ, ਜਿੰਦ ਪਾਉਣੀ, ਜੋਸ਼ ਭਰਨਾ, ਹੌਸਲਾ ਵਧਾਉਣਾ

animation ('ਐਨਿਮੇਇਸ਼ਨ) *n* ਸਜੀਵਤਾ, ਜੋਸ਼, ਉਤਸ਼ਾਹ; ਜੀਵੰਤ-ਚਿਤਰ; ਲੋਰ, ਤਰੰਗ

animosity ('ਐਨਿ'ਮੌਸਅਟਿ) *n* ਵੈਰ-ਭਾਵ, ਦੁਸ਼ਮਣੀ, ਖੁਣਸ

ankle ('ਐਂਕਲ) *n* ਗਿੱਟਾ, ਟਖਣਾ; **~t** ਪਾਜ਼ੇਬ, ਝਾਂਜਰ, ਪਾਇਲ; ਫੋਜੀ ਪੱਟੀਆਂ, ਬਾਂਕ

annals ('ਐਨਲਜ਼) *n (pl)* ਸਾਲਨਾਮਾ; ਇਤਿਹਾਸਕ ਲੇਖਾਂ ਦਾ ਸੰਗ੍ਰਹਿ, ਇਤਿਹਾਸ, ਤਾਰੀਖ

annex (ਅ'ਨੈਕਸ) *v n* ਮਿਲਾ ਲੈਣਾ, ਸੰਯੁਕਤ ਕਰਨਾ, ਸ਼ਾਮਲ ਕਰਨਾ, ਨੱਥੀ ਕਰਨਾ, ਜੋੜਨਾ; ਵਾਧਾ ਲੈਣਾ

annex (e) ('ਐਨੈਕਸ) *n* ਵਾਧਾ, ਪੂਰਕ, ਅੰਸ਼, ਅੰਤਕਾ, ਉਪਭਵਨ, ਕਿਸੇ ਮਕਾਨ ਨਾਲ ਮਿਲਦਾ ਹਿੱਸਾ, ਛੋਟਾ ਮਕਾਨ; **~ture** ਅਨੁਲੱਗ

annihilate (ਅ'ਨਾਇਅਲੇਇਟ) *v* ਮਿਟਾਉਣਾ, ਨਸ਼ਟ ਕਰਨਾ, ਜੜ੍ਹੋਂ ਪੁੱਟਣਾ ਸਰਬਨਾਸ਼ ਕਰਨਾ, ਖੈ ਕਰਨਾ, ਸੰਘਾਰਨਾ

annihilation (ਅ'ਨਾਇਅ'ਲੇਇਸ਼ਨ) *n* ਤਬਾਹੀ, ਬਰਬਾਦੀ, ਸਰਬਨਾਸ਼, ਸੱਤਿਆਨਾਸ, ਸੰਘਾਰ, ਖੈ, (ਧਰਮ) ਸਰੀਰ ਆਤਮਾ ਦਾ ਨਾਸ਼, ਪਰਲੋ, ਸੁੰਨ ਅਵਸਥਾ

anniversary ('ਐਨਿ'ਵਅ:ਸ(ਅ)ਰਿ) *n* ਵਰ੍ਹੇਗੰਢ; ਸਾਲ-ਗਿਰ੍ਹਾ, ਜਰਸੀ, ਬਰਸੀ, ਵਾਰਸ਼ਕ ਉਤਸਵ, ਸਾਲਾਨਾ ਪੂਰਬ

Anno Domini ('ਐਨਅ(ਉ)'ਡੌਮਿਨਾਇ) *(L) phr (A.D)* ਸੰਨ ਈਸਵੀ ਵਿਚ, ਈਸਵੀ ਵਿਚ, ਈਮਾ ਦੇ ਜਨਮ ਬਾਅਦ

annotate ('ਐਨਅ(ਉ)ਟੇਇਟ) *v* ਵਿਆਖਿਆ ਕਰਨੀ, ਟੀਕਾ ਕਰਨਾ

annotation ('ਐਨਅ(ਉ)'ਟੇਇਸ਼ਨ) *n* ਟੀਕਾ, ਵਿਆਖਿਆ, ਭਾਸ਼

announce (ਅ'ਨਾਉਂਸ) *v* ਐਲਾਨ ਕਰਨਾ, ਘੋਸ਼ਣਾ ਕਰਨੀ, ਖ਼ਬਰ ਦੇਣੀ, ਹੋਕਾ ਦੇਣਾ, ਸੂਚਤ ਕਰਨਾ; **~ment** ਐਲਾਨ, ਘੋਸ਼ਣਾ, ਸੂਚਨਾ, ਹੋਕਾ; **~r** ਘੋਸ਼ਕ ਅਨਾਉਂਸਰ

annoy (ਅ'ਨੌਇ) *v* ਤੰਗ ਕਰਨਾ, ਚਿੜ੍ਹਾਉਣਾ,

ਖਿਝਾਉਣਾ, ਪਰੇਸ਼ਾਨ ਕਰਨਾ, ਜ਼ਿਦ ਕਰਨਾ; ~ance ਖਿਝ, ਚਿੜ੍ਹ, ਅੜਵਾਂ, ਪਰੇਸ਼ਾਨੀ, ਛੇੜਛਾੜ, ਉਜਲਾਹਟ

annual ('ਐਨਯੁਅਲ) *a n* ਸਾਲਾਨਾ, ਵਾਰਸ਼ਕ; ਵਰਸ਼ਜੀਵੀ, ਸਾਲਾਨਾ ਪਰਚਾ

annuity (ਅ'ਨਯੂਇਟੀ) *n* ਵਾਰਸ਼ਕ ਵਜ਼ੀਫ਼ਾ, ਤਨਖ਼ਾਹ ਆਦਿ, ਵਾਰਸ਼ਕੀ, ਸਾਲਾਨਾ

annul (ਅ'ਨਅੱਲ) *v* ਰੱਦ ਕਰਨਾ, ਮਨਸੂਖ ਕਰਨਾ, ਮੇਟਨਾ, ਨਾਜਾਇਜ਼ ਕਰਾਰ ਦੇਣਾ; ~ment ਮਨਸੂਖੀ, ਰੱਦਣ, ਖੰਡਨ, ਅੰਤ

annulate ('ਐਨਯੁਲੇਇਟ) *a* ਗੋਲਾਈਦਾਰ, ਛੱਲੇਦਾਰ, ਚੂੜੀਦਾਰ

anoint (ਅ'ਨੋਇੰਟ) *v* ਚੋਪੜਨਾ, ਤੇਲ ਮਲਣਾ, ਮਾਲਸ਼ ਕਰਨੀ; ਮੁਲਾਇਮ ਬਣਾਉਣਾ

anomaly (ਅ'ਨੈਮਅਲਿ) *n* ਅਸੰਗਤੀ ਬੇਤਰਤੀਬੀ, ਅਣਮੇਲ, ਬਿਖਮਤਾ, ਅਨਿਯਮਤਤਾ

anonym ('ਐਨਅਨਿਮ) ਅਗਿਆਤ ਨਾਂ, ਉਪਨਾਮ; ~ous ਅਗਿਆਤ ਲੇਖਕ ਦਾ, ਅਨਾਮ, ਗੁਮਨਾਮ; ~ously ਗੁਮਨਾਮ ਤੌਰ ਤੇ

answer (ਆਨਸਅ*) *n v* ਜਵਾਬ, ਉੱਤਰ; ਪ੍ਰਤੀ-ਕਿਰਿਆ, ਹੱਲ, ਨਿਵਾਰਣ; ਜਵਾਬ ਦੇਣਾ, ਉੱਤਰ ਦੇਣਾ, ਹੱਲ ਕਰਨਾ, ਜਵਾਬਦੇਹ, ਜ਼ਿੰਮੇਵਾਰ ਹੋਣਾ; ~able ਜਵਾਬਦੇਹ, ਉਤਰਦਾਈ, ਜ਼ਿੰਮੇਵਾਰ

ante-room ('ਐਨਟਿਰੂਮ) *n* ਡਿਓੜੀ, ਬੈਠਕ, ਬਾਹਰਲਾ ਕਮਰਾ

anthem ('ਐਂਥਅਮ) *n* ਗੀਤ, ਤਰਾਨਾ, ਭਜਨ, ਪਰਮਾਤਮਾ ਦੀ ਉਸਤਤੀ, ਖ਼ੁਸ਼ੀ ਦਾ ਗੀਤ

anthropology ('ਐਂਥਰਅ'ਪੌਲਅਜਿ) *n* ਮਾਨਵ-ਵਿਗਿਆਨ

anti (ਐਂਟਿ) *pref* ਵਿਰੁੱਧ, ਵਿਪਰੀਤ; ~biotic ਰੋਗਾਣੂਨਾਸ਼ਕ; ਰੋਗਾਣੂਨਾਸ਼ਕ ਦਵਾਈ; ~body ਪ੍ਰਤੀ ਪਿੰਡ, ਲਹੂ ਦੇ ਅਜਿਹੇ ਅੰਸ਼ ਜੋ ਕੁਝ ਹੋਰ ਅੰਸ਼ਾਂ ਦਾ ਨਾਸ਼ ਕਰਦੇ ਹਨ; ਰੋਗਨਾਸ਼ਕ ਅੰਸ਼; ~clockwise ਪੁੱਠਾ ਗੇੜਾ

anticipant (ਐਂਟਿ'ਸਿਪਅੰਟ) *n a* ਆਸਵੰਦ

anticipate (ਐਂਟਿ'ਸਿਪੇਇਟ) *v* ਪੂਰਵ ਗਿਆਨ ਹੋਣਾ, ਅਗਾਊਂ ਜਾਣਨਾ, ਅੱਗੇ ਹੋਣਾ, ਪਹਿਲ ਕਰਨੀ, ਆਸ ਰੱਖਣੀ; ਉਡੀਕਣਾ

anticipation (ਐਂਟਿਸਿ'ਪੇਇਸ਼ਨ) *n* ਪੂਰਵ ਅਨੁਸਾਰ, ਪੂਰਵ ਧਾਰਣਾ, ਪੂਰਵ-ਗਿਆਨ; ਪੂਰਵ-ਆਸ, ਪੇਸ਼ਬੰਦੀ, ਉਡੀਕ

antipathy (ਐਂ'ਟਿਪਅਥਿ) *n* ਘਿਰਣਾ; ਵੈਰ, ਵਿਰੋਧ, ਵੈਰ-ਭਾਵ, ਦਵੈਖ-ਭਾਵ

antique (ਐਂ'ਟੀਕ) *a n* ਪੁਰਾਤਨ, ਪ੍ਰਾਚੀਨ, ਕਦੀਮੀ; ਪੁਰਾਣੇ ਢੰਗ ਦਾ, ਪਰੰਪਰਾਵਾਦੀ, ਰੂੜੀਵਾਦੀ, ਪੁਰਾਤਨ ਕਲਾ ਦੇ ਨਮੂਨੇ

antiquity (ਐਂ'ਟਿਕਵਅਟਿ) *n* ਪ੍ਰਾਚੀਨ ਕਾਲ, ਪੂਰਵ-ਕਾਲ, ਪੁਰਾਤਨਤਾ, ਪ੍ਰਾਚੀਨਤਾ, ਪ੍ਰਾਚੀਨ-ਯੁੱਗ, ਆਦਿਕਾਲ, ਪੁਰਾਣੇ ਆਦਮੀ, ਵੱਡ ਵਡੇਰੇ; ਪੁਰਾਣੇ ਰੀਤੀ ਰਿਵਾਜ, ਪਰੰਪਰਾਵਾਂ, ਪੁਰਾਣੀਆਂ ਘਟਨਾਵਾਂ, ਪ੍ਰਾਚੀਨ ਲੱਭਤਾਂ

antitheist ('ਐਂਟਿ'ਥਿਇਸਟ) *n* ਨਾਸਤਕ, ਈਸ਼ਵਰ ਵਿਰੋਧੀ, ਖ਼ੁਦਾ ਤੋਂ ਮੁਨਕਰ

antithesis (ਐਂ'ਟਿਥਿਸਿਸ) *n* ਪ੍ਰਤੀਕੂਲਤਾ, ਮੱਤਭੇਦ, ਪ੍ਰਤੀਪੱਖ, ਵਿਰੋਧ ਅਲੰਕਾਰ, ਵਿਪਰੀਤਤਾ

antonym (ਐਂਟਅਨਿਮ) *n* ਉਲਟ-ਭਾਵੀ ਸ਼ਬਦ, ਵਿਪਰੀਤ-ਅਰਥ ਬੋਧਕ ਸ਼ਬਦ, ਵਿਰੋਧੀ ਅਰਥਾਂ ਵਾਲਾ ਸ਼ਬਦ, ਵਿਪਰਜਾਝ

anxiety (ਐਡ਼'ਜ਼ਾਇਅਟਿ) *n* ਚਿੰਤਾ, ਫ਼ਿਕਰ, ਪਰੇਸ਼ਾਨੀ, ਵਿਆਕੁਲਤਾ; ਤੌਖ਼ਲਾ; ਉਤਸੁਕਤਾ, ਤਾਂਘ

anxious ('ਐਡ਼(ਕ)ਸ਼ਅਸ) *a* ਉਤਸੁਕ,

ਉਤਾਵਲਾ; ਬੇਚੈਨ, ਬੇਤਾਬ

any ('ਐਨਿ) *a pron* ਇਕ, ਕੋਈ, ਕੁਝ ਥੋੜ੍ਹਾ ਜਿਹਾ, ਕੋਈ ਵੀ, ਕੁਝ ਵੀ, ਹਰ ਇਕ, ਜੋ ਵੀ, ਜਿਹੜਾ ਵੀ; **~body** ਕੋਈ ਬੰਦਾ, ਕੋਈ ਮਨੁੱਖ, ਕੋਈ ਵੀ, ਫ਼ਲਾਣਾ-ਢਿਮਕਾ; **~how** ਕਿਸੇ ਤਰ੍ਹਾਂ, ਕਿਸੇ ਨਾ ਕਿਸੇ ਤਰੀਕੇ ਨਾਲ, ਜਿਵੇਂ ਕਿਵੇਂ ਵੀ, ਕਿਸੇ ਵੀ ਹਾਲਤ ਵਿਚ; **~thing** ਕੋਈ ਸ਼ੈ ਜਾਂ ਵਸਤੂ, ਕੋਈ ਵੀ ਚੀਜ਼, ਕੁਝ ਵੀ, ਕੋਈ ਇਕ ਚੀਜ਼, ਹਰ ਚੀਜ਼; **~where** ਕਿਧਰੇ; ਕਿਤੇ, ਕਿਸੇ ਥਾਂ, ਕਿਤੇ ਵੀ, ਹੋਰ ਥਾਂ, ਸਾਰੇ ਹੀ, ਸਭ ਥਾਂ; **at~time** ਕਿਸੇ ਵੇਲੇ, ਕਿਸੇ ਸਮੇਂ

apart (ਅ'ਪਾਟ) *adv* ਇਕ ਬੰਨੇ, ਵੱਖਰਾ, ਅੱਡ, ਲਾਂਭੇ, ਵੱਖ-ਵੱਖ, ਦੂਰੀ ਰੱਖ ਕੇ, ਫ਼ਾਸਲੇ ਉਤੇ; **set~** ਵੱਖਰਾ ਰੱਖਣਾ,ਬਚਾ ਕੇ ਰੱਖ ਲੈਣਾ

apartheid (ਅ'ਪਾਟਹੇਇਟ) *n* ਨਸਲੀ ਵਿਤਕਰਾ, ਭੇਦ ਭਾਵ ਵਾਲਾ ਵਰਤਾਉ

apartment (ਅ'ਪਾ*ਟਮਅੰਟ) *n* ਕਮਰਾ, ਕੋਠਾ, ਮਕਾਨ

apathetic ('ਐਪਅ'ਥੈਟਿਕ) *a* ਉਦਾਸੀਨ, ਲਾਪਰਵਾਹ, ਉਤਸ਼ਾਹਹੀਨ; ਨਿਰਪੇਖ, ਹਿਰਦੇਹੀਨ

apathy ('ਐਪਅਥਿ) *n* ਲਾਪਰਵਾਹੀ, ਰੁੱਖਾਪਨ, ਕੋਰਾਪਨ; ਅਲੇਪਤਾ, ਵੈਰਾਗ, ਬੇਦਿਲੀ, ਉਤਸ਼ਾਹ-ਹੀਣਤਾ, ਨਿਰਦਇਤਾ

ape (ਏਇਪ) *n v* ਇਕ ਪੂਛਹੀਣ ਬਾਂਦਰ; ਨਕਲੀਆ, ਸਾਂਗ ਲਾਉਣਾ, ਨਕਲ ਉਤਾਰਨੀ; **to play the ~** ਨਕਲ ਕਰਨਾ, ਬਾਂਦਰ ਵਾਂਗੂ ਨਕਲ ਕਰਨਾ

apex ('ਏਇਪਿਕਸ) *n* ਸਿਖਰ, ਉਤਲੀ ਨੋਕ, ਸਿਰ-ਬਿੰਦੂ, ਟੀਸੀ-ਪੱਥਰ

aphasia (ਅ'ਫ਼ਇਜ਼ਯਅ) *n* ਗੁੰਗਾਪਨ, ਦਿਮਾਗ਼ ਨੂੰ ਸੱਟ ਲੱਗਣ ਕਰਕੇ ਬੋਲਣਾ ਬੰਦ ਹੋ ਜਾਣ ਦਾ ਰੋਗ

Apollo (ਅ'ਪੌਲਅਉ) *n* ਯੂਨਾਨ ਦਾ ਸੂਰਜ ਦੇਵਤਾ; ਸੂਰਜ; ਅਤੀ ਸੁੰਦਰ ਵਿਅਕਤੀ

apologize (ਅ'ਪੌਲਅਜਾਇਜ਼) *v* ਮਾਫ਼ੀ ਮੰਗਣਾ, ਖਿਮਾਂ ਜਾਚਨਾ ਕਰਨੀ, ਭੁੱਲ ਮੰਨਣੀ

apologue ('ਐਪਅਲੌਗ) ਨੀਤੀ ਕਥਾ, ਇਖ਼ਲਾਕੀ, ਕਿੱਸਾ, ਸਿਖਆਦਾਇਕ ਕਥਾ

apology (ਅ'ਪੌਲਅਜਿ) *n* ਖਿਮਾਜਾਚਨਾ, ਭੁੱਲ ਦੀ ਸੋਧ; ਸਫ਼ਾਈ

apostle (ਅ'ਪੌਸਲ) *n* ਪੈਗ਼ੰਬਰ, ਰਸੂਲ, ਇਸਾਈ ਧਰਮ ਪਰਚਾਰਕ

apparatus ('ਐਪਅ'ਰੇਇਟਅਸ) *n* ਉਪਕਰਣ, ਵਿਗਿਆਨਕ ਜੰਤਰ ਆਦਿ, ਸਾਮਾਨ, ਸੰਦ, ਹਥਿਆਰ, ਔਜ਼ਾਰ; ਸਰੀਰ ਦੇ ਅੰਗ-ਜੋੜ

apparent (ਅੰ'ਪੈਰਅੰਟ) *a* ਦਿਸਦਾ, ਜਾਪਦਾ; ਪ੍ਰਤੱਖ, ਸਪਸ਼ਟ; **~ly** ਜ਼ਾਹਰਾ ਤੌਰ ਤੇ, ਵੇਖਣ ਵਿਚ; ਸਪਸ਼ਟ ਰੂਪ ਵਿਚ, ਵਿਖਾਵੇ ਨੂੰ

appeal (ਅ'ਪੀਲ) *n v* ਅਪੀਲ, ਪੁਨਰ-ਵਿਚਾਰ ਪ੍ਰਾਰਥਨਾ; ਪੁਨਰ-ਵਿਚਾਰ, ਅਪੀਲ ਕਰਨੀ, ਪ੍ਰਾਰਥਨਾ ਕਰਨੀ, ਮਿੰਨਤ ਕਰਨੀ; **~ing** ਦਿਲ ਖਿੱਚਵਾਂ, ਆਕਰਸ਼ਕ

appear (ਅ'ਪਿਅ*) *v* ਹਾਜ਼ਰ ਹੋਣਾ; ਪੇਸ਼ ਆਉਣਾ (ਦਾ), ਉਪਸਥਿਤ ਹੋਣਾ; ਬੈਠਣਾ (ਪਰੀਖਿਆ ਵਿਚ); **~ance** ਪ੍ਰਤੱਖਤਾ, ਆਗਮਨ, ਹਾਜ਼ਰੀ, ਉਪਸਥਿਤੀ, ਪੇਸ਼ੀ (ਦਾ); ਰੂਪ, ਸੂਰਤ, ਦਰਸ਼ਨ, ਦ੍ਰਿਸ਼ਟੀ-ਭਰਮ

appease (ਅਪੀਜ਼) *v* ਪ੍ਰਸੰਨ ਕਰਨਾ, ਮਨਾਉਣਾ, ਰਾਜ਼ੀ ਕਰਨਾ, ਸ਼ਾਂਤ ਕਰਨਾ, ਦਿਲਾਸਾ ਦੇਣਾ; ਠੰਢਾ ਕਰਨਾ, ਸੰਤੁਸ਼ਟ ਕਰਨਾ, ਪਤਿਆਉਣਾ

appellant (ਅ'ਪੈੱਲਅੰਟ) *n a* ਅਪੀਲ-ਸਬੰਧੀ, ਪੁਨਰਆਵੇਦਨ ਸਬੰਧੀ; ਅਪੀਲ-ਕਰਨਾ

appellate (ਅ'ਪੈੱਲਅਟ) *a* ਮੁੜ, ਵਿਚਾਰਨਯੋਗ,

ਪੁਨਰਵਿਚਾਰਕ, ਅਪੀਲ ਸੁਣਨ ਜਾਂ ਕਰਨ ਵਾਲਾ

append (ਅ'ਪੈਂਡ) *v* ਜੜਨਾ, ਲਾਉਣਾ, ਮਿਲਾਉਣਾ, ਨੱਥੀ ਕਰਨਾ, ਟਾਂਕਣਾ, ਸੰਯੁਕਤ ਕਰਨਾ; ~age ਜੋੜ, ਵਾਧਾ, ਸਹਾਇਕ, ਜ਼ਮੀਮਾ, ਉਪਕਰਣ, ਗੌਣ-ਅੰਗ

appendicitis (ਅ'ਪੈਂਡਿ'ਸਾਇਟਿਸ) *n* ਕੁਲੰਜ, ਅੰਤੜੀਆਂ ਦੀ ਸੋਜਸ਼

appendix (ਅ'ਪੈਂਡਿਕਸ) *n* ਅੰਤਕਾ, ਪੂਰਕ ਭਾਗ, ਜ਼ਮੀਮਾ, ਸਹਾਇਕ ਭਾਗ

appetite ('ਐਪਿਟਾਇਟ) *n* ਭੁੱਖ, ਲਾਲਸਾ, ਚਾਹ, ਤਾਂਘ

appetize ('ਐਪਿਟਾਇਜ਼) *v* ਭੁੱਖ ਲਾਉਣਾ, ਇੱਛਾ ਜਗਾਉਣੀ, ਰੁਚਤ ਕਰਨਾ

appetizing ('ਐਪਿਟਾਇਜ਼ਿਙ) *a* ਭੁੱਖ-ਵਧਾਊ

applaud (ਅ'ਪਲੈਡ) *a* ਪ੍ਰਸੰਸਾ ਕਰਨਾ, ਸਲਾਹੁਣਾ, ਤਾੜੀ ਵਜਾਉਣਾ, ਵਾਹਵਾ ਕਰਨੀ

applause (ਅ'ਪਲੈਜ਼) *n* ਪ੍ਰਸੰਸਾ, ਉਸਤਤੀ, ਸਾਬਾਸ਼, ਵਾਹ ਵਾਹ, ਤਾੜੀ

apple ('ਐਪਲ) *n* ਸੇਬ, ਸਿਊ; ~cart ਯੋਜਨਾ, ਵਿਉਂਤ, ਸਕੀਮ; ~pie order ਚੀਜ਼ਾਂ ਦਾ ਥਾਂ ਸਿਰ ਹੋਣਾ, ਪੂਰਨ ਸਾਂਝੀ, ਮੁਕੰਮਲ ਪ੍ਰਬੰਧ

appliance (ਅ'ਪਲਾਇਅੰਨਸ) *n* ਉਪਕਰਣ, ਸਾਧਨ, ਉਪਾਉ; ਪ੍ਰਯੋਗ, ਵਰਤੋਂ

applicability ('ਐਪਲਿਕਅਬਿਲਅਟਿ) *n* ਉਚਿਤਤਾ, ਅਨੁਕੂਲਤਾ, ਯੋਗਤਾ

applicable ('ਐਪਲਿਕਅਬਲ) *a* ਮੁਨਾਸਬ, ਉਚਿਤ, ਲਾਗੂ ਹੋਣ ਯੋਗ, ਅਨੁਕੂਲ, ਪ੍ਰਸੰਗ-ਅਨੁਕੂਲ, ਯੋਗ, ਠੀਕ, ਢੁੱਕਦਾ

applicant ('ਐਪਲਿਕਅੰਟ) *n* ਨਿਵੇਦਕ, ਜਾਚਕ, ਆਵੇਦਕ, ਬਿਨੈਕਾਰ, ਦਰਖ਼ਾਸਤ ਕਰਨ ਵਾਲਾ, ਬੇਨਤੀ ਕਰਨ ਵਾਲਾ; ਉਮੀਦਵਾਰ

application ('ਐਪਲਿਕੇਇਸ਼ਨ) *n* (1) ਅਰਜ਼ੀ, ਦਰਖ਼ਾਸਤ, ਬਿਨੈ-ਪੱਤਰ, ਨਿਵੇਦਨ-ਪੱਤਰ, ਪ੍ਰਾਰਥਨਾ-ਪੱਤਰ; (2) ਉਦਮ, ਉਦਯੋਗ, ਮਿਹਨਤ; (3) ਉਚਿਤਤਾ; ਪ੍ਰਸੰਗਕਤਾ, ਸੁਸੰਗਤ

applied (ਅ'ਪਲਾਇਡ) *a* ਲਾਗੂ ਕੀਤਾ ਹੋਇਆ, ਪ੍ਰਾਯੋਗਿਕ

apply (ਅ'ਪਲਾਇ) *v* (1) ਵਰਤੋਂ ਵਿਚ ਲਿਆਉਣਾ, (2) ਵਰਤਣਾ, ਲਾਗੂ ਕਰਨਾ; ਅਰਜ਼ੀ ਦੇਣੀ, ਦਰਖ਼ਾਸਤ ਦੇਣੀ, ਪ੍ਰਾਰਥਨਾ ਕਰਨੀ; (3) ਸਬੰਧਤ ਹੋਣਾ, ਸਬੰਧ ਰੱਖਣਾ, ਧਿਆਨ ਲਗਾਉਣਾ

appoint (ਅ'ਪੌਇੰਟ) *v* ਨਿਯੁਕਤ ਕਰਨਾ, ਨਿਸ਼ਚਤ ਕਰਨਾ, ਥਾਪਣਾ, ਨੌਕਰੀ ਤੇ ਲਾਉਣਾ; ਨਿਸ਼ਚਤ ਕਰਨਾ; ਸੰਕੇਤ ਕਰਨਾ; ~ed ਨਿਯੁਕਤ; ਨਿਯਤ, ਲੱਗਿਆ ਹੋਇਆ; ~ee ਨਿਯੁਕਤੀ; ਨਿਯੁਕਤ; ~ment ਨਿਯੁਕਤੀ; (ਮਿਲਣ ਦਾ) ਇਕਰਾਰ

apportion (ਅ'ਪੋਸ਼ਨ) *v* ਹਿੱਸੇ ਕਰਨਾ, ਵੰਡਣਾ, ਹਿੱਸੇ ਅਨੁਸਾਰ ਸੌਂਪਣਾ, ਬਰਾਬਰ ਬਰਾਬਰ ਹਿੱਸਾ ਦੇਣਾ; ~ment ਵੰਡ, ਤਕਸੀਮ

apposite ('ਐਪਅ(ਉ)ਜ਼ਿਟ) *a* ਯੋਗ, ਉਚਿਤ, ਢੁਕਵਾਂ

apposition ('ਐਪਅ(ਉ)'ਜ਼ਿਸ਼ਨ) *n* ਵਾਧਾ, ਕੋਲ ਕੋਲ ਰੱਖਣ ਦੀ ਕਿਰਿਆ; ਮੁਹਰਬੰਦੀ, ਕਾਰਕ ਸਬੰਧ

appraisal, appraisement (ਅ'ਪਰੇਇਜ਼ਲ, ਅ'ਪਰੇਇਜ਼ਮਅੰਟ) *n* ਮੁਲਾਂਕਣ, ਮੁੱਲ-ਨਿਰਧਾਰਨ; ਅੰਦਾਜ਼ਾ

appraise ('ਅਪਰੇਇਜ਼) *v* ਮੁੱਲ ਪਾਉਣਾ, ਅੰਕਣਾ, ਮੁਲਾਂਕਣ ਕਰਨਾ, ਅੰਦਾਜ਼ਾ ਲਗਾਉਣਾ

appreciate (ਅ'ਪਰੀਸ਼ਿਏਇਟ) *v* ਪ੍ਰਸੰਸਾ ਕਰਨੀ, ਕਦਰ ਕਰਨੀ; ਮੁਲਾਂਕਣ ਕਰਨਾ

appreciation (ਅ'ਪਰੀਸ਼ਿ'ਏਇਸ਼ਨ) *n* ਪ੍ਰਸੰਸਾ, ਵਰਤੋਂ, ਅਨੁਭਵ

apprehend ('ਐਪਰਿ'ਹੈਂਡ) *v* ਮਹਿਸੂਸ ਕਰਨਾ, ਅਨੁਭਵ ਕਰਨਾ, ਸ਼ੰਕਾ ਕਰਨਾ; ਡਰਨਾ ਜਾਂ ਡਰਾਉਣਾ, ਭੈ ਖਾਣਾ; ਬੰਦੀ ਬਣਾਉਣਾ, ਗਰਿਫ਼ਤਾਰ ਕਰਨਾ, (ਪੁਲੀਸ ਦਾ) ਫੜਨਾ

apprehensibility ('ਐਪਰਿ'ਹੌਂਸਿ'ਬਿਲਅਟਿ) *n* ਸਮਝਣਯੋਗਤਾ, ਸੁਬੋਧਤਾ; ਗੋਚਰਤਾ, ਬੋਧ, ਸਮਝ

apprehensible ('ਐਪਰਿ'ਹੌਂਸਿਬਲ) *a* ਸੁਬੋਧ, ਸਮਝਣਯੋਗ, ਗੋਚਰ, ਅਨੁਭਵ ਦੇ ਯੋਗ

apprehension ('ਐਪਰਿ'ਹੈਂਸ਼ਨ) *n* (1) ਸਮਝ, ਬੋਧ, ਸੂਝ, ਪਕੜ, ਜਾਣਕਾਰੀ; (2) ਸ਼ੰਕਾ; ਡਰ; ਤਿਹਸਾਸ, ਗਿਫ਼ਤਾਰੀ, ਪਕੜ; ਘੇਰਾ

apprentice (ਅ'ਪਰੈਂਟਿਸ) ਸਿਖਾਂਦਰੂ, ਸ਼ਾਗਿਰਦ, ਸ਼ਿਲਪ-ਸਿਖਿਆਰਥੀ

apprise (ਅ'ਪਰਾਇਜ਼) *v* ਸੂਚਨਾ ਦੇਣਾ, ਦੱਸਣਾ, ਖ਼ਬਰ ਦੇਣੀ, ਜਾਣਕਾਰੀ ਰੱਖਣਾ

approach (ਅ'ਪਰਅਉਚ) *v n* ਕੋਲ ਜਾਣਾ, ਬਰਾਬਰ ਹੋਣਾ, ਪ੍ਰਵੇਸ਼, ਹਾਜ਼ਰੀ, ਪਹੁੰਚਣਾ, ਅੱਪੜਨਾ, ਮਿਲਣਾ-ਜੁਲਣਾ ਹੋਣਾ; **~ability** ਸਮੀਪਤਾ, ਨਿਕਟਤਾ; ਮਿਲਣਸਾਰੀ, ਰਸਾਈ ਯੋਗਤਾ, ਪਹੁੰਚ

appropriate (ਅ'ਪਰਅਉਪਰਿਅਟ, ਅ'ਰਅਉਪਰਿਏਇਟ) *a* ਚੁੱਕਵਾਂ, ਉਚਿਤ, ਅਨੁਕੂਲ, ਠੀਕ, ਸਬੰਧਤ, ਉਪਯੁਕਤ

appropriation (ਅ'ਪਰਅਉਪਰਿ'ਏਇਸ਼ਨ) *n* ਵਰਤੋਂ, ਵਿਹਾਰ, ਪ੍ਰਯੋਗ, ਇਸਤੇਮਾਲ; ਮਲਕੀਅਤ, ਚੋਰੀ; ਅਨੁਕੂਲਤਾ

approval (ਅ'ਪਰੂਵ਼ਲ) *n* ਮਨਜ਼ੂਰੀ, ਸੰਮਤੀ, ਪਰਵਾਨਗੀ, ਆਗਿਆ, ਅਨੁਮਤੀ, ਪਸੰਦ

approve (ਅ'ਪਰੂਵ਼) *v* ਮਨਜ਼ੂਰ ਕਰਨਾ, ਪਰਵਾਨ ਕਰਨਾ; ਸਵੀਕਾਰ ਕਰਨਾ, ਤਾਈਦ ਕਰਨੀ; ਪਸੰਦ ਕਰਨਾ, ਠੀਕ ਸਮਝਣਾ

approximate (ਅ'ਪਰੌਕਸਿਮਅਟ, ਅ'ਪਰੌਕਸਿਮੇਇਟ) *a v* ਲਗਭਗ, ਬਿਲਕੁਲ ਨੇੜੇ, ਅਨੁਰੂਪ, ਕਰੀਬਨ, ਅੰਦਾਜ਼ਾ ਲਾਉਣਾ, ਅਨੁਮਾਨ ਲਾਉਣਾ

apt (ਐਪਟ) *a* ਯੋਗ, ਕਾਬਲ; ਉਚਿਤ, ਚੁੱਕਵਾਂ, ਠੀਕ, ਮੁਨਾਸਬ; **~ly** ਯੋਗ ਤਰੀਕੇ ਨਾਲ, ਠੀਕ ਢੰਗ ਨਾਲ, ਚਤੁਰਾਈ ਨਾਲ, ਮੁਨਾਸਬ ਤੌਰ ਤੇ; **~ness** ਯੋਗਤਾ, ਉਚਿਤਤਾ, ਚਤੁਰਤਾ; **~itude** ਯੋਗਤਾ, ਕਾਬਲੀਅਤ; ਝੁਕਾਉ, ਰੁਝਾਣ, ਰੁਚੀ

arbitrary ('ਆਬਿਟਰਅਰਿ) *a* ਆਪ-ਹੁਦਰਾ, ਮਨ ਮੰਨਣਾ, ਧੱਕੇਸ਼ਾਹੀ ਵਾਲਾ

arbitration ('ਆਬਿ'ਰੇਇਸ਼ਨ) *n* ਪੰਚ ਦਾ ਫ਼ੈਸਲਾ, ਸਾਲਸੀ-ਫ਼ੈਸਲਾ, ਵਿਚੋਲਪੁਣਾ

arbitrator ('ਆਬਿਟਰੇਇਟਅ*) *n* ਵਿਚੋਲਾ, ਸਾਲਸ, ਪੰਚ, ਨਿਰਣਾ ਕਰਨ ਵਾਲਾ

arch (ਆਚ) *n a v* (1) ਡਾਟ, ਮਹਿਰਾਬ, ਮਹਿਰਾਬਦਾਰ, (2) ਛੱਤ, ਚਾਪ, ਕੋਸ; (3) ਪ੍ਰਧਾਨ, (4) ਮਹਾਂ ਮੱਕਾਰ, ਛਟਿਆ, ਖ਼ਚਰਾ, ਚਲਾਕ, ਗੁਰੂ ਘੰਟਾਲ

archaeology (ਆਕਿ'ਔਲਅਜਿ) *n* ਪੁਰਾਤੱਤਵ ਵਿਗਿਆਨ

archetype ('ਆਕਿਟਾਇਪ) *n* ਆਦਿ ਰੂਪ, ਮੂਲ ਰੂਪ, ਅਸਲੀ ਨਮੂਨਾ; ਮੂਲ ਆਦਰਸ਼

arch-fiend ('ਆਚ'ਫ਼ੀਨਡ) *n* ਸ਼ੈਤਾਨ

ardour ('ਆਡਅ*) *n* ਤੇਜ਼ੀ, ਪ੍ਰਚੰਡਤਾ, ਤੀਬਰਤਾ, ਉਮੰਗ, ਤੇਜ਼ ਗਰਮੀ, ਲਗਨ, ਧੁਨ, ਸਰਗਰਮੀ

area ('ਏਅਰਿਆ) *n* ਖੇਤਰਫਲ, ਰਕਬਾ; ਇਲਾਕਾ; ਖੇਤਰ

arena (ਅੇ'ਰੀਨਅ) *n* ਅਖਾੜਾ, ਕਾਰਜ-ਖੇਤਰ; ਰਣ-ਖੇਤਰ, ਰੰਗ-ਭੂਮੀ

arguable ('ਆਗਯੂਅਬਲ) *a* ਵਿਵਾਦਪੂਰਨ,

ਵਿਵਾਦਯੋਗ, ਵਿਚਾਰਯੋਗ

argue ('ਆਗਯੂ) v ਦਲੀਲ ਦੇਣੀ, ਤਰਕ-ਵਿਤਰਕ ਕਰਨਾ, ਵਾਦ-ਵਿਵਾਦ ਕਰਨਾ, ਬਹਿਸ ਕਰਨੀ; ਇਤਰਾਜ਼ ਕਰਨਾ, ਵਿਰੋਧ ਕਰਨਾ; ਸਿੱਧ ਕਰਨਾ; ਸੰਕੇਤ ਦੇਣਾ

argument ('ਆਗਯੂਮਅੰਟ) n ਦਲੀਲ, ਦਾਅਵਾ, ਹੁੱਜਤ, ਤਰਕ, ਪ੍ਰਮਾਣ, ਤਰਕ-ਪ੍ਰਣਾਲੀ, ਵਾਦ-ਵਿਵਾਦ; **~ation** ਬਹਿਸ, ਵਿਵਾਦ, ਤਰਕ, ਖੰਡਨ-ਮੰਡਨ, ਤਰਕ-ਵਿਤਰਕ

arid ('ਐਰਿਡ) a ਮਾਰੂ, ਬੰਜਰ, ਵੀਰਾਨ, ਨਿਰਜਲ

arise (ਅ'ਰਾਇਜ਼) v ਉੱਠਣਾ ਉੱਠ ਖੜੋਣਾ, ਮੁੜ ਪੈਦਾ ਹੋਣਾ, ਨਿਕਲਣਾ, ਉਤਪੰਨ ਹੋਣਾ, ਜਾਗਣਾ; ਦਿਸਣਾ

arising (ਅ'ਰਾਇਜ਼ਿਙ) a ਉਤਪੰਨ, ਨਿਕਲਦਾ, ਚੜ੍ਹਦਾ, ਉੱਭਰਦਾ

aristocracy ('ਐਰਿ'ਸਟੋਕਰਅਸਿ) n ਕੁਲੀਨ-ਵਰਗ; ਕੁਲੀਨ-ਤੰਤਰ

aristocrat ('ਐਰਿਸਟਅਕਰੈਟ) n ਕੁਲੀਨ, ਰਈਸ

arithmetic (ਅ'ਰਿਥਮਅਟਿਕ) n ਹਿਸਾਬ, ਗਿਣਤੀ, ਲੇਖ; ਹਿਸਾਬ ਦੀ ਪੋਥੀ

ark ('ਆ*ਕ) n v ਪੇਟੀ, ਸੰਦੂਕ, ਬਕਸ, ਬੇੜੀ, ਨਾਵ; (ਹਜ਼ਰਤ ਨੂਹ ਦੀ ਬੇੜੀ)

arm ('ਆ*ਮ) n v ਬਾਂਹ, ਭੁਜਾ, ਬਾਜ਼ੂ, ਪਸ਼ੂ ਦੀਆਂ ਮੂਹਰਲੀਆਂ ਲੱਤਾਂ; ਰੁੱਖ ਦਾ ਮੋਟਾ ਟਾਹਣ; ਕਮੀਜ਼ ਦੀ ਬਾਂਹ; ਹਥਿਆਰ, ਸ਼ਕਤੀ; ਹਥਿਆਰ ਬੰਦ ਕਰਨਾ ਜਾਂ ਹੋਣਾ, ਸ਼ਸਤਰ ਧਾਰਣਾ; **~pit** ਕੱਛਾਂ ਬਗਲਾਂ; **~ful** ਗਲਵੱਕੜੀ ਵਿਚ ਸਮਾਉਣ ਯੋਗ; **~less** ਨਿਥਾ, ਬੇਹਥਿਆਰ, ਬਾਂਹ ਹੀਣ; **~let** ਬਾਜ਼ੂਬੰਦ

armament ('ਆ*ਮਅਮਅੰਟ) n ਜੁੱਧ ਦਾ ਸਾਮਾਨ, ਜੰਗੀ-ਸਾਮਾਨ, ਸ਼ਸਤਰਬੱਧ ਫ਼ੌਜ; ਹਥਿਆਰਬੰਦੀ, ਹਥਿਆਰਬੰਦ ਹੋਣ ਦਾ ਕੰਮ, ਸ਼ਸਤਰੀ-ਕਰਨ

armory ('ਆ*ਮਅਰਿ) n ਸ਼ਸਤਰ ਰੱਖਣ ਜਾਂ ਬਣਾਉਣ ਵਾਲਾ ਕਾਰਖ਼ਾਨਾ, ਅਸਲ੍ਹਾਖ਼ਾਨਾ

armour ('ਆ*ਮਅ) n v ਕਵਚ, ਜ਼ਰਾ ਬਕਤਰ

arms ('ਆ*ਮਜ਼) n pl ਸ਼ਸਤਰ, ਹਥਿਆਰ

army ('ਆ*ਮਿ) n ਸੈਨਾ, ਫ਼ੌਜ, ਲਸ਼ਕਰ

aroma n (ਅ'ਰਅਉਮਅ) n ਮਹਿਕ, ਸੁਗੰਧ

around (ਅ'ਰਾਉਂਡ) adv prep ਹਰ ਪਾਸੇ, ਚਾਰੇ ਪਾਸੇ, ਇੱਧਰ-ਉੱਧਰ, ਆਸਪਾਸ, ਲਗਭਗ, ਕਰੀਬ ਕਰੀਬ, ਚਾਰੇ ਪਾਸਿਓਂ ਘੇਰਿਆ

arouse (ਅ'ਰਊਜ਼) v ਜਗਾਉਣਾ, ਭੜਕਾਉਣਾ, ਉਤਾਰਨਾ, ਉਕਸਾਉਣਾ, ਕਿਰਿਆਸ਼ੀਲ ਬਣਾਉਣਾ, ਜਾਗਰਤ ਕਰਨਾ, ਜੋਸ਼ ਦਿਵਾਉਣਾ

arrange (ਅ'ਰੇਂਜਿ) v ਵਿਉਂਤਣਾ, ਵਿਉਂਤ-ਬੱਧ ਕਰਨਾ, ਤਰਤੀਬ ਦੇਣਾ; ਵਿਵਸਥਿਤ ਕਰਨਾ, ਪ੍ਰਬੰਧ ਕਰਨਾ; **~ment** ਵਿਉਂਤ, ਇੰਤਜ਼ਾਮ, ਪ੍ਰਬੰਧ, ਵਿਵਸਥਾ

array (ਅ'ਰੇਇ) v n ਸੰਵਾਰਨਾ, ਸਜਾਉਣਾ, ਅਲੰਕਰਤ ਕਰਨਾ; ਫ਼ੌਜ ਦੀ ਹਥਿਆਰਬੰਦੀ, ਫ਼ੌਜੀ ਤਾਕਤ, ਲਸ਼ਕਰ

arrear ('ਅਰਿਅ*) n ਬਕਾਇਆ ਰਕਮ, ਬਕਾਇਆ, ਉਗਰਾਹੁਣਯੋਗ ਕਰਜ਼ਾ ਜਾਂ ਧਨ; ਪਛੜਿਆ ਕੰਮ

arrest (ਅ'ਰੇੱਸਟ) v n ਬੰਦੀ ਬਣਾਉਣਾ, ਗਿਰਫ਼ਤਾਰ ਕਰਨਾ, ਖਿੱਚਣਾ, ਲੁਭਾਉਣਾ; ਗਿਰਫ਼ਤਾਰੀ, ਹਿਰਾਸਤ, ਪਕੜ

arrival (ਅ'ਰਾਇਵ੍ਲ) n ਪਹੁੰਚ, ਆਗਮਨ, ਚੁਕਾਉ ਆਮਦ, ਹਾਜ਼ਰੀ

arrive (ਅ'ਰਾਇਵ) v ਆਉਣਾ, ਪਹੁੰਚਣਾ, ਹਾਜ਼ਰ ਹੋਣਾ, ਅੱਪੜਨਾ, ਮੰਜ਼ਲ ਤੇ ਪਹੁੰਚਣਾ

arrogance ('ਐਰਅਗਾਯੰਸ) *n* ਹੰਕਾਰ, ਘਮੰਡ, ਅਭਿਮਾਨ, ਗਰਬ, ਗ਼ਰੂਰ, ਆਕੜ

arrogant ('ਐਰਅਗਅੰਟ) *a* ਮਾਣ-ਮੱਤਾ, ਹੰਕਾਰੀ, ਅਭਿਮਾਨੀ, ਗ਼ਰੂਮਾਨੀ, ਆਕੜ ਖ਼ਾਂ, ਘਮੰਡੀ

arrogate ('ਐਰਅ(ਉ)ਗੇਇਟ) *v* ਝੂਠਾ ਹੱਕ ਜਮਾਉਣ, ਝੂਠਾ ਦਾਅਵਾ ਕਰਨ

arrow ('ਐਰਅਉ) *n* ਤੀਰ, ਬਾਣ, ਕਾਨੀ; ਤੀਰ ਦਾ ਨਿਸ਼ਾਨ, ਤੀਰ ਦਾ ਚਿੰਨ੍ਹ

art (ਆ*ਟ) *n* ਕਲਾ, ਹੁਨਰ, ਸ਼ਿਲਪ; ਕਾਰੀਗਰੀ, ਉਸਤਾਦੀ, ਕੁਸ਼ਲਤਾ; ਮੱਕਾਰੀ, ਚਾਲ; **~ful** ਗੁਣੀ, ਹੁਨਰੀ; ਕਪਟੀ, ਚਾਲਬਾਜ਼, ਚੰਟ

arthritis (ਆ*ਥਰਾਇਟਅਸ) *n* ਗਠੀਆ, ਜੋੜਾਂ ਦੇ ਦਰਦ ਜਾਂ ਸੋਜਸ਼ ਦੀ ਬੀਮਾਰੀ

article ('ਆ*ਟਿਕਲ) *n v* (1) ਪਦਾਰਥ, ਵਸਤੂ, ਚੀਜ਼; (2) ਧਾਰਾ, ਦਫ਼ਾ, ਅੰਸ਼, ਭਾਗ; (3) ਲੇਖ, ਨਿਬੰਧ; ਦਫ਼ਾ ਲਗਾਉਣੀ, ਨਿਯੰਤਰਣ ਰੱਖਣਾ, ਹਿਸਿਆਂ ਵਿਚ ਵੰਡਣਾ; ਧਰਮ ਸਿਧਾਂਤ, ਸੂਤਰ, ਨਿਯਮ; ਯੁਧ-ਨਿਯਮ

articulate (ਆ*ਟਿਕਯੂਲੇਇਟ) *v a* ਗੰਢਣਾ, ਜੋੜਨਾ, ਗੰਢ ਦੇਣੀ, ਜੋੜ ਪਾਉਣਾ; ਸਾਫ਼ ਬੋਲਣਾ, ਗੰਢਦਾਰ, ਜੋੜਦਾਰ; (ਬੋਲਣ ਵਿਚ) ਸਾਫ਼-ਸਪਸ਼ਟ

articulation (ਆ*ਟਿਕਯੂਲੇ'ਇਯ਼ਨ) *n* ਜੋੜਬੰਦੀ, ਜੋੜ ਗੰਢ; ਸਪਸ਼ਟ ਪਰਗਟਾਉ

artificial ('ਆਟਿ'ਫ਼ਿਸ਼ਲ) *a* ਨਕਲੀ, ਬਣਾਵਟੀ, ਝੂਠਾ, ਅਵਸਤਵਿਕ, ਮਿਥਿਆ; **~ity** ਨਕਲ, ਝੂਠ, ਬਣਾਵਟ, ਅਵਸਤਵਿਕਤਾ

artillery (ਆ*ਟਿਲਅਰਿ) *n* ਤੋਪਖ਼ਾਨਾ

artisan ('ਆਟਿ'ਜ਼ੈਨ) *n* ਦਸਤਕਾਰ, ਸ਼ਿਲਪਕਾਰ

artist ('ਆਟਿਸਟ) *n* ਕਲਾਕਾਰ, ਕਾਰੀਗਰ, ਗੁਣੀ

artiste (ਆ*ਟੀਸਟ) *n* ਨਾਚੀ, ਗਾਇਕਾ

artistry ('ਆਟਿਸਟਰਿ) *n* ਕਲਾਕਾਰੀ, ਫ਼ਨਕਾਰੀ, ਕਲਾਕੌਸ਼ਲਤਾ, ਕਾਰੀਗਰੀ

artless ('ਆਟਲਿਸ) *a* ਕਲਹੀਣ, ਅਸੱਭਿਅ; ਅਨਾੜੀ, ਮੂਰਖ, ਘੁੱਥੂ; ਨਿਸ਼ਕਪਟ, ਛਲ ਰਹਿਤ, ਸੱਚਾ, ਸਿੱਧਾ-ਸਾਦਾ, ਭੋਲਾ-ਭਾਲਾ, ਕੁਦਰਤੀ, ਸੁਭਾਵਕ

arts (ਆ*ਟਸ) *n pl* ਲਲਿਤ ਕਲਾਵਾਂ, ਸੁੱਧ ਸਾਇੰਸਾਂ ਦੇ ਵਿਪਰੀਤ ਸਮਾਜਕ ਵਿਗਿਆਨਾਂ ਦੇ ਵਿਸ਼ੇ

as (ਐਜ਼) *a conj* ਜਿਵੇਂ, ਉਸੇ ਤਰ੍ਹਾਂ; ਕਿਉਂਕਿ, ਇਸ ਲਈ ਕਿ, ਤਾਂ ਜੋ

ascend (ਅੱਸੈਂਡ) *v* ਉਤਰਨਾ, ਉੱਪਰ ਜਠੂਨਾ, ਉਦੇ ਹੋਣਾ, ਉੱਚਾ-ਉੱਠਣਾ, ਉੱਨਤੀ ਕਰਨਾ, (ਧੁਨੀ ਜਾਂ ਅਵਾਜ਼ ਦਾ) ਉੱਚ ਹੋਣਾ, (ਤਖ਼ਤ ਤੇ) ਬੈਠਣਾ, ਬਿਰਾਜਣਾ

ascertain (ਐਸਅਾ'ਟੇਇਨ) *v* ਨਿਰਣਾ ਕਰਨਾ, ਨਿਸ਼ਚਾ ਕਰਨਾ, ਜਾਣਨਾ; ਜਾਂਚਣਾ, ਪਤਾ ਲਾਉਣਾ

ascetic (ਅ'ਸੈਟਿਕ) *n a* ਤਿਆਗੀ, ਵਿਰਾਗੀ, ਤਪੱਸਵੀ; ਇਕਾਂਤਵਾਸੀ, ਸਾਧਕ

ash (ਐਸ਼) *n* ਸੁਆਹ, ਭਸਮ, ਰਾਖ; **~tray** ਰਾਖਦਾਨੀ, ਸੁਆਹ ਪਾਉਣ ਵਾਲੀ ਤ੍ਰੇ (ਸਿਗਰਟ ਆਦਿ ਦੀ); **~es** ਅਸਥੀਆਂ, ਮੁਰਦੇ ਦੀ ਮਿੱਟੀ, ਮੁਆਦ

ashame (ਅ'ਸ਼ੇਇਮ) *v* ਸ਼ਰਮਿੰਦਾ ਕਰਨਾ ਜਾਂ ਹੋਣਾ, ਲੱਜਤ ਕਰਨਾ ਜਾਂ ਹੋਣਾ; **~d** ਪਸ਼ੇਮਾਨ, ਲੱਜਾਵਾਨ, ਸ਼ਰਮਿੰਦਾ

ashore (ਅ'ਸ਼ੋਰ) *adv* ਕਿਨਾਰੇ ਤੇ, ਤੱਟ ਉੱਤੇ, ਕੰਢੇ ਉੱਤੇ

aside (ਅ'ਸਾਇਡ) *adv n* ਅੱਡ, ਵੱਖ, ਦੂਰ, ਜੁਦਾ, ਇਲਾਵਾ, ਬਿਨਾਂ; (ਨਾਟਕ) ਇਕਾਂਤ-ਕਥਨ, ਪਰੋਖ ਜਤਨ

ask (ਆਸਕ) *v* ਪੁੱਛਣਾ, ਉੱਤਰ ਮੰਗਣਾ, ਬੇਨਤੀ

ਕਰਨਾ, ਸੱਦਾ ਦੇਣਾ, ਬੁਲਾਉਣਾ, ਜ਼ਰੂਰਤ ਸਮਝਣਾ, ਚਾਹੁਣਾ, ਮੰਗਣਾ

asleep (ਅ'ਸਲੀਪ) *adv* ਸੁੱਤਾ, ਸੁਪਤ, ਨੀਂਦਗ੍ਰਸਤ, ਨੀਂਦ ਵਿਚ

aspect ('ਐਸਪੈਕਟ) *n* ਪਹਿਲੂ, ਪੱਖ; ਦ੍ਰਿਸ਼ਟੀਕੋਣ, ਨਜ਼ਰੀਆ; ਹਾਲਤ

aspersion (ਅ'ਸਪਅ:ਸ਼ਨ) *v* ਤੁਹਮਤ, ਊਜ, ਇਲਜ਼ਾਮ

aspirant (ਅ'ਸਪਾਇਰਅੰਟ) *n* ਆਕਾਂਖੀ, ਇੱਛਾਵਾਨ, ਅਭਿਲਾਸ਼ੀ, ਉਮੀਦਵਾਰ

aspirate ('ਐਸਪਅਰੇਇਟ) *n v* (ਭਾਸ਼ਾ) ਮਹਾਂਪ੍ਰਾਣ, ਹਕਾਰ; ਬਰਤਨ ਨੂੰ ਹਵਾ ਰਹਿਤ ਕਰਨ

aspiration ('ਐਸਪਅ'ਰੇਇਸ਼ਨ) *n* ਤਾਂਘ; ਆਕਾਂਖਿਆ, ਆਰਜ਼ੂ, ਇੱਛਾ, ਅਭਿਲਾਸ਼ਾ; (ਭਾਸ਼ਾ) ਮਹਾਂ-ਪ੍ਰਾਣਤਾ, ਹਾ ਦੀ ਧੁਨੀ

aspire (ਅ'ਸਪਾਇਅ*) *v* ਇੱਛਾ ਕਰਨੀ, ਤਾਂਘਣਾ, ਆਕਾਂਖਿਆ ਕਰਨੀ

ass (ਐਸ) *n* ਖੋਤਾ, ਗਧਾ; ਮੂਰਖ ਮਨੁੱਖ, ਖਰ

assail (ਅ'ਸੇਇਲ) *v* ਧਾਵਾ ਕਰਨਾ, ਹਮਲਾ ਕਰਨਾ; ਚੜ੍ਹਾਈ ਕਰਨਾ, (ਕੰਮ ਨੂੰ) ਦ੍ਰਿੜ੍ਹਤਾ-ਪੂਰਵਕ ਕਰਨਾ

assassin (ਅ'ਸੈਸਿਨ) *n* ਕਾਤਲ, ਖ਼ੂਨੀ, ਹਤਿਆਰਾ, ਘਾਤਕ; **~ate** (ਛਿਪ ਕੇ) ਹੱਤਿਆ ਕਰਨੀ, ਵਿਸਾਹਘਾਤ ਕਰਕੇ ਮਾਰਨਾ, ਖ਼ੂਨ ਕਰਨਾ, ਮਾਰ ਦੇਣਾ; **~ation** ਛਲ-ਘਾਤ, ਗੁਪਤ-ਘਾਤ, ਕਤਲ, ਹੱਤਿਆ; (ਚਰਿੱਤਰ) ਬਦਨਾਮੀ

assault (ਅ'ਸੋਲਟ) *n v* ਧਾਵਾ, ਚੜ੍ਹਾਈ, ਹਮਲਾ; ਹਮਲਾ ਕਰਨਾ, ਧਾਵਾ ਬੋਲਣਾ; ਬਲਾਤਕਾਰ ਕਰਨਾ

assay (ਅ'ਸੇਇ) *n* ਪਰੀਖਿਆ, ਕਸਵੱਟੀ, ਪਰਖ, ਪੜਤਾਲ, ਜਾਂਚ, ਅਜ਼ਮਾਇਸ਼

assemblage (ਅਸੈਂਬਲਿਜ) *n* ਸਭਾ, ਇਕੱਠ, ਇਕੱਤਰਤਾ, ਜਮ-ਘਟਾ

assemble (ਅਸੈਂਬਲ) *v* ਇਕੱਠਾ ਕਰਨਾ, ਇਕੱਤਰ ਕਰਨਾ, ਇਕੱਠਾ ਹੋਣਾ, ਜੋੜਨਾ

assembly (ਅ'ਸੈਂਬਲਿ) *n* ਸਭਾ, ਇਕੱਠ, ਸੰਮੇਲਨ, ਮਹਿਫ਼ਲ, ਮਜਲਸ, ਸੰਘ

assent (ਅ'ਸੈਂਟ) *v n* ਹਾਮੀ ਭਰਨੀ, ਰਜ਼ਾਮੰਦ ਹੋਣਾ, ਸਹਿਮਤ ਹੋਣਾ, ਪਰਵਾਨ ਕਰਨਾ, ਕਬੂਲ ਕਰਨਾ; ਸਹਿਮਤੀ, ਮਨਜ਼ੂਰੀ

assert (ਅ'ਸਅ:ਟ) *v* ਨਿਸਚੇ ਪੂਰਵਕ ਕਹਿਣਾ, ਜੋਸ਼ ਨਾਲ ਕਹਿਣਾ; ਦਾਅਵਾ ਕਰਨਾ, ਹੱਕ ਜਮਾਉਣਾ

assertive (ਅ'ਸਅ:ਟਿਵ) *a* ਨਿਸਚੇਆਤਮਕ, ਹਠਧਰਮੀ ਵਾਲਾ; **~ness** ਦ੍ਰਿੜ੍ਹਤਾ, ਪਕਿਆਈ; ਦਾਅਵਾਗੀਰੀ

assess (ਅ'ਸੈਸ) *v* ਨਿਯਤ ਕਰਨਾ, ਨਿਰਧਾਰਨ ਨਿਸ਼ਚਤ ਕਰਨਾ, ਦੰਡ ਲਾਉਣਾ, ਕਰ ਲਾਉਣਾ, ਅਨੁਮਾਨਣਾ, ਅਨੁਮਾਨ ਲਾਉਣਾ; **~able** ਨਿਯਤ ਕਰਨ ਯੋਗ; ਟੈਕਸ ਲਾਉਣ ਯੋਗ; **~ee** ਕਰਦਾਤਾ, ਜਿਸ ਤੋਂ ਹਾਲਾ ਜਾਂ ਟੈਕਸ ਵਸੂਲਿਆ ਜਾਵੇ; **~ment** ਕਰ-ਨਿਰਧਾਰਨ, ਮੁਲਾਂਕਲ, ਲਗਾਨ, ਜਮਾਂਬੰਦੀ; **~or** (ਕਰ) ਨਿਰਧਾਰਕ, ਅਨੁਮਾਨਕਰਤਾ

assets (ਐਸੈਂਟਸ) *n pl* ਜਾਇਦਾਦ, ਕੁਲ ਅਸਾਸਾ, ਸੰਪੱਤੀ; ਵਿਸ਼ੇਸ਼ਤਾ, ਚੰਗਿਆਈ

assign (ਅ'ਸਾਇਨ) *v* ਸੌਂਪਣਾ, ਸੁਪੁਰਦ ਕਰਨਾ, ਨਿਸ਼ਚਤ ਕਰਨਾ; ਦੇਣਾ, ਵੰਡਣਾ, ਮੁਕੱਰਰ ਕਰਨਾ, ਦੱਸਣਾ, ਨਿਰਦੇਸ਼ਨ ਕਰਨਾ, ਦੇ ਦੇਣਾ; **~able** ਸੌਂਪਣ ਯੋਗ, ਨਿਸ਼ਚਤ ਕਰਨ ਯੋਗ, ਨਿਰਧਾਰਨ-ਯੋਗ; **~ment** ਸਪੁਰਦਗੀ, ਸੌਂਪਿਆ ਹੋਇਆ ਕੰਮ

assimilate (ਅ'ਸਿਮਿਲੇਇਟ) *v* ਇਕਮਿਕ ਹੋਣਾ, ਰਚਾ ਲੈਣਾ, ਸਮਾ ਜਾਣਾ, ਆਤਮਸਾਤ ਕਰਨਾ,

assist (अ'सिसट) v ਸਹਾਇਤਾ ਦੇਣੀ ਜਾਂ ਕਰਨੀ, ਸਹਿਯੋਗ ਦੇਣਾ, ਹੱਥ ਵਟਾਉਣਾ

associate (अ'ਸਅਉਸ਼ਿਏਇਟ, अ'ਸਅਉਸ਼ਿਅਟ) v n a ਰਲਾਉਣ, ਸ਼ਾਮਲ ਕਰਨ, ਸ਼ਰੀਕ ਕਰਨ, ਭਾਈਵਾਲ ਬਣਾਉਣਾ, ਸਹਿਕਾਰੀ ਬਣਨਾ; ਸਹਿਯੋਗੀ, ਸਹਿਕਾਰੀ; ਹਿੰਮਤੀਏ, ਸਹਾਇਕ

association (अ'ਸਅਉਸਿ'ਏਇਸ਼ਨ) n ਸਭਾ, ਸੰਸਥਾ, ਸਮਾਜ, ਸੰਘ; ਮੇਲ-ਜੋਲ, ਸੰਗਤ

assume (अ'ਸਯੂਮ) v ਧਾਰਨਾ, ਲੈਣਾ, ਧਾਰਨ ਕਰਨਾ, ਅਪਨਾਉਣਾ, ਹੱਥ ਵਿਚ ਲੈਣਾ; ਮੰਨਣਾ, ਫ਼ਰਜ਼ ਕਰਨਾ

assumption (अ'ਸਅੰਪਸ਼ਨ) n ਧਾਰਨਾ; ਜ਼ੁੰਮੇਵਾਰੀ ਲੈਣ ਦੀ ਕਿਰਿਆ; ਧਾਰਨ

assumptive (अ'ਸਅੰਪਟਿਵ) a ਦੰਭੀ, ਫ਼ਰਜ਼ੀ, ਕਲਪਤ; ਮੰਨਿਆ

assurance (अ'ਸ਼ੋਰਅੰਸ) n ਵਿਸ਼ਵਾਸ, ਯਕੀਨ, ਜ਼ਮਾਨਤ, ਤਸੱਲੀ, ਭਰੋਸਾ; ਬੀਮਾ

assure (अ'ਸ਼ੋ*) ਵਿਸ਼ਵਾਸ ਦਿਵਾਉਣਾ, ਭਰੋਸਾ ਦਿਵਾਉਣਾ; ਪੱਕਾ ਕਰਨਾ, ਤਸੱਲੀ ਕਰ ਲੈਣੀ

asterisk (ਐਸਟਾ(अ)ਰਿਸਕ) n v ਤਾਰਾ-ਚਿੰਨ੍ਹ; ਤਾਰੇ ਦਾ ਨਿਸ਼ਾਨ (*), ਤਾਰਿਕ, ਤਾਰਾ; ਤਾਰਾ-ਚਿੰਨ੍ਹ ਅੰਕਤ ਕਰਨਾ

asthma (ਐਸਥਮਅ) a ਦਮਾ, ਸਾਹ ਦਾ ਰੋਗ

astonish ('अ'ਸਟੋਨਿਸ਼) v ਅਚੰਭੇ ਵਿਚ ਪਾਉਣਾ, ਹੈਰਾਨ ਕਰਨਾ, ਵਿਸਮਤ ਕਰਨਾ, ਦੰਗ ਕਰਨਾ, ਹੈਰਤ ਵਿਚ ਪਾਉਣਾ; **~ed** ਹੈਰਾਨੀ ਭਰਿਆ, ਹੈਰਾਨਕੁਨ, ਅਸਚਰਜਜਨਕ, ਵਿਸਮਤ, ਹੱਕ ਬੱਕਾ, ਦੰਗ; **~ing** ਅਚੰਭਾਕਾਰੀ, ਹੈਰਾਨਕੁਨ, ਅਸਚਰਜ ਕਰਨ ਵਾਲਾ, ਵਿਸਮਾਦ ਵਿਚ ਲੈ ਜਾਣ ਵਾਲਾ; **~ment** ਹੈਰਾਨੀ, ਅਸਚਰਜਤਾ, ਅਚੰਭਾ

astound (अ'ਸਟਉਂਡ) v ਹੈਰਾਨ ਕਰਨਾ, ਹੱਕਾ ਬੱਕਾ ਕਰਨਾ, ਤ੍ਰਹ ਕੱਢਣਾ

astray (अ'ਸਟਰੇਇ) adv a ਗੁਮਰਾਹ, ਭੁੱਲਿਆ ਭਟਕਿਆ, ਔਝੜ ਪਿਆ, ਕੁਰਾਹੀਆ

astringe (अ'ਸਟਰਿੰਜ) v ਸੰਕੁਚਤ ਕਰਨਾ, ਘੁੱਟ ਕੇ ਬੰਨ੍ਹਣਾ, ਕਸਣਾ, ਸੁੰਗੜਨ

astrologer (अ'ਸਟਰੌਲਅਜਅ*) a ਜੋਤਸ਼ੀ, ਨਜੂਮੀ

astrology (अ'ਸਟਰੌਲਅਜਿ) n ਜੋਤਸ਼, ਜੋਤਸ਼ ਵਿੱਦਿਆ, ਨਜੂਮ, ਨਜੂਮ ਦਾ ਹਿਸਾਬ

astronomy (अ'ਸਟਰੌਨਅਮਿ) n ਖਗੋਲ-ਵਿਗਿਆਨ, ਤਾਰਾ-ਵਿਗਿਆਨ, ਨਛੱਤਰ ਵਿਗਿਆਨ, ਗ੍ਰਹਿਵਿਦਿਆ, ਖਗੋਲ-ਸ਼ਾਸਤਰ

asylum (अ'ਸਾਇਲਅਮ) n ਅਨਾਥ-ਆਸ਼ਰਮ, ਦੀਨ-ਆਸ਼ਰਮ, ਸ਼ਰਨ, ਪਨਾਹ, ਸਹਾਰਾ

at (ਐਟ) perp ਉੱਤੇ, 'ਤੇ, ਉੱਤੇ ਵੱਲ, ਉੱਪਰ; **~all** ਬਿਲਕੁਲ, ਹਰ ਤਰ੍ਹਾਂ; **~ home** ਉਚੇਚ ਰਹਿਤ ਦਾਅਵਤ; **~ once** ਫੌਰਨ, ਇਕ ਦਮ, ਤੁਰੰਤ; **~ one** ਸਮਝੌਤੇ ਤੇ ਸਮੰਤੀ ਨਾਲ, ਇਕਸਾਰ; **random** ਅਟਕਲ-ਪੱਚੂ; **~ sea** ਉਲਝਿਆ ਹੋਣਾ, ਸਮਝਦੇ ਨਾ ਹੋਣਾ

atheism ('ਏਇਥਿਇਜ਼(अ)ਮ) n ਨਾਸਤਕਤਾ, ਨਾਸਤਕ ਮੱਤ, ਰੱਬ ਨਾ ਮੰਨਣ ਦਾ ਵਾਦ

atheist ('ਏਇਥਿਇਸਟ) n ਨਾਸਤਕ, ਅਨੀਸ਼ਵਰਵਾਦੀ, ਕਾਫ਼ਰ, ਮੁਨਕਰ

athlete ('ਐਥਲੀਟ) n ਖਿਡਾਰੀ, ਪਹਿਲਵਾਨ, ਕਸਰਤ ਕਰਨ ਵਾਲਾ, ਰਿਸ਼ਟ ਪੁਸ਼ਟ ਆਦਮੀ, ਹੱਟਾ ਕੱਟਾ

athletic (ਐਥਲੈਟਿਕ) a n ਕਸਰਤੀ, ਸਰੀਰਕ ਕਸਰਤ ਦਾ, ਰਿਸ਼ਟ-ਪੁਸ਼ਟ, ਕਸਰਤ ਬਾਰੇ; (ਬ ਵ) ਕਸਰਤ-ਅਭਿਆਸ, ਕਸਰਤ, ਵਰਜ਼ਸ਼

atlas ('ਐਟਲਅਸ) *n* ਐਟਲਸ, ਭੂ-ਚਿਤਰਾਵਲੀ, ਮਾਨ ਚਿਤਰਾਵਲੀ, ਗਰਦਨ ਦੀ ਹੱਡੀ ਜਿਸ ਉੱਤੇ ਖੋਪੜੀ ਟਿਕੀ ਹੁੰਦੀ ਹੈ

atmophere ('ਐਟਮਅਸਫ਼ਿਅ*) *n* ਵਾਯੂ-ਮੰਡਲ, ਵਾਤਾਵਰਨ; ਹਾਲਾਤ, ਪਰਿਸਥਿਤੀਆਂ; ਆਲਾ-ਦੁਆਲਾ, ਹਵਾ, ਵਾਯੂ

atom ('ਐਟਅਮ) *n* ਪਰਮਾਣੂ, ਅਣੂ, ਕਣ, ਜ਼ੱਰਾ, ਸੂਖਮ ਅੰਸ਼; **~ic** ਪਰਮਾਣੂ ਬਾਰੇ, ਪਰਮਾਣਵੀ, ਪਰਮਾਣੂ, ਰੂਪ, ਪਰਮਾਣੂ-ਸਬੰਧੀ; ਸੂਖਮ; **~bomb** ਅਣੂ ਬੰਬ; **~y** ਪਰਮਾਣੂ; ਛੋਟੀ ਵਸਤੂ, ਪਿੰਜਰ, ਢਾਂਚਾ, ਨਿਰਬਲ ਸਰੀਰ

atone (ਅ'ਟਅਉਨ) *v* ਪ੍ਰਾਸ਼ਚਿਤ ਕਰਨਾ; **~ment** ਹਰਜਾਨਾ, ਪ੍ਰਾਸ਼ਚਿਤ(ਪ੍ਰਾ) ਸੁਲ੍ਹਾ-ਸਫ਼ਾਈ

atrocious (ਅ'ਟਰਅਉਸ਼ਅਸ) *a* ਅੱਤਿਆਚਾਰੀ, ਦੁਸ਼ਟ, ਜਾਬਰ; ਬੇਦਰਦ, ਜ਼ਾਲਮ

atrocity (ਅ'ਟਰੌਸਅਟਿ) *n* ਘੋਰ ਅੱਤਿਆਚਾਰ, ਜ਼ੁਲਮ, ਪਾਪ

attach (ਅ'ਟੈਚ) *v* ਜੋੜਨਾ ਬੰਨ੍ਹਣਾ, ਨੱਥੀ ਕਰਨਾ; ਮਿਲਾਉਣਾ; ਸੰਯੁਕਤ ਕਰਨਾ, ਸੰਮਿਲਤ ਹੋਣਾ, (ਕਾਨੂੰਨੀ ਆਧਿਕਾਰ; ਕਿਸੇ ਵਿਅਕਤੀ ਦੀ ਜਾਇਦਾਦ ਨੂੰ) ਜ਼ਬਤ ਕਰਨਾ; **~able** ਕੁਰਕੀ ਯੋਗ; **~ed** ਨਾਲ ਲੱਗਾ, ਨੱਥੀ ਕੀਤਾ, ਨਾਲ ਲੱਗਵਾਂ, ਲਾਗਲਾ; (ਕਾ) ਕੁਰਕ ਕੀਤਾ; **~ment** ਮੋਹ, ਪਰੇਮ, ਸਨੇਹ, ਨਿਸ਼ਠਾ, ਲਗਾਉ; ਸੰਜੋਜਤ ਵਸਤੂ, ਯੋਗ, ਸਬੰਧ, ਬੰਧਨ; ਕੁਰਕੀ, ਜ਼ਬਤੀ

attache (ਅ'ਟੈਸ਼ੇਇ) *n* ਰਾਜਦੂਤ-ਸਹਿਕਾਰੀ, ਅਤਾਸ਼ੇ, ਅਟੈਚੀ; **~ case** ਬਕਸਾ, ਅਟੈਚੀਕੇਸ

attack (ਅ'ਟੈਕ) *v n* ਧਾਵਾ ਬੋਲਣਾ, ਆਕਰਮਣ ਕਰਨਾ, ਚੜ੍ਹਾਈ ਕਰਨੀ; ਹਾਨੀਕਾਰਕ ਹੋਣਾ, ਦੋਸ਼ ਲਾਉਣਾ, ਹਮਲਾ, ਧਾਵਾ, ਚੜ੍ਹਾਈ, ਆਕਰਮਣ

attain (ਅ'ਟੇਇਨ) *v* ਪ੍ਰਾਪਤ ਕਰਨਾ, ਪਾ ਲੈਣਾ ਹਾਸਲ ਕਰਨਾ, ਪੁੱਜ ਜਾਣਾ, ਪਹੁੰਚਣਾ; ਸਿ ਕਰਨਾ; **~able** ਪ੍ਰਾਪਤ ਕਰਨ ਯੋਗ, ਪਾਉਣ ਯੋਗ; **~ment** ਲਾਭ, ਪ੍ਰਾਪਤੀ, ਉਪਲਬਧੀ ਸਿੱਧੀ; ਪ੍ਰਾਪਤ-ਵਸਤੂ

attempt (ਅ'ਟੈਂਪਟ) *v n* ਜਤਨ ਕਰਨਾ, ਕੋਸ਼ਿ ਕਰਨਾ, ਉੱਦਮ ਕਰਨਾ, ਜਾਂਚਣਾ, ਹਮਲਾ ਕਰਨਾ ਕੋਸ਼ਸ਼, ਜਤਨ, ਉੱਦਮ, ਪ੍ਰਯਾਸ; ਆਕਰਮਣ

attend (ਅ'ਟੈਂਡ) *v* ਹਾਜ਼ਰ ਹੋਣਾ, ਮੌਜੂਦ ਰਹਿਣਾ ਸੇਵਾ ਵਿਚ ਪੁੱਜਣਾ; ਸੇਵਾ ਕਰਨਾ, ਦਿ ਲਾਉਣਾ, ਜੁਟ ਜਾਣਾ, ਸਾਥ ਦੇਣਾ, ਸੰਗ ਕਰਨਾ ਨਾਲ ਰਹਿਣਾ; ਹੱਥ ਵਿਚ ਲੈਣਾ; **~anc** ਹਾਜ਼ਰੀ, ਮੌਜੂਦਗੀ, ਉਪਸਥਿਤੀ; ਹਾਜ਼ਰੀ; **~a** ਦਾਸ, ਨੌਕਰ, ਚਾਕਰ, ਅਰਦਲੀ, ਸੇਵਾਦਾ ਸੇਵਕ, ਸਹਿਗਾਮੀ; ਸਬੰਧਤ, ਉਪਸਥਿਤ, ਹਾਜ਼

attention (ਅ'ਟੈਂਸ਼ਨ) *n* ਧਿਆਨ, ਖ਼ਿਆਲ ਸਾਵਧਾਨੀ, ਇਕਾਗਰਤਾ, ਤਵਜੁਹ (ਵ ਸ਼ਿਸ਼ਟਾਚਾਰ, ਆਦਰ ਸਤਿਕਾਰ

attentive (ਅ'ਟੈਂਟਿਵ) *a* ਚੌਕਸ, ਸਾਵਧਾਨ, ਚੇਤ ਸਚੇਤ, ਜਾਗਰੂਕ, ਇਕਾਗਰ; **~ness** ਸਾਵਧਾਨ ਚੇਤਨਤਾ, ਇਕਾਗਰਚਿੱਤਤਾ; ਸ਼ਿਸ਼ਟਤਾ

attest (ਅ'ਟੈੱਸਟ) *v* ਤਸਦੀਕ ਕਰਨੀ, ਪ੍ਰਮਾਣ ਕਰਨਾ, ਗਵਾਹੀ ਦੇਣੀ, ਸਾਖੀ ਭਰਨਾ, ਸ ਚੁੱਕਣੀ, ਹਲਫ਼ ਲੈਣਾ; **~ation** ਪ੍ਰਮਾਣੀਕਰ ਤਸਦੀਕ, ਪ੍ਰਮਾਣ, ਸਾਖੀ, ਗਵਾਹੀ, ਪ੍ਰਮਾ ਪੱਤਰ; **~ed** ਤਸਦੀਕ ਕੀਤਾ, ਪ੍ਰਮਾਣਕ

attic (ਐਟਿਕ) *n* ਅਟਾਰੀ

attire (ਅ'ਟਾਇਅ*) *v n* ਪੁਸ਼ਾਕ ਪਹਿਨਣੀ, ਕੱ

attitude (ਐਟਿਟਯੂਡ) *n* ਰੁਖ, ਰਉਂ; ਮਨੋ-ਬਿਰ ਰਵੱਈਆ, ਵਿਹਾਰ, ਅੰਦਾਜ਼, ਬਿਰਤੀ; ਰੰਗ-ਢੰ ਵਿਚਾਰ ਭਾਵ (ਰਾਏ), ਸਥਿਤੀ

attract (ਅ'ਟਰੈਕਟ) *v* ਖਿਚਣਾ, ਆਕਰਸ਼ਤ ਕਰਨਾ, ਲੁਭਾਉਣਾ, ਮੋਹਣਾ, ਧਿਆਨ ਖਿਚਣਾ; ~ion ਆਕਰਸ਼ਣ, ਖਿੱਚ, ਮੋਹ, ਆਕਰਸ਼ਨ ਸ਼ਕਤੀ, ਕਸ਼ਸ਼; ~ive ਮਨੋਹਰ, ਆਕਰਸ਼ਕ, ਦਿਲਚਸਪ, ਮਨੋਰੰਜਕ

attribute (ਐਟਰਿਬਯੂਟ, ਅ'ਟਰਿਬਯੂਟ) *n v* ਗੁਣ, ਵਿਸ਼ੇਸ਼ਤਾ ਦੱਸਣਾ, ਸਾਰਥ ਦੱਸਣਾ, ਸਾਰਥ ਦੱਸਣਾ; ਨਾਂ ਲਗਾਉਣਾ, ਮਨਸੂਬਾ ਕਰਨਾ, ਮੱਥੇ ਮੜਨਾ

attributive (ਅ'ਟਰਿਬਯੂਟਿਵ਼) *a* ਗੁਣਵਾਚਕ

attune (ਅ'ਟਯੂਨ) *v* ਇਕ ਸੁਰ ਕਰਨਾ, ਮਿਲਾਉਣਾ; ਅਨੁਕੂਲ ਕਰਨਾ

auction ('ਓਕਸ਼ਨ) *n v* ਨੀਲਾਮੀ, ਬੋਲੀ; ਨੀਲਾਮੀ ਕਰਨਾ

audacity (ਓ'ਡੈਸਅਟਿ) *n* ਬੇਬਾਕੀ, ਦਲੇਰੀ, ਨਿਰਭੈਤਾ ਨਿਡਰਤਾ; ਢੀਠਪੁਣਾ

audible ('ਓਡਿਬਲ) *a* ਸੁਣਨ ਯੋਗ, ਸਪਸ਼ਟ, ਸ੍ਰਵਣ-ਗੋਚਰ, ਸ੍ਰਵਣੀ

audience ('ਓਡਯਅੰਸ) *n* ਸਰੋਤਾ-ਗਣ; ਸਰੋਤੇ, ਸਭਾ; ਸੁਣਵਾਈ, ਮੁਲਾਕਾਤ; ਪਾਠਕ-ਗਣ, ਦਰਸ਼ਕ-ਗਣ

audit ('ਓਡਿਟ) *n* ਲੇਖਾ-ਪਰੀਖਿਆ, ਲੇਖਾ-ਪੜਤਾਲ

auditor (ਓ'ਡਿਟਅ*) *n* ਲੇਖਾ-ਪਰੀਖਿਅਕ

auditorium ('ਓਡਿ'ਟੋਰਿਅਮ) *n* ਸਭਾਭਵਨ, ਜਲਸਾ ਘਰ, ਆਡੀਟੋਰੀਅਮ

auditory ('ਓਡਿਟ(ਅ)ਰਿ) *a* ਸੁਣਨ ਬਾਰੇ, ਸੁਣਨ ਸਬੰਧੀ, ਸ੍ਰਵਣਾਤਮਕ

augment /'ਓਗਸੈਂਟ, 'ਓਗਮਅੰਟ) *v n* ਵਧਾਉਣਾ, ਵਾਧਾ ਕਰਨਾ, ਅਧਿਕ ਕਰਨਾ, ਜ਼ਿਆਦਾ ਕਰਨਾ, ਸਵਰ-ਆਗਮ, ਵਾਧਾ, ਵ੍ਰਿਧੀ

august, August (ਓ'ਗਾਸਟ,'ਓਗਅਸਟ) *a n* ਪੂਜਨੀਕ, ਸਤਿਕਾਰ ਯੋਗ, ਉਚੀ ਸ਼ਾਨ ਵਾਲਾ, ਮਹਾਨ; ਅਗਸਤ ਮਹੀਨਾ

aunt ('ਆਂਟ) *n* ਚਾਚੀ, ਤਾਈ, ਮਾਮੀ, ਭੂਆ, ਫੁੱਫੀ, ਮਾਸੀ

aura ('ਓਰਅ) *n* ਨੂਰ, ਆਭਾ ਮੰਡਲ ਸੁਗੰਧ, ਕੰਬਣੀ, ਬਰਬਰੀ, ਝਰਨਾਟ; ਕੰਨਾਂ ਸਬੰਧੀ, ਕੰਨਾਂ ਦਾ, ਸੁਣੀ ਹੋਈ

aurora (ਓ'ਰੋਰਅ) *n* ਪ੍ਰਭਾਤ, ਪਹੁ-ਫੁਟਾਲਾ, ਤੜਕਾ, ਸਰਘੀ ਵੇਲਾ

auspice ('ਓਸਪਿਸ) *n* ਸ਼ਗਨ, ਮਹੂਰਤ; ਸ਼ੁਭ ਅਤੇ ਸ੍ਰੇਸ਼ਠ ਅਗਵਾਈ

auspicious (ਓ'ਸਪਿਸ਼ਅਸ) *a* ਸ਼ੁਭ ਲਗਨ ਵਾਲਾ, ਚੰਗੇ ਮਹੂਰਤ ਵਾਲਾ, ਸੁਲੱਖਣਾ, ਸ਼ੁਭਾਗਸ਼ਾਲੀ, ਕਲਿਆਣਕਾਰੀ, ਮੁਬਾਰਕ

austere (ਔ'ਸਟਿਅ*) *a* ਅਤੀ-ਸੰਜਮੀ, ਸਾਦਗੀ-ਪਸੰਦ; ਕੱਟੜ; ਕਠੋਰ-ਤਪੱਸਿਆ ਕਰਨਾ ਵਾਲਾ, ਵਿਤ੍ਰਿਸ਼ ਰੁਖ਼ ਵਿਤ, ਤੀਖਣ; ਗਠੀਰ

austerity (ਔ'ਸਟੈਰਅਟਿ) *n* ਸਾਦਗੀ, ਸਿੰਧਾਪਣ; ਕਠੋਰਤਾ, ਸਾਧਨ, ਤਪੱਸਿਆ, ਵਿਤ੍ਰਿਸ਼ ਸਦਾਚਾਰ

authentic (ਓ'ਥੈਂਟਿਕ) *n* ਭਰੋਸੇਯੋਗ, ਮੰਨਣ ਯੋਗ, ਵਿਸ਼ਵਾਸਪੂਰਨ, ਅਸਲੀ, ਮੌਲਕ, ਵਾਸਤਵਿਕ; ~ate ਪ੍ਰਮਾਣਤ ਕਰਨਾ; ~ity ਪ੍ਰਮਾਣਕਤਾ, ਵਾਸਤਵਿਕਤਾ, ਪ੍ਰਮਾਣਸਿੰਧਤਾ, ਸਚਾਈ

author ('ਓਥਅ*) *v* ਲੇਖਕ, ਲਿਖਾਰੀ, ਕਰਤਾ, ਰਚਨਹਾਰ, ਗ੍ਰੰਥਕਾਰ; ਮੋਢੀ, ਉਤਪਾਦਕ

authority (ਓ'ਥੋਰਿਟਅਟਿ) *n* ਅਧਿਕਾਰ, ਇਖ਼ਤਿਆਰ, ਪ੍ਰਭੁਤਾ; ਅਹੁਦੇਦਾਰ, ਪਦ-ਅਧਿਕਾਰੀ, ਪ੍ਰਮਾਣ, ਵਿਸ਼ੇਸ਼ੱਗ

authorize ('ਓਥਅਰਾਇਜ਼) *v* ਅਧਿਕਾਰ ਦੇਣਾ, ਇਖ਼ਤਿਆਰ ਦੇਣਾ, ਮੁਖ਼ਤਾਰ ਬਣਾਉਣਾ

authorship ('ਓਥਅ:ਸ਼ਿਪ) *n* ਗ੍ਰੰਥਕਾਰੀ, ਕਰਤ੍ਰਿਤਵ

auto ('ਓਟਅਓ) *n* (ਬੋਲ) ਸਵੈਚਾਲਕ ਗੱਡੀ, ਆਟੋ

autobiographer ('ਓਟਅ(ਉ)ਬਾਇ' ਔਗਰਅਫ਼ੇਅ*) *n* ਆਤਮ-ਕਥਾਕਾਰ, ਆਤਮ-ਕਥਾ-ਲੇਖਕ, ਸਵੈ-ਜੀਵਨੀਕਾਰ

autobiography ('ਓਟਅ(ਉ),ਬਾਇਅ(ਉ)ਗਰੈਫ਼ਿ) *n* ਆਪਬੀਤੀ, ਆਤਮ-ਕਥਾ, ਸਵੈਜੀਵਨੀ

autocracy (ਓ'ਟੋਕਰਅਸਿ) *n* ਖ਼ੁਦਮੁਖ਼ਤਾਰੀ, ਏਕਤੰਤਰ, ਨਿਰੰਕੁਸ਼ਤਾ; ਪ੍ਰਭਾਵ, ਦਬਦਬਾ

autocrat ('ਓਟਅ(ਉ)ਕਰੈਟ) *n* ਖ਼ੁਦਮੁਖ਼ਤਾਰ, ਬਾਦਸ਼ਾਹ, ਨਿਰੰਕੁਸ਼ ਸ਼ਾਸਕ

autograph ('ਓਟਅਗਰਾਫ਼) *n* ਆਪਣੇ ਹਸਤਾਖ਼ਰ, ਦਸਤਖ਼ਤ, ਹੱਥ-ਲਿਖਤ

automatic (ਓਟਅ'ਮੈਟਿਕ) *a* ਸਵੈਚਲਤ, ਆਪਣੇ ਆਪ ਚੱਲਣ ਜਾਂ ਕੰਮ ਕਰਨ ਵਾਲੀ

automobile ('ਓਟਅਮਅ(ਉ)ਬੀਲ) *n* ਮੋਟਰ ਜਾਂ ਕਾਰ

autonomy (ਓ'ਟੋਨਮਿ) *n* ਖ਼ੁਦਮੁਖ਼ਤਾਰੀ, ਵਿਅਕਤੀਗਤ ਸੁਤੰਤਰਤਾ, ਸਵਾਧੀਨਤਾ, ਸਵਰਾਜ

autumn ('ਓਟਅਮ) *n* ਪਤਝੜ ਦੀ ਰੁੱਤ, ਖ਼ਿਜ਼ਾਂ ਦਾ ਮੌਸਮ; ਖ਼ਰੀਫ਼ (ਫ਼ਸਲ)

auxiliary ('ਓਗ'ਜ਼ਿਲਯਅਰਿ) *n a* ਸਹਾਈ, ਉਪਕਾਰੀ, ਸਹਾਇਕ

avail (ਅ'ਵੇਇਲ) *v* ਕੰਮ ਵਿਚ ਲਿਆਉਣਾ, ਫ਼ਾਇਦਾ ਉਠਾਉਣਾ, ਮਦਦ ਦੇਣੀ, ਸਹਾਈ ਹੋਣਾ, ਕੰਮ ਆਉਣਾ; **to be of no** ~ ਕਿਸੇ ਕੰਮ ਦਾ ਨਾ ਹੋਣਾ, ਨਿਕੰਮਾ; **of no** ~ ਵਿਅਰਥ, ਨਿਸਫਲ, ਬੇਮਤਲਬ; **to** ~ **oneself of** ਤੋਂ (ਜਾਂ) ਦੇ ਲਾਭ ਉਠਾਉਣਾ; **~ability** ਪ੍ਰਾਪਤ, ਸੁਲੱਭਤਾ; ਉਪਲਬਧੀ; **~able** ਪ੍ਰਾਪਤ, ਮੌਜੂਦ, ਸੁਲੱਭ, ਲੱਭਣ, ਉਪਲਬਧ

avalanche ('ਐਵ੍ਅਲਾਂਸ਼) *n* ਬਰਫ਼ ਦਾ ਤੋਦਾ ਜੋ ਹੇਠਾਂ ਡਿਗ ਪੈਂਦਾ ਹੈ

avarice ('ਐਵ੍ਅਰਿਸ) *n* ਲੋਭ, ਲਾਲਚ, ਤ੍ਰਿਸ਼ਨਾ, ਹਿਰਸ

avenge (ਅ'ਵੈਂਜ) *v* ਬਦਲਾ ਲੈਣਾ, ਕਿੜ ਕੱਢਣੀ, ਇੰਤਕਾਮ ਲੈਣਾ

avenue ('ਐਵ੍ਅਨਯੂ) *n* ਛਾਂਦਾਰ ਮਾਰਗ, ਪ੍ਰਵੇਸ਼ ਮਾਰਗ, ਕੂੰਜ ਗਲੀ

average ('ਐਵ੍(ਅ)ਰਿਜ) *n v a* ਔਸਤ, ਮੱਧਮਾਨ, ਸਧਾਰਨਤਾ; ਔਸਤ ਕੱਢਣੀ; ਸਧਾਰਨ ਪੱਧਰ ਦਾ ਅਨੁਮਾਨ ਲਾਉਣਾ; ਸਧਾਰਨ, ਔਸਤ ਦਰਜੇ ਦਾ, ਮਾਮੂਲੀ

averse (ਅ'ਵ੍ਅ:ਸ) *a* ਵਿਰੁੱਧ, ਵਿਪਰੀਤ, ਪ੍ਰਤੀਕੂਲ, ਖਿਲਾਫ਼, ਉਲਟ

aversion (ਅ'ਵ੍ਅ:ਸ਼ਨ) *n* ਬੇਮੁਖਤਾ, ਅਰੁਚੀ, ਵਿਰਕਤੀ, ਵਿਰੋਧ, ਨਰਾਜ਼ਗੀ

avert (ਅ'ਵ੍ਅ:ਟ) *v* ਦੂਰ ਕਰਨਾ, ਫੇਰਨਾ, ਟਾਲਣਾ, ਹਟਾਉਣਾ, ਮੋੜ ਲੈਣਾ, ਫੇਰ ਦੇਣਾ, ਟਾਲ ਦੇਣਾ

aviation ('ਏਇਵ੍ਏਇਸ਼ਨ) *n* ਚਿੜੀਆਘਰ, ਵਿਮਾਨ ਸੰਚਾਲਨ, ਹਵਾਈ ਜਹਾਜ਼ ਚਲਾਉਣ ਦੀ ਕਿਰਿਆ

avication ('ਐਵ੍ਅ(ਉ)'ਕੇਇਸ਼ਨ) *n* ਪੇਸ਼ਾ, ਧੰਦਾ, ਕੰਮ; ਸ਼ੁਗਲ

avoid (ਅ'ਵੋਇਡ) *v* ਪਰਹੇਜ਼ ਕਰਨਾ; ਟਾਲਣਾ, ਬਚਣਾ, ਕਿਨਾਰਾ ਕਰਨਾ

await (ਅ'ਵੇਇਟ) *v* ਉਡੀਕਣਾ, ਇੰਤਜ਼ਾਰ ਕਰਨਾ, ਪ੍ਰਤੀਖਿਆ ਕਰਨੀ, ਰਾਹ ਤੱਕਣਾ, ਆਸਰਾ ਦੇਖਣਾ

awake (ਅ'ਵੇਇਕ) *a v* ਜਾਗਰਤ, ਜਾਗਰੁਕ, ਸਾਵਧਾਨ; ਉਠਣਾ, ਜਾਗਣਾ; ਉਤਸ਼ਾਹ ਦੇਣਾ,

ਸਾਵਧਾਨ ਹੋਣਾ, ਜਗਾਉਣਾ, ਸਚੇਤ ਕਰਨਾ, ਜਾਗਰਤ ਹੋਣਾ

award (ਅ'ਵੈ:ਡ) *v n* ਨਿਰਣਾ ਦੇਣਾ, ਪ੍ਰਦਾਨ ਕਰਨਾ, ਸਮਰਪਣ ਕਰਨਾ, ਸੌਂਪਣਾ, ਦੇਣਾ; ਪੰਚ-ਨਿਰਣਾ, ਫ਼ੈਸਲਾ; ਇਨਾਮ, ਪੁਰਸਕਾਰ, ਜੁਰਮਾਨਾ

aware (ਅ'ਵੇਇਅ*) *a* ਸਚੇਤ, ਸਾਵਧਾਨ, ਚੁਕੰਨਾ, ਹੁਸ਼ਿਆਰ, ਜਾਣਕਾਰ

away (ਅ'ਵੇਇ) *adv* ਦੂਰ, ਗ਼ੈਰਹਾਜ਼ਰ, ਪਰੇ, ਦੂਰੀ ਤੇ; ਅਲੱਗ, ਫ਼ਾਸਲੇ ਤੇ; ਨਿਰੰਤਰ, ਲਗਾਤਾਰ, ਹੋਗ਼ਾ

awe (ਓ) *n v* ਵਿਸਮਯ, ਰੁਆਬ, ਘੋਡ਼, ਡਰ; ਭਉ; ਵਿਸਮਤ ਕਰ ਦੇਣਾ, ਭੈਭੀਤ ਕਰਨਾ

awful ('ਓਫ਼ੁਲ) *a* ਡਰਾਉਣਾ, ਰੋਹਬ ਵਾਲਾ; ਆਦਰ-ਯੋਗ, ਮਹਿਮਾਪੂਰਨ, ਮਹਾਨ; ~**ly** ਡਰ ਨਾਲ, ਬਹੁਤ, ਅਧਿਕ

awhile (ਅ'ਵਾਇਲ) *adv* ਕੁਝ ਚਿਰ ਲਈ, ਥੋੜ੍ਹੀ ਦੇਰ ਲਈ

awkward ('ਓਕਵਅ*ਡ) *a* ਬੇਡੋਲ, ਕਰੂਪ, ਕੋਝਾ; ਭੱਦਾ ਅਨਾੜੀ, ਕਠਨ; ਭਿਆਨਕ, ਡਰਾਵਣਾ

awry (ਅ'ਰਾਇ) *adv* ਭੁੱਲ ਕੇ, ਟੇਢੇ ਢੰਗ ਨਾਲ

axe (ਐਕਸ) *n* ਕੁਹਾੜੀ, ਤੇਸੀ

axiom ('ਐਕਸਿਅਮ) *n* ਅਟੱਲ ਸਚਾਈ, ਪ੍ਰਮਾਣ, ਪ੍ਰਸਿੱਧ ਸਿਧਾਂਤ; ਫ਼ਾਰਮੂਲਾ, ਸੂਤਰ, ਸੂਕਤੀ, ਕਥਨ, ਵਾਕ, ਗੱਲ

axis ('ਐਕਸਿਸ) *n* ਕੇਂਦਰ, ਧੁਰਾ, ਧੁਰੀ

axle ('ਐਕਸਲ) *n* ਧੁਰਾ, ਧੁਰੀ, ਕਿੱਲੀ

ayah ('ਆਇਅ) *n* ਆਯਾ, ਦਾਈ

azure ('ਐਯ਼ਅ*) *n* ਅਸਮਾਨੀ, ਰੰਗ, ਨਿਰਮਲ ਆਕਾਸ਼, ਚਮਕਦਾਰ ਨੀਲਾ ਰੰਗ

B

B, b (ਬੀ) *n* ਰੋਮਨ ਵਰਣਮਾਲਾ ਦਾ ਦੂਜਾ ਅੱਖਰ; ਸਰਗਮ ਦੀ ਸੱਤਵੀਂ ਸੁਰ; ਦੂਜੀ ਚੀਜ਼

B. A. (ਬੀਏਇ) *a n* ਬੀ.ਏ. ਦੀ ਡਿਗਰੀ; ਬੀ.ਏ. ਪਾਸ

baa (ਬਾ) *n v* ਭੈਂ-ਭੈਂ (ਭੇਡ ਦੀ), ਮੈਂ-ਮੈਂ; ਭੈਂ-ਭੈਂ ਕਰਨਾ, ਮਿਆਂਕਣਾ, ਮਿਮਿਆਉਣਾ

babble ('ਬੈਬਲ) *v n* ਬੁੜਬੁੜਾਉਣਾ, ਲੁਤਰ-ਲੁਤਰ ਕਰਨਾ, ਟੈਂ-ਟੈਂ ਕਰਨਾ; ਬਕਣਾ; ਬੜ-ਬੜ, ਬਾਂ-ਬਾਂ, ਖੱਕੜ

babbling ('ਬੈਬਲਿਙ) *n a* ਬਕਵਾਸ, ਬੁੜਬੁੜਾਹਟ

babe ('ਬੇਇਬ) *n* ਬਾਲ, ਬਾਲਕ, ਬੱਚਾ, ਕਾਕਾ, ਕਾਕੀ, ਨਿਆਣਾ, ਗੀਗਾ, ਭੋਲਾ ਆਦਮੀ, ਅਨਾੜੀ

babel ('ਬੇਇਬਲ) *n* ਬਾਬਲ ਦਾ ਵੱਡਾ ਮੁਨਾਰਾ; ਰੌਲਾ-ਰੱਪਾ, ਕਾਵਾਂ-ਰੌਲੀ, ਚੀਕ-ਚਿਹਾੜਾ

baboon (ਬਅ'ਬੂਨ) *n* ਲੰਗੂਰ

babouche (ਬਅ'ਬੂਸ਼) *n* ਸਲੀਪਰ, ਚੱਪਲ

baby ('ਬੇਇਬਿ) *n* ਬੱਚਾ, ਬਾਲ, ਨਿੱਕੂ, ਕਾਕਾ, ਨਿਆਣਾ, ਛੋਟੂ, ਗੀਗਾ; ਕੋਈ ਬਹੁਤ ਛੋਟੀ ਚੀਜ਼

bachelor ('ਬੈਚਅਲਅ*) *n* ਕੰਵਾਰਾ, ਛੜਾ, ਬ੍ਰਹਮਚਾਰੀ; ਯੂਨੀਵਰਸਿਟੀ ਦੀ ਪਹਿਲੀ ਡਿਗਰੀ ਪ੍ਰਾਪਤ ਵਿਅਕਤੀ; (ਇਤਿ) ਜੋਧਾ, ਦੂਜੇ ਦੇ ਝੰਡੇ ਹੇਠ ਕੰਮ ਕਰਨ ਵਾਲਾ ਸੂਰਬੀਰ

back (ਬੈਕ) *n a adv* (1) ਪਿੱਠ, ਕੰਡ, ਪਿੱਛਾ (2) ਲਲਾਰੀ ਦਾ ਵੱਡਾ ਤਸਲਾ; ਤਗਾਰ; ਕੁੰਡ; ਬੱਠਲ, ਟੱਬ, ਪਹਿਲਾਂ ਜੇਹੀ ਹਾਲਤ ਵਿਚ; ਪੁੱਠਾ, ਪਿਛਲਾ; ਪਿੱਛੇ, ਪਿੱਛਾਂਹ, ਪੁਰਾਣੇ ਜ਼ਮਾਨੇ ਵਿਚ; ਸਮਰਥਨ ਕਰਨਾ, ਪਿੱਠ ਠੋਕਣੀ, ਪੁਸ਼ਟੀ ਕਰਨੀ; ਤਸਦੀਕ ਕਰਨਾ; ਪਿੱਛੇ ਹਟਣਾ; ਘੋੜਾ ਫੇਰਨਾ; ~**ground** ਪਿਛੋਕੜ, ਪਿੱਠ-ਭੂਮੀ, ਆਧਾਰ; ਪਿੱਛੇ ਦਾ ਹਿੱਸਾ; ~**log** ਰਹਿੰਦਾ ਕੰਮ; ~**side** ਪਿੱਛਾ, ਚਿੱਤੜ; ~**water** ਰੁਕਿਆ ਪਾਣੀ, ਬੰਦ ਪਾਣੀ, ਸਮੁੰਦਰ ਦੀ ਖਾੜੀ; ~**out of** ਮੁਕਰਨਾ, ਪਿੱਛੇ ਹਟਣਾ, ਆਪਣੀ ਗਲ ਤੋਂ ਫਿਰ ਜਾਣਾ; ~**up** ਪਿੱਠ ਠੋਕਣੀ, ਸਮਰਥਨ ਕਰਨਾ, ਹੌਸਲਾ ਵਧਾਉਣਾ ਸਹਾਇਤਾ ਕਰਨਾ ਹਾਮੀ ਭਰਨੀ ਸ਼ਹਿ ਦੇਣੀ; **to the ~ bone** ਪੂਰੀ ਤਰ੍ਹਾਂ; **turn one's~upon** ਪਿੱਠ ਦਿਖਾਉਣਾ, ਭੱਜ ਨਿਕਲਣਾ, ਛੱਡ ਕੇ ਨੱਠ ਜਾਣਾ ~**ing** ਆਸਰਾ, ਟੇਕ, ਹਿਮਾਇਤ, ਪੁਸ਼ਟੀ

backward ('ਬੈਕਵਅ*ਡ) *a adv* ਪਛੜਿਆ; ਪਿੱਛੇ; ਪਿੱਛਾਂਹ ਵੱਲ; ਭੈੜੀ ਹਾਲਤ ਵਿਚ; ਉਲਟਿਆ; ਪਿੱਛੇ ਰਿਹਾ; ~**classes** ਪੱਛੜੀਆਂ ਸ਼੍ਰੇਣੀਆਂ; ~**ness** ਪਛੜਾਪਣ, ਪਛੜੇਵਾਂ; ਉਲਟਾਪਣ

bacon ('ਬੇਇਕ(ਅ)ਨ) *n* ਸੂਰ ਦਾ ਮਾਸ

bacteria (ਬੈਕ'ਟਿਅਰਿਅ) (**becterium** ਦਾ *pl*) *n* ਜੀਵਾਣੂ, ਰੋਗਾਣੂ; ~**l** ਜਰਾਸੀਮੀ, ਰੋਗਾਣੂ ਸਬੰਧੀ

bad (ਬੈਡ') *a n* ਬੁਰਾ, ਖੋਟਾ, ਨਿਕੰਮਾ, ਘਟੀਆ; ਨੀਚ, ਭੈੜਾ, ਹੋਛਾ, ਕਮੀਨਾ, ਚੰਦਰਾ, ਬਦਕਾਰ; ~**ly** ਭੈੜੀ ਤਰ੍ਹਾਂ, ਬੁਰੀ ਤਰ੍ਹਾਂ; ਅਸਫਲਤਾ ਨਾਲ, ਮੰਦੇ ਹਾਲ; ਅਨਾੜੀਆਂ ਵਾਂਗ, ਗ਼ਲਤੀ ਨਾਲ; ~**ness** ਭੈੜ; ਬੁਰਾਈ, ਖੋਟ, ਬੁਰੀ ਹਾਲਤ; ਨੁਕਸ, ਦੋਸ਼, ਖ਼ਰਾਬੀ; ਘੋਟਾਪਣ, ਬਿਪਤਾ, ਦੁਰਗਤੀ, ਦੁਸ਼ਟਤਾ

badge (ਬੈਜ) *n* ਬਿੱਲਾ, ਨਿਸ਼ਾਨ, ਪ੍ਰਤੀਕ, ਪੱਟਾ

badminton ('ਬੈਡਮਿੰਟਅਨ) *n* ਬੈਡ-ਮਿੰਟਨ, ਚਿੜੀ-ਛਿੱਕਾ (ਇਕ ਖੇਡ); ਸ਼ਰਦਾਈ ਜੋ ਸ਼ਰਾਬ, ਸੋਡਾ ਤੇ ਖੰਡ ਰਲਾ ਕੇ ਬਣਦੀ ਹੈ

baffle ('ਬੈਫ਼ਲ) *v n* ਘਬਰਾਉਣਾ, ਮੱਤ ਮਾਰ ਦੇਣੀ; ਚਕਰ ਦੇਣਾ, ਰੁਕਾਵਟ ਪਾਉਣੀ, ਰੋੜਾ ਅਟਕਾਉਣਾ, ਨਿਸਫਲ ਕਰ ਦੇਣਾ; ਹੈਰਾਨ ਕਰਨ ਵਾਲਾ, ਘਬਰਾ ਦੇਣ ਵਾਲਾ, ਰੋੜਾ ਅਟਕਾਉਣ ਵਾਲਾ

bag (ਬੈਗ) *n* ਥੈਲਾ, ਥੈਲੀ, ਬੋਰਾ, ਝੋਲਾ, ਗੁੱਥੀ, ਗਾਂ ਦਾ ਲੇਵਾ; ਕੀੜਿਆਂ ਜਾਂ ਮੱਖੀਆਂ ਦੇ ਸਰੀਰ ਵਿਚ ਜ਼ਹਿਰ ਜਾਂ ਸ਼ਹਿਦ ਦੀ ਥੈਲੀ; ਅੱਖ ਦੇ ਝੱਲੇ ਉਤਰੀ ਥਾਂ; ਜਿਤਨਾ ਜਾ ਪ੍ਰਾਪਤ ਕਰਨ (ਇਨਾਮ ਦਾ), ਥੈਲੇ ਵਿਚ ਪਾਉਣਾ, ਫਸਾਉਣਾ, ਸ਼ਿਕਾਰ ਮਾਰਨਾ, ਹਥਿਆ ਲੈਣਾ, ਝੋਲ ਪੈਣੀ, ਭਟਕਣਾ; let the cat out of the~ ਭੇਦ ਖੋਲ੍ਹਣਾ, ਬਿੱਲੀ ਥੈਲਿਉਂ ਬਾਹਰ ਕੱਢਣਾ

baggage ('ਬੈਗਿਜ) *n a* ਸਫ਼ਰੀ ਸਾਮਾਨ, ਫ਼ੌਜੀ ਸਾਮਾਨ, ਮਾਲ, ਵਸਤ-ਵਲੇਵਾ, ਖੁੱਥੜ ਤੀਵੀਂ

bagging ('ਬੈਗਿੜ) *n* ਸਾਮਾਨ ਅਸਬਾਬ, ਮਾਲ-ਅਸਬਾਬ; ਬੈਗ ਬਣਾਉਣ ਵਾਲਾ ਟਾਟ

bail (ਬੇਇਲ) *n v* ਜ਼ਮਾਨਤ, ਜ਼ਾਮਨੀ; ਜ਼ਾਮਨ; ਕ੍ਰਿਕਟ ਦੀ ਖੇਡ ਵਿੱਚ ਵਿਕਟਾਂ ਦੇ ਉੱਪਰ ਦੀ ਗੁੱਲੀ; ਜ਼ਮਾਨਤ ਤੇ ਛੱਡਣਾ, ਮੁਚੱਲਕਾ ਲੈਣਾ

bailment ('ਬੇਇਲਮਅੰਟ) *n* ਜ਼ਮਾਨਤ, ਜ਼ਾਮਨੀ

bake (ਬੇਇਕ) *v* ਪਕਾਉਣਾ, ਰਾੜ੍ਹਨਾ; ਸੇਕਣਾ; ਭੁੰਨਣਾ; ਪੱਕ ਜਾਣਾ

baker ('ਬੇਇਕਅ*) *n* ਨਾਨਬਾਈ, ਤੰਦੂਰੀਆ, ਰੋਟੀ ਵਾਲਾ

balance ('ਬੈਲਅੰਸ) *n v* ਤੱਕੜੀ, ਕੰਡਾ, (ਘੜੀ ਦਾ) ਕਮਾਨੀਲੀਵਰ, ਬਾਲ ਕਮਾਨੀ; ਸੰਤੁਲਨ, ਬਰਾਬਰੀ, ਬਾਕੀ; ਬੱਚਤ; (ਜੋ) ਤੁਲਾ ਰਾਸ਼ੀ; ਕਿਸੇ ਵਸਤੂ ਦਾ ਬਾਕੀ ਭਾਗ; ਤੋਲਣਾ, ਵਜ਼ਨ ਕਰਨਾ, ਹਿਸਾਬ ਬਰਾਬਰ ਕਰਨਾ, ਇਕ ਜਿਹਾ ਕਰਨਾ, ਜੋੜ ਮਿਲਾਉਣਾ; ਡੋਲਣਾ; ~d ਸੰਤੁਲਤ; ~sheet ਆਮਦਨ-ਖਰਚ ਦਾ ਚਿੱਠਾ; lose one's~ ਡੋਲ ਜਾਣਾ, ਘਬਰਾਹਟ ਵਿਚ ਦਿਲ ਛੱਡ ਜਾਣਾ

balcony ('ਬੈਲਕਅਨਿ) *n* (ਉਪਰਲੀ ਮੰਜ਼ਲ ਦਾ) ਛੱਜਾ, ਬਾਲਕੋਨੀ

bald (ਬੋਲਡ) *a* ਗੰਜਾ, ਰੋਡਾ, ਕੋਰ, ਫਿੱਕ; ਸਰੀਰ ਤੇ ਵਿਸ਼ੇਸ਼ ਕਰਕੇ ਚਿਹਰੇ ਉਪਰ ਚਿੱਟੇ ਦਾਗ ਵਾਲਾ ਘੋੜਾ, ਪਪਹੀਟ, ਬੰਜਰ, ਗੰਜੀ ਭੋਂ; ~head ਗੰਜੇ ਸਿਰ ਵਾਲਾ; ~ness ਗੰਜ, ਰੋਡ, ਘੋਨ, ਰੁੱਖਪਣ

bale (ਬੇਇਲ) *n v* ਗੰਢ, ਪੰਡ, ਦੁੱਖ, ਪਾਪ, ਬੁਰਾਈ, ਬਿਪਤਾ, ਕਸ਼ਟ, ਕਲੇਸ਼, ਕਠਨਾਈ, ਤਕਲੀਫ਼; ਤਬਾਹੀ; ਗੰਢ ਬੰਨ੍ਹਣੀ, ਗੰਢ ਬਣਾਉਣਾ; ~ful ਮਨਹੂਸ, ਕਸ਼ਟਕਾਰੀ, ਸੋਗੀ, ਹਾਨੀਕਾਰਕ

ball (ਬੋਲ) *n v* ਗੇਂਦ, ਖੇਹਨੂੰ, ਖਿਦੋ, ਪਿੰਨਾ; (ਪਿਸਤੌਲ ਜਾਂ ਬੰਦੂਕ ਦੀ) ਗੋਲੀ, (ਤੋਪ ਦਾ) ਗੋਲਾ, ਬਰਫ਼ ਦਾ ਗੋਲਾ; ਉੱਨ ਦਾ ਗੋਲਾ, ਡੋਰ ਦਾ ਗੋਲਾ; ਅੱਖ ਦਾ ਡੇਲਾ; ਅਸਮਾਨੀ ਗ੍ਰਹਿ (ਚੰਦ, ਸੂਰਜ, ਤਾਰੇ ਆਦਿ), (ਕ੍ਰਿਕਟ ਵਿਚ) ਇੱਕ ਵਾਰ ਗੁੱਟਿਆ ਗੋਂਦ; ਬਾਲ-ਨ੍ਰਿਤ, ਵਲੇਟਣਾ, ਗੋਲ-ਮੋਲ ਹੋ ਜਾਣਾ; ਗੋਲਾ ਬਣਾਉਣਾ have the ~ at one's feet ਸਫ਼ਲਤਾ ਦਾ ਮੌਕਾ; keep the ~ rolling, keep up the ~ ਸਿਲਸਲਾ ਜਾਰੀ ਰੱਖਣਾ; ~room ਨਾਚ-ਘਰ; ~open the ~ ਨਾਚ ਆਰੰਭ ਕਰਨਾ; ਕੰਮ ਸ਼ੁਰੂ ਕਰਨਾ

ballad (ਬੈਲਅਡ) *n* ਗਾਥਾ-ਕਾਵਿ, ਜੱਜ਼ਬੇ ਭਰਿਆ ਗੀਤ, ਬੈਲੇਡ; ~monger ਭੱਟ, ਗੌਂਤਬਾਜ਼

ballet ('ਬੈਲੇਇ) *n* ਸੰਗੀਤਕ ਨਾਚ, ਰਾਸ-ਲੀਲ੍ਹਾ,

ਸਮੂਹ-ਨ੍ਰਿਤ; ~girl ਮੰਚ ਦੀ ਨਾਰੀ, ਸੰਗੀਤਕ ਨਾਟ ਦੀ ਨਰਤਕੀ

balloon (ਬਅ'ਲੂਨ) *n v* ਗੁਬਾਰਾ, ਭੁਕਾਨਾ, ਘੇਲੂਆ; ਬੁਰਜ; ਸ਼ੀਸ਼ੇ ਦਾ ਗਲੋਬ, (ਇਮਾਰਤ) ਲਾਟੂ ਜਾਂ ਗੁੰਬਦ; ਗੁਬਾਰੇ ਵਿਚ ਚੜ੍ਹਨਾ ਜਾਂ ਉਡਣਾ; ਗੁਬਾਰੇ ਵਾਂਗ ਫੁੱਲ ਜਾਣਾ

ballot ('ਬੈਲਅਟ) *n v* ਲੁਕਵੀਂ ਵੋਟ; ਗੁਪਤ ਦਿੱਤੇ ਗਏ ਮੱਤ; ਲਾਟਰੀ ਕੱਢਣ ਦਾ ਢੰਗ; ਗੁਪਤ ਰਾਇ ਦੇਣੀ, ਗੁਪਤ ਮੱਤ ਦੁਆਰਾ ਚੁਣਨਾ, ਚੋਣ ਕਰਨੀ ~box ਵੋਟ-ਸੰਦੂਕੜੀ, ਚੋਣ ਪੇਟੀ, ਬੈਲਟ ਬਾਕਸ; ~paper ਵੋਟ ਪਾਉਣ ਵਾਲੀ ਪਰਚੀ, ਗੁਪਤ ਪਰਚੀ

balm (ਬਾਮ) *n v* ਮਲ੍ਹਮ, ਖ਼ੁਸ਼ਬੂਦਾਰ ਲੇਪ; ਠੰਢ ਪਾਊ ਅਸਰ, ਤਸਕੀਨ, ਸੁਗੰਧਿਤ ਮਲ੍ਹਮ ਦਾ ਲੇਪ ਕਰਨਾ, ਤਸੱਲੀ ਦੇਣੀ, ਸੁਗੰਧ ਫੈਲਾਉਣੀ

bamboo (ਬੈਮ'ਬੂ) *n* ਬਾਂਸ, ਵੰਝ, ਵੇਟੂ; ਬਾਂਸ ਦੀ ਸੋਟੀ

ban (ਬੈਨ) *v n* ਮਨ੍ਹਾਂ ਕਰਨਾ, ਰੋਕਣਾ, ਮਨਾਹੀ ਕਰਨਾ; ਸਰਾਪ ਦੇਣਾ; ਛੇਕਣਾ; ਕਨੂੰਨੀ ਰੋਕ, ਬੰਦਸ਼, ਮਨਾਹੀ; ਲਾਨ੍ਹਤ-ਮਲਾਮਤ; ਸਰਾਪ; ਦੇਸ-ਨਿਕਾਲਾ

banal (ਬਅ'ਨਾਲ) *adv* ਤੁੱਛ, ਮਾਮੂਲੀ

banana (ਬਅ'ਨਾਨਅ) *n* ਕੇਲਾ

band (ਬੈਂਡ) *n* (1) ਵਾਜਾ, ਬੀਨ-ਵਾਜਾ, ਬੈਂਡ; ਸੰਗੀਤ-ਮੰਡਲੀ; (2) ਟੋਲੀ, ਜੱਥਾ; (3) ਪੱਟੀ, ਫੀਤਾ; ਰਪਟੀ ਪੱਟੀ; ਅੰਗੂਠੀ, ਛੱਲਾ; ਰੱਸੀ ਜਾਂ ਪੱਟੀ ਬੰਨ੍ਹਣੀ; ਸੰਗਠਨ ਕਰਨਾ, ਜਥੇਬੰਦੀ ਕਰਨੀ; ਧਾਰੀਆਂ ਪਾਉਣੀਆਂ; ~box ਕਾਗ਼ਜ਼ ਜਾਂ ਗੱਤੇ ਦਾ ਡੱਬਾ; ~master ਬੈਂਡ ਵਾਜੇ ਵਾਲਿਆਂ ਦਾ ਆਗੂ

bandage ('ਬੈਨਡਿਜ) *n v* (ਜ਼ਖ਼ਮ ਆਦਿ ਤੇ ਬੰਨ੍ਹਣ ਵਾਲੀ) ਪੱਟੀ; ਅੱਖਾਂ ਤੇ ਬੰਨ੍ਹਣ ਵਾਲੀ ਪੱਟੀ; ਪੱਟੀ ਕਰਨੀ; ਪੱਟੀ ਬੰਨ੍ਹਣੀ

bandaging (ਬੈਂਡਿਜਿਙ) *n* ਮੱਲ੍ਹਮ ਪੱਟੀ

bandit (ਬੈਂਡਿਟ) *n* ਡਾਕੂ ਡਕੈਤ, ਲੁਟੇਰਾ; ਧਾੜਵੀ

bandog (ਬੈਂਡੋਗ) *n* ਸ਼ਿਕਾਰੀ ਕੁੱਤਾ, ਖੋਜੀ ਕੁੱਤਾ

bane (ਬੇਇਨ) *n* ਜ਼ਹਿਰ, ਵਿਸ, ਵਿਹੁ; ਤਬਾਹੀ, ਬਰਬਾਦੀ; ਤਬਾਹੀ ਦਾ ਕਾਰਨ; ~ful ਜ਼ਹਿਰੀਲਾ, ਵਿਸ਼ੈਲਾ, ਵਿਹੁਲਾ, ਦੁਖਦਾਈ, ਵਿਨਾਸ਼ੀ, ਖ਼ਤਰਨਾਕ; ~fulness ਵਿਨਾਸ਼, ਖ਼ਤਰਾ, ਬਰਬਾਦੀ

bang (ਬੈਙ) *n v adv int* ਖੜਾਕ, ਖੜਕਾ, ਧਮਾਕਾ, ਬੰਦੂਕ ਚੱਲਣ ਦੀ ਅਵਾਜ਼, ਠਾਹ; ਠੋਕਣਾ, ਖੜਾਕ ਨਾਲ ਮਾਰਨਾ, ਜ਼ੋਰ ਨਾਲ ਮਾਰਨਾ, ਕੁੱਟਣਾ, ਮਾਰਨਾ-ਪਿਟਣਾ; (with a~) ਧੜੰਮ ਕਰਕੇ, ਠਾਹ ਕਰਕੇ; ਯਕਾਯਕ, ਪੂਰਾ ਪੂਰਾ, ਮੁਕੰਮਲ ਤੌਰ ਤੇ

bangle (ਬੈਙਗਲ) *n v* ਚੂੜੀ, ਵੰਗ, ਕੜਾ, ਕੰਗਣ; ~d ਚੂੜੀਦਾਰ, ਚੂੜੀਵਾਲਾ, ਕੜੇਦਾਰ

banish (ਬੈਨਿਸ਼) *v* ਦੇਸ ਨਿਕਾਲਾ ਦੇਣਾ, ਬਟਵਾਸ ਦੇਣਾ, ਦਿਲੋਂ ਕੱਢ ਦੇਣਾ, ਦੂਰ ਕਰ ਦੇਣਾ; ~ment ਦੇਸ ਨਿਕਾਲਾ, ਜਲਾਵਤਨੀ, ਨਿਰਵਾਸਨ

bank (ਬੈਙਕ) *n* (1) ਕੰਢਾ ਬਣਾਉਣਾ, ਕਿਨਾਰੇ ਦਾ ਕੰਮ ਕਰਨਾ; ਢੇਰ ਲੱਗਣਾ, ਤੇੜਾ ਬਣ ਜਾਣਾ; ਕੰਢ, ਕਿਨਾਰਾ, ਕੰਧੀ, ਥੇਹ, ਵੱਟ; ਟਿੱਬਾ; (2) ਬੈਂਕ, ਰੁਪਏ ਲੈਣ-ਦੇਣ ਦੀ ਥਾਂ, ਸ਼ਾਹੂਕਾਰਾ, ਸਰਾਫ਼ਾ; ਜੂਏ ਤੇ ਲੱਗੀ ਕੁੱਲ ਰਕਮ; to break the ~ ਜੂਏ ਵਿਚ ਜਿੱਤਣਾ; ~ on ਨਿਰਭਰ ਕਰਨਾ, ਆਸਾਂ ਬੰਨ੍ਹਣੀਆਂ, ਉਮੀਦਾਂ ਰੱਖਣੀਆਂ; ~bill ਚੈੱਕ, ਹੁੰਡੀ; ~ note ਹੁੰਡੀ; ~ paper ਬੈਂਕ ਦੇ ਨੋਟ ਜਿਹੜੇ ਲੋਕਾਂ ਵਿਚ ਚਲਦੇ ਹੋਣ, ਇਕ ਵਧੀਆ ਕਿਸਮ ਦਾ ਕਾਗ਼ਜ਼; rate ਬੈਂਕ-ਦਰ; ~er ਸ਼ਾਹੂਕਾਰ, ਮਹਾਜਨ, ਸਰਾਫ, ਬੈਂਕ ਦਾ ਪ੍ਰਬੰਧਕ; ਜੂਆ

ਖਿਡਾਉਣ ਵਾਲਾ; ~ing ਸ਼ਾਹੂਕਾਰਾ, ਬੈਂਕਿੰਗ, ਬੈਂਕ-ਵਪਾਰ

bankrupt (ਬੈਂਕਰਅੱਪਟ) *n v* ਦਿਵਾਲੀਆ, ਸੰਖਣਾ, ਹੀਣਾ; ਦਿਵਾਲਾ ਕੱਢਣਾ; ਦਿਵਾਲੀਆ ਬਣਾਉਣਾ; **~cy** ਦਿਵਾਲਾਪਨ, ਸਤਿਆਨਾਸ, ਤਬਾਹੀ, ਸੰਪੂਰਨ ਨਾਸ

banner (ਬੈਨਅ*) (ਸਮਰਾਟ, ਰਾਜਾ, ਸਰਦਾਰ ਦਾ) *n* ਝੰਡਾ, ਨਿਸ਼ਾਨ; **~ed** ਝੰਡੇ ਵਾਲਾ, ਝੰਡੇਦਾਰ; **~headline** (ਅਖ਼ਬਾਰ ਦੀ) ਵੱਡੀ ਸੁਰਖੀ

banquet (ਬੈਂਕਵਿਟ) *n v* ਮਹਾਂ-ਭੋਜ, ਦਾਅਵਤ, ਜ਼ਿਆਫ਼ਤ, ਖਾਣੇ ਵਿਚ ਹਿੱਸਾ ਲੈਣਾ, ਪਾਣਾ ਕਰਨਾ, ਪੇਟ ਭਰਨਾ

banquette (ਬੈਂਕੱਇਟ) *n* ਗੋਲੇ ਵਰ੍ਹਾਉਣ ਲਈ ਕਿਲ੍ਹੇ ਅੰਦਰ ਉਚੀ ਥਾਂ, ਫ਼ਰਾਂਸੀਸੀ ਗੱਡੀਆਂ ਵਿਚ ਡਰਾਈਵਰ ਦੇ ਪਿੱਛੇ ਬੈਠਣ ਦੀ ਥਾਂ

baptism (ਬੈਪਟਿਜ਼(ਅ)ਮ) *n* ਬਪਤਿਸਮਾ, ਇਸਾਈ ਧਰਮ ਵਿਚ ਪ੍ਰਵੇਸ਼ ਕਰਨ ਦਾ ਸੰਸਕਾਰ, ਨਾਮਕਰਨ ਸੰਸਕਾਰ, ਦੀਖਿਆ, ਪਾਹੁਲ

baptist (ਬੈਪਟਿਸਟ) *n* ਬਪਤਿਸਮਾ ਕਰਨ ਵਾਲਾ, ਇਸਾਈ ਮੱਤ ਦੀ ਦੀਖਿਆ ਦੇਣ ਵਾਲਾ

baptize (ਬੈਪਟਾਇਜ਼) *v* ਸਪਤਿਸਮਾ ਦੇਣਾ, ਅੰਮ੍ਰਿਤ ਛਕਾਉਣਾ, ਪਾਹੁਲ ਦੇਣੀ, ਸ਼ੁੱਧ ਕਰਨਾ, ਪਦਵੀ ਵਧਾਉਣੀ

bar (ਬਾ*) *n v* (1) ਸਰੀਆ, ਸੀਖ, ਸਲਾਖ, ਛੜ (ਧਾਤੂ, ਲੱਕੜੀ, ਸਾਬਣ ਆਦਿ ਦਾ) ਡੰਡਾ, (2) ਢੀਠੇ ਉਤੇ ਚਾਂਦੀ ਦੀ ਪੱਟੀ, ਰੰਗ ਆਦਿ ਦੀ ਪੱਟੀ, ਰੋਕ (ਜਿਵੇਂ ਹੁੰਗੀ ਦੀ); (3) ਸ਼ਰਾਬ ਘਰ, ਬਾਰ, ਜਲਪਾਨ ਘਰ; (4) ਵਕੀਲਾਂ ਦੀ ਸ਼੍ਰੇਣੀ; ਅਦਾਲਤ ਵਿਚ ਕੈਦੀਆਂ ਦੇ ਖੜ੍ਹੇ ਹੋਣ ਦੀ ਥਾਂ, ਮੁਜਰਮ ਦਾ ਕਟਹਿਰਾ; ਪਾਰਲੀਮੈਂਟ ਹਾਲ ਵਿਚ ਉਹ ਜੰਗਲਾ ਜਿਸ ਤੋਂ ਬਿਨਾਂ ਕੋਈ ਨਹੀਂ ਜਾ ਸਕਦਾ; ਦਾਅਵੇ ਜਾਂ ਕਾਨੂੰਨ ਦੀ ਵਰਤੋਂ ਵਿਚ ਰੁਕਾਵਟ, ਅੜਿੱਕਾ, ਅਦਾਲਤੀ ਕਾਰਵਾਈ ਰੋਕਣ ਦੀ ਬਹਿਸ; (5) (ਸੰਗੀ) ਲਿਪੀ ਵਿਚ ਤਾਲ ਲਈ ਸਿੱਧੀ ਖੜੀ ਲਕੀਰ

barb (ਬਾਬ) *n v* (1) ਮੱਛੀ ਦੇ ਬਾਰੀਕ ਕੰਡੇ, ਬਰਛੇ ਜਾਂ ਤੀਰ ਦੀ ਨੋਕ, ਸੂਲ, ਮੱਛੀ ਫੜਨ ਵਾਲੀ ਕੁੰਡੀ; (2) ਹੁੱਕ ਲਗਾਉਣਾ; ਚੋਭ, ਪੀੜ; ਸੂਲ ਚੁਭਾਉਣਾ, ਸੂਲ ਲਗਾਉਣਾ

barbarian (ਬਾਬੇਅਰਿਅਨ) *n a* ਵਹਿਸ਼ੀ, ਅਸੱਭਿਅ, ਜਾਂਗਲੀ, ਉਜੱਡ, ਗੰਵਾਰ (ਵਿਅਕਤੀ); (ਇਤਿ) ਗ਼ੈਰਕ'ਨੂੰਨੀ; ਗ੍ਰੀਏਸਿਆਈ; ਵਿਦੇਸ਼ੀ

barbaric (ਬਾਬੈਰੀਕ) *a* ਵਹਿਸ਼ੀ, ਮਲੇਛ, ਗੰਵਾਰ; ਜਾਂਗਲੀ; (ਇਤਿ) ਗ੍ਰੀਕੂਨਾਨੀ, ਗ੍ਰੀਏਸਿਆਈ; ਅਸੱਭਿਅ, ਬਰਬਰ, ਵਿਦੇਸ਼ੀ

barbarism (ਬਾਬਅਰਿਜ਼(ਅ)ਮ) *n* ਕਰੂਰਤਾ, ਵਹਿਸ਼ੀਪੁਣਾ, ਜਾਂਗਲੀਪੁਣਾ, ਉਜੱਡਪੁਣਾ, ਗੰਵਾਰਪੁਣਾ, ਅਸੱਭਿਅਤਾ, ਅਸ਼ਿਸ਼ਟਤਾ, ਅਗਿਆਨ, ਬਰਬਰ ਅਵਸਥਾ

barbarity (ਬਾਬੈਰਅਟਿ) *n* ਰਾਕਸ਼-ਪੁਣਾ, ਜ਼ੁਲਮ, ਜਬਰ, ਜਾਂਗਲੀਆਂ ਵਰਗਾ ਅੱਖੜਪਣ, ਨਿਰਦਇਆਤਾ, ਬਰਬਰਤਾ, ਅਸੱਭਿਅ ਅਵਸਥਾ; ਗੰਵਾਰੂ ਸ਼ੈਲੀ

barbarous (ਬਾਬ(ਅ)ਰਅਸ) *a* ਜਾਂਗਲੀ, ਉਜੱਡ, ਵਹਿਸ਼ੀ, ਨਿਰਦਈ, ਜ਼ਾਲਮ, ਅਸੱਭਿਅ ਸੁਭਾਅ ਵਾਲਾ, ਅਸ਼ਿਸ਼ਟ; **~ness** ਨਿਰਦਇਆਤਾ, ਅਸੱਭਿਅਤਾ, ਬਰਬਰਤਾ

barbed (ਬਾਬਡ) *a* ਕੰਡਿਆਲੀ, ਕੰਡਿਆ ਵਾਲਾ, ਉਲਝਿਆ; **~wire** ਕੰਡਿਆਂ ਵਾਲੀ ਤਾਰ, ਕੰਡਿਆਲੀ ਤਾਰ

barber (ਬਾਬਅ*) *n* ਨਾਈ, ਹੱਜਾਮ

bard (ਬਾਡ) *n* (1) ਚਾੜੀ, ਭੱਟ, ਗਵੱਈਆ;

ਪੁਰਾਤਨ ਕਵੀ, ਗੀਤਕਾਰ; (2) ਜੰਗੀ ਘੋੜੇ ਦੀ ਛਾਤੀ ਅਤੇ ਪਿੱਠ ਦੀ ਸੰਜੋਅ ਜਾਂ ਕਵਚ

bare (ਬੇਇਅ*) *a v* (1) ਨੰਗਾ, ਅਲਾਣਾ, ਅਣਕੱਜਿਆ, ਖੁੱਲ੍ਹੇ-ਮੂੰਹ, ਗੰਜਾ; (2) ਮਾਤਰ, ਕੇਵਲ, ਸੁੰਨ, ਨਿਰਾ, ਸਿਰਫ਼, ਅਲਪ; (3) ਰੁੱਖ-ਹੀਣ, ਬੰਜਰ; ਨੰਗਾ ਕਰਨਾ, ਭੇਤ ਖੋਲ੍ਹਣਾ; ਪਰਗਟ ਕਰਨਾ, ਪਰਦਾ ਲਾਹੁਣਾ, ਉਘੇੜਨਾ; ~**backed** ਬਿਨਾ ਕਾਠੀਉਂ (ਘੋੜਾ), ਅਲਾਣਾ, ਨੰਗੇ-ਪਿੱਠੇ; ~**bone** ਦੁਬਲਾ ਪਤਲਾ, ਜਿਸ ਦੀਆਂ ਹੱਡੀਆਂ ਨਿਕਲੀਆਂ ਹੋਣ; ~**footed** ਨੰਗੇ ਪੈਰ, ਨੰਗੇ ਪੈਰੀਂ; ~**headed** ਨੰਗੇ ਸਿਰ

barely (ਬੇਅ*ਲਿ) *adv* ਮਸਾਂ ਹੀ, ਮੁਸ਼ਕਲ ਨਾਲ; ਕੇਵਲ, ਮਾਤਰ; ਸਪਸ਼ਟ, ਖੁੱਲ੍ਹਮ-ਖੁੱਲ੍ਹਾ

bargain ('ਬਾ*ਗਿਨ) *n v* ਸੌਦਾ, ਸੌਦੇਬਾਜ਼ੀ, ਸੱਟਾ, ਮਾਲ, ਖਰਾ ਸੌਦਾ, ਚੰਗੀ ਖ਼ਰੀਦ; ਸੌਦਾ ਕਰਨਾ, ਮੁੱਲ ਕਰਨਾ, ਸੌਦਾ ਮੁਕਾਉਣਾ, ਤਹਿ ਕਰਨਾ, ਠਹਿਰਾਉਣਾ; **a**~ ਚੰਗਾ ਜਾਂ ਮੁਨਾਫ਼ੇ ਵਾਲਾ ਸੌਦਾ; ~**into the** ਝੁੰਗੇ ਵਿਚ, ਮੁਫ਼ਤ ਵਿਚ, ਸੀਦੀ ਵਜੋਂ; **strike a**~ ਸੌਦਾ ਪੱਕਾ ਕਰਨਾ

bark (ਬਾ:ਕ) *n v* (1) ਛਿੱਲ, ਛਿਲਕਾ, ਕੁਨੀਨ; ਖੱਲ, ਚਮੜੀ; ਰੁੱਖ ਦੀ ਛਿਲੜ ਲਾਹੁਣਾ, ਛਿਲਕਾ ਉਤਾਰਨਾ, ਤਹਿ ਜਮਾਉਣਾ; ਖਿਸਲਾ, ਛਿੱਲਣਾ; (2) ਭੌਂਕ, ਭੌਂਕਣ ਦੀ ਅਵਾਜ਼, ਬੰਦੂਕ ਚੱਲਣ ਦੀ ਅਵਾਜ਼, ਖੰਘੁਰਾ; ਭੌਂਕਣਾ, ਘੁਰਕਣਾ, ਘੁਰਕ ਕੇ ਬੋਲਣਾ, ਖੰਘੁਰਨਾ, ਚਿੜਚੜਾ ਕੇ ਜਾਂ ਚੀਹਤਾਈ ਕੇ ਲਹਿਜੇ ਵਿਚ ਬੋਲਣਾ

barley ('ਬਾ:ਲਿ) *n* ਜੌਂ, ਜੌਂ ਦਾ ਦਾਣਾ, ਜੌਂ ਦਾ ਕਸੀਰ, ਸਿੱਟਾ ਜਾਂ ਬੱਲੀ; ~ **corn** ਜੌਂ, ਜੌਂ ਦਾ ਦਾਣਾ, ਜੌਂ ਦੀ ਫ਼ਸਲ; ~ **meal** ਸੱਤੂ

barometer (ਬਅ'ਰੌਮਿਟਅ*) *n* ਘੌਰੋਮੀਟਰ, ਹਵਾ ਦਬਾ ਮਾਪਕ, ਹਵਾ ਦੇ ਦਬਾ ਨੂੰ ਮਿਣੀਦਾ ਅਤੇ ਆਉਣ ਵਾਲੇ ਮੌਸਮ ਅਤੇ ਸਮੁੰਦਰ ਤੋਂ ਉਚਾਈ ਦਾ ਪਤਾ ਲਾਉਣ ਵਾਲਾ, ਇਕ ਆਲਾ ਜਾਂ ਜੰਤਰ

baron ('ਬੈਰ(ਅ)ਨ) *n* (ਇੰਗਲੈਂਡ ਵਿਚ) ਅਮੀਰ ਨੂੰ ਲਾਰਡ ਦਾ ਖ਼ਿਤਾਬ ਮਿਲਿਆ ਹੋਵੇ, ਸਾਮੰਤ, ਜਾਗੀਰਦਾਰ, ਨਵਾਬ, ਬੈਰਨ, ਛੋਟਾ ਲਾਰਡ

barrack ('ਬੈਰਅਕ) *n v* ਸੈਨਾ ਨਿਵਾਸ, ਬੈਰਕ, ਫ਼ੌਜੀਆਂ ਦੇ ਇਕੱਠੇ ਰਹਿਣ ਲਈ ਬਣੇ ਹੋਏ ਵੱਡੇ ਕਮਰੇ, ਨਿਵਾਸ, ਬੈਰਕਾਂ ਵਿਚ ਰੱਖਣਾ, ਥਾਂ ਦੇਣੀ; (ਕ੍ਰਿਕਟ ਦੀ ਖੇਡ ਆਦਿ ਵਿਚ) ਮਖ਼ੌਲ ਕਰਨਾ, ਅਵਾਜ਼ਾਂ ਕੱਸਣੀਆਂ

barrage ('ਬੈਰਾਯ਼) *n* ਬੰਨ੍ਹ, ਬੰਦ ਬੰਦੂਕਾਂ ਦੀ ਬੁਛਾੜ, ਬਾਹੂ; ਹਮਲਾ ਕਰਨ ਅਤੇ ਰੋਕਣ ਲਈ ਬਣਾਈ ਗਈ ਰੋਕ, ਆੜ

barrel ('ਬੈਰ(ਅ)ਲ) *n v* ਪੀਪਾ, ਕੁੱਪਾ, ਘੜੀ ਦਾ ਇਕ ਪੁਰਜ਼ਾ; ਬੰਦੂਕ ਦੀ ਨਾਲੀ; ਸ਼ੇਰ ਅਤੇ ਘੋੜੇ ਦਾ ਲੱਕ ਅਤੇ ਪਿੱਠ; ਸਿੱਧਾ ਖੜਾ ਸਰੀਰ, ਪੀਪਿਆਂ ਵਿਚ ਭਰਨਾ ਜਾਂ ਰੱਖਣਾ; ~**led** ਨਲੀਦਾਰ, ਪੀਪੇ ਵਿਚ ਬੰਦ (ਸ਼ਰਾਬ); **double ~ gun** ਦੋ ਨਾਲੀ ਬੰਦੂਕ

barren ('ਬੈਰ(ਅ)ਨ) *a n* ਬਾਂਝ, ਸੰਢ; ਅਫਲ; (ਜ਼ਮੀਨ) ਬੰਜਰ, ਅਣਉਪਜਾਊ; ਵਿਅਰਥ, ਬੇਫ਼ਾਇਦਾ, ਖ਼ੁਸ਼ਕ, ਜ਼ਮੀਨ

barricade ('ਬੈਰਿ'ਕੇਇਡ) *n v* ਨਾਕਾਬੰਦੀ, ਕੱਚੀ ਮੋਰਚਾਬੰਦੀ, ਅੜਿੱਕਾ, ਆੜ, ਰੋਕ; ਨਾਕਾਬੰਦੀ ਕਰਨੀ, ਮੋਰਚਾਬੰਦੀ ਕਰਨੀ, ਕੱਚੇ ਮੋਰਚੇ ਬਣਾਉਣੇ, ਬਚਾਉ ਕਰਨਾ, (ਸੜਕ) ਰੋਕ ਦੇਣਾ, ਆੜ ਪਾਉਣੀ, ਰੁਕਾਵਟ ਪਾਉਣੀ

barrier ('ਬੈਰਿਅ)* *n v* ਰੋਕ, ਵਾੜ, ਜੰਗਲਾ, ਹੁੰਗੀ, ਫਾਟਕ, ਨੇਜ਼ਾਬਾਜ਼ੀ ਦਾ ਕਟਹਿਰਾ, ਆੜ; ਰੋਕ ਲਾਉਣੀ, ਬੰਦ ਕਰਨਾ

barring ('ਬਾਰਿਙ) *prep* ਛੱਡ ਕੇ, ਸਿਵਾਏ,

ਤੋਂ ਛੁੱਟ

barrow ('ਬੈਰਅਉ) *n* ਸਮਾਧੀਆਂ ਦਾ ਟਿੱਲਾ, ਕਬਰਾਂ ਦੇ ਉਪਰਲਾ ਮਿੱਟੀ ਦਾ ਢੇਰ

barter ('ਬਾਟਅ*) *n v* ਵੱਟਾ-ਸੱਟਾ, ਵਟਾਂਦਰਾ; ਵੱਟਾ-ਸੱਟਾ ਕਰਨਾ, ਇਕ ਚੀਜ਼ ਦੇ ਕੇ ਬਦਲੇ ਵਿਚ ਦੂਜੀ ਲੈਣੀ, ਚੀਜ਼ ਬਦਲੇ ਚੀਜ਼ ਲੈਣੀ ਦੇਣੀ

base (ਬੇਇਸ) *n adv v* ਆਧਾਰ, ਥੱਲਾ, ਤਲਾ; ਨੀਂਹ, ਬੁਨਿਆਦ; ਮੂਲ ਤੱਤ, (ਬਨ) ਜੋੜ; ਖਾਰ; (ਸੈਨਾ) ਬੇਸ, ਅੱਡਾ; ਕਮੀਨਾ, ਪਤਿਤ, ਨੀਚ; ਬਦਜ਼ਾਤ, ਥੋਂਟਾ, ਮਦਾ, ਮਾੜਾ, ਨਕਾਰਾ; ਨੀਚ ਰੱਖਣੀ, ਸਥਾਪਤ ਕਰਨਾ, ਆਧਾਰ ਬਣਾਉਣਾ, ਆਧਾਰਤ ਕਰਨਾ; ~**less** ਬੇਬੁਨਿਆਦ, ਨਿਰਮੂਲ, ਆਧਾਰਹੀਨ, ਸਾਰਹੀਣ; ~**lessness** ਨਿਰਮੂਲਤਾ; ~**ment** ਭੌਰਾ, ਤਹਿਖ਼ਾਨਾ; ਤਲ, ਥੱਲਾ

bash (ਬੈਸ਼) *v* ਜ਼ੋਰ ਨਾਲ ਮਾਰਨਾ; ~**ful** ਸ਼ਰਮਾਕਲ, ਸ਼ਰਮੀਲਾ, ਸੰਗਾਊ, ਲੱਜਾਵਾਨ; ~**fully** ਸ਼ਰਮ ਨਾਲ, ਸੰਗਦਿਆਂ; ~**ness** ਸ਼ਰਮ, ਸੰਗ, ਲੱਜਾ; ~**less** ਬੇਸ਼ਰਮ, ਬੇਹਯਾ, ਨਿਰਲੱਜ

basic (ਬੇਇਸਿਕ) *a* ਆਧਾਰੀ, ਮੂਲ, ਮੁੱਢਲਾ, ਅਰੰਭਕ, ਪ੍ਰਧਾਨ (ਧਾਤੂ); (ਰਸਾ) ਖਾਰ-ਯੁਕਤ; ~**education** ਬੁਨਿਆਦੀ ਸਿੱਖਿਆ, ਗੁੱਡਲੀ ਸਿੱਖਿਆ; ~**pay** ਮੂਲ ਤਨਖ਼ਾਹ

basin ('ਬੇਇਸਨ) *n* ਚਿਲਮਚੀ, ਹੌਦੀ, ਦੌਰ, ਬੇਸਿਨ, ਕੁੰਡ; ਗੋਲ ਜਾਂ ਅੰਡ-ਕਾਰ ਨਦੀ-ਖੇਤਰ; ਜ਼ਮੀਨ ਨਾਲ ਘਿਰੀ ਹੋਈ ਬੰਦਰਗਾਹ, ਬਣਾਉਟੀ ਬੰਦਰਗਾਹ; ਨਦੀ-ਲਾਂਘਾ, ਵਹਾਉ-ਸਥਾਨ; ਕੇਂਦਰ ਵੱਲ ਝੁਕਿਆ ਪੱਥਰਾਂ ਦਾ ਢਾਂਚਾ

basis ('ਬੇਇਸਿਸ) *n* (*pl* bases) ਨੀਂਹ, ਬੁਨਿਆਦ, ਆਧਾਰ; ਮੂਲ, ਮੂਲ-ਆਧਾਰ; ਮੂਲ ਸਿਧਾਂਤ; ਫ਼ੌਜੀ ਅੱਡਾ

bask (ਬਾਸਕ) *v* ਧੁੱਪ ਸੇਕਣੀ, ਨਿੱਘ ਮਾਨਣਾ

basket ('ਬਾਸਕਿਟ) *n v* ਟੋਕਰਾ, ਟੋਕਰੀ, ਪਟਾਰਾ, ਪਟਾਰੀ, ਛਾਬਾ, ਝਿੰਕੁ, ਚੰਗੇਰ, ਪੱਛੀ; ਕਿਸੇ ਵਸਤੂ ਨੂੰ ਟੋਕਰੀ ਵਿਚ ਰੱਖਣਾ; ਪਟਾਰੀ ਪਾਉਣਾ; ~**ball** ਖਿਦੂ-ਛਿੱਕਾ, ਗੇਂਦ, ਬਾਸਕਟ ਬਾਲ

bastard ('ਬਾਸਟਅ*ਡ) *n a* ਹਰਾਮੀ, ਨਾਜਾਇਜ਼ ਸੰਬੰਧ ਤੋਂ ਪੈਦਾ ਹੋਇਆ (ਬੱਚਾ), ਵਰਣਸੰਕਰ, ਕਮੀਨਾ, ਨੀਚ, ਹਰਾਮਜ਼ਾਦਾ, ਖੋਟਾ, ਦੋਗਲਾ

bat (ਬੈਟ) *n v* (1) ਚਮਗਿੱਦੜ, ਚਾਮ-ਚੜਿੱਕ, ਖੱਚਰ ਔਰਤ; (2) (ਕ੍ਰਿਕਟ ਦਾ) ਬੱਲਾ, ਬੈਟ; ਖੱਲੇ ਨਾਲ ਖੇਡਣਾ, ਬੱਲਾ ਮਾਰਨਾ, ਇਨਿੰਗ ਕਰਨਾ, ਵਾਰੀ ਲੈਣੀ

batch (ਬੈਚ) *n* ਜੱਥਾ, ਟੋਲੀ, ਸਮੂਹ, ਦਲ, ਰੋਟੀਆਂ ਦਾ ਪੂਰ; ਖ਼ਾਨ; (ਇਕੋ ਹੀ) ਜੱਥੇ ਵਿਚ; ਵਰਗ ਵਿਚ

bate (ਬੇਇਟ) *v n* ਸ਼ਕਤੀਹੀਨ ਹੋ ਜਾਣਾ, ਜ਼ੋਰ ਘਟ ਜਾਣਾ, ਘਟਾਉਣਾ; (1) ਚਮੜਾ ਸਾਫ਼ ਕਰਨ ਲਈ ਖਾਰ ਵਾਲਾ ਘੋਲ; (2) ਕਰੋਧ, ਗੁੱਸਾ

bath, Bath (ਬਾਥ) *n v* ਇਸ਼ਨਾਨ, ਨਹਾਉਣ, ਗੁਸਲ, ਇਸ਼ਨਾਨ ਕਰਨ ਦਾ ਪਾਣੀ; ਨਹਾਉਣ ਦਾ ਭਾਂਡਾ, ਟੱਬ; ਗੁਸਲਖ਼ਾਨਾ; ਇਸ਼ਨਾਨ ਘਰ, ਹਮਾਮ, ਇਸ਼ਨਾਨ ਕਰਨਾ, ਨਹਾਉਣਾ; ~**ing** ਨਹਾਉਣ-ਧੋਣ, ਇਸ਼ਨਾਨ; ~**room** ਗੁਸਲਖ਼ਾਨਾ, ਇਸ਼ਨਾਨ ਘਰ

bathe (ਬੇਇਦ) *v* ਇਸ਼ਨਾਨ ਕਰਨਾ ਜਾਂ ਕਰਾਉਣਾ, ਨਹਾਉਣਾ, ਨਹਾਲਣਾ; ਟੱਕੀ ਲਾਉਣੀ, ਪਾਣੀ ਨਾਲ ਧੋਣਾ, ਧੁੱਪ ਲਗਵਾਉਣਾ

batman ('ਬੈਟਮਅਨ) *n* ਫ਼ੌਜੀ ਅਫ਼ਸਰ ਦਾ ਅਰਦਲੀ

baton ('ਬੈਟ(ਅ)ਨ) *n v* ਪੁਲੀਸ ਦੇ ਸਿਪਾਹੀ ਦਾ ਡੰਡਾ, ਬੈਂਤ; (ਸੰਗੀਤ ਨਿਰਦੇਸ਼ਕ ਦੀ ਤਾਲ ਦੇਣ

batsman

ਲਈ) ਛੜੀ; ਡੰਡੇ ਨਾਲ ਮਾਰਨਾ

batsman ('ਬੈਟਸਮਅਨ) *n* ਬੱਲੇਬਾਜ਼, ਗੇਂਦ ਮਾਰਨ ਵਾਲਾ ਖਿਡਾਰੀ; ਸਮੁੰਦਰੀ ਜਹਾਜ਼ ਉੱਤੇ ਉੱਤਰਨ ਵਾਲੇ ਹਵਾਈ ਜਹਾਜ਼ ਨੂੰ ਬੱਲੇ ਨਾਲ ਸੰਕੇਤ ਕਰਨ ਵਾਲਾ

battalion (ਬੈਅ'ਟੈਲਯਅਨ) *n* (ਫ਼ੌਜੀ) ਦਸਤਾ, ਪਲਟਨ, ਸੈਨਕ ਦਲ, ਬਟੈਲੀਅਨ

batten ('ਬੈਟਨ) *v n* ਕਿਸੇ ਚੀਜ਼ ਨੂੰ ਲੱਕੜੀ ਦੀਆਂ ਫੱਟੀਆਂ ਨਾਲ ਪੱਕਾ ਕਰਨਾ, ਫ਼ਰਸ਼ ਬਣਾਉਣਾ, ਚੱਕਣ ਕੱਸਣਾ, ਪੁਸ਼ਟਾ; ਬਿਜਲੀ ਦੀਆਂ ਤਾਰਾਂ ਲਈ ਲਕੜੀ ਦੀ ਫੱਟੀ

batter ('ਬੈਟਅ*) *v n* ਫੈਂਟਣਾ; ਸੂਰਤ ਵਿਗਾੜ ਦੇਣਾ, ਤੋੜ ਦੇਣਾ; ਢਾਹ ਸੁੱਟਣਾ, ਮਾਰ ਮਾਰ ਕੇ ਡੇਗ ਦੇਣਾ, ਖੁੰਭ ਠੱਪਣੀ; ਅੱਖਰਾਂ ਦੀ ਪਲੇਟ, ਪੀਠੀ ਦਾਲ ਦੀ; ਢਾਲ, ਸਲਾਮੀ

battery ('ਬੈਟਅਰਿ) (ਸੈਨਾ) ਤੋਪਖ਼ਾਨਾ, ਮੋਰਚਾ; (ਕਾ) ਧੌਲ-ਧੱਪਾ, ਮਾਰ ਕੁੱਟ; (ਬਿਜਲੀ) ਬੈਟਰੀ

batting ('ਬੈਟਿਙ) *n* ਬੱਲਬਾਜ਼ੀ; ਰੂੰ ਦੀ ਤਹਿ

battle ('ਬੈਟਲ) *n v* ਲੜਾਈ, ਜੁੱਧ, ਸੰਗਰਾਮ; ਸੰਘਰਸ਼; ਜਿੱਤ; ਲੜਾਈ ਕਰਨਾ, ਜੁੱਧ ਵਿਚ ਸ਼ਾਮਲ ਹੋਣਾ, ਸੰਘਰਸ਼ ਕਰਨਾ, ਮੁਕਾਬਲਾ ਕਰਨਾ; **~field** ਲੜਾਈ ਦਾ ਮੈਦਾਨ ਜੁੱਧ-ਖੇਤਰ, ਰਣਭੂਮੀ

bawd (ਬੋਡ) *n* ਭੜੂਆ, ਵੇਸਵਾ, ਦੱਲੀ, ਫੱਢੇ-ਕੁੱਟਣੀ; ਗੰਦੀ ਗੱਲ, ਅਸ਼ਲੀਲ ਕਥਨ; **~iness** ਅਸ਼ਲੀਲਤਾ, ਅਸ਼ਲੀਲ ਕਥਨ

bawl (ਬੋਲ) *v* ਕੂਕਣਾ, ਚੀਕਣਾ; ਧਾਹਾਂ ਮਾਰਨੀਆਂ, ਵਿਰਲਾਪ ਕਰਨਾ; ਵਭੁ ਪੈਣਾ

bay (ਬੇਇ) *n* (1) ਖਾੜੀ, ਖਲੀਜ; (2) ਜੈ ਮਾਲਾ, ਵਿਜੈ ਮੁਕਟ, ਤੇਜ-ਪੱਤਰ; (3) (ਸੈਨਾ ਵਿਚ) ਖਾਈ (ਵਿਚ ਚੱਲਣ) ਦਾ ਰਸਤਾ; (4) ਰੇਲਵੇ-ਲਾਈਨ ਦੇ ਸ਼ੁਰੂ ਜਾਂ ਅੰਤ ਤੇ ਬਣਿਆ ਪਲੇਟਫਾਰਮ; (5) ਸ਼ਿਕਾਰੀ ਕੁੱਤਿਆਂ ਦੀ ਭੌਂਕ, ਭੌਂ-ਭੌਂ, ਭੌਂਕਣ, ਭੌਂਕਣਾ; **~salt** ਸਮੁੰਦਰੀ ਲੂਣ, ਖਾਰੀ ਲੂਣ; **be at~** ਘਿਰ ਜਾਣਾ, ਫਸ ਜਾਣਾ; **~leaf** ਤੇਜ-ਪੱਤਰ

bazooka (ਬਅ'ਜ਼ੂਕਅ) *n* ਟੈਂਕ-ਤੋੜ ਰਾਕਟ, ਬਜੂਕਾ

be (ਬੀ) *v (substantive, copulative & auxiliary)* ਹੋਣਾ, ਹਾਜ਼ਰ ਹੋਣਾ, ਜਿਉਂਦੇ ਹੋਣਾ, ਜਾਰੀ ਰਹਿਣਾ, ਆ ਪੈਣਾ, ਸੰਭਾਵਨਾ ਜਾਂ ਆਸ ਦਾ ਹੋਣਾ

beach (ਬੀਚ) *n v* ਸਮੁੰਦਰ ਜਾਂ ਦਰਿਆ ਦਾ ਕੰਢਾ, ਦਰਿਆ ਦੇ ਕਿਨਾਰੇ ਦੇ ਕੰਕਰ ਜਾਂ ਗੀਟੇ; ਕਿਨਾਰੇ ਉੱਤੇ ਲੰਗਰ ਸੁੱਟਣਾ

beacon ('ਬੀਕ(ਅ)ਨ) *n v* ਚਾਨਣ-ਮੁਨਾਰਾ, ਆਕਾਸ਼ਦੀਪ, ਪਥ-ਪਰਦਰਸ਼ਕ, ਸਿਗਨਲ-ਸਟੇਸ਼ਨ; ਪਤਾ ਦੇਣਾ, ਰੌਸ਼ਨੀ ਦਿਖਾਉਣਾ, ਰਸਤਾ ਦੱਸਣਾ, ਖ਼ਤਰਾ ਦੱਸਣ ਲਈ ਇਸ਼ਾਰਾ ਕਰਨਾ, ਅਗਵਾਈ ਕਰਨੀ; ਚਾਨਣ ਦੇ ਖੰਭੇ ਲਾਉਣੇ

bead (ਬੀਡ) *n v* ਮਣਕਾ, ਸਿਮਰਨੀ ਜਾਂ ਮਾਲਾ ਦਾ ਦਾਣਾ; ਬੂੰਦ, ਬੁਲਬੁਲਾ, ਮਣਕੇਦਾਰ ਉਸਾਰੀ; (ਬੰਦੂਕ ਦੀ) ਮੱਖੀ; ਪੂਜਾ, ਪ੍ਰਾਰਥਨਾ; ਗੁੰਦਣਾ, ਲੜੀ ਬਣਾਉਣਾ

beak (ਬੀਕ) *n* ਚੁੰਝ; ਨੁਕੀਲੀ ਨੱਕ; ਚੁੰਝੀ

beam (ਬੀਮ) *n v* (1) ਸ਼ਤੀਰ, ਬਾਲਾ; ਲੰਗਰ ਦਾ ਦਸਤਾ; ਲੱਠ, ਹਲ ਦੀ ਵੇਲ; ਤੱਕੜੀ ਦੀ ਡੰਡੀ; ਗੱਡੀ ਦਾ ਧੁਰਾ; (2) ਚਾਨਣ ਦੀ ਕਿਰਨ; ਚਿਹਰੇ ਦੀ ਰੌਣਕ, ਖ਼ੁਸ਼ੀ, ਦਮਕ; ਖਿੜਨਾ ਚਮਕਣਾ, ਜਗਮਗਾ ਉੱਠਣਾ; **~lessing** ਪ੍ਰਕਾਸ਼ਮਾਨ, ਦਮਕਦਾ; ਆਨੰਦ ਮਗਨ; **~less** ਪ੍ਰਕਾਸ਼ਰਹਿਤ

bean (ਬੀਨ) *n* ਰਵਾਂਹ, ਲੋਬੀਆ, ਸੇਮ, ਕਾਢੀ ਤੇ

ਹੋਰਨਾਂ ਪੌਦਿਆਂ ਦੇ ਬੀਜ

bear (ਬੇਅ*) *n* ਰਿੱਛ, ਭਾਲੂ; ਉਜੱਡ ਜਾਂ ਰੁੱਖਾ ਮਨੁੱਖ; (ਸੱਟਾ) ਮਾਂਦੜੀਆ; ਸਹਿਣਾ, ਸਹਾਰਨਾ, ਝੱਲਣਾ, ਭੋਗਣਾ; ਪੈਦਾ ਕਰਨਾ; ਚੁੱਕਣਾ, ਚੁੱਕ ਕੇ ਲੈ ਜਾਣਾ, ਭਾਰ ਉਠਾਉਣਾ; ਰੁਖ ਕਰਨਾ; ~**able** ਸਹਿਣਯੋਗ, ਸਹਾਰਨਯੋਗ

beard (ਬਿਅ*ਡ) *n v* ਦਾੜ੍ਹੀ, ਘੁੰਢ; ਸਖ਼ਤ ਵਾਲ; ਦਾੜ੍ਹੀ ਫੜਨਾ ਜਾਂ ਖਿੱਚਣਾ, ਨਿਰਾਦਰ ਕਰਨਾ; ਸਾਮ੍ਹਣਾ ਕਰਨਾ, ਵੰਗਾਰਨਾ

bearer ('ਬੇਅਰਅ*) *n* ਬਹਿਰਾ (ਹੋਟਲ ਦਾ); ਕੁਲੀ, ਵਾਹਕ, ਚੁੱਕਣ ਵਾਲਾ, ਕਹਾਰ, ਖਤ ਲੈ ਜਾਣ ਵਾਲਾ, ਸੇਵਕ, ਅੰਗ-ਰਖਿਅਕ; ਫਲਦਾਰ ਰੁੱਖ, ਫਲਣ ਵਾਲਾ ਪੌਦਾ

beast (ਬੀਸਟ) *n* ਪਸ਼ੂ, ਜਾਨਵਰ; ਘਿਰਨਾਯੋਗ ਮਨੁੱਖ, ਪਸ਼ੂ ਬਿਰਤੀ ਦਾ ਮਨੁੱਖ, ਜਾਂਗਲੀ, ਉਜੱਡ, ਹੈਵਾਨ; ~**ly** ਪਸ਼ੂਹਾਰ, ਪਸ਼ੂ ਵਰਗਾ; ਗੰਦਾ, ਘਿਰਨਾਯੋਗ; ਲੁਚਾ, ਵਹਿਸ਼ੀ

beat (ਬੀਟ) *v n* ਮਾਰਨਾ, ਕੁੱਟਣਾ, ਮਾਰ-ਕੁਟਾਈ ਕਰਨੀ, ਹਰਾਉਣਾ; ਜਿੱਚ ਕਰਨਾ, ਮਾਤ ਕਰਨਾ; ਪਰ ਮਾਰਨਾ, ਫੜਕਣਾ; (ਢੋਲ) ਥਪਥਪਾਉਣਾ, ਵਜਾਉਣਾ; (ਦਿਲ) ਧੜਕਣਾ; ਧਕੇਲਣਾ, ਹੱਕਣਾ; ਕੁੱਟਣਾ, ਫੁਦਕਣਾ, ਸ਼ਿਕਾਰੀ ਵਲ ਲਿਆਉਣ ਲਈ ਰੌਲਾ ਪਾਉਣਾ; ਚੋਟ, ਸੱਟ (ਢੋਲ ਜਾਂ ਨਗਾਰੇ ਉੱਤੇ); (ਬੈਂਡ ਮਾਸਟਰ ਦੇ) ਡੰਡੇ ਦੀ ਗਤੀ, ਇਸ਼ਾਰਾ; (ਘੜੀ ਆਦਿ) ਹਿਲਜੁਲ, ਦਿਲ ਦੀ ਧੜਕਣ, ਸਿਪਾਹੀ ਦੀ ਗਸ਼ਤ, ਜੇਤੂ, ਜੋਂਨ, ਫੇਰੀ; ਬਿਲਾਅ; **ing** ਟੰਡ, ਸਜ਼ਾ, ਫਿਟਕਾਰ, ਕੁੱਟ, ਪਿਟਾਈ; ~**about the bush** ਉਰਲੀਆਂ ਪਰਲੀਆਂ ਮਾਰਨੀਆਂ, ਖੱਬਲੀਆਂ ਮਾਰਨਾ; ~**back and blue** ਬਹੁਤਾ ਮਾਰਨਾ; ~**one's brains** ਮਗ਼ਜ਼ ਖਪਾਈ ਕਰਨੀ, ਸਿਰ ਖਪਾਉਣਾ; ~**the breast** ਛਾਤੀ ਪਿੱਟਣਾ, ਦੁੱਖਬਝੜੀ ਪਿੱਟਣਾ

beau (ਬਅਉ) *n* ਬਾਂਕਾ, ਛੈਲਾ, ਅਲਬੇਲਾ, ਛਬੀਲਾ, ਆਸ਼ਕ, ਦਿਲਦਾਰ, ਢੋਲਾ, ਪਰੇਮੀ; ~**ish** ਛੈਲ-ਛਬੀਲਾ, ਰੰਗ-ਰੰਗੀਲਾ; ~**monde** ਫੈਸ਼ਨੇਬਲ ਸੁਸਾਇਟੀ, ਫੈਸ਼ਨਦਾਰ ਦੁਨੀਆ, ਸੁਕੀਨ ਲੋਕ

beauteous ('ਬਯੂਟਿਅਸ) *a* (ਕਵਿਤਾ ਵਿਚ) ਰੂਪਵੰਤ, ਸੁੰਦਰ, ਸੋਹਣਾ, ਖ਼ੁਬਸੂਰਤ, ਰਸਮਈ, ਮਨੋਹਰ, ਹੁਸੀਨ

beautician ('ਬਯੂ'ਟਿਸ਼ਨ) *n* ਸ਼ਿੰਗਾਰਕਰਤਾ, ਸ਼ਿੰਗਾਰ ਕੇਂਦਰ ਨੂੰ ਚਲਾਉਣ ਵਾਲਾ

beautiful ('ਬਯੂਟਿਫ਼ੁਲ) *a* ਸੋਹਣਾ, ਸੁੰਦਰ, ਖ਼ੁਬਸੂਰਤ, ਮਨਮੋਹਣਾ, ਰੂਪਵੰਤ, ਰੂਪਵਾਨ

beauty ('ਬਯੂਟਿ) *n* ਰੂਪ, ਸੁੰਦਰਤਾ-ਖ਼ੁਬਸੂਰਤੀ, ਮਨੋਹਰਤਾ, ਰਮਣੀਕਤਾ, ਜੋਬਨ, ਹੁਸਨ; ਛਬ, ਜਮਾਲ, ਸ਼ੋਭਾ; ਪਰੀ, ਸੁੰਦਰੀ, ਸੁੰਦਰ ਗੁਣ, ਚੰਗੀ ਝਾਕੀ; ~**parlour** ਸ਼ਿੰਗਾਰ ਕਲਾ ਕੇਂਦਰ, ਫੈਸ਼ਨੇਬਲ ਵਾਲ ਬਣਾਉਣ ਦੀ ਦੁਕਾਨ, (ਇਸਤਰੀਆਂ ਦੇ) ਚਿਹਰੇ ਸੁੰਦਰ ਬਣਾਉਣ ਦੀਆਂ ਵਿਧੀਆਂ ਦੀ ਥਾਂ; ~**spot** ਦਰਸ਼ਨੀ ਥਾਂ; ਤਿਲ, ਸਰੀਰ ਦੇ ਉੱਪਰ ਸੁੰਦਰਤਾ ਦਾ ਨਿਸ਼ਾਨ

becall (ਬਿਕੋਲ) *v* ਗਾਲ੍ਹ ਕੱਢਣੀ, ਕੌੜੇ ਸ਼ਬਦ ਕਹਿਣੇ

because (ਬਿ'ਕੋਜ਼) *adv conj* ਕਿਉਂਕਿ, ਕਿਉਂਜੋ, ਇਸ ਲਈ ਕਿ, ਇਸ ਕਰਕੇ

beck (ਬੈਕ) *v n* ਸੰਕੇਤ ਕਰਨਾ, ਇਸ਼ਾਰਾ ਕਰਨਾ, ਮੂਕ ਭਾਸ਼ਾ ਵਿਚ ਆਖਣਾ; ਸਿਰ ਹਿਲਾਉਣਾ; (1) ਇਸ਼ਾਰਾ, ਗੁੱਝਾ ਇਸ਼ਾਰਾ, ਸੰਕੇਤ; ਆਦੇਸ਼, ਹੁਕਮ; (2) ਚਸ਼ਮਾ, ਪਹਾੜੀ ਨਦੀ ਜਾਂ ਨਾਲਾ; **to have at one's**~ ਇਸ਼ਾਰਿਆਂ ਤੇ ਨਚਾਉਣਾ, ਉਂਗਲੀਆਂ ਤੇ ਨਚਾਉਣਾ

becket (ਬੈਕਿਟ) *n* ਹੁੱਕ, ਖੁੰਟੀ

beckon ('ਬੈੱਕ(ਅ)ਨ) *v* ਇਸ਼ਾਰੇ ਨਾਲ ਬੁਲਾਉਣਾ, ਇਸ਼ਾਰੇ ਰਾਹੀਂ ਧਿਆਨ ਖਿਚਣਾ; ਕਿਸੇ ਨੂੰ ਇਸ਼ਾਰਾ ਕਰਨਾ

become (ਬਿ'ਕਅੱਮ) *v* ਹੋਣਾ, ਬਣ ਜਾਣਾ; ਯੋਗ ਕਰਨਾ, ਠੀਕ ਹੋਣਾ; ਜਚਣਾ, ਫਬਣਾ

becoming (ਬਿ'ਕਅੱਮਿਙ) *a* ਸੁਹਾਵਣਾ, ਫਬਵਾਂ; ਅਨੁਰੂਪ, ਉਪਯੁਕਤ, ਢੁੱਕਵਾਂ, ਉਚਿਤ; **~ly** ਯੋਗ ਤਰੀਕੇ ਨਾਲ, ਉਚਿਤ ਢੰਗ ਅਨੁਸਾਰ, ਢੁਕਵੇਂ ਤੌਰ ਤੇ, ਚੰਗੀ ਤਰ੍ਹਾਂ ਨਾਲ; **~ness** ਢੁਕਵਾਂਪਣ, ਉਚਿਤਤਾ, ਅਨੁਰੂਪਤਾ

bed (ਬੈੱਡ) *n* ਬਿਸਤਰਾ; ਵਿਛਾਈ; ਗੱਦਾ; ਸੇਜ, ਪਲੰਘ, ਚਾਰਪਾਈ, ਮੰਜਾ; ਨੀਂਹ, ਤਲਾ, ਬੁਨਿਆਦ, ਤਹਿ; ਕਿਆਰੀ; ਥੱਲ, ਤਲ; ਬਿਲੀਅਰਡ ਖੇਡ ਦੀ ਮੇਜ਼; ਤੋਪ ਗੱਡੀ ਦਾ ਵਿਚਕਾਰਲਾ ਹਿੱਸਾ; ਬਿਸਤਰੇ ਉੱਤੇ ਸੌਣਾ ਜਾਂ ਸੁਲਾਉਣਾ; ਪੌਦਾ ਲਗਾਉਣਾ, ਜਮਾਉਣਾ, ਤਹਿ ਜਮਾਉਣੀ, ਤਹਿ ਦੇਣੀ, ਤਹਿ ਜੰਮਣਾ, ਫਕਣਾ, ਜੜਨਾ; **~bug** ਖਟਮਲ; **~of roses** ਫੁੱਲਾਂ ਦੀ ਸੇਜ, ਆਨੰਦਮਈ ਅਵਸਥਾ (ਜੀਵਨ ਦੀ); **~ridden** ਰੋਗੀ, ਬੀਮਾਰ, ਮੰਜੇ ਪਿਆ; **~rock** ਦਰਿਆ ਦੀ ਤਹਿ ਵਿਚਲੀ ਚਟਾਨ; ਮੂਲ ਸਿਧਾਂਤ, ਬੁਨਿਆਦੀ ਅਸੂਲ; **~sore** ਮੰਜੇ ਤੇ ਬਹੁਤਾ ਪਏ ਰਹਿਣ ਕਰਕੇ ਹੋ ਜਾਣ ਵਾਲਾ ਜ਼ਖ਼ਮ ਜਾਂ ਆਮੁ; **~stead** ਪਲੰਘ, ਚਾਰਪਾਈ

bedaub (ਬਿ'ਡੋਬ) *v* ਰੰਗਣਾ, ਰੰਗ ਥਪਣਾ, ਰੰਗ ਚੜ੍ਹਾਉਣਾ; ਸ਼ੋਖ ਜਾਂ ਭੜਕੀਲੇ ਰੰਗਾਂ ਵਾਲੇ ਕੱਪੜੇ ਪਾਉਣਾ

bedding (ਬੈੱਡਿਙ) *n* ਬਿਸਤਰਾ, ਗੱਦਾ; ਪਰਾਲੀ

bedlam ('ਬੈੱਡਲਅਮ) *n* ਰੌਲਾ-ਰੱਪਾ, ਖਪ, (ਪ੍ਰ) ਪਾਗਲਖ਼ਾਨਾ; **~ism** ਹੁੱਲੜਬਾਜ਼ੀ; **~ite** ਝੱਲਾ, ਦਿਵਾਨਾ, ਝੌਲਾ; ਸਨਕੀ

bee (ਬੀ) *n* ਸ਼ਹਿਦ ਦੀ ਮੱਖੀ, ਮਧੂ ਮੱਖੀ; ਉਦਸੀ ਪੁਰਖ; ਮਜਲਸ, ਮਹਿਫ਼ਲ; **~hive** ਮਖੀਰ, ਮਖਿਆਲ ਖੱਗਾ, ਛੱਤਾ; **~s wax** ਮੋਮ; **~keeping** ਮਧੂ-ਮੱਖੀ ਪਾਲਣ

beef (ਬੀਫ਼) *n* (ਖਾਣ ਲਈ) ਗਾਂ, ਮੱਝ ਜਾਂ ਬੈਲ ਦਾ ਮਾਸ; (ਮਨੁੱਖਾਂ ਦੀ) ਸਰੀਰਕ ਸ਼ਕਤੀ, ਮੋਟੀ ਤਾਜ਼ੀ ਗਾਂ, ਬਲਦ; **~up** ਮਜ਼ਬੂਤ ਕਰਨਾ; **~y** ਰਿਸ਼ਟ-ਪੁਸ਼ਟ, ਪੀਡਾ, ਠੋਸ, ਮੋਟਾ ਤਾਜ਼ਾ, ਪੱਕਾ ਕਾਠੀ ਵਾਲਾ

beep (ਬੀਪ) *n* ਟੀਂ ਟੀਂ ਦੀ ਅਵਾਜ਼

beer (ਬਿਅ*) *n* ਜੌਂ ਦੀ ਸ਼ਰਾਬ, ਬੀਅਰ

beet (ਬੀਟ) *n* ਚੁਕੰਦਰ

beetle (ਬੀਟਲ) *n adv* ਹਥੌੜਾ; ਮੂੰਗਲੀ, ਮੋਹਲਾ, ਭੂੰਡ, ਬੀਂਡਾ; ਮੱਥੇ ਤੇ ਵੱਟ ਪਾਈ, ਉਲਰਿਆ; ਬਾਹਰ ਨੂੰ ਨਿਕਲੀਆਂ ਭਵਾਂ, ਅਗਾਂਹ ਨੂੰ ਵਧੀ ਹੋਈ (ਚਟਾਨ); ਸਿਰ ਤੇ ਉਲਰਨਾ

befall (ਬਿ'ਫੋਲ) *v* ਵਾਪਰਨਾ, ਬੀਤਣਾ, ਆਪਣਾ ਹੋ ਜਾਣਾ

befit (ਬਿ'ਫ਼ਿਟ) *v* ਫਬਣਾ, ਢੁਕਣਾ, ਠੀਕ ਜੱਚਣਾ; **~ting** (ਬਿ'ਫ਼ਿਟਿਙ) ਢੁਕਵਾਂ, ਠੀਕ, ਉਚਿਤ, ਯੋਗ ਉਪਯੁਕਤ

befool (ਬਿ'ਫ਼ੁਲ) *v* ਬੁੱਧੂ ਬਣਾਉਣਾ, ਮੌਜੂ ਉਡਾਉਣਾ, ਮੂਰਖ ਬਣਾਉਣਾ; ਠੱਗਣਾ, ਧੋਖਾ ਦੇਣਾ

before (ਬਿ'ਫੋ*) *adv prep conj* ਪਹਿਲਾਂ, ਅੱਗੋਂ ਪਹਿਲਾਂ ਤੋਂ, ਸਾਮੁਣੇ, ਮੂਹਰੇ, ਅੱਗੇ, ਇਸ ਤੋਂ ਪਹਿਲਾਂ ਕਿ, ਜਦ ਤਕ

befriend (ਬਿ'ਫ਼ਰੈਂਡ) *v* ਮਿੱਤਰ ਬਣਾ ਲੈਣਾ, ਦੋਸਤੀ ਕਾਇਮ ਕਰਨੀ, ਮਿੱਤਰਾਂ ਵਾਲਾ ਵਿਹਾਰ ਕਰਨਾ, ਸਹਾਇਤਾ ਕਰਨੀ, ਸਾਥ ਦੇਣਾ

beg (ਬੈਗ) *v* ਭਿੱਖ ਮੰਗਣੀ, ਤਰਲਾ ਕਰਨਾ, ਮਿੰਨਤ

ਕਰਨੀ, ਖ਼ੈਰ ਮੰਗਣਾ, ਬੇਨਤੀ ਕਰਨੀ; ਮੰਗ ਪਿੰਨ ਕੇ ਗੁਜ਼ਾਰਾ ਕਰਨਾ; ਕੁੱਤੇ ਦਾ ਅਗਲਾ ਪੈਰ ਚੁੱਕਣਾ

beget (ਬਿਗੈੱਟ) *v* ਜੰਮਣਾ, ਜਣਨਾ, ਪੈਦਾ ਕਰਨਾ, ਜਨਮ ਦੇਣਾ; ਕਾਰਣ ਹੋਣਾ

beggar (ਬੈਗਅ*) *n v* ਭਿਖਾਰੀ, ਮੰਗਤਾ; ਭਿਖ-ਮੰਗਾ, ਕੰਗਾਲ ਕਰ ਦੇਣਾ, ਮੰਗਤਾ ਬਣਾ ਦੇਣਾ, ਖ਼ਾਕ-ਝਾਹ ਕਰ ਦੇਣਾ; ਮਾਤ ਕਰਨਾ; ~s must not be choosers ਮੰਗਤਿਆਂ ਦੀ ਚੋਣ ਦੀ ਕੋਈ ਮਹੱਤਾ ਨਹੀਂ, ਪੁੰਨ ਦੀ ਗਾਂ ਦੇ ਦੰਦ ਨਹੀਂ ਵੇਖੀਦੇ; ~y ਕੰਗਾਲੀ, ਗ਼ਰੀਬੀ, ਅਤੀ ਨਿਰਧਨਤਾ; ਝਲਾਹਟ; ਫ਼ਕੀਰੀ

begin (ਬਿਗਿਨ) *v* ਸ਼ੁਰੂ ਕਰਨਾ, ਆਰੰਭ ਕਰਨਾ, ਪਹਿਲ ਕਰਨੀ, ਪਹਿਲਾ ਕਦਮ ਚੁੱਕਣਾ, ਛੋਹਣਾ; ~ner ਆਰੰਭਕ, ਮੋਢੀ, ਸ਼ੁਰੂ ਕਰਨ ਵਾਲਾ, ਛੋਹਣ ਵਾਲਾ, ਨਵ-ਸਿਖਾਂਦਰੂ, ਸਿਖੰਦਰ, ਸਿਖਾਂਦਰੂ, ਨੌਜਵਾਨ; ~ning ਆਰੰਭ, ਸ਼ੁਰੂ, ਮੁੱਢ, ਕਿਸੇ ਵਸਤੂ ਦੇ ਸ਼ੁਰੂ ਦਾ ਹਿੱਸਾ, ਮੂਲ ਕੇਂਦਰ

begone (ਬਿਗੌਨ) *v imperat* (ਪ੍ਰ) ਦੂਰ ਹੋ, ਦਫ਼ਾ ਹੋ, ਪਰੇ ਹਟ

begrudge (ਬਿ'ਗਰਅੱਜ) *v* ਈਰਖਾ ਕਰਨੀ, ਕਿਸੇ ਨਾਲ ਵੈਰ ਰੱਖਣਾ, ਦਿਲ ਵਿਚ ਕਿਸੇ ਵਿਰੁੱਧ ਰੜਕ ਰੱਖਣੀ

beguile (ਬਿ'ਗਾਇਲ) *v* ਕਪਟ ਕਰਨਾ, ਧੋਖਾ ਦੇਣਾ; ਠੱਗਣਾ; ਦਿਲ ਲੁਭਾਉਣਾ

behalf (ਬਿਹਾਫ਼) *n* ਹਿਤ, ਪੱਖ, ਸਮਰਥਨ, ਤਰਫ਼; on or in ~ of ਨਿਮਿਤ, ਦੇ ਵੱਲੋਂ; ਵਾਸਤੇ, ਲਈ, ਖ਼ਾਤਰ

behave (ਬਿ'ਹੇਇਵ) *v* ਸਲੂਕ ਕਰਨਾ, ਪੇਸ਼ ਆਉਣਾ; ਸਲੀਕਾ ਕਰਨਾ, ਕਿਸੇ ਆਦਮੀ ਜਾਂ ਮਸ਼ੀਨ ਦਾ ਠੀਕ ਕੰਮ ਕਰਨਾ

behaviour (ਬਿ'ਹੇਵਿਅਅ*) *n* ਵਤੀਰਾ, ਰਵੱਈਆ; ਵਰਤਾਉ, ਸਲੂਕ; ਢੰਗ, ਚਾਲ-ਚਲਣ, ਚਾਲ-ਢਾਲ, ਲੱਛਣ, ਚਰਿੱਤਰ, ਸ਼ਿਸ਼ਟਾਚਾਰ, ਮਸ਼ੀਨ ਜਾਂ ਕਿਸੇ ਪਦਾਰਥ ਦੇ ਕੰਮ ਕਰਨ ਦਾ ਢੰਗ

behead (ਬਿ'ਹੈੱਡ) *v* ਸਿਰ ਲਾਹੁਣਾ, ਸਿਰ ਕਲਮ ਕਰਨਾ

behest (ਬਿਹੈਸੱਟ) *n* ਹੁਕਮ, ਆਗਿਆ, ਆਦੇਸ਼, ਫ਼ਰਮਾਨ

behind (ਬਿ'ਹਾਇੰਡ) *prep adv n* ਪਿੱਛੇ, ਪਛੜਿਆ ਹੋਇਆ, ਬਾਅਦ ਵਿਚ, ਪਿੱਛੋਂ, ਥੱਲੇ, ਉਹਲੇ ਵਿਚ, ਲੁਕਿਆ ਹੋਇਆ; ਪਿਛਲਾ ਹਿੱਸਾ, ਚਿਤੜ

behold (ਬਿ'ਹਅਉਲਡ) *v* ਦੇਖਣਾ, ਤੱਕਣਾ, ਧਿਆਨ ਕਰਨਾ

being (ਬੀਇੰਙ) *n* ਹੋਂਦ, ਹਸਤੀ, ਵਿਅਕਤੀ, ਵਜੂਦ the Supreme B~ ਈਸ਼ਵਰ, ਪਰਮ ਸੱਤਾ

belated (ਬਿ'ਲੇਇਟਿਡ) *a* ਪਛੜਿਆ, ਚਿਰਕਾ ਪੁੱਜਾ, ਵਿਲੰਬਤ, ਜਿਸ ਨੂੰ ਰਸਤੇ ਵਿਚ ਰਾਤ ਪੈ ਜਾਏ, ਬਹੁਤ ਦੇਰ ਕਰ ਆਇਆ

belch (ਬੈਲੱਚ) *v n* ਡਕਾਰ ਮਾਰਨਾ, ਡਕਾਰਨਾ; ਤੜਾ-ਤੜ ਕੱਢਣਾ, ਨਸ਼ੇ ਵਿਚ ਬੁੜ-ਬੁੜਾਉਣਾ; ਗੰਦੀਆਂ ਗਾਲ੍ਹਾਂ ਕੱਢਣੀਆਂ; ਡਕਾਰ; ਗਾਰਜ, ਗਰਜ-ਬਰ

beldam(e) (ਬੈਲਡਾਅਮ) *n* ਬੁਢੰਡੀ, ਬੁੱਢੀ ਤੀਵੀਂ; ਡੈਣ, ਲੜਾਕੀ ਤੀਵੀਂ, ਭੂਤਨੀ, ਕਰੂਪ ਬੁੱਢੀ ਇਸਤਰੀ

beleaguer (ਬਿ'ਲੀਗਅ*) *v* ਘੇਰ ਲੈਣਾ, ਘੇਰਾ ਪਾਉਣਾ, ਘੇਰਨਾ

belial (ਬੀਲਯਅਲ) *n* ਦੈਂਤ, ਪਰੇਤ, ਸ਼ੈਤਾਨ,

ਰਾਕਸ਼ਸ, ਦੁਰਾਚਾਰੀ ਵਿਅਕਤੀ, ਦੁਸ਼ਟ, ਪਾਪੀ

belie (ਬੀਲਾਇ) *v* ਝੂਠ ਬੋਲਣਾ, ਝੂਠਾ ਕਰਨਾ, ਝੁਠਲਾਉਣਾ, ਨਿੰਦਾ ਕਰਨਾ, ਕਲੰਕ ਆਰੋਪਣ ਕਰਨਾ, ਵਡਾ ਨਾ ਕਰਨਾ

belief (ਬੀ'ਲੀਫ਼) *n* ਵਿਸ਼ਵਾਸ, ਨਿਸ਼ਚੇ, ਸ਼ਰਧਾ, ਭਰੋਸਾ, ਇਮਾਨ, ਵਿਚਾਰ, ਧਰਮ, ਮੱਤ, ਰਾਏ ਖ਼ਿਆਲ

believable (ਬਿ'ਲੀਵਅਬਲ) *a* ਵਿਸ਼ਵਾਸ ਕਰਨਯੋਗ, ਮੰਨਣਯੋਗ, ਭਰੋਸੇਯੋਗ

believe (ਬਿ'ਲੀਵ) *v* ਵਿਸ਼ਵਾਸ ਕਰਨਾ, ਭਰੋਸਾ ਕਰਨਾ, ਮੰਨਣਾ; ਰਾਏ ਰੱਖਣੀ, ਖ਼ਿਆਲ ਕਰਨਾ, ਸਮਝਣਾ

believer (ਬਿ'ਲੀਵਅ*) *n* ਮੰਨਣ ਵਾਲਾ; ਸ਼ਰਧਾਲੂ, ਉਪਾਸਕ, ਆਸਤਕ, ਵਿਸ਼ਵਾਸੀ, ਆਪਣੇ ਧਰਮ ਵਿਚ ਵਿਸ਼ਵਾਸ ਰੱਖਣ ਵਾਲਾ

believing (ਬਿ'ਲੀਵਿੰਡ) *a* ਵਿਸ਼ਵਾਸੀ

bell (ਬੈਲ) *n v* ਘੰਟ, ਘੰਟੀ, ਟੱਲੀ, ਘੁੰਗਰੂ, ਟੱਲ, ਅਜ਼ਿਆਲ, ਘੰਟੇ ਵਰਗੀ ਵਸਤੂ; ਬੈਰਾ; ਘੰਟੀ ਬੰਨ੍ਹਣੀ, ਘੰਟੀ ਲਾਉਣੀ; **~boy** ਹੋਟਲ ਵਿਚ ਨੋਕਰ

belladonna (ਬੈੱਲਅ'ਡੋਨਅ) *n* ਧਤੂਰਾ, ਬੈਲਡੋਨਾ, ਭਲਾਵਾ; ਮੌਸ਼ਮ (ਭਲਾਵਿਆਂ ਦੀ)

belle (ਬੈਲ) *n* ਸੁੰਦਰੀ, ਇਸਤਰੀ, ਰੂਪਵਤੀ, ਹੁਸੀਨ, ਗੋਰੀ; ਕਿਸੇ ਥਾਂ ਦੀ ਸਭ ਤੋਂ ਸੁਹਣੀ ਇਸਤਰੀ

bellicose (ਬੈੱਲਿਕਅਉਸ) *a* ਲੜਾਕਾ, ਲੜਣ ਨੂੰ ਤਿਆਰ, ਫ਼ਸਾਦੀ, ਦੰਗਈ

bellicosity (ਬੈੱਲਿਕੋਸਅਟਿ) *n* ਜੁੱਧ-ਪਰੇਮ, ਦੰਗੇਬਾਜ਼ੀ, ਲੜਾਕਾਪਣ

belligerent (ਬਿ'ਲਿਜ਼ਅਰੰਟ) *n a* ਲੜਾਕਾ, ਜੋਧਾ, ਬੀਰ, ਜੁੱਧਕਾਰ, ਦੁਸ਼ਮਨ, ਵੈਰੀ

bellow (ਬੈੱਲਅਉ) *v n* ਰੰਭਣਾ, ਅੰਙਿੰਗਣਾ, ਗੱਜਣਾ, ਭਬਕ ਮਾਰਨਾ; ਕਰੋਧ ਵਿਚ ਜ਼ੋਰ ਨਾਲ ਬੋਲਣਾ; ਚਿੱਲਾਉਣਾ, ਕੜਕਣਾ; (ਦੁੱਖ ਨਾਲ) ਚੀਖ਼ਣਾ; ਤੋਪ ਦੀ ਅਵਾਜ਼, ਗਰਜ

bellows (ਬੈੱਲਅਉਜ਼) *n pl* ਧੌਂਕਣੀ, ਫੂਕਣੀ, ਕੈਮਰੇ ਦਾ ਫੈਲਣ ਵਾਲਾ ਹਿੱਸਾ, ਵਾਜੇ ਦਾ ਪੱਖਾ, ਫੇਫੜੇ

belly (ਬੈਲਿ) *n v* ਪੇਟ, ਢਿੱਡ, ਕੁੱਖ, ਗੋਗੜ, ਉਦਰ; ਸਾਮੂਨੇ ਦਾ, ਆਂਤਰਿਕ ਜਾਂ ਖੋਖਲੇ ਦਾ ਤਲ; ਫੁੱਲਣਾ, ਹਵਾ ਭਰ ਜਾਣਾ, ਆਫਰਨਾ

belong (ਬਿ'ਲੈਙ) *v* ਸਬੰਧ ਹੋਣਾ, ਸਬੰਧਤ ਹੋਣਾ, ਕਿਸੇ ਦਾ ਹੋਣਾ, ਕਿਸੇ ਦਾ ਕਬਜ਼ਾ ਹੋਣਾ; ਵਾਸੀ ਹੋਣਾ

below (ਬਿ'ਲਅਉ) *adv prep* ਹੇਠਾਂ, ਥੱਲੇ; ਮਕਾਨ ਦੀ ਹੇਠਲੀ ਛੱਤ; ਪਾਤਾਲ ਵਿਚ, ਨੀਚਤਾ ਵਲ; **~one's breath** ਬਹੁਤ ਹੋਲੀ ਜੇਹੇ, ਧੀਮੀ ਅਵਾਜ਼ ਵਿਚ

belt (ਬੈੱਲਟ) *n v* ਪੇਟੀ, ਕਮਰਬੰਦ, ਤੜਾਗੀ; ਖੇਤਰ, ਇਲਾਕਾ, ਮੰਡਲ, ਹਲਕਾ, ਤਸਮਾ, ਮਸ਼ੀਨ ਚਲਾਉਣ ਦਾ ਪੱਟਾ; ਪੇਟੀ ਬੰਨ੍ਹਣੀ; ਬੰਨ੍ਹਣਾ; ਰੰਗ ਨਾਲ ਗੋਲ ਘੇਰਾ ਬਣਾਉਣਾ; ਪੇਟੀ ਨਾਲ ਮਾਰਨਾ

bemean (ਬਿ'ਮੀਨ) *v* ਨਿਰਾਦਰੀ ਕਰਨੀ, ਬੇਇੱਜ਼ਤੀ ਕਰਨੀ, ਪੱਤ ਲਾਹੁਣੀ

bemoan (ਬਿ'ਮਅਉਨ) *v* ਰੋਣਾ, ਪਿਟਣਾ, ਕੁਰਲਾਉਣਾ, ਵਿਰਲਾਪ ਕਰਨਾ, ਮਾਤਮ ਕਰਨਾ, ਅਫ਼ਸੋਸ ਜ਼ਾਹਰ ਕਰਨਾ

bemock (ਬਿ'ਮੋਕ) *v* ਮਖੌਲ ਕਰਨਾ, ਹਾਸਾ ਉਡਾਉਣਾ, ਖਿੱਲੀ ਉਡਾਉਣਾ, ਪਰਿਹਾਸ ਕਰਨਾ

bench (ਬੈਂਚ) *n* ਬੈਂਚ, ਕਾਠ ਦੀ ਲੰਬੀ ਕੁਰਸੀ, ਚੌਂਕੀ, ਤਖ਼ਤਪੋਸ਼; ਬਤਰੁ; ਮੰਚ; ਕਚਹਿਰੀ ਦੇ ਹਾਕਮ, ਜੱਜ, ਪੀਠ, ਅਦਾਲਤ; ਕੁੱਤਿਆਂ ਨੂੰ ਰੱਖਣ ਦਾ ਘਰ

bend (ਬੈਂਡ) v ਮੋੜਨਾ, ਫੇਰਨਾ, ਵਿੰਗਾ ਕਰਨਾ, ਝੁਕਾਉਣਾ; (ਆਦਰ ਵਜੋਂ), ਝੁਕਣਾ, ਨਿਵਣਾ, ਨਿਵਾਉਣਾ; ਲਿਫਣਾ, ਲਿਫਾਉਣਾ, ਪੱਕੀ ਕਰ ਲੈਣੀ, ਵੱਸ ਵਿਚ ਲਿਆਉਣਾ; ਗੰਢ ਮਾਰਨੀ; ਵਲ-ਵਿੰਗ; ਗੰਢ; ਕਿਸੇ ਚੀਜ਼ ਦਾ ਮੁੱਕਿਆ ਹੋਇਆ ਹਿੱਸਾ; ਟੁਕੜਾ; ਸਮਾਨਾਂਤਰ ਮੁੱਖ ਰੇਖਾਵਾਂ; ~ing ਝੁਕਾਉ

beneath (ਬਿ'ਨੀਥ) adv prep ਥੱਲੇ, ਥੱਲੇ ਵੱਲ

benediction (ਬੈਨਿ'ਡਿਕਸ਼ਨ) n ਆਸ਼ੀਰਵਾਦ, ਅਸੀਸ, ਵਰ; ਸ਼ੁਭ-ਅਸੀਸ, ਸ਼ੁਭ ਕਾਮਨਾ, ਈਸ਼ਵਰੀ ਕਿਰਪਾ, ਕਲਿਆਣ

benedictive (ਬੈਨਿ'ਡਿਕਟਿਵ੍) a ਆਸ਼ੀਰਵਾਦੀ, ਮੰਗਲਵਾਦੀ

benedictory (ਬੈਨਿ'ਡਿਕਟਅਰਿ) a ਕਲਿਆਣਕਾਰੀ; ਅਸੀਸ ਸਬੰਧੀ, ਸ਼ੁਭ-ਇੱਛਾ ਸਬੰਧੀ

benefaction (ਬੈਨਿ'ਫੈਕਸ਼ਨ) n ਪੁੰਨ, ਦਾਨ, ਉਪਕਾਰ, ਧਰਮ-ਅਰਥ ਖ਼ਰਾਇਤ, ਭਲਾਈ, ਕਲਿਆਣ, ਸਹਾਇਤਾ

benefactor (ਬੈਨਿ'ਫੈਕਟਅ*) n ਦਾਤਾ, ਦਾਨੀ; ਉਪਕਾਰੀ, ਭਲਾ ਕਰਨ ਵਾਲਾ, ਸਰਪਰਸਤ

beneficial (ਬੈਨਿ'ਫ਼ਿਸ਼ਲ) a ਗੁਣਕਾਰੀ, ਲਾਹੇਵੰਦ, ਫ਼ਾਇਦੇਮੰਦ, ਕਲਿਆਣਕਾਰੀ, ਸਹਾਇਕ, ਹਿਤਕਾਰੀ; (ਕਾ) ਜਾਇਦਾਦ ਦੇ ਲਾਭ ਨਾਲ ਸਬੰਧਤ

beneficiary (ਬੈਨਿ'ਫ਼ਿਸ਼ਅਰਿ) n a ਲਾਭ ਪ੍ਰਾਪਤ ਕਰਨ ਵਾਲਾ, ਦਾਨ ਦਾ ਪਾਤਰ; (ਕਾ) ਜਾਗੀਰਦਾਰ, ਲਾਭ ਦਾ ਹੱਕ ਲੈਣ ਵਾਲਾ

benefit (ਬੈਨਿਫ਼ਿਟ) n v ਲਾਭ, ਫ਼ਾਇਦਾ, ਨਫ਼ਾ; ਹਿਤ, ਭਲਾਈ, ਭੱਤਾ, ਵਜ਼ੀਫ਼ਾ, ਗੁਜ਼ਾਰਾ; ਭਲਾ ਕਰਨਾ, ਉਪਕਾਰ, ਫ਼ਾਇਦਾ ਪੁਚਾਉਣਾ, ਫ਼ਾਇਦਾ ਉਠਾਉਣਾ, ਲਾਭ ਲੈਣਾ

benevolence (ਬਿ'ਨੈਵ੍ਅਲਅੰਸ) n ਦਇਆਲਤਾ, ਕਿਰਪਾ, ਮਿਹਰ, ਕਿਰਪਾਲਤਾ, ਉਦਾਰਤਾ, ਪਰਉਪਕਾਰਤਾ, ਦਿਆਲੂ ਸੁਭਾਅ

benevolent (ਬਿ'ਨੈਵ੍ਅਲਅੰਟ) a ਦਇਆਵਾਨ, ਦਿਆਲੂ, ਕਿਰਪਾਲੂ, ਉਪਕਾਰੀ, ਉਦਾਰ-ਚਿੱਤ, ਹਿਤੈਸ਼ੀ, ਸ਼ੁਭ-ਚਿੰਤਕ

benight (ਬਿ'ਨਾਇਟ) v ਹਨੇਰਾ ਕਰਨਾ, ਅੰਧਕਾਰ ਫੈਲਾਉਣਾ, ਨਿਤਾਸ਼ ਕਰਨਾ

benign (ਬਿ'ਨਾਇਨ) a ਕਿਰਪਾਲੂ, ਦਿਆਲੂ, ਨੇਕ-ਦਿਲ; ਸੁਲੱਖਣਾ, ਗੁਣਕਾਰੀ; (ਬੀਮਾਰੀ) ਘੱਟ ਦੁੱਖਦਾਈ

benumb (ਬਿ'ਨੱਮ) v ਸੁੰਨ ਕਰਨਾ, ਨਕਾਰਾ ਕਰਨਾ, ਸ਼ਕਤੀਹੀਣ ਕਰਨਾ, ਅਕੜਾਉਣਾ

bequeath (ਬਿ'ਕਵੀਦ) v ਵਸੀਅਤ ਕਰ ਜਾਣਾ, ਸੰਕਲਪਣਾ; ਹਵਾਲੇ ਕਰਨਾ

bequest (ਬਿ'ਕਵੈਸ਼ੱਟ) n ਵਸੀਅਤਨਾਮਾ; ਵਸੀਅਤ, ਵਸੀਅਤ ਰਾਹੀਂ ਮਿਲਿਆ ਮਾਲ; ਵਿਰਸਾ;

berate (ਬਿ'ਰੇਇਟ) v ਝਿੜਕਣਾ, ਝਾੜਨਾ, ਧਮਕਾਣਾ, ਗੁੱਸੇ ਹੋਣਾ, ਬੁਰਾ ਭਲਾ ਕਹਿਣਾ, ਫ਼ਜੀਹਤ ਕਰਨਾ

berceuse (ਬੇਅ'ਸਅ:ਜ਼) (F) n ਲੋਰੀ

bereav (ਬਿ'ਰੀਵ੍) v ਮਰ ਜਾਣਾ (ਕਿਸੇ ਸਬੰਧੀ ਪਿਆਰੇ ਦਾ) ਘੋਰ ਲੈਣਾ, ਵਿਯੁਕਤਾ ਕਰਨਾ, ਵਾਂਝਿਆਂ ਕਰਨਾ; ~ment ਸੋਗ, ਮਾਤਮ (ਮੋਤ ਉਤੇ)

bereft (ਬਿ'ਰੈਫ਼ੱਟ) a ਵਾਂਝਾ, ਵੰਚਤ, (ਇਕੱਲਾ) ਛੱਡਿਆ, ਨਿਆਸਰਾ, ਸੋਕ-ਅਵੱਸਥਾ ਵਿਚ

berg (ਬਅਰਗ) n ਬਰਫ਼ ਦਾ ਤੋਦਾ

berm (ਬਅਰਮ) n ਪਟੜੀ, ਸੜਕ ਜਾਂ ਨਹਿਰ ਦਾ ਕਿਨਾਰਾ

berry (ਬੈਰਿ) *n v* ਬੇਰ, ਰਸ-ਭਰੀ, ਕਟਕ ਦਾ ਬੀਂ, ਦਾਣਾ, ਇਕ ਕਿਸਮ ਦੀ ਮੱਛੀ ਦਾ ਅੰਡਾ; ਫਲ ਲੱਗਣਾ; ਬੇਰ ਚੁਗਣਾ

berserk (ਬਅ'ਜ਼ਅਰਕ) *a* ਪਾਗਲ, ਵਹਿਸ਼ੀ, ਜਨੂੰਨੀ

berth (ਬਅਰਥ) *n v* (ਜਹਾਜ਼ ਜਾਂ ਰੇਲ ਵਿਚ) ਸੌਣ ਲਈ ਥਾਂ; ਬਰਥ, ਸਮੁੰਦਰੀ ਜਹਾਜ਼ ਦੇ ਲੰਗਰ ਲਾਉਣ ਦੀ ਥਾਂ; (ਕਿਸੇ ਚੀਜ਼ ਲਈ) ਠੀਕ ਥਾਂ, ਨੌਕਰੀ, ਆਸਾਮੀ; (ਠੀਕ ਥਾਂ ਤੇ) ਲੰਗਰ ਸੁੱਟਣਾ, ਸੌਣ ਲਈ ਥਾਂ ਦੇਣੀ, ਟਿਕਾਣਾ ਕਰਨਾ

beseech (ਬਿ'ਸੀਚ) *v* ਬੇਨਤੀ ਕਰਨਾ, ਪ੍ਰਾਰਥਨਾ ਕਰਨਾ, ਤਰਲੇ ਕਰਨੇ, ਮਿੰਨਤ ਕਰਨੀ

beset (ਬਿ'ਸੈੱਟ) *v* ਘੇਰ ਲੈਣਾ; ਰਾਹ ਰੋਕ ਲੈਣਾ, ਮੱਲ ਲੈਣਾ; ਹੱਲਾ ਕਰਨਾ, ਟੁੱਟ ਕੇ ਜਾ ਪੈਣਾ; ਕਾਬੂ ਪਾ ਲੈਣਾ; ਜਿਚ ਕਰਨਾ

beside (ਬਿ'ਸਾਇਡ) *prep* ਨੇੜੇ, ਪਾਸ, ਕੋਲ, ਆਸ ਪਾਸ, ਕਿਨਾਰੇ ਦੇ

besides (ਬਿ'ਸਾਇਡਜ਼) *prep adv* ਇਸ ਤੋਂ ਛੁੱਟ, ਇਸ ਤੋਂ ਇਲਾਵਾ, ਨਾਲੇ, ਹੋਰ, ਸਿਵਾਏ, ਅਤਿਰਿਕਤ

besiege (ਬਿ'ਸੀਜ) *v* ਘੇਰਾ ਪਾਉਣਾ, ਘੇਰਨਾ, ਘੇਰ ਲੈਣਾ, ਭੀੜ ਕਰਨੀ; **~ment** ਘੇਰਾ, ਕਿਲ੍ਹਾਬੰਦੀ

besigh (ਬਿ'ਸਾਇ) *v* ਠੰਢਾ ਸਾਹ ਲੈਣਾ, ਆਹ ਭਰਨੀ

besmear (ਬਿ'ਸਮਿਅਰ) *v* ਲੇਪ ਕਰਨਾ, ਚੋਪੜਨਾ, ਪੋਚਣਾ, ਮਲਣਾ, ਧੱਬਾ ਲਾਉਣਾ, ਕਾਲਖ ਲਾਉਣੀ, ਕਲੰਕਤ ਕਰਨਾ

bespectecled (ਬਿ'ਸਕਪੈੱਕਟਅਲੇਡ) *a* ਐਨਕ ਵਾਲਾ, ਐਨਕਦਾਰ ਚਸ਼ਮਾ ਪਹਿਨੇ ਹੋਏ

best (ਬੈਸੱਟ) *a adv* (superl of *good,*
well) ਸਭ ਤੋਂ ਚੰਗਾ, ਚੰਗੇ ਤੋਂ ਚੰਗਾ; ਵਧੀਆ, ਸ੍ਰੇਸ਼ਟ, ਪਰਮ; ਸਭ ਤੋਂ ਚੰਗੀ ਤਰ੍ਹਾਂ; **be at one's ~** (ਹੁਨਰ) ਸਿਖਰ ਤੇ ਹੋਣਾ; **make the ~ of things** ਹਰ ਅਵਸਥਾ ਤੋਂ ਲਾਭ ਉਠਾਉਣਾ; ਕਿਸੇ ਕਿਸਮ ਦਾ ਕੰਮ ਕੱਢਣਾ

bestain (ਬਿ'ਸਟੇਇਨ) *v* ਦਾਗ਼ ਲਾਉਣਾ, ਧੱਬਾ ਲਾਉਣਾ, ਕਲੰਕਤ ਕਰਨਾ

bestow (ਬਿ'ਸਟਅਉ) *v* ਪ੍ਰਦਾਨ ਕਰਨਾ, (ਭੇਟਾ) ਦੇਣਾ, ਅਰਪਣ ਕਰਨਾ; ਬਖ਼ਸ਼ਣਾ, ਜਮ੍ਹਾਂ ਕਰਨਾ, ਟਿਕਾਉਣਾ

bet (ਬੈੱਟ) *n v* ਸ਼ਰਤ; ਦਾਉ, ਬਾਜ਼ੀ; ਸ਼ਰਤ ਲਾਉਣਾ, ਬਾਜ਼ੀ ਲਾਉਣੀ, ਜੂਆ ਖੇਡਣਾ

betel ('ਬੀਟਲ) *n* ਪਾਨ-ਪੱਤਾ, ਤੰਬੋਲ; **~nut** ਸੁਪਾਰੀ

betray (ਬਿ'ਟਰੇਇ) *v* ਵਿਸ਼ਵਾਸਘਾਤ ਕਰਨਾ, ਬੇਵਫ਼ਾਈ ਕਰਨਾ; ਧਰੋਹ ਕਰਨਾ, ਭੇਤ ਖੋਲ੍ਹਣਾ, ਪਰਗਟ ਕਰਨਾ; **~al** ਵਿਸ਼ਵਾਸਘਾਤ; ਧਰੋਹ ਬੇਵਸਾਹੀ; ਭੇਤ ਖੋਲ੍ਹਣਾ; **~er** ਵਿਸ਼ਵਾਸਘਾਤੀ ਵਿਸ਼ਵਾਸਘਾਤਕ, ਧਰੋਹੀ

betroth (ਬਿ'ਟਰਅਉਦ) *v* ਮੰਗਣੀ ਕਰਨੀ; **~al** ਮੰਗਣੀ, ਕੁੜਮਾਈ, ਸਗਾਈ, ਸ਼ਗਨ

better (ਬੈੱਟਅ*) *adv. adv. n v* ਚੰਗੇਰਾ ਭਲੇਰਾ, ਬਿਹਤਰ; ਚੰਗੇਰਾ ਬਣਾਉਣਾ, ਸੁਧਾਰ ਕਰਨਾ; ਉੱਨਤੀ ਕਰਨਾ, (ਕਿਸੇ ਨਾਲੋਂ) ਵਧ ਜਾਣਾ **~ment** ਭਲਾਈ, ਸੁਧਾਰ, ਉੱਨਤੀ, ਬਿਹਤਰੀ

between (ਬਿਟਵੀਨ) *a prep* ਵਿਚ, ਵਿਚਕਾਰ ਮੱਧ ਵਿਚ, ਵਿਚ-ਵਿਚਾਲੇ, ਦਰਮਿਆਨ, ਅੰਦਰ ਆਪੇ ਵਿਚ

beverage (ਬੇੱਵ੍(ਅ)ਰਿਜ) *n* ਸ਼ਰਬਤ, ਪੀਣ ਵਾਲੀ ਚੀਜ਼ (ਸ਼ਰਾਬ ਆਦਿ)

beware (ਬਿ'ਵੇਅ*) *v* ਸਚੇਤ ਰਹਿਣਾ, ਖ਼ਬਰਦਾਰ

ਰਹਿਣਾ, ਚੌਕਸ ਰਹਿਣਾ, ਸਾਵਧਾਨ ਹੋਣਾ

bewilder (ਬਿ'ਵਿਲਡਅ*) v ਬੌਂਦਲਾਉਣਾ, ਭਰਕਾਉਣਾ; ਉਲਝਣ ਵਿਚ ਪਾਉਣਾ ਖ਼ਬਰਾ ਦੇਣਾ, ਹੈਰਾਨ ਕਰਨਾ, ਮੱਤ ਮਾਰ ਦੇਣੀ, ਭੁਲਾਉਣਾ, ਬਟਕਾਉਣਾ; **~ed** ਘਬਰਾਇਆ, ਵਿਆਕੁਲ; **~ment** ਘਬਰਾਹਟ, ਪਰੇਸ਼ਾਨੀ, ਹੈਰਾਨੀ, ਵਿਆਕੁਲਤਾ

beyond (ਬਿ'ਯੌਂਡ) adv prep n ਪਰਲੇ ਪਾਸੇ, ਪਾਰ, ਦੂਜੇ ਪਾਸੇ, ਉਸ ਪਾਸੇ; ਉਧਰ, ਪਰ੍ਹਾਂ; ਤੋਂ ਵਧੇਰੇ, ਪਹੁੰਚ ਤੋਂ ਬਾਹਰ, ਅਧਿਕ; ਅੱਗਾ

bi (ਬਾਇ) prefix ਦੋ ਗੁਣਾ, ਦੋ ਗੁਨੀ (ਵਸਤੂ), ਦੋ ਵਾਰ ਹੋਣ ਵਾਲਾ

biangular ('ਬਾਈ'ਐਂਗਯੁਲਅ*) a ਦੋ ਕੋਣੀ, ਦੋ ਕੋਣਾਂ ਵਾਲਾ

biannual ('ਬਾਈ'ਐਨੁਅਲ) a ਸਾਲ ਵਿਚ ਦੋ ਵਾਰੀ, ਛਿਮਾਹੀ

bias (ਬਾਇਅਸ) n v ਪੱਖਪਾਤ, ਪੜ੍ਹੇਬਾਜ਼ੀ, ਤਰਫਦਾਰੀ, ਲਿਹਾਜ਼, ਪੱਖ ਪਾਲਣਾ, ਨਾਜਾਇਜ਼ ਪ੍ਰਭਾਵ ਪਾਉਣਾ

bibilographer ('ਬਿਬਲਿਔਗਰਅਫ਼*) n ਪੁਸਤਕ ਸੂਚੀਕਾਰ; ਗ੍ਰੰਥ-ਵਿਗਿਆਨੀ

bibilography ('ਬਿਬਲਿ'ਔਗਰਅਫ਼ਿ) n ਪੁਸਤਕ-ਸੂਚੀ, ਗ੍ਰੰਥ-ਸੂਚੀ, ਪੁਸਤਕਮਾਲਾ

bicoloured ('ਬਾਇ'ਕਲਅੱਡ) a ਦੋ-ਰੰਗਾ, ਦੋ ਰੰਗਾਂ ਵਾਲਾ

bicycle (ਬਾਇਸਿਕਲ) v ਸਾਈਕਲ, ਬਾਈਸਿਕਲ ਚਲਾਉਣਾ

bid (ਬਿਡ) n v (ਨੀਲਾਮੀ ਦੀ) ਬੋਲੀ; ਸੱਦਾ, ਬੁਲਾਵਾ; ਹੁਕਮ ਦੇਣਾ, ਸੱਦਾ ਦੇਣਾ, ਨਿਮੰਤਰਤ ਕਰਨਾ; ਨੀਲਾਮੀ ਵਿਚ ਬੋਲੀ ਦੇਣੀ, (ਤਾਸ਼ ਦੀ ਖੇਡ ਵਿਚ) ਸਰਾਂ ਮਿਥਣੀਆਂ, ਤੁਰਮ ਬੋਲਣਾ,

ਬੁਰਦ ਲਾਉਣੀ, (ਵਿਦਾਈ ਵੇਲੇ) ਨਮਸਕਾਰ ਕਹਿਣਾ; **~der** ਬੋਲੀ ਦੇਣ ਵਾਲਾ

biennial (ਬਾਇ'ਐਨਿਅਲ) a ਦੋ ਸਾਲ ਵਿਚ ਹੋਣ ਵਾਲਾ, ਦੋ-ਬਰਸੀ, ਦੋ-ਸਾਲਾ ਬਿਰਛ ਜਾਂ ਪੋਦਾ ਜਿਹੜਾ ਦੋ ਵਰ੍ਹੇ ਰਹੇ ਜਾਂ ਦੂਜੇ ਸਾਲ ਫੁੱਲ ਤੇ ਫਲ ਦੇਵੇ

bier (ਬਿਅ*) ਅਰਬੀ, ਮੁਰਦਾ ਲੈ ਜਾਣ ਵਾਲੀ ਗੱਡੀ, ਜਨਾਜ਼ਾ, ਤਖ਼ਤਾ, ਤਾਬੂਤ, ਸਿਥਾਨ

bifurcate ('ਬਾਇਫ਼ਅਕੇਇਟ) v a ਦੋ ਹਿੱਸਿਆਂ ਵਿਚ ਵੰਡਣਾ, ਦੋ ਫਾਂਟਾਂ ਕਰਨੀਆਂ, ਦੁਫਾਂਟਣਾ, ਦੁਫੱੜ ਕਰਨਾ ਜਾਂ ਹੋਣਾ, ਦੋਫਾੜਾ

bifurcation ('ਬਾਇਫ਼ਅਾ'ਕੇਇਸ਼ਨ) n ਦੁਸਾਂਗ, ਦੁਫੱਟਣ; ਫਾਂਟ, ਦੋ ਸ਼ਾਖਾਂ ਵਿਚ ਵੰਡ, ਦੋ ਸ਼ਾਖਾਂ ਜਾਂ ਉਨ੍ਹਾਂ ਵਿਚੋਂ ਇਕ

big (ਬਿਗ) a v ਵੱਡਾ, ਵਿਸ਼ਾਲ; ਮਹਾਨ, ਮੁਖੀਆ; ਫੁੱਲਿਆ; ਉਭਰਿਆ; ਪੂਰਨ, ਉਦਾਰ; ਉੱਚਾ; **~bellied** ਗਰਭਵਤੀ; **~talk** ਸ਼ੇਖ਼ੀ ਮਾਰਨਾ;

bigamy ('ਬਿਗਅਮਿ) n ਦੁਪਤਨੀਤਵ, ਇਕ ਪਤੀ ਦਾ ਪਤਨੀ ਦੇ ਹੁੰਦੇ ਹੋਏ ਦੂਜਾ ਵਿਆਹ

bigot ('ਬਿਗਅਟ) n ਕੱਟੜਪੰਥੀ, ਤੁਅੱਸਬੀ, ਹਠਧਰਮੀ; **~ry** ਕੱਟੜਪੁਣਾ, ਤੁਅੱਸਬ, ਹਠਧਰਮੀ

billingual (ਬਾਇ'ਲਿੰਗਵਅਲ) a ਦੁਭਾਸ਼ੀਆ, ਦੋ ਭਾਸ਼ਾਵਾਂ ਲਿਖਣ, ਬੋਲਣ ਜਾਂ ਜਾਨਣ ਵਾਲਾ

bill (ਬਿਲ) n (1) ਬੀਜਕ, ਹੁੰਡੀ, ਹਿਸਾਬ ਦੀ ਪਰਚੀ, ਰਸੀਦ, ਬਿਲ; (2) ਵਿਧੇਕ (ਕਾ); (3) ਇਸ਼ਤਿਹਾਰ; (4) ਗੰਡਾਸਾ, ਫਰਸਾ, ਲੰਗਰ ਦੀ ਫਾਲ ਦੀ ਨੋਕ; ਚੁੰਝਾਂ ਭਰਨੀਆਂ, ਲਾਡ ਕਰਨਾ, ਚੁੰਮਣਾ-ਚੱਟਣਾ; **~and coo** ਪਿਆਰ ਕਰਨਾ, ਕਲੋਲ ਕਰਨਾ, ਇਕ ਦੂਜੇ ਨੂੰ ਚੁੰਮਣਾ; **~book** ਵਹੀ ਖਾਤਾ, ਬਿਲ ਕੱਟਣ ਵਾਲੀ ਕਾਪੀ; **~of exchange** ਹੁੰਡੀ; **~sticking** ਇਸ਼ਤਿਹਾਰ ਲਾਉਣਾ

billion ('ਬਿਲਯਅਨ) n ਇਕ ਅਰਬ

binary ('ਬਾਇਨਅਰਿ) a n ਦੂਹਰਾ, ਜੋੜੇਦਾਰ, ਦੋ-ਅੰਗੀ, ਯੁਗਮ; **~system** ਦੋ ਆਧਾਰੀ ਪ੍ਰਣਾਲੀ

bind (ਬਾਈਂਡ) v ਜਿਲਦ ਬੰਨ੍ਹਣਾ, ਪੱਟੀ ਬੰਨ੍ਹਣਾ, ਗੋਟਾ ਕਿਨਾਰੀ ਲਗਾਉਣਾ, ਅਧਿਕਾਰ ਨੂੰ ਵਰਤਣਾ, ਲਾਗੂ ਕਰਨਾ, ਪੱਕਾ ਕਰਨਾ, ਪੱਕਾ ਕਰਾਉਣਾ; ਜੁੜਨਾ, ਸੰਯੁਕਤ ਹੋਣਾ; **~er** ਬੰਨ੍ਹਣ ਵਾਲਾ, ਜਿਲਦਸਾਜ਼; ਅਖ਼ਬਾਰ ਜਾਂ ਕਾਗਜ਼ਾਂ ਨੂੰ ਰੱਖਣ ਲਈ ਫ਼ਾਈਲ; **~ing** ਜਿਲਦਸਾਜ਼ੀ, ਪੱਟੀ, ਗੋਟਾ, ਬੰਧਨ, ਬੰਦਸ਼

binocular ('ਬਿ'ਨੋਕਅਲਕ) n ਦੂਰਬੀਨ, ਦੋ-ਨੇਤਰੀ, ਦੋ-ਅੱਖੀ

bio ('ਬਾਇਅਉ) ਜੀਵ, ਜਾਨਦਾਰ, ਪ੍ਰਾਣੀ; **~chemistry** ਜੀਵ-ਰਸਾਇਣਕੀ; **~physics** ਜੀਵ-ਭੌਤਕੀ; **~scope** ਚਲ-ਚਿੱਤਰਪਟ

biography (ਬਾਇ'ਔਗਰਅਫ਼ਿ) n ਜੀਵਨੀ, ਜੀਵਨਚਿਰਤਾਂਤ, ਜੀਵਨ-ਕਥਾ, ਜੀਵਨ-ਚਰਿੱਤਰ

biology (ਬਾਇ'ਔਲਅਜਿ) n ਜੀਵ-ਵਿਗਿਆਨ

bipartite ('ਬਾਈ'ਪਾਟਾਇਟ) a ਦੋ-ਪੱਖਾ, ਦੋ-ਭਾਰੀ, ਦੋ-ਖੰਡੜੀਆ

bipartition ('ਬਾਇਪਾ'ਟਿਸ਼ਨ) n ਦੋ-ਹਿੱਸਿਆਂ ਵਿਚ ਵੰਡ, ਦੁਭਾਜਨ

bipolar (ਬਾਇ'ਪਅਉਲਅ*) a ਦੋ-ਧਰੁਵੀ

bird (ਬਅ'ਡ) n v ਪੰਛੀ, ਪੰਖੇਰੂ, ਮੁਟਿਆਰ; (ਅਪ) ਚੂਚਾ, ਕੁੜੀ; ਪੰਛੀਆਂ ਦਾ ਸ਼ਿਕਾਰ ਕਰਨਾ ਜਾਂ ਫਸਾਉਣਾ; **~'s eye view** ਪੰਛੀ-ਝਾਤ

birth (ਬਅ:ਥ) n ਜਨਮ, ਪੈਦਾਇਸ਼ ਜੂਨ, ਉਤਪਤੀ, ਆਰੰਭ, ਮੂਲ; ਨਸਲ, ਜਾਤੀ; ਕੁਲੀਨਤਾ; **~control** ਸੰਤਾਨ-ਸੰਜਮ; **~day** ਜਨਮ-ਦਿਨ, ਵਰ੍ਹੇ-ਗੰਢ; **~place** ਜਨਮ-ਭੂਮੀ, ਜਨਮ-ਸਥਾਨ; **~rate** ਜੰਮਣ-ਦਰ, ਜਨਮ ਦਰ; **~right** ਜਮਾਂਦਰੂ ਹੱਕ, ਪੈਦਾਇਸ਼ੀ ਹੱਕ

biscuit (ਬਿਸਕਿਟ) n ਬਿਸਕੁਟ, ਖਟਾਈ

bisect (ਬਾਇ'ਸੈਕਟ) v ਦੋ-ਟੁੱਕ ਕਰਨਾ, ਅੱਧੋ-ਅੱਧ ਕਰਨਾ, ਦੋ ਹਿੱਸਿਆਂ ਵਿਚ ਕੱਟਣਾ, ਵਿਚੋਂ ਟੁੱਕਣਾ

bishop ('ਬਿਸ਼ਅਪ) n (1) ਵੱਡਾ ਪਾਦਰੀ, ਬਿਸ਼ਪ; (2) ਮਸਾਲੇਦਾਰ ਸ਼ਰਾਬ; ਟੋਪੀ ਵਰਗੀ ਸ਼ਕਲ ਦਾ, (ਸ਼ਤਰੰਜ ਵਿਚ) ਫ਼ੀਲਾ

bit (ਬਿਟ) n v (1) ਟੁਕੜਾ, ਟੋਟਾ; ਗਰਾਹੀ, ਬੁਰਕੀ, ਟੁਕਰ, ਟੁਕ; (2) ਛੋਟਾ ਸਿੱਕਾ; (3) ਲਗਾਮ ਦਾ ਕੜਿਆਲਾ, ਚਾਬੀ ਦੇ ਦੰਦ; ਸੰਨ੍ਹੀ ਦਾ ਸਿਰਾ; ਵਰਮੇ ਦੀ ਅਣੀ, ਨੋਕ, ਸਿਰਾ; ਰੋਕ, ਲਗਾਮ ਦਾ ਆਦੀ ਬਣਾਉਣਾ; ਕਾਬੂ ਪਾਉਣਾ, ਰੋਕਣਾ, ਵੱਸ ਵਿਚ ਕਰਨਾ

bitch (ਬਿਚ) n ਕੁੱਤੀ; ਲੁੱਚਕੀ; ਲੁੱਚੀ ਰੰਨ

bite (ਬਾਇਟ) n v ਕੱਟਣਾ, ਵੱਢਣਾ, ਦੰਦੀ ਵੱਢਣੀ; ਤੋੜਨਾ, ਡੰਗਣਾ; ਚਾਰੇ ਤੇ ਮੂੰਹ ਮਾਰਨਾ; ਘੋਰਨਾ ਖਾਣਾ

biting ('ਬਾਇਟਿੰਡ) a ਤੇਜ਼, ਤਿੱਖਾ, ਤੀਬਰ ਵੱਢਦਾ, ਚੁੱਭਵਾਂ, ਕਾਟਵਾਂ

bitter (ਬਿਟਅ*) a ਕੌੜਾ ਤਿੱਖਾ, ਕੁੜੱਾਂਗਾ; ਦੁਖਾਵ **~ness*** ਕਟੂਤਾ, ਤੀਖਣਤਾ, ਕਠੋਰਤਾ, ਕੁੜੱੱਤਣ ਤਿੱਖਾਪਣ

bi-weekly ('ਬਾਇ'ਵਿਕਲਿ) a ਦੋ-ਸਪਤਾਹਕ

bizarre (ਬਿ'ਜ਼ਾ*) a ਅਦਭੁਤ, ਅਨੋਖਾ, ਵਿਲੱਖਣ

black (ਬਲੈਕ) a n v ਕਾਲਾ, ਮੁਸ਼ਕੀ, ਧੁੰਦਲਾ ਮੈਲਾ, ਗੰਦਾ, ਮਲੀਨ (ਕੱਪੜਾ, ਹੱਥ); ਹਨੇਰਾ ਪਾਪੀ, ਅਤੀਅੰਤ ਬੁਰਾ; ਨਿਰਾਸ਼ਾਜਨਕ ਡਰਾਉਣਾ; ਧੱਬਾ; ਕਾਲਖ, ਕਾਲਾ ਰੰਗ; ਕਾਲਾ ਹਬਸ਼ੀ; ਕਾਲੀ ਚਮੜੀ ਵਾਲਾ; ਕਾਲਾ ਕਰਨ ਰੰਗ ਚੜ੍ਹਾਉਣਾ, ਕਾਲੀ ਪਾਲਸ਼ ਕਰਨਾ; **~a**

blue ਮਾਰ ਕੁਟਾਈ ਨਾਲ ਪਏ ਨੀਲ; ~ and white ਸਾਦਾ, ਲਿਖਿਆ ਹੋਇਆ, ਸਿਆਹੀ ਨਾਲ ਲਿਖਿਆ; ਕਾਲੀ ਅਤੇ ਚਿੱਟੀ ਤਸਵੀਰ; ~art ਜਾਦੂ; ਟੂਣਾ; ~board ਬਲੈਕ ਬੋਰਡ; ~draught ਜੁਲਾਬ; ~list ਅਪਰਾਧੀਆਂ ਦੀ ਸੂਚੀ, ਕਾਨੂੰਨ ਤੋੜਨ ਵਾਲਿਆਂ ਦੀ ਸੂਚੀ, ਸ਼ੱਕੀ ਲੋਕਾਂ ਦੀ ਸੂਚੀ; ~mail ਭੇਤ ਲੁਕਾਈ ਰੱਖਣ ਦੀ ਵੱਢੀ, ਬਲੈਕਮੇਲ; ~market ਚੋਰ-ਬਜ਼ਾਰੀ; ~out ਆਰਜ਼ੀ ਹਨੇਰਾ, ਬਲੈਕ ਆਊਟ; ਚੇਤਨਾ ਸ਼ਕਤੀ ਦਾ ਅਭਾਵ, ਨ੍ਹੇਰਨੀ; ~smith ਲੁਹਾਰ; ~en ਜਾਣਾ ਕਰਨ ਜਾਂ ਹੋਣ, ਕੰਲਕ ਲਗਾਉਣਾ, ਬਦਨਾਮੀ ਕਰਨੀ, ਨਿੰਦਣਾ, ਬੁਰਾ ਕਹਿਣਾ; ~ness ਅੰਧਕਾਰ, ਕਾਲਾਪਣ, ਸਿਆਹੀ, ਕਾਲਿਮਾ

bladder (ਬਲੈਡਅਰ) n ਬੁਕਨਾ; ਫੁੱਲੀ ਹੋਈ ਖ਼ਾਲੀ ਚੀਜ਼, ਬਲੈਡਰ; ਮਸਾਨਾ, ਹਵਾ ਦਾ ਥੈਲਾ, ਫਲੂਸ; ਗਾਲੂੜੀ ਮਨੁੱਖ, ਬਾਤੂਨੀ

blade (ਬਲੇਇਡ) n ਪੱਤਰ, ਪੱਤੀ, ਤ੍ਰਿਣ; (ਚਾਕੂ, ਤਲਵਾਰ, ਛੁਰੀ, ਕਹੀ, ਚੱਪੂ ਆਦਿ ਦਾ) ਫਲ; ਤਲਵਾਰ, (ਹਜਾਮਤ ਕਰਨ ਵਾਲਾ) ਬਲੇਡ; ਘੱਲੇ ਜਾਂ ਚੱਪੂ ਦੀ ਬਾਪੀ; ਮੋਢੇ ਦੀ ਚੌੜੀ ਹੱਡੀ; ਤਿਖਾ ਬੰਦਾ, ਛੁਰੀ

blame (ਬਲੇਮ) v n ਦੋਸ਼ ਲਾਉਣਾ, ਦੋਸ਼ ਥੱਪਣਾ, ਭੰਡਣਾ, ਊਜ ਲਾਉਣੀ, ਨਿੰਦਾ ਕਰਨੀ, ਅਪਰਾਧੀ ਠਹਿਰਾਉਣਾ; ਦੋਸ਼, ਐਬ, ਇਲਜ਼ਾਮ; ~less ਬਿਦੋਸ਼ਾ, ਨਿਰਦੋਸ਼, ਬੇਕਸੂਰ, ਨਿਰਦੋਸ਼

blandish (ਬਲੈਂਡਿਸ਼) v ਪਸਮਾਉਣਾ, ਭਰਮਾਉਣਾ, ਚਾਪਲੂਸੀ ਕਰਨਾ

blank (ਬਲੈਂਕ) n a ਖ਼ਾਲੀਪਨ, ਕੋਰਾ, ਸਾਦਾ (ਕਾਗ਼ਜ਼), ਖ਼ਾਲੀ, ਫੋਕਾ, ਬਿਨਾ ਦਸਤਖਤ ਤੋਂ; ਉੱਕਾ, ਨਿਰਾ; ~cheque ਕੋਰਾ ਚੈੱਕ; ~ness ਖ਼ਾਲੀਪਨ, ਕੋਰਾਪਨ, ਸਾਦਾਪਨ; ਘਬਰਾਹਟ

blanket ('ਬਲੈਂਕਿਟ) n v ਕੰਬਲ, ਝੁੱਲ, ਕੰਬਲ ਨਾਲ ਕੱਜਣਾ; ਹਵਾ ਰੋਕਣੀ

blaspheme (ਬਲੈਸ'ਫ਼ੀਮ) v ਬੇਅਦਬੀ ਕਰਨੀ, ਕੁਫ਼ਰ ਤੋਲਣਾ, ਕੁਫ਼ਰਾਮੀ ਗੱਲਾਂ ਕਰਨੀਆਂ, ਬੇਅਦਬੀ ਦੇ ਸ਼ਬਦ ਵਰਤਣੇ

blasphemous (ਬਲੈਸਫ਼ਅਮਅਸ) a ਰੱਬ-ਨਿੰਦਕ, ਪਖੰਡੀ; ਕਾਫ਼ਰ, ਕੁਫ਼ਰੀ

blasphemy ('ਬਲੈਸਫ਼ਅਮਿ) n ਕੁਫ਼ਰ, ਕੁਫ਼ਰ ਦੇ ਲਫ਼ਜ਼, ਬੇਅਦਬੀ

blast (ਬਲਾਸਟ) n v (ਹਵਾ ਦਾ ਤੇਜ਼) ਬੁੱਲਾ, ਝੋਕਾਂ; ਬੰਬ ਦੇ ਫਟਣ ਦਾ ਧਮਾਕਾ, ਭੜਕ; (ਬਾਰੂਦ ਨਾਲ) ਉਡਾਉਣਾ; ਸਾੜ ਸੁਆਹ ਕਰਨਾ, ਝੁਲਸਾਉਣਾ, ਝੁਲਸ ਦੇਣਾ

blatancy ('ਬਲੇਇਟਅੰਸਿ) n ਹੁੱਲੜਬਾਜ਼ੀ, ਸ਼ੋਰ-ਸ਼ਰਾਬਾ

blatant ('ਬਲੇਇਟਅੰਟ) a ਰੋਲਾ-ਪਾਊ, ਖੱਪ ਪਾਊਣ ਵਾਲਾ

blaze (ਬਲੇਇਜ਼) n v ਭਾਂਬੜ, ਲਾਟ, ਲਪਟ, ਲੂੰਬਾ, ਜੋਸ਼, ਭੜਕ; ਤੜਕ-ਭੜਕ, ਠਾਠ-ਬਾਠ, ਜਗ-ਮਗ, ਚਕਾਚੌਂਧ, ਲਾਟਾਂ ਨਾਲ ਬਲਣਾ; ਜੋਸ਼ ਵਿਚ ਲਾਉਣਾ, ਭੜਕ ਉੱਠਣਾ; ਚਮਕ ਪੈਣਾ

bleach (ਬਲੀਚ) v n ਰੰਗ ਉਡਾਉਣਾ, ਖੁੰਭ ਕਰਨਾ, ਚਿਟਿਆਉਣਾ; ਚਿਟਾ ਕਰਨ ਪੇਣ ਦਾ ਮਸਾਲਾ; ~ing ਸਫ਼ੈਦ ਕਰਨ ਦੀ ਕਿਰਿਆ, ਕੱਪੜਿਆਂ ਨੂੰ ਸਫ਼ੈਦ ਕਰਨ ਦੀ ਕਲਾ; ~ing-power (ਰਸਾ) ਕਲੋਰੀਨ ਅਤੇ ਆਕਸੀਜਨ ਦਾ ਮਿਸ਼ਰਣ, ਚੂਨੇ ਦਾ ਕਲੋਰਾਇਡ, ਰੰਗ ਉਡਾਊਣ ਵਾਲਾ ਪਾਊਡਰ, ਮਿੱਠਾ ਸੋਡਾ

bleak (ਬਲੀਕ) a n ਵੀਰਾਨ, ਬੇਰੰਗ, ਫਿੱਕਾ, ਪੀਲਾ; ਉਦਾਸ, ਉਤਸ਼ਾਹਹੀਨ; ਠੰਢਾ, ਨੰਗਾ,

bleed

ਖੁੱਲ੍ਹ (ਮੈਦਾਨ ਆਦਿ); ਭਿੰਨ-ਭਿੰਨ ਪ੍ਰਕਾਰ ਦੀਆਂ ਛੋਟੀਆਂ ਮੱਛੀਆਂ

bleed (ਬਲੀਡ) *v* ਲਹੂ ਵਗਣਾ ਜਾਂ ਵਗਾਉਣਾ; ਖੂਨ ਹੋਣਾ, ਲਹੂ ਚੁਸਣਾ

blench (ਬਲੈਂਚ) *v* ਝਿਜਕਣਾ, ਸਹਿਮਣਾ, ਸੰਕੋਚ ਵਿਚ ਹੋਣਾ, ਪਿੱਛੇ ਹਟਣਾ; ਜਾਣ ਬੁੱਝ ਕੇ ਅਨਜਾਣ ਬਣਨਾ, ਅੱਖ ਬਟਾਉਣਾ, ਕੰਨੀ ਕਤਰਾਉਣਾ; ਟਾਲਣਾ

blend (ਬਲੈਂਡ) *v n* ਰਲਾਉਣਾ; ਘੋਲਣਾ, ਘੁਲਣਾ, ਮਿਲਾਉਣਾ; ਇਕ ਦੂਜੇ ਵਿਚ ਮਿਲਾਵਟ

bless (ਬਲੈੱਸ) *v* ਅਸੀਸ ਦੇਣੀ, ਵਰ ਦੇਣਾ, ਆਸ਼ੀਰਵਾਦ ਦੇਣੀ (ਪਿਤਾ, ਭਾਈ ਆਦਿ ਦੀ), ਰੱਬੀ ਮਿਹਰ ਮੰਗਣੀ; ਨਿਹਾਲ ਕਰਨਾ, ਕਰਨੀ; ~ed ਪਵਿੱਤਰ, ਪਾਵਨ, ਮੁਬਾਰਕ, ਪੁਨੀਤ, ਧੰਨ, ਸੁਭਾਗਾਸ਼ਾਲੀ; ਪੂਜਨੀਕ; ~ing ਅਸੀਸ, ਅਸ਼ੀਰਵਾਦ, ਵਰਦਾਨ, ਬਰਕਤ, ਦੁਆ, ਰਹਿਮਤ, ਮਿਹਰ, ਫ਼ਜ਼ਲ

blind (ਬਲਾਇੰਡ) *a v n* ਅੰਨ੍ਹਾ, ਨੇਤਰਹੀਨ, ਮਨਾਖਾ; ਅਗਿਆਨੀ, ਬੁੱਧੂ; ਅੰਨ੍ਹੇ-ਵਾਹ, ਬੇਅਰਥ; ਅੰਧਾ ਕਰਨਾ; ਧੋਖਾ ਦੇਣਾ; ~born ਜਨਮਾਂਧ, ਜਨਮ ਤੋਂ ਅੰਨ੍ਹਾ; ~follower ਪਿੱਛ-ਲੱਗਾ, ਬਿਨਾਂ ਸੋਚੇ ਸਮਝੇ ਪਿੱਛੇ ਲੱਗਣ ਵਾਲਾ, ਅੰਧ ਵਿਸ਼ਵਾਸੀ; ~ly ਅੱਖਾਂ ਬੰਦ ਕਰਕੇ, ਬਿਨਾਂ ਸੋਚੇ ਸਮਝੇ; ~ness ਅੰਨ੍ਹਾਪਣ, ਮੂਰਖਤਾ, ਅਗਿਆਨ, ਦ੍ਰਿਸ਼ਟੀ-ਹੀਣਤਾ, ਅਸਾਵਧਾਨੀ

blink (ਬਲਿੰਕ) *v n* ਅੱਖ ਝਮਕਣੀ, ਝਲਕਾਰਾ ਮਾਰਨਾ, ਪਲਕ ਮਾਰਨਾ; ਧਿਆਨ ਨਾ ਦੇਣਾ, ਟਾਲਣਾ, ਨਜ਼ਰੋਂ ਉਹਲੇ ਕਰ ਜਾਣਾ; ਝਲਕ, ਝਲਕਾਰਾ, ਦੂਰ ਦੀ ਬਰਫ਼ ਦਾ ਲਿਸ਼ਕਾਰਾ

bliss (ਬਲਿਸ) *n* ਆਨੰਦ, ਸਰੂਰ, ਆਤਮਕ ਸੁਖ; ਸੁਰਗਾ; ~ful ਆਨੰਦਪੂਰਨ, ਆਨੰਦਤ, ਸੁਖੀ,

blood

ਮਗਨ, ਵਿਸਮਾਦੀ; ~fully ਪਰਮਆਨੰਦੀ ਸਥਿਤੀ ਵਿਚ, ਆਨੰਦਪੂਰਵਕ ਹਾਲਤ ਵਿਚ

blitz (ਬਲਿਟਸ) *n v* ਤਗੜਾ ਤੇ ਅਚਾਨਕ ਹਮਲਾ, ਤਿੱਖਾ ਹਮਲਾ, (ਰਾਜਨੀਤੀ ਵਿਚ) ਡੂੰਘੀ ਚਾਲ; ਹਮਲੇ ਨਾਲ ਤਬਾਹੀ ਕਰਨੀ

blizzard ('ਬਲਿਜ਼ਅਡ) *n* ਬਰਫ਼ ਦਾ ਤੇਜ਼ ਤੂਫ਼ਾਨ, ਬਰਫ਼ੀਲਾ ਤੂਫ਼ਾਨ, ਬਰਫ਼ਾਨੀ ਹਨੇਰੀ

bloc (ਬਲੌਕ) *n* ਦਲ, ਗੁੱਟ, (ਰਾਜਸੀ) ਦਲਾਂ ਦਾ ਸੰਗਠਨ

block (ਬਲੌਕ) *n v* (ਲੱਕੜ ਦਾ) ਅੱਡਾ (ਜਿਸ ਉੱਤੇ ਰੱਖ ਕੇ ਲੱਕੜ ਰੰਦਦੇ ਜਾਂ ਠੋਕਦੇ ਹਨ); ਮਕਾਨਾਂ ਦਾ ਸਿਲਸਿਲਾ, ਬਲਾਕ, ਮੁਹੱਲਾ; ਰੋਕ; (ਪਾਰਲੀਮੈਂਟ) ਬਿਲ ਦਾ ਵਿਰੋਧ ਕਰਨ ਦੀ ਸੂਚਨਾ; ਅਟਕਾਉਣਾ, ਰੋਕ ਪਾਉਣੀ, ਰੋਕਣਾ, ਘੇਰਨਾ, ਬੰਦ ਕਰਨਾ; ~ade ਘੇਰਾ, ਨਾਕਾਬੰਦੀ, ਡੱਕਾ; ਘੇਰਾ ਘੱਤਣਾ, ਨਾਕਾਬੰਦੀ ਕਰਨੀ, ਡੱਕਾ ਲਾਉਣਾ, ਰੋਕਣਾ, ਰਾਹ ਰੋਕਣਾ; ~ed ਰੁਕਿਆ ਹੋਇਆ; ~head ਮੂਰਖ, ਉਤ, ਉੱਲੂ-ਬਾਟਾ, ਮੂੜ੍ਹ; ~ish ਮੂਰਖ, ਬੁੱਧੂ, ਹਠੀ, ਕਠੋਰ ਹਿਰਦਾ

blood (ਬਲਅੱਡ) *n v* ਲਹੂ, ਖ਼ੂਨ; ਰੱਤ; ਅੰਗੂਰ ਜਾਂ ਕਿਸੇ ਬੂਟੇ ਦਾ ਰਸ; ਨਸਲ, ਵੰਸ਼; ਉਕਸਾਉਣਾ, ਉਤੇਜਤ ਕਰਨਾ; ~is thicker than water ਆਪਣਾ ਆਪਣਾ ਗ਼ੈਰ ਗ਼ੈਰ; ~pressure ਬਲੱਡ-ਪ੍ਰੈਸ਼ਰ, ਲਹੂ ਦਾ ਦਬਾ; ~shed ਖ਼ੂਨ-ਖ਼ਰਾਬਾ; ~sucker ਰੱਤ-ਪੀਣਾ, ਲਹੂ-ਚੂਸ, ਜੋਕ, ਜਾਬਰ, ਜ਼ਰਵਾਣਾ, ਜ਼ਾਲਮ; ~thirsty ਲਹੂ-ਤਿਹਾਇਆ, ਖ਼ੂਨੀ, ਜ਼ਾਲਮ; ~worm ਲਾਲ ਕੀੜਾ; blue~ ਉੱਚੇ ਖ਼ਾਨਦਾਨ ਵਿਚ ਪੈਦਾਇਸ਼, ਕੁਲੀਨਤਾ; half~ ਸੌਤੇਲਾ; hot~ed ਅਤੀ ਕਰੋਧੀ; young~ ਨਵਯੁਵਕ, ਨਵਾਂ ਸਦੱਸ

bloom (ਬਲੂਮ) *n v* ਫੁੱਲ, ਪੁਸ਼ਪ; ਬਹਾਰ; ਜੋਬਨ, ਜਵਾਨੀ, ਚਮਕ, ਤੇਜ, ਲਾਲੀ, ਰੌਣਕ, ਤਾਜ਼ਗੀ; ਮੁਨੱਕਾ ਕਿਸ਼ਮਿਸ਼; ਫੁੱਲਣਾ, ਪੂਰੇ ਜੋਬਨ ਵਿਚ ਆਉਣਾ, ਪ੍ਰਫੁੱਲਤ ਹੋਣਾ, ਬਹਾਰ ਆਉਣੀ; ~y ਪ੍ਰਫੁੱਲਤ, ਖਿੜਿਆ

blossom ('ਬਲੌਸ(ਅ)ਮ) *n v* ਬੂਟੇ ਦੀ ਕਲੀ, ਸ਼ਗੂਫ਼ਾ; ਹੋਣਹਾਰਪੁਣਾ, ਵਧਣ ਮੌਲਣ ਦੇ ਦਿਨ, ਜੋਬਨ; ਖਿੜਨਾ (ਫੁੱਲ ਦਾ), ਫੁੱਲ ਲੱਗਣੇ

blot (ਬਲੌਟ) *n v* ਧੱਬਾ, ਡੱਬ, ਦਾਗ਼; ਕਲੰਕ, ਦੋਸ਼, ਔਗੁਣ, ਨੁਕਸ, ਐਬ, ਧੱਬਾ ਲੱਗਣਾ; ਧੱਬੇ ਲਾਉਣਾ; ਸਿਆਹੀ-ਚੂਸ ਨਾਲ ਸੁਕਾਉਣਾ

blow (ਬਲਅਉ) *v* (ਹਵਾ ਦਾ) ਚੱਲਣਾ, ਝੁੱਲਣਾ, ਰੁਮਕਣਾ; ਆਰਗਨ ਵਾਜਾ ਵਜਾਉਣਾ; ਧੌਂਕਣੀ ਨਾਲ ਹਵਾ ਦੇਣਾ, ਧੌਂਕਣਾ; ਸਾਹ ਬਾਹਰ ਕੱਢਣਾ, ਫੂਕ ਮਾਰਨਾ; ਉਡਾਉਣਾ; ਪਿਚਕਾਰਨਾ; ~out ਬੁਝਾਉਣਾ; ~pipe ਫੂਕਨੀ, ਧੌਂਕਣੀ

blowze (ਬਲਅਉਜ਼) *n* ਕੋਝੀ ਔਰਤ

blue (ਬਲੂ) ਨੀਲਾ, ਅਸਮਾਨੀ; ਨੀਲਾ ਰੰਗ; ਨੀਲ; ਨੀਲੱਤਣ, ਨੀਲਾ, ਕੱਪੜਾ, ਅਸਮਾਨ; ਸਮੁੰਦਰ; ~moon ਅਲਪਟੀ ਘਟਨਾ; once in a ~moon ਕਦੇ ਕਦੇ, ਭੁੱਲੇ ਭਟਕੇ

bluff (ਬਲਅੱਫ) *v n* ਉੱਲੂ ਬਣਾਉਣਾ, ਮੂਰਖ ਬਣਾਉਣਾ, ਰੋਅਬ ਪਾਉਣ ਦੀ ਨੀਤੀ ਅਪਨਾਉਣਾ; ਗਿੱਦੜ ਭਬਕੀ, ਫੋਕੀ ਧੌਂਸ

blunder ('ਬਲਅੰਡਅ*) *v n* ਭਾਰੀ ਭੁੱਲ ਕਰਨੀ, ਗੜਬੜ ਕਰਨੀ, ਵਿਗਾੜ ਦੇਣਾ, ਖ਼ਰਾਬ ਕਰਨਾ; ਭਾਰੀ ਭੁੱਲ, ਗ਼ਲਤੀ, ਦੋਸ਼; ਅਸ਼ੁੱਧੀ

blunt (ਬਲਅੰਟ) *a n v* ਖੁੰਢਾ, ਕੁੰਦ; ਦੋ-ਟੁੱਕ; ਕੋਰਾ, ਰੁੱਖਾ, ਖਰਾ-ਖਰਾ, ਮੂੰਹ-ਫੱਟ, ਮੋਟੀ ਖੁੰਡਾਈ, ਛੋਟਾ ਸੂਆ; ਨਕਦ ਮਾਲ; ਖੁੰਢਾ ਕਰਨਾ, ਮੱਠ ਮਾਰਨਾ; ਕਮਜ਼ੋਰ ਕਰਨਾ; ~ness ਖੁੰਢਾਪਣ, ਸਪਸ਼ਟਵਾਦਤਾ; ਔਖੜਪਣ

blur (ਬਲਅ:*) *n v* ਧੁੰਦਲਾਪਣ, ਅਸਪਸ਼ਟਤਾ; ਸਿਆਹੀ ਆਦਿ ਦਾ ਦਾਗ਼, ਧੱਬਾ; ਧੁੰਦਲਾਪਣ, ਧੁੰਦਲਾ ਕਰ ਦੇਣਾ, ਅਸਪਸ਼ਟ ਕਰਨਾ; ਧੱਬੇ ਪੈਣੇ

blush (ਬਲਅੱਸ਼) *n v* ਸ਼ਰਮਾ ਜਾਣਾ, ਸ਼ਰਮਾਉਣਾ, ਲਜਾਉਣਾ, ਸੰਕੋਚਣਾ; ਸ਼ਰਮ ਦੀ ਲਾਲੀ; ਝਲਕ, ਝਾਂਕੀ; ~ing ਲੱਜਾਇਆ

board (ਬੋ:ਡ) *n v* ਬੋਰਡ, ਪਟੜਾ, ਫੱਟਾ, ਤਖਤਾ; ਜਹਾਜ਼ ਦਾ ਤਖ਼ਤਾ; ਰੰਗ-ਮੰਚ; ਮੰਡਲੀ; ਫੱਟਿਆਂ ਨਾਲ ਕੱਜਣਾ; ਗੱਡੀ ਜਾਂ ਜਹਾਜ਼ ਤੇ ਚੜ੍ਹਨਾ

boast (ਬਅਉਸਟ) *n v* ਸ਼ੇਖੀ, ਡੀਂਗ, ਫੜ੍ਹ; ਡੀਂਗ ਮਾਰਨੀ, ਸ਼ੇਖੀ ਮਾਰਨੀ, ਫੜ੍ਹ ਮਾਰਨੀ; ~ful ਸ਼ੇਖੀ-ਖ਼ੋਰਾ, ਹੰਕਾਰੀ, ਫੜ੍ਹ-ਮਾਰ, ਗੱਪੀ; ~ing ਸ਼ੇਖੀਬਾਜ਼ੀ, ਡੀਂਗਬਾਜ਼ੀ

boat (ਬਅਉਟ) *n v* ਬੇੜੀ, ਕਿਸ਼ਤੀ, ਨਾਵ, ਜਹਾਜ਼; ਬੇੜੀ ਵਿਚ ਜਾਣਾ, ਬੇੜੀ ਦੀ ਸੈਰ ਕਰਨੀ, ਬੇੜੀ ਚਲਾਉਣਾ; ~man ਮੱਲਾਹ, ਖੇਵਟ; ਮਾਂਝੀ

bob (ਬੌਬ) *n v* ਵਾਲਾਂ ਦੀ ਲਟ, ਪਟੇ, ਲਟਕਣ; ਪਟੇ ਰੱਖਣੇ, ਛਾਂਗਣੇ ਮੂੰਹ ਨਾਲ ਫੜਨਾ, ਉਛਲਣਾ, ਕੁੱਦਣਾ, ਭੁੜਕਣਾ, ਟੱਪਣਾ; ~tail ਦੁਮਕਟੀ; ਦੁਹਾਟਣ (ਪਸ਼ੂ)

bodice ('ਬੌਡਿਸ) *n* ਚੋਲੀ, ਅੰਗੀ, ਕੁੜਤੀ, ਬੰਡੀ

body ('ਬੌਡਿ) *n v* ਸਰੀਰ, ਤਨ, ਦੇਹ, ਪਿੰਡਾ; ਮਨੁੱਖ, ਬੰਦਾ, ਵਿਅਕਤੀ; ਲਾਸ਼, ਲੋਥ, ਲਿਖਤ ਜਾਂ ਮਜ਼ਮੂਨ ਦਾ ਪ੍ਰਧਾਨ ਅੰਗ; ਚੋਲੀ, ਧੜ; ਰੂਪ ਦੇਣਾ, ਆਕਾਰ ਚਿਤਵਨਾ, ਵਜੂਦ ਵਿਚ ਲਿਆਉਣਾ; ~guard ਅੰਗ-ਰੱਖਿਅਕ, ਬਾਡੀਗਾਰਡ

bogie ('ਬਅਉਗਿ) *n* ਬੋਗੀ, ਰੇਲ ਦਾ ਡੱਬਾ

bogle ('ਬਅਉਗਲ) *n* ਭੂਤ, ਪਰੇਤ, ਹਊਆ; ਧੋਖਾ; ਚਿੜੀਆਂ ਨੂੰ ਡਰਾਉਣ ਲਈ ਖੇਤ ਵਿਚ

ਰੱਖੀ ਵਸਤੂ

bogus ('ਬਅਉਗਸ) *a* ਬਣਾਉਟੀ, ਨਕਲੀ, ਜਾਅਲੀ, ਮਿਥਿਆ, ਝੂਠੀ; ਨਿਕੰਮਾ

boil (ਬੋਇਲ) *n v* ਫ਼ੋੜਾ, ਉਠਾਅ; ਉਬਲਣਾ, ਉਬਾਲਣਾ, ਖੋਲਣਾ, ਉਬਾਲਾ ਆਉਣਾ; ਜੋਸ਼ ਖਾਣਾ; ਕੜ੍ਹਨ, ਕਾੜ੍ਹਨ; • ਉਬਾਲਾ, ਉਬਾਲ; ਉਬਾਲ-ਦਰਜਾ; **~er** ਉਬਲਣ ਵਾਲਾ ਵੱਡਾ ਪਤੀਲਾ; ਭੱਠੀ

bold (ਬਅਉਲਡ) *a* ਦਲੇਰ, ਬਹਾਦਰ; ਹਿੰਮਤੀ, ਪਠੱਲੇਦਾਰ, ਜ਼ੋਰਦਾਰ, ਗਤੀਸ਼ੀਲ, ਬੇ-ਬਾਕ; ਸਪਸ਼ਟ; **~ness** ਹੌਂਸਲਾ; ਸਾਹਸ, ਨਿਡਰਤਾ, ਦਲੇਰੀ, ਸਪਸ਼ਟਤਾ

bolt (ਬਅਉਲਟ) *n v* ਚਿਟਕਨੀ; ਜੰਦਰੇ ਦੀ ਛੜ੍ਹ; ਕਾਬਲਿਆਂ ਨਾਲ ਕੱਸਣਾ; ਚਿਟਕਨੀ ਮਾਰਨੀ, ਬੰਦ ਕਰਨਾ (ਦਰਵਾਜ਼ਾ), ਨੱਠ ਜਾਣਾ, ਨਿਗਲ ਜਾਣਾ, ਹੜੱਪ ਕਰ ਜਾਣਾ; **~from the blue** ਦੈਵੀ ਆਪੱਤੀ, ਅਚਿੰਤੇ ਬਾਜ, ਅਚਾਨਕ, ਘਟਨਾ, ਅਚਨਚੇਤ ਮੁਸੀਬਤ

bomb (ਬੌਮ) *n v* ਬੰਬ ਦਾ ਗੋਲਾ; ਬੰਬ ਮਾਰਨਾ, ਬੰਬਾਰੀ ਕਰਨਾ, ਬੰਬ ਚਲਾਉਣਾ, ਗੋਲੇ ਵਰ੍ਹਾਉਣਾ; **~ard** ਬੰਬ ਮਾਰ ਕੇ ਨਾਸ ਕਰਨਾ, ਗੋਲੀਆਂ ਜਾਂ ਗੋਲੇ ਵਰ੍ਹਾਉਣਾ, ਗੋਲਾਬਾਰੀ ਕਰਨੀ; **~er** ਬੰਬਾਰੀ ਕਰਨ ਵਾਲਾ ਜਹਾਜ਼, ਗੋਲਾ ਮਾਰ, ਬੰਬ ਸੁੱਟਣ ਵਾਲਾ ਫੌਜੀ

bonafide ('ਬਅਉਨ'ਅਫ਼ਾਇਡ) *a* ਅਸਲੀ, ਵਾਸਤਵਿਕ, ਪ੍ਰਮਾਣਕ, ਸਦਭਾਵੀ, ਨਿਸ਼ਕਪਟ

bonanza (ਬਅ(ਉ)'ਨੈਂਜ਼ਅ) *n* ਗੱਫਾ

bond (ਬੌਂਡ) *n v* (1) ਸਬੰਧ, ਜੋੜ; (2) ਬੰਨ੍ਹਣ, ਕੈਦ; (3) ਇਕਰਾਰਨਾਮਾ, ਮੁਚੱਲਕਾ, ਲਿਖਤ, ਅਸ਼ਟਾਮ, ਬਾਂਡ; ਬੰਨ੍ਹਣਾ, ਜੋੜਨਾ; ਉਧਾਰ ਲਿਖਤ ਕਰਨਾ; ਚੁੰਗੀ ਲੱਗਣ ਵਾਲੇ ਮਾਲ ਨੂੰ ਮਾਲਗੁਦਾਮ ਵਿਚ ਬੰਦ ਰੱਖਣਾ; **~holder** ਬਾਂਡਧਾਰੀ, ਜਿਸ ਪਾਸ ਇਕਰਾਰਨਾਮੇ ਦੀ ਲਿਖਤ ਹੋਵੇ; **~age** ਬੰਨ੍ਹਣ, ਬੰਦਸ਼, ਬੰਧੇਜ, ਬੰਦੀ, ਪਾਬੰਦੀ, ਅਧੀਨਤਾ, ਦਾਸਤਾ, ਗ਼ੁਲਾਮੀ, ਕੈਦ; **~man** ਦਾਸ, ਗ਼ੁਲਾਮ; **~woman** ਦਾਸੀ

bone (ਬਅਉਨ) *n v* ਹੱਡੀ, ਅਸਥੀ; ਪਸ਼ੂਆਂ ਦੇ ਸੁੱਕੇ ਪਿੰਜਰ, ਅਸਥੀਆਂ, ਕੁੱਲ; (ਅਪ) ਚੋਰੀ ਕਰਨਾ, ਚੁਰਾਉਣਾ; **~head** (ਅਪ) ਮੂਰਖ, ਬੁੱਧੂ, ਮੂਤ੍ਰ ਵਿਅਕਤੀ, ਉੱਲੂ; **~of contention** ਲੜਾਈ-ਝਗੜੇ ਦੀ ਜੜ੍ਹ; **flesh and~** ਹੱਡੀਆਂ ਦੀ ਮੁੱਠ

bonfire ('ਬੌਨ'ਫ਼ਾਇਅ*) *n* ਧੂੰਈ; ਲੋਹੜੀ, ਉਸਤਵ-ਅਗਨੀ, ਪੁਰਬ-ਅਗਨੀ, ਭਾਂਬੜ; ਕੂੜਾ-ਕਰਕਟ ਸਾੜਨ ਲਈ ਬਾਘੀ ਅੱਗ

bonne (ਬੌਨ) *n* ਖਿਡਾਵੀ, ਨੌਕਰਾਨੀ, ਆਯਾ, ਦਾਸੀ

bonnet ('ਬੌਨਿਟ) *n v* ਤੀਵੀਆਂ ਦੀ ਅੰਗਰੇਜ਼ੀ ਟੋਪੀ, ਮਰਦਾਂ ਦੀ ਟੋਪੀ, ਬੋਨਟ; ਸਿਰ ਤੇ ਟੋਪੀ ਰਖਣੀ; ਟੋਪੀ ਨਾਲ ਮੂੰਹ ਢਕਣਾ, ਅੱਖਾਂ ਤੀਕ ਖਿੱਚ ਕੇ ਟੋਪੀ ਲਿਆਉਣੀ

bonny ('ਬੌਨਿ) *a* ਸੋਹਣਾ, ਸੁੰਦਰ; ਅਲਬੇਲਾ

bonus ('ਬਅਉਨਸ) *n* ਬੋਨਸ, ਵਾਧੂ ਨਫ਼ਾ, ਝੁੰਗਾ

bon voyage ('ਬੌਨਵੁਅ'ਯਾਯ਼) *(F)* ਰੱਬ ਰਾਖਾ! ਅਲਵਿਦਾ! ਯਾਤਰਾ ਸਬੰਧੀ ਸ਼ੁਭ ਕਾਮਨਾਵਾਂ

bony ('ਬਅਉਨਿ) *a* ਹੱਡੀ, ਹੱਡੀ ਵਰਗਾ, ਨਿਰਾ ਹੱਡੀਆਂ ਦਾ, ਦੁਬਲਾ-ਪਤਲਾ, ਕਮਜ਼ੋਰ

boo (ਬੂ) *n v int* ਅਨਾੜੀ, ਬੇਸਮਝ, ਮੂਰਖ, ਘਿਰਨਾ ਸੂਚਕ ਸ਼ਬਦ (ਕਹਿਣਾ), ਧਿੱਕ ਕਰਨਾ, ਧਿੱਕਾਰਨਾ, ਛੀ ਛੀ (ਕਰਨਾ), ਉਇ ਉਇ! ਹੂਸ਼ (ਕਰਨਾ)

booby ('ਬੁਬਿ) *n* ਬੁੱਧੂ, ਸਿੰਧੜ, ਡੋਲਾ, ਲੋਲ੍ਹਾ, ਹੰਸ ਜਾਤੀ ਦੀ ਕਿਸਮ ਦਾ ਇਕ ਸਮੁੰਦਰੀ ਪੰਛੀ

boodle ('ਬੂਡਲ) *n* ਭੀੜ, ਜੁੰਡੀ, ਦਲ, ਸਮੂਹ, ਝੁੰਡ

boohoo ('ਬੂਹੂ) *n v* ਕੁਰਲਾਹਟ, ਹਾਲਦੁਹਾਈ, ਗਲਾ ਫਾੜ ਕੇ ਰੋਣ ਦੀ ਧੁਨੀ; ਕੁਰਲਾਉਣਾ, ਉੱਚੀ ਉੱਚੀ ਰੋਣਾ

book (ਬੁਕ) *n v* ਪੁਸਤਕ, ਕਿਤਾਬ, ਪੋਥੀ; ਗ੍ਰੰਥ; ਤਾਲਿਕਾ, ਸੂਚੀ; ਧਾਰਮਕ ਗ੍ਰੰਥ; ਵਹੀ, ਵਹੀ ਖਾਤਾ; ਅੰਕਤ ਕਰਨਾ, ਰਜਿਸਟਰ ਤੇ ਚਾੜ੍ਹਨਾ, ਨਿਯਤ ਕਰਨਾ, ਬੁੱਕ ਕਰਨਾ, ਨਾਂ ਲਿਖ ਲੈਣਾ; ਪੇਸ਼ਗੀ ਨਿਯਤ ਕਰਨਾ; **~binder** ਜਿਲਦਸਾਜ਼; **~binding** ਜਿਲਦਸਾਜ਼ੀ; **~case** ਕਿਤਾਬ-ਦਾਨ, ਕਿਤਾਬਾਂ ਦੀ ਅਲਮਾਰੀ; **~keeper** ਹਿਸਾਬ-ਕਿਤਾਬ ਰੱਖਣ ਵਾਲਾ; **~keeping** ਵਹੀ-ਖਾਤਾ, ਹਿਸਾਬ-ਕਿਤਾਬ; **~let** ਕਿਤਾਬਚਾ; **~of fate** ਕਰਮ-ਲੇਖਾ, ਕਰਮਾਂ ਦੇ ਲੇਖ; **~post** ਬੁਕ ਪੋਸਟ, ਡਾਕ ਰਾਹੀਂ ਛਪੀ ਕਿਤਾਬ ਆਦਿ ਭੇਜਣਾ; **~seller** ਕਿਤਾਬਾਂ ਵੇਚਣ ਵਾਲਾ, ਕੁਤਬ-ਫ਼ਰੋਸ਼; **~shelf** ਕਿਤਾਬਾਂ ਦੀ ਦੁਕਾਨ; **~worm** ਕਿਤਾਬੀ ਕੀੜਾ, ਪੜਾਕੂ; **bring to~** ਗ਼ਲਤੀ ਲਈ ਸਜ਼ਾ ਦੇਣੀ; ਜਵਾਬਦੇਹੀ ਕਰਨੀ; **be in bad ~s** ਕਿਸੇ ਦੀਆਂ ਨਜ਼ਰਾਂ ਵਿਚ ਗਿਰ ਜਾਣਾ; **~ing-clerk** ਟਿਕਟ-ਬਾਬੂ

boom (ਬੂਮ) *n v* ਗਰਜ, ਗਰੂੰਜ, ਤੇਜ਼ੀ, ਚੜ੍ਹਤ, ਬੰਦਰਗਾਹੀ ਰੋਕ, ਗੱਜਣਾ

boon (ਬੂਨ) *n* ਵਰ; ਵਰਦਾਨ, ਸੁਗਾਤ, ਦਾਨ, ਅਸੀਸ; (ਅਪ) ਪ੍ਰਾਰਥਨਾ, ਬੇਨਤੀ

boor (ਬੁਅ*) *n* ਉਜੱਡ, ਗੰਵਾਰ, ਅਸਭਿਅ, ਪੇਂਡੂ, ਅਵੈੜਾ **~ish** ਗੰਵਾਰੀ; ਉਜੱਡ, ਜੰਗਲੀ; **~ishness** ਗੰਵਾਰਪੁਣਾ; ਉਜੱਡਪੁਣਾ

boost (ਬੂਸਟ) *n v* ਵਾਧਾ, ਇਸ਼ਤਿਹਾਰਬਾਜ਼ੀ, ਢੰਡੋਰਾ ਪਿੱਟਣਾ, ਗੁਣ-ਗਾਇਨ ਕਰਨਾ, ਵਧਾ ਚੜ੍ਹਾ ਕੇ ਦੱਸਣਾ, ਵਡਿਆਉਣਾ

booster ('ਬੂਸਟਅ*) *n* ਸ਼ਕਤੀਵਰਧਕ, ਬੂਸਟਰ; ਹੌਸਲੇਰੀ ਦੇਣ ਵਾਲਾ

boot (ਬੂਟ) *n v* ਬੂਟ, (ਠੁੰਡ) ਮਾਰਨਾ, ਜੁੱਤੀ ਪਾਉਣੀ; **~legger** ਸ਼ਰਾਬ ਨੂੰ ਚੋਰੀ ਛਿਪੇ ਲਿਆਉਣ ਤੇ ਵੇਚਣ ਵਾਲਾ; ਸ਼ਰਾਬ ਦਾ ਚੋਰ ਵਪਾਰੀ; **~legging** ਨਾਜਾਇਜ਼ ਸ਼ਰਾਬ ਦਾ ਵਪਾਰ; **~licker** ਚਾਪਲੂਸ, ਖ਼ੁਸ਼ਾਮਦੀ, ਜੁੱਤੀਚੱਟ

booth (ਬੂਦ) *n* ਬੂਥ, ਖੇਖਾ, ਸਟਾਲ, ਅਸਥਾਈ ਨਿਵਾਸ, ਛੱਪਰ, ਅਸਥਾਈ ਦੁਕਾਨ; ਮੇਲੇ ਦੀ ਹੱਟੀ, ਡੇਰਾ

booty ('ਬੂਟਿ) *n* ਲੁੱਟ, ਲੁੱਟ ਦਾ ਮਾਲ; ਲਾਭ, ਫ਼ਾਇਦਾ

border ('ਬੋਡਅ*) *n a v* ਸਰਹੱਦ, ਸੀਮਾ, ਹੱਦ, ਕਿਨਾਰਾ, ਹਾਸ਼ੀਆ; ਹੱਦਬੰਦੀ ਕਰਨੀ, ਵਲਣਾ, ਵਾੜ ਲਗਾਉਣਾ, ਹਾਸ਼ੀਆ ਲਾਉਣਾ, ਕਿਨਾਰੀ ਲਾਉਣੀ, ਮਗਜ਼ੀ ਲਾਉਣੀ; ਮਿਲਾਉਣਾ, ਜੋੜਨਾ, ਲਗਾਉਣਾ, ਸੰਜੋਗ ਕਰਨਾ

bore (ਬੋ:) *v n* (1) ਛੇਕ ਕਰਨਾ, ਵਰਮੇ ਨਾਲ ਮੋਰੀ ਕੱਢਣੀ, ਵਰਮਾਉਣਾ, ਖੋਖਲਾ ਕਰਨਾ, (ਖੂਹ) ਪੁੱਟਣਾ, ਰਾਹ ਬਣਾਉਣਾ; (2) ਤੰਗ ਕਰਨਾ, ਮਗਜ਼-ਚੱਟਣਾ, ਅਕਾਉਣਾ, ਪਰੇਸ਼ਾਨ ਕਰਨਾ; ਛੇਕ, ਮੋਰੀ; ਬੰਦੂਕ ਦੀ ਨਾਲੀ ਦਾ ਵਿਆਸ; ਪਾਣੀ ਦਾ ਪਤਾ ਲਗਾਉਣ ਲਈ ਜ਼ਮੀਨ ਵਿਚ ਕੀਤੀ ਗਈ ਮੋਰੀ; ਖੇਚ-ਤਬੇਲਾ, ਮਗਜ਼-ਚੱਟ, ਤੰਗ ਕਰਨ ਵਾਲਾ, ਬਾਤੂਨੀ; **~dom** ਅਕੇਵਾਂ, ਉਕਤਾਹਟ

boring ('ਬੋਰਿੰਗ) *a* ਨੀਰਸ

borough ('ਬਅੱਰਅ) *n* (ਪੁਰਾਣਾ ਅਰਥ) ਆਬਾਦੀ, ਨਗਰ; (ਸੰਸਦ ਆਦਿ) ਚੋਣ ਹਲਕਾ

borrow ('ਬੌਰਅਉ) *v* ਉਧਾਰ ਲੈਣਾ; ਕਰਜ਼ਾ ਲੈਣਾ; ਮਾਂਗਵਾਂ ਲੈਣਾ; ਅਪਣਾਉਣਾ; **~er** ਉਧਾਰ ਲੈਣ ਵਾਲਾ, ਕਰਜ਼ਦਾਰ

bosom ('ਬੁਜ਼(ਅ)ਮ) *n* ਸੀਨਾ, ਛਾਤੀ, ਦਿਲ; ਅੰਦਰਲਾ ਹਿੱਸਾ; ਆਲਿੰਗਨ; ਖ਼ਿਆਲ

botany ('ਬੌਟਅਨਿ) *n* ਬਨਸਪਤੀ-ਵਿਗਿਆਨ

bote (ਬਅਉਟ) *n* ਮੁਆਵਜ਼ਾ, ਨੁਕਸਾਨ ਦੀ ਤਲਾਫ਼ੀ, ਨੁਕਸਾਨ ਦੀ ਪੂਰਤੀ

bother (ਬੌਦਅ*) *v n* ਔਖਾ ਕਰਨਾ· ਵਿਆਕੁਲ ਕਰਨਾ, ਅਕਾਉਣਾ, ਕਸ਼ਟ ਉਠਾਉਣਾ, ਜਿੱਚ ਕਰਨਾ, ਖਿਝਣਾ; ਝਮੇਲਾ, ਬਖੇੜਾ, ਪਰੇਸ਼ਾਨੀ, ਕਸ਼ਟ, ਜ਼ਹਿਮਤ; **~ation** ਚਿੰਤਾ, ਝੰਜਟ, ਝਮੇਲਾ, ਬਖੇੜਾ, ਅਕੇਵਾਂ ਸਿਰ-ਖਪਾਈ

bottle (ਬੌਟਲ) *n* ਬੋਤਲ, ਸ਼ੀਸ਼ੀ, ਕੁੱਪੀ; ਬੋਤਲ ਵਿਚ ਬੰਦ ਕਰਨਾ; (ਕਿਸੇ ਵਿਅਕਤੀ ਨੂੰ) ਉੱਤੋਂ ਜਾ ਫੜਨਾ, ਝਪਟਣਾ

bottom (ਬੌਟ(ਅ)ਮ) *n a v* ਤਹਿ, ਆਧਾਰ ਪੇਂਦਾ; (ਕੁਰਸੀ ਆਦਿ ਦੀ) ਚਿੱਤੜ, ਆਸਣ; **~neck** ਭੀੜਾ ਰਾਹ; ਰੁਕਾਵਟ, ਅੜਚਣ ਨੀਂਹ, ਗਹਿਰਾਈ; ਸਹਿਣ-ਸ਼ੀਲਤਾ; ਬੁਨਿਆਦੀ, ਆਧਾਰਕ, ਸਭ ਤੋਂ ਹੇਠਲਾ, ਅੰਤਮ, ਅਖੀਰੀ, ਪਿਛਲਾ, ਛੇਕੜਲਾ; ਟਿਕਣਾ, ਆਧਾਰਤ ਕਰਨਾ, ਤਹਿ ਤਕ ਪੁੱਜਣਾ, ਵਾਸਤਵਿਕ ਗੱਲ ਨੂੰ ਲਤਣਾ; **~less** ਨਿਰਾਧਾਰ, ਬੇ-ਬੁਨਿਆਦ, ਬੇਪੇਂਦਾ, ਅਥਾਹ, ਅਗਮ, ਅਸਗਾਹ, ਅਤਲ

bough (ਬਾਓ) *n* ਟਾਹਣੀ, ਡਾਲੀ, ਸ਼ਾਖ਼ਾ, ਲਗਰ; ਜਹਾਜ਼ ਦੇ ਦੋਵੇਂ ਪਾਸਿਆਂ ਦਾ ਹਿੱਸਾ

boulder (ਬਅਉਲਡਅ*) *n* ਗੋਲ ਪੱਥਰ

boulevard (ਬੂਲਅਵ੍ਹਾਡ) *(F) n* ਛਾਂਦਾਰ ਸੜਕ; ਜਰਨੈਲੀ ਸੜਕ, ਸ਼ਾਹ ਰਾਹ

bounce (ਬਾਉਂਸ) *v n adv* ਟੱਪਣਾ, ਉਛਲਣਾ, ਉਭਰਨਾ; ਕੁੜਕਣਾ; ਗੁੱਸੇ ਜਾਂ ਜੋਸ਼ ਵਿਚ ਉਛਲ ਪੈਣਾ; ਡੀਂਗ ਮਾਰਨੀ, ਫੜ ਮਾਰਨੀ; ਟੱਪੀ; ਫੜ੍ਹ, ਅੱਤਕਥਨੀ; **~r** ਗੱਪੀ, ਸ਼ੇਖ਼ੀ-ਖੋਰ, ਝੂਠਾ ਭਾਸ਼ਣ, ਨਾਟਕ ਵਿਚ ਸ਼ੋਰ-ਸ਼ਰਾਬਾ ਬੰਦ ਕਰਾਉਣ ਵਾਲਾ ਪਹਿਰੇਦਾਰ

bound (ਬਾਉਂਡ) *n v* ਹੱਦ, ਸੀਮਾ, ਬੰਨਾ; ਰੁਕਾਵਟ; ਟੱਪੀ, ਟਪੋਸੀ, ਛਲਾਂਗ, ਚੌਕੜੀ, ਉਛਾਲ ਹਦੱਾਂ ਬੰਨ੍ਹਣੀਆਂ, ਪ੍ਰਤੀਬੰਧ ਲਗਾਉਣਾ, ਹੱਦਬੰਦੀ ਕਰਨੀ, ਘੇਰਨਾ, ਸੀਮਾ ਨਿਰਧਾਰਤ ਕਰਨਾ, ਕੁੱਦਣਾ, ਉਛਲਣਾ, ਟੱਪਣਾ, ਛਾਲ ਮਾਰਨਾ, ਚੌਕੜੀ ਮਾਰਨਾ; ਟੱਪਾ ਖਾਣਾ; ਬੰਨ੍ਹਿਆ ਹੋਇਆ, ਮਜਬੂਰ; **out of ~s** ਸੀਮਾ ਤੋਂ ਬਾਹਰ, ਵਿਵਰਜਤ; **~ary** ਸਰਹੱਦ, ਸੀਮਾ, ਹੱਦ ਦੀ ਨਿਸ਼ਾਨੀ ਜਾਂ ਲੀਕ, ਹੱਦ-ਬੰਨਾ, ਕਿਨਾਰਾ, ਵੱਟ, ਵਾੜ

bounteous (ਬਾਉਂਟਿਅਸ) *a* ਦਿਆਲੂ, ਦਾਨੀ, ਸਖੀ, ਉਦਾਰ, ਕਿਰਪਾਲੂ, ਪਰਉਪਕਾਰੀ; **~ness** ਉਦਾਰਤਾ, ਕਿਰਪਾਲਤਾ

bountiful (ਬਾਉਂਟਿਫ਼ੁਲ) *a* ਕਾਫ਼ੀ, ਚੋਖਾ ਸਾਰਾ; ਦਿਆਲੂ, ਖੁੱਲ੍ਹਦਿਲਾ ਕਿਰਪਾਲੂ, ਹਿਤਕਾਰੀ, ਪਰਉਪਕਾਰੀ

bounty (ਬਾਉਂਟਿ) *n* ਦਾਤ, ਬਖ਼ਸ਼ੀਸ਼; ਉਦਾਰਤਾ, ਖੁੱਲ੍ਹ-ਦਿਲੀ, ਸਰਕਾਰੀ ਮਦਦ, ਆਰਥਕ ਸਹਾਇਤਾ

bouquet (ਬੁ'ਕੇਇ) *n* ਗੁਲਦਸਤਾ, ਬੁਕੇ; ਸ਼ਰਾਬ ਦੀ ਸੁਗੰਧੀ

bourgeois ('ਬੋਯ਼ਵਾ) *n a* ਮੱਧਵਰਗੀ ਪਰੰਪਰਾਵਾਦੀ ਵਿਅਕਤੀ, ਮੱਧ ਸ਼੍ਰੇਣੀ ਦਾ ਸਦੱਸ

boutique (ਬੂ'ਟੀਕ) *n* ਫ਼ੈਸ਼ਨਦਾਰ ਕੱਪੜਿਆਂ ਦੀ ਹੱਟੀ, ਬੁਟੀਕ

bow (ਬਅਉ) *n v* (1) ਕਮਾਨ, ਧਨੁਖ, ਕੁਮਾਣੀ; (2) ਅਸਮਾਨੀ ਪੀਂਘ, ਇੰਦਰ ਧਨੁਖ; (3) ਪ੍ਰਣਾਮ, ਨਮਸਕਾਰ, ਸਿਰ-ਝੁਕਾਈ;

bowel

ਨਿਵਣਾ, ਸਿਜਦਾ ਕਰਨ, ਪ੍ਰਣਾਮ ਕਰਨ, ਝੁਕਣਾ, ਸਲਾਮ ਕਰਨਾ, ਕੋਡਾ ਹੋਣਾ, ਸਿਜਦਾ; ~**man** ਤੀਰ-ਅੰਦਾਜ਼

bowel (ਬਾਊਅਲ) *n* ਆਂਦਰ, ਆਂਤੜੀ, (*in pl*) ਆਂਦਰਾਂ, ਆਂਤੜੀਆਂ, ਸਰੀਰ ਦਾ ਅੰਦਰਲਾ ਹਿੱਸ; ਕਿਸੇ ਵਸਤੂ ਦਾ ਅੰਦਰਲਾ ਭਾਗ; ਕੋਮਲ ਭਾਵ, ਦਇਆ, ਤਰਸ

bowl (ਬਅਉਲ) *n* ਕਟੋਰਾ, ਪਿਆਲਾ, ਠੂਠਾ, ਛੰਨਾ, ਚਿੱਪੀ; ਲੱਕੜ ਦੀ ਬਣੀ ਅਜੇਹੀ ਗੇਂਦ; ਡਿੱਕ ਡਿੱਕ ਦੀ ਖੇਡ ਖੇਡਣੀ, (ਕ੍ਰਿਕਟ ਵਿਚ) ਗੇਂਦ ਸੁੱਟਣੀ; ~**er** ਗੇਂਦਸਾਜ਼, ਬਾਉਲਰ; **ing** ਗੇਂਦਬਾਜ਼ੀ

box (ਬੌਕਸ) *n v* (1) ਸੰਦੂਕ, ਸੰਦੂਕੜੀ, ਪੇਟੀ, ਡੱਬਾ, ਤਿਜੋਰੀ, ਬਕਸਾ, (2) ਨਾਟਕਘਰ, ਸ਼ਰਾਬਖ਼ਾਨੇ ਜਾਂ ਹੋਟਲ ਵਿਚ ਬੈਠਣ ਦਾ ਵੱਖਰਾ ਕਮਰਾ, ਮੁਜਰਮ ਦਾ ਕਟਹਿਰਾ; (3) ਘਸੁੰਨ, ਮੁੱਕਾ, ਚਪੇੜ, ਥੱਪੜ, ਤਮਾਚਾ, ਚਾਂਟਾ; ਸੰਦੂਕ ਵਿਚ ਰੱਖਣਾ, (ਅਦਾਲਤ) ਵਿਚ ਕਾਗ਼ਜ਼ ਦਾਖਲ ਕਰਨੇ, ਖ਼ਾਨਿਆਂ ਵਿਚ ਵੰਡਣਾ; ਚਪੇੜ ਮਾਰਨੀ, ਮੁੱਕੇਬਾਜ਼ੀ ਦੀ ਖੇਡ ਵਿਚ ਘਸੁੰਨ ਮਾਰਨੇ; ~**er** ਮੁੱਕੇ-ਬਾਜ਼; ਦਰਮਿਆਨੇ ਕੱਦ ਦਾ ਚਿਕਣੇ ਵਾਲਾਂ ਵਾਲਾ ਇਕ ਕੁੱਤਾ; ~**ing** ਮੁੱਕੇਬਾਜ਼ੀ; ~**box-office** (ਬੌਕਸ-ਔਫਿਸ) (ਥੀਏਟਰ ਦਾ) ਟਿਕਟ-ਘਰ

boy (ਬੌਇ) *n* ਮੁੰਡਾ, ਲੜਕਾ, ਨੱਢਾ; ਛੋਟੂ; ਬੈਰਾ, ਨੌਕਰ; ~**hood** ਲੜਕਪਨ; ~**ish** ਮੁੰਡਿਆਂ ਵਰਗਾ, ਬਚਗਾਨਾ, ਬੱਚਿਆਂ ਵਾਂਗ; ~**ishness** ਸਾਹਸ, ਮੁੰਡਪੁਣਾ, ਲੜਕਪਨ, ਬਚਗਾਨਾਪਨ

boycott ('ਬੌਇਕੌਟ) *v n* ਛੇਕਣਾ, ਭਾਈਚਾਰੇ ਜਾਂ ਬਰਾਦਰੀ ਵਿੱਚੋਂ ਕੱਢ ਦੇਣਾ; ਬਾਈਕਾਟ ਕਰਨਾ; ਬਾਈਕਾਟ; ਕੱਟੀ

bra (ਬਰਾ) *n* (ਬੋਲ) ਅੰਗੀ

brace (ਬਰੇਇਸ) *v n* ਬੰਨ੍ਹਣਾ, ਕਸਣਾ, ਜਕੜਣਾ;

brave

(ਆਪਣੇ ਆਪ ਨੂੰ) ਤਕੜਾ ਜਾਂ ਤਿਆਰ ਕਰਨਾ, ਤੁੰਨਣਾ; ਤਣੀ, ਡੋਰੀ, ਪੱਟੀ, ਪਤਲੂਨ ਦੇ ਗੈਲਸ; ਜਕੜਨ, ਚਿੰਨ੍ਹ (), {} ਜੋੜ; ~**let** ਕੰਗਣ, ਚੂੜੀ; ਹੱਥਕੜੀ

bracket ('ਬਰੈਕਿਟ) *n v* ਕਮਾਨੀ ਦਾ ਨਿਸ਼ਾਨ ਜਿਸ ਵਿਚ ਸ਼ਬਦਾਂ ਜਾਂ ਅੰਕਾਂ ਨੂੰ ਘੇਰਿਆ ਜਾਂਦਾ ਹੈ : (), {}, []; ਚਾਂਦਮਾਰੀ ਵਿਚ ਦੋ ਬਿੰਦੂਆਂ ਦੀ ਦੂਰੀ, ਤੋਪਗੱਡੀ ਦੀ ਟੇਕ, ਥੈਕਟ, ਕਮਾਨੀ, ਦੀਵਾਰਗੀਰ; ਗੁੱਟਬੰਦੀ ਕਰਨਾ

brain (ਬਰੇਇਨ) *n v* ਦਿਮਾਗ਼, ਮਗ਼ਜ਼, ਭੇਜਾ; ਅਕਲ, ਮੱਸ, ਚਿਤ, ਖੁੱਪੀ; ਸਚ ਸ਼ਕਤੀ, ਬੋਧਕ-ਸ਼ਕਤੀ; ਵਿਚਾਰ ਕੇਂਦਰ; ~**less** ਮੂਰਖ, ਮੂੜ੍ਹ, ਬੇਅਕਲ, ਬੁੱਧੂ

brake (ਬਰੇਇਕ) *v n* ਸਣ ਕੁੱਟਣੀ; ਬਰੇਕ ਲਾਉਣੀ; ਪਹੀਏ ਆਦਿ ਨੂੰ ਰੋਕਣਾ, ਰੋਕ ਲਗਾਉਣਾ, ਸਣ ਆਦਿ ਕੁੱਟਣ ਦਾ ਜੰਤਰ, ਦੰਦਲ-ਮੁੰਗਲੀ, ਬਰੇਕ, ਰੋਕ, ਹੋੜਾ, ਅਟਕਨੀ

branch (ਬਰਾਂਚ) *n v* ਟਾਹਣੀ, ਸ਼ਾਖ, ਡਾਲੀ, ਕਿਸੇ ਸਭਾ, ਬੈਂਕ ਆਦਿ ਦੀ ਸ਼ਾਖਾ; ਸ਼ਾਖ ਨਿਕਲਣੀ, ਟਹਿਣੀਆਂ ਵਿਚ ਜਾਂ ਸ਼ਾਖਾਵਾਂ ਵਿਚ ਵੰਡਣਾ; ਵੇਲ ਬੂਟੇ ਕੱਢਣਾ

brand (ਬਰੈਂਡ) *n v* ਮਾਰਕਾ; ਛਾਪ; ਹੁਆਤੀ, ਬਲਦੀ ਲੱਕੜ, ਮਸ਼ਾਲ; ਮਾਰਕਾ ਲਾਉਣ ਵਾਲੀ ਗਰਮ ਛਾਪ; ਕਲੰਕ ਦਾ ਟਿੱਕਾ; ਦਾਗ਼ਣਾ, ਡੰਮ੍ਹਣਾ, ਤੱਤੇ ਲੋਹੇ ਨਾਲ ਨਿਸ਼ਾਨ ਲਾਉਣਾ, ਮਨ ਵਿਚ ਬਿਠਾਉਣਾ, ਪੱਕਾ ਕਰਨਾ, ਕਲੰਕਤ ਕਰਨਾ; ~**new** ਅਤਿ-ਨਵੀਨ, ਨਵਾਂ ਨਿਛੋਹ, ਨਵਾਂ ਨਿਕੋਰ

brass (ਬਰਾਸ) *n* ਪਿੱਤਲ; ਪਿੱਤਲ ਦਾ ਪੱਤਰਾ; ਰੁਪਿਆ ਪੈਸਾ; ਢੀਠਪੁਣਾ, ਬੇ-ਹਯਾਈ

brave (ਬਰੇਇਵ) *a n v* ਦਲੇਰ, ਸੂਰਵੀਰ, ਵਰਿਆਮ, ਸੂਰਾ, ਤਕੜਾ, ਹਿੰਮਤੀ, ਬਹਾਦਰ,

ਸਾਹਸੀ; ਟਾਕਰੇ ਤੇ ਡਟ ਜਾਣਾ

bravo (ਬਰਾ'ਵ਼ੁਅਓ) *int n* (1) ਵਾਹ-ਵਾ! ਘੱਲੇ ਘੱਲੇ! ਸ਼ਾਵਾ! ਸ਼ਾਵਾ! ਸ਼ਾਬਾਸ਼! (2) ਹਤਿਆਰਾ, ਡਾਕੂ, ਪੇਸ਼ਾਵਰ ਖ਼ੂਨੀ

breach (ਬਰੀਚ) *n v* ਉਲੰਘਣ, ਭੰਗ, ਨੇਮ-ਭੰਗ; ਮੋਰੀ, ਪਾੜਾ, ਲੜਾਈ-ਝਗੜਾ, ਵਿਗਾੜ; (ਸਮੁੰਦਰੀ) ਲਹਿਰਾਂ ਦਾ ਟਕਰਾਉਣਾ, ਦਰਾੜ ਪੈਦਾ ਕਰਨਾ; **~of the peace** ਸ਼ਾਂਤੀ-ਭੰਗ, ਦੰਗਾ, ਫ਼ਸਾਦ

bread (ਬਰੈੱਡ) *n* ਰੋਟੀ, ਡਬਲ ਰੋਟੀ; ਰੋਜ਼ੀ, ਉਪਜੀਵਕਾ, ਗੁਜ਼ਾਰਾ; **~and butter** ਰੋਜ਼ੀ-ਰੋਟੀ, ਦਾਲ ਫੁਲਕਾ, ਉਪਜੀਵਕਾ

breadth (ਬਰੈੱਟਥ) *n* ਚੌੜਾਈ, ਬਰ, ਅਰਜ਼ ਪੱਟ (ਕੱਪੜੇ ਦਾ), ਪਾਟ; ਪੇਟ (ਨਦੀ ਦਾ); ਦੂਰੀ, ਵਿੱਥ, ਫ਼ਾਸਲਾ, ਵਿਸਤਾਰ

break (ਬਰੇਇਕ) *v* ਤੋੜਨਾ, ਭੰਨਣਾ, ਟੁੱਟਣਾ, ਭੱਜਣਾ, ਟੋਟੇ ਕਰਨਾ, ਚੂਰ ਚੂਰ ਕਰਨਾ; ਭੰਗ ਕਰਨਾ, ਖੰਡਤ ਕਰਨਾ, ਉਲੰਘਣਾ; ਉਜਾੜਣਾ; ਤੋੜਨਾ, ਰੋਕਣਾ ਜਾਂ ਟੋਕਣਾ, ਪ੍ਰਭਾਵਹੀਣ ਹੋਣਾ; ਤਰੱਟੀ ਚੋਂਜ ਹੋਈ ਜਾਂ ਕਰਨੀ; ਰੁਕਣਾ, ਮੁੱਕ ਜਾਣਾ, ਬੰਦ ਹੋਣਾ; **~able** ਟੁੱਟਣ-ਭੁੱਟਣ ਵਾਲਾ, ਫੁੱਟਲ; ਟੁੱਟਣ-ਭੁੱਟਣ ਵਾਲੀਆਂ ਚੀਜ਼ਾਂ **~down** ਨਾਸ, ਫਹਿ-ਫੇਰੀ, ਰੁਕਾਵਟ, ਠਹਿਰਾਉ, (ਸਿਹਤ ਦੀ) ਖੀਣਤਾ, ਨਿਸੱਤਾ, ਭੰਗ ਹੋ ਜਾਣਾ; ਬੰਦ ਹੋ ਜਾਣਾ; **~news** ਖ਼ਬਰ ਦੇਣਾ; **~open** (ਦਰਵਾਜ਼ਾ) ਤੋੜ ਕੇ ਅੰਦਰ ਆਉਣਾ; **~up** ਕਮਜ਼ੋਰ ਹੋਣਾ, ਨਿਰਬਲ ਹੋਣਾ, ਚੂਰ ਹੋਣਾ, ਥੱਕ-ਟੁੱਟ ਜਾਣਾ, ਖਿੰਡ-ਪੁੰਡ ਜਾਣਾ, ਵਿਵਰਨ, ਅੰਗ, ਨਿਖੇੜ

breakfast ('ਬਰੈੱਕਫ਼ਅਸਟ) *n v* ਨਾਸ਼ਤਾ; ਛਾਹ ਵੇਲਾ; ਨਾਸ਼ਤਾ ਕਰਨਾ ਜਾਂ ਕਰਵਾਉਣਾ, ਛਾਹ ਵੇਲਾ ਖਾਣਾ ਜਾਂ ਖਵਾਉਣਾ

breast (ਬਰੈੱਸਟ) *n v* ਛਾਤੀ, ਹਿੱਕ, ਸੀਨਾ, ਥਣ, ਦੁੱਧੀ; ਹਿਰਦਾ; ਦਿਲ, ਵਲਵਲਾ, ਭਾਵਨਾਵਾਂ; ਸਾਮ੍ਹਣਾ ਕਰਨਾ, ਆਹਮੋ-ਸਾਹਮਣੇ ਹੋਣਾ; ਬਹਿਸ ਕਰਨਾ

breath (ਬਰੈੱਥ) *n* ਸਾਹ, ਦਮ, ਸੁਆਸ, ਪ੍ਰਾਣ, ਹਵਾ ਦਾ ਬੁੱਲ੍ਹਾ; ਫੂਕ; ਮੂੰਹ ਦੀ ਹਵਾੜ, ਫੁਸ-ਫੁਸ; ਛਿਣ, ਪਲ; **~less** ਨਿਰਜੀਵ, ਬੇਜਾਨ, ਬੇਦਮ, ਮਰਿਆ ਹੋਇਆ, ਟੁੱਟੇ ਸਾਹ, ਸਾਹੋ-ਸਾਹ, ਹੌਂਕਦਾ, ਹੁਸੜਵਾਂ

breathe ('ਬਰੀਦ) *v* ਸਾਹ ਲੈਣਾ, ਜੀਊਂਦੇ ਹੋਣਾ, ਜੀਉਣਾ; ਪਰਗਟ ਕਰਨਾ; ਮਹਿਕਣਾ

breech (ਬਰੀਚ) *n v* (ਪੁ) ਚਿੱਤੜ, ਪਿੱਛਾ; ਬੰਦੂਕ, ਤੋਪ ਦਾ ਪਿੱਛਲਾ ਹਿੱਸਾ; ਬਿਰਜਮ ਪਾਉਣੀ

breed (ਬਰੀਡ) *v n* ਜਣਨਾ, (ਸੰਤਾਨ) ਜਮਾਉਣਾ, ਜਨਮ ਦੇਣਾ, ਉਪਜਾਉਣਾ, ਗਰਭਿਤ ਹੋਣਾ, ਉਤਪਾਦਨ ਕਰਨਾ, ਫਲ ਹੋਣਾ, ਪਾਲਣਾ, ਵਧਾਉਣਾ, ਫੈਲਾਉਣਾ; ਸਿਧਾਉਣਾ, ਤਿਆਰ ਕਰਨਾ; ਸਿਖਾਉਣਾ, ਪੜ੍ਹਾਉਣਾ, ਤਿਆਰ ਕਰਨਾ; ਉਠਣਾ, ਨਿਕਲਣਾ; ਨਸਲ, ਜਾਤੀ

breeze (ਬਰੀਜ਼) *n* (1) ਰੁਮਕਦੀ ਹਵਾ, ਮੱਠੀ ਹਵਾ; (2) ਵੱਡ-ਮੱਖੀ, ਮੱਖ; ਇਕ ਵੱਡੀ ਮੱਖੀ; (ਬੋਲ) ਨੋਕ-ਝੋਂਕ

brethren ('ਬਰੈੱਦਰਅਨ) *n* ਭਾਈਬੰਦ, ਧਰਮ ਭਾਈ

brevity (ਬਰੈੱਵ਼ਅਟਿ) *v n* ਸੰਖੇਪਤਾ, ਥੁੜ੍ਹ, ਛੋਟੀ ਅਵਧੀ, ਅਲਪਕਾਲ

bribe (ਬਰਾਇਬ) *n v* ਰਿਸ਼ਵਤ, ਵੱਢੀ; ਵੱਢੀ ਦੇਣੀ ਲੋੜ ਦੇਣਾ, ਮੁੱਠੀ ਗਰਮ ਕਰਨੀ; **~ry** ਰਿਸ਼ਵਤ ਖੋਰੀ

brick (ਬਰਿਕ) *n v* ਇੱਟ, ਇੱਟਾਂ ਨਾਲ ਚਿਣਾਈ ਕਰਨੀ, ਇੱਟਾਂ ਨਾਲ ਭਰ ਦੇਣਾ; **~bat** ਹੋਣਾ,

ਵੀਮ; ਨਿਰਾਦਰੀ; ~kiln ਇੱਟਾਂ ਦਾ ਭੱਠਾ; ~work ਚਿਣਾਈ, ਇੱਟਾਂ ਦੀ ਉਸਾਰੀ

bride (ਬਰਾਇਡ) *n v* ਵਹੁਟੀ, ਲਾੜੀ, ਵਿਆਂਹਦੜ, ਦੁਲਹਨ; ਸੱਜ-ਵਿਆਹੀ (ਨਾਟਕ ਵਿਚ) ਵਹੁਟੀ ਦਾ ਰੂਪ ਧਾਰਨ ਕਰਨ ਜਾਂ ਕਰਾਉਣ; ~groom ਵਰ, ਦੂਲਾ, ਲਾੜਾ, ਨੌਂਗਰ

bridge (ਬਰਿਜ) *n v* ਪੁਲ; ਜਹਾਜ਼ ਦੇ ਅਧਿਕਾਰੀ ਲਈ ਵਿਚਕਾਰਲਾ ਬਣੂਾ, ਸਾਰੰਗੀ ਆਦਿ ਦੀ ਘੋੜੀ, (ਨੱਕ ਦੀ) ਘੋੜੀ, ਝਿਜ, ਤਾਸ਼ ਦੀ ਇਕ ਖੇਡ, ਪੁਲ ਬੰਨ੍ਹਣਾ; ਪੁਲ ਬੰਨ੍ਹ ਕੇ ਪਾਰ ਕਰਨ

bridle ('ਬਰਾਇਡਲ) *n v* ਲਗਾਮ; ਕਾਬੂ, ਰੋਕ; ਲੰਗਰ ਦੀ ਜੰਜੀਰ; ਲਗਾਮ ਪਾਉਣੀ ਜਾਂ ਚਾੜ੍ਹਨੀ, ਕਾਬੂ ਕਰਨਾ, ਰੋਕਣਾ

brief (ਬਰੀਫ਼) *a n v* ਸਾਰ, ਬਿਊਰਾ, ਖੁਲਾਸਾ; ਸੰਖੇਪ, ਸੰਕੁਚਤ, ਮੋਟਾ-ਮੋਟਾ, ਦੋ ਹਰਫ਼ੀ, ਬੋਟੂ-ਚਿਰਾ; (ਕ) ਵਕੀਲਾਂ ਲਈ ਕਿਸੇ ਮੁਕੱਦਮੇ ਦੇ ਮੋਟੇ ਮੋਟੇ ਨੁਕਤੇ; (ਪੋਪ ਵੱਲੋਂ) ਹੁਕਮਨਾਮਾ,

brigade (ਬਰਿ'ਗੇਇਡ) *n v* ਫ਼ੌਜ ਦੀ ਟੁਕੜੀ; ਸੰਗਠਤ ਜੱਥਾ; ਬਰਿਗੇਡ ਬਣਾਉਣਾ; ਪਲਟਣ ਦੇ ਰੂਪ ਵਿਚ ਸੰਗਠਤ ਕਰਨ

brigand ('ਬਰਿਗਅੰਡ) *n* ਡਕੈਤ, ਡਾਕੂ, ਧਾੜਵੀ, ਰਾਹ-ਮਾਰ

bright (ਬਰਾਇਟ) *a adv* ਟਮਕਦਾ, ਲਿਸ਼ਕਦਾ, ਰੋਸ਼ਨ, ਸਾਫ਼, ਭੜਕੀਲਾ, ਚਮਕਦਾਰ, ਹਸਮੁਖ, ਤੇਜਸਵੀ, ਉਜਲ; ਉਤਸ਼ਾਹੀ, ਚੜ੍ਹਦੀਆਂ ਕਲਾਂ ਵਿਚ; ~en ਚਮਕਾਉਣਾ ਜਾਂ ਚਮਕਣਾ, ਲਿਸ਼ਕਾਉਣਾ ਜਾਂ ਲਿਸ਼ਕਣਾ, ਪ੍ਰਕਾਸ਼ਮਾਨ ਕਰਨਾ ਜਾਂ ਹੋਣਾ, ~ness ਖ਼ੁਸ਼ਦਿਲੀ; ਪ੍ਰਕਾਸ਼ ਤੇਜ, ਨਿਰਮਲਤਾ, ਉਜਲਪਣ, ਚਮਕ, ਚਮਕ-ਦਮਕ, ਤੜਕ-ਭੜਕ

brilliance ('ਬਰਿਲਯੰਸ) *n* ਚਮਕ, ਦਮਕ, ਛਬ, ਆਭਾ, ਝਲਕ, ਪ੍ਰਤਿਭਾ

brilliant ('ਬਰਿਲਯੰਟ) *a n* ਚਮਕੀਲਾ, ਭੜਕੀਲਾ, ਚਮਕਦਾਰ, ਰੋਸ਼ਨ; ਬੁੱਧੀਮਾਨ ਹਸਮੁਖ; ਪ੍ਰਸਿੱਧ, ਸ਼ੋਖ,

brindled ('ਬਰਿੰਡਲਡ) *a* ਚਿਤ-ਕਬਰਾ, ਡੱਬ-ਖੜੱਬਾ

bring (ਬਰਿੰਗ) *v* ਲਿਆਉਣਾ, ਲੈ ਜਾਣਾ, ਢੋਣਾ, ਉਪਜਾਉਣਾ, ਪੇਸ਼ ਕਰਨਾ, ਸਾਮ੍ਹਣੇ ਰੱਖਣਾ, ਪ੍ਰਸਤੁਤ ਕਰਨਾ; ~about ਕਾਰਨ ਹੋਣਾ, (ਨੂੰ) ਵਜੂਦ ਵਿਚ ਲਿਆਉਣਾ; (ਜਹਾਜ਼ ਨੂੰ) ਮੋੜਨਾ; ~down ਮਾਨ ਘਟਾਉਣਾ, (ਕੀਮਤ) ਘੱਟ ਕਰਨਾ, ਮਾਰ ਮੁਕਾਉਣਾ, ਸੱਟ ਮਾਰਨੀ, ਸਜ਼ਾ ਦਿਵਾਉਣੀ; ~forth ਜਣਨਾ, ਪੈਦਾ ਕਰਨਾ, ਸਾਮ੍ਹਣੇ ਲਿਆਉਣਾ; ~forward ਅੱਗੇ ਲਿਆਉਣਾ, (ਕਿਤਾਬ ਦੇ) ਅਗਲੇ ਸਫ਼ੇ ਉੱਤੇ ਲਿਆਉਣਾ; ~home to ਸਿੱਧ ਕਰਨਾ, ਪੂਰੀ ਤਰ੍ਹਾਂ ਸਮਝਾ ਦੇਣਾ, ਦਿਮਾਗ ਵਿਚ ਬਿਠਾ ਦੇਣਾ; ~off ਸਫਲ ਬਣਾਉਣਾ; ਬਚਾ ਲਿਆਉਣਾ; ~out (ਪੁਸਤਕ ਦਾ) ਪ੍ਰਕਾਸ਼ਤ ਕਰਨਾ; ਕੱਢਣਾ, ਨਸ਼ਰ ਕਰਨਾ, ਸਾਫ਼ ਸਾਫ਼ ਪਰਗਟ ਕਰਨਾ, ਭਾਂਡਾ ਫੋੜਨਾ; ~up ਉਗਾਉਣਾ, ਪਾਲਣਾ, ਪੋਸਣਾ, ਸਿਖਾਉਣਾ; ਮੁਕੱਦਮਾ ਚਲਾਉਣਾ

brinjal ('ਬਰਿੰਜਲ) *n* ਬੈਂਗਣ, ਵਤਾਊਂ

brink (ਬਰਿੰਕ) *n* ਕੰਢਾ; ਸਿਰਾ

brisk (ਬਰਿਸਕ) *a v* ਤੇਜ਼, ਕਿਰਿਆਸ਼ੀਲ, ਚੁਸਤ, ਛੁਹਲਾ, ਫੁਰਤੀਲਾ, ਚਲਾਕ, ਜੋਸ਼ ਦੇਣ ਵਾਲਾ; ਤੇਜ਼ ਹੋਣਾ ਜਾਂ ਕਰਨਾ, ਫੁਰਤੀਲਾ ਹੋਣਾ ਜਾਂ ਕਰਨਾ; ~ness ਸਫੁਰਤੀ, ਤੀਬਰਤਾ, ਤੇਜ਼ੀ, ਚੁਸਤੀ, ਫੁਰਤੀ

bristle ('ਬਰਿਸਲ) *n v* ਕਰੜਾ ਵਾਲ, ਮੋਟਾ ਜਾਂ ਖਰਵਾ ਵਾਲ, ਸੂਰ ਦਾ ਵਾਲ; ਕਰੜਾ ਜਾਂ ਖਰਵਾ

ਹੋ ਜਾਣਾ, ਗੁੱਸੇ ਨਾਲ ਲੂੰ ਖੜ੍ਹੇ ਹੋ ਜਾਣੇ, ਤਾਅ ਵਿਚ ਆ ਜਾਣਾ

British ('ਬਰਿਟਿਸ਼) *a* ਬਰਤਾਨਵੀ, ਬਰਤਾਨੀਆ ਦਾ, ਅੰਗਰੇਜ਼ਾਂ ਦਾ; ~**er** ਬਰਤਾਨੀਆ ਦਾ ਵਸਨੀਕ

brittle ('ਬਰਿਟਲ) *a* ਭੁਰਭੁਰਾ, ਕੁੜਕਵਾਂ, ਕੁੜਕੀਲਾ, ਕਮਜ਼ੋਰ, ਮਾੜਾ, ਟੁੱਟ ਜਾਣ ਵਾਲਾ, ਨਾਸ਼ਵਾਨ; ~**ness** ਭੁਰਭੁਰਾਪਣ, ਥੋਲਰਕਪਣ, ਕਮਜ਼ੋਰੀ

broad (ਬਰੋਡ) *a n adv* ਚੌੜਾ, ਖੁੱਲ੍ਹਾ, ਮੋਕਲਾ, ਵਿਸਤਰਤ; ਪੂਰਨ, ਭਰਿਆ; ਸਪੱਸ਼ਟ; ਚੌੜਾ ਹਿੱਸਾ, ਖਿਲਾਰ; ਚੌੜਾਈ ਦੇ ਰੁਖ, ਚੌੜੇ ਦਾਅ, ਖੁੱਲ੍ਹ-ਦਿਲਾ, ਉਦਾਰ; ~**based** ਚੌੜੇ ਆਧਾਰ ਤੇ, ਉਦਾਰ (ਦਿਲ ਦਾ), ਜਿਸਦੇ ਵਿਚ ਸੰਕੀਰਣਤਾ ਨਹੀਂ ਹੈ; ~**daylight** ਦਿਨਦੀਵੀਂ, ਦਿਨ ਦਿਹਾੜੇ; ~**facts** ਮੋਟੀਆਂ ਮੋਟੀਆਂ ਗੱਲਾਂ ਦਾ ਤੱਥ; ~**minded** ਖੁੱਲ੍ਹ-ਦਿਲਾ, ਉਦਾਰ, ਫਰਾਖ਼ ਦਿਲ; ~**ly** ਮੋਟੇ ਤੌਰ ਤੇ

broadcast ('ਬਰੋਡਕਾਸਟ) *n v* ਪ੍ਰਸਾਰਤ ਕਰਨਾ; ਖ਼ਬਰ ਫੈਲਾਉਣਾ ਮਸ਼ਹੂਰ ਕਰਨਾ; ਪ੍ਰਸਾਰਨ, ਪ੍ਰਸਾਰ, ਧੁੱਡਕਾਸਟ; ਖਿਲਾਰਨਾ

brochure (ਬਰਅਉਸ਼ਅ*) *n* ਕਿਤਾਬਚਾ, ਚੁਵਰਕੀ, ਪੈਂਫ਼ਲਿਟ, ਬਰੋਸ਼ਰ

brokage ('ਬਰਉਕਿਜ) *n* ਦਲਾਲੀ, ਆੜ੍ਹਤ

broker ('ਬਰਅਉਕਅ*) ਦਲਾਲ, ਆੜ੍ਹਤੀ, ਏਜੰਟ; ਕਬਾੜੀਆ

bronze ('ਬਰੌਂਜ਼) *n a v* ਕਾਂਸਾ, ਕਹਿਆ, ਕਾਂਸੀ; ਕਾਂਸੇ ਦਾ, ਕਾਂਸੇ ਵਰਗਾ; ਕਾਂਸੇ ਵਰਗਾ ਬਣਾਉਣਾ, ਕਾਂਸੇ ਦਾ ਰੰਗ ਦੇਣਾ, ਭੂਰਾ ਤੇ ਲਾਲ ਕਰਨਾ

brook (ਬਰੁਕ) *n v* ਨਾਲਾ, ਛੋਟੀ ਨਦੀ, ਚੋਅ, ਵੇਈਂ; ਬਰਦਾਸ਼ਤ ਕਰਨਾ, ਸਹਿਣਾ, ਸਹਿ ਜਾਣਾ, ਸਹਾਰਨਾ, ਝੱਲਣਾ, ਜਰ ਜਾਣਾ; ~**let** ਛੋਟਾ ਨਾਲਾ, ਵੇਈਂ

broom (ਬਰੂਮ) *n* ਬੁਹਾਰੀ, ਝਾੜੂ; ਬੁਹਕਰ ਮਾਰਨੀ ਜਾਂ ਦੇਣੀ, ਮਾਂਜਾ ਮਾਰਨਾ

brothel ('ਬਰੌਥਲ) *n* ਚਕਲਾ, ਕੰਜਰਖ਼ਾਨਾ, ਕੋਠਾ

brother ('ਬਰਅੱਦਅ*) *n* ਭਰਾ, ਭਾਈ, ਵੀਰ, ਸਾਥੀ, ਗੁੱਟੂ, ਮਿੱਤਰ, ਸਹਿਯੋਗੀ, ਧਰਮ ਭਰਾ, ਦੇਸ ਵਾਸੀ, ਹਮਵਤਨ; ~**in-law** ਜੀਜਾ, ਭਣਵੱਈਆ, ਸਾਲਾ; ਜੇਠ, ਦਿਉਰ; ਸਾਂਢੂ ਨਨਾਣਵੱਈਆ; **half**-ਮਤੇਆ ਭਰਾ; ~**hood** ਭਾਈਚਾਰਾ, ਭਾਈਬੰਦੀ, ਬਰਦਰੀ, ਸ਼ਰੀਕਾ

brown (ਬਰਾਉਨ) *a n v* ਭੂਰਾ, ਖ਼ਾਕੀ, ਬਦਾਮੀ, ਸਾਂਉਲਾ, ਤਾਂਬੇ ਦਾ ਸਿੱਕਾ; ਭੂਰੇ ਜਾਂ ਖ਼ਾਕੀ ਕੱਪੜੇ; ਭੂਰਾ ਰੋਗਨ; ਭੂਰਾ ਕਰਨਾ

bruise (ਬਰੂਜ਼) *n v* ਰਗੜ, ਝਰੀਟ, ਘਸਰ, ਲਾਗਾ, ਸੱਟ ਲੱਗਣ ਕਰਕੇ ਪਿਆ ਨੀਲ, ਦਾਗ਼; ਰਗੜ ਮਾਰਨੀ, ਝਰੀਟ ਪੈਣੀ; ਘਸਰ ਲੱਗਾਉਣੀ; ਦਰੜ ਦੇਣਾ, ਲਿਤਾੜ ਦੇਣਾ, ਚੂਰ ਕਰ ਦੇਣਾ, ਫੇਹ ਸੁੱਟਣਾ; ਲੱਕੜੀ ਜਾਂ ਧਾਤ ਉੱਤੇ ਨਿਸ਼ਾਨ ਬਣਾਉਣਾ; ~**r** ਇਨਾਮੀ, ਮੁਕਾਬਲਾ ਕਰਨ ਵਾਲਾ, ਇਨਾਮੀ ਦੰਗਲ ਲੜਨ ਵਾਲਾ, ਪੇਸ਼ਾਵਰ ਮੁੱਕੇਬਾਜ਼, ਪਹਿਲਵਾਨ, ਮੱਲ

brush (ਬਰਅੱਸ਼) *v n* ਬੁਰਸ਼ ਕਰਨਾ, ਬੁਰਸ਼ ਨਾਲ ਸਾਫ਼ ਕਰਨਾ ਜਾਂ ਚਮਕਾਉਣਾ; ਪੂੰਝਣਾ, ਸੰਵਾਰਨਾ, ਝਾੜਨਾ; ਝਾੜ ਬੁਰਸ਼, ਕੁਚੀ, ਜੁਲਾਹੇ ਦਾ ਕੁੱਚ, ਚਿਤਰਕਾਰ ਦੀ ਵਾਲਾਂ ਵਾਲੀ ਲੇਖਣੀ

brutal ('ਬਰੂਟਲ) *a* ਜੰਗਲੀ, ਵਹਿਸ਼ੀ, ਬੇਰਹਿਮ, ਕਰੂਰ, ਅਤਿਆਚਾਰੀ, ਜ਼ਾਲਮ; ~**ity** ਨਿਰਦਇਤਾ, ਦਰਿੰਦਗੀ, ਜ਼ੁਲਮ, ਅਤਿਆਚਾਰ, ਕਰੂਰਤਾ

brute (ਬਰੂਟ) *n* ਨਿਰਦਈ ਵਿਅਕਤੀ; ਦਰਿੰਦਾ, ਕਰੂਰ

bubble ('ਬਅੱਬਲ) *n v* ਬੁਲਬੁਲਾ; ਉਬਾਲ, ਧੋਖਾ,

ਪਰਪੰਚ, ਖ਼ਿਆਲੀ ਮਹਿਲ; ਬੁਲਬੁਲੇ ਨਿਕਲਣੇ; ਬੁਲਬੁਲੀਆਂ ਪਾਉਣੀਆਂ, ਉੱਭਲਣਾ

buck (ਬਅੱਕ) *n v* ਚਿਕਾਰਾ, ਚੀਤਲ; ਹਿਰਨ; ਮਰਦ; ਬਾਂਕਾ, ਛੈਲ ਮਨੁੱਖ; ਹਰਨ-ਚੌਕੜੀ ਭਰਨੀ, (ਘੋੜੇ ਦਾ) ਸੀਖ਼ ਪਾ ਹੋਣਾ; ਧੁੱਸ ਮਾਰਨੀ; ਉਤਸ਼ਾਹਤ ਹੋਣਾ, ਖ਼ੁਸ਼ੀ ਨਾਲ ਭਰ ਜਾਣਾ, ਜੋਸ਼ ਵਿਚ ਆਉਣਾ; ~up ਹੌਸਲਾ ਵਧਾਉਣਾ, ਜੋਸ਼ ਦਿਵਾਉਣਾ, ਹੱਲਾਸ਼ੇਰੀ ਦੇਣੀ

bucket ('ਬਅੱਕਿਟ) *n v* ਬਾਲਟੀ, ਡੋਲ; ਡੋਲ ਨਾਲ ਪਾਣੀ ਕੱਢਣਾ; ਘੋੜਾ ਸਰਪਟ ਦੁੜਾਉਣਾ; ਬੇੜੀ ਨੂੰ ਕਾਹਲੀ ਚੱਪੂ ਨਾਲ ਚਲਾਉਣਾ; **kick the~** ਮਰ ਜਾਣਾ

buckle ('ਬਅੱਕਲ) *n v* ਬਕਸੂਆ; ਬਕਲ; ਬਕਸੂਆ ਲਾਉਣਾ, ਬਕਸੂਏ ਨਾਲ ਜੋੜਨਾ

buckram ('ਬਅੱਕਰਅਮ) *n a v* ਬੁਕਰਮ, ਮੋਟਾ ਤੇ ਕਰੜਾ ਕੱਪੜਾ, ਸਖ਼ਤ ਪਾਬੰਦੀ (ਵਰਤਾਉ ਵਿਹਾਰ ਵਿਚ) ਕਰੜਾਈ, ਨੇਮਬੱਧਤਾ, ਆਕੜ, ਰੁਖਾਈ; ਪੀੜਾ, ਸਖ਼ਤ, ਪੱਕਾ

bud (ਬਅੱਡ) *n v* ਕਲੀ, ਡੋਡੀ, ਕਲੀਆਂ ਨਿਕਲਣੀਆਂ, ਕਰੁੰਬਲਾਂ ਫੁੱਟਣੀਆਂ; ਵਿਕਾਸ ਦਾ ਆਰੰਭ ਕਰਨਾ, (ਬਾਗ਼ਬਾਨੀ) ਕਲਮ ਲਾਉਣੀ; *nip in the~* ਆਰੰਭ ਵਿਚ ਹੀ ਦਬਾ ਦੇਣਾ

budge (ਬਅੱਜ) *v* ਹਟਣਾ, ਖਿਸਕਣਾ, ਟਲਣਾ, ਸਰਕਣਾ; ਹਟਾਉਣਾ ਸਰਕਾਉਣਾ, ਟਾਲਣਾ

budget ('ਬਅੱਜਿਟ) *n* ਆਮਦਨੀ ਤੇ ਖ਼ਰਚ ਦਾ ਬਿਓਰਾ, ਆਮਦਨੀ-ਖ਼ਰਚ ਦਾ ਅਨੁਮਾਨ, ਸਾਲਾਨਾ ਆਮਦਨੀ-ਖ਼ਰਚ ਦਾ ਅਨੁਮਾਨਤ ਬਿਓਰਾ, ਬਜਟ; ਕਿਸੇ ਝੋਲੇ ਜਾਂ ਗੰਢ ਵਿਚ ਪਾਈਆਂ ਵਸਤੂਆਂ; **~esimate** ਬਜਟ-ਅਨੁਮਾਨ

buffalo ('ਬਅੱਫ਼ਅਲਏੁ) *n* ਸੈਂਹ, ਮੱਝ, ਸੰਢਾ, ਸੈਂਹਾਂ

buffer ('ਬਅੱਫ਼ਅ*) ਪੁਰਾਤਨਵਾਦੀ, ਦਕਿਆਨੂਸੀ, ਆਲਸੀ ਆਦਮੀ; **~state** ਦੋ ਵਿਰੋਧੀ ਰਾਜਾਂ ਦਰਮਿਆਨ ਇਕ ਨਿਰਪੱਖ ਦੇਸ

buffet ('ਬਅੱਫ਼ਿਟ) *n v* ਘਸੁੰਨ, ਮੁੱਕੀ; ਸੱਟ; ਲਹਿਰਾਂ ਦਾ ਥਪੇੜਾ; (ਚੀਨੀ ਦੇ) ਭਾਂਡਿਆਂ ਦੀ ਅਲਮਾਰੀ; ਮੇਜ਼ ਤੇ ਰੱਖੇ ਹੋਏ ਖਾਣੇ ਨੂੰ ਆਪਣੀ ਮਰਜ਼ੀ ਨਾਲ ਲੈਣਾ; ਘਸੁੰਨ ਮਾਰਨਾ, ਘਸੁੰਨ ਵੱਜਣਾ

buffoon (ਬਅ'ਫ਼ੂਨ) *n v* ਵਿਦੂਸ਼ਕ, ਨਕਲੀਆ, ਭੰਡ; ਮਸਖ਼ਰਾ; ਮਸ਼ਕਰੀ ਕਰਨੀ, ਮਖੌਲ ਕਰਨਾ, ਨਕਲ ਲਾਹੁਣੀ, ਹਾਸਾ ਕਰਨਾ; **~ery** ਹਾਸਾ-ਠੱਠਾ, ਮਖੌਲਬਾਜ਼ੀ, ਭੰਡਬਾਜ਼ੀ

bug (ਬਅੱਗ) *n* ਖਟਮਲ; ਖਬਤ, ਖ਼ੁਫ਼ੀਆ ਮਾਈਕ੍ਰੋਫ਼ੋਨ

bugger ('ਬਅੱਗਅ*) *n* (ਗਾਲ੍ਹ ਵਜੋਂ) ਮੁੰਡੇਬਾਜ਼, ਸ਼ੈਤਾਨ, ਲੁੱਚਾ, ਬਦਮਾਸ਼

buggy ('ਬਅੱਗਿ) *n a* (1) ਬੱਘੀ, ਪਾਲਕੀ, ਗੱਡੀ; (2) ਖਟਮਲ ਵਾਲਾ, ਮਾਠੂਆਂ ਭਰਿਆ

bugle ('ਬਯੂਗਲ) *n v* ਬਿਗਲ; (ਵਜਾਉਣਾ) ਬਿਗਲ ਵਜਾ ਕੇ ਸਾਵਧਾਨ ਕਰਨਾ

build (ਬਿਲਡ) *n v* ਬਣਤਰ, ਨਿਰਮਾਣ-ਸ਼ੈਲੀ, ਨਿਰਮਾਣ, ਕਾਠੀ; ਬਣਾਉਣਾ, ਰਚਣਾ, ਨਿਰਮਾਣ ਕਰਨਾ, ਘਰ ਬਣਾਉਣਾ; **~er** ਰਾਜ, ਉਸਾਰੀ ਦੇ ਕੰਮ ਦਾ ਮਾਹਰ, ਉਸਰੱਈਆ, ਨਿਰਮਾਤਾ

building ('ਬਿਲਡਿਙ) *n* ਇਮਾਰਤ, ਭਵਨ, ਮਕਾਨ, ਘਰ; ਉਸਾਰੀ, ਨਿਰਮਾਣ

bulb (ਬਅੱਲਬ) *n v* ਬਲਬ, ਬਿਜਲੀ ਦਾ ਲਾਟੂ; ਗੰਢੀ, ਗੰਢ ਬੱਝਣੀ; ਗੰਢੇ ਵਰਗਾ ਫੁੱਲਾ ਹੋਣਾ, ਖੁੰਡੀ ਬਣਨੀ

bulge (ਬਅੱਲਜ) *v n* ਉੱਭਰਨਾ, ਫੁੱਲਣਾ, ਸੁੱਜਣਾ; ਅਗਾਂਹ ਵਧੇ ਹੋਣਾ; ਫੁਲਾਉਣਾ, ਵਧਾਉਣਾ,

bulginess

ਪਸਾਰਨਾ; ਉਭਾਰ, ਕੁੱਬ, ਬਾਹਰ ਨੂੰ ਵਧਿਆ ਹਿੱਸਾ, ਸੋਜ, ਫੁਲਾਉ

bulginess (ਬਅੱਲਜਿਨਿਸ) *n* ਉਭਾਰ, ਫੁਲਾਹਟ

bulk (ਬਅੱਲਕ) *n v* ਮਿਕਦਾਰ ਮਾਤਰਾ; ਭਾਰ, ਵਿਸਤਾਰ, ਜਹਾਜ਼ ਦਾ ਭਾਰ, ਖੇਪ, ਸਮੂਹ; ਢੇਰ; ਡੀਲ, ਕੱਦ-ਬੁੱਤ, ਆਕਾਰ; ਅਧਿਕ ਭਾਗ, ਅਧਿਕ ਮਾਤਰਾ, ਵੱਡਾ ਆਕਾਰ, ਭਾਰਾ ਸਰੀਰ; in ~ਭਾਰੀ ਮਾਤਰਾ ਵਿਚ; ~y ਵੱਡੇ ਆਕਾਰ ਵਾਲਾ, ਭਾਰਾ, ਵਿਸ਼ਾਲ, ਵੱਡਾ, ਮੋਟਾ-ਤਾਜ਼ਾ

bull (ਬੁਲ) *n* ਸਾਨ੍ਹ, ਬਲਦ, ਢੱਗਾ; ਵ੍ਹੇਲ ਮੱਛੀ ਦਾ ਨਰ; ਤੇਜ਼ੜੀਆ, ਸੱਟੇਬਾਜ਼, ਭਾਅ ਤੇਜ਼ ਕਰਨ ਵਾਲਾ; ਪੋਪ ਦਾ ਫ਼ਰਮਾਨ, ਕੀਮਤਾਂ ਚੜ੍ਹਾਉਣਾ, ਸੱਟੇ ਵਿਚ ਭਾਅ ਚੜ੍ਹਾਉਣੇ ~**bitch** ਜੁਆਨ ਕੁੱਤੀ; ~**calf** ਵੱਛਾ, ਵਹਿੜਕਾ; ਸਿੰਘੜਾ, ਸਿਪਾਰ; ~**dog** ਬੁਲੀ ਕੁੱਤਾ, ਇਕ ਵੱਡੇ ਸਿਰ ਵਾਲਾ ਕੁੱਤਾ; ਜ਼ਿੱਦੀ ਮਨੁੱਖ, ਗਲ ਪੈਣ ਵਾਲਾ ਲੜਾਕਾ, ਆਦਮੀ; ~**dozer** ਭੋਂ ਪੱਧਰੀ ਕਰਨ ਵਾਲੀ ਮਸ਼ੀਨ; ~**headed** ਹਠੀ, ਜ਼ਿੱਦੀ

bullet (ਬੁਲਿਟ) *n* ਬੰਦੂਕ, ਪਿਸਤੌਲ, ਮਸ਼ੀਨਗਨ ਆਦਿ ਦੀ ਗੋਲੀ; ~**proof** ਜਿਸ ਉੱਤੇ ਗੋਲੀ ਅਸਰ ਨਾ ਕਰ ਸਕੇ

bulletin (ਬੁਲਅਟਿਨ) *n* ਸੂਚਨਾ ਪੱਤਰ, ਸਰਕਾਰੀ ਸੂਚਨਾ, ਮਹੱਤਵ ਪੂਰਨ ਘਟਨਾਵਾਂ ਬਾਰੇ ਜਾਂ ਕਿਸੇ ਰੋਗੀ ਦੀ ਹਾਲਤ ਬਾਰੇ ਸੂਚਨਾ, ਬੁਲੇਟਿਨ

bullion (ਬੁਲਯਅਨ) *n a* ਸ਼ੁੱਧ ਸੋਨਾ ਜਾਂ ਚਾਂਦੀ; ਸੋਨੇ ਜਾਂ ਚਾਂਦੀ ਦੀ ਇੱਟ; ਧਾਤੀ ਮੁਦਰਾ; ਸਰਾਫ਼ਾ

bullock (ਬੁਲਅਕ) *n* ਬਲਦ, ਢੱਗਾ, ਬੋਲਦ

bully (ਬੁਲਿ) *n v* ਧੌਂਸਬਾਜ਼ ਗੁੰਡਾ, ਲੜਾਕਾ, ਦੱਲਾ, ਭੜੂਆ, ਧੱਕੇਸ਼ਾਹੀ ਕਰਨ ਵਾਲਾ; ਗੁੰਡਾਗਰਦੀ ਕਰਨੀ, ਧੱਕੇਸ਼ਾਹੀ ਕਰਨੀ, ਡਰਾਉਣਾ, ਧਮਕਾਉਣਾ, ਧੌਂਸ ਜਮਾਉਣੀ

384

burden

bumper ('ਬਅੱਮਪਅ*) *n* ਟੱਕਰ, ਰੋਕ; ਬੰਪਰ, ਮੋਟਰ ਦੇ ਅੱਗੇ ਲੱਗੀ ਟੱਕਰ-ਰੋਕ ਫੱਟੀ; ਬੁਝੁਕਣ ਵਾਲਾ; ~**crop** ਭਰਵੀਂ ਫ਼ਸਲ

bun (ਬਅੱਨ) *n* ਬੰਦ, ਮਿੱਠੀ ਡਬਲ ਰੋਟੀ; ਜਲੇਬੀ ਜੁੜ੍ਹਾ; ਸਹੇ ਦੀ ਪੂਛ

bunch ('ਬਅੰਚ) *n v* ਗੁੱਛਾ, ਝੁੰਡ, ਗੁੱਟ, ਸਮੂਹ, ਜੱਥਾ, ਟੋਲੀ; ਗੁੱਛਾ ਬਣਾਉਣਾ; ਕੱਪੜੇ ਸੰਭਾਲਣੇ ਜਾਂ ਇਕੱਠੇ ਕਰਨੇ; ਇਕੱਠੇ ਹੋਣਾ, ਜੁੜਨਾ; ~**of fives** ਮੁੱਠੀ, ਪੰਜਾ; ~**of flowers** ਗੁਲਦਸਤਾ

bundle ('ਬਅੰਡਲ) *n v* ਗੰਢ, ਪੰਡ, ਗੰਢੜੀ, ਪੋਟਲੀ, ਬੰਡਲ, ਬੱਘਾ; ਗੰਢ ਬੰਨ੍ਹਣੀ, ਪੁਲਾ ਬੰਨ੍ਹਣਾ; ਇਕ ਥਾਂ ਇਕੱਠੇ ਕਰਕੇ ਬੰਨ੍ਹਣਾ

bungalow ('ਬਅੱਨ੍ਗਰਅਲਅਉ) *n* ਬੰਗਲਾ, ਕੋਠੀ, ਮਹਿਮਾਨ-ਘਰ

bungle ('ਬਅੱਨ੍ਗਲ) *n v* ਖ਼ਰਾਬੀ, ਵਿਗਾੜ, ਵੱਡੀ ਭੁੱਲ; ਅਨਾੜੀਪਨ; ਕੰਮ ਵਿਗਾੜਨਾ, ਗੜਬੜ ਕਰਨਾ, ਚੋਂਚ-ਰੁਪੱਟ ਕਰਨਾ; ~**r** ਅਨਾੜੀ, ਵਿਗਾੜੂ, ਬੁੱਧੂ, ਚੋਂਚ-ਚਾਨਲ, ਕੁਚੱਜਾ

bungling ('ਬਅੱਨ੍ਗਲਿਙ) *n* ਗੜਬੜ, ਗੋਲ-ਮਾਲ

buoy (ਬੋਇ) *n v* ਤਰਦਾ ਪੀਪਾ ਜਾਂ ਢੋਲ, ਤਰਿੰਦਾ; ਤਰਦੇ ਰਖਣਾ; ਸੰਭਾਲਣਾ, ਹੌਸਲਾ ਵਧਾਉਣਾ; ~**ancy** ਤੈਰਨ ਦੀ ਸ਼ਕਤੀ, ਤਰਨਸ਼ੀਲਤਾ; ਲਚਕ; ਉਤਸ਼ਾਹ, ਚਾਅ, ਉਮੰਗ, ਤਰੰਗ; ~**ant** ਤਰਨਯੋਗ, ਤਰਨਸ਼ੀਲ, ਤਰਨਹਾਰ; ਹੌਲਾ, ਛੱਲਾ, ਲਚਕਦਾਰ, ਚੁਸਤ, ਉੱਭਰਵਾਂ, ਮੌਜੀ, ਪ੍ਰਸੰਨਚਿੱਤ, ਖ਼ੁਸ਼ਦਿਲ

burden ('ਬਅːਡਨ) *n v* ਭਾਰ; ਬੋਝ, ਵਜ਼ਨ, ਜ਼ੁੰਮੇਵਾਰੀ ਰਾਗ ਜਾਂ ਗੀਤ ਦੀ ਟੇਕ; ਭਾਸ਼ਨ ਆਦਿ ਦਾ ਕੇਂਦਰੀ ਭਾਵ; ਭਾਰ ਲੱਦਣਾ, ਭਾਰ ਪਾਉਣਾ, ਦਬਾਉਣਾ, ਜ਼ੁੰਮੇਵਾਰੀ ਪਾਉਣਾ, ਦੁਖੀ ਕਰਨਾ, ਕਸ਼ਟ ਦੇਣਾ

bureau ('ਬਯੂਅਰਅਉ) *n* (*pl~x*) ਦਫ਼ਤਰ, ਸਰਕਾਰੀ ਮਹਿਕਮਾ, ਰਾਜਕੀ ਵਿਭਾਗ, ਕੇਂਦਰ, ਕਾਰਿਆਲਾ, ਬਿਉਰੋ; ਕਈਆਂ ਖ਼ਾਨਿਆਂ ਵਾਲਾ ਮੇਜ਼, ਲਿਖਣ ਦੀ ਥਾਂ; **~cracy** ਅਫ਼ਸਰਸ਼ਾਹੀ, ਲਾਲ ਫ਼ੀਤਾ ਸ਼ਾਹੀ, ਅਧਿਕਾਰੀ-ਵਰਗ, ਅਫ਼ਸਰ ਲੋਕ; **~crat** ਅਫ਼ਸਰਸ਼ਾਹ,

burial ('ਬੇਰਿਅਲ) *n* ਮੁਰਦਾ ਦਫ਼ਨਾਉਣ ਦੀ ਰਸਮ, ਮੁਰਦਾ ਦਾਬੋਟ ਦੀ ਕਿਰਿਆ; ਅਰਥੀ; ਜਨਾਜ਼ਾ; ਅੰਤਮ ਸੰਸਕਾਰ

burn *v n* ਬਾਲਣਾ, ਸਾੜਨਾ, ਲੂਹਣਾ, ਮਘਾਉਣਾ, ਜਗਾਉਣਾ, ਭੜਕਾਉਣਾ, ਬਲਣਾ, ਲੁਸਣਾ, ਸੜਨਾ, ਡੰਮ੍ਹ ਲਾਉਣਾ, ਦਾਗ਼ ਦੇਣਾ, ਦਾਗ਼ਣਾ; ਸਾੜ, ਲੂਸ, ਡੰਮ੍ਹ, ਦਾਗ਼; **~ing** ਸੜਨ, ਜਲਣ, ਸਾੜਾ, ਦਾਹ, ਝੁਲਸ; ਤਪਦਾ, ਮਘਦਾ; (ਇੱਛਾ) ਤੀਬਰ; **~glass** ਆਤਸ਼ੀ ਸ਼ੀਸ਼ਾ; **~one's fingers** ਕਿਸੇ ਦੂਜੇ ਦੇ ਝਗੜੇ ਵਿਚ ਪੈ ਕੇ ਨੁਕਸਾਨ ਉਠਾਉਣਾ; **~out** ਸਭ ਕੁਝ ਸਾੜ ਟੁਕ ਦੇਣਾ; **~the candle at both ends** ਦੁਹੀਂ ਹੱਥੀਂ ਲੁਟਾਉਣਾ, ਬਹੁਤ ਜ਼ਿਆਦਾ ਖ਼ਰਚ ਕਰਨਾ; **~the mid night oil** ਰਾਤ ਨੂੰ ਬਹੁਤ ਦੇਰ ਨਾਲ ਕੰਮ ਕਰਨਾ

bursar ('ਬਅਃਸਅ*) *n* ਖ਼ਜ਼ਾਨਚੀ, ਵਜ਼ੀਫ਼ਾ ਲੈਣ ਵਾਲਾ ਵਿਦਿਆਰਥੀ, ਭਰਸਰ

burst (ਬਅਃਸਟ) *v n* ਫਟਣਾ, ਵਿਸਫ਼ੋਟ ਹੋਣਾ, ਪਾਟਣਾ, ਫੁੱਟਣਾ, ਢਿਸ ਜਾਣਾ, ਧਮਾਕਾ ਪੈਣਾ; ਬੜੇ ਵੇਗ ਨਾਲ ਖੁੱਲ੍ਹਣਾ, ਪਾੜ ਕੇ ਨਿਕਲ ਜਾਣਾ; ਧਮਕੇ ਨਾਲ ਪਾਟਣਾ; ਵਿਸਫ਼ੋਟ, ਉਛਾਲ ਭੜਕ, ਪੜਾਕਾ, ਫਟਣ, ਪਾਟਣ; ਮਨੋਭਾਵਾਂ ਦਾ ਅਚਾਨਕ ਵਿਸਫ਼ੋਟ; **~into laughter** ਖਿੜ-ਖਿੜ ਕੇ ਹੱਸ ਪੈਣਾ **~into tears** ਫੁੱਟ-ਫੁੱਟ ਕੇ ਰੋਣਾ; **~out** ਫੁੱਟ ਪੈਣਾ, ਚਾਂਘਾਂ ਮਾਰਨੀਆਂ, ਚੀਕ ਉੱਠਣਾ, ਛਿੜ ਪੈਣਾ, (ਬੀਮਾਰੀ) ਫੁੱਟ ਪੈਣੀ; **~sides with laughing** ਹੱਸਦਿਆਂ ਹੱਸਦਿਆਂ ਢਿੱਡ ਪੀੜ ਪੈ ਜਾਣੀ, ਹੱਸਦਿਆਂ ਵੱਖੀਆਂ ਟੁੱਟਣੀਆਂ; **~up** ਫਟ ਜਾਣਾ, ਖੁੱਲ੍ਹ ਜਾਣਾ, ਧਮਾਕਾ ਹੋਣਾ, ਵਿਸਫ਼ੋਟ ਹੋਣਾ; ਤਬਾਹ ਹੋ ਜਾਣਾ; **~with joy** ਖ਼ੁਸ਼ੀ ਵਿਚ ਫੁਲੇ ਨਾ ਸਮਾਉਣਾ

bury ('ਬੈਰਿ) *v* ਦੱਬਣਾ, ਗੱਡਣਾ, ਦਫ਼ਨਾਉਣਾ, ਦਫ਼ਨ ਕਰਨਾ; ਭੁਲਾ ਦੇਣਾ, ਮਿੱਟੀ ਹੇਠਾਂ ਢੱਕ ਦੇਣਾ, ਪੂਰ ਦੇਣਾ; **~alive** ਜੀਉਂਦਾ ਦਫ਼ਨ ਕਰ ਦੇਣਾ, ਦੱਬਾ ਦੇਣਾ; **~the hatchet** ਵੈਰ ਮੁਕਾਉਣਾ, ਤਲਵਾਰ ਮਿਆਨੇ ਪਾਉਣਾ

bus (ਬਅੱਸ) *n* ਬਸ, ਲਾਰੀ, ਮੋਟਰ-ਗੱਡੀ; **miss the~** ਮੌਕਾ ਖੁੰਝਾ ਦੇਣਾ, ਉੱਕ ਜਾਣਾ

bush (ਬੁਸ਼) *n* ਝਾੜੀ, ਝਾੜੀਆਂ ਦੀ ਝੰਗੀ, ਇਸ਼ਕ ਪੇਚੇ ਦੀ ਵੇਲ ਦਾ ਗੁੱਛਾ ਸੰਘਣੇ ਲੱਛੇਦਾਰ ਵਾਲ, ਝਾਟਾ, ਸੰਘਣੀਆਂ ਮੁੱਛਾਂ; **~fighter** ਛਾਪਾਮਾਰ, ਲੁਕ-ਛੁਪ ਕੇ ਲੜਾਈ ਕਰਨ ਵਾਲਾ, ਚੋਰ-ਲੜਾਈ ਲੜਨ ਵਾਲਾ, ਗੁਰੀਲਾ; **~fighting** ਛਾਪਾਮਾਰ ਲੜਾਈ; ਗੁਰੀਲਾ ਜੁੱਧ; **beat about the~** ਉਰਲੀਆਂ-ਪਰਲੀਆਂ ਮਾਰਨੀਆਂ; **~y** ਝਾੜੀਦਾਰ, ਸੰਘਣਾ

business ('ਬਿਜ਼ਨਿਸ) *n* ਵਣਜ-ਵਪਾਰ; ਪੇਸ਼ਾ, ਕਾਰੋਬਾਰ; ਕੰਮ, ਧੰਦਾ, ਵਿਹਾਰ, ਕੰਮ-ਕਾਰ; ਮਾਮਲਾ, ਰੁਝੇਵਾਂ; ਕੰਮਕਾਜ; ਮਤਲਬ, ਕਾਰਜ-ਕਰਮ; ਵਿਹਾਰ, ਲੈਣ-ਦੇਣ; ਕਾਰਜ ਦੀ ਗਤੀ-ਵਿਧੀ; **~man** ਵਪਾਰੀ, ਕਾਰੋਬਾਰੀ ਆਦਮੀ, ਵਿਹਾਰ ਵਿਚ ਤਜਰਬਾਕਾਰ; **has no~to** (ਉਸ ਦਾ) ਕੋਈ ਵਾਸਤਾ ਨਹੀਂ, ਕੋਈ ਹੱਕ ਨਹੀਂ

bust (ਬਅੱਸਟ) *n v* ਵਿਅਕਤੀ ਦਾ ਧੜ, ਬੁੱਤ; ਪੁਲੀਸ ਵੱਲੋਂ ਛਾਪਾ ਮਾਰ ਕੇ ਫੜਨਾ

busy ('ਬਿਜ਼ਿ) *a v* ਮਸਰੂਫ਼, ਰੁੱਝਾ ਹੋਇਆ, ਲੱਗਾ

but

ਹੋਇਆ, ਵਿਆਸਤ; ਆਹਰੀ, ਲੀਨ, ਮਗਨ; ਰੁੱਝਣਾ, ਆਹਰੇ ਲਾਉਣਾ, ਜਾਂ ਲੱਗਣਾ, ਕੰਮ ਵਿਚ ਜੁਟਣਾ

but (ਬੱਟ) *conj, prep, adv. n* ਇਤਰਾਜ਼, ਆਪੱਤੀ; ਕਿੰਤੂ, ਲੇਕਿਨ, ਕੇਵਲ; ਫਿਰ ਵੀ, ਤਾਂ ਵੀ; ਪਰ ਇਸ ਦੇ ਨਾਲ ਹੀ, ਪਰ ਫਿਰ ਵੀ; ਆਰੋਪ

butcher (ਬੁਚਅ*) *n v* ਕਸਾਈ, ਝਟਕਈ, ਬੁੱਚੜ; ਜਲਾਦ; ਝਟਕਾਉਣਾ, ਹੱਤਿਆ ਕਰਨੀ, ਖੂਨ ਕਰਨਾ, ਮਾਰ ਸੁੱਟਣਾ, ਕੋਹਣਾ; ਕਰੜੀ ਨੁਕਤਾ-ਚੀਨੀ ਕਰਨਾ; **~y** ਬੁਚੜਖ਼ਾਨਾ, ਕਸਾਈਪੁਣਾ, ਖ਼ੂਨ-ਖ਼ਰਾਬਾ, ਨਿਰਦਇਤਾ ਪੂਰਵਕ ਹਤਿਆ, ਵੱਢ-ਟੁੱਕ

butler ('ਬਅੱਟਲਅ*) *n* ਖਾਨਸਾਮਾ, ਨੌਕਰਾਂ ਦਾ ਮੁਖੀ, ਸ਼ਰਾਬਖ਼ਾਨੇ ਦਾ ਕਰਮਚਾਰੀ, ਰਕਬਦਾਰ ਭੰਡਾਰੀ, ਖ਼ਰੀਦੀ; **~y** ਭੰਡਾਰ, ਲੰਗਰ

butt (ਬੱਟ) *n v* ਪੀਪਾ, ਕੁੰਦਾ; ਟੱਕਰ, ਧੱਕਾ; ਚਾਂਦਮਾਰੀ ਦਾ ਮੈਦਾਨ; ਕਿਸੇ ਹਥਿਆਰ ਜਾਂ ਸੰਦ ਦਾ ਮੋਟਾ ਸਿਰਾ; ਹਾਸੇ-ਠੱਠੇ ਦਾ ਸੱਜਣ ਜਿਸ ਦਾ ਮਖੌਲ ਉਡਾਇਆ ਜਾਵੇ; ਸਿਰ ਦੀ ਟੱਕਰ ਮਾਰਨੀ, ਧੱਕਣਾ; ਬਾਹਰ ਕੱਢਣਾ

butter ('ਬਅੱਟਅ*) *n v* ਮੱਖਣ, ਸੱਖਣੀ; ਚੋਪੜਨਾ, ਮੱਖਣ ਛੱਡਣਾ; ਚਾਪਲੂਸੀ ਕਰਨੀ, ਚਿਕਨੀਆਂ ਚੋਪੜੀਆਂ ਗੱਲਾਂ ਕਰਨੀਆਂ; **~milk** ਲੱਸੀ, ਛਾਹ

butterfly ('ਬਅੱਟਅਫ਼ਲਾਇ) *n* ਤਿਤਲੀ; ਭੰਬੀਰੀ, ਦਿਲ ਡੁੱਬਣ ਦਾ ਭਾਵ

buttock ('ਬਅੱਟਅਕ) *n v* ਚਿੱਤੜ, ਪਿੱਛਾ, ਪੁੱਠਾ; ਘੋਲ (ਕੁਸ਼ਤੀ) ਦਾ ਇਕ ਦਾਅ; ਪੱਟਾਂ ਤੋਂ ਫੜ ਕੇ ਸੁੱਟ ਦੇਣਾ, ਚਿੱਤੜਾਂ ਭਾਰ ਸੁੱਟਣਾ, ਚੁੱਕ ਕੇ ਮਾਰਨਾ

button (ਬਅੱਟਨ) *n v* ਬਟਨ, ਬੀੜਾ, ਗੁਦਾਮ ਝੋੜੀ, ਅਲਖਿਣੀ ਖੁੰਭ; ਬਟਨ ਬੰਦ ਕਰਨੇ; **~hole** ਕਾਜ, ਬਟਨ ਮਾਰਨ ਵਾਲਾ ਸੁਰਾਖ਼

by(e)

buy (ਬਾਇ) *n v* ਖ਼ਰੀਦ, ਸੌਦਾ, ਮੁੱਲ; ਖ਼ਰੀਦਣਾ, ਮੁੱਲ ਲੈਣਾ, ਪ੍ਰਾਪਤ ਕਰਨਾ, ਕਿਸੇ ਨੂੰ ਵੱਢੀ ਦੇ ਕੇ ਆਪਣੇ ਨਾਲ ਮਿਲਾ ਲੈਣਾ; **~off** ਕੁਝ ਦੇ ਕੇ ਜਾਨ ਛੁਡਾ ਲੈਣੀ; **~over** ਰਿਸ਼ਵਤ ਦੇ ਕੇ ਆਪਣੇ ਵੱਲ ਕਰ ਲੈਣਾ; **~up** ਸਾਰਾ ਮਾਲ ਖ਼ਰੀਦ ਲੈਣਾ; **a good ~** ਖ਼ਰਾ ਸੌਦਾ; **~er** ਖ਼ਰੀਦਾਰ, ਗਾਹਕ

buzz (ਬਅੱਜ਼) *n v* ਸ਼ਹਿਦ ਦੀ ਮੱਖੀ ਆਦਿ ਦੀ ਗੂੰਜ, ਭਿਣਕ, ਭਿਣਕਾਰ, ਭਿਣਭਿਣਾਹਟ; ਭਿਣਕਣਾ, ਭਿਣ-ਭਿਣ ਕਰਨਾ, ਗੁਟਗੁਟਾਉਣਾ; ਗਟ ਗਟ ਪੀ ਜਾਣਾ; ਚੜ੍ਹਾ ਜਾਣਾ (ਸ਼ਰਾਬ)

buzzer ('ਬਅੱਜ਼ਅ*) *n* ਸੀਟੀ, ਜਹਾਜ਼ ਦਾ ਭੌਂਪੂ; ਭਿਣਕਣ ਵਾਲਾ; ਸਿਗਨੇਲਰ

by (ਬਾਇ) *adv prep a* ਤੋਂ, ਥੋਂ, ਤਕ, ਤੋੜੀ; ਦੁਆਰਾ, ਹੱਥੀਂ; ਕੋਲੋਂ, ਨਾਲ ਹੀ; ਕੋਲ, ਨੇੜੇ, ਲਾਗੇ, ਵੱਲ, ਬੰਨੇ, ਪਾਸੇ, ਨਾਲ ਨਾਲ, ਵਿਚੋਂ ਦੀ; **~all means** ਜ਼ਰੂਰ, ਅਵੱਸ਼, ਨਿਸ਼ਚੇ ਹੀ, ਹਰ ਹੀਲੇ; **~gone** ਬੀਤਿਆ ਕਾਲ, ਭੂਤਕਾਲ, ਅਤੀਤ, ਪੁਰਾਣਾ; **~heart** ਜ਼ਬਾਨੀ, ਮੂੰਹ ਜ਼ਬਾਨੀ; **~lane** ਗਲੀ, ਵੱਡੀ ਗਲੀ ਵਿਚੋਂ ਨਿਕਲੀ ਛੋਟੀ ਗਲੀ, ਇਕ ਪਾਸੇ ਦੀ ਛੋਟੀ ਗਲੀ; **~name** ਉਪ-ਨਾਮ, ਅੱਲ; **~pass** ਫਿਰਨੀ, ਲਾਂਭਵੀਂ ਸੜਕ, ਇਕ ਪਾਸੇ ਦਾ ਰਾਹ, ਉਪ-ਮਾਰਗ, ਸਿੱਧਾ ਰਸਤਾ; **~path** ਪਗ-ਡੰਡੀ, ਇਕ ਪਾਸੇ ਦਾ ਰਾਹ, ਉਪਮਾਰਗ, ਸਿੱਧੀ ਡੰਡੀ; **~product** ਗੌਣ-ਉਪਜ, ਨਾਲ ਲਗਦੀ ਪੈਦਾਵਾਰ; **~way** ਉਪਮਾਰਗ; **~word** ਲੋਕੋਕਤੀ, ਕਹਾਵਤ, ਅਖਾਣ

by(e) (ਬਾਇ) *a* ਉਪ, ਇਤਫ਼ਾਕੀਆ, ਜ਼ਿਮਨੀ; **~election** ਉਪਚੋਣ, ਜ਼ਿਮਨੀ ਚੋਣ; **~law** ਉਪ-ਨਿਯਮ, ਜ਼ਿਮਨੀ-ਕਾਨੂੰਨ; **~bye** ਰੱਬ ਰਾਖਾ, ਅਲਵਿਦਾ!

C

C, c (ਸੀ) *n* ਰੋਮਨ ਵਰਣਮਾਲਾ ਦਾ ਤੀਜਾ ਅੱਖਰ; ਤੀਜਾ ਮਨੁੱਖ ਜਾਂ ਤੀਜੀ ਗੱਲ

cab (ਕੈਬ) *n v* ਭਾੜੇ ਦੀ ਗੱਡੀ, ਟੈਕਸੀ, ਯੱਕੇ, ਬੱਘੀ ਵਿਚ ਜਾਣਾ ਜਾਂ ਉਸਨੂੰ ਚਲਾਉਣਾ; ~**man** ਕੋਚਵਾਨ, ਟੈਕਸੀ-ਡਰਾਇਵਰ, ਟੈਕਸੀ ਵਾਲਾ, ਯੱਕੇ ਵਾਲਾ; ਬੱਘੀ ਵਾਲਾ

cabaret ('ਕੈਬਅਰੇਇ) *n* ਰੈਸਟੋਰਾਂ ਵਿਚ ਨਾਚ ਰੰਗ, ਮਨੋਰੰਜਨ-ਕਾਰਜ, ਕੈਬਰੇ ਨਾਚ; ਸ਼ਰਾਬਖ਼ਾਨਾ, ਸੈਖਾਨਾ

cabbage ('ਕੈਬਿਜ਼) *n* ਬੰਦ ਗੋਭੀ, ਪੱਤ ਗੋਭੀ

cabin ('ਕੈਬਿਨ) *n v* ਕੋਠੜੀ, ਝੁੱਗੀ, ਹੁਜਰਾ, ਝੌਂਪੜੀ; ਜਹਾਜ਼ ਦਾ ਖਾਣ ਜਾਂ ਸੌਣ ਦਾ ਕਮਰਾ, ਕੈਬਿਨ; (ਕੈਬਿਨ ਵਿਚ) ਬੰਦ ਕਰਨਾ, ਤੁੰਨਣ, ਤੰਗ ਥਾਂ ਵਿਚ ਭਰਨਾ

cabinet ('ਕੈਬਿਨਿਟ) *n* (1) ਛੋਟਾ ਕਮਰਾ, ਹੁਜਰਾ, ਖ਼ਿਲਵਤ-ਖ਼ਾਨਾ, ਨਿੱਜੀ ਕਮਰਾ; (2) ਛੋਟੀ ਅਲਮਾਰੀ, ਦਰਾਜ਼ਾਂ ਵਾਲਾ ਸੰਦੂਕ; (3) ਕਾਬੀਨਾ, ਵਜ਼ਾਰਤ, ਮੰਤਰੀ-ਮੰਡਲ; ਦੀਵਾਨ-ਖ਼ਾਸ

cable ('ਕੇਇਬਲ) *n* ਤਾਰ, ਸੰਗਲੀ, ਰੱਸੀ; ਸਮੁੰਦਰੀ-ਤਾਰ; (ਮੁੰਜ ਦਾ) ਮੋਟਾ ਰੱਸਾ, ਲੰਗਰ ਦਾ ਸੰਗਲ ਜਾਂ ਰੱਸਾ; ਵਲਦਾਰ ਨੱਕਾਸ਼ੀ; ਤਾਰ ਕਸਣਾ, ਰੱਸੀ ਕਸਣਾ ਸਮੁੰਦਰੀ ਤਾਰ ਦੇਣੀ, ਰੱਸੀ ਜਾਂ ਸੰਗਲ ਨਾਲ ਬੰਨ੍ਹਣਾ

cackle (ਕੈਕਲ) *v n* ਕੁੜ ਕੁੜ ਕਰਨਾ, ਕੁੜ-ਕੁੜਾਉਣਾ; ਬਕਵਾਸ ਕਰਨੀ; ਸ਼ੇਖੀ ਮਾਰਨੀ, ਗੱਪ ਮਾਰਨੀ; ਬਕਵਾਸ, ਸ਼ੇਖੀ, ਗੱਪ, ਬਕ-ਬਕ, ਗੱਪ-ਸੜੱਪ

cactus (ਕੈਕਟਸ) *n* ਥੋਹਰ, ਨਾਗ-ਫਨੀ

cad (ਕੈਡ) *n* ਕਮੀਨਾ, ਉਜੱਡ ਬੰਦਾ; ਬਸ ਦਾ ਕੰਡਕਟਰ; ਮੰਡੂ

cadet (ਕਅ'ਡੈਟ) *n* ਫ਼ੌਜੀ ਸਕੂਲ ਦਾ ਵਿਦਿਆਰਥੀ, ਸੈਨਾ-ਸਿਖਿਆਰਥੀ, ਕੈਡਿਟ ਛੋਟਾ ਪੁੱਤਰ ਜਾਂ ਛੋਟਾ ਭਰਾ; ~**corps** ਫ਼ੌਜੀ ਸਕੂਲ ਦੇ ਵਿਦਿਆਰਥੀਆਂ ਦੀ ਕੰਪਨੀ, ਕੈਡਿਟ ਕੋਰ

cadre ('ਕਾਡਅ*) *n* ਸ਼ੇਨੀ, ਵਰਗ, ਸੰਗਠਨ, ਢਾਂਚਾ; ਸਥਾਈ ਅਮਲਾ, ਰੂਪ-ਰੇਖਾ, ਨਫ਼ਰੀ

cafe ('ਕੈਫ਼ੇਇ) *n* (F) ਕਾਹਵਾ, ਕਾਫ਼ੀ; ਕਾਹਵਾਖ਼ਾਨਾ, ਵਿਸ਼ਰਾਮ ਘਰ, ਕਾਫ਼ੀ ਹਾਊਸ, ਰੈਸਟੋਰਾਂ, ਕੈਫ਼ੇ; ~**teria** ਭੋਜਨ-ਭੰਡਾਰ, ਅੰਨ-ਪੂਰਨਾ, ਰੈਸਟੋਰਾਂ

cage (ਕੇਇਜ) *n v* ਪਿੰਜਰਾ; ਕੈਦਖ਼ਾਨਾ ਕਟਿਹਰਾ, ਜੰਗਲਾ; ਪਿੰਜਰੇ ਪਾਉਣਾ, ਜੇਲ੍ਹ ਵਿਚ ਬੰਦ ਕਰਨਾ, ਕੈਦੀ ਬਣਾਉਣਾ

cajole (ਕਅ'ਜਅਉਲ) *v* ਫੁਸਲਾਉਣਾ, ਪਸਮਾਉਣਾ, ਪਤਿਆਉਣਾ; ਚਾਪਲੂਸੀ ਕਰਨੀ, ਪੁਚਕਾਰਨਾ, ਖ਼ੁਸ਼ਾਮਦ ਕਰਨੀ; ਝਾਸਾਂ ਦੇਣਾ; ~**ment**, ~**ry** ਚਾਪਲੂਸੀ, ਫੁਲਾਹੁਣੀ, ਬੁੱਤੀ

cake (ਕੇਇਕ) *n* ਕੇਕ, ਟਿੱਕੀ, ਕੁਲਚਾ, ਸਿੱਠੀ ਰੋਟੀ, ਮੱਠੀ, ਮੰਨ, (ਕਿਸੇ ਚੀਜ਼ ਦੀ) ਚਾਕੀ; **charity**~ (ਸਾਧੂ ਫ਼ਕੀਰ ਨੂੰ ਭਿੱਖਿਆ ਵਿਚ ਦਿੱਤੀ ਹੋਈ ਰੋਟੀ) ਸਧੁਕੜ, ਹੁੰਦ; **to take the**~ ਟਿੱਕੀ ਜਾਂ ਪੇੜੀ ਬਣਾਉਣਾ, ਟਿੱਕੀਆਂ ਜਮਾਉਣੀਆਂ, ਚਪੜੀ ਜਮਾਉਣੀ, ਪੇਪੜੀ ਬੱਝਣੀ ਬਾਜ਼ੀ ਲੈ ਜਾਣਾ, ਨਾਮਣਾ ਖੱਟਣਾ

calamity (ਕਅ'ਲੈਮਅਟਿ) *n* ਬਿਪਤਾ, ਮੁਸੀਬਤ, ਰੱਬੀ ਕਹਿਰ, ਕਸ਼ਟ, ਬਦਬਖ਼ਤੀ

calcify (ਕੈਲਸਿਫ਼ਾਇ) v ਪਥਰਾ ਜਾਣਾ, ਕਰੜਾ ਹੋ ਜਾਣਾ, ਸਖ਼ਤ ਕਰਨਾ, ਚੂਨਾ ਬਣ ਜਾਣਾ

calcium (ਕੈਲਸ਼ਿਅਮ) n ਚੂਨੇ ਦੀ ਕਿਸਮ, ਚੂਨੇ ਦਾ ਸਾਰ, ਕੈਲਸ਼ਿਅਮ

calculate (ਕੈਲਕਯੂਲੇਇਟ) v ਗਿਣਨਾ, ਲੇਖਾ ਕਰਨਾ, ਜਾਚਣਾ, ਹਿਸਾਬ ਲਾਉਣਾ, ਗਿਣਤੀ ਕਰਨਾ, ਅਨੁਮਾਨ ਲਾਉਣਾ, ਹਾਜ਼ਣਾ, ਅੰਕਣਾ, ਕਿਆਸ ਕਰਨਾ, ਵਿਚਾਰਨਾ

calculating (ਕੈਲਕਯੂਲੇਇਟਿੰਙ) a ਹਿਸਾਬੀ, ਗਿਣਤੀਆਂ ਗਿਣਨ ਵਾਲਾ, ਸੁਆਰਥੀ, ਮਤਲਬੀ

calculation (ਕੈਲਕਯੂ'ਲੇਇਸ਼ਨ) n ਅਨੁਮਾਨ, ਗਿਣਤੀ, ਗਣਨਾ, ਹਿਸਾਬ, ਅੰਦਾਜ਼ਾ, ਤਖ਼ਮੀਨਾ, ਕਿਆਸ, ਲੇਖ-ਜੋਖ, ਅੱਟਾ-ਸੱਟਾ; ਸੋਚ-ਵਿਚਾਰ

calculative (ਕੈਲਕਯੂਲਅਟਿਵ) a ਗਿਣਤੀ-ਸਬੰਧੀ, ਹਿਸਾਬੀ

calculator (ਕੈਲਕਯੂਲੇਇਟਅ*) n ਹਿਸਾਬੀ, ਅਨੁਮਾਨ ਲਾਉਣ ਵਾਲੀ, ਹਿਸਾਬੀ ਮਸ਼ੀਨ, ਸਵਾਲ ਕੱਢਣ ਵਾਲੀ ਮਸ਼ੀਨ; ਗਣਨ-ਜੰਤਰੀ; ~y ਗਣਨਾ-ਸਬੰਧੀ, ਗਿਣਤੀ-ਸਬੰਧੀ, ਗਣਨਾਤਮਕ

calculous (ਕੈਲਕਯੂਲਅਸ) a ਪੱਥਰੀਲਾ, ਕੰਕਰੀਲਾ, ਪੱਥਰੀ ਦਾ ਰੋਗੀ, ਪੱਥਰੀ ਦੀ ਬੀਮਾਰੀ ਦਾ

calculus (ਕੈਲਕਯੂਲਅਸ) n (ਚਿਕਿ) ਪੱਥਰੀ, ਗਣਿਤ ਦੀ ਇਕ ਸ਼ਾਖਾ, ਕੈਲਕੂਲਸ

calendar (ਕੈਲਿਨਡਅ*) n v ਜੰਤਰੀ, ਪੱਤਰੀ, ਕੈਲੰਡਰ, ਤਾਰੀਖ਼ਾਂ ਦਾ ਹਿਸਾਬ-ਕਿਤਾਬ, ਨਿਯਮਾਵਲੀ; ਡਾਇਰੀ; ਦਰਜ ਕਰਨਾ, ਰਜਿਸਟਰ ਵਿਚ ਚੜ੍ਹਾਉਣਾ, ਸੂਚੀ ਬਣਾਉਣੀ, ਤਰਤੀਬ ਦੇਣੀ, ਵਿਉਂਤ ਅਨੁਸਾਰ ਕਰਨਾ

calf (ਕਾਫ਼) n ਵੱਛਾ, ਵੱਛੀ, ਕੱਟਾ, ਕੱਟੀ, ਵਛੇਰਾ, ਵਹਿੜਕਾ, ਹਾਥੀ ਦਾ ਬੱਚਾ, (ਹਿਰਨੇਟਾ); ਅਲੂਣ ਵਿਅਕਤੀ; **~'s teeth** ਦੁੱਧ ਦੇ ਦੰਦ; **cow in-, cow with~** ਸੂਣ ਵਾਲੀ ਗਾਂ; **moon-~** ਜਮਾਂਦਰੂ ਮੂਰਖ

calibre, caliber (ਕੈਲਿਬਅ*) n ਯੋਗਤਾ ਹੈਸੀਅਤ, ਅਖ਼ਲਾਕੀ ਪੱਧਰ, ਵਿਆਸ, ਬੋਰ

call (ਕੋਲ) v n ਬੁਲਾਉਣਾ, ਪੁਕਾਰਨਾ, ਜ਼ੋਰ ਨਾਲ ਚੀਕਣਾ, ਹਾਜ਼ਰੀ ਬੋਲਣਾ, ਸੱਦਣਾ, ਬੁਲਾ ਘੱਲਣਾ ਬਿਆਨ ਕਰਨਾ; ਚਹਿਚਾਟ; ਥਿਗਲ, ਜ਼ਰੂਰਤ ਹੁਕਮ, ਦੁਹਾਈ; ਅਵਾਜ਼, (ਟੈਲੀਫ਼ੋਨ ਦੀ) ਕਾਲ ਰਸਮੀ ਮੁਲਾਕਾਤ; ਕਸ਼ਸ਼, ਬੁਲਾਵਾ; **~a meeting** ਬੈਠਕ ਬੁਲਾਉਣਾ, ਇਕੱਤਰਤਾ ਕਰਨੀ; **~a spade a spade** ਸਾਫ਼-ਸਾਫ਼ ਆਖਣਾ, ਕਾਂ ਨੂੰ ਕਾਣਾ ਆਖਣਾ, ਸੱਚ-ਪੁੱਤਰ ਹੋਣਾ; **~at** ਮਿਲਣ ਜਾਣਾ; **~ boy** ਨੌਕਰ; **~for** ਮੰਗਣਾ, ਆਉਣਾ, ਫ਼ਰਮਾਇਸ਼ ਕਰਨੀ, ਸੰਗ ਕਰਨੀ; **~gi** ਕਾਲ ਗਰਲ, ਨੰਚਨੀ; **~in** (ਡਾਕਟਰ ਆਦਿ ਇਲਾਜ ਲਈ ਸੱਦਣਾ, ਵਾਪਸ ਲੈਣਾ; **~i question** (ਤੇ) ਕਿੰਤੂ ਕਰਨਾ; **~money** (ਬੈਂਕ ਕਰਜ਼ਾ ਜਾਚਨ-ਰਾਸ਼ੀ; **~names** ਗਾਲੀਆ ਦੇਣਾ, ਗਾਲਾਂ ਕੱਢਣੀਆਂ, ਬੁਰਾ ਭਲਾ ਆਖਣਾ **~on** ਮਿਲਣਾ, ਮਿਲਣ ਜਾਣਾ; **~ou** ਲਲਕਾਰਨਾ, ਵੰਗਾਰਨਾ, ਚੁਣੌਤੀ ਦੇਣਾ; **~not** ਬੁਲਾਵਾ, ਸੱਦਾ, ਚੇਤਾਵਨੀ; **~sign** ਨਾਮ-ਸੰਕੇਤ ਨਾਮ-ਚਿੰਨ੍ਹ; **~woman** ਦਾਈ; **~of natur** (ਟੱਟੀ ਪਿਸ਼ਾਬ ਦੀ) ਹਾਜਤ; **~roll** ਹਾਜ਼ਰੀ

calligrapher (ਕਅ'ਲਿਗਰਅਫ਼ਅ*) n ਸੁਲੇਖਕ ਸੁਲਿਪਿਕਾਰ, ਖ਼ੁਸ਼ਨਵੀਸ

calligraphist (ਕਅਲਿ'ਗਰਅਫ਼ਿਸਟ) n ਸੁਲੇਖਕ ਕਾਤਬ, ਖ਼ੁਸ਼ਨਵੀਸ

calligraphy (ਕਅ'ਲਿਗਰਅਫ਼ਿ) n ਸੁਲੇਖ, ਸੁਲੇਖ ਕਲਾ, ਸੁੰਦਰ ਲਿਖਾਈ, ਖ਼ੁਸ਼ਖ਼ਤੀ, ਖ਼ੁਸ਼ਨਵੀਸੀ

calling (ਕੋਲਿਙ) *n* ਬੁਲਾਵਾ, ਰੱਬੀ ਰਜ਼ਾ, ਬਾਣਾ, ਪੇਸ਼ਾ, ਧੰਦਾ, ਨੇਕ ਪੇਸ਼ਾਵਾਰ ਲੋਕ ਜਾਂ ਕਿਸੇ ਖ਼ਾਸ ਕਿੱਤੇ ਨਾਲ ਸਬੰਧਤ ਪੁਰਸ਼; **~list** ਅਤਿਥੀ-ਸੂਚੀ, ਵਿਜ਼ਿਟਿੰਗ-ਲਿਸਟ

callous (ਕੈਲਅਸ) *a* ਕਠੋਰ, ਨਿਰਦਈ, ਪੱਥਰ-ਚਿੱਤ, ਕਰੂਰ, ਬੇਰਹਿਮ, ਬੇਦਰਦ, ਸੰਗਦਿਲ; **~ness** ਨਿਰਦਇਤਾ, ਕਠੋਰਤਾ, ਸਖ਼ਤੀ, ਬੇਰਹਿਮੀ, ਕਰੜਾਈ, ਬੇਦਰਦੀ, ਸੰਗਦਿਲੀ

calm (ਕਾਮ) *n a v* ਸ਼ਾਂਤੀ, ਚੈਨ, ਖ਼ਮੋਸ਼ੀ, ਸਥਿਰਤਾ, ਟਿਕਾਉ, ਅਡੋਲਤਾ, ਸਕੂਨ; ਸ਼ਾਂਤ, ਚੁੱਪ, ਖ਼ਮੋਸ਼; ਸ਼ਾਂਤ ਕਰਨਾ, ਚੁੱਪ ਕਰਾਉਣਾ, ਟਿਕਾਉਣਾ, ਤਸੱਲੀ ਦੇਣੀ, ਖ਼ਮੋਸ਼ ਹੋਣਾ; **~ly** ਧੀਰਜ ਨਾਲ, ਸ਼ਾਂਤੀ ਨਾਲ, ਸਹਿਜ ਨਾਲ; **~ness** ਸ਼ਾਂਤੀ, ਖ਼ਮੋਸ਼ੀ, ਸਕੂਨ, ਧੀਰਜ, ਸਥਿਰਤਾ

camel (ਕੈਮਲ) *n* ਊਠ; ਇਕ ਮਸ਼ੀਨ ਜਿਸ ਨਾਲ ਸਮੁੰਦਰੀ ਜਹਾਜ਼ ਨੂੰ ਘੱਟ ਡੂੰਘੇ ਪਾਣੀ ਵਿਚ ਚਲਾਇਆ ਜਾਂਦਾ ਹੈ;

camouflage (ਕੈਮਅਫ਼ਲਾਯ੍ਹ) *n v* ਭੁਲਾਂਦਰਾ, ਛਲ ਦਾ ਪਰਦਾ, ਭੁਲਾਂਦਰੇ ਰਾਹੀਂ ਲੁਕਾਉਣਾ

camp (ਕੈਂਪ) *n v* ਡੇਰਾ, ਪੜਾਉ, ਛਾਉਣੀ, ਤੰਬੂ, ਸਫ਼ਰੀ ਜੀਵਨ, ਧੜਾ, ਪੱਖ; ਸੈਨਾ, ਕੈਂਪ; ਪੜਾਉ ਕਰਨਾ, ਤੰਬੂ ਲਾਉਣਾ; ਡੇਰਾ ਕਰਨਾ, ਛਾਉਣੀ ਪਾਉਣੀ

campaign (ਕੈਂਪੇਇਨ) *n v* ਅੰਦੋਲਨ; ਜੰਗ, ਮੁਹਿੰਮ, ਜੱਦ-ਜਹਿਦ, ਲੜਾਈ, ਫ਼ੌਜੀ ਕਾਰਵਾਈ, ਜਥੇਬੰਦ ਕਾਰਵਾਈ, ਮਹਾਨ ਉੱਦਮ, ਜੱਦ-ਜਹਿਦ ਵਿਚ ਸ਼ਾਮਲ ਹੋਣਾ, ਸੰਘਰਸ਼ ਵਿਚ ਪੈਣਾ, ਅੰਦੋਲਨ ਚਲਾਉਣਾ; **~er** ਅੰਦੋਲਨਕਾਰੀ, ਮੁਹਿੰਮਬਾਜ਼, ਘੁਲਾਟੀਆ

camphor (ਕੈਮਫ਼ਅ*) *n* ਕਪੂਰ, ਮੁਸ਼ਕ ਕਾਫ਼ੂਰ

campus (ਕੈਂਪਅਸ) *n* ਇਹਾਤਾ (ਸਕੂਲ, ਕਾਲਜ, ਜਾਂ ਯੂਨੀਵਰਸਿਟੀ ਦਾ) ਕੈਂਪਸ, ਸਿੱਖਿਆ-ਸੰਸਥਾ, ਕਾਲਜ

can (ਕੈਨ) *n v aux* ਕੁੱਪਾ, ਡੋਲ, ਕਨਸਤਰ, ਪੀਪਾ, ਡੱਬਾ ਪੀਪੇ ਵਿਚ ਭਰਨਾ, ਡੋਲ ਭਰਨਾ, ਡੱਬੇ ਵਿਚ ਬੰਦ ਕਰਨਾ; ਸਕਣਾ, ਯੋਗ ਹੋਣਾ, ਹੋ ਸਕਣਾ, ਸੰਭਵ ਹੋਣਾ

canal (ਕਅਨੈਲ) *n v* ਨਹਿਰ, ਆਡ, ਸਰੀਰ ਦੇ ਅੰਦਰ ਭੋਜਨ ਜਾਂ ਹਵਾ ਵਾਲੀ ਨਾਲੀ; ਨਹਿਰ ਪੁੱਟਣੀ, ਨਹਿਰ ਕੱਢਣੀ; **~lize** ਆਡ ਜਾਂ ਨਹਿਰ ਦੀ ਖੁਦਾਈ ਕਰਨੀ, ਦਰਿਆ ਵਿਚੋਂ ਨਹਿਰ ਕੱਢਣੀ

cancel (ਕੈਂਸਲ) *v n* ਰੱਦ ਕਰਨਾ, ਮੇਟਣਾ ਕੱਟ ਫੇਰਨਾ, ਕੱਟਣਾ, ਲੀਕ ਫੇਰਨੀ, ਮਿਟਾ ਦੇਣਾ, ਮਨਸੂਖ਼ ਕਰਨਾ; ਵਿਅਰਥ ਠਹਿਰਾਉਣਾ; ਰੱਦ; **~lation** ਮਨਸੂਖ਼ੀ, ਨਕਾਰਨ, ਕਾਟ, ਕੱਟ, ਰੋਕੀਕਰਨ

cancer (ਕੈਂਸਅ*) *n* ਕੈਂਸਰ, ਰਾਜਫੋੜਾ; ਤੇਜ਼ੀ ਵਾਦੀ ਜੋ ਨਾਸੂਰ ਬਣ ਕੇ ਚੰਬੜਾ ਜਾਵੇ; ਬਰਦੰਰ ਫੋੜਾ; ਕਰਕ ਰਾਸ਼ੀ

candid (ਕੈਂਡਿਡ) *a* ਨਿਰਪੱਖ, ਨਿਸ਼ਕਪਟ, ਖਰਾ, ਸਪਸ਼ਟ, ਸੱਚਾ, ਸਾਫ਼ ਦਿਲ, ਸਾਫ਼-ਗੋ, ਨਿਰਛਲ; **~ly** ਸਾਫ਼ ਸਾਫ਼, ਸਫ਼ਾਈ ਨਾਲ, ਬਿਨਾ ਲੱਗਲਬੇੜ ਦੇ, ਖੇਲ੍ਹਾਂਗਾ ਹੋ ਕੇ; **~ness** ਸਾਫ਼-ਗੋਈ, ਸਾਫ਼-ਦਿਲੀ, ਸਚਾਈ, ਨਿਸ਼ਕਪਟਤਾ

candidate (ਕੈਂਡਿਡਅਟ) *n* ਉਮੀਦਵਾਰ; ਪਰੀਖਿਆਰਥੀ, ਚੋਣ ਉਮੀਦਵਾਰ; ਤਲਬਗਾਰ

candidature (ਕੈਂਡਿਡਅਚਅ*) *n* ਪਾਤਰਤਾ, ਉਮੀਦਵਾਰ ਹੋਣ ਦੀ ਸਥਿਤੀ

candle (ਕੈਂਡਲ) *n* ਮੋਮਬੱਤੀ; ਦੀਵਾ

candy (ਕੈਂਡੀ) *n v* ਮਿਸਰੀ, ਖੰਡ ਦੀ ਗੋਲੀ; ਮਿਸਰੀ ਬਣਾਉਣਾ

cane (ਕੇਇਨ) *n v* ਗੰਨਾ, ਨੜਾ, ਬਾਂਸ ਆਦਿ;

caning ('ਕੇਨਿਡ਼) *n* ਦੰਡ ਦੇਣ ਦੀ ਕਿਰਿਆ, ਬੈਂਤ ਲਗਾਉਣ ਦਾ ਕੰਮ, ਬੈਂਤ ਬੁਣਨ ਦਾ ਅਮਲ

canister ('ਕੈਨਿਸਟਅ*) ਧਾਤ ਦਾ ਛੋਟਾ ਡੱਬਾ, ਕਨਸਤਰ, ਪੀਪਾ; ਭੇਟਾ-ਪਾਤਰ, ਦਾਨ-ਪਾਤਰ

cannibal ('ਕੈਨਿਬਲ) *n a* ਆਦਮ-ਖੋਰ, ਮਾਸਖਾਣਾ, ਮਰਦਮ-ਖ਼ੋਰ

canning ('ਕੈਨਿਡ਼) *n* ਡੱਬੇਬੰਦੀ

cannon ('ਕੈਨਅਨ) *n v* ਤੋਪ, ਤੋਪਖ਼ਾਨਾ, ਧੁਰੇ ਉੱਤੇ ਆਪਣੇ ਆਪ ਘੁੰਮਣ ਵਾਲਾ ਵੇਲਣ, ਕੁੰਜੀ ਦੀ ਨਾਲੀ, ਬਿਲੀਅਰਡ ਖੇਡਣ ਸਮੇਂ ਇਕੋ ਵੇਲੇ ਦੋ ਗੋਂਦਾਂ ਦੀ ਮਾਰ; ਟੇਢਾ ਟਕਰਾਉਣਾ, ਦੋ-ਗੋਂਦੀ ਮਾਰ ਮਾਰਨਾ, ਦੋ ਗੋਂਦਾਂ ਨੂੰ ਇੱਕਠਾ ਮਾਰਨਾ; **~ball** ਤੋਪ ਦਾ ਗੋਲਾ

canon ('ਕੈਨਅਨ) *n* ਧਾਰਮਕ ਸਿਧਾਂਤ; ਧਰਮ-ਸੂਤਰ, ਧਰਮ-ਆਦੇਸ਼, ਧਾਰਮਕ ਨਿਯਮ, ਵਿਧਾਨ; ਮਾਨਦੰਡ; ਇਸਾਈਆਂ ਦੀ ਨਮਾਜ਼ ਦਾ ਪਵਿੱਤਰ ਭਾਗ; ਛਾਪੇ ਦੇ ਸਭ ਤੋਂ ਵੱਡੇ ਅੱਖਰ; ਪਾਦਰੀਆਂ ਦੀ ਸਤਾ ਦਾ ਸਦੇਸ਼; ਘੰਟਾ ਲਟਕਾਉਣ ਵਾਲਾ ਕੜਾ; ਸੰਗੀਤ ਵਿਚ ਇਕ ਰੀਤ; **~ical** ਧਾਰਮਕ ਆਗਿਆ ਦੁਆਰਾ ਨਿਯਤ, ਸ਼ਰੁਈ, ਦੀਨੀ, ਮਜ਼ਹਬੀ; ਧਾਰਮਕ ਗ੍ਰੰਥ ਅਥਵਾ ਪੁਸਤਕ ਦਾ ਭਾਗ; **~ically** ਮਰਯਾਦਾ ਪੂਰਵਕ, ਨੇਮ ਅਨੁਸਾਰ

canopy ('ਕੈਨਅਪਿ) *n v* ਛੱਤਰ; ਮੰਡਪ, ਤੰਬੂ, ਚੰਦੋਆ, ਬਾਰੀ ਦਾ ਛੱਜਾ; ਚੰਦੋਆ ਤਾਨਣਾ; ਛੱਤਰ ਤਾਨਣਾ, ਛੱਪਰ ਬਣਾਉਣਾ, ਤੰਬੂ ਲਾਉਣਾ

canteen (ਕੈਨ'ਟਿਨ) *n* ਚਾਹ ਪਾਣੀ ਦੀ ਦੁਕਾਨ, ਭੋਜਨ ਭੰਡਾਰ, ਅੰਨਪੂਰਨਾ; ਫ਼ੌਜੀਆਂ ਲਈ ਰਸਦ ਤੇ ਸ਼ਰਾਬ ਦੀ ਦੁਕਾਨ, ਸੈਖਨਾ; ਜਲ-ਪਾਤਰ

canton ('ਕੈਨਟੌਨ) *n v* ਪ੍ਰਾਂਤ, ਸੂਬਾ, ਪ੍ਰਦੇਸ਼, ਇਲਾਕਾ, ਪਰਗਣਾ; ਛਾਉਣੀ, ਸਵਿਟਜ਼ਰਲੈਂਡ ਦੀ ਇਕ ਰਿਆਸਤ; ਛਿਰਕਾ, ਕੌਮ; ਪਰਗਣਿਆਂ ਜਾਂ ਜ਼ਿਲ੍ਹਿਆਂ ਵਿਚ ਵੰਡਣਾ, ਛਾਉਣੀ, (ਸਿਪਾਹੀਆਂ ਨੂੰ) ਠਹਿਰਾਉਣਾ; **~ment** ਛਾਉਣੀ ਵੱਡਾ ਕੈਂਪ, ਫ਼ੌਜ, ਲਸ਼ਕਰ

canvas ('ਕੈਨਵ੍ਅਸ) *n v* ਬੋਰਾ, ਟਾਟ, ਤਿਰਪਾਲ, ਮੋਟਾ ਸੂਤੀ ਕੱਪੜਾ, ਦੌੜ ਵਾਲੀ ਕਿਸ਼ਤੀ ਦਾ ਛੱਤਦਾਰ ਕਿਨਾਰਾ; ਤੰਬੂ; ਸ਼ਾਸਤਰਾਰਥ, ਵਾਦ-ਵਿਵਾਦ, ਬਹਿਸ, ਮਤ, ਵੋਟ, ਵੋਟਾਂ ਮੰਗਣਾ, ਜਾਚਨਾ ਕਰਨੀ; **~er** ਵੋਟ ਜਾਂ ਮੱਤ ਚਾਹੁਣ ਵਾਲਾ, ਜਾਚਕ, ਮੱਤ-ਸੰਗ੍ਰਾਹਕ; **~ing** ਕਨਵੈਸਿੰਗ, ਵੋਟ ਦੀ ਮੰਗ, ਮੱਤ-ਸੰਗ੍ਰਹ ਦਾ ਜਤਨ, ਜਾਚਨਾ

cap (ਕੈਪ) *n* ਟੋਪੀ, ਕੁਲ੍ਹਾ; ਟੋਪ, ਸਿਖਰ; ਢੱਕਣ, ਉਛਾੜ, ਝਿਲਾਫ਼; ਸਰਦਾਰ, ਮੁਖੀਆ; ਟੋਪੀ ਪਹਿਨਣਾ ਜਾਂ ਪਹਿਨਾਉਣਾ; ਬੰਦੂਕ ਉੱਤੇ ਟੋਪੀ ਚੜ੍ਹਾਉਣਾ; ਸਲਾਮ ਕਰਨੀ, ਪਦਵੀ ਪ੍ਰਦਾਨ ਕਰਨਾ; ਚੋਟੀ ਤੇ ਹੋਣਾ; ਠੋਕਰ ਲਗਾ ਦੇਣਾ, ਚੋਟ ਖਾ ਲੈਣਾ

capabillity ('ਕੇਇਪਿਅ'ਬਿਲਅਟਿ) *n* ਯੋਗਤਾ, ਸਮਰੱਥਾ, ਪੁੱਜਤ, ਲਿਆਕਤ

capable ('ਕੇਇਪਅ'ਬਲ) *a* ਯੋਗ, ਸਮਰੱਥ, ਬਲਵਾਨ, ਲਾਇਕ, ਗੁਣੀ, ਗੁਣਵੰਤ

capacity (ਕਅ'ਪੈਸਅਟਿ) *n* ਸਮਰੱਥਾ, ਗ੍ਰਹਿਣ-ਸ਼ਕਤੀ, ਯੋਗਤਾ, ਗੁੰਜਾਇਸ਼; ਸਮਾਈ, ਦਰਜਾ, ਪਦ, ਹੈਸੀਅਤ

cape (ਕੇਇਪ) *n* ਛਤਰੀ; ਬਾਹਵਾਂ ਤੋਂ ਬਿਨਾਂ ਕੋਟ, ਅੰਤਰੀਪ

capital ('ਕੈਪਿਟਲ) *n a* ਮੂਲ-ਧਨ, ਪੂੰਜੀ, ਸਰਮਾਇਆ, ਲਾਗਤ; ਰਾਜਧਾਨੀ; ਥੰਮ੍ਹ ਦਾ ਉੱਪਰਲਾ ਹਿੱਸਾ, (ਸਜ਼ਾ) ਘਾਤਕ, ਪ੍ਰਧਾਨ, ਮਹੱਤਪੂਰਨ, ਸਰਵੋਤਮ; **~ism** ਪੂੰਜੀਵਾਦ,

ਸਰਮਾਏਦਾਰੀ; ~**ist** ਪੂੰਜੀਵਾਦੀ, ਪੂੰਜੀਪਤੀ, ਸਰਮਾਏਦਾਰ; ~**ization** ਪੂੰਜੀਕਰਣ, ਪੂੰਜੀ-ਸੰਗ੍ਰਹਣ

capitation ('ਕੈਪਿ'ਟੇਇਸ਼ਨ) *n* ਨੀਯਤ (ਫ਼ੀਸ, ਮਸੂਲ ਆਦਿ); ~**tax** ਨੀਯਤਕਰ

capitulate (ਕਅ'ਪਿਅਚੁਲੇਇਟ) *v* ਆਤਮ-ਸਮਰਪਣ ਕਰਨਾ, ਅਧੀਨ ਹੋ ਜਾਣਾ, ਹਥਿਆਰ ਸੁੱਟ ਦੇਣੇ (ਕੁਝ ਸ਼ਰਤ ਤੇ)

capitulation (ਕਅ'ਪਿਚੁ'ਲੇਇਸ਼ਨ) *n* ਸਮਝੌਤਾ; ਸ਼ਰਤਾਂ ਅਧੀਨ ਸਮਰਪਣ ਸੰਧੀ; ਸਿਰਲੇਖਬੰਦੀ

caprice (ਕਅ'ਪਰੀਸ) *n* ਤਰੰਗ, ਮੌਜ, ਲਹਿਰ; ਚਪਲਤਾ, ਚੰਚਲਤਾ; ਸਨਕ

capricious (ਕਅ'ਪਰਿਸ਼ਅਸ) *a* ਤਰੰਗੀ, ਮੌਜੀ, ਲਹਿਰੀ, ਵਹਿਮੀ; ਸਨਕੀ; ~**ness** ਚੰਚਲਤਾ, ਅਸਥਿਰਤਾ, ਮਨਮੌਜੀਪਣ, ਸਨਕਪੁਣਾ

capricorn ('ਕੈਪਰਿਕੋਨ) *n* ਮਕਰ ਰਾਸ਼ੀ

capsize (ਕੈਪ'ਸਾਇਜ਼) *v* (ਜਹਾਜ਼, ਕਿਸ਼ਤੀ ਦਾ) ਡੁੱਬਣਾ, ਉਲਟਾ ਹੋਣਾ, ਉਲਟਣਾ, ਪਲਟਣਾ

capsule ('ਕੈਪਸਯੂਲ) *n* ਝਿੱਲੀਦਾਰ ਥੈਲੀ; ਬੀਜ-ਕੋਸ਼; ਝਿੱਲੀ ਦੀ ਡੱਬੀ; ਫਲੀ, ਖੋਲ, ਲਿਫ਼ਾਫ਼ਾ; ਗ਼ਿਲਾਫ਼; ਡੋਡਾ, ਡੋਡੀ; ਕੈਪਸੂਲ

captain ('ਕੈਪਟਿਨ) *n v* ਕਪਤਾਨ, ਆਗੂ; ਨਾਇਕ, ਸੈਨਾ ਦਾ ਅਫ਼ਸਰ, ਸਰਦਾਰ; ਖਾਣਾਂ ਦਾ ਮੈਨੇਜਰ; ਫੋਰਮੈਨ; ਅਗਵਾਈ ਕਰਨਾ, ਮਾਰਗ-ਪਰਦਰਸ਼ਨ ਕਰਨਾ, ਰਹਿਨੁਮਾਈ ਕਰਨਾ, ਕਪਤਾਨੀ ਕਰਨਾ

caption ('ਕੈਪਸ਼ਨ) *n* ਸੁਰਖ਼ੀ, ਪੁਸਤਕ ਦਾ ਸਿਰਲੇਖ; ਕਾਨੂੰਨੀ ਗਰਿਫ਼ਤਾਰੀ, ਪਕੜ

captivate ('ਕੈਪਟਿਵ੍ਹੇਇਟ) *v* ਬੰਦੀ ਬਣਾਉਣਾ, ਕੈਦ ਕਰਨਾ, ਮੋਹ ਲੈਣਾ, ਮੋਹਣਾ, ਆਕਰਸ਼ਤ ਕਰਨਾ, ਖਿੱਚ ਲੈਣਾ

captivating ('ਕੈਪਟਿਵ੍ਹਇਟਿਙ) *a* ਮਨੋਹਰ, ਮਨਮੋਹਕ, ਆਕਰਸ਼ਕ

captivation ('ਕੈਪਟਿਵ੍ਹਇਸ਼ਨ) *n* ਮੋਹਨ, ਮਨਮੋਹਕਤਾ, ਆਕਰਸ਼ਣ; ਬੰਦੀਕਰਨ

captivity (ਕੈਪ'ਟਿਵ੍ਹਅਟਿ) *n* ਬੰਦੀਖ਼ਾਨਾ, ਕੈਦ, ਹਿਰਾਸਤ; ਗ਼ੁਲਾਮੀ

capture ('ਕੈਪਚਅ*) *n v* ਕਬਜ਼ਾ, ਗਰਿਫ਼ਤਾਰੀ; ਜਿੱਤਣਾ, ਕਬਜ਼ਾ ਕਰਨਾ

car (ਕਾ*) *n* ਮੋਟਰ ਕਾਰ, ਗੱਡੀ, ਰਥ, ਰੇਲ ਦਾ ਡੱਬਾ, ਉਡਣ-ਖਟੋਲੇ ਦਾ ਝੂਲਾ

carat ('ਕੈਰਅਟ) *n* ਸੋਨੇ ਤੇ ਹੀਰੇ ਤੋਲਣ ਦਾ ਤੋਲ, 3½ ਗ੍ਰੇਨ ਸੋਨੇ ਦੀ ਸ਼ੁੱਧਤਾ ਦਾ ਮਾਪ

caravan ('ਕੈਰਅਵ੍ਹੈਨ) *n* ਕਾਫ਼ਲਾ, ਕਾਰਵਾਨ, ਬੰਦਗੱਡੀ, ਚੱਲਦਾ ਫਿਰਦਾ ਘਰ

carbon ('ਕਾ*ਬਅਨ) *n* ਕਾਰਬਨ; ਕੋਲਾ, ਕੋਇਲਾ; ਕਾਲਖ, ਸੜੀਆਂ ਹੱਡੀਆਂ, ਪੱਥਰ ਦਾ ਕੋਲਾ, ਲੱਕੜ ਦਾ ਕੋਲਾ

carcass, carcase ('ਕਾ*ਕਅਸ) *n* ਲੋਥ, ਲਾਸ਼, ਮੁਰਦਾਰ, ਪਿੰਜਰ, ਢਾਂਚਾ

card (ਕਾ*ਡ) *n v* ਪਿੰਜਣਾ, ਧੁਣਕੁਣਾ, (ਪਿੰਜਣ ਵਾਲਾ) ਤਾੜਾ, ਧੁਣਕੁਲੀ, ਉੱਨ ਸਾਫ਼ ਕਰਨ ਵਾਲਾ ਕੰਘਾ; (ਤਾਸ਼ ਦੇ) ਪੱਤੇ, ਮੋਟੇ ਕਾਗ਼ਜ਼ ਦਾ ਟੁਕੜਾ; ਪੋਸਟ-ਕਾਰਡ, ਇਸ਼ਤਿਹਾਰ, ਉੱਨ ਸਾਫ਼ ਕਰਨੀ; ~**board** ਗੱਤਾ, ਮੋਟਾ ਕਾਗ਼ਜ਼; **post~** ਪੋਸਟ ਕਾਰਡ, ਕਾਰਡ **wedding** ਵਿਵਾਹ-ਪੱਤਰ ~**s** ਤਾਸ਼

cardamom ('ਕਾ*ਡਅਮਅਮ) *n* ਇਲਾਇਚੀ

cardiac ('ਕਾ*ਡਿਐਕ) *n* ਦਿਲ-ਸਬੰਧੀ, ਦਿਲੀ, ਹਿਰਦੇ ਦਾ, ਦਿਲ ਲਈ ਗੁਣਕਾਰੀ ਦਵਾਈ

cardinal ('ਕਾ*ਡਿਨਲ) *a n* ਮੌਲਕ, ਪ੍ਰਧਾਨ, ਮਹੱਤਵਪੂਰਣ, ਮੂਲ; ਛੋਟੀ ਲਾਲ ਚਿੜੀ; ਗਿਰਜੇ

cardiogram / **cart**

ਦਾ ਮੁਖੀ, ਕਾਰਡੀਨਲ ਪਾਦਰੀ

cardiogram ('ਕਾ*ਡਿਆ(ਉ)ਗਰੈਮ) *n* ਹਿਰਦੇ-ਚਿੱਤਰ, ਦਿਲ-ਗਤੀ ਲੇਖ

cardiograph ('ਕਾ*ਡਿਆ(ਉ)ਗਰਾਫ਼) *n* ਹਿਰਦੇ ਦੀ ਧੜਕਣ ਜਾਣਨ ਵਾਲਾ ਜੰਤਰ

cardiology (ਕਾ*ਡਿ'ਔਲਅਜਿ) *n* ਹਿਰਦੇ-ਵਿਗਿਆਨ

care (ਕੇਅ*) *n* ਪਰਵਾਹ, ਧਿਆਨ, ਖ਼ਬਰਦਾਰੀ, ਚੌਕਸੀ, ਫ਼ਿਕਰ, ਤੱਰਦਦ, ਚਿੰਤਾ, ਸੋਚ, ਜ਼ੁੰਮੇਵਾਰੀ, ਡਰ, ਮਾਰਫ਼ਤ; ਚਿੰਤਾ ਕਰਨਾ, ਫ਼ਿਕਰ ਕਰਨਾ, ਤੱਰਦਦ ਕਰਨਾ, ਸੰਭਾਲ ਕਰਨਾ, ਚੌਕਸ ਹੋਣਾ; ਪਿਆਰ ਕਰਨਾ, ਚਾਹੁਣਾ; ਰੋਗਾਂ ਦੀ ਦੇਖ ਭਾਲ ਕਰਨੀ; ਆਦਰ ਕਰਨਾ; **~of, c/o** ਮਾਰਫ਼ਤ, ਦੁਆਰਾ, ਰਾਹੀਂ; **~taker** ਰਖਵਾਲਾ, ਨਿਗਰਾਨ, ਕਾਰਿੰਦਾ; **take~of** ਸੰਭਾਲਣਾ, ਧਿਆਨ ਰਖਣਾ, ਖਬਰ ਲੈਣੀ; **~ful** ਸਚੇਤ, ਸੁਚੱਜਾ, ਸਾਵਧਾਨ ਖ਼ਬਰਦਾਰ; **~fulness** ਸਾਵਧਾਨੀ, ਸਤਰਕਤਾ, ਹੁਸ਼ਿਆਰੀ, ਖ਼ਬਰਦਾਰੀ; **~less** ਬੇਫ਼ਿਕਰ, ਬੇਪਰਵਾਹ, ਅਚੇਤ ਅਸਾਵਧਾਨ, ਅਣਗਹਿਲਾ, ਲਾਪਰਵਾਹ, ਬੇਖ਼ਬਰ, ਅਟਕਲ-ਪੱਚੂ; **~lessness** ਲਾਪਰਵਾਹੀ, ਬੇਪਰਵਾਹੀ, ਅਸਾਵਧਾਨੀ, ਨਿਸਚਿੰਤਤਾ

career (ਕਅ'ਰਿਅ*) *n v* ਵਿਵਸਾਇ, ਰੋਜ਼ੀ, ਪੇਸ਼ਾ, ਚਰਿੱਤਰ, ਚਲਣ; ਜੀਵਨ-ਯਾਤਰਾ; ਗਤੀ, ਰੌ, ਚਾਲ, ਰਿਵਾਜ

caress (ਕਅ'ਰੈੱਸ) *n v* ਲਾਡ, ਦਿਲਾਸਾ, ਪੁਚਕਾਰ, ਪਲੋਸਨਾ, ਲਾਡ ਲਡਾਉਣਾ, ਦਿਲਾਸਾ ਦੇਣਾ, ਪੁਚਕਾਰਨਾ

cargo ('ਕਾ*ਗਅਉ) *n* ਜਹਾਜ਼ ਦਾ ਮਾਲ, ਲੱਦ, ਭਾਰ

caricature ('ਕੈਰਿਕਅਚੁਅ*) *n v* ਵਿਅੰਗਾ-ਚਿੱਤਰਣ, ਉਪਹਾਸ, ਨਕਲ, ਕਾਰਟੂਨ, ਵਿਅੰਗ-ਚਿੱਤਰ ਖਿਚਣਾ, ਕਾਰਟੂਨ ਬਣਾਉਣਾ, ਸਾਂਗ ਲਾਉਣਾ

carnage ('ਕਾ*ਨਿਜ) *n* ਕਤਲਾਮ, ਖ਼ੂਨ ਖ਼ਰਾਬਾ, ਹੱਤਿਆ ਕਾਂਡ

carnal ('ਕਾ*ਨਲ) *n* ਭੋਗਵਿਲਾਸੀ, ਕਾਮੁਕ, ਵਿਸ਼ਈ, ਸਰੀਰਕ ਵਿਸ਼ਿਆਂ ਅਤੇ ਭੋਗਾਂ ਸਬੰਧੀ; ਸੰਸਾਰਕ, ਭੌਤਕ

carnival ('ਕਾ*ਨਿਵ਼ਲ) *n* ਇਕ ਇਸਾਈ ਤਿਉਹਾਰ; ਜਸ਼ਨ; ਰੰਗ ਰਲੀਆਂ, ਮੌਜ

carpenter ('ਕਾ*ਪੈਂਟਅ*) *n v* ਤਰਖਾਣ, ਲਕੜੀ ਦਾ ਕੰਮ ਕਰਨ ਵਾਲਾ; ਤਰਖਾਣਾ ਕੰਮ ਕਰਨਾ

carpentry ('ਕਾ*ਪੈਂਟਰਿ) *n* ਤਰਖਾਣਾ ਕੰਮ, ਲੱਕੜੀ ਦਾ ਕੰਮ

carpet ('ਕਾ*ਪਿਟ) *n v* ਗ਼ਾਲੀਚਾ, ਕਾਲੀਨ, ਦਰੀ, ਫ਼ਰਸ਼, ਫੁੱਲਾਂ ਜਾਂ ਘਾਹ ਦਾ ਪਲਾਟ; ਦਰੀ ਵਿਛਾਉਣਾ; ਫ਼ਰਸ਼ ਵਿਛਾਉਣਾ; (ਨੌਕਰ ਦੀ) ਝਾੜ-ਝੰਭ ਕਰਨੀ

carriage ('ਕੈਰਿਜ) *n* ਗੱਡੀ, ਬੱਘੀ; ਭਾੜਾ, ਢੁਆਈ, ਬੰਦੋਬਸਤ, ਇੰਤਜ਼ਾਮ; ਢੰਗ, ਅੰਦਾਜ਼

carrier (ਕੈਰਿਅ*) *n* ਢਕਣ ਵਾਲਾ, ਭਾੜੇ ਵਾਲਾ, ਗੱਡੀ ਵਾਲਾ, ਭਾਰ ਢੋਣ ਵਾਲਾ; ਕੁਲੀ, ਪਾਂਡੀ, ਮਜ਼ਦੂਰ; ਬਾਈਸਿਕਲ ਦੇ ਪਿੱਛੇ ਭਾਰ ਰੱਖਣ ਲਈ ਥਾਂ, ਕੈਰੀਅਰ

carrot ('ਕੈਰਅਟ) *n* ਗਾਜਰ

carry ('ਕੈਰਿ) *v* ਢੋਣਾ, ਲੈ ਜਾਣਾ, ਪਹੁੰਚਾਉਣਾ; ਜਿੱਤਣਾ; **~off** ਲੈ ਭੱਜਣਾ, ਭਜਾ ਕੇ ਲੈ ਜਾਣਾ, ਜਿੱਤਣਾ; **~on** ਜਾਰੀ ਰੱਖਣਾ, ਚੱਲਦੇ ਜਾਣਾ; **~out** ਆਗਿਆ ਦੀ ਪਾਲਣਾ ਕਰਨਾ

cart (ਕਾ:ਟ) *n* ਗੱਡਾ, ਛਕੜਾ; ਗੱਡੇ ਲੱਦਣਾ, ਲੱਦ ਕੇ ਲੈ ਜਾਣਾ; **~horse** ਟੱਟੂ; **bullock~** ਬੈਲ-

cartographer

ਗੱਡੀ, ਬਹਿਲੀ; ~**hand** ਹੱਥ-ਗੱਡੀ, ਰੇੜ੍ਹੀ; ~**age** ਭਾੜਾ

cartographer (ਕਾ'ਟੋਗਰਅਫ਼ਅ*) *n* ਨਕਸ਼ਾ-ਨਵੀਸ, ਨਕਸ਼ਾ-ਨਿਗਾਰ, ਨਕਸ਼ੇ ਬਣਾਉਣ ਵਾਲਾ

cartography (ਕਾ'ਟੋਗਰਅਫ਼ਿ) *n* ਨਕਸ਼ਾ-ਨਵੀਸੀ, ਨਕਸ਼ਾ-ਨਿਗਾਰੀ, ਨਕਸ਼ੇ ਬਣਾਉਣ ਦੀ ਵਿੱਦਿਆ

cartoon (ਕਾ'ਟੂਨ) *n v* ਕਾਰਟੂਨ, ਵਿਅੰਗ-ਚਿਤਰ; ਕਾਰਟੂਨ ਬਣਾਉਣਾ, ਵਿਅੰਗ-ਚਿਤਰ ਬਣਾਉਣਾ

cartridge ('ਕਾਟਰਿਜ) *n* ਕਾਰਤੂਸ, ਗੋਲੀਆਂ (ਸੰਦੂਕ ਆਦਿ ਦੀਆਂ); **blank~** ਠੋਕਾ ਕਾਰਤੂਸ

carve (ਕਾਵ਼) *v* ਘੜਨਾ, ਤਰਾਸ਼ਣਾ, ਉਕਰਨਾ, ਸਜਾਉਣਾ, ਛੋਟੇ ਛੋਟੇ ਟੁਕੜੇ ਕਰਨਾ, ਖੋਦਣਾ; ~**in** ਖੋਦ ਕੇ ਬਣਾਉਣਾ

carving ('ਕਾਵ਼ਿੰਙ) *n* ਮੂਰਤੀ-ਕਲਾ, ਸੰਗ-ਤਰਾਸ਼ੀ, ਖੁਦਣ-ਕਲਾ; ਨੱਕਾਸ਼ੀ; ਤਰਾਸ਼, ਕਾਟ

case (ਕੇਇਸ) *n v* ਮਾਮਲਾ, ਮੁਕਦਮਾ, ਹਾਲਤ, ਸੂਰਤ, ਸਥਿਤੀ, ਕੈਫ਼ੀਅਤ; ਰੋਗੀ ਦੀ ਦਸ਼ਾ; ਘਟਨਾ; ਦਾਅਵਾ, ਖੋਲ, ਡੱਬਾ; (ਭਾਸ਼ਾ) ਕਾਰਕ; ਖੋਲ ਚੜ੍ਹਾਉਣਾ, ਗ਼ਿਲਾਫ਼ ਚੜ੍ਹਾਉਣਾ, ਡੱਬੇ ਜਾਂ ਸੰਦੂਕ ਵਿਚ ਬੰਦ ਕਰਨਾ; ~**history** (ਚਿਕਿ) ਰੋਗ ਇਤਿਰੰਜ; ~**as the~ may bo** ਜੋ ਵੀ ਹੋਵੇ; ਜਿਸ ਤਰ੍ਹਾਂ ਵੀ ਹੋਵੇ, ਦਸ਼ਾ ਅਨੁਸਾਰ; **in any~** ਹਰ ਹਾਲਤ ਵਿਚ, ਹਰ ਹੀਲੇ; **in~** ਜੇ, ਜੇਕਰ; **in-if** ਅਜਿਹਾ ਹੋਇਆ ਤਾਂ, ਜੇ, ਅਗਰ; **in~of** ਇਸ ਦਸ਼ਾ ਵਿਚ, ਅਜਿਹਾ ਹੋਣ ਤੇ, ਅਵਸਥਾ ਵਿਚ; **in that~** ਅਜਿਹੀ ਹਾਲਤ ਵਿਚ; **in the~of** ਬਾਰੇ, ਸਬੰਧੀ, ਬਾਬਤ; **make out one's~** ਆਪਣੇ ਪੱਖ ਵਿਚ ਦਲੀਲਾਂ ਦੇਣੀਆਂ; ~**ment** ਖਿੜਕੀ

cash (ਕੈਸ਼) *n v* ਰੋਕੜ, ਨਕਦ, ਨਕਦੀ ਕਰਵਾਉਣਾ; ~**account** ਰੋਕੜ-ਲੇਖਾ; ~**book** ਲੇਖਾ-ਵਹੀ, ਵਹੀ-ਖਾਤਾ, ਰੋਕੜ; ~**crop** ਵਪਾਰਕ ਫ਼ਸਲ; ~**deposit** ਨਕਦ ਜਮ੍ਹਾਂ; ~**memo** ਨਕਦੀ ਦੀ ਰਸੀਦ

cashier (ਕੈ'ਸ਼ਿਅ*) *n v* ਖ਼ਜ਼ਾਨਚੀ, ਰੋਕੜੀਆ; ਖ਼ਾਰਜ ਕਰਨਾ, ਨਾਉਂ ਕਟੱਣਾ; ਰੱਦ ਕਰਨਾ, ਮੌਕੂਫ਼ ਕਰਨਾ, ਬਰਖ਼ਾਸਤ ਕਰਨਾ

casino (ਕਅ'ਸੀਨਅਉ) *n* ਜੂਆਖ਼ਾਨਾ; ਤਾਸ਼ ਦਾ ਪੁਰਾਣਾ ਖੇਲ

cask (ਕਾਸਕ) *n* (ਲੱਕੜ ਦੀ) ਪੀਪਾ, ਲੱਕੜ ਦਾ ਛੋਟਾ ਢੋਲ

cast (ਕਾਸਟ) *v n* ਸੁੱਟਣਾ; ਦਫ਼ਾ ਕਰਨਾ; ਹਿਸਾਬ ਲਗਾਉਣਾ, ਜੋੜਨਾ, ਗਿਣਨਾ, ਢਾਲਣਾ (ਪਿਘਲੀ ਹੋਈ ਧਾਤ ਦਾ); ਪਾਉਣਾ (ਵੋਟ), ਮੁਕੱਦਮਾ ਜਿੱਤਣਾ; ਆਕਾਰ, ਰੂਪ, ਪ੍ਰਕਾਰ; ਜੋੜ; ਹਿਸਾਬ; ਢਲਾਈ; ~**down** ਉਦਾਸ, ਦਿਲਗੀਰ; ~**about** ਹੱਥ ਪੈਰ ਮਾਰਨੇ, ਭਾਲਣਾ; ~**a vote** ਵੋਟ ਪਾਉਣੀ, ਪਰਚੀ ਪਾਉਣੀ; ~**iron** ਢਲਿਆ ਲੋਹਾ; ਢਾਲੇ ਹੋਏ ਲੋਹੇ ਦਾ; ਸਖ਼ਤ, ਕਠੋਰ, ਕਰੜਾ

casting ('ਕਾਸਟਿਙ) *n* ਢਲਾਈ, ਢਲੀ ਹੋਈ ਚੀਜ਼; ਪਾਤਰ-ਵੰਡ; ~**vote** ਨਿਰਣਾਇਕ ਵੋਟ, ਸਭਾਪਤੀ ਦਾ ਵੋਟ ਜੋ ਦੋ ਬਰਾਬਰ ਪੱਖਿਆਂ ਦਾ ਫ਼ੈਸਲਾ ਕਰਵਾ ਦੇਵੇ

caste (ਕਾਸਟ) *n* ਵਰਣ, ਜਾਤ, ਜਾਤ-ਪਾਤ, ਕੌਮ, ਫ਼ਿਰਕਾ, ਬਰਾਦਰੀ; (ਦੂਜੇ ਦੇਸ਼ਾਂ ਵਿਚ) ਵਰਗ, ਸਮੂਹ; ~**system** ਜਾਤੀ-ਪ੍ਰਥਾ, ਜਾਤੀ ਪ੍ਰਣਾਲੀ; ~**less** ਜਾਤ ਪਾਤ ਤੋਂ ਰਹਿਤ ਵਰਣਹੀਨ

castigate ('ਕੈਸਟਿਗੇਇਟ) *v* ਫਿਟਕਾਰਨਾ; ਝਾੜਨਾ, ਚੰਡਣਾ

castigation ('ਕੈਸਟਿ'ਗੇਇਸ਼ਨ) *n* ਫਿਟਕਾਰ, ਤਾੜਨਾ, ਕੁੱਟ, ਸੁਧਾਰ, ਸੁਧਾਈ

castle ('ਕਾਸਲ) *n v* ਕਿਲ੍ਹਾ, ਗੜ੍ਹ, ਕੋਟ, ਸ਼ਤਰੰਜ ਦਾ ਰੁਖ਼; ਰੁਖਬੰਦੀ ਕਰਨੀ; **build ~s in the air** ਹਵਾਈ ਕਿਲ੍ਹੇ ਉਸਾਰਨੇ, ਖ਼ਿਆਲੀ ਪੁਲਾਉ ਪਕਾਉਣੇ

casual ('ਕੈਯੂਅਲ) *a n* ਇਤਫ਼ਾਕੀਆ, ਅਚਨਚੇਤੀ, ਸਬੱਬੀ, ਅਚਾਨਕ, ਬੇਕਾਇਦਾ; ਅਨਿਯਮਤ, ਅਸਾਵਧਾਨ ਬੇਢੰਗਾ; **~labourer** ਦਿਹਾੜੀਦਾਰ, ਕੱਚਾ ਮਜ਼ਦੂਰ; **~ly** ਸਬੱਬੀ, ਕਦੇ ਕਦੇ, ਅਚਾਨਕ ਹੀ

casualties ('ਕੈਯੂਅਲਟਿਜ਼) *n* ਮਰੇ ਹੋਏ ਜਾਂ ਘਾਇਲ ਹੋਏ ਆਦਮੀਆਂ ਦੀ ਸੰਖਿਆ

casualty (ਕੈਯੂਅਲਟਿ) *n* ਦੁਰਘਟਨਾ, ਹਾਦਸਾ; ਮੁਸੀਬਤ; ਖਾਤਨਾ; (ਜੁੱਧ ਵਿਚ) ਮਰਿਆਂ ਦੀ ਸੂਚੀ, ਘਾਇਲ ਲੋਕ; **~ward** ਅਚਾਨਕ ਘਾਇਲ ਹੋਏ ਲੋਕਾਂ ਦਾ ਵਾਰਡ

cat (ਕੈਟ) *n v* ਬਿੱਲੀ; ਬਿੱਲੀ-ਪਰਵਾਰ ਦੇ ਜਾਨਵਰ; ਲੜਾਕੀ ਰੰਨ, ਲੰਗਰ ਚੁੱਕਣ ਵਾਲਾ ਜਹਾਜ਼ੀਰ ਉਲਟੀ ਕਰਨੀ; ਲੰਗਰ ਚੁੱਕਣਾ; **~and dog life** ਕੁੱਤਿਆਂ ਬਿੱਲਿਆਂ ਵਾਲਾ ਜੀਵਨ, ਕਲਾ ਕਲੇਸ਼ ਦਾ ਜੀਵਨ; **~eyed** ਜੋ ਹਨੇਰੇ ਵਿਚ ਵੇਖ ਸਕੇ; **wild~** ਸ਼ੇਰ, ਚੀਤਾ ਆਦਿ

catalogue ('ਕੈਟਲੌਗ) *n v* ਨਾਮਾਵਲੀ, ਸੂਚੀ-ਪੱਤਰ, ਪੁਸਤਕ ਸੂਚੀ, ਸਾਰਨੀ, ਤਾਲਿਕਾ; ਫ਼ਹਿਰਿਸਤ; ਸੂਚੀ ਬਣਾਉਣਾ, ਫ਼ਹਿਰਿਸਤ ਵਿਚ ਦਰਜ ਕਰਨਾ

cataract ('ਕੈਟਅਰੈਕਟ) *n* ਮੋਤੀਆ ਬਿੰਦ ਝਰਨਾ, ਆਬਸ਼ਾਰ, ਪਾਣੀ ਦੀ ਚਾਦਰ, ਮੋਹਲੇਧਾਰ ਵਰਖਾ

catarrh (ਕਅ'ਟਾ*) *n* ਨਜ਼ਲਾ, ਜ਼ੁਕਾਮ, ਰੇਸ਼ਾ

catastrophe (ਕਅ'ਟੈਸਟਰਅਫ਼ਿ) *n* ਬਿਪਤਾ, ਆਫ਼ਤ, ਘੱਲੂਘਾਰਾ, ਅਨਰਥ, ਕਹਿਰ, ਉਥਲ-ਪੁਥਲ; ਬਿਪਤਾ ਭਰਿਆ ਅੰਤ, ਤਬਾਹੀ, ਨਾਟਕ ਦਾ ਦੁਖਾਂਤ

catastrophic, -al ('ਕੈਟਅ'ਸਟਰੌਫ਼ਿਕ, ਕੈਟਅ'- ਸਟਰੌਫ਼ਿਕਲ) *a* ਬਿਪਤਾਪੂਰਨ, ਤਬਾਹਕਾਰੀ

catch (ਕੈਚ) *v n* ਫੜਨਾ, ਫੜ ਲੈਣਾ, ਥੰਮ੍ਹਣਾ, ਫਾਹੁਣਾ, ਗਿਰਫ਼ਤਾਰ ਕਰਨਾ, ਝਪਟਾ, ਧਰਨਾ; ਝੁੱਪ ਲੈਣਾ; ਪਕੜ, ਫੜਾਈ; ਗਿਰਫ਼ਤਾਰੀ ਕ੍ਰਿਕਟ ਵਿਚ ਗੇਂਦ ਬੋਚ; ਅੜਿੱਕਾ, ਅੜਾਉਣੀ, ਹਟਕੋਰਾ, ਫਾਹੁਣ ਯੋਗ ਆਦਮੀ, ਚੰਗਾ ਸ਼ਿਕਾਰ; **~ment** ਅਜਿਹਾ ਖੇਤਰ ਜਿਥੇ ਮੀਂਹ ਦਾ ਪਾਣੀ ਵਹਿ ਕੇ ਨਦੀ ਵਿਚ ਆਏ; **~word** ਸੂਚਕ ਸ਼ਬਦ, ਪੰਨੇ ਦੇ ਸਿਰੇ ਤੇ ਲਿਖਿਆ ਆਰੰਭਕ ਤੇ ਅੰਤਮ ਸ਼ਬਦ, ਨਾਅਰਾ; ਸੂਤਰ

catching ('ਕੈਚਿੰਗ) *a n* ਦਿਲ ਖਿਚਵਾਂ, ਆਕਰਸ਼ਤ; ਅਸਰਦਾਇਕ; ਪਕੜ; ਗ੍ਰਾਹੀ

categorisation ('ਕੈਟਅਗਅਰਾਇ'ਜ਼ੇਇਸ਼ਨ) *n* ਵਰਗੀਕਰਨ, ਪ੍ਰਕਾਰ-ਵੰਡ

categorise ('ਕੈਟਅਗਅਰਾਇਜ਼) *v* ਵਰਗੀਕ੍ਰਿਤ ਕਰਨਾ, ਵੰਡ ਕਰਨੀ, ਵੰਡਣਾ

category ('ਕੈਟਗਅਰਿ) *n* ਸ਼੍ਰੇਣੀ

cater ('ਕੇਇਟਅ*) *v* ਭੋਜਨ ਦਾ, ਪ੍ਰਬੰਧ ਕਰਨਾ, ਲੋੜ ਪੂਰੀ ਕਰਨਾ; **~er** ਭੰਡਾਰੀ, ਭੋਜਨ ਵੰਡਣ ਵਾਲਾ, ਭੋਜਪ੍ਰਬੰਧਕ; **~ing** ਭੋਜਨ-ਪ੍ਰਬੰਧ, ਆਹਾਰ-ਪ੍ਰਦਾਨ, ਖਿਲਾਈ

catharsis (ਕਅ'ਥਾਸਿਸ) *n* ਜੁਲਾਬ, ਵਿਰੇਚਨ, ਜ਼ੋਖ; ਸਰੀਰ-ਸੁੱਧੀ; ਭਾਵ-ਵਿਰੇਚਨ

cattle ('ਕੈਟਲ) *n* ਪਸ਼ੂ, ਡੰਗਰ, ਵੱਗ; ਮਾਲ

cauliflower ('ਕੌਲਿ'ਫ਼ਲਾਉਅ*) *n* ਫੁੱਲ ਗੋਭੀ

causal ('ਕੋਜ਼ਲ) *a* ਕਾਰਨਵਾਦੀ, ਕਾਰਨ-ਸਬੰਧੀ, ਕਾਰਨ

causative ('ਕੋਜ਼ਅਟਿਵ) *n* (ਬੋਲ) ਕਾਰਨਿਕ, ਕਾਰਨਕਾਰੀ, ਕਾਰਨਵਾਚਕ; ਪਰੇਨਾਰਥਕ

cause (ਕੌਜ਼) *n v* ਕਾਰਨ, ਸਬੱਬ, ਵਜ੍ਹਾ, ਮੂਲ ਕਰਤਾ; ਉਦੇਸ਼, ਪ੍ਰਯੋਜਨ, ਦਾਅਵਾ, ਪੱਖ; **final~** ਅੰਤਮ ਉਦੇਸ਼; **first~** ਮੂਲ ਕਾਰਨ; ਸਿਰਜਨਹਾਰ, ਪਰਮਾਤਮਾ; **show~** ਕਾਰਨ ਦੱਸਣਾ; ਕਰਾਉਣਾ, ਕਰਵਾਉਣਾ; ਪੈਦਾ ਕਰਨਾ; ਬਣਾ ਲੈਣਾ

caution ('ਕੋਸ਼ਨ) *v* ਖ਼ਬਰਦਾਰੀ, ਸਾਵਧਾਨੀ, ਚੌਕਸੀ, ਚੇਤਾਵਨੀ; ਸਿਆਣਪ; ਚੇਤਾਵਨੀ ਦੇਣੀ, ਜਤਲਾਉਣਾ, ਖ਼ਬਰਦਾਰ ਕਰਨਾ, ਆਗਾਹ ਕਰਨਾ

cautious ('ਕੌਸ਼ਅਸ) *a* ਸਾਵਧਾਨ, ਚੌਕਸ, ਖ਼ਬਰਦਾਰ, ਸਿਆਣਾ; **~ly** ਸਾਵਧਾਨੀ ਨਾਲ, ਖ਼ਬਰਦਾਰ ਹੋ ਕੇ, ਸੋਚ ਸਮਝ ਕੇ, ਧਿਆਨ ਨਾਲ; **~ness** ਹੁਸ਼ਿਆਰੀ, ਚੌਕਸੀ, ਖ਼ਬਰਦਾਰੀ, ਨਿਪੁੰਨਤਾ

cavalry ('ਕੈਵ'ਅ'ਰਿ) ਘੁੜਸਵਾਰ ਸੈਨਾ, (ਸਵਾਰਾਂ ਦਾ) ਰਸਾਲਾ

cave (ਕੇਇਵ਼) *n v int* ਗੁਫ਼ਾ, ਕੰਦਰਾ; ਪੇਹ, ਗ੍ਹਾਰ; ਗੁਟਬੰਦੀ; ਗੁਫ਼ਾ ਪੁੱਟਣੀ, ਪੋਲਾ ਕਰਨਾ; ਗੁੱਟ ਬਣਾਉਣਾ, ਅਧੀਨ ਹੋ ਜਾਣਾ; ਹਾਰ ਮੰਨਣੀ, ਵਿਗਾੜ ਦੇਣਾ; (ਸਕੂਲ ਵਿਚ ਅਧਿਆਪਕ ਦੇ ਆਉਣ ਦੀ ਸੂਚਨਾ ਮੁੰਡਿਆਂ ਵੱਲੋਂ) ਹੁਸ਼ਿਆਰ! ਸਾਵਧਾਨ! ਖ਼ਬਰਦਾਰ!

cavern ('ਕੈਵ਼(ਅ)ਨ) *n v* ਕੰਦਰਾ, ਖੁੰਦਰ, ਗੁਫ਼ਾ (ਕਾਵਿਆਈ); ਗੁਫ਼ਾ ਖੋਦਣਾ ਜਾਂ ਬਣਾਉਣਾ; ਕੰਦਰਾਂ ਵਿਚ ਬੰਦ ਕੇ ਰੱਖਣਾ

ceiling ('ਸਿਲਿਙ) *n* ਛੱਤ, ਅੰਦਰਲੀ ਛੱਤ, ਮੁੱਲ ਜਾਂ ਮਜ਼ਦੂਰੀ ਆਦਿ ਦੀ ਅੰਤਮ ਸੀਮਾ

celebrate ('ਸੈਲਿਬਰੇਇਟ) *v* (ਤਿਉਹਾਰ, ਦਿਨ) ਮਨਾਉਣਾ, ਜਸ਼ਨ ਮਨਾਉਣਾ; ਸਮਾਰੋਹ ਕਰਨਾ, ਉਤਸਵ ਮਨਾਉਣਾ, (ਧਾਰਮਕ ਰੀਤ) ਅਦਾ ਕਰਨੀ, ਪੂਜਣਾ, ਕੀਰਤੀ ਕਰਨਾ; ਜਸ ਫੈਲਾਉਣਾ, ਪ੍ਰਸਿੱਧ ਕਰਨਾ

celebrity (ਸਿ'ਲੈਬਰਅਟਿ) *n* ਜਸ, ਪ੍ਰਸਿੱਧੀ, ਪ੍ਰਸਿੱਧ ਵਿਅਕਤੀ

celestial (ਸਿ'ਲੈਸਟਅਲ) *a* ਆਕਾਸ਼ੀ, ਅਸਮਾਨੀ, ਪਵਿੱਤਰ, ਸਵਰਗੀ, ਸੁੰਦਰ, ਬ੍ਰਹਮ ਲੋਕੀ

celibacy ('ਸੈਲਿਬਅਸਿ) *n* ਕੁਆਰਾਪਣ, ਜਤ-ਸਤ, ਬ੍ਰਹਮਚਾਰੀ-ਜੀਵਨ

celibate ('ਸੈਲਿਬਅਟ) *n a* ਬ੍ਰਹਮਚਾਰੀ, ਜਤੀ-ਸਤੀ, ਕੁਆਰਾ; ਅਣ-ਵਿਆਹਿਆ (ਪੁਰਸ਼), ਅਵਿਵਾਹਤ (ਜੀਵਨ)

cell (ਸੈੱਲ) *n* ਕੋਠੜੀ; ਇਕ ਖੋਲ; ਕੋਸ਼ਾਣ, ਕੋਸ਼ਿਕਾ, ਕੁਟੀਆ, ਕੁਟੀਰ; ਸਮਾਧੀ; ਕਬਰ; **condemned~** ਕਾਲ-ਕੋਠੜੀ; **~er** ਤਹਿਖ਼ਾਨਾ, ਧਰਤੀ ਹੇਠਲਾ ਗੁਦਾਮ

cellular ('ਸੈੱਲਯੁਲਅ*) *a* ਖ਼ਾਨੇਦਾਰ, ਛੇਕਾਂ ਵਾਲਾ, ਜਾਲੀਦਾਰ

cement ('ਸਿ'ਮੈਂਟ) *n v* ਸੀਮਿੰਟ; ਜੋੜਨ ਦਾ ਮਸਾਲਾ; ਦੰਦ ਦਾ ਸਖ਼ਤ ਆਵਾਰਣ; ਸੀਮਿੰਟ ਲਗਾਉਣਾ

cemetery ('ਸੈਮਿਟਰਿ) *n* ਸ਼ਮਸ਼ਾਨ, ਕਬਰਸਤਾਨ

censor ('ਸੈਨਸਅ*) *n v* ਦੋਸ਼-ਨਿਰੀਖਕ, ਪੁਸਤਕਾਂ, ਸਮਾਚਾਰਾਂ ਆਦਿ ਦਾ ਸੈਂਸਰ, ਦੋਸ਼ ਲੱਭਣਾ, ਪੜਤਾਲਣਾ

censure ('ਸੈਂਨਸ਼ਅ*) *n v* ਨਿੰਦਾ, ਕਲੰਕ, ਮੁਜ਼ੰਮਤ; ਤਿਰਸਕਾਰ, ਝਿੜਕ, ਫਿਟਕਾਰ; ਨਿੰਦਾ ਕਰਨਾ, ਦੋਸ਼ ਕੱਢਣਾ, ਮੁਜ਼ੰਮਤ ਕਰਨਾ, ਦੋਸ਼ ਲਗਾਉਣਾ

census ('ਸੈਨਸਅਸ) *n* ਮਰਦਮ ਸ਼ੁਮਾਰੀ, ਜਨ-ਗਣਨਾ

centenary (ਸੈਂ'ਟੀਨਅਰਿ) *n a* ਸ਼ਤਾਬਦੀ ਸਮਾਰੋਹ; ਸੌ ਬਰਸੀ, ਸੌ ਸਾਲਾ ਉਤਸਵ

center (ਸੈਂਟਅ*) *n* (ਪ੍ਰ) ਕਮਰਬੰਦ

centigram ('ਸੈਂਟਿਗਰੈਮ) *n* ਸੈਂਟੀਗ੍ਰਾਮ, ਗ੍ਰਾਮ ਦਾ

ਸੌਂਵਾਂ ਭਾਗ

centimetre ('ਸੈਂਟਿ'ਮੀਟਅ*) *n* ਸੈਂਟੀਮੀਟਰ, ਮੀਟਰ ਦਾ ਸੌਂਵਾਂ ਭਾਗ

centipede ('ਸੈਂਟਿਪੀਡ) *n* ਕੰਨ ਖਜੂਰਾ

central ('ਸੈਂਟਰਲ) *a* ਕੇਂਦਰੀ ਵਿਚਕਾਰਲਾ, ਮੱਧਵਰਤੀ; ਪ੍ਰਧਾਨ, ਸਰਵ, ਪ੍ਰਮੁੱਖ, ਮੁੱਖ; ਸਿਰੋਮਣੀ, ਵੱਡਾ; ~ideal ਕੇਂਦਰੀ ਭਾਵ; ~ization ਕੇਂਦਰੀਕਰਨ; ~ly ਕੇਂਦਰ ਵਿਚ, ਕੇਂਦਰ ਤੋਂ

centre (ਸੈਂਟਅ*) *n a v* ਕੇਂਦਰ, ਮੱਧਵਰਤੀ ਭਾਗ, ਮਰਕਜ਼, ਕੇਂਦਰੀ ਨੁਕਤਾ; ਵਿਚਕਾਰਲੀ ਥਾਂ; ਕੇਂਦਰੀ, ਮਰਕਜ਼ੀ; ਕੇਂਦਰ ਵਿਚ ਕਰਨਾ, ਕੇਂਦਰਤ ਕਰਨਾ, ਇੱਕਠਾ ਕਰਨਾ; **~of gravity** ਗੁਰੁਤਾ-ਕੇਂਦਰ

centrifugal (ਸੈਂ'ਟਰਿਫ਼ਯੂਗਲ) *a* ਵਿਕੇਂਦਰੀ, ਕੇਂਦਰੀ ਤੋਂ ਖਿੰਡਣ ਜਾਂ ਪਸਰਨ ਵਾਲੀ, ਅਪਕੇਂਦਰੀ; **~force** ਅਪਕੇਂਦਰ ਸ਼ਕਤੀ, ਜਿਸ ਸ਼ਕਤੀ ਨਾਲ ਕੋਈ ਚੀਜ਼ ਆਪਣੇ ਕੇਂਦਰ ਤੋਂ ਬਾਹਰ ਜਾਂਦੀ ਹੈ

centripetal (ਸੈਂ'ਟਰਿਪਿਟਲ) *a* ਕੇਂਦਰਮੁਖੀ, ਕੇਂਦਰ ਵੱਲ ਲੈ ਜਾਣ ਵਾਲੀ

century ('ਸੈਂਚੁਰਿ) *n* ਸੈਂਕੜਾ, ਸ਼ਤਕ, ਸਦੀ, ਸੌ ਵਰ੍ਹੇ ਦਾ ਸਮਾਂ, ਸ਼ਤਾਬਦੀ

cereal ('ਸਿਅਰਿਅਲ) *n a* ਅਨਾਜ, ਗੱਲਾ; ਅੰਨ ਸਬੰਧੀ, ਅੰਨ ਦਾ

cerebral ('ਸੈਰਿਬਰ(ਅ)ਲ) *a* ਦਿਮਾਗ਼ ਦਾ, ਦਿਮਾਗ਼ੀ, ਮੁਰਦਨੀ

ceremonial ('ਸੈਰਿ'ਮਅਉਨਯਅਲ) *a n* ਰਸਮੀ, ਉਪਚਾਰਕ ਰੀਤੀ-ਅਨੁਸਾਰ, ਰੀਤੀਬੱਧ, ਮਰਯਾਦਾ-ਪੂਰਬਕ, ਸਮਾਰੋਹ-ਸਬੰਧੀ; ਰੀਤੀ-ਪਾਲਣ, ਪ੍ਰਥਾ, ਦਸਤੂਰ, ਸੰਸਕਾਰ, ਕਰਮਕਾਂਡ ਜਾਂ ਸੰਸਕਾਰ ਦੀ ਪੋਥੀ; **~ly** ਰਸਮੀ ਤੌਰ ਤੇ, ਰੀਤੀ ਅਨੁਸਾਰ

ceremonious ('ਸੈਰਿ'ਮਅਉਨਯਅਸ) *a* ਰਸਮੀ, ਉਪਚਾਰਕ, ਰਸਮਪੂਰਬਕ, ਰੀਤ-ਪੁਜਾਰੀ

ceremony ('ਸੈਰਿਮਅਨਿ) *n* ਧਾਰਮਕ ਰੀਤ, ਰਸਮ, ਵਿਧੀ, ਸੰਸਕਾਰ; ਸ਼ਿਸ਼ਟਾਚਾਰ

certificate ('ਸਅ*'ਟਿਫ਼ਿਕਅਟ, ਸਅ*'ਟਿਫ਼ਿਕੇਇਟ) *n v* ਸਨਦ, ਪ੍ਰਮਾਣ-ਪੱਤਰ, ਸਰਟਿਫ਼ਿਕੇਟ, ਪ੍ਰਸੰਸਾ-ਪੱਤਰ; ਸਨਦ ਦੇਣੀ, ਤਸਦੀਕ ਕਰਨਾ

certification ('ਸਅ*:ਟਿਫ਼ਿ'ਕੇਇਸ਼ਨ) *n* ਪ੍ਰਮਾਣੀਕਰਨ

certified ('ਸਅ*:ਟਿਫ਼ਾਇਡ) *a* ਪ੍ਰਮਾਣਤ, ਤਸਦੀਕਸ਼ੁਦਾ

certify ('ਸਅ*:ਟਿਫ਼ਿਇ) *v* ਪ੍ਰਮਾਣਤ ਕਰਨਾ, ਪ੍ਰਮਾਣ-ਪੱਤਰ ਦੇਣਾ, ਪ੍ਰਮਾਣ-ਸਹਿਤ ਆਖਣਾ, ਵਿਸ਼ਵਾਸ ਦਿਵਾਉਣਾ

cess (ਸੈੱਸ) *n v* ਕਰ, ਉਪਕਰ, ਚੁੰਗੀ, ਮਹਿਸੂਲ, ਸਥਾਨਕ ਕਰ; ਕਰ ਲਾਉਣਾ, ਚੁੰਗੀ ਲਾਉਣਾ

cessation (ਸੈਸੇਇਸ਼ਨ) *n* ਠਹਿਰਾਉ, ਅੰਤ, ਖ਼ਾਤਮਾ, ਮੁਕ-ਚੁਕ, (ਜੰਗ ਦੀ) ਬੰਦੀ

chafe (ਚੇਇਫ਼) *n v* ਖਿਝ; ਰਗੜ; ਖਿਝਣਾ, ਖਿਝਾਉਣਾ, ਮਾਲਸ਼ ਕਰਨਾ, ਸਲਣਾ; ਖੁਜਲਾਉਣਾ, ਮਲਣ ਜਾਂ ਰਗੜਨ ਨਾਲ ਸ਼ਰੀਰ ਦਾ ਛਿਲਿਆ ਜਾਣਾ, ਚਿੜ੍ਹਨਾ, ਚਿੜ੍ਹਾਉਣਾ

chaff (ਚੈਫ਼) *n v* ਤੂੜੀ, ਛਾਲੂਰ, ਫੱਕ; ਘਾਹ-ਫੂਸ, ਕੱਖ-ਕਾਣ; ਛੇੜਨਾ, ਮੌਜ ਉਡਾਉਣਾ, (ਘਾਹ) ਕਟਣਾ, ਛੇੜਾਂ ਕਰਨੀਆ

chain (ਚੇਇਨ) *n v* ਬੰਧਨ, ਬੇੜੀ, ਹਥਕੜੀ, ਸੰਗਲ, ਜੰਜੀਰ, ਹਾਰ, ਲੜੀ, ਸਿਲਸਿਲਾ, ਜੰਜੀਰ ਨਾਲ ਬੰਨ੍ਹਣਾ, ਸੰਗਲੀ ਪਾਉਣੀ, ਹੱਥਕੜੀ ਲਾਉਣੀ, ਬੰਧਨ ਪਾਉਣੇ, ਕੁੰਡੀ ਲਾਉਣੀ; **~smoker** ਲਗਾਤਾਰ ਸਿਗਰਟ ਪੀਣ ਵਾਲਾ

chair (ਚੇਅ*) *n v* ਕੁਰਸੀ, ਚੌਕੀ, ਗੱਦੀ; ਸਭਾਪਤੀ

ਮੁਖੀ, (ਪ੍ਰ) ਪਾਲਕੀ, ਡੋਲੀ; ਪੀਠ; ਪ੍ਰਧਾਨਗੀ ਦੀ ਕੁਰਸੀ ਤੇ ਬਿਠਾਉਣਾ; ਅਧਿਕਾਰੀ ਬਣਾਉਣਾ; ਗੱਦੀ ਤੇ ਬਿਠਾਉਣਾ; ~man ਸਭਾਪਤੀ, ਸਦਰ, ਪ੍ਰਧਾਨ, ਚੇਅਰਮੈਨ, ਰੋਗੀ ਦੀ ਪਹੀਆਂ ਵਾਲੀ ਕੁਰਸੀ ਦਾ ਰੱਖਿਅਕ; ~ship ਪ੍ਰਧਾਨਗੀ; ~person ਪ੍ਰਧਾਨ, ਸਦਰ

chaise (ਸ਼ੇਇਜ਼)*n* ਸੈਰ-ਗੱਡੀ, ਬੱਘੀ, ਸਵਾਰੀ ਬੱਘੀ

chalk (ਚੋਕ) *n v* ਚਾਕ, ਖੜੀਆ ਮਿੱਟੀ, ਚਾਕ ਦੀ ਡਲੀ; ਖੜੀਆ ਮਿੱਟੀ ਮਲਣੀ; ~out ਖ਼ਾਕਾ ਖਿਚਣਾ, ਯੋਜਨਾ ਬਣਾਉਣੀ, ਰੂਪ-ਰੇਖਾ, ਤਿਆਰ ਕਰਨੀ

challan ('ਚਅੱਲਅਨ) *n* ਚਲਾਨ

challenge ('ਚੈਲਿਨਜ) *n* ਚੁਣੌਤੀ, ਲਲਕਾਰ, ਵੰਗਾਰ, ਮੰਗ; ਇਤਰਾਜ਼, ਉਜ਼ਰ; ਲਲਕਾਰਨ, ਵੰਗਾਰਨ, ਚੁਣੌਤੀ ਦੇਣਾ; ਉਜ਼ਰ ਕਰਨਾ; ਧਿਆਨ ਦੀ ਮੰਗ ਕਰਨੀ

chamber ('ਚੇਇਮਬਅ*) *n* ਕਮਰਾ, ਸਦਨ, ਮੰਡਲ, ਜੱਜ ਦਾ ਨਿਜੀ ਕਮਰਾ; ਸੰਸਦ-ਭਵਨ, ਸਭਾ-ਭਵਨ, ਘੁਰਨਾ

champagne ('ਸ਼ੌਂ'ਪੇਇਨ) *n* ਸ਼ੈਮਪੇਨ, ਫ਼ਰਾਂਸ ਵਿਚ ਬਣੀ ਸ਼ਰਾਬ

champion ('ਚੈਂਪਯਅਨ) *n* ਚੈਂਪੀਅਨ, ਜੋਧਾ, ਬਲੀ, ਸੂਰਮਾ ਮਲ; ਪੱਖੀ, ਹਿਮਾਇਤੀ, ਸਮਰਥਕ, ਹਾਮੀ; ਸਰਬ ਸਮੱਰਥ ਕਰਨਾ, ਪੱਖ ਪੂਰਨਾ, ਹਾਮੀ ਭਰਨੀ

chance (ਚਾਂਸ) *n* ਮੌਕਾ, ਅਵਸਰ ਸੰਭਾਵਨਾ; ਸੰਜੋਗ; ਇਤਫ਼ਾਕ, ਦੈਵ ਘਟਨਾ, ਭਾਗ, ਸਬੱਬ, ਭਾਣਾ; ਸੰਜੋਗ ਨਾਲ ਹੋ ਜਾਣਾ; ਅਚਾਨਕ ਵਾਪਰ ਜਾਣਾ, ਜੋਖ਼ਮ ਉਠਾਉਣਾ, ਭਾਗ ਅਜ਼ਮਾਉਣਾ; **by**~ ਸਹਿਜ ਸੁਭਾਅ ਦੈਵਨੇਤ ਨਾਲ, ਰੱਬ ਸਬੱਬੀ; **take one's**~ ਕਿਸਮਤ ਅਜ਼ਮਾਉਣਾ

chancellor ('ਚਾਂਸਅਲਅ*) *n* ਕੁਲਪਤੀ, ਕੁਨਹੀਪਤੀ; (ਜਰਮਨੀ ਵਿਚ) ਪ੍ਰਧਾਨ ਮੰਤਰੀ; **vice**~ ਕੁਲਪਤਿ, ਉਪਕੁਲਪਤੀ

chance-medley ('ਚਾਨਸ'ਮੈਂਡਲਿ) *n* (ਕ਼ਾ) ਅਣਜਾਣਪੁਣੇ ਵਿਚ ਕੀਤਾ ਗਿਆ ਅਪਰਾਧ ਅਚਿੰਤੀ ਹੱਤਿਆ, ਅਣਗਹਿਲੀ, ਅਸਾਵਧਾਨੀ

chandelier ('ਸ਼ੈਂਡਅ'ਲਿਅ*) *n* ਝਾੜ-ਫ਼ਾਨੂਸ

change (ਚੇਇੰਜ) *n v* ਬਦਲੀ, ਤਬਦੀਲੀ, ਪਰਿਵਰਤਨ, ਉਲਟ ਫੇਰ, ਫ਼ਰਕ; ਹੇਰ ਫੇਰ ਰੇਜ਼ਗਾਰੀ, ਭਾਨ; ਬਦਲਣਾ, ਅਦਲਾ-ਬਦਲੀ ਕਰਨੀ, ਹੇਠ ਉੱਪਰ ਕਰਨਾ; ਪਰਿਵਰਤਨ ਕਰਨਾ; ਲੈਣ-ਦੇਣ ਕਰਨਾ, ਨੋਟ ਜਾਂ ਸਿੱਕਾ ਤੁੜਾਉਣਾ; ਚੰਨ ਦਾ ਘਟਣਾ ਵਧਣਾ

changing ('ਚੇਇੰਜਿਙ) *a* ਬਦਲਣ ਵਾਲਾ, ਪਰਿਵਰਤਨਸ਼ੀਲ

channel ('ਚੈਨਲ) *n v* ਖਾੜੀ, ਨਹਿਰ, ਨਾਲਾ, ਖਾਲ, ਨਾਲੀ, ਆੜ, ਪ੍ਰਣਾਲੀ; ਨਲਕਾ; ਮਾਰਗਾ, ਦਿਸ਼ਾ ਸਾਧਨ, ਮਾਧਿਅਮ, ਨਾਲੀ ਬਣਾਉਣਾ, ਨਹਿਰ ਕੱਢਣੀ, ਹਾਸ਼ੀਆ ਬਣਾਉਣਾ; **~led** ਨਾਲੀਦਾਰ

chant (ਚਾਂਟ) *n v* ਗੀਤ, ਭਜਨ, ਮੰਤਰ; ਉਸਤਤੀ; ਗੀਤ ਗਾਉਣਾ, ਭਜਨ ਗਾਉਣੇ, ਮੰਤਰ, ਉਚਾਰਨੇ, ਗਾਉਣਾ

chaos (ਕਇਔਸ) *n* ਅਫਰਾਤਫਰੀ, ਘੇਤਰਤੀਬੀ, ਘੁੰਦਕਾਰਾ, ਉਘੜ ਧੁੰਮੀ

chaotic (ਕੇਇ'ਔਟਿਕ) *a* ਗੜਮੜ, ਘੜਮਸ ਵਾਲਾ, ਉੱਘੜ-ਦੁੱਘੜ; ਅਵਿਵਸਥਿਤ

chap (ਚੈਪ) *n v* (ਬੋਲ) ਛੋਕਰਾ, ਮਨੁੱਖ; ਦਰਾੜ; ਬਿਆਈ; ਜਬਾੜ੍ਹਾ, ਹੜਬਾਂ; ਫਟਣਾ, ਫੁੱਟਣਾ, ਤਿੜਕਣਾ, ਟੁੱਟਣਾ, ਤਰੇੜ ਆਉਣੀ

chapel ('ਚੈਪਲ) *n* ਪ੍ਰਾਰਥਨ ਘਰ, ਪੂਜਾ ਸਥਾਨ; ਰੋਮਨ ਕੈਥੋਲਿਕ ਗਿਰਜਾ

chaplain ('ਚੈਪਲਿਨ) *n* ਪੁਰੋਹਤ, ਗਿਰਜੇ ਦਾ ਪਾਦਰੀ

chaplet ('ਚੈਪਲਿਟ) *n* ਮੁਕਟ, ਸਿਹਰਾ, ਹਾਰ, ਪੁਸ਼ਪ-ਮਾਲਾ; ਛੋਟਾ ਗਿਰਜਾ

chapman ('ਚੈਪਮਅਨ) *n* ਫੇਰੀਵਾਲਾ

chapter (ਚੈਪਟਅ*) *n* ਅਧਿਆਇ, ਕਾਂਡ, ਖੰਡ, ਪ੍ਰਕਰਣ, ਪਰਿਛੇਦ; ਪਾਦਰੀ-ਸੰਘ; ਸੰਸਦ ਦਾ ਅਧਿਨਿਯਮ

character (ਕੈਰਅਕਟਅ*) *n v* ਚਰਿੱਤਰ, ਵਿਅਕਤੀਗਤ ਵਿਸ਼ੇਸ਼ਤਾ, ਆਚਾਰ, ਆਚਰਨ, ਸਦਾਚਾਰ, ਖ਼ਸਲਤ, ਫ਼ਿਤਰਤ, ਸੁਭਾਉ, ਲੱਛਣ, ਚਿੰਨ੍ਹ, ਵਿਸ਼ੇਸ਼ ਗੁਣ, ਵਚਿੱਤਰਤਾ, ਪ੍ਰਕਾਰ, ਸ਼ੈਲੀ; ਪ੍ਰਸਿੱਧੀ, ਮਾਣ-ਮਰਯਾਦਾ; ਨੇਕਨਾਮੀ; ਅੱਖਰ, ਹਰਫ਼; ਉਕਰਨਾ; **~istic** ਖ਼ਾਸਾ, ਲੱਛਣ ਵਿਸ਼ੇਸ਼ਤਾ, ਸਿਫ਼ਤ, ਖ਼ਾਸੀਅਤ, ਸੁਭਾਉ; ਚਿੰਨ੍ਹ, ਲੱਛਣ; **~rize** ਵਿਸ਼ੇਸ਼ਤਾ ਦਾ ਵਰਣਨ ਕਰਨਾ, ਲੱਛਣ-ਚਿੱਤਰਨ ਕਰਨਾ; **~less** ਚਰਿੱਤਰਹੀਨ, ਬਦਚਲਨ,

charcoal (ਚਾਕਅਉੁਲ) *n* ਲੱਕੜੀ ਦਾ ਕੋਲਾ, ਕੋਲਾ; ਅੰਗਾਰ

charge (ਚਾਜ) *n v* ਬੋਝ, ਭਾਰ, ਖ਼ਰਚਾ, ਲਾਗਤ; ਜ਼ੁੰਮੇਵਾਰੀ, ਫ਼ਰਜ਼ ਸੌਂਪਣਾ, ਰੱਖਿਆ, ਸੰਭਾਲ, ਅਮਾਨਤ, ਤੁਹਮਤ, ਹੱਲਾ, ਕਾਰਤੂਸ, ਬਾਰੂਦ ਗੋਲੀ, ਸਿੱਕਾ; (ਬਿਜਲੀ) ਚਾਰਜ; ਪੂਰਾ ਪੂਰਾ ਬਕਣਾ; ਮੁੱਲ ਮੰਗਣਾ, ਖ਼ਰਚਾ ਪਾਉਣਾ; ਧਾਵਾ ਕਰਨਾ; ਦੋਸ਼ੀ ਠਹਿਰਾਉਣਾ; ਜ਼ੁੰਮੇਵਾਰੀ ਸੌਂਪਣੀ; ਸੰਭਾਲਣਾ, ਕੰਮ ਸੌਂਪਣਾ; **~able** ਹਿਸਾਬ ਵਿਚ ਗਿਣਨਯੋਗ, ਭਰਨਯੋਗ, ਦੋਸ਼ਣਯੋਗ, ਆਰੋਪਣਯੋਗ; ਮਹਿੰਗਾ; ਖ਼ਰਚਣਯੋਗ; **~less** ਕਲੰਕਰਹਿਤ; **~ness** ਵਸੂਲੀ

charge d'affaires (ਸ਼ਾਯੋਇਡੈ*ਫੇਅ*) ਉਪ-ਰਾਜਦੂਤ

chariot (ਚੈਰਿਅਟ) *n v* ਰਥ, ਸੂਰਜ ਦਾ ਰਥ; ਰਥ ਵਿਚ ਲੈ ਜਾਣਾ, ਰਥ; **~eer** ਸਾਰਥੀ, ਰਥਵਾਨ

charitable (ਚੈਰਿਟਅਬਲ) *a* ਖ਼ਰੈਤੀ; ਖੁੱਲ੍ਹ-ਦਿਲਾ; ਦਾਨੀ, ਉਪਕਾਰੀ, ਸਖ਼ੀ; ਦਿਆਆਵਾਨ, ਕਿਰਪਾਲੂ, ਉਦਾਰ

charity (ਚੈਰਅਟਿ) *n* ਪਰਉਪਕਾਰ, ਕਿਰਪਾ, ਉਦਾਰਤਾ, ਦਿਆਲਤਾ, ਦਇਆ; ਦਾਨ, ਭਿੱਖਿਆ

charm (ਚਾ*ਮ) *n v* ਮਨੋਹਰਤਾ, ਲੁਭਾਇਮਾਨਤਾ, ਜਾਦੂ, ਮੰਤਰ, ਤਲਿਸਮ, ਤਵੀਤ, ਖਿੱਚ, ਕਸ਼ਸ਼; ਮੋਹ ਲੈਣਾ; ਖ਼ੁਸ਼ ਕਰਨਾ, ਆਨੰਦ ਦੇਣਾ, ਵੱਸ ਵਿਚ ਕਰਨਾ; ਜਾਦੂ ਦੀ ਸ਼ਕਤੀ ਪ੍ਰਾਪਤ ਕਰਨੀ; **~ing** ਮਨੋਹਰ, ਸੁਹਾਵਣਾ, ਦਿਲਕਸ਼, ਮਨਮੋਹਕ, ਸੁੰਦਰ

chart (ਚਾ*ਟ) *n v* ਚਾਰਟ, ਜਹਾਜ਼ੀਆਂ ਦਾ ਸਮੁੰਦਰੀ ਨਕਸ਼ਾ; ਰੇਖ-ਚਿੱਤਰ, ਸਾਰਨੀ, ਨਕਸ਼ਾ ਬਣਾਉਣਾ

charter (ਚਾਟਅ*) *n v* ਸਨਦ, ਫ਼ਰਮਾਨ, ਅਧਿਕਾਰ ਪੱਤਰ, ਪੱਟਾ, ਆਧਾਰ; ਸਨਦ ਦੇਣੀ, ਅਧਿਕਾਰ ਪੱਤਰ ਦੇਣਾ; ਪਰਵਾਨਾ ਦੇਣਾ; **~ed accountant** ਅਧਿਕ੍ਰਿਤ ਲੇਖਾਕਾਰ, ਚਾਰਟਰਡ ਅਕਾਊਂਟੈਂਟ

chase (ਚੇਇਸ) *n v* ਸ਼ਿਕਾਰ; ਬੀੜ, ਸ਼ਿਕਾਰਗਾਹ; ਪਿੱਛਾ; (ਛਪਾਈ ਵਿਚ) ਟਾਈਪ ਨੂੰ ਕਸਣ ਵਾਲਾ ਢਾਂਚਾ; ਪਿੱਛਾ ਕਰਨਾ, ਪਿੱਛੇ ਭੱਜਣਾ; ਫ਼ਰਮਾ ਕਸਣਾ; ਨੱਕਾਸ਼ੀ ਕਰਨਾ; ਸ਼ਿੰਗਾਰਨਾ

chaste (ਚੇਇਸਟ) *a* ਪਵਿੱਤਰ, (ਅ) ਸੁੱਚਾ, ਅਛੋਹ, ਨਿਰਮਲ, ਖ਼ਾਲਸ; ਸਤਵੰਤੀ, ਕੁਆਰਾ, ਅਲੱਗਣ

chastise (ਚੈ*ਸਟਾਇਜ਼) *v* ਦੰਡ ਦੇਣਾ, ਸਜ਼ਾ ਦੇਣੀ,

ਚੰਡਣਾ, ਖੁੰਭ ਠੱਪਣੀ, ਤਾੜਨਾ ਕਰਨੀ, ਸਿੱਧਾ ਕਰਨਾ

chastity (ਚੈਸਟਅਟਿ) *n* ਪਵਿੱਤਰਤਾ, ਸ਼ੁੱਧਤਾ, ਸਤ, ਕੁਆਰਾਪਣ; ਸ਼ੈਲੀ ਦੀ ਸ਼ੁੱਧੀ

chat (ਚੈਟ) *n* ਗੱਪ, ਬਾਤਚੀਤ, ਗੱਲ-ਕੱਥ, ਗੱਲਬਾਤ

chatter (ਚੈਟਅ*) *n v* ਗੱਪ, ਗੜਬੜ, ਬਕਵਾਸ; ਟੀਂ ਟੀਂ ਕਰਨਾ, ਟਰ ਟਰ ਕਰਨਾ, ਦੰਦ ਕਰੀਚਣੇ, ਪੁਰਜ਼ਿਆਂ ਦਾ ਕਿੜ ਕਿੜ ਕਰਨਾ; **~box** ਬਕਵਾਸੀ, ਗਲਪਫੜ; ਬਾਤੂਨੀ, ਗੱਪੀ

chauffeur (ਸ਼ਅਉਫ਼ਅ*) *n* ਸ਼ੱਫਰ, ਪੇਸ਼ਾਵਰ ਕਾਰ-ਡਰਾਈਵਰ

chauvinism (ਸ਼ਅਉਵਿਨਿਜ਼(ਅ)ਮ) *n* ਕੱਟੜਪੁਣਾ, ਘੋਰ ਦੇਸ਼ ਭਗਤੀ

chauvinist (ਸ਼ਅਉਵਿਨਿਸਟ) *n* ਕੱਟੜ ਦੇਸ਼ ਪਰੇਮੀ

cheap (ਚੀਪ) *a* ਸਸਤਾ, ਸੁਵੱਲਾ, ਸੁਲੱਭ, ਸਹਿਜੇ ਹੀ ਪਰਾਪਤ; ਨਿਕੰਮਾ, ਹੋਛਾ; ਮਹੱਤਵਹੀਣ; **~ly** ਸਸਤੇ ਭਾਅ ਵਿਚ, ਘਟੀਆ ਤਰੀਕੇ ਨਾਲ, ਸਸਤੇ ਢੰਗ ਨਾਲ; **~ness** ਸਸਤਾਪਣ, ਸੁਲੱਭਤਾ, ਘਟੀਆਪਨ

cheat (ਚੀਟ) *n a v* ਠੱਗੀ, ਧੋਖਾ, ਫ਼ਰੇਬ, ਛਲ; ਕਪਟ; ਠੱਗ, ਦਗ਼ੋਬਾਜ਼, ਕਪਟੀ, ਫ਼ਰੇਬੀ; ਧੋਖਾ ਦੇਣਾ, ਬੇਈਮਾਨੀ ਕਰਨੀ, ਛਲਣਾ, ਝਾਂਸਾ ਦੇਣਾ; **~er** ਧੋਖੇਬਾਜ਼, ਕਪਟੀ, ਛਲ ਕਰਨ ਵਾਲਾ, ਠੱਗ; **~ing** ਧੋਖੇਬਾਜ਼ੀ

check (ਚੈਕ) *n v* ਰੋਕ, ਸੰਜਮ, ਅਟਕਾਅ, ਠੱਲ੍ਹ, ਰੋਕਣਾ, ਝਿੜਕ; ਨਿਰੀਖਣ, ਜਾਂਚ, ਪੜਤਾਲ; ਚਾਰਖ਼ਾਨਾ ਕੱਪੜਾ; ਸੰਭਲਣਾ, ਜਾਂਚ ਪੜਤਾਲ ਕਰਨੀ

cheek (ਚੀਕ) *n* ਗੱਲ੍ਹ, ਰੁਖ਼ਸਾਰ; **~ness** ਗੁਸਤਾਖ਼ੀ

cheer (ਚਿਅ*) *n v* ਖ਼ੁਸ਼ੀ; ਘੱਲੇ-ਘੱਲੇ, ਖ਼ੁਸ਼ੀ ਪਰਗਟ ਕਰਨ ਵਾਲੇ ਸ਼ਬਦ; ਘੱਲੇ-ਘੱਲੇ ਕਰਨਾ, ਢਾਰਸ ਦੇਣਾ, ਪ੍ਰਸੰਨ ਕਰਨਾ; **~up** ਖ਼ੁਸ਼ ਹੋਣਾ, ਚੜ੍ਹਦੀ ਕਲਾ ਵਿਚ ਆਉਣਾ; **~ful** ਖ਼ੁਸ਼, ਪ੍ਰਫੁੱਲਤ, ਆਨੰਦ, ਹਸਦਾ-ਰਸਦਾ, ਹਸਮੁਖ, ਟਹਿਕਦਾ ਹੋਇਆ, ਆਨੰਦਕਾਰਕ, ਆਨੰਦ ਦੇਣ ਵਾਲਾ; **~fully** ਚਾਈਂ ਚਾਈਂ, ਖ਼ੁਸ਼ੀ ਖ਼ੁਸ਼ੀ, ਚਾਅ ਨਾਲ, ਦਿਲ ਨਾਲ; **~fulness** ਖ਼ੁਸ਼ੀ, ਟਹਿਕ, ਆਨੰਦ, ਪ੍ਰਸੰਨਤਾ; **~less** ਉਦਾਸ, ਨਿਮੋਝੂਣਾ, ਘੇ-ਰੌਂਣਕ, ਮੁਰਝਾਇਆ (ਚਿਹਰਾ)

cheese (ਚੀਜ਼) *n* ਪਨੀਰ; **bread and ~**-ਦਾਲ-ਰੋਟੀ

chef (ਸ਼ੈੱਫ) *n* ਖਾਨਸਾਮਾ, ਮੁੱਖ ਰਸੋਈਆ

chemical (ਕੈ'ਮਿਕਲ) *a n* ਰਸਾਇਣਕ, ਰਸਾਇਣ; ਰਸਾਇਣਕ ਪਦਾਰਥ

chemist (ਕੈ'ਮਿਸਟ) *n* ਰਸਾਇਣ ਵਿੱਦਿਆ ਨੂੰ ਜਾਣਨ ਵਾਲਾ, ਦਵਾਈਆਂ ਵੇਚਣ ਵਾਲਾ, ਦਵਾਫ਼ਰੋਸ਼, ਕੈਮਿਸਟ; **~ry** ਰਸਾਇਣ-ਵਿਗਿਆਨ, ਰਸਾਇਣਕੀ

cheque (ਚੈੱਕ) *n* ਚੈੱਕ, ਹੁੰਡੀ; **~book** ਚੈੱਕਾਂ ਦੀ ਕਾਪੀ; **blank~** ਕੋਰਾ ਚੈੱਕ; **crossed~** ਰੇਖਾ-ਅੰਕਤ ਚੈੱਕ, ਨਕਦ ਭੁਗਤਾਨ ਦੀ ਥਾਂ ਖਾਤੇ ਵਿਚ ਜਮ੍ਹਾ ਹੋਣ ਵਾਲਾ ਚੈੱਕ

cherish (ਚੈ'ਰਿਸ਼) *v* ਪਾਲਣ-ਪੋਸਣ ਕਰਨਾ, ਕਦਰ ਕਰਨੀ, ਹਿਤ ਕਰਨਾ, ਦਿਲ ਵਿਚ ਥਾਂ ਦੇਣੀ, ਨਿਵਾਜਣਾ

chess (ਚੈੱਸ) *n* ਸ਼ਤਰੰਜ; **~board** ਸ਼ਤਰੰਜ ਦੀ ਬਿਸਾਤ, ਸ਼ਤਰੰਜੀ; **~men** ਮੋਹਰੇ, ਗੋਟ

chest (ਚੈੱਸਟ) *n* ਛਾਤੀ, ਸੀਨਾ, ਹਿੱਕ; ਪੇਟੀ, ਸੰਦੂਕ, ਸੰਦੂਕਚੀ, ਦਰਾਜ਼ਾਂ ਵਾਲੀ ਅਲਮਾਰੀ

chew (ਚੂ) *n v* ਗੋਲੀ; ਚਿੱਥਣਾ, ਚਬਾਉਣਾ,

ਉਗਾਲੀ ਕਰਨੀ

chicken (ਚਿਕਿਨ) *n* ਕੁੜ੍ਹਾ; **~hearted** ਕਾਇਰ, ਡਰਪੋਕ; **~pox** ਛੋਟੀ ਮਾਤਾ

chickling (ਚਿਕਲਿੰਡ) *n* ਕੁੜ੍ਹਿਆਂ ਦਾ ਚੋਗਾ

chide (ਚਾਇਡ) *v* ਡਾਂਟਣਾ, ਝਾੜਨਾ

chiding (ਚਾਇਡਿੰਡ) *n* ਡਾਂਟ, ਝਾੜ, ਝਿੜਕ, ਘੁਰਨੀ

chief (ਚੀਫ਼) *n* ਪ੍ਰਧਾਨ, ਪ੍ਰਮੁੱਖ, ਮੁਖੀ; **~dom** ਸਰਦਾਰੀ, ਚੌਧਰ; **~tain** ਮੁਖੀਆ

child (ਚਾਇਲਡ) *n* ਬਾਲ, ਬੱਚਾ, ਬਾਲਕ, ਕਾਕਾ, ਮੁੰਡਾ, ਔਂਤਰਾ; ਸੰਤਾਨ, ਵੰਸ਼; **~bed** (ਪ੍ਰ) ਜਣੇਪਾ; **'s play** ਸੌਖਾ ਕੰਮ, ਬੱਚਿਆਂ ਦਾ ਖੇਲ; **with~** ਗਰਭਵਤੀ; **~hood** ਬਚਪਨ, ਬਾਲਪਨ, ਬਾਲ-ਅਵਸਥਾ, ਛੋਟੀ ਉਮਰ; **~ish** ਬਚਗਾਨਾ, ਬੱਚੇ ਵਾਂਗ **~like** ਸਰਲ, ਭੋਲਾ; **~ness** ਬਚਗਾਨਾਪਨ

chill (ਚਿਲ) *n a v* ਸੀਤ, ਠੰਢ, ਸਰਦੀ, ਪਾਲਾ, ਕਾਂਬਾ, ਉਤਸ਼ਾਹਹੀਣਤਾ, ਉਦਾਸੀ; ਠੰਢਾ; ਠੰਢ ਲੱਗ ਜਾਣੀ, ਠਰਨਾ, ਸੁਸਤ ਹੋਣਾ, ਦਿਲ ਢਾਹੁਣਾ, ਨਿਰਾਸ ਹੋਣਾ; **~y** ਸੀਤ, ਠੰਢਾ, ਠਰਿਆ, (ਸੁਭਾਅ ਦਾ), ਰੁੱਖਾ, ਉਦਾਸੀਨ

chilli (ਚਿਲਿ) *n* ਸੁੱਕੀ ਲਾਲ ਮਿਰਚ

chimney (ਚਿਮਨਿ) *n* ਚਿਮਨੀ, ਅੰਗੀਠੀ, ਧੂੰਆਂ ਨਿਕਲਣ ਵਾਲੀ ਥਾਂ, ਤੰਗ ਦਰਾੜ

chimpanzee (ਚਿਮਪਅੰਜ਼ੀ) *n* ਬਾਂਦਰ ਦੀ ਇਕ ਨਸਲ, ਚਿੰਪੰਜ਼ੀ

chin (ਚਿਨ) *n* ਠੋਡੀ

chink (ਚਿੰਕ) *n v* ਝਰੋਖਾ, ਛੇਕ, ਮੋਰੀ, ਝਨਕਾਰ; ਛਣਕਣਾ, ਟੁਣਕਣਾ, ਟੁਣਕਾਰ ਹੋਣੀ

chip (ਚਿਪ) *n* ਟੁਕੜਾ, ਛਿਲਤਰ, ਗੀਟਾ, ਪਾਥੀ;

chirp (ਚਅ:ਪ) *n* ਚਹਿਚਹਾਟ, ਚੀਂ ਚੀਂ, ਚੂੰ ਚੂੰ; ਚੀਂ ਚੀਂ ਕਰਨਾ, ਚਹਿਚਹਾਉਣਾ,

chirrup (ਚਿਰਅਪ) *v* ਚੂੰ ਚੂੰ ਕਰਨਾ; ਪੁਚਕਾਰਨਾ

chisel (ਚਿਜ਼ਲ) *n v* ਛੈਣੀ, ਚੋਰਸੀ, ਚੱਕੀ-ਰਾਹਾ; ਛਿੱਲਣਾ, ਘੜਨਾ; ਧੋਖਾ ਦੇਣਾ, ਠੱਗ ਲੈਣਾ

chit-chat (ਚਿਟਚੈਟ) *n* ਗੱਪ-ਸ਼ੱਪ, ਗਲਬਾਤ

chivalrous (ਸ਼ਿਵਲਰਅਸ) *a* ਬੀਰ, ਸੂਰਬੀਰ, ਬੀਰ ਕਾਲ ਦਾ; ਸੱਭਿਆ; ਸੁਆਰਥਹੀਨ, ਉਦਾਰ, ਨਿਸ਼ਕਾਮ

chivalry (ਸ਼ਿਵਲਰਿ) *n* ਘੋੜਸਵਾਰ, ਘੋੜਸਵਾਰਾਂ ਦਾ ਰਿਸਾਲਾ; ਸ਼ਿਸ਼ਟ ਜੋਧਾ, ਬੀਰਤਾ, ਸੂਰਬੀਰਤਾ

chock (ਚੌਕ) *n* ਗੁਟਕਾ, ਲੱਕੜ ਦਾ ਟੁਕੜਾ

chocolate (ਚੌਕ(ਅ)ਲਅਟ) *n a* ਚਾਕਲੇਟ (ਖਾਣ ਵਾਲੀ); ਗੁੜ੍ਹਾ ਲਾਖ ਜਾਂ ਕਥਈ (ਰੰਗ)

choice (ਚੌਇਸ) *n a* ਚੋਣ, ਚੁਣੀ ਹੋਈ ਚੀਜ਼, ਪਸੰਦ, ਛਾਂਟ; ਵਧੀਆ, ਸੰਗਤ; **at ~** ਇੱਛਾ ਅਨੁਸਾਰ, ਮਰਜ਼ੀ ਨਾਲ

choke (ਚਾਉਕ) *v n* ਗਲ ਘੁੱਟਣਾ; ਤੁੜਕਣਾ, ਬੰਦ ਕਰਨਾ, ਥਰ ਦੇਣਾ, ਸਾਹ ਰੋਕਣਾ; ਰੋਕਣਾ, ਰੋਕ, ਰੁਕਾਵਟ; ਚੋਕ

cholera (ਕੌਲਅਰਅ) *n* ਹੈਜ਼ਾ

choleric ('ਕੌਲਅਰਿਕ) *a* ਚਿੜਚੜਾ, ਸੜੀਅਲ, ਖਿਝੂ, ਗੁਸੈਲ, ਕਰੋਪੀ, ਤੇਜ਼ ਮਿਜ਼ਾਜ

choose (ਚੂਜ਼) *v* ਚੁਣਨਾ, ਨਿਸ਼ਚਤ ਕਰਨਾ; **~r** ਚੋਣਕਾਰ, ਚੁਨਣ ਵਾਲਾ, ਪਸੰਦ ਕਰਨ ਵਾਲਾ; **~y** (ਬੋਲ) ਵਹਿਮੀ, ਸਨਕੀ

chop (ਚੌਪ) *n v* ਮਾਸ ਦਾ ਟੁਕੜਾ, ਵੱਢ, ਫੱਟ; ਕੱਟਣਾ, ਵੱਢਣਾ, ਟੁਕੜੇ ਟੁਕੜੇ ਕਰਨਾ, ਕੀਮ ਕਰਨਾ; (ਗੱਲ) ਟੋਕਣਾ; **~in** ਗੱਲ ਕੱਟਣੀ ਬਦਲ ਜਾਣਾ, ਬਦਸੀ ਕਰਨੀ, ਚੰਚਲ ਹੋਣਾ ਅਸਥਿਰ ਹੋਣਾ; **~about, -round** ਦਿਸ਼ਾ ਬਦਲ ਦੇਣਾ, ਰੁਖ ਬਦਲ ਦੇਣਾ

chopper ('ਚੋਪਅ') *n* ਛੋਟੀ ਕੁਹਾੜੀ, ਗੰਡਾਸਾ, ਟੇਕਾ

choppy ('ਚੋਪਿ) *a* (ਸਮੁੰਦਰ) ਤੂਫ਼ਾਨੀ

choral ('ਕੋਰ(ਅ)ਲ) *a* ਸਮੂਹ-ਗਾਨ ਸਬੰਧੀ

chord (ਕੋਡ) *n* ਤੰਦ, ਤਾਰ, ਡੋਰੀ, ਵਤਰ

chore (ਚੋ*) *n* ਛੋਟਾ ਮੋਟਾ, ਕੰਮ, ਨਿਤ ਦਾ ਕੰਮ

choreograph ('ਕੋਰਿਅਗਰਾਫ਼਼਼ਿ) *n* ਨ੍ਰਿਤ-ਲੇਖ; ~**y** ਨ੍ਰਿਤਲੇਖਨ

chorus ('ਕੋਰਅਸ) *n* ਸਮੂਹ-ਗਾਨ, ਸਹਿਗਾਨ, ਜੋਗੀਆਂ ਵਾਲਾ ਗੀਤ, ਨਾਚ ਮੰਡਲੀ ਦਾ ਗੀਤ

Christ (ਕਰਾਇਸਟ) *n* ਹਜ਼ਰਤ ਈਸਾ, ਈਸਾ ਮਸੀਹ, ਯਸੂਹ-ਮਸੂਹ; ~**hood** ਮਸੀਹਪਣ

Christian ('ਕਰਿਸਚਨ) *n* ਇਸਾਈ, ਮਸੀਹੀ ਯਸੂਹੀ; ~**era** ਸੰਨ ਈਸਵੀ; ~**ity** ਇਸਾਈ ਮੱਤ, ਮਸੀਹੀ ਧਰਮ

Christmas ('ਕਰਿਸਮਅਸ) (*Xmas*) *n* ਕ੍ਰਿਸਮਿਸ, ਇਸਾਈਆਂ ਦਾ ਦਿਨ 25 ਦਸੰਬਰ; ~**day** ਹਜ਼ਰਤ ਈਸਾ ਦਾ ਜਨਮ ਦਿਨ, ਵੱਡਾ ਦਿਨ

chronic ('ਕਰੌਨਿਕ) *a* ਪੁਰਾਣਾ, ਦਾਇਮੀ, ਚਿਰਕਾਲੀਨ, ਪੱਕਾ

chronicle ('ਕਰੌਨਿਕਲ) *n v* ਰੋਜ਼ਨਾਮਚਾ, ਰੋਜ਼ਨਾਮਾ, ਬਿਰਤਾਂਤ; ਰੋਜ਼ਨਾਮਚਾ ਲਿਖਣਾ, ਕਹਾਣੀ ਲਿਖਣਾ

Chronicles ('ਕਰੌਨਿਕਲਜ਼) *n* ਬਾਈਬਲ ਦੇ ਦੋ ਅਧਿਆਇ

chronological ('ਕਰੌਨਅ'ਲੌਜਿਕਲ) *a* ਕਾਲ-ਕ੍ਰਮਕ

chronology (ਕਰਅ'ਨੌਲੋਜਿ) *n* ਕਾਲਕ੍ਰਮ ਅਨੁਸਾਰ ਲਿਖਣਾ, ਰੋਜ਼ਨਾਮਚਾ ਲਿਖਣਾ

chuck (ਚੱਕ) *int v* ਠੱਕ ਠੱਕ, ਕੱਟ ਕੱਟ, ਕੜ ਕੜ; ਝਟਕਾਉਣਾ, ਪਰੇ ਸੁਟਣਾ, ਪਰੇ ਮਾਰਨਾ, ਭੁਆ ਕੇ ਸੁੱਟਣਾ; ਕੁਕੜੀਆਂ ਨੂੰ ਸੱਦਣ ਦੀ ਅਵਾਜ਼; ਝਟਕਾ; ਪਿਆਰਾ, ਯਾਰ, ਪਿਆਰ ਤੇ ਲਾਡ ਵਾਲਾ ਸ਼ਬਦ; ~**away** ਬਰਬਾਦ ਕਰਨਾ, ਗੁਆਉਣਾ; ~**out** (ਬੋਲ) ਗਿਰਹੀਂਓ ਫੜ ਕੇ ਬਾਹਰ ਕੱਢਣਾ, ਧੱਕੇ ਦੇਣਾ; ~**up** ਛੱਡ ਦੇਣਾ, ਗਾਲਾਂ ਲਾਹੁਣਾ; ~**y** ਪਿਆਰਾ ਬੇਟਾ

chuckle ('ਚਅੱਕਲ) *n v* ਮਿੰਨ੍ਹਾ ਮਿੰਨ੍ਹਾ ਹਾਸਾ; ਕੁਕੜੀਆਂ ਦੀ ਕੁੜ ਕੁੜ; ਕੁੜ ਕੁੜ ਕਰਨਾ; ਮੂੰਹ ਬੰਦ ਕਰ ਕੇ ਹੱਸਣਾ; ~**head**, ~**headed** ਬੁੱਧੂ, ਮੂਰਖ, ਮੋਟੀ ਮੱਤ ਵਾਲਾ

chuff (ਚਅੱਫ) *n* ਵਿਦੂਸ਼ਕ

chum (ਚਅੱਮ) *n* ਆੜੀ, ਲੰਗੋਟੀਆ ਯਾਰ; ~**up with** ਗੂੜ੍ਹੀ ਮਿੱਤਰਤਾ ਹੋਣੀ, ਗਹਿਰੀ ਦੋਸਤੀ ਹੋਣੀ; ~**my** ਮਿੱਤਰ, ਯਾਰ, ਸਾਥੀ; ਮਿਲਣਸਾਰ

chunk (ਚਅੱਕ) *a* ਮੋਟਾ ਟੁਕੜਾ, ਕੱਟਲਾ, ਫਾਂਕ,

chunky ('ਚਅੱਕਿ) *a* ਮੋਟੂ

church (ਚਅ:ਚ) *n* ਗਿਰਜਾ ਘਰ, ਕਲੀਸਾ; ਪਰਮ-ਸਥਾਨ; ਇਸਾਈ ਲੋਕ; ~**ing** ਪੂਜਨ; ~**man** ਪਾਦਰੀ

churl (ਚਅ:ਲ) *n* ਉਜੱਡ, ਪੇਂਡੂ, ਘਟੀਆ, ਬਦਤਮੀਜ਼, ਕੰਜੂਸ, ਮੱਖੀ-ਚੂਸ; ~**ish** ਉਜੱਡ, ਅੱਖੜ, ਗੰਵਾਰ, ਅਸ਼ਿਸ਼ਟ; ~**ishness** ਕੰਜੂਸੀ; ਅਸ਼ਿਸ਼ਟਤਾ, ਅੱਖੜਪਣ, ਉਜੱਡਤਾ

churn (ਚਅ:ਨ) *n v* ਚਾਟੀ; ਦੁੱਧ ਰਿੜਕਣਾ, ਦੁੱਧ ਵਿਲੋਣਾ

cigar (ਸਿ'ਗਾ*) *n* ਸਿਗਾਰ, ਚੁਰਟ

cigarette ('ਸਿਗਅ'ਰੈਟ) *n* ਸਿਗਰਟ

cine ('ਸਿਨਿ) *a* ਸਿਨੇਮਾ-ਸਬੰਧੀ, ਫ਼ਿਲਮ ਦਾ

cinema ('ਸਿਨਅਮਅ) *n* ਸਿਨੇਮਾ, ਚਲ-ਚਿੱਤਰ, ਚਲਦੀਆਂ ਮੂਰਤਾਂ ਵਾਲਾ ਨਾਟਕ; ਸਿਨੇਮਾ-ਘਰ

cipher (ਸਾਇਫ਼ਅ*) *n* ਸੂਨ, ਨਿਕੰਮਾ, ਨਾਚੀਜ਼, ਜ਼ੀਰੋ, ਗੁਪਤ ਲਿਖਤ; ਹਿਸਾਬ ਲਾਉਣਾ; ਕਢਣਾ; ਜੋੜਨਾ

circle (ਸਅਃਕਲ) *n* ਗੋਲ ਚੱਕਰ, ਗੋਲ ਦਾਇਰਾ; ਪਰਿਕਰਮਾ, ਕੁੰਡਲ, ਛੱਲਾ, ਚੱਕਰ; ਮੰਡਲ; ਖੇਤਰ, ਹਲਕਾ; ਘੇਰਨਾ, ਵਲਣਾ, ਚੱਕਰ ਲਾਉਣਾ, ਘੁੰਮਣਾ

circuit ('ਸਅਃਕਿਟ) *n* ਘੇਰਾ, ਚੱਕਰ, ਦਾਇਰਾ; ਪਰਿਕਰਮਾ; ਵਲਾਵੇਂਦਾਰ ਸ਼ਫ਼ਰ; ਹਲਕਾ; ਘੇਰਨਾ, ਵਲਣਾ, ਚੱਕਰ ਲਾਉਣਾ, ਘੁੰਮਣਾ, ਦੌਰਾ; **short~** ਬਿਜਲੀ ਦੀ ਰੋਂ ਜਾਂ ਧਾਰਾ ਦੀ ਰੁਕਾਵਟ

circular (ਸਅਃਕਯੁਲਅ*) *a n* ਗੋਲ, ਚੱਕਰਦਾਰ; ਗਸ਼ਤੀ ਪੱਤਰ; **~letter** ਗਸ਼ਤੀ ਚਿੱਠੀ

circulate ('ਸਅਃਕਯੁਲੇਇਟ) *v* ਭੇਜਣਾ, ਘੁਮਾਉਣਾ, ਪ੍ਰਚਾਰ ਕਰਨਾ, ਸੰਚਾਰ ਕਰਨਾ; ਪ੍ਰਚਲਤ ਹੋਣਾ, ਦੌਰ ਚੱਲਣਾ, ਚੱਕਰ ਮਾਰਨਾ

circulating ('ਸਅਃਕਯੁਲੇਇਟਿਙ) *a* ਗਸ਼ਤੀ, ਘੁੰਮਦਾ

circulation ('ਸਅਃਕਯੁ'ਲੇਇਸ਼ਨ) *n* ਦੌਰਾ (ਖੂਨ ਦਾ), ਚੱਕਰ, ਗਸ਼ਤ, ਵਿੱਕਰੀ (ਅਖ਼ਬਾਰ, ਕਿਤਾਬਾਂ ਆਦਿ ਦੀ)

circumference (ਸਅ*ਕੱਅਸਫ਼(ਅ)ਰਅੰਸ) *n* ਘੇਰਾ ਘੇਰ, ਚੁਗਿਰਦਾ, ਮੰਡਲ, ਦਾਇਰਾ

circumscribe ('ਸਅਃਕਅਮਸਕਰਾਇਬ) *v* ਘੇਰਨਾ, ਅਹਾਤਾਬੰਦੀ ਕਰਨਾ, ਸੀਮਾਬੱਧ ਕਰਨਾ; ਸੀਮਤ ਕਰਨਾ, ਸੀਮਾ ਨਿਸ਼ਚਤ ਕਰਨਾ, ਨਿਯਮਤ ਕਰਨਾ

circumstance ('ਸਅਃਕਅਮਸਟਅੰਸ) *n* ਹਾਲਾਤ, ਸੂਰਤ, ਅਵਸਥਾ, ਸਥਿਤੀ, ਵਾਤਾਵਰਨ, ਦਸ਼ਾ; **under no ~s** ਕਦਾਚਿਤ ਨਹੀਂ, ਕਿਸੇ ਸੂਰਤ ਵੀ ਨਹੀਂ

circumstantial ('ਸਅਃਕਅਮ'ਸਟੈਂਸ਼ਲ) *a* ਇਤਫ਼ਾਕੀਆ, ਅਚਾਨਕ; ਵੇਰਵੇ-ਸਹਿਤ; ਤਫ਼ਸੀਲਵਾਰ; ਪ੍ਰਸੰਗਕ; **~ity** ਸੰਯੋਗਤਾ; ਵਿਵਰਣਾਤਮਕਤਾ; **~ly** ਅਚਾਨਕ ਹੀ, ਸੰਯੋਗਵਸ

circumvent ('ਸਅਃਕਅਮ'ਵੈਂਟ) *v* ਫਾਹੁਣਾ, ਫਸਾਉਣਾ, ਛਲ ਖੇਡਣਾ, ਧੋਖਾ ਦੇਣਾ, ਝਾਂਸਾ ਦੇਣਾ

circus (ਸਅਃਕਸ) *n* ਸਰਕਸ, ਚੁਗਾਨ, ਗੋਲ ਅਖਾੜਾ, ਰੰਗ-ਮੰਡਲ

cistern ('ਸਿਸਟਅਨ) *n* ਪਾਣੀ ਦੀ ਟੈਂਕੀ, ਹੌਜ਼, ਕੁੰਡ

citadel ('ਸਿਟਅਡ(ਅ)ਲ) *n* ਗੜ੍ਹੀ, ਕਿਲ੍ਹਾ, ਕੋਟ; ਅੰਤਮ ਆਸਰਾ; ਓਟ, ਪਨਾਹ

citation (ਸਾਇਟੇਇਸ਼ਨ) *n* ਹਵਾਲਾ ਪ੍ਰਸੰਗ, ਸੰਦਰਭ; ਸੋਢਾ ਪੱਤਰ; ਪ੍ਰਮਾਣ, ਨਜ਼ੀਰ; ਸੱਦਾ

cite (ਸਇਟ) *v n* ਸੱਦਣਾ, ਹਵਾਲਾ ਦੇਣਾ, ਮਿਸਾਲ ਦੇਣੀ, ਉਦਾਹਰਨ ਦੇਣਾ; ਸੱਦ, ਬੁਲਾਵਾ, ਹਵਾਲਾ, ਉਦਾਹਰਨ; ਮਿਸਾਲ

citizen ('ਸਿਟਿਜ਼ਨ) *n* ਨਾਗਰਿਕ, ਸ਼ਹਿਰੀ ਨਿਵਾਸੀ; **~ship** ਨਾਗਰਿਕਤਾ, ਸ਼ਹਿਰੀਅਤ, ਸ਼ਹਿਰੀ ਅਧਿਕਾਰ

city ('ਸਿਟਿ) *n* ਨਗਰ, ਸ਼ਹਿਰ, ਵੱਡਾ ਕਸਬਾ

civic ('ਸਿਵ੍ਕਿ) *a* ਨਾਗਰਿਕਤਾ ਸਬੰਧੀ, ਸ਼ਹਿਰੀਅਤ ਸਬੰਧੀ; ਨਾਗਰਿਕਤਾ, ਨਗਰ-ਸਬੰਧੀ, ਨਗਰ-ਪਾਲਕਾ ਸਬੰਧੀ; **~s** ਨਾਗਰਿਕ-ਸ਼ਾਸਤਰ

civil ('ਸਿਵ੍ਲ) *a* ਸੱਭਿਆ, ਸ਼ਿਸ਼ਟ; ਵਿਨੀਤ; ਅਸੈਨਕ, ਵਿਹਾਰਕ, ਦੀਵਾਨੀ; ਗ਼ੈਰ-ਫ਼ੌਜਦਾਰੀ; ਸਮਾਜਕ, ਦੀਵਾਨੀ, ਗ਼ੈਰ-ਫ਼ੌਜਦਾਰੀ; ਸਮਾਜਕ, ਕਾਨੂੰਨੀ; **~disobedience** ਸਤਿਆਗ੍ਰਹਿ, ਸਿਵਲ ਨਾਫ਼ਰਮਾਨੀ, ਨਾ ਮਿਲਵਰਤਨ; **~law** ਦੀਵਾਨੀ ਕਾਨੂੰਨ, ਨਾਗਰਿਕ ਕਾਨੂੰਨ; **~marriage** ਅਦਾਲਤੀ ਵਿਆਹ, ਸਿਵਲ ਮੈਰਿਜ;

~rights ਨਾਗਰਿਕ ਅਧਿਕਾਰ; ~servant ਰਾਜ ਅਧਿਕਾਰੀ; ~service ਸਰਕਾਰੀ ਨੌਕਰੀ, ਰਾਜ ਸੇਵਾ; ਸਿਵਲ-ਸਰਵਿਸ; ~war ਖ਼ਾਨਾ ਜੰਗੀ, ਘਰੇਲੂ ਯੁੱਧ, ਗ੍ਰਹਿ ਯੁੱਧ ~ian ਪ੍ਰਬੰਧ ਵਿਭਾਗ ਦਾ ਕਰਮਚਾਰੀ, ਅਸੈਨਕ ਅਧਿਕਾਰੀ; ਅਸੈਨਕ; ~ization ਸੱਭਿਅਤਾ, ਤਹਿਜ਼ੀਬ, ਸੁਘੜਤਾ, ਸੁਰੱਜ, ਮਨੁੱਖਤਾ; ਸ਼ਿਸ਼ਟਤਾ; ~ize ਸੱਭਿਅਤਾ ਸਿਖਾਉਣੀ, ਸੁਧਾਰਨ, ਸੁੱਘੜ ਬਣਾਉਣ, ਤਹਿਜ਼ੀਬ ਸਿਖਾਉਣ; ~ized ਸੱਭਿਆ, ਨਿਮਰ

clad (ਕਲੈਡ) a ਕੱਪੜੇ, ਪਾਏ ਹੋਏ, ਵਸਤਰਾਂ ਨਾਲ ਸਜੇ ਹੋਏ

claim (ਕਲੇਇਮ) n v ਹੱਕ, ਮੰਗ, ਮੁਤਾਲਬਾ, ਦਾਅਵਾ, ਹੱਕ ਜਮਾਉਣਾ, ਮੁਤਾਲਬਾ ਕਰਨਾ, ਦਾਅਵਾ ਕਰਨਾ; ~able ਹੱਕ ਯੋਗ, ਦਾਅਵੇਯੋਗ, ਆਦੇਸ਼ਯੋਗ; ~ant ਹੱਕਦਾਰ, ਦਾਅਵੇਦਾਰ

clamminess ('ਕਲੈਮਿਨੇਸ) n ਚਿਪਚਿਪਾਹਟ, ਲੇਸਲਾਪਣ

clamour ('ਕਲੈਮਅ*) n v ਰੌਲਾ-ਰੱਪਾ, ਦੁਹਾਈ, ਚੀਕ-ਚਿਹਾੜਾ ਪਾਉਣਾ, ਘੱਥ ਪਾਉਣੀ

clamp (ਕਲੈਂਪ) n v ਜੋੜ, ਸ਼ਿਕੰਜਾ; ਢੇਰ; ਪੱਤਰਾ ਚੜ੍ਹਾਉਣਾ; ਸ਼ਿਕੰਜਾ ਕਸਣਾ; ਢੇਰ ਲਗਾਉਣਾ; ~ed ਕੀਲਿਆ, ਜਕੜਿਆ

clan (ਕਲੈਨ) n ਫ਼ਿਰਕਾ, ਕਬੀਲਾ, ਬਰਾਦਰੀ

clap (ਕਲੈਪ) n v ਤਾੜੀ, ਦਸਤਕ; ਤਾੜੀਆਂ ਮਾਰਨ, ਦਸਤਕ ਦੇਣਾ, ਥਪਥਪਾਉਣਾ; ~eyes on ਨਜ਼ਰ ਪੈਣਾ, ਦੇਖਣਾ

clarification ('ਕਲੈਰਿਫ਼ਿ'ਕੇਇਸ਼ਨ) n ਸਪਸ਼ਟੀਕਰਨ, ਸਫ਼ਾਈ

clarify ('ਕਲੈਰਿਫ਼ਾਇ) v ਸਪਸ਼ਟ ਕਰਨਾ, ਖੋਲ੍ਹ ਕੇ ਦੱਸਣਾ, ਸਾਫ਼ ਕਰਨਾ, ਛਾਂਟਣਾ, ਸਾਫ਼ ਹੋਣਾ, ਸੁਲਝਣਾ

clarity ('ਕਲੈਰਅਟਿ) n ਸਪਸ਼ਟਤਾ, ਸਫ਼ਾਈ, ਸ਼ੁੱਧਤਾ, ਸੁਅੱਛਤਾ, ਨਿਰਮਲਤਾ

clash (ਕਲੈਸ਼) n v ਟੱਕਰ, ਟਕਰਾ, ਲੜਾਈ, ਝੜਪ, ਮੁੱਠ-ਭੇੜ, ਖਟਪਟ, ਰੁਕਾਵਟ, ਹਮਲਾ; ਟਕਰਾਉਣਾ; ਲੜਨਾ; ਖਟਪਟਾਉਣਾ; ਰੋਕਣਾ, ਹਮਲਾ ਕਰਨਾ

clasp (ਕਲਾਸਪ) n v ਕੁੰਡਾ, ਬਕਸੂਆ; ਪਕੜ, ਜੱਫੀ, ਗਲਵਕੜੀ; ਬੰਦ ਕਰਨਾ, ਬੰਨ੍ਹਣਾ, ਬਕਸੂਆ ਲਾਉਣਾ, ਜੱਫੀ ਪਾਉਣਾ, ਘੁੱਟਣਾ, ਗਲ ਲਾਉਣਾ

class (ਕਲਾਸ) n v ਵਰਗ, ਸ਼੍ਰੇਣੀ; ਜਾਤ, ਦਰਜਾ, ਵਰਗੀਕਰਨ ਕਰਨਾ; ਜਮਾਤ ਵੰਡ ਕਰਨਾ, ਦਰਜੇਵਾਰ ਕਰਨਾ; ~fellow ਜਮਾਤੀ, ਹਮਜਮਾਤ, ਸਹਿਪਾਠੀ; ~room ਅਧਿਐਨ-ਕਮਰਾ, ਕਲਾਸ ਰੂਮ

classic ('ਕਲੈਸਿਕ) a n ਉੱਤਮ, ਟਕਸਾਲੀ, ਸ੍ਰੇਸ਼ਠ; ਸਨਾਤਨੀ; ਕਿਸੇ ਦੇਸ਼ ਦਾ ਪੁਰਾਤਨ ਸਾਹਿਤ; ਯੂਨਾਨੀ ਜਾਂ ਲਾਤੀਨੀ ਜਾਂ ਸੰਸਕ੍ਰਿਤ ਭਾਸ਼ਾ

classification ('ਕਲੈਸਿਫ਼ਿ'ਕੇਇਸ਼ਨ) n ਵਰਗੀਕਰਨ, ਸ਼੍ਰੇਣੀਕਰਨ

classifier ('ਕਲੈਸਿਫ਼ਿਅ*) n ਸ਼੍ਰੇਣੀ ਜਾਂ ਵਰਗ ਵਿਚ ਰੱਖਣ ਵਾਲਾ, ਕ੍ਰਮਬੱਧ ਕਰਨ ਵਾਲਾ

classify ('ਕਲੈਸਿਫ਼ਾਇ) v ਵਰਗੀਕਰਨ ਕਰਨਾ, ਸ਼੍ਰੇਣੀ ਬੱਧ ਕਰਨਾ, ਦਰਜਾਬੰਦੀ ਕਰਨਾ

clatter ('ਕਲੈਟਅ*) v n ਖੜਕਣਾ, ਖੜਕਾਉਣਾ, ਰੌਲਾ ਪੈਣਾ, ਬਕਬਕ ਕਰਨਾ, ਖੜਕਾਟ, ਰੌਲਾ, ਬਕਵਾਸ

clause (ਕਲਾਜ਼) n ਉਪਵਾਕ, ਛੋਟਾ ਵਾਕ; ਦਫ਼ਾ, ਸ਼ਰਤ

claw (ਕਲਾ) n ਪੰਜਾ, ਪੌਂਚਾ, ਨਹੁੰਦਰ; ਸੰਨੀ

clay (ਕਲੇਇ) n ਪਾਂਡੂ, ਚੀਕਣੀ ਮਿੱਟੀ; ~pipe ਮਿੱਟੀ ਦਾ ਹੁੱਕਾ ਜਾਂ ਪਾਈਪ

clean (ਕਲੀਨ) *a adv v n* ਸਾਫ਼, ਸੁਥਰਾ, ਸੁਅੱਛ, ਉਜਲ, ਨਿਰਮਲ, ਬੇਦਾਗ਼, ਉੱਤਮ; ਸਰਾਸਰ, ਨਿਰੋਲ ਸਫ਼ਾਈ ਨਾਲ; ਸਾਫ਼ ਕਰਨਾ, ਮਾਂਜਣਾ; ਉੱਜਲਾ ਕਰਨਾ, ਝਾੜਨਾ, ਸਫ਼ਾਈ, ਝਾੜ-ਪੂੰਝ; ~**tongue** ਸ਼ੁੱਧ ਬਚਨ ਬੋਲਣੇ; ~**er** ਸਾਫ਼ ਕਰਨ ਵਾਲਾ, ਝਾੜੂ ਦੇਣ ਵਾਲਾ; ਕੱਪੜੇ ਡਰਾਈਕਲੀਨ ਕਰਨ ਵਾਲਾ; ~**ing** ਸਫ਼ਾਈ; ~**liness** ਸਫ਼ਾਈ, ਸਫ਼ਾਈ ਪਸੰਦੀ; ~**ness** ਪਵਿੱਤਰਤਾ, ਨਿਰਮਲਤਾ, ਸੁਅੱਛਤਾ; ~**se** ਸਾਫ਼ ਕਰਨਾ, ਸ਼ੁੱਧ ਕਰਨਾ, ਝਾੜਨਾ, ਪੂੰਝਣਾ, ਮਾਂਜਣਾ, ਧੋਣਾ, ਪਵਿੱਤਰ ਕਰਨਾ

clear (ਕਲਿਅ*) *a v* ਸਾਫ਼, ਨਿਰਮਲ, ਬੇਦਾਗ਼, ਖ਼ਾਲਸ, ਸੁਅੱਛ, ਸਪੱਸ਼ਟ, ਪਰਗਟ; ਨਿਖੱਰਨਾ, ਸਾਫ਼ ਕਰਨਾ, ਸਾਫ਼ ਹੋਣਾ, ਨਿਰਮਲ ਹੋਣਾ, ਭੁਲੇਖਾ ਦੂਰ ਕਰਨਾ, ਨਿਰ-ਅਪਰਾਧ ਠਹਿਰਾਉਣਾ, ਰਿਹਾ ਕਰਨਾ; ~**ance** ਸਪੱਸ਼ਟਤਾ, ਸਫ਼ਾਈ; ਭੁਗਤਾਨ; ਭੁਗਤਾਨ ਪੱਤਰ, ਜਹਾਜ਼ ਖ਼ਾਲੀ ਹੋਣ ਦਾ ਪ੍ਰਮਾਣ-ਪੱਤਰ, ਸੋਧਨ; ਮਾਲ ਦਾ ਨਿਕਾਸ, ਡਾਕ ਦਾ ਨਿਕਾਸ; ~**away** ਲਾਂਭੇ ਕਰਨਾ, ਹਟਾਉਣਾ, ਅੱਖਾਂ ਤੋਂ ਦੂਰ ਹੋ ਜਾਣਾ; ~**ing** ਨਿਕਾਸੀ; ~**ly** ਸਾਫ਼ ਸਾਫ਼ ਸਚਮੁਚ, ਸਪੱਸ਼ਟਤਾ ਪੂਰਵਕ; ~**ness** ਸਫ਼ਾਈ, ਸੁਅੱਛਤਾ, ਸਪੱਸ਼ਟਤਾ, ਨਿਰਵਿਘਨਤਾ; ~**off** ਛੁਟਕਾਰਾ ਪਾਉਣਾ, ਖ਼ਲਾਸੀ ਪਾਉਣਾ; ~**up** ਹੱਲ ਕਰਨਾ, ਨਿੱਤਰ ਆਉਣਾ; ~**conscience** ਸਾਫ਼, ਜ਼ਮੀਰ; ~**sighted** ਤੇਜ਼ ਨਜ਼ਰ, ਤੀਬਰ ਦ੍ਰਿਸ਼ਟੀ

cleavage ('ਕਲੀਵਿਜ) *n* ਚੀਰ, ਦਰਜ, ਵਿੱਥ; ਪਾੜਾ

cleave (ਕਲੀਵ਼) *v* ਚੀਰਨਾ, ਪਾੜਨਾ, ਵਫ਼ਾਦਾਰ ਰਹਿਣਾ, ਡਟੇ ਰਹਿਣਾ

cleft (ਕਲੈਫ਼ਟ) *n* ਦਰਾੜ, ਤੇੜ, ਦਰਜ, ਚੀਰ

clemency ('ਕਲੈਮਂਅੰਸਿ) *a* ਨਰਮ-ਦਿਲੀ, ਉਦਾਰਤਾ, ਕਿਰਪਾ, ਦਇਆ, ਰਹਿਮ, ਤਰਸ

clement ('ਕਲੈਮਅੰਟ) *a* ਨਰਮ-ਦਿਲ, ਕਿਰਪਾਲੂ, ਉਦਾਰ, ਦਇਆਮਈ

clergy ('ਕਲਅਃਜਿ) *n* ਪਾਦਰੀ-ਵਰਗਾ, ਪਰੋਹਤ-ਵਰਗਾ; ਪਾਦਰੀ ਜਾਂ ਪਰੋਹਤ ਦਾ ਅਧਿਕਾਰ; ~**man** ਪਾਦਰੀ

cleric ('ਕਲੈਰਿਕ) *n a* ਪਾਦਰੀ, ਪਰੋਹਤ; ਪਾਦਰੀਆਂ ਦਾ, ਪਾਦਰੀ-ਵਰਗ-ਸਬੰਧੀ; ~**al** ਪਾਰਲੀਮੈਂਟ ਆਦਿ ਵਿਚ ਪਾਦਰੀ-ਵਰਗ ਦਾ ਮੈਂਬਰ ਜਾਂ ਸਦੱਸ; ਕਲਰਕੀ, ਕਲਰਕ ਸਬੰਧੀ; ਪਾਦਰੀ ਦਾ

clerk (ਕਲ*ਕ) *a* ਮੁਨਸ਼ੀ, ਬਾਬੂ; ਲੇਖਕ; ਕਲਰਕ, ਪਾਦਰੀ; **great**~ (ਪ੍ਰ) ਮਹਾਨ ਵਿਦਵਾਨ

clever (ਕਲੈੱਵ਼ਅ*) *n* ਚੁਸਤ, ਹੁਸ਼ਿਆਰ, ਸਚੇਤ, ਸਿਆਣਾ; ਚੰਟ, ਚਤਰ, ~**ness** ਚਤਰਾਈ, ਚੁਸਤੀ, ਹੁਸ਼ਿਆਰੀ, ਚਲਾਕੀ, ਪ੍ਰਵੀਣਤਾ, ਸਾਵਧਾਨੀ

cliche ('ਕਲੀਸ਼ੇਇ) *n* ਘਸੇ-ਪਿਟੇ ਸ਼ਬਦ

cliff (ਕਲਿਫ਼) *n* ਟਿੱਲਾ, ਚਟਾਨ, ਢਲਵਾਨ, ਢਿੰਗ

climate ('ਕਲਾਇਮਇਟ) *n* ਜਲਵਾਯੂ, ਪੌਣ-ਪਾਣੀ, ਆਬੋ-ਹਵਾ; ਵਾਤਾਵਰਣ, ਮਾਹੌਲ

climatic (ਕਲਾਇ'ਮੈਟਿਕ) *a* ਜਲਵਾਯੂ-ਸਬੰਧੀ

climax ('ਕਲਾਇਮੈਕਸ) *n* ਸਿਖਰ, ਟੀਸੀ, ਤੇਜ਼ ਚਰਮ ਸੀਮਾ, ਚਰਮ ਬਿੰਦੂ

climb (ਕਲਾਇਮ) *n v* ਚੜ੍ਹਾਈ; ਉਤਕਰਸ਼ ਚੜ੍ਹਨਾ, ਉੱਨਤੀ ਕਰਨੀ; ~**er** (ਪਹਾੜ ਉੱਤੇ) ਚੜ੍ਹਨ ਵਾਲਾ, ਉੱਨਤੀ ਕਰ ਰਿਹਾ ਵਿਅਕਤੀ

cling (ਕਲਿਙ) *v* ਚੰਬੜਨਾ, ਲੱਗੇ ਰਹਿਣਾ ਚਿਪਕਣਾ, ਲਿਪਟਣਾ; ਵਫ਼ਾਦਾਰ ਰਹਿਣਾ, ਡਟੇ ਰਹਿਣਾ

clinic ('ਕਲਿਨਿਕ) *n* ਚਕਿਤਸ਼ਾਲਾ, ਕਲੈਨਿਕ

clip (ਕਲਿਪ) *n v* ਹੁੰਢੀ, ਕਲਿਪ, ਚੁਟਕੀ; ਕੱਟ-ਛਾਂਟ; ਫੜਨਾ, ਕਸ ਕੇ ਫੜਨਾ, ਕੱਟ-ਛਾਂਟ ਕਰਨਾ; **~per** ਕੈਂਚੀ, ਕਾਤ; **~ping** ਕਟਾਈ, ਕੁਤਰਨ, ਕਾਤਰ, ਛੰਟਾਈ

clique (ਕਲੀਕ) *n* ਢਾਣੀ, ਜੁੰਡੀ, ਗੁਟ

cloak (ਕਲਅਉਕ) *n v* ਚੋਗਾ, ਅੰਗਰਖਾ, ਲਬਾਦਾ; ਆੜ, ਓਟ, ਚੋਗਾ ਪਾਉਣਾ, ਢੱਕਣਾ; **~room** ਕਲੋਕ ਰੂਮ, ਸਾਮਾਨ ਰੱਖਣ ਵਾਲਾ ਕਮਰਾ

clock (ਕਲੋਕ) *n* ਵੱਡੀ ਘੜੀ, ਦੀਵਾਰ-ਘੜੀ; **~tower** ਘੰਟਾ ਘਰ; **~wise** ਸਿੱਧਾ ਗੇੜਾ

clod (ਕਲੋਡ) *n v* (ਮਿੱਟੀ ਦਾ) ਢੇਲਾ, ਡਲਾ, ਡਲਾ ਮਾਰਨਾ; **the~** ਧਰਤੀ, ਜ਼ਮੀਨ

clog (ਕਲੋਗ) *n v* ਢਾਹਾ; ਅੜੰਗਾ; ਖੜਾਵਾਂ; ਅੜਿੱਕਾ, ਅਟਕਾਉ, ਰੁਕਾਵਟ, ਰੋਕਣਾ; ਅੱਟ ਜਾਣਾ

close (ਕਲਅਉਸ) *a adv n v* ਗੁਪਤ, ਗੁੜ੍ਹ; ਨੇੜੇ, ਨਿਕਟ, ਪਾਸ; ਘਣਾ, ਘਨਿਸ਼ਠ; ਬੰਦ; ਤੰਗ, ਭੀੜਾ, ਸੌੜਾ, ਸੰਕੀਰਣ; ਸੰਕੁਚਤ; ਸੂਮ; ਸੀਮਤ; ਮੁੰਦਣਾ, ਮੀਟਣਾ, ਭੇੜਨਾ, ਬੰਦ ਕਰਨਾ, ਨੇੜੇ ਆਉਣਾ; ਭਿੜਨਾ, ਭਿੜਾਉਣਾ, ਮਿਲਣਾ, ਮਿਲ ਜਾਣਾ, ਜੜਨਾ, ਜੋੜਨਾ; **~air** ਬੰਦ, ਹੁੰਮਸ, ਹੁਸੜ ਘੁਟਣ; **~by** ਨੇੜੇ; **~fisted** ਕੰਜੂਸ, ਮੱਖੀ ਚੂਸ; **~at hand** ਪਾਸ ਹੀ, ਨੇੜੇ ਹੀ; **~in** ਪਾਸ ਆਉਣਾ, ਹੌਲੀ-ਹੌਲੀ ਕੰਮ ਹੋਣਾ, ਘੇਰਨਾ, ਅਹਾਤਾਬੰਦੀ ਕਰਨਾ; **~ly** ਧਿਆਨਪੂਰਵਕ, ਬਾਰੀਕੀ ਨਾਲ; ਪਾਸ ਪਾਸ, ਕਰੀਬ ਕਰੀਬ; **~ness** ਨਿਕਟਤਾ, ਸਮੀਪਤਾ, ਜੋੜ; ਸਮਾਪਤੀ; ਹੁੰਮਸ, ਘੁਟਣ

closet ('ਕਲੋਜ਼ਿਟ) *n* ਕੋਠੜੀ, ਕਮਰਾ, ਖਿਲਵਗਾਹ; ਬਰਤਨਾਂ ਦੀ ਅਲਮਾਰੀ

closure ('ਕਲਅਉਯ਼ਅ') *n v* ਬੰਦਸ਼, ਪਾਬੰਦੀ, ਰੋਕ, ਇਹਾਤਾ; ਰੋਕਣਾ, ਬੰਦ ਕਰਨਾ

clot (ਕਲੋਟ) *n v* ਫੁੱਟ, ਫੁੱਟੀ, ਗੱਤਲਾ; ਘਟਚੱਕਰ, ਫੁੱਟੀ ਹੋਣਾ, ਜੰਮ ਜਾਣਾ; **~of blood** ਖੂਨ ਦਾ ਗੱਤਲਾ; **~ted hair** ਜਟਾਜੂਟ

cloth (ਕਲੋਥ) *n* ਕੱਪੜੇ, ਵਸਤਰ, ਜਾਮਾ, ਪੁਸ਼ਾਕ ਲਈ ਕੱਪੜਾ, ਪੱਟੂ, ਸ਼ਾਲ; **table~** ਮੇਜ਼ ਪੋਸ਼; **the~** ਪਾਦਰੀ ਦਾ ਪਦ

clothe (ਕਲਅਉਦ) *v* ਕੱਪੜੇ ਪਹਿਨਾਉਣਾ; ਕੱਜਣਾ, ਢਕਣਾ

clothier ('ਕਲਅਉਦਿਅ') *n* ਜੁਲਾਹਾ; ਬਜਾਜ, ਵਸਤਰ-ਵਪਾਰੀ

clothing ('ਕਲਅਉਦਿੰਙ) *n* ਪੁਸ਼ਾਕ, ਵਸਤਰ

cloud (ਕਲਾਉਡ) *n v* ਬੱਦਲ, ਮੇਘ, ਘਟ ਘਟਾ; ਗਰਦ, ਧੁੰਦਲਕਾ; ਧੁੰਦਲਾਪਨ, ਬੱਦਲ ਛਾ ਜਾਣੇ, ਘਟਾ ਉਠਨੀ, ਨਿਰਾਸ ਹੋਣਾ; **~burst** ਮੂਸਲਾਧਾਰ ਵਰਖਾ, ਤੁਫ਼ਾਨੀ ਛਹਿਬਰ; **~of words** ਵਾਕ-ਜਾਲ, ਸ਼ਬਦ-ਅੜੰਬਰ, ਵਾਕ ਛਲ; **in the~** ਅਵਾਸਤਵਿਕ, ਕਲਪਨਾ ਵਿਚ

clout (ਕਲਾਉਟ) *n v* ਟਾਕੀ, ਚੀਥੜਾ, ਪੁੰਝਣ, ਪੋਚੜਾ, ਸਾਢੀ; ਕੀਲਾ, ਟਾਕੀ ਲਾਉਣਾ, ਚੀਥੜਾ ਗੰਢਣਾ, ਪੁੰਝਣਾ

clown (ਕਲਾਉਨ) *n* ਉਜੱਡ, ਅਨਘੜ; ਗੰਵਾਰ, ਭੰਡ, ਨਕਲੀਆ, ਮਸਖ਼ਰਾ, ਵਿਦੂਸ਼ਕ; **~ish** ਅੱਖੜ, ਉਜੱਡ, ਮਜ਼ਾਕੀਆ, ਅਸੱਭਿਅ

club (ਕਲੱਬ) *n v* ਕਲੱਬ, ਸਭਾ, ਡੰਡਾ, ਸੋਟਾ, ਲੱਠ, ਚਿੜੀਏ ਦਾ ਪੱਤਾ; ਡੰਡੇ ਮਾਰਨਾ, ਕੁੱਟਣਾ; ਜੋੜਨਾ, ਮਿਲਨਾ, ਸ਼ਾਮਲ ਹੋਣਾ, ਲਾਭ ਪਹੁੰਚਾਉਣਾ **~law** ਜਬਰਦਸਤੀ, ਡੰਡੇ ਦਾ ਕਾਨੂੰਨ; **~s** ਚਿੜੀਏ ਦਾ ਰੰਗ, ਚਿੜੀਆ

clue (ਕਲੂ) *n* ਊਘ-ਸੂਘ, ਭਿਣਕ, ਪਤਾ, ਨਿਸ਼ਾਨ; **~less** ਘੋਣਿਸ਼ਾਨ; ਲਾਪਤਾ

clump ('ਕਲਅੰਪ) *n v* ਸਮੂਹ; ਝੁਰਮਟ; ਸੁੰਕਾ; ਘਸੁੰਨ; ਸੰਘਣੇ ਬਿਰਛ ਲਗਾਉਣਾ; ਢੇਰ ਲਗਾਉਣਾ, ਜੁੱਤੀ ਨੂੰ ਦੋਹਰਾ ਤਲਾ ਲਗਾਉਣਾ; ਘਸੁੰਨ ਮਾਰਨਾ

clumsily ('ਕਲਅੱਸਜ਼ਿਲਿ) *adv* ਬੇਢੰਗੇ ਢੰਗ ਨਾਲ, ਕੁਚੱਜਪੁਣੇ ਨਾਲ

clumsiness ('ਕਲਅੱਮਜ਼ਿਨਇਸ) *n* ਬੱਦੀਪਨ, ਅਨਾੜੀਪਨ, ਘੇਰੰਗਾਪਨ, ਅੱਖੜਪਨ

clumsy ('ਕਲਅੱਮਜ਼ਿ) *a* ਕੁਢੱਬਾ, ਘੇਢੰਗਲ, ਬੇਢੰਗਾ, ਅੱਖੜ, ਭੱਦਾ, ਅਨਾੜੀ, ਫੂਹੜ

cluster ('ਕਲਅੱਸਟਅ*) *n v* ਝੁਰਮਟ, ਝੁੰਮਰ, ਗੁੱਛਾ, ਝੰਡ, ਝੁਮਕਾ; ਸਮੂਹ; ਝੁੰਡ ਬਣਾਉਣਾ, ਇਕੱਠਾ ਹੋਣਾ, ਜਮ੍ਹਾ ਕਰਨਾ ਜਾਂ ਹੋਣਾ

clutch (ਕਲਅੱਚ) *n v* ਪਕੜ, ਪੰਜਾ, ਸ਼ਿਕੰਜਾ, ਕਲੱਚ; ਝਪਟਣਾ, ਘੁੱਟ ਕੇ ਫੜਨਾ, ਜਕੜ ਲਾਉਣੀ

Co (ਕਅਉ) *perf* ਨਾਲ; ਸਹਿ, ਕੰਪਨੀ ਦਾ ਸੰਖਿਪਤ ਰੂਪ; ~**author** ਸਹਿ-ਲੇਖਕ

coach (ਕਅਉਚ) *n v* (ਸ਼ਾਹੀ) ਗੱਡੀ, ਸਵਾਰੀ ਗੱਡੀ, ਰੇਲ ਦਾ ਡੱਬਾ; ਸਮੁੰਦਰੀ ਜਹਾਜ਼ ਦਾ ਪਿਛਲਾ ਕਮਰਾ; ਘਰ ਪੜ੍ਹਾਉਣ ਵਾਲਾ ਅਧਿਆਪਕ; ਘਰ ਪੜ੍ਹਾਉਣਾ, ਖੇਡਣਾ ਸਿਖਾਉਣਾ; ~**man** ਕੋਚਵਾਨ, ਸਾਈਸ, ਚਾਲਕ; ~**manship** ਕੋਚਵਾਨੀ, ਸਾਈਸੀ

coal (ਕਅਉਲ) *n v* ਖਣਿਜੀ ਕੋਲਾ, ਪੱਥਰ ਦਾ ਕੋਲਾ; ~**bed** ਕੋਲੇ ਦੀ ਤਹਿ; ~**black** ਕਾਲਾ-ਸਿਆਹ, ਕਾਲਾ ਧੁੱਤ; ~**dust** ਕੋਲੇ ਦਾ ਚੂਰਾ, ਕੇਰੀ; ~**field** ਕੋਲਾ-ਖੇਤਰ, ਕੋਲੇ ਦੀ ਖਾਣ; ~**pit** ਕੋਲੇ ਦੀ ਖਾਣ; ~**tar** ਲੁੱਕ, ਤਾਰਕੋਲ

coalition ('ਕਅਉਅ'ਲਿਸ਼ਨ) *n* ਮੇਲ; ਸੰਯੋਗ, ਸੰਧੀ, ਸੰਯੁਕਤ, ਮਿਲਾਪ, ਸਹਿਯੋਗ, ਸਹਿਮਿਲਨ, ਗਠਬੰਧਨ, ਕੋਲੀਸ਼ਨ

coarse (ਕੋ*ਸ) *a* ਘਟੀਆ, ਮੋਟਾ, ਖੁਰਦਰਾ, ਤੁੱਛ, ਸਧਾਰਨ, ਗੰਵਾਰ, ਅਸੱਭਿਆ, ਅੱਖੜ ਅਨਾੜੀ, ਭੱਦਾ

coast (ਕਅਉਸਟ) *n v* ਸਮੁੰਦਰੀ ਤਟ, ਸਮੁੰਦਰੀ ਕੰਢਾ; ਤਟ ਦੇ ਨਾਲ ਨਾਲ ਜਾਣਾ; ~**guard** ਤੱਟ-ਰੱਖਿਅਕ ਪੁਲੀਸ; ~**line** ਤੱਟ-ਰੇਖਾ; ~**al** ਤਟਵਰਤੀ, ਤਟੀ, ਸਾਹਲੀ, ਕਿਨਾਰੇ ਦਾ

coat (ਕਅਉਟ) *n v* ਕੋਟ; ਪਰਦਾ, ਝਿੱਲੀ; ਮੁਲੰਮਾ; ਉੱਪਰਲੀ ਤਹਿ, ਢਕੇ ਹੋਣਾ, ਮੁਲੰਮਾ ਕਰਨਾ, ਤਹਿ ਚੜ੍ਹਾਉਣਾ, ਪੋਚਣਾ, ਕਲੀ ਕਰਨਾ; ~**ed** ਕੋਟਧਾਰੀ, ਢੱਕਿਆ, ਪੋਚਿਆ, ਛਿਲਕੇਦਾਰ; **turn one's~** ਨਮਕਹਰਾਮੀ ਕਰਨਾ, ਗ਼ਦਾਰੀ ਕਰਨਾ

coax (ਕਅਉਕਸ) *v* ਪਰਚਾਉਣਾ, ਵਲਾਉਣਾ, ਦਿਲਾਸਾ ਦੇਣਾ, ਮਨਾਉਣਾ; ਵਰਗਲਾਉਣਾ

cobble ('ਕੌਬਲ) *v* ਗੰਢਣਾ, ਗੰਢ ਤੁਪ ਕਰਨਾ, ਜੁੱਤੀਆਂ ਸਿਉਣਾ; ~**r** ਮੋਚੀ, ਜੁੱਤੀਆਂ ਗੰਢਣ ਜਾਂ ਸਿਉਣ ਵਾਲਾ

cobra ('ਕਅਉਬਰਅ) *n* ਫਨੀਅਰ ਕਾਲਾ ਨਾਗ

cobweb ('ਕੌਬਵੈੱਬ) *n a* ਮੱਕੜੀ ਦਾ ਜਾਲਾ, ਜਾਲ, ਫੰਦਾ; ਧੋਖਾ; ਸ਼ਬਦਜਾਲ; ਕਮਜ਼ੋਰ, ਪਤਲਾ

cock (ਕੌਕ) *n* ਕੁੱਕੜ, ਮੁਰਗ਼ਾ; ਟੂਟੀ; ਘੋੜਪੇਚ; ਉਟਪਟਾਂਗ ਗੱਲ; ਤਾਨਣਾ, ਖੜਾ ਕਰਨਾ, ਚੜ੍ਹਾਉਣਾ (ਬੰਦੂਕ ਦਾ ਘੋੜਾ); ~**and bull story** ਬਣਾਉਟੀ ਕਹਾਣੀ, ਮਨਘੜਤ ਕਹਾਣੀ, ~**eyed** ਭੈਂਗਾ, ਲਾਂਵਾ, ਮੂੜ੍ਹ, ਹਾਸੋਹੀਣਾ; ~**pit** ਕੁੱਕੜਾਂ ਦਾ ਅਖਾੜਾ; ਅਖਾੜਾ; ਹਵਾਈ ਜਹਾਜ਼ ਵਿਚ ਚਾਲਕ ਦੇ ਬੈਠਨ ਦੀ ਥਾਂ

cockroach ('ਕੌਕਰਅਉਚ) *n* ਤਿਲਚਟਾ, ਕਾਕਰੋਚ

cocktail ('ਕੌਕਟੇਇਲ) *n a* ਕਾਕਟੇਲ, ਰਲੀ ਮਿਲੀ ਸ਼ਰਾਬ; ਇਕ ਪ੍ਰਕਾਰ ਦਾ ਭੋਰ;

coco ('ਕਅਉਕਅਉ) *n* ਗਿਰੀ, ਖੋਪਾ, ਨਾਰੀਅਲ

code ('ਕਾਉਡ) *n* ਕੋਡ, ਨਿਆਇ-ਸ਼ਾਸਤਰ, ਸਦਾਚਾਰ ਦੇ ਨਿਯਮ; ਸੰਹਿਤਾ, ਕਾਨੂੰਨ ਦਾ ਗ੍ਰੰਥ, ਨਿਯਮਾਂਵਲੀ, ਵਿਧਾਨਾਂ ਜਾਂ ਨਿਯਮਾਂ ਦਾ ਸੰਗ੍ਰਹਿ; ਸੁਕੇਤ-ਪੱਧਤੀ; ਸੰਖਿਪਤ ਨਾਂ, ਸੰਕੇਤਾਵਲੀ; ਗੁਪਤ-ਦੇਸ਼; ਸੰਕੇਤਬੱਧ ਕਰਨਾ, ਸੰਖਿਪਤ ਕਰਨਾ; **~words** ਸੰਕੇਤ-ਸ਼ਬਦ, ਸੰਕੇਤ

codification ('ਕਾਉਡਿਫ਼ਿ'ਕੇਇਸ਼ਨ) *n* ਨਿਯਮ-ਵਿਵਸਥਾ, ਕਾਨੂੰਨੀ-ਵਿਵਸਥਾ; ਸੰਹਿਤਾਕਰਨ

codified ('ਕਾਉਡਿਫ਼ਾਇਡ) *a* ਵਿਵਸਥਿਤ, ਨਿਯਮਬੱਧ, ਸੰਹਿਤਾ, ਸੰਹਿਤਾਬੱਧ

codifier ('ਕਾਉਡਿਫ਼ਾਇਅ*) *n* ਸੰਹਿਤਾਕਾਰ

codify ('ਕਾਉਡਿਫ਼ਾਇ) *v* ਨਿਯਮਤ ਕਰਨਾ, ਨਿਯਮਬੱਧ ਕਰਨਾ, ਸੰਗ੍ਰਹ ਕਰਨਾ, ਸੰਹਿਤਾਕਰਨ ਕਰਨਾ

co-education ('ਕਾਉਐਡਯੂ'ਕੇਇਸ਼ਨ) *n* ਸਾਂਝੀ ਸਿੱਖਿਆ, ਸਹਿ-ਸਿੱਖਿਆ

coerce (ਕਾਉ'ਅ:ਸ) *v* ਦਬਾਉਣਾ, ਜ਼ਬਰ ਕਰਨਾ, ਬੇਵੱਸ ਕਰਨਾ

corecion (ਕਾਉ'ਅ:ਸ਼ਨ) *n* ਦਾਬਾ, ਦਬਾਉ, ਜ਼ਬਰ, ਜ਼ਬਰਦਸਤੀ, ਵਧੀਕ, ਹਿੰਸਾ

coercive (ਕਾਉ'ਅ:ਸਿਵ਼) *a* ਦਬਾਉ, ਬਲਯੁਕਤ, ਬਲਾਤਕਾਰੀ, ਦਮਨਸ਼ੀਲ; **~ness** ਬਲ-ਪ੍ਰਯੋਗ, ਦਬਾਉ, ਦਮਨ

coexist ('ਕਾਉਇਗ'ਜ਼ਿਸਟ) *v* ਇਕ ਹੀ ਕਾਲ ਵਿਚ ਵਿਦਮਾਨ ਹੋਣਾ, ਸਮਕਾਲੀ ਹੋਣਾ; **~ence** ਸਹਿਹੋਂਦ, ਸਹਿਅਸਤਿਤਵ, ਸਹਿਭਾਵ, ਸਮਕਾਲੀ ਵਿਦਮਾਨਤਾ; **~ent** ਸਮਕਾਲੀਨ

coffee ('ਕੌਫ਼ਿ) *n* ਕਾਫ਼ੀ, ਕਾਹਵਾ, ਕਾਫ਼ੀ ਦਾ ਬੂਟਾ

coffer ('ਕੌਫ਼ਅ*) *n v* ਤਿਜੋਰੀ, ਖ਼ਜ਼ਾਨੇ ਵਾਲੀ ਅਲਮਾਰੀ, ਖ਼ਜ਼ਾਨਾ, ਕੋਸ਼, ਜਮ੍ਹਾ ਰੱਖਣਾ, ਤਿਜੋਰੀ ਵਿਚ ਬੰਦ ਕਰਨਾ

coffin ('ਕੌਫ਼ਿਨ) *n* ਤਾਬੂਤ; ਨਿਕੰਮਾ ਜਹਾਜ਼, ਘੋੜੇ ਦਾ ਸੁੰਮ

cognition (ਕੌਗ'ਨਿਸ਼ਨ) *n* ਬੋਧ, ਗਿਆਨ, ਅਨੁਭਵ; ਸੰਕਲਪ; **~al** ਬੋਧਾਤਮਕ ਗਿਆਨ ਸਬੰਧੀ, ਅਨੁਭੂਤੀ ਜਾਂ ਧਾਰਨਾ ਸਬੰਧੀ

cognizance ('ਕੌਗਨਿਜ਼ਅੰਸ) *n* ਗਿਆਨ; ਪਛਾਣ; ਧਿਆਨ; ਲੱਛਣ, ਚਿੰਨ੍ਹ, ਕਾਨੂੰਨੀ ਅਧਿਕਾਰ ਦਾ ਪ੍ਰਯੋਗ

cohabit (ਕਾਉ'ਹੈਬਿਟ) *v* ਪਤੀ ਪਤਨੀ ਦੀ ਤਰ੍ਹਾਂ ਰਹਿਣਾ, ਗ੍ਰਹਿਵਾਸ ਕਰਨਾ, **~ation** ਸੰਭੋਗ, ਸਹਿਵਾਸ

co-heir, -ess ('ਕਾਉ'ਏਅ*'ਕਾਉ'ਏਅਰਿਸ) *n* ਬਰਾਬਰ ਦਾ ਹੱਕਦਾਰ, ਹਮਵਾਰਸ, ਵਿਰਸੇ ਦਾ ਹੱਕਦਾਰ

cohere (ਕਅ(ਉ)'ਹਿਅ*) *v* ਚੰਬੜਨਾ, ਜੁੜਨਾ, ਇਕਸਾਰ ਹੋਣਾ, ਸੰਯੁਕਤ ਹੋਣਾ; **~nce, ~ncy** ਸੰਮਤੀ, ਸੰਸ਼ਲੇਸ਼ਣ, ਇਕੱਠ, ਇਕਤਰਤਾ, ਇਕਸਾਰਤਾ; **~nt** ਉਚਿਤ, ਸੰਯੁਕਤ, ਚਿਪਕਿਆ, ਚੰਬੜਿਆ, ਜੁੜਿਆ, ਜੰਮਿਆ

cohesion (ਕਅ(ਉ)'ਹੀਯ਼ਨ) *n* ਜੋੜ, ਮੇਲ, ਸੰਯੋਗ, ਸੰਯੁਕਤ ਹੋਣ ਦੀ ਪ੍ਰਵਿਰਤੀ

coil (ਕੌਇਲ) *v n* ਕੁੰਡਲ ਬਣਾਉਣੇ, ਵਲ ਪਾਉਣੇ, ਪੇਚ ਪਾਉਣੇ; ਕੁੰਡਲ, ਵਲ, ਪੇਚ, ਲੱਛਾ, ਅੱਟੀ, ਕੁੰਡਲੀ

coin (ਕੌਇਨ) *n v* ਸਿੱਕਾ, ਰੁਪਈਆ, ਪੈਸਾ, ਧਨ, ਮੁਦਰਾ; ਸਿੱਕਾ ਢਾਲਣਾ ਜਾਂ ਬਣਾਉਣਾ, ਘੜਨਾ, ਟਕਸਾਲਣਾ; **false~** ਖੋਟਾ ਸਿੱਕਾ, ਜਾਅਲੀ ਸਿੱਕਾ; **~age** ਸਿੱਕਾ ਢਲਾਈ, ਪ੍ਰਚਲਤ ਸਿੱਕਾ ਜਾਂ ਮੁਦਰਾ; ਸਿੱਕੇ; ਘੜੇ ਹੋਏ ਸ਼ਬਦ; **~less** ਨਿਰਧਨ, ਕੰਗਾਲ, ਗ਼ਰੀਬ

coincide ('ਕਅਉਿਨ'ਸਾਇਡ) v ਇਕੇ ਸਮੇਂ ਵਾਪਰਨਾ, ਰਲਣਾ-ਮਿਲਣਾ, ਮੇਲ ਖਾਣਾ, ਠੀਕ ਬੈਠਣਾ; ਸਮਕਾਲੀ ਹੋਣਾ; ਅਨੁਰੂਪ ਹੋਣਾ; ~nce ਨ, ਮੇਲ, ਸੰਜੋਗ, ਸੰਕਾ-ਮੇਲ; ਅਨੁਰੂਪਤਾ; ~nt ਸੰਜੋਗੀ, ਮਿਲਦਾ-ਜੁਲਦਾ; ~ntal ਸੰਜੋਗੀ, ਸੁਭਾਵਕ, ਉਸੇ ਥਾਂ ਜਾਂ ਉਸੇ ਸਮੇਂ, ਸਮਕਾਲੀ

coir ('ਕੋਇਅ*) n ਨਾਰੀਅਲ ਦੇ ਰੇਸ਼ੇ, ਕੋਇਰ

coke (ਕਅਉਕ) n ਕੋਕ, ਪੱਥਰ ਦਾ ਕੋਲਾ, ਪੱਥਰੀ ਕੋਲਾ; ਇਕ ਪੇਯ

cold (ਕਅਉਲਡ) n a ਠੰਢ, ਸਰਦੀ, ਨਜ਼ਲਾ, ਜ਼ੁਕਾਮ; ਠੰਢਕ; ਠੰਢਾ, ਸੀਤ, ਸੀਤਲ, ਸਰਦ; ਰੁੱਖਾ, ਅਰੋਚਕ, ਕੋਰਾ, ਪ੍ਰਤੀਕੂਲ; ~**blooded** ਨਿਰਦਈ, ਬੇਦਰਦ; ~**bloodedness** ਨਿਰਦਇਤਾ, ਨਿਸ਼ਠੁਰਤਾ, ਬੇਰਹਿਮੀ; ~**steel** ਤਲਵਾਰ, ਸੰਗੀਨ ਆਦਿ; ~**war** ਸੀਤ ਜੁੱਧ, ਠੰਢੀ-ਜੰਗ; **give the~ shoulder (to)** ਬੇਰੁਖ਼ੀ ਵਰਤਣਾ

collaborate (ਕਅ'ਲੈਬਅਰੇਇਟ) v ਸਹਿਯੋਗ ਦੇਣਾ, ਨਾਲ ਮਿਲ ਕੇ ਕੰਮ ਕਰਨਾ, ਹੱਥ ਵਟਾਉਣਾ, ਮਿਲਵਰਤਣ ਕਰਨਾ, ਸਾਥ ਦੇਣਾ

collaboration (ਕਅ'ਲੈਬਅ'ਰੇਇਸ਼ਨ) n ਸਹਿਕਾਰਤਾ, ਸਹਿਯੋਗ ਜਾਂ ਮਿਲਵਰਤਨ, ਹੱਥ ਵਟਾਈ, ਸਾਂਝੀ ਪੈਦਾਵਾਰ

collapse (ਕਅ'ਲੈਪਸ) v n ਪੜੱਮ ਕਰਕੇ ਡਿੱਗ ਪੈਣਾ, ਹਿੰਮਤ ਹਾਰਨੀ, ਬੈਠ ਬਹਿ ਜਾਣਾ, ਬੇਹੋਸ਼ ਹੋ ਜਾਣਾ; ਨਸ਼ਟ ਹੋਣਾ, ਢਹਿ ਜਾਣਾ; ਗਿਰਾਵਟ, ਪਤਨ;

collar (ਕੋਲਅ*) v n ਹਸਲੀ, ਕੰਠ, ਗੁਲੂਬੰਦ, ਕਾਲਰ, ਗਲ ਪੈਣਾ, ਗਿਚੀਉਂ ਫੜਨਾ, ਪੇਟੇ ਪਾ ਲੈਣਾ; ਝੋਹਣਾ; ਗਰਿਫ਼ਤਾਰ ਕਰਨਾ; ~**bone** ਹਸਲੀ

colleague (ਕੋਲੀਗ) n ਸਹਿਕਾਰੀ, ਸਹਿਯੋਗੀ, ਸਾਥੀ, ਭਾਈਵਾਲ

collect (ਕਅਲੇਕਟ) v n ਜੁੜਨਾ, ਜੋੜਨਾ, ਸੰਗ੍ਰਹ ਕਰਨਾ, ਇਕੱਤਰ ਕਰਨਾ, ਇਕੱਠਾ ਕਰਨਾ, ਜਮ੍ਹਾ ਕਰਨਾ, ਵਸੂਲ ਕਰਨਾ, ਉਗਰਾਹੁਣਾ; ਇਸਾਈਆਂ ਦੀ ਅਰਦਾਸ ਜੋ ਉਹ ਪਾਠ ਤੋਂ ਪਿਛੋਂ ਕਰਦੇ ਹਨ; ~**ed** ਇਕੱਤਰਤ, ਸੰਗ੍ਰਹਤ; ਸ਼ਾਂਤ, ਧੀਰਜਵਾਨ; ~**ion** ਜੋੜ, ਇਕੱਠ; ਉਗਰਾਹੀ; ਇਕੱਤਰੀਕਰਨ, ਸਮੂਹ, ਢੇਰ, ਅੰਬਾਰ; ਇਕੱਠ

collective (ਕਅ'ਲੇਕਟਿਵ) adv ਇਕੱਤਰਤ, ਸਮੂਹਕ, ਇਕੱਠਾ, ਰਲਵਾਂ, ਸਮੁੱਚਾ; ~**ly** ਇਕੱਠੇ ਹੋ ਕੇ, ਰਲ ਕੇ, ਸਮੁੱਚੇ ਤੌਰ ਤੇ, ਸਮੂਹਕ ਤੌਰ ਤੇ

collector (ਕਅ'ਲੇਕਟਆ*) n ਜ਼ਿਲੇ ਦਾ ਮੁਖੀ, ਕੁਲੈਕਟਰ, ਡਿਪਟੀ ਕਮਿਸ਼ਨਰ, ਉਗਰਾਹੀ ਕਰਨ ਵਾਲਾ, ਵਸੂਲ ਕਰਨ ਵਾਲਾ, ਇੱਕਠਾ ਕਰਨ ਵਾਲਾ; ਮਸ਼ੀਨ ਦਾ ਇਕ ਪੁਰਜਾ; ~**ate** ਕੁਲੈਕਟਰੀ

college (ਕੋਲਿਜ) n ਮਹਾਂ-ਵਿਦਿਆਲਾ, ਕਾਲਜ

collegian (ਕਅ'ਲੀਜਅਨ) n ਕਾਲਜ ਦਾ ਵਿਦਿਆਰਥੀ, ਕਿਸੇ ਕਾਲਜ ਦਾ ਸਦੱਸ

collegiate (ਕਅ'ਲੀਜਿਏਟ) a v ਕਾਲਜ-ਸਬੰਧੀ, ਕਾਲਜ ਦਾ; ਕਾਲਜ ਦਾ ਪਦ ਦੇਣਾ, ਕਾਲਜ ਦੀ ਸਥਿਤੀ ਪ੍ਰਦਾਨ ਕਰਨਾ, ਕਾਲਜ ਬਣਾਉਣਾ

collide (ਕਅ'ਲਾਇਡ) n ਭਿੜਨਾ, ਟੱਕਰਨਾ, ਟਕਰਾਉਣਾ, ਟੱਕਰ ਖਾਣਾ, ਵਿਰੋਧ ਹੋਣਾ, ਮੁੰਠ-ਭੇੜ ਹੋਣਾ

colliery (ਕੋਲਿਯਅਰਿ) n ਕੋਲੇ ਦੀ ਖਾਨ, ਕੋਲਰੀ

collision (ਕਅਲਿਯ਼ਨ) n ਭੇੜ, ਟੱਕਰ, ਟਕਰ, ਮੁੰਠ-ਭੇੜ, ਸੰਘਰਸ਼

collocation (ਕਲਅ(ਉ)'ਕੇਇਸ਼ਨ) n ਸ਼ਬਦ-ਕ੍ਰਮ

colloquial (ਕਅ'ਲਅਉਕਵਿਅਲ) *a* ਲੋਕਕ, ਗੱਲ-ਬਾਤੀ, ਬੋਲਚਾਲੀ

collusion (ਕਅ'ਲੂਯ਼ਨ) *n* ਗੱਠ-ਜੋੜ, ਗਾਂਢਾ-ਸਾਂਢਾ

collusive (ਕਅ'ਲੂਸਿਵ) *a* ਫ਼ਰੇਬੀ, ਕਪਟਪੂਰਨ

colonel (ਕਅ:ਨਲ) *n* ਕਰਨੈਲ, ਕਰਨਲ

colonial (ਕਅ'ਲਅਉਨਯਅਲ) *n* ਬਸਤੀਵਾਦੀ; **~ism** ਬਸਤੀਵਾਦ

colonization (ਕੌਲਅਨਾਇ'ਜ਼ੇਇਸ਼ਨ) *a n* ਬਸਤੀਕਰਨ, ਨੋਅਬਾਦਕਾਰੀ

colonize (ਕੌਲਅਨਾਇਜ਼) *n* ਨਵੀਂ ਬਸਤੀ ਵਸਾਉਣਾ, ਨਵੀਂ ਧਾਂ ਜਾ ਕੇ ਵਸ ਜਾਣਾ

colony (ਕੌਲਅਨਿ) *n* ਨਵੀਂ ਅਬਾਦੀ, ਬਸਤੀ, ਛਾਉਣੀ

colour (ਕਅੱਲਅ) *n v* ਰੰਗ, ਚਿਹਰੇ ਦੀ ਰੰਗਤ, ਰੰਗ-ਰੂਪ, ਸ਼ਕਲ-ਸੂਰਤ, ਬਾਣਾ; ਝੰਡਾ; ਬਿੱਲਾ, ਵਰਦੀ; ਰੰਗਣਾ, ਰੰਗ ਭਰਨਾ, ਸਚਾਈ ਨੂੰ ਛਿਪਾਉਣਾ, ਝੂਠਾ ਕਥਨ ਕਰਨਾ; ਲੱਜਾਉਣਾ; ਪ੍ਰਭਾਵ ਛੱਡਣਾ; **~able** ਮਨੋਹਰ, ਰਮਣੀਕ, ਨਕਲੀ, ਜਾਅਲੀ; **~ed** ਰੰਗੀਨ, ਰੰਗਿਆ; **~ful** ਰੰਗੀਨ, ਮਨੋਰੰਜਕ, ਸੁਦਰਸ਼ਨ, ਮੋਹਕ; **~less** ਬੇਰੰਗ, ਰੰਗਹੀਨ ਵਰਣਹੀਨ, ਪੀਲਾ, ਜ਼ਰਦ; ਫਿੱਕਾ, ਉਦਾਸੀਨ, ਰੁੱਖਾ; **~lessness** ਰੰਗਹੀਨਤਾ, ਉਦਾਸੀਨਤਾ, ਫਿੱਕਾਪਣ, ਰੁੱਖਾਪਣ, ਪੀਲਾਪਣ

column (ਕੌਲਅਮ) *n* ਥੰਮ੍ਹ, ਖੰਭਾ, ਕੋਲਾ, ਲਾਠ; ਆਸਰਾ, ਟੇਕ; ਫ਼ੌਜ ਦੀ ਸਫ਼; (ਅਖ਼ਬਾਰ ਦਾ) ਕਾਲਮ; ਜਹਾਜ਼ਾਂ ਦਾ ਬੇੜਾ

columnist (ਕੌਲਅਮਨਿਸਟ) *n* ਕਿਸੇ-ਸਮਾਚਾਰ-ਪੱਤਰ ਵਿਚ ਲਗਾਤਾਰ ਲਿਖਣ ਵਾਲਾ, ਕਾਲਮਨਵੀਸ

coma (ਕਅਉਮਅ) *n* ਡੂੰਘੀ ਬੇਹੋਸ਼ੀ

comb (ਕਅਉਮ) *n v* ਕੰਘੀ, ਕੰਘਾ; ਕੁੱਕੜ ਦੀ ਕਲਗੀ, ਸ਼ਹਿਦ ਦਾ ਛੱਤਾ; ਕੁੱਚ ਫੇਰਨਾ, ਕੰਘੀ ਕਰਨਾ, ਸਾਫ਼ ਕਰਨਾ

combat (ਕੌਬੈਟ) *n v* ਲੜਾਈ, ਮੁੰਠਭੇੜ, ਟੱਕਰ; ਭਿੜਨਾ, ਖ਼ੁਲਣਾ, ਲੜਨਾ, ਮੁਕਾਬਲਾ ਕਰਨਾ; **~ive** ਲੜਾਕਾ, ਰਣਸ਼ੀਲ

combination (ਕੌਂਬਿ'ਨੇਇਸ਼ਨ) *n* ਸੁਮੇਲ; ਜੋੜ, ਜੁੱਟ, ਮੇਲ, ਸੰਜੋਗ, ਇਕੱਠ

combine (ਕਅ'ਬਾਇਨ) *v* ਜੋੜਨਾ, ਮੇਲਣਾ, ਇਕੱਠਾ ਕਰਨਾ; **~d** ਸੰਯੁਕਤ, ਮਿਲਿਆ, ਸੰਜੋਜਤ

come (ਕਅੱਮ) *v* ਆਉਣਾ, ਚੱਲਣਾ, ਅੱਗੇ ਵਧਣਾ, ਵਾਪਰਨਾ, ਹੋਣਾ, ਨਿਕਲਣਾ, ਨਿਕਾਸ ਹੋਣਾ; **~about** ਵਾਪਰਨਾ, ਬੀਤਣਾ, ਹੋਣਾ; **~across** ਮਿਲਣਾ, ਰੂ-ਬਰੂ ਹੋਣਾ, ਭੇਂਟ ਕਰਨਾ; **~along** ਕਿਸੇ ਨਾਲ ਜਾਣਾ, ਸਾਥ ਦੇਣਾ; **~at** ਗੱਲ ਸਮਝਣਾ, ਪਹੁੰਚਣਾ; **~by** ਹੱਥ ਆਉਣਾ, ਪ੍ਰਾਪਤ ਕਰਨਾ; **~forward** ਸਾਮ੍ਹਣੇ ਆਉਣਾ; **~in** ਅੰਦਰ ਆਉਣਾ, ਘੁਸਣਾ, ਪ੍ਰਵੇਸ਼ ਕਰਨਾ; **~into** ਪ੍ਰਾਪਤ ਕਰਨਾ, ਪਾਉਣਾ; **~into force** ਲਾਗੂ ਹੋਣਾ; **~out** ਹੜਤਾਲ ਕਰਨੀ, ਕੰਮ ਛੱਡਣਾ, ਪ੍ਰਕਾਸ਼ਤ ਹੋਣਾ; ਸਫਲ ਹੋਣਾ, ਕਾਮਯਾਬ ਹੋਣਾ; **~to** ਹੋਸ਼ ਵਿਚ ਆਉਣਾ, **~to an end** ਖ਼ਤਮ ਹੋ ਜਾਣਾ, ਸਮਾਪਤ ਹੋਣਾ; **~up** ਚੜ੍ਹਨਾ; **~upon** ਅਚਾਨਕ ਹਮਲਾ ਕਰਨਾ

comedian (ਕਅ'ਮੀਡਯਅਨ) *n* ਕਾਮੇਡੀ (ਸੁਖਾਂਤ ਨਾਟਕ) ਦਾ ਅਭਿਨੇਤਾ ਜਾਂ ਲੇਖਕ; ਭੰਡ, ਨਕਸ਼ੀਆ

comedy (ਕੌਮਅਡਿ) *n* ਨਾਚ-ਰੰਗ, ਦਿਲਲੱਗੀ, ਸੁਖਾਂਤ ਨਾਟਕ, ਕਾਮਦੀ

comely (ਕਅਮੱਲਿ) *a* ਸੋਹਣੀ (ਵਿਸ਼ੇਸ਼ ਕਰਕੇ ਜਨਨੀ)

comfort (ਕਅਮੱਫ਼ਅ*ਟ) *n v* ਸੁਖ, ਆਰਾਮ,

ਇਤਮੀਨਾਨ, ਦਿਲਾਸਾ, ਸੰਤੋਖ; ਸੁਖ ਦੇਣਾ, ਆਰਾਮ ਪਹੁੰਚਾਉਣਾ, ਦਿਲਾਸਾ ਦੇਣਾ, ਤਸੱਲੀ ਦੇਣੀ; ~able ਸੁਖਦਾਇਕ, ਆਰਾਮਦੇਹ, ਧੀਰਜ-ਬੰਨ੍ਹਾਊ, ਸੁਖੀ, ਮੌਜੀ, ਕਾਫ਼ੀ, ਖਾਸੀ; ~ably ਸੌਖ ਨਾਲ, ਆਰਾਮ ਨਾਲ, ਤਸੱਲੀ ਨਾਲ; ~less ਸੁਖ-ਰਹਿਤ, ਦੁਖੀ, ਸੰਤੋਖ-ਹੀਣ

comic (ਕੌਮਿਕ) *a* ਸੁਖਾਂਤਕ, ਸੁਖਾਂਤ, ਹਸਾਉਣਾ, ਮਸ਼ਕਰੀ ਭਰਿਆ; **~opera** ਹਾਸ-ਰਸੀ ਸੰਗੀਤ-ਨਾਟ; **~al** ਹਾਸਪੂਰਨ, ਵਚਿਤੱਰ; ਅਨੋਖਾ, ਨਿਰਾਲਾ

coming (ਕਅੱਮਿਙ) *n a* ਆਗਮਨ, ਭਾਵੀ, ਆਗਾਮੀ

command (ਕਅ'ਮਾਂਡ) *v n* ਆਗਿਆ ਦੇਣੀ, ਹੁਕਮ ਕਰਨਾ, ਕਮਾਨ ਕਰਨੀ, ਕਾਬੂ ਕਰਨਾ; ਆਗਿਆ, ਹੁਕਮ, ਆਦੇਸ਼, ਕਮਾਨ, ਨਿਯੰਤਰਣ; **at~** ਮੁੱਠੀ ਵਿਚ, ਇਖ਼ਤਿਆਰ ਵਿਚ

commander (ਕਅ'ਮਾਂਡਅ*) *n* ਸੈਨਾਪਤੀ, ਫ਼ੌਜਦਾਰ, ਕਮਾਂਡਰ; ਨਾਈਟ ਦੀ ਉੱਚੀ ਉਪਾਧੀ; ਮੁੱਖ ਸੈਨਾਪਤੀ

commandment (ਕਅ'ਮਾਂ(ਡ)ਮਅੰਟ) *n* ਰੱਬੀ ਹੁਕਮ, ਧਾਰਮਕ ਨਿਯਮ

commando (ਕਅ'ਮਾਂਡਅਓ) *n* ਛਾਪਾਮਾਰ ਸੈਨਕ, ਕਮਾਂਡੋ

commemorable (ਕਅ'ਮੈਮੱਅਰਅਬਲ) *a* ਯਾਦਗਾਰੀ, ਸਮਰਣੀਜ

commemorate (ਕਅ'ਮੈਮੱਅਰੇਇਟ) *v* (ਕਿਸੇ ਦੀ ਯਾਦ) ਮਨਾਉਣਾ, ਯਾਦਗਾਰ ਕਾਇਮ ਕਰਨਾ; ਸਮਾਰਕ ਹੋਣਾ, ਯਾਦ ਕਰਨਾ

commemoration (ਕਅ'ਮੈਮੱਅਰੇਇਸ਼ਨ) *n* ਯਾਦਗਾਰ, ਯਾਦਗਾਰੀ ਕਾਰਜ

commence (ਕਅ'ਮੈਂਸ) *v* ਸ਼ੁਰੂ ਕਰਨਾ, ਆਰੰਭਣਾ, ਛੋਹਣਾ, ਚਲਾਉਣਾ, ਚਲੱਣਾ, ਸ਼ੁਰੂ ਹੋਣਾ; **~ment** ਸ਼ੁਰੂ, ਮੁੱਢ, ਆਰੰਭ

commend (ਕਅ'ਮੈਂਡ) *v* ਸੌਂਪਣਾ, ਸਪੁਰਦ ਕਰਨਾ, ਹੱਥ ਵਿਚ ਦੇਣਾ; ਪ੍ਰਸੰਸਾ ਕਰਨਾ, ਸ਼ਲਾਘਾ ਕਰਨਾ; **~able** ਸੌਂਪਣਯੋਗ, ਸ਼ਲਾਘਾਯੋਗ, ਸਪੁਰਦ ਕਰਨਯੋਗ, ਆਦਰਯੋਗ; **~ation** ਸ਼ਲਾਘਾ, ਵਡਿਆਈ, ਪ੍ਰਸੰਸਾ, ਸਿਫ਼ਾਰਿਸ਼

commensurate (ਕਅ'ਮੈਂਸ਼ੁ(ਅ)ਰਅਟ) *a* ਸਮਾਨ, ਅਨੁਕੂਲ, ਅਨੁਰੂਪ, ਬਰਾਬਰ

comment ('ਕੌਮੈਂਟ) *n* ਟਿੱਪਣੀ, ਰਾਏ; ਟੀਕਾ ਟਿੱਪਣੀ ਕਰਨੀ, ਰਾਏ ਦੇਣੀ; **~ary** ਵਿਆਖਿਆ, ਭਾਸ਼ਟ, ਟਿੱਪਣੀ, ਸਮਾਲੋਚਨਾ; **~ator** ਟਿੱਪਣੀਕਾਰ

commerce ('ਕੌਮਅ:ਸ) *n* ਵਣਜ, ਵਪਾਰ, ਤਜਾਰਤ, ਸੰਪਰਕ, ਮੇਲ-ਜੋਲ; ਤਾਸ਼ ਦੀ ਇਕ ਖੇਡ

commercial (ਕਅ'ਮਅ:ਸ਼ਲ) *a* ਵਣਜ-ਸਬੰਧੀ, ਵਿਹਾਰਕ, ਵਪਾਰਕ, ਤਜਾਰਤੀ

commission (ਕਅ'ਮਿਸ਼ਨ) *n v* ਦਲਾਲੀ, ਆੜ੍ਹਤ; ਆਦੇਸ਼, ਹਿਦਾਇਤ, ਹੁਕਮ; ਆਯੋਗ, ਅਧਿਕਾਰੀ-ਵਰਗ; ਅਧਿਕਾਰ ਪ੍ਰਦਾਨ ਕਰਨਾ, ਇਖ਼ਤਿਆਰ ਦੇਣਾ, ਮੁਖਤਿਆਰ ਬਣਾਉਣਾ, ਕਮਿਸ਼ਨ ਦੇਣਾ; ਅਫ਼ਸਰ ਬਣਾਉਣਾ; **~ed** ਨਿਯੁਕਤ, ਅਧਿਨਿਯਤ, ਕਮਿਸ਼ਨ ਦੁਆਰਾ ਪਰਾਪਤ; **~er** ਆਯੁਕਤ, ਕਮਿਸ਼ਨਰ; **~agent** ਆੜ੍ਹਤੀਆ

commit (ਕਅ'ਮਿਟ) *v* ਵਚਨਬੱਧ ਕਰਨਾ, ਸੌਂਪਣਾ, ਹਵਾਲੇ ਕਰਨਾ, ਸਪੁਰਦ ਕਰਨਾ, ਪਾਬੰਦ ਹੋਣਾ, ਅਰਪਣ ਕਰਨਾ; **~ment** ਪ੍ਰਤੀਬੱਧਤਾ, ਵਚਨ-ਬੱਧਤਾ ਪਾਬੰਦੀ, ਕੈਦ, ਵਚਨ, ਬੰਧਨ; **~ted** ਵਚਨਬੱਧ, ਪ੍ਰਤੀਬੱਧ

committee (ਕਅ'ਮਿਟਿ) *n* ਸਮਿਤੀ, ਸਭਾ, ਕਮੇਟੀ, ਵਿਸ਼ੇਸ਼ ਉਦੇਸ਼ ਲਈ ਸਥਾਪਤ ਸਭਾ,

joint ~ ਸੰਯੁਕਤ ਕਮੇਟੀ; **standing~** ਸਥਾਈ ਸਮਿਤਿ

commode (ਕਅ'ਮਅਉਡ) *n* ਦਰਾਜ਼ਾਂ ਵਾਲਾ ਸੰਦੂਕ, ਪੇਟੀ, ਸ਼ਿੰਗਾਰ ਦੀ ਅਲਮਾਰੀ; ਟੱਟੀ ਪਿਸ਼ਾਬ ਵਾਲਾ ਬਰਤਨ, ਕਮੋਡ

commodity (ਕਅ'ਮੌਡਅਟਿ) *n* ਚੀਜ਼, ਪਦਾਰਥ, ਜਿਨਸ, ਵਪਾਰ ਦੀ ਵਸਤੂ, ਉਪਯੋਗੀ ਵਸਤੂ

common (ਕੌਅਮਨ) *a n* ਸਧਾਰਨ, ਸਾਂਝਾ, ਆਮ, ਅਵਾਮੀ, ਮਾਮੂਲੀ, ਸੁਲਭ, ਸੰਜੁਕਤ; ਸਾਮਲਾਤ, ਸਾਂਝੀ ਜ਼ਮੀਨ; **~gender** ਨਪੁੰਸਕ ਲਿੰਗ; **~market** ਸਾਂਝੀ ਮੰਡੀ; **~room** ਬੈਠਕ, **ਸਾਂਝਾ** ਕਮਰਾ; **~sense** ਆਮ ਸਮਝ, ਸਧਾਰਨ ਸੂਝ; **~wealth** ਰਾਸ਼ਟਰ-ਮੰਡਲ

commotion (ਕਅ'ਮਅਉਸ਼ਨ) *n* ਰੌਲਾ, ਹਫੜਾ-ਦਫੜੀ, ਗੜਬੜ, ਉਲਝ, ਹਲਚਲ, ਖਲਬਲੀ

communal ('ਕੌਮਯੁਨਲ) *a* ਫ਼ਿਰਕੂ, ਸੰਪਰਦਾਇਕ; ਸਰਵਜਨਕ, ਅਵਾਮੀ; **~ism** ਫ਼ਿਰਕਾਪਰਸਤੀ, ਫ਼ਿਰਕੂਪੁਣਾ, ਸੰਪਰਦਾਇਕਤਾ

commune (ਕਅਮਯੂਨ) *n v* ਪਰਗਣਾ, ਪੰਚਾਇਤ; ਭੇਦ ਭਰੀ ਗਲ ਕਰਨੀ

communicabillity (ਕਅ'ਮਯੁਨਿਕਅ-'ਬਿਲਅਟਿ) *n* ਸੰਚਾਰਨ-ਯੋਗਤਾ, ਸੰਚਾਰਤਾ, ਸੰਵਾਦਸ਼ੀਲਤਾ

communicable (ਕਅ'ਮਯੁਨਿਕਅਬਲ) *a* ਸੰਚਾਰੀ, ਸੂਚਨਾਯੋਗ, ਦੱਸਣਯੋਗ, ਪਤਾ ਦੇਣ ਦੇ ਯੋਗ, ਕਥਨਯੋਗ

communicate (ਕਅ'ਮਯੁਨਿਕੇਇਟ) *v* ਸੰਚਾਰਨ, ਸੂਚਤ ਕਰਨਾ, ਖ਼ਬਰ ਦੇਣੀ, ਆਵਾਜਾਈ ਦਾ ਸਾਧਨ ਪੈਦਾ ਕਰਨਾ

communication (ਕਅ'ਮਯੁਨਿ'ਕੇਇਸ਼ਨ) *n* ਸੰਚਾਰ, ਸੂਚਨਾ, ਖ਼ਬਰ, ਪਹੁੰਚ, ਆਵਾਜਾਈ, ਪ੍ਰਚਾਰ, ਪ੍ਰਚਲਨ, ਸੰਪਰਕ

communicative (ਕਅਮ'ਯੂਨਿਕਅਟਿਵ੍) *a* ਖ਼ਬਰ ਪੁਚਾਉਣ ਵਾਲਾ, ਸੰਚਾਰੀ, **~ness** ਖੁੱਲ੍ਹੀਆਂ ਗੱਲਾਂ ਕਰਨ ਦਾ ਭਾਵ

communion (ਕਅ'ਮਯੂਨਯਅਨ) *n* ਭਾਈਚਾਰਾ, ਸੰਪਰਦਾਈ, ਸੰਗਤ; (ਇਸਾਈ ਮੱਤ) ਰੱਬੀ-ਭੋਜ; ਸੰਪਰਕ, ਸਾਂਝ, ਰਾਬਤਾ

communique (ਕਅ'ਮਯੂਨਿਕੇਇ) *n* ਸਰਕਾਰੀ ਐਲਾਨ, ਅਧਿਕਾਰਤ ਘੋਸ਼ਣਾ

communism ('ਕੌਮਯੁਨਿਜ਼(ਅ)ਮ) *n* ਸਾਮਵਾਦ, ਸਾਮਵਾਦੀ ਅੰਦੋਲਨ

communist ('ਕੌਮਯੁਨਿਸਟ) *n* ਸਾਮਵਾਦੀ, ਸਾਂਝੀਵਾਲ, ਕਮਿਊਨਿਸਟ

community (ਕਅ'ਮਯੂਨਅਟਿ) *n* ਭਾਈਚਾਰਾ, ਬਰਾਬਰੀ, ਫ਼ਿਰਕਾ, ਸੰਪਰਦਾਇ; ਸਮਾਜ, ਸਮੂਹ; ਰਾਜਨੀਤਕ, ਸਮਾਜਕ ਅਤੇ ਨਾਗਰਿਕ ਸੰਗਠਨ

communize ('ਕੌਮਯੁਨਾਇਜ਼) *v* ਸਮੂਹੀਕਰਨ ਕਰਨਾ, ਸਮਾਜੀਕਰਨ ਕਰਨਾ

commutable (ਕਅ'ਮਯੂਟਅਬਲ) *a* ਵਟਾਉਣਯੋਗ

commutation (ਕੌਮਯੂ'ਟੇਇਸ਼ਨ) *n* ਵਟਾਅ

commute (ਕਅ'ਮਯੂਟ) *v* ਬਦਲਣਾ, ਵਟਾ ਲੈਣਾ; **~r** ਰੋਜ਼ਾਨਾ ਯਾਤਰੀ

compact (ਕਅਂਪੈਕਟ) *a n* ਪੁਖਤਾ, ਪੱਕਾ, ਦ੍ਰਿੜ, ਠੋਸ, ਸੰਖਿਪਤ; ਚੁਸਤ (ਸ਼ੈਲੀ); ਸੰਧੀ, ਮੁਆਹਿਦਾ

companion (ਕਅਂਪੈਨਯਅਨ) *n v* ਸਾਥੀ, ਸੰਗੀ, ਯਾਰ, ਬੇਲੀ, ਆੜੀ, ਸਹਿਕਾਰੀ, ਸਹਾਇਕ; ਸਾਂਝੀ, ਹਿੱਸੇਦਾਰ; ਸਾਥ ਦੇਣਾ, ਨਾਲ ਹੋਣਾ, ਜੋੜ ਮਿਲਾਉਣਾ, ਸਾਥ ਨਿਭਾਉਣਾ; **~ship** ਜੋਟੀ, ਯਾਰੀ, ਸਾਥ, ਸੰਗਤ, ਭਾਈਵਾਲੀ; **bad~** ਕੁਸੰਗ, ਕੁਸੰਗਤ, ਮਾੜੀ ਸੰਗਤ

comparable ('ਕੌਂਪ(ਅ)ਰਅਬਲ) *a* ਸਮਾਨ, ਸਦ੍ਰਿਸ਼, ਬਰਾਬਰ ਦਾ, ਨਾਲ ਦਾ, ਮੁਕਾਬਲੇ ਦਾ, ਟਾਕਰੇ ਦਾ, ਮੇਚਵਾਂ

comparative (ਕਅੰਪੈਰਅਟਿਵ਼) *a* ਤੁਲਨਾਤਮਕ; ਤੁਲਨਾਵਾਚੀ; ਮੁਕਾਬਲੇ ਦਾ; ~**ly** ਤੁਲਨਾਤਮਕ ਤੌਰ ਤੇ, ਮੁਕਾਬਲਤਨ

compare (ਕਅੰਮ'ਪੇਅ*) *v* ਤੁਲਨ ਕਰਨਾ, ਉਪਮਾ ਕਰਨਾ, ਟਾਕਰ ਕਰਨਾ, ਮੁਕਾਬਲਾ ਕਰਨਾ, ਬਰਾਬਰੀ ਕਰਨਾ, ਤੁਲਨਾ ਹੋਣਾ, ਮਿਲਾਉਣਾ, ਮੇਲਾਨ ਕਰਨਾ; ਜਾਂਚਣਾ

comparison (ਕਅੰਪੈਰਿਸਨ) *n* ਤੁਲਨਾ, ਉਪਮਾ, ਬਰਾਬਰੀ, ਮੁਕਾਬਲਾ, ਟਾਕਰਾ, ਉਦਾਹਰਨ, ਮਿਸਾਲ, ਦ੍ਰਿਸ਼ਟਾਂਤ; **in~with** ਤੁਲਨਾ ਵਿਚ, ਮੁਕਾਬਲੇ ਵਿਚ

compart (ਕੰਪਾ*ਟ) *v* ਵਖ ਵਖ ਕਰਨਾ, ਅਲਗ ਅਲਗ ਟੁਕੜਿਆਂ ਵਿਚ ਵੰਡਣਾ; ~**ment** ਕਮਰਾ, ਡੱਬਾ, ਪਰੀਖਿਆ, ਵਿਚ ਕੰਪਾਰਟਮੈਂਟ, ਪਰਿਪੂਰਕ ਪਰੀਖਿਆ

compass ('ਕੰਮ੍ਪਅਸ) *n v* ਕੁਤਬਨੁਮਾ, ਦਿਸ਼ਾਸੂਚਕ; ਕੰਪਾਸ, ਪਰਕਾਰ, ਚੱਕਰ, ਘੇਰਨਾ, ਵਲਣਾ, ਚੱਕਰ ਕੱਟਣਾ

compassion (ਕਅੰ'ਪੈਸ਼ਨ) *n* ਦਇਆ, ਕਿਰਪਾ, ਤਰਸ, ਦਰਦ, ਰਹਿਮ, ਰਹਿਮਦਿਲੀ; ~**ate** ਦਇਆ-ਵਾਨ, ਕਿਰਪਾਲੂ, ਦਿਆਲੂ; ਦਇਆ ਕਰਨੀ, ਤਰਸ ਕਰਨਾ, ਰਹਿਮ ਖਾਣਾ; ~**ness** ਦਇਆਸ਼ੀਲਤਾ, ਦਇਆਲਤਾ, ਕਰੁਣਾ

compatibility (ਕਅੰਪੈਟਅ'ਬਿਲਅਟਿ) *n* ਸੰਗਤੀ, ਅਨੁਕੂਲਤਾ, ਅਨੁਰੂਪਤਾ

compatible (ਕਅੰ'ਪੈਟਅਬਲ) *a* ਅਨੁਕੂਲ, ਅਨੁਰੂਪ, ਯੋਗ, ਢੁੱਕਵਾਂ, ਮੁਨਾਸਬ, ਮੁਆਫ਼ਕ,

compatriot (ਕਅੰ'ਪੈਟਿਰਿਅਟ) *n* ਹਮ-ਵਤਨੀ, ਵਤਨੀ, ਦੇਸ਼ਵਾਸੀ

compel (ਕਅੰ'ਪੈੱਲ) *v* ਮਜਬੂਰ ਕਰਨਾ, ਦਬਾਉਣਾ, ਲਾਚਾਰ ਕਰਨਾ, ਬੇਵੱਸ ਕਰਨਾ

compelling (ਕਅੰ'ਪੈੱਲਿਙ) *a* (ਕਹਾਣੀ ਆਦਿ) ਰੋਮਾਂਚਕਾਰੀ, ਜ਼ੋਰਦਾਰ, ਜ਼ੋਰਪਾਊ

compensate ('ਕੌਂਪੈੱਨਸੇਇਟ) *v* ਮੁਆਵਜ਼ਾ ਦੇਣਾ, ਇਵਜ਼ਾਨਾ ਦੇਣਾ, ਭਰਨਾ, ਘਾਟਾ ਪੂਰਾ ਕਰਨਾ, ਮੁਜਰਾਈ ਲੈਣਾ

compensation ('ਕੌਂਪੈੱਨਸੇਇਸ਼ਨ) *n* ਪੂਰਤੀ, ਧਨਪੂਰਤੀ, ਇਵਜ਼ਾਨਾ, ਮੁਆਵਜ਼ਾ, ਹਾਨੀ-ਪੂਰਤੀ

compensatory ('ਕੈਂਪਅੰਨ'ਸੇਇਟ(ਅ)ਰਿ) *a* ਮੁਜਰਾਈ ਪੂਰਕ, ਹਾਨੀਪੂਰਕ

compere ('ਕੌਂਪੇਅ*) *n v* (ਗੋਸ਼ਟੀ ਆਦਿ ਦਾ) ਸੰਚਾਲਕ; ਸੰਚਾਲਨ ਕਰਨਾ

compete (ਕਅੰ'ਪੀਟ) *v* ਟਾਕਰਾ ਕਰਨਾ, ਰੀਸ ਕਰਨਾ; ਬਰਾਬਰੀ ਕਰਨਾ, ਮੁਕਾਬਲਾ ਕਰਨਾ, ਪ੍ਰਤੀਯੋਗਤਾ ਕਰਨਾ

competency ('ਕੌਂਮਪਿਟਅੰਸਿ) *n* ਯੋਗਤਾ, ਸਮੱਰਥਾ, ਸ਼ਕਤੀ

competent (ਕੌਂਮਪਿਟ(ਅ)ਟ) *a* ਯੋਗ, ਢੁਕਵਾਂ, ਸਮੱਰਥ, ਸ਼ਕਤੀਵਾਨ

competing (ਕਅੰ'ਪੀਟਿਙ) *a* ਪ੍ਰਤੀਯੋਗੀ

competition ('ਕੌਂਪਿ'ਟਿਸ਼ਨ) *n* ਮੁਕਾਬਲਾ, ਬਰਾਬਰੀ, ਪ੍ਰਤੀਯੋਗਤਾ, ਟਾਕਰਾ

competitive (ਕਅੰ'ਪੈੱਟਅਟਿਵ਼) *a* ਪ੍ਰਤੀਯੋਗਤਾਮੂਲਕ, ਮੁਕਾਬਲੇ ਦਾ

compilation ('ਕੌਂਪਿ'ਲੇਇਸ਼ਨ) *n* ਸੰਗ੍ਰਹ, ਸੰਕਲਨ, ਸੰਪਾਦਨ

compile (ਕਅੰ'ਪਾਇਲ) *v* ਸੰਕਲਨ ਕਰਨਾ, ਸੰਗ੍ਰਹ ਕਰਨਾ, ਰਚਨਾ ਕਰਨਾ, ਇਕੱਤਰ ਕਰਨਾ, (ਕ੍ਰਿਕਟ ਵਿਚ) ਦੇਰ ਤਕ ਖੇਡਣਾ ਤੇ ਦੌੜਾਂ ਬਣਾਉਣਾ;

~d ਸੰਕਲਨ, ਸੰਪਾਦਤ, ਰਚਿਤ; ~r ਸੰਕਲਨ-ਕਰਨ, ਰਚਨਾਕਾਰ

complacence (ਕਅਾਂਪਲੇਇਸੰਸ) *a* ਸੰਤੁਸ਼ਟਤਾ; ਤ੍ਰਿਪਤੀ; ਤਸੱਲੀ, ਸ਼ਾਂਤੀ, ਇਤਮੀਨਾਨ; ਖ਼ੁਸ਼ੀ

complacent (ਕਅਾਂਲੇਇਸੰਟ) *a* ਸੰਤੁਸ਼ਟ, ਤ੍ਰਿਪਤ

complain (ਕਅ'ਪਲੇਇਨ) *v* ਗਿਲਾ ਕਰਨਾ, ਸ਼ਿਕਵਾ ਕਰਨਾ, ਸ਼ਿਕਾਇਤ ਕਰਨੀ, ਫ਼ਰਿਆਦ ਕਰਨਾ, ਰੋਲਾ-ਪਾਉਣਾ; ~ant ਫ਼ਰਿਆਦੀ, ਸ਼ਿਕਾਇਤ ਕਰਨ ਵਾਲਾ, ਮੁਦੱਈ; ~t ਗਿਲਾ, ਫ਼ਰਿਆਦ, ਸ਼ਿਕਾਇਤ, ਸ਼ਿਕਵਾ

complement (ਕੌਂਪਲਿਮੰਟ, 'ਕੌਂਮਪਲਿਮੰਟ) *n v* ਪੂਰਕ, ਪੂਰਤੀ ਕਰਨਾ, ਪੂਰਾ ਕਰਨਾ, ਖ਼ੁਸ਼ਹਾਲ ਬਣਾਉਣਾ

complementary ('ਕੌਂਲਿ'ਮੈਂਟ(ਅ)ਰਿ) *a* ਪੂਰਕ, ਪੂਰਾ ਕਰਨ ਵਾਲਾ, ਸਹਾਇਕ

complete (ਕਅਾਂ'ਪਲੀਟ) *v* ਪੂਰਾ ਕਰਨਾ, ਪੂਰਤੀ ਕਰਨਾ, ਸੰਪੰਨ ਕਰਨਾ; ਮੁਕਾਉਣਾ, ਸਮਾਪਤ ਕਰਨਾ, ਭੋਗ ਪਾਉਣਾ, ਸਿਰੇ ਚੜ੍ਹਾਉਣਾ; ~ness ਪੂਰਨਤਾ, ਸਮਾਪਤੀ, ਸੰਪੰਨਤਾ

completion (ਕਅਾਂ'ਪਲੀਸ਼ਨ) *n* ਪੂਰਤੀ, ਪੂਰਨਤਾ, ਤਕਮੀਲ, ਸਮਾਪਤੀ

complex ('ਕੌਂਪਲਕਸ) *n a* (1) ਗੁੰਝਲ, ਉਲਝਣ, ਪੇਚੀਦਾ ਮਾਮਲਾ, ਜਟਿਲ ਗੱਲ; (2) ਭਵਨ-ਸਮੂਹ; (3) ਮਨੋਗ੍ਰੰਥੀ; ਗੁੰਝਲਦਾਰ, ਜਟਿਲ, ਉਲਝਿਆ, ਪੇਚੀਦਾ

complexion (ਕਅਾਂ'ਪਲੇੱਕਸ਼ਨ) *n* ਰੰਗ-ਢੰਗ, ਚੇਹਰਾ-ਮੁਹਰਾ, ਰੰਗ-ਰੂਪ, ਸਰੂਪ

complexity (ਕਅਾਂ'ਪੈਲਕਸਅਟਿ) *n* ਉਲਝਣ, ਉਲਝਾਉ, ਜਟਿਲਤਾ, ਪੇਚੀਦਗੀ, ਗੁੰਝੀ

compliance ('ਕਅਾਂਪਲਾਇਅੰਸ) *n* ਆਗਿਆ-ਪਾਲਨ, ਹੁਕਮ ਦੀ ਤਾਮੀਲ, ਫ਼ਰਮਾਬਰਦਾਰੀ; ਸੰਮਤੀ

complicate ('ਕੌਂਪਲਿਕੇਇਟ) *v* ਉਲਝਾਉਣਾ, ਜਟਿਲ ਬਣਾਉਣਾ, ਪੇਚੀਦਾ ਬਣਾਉਣਾ; ~d ਪੇਚੀਦਾ, ਗੁੰਝਲਦਾਰ, ਉਲਝਿਆ, ਪੇਚਦਾਰ, ਜਟਿਲ

complication ('ਕੌਂਪਲਿ'ਕੇਇਸ਼ਨ) *n* ਉਲਝਨ, ਗੁੰਝਲ, ਜਟਿਲਤਾ, ਜਟਿਲ ਪ੍ਰਸ਼ਨ, ਗੁੰਝੀ

compliment (ਕੌਂਪਲਿਮੰਟ, ਕੌਂਮਪਲਿਮੰਟ) *n v* (*in pl*) ਸ਼ੁਭ ਕਾਮਨਾਵਾਂ, ਸ਼ਲਾਘਾ, ਸਲਾਹੁਤਾ, ਆਦਾਬ, ਵਡਿਆਈ; (ਪ੍ਰ) ਸੁਗਾਤ; ਸ਼ਲਾਘਾ ਕਰਨਾ, ਸਲਾਹੁਣਾ, ਅਦਬ ਸਲਾਮ ਬੁਲਾਉਣਾ; ਸੁਗਾਤ ਦੇਣੀ; ~ary ਪ੍ਰਸੰਸਾਮਈ, ਸਨਮਾਨ-ਸੂਚਕ, ਅਭਿਨੰਦਨੀ

component (ਕਅਾਂ'ਪਅਉਨੰਟ) *n* ਅੰਗ, ਹਿੱਸਾ, ਭਾਗ, ਜੁੱਜ

compose (ਕੰਪਅਉਜ਼) *v* ਸੁਆਰਨਾ, ਲਿਖਣਾ, ਸਾਹਿਤ-ਸਿਰਜਨਾ ਕਰਨੀ, ਰਚਨਾ ਕਰਨੀ, ਨਿਰਮਾਣ ਕਰਨਾ; ਇੱਕਤਰ ਕਰਨਾ; ਕੰਪੋਜ਼ ਕਰਨਾ; ਛਾਪੇ ਦੇ ਅੱਖਰ ਜੋੜਨਾ, ਵਿਵਸਥਿਤ ਕਰਨਾ, ਵਿਉਂਤ ਨਾਲ ਰਖਣਾ; ਸੰਗੀਤ ਵਿਚ ਧੁਨ ਬਣਾਉਣਾ; ਸ਼ਾਂਤ ਕਰਨਾ; ~d ਸ਼ਾਂਤ, ਅਡੋਲ; ~dness ਸ਼ਾਂਤੀ, ਗੰਭੀਰਤਾ, ਇਤਮੀਨਾਨ; ~r ਸੰਗੀਤਕਾਰ, ਲੇਖਕ, ਰਚਨਾਕਾਰ, ਕਵੀ, ਰਚੇਤਾ

composing (ਕਅਾਂ'ਪਅਉਜ਼ਿਙ) *n* ਰਚਨ, ਟਾਈਪ ਨੂੰ ਜੋੜਨ ਦੀ ਕਿਰਿਆ, ਕੰਪੋਜ਼ਿੰਗ

composite (ਕੌਂਪਅਜ਼ਿਟ) *n* ਸੰਘਟਤ, ਮਿਸ਼ਰਤ, ਸੰਯੋਜਤ; ~**interest** ਮਿਸ਼ਰਤ ਵਿਆਜ; ~**sentence** ਸੰਯੁਕਤ ਵਾਕ; ~**word** ਸਮਾਸੀ ਸ਼ਬਦ

comprehend ('ਕੌਂਪਰਿ'ਹੈਂਡ) *v* ਸੰਮਿਲਤ ਕਰਨਾ, ਗ੍ਰਹਿਤ ਕਰਨਾ, ਮਿਲਾਉਣਾ; ਅਨੁਭਵ ਕਰਨਾ, ਸਮਝਣਾ

comprise (ਕਅੰ'ਪਰਾਇਜ਼) *n* ਸ਼ਾਮਲ ਕਰਨਾ, ਮਿਲਾਉਣਾ, ਅੰਦਰ ਸਮਾਉਣਾ; ਧਾਰਨ ਕਰਨਾ

compulsion (ਕਅੰ'ਪਅੱਲਸ਼ਨ) *n* ਜ਼ੋਰਾਵਰੀ, ਜ਼ਬਰਦਸਤੀ, ਜ਼ਬਰ, ਜ਼ੋਰ, ਬੰਧਨ, ਦਬਾਉ, ਬੇਵਸੀ, ਮਜਬੂਰੀ

compulsorily (ਕਅੰ'ਪਅੱਲਸਅਰਅਲਿ) *a* ਜ਼ਬਰਦਸਤੀ ਨਾਲ, ਬਲਪੂਰਵਕ, ਮਜਬੂਰਨ

compulsory (ਕਅੰ'ਪਅੱਲਸ(ਅ)ਰਿ) *a* ਜ਼ਰੂਰੀ, ਅਵੱਸ਼ਕ, ਲਾਜ਼ਮੀ, ਅਨਿਵਾਰੀ; ਜ਼ਬਰੀ

compute (ਕਅੰ'ਪਯੂਟ) *v* ਲੇਖਾ ਕਰਨਾ, ਗਿਣਨਾ, ਹਿਸਾਬ ਲਾਉਣਾ, ਗਿਣਤੀ ਵਿਚ ਲਿਆਉਣਾ; ~r, computor ਹਿਸਾਬ ਲਗਾਉਣ ਵਾਲਾ, ਗਣਕ, ਕੰਪਿਊਟਰ

computing (ਕਅੰ'ਪਯੂਟਿਙ) *n* ਗਿਣਤੀ, ਗਣਨਾ, ਹਿਸਾਬ

comrade ('ਕੌਮਰੇਡਿ) *n* ਸੰਗੀ, ਸਾਥੀ, ਯਾਰ, ਹਮਦਮ, ਮਿੱਤਰ, ਕਾਮਰੇਡ; ~ship ਸੰਗ; ਸਾਥ, ਯਾਰੀ, ਦੋਸਤੀ, ਮਿੱਤਰਤਾ

conceal (ਕਅਨ'ਸੀਲ) *v* ਗੁਪਤ ਰੱਖਣਾ, ਲੁਕਾਉਣਾ, ਛੁਪਾਉਣਾ, ਢਕਣਾ, ਉਹਲੇ ਰੱਖਣਾ

concede (ਕਅਨ'ਸੀਡ) *v* ਮੰਨਣਾ, ਮਨਜ਼ੂਰ ਕਰਨਾ, ਸਵੀਕਾਰ ਕਰਨਾ, ਕਬੂਲ ਕਰਨਾ; ਪ੍ਰਦਾਨ ਕਰਨਾ

concentrate ('ਕੌਨਸ(ਅ)ਨਟਰੇਇਟ) *v* ਕੇਂਦਰਤ ਕਰਨਾ, ਸਹਿ-ਕੇਂਦਰ ਹੋਣਾ, ਇਕਾਗਰ ਹੋਣਾ, ਸੰਘਣਾ ਕਰਨਾ, ਗਾੜ੍ਹਾ ਕਰਨਾ ~d ਕੇਂਦਰਤ, ਸੰਘਣਾ

concentration ('ਕੌਨਸ(ਅ)ਨ'ਟਰੇਇਸ਼ਨ) *n* ਕੇਂਦਰੀ-ਕਰਨ, ਸਹਿ-ਕੇਂਦਰੀਕਰਨ, ਇਕੱਤਰੀਕਰਨ, ਟਿਕਾਉ

concept ('ਕੌਨਸੈਂਪਟ) *n* ਸੰਕਲਪ, ਧਾਰਨਾ, ਸੰਬੋਧ; ~ion ਧਾਰਨਾ, ਖ਼ਿਆਲ, ਅਨੁਭਵ, ਗਰਭ-ਧਾਰਨ, ਗਰਭਾਧਾਨ

conceptive (ਕਅਨ'ਸੈਂਪਟਿਵ) *a* ਖ਼ਿਆਲੀ, ਅਨੁਭਵੀ, ਗਰਭ-ਸਬੰਧੀ

conceptual (ਕਅਨ'ਸੈਂਪਚੁਅਲ) *a* ਧਾਰਨਾ ਸਬੰਧੀ, ਸੰਕਲਪਵਾਦੀ, ਤਸੱਵਰੀ

concern (ਕਨੰ'ਸਅਃਨ) *v* ਸਬੰਧ ਰੱਖਣਾ, ਸਰੋਕਾਰ ਜਾਂ ਵਾਸਤਾ ਰੱਖਣਾ, ਵਾਹ ਪੈਣਾ, ਲਗਾਉ ਰੱਖਣਾ; ਦਿਲਚਸਪੀ ਲੈਣਾ; ਫ਼ਿਕਰ ਕਰਨਾ; ~ed ਸਬੰਧਤ, ਪ੍ਰਸੰਗਬੱਧ ਚਿੰਤਤ, ਚਿੰਤਾਤੁਰ; ~ing ਬਾਬਤ, ਬਾਰੇ, ਸਬੰਧਤ, ਵਿਸ਼ੇ ਵਿਚ, ਪ੍ਰਤੀ

concession (ਕਅਨ'ਸੈਸ਼ਨ) *n* ਛੋਟ, ਰਿਆਇਤ, ਸਵੀਕਾਰਨਾ, ਮਾਫ਼ੀ

concise (ਕਅਨ'ਸਾਇਸ) *a* ਸੰਖੇਪ, ਛੋਟਾ ~ly ਸੰਖਿਪ ਢੰਗ ਨਾਲ; ~ness ਸੰਖਿਪਤਤਾ

conclave ('ਕੌਙਕਲੇਇਵ) *n* ਪੋਪ ਦੀ ਚੋਣ ਲਈ ਵੱਡੇ ਪਾਦਰੀਆਂ ਦਾ ਇਕੱਠ; ਮੁੱਖ ਰਾਜਨੀਤਕ ਪਾਰਟੀਆਂ ਦੇ ਅਗੂਆਂ ਦਾ ਇਕੱਠ

conclude (ਕਅਨ'ਕਲੂਡ) *v* ਭੋਗ ਪਾਉਣਾ, ਨਿਬੇੜਨਾ, ਮੁਕਾਉਣਾ, ਖ਼ਤਮ ਕਰਨਾ, ਪੂਰਾ ਕਰਨਾ, ਸਿਰੇ ਚਾੜ੍ਹਨਾ; ~d ਸਮਾਪਤ, ਨਿਸ਼ਚਤ

concluding (ਕਅਨ'ਕਲੂਡਿਙ) *a* ਸਮਾਪਤੀ (ਸਮਾਰੋਹ ਆਦਿ); ਅੰਤਮ (ਟਿੱਪਣੀ ਆਦਿ)

conclusion (ਕਅਨ'ਕਲੂਯਨ) *n* ਸਿੱਟਾ, ਨਤੀਜਾ, ਪਰਿਣਾਮ; ਅੰਤ, ਸਮਾਪਤੀ, ਨਿਸ਼ਰਾ; ਨਿਸ਼ਕਰਸ਼; in ~ ਉਝਕ, ਅੰਤ ਵਿਚ

concoct ('ਕਅਨ'ਕੌਕਟ) *v* ਮਨੋਂ ਘੜਨਾ, ਜੋੜਨਾ, ਮਨੋਂ ਬਣਾਉਣਾ ~ed ਮਨਘੜਤ, ਘੜੀ ਹੋਈ, ਜੋੜੀ ਹੋਈ

concord (ਕੌਙਕੋ*ਡ) *n* ਸਮਝੌਤਾ, ਸੰਧੀ; ਮੇਲ-ਮਿਲਾਪ, ਤਰਕੀਬ, ਸਹਿਮਤੀ, ਮਿੱਤਰਤਾ; ਤਾਲ-ਮੇਲ ~ance ਏਕਤਾ, ਸਹਿਮਤੀ, ਸਮਾਨਤਾ,

ਸਮਤਾ, ਸਦ੍ਰਿਸ਼ਤਾ, ਅਨੁਕੂਲਤਾ; ਅਨੁਕ੍ਰਮਿਕਤਾ

concrete ('ਕੌਂਕਰੀਟ) *a n v* ਪੱਕਾ, ਠੋਸ, ਨਿਗਰ ਪਦਾਰਥ; ਨਿਗਰੇਪੁਣਾ; **~ness** ਪਕਿਆਈ, ਸਖ਼ਤਾਈ, ਠੋਸਪਣ

concur (ਕਅਨ'ਕਅ*) *v* ਸੰਮਤੀ ਰੱਖਣਾ, ਸਹਿਮਤ ਹੋਣਾ, ਰਾਇ ਮੇਲਣੀ, ਇਕ ਮਤ ਹੋਣਾ, ਅਨੁਕੂਲ ਹੋਣਾ; **~rence** ਸੰਮਤੀ, ਸਹਿਮਤੀ, ਮਨਜ਼ੂਰੀ, ਮਿਲਵਰਤਨ; **~rent** ਸਮਕਾਲੀ, ਸਹਿਵਰਤੀ, (ਸਜ਼ਾਵਾਂ) ਇਕੋ ਵੇਲੇ ਲਾਗੂ ਹੋਣ ਵਾਲੀਆਂ, ਸਹਿਗਾਮੀ ਅਨੁਸਾਰੀ, ਸੰਮਤੀ ਰੱਖਣ ਵਾਲਾ; ਸਮਾਨ; ਸਮਾਨਾਂਤਰ ਪਰਿਸਥਿਤੀ

condemn (ਕਅਨ'ਡੇਮ) *v* ਦੁਰਕਾਰਨਾ, ਤਿਰਸਕਾਰਨਾ, ਭੰਡਣਾ, ਰੱਦ ਕਰਨਾ; ਅਪਰਾਧੀ ਠਹਿਰਾਉਣਾ, ਦੋਸ਼ ਥੱਪਣਾ, ਸਜ਼ਾ ਸੁਣਾਉਣਾ; (ਵਿਰੁੱਧ) ਨਿਰਣਾ ਦੇਣਾ, ਬੁਰਾ-ਭਲਾ ਕਹਿਣਾ; **~able** ਦੰਡ ਦੇਣਯੋਗ, ਤਿਰਸਕਾਰ ਕਰਨਯੋਗ, ਨਿੰਦਣਯੋਗ; **~ation** ਦੰਡ-ਆਗਿਆ, ਸਜ਼ਾ ਦਾ ਹੁਕਮ; ਦੁਸ਼ਟ, ਨਿੰਦਾ; **~ed** ਦੰਡਤ, ਨਿੰਦਤ; ਨਿਕੰਮਾ, ਨਕਾਰਾ, ਨਿਸਿੱਧ

condensation ('ਕੇਨਡੇਨ'ਸੇਇਸ਼ਨ) *n* ਸੰਖੇਪਤਾ, ਗਾੜ੍ਹਪਣ, ਸੰਘਣਾਪਣ, ਘਾਣ

condense (ਕਅਨ'ਡੈਂਸ) *v* ਸੰਖੇਪ ਕਰਨਾ, ਛੋਟਾ ਕਰਨਾ, ਗਾੜ੍ਹਾ ਕਰਨਾ, ਬੱਦਲਾਂ ਦਾ ਘੁਲਣਾ; **~d** ਸੰਖਿਪਤ, ਘਟੀਕ੍ਰਿਤ

condiment ('ਕੌਂਡਿਮਅੰਟ) *n* ਅਚਾਰ; **~al** ਮਸਾਲੇਦਾਰ, ਚਟਪਟਾ

condition (ਕਅਨ'ਡਿਸ਼ਨ) *n v* ਅਵਸਥਾ, ਦਸ਼ਾ, ਸਥਿਤੀ, ਹਾਲਤ, ਹਾਲ; ਪਰਿਸਥਿਤੀ; ਸ਼ਰਤ, ਪ੍ਰਤੀਬੰਧ; ਹੈਸੀਅਤ, ਡੀਲ-ਡੌਲ, ਰੰਗ-ਢੰਗ, (ਦਸ਼ਾ) ਠੀਕ ਕਰਨਾ, ਅਨੁਕੂਲ ਕਰਨਾ, ਗਿਝਾਉਣਾ, ਆਦਤ ਪਾਉਣਾ, ਸ਼ਰਤ ਲਾਉਣਾ; **~al** ਸ਼ਰਤਬੰਦ, ਸ਼ਰਤੀਆ, ਮਸ਼ਰੂਤ, **~ed** ਅਨੁਕੂਲ, ਆਦੀ

condole (ਕਅਨ'ਡਅਉਲ) *v* ਅਫ਼ਸੋਸ ਕਰਨਾ, ਮਾਤਮ-ਪੁਰਸੀ ਕਰਨਾ, ਹਮਦਰਦੀ ਪਰਚਾਉਣੀ ਕਰਨੀ; **~nce** ਅਫ਼ਸੋਸ, ਮਾਤਮ, ਮਾਤਮਪੁਰਸੀ, ਪਰਚਾਉਣੀ, ਸੋਗ

condone (ਕਅਨ'ਡਅਉਨ) *v* ਛੋਟ ਦੇਣੀ, ਮਾਫ਼ ਕਰਨਾ ਜਾਣ ਦੇਣਾ, ਨਜ਼ਰਅੰਦਾਜ਼ ਕਰਨਾ

conduct ('ਕੌਂਡਅੱਕਟ) *n* ਵਤੀਰਾ, ਰਵੱਈਆ, ਚਾਲ-ਚਲਨ, ਆਚਰਨ, ਆਚਾਰ-ਵਿਹਾਰ, ਪ੍ਰਣਾਲੀ, ਪੱਧਤੀ

confederation (ਕਅਨ'ਫ਼ੈੱਡਅ'ਰੇਇਸ਼ਨ) *n* ਮਹਾਂਸੰਘ

confer (ਕਅਨ'ਡ਼ਅ:*) *v* (ਡਿਗਰੀ, ਪਦਵੀ, ਬਿੱਲਾ, ਖ਼ਿਤਾਬ) ਦੇਣਾ, ਪ੍ਰਦਾਨ ਕਰਨਾ; ਸਲਾਹ ਕਰਨੀ, ਮਸ਼ਵਰਾ ਕਰਨਾ

conference ('ਕੌਂਡ਼(ਅ)ਰਅੰਸ) *n* ਸੰਮੇਲਨ, ਕਾਨਫ਼ਰੰਸ, ਜਲਸਾ; ਸਲਾਹ, ਮਸ਼ਵਰਾ

conferment (ਕਅਨ'ਡ਼ਅ'ਮਅੰਟ) *n* ਪ੍ਰਦਾਨ, ਉਪਹਾਰ; ਭੇਟ

confess (ਕਅਨ'ਡ਼ੈਸ) *v* (ਅਪਰਾਧ) ਇਕਬਾਲ ਕਰਨਾ, ਮੰਨ ਜਾਣਾ; ਪਛਤਾਵਾ ਕਰਨਾ, ਤੋਬਾ ਕਰਨੀ, ਕਬੂਲਣਾ

confession (ਕਅਨ'ਡ਼ੈਸ਼ਨ) *n* ਇਕਬਾਲ, ਤੋਬਾ

confidant ('ਕੌਂਡਿ'ਡੈਂਟ) *n* ਵਿਸ਼ਵਾਸਪਾਤਰ, ਭਰੋਸੇਯੋਗ ਪੁਰਸ਼, ਹਮਰਾਜ਼, ਰਾਜ਼ਦਾਨ

confide (ਕਅਨ'ਡ਼ਾਇਡ) *v* ਵਿਸਾਹ ਖਾਣਾ, ਭਰੋਸਾ ਕਰਨਾ, ਭੇਤੀ ਬਣਾਉਣਾ, ਸੌਂਪਣਾ, ਹਵਾਲੇ ਕਰਨਾ; **~nce** ਵਿਸ਼ਵਾਸ, ਵਿਸਾਹ, ਭਰੋਸਾ, ਯਕੀਨ, ਪ੍ਰਤੀਤੀ, ਧੀਆ; **~nt** ਭਰੋਸਾ ਕਰਨ ਵਾਲਾ, ਭੇਤੀ, ਮਹਿਰਮ, ਵਿਸ਼ਵਾਸੀ, ਵਿਸ਼ਵਾਸ-ਪੂਰਨ; **~ntial** ਗੁਪਤ, ਗੁੱਝਾ, ਰਹੱਸਮਈ, ਭੇਤਵਾਲੀ

configuration (ਕਅਨ'ਫ਼ਿਗਅਰਏਸ਼ਨ) *n* ਰੂਪ, ਡੀਲ-ਡੌਲ, ਰੂਪ-ਰੇਖਾ, ਨੁਹਾਰ, ਵਜ਼ੂ-ਕਟੂ

configure (ਕਅਨ'ਫ਼ਿਗਾ*) *v* ਰੂਪ ਦੇਣਾ, ਸ਼ਕਲ ਬਣਾਉਣੀ, ਸ਼ਕਲ ਦੇਣੀ, ਢਾਂਚਾ ਬਣਾਉਣਾ

confine ('ਕੌਨਫ਼ਾਇਨ, ਕਅਨ'ਫ਼ਾਇਨ) *n (in pl) v* ਹੱਦ, ਹੱਦ-ਬੰਨਾ, ਸੀਮਾਂਤ, ਸੀਮਾ, ਹੱਦ ਅੰਦਰ ਕਰਨਾ, ਸੀਮਾ-ਬੱਧ ਕਰਨਾ, ਘੇਰੇ ਵਿੱਚ ਰੱਖਣਾ, ਕੈਦ ਕਰਨਾ, ਰੋਕ ਰੱਖਣਾ, ਅਟਕਾਉਣਾ; ~d ਸੀਮਤ, ਘਿਰਿਆ, ਬੰਦ, ਸੰਕੀਰਣ

confirm (ਕਅਨ'ਫ਼ਅ:ਮ) *v* ਪੁਸ਼ਟੀ ਕਰਨੀ, ਹਾਮੀ ਭਰਨੀ, ਪੱਕਾ ਕਰਨਾ, ਸਥਾਈ ਕਰਨਾ, ਤਸਦੀਕ ਕਰਨਾ, ਮਨਜ਼ੂਰੀ ਦੇਣਾ; ~ation ਪੁਸ਼ਟੀ, ਪੁਸ਼ਟੀਕਰਨ, ਤਸਦੀਕ, ਸਮਰਥਨ, ਮਨਜ਼ੂਰੀ, ਨਾਮਕਰਨ ਸੰਸਕਾਰ; ~ative, ~atory ਪੁਸ਼ਟੀਕਾਰਕ, ਸਮਰਥਕ, ਤਾਈਦੀ, ਹਿਮਾਇਤੀ

confiscate ('ਕੌਨਫ਼ਿਸਕੇਇਟ) *v* ਜ਼ਬਤ ਕਰਨਾ, ਕੁਰਕ ਕਰਨਾ, ਖੋਹ ਲੈਣਾ; ~d ਜ਼ਬਤ ਕੀਤਾ, ਕੁਰਕ ਕੀਤਾ, ਖੋਹਿਆ

confiscation ('ਕੌਨਫ਼ਿਸਕੇਅਨ) *n* ਜ਼ਬਤੀ, ਕੁਰਕੀ

confix (ਕਅਨ'ਫ਼ਿਕਸ) *v* ਦ੍ਰਿੜ੍ਹ ਕਰਨਾ, ਪੱਕਾ ਕਰਨਾ, ਮਜ਼ਬੂਤੀ ਨਾਲ ਜਮਾਉਣਾ

conflict ('ਕੌਨਫ਼ਲਿਕਟ, ਕਅ'ਫ਼ਲਿਕਟ) *n v* ਟਕਰਾ, ਕਸ਼ਮਕਸ਼, ਸੰਘਰਸ਼, ਮੁਕਾਬਲਾ, ਵਿਰੋਧ, ਦਵੰਦ, ਘਚੇੜਾ, ਝਗੜਾ, ਟਾਕਰਾ ਕਰਨਾ, ਟੱਕਰਨਾ, ਵਿਰੋਧ ਕਰਨਾ, ਝਗੜਨਾ, ਮੁਕਾਬਲਾ ਹੋਣਾ; ~ing ਵਿਪਰੀਤ, ਪ੍ਰਤੀਕੂਲ, ਪਰਸਪਰ ਵਿਰੋਧੀ ਵਿਵਾਦਗ੍ਰਸਤ; ~ion ਵਿਰੋਧ, ਵਿਵਾਦ, ਕਲਹ, ਟੱਕਰ, ਮੁੱਠ-ਭੇੜ ਪ੍ਰਤੀਕੂਲਤਾ; ~ive ਵਿਵਾਦਗ੍ਰਸਤ, ਪ੍ਰਤੀਕੂਲ, ਪਰਸਪਰ ਵਿਰੋਧੀ

confluence ('ਕੌਨਫ਼ਲੂਅੰਸ) *n* ਸੰਗਮ, ਮੇਲ, ਵੇਣੀ

conform (ਕਅਨ'ਫ਼ੋਮ) *v* ਅਨੁਕੂਲ ਕਰਨਾ, ਇਕ ਸੁਰ ਹੋਣਾ, ਇਕਸਾਰ ਦੇਣਾ, ਅਨੁਸਾਰ ਕਰਨਾ, ਅਨੁਕੂਲ ਹੋਣਾ; ~ation ਅਨੁਕੂਲੀਕਰਨ, ਅਨੁਰੂਪ, ਸਦ੍ਰਿਸ਼ਤਾ, ਬਣਾਵਟ, ਢਾਂਚਾ

conformity (ਕਅਨ'ਫ਼ੋਮਅਟਿ) *n* ਅਨੁਕੂਲਤ, ਅਨੁਰੂਪਤਾ, ਅਨੁਸਾਰਤਾ, ਮੇਲ, ਪੈਰਵੀ, ਤਾਮੀਲ, ਅਗਿਆਕਾਰਤਾ

confuse (ਕਅਨ'ਫ਼ਯੂਜ਼) *v* ਮੱਤ ਮਾਰ ਦੇਣੀ, ਭੁਚਲਾਉਣਾ, ਉਲਝਾਉਣਾ, ਪਰੇਸ਼ਾਨ ਕਰਨਾ; ~d ਪਰੇਸ਼ਾਨ, ਘਬਰਾਇਆ ਹੋਇਆ, ਉਲਝਿਆ ਹੋਇਆ

confusing (ਕਅਨ'ਫ਼ਯੂਜ਼ਿਙ) *a* ਪਰੇਸ਼ਾਨੀ ਵਾਲਾ, ਚਕਰਾਉਣ ਵਾਲਾ, ਉਲਝਾਉਣ ਵਾਲੀ, ਭਰਮਕਾਰੀ

confusion (ਕਅਨ'ਫ਼ਯੂਜ਼ਨ) *n* ਘਬਰਾਹਟ, ਅਫ਼ਰਾਤਫ਼ਰੀ, ਹਫ਼ੜਾ ਦਫ਼ੜੀ, ਪਰੇਸ਼ਾਨੀ

congenial (ਕਅਨ'ਜੀਨਯਅਲ) *a* ਹਮਦਰਦ, ਅਨੁਸਾਰੀ, ਸੁਹਾਵਣਾ, ਅਨੁਕੂਲ, ਸੁਖਾਉਂਦਾ, ਮਨਪਸੰਦ; ~ity ਉਚਿਤਤਾ, ਸਮਾਨਤਾ, ਹਮਜਿਨਸੀ

congratulate (ਕਅਨ'ਗਰੈਚੁਲੇਇਟ) *v* ਵਧਾਈ ਦੇਣੀ, ਮੁਬਾਰਕ ਦੇਣੀ

congratulation (ਕਅਨ'ਗਰੈਚੁ'ਲੇਇਸ਼ਨ) *n* ਵਧਾਈ, ਮੁਬਾਰਕ, ਮੁਬਾਰਕਬਾਦ

congruity (ਕੌਙ'ਗਰੂਅਟਿ) *n* ਇਕਸਾਰਤਾ, ਸਮਰੂਪਤਾ, ਅਨੁਰੂਪਤਾ, ਸਦ੍ਰਿਸ਼ਟਤਾ, ਸੰਗਤੀ

congruous ('ਕੌਙ'ਗਰੂਅਸ) *a* ਉਚਿਤ, ਚੁੱਕਵਾਂ, ਅਨੁਰੂਪ, ਅਨੁਕੂਲ, ਸਦ੍ਰਿਸ਼, ਯੁਕਤ

conjugation ('ਕੌਨਜੁ'ਗੇਇਸ਼ਨ) *n* ਸਬੰਧ, ਸੰਯੋਗ, ਮੇਲ, ਜੋੜ, ਸੰਯੋਜਨ, ਰੂਪ-ਸਾਧਨ; ਧਾਤੂ ਰੂਪ; ਕਿਰਿਆ-ਰੂਪ; ਭੋਗ, ਮੈਥਨ, ਜੜਾਈ, ਪੋਟ

conjure (ਕਅਨ'ਜੂਅ*) *v* ਵਾਸਤਾ ਪਾਉਣਾ,

ਬੇਨਤੀ ਕਰਨਾ, ਅਪੀਲ ਕਰਨਾ; ਜਾਦੂ ਕਰਨਾ, ਰੂਹਾਂ ਨੂੰ ਬੁਲਾਉਣਾ

connect (ਕਅ'ਨੈਕਟ) v ਜੋੜਨਾ, ਜੁੜਨਾ, ਗੰਢਣਾ, ਸਬੰਧ ਪੈਦਾ ਕਰਨਾ, ਮੇਲਣ; ~**ed** ਸਬੰਧਤ, ਜੁੜਿਆ, ਸੰਯੁਕਤ

connote (ਕਅ'ਨਅਉਟ) v ਸੰਕੇਤ ਕਰਨਾ, ਭਾਵ ਪਰਗਟ ਕਰਨਾ, ਜਤਲਾਉਣਾ

conquer (ਕੌਙਕਅ*) v ਫ਼ਤਿਹ ਕਰਨਾ, ਸਰ ਕਰਨਾ, ਜਿੱਤਣਾ, ਅਧੀਨ ਕਰਨਾ; ~**or** ਜੇਤੂ, ਵਿਜਈ, ਵਿਜੇਤਾ

conquest ('ਕੌਙਕਵੈੱਸਟ) n ਜਿੱਤ, ਫ਼ਤਿਹ, ਵਿਜੈ

conscience ('ਕੌਨਸ(ਅੇ)ਸ) n ਜ਼ਮੀਰ, ਈਮਾਨ, ਅੰਤਹਕਰਣ, ਅੰਤਰ ਆਤਮ; ~**less** ਬੇਈਮਾਨ, ਅਵਿਵੇਕੀ, ਬੇਜ਼ਮੀਰ; ~**ly** ਈਮਾਨਦਾਰੀ ਨਾਲ ਵਿਵੇਕਪੂਰਵਕ; ~**ness** ਈਮਾਨਦਾਰੀ, ਜ਼ਮੀਰ, ਸਾਤਵਿਕਤਾ

conscious ('ਕੌਨਸ਼ਅਸ) a ਚੇਤਨ, ਸਚੇਤ, ਸੋਝੀਵਾਨ; ~**ness** ਚੇਤਨਤਾ, ਜਾਣਕਾਰੀ; ਨਿਪੁੰਨਤਾ, ਸੋਝੀ, ਚੇਤਨਾ; ਜਾਣਕਾਰੀ, ਗਿਆਨ, ਅਨੁਭਵ

consecutive ('ਕਅਨ'ਸੈਕਯੁਟਿਵ) a ਲਗਾਤਾਰ, ਸਿਲਸਿਲੇਵਾਰ, ਪੁੜੀਵਾਰ, ਲਾਗਵਾਂ; ਨਿਰੰਤਰ; ~**ly** ਉਪਰੋਥਲੀ, ਨਾਲੋ ਨਾਲ, ਸਿਲਸਲੇਵਾਰ, ਲਗਾਤਾਰ

consensus (ਕਅਨ'ਸੈਨਸਅਸ) n ਸਹਿਮਤੀ, ਸਰਵਸੰਮਤੀ, ਏਕਤਾ

consent (ਕਅਨ'ਸੈਂਟ) n v ਰਜ਼ਾਮੰਦੀ, ਸਹਿਮਤੀ, ਸੰਮਤੀ, ਮਨਜ਼ੂਰੀ, ਆਗਿਆ; ਰਜ਼ਾਮੰਦ ਹੋਣਾ, ਮਨਜ਼ੂਰੀ ਦੇਣੀ, ਸਲਾਹ ਦੇਣੀ, ਸਹਿਮਤ ਹੋਣਾ, ਸਵੀਕਾਰ ਕਰਨਾ, ਮੰਨ ਲੈਣਾ

consequence ('ਕੌਨਸਿਕਵਅੰਸ) n ਸਿੱਟਾ, ਫਲ, ਪਰਿਣਾਮ, ਮਹੱਤਾ, ਮਹਤਵ

consequent ('ਕੌਨਸਿਕਵਅੰਟ) n ਸਿੱਟਾ, ਨਤੀਜਾ, ਫਲ; ~**ly** ਸਿੱਟੇ ਵਜੋਂ, ਨਤੀਜੇ ਦੇ ਤੌਰ ਤੇ, ਫਲਸਰੂਪ

consider (ਕਅਨ'ਸਿਡਅ*) v ਸੋਚਣਾ, ਵਿਚਾਰਨਾ, ਗੌਲਣਾ, ਧਿਆਨ ਦੇਣਾ, ਸਮਝਣਾ; ~**able** ਸੋਚਣਯੋਗ, ਵਿਚਾਰਨਯੋਗ, ਗੌਰ ਕਰਨਯੋਗ; ਕਾਫ਼ੀ, ਬਹੁਤ; ~**ably** ਢੇਰ ਸਾਰਾ, ਬਹੁਤ ਸਾਰਾ, ਅਤੀਅੰਤ, ਅਤੀਅਧਿਕ; ~**ate** ਸਚੇਤ, ਦੂਰਦਰਸ਼ੀ

consideration (ਕਅਨ'ਸਿਡਅ'ਰੇਇਸ਼ਨ) n ਵਿਚਾਰ, ਖ਼ਿਆਲ, ਗੌਰ, ਧਿਆਨ, ਗੰਭੀਰ ਚਿੰਤਨ; **in ~ of** ਨੂੰ ਧਿਆਨ ਵਿਚ ਰਖਦਿਆਂ; **take into ~** ਵਿਚਾਰ ਅਧੀਨ ਕਰਨਾ, ਗੌਰ ਕਰਨਾ; ਧਿਆਨ ਦੇਣਾ; **under~** ਵਿਚਾਰ-ਅਧੀਨ

consign (ਕਅਨ'ਸਾਇਨ) v ਸੌਂਪਣਾ, ਬਖ਼ਸ਼ਣਾ, ਹਵਾਲੇ ਕਰਨਾ, ਭੇਜਣਾ; ~**ee** ਪ੍ਰਾਪਤ ਕਰਨ ਵਾਲਾ, (ਪਾਰਸਲ) ਪ੍ਰਾਪਤ ਕਰਨ ਵਾਲਾ; ~**ment** ਮਾਲ ਭਿਜਵਾਈ, ਸਪੁਰਦਗੀ, ਸੌਂਪਿਆ ਗਿਆ ਮਾਲ

consist (ਕਅਨ'ਸਿਸਟ) v ਬਣਨਾ, ਬਣਿਆ ਹੋਣਾ, ਸ਼ਾਮਲ ਹੋਣਾ; ~**ence** ਘਣਤਾ, ਠੋਸਪਣ, ਪਕਿਆਈ, ਦ੍ਰਿੜ੍ਹਤਾ; ~**ent** ਦ੍ਰਿੜ੍ਹ, ਸਥਿਰ, ਅਟੱਲ; ਅਨੁਕੂਲ

consolation ('ਕੌਨਸਅ'ਲੇਇਸ਼ਨ) n ਦਿਲਾਸਾ, ਧਰਵਾਸ, ਧੀਰਜ, ਢਾਰਸ, ਤਸੱਲੀ

console (ਕਅਨ'ਸਅਉਲ) v ਦਿਲਾਸਾ ਦੇਣਾ, ਢਾਰਸ ਦੇਣਾ, ਧੀਰਜ ਬੰਨ੍ਹਾਉਣਾ, ਤਸੱਲੀ ਦੇਣੀ

consolidation (ਕਅਨ'ਸੌਲਿ'ਡੇਇਸ਼ਨ) n ਚੱਕਬੰਦੀ, ਮੁਰੱਬਾਬੰਦੀ

consonant ('ਕੌਨਸਅੰਟ) a n ਇਕ-ਸੁਰ, ਥੁੱਕਦਾ, ਸੁਰੀਲਾ, ਮਧੁਰ; ਵਿਅੰਜਨ

consort ('ਕਨਸੋਟ) n v ਪਤੀ ਜਾਂ ਪਤਨੀ,

ਹਮਰਾਹੀ; ਸਾਥੀ ਜਹਾਜ਼

conspicuous (ਕਅਨ'ਸਪਿਕਯੂਅਸ) *a* ਉੱਘਾ, ਪ੍ਰਤੱਖ, ਪਰਗਟ, ਸਪਸ਼ਟ, ਵਿਅਕਤ

conspiracy (ਕਅਨ'ਸਪਿਰਅਸਿ) *n* ਸਾਜ਼ਸ, ਸਾਜ਼ਬਾਜ਼

conspire (ਕਅਨ'ਸਪਾਇਅ*) *v* ਸਾਜ਼ਸ਼ ਕਰਨ, ਮਨਸੂਬਾ ਬਣਾਉਣਾ, ਵਿਦਰੋਹ ਕਰਨਾ, ਸੰਮਿਲਤ ਹੋਣਾ

constable ('ਕਅਨਸਟਅਬਲ) *n* ਪੁਲੀਸ ਦਾ ਸਿਪਾਹੀ, ਕਾਨਸਟੇਬਲ, ਪੁਲਸੀਆ

constant ('ਕੌਨਸਟਅੰਟ) *a n* ਥਿਰ, ਸਥਿਰ, ਸਥਾਈ, ਪੱਕਾ, ਦ੍ਰਿੜ੍ਹ, ਅਡੋਲ, ਨਿਰੰਤਰ, ਲਗਾਤਾਰ, ਵਫ਼ਾਦਾਰ; ਸੱਚਾ, ਥਿਰ ਜਾਂ ਸਥਾਈ ਸੰਖਿਆ (ਗਣਿ), ਪੱਕਾ ਨਾਪ; **~ly** ਲਗਾਤਾਰ, ਨਿਰੰਤਰ, ਨਿਤ, ਹਰਦਮ, ਮੁਤਵਾਤਰ

constipation ('ਕੌਨਸਟਿ'ਪੇਇਸ਼ਨ) *n* ਕਬਜ਼ੀ, ਕਬਜ਼

constituency (ਕਅਨ'ਸਟਿਟਯੁਅੰਸਿ) *a n* ਚੋਣ-ਖੇਤਰ, ਚੋਣ-ਹਲਕਾ, ਖ਼ਰੀਦਾਰ ਲੋਕ, ਗਾਹਕ-ਵਰਗ

constituent (ਕਅੰਨ'ਸਟਿਯੁਅੰਟ) *a n* ਸੰਘਟਕ; **~d** ਸਥਾਪਤ, ਸੰਗਠਤ, ਨਿਯੁਕਤ, ਸੰਸਥਾਪਤ

constitute ('ਕੌਨਸਟਿਟਯੂਟ) *v* ਬਣਾਉਣਾ, ਖੜ੍ਹਾ ਕਰਨਾ, ਕਾਨੂੰਨੀ ਰੂਪ ਦੇਣਾ, ਸਥਾਪਤ ਕਰਨਾ, ਵਿਧਾਨਕ ਰੂਪ ਦੇਣਾ, ਸੰਸਥਾਪਨ ਕਰਨਾ

constitution ('ਕੌਨਸਟਿ'ਟਯੂਸ਼ਨ) *n* ਸੰਵਿਧਾਨ, ਸੰਗਠਨ, ਦਸ਼ਾ; ਪੱਧਤੀ, ਰੀਤ; ਸਰੀਰ ਰਚਨਾ, ਗਠਨ, ਬਣਾਵਟ; ਅਸੂਲ, ਸਿਧਾਂਤ

constrain (ਕਅਨ'ਸਟਰੇਇਨ) *v* ਰੋਕਣਾ, ਪਾਬੰਦੀ ਲਾਉਣੀ, ਮਜ਼ਬੂਰ ਕਰਨਾ; **~t** ਰੁਕਾਵਟ, ਮਜਬੂਰੀ, ਪਾਬੰਦੀ, ਬੰਦਸ਼, ਨਿਜੰਤਰਨ

constrict (ਕਅਨ'ਸਟਰਿਕਟ) *v* ਸਮੇਟਣਾ, ਸੁੰਗੋੜਨਾ, ਖਿੱਚਣਾ, ਦੱਬਣਾ; ਵਲਣਾ; **~ion** ਖਿਚਾਉ, ਦਬਾਅ, ਕਸ, ਸੰਕੀਰਣਤਾ

construct (ਕਅਨ'ਸਟਰਅੱਕਟ) *v* (ਇਮਾਰਤ) ਉਸਾਰਨਾ, ਰਚਨਾ ਕਰਨਾ, ਨਿਰਮਾਣ ਕਰਨਾ, ਵਾਕ ਬਣਾਉਣਾ; ਖਾਨਾ ਖਿਚਣਾ; **~ed** ਤਿਆਰ, ਰਚਿਤ, ਨਿਰਮਿਤ; **~ion** ਉਸਾਰੀ, ਕਰਨਾ, ਬਣਾਵਟ, ਨਿਰਮਤ ਵਸਤ; ਸ਼ਬਦ-ਯੋਜਨਾ; **~ive** ਉਸਾਰੂ, ਰਚਨਾਤਮਕ, ਨਿਰਮਾਣਸ਼ੀਲ, ਵਾਸਤਵਿਕ

consult (ਕਅਨ'ਸੱਅਲਟ) *v* ਸੰਮਤੀ ਲੈਣੀ, ਮਸ਼ਵਰਾ ਲੈਣਾ, ਰਾਇ ਲੈਣੀ, ਸਲਾਹ ਲੈਣੀ, ਵਿਚਾਰ ਕਰਨੀ; **~ant** ਸਲਾਹਕਾਰ; **~ation** ਰਾਇ, ਸਲਾਹ, ਮਸ਼ਵਰਾ, ਸੋਚ-ਵਿਚਾਰ

consume (ਕਅਨ'ਸਯੂਮ) *v* ਖਪਾ ਦੇਣਾ, ਖ਼ਰਚ ਕਰ ਦੇਣਾ, ਖਪਤ ਕਰਨਾ, ਵਰਤ ਲੈਣਾ, ਉਡਾਉਣਾ; **~d** ਖਪਤ ਕੀਤਾ; **~r** ਖਪਤਕਾਰ, ਉਪਭੋਗਤਾ, ਗ੍ਰਾਹਕ

consuming (ਕਅਨ'ਸਯੁਮਿਙ) *a* ਉਪਭੋਗੀ

consumption (ਕਅਨ'ਸੱਅਪਸ਼ਨ) *n* ਖਪਤ, ਉਪਭੋਗ, ਖਪਾ, ਖ਼ਰਚ; ਉਜਾੜਾ, ਵਿਨਾਸ਼

contact ('ਕੌਨਟੈਕਟ) *n v* ਵਾਹ, ਮੇਲ; ਸੰਪਰਕ, ਛੋਹ, ਸਬੰਧ, ਵਾਹ ਪੈਣਾ, ਮਿਲਣਾ, ਛੋਹਣਾ, ਪੰਦ ਚੜ੍ਹਨੀ

contagious (ਕਅਨ'ਟੇਇਜਅਸ) *n* ਛੂਤਕਾਰੀ, ਲਾਗ ਵਾਲਾ

contain (ਕਅਨ'ਟੇਇਨ) *v* ਸ਼ਾਮਲ ਕਰਨਾ, ਘੇਰਨਾ, ਰੱਖਣਾ, ਘਿਰੇ ਹੋਣਾ; ਗਰਭਿਤ ਹੋਣਾ; **~er** ਡੱਬਾ, ਬਕਸ; **~ed** ਸ਼ਾਮਲ, ਸੰਮਿਲਤ

contaminate (ਕਅਨ'ਟੈਮਿਨੇਇਟ) *n* ਭ੍ਰਿਸ਼ਟ ਕਰਨਾ, ਭਿੱਟਣਾ, ਵਿਗਾੜਨਾ, ਗੰਦਾ ਕਰਨਾ ਦੂਸ਼ਤ ਕਰਨਾ

contamination (ਕਅਨ'ਟੈਮਿ'ਨੇਇਸ਼ਨ) *n* ਭਿੱਟ

ਛੂਤ, ਦੂਸ਼ਨ ਭ੍ਰਿਸ਼ਟਤਾ, ਮਿਲਾਵਟ, ਖੋਟ

contemplate (ਕੌਨਟਅੱਪਲੇਇਟ) v ਧਿਆਉਣਾ, ਕਲਪਨਾ ਕਰਨਾ, ਸੋਚਣਾ, ਵਿਚਾਰਨਾ, ਇਰਾਦਾ ਕਰਨਾ, ਇੱਛਾ ਰੱਖਣਾ

contemplation (ਕੌਨਟਅੱਪਲੇਇਸ਼ਨ) n ਧਿਆਨ, ਕਲਪਨਾ, ਸੋਚ, ਵਿਚਾਰ

contemplative (ਕੌਨਟਅੱਪਲੇਇਟਿਵ) a ਧਿਆਨੀ, ਅੰਤਰ ਧਿਆਨੀ, ਚਿੰਤਨਸ਼ੀਲ, ਸੋਚਵਾਨ, ਵਿਚਾਰਸ਼ੀਲ

contemporary (ਕੌਨਅੱਨਟੈੱਪ(ਅ)ਰ(ਅ)ਰਿ) a ਸਮਕਾਲੀ, ਸਮਕਾਲੀਨ; ਸਮਕਾਲਕ; ਹਾਈ

contempt (ਕਅਨਟੈੱਪਟ) n ਘਿਰਣਾ, ਨਫ਼ਰਤ, ਤਿਰਸਕਾਰ, ਅਪਮਾਨ, ਅਵੱਗਿਆ; ~of court ਹਤੱਕ ਅਦਾਲਤ, ਅਦਾਲਤ ਦਾ ਅਪਮਾਨ; ~ible ਘਿਰਣਾਯੋਗ, ਤੁੱਛ, ਨੀਚ, ਕੀਰ; ~uous ਘਿਰਣਾ ਭਰੀ, ਹਤੱਕ ਭਰੀ

contend (ਕਅਨਟੈਂਡ) v ਬਹਿਸ ਕਰਨਾ, ਵਾਦ-ਵਿਵਾਦ ਕਰਨਾ, ਸੰਘਰਸ਼ ਕਰਨਾ, ਹੱਥ-ਪੈਰ ਮਾਰਨਾ, ਝਗੜਨਾ, ਝੜਪਣਾ, ਉਜ਼ਰ ਕਰਨਾ

content (ਕੌਨਟੈਂਟ) n v ਤੱਤ, ਅੰਸ਼; (ਪੁਸਤਕ ਆਦਿ ਦਾ) ਵਿਸ਼ਾ ਵਸਤੂ; ਸਮਗਰੀ; ਸਬਰ, ਤ੍ਰਿਪਤੀ, ਸੰਤੁਸ਼ਟੀ; ਸੰਤੋਖੀ, ਸੰਤੁਸ਼ਟ, ਰਾਜ਼ੀ, ਤ੍ਰਿਪਤ ਕਰਨਾ, ਰਜਾਣਾ, ਰੀਝਾਉਣਾ, ਰਜ਼ਾਮੰਦ ਕਰਨਾ; table of ~s ਵਿਸ਼ੇ-ਸੂਚੀ; ~ed ਤ੍ਰਿਪਤ, ਸੰਤੁਸ਼ਟ, ਰੱਜਿਆ, ਪ੍ਰਸੰਨ

contention (ਕਅਨਟੈਨਸ਼ਨ) n ਮੁਕਾਬਲਾ, ਟਾਕਰਾ; ਵਾਦ-ਵਿਵਾਦ, ਵਿਵਾਦਗ੍ਰਸਤ ਵਿਸ਼ਾ; ਤਕਰਾਰ, ਰੇੜਕਾ

contentious (ਕਅਨਟੈਂਸ਼ਅਸ) a ਵਿਵਾਦਪੂਰਨ, ਝਗੜੇ ਭਰਿਆ

contest (ਕੌਨਟੈੱਸਟ, ਕਅਨਟੈੱਸਟ) n v ਸੰਘਰਸ਼, ਮੁਕਾਬਲਾ, ਦਵੰਦ, ਪ੍ਰਤੀਯੋਗਤਾ, ਟਾਕਰਾ, ਵਿਵਾਦ; ਝਗੜਾ; ਜੱਦੋ-ਜਹਿਦ ਕਰਨਾ, ਵਿਰੋਧ ਕਰਨਾ, ਬਹਿਸ ਕਰਨਾ, ਝਗੜਨਾ; ~ant ਪ੍ਰਤੀਯੋਗੀ, ਵਿਵਾਦ ਕਰਨ ਵਾਲਾ

context (ਕੌਨਟੈੱਕਸਟ) n ਪ੍ਰਸੰਗ, ਵਿਸ਼ਾ, ਸੰਦਰਭ

contextual (ਕਅਨਟੈੱਕਸਟਯੂਅਲ) a ਸੰਬਧਤ, ਪ੍ਰਸੰਗ ਸਰਬੰਧੀ

contiguity ('ਕੌਨਟਿ'ਗਯੂਅਟਿ) n ਨਿਕਟਤਾ, ਮੇਲ, ਲਗਾਉ, ਰਾਬਤਾ

contiguous (ਕਅਟ'ਟਿਗਯੂਅਸ) a ਨੇੜੇ ਦਾ, ਨਿਕਟਵਰਤੀ, ਜੁੜਿਆ

contingent (ਕਅਨ'ਟਿਨਜਅੰਟ) a ਸਬੰਧੀ, ਇਤਫ਼ਾਕੀਆ, ਅਚਾਨਕ

continual (ਕਅਨ'ਟਿਨਯੂਅਲ) a ਜਾਰੀ, ਲਗਾਤਾਰ, ਅਖੰਡ, ਨਿਰੰਤਰ; ~ly ਲਗਾਤਾਰ, ਇਕ ਰਸ, ਹਰ ਸਮੇਂ, ਨਿਰੰਤਰ

continuance (ਕਅਨ'ਟਿਨਯੂਅੰਸ) n ਲਗਾਤਾਰਤਾ, ਨਿਰੰਤਰਤਾ; ਸਿਲਸਲਾ, ਲੜੀ

continuation (ਕਅਨ'ਟਿਨਯੂ'ਏਇਸ਼ਨ) n ਲਗਾਤਾਰਤਾ, ਲੜੀਬੱਧਤਾ, ਪੁਨਰ-ਆਰੰਭ

continue (ਕਅਨ'ਟਿਨਯੂ) v ਜਾਰੀ ਰੱਖਣਾ, ਜਾਰੀ ਰਹਿਣਾ, ਚਾਲੂ ਰੱਖਣਾ, ਰੋਕ ਰੱਖਣਾ, ਠਹਿਰਾਉਣਾ; ~d ਲਗਾਤਾਰ, ਨਿਰੰਤਰ

continuity (ਕੌਨਟਿ'ਨਯੂਅਟਿ) n ਲਗਾਤਾਰਤਾ, ਅਖੰਡਤਾ, ਨਿਰੰਤਰਤਾ, ਰਵਾਨੀ

continuous (ਕਅਨ'ਟਿਨਯੂਅਸ) adv ਲਗਾਤਾਰ, ਅਟੁੱਟ, ਅਖੰਡ, ਨਿਰੰਤਰ, ਨਿਰਵਿਘਨ; ~ly ਲਗਾਤਾਰ, ਅਟੁੱਟ ਤਰੀਕੇ ਨਾਲ, ਸਦਾ, ਨਿਰੰਤਰ

contraception (ਕੌਨਟਰਅ'ਸੈੱਪਸ਼ਨ) n ਗਰਭ ਰੋਕ, ਗਰਭ ਨਿਰੋਧ

contraceptive ('ਕੌਨਟਰਾ'ਸੈੱਪਟਿਵ) *n* ਗਰਭ ਰੋਕੂ, ਗਰਭ ਨਿਰੋਧਕ

contract (ਕੌਨਟਰੈਕਟ, ਕਆਨ'ਟਰੈਕਟ) *n v* ਠੇਕਾ, ਇਕਰਾਰਨਾਮਾ, ਇਕਰਾਰ; ਠੇਕਾ ਦੇਣਾ ਜਾਂ ਲੈਣਾ; ਸੁੰਗੜਨਾ, ਸਿਮਟਣਾ, ਸੰਕੋਚ ਕਰਨਾ, ਸਕੁੰਚਤ ਕਰਨਾ; ਮਰੋੜਨਾ; **~ion** ਸੰਕੋਚ, ਸੁੰਗੇੜ, ਸੁੰਗੜਨ, ਸੁੰਗੜਾਉ; ਸੰਖੇਪ; ਠੇਕਾ ਕਰਨ ਦੀ ਕਿਰਿਆ; ਸੰਕੀਰਨਤਾ; ਖਿਚੋ, ਕਸ; **~or** ਠੇਕੇਦਾਰ, ਸੰਖਿਪਤ ਕਰਨ ਵਾਲਾ

contradict (ਕੌਨਟਰਾ'ਡਿਕਟ) *v* ਖੰਡਨ ਕਰਨਾ, ਰਦ ਕਰਨਾ, ਤਰਦੀਦ ਕਰਨੀ, ਮੁਕਰਨਾ, ਵਿਰੁੱਧ ਆਖਣਾ; **~ion** ਖੰਡਨ, ਇਨਕਾਰ, ਭਾਂਜੀ, ਵਿਰੋਧ, ਤਰਦੀਦ; **~ory** ਖੰਡਨਾਤਮਕ, ਅੰਤਰ-ਵਿਰੋਧੀ, ਪਰਸਪਰ ਵਿਰੁੱਧ, ਅਸੰਗਤ, ਉਲਟਾ

contrary (ਕੌਂਟਰਅਰਿ, ਕਆਂ'ਟਰੇਅਰਿ) *n a* ਪ੍ਰਤੀਕੂਲਤਾ, ਵਿਰੋਧ, ਵਿਪੱਖ, ਵਿਪਰੀਤਤਾ, ਉਲਟਾਪਣ; ਉਲਟਾ, ਪ੍ਰਤੀਕੂਲ, ਵਿਰੋਧੀ, ਅਸੰਗਤ

contrast (ਕੌਂਟਰਾਸਟ, ਕਆਂ'ਟਰਾਸਟ) *n v* ਟਾਕਰਾ, ਅੰਤਰ, ਭਿੰਨਤਾ, ਫ਼ਰਕ, ਭਿੰਨ-ਭੇਦ; ਅੰਤਰ ਹੋਣਾ, ਭਿੰਨਤਾ ਦੱਸਣੀ, ਵਖਰਾਉਣ; **~ing** ਵਿਰੋਧੀ, ਵਿਖਮ

contravene ('ਕੌਨਟਰਾ'ਵੀਨ) *v* ਹੁਕਮ ਅਦੂਲੀ ਕਰਨੀ, ਤੋੜਨਾ; ਖੰਡਨ ਕਰਨਾ, ਮੱਤ-ਭੇਦ ਹੋਣਾ; ਵਿਵਾਦ ਕਰਨਾ, ਟੇਕਣਾ

contravening (ਕੌਂਟਰਾ'ਵੀਨਿੰਡ) *a* ਪਰਸਪਰ ਵਿਰੋਧੀ

contribute (ਕਆਂ'ਟਰਿਬਯੂਟ) *v* ਚੰਦਾ ਦੇਣਾ, ਹਿੱਸਾ ਪਾਉਣਾ, (ਪੱਤਰ-ਪੱਤਰਕਾਵਾਂ ਨੂੰ) ਲੇਖ ਭੇਜਣਾ, ਪ੍ਰਦਾਨ ਕਰਨਾ

contribution (ਕਆਂ'ਟਰਿਬਯੂਸ਼ਨ) *n* ਚੰਦਾ, ਲੇਖ, ਸਹਾਇਤਾ, ਜ਼ਖ਼ੀਆ, ਮਸੂਲ, ਯੋਗ-ਦਾਨ

contributor (ਕਆਂ'ਟਰਿਬਯੂਟ*) *n* ਲੇਖ ਭੇਜਣ ਵਾਲਾ, ਯੋਗਦਾਨੀ, ਸਹਾਇਕ

control (ਕਆਨ'ਟਰਅਉਲ) *n v* ਕੰਟਰੋਲ, ਕਾਬੂ, ਵਸ, ਇਖਤਿਆਰ, ਨਿਗਰਾਨੀ, ਸ਼ਾਸਨ, ਜ਼ਬਤ; ਕਾਬੂ ਵਿਚ ਰੱਖਣਾ, ਬੰਨ੍ਹਣਾ, ਰੋਕਣਾ, ਸੰਜਮ ਕਰਨਾ, ਵੱਸ ਵਿਚ ਕਰਨਾ; **~ler** ਕੰਟਰੋਲਰ, ਨਾਜ਼ਰ

controversial (ਕੌਂਟਰਅ'ਵਅਃਸ਼ਲ) ਵਿਵਾਦਪੂਰਨ, ਬਹਿਸ-ਗੋਚਰਾ, ਤਕਰਾਰ ਵਾਲਾ, ਵਿਵਾਦਗ੍ਰਸਤ

controversy (ਕੌਂਟਰਅਵ੍ਅਃਸਿ) *n* ਝਗੜਾ, ਵਿਵਾਦ, ਚਰਚਾ, ਵਾਦ-ਵਿਵਾਦ, ਪ੍ਰਤੀਵਾਦ

convene (ਕਅਨ'ਵੀਨ) *v* ਸਮਾਗਮ ਬੁਲਾਉਣਾ ਇਕੱਠਾ ਕਰਨਾ, ਇਕੱਠੇ ਹੋਣਾ, ਜਲਸਾ ਕਰਨਾ ਸੱਦਣਾ; **~d** ਬੁਲਾਇਆ ਗਿਆ, ਆਯੋਜਤ; **~r** ਆਯੋਜਕ, ਸਮਾਗਮਕਰਤਾ, ਸੰਯੋਜਕ

convenience (ਕਅਨ'ਵੀਨਯਅੰਸ) *n* ਸਹੂਲਤ ਆਰਾਮ, ਸੌਖ, ਲਾਭ, ਸੁੱਖ, ਸੁਵਿਧਾ

convenient (ਕਅਨ'ਵੀਨਯਅੰਟ) *a* ਆਰਾਮਦੇਹ ਸਰਲ, ਸੌਖਾ, ਲਾਹੇਵੰਦ; ਸੁਖਾਲਾ, ਅਨੁਕੂਲ ਉਚਿਤ, ਸੁਵਿਧਾਜਨਕ

convention (ਕਅਨ'ਵੈਨਸ਼ਨ) *n* ਸਮਾਗਮ ਸੰਮੇਲਨ, ਸਭਾ, ਸੰਸਦ; ਸਮਝੌਤਾ, ਦਸਤੂਰ, ਪ੍ਰਥਾ ਮਰਯਾਦਾ, ਸੰਧੀ, ਜਨ-ਸਮਿਤੀ, ਇਕਰਾਰਨਾਮਾ

conventional (ਕਅਨ'ਵੈਨੱਸ਼ਅਨਲ) *a* ਰਸਮ ਰਿਵਾਜੀ, ਰਵਾਇਤੀ, ਰੀਤਵਾਦੀ, ਰੂੜ੍ਹੀਵਾਦੀ ਮਰਯਾਦਾ-ਪੂਰਨ, ਪਰੰਪਰਾਗਤ; **~ly** ਰੀਤ ਅਨੁਸਾਰ, ਪ੍ਰਥਾ ਅਨੁਸਾਰ

conversant (ਕਅਨ'ਵਅਃਸਅੰਟ) *a* ਜਾਣਕਾਰ ਵਾਕਫ਼, ਜਾਣੂ, ਵਾਕਫ਼ਕਾਰ, ਪਰਿਚਿਤ, ਨਿਪੁੰ

conversation (ਕੌਨਵ੍ਅ'ਸੇਇਸ਼ਨ)

ਵਾਰਤਾਲਾਪ, ਗੱਲਬਾਤ, ਗੱਲ-ਕੱਥ, ਗੁਫ਼ਤਗੂ

converse (ਕਅਨ'ਵਅ:ਸ, ਕੈਨਵਅ:ਸ) *v n a* ਗੱਲਾਂ ਕਰਨੀਆਂ, ਵਾਰਤਾਲਾਪ ਕਰਨੀ; ਉਲਟਾ ਮਸਲਾ, ਪਲਟਾ, ਉਲਟ, ਉਲਟਾ, ਸੁਧਾ, ਪੁੱਠ, ਵਿਪਰੀਤ

conversion (ਕਅਨ'ਵਅ:ਸ਼ਨ) *n* ਰੂਪਾਂਤਰਨ, ਧਰਮ ਦੀ ਬਦਲੀ, ਧਰਮ-ਪਰਿਵਰਤਨ, ਪਰਿਵਰਤਨ

convert (ਕੌਨਵਅ:ਟ, ਕਅਨ'ਵਅ:ਟ) *n v* ਨਵ-ਧਰਮੀ, ਧਰਮ ਬਦਲਾਊਣਾ, ਧਰਮ ਵਿਚ ਸ਼ਾਮਲ ਕਰਨ; (ਵਿਚ) ਬਦਲਣਾ; **~ed** ਪਰਿਵਰਤਤ, ਰੂਪਾਂਤਰਤ

convex (ਕੌਨ'ਵੈਕਸ) *a* ਉਭਰਿਆ, ਕੁੱਬਾ, ਕੁਬੰਦਾਰ, ਉਤੱਲ; ਉਭਾਰ, ਕੁੱਬ

convey (ਕਅਨ'ਵੇਇ) *v* ਲੈ ਜਾਣਾ, ਅਪੜਾ ਦੇਣਾ; ਪਹੁੰਚਾਉਣਾ, ਕਿਸੇ ਦੇ ਹੱਥੀਂ ਘੱਲਣਾ; ਹੱਥ ਬਦਲਣ; **~ance** ਗੱਡੀ, ਢੁਆਈ, ਵਾਹਣ

convict (ਕਅਨ'ਵਿਕਟ, ਕੌਨਵਿਕਟ) *v n* ਦੋਸ਼ੀ ਠਹਿਰਾਉਣਾ, ਸਜ਼ਾ ਸੁਣਾਉਣਾ; ਮੁਜਰਮ, ਕਸੂਰਵਾਰ, ਅਪਰਾਧੀ, ਦੋਸ਼ੀ

convince (ਕਅਨ'ਵਿੰਸ) *v* ਨਿਸ਼ਚਾ ਕਰਵਾਉਣਾ, ਮਨਵਾਉਣਾ, ਮੰਨ ਲੈਣਾ

convincible (ਕਅਨ'ਵਿੰਸਾਇਬਲ) *a* ਯਕੀਨ ਕਰਨ ਲਈ ਤਿਆਰ, ਮੰਨ ਲੈਣ ਵਾਲਾ, ਮੰਨਣਯੋਗ

convincing (ਕਅਨ'ਵਿੰਸਿਙ) *a* ਮੰਨਣਯੋਗ, ਯਕੀਨੀ, ਵਿਸ਼ਵਾਸਮਈ

convocation (ਕੈਨਵਅ(ਉ)ਕੇਇਸ਼ਨ) *n* ਦੀਖਿਆਂਤ-ਸਮਾਰੋਹ, ਪਾਦਰੀਆਂ ਦਾ ਜਲਸਾ; ਸੱਦਾ, ਸਮਾਗਮ, ਸੰਮੇਲਨ, ਸਮਾਰੋਹ

onvoy ('ਕੌਨਵੋਇ) *n v* ਵਪਾਰਕ ਬੇੜਾ, ਰੱਖਿਅਕ ਬੇੜਾ; ਫ਼ੌਜੀ ਦਸਤਾ ਜਾਂ ਰਸਦ ਦੇ ਸਾਮਾਨ ਦਾ ਕਾਫ਼ਲਾ; ਨਿਗਰਾਨੀ; ਰੱਖਿਆ ਵਾਸਤੇ ਨਾਲ ਜਾਣਾ, ਪਰਾਹੁਣਿਆਂ ਦੀ ਅਗਵਾਈ ਕਰਨੀ

cook (ਕੁਕ) *v n* ਰੋਟੀ ਪਕਾਉਣੀ, ਭੋਜਨ ਬਣਾਉਣਾ, ਪੱਕਣਾ, ਪਕਾਉਣਾ; ਮਨਘੜਤ ਗੱਲ ਕਰਨੀ; ਰਸੋਈਆ, ਲਾਂਗਰੀ, ਬਾਵਰਚੀ

cool (ਕੂਲ) *n a v* ਠੰਢ, ਸੀਤਲਤਾ; ਠੰਢਾ, ਠਰੁੰਮੇ ਵਾਲਾ, ਸ਼ਾਂਤ, ਮੰਦ, ਉਤਸਾਹਹੀਣ, ਉਦਾਸੀਨ, ਸੀਤਲ, ਸੀਤ; ਠੰਢਾ ਹੋਣਾ, ਧੀਮਾ ਕਰਨਾ, ਠਰੁੰਮਾ ਦੇਣਾ, ਠਰੁੰਮਾ ਰੱਖਣਾ; **~headed** ਸ਼ਾਂਤ, ਧੀਰਜਵਾਨ, ਠੰਢੇ ਦਿਲ ਵਾਲਾ; **~ness** ਠੰਢਕ, ਸੀਤਲਤਾ

coolie (ਕੂਲਿ) *n* ਪਾਂਡੀ, ਕੁਲੀ, ਪੱਲੇਦਾਰ

co-operate (ਕਅਉ'ਔਪਅਰੇਇਟ) *v* ਮਿਲ ਕੇ ਕੰਮ ਕਰਨਾ, ਸਹਿਕਾਰੀ ਹੋਣਾ, ਸਹਿਯੋਗ ਦੇਣਾ, ਮਿਲਵਰਤਨ ਕਰਨੀ

co-operation (ਕਅਉ'ਔਪਅ'ਰੇਇਸ਼ਨ) *n* ਮਿਲਵਰਤਨ, ਸਹਿਕਾਰਤਾ, ਸਹਿਯੋਗ, ਮੇਲ-ਮਿਲਾਪ

co-operative (ਕਅਉ'ਔਪ(ਅ)ਰਅਟਿਵ) *a* ਸਹਿਕਾਰੀ, ਸਹਿਯੋਗੀ; **~bank** ਸਹਿਕਾਰੀ ਬੈਂਕ, ਜ਼ਿੰਮੀਦਾਰ ਬੈਂਕ

co-opt (ਕਅਉ'ਔਪਟ) *v* ਨਾਮਜ਼ਦ ਕਰਨਾ, ਨਿਯੁਕਤ ਕਰਨਾ, ਨਾਲ ਰਲਾ ਲੈਣਾ, ਸੰਯੁਕਤ ਕਰਨਾ; **~ed** ਨਿਯੁਕਤ, ਜੋੜਿਆ, ਨਾਮਜ਼ਦ ਕੀਤਾ ਹੋਇਆ

co-ordinate (ਕਅਉ'ਓਡਨਅਟ, ਕਅਉ'ਓਡਅਨਅਟ, ਕਅਉ'ਓਡਿਨੇਇਟ) *a n v* ਸਮਾਨ, ਤੁਲ ਬਰਾਬਰ; ਇਕਸਾਰ; ਉਪਵਾਕ; ਸਮਾਨ ਕਰਨਾ, ਬਰਾਬਰ ਕਰ ਦੇਣਾ; ਇਕਸਾਰ ਕਰਨਾ, ਅਨੁਸਾਰਨਾ

co-ordination (ਕਅਉ'ਓਡਿ'ਨੇਇਸ਼ਨ) *n* ਤਾਲ-

ਮੇਲ, ਅਨੁਸਰਨ, ਇਕਸਾਰਤਾ, ਮੇਲ

co-ordinator (ਕਆਉੂ'ਉਡ਼ਨੇਟਅ*) *n* ਸੰਯੋਜਕ, ਤਾਲਮੇਲ ਕਰਨ ਵਾਲਾ

copper (ਕੋਪਅ*) *n a* ਤਾਂਬਾ; ਪੈਸਾ, ਪੁਲਸੀਆ; ~**smith** ਠਠਿਆਰ

copra (ਕੋਪਰਾ) *n* ਖੋਪਾ

copulate (ਕੋਪਯੁਲੇਇਟ) *v* ਸੰਭੋਗ ਕਰਨਾ, ਮੈਥੁਨ ਕਰਨਾ, ਸਹਿਵਾਸ ਕਰਨਾ

copulation (ਕੋਪਯੁ'ਲੇਇਸ਼ਨ) *n* ਸੰਜੋਗ, ਜੋੜ-ਮੇਲ, ਸੰਭੋਗ; ਮੈਥੁਨ, ਸਹਿਵਾਸ

copy (ਕੋਪਿ) *n v* ਉਤਾਰਾ, ਕਾਪੀ, ਨਕਲ, ਪਰਤ; ਉਤਾਰਨਾ, ਉਤਾਰਾ ਲਾਹੁਣਾ, ਕਾਪੀ ਕਰਨੀ, ਨਕਲ ਉਤਾਰਨੀ, ਪਰਤ ਤਿਆਰ ਕਰਨੀ, ਨਕਲ ਮਾਰਨੀ; ~**right** ਉਤਾਰਾ ਅਧਿਕਾਰ, ਕਾਪੀਰਾਈਟ; ~**ist** ਨਕਲ-ਨਵੀਸ, ਨਕਲ-ਉਤਾਰ; ਨਕਲਚੀ

coquetry (ਕੋਕਿਟਰਿ) *n* ਨਖ਼ਰਾ, ਨਖ਼ਰੇਬਾਜ਼ੀ, ਚੁਹਲ

coquette (ਕੋ'ਕੇਟ) *n* ਨਖ਼ਰੇਬਾਜ਼, ਚੋਂਚਲੇਬਾਜ਼, ਅਲਬੇਲਾ, ਬਾਂਕਾ

coral (ਕੋਰ(ਅ)ਲ) *n* ਮੂੰਗਾ

cord (ਕੋਡ) *n v* ਰੱਸੀ, ਡੋਰੀ, ਰੱਸਾ, ਪੱਠਾ; ਤੜ ਬੰਨ੍ਹਣਾ, ਜਕੜਨਾ

cordial (ਕੋਡਯਅਲ) *a n* ਦਿਲੀ, ਹਾਰਦਿਕ; ਨਿਸ਼ਕਪਟ, ਦੋਸਤਾਨਾ, ਸਨੇਹਪੂਰਨ, ਨਿੱਘ; ~**ly** ਦਿਲੋਂ, ਪਰੇਮ ਨਾਲ, ਸੁਹਿਰਦਤਾ ਨਾਲ

core (ਕੋ*) *n v* ਗਿਰੀ, ਮਜ਼ਗ, ਗੁੱਦਾ, ਗੁਲੀ, ਸਾਰ, ਤੱਤ, ਗੁੱਦਾ ਕੱਢਣਾ

co-relation (ਕਾਓੂਰਿ'ਲੇਇਸ਼ਨ) *n* ਆਪਸੀ ਸਬੰਧ, ਪਰਸਪਰ ਸਬੰਧ

cork (ਕੋਕ) *n a v* ਕਾਕ, ਡੱਟ; ਕਾਕ ਦਾ, ਕਾਕ ਤੋਂ ਬਣਿਆ; ਕਾਕ ਲਾਉਣਾ, ਡੱਟ ਦੇਣਾ, ਟੇਢਾ ਚੱਲਣਾ, ਰੋਕਣਾ

corn (ਕੋਨ) *n v* ਦਾਣੇ, ਅੰਨ, ਅਨਾਜ, (US) ਮੱਕੀ; ਨਮਕ ਛਿੜਕਨਾ; ~**flour** (ਮੱਕੀ ਆਦਿ ਦਾ) ਆਟਾ

corner (ਕੋ*ਨਅ*) *n v* ਨੁੱਕਰ, ਗੁੱਠ, ਖੁੰਜਾ, ਕੋਨਾ ਗੋਸ਼ਾ, ਗੁਪਤ ਥਾਂ; ਨੁੱਕਰਾਂ ਕੱਢਣੀਆਂ, ਘੇਰ ਲੈਣਾ; ~**boy** ਅਵਾਰਾ, ਲੋਫਰ

coronation (ਕੋਰਅ'ਨੇਇਸ਼ਨ) *n* ਰਾਜ ਤਿਲਕ ਤਖ਼ਤ ਨਸ਼ੀਨੀ, ਤਾਜਪੋਸ਼ੀ ਦੀ ਰਸਮ

corporation (ਕੋ*ਪਅ'ਰੇਇਸ਼ਨ) *n* ਨਿਗਮ, ਮਹਾਂ ਨਗਰ ਸਭਾ, ਕਾਰਪੋਰੇਸ਼ਨ; ~**municipal** ਨਗਰਪਾਲਕਾ, ਨਿਗਮ

corps (ਕੋ*) *n* ਪਲਟਨ, ਫ਼ੌਜ ਦਾ ਦਸਤਾ, ਕੋਰ

corpse (ਕੋ*ਪਸ) *n* ਲੋਥ, ਲਾਸ਼, ਮਿਰਤਕ ਸਰੀਰ

corpus (ਕੋ*ਪਅਸ) *n* ਸਰੀਰ, ਦੇਹ, ਪੁਸਤਕਾਂ ਦਾ ਸੰਗ੍ਰਹ

correct (ਕਅ'ਰੇਕੱਟ) *a v* ਸਹੀ, ਸਿੱਧ, ਠੀਕ, ਚੁੱਕਵਾਂ ਉਚਿਤ, ਸ਼ੁੱਧ; ਸਹੀ ਕਰਨਾ, ਠੀਕ ਕਰਨਾ, ਯੋਗ ਬਣਾਉਣਾ, ਸੁਆਰਨਾ, ਸੁਪਾਰਨਾ; ~**ion** ਸੁਧਾਈ ਸੋਧ, ਸੰਸ਼ੋਧਨ, ਦਰੁਸਤੀ, ਸੁਧਾਰ, ਝਿੜਕ

correlate ('ਕੋਰਅਲੇਇਟ) *v* ਸਹਿ-ਸਬੰਧਤ ਹੋਣ ਪਰਸਪਰ ਸਬੰਧ ਕਾਇਮ ਕਰਨਾ, ਦੋ ਚੀਜ਼ਾਂ ਦ ਇਕ ਦੂਜੇ ਦੇ ਸਹਾਰੇ ਹੋਣਾ

correlation ('ਕੋਰਅ'ਲੇਇਸ਼ਨ) *n* ਪਰਸਪ ਸਬੰਧ, ਆਪਸੀ ਮੇਲ, ਸਹਿ-ਸਬੰਧ

correspond ('ਕੋਰਿ'ਸਪੌਂਡ) *v* ਅਨੁਸਾਰੀ ਹੋਣਾ, ਜੋ ਹੋਣਾ, ਬਰਾਬਰ ਹੋਣਾ; ਚਿੱਠੀ ਪੱਤਰ ਲਿਖਣ ~**ence** ਅਨੁਸਰਨ; ਲਿਖਤ-ਪੜ੍ਹਤ, ਪੱਤ ਵਿਹਾਰ, ਚਿੱਠੀ ਚਪੱਠੀ, ~**ent** ਅਨੁਸਾਰੀ; ਪੱਤਰ ਪੇਰਕ; ਨਾਮਾਨਿਗਾਰ, ਸੰਵਾਦਦਾਤਾ; ਆੜ੍ਹਤੀਅ

corrigendum ('ਕੋਰਿ'ਜੇਂਡਅਮ) *n* ਸ਼ੁੱਧੀ ਸੂਚ

ਸੂਚੀ ਪੱਤਰ, ਸੰਸ਼ੋਧਨ, ਸੁਧਾਰ

corroborate (ਕਅ'ਰੌਬਅਰੇਇਟ) *v* ਪ੍ਰੋੜ੍ਹਤਾ ਕਰਨੀ, ਪੱਕਾ ਕਰਨਾ, ਤਸਦੀਕ ਕਰਨੀ, ਤਾਈਦ ਕਰਨੀ, ਹਾਮੀ ਭਰਨੀ

corroborator (ਕਅ'ਰੌਬਅਰੇਇਟਅ*) *n* ਪੁਸ਼ਟੀਕਾਰ, ਪੁਸ਼ਟੀ ਕਰਨ ਵਾਲਾ, ਸਾਖੀ, ਸਮਰਥਕ

corrupt (ਕਅ'ਰਅੱਪਟ) *a* ਵੱਢੀ-ਖੋਰ, ਹਰਾਮ-ਖੋਰ, ਖੋਟਾ, ਮਾੜਾ; ਰਿਸ਼ਵਤਖੋਰ, ਬਦਕਾਰ; ਵੱਢੀ ਦੇਣੀ; ਵਿਗਾੜਨਾ, ਖਰਾਬ ਹੋਣਾ, ਰੁਕਣਾ; ~ion ਵੱਢੀਖੋਰੀ, ਹਰਾਮਖੋਰੀ, ਖ਼ਰਾਬੀ, ਰਿਸ਼ਵਤ ਖੋਰੀ; ਅਪਭ੍ਰਸ਼ਟ ਸ਼ਬਦ

cortege (ਕੋ*ਟਿਏਜ਼) *n* ਨੌਕਰ-ਚਾਕਰ, ਅਮਲਾ-ਫੈਲਾ

cosmetic (ਕੌਜ਼'ਮੈਟਿਕ) *a n* ਸ਼ੋਭਾਜਨਕ, ਸ਼ਿੰਗਾਰ ਪੂਰਨ

cosmic ('ਕੌਜ਼ਮਿਕ) *a* ਬ੍ਰਹਿਮੰਡੀ

cosmonaut (ਕੌਜ਼ਮਅਨੌਟ) *n* ਪੁਲਾੜ ਯਾਤਰੀ

cosmopolitan ('ਕੌਜ਼ਮਆ'ਪੌਲਿਟ(ਅ)ਨ) *n* ਵਿਸ਼ਵਪਰੇਮੀ, ਵਿਸ਼ਵ ਨਾਗਰਿਕ

cosmos ('ਕੌਜ਼ਮੌਸ) *n* ਬ੍ਰਹਿਮੰਡ, ਸੰਸਾਰ, ਸ੍ਰਿਸ਼ਟੀ, ਵਿਆਪਕਤਾ

cost (ਕੌਸਟ) *n v* ਮੁੱਲ, ਲਾਗਤ, ਦਾਮ, ਕੀਮਤ, ਖ਼ਰਚ; ਮੁੱਲ ਤਾਰਨਾ, ਪੈਸੇ ਖ਼ਰਚ ਕਰਨੇ, ਮੁੱਲ ਕਰਾਉਣਾ, ਕੀਮਤ ਨਿਸ਼ਚਤ ਕਰਨੀ; ~ac- countant ਲਾਗਤ-ਲੇਖਾਕਾਰ, ਮੁਨੀਮ, ਤਾਲੁਕ; ~book ਖਾਤ-ਖਾਤਾ, ਖਦਾਨ-ਖਾਤਾ; at the ~ of ਨੁਕਸਾਨ ਸਹਿ ਕੇ; at all ~s ਹਰ ਹਾਲਤ ਵਿਚ; ~less ਅਣਮੁੱਲਾ, ਮੁਫ਼ਤ; ~ly ਬਹੁਮੁੱਲਾ, ਕੀਮਤੀ, ਵਡਮੁੱਲਾ, ਮਹਿੰਗਾ

cosy ('ਕਅਉਜ਼ਿ) *a n* ਸੁਖਦਾਈ (ਥਾਂ), ਨਿੱਘਾ, ਆਰਾਮ ਦੇਹ; ਸਨੇਹਪੂਰਨ

cot (ਕੌਟ) *n* ਮੰਜਾ, ਮੰਜੀ, ਬੱਚਿਆਂ ਦਾ ਝੂਲਾ, ਖਟੋਲਾ

coterie (ਕਅਉਟਰਿ) *n* ਜੁੰਡਲੀ, ਚੰਡਾਲ-ਚੌਕੜੀ, ਟੋਲਾ

cottage ('ਕੌਟਿਜ) *n* ਕੁੱਟੀ, ਕੁਟੀਆ, ਛੱਪਰ, ਝੁੱਪੜੀ, ਛੋਟਾ ਘਰ, ਪੇਂਡੂ ਮਕਾਨ

cotton ('ਕੌਟਨ) *n v* ਰੂੰ, ਢੰਬਾ, ਕਪਾਹ, ਸੂਤ, ਧਾਗਾ, ਸੂਤੀ ਧਾਗਾ, ਸੂਤੀ ਕੱਪੜ; ਸੰਮਤੀ ਹੋਣੀ, ਸੁਰਮੇਲ ਹੋਣਾ, ਰਾਇ ਮਿਲਣੀ; ~cake ਖਲ (ਵੜੇਵਿਆਂ ਦੀ); ~yarn ਧਾਗਾ

cough (ਕੌਫ) *n v* ਖੰਘ, ਖਾਂਸੀ; ਖੰਘਾਰ; ਖੰਘਣਾ, ਖੰਘੂਰਾ ਮਾਰਨਾ, ਖੰਘਾਰਨਾ, ਖਉ ਖਉ ਕਰਨਾ

council ('ਕਾਉਂਸਲ) *n* ਕੌਂਸਲ, ਸਭਾ, ਪਰਿਸ਼ਦ, ਕਮੇਟੀ, ਸਮਿਤੀ

counsel ('ਕਾਉਂਸਲ) *n* ਮਸ਼ਵਰਾ, ਸਲਾਹ; ਕਾਨੂੰਨੀ ਸਲਾਹਕਾਰ, ਵਕੀਲ; ਸਲਾਹ ਦੇਣਾ, ਮਸ਼ਵਰਾ ਦੇਣਾ, ਰਾਇ ਦੇਣਾ, ਸਮਝਾਉਣਾ; ~lor ਸਲਾਹਕਾਰ, ਉਪਦੇਸ਼ਕ, ਵਕੀਲ

count (ਕਾਉਂਟ) *n v* ਗਿਣਤੀ, ਗਣਨਾ; ਸੰਖਿਆ, ਤਾਦਾਦ; ਕੁੱਲ ਜੋੜ, ਪੂਰਨ ਸੰਖਿਆ; ਲੇਖਾ, ਹਿਸਾਬ; ਮੁਆਮੀ; ~less ਅਣਗਿਣਤ; ਅਸੰਖ, ਸੰਖਿਆਤੀਤ, ਬੇਹਿਸਾਬ, ਬੇਸ਼ੁਮਾਰ; ਗਿਣਤੀ ਹਿਸਾਬ ਕਰਨਾ, ਹਿਸਾਬ ਲਗਾਉਣਾ ਗਿਣਤੀ ਕਰਨਾ, ਸ਼ੁਮਾਰ ਕਰਨਾ, ਸੋਚਣਾ, ਵਿਚਾਰਨਾ, ਖ਼ਿਆਲ ਕਰਨਾ

counter (ਕਾਉਂਟ*) *n a v* (ਬੈਂਕ, ਦੁਕਾਨ ਆਦਿ ਦਾ) ਕਾਊਂਟਰ; ਜੁੱਤੀ ਦੀ ਅੱਡੀ; ਗਿਨਣ ਵਾਲਾ; ਵਿਪਰੀਤ, ਉਲਟਾ, ਪ੍ਰਤੀਕੂਲ, ਵਿਰੋਧੀ; ਦੋਹਰਾ; ਵਿਰੋਧ ਕਰਨਾ; ਰੱਦ ਕਰਨਾ; ਰੋਕਣਾ; ਵਿਪਰੀਤ ਚਲਣਾ; ~action ਰੋਕ, ਰੁਕਾਵਟ, ਵਿਰੋਧ;

~attack ਜਵਾਬੀ ਹਮਲਾ; ~sign ਪ੍ਰਤੀਪੁਸ਼ਟੀ ਕਰਨਾ

country ('ਕਅੰਟਰਿ) n ਦੇਸ਼, ਮੁਲਕ, ਵਤਨ; ਰਾਸ਼ਟਰ, ਪਿੰਡ, ਦੇਹਾਤੀ ਖੇਤਰ; ~side ਪਿੰਡ ਦਾ ਇਲਾਕਾ, ਪਿੰਡ

coup (ਕੂ) n ਚਾਲ, ਕਾਰੀ ਚੋਟ, ਰਾਜ ਪਲਟਾ

coup d'etat ('ਕੂਡੇਇ'ਟਾ) (F) n ਰਾਜ ਪਲਟਾ, ਰਾਜਗਰਦੀ

couple ('ਕਅੱਪਲ) n v ਜੋੜਾ, ਪਤੀ-ਪਤਨੀ, ਲਾੜਾ ਲਾੜੀ, ਦੰਪੱਤੀ; ਗੰਢਣਾ, ਸਬੰਧ ਜੋੜਨਾ, ਸੰਭੋਗ ਕਰਨਾ

couplet ('ਕਅੱਪਲਿਟ) ਬੈਂਤ, ਦੋਹਰਾ

coupon ('ਕੂਪੌਨ) n ਕੂਪਨ, ਪਰਚੀ, ਟਿਕਟ

courage ('ਕਅੱਰਿਜ) n ਹਿੰਮਤ, ਸਾਹਸ, ਹੌਸਲਾ, ਜਿਗਰਾ, ਹੀਆ, ਮਰਦਾਨਗੀ, ਬਹਾਦਰੀ

courageous (ਕਅ'ਰੇਇਜਅਸ) a ਸਾਹਸੀ, ਜਿਗਰੇ ਵਾਲਾ, ਹਿੰਮਤੀ, ਬਹਾਦਰ, ਦਲੇਰ ਦਿਲਾਵਰ; ~ness ਦਲੇਰੀ, ਨਿਰਭੀਰਤਾ, ਸਾਹਸ, ਹਿੰਮਤ, ਹੀਆ

courier (ਕੁਰਿਅ*) n ਹਰਕਾਰਾ

course (ਕੋ*ਸ) n ਪਾਠ-ਕ੍ਰਮ ਚਾਲ, ਰਫ਼ਤਾਰ; ਰਾਹ, ਰਵੱਸ਼; ਖੋਡ-ਦੋੜ ਦਾ ਮੈਦਾਨ; ਦਿਸ਼ਾ; ਪਾਣੀ ਦਾ ਰਾਹ, ਖਾਣੇ ਦਾ ਦੋਰ; ਰੀਤ, ਰਸਮ, ਮਾਹਵਾਰੀ; ~of action ਕਿਰਿਆ-ਵਿਧੀ; of ~ ਕੁਦਰਤੀ, ਨਿਸ਼ਚੇ ਹੀ

court (ਕੋ*ਟ) n v (1) ਵਿਹੜਾ, ਆਂਗਣ; (2) ਟੈਨਿਸ ਖੇਡਣ ਦਾ ਮੈਦਾਨ; (3) ਸ਼ਾਹੀ ਦਰਬਾਰ, ਦਰਬਾਰੀ, ਖ਼ੁਸ਼ਾਮਦ ਕਰਨੀ, ਚਾਪਲੂਸੀ ਕਰਨੀ, ਰੀਝਾਉਣਾ, ਪਰੇਮ ਕਰਨਾ; (4) ਅਦਾਲਤ, ਕਚਹਿਰੀ; ~yard ਵਿਹੜਾ, ਆਂਗਣ, ਦਲਾਨ, ਘਰ ਦੇ ਬਾਹਰ ਦੇ ਸਿਹਨ; civil~ ਦੀਵਾਨੀ ਅਦਾਲਤ; criminal ਫ਼ੋਜਦਾਰੀ ਅਦਾਲਤ; high~ ਹਾਈਕੋਰਟ, ਉਚ ਨਿਆਇਆਲਾ; supreme~ ਸੁਪਰੀਮ ਕੋਰਟ, ਸਰਵ-ਉਚ ਨਿਆਇਆਲਾ; ~ship ਵਿਆਹ ਤੋਂ ਪਹਿਲਾਂ ਪਿਆਰ

courteous ('ਕਅ:ਟਯਅਸ) a ਸ਼ਿਸ਼ਟ, ਨਿਮਰ, ਭੱਦਰ, ਮਿਲਣਸਾਰ; ਮੁਲਾਹਜ਼ੇਦਾਰ, ਧੀਮਾ

courtesy ('ਕਅ:ਟਿਸਿ) n ਮੂੰਹ-ਮੁਲਾਹਜ਼ਾ, ਸ਼ਿਸ਼ਟਤਾ, ਭੱਦਰਤਾ, ਨਿਮਰਤਾ, ਸ਼ਰਾਫਤ

cousin ('ਕਅੱਜ਼ਨ) n ਮਸੇਰ, ਫਫੇਰ, ਚਚੇਰੇ ਭਰਾ ਜਾਂ ਭੈਣ

covenant ('ਕਅਵਨਅੰਟ) n v ਪ੍ਰਤਿੰਗਿਆ; ਇਕਰਾਰ ਨਾਮਾ; ਇਕਰਾਰ ਕਰਨਾ

cover ('ਕਅੱਵ*) n v ਢੱਕਣ, ਕੱਜਣ, ਉਢਾਉਣ ਗਿਲਾਫ, ਲਿਫ਼ਾਫ਼ਾ, ਮੇਜ਼ਪੋਸ਼ ਆਤ, ਓਟ, ਰੋਕ; ਢਕਣਾ, ਕੱਜਣਾ, ਲੁਕਾਉਣਾ, ਛੁਪਣਾ; ਛਾ ਜਾਣਾ; ਕਾਫ਼ੀ ਹੋਣਾ, ਘਟਨਾ, ਅੰਡੇ ਸਿਉਣਾ; ਸ਼ਾਮਲ ਹੋਣਾ; (ਫ਼ਾਸਲਾ ਤੈ ਕਰਨਾ; (ਵਿਸ਼ਾ ਆਦਿ) ਨਿਭਾਉਣਾ; ~ed ਢਕਿਆ ਹੋਇਆ, ਅੰਤਰਗਤ; ~ing ਚਾਦਰ, ਪਰਦਾ, ਆਵਰਣ; ~let ਗਿਲਾਫ, ਉਢਾਣ, ਚਾਦਰ

covert ('ਕਅਵਅਟ, 'ਕਅੱਵ*) a n ਲੁਕਵਾਂ, ਗੁੱਝਾ, ਗੁਪਤ, ਝਾੜੀ; ਓਟ, ਪਨਾਹ, ਆਸਰਾ; ~ure ਆਸਰਾ, ਪਨਾਹ; ਸੁਹਾਗ

covet ('ਕਅੱਵਿਟ) v ਲੋਡੀ ਹੋਣਾ, ਹਿਰਸ ਕਰਨੀ; ਤਮਾਂ ਕਰਨੀ, ਲਾਲਚ ਕਰਨਾ, ਚਾਹੁਣ; ~ous ਲੋੜੀ, ਹਿਰਸੀ, ਲਾਲਚੀ, ਹਵਸੀ

cow (ਕਾਊ) n v ਗਾਂ, ਗਊ, ਢੱਗੀ; ਡਰਾਉਣਾ, ਧਮਕਾਉਣਾ, ਜ਼ਰਕਾਉਣਾ, ਰੋਹਬ ਦੇਣਾ; ~boy ਗਵਾਲਾ, ਚਾਕ, ਪਾਲੀ, ਵਾਗੀ, ਛੇਡੂ, ਚਰਵਾਹਾ; ~dung ਗੋਹਾ, ਗੋਬਰ; ~herd ਚਰਵਾਹਾ

coward ('ਕਾਊਅਡ) n a ਡਰਾਕਲ, ਡਰੂ, ਡਰਪੋਕ ਕਾਇਰ, ਬੁਜ਼ਦਿਲ

coy (ਕੌਇ) *a* ਸੰਗਾਉ, ਸ਼ਰਮਾਕਲ, ਲੱਜਾਵਾਨ; (ਥਾਂ) ਲੁਕਵੀਂ, ਇਕਵਾਂਝੀ

crab (ਕਰੈਬ) *n v* ਕੇਕੜਾ, ਜੰਗਲੀ ਸਿਉ; ਸੜੀਅਲ, ਭਾਰ ਚੁੱਕਣ ਵਾਲਾ ਜੰਤਰ; ਨਿੰਦਾ ਕਰਨੀ; ਖਿਝਾਣਾ, ਪੰਜੇ ਮਾਰਨ, ਧੱਜੀਆਂ ਉਡਾਉਣੀਆਂ

crack (ਕਰੈਕ) *n a v* ਦਰਜ, ਤੇੜੇ, ਦਰਾੜ, ਫੱਟ, ਧਮਾਕਾ, ਕੜਕ; ਚੋਟਵਾਂ, ਜ਼ੋਰ ਦਾ; ਨਿਪੁੰਨ; ਕੜਕਾਉਣਾ, ਤਿੜਕਾਉਣਾ, ਫੱਟ ਲਾਉਣਾ, ਤੇੜੇ ਪਾਉਣੀ; ਕੜਕਣਾ; ~a joke ਠੱਠਾ-ਮਜ਼ਾਕ ਕਰਨਾ, ਮਖੌਲ ਕਰਨਾ; ~ed (ਅਾਡ) ਪਾਗਲ, ਉਨਮੱਤ; ~er ਪਟਾਕਾ, ਤਿੜਤਿੜੀ, ਧਮਾਕਾ, ਗੋਲਾ (ਆਤਸ਼-ਬਾਜ਼ੀ); ਕਰਾਰਾ ਬਿਸਕੁਟ; ~ers (ਅਪ) ਝੱਲਾ, ਸਨਕੀ

cradle ('ਕਰੇਇਡਲ) *n v* ਝੂਲ਼ਾ; ਖਟੋਲਾ, ਪੰਘੂੜਾ; ਪੰਘੂੜੇ ਵਿਚ ਪਾਉਣਾ, ਪਾਲਣ ਪੋਸ਼ਣ ਕਰਨਾ; a child in~ ਦੁੱਧ ਪੀਂਦਾ ਬੱਚਾ; from the-~ ਬਚਪਨ ਤੋਂ

craft (ਕਰਾਫ਼ਟ) *n* ਪੇਸ਼ਾ, ਧੰਦਾ, ਸ਼ਿਲਪਕਾਰੀ, ਹੁਨਰਮੰਦੀ, ਕਾਰੀਗਰੀ, ਹਵਾਈ ਜਹਾਜ਼; ~sman ਸ਼ਿਲਪਕਾਰ, ਸ਼ਿਲਪੀ, ਦਸਤਕਾਰ, ਕਾਰੀਗਰ; ~smanship ਦਸਤਕਾਰੀ, ਕਾਰੀਗਰੀ; ~y ਚਾਲਬਾਜ਼, ਛਲੀਆ, ਕਪਟੀ, ਫ਼ਰੇਬੀ, ਮੱਕਾਰ; ਨਿਪੁੰਨ

cram (ਕਰੈਮ) *n v* ਭੀੜ, ਜਮਘਟਾ; ਝੂਠ; ਘੋਟ, ਰੱਟਾ; ਤੁੰਣਨਾ, ਠੂੰਸਣਾ, ਰਟਣਾ, ਘੋਟਾ ਲਾਉਣਾ; ~mer ਘੋਟੂ, ਰੱਟੂ

crane (ਕਰੇਨ) *n v* ਭਾਰ ਆਦਿ ਚੁੱਕਣ ਵਾਲਾ ਜੰਤਰ, ਕਰੇਨ; ਸਾਰਸ, ਲਮਢੀਂਗ; ਕਰੇਨ ਨਾਲ ਭਾਰ ਚੁੱਕਣਾ; ਸਾਰਸ ਵਾਂਗ ਧੌਣ ਅੱਗੇ ਨੂੰ ਕਰਨਾ

crank (ਕਰੈਂਕ) *n v a* ਪੁਰੇ ਦੀ ਕੂਹਣੀ ਦਾ ਸਿਰਾ, ਗੱਲ ਦਾ ਫੇਰ ਜਾਂ ਪੇਚ, ਕੂਹਨੀਦਾਰ ਬਣਾਉਣਾ, ਮੋੜਨਾ; (ਮਸ਼ੀਨਰੀ) ਢਿੱਲੀ; ਖ਼ਬਤੀ; ~y ਢਿੱਲਾ, ਕਮਜ਼ੋਰ, ਥੋੜਾ, ਖ਼ਬਤੀ, ਪਾਗਲ, ਸਨਕੀ, ਵਹਿਮੀ

crash (ਕਰੈਸ਼) *n v* ਤਬਾਹੀ, ਬਰਬਾਦੀ, ਧਮਾਕਾ, ਡਿੱਗਣਾ, ਟੁੱਟਣਾ

crave (ਕਰੇਇਵ) *v* ਲਾਲਸਾ ਕਰਨਾ, ਤਰਸਣਾ, ਜਾਚਨਾ ਕਰਨੀ, ਤਰਲਾ ਕਰਨਾ

craving ('ਕਰੇਇਵਿੰਡ) *n* ਲਾਲਸਾ, ਅਭਿਲਾਸ਼ਾ, ਸਿੱਕ, ਤਾਂਘ, ਲਲੂਕ

crawl *v n* ਹੌਲੀ ਹੌਲੀ ਟੁਰਨਾ, ਪੇਟ ਦੇ ਭਾਰ ਟੁਰਨਾ; ਥੋੜੇ ਪਾਣੀ ਵਾਲਾ ਟੋਭਾ (ਮੱਛੀਆਂ ਫੜਨ ਲਈ)

craze (ਕਰੇਇਜ਼) *v n* ਮੱਤ ਮਾਰਨੀ, ਪਾਗਲ ਬਣਾ ਦੇਣਾ; ਵਹਿਮ, ਸਨਕ, ਖ਼ਬਤ, ਪਾਗਲਪਨ

crazy ('ਕਰੇਇਜ਼ਿ) *a* ਖ਼ਬਤੀ, ਸ਼ੁਦਾਈ, ਝੱਲਾ, ਕਮਲਾ, ਠਰਕੀ, ਸਨਕੀ

cream (ਕਰੀਮ) *n v* ਮਲਾਈ, ਕਰੀਮ; ਸਾਰ, ਤੱਤ; ਮਲਾਈ ਆਉਣੀ; ਤੱਤ ਕੱਢਣਾ, ਨਿਚੋੜ ਕੱਢਣਾ

crease (ਕਰੀਸ) *n v* ਵੱਟ, ਕਰੀਜ਼, ਸਲਵਟ; ਸਿਕਨ; ਵੱਟ ਪਾਉਣੇ ਜਾਂ ਪੈਣੇ, ਗਲਵਟ ਪਾਉਣੇ

creasy ('ਕਰੀਸਿ) *a* ਭਾਨ ਵਾਲਾ, ਵੱਟਦਾਰ, ਝੁਰੜੀਆਂ ਵਾਲਾ

create (ਕਰੀ'ਏਇਟ) *v* ਉਤਪੰਨ ਕਰਨਾ, ਬਣਾਉਣਾ, ਉਪਜਾਉਣਾ, ਰਚਣਾ, ਸਿਰਜਣਾ

creation (ਕਰਿ'ਏਇਸ਼ਨ) *n* ਉਪਜ, ਰਚਨਾ, ਸਿਰਜਣਾ, ਉਤਪਤੀ, ਸ੍ਰਿਸ਼ਟੀ

creative (ਕਰੀ'ਏਇਟਿਵ) *a* ਸਿਰਜਣਾਤਮਕ, ਰਚਨਾਤਮਕ, ਸਿਰਜਨਸ਼ੀਲ, ਉਤਪਾਦਕ

creator (ਕਰਿ'ਏਇਟਅ*) *n* ਸਿਰਜਨਹਾਰ,

ਸਿਸ਼ਟਾ, ਕਰਤਾਰ, ਜਨਮਦਾਤਾ

creature ('ਕਰੀਚਅ*) *n* ਜੀਵ, ਜੀਉੜਾ, ਪ੍ਰਾਣੀ

creche (ਕਰੈੱਸ਼) *n* ਬਾਲਵਾੜੀ

credential (ਕਰਿ'ਡੈਂਸ਼ਲ) *n* ਪਰੀਚੇ ਪੱਤਰ, ਸਨਦ, ਜਾਣ ਪਛਾਣ ਦੀ ਚਿੱਠੀ, ਵਸੀਕਾ

credibility ('ਕਰੈੱਡਅ'ਬਿਲਅਟਿ) *n* ਸ਼ਾਖ, ਪ੍ਰਤੀਤ

credible ('ਕਰੈੱਡਿਅਬਲ) *a* ਮੰਨਣਯੋਗ, ਭਰੋਸੇਯੋਗ, ਇਤਬਾਰੀ, ਵਿਸ਼ਵਾਸਯੋਗ

credit ('ਕਰੈੱਡਿਟ) *n v* ਭਰੋਸਾ, ਇਤਬਾਰ, ਯਕੀਨ, ਸਾਖ; ਭਰੋਸਾ ਕਰਨਾ, ਇਤਬਾਰ ਕਰਨਾ, ਮੰਨ ਲੈਣਾ, ਲੇਖੇ ਵਿਚ ਜੋੜਨਾ, ਖਾਤੇ ਵਿਚ ਜਾਮੁਂ ਕਰਨਾ; ~**account** ਵਹੀ-ਖਾਤਾ; ~**bill** ਹੁੰਡੀ; **letter of**~ ਹੁੰਡੀ; ~**able** ਸ਼ੋਭਨੀਕ, ਪ੍ਰਸੰਸਾਯੋਗ ਵਡਿਆਉਣ ਯੋਗ; ~**or** ਲੈਣਦਾਰ, (ਸ਼ਾਹੂਕਾਰ)

creed (ਕਰੀਡ) *n* ਦੀਨ, ਮੱਤ, ਧਰਮ, ਸੰਪਰਦਾਇ

creep (ਕਰੀਪ) *n v* ਝੁਟਝੁਟੀ; ਖਿਸਰਨਾ, ਪੇਟ ਦੇ ਭਾਰ ਟੁਰਨਾ, ਹੌਲੀ ਹੌਲੀ ਟੁਰਨਾ, ਜੂੰ ਦੀ ਟੋਰ ਟੁਰਨਾ, ਘਸਣਾ; ~**er** ਘਸਰ ਕੇ ਟੁਰਨ ਵਾਲਾ, ਵੇਲ; ~**y** ਘਸ ਦੇ ਟੁਰਨ ਵਾਲਾ; ਪੇਟ ਦੇ ਭਾਰ ਟੁਰਨ ਵਾਲਾ, ਸਰੀਰ ਨੂੰ ਸੁੰਨ ਕਰ ਦੇਣ ਵਾਲਾ, ਲੂੰ ਕੰਡੇ ਖੜ੍ਹੇ ਕਰਨ ਵਾਲਾ; ਸ਼ੰਕਾਜਨਕ

cremate (ਕਰਿ'ਮੇਇਟ) *v* ਸਸਕਾਰ ਕਰਨਾ, ਦਾਗ ਦੇਣਾ

cremation (ਕਰਿ'ਮੇਇਸ਼ਨ) *n* ਦਾਹ-ਸਸਕਾਰ, ਦਾਹ-ਕਿਰਿਆ

crematory (ਕਰਿਮਅਟਰਿ) *n* ਸ਼ਮਸ਼ਾਨ ਭੂਮੀ

crematorium ('ਕਰੈੱਮਅ'ਟੋਰਿਅਮ) *n* ਸ਼ਮਸ਼ਾਨ ਘਾਟ

crest (ਕਰੈੱਸਟ) *n* ਚੋਟੀ, ਸਿਖਰ; ਕਲਗੀ, ਤਾਜ

crew (ਕਰੂ) *n* ਜਹਾਜ਼ੀ ਅਮਲਾ, ਮੱਲਾਹ; ਟੋਲਾ, ਜੱਥਾ

cricket ('ਕਰਿਕਿਟ) *n* ਕ੍ਰਿਕਟ, ਬੱਲੇ ਤੇ ਗੇਂਦ ਦੀ ਖੇਡ; ਟਿੱਡਾ, ਝੀਂਗਰ

crime (ਕਰਾਇਮ) *n v* ਜੁਰਮ, ਦੋਸ਼, ਅਪਰਾਧ, ਕਾਨੂੰਨ ਵਿਰੁੱਧ ਕੰਮ; ਦੋਸ਼ੀ ਠਹਿਰਾਉਣਾ, ਦੋਸ਼ ਮੜਨਾ

criminal ('ਕਰਿਮਿਨਲ) *n a* ਮੁਜਰਮ, ਦੋਸ਼ੀ, ਅਪਰਾਧੀ, ਗੁਨਾਹਗਾਰ, (ਮੁਕੱਦਮਾ) ਫ਼ੌਜਦਾਰੀ

crimson ('ਕਰਿਮਜ਼ਨ) *n a v* ਉਦਾ ਰੰਗ, ਕਿਰਮਚੀ ਰੰਗ, ਗੁੜ੍ਹਾ ਲਾਲ ਰੰਗ; ਅਰਗਵਾਨੀ, ਗੁੜ੍ਹਾ ਲਾਲ ਰੰਗਣਾ

cripple ('ਕਰਿਪਲ) *v n* ਲੂਲ੍ਹਾ, ਟੁੰਡਾ, ਲੰਜਾ, ਲੰਗੜਾ; ਲੰਗੜਾ ਕੇ ਟੁਰਨਾ, ਨਿਰਬਲ ਕਰਨਾ, ਵਿਗਾੜਨਾ

crisis ('ਕਰਾਇਸਿਸ) *n* ਸੰਕਟ, ਔਖੀ ਘੜੀ

crisp (ਕਰਿਸਪ) *a n v* ਖਸਤਾ, ਭੁਰਭੁਰਾ, ਮੁਰਮਰਾ, ਕਰਾਰਾ, ਫੁਰਤੀਲਾ, ਵਾਲ ਘੁੰਗਰਾਲੇ ਬਣਾਉਣਾ; ~**ate** ਵਲਦਾਰ, ਲਹਿਰੀਆ, ਘੁੰਗਰਾਲਾ

criterion (ਕਰਾਇ'ਟਿਅਰਿਅਨ) *n* ਮਾਪ-ਦੰਡ, ਕਸੌਟੀ, ਪਰਖ

critic ('ਕਰਿਟਿਕ) *n* ਆਲੋਚਕ, ਨੁਕਤਾਚੀਨ, ਸਮਾ-ਲੋਚਕ, ਸਮੀਖਿਆਕਾਰ; ~**al** ਆਲੋਚਨਾਤਮਕ, ਸਮਾਲੋਚਨਾਤਮਕ, ਸੰਕਟਮਈ, ਖ਼ਤਰਨਾਕ, ਨਾਜ਼ਕ; ~**ism** ਆਲੋਚਨਾ, ਸਮਾਲੋਚਨਾ; ਪੜਚੋਲ, ਸਮੀਖਿਆ, ਨੁਕਤਾਚੀਨੀ; ~**ize** ਨੁਕਤਾਚੀਨੀ ਕਰਨੀ, ਆਲੋਚਨਾ ਕਰਨੀ, ਛਾਣ-ਬੀਣ ਕਰਨੀ, ਨੁਕਸ ਕੱਢਣੇ

critique (ਕਰਿ'ਟੀਕ) *n* ਆਲੋਚਨਾਤਮਕ ਵਿਸ਼ਲੇਸ਼ਣ

crockery ('ਕਰੌਕਅਰਿ) *n* ਮਿੱਟੀ ਜਾਂ ਚੀਨੀ ਦੇ ਭਾਂਡੇ, ਪਿਆਲੇ ਪਿਆਲੀਆਂ, ਕ੍ਰਾਕਰੀ

crocodile ('ਕਰੌਕਅਡਾਇਲ) *n* ਮਗਰਮੱਛ, ਘੜਿਆਲ, ਸੰਸਾਰ

crone (ਕਰਅਉਨ) *n* ਬੁੱਢੀ ਠੇਰੀ, ਬੁੱਢੜੀ

crony ('ਕਰਅਉਨਿ) *n* ਲੰਗੋਟੀਆ ਯਾਰ, ਜਿਗਰੀ ਦੋਸਤ

crop (ਕਰੌਪ) *n v* ਫ਼ਸਲ; ਅਨਾਜ; ਖੇਤੀ ਕੱਟਣਾ, (ਫ਼ਸਲ) ਵੱਢਣਾ, ਕਤਰਨਾ, ਛਾਂਗਣਾ; ~**up** ਪਰਗਟ ਹੋਣਾ, ਪੈਦਾ ਹੋਣਾ, ਨਿਕਲਣਾ

cross (ਕਰੌਸ) *n v* ਸੂਲੀ, ਸਲੀਬ, ਫਾਂਸੀ; ਇਸਾਈ ਧਰਮ; ਤਸੀਹਾ, ਬਿਪਤਾ, ਕਸ਼ਟ; ਦੋਗਲਾ ਪਸ਼ੂ; ਜੋਬ; ਉੱਗੀ; ਕਟਣਾ, ਕਾਟਾ ਮਾਰਨਾ, ਉਲੀਕਣਾ, ਪਾਰ ਕਰਨਾ, ਲੰਘਣਾ, ਰਾਹ ਵਿਚ ਮਿਲਣਾ; ਸੂਲੀ ਜਾਂ ਸਲੀਬ ਬਣਾਉਣਾ, ਦੋਗਲਾ ਕਰਨਾ; ਉਲਟ, ਵਿਰੁੱਧ, ਟੇਢਾ, ਆੜਾ, ਕਾਟਵਾਂ, ਸਲੀਬੀ, ਚਿੜਚੜਾ, ਕੋਝਾ; ~**breed** ਦੋਗਲਾ; ~**examination** ਜਿਰਾ, ਪੁੱਛ ਗਿੱਛ; ~**legged** ਚੌਕੜੀ ਮਾਰ ਕੇ ਬੈਠਣਾ; ~**question** ਪ੍ਰਤੀ-ਪ੍ਰਸ਼ਨ ਕਰਨਾ; ਜਿਰਾ ਕਰਨਾ; ~**road** ਚੌਰਾਹਾ; ~**way** ਪਗਡੰਡੀ; ~**word** ਸ਼ਬਦ-ਪਹੇਲੀ, ਸ਼ਬਦ-ਅੜਾਉਣੀ

crow (ਕਰਅਉ) *n v* ਕਾਂ, ਕਾਂਗ, ਕਊਆ; ਬਾਂਗ; ਕੁੱਕੜ ਦਾ ਬਾਂਗ ਦੇਣਾ

crowd (ਕਰਅਉਡ) *n v* ਭੀੜ, ਜਮਘਟਾ, ਖਲਕਤ, ਬਾੜ, ਭਰਮਟ, ਟੋਲੀ, ਗੁਟ; ਭੀੜ ਹੋਣੀ ਜਾਂ ਕਰਨੀ, ਭਰਮਟ ਪੈਣਾ

crown (ਕਰਅਉਨ) *n v* ਮੁਕਟ, ਤਾਜ, ਸਿਹਰਾ, ਇਕ ਅੰਗਰੇਜ਼ੀ ਸਿੱਕਾ; ਟੱਟ, ਟੱਟੀ, ਚੂੰਡਾ, ਟੀਸੀ, ਚੋਟੀ; 15"×19" ਦਾ ਕਾਗ਼ਜ਼; ਦੰਦ ਦਾ ਮਸੂੜੇ ਤੋਂ ਬਾਹਰ ਦਾ ਭਾਗ; ਆਦਰਸ਼ ਸਥਿਤੀ; ਮੁਕਟ ਪੁਆਉਣਾ, ਸਿਹਰਾ ਬੰਨ੍ਹਣਾ, ਵਡਿਆਉਣਾ, ਦੰਦ ਮੜ੍ਹਾਉਣਾ

crumble (ਕਰਅੰਬਲ) ਚੂਰਾ ਚੂਰਾ ਹੋਣਾ, ਭੋਰਨਾ, ਭੁਰਨਾ, ਟੁੱਟਣਾ, ਤੋੜਨਾ

crusade (ਕਰੁ'ਸੇਇਡ) *n v* ਧਰਮ ਜੁੱਧ, ਮਸੀਹੀ ਜਹਾਦ; ਧਰਮ ਜੁੱਧ ਕਰਨਾ

crush ('ਕਰਅੱਸ਼) *v n* ਦਲਣਾ, ਦਰੜਨਾ; ਕੁਚਲਣਾ, ਚੂਰ ਕਰਨਾ, ਮਸਲਣਾ; ਭੀੜ-ਭੜੱਕਾ, ਜਮਘਟਾ

crux ('ਕਰਅੱਸ) *n* ਖੁੰਢੀ, ਗੁੱਥੀ, ਮੂਲ ਸਮੱਸਿਆ; ਪੇਚੀਦਾ ਮਾਮਲਾ

cry (ਕਰਾਇ) *n v* ਚੀਕ, ਕੂਕ, ਸ਼ੋਰ, ਚੀਂਘਿਆੜ, ਰੋਣ, ਪੁਕਾਰ, ਫ਼ਰਿਆਦ, ਕੁਰਲਾਹਟ, ਲਲਕਾਰ, ਨਾਅਰਾ; ਚੀਕਣਾ, ਕੂਕਣਾ, ਚਾਂਘਿਆੜਨਾ, ਰੋਣਾ, ਵਿਲਕਣਾ, ਪੁਕਾਰਨਾ, ਢੰਡੋਰਾ ਕਰਨਾ, ਉੱਚੀ ਅਵਾਜ਼ ਦੇਣੀ; ~**down** ਨਿੰਦਣਾ, ਭੰਡਣਾ; ~**ing need** ਸਖ਼ਤ ਲੋੜ; ~**up** ਵਧਾ ਚੜ੍ਹਾ ਕੇ ਦੱਸਣਾ, ਸੋਹਿਲੇ ਗਾਉਣੇ

crystal ('ਕਰਿਸਟਲ) *n a* ਰਵਾ, ਬਲੋਰੀ, ਰਵੇਦਾਰ, ਪਾਰਦਰਸ਼ੀ ਸ਼ੀਸ਼ਾ

cub (ਕਅੱਬ) *n* ਕਤੂਰਾ, ਬੱਚਾ (ਸ਼ੇਰ, ਰਿੱਛ ਜਾਂ ਕੁੱਤੇ ਦਾ), ਅੱਲੜ੍ਹ ਮੁੰਡਾ, ਸਕਾਊਟ ਬੱਚਾ; ਸਿਖਾਂਦਰੂ ਪੱਤਰਕਾਰ; ਬੱਚਾ ਜਣਨਾ

cube (ਕਯੂਬ) *n* ਘਣ, ਛੇ-ਬਾਹੀ ਆਕਾਰ, ਘਣਾਕਾਰ

cubicle (ਕਯੂਬਿਕਲ) *n* ਵਿਦਿਆਰਥੀਆਂ ਦਾ ਸੌਣ ਕਮਰਾ

cuckold ('ਕਅੱਕਅਉਲਡ) *n* ਭੜਵਾ

cuckoo ('ਕੁਕੂ) *n* ਬਘਿਹਾ, ਕੋਇਲ

cucumber ('ਕਯੂਕਅੱਮਬਅ') *n* ਖੀਰਾ, ਤਰ

cuddle ('ਕਅੱਡਲ) *v n* ਗਲ ਲਾਉਣਾ, ਲਾਡ ਪਿਆਰ ਕਰਨਾ, ਜੱਫੀ ਪਾਉਣਾ; ਜੱਫੀ, ਆਲਿੰਗਨ

cudgel ('ਕਅੱਜ(ਅ)ਲ) *n v* ਸੋਟਾ, ਡੰਡਾ; ਡੰਡੇ ਮਾਰਨਾ

cue (ਕਯੂ) *n* ਸੰਕੇਤ, ਇਸ਼ਾਰਾ; ਗੁਤ

culminate ('ਕੱਅਲਮਿਨੇਇਟ) *v* ਸਿਖਰ ਤੇ ਪੁੱਜਣਾ, ਉੱਚਾ ਹੋਣਾ; ਨਤੀਜਾ ਹੋਣਾ

culmination ('ਕੱਅਲਮਿ'ਨੇਇਸ਼ਨ) *n* ਟੀਸੀ, ਸਿਖਰ; ਨਤੀਜਾ, ਸਿੱਟਾ

culpable ('ਕੱਅਲਪਅਬਲ) *a* ਦੋਸ਼ਪੂਰਨ, ਅਪਰਾਧੀ

culprit ('ਕੱਅਲਪਰਿਟ) *n* ਦੋਸ਼ੀ, ਅਪਰਾਧੀ, ਮੁਜਰਮ

cult (ਕੱਅਲਟ) *n* ਦੀਨ, ਮਾਰਗ, ਸੰਪਰਦਾਇ, ਧਰਮ, ਰੀਤ, ਪੂਜਾ-ਪੱਧਤੀ

cultivate ('ਕੱਅਲਟਿਵੇਇਟ) *v* ਵਾਹੁਣਾ, ਖੇਤੀ ਕਰਨੀ, ਸੁਆਰਨਾ, ਸਿੱਖਿਆ ਦੇਣਾ, ਧਰਤੀ ਤਿਆਰ ਕਰਨੀ

cultivation ('ਕੱਅਲਟਿ'ਵੇਇਸ਼ਨ) *n* ਵਾਹੀ ਖੇਤੀ, ਕਾਸ਼ਤ

cultural ('ਕੱਅਲਚ(ਅ)ਰ(ਅ)ਲ) *a* ਸਾਂਸਕ੍ਰਿਤਕ, ਸੱਭਿਆਚਾਰਕ

culture ('ਕੱਅਲਚਆ*) *n v* ਸੰਸਕ੍ਰਿਤੀ, ਸੱਭਿਆਚਾਰ, ਕਾਸ਼ਤਕਾਰੀ; ਖੇਤੀ ਕਰਨੀ, ਜੋਤਣਾ; ~d ਸੁਸੰਸਕ੍ਰਿਤ, ਸੱਭਿਅ, ਕੋਮਲ ਭਾਵਾਂ ਦਾ ਸੁਆਮੀ, ਸੱਭਿਆਵਾਨ; ਬੀਜੀ ਹੋਈ ਜ਼ਮੀਨ

culvert ('ਕੱਅਲਵਅ:ਟ) *n* (ਸੜਕ ਆਦਿ ਦੀ) ਪੁਲੀ

cumber ('ਕੱਅਮਬਅ*) *v n* ਭਾਰ ਪਾਉਣਾ, ਰੁਕਾਵਟ ਪਾਉਣਾ; ਬੋਝ, ਰੁਕਾਵਟ

cumulate (ਕਯੂਮਯੁਲੇਇਟ) *v a* ਇਕੱਠਾ ਕਰਨਾ, ਜਮ੍ਹਾਂ ਕਰਨਾ, ਢੇਰ ਲਗਾਉਣਾ; ਇਕੱਤਰਤ, ਜਮ੍ਹਾਂ, ਢੇਰ ਕੀਤਾ, ਸੰਚਤ

cumulation (ਕਯੂਮਯੁ'ਲੇਇਸ਼ਨ) *n* ਸਮੂਹ, ਢੇਰ, ਇਕੱਤਰੀਕਰਨ

cumulative (ਕਯੂਮਯੁਲ(ਅ)ਟਿਵ) *a* ਸਮੁੱਚਾ, ਇੱਕਠਾ, ਸੰਚਤ

cunning (ਕੱਅਨਇਙ) *a n* ਚਲਾਕ, ਚੁੰਟ, ਘਾਗ, ਉਸਤਾਦ, ਮੱਕਾਰ; ਚਲਾਕੀ, ਉਸਤਾਦੀ, ਮੱਕਾਰੀ

cup (ਕੱਅਪ) *n* ਪਿਆਲਾ, ਛੰਨ, ਠੂਠਾ, ਜਾਮ, ਕੱਪ; in one's ~s ਸ਼ਰਾਬ ਦੇ ਨਸ਼ੇ ਵਿਚ, ਮਦਹੋਸ਼

cupboard (ਕੱਅਬਅੜ) *n* ਭਾਂਡਿਆਂ ਤੇ ਭੋਜਨ ਦੀ ਅਲਮਾਰੀ

cupid (ਕਯੂਪਿਡ) *n* ਕਾਮਦੇਵ, ਸੁੰਦਰ ਮੁੰਡਾ, ਕਾਮ ਦਾ ਰੋਮਨ ਦੇਵਤਾ

curable (ਕਯੂਅਰਅਬਲ) *a* ਠੀਕ ਹੋਣ ਜੋਗ, ਇਲਾਜ ਜੋਗ

curative ('ਕਯੂਅਰਅਟਿਵ) *adv. n* ਰੋਗਨਾਸ਼ਕ (ਦਵਾਈ)

curator (ਕਯੂ'ਰੇਇਅ*) *n* ਰੱਖਿਅਕ, ਪ੍ਰਬੰਧਕ, ਵਿਵਸਥਾਪਕ

curb (ਕਅ:ਬ) *n v* ਗੰਢ, ਰੋਕ, ਅੜਾਉਣੀ, ਰੋਕਣਾ, ਖੜੀ ਪਾਉਣੀ

curd (ਕਅ:ਡ) *n* ਦਹੀ

cure (ਕਯੂਅ*) *n v* ਇਲਾਜ, ਚਿਕਿਤਸਾ, ਉਪਾਯ, ਤੰਦਰੁਸਤੀ, ਅਰੋਗਤਾ; ਇਲਾਜ ਕਰਨਾ; ਦਵਾਈ ਦੇਣੀ, ਤੰਦਰੁਸਤ ਹੋਣਾ; ~less ਲਾਇਲਾਜ, ਅਸਾਧ, ਨਿਰਉਪਾਇ

curfew (ਕਅ:ਫ਼ਯੂ) *n* ਕਰਫ਼ਿਊ, ਘਰਬੰਦੀ ਦਾ ਹੁਕਮ; ~order ਕਰਫ਼ਿਊ ਦਾ ਹੁਕਮ

curio (ਕਯੂਅਰਿਅਉ) *n* ਅਨੋਖੀ ਕਲਾਕ੍ਰਿਤ

curiosity (ਕਯੂਅਰਿ'ਔਸਟਿ) *n* ਉਤਸੁਕਤਾ, ਪ੍ਰਬਲ ਇੱਛ, ਜਿਗਿਆਸਾ, ਉਤਕੰਠਾ; ਅਨੋਖਪਣ

curious (ਕਯੂਅਰਿਅਸ) *a* ਜਿਗਿਆਸੂ, ਅਨੋਖਾ, ਨਿਆਰਾ, ਵਿਸਮੈਜਨਕ, ਉਤਸੁਕ

curl (ਕਅ:ਲ) *n v* ਵਾਲਾਂ ਦਾ ਛੱਲਾ, ਘੁਰਗੂ ਜਾਂ ਪੇਚ, ਲਿਟ ਜ਼ੁਲਫ਼; ਦੇ ਕੁੰਡਲ ਬਣਾਉਣੇ

currency (ਕਅਰ(ਅ)ਨਸਿ) *n* ਪ੍ਰਚਲਤ ਮੁਦਰਾ, ਸਿੱਕਾ, ਕਰੰਸੀ; ਪ੍ਰਸਾਰ, ਰਿਵਾਜ;

current ('ਕਅਰ(ਅ)ਨਟ) *a n* ਜਾਰੀ ਮੌਜੂਦਾ, ਵਰਤਮਾਨ, ਆਧੁਨਿਕ, ਵਿਦਮਾਨ, ਪ੍ਰਚਲਤ, ਚਲੰਤ, ਚਾਲੂ, ਪਰਵਾਹ, ਬਿਜਲੀ ਦੀ ਧਾਰਾ, ਕਰੰਟ, ਵੇਗ, ਗਤੀ; ~**account** ਚਾਲੂ ਲੇਖਾ

curriculum (ਕਅ'ਰਿਕਯਅਲਅਮ) *n* ਪਾਠਕ੍ਰਮ

curry (ਕਅੱਰਿ) *n v* ਸ਼ੋਰਬਾ; ਸ਼ੋਰਬਾ ਤਿਆਰ ਕਰਨਾ

curse (ਕਅ:ਸ) *n* ਫਿਟਕਾਰ, ਧਿਕਾਰ; ਫਿਟਕਾਰ ਦੇਣਾ, ਧਿਰਕਾਰਨਾ, ਸਰਾਪਣਾ

cursory (ਕਅ:ਸ:ਮ(ਅ)ਰਿ) *a* ਸਰਸਰੀ, ਕਾਹਲੀ ਦਾ

curtail (ਕਅ:'ਟੇਇਲ) *v* ਕੱਟਣਾ, ਛਾਂਟਣਾ, ਘਟਾਉਣਾ, ਸੰਖੇਪ ਕਰਨਾ; ~**ment** ਕਾਂਟ-ਛਾਂਟ, ਘਾਟਾ, ਛਾਂਟੀ, ਸੰਖੇਪਤਾ

curtain ('ਕਅ:ਟਨ) *n v* ਪਰਦਾ, ਓਹਲਾ, ਚਿਕ ਪਰਦਾ ਢੇਰਨਾ; ਓਹਲਾ ਕਰਨਾ

curvature (ਕਅ:ਵਅਚਰਅ) *n* ਮੋੜ, ਵਿੰਗ, ਵਕਰਤਾ

curve ('ਕਅ:ਵ) *n v* ਮੋੜ, ਗੋਲਾਈ, ਵਿੰਗ, ਖਮ, ਵਕਰ; ਮੋੜਨਾ, ਗੋਲ ਕਰਨਾ; ~**d** ਟੇਢਾ ਵਿੰਗਾ, ਵਕਰ

cushion ('ਕੁਸ਼ਨ) *n v* ਗੱਦਾ, ਗਾਤਲਾ, ਗੱਦਾ ਲਾਉਣਾ, ਗੁਦਗੁਦ ਕਰਨਾ

cushy ('ਕੁਸ਼ਿ) *a* ਸੌਖਾ (ਕੰਮ), ਆਨੰਦਮਈ, ਸੁਖਦਾਇਕ

custard ('ਕਅਸਟਅ:ਡ) *n* ਫਿਰਨੀ, ਚੌਲਾਂ ਦੇ ਆਟੇ ਅਤੇ ਦੁੱਧ ਦੀ ਖੀਰ, ਕਸਟਰਡ

custodian (ਕਅਸਟਅਉਡਯਅਨ) *n* ਨਿਗਰਾਨ, ਰਖਵਾਲਾ, ਦਰੋਗਾ

custody ('ਕਅਸਟਅਡਿ) *n* ਹਿਰਾਸਤ, ਕੈਦ, ਸਪੁਰਦਗੀ, ਨਿਗਰਾਨੀ; **take into**~ ਕੈਦ ਕਰਨਾ, ਹਿਰਾਸਤ ਵਿਚ ਲੈਣਾ

custom ('ਕਅਸਟਅਮ) *n* (1) ਰੀਤ, ਰਿਵਾਜ, ਪ੍ਰਥਾ; ਨਿਤਨੇਮ; (2) ਵਤੀਰਾ; ਗਾਹਕੀ; (3) ਚੁੰਗੀ, ਅਯਾਤ-ਕਰ, ~**er** ਗਾਹਕ, ਖ਼ਰੀਦਾਰ, ਆਸਾਮੀ

cut (ਕਅੱਟ) *v n* ਕਟਣਾ, ਵਢੱਣਾ, ਟੁੱਕਣਾ, ਟੱਕ ਲਾਉਣਾ, ਘਾਉ ਲਾਉਣਾ, ਕਲਮ ਕਰਨਾ, ਛਿਲਣਾ, ਚੀਰਨਾ; ਘਟਾਉਣਾ, ਘੱਟ ਕਰਨਾ, ਟੱਕ, ਵੱਢ, ਚੀਰ, ਫੱਟ, ਕਾਂਟ-ਛਾਂਟ, ਘਾਉ; ~**out** ਗਾਤ ਨੂੰ ਕੱਟ ਕੇ ਬਣਾਇਆ ਵਿਅਕਤੀ ਆਦਿ ਦੀ ਬੁੱਤ, ਕਟ-ਆਊਟ; ~**off** ਵੱਖ ਕਰਨਾ; ਟੋਕਣਾ

cutler ('ਕਅਟਲਅ*) *n* ਛੁਰੀਸਾਜ਼; ~**y** ਛੁਰੀਸਾਜ਼ੀ; ਛੁਰੀ ਕਾਂਟੇ

cutlet ('ਕਅਟਲਿਟ) *n* ਕਤਲਾ, ਕਤਲੰਮਾ

cutter ('ਕਅਟਅ*) *n* ਟੇਕਾ; ਦਰਜ਼ੀ; ਕਤਿਆ, ਕੈਂਚੀ

cutting ('ਕਅੱਟਿਙ) *n* ਕਟਾਈ, ਕਾਤਰ, ਟੋਟਾ

cycle ('ਸਾਇਕਲ) *n v* ਚੱਕਰ, ਦੌਰ, ਗਾਰਦਿਸ਼; ਸਾਈਕਲ; ਫਿਰਨਾ, ਚੱਕਰ ਲਾਉਣੇ, ਬਾਈਸਿਕਲ ਚਲਾਉਣਾ

cyclist ('ਸਾਇਕਲਿਸਟ) *n* ਸਾਈਕਲ ਸਵਾਰ

cyclone ('ਸਾਇਕਲਅਉਨ) *n* ਸਮੁੰਦਰੀ ਝੱਖੜ, ਸਾਗਰੀ ਤੂਫ਼ਾਨ, ਚੱਕਰਦਾਰ ਹਵਾ

cylinder ('ਸਿਲਿੰਡਅ*) *n* ਵੇਲਣ, ਵੇਲਣਾਕਾਰ ਪਦਾਰਥ; ਸਿਲੰਡਰ

cynic ('ਸਿਨਿਕ) *n* ਸਨਕੀ ਵਿਅਕਤੀ, ਨੋਕ-ਚੜ੍ਹੂ ਵਿਅਕਤੀ; ~**al** ਰੁੱਖਾ, ਸਨਕੀ, ਤੁਰਸ਼

cypher, cipher (ਸਾਇਫਅ*) *n* ਸਿਫ਼ਰ, ਬਿੰਦੀ

D

D, d (ਡੀ) *n* ਰੋਮਨ ਵਰਣਮਾਲਾ ਦਾ ਚੌਥਾ ਵਰਣ ਜਾਂ ਅੱਖਰ; 500 ਦਾ ਚਿੰਨ੍ਹ

dabble ('ਡੈਬਲ) *v* ਕੁਚੱਜ ਮਾਰਨਾ, ਪਾਣੀ ਵਿਚ ਹੱਥ ਪੈਰ ਮਾਰਨਾ, ਛਿੜਕਣਾ, ਛਿੱਟੇ ਮਾਰਨਾ, ਗਿੱਲਾ ਕਰਨਾ, ਖੰਗੋਲਣਾ, ਪਾਣੀ ਵਿਚੋਂ ਕੱਢਣਾ

dacoit (ਡਅ'ਕੋਇਟ) *n* ਡਾਕੂ, ਡਕੈਤ; **~y** ਡਾਕਾ, ਡਕੈਤੀ, ਧਾੜਾ

dad (ਡੈਡ) *n* ਬਾਪੂ, ਬਾਪਾ, ਅੱਬਾ; *daddy, dada* ਵੀ

daddle (ਡੈਡਲ) *v* ਡਗਮਗਾਉਣਾ; ਲੜਖੜਾ ਕੇ ਟੁਰਨਾ, ਝੂਮ ਝੂਮ ਕੇ ਚੱਲਣਾ

daffodil ('ਡੈਫ਼ਅਡਿਲ) *n* ਨਰਗਸੀ ਫੁੱਲ; ਹਲਕਾ ਪੀਲਾ ਰੰਗ

dagger (ਡੈਗਾਗ*) *n* ਛੁਰਾ, ਖੰਜਰ, ਕਟਾਰ; *at ~s drawn* ਜਾਨੀ ਦੁਸ਼ਮਨ, ਕੱਟੜ ਵੈਰੀ

daily ('ਡੇਇਲਿ) *adv a* ਰੋਜ਼, ਨਿੱਤ ਨਿੱਤ, ਰੋਜ਼ਾਨਾ; ਨਿਰੰਤਰ, ਦੈਨਕ (ਪੱਤਰ), ਦਿਹਾੜੀਦਾਰ

dairy ('ਡੇਅਰਿ) *n* ਦੁੱਧ-ਘਰ, ਦੁੱਧ-ਮੱਖਣ ਆਦਿ ਦੀ ਦੁਕਾਨ, ਡੇਅਰੀ

dais ('ਡੇਇਸ) *n* ਮੰਚ, ਚਬੂਤਰਾ, ਥੜ੍ਹਾ

dak (ਡਾਕ) *n* ਡਾਕ (ਵਿਭਾਗ)

dakota (ਡਅ'ਕਅਉਟਅ) *n* ਛੋਟਾ ਹਵਾਈ ਜਹਾਜ਼

dale (ਡੇਇਲ) *n* ਘਾਟੀ, ਵਾਦੀ, ਦੂਨ

dally (ਡੈਲਿ) *v* ਸਮਾਂ ਗੁਆਉਣਾ; ਨਖਰੇ ਕਰਨਾ; ਟਾਲਣਾ, ਢਿੱਲ ਕਰਨਾ; ਕਲੋਲ ਕਰਨਾ, ਚੋਹਲ ਕਰਨਾ

dam (ਡੈਮ) *n v* ਡੈਮ, ਬੰਨ੍ਹ, ਰੋਕਿਆ ਪਾਣੀ; ਬੰਨ੍ਹ ਬੰਨ੍ਹਣਾ, ਡੈਮ ਉਸਾਰਨਾ

damage ('ਡੈਮਿਜ) *n* ਹਾਨੀ ਪੂਰਤੀ, ਨੁਕਸਾਨ; ਹਰਜਾਨਾ, ਚੱਟੀ; **~able** ਹਾਨੀਕਾਰਕ, ਟੁੱਟਣਹਾਰ

dame (ਡੇਇਮ) *n* (ਉਪਾਧੀ ਵਜੋਂ) ਸਰਦਾਰਨੀ

damn (ਡੈਮ) *n v* ਫਿਟਕਾਰ, ਨਿੰਦਾ, ਧਿੱਕਾਰ, ਲਾਨ੍ਹਤ; ਫਿਟਕਾਰ ਪਾਉਣੀ; **~ation** ਫਿਟਕਾਰ, ਲਾਨ੍ਹਤ, ਧਿਰਕਾਰ, ਬਦਅਸੀਸ; **~atory** ਧਿਰਕਾਰ ਭਰਿਆ, ਘਿਰਣਾਪੂਰਨ, ਨਿੰਦਾਪੂਰਨ; **~ed** ਧਿਰਕਾਰਿਆ, ਰੱਦ ਕੀਤਾ, ਦੁਰਕਾਰਿਆ, ਨਿੰਦਤ, ਅਤੀਅੰਤ, ਅਤਿ ਅਧਿਕ

damsel ('ਡੈਮਜ਼ਲ) *n* ਮੁਟਿਆਰ, ਨੱਢੀ, ਕੁਆਰੀ, ਕੰਨਿਆ

damson ('ਡੈਮਜ਼(ਅ)ਨ) *n a* ਆਲੂਬੁਖ਼ਾਰਾ

dance (ਡਾਂਸ) *n v* ਨਾਚ, ਨ੍ਰਿਤ; ਨਾਚ ਕਰਨਾ, ਨੱਚਣਾ, ਮੁਜਰਾ ਕਰਨਾ, ਨਚਾਉਣਾ; **~r** ਨ੍ਰਿਤਕਾਰ, ਨਾਚੀ, ਨਰਤਕੀ

dancing ('ਡਾਂਸਿਙ) *n* ਨਾਚ-ਕਲਾ, ਨ੍ਰਿਤ-ਕਲਾ; **~girl** ਨਾਚੀ, ਨਰਤਕੀ

dandruff ('ਡੈਨਡਰਿਫ਼) *n* ਸਿੱਕਰੀ, ਕਰ

dandy (ਡੈਂਡਿ) *n* ਵਿਸ਼ੇਸ਼ ਕਿਸਮ ਦੇ ਮਸਤੂਲ ਦਾ ਜਹਾਜ਼, ਛੈਲ ਛਬੀਲਾ, ਬਾਂਕਾ

danger ('ਡੇਇੰਜਅ*) *n* ਭੈ, ਖ਼ਤਰਾ, ਖਟਕਾ, ਜੋਖ਼ਮ; **~ous** ਖ਼ਤਰਨਾਕ, ਭਿਆਨਕ, ਭਿਅੰਕਰ, ਡਰਾਉਣਾ

dangle ('ਡੈਂਗਲ) *v* ਪਿੱਛੇ ਪਿੱਛੇ ਫਿਰਨਾ; ਲਟਕਾਉਣਾ, ਲਟਕਣਾ; **~r** (ਆਸ਼ਕ ਆਦਿ) ਪਿੱਛਲਗ

dare (ਡੇਅ*) *v* ਹੌਸਲਾ ਕਰਨਾ, ਹਿੰਮਤ ਕਰਨੀ, ਸਾਹਸ ਕਰਨਾ

daring ('ਡੇਅਰਿਙ) *n a* ਦਲੇਰੀ, ਵੀਰਤਾ, ਬਹਾਦਰੀ, ਜੇਰਾ, ਹਿੰਮਤ, ਜਿਗਰੇ ਵਾਲਾ, ਨਿਡਰ, ਹਿੰਮਤੀ

dark (ਡਾਕ) *n a* ਅੰਧਕਾਰ, ਹਨੇਰਾ, ਅਗਿਆਨ, ਸਿਆਹ, ਕਾਲਾ, ਸਾਂਵਲਾ; ਅਸਪਸ਼ਟਤਾ, ਭਿਆਨਕ, ਧੁੰਧਲਾ, ਉਦਾਸ, ਗੁਪਤ; ~**blue** ਗੂੜ੍ਹਾ ਨੀਲਾ; **in the**~ ਬੇਖ਼ਬਰ, ਅਨਜਾਣ; ~**en** ਧੁੰਦਲਾ ਕਰਨਾ, ਕਾਲਾ ਕਰਨਾ, ਅੰਨ੍ਹਾ ਕਰਨਾ, ਘਬਰਾਉਣਾ; ~**ness** ਹਨੇਰਾਪਨ, ਧੁੰਦਲਾਪਨ, ਅੰਧਕਾਰ, ਅਗਿਆਨ

darling ('ਡਾਲਿਙ) *n a* ਪਿਆਰਾ, ਪ੍ਰੀਤਮ, ਪ੍ਰਿਅ, ਲਾਡਲਾ, ਦੁਲਾਰਾ

darn (ਡਾ*ਨ) *v n* ਰਫ਼ੂ ਕਰਨਾ, ਜਾਲੀ ਪਾਉਣਾ; ~**ing** ਰਫ਼ੂ, ਰਫ਼ੂਗਰੀ

dart (ਡਾਟ) *n v* ਤੀਰ, ਬਰਛੀ; ਭਾਲਾ; ਬਾਣ; ਤੀਰ ਮਾਰਨਾ, ਬਰਛੀ ਮਾਰਨਾ, ਤੇਜ਼ੀ ਨਾਲ ਵਧਣਾ

dash (ਡੈਸ਼) *n v* ਵਕਫ਼ਾ, ਵਾਕ ਛੋਡਣ ਦਾ ਨਿਸ਼ਾਨ (—), ਅਲਪ ਮਾਤਰਾ; ਕਲਮ ਦੀ ਝਰੀਟ, ਰੰਗ ਦਾ ਛਿੱਟਾ; ਚੁਟਕੀ; ਪਾਣੀ ਦੀਆਂ ਛੱਲਾਂ ਦੀ ਅਵਾਜ਼; ਤੁਰਤ-ਫੁਰਤ ਕੰਮ; ਚੜ੍ਹਾਈ, ਧਾਵਾ; ਡੈਸ਼ ਲਾਉਣਾ; ਟੱਕਰ ਖਾਣਾ, ਟਕਰਾਉਣਾ ਦਬਾਉਣਾ, ਤੇਜ਼ਨਾ, ਜ਼ਮੀਨ ਵਿਚ ਮਿਲਾ ਦੇਣਾ; ਤੇਜ਼ੀ ਨਾਲ ਡਿੱਗਣਾ; ~**ing** ਉਦਮੀ, ਸ਼ਾਨ ਵਿਖਾਉਣ ਵਾਲਾ

data ('ਡੇਇਟਾ) *n* (*datum* ਦਾ ਬ ਵ), ਸਮਗਰੀ, ਆਧਾਰ, ਅੰਕੜੇ

date (ਡੇਇਟ) *n v* ਤਿਥੀ, ਮਿਤੀ, ਤਾਰੀਖ਼; ਤਾਰੀਖ਼ ਪਾਉਣੀ; ਖਜੂਰ, ਛੁਹਾਰਾ; ~**d** ਮਿਤੀ-ਯੁਕਤ; ~**less** ਬੇਤਾਰੀਖ਼; ਆਦਿ, ਪੁਰਾਣਾ

dative ('ਡੇਇਟਿਵ਼) *n a* ਸੰਪਰਦਾਨ ਕਾਰਕ

daub (ਡੋਬ) *v n* ਪੋਚਣਾ, ਲਿੱਬੜਨਾ, ਲਬੇੜਨਾ; ਪੋਚਾ, ਭੱਦਾ ਚਿਤਰ

daughter ('ਡੋਟਾ*) *n* ਪੁੱਤਰੀ, ਬੇਟੀ, ਧੀ, ਲੜਕੀ, ਜਾਈ; ~**in-law** ਨੂੰਹ

daunt (ਡੋਂਟ) *v* ਹਿੰਮਤ ਤੋੜਨਾ; ਡਾਂਟਣਾ, ਧਮਕਾਉਣਾ, ਭੈ ਦੇਣਾ; ~**less** ਨਿਡਰ, ਨਿਧੜਕ

dawdle (ਡੋਡਲ) *v* ਸਮਾਂ ਨਸ਼ਟ ਕਰਨਾ, ਅਵਾਰਾ ਘੁੰਮਣਾ, ਬੇਕਾਰ ਫਿਰਨਾ; ਸੁਸਤੀ ਕਰਨਾ

dawn (ਡੋਨ) *n v* ਪ੍ਰਭਾਤ, ਸਰਘੀ ਵੇਲਾ, ਪਹੁਫੁਟਾਲਾ, ਤੜਕਾ, ਪ੍ਰਾਤਕਾਲ; ਸਵੇਰ ਹੋਣਾ; ਦਿਸਣਾ, ਆਰੰਭ ਹੋਣਾ

day (ਡੇਇ) *n* ਦਿਨ, ਦਿਵਸ, ਵਾਰ; ਸਵੇਰ; ਅੱਠ ਪਹਿਰ, ਨਿਸ਼ਚਤ ਮਿਤੀ; ਦੌਰ, ਯੁੱਗ; ~**book** ਰੋਜ਼-ਨਾਮਚਾ; ~**break** ਪ੍ਰਭਾਤ, ਪਹੁ-ਫੁਟਾਲਾ; ~**light** ਚਾਨਣ, ਧੁੱਪ, ਤੜਕਾ; ~**long** ਸਾਰਾ ਦਿਨ; *better*~ **s** ਖ਼ੁਸ਼ਹਾਲੀ ਦਾ ਸਮਾਂ, ਚੰਗੇ ਦਿਨ

daze (ਡੇਇਜ਼) *v n* ਚਕਰਾ ਦੇਣਾ, ਚਲਿਤ ਕਰ ਦੇਣਾ, ਹੱਕਾ-ਬੱਕਾ ਕਰ ਦੇਣਾ, ਚੁੰਧਿਆ ਦੇਣਾ; ਹੈਰਾਨੀ

dazzle (ਡੈਜ਼ਲ) *v* ਚੁੰਧਿਆਉਣਾ, ਚਕਚੌਂਧ ਕਰਨਾ, ਚਕਰਾ ਦੇਣਾ, ਹੈਰਾਨ ਕਰਨਾ

dazzling (ਡੈਜ਼ਲਿਙ) *a* ਚੁੰਧਿਆ ਦੇਣ ਵਾਲਾ, ਪਰੇਸ਼ਾਨ ਕਰਨ ਵਾਲਾ

dead (ਡੈਡ) *a adv* ਮਰਿਆ, ਮਿਰਤਕ, ਮੁਰਦਾ; ਨਿਰਜੀਵ; ਅਚੇਤਨ, ਬੇਸੁਧ; ਅਪ੍ਰਚਲਤ, ਪ੍ਰਭਾਵਹੀਨ, ਬੀਤਿਆ, ਪੁਰਾਣਾ; ਪੂਰੇ ਤੌਰ ਤੇ, ਬਿਲਕੁਲ, ਸਰਾਸਰ; ~**against** ਸਖ਼ਤ ਵੈਰੀ, ਜਾਨੀ ਦੁਸ਼ਮਨ; ~**end** ਅੰਤਮ ਸਿਰਾ, ਬੰਦ ਗਲੀ; ~**hours** ਅੱਧੀ ਰਾਤ; ~**language** ਅਪ੍ਰਚਲਤ ਭਾਸ਼ਾ; ~**lock** ਅੜਿੱਕਾ; ~**shot** ਚੰਗਾ ਨਿਸ਼ਾਨਚੀ; ~**stock** ਡੁੱਬੀ ਰਕਮ, ਬੇਕਾਰ ਮਾਲ; ~**sure** ਪੱਕਾ ਨਿਸ਼ਚਾ; ~**wood** ਮਰਿਆ ਸੱਪ,

ਵਾਯੂ ਦਾ ਭਾਰ; ~en ਮਾਰਨਾ, ਅਚੇਤ ਕਰਨਾ, ਸੁੰਨ ਕਰਨਾ; ਘਟ ਕਰ ਦੇਣਾ; ~ly ਮੌਤ ਵਰਗੀ, ਅਤੀਅੰਤ, ਬਿਲਕੁਲ

deaf (ਡੈੱਫ਼) *a* ਬੋਲਾ; ਡੋਰਾ; ਬਹਿਰਾ, ਲਾਪਰਵਾਹ; ~mute ਗੁੰਗਾ-ਬੋਲਾ ਆਦਮੀ; ~en ਬੋਲਾ ਕਰਨਾ, ਕੰਨ ਪਾੜ ਦੇਣੇ; (ਅਵਾਜ਼) ਨਾ ਸੁਣਨ ਦੇਣੀ

deal (ਡੀਲ) *n v* ਸੌਦਾ; ਹਿੱਸਾ, ਵੰਡਾਰਾ; ਵਰਤਾਉ ਕਰਨਾ; ਸਲੂਕ ਕਰਨਾ, ਸੌਦਾ ਕਰਨਾ; ~er ਵਪਾਰੀ, ਦੁਕਾਨਦਾਰ, ਵਿਕਰੇਤਾ; ~ing ਲੈਣ-ਦੇਣ, ਕਾਰੋਬਾਰ, ਵਣਜ; ਵਪਾਰ; ਵਰਤਾਉ

dean (ਡੀਨ) *n* (ਯੂਨੀਵਰਸਿਟੀ ਵਿਚ) ਡੀਨ; ਵੱਡਾ ਪਾਦਰੀ, ਮੱਠ-ਅਧਿਕਾਰੀ

dear (ਡਿਅ*) *a* ਪਿਆਰਾ, ਦੁਲਾਰਾ, ਲਾਡਲਾ, ਚਹੇਤਾ; ਮਹਿੰਗਾ; ~ness ਪ੍ਰੀਤ, ਪਰੇਮ, ਪਿਆਰ, ਮਹਿੰਗਾਈ

dearth (ਡਅ:ਥ) *n* ਥੁੜ, ਕਮੀ, ਘਾਟ, ਤੋੜਾ, ਕਿੱਲਤ

death (ਡੈਥ) *n* ਦੇਹਾਂਤ, ਮੌਤ, ਮਿਰਤੂ; ~sentence ਮੌਤ ਦੀ ਸਜ਼ਾ, ਮਿਰਤੂ ਦੰਡ; ~less ਅਮਰ, ਸਦੀਵੀ

debacle (ਡੇਇ'ਬਾਕਲ) *n* ਪਤਨ, ਜ਼ਵਾਲ; ਭਾਜੜ

debar (ਡਿ'ਬਾ*) *n* ਵਰਜਣਾ, ਮਨ੍ਹਾਂ ਕਰਨਾ, ਰੋਕਣਾ; ਖ਼ਾਰਜ ਕਰਨਾ; ਅੜਚਨ ਪਾਉਣੀ; ~red ਵਰਜਤ, ਵਿਵਰਜਤ; ਰੋਕਿਆ

debase (ਡਿ'ਬੇਇਸ) *v* ਮਿਲਾਵਟ ਕਰਨੀ, ਖੋਟ ਰਲਾਉਣੀ; ਮੁੱਲ ਘਟਾਉਣਾ; ਦਰਜਾ ਘੱਟ ਕਰਨਾ, ਆਦਰ ਮਾਨ ਘਟਾਉਣਾ, ਵਿਗਾੜਨਾ; ~ment ਮਿਲਾਵਟ, ਖ਼ਰਾਬੀ, ਨੁਕਸ, ਵਿਗਾੜ, ਬੇਕਦਰੀ, ਨਿਰਾਦਰ

debatable (ਡਿ'ਬੇਇਟਅਬਲ) *a* ਵਿਵਾਦਗ੍ਰਸਤ, ਬਹਿਸਯੋਗ, ਸ਼ਕੀ, ਸ਼ੰਕਾਪੂਰਨ

debate (ਡਿ'ਬੇਇਟ) *n v* ਬਹਿਸ, ਵਾਦ-ਵਿਵਾਦ, ਵਿਚਾਰ-ਵਟਾਂਦਰਾ; ਵਿਵਾਦ ਕਰਨਾ, ਤਕਰਾਰ ਕਰਨਾ

debauch (ਡਿ'ਬੋਚ) *n v* ਭ੍ਰਿਸ਼ਟ, ਲੁੱਚਾ, ਬਦਮਾਸ਼ੀ ਕਰਨੀ, ਬਦਕਾਰੀ ਕਰਨਾ, ਅਵਾਰਾ ਬਣਾਉਣਾ; ਸਤ ਭੰਗ ਕਰਨਾ; ਫੁਸਲਾਉਣਾ; ~edness ਭ੍ਰਿਸ਼ਟਤਾ, ਚਰਿੱਤਰਹੀਨਤਾ; ~ery ਕਾਮ ਵਾਸ਼ਨਾ, ਅੱਯਾਸ਼ੀ, ਵਿਸ਼ਯ ਭੋਗ

debenture (ਡਿ'ਬੇਨੱਚਅ*) *n* ਇਕਰਾਰਨਾਮਾ; ਤਮਸਕ, ਰਿਣ ਪੱਤਰ

debit (ਡੈੱਬਿਟ) *n v* ਖ਼ਰਚ, ਉਧਾਰ, ਕਰਜ਼ਾ, ਰਿਣ, ਉਧਾਰ ਖਾਤਾ

debonair (ਡੈੱਬੱਅ'ਨੇਅ*) *a* ਨਿਮਰ, ਸੱਜਣ, ਭੱਦਰ, ਮਿਲਣਸਾਰ, ਸੁਸ਼ੀਲ

debris (ਡੇਇਬਰੀ) *n* ਮਲਬਾ, ਇੱਟਾਂ ਰੋੜੇ

debt (ਡੈੱਟ) *n* ਕਰਜ਼, ਰਿਣ, ਦੇਣਦਾਰੀ, ਉਧਾਰ; ~of nature ਮੌਤ; ~ee ਸਾਹੂਕਾਰ, ਰਿਣਦਾਤਾ; ~or ਦੇਣਦਾਰ, ਕਰਜ਼ਦਾਰ, ਰਿਣੀ

decade (ਡੈਕੇਇਡ) *n* ਦਹਾਕਾ, ਦਸ਼ਕ, ਦਹਾਈ

decamp (ਡਿ'ਕੈਂਪ) *v* ਅਚਾਨਕ ਭੱਜ ਜਾਣਾ, ਰਫੂ ਚੱਕਰ ਹੋ ਜਾਣਾ, ਕੁਝ ਚੁਰਾ ਕੇ ਨੱਸ ਜਾਣਾ, ਡੇਰਾ ਚੁੱਕਣਾ, ਲੋਪ ਹੋਣਾ; ~ment ਕੂਚ, ਰਵਾਨਗੀ, ਫਰਾਰੀ, ਪਲਾਇਨ

decay (ਡਿ'ਕੇਇ) *v n* ਪਤਿਤ ਹੋਣਾ, ਨਾਸ ਹੋਣਾ, ਖ਼ਰਾਬ ਹੋਣਾ, ਘਟਾਉਣਾ; ਤਬਾਹੀ, ਬਰਬਾਦੀ, ਜ਼ਵਾਲ, ਪਤਨ, ਨਾਸ

decease (ਡਿ'ਸੀਸ) *n v* ਮੌਤ, ਮਿਰਤੂ, ਦੇਹਾਂਤ, ਮਰਨਾ, ਸੁਰਗਵਾਸ ਹੋਣਾ; ~d ਮਿਰਤਕ, ਸੁਰਗਵਾਸੀ

deceit (ਡਿ'ਸੀਟ) *n* ਕਪਟ, ਧੋਖਾ, ਛਲ, ਫਰੇਬ,

~ful ਛਲੀਆ, ਕਪਟੀ, ਮੱਕਾਰ, ਧੋਖੇਬਾਜ਼, ਚਾਲਬਾਜ਼; ~fulness ਕਪਟਪੂਰਨਤਾ, ਛਲ, ਦਗਾ, ਮੱਕਾਰੀ, ਧੋਖੇਬਾਜ਼ੀ, ਚਾਲਬਾਜ਼ੀ

deceive (ਡਿ'ਸੀਵ਼) v ਧੋਖ ਦੇਣਾ, ਛਲ ਕਰਨਾ, ਛਲਣਾ, ਵਿਸ਼ਵਾਸਘਾਤ ਕਰਨਾ; ~r ਠੱਗ, ਕਪਟੀ, ਮੱਕਾਰ, ਧੋਖੇਬਾਜ਼, ਦਗ਼ਾਬਾਜ਼

december (ਡਿ'ਸੈਂਬਅ*) n ਅੰਗਰੇਜ਼ੀ ਸਾਲ ਦਾ ਬਾਰ੍ਹਵਾਂ ਮਹੀਨਾ, ਦਸੰਬਰ

decency (ਡੀਸੰਸਿ) n ਸੁਸ਼ੀਲਤਾ, ਸ਼ਿਸ਼ਟਤਾ; ਸੁਘੜਤਾ, ਭਲਮਾਨਸੀ, ਮਰਜਾਦਾ

decent (ਡੀਸੰਟ) a ਸੁਘੜ, ਭਲਾ, ਮਾਊ, ਭਲਮਾਨਸ, ਸੁਸ਼ੀਲ, ਚੰਗਾ, ਚੋਖਾ

decentralize (ਡੀ'ਸੈਂਟਰਅਲਇਜ਼) v ਵਿਕੇਂਦਰੀਕਰਨ ਕਰਨਾ, ਵਿਕੇਂਦਰਤ ਕਰਨਾ; ~d ਵਿਕੇਂਦਰੀਭਿਤ, ਵਿਕੇਂਦਰਤ

deceptible (ਡਿ'ਸੈਪਟਅਬਲ) n ਛਲਣਯੋਗ

deception (ਡਿ'ਸੈਪੱਸ਼ਨ) n ਕਪਟ, ਛਲ, ਧੋਖਾ, ਝਾਂਸਾ

deceptive (ਡਿ'ਸੈਪਟਿਵ਼) a ਭਰਮਪੂਰਨ, ਕਪਟ-ਪੂਰਨ, ਝੂਠਾ

decide (ਡਿ'ਸਾਇਡ) v ਫ਼ੈਸਲਾ ਦੇਣਾ, ਨਿਰਾ ਕਰਨਾ, ਨਿਸ਼ਚਤ ਕਰਨਾ, ਤੈ ਕਰਨਾ,

deciding (ਡਿ'ਸਾਇਡਿਙ) a ਨਿਸ਼ਚੇਕਾਰੀ; ਨਿਰਨਾਤਮਕ

decimal (ਡੈੱਸਿਮਲ) n a ਦਸ਼ਮਲਵ, ਇਸ਼ਾਰੀਆ, ਦਸ਼ਾਂਸ਼ਕ, ਦਸ਼ਮਕ, ਦਸ਼ਾਂਸ਼; ~system ਦਸ਼ਮਲਵ ਪ੍ਰਣਾਲੀ

decipher (ਡਿ'ਸਾਇਫ਼ਅ*) n v ਗੁਝ ਜਾਂ ਗੁਪਤ ਲੇਖ ਜਾਂ ਲਿਪੀ ਦੀ ਵਿਆਖਿਆ, ਗੁਪਤ ਲੇਖ ਵਾਚਣਾ

decision (ਡਿ'ਸਿਯ਼ਨ) n ਨਿਰਾ, ਫ਼ੈਸਲਾ, ਨਿਸ਼ਚਾ, ਨਿਬੇੜਾ

decisive (ਡਿ'ਸਾਇਸਿਵ਼) a ਫ਼ੈਸਲਾਕੁਨ, ਨਿਸ਼ਚੇਕਾਰੀ, ਨਿਰਣਾਇਕ, ਨਿਸ਼ਚਤ; ~ness ਨਿਸ਼ਚਤਤਾ, ਨਿਸ਼ਚਤਮਕਤਾ, ਨਿਰਣਾਇਕਤਾ

deck (ਡੈੱਕ) n v ਜਹਾਜ਼ ਦਾ ਫ਼ਰਸ਼, ਡੈੱਕ; ਜ਼ਮੀਨ; ਛਾ ਜਾਣਾ, ਢਕ ਲੈਣਾ; ਅਲੰਕਰਤ ਕਰਨਾ, ਸ਼ਿੰਗਾਰਨਾ

declaim (ਡਿ'ਕਲੇਇਮ) v ਭਾਸ਼ਣ ਦੇਣਾ, ਜੋਸ਼ੀਲੀ ਤਕਰੀਰ ਕਰਨੀ

declamation (ਡੈੱਕੱਲਆ'ਮੇਇਸ਼ਨ) n ਭਾਵੁਕ ਭਾਸ਼ਣ; ਭਾਸ਼ਣਬਾਜ਼ੀ; ਅਲੰਕਾਰਮਈ ਵਿਆਖਿਆਨ

declaration (ਡੈੱਕੱਲਅ'ਰੇਇਸ਼ਨ) n ਐਲਾਨ, ਘੋਸ਼ਣਾ-ਪੱਤਰ, ਮਹਿਸੂਲੀ ਮਾਲ ਦਾ ਵਿਵਰਨ

declaratory (ਡਿ'ਕਲੈਰਅਟ(ਅ)ਰਿ) a ਘੋਸ਼ਕ, ਸੂਚਕ, ਪ੍ਰਕਾਸ਼ਕ

declare (ਡਿ'ਕਲੇਅ*) v ਐਲਾਨ ਕਰਨਾ, ਘੋਸ਼ਣਾ ਕਰਨਾ, ਬਿਆਨ ਦੇਣਾ, ਸੂਚਤ ਕਰਨਾ, ਮਹਿਸੂਲੀ ਮਾਲ ਦਾ ਵਿਵਰਨ ਦੇਣਾ; ~d ਐਲਾਨ ਸ਼ੁਦਾ, ਘੋਸ਼ਤ

declass (ਡੀ'ਕਲਾਸ) v ਛੇਕਣਾ, ਜਮਾਤ ਜਾਂ ਜਾਤੀ ਵਿਚੋਂ ਕੱਢਣਾ, ਹੁੱਕਾ-ਪਾਣੀ ਬੰਦ ਕਰਨਾ

decline (ਡਿ'ਕਲਾਇਨ) n v ਪਤਨ, ਗਿਰਾਵਟ, ਨਿਘਾਰ, ਉਤਰਾਅ;(ਭਾਅ ਦਾ) ਮੰਦਾ, ਅੰਤਮ ਘੜੀ, ਪਤਨ ਵਲ ਜਾਣਾ; ਕੀਮਤਾਂ ਘਟੀਆਂ, ਭਾਅ ਮੰਦੇ ਹੋਣੇ, ਢਲਣਾ, ਢਾਲਣਾ, ਝੁਕਾਉਣਾ; ~on ਉਤਰਨਾ

declining (ਡਿ'ਕਲਾਇਨਿਙ) a ਢਲਵਾਂ, ਢਾਲਦਾਰ, ਪਤਨਸ਼ੀਲ

decode (ਡੀ'ਕਅਉਡ) v ਗੁਪਤਲੇਖ ਪੜ੍ਹਨਾ, ਸੰਕੇਤ-ਵਾਚਨਾ

decompose (ਡੀਕਅੰ*ਪਅਉਜ਼) v ਅੰਗ-ਨਿਖੇੜ ਕਰਨਾ, ਅਲੱਗ ਕਰਨਾ, ਵਿਸ਼ਲੇਸ਼ਣ ਕਰਨਾ; ਗਲਣਾ, ਸੜਨਾ, ਗਲਾਉਣਾ

decomposition (ਡੀਕੰਪਅ'ਜ਼ਿਸ਼ਨ) v ਵਿਘਟਣ; ਵਿਸ਼ਲੇਸ਼ਣ, ਸੜਣ, ਗਲਣ

decontaminate (ਡੀਕਅਨ'ਟੈਮਿਨੇਇਟ) v ਰੋਗਾਣੂਰਹਿਤ ਕਰਨਾ, ਸ਼ੁੱਧ ਕਰਨਾ, ਦੋਸ਼-ਮੁਕਤ ਕਰਨਾ

decontamination (ਡੀਕੰਟੈਮਿਨੇਸ਼ਨ) n ਨਿਰਦੋਸ਼ੀਕਰਣ, ਸ਼ੁਧੀਕਰਣ, ਦੋਸ਼ਮੁਕਤੀ

decontrol (ਡੀਕੰਟਰਅਉਲ) n v ਕੰਟਰੋਲ, ਨਿਵਾਰਨ, ਵਿਨਿਯੰਤਰਣ, ਅਪਨਿਯੰਤਰਣ ਕਰਨਾ

decor (ਡੇਇਕੋ*) n ਸ਼ਿੰਗਾਰ, ਸਜਾਵਟ; **~ate** ਸ਼ਿੰਗਾਰਨਾ, ਸਜਾਉਣਾ, ਸੰਵਾਰਨਾ, ਤਮਗਾ ਦੇਣਾ; **~ation** ਸਜਾਵਟ, ਸ਼ਿੰਗਾਰ, ਅਲੰਕਰਣ, ਅਲੰਕਾਰ; ਸਾਜ਼; ਤਮਗਾ

decorum (ਡਿ'ਕੋਰਅਮ) n ਮਰਯਾਦਾ, ਸੁਘੜਤਾ, ਵਿਹਾਰਸ਼ੀਲਤਾ, ਸੁੱਚਜਤਾ

decoy (ਡੀ'ਕੋਇ, ਡਿ'ਕੋਇ) n v ਫੰਦਾ, ਚਾਰਾ, ਫਸਾਉਣਾ, ਧੋਖੇ ਨਾਲ ਫੜਨਾ, ਘੇਰਨਾ, ਧੋਖਾ ਦੇਣਾ

decrease (ਡੀ'ਕਰੀਸ, ਡ਼ਿਕਰੀਸ) v n ਘੱਟ ਕਰਨਾ, ਘਟਾਉਣਾ; ਕਮੀ, ਘਾਟਾ; **~d** ਘਟਿਆ

decree (ਡਿ'ਕਰੀ) n v ਫ਼ਰਮਾਨ, ਹੁਕਮ; ਰਜ਼ਾ, ਡਿਗਰੀ; ਰਾਜ-ਆਗਿਆ; ਹੁਕਮ ਦੇਣਾ, ਫ਼ਰਮਾਨ ਜਾਰੀ ਕਰਨਾ, ਆਗਿਆ ਦੇਣੀ, ਡਿਗਰੀ ਕਰਨੀ

decrown (ਡੀ'ਕਰਾਉਨ) v ਤਾਜ ਉਤਾਰਨਾ, ਤਾਜਹੀਨ ਕਰਨਾ

decry (ਡ਼ਿ'ਕਰਾਇ) v ਨਿੰਦਿਆ, ਭੰਡਣਾ, ਦੋਸ਼ ਲਗਾਉਣਾ, ਕੋਸਣਾ

dedicate (ਡੇਡਿਕੇਇਟ) v ਭੇਟਾ ਕਰਨਾ, ਅਰਪਣ ਕਰਨਾ; ਸਮਰਪਣ ਕਰਨਾ, ਪ੍ਰਦਾਨ ਕਰਨਾ, ਨਿਛਾਵਰ ਕਰਨਾ, ਸੌਂਪਣਾ; **~d** ਭੇਟਾ ਕੀਤਾ, ਸਮਰਪਤ; ਸਿਦਕਵਾਨ

dedication (ਡੈਡਿਕੇ'ਇਸ਼ਨ) n ਭੇਟਾ, ਨਜ਼ਰ, ਸਮਰਪਣ, ਸ਼ਰਧਾ

deduct (ਡਿ'ਡਅੱਕਟ) v ਘਟਾਉਣਾ, ਘਟਾ ਦੇਣਾ; ਕਟੌਤੀ ਕਰਨਾ, ਕੱਟਣਾ, ਅਨੁਮਾਨ ਕਰਨਾ; **~ion** ਕਟੌਤੀ, ਕਾਟ, ਛੋਟ; ਸਿੱਟਾ

deed (ਡੀਡ) n ਕੰਮ, ਕਾਰਜ; ਕਰਨੀ; ਦਸਤਾਵੇਜ਼, ਲਿਖਤ, ਪੱਟਾ

deem (ਡੀਮ) v ਵਿਚਾਰ ਕਰਨਾ, ਗਿਣਨਾ, ਸੋਚਣਾ, ਮੰਨਣਾ, ਸਮਝਣਾ, ਅਨੁਭਵ ਕਰਨਾ, ਅਨੁਮਾਨ ਲਾਉਣਾ

deep (ਡੀਪ) a n adv ਡੂੰਘਾ, ਅਗਾਧ, ਗੰਭੀਰ, ਗਹਿਰਾ; ਘਣਾ; ਡੁੱਬਿਆ, ਸ਼ੋਖ਼ (ਰੰਗ), ਤੀਬਰ; ਅਤੀਅੰਤ, ਅਧਿਕ; ਸਾਗਰ, ਸਮੁੰਦਰ ਦਾ ਡੂੰਘਾ ਹਿੱਸਾ; ਗਹਿਰਾਈ ਵਿਚ; **~learning** ਅਥਾਹ ਵਿਦਵਤਾ, ਡੂੰਘਾ ਗਿਆਨ; **~interest** ਡਾਢੀ ਦਿਲਚਸਪੀ; **~rooted** ਡੂੰਘਾ, ਗਹਿਰਾ; **in~waters** ਸੰਕਟ ਵਿਚ ਫਸਿਆ; **the~** ਸਮੁੰਦਰ, ਸਾਗਰ, ਖੱਡਾ, ਟੋਆ

deer (ਡ਼ਿਅ*) n ਹਿਰਨ, ਮਿਰਗਾ

deface (ਡਿ'ਫ਼ੇਇਸ) v ਰੂਪ ਵਿਗਾੜਨਾ, ਕਰੂਪ ਕਰਨਾ, ਮਿਟਾਉਣਾ, ਬਦਨਾਮ ਕਰਨਾ; **~d** ਵਿਗੜਿਆ, ਕਰੂਪ, ਵਿਕਿਰਤ

defacto (ਡੇਏ'ਫ਼ੈਕਟਅੋ) adv ਯਥਾਰਥ ਵਿਚ

defalcate (ਡੇਇ'ਫ਼ੈਲਕੇਇਟ) v ਗ਼ਬਨ ਕਰਨਾ ਖਾ ਜਾਣਾ, (ਰੁਪਏ ਦੀ) ਖਿਆਨਤ ਕਰਨੀ ਹੜਪਣਾ, ਗੋਲਮਾਲ ਕਰਨਾ, ਮਾਰ ਲੈਣਾ

defalcation (ਡੀਫ਼ੈਲ'ਕੇਇਸ਼ਨ) n ਗ਼ਬਨ, ਖ਼ਾਲਾ ਮਾਲਾ, ਵਿਸ਼ਵਾਸਘਾਤ

defamation (ਡੇਫ਼ੱਅ'ਮੇਇਸ਼ਨ) *n* ਬਦਨਾਮੀ, ਨਿਰਾਦਰ, ਤੌਹੀਨ, ਮਾਨ-ਹਾਨੀ, ਹੱਤਕ, ਬੇਇੱਜ਼ਤੀ

defamatory (ਡਿ'ਫ਼ੈਮਅਟ(ਇ)ਰਿ) *a* ਬਦਨਾਮੀ ਵਾਲਾ, ਬਦਨਾਮੀ ਦਾ, ਕਲੰਕਤਕਾਰੀ

defame (ਡਿ'ਫ਼ੇਇਮ) *v* ਬਦਨਾਮ ਕਰਨਾ, ਨਿਰਾਦਰ ਕਰਨਾ, ਭੰਡੀ ਕਰਨੀ, ਨਿੰਦਾ ਕਰਨਾ

default (ਡਿ'ਫ਼ੋਲਟ) *n v* ਉਕਾਈ, ਤਰੁਟੀ, ਭੁੱਲ ਚੁੱਕ; ਅਣਗਹਿਲੀ ਕਰਨੀ, ਅਦਾਲਤ ਵਿਚ ਹਾਜ਼ਰ ਨਾ ਹੋਣਾ, ਪੈਰਵੀ ਨਾ ਕਰਨੀ; ਹਿਸਾਬ ਨਾ ਚੁਕਾਉਣਾ; ~ed ਅਸੁੱਧ, ਦੋਸ਼ਪੂਰਨ (ਬੀਮਾ, ਨਿੱਝਕ ਆਦਿ); ~er (ਅਦਾਲਤ ਵਿਚ) ਗ਼ੈਰ-ਹਾਜ਼ਰ ਧਿਰ; ਭੁਗਤਾਨ ਤੋਂ ਖੁੰਝਣ ਵਾਲਾ

defeat (ਡਿ'ਫ਼ੀਟ) *n v* ਹਾਰ, ਅਸਫਲਤਾ, ਸ਼ਿਕਸਤ, ਹਰਾਉਣਾ, ਨਿਸਫਲ ਕਰਨਾ; ਪਿੱਠ ਲਾਉਣੀ; ~d ਹਾਰਿਆ, ਪਰਾਜਿਤ

defect (ਡਿਫ਼ੈਕਟ) *n* ਔਗੁਣ, ਵਿਕਾਰ, ਤਰੁਟੀ, ਦੋਸ਼, ਐਬ, ਨੁਕਸ, ਖ਼ਾਮੀ, ਖ਼ਰਾਬੀ, ਕਲੰਕ, ਕਮੀ; ~ion ਪੱਖ-ਤਿਆਗ, ਧਰਮ-ਤਿਆਗ, ਦਲ-ਤਿਆਗ

defective (ਡਿ'ਫ਼ੈਕਟਿਵ) *a* ਨੁਕਸਦਾਰ, ਦੋਸ਼ਪੂਰਨ, ਤਰੁਟੀਪੂਰਨ, ਘੱਟਾ, ਦਾਗ਼ੀ, ਅਪੂਰਨ

defector (ਡਿ'ਫ਼ੈਕਟਅ*) *n* ਦਲਬਦਲੂ

defence (ਡਿ'ਫ਼ੈਂਸ) *n* ਰੱਖਿਆ, ਸੁਰੱਖਿਆ, ਪ੍ਰਤੀਵਾਦ ਲੇਖ, ਬਚਾਉ, ਰੋਕ, ਆੜ, ਓਟ, ਕਿਲ੍ਹਾ-ਬੰਦੀ; **line of~** ਮੋਰਚਾਬੰਦੀ

defend (ਡਿ'ਫ਼ੈਂਡ) *v* ਰੱਖਿਆ ਕਰਨਾ, ਬਚਾਉ ਕਰਨਾ; ਪ੍ਰਤੀਵਾਦ ਕਰਨਾ, ਪੱਖ-ਪੁਸ਼ਟੀ ਕਰਨੀ; ਸਫ਼ਾਈ ਪੇਸ਼ ਕਰਨਾ, ਮੁਕੱਦਮੇ ਦੀ ਜਵਾਬਦੇਹੀ ਕਰਨਾ; ਉਜਰਦਾਰੀ ਕਰਨਾ; ~**able** ਰੱਖਿਆ ਕਰਨ ਯੋਗ

defensive (ਡਿ'ਫ਼ੈਂਸਿਵ) *n a* ਬਚਾਉ, ਰੱਖਿਆ, ਰੱਖਿਅਕ, ਰੱਖਿਆਤਮਕ

defer (ਡਿ'ਫ਼ਅ*) *v* ਟਾਲਣਾ, ਲਮਕਾਉਣਾ; ਮੁਲਤਵੀ ਕਰਨਾ, ਸਥਗਿਤ ਕਰਨਾ; ~**ment** ਦੇਰੀ, ਸਥਗਨ; ~**red** ਮੁਲਤਵੀ ਕੀਤਾ ਗਿਆ, ਸਥਗਿਤ

deference (ਡੈਫ਼(ਅ)ਰ(ਅ)ਨਸ) *n* ਸਨਮਾਨ, ਆਦਰ, ਇੱਜ਼ਤ, ਲਿਹਾਜ਼, ਸਤਿਕਾਰ

deferent (ਡੈਫ਼(ਅ)ਰਅੰਟ) *a* ਸਨਮਾਨਤ

deferential (ਡੈਫ਼ਅ'ਰੈਂਸ਼ਲ) *a* ਆਦਰਪੂਰਨ, ਆਦਰਯੋਗ, ਮਾਨਯੋਗ

defiant (ਡਿ'ਡਫ਼ਾਇਅੰਟ) *a* ਵਿਰੋਧੀ, ਅਗਿਆਕਾਰੀ, ਗੁਸਤਾਖ਼

deficiency (ਡਿ'ਫ਼ਿਸ਼ਂਸਿ) *n* ਅਪੂਰਨਤਾ, ਟੋਟਾ, ਕਮੀ, ਕਸਰ, ਅਧੂਰਾਪਣ, ਨੁਕਸ, ਅਭਾਵ

deficient (ਡਿ'ਫ਼ਿਸ਼ਂਟ) *a* ਥੋੜ੍ਹਾ, ਘੱਟ, ਅਧੂਰਾ, ਅਪੂਰਨ, ਊਣਾ, ਦੋਸ਼ਪੂਰਨ

deficit ('ਡੈਫ਼ਿਸਿਟ) *n* ਘਾਟਾ, ਟੋਟਾ, ਕਮੀ, ਨੁਕਸਾਨ, ਕਸਰ

defile (ਡਿ'ਫ਼ਾਇਲ, 'ਡੀਫ਼ਾਇਲ) *v n* ਪਾਲ ਵਿਚ ਹੋ ਕੇ ਚੱਲਣਾ; ਤੰਗ ਰਸਤਾ, ਸੰਕੀਰਣ ਘਾਟੀ, ਸੌੜਾ ਰਾਹ; ਭ੍ਰਿਸ਼ਟ ਕਰਨਾ, ਸਤ ਭੰਗ ਕਰਨਾ, ਅਪਵਿੱਤਰ ਕਰਨਾ, ਭਿੱਟਣਾ, ਦੂਸ਼ਤ ਕਰਨਾ; ~**d** ਦੂਸ਼ਤ, ਕਲੰਕਤ, ਭ੍ਰਿਸ਼ਟ, ਅਪਵਿੱਤਰ; ~**ment** ਅਪਵਿੱਤਰਤਾ, ਦੂਸ਼ਣ, ਭ੍ਰਿਸ਼ਟਤਾ, ਪਲੀਤੀ ਭਿੱਟ

definable (ਡਿ'ਫ਼ਾਇਨਅਬਲ) *a* ਪਰਿਭਾਸ਼ੀ; ਸਪਸ਼ਟ ਕਰਨ ਯੋਗ; ਪਰਿਭਾਸ਼ਾ

define (ਡਿ'ਫ਼ਾਇਨ) *v* ਪਰਿਭਾਸ਼ਾ ਦੇਣਾ, ਲੱਛਣ ਦਰਸਾਣਾ, ਸਪਸ਼ਟ ਅਰਥ ਦੱਸਣਾ, ਸੀਮਾ-ਅੰਕਤ ਕਰਨਾ; ~**d** ਪਰਿਭਾਸ਼ਤ, ਨਿਰਧਾਰਤ

definite ('ਡੈਫ਼ਿਨਿਟ) *a* ਨਿਸ਼ਚਤ, ਨਿਯਤ, ਸਪਸ਼ਟ, ਸੀਮਾਬੱਧ ਨਿਰੀਤ, ਮੁਕੱਰਰ; ~**ly** ਸਪਸ਼ਟ ਤੌਰ ਤੇ, ਬਿਲਕੁਲ

definition ('ਡਿਫ਼ਿ'ਨਿਸ਼ਨ) *n* ਪਰਿਭਾਸ਼ਾ,

ਵਿਆਖਿਆ, ਲੱਛਣ, ਅਰਥ ਨਿਰੂਪਣ

definitive (ਡਿ'ਫ਼ਿਨਿਟਿਵ੍) *a* ਨਿਯਤ, ਨਿਸ਼ਚਤ; ਨਿਰਣਾਤਮਕ

deflate (ਡਿ'ਫ਼ਲੇਇਟ) *v* ਵਧੇ ਮੁੱਲ ਨੂੰ ਘਟਾਉਣਾ, ਮੁਦਰਾ-ਸਫੀਤੀ ਵਿੱਚ ਕਮੀ ਕਰਨਾ; ਫੁਸ ਕਰਨਾ, ਹਵਾ ਕੱਢਣਾ

deflation (ਡਿ'ਫ਼ਲੇਇਸ਼ਨ) *n* ਮੁਦਰਾ-ਸਫੀਤੀ ਵਿੱਚ ਕਮੀ, ਵਧੀਆਂ ਕੀਮਤਾਂ ਦਾ ਘਟਣਾ, ਹਵਾ ਕੱਢਣ ਦੀ ਕਿਰਿਆ

deflect (ਡਿ'ਫ਼ਲੈੱਕਟ) *v* ਲਾਂਭੇ ਮੁੜਨਾ, ਥਿੜਕਣਾ, ਮੁੜਨਾ; ~ion, deflexion ਪੱਥ-ਵਿਚਲਣ, ਚੁੰਬਕੀ ਸੂਈ ਦਾ ਕੇਂਦਰ-ਬਿੰਦੂ ਤੋਂ ਹਟਾਉ

deforest ('ਡੀ'ਫ਼ੌਰਿਸਟ) *v* ਜੰਗਲ ਕੱਟਣੇ; ~ation (ਡੀ'ਫ਼ੌਰਿਸਟੇਇਸ਼ਨ) *n* ਜੰਗਲ ਵੱਢਣ

deform (ਡਿ'ਫ਼ੌਮ) *v* ਕਰੂਪ ਕਰਨਾ, ਰੂਪ ਵਿਗਾੜਨਾ, ਸ਼ਕਲ ਵਿਗਾੜਨੀ, ਬੇਢੰਗਾ ਕਰਨਾ; ~ation ਕਰੂਪਤਾ, ਬਦਸੂਰਤੀ, ਵਿਰੂਪਤਾ, ਬੱਜ, ਸ਼ਬਦ ਦਾ ਵਿਗੜਿਆ ਰੂਪ; ~ed ਬੇਢੰਗਾ, ਬੇਡੋਲ, ਵਿਰੂਪਤ

defraud (ਡਿ'ਫ਼ਰੋਡ) *v* ਛਲ ਕਰਨਾ, ਧੋਖਾ ਕਰਨਾ, ਕਪਟ ਕਰਨਾ, ਠੱਗਣਾ, ਹੱਕ ਮਾਰਨਾ

deft (ਡੈੱਫ਼ਟ) *a* ਹੁਸ਼ਿਆਰ, ਚਤਰ, ਨਿਪੁੰਨ, ਪ੍ਰਵੀਨ, ਕੁਸ਼ਲ, ਚਲਾਕ; ~ness ਨਿਪੁੰਨਤਾ, ਚਤਰਤਾ, ਚਲਾਕੀ, ਹੁਸ਼ਿਆਰੀ

defuse ('ਡੀ'ਫ਼ਯੂਜ਼) *v* ਸੰਕਟ ਟਾਲਣਾ; (ਬੰਬ) ਨਕਾਰਾ ਕਰਨਾ

defy (ਡਿ'ਫ਼ਾਇ) *v* ਵਿਰੋਧ ਕਰਨਾ, ਅਵੱਗਿਆ ਕਰਨਾ, ਆਗਿਆ ਨੂੰ ਉਲੰਘਣਾ, ਉਪੇਖਿਆ ਕਰਨਾ, ਵੰਗਾਰਨਾ

degenerate ('ਡਿ'ਜੇਨਅਰਅਟ) *a v n* ਪਤਿਤ, ਹੀਣਾ, ਚਰਿਤ੍ਰਹੀਨ, ਭ੍ਰਿਸ਼ਟ, ਨੀਚ; ਨਿਘਰਿਆ, ਵਿਗੜਿਆ; ਪਤਿਤ ਹੋਣਾ; ਪਤਿਤ ਪੁਰਸ਼

degeneration ('ਡਿ'ਜੇਨਅ'ਰੇਇਸ਼ਨ) *n* ਗਿਰਾਵਟ, ਹਾ੍ਸ, ਪਤਨ, ਅਧੋਗਤੀ

degradation ('ਡੇਗਰਅ'ਡੇਇਸ਼ਨ) *n* ਅਧੋਗਤੀ, ਪਤਨ, ਗਿਰਾਵਟ

degrade (ਡਿ'ਗਰੇਇਡ) *v* ਪਦ ਘਟਾਉਣਾ, ਅਪਮਾਨ ਕਰਨਾ, ਨਿਰਾਦਰ ਕਰਨਾ; ਨੈਤਕ ਪਤਨ ਹੋਣਾ, ਵਿਗਾੜਨਾ, ਪਤਿਤ ਕਰਨਾ, ਭ੍ਰਿਸ਼ਟ ਕਰਨਾ

degrading (ਡਿ'ਗਰੇਇਡਿੰਡ) *a* ਅਪਮਾਨਜਨਕ, ਹੀਣਤਾ ਭਰਿਆ, ਬੁਰਾ, ਹੱਤਕ ਭਰਿਆ, ਬੇਇੱਜ਼ਤੀ ਵਾਲਾ

degree (ਡਿ'ਗਰੀ) *n* ਦਰਜਾ, ਪਦਵੀ, ਮਾਤਰਾ ਡਿਗਰੀ, ਸਨਦ; ਤਾਪਮਾਨ ਦੀ ਇਕਾਈ ਉਪਾਧੀ; (ਵਿਆ) ਕੋਟੀ

degression (ਡਿ'ਗਰੈੱਸ਼ਨ) *n* ਗਿਰਾਵਟ, ਜਵਾਲ ਪਤਨ

dehumanize ('ਡੀ'ਹਯੂਮਅਨਾਇਜ਼) *v* ਅਮਾਨਵ ਬਣਾਉਣਾ, ਹੀਣਾ ਕਰਨਾ, ਅਸੱਭਿਯ ਬਣਾਉਣਾ

deil (ਡੀਲ) *n* ਭੂਤ-ਪਰੇਤ, ਜਿੰਨ, ਚੁੜੇਲ

deity ('ਡੀਇਟਿ) *n* ਦੇਵਤਵ, ਦੇਵ ਸਰੂਪ, ਦੇਵਤਾ The D~ ਈਸ਼ਵਰ, ਰਚਨਹਾਰ, ਕਰਤਾਰ, ਕਰਤਾਪੁਰਖ

deject ('ਡਿ'ਜੈੱਕਟ) *v* ਦਿਲ ਤੋੜਨਾ, ਉਦਾਸ ਕਰਨਾ, ਦਿਲ ਖੱਟਾ ਕਰਨਾ, ਬੇਦਿਲ ਹੋਣਾ; ~ed ਉਦਾਸ, ਨਿੰਮੋਝੂਣਾ, ਉਦਾਸੀਨ; ~ion ਨਿਰਾਸਤਾ, ਉਦਾਸੀ, ਖਿੰਨਤਾ, ਗਿਲਾਨੀ

de jure ('ਡੇਇ'ਜੂਅ(ਰਿ) (L) *a* ਕਾਨੂੰਨੀ ਅਧਿਕਾਰ ਅਨੁਸਾਰ

delay (ਡਿ'ਲੇਇ) *v n* ਦੇਰ ਕਰਨਾ, ਰੁਕਾਵ ਪਾਉਣਾ, ਟਾਲਣਾ, ਲਮਕਾਉਣਾ; ਦੇਰ, ਰੁਕਾਵ

delegate ('ਡੇਲਿਗਾਇਟ, ਡੈਲਿਗਾਿਟ) *v*

ਪ੍ਰਤਿਨਿਧ ਬਣਾਉਣਾ, ਮੁਖ਼ਤਿਆਰ ਕਰਨਾ; ਪ੍ਰਤਿਨਿਧ, ਏਲਚੀ, ਮੁਖ਼ਤਿਆਰ, ਡੈਲੀਗੇਟ

delegation (‘ਡੈਲਿ’ਗੇਇਸ਼ਨ) *n* ਪ੍ਰਤਿਨਿਧ-ਮੰਡਲ, ਵਫ਼ਦ, ਅਧਿਕਾਰ-ਸੌਂਪਣਾ, ਸੁਪਰਦਗੀ

delete (ਡਿ’ਲੀਟ) *v* ਕੱਟਣਾ; ਮੇਟਣਾ, ਲੀਕ ਫੇਰਨੀ, ਰੱਦ ਕਰਨਾ; ~d ਕੱਟਿਆ

deletion (ਡਿ’ਲੀਸ਼ਨ) *n* ਕਾਟ, ਛਾਂਟ

deliberate (ਡਿ’ਲਿਬਅਰੇਇਟ) *v a* ਵਿਚਾਰ ਕਰਨਾ, ਸੋਚਣਾ, ਚਿੰਤਨ ਕਰਨਾ, ਵਿਚਾਰਨਾ, ਸਲਾਹ ਮਸ਼ਵਰਾ ਕਰਨਾ, ਰਾਇ ਲੈਣਾ

deliberation (ਡਿ’ਲਿਬਅ’ਰੇਇਸ਼ਨ) *n* ਸੋਚ-ਵਿਚਾਰ, ਸਲਾਹ-ਮਸ਼ਵਰਾ, ਵਾਦ-ਵਿਵਾਦ, ਚਰਚਾ, ਬਹਿਸ

deliberative (ਡਿ’ਲਿਬ(ਅ)ਰਟਿਵ) *a* ਵਿਚਾਰਾਤਮਕ, ਵਿਚਾਰਪੂਰਨ

delecacies (‘ਡੈਲਿਕਅਸਿਜ਼) *n* ਸੁਆਦਲੀਆਂ ਚੀਜ਼ਾਂ, ਨਿਆਮਤਾਂ, ਸੁਆਦੀ ਭੋਜਨ

delicacy (‘ਡੈਲਿਕਅਸਿ) *n* ਸੁਖਮਤਾ, ਬਾਰੀਕੀ, ਮਧੁਰਤਾ, ਕੋਮਲਤਾ, ਨਜ਼ਾਕਤ, ਸੁਆਦੀ ਭੋਜਨ

delicate (ਡੈਲਿਕਅਟ) *a* ਨਾਜ਼ੁਕ, ਕੋਮਲ; ਸੁਖਮ-ਗ੍ਰਾਹੀ, ਸੰਵੇਦਨਸ਼ੀਲ, ਸੁਖਮ, ਬਾਰੀਕ, ਹਲਕਾ (ਹੱਥ), ਸੁਆਦੀ (ਭੋਜਨ); ਸ਼ਰਮੀਲਾ, ਮਲੂਕ, ਕੂਲਾ

delicious (ਡਿ’ਲਿਸ਼ਿਅਸ) *a* ਸੁਆਦੀ, ਰਸੀਲਾ, ਮਿੱਠਾ, ਮਜ਼ੇਦਾਰ

delight (ਡਿਲਾਇਟ) *n a* ਪ੍ਰਸੰਨਤਾ, ਖ਼ੁਸ਼ੀ, ਆਨੰਦ; ਖ਼ੁਸ਼ ਹੋਣਾ, ਪ੍ਰਸੰਨ ਹੋਣਾ, ਆਨੰਦਤ ਹੋਣਾ; ~ed ਖ਼ੁਸ਼, ਪ੍ਰਸੰਨ; ~ful ਆਨੰਦਮਈ, ਦਿਲਚਸਪ, ਰਸੀਲਾ, ਰਮਤੀਕ; ~some ਆਨੰਦਦਾਇਕ

delimitate (ਡਿ’ਲਿਮਿਟੇਇਟ) *v* ਹੱਦਬੰਦੀ ਕਰਨਾ, ਸੀਮਾਬੱਧ ਕਰਨਾ

delimitation (ਡਿ’ਲਿਮਿ’ਟੇਇਸ਼ਨ) *n* ਹੱਦਬੰਦੀ, ਸੀਮਾ-ਨਿਰਧਾਰਨ, ਸੀਮਾ-ਨਿਰਦੇਸ਼ਨ

delineable (ਡਿ’ਲਿਨਿਅਬਲ) *a* ਰੂਪ-ਰੇਖਯੋਗ, ਵਰਨਣਯੋਗ

delineate (ਡਿ’ਲਿਨਿਏਇਟ) *v* ਵਰਨਣ ਕਰਨਾ, ਬਿਆਨ ਕਰਨਾ, ਰੇਖਾਂਤਰ ਕਰਨਾ, ਨਕਸ਼ਾ ਖਿੱਚਣਾ

delineation (ਡਿ’ਲਿਨਿ’ਏਇਸ਼ਨ) *n* ਚਿਤਰਨ, ਬਿਆਨ, ਰੂਪ-ਰੇਖਾ, ਖ਼ਾਕਾ, ਵਰਨਣ, ਉੱਲੇਖ, ਬਿਰਤਾਂਤ

delinquency (ਡਿ’ਲਿਙਕਵਅੰਸਿ) *n* ਖ਼ਤਾ, ਦੋਸ਼; ਭੁੱਲ; ਕੁਕਰਮ, ਅਪਰਾਧ

delinquent (ਡਿ’ਲਿਙਕਵਅੰਟ) *n* ਅਪਰਾਧੀ, ਕਸੂਰਵਾਰ, ਖ਼ਤਾਵਾਰ

deliquesce (‘ਡੈਲਿ’ਕਵੈੱਸ) *v* ਤਰਲ ਹੋਣਾ, ਪਤਲਾ ਹੋ ਜਾਣਾ, ਪਿਘਲਣਾ, ਪਸੀਜਣਾ, ਘੁਲ ਜਾਣਾ; ~nce ਤਰਲਤਾ, ਦਵਤਾ; ਪਤਲਾਪਣ

delirium (ਡਿ’ਲਿਰਿਅਮ) *n* ਸਰਸਾਮ; ਬਕਝਵਾਦ; ਉਨਮਾਦ

deliver (ਡਿ’ਲਿਵਅ*) *v* (ਡਾਕ) ਵੰਡਣਾ; (ਚਿੱਠੀ) ਦੇਣਾ, ਸਪੁਰਦ ਕਰਨਾ, (ਭਾਸ਼ਨ) ਦੇਣਾ, ਉਤਪੰਨ ਕਰਨਾ, ਜਨਮ ਦੇਣਾ; ~y ਸੁਪਰਦਗੀ, (ਡਾਕ ਆਦਿ ਦੀ) ਵੰਡ, ਛੁਟਕਾਰਾ, ਅਰਪਣ, ਪ੍ਰਦਾਨ

dell (ਡੈੱਲ) *n* ਵਾਦੀ, ਘਾਟੀ, ਦੂਨ, ਖੱਡ

delta (ਡੈੱਲਟਅ) *n* ਯੂਨਾਨੀ ਵਰਨਮਾਲਾ ਦਾ ਚੌਥਾ ਅੱਖਰ, ਡੈਲਟਾ, ਦਹਾਨਾ

delude (ਡਿ’ਲੂਡ) *v* ਭਰਮਾਉਣਾ, ਧੋਖਾ ਦੇਣਾ, ਛਲਣਾ, ਸਬਜ਼ ਬਾਗ਼ ਦਿਖਾਉਣਾ, ਬਹਿਕਾਉਣਾ

delusion (ਡੈ’ਲੂਯ਼ਨ) *n* ਵਹਿਮ, ਭੁਲੇਖਾ, ਮਾਇਆ-ਜਾਲ

delusive (ਡਿ’ਲੀਸਿਵ੍) *a* ਭਰਮਪੂਰਨ, ਮਾਇਆਵੀ

deluxe (ਡਲ'ਅਕਸ) *(F) a adv* ਬਹੁਤ ਵਧੀਆ, ਸ਼ਾਨਦਾਰ (ਢੰਗ ਨਾਲ)	**demonetization** ('ਡੀ'ਮਅੱਨਿਟਾਇ'ਜ਼ਇਸ਼ਨ) *n* ਸਿੱਕੇ ਦਾ ਅਪ੍ਰਚਲਕਰਨ
delve (ਡੈਲਵ੍) *v* ਪੁੱਟਣਾ, ਖੋਜ ਕਰਨਾ, ਛਾਣਬੀਨ ਕਰਨੀ, ਡੁਬਕੀ ਲਾਉਣੀ, (ਸੜਕ ਆਦਿ ਦਾ) ਅਚਾਨਕ ਧਸ ਜਾਣਾ, ਬੈਠ ਜਾਣਾ, ਪ੍ਰਵੇਸ਼	**demonetize** ('ਡੀ'ਮਅੱਨਿਟਾਇਜ਼) *v* ਸਰਕਾਰੀ ਸਿੱਕੇ ਨੂੰ ਚੱਲਣ ਤੋਂ ਹਟਾਉਣਾ, ਵਿਮੁਦਰੀਕਰਨ ਕਰਨਾ
demagogue ('ਡੈੱਮਅਗੋੱਗ) *n* ਸ਼ਬਦ-ਆਡੰਬਰੀ, ਉਸਟੰਡਬਾਜ਼ੀ; ਸਿਆਸੀ ਆਗੂ	**demoniac** (ਡਿ'ਮਅਉਨਿਐਕ) *a* ਦਾਨਵੀ, ਰਾਖਸ਼ੀ; ~al ਅਸੁਰੀ; ਦਾਨਵੀ; ਰਾਖਸ਼ੀ
demagogy ('ਡੈੱਮਅਗੋੱਗਿ) *n* ਨੇਤਾਗੀਰੀ, ਘਟੀਆ ਲੀਡਰੀ	**demonic** (ਡੀ'ਮੌਨਿਕ) *a* ਭੂਤਗ੍ਰਸਤ; ਪਿਸ਼ਾਚਗ੍ਰਸਤ
demand (ਡਿ'ਮਾਂਡ) *n v* ਮੰਗ, ਲੋੜ, ਜ਼ਰੂਰਤ, ਦਾਅਵਾ, ਅਵੱਸ਼ਕਤਾ ਹੋਈ, ਮੰਗ ਕਰਨਾ, ਮੰਗਣਾ	**demonstrate** ('ਡੈੱਮਅਨਸਟਰੇਇਟ) *v* ਪਰਦਰਸ਼ਤ ਕਰਨਾ, ਨੁਮਾਇਸ਼ ਕਰਨਾ, ਮੁਜ਼ਾਹਰਾ ਕਰਨਾ, ਵਿਖਾਲਾ ਕਰਨਾ, ਪਰਦਰਸ਼ਨ ਕਰਨਾ, ਵਿਆਖਿਆ ਕਰਨਾ, ਸਿੱਧ ਕਰਨਾ, ਪ੍ਰਮਾਣਤ ਕਰਨਾ
demarcate ('ਡੀਮਾ*ਕੇਇਟ) *v* ਹੱਦ-ਬੰਦੀ ਕਰਨਾ, ਨਿਸ਼ਾਨਦੇਹੀ ਕਰਨਾ, ਸੀਮਾ ਨਿਸ਼ਚਤ ਕਰਨਾ; ~d ਨਿਸ਼ਚਤ, ਨਿਰਧਾਰਤ, ਸੀਮਾਂਕਤ	
demarcation ('ਡੀਮਾ*ਕੇਇਸ਼ਨ) *n* ਹੱਦਬੰਦੀ, ਸੀਮਾ-ਨਿਰਧਾਰਨ, ਸੀਮਾ-ਅੰਕਣ	**demonstration** ('ਡੈੱਮਅਨ'ਸਟਰੇਇਸ਼ਨ) *v* ਪਰਦਰਸ਼ਨ, ਨੁਮਾਇਸ਼, ਮੁਜ਼ਾਹਰਾ, ਸਪਸ਼ਟੀਕਰਨ, ਵਿਆਖਿਆ
demerit (ਡੀ'ਮੈਰਿਟ) *v* ਔਗੁਣ; ਅਯੋਗਤਾ; ਨੁਕਸ, ਖ਼ਰਾਬੀ	**demonstrator** (ਡੈੱਮਅਨਸਟਰੇਇਟਅ*) *n* ਪਰਦਰਸ਼ਕ, ਮੁਜ਼ਾਹਰੇ ਵਿਚ ਹਿੱਸਾ ਲੈਣ ਵਾਲਾ, ਨਿਰਦੇਸ਼ਕ, ਪ੍ਰਤੀਪਾਦਕ, ਡਿਮਾਨਸਟਰੇਟਰ
demise (ਡਿ'ਮਾਇਜ਼) *v n* ਇੰਤਕਾਲ ਕਰਨਾ, ਮੌਤ, ਦੇਹਾਂਤ, ਚਲਾਣਾ, ਵਸੀਅਤ ਕਰਨੀ,	
demit (ਡਿ'ਮਿਟ) *v* ਤਿਆਗਣਾ, ਅਸਤੀਫ਼ਾ ਦੇਣਾ	**demoralization** (ਡਿ'ਮੌਰਅਲਾਇਜ਼ੇਇਸ਼ਨ) *n* ਸਦਾਚਾਰਕ ਗਿਰਾਵਟ, ਨੈਤਕ ਪਤਨ, ਉਤਸਾਹ-ਭੰਗ, ਬੇਦਿਲੀ
democracy (ਡਿ'ਮੌਕਰਅਸਿ) *n* ਲੋਕਤੰਤਰ, ਜਨਤੰਤਰ, ਪਰਜਾਤੰਤਰ, ਗਣਰਾਜ	
democrat ('ਡੈੱਮਅਕਰੈਟ) *n* ਲੋਕਤੰਤਰਵਾਦੀ, ਗਣ-ਤੰਤਰਵਾਦੀ, ਲੋਕਰਾਜੀ; ~ic ਲੋਕਤੰਤਰਾਤਮਕ, ਗਣਤੰਤਰਾਤਮਕ, ਜਮਹੂਰੀ, ਲੋਕਰਾਜੀ	**demoralize** (ਡਿ'ਮੌਰਅਲਾਇਜ਼) *v* ਚਰਿੱਤਰ ਭ੍ਰਿਸ਼ਟ ਕਰਨਾ, ਚਰਿੱਤਰਹੀਨ ਕਰਨਾ, ਨੈਤਕ ਪਤਨ ਕਰਨਾ, ਵਿਗਾੜਨਾ, ਨਿਰਉਤਸ਼ਾਹ ਕਰਨਾ, ਬੇਦਿਲ ਕਰਨਾ, ਮਨੋਬਲ ਡੇਗਣਾ
demolish (ਡਿ'ਮੌਲਿਸ਼) *v* ਢਾਹੁਣਾ, ਨਸ਼ਟ ਕਰਨਾ, ਪੁੱਟ ਸੁੱਟਣਾ, ਤੋੜਨਾ, ਨਿਗਲ ਜਾਣਾ, ਖਾ ਜਾਣਾ; ~ment, demoilition ਨਾਸ਼, ਵਿਨਾਸ਼; ਖੰਡਨ	**demote** ('ਡੀ'ਮਅਉਟ) *v* ਪਦ ਘਟਾਉਣਾ, ਅਵੱਨਤ ਕਰਨਾ; ~d ਅਵੱਨਤ
demon ('ਡੀਮਅਨ) *n* ਰਾਖਸ਼, ਸ਼ੈਤਾਨ, ਜਿੰਨ, ਦਾਨਵ, ਅਸੁਰ	**demotion** ('ਡੀ'ਮਅਉਸ਼ਨ) *n* ਪਦ ਘਟਾਈ, ਅਵਨਤਿ
	demur (ਡਿ'ਮਯੂਅ:) *v n* ਇਤਰਾਜ਼ ਕਰਨਾ, ਉਜ਼ਰ

करना, आपੱती करनी; ਇਤਰਾਜ਼, ਉਜ਼ਰ; ~rage ਦੇਰੀ, ਅਟਕਾਉ, ਮਾਲ ਛੁਡਾਉਣ ਵਿਚ ਦੇਰੀ ਦਾ ਹਰਜਾਨਾ

demure (ਡਿ'ਮਯੂਅ*) *n* ਸ਼ਰਮਾਕਲ, ਸੰਗਾਊ, ਸੰਕੋਚੀ, ਸ਼ਾਂਤ, ਧੀਰਜਵਾਨ

demy (ਡਿ'ਮਾਇ) *n* ਕਾਗ਼ਜ਼ ਦਾ ਇਕ ਨਾਪ (17½ x 22½)

den (ਡੈਨ) *n* ਖੋਹ, ਘੁਰਨਾ, ਚੋਰਾਂ ਦਾ ਅੱਡਾ, ਛੋਟੀ ਗੰਦੀ ਕੋਠੜੀ, ਗੁਫ਼ਾ

dengue (ਡਿ'ਙਗਿ) *n* ਹੱਡ-ਭੰਨਵਾਂ ਬੁਖ਼ਾਰ

denial (ਡਿ'ਨਾਇਲ) *n* ਇਨਕਾਰ, ਨਾਂਹ, ਖੰਡਤ, ਨਾਮਨਜ਼ੂਰੀ

denied (ਡੇ'ਨਾਇਡ) *v* ਵਾਂਝਾ ਰੱਖਿਆ ਗਿਆ, ਵੰਚਤ

denigrate ('ਡੈਨਿਗਰੇਇਟ) *v* ਅਪਮਾਨ ਕਰਨਾ, ਭੰਡੀ ਕਰਨੀ, ਦਾਗ਼ ਲਾਉਣਾ, ਕਲੰਕਤ ਕਰਨਾ

denigration ('ਡੈਨਿ'ਗਰੇਇਸ਼ਨ) *n* ਨਿੰਦਾ, ਬਦਨਾਮੀ, ਅਪਜਸ, ਅਪਮਾਨ, ਭੰਡੀ

denim (ਡੈਨਿਮ) *n* ਮੋਟਾ, ਠੁਸ੍ਹ ਤੇ ਰੰਗਦਾਰ ਸੂਤੀ ਕੱਪੜਾ

denominate (ਡਿ'ਨੌਮਿ'ਨੇਇਟ) *v* ਨਾਂ ਰੱਖਣਾ, ਨਾਮਕਰਨ ਕਰਨਾ, ਮੰਗਿਆ ਦੇਈ, ਨੋ ਨਾਲ ਬੁਲਾਉਣਾ, ਬੁਲਾਉਣਾ, ਕਹਿਣਾ

denomination (ਡਿ'ਨੌਮਿ'ਨੇਇਸ਼ਨ) *n* ਨਾਂ, ਸੰਗਿਆ, ਉਪਾਧੀ, (ਅਰਥ) ਮੁੱਲ-ਅੰਕ; ਜਾਤੀ; ਪੰਥ; ਸ਼੍ਰੇਣੀ, ਧਾਰਮਕ ਸੰਪਰਦਾਇ, ਫ਼ਿਰਕਾ

denotation ('ਡੀਨਾ(ਉ)'ਟੇਇਸ਼ਨ) *n* ਨਾਂ ਸੰਗਿਆ, ਪ੍ਰਤੀਕ-ਕਥਨ, ਚਿੰਨ੍ਹਾਂ ਦੁਆਰਾ ਪਰਗਟੀਕਰਨ

denotative (ਡਿ'ਨਾਉਟਅਟਿਵ) *a* ਵਾਚਕ, ਨਿਰਦੇਸ਼ਕ, ਸੂਚਕ, ਵਸਤੂਵਾਚੀ

denote (ਡਿ'ਨਅਉਟ) *v* ਨਾਂ ਦੇਣਾ; ਅਰਥ ਦੇਣਾ; ਦੱਸਣਾ, ਵਿਅਕਤ ਕਰਨਾ, ਸੰਕੇਤ ਕਰਨਾ

denounce (ਡਿ'ਨਾਉਂਸ) *n* ਬੁਰਾਈ ਕਰਨਾ, ਦੋਸ਼ ਥੱਪਣਾ; ਬਦਅਸੀਸ ਦੇਣੀ, ਸੰਧੀ ਤੋੜਨ ਦੀ ਸੂਚਨ ਦੇਣਾ; ਭਵਿੱਖਬਾਣੀ ਕਰਨਾ

dense (ਡੈਂਸ) *a* ਸੰਘਣਾ, ਘਣਾ; ਗਾੜ੍ਹਾ; ਜੜ੍ਹ, ਬੁੱਧੂ

density ('ਡੈਂਸਅਟਿ) *n* ਸੰਘਣਾਪਣ, ਗਾੜ੍ਹਾਪਣ, ਘਣਤਾ; ਬੁੱਧੂਪਣਾ

dental ('ਡੈਂਟਲ) *a* ਦੰਦਾਂ ਸਬੰਧੀ, ਦੰਦਾ ਦੇ ਇਲਾਜ ਸਬੰਧੀ; ਦੰਤੀ

dentist ('ਡੈਨਟਿਸਟ) *n* ਦੰਦਾਂ ਦਾ ਡਾਕਟਰ, ਦੰਦ-ਸਾਜ਼

denture ('ਡੈਂਚਅ*) *n* ਦੰਦ-ਮਾਲਾ, ਬਣਾਉਟੀ ਦੰਦ

denude (ਡਿ'ਨਯੂਡ) *v* ਵਸਤਰਹੀਨ ਕਰਨਾ, ਨੰਗਾ ਕਰਨਾ, ਨੰਗਿਆਉਣਾ

denunicate (ਡਿ'ਨਅੰਸਿਏਇਟ) *v* ਨਿੰਦਣਾ, ਤਿਰਸਕਾਰਨਾ, ਫਿਟਕਾਰਨਾ, ਲਾਹ-ਪਾਹ ਕਰਨਾ

denunciation (ਡਿ'ਨਅੰਸਿ'ਏਇਸ਼ਨ) *n* ਫਿਟਕਾਰ, ਨਿੰਦਾ, ਦੋਸ਼-ਆਰੋਪਣ

deny (ਡਿ'ਨਾਇ) *v* ਅਸਵੀਕਾਰ ਕਰਨਾ, ਨਾਮਨਜ਼ੂਰ ਕਰਨਾ, ਨਾਂਹ ਕਰਨੀ, ਮੁੱਕਰਨਾ, ਖੰਡਨ ਕਰਨਾ

depart (ਡਿ'ਪਾਟ) *v* ਵਿੱਛੜਨਾ, ਵਿਦਾ ਹੋਣਾ, ਤੁਰ ਜਾਣਾ, ਪਰਲੋਕ ਸਿਧਾਰਨਾ, ਚਲਾਣਾ ਕਰਨਾ

department (ਡਿ'ਪਾਟਮੈਂਟ) *n* ਵਿਭਾਗ, ਮਹਿਕਮਾ, ਮੰਡਲ; ਅੰਗ; ~al ਵਿਭਾਗੀ, ਮਹਿਕਮੇ ਸਬੰਧੀ; ਵਿਸ਼ੇ ਸਬੰਧੀ

departure (ਡਿ'ਪਾਚਅ*) *n* ਚਲਾਣਾ, ਵਿਦਾਇਗੀ, ਕੂਚ, ਰਵਾਨਗੀ; ਮੌਤ

depend (ਡਿ'ਪੈਂਡ) *v* ਨਿਰਭਰ ਹੋਣਾ, ਆਸਰੇ ਹੋਣਾ,

depict | 440 | **depth**

ਅਧੀਨ ਹੋਣਾ, ਆਸਰਤ ਹੋਣਾ, ਅਵਲੰਬਤ ਹੋਣਾ; ~**able** ਵਿਸ਼ਵਾਸਯੋਗ, ਭਰੋਸੇਯੋਗ, ਨਿਰਭਰ ਰਹਿਣਯੋਗ, ਆਸਰੇਯੋਗ; ~**ant** ਆਸਰਤ, ਨਿਰਭਰ, ਅਧੀਨ, ਅਵਲੰਬੀ, ਸੇਵਕ; ~**ence** ਨਿਰਭਰਤਾ, ਆਸਰਾ, ਭਰੋਸਾ, ਵਿਸਾਹ; ਅਧੀਨਤਾ

depict (ਡਿ'ਪਿਕਟ) *v* ਚਿੱਤਰਨਾ, ਵਰਣਨ ਕਰਨਾ, ਦਰਸਾਉਣਾ, ਚਿੱਤਰਤ ਕਰਨਾ; ~**ion** ਚਿੱਤਰਣ, ਵਰਣਨ, ਪ੍ਰਸਤੁਤੀਕਰਨ

depilate ('ਡੈਪਿਲੇਇਟ) *v* ਵਾਲ ਲਾਹੁਣਾ, ਮੁੰਨਣਾ

deplete (ਡਿ'ਪਲੀਟ) *v* ਕਿਸੇ ਅੰਗ ਵਿਚੋਂ ਲਹੂ ਕੱਢਣਾ, ਖ਼ਾਲੀ ਕਰਨਾ, ਖ਼ਰਚ ਕਰਨਾ

deplorable (ਡਿ'ਪਲੋਰਅਬਇਲ) *a* ਦੁਖਦਾਇਕ, ਸ਼ੋਕਪੂਰਨ, ਭੈੜਾ, ਖ਼ਰਾਬ

deplore (ਡਿ'ਪਲੋ*) *v* ਸ਼ੋਕ ਕਰਨਾ, ਅਫ਼ਸੋਸ ਕਰਨਾ, ਹੱਥ ਮਲਣੇ

deploy (ਡਿ'ਪਲੋਇ) *v* ਪੰਗਤੀਬੱਧ ਕਰਨਾ, (ਫ਼ੌਜ ਦੀ) ਪਰੂਬੰਦੀ ਕਰਨਾ; ~**ed** ਪੰਗਤੀਬੱਧ, ਲਾਮਬੱਧ; ~**ment** ਪਾਬੰਦੀ, ਪਰੂਬੰਦੀ

deponent (ਡਿ'ਪਅਉਨਅੰਟ) *n a* ਹਲਫ਼ੀਆ ਬਿਆਨ ਦੇਣ ਵਾਲਾ, ਸ਼ਾਹਦ; ਅਭਿਸਾਕਸ਼ੀ

deport (ਡਿ'ਪੋਟ*) *v* ਦੇਸ਼ ਨਿਕਾਲਾ ਦੇਣਾ, ਜਲਾਵਤਨ ਕਰਨਾ

depose (ਡਿ'ਪਅਉਜ਼) *n* ਬੇਦਖ਼ਲ ਕਰਨਾ, ਰਾਜ-ਗੱਦੀ ਤੋਂ ਲਾਹੁਣਾ, ਹਲਫ਼ੀਆ ਬਿਆਨ ਦੇਣਾ;

deposit (ਡਿ'ਪੌਜ਼ਿਟ) *n v* ਜਮ੍ਹਾ ਰਕਮ, ਅਮਾਨਤ; ਰੇਤ ਜਾਂ ਮਿੱਟੀ ਆਦਿ ਦਾ ਜਮਾਉ, ਸਾਈ, ਧਰੋਹਰ; ਜਮ੍ਹਾਂ ਕਰਾਉਣਾ, ਸਾਈ ਦੇਣੀ, ਗਿਰਵੀ ਰੱਖਣਾ, ਪੇਸ਼ਗੀ ਦੇਣੀ, ਬਿਆਨਾ ਦੇਣਾ; ~**ory** ਬੈਂਕ, ਗੁਦਾਮ, ਭੰਡਾਰ, ਸੰਗ੍ਰਹਿਸਥਾਨ, ਮਾਲਖ਼ਾਨਾ, ਖ਼ਜ਼ਾਨਾ

deposition ('ਡੈਪਅ'ਜ਼ਿਸ਼ਨ) *n* ਜਮ੍ਹਾਂ; ਅਮਾਨਤ, ਧਰੋਹਰ, ਰਾਜ ਤੋਂ ਵੰਚਤ ਕਰਨਾ, ਗਵਾਹੀ, ਹਲਫ਼ੀਆ ਬਿਆਨ; ਸਰਮਾਇਆ, ਬਿਆਨਾ, ਸਾਈ

depot ('ਡੈਪਅਉ) *n* ਗੁਦਾਮ, ਡੀਪੂ, ਮਾਲਖ਼ਾਨਾ, ਭੰਡਾਰ, ਕੋਠੀ; ਰੰਗਰੂਟਾਂ ਦੀ ਸਿਖਲਾਈ ਵਾਲੀ ਥਾਂ

depreciate (ਡਿ'ਪਰੀਸ਼ਿਏਇਟ) *v* (ਘਸਾਈ ਕਰਨਾ) ਕਦਰ ਘਟਾਉਣੀ ਜਾਂ ਘਟਣੀ, ਮੰਦਾ ਸਮਝਣਾ, (ਰੁਪਏ ਦੀ ਕੀਮਤ) ਘਟਾਉਣੀ ਜਾਂ ਘਟਣੀ, ਮੁੱਲ ਗਿਰਾਉਣਾ ਜਾਂ ਗਿਰਨਾ, ਭਾਅ ਗਿਰਨੇ ਜਾਂ ਗਿਰਾਉਣੇ; ਤੁੱਛ ਸਮਝਣਾ, ਹੇਠੀ ਕਰਨੀ ਜਾਂ ਹੋਣੀ

depreciation (ਡਿ'ਪਰੀਸਿ'ਏਇਸ਼ਨ) *n* ਬੇਕਦਰੀ, ਮੰਦੀਕਰਨ, ਮੁੱਲ-ਘਾਟਾ; ਉਪੇਖਿਆ, ਭਾਅ ਵਿਚ ਕਮੀ, ਮੁੱਲ-ਹ੍ਰਾਸ; ਘਸਾਈ

depress (ਡਿ'ਪਰੈੱਸ) *v* (ਦਿਲ) ਢਾਹੁਣਾ, ਨੀਵਾਂ ਕਰਨਾ; ਬਜ਼ਾਰ ਮੰਦਾ ਕਰਨਾ, ਵਪਾਰ ਦੀ ਸਰਗਰਮੀ ਘੱਟ ਕਰਨਾ; ਉਦਾਸ ਕਰਨਾ, ਦੁਖੀ ਕਰਨਾ, ਖਿੰਨ ਕਰਨਾ; ~**ed** ਉਦਾਸ, ਦੁਖੀ, ਖਿੰਨ; ਦਲਿਤ; ~**ion** ਉਦਾਸੀ, ਬੇਦਿਲੀ, ਵਿਸ਼ਾਦ, ਨਿਰਉਤਸਾਹ, ਮੰਦਵਾੜਾ, ਪਤਨ, ਟੋਆ, ਸੁਰ ਵਿਚ ਹਲਕਾਪਣ, (ਹਵਾ ਦੇ ਦਬਾ ਦਾ) ਘਟਾਉ

deprivation ('ਡੈਪਰਿ'ਵੇਇਸ਼ਨ) *n* ਵੰਚਨ, ਬਰਤਰਫ਼ੀ, ਵਿਗੋਚਾ, ਮੌਕੂਫ਼ੀ, ਹਾਨੀ, ਲੋਪ

depute (ਡਿ'ਪਯੂਟ) *v* ਨਿਯੁਕਤ ਕਰਨਾ, ਪ੍ਰਤੀਨਿਧ ਨਿਯੁਕਤ ਕਰਨਾ, (ਅਧਿਕਾਰ ਆਦਿ) ਸੌਂਪਣਾ, ਸਪੁਰਦ ਕਰਨਾ, ਮੁਖ਼ਤਿਆਰ ਕਰਨਾ

deprive (ਡਿ'ਪਰਾਇਵ) *v* ਵੰਚਤ ਕਰਨਾ, ਵਾਂਝਿਆਂ ਕਰਨਾ, ਖੋਹ ਲੈਣਾ, ਹਟਾਉਣਾ, ਲੁੱਟ ਲੈਣਾ; ~**d** ਰਹਿਤ, ਵਿਹੂਣਾ, ਵਾਂਝਾ, ਵੰਚਤ

depth (ਡੈੱਪਥ) *n* ਡੂੰਘਾਈ, ਗਹਿਰਾਈ, ਡੂੰਘਾ ਪਾਣੀ, ਡੂੰਮ, ਗੰਭੀਰਤਾ; ਸੂਖਮ ਬੁੱਧੀ

deputation ('ਡੈਪਯੁ'ਟੇਇਸ਼ਨ) *n* ਪ੍ਰਤੀਨਿਧ ਮੰਡਲ, ਵ੍ਫਦ, ਪ੍ਰਤੀਨਿਯੁਕਤੀ

depute (ਡਿ'ਪਯੂਟ) *v* ਪ੍ਰਤੀਨਿਯੁਕਤ ਕਰਨਾ, ਪ੍ਰਤੀਨਿਧ ਨਿਯੁਕਤ ਕਰਨਾ, ਸਪੁਰਦ ਕਰਨਾ, ਮੁਖ਼ਤਿਆਰ ਕਰਨਾ (ਅਧਿਕਾਰ) ਸੌਂਪਣਾ; **~d** ਪ੍ਰਤੀਨਿਯੁਕਤ

deputy ('ਡੈਪਯੁਟਿ) *n* ਸਹਿ, ਉਪ, ਸਹਿਕਾਰੀ, ਨਾਇਬ

derail (ਡਿ'ਰੇਇਲ) *v* ਪਟੜੀ ਤੋਂ ਲਾਹੁਣਾ; ਪਟੜੀ ਤੋਂ ਉਤਰ ਜਾਣਾ, ਅਸਲੀ ਰਾਹ ਤੋਂ ਉੱਖੜ ਜਾਣਾ

derange (ਡਿ'ਰੇਇੰਜ) *v* ਉਲਟ-ਪੁਲਟ ਕਰਨਾ, ਬੁੱਧੀ ਭ੍ਰਿਸ਼ਟ ਕਰਨਾ, ਪਾਗਲ ਕਰ ਦੇਣਾ, ਅੜਚਨ ਪਾਉਣੀ; **~d** ਉਲਟਾ-ਪੁਲਟਾ, ਬੇਤਰਤੀਬ, ਪਾਗਲ, ਵਿਆਕੁਲ; **~ment** ਉਲਟ-ਪੁਲਟ, ਬੇਤਰਤੀਬਾ, ਫ਼ਤੂਰ

derivation ('ਡੈਰਿ'ਵੇਇਸ਼ਨ) *n* ਵਿਉਤਪਤੀ, ਮੂਲ, ਸਰੋਤ

derivative (ਡਿ'ਰਿਵਅਟਿਵ੍) *a n* ਵਿਉਤਪਤ, (ਸ਼ਬਦ), ਵਿਉਤਪੰਨ ਤੱਤ

derive (ਡਿ'ਰਾਇਵ੍) *v* ਕੱਢਣਾ, ਉਤਪਤੀ ਹੋਣੀ, ਵਿਉਤਪੰਨ ਹੋਣਾ, ਮੂਲ ਲੱਭਣਾ, (ਸ਼ਬਦਾਂ ਦੀ) ਵਿਉਪਤੀ ਲੱਭਣੀ; **~d** ਉਤਪੰਨ, ਵਿਉਤਪੰਨ, ਵਿਉਤਪਾਦਤ

derogate ('ਡੈਰੌ(ਉ)ਗੇਇਟ) *v* ਘਟਾਉਣਾ, ਕਮੀ ਕਰਨਾ, ਅਪਮਾਨ ਕਰਨਾ, ਵੱਟਾ ਲਾਉਣਾ, ਨਿਕਦਰੀ ਹੋਣਾ, ਹੇਠੀ ਹੋਣੀ, ਅਪਮਾਨਤ ਹੋਣਾ

derogation ('ਡੈਰੌ(ਉ)'ਗੇਇਸ਼ਨ) *n* ਅਲਪੀਕਰਨ, ਪਤਨ, ਨਿਕਦਰੀ, ਹੇਠੀ, ਗੌਰਵਹੀਨਤਾ, ਅਪਮਾਨ

derogatory (ਡਿ'ਰੌਗਾਟ(ਅ)ਰਿ) *a* ਅਪਮਾਨਜਨਕ, ਹੇਠੀ ਵਾਲੀ, ਸ਼ਾਨ ਵਿਰੋਧ

descend (ਡਿ'ਸੈਂਡ) *v* ਲਹਿਣਾ, ਲੱਖਣਾ, ਉਤਰਨਾ, ਡਿਗਣਾ, ਆ ਪੈਣਾ; ਪੈਣਾ, ਘਟਣਾ (ਵਰਨਣ ਵਿਚ), ਵੰਸ਼-ਕ੍ਰਮ ਅਨੁਸਾਰ ਆਉਣਾ, ਉਤਰ ਆਉਣਾ; **~ant** ਵੰਸ਼, ਔਲਾਦ, ਸੰਤਾਨ, ਜਾਨਸ਼ੀਨ

descent (ਡੈ'ਸੈਂਟ) *n* ਉਤਰਾਈ, ਢਲਵਾਣ, ਲਹਾਈ; ਅਚਾਨਕ ਹੱਲਾ; ਵੰਸ਼, ਕੁਲ, ਪੀੜ੍ਹੀ; ਉਤਪਤੀ, ਉਦਭਵ

describe (ਡਿ'ਸਕਰਾਇਬ) *v* ਵਰਨਣ ਕਰਨਾ, ਬਿਆਨ ਕਰਨਾ, ਉਲੀਕਣਾ, ਚਿਤਰਨਾ, ਅੰਕਤ ਕਰਨਾ, ਬਖਾਨਣਾ

description (ਡਿ'ਸਕਰਿਪਸ਼ਨ) *n* ਵਰਨਣ, ਬਿਆਨ, ਨਿਰੂਪਣ, ਵਿਵਰਨ, ਭਾਂਤ, ਵੰਨਗੀ, ਪ੍ਰਕਾਰ, ਸ੍ਰੇਣੀ

descriptive (ਡਿ'ਸਕਰਿਪਟਿਵ੍) *a* ਵਰਨਨਾਤਮਕ, ਚਿਤਰਨਾਤਮਕ, ਬਿਆਨੀਆ; **~ness** ਵਰਨਨਾਤਮਕਤਾ, ਬਿਆਨ

desert ('ਡੈਜ਼ਅਟ, ਡਿ'ਜ਼ਅ:ਟ) *n* ਰੇਗਿਸਤਾਨ, ਮਾਰੂਥਲ, ਸੁਨਸਾਨ, ਉਜਾੜ, ਵੀਰਾਨ; ਧੋਖਾ ਦੇਣਾ, ਅਲੱਗ ਹੋਣਾ; **~ed** ਤਿਆਗਿਆ, ਇਕੱਲਵਾਂਝਾ

deserve (ਡਿ'ਜ਼ਅ:ਵ੍) *v* ਸੁਯੋਗ ਹੋਣਾ, ਕਾਬਲ ਹੋਣਾ, ਪਾਤਰ ਹੋਣਾ, ਅਧਿਕਾਰੀ ਹੋਣਾ, ਲਾਇਕ ਹੋਣਾ

deserving (ਡਿ'ਜ਼ਅ:ਵਿਙ) *a* ਅਧਿਕਾਰੀ, ਹੱਕਦਾਰ, ਸੁਪਾਤਰ, ਸੁਯੋਗ

design (ਡਿ'ਜ਼ਾਇਨ) *v n* (ਚਿਤਰ ਦੀ) ਰੂਪ ਰੇਖਾ ਬਣਾਉਣਾ, (ਭਵਨ ਮਕਾਨ ਆਦਿ ਦਾ) ਖ਼ਾਕਾ ਖਿਚਣਾ, ਕਥਾਨਕ ਜਾਂ ਆਧਾਰ ਸੋਚਣਾ, ਰੂਪ-ਰੇਖਾ ਬਣਾਉਣਾ, ਵਿਉਂਤ ਕਰਨੀ, ਇਰਾਦਾ ਕਰਨਾ, ਉਪਾਉ ਕਰਨਾ; ਆਕਾਰ, ਸਾਂਚਾ, ਢਾਂਚਾ, ਰੂਪ-ਰੇਖਾ, ਖ਼ਾਕਾ; ਨਮੂਨਾ, ਉਦੇਸ਼, ਮਨਸੂਬਾ; ਸਾਜ਼ਸ਼; **~ed** ਬਣਾਇਆ ਗਿਆ, ਕਲਪਤ, ਰੂਪਅੰਕਤ

designate (ਡੈੱਜ਼ਿਗਨੇਇਟ) *v a* ਨਿਯਤ ਕਰਨਾ, ਨਾਂ ਰੱਖਣਾ, ਮਨੋਨੀਤ ਕਰਨਾ, ਨਿਰਦਿਸ਼ਟ ਨਾਂ, ਮਨੋਨੀਤ

designation ('ਡੈੱਜ਼ਿਗਾ'ਨੇਇਸ਼ਨ) *n* ਨਾਂ, ਪਦਵੀ, ਅਹੁਦਾ, ਮਨੋਨੀਤ, ਪਦ-ਸੰਗਿਆ

desirable (ਡਿ'ਜ਼ਾਇਅਰਅਬਲ) *a* ਉਚਿੱਤ, ਲੋੜੀਂਦਾ, ਵਾਜਬੀ, ਮਨ-ਭਾਉਂਦਾ, ਵਾਂਛਤੀ

desire (ਡਿ'ਜ਼ਾਇਅ*) *n* ਚਾਹ, ਖ਼ਾਹਸ਼, ਇੱਛਾ, ਅਭਿਲਾਸ਼ਾ, ਕਾਮਨਾ, ਮਨੋਰਥ; ਚਾਹੁਣਾ, ਖ਼ਾਹਸ਼ ਕਰਨਾ, ਮੰਗ ਕਰਨਾ

desirous (ਡਿ'ਜ਼ਾਇਅਰਸ) *a* ਅਭਿਲਾਸ਼ੀ, ਇੱਛਕ, ਚਾਹਵਾਨ, ਇੱਛਾਵਾਨ, ਖ਼ਾਹਸ਼ਮੰਦ

desist (ਡਿ'ਜ਼ਿਸਟ) *v* ਹਟ ਜਾਣਾ, ਬਾਜ ਰਹਿਣਾ, ਗੁਰੇਜ ਕਰਨਾ, ਹੱਥ ਖਿੱਚਣਾ

desk (ਡੈੱਸਕ) *n* ਮੇਜ਼, ਡੈੱਸਕ; **~man** ਉਪ-ਸੰਪਾਦਕ; **the~** ਸਾਹਿਤਕ ਕੰਮ, ਦਫ਼ਤਰੀ ਕੰਮ

desolate (ਡੈੱਸਅਲਅਟ, 'ਡੈੱਸਅਲੇਇਟ) *a v* ਇੱਕਲਾ, ਲੁਗਾ; ਬੇਕਸ; ਉਜਾੜ, ਸੁੰਨਾ, ਵੀਰਾਨ, ਬੰਜਰ, ਗ਼ੈਰ-ਆਬਾਦ; ਉਜਾੜਨਾ, ਵੀਰਾਨ ਕਰਨਾ, ਗ਼ੈਰ-ਆਬਾਦ ਕਰਨਾ; ਦਿਲ ਤੋੜਨਾ, ਉਦਾਸ ਕਰਨਾ

desolation ('ਡੈੱਸਅਲੇਇਸ਼ਨ) *n* ਬਰਬਾਦੀ, ਵੀਰਾਨੀ, ਉਜਾੜ; ਉਦਾਸੀ, ਵਿਸ਼ਾਦ, ਨਿਰਾਸਤਾ

despair (ਡਿ'ਸਪੇਅ*) *n v* ਨਿਰਾਸ਼ਤਾ, ਆਸਹੀਣਤਾ; ਨਿਰਾਸ਼ ਹੋਣਾ, ਢੇਰੀ ਢਾਹ ਬੈਠਣਾ, ਉਮੀਦ ਛੱਡ ਬੈਠਣਾ

despatch (ਡਿ'ਸਪੇਚ) *v n* ਭੇਜਣਾ, ਘੱਲਣਾ, ਰਵਾਨਾ ਕਰਨਾ; ਮਾਰ ਮੁਕਾਉਣਾ; ਰਵਾਨਗੀ; ਖ਼ਾਤਮਾ; ਤੇਜ਼ੀ, ਫੁਰਤੀ, ਕਾਹਲ; ਸਰਕਾਰੀ ਚਿੱਠੀ; ਵੇਖੋ dispatch

desperate ('ਡਸਪ(ਅ)ਰਅਟ) *a* ਨਿਰਾਸ਼, ਬਿਲਕੁਲ ਮਾਯੂਸ, ਜਾਨ ਦੀ ਬਾਜ਼ੀ ਖੇਡਣ ਵਾਲਾ, ਸਿਰਲਥ, ਨਿਹੰਗ, ਖ਼ਤਰਨਾਕ; **~ness, desperation** ਨਿਰਾਸ਼ਤਾ, ਬੇਚਾਰਗੀ; ਨਿਧੜਕਤਾ

despise (ਡਿ'ਸਪਾਇਜ਼) *v* ਨੀਚ ਸਮਝਣਾ, ਘਿਰਨਾ ਕਰਨਾ, ਤੁੱਛ ਸਮਝਣਾ, ਤਿਰਸਕਾਰ ਕਰਨਾ; **-dness** ਨੀਚਤਾ, ਘਿਰਨਾ, ਤੁੱਛਤਾ, ਤਿਰਸਕਾਰ

despite (ਡਿ:ਸਪਾਇਟ) *n prep* ਈਰਖਾ, ਕੀਨਾ, ਦਵੈਸ਼, ਘਿਰਨਾ; (ਪ੍ਰ) ਤਿਰਸਕਾਰ, ਬਾਵਜੂਦ, ਹੁੰਦੇ ਹੋਏ, ਹੋਣ ਦੇ ਬਾਵਜੂਦ; **~ful** ਦਵੇਸ਼ੀ, ਅਤਿਆਚਾਰੀ, ਅਪਮਾਨਜਨਕ, ਤਿਰਸਕਾਰਪੂਰਨ

despond (ਡਿ'ਸਪੌਂਡ) *v n* ਹਿੰਮਤ ਹਾਰਨਾ, ਦਿਲ ਹਾਰਨਾ, ਨਿਰਾਸ਼ ਹੋਣਾ, ਉਚਾਟ ਹੋਣਾ; ਉਦਾਸੀ, ਨਿਰਾਸ਼ਾ, ਨਿਰਾਸ਼ਤਾ (ਪ੍ਰ)

desitination ('ਡੈੱਸਟਿਨੇਇਸ਼ਨ) *n* ਮੰਜ਼ਲ, ਲਕਸ਼, ਨਿਯਤ ਥਾਂ, ਟਿਕਾਣਾ, ਮੰਜ਼ਲ, ਭਾਗ, ਸੰਯੋਗ

destiny ('ਡੈੱਸਟਿਨਿ) *n* ਤਕਦੀਰ, ਹੋਣੀ, ਸੰਯੋਗ, ਪ੍ਰਾਲਬਧ, ਤਕਦੀਰ, ਨਸੀਬ, ਭਾਗ

destitute ('ਡੈੱਸਟਿਟਯੂਟ) *a* ਵਾਂਝਿਆ, ਵਿਰਵਾ, ਵਰਜਤ, ਅਨਾਥ, ਮੁਥਾਜ, ਬੁਭਿਆ, ਸਾਧਨਹੀਨ

destroy (ਡਿ'ਸਟਰੌਇ) *v* ਬਰਬਾਦ ਕਰਨਾ, ਉਜਾੜਨਾ, ਵਿਅਰਥ ਕਰਨਾ, ਫਨਾ ਕਰਨਾ; ਅੰਤ ਕਰਨਾ, ਮੇਟਣਾ, ਨਾਸ ਕਰਨਾ; **~er** ਨਸ਼ਟ; ਪਤਿਤ

destruction (ਡਿ'ਸਟਰਅੱਕਸ਼ਨ) *n* ਬਰਬਾਦੀ, ਤਬਾਹੀ, ਉਜਾੜਾ, ਵਿਨਾਸ਼

destructive (ਡਿ'ਸਟਰਅੱਕਟਿਵ੍) *a* ਵਿਨਾਸ਼ਕਾਰੀ, ਨਾਸ਼ਕ, ਤਬਾਹਕੁਨ, ਸੰਘਾਰਨੀ, ਮੁਹਲਕ, ਤਖ਼ਰੀਬੀ, ਨਾਸ਼ਾਤਮਕ

detach (ਡਿ'ਟੈਚ) *v* ਨਿਖੇੜਨ, ਅੱਡ ਕਰਨਾ, ਜੁਦਾ ਕਰਨਾ, ਵੱਖਰਾ ਕਰਨਾ, ਅਲਗ ਕਰਨਾ; **~ed** ਦੂਜਿਆਂ ਤੋਂ ਵੱਖਰਾ, ਅੱਡਰਾ; ਨਿਰਪੱਖ; **~ment**

ਨਿਰਲੇਪਤਾ, ਵੈਰਾਗ, ਵਿਚਾਰ-ਸੁਤੰਤਰਤਾ; ਟੁਕੜੀ

detail (ਡੀਟੇਇਲ) *n v* ਵਿਸਤਾਰ, ਵਿਵਰਨ, ਵੇਰਵਾ; ਤਫ਼ਸੀਲ; ਦਸਤਾ; ਅੰਸ਼, ਵਿਸਤਾਰ ਨਾਲ ਵਰਨਨ ਕਰਨਾ; ਵੇਰਵਾ ਦੇਣਾ, ਖੋਲ੍ਹ ਕੇ ਲਿਖਣਾ; **~ed** ਵਿਸਤਾਰਤ, ਵਿਸਤਾਰ-ਪੂਰਵਕ, ਵਿਵਰਨ ਸਹਿਤ

detain (ਡਿ'ਟੇਇਨ) *v* ਰੋਕਣਾ, ਅਟਕਾਉਣਾ, ਬਿਠਾਈ ਰੱਖਣਾ, ਇੰਤਜ਼ਾਰ ਕਰਾਉਣਾ; ਬੰਨ੍ਹ ਰੱਖਣਾ, ਕੈਦ ਕਰਨਾ, ਨਜ਼ਰਬੰਦ ਕਰਨਾ; **~ed** ਰੋਕਿਆ, ਡੱਕਿਆ, ਨਜ਼ਰਬੰਦ

detect (ਡਿ'ਟੈਕੱਟ) *v* ਖੋਜ ਕੱਢਣਾ, ਸੂਹ ਕੱਢਣੀ, ਪਤਾ ਲਗਾਉਣਾ; ਤਾੜ ਲੈਣਾ; **~able** ਖੋਜਣਯੋਗ, ਸੂਹ ਕੱਢਣਯੋਗ, ਫੜਨਯੋਗ; **~ion** ਖੋਜ, ਪਕੜ, ਸੂਹ, ਲਭਾਈ; **~ive** ਖੋਜੀ, ਜਾਸੂਸ, ਗੁਪਤਚਰ, ਸੂਹੀਆ

detention, **detainment** (ਡਿ'ਟੈਨੱਸ਼ਨ, ਡਿ'ਟੇਇਨਮੇਂਟ) *n* ਦੇਰ; ਅਟਕਾ, ਰੋਕ, ਨਜ਼ਰਬੰਦੀ, ਗਰਿਫ਼ਤਾਰੀ

detenu, detinu ('ਡੇਇਟਾਅਨੂ) *n* ਨਜ਼ਰਬੰਦ, ਬੰਦੀ

deter (ਡਿ'ਟਅ:*) *v* ਰੋਕਣਾ, ਠਾਕਣਾ, ਬਾਜ਼ ਰੱਖਣਾ; **~ed** ਰੋਕਿਆ ਜਾਂ ਰੁਕਿਆ

deteriorate (ਡਿ'ਟਿਅਰਿਏਇਟ) *v* ਵਿਗਾੜਨਾ ਜਾਂ ਵਿਗੜਨਾ, ਖ਼ਰਾਬ ਕਰਨਾ

deterioration (ਡਿ'ਟਿਅਰਿਅ'ਰੇਇਸ਼ਨ) *n* ਵਿਗਾੜ, ਖ਼ਰਾਬੀ, ਗਿਰਾਵਟ, ਪਤਨ; ਗਲਣ

determinant (ਡਿ'ਟਅ:ਮਿਨੇਂਟ) *a* ਨਿਰਣਾਇਕ, ਨਿਰਧਾਰਕੀ; **~al** ਨਿਰਣੇਆਤਮਕ, ਨਿਰਧਾਰਨ ਸਬੰਧੀ, ਨਿਸ਼ਚਾਤਮਕ

determinate (ਡਿ'ਟਅ:'ਮਿਨਾਟ) *a* ਨਿਸ਼ਚਤ, ਨਿਰਧਾਰੀ, ਨਿਰਧਾਰਤ; **~ness** ਸਥਿਰਤਾ, ਨਿਸ਼ਚਤਤ

determination (ਡਿ'ਟਅ:ਮਿਨੇਇਸ਼ਨ) *n* ਪੱਕਾ ਇਰਾਦਾ, ਦ੍ਰਿੜਤਾ, ਨਿਸ਼ਚਾ; ਪਰਿਭਾਸ਼ਾ, ਸੀਮਾ-ਨਿਰਧਾਰਨ; ਜਾਂਚ

determine (ਡਿ'ਟਅ:ਮਿਨ) *v* ਪੱਕਾ ਇਰਾਦਾ ਕਰਨਾ, ਨਿਸਚਾ ਕਰਨਾ, ਠਾਨਣਾ (ਕਾ), ਸੀਮਤ ਕਰਨਾ, ਠਹਿਰਾਉਣਾ, ਫ਼ੈਸਲਾ ਕਰਨਾ, ਨਿਰਣਾ ਕਰਨਾ, ਤਸ਼ਖ਼ੀਸ ਕਰਨਾ; **~d** ਪੱਕਾ, ਦ੍ਰਿੜ੍ਹ, ਅਟੱਲ; ਨਿਸ਼ਚਤ, ਨਿਰਧਾਰਤ, ਸੀਮਤ, ਨਿਰਣੀਤ

deterred (ਡਿ'ਟਅ:ਡ) *a* ਰੋਕਿਆ ਜਾਂ ਰੁਕਿਆ

deterrence, determent (ਡਿ'ਟੈਰੇਂਅੱਸ, ਡਿ'ਟਅ:ਮਅੰਟ) *n* ਰੋਕ, ਰੁਕਾਵਟ, ਠੱਲ੍ਹ

detest (ਡਿ'ਟੈੱਸਟ) *v* ਘਿਰਣਾ ਕਰਨੀ, ਤਿਰਸਕਾਰਨਾ; **~ation** ਘਿਰਣਾ, ਤਿਰਸਕਾਰ, ਗਿਲਾਨੀ

dethrone (ਡਿਥਰਅਉਨ) *v* ਗੱਦੀਓਂ ਲਾਹੁਣਾ, ਪਰਭਾਵ ਜਾਂ ਜ਼ੋਰ ਘੱਟ ਕਰਨਾ

detriment ('ਡੇਂਟਰਿਮਅੰਟ) *n* ਹਾਨੀ, ਨੁਕਸਾਨ, ਹਰਜਾ; **~al** ਹਾਨੀਕਾਰਕ, ਬਾਧਕ

deuce (ਡਯੂਸ) *n* (ਤਾਸ਼ ਦੀ) ਦੁੱਕੀ; (ਟੈਨਿਸ) ਦੋਹਾਂ ਦੀ ਬਰਾਬਰੀ; ਮੁਸੀਬਤ, ਬਲਾ, ਆਫ਼ਤ; **~d** ਦਾਨਵੀ, ਵਹਿਸ਼ੀ; ਵਿਆਕੁਲਤਾ ਨਾਲ

devaluation (ਡੀ'ਵੈਲਯੂ'ਏਇਸ਼ਨ) *n* ਵਿਮੁੱਲਣ, ਅਵਮੁੱਲਨ

devalue ('ਡੀ'ਵੈਲਯੂ) *v* ਮੁਦਰਾ ਦਾ ਮੁੱਲ ਘਟਾਉਣਾ, ਵਿਮੁੱਲਣ ਕਰਨਾ, ਨਸ਼ਟ ਕਰਨਾ, ਤਬਾਹ ਕਰਨਾ

devastate ('ਡੇਂਵੱਅਸਟੇਇਟ) *v* ਉਜਾੜਨਾ, ਬਰਬਾਦ ਕਰਨਾ, ਵੀਰਾਨ ਕਰਨਾ, ਨਸ਼ਟ ਕਰਨਾ, ਤਬਾਹ ਕਰਨਾ

devastation ('ਡੇਂਵੱਅਸ'ਟੇਇਸ਼ਨ) *n* ਉਜਾੜ,

ਤਬਾਹੀ, ਬਰਬਾਦੀ, ਵੀਰਾਨੀ, ਉਜਾੜ, ਵਿਨਾਸ਼

develop (ਡਿ'ਵੈੱਲਅਪ) *v* ਵਧਾਉਣਾ ਜਾਂ ਵਧਣਾ, ਵਿਕਾਸ ਕਰਨਾ ਦਾਂ ਹੋਣਾ, ਉਨਤੀ ਕਰਨੀ ਜਾਂ ਹੋਣੀ; ਪ੍ਰਕਾਸ਼ਤ ਕਰਨਾ, ਫੋਟੋ ਧੋਣਾ; ਦਿਖਲਾਉਣਾ, ਪਰਦਰਸ਼ਤ ਕਰਨਾ; ਪ੍ਰੰਗਾਰਨਾ; ~ed ਵਿਕਸਤ, ਉੱਨਤ, ਪ੍ਰਫੁਲਤ, ਵਧਿਆ ਫੁੱਲਿਆ; ~ing ਵਿਕਾਸਸ਼ੀਲ, ਵਿਕਾਸੀ; ~ment ਵਿਕਾਸ, ਉੱਨਤੀ, ਤਰੱਕੀ; ਵਾਧਾ, ਪ੍ਰਖਤਰਗੀ; (ਫੋਟੋ) ਧੁਲਾਈ

deviate ('ਡੀਵਿ'ਏਇਟ) *v* (ਮਾਰਗ, ਸ਼ਾਸਨ, ਸੱਚਾਈ ਆਦਿ ਤੋਂ) ਹਟਣਾ, ਫਿਰ ਜਾਣਾ, ਭਟਕਣਾ, ਉਲੰਘਣ ਕਰਨਾ; ~d ਵਿਚਲਤ, ਪਥ-ਭ੍ਰਿਸ਼ਟ

deviation ('ਡਿ'ਵਿ'ਏਇਸ਼ਨ) *n* ਭਟਕਣ, ਖਿਝਕਣ, ਪਹਨ, ਪਥ-ਭ੍ਰਸ਼ਟਤਾ, ਵਿਚਲਣ

device (ਡਿ'ਵਾਇਸ) *n* ਵਿਉਂਤ, ਢੰਗ, ਜੁਗਤ, ਤਰਕੀਬ, ਉਪਾਉ; ਮਰਜ਼ੀ, ਖ਼ੁਸ਼ੀ, ਇੱਛਿਆ; ਖ਼ਾਕਾ, ਚਿੱਤਰ

devil, The devil ('ਡੈੱਵ਼ਲ) *n* ਸ਼ੈਤਾਨ, ਅਸੁਰ, ਇਬਲੀਸ, ਪਰੇਤ, ਬਦਮਾਸ਼, ਭਾੜੇ ਦਾ ਟੱਟੂ; ~ish ਸ਼ੈਤਾਨੀ, ਅਸੁਰੀ; ਭਿਆਨਕ; ਸਖ਼ਤ, ਅਤੀਅੰਤ; ~ishness ਸ਼ੈਤਾਨੀ, ਰਾਖ਼ਸ਼ਪੁਣਾ, ਪਿਸ਼ਾਚਤਾ

devolve (ਡਿ'ਵੌਲਵ) *v* ਸਪੁਰਦ ਕਰਨਾ ਜਾਂ ਹੋਣਾ, ਸੌਂਪਣਾ; ਹਵਾਲੇ ਕਰਨਾ ਜਾਂ ਹੋਣਾ ਵਿਰਸੇ ਵਿਚ ਮਿਲਣਾ

devote (ਡਿ'ਵੈਉਟ) *v* ਭੇਟਾ ਕਰਨਾ, ਸਮਰਪਣ ਕਰਨਾ, ਅਰਪਣ ਕਰਨਾ; ~d ਅਰਪਿਆ, ਵਕਫ਼ ਕੀਤਾ ਹੋਇਆ; ਸ਼ਰਧਾਵਾਨ; ਦ੍ਰਿੜ ਭਗਤ; ਉਪਾਸ਼ਕ; ~dness ਸਮਰਪਣ, ਆਤਮ-ਸਮਰਪਣ, ਭਗਤੀ, ਸ਼ਰਧਾ, ਅਨੁਰਾਗ; ~e ਸ਼ਰਧਾਲੂ, ਉਪਾਸ਼ਕ, ਭਗਤ

devotion (ਡਿ'ਵ਼ਊਸ਼ਨ) *n* ਸ਼ਰਧਾ, ਭਗਤੀ, ਸਿਦਕ, ਭਗਤੀ ਭਾਵ, ਪਰੇਮ; ~al ਧਾਰਮਕ, ਭਗਤੀ ਸਬੰਧੀ, ਸ਼ਰਧਾਮਈ

dew (ਡਯੂ) *n v* ਤਰੇਲ, ਓਸ, ਸ਼ਬਨਮ, ਤੁਸ਼ਾਰ; ਟੇਪੇ, ਤਰ ਕਰਨਾ, ਤਰੇਲ ਦਾ ਬਣਨਾ

dexterous ('ਡੈਕਸਟ(ਅ)ਰਅਸ) *a* ਨਿਪੁੰਨ, ਚਤਰ, ਉਸਤਾਦ, ਫੁਰਤੀਲਾ; ਸੱਜੇ ਹੱਥਾ, ਸਿੱਧ ਹੱਥਾ

diabetes ('ਡਾਇਅ'ਬੀਟੀਜ਼) *n* ਸ਼ਕਰ ਰੋਗ, ਜ਼ਿਆਬਤੀਸ

diabetic ('ਡਾਇਅ'ਬੈਟਿਕ) *n a* ਜ਼ਿਆਬਤੀਸ, ਸ਼ਕਰ-ਰੋਗੀ, ਸ਼ਕਰ-ਰੋਗ ਸਬੰਧੀ

diabolic, -al ('ਡਾਇਅ'ਬੌਲਿਕ, ਡਾਇਅ'ਬੌਲਿਕਲ) *a* ਸ਼ੈਤਾਨੀ, ਸ਼ੈਤਾਨ ਵਾਂਗੂ, ਰਾਖ਼ਸ਼ੀ; ਨਿਰਦਈ, ਪਾਪੀ; ਦੁਸ਼ਟ

diacritic ('ਡਾਇਅ'ਕਰਿਟਿਕ) *n* ਭੇਦ-ਸੂਚਕ

diagnose ('ਡਾਇਅਗਨਅਉਜ਼) *v* (ਰੋਗ), ਤਸ਼ਖ਼ੀਸ ਕਰਨੀ, ਜਾਂਚ ਕਰਨਾ, ਲਖਣਾ

diagnosis (ਡਾਇਅਗਨਅਉਸਿਸ) *n* ਰੋਗ ਦੀ ਪਛਾਣ, ਤਸ਼ਖ਼ੀਸ; ਰੋਗ ਦਾ ਵਰਨਣ

diagnostic ('ਡਾਇਅਗਾ'ਨੌਸਟਿਕ) *a n* ਤਸ਼ਖ਼ੀਸੀ, ਤਸ਼ਖ਼ੀਸ ਸਬੰਧੀ; ਬੀਮਾਰੀ ਦੇ ਚਿੰਨ੍ਹ, ਰੋਗ-ਲੱਛਣ

diagonal (ਡਾਇ'ਐਗਅਨਲ) *a n* ਆਡਾ, ਟੇਡਾ, (ਰੇਖਾ) ਦੂਸਾਰ, ਕਰਨ ਰੇਖਾ

diagram ('ਡਾਇਅਗਰੈਮ) *n* ਖ਼ਾਕਾ, ਨਕਸ਼ਾ, (ਰੇਖਾ) ਸ਼ਕਲ, ਰੇਖ-ਚਿਤਰ

dial ('ਡਾਇ(ਅ)ਲ) *n v* ਅੰਕ-ਪਟ, (ਘੜੀ ਦਾ ਫੋਨ ਦਾ) ਡਾਇਲ; ਭਾੜ ਦਾ ਮਾਪਕ; ਟੈਲੀਫ਼ੋਨ ਕਰਨਾ, ਡਾਇਲ ਕਰਨਾ, ਨੰਬਰ ਫੇਰਨਾ

dialect ('ਡਾਇਲੈੱਕਟ) *n* ਉਪਭਾਸ਼ਾ, ਬੋਲੀ

dialogue ('ਡਾਇਅਲੌਗ) *n* ਵਾਰਤਾਲਾਪ,

ਗੱਲਬਾਤ; ਸੰਬਾਦ

diameter (ਡਾਇ'ਐਮਿਟਅ*) *n* ਵਿਆਸ; ਨਾਪ ਦੀ ਇਕਾਈ

diamond ('ਡਾਇਅਮੰਡ) *n v* ਹੀਰਾ (ਤਾਸ਼ ਵਿਚ) ਇੱਟ ਦਾ ਪੱਤਾ (ਰੰਗ); ਹੀਰਿਆਂ ਨਾਲ ਜੜਿਆ, ਜੜਾਉ

dirarrhoea ('ਡਾਇਅ'ਰਿਅ) *n* ਦਸਤ, ਪੇਚਸ਼, ਮਰੋੜ, ਅਤਿਸਾਰ; (ਡੰਗਰਾਂ ਦੀ) ਮੋਕ

diary ('ਡਾਇਅਰਿ) *n* ਰੋਜ਼ਨਾਮਚਾ, ਦੈਨਕੀ, ਡਾਇਰੀ, ਪਤਰੀ, ਜੰਤਰੀ

dice ('ਡਾਇਸ) *n pl/v* ਗੋਟੀਆਂ, ਗੋਟਾਂ, ਚੌਪੜ, (ਪਾਸਾ ਆਦਿ) ਖੇਡਣਾ; ਮਾਸ ਦੇ ਚੌਰਸ ਟੁਕੜੇ ਕਰਨਾ; ~r ਚੌਪੜ ਖਿਡਾਰੀ, ਜੁਆਰੀਆ, ਜੁਦੇਬਾਜ਼

dichotomy (ਡਾਇ'ਕੌਟਅਮਿ) *n* ਦੁਵੰਡ, ਦੁਫਾੜ, ਦੋ ਟੁਕ

dictate (ਡਿਕ'ਟੇਇਟ,'ਡਿਕਟੇਇਟ) *v n* ਬੋਲ ਕੇ ਲਿਖਾਉਣਾ; ਹੁਕਮ ਚਲਾਉਣਾ, ਬੋਲੇ ਅਨੁਸਾਰ ਲਿਖਤ; ਹੁਕਮ, ਆਦੇਸ਼

dictation (ਡਿਕ'ਟੇਇਸ਼ਨ) *n* ਇਮਲਾ; ਆਦੇਸ਼, ਹੁਕਮ

dictator ('ਡਿਕ'ਟੇਇਟਅ*) *n* ਕੁਲਮੁਖਤਾਰ, ਨਿਰੰਕੁਸ਼ ਸ਼ਾਸਕ, ਤਾਨਾਸਾਹੀ, ਬੋਲ ਕੇ ਲਿਖਾਉਣ ਵਾਲਾ

diction ('ਡਿਕਸ਼ਨ) *n* ਲਿਖਣ ਸ਼ੈਲੀ; ਬੋਲਿਆ ਵਾਕ; ਭਾਸ਼ਾ, ਭਾਸ਼ਾ ਦੀ ਸ਼ੈਲੀ; ਸ਼ਬਦ-ਚੋਣ, ਸ਼ਬਦ-ਯੋਜਨਾ; ~ary ਸ਼ਬਦ-ਕੋਸ਼, ਕੋਸ਼

dictum ('ਡਿਕਟਅਮ) *n* ਅਖਾਣ, ਕਹਾਵਤ, ਉਕਤੀ

didactic (ਡਿ'ਡੈਕਟਿਕ) *a* ਉਪਦੇਸ਼ਾਤਮਕ, ਸਿੱਖਿਆ-ਦਾਇਕ, ਸਿੱਖਿਆਤਮਕ; ~ism ਉਪਦੇਸ਼ਾਤਮਕਤਾ, ਸਿੱਖਿਆਵਾਦ

die (ਡਾਇ) *n v* ਪਾਸਾ (ਜੁਏ ਵਿਚ) ਗੀਟੀ, ਮੋਹਰ, ਪਾਸੇ ਦੀ ਖੇਡ; ਠੱਪਾ; ਮਰਨਾ, ਮਰ ਜਾਣਾ, ਚਲਾਣਾ ਕਰਨਾ, ਮਿਟ ਜਾਣਾ, ਖਤਮ ਹੋਣਾ, (ਬੁਟਿਆਂ ਦਾ) ਮੁਰਝਾ ਜਾਣਾ, ਕੁਮਲਾ.ਜਾਣਾ

diet (ਡਾਇਟ) *n v* ਖੁਰਾਕ, ਆਹਾਰ; ਨਿਯਮਤ ਭੋਜਨ; ਪਰਹੇਜ਼ ਵਾਲੀ, ਖੁਰਾਕ ਦੇਣੀ; ਸੱਭ, ਸਭਾ, ਮਜਲਸ

dietician (ਡਾਇਅ'ਟਿਸ਼ਨ) *n* ਆਹਾਰ-ਵਿਗਿਆਨੀ

differ ('ਡਿਫਅ*) *v* ਫ਼ਰਕ ਹੋਣਾ, ਅੰਤਰ ਹੋਣਾ, ਵੱਖ ਵੱਖ ਹੋਣਾ, ਭੇਦ ਹੋਣਾ

difference ('ਡਿਫ਼ਰ(ਅ)ਨਸ) *n* ਫ਼ਰਕ, ਅੰਤਰ, ਵਿੱਥਕਾਣ, ਵਖਰੇਵਾਂ, ਭੇਦ, ਭਿੰਨਤਾ; ਅਸਹਿਮਤੀ, ਮੱਤਭੇਦ, ਝਗੜਾ, ਵਿਵਾਦ; ਵਿਰੋਧ, ਪਾੜਾ; ਵਿਅਕਤੀਗਤ ਜਾਂ ਜਾਤੀਗਤ ਵਿਸ਼ੇਸ਼ਤਾ

different ('ਡਿਫ਼ਰ(ਅ)ਨਟ) *a* ਵੱਖਰਾ, ਭਿੰਨ, ਹੋਰ, ਦੂਜਾ; ਅਸਮਾਨ, ਬੇਜੋੜ, ਬੇਮੇਲ; ~iation ਭਿੰਨਤਾ, ਵਖਰੇਵਾਂ, ਵਿਤਕਰਾ, ਵਿਭੇਦੀਕਰਨ

difficult ('ਡਿਫ਼ਿਕ(ਅ)ਲਟ) *a* ਔਖਾ, ਕਠਨ, ਮੁਸ਼ਕਲ, ਕਰੜਾ; ਟੇਢਾ

diffidence (ਡਿਫ਼ਿਡਅੰਸ) *n* ਝਿਜਕ, ਝਾਕਾ, ਸੰਕੋਚ, ਸੰਗ, ਆਸ਼ੰਕਾ; ਆਤਮ-ਸੰਦੇਹ, ਆਪਣੇ ਆਪ ਉੱਤੇ ਵਿਸ਼ਵਾਸ ਨਾ ਹੋਣ ਦੀ ਹਾਲਤ; ਸੰਗਾਊਪਣ, ਢਾਰਾ ਗਿਲਪਣ

diffident (ਡਿਫ਼ਿਡਅੰਟ) *a* ਸੰਗਾਊ, ਸ਼ਰਮਾਕਲ, ਸੰਕੋਚਵਾਨ, ਬੇਹੋਸਲਾ; ਅਵਿਸ਼ਵਾਸੀ, ਆਤਮ ਵਿਸ਼ਵਾਸਹੀਣ

diffuse (ਡਿ'ਫ਼ਯੂਜ਼) *v a* ਖਿਲਾਰਨਾ ਜਾਂ ਖਿੱਲਰਨਾ, ਖਿਲਰਵਾਂ, ਵਿਸਤਰਤ, ਵਿਸਤਾਰਸ਼ੀਲ; ~d ਫੈਲਿਆ, ਵਿਸਤਰਤ, ਵਿਆਪਤ

diffusible (ਡਿ'ਫ਼ਯੂਜ਼ਅਬਲ) *a* ਖਿਲਰਨਯੋਗ ਪ੍ਰਸਾਰਨਯੋਗ

diffusion (ਡਿ'ਫ਼ਯੂਜ਼ਨ) *n* ਖਿਲਾਰ, ਫੈਲਾਉ,

ਪ੍ਰਸਾਰਨ, ਵਿਆਪਕਤਾ

dig (ਡਿਗ) *v n* ਪੁੱਟਣਾ; ਟੋਆ ਕੱਢਣਾ, ਕੱਢ ਕੇ ਸੁੱਟਣਾ, ਖੁਰਨ, ਚੋਭਣਾ, ਖੋਜ ਕਰਨੀ; ਪੁਟਾਈ, ਗੋਡੀ; ਹੁੱਝ, ਠੁੰਗਾ

digamy ('ਡਿਗਾਅਮਿ) *n* ਦੋ-ਵਿਆਹ

digest (ਡਿ'ਜੈੱਸਟ, 'ਡਾਇਜੈੱਸਟ) *v n* ਪਚਾਉਣਾ, ਹਜ਼ਮ ਕਰਨਾ, ਹਜ਼ਮ ਹੋਣਾ; ਸਹਿ ਜਾਣਾ, ਜਰ ਜਾਣਾ, ਨਾਲ ਮਿਲਾ ਲੈਣਾ; ਸੰਖੇਪ; ਸੰਖਿਪਤ, ਪੁਸਤਕ, ਖੁਲਾਸਾ; ~**ion** ਪਾਚਨ-ਸ਼ਕਤੀ, ਹਾਜ਼ਮਾ; ~**ive** ਪਚਾਉ, ਹਾਜ਼ਮੇਦਾਰ, ਹਾਜ਼ਮੇ ਲਈ ਚੰਗਾ, ਪਾਚਕ, ਪਾਚਨਸ਼ੀਲ

digit ('ਡਿਜਿਟ) *n* 0 ਤੋਂ 9 ਤਕ ਦਾ ਕੋਈ ਅੰਕ, ਅੰਕੜਾ; ਹੱਥ ਜਾਂ ਪੈਰ ਦੀ ਉਂਗਲ

dignify (ਡਿਗਨਿਫ਼ਾਇ) *n* ਵਡਿਆਉਣਾ, ਮਾਨ ਦੇਣਾ, ਸਨਮਾਨਤ ਕਰਨਾ, ਸ਼ਾਨ ਵਧਾਉਣੀ

dignitary (ਡਿਗਨਿਟ(ਅ)ਰਿ) *n* ਉੱਚੀ ਪਦਵੀ ਵਾਲਾ ਵਿਅਕਤੀ, ਪਤਵੰਤਾ

dignity ('ਡਿਗਨਅਟਿ) *n* ਮਾਨ, ਵਡਿਆਈ, ਪਰਤਿਸ਼ਠਾ, ਗੌਰਵ, ਪ੍ਰਤਾਪ, ਸਨਮਾਨ, ਸ਼ਾਨ

dilapidate ('ਡਿ'ਲੈਪਿਡੇਇਟ) *v* ਤੋੜਨਾ, ਭੰਨਣਾ, ਟੁੱਟ ਭੱਜ ਜਾਣਾ, ਉਜਾੜਨਾ ਜਾਂ ਉੱਜੜਨਾ, ਨਾਸ ਕਰਨਾ ਜਾਂ ਹੋਣਾ; ~**d** ਟੁੱਟਾ ਭੱਜਾ; ਭੈੜੀ ਹਾਲਤ ਵਿਚ, ਉਜੜਿਆ, ਖ਼ਸਤਾ ਹਾਲ

dilemma (ਡਿ'ਲੈੱਮਅ) *n* ਦੁਬਧਾ, ਦੁਵੱਲੀ ਔਕੜ, ਦੁਚਿੱਤੀ; ਪਰੇਸ਼ਾਨੀ

dilligence ('ਡਿਲਿਜਅੰਸ) *n* ਮਿਹਨਤ, ਘਾਲ, ਪਰਿਸ਼੍ਰਮ, ਉੱਦਮ

dilligent ('ਡਿਲਿਜਅੰਟ) *a* ਮਿਹਨਤੀ, ਪਰਿਸ਼੍ਰਮੀ, ਉੱਦਮੀ

dilly ('ਡਿਲਿ) *n* ਗੱਡੀ, ਥੈਲਾ, ਝੋਲਾ; ~**dally** ਢਿੱਲ-ਮੱਠ ਕਰਨੀ, ਟਾਲ-ਮਟੋਲ ਕਰਨਾ;

ਅਵਾਰਾਗਰਦੀ ਕਰਨਾ

dilute (ਡਾਇ'ਲਯੂਟ) *v a* ਪਤਲਾ ਕਰਨਾ, ਪਾਣੀ ਮਿਲਾ ਕੇ ਮੱਧਮ ਕਰਨਾ; (ਰੰਗ) ਫਿੱਕਾ ਕਰਨਾ; ਮੱਠਾ ਪਾ ਦੇਣਾ; ਹਲਕਾ, ਫਿੱਕਾ (ਰੰਗ); ਸੁਆਦਹੀਣ, ਪਤਲਾ

dim (ਡਿਮ) *a v* ਨਿੰਮ੍ਹਾ, ਮੱਧਮ; ਧੁੰਦਲਾ, ਅਸਪਸ਼ਟ, ਫਿੱਕਾ; ਨਿੰਮ੍ਹਾ ਕਰਨਾ ਜਾਂ ਹੋਣਾ

dimension (ਡਿ'ਮੈਨੱਸ਼ਨ) *n* ਪਰਿਮਾਪ, (ਲੰਬਾਈ-ਚੌੜਾਈ) ਆਯਾਮ; ~**al** ਨਾਪ ਸਬੰਧੀ, ਆਕਾਰ ਜਾਂ ਵਿਸਤਾਰ ਬਾਰੇ

diminish (ਡਿ'ਮਿਨਿਸ਼) *v* ਘਟਾਉਣਾ ਜਾਂ ਘਟਣਾ, ਸੰਖਿਪਤ ਕਰਨਾ; ਮੱਠਾ ਪੈਣਾ ਜਾਂ ਹੋਣਾ; ~**ing** ਹ੍ਰਾਸਮਾਨ, ਘਟਣ ਵਾਲਾ

dimple ('ਡਿੰਪਲ) *n* ਠੋਡੀ ਦਾ ਡੂੰਘ, (ਹੱਸਣ ਲੱਗਿਆਂ) ਗੱਲ੍ਹਾਂ ਵਿਚ ਪੈਂਦਾ ਟੋਆ; ਟੋਆ ਪੈਣਾ, ਡੂੰਘ ਬਣਨਾ

dimply ('ਡਿੰਪਲਿ) *a* ਡੂੰਘਦਾਰ, ਲਹਿਰਦਾਰ

din (ਡਿਨ) *n v* ਰੌਲਾ, ਸ਼ੋਰ; ਰੌਲਾ ਪਾਉਣਾ, ਸ਼ੋਰ ਕਰਨਾ, ਸਿਰ ਖਾਣਾ, ਕੰਨ ਖਾਣੇ, ਬੋਲ ਬੋਲ ਕੇ ਅਕਾ ਦੇਣਾ

dinar ('ਡੀਨਾ*) *n* ਦਿਨਾਰ (ਇਕ ਕੁਵੈਤੀ, ਇਰਾਕੀ ਅਤੇ ਇਰਾਨੀ ਸਿੱਕਾ)

dine (ਡਾਇਨ) *v* ਰੋਟੀ ਖਾਣੀ, ਭੋਜਨ ਕਰਨਾ, ਖਾਣਾ ਖਾਣਾ

dinner ('ਡਿਨਅ*) *n* ਸ਼ਾਮ ਦੀ ਦਾਅਵਤ, ਰਾਤ ਦਾ ਭੋਜਨ

dip (ਡਿਪ) *n* ਡੋਬਣਾ, ਡੋਬਾ ਦੇਣਾ; ਡੋਬ ਕੇ ਰੰਗਣਾ; ਡੁੱਬਣਾ, ਲਹਿਣਾ; ਕੜਛੀ ਨਾਲ ਕੱਢਣਾ, (ਝੰਡੇ, ਜਹਾਜ਼ ਦੇ ਪੱਲੇ ਜਾਂ ਤੱਕੜੀ ਨੂੰ) ਨੀਵਾਂ ਕਰਨਾ

diphtheria, diphtheritis (ਡਿਫ਼'ਥਿਅਰਿਅ, ਡਿਫ਼-ਥੇਰਾਇਟਿਸ) *n* ਗਲਘੋਟੂ ਰੋਗ

diphthong ('ਡਿਫ਼ਥੋਂਙ) *n* ਸੰਯੁਕਤ ਸਵਰ, ਸੰਧੀਸਵਰ

diploma (ਡਿ'ਪਲਅਓਮਅ) *n* ਸਨਦ, ਪ੍ਰਮਾਣ ਪੱਤਰ; ਰਾਜ ਪੱਤਰ, ਅਧਿਕਾਰ ਪੱਤਰ

diplomacy (ਡਿ'ਪਲੋਮਅਸਿ) *n* ਰਾਜਨੀਤੀ, ਜੁਗਤ, ਚਤਰਤਾ; ਕੂਟਨੀਤੀ

diplomat ('ਡਿਪਲਅਮੈਟ) *n* ਨੀਤੀਵਾਨ, ਸਫ਼ੀਰ, ਰਾਜਦੂਤ

dire ('ਡਾਇਅ*) *a* ਤੀਬਰ, ਘੋਰ, ਭਿਅੰਕਰ

direct (ਡਿ'ਰੈਕਟ) *v a adv* ਆਗਿਆ ਦੇਣੀ; ਨਿਰਦੇਸ਼ਨ ਦੇਣਾ, ਚਲਾਉਣਾ; ਪਿਆ ਪ੍ਰਾਪਨ ਕਰਨਾ; ਹੁਕਮ ਦੇਣਾ, ਆਦੇਸ਼ ਦੇਣਾ; ਸਿੱਧਾ, ਬਿਲਕੁਲ, ਕਤਈ, ਸਪੱਸ਼ਟ, ਸਰਲ, ਖਰਾ, ਠੀਕ; ਤੁਰਤ; **~action** ਅਮਲੀ ਕਾਰਵਾਈ

direction (ਡਿ'ਰੈਕਸ਼ਨ) *n* ਸੰਚਾਲਨ, ਨਿਰਦੇਸ਼ਨ, ਨਿਗਰਾਨੀ, ਆਦੇਸ਼; ਦਿਸ਼ਾ, ਪਹਿਲੂ

directive (ਡਿ'ਰੈਕਟਿਵ) *n a* ਨਿਰਦੇਸ਼; ਨਿਰਦੇਸ਼ਕ, ਮਾਰਗਦਰਸ਼ਕ, ਸੂਚਕ

director (ਡਿ'ਰੈਕਟਅ*) *n* ਨਿਰਦੇਸ਼ਕ, ਸੰਚਾਲਕ, ਸੂਤਰਧਾਰ, (ਫ਼ਿਲਮ) ਨਿਰਦੇਸ਼ਕ, ਨਿਰਮਾਤਾ; **~ate** ਪ੍ਰਬੰਧ ਸੰਚਾਲਕ, ਨਿਰਦੇਸ਼ਕ ਦਾ ਦਫ਼ਤਰ, ਅਧਿਕਰਨ ਸੰਮਤੀ, ਸੰਚਾਲਕ-ਮੰਡਲੀ, ਸੰਚਾਲਕ-ਪਦ; **~ship** ਸੰਚਾਲਕਤਾ, ਨਿਰਦੇਸ਼ਕਤਵ, ਸੰਚਾਲ੍ਰਪਦ; **~y** ਨਿਰਦੇਸ਼ਤਾ, ਡਾਇਰੈਕਟਰੀ, ਨਿਯਮਾਵਲੀ, ਰਾਹਨਾਮਾ; ਸੰਚਾਲਕ ਮੰਡਲ

direful ('ਡਾਇਅਫ਼ੁਲ) *a* ਘੋਰ, ਭਿਅੰਕਰ

dirt (ਡਅ:ਟ) *n v* ਧੂੜ, ਚਿੱਕੜ, ਮੈਲ, ਮਲ, ਕੂੜਾ ਕਰਕਟ, ਗੰਦਗੀ; **~y** ਮੈਲਾ, ਗੰਦਾ, ਕਲੰਕਿਤ, ਅਪਵਿੱਤਰ, ਗੰਧਲਿਆ, ਮਿਟਿਆਲਾ; ਖ਼ਰਾਬ

disability ('ਡਿਸਅ'ਬਿਲਅਟਿ) *n* ਅਯੋਗਤਾ, ਅਸਮਰੱਥ; ਅੰਗਹੀਣਤਾ, ਅਪਾਹਜਪੁਣਾ

disable (ਡਿਸ'ਏਇਬਲ) *v* ਅਯੋਗ ਠਹਿਰਾਉਣਾ, ਅਸਮਰੱਥ ਘੋਸ਼ਤ ਕਰਨਾ; ਅੰਗਹੀਣ ਕਰਨਾ, ਨਕਾਰਾ ਕਰਨਾ, ਅਪਾਹਜ ਬਣਾ ਦੇਣਾ; **~d** ਅੰਗਹੀਣ, ਨਾਕਾਮ, ਅਪੰਗ, ਅਪਾਹਜ; **~ment** ਅਸਮਰੱਥਤਾ, ਅਸ਼ਕਤੀ, ਅਯੋਗਤਾ, ਅੰਗਹੀਣਤਾ

disadvantage ('ਡਿਸਅਡ'ਵਾਂਟਿਜ) *n* ਹਾਨੀ, ਘਾਟਾ, ਨੁਕਸਾਨ; ਦਿੱਕਤ, ਔਖਿਆਈ

disagree ('ਡਿਸਅ'ਗਰੀ) *v* ਮੱਤ-ਭੇਦ ਰੱਖਣਾ, ਅਸੰਮਤੀ ਰੱਖਣਾ, ਅਸਹਿਮਤ ਹੋਣਾ

disallow ('ਡਿਸਅ'ਲਾਉ) *v* ਅਸਵੀਕਾਰ ਕਰਨਾ, ਆਗਿਆ ਨਾ ਦੇਣੀ, ਮਨ੍ਹਾਂ ਕਰਨਾ, ਨਾਮਨਜ਼ੂਰ ਕਰਨਾ; **~ed** ਨਾ-ਮਨਜ਼ੂਰ, ਅਸਵੀਕ੍ਰਿਤ

disappear ('ਡਿਸਅ'ਪਿਅ*) *v* ਲੁਕਣਾ, ਲੋਪ ਹੋਣਾ, ਅੱਖਾਂ ਤੋਂ ਉਹਲੇ ਹੋਣਾ, ਗੁਆਚਣਾ, ਛਿਪ ਜਾਣਾ, ਮਿਟ ਜਾਣਾ, ਗ਼ਾਇਬ ਹੋ ਜਾਣਾ; **~ance** ਲੋਪ, ਉਹਲੇ, ਓਟ, ਅਦਿ੍ਸ਼ਟਤਾ

disappoint ('ਡਿ'ਸਅ'ਪੋਇੰਟ) *v* ਨਿਸਫਲ ਕਰਨਾ, ਆਸ ਭੰਗ ਕਰਨੀ, ਆਸ ਤੋੜਨੀ, ਨਿਰਾਸ਼ ਕਰਨਾ; **~ed** ਨਿਰਾਸ਼, ਮਾਯੂਸ, ਨਾਉਮੀਦ; **~ment** ਨਿਰਾਸ਼ਤਾ, ਨਿਰਾਸ਼ਾ

disapproval ('ਡਿਸਅ'ਪਰੁਵ੍ਲ) *n* ਅਸੰਮਤੀ, ਨਾਮਨਜ਼ੂਰੀ, ਨਾ ਪਾਂਤਰਤਾ

disapprove ('ਡਿਸਅ'ਪਰੁਵ) *v* ਅਪ੍ਰਵਾਨ ਕਰਨਾ, ਅਸੰਮਤੀ ਪਰਗਟ ਕਰਨੀ, ਵਿਰੋਧ ਕਰਨਾ, ਨਾ ਪਸੰਦ ਕਰਨਾ

disarm (ਡਿਸ'ਆਮ) *v* ਸ਼ਸਤਰਹੀਨ ਕਰਨਾ, ਬੇਬਸ ਕਰਨਾ, ਨਿਹੱਥਾ ਕਰਨਾ; **~ament** ਨਿਸ਼ਸਤਰੀਕਰਨ, ਸ਼ਸਤਰਹੀਨਤਾ, ਸ਼ਸਤਰ-ਤਿਆਗ; **~ed** ਨਿਹੱਥਾ, ਬੇਬਸ

disarrange ('ਡਿਸਅ'ਰੇਇੰਜ) *v* ਬੇਤਰਤੀਬ ਕਰਨਾ, ਅੱਗੇ ਪਿੱਛੇ ਕਰ ਦੇਣਾ, ਉਲਟ-ਪੁਲਟ

disarray | 448 | **discourage**

ਕਰ ਦੇਣਾ; ~ment ਬੇਤਰਤੀਬੀ, ਉਲਟ-ਪੁਲਟ, ਅਵਿਵਸਥਾ, ਗੜਬੜ

disarray ('ਡਿਸਅਰੇਇ) *n v* ਬੇਤਰਤੀਬੀ, ਗੜਬੜ ਉਲਟ-ਪੁਲਟ, ਉਲਟ-ਪੁਲਟ ਕਰਨਾ, ਅੱਗੇ ਪਿੱਛੇ ਕਰ ਦੇਣਾ

disassociate (ਡਿਸਅ'ਸ਼ਿਏਇਟ) *v* ਅੱਲਗ ਹੋ ਜਾਣਾ, ਨਾਤਾ ਤੋੜ ਦੇਣਾ, ਸਬੰਧ ਤੋੜ ਲੈਣਾ

disaster (ਡਿ'ਜ਼ਾਸਟਅ*) *n* ਬਿਪਤਾ, ਮੁਸੀਬਤ, ਸ਼ਾਮਤ, ਆਫ਼ਤ, ਸੰਕਟ; ~ous ਬਿਪਤਾ ਵਾਲਾ, ਮੰਦ ਭਾਗਾ, ਸੰਕਟ ਵਾਲਾ, ਘੋਰ

disband (ਡਿਸਬੈਂਡ) *n* (ਸੈਨਾ, ਪਲਟਨ) ਤੋੜ ਦੇਣੀ, ਲਾਮਬੰਦੀ ਸਮਾਪਤ ਕਰ ਦੇਣੀ, ਖਿੰਡਾ ਦੇਣਾ, ਭੰਗ ਕਰ ਦੇਣਾ, ਬਰਖ਼ਾਸਤ ਕਰ ਦੇਣਾ

disbelief ('ਡਿਸਬਿ'ਲੀਫ਼) *n* ਅਵਿਸ਼ਵਾਸ, ਬੇਯਕੀਨੀ, ਬੇਇਤਬਾਰੀ, ਬੇਪ੍ਰਤੀਤੀ, ਨਾਸਤਕਤਾ

disbelieve 'ਡਿਸਬਿ'ਲੀਵ੍) *v* ਅਵਿਸ਼ਵਾਸ ਕਰਨਾ, ਨਾ ਮੰਨਣਾ

disburse (ਡਿਸ'ਬਅ:ਸ) *v* ਖ਼ਰਚ ਕਰਨਾ, ਖ਼ਰਚਣਾ, ਭੁਗਤਾਨ ਕਰਨਾ, ਅਦਾਇਗੀ ਕਰਨਾ, ਵੰਡਣੀ; ~ment ਭੁਗਤਾਨ, ਅਦਾਇਗੀ, ਖ਼ਰਚ

disc (ਡਿਸਕ) *n* ਤਵਾ, ਚੱਕਲੀ, ਤਸ਼ਤਰੀ

discard (ਡਿਸ'ਕਾਡ) *v n* ਸੁੱਟ ਪਾਉਣਾ, ਛੱਡ ਦੇਣਾ, ਬਰਖ਼ਾਸਤ ਕਰਨਾ, ਕੱਢ ਦੇਣਾ

discern (ਡਿ'ਸਅ:ਨ) *v* ਵੇਖ ਲੈਣਾ, ਸਮਝ ਜਾਣਾ, ਜਾਣ ਲੈਣਾ, ਤਾੜ ਲੈਣਾ; ਜਾਂਚਣਾ

discharge (ਡਿਸ'ਚਾ*ਜ, 'ਡਿਸਚਾ*ਜ) *v n* ਬਰਖ਼ਾਸਤ ਕਰਨਾ, ਕੱਢ ਦੇਣਾ; (ਫ਼ਰਜ਼) ਨਿਭਾਉਣਾ, ਛੁਟਣਾ, (ਜਹਾਜ਼ ਆਦਿ ਤੋਂ) ਮਾਲ ਲਾਹੁਣਾ; (ਦਰਿਆ ਦਾ) ਸਮੁੰਦਰ ਵਿਚ ਡਿੱਗਣਾ; (ਕ) ਰਿਹਾ ਕਰਨਾ; ਬਿਜਲੀ ਖ਼ਾਰਜ ਕਰਨੀ; ਪਾਕ ਨਿਕਲਣਾ; (ਤੋਪ ਆਦਿ) ਦਾਗ਼ਣਾ ਜਾਂ ਚਲਾਉਣਾ, (ਰੋਗੀ ਨੂੰ) ਹਸਪਤਾਲ ਵਿਚੋਂ ਜਾਣ ਦੀ ਆਗਿਆ ਦੇਣੀ; (ਨੌਕਰੀ ਤੋਂ) ਬਰਖ਼ਾਸਤਗੀ; ਰਿਹਾਈ, ਛੁਟਕਾਰਾ; ਫ਼ਰਜ਼ ਦਾ ਪਾਲਣ; ਤੋਪ ਆਦਿ ਦਾ ਫ਼ਾਇਰ; ਕਰਜ਼ ਦੀ ਅਦਾਇਗੀ; ਨਾਂ-ਕਟਾਈ; ~d ਦੋਸ਼ ਮੁਕਤ, ਸੇਵਾ ਮੁਕਤ

disciple (ਡਿ'ਸਾਇਪਲ) *n* ਚੇਲਾ, ਮੁਰੀਦ, ਸ਼ਿਸ਼, ਅਨੁਯਾਈ, ਸ਼ਾਗਿਰਦ

disciplinary ('ਡਿਸਿਪਲਿਨ(ਅ)ਰਿ) *a* ਅਨੁਸ਼ਾਸਨ-ਸਬੰਧੀ, ਨਿਯਮ ਪਾਲਣ ਸਬੰਧੀ, ਅਨੁਸ਼ਾਸਕ

discipline (ਡਿਸਿਪਲਿਨ) *n v* ਅਨੁਸ਼ਾਸਨ, ਜ਼ਬਤ, ਨਿਯਮ-ਪਾਲਣ; ਸੰਜਮ; ਵਿਸ਼ਾ-ਖੇਤਰ; ਨਿਯੰਤਰਣ; ਅਨੁਸ਼ਾਸਨ ਵਿਚ ਰੱਖਣਾ, ਸੰਜਮ ਵਿਚ ਰੱਖਣਾ, ਨਿਯਮਬੱਧ ਰੱਖਣਾ; ~d ਅਨੁਸ਼ਾਸਤ, ਨਿਯੰਤਰਤ

disclose (ਡਿਸ'ਕਲਅਉਜ਼) *v* ਪਰਗਟ ਕਰਨਾ, ਜ਼ਾਹਰ ਕਰਨਾ, ਖੋਲ੍ਹਣਾ (ਭੇਦ ਆਦਿ), ਉਘਾੜਨਾ, ਦੱਸਣਾ

disclosure (ਡਿਸ'ਕਲਅਉਜ਼ਅ*) *n* ਪਰਗਟਾਉ, ਉਘਾੜ, ਖੋਲ੍ਹਿਆ ਭੇਦ

discord ('ਡਿਸਕੋਡ, ਡਿ'ਸਕੋਡ) *n v* ਅਸਹਿਮਤੀ, ਮੱਤਭੇਦ, ਅਣ-ਬਣ, ਫੁੱਟ, ਕਲਹ, ਝਗੜਾ; ਅਸਹਿਮਤ ਹੋਣਾ; ਮੱਤਭੇਦ ਹੋਣਾ

discount (ਡਿਸਕਾਉਂਟ, ਡਿ'ਸਕਾਉਂਟ) *n v* ਕਟੌਤੀ, ਵੱਟਾ ਲਾਉਣਾ, ਕਾਟ ਕਰਨੀ; ਘਟਾਉਣਾ, ਕੱਢਣਾ, ਛੇਤੀ (ਮਾਲ) ਵੇਚਣ ਲਈ ਘੱਟ ਲਾਭ ਤੇ ਦੇ ਦੇਣਾ; ਗਿਣਤੀ ਵਿਚ ਨਾ ਰੱਖਣਾ; ਹੁੰਡੀ ਲੈਣੀ, ਹਿਸਾਬ ਵਿਚੋਂ ਕੱਢ ਦੇਣਾ

discourage (ਡਿ'ਸਕਅੱਰਿਜ) *v* ਦਿਲ ਢਾਹੁਣ, ਉਤਸ਼ਾਹਹੀਣ ਕਰਨਾ, ਹੌਸਲਾ ਢਾਹੁਣਾ, ਹਿੰਮਤ ਤੋੜਨੀ, ਨਿਰਾਸ ਕਰਨਾ; ~d ਨਿਰਉਤਸ਼ਾਹਤ, ਨਿਰਾਸ; ~ment ਉਤਸ਼ਾਹਭੰਗ, ਦਿਲਢਾਹੀ

ਅਸਮਰਥਨ, ਹੌਂਸਲਾ ਸ਼ਿਕਨੀ

discouraging (ਡਿ'ਸਕਅੱਰਿਜ਼ਿਡ਼) *a* ਨਿਰਉਤਸ਼ਾਹ ਕਰਨ ਵਾਲਾ, ਦਿਲ ਢਾਹੁਣ ਵਾਲਾ

discourse ('ਡਿਸਕੋ:ਸ) *n v* ਪ੍ਰਵਚਨ, ਵਾਰਤਾਲਾਪ, ਵਿਆਖਿਆਨ, ਭਾਸ਼ਨ, ਪ੍ਰੋਕਤਿ

discourteous (ਡਿਸ'ਕਯਾ:ਟਯਸ) *a* ਬਦਤਮੀਜ਼, ਅਸਭਿਯ, ਉਜੱਡ, ਅਸ਼ਿਸ਼ਟ; ~ly ਬਦਤਮੀਜ਼ੀ ਨਾਲ, ਅਸਭਿਯ ਢੰਗ ਨਾਲ; ~ness ਅਸ਼ਿਸ਼ਟਤਾ, ਬਦਤਮੀਜ਼ੀ, ਬੇਲਿਹਾਜ਼ੀ, ਉਜੱਡਤਾ, ਕੋਰਪਣ

discourtesy (ਡਿਸ'ਕਯਾ.ਟਿਸਿ) *n* ਅਸ਼ਿਸ਼ਟਾਚਾਰ, ਦੁਸ਼ੀਲਤਾ

discover (ਡਿ'ਸਕਅੱਵਅ) *v* ਖੋਜ ਕਰਨੀ, ਲੱਭ ਲੈਣਾ, ਪਰਗਟ ਕਰਨਾ, ਭੇਦ ਖੋਲ੍ਹਣਾ, ਪਤਾ ਕਰਨਾ, ਬਾਹਰ ਕੱਢਣਾ, ਜਾਣ ਲੈਣਾ, ਪੋਲ ਖੋਲ੍ਹਣਾ; ~er ਖੋਜੀ, ਢੂੰਡਾਊ, ਗਿਆਤਾ; ~y ਲੱਭਤ, ਖੋਜ, ਸੋਧ, ਪ੍ਰਾਪਤੀ; ਸਪਸ਼ਟੀਕਰਨ

discredit (ਡਿਸ'ਕਰੈਡਿਟ) *n v* ਬੇਇਤਬਾਰੀ, ਅਪ੍ਰਤਿਸ਼ਠਾ, ਬਦਨਾਮੀ ਵਾਲੀ ਗੱਲ, ਬੇਪ੍ਰਤੀਤੀ ਕਰਨੀ, ਸ਼ਾਖ ਘਟਾਉਣੀ

discreet (ਡਿ'ਸਕਰੀਟ) *a* ਸਿਆਣਾ, ਸੂਝਵਾਨ, ਵਿਹਤਵਾਨ, ਸਾਵਧਾਨ, ਗੰਭੀਰ

discrepancy (ਡਿ'ਸਕਰੈਪੰਸਿ) *n* ਭੁੱਲ, ਫ਼ਰਕ, ਅੰਤਰ, ਭੇਦ

discrete (ਡਿ'ਸਕਰੀਟ) *a* ਵੱਖਰਾ, ਅਲੱਗ, ਭਿੰਨ, ਖੰਡਤ

discretion (ਡਿ'ਸਕਰੈੱਸ਼ਨ) *n* ਸੂਝ, ਸਿਆਣਪ, ਵਿਵੇਕ, ਵਿਚਾਰਸ਼ੀਲਤਾ; ~ary ਇੱਛਾ ਅਨੁਸਾਰ, ਇਖ਼ਤਿਆਰੀ, ਸਵੈਧੀਨ

discriminate (ਡਿਸਕਰਿਮਿਨਏਟ) *v* ਫ਼ਰਕ ਕੱਢਣਾ, ਨਿਤਾਰਾ ਕਰਨਾ, ਸੂਖਮ ਭੇਦ ਰੱਖਣਾ, ਵਿਸ਼ੇਸ਼ਤਾ ਦੱਸਣੀ, ਨਿਖੇੜਨਾ, ਅੰਤਰ ਹੋਣਾ, ਫ਼ਰਕ ਹੋਣਾ

discrimination (ਡਿ'ਸਕਰਿਮਿ'ਨੇਇਸ਼ਨ) *n* ਸੂਝ, ਵਿਵੇਕ, ਤਮੀਜ਼, ਵਿਤਕਰਾ, ਭੇਦ-ਭਾਵ, ਪੱਖ-ਪਾਤ; ਵਖਰੇਵਾਂ

discriminatory (ਡਿ'ਸਕਰਿਮਿਨਅਟ(ਅ)ਰਿ) *a* ਵਿਭੇਦਕ, ਵਿਤਕੇਦਾਰ, ਪੱਖਪਾਤੀ

discursion (ਯਡਿ'ਸਕਯਾ:ਸ਼ਨ) *n* ਵਿਵਾਦ, ਬਹਿਸ, ਤਰਕਯੁਕਤ ਵਾਰਤਾ

discursive (ਡਿ'ਸਕਯਾ:ਸਿਵ਼) *a* ਉਕਤੀ-ਪੂਰਨ, ਤਰਕਪੂਰਨ, ਲੰਬਾ ਚੈੜਾ; ਅਸੰਗਤ; ~ly ਦਲੀਲ ਨਾਲ; ਬੇਤੁਕੇ ਢੰਗ ਨਾਲ; ~ness ਤਰਕਪੂਰਨਤਾ, ਵਲ-ਫੇਰ, ਅਸੰਗਤੀ

discuss (ਡਿ'ਸਕਅੱਸ) *v* ਵਿਚਾਰਨਾ, ਵਿਚਾਰ ਵਿਮਰਸ਼ ਕਰਨਾ; ਤਰਕ ਕਰਨਾ, ਚਰਚਾ ਕਰਨੀ, ਬਹਿਸ ਕਰਨੀ; ~ion ਬਹਿਸ, ਵਾਦ-ਵਿਵਾਦ, ਵਿਚਾਰ-ਵਟਾਂਦਰਾ, ਚਰਚਾ

disease (ਡਿ'ਜ਼ੀਜ਼) *n* ਰੋਗ, ਬੀਮਾਰੀ, ਮਰਜ਼ ਦੋਸ਼; ~d ਰੋਗੀ, ਬੀਮਾਰ, ਮਰੀਜ਼, ਅਸੁਅਸਥ, ਰੋਗ-ਗ੍ਰਸਤ; ਦੂਸ਼ਤ

disfigure (ਡਿਸ'ਫ਼ਿਗਆ*) *v* ਸ਼ਕਲ ਵਿਗਾੜਨੀ, ਕਰੂਪ ਕਰ ਦੇਣਾ, ਧੱਬਾ ਲਾਉਣੀ, ਵਿਗਾੜਨਾ, ਬਦਸੂਰਤ ਬਣਾ ਦੇਣਾ

disfranchise (ਡਿਸ'ਫ਼ਰੈਨਚਾਇਜ਼) *v* ਵੋਟ ਦਾ ਹੱਕ ਖੋਹ ਲੈਣਾ, ਨਾਗਰਿਕਤਾ ਦੇ ਅਧਿਕਾਰ ਤੋਂ ਵਾਂਝਿਆ ਕਰ ਦੇਣਾ

disforest (ਡਿਸ'ਫ਼ੋਰਿਸਟ) *v* ਜੰਗਲ ਕੱਟਣਾ

disgrace (ਡਿਸ'ਗਰੇਇਸ) *n v* ਬੇਇਜ਼ੱਤੀ, ਬਦਨਾਮੀ, ਨਮੋਸ਼ੀ, ਨਿਰਾਦਰ; ਬੇਇੱਜ਼ਤੀ ਕਰਨੀ, ਨਿਰਾਦਰ ਕਰਨਾ, ਪਤ ਲਾਹੁਣੀ

disguise (ਡਿਸ'ਗਾਇਜ਼) *v n* ਭੇਸ ਬਦਲਣਾ ਜਾਂ

ਵਟਾਉਣਾ; ਲੁਕਾਉਣਾ; ਸਾਂਗ ਰਚਣਾ, ਢੋਂਗ ਰਚਣਾ; ਭੇਸ; ਛਲ

disgust (ਡਿਸ'ਗਾਸਟ) *n v* ਉਪਰਾਮਤਾ, ਅਰੁਚੀ, ਉਚਾਟ, ਉਕਤਾਹਟ; ਉਚਾਟ ਕਰਨਾ, ਅਕਾ ਦੇਣਾ; ~ed ਉਚਾਟ, ਉਪਰਾਮ, ਅੱਕਿਆ, ਉਕਤਾਉਆ; ~ful ਘਿਣਾਉਣਾ, ਅਕਾਊ, ਉਕਤਾਊ

dish (ਡਿਸ਼) *n v* ਪਿਆਲੀ, ਕੌਲੀ, ਡੂੰਘਾ ਕਟੋਰਾ, ਪਰੋਸਿਆ ਭੋਜਨ; ਪਰੋਸਣਾ; (ਅਪ) ਠੱਗਣਾ, ਧੋਖਾ ਦੇਣਾ; ਚਿਥ ਪੈਣਾ; ~out ਵੰਡਣਾ

disharmony (ਡਿਸ'ਹਾਮਅਨਿ) *n* ਸੁਰਹੀਣਤਾ, ਅਣਜੋੜ, ਬੇਸੁਰਾਪਣ, ਅਸੰਗਤੀ

dishearten (ਡਿਸ'ਹਾਟਨ) *v* ਨਿਰਾਸ਼ ਕਰਨਾ, ਨਿਰਉਤਸਾਹ ਕਰਨਾ, ਦਿਲ ਢਾਹੁਣਾ, ਹਿੰਮਤ ਤੋੜਨੀ, ਡੁਲਾਉਣਾ; ~ment ਨਿਰਾਸ਼ਾ, ਉਤਸਾਹਹੀਣਤਾ

dishonest (ਡਿਸ'ਔਨਿਸਟ) *a* ਖੋਟਾ, ਕਪਟੀ, ਬੇਈਮਾਨ ਧੋਖੇਬਾਜ਼

dishonour (ਡਿਸ'ਔਨਅ*) *v n* ਬੇਇੱਜ਼ਤੀ ਕਰਨੀ, ਨਿਰਾਦਰ ਕਰਨਾ, ਅਪਮਾਨ ਕਰਨਾ, ਪਤ ਲਾਹੁਣਾ; ਵਾਪਸ ਮੋੜ ਦੇਣਾ; ਨਿਰਾਦਰ, ਅਪਮਾਨ; ~ed ਅਪਮਾਨਤ, ਨਾਮਨਜ਼ੂਰ

disintergation (ਡਿਸ'ਇਨਟਿ'ਗਰੇਇਸ਼ਨ) *n* ਵਿਭਾਜਨ, ਅਵਛੇਦਨ, ਖੰਡਨ, ਵਿਯੋਜਨ

dislike (ਡਿਸ'ਲਾਇਕ) *v n* ਘਿਰਣਾ ਕਰਨੀ, ਨਫ਼ਰਤ ਕਰਨੀ, ਬੁਰਾ ਲੱਗਣਾ, ਨਾ ਪਸੰਦ ਕਰਨਾ, ਘਿਰਣਾ, ਨਫ਼ਰਤ

dislocate ('ਡਿਸਲਅ(ਉ)ਕੇਇਟ) *v* ਜੋੜ ਅਲੱਗ ਕਰਨੀ, ਸਰਕਾਉਣਾ, ਥਾਂ ਤੋਂ ਹਟਾਉਣਾ; ਸੋਚ ਆਉਣੀ; (ਕਿਸੇ ਅੰਗ ਨੂੰ) ਅਲੱਗ ਅਲੱਗ ਕਰਨਾ; ਉਲਟ-ਪੁਲਟ ਕਰਨਾ

dislocation ('ਡਿਸਲਅ(ਉ)'ਕੇਇਸ਼ਨ) *n* ਹੱਡੀ ਦੀ ਉਤਰਾਈ, ਸੋਚ; ਉਲਟ-ਪੁਲਟ, ਖਲਲ, ਗੜਬੜ, ਖ਼ਰਾਬੀ; ਵਿਸਥਾਪਨ

dislodge (ਡਿਸ'ਲੌਜ) *v* ਕੱਢ ਦੇਣਾ, ਉਖਾੜਨਾ, ਮੋਰਚੇ ਤੋਂ ਹਟਾਉਣਾ, ਪੁੱਟ ਸੁੱਟਣਾ

disloyal ('ਡਿਸ'ਲੋਇ(ਅ)ਲ) *a* ਗ਼ੱਦਾਰ; ਬਾਗ਼ੀ; ਧੋਖੇਬਾਜ਼

dismal ('ਡਿਜ਼ਮ(ਅ)ਲ) *a* ਸੋਗਮਈ, ਦੁੱਖਮਈ, ਉਦਾਸੀਨ, ਬਦਕਿਸਮਤ, ਬੇਰੌਣਕ, ਸੁਨਸਾਨ, ਵੀਰਾਨ, ਉਜਾੜਿਆ-ਪੁੰਜਾੜਿਆ, ਭਿਆਨਕ, ਡਰਾਉਣਾ

dismantle (ਡਿਸ'ਮੈਂਟਲ) *v* ਵੰਚਤ ਕਰਨਾ, (ਮੋਰਚਾਬੰਦੀ ਆਦਿ ਨੂੰ) ਤੋੜ ਦੇਣਾ; (ਜਹਾਜ਼ ਨੂੰ) ਮਸਤੂਲ, ਤੋੜ ਫੋੜ ਦੇਣਾ, ਉਧੇੜਨਾ

dismay (ਡਿਸ'ਮੇਇ) *v* ਮਸਤੂਲ-ਰਹਿਤ ਕਰਨਾ

dismember (ਡਿਸ'ਮੈਂਬਅ*) *v* ਟੁਕੜੇ ਟੁਕੜੇ ਕਰਨਾ, ਬੰਦ ਬੰਦ ਕੱਟਣੇ, ਅੰਗ-ਭੰਗ ਕਰਨਾ; ਵੰਡ ਦੇਣਾ, (ਦੇਸ਼ ਦਾ) ਬਟਵਾਰਾ ਕਰਨਾ; ~ment ਵਿਭਾਜਨ

dismiss (ਡਿਸ'ਮਿਸ) *v* ਮੌਕੂਫ਼ ਕਰਨਾ, ਕੱਢ ਦੇਣਾ, ਬਰਖ਼ਾਸਤ ਕਰਨਾ, ਨੌਕਰੀਉਂ ਕੱਢ ਦੇਣਾ ਸਾਮੂਹਿਓ ਹਟਾ ਦੇਣਾ, ਮੁਕੱਦਮਾ ਖ਼ਾਰਜ ਕਰਨਾ; ਜ਼ੋਰ ਦੀ ਹਿੱਟ ਲਾਉਣੀ

dismount (ਡਿਸ'ਮਾਉਂਟ) *v* ਘੋੜੇ ਤੋਂ ਉਤਰਨਾ, ਘੋੜੇ ਤੋਂ ਡੇਗ ਦੇਣਾ; ਉਤਰਾਈ;

disobedience (ਡਿਸਅ'ਬੀਡਯਅੰਸ) *n* ਆਗਿਆ-ਭੰਗ, ਅਵੱਗਿਆ, ਨਾ-ਫ਼ਰਮਾਨੀ, ਨਿਯਮ-ਉਲੰਘਣ, ਹੁਕਮ-ਅਦੂਲੀ

disobedient (ਡਿਸਅ'ਬੀਡਯਅੰਟ) *a* ਆਕੀ, ਅਵੱਗਿਆਕਾਰੀ, ਨਾਬਰ

disobey (ਡਿਸਅ'ਬੋਇ) *v* ਆਗਿਆ ਭੰਗ ਕਰਨੀ, ਅਵੱਗਿਆ ਕਰਨੀ, ਨਿਯਮ ਤੋੜਨਾ, ਹੁਕਮ ਨਾ

ਮੰਨਣਾ, ਨਾ-ਫ਼ਰਮਾਨੀ ਕਰਨੀ

disorder (ਡਿਸ'ਓਡਅ*) n ਬੇਤਰਤੀਬੀ, ਉਲਟ-ਪੁਲਟ, ਗੜਬੜ; ਹਲਚਲ; ਰੋਗ; ਉਲਟ-ਪੁਲਟ ਕਰਨ; ~ly ਬੇਤਰਤੀਬ; ਉਂਗੜ-ਦੁੱਗੜ; ਅਨਿਯਮਤ, ਬੇਜ਼ਾਬਤਾ, ਬੇ-ਲਗਾਮ, ਹਫੜਾ-ਦਫੜੀ ਭਰਿਆ

disown (ਡਿਸ'ਅਉਨ) v ਛੱਡਣਾ, ਇਨਕਾਰ ਕਰਨੀ, ਮੁੱਕਰਨਾ, ਨਾ ਮੰਨਣਾ, ਨਾ ਅਪਣਾਉਣਾ, ਤਿਆਗਣਾ; ~ed ਤਿਆਗਿਆ

dispel (ਡਿ'ਸਪੈੱਲ) v (ਭਰਮ ਜਾਂ ਭੈ ਜਾਂ ਹਨੇਰਾ) ਨਿਵਿਰਤ ਕਰਨ, ਹਟਾਉਣਾ, ਮਿਟਾਉਣਾ, ਦੂਰ ਕਰਨਾ, ਕੱਢਣਾ

dispensable (ਡਿ'ਸਪੈਂਸੇਬਲ) a (ਕਨੂੰਨ ਜਾਂ ਰਸਮ) ਬੇ-ਲੋੜ, ਗ਼ੈਰਜ਼ਰੂਰੀ; ਛੱਡੇ ਜਾਣ ਯੋਗ

dispensary (ਡਿ'ਸਪੈਂਨਸ(ਅ)ਰਿ) n ਦਵਾਖ਼ਾਨਾ, ਸ਼ਫ਼ਾਖ਼ਾਨਾ

dispense (ਡਿ'ਸਪੈਂਸ) v ਵੰਡਣਾ, ਤਕਸੀਮ ਕਰਨਾ, ਨੁਸਖ਼ੇ ਅਨੁਸਾਰ ਦਵਾਈ ਬਣਾਉਣੀ; (ਪਾਪਾਂ ਤੋਂ) ਛੋਟ ਦੇਣੀ, ਮਾਫ਼ੀ ਦੇਣੀ, ਛੱਡਣਾ, ਤਿਆਗਣਾ; (ਨੌਕਰੀ ਤੋਂ) ਛੁੱਟੀ ਦੇਣੀ

disperse (ਡਿ'ਸਪਅ:ਸ) v (ਰੋਸ਼ਨੀ) ਫੈਲਾਉਣਾ; ਖਿੰਡਾਉਣਾ, ਖਿੰਡਣਾ; ਸਭਾ ਉਠਾਉਣੀ

displace (ਡਿਸ'ਪਲੇਇਸ) v ਥਾਂ ਤੋਂ ਹਟਾਉਣਾ, ਸਰਕਾਉਣਾ, ਉਰੇ ਪਰੇ ਕਰਨਾ; ਥਾਂ ਮੱਲਣੀ, ਪਦਵੀ ਤੋਂ ਲਾਹੁਣਾ

display (ਡਿ'ਸਪਲੇਇ) v ਵਿਖਾਲਣਾ, ਦੱਸਣਾ, ਸਾਮ੍ਹਣੇ ਲਿਆਉਣਾ; ਵਿਖਾਲਾ ਕਰਨਾ, ਨੁਮਾਇਸ਼ ਕਰਨਾ; ~ed ਪਰਦਰਸ਼ਤ, ਫੈਲਾਇਆ, ਦਿਖਾਇਆ

displease (ਡਿਸ'ਪਲੀਜ਼) v ਨਾਰਾਜ਼ ਕਰਨਾ, ਰੁਸਾਉਣਾ, ਚਿੜਾਉਣਾ; ~d ਨਾਰਾਜ਼, ਨਾਖ਼ੁਸ਼, ਰੁੱਸਿਆ, ਅਪ੍ਰਸੰਨ

displeasing (ਡਿ'ਪਲੀਜ਼ਿਙ) a ਅਟਸੁਖਾਵਾਂ, ਅਰੋਚਕ, ਅਸੰਤੋਖਜਨਕ, ਅਪ੍ਰਿਯ

displeasure (ਡਿਸ'ਪਲੈੱਯੂਅ*) n ਨਾਰਾਜ਼ਰੀ, ਗੁੱਸਾ, ਬੇਆਰਾਮੀ, ਅਸੰਤੋਖ, ਅਪ੍ਰਸੰਨਤਾ

disposal (ਡਿ'ਸਪਅਉਜ਼ਲ) n ਸਪੁਰਦਗੀ, ਸੌਂਪਣੀ, ਸਮਰਪਣ, ਨਿਬੇੜਾ, ਨਿਪਟਾਰਾ, ਇਖ਼ਤਿਆਰ; ਇੰਤਜ਼ਾਮ; ਵਿੱਕਰੀ

disposable (ਡਿ'ਸਪਅਉਜ਼ਅਬਲ) adv ਇਕ ਵਾਰੀ ਵਰਤ ਕੇ ਸੁੱਟਣ ਯੋਗ

dispose (ਡਿ'ਸਪਅਉਜ਼) v ਥਾਂ ਸਿਰ ਜਾਂ ਨੁੱਕ ਸਿਰ ਰੱਖਣਾ; ਟਿਕਾਉਣਾ, ਚਾਲਣਾ, ਰੁਚੀ ਪੈਦਾ ਕਰਨੀ; ਵਿੱਕਰੀ ਕਰਨੀ; ਸਮਾਪਤ ਕਰਨਾ, ਨਸ਼ਟ ਕਰਨਾ, ਮਾਰ ਦੇਣਾ; ਫ਼ੈਸਲਾ ਕਰਨਾ, ਨਿਪਟਾਉਣਾ, ਤੇ ਕਰਨਾ, ਨਿਰਣਾ ਕਰਨਾ

disposition (ਡਿਸਪਅ'ਜ਼ਿਸ਼ਨ) n ਸੁਭਾਅ, ਮਿਜ਼ਾਜ, ਰੁਚੀ, ਤਬੀਅਤ; ਪ੍ਰਕਿਰਤੀ; ਵਿਉਂਤ, ਪ੍ਰਬੰਧ; ਅਧਿਕਾਰ

disproportion (ਡਿਸਪਰਅ'ਪੋਸ਼ਨ) n ਅਨੁਪਾਤ-ਹੀਣਤਾ, ਬੇਮੇਲ, ਅਸੰਗਤੀ; ~ate ਬੇਢੰਗਾ, ਵਿਖਮ, ਬੇਮੇਲ, ਬੇਢੋਲ, ਬੇਜੋੜ, ਅਨੁਪਾਤਹੀਣ; ~ately ਬੇਮੇਲਵੇਂ ਢੰਗ ਨਾਲ, ਅਨੁਪਾਤਹੀਣਤਾ ਨਾਲ

disprove (ਡਿਸ'ਪਰੂਵ) v ਗ਼ਲਤ ਸਾਬਤ ਕਰਨਾ, ਖੰਡਨ ਕਰਨਾ, ਝੂਠ ਸਾਬਤ ਕਰਨਾ, ਰੱਦ ਕਰਨਾ, ਝੁਠਲਾਉਣਾ

disputable (ਡਿ'ਸਪਯੂਟਅਬਲ) a ਵਿਵਾਦਪੂਰਨ, ਸ਼ੱਕੀ, ਸੰਦੇਹੀ

dispute (ਡਿ'ਸਪਯੂਟ) v ਵਿਵਾਦ ਕਰਨਾ; ਝਗੜਾ ਕਰਨਾ, ਹੁੱਜਤ ਕਰਨੀ; ਬਹਿਸਣਾ, ਸੰਦੇਹ ਪਰਗਟ ਕਰਨਾ

disqualification (ਡਿਸ'ਕਵੋਲਿਫ਼ਿ'ਕੇਇਸ਼ਨ) n

disqualified *n* ਅਯੋਗਤਾ, ਨੁਕਸ, ਖਾਮੀ, ਕਮੀ, ਔਗੁਣ

disqualified (ਡਿਸ'ਕਵੌਲਿਫ਼ਾਇਡ) *a* ਅਯੋਗ ਕਰਾਰ ਦਿੱਤਾ ਗਿਆ, ਅਯੋਗ

disqualify (ਡਿਸ'ਕਵੌਲਿਫ਼ਾਇ) *v* ਅਯੋਗ ਕਰਨਾ ਜਾਂ ਠਹਿਰਾਉਣਾ, (ਕ) ਅਧਿਕਾਰ ਖੋਹ ਲੈਣਾ

disregard (ਡਿਸਰਿ'ਗਾਡ) *v n* ਧਿਆਨ ਨ ਦੇਣਾ, ਅੱਖਾਂ ਤੋਂ ਓਹਲੇ ਕਰਨਾ, ਪਰਵਾਹ ਨਾ ਕਰਨੀ, ਗ਼ਫ਼ਲਤ, ਅਣਗਹਿਲੀ, ਅਣਸੁਣੀ, ਅੱਵਗਿਆ, ਅਨਾਦਰ, ਉਪੇਖਿਆ

disrespect (ਡਿਸ'ਰਿਸਪੈੱਕਟ) *n v* ਅਨਾਦਰ, ਬੇਅਦਬੀ, ਗੁਸਤਾਖੀ; ਅਨਾਦਰ ਕਰਨਾ, ਅਪਮਾਨ ਕਰਨਾ

disrupt (ਡਿਸ'ਰਅੱਪਟ) *v* ਗੜਬੜੀ ਪਾਉਣੀ, ਫੁੱਟ ਪਾਉਣੀ, ਭੰਗ ਕਰਨਾ; ਚੀਰਨਾ; ~ion ਤੋੜ-ਫੋੜ, ਪਾੜਾ, ਵਿਘਨ, ਗੜਬੜ; ~ive ਫੁੱਟ ਪਾਊ; ਵਿਘਟਨਕਾਰੀ, ਵਿਨਾਸ਼ਕ

dissatisfaction (ਡਿਸ'ਸੈਟਿਸ'ਫ਼ੈਕਸ਼ਨ) *n* ਅਤ੍ਰਿਪਤੀ, ਅਸੰਤੋਸ਼, ਬੇਚੈਨੀ, ਨਾਰਾਜ਼ਗੀ

dissatisfied (ਡਿਸ'ਸੈਟਿਸ'ਫ਼ੈਇਡ) *a* ਅਸੰਤੋਖਜਨਕ, ਅਤ੍ਰਿਪਤਕਾਰੀ

dissatisfy (ਡਿਸ'ਸੈਟਿਸਫ਼ਾਇ) *v* ਅਸੰਤੁਸ਼ਟ ਕਰਨਾ, ਅਤ੍ਰਿਪਤ ਕਰਨਾ; ਨਾਖ਼ੁਸ਼ ਕਰਨਾ, ਨਾਰਾਜ਼ ਕਰਨਾ

dissect (ਡਿ'ਸੈੱਕਟ) *v* ਬੰਦ ਬੰਦ ਕੱਟਣਾ, ਅੰਗ ਅੰਗ ਵੱਖ ਕਰਨਾ, ਚੀਰਨਾ, ਵਿਸ਼ਲੇਸ਼ਣ ਕਰਨਾ; ਛਾਣਬੀਣ ਕਰਨੀ; ~ion ਅੰਗ-ਵਿਛੇਦ, ਚੀਰ-ਫ਼ਾੜ, ਵਿਸ਼ਲੇਸ਼ਣ ਸੂਖਮ ਪਰੀਖਿਆ ਛਾਣਬੀਣ

disseminate (ਡਿ'ਸੈਮਿਨੇਇਟ) *v* ਖਿਲਾਰਨਾ, ਬੀਜਣਾ, ਬਿਖੇਰਨਾ; ਪ੍ਰਚਾਰ ਕਰਨਾ, ਪ੍ਰਸਾਰ ਕਰਨਾ

dissemination (ਡਿਸ'ਸੈੱਮਿ'ਨੇਇਸ਼ਨ) *n* ਖਿਲਾਰ, ਬੀਜਣ ਦੀ ਕਿਰਿਆ, ਵਿਕੀਰਣ; ਪ੍ਰਸਾਰ, ਪ੍ਰਚਾਰ, ਪ੍ਰਸਾਰਣ

dissent (ਡਿ'ਸੈਂਟ) *v* ਅੰਗੀਕਾਰ ਨਾ ਕਰਨਾ, ਨ ਮੰਨਣਾ, ਇਨਕਾਰ ਕਰਨਾ, ਮੱਤਭੇਦ ਰੱਖਣਾ ਅਸੰਮਤੀ ਰੱਖਣਾ; ਮੱਤਭੇਦ; ਅਸਹਿਮਤੀ; ~ient ਅਸਹਿਮਤ, ਭਿੰਨ ਮੱਤਪ੍ਰਕਾਸ਼ਕ, ਬਹੁਮਤ ਵਿਰੋਧੀ

dissert (ਡਿ'ਸਅਃਟ) *v* ਸਪੱਸ਼ਟ ਵਿਆਖਿਆ ਕਰਨਾ, ਵਿਸਤਰਤ ਵਿਵੇਚਨ ਕਰਨਾ, ਵਿਵਰਣ ਦੇਣਾ, ਬਹਿਸ ਕਰਨਾ, ਵਿਚਾਰ ਵਿਮਰਸ਼ ਕਰਨਾ

dissertation (ਡਿ'ਸਅਃਟੇਸ਼ਨ) *a* ਖੋਜ-ਨਿਬੰਧ ਰਚਨਾ; ਵਿਵੇਚਨ, ਨਿਰੂਪਣ, ਵਿਆਖਿਆ ਵਿਚਾਰ-ਪ੍ਰਬੰਧ

dissidence (ਡਿਸਿਡਅੰਸ) *n* ਮੱਤਭੇਦ, ਵਿਰੋਧ ਅਸੰਮਤੀ, ਅਸਹਿਮਤੀ

dissident ('ਡਿਸਿਡਅੰਟ) *a n* ਵਿਰੋਧੀ, ਮਤਭੇਦੀ ਮੱਤਭੇਦ ਰੱਖਣ ਵਾਲਾ, ਅਸੰਮਤੀ ਰਖਣ ਵਾਲਾ

dissimilar (ਡਿ'ਸਿਮਿਲਅ*) *n* ਵਿਜਾਤੀ, ਭਿੰਨ ਅਸਾਵਾਂ, ਵੱਖਰਾ, ਵਿਖਮ, ਅਸਮਾਨ, ਅਸਮਰੂ

dissimilate (ਡਿ'ਸਿਮਿਲੇਇਟ) *n* (ਭਾਸ਼ਾ) ਅੱਖਰ ਨੂੰ ਬਦਲਣਾ, ਧੁਨੀ-ਭੇਦ ਕਰਨਾ, ਅਸਮ ਕਰਨ

dissimilation (ਡਿ'ਸਿ'ਮਿਲੇਇਸ਼ਨ) *n* ਧੁਨੀ-ਭੇਦ ਅਸਮਤਾ

dissolute (ਡਿਸਅਲੂਟ) *a* ਅਵਾਰਾ, ਲੁੱਚਾ, ਲੰਪਟ ਵੈਲੀ, ਬਦਕਾਰ, ਵਿਸ਼ਈ; ਦੁਰਾਚਾਰੀ, ਲਫੰਗਾ ਬਦਚਲਨ

dissolution (ਡਿਸਅ'ਲੂਸ਼ਨ) *n* ਦ੍ਵੀਕਰ ਵਿਲੋਪ; ਵਿਘਟਨ, ਖ਼ਾਤਮਾ, ਲੋਪ

dissolve (ਡਿ'ਜ਼ੌਲਵ) *v* ਘੋਲਣਾ, ਖਲਤ ਗਾਲਣਾ; ਗਲਣਾ, ਪੰਘਾਰਨਾ, ਪੰਘਰਨ ਪਿਘਲਾਉਣਾ, ਪਿਘਲਣਾ; ਵਿਘਟਨ ਕਰਨ ਤੋੜਨਾ, ਅੰਤ ਕਰਨਾ, (ਮਸਲਾ) ਹੱਲ ਕਰਨ ਤੈਅ ਕਰਨਾ, ਮਿਟਾਉਣਾ; ~d ਘੁਲਿਆ

ਘੁਲਿਆ, ਵਿਲੀਨ

distance (ਡਿਸਟਅੰਸ) *n* ਵਿੱਥ, ਫ਼ਾਸਲਾ, ਵਾਟ, ਪੰਥ, ਪੈਂਡਾ; ਪਾੜਾ, ਅੰਤਰ; ਮੁੱਦਤ; ਦੂਰ ਰੱਖਣਾ, ਪਿੱਛੇ ਛੱਡ ਜਾਣਾ, ਅਗੇ ਲੰਘ ਜਾਣਾ

distant (ਡਿਸਟਅੰਟ) *a* ਦੁਰੇਡਾ, ਪਰੇਡਾ, ਦੂਰਵਰਤੀ, ਵਿੱਥ ਉੱਤੇ; ਨਿੱਘ-ਰਹਿਤ

distemper (ਡਿ'ਸਟੈਂਪਅ*) *n v* ਵਿਕਾਰ, ਬਦਮਜ਼ਾਜ਼ੀ; ਪੱਕਾ ਪਲਸਤਰੀ ਰੰਗ, ਆਬਾਦਾਰ ਪਲਸਤਰ; ਪੱਕਾ ਰੰਗਦਾਰ ਪਲਸਤਰ ਕਰਨਾ, ਸਿਹਤ ਵਿਗਾੜਨੀ, ਦਿਮਾਗੀ ਸੰਤੁਲਨ ਵਿਗਾੜਨਾ; ~ed ਉਲਟਾ-ਪੁਲਟਾ, ਅਸਤ-ਵਿਅਸਤ, ਕ੍ਰਮਹੀਣ, ਅਵਿਵਸਥਿਤ; ਅਸੰਜਮੀ, ਘੇਰੈਣ

distil (ਡਿ'ਸਟਿਲ) *v* ਚੋਣਾ, ਟਪਕਣਾ, ਰਿਸਣਾ; ਨਿਚੋੜਨਾ, ਖਿੱਚਣਾ, (ਅਰਕ, ਸੱਤ, ਸ਼ਰਾਬ) ਕੱਢਣਾ, ਨਿਕਲਣਾ; ਛਣਨਾ; ~ler ਆਬਕਾਰ, ਅਰਕ ਜਾਂ ਸ਼ਰਾਬ ਕੱਢਣ ਵਾਲਾ, ਸ਼ੁਰਾਕਾਰ; ~lery ਸ਼ਰਾਬ ਦੀ ਭੱਠੀ ਜਾਂ ਕਾਰਖ਼ਾਨਾ

distinct (ਡਿ'ਸਟਿਙਕਟ) *a* ਵੱਖਰਾ, ਅੱਡ, ਭਿੰਨ, ਨਿਵੇਕਲਾ, ਨਿਆਰਾ; ਸਪਸ਼ਟ, ਨਿਸ਼ਚਤ; ਵਿਅਕਤੀਗਤ; ~ion ਵਖਰੇਵਾਂ, ਫ਼ਰਕ, ਭਿੰਨਤਾ, ਭੇਦ, ਨਿਖੇੜਾ, ਵਿਸ਼ੇਸ਼ਤਾ; ਮਹੱਤਾ, ਪ੍ਰਸਿੱਧੀ, ਵਡਿਆਈ, ਉੱਚ ਪਦਵੀ, ਮਹੱਤਬਾ, ਮ੍ਰਿਤਬਾ; ਵਿਅਕਤਿਤਵ; ~ive ਵਿਸ਼ੇਸ਼, ਨਿਵੇਕਲਾ, ਖ਼ਾਸ, ਅਲੌਕਕ, ਅਲੱਗ, ਭਿੰਨ; ਮੁੱਖ, ਪ੍ਰਮੁੱਖ; ~iveness ਵਿਸ਼ੇਸ਼ਤਾ, ਅਲੌਕਕਤਾ, ਭੇਦ, ਭਿੰਨਤਾ, ਵੱਖਰੇਵਾਂ, ਪ੍ਰਮੁੱਖਤਾ

distinguish (ਡਿ'ਸਟਿਙਗਵਿਸ਼) *v* ਵੱਖਰਾਉਣਾ, ਭਿੰਨ ਦਰਸਾਉਣਾ, ਫ਼ਰਕ ਦੇਣਾ, ਨਿਖੇੜ ਕਰਨਾ, ਛਾਂਟਣਾ, ਛਾਣਨਾ, ਉਘਾੜਨਾ, ਪ੍ਰਸਿੱਧ ਹੋਣਾ, ਪਰਗਟ ਹੋਣਾ; ~ed ਚੋਣਵਾਂ, ਉਘਾ, ਪ੍ਰਸਿੱਧ, ਨਾਮੀ, ਨਾਮਵਰ, ਪ੍ਰਤਿਸ਼ਠਤ; ਵਿਸ਼ੇਸ਼, ਵਿੱਲਖਣ,

ਅਦਭੁਤ

distort (ਡਿ'ਸਟੋ'ਟ) *v* ਵਿਗਾੜਨਾ, ਮੋੜਨਾ-ਤੋੜਨਾ, ਭੰਨ-ਤੋੜ ਦੇਣਾ, ਗ਼ਲਤ ਬਿਆਨੀ ਕਰਨਾ; ਵਿਕ੍ਰਿਤ ਕਰਨਾ, ਵਿਰੂਪ ਕਰ ਦੇਣਾ, ਹੁਲੀਆ ਵਿਗਾੜਨਾ; ~ed ਵਿਗੜਿਆ, ਵਿਕ੍ਰਿਤ, ਵਿਰੂਪਤ; ~ion ਵਿਗਾੜ, ਮੋੜ-ਤਰੋੜ, ਭੰਨ-ਤੋੜ, ਗ਼ਲਤ-ਬਿਆਨੀ, ਵਿਕਾਰ, ਵਿਰੂਪੀਕਰਨ, ਵਿਰੂਪਣ, ਕਰੂਪੀਕਰਨ

distract (ਡਿ'ਸਟਰੈਕਟ) *v* ਧਿਆਨ-ਹਟਾਉਣਾ, ਉਚਾਟ ਕਰਨਾ, ਖ਼ਬਰਾ ਦੇਣਾ, ਚਿੱਤ ਭਰਮਾਉਣਾ, ਚਕਰਾ ਦੇਣਾ, ਵਿਆਕੁਲ ਕਰਨਾ; ~ion ਬਾਂਦਿਆਨੀ, ਉਲਝਣ, ਵਿਆਕੁਲਤਾ, ਜਿੱਚੀ; ਵਿਘਨ, ਰੁਕਾਵਟ, ਖਲਲ, ਹਰਜ; ਦਿਲ-ਭੁਲਾਵਾ; ਉਨਮਾਦ, ਪਾਗਲਪਨ

distress (ਡਿ'ਸਟਰੈੱਸ) *n v* ਦੁੱਖ, ਕਲੇਸ਼, ਕਸ਼ਟ, ਬਿਪਤਾ, ਤੰਗੀ, ਦਿੱਕਤ; ਆਪੱਤੀ; ਪੀੜਤ ਕਰਨਾ, ਕਲਪਾਉਣਾ, ਦੁਖਾਉਣਾ, ਸਤਾਉਣਾ, ਤੰਗ ਕਰਨਾ; ~ed ਦੁਖੀ, ਪੀੜਤ, ਚਿੰਤਾਤੁਰ

distributary (ਡਿ'ਸਰਿਬਯੁਟ(ਅ)ਰਿ) *n* ਨਦੀ ਜਾਂ ਨਹਿਰ ਦੀ ਸ਼ਾਖ਼, ਸਹਾਇਕ ਨਦੀ, ਰਜਵਾਹਾ

distribute (ਡਿ'ਸਟਰਿਬਯੂਟ) *v* ਵੰਡਣਾ, ਵਰਤਾਉਣਾ, ਵਿਕੀਰਨ ਕਰਨਾ; ਖਿਲਾਰਨਾ; ਵਿਭਾਜਨ ਕਰਨਾ, ਬਟਵਾਰਾ ਕਰਨਾ; ਕ੍ਰਮਵਾਰ ਕਰਨਾ; ~d ਵੰਡਿਆ, ਵਿਭਾਜਤ, ਕ੍ਰਮਬੱਧ

distribution (ਡਿਸਟਰਿ'ਬਯੂਸ਼ਨ) *n* ਵਿਭਾਜਨ, ਵਿਭਾਗੀ, ਵੰਡ, ਬਟਵਾਰਾ, ਵਿਭਾਜਨ-ਕ੍ਰਮ

disrtibutor (ਡਿ'ਸਟਰਿਬਯੂਟਅ*) *n* ਵਰਤਾਵਾ, ਵੰਡਣ ਵਾਲਾ, ਵਿਤਰਕ, ਵਿਭਾਜਕ, ਵੰਡਾਵਾ; ਥੋਕ ਵਪਾਰੀ

district (ਡਿਸਟਰਿਕਟ) *n v* ਜ਼ਿਲ੍ਹਾ, ਇਲਾਕਾ, ਹਲਕਾ, ਮੰਡਲ, ਭੂਖੰਡ; ਤਅੱਲੁਕਾ; ਚੋਣ-ਖੇਤਰ ਜਨਪਦ

disturb (ਡਿ'ਸਟਾਃਬ) v ਵਿਘਨ ਪਾਉਣਾ, ਦਖ਼ਲ ਦੇਣਾ, ਹਲਚਲ ਮਚਾਉਣੀ, ਅਸ਼ਾਂਤ ਕਰਨਾ, ਬੇਚੈਨ ਕਰਨਾ, ਉਲਟ ਪੁਲਟ ਕਰ ਦੇਣਾ; **~ance** ਵਿਘਨ, ਹਲਚਲ, ਫ਼ਸਾਦ, ਦਖ਼ਲ ਅਸ਼ਾਂਤੀ; ਵਿਆਕੁਲਤਾ, ਖਲਬਲੀ, ਉਪੱਦਰ, ਹੁੱਲੜ, ਦੰਗਾ, ਵਿਦਰੋਹ; **~ed** ਅਸ਼ਾਂਤ, ਵਿਆਕੁਲ, ਘਾਬਰਿਆ, ਬੇਚੈਨ

ditch (ਡਿਚ) a v ਖਾਈ, ਖੱਡ; ਖਾਈ ਪੁੱਟਣਾ, ਅੱਧ-ਵਿਚਾਲੇ ਛੱਡਣਾ

ditto (ਡਿਟਅਓ) a v ਉਪਰੋਕਤ, ਪਹਿਲੇ ਦੀ ਨਕਲ; ਹਾਂ ਵਿਚ ਹਾਂ ਮਿਲਾਉਣੀ, ਪੁਸ਼ਟੀ ਕਰਨੀ

ditty (ਡਿਟਿ) n ਟੱਪਾ, ਛੋਟਾ ਗੀਤ

dive (ਡਾਇਵ) v n ਟੁੱਭੀ ਮਾਰਨੀ, ਗੋਤਾ ਮਾਰਨਾ, ਡੁਬਕੀ ਲਾਉਣੀ, ਮਨ ਵਿਚ ਝਾਤੀ ਮਾਰਨਾ; ਟੁੱਭੀ, ਗੋਤਾ, ਡੁਬਕੀ, ਤਖ਼ਿਸ਼ਨਾ

diverge (ਡਾਇ'ਵ਼ਅਃਜ*) v ਵੱਖ ਹੋਣਾ, ਅਪਸਰਣ ਕਰਨਾ, ਵਿਚਲਤ ਹੋਣਾ, ਭਟਕਾਉਣਾ, ਭਟਕਣਾ; ਰੁਖ ਫੇਰਨਾ; **~nce** ਅਪਸਰਣ; ਭਟਕਣ; **~nt** ਅਪਸਾਰੀ, ਭਟਕਣ ਵਾਲਾ, ਬਹਿਕਾਉਣ ਵਾਲਾ; ਭਿੰਨ, ਵਿਰੁੱਧ

diverse (ਡਾਇ'ਵ਼ਅਃਸ) a ਵੱਖ ਵੱਖ, ਭਿੰਨ ਭਿੰਨ, ਤਰ੍ਹਾਂ ਤਰ੍ਹਾਂ ਦਾ ਵੰਨ-ਸੁਵੰਨਾ, ਅਸਮਾਨ, ਰੰਗ-ਬਰੰਗਾ

diversion (ਡਾਇ'ਵ਼ਅਃਸ਼ਨ) n ਮੋੜ; ਵਿਚਲਨ, ਬਹਿਕਾਉ, ਭਟਕਣ, ਦਿਲ ਭੁਲਾਵਾ, ਵਿਲਾਸ

diversity (ਡਾਇਵ਼ਅਃਸਅਟਿ) n ਭੇਦ, ਵਿਭਿੰਨਤਾ, ਵੰਨ-ਸੁਵੰਨਤਾ, ਅਨੇਕ ਰੂਪਤਾ, ਵਿਵਿਧਤਾ, ਰੰਗ-ਬਰੰਗਾਪਣ

divert (ਡਾਇ'ਵ਼ਅਃਟ) v ਮੋੜਨਾ, ਫੇਰਨਾ, ਪਰ੍ਹੇ ਹਟਾਉਣਾ; ਟਾਲਣਾ; ਖ਼ੁਸ਼ਾਉਣਾ, ਦੂਰ ਕਰਨਾ, ਰੁਖ ਬਦਲਣਾ, ਵਰਾਉਣਾ, ਮਨੋਰੰਜਨ ਕਰਨਾ

divest (ਡਾਇ'ਵ਼ੈਸਟ) v ਨੰਗਾ ਕਰਨਾ ਵਸਤਰਹੀਨ ਕਰਨਾ; ਵੰਚਤ ਕਰਨਾ, ਅਧਿਕਾਰ ਖੋਹ ਲੈਣਾ

divide (ਡਿ'ਵ਼ਾਇਡ) n v ਵੰਡ; ਵਟ, ਬੰਨ੍ਹੀ; ਵੰਡਣਾ ਵਿਭਾਜਤ ਕਰਨਾ, ਫੁੱਟ ਪਾਉਣਾ, ਧਿਆਨ ਵਟਾਉਣਾ, ਹਿੱਸਾ ਵੰਡਣਾ; ਵੰਡਣਾ, ਤਕਸੀਮ ਕਰਨਾ; **~d** ਵੰਡਿਆ ਹੋਇਆ, ਵਿਭਾਜਤ, ਵੱਖ

dividend (ਡਿ'ਵ਼ਿਡਅੰਡ) n (ਗਣਿਤ) ਵਾਂਡੂ, ਭਾਜ-ਅੰਕ, ਲਾਭ-ਅੰਸ਼

divider (ਡਿ'ਵ਼ਿਡਇਅ*) n ਪਾਟੂ, ਵਿਭਾਜਕ

dividing (ਡਿ'ਵ਼ਾਇਡਿਙ) a ਵਿਭਾਜਕ

divine (ਡਿ'ਵ਼ਾਇਨ) a n v ਇਸ਼ਵਰੀ; ਰੱਬੀ ਇਲਾਹੀ, ਦੈਵੀ, ਰੂਹਾਨੀ, ਪਵਿੱਤਰ, ਧਾਰਮਕ **~ness** ਦੈਵਤਵ, ਦੈਵੀਪਣ; ਪਵਿੱਤਰਤਾ

divinity (ਡਿ'ਵ਼ਿਨਅਟਿ) n ਦੇਵਤਵ, ਦਿੱਵੀਕਰਨ ਦਿਵਤਾ, ਇਸ਼ਵਰਤਾ; ਪੂਜਨੀਕ ਵਿਅਕਤੀ ਧਾਰਮਕਤਾ

divisible (ਡਿ'ਵ਼ਿਜ਼ਿਅਬਲ) a ਵੰਡਣਯੋਗ, ਭਾਗ ਹੋਣ ਯੋਗ, ਵਿਭਾਜੀ

division (ਡਿ'ਵ਼ਿਯ਼ਨ) n ਵੰਡ, ਖੰਡਨ; ਵਿਭਾਜਨ ਬਟਵਾਰਾ; ਵਰਗੀਕਰਨ, ਵਰਗ; ਤਕਸੀਮ ਭਾਗ, ਸੀਮਾ, ਹੱਦ; ਖੰਡ; ਸੈਨਾ-ਦਲ, ਟੁਕੜੀ ਡਿਵੀਜ਼ਨ; ਦਰਜਾ, ਸ਼੍ਰੇਣੀ; **~al** ਵਿਭਾਗੀ, ਮੰਡਲੀ ਅਰਥ ਭੇਦ

divorce (ਡਿ'ਵ਼ੋਸ) n ਤਲਾਕ, ਤਿਆਗ; ਤਲਾਕ ਦੇਣਾ, ਸਬੰਧ ਤੋੜਨਾ; **~e** ਤਲਾਕਸ਼ੁਦਾ ਵਿਅਕਤੀ ਤਲਾਕਸ਼ੁਦਾ ਔਰਤ

divulge (ਡਾਇ'ਵ਼ਅਲਜ) v (ਭੇਦ) ਖੋਲ੍ਹਣਾ, ਨਸ਼ਰ ਕਰਨਾ, ਉਘਾੜਨਾ, ਪਰਗਟ ਕਰਨਾ, ਜ਼ਾਹਰ ਕਰਨਾ **~nce** ਉਘਾੜ, ਪਰਗਟਾਵਾ, ਪ੍ਰਚਾਰ-ਪ੍ਰਸਾਰ

do (ਡੁ) v aux subst ਸਰਗਮ ਦਾ ਪਹਿਲਾ ਸੁਰ

ਕਰਨ, ਪ੍ਰਦਾਨ ਕਰਨਾ, ਦੇ ਦੇਣਾ, ਸੰਪਾਦਨ ਕਰਨ, ਸੰਪੰਨ ਕਰਨਾ, ਪਾਲਣ ਕਰਨਾ; ਪੂਰਾ ਕਰਨਾ, ਮੁਕੰਮਲ ਕਰਨਾ, ਮੁਰੰਮਤ ਕਰਨੀ; ਪਕਾਉਣਾ, ਪ੍ਰਸ਼ਨ ਹੱਲ ਕਰਨਾ, ਸੰਮਸਿਆ ਸੁਲਝਾਉਣੀ; ਅਨੁਵਾਦ ਕਰਨਾ; ਕੰਮ ਕਰਨਾ, ਵਧਣਾ, ਬੰਦ ਕਰਨਾ; ਚਲਾਉਣਾ, ਗੁਜ਼ਾਰਨਾ; ਉਪਯੁਕਤਾ ਕਰਨਾ, ਠੀਕ ਹੋਣਾ; ~away ਛੁਟਕਾਰਾ ਪਾਉਣਾ, ਮੌਤ ਦੇ ਘਾਟ ਉਤਾਰਨਾ; well-to ~ ਧਨਵਾਨ, ਖਾਂਦਾ-ਪੀਂਦਾ

doctor (ਡੋਕਟਅ*) *n* ਚਿਕਿਤਸਕ, ਡਾਕਟਰ; ਹਕੀਮ, ਵੈਦ; ਪੰਡਤ, ਵਿਦਵਾਨ, (ਅਪ, ਨੌ) ਰਸੋਈਆ; ਡਾਕਟਰ ਦੀ ਉਪਾਧੀ ਦੇਣਾ; ~ate ਡਾਕਟਰ ਦੀ ਉਪਾਧੀ

doctrine (ਡੋਕਟਰਿਨ) *n* ਸਿੱਖਿਆ, ਵਿੱਦਿਆ, ਵਾਦ, ਮੱਤ, ਪੰਥ, ਸਿਧਾਂਤ, ਅਸੂਲ

document (ਡੋਕਯੁਮਅੰਟ, 'ਡੋਕਯੁਮੈਂਟ) *n v* ਲਿਖਤ, ਦਸਤਾਵੇਜ਼; ਲਿਖਤੀ, ਪ੍ਰਮਾਣ, ਲੇਖ-ਪੱਤਰ; ~ary ਲੇਖ-ਬੱਧ, ਦਸਤਾਵੇਜ਼ੀ, ਤਹਿਰੀਰੀ, (ਵਾਕਿਆਤੀ ਜਾਂ ਦਸਤਾਵੇਜ਼ੀ) ਫ਼ਿਲਮ, ਵਰਿਤ-ਚਿੱਤਰ; ~ation (ਦਸਤਾਵੇਜ਼ ਦੁਆਰਾ) ਪ੍ਰਮਾਣ, ਸਬੂਤ; ਪ੍ਰਸਤੁਤੀਕਰਨ, ਪ੍ਰਸਾਰਨ

dodge (ਡੋਜ) *n* ਟਾਲ-ਮਟੋਲ, ਘੁਸਾਉ, ਝਾਸਾ, ਚਲਾਕੀ; ਥਾਂ ਬਦਲ ਦੇਣਾ, ਪੈਂਤੜਾ ਬਦਲਣਾ, ਖਿਸਕਣਾ, ਕਤਰਾਉਣਾ, ਟਾਲ-ਮਟੋਲ ਕਰਨਾ; ਵਾਕ-ਚਾਤਰੀ ਕਰਨੀ, ਉਸਤਾਦੀ ਦਿਖਾਉਣਾ; ਫਿਰਾ ਕੇ ਸਵਾਲ ਪੁੱਛਣਾ

doer (ਡੂਅ*) *n* ਕਰਤਾ, ਕਾਰਕ, ਕਾਰਿੰਦਾ; ਦਾਤਾ, ਸੁਧਾਰਕ; ਹੱਲ ਕਰਨ ਵਾਲਾ

dog (ਡੋਗ) *n v a* ਕੁੱਕਰ, ਕੁੱਤਾ; ਤੁੱਛ ਵਿਅਕਤੀ, ਨਿਕੰਮਾ ਆਦਮੀ; ਖੋਜ ਕਰਨਾ, ਪਤਾ ਲਾਉਣਾ, ਸੁਰਾਗ ਲਾਉਣਾ, ਪਿੱਛਾ ਕਰਨਾ; ਫੜਨਾ; ਘਟੀਆ, ਬਿਲਕੁਲ; go to the ~s ਨਸ਼ਟ ਹੋਣਾ, ਅਧੋਗਤ ਹੋਣਾ

dogma (ਡੋਗਮਾ) *n* ਮੱਤ-ਸਿਧਾਂਤ, ਧਰਮ-ਸਿਧਾਂਤ; ਹਠ ਧਰਮੀ; ~tic ਸਿਧਾਂਤਆਤਮਕ, ਰੂੜ੍ਹੀਬੱਧ, ਹਠਧਰਮੀ

doldrums (ਡੋਲਡਰਅਮਜ਼) *n* ਉਦਾਸੀ, ਖੜੋਤ, ਢਹਿੰਦੀ ਕਲਾ, ਵਿਸ਼ਾਦ; ਸੁੰਨ-ਖੰਡ

dole (ਡਾਓਲ) *n v* ਰੰਜ, ਦੁੱਖ, ਸ਼ੋਕ, ਉਦਾਸੀ; ਕਲੇਸ਼; ਦਾਨ, ਤੁੱਛ ਦਾਨ; (ਪ੍ਰ) ਕਿਸਮਤ, ਵਿਭਾਗ, ਤੁੱਛ ਅੰਸ਼; ਦਾਨ ਕਰਨਾ, ਵੰਡਣਾ

doll (ਡੋਲ) *n v* ਪੁਤਲੀ, ਗੁੱਡੀ, ਗੁੱਡਾ, ਸਜਣਾ, ਸਜਾਉਣਾ, ਸਿੰਗਾਰਨਾ, ਬਣਨਾ-ਠਣਨਾ

dolly (ਡੋਲਿ) *n* ਪੁਤਲੀ, ਗੁੱਡਾ, ਗੁੱਡੀ

domain (ਡਅ(ਉ)ਮੇਇਨ) *n* ਇਲਾਕਾ, ਜਾਗੀਰ, ਪ੍ਰਦੇਸ਼; ਕਾਰਜ-ਖੇਤਰ

dome (ਡਅਓਮ) *n* ਗੁੰਬਦ, ਮਮਟੀ; ਮਹਿਲ, ਹਵੇਲੀ; ਸਿਖਰ, ਗੋਲ ਚੋਟੀ; ~d ਗੁੰਬਦਦਾਰ, ਮਮਟੀਵਾਲਾ, ਗੁਮਟੀਦਾਰ

domestic (ਡਅ(ਉ)'ਮੈਸਟਿਕ) *a n* ਘਰੋਗੀ, ਪਰਵਾਰਕ, ਘਰੇਲੂ; ਦੇਸੀ

domicile (ਡੋਮਿਸਾਇਲ) *n v* ਪੱਕਾ ਨਿਵਾਸ, ਘਰ, ਨਿਵਾਸ-ਸਥਾਨ, ਵਤਨ; ਵਸਣਾ, ਨਾਗਰਿਕਤਾ ਪ੍ਰਾਪਤ ਕਰਨਾ

dominance, domination (ਡੋਮਿਨਅੰਸ, ਡੋਮਿ'ਨੇਇਸ਼ਨ) *n* ਪ੍ਰਬਲਤਾ, ਬੋਲਬਾਲਾ

dominant (ਡੋਮਿਨਅੰਟ) *a n* ਪ੍ਰਮੁੱਖ, ਪ੍ਰਬਲ; ਪ੍ਰਭੂਤਸ਼ਾਲੀ;

dominate (ਡੋਮਿਨੇਇਟ) *v* ਪ੍ਰਭੂਤਾ ਜਮਾਉਣਾ, ਅਧਿਕਾਰ ਰੱਖਣਾ; ਪ੍ਰਬਲ ਹੋਣਾ, ਛਾ ਜਾਣਾ; ਹਾਵੀ ਹੋਣਾ

dominion (ਡਅ'ਮਿਨਯਅਨ) *n* ਪ੍ਰਭੂਤਾ, ਸੱਤਾ,

ਅਧਿਕਾਰ, ਮਲਕੀਅਤ, ਰਿਆਸਤ; ਬਾਦਸ਼ਾਹੀ; ਅਮਲਦਾਰੀ, ਇਲਾਕਾ

don (ਡੌਨ) *n* (ਸੰਬੋਧਨ ਵਜੋਂ) ਸ੍ਰੀਮਾਨ, ਸਾਹਿਬ, ਸਰਦਾਰ, ਭੱਦਰ ਪੁਰਸ਼, ਪ੍ਰਮੁੱਖ ਵਿਅਕਤੀ, ਪ੍ਰਸਿੱਧੀ-ਪ੍ਰਾਪਤ ਮਨੁੱਖ, ਵਿਸ਼ਵਵਿਦਿਆਲੇ ਦਾ ਅਧਿਅਕਸ਼ ਜਾਂ ਅਧਿਆਪਕ

donate (ਡਅ(ਓ)'ਨੇਇਟ) *v* ਦਾਨ ਕਰਨਾ, ਦਾਨ ਦੇਣਾ, ਪ੍ਰਦਾਨ ਕਰਨਾ, ਭੇਂਟ ਕਰਨਾ

donation (ਡਅ(ਓ)'ਨੇਇਸ਼ਨ) *v* ਦਾਨ, ਭੇਟਾ, ਚੰਦਾ; ਭੇਂਟ, ਉਪਹਾਰ

donkey (ਡੌਂਕਿ) *n a* ਖੋਤਾ, ਗਧਾ, ਖਰ; ਅੜਿਆਲ ਮੂਨੁੱਖ, ਨਿਰਬੋਧ ਵਿਅਕਤੀ

donor (ਡਅਉਨਅ*) *n* ਦਾਨੀ, ਦਾਤਾ, ਖ਼ੂਨ ਦਾਨ ਕਰਨ ਵਾਲਾ

doom (ਡੂਮ) *n v* ਤਕਦੀਰ, ਪਰਲੋ, ਵਿਨਾਸ਼, ਤਬਾਹੀ, ਬਰਬਾਦੀ; ਅੰਤ, ਮਿਰਤੂ, ਮੌਤ ਦੇ ਮੂੰਹ ਪਕੌਣਾ, ਨਿਯੁਕਤ ਕਰਨਾ, ਸਜ਼ਾ ਦਾ ਹੁਕਮ ਸੁਣਾਉਣਾ; **~s day** ਕਿਆਮਤ ਦਾ ਦਿਨ, ਪਰਲੋ ਦਾ ਦਿਨ

door (ਡੋ*) *n* ਬੂਹਾ, ਦਰਵਾਜ਼ਾ, ਦੁਆਰ, ਕਿਵਾੜ, ਕਪਾਟ; ਪ੍ਰਵੇਸ਼-ਪਥ, ਪ੍ਰਵੇਸ਼ ਮਾਰਗ; **~keeper** ਦੁਆਰਪਾਲ, ਦਰਬਾਨ; **~mat** ਪਾਇਦਾਨ

dormitory (ਡੋ*ਮਅਟਰਿ) *n* ਸੌਣ-ਕਮਰਾ (ਬੋਰਡਿੰਗ ਵਿਚ)

dose (ਡਅਉਜ਼) *n v* (ਦਵਾਈ ਦੀ) ਖ਼ੁਰਾਕ, ਮਾਤਰਾ; ਖ਼ਸ਼ਾਮਦ, ਮਿਸ਼ਰਣ ਬਣਾਉਣਾ; ਦਵਾ ਦੇਣੀ; ਖ਼ੁਰਾਕ ਪਿਆਉਣੀ

dossier (ਡੌਸਿਏਇ*) *n* ਮਿਸਲ, ਕਾਗ਼ਜ਼ਾਂ ਦੀ ਫ਼ਾਈਲ; ਚਾਲ-ਚਲਣ ਦਾ ਲਿਖਤੀ ਵੇਰਵਾ, ਗੁਪਤ ਫ਼ਾਈਲ

dot (ਡੌਟ) *n v* ਨੁਕਤਾ, ਬਿੰਦੀ, ਬਿੰਦੂ; (ਸੰਗੀ) ਚਿੰਨ੍ਹ; (ਟੈਲੀਗ੍ਰਾਫ਼ੀ) ਸੰਕੇਤ ਚਿੰਨ੍ਹ, ਨਿੱਕੀ ਚੀਜ਼; ਬਿੰਦੀ, ਲਾਉਣੀ, ਨੁਕਤਾ ਲਾਉਣਾ; ਚਿਤਰਨਾ, ਨਿਸ਼ਾਨਾ ਮਾਰਨਾ

double (ਡਅੱਬਲ) *n v a* ਪ੍ਰਤੀਰੂਪ, ਪ੍ਰਤੀ ਮੂਰਤੀ, ਨਕਲ; ਦੁਗਣਾ; ਦੂਹਰਾ; ਧੋਖੇਬਾਜ਼, ਕਪਟੀ, ਦੁਗਣਾ ਕਰਨਾ ਜਾਂ ਹੋਣਾ, ਦੂਹਰਾ ਕਰਨਾ; ਤਹਿ ਕਰਨਾ, ਕਸ ਕੇ ਫੜ੍ਹਨਾ, ਗੋਲ ਦਾ ਟੱਪਾ ਖਾਣਾ, ਪਲਟਾਉਣਾ; ਦੂਣਾ, ਦੁੱਗਣਾ, ਦੂਹਰਾ, ਡਬਲ ਸੰਦੇਹਪੁਰਨ, ਦੇ-ਅਰਥਕ; ਦੇ-ਰੰਗਾ; ਦੁਗਣੀ ਸ਼ਕਤੀ ਵਾਲਾ; ਮੱਕਾਰ; **~edged** ਦੋ-ਧਾਰੀ, ਦੋ-ਰੂਪੀ, ਦੋ-ਅਕਖਰ; **~faced** ਕਪਟੀ, ਕੁਟਿਲ, ਛਲੀਆ, ਮੱਕਾਰ, ਦੁਬਾਜਰਾ

doubt (ਡਾਉਟ) *n* ਸ਼ੱਕ, ਸ਼ੰਕਾ, ਸੰਦੇਹ, ਸ਼ੁਬ੍ਹਾ, ਬੇ-ਵਸਾਹੀ; ਅਵਿਸ਼ਵਾਸ, ਖਟਕਾ; ਸ਼ੱਕ ਕਰਨਾ, ਦੁਬਧਾ ਵਿਚ ਹੋਣਾ; ਵਿਚਾਰ ਕਰਨਾ, ਡਰਨਾ; **~ful** ਸ਼ੱਕ ਵਾਲਾ, ਸ਼ੰਕਾ ਭਰਿਆ, ਸੰਦੇਹਪੁਰਨ, ਝੌਰਕਨੀਕੀ, ਸੰਦਿਗਧ

dove (ਡਅੱਵ) *n* ਘੁੱਗੀ, ਕੁਮਰੀ, ਫ਼ਾਖ਼ਤਾ, ਦਿਵ-ਆਤਮਾ

down (ਡਾਊਨ) *v adv a* ਡੇਗ ਦੇਣਾ, ਪਟਕਾ ਦੇਣਾ, ਹਰਾਉਣਾ; ਅਧੋਗਤੀ; ਹੇਠਾਂ, ਥੱਲੇ; ਉਦਾਸ, ਦਿਲਗੀਰ ਮਸੋਸਿਆ, ਨਿਵਾਣ; **get~** ਉਤਰਨਾ **shout~** ਚਿਲਾ ਚਿਲਾ ਕੇ ਚੁਪ ਕਰਾ ਦੇਣਾ; **~fall** ਗਿਰਾਵਟ, ਅਵਨਤੀ, ਤਬਾਹੀ, ਬਰਬਾਦੀ, ਨਾਸ, (ਮੀਂਹ ਦੀ) ਬੁਛਾੜ, ਫੰਡ, ਵਾਛੜ; **~grade** ਪਦ-ਅਵਨਤੀ, ਦਰਜਾ ਘਟਾਉਣਾ; **~pour** ਮੋਹਲੇਧਾਰ ਮੀਂਹ, ਬੁਛਾੜ, ਝੜੀ; **~stairs** ਹੇਠਲੀ ਛੱਤ ਉੱਤੇ; **~trodden** ਕੁਚਲਿਆ, ਦਲਿਤ ਲਿਤਾੜਿਆ, ਦਬਿਆ, ਪੀੜਤ; **~ward** ਪਤਨਸ਼ੀਲ, ਅਧੋਮੁਖੀ, ਨੀਵੇਂ ਪਾਸੇ; **up and ~**ਇੱਧਰ-ਉੱਧਰ; ਅੱਗੇ ਪਿੱਛੇ, ਉੱਪਰ-ਹੇਠਾਂ

dowry ('ਡਾਉਰਿ) *n* ਦਹੇਜ-ਦਾਜ, ਕੰਨਿਆ-ਦਾਨ

doze (ਡਅਊਜ਼) *n v* ਉਂਘ, ਝਪਕੀ, ਹਲਕੀ ਨੀਂਦ

dozen ('ਡਅੱਜ਼ਨ) *n* ਦਰਜਨ, ਬਾਰ੍ਹਾਂ

draft (ਡਰਾਫ਼ਟ) *n v* ਫ਼ੌਜੀ ਟੁਕੜੀ, ਦਸਤਾ; ਡਰਾਫ਼ਟ; ਖਰੜਾ, ਢਾਂਚਾ, ਰੂਪ-ਰੇਖਾ; ਢਾਂਚਾ ਬਣਾਉਣਾ

draftsman ('ਡਰਾਫ਼ਟਸਮਅਨ) *n* ਨਕਸ਼ਾਨਵੀਸ, ਮਾਨਚਿਤਰਕਾਰ, ਰੇਖਾਕਾਰ, ਨਕਸ਼ਾ ਬਣਾਉਣ ਵਾਲਾ, ਮਸੌਦਾਕਾਰ

drag (ਡਰੈਗ) *v n* ਘਸੀਟਣਾ, ਖਿੱਚਣਾ, ਔਖੇ ਚੱਲਣਾ; ਜਾਲ ਸੁੱਟਣਾ; ਸੁਹਾਗਾ, ਫੱਟੂ, ਕਰਾਹ; ਅੜਿੱਕਾ; ~**on** ਘਸੀਟਦੇ ਜਾਣਾ; ~**out** ਲਮਕਾਉਣਾ, ਲੰਬਾ ਕਰਨਾ, ਦੇਰ ਲਗਾਉਣਾ; ~**up** ਸਖ਼ਤ ਵਰਤਾਉ ਕਰਨਾ

drain (ਡਰੇਇਨ) *v n* ਪਾਣੀ ਕੱਢਣਾ, ਨਿਚੋੜਨਾ; ਕੱਢਣਾ; ਚੋਣਾ; ਨਾਲੀ, ਵਹਿਣੀ, ਮੋਰੀ, ਨਿਕਾਸ; ~**age** ਨਿਕਾਸ-ਪ੍ਰਬੰਧ,ਜਲ-ਪ੍ਰਣਾਲੀ, ਵਹਿਣੀਆਂ

drama (ਡਰਾਮਅ) ਨਾਟਕ, ਰੂਪਕ, ਸਾਂਗ, ਰਾਸ; ਨਾਟਕ ਕਲਾ; ~**itc** ਨਾਟਕ ਸਬੰਧੀ, ਨਾਟਕੀ; ਅਨੋਖਾ ਵੱਖਿਤਰ, ਅਚਾਨਕ; ~**tist** ਨਾਟਕਕਾਰ

drastic ('ਡਰੈਸਟਿਕ) *a* ਕਠੋਰ, ਕਰੜਾ, ਸਖ਼ਤ, ਉਗਰ, ਪ੍ਰਚੰਡ

draught (ਡਰਾਫ਼ਟ) *n v* ਖਿਚਾਈ, ਘਸੀਟ; ਭਾਰ ਢੁਆਈ; ਘੁੱਟ (ਪਾਣੀ ਆਦਿ ਦਾ); ਦਵਾਈ (ਪੀਣ ਵਾਲੀ) ਦੀ ਇਕ ਖ਼ੁਰਾਕ; ਢਾਂਚਾ, ਖ਼ਾਕਾ, ਨਕਸ਼ਾ, ਰੂਪ-ਰੇਖਾ; ਖਰੜਾ; ਫ਼ੌਜੀ ਟੁਕੜੀ, ਫ਼ੌਜੀ ਦਸਤਾ; ਹੁੰਡੀ, ਚੈਕ; ਛਾਂਟਣਾ; ਢਾਂਚਾ ਬਣਾਉਣਾ; ~**sman** ਨਕਸ਼ਾਨਵੀਸ, ਖਰੜਾ ਲੇਖਕ, ਰੂਪ ਰੇਖਾ ਖਿੱਚਣ ਵਾਲਾ

draw (ਡਰੋ) *n v* ਖਿਚ; ਖਿਚਾਈ; (ਗਾਹਕਾਂ ਨੂੰ) ਖਿੱਚਣ ਵਾਲੀ ਵਸਤੂ, ਲਾਟਰੀ, ਖਿੱਚਣਾ, ਧੂਹਣਾ, ਘਸੀਟਣਾ; ਛੋਟਾ, ਖਿਚ ਪਾਉਣਾ, ਖਿੱਚੇ ਜਾਣਾ, ਆਕਰਸ਼ਤ ਹੋਣਾ, ਇਕੱਤਰ ਹੋਣਾ, ਇਕੱਠੇ ਹੋਣਾ; ਰਜ਼ਾਮੰਦ ਕਰਨਾ; (ਖੂਹ ਵਿਚੋਂ ਪਾਣੀ) ਕੱਢਣਾ; ਸਤ ਜਾਂ ਰਸ ਕੱਢਣਾ; (ਸਰੀਰ ਵਿਚੋਂ ਲਹੂ) ਕੱਢਣਾ; ਪ੍ਰਾਪਤ ਕਰਨਾ, ਗ੍ਰਹਿਣ ਕਰਨਾ; (ਤਾਸ਼ ਵਿਚ) ਪੱਤਾ ਕਢਵਾਉਣਾ; ਅਨੁਮਾਨ ਲਾਉਣਾ, (ਨਕਸ਼ਾ ਆਦਿ) ਖਿਚਣਾ, (ਤਸਵੀਰ) ਬਣਾਉਣੀ, ਦਸਤਾਵੇਜ਼ ਤਿਆਰ ਕਰਨਾ; ਬਰਾਬਰੀ ਵਿਖਾਉਣੀ, ਹਿੱਲਣਾ-ਜੁੱਲਣਾ, ਚਲੱਣਾ; ਨੇੜੇ ਆ ਪੁੱਜਣਾ; ~**attention** ਧਿਆਨ ਖਿੱਚਣਾ; ~**back** ਘਾਟ, ਕਮੀ, ਤਰੁੱਟੀ, ਨਿਊਨਤਾ, ਨੁਕਸ, ਐਬ

drawee (ਡਰੋ'ਈ) *n* ਹੁੰਡੀ-ਗਾਹਕ

drawer (ਡਰੋ*) *n* (ਮੇਜ਼ ਆਦਿ ਦਾ) ਖ਼ਾਨਾ, ਦਰਾਜ਼, ਗਾਹਕ, ਹੁੰਡੀਕਰਤਾ; ਛੋਟਾ ਵਾਲਾ

drawing (ਡਰੋਇੰਡ) *n* ਨਕਸ਼ਾਕਸ਼ੀ; ਖਿੱਚਣ, ਨਕਸ਼ਾ, ਖ਼ਾਕਾ, ਢਾਂਚਾ; ਚਿੱਤਰ, ਤਸਵੀਰ; ਚਿੱਤਰ-ਵਿੰਦਿਆ; ~**room** ਬੈਠਕ; ਦਰਬਾਰ ਭਵਨ

dray (ਡਰੇਇ) *n* ਠੇਲ੍ਹਾ, ਰੇੜ੍ਹਾ

dread (ਡਰੈੱਡ) *v n a* ਡਰਨਾ, ਸਹਿਮਣਾ, ਭੈ ਖਾਣਾ; ਭੈ, ਡਰ, ਆਤੰਕ, ਖ਼ਤਰਾ; ਡਰਾਉਣੀ ਵਸਤੂ; ਭਿਆਨਕ, ਡਰਾਉਣਾ; ~**ful** ਭਿਆਨਕ, ਡਰਾਉਣਾ, ਖੌਫ਼ਨਾਕ, ਆਤੰਕਮਈ

dream (ਡਰੀਮ) *n v* ਸੁਪਨਾ; ਕਪੋਲ ਕਲਪਨਾ; ਸੁਪਨੇ ਵੇਖਣਾ, ਖਿਆਲੀ ਪਲਾਉ ਪਕਾਉਣੇ, ਵਿਚਾਰਾਂ ਵਿਚ ਡੁੱਬੇ ਰਹਿਣਾ

dreary ('ਡਰਿਅਰਿ) *a* ਵਿਰਾਨ, ਉਜਾੜ, ਸੁਨਸਾਨ, ਉਦਾਸ, ਫਿੱਕਾ, ਨੀਰਸ

dredge (ਡਰੈੱਜ) *n v* ਸਮੁੰਦਰ ਜਾਂ ਦਰਿਆ ਦੀ ਤਹਿ ਵਿਚੋਂ ਗਾਰਾ ਕੱਢਣ ਵਾਲਾ ਜੰਤਰ; ਝਾਮ; ਇਸ ਜੰਤਰ ਨਾਲ ਗਾਰਾ ਕੱਢਣਾ; (ਕਿਸੇ ਚੀਜ਼ ਉੱਤੇ ਆਟਾ, ਮੈਦਾ ਆਦਿ) ਛਿੜਕਣਾ

drench (ਡਰੈਨੱਚ) *v n* ਭਿਉਂ ਦੇਣਾ, ਤਰੋ ਤਰ ਕਰ ਦੇਣਾ, ਮੋਹਲੇਧਾਰ ਮੀਂਹ; ਪਸ਼ੂਆਂ ਦੀ ਦਵਾਈ ਦੀ ਖ਼ੁਰਾਕ

dress (ਡਰੈੱਸ) *v n* ਕੱਪੜੇ ਪਾਉਣੇ; (ਜ਼ਖ਼ਮ ਆਦਿ ਉੱਤੇ) ਪੱਟੀ ਬੰਨ੍ਹਣੀ; ਸਜਾਉਣਾ, ਵਾਲ ਸੰਵਾਰਨੇ, ਕੰਘੀ-ਪੱਟੀ ਕਰਨੀ; ਈਸਤਰੀ ਕਰਨਾ; ਪੁਸ਼ਾਕ, ਕੱਪੜੇ, ਵਰਦੀ, ਵਸਤਰ, ਵੇਸ, ਬਾਣਾ, ਬਾਹਰੀ ਰੂਪ, ਭੇਸ, ਰੂਪ-ਰੰਗ; **~circle** ਰੰਗ-ਭਵਨ, (ਥੀਏਟਰ) ਦੀ ਗੈਲਰੀ; **~ed** ਚੰਗੇ ਕੱਪੜੇ ਪਹਿਨੇ ਹੋਏ; **~er** ਸ਼ਿੰਗਾਰ ਮੇਜ਼, ਮਲ੍ਹਮ-ਪੱਟੀ ਕਰਨ ਵਾਲਾ, ਵਸਤਰ ਆਦਿ ਪਵਾਉਣ ਵਾਲਾ, ਬੂਟਿਆਂ ਨੂੰ ਕੱਟਣ-ਛਾਂਟਣ ਵਾਲਾ **~maker** ਦਰਜ਼ੀ, ਦਰਜ਼ਨ; **~up** ਭੇਸ ਬਣਾਉਣਾ

dressing ('ਡਰੈੱਸਿੰਛ) *n* ਮਲ੍ਹਮ ਪੱਟੀ; ਪੁਸ਼ਾਕ ਆਦਿ ਪਹਿਨਣ, ਬੂਟਿਆਂ ਨੂੰ ਛਾਂਟਣ, ਰੁੱਖੀ ਪਾਉਣ; **~room** ਸ਼ਿੰਗਾਰ-ਕਮਰਾ

drift (ਡਰਿਫ਼ਟ) *n v* ਵਹਿਣ, ਵਹਾ, ਰੋੜ੍ਹ; ਧਾਰ; ਵੰ; ਇਕੱਠਾ ਕਰਨਾ; ਵਰਮਾ ਮਾਰਨਾ, ਛੇਕ ਕਰਨਾ, ਛੇਕ ਕੱਢਣਾ

drill (ਡਰਿਲ) *n v* ਵਰਮਾ; ਕਵਾਇਦ, ਡ੍ਰਿਲ, ਕਰੜਾ ਅਨੁਸ਼ਾਸਨ; ਵਰਮੇ ਨਾਲ ਛੇਕ ਕੱਢਣਾ; ਡ੍ਰਿਲ ਕਰਨਾ

drink (ਡਰਿੰਕ) *v n* ਪੀਣਾ; ਸ਼ਰਾਬ ਪੀਣਾ; ਪਾਣੀ ਧਾਣੀ, ਸ਼ਰਬਤ, ਜਲਪਾਨ, ਸ਼ਰਾਬ, ਨਸ਼ਾ-ਪਾਣੀ, ਦਾਰੂ; ਪੈਗ; **~ing water** ਪੀਣ ਵਾਲਾ ਪਾਣੀ

drip (ਡਰਿਪ) *v n* ਚੋਣਾ, ਚੋਆ ਪੈਣਾ, ਰਿਸਣਾ; ਚੋਆ

drive (ਡਰਾਇਵ) *v n* (ਮੋਟਰ ਆਦਿ) ਚਲਾਉਣਾ; ਹਿੱਕਣਾ, ਟੇਕਣਾ; ਸੁੱਟਣਾ, ਧੱਕਣਾ; ਠੋਕਣਾ (ਕਿੱਲਾ, ਕਿੱਲ ਆਦਿ), ਗੱਡਣਾ, ਛੇਕ ਕਰਨਾ; (ਕ੍ਰਿਕਟ) ਗੇਂਦ ਅਗੇ ਸੁੱਟਣੀ; ਸ਼ਕਤੀ, ਸਾਹਸ, ਉੱਦਮ, ਧੱਕਾ, ਝਟਕਾ; ਮੋਟਰ ਦਾ ਰਸਤਾ ਜਾਂ ਸਫ਼ਰ; **~at** ਮਤਲਬ ਹੋਣਾ, ਭਾਵ ਹੋਣਾ; **~away** ਪਰ੍ਹੇ ਕਰਨਾ, ਭਜਾਉਣਾ, ਨਠਾਉਣਾ

drizzle ('ਡਰਿਜ਼ਲ) *v n* ਨਿੱਕਾ ਨਿੱਕਾ ਮੀਂਹ ਵਰ੍ਹਨਾ, ਕਿਣ-ਮਿਣ ਹੋਣੀ; ਫੁਹਾਰ ਪੈਣੀ; ਫੁਹੂ, ਨਿੱਕਾ ਨਿੱਕਾ ਮੀਂਹ

drop (ਡਰੌਪ) *v n* ਡਿਗਣਾ, ਡੇਗਣਾ; ਚੋਣਾ, ਚੁਆਉਣਾ; ਲਹਿ ਜਾਣਾ, ਘਟਣਾ; ਪੱਛੜਣਾ, ਹੇਠਾਂ ਨੂੰ ਜਾਣਾ, ਮਰਨਾ, ਮਰ ਜਾਣਾ; ਸਮਾਪਤ ਹੋਣਾ, ਖ਼ਤਮ ਹੋ ਜਾਣਾ; (ਕੀਮਤਾਂ ਦਾ) ਡਿੱਗਣਾ, ਘੱਟ ਹੋਣਾ; ਹੇਠੁ ਸੁੱਟਣਾ; ਛੱਡ ਦੇਣਾ, ਤਿਆਗਣਾ; ਸੂਆ (ਭੇਡ, ਬੱਕਰੀ ਆਦਿ ਦਾ); ਕਣੀ, ਛਿੱਟ, ਬੂੰਦ, ਤੁਪਕਾ, ਘੁਟ, (ਦਵਾਈ ਦੀ) ਬੋਤੀ ਜੋਈ ਮਾਤਰਾ (ਬ ਵ) ਤਰਲ ਦਵਾਈ; ਸਮਾਜੀ ਗਿਰਾਵਟ ਉਤਾਰ; ਮੰਦਾ ਪੈ ਰਿਹਾ ਪਦਾਰਥ

drought, drouth ('ਡਰਾਉਟ) *n* ਔੜ, ਸੋਕਾ, ਟੇਹ, ਪਿਆਸ, ਖ਼ੁਸ਼ਕੀ

drown (ਡਰਾਉਨ) *v* ਡੁੱਬਣਾ, ਡੋਬਣਾ; ਡੁੱਬ ਕੇ ਮਰਨਾ, ਗੋਤਾ ਦੇਣਾ, ਪਾਣੀ ਵਿਚ ਸੁੱਟਣਾ; ਪੂਰਾ ਭਿਉਂ ਦੇਣਾ, ਤਰ ਕਰ ਦੇਣਾ

drowse (ਡਰਾਉਜ਼) *v* ਉਂਘਣਾ, ਨਿੰਦਰਾਉਣਾ, ਨੀਂਦ ਲਿਆਉਣੀ; ਉਂਘਦਿਆਂ ਸਮਾਂ ਲੰਘਾਉਣਾ; ਆਲਸ ਪਾਉਣਾ, ਸੁਸਤੀ ਛਾਉਣੀ ਉਂਘ

drowsiness ('ਡਰਾਉਜ਼ਿਨਿਸ) *n* ਸੁਸਤੀ, ਆਲਸ, ਉਂਘ

drowsy ('ਡਰਾਉਜ਼ੀ) *a* ਉਂਘਦਾ, ਨਿੰਦਰਾਇਆ; ਆਲਸ ਵਿਚ; ਸੁਸਤ ਪਿਆ

drudge ('ਡਰੱਜ) *v n* ਮਿਹਨਤ ਕਰਨੀ, ਜਾਨ ਮਾਰ ਕੇ ਕੰਮ ਕਰਨਾ, ਕਾਮਾ, ਭਾੜੇ ਦਾ ਟੱਟੂ, ਵਗਾਰ ਵਿਚ ਕੰਮ ਕਰਨ ਵਾਲਾ, ਸੇਵਕ; ਗ਼ੁਲਾਮ; **~ry** ਮਜ਼ਦੂਰੀ; ਗ਼ੁਲਾਮੀ; ਸਖ਼ਤ ਮਿਹਨਤ, ਹੱਡ

ਭੰਨਵੀਂ ਕਾਰ; ਵਗਾਰ

drug (ਡਰਅੱਗ) *n v* ਦਵਾਈ, ਔਸ਼ਧੀ, ਔਖਧ, ਜੜੀ ਬੂਟੀ, ਅਮਲ; ਦਵਾ ਦੇਣਾ ਪਿਆਉਣਾ, ਦਵਾਈਆਂ ਮਿਲਾਉਣਾ; ~gist ਦਵਾ ਫ਼ਰੋਸ਼, ਪੰਸਾਰੀ, ਦਵਾਈਆਂ ਵਟਾਉਣ ਵਾਲਾ, ਅਤਰ

drum (ਡਰੱਮ) *n v* ਢੋਲ, ਢੋਲਕੀ, ਨਗਾਰਾ; ਦਮਾਮਾ; ਕੰਨ ਦਾ ਪਰਦਾ; ਪੀਪਾ, ਬੰਮੂ ਦਾ ਉਤਲਾ ਭਾਗ; ਢੋਲ ਵਜਾਉਣਾ, ਠੱਕ-ਠੱਕ ਕਰਨਾ, ਲਗਾਤਾਰ ਠੋਕਣਾ

drunkard (ਡਰਅੱਕਅਡ਼) ਨਸ਼ੱਈ, ਨਸ਼ੇਬਾਜ਼, ਸ਼ਰਾਬੀ, ਸ਼ਰਾਬਖੋਰ

dry (ਡਰਾਇ) *a* ਸੁੱਕਾ, ਖ਼ੁਸ਼ਕ; ਲੂਹਿਆ, ਰੁੱਖਾ, ਕੋਰਾ, ਫਿੱਕਾ, ਫੋਕਾ, ਖਰਵਾਂ; ~fruit ਸੁੱਕਾ ਮੇਵਾ ~ness ਖ਼ੁਸ਼ਕੀ, ਨੀਰਸਤਾ; ਨਿਰਲਜਤਾ

dual ('ਡਯੂਅਲ) *a n* ਦੂਹਰਾ; ਦੂਣਾ; ਦੁਵੱਲੀ; ~ism ਦਵੈਤਵਾਦ; ਦਵੈਤ

dubious ('ਡਯੂਬਯਅਸ) *a* ਸੰਦੇਹ-ਜਨਕ, ਅਸਪਸ਼ਟ; ਪੁੰਦਲਾ, ਅਨਿਸ਼ਚਤ, ਦੋ-ਅਰਥੀ, ਸ਼ੰਕੇ ਵਾਲਾ

duck (ਡਅੱਕ) *n v* ਬੱਤਖ, ਮੁਰਗਾਬੀ; ਮੋਟਾ ਸੂਤੀ ਕਪੜਾ; ਕਬੂਤਰੀ; ਚੁੰਭੀ ਮਾਰਨੀ, ਗੋਤਾ ਮਾਰਨਾ; ਸਿਰ ਨਿਵਾਉਣਾ, ਗੋਤਾ ਦੇਣਾ, ਚੁੰਭੀ ਲਵਾਉਣੀ

due (ਡਯੂ) *a adv n* ਦੇਣਯੋਗ ਬਕਾਇਆ, ਉਚਿਤ, ਮੁਨਾਸਬ, ਨਿਸ਼ਚਤ, ਦੀ ਵਜਾ ਨਾਲ, ਦੇ ਕਾਰਨ, ਬਿਲਕੁਲ, ਸਿੱਧਾ, ਹੱਕ, ਅਧਿਕਾਰ; ਦਾਅਵਾ; ਉਧਾਰ, ਕਰਜਾ; ਮਹਿਸੂਲ

duel ('ਡਯੂਅਲ) *n v* ਦਵੰਦ, ਦਵੱਲੀ ਲੜਾਈ;

duffer ('ਡਅੱਫ਼ਅ*) *n* ਨਿਕੰਮਾ ਆਦਮੀ, ਲੋੜ੍ਹੂ, ਬੰਦਾ, ਬੁੱਧੂ, ਬਗਲੋਲੜ

dull (ਡਅੱਲ) *a v* ਮੋਟੀ ਮੱਤ ਵਾਲਾ, ਮੂਰਖ, ਮੁਠ; ਖੁੰਢਾ; ਸੁਸਤ, ਮੱਠਾ, ਢਿੱਲਾ; ਜੜ੍ਹ, ਪੁੰਦਲਾ; ਮੱਤ ਮਾਰ ਦੇਣੀ, ਮੂਰਖ ਬਣਾ ਦੇਣਾ; ਖੁੰਢਾ ਕਰਨਾ, ਮਾਂਦਾ ਪਾ ਦੇਣਾ, ਫਿੱਕਾ ਹੋਣਾ, ਬੇ-ਸੁਆਦ ਹੋਣਾ; ਫਿੱਕਾ ਜਾਂ ਤੇਜਹੀਣ ਹੋਣਾ; ~ard ਮੂਰਖ ਮਨੁੱਖ, ਮੂੜ੍ਹ ਵਿਅਕਤੀ, ਮੱਤਹੀਨ ਬੰਦਾ, ਮੋਟੀ ਮੱਤ ਵਾਲਾ ਆਦਮੀ, ਬੁੱਧੂ, ਲੋੜ੍ਹੂ

duly ('ਡਯੂਲਿ) *adv* ਉਚਿਤ ਰੂਪ ਵਿਚ, ਠੀਕ-ਠੀਕ, ਕਾਇਦੀ, ਤੌਰ ਤੇ, ਯਥਾ ਸਮੇਂ, ਯਥਾ ਸੰਭਵ

dumb (ਡਅੱਮ) *adv* ਗੂੰਗਾ, ਚੁੱਪ, ਹੈਰਾਨ-ਪਰੇਸ਼ਾਨ, ਹੱਕਾ-ਬੱਕਾ; ਮੂਰਖ, ਉਜੱਡ; ਬੇਜ਼ਬਾਨ ਬਣਾ ਦੇਣਾ, ਗੂੰਗਾ ਬਣਾ ਦੇਣਾ; ਚੁੱਪ ਕਰ ਦੇਣਾ; ~found ਗੂੰਗਾ ਕਰ ਦੇਣਾ, ਚੁੱਪ ਕਰ ਦੇਣਾ, ਘਬਰਾ ਦੇਣਾ

dummy ('ਡਅੱਮਿ) *n a* ਮਿੱਟੀ ਦਾ ਮਾਧੋ, ਕਠਪੁਤਲੀ; ਮੂਰਖ, ਮੋਟੀ ਮੱਤ ਵਾਲਾ, ਕਾਠ ਦਾ ਉੱਲੂ, ਮਨਵੀ, ਬੁੱਤ, ਲੱਕੜੀ ਦਾ ਢਾਂਚਾ, ਬਣਾਉਟੀ, ਨਕਲੀ, ਜਾਅਲੀ, ਫਰਜ਼ੀ, ਕਲਪਤ

dump (ਡਅੱਪ) *v n* ਢੇਰ ਲਾਉਣਾ; (ਕੂੜਾ ਆਦਿ) ਇਕ ਥਾਂ ਸੁੱਟਣਾ, ਜਮ੍ਹਾਂ ਕਰਨਾ; ਪੱਕਾ, ਠੇਕਰ, ਠੁੰਡਾ; ਧਮਾਕਾ, ਪਤੱਣ ਦਾ ਆਵਾਜ਼; ਕੋਈ ਤੁੱਛ ਵਸਤੂ, ਛੋਟੀ ਮੋਟੀ ਚੀਜ਼

dunce (ਡਅੱਸ) *n* ਮੂਰਖ ਮਨੁੱਖ, ਮੂੜ੍ਹ, ਘੁੱਗੂ, ਭੌਂਦੂ, ਉਜੱਡ

dunderhead ('ਡਅੱਡਅਹੈੱਡ) *n* ਖਰ ਦਿਮਾਗ, ਭੌਂਦੂ

dung (ਡਅੱਡ) *n* ਗੋਹਾ, ਲਿੱਦ; ਰੂੜੀ; ਗੰਦ-ਮੰਦ; ਰੂੜੀ ਪਾਉਣੀ

duo (ਡਯੂਅਉ) *n* ਜੋੜਾ, ਸੰਗੀਤੱਗਾਂ ਦੀ ਜੋੜੀ

dupe (ਡਯੂਪ) *v n* ਧੋਖਾ ਦੇਣਾ; ਠੱਗਣਾ; ਛਲਣਾ, ਮੁੰਠਣਾ; ਮੁੱਛਣਾ; ਬੋਲਾ-ਪਾਤਸ਼ਾਹ, ਧੋਖੇ ਦਾ ਸ਼ਿਕਾਰ; ਸਿੱਧਰ ਮਨੁੱਖ

duplex ('ਡਯੂਪਲੈੱਕਸ) *a v* ਦੋਹਰਾ, ਦੂਣਾ, ਦੁੱਗਣਾ; ਦੁਤਰਫੀ, ਦੁਹਰਾਉਣਾ; ਦੁੱਗਣਾ ਕਰਨਾ

duplicate (ਡਯੂਪਲਿਕੇਇਟ) *a n v* ਦੂਹਰਾ, ਜੋੜਾ; ਹੂਬਹੂ, ਉਹੋ ਜੇਹਾ, (ਕਿਸੇ ਦੂਜੇ) ਵਰਗਾ, ਪ੍ਰਤੀਰੂਪ; ਉਤਾਰਾ, ਨਕਲ, ਪ੍ਰਤੀਲਿਪੀ

duplicating ('ਡਯੂਪਲਿਕੇਇਟਿੰਡ) *n* ਪ੍ਰਤੀਲਿਪੀਕਰਨ, ਉਤਾਰਾਕਰਨ

duplication ('ਡਯੂਪਲਿ'ਕੇਇਸ਼ਨ) *n* ਉਤਾਰਾ ਕਰਨ, ਪ੍ਰਤੀਲਿਪੀਕਰਨ; ਦੁਗਣਾ ਕਰਨ

duplicity (ਡਯੂ'ਪਲਿਸਅਟਿ) *n* ਧੋਖੇਬਾਜ਼ੀ, ਚਾਲਬਾਜ਼ੀ, ਛਲ, ਕਪਟ, ਦੁਰੰਗੀ, ਦੁਬਾਜਰਾਪਣ

durability (ਡਯੂਅਰਅ'ਬਿਲਅਟਿ) *n* ਪਕਿਆਈ, ਹੰਢਣਸਾਰਤਾ, ਪਾਏਦਾਰੀ, ਸਥਿਰਤਾ, ਟਿਕਾਉ

durable ('ਡਯੂਅਰਅਬਲ) *a* ਹੰਢਣਸਾਰ, ਪਾਇਦਾਰ, ਪੱਕਾ, ਚਿਰ-ਸਥਾਈ

duration (ਡਯੂ'ਰੇਇਸ਼ਨ) *n* ਮਿਆਦ, ਅਵਧੀ, ਮੁਕਰਰ ਸਮਾਂ, ਨਿਸ਼ਚਤ ਸਮਾਂ

duress (ਡਯੂ(ਅ)'ਰਿਸ) *n* ਨਜਾਇਜ਼ ਦਬਾਉ; ਧਮਕੀ, ਸਖ਼ਤੀ, ਧੱਕਸ਼ਾਹੀ

during ('ਡਯੂਅਰਿੰਡ) *perp* ਦੇ ਵਿਚ, ਵਿਚ, ਸਮੇਂ ਵਿਚ, ਤਕ, ਵੇਲੇ, ਵੇਲੇ ਤਕ, ਤਦ ਤਕ, ਜਦ ਤਕ, ਦੌਰਾਨ

dusk (ਡਅੱਸਕ) *n v* ਘੁਸਮੁਸਾ; ਧੁੰਦਲਾਪਣ, ਤ੍ਰਿਕਾਲਾਂ, ਸੰਧਿਆ, ਹਨੇਰਾ ਹੋਣਾ, ਧੁੰਦਲਾ ਹੋਣਾ

dust (ਡਅੱਸਟ) *n v* ਧੂੜ, ਘੱਟਾ, ਮਿੱਟੀ, ਗਰਦਾ, ਖੇਹ, ਕੂੜਾ ਕਰਕਟ; ਫੁੱਲਾਂ ਦਾ ਬੂਰ, ਪਰਾਗ, ਕੇਸਰ; ਮਨੁੱਖੀ ਸਰੀਰ, ਗੜਬੜ, ਰੌਲਾਗੋਲਾ, ਝੰਬੇਲਾ; (ਅਪ) ਧੂੜ ਝਾੜਨਾ, ਸਫ਼ਾਈ ਕਰਨਾ; ਧੂੜ ਪਾਉਣੀ, ਖੇਹ ਉਡਾਉਣਾ, ਮਿੱਟੀਓ-ਮਿੱਟੀ ਕਰਨਾ; ਛਿੜਕਣਾ, ਪੂੜਨਾ; ~**bin** ਕੂੜਾਦਾਨ; ~**colour** ਹਲਕਾ ਭੂਰਾ; ~**er** ਝਾੜਨ, ਪਰੋਲਾ ਝਾੜਨ ਵਾਲਾ

duty ('ਡਯੂਟਿ) *n* ਫ਼ਰਜ਼, ਕਰਤੱਵ; ਕੰਮ, ਸੇਵਾ, ਫ਼ਰਜ਼ ਦੀ ਅਦਾਇਗੀ; ਇਖ਼ਲਾਕੀ ਪਾਬੰਦੀ; ਮਹਿਸੂਲ, ਚੁੰਗੀ

dwarf (ਡਵੋਰਫ਼) *n v a* ਬੌਣਾ, ਠਿਗਣਾ, ਗਿਠਮੁੱਠੀਆ, ਨਿੱਕ ਬਣਾਉਣਾ ਜਾਂ ਕਰਨਾ; ~**ish** ਕੁਝ ਛੋਟਾ, ਬੌਣੇ ਵਰਗਾ, ਨਿੱਕ, ਛੁਟੇਰਾ

dwell (ਡਵੈੱਲ) *v* ਰਹਿਣਾ, ਵਸਣਾ, ਰਿਹਾਇਸ਼ ਕਰਨਾ, ਧਿਆਨ ਜਮਾਉਣਾ, ਧਿਆਨ ਕੇਂਦਰਤ ਕਰਨਾ; ~**er** ਵਾਸੀ, ਨਿਵਾਸੀ, ਵਸਨੀਕ, ਬਾਸ਼ਿੰਦਾ; ~**ing** ਨਿਵਾਸ, ਰਿਹਾਇਸ਼, ਵਾਸਾ, ਵਸੇਬਾ, ਨਿਵਾਸ-ਸਥਾਨ, ਰਿਹਾਇਸ਼ ਦੀ ਜਗ੍ਹਾ

dwindle (ਡਵਿੰਡਲ) *v* ਘੱਟ ਹੋਣਾ, ਘਟਦੇ ਜਾਣਾ, ਸੁੰਗੜਨਾ, ਘੁਲਣਾ; ਢਲਣਾ; ਪਤਲੇ ਹੋਣਾ, ਮਾੜੇ ਪੈਣਾ; ਮਹੱਤਾ ਜਾਂਦੀ ਰਹਿਣੀ, ਸਿਤਾਰਾ ਢਲਣਾ

dye (ਡਾਇ) *n v* ਰੰਗ, ਰੰਗ ਚਾੜ੍ਹਨ ਵਾਲੀ ਚੀਜ਼, ਰੰਗ ਚਾੜ੍ਹਨ ਵਾਲਾ ਮਸਾਲਾ; ਰੰਗਣਾ, ਰੰਗ ਲਾਉਣਾ ~**r** ਲਲਾਰੀ, ਰੰਗਸਾਜ, ਰੰਗਰੇਜ਼

dying ('ਡਾਇਇੰਡ) *n* ਮਰਨ; ਖ਼ਾਤਮਾ, ਅੰਤ

dynamic (ਡਾਇ'ਨੈਮਿਕ) *n a* (ਸੰਚਾਲਕ) ਸ਼ਕਤੀ, ਵੇਗ, ਗਤੀ; ਗਤੀ-ਆਤਮਕ, ਗਤੀਸ਼ੀਲ, ਵੇਗਵਾਨ, ਸ਼ਕਤੀਮਾਨ, ਪ੍ਰਭਾਵਸ਼ੀਲ, ਗਤੀ-ਵਿਗਿਆਨ ਸਬੰਧੀ

dynamite (ਡਾਇਨਅਮਾਇਟ) *v n* ਬਾਰੂਦ ਨਾਲ ਉਡਾਉਣਾ, (ਵਿਸ਼ੇਸ਼ ਪ੍ਰਕਾਰ ਦਾ) ਬਾਰੂਦ

dynasty (ਡਿਨਅਸਟਿ) *n* ਰਾਜਵੰਸ਼, ਸ਼ਾਹੀ ਖ਼ਾਨਦਾਨ, ਸ਼ਾਹੀ ਘਰਾਣਾ

dysentery ('ਡਿਸੰਟਰਿ) *n* ਪੇਚਿਸ਼, ਮਰੋੜ, ਸੰਗ੍ਰਹਿਣੀ, ਅਤਿਸਾਰ

E

E, e (ਈ) n ਰੋਮਨ ਵਰਨਮਾਲਾ ਦਾ ਪੰਜਵਾਂ ਅੱਖਰ

each (ਈਚ) a pron ਹਰ, ਹਰ ਇਕ, ਪ੍ਰਤੀ, ਫ਼ੀ, ਇਕ ਇਕ, ਹਰੇਕ

eager ('ਈਗਅ*) a ਅਭਿਲਾਸ਼ੀ, ਉਤਸ਼ਾਹੀ, ਤਾਂਘੀ, ਜੋਸ਼ੀਲਾ, ਮੁਸ਼ਤਾਕ, ਵਿਆਕੁਲ; **~ness** ਅਭਿਲਾਸ਼ਾ, ਉਤਸ਼ਾਹ, ਰੀਝ, ਤਾਂਘ, ਸਰਗਰਮੀ

eagle ('ਈਗਲ) n ਉਕਾਬ, ਸ਼ਾਹੀਨ; **~eyed** ਤੱਖਣ ਦ੍ਰਿਸ਼ਟੀ ਵਾਲਾ, ਬਾਜ਼ ਨਜ਼ਰ

ear (ਇਅ*) n ਕੰਨ; ਸੁਣਨ ਦੀ ਯੋਗਤਾ; ਕਣਕ ਜਾਂ ਹੋਰ ਅਨਾਜ ਦੀ ਬੱਲੀ, ਸਿੱਟਾ; **~drum** ਕੰਨਾਂ ਦਾ ਪੜਦਾ; **~ring** ਕੰਨਾਂ ਦੀਆਂ ਵਾਲੀਆਂ, ਮੁੰਦਰਾਂ; **~wax** ਕੰਨਾਂ ਦੀ ਮੈਲ; **give~ to** ਧਿਆਨ ਦੇਣਾ

early ('ਅ:ਲਿ) a adv ਅਗੇਤਾ, ਸੁਵੇਲੇ, ਪਹਿਲਾਂ, ਛੇਤੀ, ਆਰੰਭਕ, ਮੁਢਲਾ, ਪੁਰਾਤਨ

earn (ਅ:ਨ) v ਖੱਟਣਾ, ਕਮਾਉਣਾ, ਪ੍ਰਾਪਤ ਕਰਨਾ; ਪੈਦਾ ਕਰਨਾ; **~ed** ਕਮਾਇਆ, ਪ੍ਰਾਪਤ, **~ing** ਆਮਦਨੀ, ਕਮਾਈ

earnest ('ਅ:ਨਿਸਟ) a n ਗੰਭੀਰ, ਉਦਮੀ, ਤੀਬਰ, ਸੱਚਾ; ਗੰਭੀਰਤਾ, ਸਾਈ, ਬਿਆਨਾ; **~ly** ਗੰਭੀਰਤਾ ਨਾਲ, ਸੱਚੇ ਦਿਲੋਂ; **~ness** ਗੰਭੀਰਤਾ, ਸੰਜੀਦਗੀ, ਸਚਾਈ

earth (ਅ:ਥ) n v ਭੁਈਂ, ਭੌਂ, ਧਰਤੀ, ਜ਼ਮੀਨ, ਪ੍ਰਿਥਵੀ, ਭੂਮੀ, ਖ਼ਾਕ; ਮੁਲਕ, ਦੰਬਣਾ, ਧਰਤੀ ਹੇਠਾਂ ਲੁਕਾਉਣਾ; **~en** ਮਿੱਟੀ ਦਾ ਬਣਿਆ, ਕੱਚਾ, ਮਿਟਿਆਲਾ; **~en ware** ਮਿੱਟੀ ਦੇ ਭਾਂਡੇ; **~quake** ਭੁਚਾਲ, ਭੂ-ਕੰਪ

ease (ਈਜ਼) n v ਸੌਖ, ਆਰਾਮ, ਤਸਕੀਨ; ਸੁਖ ਦੇਣਾ, ਸੌਖੇ ਹੋਣਾ, ਸੁਸਤਾਉਣਾ, ਢਿੱਲਾ ਕਰਨਾ;

stand at~ (ਸੈਨਕ ਆਦੇਸ਼) ਸੌਖੇ ਖੜੋਵੋ! **~ness** ਸੁਗਮਤਾ, ਸੁਖੈਨਤਾ, ਸੌਖ, ਸਰਲਤਾ; ਚੈਨ, ਸੁਖ

east (ਈਸਟ) n a adv ਪੂਰਬ, ਪੂਰਬ ਕੇ ਦੇਸ਼, ਚੜ੍ਹਦਾ ਪਾਸਾ; **~ern** ਪੂਰਬੀਆ, ਪੂਰਬੀ

easter (ਈਸਟ*) n ਇਸਾਈਆਂ ਦਾ ਤਿਉਹਾਰ, ਹਜ਼ਰਤ ਈਸਾ ਦਾ ਮੁੜ ਜੀਵਤ ਹੋਣ ਦਾ ਦਿਵਸ

easy ('ਈਜ਼ੀ) a n adv ਸੌਖਾ, ਸੁਖਾਲਾ, ਸੁਖੈਨ, ਸਹਿਲਾ, ਸਹਿਲ, ਸੁਗਮ; ਸੁਖੀ, ਸੁਖਾਵਾਂ, ਸੁਖਦਾਈ, ਬੇਫ਼ਿਕਰ; ਉਹ ਜਿਨਸ ਜਿਸ ਦੀ ਮੰਗ ਘੱਟ ਹੋਵੇ; ਆਸਾਨੀ ਨਾਲ, ਸਰਲਤਾ ਨਾਲ ਸੁਵਿਧਾਪੂਰਵਕ; **~chair** ਆਰਾਮ ਕੁਰਸੀ; **~going** ਸੁੱਖ ਰਹਿਣਾ, ਆਰਾਮ ਤਲਬ; **take it~** ਘਬਰਾਉ ਨਹੀਂ, ਤਸੱਲੀ ਰੱਖੋ

eat (ਈਟ) v ਖਾਣਾ, ਚੱਬਣਾ, ਨਿਗਲਣਾ, ਹਜ਼ਮ ਕਰਨਾ; **~away** ਖਾ ਜਾਣਾ; **~humble pie** ਜ਼ਲੀਲ ਹੋਣਾ; **~one's heart out** ਅੰਦਰ-ਅੰਦਰ ਕੁੜ੍ਹਨਾ; **~able** ਖਾਧ-ਪਦਾਰਥ; **~ing house** ਢਾਬਾ, ਅੰਨਪੂਰਨਾ

eccentric (ਇਕ'ਸੈਂਟਰਿਕ) n a ਵਿਕੇਂਦਰੀ ਚੱਕਰ, ਅਕੇਂਦਰੀ; ਖਬਤੀ, ਵਹਿਮੀ, ਵਚਿੱਤਰ

echo ('ਐੱਕਅਉ) n v ਗੂੰਜ, ਧੁਨੀ, ਪ੍ਰਤੀਧੁਨੀ; ਗੂੰਜਣਾ, ਗੂੰਜਾਉਣਾ

eclipse (ਇ'ਕਲਿਪਸ) n v ਗ੍ਰਹਿਣ; ਤੇਜ ਘਟਾਉਣਾ, ਮਾਨ ਘਟਾਉਣਾ

ecological ('ਇਕਅ'ਲੌਜਿਕਲ) a ਪਰਿਆਵਰਤਕ

ecology (ਈ'ਕੌਲਅਜਿ) n ਵਾਤਾਵਰਣ ਵਿਗਿਆਨ, ਪਰਿਆਵਰਤ ਵਿਗਿਆਨ

economic ('ਈਕਅ'ਨੌਮਿਕ) *a* ਆਰਥਕ, ਕਿਫ਼ਾਇਤੀ, ਮਾਲੀ ਲਾਭਦਾਇਕ; ~al ਸਸਤਾ; ~s ਅਰਥ-ਸ਼ਾਸਤਰ

economist (ਇ'ਕੌਨਅਮਿਸਟ) *n* ਅਰਥ-ਸ਼ਾਸਤਰੀ, ਅਰਥ-ਵਿਗਿਆਨੀ

economize (ਇ'ਕੌਨਅਮਾਇਜ਼) *v* ਬਚਾਉਣਾ, ਬੱਚਤ ਕਰਨਾ, ਸੰਜਮ ਕਰਨਾ

economy (ਇ'ਕੌਨਅਮਿ) *n* ਅਰਥ-ਪ੍ਰਬੰਧ, ਆਰਥਕ ਦਸ਼ਾ, ਬੱਚਤ

ecstasy ('ਐਕਸਟਅਸਿ) *n* ਉਤਸਾਹ, ਤਰੰਗ, ਪਰਮਾਨੰਦ

ecstatic (ਇਕ'ਸਟੈਟਿਕ) *a* ਉਤਸਾਹਪੂਰਨ, ਮਸਤ, ਤਰੰਗਮਈ

edacious (ਇ'ਡੇਇਸ਼ਅਸ) *a* ਖਾਊ-ਪੀਊ, ਪੇਟੂ, ਲਾਲਚੀ, ਭੁੱਖੜ, ਲੋੜੀ

edacity (ਇ'ਡੈਸਅਟਿ) *n* ਭੁੱਖਾਪਣ, ਲਾਲਚੀਪਣ, ਪੇਟੂਪਣ

edge (ਐਜ) *n v* ਹਾਸ਼ੀਆ; ਝਾਲਰ; ਦੌਰ, ਕੰਢਾ, ਧਾਰ, ਕਿਨਾਰਾ; ਹਾਸ਼ੀਆ ਲਾਉਣਾ, ਧਾਰ ਬਣਾਉਣਾ; ਕੰਨੀ ਕਤਰ ਕੇ ਟੁਰਨਾ, ਤਿੱਖਾਰਉਣਾ, ਉਕਸਾਉਣਾ ~d ਤਿੱਖਾ; ਕਿਨਾਰੇਦਾਰ ~less ਖੁੰਢਾ, ਕੁੰਠਤ

edible ('ਐਡ੍ਰਿਬਲ) *a* ਖਾਣਯੋਗ, ਸੁਆਦਲਾ

edify ('ਐਡ੍ਰਿਫ਼ਾਇ) *v* (ਜੀਵਾਂ ਦਾ) ਉਧਾਰ ਕਰਨਾ, ਸਿੱਖਿਆ ਦੇਣੀ, ਚਿਤਾਉਣਾ; ~ing ਗਿਆਨ-ਵਰਧਕ, ਉਪਦੇਸ਼ਕ

edit ('ਐਡਿਟ) *v* ਸੰਪਾਦਨ ਕਰਨਾ, ਕਾਟ ਛਾਂਟ ਕਰਨਾ; ~ing ਸੰਪਾਦਨ; ~ion ਸੰਸਕਰਨ, ਸੰਪਾਦਨ, ਜਿਲਦ, ਪ੍ਰਕਾਸ਼ਨ; ~or ਸੰਪਾਦਕ; ~orial ਸੰਪਾਦਕੀ

educand ('ਐਜੁਕਅੰਡ) *n* ਚੇਲਾ, ਸ਼ਿਸ਼, ਸਿੱਖਿਆਰਥੀ

educate ('ਐਜੁਕੇਇਟ) *v* ਸਿਖਾਉਣਾ, ਪੜ੍ਹਾਉਣਾ, ਵਿੱਦਿਆ ਦੇਣਾ; ~d ਸਿੱਖਿਅਤ, ਸਿਖਾਇਆ, ਪੜ੍ਹਿਆ-ਲਿਖਿਆ

education ('ਐਜੁ'ਕੇਇਸ਼ਨ) *n* ਸਿੱਖਿਆ, ਪੜ੍ਹਾਈ-ਲਿਖਾਈ; ~al ਸਿੱਖਿਆ ਸਬੰਧੀ, ਵਿੱਦਿਅਕ

educator ('ਐਜੁਕੇਟਿਅ*) *n* ਸਿੱਖਿਅਕ, ਅਧਿਆਪਕ

efface (ਇ'ਫ਼ੇਇਸ) *v* ਮੇਸਣਾ, ਮਾਤ ਪਾਉਣਾ, ਕਲਮ ਫੇਰਨੀ; ਮਲੀਆਮੇਟ ਕਰਨਾ, ਨੇਸਤੇ-ਨਾਬੂਦ ਕਰਨਾ, ਭੁਲਾ ਦੇਣਾ; ~ment ਮਲੀਆ-ਮੇਟ, ਨੇਸਤੇ-ਨਾਬੂਦ, ਫ਼ਨ੍ਹਾ, ਨਾਸ

effect (ਇ'ਫ਼ੈਕਟ) *n v* ਸਿੱਟਾ, ਫਲ, ਅਸਰ, ਤਾਸੀਰ, ਨਤੀਜਾ, ਕਮਾਲ, ਉਦੇਸ਼, ਮਾਲ, ਵਸਤੂ; ਕਰ ਦਿਖਾਉਣਾ, ਪੂਰਾ ਕਰਨਾ, ਪੈਦਾ ਕਰਨਾ; ~ive ਪ੍ਰਭਾਵਸ਼ਾਲੀ, ਕਾਰਗਰ, ਸਾਰਥਕ, ਸ਼ਕਤੀਮਾਨ; ਅਸਰਦਾਰ

efficiency (ਇ'ਫ਼ਿਸ਼ਅੰਸਿ) *n* ਸਮਰੱਥਾ, ਕੁਸ਼ਲਤਾ, ਨਿਪੁੰਨਤਾ, ਯੋਗਤਾ, ਕਮਾਲ ਕਾਬਲੀਅਤ

efficient (ਇ'ਫ਼ਿਸ਼ਅੰਟ) *a* ਸਮਰੱਥ, ਨਿਪੁੰਨ, ਪ੍ਰਵੀਣ, ਗੁਣਕਾਰੀ, ਲਾਇਕ, ਕਾਮਲ

effigy ('ਐਫ਼ਿਜਿ) *n* ਪੁਤਲਾ, ਗੁੱਡਾ, ਮੂਰਤੀ

effloresce (ਐਫ਼ਲੋ'ਰੈਸ) *v* ਕਲੀਆਂ ਖਿੜਨੀਆਂ, ਫੁੱਲਣਾ, ਜੋਬਨ ਤੇ ਆ ਜਾਣਾ; ~nce (ਫੁੱਲਾਂ ਦਾ) ਖੇੜਾ, ਖਿੜਨ, ਸ਼ਗੁਫ਼ਤਗੀ; ~nt ਖਿੜਿਆ, ਫੁੱਲਾਂ ਲੱਦਿਆ

effluence ('ਐਫ਼ਲੂਅੰਸ) *n* ਨਿਕਾਸ, ਬਹਾਉ, ਹੌਂ

effort ('ਐਫ਼ਅ*ਟ) *n* ਜਤਨ, ਘਾਲ, ਕੋਸ਼ਸ਼, ਨੱਠ-ਭੱਜ, ਸਰਗਰਮੀ

egalitarian (ਇ'ਗੈਲਿ'ਟੇਅਰਿਅਨ) *a* ਸਮਾਨਤਾਵਾਦੀ

egg (ਐਗ) *n v* ਅੰਡਾ, ਆਂਡਾ; ਚੁੱਕਣਾ, ਉਕਸਾਉਣਾ; in the~ ਗਰਭ ਵਿਚ, ਸ਼ੁਰੂ ਦੀ ਹਾਲਤ ਵਿਚ

ego ('ਐਗਅਉ) *n* ਆਪਾ, ਅਹੰ, ਖ਼ੁਦੀ, ਹਉਮੈ, ਅਹੰਕਾਰ; ~ism ਅਹੰਕਾਰਵਾਦ, ਹਉਮੈਵਾਦ, ਅਹੰਵਾਦ; ~ist ਅਹੰਕਾਰੀ, ਹਉਮੈਵਾਦੀ, ਖ਼ੁਦਗਰਜ਼

either ('ਆਇਦਅ*) *pron a adv* ਜਾਂ ਤਾਂ, ਭਾਵੇਂ, ਇਹ, ਇਕ ਤਾਂ, ਦੋ ਵਿੱਚੋ ਇਕ, ਕੋਈ ਇਕ; ਦੋਹਾਂ ਹਾਲਤਾਂ ਵਿਚ

ejaculate (ਇ'ਜੈਕਯੁਲੇਇਟ) *v* ਛੁਟਣਾ, ਖ਼ਲਾਸ ਕਰਨਾ, ਛੁੱਟ ਪੈਣਾ, ਬੋਲ ਉੱਠਣਾ, ਜਪਣਾ, ਬਾਹਰ ਕੱਢਣਾ

ejaculation (ਇ'ਜੈਕਯੁ'ਲੇਇਸ਼ਨ) *n* ਬਾਹਰ ਨਿਕਲਨ, ਛੁਟਨ

eject (ਇ'ਜੈਕਟ, 'ਈਜੈਕਟ) *v n* ਬਾਹਰ ਕੱਢਣਾ; ਬੇਦਖ਼ਲ ਕਰਨਾ, ਖ਼ਾਰਜ ਕਰਨਾ, ਹਟਾ ਦੇਣਾ; ~ion ਕਢਾਈ, ਬੇਦਖ਼ਲੀ, ਹੁਕਮਨਾਮਾ ਬੇਦਖ਼ਲੀ, ਦੇਸ਼-ਨਿਕਾਲਾ, ਜਲਾਵਤਨੀ; ~ment ਬੇਦਖ਼ਲੀ

elaborate (ਇ'ਲੈਬ(ਅ)ਰਅਟ, ਇ'ਲੈਬਅਰੇਇਟ) *a v* ਵਿਸਤਰਤ; ਜਟਲ, ਵਿਸਤਾਰ ਸਹਿਤ ਦੱਸਣਾ

elaboration (ਇ'ਲੈਬਅ'ਰੇਇਸ਼ਨ) *n* ਵਿਸਤਾਰ, ਸੰਪੰਨਤਾ

elastic (ਇ'ਲੈਸਟਿਕ) *a* ਲਚਕਵਾਂ, ਛਿਲਕਵਾਂ, ਸੌਜੀ, ਤਰੰਗੀ; ਲਚਕਦਾਰ, ਲਚਕੀਲਾ

elasticity ('ਇਲ'ਸਟਿਸਅਟਿ) *n* ਲਚਕ, ਅਨੁਕੂਲਨ-ਸ਼ੀਲਤਾ

elbow ('ਐਲਬਅਉ) *n* ਕੁਹਣੀ, ਅਰਕ, ਕੁਹਣੀ-ਮੋੜ; ਕੁਹਣੀ ਮਾਰਨੀ, ਘੁਸਰਣਾ, ਹੁੱਜ ਮਾਰਨਾ; at one's~ ਕੋਲ ਹੀ, ਨੇੜੇ ਹੀ

elder *a n* ਵਡੇਰਾ (ਆਦਮੀ), ਵੱਡ-ਵਡੇਰਾ, ਵਡਿਕਾ; ਬਜ਼ੁਰਗਾ; ~erly ਬੁੱਢਾ, ਵੱਡੀ ਉਮਰ ਦਾ, ਪੁਰਾਣੇ ਸਮੇਂ ਦਾ

El Dorado (ਐੱਲਡਅ'ਰਾਡਅਉ) *n* ਸਵਰਨ-ਭੂਮੀ, ਸੋਨ ਨਗਰੀ; ਸੋਨੇ ਦੀ ਕਲਪਤ ਨਗਰੀ

elect (ਇ'ਲੈੱਕਟ) *v* ਚੁਣ ਲੈਣਾ, ਚੁਣਨਾ, ਚੋਣ ਕਰਨੀ; ਚੋਟਵਾਂ, ਚੁਣਵਾਂ, ਵਧੀਆ, ਨਾਮਜ਼ਦ; ~ed ਚੁਣਿਆ, ਨਿਰਵਚਤ

election (ਇ'ਲੈੱਕਸ਼ਨ) *n* ਚੋਣ, ਨਿਰਵਾਚਨ

electoral (ਇ'ਲੈੱਕਟ(ਅ)ਰ(ਅ)ਲ) *a* ਚੋਣ-ਸਬੰਧੀ, ਨਿਰਵਾਚਨ

electorate (ਇ'ਲੈੱਕਟ(ਓ)ਰਅਟ) *n a* ਚੋਣ-ਹਲਕਾ, ਚੋਣ ਖੇਤਰ; ਚੋਣਕਾਰ, ਵੋਟਰ

electric (ਇ'ਲੈੱਕਟਰਿਕ) *n* ਬਿਜਲੀ; ਬਿਜਲੀ ਦਾ, ਬਿਜਲੀ ਨਾਲ ਸਬੰਧਤ; ~al ਬਿਜਲਈ; ਦਾਮਨਿਕ, ਬਰਕੀ; ~ity ਬਿਜਲੀ, ਦਾਮਨੀ, ਬਰਕ

electrification (ਇ'ਲੈੱਕਟਰਿਫ਼ਿ'ਕੇਇਸ਼ਨ) *n* ਬਿਜਲੀਕਰਨ

electrify (ਇ'ਲੈੱਕਟਰਿਫ਼ਾਇ) *v* ਬਿਜਲੀ ਪਹੁੰਚਾਉਣੀ; ਉਤੇਜਤ ਕਰਨਾ

electrocute (ਇ'ਲੈੱਕਟਰਅਕਯੂਟ) *n* ਬਿਜਲੀ ਨਾਲ ਮਰਨਾ

electrocution (ਇ'ਲੈੱਕਟਰਅ'ਕਯੂਸ਼ਨ) *n* ਬਿਜਲੀ ਦੁਆਰਾ ਮੌਤ

elegance, elegancy ('ਐ'ਲਿਗਅੰਸ, 'ਐੱਲਿਗਅੰਸਿ) *n* ਛਬ, ਸ਼ਾਨ, ਸ਼ੋਭਾ, ਠਾਠ-ਬਾਠ

elegant ('ਐੱਲਿਗਅੰਟ) *a* ਛਬੀਲਾ, ਸ਼ਾਨਦਾਰ

element ('ਐੱਲਿਮਅੰਟ) *n* ਤੱਤ, ਸਾਰ, ਸਾਰ-ਤੱਤ, ਅੰਸ਼, ਹਿੱਸਾ, ਮੂਲ, ਅਸਲਾ; ~ary ਮੁੱਢਲਾ, ਆਧਾਰੀ, ਮੂਲ, ਆਰੰਭਕ, ਮੌਲਕ

elephant ('ਐੱਲਿਫ਼ਅੰਟ) *n* ਹਾਥੀ, ਪੀਲ ਜਾਂ ਫ਼ੀਲ, ਗਜ; ~driver ਮਹਾਵਤ

elevate ('ਐੱਲਿਵੇਇਟ) *v* ਉਚਿਆਉਣਾ,

elevation — ਵਡਿਆਉਣਾ, ਉੱਚਾ ਚੁੱਕਣਾ; ਪਦਵੀ ਉੱਚੀ ਕਰਨੀ, ਤਰੱਕੀ ਦੇਣੀ

elevation (ਐੱਲਿ'ਵ੍ਹੇਇਸ਼ਨ) n ਉੱਚਾਈ, ਵਡਿਆਈ, ਉਚਾਣ, ਬੁਲੰਦੀ; ~d ਉੱਨਤ, ਉੱਚ ਉਥਾਪਤ

elevator (ਐੱਲਿਵ੍ਹੇਇਟਅ*) n ਉੱਚਾ ਚੁੱਕਣ ਵਾਲਾ ਲਿਫਟ

eleven (ਇ'ਲੈੱਵੰਨ) a n ਗਿਆਰਾਂ, ਇਕਾਦਸ਼, ਯਾਰ੍ਹਾਂ; ~th ਗਿਆਰਵਾਂ, ਯਾਰ੍ਹਵਾਂ

elf (ਐੱਲਫ਼) n ਪਰੇਤ, ਛਲੇਡਾ, ਪਰੀ, ਜਿਨੂਰਾ; ਬੌਣਾ

elicit (ਇ'ਲਿਸਿਟ) v ਕਢਵਾ ਲੈਣਾ, ਗੱਲ ਕਢਵਾ ਲੈਣੀ, ਸਿੱਟਾ ਕੱਢਣਾ

eligibility ('ਐੱਲਿਜਅ'ਬਿਲਅਟਿ) n ਪਾਤਰਤਾ, ਹੱਕ, ਯੋਗਤਾ, ਕਾਬਲੀਅਤ

eligible ('ਐੱਲਿਜਅਬਲ) a ਪਾਤਰ, ਲਾਇਕ

eleminate (ਇ'ਲੀਮਿਨੇਇਟ) v ਕੱਢ ਦੇਣਾ, ਕੱਟ ਦੇਣਾ, ਕੰਢਾ ਕੱਢ ਦੇਣਾ, ਵਿਚੋਂ ਕੱਢਣਾ, ਖ਼ਾਰਜ ਕਰਨਾ

elimination (ਇ'ਲਿਮਿਨੇਸ਼ਨ) n ਨਿਕਾਸ, ਲੋਪ

elision (ਇ'ਲਿਯ਼ਨ) n ਛੋਟ, ਲੋਪ, ਅੱਖਰ-ਲੋਪ, ਸਵਰ-ਲੋਪ

elite (ਏਇ'ਲੀਟ) (F) n ਸ੍ਰੇਸ਼ਠ ਵਰਗ

elixir (ਇ'ਲਿਕਸਅ*) n ਸੰਜੀਵਨੀ, ਅਕਸੀਰ, ਸ਼ਰਬਤ

elk (ਐੱਲਕ) n ਬਾਰਾਸਿੰਗਾ

elocution (ਐੱਲਅ'ਕਯੂਸ਼ਨ) n ਭਾਸ਼ਟਕਲਾ, ਭਾਸ਼ਟ-ਕਾਰੀ; ~ary ਸੁਵਕਤਤਾ

elongate ('ਈਲੌਂਡਗੋਇਟ) v ਵਧਾਉਣਾ, ਫੈਲਾਉਣਾ, ਲੰਬਾ ਕਰਨਾ, ਪਤਲਾ ਹੋਣਾ; ~d ਥਿਆਇਆ, ਦੀਰਘਕ੍ਰਿਤ, ਪਰਸਾਰਿਆ

elongation ('ਇਲੌਂਡ'ਗੋਇਸ਼ਨ) n ਫੈਲਾਉ, ਲੰਬਾਨ, ਖਿਚਾਉ, ਵਿਸਤਰਤੀ

elope (ਇ'ਲਅਉਪ) v ਉੱਧਲਣਾ, ਲੋਪ ਹੋਣਾ, ਚੋਰੀ ਭੱਜ ਨਿਕਲਣਾ, ਫ਼ਰਾਰ ਹੋਣਾ; ~ment ਉਧਾਲਾ

eloquence ('ਐੱਲਅਕਵਅੰਸ) a ਸੁਭਾਸ਼ਤਾ, ਖੁਸ਼-ਬਿਆਨੀ

eloquent ('ਐੱਲਅ'ਕਵਅੰਟ) a ਸੁਭਾਸ਼ੀਆ, ਖੁਸ਼-ਬਿਆਨ

else (ਐੱਲਸ) adv ਕੋਈ ਹੋਰ, ਹੋਰ ਭੀ, ਪਰ ਨਹੀਂ ਤਾਂ, ਵਰਨਾ, ਜਾਂ; ~where ਹੋਰ ਤਾਂ, ਦੂਜੇ ਢੰਗ ਨਾਲ; ~wise ਨਹੀਂ ਤਾਂ, ਦੂਜੇ ਢੰਗ ਨਾਲ; what~ ਹੋਰ ਕੀ?

elucidate (ਇ'ਲੂਸਿਡੇਇਟ) v ਵਿਆਖਿਆ ਕਰਨੀ, ਸਪਸ਼ਟੀਕਰਨ ਕਰਨਾ; ਚਾਨਣ ਪਾਉਣ

elucidation (ਇ'ਲੂਸਿਡੇਇਸ਼ਨ) n ਵਿਆਖਿਆ ਵਿਸਤਾਰ, ਸਪਸ਼ਟੀਕਰਨ, ਵਿਵਰਣ

elucidative, elucidatory (ਇ'ਲੂਸਿਡੇਇਟਿਵ੍ਹ ਇ'ਲੂਸਿਡੇਇਟ(ਅ)ਰਿ) a ਵਿਆਖਿਆਤਮਕ ਵਿਸਤਰਤ, ਸਪਸ਼ਟੀਕ੍ਰਿਤ

elude (ਇ'ਲੂਡ) v ਖਿਸਕ ਜਾਣਾ, ਟਾਲ ਜਾਣਾ ਅੱਖ ਬਚਾ ਕੇ ਨਿਕਲ ਜਾਣਾ, ਬਚ ਨਿਕਲਣਾ

elusion (ਇ'ਲੂਯ਼ਨ) n ਖੁਸਾਈ, ਅੱਖ ਬਚਾਈ ਧੋਖਾ, ਮੁਗਾਲਤਾ

elusive (ਇ'ਲੂਸਿਵ੍ਹ) a ਹੱਥ ਨਾ ਆਉਣ ਵਾਲਾ ਤਿਲਕਵਾਂ; ~ness ਕਪਟ; ਛਲ, ਭਰਾਂਤੀ ਬਚਾਉ

emaciate (ਇ'ਮੇਇਸ਼ਿਏਇਟ) v a ਲਿੱਸਾ ਹੋਣ ਨਿਰਬਲ ਹੋਣਾ, ਸੁੱਕਣਾ, ਘੁਲਣਾ, ਕਮਜ਼ੋਰ ਪੈਣ ਨਿਰਬਲ, ਦੁਬਲਾ-ਪਤਲਾ, ਸੁੱਕਿਆ, ਕਮਜ਼ੋਰ

emaciation (ਇ'ਮੇਇਸ਼ਿ'ਏਇਸ਼ਨ) n ਨਿਰਬਲਤ ਦੁਬਲਾਪਣ, ਨਿਤਾਣਤਾ, ਸਿਥਲਤਾ, ਕਮਜ਼ੋਰੀ

emaculate (ਇ'ਮੈਕਯੁਲੇਇਟ) v ਦਾ

ਹਟਾਉਣਾ, ਧੱਬਾ ਹਟਾਉਣਾ (ਚਿਹਰੇ ਤੋਂ)

emancipate ('ਇ'ਮੈਂਸਪੇਇਟ) v ਛੁਡਾਉਣਾ, ਸੁਤੰਤਰ ਕਰਵਾਉਣਾ; ਬਰੀ ਕਰਨਾ, ਛੁਟਕਾਰਾ ਦੇਣਾ, ਨਿਸਤਾਰਾ ਕਰਨਾ

emancipation (ਇ'ਮੈਂਸਿ'ਪੇਇਸ਼ਨ) n ਮੁਕਤੀ, ਛੁਟਕਾਰਾ, ਨਿਸਤਾਰਾ, ਖ਼ਲਾਸੀ, ਨਿਜਾਤ

emancipatory (ਇ'ਮੈਂਸਿ'ਪੇਇਟਅਰਿ) a ਮੁਕਤੀ-ਸਬੰਧੀ, ਛੁਟਕਾਰੇ-ਸਬੰਧੀ, ਉੱਧਾਰਕ

emasculate (ਇ'ਮੈਸਕਯੁਲਿਟ, ਇ'ਮੈਸਕਯੁਲੇਇਟ) a ਖੱਸੀ; ਹਿਜੜਾ, ਨਾਮਰਦ; ਨਪੁੰਸਕ, ਨਿਤਾਣਾ; ਖੱਸੀ ਕਰਨਾ, ਨਸਪੁੰਕ ਕਰਨਾ; ਕਮਜ਼ੋਰ ਕਰਨਾ, ਨਿਤਾਣਾ ਕਰਨਾ

emasculation (ਇ'ਮੈਸਕਯੁ'ਲੇਇਸ਼ਨ) n ਖੱਸੀਪੁਣਾ, ਨਪੁੰਸਕਤਾ, ਨਿਤਾਣਤਾ, ਨਾਮਰਦੀ

embalm (ਇਮ'ਬਾਮ) v ਲਾਸ਼ ਨੂੰ ਸੁਰੱਖਿਅਤ ਰੱਖਣ ਲਈ ਮਸਾਲੇ ਲਾਉਣੇ; ਸੁਗੰਧਤ ਕਰਨਾ, ਸੁੱਰਖਿਅਤ

embank (ਇਮ'ਬੈਙਕ) n ਬੰਨ੍ਹ ਬੰਨ੍ਹਣਾ; ਪਟੜੀ ਬੰਨ੍ਹਣੀ, ਦਰੇਸੀ ਬਣਾਉਣੀ; ~ment ਬੰਨ੍ਹ, ਪਟੜੀ, ਦਰੇਸੀ

embargo (ਐੱਮ'ਬਾ*ਅਓ) n v ਵਪਾਰ ਦੀ ਮਨਾਹੀ, ਨਾਕਾਬੰਦੀ; ਅਧਿਕਾਰ ਵਿਚ ਲੈਣਾ, ਨਾਕਾਬੰਦੀ ਕਰਨਾ

embarrass (ਇ'ਮਬੈਰਅਸ) v ਪਰੇਸ਼ਾਨੀ ਵਿਚ ਪਾਉਣਾ; ਉਲਝਾਉਣਾ, ਪਰੇਸ਼ਾਨ ਕਰਨਾ, ਭੇਜਾ ਪਾਉਣਾ; ~ing ਪਰੇਸ਼ਾਨਕਾਰੀ; ~ment ਉਲਝਣ, ਅੜਿੱਕਾ, ਪਸ਼ੇਮਾਨੀ, ਘਬਰਾਹਟ

embassy ('ਐੱਮਬਅਸਿ) n ਸਿਫ਼ਾਰਤਖ਼ਾਨਾ, ਦੂਤਾਵਾਸ, ਸਿਫ਼ਾਰਤ

embellish (ਇਮ'ਬੇਲਿਸ਼) v ਸ਼ਿੰਗਾਰਨਾ, ਸਜਾਉਣਾ

embezzie (ਇਮ'ਬੈੱਜ਼ਲ) v ਗ਼ਬਨ ਕਰਨਾ, ਖੁਰਦ-ਬੁਰਦ ਕਰਨਾ, ਘਾਲਾ-ਮਾਲਾ ਕਰਨਾ, ਗੋਲ-ਮਾਲ ਕਰਨਾ

emblem ('ਐੱਮਬਲਅਮ) v n ਨਿਸ਼ਾਨ, ਚਿੰਨ੍ਹ, ਅਲਾਮਤ; ਨਿਸ਼ਾਨ ਬਣਾਉਣਾ, ਪ੍ਰਤੀਕ ਰਾਹੀਂ ਪਰਗਟ ਕਰਨਾ

embodiment (ਇਮ'ਬੌਡਿਮਅੰਟ) n ਸਾਕਾਰ ਰੂਪ; ਪ੍ਰਤੱਖ ਰੂਪ, ਸਾਖਿਆਤ ਦਰਸ਼ਨ, ਰੂਪ, ਪੁੰਜ

embody (ਇਮ'ਬੌਡਿ) v ਸਾਕਾਰ ਕਰਨਾ, ਰੂਪ ਦੇਣਾ; ਨਿਰੂਪਣ ਕਰਨਾ, ਸ਼ਾਮਲ ਕਰਨਾ; ਵਿਚਾਰ ਨੂੰ ਪਰਗਟ ਰੂਪ ਦੇਣਾ, ਅਸੂਲ ਨੂੰ ਅਮਲ ਵਿਚ ਲਿਆਉਣਾ

embrace (ਇਮ'ਬਰੇਇਸ) v n ਜੱਫੀ ਪਾਉਣੀ, ਗਲ ਲਾਉਣਾ; ਧਾਰਨ ਕਰਨਾ, ਗ੍ਰਹਿਣ ਕਰਨਾ; ਜੱਫੀ, ਗਲਵੱਕੜੀ; ਧਾਰਤਾ

emerge (ਇ'ਮਅ:ਜ) v ਫੁੱਟਣਾ, ਉਭਰਨਾ, ਪਰਗਟ ਹੋਣਾ; ~nce ਨਿਕਾਸ, ਉਭਾਰ, ਉਗਮਣ, ਪਰਗਟਾਉ

emergency (ਇੱਸਅਃਜਅੰਸੀ) n ਸੰਕਟ, ਔਖਾ ਸਮਾਂ, ਅਪਾਤਕਾਲ, ਇਤਫ਼ਾਕੀਆ ਲੋੜ

emeritus (ਇ'ਮੈ*ਟਿਅਸ) a ਸਨਮਾਨਤ ਪੈਨਸ਼ਨ ਪ੍ਰਾਪਤ, ਸੇਵਾਮੁਕਤ, ਅਵਕਾਸ਼ ਪ੍ਰਾਪਤ (ਅਧਿਆਪਕ)

emigrant ('ਐੱਮਿਗਰਅੰਟ) a n ਪਰਵਾਸੀ, ਪਰਦੇਸ ਵਾਸੀ

emigration ('ਐੱਮਿ'ਗਰੇਇਸ਼ਨ) n ਪਰਵਾਸ, ਹਿਜਰਤ, ਜਲਾਵਤਨ

eminence ('ਐੱਮਿਨਅੰਸ) n ਸਿਖਰ, ਟਿੱਲਾ, ਉਚਾਈ; ਮਹਾਨਤਾ; ਵਡਿਆਈ; ਨਾਮਵਰੀ; ਗੌਰਵ; ਪ੍ਰਸਿੱਧੀ, ਸ੍ਰੇਸ਼ਠਤਾ

eminent ('ਐੱਮਿਨਅੰਟ) a ਉੱਚ ਕੋਟੀ ਦਾ, ਪ੍ਰਤਾਪੀ,

ਮਹਾਨ, ਉੱਘਾ; ਬੁਲੰਦ, ਮੁਮਤਾਜ਼; ਨੁਮਾਇਆਂ, ਪ੍ਰਸਿੱਧ, ਗੌਰਵਸ਼ਾਲੀ

emissary ('ਐਮਿਸ(ਅ)ਰਿ) *n* ਦੂਤ, ਕਾਸਦ, ਸਫ਼ੀਰ, ਏਲਚੀ

emission (ਇ'ਮਿਸ਼ਨ) *n* ਨਿਕਾਸ, ਉਦਗਾਰ, (ਮਨੋ) ਸੁਪਨ-ਦੋਸ਼

emit (ਇ'ਮਿਟ) *v* (ਪ੍ਰਕਾਸ਼ ਦੀਆਂ ਕਿਰਨਾਂ) ਛੱਡਣਾ, ਕੱਢਣਾ

emolument (ਇ'ਮੋਲਯੁਮਅੰਟ) *n* ਵੇਤਨ, ਤਨਖ਼ਾਹ, ਤਲਬ

emotion (ਇ'ਮਅਉਸ਼ਨ) *n* ਤਰੰਗ, ਭਾਵ, ਵਲਵਲਾ, ਜਜ਼ਬਾ, ਜੋਸ਼, ਉਤੇਜਨਾ, ਸੰਵੇਗ; ~al ਭਾਵੁਕ, ਉਤੇਜਤ, ਭਾਵਪੂਰਨ

emotive (ਇ'ਮਅਉਟਿਵ) *a* ਭਾਵਾਤਮਕ

empathy ('ਐਮਪਅਥਿ) *n* (ਦਰਸ਼) ਹਮਦਰਦੀ, ਸਹਾਨਭੂਤੀ

emperor ('ਐਮਪ(ਅ)ਰਅ*) *n* ਸਮਰਾਟ, ਸ਼ਹਿਨਸ਼ਾਹ, ਸੁਲਤਾਨ, ਬਾਦਸ਼ਾਹ

emphasis ('ਐਮਫ਼ਅਸਿਸ) *n* ਬਲ, ਜ਼ੋਰ

emphasize ('ਐਮਫ਼ਅਸਾਇਜ਼) *v* ਜ਼ੋਰ ਦੇਣਾ, ਦਬਾਉ ਦੇਣਾ

emphatic (ਇਮ'ਫ਼ੈਟਿਕ) *a* ਜ਼ੋਰਦਾਰ, ਪ੍ਰਭਾਵਸ਼ਾਲੀ, ਦ੍ਰਿੜ੍ਹ; (ਵਿਆ) ਦਬਾਵਾਚਕ

empire ('ਐਮਪਾਇਅ*) *n* ਸਾਮਰਾਜ, ਸਲਤਨਤ, ਬਾਦਸ਼ਾਹੀ

empiric (ਇਮ'ਪਿਰਿਕ) *a n* ਅਮਲੀ, ਪ੍ਰਯੋਗਕ; ਸਿਖਾਂਦਰੂ, ਵੈਦੜਾ, ਨੀਮ-ਹਕੀਮ; ~al ਅਨੁਭਾਵਕ, ਅਨੁਭਵਵਾਦੀ, ਪ੍ਰਯੋਗ-ਸਿੱਧ

emplane (ਇਮ'ਪਲੇਇਨ) *v* ਹਵਾਈ ਜਹਾਜ਼ ਵਿਚ ਸਵਾਰ ਹੋਣਾ ਜਾਂ ਮਾਲ ਲੱਦਣਾ

employ (ਇਮ'ਪਲੋਇ) *v* ਭਰਤੀ ਕਰਨਾ, ਕੰਮ ਦੇਣਾ, ਰੁਜ਼ਗਾਰ ਉੱਤੇ ਲਾਉਣਾ; ਪ੍ਰਯੋਗ ਕਰਨਾ, ਵਰਤਣਾ; ~ed ਨਿਯੁਕਤ, ਲੱਗਿਆ, ਰੁੱਝਿਆ; ~ee ਨੌਕਰ, ਮੁਲਾਜ਼ਮ, ਕਰਮਚਾਰੀ; ~er ਮਾਲਕ, ਸੁਆਮੀ; ~ment ਨੌਕਰੀ, ਤਨਖ਼ਾਹ ਵਾਲੀ ਮੁਲਾਜ਼ਮਤ, ਰੁਜ਼ਗਾਰ, ਪੇਸ਼ਾ

emporium (ਐਮ'ਪੋਰਿਅਮ) *n* ਹੱਟ, ਤਿਜਾਰਤਗਾਹ, ਬਜ਼ਾਰ

empower (ਇਮ'ਪਾਉਅ*) *v* ਇਖ਼ਤਿਆਰ ਦੇਣਾ, ਅਧਿਕਾਰ ਸੌਂਪਣਾ, ਸੱਤਾ ਦੇਣੀ, ਮੁਖ਼ਤਿਆਰ ਬਣਾਉਣਾ

empress ('ਐਮਪਰਿਸ) *n* ਮਹਾਰਾਣੀ, ਮਲਕਾ, ਸਮਰਾਟ ਦੀ ਪਤਨੀ

emptiness ('ਐਮ(ਪ)ਟਿਨਿਸ) *n* ਸੁੰਞਾਪਣ, ਵਿਹਲ, ਖ਼ਲਾਅ, ਥੋਥਾਪਣ, ਸੱਖਣਾਪਣ

empty ('ਐਮ(ਪ)ਟਿ) *a v* ਵਿਹਲਾ, ਸੱਖਣਾ, ਸੁੰਞਾ, ਖ਼ਾਲੀ, ਥੋਥਾ, ਫੋਕਾ, ਭੁੱਖਾ, ਨਿਕੰਮਾ, ਨਿਰਥਕ; ਖਾਲੀ ਕਰਨਾ, ਖ਼ਾਲੀ ਹੋਣਾ

emulate ('ਐਮਯੁਲੇਇਟ) *v* ਰਸ਼ਕ ਕਰਨਾ, ਬਰਾਬਰੀ ਕਰਨੀ, ਰੀਸ ਕਰਨੀ, ਹੋੜ ਕਰਨਾ

emulation ('ਐਮਯੁ'ਲੇਇਸ਼ਨ) *n* ਬਰਾਬਰੀ, ਮੁਕਾਬਲਾ, ਰੀਸ, ਰਸ਼ਕ

enable (ਇ'ਨੇਇਬਲ) *v* ਯੋਗ ਬਣਾਉਣਾ, ਸਮੱਰਥ ਕਰਨਾ, ਕਾਬਲ ਕਰਨਾ

enact (ਇ'ਨੈਕਟ) *v* ਕਾਨੂੰਨ ਪਾਸ ਕਰਨਾ, ਬਣਾਉਣਾ, (ਨਾਟਕ) ਖੇਡਣਾ, ਐਕਟਿੰਗ ਕਰਨਾ; ~ment ਕਾਨੂੰਨ ਦਾ ਰੂਪ

enamel (ਇ'ਨੈਮਲ) *n v* ਮੁਲੰਮਾ, ਝਾਲ, ਮੀਨਾਕਾਰੀ; ਮੁਲੰਮਾ ਕਰਨਾ, ਝਾਲ ਫੇਰਨੀ, ਮੀਨਾਕਾਰੀ ਕਰਨੀ

en bloc (ਆਨ'ਬਲੈਕ) (*F*) *a* ਸਮੂਹਕ, ਰੂਪ ਵਿਚ ਸਾਰੇ ਦੇ ਸਾਰੇ

encage, incage (ਇਨ'ਕੇਇਜ) *v* ਪਿੰਜਰੇ ਵਿਚ ਰੱਖਣਾ, ਬੰਦ ਕਰਨਾ, ਕੈਦ ਕਰਨਾ

encamp (ਇਨ'ਕੈਂਪ) *v* ਡੇਰਾ ਜਾਂ ਛਾਉਣੀ ਪਾਉਣਾ, ਪੜਾਉ ਪਾਉਣਾ, ਪੜਾ ਵਿਚ ਠਹਿਰਨਾ, ਤੰਬੂ ਖੜ੍ਹਾ ਕਰਨਾ; ~ment ਛਾਉਣੀ, ਡੇਰਾ, ਪੜਾਉ, ਤੰਬੂ, ਖ਼ੇਮਾ

encase, incase (ਇਨ'ਕੇਇਸ) *v* ਢਕਣਾ, ਬਕਸੇ ਵਿਚ ਰੱਖਣਾ, ਲਪੇਟਣਾ, ਖ਼ਾਨੇ ਵਿਚ ਰੱਖਣਾ

encash (ਇਨ'ਕੈਸ਼) *v* ਨਕਦ ਰੁਪਏ ਦੇਣਾ, ਹੁੰਡੀ ਜਾਂ ਚੈੱਕ ਤੁੜਾਉਣਾ, ਵਸੂਲਣਾ

encave (ਇਨ'ਕੇਇਵ) *v* ਗੁਫ਼ਾ ਵਿਚ ਲੁਕਾਉਣਾ, ਕੰਦਰਾਂ ਵਿਚ ਰੱਖਣਾ

enchain (ਇਨ'ਚੇਇਨ) *v* ਜ਼ੰਜੀਰ ਨਾਲ ਬੰਨ੍ਹਣਾ; ਕੜੀ-ਬੱਧ ਕਰਨਾ, ਕਸ ਕੇ ਬੰਨ੍ਹਣਾ; ਧਿਆਨ ਖਿਚਣਾ, ਵੱਸ ਵਿਚ ਕਰਨਾ

enchant (ਇਨ'ਚਾਂਟ) *v* ਜਾਦੂ ਕਰਨਾ, ਟੂਣਾ ਕਰਨਾ ਲੁਭਾਉਣਾ, ਰੀਝਾਉਣਾ, ਮੁਗਧ ਕਰਨਾ; ~ing ਮੋਹਕ, ਦਿਲਕਸ਼; ~ment ਜਾਦੂ, ਟੂਣਾ, ਇੰਦਰਜਾਲ, ਸੰਮੋਹਨ ਮਾਇਆ

encharge (ਇਨ'ਚਾਜ) *v* ਸੌਂਪਣਾ, ਸਪੁਰਦ ਕਰਨਾ

encircle (ਇਨ'ਸਅ:ਕਲ) *v* ਵਲ ਲੈਣਾ, ਘੇਰ ਲੈਣਾ, ਵਲਗਣਾ, ਬੰਦ ਕਰਨਾ, ਘੇਰਾ ਪਾਉਣਾ, ਵਾੜ ਲਾਉਣਾ

enclose, inclose (ਇਨ'ਕਲਅਉਜ਼) *v* ਘੇਰਨਾ, ਬੰਦ ਕਰਨਾ, ਵਾੜ ਲਗਾਉਣਾ; ~d ਘੇਰਿਆ, ਬੰਦ, ਨੱਥੀ ਕੀਤਾ

enclosure (ਇਨ'ਕਲਅਉਯ਼ਅ*) *n* ਵਲਗਣ, ਘੇਰਾ, ਵਾੜ, ਇਹਾਤਾ; ਨੱਥੀ ਕਾਗ਼ਜ਼; ਸਹਿ-ਪੱਤਰ

enclothe (ਇਨ'ਕਲਅਉਦ) *v* ਕੱਪੜੇ ਪੁਆਉਣਾ, ਵਸਤਰ ਪਹਿਨਾਉਣਾ

encode (ਇਨ'ਕਅਉਡ) *v* ਕੋਡ ਵਿਚ ਬਦਲਣਾ

encompass (ਇਨ'ਕਅੱਮਪਅਸ) *v* ਘੇਰ ਲੈਣਾ, ਸ਼ਾਮਲ ਕਰਨਾ, ਵਿਆਪਤ ਕਰਨਾ, ਵਲ੍ਹੇਟਣਾ, ਧਰਨਾ

encore ('ਔਂਕੋ*') *int* ਮੁਕਰਰ

encounter (ਇਨ'ਕਾਉਂਟਅ*) *n v* ਟਾਕਰਾ, ਮੁਕਾਬਲਾ, ਮੁੱਠ-ਭੇੜ, ਸੰਗਰਾਮ, ਸਮਾਗਮ, ਅਚਾਨਕ, ਮੇਲ; ਟਾਕਰਾ ਕਰਨਾ, ਜੂਝਣਾ, ਭਿੜਨਾ, ਲੜਨਾ

encourage (ਇਨ'ਕਅੱਰਿਜ) *v* ਉਤਸ਼ਾਹ ਦੇਣਾ, ਦਿਲ ਵਧਾਉਣਾ, ਹੌਂਸਲਾ ਦੇਣਾ, ਚੁੱਕ ਦੇਣੀ, ਪਿੱਠ ਠੋਕਣੀ, ਪਰੇਰਨਾ ਦੇਣੀ, ਉਕਸਾਉਣਾ; ~ment ਉਤਸ਼ਾਹ, ਧਰਵਾਸ, ਪਰੇਰਨਾ

encouraging (ਇਨ'ਕਅੱਰਿਜਿਡ) *a* ਉਤਸ਼ਾਹਜਨਕ

encroach (ਇਨ'ਕਰਅਉਚ) *v* (ਅਯੋਗ) ਦਖ਼ਲ ਦੇਣਾ, ਅਨੁਚਿਤ ਅਧਿਕਾਰ ਜਮਾਉਣਾ, ਲੱਤ ਅੜਾਉਣੀ; ~ment ਅਯੋਗ ਦਖ਼ਲ, ਨਾਜਾਇਜ਼ ਕਬਜ਼ਾ

encumber (ਇਨ'ਕਅੱਮਬਅ*) *v* ਭਾਰ ਪਾਉਣਾ; ਰੋੜਾ ਅਟਕਾਉਣਾ, ਵਿਘਨ ਪਾਉਣਾ, ਅਟਕਾਉਣਾ; ਕਰਜ਼ਾਈ ਕਰਨਾ

encumbrance (ਇਨ'ਕਅੱਮਬਰਅੱਸ) *n* ਭਾਰ, ਬੋਝ, ਵਿਘਨ, ਦੁੱਖ, ਰੋੜਾ

encyclopaedia (ਇਨ'ਸਾਇਕਲਅ(ਉ)'ਪੀਡ-ਯਅ) *n* ਵਿਸ਼ਵ-ਕੋਸ਼

end (ਔਂਡ) *n v* ਅੰਤ, ਸੀਮਾ, ਹੱਦ, ਸਿਰਾ; ਟੋਟਾ; ਸਮਾਪਤੀ, ਬਰਬਾਦੀ, ਮਿਰਤੂ, ਨਤੀਜਾ, ਉਦੇਸ਼, ਮਨੋਰਥ; ਸਮਾਪਤ ਕਰਨਾ, ਅੰਤ ਕਰਨਾ, ਪੂਰਾ ਕਰਨਾ, ਨਸ਼ਟ ਕਰਨਾ, ਖ਼ਤਮ ਹੋਣਾ, ਨਤੀਜਾ ਨਿਕਲਣਾ, ਸਿੱਟਾ ਕੱਢਣਾ; **in the~** ਆਖ਼ਰਕਾਰ, ਅੰਤ ਨੂੰ; **make both~s meet** ਡੰਗ

ਟਪਾਉਣਾ, ਗੁਜ਼ਾਰਾ, ਕਰਨਾ; ~less ਅੰਤਹ, ਅਪਾਰ, ਨਿਰੰਤਰ, ਬੇ-ਇੰਤਹਾ

endanger (ਇਨ'ਡੇਂਜਿਅਅ*) *n* ਖ਼ਤਰੇ ਵਿਚ ਪਾਉਣਾ, ਆਪੱਤੀ ਵਿਚ ਪਾਉਣਾ

endear (ਇਨ'ਡਿਅ*) *v* ਪਿਆਰਾ ਬਣਾਉਣਾ, ਲਾਡਲਾ ਬਣਾਉਣਾ; ~ment ਪ੍ਰੀਤ, ਪਿਆਰ, ਪਰੇਮ, ਲਾਡ-ਦੁਲਾਰ

endeavour (ਇਨ'ਡੈੱਵਅ*) *n v* ਜਤਨ, ਘਾਲ, ਹੰਭਲਾ, ਵਾਹ, ਜਾਨਮਾਰੀ, ਉੱਦਮ, ਕੋਸ਼ਸ਼; ਜਤਨ ਕਰਨਾ, ਉੱਦਮ ਕਰਨਾ

endorse (ਇਨ'ਡੋਸ) *v* ਸਕਾਰਨਾ, ਤਸਦੀਕ ਕਰਨੀ, ਪਿੱਠਾਂਕਣ ਕਰਨ, ਪੁਸ਼ਟੀ ਕਰਨੀ; ~ment ਸਹੀ, ਤਸਦੀਕ, ਪਿੱਠਾਂਕਣ, ਸਮਰਥਨ, ਅਨੁਮੋਦਨ

endow (ਇਨ'ਡਾਉ) *v* ਭੇਟਾ ਕਰਨਾ, ਨਾਉਂ ਲਾਉਣਾ ਵਕਫ਼ ਕਰਨਾ, ਧਰਮ ਅਰਥ ਦੇਣਾ, ਦਾਨ ਦੇਣਾ, ਭੇਟ ਦੇਣਾ, ਸਮੱਰਥ ਬਣਾਉਣਾ; ~ment ਧਰਮ ਅਰਥ ਭੇਟਾ, ਧਰਮਦਾਨ; ਦਹੇਜ, ਸਮੱਰਥਾ, ਪ੍ਰਤਿਭਾ; ਯੋਗਤਾ

endurance (ਇਨ'ਡਯੂਅਰਨਸ) *n* ਜੇਰਾ, ਸਹਾਰਨ-ਸ਼ਕਤੀ, ਧੀਰਜ, ਸਹਿਣਸ਼ੀਲਤਾ, ਬੁਰਦਬਾਰੀ, ਸਬਰ

endure (ਇਨ'ਡਯੂਅ*) *v* ਭੋਗਣਾ, ਸਹਾਰਨਾ, ਝੱਲਣਾ, ਸਹਿਣਾ, ਭੁਗਤਣਾ, ਟਿਕਣਾ, ਠਹਿਰੇ ਰਹਿਣਾ

enduring (ਇਨ'ਡਯੂਅਰਿੰਡ) *a* ਚਿਰਸਥਾਈ, ਟਿਕਾਊ, ਸਹਿਣਸ਼ੀਲ

enemy (ਐੱਨਅਮਿ) *n a* ਵੈਰੀ, ਦੁਸ਼ਮਣ, ਵਿਪੱਖੀ, ਸ਼ੱਤਰੂ, ਵਿਰੋਪੀ

energetic (ਐੱਨਅ'ਜੈੱਟਿਕ) *n a* ਤੇਜਵਾਨ, ਬਲਵਾਨ, ਪ੍ਰਬੱਲ, ਸ਼ਕਤੀਸ਼ਾਲੀ, ਮਿਹਨਤੀ, ਉਤਸ਼ਾਹੀ

energize (ਐੱਨਅ:ਜਾਇਜ਼) *v* ਸ਼ਕਤੀ ਦਾ ਸੰਚਾਰ ਕਰਨ, ਬਲ ਪ੍ਰਦਾਨ ਕਰਨਾ, ਸ਼ਕਤੀ ਭਰਨਾ; ਜਾਨ ਪਾ ਦੇਣਾ

energy (ਐੱਨਅ:ਜਿ) *n* ਬਲ, ਜ਼ੋਰ, ਸ਼ਕਤੀ, ਦਮ, ਊਰਜਾ, ਤੇਜ, ਜੀਵਨ-ਸ਼ਕਤੀ ਕਿਰਿਆਸ਼ੀਲਤਾ, ਯੋਗਤਾ

enfeeble (ਇਨ'ਫ਼ੀਬਲ) *v* ਸ਼ਕਤੀਹੀਨ ਕਰਨਾ, ਨਿਤਾਣਾ ਕਰਨਾ, ਦੁਰਬਲ ਕਰਨਾ

enfold, infold (ਇਨ'ਫ਼ਅਉਲਡ) *v* ਜੱਫੀ ਵਿਚ ਲੈਣਾ, ਗਲ ਲਾਉਣਾ, ਘੁੱਟਣਾ, ਵਲੇਟਣਾ, ਤਹਿ ਕਰਨਾ

enforce (ਇਨ'ਫ਼ੋਸ) *v* ਚਾਲੂ ਕਰਨਾ, ਲਾਗੂ ਕਰਨਾ, ਹੁਕਮ ਜਾਂ ਕਾਨੂੰਨ ਅਮਲ ਵਿਚ ਲਿਆਉਣਾ, ਜਾਰੀ ਕਰਨਾ, ਪ੍ਰਚਲਤ ਕਰਨਾ, (ਹੁਕਮ) ਚਲਾਉਣਾ; ~ment ਪ੍ਰਦਾਨ, ਦ੍ਰਿੜ੍ਹੀਕਰਨ, ਪਾਲਣ, ਤਾਮੀਲ

enfranchise (ਇਨ'ਫ਼ਰੈਨਚਾਇਜ਼) *v* ਆਜ਼ਾਦ ਕਰਨਾ, ਰਿਹਾ ਕਰਨਾ; ਸ਼ਹਿਰੀ ਹੱਕ ਦੇਣੇ, ਵੋਟ ਦਾ ਹੱਕ ਦੇਣਾ; ~ment ਮੁਕਤੀਦਾਨ, ਵੋਟ ਅਧਿਕਾਰ

engage (ਇਨ'ਗੇਇਜ) *v* ਵਚਨ-ਬੱਧ ਹੋਣਾ, ਇਕਰਾਰ; ~d ਰੁੱਝਿਆ; ਮੰਗਣੀ, ਕੁੜਮਾਈ ਕਰਨੀ, ਕੰਮ ਤੇ ਲਾ ਦੇਣਾ; ਅਹਾਰੇ ਲਾਉਣਾ, ਜੁਟ ਜਾਣਾ, ਲਾ ਰੱਖਣਾ, ਕੱਸ ਕੇ ਫੜਨਾ; ਭਿੜਨਾ; ~ment ਇਕਰਾਰ, ਵਚਨ-ਬੰਧੇਜ; ਰੁਝੇਵਾਂ, ਕੰਮ, ਪੰਦਾ; ਸੰਗਨੀ, ਕੁੜਮਾਈ; ਸੱਮਠ-ਭੇੜ, ਝੜਪ

engender (ਇਨ'ਜੈੱਡਅ*) *v* ਪੈਦਾ ਕਰਨਾ, ਉਤਪੰਨ ਕਰਨਾ, ਬੱਚਾ ਜਣਨਾ

engine (ਐੱਨਜਿਨ) *n v* ਇੰਜਣ, ਕਲ, ਮਸ਼ੀਨ, ਜੰਤਰ

engineer (ਐੱਨਜਿ'ਨਿਅ*) *n v* ਇੰਜਣਸਾਜ,

engrave ਇੰਜੀਨੀਅਰ, ਨਿਰਮਾਤਾ; ਨਿਰਮਾਨ ਕਰਨਾ, ਇੰਜੀਨੀਅਰੀ ਦਾ ਕੰਮ ਕਰਨਾ, ਕਾਢ ਕੱਢਣੀ, ਪ੍ਰਬੰਧ ਕਰਨਾ, ਜੁਗਤ ਕੱਢਣੀ, ਮਨਸੂਬਾ ਬੰਨ੍ਹਣਾ; ~ing ਇੰਜੀਨੀਅਰੀ, ਜੰਤਰਸ਼ਾਸਤਰ

engrave (ਇਨ'ਗਰੇਇਵ) v ਮੀਨਾਕਾਰੀ ਕਰਨਾ, ਨੱਕਾਸ਼ੀ ਕਰਨਾ, ਉਘਾੜਨਾ, ਉਕਰਨਾ

engraving (ਇਨ'ਗਰੇਇਵਿਙ) n ਖੁਦਾਇ, ਨੱਕਾਸ਼ੀ, ਖੁਟਨ

engross (ਇਨ'ਗਰਅਉਸ) v ਮੋਟੇ ਅੱਖਰਾਂ ਵਿਚ ਲਿਖਣਾ, ਕਾਨੂੰਨ ਦੇ ਰੂਪ ਵਿਚ ਜ਼ਾਹਰ ਕਰਨਾ, ਸਾਰਾ ਭੰਡਾਰ ਖ਼ਰੀਦ ਲੈਣਾ; ਧਿਆਨ ਵਿਚ ਲੀਨ ਕਰਨਾ

engulf (ਇਨ'ਗਅੱਲਫ਼) v ਲਪੇਟ ਵਿਚ ਲੈਣਾ; ~ed ਲੀਨ, ਇਕਾਗਰਚਿਤ, ਮਗਨ

enhance (ਇਨ'ਹਾਂਸ) v ਵਧਾਉਣਾ, (ਕੀਮਤ) ਚੜ੍ਹਾਉਣੀ, ਉੱਚਾ ਕਰਨਾ; ~ment ਵਾਧਾ, ਵਧਾ-ਚੜ੍ਹਾ, ਤੀਬਰਤਾ

enigma (ਇ'ਨਿਗਮਅ) n ਬੁਝਾਰਤ, ਅੜਾਉਣੀ, ਪਹੇਲੀ, ਉਲਝਣ

enigmatic ('ਇਨਿਗ'ਮੈਟਿਕ) a ਗੁੱਝਾ, ਪੇਚੀਦਾ

enjoin (ਇਨ'ਜੋਇਨ) v ਲਾਗੂ ਕਰਨਾ, ਨਿਰਧਾਰਤ ਕਰਨਾ, ਹੁਕਮ ਦੇਣਾ, ਨਿਰਦੇਸ਼ ਕਰਨਾ

enjoy (ਇਨ'ਜੋਇ) v ਭੋਗਣਾ, ਮਾਣਨਾ, ਅਨੰਦ ਲੁੱਟਣਾ, ਉਪਭੋਗ ਕਰਨਾ; ਲਾਭ ਉਠਾਉਣਾ; ~ment ਵਾਧਾ, ਸਮਰਿਧੀ, ਸੰਪੰਨਤਾ

enkindle (ਇਨ'ਕਿੰਡਲ) v ਪ੍ਰਚੰਡ ਕਰਨਾ, ਭੜ-ਕਾਉਣਾ, ਉਤੇਜਤ ਕਰਨਾ, ਜਲਾਉਣਾ, ਭਾਵਾਂ ਨੂੰ ਤੀਬਰ ਕਰਨਾ, ਅੱਗ ਲਾਉਣਾ

enlarge (ਇਨ'ਲਾਜ) v ਵਧਾਉਣਾ, ਫੈਲਾਉਣਾ, ਵਿਸਤਰਤ ਕਰਨਾ, ਇਜ਼ਾਫ਼ਾ ਕਰਨਾ, (ਫੋਟੋ) ਵੱਡੀ ਕਰਨੀ; ~ment ਵਾਧਾ, ਵ੍ਰਿਧੀ, ਫੈਲਾਉ

enlighten (ਇਨ'ਲਾਇਟਨ) v ਸਿੱਖਿਆ ਦੇਣਾ, ਪ੍ਰਕਾਸ਼ ਪਾਉਣਾ, ਸਪਸ਼ਟ ਕਰਨਾ, ਉਪਦੇਸ਼ ਦੇਣਾ, ਗਿਆਨ ਦੇਣਾ; ~ed ਪ੍ਰਬੁੱਧ, ਪ੍ਰਕਾਸ਼ਤ, ਗਿਆਨ-ਉੱਦੀਪਤ; ~ment ਬੋਧ, ਗਿਆਨ ਪ੍ਰਕਾਸ਼ਨ, ਸਪਸ਼ਟੀਕਰਨ, ਗਿਆਨ ਦਾਨ

enlist (ਇਨ'ਲਿਸਟ) v ਸੂਚੀਬੱਧ ਕਰਨਾ, ਭਰਤੀ ਕਰਨਾ ਜਾਂ ਹੋਣਾ; ਸਹਿਯੋਗ ਪ੍ਰਾਪਤ ਕਰਨਾ; ~ment ਭਰਤੀ

enmity ('ਐੱਨਮਅਟਿ) n ਵੈਰ, ਦੁਸ਼ਮਨੀ, ਰੰਜ਼ਕ, ਵੈਰ-ਭਾਵ, ਵਿਰੋਧ

enormous (ਇ'ਨੋਮਅਸ) a ਵੱਡਾ ਸਾਰਾ, ਮਹਾਨ, ਭੀਸ਼ਣ, ਅਤਿਅਧਿਕ, ਅਸਾਧਾਰਨ

enough (ਇ'ਨਅੱਫ) a adv int ਚੋਖਾ, ਕਾਫ਼ੀ, ਉਚਿਤ; ਬਹੁਤ ਸਾਰਾ, ਬੱਸ! ਹੱਦ ਹੋ ਗਈ

eouire, Iouire (ਇਨ'ਕਵਾਇਅ*) v ਜਾਂਚ ਕਰਨਾ, ਪੁੱਛ ਗਿੱਛ ਕਰਨਾ, ਪੁੱਛਣਾ

eouiry, Iouiry (ਇਨ'ਕਵਾਇਅਰਿ) n ਪੁੱਛ ਗਿੱਛ, ਜਾਂਚ, ਖੋਜ, ਤਹਿਕੀਕਾਤ

enrich (ਇਨ'ਰਿਚ) v ਸੰਪੰਨ ਬਣਾਉਣਾ, ਨਿਹਾਲ ਕਰ ਦੇਣਾ, ਵਧੀਆ ਬਣਾਉਣਾ; ਸਮਰਿਧ ਬਣਾਉਣਾ; ਜ਼ਰਖੇਜ਼ ਕਰਨਾ; ਅਲੰਕਰਤ ਕਰਨਾ, ਸਜਾਉਣਾ; ~ment ਵਾਧਾ, ਸਮਰਿਧੀ, ਸੰਪੰਨਤਾ

enrol, enroll (ਇਨ'ਰਅਉਲ) v ਨਾਂ ਚੜ੍ਹਾਉਣਾ, ਦਰਜ ਕਰਨਾ, ਦਾਖ਼ਲ ਕਰਨਾ, ਭਰਤੀ ਕਰਨਾ; ~ment ਇੰਦਰਾਜ, ਦਾਖ਼ਲਾ, ਭਰਤੀ, ਸੂਚੀ, ਫ਼ਰਦ

en route (ਆਨ'ਰੂਟ) (F) adv ਬਰਸਤਾ, ਰਾਹ ਜਾਂਦਿਆਂ

enshrine (ਇਨ'ਸ਼ਰਾਇਨ) v ਪਵਿੱਤਰ ਥਾਂ ਤੇ ਰੱਖਣਾ, ਪਵਿੱਤਰ ਸਮਝ ਕੇ ਸੁਰੱਖਿਅਤ ਰੱਖਣਾ

enslave (ਇਨ'ਸਲੇਇਵ) v ਗ਼ੁਲਾਮ ਬਣਾਉਣਾ, ਵੱਸ ਵਿਚ ਕਰਨਾ; ~ment ਗ਼ੁਲਾਮੀ, ਦਾਸਤਾ

ensue (ਇਨ'ਸਯੂ) v ਸਿੱਟਾ ਨਿਕਲਣਾ, ਖੋਜ ਕਰਨਾ, ਪਿੱਛਾ ਕਰਨਾ, ਪਿੱਛੇ ਚੱਲਣਾ

ensuing (ਇਨ'ਸਯੂਇਙ) a ਆਗਾਮੀ, ਆਉਣ ਵਾਲਾ, ਉੱਤਰ-ਕਾਲੀਨ

entangle (ਇਨ'ਟੈਙਗਲ) v ਉਲਝਾਉਣਾ, ਫਸਾ ਲੈਣਾ, ਅੜਾਉਣਾ, ਹੈਰਾਨ ਪਰੇਸ਼ਾਨ ਕਰਨਾ; ~ment ਉਲਝੇਵਾਂ, ਝਮੇਲਾ, ਜੰਜਾਲ, ਅੜਿਚਣ

enter ('ਐਨਟਅ*) v ਵੜਨਾ, ਅੰਦਰ ਆਉਣਾ, ਦਾਖ਼ਲ ਹੋਣਾ, ਪ੍ਰਵੇਸ਼ ਕਰਨਾ, ਖੁਸ਼ਣਾ, ਦਰਜ ਕਰਨਾ; ਨਾਂ ਲਿਖਣਾ, ਦਾਖ਼ਲਾ ਕਰਨਾ, ਕਦਮ ਰੱਖਣਾ

enterprise ('ਐਨਟਅ*ਪਰਾਇਜ਼) n ਮੁਹਿੰਮ, ਔਖਾ ਕੰਮ, ਉਦਯੋਗ, ਉੱਦਮ, ਹਿੰਮਤ, ਹੌਂਸਲਾ

enterprising ('ਐਨਟਅ*ਪਰਾਇਜ਼ਿਙ) a ਉੱਦਮੀ, ਉਦਯੋਗੀ, ਮਨਚਲਾ, ਦਲੇਰ

entertain ('ਐਨਟਅ'ਟੇਇਨ) v ਚੱਲਣਾ ਜਾਰੀ ਰੱਖਣਾ; ਆਉ-ਭਗਤ ਕਰਨੀ, ਪਰਚਾਉਣਾ, ਧਾਰਨਾ; ~ing ਮਨੋਰੰਜਕ, ਦਿਲਚਸਪ, ਰੋਚਕ; ~ment ਖ਼ਾਤਰ ਆਉ-ਭਗਤ, ਦਿਲ-ਪਰਚਾਵਾ, ਮੌਜ-ਮੇਲਾ, ਮਨੋਰੰਜਨ

enthrone (ਇਨ'ਥਰਅਉਨ) v ਗੱਦੀ ਉੱਤੇ ਬਿਠਾਉਣਾ, ਤਖ਼ਤ ਤੇ ਬਿਠਾਉਣਾ

enthuse (ਇਨ'ਥਯੂਜ਼) v ਜੋਸ਼ ਦੁਆਉਣਾ; ਉਤਸਾਹਤ ਕਰਨਾ, ਉਮੰਗ ਪੈਦਾ ਕਰਨੀ, ਉਤਸ਼ਾਹਤ ਹੋਣਾ

enthusiasm (ਇਨ'ਥਯੂਜ਼ਿਐਜ਼(ਅ)ਮ) n ਜੋਸ਼, ਉਤਸਾਹ, ਸਰਗਰਮੀ, ਉਮਾਹ, ਉਮੰਗ, ਜਲਾਲ

enthusiast (ਇਨ'ਥਯੂਜ਼ਿਐਸਟ) n ਉਤਸਾਹੀ, ਉਤਸੁਕ, ਅਨੁਰਾਗੀ, ਜੋਸ਼ੀਲਾ (ਵਿਅਕਤੀ); ~ic, ~ical ਜੋਸ਼ੀਲਾ, ਉਤਸਾਹੀ, ਸਰਗਰਮ, ਪੁਰਜੋਸ਼, ਉਮੰਗੀ, ਅਨੁਰਾਗੀ

entice (ਇਨ'ਟਾਇਸ) v ਲੁਭਾਉਣਾ, ਭਰਮਾਉਣਾ, ਵਰਗਲਾਉਣਾ, ਬਹਿਕਾਉਣਾ, ਫਸਾਉਣਾ

entire (ਇਨ'ਟਾਇਅ*) a n ਸਾਰਾ, ਸਮੁੱਚਾ, ਸਾਬਤ, ਸਗਲ, ਸਮਗਰ, ਸਕਲ, ਸਮਸਤ, ਜਿਉਂ ਦਾ ਤਿਉਂ, ਸ਼ੁੱਧ

entitle ('ਐਨਟਾਇਟਲ) v ਸਿਰਲੇਖ ਦੇਣਾ, ਨਾਂ ਰੱਖਣਾ, ਖ਼ਿਤਾਬ ਦੇਣਾ, ਹਕ ਦੇਣਾ; ~d ਅਧਿਕਾਰੀ, ਹੱਕਦਾਰ, ਅਧਿਪਿਤ; ਸ਼ੀਰਸ਼ਕ

entity ('ਐਨਟਅਟਿ) n ਹੋਂਦ, ਹਸਤੀ, ਜ਼ਾਤ, ਅਸਤਿਤਵ; ਅਸਲੀਅਤ, ਮੌਜੂਦਗੀ, ਵਜੂਦ

entomology ('ਐਨਟਅ(ਉ)'ਮੌਲਅਜਿ) n ਕੀਟ-ਵਿਗਿਆਨ

entrance ('ਐਨਟਰ(ਅ)ਨਸ) n ਦਾਖ਼ਲਾ, ਪ੍ਰਵੇਸ਼, ਪ੍ਰਵੇਸ਼-ਦੁਆਰ

entrap (ਇਨ'ਟਰੈਪ) v ਜਾਲ ਵਿਚ ਫਸਾਉਣਾ, ਮੁਗਧ ਕਰਨਾ, ਖਿਚਣਾ, ਬਹਿਕਾਉਣਾ

entreat (ਇਨ'ਟਰੀਟ) v ਮਿੰਨਤ ਕਰਨੀ, ਹਾੜੇ ਕੱਢਣੇ, ਤਰਲਾ ਕਰਨਾ, ਵਾਸਤਾ ਪਾਉਣਾ, ਗਿੜਗਿੜਾਉਣਾ

entrench (ਇਨ'ਟਰੈਨੱਚ) v ਮੋਰਚਾ ਬੰਨ੍ਹਣਾ, ਪੈਰ ਜਮਾਉਣਾ, ਡਟ ਜਾਣਾ

entrepreneur ('ਐਨਟਰਅਪਰਅ'ਨਅ:*) n ਉੱਦਮਕਰਤਾ, ਉਦਯੋਗਪਤੀ, ਕਾਰਖ਼ਾਨੇਦਾਰ ~ship ਉੱਦਮ

entrust (ਇਨ'ਟਰਅੱਸਟ) v ਸਪੁਰਦ ਕਰਨਾ ਸੌਂਪਣਾ

entry ('ਐਨਟਰਿ) n ਦਾਖ਼ਲਾ, ਆਮਦ, ਰਸਾਈ ਪ੍ਰਵੇਸ਼, (ਕਾ) ਦਖ਼ਲ, ਕਬਜ਼ਾ, ਲਾਂਘਾ, ਪ੍ਰਵੇਸ਼ ਦੁਆਰ; ਇੰਦਰਾਜ

enumerate (ਇ'ਨਯੂਮਅਰੇਇਟ) v ਗਿਣਨਾ ਗਿਣਤੀ ਕਰਨੀ; ਨਿਰਦੇਸ਼ ਕਰਨਾ, ਵਿਵਰਨ ਦੇਣ

ਸ਼ੁਮਾਰ ਕਰਨਾ

enumeration (ਇ'ਨਯੂਮਅ'ਰੇਇਸ਼ਨ) *n* ਗਿਣਤੀ, ਗਣਨਾ, ਸ਼ੁਮਾਰ, ਨਿਰਦੇਸ਼ਨ

enunicate (ਇ'ਨਅੰਨਸਿਏਇਟ) *v* ਘੋਸ਼ਣਾ ਕਰਨੀ, ਐਲਾਨ ਕਰਨਾ, ਉਚਾਰਨ ਕਰਨਾ, ਉਚਾਰਨਾ

enunciation (ਇ'ਨਅੰਨਸਿ'ਏਇਸ਼ਨ) *n* ਕਥਨ, ਉਚਾਰਨ, ਵਰਣਨ, ਪ੍ਰਸਤੁਤੀਕਰਨ

envelop (ਇਨ'ਵੈਅਲਪ) *v* ਵਲ੍ਹੇਟਣਾ, ਵਿਹਣਾ, ਢਕਣਾ, ਕੱਜਣਾ, ਲਿਫ਼ਾਫ਼ੇ ਵਿਚ ਪਾਉਣਾ; ~ment ਵਿਤਾਰ, ਲਪੇਟ, ਘੇਰਾ, ਆਵੇਸ਼ਣ

envelope (ਐਨਵ੍ਅਲਅਉਪ) *n* ਲਿਫ਼ਾਫ਼ਾ, ਆਵਰਣ

enviable (ਐਨਵ੍ਇਅਬਲ) *a* ਰਸ਼ਕਯੋਗ, ਰੀਸਯੋਗ, ਈਰਖਾਯੋਗ

environment (ਇਨ'ਵ੍ਹਾਇਅਰ(ਅ)ਨਮੈਂਟ) *n* ਵਾਤਾਵਰਣ, ਚੁਗਿਰਦਾ, ਪਰਿਸਥਿਤੀ, ਵਾਯੂਮੰਡਲ, ਚੁਫੇਰਾ; ਦੁਆਲਾ, ਪਰਿਵੇਸ਼; ਮਾਹੌਲ; ~al ਵਾਤਾਵਰਣ ਸਬੰਧੀ, ਵਾਯੂਮੰਡਲ ਸਬੰਧੀ, ਪਰਿਸਥਿਤੀ ਸਬੰਧੀ

envisage (ਇਨ'ਵ੍ਹਿਜ਼ਿਜ਼) *v* ਸਾਮੂਣੇ ਹੋਣਾ ਰੁਬਰੁ ਹੋਣਾ; ਵਿਚਾਰ ਵਿਚ ਲਿਆਉਣਾ

envoy (ਐਨਵੌਇ) *n* ਕਾਸਦ, ਪ੍ਰਤੀਨਿਧ; ਏਲਚੀ, ਛੋਟਾ ਸਫ਼ੀਰ ਜਾਂ ਦੂਤ

envy (ਐਨਵ੍ਹਿ) *n v* ਸਾੜਾ, ਈਰਖਾ, ਈਰਖਾ ਕਰਨੀ, ਹਸਦ ਕਰਨਾ

enzyme (ਐਨਜ਼ਾਇਮ) *n* ਪਾਚਕ ਰਸ, ਰਸਾਇਣੀ ਖ਼ਮੀਰ

epic (ਐਪਿਕ) *n a* (ਕਾਵਿ) ਮਹਾਂਕਾਵਿਕ, ਬੀਰਕਾਵਿ, ਵੀਰ-ਗਾਥਾ; ~al ਮਹਾਂਕਾਵਿਕ, ਮਹਾਂਕਾਵਿ ਸਬੰਧੀ

epidemic (ਐਪਿ'ਡੈਮਿਕ) *n a* ਵਿਆਪਕ ਬੀਮਾਰੀ, ਮਹਾਂਮਾਰੀ, ਛੂਤ ਰੋਗ, ਸੰਚਾਰੀ

epilepsy ('ਐਪਿਲੈੱਪਸਿ) *n* ਮਿਰਗੀ, ਮੂਰਛਾ ਰੋਗ

epilogue ('ਐਪਿਲੌਗ) *n* ਉਪਸੰਹਾਰ, ਸਾਹਿਤ-ਰਚਨਾ ਦਾ ਅੰਤਮ ਭਾਗ

episode ('ਐਪਿਸਅਉਡ) *n* ਪ੍ਰਸੰਗ, ਉਪ-ਕਥਾ; ਕਥਾ-ਮਾਲਾ; ਸੰਜੋਗੀ ਘਟਨਾ

epitaph ('ਐਪਿਟਾਫ਼) *n* ਸਮਾਪੀ-ਲੇਖ, ਸਿਮਰਤੀ-ਲੇਖ, ਕਬਰ ਦਾ ਕਤਬਾ

epithet ('ਐਪਿਥੈੱਟ) *n* ਵਿਸ਼ੇਸ਼ਣ, ਉਪਾਧੀ, ਉਪਨਾਮ

epitome (ਇ'ਪਿਟਅਮਿ) *n* ਪੁਸਤਕ ਦਾ ਸਾਰ, ਖ਼ੁਲਾਸਾ, ਤੱਤ, ਅੰਸ਼ ਸਾਰਾਂਸ਼, ਨਿਚੋੜ

epitomize (ਇ'ਪਿਟਅਮਾਇਜ਼) *v* ਤੱਤ ਕੱਢਣਾ, ਸੰਖੇਪ ਕਰਨਾ, ਸਾਰ ਸੰਗ੍ਰਹ ਕਰਨਾ

epoch ('ਈਪੱਕ) *n* ਯੁੱਗ, ਕਾਲ, ਜ਼ਮਾਨਾ, ਦੌਰ

equal ('ਈਕਵ(ਅ)ਲ) *a n v* ਸਮ, ਤੁੱਲ, ਸਮਰੂਪ ਇਕਰੂਪ, ਸੰਤੁਲਤ, ਸਮਾਨ ਹੋਣਾ, ਬਰਾਬਰੀ ਕਰਨਾ, ਇਕੇ ਜਿਹਾ ਕਰਨਾ; ~ity ਬਰਾਬਰੀ, ਤੁੱਲਤਾ, ਸਮਾਨਤਾ, ਸਮਤਾ; ~ize ਬਰਾਬਰ ਕਰਨਾ, ਸਮੀਕਰਨ ਕਰਨਾ

equate (ਇ'ਕਵੇਇਟ) *v* ਬਰਾਬਰ ਕਰਨਾ, ਬਰਾਬਰੀ ਦੱਸਣੀ, ਸਮੀਕਰਨ ਕਰਨਾ, ਸਮੀਕ੍ਰਿਤ ਕਰਨਾ, ਤੁੱਲਤਾ ਦਿਖਾਉਣੀ, ਸਮਾਨ ਰੂਪ ਮੰਨਣਾ

equation (ਇ'ਕਵੇਇਸ਼ਨ) *n* ਸਮੀਕਰਨ, ਤੁੱਲਕਰਨ; ਸੰਤੁਲਨ, ਬਰਾਬਰੀ, (ਗਣਿ)

equator (ਇ'ਕਵੇਇਟਅ*) *n* ਭੂ-ਮੱਧ-ਰੇਖਾ

equilibrium ('ਈਕਵਿ'ਲਿਬਰਿਅਮ) *n* ਸਮਤੋਲ, ਸੰਤੁਲਨ, ਸੰਤੁਲਨ ਅਵਸਥਾ, ਤੁੱਲ ਭਾਰਤਾ

equip (ਇ'ਕਵਿਪ) *v* ਲੈਸ ਕਰਨਾ, ਸਾਜ਼ੋ-ਸਮਾਨ ਦਾ

ਪ੍ਰਬੰਧ ਕਰਨਾ, ਸੰਦਬੱਧ ਕਰਨਾ, ਸੁਆਰਨਾ, ਸਜਾਉਣਾ; ਤਿਆਰ ਕਰਨਾ, ਠੀਕ ਠਾਕ ਕਰਨਾ; ~**ped** ਸੁਸੱਜਤ, ਸਾਜ਼-ਸਾਮਾਨ ਨਾਲ ਲੈਸ; ~**ment** ਸਮਗਰੀ, ਸਾਜ਼ੋ-ਸਾਮਾਨ, ਬੋਰੀਆ-ਬਿਸਤਰਾ

equity ('ਐੱਕਵਅਟਿ) *n* ਨਿਆਂ, ਹੱਕ; ਨਿਰਪੱਖਤਾ; (ਕਾ) ਸੁਨੀਤੀ, ਉਹ ਹੁੰਡੀਆਂ ਜਾਂ ਸ਼ੇਅਰ ਜਿਨ੍ਹਾਂ ਤੇ ਨਿਸ਼ਚਤ ਸੂਦ ਨਹੀਂ ਮਿਲਦਾ

equivalence (ਇ'ਕਵਿਵ੍ਅਲਅੰਸ) *n* ਤੁੱਲਤਾ, ਸਮਾਨਤਾ, ਸਮਾਨਾਰਥਕਤਾ, ਸਮਫਲਤਵ, ਸਮੂਲਤਾ

equivalent (ਇ'ਕਵਿਵ੍ਅਲਅੰਟ) *n a* ਤੁੱਲਾ ਰਾਸ਼ੀ, ਪਰਯਾਯ, ਤੁੱਲਾਰਥ ਸ਼ਬਦ; ਸਮਾਨ ਸਮਮੁੱਲ, ਸਮਪ੍ਰਭਾਵੀ, ਤੁੱਲਾਰਥਕ, ਸਮਾਨਾਰਥਕ

era ('ਇਅਰਅ) *n* ਸਮਤ, ਸੰਨ, ਸਾਕਾ

eradicate (ਇ'ਰੈਡਿਕੇਇਟ) *v* ਜੜ੍ਹੋਂ ਉਘੇੜਨਾ ਨਸ਼ਟ ਕਰਨਾ, ਨਿਰਮੂਲ ਕਰਨਾ, ਕੱਢ ਦੇਣਾ, ਹਟਾ ਦੇਣਾ, ਉਜਾੜਨਾ

eradication (ਇ'ਰੈਡਿ'ਕੇਇਸ਼ਨ) *n* ਮਲੀਆਮੇਟ, ਸਫ਼ਾਈ, ਖ਼ਾਤਮਾ, ਸਤਿਆਨਾਸ

erase (ਇ'ਰੇਇਜ਼) *v* ਰਬੜ ਨਾਲ ਮਿਟਾਉਣਾ, ਖੁਰਚਣਾ, ਪੂੰਝਣਾ, ਮੇਸਣਾ; ~**r** ਰਬੜ (ਮਿਟਾਉਣ ਵਾਲੀ), ਖੁਰਚਣੀ

erect (ਇ'ਰੈੱਕਟ) *v a* ਸਿੱਧਾ ਕਰਨਾ, ਖੜ੍ਹਾ ਕਰਨਾ, ਉਠਾਉਣਾ, ਨਿਰਮਾਣ ਕਰਨਾ, ਖਲੋਤਾ, ਖੜ੍ਹਾ, ਰੋਮਾਂਚਤ; ~**ion** ਨਿਰਮਾਣ, ਉਠਾਨ, ਖੜਾ ਕਰਨ, ਰਚਨਾ, ਸੰਸਥਾਪਨ; ਇਮਾਰਤ

erode (ਇ'ਰਅਉਡ) *v* ਫਹਿਣਾ, ਖੋਰਨਾ, ਨਸ਼ਟ ਕਰਨਾ, ਹੌਲੀ ਹੌਲੀ ਖੈ ਕਰਨਾ, ਚੱਟ ਜਾਣਾ; ਖਾ ਜਾਣਾ

erosion (ਇ'ਰਅਉਯ਼ਨ) *n* ਢਾਹ, ਖੋਰ, ਕਾਟ, ਖੈ, ਖੈ ਕਰਨ

erotic (ਇ'ਰੌਟਿਕ) *n a* ਸ਼ਿੰਗਾਰ-ਕਾਵਿ, ਪਰੇਮ-ਕਾਵਿ; ਇਸ਼ਕੀਆ, ਸ਼ਿੰਗਾਰਾਤਮਕ; ਪਰੇਮਾਤਮਕ, ਕਾਮੁਕ, ਵਾਸ਼ਨਾ-ਪੂਰਨ

err (ਅ:*) *v* ਗ਼ਲਤੀ ਕਰਨੀ, ਭੁੱਲ ਕਰਨੀ; ਅਸ਼ੁੱਧ ਹੋਣਾ, ਭੁੱਲ ਹੋਣੀ; ~**ata** *pl* ਸ਼ੁੱਧੀ-ਪੱਤਰ ਅਸ਼ੁੱਧ ਲਿਖਤ, ਅਸ਼ੁੱਧੀ ਲਿਖਤ; ~**atic** ਅਨਿਸ਼ਚਤ, ਅਨਿਯਤ, ਡਾਵਾਂਡੋਲ, ਚੰਚਲ, ਬੇਕਾਇਦਾ, ਅਸਥਿਰ, ਕਮਹੀਣ; ~**oneous** ਅਸ਼ੁੱਧ, ਗ਼ਲਤ, ਭਰਾਂਤੀਪੂਰਨ ਤਰੁਟੀਪੂਰਨ, ਮਿਥਿਆ; ~**or** ਅਸ਼ੁੱਧੀ, ਗ਼ਲਤੀ, ਗ਼ਲਤ ਗੱਲ, ਭੁੱਲ; ਦੋਸ਼

erupt (ਇ'ਰਅੱਪਟ) *v* (ਮਸੂੜ੍ਹਿਆਂ ਵਿਚੋਂ ਲਹੂ ਦਾ) ਫੁੱਟ ਨਿਕਲਣਾ, (ਜੁਆਲਾਮੁਖੀ ਪਹਾੜ ਦੀ) ਫੁੱਟ ਪੈਣਾ; ~**ion** ਸਫੋਟ, ਵਿਸਫੋਟ, ਫੋੜਾ; ਨਿਕਾਸ

escalator ('ਐੱਸਕਅਲੇਇਟਅ*) *n* ਬਿਜਲਈ ਪੌੜੀ, ਟੁਰਦੀ ਪੌੜੀ

escape (ਇ'ਸਕੇਇਪ) *n v* ਪਲਾਇਨ, ਬਚਾਉ; ਛੁਟਕਾਰਾ; ਫਰਾਰ ਹੋਣਾ, ਭੱਜਣਾ; ਸਾਫ਼ ਬਚਣਾ

escapism (ਇ'ਸਕੇਇਪਿਜ਼(ਅ)ਮ) *n* ਪਲਾਇਨਵਾਦ, ਭਾਂਜਵਾਦ

escapist (ਇ'ਸਕੇਇਪਿਸਟ) *n* ਪਲਾਇਨਵਾਦੀ

eschew (ਇਸ'ਚੂ) *v* (ਤੋਂ) ਪਰਹੇਜ਼ ਕਰਨਾ, ਬਾਝ ਰਹਿਣਾ

escort ('ਐੱਸਕੋਟ, ਇ'ਸਕੋਟ) *n v* ਰੱਖਿਅਕ, ਰਖਵਾਲਾ, ਰਾਖੀ; ਪਹਿਰਾ; ਰੱਖਿਆ ਕਰਨੀ, ਅਗਵਾਈ ਕਰਨੀ

esoteric ('ਐੱਸਅ(ਉ)'ਟੈਰਿਕ) *a* ਗੂੜ੍ਹ, ਗੁਪਤ, ਬਾਤਨੀ

especial (ਇ'ਸਪੈੱਸ਼ਲ) *a* ਉੱਤਮ, ਪ੍ਰਮੁੱਖ; ਖ਼ਾਸ, ਵਿਸ਼ੇਸ਼

espionage ('ਐੱਸਪਿਅਨਾਯ਼) *n* (ਜਾਸੂਸਾਂ ਵਲੋਂ

ਕੀਤੀ), ਤੋੜ-ਫੋੜ

espousal (ਇ'ਸਪਉਜ਼ਲ) *n* ਹਿਮਾਇਤ, ਵਕਾਲਤ, ਵਿਆਹ, ਨਿਕਾਹ; ਮੰਗਣੀ

espy (ਇ'ਸਪਾਇ) *v* ਤਾੜਨਾ, ਪਤਾ ਲਗਾਉਣ, ਭੇਦ ਪਾਉਣਾ

esquire (ਇ'ਸਕਵਾਇਅ*) *n* ਨਾਂ ਦੇ ਸਨਮਾਨਾਰਥ ਪਦ, ਪਿੱਛੇ ਲਿਖਿਆ ਜਾਂਦਾ ਹੈ, ਸਰਦਾਰ ਜੀ ਸ੍ਰੀਮਾਨ ਆਦਿ

essay ('ਐੱਸੇਇ, ਐੱਸੇ) *n v* ਨਿਬੰਧ, ਸਾਹਿਤਕ ਰਚਨਾ ਜਾਂ ਲੇਖ, ਜਤਨ; ਪਰਖ, ਜਾਂਚ; ਪਰਖਣਾ, ਕਸਣਾ, ਕੋਸਸ ਕਰਨੀ; ~**ist** ਨਿਬੰਧਕਾਰ, ਨਿਪੰਧ ਲੇਖਕ

essence ('ਐੱਸਅੰਸ) *a n* ਸਾਰ, ਮੂਲ, ਮੂਲ ਪ੍ਰਕਿਰਤੀ, ਖ਼ਾਸੀਅਤ; ਤੱਤ, ਮੂਲ ਵਸਤੂ, ਮਹਿਕ, ਖ਼ੁਸ਼ਬੂ

essential (ਇ'ਸੈਂਸ਼ਲ) *a n* ਮੂਲ; ਅਵੱਸ਼ਕ, ਤਾਤਵਕ, ਸਾਰਭੂਤ, ਵਾਸਤਵਿਕ; ~**ly** ਜ਼ਰੂਰੀ ਹੀ, ਅਵੱਸ਼ਕ ਰੂਪ ਨਾਲ, ਯਥਾਰਥਕ ਰੂਪ ਨਾਲ

establish (ਇ'ਸਟੈਬਲਿਸ਼) *v* ਸਥਾਪਤ ਕਰਨਾ, ਜਮਾਉਣਾ, ਬਾਪਨਾ, ਬਿਠਾਉਣਾ, ਸਿੱਧ ਕਰਨਾ, ਸਾਬਤ ਕਰਨਾ, ਨੀਂਹ ਰੱਖਣੀ; ~**ed** ਸਥਾਪਤ, ਸਿੱਧ, ਪ੍ਰਮਾਣਤ, ਸਰਵਸੰਮਤ; ~**ment** ਸੰਸਥਾਪਨ, ਕਾਇਮੀ, ਚਾਕਰ ਮੰਡਲ, ਦਫ਼ਤਰ ਦਾ ਅਮਲਾ; ਵਪਾਰੀ ਫ਼ਰਮ, ਘਰ-ਬਾਰ, ਘਰ-ਗ੍ਰਹਿਸਥੀ

estate (ਇ'ਸਟੇਇਟ) *n* ਜਾਇਦਾਦ; ਇਲਾਕਾ, ਜਾਗੀਰ, ਸ਼ਾਸਕ ਵਰਗ, (ਪ੍ਰ) ਦਸ਼ਾ, ਹਾਲਤ, ਸੰਪਤੀ, ਜਾਗੀਰ, ਰਿਆਸਤ

esteem (ਇ'ਸਟੀਮ) *v n* ਆਦਰ ਮਾਨ ਕਰਨਾ, ਚੰਗਾ ਸਮਝਣਾ, ਖ਼ਿਆਲ ਕਰਨਾ; ਆਦਰ ਸਨਮਾਨ, ਮਾਣ

estimate ('ਐੱਸਟਿਮਅਟ, 'ਐੱਸਟਿਮੇਇਟ) *n v* ਅਨੁਮਾਨ (ਗਿਣਤੀ, ਮਿਕਦਾਰ, ਰਕਮ ਆਦਿ ਦਾ) ਤਖ਼ਮੀਨਾ, ਅੱਟਾ ਸੱਟਾ, ਅੰਦਾਜ਼ਾ ਲਾਉਣਾ, ਅਨੁਮਾਨ ਲਾਉਣਾ

estimation ('ਐੱਸਟਿ'ਮੇਇਸ਼ਨ) *n* ਪਰਿਮਾਪ, ਮੁੱਲਾਂਕਣ, ਅਨੁਮਾਨ, ਅਟਕਲ ਮੱਤ, ਮੂਲ ਨਿਰੂਪਣ

estrange (ਇ'ਸਟਰੇਇੰਜ) *v* ਰੁਸਾਉਣਾ, ਨਾਰਾਜ਼ ਕਰਨਾ, ਚਿੱਤ ਹਟਾਉਣਾ, ਬੇਮੁਖ ਕਰਨਾ

eternal (ਇ'ਟਅ:ਨਲ) *a* ਅਮਰ, ਸਨਾਤਨ, ਨਿੱਤ, ਨਿਰੰਤਰ

eternity (ਇ'ਟਅ:ਨਅਟਿ) *n* ਸਦੀਵਤਾ, ਅਨੰਤਤਾ, ਅਸਿੰਟ ਸਚਾਈ

ether ('ਇਥਅ*) *n* ਆਕਾਸ਼, ਆਕਾਸ਼ ਤੋਂ ਪਰ੍ਹੇ ਆਕਾਸ਼, ਬੇਹੋਸ਼ ਕਰ ਦੇਣ ਵਾਲੀ ਦਵਾਈ; ਇਕ ਰਸਾਇਣਕ ਪਦਾਰਥ

ethic, ethics ('ਐੱਥਿਕ, 'ਐੱਥਿਕਸ) *n* ਨੀਤੀ ਵਿਗਿਆਨ; ਨੈਤਕਤਾ, ਨੈਤਕਨਿਯਮ; ਸਦਾਚਾਰ; ~**al** ਨੈਤਕ, ਨੀਤੀ-ਸ਼ਾਸਤਰੀ; ਆਚਾਰਕ

ethnic ('ਐੱਥਨਿਕ) *a* ਜਾਤੀ, ਨਸਲੀ; ਨਾਸਤਕ

etiquette ('ਐੱਟਿਕੈੱਟ) *n* ਸ਼ਿਸ਼ਟਾਚਾਰ, ਲੋਕਾਚਾਰ, ਸੁਚੱਜ, ਸੱਭਿਆਚਾਰ, ਵਿਧੀ; ਅਦਬੋ-ਆਦਬ; ਦਰਬਾਰੀ ਅਦੋ ਆਦਾਬ, ਤਕੱਲਫ਼

eulogize ('ਯੂਲਅਜਾਇਜ਼) *n* ਉਸਤਤੀ ਕਰਨੀ, ਜਸ ਗਾਉਣਾ, ਕੀਰਤੀ ਕਰਨੀ

eulogy ('ਯੂਲਅਜਿ) *n* ਉਸਤਤੀ, ਪ੍ਰਸੰਸਾ, ਵਡਿਆਈ; ਕਸੀਦਾ, ਕੀਰਤੀ, ਸਲਾਹੁਤਾ

eunuch ('ਯੂਨਅਕ) *n* ਹੀਜੜਾ, ਖ਼ੁਸਰਾ, ਜਟਖਾ; ਨਾਮਰਦ

euphony ('ਯੂਫ਼ਅਨਿ) *n* ਮਧੁਰ ਧੁਨ, ਸੁਰਸੋਤਾ, ਸੁਰੀਲਾਪਨ, ਸੁਸ਼ਬਦ

evacuate (ਇ'ਵੈਕਯੁਏਇਟ) *v* ਕੱਢਣਾ, ਖ਼ਾਲੀ

evacution | 474 | exact

ਕਰਨਾ; ਛੱਡ ਦੇਣਾ, ਪਰ੍ਹੇ ਲਿਜਾਣਾ, ਪਰਿਤਿਆਗ ਕਰਨਾ, ਹਟਾਉਣਾ; ਵਿਰੇਚਨ ਕਰਨਾ

evacution (ਇ'ਵੈਕਯੂ'ਏਇਸ਼ਨ) *n* ਨਿਕਾਸ, ਤਿਆਗ, ਮਲ ਤਿਆਗ

evade (ਇ'ਵੇਇਡ) *v* ਟਾਲ ਜਾਣਾ, ਬਚ ਜਾਣਾ, ਟਾਲਮਟੋਲ ਕਰਨਾ, ਭੱਜਣਾ, ਖਿਸਕਣਾ

evaluation (ਇ'ਵੈਲਯੂ'ਏਇਸ਼ਨ) *n* ਮੁੱਲ-ਨਿਰਧਾਰਨ

evaporate (ਇ'ਵੈਪਅਰੇਇਟ) *v* ਭਾਫ਼ ਬਣਨਾ, ਭਾਫ਼ ਬਣਾਉਣਾ, ਲੋਪ ਹੋ ਜਾਣਾ, ਨਮੀਂ ਜਾਂ ਤਰੀ ਕੱਢ ਦੇਣੀ

evoporation (ਇ'ਵੈਪਅ'ਰੇਇਸ਼ਨ) *n* ਵਾਸ਼ਪਨ, ਵਾਸ਼ਪੀਕਰਨ, ਭਾਫਣ; ਭਾਫ਼

evasion (ਇ'ਵੇਇਯ਼ਨ) *a* ਟਾਲਮਟੋਲ, ਬਹਾਨਾ, ਬੂਤਾ

evasive (ਇ'ਵੇਇਸਿਵ) *a* ਛਲੀ, ਕਪਟੀ, ਟਾਲੂ

Eve (ਈਵ) *n* (1) ਹੱਵਾ, ਆਦਿ ਨਾਰੀ; (e~) (2) ਔਰਤ; (3) ਪੁਰਬ, ਦਿਵਸ, ਘਟਨਾ ਵਿਸ਼ੇਸ਼; ਸੰਧਿਆ; ਪੁਰਬ-ਸੰਧਿਆ

even ('ਈਵਨ) *adv* ਇਕ ਰਸ, ਸਮਤਲ, ਸਮ, ਬਰਾਬਰ, ਬਿਨਾ ਰਿਆਇਤ; ਸ਼ਾਂਤ; ਜੋੜਾ, ਯੁਗਮ, ਜੁਫ਼ਤ; ਭੀ, ਵੀ, ਤਕ, ਇਥੋਂ ਤਕ ਕਿ

evening ('ਈਵਨਿੰਢ) *n* ਸੰਝ, ਸੰਧਿਆ, ਸ਼ਾਮ

event (ਇ'ਵੈਂਟ) *n* ਘਟਨਾ, ਵਾਰਦਾਤ, ਮਹੱਤਵਪੂਰਨ ਵਾਕਿਆ

eventual (ਇ'ਵੈਨੰਚੁਅਲ) *a* ਅੰਤਮ, ਆਖ਼ਰੀ, ਸੰਭਾਵਤ; **~ity** ਸੰਭਾਵਨਾ, ਸੰਭਵ ਘਟਨਾ; **~ly** ਆਖ਼ਰਕਾਰ, ਅੰਤ ਵਿਚ

ever ('ਐੱਵਅ*) *adv* ਨਿੱਤ, ਨਿਰੰਤਰ; ਸਦਾ ਸਦੀਵੀ, ਲਗਾਤਾਰ, ਕਦੇ, ਕਿਸੇ ਵੇਲੇ, ਹਰ ਵੇਲੇ; **~after** ਉਦੋਂ ਤੋਂ, ਉਦੋਂ ਲੈ ਕੇ; **~green** ਸਦਾ-ਬਹਾਰ, ਬਾਰਾ ਮਾਸੀ; **~lasting** ਨਿੱਤਤਾ, ਸਥਾਈ, ਨਿੱਤ, ਅੰਨਤ, ਅਜਰ, ਚਿਰਸਥਾਈ; **for~** ਸਦਾ ਲਈ

every ('ਐੱਵਰਿ) *a* ਹਰ, ਹਰ ਇਕ, ਪ੍ਰਤੀ, ਪ੍ਰਤੀ ਇਕ, ਇਕ ਇਕ

evict (ਇ'ਵਿਕਟ) *v* (ਮਜ਼ਾਰੇ ਨੂੰ) ਬੇਦਖ਼ਲ ਕਰਨਾ, ਕੱਢ ਦੇਣਾ; **~ion** ਬੇਦਖ਼ਲੀ

evidence ('ਐੱਵਿਡਅੰਸ) *a* ਸਪਸ਼ਟਤਾ; ਸੰਕੇਤ, ਪਰਮਾਣ, ਗਵਾਹੀ, ਸ਼ਹਾਦਤ, ਸਬੂਤ; ਪਰਮਾਣਤ ਕਰਨਾ, ਪਰਗਟ ਕਰਨਾ, ਸਾਬਤ ਕਰਨਾ, ਸ਼ਹਾਦਤ ਦੇਣਾ

evident ('ਐੱਵਿਡਅੰਟ) *a* ਪ੍ਰਤੱਖ ਜ਼ਾਹਰ, ਖੁੱਲ੍ਹਾ, ਸਪਸ਼ਟ

evil ('ਇਵਲ) *a n* ਬੁਰਾ, ਮੰਦਾ, ਮਨਹੂਸ, ਨਕਾਰਾ, ਹਾਨੀਕਾਰਕ, ਬਦੀ, ਗੁਨਾਹ, ਬੁਰਾਈ; **~doer** ਬਦਕਾਰ, ਦੁਸ਼ਟ

evocation ('ਐੱਵਅ(ਉ)'ਕੇਇਸ਼ਨ) *n* ਜਜ਼ਬਾਤ ਦਾ ਉਭਾਰ, ਸੱਦਾ, ਪੁਕਾਰ

evocative, evocatory (ਇ'ਵੌਕਅਟਿਵ ਇ'ਵੌਕਅਟਰਿ) *a* ਭਾਵਨਾਮਈ, ਭਾਵਨਾਉਪਜਾਇਕ

evoke (ਇਵ਼ਅਉਕ) *v* ਬੁਲਾਉਣਾ, ਸੱਦਣਾ, (ਜਜ਼ਬਾਤ) ਉਭਾਰਨਾ, ਵੱਡੀ ਅਦਾਲਤ ਵਿਚ ਤਲਬ ਕਰਨਾ, ਚੇਤਨ ਕਰਨਾ, ਜਗਾਉਣਾ

evolution ('ਈਵਅ'ਲੂਸ਼ਨ) *n* ਵਿਕਾਸ, ਚਾਲ

evolve (ਇ'ਵੌਲਵ) *v* ਉਤਪੰਨ ਕਰਨਾ; ਫੈਲਾਉਣਾ, ਫੈਲਣਾ, ਤਰਤੀਬ ਦੇਣਾ; (ਗਰਮੀ ਦਾ) ਖ਼ਾਰਜ ਕਰਨਾ; ਵਿਕਾਸ ਕਰਨਾ, ਪੁਸ਼ਟੀ ਹੋਣੀ, ਵਧਾਉਣਾ, ਵੱਧਣਾ

exact (ਇਗ'ਜ਼ੈਕਟ) *a v* ਠੀਕ, ਸਹੀ, ਜਚਵਾਂ, ਢੁਕਵਾਂ, ਸੁਨਿਸ਼ਚਿਤ; ਕਠੋਰ, ਤਕਾਜ਼ਾ ਕਰਨਾ,

exaggerate ਜ਼ੋਰ ਪਾਉਣਾ; ~ly ਐਨ, ਬਰਾਬਰ, ਠੀਕ ਵਕਤ, ਉੱਤੇ, ਦਰੁਸਤ

exaggerate (ਇਗ'ਜ਼ੈਜਅਰੇਇਟ) v ਅੱਤਕਥਨੀ ਕਰਨੀ, ਵਧਾ ਚੜ੍ਹਾ ਕੇ ਦੱਸਣਾ, ਮਿਰਚ ਮਸਾਲਾ ਲਾ ਕੇ ਦੱਸਣਾ

exaggeration (ਇਗ'ਜ਼ੈਜਅ'ਰੇਇਸ਼ਨ) n ਅੱਤਕਥਨੀ, ਮੁਬਾਲਗਾ, ਵਾਕ-ਵਿਸਤਾਰ

exalt (ਇਗਾ'ਜ਼ੋਲਟ) v ਵਧਾਉਣਾ, ਉਚਿਆਉਣਾ, ਉੱਚਾ ਕਰਨਾ, ਵਡਿਆਈ ਕਰਨੀ; ਉਸਤਤੀ ਕਰਨੀ; ~ation ਉਚਾਣ, ਉੱਚਪਦ, ਉੱਨਤੀ, ਉਨ੍ਹਤਾ, ਪੁਲਕਿਤੀ, ਆਨੰਦ, ਉੱਲਾਸ, ਉਮੰਗ; ਤੀਬਰਤਾ

examination (ਇਗ'ਜ਼ੈਮਿ'ਨੇਇਸ਼ਨ) n ਪਰੀਖਿਆ, ਇਮਤਿਹਾਨ, ਪਰਖ; ਨਿਰੀਖਣ; ਮੁਆਇਨਾ, ਜਾਂਚ-ਪੜਤਾਲ

examine (ਇਗਾ'ਜ਼ੈਮਿਨ) n ਪੜਤਾਲਣਾ, ਪਰੀਖਿਆ ਲੈਣੀ, ਜਾਂਚ ਕਰਨੀ, ਪਰਖਣਾ; ਪੜਤਾਲ ਕਰਨੀ; ਛਾਣਬੀਣ ਕਰਨੀ; ਜਾਂਚ ਕਰਨੀ, ਪੁੱਛ-ਗਿੱਛ ਕਰਨੀ; ~e ਪਰੀਖਿਆਰਥੀ; ~r ਪਰੀਖਿਅਕ, ਪੜਤਾਲੀਆ

example (ਇਗਾ'ਜ਼ਾਂਪਲ) n ਦ੍ਰਿਸ਼ਟਾਂਤ, ਉਦਾਹਰਨ, ਮਿਸਾਲ; ਨਮੂਨਾ

exasperate (ਇਗਾ'ਜ਼ੈਸਪਅਰੇਇਟ) v ਖਿਝਾਉਣਾ, ਉਤੇਜਤ ਕਰਨਾ, ਕਰੋਧ ਦੁਆਉਣਾ, ਚਿੜਾਉਣਾ, ਅੱਗ ਬਗੋਲਾ ਕਰਨਾ

excavate ('ਔਕਸਕਅਵੇਇਟ) v ਖੋਦਣਾ, ਪੁੱਟਣਾ, ਖੁੰਦਣਾ; ਖ਼ਾਲੀ ਕਰਨਾ; ਪੋਲਾ ਕਰਨਾ, ਥੋਥਾ ਕਰਨਾ

exceed (ਇਕ'ਸੀਡ) v ਵਧ ਜਾਣਾ, ਅੱਗੇ ਨਿਕਲ ਜਾਣਾ, ਅੰਤ ਕਰਨੀ, ਹੱਦ ਟੱਪਣੀ, ਮਾਤ ਕਰਨਾ, ਉਲੰਘਣਾ; ~ingly ਅਤੀ ਅਧਿਕ; ਬਹੁਤ, ਬੇਹੱਦ, ਬਹੁਤ ਹੀ

excellence (ਇਕ'ਸੈੱਲਇੰਸ) v ਅੱਗੇ ਨਿਕਲ ਜਾਣਾ, ਵਧ ਜਾਣਾ, ਬਾਜ਼ੀ ਲੈ ਜਾਣਾ, ਮਾਤ ਕਰਨਾ

excellent (ਇਕ'ਸੈੱਲਇੰਟ) a ਉਤਕ੍ਰਿਸ਼ਟ, ਪਰਮ, ਸ਼੍ਰੇਸ਼ਠ, ਉੱਤਮ, ਮਹੱਤਵ-ਪੂਰਨ, ਪ੍ਰਤਿਸ਼ਠਤ

except (ਇਕਸੈੱਪਟ) v perp ਛੱਡਣਾ, ਗਿਣਤੀ ਵਿਚ ਨਾ ਲਿਆਉਣਾ, ਆਪੱਤੀ ਕਰਨੀ, ਇਤਰਾਜ਼ ਕਰਨਾ, ਕੱਢਣਾ; ਪਰੰਤੂ; ~ion ਵਰਜਨ, ਵਿਵਰਜਨ, ਛੋਟ, ਤਿਆਗ; ~ional ਅਸਧਾਰਨ, ਅਨੋਖਾ

excerpt ('ਐਕਸਅਪਟ, ਇਕ'ਸਅਪਟ) n v ਪੁਸਤਕ ਵਿਚੋਂ ਹਵਾਲਾ, ਟੁਕ, ਪੁਸਤਕ, ਸੰਕਲਨ; ਚੋਟ, ਖ਼ੁਲਾਸਾ ਕਰਨਾ, ਚੋਟ ਕਰਨਾ

excess (ਇਕ'ਸੈੱਸ) n a ਅੱਤਿਆਚਾਰ; ਵਧੀਕੀ, ਵਾਧਾ, ਅਧਿਕਤਾ, ਬਹੁਤਾਤ; ~ive ਅਤੀ, ਅਤੀਅੰਤ, ਬੇਹਿਸਾਬ, ਬੇਸ਼ੁਮਾਰ

exchange (ਇਕਸ'ਚੇਇੰਜ) n v (1) ਤਬਾਦਲਾ ਵਟਾਂਦਰਾ, ਸਿੱਕੇ ਦਾ ਵਟਾਂਦਰਾ, ਹੁੰਡੀ ਦੁਆਰਾ ਲੈਣ-ਦੇਣ, ਆਦਾਨਪ੍ਰਦਾਨ; (2) ਕੇਂਦਰ; ਵਟਾਂਦਰਾ ਕਰਨਾ, ਬਦਲਣਾ, ਲੈਣ ਦੇਣ ਕਰਨਾ, ਨਿਗਾਹਾਂ ਮਿਲਾਉਣੀਆਂ

exchequer (ਇਕਸ'ਚੈੱਕਅ*) n ਰਾਜ-ਕੋਸ਼, ਗਰਜਾਰੀ ਖ਼ਜ਼ਾਨਾ, ਮਹਿਕਮਾ ਮਾਲ, ਵਿੱਤ-ਵਿਭਾਗ

excise ('ਔਕਸਾਇਜ਼, ਔਕ'ਸਾਇਜ਼) v ਉਤਪਾਦਨ ਕਰ, ਚੁੰਗੀ, ਸਰਕਾਰੀ ਮਹਿਸੂਲ, ਆਬਕਾਰੀ; ਚੁੰਗੀ ਲੈਣਾ, ਮਹਿਸੂਲ ਲੈਣਾ; ਕੱਟ ਦੇਣਾ, ਉੱਡਾ ਦੇਣਾ

excite (ਇਕ'ਸਾਇਟ) v ਉਕਸਾਉਣਾ, ਉਭਾਰਨਾ, ਗਰਮਾਉਣਾ, ਟੁੰਬਣਾ; ਭੜਕ ਪੈਣਾ, ਗਰਮ ਹੋ ਜਾਣਾ; ~ment ਜੋਸ਼, ਖਲਬਲੀ ਉਤੇਜਨਾ, ਆਵੇਸ਼, ਸਨਸਨੀ

exciting (ਇਕ'ਸਾਇਟਿੰਡ) a ਭੜਕਾਉਣ ਵਾਲਾ, ਉਕਸਾਉਣ ਵਾਲਾ, ਉਤੇਜਕ

exclaim (ਇਕ'ਸਕਲੇਇਮ) v ਪੁਕਾਰ ਉੱਠਣਾ, ਚੀਕ ਉਠਣਾ, ਦੁਹਾਈ ਪਾਉਣਾ

exclamation ('ਐੱਕਸਕਲਅ'ਮੇਇਸ਼ਨ) n ਪੁਕਾਰ, ਦੁਹਾਈ, ਹਾਏ ਹਾਏ; ਵਿਸਮਕ ਚਿੰਨ੍ਹ

exclamatory (ਐੱਕ'ਸਕਲੈਮਅਟ(ਅ)ਰਿ) a ਅਸਚਰਜ-ਜਨਕ, ਵਿਸਮੈ-ਜਨਕ

exclude (ਇਕ'ਸਕਲੂਡ) v ਬਾਹਰ ਰੱਖਣਾ, ਪਰੇ ਰੱਖਣਾ, ਕੱਢ ਦੇਣਾ; ਛੱਡ ਦੇਣਾ; ਰੋਕਣਾ

excluding (ਇਕ'ਸਕਲੂਡਿਙ) n ਬਿਨਾ, ਤੋਂ ਰਹਿਤ, ਨੂੰ ਛੱਡ ਕੇ

exclusion (ਇਕ'ਸਕਲੂਯ਼ਨ) n ਵਰਜਨ, ਅਲਹਿਦਗੀ

exclusive (ਇਕ'ਸਕਲੂਸਿਵ਼) a ਨਿਵੇਕਲਾ; ਰਾਖਵਾਂ; ਵੱਖਰਾ

excreta (ਇਕ'ਸਕਰੀਟਅ) n pl ਵਿਸ਼ਟਾ, ਗੋਹਾ, ਮਲ-ਮੂਤਰ, ਟੱਟੀ

excrete (ਇਕ'ਸਕਰੀਟ) v ਵਿਸ਼ਟਾ, ਗੋਹਾ, ਸੈਲਾ ਆਦਿ ਤਿਆਗਣਾ, ਟੱਟੀ ਕਰਨਾ, ਹੱਗਣਾ

excretion (ਇਕ'ਸਕਰੀਸ਼ਨ) n ਮਲ-ਮੂਤਰ

excurse (ਇਕ'ਸਕਅਃਸ) v ਮਟਰ-ਗਸ਼ਤ ਕਰਨੀ, ਘੁੰਮਣਾ, ਸੈਰ-ਸਪਾਟਾ ਕਰਨਾ

excursion (ਇਕ'ਸਕਅਃਸ਼ਨ) n ਸਫ਼ਰ; ਸੈਰ-ਸਪਾਟਾ, ਹਵਾਖੋਰੀ, ਮਟਰ-ਗਸ਼ਤ, ਭ੍ਰਮਣ

excursive (ਇਕ'ਸਕਅਃਸਿਵ਼) a ਭ੍ਰਮਣਸ਼ੀਲ, ਸੈਲਾਨੀ

excuse (ਇਕ'ਸਕਯੂਸ) n v ਦੋਸ਼-ਮੁਕਤੀ, ਖਿਮਾ, ਬਹਾਨਾ; ਖਿਮਾ ਕਰਨਾ, ਉਜ਼ਰ ਕਰਨਾ, ਖਿਮਾ ਮੰਗਣੀ

execrate (ਐੱਕਸਿਕਰੇਇਟ) v ਅਤੀਅੰਤ ਘਿਰਣਾ ਕਰਨਾ, ਸਰਾਪ ਦੇਣਾ, ਸਰਾਪਣਾ, ਕੋਸਣਾ, ਲਾਨ੍ਹਤ ਪਾਉਣਾ

execration (ਐੱਕਸਿ'ਕਰੇਇਸ਼ਨ) n ਘਿਰਣਾ, ਨਫ਼ਰਤ, ਲਾਨ੍ਹਤ, ਦੁਰਾਸੀਸ, ਸਰਾਪ

execute (ਐੱਕਸਿਕਯੂਟ) v ਲਾਗੂ ਕਰਨਾ; ਪਾਲਣਾ ਕਰਨੀ, ਅਮਲ ਕਰਨਾ; ਬਜਾ ਲਿਆਉਣਾ; ਲਿਖ ਦੇਣਾ, ਸਹੀ ਪਾਉਣੀ; ਜਾਇਦਾਦ ਜਾਂ ਮੁਲਕ ਦੇ ਦੇਣਾ; ਕਰਤੱਵ ਪਾਲਣਾ, ਫਾਂਸੀ ਦੇਣਾ, (ਸੰਗੀ) ਵਜਾਉਣਾ

execution (ਐੱਕਸਿ'ਕਯੂਸ਼ਨ) n ਪਾਲਣ, ਮੂਰਤੀ, ਤਾਮੀਲ; ਨਿਬਾ, ਚੁਸਤੀ, ਹੁਸ਼ਿਆਰੀ, ਜਬਤ; ਪ੍ਰਾਣ-ਦੰਡ, ਸੂਲੀ, ਫਾਂਸੀ

executive (ਇਗ'ਜ਼ੈੱਕਯੂਟਿਵ਼) a n· ਪ੍ਰਬੰਧਕ, ਪ੍ਰਬੰਧ-ਅਧਿਕਾਰੀ

exegesis (ਐੱਕਸਿ'ਜੀਸਿਸ) n ਵਿਆਖਿਆ, ਟੀਕਾ; ਭਾਸ਼

exemplify (ਇਗ'ਜ਼ੈੱਮਪਲਿਫ਼ਾਇ) v ਦਿਸ਼ਟਾਂਤ ਦੁਆਰਾ, ਮਿਸਾਲ ਦੇਣਾ, ਮਿਸਾਲ ਬਣਨਾ,

exempt (ਇਗ'ਜ਼ੈੱਂਪਟ) a n v ਮੁਕਤ, ਰਿਹਾ, ਛੱਡਿਆ ਹੋਇਆ; ਮੁਕਤ ਕਰਨਾ, ਛੱਡ ਦੇਣਾ

exercise (ਐੱਕਸਅਃਸਾਇਸ) n v ਪ੍ਰਯੋਗ; ਅਭਿਆਸ, ਮਸ਼ਕ, ਕਸਰਤ; ਪ੍ਰਸ਼ਨਮਾਲਾ, ਪੂਜਾ-ਪਾਠ, ਪ੍ਰਯੋਗ ਕਰਨਾ; ਅਭਿਆਸ ਕਰਨਾ; ਸੇਵਨ ਕਰਨਾ, ਕਸਰਤ ਕਰਨੀ; ਸਿੱਖਿਆ ਦੇਣੀ; ਵਰਤੋਂ ਕਰਨੀ

exert (ਇਗ'ਜ਼ਅਃਟ) v ਜ਼ੋਰ ਮਾਰਨਾ; ਕੰਮ ਲੈਣਾ, ਪ੍ਰਯਤਨ ਕਰਨਾ, ਚੇਸ਼ਟਾ ਕਰਨੀ, ਪ੍ਰਯਾਸ ਕਰਨਾ; ~ion ਪ੍ਰਯਤਨ, ਜਤਨ, ਪਰਿਸ਼ਰਮ, ਉਦੱਮ, ਕੋਸ਼ਸ਼, ਸਰਗਰਮੀ

exgratia (ਐੱਕਸ'ਗਰੇਇਸ਼ਅ) (L) (phr) ਬਖ਼ਸ਼ਸ਼ ਵਜੋਂ

exhale (ਐੱਕਸ'ਹੇਇਲ) v (ਧੂੰਆਂ ਜਾਂ ਹਵਾ) ਬਾਹਰ ਕੱਢਣਾ, ਸਾਹ ਬਾਹਰ ਕੱਢਣਾ, ਹੌਲੀ ਹੌਲੀ

ਬੋਲਣਾ, ਪ੍ਰਾਣ ਤਿਆਗਣੇ

exhaust (ਇਗਜ਼ੋਸਟ) *v n* ਸੋਖਤਾ ਕਰਨਾ; ਖ਼ਰਚ ਕਰ ਦੇਣਾ, ਸਿਲੰਡਰ ਵਿਚੋਂ ਭਾਫ਼ ਦਾ ਨਿਕਲਣਾ; ~**ion** ਸਖਣਾਪਣ, ਨਿਕਾਸ; ਖੀਣਤਾ, ਥਕਾਵਟ

exhibit (ਇਗਜ਼ਿਬਿਟ) *v* ਵਿਖਾਉਣਾ, ਪਰਗਟ ਕਰਨਾ, ਪੇਸ਼ ਕਰਨਾ, ਨੁਮਾਇਸ਼ ਕਰਨੀ; ਉਜਾਗਰ ਕਰਨਾ; ~**ion** ਪਰਦਰਸ਼ਨ, ਪ੍ਰਤੱਖ, ਨਿਰੂਪਣ, ਪਰਦਰਸ਼ਨੀ, ਨੁਮਾਇਸ਼; ~**ive** ਵਿਸਤਰਤ, ਵਿਆਪਕ, ਪੂਰਨ, ਸਰਵਾਂਗੀਨ

exhilarate (ਇਗਜ਼ਿਲਅਰੇਇਟ) *v* ਆਨੰਦ ਕਰਨਾ, ਹੁਲਸਾਉਣਾ, ਮਗਨ ਕਰਨਾ, ਖ਼ੁਸ਼ ਕਰਨਾ

exhilaration (ਇਗਜ਼ਿਲਅ'ਰੇਇਸ਼ਨ) *n* ਪ੍ਰਫੁਲਤਾ, ਆਹਲਾਦ, ਉਲੱਾਸ, ਖੇੜਾ, ਆਨੰਦ

exigence, exigency (ਐਕਸਿਜਅੰਸ, ਐਕਸਿਜਅੰਸਿ) *n* ਸਖ਼ਤ ਲੋੜ; ਮੁਤਾਲਬਾ; ਫੌਰੀ ਲੋੜ, ਐਕੜ

exile (ਐਕ'ਸਾਇਲ) *n v* ਦੇਸ਼-ਨਿਕਾਲਾ, ਪਰਵਾਸ, ਜਲਾਵਤਨੀ, ਬਨਵਾਸੀ ਬਨਵਾਸ, ਜਲਾਵਤਨ (ਮਨੁੱਖ); ਦੇਸ਼ ਨਿਕਾਲਾ ਦੇਣਾ, ਜਲਾਵਤਨ ਕਰਨਾ; ਜਲਾਵਤਨ

exist (ਇਗਜ਼ਿਸਟ) *v* ਹੋਣਾ, ਮੌਜੂਦ ਹੋਣਾ, ਰਹਿਣਾ, ਅਸਤਿਤਵ ਰੱਖਣਾ, ਘਟਤ ਹੋਣਾ; ~**ence** ਹੋਂਦ, ਮੌਜੂਦਗੀ; ਹਸਤੀ, ਪੈਦਾਇਸ਼, ਅਸਤਿਤਵ, ਪ੍ਰਾਣ, ਜੀਵ; ~**ent** ਵਿੱਦਮਾਨ, ਵਰਤਮਾਨ, ਵਾਸਤਵਿਕ, ਜੀਵਤ, ਪ੍ਰਚਲਤ

exit (ਐਕਸਿਟ) *n* ਪ੍ਰਸਥਾਨ; ਕੂਚ; ਵਿਦਾ, ਨਿਕਾਸ, ਬਾਹਰ ਜਾਣ ਦਾ ਰਸਤਾ

exodus (ਐਕਸਅਡਅਸ) *n* ਨਿਕਾਸ, ਕੂਚ, ਪਰਦੇਸ-ਜਾਣ, ਹਿਜਰਤ

ex-officio (ਐਕਸਅ'ਫ਼ਿਸ਼ਿਅਉ) (*L*) *a* ਅਹੁਦੇ ਦੇ ਨਾਤੇ, ਪਦ ਅਨੁਸਾਰ

exonerate (ਇਗਜ਼ੋਨਅਰੇਇਟ) *v* ਭਾਰ ਮੁਕਤ ਕਰਨਾ, ਨਿਵਿਰਤ ਕਰਨਾ, ਭਾਰ ਲਾਹੁਣਾ; ਨਿਰਦੋਸ਼ ਠਹਿਰਾਉਣਾ; (ਸੇਵਾ ਤੋਂ) ਛੁੱਟੀ ਦੇਣੀ

exorbitant (ਇਗਜ਼ੋ*ਬਿਟਅੰਟ) *a* ਬੇਜਾ, ਅਨੁਚਿਤ, ਅਤੀਅੰਤ

exotic (ਇਗਜ਼ੋਟਿਕ) *a* ਬਿਦੇਸ਼ੀ; ਵਚਿੱਤਰ

expand (ਇਕ'ਸਪੈਂਡ) *v* ਚਾਰੇ ਪਾਸੇ ਫੈਲਣਾ, ਵਿਆਖਿਆ ਕਰਨੀ, ਵਧਣਾ, ਵਧਾਉਣਾ, ਫੁਲਾਉਣਾ, ਪਸਾਰਨਾ

expansion (ਐਕ'ਸਪੈਨਸ਼ਨ) *n* ਫੈਲਾਉ; ਕਾਰੋਬਾਰ ਦਾ ਫੈਲਾਉ; ਵਿਸਤਾਰ ਪ੍ਰਚਾਰ, ਵਿਆਪਤੀ

expatiate (ਐਕ'ਸਪੇਇਸ਼ਿਏਇਟ) *v* (ਕਿਸੇ ਵਿਸ਼ੇ ਉੱਤੇ) ਰੱਜ ਕੇ ਬੋਲਣਾ; ਬੇਰੋਕ-ਟੋਕ ਘੁੰਮਣਾ, ਫਿਰਨਾ, ਵਿਚਰਨਾ

expatriate (ਐਕਸ'ਪੈਟਰਿਏਇਟ, ਐਕਸ'ਪੈਟਰਿਅਟ) *v a* ਪਰਵਾਸ ਕਰਨਾ, ਦੇਸ਼ ਤਿਆਗ ਕਰਨਾ, ਦੇਸ਼ ਨਿਕਾਲਾ ਦੇਣਾ, ਪਰਵਾਸੀ, ਜਲਾਵਤਨੀ

expatriation (ਐਕਸ'ਪੈਟਰਿ'ਏਇਸ਼ਨ) *n* ਪਰਵਾਸ, ਦੇਸ਼ਤਿਆਗ, ਦੇਸ਼-ਨਿਕਾਲਾ

expect (ਇਕ'ਸਪੈਕਟ) *v* ਆਸ ਰੱਖਣੀ; ਉਮੀਦ ਕਰਨੀ, ਰਾਹ ਵੇਖਣਾ, ਉਡੀਕਣਾ, ਖ਼ਿਆਲ ਕਰਨਾ; ~**ancy** ਆਸ਼ਾ, ਸੰਭਾਵਨਾ, ਭਵਿੱਖ, ਆਸ, ਉਮੀਦਵਾਰੀ; ~**ant mother** ਗਰਭਵਤੀ ਇਸਤਰੀ

expedience, expediency (ਇਕ'ਸਪੀਡਯਅੰਸ, ਇਕ'ਸਪੀਡਯਅੰਸਿ) *n* ਉਪਯੋਗਤਾ, ਉਚਿਤਤਾ; ਹਿਕਮਤ; ਸਿਆਣਪ

expedient (ਇਕ'ਸਪੀਡਯਅੰਟ) *n a* ਉਪਯੋਗੀ

expedite (ਐਕਸਪਿਡਾਇਟ) *v* (ਕੰਮ) ਛੇਤੀ ਕਰ ਦੇਣਾ, ਤੁਰਤ ਕਰਨਾ, ਝਟਪਟ ਕਰਨਾ, ਸੀਘਰ

ਘੱਲਣਾ

expedition (ਐਕਸਪਿ'ਡਿਸ਼ਨ) *n* ਮੁਹਿੰਮ, ਚੜ੍ਹਾਈ

expel (ਇਕ'ਸਪੈੱਲ) *v* ਜ਼ੋਰ ਨਾਲ ਬਾਹਰ ਕੱਢਣਾ, ਬਰਾਦਰੀ ਜਾਂ ਸਕੂਲ ਅਥਵਾ ਕਾਲਜ ਵਿਚੋਂ ਕੱਢ ਦੇਣਾ, ਛੇਕਣਾ, ਨਾਂ ਕੱਟ ਦੇਣਾ, ਖ਼ਾਰਜ ਕਰਨਾ

expend (ਇਕ'ਸਪੈਂਡ) *v* ਪ੍ਰਯੋਗ ਕਰ ਲੈਣਾ, ਖ਼ਰਚ ਕਰਨਾ, ਲਗਾਉਣਾ, ਖਪਾਉਣਾ; ~iture ਖ਼ਰਚ, ਖਪਾਉ, ਖ਼ਰਚੀ ਰਕਮ

expense (ਇਕ'ਸਪੈਂਸ) *n* ਖ਼ਰਚ, ਮੁੱਲ, ਲਾਗਤ

expensive (ਇਕ'ਸਪੈਂਸਿਵ੍) *a* ਮਹਿੰਗਾ, ਕੀਮਤੀ, ਮੁੱਲਵਾਨ, ਖ਼ਰਚੀਲਾ

experience (ਇਕ'ਸਪਿਅਰਿਅੰਸ) *n v* ਅਨੁਭਵ, ਤਜਰਬਾ, ਅਨੁਭਵ ਕਰਨਾ, ਸਿੱਖਣਾ, ਮਾਲੂਮ ਕਰਨਾ, ਪਰਖਣਾ, ਮਹਿਸੂਸ ਕਰਨਾ; ~d ਅਨੁਭਵੀ, ਤਜਰਬੇਕਾਰ, ਕੁਸ਼ਲ

experiment (ਇਕ'ਸਪੈਰਿਮੇੰਟ, ਇਕ'ਸਪੈਰਿਮੈਂਟ) *n v* ਪ੍ਰਯੋਗ, ਤਜਰਬਾ, ਜਾਂਚ, ਪਰਖ; ਪ੍ਰਯੋਗ ਕਰਨਾ, ਤਜਰਬਾ ਕਰਨਾ, ਪਰੀਖਿਆ ਕਰਨੀ, ਜਾਂਚਣਾ; ~al ਪ੍ਰਯੋਗਾਤਮਕ ਅਨੁਭੁਤੀਮੂਲਕ,

expert (ਐੱਕਸਪਅ:ਟ) *a* ਮਾਹਰ, ਵਿਸ਼ੇਸ਼ੱਗ

expertise (ਐੱਕਸਪਅ:ਟੀਜ਼) *n* ਨਿਪੁੰਨਤਾ, ਵਿਸ਼ੇਸ਼ੱਗਤਾ, ਮੁਹਾਰਤ

expire (ਇਕ'ਸਪਾਇਅ*) *v* (ਫੇਫੜਿਆਂ ਦੀ) ਹਵਾ ਬਾਹਰ ਕੱਢਣੀ; (ਅੰਗ ਦਾ) ਬੁਝ ਜਾਣਾ; ਮਰਨਾ, ਖ਼ਤਮ ਹੋਣਾ

expiry (ਇਕ'ਸਪਾਇਅਰਿ) *n* ਅੰਤ, ਖ਼ਾਤਮਾ

explain (ਇਕ'ਸਪਲੇਇਨ) *v* ਵਿਆਖਿਆ ਕਰਨੀ, ਸਪਸ਼ਟ ਕਰਨਾ, ਵਿਸਤਾਰ ਨਾਲ ਸਮਝਾਉਣਾ, ਜਵਾਬਦੇਹੀ ਕਰਨੀ, ਸਫ਼ਾਈ ਦੇਣਾ

explanation (ਐੱਕਸਪਲ'ਨੇਇਸ਼ਨ) *n* ਵੇਰਵਾ, ਵਿਆਖਿਆਤਮਕ, ਸਪਸ਼ਟੀਕਰਨ, ਸਫ਼ਾਈ, ਜਵਾਬ ਤਲਬੀ

explanatory (ਇਕ'ਸਪੈਲਨਅਟ(ਅ)ਰਿ) *a* ਵਿਆਖਿਆਤਮਕ, ਸਪਸ਼ਟੀਕਰਨ, ਵੇਰਵੇਪੂਰਨ

explicable (ਇਕ'ਸਪਲਿਕਅਬਲ) *a* ਵਿਆਖਿਆ ਯੋਗ, ਸਪਸ਼ਟ ਕਰਨ ਯੋਗ

explicate (ਐੱਕਸਪਲਿਕੇਇਟ) *v* ਸਪਸ਼ਟ ਕਰਨਾ, ਅਰਥ ਖੋਲ੍ਹਣਾ, ਸਮਝਾਉਣਾ

explication (ਐੱਕਸਪਲਿ'ਕੇਇਸ਼ਨ) *n* ਸਪਸ਼ਟੀਕਰਨ, ਅਰਥ-ਵਿਸਤਾਰ

explicit (ਇਕ'ਸਪਲਿਸਿਟ) *n a* ਸੁਸਪਸ਼ਟ, ਸਾਫ਼, ਖਰਾ

explode (ਇਕ'ਸਪਲਅਉਡ) *v* ਵਿਸਫੋਟ ਹੋਣਾ, ਆਵਾਜ਼ ਜਾਂ ਧਮਾਕੇ ਨਾਲ ਫਟਣਾ; ਖੰਡਨ ਕਰਨਾ; ਬਦਨਾਮ ਕਰਨਾ

exploit (ਐੱਕਸਪਲੋਇਟ) *n v* ਵਰਤਨਾ, ਸ਼ੋਸ਼ਣ ਕਰਨਾ, ਲੁੱਟ ਕਰਨੀ, ਆਪਣਾ ਮਤਲਬ ਕੱਢਣਾ; ~ation ਦੁਰ-ਉਪਯੋਗ; ਸ਼ੋਸ਼ਣ

exploration (ਐੱਕਸਪਲੇਅ'ਰੇਇਸ਼ਨ) *n* ਖੋਜ, ਛਾਣਬੀਣ, ਖੋਜ ਪੜਤਾਲ

explore (ਇਕ'ਸਪਲੋ*) *v* ਜਾਂਚ ਪੜਤਾਲ ਕਰਨੀ, ਛਾਣਬੀਣ ਕਰਨੀ, ਖੋਜ ਕੱਢਣੀ, ਢੂੰਡ ਭਾਲ ਕਰਨੀ, ਟੋਹਣਾ, ਖੋਜਣਾ, ਗਾਹਣਾ

explosion (ਇਕ'ਸਪਲਅਉਯਨ) *n* ਧਮਾਕਾ, ਭੜਾਕਾ; ਸਫੋਟ, ਵਿਸਫੋਟ; ਕਰੋਧ ਨਾਲ ਭੜਕ ਉੱਠਣਾ

explosive (ਇਕ'ਸਪਲਉਸਿਵ) *n* ਸਫੋਟਕ ਪਦਾਰਥ; ਸਫੋਟਕ ਧੁਨੀ; ਸਫੋਟਕ; ਵਿਸਫੋਟਕ

exponent (ਇਕ'ਸਪਅਉਨਅੰਟ) *n* ਵਿਆਖਿਆਤਾ, ਵਿਆਖਿਆਕਾਰ, ਪੈਰੋਕਾਰ

export (ਐੱਕਸਪੋਟ, ਇਕ'ਸਪੋਟ) *n v* ਨਿਰਯਾਤ, ਬਰਾਮਦ, ਬਾਹਰ ਘੱਲਣਾ, ਨਿਰਯਾਤ ਕਰਨਾ

expose (ਇਕ'ਸਪਅਉਜ਼) v ਨੰਗਾ ਰੱਖਣਾ, ਖੁੱਲ੍ਹਾ ਛੱਡਣਾ, ਬਰਬਾਦ ਹੋਣ ਦੇਣਾ; ਨੁਮਾਇਸ਼ ਲਈ ਰੱਖਣਾ; (ਭੇਦ) ਪਰਗਟ ਕਰਨਾ, ਨਸ਼ਰ ਕਰਨਾ

exposition (ਐਕਸਪਅ(ਉ)ਜ਼ਿਸ਼ਨ) n ਸਪਸ਼ਟੀਕਰਨ, ਪ੍ਰਤੀਪਾਦਨ, ਪ੍ਰਸਤੁਤੀਕਰਨ, ਭਾਸ਼, ਆਲੋਚਨਾ, ਟੀਕਾ, ਵਿਆਖਿਆ

exposure (ਇਕ'ਸਪਅਉਯਅ*) n ਭੇਦ ਆਦਿ ਦਾ ਪਰਗਟੀਕਰਨ, ਪੱਖ, ਹਵਾ ਲੁਆਉਣ; ਪਰਗਟਾਉ, ਪ੍ਰਭਾਵ; (ਫੋਟੋ) ਪ੍ਰਕਾਸ਼ਨ

expound (ਇਕ'ਸਪਾਉਂਡ) v ਵਿਆਖਿਆ ਕਰਨੀ, ਬਿਆਨ ਕਰਨਾ, ਸਪਸ਼ਟ ਕਰਨਾ, ਪਰਗਟ ਕਰਨਾ, ਵਿਸਤਾਰ ਨਾਲ ਦੱਸਣਾ

express (ਇਕ'ਸਪਰੈੱਸ) n v a adv ਅਤਿਵਿਅਕਤ ਕਰਨਾ, ਪਰਗਟ ਕਰਨਾ, ਸੂਚਤ ਕਰਨਾ, ਘੋਲੁਣਾ, ਜ਼ਾਹਰ ਕਰਨਾ, ਨਿਚੋੜਨਾ; ਅਤਿਵਿਅਕਤ, ਸਪਸ਼ਟ, ਸਾਫ਼, ਸਟੀਕ, ਠੀਕ, ਤੇਜ਼ੀ ਨਾਲ; ~ion ਅਤਿਵਿਅੰਜਨਾ, ਅਤਿਵਿਅਕਤੀ, ਪਦਾਵਲੀ, ਕਥਨ, ਮੁਹਾਵਰਾ, ਵਿਅੰਜਨਸ਼ੈਲੀ, ਭਾਵ-ਅਤਿਵਿਅਕਤੀ; ~ive ਅਤਿਵਿਅੰਜਨਾਤਮਕ, ਅਰਥ-ਪੂਰਨ, ਭਾਵ-ਪੂਰਨ, ਵਿਅੰਜਕ

expulsion (ਇਕ'ਸਪਲਸ਼ਨ) n ਬਾਹਰ ਕੱਢਣ ਦੇਣ, ਨਿਰਵਾਸਨ

expunge (ਇਕ'ਸਪਅੰਨਜ) v ਕੱਢ ਦੇਣਾ, ਰੱਦ ਕਰਨਾ, ਲੋਪ ਕਰਨਾ, ਕੱਟ ਦੇਣਾ, ਮਿਟਾ ਦੇਣਾ

exquisite (ਐਕਸਕਵਿਜ਼ਿਟ) a n ਉੱਤਮ, ਨਫ਼ੀਸ, ਤੇਜ, ਤੀਬਰ, ਬਾਂਕਾ

extempore (ਐਕ'ਸਟੈਂਪਅਰਿ) adv a ਤਤਕਾਲਕ ਭਾਸ਼ਨ, ਬਿਨਾ ਸੋਚੇ, ਬਿਨਾ ਤਿਆਰੀ ਤੋਂ ਦਿੱਤਾ ਗਿਆ (ਭਾਸ਼ਣ)

extemporize (ਇਕ'ਸਟੈਂਪਅਰਾਇਜ਼) v ਪਹਿਲਾਂ ਸੋਚੇ ਬਿਨਾ ਬੋਲਣਾ, ਸਮੇਂ ਦੇ ਅਨੁਸਾਰ ਬੋਲ ਜਾਣਾ, ਬਿਨਾ ਤਿਆਰੀ ਬੋਲਣਾ

extend (ਇਕ'ਸਟੈਂਡ) v ਪੂਰਾ ਫੈਲਾਉਣਾ, ਵਿਸਤਾਰ ਸਹਿਤ ਲਿਖਣਾ; ਪਹੁੰਚਣਾ, ਪਹੁੰਚਾਉਣਾ; (ਮਿਆਦ) ਵਧਾਉਣਾ

extension (ਇਕ'ਸਟੈਂਨਸ਼ਨ) n ਵਾਧਾ, ਵਿਸਤਾਰ, ਮਿਆਦ ਵਿਚ ਵਾਧਾ, ਪ੍ਰਸਾਰ

extensive (ਇਕ'ਸਟੈਂਨਸਿਵ੍) n ਵਿਆਪਕ, ਵਿਸਤਰਤ, ਵਿਸ਼ਾਲ, ਵੱਡਾ

extent (ਇਕ'ਸਟੈਂਟ) n ਸੀਮਾ, ਹੱਦ, ਵਿਸਤਾਰ, ਫੈਲਾਉ

exterior (ਇਕ'ਸਟਿਅਰਿਅ*) a n ਬਾਹਰੀ, ਬਾਹਰਲਾ, ਖਾਰਜੀ, ਬੈਰੁਨੀ

exterminate (ਇਕ'ਸਟਅਃਮਿਨੇਇਟ) v ਜੜ੍ਹੋਂ ਪੁੱਟਣਾ, ਨਸ਼ਟ ਕਰਨਾ, ਮਿਟਾਉਣਾ, ਉਖੇੜਨਾ, ਬਰਬਾਦ ਕਰਨਾ

external (ਇਕ'ਸਟਅਃਨਲ) n a ਬਾਹਰੀ, ਬੈਰੁਨੀ, ਵਿਦੇਸ਼ੀ ਪਰਰਾਸ਼ਟਰੀ

extinct (ਇਕ'ਸਟਿਙ(ਕ)ਟ) a ਬੁਝਿਆ, ਨਸ਼ਟ, ਮੁਰਦਾ; ਲੁਪਤ, ਅਪ੍ਰਚਲਤ; ~ion ਲੋਪ, ਨਾਸ, ਨਿਰਵਾਣ; ਪਰਿਸਮਾਪਤੀ, ਸੱਤਿਆਨਾਸ, ਵਿਨਾਸ਼

extinguish (ਇਕ'ਸਟਿਙਗਵਿਸ਼) v ਬੁਝਾਉਣਾ, ਮਿਟਾਉਣਾ, ਦਬਾ ਦੇਣਾ, ਦਮਨ ਕਰਨਾ, ਠੰਡਾ ਕਰਨਾ; ~er ਵਿਨਾਸ਼-ਕਰਤਾ, ਬੁਝਾਉਣ ਵਾਲਾ, ਅਗਨੀ ਰੋਧਕ

extort (ਇਕ'ਸਟੇਟ) v (ਸ਼ਬਦਾਂ ਦੇ ਅਰਥਾਂ ਨੂੰ) ਤੋੜਨਾ ਮਰੋੜਨਾ, (ਅੱਖਰਾਂ ਦੇ) ਘੁਮਾ ਫਿਰਾ ਕੇ ਸਿੱਟੇ ਕੱਢਣੇ, ਖਿੱਚੋਤਾਣ ਕਰਕੇ ਅਰਥ ਕੱਢਣੇ

extra (ਐਕਸਟਰਅ) n a adv ਵਾਧੂ ਤੇ ਫ਼ਾਲਤੂ ਚੀਜ਼, ਅਧਿਕ ਵਸਤੂ, ਫ਼ਾਲਤੂ, ਵਾਧੂ, ਵਿਸ਼ੇਸ਼, ਵੱਡਾ; ਸਧਾਰਨ ਤੋਂ ਅਧਿਕ, ਅਤੀ, ਜ਼ਿਆਦਾ

extract (ਐਕੱਸਟਰੈਕਟ) *n v* ਰਸ, ਤੱਤ, ਨਿਚੋੜ, ਸਤ, ਅਰਕ; ਸਿੱਟਾ, ਸਾਰ, ਸਾਰਾਂਸ਼, ਸੰਖੇਪ, ਖ਼ੁਲਾਸਾ; ਅਰਕ ਕੱਢਣਾ, ਸਾਰ ਕੱਢਣਾ, ਨਿਚੋੜਨਾ, ਬਲ ਨਾਲ ਹਟਾਉਣਾ, ਦੰਦ ਕੱਢਣਾ (ਉਘੇੜਨਾ)

etraneous (ਇਕਸਟਰੇਇਨਯਅਸ) *a* ਭਿੰਨ; ਅਸੰਬੰਧ, ਅਸੰਗਤ, ਬਾਹਰੀ

extraordinary (ਇਕ'ਸਟਰੋਡਨਰਿ) *n a* ਵਿਸ਼ੇਸ਼, ਅਸਾਧਾਰਨ, ਵਿਲੱਖਣ, ਅਨੋਖਾ, ਨਿਰਾਲਾ, ਮਹਾਨ

extravagance (ਇਕ'ਸਟਕੈਵ੍ਅਗਅੰਸ) *n* ਫ਼ਜ਼ੂਲ ਖ਼ਰਚੀ, ਫ਼ਜ਼ੂਲੀਅਤ, ਬੇਤੁਕਾਪਨ

extravagant (ਇਕ'ਸਟਰੈਵ੍ਅਗਅੰਟ) *a* ਫ਼ਜ਼ੂਲ-ਖ਼ਰਚ, ਉਡਾਊ, ਖ਼ਰਚੀਲਾ

extravaganza (ਐੱਕ'ਸਟਰੈਵ੍ਅ'ਗੈਂਜ਼ਅ) *n* ਅਲੋਕਕਤਾ, ਧੂਮ-ਧੱੜਕਾ

extreme (ਇਕ'ਸਟਰੀਮ) *a n* ਅਧਿਕ, ਅੰਤਮ, ਆਖ਼ਰੀ ਸਿਰੇ ਦਾ, ਕੱਟੜ, ਸੰਕੀਰਣ, ਇੰਤਹਾਪਸੰਦ, ਚਰਮਸੀਮਾ, ਹੱਦ, ਸਿਰਾ; **~ly** ਬਹੁਤ ਹੀ ਹੱਦ ਤੋ ਜ਼ਿਆਦਾ, ਅਤੀਅਧਿਕ, ਬੇਹੱਦ; **~ness** ਅੱਤਤਾ, ਬਹੁਤਾਤ, ਚਰਮਸਥਿਤੀ; ਉਗਰਤਾ

extremism (ਇਕ'ਸਟਰੀਮਿਜ਼(ਅ)ਮ) *n* ਅੱਤਵਾਦ, ਇੰਤਹਾਪਸੰਦੀ

extremist (ਇਕ'ਸਟਰੀਮਿਸਟ) *n* ਕੱਟੜ, ਇੰਤਹਾਪਸੰਦ, ਉਗਰਵਾਦੀ, ਅੱਤਵਾਦੀ

extremity (ਇਕ'ਸਟਰੈੱਮਅਟਿ) *n* ਸਿਰਾ, ਹੱਦ, ਤੇਜ਼ੀ, ਤੀਬਰਤਾ; (*In pl*) ਹੱਥ ਪੈਰ

extricate ('ਐੱਕਸਟਰਿਕੇਇਟ) *v* ਨਿਸਤਾਰਨ, ਛੁਡਾਉਣਾ, ਉਧਾਰ ਕਰਨਾ, ਮੁਕਤ ਕਰਨਾ, ਸੁਲਝਾਉਣਾ

extrication ('ਐੱਕਸਟਰਿ'ਕੇਇਸ਼ਨ) *n* ਨਿਸਤਾਰਾ, ਛੁਟਕਾਰਾ, ਮੁਕਤੀ, ਸੁਲਝਾਉ

extrinsic (ਐੱਕ'ਸਟਰਿੰਸਿਕ) *a* ਅਣਅਵੱਸ਼ਕ, ਅਪ੍ਰਧਾਨ, ਗ਼ੈਰ-ਜ਼ਰੂਰੀ; ਬਾਹਰੀ, ਅਸੰਬਧਤ

extrovert ('ਐੱਕਸਟਰਅ(ਉ)ਵ੍ਅ:ਟ) *v n* ਬਾਹਰ ਵੱਲ ਨਿਕਲਨਾ, ਬਾਹਰਮੁਖੀ

exuberant (ਇਗ'ਜ਼ੂਬ(ਅ)ਰਅੰਟ) *a* ਸੰਪੰਨ, ਸਮਰਿਧ, ਬਹੁਤ ਜ਼ਿਆਦਾ; ਜ਼ਿੰਦਾ-ਦਿਲ, ਉੱਲਾਸ-ਪੂਰਨ, ਓਜਪੂਰਨ, ਸ਼ਬਦ-ਆਡੰਬਰਪੂਰਨ (ਭਾਸ਼ਾ); ਤੀਬਰ, ਭਰਪੂਰ

exuberate (ਇਗ'ਜ਼ੁਯਬਰੇਇਟ) *v* ਡੁੱਲ੍ਹ ਡੁੱਲ੍ਹ ਪੈਣਾ; ਸਮਰਿਧ ਜਾਂ ਪਰਿਪੂਰਨ ਹੋਣਾ, ਬਹੁਲਤਾ ਹੋਣੀ, ਭਰਪੂਰ ਹੋਣਾ, ਹਰਿਆ ਭਰਿਆ ਹੋਣਾ

eye (ਆਇ) *n* ਅੱਖ, ਨੈਣ, ਨੇਤਰ, ਦ੍ਰਿਸ਼ਟੀ; ਅੱਖ ਦਾ ਤਾਰਾ; ਧਿਆਨ, ਮੋਰ ਦੇ ਖੰਭਾਂ ਦੀ ਟਿੱਕੀ; **~ball** ਅੱਖ ਦਾ ਡੇਲਾ, ਆਨਾ; **~brow** ਭਾਉਂ, ਭਰਵੱਟਾ; **~drop** ਅੱਥਰੂ, ਹੰਝੂ; **~lash** ਝਿੰਮਣੀ, ਪਲਕ; **~lid** ਪਪੋਟਾ, ਅੱਖ ਦਾ ਉਪਰਲਾ ਪਰਦਾ; **~sight** ਨਜ਼ਰ, ਜੋਤ, ਬੀਨਾਈ, ਦ੍ਰਿਸ਼ਟੀ; **~wash** ਅੱਖਾਂ ਦੀ ਦਾਰੂ; ਮੂੰਹ ਰੱਖਣੀ, ਉਪਰੀ ਫੱਕੋਸਲਾ; **~witness** ਸਾਖੀ, ਚਸ਼ਮਦੀਦ ਗਵਾਹ

F

F, f (ਐੱਫ਼) *n* ਰੋਮਨ ਵਰਨਮਾਲਾ ਦਾ ਛੇਵਾਂ ਅੱਖਰ; (ਸੰਗੀ) ਚੌਥੀ ਸੁਰ

fable ('ਫ਼ੇਇਬਲ) *n v* ਪੁਰਾਤਨ ਕਥਾ, ਕਿੱਸਾ, ਕਹਾਣੀ; (ਨਾਟਕ ਦਾ) ਕਥਾਨਕ, ਪਸ਼ੂ-ਪੰਛੀਆਂ ਦੀ ਸਿੱਖਿਆਦਾਇਕ ਕਹਾਣੀ (ਪੰਚਤੰਤਰ ਦੀ ਵਾਰਤਾ); ਬਣਾਵਟੀ ਕਿੱਸਾ ਦੱਸਣਾ, ਮਨਘੜਤ ਕਹਾਣੀ ਸੁਣਾਉਣੀ; ਕਲਪਨ ਵਾਰਤਾ ਪੇਸ਼ ਕਰਨੀ

fabric ('ਫ਼ੈਬਰਿਕ) *n* ਢਾਂਚਾ, ਫ਼ਰੇਮ; ਉਸਾਰੀ; ਬੁਣਤੀ ਕੱਪੜਾ

fabricate ('ਫ਼ੈਬਰਿਕੇਇਟ) *v* ਬਣਾਉਣਾ, ਘੜਨਾ, ਉਣਨਾ, ਨਿਰਮਾਣ ਕਰਨਾ, ਰਚਨਾ ਕਰਨੀ; ਬਣਾਉਟੀ ਗੱਲ ਘੜਨੀ, ਜਾਅਲਸਾਜ਼ੀ ਕਰਨੀ; **~d** ਘੜੀ ਹੋਈ, ਝੂਠੀ, ਕੂੜੀ

fabrication ('ਫ਼ੈਬਰਿ'ਕੇਇਸ਼ਨ) *n* ਬਣਾਉਟੀ, ਗੱਲ, ਝੂਠੀ ਕਹਾਣੀ; ਮਨਘੜਤ ਬਿਰਤਾਂਤ, ਜਾਅਲਸਾਜ਼ੀ

fabricator ('ਫ਼ੈਬਰਿਕੇਇਟਅ*) *n* ਝੂਠਾ, ਧੋਖੇਬਾਜ਼, ਮਿਥਿਆਵਾਦੀ

fabulous ('ਫ਼ੈਬਯੁਲਅਸ) *a* ਝੂਠਾ, ਕਲਪਤ, ਨਿਰਾਧਾਰ, ਮਿਥਿਆਕਾਰੀ, ਚਮਤਕਾਰੀ

face (ਫ਼ੇਇਸ) *n v* ਚਿਹਰਾ-ਮੋਹਰਾ, ਮੂੰਹਾਂਦਰਾ, ਮੂੰਹ-ਮੱਥਾ, ਮੂੰਹ, ਮੁੱਖ, ਹੁਲੀਆ, ਨੁਹਾਰ, ਦਿਖਾਵਾ, ਟੀਪ-ਟਾਪ; ਸਾਮ੍ਹਣੇ ਆਉਣਾ; ਮੁਕਾਬਲਾ ਕਰਨਾ, ਡਟੇ; ਰਹਿਣਾ; **~cloth** ਕੱਫ਼ਨ, ਮੂੰਹ ਧੋਣ ਲਈ ਪ੍ਰਯੋਗ ਕੀਤਾ ਕੱਪੜਾ; **~down** (ਸਖ਼ਤੀ ਨਾਲ) ਦੇਖਣ ਨਾਲ ਹੀ ਸ਼ਰਮਿੰਦਾ ਕਰਨਾ; **~lifting** ਪੋਚਾ ਪਾਚੀ; **~value** ਅੰਕਤ ਮੁੱਲ, ਪ੍ਰਤੱਖ ਮੁੱਲ; **~to** ਆਮ੍ਹਣੇ-ਸਾਮ੍ਹਣੇ; **having two ~s** ਬਹੁਰੂਪੀਆ ਹੋਣਾ, ਆਪਣੀ ਗੱਲ ਵਿਚ ਸੱਚਾ ਨਾ ਹੋਣਾ; **on the ~of it** ਜ਼ਾਹਰਾ ਤੌਰ ਤੇ, ਉਪਰੇ ਤੌਰ ਤੇ; **pull a long ~** ਮੂੰਹ ਬਣਾਉਣਾ, ਮੂੰਹ ਫੁਲਾਉਣਾ; **show one's~** ਹਾਜ਼ਰ ਹੋਣਾ

facet ('ਫ਼ੈਸਿਟ) *n* ਮੱਥਾ, ਪੱਖ, ਪਹਿਲੂ

facial ('ਫ਼ੇਇਸ਼ਲ) *a* ਮੂੰਹ ਦਾ, ਚਿਹਰੇ ਦਾ

facile ('ਫ਼ੈਮ'ਇਲ) *a* ਸੁਖਾਲਾ, ਸੌਖਾ, ਸਰਲ, ਆਸਾਨ, ਸੁਗਮ, ਸਿੱਧਾ; ਨੇਕ, ਸਰਲ ਸੁਭਾਅ, ਉਦਾਰ, ਬਲਮਾਨਸ, ਨਿਮਰਤਾ ਵਾਲਾ

facilitate (ਫ਼ਅ'ਸਿਲਿਟੇਇਟ) *v* ਸੁਖਾਲਾ ਕਰਨਾ, ਸਰਲ ਕਰ ਦੇਣਾ, ਸੁਵਿਧਾ ਦੇਣੀ, ਸਹੂਲਤ ਦੇਣੀ

facility (ਫ਼ਅ'ਸਿਲਅਟਿ) *n* ਸਹੂਲਤ, ਸੌਖ, ਸੁਵਿਧਾ, ਆਸਾਨੀ; ਲਚਕ; ਮੁਹਾਰਤ

facing ('ਫ਼ੇਇਸਿਙ) *n* ਮੋਹਰਾ, ਅਗਾੜੀ, ਮੱਥਾ

facsimile (ਫ਼ਕ'ਸਿਮਿਲਿ) *n v* ਹੂਬਹੂ ਨਕਲ, ਪ੍ਰਤੀਲਿਪੀ, ਪ੍ਰਤੀਰੂਪ; ਉਤਾਰਾ ਕਰਨਾ, ਪ੍ਰਤੀਲਿਪੀ ਬਣਾਉਣੀ; **~signature** ਚਿਤਰ-ਹਸਤਾਖ਼ਰ

fact (ਫ਼ੈਕਟ) *n* ਤੱਥ, ਭੱਤ, ਸਚਾਈ, ਅਸਲੀਅਤ ਵਾਸਤਵਿਕਤਾ, ਯਥਾਰਥਤਾ, ਹਕੀਕਤ; **in~** ਅਸਲ ਵਿਚ, ਦਰਅਸਲ, ਸੰਖੇਪ ਵਿਚ

faction ('ਫ਼ੈਕਸ਼ਨ) *n* ਧੜਾ, ਫ਼ਿਰਕਾ, ਸਿਰ, ਪਾਸਾ, ਪੱਖਪਾਤ; **~al, factious** ਧੜੇਬਾਜ਼ੀ ਵਾਲਾ, ਪੱਖਪਾਤੀ, ਦਲ ਸਬੰਧੀ, ਫ਼ਸਾਦੀ, ਉਪੱਦਰ ਮਚਾਉ; **~alism** ਦਲਬੰਦੀ, ਗੁਟਬੰਦੀ, ਧੜੇਬਾਜ਼ੀ; **~ary** ਧੜੇਬਾਜ਼, ਗੁੱਟਬਾਜ਼

factitious (ਫ਼ੈਕ'ਟਿਸ਼ਅਸ) *a* ਨਕਲੀ, ਜਾਅਲੀ, ਕ੍ਰਿਤਿਮ, ਬਣਾਉਟੀ, ਕਲਪਤ

factor ('ਫ਼ੈਕਟਅ*) *n* ਗੁਟਲਪੰਡ, **ਗੁਣ**, ਗਨਿਕ,

factory

ਕਾਰਕ, ਉਪਾਦਾਨ, ਭਾਗ, ਪੱਖ, ਅੰਗ, ਅੰਸ਼; ਕਾਰਿੰਦਾ, ਆੜ੍ਹਤੀ; ਪ੍ਰਤੀਨਿਧ; ~ise ਗੁਣਨਖੰਡ ਕਰਨਾ, ਜੁਜ਼ ਬਣਾਉਣੇ, ਵਿਭਾਗ ਕਰਨਾ

factory ('ਫ਼ੈਕਟ(ਅ)ਰਿ) *n* ਕਾਰਖ਼ਾਨਾ

factual ('ਫ਼ੈਕਚੁਅਲ) *a* ਵਾਸਤਵਿਕ, ਯਥਾਰਥ, ਤੱਤ

faculty ('ਫ਼ੈਕਅਲਟਿ) *n* ਯੋਗਤਾ, ਕਾਰਜਕੁਸ਼ਲਤਾ, ਪ੍ਰਬੰਧ ਦੀ ਯੋਗਤਾ; ਮਾਨਸਕ ਸ਼ਕਤੀ; ਵਿੱਦਿਆ-ਵਿਭਾਗ, ਫ਼ੈਕਲਟੀ, (ਯੂਨੀਵਰਸਿਟੀ ਦਾ) ਪਰਤਾਗਾ

fade (ਫ਼ੈਇਡ) *v* ਬਣਾਉਟੀ, ਮੁਰਝਾਉਣਾ, ਕੁਮਲਾਉਣਾ, ਸੁੰਕਣਾ, ਫਿੱਕਾ ਪੈਣਾ, ਪੀਲਾ ਹੋ ਜਾਣਾ, ਝੂੰ ਜਾਣਾ, ਰੰਗ ਉੱਡਣਾ, ਹੋਲੀ ਹੋਲੀ ਲੋਪ ਹੋਣਾ, ਰੰਗ ਉਡਾਉਣਾ, ਘੱਟ ਹੋਣਾ, ਮਾੜਾ ਪੈਣਾ; ~less ਸਦਾ-ਬਹਾਰ, ਹਰਿਆ-ਭਰਿਆ

faecal ('ਫ਼ੀਕਲ) *a* ਗੰਦ ਦਾ, ਵਿਸ਼ਟਾ ਦਾ, ਕੀਟ ਦਾ; ~matter ਗੰਦ, ਟੱਟੀ

fag (ਫ਼ੈਗ) *n v* ਮਿਹਨਤ, ਕਠਨ ਪਰਿਸ਼ਰਮ, ਵਗਾਰ ਦਾ ਕੰਮ, ਵਾਪੂ ਵਗਾਰ, ਚੱਟੀ ਦਾ ਕੰਮ; ਥੱਕ ਜਾਣਾ, ਥਕਾ ਦੇਣਾ, ਵਗਾਰ ਦਾ ਕੰਮ ਕਰਨਾ; ਸਖ਼ਤ ਮਿਹਨਤ ਕਰਨੀ, ਜਾਨ ਮਾਰ ਕੇ ਕੰਮ ਕਰਨਾ, ਬਹੁਤ ਕਸ਼ਟ ਸਹਿਣਾ; ਸਿਥਲ ਕਰ ਦੇਣਾ; ~end ਆਖ਼ਰੀ ਹਿੱਸਾ, ਨਿਕੰਮਾ, ਭਾਗ ਜਾਂ ਸਿਰਾ

fail (ਫ਼ੈਇਲ) *n v* ਨਿਰਸੰਦੇਹ; ਅਸਫਲਤਾ, ਅਸਫਲ ਹੋਣਾ, ਸਿਰੇ ਨਾ ਚੜ੍ਹਨਾ, (ਕੋਈ ਕੰਮ) ਨਾ ਕਰ ਸਕਣਾ, ਹਾਰ ਜਾਣਾ, ਉੱਕਣਾ, ਟੁੱਟ ਜਾਣਾ, ਦੀਵਾਲਾ ਨਿਕਲਣਾ, ਘੱਟ ਹੋਣਾ, ਪੂਰਾ ਨਾ ਉਤਰਨਾ, ਹਿੰਮਤ ਹਾਰ ਜਾਣਾ, ਨਸ਼ਟ ਹੋ ਜਾਣਾ, ਨਿਰਾਸ਼ ਕਰਨਾ; ~ing ਘਾਟ, ਕਮੀ, ਕਮਜ਼ੋਰੀ, ਦੁਰਬਲਤਾ, ਉਕਾਈ, ਢਿੱਲ, ਭੁੱਲ, ਕਸੂਰ; ~ure ਅਸਫਲਤਾ, ਨਾਕਾਮਯਾਬੀ, ਹਾਰ, ਨਾਕਾਮੀ, ਉਕਾਈ, ਭੁੱਲ; ਘਾਟਾ, ਟੋਟਾ, ਘਾਟ, ਅਭਾਵ; ਹਾਰਿਆ ਹੋਇਆ, ਨਿਸਫਲ ਜਤਨ, ਨੁਕਸਾਨ; ਦੀਵਾਲਾ; without~ ਨਿਸ਼ਚਤ ਰੂਪ ਨਾਲ, ਜ਼ਰੂਰੀ, ਅਵੱਸ਼ਕ

faint (ਫ਼ੈਇੰਟ) *a n v* ਮੱਧਮ, ਧੀਮਾ, ਫਿੱਕਾ, ਅਸਪਸ਼ਟ, ਕਮਜ਼ੋਰ, ਨਿਢਾਲ, ਬੇਹੋਸ਼, ਮੂਰਛਾ, ਬੇਸੁਰਤੀ, ਗ਼ਸ਼; ਬੇਸੁਰਤ ਹੋਣਾ, ਗ਼ਸ਼ ਪੈਣੀ, ਮੂਰਛਾ ਆਉਣੀ, ਸਿਥਲ ਪੈਣਾ, ਨਿਢਾਲ ਹੋ ਜਾਣਾ, ਹਿੰਮਤ ਹਾਰਨਾ, ਹੌਸਲਾ ਛੱਡਣਾ, ਡਰ ਜਾਣਾ, ਕਾਇਰਤਾ ਵਿਖਾਉਣਾ; ~heart ~hearted ਡਰਪੋਕ, ਕਾਇਰ, ਕਮਜ਼ੋਰ

fair (ਫ਼ੇਅ*) *n a v* (1) ਮੇਲਾ, ਨੁਮਾਇਸ਼, ਮੰਡੀ; (2) ਤੀਵੀਂ, ਜ਼ਨਾਨੀ; ਸੋਹਣਾ, ਸੁੰਦਰ, ਸਾਫ਼, ਉਜਲ, ਸੁਥਰਾ, ਬੇਦਾਗ਼, ਨਿਆਂਕਾਰੀ, ਨਿਰਪੱਖ, ਵਾਜਬ, ਉਚਿਤ, ਮੁਨਾਸਬ, ਜਚਵਾਂ, ਨਾਜ਼ੁਕ, ਸਧਾਰਨ ਸਤਰ ਦਾ; ਔਸਤ ਦਰਜੇ ਦਾ; ਅਨੁਕੂਲ ਹੋਣਾ, ਠੀਕ ਬੈਠਣਾ, ਰਾਸ ਹੋਣਾ; ਠੀਕ ਠੀਕ ਨਕਲ ਉਤਾਰਨਾ; ~ and square ਈਮਾਨਦਾਰ, ਸਾਫ਼ ਨੀਤ ਵਾਲਾ; ~copy ਸੁੱਧ ਪ੍ਰਤਿ; ~minded ਨਿਰਪੱਖ; the ~sex ਨਾਰੀ ਜਾਤੀ; ~ness ਨਿਰਪੱਖਤਾ, ਹੱਕ-ਨਿਆਂ, ਸੁਅੱਛਤਾ, ਸੁੰਦਰਤਾ

fairy ('ਫ਼ੇਅਰਿ) *n a* ਪਰੀ, ਅਪੱਛਰਾ, ਸੁੰਦਰ ਮੁਟਿਆਰ; ਫ਼ਰਜ਼ੀ, ਖ਼ਿਆਲੀ; ਜਾਦੂ ਦੀ; ਮੋਹਣੀ, ਕੋਮਲ ਨਾਜ਼ੁਕ; ~tale ਪਰੀ-ਕਥਾ, ਅਦਭੁਤ ਕਹਾਣੀ, ਕਲਪਤ ਕਿੱਸਾ

fait accompli ('ਫ਼ੇਇਟਆ'ਕੌਂਪਲੀ) (F) *n* ਨਜਿੱਠਿਆ ਮਾਮਲਾ

faith (ਫ਼ੈਇਥ) *n int v* ਧਰਮ, ਮੱਤ, ਸ਼ਰਧਾ, ਨਿਸ਼ਚਾ ਵਿਸ਼ਵਾਸ, ਈਮਾਨ, ਭਰੋਸਾ; in good~ ਸਚਾਈ ਨਾਲ, ਨਿਸ਼ਚੇ ਨਾਲ, ਈਮਾਨਦਾਰੀ ਨਾਲ; ~ful ਨਿਸ਼ਠਾਵਾਨ, ਦੀਨਦਾਰ, ਸਿਦਕੀ, ਵਫ਼ਾਦਾਰ,

ਵਿਸ਼ਵਾਸਪਾਤਰ, ਭਰੋਸੇਯੋਗ; ~less ਸ਼ਰਧਾਹੀਨ, ਧਰਮਹੀਨ, ਨਾਸਤਕ, ਕਾਫ਼ਰ, ਬੇਈਮਾਨ, ਬਦਨੀਤ, ਵਿਸ਼ਵਾਸਘਾਤੀ

fake (ਫ਼ੇਇਕ) *n* ਨਕਲੀ ਮਾਲ, ਛਲ, ਕਪਟ, ਧੋਖਾ, ਚਾਲਬਾਜ਼ੀ

falcon ('ਫ਼ੋਲਕਅਨ) *n* ਬਾਜ਼, ਸ਼ਿਕਰਾ

fall (ਫ਼ੋਲ) *v n* ਡਿਗਣਾ, ਢਹਿਣਾ, ਲਹਿਣਾ, ਉੱਤਰਨਾ, ਝੜਨਾ, ਉੱਖੜ ਕੇ ਡਿਗਣਾ, ਟੁੱਟ ਕੇ ਡਿਗਣਾ, ਵਾਪਰਨਾ; ਨੀਵੀਂ ਹੋਣਾ; ਮੂੰਹ ਭਾਰ ਡਿਗਣਾ, ਮੁਸੀਬਤ ਵਿਚ ਭਗਾ, ਨਿਰਾਸ਼ਟ, ਪੈਣਾ; ਉਤਾਰ, ਢਲਾਨ, ਨਿਵਾਣ, ਢਾਲ; ਝਰਨਾ, ਆਬਸ਼ਾਰ; ~across ਕਿਸੇ ਨਾਲ ਅਚਾਨਕ ਮੁਲਾਕਾਤ ਹੋ ਜਾਣੀ; ~off ਘੱਟ ਹੋਣਾ; ~out ਵਾਪਰਨਾ; ਛੱਡ ਦੇਣਾ; ~short ਥੁੜਨਾ, ਘੱਟ ਹੋ ਜਾਣਾ; ~upon ਹਮਲਾ ਕਰਨਾ, ਤਿੱਤਣਾ; to ~ a prey to ਸ਼ਿਕਾਰ ਹੋ ਜਾਣਾ, ਕਿਸੇ ਹੱਥੀਂ ਚੜ੍ਹ ਜਾਣਾ, ਵਾਦੀ ਹੋ ਜਾਣਾ

fallacy ('ਫ਼ੈਲਅਸਿ) *n* ਭੁਲਾਵਾ, ਭਰਮ, ਧੋਖਾ, ਛਲ, ਭਰਾਂਤੀ, ਫ਼ਰੇਬ, ਭੁਲੇਖਾ, ਵਾਕਛਲ, ਮਿਥਿਆ ਗਿਆਨ

false (ਫ਼ੋਲਸ) *a adv* ਝੂਠਾ, ਕੂੜਾ; ਨਕਲੀ, ਜਾਲ੍ਹੀ, ਖੋਟਾ, ਬੇਵਫ਼ਾ, ਦਗ਼ਾਬਾਜ਼, ਕਪਟੀ; ਧੋਖੇ ਨਾਲ, ਦਗ਼ਾ ਕਰਕੇ; ~hood, ~ness ਝੂਠ, ਧੋਖ, ਫ਼ਰੇਬ, ਦਗ਼ਾ, ਕਪਟਤਾ; ਝੂਠ-ਮੂਠ, ਝੂਠੀ ਗੱਲ

falsify ('ਫ਼ੋਲਸਿਫ਼ਾਇ) *v* ਝੂਠਾ ਸਿੱਧ ਕਰਨਾ, ਝੁਠਲਾਉਣਾ, ਅਸ਼ੁੱਧ ਕਰਨਾ, ਵਿਗਾੜਨਾ, ਦੂਸ਼ਤ ਕਰਨਾ

fame (ਫ਼ੇਇਮ) *n* ਜਸ, ਮਸ਼ਹੂਰੀ, ਪ੍ਰਸਿੱਧੀ, ਨੇਕਨਾਮੀ, ਕੀਰਤੀ; ~d ਮਸ਼ਹੂਰ, ਪ੍ਰਸਿੱਧ, ਜਸ-ਪ੍ਰਾਪਤ

familiar (ਫ਼ਅ'ਮਿਲਯਅ*) *a n* ਜਾਣੂ, ਪਰਿਚਿਤ, ਵੇਖਿਆ-ਚਾਖਿਆ; ਸਧਾਰਨ, ਮਾਮੂਲੀ, ਪ੍ਰਚਲਤ; ਬੇ-ਤਕੱਲੁਫ਼, ਨਿਸ਼ੰਕ; ~ity ਜਾਣ-ਪਛਾਣ, ਵਾਕ-ਫ਼ੀਅਤ, ਪਰਿਚੈ; ਅਪੱਣਤ, ਬੇ-ਤਕੱਲੁਫ਼ੀ; ~ize ਵਾਕਫ਼ੀਅਤ ਕਰਾ ਦੇਣੀ, ਜਾਣ-ਪਛਾਣ ਕਰਵਾਉਣੀ; ਅਭਿਆਸ ਕਰਾਉਣਾ; ਮਸ਼ਹੂਰ ਕਰਨਾ

family ('ਫ਼ੈਮ(ਅ)ਲਿ) *n* ਟੱਬਰ, ਪਰਵਾਰ, ਕੁਟੰਬ, ਕੋੜਮਾ; ਖ਼ਾਨਦਾਨ, ਘਰਾਣਾ; ~man ਟੱਬਰਦਾਰ, ਗ੍ਰਹਿਸਤੀ; ~tree ਬੰਸਾਵਲੀ, ਕੁਰਸੀਨਾਮਾ; in the~ way ਗਰਭਵਤੀ

famine ('ਫ਼ੈਮਿਨ) *n* ਕਾਲ, ਕਹਤ; ਥੁੜ, ਟੋਟ, ਅਭਾਵ; ~stricken ਕਾਲ-ਪੀੜਤ, ਕਾਲ ਦੇ ਮਾਰੇ; ~ment ਭੁਖਮਰੀ, ਕਾਲ ਪੀੜਾ

famous ('ਫ਼ੇਇਮਅਸ) *a* ਮਸ਼ਹੂਰ, ਪ੍ਰਸਿੱਧ, ਨਾਮੀ; ਵਧੀਆ

fan (ਫ਼ੈਨ) *n v* (1) ਪੱਖਾ; ਅਨਾਜ ਉਡਾਉਣ ਵਾਲੀ ਮਸ਼ੀਨ; (2) ਪਰੇਮੀ, ਰਸੀਆ, ਚੇਟਕੀ; ਪੱਖਾ ਝੱਲਣਾ; ਅੱਗ ਬਾਲਣ ਲਈ ਹਵਾ ਕਰਨੀ, ਅੱਗ ਭੜਕਾਉਣਾ, ਉੱਤੇਜਤ ਕਰਨਾ; ~out (ਸੈਨਾ ਆਦਿ ਦਾ) ਖਿਲਰ ਜਾਣਾ

fanatic (ਫ਼ਅ'ਨੈਟਿਕ) *a n* ਹਠ-ਧਰਮੀ, ਤੁਅੱਸਬੀ, ਜਨੂਨੀ; ~al ਕੱਟੜ, ਉਨਮਾਦਮਈ; ~ism ਧਰਮ-ਉਨਮਾਦ, ਕੱਟੜਤਾ; ਹਠ-ਧਰਮੀ; ਦੀਵਾਨਾਪਨ

fanciful ('ਫ਼ੈਂਸਿਫ਼ੁਲ) *a* ਖ਼ਿਆਲੀ, ਕਾਲਪਨਕ, ਵਹਿਮੀ, ਬਣਾਉਟੀ, ਵਚਿੱਤਰ, ਅਨੋਖਾ, ਮੌਜੀ, ਸਨਕੀ

fancy ('ਫ਼ੈਂਸਿ) *n a v* ਖ਼ਿਆਲ, ਭਾਵਨਾ, ਅਨੁਮਾਨ, ਕਲਪਨਾ, ਕਿਆਸ; ਭਰਮ, ਮਾਇਆ, ਵਹਿਮ, ਸਨਕ; ਕਲਪਤ, ਤੱਤਹੀਣ, ਮੌਜੀ, ਸਨਕੀ, ਵਹਿਮੀ; ਵਿਚਾਰਨਾ, ਖ਼ਿਆਲ ਕਰਨਾ, ਕਲਪਨਾ

ਕਰਨੀ, ਕਿਆਸ ਕਰਨ, ਮਨ ਵਿਚ ਕਲਪਤ ਚਿਤਰ ਬਣਾਉਣਾ; ~dress ਸਾਂਗ-ਵਸਤਰ; ~fair ਮੀਨਾ-ਬਜ਼ਾਰ; ~man ਦੱਲਾ, ਭੜੂਆ; ~woman ਰੰਡੀ, ਬਜ਼ਾਰੀ ਤੀਵੀਂ, ਬਦਚਲਨ ਵਿਸਤਰੀ

fantasy, phantasy ('ਫ਼ੈਂਟਅਸਿ) *n* ਕਲਪਨਾ-ਸ਼ਕਤੀ; ਤਰੰਗ, ਮਨਮੌਜ, ਸਨਕ

far (ਫ਼ਾ*) *adv a n* ਦੂਰ, ਦੂਰਭੇ, ਬਹੁਤ ਦੂਰ; ਬਹੁਤ ਜ਼ਿਆਦਾ, ਬੜਾ; ਗ਼ਾਇਬ, ਲੁਪਤ; ਕਲਪਨਾਮਈ, ਦੂਰੋਂ, ਦੂਰੀ ਤੋਂ; ਦੂਰ ਦਾ, ਦੂਰਵਰਤੀ; ~and near ਹਰੇਕ ਥਾਂ ਤੇ, ਚਾਰੇ ਪਾਸੇ; ~away ਬਹੁਤ ਦੂਰ, ਦੂਰ ਸਾਰੇ, ਪਰੇ-ਪਰੇਡੇ; ~reaching ਦੂਰਗਾਮੀ; ~sighted ਦੂਰ-ਅੰਦੇਸ਼, ਦੂਰ-ਦਰਸ਼ੀ

farce (ਫ਼ਾ*ਸ) *n v* ਨਕਲ, ਸਾਂਗ, ਹਾਸਾ ਠੱਠਾ, ਮਸ਼ਕਰੀ, ਮਖ਼ੌਲ; ਮਸਾਲੇਦਾਰ ਬਣਾਉਣਾ, ਹਾਸਰਸੀ ਬਣਾਉਣਾ

fare (ਫ਼ੇਅ*) *n v* ਭਾੜਾ, ਕਿਰਾਇਆ (ਸਫ਼ਰ); ਖ਼ੁਰਾਕ, ਪੈਂਡਾ ਕਰਨਾ, ਸਫ਼ਰ ਕਰਨਾ, ਨਿਭਣਾ; ਭੋਜਨ ਖਾਣਾ

farewell ('ਫ਼ੇਅ*ਵੈੱਲ) *n int* ਵਿਦਾ, ਵਿਦਾਇਗੀ, ਅਲਵਿਦਾ

farm (ਫ਼ਾ*ਮ) *n v* ਖੇਤ, ਖੇਤੀ, ਸ਼ਿਸ਼ੂ-ਨਿਕੇਤਨ; ਪਟਾ, ਠੇਕਾ; ਖੇਤੀ ਕਰਨਾ, ਵਾਹੀ ਕਰਨਾ; ਠੇਕਾ ਲੈਣਾ; ~house ਖੇਤ ਵਿਚਲਾ ਮਕਾਨ, ਹਵੇਲੀ; ~er ਕਿਸਾਨ, ਜ਼ਿਮੀਂਦਾਰ, ਕਾਸ਼ਤਕਾਰ, ਵਾਹੀਕਾਰ, ਕ੍ਰਿਸ਼ਕ; ~ing ਵਾਹੀ-ਜੋਤੀ, ਖੇਤੀ, ਕਾਸ਼ਤਕਾਰੀ, ਕਿਰਸਾਣੀ

farther ('ਫ਼ਾ*ਦਅ*) *a adv* ਵਧੇਰੇ, ਵੱਧ, ਹੋਰ ਜ਼ਿਆਦਾ, ਭੀ, ਵੀ, ਅਤੇ ਇਸ ਤੋਂ ਇਲਾਵਾ, ਅਗੇਰੇ, ਹੋਰ ਅੱਗੇ; ~most ਸਭ ਤੋਂ ਦੂਰ, ਦੂਰਤਮ, ਦੂਰਵਰਤੀ

farthest ('ਫ਼ਾਦਿਸਟ) ਸਭ ਤੋਂ ਦੂਰੇਡਾ

fascinate ('ਫ਼ੈਸਿਨੇਇਟ) *v* ਮੋਹ ਲੈਣਾ, ਮੁਗਧ ਕਰਨਾ, ਮੋਹਤ ਕਰਨਾ; ਵੱਸ ਵਿਚ ਕਰ ਲੈਣਾ ਬੁਰੀ ਨਜ਼ਰ ਰੱਖਣੀ, ਧਿਆਨ ਆਕਰਸ਼ਤ ਕਰਨ

fascinating ('ਫ਼ੈਸਿਨੇਇਟਿਙ) *a* ਮਨਮੋਹਣਾ ਦਿਲ-ਖਿੱਚਵਾਂ, ਮਨੋਹਰ, ਰੀਝਾਉਣਾ, ਆਕਰਸ਼ਕ

fascination ('ਫ਼ੈਸਿ'ਨੇਇਸ਼ਨ) *n* ਖਿੱਚ ਆਕਰਸ਼ਨ, ਵਸ਼ੀਕਰਨ

fashion ('ਫ਼ੈਸ਼ਨ) *n v* ਵੇਸ, ਭੇਸ, ਸਜਪਜ, ਢੰਗ ਰੂਪ, ਪ੍ਰਕਾਰ, ਸ਼ੈਲੀ, ਪਰਟਾਲੀ, ਪ੍ਰਥਾ, ਰੀਤ, ਰਸਮ ਬਣਾਉਣਾ, ਸਜਾਣਾ, ਢਾਲਣਾ; ~able ਫ਼ੈਸ਼ਨ ਪਰਸਤ, ਆਧੁਨਿਕ ਜੀਵਨ ਵਾਲਾ ਵਿਅਕਤੀ ਪ੍ਰਚਲਤ ਸ਼ੈਲੀ, ਅਧੁਨਾਈ, ਸ਼ੋਭਾਚਾਰੀ, ਲੋਕਚਾਰੀ

fast (ਫ਼ਾਸਟ) *n a adv. v* ਵਰਤ, ਨਾਗ਼ਾ, ਢਾਕ ਰੋਜ਼ਾ, ਉਪਵਾਸ; ਤੇਜ਼, ਤਿੱਖਾ; ਕੱਸਿਆ, ਕਸ ਬੱਧਾ; ਪੱਕਾ (ਰੰਗ ਆਦਿ), ਝਟਪਟ, ਤੁਰਤ, ਛੇਤ ਛੇਤੀ; ਨੇੜੇ, ਕੋਲ, ਦ੍ਰਿੜ੍ਹਤਾ ਨਾਲ, ਕਸ ਕੇ, ਵਰ ਰੱਖਣਾ, ਰੋਜ਼ਾ ਰੱਖਣਾ; ~friend ਪੱਕਾ ਮਿੱਤਰ ਜਿਗਰੀ ਦੋਸਤ; ~en ਬੰਨ੍ਹਣਾ, ਜਕੜਨ ਜੁੜਨਾ, ਪੱਕਾ ਹੋਣਾ, ਮਜ਼ਬੂਤ ਹੋਣਾ, ਸਥਾਪ ਹੋਣਾ, ਅਧਿਕਾਰ ਕਰਨਾ; ਕਬਜ਼ਾ ਜਮਾ ਲੈਣ ~ener ਕਸਣ ਵਾਲਾ, ਜਕੜਨੀ, ਗੁੱਠ ਚਿਟਕਣੀ, ਬੰਨ੍ਹਣ ਵਾਲਾ; ~ness ਤੇਜ਼ ਸ਼ੀਘਰਤਾ, ਦ੍ਰਿੜ੍ਹਤਾ

fat (ਫ਼ੈਟ) *a n v* ਮੋਟਾ, ਮੋਟਾ-ਤਾਜ਼ਾ, ਪਲਿਆ ਹੋਇਆ, ਭਾਰੀ (ਜ਼ਮੀਨ); ਮੋਟੀ ਅਕਲ ਵਾਲ ਗੰਵਾਰ, ਘੁੱਥੂ

fatal ('ਫ਼ੇਇਟਲ) *a* ਘਾਤਕ, ਕਾਰੀ, ਸ ਹਤਿਆਰਾ, ਹਾਨੀਕਾਰਕ; ~ity ਵਿਨਾਸ਼ੀ ਪ੍ਰਥਾ ਵਿਨਾਸ਼ਕਤਾ, ਬਿਪਤਾ, ਕਸ਼ਟ

fate (ਫ਼ੇਇਟ) *n v* ਭਾਗ, ਲੇਖ, ਮੁਕੱਦਰ, ਨਸ ਕਿਸਮਤ, ਤਕਦੀਰ

father ('ਫਾਦਅ*) *n v* ਪਿਤਾ, ਬਾਪ, ਪਿਓ; ਵਡੇਰਾ, ਜਨਮਦਾਤਾ, ਪ੍ਰਮੁੱਖ ਵਿਅਕਤੀ, (F~) ਪਰਮਾਤਮਾ; ਲਾਟ ਪਾਦਰੀ ਦਾ ਖ਼ਿਤਾਬ; ਜਨਮ ਦੇਣਾ, ਪੈਦਾ ਕਰਨਾ; ਪਿਤਾ ਬਣਨਾ; ~**in law** ਸਹੁਰਾ; ~**less** ਅਨਾਥ, ਯਤੀਮ; **grand**~ ਦਾਦਾ, ਨਾਨਾ, ਪੁਰਖਾ

fathom ('ਫੈਦਅਮ) *n v* ਪਾਣੀ ਦੀ ਡੂੰਘਾਈ ਨਾਪਣੀ, ਥਾਹ ਲੈਣੀ, ਤਹਿ ਤਕ ਪੁੱਜਣਾ; ਬਾਹਵਾਂ ਨਾਲ ਘੇਰ ਲੈਣਾ; ~**less** ਅਥਾਹ, ਅਤਲ

fatigue (ਫਅ'ਟੀਗ) *n v* ਥਕੇਵਾਂ, ਥਕਾਵਟ, ਵਗਾਰ, ਸਿਥਲ ਕਰ ਦੇਣਾ; ਧਾਤ ਨੂੰ ਕੁੱਟ ਕੁੱਟ ਕੇ ਪਤਲਾ ਕਰ ਦੇਣਾ

fatty (ਫੈਟੀ) *a n* ਚਰਬੀਲਾ, ਮੋਟਾ ਤਾਜ਼ਾ

fault (ਫੋਲਟ) *n v* ਭੁੱਲ, ਗ਼ਲਤੀ, ਕਸੂਰ, ਦੋਸ਼, ਨੁਕਸ, ਤੇੜ; ਦਰਾੜ ਪਾਉਂਟੀ, ਟੁੱਟ ਜਾਣਾ; ~**finding** ਨੁਕਤਾਚੀਨੀ, ਦੋਸ਼ ਦੇਖਣ ਦੀ ਰੁਚੀ; ~**less** ਬੇਕਸੂਰ, ਨਿਰਦੋਸ਼, ਨਿਸ਼ਕਲੰਕ; ~**y** ਅਸ਼ੁੱਧ, ਗ਼ਲਤ, ਨੁਕਸਦਾਰ, ਦੋਸ਼ਪੂਰਨ, ਦੋਸ਼ੀ, ਕਸੂਰਵਾਰ

fauna (ਫੋਨਅ) *n pl* ਜੀਵ ਜੰਤੂ; ਜੀਵ ਜੰਤੂ ਵਰਗਾ, ਜੀਵ-ਸ਼ਾਸਤਰ

favour ('ਫੇਇਵ੍ਅ*) *n v* ਉਪਕਾਰ, ਲਿਹਾਜ਼, ਪੱਖਧਾਰੀ ਰਿਆਇਤ; ਅਨੁਕੂਲਤਾ; ਮੂੰਹ-ਮੁਹਾਂਦਰਾ, ਚਿਹਰਾ-ਮੁਹਰਾ; ਲਿਹਾਜ਼ ਕਰਨਾ, ਤਰਫ਼ਦਾਰੀ ਕਰਨੀ, ਅਨੁਕੂਲਤਾ ਪਰਗਟ ਕਰਨੀ; ਮਿਹਰਬਾਨੀ ਕਰਨੀ; ਸਵੀਕਾਰ ਕਰਨਾ, ਸਰਲ ਕਰ ਦੇਣਾ, ਸਹਾਰਾ ਦੇਣਾ; ~**able** ਅਨੁਕੂਲ, ਸਹਾਇਕ, ਹਿਤਕਾਰੀ, ਮੁਆਫ਼ਕ, ਉਪਕਾਰਕ; ~**ite** ਲਾਡਲਾ, ਮੂੰਹ ਚੜ੍ਹਿਆ, ਲਿਹਾਜ਼ੀ, ਵਿਸ਼ੇਸ਼ ਨਿਕਟਵਰਤੀ ਵਿਅਕਤੀ; ਪਿਆਰਾ, ਮਨਪਸੰਦ, ਮਨਭਾਉਂਦਾ; ~**itism** ਤਰਫ਼ਦਾਰੀ, ਪੱਖਪਾਤ, ਲਿਹਾਜ਼, ਮੁਲਾਹਜ਼ਾ

fawn (ਫੋਨ) *n v* ਹਿਰਨ ਦਾ ਬੱਚਾ, ਹਿਰਨੋਟਾ; ਲਾਡਕਰਨਾ; ਚਾਪਲੂਸੀ ਕਰਨੀ; ~**ing** ਖ਼ੁਸ਼ਾਮਦੀ, ਚਾਪਲੂਸ; ਖ਼ੁਸ਼ਾਮਦ, ਚਾਪਲੂਸੀ

fear (ਫ਼ਿਅ*) *n v* ਡਰ, ਭੈ, ਪਰੇਸ਼ਾਨੀ; ਡਰਨਾ ਜਾਂ ਡਰਾਉਣਾ, ਭੈਭੀਤ ਕਰਨਾ, ਸ਼ੰਕਾ ਹੋਣਾ; ਰੱਬ ਤੋਂ ਡਰਨਾ; ~**ful** ਡਰਾਉਣਾ, ਭਿਅੰਕਰ, ਭਿਆਨਕ, ਖੌਫ਼ਨਾਕ; ~**less** ਨਿਡਰ, ਨਿਡਰਕ, ਦਲੇਰ

feasibility ('ਫ਼ੀਜ਼ਅ'ਬਿਲਟੀ) *n* ਸੰਭਵਤਾ, ਯੋਗਤਾ, ਨਿਬੜਯੋਗਤਾ

feasible ('ਫ਼ੀਜ਼ਅਬਲ) *a* ਹੋਣ ਯੋਗ, ਉਚਿਤ, ਨਿਬੜਯੋਗ, ਉਪਯੋਗੀ

feast (ਫ਼ੀਸਟ) *n v* ਪਰੀਤੀਭੋਜ, ਦਾਅਵਤ, ਭੰਡਾਰਾ, ਜ਼ਿਆਫ਼ਤ, ਤਿਉਹਾਰ, ਪੁਰਬ, ਉਤਸਵ, ਧਾਰਮਕ ਉਤਸਵ; ਰਜ ਕੇ ਖਾਣਾ ਜਾਂ ਖਵਾਉਣਾ, ਤ੍ਰਿਪਤ ਕਰਨਾ, ਭੰਡਾਰਾ ਕਰਨਾ, ਪੁਰਬ ਮਨਾਉਣਾ

feat (ਫ਼ੀਟ) *n a* ਸਾਹਸੀ ਕੰਮ, ਅਸਧਾਰਨ ਕੰਮ, ਅਸਚਰਜ ਕੰਮ, ਕਮਾਲ, ਕਾਰੀਗਰੀ, ਹੱਥ ਦੀ ਸਫ਼ਾਈ; ਪ੍ਰਵੀਨ, ਨਿਪੁੰਨ, ਚੁਸਤ, ਫ਼ੁਰਤੀਲਾ

feather ('ਫ਼ੈਦਅ*) *n v* ਖੰਭ, ਪਰ; ਬਹੁਤ ਹੌਲੀ ਵਸਤੂ; ਖੰਭ ਲਾਉਣਾ, ਖੰਭ ਚਿਪਕਾਉਣਾ; **in high**~ ਬੜੇ ਜੋਸ਼ ਵਿਚ, ਪੂਰੇ ਉਤਸ਼ਾਹ ਨਾਲ

feature ('ਫ਼ੀਚਅ*) *n* ਚਿਹਰਾ-ਮੁਹਰਾ, ਹੁਲੀਆ, ਰੂਪ, ਰੰਗ-ਰੂਪ, ਨਕਸ਼, ਸ਼ਕਲ-ਸੂਰਤ; ਵਿਸ਼ੇਸ਼ਤਾ, ਲੱਛਣ; (ਅਖ਼ਬਾਰ ਦਾ) ਵਿਸ਼ੇਸ਼ ਲੇਖ; ਪ੍ਰਮੁੱਖ ਹੋਣਾ, ਰੂਪ ਦੇਣਾ, ਸ਼ਕਲ ਦੇਣੀ, ਰੂਪ-ਰੇਖਾ ਬਣਾਉਣੀ, ਨਕਸ਼ਾ ਖਿਚਣਾ, ਖ਼ਾਕਾ ਜਾਂ ਢਾਂਚਾ ਤਿਆਰ ਕਰਨਾ; ~**film** ਕਥਾ-ਚਿੱਤਰ; ~**less** ਆਕ੍ਰਿਤੀਹੀਨ, ਆਕਰਸ਼ਣਹੀਨ, ਫਿੱਕਾ ਤੇ ਕੋਝਾ, ਅਟਪਟ ਜਿਹਾ

federal ('ਫ਼ੈਡ(ਅ)ਰ(ਅ)ਲ) *a* ਸੰਘੀ

federation ('ਫ਼ੈਡਅ'ਰੇਇਸ਼ਨ) *n* ਸੰਘ, ਸੰਗਠਨ, ਸੰਧੀ

fee (ਫ਼ੀ) *n* ਫ਼ੀਸ, ਉਜਰਤ, ਮਿਹਨਤਾਨਾ,

feeble (ਫ਼ੀਬਲ) *a* ਕਮਜ਼ੋਰ, ਮਾੜ੍ਹਾ, ਨਿਰਬਲ ਦੁਰਬਲ, ਲਿੱਸਾ, ਬੁੱਧੀਹੀਣ, ਪ੍ਰਭਾਵਹੀਣ

feed (ਫ਼ੀਡ) *v n* ਖੁਆਉਣਾ, ਚੋਗਾ ਪਾਉਣਾ, ਚਰਨਾ, ਚੁਗਣਾ, ਹਿੰਮਤ ਪੂਰੀ ਕਰਨੀ; ਖ਼ੁਰਾਕ, ਗ਼ਿਜ਼ਾ, ਭੋਜਨ; **~back** ਪਰਤੀ ਸੂਚਨਾ,

feel (ਫ਼ੀਲ) *v n* ਟੋਹਣਾ; ਅਨੁਭਵ ਕਰਨਾ, ਮਹਿਸੂਸ ਕਰਨਾ, ਟਟੋਲਣਾ, ਟੋਹ ਕੇ ਲੱਭਣਾ; ਜਾਪਣਾ, ਪ੍ਰਤੀਤ ਹੋਣਾ, ਭਾਸਣਾ; ਸਮਝਣਾ; ਜਾਂਚ ਪੜਤਾਲ ਕਰਨੀ, ਸੂਝ ਹੋਣੀ, ਪਤਾ ਹੋਣਾ; ਪ੍ਰਭਾਵਤ ਹੋਣਾ; ਵਿਸ਼ਵਾਸ ਹੋਣਾ; ਸਪਰਸ਼, ਪਰਖ, ਛੁਹ ਦੁਆਰਾ ਪੜਤਾਲ; **~the pulse of** ਨਬਜ਼ ਵੇਖਣੀ, ਭੇਦਾਂ ਜਾਂ ਵਿਚਾਰਾਂ ਨੂੰ ਸਮਝਣਾ; **~ing** ਭਾਵ, ਇਹਸਾਸ, ਵਿਚਾਰ, ਜਜ਼ਬਾ; ਦਰਦ, ਵੇਦਨਾ; ਹਮਦਰਦੀ, ਵਿਸ਼ਵਾਸ

feign (ਫ਼ੇਇਨ) *v* ਬਹਾਨਾ ਕਰਨਾ, ਮਕਰ ਕਰਨਾ, ਮਚਲੇ ਹੋਣਾ; ਘੜਨਾ

felicitate (ਫ਼ਲ'ਲਿਸਿਟੇਇਟ) *v* ਵਧਾਈ ਦੇਣੀ; ਪਰਸੰਨ ਕਰਨਾ, ਨਿਹਾਲ ਕਰਨਾ, ਅਭਿਨੰਦਨ ਕਰਨਾ

felicitation (ਫ਼ਅ'ਲਿਸਿ'ਟੇਇਸ਼ਨ) *n* ਵਧਾਈ, ਮੁਬਾਰਕਬਾਦ, ਅਭਿਨੰਦਨ

felicity (ਫ਼ਅ'ਲਿਸਅਟਿ) *n* ਆਨੰਦ, ਪਰਮਾਨੰਦ, ਹੁਲਾਸ, ਸੁਭਾਗ

fellow ('ਫ਼ੈੱਲਅਉ) *n* ਸਾਥੀ, ਜੋਟੀਦਾਰ, ਸਹਿਯੋਗੀ, ਸੰਗੀ, ਆੜੀ, ਦੋਸਤ, ਭਾਈ-ਬੰਦ; ਸਮਕਾਲੀ, (ਯੂਨੀਵਰਸਿਟੀ ਦਾ) ਫ਼ੈਲੋ, ਬੰਦਾ; **~ship** ਭਾਈਚਾਰਾ, ਬਰਾਦਰੀ, ਭਿਆਲੀ, ਮਿੱਤਰਤਾ, ਮਿੱਤਰ-ਭਾਵ; ਸਾਥੀ-ਸੰਖ; ਕਾਲਜ ਜਾਂ ਯੂਨੀਵਰਸਿਟੀ ਦਾ ਵਜ਼ੀਫ਼ਾ; ਯੂਨੀਵਰਸਿਟੀ ਦੀ ਸਦੱਸਤਾ

female ('ਫ਼ੀਮੇਇਲ) *n a* ਮਦੀਨ, ਮਾਦਾ, ਇਸਤਰੀ, ਮਹਿਲਾ, ਔਰਤ; ਜ਼ਨਾਨਾ; **~friend** ਸਹੇਲੀ, ਸਖੀ

feminine ('ਫ਼ੈਮਿਨਿਨ) *a* ਜ਼ਨਾਨਾ, ਤੀਵੀਆਂ ਦਾ; ਜਨਨਖ਼, ਤੀਵੀਆਂ ਵਰਗਾ

femininity, feminism, femineity ('ਫ਼ੈਮਿ-ਨਿਨਅਟਿ, 'ਫ਼ੈਮਿਨਿਜ਼(ਅ)ਮ, 'ਫ਼ੈਮਿਨੀਅਟਿ) *n* ਨਾਰੀਤਵ, ਇਸਤਰੀਪਨ, ਨਾਰੀਪਨ, ਇਸਤਰੀ-ਵਾਦ

feminist ('ਫ਼ੈਮਿਨਿਸਟ) *a* ਨਾਰੀਵਾਦੀ; ਨਾਰੀਅ ਸਬੰਧੀ

fence (ਫ਼ੈਂਸ) *n v* ਵਾੜ, ਜੰਗਲਾ, ਵਲਗਣ, ਘੇਰਾ ਅਹਾਤਾ; ਪੈਂਤੜਾ; ਪੱਟਾ; ਘੇਰਾ ਵਲਣਾ; ਵਲਗਣ ਬਣਾਉਣਾ, ਵਾੜ ਲਾਉਣਾ; ਬਚਾ ਕਰਨਾ ਗਟਕਾ ਖੇਡਣਾ, ਚੋਰੀ ਦਾ ਮਾਲ ਖ਼ਰੀਦਣਾ ਵੇਚਣਾ

fencing ('ਫ਼ੈਂਸਿਙ) *n* ਜੰਗਲਾ, ਵਾੜ, ਘੇਰ ਚਾਰਦੀਵਾਰੀ; ਚੋਰੀ ਦੇ ਸਾਮਾਨ ਦਾ ਗੁਦਾਮ ਗਟਕਾ

fend (ਫ਼ੈਂਡ) *v* ਪ੍ਰਬੰਧ ਕਰਨਾ, ਇਕੱਤਰ ਕਰਨ ਬਚਾਉਣਾ, ਰੱਖਿਆ ਕਰਨੀ, ਸੰਭਾਲ ਕੇ ਰੱਖਣ ਬਚਾ ਕੇ ਰੱਖਣਾ; ਨਿਵਾਰਣ ਕਰਨਾ, ਹਟਾਉਣ ਦੂਰ ਭਜਾ ਦੇਣਾ

ferment ('ਫ਼ਅਃਮੈਂਟ, ਫ਼ਅ'ਮੈਂਟ) *n v* ਖ਼ਮੀ ਜਾਮਣ, ਉਬਾਲ, ਗੜਬੜ; ਉਬਲਣਾ, ਖ਼ਮ ਉਠਣਾ, ਉਤੇਜਤ ਕਰਨਾ, ਫ਼ਸਾਦ ਕਰਾਉਣ ਜੋਸ਼ ਵਿਚ ਆਉਣਾ, ਤੜਕ ਉੱਠਣਾ; **~atio** ਖ਼ਮੀਰ, ਜਾਮਣ, ਉਬਾਲ, ਉਤੇਜਨਾ; ਫ਼ਸਾਦ

ferocious (ਫ਼ਅ'ਰਅਉਸ਼ਅਸ) *a* ਵਹਿਸ਼ੀ, ਹਿੰਸ ਦਰਿੰਦਾ, ਖੂੰਖ਼ਾਰ, ਕਰੂਰ, ਭਿਅੰਕਰ, ਘੇਰਹਿਮ

ferocity (ਫ਼ਅ'ਰੌਸਅਟਿ) *n* ਵਹਿਸ਼ੀਪ

ਨਿਰਦਇਤਾ, ਕਰੂਰਤਾ, ਹਿੰਸਕਤਾ, ਜੰਗਲੀਪਨ

ferry ('ਫ਼ੈਰਿ) *n v* ਪੱਤਣ, ਘਾਟ, ਬੇੜੀ-ਘਾਟ, ਬੇੜੀ; ਬੇੜੀ ਦਾ ਭਾੜਾ; ਬੇੜੀ ਵਿਚ ਪਾਰ ਜਾਣਾ, ਬੇੜੀ ਵਿਚ ਪਾਰ ਲੈ ਜਾਣਾ; ਹਵਾਈ; **~boat** ਯਾਤਰੀਆਂ ਦੀ ਬੇੜੀ, ਪੱਤਣ ਦੀ ਬੇੜੀ, ਘਾਟ ਵਾਲੀ ਨੌਕਾ; **~man** ਮਾਂਝੀ, ਪਾਤਣੀ

fertile ('ਫ਼ਅਃਟਾਇਲ) *a* ਉਪਜਾਊ, ਜ਼ਰਖੇਜ਼, ਫਲਦਾਇਕ; ਬਹੁਜਨਨੀ

fertility (ਫ਼ਅ'ਟਿਲਅਟਿ) *n* ਉਪਜਾਊਪਣ, ਉਪਜਾਊ-ਸ਼ਕਤੀ, ਜਟਨ-ਸ਼ਕਤੀ, ਜ਼ਰਖੇਜ਼ੀ

fertilize ('ਫ਼ਅਃਟਅਲਾਇਜ਼) *v* ਉਪਜਾਊ ਬਣਾਉਣਾ, ਫਲਦਾਰ ਬਣਾਉਣਾ; ਜ਼ਰਖੇਜ਼ ਕਰਨਾ; **~or** ਰੂੜੀ, ਪਾਦ

fervent ('ਫ਼ਅਃਵ੍ਅੰਟ) *a* ਪ੍ਰਚੰਡ, ਜੋਸ਼ੀਲਾ ਗਰਮਾਗਰਮ, ਭਖਦਾ, ਤੱਤਾ

fervid ('ਫ਼ਅਃਵ੍ਇਡ) *a* ਉਤਸੁਕ, ਪ੍ਰਚੰਡ, ਮਘਦਾ; **~ness** ਉਤਸੁਕਤਾ, ਪ੍ਰਚੰਡਤਾ; ਉਤਕੰਠਾ

fervour, fervency ('ਫ਼ਅਃਵ਼੍ਅ*, 'ਫ਼ਅਃਵ਼੍ਅੰਸਿ) *n* ਤੀਬਰਤਾ, ਪ੍ਰਚੰਡਤਾ, ਉਤਸਾਹ, ਗਰਮੀ, ਤਪਸ਼, ਤਾਅ

festival ('ਫ਼ਐਸਟਅਵ੍ਅਲ) *n a* ਉਤਸਵ, ਪੁਰਬ, ਤਿਉਹਾਰ, ਜਸ਼ਨ

festive ('ਫ਼ੈਸਟਿਵ੍) *a* ਖ਼ੁਸ਼ ਖ਼ੁਸ਼, ਰੰਗੀਨਤ, ਪਰਸੰਨ, ਖ਼ੁਸ਼ੀ ਵਾਲਾ, ਅਨੰਦਦਾਇਕ; ਜ਼ਿੰਦਾ-ਦਿਲ, ਵਿਨੋਦੀ

festivity (ਫ਼ੈਸ'ਟਿਵ੍ਅਟਿ) *n* ਰੌਣਕ, ਸਜ-ਧਜ, ਰੰਗ-ਰਲੀਆਂ; ਉਤਸਵ, ਪੁਰਬ, ਤਿਉਹਾਰ, ਮੇਲਾ, ਰਾਗਾ-ਰੰਗ, ਜਸ਼ਨ

festoon (ਫ਼ੈਸ'ਟੂਨ) *n v* ਹਾਰ, ਸਜਾਵਟ ਲਈ ਲਾਈਆਂ ਝੰਡੀਆਂ; ਹਾਰਾਂ, ਝੰਡੀਆਂ ਆਦਿ ਨਾਲ ਸਜਾਉਣਾ, ਹਾਰ ਪਾਉਣਾ

fetch (ਫ਼ੈਂਚ) *v n* ਲਿਆਉਣਾ, ਚੁੱਕਣਾ; ਮੁੱਲ ਮਿਲਣਾ, ਕੁਝ ਪ੍ਰਾਪਤ ਹੋਣਾ; ਪ੍ਰਭਾਵਤ ਹੋਣਾ; ਧੋਖਾ, ਕਪਟ, ਫ਼ਰੇਬ, ਹੱਥਫੇਰੀ

fete (ਫ਼ੇਇਟ) *n v* ਉਤਸਵ; ਮੇਲਾ; ਤਿਉਹਾਰ ਜਾਂ ਉਤਸਵ ਮਨਾਉਣਾ, ਮੌਜ-ਮੇਲਾ ਕਰਨਾ; ਮੇਲਾ ਲਾਉਣਾ

fetter ('ਫ਼ੈੱਟਅ*) *n v* ਬੇੜੀ, ਪੈਂਖੜ, ਰੋਕ, ਰੁਕਾਵਟ, ਗਰਿਫ਼ਤਾਰੀ, ਬੇੜੀ ਪਾਉਣਾ, ਬੰਧਨ ਲਾਉਣਾ, ਬੰਨ੍ਹ ਦੇਣਾ

feud (ਫ਼ਯੂਡ) *n* ਖ਼ਾਨਦਾਨੀ ਵੈਰ, ਜੱਦੀ ਦੁਸ਼ਮਣੀ, ਦੰਗਾ, ਦੁਸ਼ਮਣੀ; ਜਾਗੀਰ; **~al** ਜਾਗੀਰੀ, ਸਾਮੰਤ-ਵਾਦੀ, ਸਾਮੰਤੀ, ਭੂਪਵਾਦੀ; **~alism** ਜਾਗੀਰ-ਦਾਰੀ, ਥਿਸਵੇਦਾਰੀ, ਸਾਮੰਤਵਾਦ, ਰਾਜਵਾੜਾਸ਼ਾਹੀ; **~alist** ਜਾਗੀਰਦਾਰ, ਸਾਮੰਤਵਾਦੀ

fever ('ਫ਼ੀਵ੍ਅ*) *n v* ਤਾਪ, ਬੁਖ਼ਾਰ, ਉਤੇਜਨਾ; ਤਾਪ ਚੜ੍ਹਾਉਣਾ; **~ish** ਤਾਪਲ, ਸਰਗਰਮ, ਭਖਦਾ

few (ਫ਼ਯੂ) *a n* ਕੁਝ, ਥੋੜ੍ਹੇ ਜਿਹੇ, ਕੁਝ ਕੁ, ਕੋਈ ਕੋਈ, ਟਾਂਵਾਂ ਟਾਂਵਾਂ, ਇਕ ਅੱਧਾ; **not a~** ਬਹੁਤ ਸਾਰੇ; **the~** ਕੁਝ ਥੋੜ੍ਹੀ ਗਿਣਤੀ ਦੇ, ਚੋਣਵੇਂ

fiasco (ਫ਼ਿ'ਐਸਕਅਓ) *n v* ਅਸਫਲਤਾ, ਨਾਕਾਮਯਾਬੀ, ਬਹੁਤ ਬੁਰੀ ਵਿਫਲਤਾ

fiat ('ਫ਼ਾਇਐਟ) *n v* ਹੁਕਮ, ਫ਼ਰਮਾਨ, ਆਗਿਆ, ਆਦੇਸ਼; ਅਧਿਕਾਰ ਦੇਣਾ, ਮੁਖਤਿਆਰ ਬਣਾਉਣਾ

fibre ('ਫ਼ਾਇਬਅ*) *n* ਰੇਸ਼ਾ; ਸੂਤ, ਤੰਦ; ਢੰਗ, ਢਾਂਚਾ, ਸ਼ਕਲ; ਸੁਭਾਉ; **~d** ਰੇਸ਼ੇਦਾਰ, ਤੰਦਾਂ ਵਾਲਾ, ਤਾਰਦਾਰ

fibrous ('ਫ਼ਿਬਿਰਅਸ) *a* ਰੇਸ਼ੇਦਾਰ; ਪੱਕਾ, ਮਜ਼ਬੂਤ

fickle ('ਫ਼ਿਕਲ) *a* ਚੰਚਲ, ਅਸਥਿਰ, ਚਪਲ, ਡੋਲਵਾਂ, ਪਰਿਵਰਤਨਸ਼ੀਲ; **~minded** ਚੰਚਲ

ਮਨ ਵਾਲਾ, ਅਟਿਕਵਾਂ ਵਿਅਕਤੀ; ~ness ਚੰਚਲਤਾ, ਅਸਥਿਰਤਾ

fiction (ਫ਼ਿਕਸ਼ਨ) *n* ਗਲਪ, ਨਾਵਲ ਕਹਾਣੀ ਆਦਿ ਕਥਾ-ਸਾਹਿਤ; ਕਲਪਤ ਕਥਾ, ਝੂਠਾ ਕਿੱਸਾ, ਕਲਪਨਾ, ਗੱਪ, ਝੂਠ; ~al ਗਲਪਈ, ਕਲਪਤ, ਕਹਾਣੀ ਜਾਂ ਨਾਵਲ ਸਬੰਧੀ

fictitious (ਫ਼ਿਕ'ਟਿਸ਼ਅਸ) *a* ਬਣਾਉਟੀ, ਨਕਲੀ, ਖੋਟਾ, ਫ਼ਰਜ਼ੀ, ਕਲਪਤ, ਅਵਾਸਤਵਿਕ,

fidelity (ਫ਼ਿ'ਡੇਲਅਟਿ) *n* ਵਫ਼ਾਦਾਰੀ, ਨਿਸ਼ਠਾ; ਦ੍ਰਿੜ੍ਹਤਾ; ਸਥਿਰ ਵਿਸ਼ਵਾਸ, ਪੱਕੀ ਸ਼ਰਧਾ

fie (ਫ਼ਾਇ) *int* ਫਿੱਟੇ ਮੂੰਹ, ਲਖ ਲਾਨ੍ਹਤ, ਧਿੱਕਾਰ

fief (ਫ਼ੀਫ਼) *n* ਜਾਗੀਰ

field (ਫ਼ੀਲਡ) *n v* (1) ਖੇਤ, ਚਰਾਗਾਹ; ਭੋਂ, ਜ਼ਮੀਨ; (2) ਰਣਭੂਮੀ, ਜੁੱਧ-ਖੇਤਰ; (3) ਹਾਕੀ, ਫੁਟਬਾਲ, ਕ੍ਰਿਕਟ ਆਦਿ ਖੇਡਾਂ ਦੇ ਮੈਦਾਨ; ਗੇਂਦ ਰੋਕਣਾ ਤੇ ਮੋੜਨਾ; ਖਿਡਾਰੀਆਂ ਨੂੰ ਹੱਲਾ ਸ਼ੇਰੀ ਦੇਣੀ, ਉਤਸ਼ਾਹ ਵਧਾਉਣਾ, ਕਾਰਜ ਕਰਨਾ; hold the~ ਡਟੇ ਰਹਿਣਾ, ਪੈਰ ਪਿੱਛੇ ਨਾ ਕਰਨਾ; keep the~ ਅੰਦੋਲਨ ਜਾਰੀ ਰੱਖਣਾ, ਆਪਣੀ ਗੱਲ ਪੱਕੀ ਕਰਨਾ; take the~ ਮੈਦਾਨ ਵਿਚ ਨਿਤਰਨਾ, ਲੜਾਈ ਸ਼ੁਰੂ ਕਰਨੀ

fiend (ਫ਼ੀਂਡ) *n* ਭੂਤਨਾ, ਪਰੇਤ; ਸ਼ੈਤਾਨ, ਦੁਸ਼ਟ, ਚੰਡਾਲ, ਉਪੱਦਰੀ

fierce (ਫ਼ਿਅਃਸ) *a* ਤੀਬਰ, ਤੁੰਦ, ਪ੍ਰਚੰਡ; ਘੋਰ, ਉਗਰ ਭਿਆਨਕ, ਕਰੂਰ; ਜੋਸ਼ੀਲਾ, ਨਿਰਦਈ, ਬੇਰਹਿਮ

fiery ('ਫ਼ਾਇਅਰਿ) *a* ਅਗਨਮਈ, ਦਗਦਾ, ਭਖਦਾ; ਜੋਸ਼ੀਲਾ, ਲੜਾਕਾ, ਅੰਗ ਦੀ ਨਾੜ, ਕਰੋਪੀ; ਅੰਗ ਵਰਗਾ, ਤਪਦਾ, ਲਾਲ ਅੰਗਾਰ; ਭੜਕਾਊ, ਉਤੇਜਤ ਕਰਨ ਵਾਲਾ, ਅੰਗ ਵਾਂਗ ਭਖਾ ਦੇਣ ਵਾਲਾ; ਧੂੰਆਂਧਾਰ (ਭਾਸ਼ਣ)

fiesta (ਫ਼ਿ'ਐੱਸਟਾ) *n* ਮੇਲਾ

fifteen ('ਫ਼ਿਫ਼'ਟੀਨ) *a n* ਪੰਦਰ੍ਹਾਂ; ~th ਪੰਦਰਵਾਂ

fifth (ਫ਼ਿਫ਼ਥ) *a n* ਪੰਜਵਾਂ; ਪੰਜ ਤਾਰੀਖ਼; ਪੰਜਵੀਂ ਥਿਤ, ਪੰਜਵੀਂ ਸੁਰ (ਰਾਗ ਵਿਚ), ਪੰਚਮ; ਘਟੀਆ ਚੀਜ਼, ਰੱਦੀ ਵਸਤੂ; ~column ਦੇਸ਼ਧਰੋਹੀ ਸੰਸਥਾ, ਘਰ ਦਾ ਭੇਤੀ, ਦੇਸ਼ਧਰੋਹੀ; ~columnist ਦੇਸ਼ਧਰੋਹੀ, ਗੱਦਾਰ

fifty ('ਫ਼ਿਫ਼ਟਿ) *a n* ਪੰਜਾਹ (50), ਪੰਜਾਹਵਾਂ ਦਾ ਸਮੂਹ; ਬਹੁਤ ਸਾਰੇ, ਕਈ, ਲੋੜ ਤੋਂ ਵਧੇਰੇ

fig (ਫ਼ਿਗ) *n* (1) ਅੰਜੀਰ, ਮਾਮੂਲੀ ਚੀਜ਼, ਤੁੱਛ ਵਸਤੂ; (2) ਹਾਲਤ, ਦਸ਼ਾ, ਅਵਸਥਾ

fight (ਫ਼ਾਇਟ) *n v* ਲੜਨਾ, ਝਗੜਨਾ, ਜੁੱਧ ਕਰਨਾ, ਜੰਗ ਕਰਨਾ; ਟੱਕਰ ਲੈਣੀ, ਮੁਕਾਬਲਾ ਕਰਨਾ; ਮੁਕੱਦਮਾ ਲੜਨਾ; ਘੁਲਣਾ; ਲੜਾਈ ਮੁੱਠ-ਭੇੜ, ਟੱਕਰ, ਕੁਸ਼ਤੀ, ਜੁੱਧ, ਜੰਗ, ਸੰਘਰਸ਼, ਜਤਨ; ਲਗਾਤਾਰ ਕੋਸ਼ਸ਼; ~out ਲੜ ਝਗੜ ਕੇ ਮਾਮਲਾ ਨਜਿੱਠਣਾ; ~er ਜੋਧਾ, ਲੜਾਕਾ, ਸੂਰਬੀਰ

figment ('ਫ਼ਿਗਮਅੰਟ) *n* ਕਲਪਨਾ, ਵਹਿਮ, ਮਨਘੜਤ, ਬਿਆਨ

figure ('ਫ਼ਿਗਅ*) *n v* ਸ਼ਕਲ, ਖ਼ਾਕਾ, ਆਕਾਰ, ਬਾਹਰੀ ਰੂਪ, ਸਰੀਰ, ਡੌਲ, ਕਾਠੀ, ਮੂਰਤੀ, ਬੁੱਤ; (ਗਣਿਤ ਆਦਿ ਵਿਚ) ਸੰਖਿਆ, ਗਿਣਤੀ; ਅੰਗ, ਚਿੰਨ੍ਹ, ਛਾਪ, ਉਪਮਾ, ਅੱਲੰਕਾਰ, ਸਦ੍ਰਿਸ਼ਤਾ; ਅਨੁਮਾਨ; ਵੇਲ-ਬੂਟੇ ਪਾਉਣੇ; ਗਿਣਤੀ ਕਰਨੀ; ਕੁੱਲ ਜੋੜ ਕਰਨਾ; ~head ਦਿਖਾਵੇ ਦਾ ਮੁੱਖੀ, ਨਾਂ ਦਾ ਪ੍ਰਧਾਨ, ~of speech ਅੱਲੰਕਾਰ (ਰੁਪਕ, ਅਤਕਥਨੀ ਆਦਿ); ~less ਨਿਰਾਕਾਰ, ਆਕਾਰਹੀਨ, ਬੇਢੰਗਾ, ਭੱਦਾ, ਬੇਡੌਲ

filament ('ਫ਼ਿਲਅਮਅੰਟ) *n* ਰੇਸ਼ਾ, ਤਾਰ, ਤੰਦ, ਸੂਤ; ਪਰਾਗ ਕੇਸਰ, ਕਿੰਜਲਕ; ਬਲਬ ਦੀ ਤਾਰ; ~ary ਰੇਸ਼ੇ ਦਾ, ਤੰਦਾਂ ਵਾਲਾ; ਕੇਸਰ ਜਾਂ ਕਿੰਜਲਕ ਵਾਲਾ

file (ਫ਼ਾਇਲ) *n v* ਫ਼ਾਇਲ, ਪੁਲੰਦਾ, ਮਿਸਲ; ਪੰਗਤੀ, ਕਤਾਰ, ਖ਼ਾਨੇ, ਘਰ, ਰੇਤੀ ਚੋਸਾ; ਕਪਟੀ ਮਨੁੱਖ, ਚਲਾਕ ਬੰਦਾ; ਨੱਥੀ ਕਰਨਾ ਕ੍ਰਮਵਾਰ ਕਾਗ਼ਜ਼ ਰੱਖਣਾ; ਮਿਸਲ ਬਣਾਉਣੀ, ਰੇਤੀ ਨਾਲ ਪੱਧਰਾ ਕਰਨਾ; ਸਾਫ਼ ਕਰਨਾ; ਸੁਧਾਰਨਾ, ਮੁਲਾਇਮ ਕਰਨਾ, ਰਗੜਨਾ, ਘਿਸਾਉਣਾ; ਪਾਲ ਬੰਨ੍ਹਣੀ, ਪੰਗਤੀਆਂ ਵਿਚ ਕੂਚ ਕਰਨਾ; **~a suit** ਦਾਵਾ ਦਾਇਰ ਕਰਨਾ; **rank and~** ਪਿਛਲੱਗ, ਆਮ ਲੋਕ, ਸਰਬ

fill (ਫ਼ਿਲ) *v n* ਭਰਨਾ, ਭਰ ਜਾਣਾ, ਪੂਰਾ ਕਰਨਾ, ਪੂਰਨਾ, ਪੂਰੇ ਜਾਣਾ, ਦਫ਼ਤਰ ਦੇ ਕੰਮ ਨਿਭਾਉਣੇ; ਕਿਸੇ ਅਹੁਦੇ ਤੇ ਹੋਣਾ; ਰੱਜ ਕੇ ਖਾਣਾ, ਤੁਸਣਾ; ਪੂਰਤੀ, ਮਾਪ, ਭਰਤੀ, ਰੱਜ, ਤ੍ਰਿਪਤੀ; **~in** ਖ਼ਾਨਾ ਪੂਰੀ ਕਰਨਾ, ਲਿਖਣਾ; **~up** ਪੂਰੀ ਤਰ੍ਹਾਂ ਭਰ ਜਾਣਾ, ਵੱਡਾ ਹੋ ਜਾਣਾ, ਖ਼ਾਲੀ ਥਾਂ ਨੂੰ ਭਰਨਾ; **~er** ਭਰਨ ਵਾਲਾ, ਪੂਰਕ; **~ing** ਭਰਤ, ਭਰਾਈ; ਦੰਦ ਵਿਚ ਭਰੀ ਗਈ ਵਸਤੂ

fillet (ਫ਼ਿਲਿਟ) *n v* ਕਿਸੇ ਚੀਜ਼ ਦਾ ਪਤਲਾ ਜਿਹਾ ਟੁਕੜਾ, ਸਿਰ ਨੂੰ ਬੰਨ੍ਹਣ ਲਈ ਫੀਤਾ, ਪਰਾਂਦਾ, ਜਾਨਵਰਾਂ ਦੀ ਕਮਰ, ਕੁੱਲ੍ਹਾ, ਸਿਰ ਉੱਤੇ ਪੱਟੀ, ਫੀਤਾ ਆਦਿ ਬੰਨ੍ਹਣਾ, ਮੱਛੀ ਦੇ ਟੁਕੜੇ ਕਰਨੇ

fillip (ਫ਼ਿਲਿਪ) *n v* ਠੋਲ੍ਹਾ ਮਾਰਨਾ, ਉਂਗਲ ਦੀ ਚੁਟਕੀ; ਹਿਲਕੋਰਨਾ; ਪਰੇਰਨਾ, ਉਕਸਾਹਟ; ਹੱਲਾਸ਼ੇਰੀ ਦੇਣੀ; ਨਹੁੰ ਜਾਂ ਉਂਗਲ ਦਾ ਟੁਣਕਾ ਮਾਰਨਾ

film (ਫ਼ਿਲਮ) *n v* ਚਲਚਿੱਤਰ; ਫ਼ਿਲਮ, ਪਰਦਾ, ਝਿੱਲੀ, ਪਤਲੀ, ਤਹਿ; ਅੱਖ ਦਾ ਜਾਲਾ; ਫ਼ਿਲਮ ਬਣਾਉਣਾ

filter ('ਫ਼ਿਲਟਅ*) *n v* ਤਰਲ ਪਦਾਰਥਾਂ ਨੂੰ ਛਾਣਨ ਵਾਲਾ ਜੰਤਰ, ਪੁਣਨਾ, ਛਾਣਨਾ (ਤਰਲ ਪਦਾਰਥ ਦਾ), ਸਾਫ਼ ਕਰਨਾ; ਛਟ ਕੇ ਲੰਘਣਾ, ਚੋਣਾ, ਚੁਆਉਣਾ; ਫੁੱਟ ਕੇ ਨਿਕਲਣਾ; ਫੁੱਟ ਨਿਕਲਣਾ

filth (ਫ਼ਿਲਥ) *n* ਗੰਦ, ਗੰਦ-ਮੰਦ, ਗੰਦਗੀ, ਮੈਲ; ਮਲ ਰੂੜੀ, ਕੂੜਾ; ਅਸ਼ਲੀਲਤਾ, ਭ੍ਰਿਸ਼ਟਤਾ

filtrate ('ਫ਼ਿਲਟਰੇਇਟ) *n v* ਪੁਣ ਕੇ ਸਾਫ਼ ਕੀਤੀ ਸ਼ਰਾਬ; ਪੁਣਨਾ, ਸਾਫ਼ ਕਰਨਾ

filtration ('ਫ਼ਿਲਟ'ਰੇਇਸ਼ਨ) *n* ਛਟਾਈ, ਛਾਣਨ

fin (ਫ਼ਿਨ) *n* ਮੱਛੀ ਦਾ ਖੰਭ, ਖੰਭ

final ('ਫ਼ਾਇਨਲ) *a n* ਫ਼ੈਸਲਾਕੁਨ, ਅੰਤਮ, ਅੰਤਲਾ; **~e** (ਸੰਗੀ) ਅੰਤਮ, ਗਤੀ, (ਨਾਟਕ) ਅੰਤਮ ਝਾਕੀ, ਅੰਤ, ਸਮਾਪਤੀ; **~ly** ਆਖ਼ਰ ਵਿਚ, ਅੰਤਮ ਰੂਪ ਵਿਚ

finance (ਫ਼ਾਇਨੈਂਸ) *a* ਵਿੱਤ, ਅਰਥ, ਮਾਲ, ਪੂੰਜੀ, ਆਰਥਕ ਸਾਧਨ; ਆਰਥਕ ਪ੍ਰਬੰਧ; ਪੂੰਜੀ ਲਾਉਣੀ, (ਕਿਸੇ ਵਿਹਾਰ ਵਿਚ) ਪੈਸਾ ਲਾਉਣਾ, ਆਰਥਕ ਪ੍ਰਬੰਧ ਕਰਨਾ, ਪੂੰਜੀ ਇਕੱਤਰ ਕਰਨਾ; **~r** ਸ਼ਾਹੂਕਾਰ, ਪੂੰਜੀਪਤੀ, ਸਰਮਾਏਦਾਰ

financial (ਫ਼ਾਇਨੈਂਸ਼ਲ) *a* ਆਰਥਕ, ਮਾਲੀ ਵਿੱਤ ਸਬੰਧੀ, ਆਮਦਨੀ ਬਾਰੇ

financier (ਫ਼ਾਇਨੈਂਸਿਅ*) *n* ਆਰਥਕ ਪ੍ਰਬੰਧ ਵਿਚ ਪ੍ਰਵੀਣ, ਪੂੰਜੀਕਾਰ, ਸ਼ਾਹੂਕਾਰ, ਸਰਮਾਏਦਾਰ, ਕੋਸ਼-ਅਧਿਅਕਸ਼

find (ਫ਼ਾਇੰਡ) *v* ਲੱਭਣਾ, ਪ੍ਰਾਪਤ ਕਰਨਾ, ਖੋਜ ਲੱਗਣਾ, ਮਾਲੂਮ ਹੋਣਾ, ਜਾਣਨਾ; ਖੋਜ ਕਰਨੀ; ਵੇਖਣਾ, ਨਜ਼ਰ ਆਉਣਾ; ਅਨੁਭਵ ਕਰਨਾ, ਮਹਿਸੂਸ ਕਰਨਾ, ਸਮਝਣਾ; **~fault with** ਨੁਕਸ ਕੱਢਣੇ; **~ing** ਨਿਰਨਾ, ਉਪਲਬਧੀ, ਨਿਸ਼ਕਰਸ਼, ਖੋਜ

fine (ਫ਼ਾਇਨ) *n v* ਜੁਰਮਾਨਾ, ਚੱਟੀ, ਤਾਵਾਨ; ਨਜ਼ਰਾਨਾ; ਜੁਰਮਾਨਾ ਕਰਨਾ; ਚੰਗਾ, ਵਧੀਆ, ਉੱਤਮ; ਸੋਹਣਾ, ਮਨੋਹਰ, ਨਿਰਦੋਸ਼, ਨਿਰਮਲ, ਸ਼ੁੱਧ, ਚੁਸਤ; ਟੀਪ-ਟਾਪ ਵਾਲਾ, ਭੜਕੀਲਾ;

ਪਤਲਾ, ਬਾਰੀਕ, ਮਹੀਨ, ਸੂਖਮ; ਨੋਕਦਾਰ, ਤੇਜ਼, ਤਿੱਖਾ; ~**art** ਲਲਿਤ ਕਲਾ

finger ('ਫ਼ਿੰਗਰਾ*) *n v* ਉਂਗਲ, ਉਂਗਲੀ; ~**print** ਉਂਗਲਾਂ ਦੇ ਨਿਸ਼ਾਨ

finish ('ਫ਼ਿਨਿਸ਼) *v n* ਪੂਰਾ ਕਰਨਾ, ਸਮਾਪਤ ਹੋਣਾ, ਮੁੱਕਣਾ ਜਾਂ ਮੁਕਾਉਣਾ, ਸਿਰੇ ਚਾੜ੍ਹਨਾ, ਬਣਾਉਣਾ, ਸਜਾਉਣਾ; ਅੰਤ, ਸਮਾਪਤੀ, ਖ਼ਾਤਮਾ; ~**ed** ਸਮਾਪਤ, ਸੰਪੂਰਨ, ਤਿਆਰ

finite ('ਫ਼ਾਇਨਾਇਟ) *a* ਸੀਮਤ, ਸੀਮਾਬੱਧ, ਨਿਸ਼ਚਤ; ਅਜਿਹੀ ਕਿਰਿਆ

fire (ਫ਼ਾਇਅ*) *n v* ਅੱਗ, ਅਗਨੀ; ਭਾਂਬੜ ਅੰਗਾਰਾ; ਤਪਸ਼, ਸਾੜ; ਅੱਗ ਲਗਾਣਾ, ਭੜਕ ਉੱਠਣਾ; ਤੋਪ ਦਾਗਣੀ, ਗੋਲੀ ਚਲਾਉਣੀ, ਅੱਗ ਦੇਣੀ; ~**place** ਚੁੱਲ੍ਹਾ; ~**work** ਆਤਸ਼ਬਾਜ਼ੀ; **catch**~, **take**~ ਅੱਗ ਲੱਗਣਾ

firing ('ਫ਼ਾਇਰਿੰਡ਼) *n* ਗੋਲਾਬਾਰੀ, ਭਾਂਬੜ, ਜਲਾਉਣ ਦਾ ਲੱਕੜੀ

firm (ਫ਼ਅ:ਮ) *n a v* ਵਪਾਰੀ-ਸੰਸਥਾ, ਕੰਪਨੀ; ਪੱਕਾ, ਦ੍ਰਿੜ, ਮਜ਼ਬੂਤ, ਤਕੜਾ; ਨਿਸ਼ਚਤ; ਕਰੜਾ ਦ੍ਰਿੜ ਕਰਨਾ, ਠੋਸ ਕਰਨਾ; ~**ness** ਪਕਿਆਈ, ਦ੍ਰਿੜਤਾ

first (ਫ਼ਅ:ਸਟ) *n a adv* ਪਹਿਲੀ ਤਾਰੀਖ਼; ਪਹਿਲਾ ਸਥਾਨ; ਵਧੀਆ ਕਿਸਮ; ਪਹਿਲਾ; ਪ੍ਰਮੁੱਖ, ਪ੍ਰਧਾਨ; ਪ੍ਰਾਰੰਭਕ, ਸਭ ਤੋਂ ਪਹਿਲਾਂ; ~**aid** ਫੱਟਣ ਦਾ ਆਰੰਭਕ ਇਲਾਜ, ਤੁਰਤ ਸਹਾਇਤਾ; ~**born** ਪਲੇਠੀ ਦਾ ਜੇਠਾ; ~**day** ਐਤਵਾਰ; ~**person** (ਵਿਆ) ਉੱਤਮ ਪੁਰਖ; ~**rate** ਵਧੀਆ, ਸ੍ਰੇਸ਼ਠ, ਉੱਤਮ; ~**ly** ਸਭ ਤੋਂ ਪਹਿਲਾਂ, ਅੱਵਲ

fisc, fisk (ਫ਼ਿਸਕ) *n* ਸਰਕਾਰੀ ਖ਼ਜ਼ਾਨਾ; ~**al** ਆਰਥਕ, ਵਿੱਤ ਸਬੰਧੀ, ਰਾਜ ਦੋਸ਼ ਸਬੰਧੀ

fish (ਫ਼ਿਸ਼) *n v* ਮੱਛੀ, ਮੱਛੀ ਦਾ ਮਾਸ; ਮੱਛੀਆਂ ਫੜਨਾ, (ਪਾਣੀ ਦੀ ਤਹਿ ਵਿਚੋਂ) ਮੱਛੀਆਂ, ਮੋਤੀ, ਮੂੰਗੇ ਆਦਿ ਕੱਢ ਲਿਆਉਣਾ; ~**in troubled waters** ਬਿਪਤਾ ਵੇਲੇ ਆਪਣਾ ਕੰਮ ਕੱਢਣਾ, ਗੜਬੜ ਵਿਚ ਆਪਣਾ ਦਾਅ ਲਾਉਣਾ; ~**market** ਮੱਛੀ ਬਜ਼ਾਰ, ਰੌਲੇ ਵਾਲੀ ਥਾਂ; ~**monger** ਮੱਛੀ ਵੇਚਣ ਵਾਲਾ; ~**erman** ਮਾਛੀ; ~**ery** ਮੱਛੀਆਂ ਵਾਲੀ ਥਾਂ, ਮੱਛੀ ਫੜਨ ਦਾ ਪੇਸ਼ਾ ਜਾਂ ਵਿਹਾਰ, ਮੱਛੀਆਂ ਦਾ ਵਣਜ

fist (ਫ਼ਿਸਟ) *n v* ਮੁੱਕੀ, ਘਸੁੰਨ; ਮੁੱਕੀ ਮਾਰਨੀ

fistula ('ਫ਼ਿਸਟਯੂਲ) *n* ਭਗੰਦਰ, ਡੂੰਘਾ ਜ਼ਖ਼ਮ

fit (ਫ਼ਿਟ) *a n adv v* (1) ਯੋਗ, ਢੁੱਕਵਾਂ, ਜੱਚਵਾਂ, ਤੰਦਰੁਸਤ, ਸੁਅਸਥ; (2) ਬੀਮਾਰੀ ਦਾ ਦੌਰਾ, ਬੇਹੋਸ਼ੀ, ਡ਼ੋਬ; ਤਰੰਗ; ਯੋਗਤਾ ਦੇਣੀ; ਠੀਕ-ਠਾਕ ਜੜ ਦੇਣਾ; ਠੀਕ ਬੈਠਣਾ, ਜਚਣਾ, ਮੁਨਾਸਬ ਹੋਣਾ, ਅਨੁਕੂਲ ਹੋਣਾ, ਫ਼ਿਟ ਹੋਣਾ; ~**ness** ਉਚਿਤਤਾ, ਸੰਗਤੀ, ਅਨੁਰੂਪਤਾ; ~**ting** (ਬ ਵ) ਸਾਮਾਨ, ਸਾਜ਼ ਸਾਮਾਨ; ਠੀਕ ਉਚਿਤ, ਯੋਗ, ਢੁਕਵਾਂ ਮੁਨਾਸਬ

five (ਫ਼ਾਇਵ) *a n* ਪੰਜ; ਪਾਂਜਾ; ਪੰਜ ਦੀ ਸੰਖਿਆ; ~**fold** ਪੰਜ ਗੁਣਾ; ~**o'clock** ਪੰਜ ਵਜੇ

fix (ਫ਼ਿਕਸ) *v n* ਨਿਸ਼ਚਤ ਕਰਨਾ, ਨਿਰਧਾਰਤ ਕਰਨਾ, ਮਿਥਣਾ, ਨਿਯਤ ਕਰਨਾ; ਪੱਕਾ ਕਰਨਾ; ਕਰੜੇ ਹੋਣਾ, ਪਥਰਾ ਜਾਣਾ, ਤਿਆਰ ਕਰਨਾ, ਅਹੁਦਾ ਸੰਭਾਲਣਾ, ਰਾਏ ਕਾਇਮ ਕਰਨਾ, ਫ਼ੈਸਲਾ ਕਰਨਾ; ਪੂਰਾ ਕਰਨਾ; ਨਿਯੁਕਤ ਕਰਨਾ; ਔਖ, ਔਕੜ, ਉਲਝਣ, ਜੰਜਾਲ; ਕਠਨਾਈ; ~**ation** ਸਥਿਰੀਕਰਨ, ਸਥਿਰਤਾ, ਦ੍ਰਿੜ੍ਹਤਾ, ਪਕਿਆਈ; ਟਿਕਟਿਕੀ; ~**ed** ਨਿਸ਼ਚਤ, ਸਥਿਰ, ਨਿਯਤ, ਮਿਆਦੀ; ~**edness** ਦ੍ਰਿੜ੍ਹਤਾ, ਸਥਿਰਤਾ, ਅਚਲਤਾ

fizzle ('ਫ਼ਿਜ਼ਲ) v n ਸੂੰ ਸੂੰ ਕਰਕੇ ਨਿਕਲਣਾ, ਠੁਸ ਹੋ ਜਾਣਾ; ਅਸਫਲਤਾ; ~**out** ਅਸਫਲ ਹੋਣਾ, ਠੁਸ ਹੋਣਾ

flag (ਫ਼ਲੈਗ) n v (1) ਝੰਡਾ; ਫ਼ਾਇਲ ਵਿਚ ਨਿਸ਼ਾਨੀ ਲਈ ਲਾਈ ਪਰਚੀ; (2) ਫ਼ਰਸ਼ ਵਿਚ ਲਾਉਣ ਵਾਲੀ ਸਿਲ ; ਫ਼ਰਸ਼ੀ ਪੱਥਰ (3) ਪੰਛੀ ਦੇ ਖੰਭ ਦੀ ਬਣੀ ਕਲਮ ; (4) ਝੰਡਾ ਲਾਉਣਾ, ਝੰਡਾ ਚੜ੍ਹਾਉਣਾ; (5) ਪੱਥਰ ਦੀਆਂ ਬਣੀਆਂ ਸਿਲਾਂ ਫ਼ਰਸ਼ ਵਿਚ ਲਾਉਣੀਆਂ (6) ਉਤਸ਼ਾਹਹੀਣ ਹੋਣਾ, ਸਿਥਲ ਹੋ ਜਾਣਾ, ਮੁਰਝਾਉਣਾ, ਦਿਲਚਸਪੀ ਨਾ ਰਹਿਣੀ

flake (ਫ਼ਲੇਇਕ) n v ਝੂਰਾ, ਫੰਭਾ, ਪੇਪੜੀ, ਪਤਲੀ ਪਰਤ; ਥੋੜ੍ਹਾ ਥੋੜ੍ਹਾ ਕਰਕੇ ਬਾਹਰ ਨਿਕਲਣਾ, ਟੋਟੇ ਟੋਟੇ ਕਰਕੇ ਬਾਹਰ ਕੱਢਣਾ

flambeau ('ਫ਼ਲੈਮਬਅਉ) n ਮਸ਼ਾਲ, ਬੱਤੀ

flamboyance, flamboyancy (ਫ਼ਲੈਮ'ਬੋਇਅੰਸ, ਫ਼ਲੈਮ'ਬੋਇਅੰਸਿ) n ਭੜਕੀਲਾਪਣ, ਤੜਕ-ਭੜਕ

flame (ਫ਼ਲੇਇਮ) n v ਭਾਂਬੜ, ਲਾਟ, ਜੋਤ; ਤੇਜ਼ ਰੌਸ਼ਨੀ; ਬਲਣਾ, ਬਲ ਉੱਠਣਾ, ਲਾਟਾਂ ਉੱਠਣੀਆਂ, ਕਰੋਧ ਨਾਲ ਭੜਕ ਉੱਠਣਾ

flank (ਫ਼ਲੈਂਕ) n v ਵੱਖੀ, ਪਾਸਾ, ਫ਼ੌਜ ਦੀ ਟੁਕੜੀ ਦੇ ਗੱਠੇ ਘੋੜੇ ਦਾ ਪਾਸਾ; ਇਕ ਕਿਨਾਰਾ, ਦਿਸ਼ਾ, ਫ਼ੌਜ ਦੇ ਕਿਸੇ ਪਾਸੇ ਨੂੰ ਮਜ਼ਬੂਤ ਕਰਨਾ

flannel ('ਫ਼ਲੈਨਲ) n a ਫ਼ਲਨੈੱਟ, ਇਕ ਪ੍ਰਕਾਰ ਦਾ ਉਨੀ ਕੱਪੜਾ, ਫ਼ਲਨੈੱਟ ਦੇ ਕੱਪੜੇ; ਫ਼ਲਨੈੱਟ ਦੀਆਂ ਪੱਟੀਆਂ

flap (ਫ਼ਲੈਪ) v n ਫੜਫੜਾਉਣਾ, ਖੰਭ ਮਾਰਨੇ, ਖੰਭ ਫਟਕਣੇ; ਥਪਕਣਾ, ਉਡਾਉਣਾ; ਗੜ੍ਹੇ ਕੱਢਣੇ; ਡੋਲਣਾ, ਝੂਲਣਾ

flare (ਫ਼ਲੇਅ*) v n ਭੜਕੰਣਾ, ਭੜਕ ਉੱਠਣਾ, ਚਮਕਣਾ; ਫੁੱਲਣਾ, ਖਿਲਰਨਾ, ਫਲਾਉਣਾ; ਸੜਨਾ; ਭਾਂਬੜ, ਭੜਕ; ਤਿੱਖੀ ਰੌਸ਼ਨੀ, ਪ੍ਰਕਾਸ਼-ਗੋਲਾ, ਅੱਖਾਂ ਚੁੰਧਿਆ ਦੇਣ ਵਾਲਾ ਪ੍ਰਕਾਸ਼; ਤੜਕ ਭੜਕ, ਆਡੰਬਰ

flash (ਫ਼ਲੈਸ਼) v n a ਚਮਕਣਾ, ਲਿਸ਼ਕਣਾ, ਭੜਕ ਉੱਠਣਾ; ਅਚਾਨਕ ਚਮਕ ਪੈਣਾ; ਤੇਜ਼ੀ ਨਾਲ ਚੱਲਣਾ; ਚਮਕ, ਲਿਸ਼ਕ, ਝਲਕਾਰਾ, ਚਾਨਣ ਦੀ ਲਪਟ; ਅਤਿਮਾਨ ਭਰੀ ਗੱਲ-ਬਾਤ ਬਣਾਉਟੀ; ਭੜਕੀਲਾ; ~**house** ਰੰਡੀਖ਼ਾਨਾ

flask (ਫ਼ਲਾਸਕ) n ਸੁਰਾਹੀ, ਝੱਜਰ

flat (ਫ਼ਲੈਟ) n a adv v (1) ਇਕ ਹੀ ਛੱਤ ਦੇ ਰਿਹਾਇਸ਼ੀ ਕਮਰਿਆਂ ਦੀ ਪਾਲ; ਰਹਿਤ ਵਾਲਾ ਕਮਰਾ; (2) ਪੱਧਰਾ, ਮੈਦਾਨ; ਹਥੇਲੀ; ਫ਼ਰਸ਼; ਖਿਲਰਿਆ; ਸਪਸ਼ਟ, ਸਾਫ਼; ਪ੍ਰਭਾਵਹੀਣ, ਸ਼ਕਤੀਹੀਣ, ਨਿਰਬਲ; ਮੁਲਾਇਮ ਕਰਨਾ, ਚੀਕਣਾ ਕਰਨਾ

flatter ('ਫ਼ਲੈਟਅ*) v n ਝੂਠੀ ਪ੍ਰਸੰਸਾ ਕਰਨੀ; ਚਾਪਲੂਸੀ ਕਰਨੀ, ਖ਼ੁਸ਼ਾਮਦ ਕਰਨੀ; ਝੂਠੀ ਆਸ ਬਨਾਉਣੀ; ~**y** ਖ਼ੁਸ਼ਾਮਦ, ਚਾਪਲੂਸੀ, ਝੂਠੀ ਪ੍ਰਸੰਸਾ

flatulent ('ਫ਼ਲੈਟਯੁਲਅੰਟ) a ਵਾਈ ਵਾਲਾ, ਬਾਦੀ, ਹਵਾ ਪੈਦਾ ਕਰਨ ਵਾਲਾ; ਫੁੱਲਿਆ; ਬਹਾਨੇ ਖੋਰ, ਕਪਟੀ

flavour ('ਫ਼ਲੇਇਵਅ*) a ਸੁਆਦ, ਸ਼ੀਰੀ ਮਹਿਕ, ਰਸ, ਲੱਜ਼ਤ; ਸੁਗੰਧਤ ਕਰਨਾ; ~**less** ਸੁਆਦਹੀਨ, ਬੇਸੁਆਦ, ਬੇਲੱਜ਼ਤ

flavorous (ਫ਼ਲੇਇਵਅਰਅਸ) a ਸੁਆਦੀ, ਮਹਿਕਦਾਰ, ਸ਼ੀਰੀ, ਖ਼ੁਸ਼ਬੂਦਾਰ

flaw (ਫ਼ਲੋ) n v ਦੋਸ਼, ਨੁਕਸ, ਔਗੁਣ, ਤਰੁਟੀ, ਕਮੀ, ਘਾਟ, ਤੇੜ, (ਕਾ) ਕਲੰਕ, ਵਿਗਾੜਨਾ, ਨੁਕਸ ਪੈਦਾ ਕਰਨਾ; ~**less** ਬੇਨੁਕਸ, ਬੇਐਬ, ਬੇਦਾਗ਼, ਨਿਸ਼ਕਲੰਕ

flawn (ਫ਼ਲੈਨ) *n* ਤਲਣ ਵਾਲਾ ਭਾਂਡਾ, ਕੜਾਹੀ, ਖੁੱਲ੍ਹਾ ਪਤੀਲਾ

flay (ਫ਼ਲੇਇ) *v* ਖੱਲ ਲਾਹੁਣੀ, ਛਿੱਲਣਾ, ਉਰੇੜਨਾ; ਕਰੜੀ ਆਲੋਚਨਾ ਕਰਨੀ, ਛਾਂਟ ਕੇ ਠੀਕ ਕਰਨਾ

flee (ਫ਼ਲੀ) *v* ਨਸ ਜਾਣਾ; ਫ਼ਰਾਰ ਹੋ ਜਾਣਾ; ਖਿਸਕ ਜਾਣਾ, ਲੋਪ ਹੋ ਜਾਣਾ, ਕਤਰਾਉਣਾ, ਤਿਆਗਣਾ

fleece (ਫ਼ਲੀਸ) *n v* ਉੱਨ, ਪਸ਼ਮ, ਇਕ ਵਾਰੀ ਵਿਚ ਲਾਹੀ ਹੋਈ ਉੱਨ; ਲੱਛਾ, ਡਿੱਗਦੀ ਹੋਈ ਬਰਫ਼ ਆਦਿ; ਉੱਨ ਲਾਹੁਣੀ, ਭੇਡ, ਬੱਕਰੀ ਆਦਿ ਮੁੰਨਣੀ; ਠੱਗ ਲੈਣਾ, ਮੁੰਨਣਾ, ਛਿਲ ਲਾਹੁਣੀ, ਖੋਹ ਲੈਣਾ

fleet (ਫ਼ਲੀਟ) *n a v* (1) ਜਹਾਜ਼ੀ ਬੇੜਾ, ਬੱਸਾਂ ਜਾਂ ਟੈਕਸੀਆਂ ਆਦਿ ਦਾ ਸਮੂਹ, ਫ਼ਰਾਰ ਹੋ ਜਾਣਾ, ਚੁਸਤ; (2) ਖਾੜੀ

flesh (ਫ਼ਲੈੱਸ਼) *n a v* (ਕੱਚਾ) ਮਾਸ, ਗੋਸ਼ਤ, ਮੁਟਾਪਾ, ਚਰਬੀ; ਸਰੀਰ, ਸਿਖਾਉਣਾ; ਮੂੰਹ ਨੂੰ ਲਹੂ ਲਾਉਣਾ; **~and blood** ਵਾਸਤਵਿਕ ਰੂਪ ਵਿਚ ਜੀਵਤ

flex (ਫ਼ਲੈਕਸ) *n v* ਬਿਜਲੀ ਦੀ ਲਚਕਦਾਰ ਤਾਰ; **~ibility** ਲਚਕ, ਨਿਮਰਤਾ; **~ible** ਲਿਫਵਾਂ, ਲਚਕਦਾਰ; ਮੌਕੇ ਦੇ ਮੁਤਾਬਕ ਢਾਲ ਲੈਣਾ

flick (ਫ਼ਲਿਕ) *n v* ਹੌਲਾ ਜੇਹਾ ਧੱਕਾ; ਝਟਕਾ; ਸੱਟ ਮਾਰਨੀ, ਚਾਬਕ ਮਾਰਨਾ; ਝਾੜਨਾ, ਝਟਕ ਦੇਣਾ, ਤਿਛਤਿਛ ਕਰਨਾ

flight (ਫ਼ਲਾਇਟ) *n v* ਉਡਾਰੀ, ਉਡਾਣ, ਭਾਜੜ, ਪਲਾਇਟ, ਬਾਜ਼ ਦੀ ਸ਼ਿਕਾਰ ਉੱਤੇ ਝਪਟ

flimsy (ਫ਼ਲਿਮਜ਼ਿ) *n a* ਪਤਲਾ ਕਾਗਜ਼; ਨਿਗੂਣਾ, ਤੁੱਛ

flinch (ਫ਼ਲਿੰਚ) *v* ਘਬਰਾਉਣਾ, ਬੇਚੈਨ ਹੋਣਾ, ਅਸ਼ਾਂਤ ਹੋਣਾ, ਹਾਰ ਮੰਨਣਾ, ਪਿੱਠ ਦਿਖਾਉਣੀ

fling (ਫ਼ਲਿੰਙ) *v n* ਵਗਾਹ ਕੇ ਮਾਰਨਾ, ਸੁੱਟ ਦੇਣਾ, ਚੁੱਕ ਕੇ ਮਾਰਨਾ; ਗਾਲ੍ਹ ਕੱਢਣੀ; ਡਾਂਟਣਾ, ਬੁਰਾ ਭਲਾ ਕਹਿਣਾ, ਝਪਟ, ਵੇਗਮਈ ਚਾਲ

flip (ਫ਼ਲਿਪ) *v n* ਉਂਗਲੀਆਂ ਨਾਲ ਉਛਾਲਣਾ; ਹੌਲੀ ਜੇਹੀ ਉਂਗਲ ਮਾਰਨੀ; ਧੱਕਾ, ਤੁਣਕਾ, ਝਟਕਾ

flirt (ਫ਼ਲਅ:ਟ) *v n* ਨਖ਼ਰੇ ਕਰਨਾ, ਚੁਹਲ-ਮੁਹਲ ਕਰਨਾ; ਅੱਖ-ਮਟੱਕਾ ਕਰਨਾ; ਨਾਜ਼ੋ, ਚੋਚਲੋ; **~ation** ਨਖ਼ਰੇਬਾਜ਼ੀ, ਪਿਆਰ ਦਾ ਦਿਖਾਵਾ

flisk (ਫ਼ਲਿਸਕ) *v n* ਬੇਚੈਨ ਹੋਣਾ, ਇੱਧਰ ਉੱਧਰ ਨੱਚਣਾ, ਟੱਪਣਾ; ਵਹਿਮ, ਖ਼ਬਤ

flit (ਫ਼ਲਿਟ) *v n* ਛੋਟੀ ਉਡਾਰੀ ਮਾਰਨੀ, ਸਰਕਣਾ, ਖਿਸਕਣਾ; ਨੱਸ ਜਾਣਾ, ਘੁੰਮਣਾ

float (ਫ਼ਲਅਉਟ) *v n* ਤਾਰਨਾ, ਠੇਲ੍ਹਣਾ, ਵਹਾਉਣਾ, ਵਹਿਣ ਦੇ ਨਾਲ ਤਰਨਾ; **~able** ਤਰਨਯੋਗ

floating (ਫ਼ਲਅਉਟਿਙ) *a* ਤਰਦਾ, ਤਿੱਲ੍ਹਦਾ, ਪਾਣੀ ਨਾਲ ਵਹਿੰਦਾ; ਅਸਥਿਰ

flock (ਫ਼ਲੌਕ) *n v n* ਇੱਜੜ, ਸਮੂਹ, ਝੁੰਡ; (ਮਨੁੱਖਾਂ ਦਾ) ਜੱਥਾ, ਟੋਲਾ; ਰੂੰ ਜਾਂ ਉੱਨ ਦਾ ਫਹਿਆ ਜਾਂ ਗੋਹੜਾ, ਛੱਟੀ, ਗੁੰਛ, ਲਿਟ; (ਬ ਵ) ਗੱਦੇ-ਗੱਦੀਆਂ ਨੂੰ ਭਰਨ ਲਈ ਵਰਤੇ ਜਾਣ ਵਾਲੇ ਬਚੀ-ਖੁਚੀ ਉੱਨ ਦੇ ਗੁੱਛੇ; ਕਾਗ਼ਜ਼ ਬਣਾਉਣ ਲਈ ਵਰਤਿਆ ਜਾਣ ਵਾਲਾ ਉੱਨ ਦਾ ਲੋਂਗੜ; ਇਕੱਤਰ ਹੋਣਾ, ਇਕੱਠੇ ਹੋਣਾ,

flog (ਫ਼ਲੌਗ) *v* ਚਾਬਕ ਮਾਰਨਾ, ਛਮਕਾ ਮਾਰਨੀਆਂ, (ਘੋੜੇ ਨੂੰ) ਹਿੱਕਣਾ; ਝੰਬਣਾ

flood (ਫ਼ਲਅੱਡ) *n v* ਹੜ੍ਹ; ਕਾਂਗ; ਹੜ੍ਹ ਆ ਜਾਣਾ, ਹੜ੍ਹ ਲਿਆਉਣਾ; ਡੋਬ ਦੇਣਾ; ਪਾਣੀ ਪਾਣੀ ਕਰ ਦੇਣਾ; **~gate** ਮੋਘਾ, ਨਹਿਰ ਦਾ ਫਾਟਕ; **~light** ਪ੍ਰਕਾਸ਼ ਪੁੰਜ ਰੋਸ਼ਨੀ

floor (ਫ਼ਲੋ*) *n v* ਫ਼ਰਸ਼; ਥੱਲਾ, ਤਹਿ; ਧਰਤੀ-ਤਲ,

ਮੰਜ਼ਲ, ਸਭਾ-ਸਦਨ, ਮੰਚ; ਫ਼ਰਸ਼ ਬਣਾਉਣਾ, ਵਿਆਕੁਲ ਕਰ ਦੇਣਾ

flop (ਫ਼ਲੌਪ) *n v* ਧਰੰਮ ਦੀ ਅਵਾਜ਼; ਠੁੱਸ, ਤਿਰਛਕਿਸ, ਅਸਫਲਤਾ; ਧਰੰਮ ਕਰਕੇ ਡਿਗਣਾ

flora (ਫ਼ਲੋਰਾ) *n* ਕਿਸੇ ਇਲਾਕੇ ਜਾਂ ਸਮੇਂ ਦੀ ਬਨਸਪਤੀ (F) ਫੁੱਲਰਾਣੀ; **~design** ਫੁੱਲਕਾਰੀ; **~l** ਫੁੱਲਾਂ ਸਬੰਧੀ, ਫੁੱਲਾਂ ਦਾ; ਬਨਸਪਤੀ ਬਾਰੇ

florist (ਫ਼ਲੋਰਿਸਟ) *n* ਫੁੱਲ-ਵਿਗਿਆਨੀ; ਫੁੱਲ ਵੇਚਣ ਵਾਲਾ

flour (ਫ਼ਲਾਉਅ*) *n v* ਆਟਾ, ਮੈਦਾ; **~mill** ਆਟਾ ਪੀਹਣ ਦੀ ਚੱਕੀ

flourish (ਫ਼ਲਅੌਰਿਸ਼) *v n* ਵਧਣਾ; ਜੋਬਨ ਵਿਚ ਹੋਣਾ; ਹਰੇ ਭਰੇ ਹੋਣਾ; ਵਿਕਾਸ, ਵਾਧਾ, ਪਰਤਾਪ, ਖੁਸ਼ਹਾਲੀ

flout (ਫ਼ਲਾਉਟ) *v n* ਅਵੱਗਿਆ ਕਰਨੀ, ਹੁਕਮ ਅਦੂਲੀ ਕਰਨਾ, ਹੁਕਮ ਅਦੂਲੀ, ਉਲੰਘਣਾ

flow (ਫ਼ਲਅਉ) *v n* ਵਗਣਾ, ਵਹਿਣਾ, ਫੁੱਟਣਾ, ਫੁੱਟ ਨਿਕਲਣਾ; ਖ਼ੂਨ ਦਾ ਸਰੀਰ ਵਿਚ ਦੌਰਾ ਕਰਨਾ; ਛਲਕ ਪੈਣਾ, ਉਛਲ ਕੇ ਵਗਣਾ; ਰਵਾਨੀ; ਪਾਣੀ ਦਾ ਚੜ੍ਹਾ; **~ing** ਪਰਵਾਹਪੂਰਨ, ਸਰਲ

flower (ਫ਼ਲਾਉਅ*) *n v* ਫੁੱਲ, ਪੁਸ਼ਪ, ਕਲੀ; ਵਿਕਾਸ, ਜੋਬਨ; ਤੱਤ, ਸਾਰ, ਫੁੱਲਣਾ, ਖਿੜਨਾ, ਫੁੱਲ ਲਾਉਣੇ, ਖਿੜਨ ਦੇਣਾ; ਕੱਪੜੇ ਆਦਿ ਉੱਤੇ ਬੂਟੀਆਂ ਕੱਢਣੀਆਂ, ਫੁੱਲਾਂ ਨਾਲ ਸਜਾਉਣਾ; ਖ਼ਮੀਰ ਦਾ ਝੱਗ ਛੱਡਣਾ; **~bed** ਫੁੱਲਾਂ ਦੀ ਕਿਆਰੀ, **~bud** ਕਲੀ; **~pot** ਗਮਲਾ; **~et** ਛੋਟਾ ਫੁੱਲ, ਨਿੱਕਾ ਜਿਹਾ ਫੁੱਲ

flu (ਫ਼ਲੂ) *n* ਫ਼ਲੂ ਰੋਗ, ਇਨਫਲੂੰਜ਼ਾ

fluctuating (ਫ਼ਲਅੱਕਚੁਏਟਿੰਡ) *a* ਅਸਥਿਰ, ਚੰਚਲ, ਘਟਦਾ-ਵਧਦਾ, ਉਤਰਦਾ-ਚੜ੍ਹਦਾ

fluctuation (ਫ਼ਲਅੱਕਚੁ'ਏਇਸ਼ਨ) *n* ਅਸਥਿਰਤਾ, ਉਤਾਰ-ਚੜ੍ਹਾਉ, ਘਾਟਾ-ਵਾਧਾ, ਅਨਿਯਮਤਤਾ

fluency (ਫ਼ਲੂਅੰਸਿ) *n* ਰਵਾਨੀ, ਇਕਸਾਰ ਵਹਾ, ਬੇਅਟਕ ਚਾਲ

fluent ('ਫ਼ਲੂਅੰਟ) *a* (ਭਾਸ਼ਨ ਜਾਂ ਸ਼ੈਲੀ) ਰਵਾਂ, ਸਰਲ ਪਰਵਾਹਸ਼ੀਲ

fluid (ਫ਼ਲੂਇਡ) *a n* ਤਰਲ, ਦ੍ਰਵ; **~ity** ਤਰਲਤਾ, ਦ੍ਰਵਤਾ

flush (ਫ਼ਲਅੱਸ਼) *v n a* (1) ਪੰਛੀਆਂ ਨੂੰ ਉਡਾਉਣਾ, ਉੱਡ ਜਾਣਾ, ਖੰਭ ਖੋਲ੍ਹ ਕੇ ਉੱਡਣਾ; (2) (ਨਾਲੀ ਆਦਿ ਨੂੰ) ਪਾਣੀ ਨਾਲ ਧੋਣਾ, ਪਾਣੀ ਵਗਾਉਣਾ; ਖੇਤ ਨੂੰ ਪਾਣੀ ਨਾਲ ਭਰ ਦੇਣਾ, ਤਰੋ-ਤਰ ਕਰ ਦੇਣਾ, (ਚਿਹਰੇ ਦਾ) ਲਾਲ ਹੋ ਜਾਣਾ, ਚਮਕਣਾ, ਚਮਕਾਉਣਾ, ਤਾਜ਼ਗੀ; ਲਾਲੀ, ਚਮਕ; ਚਿਹਰੇ ਦੀ ਲਾਲੀ, ਸਮਰਿਧ; (3) ਤਾਸ਼ ਦੀ ਇਕ ਖੇਡ

flute (ਫ਼ਲੂਟ) *n v* ਵੰਝਲੀ, ਬੰਸਰੀ, ਬੰਸਰੀ ਤੋਂ ਕੋਈ ਸੁਰ ਕੱਢਣੀ

flutter (ਫ਼ਲਅੱਟਅ*) *v n* ਖੰਭ ਮਾਰਨਾ, ਖੰਭ ਫੜਫੜਾਉਣਾ, ਝੰਡੇ ਦਾ ਲਹਿਰਾਨਾ; ਘੇਚੈਨ ਕਰਨਾ, ਪਰੇਸ਼ਾਨ ਕਰਨਾ, ਤੜਫਟਨਾ; ਫੜਫੜਾਹਟ, ਫ਼ਰਾਟਾ, ਝੰਡੇ ਆਦਿ ਦੇ ਲਹਿਰਨ (ਦੀ ਕਿਰਿਆ), ਕੰਬਾ; ਉਤੇਜਨਾ, ਮਾਨਸਕ ਵੇਗ

flux (ਫ਼ਲਅੱਕਸ) *v n* ਦ੍ਰਵਤ ਕਰਨਾ, ਪਾਣੀ ਵਰਗਾ ਬਣਾਉਣਾ; ਪੰਘਰਨਾ, ਗਾਲਣਾ; ਬੜੀ ਮਾਤਰਾ ਵਿਚ ਵਗਣਾ; ਖ਼ੂਨ ਵਗਣਾ; ਮੋਕ, ਦਸਤ, ਪੇਚਸ, ਝੁਕਣੀ

fly (ਫ਼ਲਾਇ) *n v a* ਮੱਖੀ; ਉੱਡਣਾ, ਉਡਾਉਣਾ, ਹਵਾਈ ਜਹਾਜ਼ ਵਿਚ ਸਫ਼ਰ ਕਰਨਾ; ਲਹਿਰਾ-ਉਣਾ; ਫੁਰਤੀ ਨਾਲ ਲੰਘ ਜਾਣਾ; ਨੱਸ ਕੇ ਨਿਕਲ ਜਾਣਾ, ਤੀਰ ਹੋ ਜਾਣਾ; ਸਾਵਧਾਨ, ਖ਼ਬਰਦਾਰ,

ਸਚੇਤ; ~at upon ਟੁੱਟ ਕੇ ਪੈ ਜਾਣਾ; ~ing bridge ਕਿਸ਼ਤੀਆਂ ਦਾ ਆਰਜੀ ਪੁਲ; ~ing club ਹਵਾਈ ਜਹਾਜ਼ਾਂ ਨੂੰ ਚਲਾਉਣ ਦੀ ਸਿਖਲਾਈ ਦੀ ਸੰਸਥਾ ਜਾਂ ਸਕੂਲ; ~ing colours ਸ਼ਾਨਦਾਰ ਸਫਲਤਾ; ~in the face of ਨਿਰਾਦਰ ਕਰਨਾ, ਗੁਸਤਾਖ਼ੀ ਕਰਨਾ; ~out ਗੁੱਸਾ ਕਰਨਾ; ~past ਹਵਾਈ ਜਹਾਜ਼ ਦੀ ਸਲਾਮੀ

foam (ਫ਼ਅਉਮ) *n v* ਝੱਗ; ਝੱਗ ਛੱਡਣੀ; ਪਾਣੀ ਆਦਿ ਉੱਤੇ ਝੱਗ ਆਉਣੀ; ~y ਝੱਗਦਾਰ

focal (ਫ਼ਅਉਕਲ) *a* ਇਕੱਤਰਤ, ਨਾਭੀ ਸਬੰਧੀ, ਕੇਂਦਰ ਬਿੰਦੂ ਸਬੰਧੀ, ਫੋਕਸੀ

focus (ਫ਼ਅਉਕਸ) *n v* ਧਰੁਵ-ਬਿੰਦੂ, ਕਾਰਜ-ਕੇਂਦਰ, ਮੁੱਖ ਖੇਤਰ; (ਰੋਗ ਆਦਿ ਦਾ) ਕੇਂਦਰਤ ਕਰਨਾ, ਕੇਂਦਰ ਵੱਲ ਫੇਰਨਾ, ਫੋਕਸ ਹੇਠ ਲੈਣਾ

fodder (ਫ਼ੋਡਅ*) *n v* ਪਸ਼ੂਆਂ ਦਾ ਚਾਰਾ, ਤੂੜੀ; ਚਾਰਾ ਦੇਣਾ

foe (ਫ਼ਅਉ) *n* (ਕਾਵਿ) ਵੈਰੀ, ਸ਼ੱਤਰੂ, ਦੁਸ਼ਮਨ

f(o)etal (ਫ਼ੀਟਲ) *a* ਗਰਭ-ਸਬੰਧੀ, ਗਰਭਸਥ, ਭਰੂਣ-ਸਬੰਧੀ; ~period ਗਰਭ-ਅਵਧੀ, ਗਰਭ-ਸਮਾਂ

foetation (ਫ਼ੀ'ਟੇਇਸ਼ਨ) *n* ਗਰਭ-ਅਵਸਥਾ, ਗਰਭ-ਧਾਰਨ

foetus ('ਫ਼ੀਟਅਸ) *n* ਗਰਭ-ਅਵਸਥਾ, ਚਾਰ ਮਹੀਨਿਆਂ ਤੋਂ ਜਨਮ ਤਕ ਦਾ ਗਰਭ ਵਿਚ ਬੱਚਾ

fog (ਫ਼ੋਗ) *n v* ਧੁੰਦ, ਕੁਹਰ, ਕੁਹਾਸਾ; ਧੁੰਦਲਾ ਕਰਨਾ, ਢਕੇ ਜਾਣਾ, ਹੈਰਾਨ ਕਰ ਦੇਣਾ; ~in ਪਰੇਸ਼ਾਨ, ਘਬਰਾਇਆ, ਹੈਰਾਨ; ~gy ਧੁੰਦਲਾ, ਅਸਪੱਸ਼ਟ

foil (ਫ਼ੋਇਲ) *n v* (1) ਪੱਤਰਾ, ਸੋਨੇ ਚਾਂਦੀ ਆਦਿ ਨੂੰ ਕੁਟਕੇ ਬਣਾਏ ਵਰਕ; ਖਿੜਕੀ ਦੀ ਉਤਲੀ ਡਾਟ (2) ਖੁੰਢੀ ਤਲਵਾਰ; ਅਸਫਲਤਾ, ਹਾਰ, ਬੇਅਸਰ ਕਰ ਦੇਣਾ, ਹਰਾ ਦੇਣਾ; ਮਾਰ ਕੇ ਭਜਾ ਦੇਣਾ

fold (ਫ਼ਅਉਲਡ) *n v* (1) ਵਾੜਾ; ਕੋਈ ਧਰਮ-ਸੰਘ, ਪੰਥ, ਤਹਿ ਕਰਨਾ, ਮੋੜਨਾ, ਮੁੜਨਾ, ਦੋਹਰਾ ਕਰਨਾ; ਮੋੜ ਪਾ ਕੇ ਦੋਹਰਾ ਕਰਨਾ; ਢਕਣਾ, ਵਲੇਟਣਾ, ਲਪੇਟਣਾ; (ਹੱਥ) ਜੋੜਣੇ; ਚਿਥੜਨਾ, (2) ਮੋੜ, ਪਰਤ; ਤਹਿ, ਵਲੇਟ, ਲਪੇਟ, ਕੁੰਡਲ, ਬੰਦ ਕਰਨਾ; ~er ਮੋੜਨ ਵਾਲਾ, ਦੋਹਰਾ ਕਰਨ ਵਾਲਾ, ਤਹਿ ਲਾਉਣ ਵਾਲਾ; ~ing ਮੋੜ, ਤਹਿ, ਸਲਵਟ, ਠੱਪਵਾਂ, ਮੁੜਵਾਂ, ਫੋਲਡਿੰਗ

folio (ਫ਼ਅਉਲਿਅਉ) *n v* ਪੰਨਾ, ਸਫ਼ਾ; ਪੰਨੇ ਲਗਾਉਣਾ

folk (ਫ਼ਅਉਕ) *n* ਲੋਕ, ਜਨਤਾ; ~lore ਲੋਕ-ਪਰੰਪਰਾ, ਲੋਕ-ਵਾਰਤਾ, ਲੋਕ-ਕਥਾ, ਲੋਕਧਾਰਾ; ~song ਲੋਕ-ਗੀਤ

follow (ਫ਼ੋਲਅਉ) *v* ਪਿੱਛਾ ਕਰਨਾ, ਪਿੱਛੇ ਲੱਗਣਾ; ਪਿੱਛੇ ਆਉਣਾ; ਆਗਿਆ ਦਾ ਪਾਲਣ ਕਰਨਾ; ਪੇਸ਼ਾ ਅਪਨਾਉਣਾ; (ਕਿਸੇ ਵਿਚਾਰ ਜਾਂ ਗੱਲ ਤੇ) ਦ੍ਰਿੜ੍ਹ ਰਹਿਣਾ; ਪਾਲਣਾ ਕਰਨੀ; ~on (ਕ੍ਰਿਕਟ) ਪਹਿਲੀ ਵਾਰੀ ਦੇ ਮੁਕਾਬਿਦਾਂ ਹੀ ਦੂਜੀ ਵਾਰੀ ਦੀ ਖੇਡ; ~up ਕਿਸੇ ਕਾਰਜ ਨੂੰ ਸਿਰੇ ਚਾੜਨ ਲਈ ਪਿੱਛੇ ਲੱਗੇ ਰਹਿਣਾ; ~er ਸ਼ਰਧਾਲੂ, ਸੇਵਕ; ਅਨੁਯਾਈ, ਚੇਲਾ; ਸੈਨਾ ਵਿਚ ਧੋਬੀ, ਨਾਈ, ਲਾਂਗਰੀ ਆਦਿ ਗੈਰ-ਲੜਾਕੇ ਕਰਮਚਾਰੀ; ~ing ਸਿੱਖੀ, ਸੇਵਕੀ, ਉੱਮਤ, ਅਨੁਯਾਈ-ਸਮੂਹ; ਹੇਠ ਲਿਖਿਆ, ਪਿੱਛੇ ਆਉਣ ਵਾਲਾ, ਨਿਮਨਲਿਖਤ

folly ('ਫ਼ੋਲਿ) *n* ਮੂਰਖਤਾ, ਬੇਵਕੂਫ਼ੀ, ਅਗਿਆਨ, ਹਾਸੋਹੀਣੀ, ਗੱਲ

foment (ਫ਼ਅ(ਉ)ਮੈਂਟ) *v* ਸੇਕਣਾ, ਟਕੋਰ ਕਰਨੀ, ਤੱਤੇ ਪਾਣੀ ਨਾਲ ਧੋਣਾ ਜਾਂ ਸੇਕਣਾ; ਉਤੇਜਤ

ਕਰਨਾ, ਭੜਕਾਉਣਾ, ਉਕਸਾਉਣਾ

fond (ਫ਼ੌਂਡ) *a* ਪਰੇਮੀ, ਚਾਹਵਾਨ, ਲਾਡਲੀ; ਸਿੰਘੜ; ~**ie** ਲਾਡ ਕਰਨਾ, ਪੁਚਕਾਰਨਾ, ਪਿਆਰ ਨਾਲ ਘੁੱਟਣਾ; ~**ling** ਪਿਆਰਾ ਬੱਚਾ, ਲਾਡਲਾ, ਦੁਲਾਰਾ; ~**ness** ਪਰੇਮ, ਚਾਅ, ਮੋਹ

food (ਫ਼ੂਡ) *n* ਅੰਨ, ਖ਼ੁਰਾਕ, ਭੋਜਨ, ਆਹਾਰ, ਖਾਣਾ

fool (ਫ਼ੂਲ) *n a v* ਮੂਰਖ, ਮੂੜ੍ਹ, ਬੁੱਧੂ, ਬੇਵਕੂਫ਼, ਠੱਗਣਾ; ਬੇਵਕੂਫ਼ ਬਣਾਉਣਾ; ~**s paradise** ਹਵਾਈ ਮਹਿਲ; ~**ish** ਮੂਰਖ, ਬੇਅਕਲ, ਬੁੱਧੂ, ਮੰਤਹੀਣ; ~**ishness** ਮੂਰਖਤਾ, ਊਜੱਡਤਾ, ਮੂੜ੍ਹਤਾ, ਬੇਵਕੂਫ਼ੀ

foot (ਫ਼ੁੱਟ) *n v* ਪੈਰ, ਚਰਨ, ਪਗ, ਖ਼ੁਰ; ਪੈਦਲ ਫ਼ੌਜ; ਧਾਵਾ; ਫ਼ੁੱਟ (12 ਇੰਚ ਦਾ ਨਾਪ); ਲੱਤ ਮਾਰਨਾ, ਠੁੰਡਾ ਮਾਰਨਾ; ~**board** ਪਾਏਦਾਨ; ~**fall** ਪੈਰਾਂ ਦੀ ਆਵਾਜ਼, ਟੁਰਨ ਦੀ ਆਵਾਜ਼; ~**man** ਪਿਆਦਾ, ਪੈਦਲ ਫ਼ੌਜ ਦਾ ਫ਼ੌਜੀ, ਬਾਵਰਦੀ ਨੌਕਰ; ~**path** ਪਟੜੀ, ਪਗਡੰਡੀ, ਡੰਡੀ; ~**rest** ਪਾਏਦਾਨ; ~**rule** ਫ਼ੁੱਟਾ; ~**step** ਚਾਲ; ਕਦਮ; ਪਾਏਦਾਨ; ~**wear** ਜੁੱਤੀ, ਬੂਟ; **have one~ in grave** ਮੌਤ ਨੇੜੇ ਹੋਣਾ, ਕਬਰ ਵਿਚ ਲੱਤਾਂ ਹੋਣੀਆਂ; **put one's best~foremost** ਪੂਰਾ ਜਤਨ ਕਰਨਾ; ~**ing** ਪਕੜ, ਪੈਰ-ਜਮਾ, ਪੈਂਡਾ, ਆਧਾਰ, ਸਬੰਧ, ਨਾਤਾ, ਹੈਸੀਅਤ

footle ('ਫ਼ੂਟਲ) *n v* (ਅਪ) ਮੂਰਖਤਾ, ਮੂੜ੍ਹਤਾ, ਬੇਵਕੂਫ਼ੀ, ਨੀਚ ਕੰਮ ਕਰਨਾ

for (ਫ਼ੋ*) *prep conj* ਵਾਸਤੇ, ਲਈ, ਜੋਗ, ਕਿਉਂਕਿ, ਦੀ ਥਾਂ; ਮੁਕਾਬਲੇ ਵਿਚ; ਖ਼ਾਤਰ; ਵੱਲ ਨੂੰ, ਪਾਸ ਨੂੰ; ~**good** ਸਦਾ ਲਈ; ~**the present** ਅਜੇ, ਹਾਲਾਂ, ਹਾਲੀਂ; **once ~ all** ਸਦਾ ਲਈ, ਹਮੇਸ਼ਾ ਵਾਸਤੇ; **take ~ granted** ਯਕੀਨ ਕਰ ਲਵੇ, ਪੱਕਾ ਸਮਝੋ; **word ~word** ਲਫ਼ਜ਼-ਬ-ਲਫ਼ਜ਼, ਅੱਖਰੋਂ-ਅੱਖਰੀ, ਸ਼ਾਬਦਕ

forbear (ਫ਼ੋ'ਬੇਅ*) *v* ਸਹਿ ਜਾਣਾ, ਸਹਾਰਾ ਲੈਣਾ, ਧੀਰਜ ਰੱਖਣਾ; ਬਚਾਉਣਾ; ~**ance** ਧੀਰਜ, ਹੌਸਲਾ, ਜੇਰਾ, ਬਚਾਉ; ~**ing** ਸਹਿਨਸ਼ੀਲ, ਖਿਮਾਸ਼ੀਲ, ਧੀਰਜਵਾਨ

forbid (ਫ਼ਅ'ਬਿਡ) *v* ਰੋਕਣਾ; ਵਰਜਣਾ, ਹੋੜਨਾ, ਮਨ੍ਹਾ ਕਰਨਾ; ~**den** ਵਰਜਤ

force (ਫ਼ੋ:ਸ) *n v* ਸ਼ਕਤੀ, ਤਾਕ਼ਤ, ਜ਼ੋਰ, ਬਲ; ਫ਼ੌਜੀ ਟਕੜੀ, ਪਲੀਸ; ਜੋਸ਼, ਆਵੇਗ, ਪਰੰਚੰਡਤਾ; ਪੱਕਾ ਦੇਣਾ, ਸਵੀਕਾਰ ਕਰਨ ਲਈ ਮਜਬੂਰ ਕਰਨਾ; ਖੋਹ ਲੈਣਾ, ਧੱਕੇ ਨਾਲ ਲੈ ਲੈਣਾ; **in great ~** ਸ਼ਕਤੀਪੂਰਨ, ਚੜ੍ਹਦੀ ਕਲਾ ਵਿਚ; ~**ful** ਜ਼ੋਰਦਾਰ, ਪੜ੍ਹੱਲੇਦਾਰ, ਸ਼ਕਤੀਸ਼ਾਲੀ

forcible (ਫ਼ੋ:ਸਾਬਲ) *a* ਬਲਪੂਰਨ, ਪਰਬਲ, ਜ਼ਬਰਦਸਤੀ, ਜਬਰੀ

ford (ਫ਼ੋਡ) *n v* ਪੱਤਣ, ਲਾਂਘਾ; ਪਾਰ ਕਰਨਾ, ਪਾਰ ਲੰਘਣਾ; ~**able** ਪਾਰ ਲੰਘਣ ਯੋਗ

fordo (ਫ਼ੋ'ਡੂ) *v* ਨਸ਼ਟ ਕਰਨਾ, ਤਬਾਹ ਕਰਨਾ

fordone (ਫ਼ੋ'ਡਅੱਨ) *a* ਥੱਕਿਆ, ਹੁੱਸਿਆ, ਥੱਕਿਆ ਟੁੱਟਿਆ, ਨਸ਼ਟ

fore (ਫ਼ੋ*) *adv prep a n* ਸਾਮ੍ਹਣੇ, ਅੱਗੇ; ਮੂਹਰੇ; ~**bear** ਪਿਤਰ, ਵੱਡੇਰੇ, ਪੂਰਵਜ, ਬਾਪ-ਦਾਦੇ; ~**cast** ਪਹਿਲਾਂ, ਤੋਂ ਲਾਇਆ ਕਿਆਸ, ਪੇਸ਼ੀਨਗੋਈ, ਪੂਰਵ-ਅਨੁਮਾਨ; ਅਗੇਤਾ ਕਿਆਸ ਕਰਨਾ, ਪੂਰਵ-ਕਲਪਨਾ ਕਰਨੀ; ~**father** ਵੱਡੇਰੇ, ਬਜ਼ੁਰਗ, ਦਾਦੇ-ਪੜਦਾਦੇ, ਪੂਰਵਜ, ਪਿਤਰ; ~**finger** ਅਗਰੀ ਉਂਗਲ, ਅੰਗੂਠੇ ਨਾਲ ਦੀ ਉਂਗਲ ਤਰਜਨੀ; ~**front** ਸਭ ਤੋਂ ਅਗਲਾ ਹਿੱਸਾ, ਮੂਹਰਲਾ ਭਾਗ; ~**go** ਪਹਿਲਾਂ ਹੋਣਾ, ਸਮੇਂ ਜਾਂ ਸਥਾਨ ਵਿਚ ਅੱਗੇ ਹੋਣਾ; ਛੱਡਣਾ,

ਤਿਆਗਣਾ; ~going ਉਪਰੋਕਤ, ਉੱਪਰਲਾ, ਉੱਤੇ ਆਇਆ, ਪੂਰਵਵਰਣਤ; ~gone ਅਗੇਤਰਾ, ਪਹਿਲਾਂ ਹੀ, ਪੂਰਵ ਨਿਸਚਤ; ~ground ਅਗਵਾੜਾ, ਅਗਰ ਭੂਮੀ; ~head ਮੱਥਾ, ਮਸਤਕ; ~man ਫੋਰਮੈਨ, ਮਜ਼ਦੂਰਾਂ ਦਾ ਦਰੋਗਾ, ਅਧਿਕਕਸ਼, ਸਰਦਾਰ, ਮੁਖੀ; ~most ਪ੍ਰਮੁੱਖ, ਪ੍ਰਧਾਨ, ਪਹਿਲਾ; ਸਭ ਤੋਂ ਪਹਿਲਾ; ~noon ਦੁਪਹਿਰ ਤੋਂ ਪਹਿਲਾਂ ਦਾ ਵੇਲਾ, ਪੂਰਵ ਦੁਪਹਿਰ; ~run ਪੂਰਵ ਸੂਚਨਾ ਦੇਣੀ, ਪਹਿਲਾਂ ਆਉਣਾ, ਅਗਵਾਈ ਕਰਨੀ; ~shore ਮੰਡ, ਕਛਾਰ; ~side ਅਗਲਾ ਹਿੱਸਾ, ਅਗਲਾ ਭਾਗ; ~sight ਦੂਰ-ਦ੍ਰਿਸ਼ਟੀ, ਦੂਰ-ਅੰਦੇਸ਼ੀ, ਦੂਰ-ਦ੍ਰਿਸ਼ਟਤਾ, ਦੂਰ ਦੀ ਸੋਝੀ; ਭਵਿੱਖ ਦੀ ਚਿੰਤਾ; ~sighted ਦੂਰ-ਦਰਸ਼ੀ, ਦੂਰ-ਅੰਦੇਸ਼ੀ, ਲੰਮੀ; ਸੋਚ ਵਾਲਾ; ~stall ਪੇਸ਼ਬੰਦੀ ਕਰਨਾ, ਰੋਕ ਦੇਣਾ; ~tell ਅਗੋਂ ਦੱਸ ਦੇਣਾ, ਭਵਿੱਖਬਾਣੀ ਕਰਨੀ, ਪੇਸ਼ੀਨਗੋਈ ਕਰਨੀ; ~teller ਭਵਿੱਖਬਾਣੀ-ਕਰਤਾ, ਜੋਤਸ਼ੀ; ~warning ਪੂਰਵ-ਚਿਤਾਵਨੀ, ਪੂਰਵ-ਸਾਵਧਾਨੀ, ਖ਼ਬਰਦਾਰੀ; ~word ਪੁਸਤਕ ਦਾ ਮੁੱਖਬੰਦ, ਭੂਮਕਾ, ਪ੍ਰਸਤਾਵਨਾ

foreign (ਫ਼ੌਰਨ) *a n* ਵਿਦੇਸ਼ੀ (ਬਿਦੇਸ਼ੀ), ਪਰਦੇਸੀ, ਵਲਾਇਤੀ, ਬਾਹਰਲਾ, ਉਪਰਾ, ਬਿਗਾਨਾ; ਅਜੋੜ, ਅਮੇਲ

forensic (ਫਅ'ਰੈਂਸਿਕ) *a* ਅਪਰਾਧ ਦੀ ਵਿਗਿਆਨਕ ਜਾਂਚ ਸਬੰਧੀ

forest ('ਫੋਰਿਸਟ) *n v* ਜੰਗਲ, ਵਨ, ਬੀੜ; ਜੰਗਲ ਲਾਉਣਾ; ~ation ਜੰਗਲਾਉਣਾ; ~ry ਵਣ-ਵਿਗਿਆਨ; ਜੰਗਲੀ ਇਲਾਕਾ

forever (ਫਅ'ਰੈਵ਼ਅ*) *adv* ਹਮੇਸ਼ਾ, ਸਦਾ ਲਈ, ਸਰਬਥਾ; ~more ਜ਼ਰੂਰ ਹੀ, ਅਨੰਤ ਕਾਲ ਤਕ

forfeit ('ਫ਼ੋ*ਫ਼ਿਟ) *v a n* ਗੁਆ ਬੈਠਣਾ, ਵਾਂਝਿਆਂ ਹੋ ਜਾਣਾ; ਖੁਹਾ ਲੈਣਾ; ਜੁਰਮਾਨਾ ਭਰਨਾ, ਜਬਤ ਕੀਤਾ, ਖੋਹਿਆ ਗਿਆ, ਦੰਡ, ਜੁਰਮਾਨਾ

forfend (ਫ਼ੋ'ਫ਼ੈਂਡ) *v* ਰੋਕਣਾ, ਟਾਲਣਾ, ਦੂਰ ਰੱਖਣਾ, ਹਟਵਾਂ ਰੱਖਣਾ, ਟਾਲ ਦੇਣਾ

forfex ('ਫ਼ੋ*ਫ਼ੈਕਸ) *n* ਕੈਂਚੀ

forgather (ਫ਼ੋ'ਗੈਦਅ*) *v* ਇਕੱਤਰ ਹੋਣਾ, ਇੱਕਠੇ ਹੋ ਕੇ ਬੈਠਣਾ; ਸਮਾਗਮ ਕਰਨਾ

forge (ਫ਼ੋ:ਜ) *v n* ਘੜਨਾ, ਅੱਗ ਨਾਲ ਗਰਮ ਕਰਕੇ ਅਤੇ ਕੁੱਟ ਕੇ ਕੋਈ ਰੂਪ ਦੇਣਾ; ਨਕਲੀ ਬਣਾਉਣਾ; ਹੌਲੀ ਹੌਲੀ ਜਾਂ ਕਠਿਨਾਈ ਨਾਲ ਅਗਾਂਹ ਵਧਣਾ; ਜਾਅਲੀ, ਲੁਹਾਰ ਦੀ ਭੱਠੀ; ~d ਜਾਅਲੀ, ਨਕਲੀ; ~r ਲੁਹਾਰ, ਠਠਿਆਰ; ਜਾਅਲਸਾਜ਼, ਦਗ਼ਾਬਾਜ਼; ~ry ਜਾਅਲੀ ਦਸਤਖ਼ਤ ਜਾਂ ਦਸਤਾਵੇਜ਼, ਜਾਅਲਸਾਜ਼ੀ, ਕਪਟ, ਫ਼ਰੇਬ

forget (ਫ਼ਅ'ਗੈੱਟ) *v* ਭੁੱਲਣਾ, ਵਿਸਾਰ ਦੇਣਾ; ਖ਼ਿਆਲ ਛੱਡ ਦੇਣਾ; ਉਪੇਖਿਆ ਕਰਨੀ; ~ful ਭੁਲੱਕੜ, ਭੁੱਲੜ

forgive (ਫ਼ਅ'ਗਿਵ਼) *v* ਮਾਫ਼ ਕਰਨਾ, ਖ਼ਿਮਾ ਕਰਨਾ, ਬਖ਼ਸ਼ ਦੇਣਾ; ~ness ਮਾਫ਼ੀ, ਖ਼ਿਮਾ, ਛੁਟਕਾਰਾ

forgiving (ਫ਼ਅ'ਗਿਵ਼ਿੰਡ) *n* ਬਖ਼ਸ਼ਣਹਾਰ, ਖ਼ਿਮਾਸ਼ੀਲ

forgo (ਫ਼ੋ'ਗਅਉ) *v* (ਹੱਕ, ਦਾਅਵਾ ਆਦਿ) ਛੱਡ ਦੇਣਾ, ਤਿਆਗ ਦੇਣਾ

fork (ਫ਼ੋ:ਕ) *n v* ਕੰਟਾ (ਖਾਣੇ ਲਈ ਵਰਤਣ ਵਾਲਾ); ਤ੍ਰੰਗਲੀ, ਸਾਂਗਾਂ ਹੋਈਆਂ ਜਾਂ ਫੁੱਟੀਆਂ; ਸਾਂਗਾਂ ਵਾਲੇ ਸੰਦ ਨਾਲ ਤੋਂ ਪੋਸੀ ਕਰਨੀ

forlorn (ਫ਼ਅ'ਲੋ:ਨ) *a* ਬੇਸਹਾਰਾ, ਨਿਆਸਰਾ, ਦੀਨ, ਅਨਾਥ; ਸੱਖਣਾ, ਬੇਆਬਾਦ

form (ਫ਼ੋ:ਮ) *n v* ਰੂਪ, ਸ਼ਕਲ, ਸੂਰਤ, ਆਕਾਰ,

formal

ਡੋਲ, ਢਾਂਗਾ, ਬਟਾਵਟ; ਸ਼ੇਣੀ; ਛਾਪੇਖ਼ਾਨੇ ਦਾ ਫ਼ਰਮ; ਨਿਯਮਾਨੁਕੂਲ ਲਿਖਤ ਜਾਂ ਦਸਤਾਵੇਜ਼, ਕਿਸਮ, ਪ੍ਰਕਾਰ; ਸ਼ਬਦਾਂ ਦੀ ਰਚਨਾ; ਕੋਈ ਰੂਪ ਦੇਣਾ ਜਾਂ ਬਣਾਉਣਾ, ਢਾਲਣਾ; **~ed** ਰਚਿਤ, ਨਿਰਮਤ, ਬਣਿਆ; **~less** ਨਿਰਾਕਾਰ, ਨਿਰੂਪ, ਆਕਾਰਹੀਨ, ਰੂਪਹੀਨ

formal ('ਫ਼ੋ:ਮਲ) *a* ਰਸਮੀ, ਰਿਵਾਜੀ, ਲੋਕਾਚਾਰ ਵਾਲਾ, ਉਚੇਚਤਾਪੂਰਨ; **~ise /-ize** ਰੀਤ ਅਨੁਸਾਰ ਕਰਨਾ, ਵਿਸ਼ੇਸ਼ ਆਕਾਰ ਜਾਂ ਰੂਪ ਦੇਣਾ; **~ism** ਲੋਕਾਚਾਰ, ਉਚੇਚ, ਸ਼ਿਸ਼ਟਾਚਾਰ ਬਾਰੇ ਕਠੜਾਈ; ਰੂਪਵਾਦ; **~ly** ਰੀਤ ਨਾਲ, ਇੱਧੀਧੀਵਤ ਰੂਪ ਵਿਚ, ਰਸਮੀ ਤਰੀਕੇ ਨਾਲ; **~ity** ਦਸਤੂਰ, ਰੀਤ, ਰਸਮ, ਮਰਯਾਦਾ; ਉਚੇਚ, ਤਕੱਲਫ਼

format ('ਫ਼ੋ:ਮੈਟ) *n* ਕਿਤਾਬ ਦਾ ਬਾਹਰੀ ਰੂਪ, ਪੁਸਤਕ ਦਾ ਫ਼ਰਮਾ

formation (ਫ਼ੋ'ਮੇਇਸ਼ਨ) *n* ਬਣਾਵਟ, ਰਚਨਾ, ਨਿਰਮਾਣ; ਚਟਾਨਾਂ ਦਾ ਜਮਾਉ

formative ('ਫ਼ੋ:ਮਅਟਿਵ) *n a* ਬਣਾਉਣ ਵਾਲਾ, ਤਰਤੀਬ ਦੇਣ ਵਾਲਾ; ਰਚਨਾਤਮਕ, ਨਿਰਮਾਣਾਤਮਕ

former ('ਫ਼ੋ:ਮਅ*) *a pron* ਪਹਿਲਾਂ, ਪੂਰਵਲਾ, ਭੂਤਪੂਰਵ

formidable ('ਫ਼ੋ:ਮਿਡਅਬਲ) *a* ਡਰਾਉਣਾ, ਤਿਆਨਕ, ਬਹੁਤ ਵੱਡਾ; ਪਰਬਲ

formula ('ਫ਼ੋ:ਮਯੁਲਅ) *n* ਗੁਰ, ਸੂਤਰ, ਫ਼ਾਰਮੂਲਾ; ਦਸਤੂਰ, ਰੀਤੀ, ਵਿਧੀ, ਨਿਯਮ; **~tion** ਵਿਵਸਥਿਤ ਕਰਨ; ਸਥਾਪਨਾ; ਸੂਤਰੀਕਰਨ

formulise ('ਫ਼ੋ:ਮਯੁਲਾਇਜ਼) *v* ਨਿਯਮਿਤ ਰੂਪ ਵਿਚ ਕਹਿਣਾ, ਸੂਤਰਬੱਧ ਕਰਨਾ

formulism ('ਫ਼ੋ:ਮਯੁਲਿਜ਼(ਅ)ਮ) *n* ਰੂੜ੍ਹੀਵਾਦ,

formulist ('ਫ਼ੋ:ਮਯੁਲਿਸਟ) *n* ਰੂੜ੍ਹੀਵਾਦੀ

forward

forsake (ਫ਼ਅ'ਸੇਇਕ) *v* ਛੱਡ ਦੇਣਾ, ਤਿਆਗਣਾ, ਛੱਡ ਬੈਠਣਾ; ਸਿੱਤਰਤਾ ਤੋੜ ਲੈਣੀ; **~n** ਤਿਆਗਿਆ, ਛੱਡਿਆ

fort (ਫ਼ੋ:ਟ) *n* ਕਿਲ੍ਹਾ, ਗੜ੍ਹ, ਦੁਰਗ, ਕੋਟ; **~ification** ਮਜ਼ਬੂਤੀ, ਪ੍ਰਸ਼ਟੀਕਰਨ; ਕਿਲ੍ਹੇਬੰਦੀ, ਮੋਰਚਾਬੰਦੀ; **~ify** ਕਿਲ੍ਹੇਬੰਦੀ ਕਰਨੀ, ਮੋਰਚਾਬੰਦੀ ਕਰਨੀ; **~itude** ਹਿੰਮਤ, ਹੌਸਲਾ, ਸਾਹਸ, ਸਹਿਨਸ਼ਕਤੀ, ਤਾਕਤ, ਜਿਗਰਾ; **~ress** ਗੜ੍ਹੀ, ਕੋਟ

forte ('ਫ਼ੋ:ਟੇਇ) *n* ਕਿਸੇ ਮਨੁੱਖ ਦਾ ਕੋਈ ਵਿਸ਼ੇਸ਼ ਗੁਣ, ਕੋਈ ਇਖ਼ਲਾਕੀ ਜਾਂ ਦਿਮਾਗ਼ੀ ਸ਼ਕਤੀ; ਤਲਵਾਰ ਦਾ ਉੱਪਰਲਾ ਭਾਗ

forth (ਫ਼ੋ:ਥ) *adv* ਅਗਾਂਹ, ਅੱਗੇ ਵੱਲ; ਅਗਾਂਹ ਨੂੰ, ਹੁਣ ਤੋਂ, ਬਾਹਰ, ਅੱਗੇ; ਅਗਾੜੀ; **~coming** ਆਉਣ ਵਾਲਾ, ਅਗਾਂਹ ਨੂੰ ਹੋਣ ਵਾਲਾ, ਆਗਾਮੀ; **~right** ਸਿੱਧਾ ਰਾਹ; ਪ੍ਰਵੀਣ, ਚਤੁਰ, ਅਟਲ, ਸਪਸ਼ਟ, ਖਰਾ, ਖਰੀ ਖਰੀ ਕਹਿਣ ਵਾਲਾ, ਮੂੰਹਫਟ; ਤੁਰਤ; **~with** ਤੁਰਤ, ਫੌਰਨ, ਝਟਪਟ, ਹੁਣੇ, ਇਸੇ ਵੇਲੇ

fortunate ('ਫ਼ੋ:ਚਅਨਅਟ) *a* ਸੁਭਾਗਾ, ਚੰਗੀ ਕਿਸਮਤ ਵਾਲਾ, ਭਾਗਾਂ ਵਾਲਾ, ਨਸੀਬਾਂ ਵਾਲਾ, ਖ਼ੁਸ਼ਕਿਸਮਤ

fortune ('ਫ਼ੋ:ਚੂਨ) *n* ਕਿਸਮਤ, ਭਾਗ, ਨਸੀਬ, ਹੋਣੀ; **~teller** ਜੋਤਸ਼ੀ, ਨਜੂਮੀ

fortunize ('ਫ਼ੋ:ਟਅਨਾਇਜ਼) *v* ਸੁਖੀ ਬਣਾਉਣਾ, ਸੁਖ ਦੇਣਾ

forum ('ਫ਼ੋਰਅਮ) *n* ਲੋਕ-ਚਰਚਾ ਦੀ ਥਾਂ, ਗੋਸ਼ਟੀ-ਸਥਾਨ, ਗੋਸ਼ਟੀ, ਸਮਾਰੋਹ, ਜਨ-ਸਭਾ, ਚੌਪਾਲ, ਅਖਾੜਾ, ਅਦਾਲਤ

forward ('ਫ਼ੋ:ਵਡ) *a n adv v* ਅਗਲਾ, ਮੁਹਰਲਾ, ਅਗੇਤਰਾ, ਅਗਾਂਹ ਵਧਿਆ ਹੋਇਆ,

fossil / 498 / **frame**

ਪਹਿਲੇ ਸਮੇਂ ਦਾ; ਮੁਹਰੇ ਲਾਉਣਾ, ਅੱਗੇ ਵਧਾਉਣਾ; ਅਗਾਂਹ ਭੇਜਣਾ, ਅੱਗੇ ਟੋਰਨਾ; ਉੱਨਤੀ ਦੀ ਚਾਲ ਤੇਜ਼ ਕਰਨੀ; (ਚਿੱਠੀ ਆਦਿ) ਅਗਲੇ ਪਤੇ ਤੇ ਭੇਜਣੀ; ਘੱਲਣਾ, ਰਵਾਨਾ ਕਰਨਾ

fossil ('ਫ਼ੌਸਲ) *a n* ਪਥਰਾਇਆ, ਪਥਰਾਈ, ਰੂੜ੍ਹੀਵਾਦੀ; **~ize** ਪਥਰਾਉਣਾ, ਪੱਥਰਾਏ ਜਾਣਾ, ਪੱਥਰ ਰੂਪ ਕਰਨਾ ਜਾਂ ਹੋਣਾ

foster ('ਫ਼ੌਸਟਅ*) *v a* ਪਾਲਣਾ-ਪੋਸਣਾ, ਪਾਲਣਾ ਕਰਨੀ; ਦੁੱਧ ਚੁੰਘਾਉਣਾ; ਅਗਾਂਹ ਵਧਾਉਣਾ; **~er** ਪਾਲਕ, ਪੋਸ਼ਕ, ਪਰੋਤਸ਼ਾਹਕ

foul (ਫ਼ਾਊਲ) *a n adv v* ਗੰਦਾ, ਮੈਲਾ, ਲਿਥੜਿਆ, ਅਪਵਿੱਤਰ, ਬਦਬੂਦਾਰ; ਗੰਦ ਬਕਣ ਵਾਲਾ; ਬਦਸੂਰਤ, ਕੋਝੀ ਸੂਰਤ ਵਾਲਾ; ਖੇਡ ਦੇ ਨਿਯਮਾਂ ਦੇ ਵਿਰੁੱਧ, ਅਨੋਮਾ; **~play** ਧੋਖੇਬਾਜ਼ੀ; **through fair and~** ਜਿਵੇਂ ਕਿਵੇਂ

found (ਫ਼ਾਊਂਡ) *v* ਨੀਂਹ ਰੱਖਣੀ, ਮਕਾਨ (ਆਦਿ) ਬਣਾਉਣਾ, ਆਰੰਭ ਕਰਨਾ, ਉਸਾਰਨਾ, ਸਥਾਪਨਾ ਕਰਨੀ; ਕੋਈ ਸੰਸਥਾ ਆਰੰਭ ਕਰਨੀ, ਖੜ੍ਹੀ ਕਰਨੀ; ਕਾਇਮ ਕਰਨੀ, ਨੀਂਹ ਜਾਂ ਆਧਾਰ ਹੋਣਾ; ਆਸ਼ਰਤ ਹੋਣਾ; (ਧਾਤ ਆਦਿ ਨੂੰ) ਗਾਲ ਕੇ ਢਾਲਣਾ, ਢਲਾਈ ਕਰਨੀ; **~ation** ਨੀਂਹ, ਬੁਨਿਆਦ; ਆਧਾਰ, ਸਹਾਰਾ; ਨਿਰਮਾਣ, ਰਚਨਾ, ਆਰੰਭ; ਮੂਲ ਸਿਧਾਂਤ; **~ation stone** ਨੀਂਹ-ਪੱਥਰ; **~er** ਨੀਂਹ ਰੱਖਣ ਵਾਲਾ, ਆਰੰਭ ਕਰਨ ਵਾਲਾ, ਮੋਢੀ, ਸੰਚਾਲਕ

foundling ('ਫ਼ਾਊਨਡਲਿੰਡ) *n* ਅਨਾਥ, ਯਤੀਮ

fount ('ਫ਼ਾਊਂਟ) *n* ਇਕੋ ਸਾਈਜ਼ (ਨਾਪ) ਦੇ ਅੱਖਰ, ਟਾਈਪ-ਵਰਗ, ਲੈਂਪ (ਲਾਲਟੇਨ) ਦਾ ਥੱਲਾ ਜਿਸ ਵਿੱਚ ਤੇਲ ਭਰਿਆ ਜਾਂਦਾ ਹੈ; ਸਰੋਤ

fountain ('ਫ਼ਾਊਨਟਿਨ) *n* ਫੁਹਾਰਾ, ਫ਼ਰਨਾ, ਚਸ਼ਮਾ; ਸੋਮਾ; **~head** ਮੂਲ ਸਰੋਤ, ਮੁੱਢ; ਮੂਲ ਕਾਰਨ

four (ਫ਼ੋ*) *n a* ਚਾਰ ਦੀ ਗਿਣਤੀ; **~fold** ਚਾਰ ਗੁਣਾ; **~square** ਸਥਿਰ, ਮਜ਼ਬੂਤ; ਵਰਗਾਕਾਰ; **~th** ਚੌਥਾ; (ਬ ਵ) ਚੌਥੇ ਦਰਜੇ ਦੀਆਂ ਵਸਤਾਂ

fourteen ('ਫ਼ੋ'ਟੀਨ) *a* ਚੌਦਾਂ (14); **~th** ਚੌਦਵਾਂ

fox (ਫ਼ੌਕਸ) *n v* ਲੂੰਬੜ, ਲੂੰਬੜੀ; ਚਲਾਕ ਆਦਮੀ, ਘਾਗ, ਚਲਤਾ ਪੁਰਜਾ; ਚਲਾਕੀ ਕਰਨੀ; ਧੋਖਾ ਦੇਣਾ, ਛਲ ਕਰਨਾ; **~iness** ਚਾਲਬਾਜ਼ੀ, ਮੱਕਾਰੀ, ਚਲਾਕੀ

fraction ('ਫ਼ਰੈਕਸ਼ਨ) *n* ਹਿੱਸਾ, ਭਾਗ, ਖੰਡ, ਅੰਸ਼, ਟੁਕੜਾ; **~al** ਬਟੇ ਵਾਲਾ, ਭਿੰਨਾਤਮਕ, ਕਸਰ, ਨਿਗੁਣਾ

fracture ('ਫ਼ਰੈਕਚਅ*) *n v* ਹੱਡੀ ਟੁੱਟਣਾ, ਹੱਡੀ ਤਿੜਕਣਾ; ਹੱਡੀ ਦਾ ਟੁੱਟਣ

fragile ('ਫ਼ਰੈਜਾਇਲ) *a* ਨਾਜ਼ਕ, ਕਮਜ਼ੋਰ, ਭੁਰਭੁਰਾ

fragility (ਫ਼ਰਅ'ਜਿਲਅਟਿ) *n* ਭੁਰਭੁਰਾਪਣ, ਟੁੱਟਪੁਣਾ

fragment ('ਫ਼ਰੈਗਮਅੰਟ) *n* ਟੋਟਾ, ਟੁਕੜਾ, ਫਾੜ, ਖੰਡ, ਅੰਸ਼, ਭਾਗ; **~ary** ਟੋਟੇ ਟੋਟੇ, ਵੱਖੋ-ਵੱਖ, ਖੰਡਤ

fragmentation ('ਫ਼ਰੈਗਮੈਨ'ਟੇਇਸ਼ਨ) *n* ਟੋਟੇ ਟੋਟੇ ਹੋਣਾ, ਵਿਖੰਡਨ

fragrance ('ਫ਼ਰੇਇਗਰਅੰਸ) *a* ਖ਼ੁਸ਼ਬੂ, ਮਿੱਠੀ ਸੁਗੰਧ, ਮਹਿਕ

fragrant ('ਫ਼ਰੇਇਗਰਅੰਟ) *a* ਖ਼ੁਸ਼ਬੂਦਾਰ, ਮਹਿਕਦਾ

frail (ਫ਼ਰੇਇਲ) *a* ਕਮਜ਼ੋਰ, ਮਾੜਾ, ਲਿੱਸਾ; **~ty** ਕਮਜ਼ੋਰੀ, ਦੁਰਬਲਤਾ; ਔਗੁਣ ਕਰਨ ਵਾਲੀ ਰੁਚੀ

frame (ਫ਼ਰੇਇਮ) *v n* ਬਣਾਉਣਾ, ਘੜਨਾ, ਸਾਜਣਾ; ਜੜਨਾ, ਠੋਕਣਾ, ਠੀਕ ਬੈਠਾਉਣਾ; ਢਾਲਣਾ; (ਕਿਸੇ ਨੂੰ ਕਿਸੇ ਕੰਮ ਲਈ) ਤਿਆਰ ਕਰਨਾ; ਸੋਚਣਾ;

ਕਲਪਨਾ ਕਰਨੀ; ਢਾਂਚਾ, ਪਿੰਜਰ, ਚੁਗਾਠ, ਚੌਖਟਾ; ਹਾਲਤ, ਦਸ਼ਾ; ਕਾਠੀ, ਸਰੀਰ, ਕਾਇਆ; ਰਚਨਾ, ਨਿਰਮਾਣ, ਬਣਾਵਟ; ~work ਢਾਂਚਾ, ਚੌਖਟਾ

franc (ਫ਼ਰੈਂਕ) *n* ਫ਼ਰਾਂਸ ਦਾ ਇਕ ਸਿੱਕਾ, ਫ਼ਰਾਂਕ

franchise ('ਫ਼ਰੈਨਚਾਇਜ਼) *n* ਵੋਟ ਦੇਣ ਦਾ ਅਧਿਕਾਰ, ਮੱਤ-ਅਧਿਕਾਰ, ਨਾਗਰਿਕਤਾ

frank (ਫ਼ਰੈਂਕ) *a v n* ਬੇਲਾਗ, ਨਿਰਛਲ, ਸਾਫ਼-ਸਾਫ਼, ਖਰਾ, ਬੇਲਾਗ, ਭੋਲਾ, ਸਾਦਾ

frantic ('ਫ਼ਰੈਨਟਿਕ) *a* ਕਰੋਧ ਨਾਲ ਭਰਿਆ; ਦੀਵਾਨਾ, ਬਦਹਵਾਸ, ਉਤੇਜਨਾ ਪੂਰਨ

franternal (ਫ਼ਰਾ'ਟਅਃਨਲ) *a.* ਭਰਾਦਰਾਨਾ, ਸੁਹਿਰਦਕ, ਭਾਈਬੰਦੀ ਦਾ

fraternity (ਫ਼ਰਾ'ਟਅਃਨਟਿ) *n* ਭਾਈਚਾਰਾ, ਭਾਈਬੰਦੀ, ਬਰਾਤਰੀ-ਭਾਵ, ਮੰਡਲੀ

fraternize ('ਫ਼ਰੈਟਅਨਾਇਜ਼) *v* ਭਾਈਚਾਰਾ ਪਾਉਣਾ, ਭਾਈਬੰਦੀ ਕਰਨੀ, ਮੇਲਜੋਲ ਕਰਨਾ, ਮਿਲਣਾ-ਜੁਲਣਾ

fraud (ਫ਼ਰੋਡ) *n* ਧੋਖਾ, ਛਲ, ਫ਼ਰੇਬ, ਕਪਟ, ਚਾਲਬਾਜ਼ੀ; ਚਾਤਰੀ, ਛਲ, ਠੱਗੀ; ~ulence ਧੋਖੇਬਾਜ਼ੀ, ਮੱਕਾਰੀ, ਕਪਟਤਾ, ਚਾਲਬਾਜ਼ੀ, ਛਲ; ~ulent ਮੱਕਾਰੀ ਵਾਲੀ, ਕਪਟੀ, ਫ਼ਰੇਬੀ, ਛਲਿਆ, ਮੱਕਾਰ, ਧੋਖੇਬਾਜ਼

fray ('ਫ਼ਰੇਇ) *v n* ਝਗੜਾ, ਕਲਹ, ਹੰਗਾਮਾ, ਬਖੇੜਾ, ਦੰਗਾ, ਫ਼ਸਾਦ, ਸ਼ੋਰ-ਸ਼ਰਾਬਾ; ਪਤਲਾ ਕਰਨਾ, ਰਗੜਨਾ

freak (ਫ਼ਰੀਕ) *n* ਖ਼ਿਆਲ, ਤਰੰਗ, ਮੌਜ, ਵਹਿਮ, ਖਬਤ, ਅਜੂਬਾ

free (ਫ਼ਰੀ) *a* ਆਜ਼ਾਦ, ਸੁਤੰਤਰ, ਸਵਾਧੀਨ; ਸਪਸ਼ਟ, ਸਾਫ਼; ਖੁੱਲ੍ਹਾ-ਡੁੱਲ੍ਹਾ, ਬੰਧਨਹੀਨ; (ਹਵਾ) ਤੁਕਾਂਤ ਰਹਿਤ; ਛੁੱਟਿਆ; ਮੁਫ਼ਤ;, ਢੀਠ, ਨਿਰਲੱਜ, ਬੇ-ਹਯਾ; ਬੇ-ਧੜਕ; ~forall ਖੁੱਲ੍ਹੀ ਲੜਾਈ, ਲੱਗਦੀ ਲਾਉਣਾ; ~hold ਪੂਰੀ ਮਾਲਕੀ; ~thinker ਸੁਤੰਤਰ ਚਿੰਤਕ; ਆਜ਼ਾਦ ਖਿਆਲ; ~trade ਖੁੱਲ੍ਹਾ ਵਪਾਰ ~dom ਆਜ਼ਾਦੀ, ਸੁਤੰਤਰਤਾ, ਸਵਾਧੀਨਤਾ

freeze (ਫ਼ਰੀਜ਼) *v* ਜੰਮ ਕੇ ਬਰਫ਼ ਬਣ ਜਾਣਾ; ਠੰਡਾ ਹੋ ਜਾਣਾ; ਸਰਦੀ ਦੇ ਕਾਰਨ ਆਕੜ ਜਾਣਾ; ~r ਬਰਫ਼ ਜਮਾਉਣ ਦਾ ਜੰਤਰ; (ਫ਼ਰਿੱਜ ਦਾ) ਬਰਫ਼ ਜਮਾਉਣ ਦਾ ਖ਼ਾਨਾ

freezing ('ਫ਼ਰੀਜ਼ਿੰਡ) *a* ਬਹੁਤ ਠੰਢਾ; ~point ਜਮਾਓ ਦਰਜਾ, ਯਖੀਲ ਦਰਜਾ, ਹਿਮਾਂਕ

freight (ਫ਼ਰੇਇਟ) *n v* ਭਾੜਾ, ਮਾਲ-ਢੁਆਈ ਸਾਮਾਨ ਭੇਜਣ ਦਾ ਕਿਰਾਇਆ; ~age ਭਾੜਾ, ਮਾਲ ਲੈ ਜਾਣ ਦਾ ਕਿਰਾਇਆ, ਮਹਿਸੂਲ; ~er ਮਾਲ-ਵਾਹਕ ਜਹਾਜ਼

French (ਫ਼ਰੈਂਚ) *a n* ਫ਼ਰਾਂਸੀਸੀ ਭਾਸ਼ਾ, ਬੋਲੀ; ~bean ਲੋਬੀਆ; ~letter ਨਿਰੋਧ

frenzy ('ਫ਼ਰੈਂਜ਼ਿ) *n v* ਝੱਲ, ਜਨੂਨ, ਸਨਕ

frequency ('ਫ਼ਰਿਕਵੰਸਿ) *n* ਵਾਰਵਾਰਤਾ, ਗਿਣਤੀ ਦਾ ਅਨੁਪਾਤ

frequent ('ਫ਼ਰਿਕਵਅਨਟ) *a v* ਵਾਰ-ਵਾਰ ਆਉਣ ਵਾਲਾ, ਆਮ, ਬਹੁਤ; (ਨਬਜ਼) ਤੇਜ਼, ਤੀਬਰ; ਅਕਸਰ, ਆਮ ਪ੍ਰਚਲਤ; ਘੜੀ-ਮੁੜੀ ਜਾਣਾ, ਬਾਰੰਬਾਰ ਜਾਣਾ

fresh (ਫ਼ਰੈੱਸ਼) *a adv a* ਨਿਰਮਲ, ਚਮਕਦਾਰ (ਚਿਹਰਾ-ਮੁਹਰਾ); ਤਾਜ਼ਾ, ਜੋ ਬਾਸੀ ਨਾ ਹੋਵੇ (ਖਾਣਾ); ਤਾਜ਼ਾ ਰੁਸਤ, ਫੁਰਤੀਲਾ; ਨਵਾਂ ਆਧੁਨਿਕ; (ਜਲਵਾਯੂ) ਕੱਚਾ; ਵਗਦਾ (ਪਾਣੀ); ਅਗਲਾ, ਹੋਰ ਨਵਾਂ; ~en ਤਾਜ਼ਾ ਦਮ ਹੋਣਾ ਜਾਂ ਕਰਨਾ, ਤਾਜ਼ਾ ਹੋਣਾ ਜਾਂ ਕਰਨਾ; ~er ਨਵਾਂ ਵਿਅਕਤੀ; ਨਵਾਂ ਵਿਦਿਆਰਥੀ

fret (ਫ਼ਰੈੱਟ) *v n* (1) ਤੰਗ ਕਰਨਾ, ਗੱਸਾ

ਦਿਵਾਉਣਾ, ਖਿਝਾਉਣਾ; ਕੁਤਰਨਾ, ਰਗਾਉਣਾ; (2) ਨੱਕਾਸ਼ੀ ਕਰਨੀ, ਚਿੱਤਰਕਾਰੀ ਕਰਨੀ; ਜਾਲੀਦਾਰ ਨੱਕਾਸ਼ੀ; ~ful ਖਿਝ, ਪਰੇਸ਼ਾਨੀ, ਝੁੰਝਲਾਹਟ, ਝੁਰਝੁੜਪੁਣ, ਕਰੋਧ, ਚਿੜਚਿੜਾਪਣ

fricative ('ਫ਼ਰਿਕਅਟਿਵ਼) *a n* (ਭਾਸ਼ਾ) ਸੰਘਰਸ਼ੀ, ਘਰਸ਼ੀ

friction ('ਫ਼ਰਿਕਸ਼ਨ) *n* ਰਗੜ, ਘਿਸਰ, ਮਾਲਸ਼, ਘਰਸ਼ਟ, ਸੰਘਰਸ਼, ਮੱਤਭੇਦ, ਝਗੜਾ; ~al ਰਗੜ-ਸਬੰਧੀ, ਰਗੜਵਾਲਾ, ਘਰਸ਼ੀ, ਸੰਘਰਸ਼ੀ

Friday ('ਫ਼ਰਾਇਡਿ) *n* ਸ਼ੁੱਕਰਵਾਰ

friend (ਫ਼ਰੈਂਡ) *n v* ਯਾਰ, ਦੋਸਤ, ਮਿੱਤਰ, ਮਿੱਤਰ ਬਣਾਉਣਾ, ਸਹਾਇਤਾ ਦੇਣੀ; ~less ਮਿੱਤਰਹੀਣ, ਬੇਮਦਦਗਾਰ; ~ly ਮਿੱਤਰਤਾ-ਪੂਰਨ, ਦੋਸਤਾਨਾ, ਅਪੱਣਤਵਾਲਾ; ~ship ਮਿੱਤਰਤਾ, ਦੋਸਤੀ, ਯਾਰੀ

frig, fridge (ਫ਼ਰਿਜ) *n* ਫ਼ਰਿੱਜ, ਰੈਫ਼ਰਿਜਰੇਟਰ, ਚੀਜ਼ਾਂ ਠੰਢੀਆਂ ਰੱਖਣ ਲਈ ਬਿਜਲੀ ਦੀ ਅਲਮਾਰੀ, ਠੰਢਾ, ਠੰਢਾ-ਠਾਰ ਜੰਮਿਆ; ਰੁੱਖਾ, ਫਿੱਕਾ

frigate ('ਫ਼ਰਿਗਅਟ) *n* ਗਸ਼ਤੀ ਜਹਾਜ਼; ਤੋਪਾਂ ਵਾਲਾ ਜੰਗੀ ਜਹਾਜ਼

fright (ਫ਼ਰਾਇਟ) *n v* ਭੈ, ਡਰ, ਡਰਾਉਣਾ ਭੈਭੀਤ ਕਰਨਾ; ~ened ਭੈਭੀਤ, ਸਹਿਮਿਆ, ਡਰਿਆ; ~ful ਭਿਆਨਕ, ਡਰਾਉਣਾ, ਭਿਅੰਕਰ, ਭੈਭੀਤ

frill (ਫ਼ਰਿਲ) *n v* ਝਾਲਰ, ਕੰਨੀ, ਪਲੇਟ, ਪਸ਼ੂਆਂ ਵਿਖਾਵਾ, ਟੀਪ-ਟਾਪ; ਝਾਲਰ ਲਾਉਣੀ, ਕਿਨਾਰੀ ਲਾ ਕੇ ਸਜਾਉਣਾ; ਵਿਖਾਵਾ ਕਰਨਾ, ਅੱਡੋਕਵੀਂ ਸਜਾਵਟ ਕਰਨੀ

fringe (ਫ਼ਰਿੰਜ) *n v* ਕੱਲੀ, ਕਿਨਾਰੀ, ਮਗਜ਼ੀ, ਕੋਰ, ਝਾਲਰ; ਹਾਸ਼ੀਆ, ਕਿਨਾਰਾ, ਕੰਨੀ ਜਾਂ ਕਿਨਾਰੀ ਲਾਉਣੀ, ਮਗਜ਼ੀ ਲਾਉਣੀ

frizzle ('ਫ਼ਰਿਜ਼ਲ) *n v* ਕੁੰਡਲਦਾਰ ਵਾਲ, ਘੁੰਗਰਾਲੇ ਵਾਲ ਘੁੰਗਰਾਲੇ ਬਣਾਉਣੇ ਵਾਲਾਂ ਵਿਚ ਕੁੰਡਲ ਬਣਾਉਣੇ

fro (ਫ਼ਰਅਉ) *adv prep* ਪਰੇ, ਪਿੱਛੇ; ਪਿੱਛੇ ਵੱਲ

frock (ਫ਼ਰੌਕ) *n v* ਬੱਚੇ ਦੀ ਵਿਸ਼ੇਸ਼ ਕਮੀਜ਼, ਫ਼ਰਾਕ; ਇਸਾਈ ਸਾਧੂਆਂ ਦਾ ਲੰਮਾ ਚੋਗਾ

frog (ਫ਼ਰੌਗ) *n* ਡੱਡੂ, ਦਾਦਰ, ਮੇਂਡਕ; ~man ਗੋਤਾਖ਼ੋਰ

frolic ('ਫ਼ਰੌਲਿਕ) *n v a* ਕਲੋਲ, ਚੋਜ, ਆਨੰਦ, ਪ੍ਰਸੰਨਤਾ, ਹੰਗ-ਰਲੀਆਂ, ਚੁਲਬੁਲਾਹਟ, ਚੰਚਲਤਾ, ਖੇਡ-ਕੁੱਦ; ਕਲੋਲਾਂ ਕਰਨੀਆਂ, ਟੱਪਣਾ, ਨੱਚਣਾ, ਖ਼ੁਸ਼ੀਆਂ ਮਨਾਉਣੀਆਂ; ਕਲੋਲੀ, ਆਨੰਦਤ, ਪ੍ਰਸੰਨ, ਚੁਲਬੁਲਾ, ਚੰਚਲ, ਖਿੜਵਾ

from (ਫ਼ਰੌਮ) *perp* ਤੋਂ, ਆਰੰਭ ਤੋਂ, ਦੂਰੀ ਉੱਤੇ, ਤੋਂ ਲੈ ਕੇ, ਕੋਲੋਂ, ਪਾਸੋਂ, ਰਾਹੀਂ, ਵਿੱਚੋਂ; ~day to day ਹਰ ਰੋਜ਼, ਪ੍ਰਤਿਦਿਨ

front (ਫ਼ਰਅੰਟ) *n v* ਅੱਗਾ, ਅਗਾੜੀ, ਮੂਹਰਾ, ਮੱਥਾ, ਸਨਮੁਖ ਭਾਗ, ਮੋਰਚਾ, ਸੰਗਠਤ ਸੰਸਥਾ; ਮੂੰਹ, ਮਸਤਕ, ਲਲਾਟ, ਮੱਥਾ; ਅੱਗੇ ਹੋਣਾ, ਅਗਾੜੀ ਹੋਣਾ, ਸਨਮੁਖ ਹੋਣਾ, ਮੂੰਹ ਕਰਨਾ, ਸਾਮ੍ਹਣਾ ਕਰਨਾ, ਭਿੜਨਾ, ਡਟਣਾ; ~age ਮੁੱਖ-ਦਿਸ਼ਾ, ਮਕਾਨ ਦੀ ਅਗਾੜੀ; ਮੁੱਖ ਭਾਗ, ਖ਼ਾਸ ਹਿੱਸਾ; ~al ਸਾਮ੍ਹਣੇ ਦਾ, ਮੱਥੇ ਦਾ, ਅਗਾੜੀ ਵਾਲਾ, ਸਿੱਧਾ, ਸ਼ਿੰਗਾਰ-ਪੱਟੀ

frontier ('ਫ਼ਰਅੰਨ,ਟਿਅ*) *n* ਹੱਦ, ਸਰਹੱਦ, ਸੀਮਾ, ਸੂਬਾ ਜਾਂ ਪ੍ਰਾਂਤ; ਮੁੱਢਲਾ

frost (ਫ਼ਰੌਸਟ) *n v* ਕੱਕਰ, ਕੋਰਾ, ਤੁਖਾਰ ਪਾਲਾ, ਉਤਸ਼ਾਹਹੀਣਤਾ, ਫਿੱਕਾ, ਸੜ ਜਾਣਾ; ਕੋਰੇ ਨਾਲ ਢੱਕਿਆ ਜਾਣਾ; ~y ਕੱਕਰੀਲਾ; ਰੁੱਖਾ, ਕੋਰਾ

frown (ਫ਼ਰਾਉਨ) *n v* ਤਿਊੜੀ, ਮੱਥੇ ਦੇ ਵੱਟ, ਚੜ੍ਹੀ ਹੋਈ ਭੌਂ; ਨਰਾਜ਼ਗੀ; ਕਰੋਧ; ਤਿਊੜੀ ਚੜ੍ਹਾਉਣਾ, ਕੌੜ੍ਹਣਾ, ਮੱਥੇ ਵੱਟ ਪਾਉਣਾ, ਭੌਂਹਾਂ (ਭਵਾਂ) ਚੜ੍ਹਾਉਣਾ

fruit (ਫ਼ਰੂਟ) *n v* ਫਲ, ਮੇਵਾ, ਪਰਿਣਾਮ, ਸੰਤਾਨ; ਆਮਦਨੀ; ਫਲਣਾ, ਫਲ ਦੇਣਾ; **~arain** ਫਲਾਹਾਰੀ; **~ful** ਉਪਜਾਊ; ਸਫਲ, ਸਾਰਥਕ, ਸਕਾਰਥਕ; ਲਾਭਦਾਇਕ, ਉਤਪਾਦਕ; **~less** ਬਾਂਝ, ਬੇਫਲ, ਨਿਸਫਲ, ਫਲਹੀਨ, ਨਿਰਾਰਥਕ, ਫ਼ਜ਼ੂਲ

frustrate (ਫ਼ਰਅੱਸਟਰੇਇਟ) *v* ਨਿਰਾਸ਼ ਕਰਨਾ, ਮਾਯੂਸ ਕਰਨਾ; ਆਸ ਭੰਗ ਕਰਨਾ, ਨਿਸਫਲ ਕਰਨਾ, ਤੋੜ ਦੇਣਾ

frustration (ਫ਼ਰਅੱਸਟਰੇਇਸ਼ਨ) *n* ਨਿਰਾਸਤਾ, ਦਰਿੰਦੀ ਕਲਾ, ਵਿਸ਼ਾਦ, ਨਿਗ਼ਾਬਲੂਤਾ, ਕੁੰਠਾ, ਨਿਰਾਸ਼ਾ

fry (ਫ਼ਰਾਇ) *n v* ਭੁੰਨਿਆ, ਮਾਸ, ਤਲਿਆ ਮਾਸ; ਭੁੰਨਣਾ, ਭੁੰਜਣਾ, ਤਲਣਾ; **~ing** ਤਲੀ ਚੀਜ਼, ਭੁੰਨੀ ਵਸਤੂ

fuddle ('ਫ਼ਅੱਡਲ) *n v* ਮਸਤੀ, ਨਸ਼ਾ; ਵਿਆਕੁਲਤਾ; ਮਸਤ ਕਰਨਾ, ਮਖਮੂਰ ਕਰਨਾ, ਮਦਹੋਸ਼ ਕਰਨਾ ਜਾਂ ਹੋਣਾ, (ਸ਼ਰਾਬ ਪਿਆ ਕੇ) ਬੇਸੁਧ ਕਰ ਦੇਣਾ ਜਾਂ ਹੋਣਾ; ਬਹੁਤ ਸ਼ਰਾਬ ਪੀਣੀ ਜਾਂ ਪਿਆਉਣੀ, ਵਿਆਕੁਲ ਕਰਨਾ

fudge (ਫ਼ਅੱਜ) *n v* ਛੋਟਾ ਕਿੱਸਾ; ਫ਼ਜ਼ੂਲ ਗੱਲਾਂ, ਖਖੇੜ, ਗੱਪ, ਨਿਰਾਰਥਕ ਵਾਰਤਾਲਾਪ; ਝਪਾਨੀਆਂ ਛਪਦੀਆਂ ਪ੍ਰਕਾਸ਼ਤ ਸਮਾਚਾਰ; ਦੁੱਧ ਖੰਡ ਦੇ ਦਾਣਿਆਂ ਨਾਲ ਬਣਿਆ ਭੋਜਨ; ਕੁੱਰਚਜ ਘੋਲਣਾ

fudgy (ਫ਼ਅੱਜਿ) *a* ਬੇਡਾ, ਬੁਰਾ, ਕਰੂਪ

fuel (ਫ਼ਯੂਅਲ) *n v* ਬਾਲਣ, ਲੱਕੜੀ; ਉਤੇਜਨਾ, ਭੜਕਾਊ ਪਦਾਰਥ; ਬਾਲਣ ਪਾਉਣਾ

fulfil (ਫ਼ੁਲ'ਫ਼ਿਲ) *v* (*U S fulfill*) ਭਰਨਾ; ਪੂਰਾ ਕਰਨਾ; ਪੂਰਨ ਕਰਨਾ, (ਵਚਨ ਆਦਿ) ਪਾਲਣਾ, ਨਿਬਾਹੁਣਾ, ਸੰਤੁਸ਼ਟ ਕਰਨਾ, ਹੋਣਾ, ਸਿੱਧ ਕਰਨਾ; **~ment** ਪੂਰਤੀ, ਪੂਰਨਤਾ, ਸੰਪੰਨਤਾ, ਸੰਤੁਸ਼ਟੀ, ਪਾਲਣਾ

fulgency ('ਫ਼ਅੱਲਜਅੰਸਿ) *n* ਚਮਕ, ਚਮਕੀਲਾਪਣ, ਉਜਲਤਾ, ਆਭਾ

fulgent ('ਫ਼ਅੱਲਜਅੰਟ) *a* ਚਮਕਦਾਰ, ਚਮਕੀਲਾ, ਉਜਲਾ

fulgor ('ਫ਼ਅੱਲਗਾਰ) *n* ਚਮਕ, ਆਭਾ, ਕਾਂਤੀ; **~ous** ਚਮਕਦਾਰ, ਚਕਚੌਂਧ ਕਰਨ ਵਾਲਾ

full (ਫ਼ੁਲ) *a* ਪੂਰਨ, ਭਰਪੂਰ, ਪੂਰਾ; ਸ਼ਰਾਬੋਰ, ਅਧਿਕ; ਫੁੱਲਿਆ, (ਮਨੁੱਖ) ਰੱਜਿਆ; ਤੀਬਰ, ਪ੍ਰਚੰਡ, ਕਲਫ਼ ਲਾਉਣਾ; **~er** ਧੋਬੀ, ਕੱਪੜਿਆਂ ਨੂੰ ਕਲਫ਼ ਲਾਉਣ ਵਾਲਾ, ਲਿਬਾਈ, **~ness, fulness** ਭਰਪੂਰਤਾ, ਪੂਰਨਤਾ, ਸੰਪੂਰਨਤਾ, ਸਮਗਰਤਾ, ਬਹੁਲਤਾ; **~y** ਪੂਰਾ ਪੂਰਾ, ਪੂਰੀ ਤਰ੍ਹਾਂ, ਪੂਰਨ ਤੌਰ ਤੇ, ਸਾਰੇ ਦਾ ਸਾਰਾ

fume (ਫ਼ਯੂਮ) *v n* ਵਾਸ਼ਪ, ਭਾਫ਼; ਕਰੋਧ ਦਾ ਆਵੇਸ਼; ਧੂਣੀ ਦੇਣੀ, ਧੂੰਆਂ ਕਰਨਾ, ਭਾਫ਼ ਕੱਢਣਾ; ਗੁੱਸੇ ਹੋਣਾ

fumigate (ਫ਼ਯੂਮਿਗੇਇਟ) *v* ਧੂਣੀ ਦੇਣੀ

fumigation ('ਫ਼ਯੂਮਿ'ਗੇਇਸ਼ਨ) *n* ਧੂਣੀ, ਧੂਪ, ਧੂੰਆਂ ਕਰਨ ਦੀ ਕਿਰਿਆ

fumy ('ਫ਼ਯੂਮਿ) *a* ਧੂੰਆਂਦਾਰ, ਵਾਸ਼ਪਯੁਕਤ, ਭਾਫ਼ ਵਾਲਾ

fun (ਫ਼ਅੱਨ) *n v* ਖੇਡ, ਤਮਾਸ਼ਾ, ਕੌਤਕ, ਕ੍ਰੀੜਾ, ਸਾਂਗ, ਹਾਸਾ-ਠੱਠਾ, ਦਿਲਲਗੀ; ਖੇਡ ਤਮਾਸ਼ਾ ਕਰਨਾ, ਹਾਸਾ ਉਡਾਉਣਾ, ਉੱਲੂ ਬਣਾਉਣਾ; **~fair** ਮੇਲਾ

function (ਫ਼ਅੱਙਕਸ਼ਨ) *n v* (1) ਸਮਾਗਮ, ਸਮਾਰੋਹ, ਉਤਸਵ, ਸਮਾਜਕ ਸੰਮੇਲਨ, ਅਧਿਕਾਰ; (2) ਕੰਮ, ਕ੍ਰਿਤ, ਕਰਮ, ਕੰਮ ਕਰਨਾ, ਕਰਤੱਵ ਪਾਲਣਾ; **~al** (ਰੋਗ) ਕਿਰਿਆਸ਼ੀਲ, ਕਾਰਜਾਤਮਕ; ਬਿਰਤੀ ਮੂਲਕ; ਫਲ ਸਬੰਧੀ

fund (ਫ਼ੰਡ) *n v* ਖ਼ਜ਼ਾਨਾ, ਪੂੰਜੀ, ਸਰਮਾਇਆ, ਧਨ-ਕੋਸ਼; ਰਕਮ, ਰਾਸ਼ੀ, ਭੰਡਾਰ; ਇਕੱਤਰ ਕਰਨਾ, ਜਮ੍ਹਾਂ ਕਰਨਾ, ਸੰਚਤ ਕਰਨਾ, ਰੁਪਈਆ ਲਾਉਣਾ

fundamental (ਫ਼ੰਡਅਮੇਂਟਲ) *n a* ਮੂਲ ਤੱਤ, ਸਾਰ, ਮੂਲ ਸਿਧਾਂਤ, ਆਧਾਰੀ ਨਿਯਮ; ਮੌਲਕ, ਮੂਲਭੂਤ, ਪ੍ਰਮੁਖ ਮੁਖੀ; ~alism ਮੂਲਵਾਦ; ~ally ਮੁਖ ਰੂਪ ਵਿਚ, ਮੌਲਕ ਰੂਪ ਵਿਚ, ਬੁਨਿਆਦੀ ਤੌਰ ਤੇ

funeral (ਫ਼ਯੂਨ(ਅ)ਨ(ਅ)ਲ) *n a* ਜਨਾਜ਼ਾ, ਅੰਤਮ ਸੰਸਕਾਰ, ਦਾਹ ਸੰਸਕਾਰ, ਕਿਰਿਆ ਕਰਮ; ਮਾਤਮੀ

fungus (ਫ਼ੰਡਗਅਸ) *n pl* ਉੱਲੀ; ਖੁੰਭ ਵਾਂਗ ਉੱਗ ਪੈਣ ਦਾ ਭਾਵ, ਖੁੰਭ

funicle (ਫ਼ਯੂਨਿਕਲ) *n* ਡੋਰੀ, ਰੱਸੀ, ਸੂਤ ਦੀ ਤੰਦ

funnel (ਫ਼ੰਨਲ) *n* ਪੂਆਰਾ; ਪੂੰ-ਕਸ਼; ਝਰੋਖਾ, ਖਿੜਕੀ, ਰੋਸ਼ਨਦਾਨ

funny (ਫ਼ੰਨਿ) *n a* ਛੋਟੀ ਕਿਸ਼ਤੀ; ਹਾਸੇ ਭਰਿਆ, ਕੌਤਕੀ, ਰਸਕ; ਅਜੀਬ, ਨਿਰਾਲਾ

fur (ਫ਼ਅ:*) *n* ਪੋਸਤੀਨ, ਖੱਲ ਦਾ ਅਸਤਰ; ਖੱਲ ਦਾ ਕੱਪੜਾ

furiosity (ਫ਼ਯੂਰਿ'ਔਸਅਟਿ) *n* ਕਰੋਧ, ਪਾਗਲਪਨ, ਵਿਆਕੁਲਤਾ

furious (ਫ਼ਯੂਅਰਿਅਸ) *a* ਤੇਜ਼, ਕਰੋਧ-ਗ੍ਰਸਤ, ਪ੍ਰਚੰਡ, ਤੀਬਰ, ਭਿਅੰਕਰ

furl (ਫ਼ਅ:ਲ) *v* ਵਲ੍ਹੇਟਣਾ, ਤਹਿ ਕਰਨਾ; ਸੁੰਗੇੜਨਾ, ਤਰੋੜਨਾ ਮਰੋੜਨਾ; ਬੰਦ ਹੋਣਾ

furlong (ਫ਼ਅ:ਲੌਂਡ) *n* ਫਰਲਾਂਗ, ਮੀਲ ਦਾ ਅੱਠਵਾਂ ਭਾਗ, 220 ਗਜ਼ ਦੀ ਲੰਬਾਈ

furlough (ਫ਼ਅ:ਲਅਉ) *n* ਲੰਮੀ ਛੁੱਟੀ, ਆਰਜ਼ੀ ਬੇਰੁਜ਼ਗਾਰੀ

furnace ('ਫ਼ਅ:ਨਿਸ) *n v* ਭੱਠੀ, ਤੰਦੂਰ, ਅੰਗੀਠੀ, ਭੱਠੀ ਵਿਚ ਤਾਅ ਦੇਣਾ

furnish ('ਫ਼ਅ:ਨਿਸ਼) *v* ਸਜਾਉਣਾ, ਜੁਗਤ ਨਾਲ ਰੱਖਣਾ, ਜੁਟਾਉਣਾ, ਪੇਸ਼ ਕਰਨਾ, ਪ੍ਰਸਤੁਤ ਕਰਨਾ, ਦੇਣਾ, ਲਿਆ ਦੇਣਾ

furniture ('ਫ਼ਅ:ਨਿਚਅ*) *n* ਸਜਾਵਟ-ਸਮਗਰੀ, ਕੁਰਸੀਆਂ-ਮੇਜ਼ ਆਦਿ; ਘਰ ਦੇ ਅੰਦਰ ਦਾ ਸਮਾਨ

furore ('ਫ਼ਯੂ(ਅ)ਰੋਰਿ) *n* ਹਲਚਲ, ਹੰਗਾਮਾ, ਕੁਹਰਾਮ

furrow ('ਫ਼ਅਰਅਉ) *n v* ਸਿਆੜ; ਪਹੀਏ ਦੀ ਲੀਹ, ਨਾਲੀ, ਲੀਕ, ਡੂੰਘੀ, ਝਰੀ; ਪਹਾੜਾਂ ਵਿਚ ਖੁੱਡ੍ਹ ਹਿੱਸਾ; ਲੀਕ ਪਾਉਂਟੀ, ਝਰੀਆਂ ਪਾਉਣਾ, ਝਰੀਦਾਰ ਬਣਾਉਣਾ

further ('ਫ਼ਅ:ਦਅ*) *v a adv* ਅੱਗੇ ਵਧਾਉਣਾ; ਉਤਸ਼ਾਹਤ ਕਰਨਾ, ਉੱਨਤ ਕਰਨਾ; ਅਗਲਾ, ਅਗਰੇ ਹੋਰ ਦੂਰ, ਇਸ ਤੋਂ ਅੰਗੇ; ਹੋਰ ਦੂਰ, ਇਸ ਤੋਂ ਅੰਗੇ; ਹੋਰ ਅੰਗੇ; ਇਸ ਤੋਂ ਪਰੇ; ~more ਇਸ ਤੋਂ ਇਲਾਵਾ; ~most ਦੂਰਤਮ, ਬਹੁਤ ਦੂਰ, ~ance ਉੱਨਤੀ, ਵਾਧਾ

fury ('ਫ਼ਯੂਅਰਿ) *n* ਭਿਅੰਕਰ ਕਰੋਧ; ਪ੍ਰਬਲਤਾ, ਤੀਬਰਤਾ, ਚੰਡੀ, ਜੁੱਧ ਦੀ ਉਗਰਤਾ

fuse (ਫ਼ਯੂਜ਼) *n v* ਫ਼ਿਊਜ਼ ਪਲੀਤਾ, ਪਟਾਖਾ ਜਾਂ ਵਿਸਫੋਟਸ਼ੀਲ ਪਦਾਰਥ ਨਾਲ ਲੱਗੀ ਡੋਰੀ, ਬੱਤੀ, ਨਲਕੀ; ਗਾਲਣਾ, ਪਿਘਲਾਉਣਾ, ਪੰਘਾਰਨਾ; ਪਲੀਤਾ ਦਾਗਣਾ

fusion ('ਫ਼ਯੂਯਨ) *n* ਮਿਸ਼ਰਨ; ਇਕਰੂਪਤਾ; ਦ੍ਰਵਤ ਪਦਾਰਥਾਂ ਦਾ ਮੇਲ; (ਭਾਸ਼ਾ) ਸੰਸ਼ਲੇਸ਼ਨ

fuss (ਫ਼ੱਸ) *n v* ਹਲਚਲ, ਖਲਬਲੀ, ਗੜਬੜ ਕਰਨਾ, ਹਲਚਲ ਮਚਾਉਣਾ, ਹੱਲਾ-ਗੁੱਲਾ ਕਰਨਾ; ~iness ਖਲਬਲੀ, ਗੜਬੜ; ~y ਹਲਚਲ

करन वाला, रौला पाਉਣ ਵਾਲਾ; ਹੰਗਾਮਾ ਮਚਾਉਣ ਵਾਲਾ, ਗੜਬੜ ਕਰਨ ਵਾਲਾ

futile ('ਫਯੂਟਾਇਲ) *a* ਵਿਅਰਥ, ਨਿਰਰਥਕ, ਤੁੱਛ, ਬੇਕਾਰ

futility (ਫਯੂ'ਟਿਲਅਟਿ) *n* ਵਿਅਰਥਤਾ, ਨਿਰਰਥਕਤਾ, ਤੁੱਛਤਾ

future ('ਫਯਚਾ*) *n a* ਭਵਿੱਖ, ਉੱਤਰਕਾਲ, ਭਵਿੱਖ ਕਾਲ

futurism ('ਫਯੂਅਰਿਜ਼(ਅ)ਮ) *n* ਭਵਿੱਖਵਾਦ

futurist ('ਫਯੂਚਅਰਿਸਟ) *n* ਭਵਿੱਖਵਾਦੀ

fuzz (ਫਅੱਜ਼) *n* ਲੂੰਈ, ਨਰਮ ਤੇ ਘੁੰਘਰਾਲੇ ਵਾਲ; ~**y** ਲੂੰਇਦਾਰ, ਅਸਪਸ਼ਟ, ਧੁੰਦਲਾ; ਧੱਬੇਦਾਰ

G

G, g (ਜੀ) *n* ਰੋਮਨ ਵਰਣਮਾਲਾ ਦਾ ਸੱਤਵਾਂ ਅੱਖਰ; (ਸੰਗੀ) ਸਪਤਕ ਦੀ ਪੰਜਵੀਂ ਸੁਰ

gab (ਗੈਬ) *n* ਬਕਵਾਸ, ਬਕ-ਬਕ, ਗੱਪ-ਸ਼ੱਪ; ~**ble** ਬਕਣਾ, ਬਕ-ਬਕ ਕਰਨਾ, ਬੁੜਬੁੜਾਉਣਾ, ਗਰਬਲ-ਗਰਬਲ ਕਰਨਾ; ਬਕਵਾਸ, ਬੜ-ਬੜਾਹਟ, ਬਕ-ਬਕ

gaby ('ਗੇਇਬਿ) *n* ਮੂਰਖ, ਬੁੱਧੂ, ਬੇਵਕੂਫ਼, ਅਹਿਮਕ (ਵਿਅਕਤੀ)

gad (ਗੈਡ) *v* ਭਟਕਣਾ, ਅਵਾਰਾ ਫਿਰਨਾ, ਟੱਕਰਾਂ ਮਾਰਦੇ ਫਿਰਨਾ

gaffe (ਗੈਫ਼) *n* ਵੱਡੀ ਭੁੱਲ

gaffer ('ਗੈਫ਼ਅ*) *n* ਚੌਧਰੀ, ਸਰਦਾਰ, ਆਗੂ, ਮੁਖੀਆ; ਬਿਰਧ ਪੁਰਸ਼, ਬੁੱਢਾ; ਬੁੱਧੂ, ਗੰਵਾਰ

gag (ਗੈਗ) *n v* ਮੂੰਹ ਵਿਚ ਤੁੰਨਿਆ ਕੱਪੜਾ, ਬੁੱਝਾ; ਮਖ਼ੌਲ, ਮਜ਼ਾਕ; ਮੂੰਹ ਬੰਦ ਕਰਨਾ, ਚੁੱਪ ਕਰਾਉਣਾ; ਝੂਠ ਬੋਲਣਾ, ਪਖੰਡ ਰਚਣਾ

gaga ('ਗਾਗਾ) *a* ਮੂਰਖ, ਗੰਵਾਰ, ਬੇਵਕੂਫ਼

gaiety ('ਗੇਇਅਟਿ) *n* ਜਸ਼ਨ, ਧੂਮ-ਧਾਮ ਦਾ ਅਵਸਰ, ਰੰਗ ਰਲੀਆਂ, ਆਨੰਦ, ਦਿਲਲਗੀ, ਚਮਕ-ਦਮਕ

gain (ਗੇਇਨ) *v n* ਲਾਭ ਹੋਣਾ ਜਾਂ ਲੈਣਾ, ਵਾਧਾ ਹੋਣਾ; ਖੱਟਣਾ, ਕਮਾਉਣਾ, ਲਾਭ, ਵਾਧਾ; ਮੁਨਾਫ਼ਾ; ~**ings** ਪ੍ਰਾਪਤੀਆਂ, ਸਫਲਤਾਵਾਂ, ਉਪਲਬਧੀਆਂ

gait (ਗੇਇਟ) *n* ਚਾਲ, ਚਾਲ-ਢਾਲ, ਟੋਰ, ਚੱਲਣ ਦਾ ਅੰਦਾਜ਼

gala ('ਗਾਲਅ) *n* ਪੁਰਬ, ਤਿਉਹਾਰ, ਉਤਸਵ, ਜਸ਼ਨ, ਸਮਾਰੋਹ

galaxy ('ਗੈਲਅਕਸਿ) *n* ਆਕਾਸ਼, ਗੰਗਾ, ਕਹਿਕਸ਼ਾ; ਰਤਨ-ਮੰਡਲ; ਇੰਦਰ ਦਾ ਅਖਾੜਾ; ਮਹਾਂਪੁਰਸ਼

gale (ਗੇਇਲ) *n* ਝੱਖੜ, ਬਹੁਤ ਤੇਜ਼ ਹਵਾ, ਸਮੀਰ

gall (ਗੋਲ) *n v* ਪਿੱਤਾ; ਕਿੜ, ਕੀਨਾ; ਛਾਲਾ, ਫਫੋਲਾ, ਘਾਉ; ਰਗੜ, ਜ਼ਖ਼ਮ ਹੋਣਾ, ਤੰਗ ਕਰਨਾ, ਜ਼ਲੀਲ ਕਰਨਾ, ਹੈਰਾਨ ਕਰਨਾ; ~**bladder** ਪਿੱਤ ਦੀ ਪੱਥਰੀ; ~**stone** ਪਿੱਤੇ ਦੀ ਪੱਥਰੀ

gallant ('ਗੈਲਅੰਟ) *a n* ਸੂਰਮਾ, ਜਾਨਬਾਜ਼, ਜਵਾਨ-ਮਰਦ, ਸੁਕੀਨ, ਦਰਸ਼ਨੀ, ਸ਼ਾਨਦਾਰ, ਨਫ਼ੀਸ, ਬਾਂਕਾ, ਆਸ਼ਕ ਮਿਜ਼ਾਜ, ਰਸੀਆ; ~**ry** ਬਹਾਦਰੀ, ਵੀਰਤਾ, ਦਿਖਾਵਾ

gallery ('ਗੈਲਅਰਿ) *n* ਛੱਜਾ, ਬਰਾਂਡਾ, ਦਲਾਨ, ਬਰਮਦਾ; ਚਿੱਤਰਸ਼ਾਲਾ, ਚਿਤਰ ਪਰਦਰਸ਼ਨੀ-ਕਮਰਾ, ਰੰਗ ਮਹਿਲ, (ਥੀਏਟਰ) ਗੈਲਰੀ

gallop ('ਗੈਲਅਪ) *n v* ਸਰਪਟ, ਸਰਪਟ ਚੌਂਕੜੀ, ਵੇਗ ਦੀ ਦੌੜ, ਸਰਪਟ ਸਵਾਰੀ; ਸਰਪਟ ਦੌੜਨਾ ਜਾਂ ਦੁੜਾਉਣਾ

gallows ('ਗੈਲਅਉਜ਼) *n pl* ਫਾਂਸੀ ਦਾ ਤਖ਼ਤਾ, ਸੂਲੀ, ਫਾਂਸੀ ਦੀ ਸਜ਼ਾ

gamble ('ਗੈਮਬਲ) *v n* ਜੂਆ ਖੇਡਣਾ, ਜੋਖਮ ਉਠਾਉਣਾ, ਜੂਆਬਾਜ਼ੀ; ਜੋਖਮ ਦਾ ਕੰਮ; ~**r** ਜੁਆਰੀ

gambling ('ਗੈਂਬਲਿਙ) *n* ਜੂਆ

game (ਗੇਇਮ) *n v a* ਖੇਡ, ਬਾਜ਼ੀ; ਦਿਲਲਗੀ, ਜੂਏ ਵਿਚ ਉਡਾਉਣਾ; ਸਾਹਸੀ, ਦਲੇਰ, ਲੜਾਕਾ, ਲੰਗੜਾ; ~**ster** ਸ਼ਿਕਾਰੀ, ਜੁਆਰੀ, ਖਿਡਾਰੀ

gammy ('ਗੈਮਿ) *a* (ਅਪ) ਲੰਗੜਾ

gamut ('ਗੈਮਅਟ) *n* ਖੇਤਰ, ਸਰਗਮ, ਸੰਪੂਰਨ

ਸੁਰ; ਧੁਨੀ ਜਾਂ ਸਾਜ਼ ਦਾ ਘੇਰਾ ਜਾਂ ਵਿਤ

ander ('ਗੈਂਡਅ*) *n* (ਨਰ) ਹੰਸ; ਮੂਰਖ, ਬੁੱਧੂ

ang (ਗੈਂਗ) *n* ਟੋਲੀ, ਮੰਡਲੀ, ਦਲ, ਝੁੰਡ, ਜੁੱਟ, ਜੁੰਡਲੀ

aol, jail (ਜੋਇਲ) *n v* ਜੇਲ੍ਹ, ਜੇਲ੍ਹਖ਼ਾਨਾ, ਕਾਰਾਵਾਸ, ਬੰਦੀਖ਼ਾਨਾ; ਕੈਦ, ਜੇਲ੍ਹ ਭੇਜਣਾ, ਜੇਲ੍ਹ ਵਿਚ ਬੰਦ ਕਰਨਾ; ~**bird** ਆਦੀ ਕੈਦੀ, ਪੁਰਾਣਾ ਬਦਮਾਸ਼, ਨਿਤ ਦਾ ਅਪਰਾਧੀ; ~**er** ਜੇਲ੍ਹ ਦਾ ਵੱਡਾ ਅਫ਼ਸਰ, ਦਰੋਗ਼ਾ; ਜੇਲ੍ਹਰ

ap (ਗੈਪ) *n* ਅੰਤਰ, ਵਿੱਥ, ਫ਼ਰਕ

arage ('ਗੈਰਾਯ਼) *n* ਮੋਟਰ ਘਰ, ਗੋਟਯਮਾਨਾ, ਗਾਰਜ

arb (ਗਾਬ) *n* ਵੇਸ, ਪਹਿਰਾਵਾ, ਵਸਤਰ, ਪੁਸ਼ਾਕ

arbage ('ਗਾਬਿਜ) *n* ਕੂੜਾ, ਗੰਦਗੀ, ਮੈਲ, ਮਲ, ਰੱਦੀ, ਗੰਦ-ਮੰਦ

arble ('ਗਾਬਲ) *v* ਸਭ ਤੋਂ ਚੰਗੀ ਚੀਜ਼ ਛਾਂਟ ਲੈਣਾ ਦਾ ਚੋਰੀ ਚੁੱਕ ਲੈਣਾ; ਛਾਂਟਨਾ, ਛਾਂਟ-ਬੀਣ ਕਰਨਾ

arden ('ਗਾ*ਡਨ) *n v* ਫ਼ੁਲਵਾੜੀ, ਬਗ਼ੀਚਾ, ਗੁਲਸ਼ਨ ਗੁਲਜ਼ਾਰ; ~**er** ਮਾਲੀ, ਬਾਗ਼ਬਾਨ

argle ('ਗਾ*ਗਲ) *v n* ਗ਼ਰਾਰੇ ਕਰਨਾ; ਗ਼ਰਾਰਾ, ਕੁੱਲਾ

arland ('ਗਾ*ਲਅੰਡ) *n v* ਮਾਲਾ, ਹਾਰ, ਗਜਰਾ, ਸਿਹਰਾ; ਹਾਰ ਪਾਉਣਾ

arlic ('ਗਾਲਿਕ) *n* ਲਸਣ, ਥੋਮ

arment ('ਗਾਰਮੰਟ) *n v* ਵੇਸ, ਲਿਬਾਸ, ਪੁਸ਼ਾਕ, ਕੱਪੜੇ, ਵਸਤਰ, ਕੱਪੜੇ ਪੁਆਉਣਾ, ਵੇਸ ਧਾਰਨਾ, ਪੁਸ਼ਾਕ ਪਹਿਨਾ

arner ('ਗਾਨਅ*) *n v* (ਕਣਕ ਦਾ) ਕੋਠਾ, ਸਟੋਰ, ਜ਼ਖ਼ੀਰਾ, ਗੁਦਾਮ; ਇਕੱਤਰ ਕਰਨਾ, ਅਨਾਜ ਭਰਨਾ

arnet ('ਗਾਨਿਟ) *n* ਲਾਲ ਜਵਾਹਰ, ਲਾਲ ਮਣੀ; ਲਹੂ-ਰੰਗਾ ਕੀਮਤੀ ਪੱਥਰ

garnish ('ਗਾਨਿਸ਼) *v n* ਸਜਾਉਣਾ ਖਾਣਾ ਲਗਾਉਣਾ; ਚਮਕਾਉਣਾ; ਸੰਮਨ ਤਾਮੀਲ ਕਰਨਾ, ਸਿੰਗਾਰ, ਸਜਾਵਟ, ਨਕਸ਼-ਨਿਗਾਰ

garrison ('ਗੈਰਿਸਨ) *n v* ਸ਼ਹਿਰ ਜਾਂ ਕਿਲ੍ਹੇ ਦੀ ਰੱਖਿਆ ਕਰਨ ਵਾਲੀ ਫ਼ੌਜ, ਰੱਖਿਆ ਸੈਨਾ, ਮੋਰਚਾਬੰਦੀ ਕਰਨਾ, ਕਿਲ੍ਹੇਬੰਦੀ ਕਰਨਾ

garrulous ('ਗੈਰਅਲਅਸ) *a* ਗੱਪੀ, ਗਾਲੜੀ, ਬਾਤੂਨੀ, ਗੱਪਣ-ਸੰਖ, ਗੱਪੋੜੀ

gas (ਗੈਸ) *n v* (ਬੋਲ) ਗੈਸ, ਪੈਟਰੋਲ, ਗੈਸੋਲੀਨ; ਗੈਸ ਛੱਡਣਾ ਦੂਣ; ਗੈਸ ਦੇਣਾ ਜਾਂ ਪਛਾਉਣਾ; ~**sy** ਗੈਸ ਨਾਲ ਭਰਿਆ, ਫੁੱਲਿਆ; ਗਾਲੜੀ, ਗੱਪੀ, ਬਾਤੂਨੀ; ਸ਼ਬਦ-ਬਹੁਲਤਾ

gasolene, gasoline ('ਗੈਸਅ(ਉ)ਲੀਨ) *n* (ਅਮਰੀਕੀ) ਪੈਟਰੋਲ, ਪੈਟਰੋਲੀਅਮ ਤੋਂ ਪ੍ਰਾਪਤ ਤਰਲ ਵਸਤੂ, ਗੈਸੋਲੀਨ

gastric ('ਗੈਸਟਰਿਕ) *a* ਪੇਟ ਦਾ, ਮਿਹਦੇ ਦਾ, ਢਿੱਡ ਸਬੰਧੀ, ਜਠਰੀ

gate (ਗੇਇਟ) *n* ਲਾਂਘਾ, ਫਾਟਕ, ਕਿਵਾੜ, ਕਪਾਟ; ਰਾਹ, ਰਸਤਾ, ਦੱਰਾ, ਘਾਟੀ ਲੱਕੜ ਜਾਂ ਲੋਹੇ ਦਾ ਜੰਗਲਾ

gather ('ਗੈਦਅ*) *v* ਇੱਕਠਠ ਕਹਲਾ, ਜਮ੍ਹਾਂ ਕਰਨਾ, ਬਟੋਰਨਾ; ਪ੍ਰਾਪਤ ਕਰਨਾ, ਇਕੱਠੇ ਹੋਣਾ, ਸੰਗਠਤ ਹੋਣਾ, ਧਨ ਜੋੜਨਾ, ਵਧਣਾ

gaud (ਗੋਡ) *n pl* ਭੜਕੀਲੇ ਕੱਪੜੇ, ਨੁਮਾਇਸ਼ੀ ਜੇਵਰ ਜਾਂ ਲਿਬਾਸ; ਭੜਕੀਲੀਆਂ ਚੀਜ਼ਾਂ; ਉਤਸਵ, ਸਮਾਰੋਹ, ਧੂਮ-ਧਾਮ; ਰੰਗ ਰਲੀਆਂ

gauge (ਗੇਇਜ) *n v* ਮਾਪ, ਪੈਮਾਨਾ, ਸਮਰੱਥਾ, ਗੁੰਜਾਇਸ਼, ਮਿਕਦਾਰ, ਵਿਸਤਾਰ, ਰੇਲ ਦੀ ਪਟੜੀ ਦੀ ਚੌੜਾਈ ਜਾਂ ਅੰਤਰ; ਸਮਾਈ ਨਾਪਣੀ, ਗੁੰਜਾਇਸ਼ ਮਾਲੂਮ ਕਰਨੀ, ਇਕੋ ਜਿਹੀ ਕਰਨੀ;

ਅਨੁਮਾਨ ਲਗਾਉਣਾ, ਜਾਂਚਣਾ, ਅੰਦਾਜ਼ਾ ਕਰਨਾ

gaunt (ਗੌਂਟ) *a* ਦੁਬਲਾ, ਪਤਲਾ ਮਰੀਅਲ; ਬੰਜਰ

gauzy ('ਗੋਜ਼ਿ) *a* ਜਾਲੀਦਾਰ

gay (ਗੇਇ) *a n* ਖ਼ੁਸ਼, ਹੱਸਮੁਖ; ਭੜਕੀਲਾ

gaze (ਗੇਇਜ਼) *v n* ਘੂਰਨਾ, ਤਾੜਨਾ, ਟਿਕਟਿਕੀ ਲਾ ਕੇ ਵੇਖਣਾ, ਦ੍ਰਿਸ਼ਟੀ ਜਮਾਉਣੀ, ਧਿਆਨ ਨਾਲ ਵੇਖਣਾ; ਟਿਕਟਿਕੀ, ਤਾਕ

gazette (ਗਅ'ਜ਼ੈੱਟ) *n v* ਰੋਜ਼ਨਾਮਾ, ਰਾਜ-ਪੱਤਰ, ਘੋਸ਼ਣਾ-ਪੱਤਰ, ਸੂਚਨਾ-ਪੱਤਰ, ਸਮਾਚਾਰ ਪੱਤਰਿਕਾ

gear (ਗਿਅ*) *n v* (ਪ੍ਰ) ਸਾਮਾਨ, ਵਸਤਰ; ਸਮਗਰੀ, ਬਰਤਨ, ਭਾਂਡਾ, ਪੁਰਜ਼ੇ, ਕਲ, ਔਜ਼ਾਰ; ਮਸ਼ੀਨ ਵਿਚ ਪੁਰਜ਼ੇ ਜੋੜਨਾ ਜਾਂ ਲਗਾਉਣਾ, ਸਾਜ਼ ਲਗਾਉਣਾ

gem (ਜੈੱਮ) *n* ਹੀਰਾ, ਨਗ, ਨਗੀਨਾ, ਇਕ ਕੀਮਤੀ ਪੱਥਰ, ਜਵਾਹਰ, ਰਤਨ, ਮਣੀ

gaminate ('ਜੈੱਮਿਨੇਇਟ) *v a* ਦੁਗਣਾ ਕਰਨਾ, ਦੁਹਰਾਉਣਾ; ਜੋੜਾ, ਜੁੱਟ, ਜੁੱਟਾਂ ਵਿਚ ਬੱਝਾ

gemination ('ਜੈੱਮਿ'ਨੇਇਸ਼ਨ) *a* ਜੋੜਿਆਂ ਵਿਚ ਰੱਖਣਾ, ਯੁਗਮੀਕਰਨ; (ਭਾਸ਼ਾ) ਦੁੱਤੀਕਰਨ

Gemini ('ਜੈੱਮਿਨਾਇ) *n* ਮਿਥੁਨ ਰਾਸ਼ੀ

gender ('ਜੈਂਡਅ*) *n* (ਵਿਆ) ਲਿੰਗ

genealogical ('ਜੀਨਯਅ'ਲੋਜਿਕਲ) *a* ਵੰਸ਼-ਪਰੰਪਰਾਗਤ, ਬੰਸਾਵਲੀ ਸਬੰਧੀ

general ('ਜੈਨ(ਅ)ਰ(ਅ)ਲ) *a n* ਆਮ, ਸਧਾਰਨ, ਵਿਆਪਕ, ਪ੍ਰਚਲਤ; ਸਿਪਾਹਸਲਾਰ; **~ization** ਸਧਾਰਨੀਕਰਨ; ਸਧਾਰਨ, ਅਨੁਮਾਨ; **~ize** ਸਧਾਰਨੀਕਰਨ ਕਰਨਾ; ਸਧਾਰਨ ਭਾਵ ਪ੍ਰਦਾਨ ਕਰਨਾ, ਸਧਾਰਨ ਨਿਯਮ ਤੋਂ ਨਿਰਣਾ ਕੱਢਣਾ; ਆਮ ਵਰਤੋਂ ਵਿਚ ਲਿਆਉਣਾ; ਅਸਪਸ਼ਟ ਬੋਲਣਾ ਜਾਂ ਆਖਣਾ; **~ized** ਵਿਆਪਕ, ਸਧਾਰਨੀਕ੍ਰਿਤ; **~ly** ਆਮ ਤੌਰ ਤੇ, ਸਧਾਰਨ, ਨਿਯਮ ਦੇ ਰੂਪ ਵਿਚ; ਸਧਾਰਨ ਅਰਥਾਂ ਵਿਚ, ਸਰਸਰੀ ਤੌਰ ਤੇ, ਵਿਆਪਕ ਰੂਪ ਵਿਚ, ਅਕਸਰ

generate ('ਜੈੱਨਅਰੇਇਟ) *v* ਪੈਦਾ ਕਰਨਾ ਉਤਪੰਨ ਕਰਨਾ, ਉਪਜਾਉਣਾ

generating ('ਜੈੱਨਅਰੇਇਟਿਙ) *n a* ਉਤਪਾਦਕ ਜਨਕ

generation ('ਜੈੱਨਅ'ਰੇਇਸ਼ਨ) *a* ਨਸਲ, ਪੀੜ੍ਹੀ ਸੰਤਾਨ, ਵੰਸ਼; ਪੈਦਾਇਸ਼, ਉਤਪਾਦਨ, ਜਣਨ

generative ('ਜੈੱਨਅਰਅਟਿਵ਼) *a* ਉਪਜਾਊ ਜਣਨਸ਼ੀਲ, ਉਤਪਾਦਕ

generator ('ਜੈੱਨਅਰੇਇਟਅ*) *n* ਉਪਜਾਉਣ ਵਾਲਾ, ਉਤਪਾਦਕ, ਜਨਮ ਦਾਤਾ; (ਵਾਸ਼ਪ ਬਿਜਲੀ, ਗੈਸ ਆਦਿ ਦਾ) ਉਤਪਾਦਕ ਜੰਤਰ ਜੈਨਰੇਟਰ

generic (ਜਿਨੈੱਰਿਕ) *a* ਆਮ, ਸਧਾਰਨ; ਜਿਨਸਨ ਵਰਗੀ, ਜਾਤੀਗਤ; ਵਿਆਪਕ

generosity ('ਜੈੱਨਅ'ਰੌਸਅਟਿ) *n* ਉਦਾਰਤ ਸਖ਼ਾਵਤ, ਦਾਨ-ਪੁੰਨ

generous ('ਜੈੱਨਅਰਅਸ) *a* ਉਦਾਰ, ਸਖ਼ ਦਾਨੀ, ਖੁੱਲ੍ਹ-ਦਿਲਾ(ਮਨੁੱਖ), ਦਾਨਸ਼ੀਲ

genetic (ਜਿਨੈਟਿਕ) *a* ਜਨਣ ਬਾਰੇ, ਉਤਪ ਸਬੰਧੀ, ਆਨੁਵੰਸ਼ਕ

genius ('ਜੀਨਯਅਸ) *n* ਪ੍ਰਤਿਭਾ, ਕੁਦਰਤ ਯੋਗਤਾ, ਪ੍ਰਤਿਭਾਸ਼ੀਲ ਵਿਅਕਤੀ; ਸਹਿਜਯੋਗਤ ਭਾਸ਼ਾ ਦੇ ਮੂਲ ਤੱਤ, ਕਿਸੇ ਕਾਨੂੰਨ ਦੀ ਪੱਧ

genocide ('ਜੈੱਨਅ(ਉ)ਸਾਇਡ) *n* ਕੁਲ-ਨਾਸ਼ ਨਸਲਕੁਸ਼ੀ

genre ('ਯ਼ਾਨਰਅ) *n* ਪ੍ਰਕਾਰ, ਕਿਸਮ, ਭੇਦ; ਸ਼ੈਲ ਢੰਗ, ਸਾਹਿਤ ਰੂਪ

gentle ('ਜੈਂਟਲ) *a n* ਭੱਦਰ, ਪਤਵੰਤਾ, ਕੁਲਵੰਤ ਕੁਲੀਨ, ਖ਼ਾਨਦਾਨੀ; ਧੀਮਾ, ਨਰਮ, ਹਲੀਮ

entleman ('ਜੈਂਟਲਮਅਨ) n ਸੱਜਣ, ਭੱਦਰ ਪੁਰਸ਼, ਰਈਸ; ਸਰਦਾਰ; ~like ਸੱਭਿਅ, ਸ਼ਿਸ਼ਟ, ਵਿਨੀਤ, ਸਾਊਆਂ ਵਰਗਾ; ~liness ਸ਼ਿਸ਼ਟਤਾ, ਕੁਲੀਨਤਾ, ਸੱਜਣਤਾ, ਸ਼ਰਾਫ਼ਤ, ਰਈਸੀ

ਦਇਆਵਾਨ, ਨਰਮ ਦਿਲ, ਕੋਮਲ, ਕਿਰਪਾਲੂ; ~ness ਨਰਮੀ, ਨਿਮਰਤਾ, ਕੋਮਲਤਾ, ਭੱਦਰਤਾ

ently ('ਜੈਂਟਲਿ) adv ਨਰਮੀ ਨਾਲ, ਹੌਲੇ ਜਿਹੇ, ਧੀਰੇ-ਧੀਰੇ

entry ('ਜੈਂਟਰਿ) n ਭੱਦਰ ਪੁਰਸ਼, ਭਲੇਮਾਨਸ

enuine ('ਜੈਨੁਇਨ) a ਅਸਲੀ, ਖਰਾ, ਯਥਾਰਥਕ, ਵਾਸਤਵਿਕ, ਸੱਚਾ; ~ness ਵਾਸਤਵਿਕਤਾ, ਅਸਲੀਅਤ, ਮੌਲਿਕਤਾ, ਵਿਸ਼ੁੱਧਤਾ, ਸੱਚਾਪਣ, ਖਰਾਪਣ

enus ('ਜੀਨਅਸ) n ਸ਼੍ਰੇਣੀ, ਵਰਗ, ਜਾਤੀ, ਤਬਕਾ, ਜਿਨਸ, ਕਬੀਲਾ, ਕਿਸਮ; ਭੇਦ; ਪ੍ਰਕਾਰ, ਕ੍ਰਮ

eography (ਜਿਔਗਰਅਫ਼ਿ) n ਭੂਗੋਲ, ਜੁਗਰਾਫ਼ੀਆ, ਭੂਮੀ ਬਿਰਤਾਂਤ

eological ('ਜਿਆ(ਉ)ਲੌਜਿਕਲ) a ਭੂ-ਵਿਗਿਆਨਕ, ਭੂ-ਗਰਭੀ

eologist (ਜਿ'ਔਲਅਜਿਸਟ) n ਭੂ-ਵਿਗਿਆਨਕ

eology (ਜਿ'ਔਲਅਜਿ) n ਭੂ-ਵਿਗਿਆਨ

eometric, -al (ਜਿਅ(ਉ)'ਮੈਟਰਿਕ, ਜਿਅ(ਉ)'ਮੈਟਰਿਕਲ) a ਜਿਆਮਿਤੀ, ਰੇਖਾ-ਗਣਿਤ

eometry (ਜਿ'ਔਮਅਟਰਿ) n ਰੇਖਾ-ਗਣਿਤ, ਭੂ-ਮਿਤੀ; ਰੇਖਕੀ, ਜਿਆਮਿਤੀ

erm (ਜਅ:ਮ) n ਕਿਰਮ, ਕੀਟਾਣੂ, ਜੀਵਾਣੀ, ਰੋਗਾਣੂ, ਸੂਖਮ ਜੰਤੂ, ਮੂਲ ਸਿਧਾਂਤ, ਸਰੋਤ; ~inate ਉਪਜਣਾ ਜਾਂ ਉਪਜਾਉਣਾ, ਉੱਗਣਾ ਜਾਂ ਉਗਾਉਣਾ, ਉਤਪੰਨ ਹੋਣਾ ਜਾਂ ਕਰਨਾ, ਨਿਕਲਣਾ ਜਾਂ ਪੈਦਾ ਕਰਨਾ; ~ination ਪ੍ਰਗਮਣ, ਅੰਕੁਰਣ, ਉਦਭਵ, ਉਪਜਣ; ~inator ਉਤਪੰਨ ਕਰਨ ਵਾਲਾ, ਉਗਾਉਣ ਵਾਲਾ

gerund ('ਜੈਰਅੰਡ) n (ਵਿਆ) ਕਿਰਿਆ-ਵਾਚੀ ਨਾਂਵ, ਅੰਗਰੇਜ਼ੀ ਕਿਰਿਆ ਵਿਚ ਜੋੜ ਕੇ ਬਣਾਇਆ ਗਿਆ ਨਾਉਂ

gest, geste ('ਜੈਸਟ) n ਸੰਕੇਤ, ਇਸ਼ਾਰਾ ਵਿਹਾਰ, ਵਰਤਾਉ, ਸਲੂਕ, ਆਚਰਨ

gestation (ਜੈਸ'ਟੇਇਸ਼ਨ) n ਗਰਭ-ਅਵਸਥਾ, ਗਰਭ-ਕਾਲ, ਗਰਭ, ਹਮਲ

gestioulate (ਜੈਸਟਿਕਯੁਲੇਇਟ) v ਅੰਗਾਂ ਨੂੰ ਹਿਲਾ ਕੇ ਸੰਕੇਤ ਕਰਨਾ, ਅਭਿਨੈ ਕਰਨਾ, ਹਾਵ-ਭਾਵ ਵਿਅਕਤ ਕਰਨਾ

gesture ('ਜੈੱਸਚਅ*) n ਇਸ਼ਾਰਾ, ਸੈਨਤ, ਇੰਗਿਤ; ਸੰਕੇਤ, ਹਾਵ-ਭਾਵ ਦਰਸਾਉਣ ਲਈ ਸਰੀਰ ਦੇ ਅੰਗਾਂ ਦਾ ਪ੍ਰਯੋਗ

get (ਗੈਟ) v ਲੈਣਾ, ਪ੍ਰਾਪਤ ਕਰਨਾ, ਉਪਲਬਧ ਕਰਨਾ, ਮਿਲਣਾ, ਵਸੂਲ ਕਰਨਾ, ਰੱਖਣਾ, ਮਾਲੂਮ ਕਰਨਾ, ਲੱਗ ਜਾਣਾ, ਸਹਿਣਾ; ਭੁਗਤਣਾ; ਪਕੜਨਾ, ਫਸਾਉਣਾ; ਸਮੇਟਣਾ, ਬਟੋਰਨਾ, ਬੇਵੱਸ ਕਰ ਦੇਣਾ, ਜਣਨਾ, ਬੱਚਾ ਦੇਣਾ; ਤਿਆਰ ਕਰਨਾ; ਹੋ ਜਾਣਾ; ~along ਨਿਰਵਾਹ ਕਰਨਾ; ~on ਪਹਿਨਣਾ; ਕੰਮ ਚਲਾਉਣਾ, ਗੁਜ਼ਾਰਾ ਕਰਨਾ, ਤਰੱਕੀ ਕਰਨਾ

geyser ('ਗੀਜ਼ਅ*) n ਪਾਣੀ ਦਾ ਚਸ਼ਮਾ; ਹਮਾਮ

ghastly ('ਗਾਸਟਲਿ) a ਭਿਆਨਕ, ਡਰਾਉਣਾ; ਬੀਭਤਸ, ਬੁਰਾ

ghost ('ਗਅਉਸਟ) n ਜਿੰਨ, ਪਰੇਤ, ਭੂਤ, ਰੂਹ, ਵਹਿਮ, ਪ੍ਰਤੀਛਾਇਆ, ਪਰਛਾਵਾਂ, ਛਾਇਆ, ਪਿੰਜਰ; ਗੁਪਤ ਲੇਖਕ; ~ly (ਪ੍ਰ) ਰੂਹਾਨੀ, ਆਤਮਕ, ਮਜ਼ਹਬੀ, ਦੀਨੀ, ਗ਼ੈਰ-ਸਰੀਰੀ, ਭੂਤ-ਪਰੇਤ ਸਬੰਧੀ, ਭੂਤ ਵਰਗਾ

giant ('ਜਾਇਐਂਟ) *n* a ਰਾਖਸ਼, ਦੈਂਤ, ਦੇਊ, ਦਾਨਵ; ਅਸਧਾਰਨ ਸ਼ਕਤੀ

giddy ('ਗਿਡਿ) *a v* ਜਿਸ ਦਾ ਸਿਰ ਚਕਰਾਉਂਦਾ ਹੋਵੇ, ਚਲਿਤਕਾਰੀ, ਬੇਸੁਧ, ਹੋਛਾ; ਚਕਰਾਉਣਾ, ਘੇਰਨੀ, ਪੈਣੀ, ਬੇ-ਸੁਧ ਹੋਣਾ

gift (ਗਿਫ਼ਟ) *n v* ਬਖ਼ਸ਼ਸ਼, ਦਾਨ, ਉਪਹਾਰ, ਤੋਹਫ਼ਾ, ਨਜ਼ਰਾਨਾ, ਸੁਗਾਤ, ਚੋਆ; (ਕ) ਦਾਨ, ਭੇਂਟ ਕੁਦਰਤੀ ਕਮਾਲ; ਦਾਨ ਦੇਣਾ, ਸੁਗਾਤ ਵਜੋਂ ਦੇਣਾ; **~ed** ਗੁਣੀ, ਪ੍ਰਤਿਭਾਸ਼ਾਲੀ, ਗੁਣਵਾਨ, ਵਰੋਸਾਇਆ

gig (ਗਿਗ) *n* ਤਾਂਗਾ, ਟਮਟਮ, ਹੌਲੀ, ਬੇੜੀ, ਹਲਕੀ ਕਿਸ਼ਤੀ

gigantic (ਜਾਇ'ਗੈਂਟਿਕ) *a* ਬਹੁਤ ਵੱਡਾ, ਦਿਉ-ਕੱਦ; ਸ਼ਾਨਦਾਰ, ਬਹੁਤ ਭਾਰੀ, ਵਿਰਾਟ

giggle ('ਗਿਗਲ) *v n* ਬਦ-ਤਮੀਜ਼ੀ ਨਾਲ ਹੱਸਣਾ, ਦੰਦ ਕੱਢਣਾ; ਖੀ-ਖੀ ਕਰਨਾ, ਹਿਚ- ਹਿਚ ਕਰਨਾ; ਹਿਚ-ਹਿਚ, ਅਸ਼ਿਸ਼ਟ ਹਾਸਾ

gigolo ('ਜਿਗਅਲਅਉ) *n* ਭਾੜੇ ਦਾ ਯਾਰ

gild (ਗਿਲਡ) *v n* ਸੋਨੇ ਦੀ ਝਾਲ ਚੜ੍ਹਾਉਣੀ, ਸੋਨੇ ਦਾ ਪੱਤਰਾ ਮੜ੍ਹਨਾ, ਮੁਲੰਮਾ ਕਰਨਾ; ਪੈਸਿਆਂ ਨਾਲ ਐਬ ਕੱਜਣੇ, ਸ਼ਬਦ-ਆਡੰਬਰ ਕਰਨਾ; ਸ਼ਬਦਾਂ ਨਾਲ ਸਜਾਵਟ ਕਰਨੀ; ਖ਼ੱਸੀ ਘੋੜਾ

gilt (ਗਿਲਟ) *n a* (1) ਮੁਲੰਮਾ, ਝੋਲ; ਉਪਰੀ ਸੁੰਦਰਤਾ (2) ਸੂਰ ਦਾ ਮਾਦਾ ਬੱਚਾ

gimmick (ਗਿਮਿਕ) *n* (ਅਪ) ਚੁਕੰਨਸ਼ਾਲਾ, ਢਕਵੰਜ

gin (ਜਿਨ) *n v* (1) ਫੰਦਾ, ਜਾਲ, ਕੁੜੱਕੀ ਵੇਲਣਾ, ਭਾਰ ਚੁੱਕਣ ਵਾਲਾ ਵਿਸ਼ੇਸ਼ ਜੰਤਰ; ਫੰਦੇ ਵਿਚ ਫਸਾਉਣਾ; ਜਾਲ ਵਿਚ ਪਕੜਨਾ; (2) ਇਕ ਕਿਸਮ ਦੀ ਸ਼ਰਾਬ, ਜਿਨ

ginger ('ਜਿੰਜਅ*) *n v* ਅਦਰਕ, ਸੁੰਢ, ਜੋਸ਼; ਉਤਸ਼ਾਹ, ਉਤੇਜਨਾ; ਉਬਾਰਨਾ, ਉਕਸਾਉਣਾ; ਘੋੜੇ ਨੂੰ ਚਾਬੁਕ ਲਾਉਣਾ; **dry~** ਸੁੰਢ

gingerly ('ਜਿੰਜਅਃਲਿ) *a adv* ਸੰਕੇਤ ਸਹਿ, ਬੜੀ ਸਾਵਧਾਨੀ ਨਾਲ, ਡਰਦੇ ਡਰਦੇ; ਸੰਤਬਲ

gipsy, gypsy ('ਜਿਪਸਿ) *n* ਖ਼ਾਨਾਬਦੋਸ਼ ਜਾਤ ਚੰਗੜ; ਸਿਕਲੀਗਰ, ਸ਼ਰਾਰਤੀ, ਚੰਚਲ, ਨਖ਼ਰੇ

gird (ਗਅਃਡ) *v n v* (1) ਮਜ਼ਾਕ ਕਰਨਾ; ਤਾਅ ਮਾਰਨਾ, ਅਵਾਜ਼ ਕਸਣਾ; (2) ਪੇਟੀ ਕੱਸਣ ਕਮਰਬੰਦ ਆਦਿ ਚਾਰੇ ਪਾਸੋਂ ਲਪੇਟਣਾ, ਪੇ ਬੰਨ੍ਹਣੀ; ਪੱਕਾ ਕਰਨਾ; ਜਕੜਨਾ; ਮਜ਼ਾਕ, ਵਿਅੰ ਹਾਸਾ-ਠੱਠਾ; **~le** ਪੇਟੀ, ਕਮਰਬੰਦ; ਘੇਰਾ, ਦਰਖ਼ ਦੀ ਛਾਲ, ਚਿੱਪਣੀ; ਪੇਟੀ ਬੰਨ੍ਹਣਾ

girder ('ਗਅਃਡਅ*) *n* ਸ਼ਤੀਰ, ਕੜੀ; ਲੋਹੇ ਫੌਲਾਦ ਦਾ ਗਾਰਡਰ; ਛੱਤ ਜਾਂ ਪੁਲ ਦੀ ਡ

girl (ਗਅਃਲ) *n* ਲੜਕੀ, ਬੱਚੀ, ਕੁੜੀ, ਨੱ ਮੁਟਿਆਰ, ਕੰਨਿਆ; ਛੋਕਰੀ; **~hood** ਬਾ ਅਵਸਥਾ, ਕੰਨਿਆਪਣ

gist (ਜਿਸਟ) *n* ਨਚੋੜ; ਭਾਵ, ਸਾਰ, ਸਾਰੰਸ਼

give (ਗਿਵ) *v* ਦੇਣਾ, ਭੇਟ ਕਰਨਾ, ਪੇਸ਼ ਕਰਨ ਪਿਲਾਉਣਾ (ਦਵਾਈ); ਪਰਗਟ ਕਰਨਾ; ਕਾਰ ਹੋਣਾ; ਮੁਕੱਰਰ ਕਰਨਾ, ਰੱਖਣਾ (ਨਾਂ); ਪੈ ਕਰਨਾ, ਦੇਣਾ, ਨਿਕਲਣਾ; ਡਿਗ ਪੈਣਾ, ਬੈ ਜਾਣਾ; **~away** ਭੇਦ ਖੋਲ੍ਹ ਦੇਣਾ; ਪ੍ਰਦਾ ਕਰਨਾ; ਝੁਕ ਜਾਣਾ; **~n** ਦਿੱਤਾ, ਪ੍ਰਦੱਤ

giving ('ਗਿਵਿੰਡ) *n a* ਦਿੱਤੀ ਹੋਈ ਵਸ ਸਮਰਪਿਤ; ਦੇਣ ਵਾਲਾ, ਪ੍ਰਦਾਤਾ

glacier ('ਗਲੇਇਸ਼ਯਅ*) *a* ਬਰਫ਼ਾਨੀ, ਬਰਫ਼ੀ

glad (ਗਲੈਡ) *a* ਖ਼ੁਸ਼, ਪ੍ਰਸੰਨ, ਆਨੰਦਤ, ਤੁਸ਼ ਪ੍ਰਸੰਨ-ਚਿੱਤ; **~den** ਖ਼ੁਸ਼ ਕਰਨਾ, ਪ੍ਰਸੰਨ ਕਰ ਸੰਤੁਸ਼ਟ ਕਰਨਾ; **~dening** ਆਨੰਦਾਇ ਪ੍ਰਸੰਨਤਾਦਾਇਕ; **~some** ਖ਼ੁਸ਼, ਪ੍ਰਸੰਨ, ਸੰਤੁ

glamorous (ਗਲੈਮਅਰਅਸ) *a* ਦਿਲਖਿੱਚਵ

ਠਾਠਦਾਰ, ਆਕਰਸ਼ਕ, ਮਨਮੋਹਣਾ, ਮੋਹਕ

glamour (ਗਲੈਮਅ*) n v ਠਾਠ-ਬਾਠ, ਆਕਰਸ਼ਟ; ਜਾਦੂ; ਮੋਹ ਲੈਣਾ; ਆਕਰਸ਼ਟ ਕਰਨਾ, ਜਾਦੂ ਕਰਨਾ

glance (ਗਲਾਂਸ) n v ਝਾਤ, ਤੱਕਣੀ, ਉੱਡਦੀ ਨਜ਼ਰ; ਚਮਕ; ਵੇਖਣਾ, ਨਜ਼ਰ ਮਾਰਨੀ; ਝਾਤ ਮਾਰਨਾ, ਚਮਕਣਾ, ਲਿਸ਼ਕਣਾ

gland (ਗਲੈਂਡ) n ਗਿਲਟੀ, ਗਲੈਂਡ, ਗੰਢੀ

glare (ਗਲੇਅ*) v n ਘੂਰੀ ਪਾ ਕੇ ਵੇਖਣਾ, ਅੱਖਾਂ ਗੱਡ ਕੇ ਤੱਕਣਾ; ਲਿਸ਼ਕਾਰਾ ਮਾਰਨਾ; ਤੇਜ਼ ਰੋਸ਼ਨੀ, ਚਮਕ, ਤਿੱਖਾ ਪ੍ਰਕਾਸ਼, ਅੱਖਾਂ ਚੁੰਧਿਆ ਦੇਣ ਵਾਲੀ ਰੋਸ਼ਨੀ

glaring ('ਗਲੇਅਰਿੰਡ) a ਪ੍ਰਤੱਖ, ਸੁਸਪਸ਼ਟ, ਚਮਕਦਾਰ, ਉੱਜਲ, ਉੱਘੜਵਾਂ

glass (ਗਲਾਸ) n v ਸ਼ੀਸ਼ਾ, ਕੱਚ, ਸ਼ੀਸ਼ੇ ਦਾ ਗਲਾਸ, ਆਇਨਾ, ਸ਼ੀਸ਼ਾ ਜੜਨਾ; ਪ੍ਰਤੀਬਿੰਬ ਸੁੱਟਣਾ; ਸ਼ੀਸ਼ੇ ਵਿਚ ਬੰਦ ਕਰਨਾ

glaucoma (ਗਲੋ'ਕਅਉਮਅ) n ਮੋਤੀਆ ਬਿੰਦ

glaze (ਗਲੇਇਜ਼) v n ਸ਼ੀਸ਼ੇ ਜੜਨੇ, ਲਿਸ਼ਕਾਉਣਾ, ਰਗੜ ਕੇ ਚਮਕਾਉਣਾ; ਪਾਲਿਸ਼ ਜਾਂ ਰੋਗਨ ਕਰਨਾ; ਸ਼ੀਸ਼ੇ ਦਾ ਰੋਗਨ ਫੇਰਨਾ, (ਅੱਖ) ਪਥਰਾ ਜਾਣੀ, ਤੇਜਹੀਣ ਹੋ ਜਾਣੀ; ਪਾਲਸ਼, ਰੋਗਨ, ਸ਼ੀਸ਼ੇ ਦਾ ਪਾਣੀ, ਕਿਸੇ ਚਮਕਦਾਰ ਚੀਜ਼ ਦਾ ਪਾਣੀ; ਚਿਕਨਾਈ; ਚਮਕ, ਲਿਸ਼ਕ ਅੱਖ ਦਾ ਜਾਲਾ; ~d ਚਮਕੀਲਾ, ਚਮਕਾਈ ਹੋਈ, ਚਮਕਦਾਰ; ਸ਼ੀਸ਼ੇਦਾਰ

gleam (ਗਲੀਮ) n v ਝਲਕ, ਲਿਸ਼ਕਾਰਾ, ਚਮਕ, ਆਬ; ਝਲਕ ਦੇਣੀ, ਲਿਸ਼ਕਾਰਾ ਮਾਰਨਾ

glide (ਗਲਾਇਡ) v n ਸਰਕਣਾ, ਤਿਲਕਣਾ, ਹੌਲੀ-ਹੌਲੀ ਖਿਸਕਣਾ, ਵਗਣਾ; ਹੌਲੀ ਲੰਘਣਾ, ਹੌਲੀ ਵਗਣਾ; ਗਾਉਂਦਿਆਂ-ਗਾਉਂਦਿਆਂ ਸੁਰ ਜਾਂ ਤਰਜ਼ ਬਦਲਣਾ; ~r ਹਲਕਾ ਜਿਹਾ ਹਵਾਈ ਜਹਾਜ਼, ਗਲਾਈਡਰ

glimmer (ਗਲਿਮਅ*) v n ਝਿਲਮਿਲਾਉਣਾ, ਝਿਲਮਿਲ ਝਿਲਮਿਲ ਕਰਨਾ, ਟਿਮਟਿਮਾਉਣਾ, ਝਿਲਮਿਲ, ਟਿਮਟਿਮਾਹਟ, ਝਲਕ

glimpse (ਗਲਿੰਪਸ) n v ਝਲਕ, ਝਾਕੀ, ਨਜ਼ਰ, ਛਿਣ; ਝਲਕ ਦੇਣੀ, ਝਾਤ ਪਾਉਣੀ, ਸਰਸਰੀ ਨਜ਼ਰ ਮਾਰਨੀ, ਝਲਕ ਵਿਖਾਉਣੀ

glitter ('ਗਲਿਟਅ*) v n ਲਿਸ਼ਕਣਾ, ਜ਼ੋਰ ਦੀ ਚਮਕ ਮਾਰਨੀ, ਜਗਮਗ ਜਗਮਗ ਕਰਨਾ; ਭੜਕਣਾ; ਭੜਕੀਲਾ ਹੋਣਾ, ਲਿਸ਼ਕ, ਚਮਕ, ਜਗਮਗਾਹਟ

glitz (ਗਲਿਟਸ) n ਤੜਕ-ਭੜਕ

global ('ਗਲਅਉਬਲ) a ਵਿਸ਼ਵ ਵਿਆਪੀ, ਸਰਬ ਵਿਆਪੀ, ਵਿਆਪਕ

globe (ਗਲਅਉਬ) n ਭੂ-ਮੰਡਲ, ਧਰਤੀ ਦਾ ਇਕ ਗੋਲੇ ਉੱਤੇ ਬਣਾਇਆ ਨਕਸ਼ਾ; ਧਰਤੀ, ਪ੍ਰਿਥਵੀ, ਨਛੱਤਰ

gloom (ਗਲੂਮ) n v ਹਨੇਰਾ, ਧੁੰਦਲਾਪਣ; ਅਸਪਸ਼ਟਤਾ, ਉਦਾਸੀ, ਨਿਰਾਸ਼; ਧੁੰਦਲਾ ਕਰ ਦੇਣਾ, ਨਿਰਾਸ਼ ਕਰ ਦੇਣਾ; ਉਦਾਸ ਹੋ ਜਾਣਾ; ~y ਉਦਾਸ, ਅਸੰਤੁਸ਼ਟ; ਅੰਧਕਾਰਪੂਰਨ, ਉਦਾਸੀਨ, ਗ਼ਮਗੀਨ

glorification ('ਗਲੋਰਿਫ਼ਿ'ਕੇਇਸ਼ਨ) n ਸ਼ੋਭਾ, ਪ੍ਰਸੰਸਾ, ਉਸਤਤੀ, ਮਹਿਮਾ, ਵਡਿਆਈ

glorify ('ਗਲੋਰਿਫ਼ਾਇ) v ਵਡਿਆਉਣਾ, ਮਹਿਮਾ ਦੱਸਣੀ; ਗੌਰਵਮਈ ਬਣਾਉਣਾ, ਗੁਣ ਗਾਉਣੇ, ਜਸ ਗਾਉਣਾ

glorious ('ਗਲੋਰਿਅਸ) a ਸ਼ਾਨਦਾਰ, ਪ੍ਰਤਾਪੀ, ਤੇਜਸਵੀ; ਮਹਾਨ; ਸਨਮਾਨਯੁਕਤ, ਮਹਿਮਾ ਵਾਲਾ

glory ('ਗਲੋਰਿ) n ਵਡਿਆਈ, ਸ਼ਾਨ, ਮਹਿਮਾ,

ਤੇਜ ਪ੍ਰਤਾਪ, ਗੌਰਵ

gloss (ਗਲੋਸ) *n v* (1) ਟਿੱਪਣੀ, ਵਿਆਖਿਆ, ਟੀਕਾ, ਸ਼ਬਦਾਂ ਦਾ ਕੋਸ਼; (2) ਲਿਸ਼ਕ, ਚਮਕ-ਦਮਕ; ਮੁਲੰਮਾ; ਚਮਕਦਾਰ ਬਣਾਉਣਾ, ਲਿਸ਼ਕਾਉਣਾ, ਤੇਜ਼-ਮਰੋੜ ਕਰਨੇ, ਹੋਰ ਦੇ ਹੋਰ ਅਰਥ ਕੱਢਣੇ; ~**ary** ਔਖੇ ਸ਼ਬਦਾਂ ਦੀ ਅਰਥਾਵਲੀ, ਪਰਿਭਾਸ਼ਕ ਸ਼ਬਦਾਵਲੀ

glottis ('ਗਲੌਟਿਸ) *n* ਘੰਡੀ ਦਾ ਮੂੰਹ, ਕੰਠਦੁਆਰ

glove (ਗਲਅੱਵ) *n v* ਦਸਤਾਨਾ; ਬਾਕਸਿੰਗ (ਮੁੱਕੇਬਾਜ਼ੀ) ਵਿਚ ਪਾਇਆ ਜਾਣ ਵਾਲਾ ਚਮੜੇ ਦਾ ਦਸਤਾਨਾ

glow (ਗਲਅਉ) *v n* ਚਮਕਣਾ, ਦਮਕਣਾ, ਭਖਣਾ, ਲਾਲ ਹੋਣਾ, ਪ੍ਰਫੁਲਤ ਹੋਣਾ; ਚਮਕ, ਲਾਲੀ, ਚਾਉ, ਜੋਸ਼, ਆਵੇਸ਼; ~**ing** ਪ੍ਰਦੀਪਤ, ਉੱਜਲ, ਸ਼ੋਖ਼; ~**worm** ਟਟਹਿਣਾ, ਜੁਗਨੂੰ

glue (ਗਲੂ) *n v* ਸਰੇਸ਼, ਗੂੰਦ (ਚਿਪਕਾਉਣ ਵਾਲੀ), ਗੂੰਦ ਨਾਲ ਚਿਪਕਾਉਣਾ, ਪੱਕੀ ਤਰ੍ਹਾਂ ਬੰਦ ਕਰਨਾ; ~**pot** ਗੁੰਦਦਾਨੀ; ~**y** ਚਿਪਚਿਪਾ, ਚਿਪਕਾਉਣ ਵਾਲਾ

gnash (ਨੈਸ਼) *v* ਦੰਦ ਪੀਹਣੇ, ਦੰਦ ਕਰੀਚਣੇ, ਕਚੀਚੀ ਵੱਟਣੀ

gnaw (ਨੋ) *v* ਟੁੱਕਣਾ, ਕੁਤਰਨਾ, ਚੱਬਦੇ ਰਹਿਣਾ; ਘੁਣ ਵਾਂਗ ਲੱਗਣਾ, ਦੁੱਖ ਦੇਣਾ, ਹੌਲੀ ਹੌਲੀ ਨਾਸ ਕਰਨਾ

go (ਗਅਉ) *v* ਜਾਣਾ, ਚਲੇ ਜਾਣਾ, ਟੁਰਨਾ, ਰਵਾਨਾ ਹੋਣਾ; ਪ੍ਰਸਥਾਨ ਕਰਨਾ; ਫ਼ਾਇਰ ਹੋਣਾ, ਚੱਲਣਾ; ~**ahead** ਅੱਗੇ ਵਧਣ ਦਾ ਸੰਕੇਤ; ~**between** ਵਿਚੋਲਾ, ਪੰਚ, ਦਲਾਲ; ~**by** ਅਨੁਸਰਣ ਕਰਨਾ, ਦੇ ਵੱਲ ਚੱਲਣਾ; ~**off** ਨੱਠ ਜਾਣਾ, ਨਿਕਲ ਜਾਣਾ, ਬੰਦੂਕ ਆਦਿ ਦਾ ਚੱਲਣਾ, ਫ਼ਾਇਰ ਹੋਣਾ; ਗੁੰਮ ਹੋ ਜਾਣਾ, ਚਲਾਣਾ ਕਰ ਜਾਣਾ; ~**er** ਚੱਲਣ ਵਾਲਾ, ਟੁਰਨ(ਤੁਰਨ) ਵਾਲਾ; ਹਿੰਮਤੀ ਮਨੁੱਖ, ਇਰਾਦੇ ਦ ਪੱਕਾ; ~**ing** ਚਾਲ, ਗਮਨ, ਜਾਣ, ਰਵਾਨਗ ਪ੍ਰਸਥਾਨ

goal (ਗਅਉਲ) *n* ਟੀਚਾ, ਨਿਸ਼ਾਨਾ, ਉਦੇਸ਼ (ਫੁੱਟਬਾਲ, ਹਾਕੀ ਆਦਿ ਵਿਚ) ਬਾਜ਼ੀ, ਗੋਲ ਦੌੜ ਸਮਾਪਤ ਹੋਣ ਵਾਲੀ ਥਾਂ; ~**keepe** (ਫੁੱਟਬਾਲ ਜਾਂ ਹਾਕੀ ਦੀ ਖੇਡ ਵਿਚ) ਗੋਲਚੀ ਗੋਲੀ

goat (ਗਅਉਟ) *n* ਬੱਕਰੀ, ਬੱਕਰਾ; ਕਾਮੀ ਜ ਵਿਭਚਾਰੀ ਵਿਅਕਤੀ; ਮਕਰ ਰਾਸ਼ੀ ਦਾ ਚਿੰਨ੍ ~**y** ਦੁਰਾਚਾਰੀ

gobble ('ਗੌਬਲ) *v* ਕਾਹਲੀ ਕਾਹਲੀ ਖਾਣਾ, ਹਪੂ ਹਪੂ ਕਰਕੇ ਖਾਣਾ, ਹੜੱਪ ਕਰ ਜਾਣਾ; ਗੁੱਸੇ ਵਿਚ ਕੜਕਣਾ

God (ਗੌਡ) *n* ਭਗਵਾਨ, ਖ਼ੁਦਾ, ਰੱਬ; **G-forsaken** ਰੱਬ ਮਾਰਿਆ, ਅਭਾਗਾ, ਗੁਣਹੀਨ **G~fearing** ਰਹਿਮ-ਦਿਲ, ਖ਼ੁਦਾ ਤਰਸ

god *n* ਦੇਵ, ਦੇਵਤਾ, ਮੂਰਤੀ, ਬੁੱਤ; ~**dess** ਦੇਵੀ ਪੂਜਣਯੋਗ ਇਸਤਰੀ; ~**father** ਧਰਮ ਪਿਤਾ ਮੋਢੀ; ~**less** ਨਾਸਤਕ, ਮੁਨਕਰ, ਬੇਦੀਨ, ਪਾਪੀ ਦੁਸ਼ਟ; ~**ly** ਪਵਿੱਤਰ, ਧਰਮਾਤਮਾ, ਧਰਮੀ

godown ('ਗਅਉਡਾਉਨ) *n* ਗੁਦਾਮ, ਭੰਡਾਰ ਮਾਲਖ਼ਾਨਾ

goggle ('ਗੌਗਲ) *v n pl* ਤਿਰਛੀ ਅੱਖ ਨਾਲ ਵੇਖਣਾ, ਘੂਰ ਕੇ ਵੇਖਣਾ, ਕਨਖੀਆਂ ਨਾਲ ਵੇਖਣਾ, ਡੇਲੇ ਘੁਮਾਉਣੇ; ਚਸ਼ਮਾ, ਧੁੱਪ-ਐਨਕ

Golconda (ਗੌਲ'ਕੌਨਡਅ) *n* (ਅਲੰਕਾਰ ਵਜੋਂ ਧਨ ਦੀ ਖਾਣ, ਧਨ-ਕੁਬੇਰ

gold (ਗਅਉਲਡ) *n a* ਸੋਨਾ, ਧਨ, ਮਾਲ, ਦੌਲਤ ਸੋਨੇ ਦਾ ਸਿੱਕਾ; ਸੁਨਹਿਰੀ ਰੰਗ; ਸੋਨੇ ਦਾ ਪਾਣੀ ਸ਼ਾਨਦਾਰ ਚੀਜ਼; ਸੁਨਹਿਰੀ; ~**en** ਸੁਨਹਿਰ, ਸੋਨੇ

ਵਰਗਾ; ਅਮੋਲਕ, ਬਹੁਮੁੱਲਾ; ~leaf ਸੋਨੇ ਦਾ ਵਰਕ; ~smith ਸੁਨਿਆਰ

ood (ਗੁਡ) *a n* ਚੰਗਾ, ਅੱਛਾ, ਨੇਕ, ਸਦਾਚਾਰੀ, ਭਲਾ; ਸੋਹਣਾ, ਉਚਿਤ, ਮੁਨਾਸਬ, ਕਾਬਲ; ਗੁਣਕਾਰੀ, ਲਾਭਦਾਇਕ, ਗੁਣਵਾਨ, ਸਿੱਧਾ-ਸਾਦਾ; ਦਇਆਵਾਨ; ਕਾਢੀ, ਬਘੇਰਾ; ਪੁੰਨ, ਧਰਮ; ~bye ਨਮਸਤੇ; ਸ਼ੁਭ ਵਿਦਾਇਗੀ, ਰੱਬ-ਰਾਖਾ; ~for nothing ਨਿਕੰਮਾ, ਵਿਅਰਥ; ~looking ਸੋਹਣਾ, ਸੁਨੱਖਾ, ਦਰਸ਼ਨੀ; ~morning ਸ਼ੁਭ ਪ੍ਰਭਾਤ, ਨਮਸਤੇ; ~natured ਚੰਗੇ ਸੁਭਾਅ ਵਾਲ਼ਾ, ਨੇਕ, ਮੁਸ਼ੀਲ, ਭਲਾ; ~night ਸ਼ੁਭ ਰਾਤਰੀ, ਨਮਸਤੇ; ~will ਸ਼ੁਭ ਇੱਛਾ, ਸਦਭਾਵਨਾ, ਸਦਭਾਵ; ~ly ਸੋਹਣਾ, ਸੁੰਦਰ; ਉੱਤਮ, ਮਹਾਨ; ਕਾਢੀ; ~ness ਨੇਕੀ, ਚੰਗਿਆਈ, ਭਲਾਈ, ਸ੍ਰੇਸ਼ਠਤਾ; ਉਦਾਰਤਾ

ody -goody ('ਗੁਡਿ,ਗੁਡਿ) *n* ਬਣਾਵਟੀ ਤੌਰ ਵਿਚ ਭਲਾ ਚਾਹੁਣ ਵਾਲਾ, ਭਲਾਈ ਕਰਨ ਦਾ ਵਿਖਾਵਾ ਕਰਨ

ose (ਗੂਸ) *n* ਹੰਸ, ਹੰਸਣੀ; ਸਿੱਧੜ, ਮੂਰਖ, ਬੁੱਧੂ

rge (ਗੋਜ) *n v* ਖੱਡ, ਡੂੰਘੀ ਘਾਟੀ; ਪਹਾੜਾਂ ਵਿਚੋਂ ਤੰਗ ਰਸਤਾ; ਮੱਛੀ ਦੀ ਖੁਰਾਕ; ਕਿਲ੍ਹੇ ਦਾ ਪਿਛਲਾ ਦਰਵਾਜ਼ਾ, ਬੁਰਜ ਦਾ ਰਸਤਾ; ਤੁਕਣਾ, ਗਲ ਤਕ ਭਰ ਦੇਣਾ; ਬਹੁਤ ਖਾਣਾ

rgeous (ਗੋਜਅਸ) *a* ਸ਼ਾਨਦਾਰ, ਭੜਕੀਲਾ, ਉੱਜਲ, ਸੱਜਿਆ, ਫੱਬਿਆ, ਅਲੰਕਰਤ, ਚਮਕਦਾਰ, ਲਿਸ਼ਕਦਾ

rilla (ਗਾ'ਰਿਲਅ) *n* ਬਣ ਮਾਣਸ; ਵਹਿਸ਼ੀ ਬੰਦਾ

spel ('ਗੋਸਪਲ) *n* ਇੰਜੀਲ, ਬਾਈਬਲ, ਈਸਾਈਆਂ ਦਾ ਧਰਮ-ਗ੍ਰੰਥ; ਈਸਾ ਦੁਆਰਾ ਪਰਗਟ ਕੀਤਾ ਸ਼ੁਭ ਸਮਾਚਾਰ; ਮੱਤ, ਈਮਾਨ, ਧਰਮ-ਸਿਧਾਂਤ

gossip ('ਗੌਸਿਪ) *n v* ਗੱਪ, ਗੱਪ-ਸ਼ੱਪ, ਵਾਧੂ ਗੱਲ; ਗੱਪੀ, ਗਾਲੜੀ; ਗੱਪਾਂ ਮਾਰਨੀਆਂ, ਫ਼ਜ਼ੂਲ ਬਕਵਾਸ ਕਰਨਾ; ~y ਗੱਪੀ, ਗਾਲੜੀ, ਬਕਵਾਸੀ

gourmand ('ਗੁਅਮਅੰਡ) *n* ਪੇਟੂ, ਚਟੋਰਾ

gout (ਗਾਉਟ) *n* ਗਠੀਆ, ਜੋੜਾਂ ਵਿਚ ਪੀੜ ਤੇ ਸੋਜ ਦਾ ਰੋਗ

govern ('ਗਾਅੱਵਨ) *v* ਪ੍ਰਬੰਧ ਕਰਨਾ, ਇੰਤਜ਼ਾਮ ਕਰਨਾ; ਰਾਜ ਪ੍ਰਬੰਧ ਕਰਨਾ, ਰੱਖਣਾ; ~ed ਸ਼ਾਸਤ, ਅਧੀਨ, ਨਿਯੰਤਰਤ; ~ess ਅਧਿਆਪਕਾ, ਮਾਸਟਰਨੀ, ਉਸਤਾਨੀ; ਸ਼ਾਸਕਾ; ~ment ਸਰਕਾਰ, ਰਾਜ, ਹਕੂਮਤ, ਗੌਰਮਿੰਟ, ਸ਼ਾਸਨ; ~or ਰਾਜਪਾਲ, ਪ੍ਰਦੇਸ਼ਪਾਲ, ਹਾਕਮ, ਸੂਬੇਦਾਰ

gown (ਗਾਉਨ) *n v* ਚੋਲਾ, ਖੁੱਲ੍ਹਾ ਤੇ ਲੰਮਾ ਕੁੜਤਾ; ਫਰਾਕ-ਕੋਟ; ਗਾਉਨ

grab (ਗਰੈਬ) *v n* ਲੁੱਟਣਾ, ਝਪੱਟ ਮਾਰਨੀ; ਝਪਟ ਕੇ ਫੜਨਾ; ਲੁੱਟ-ਖਸੁੱਟ ਜਾਂ ਝਪਟ; ਗਰਿਫ਼ਤ, ਦਸਤ-ਦਰਾਜ਼ੀ

grace (ਗਰੇਇਸ) *n v* ਸੁੰਦਰਤਾ, ਛਬ, ਸ਼ੋਭਾ, ਅਦਾ, ਖ਼ੂਬੀ, ਹੁਸਨ, ਅੰਦਾਜ਼; ਬਖ਼ਸ਼ਸ਼, ਰਿਆਇਤ; ਰੱਬੀ ਮਿਹਰ, ਖ਼ੁਦਾਈ ਕਰਮ; ਸਜਾਉਣਾ, ਸ਼ਿੰਗਾਰਨਾ; 'ਮਾਣ ਬਖ਼ਸ਼ਣਾ; ~ful ਸੁੰਦਰ, ਛਬੀਲਾ, ਹੁਸੀਨ, ਖ਼ੂਬਸੂਰਤ, ਦਿਲਰੁਬਾ; ~less ਅਸੁੰਦਰ, ਛਬੀਹੀਣ, ਕੋਝਾ, ਢੂਢਾ; ਨਿਰਲੱਜ

gracious ('ਗਰੇਇਸ਼ਅਸ) *a* ਮਿਹਰਬਾਨ, ਦਿਆਲੂ, ਬਖ਼ਸ਼ਿੰਦ; ਸੁੰਦਰ; ਧਾਰਮਕ; ਕਾਮਲ

gradation (ਗਰਅ'ਡੇਇਸ਼ਨ) *n* ਦਰਜੇਬੰਦੀ, ਗੁੱਢਬੰਦੀ, ਦਰਜੇ ਅਨੁਸਾਰ ਦਿੱਤੀ ਗਈ ਤਰਤੀਬ; ~al ਦਰਜੇਬੰਦੀ ਸਬੰਧੀ, ਕ੍ਰਮਬੰਦੀ ਦਾ, ਗੁੱਢਬੰਦੀ ਨਾਲ ਸਬੰਧਤ

grading ('ਗਰੇਇਡਿਙ) *n* ਦਰਜਾਬੰਦੀ, ਸ੍ਰੇਟੀਕਰਨ, ਕੋਟੀਕਰਨ, ਕੋਟੀ-ਕ੍ਰਮ; ਨਿਰਧਾਰਨ

gradual ('ਗਰੇਜੁਅਲ) *a n* ਦਰਜੇਵਾਰ, ਸਿਲਸਲੇਵਾਰ; ਗਿਰਜੇ ਵਿਚ ਗਾਏ ਜਾਣ ਵਾਲੇ ਵਿਸ਼ੇਸ਼ ਗੀਤ; **~ly** ਹੌਲੀ-ਹੌਲੀ ਸਹਿਜੇ-ਸਹਿਜੇ

graduate ('ਗਰੇਜੂਅਟ, 'ਗਰੇਜੂਏਇਟ) *n v* ਸਨਦਯਾਫ਼ਤਾ (ਵਿਅਕਤੀ); ਡਿਗਰੀ ਪ੍ਰਾਪਤ ਕਰਨੀ, ਸਨਦ ਲੈਣੀ; ਦਰਜੇ ਲਾਉਣੇ

graduation ('ਗਰੇਜੁ'ਏਇਸ਼ਨ) *n* ਡਿਗਰੀ ਪ੍ਰਾਪਤ ਕਰਨ ਦਾ ਕਾਰਜ, ਅੰਕ ਲਾਉਣ

grain (ਗਰੇਇਨ) *n v* ਦਾਣਾ, ਅਨਾਜ; ਬੀ, ਤੁਖ਼ਮ; ਟੁਕੜਾ, ਕਿਨਕਾ, ਜ਼ੋਰ ਜਾਂ ਦਾਣੇਦਾਰ ਬਣਾਉਣਾ; ਲਾਲ ਰੰਗ ਚਾੜ੍ਹਨ; ਖੱਲ ਦੇ ਵਾਲ ਉਤਾਰਨੇ

gram (ਗਰੈਮ) *n* (1) ਛੋਲੇ; ਘੋੜਿਆਂ ਦਾ ਦਾਣਾ; ਗੁੱਸਾ; (2) ਗਰਾਮ; ਕਿਲੋਗ੍ਰਾਮ ਦਾ ਹਜ਼ਾਰਵਾਂ ਹਿੱਸਾ

grammar ('ਗਰੈਮਅ*) *n* ਵਿਆਕਰਨ; (ਵਿਆਕਰਨ ਦੀ) ਪੁਸਤਕ; ਵਿਆਕਰਨ ਦੇ ਸਿਧਾਂਤਾਂ ਦਾ ਪ੍ਰਯੋਗ, ਭਾਸ਼ਾ ਦੇ ਮੁਹਾਵਰੇ; **~ian** ਵਿਆਕਰਨ ਸ਼ਾਸਤਰੀ, ਵਿਆਕਰਨ ਆਚਾਰੀਆ

grammatical (ਗਰਅ'ਮੈਟਿਕਲ) *a* ਵਿਆਕਰਨਕ

granary ('ਗਰੈਨਅਰਿ) *n* ਅਨਾਜ-ਭੰਡਾਰ, ਅਨਾਜ ਦਾ ਗੁਦਾਮ, ਭੜੋਲਾ, ਬੁਖਾਰੀ

grand (ਗਰੈਂਡ) *a* ਸ਼ਾਨਦਾਰ; ਅਸਲੀ; ਠਾਠ-ਬਾਠ ਵਾਲਾ, ਉੱਚਾ, ਵੱਡਾ; **~eur** ਵਡਿਆਈ, ਸ਼ੋਭਾ, ਸ਼ਾਨ, ਚੜ੍ਹਤ, ਮਹਿਮਾ, ਤੇਜ, ਪ੍ਰਤਾਪ, ਪ੍ਰਤਿਸ਼ਠਾ

granite ('ਗਰੈਨਿਟ) *n* ਇਕ ਸਖ਼ਤ ਦਾਣੇਦਾਰ ਪੱਥਰ

granny ('ਗਰੈਨਿ) *n* (ਮੋਹ ਨਾਲ) ਦਾਦੀ ਜਾਂ ਨਾਨੀ; ਬੁੱਢੀ ਤੀਵੀਂ

grant (ਗਰਾਂਟ) *v n* ਮਨਜ਼ੂਰ ਕਰਨਾ; ਕਬੂਲ ਕਰਨਾ; ਮੰਨ ਲੈਣਾ, ਅਤਾ ਕਰਨਾ, ਬਖ਼ਸ਼ਣਾ; ਅਨੁਦਾਨ, ਮਾਫ਼ੀ, ਸਰਕਾਰੀ ਸਹਾਇਤਾ; ਮਨਜ਼ੂ

grape ('ਗਰੇਇਪ) *n* ਅੰਗੂਰ, ਦਾਖ

grapevine ('ਗਰੇਇਪਵਾਇਨ) *n* ਅੰਗੂਰੀ ਸ਼ਰਾਬ ਅਫ਼ਵਾਹ

graph (ਗਰਾਫ਼) *n v* ਰੇਖਾ, ਖ਼ਾਕਾ; ਚਿੱਤਰ; ~ ਨਕਸ਼ੇ ਦਾ, ਲਿਖਤ ਸਬੰਧੀ, ਚਿੱਤਰਕਾਰੀ ਤੇ ਝੋ ਤਰਾਸ਼ੀ ਸਬੰਧੀ, ਹੂਬਹੂ

grapple ('ਗਰੈਪਲ) *n v* ਕੁੰਡਾ, ਕਮੰਦ; ਮੁੱਠ-ਭੇੜ ਹੱਥੋ-ਪਾਈ; ਫੜਨਾ, ਉਲਝਾਉਣਾ, ਗੁੱਥਮ-ਗੁੱ ਹੋਣਾ, ਹੱਥੋ-ਪਾਈ ਕਰਨੀ

grasp (ਗਰਾਸਪ) *v n* ਝਪਟ ਮਾਰਨੀ, ਝਪਟਾ ਘੁੱਟ ਕੇ ਫੜਨਾ; ਕਾਬੂ, ਕਬਜ਼ਾ, ਪਕੜ; **~in** ਪਕੜ, ਲਾਲਚੀ

grass (ਗਰਾਸ) *n v* ਘਾਹ, ਚਾਰਾ; ਚਰਾਗਾ **~roots** ਜਨ ਸਧਾਰਨ, ਆਧਾਰ, ਬੁਨਿਆਦ; ~ ਹਰਾ-ਭਰਾ, ਘਾਹ ਵਾਲਾ

grateful ('ਗਰੇਇਟਫ਼ੁਲ) *a* ਸਵੀਕਾਰ ਕਰਨ ਯੋ ਸੁਹਾਵਣਾ, ਦਿਲ-ਪਸੰਦ; ਧੰਨਵਾ ਇਹਸਾਨਮੰਦ, ਕ੍ਰਿਤੱਗ, ਆਭਾਰੀ; **~ne** ਕ੍ਰਿਤੱਗਤਾ, ਇਹਸਾਨਮੰਦੀ, ਆਭਾਰ

gratification ('ਗਰੈਟਿਫ਼ਿ'ਕੇਇਸ਼ਨ) *n* ਇੱਕ ਪੂਰਤੀ, ਖ਼ੁਸ਼ੀ, ਪ੍ਰਸੰਨਤਾ, ਤ੍ਰਿਪਤੀ, ਤੁਸ਼ਟੀ; ਵੰ

gratify ('ਗਰੈਟਿਫ਼ਾਇ) *v* ਰੀਝਾਉਣਾ, ਰੀਝ ਪੂ ਕਰਨੀ, ਖ਼ੁਸ਼ ਕਰਨਾ; ਫ਼ੀਸ ਦੇਣੀ, ਮੁੱਠੀ ਗਰ ਕਰਨੀ, ਵੱਢੀ ਦੇਣੀ

gratis ('ਗਰੇਇਟਿਸ) *adv a* ਇਨਾਮ ਵਿ ਦਿੱਤਾ, ਪੁਰਸਕਾਰ ਵਜੋਂ ਦਿੱਤਾ; ਬਿਨਾ ਮੁੱਲ ਮੁਫ਼ਤ, ਨਿਰਮੁੱਲ

gratitude ('ਗਰੈਟਿਟਯੂਡ) *n* ਸ਼ੁਕਰੀਆ, ਧੰਨਵ ਸ਼ੁਕਰ, ਇਹਸਾਨ, ਕਿਰਪਾ, ਇਹਸਾਨਮੰਦੀ

gratutious (ਗਰਅਾ'ਟਯੂਇਟਅਸ) *a* ਬਿਨਾ ਮੁੱਲ ਤੋਂ ਪ੍ਰਾਪਤ, ਮੁਫਤ ਦਾ, ਅਣਕਮਾਇਆ, ਵਿਅਰਥ, ਫੋਕਟ, ਬਿਨਾ ਅਧਿਕਾਰ

gratuity (ਗਰਅਾ'ਟਯੂਅਟਿ) *n* ਧੰਨ-ਦਾਨ; ਉਪਦਾਨ; ਮਜ਼ਦੂਰੀ, ਤਨਖ਼ਾਹ

grave (ਗਰੇਇਵ) *n v a* (1) ਕਬਰ, ਸਮਾਧ, ਮੜ੍ਹੀ, ਸੁਨਸਾਨ ਥਾਂ; ਮਿਰਤੂ, ਅੰਤ, ਨਾਸ, (2) ਦੱਬਣਾ, ਦਫ਼ਨਾਉਣਾ; ਤਰਾਸ਼ਣਾ, ਰੂਪ ਬਣਾਉਣਾ, ਨੱਕਾਸ਼ੀ ਕਰਨੀ, ਉੱਕਰਨਾ; (3) ਗੰਭੀਰ, ਭਾਰੀ, ਮਹਾਨ, ਜ਼ਰੂਰੀ, ਪੀਰਜਵਾਨ, ਸੰਗੀਨ, ਭਿਆਨਕ, ਗ਼ਮਨਾਉਣ, ਸਮਝ, ਗੰਜੀਦਾ; **olothes** ਕਫ਼ਨ, ਖੱਫਣ; **~yard** ਮੜ੍ਹੀਆਂ, ਕਬਰਸਤਾਨ

gravitate ('ਗਰੈਵਿਟੇਇਟ) *v* ਆਕਰਸ਼ਟ-ਕੇਂਦਰ ਵੱਲ ਖਿਚਣਾ, ਆਕਰਸ਼ਤ ਹੋਣਾ, ਥੱਲੇ ਵੱਲ ਝੁਕਣਾ

gravitation ('ਗਰੈਵਿ'ਟੇਇਸ਼ਨ) *n* ਗੁਰੂਤਾ ਖਿੱਚ, ਕੇਂਦਰੀ ਖਿੱਚ, ਖਿਚਾਉ, ਕਸ਼ਸ਼, ਆਕਰਸ਼ਣ ਸ਼ਕਤੀ; **~al** ਗੁਰੂਤਾ ਖਿੱਚ ਸੰਬੰਧੀ, ਆਕਰਸ਼ਕ, ਕਸ਼ਸ਼ ਭਰਿਆ

gravity ('ਗਰੈਵ੍ਅਟਿ) *n* ਆਕਰਸ਼ਣ-ਸ਼ਕਤੀ, ਭੂਮੀ ਦੀ ਖਿੱਚ, ਗੁਰੂਤਾ; ਗੁਰੂਤਵ, ਭਾਰ, ਭਾਰਾਪਣ, ਗੰਭੀਰਤਾ; ਅਹਿਮਿਅਤ, ਸੰਜੀਦਗੀ

graze (ਗਰੇਇਜ਼) *n v* ਛਿੱਲਣਾ, ਛਿੱਲਿਆ ਜਾਣਾ; ਪਸ਼ੂਆਂ ਨੂੰ ਚਾਰਨਾ, ਘਾਹ ਚਾਰਨਾ

grazing ('ਗਰੇਇਜ਼ਿਙ) *n* ਚਰਾਈ, ਚਰਾਗਾਹ, ਚਰਾਂਦ; ਚਰਵਾਹਗਿਰੀ

grease (ਗਰੀਸ, ਗਰੀਜ਼) *n v* ਚਰਬੀ; ਸਨੇਹ; ਚਿਕਨਾਈ, ਗਰੀਜ਼ੀ ਚਰਬੀ ਲਾਉਣੀ; ਚੀਕਣਾ ਕਰਨਾ; ਗਰੀਜ਼ ਲਾਉਣੀ

great (ਗਰੇਇਟ) *n a* ਉੱਤਮ, ਮਹਾਨ, ਅਸਧਾਰਨ, ਤੇਜਵਾਨ, ਸ਼ਾਨਦਾਰ; ਪ੍ਰਮੁੱਖ; ਅਸਧਾਰਨ; ਸੰਪੰਨ; **~ness** ਮਹਾਨਤਾ, ਗੁਰੁਤਾ, ਗੌਰਵਤਾ, ਵਡਿਆਈ

greed (ਗਰੀਡ) *n* ਲੋਭ, ਲਾਲਚ, ਹਿਰਸ, ਤਮ੍ਹਾਂ; **~y** ਲੋਭੀ, ਲਾਲਚੀ, ਹਿਰਸੀ; ਪੇਟੂ, ਭੁੱਖਾ

green (ਗਰੀਨ) *a n v* ਹਰਾ, ਸਾਵਾ, ਹਰਿਆ-ਭਰਿਆ, ਹਰਿਆਲਾ, ਸਬਜ਼, ਨਰਮ, ਮੁਲਾਇਮ; ਅਨਾੜੀ; ਜਿਉਂਦਾ ਜਾਗਦਾ, ਤਾਜ਼ਾ (ਜ਼ਖ਼ਮ ਲਈ), ਸਾਗ ਸਬਜ਼ੀ; ਘਾਹ ਦਾ ਮੈਦਾਨ; ਜੋਬਨ, ਉਤਪਾਦਨ-ਸ਼ਕਤੀ; ਹਰਾ ਹੋਣਾ, ਹਰਾ ਕਰਨਾ, ਹਰੇ ਹੰਗ ਵਿਚ ਰੰਗਣਾ, ਠੱਗਣਾ, ਲੁੱਟਣਾ; **~eye** ਈਰਖਾ, ਜਲਣ, ਦਵੈਖ; **~grocer** ਕੁੰਜੜਾ, ਸਬਜ਼ੀ ਵਾਲਾ; **~horn** ਅਨਾੜੀ, ਅੱਲ੍ਹੜ; **~room** ਨੇਪਥਸ਼ਾਲਾ, ਸ਼ਿੰਗਾਰ ਕਮਰਾ; **~ery** ਹਰਿਆਲੀ, ਬਨਸਪਤੀ, ਸਬਜ਼ੀ, ਤਰਕਾਰੀ

greet (ਗਰੀਟ) *v* ਸੁਆਗਤ ਕਰਨਾ, ਜੈ ਜੈ ਕਾਰ ਕਰਨੀ, ਸ਼ਾਬਾਸ਼ ਦੇਣੀ; ਆਦਾਬ ਕਰਨਾ, ਪ੍ਰਣਾਮ ਕਰਨਾ, ਨਸਮਕਾਰ ਕਰਨਾ, ਸਲਾਮ ਕਰਨਾ; **~ing** ਨਮਸਕਾਰ, ਪ੍ਰਣਾਮ, ਸੁਆਗਤ, ਹਰਸ ਧੁਨੀ

grenade (ਗਰਅ'ਨੇਇਡ) *n* ਬਾਰੂਦ ਦਾ ਹੱਥ-ਗੋਲਾ; ਕੱਚ ਦਾ ਬੰਬ

grey, gray (ਗਰੇਇ) *n v a* ਸਲੇਟੀ; ਸਲੇਟੀ ਕਰਨਾ ਜਾਂ ਹੋਣਾ, ਮਿਟਿਆਲਾ, ਭੂਰਾ, ਸੁਆਹ ਰੰਗਾ; ਉਦਾਸ; ਬੁੱਢਾ ਹੁੰਦਾ ਹੋਇਆ; ਸਿਆਣਾ, ਪੁਰਾਣੇ ਜ਼ਮਾਨੇ ਦਾ; **~hound** ਸ਼ਿਕਾਰੀ ਕੁੱਤਾ; **~ness** ਭੂਰਾਪਣ, ਧੁੰਦਲਾਪਣ

grief (ਗਰੀਫ਼) *n* ਸੋਗ, ਗ਼ਮ, ਸ਼ੋਕ, ਅਫ਼ਸੋਸ, ਦੁੱਖ

grievance ('ਗਰੀਵ੍ਅੰਸ) *n* ਸ਼ਿਕਾਇਤ, ਗਿਲਾ, ਉਲਾਂਭਾ; ਔਕੜ, ਔਖਿਆਈ, ਬਿਪਤਾ

grieve (ਗਰੀਵ੍) *v* ਦੁੱਖ ਦੇਣਾ ਜਾਂ ਦੁਖੀ ਹੋਣਾ, ਦਿਲ ਦੁਖਾਉਣਾ ਜਾਂ ਦੁਖਣਾ, ਸੋਗ ਪਾਉਣਾ ਜਾਂ ਪੈਣਾ

grievous ('ਗਰੀਵ੍ਅਸ) *a* ਦੁਖਦਾਇਕ, ਸਖ਼ਤ,

ਘੋਰ, ਹਾਨੀਕਾਰਕ, ਦੁਸ਼ਟ; ਡਾਢਾ

grill (ਗਰਿਲ) *n v* ਮਾਸ ਭੁੰਨਣ ਲਈ ਸੀਖਦਾਰ ਚੁੱਲ੍ਹਾ; ਭੁੰਨਣਾ, ਕਬਾਬ ਕਰਨਾ; ਕਰੜੀ ਪੁੱਛ-ਗਿੱਛ ਕਰਨਾ

grim (ਗਰਿਮ) *a* ਨਿਰਦਈ, ਸਖ਼ਤ, ਕਰੜਾ, ਕਠੋਰ; ਡਰਾਉਣਾ, ਭਿਆਨਕ, ਦੁਖੀ, ਕਰੂਪ; ~y ਮੈਲਾ, ਗੰਦਾ, ਕਾਲਖ ਨਾਲ ਭਰਿਆ

grind (ਗਰਾਇੰਡ) *v n* ਪੀਹਣਾ; ਚੱਬਣਾ; ਪਿਹਾਉਣਾ, ਸਾਣ ਚੜ੍ਹਾਉਣਾ; ਜ਼ੁਲਮ ਕਰਨਾ, ਸਤਾਉਣਾ; ਤਿੱਖਾ ਕਰਨਾ, ਤੇਜ਼ ਕਰਨਾ; ਚੱਕੀ ਪੀਹਣ; ~**er** ਪੀਹਣ ਵਾਲਾ; ਪੀਹਣ ਦੀ ਮਸ਼ੀਨ, ਗਰਾਈਂਡਰ; ਸਾਣ ਦੀ ਮਸ਼ੀਨ; ~**stone** ਸਾਣ, ਸਾਣ ਲਾਉਣ ਦਾ ਪੱਥਰ

grip (ਗਰਿਪ) *n v* ਪਕੜ, ਪੰਜਾ; ਕਬਜ਼ਾ; ਮੁਹਾਰਤ, ਦਸਤਰ, ਹੱਥਾ, ਮੁੱਠਾ; ਮਜ਼ਬੂਤੀ ਨਾਲ ਪਕੜਨਾ, ਡੂੰਘੀ ਪਕੜ ਰੱਖਣਾ, ਮੁੱਠੀ ਵਿਚ ਲੈਣਾ, ਜਕੜ ਕੇ ਫੜਨਾ

gripe (ਗਰਾਇਪ) *v n* ਕਸ ਕੇ ਫੜਨਾ, ਪੱਕਾ ਜਕੜਨਾ, ਦਬੋਚਣਾ; ਅੱਤਿਆਚਾਰ ਕਰਨਾ, ਤਕਲੀਫ਼ ਦੇਣੀ; ਕਸ਼ਟ ਦੇਣਾ; ਦਬਾਉਣਾ, ਮਰੋੜਨਾ; ਮਰੋੜ ਪੈਣਾ

groan (ਗਰਅਉਨ) *v n* ਕਰਾਹੁਣਾ, ਤੜਫਣਾ, ਤਾਂਘਣਾ, ਹਉਕਾ ਲੈਣਾ, ਆਹ ਭਰਨੀ, ਲਾਲਸਾ ਕਰਨੀ; ਅੰਦਰੋਂ ਦੁੱਖ ਹੋਣਾ; ਕਰਾਹ, ਚੀਸ, ਤੜਪ, ਹਉਕਾ, ਆਹ

grocer ('ਗਰਅਉਸਅ*) *n* ਪਨਸਾਰੀ, ਕਰਿਆਨੇ ਵਾਲਾ, ਪਰਚੂਨੀਆ, ਹੱਟਵਾਣੀਆ; ~**y** ਪਨਸਾਰੀ ਦੀ ਦੁਕਾਨ, ਕਰਿਆਨੇ ਦੀ ਹੱਟੀ, ਕਰਿਆਨੇ ਦਾ ਸਾਮਾਨ

groom (ਗਰੂਮ) *n v* ਲਾੜਾ, ਦੁਲ੍ਹਾ, ਵਰ; ਦਰੋਗਾ; ਘੋੜੇ ਦਾ ਸਾਈਸ; ਦਾਣਾ-ਘਾਹ ਪਾਉਣਾ,

ਦੇਖ-ਭਾਲ ਕਰਨੀ, ਸਾਈਸੀ ਕਰਨੀ

gross (ਗਰਅਉਸ) *n a* ਗੁਰਸ, ਬਾਰਾਂ ਦਰਜਨ, ਸੰਪੂਰਨ, ਭਰਿਆ, ਵਾਯੂ, ਅਤੀ ਅਧਿਕ; ਮੋਟਾ, ਫੁੱਲਿਆ; (ਗ਼ਲਤੀ ਆਦਿ) ਸਖ਼ਤ, ਭਾਰੀ; ਸਮੁੱਚਾ, ਕੁੱਲ, ਸਾਰਾ, ਸਮਸਤ; ਮੋਟਾ, ਭੱਦਾ, ਗੰਵਾਰ, ਅਸ਼ਲੀਲ, ਅਸ਼ਿਸ਼ਟ, ਗਾਲੀਜ਼; ਮੈਲਾ, ਖ਼ਰਾਬ (ਖਾਣਾ); ਸੁਸਤ

grotto ('ਗਰੌਟਅਉ) *n* ਸੁੰਦਰ ਗੁਫ਼ਾ ਜਾਂ ਗ਼ਾਰ, ਸੁੰਦਰ ਦ੍ਰਿਸ਼ਾਂ ਵਾਲੀ ਕੰਦਰਾ

ground (ਗਰਾਉਂਡ) *n v* ਭੋਂ, ਜ਼ਮੀਨ, ਮੈਦਾਨ; ਧਰਤੀ, ਧਰਾਤਲ, ਤਲ, ਭੂਮੀ; ਨੀਂਹ, ਆਧਾਰ; ਨੀਂਹ ਰੱਖਣੀ; ਨੀਂਹ ਪੱਕੀ ਕਰਨੀ; ਜ਼ਮੀਨ ਉੱਤੇ ਉੱਤਰਨਾ; ~**floor** ਹੇਠਲੀ ਮੰਜ਼ਲ; ~**(s)man** ਕ੍ਰਿਕਟ ਦੇ ਮੈਦਾਨ ਦੀ ਦੇਖ-ਭਾਲ ਕਰਨ ਵਾਲਾ; ~**nut** ਮੂੰਗਫਲੀ; ~**ing** ਮੁਢਲੀ ਸਿੱਖਿਆ, ਬੁਨਿਆਦੀ ਤਾਲੀਮ

group (ਗਰੂਪ) *n v* ਸਮੂਹ ਝੁੰਡ, ਮੰਡਲੀ, ਟੋਲੀ, ਢਾਣੀ, ਸੰਸਥਾ, ਜਮਾਤ; ਜੱਥਾ, ਇਕੱਠ; ਇਕੱਤਰ ਕਰਨਾ ਜਾਂ ਹੋਣਾ, ਜਮਾਂ ਕਰਨਾ ਜਾਂ ਹੋਣਾ, ਵਰਗੀਕਰਨ ਕਰਨਾ; ~**ing** ਵਰਗੀਕਰਨ, ਸਮੂਹਣ, ਸਮੂਹੀਕਰਨ, ਵਰਗਵੰਡ

grouse (ਗਰਾਉਸ) *v n* ਸ਼ਿਕਾਇਤ ਜਾਂ ਗਿਲਾ ਕਰਨਾ; ਸ਼ਿਕਾਇਤ, ਅਸੰਤੋਸ਼, ਗਿਲਾ

grove (ਗਰਅਉਵ) *n* ਦਰਖ਼ਤਾਂ ਦਾ ਸਮੂਹ, ਝਿੜੀ, ਕੁੰਜ, ਉਪਵਣ

grovel ('ਗਰਅਉਵ਼ਲ) *v* ਰੀਂਗਣਾ, ਗੋਡੇ ਟੇਕਣਾ, ਗਿੜਗਿੜਾਉਣਾ

grow (ਗਰਅਉ) *v* ਉੱਗਣਾ, ਫੁੱਟਣਾ; ਉਪਜਾਉਣਾ, ਪੈਦਾ ਕਰਨਾ; ਵੱਡਾ ਹੋਣਾ; ਉਗਾਉਣਾ; ~**er** ਕਿਸਾਨ, ਕਾਸ਼ਤਕਾਰ; ~**ing** ਵੱਧਦਾ ਹੋਇਆ, ਵਰਧਮਾਨ, ਵਿਕਾਸਸ਼ੀਲ; ~**th** ਜਨਮ,

ਉਤਪਤੀ; ਫ਼ਸਲ; ਤਰੱਕੀ, ਵਿਕਾਸ, ਵਾਧਾ, ਖੇਤੀ, ਕਾਸ਼ਤ, ਉਪਜ

growl (ਗਰਾਉੱਲ) *n v* ਬੁੜਬੁੜਾਹਟ, ਗੜਗੜਾਹਟ; ਗਿਲਾ, ਸ਼ਿਕਾਇਤ; ਬੁੜਬੁੜਾਉਣਾ, ਸ਼ਿਕਾਇਤ ਕਰਨੀ, ਗਿਲਾ ਕਰਨਾ; **~er** ਗਰਜਣ ਵਾਲਾ; ਬੁੜਬੁੜਾਉਣ ਵਾਲਾ; ਚੁਪਹੀਆ ਗੱਡੀ

grub (ਗਰੱਬ) *v n* ਉਖਾੜਨਾ, (ਜੜ੍ਹਾਂ ਆਦਿ ਭੂਮੀ ਤੋਂ) ਬਾਹਰ ਕੱਢਣਾ; ਭਾਲਣਾ, ਛਾਣਬੀਣ ਕਰਨੀ, ਖੋਜਣਾ; ਕਿਰਾਏ ਦਾ ਘੋੜਾ ਜਾਂ ਟੱਟੂ; (ਪ੍ਰਚਲਤ) ਭੋਜਨ, ਦਾਣਾ; ਮਜ਼ਦੂਰ; ਬੰਟਾ

grudge (ਗਰੱਜ) *v n* (ਕੋਈ ਚੀਜ਼ ਦੇਣ ਤੋਂ) ਸੰਕੋਚ ਕਰਨਾ, ਮੰਗਣਾ, ਖਾਰ ਖਾਣੀ, ਖੁਣਸ ਖਾਣਾ; ਰੜਕ, ਲਾਗ, ਵੈਰ-ਭਾਵ

gruesome ('ਗਰੂਸਅਮ) *a* ਭਿਆਨਕ, ਭੀਸ਼ਣ, ਡਰਾਉਣਾ; ਬਹੁਤ ਬੁਰਾ

grumble ('ਗਰਅੰਬਲ) *n v* ਬੁੜ ਬੁੜ; ਚਿੜ ਚਿੜ; ਗਿਲਾ, ਸ਼ਿਕਾਇਤ, ਸ਼ਿਕਵਾ; ਬੁੜ-ਬੁੜਾਉਣਾ; ਚਿੜਚੜਾਉਣਾ, ਚਿੜਨਾ

guarantee ('ਗੈਰਅੰਟੀ) *n v* ਜ਼ਾਮਨ, ਜ਼ੁੰਮੇਵਾਰ; ਜ਼ਮਾਨਤ, ਗਾਰੰਟੀ; ਜ਼ਾਮਨ ਹੋਣਾ, ਜ਼ੁੰਮੇਵਾਰੀ ਲੈਣਾ, ਗਾਰੰਟੀ ਦੇਣਾ

guarantor ('ਗੈਰਅੰਟੇ*) *n* ਜ਼ਾਮਨ, ਜ਼ੁੰਮੇਵਾਰ, ਗਾਰੰਟੀ ਦੇਣ ਵਾਲਾ

guaranty ('ਗੈਰਅੰਟਿ) *n* ਜ਼ਮਾਨਤ, ਜ਼ਮਾਨਤਨਾਮਾ, ਜ਼ਾਮਨੀ

guard (ਗਾਡ) *n v* ਚੌਕੀਦਾਰ, ਪਹਿਰੇਦਾਰ, ਸੰਤਰੀ, ਰੁਕਾਵਟ, ਕਟਹਿਰਾ, ਰੇਲ ਦਾ ਗਾਰਡ; ਸਾਵਧਾਨੀ, ਚੌਕਸੀ, ਖ਼ਬਰਦਾਰੀ, ਪਹਿਰੇਦਾਰੀ; ਚੌਕੀਦਾਰੀ ਕਰਨਾ, ਰਖਵਾਲੀ ਕਰਨੀ, ਨਿਗਰਾਨੀ ਰੱਖਣੀ, ਸਾਵਧਾਨੀ ਵਰਤਣੀ; **~ed** ਸੁਰੱਖਿਅਤ, ਸਚੇਤ, ਸਾਵਧਾਨ, ਚੁਕੰਨਾ

guardian ('ਗਾਡਯਅਨ) *n* ਰੱਖਿਅਕ, ਰਖਵਾਲਾ; ਵਾਲੀ, ਸਰਬਰਾਹ, ਸਰਪਰਸਤ, ਗਾਰਡੀਅਨ

guava ('ਗਵਾਵਅ) *n* ਅਮਰੂਦ (ਫਲ ਜਾਂ ਦਰਖਤ)

guess (ਗੈਸ) *v n* ਅਨੁਮਾਨ ਲਾਉਣਾ; ਅੰਦਾਜ਼ਾ ਲਾਉਣਾ; ਅੱਟਾ-ਸੱਟਾ ਲਾਉਣਾ; ਰਾਇ ਕਾਇਮ ਕਰਨਾ, ਖ਼ਿਆਲ ਕਰਨਾ; ਭਾਂਪਣਾ; **~work** ਅਟਕਲ-ਪੱਚੁ, ਅਨੁਮਾਨ ਉੱਤੇ ਆਧਾਰਤ ਕਾਰਵਾਈ

guest (ਗੈੱਸਟ) *n* ਪਰਾਹੁਣਾ, ਮਹਿਮਾਨ, ਅਤਿਥੀ; **~house** ਨਿਵਾਸ-ਸਥਾਨ, ਮਹਿਮਾਨਖ਼ਾਨਾ

guidance ('ਗਾਇਡੰਸ) *n* ਅਗਵਾਈ, ਅਗਵਾਨੀ, ਰਾਹ-ਦਿਖਾਈ, ਮਾਰਗ-ਦਰਸ਼ਨ, ਨਿਰਦੇਸ਼, ਰਹਿਨੁਮਾਈ, ਰਾਹਬਰੀ

guile (ਗਾਇਲ) *n* ਧੋਖਾ, ਛਲ, ਫ਼ਰੇਬ, ਚਲਾਕੀ, ਮੱਕਾਰੀ; **~ful** ਕਪਟੀ, ਮੱਕਾਰ, ਦਗ਼ਾਬਾਜ਼

guillotine ('ਗਿਲਅ'ਟੀਨ) *n v* ਫਾਂਸੀ ਦੇਣ ਦਾ ਇਕ ਜੰਤਰ, ਸਿਰ-ਕੱਟ ਟੋਕਾ, (ਡਾਕਟਰੀ) ਚੀਰਫਾੜ ਦਾ ਜੰਤਰ

guilt (ਗਿਲਟ) *n* ਦੋਸ਼, ਅਪਰਾਧ, ਕਸੂਰ, ਗੁਨਾਹ, ਖ਼ਤਾ, ਜੁਰਮ; **~less** ਨਿਰਦੋਸ਼, ਬੇਗੁਨਾਹ, ਮਾਸੂਮ, ਨਿਰਅਪਰਾਧ; **~y** ਪਾਪੀ, ਦੋਸ਼ੀ, ਅਪਰਾਧੀ, ਮੁਜਰਮ, ਖ਼ਤਾਵਰ, ਗੁਨਾਹਗਾਰ, ਕਸੂਰਵਾਰ

guinea ('ਗਿਨਿ) *n* (ਇਤਿ) ਇਕ ਸੋਨੇ ਦਾ ਸਿੱਕਾ, ਅਸ਼ਰਫ਼ੀ

guise (ਗਾਇਜ਼) *n* (ਪ੍ਰ) ਲਿਬਾਸ, ਪੁਸ਼ਾਕ, ਭੇਸ, ਰੂਪ; ਬਾਹਰੀ ਰੂਪ, ਬਾਹਰੀ ਦਸ਼ਾ; ਸਾਂਗ

gulf (ਗਅੱਲਫ) *n v* ਖਾੜੀ, ਡੂੰਘੀ ਖੱਡ; ਪਾੜਾ; ਭੰਵਰ; ਗਰਦਾਬ; ਸਮੁੰਦਰ, ਸਾਗਰ

gulp (ਗਅੱਲਪ) *v n* ਨਿਗਲਣਾ, ਹੜੱਪ ਕਰ ਜਾਣਾ, ਦਮ ਘੁੱਟਣਾ; ਨਿਗਲਣਾ, ਡੀਕ, ਸੁੜਾਕਾ

gum (ਗਅੱਮ) *n v* (1) ਮਸੂੜਾ, ਬੂਟ (2) ਗੂੰਦ,

gun

ਚੀਜ਼, ਸਰੇਸ਼; ਚੋਟਾ; ਚਿਪਕਾਉਣਾ, ਚੇਪਣਾ, ਜੋੜਨਾ; ਗੂੰਦ ਨਾਲ ਪੱਕਾ ਕਰਨਾ; **~my** ਲੇਸਲਾ, ਚਿਪਚਪਾ, ਗੂੰਦ ਵਾਲਾ, ਸੁੱਜਿਆ, ਫੁੱਲਿਆ

gun (ਗਅੱਨ) *n* ਬੰਦੂਕ, ਤੋਪ; ਰਾਈਫਲ, ਤੁਫੰਗ; **~man** ਸ਼ਸਤਰਧਾਰੀ ਡਾਕੂ; ਅਰਦਲੀ; ਬੰਦੂਕਚੀ; **~powder** ਬਾਰੂਦ, ਦਾਰੂ-ਸਿੱਕਾ; **~ner** ਬੰਦੂਕਚੀ, ਤੋਪਚੀ, ਗੋਲਾਂਦਾਜ਼

gunny ('ਗਅੱਨਿ) *n* ਟਾਟ ਦਾ ਥੈਲਾ, ਬੋਰਾ, ਬੋਰੀ, ਗੂਣ

gurgle ('ਗਅਃਗਲ) *n v* ਗਰਾਰੇ, ਗੁੜਗੁੜਾਉਣਾ; ਗੁੜ ਗੁੜ ਕਰਨਾ

gush (ਗਅੱਸ਼) *n v* ਉਮਾਹ; ਜੋਸ਼, ਭਾਵ-ਵੇਗ; ਉਛਲਣਾ, ਫੁੱਟ ਨਿਕਲਣਾ, ਉਛਾਲਣਾ, ਫੁਹਾਰਾ ਬਣਾਉਣਾ

gust (ਗਅੱਸਟ) *n* (1) (ਹਵਾ, ਧੂੰਆਂ) ਜ਼ੋਰ ਦਾ ਝੋਂਕਾ, ਝੱਖੜ, ਪ੍ਰਬਲ ਆਵੇਗ, ਜੋਸ਼, ਉਮੰਗ; (ਸਧਾਰਨ) ਜੋਸ਼, ਜ਼ੋਰ, ਝਪਟ (2) ਸੌਂਦਰਯ-ਬੋਧ, ਲੱਜ਼ਤ, ਸੁਗੰਧ; **~y** ਜੋਸ਼ੀਲਾ

gut (ਗਅੱਟ) *n v* ਆਂਦਰਾਂ, ਅੰਤੜੀਆਂ; ਮਿਹਦੇ ਦੀ ਨਾਲੀ, (ਬ ਵ) ਮਿਹਦਾ; ਤੰਦਾਂ; ਤੰਗ ਰਸਤਾ, ਖਾਈ; ਨਦੀ ਦਾ ਮੋੜ; ਪਾਣੀ ਦੀ ਤੰਗ ਨਾਲੀ; ਜਾਨ, ਹਿੰਮਤ, ਹੀਆ; ਆਂਦਰਾਂ ਕੱਢ ਕੇ ਸਾਫ਼ ਕਰਨਾ (ਮੱਛੀ); ਲਾਲਚ ਨਾਲ ਖਾਣਾ, ਹੜੱਪਣਾ; (ਪੁਸਤਕ ਆਦਿ ਦਾ) ਸਾਰ ਭਾਵ ਜਾਂ ਤੱਤ ਕੱਢ ਲੈਣਾ; (ਸਾਮਾਨ) ਲੁੱਟ ਲੈ ਜਾਣਾ, ਨਸ਼ਟ ਕਰ ਦੇਣਾ

guy (ਗਾਇ) *n v* (1) ਜਹਾਜ਼ ਦਾ ਰੱਸਾ (2) ਹਊਆ; (3) ਬੰਦਾ, ਜਟਾ, ਸਾਥੀ; ਠੱਠਾ ਕਰਨਾ, ਮਜ਼ਾਕ ਉਡਾਉਣਾ, ਖਿਸਕ ਜਾਣਾ, ਪੁਤਲਾ ਬਣਾਉਣਾ

gymnast (ਜਿਮਨੈਸਟ) *n* ਕਸਰਤੀ, ਜਿਮਨਾਸਟਿਕ ਦਾ ਮਾਹਰ, ਵਰਜ਼ਸ਼ ਦਾ ਮਾਹਰ

gynaecology (ਗਾਇਨਅ'ਕੌਲਅਜਿ) *n* ਨਾਰੀ-ਰੋਗ-ਵਿਗਿਆਨ

gyve (ਜਾਇਵ੍) *n v* ਰੁਕਾਵਟ, ਬਾਧਾ; ਹੱਥਕੜੀ, ਬੇੜੀ, ਜ਼ੰਜੀਰ; ਰੁਕਾਵਟ ਪਾਉਣੀ, ਮੁਸ਼ਕਾਂ ਕੱਸਣਾ

H

H, h (ਏਇਚ) *n* ਰੋਮਨ ਵਰਟਮਾਲਾ ਦਾ ਅੱਠਵਾਂ ਅੱਖਰ

ha (ਹਾ) *int* ਉਹ, ਓਹੋ, ਹਾਏ

habeas corpus (ਹੇਇਬਯਅਸ 'ਕੋਂਪਅਸ) *n* (ਕਾ) ਦੋਸ਼ੀ ਨੂੰ ਅਦਾਲਤ ਦੇ ਸਾਮ੍ਹਣੇ ਪੇਸ਼ ਕਰਨ ਦਾ ਲਿਖਤੀ ਆਦੇਸ਼, ਜਿਸਮਾਨੀ ਹਾਜ਼ਰੀ

haberdasher (ਹੈਬਅਡੈਸ਼ਅ*) *n* ਮਨਿਆਰ, ਖ਼ਮਾਤੀ, ਕਰਿਆਨੇ ਦਾ ਦੁਕਾਨਦਾਰ, ਫੁਟਕਲ ਮਾਲ ਵੇਚਣ ਵਾਲਾ

habit ('ਹੈਬਿਟ) *n* ਆਦਤ, ਇੱਲਤ, ਸੁਭਾਅ, ਵਿਹਾਰ, ਚਾਲ-ਢਾਲ, ਢੰਗ, ਰਹਿਣ, ਵਸੇਬਾ ਕਰਨ, ਰਿੰਝਣਾ; **~ability** ਵਾਸਯੋਗਤਾ, ਰਿਹਾਇਸ਼ਯੋਗਤਾ; ਰਚ **~able** ਵੱਸੋਂ ਅਨੁਕੂਲ, ਰਹਿਣ ਯੋਗ; **~ual** ਪ੍ਰਚਲਤ, ਸੁਭਾਵਕ, ਵਿਹਾਰਕ; ਅਭਿਆਸੀ, ਆਦੀ, ਪੁਰਾਣਾ; **~uate** ਗਿਝਾਉਣਾ, ਆਦਤ ਬਣਾਉਣਾ, ਸਿਖਾਉਣਾ; **~uation** ਵਾਦੀ, ਗੋਝ, ਆਦੀ ਹੋਣ; **~ude** ਰੀਤ, ਗੋਝ, ਰਿਵਾਜ, ਸੁਭਾਅ, ਸਰੀਰਕ ਜਾਂ ਮਾਨਸਕ ਬਣਤਰ

hackney ('ਹੈਕਨਿ) *n v* ਟੱਟੂ, ਭਾੜੇ ਦਾ ਟੱਟੂ; ਮਜ਼ਦੂਰ; ਕਿਰਾਏ ਉੱਤੇ ਦੇਣਾ, ਆਮ ਕਰ ਦੇਣਾ; **~ed** ਜੀਰਣ, ਜਰਜਰ, ਸਿਥਲ, ਸਧਾਰਨ; ਭਾੜੇ ਦਾ; ਬਜ਼ਾਰੀ, ਚਾਲੂ, ਘਸਿਆ ਪਿਟਿਆ

haemoglobin (ਹੀਮਅ(ਉ)'ਗਲਅਉਬਿਨ) *n* ਰਕਤਾਣੂ

haemorrhage, hemorrhage ('ਹੈੱਮਅਰਿਜ) *n* ਰਕਤ-ਪਰਵਾਹ

hag (ਹੈਗ) *n* ਬੁੱਢੜੀ, ਕਰੂਪ ਬੁੱਢੀ ਤੀਵੀਂ, ਚੁੜੇਲ, ਭੂਤਨੀ

haggard ('ਹੈਗਅਡ) *a n* ਮਾੜੂਆ; ਮੰਦੇ ਹਾਲ, ਥੱਕਿਆ-ਹਾਰਿਆ; ਚਿਹਰਾ ਝੁੰਬਿਆ; ਜੰਗਲੀ ਬਾਜ਼

haggle ('ਹੈਗਲ) *v n* (ਮੁੱਲ ਕਰਦਿਆਂ) ਝੇੜਾ ਪਾਉਣਾ, ਝਗੜਨਾ, ਮੁੱਲ ਕਰਨਾ; ਝਗੜਾ

hail (ਹੇਇਲ) *n v* (1) ਗੜਾ, ਵਾਛੜ; ਗਾਲ੍ਹਾਂ; ਗੜੇ ਪੈਣੇ, ਸਵਾਲਾਂ ਆਦਿ ਦੀ ਵਾਛੜ ਕਰਨੀ (2) ਨਮਸਕਾਰ, ਸ਼ਾਬਾਸ਼, ਧੰਨ ਧੰਨ; ਸ਼ਾਬਾਸ਼ ਦੇਣਾ, ਬੱਲੇ ਬੱਲੇ ਕਹਿਣਾ, ਸੁਆਗਤ ਕਰਨਾ, ਜੀਉ ਆਇਆਂ, ਆਖਣਾ; **~storm** ਗੜਿਆਂ ਦਾ ਤੂਫ਼ਾਨ

hair (ਹੇਅ*) *n* ਵਾਲ, ਕੇਸ, ਲੂੰ, ਰੋਮ; ਜੱਤ, ਉੱਨ, ਪਸ਼ਮ; **~breadth** ਵਾਲ ਭਰ, ਜ਼ਰਾ ਜਿੰਨਾ, ਬਿਲਕੁਲ ਮਾਮੂਲੀ ਫ਼ਾਸਲਾ; **~raising** ਰੋਮਾਂਚਕਾਰੀ; **~less** ਗੰਜਾ, ਰੋਡਾ, ਘੋਨਾ, ਵਾਲਰਹਿਤ; **~y** ਵਾਲਦਾਰ, ਸੰਘਣੇ ਵਾਲ

hale (ਹੇਲ) *a v* ਤੰਦਰੁਸਤ, ਨਿਰੋਗ, ਤਕੜਾ, ਰਿਸ਼ਟ-ਪੁਸ਼ਟ, ਮੋਟਾ-ਤਾਜ਼ਾ; ਬਦੋਬਦੀ ਘਸੀਟਣਾ; **~and hearty** ਰਾਜ਼ੀ-ਬਾਜ਼ੀ, ਤੰਦਰੁਸਤ, ਤਕੜਾ; **~ness** ਰਿਸ਼ਟ-ਪੁਸ਼ਟਤਾ, ਤੰਦਰੁਸਤੀ, ਹੱਟਾ-ਕੱਟਾਪਣ

half (ਹਾਫ਼) *n a adv* ਅੱਧ, ਅੱਧਾ; ਛਿਮਾਹੀ; **~ and ~** ਅੱਧੋ-ਅੱਧ, ਅੱਧਾ-ਅੱਧਾ, ਬਰਾਬਰ-ਬਰਾਬਰ, ਇਕੋ ਜਿਹਾ; **~baked** ਅੱਧ-ਪੱਕਾ ਅੱਧ-ਕੱਚਾ; **~brother, ~sister** ਮਤਰੇਇਆ ਭਰਾ, ਭੈਣ; **~hearted** ਬੋਦਿਲਾ, ਉਤਸ਼ਾਹਹੀਣ; **~mast** ਅੱਧੀ ਉਚਾਈ ਤੋਂ, ਸੋਗ ਵਜੋਂ ਝੰਡੇ ਦਾ ਝੁਕਾਉ; **~witted** ਮੂਰਖ, ਵਲੱਲਾ, ਬੁੱਧੂ, ਭੋਂਦੂ, ਸੁਦਾਈ; **better~** ਘਰ ਵਾਲੀ, ਇਸਤਰੀ, ਤੀਵੀਂ, ਵਹੁਟੀ

hall (ਹੌਲ) *n* ਵੱਡਾ ਕਮਰਾ, ਹਾਲ; ਵੱਡਾ ਮਕਾਨ,

ਦੀਵਾਨਖ਼ਾਨਾ, ਮਹੱਲ; ਸਤਾ ਭਵਨ; ~mark ਪ੍ਰਮਾਣਕਤਾ ਦਾ ਚਿੰਨ੍ਹ

hallo (ਹਅ'ਲਅਉ) *int v* ਸੰਬੋਧਨ ਕਰਨ ਲਈ ਜਾਂ ਹੈਰਾਨੀ ਪਰਗਟ ਕਰਨ ਲਈ ਬੋਲਿਆ ਜਾਣ ਵਾਲਾ ਸ਼ਬਦ, ਹੇ, ਜੀ, ਓ, ਹੋ; ਹਾਕ ਮਾਰਨ, ਬੁਲਾਉਣਾ, ਪੁਕਾਰਨਾ; ਕੁੱਤੇ ਨੂੰ ਤੂ-ਤੂ ਕਰਨਾ, ਲਲਕਾਰਨਾ; ਵਾਵੇਲਾ ਮਚਾਣਾ, ਸ਼ੋਰ ਪਾਉਣਾ

hallow ('ਹੈਲਅਉ) *n v* ਸੰਤ, ਸਾਧੂ, ਮਹਾਤਮਾ; (1) ਪੂਜਣਾ, ਪਵਿੱਤਰ ਕਰਨਾ; (2) ਉਤੇਜਤ ਕਰਨਾ, ਲਲਕਾਰਦੇ ਹੋਏ ਪਿੱਛਾ ਕਰਨਾ

hallucinate (ਹਅ'ਲੂਸਿਨੇਇਟ) *v* ਉਲਟੇ ਰਾਹ ਪੈਣਾ, ਭਰਾਂਤੀ ਜਾਂ ਛਾਇਆ ਪੈਣੀ

hallucination (ਹਅ'ਲੂਸਿ'ਨੇਇਸ਼ਨ) *n* ਅੱਖਾਂ ਦਾ ਧੋਖਾ, ਵਹਿਮ, ਮਨੋਭਰਾਂਤੀ

halo ('ਹੇਇਲਅਉ) *n v* ਪ੍ਰਭਾ-ਮੰਡਲ, ਪ੍ਰਕਾਸ਼-ਕੁੰਡਲ, ਪਰਵਾਰ, ਹਾਲਾ; ਚਾਨਣ ਦਾ ਘੇਰਾ ਪਾਉਣਾ, ਵਡਿਆਈ ਦੇਣੀ, ਜਸ ਕਰਨਾ

halt (ਹੌਲਟ) *n v a* ਠਹਿਰ, ਡੇਰਾ, ਮੁਕਾਮ, ਮੰਜ਼ਲ; ਰੋਕ, ਠਹਿਰਾਉ, ਰੁਕਣਾ, ਅਟਕਣਾ, ਠਹਿਰਨਾ, ਕੰਮ ਬੰਦ ਕਰਨਾ, ਪੜਾਉ ਕਰਨਾ; ~ing ਲੰਗੜਾਪਨ, ਵਿਰਾਮ, ਠਹਿਰ; ~ingly ਰੁਕ ਰੁਕ ਕੇ

halve (ਹਾਵ) *v* ਅੱਧੇ-ਅੱਧ ਕਰਨਾ; ਦੋ ਟੋਟੇ ਕਰਨਾ, ਬਰਾਬਰ ਦਾ ਸਾਂਝੀਵਾਲ ਹੋਣਾ

hamburgh (ਹੈਮਬਅ:ਗ) *n* ਕਾਲਾ ਅੰਗੂਰ, ਅੰਗੂਰ ਦੀ ਇਕ ਪ੍ਰਕਾਰ; ਇਕ ਵਿਸ਼ੇਸ਼ ਨਸਲ ਦਾ ਕੁੱਕੜ; ਗਾਂ ਦੇ ਮਾਸ ਦਾ ਕੀਮਾ; **~er** ਇਕ ਖ਼ਾਸ ਪਦਾਰਥ

hamlet (ਹੈਮਲਿਟ) *n* ਛੋਟਾ ਪਿੰਡ, ਪਿੰਡੋਰੀ

hammer ('ਹੈਮਅ*) *n v* ਹਥੌੜਾ; ਮੁੰਗਲੀ; ਨੀਲਾਮੀ ਵੇਲੇ ਘੜਿਆਲ ਉੱਤੇ ਮਾਰੀ ਜਾਣ ਵਾਲੀ ਮੁੰਗਲੀ, ਹਥੌੜਾ ਮਾਰਨਾ; ਠੋਕਣਾ, ਗੋਡਣਾ

hamper ('ਹੈਂਪਅ*) *n v* (1) ਛਾਬਾ (2) ਰੁਕਾਵਟ,

ਰੋਕ, ਪ੍ਰਤਿਬੰਧ; (3) ਜਹਾਜ਼ ਦਾ ਭਾਰਾ ਸਾਮਾਨ, ਰੁਕਾਵਟ ਪਾਉਣੀ, ਅੜਿੱਕਾ ਡਾਹੁਣਾ, ਰੋਕਣਾ

hand (ਹੈਂਡ) *n v* ਹੱਥ, ਦਸਤ; ਪਸ਼ੂਆਂ ਦਾ ਅਗਲਾ ਪੈਰ; ਲਿਖਾਈ; ਦਸਤਖ਼ਤ; ਸੂਈ; ਪ੍ਰਭਾਵ, ਸੱਤਾ, ਪਾਸਾ, ਦਿਸ਼ਾ; ਹੱਥ ਦੇਣਾ, ਸੌਂਪਣਾ, ਦੇ ਦੇਣਾ; ਵਿਰਾਸਤ ਦੇ ਰੂਪ ਵਿਚ ਦੇ ਦੇਣਾ; ਬਖ਼ਸ਼ ਦੇਣਾ; **~and foot** ਪੂਰੀ ਤਰ੍ਹਾਂ, ਪੱਕਾ ਕਰਕੇ (ਬੰਨ੍ਹਣਾ); **~bill** ਇਸ਼ਤਿਹਾਰ, ਪਰਚਾ, ਦਫ਼ਤਰੀ; **~book** ਕਿਤਾਬੜੀ, ਛੋਟੀ ਜਿਹੀ ਕਿਤਾਬ; **~cuff** ਹੱਥਕੜੀ; ਹੱਥਕੜੀ ਲਾਉਣੀ; **~ in** ਇਕ ਦੂਜੇ ਦਾ ਹੱਥ ਫੜੀ, ਹੱਥ ਵਿਚ ਹੱਥ ਪਾਈ; **~shake** ਹੱਥ ਮਿਲਾਉਣਾ; **~s up** ਵਿਰੋਧੀ ਨੂੰ ਹਥਿਆਰ ਸੁੱਟਣ ਜਾਂ ਹੱਥ ਖੜੇ ਕਰਨ ਦਾ ਹੁਕਮ; **~ to** ਹੱਥੋ-ਹੱਥੀ, ਹੱਥੋ-ਹੱਥ, ਆਮ੍ਹੋ-ਸਾਮ੍ਹਣੇ; **~writing** ਲਿਖਤ, ਹੱਥ ਦੀ ਲਿਖਾਈ; ਲਿਖਣ ਦਾ ਢੰਗ; **~ful** ਬੁੱਕ ਭਰ; ਰੁੱਗ ਭਰ, ਮੁੱਠ ਭਰ; ਬਹੁਤ ਥੋੜੇ, ਥੋੜੀ ਗਿਣਤੀ; ਔਖਾ ਕੰਮ

handicap (ਹੈਂਡਿਕੈਪ) *n v* ਅਪੰਗਤਾ; ਸੀਮਾ ਕਮਜ਼ੋਰੀ, ਅੜਚਨ, ਪਾਬੰਦੀ ਲਾਉਣੀ, ਅਸੁਵਿਧਾ ਕੋਈ ਰੁਕਾਵਟ ਜਾਂ ਪ੍ਰਤੀਬੰਧ ਲਾਉਣਾ

handicraft ('ਹੈਂਡਿਕਰਾਫ਼ਟ) *n* ਦਸਤਕਾਰੀ, ਹੱਥ-ਸ਼ਿਲਪ, ਕਾਰੀਗਰੀ; ਹੁਨਰ-ਸ਼ਿਲਪ-ਵਿੰਦਿਆ

handiwork ('ਹੈਂਡਿ,ਵਅ:ਕ) *n* ਦਸਤਕਾਰੀ, ਹੱਥ-ਸ਼ਿਲਪ, ਹੱਥ ਦਾ ਧੰਦਾ

handkerchief ('ਹੈਙਕਅਚਿਫ਼) *n* ਰੁਮਾਲ

handle ('ਹੈਂਡਲ) *n v* ਹੱਥਾ, ਦਸਤਾ; ਮੁੱਠਾ, ਕਬਜ਼ਾ; ਸੰਭਲਣਾ, ਪ੍ਰਬੰਧ ਕਰਨਾ, ਚਲਾਉਣਾ, ਨਿਬਾਉਣਾ

handsome ('ਹੈਨਸਅਮ) *a* ਸੋਹਣਾ, ਸੁਨੱਖਾ, ਰੂਪਵਾਨ, ਸੁੰਦਰ, ਖ਼ੂਬਸੂਰਤ; ਚੋਖਾ, ਚੰਗਾ; **~ness** ਸੁੰਦਰਤਾ, ਖ਼ੂਬਸੂਰਤੀ, ਉਦਾਰਤਾ

hang (ਹੈਙ) *n v* ਲਟਕਣ; ਢਾਲ, ਝੁਕਾਉ, ਲਮਕਾਉ,

ਲਟਕਾਉ; ਗ੍ਰਹਿਣ ਕਰਨ ਦਾ ਭਾਵ, ਟੰਗਣਾ, ਲਮਕਾਉਣਾ; ~man ਜੱਲਾਦ

hanky ('ਹੈਂਕਿ) n ਰੁਮਾਲ

hap (ਹੈਪ) n v ਸੰਜੋਗ, ਢੋਅ ਅਵਸਰ ਹੋਣਾ, ਅਚਾਨਕ ਹੋ ਜਾਣਾ, ਇਤਫ਼ਾਕੀਆ ਹੋਣਾ, ਢੋਅ-ਢੁੱਕਣਾ; ~hazard ਸੰਜੋਗਮਾਤਰ, ਇਤਫ਼ਾਕ, ਸੰਜੋਗੀ, ਇਤਫ਼ਾਕੀਆ, ਅਵਿਵਸਥਿਤ, ਉਲਝਲੂਲ

happen ('ਹੈਪ(ਅ)ਨ) v ਹੋਣਾ, ਵਾਪਰਨਾ, ਘਟਣਾ, ਪੇਸ਼ ਆਉਣਾ, ਸਾਮ੍ਹਣੇ ਆਉਣਾ, ਵਰਤਣਾ; ~ed ਘਟਿਤ, ਬੀਤਿਆ, ਵਾਪਰਿਆ; ~ing ਘਟਣਾ, ਵਾਪਰਤ

happiness ('ਹੈਪਿਨਿਸ) n ਖ਼ੁਸ਼ਹਾਲੀ, ਸਮਰਿਧੀ, ਖ਼ੁਸ਼ੀ, ਪ੍ਰਸੰਨਤਾ, ਸੁਖ, ਆਨੰਦ, ਚੈਨ

happy ('ਹੈਪਿ) a ਪ੍ਰਸੰਨ, ਖ਼ੁਸ਼, ਆਨੰਦ; ਸੁਖੀ, ਰਾਜ਼ੀਬਾਜ਼ੀ

harass ('ਹੈਰਅਸ) v ਤੰਗ ਕਰਨਾ, ਦਿਕ ਕਰਨਾ, ਜਿਚ ਕਰਨਾ, ਸਤਾਉਣਾ, ਦੁੱਖ ਦੇਣਾ; ~ment ਪਰੇਸ਼ਾਨੀ, ਕਲੇਸ਼, ਤਕਲੀਫ਼

harbour ('ਹਾਬਅ*) n v ਬੰਦਰਗਾਹ, ਗੋਦੀ, ਆਸਰਾ, ਸਹਾਰਾ, ਆਸਰਾ ਦੇਣਾ, ਪਨਾਹ ਦੇਣੀ; ਥਾਂ ਦੇਣੀ; ਬੰਦਰਗਾਹ ਵਿਚ ਰੁਕਣਾ, ਲੰਗਰ ਸੁੱਟਣਾ

hard (ਹਾ'ਡ) a ਕਰੜਾ, ਗਾੜ੍ਹਾ, ਪੱਕਾ, ਠੋਸ, ਪੀੜਾ, ਔਖਾ, ਕਠਨ, ਮੁਸ਼ਕਲ; ਨਿਰਦਈ; ਠੋਰ, ਸਖ਼ਤ; ~bitten ਹਠੀਲਾ, ਹਠੀ, ਘੁਲਾਟੀਆ; ~headed ਅਡੋਲਵ੍ਰਕ; ਕਿਰਿਆਸ਼ੀਲ, ਮਿਹਨਤੀ; ~hearted ਸਖ਼ਤ ਦਿਲ, ਨਿਰਦਈ, ਬੇਰਹਿਮ; ~labour ਮੁਸ਼ੱਕਤ, ਸਖ਼ਤ ਮਿਹਨਤ ~of hearing ਬੋਲ਼ਾ, ਜਿਸ ਨੂੰ ਉੱਚਾ ਸੁਣਦਾ ਹੋਵੇ; ~times ਔਖੇ ਦਿਨ, ਬੇਰੁਜ਼ਗਾਰੀ ਦਾ ਸਮਾਂ; ~up (ਪੈਸੇ ਦੀ) ਤੰਗੀ, ਔਖ; ~en ਸਖ਼ਤ ਕਰਨਾ, ਕਠੋਰ ਕਰਨਾ, ਦਿੜ੍ਹ ਕਰਨਾ, ਪੱਕਾ ਕਰਨਾ; ~ened ਦਿੜ੍ਹ, ਪੱਕਾ,

ਕਠੋਰ, ਸਖ਼ਤ; ~lines ਮੰਦਭਾਗੀ, ਬਦਕਿਸਮਤੀ; ~ly ਮਸਾਂ, ਮਸਾਂ ਜਿਹੇ, ਸ਼ਾਇਦ ਹੀ; ~ness ਕਠੋਰਤਾ, ਕਰੜਾਈ; ~ship ਤੰਗੀ, ਔਖਿਆਈ, ਮੁਸੀਬਤ, ਬਿਪਤਾ; ਕਸ਼ਟ; ~ware ਧਾਤ ਦਾ ਸਾਮਾਨ; ਹਥਿਆਰ; ਕੰਪਿਊਟਰ ਦੀ ਮਸ਼ੀਨਰੀ; ~water ਭਾਰਾ ਪਾਣੀ; ~y ਕਰੜਾ, ਸਖ਼ਤ, ਤਕੜਾ, ਮਜ਼ਬੂਤ, ਹਿੰਮਤੀ, ਦਲੇਰ; ਨਿਡਰ

hare (ਹੇਅ*) n ਸੇਹਾ, ਖ਼ਰਗੋਸ਼

harem ('ਹਾਰੀਮ) n ਰਨਵਾਸ, ਜ਼ਨਾਨਖ਼ਾਨਾ, ਹਰਮ

harm (ਹਾਮ) n v ਹਾਨੀ, ਨੁਕਸਾਨ; ਨੁਕਸਾਨ ਕਰਨਾ, ਹਾਨੀ ਪਹੁਚਾਉਂਣੀ; ਕਸ਼ਟ ਦੇਣਾ; ~ful ਹਾਨੀਕਾਰਕ, ਦੁੱਖਦਾਈ

harmonic (ਹਾ'ਮੌਨਿਕ) a ਸੁਰਮੇਲ ਵਾਲਾ, ਸਮਸਵਰ; ਇਕ ਸੁਰ, ਇਕਤਾਲ

harmonious (ਹਾ'ਮਅਉਨਯਅਸ) a ਮਿਲਵਾਂ, ਇਕਸਾਰਤਾ ਵਾਲਾ ਇਕ ਸੁਰ, ਇਕ ਤਾਲ; ਸੁਰੀਲਾ

hormonize ('ਹਾ'ਮਅਨਾਇਜ਼) v ਇਕਸੁਰ ਕਰਨਾ, ਇਕਸਾਰਤਾ ਲਿਆਉਣੀ ਸੰਗਤ ਕਰਨਾ, ਸੁਰਾਂ ਮਿਲਾਉਣੀਆਂ

harmony ('ਹਾ'ਮਅਨਿ) n ਇਕਸੁਰਤਾ, ਇਕਸਾਰਤਾ, ਸੁਰਮੇਲ, ਸੰਗਤੀ; ਸਮਤਾਲ

harp (ਹਾ'ਪ) n v (ਸਿਤਾਰ ਵਰਗਾ) ਵਾਜਾ, ਦਿਲਰੁਬਾ; ਇਹ ਸਾਜ਼ ਵਜਾਉਣਾ; ~er ਸਿਤਾਰ ਵਜਾਉਣ ਵਾਲਾ

harry ('ਹੈਰਿ) v ਉਜਾੜਨਾ, ਤਬਾਹ ਕਰਨਾ, ਵੀਰਾਨ ਕਰਨਾ, ਲੁੱਟ-ਮਾਰ ਮਚਾਉਣਾ; ਦਿਕ ਕਰਨਾ

harsh (ਹਾ'ਸ਼) a ਰੁੱਖ, ਸਖ਼ਤ, ਖਰਵਾ, ਕਰਖ਼ਤ, ਕਰੜਾ, ਨਾਪਸੰਦ, ਸਖ਼ਤ ਦਿਲ, ਪੱਥਰ ਚਿਤ

harvest ('ਹਾਵਿਸਟ) n v ਪੱਕੀ ਹੋਈ ਫ਼ਸਲ, ਉਪਜ ਝਾੜ; ਫ਼ਸਲ ਕੱਟਣੀ, ਵਾਢੀ ਕਰਨੀ,

ਫ਼ਸਲ ਇਕੱਠੀ ਕਰਨੀ

hashish ('ਹੈਸ਼ੀਸ਼) *n* ਹਸ਼ੀਸ਼, ਗਾਂਜਾ

haste (ਹੇਇਸਟ) *n v* ਕਾਹਲ, ਛੇਤੀ, ਉਤਾਵਲ, ਜਲਦੀ, ਤੇਜ਼ੀ; ਕਾਹਲ ਕਰਨੀ, ਉਤਾਵਲ ਕਰਨੀ; ~n ਕਾਹਲ ਕਰਨੀ, ਛੇਤੀ ਕਰਨੀ, ਕਾਹਲਾ ਟੁਰਨਾ

hasty ('ਹੇਇਸਟਿ) *a* ਕਾਹਲਾ, ਉਤਾਵਲਾ, ਤੇਜ਼, ਤਿਖਾ; ਚਿੜਚੜਾ, ਉਜੱਡ

hat (ਹੈਟ) *n* ਟੋਪ, ਟੋਪੀ, ਅੰਗਰੇਜ਼ੀ ਟੋਪ

hatchet ('ਹੈਚਿਟ) *n* ਕੁਹਾੜੀ, ਗੰਡਾਸਾ

hate (ਹੇਇਟ) *n v* ਘਿਰਣਾ, ਨਫ਼ਰਤ, ਤਿਰਸਕਾਰ; ਘਿਰਣਾ ਕਰਨੀ, ਨਫ਼ਰਤ ਕਰਨੀ; ~ful ਘਿਰਣਾਯੋਗ, ਘਿਰਣਾਜਨਕ

hatred ('ਹੇਇਟਰਿਡ) *n* ਘਿਰਣਾ, ਨਫ਼ਰਤ, ਦਵੈਖ

haughty ('ਹੋਟਿ) *a* ਘਮੰਡੀ, ਅਭਿਮਾਨੀ, ਹੰਕਾਰੀ

haul (ਹੋਲ) *v n* ਖਿਚਣਾ, ਧੂਹਣਾ, ਘਸੀਟਣਾ; ਖਿੱਚ, ਘਸੀਟ; ਲੱਭਤ; ~age ਖਿਚਾਈ; ਢੁਹਾਈ; ਘਸੀਟ

haunt (ਹੋਂਟ) *v n* ਘੜੀ ਮੁੜੀ ਆਉਣਾ, ਮੁੜ ਮੁੜ ਆਉਣਾ, ਆਉਣ ਜਾਣ ਰੱਖਣਾ; ਭੂਤ-ਵਾਸ, ਭੂਤ-ਘਰ, ਅੱਡਾ

have (ਹੈਵ) *v aux n* ਕੋਲ ਹੋਣਾ, ਅਧਿਕਾਰ ਵਿਚ ਹੋਣਾ; ਲੈਣਾ, ਫੜਨਾ, ਪ੍ਰਾਪਤ ਕਰਨੀ; ਪਾਣਾ; ਧਨਵਾਨ, ਛਲ, ਕਪਟ; ~not (usu. in *pl*) (ਬੋਲ) ਨਿਰਧਨ, ਗ਼ਰੀਬ

haven ('ਹੇਇਵਨ) *n* ਬੰਦਰਗਾਹ; ਪਨਾਹਗਾਹ

having ('ਹੈਵ਼ਿਙ) *n* ਧਨ-ਸੰਪੱਤੀ, ਜਾਇਦਾਦ, ਸਮਗਰੀ, ਸਾਮਾਨ, ਅਸਬਾਬ

havoc ('ਹੈਵ਼ਅਕ) *n* ਤਬਾਹੀ, ਬਰਬਾਦੀ, ਵਿਨਾਸ਼, ਸਰਵਨਾਸ਼, ਪਰਲੋ

hawk (ਹੋਕ) *n v* ਬਾਜ਼, ਸ਼ਿਕਰਾ; ਜਾਬਰ ਅਤਿਆਚਾਰੀ, ਡਾਕੂ, ਲੁਟੇਰਾ; ~er ਫੇਰੀ ਵਾਲਾ, ਡੋਲੀ ਵਾਲਾ

hay (ਹੇਇ) *n* ਸੁੱਕਾ ਘਾਹ, ਤੂੜੀ

hazard ('ਹੈਜ਼ਡ) *n v* ਸੰਕਟ, ਖ਼ਤਰਾ; ਦੈਵਨੇਤ, ਘਟਨਾ, ਸੌਕਾ; ਪਾਸੇ ਦੀ ਇਕ ਖੇਡ, ਜੂਆ; ਸੰਕਟ ਵਿਚ ਫਸਾਉਣਾ, ਦਿਲ ਤਕੜਾ ਕਰ ਕੇ ਆਖਣਾ; ~ous ਸੰਕਟਮਈ; ਜੋਖੋਂ ਵਾਲਾ, ਬਿਪਤਾਪੂਰਨ, ਖ਼ਤਰਨਾਕ

haze (ਹੇਇਜ਼) *n v* ਧੁੰਦ, ਕੁਹਰਾ; ਧੁੰਦਲਾਪਣ; ਪਰੇਸ਼ਾਨੀ, ਨਿਰਾਸਤਾ; ਧੁੰਦਲਾ ਕਰਨਾ, ਧੁੰਦ ਪਾਉਣੀ; ਤੰਗ ਕਰਨਾ

hazy ('ਹੇਇਜ਼ਿ) *a* ਧੁੰਦਲਾ, ਅਸਪਸ਼ਟ, ਸ਼ੱਕ ਵਾਲਾ

head (ਹੈੱਡ) *n v* (1) ਸਿਰ, ਸੀਸ, ਖੋਪੀ; (ਸਿੱਕੇ ਉੱਤੇ ਬਣਿਆ) ਚਿਹਰਾ; ਸਿਰਾ ਜਾਂ ਅਗਲਾ ਹਿੱਸਾ; (2) ਸਰਦਾਰ, ਮੁਖੀਆ, ਪ੍ਰਧਾਨ, ਮੁੱਖ ਅਧਿਕਾਰੀ; ਸਿਰਲੇਖ; ਵਿਅਕਤੀ, ਜਣਾ; ਨੋਕ ਕੱਢਣੀ, ਸਿਰ ਬਣਾਉਣਾ, ਮੂੰਹ ਬਣਾਉਣਾ; ਛਾਂਗਣਾ, ਲਾਪਰਨਾ, ਅੱਗੇ ਹੋਣਾ; ਸਿਰਲੇਖ ਹੋਣਾ; ਉੱਨਤੀ ਕਰਨੀ; ਸਿਖਰ ਤੇ ਪੁੱਜਣਾ; ~ache ਸਿਰ-ਪੀੜ; ਸਿਰਦਰਦੀ, ਔਖੀ ਸਮੱਸਿਆ; ~line ਸੁਰਖ਼ੀ; ~master ਵੱਡਾ ਮਾਸਟਰ, ਮੁੱਖ ਅਧਿਆਪਕ; ~quarters ਮੁੱਖ ਦਫ਼ਤਰ, ਦਫ਼ਤਰ ਸਦਰ; ~man ਜੱਲਾਦ; ~ing ਸਿਰਲੇਖ, ਸੁਰਖ਼ੀ, ਸ਼ੀਰਸ਼ਕ, ਉਨਵਾਨ; ~ship ਸਰਦਾਰੀ, ਮੁਖੀ ਦਾ ਪਦ; ~y ਪ੍ਰਚੰਡ, ਪ੍ਰਬਲ, ਵੇਗਵਾਨ

heal (ਹੀਲ) *v* ਤੰਦਰੁਸਤ ਹੋਣਾ ਜਾਂ ਕਰਨਾ, ਰਾਜ਼ੀ ਹੋਣਾ ਜਾਂ ਕਰਨਾ, ਜ਼ਖ਼ਮ ਭਰਨਾ

health (ਹੈੱਲਥ) *n* ਸਿਹਤ, ਤੰਦਰੁਸਤੀ, ਸੁਅਸਥ, ਅਰੋਗਤਾ; ~y ਸਿਹਤਮੰਦ, ਨਿਰੋਗ, ਸੁਅਸਥ

heap (ਹੀਪ) *n v* ਢੇਰ, ਢੇਰੀ, ਸਮੂਹ, ਜ਼ਖੀਰਾ; ਢੇਰ ਲਾਉਣਾ, ਇਕੱਤਰ ਕਰਨਾ, ਜਮ੍ਹਾਂ ਕਰਨਾ

hear (ਹਿਅ*) *v* ਸੁਣਨਾ; ਸੁਣ ਲੈਣਾ; ਕੰਨ ਲਾਉਣਾ; ~say ਅਫ਼ਵਾਹ, ਸੁਣੀ-ਸੁਣਾਈ ਗੱਲ; ~ing

~ing ਸੁਣਵਾਈ; ਪੇਸ਼ੀ

hearse (ਹਅ:ਸ) *n* ਬਬਾਣ, ਲਾਸ਼ ਲੈ ਜਾਣ ਵਾਲੀ ਗੱਡੀ

heart (ਹਾ'ਟ) *n* ਦਿਲ, ਜੀਅ, ਮਨ, ਹਿਰਦਾ; ਛਾਤੀ, ਸੀਨਾ; ਹੌਸਲਾ, ਦਲੇਰੀ, ਸਾਹਸ; ~**and soul** ਜੋਸ਼ ਨਾਲ, ਉਤਸ਼ਾਹ ਨਾਲ, ਤਨੋਮਨੋ; ~**beat** ਦਿਲ ਦੀ ਧੱਕਪਣ; ~**breaking** ਦਿਲ-ਤੋੜ; ~**burning** ਸਾੜਾ, ਈਰਖਾ, ਦਵੈਖ; ~**felt** ਸੱਚੇ ਦਿਲੋਂ, ਹਾਰਦਿਕ; ~**of hearts** ਸੱਚੇ ਦਿਲ ਨਾਲ; ~**rending** ਅਤੀ ਦੁਖਦਾਈ, ਹਿਰਦੇ-ਵੇਧਕ; ~**less** ਬੇਰਹਿਮ, ਨਿਰਦਈ, ਪੱਥਰ-ਦਿਲ; ~**en** ਉਤਸ਼ਾਹਤ ਕਰਨ, ਢਾਰਸ ਦੇਣਾ, ਦਿਲ ਵਧਾਉਣਾ; ~**ily** ਖ਼ੁਸ਼ੀ ਖ਼ੁਸ਼ੀ, ਸੱਚੇ ਦਿਲੋਂ; ਜੀ ਖੋਲ੍ਹ ਕੇ

hearth (ਹਾ'ਥ) *n* ਚੁੱਲ੍ਹਾ, ਅੰਗੀਠੀ, ਘਰਬਾਰ, ਬਾਲ-ਬੱਚੇ, ਪਰਵਾਰ

heat (ਹੀਟ) *n v* ਗਰਮੀ, ਤਾਅ, ਤਪਸ਼; ਹੁਨਾਲ; ਜੋਸ਼, ਉਤੇਜਨਾ, ਕਰੋਧ, ਰੋਸ; ਤਪਾਉਣਾ, ਤੱਤਾ ਕਰਨਾ, ਬਖ਼ਸਉਣਾ, ਸੇਕਣਾ; ਤਪਣਾ; ਭੜਕਣਾ; ਗੁੱਸੇ ਵਿਚ ਆਉਣਾ; ~**stroke** ਲੂ-ਲਗਣਾ; ~**ed** ਤਪਤ, ਉਤੇਜਤ

heave (ਹੀਵ) *n v* ਲੰਮਾ ਸਾਹ, ਹਉਕਾ; ਉਤਾਰ; ਹਉਕਾ ਭਰਨਾ, ਠੰਢਾ ਸਾਹ ਲੈਣਾ

heaven (ਹੈੱਵਨ) *n* ਸੁਰਗ; ਬਹਿਸ਼ਤ, ਜੰਨਤ, ਦੇਵ-ਲੋਕ; ਈਸ਼ਵਰ; ਅੰਬਰ, ਆਕਾਸ਼, ਅਸਮਾਨ, ਵਾਯੂ-ਮੰਡਲ; ~**ly** ਦਿਵਯ, ਸੁਰਗੀ; ਆਕਾਸ਼ੀ, ਆਸਮਾਨੀ; ਚੰਗਾ, ਵਧੀਆ

heaviness (ਹੈੱਵਿਨਿਸ) *n* ਭਾਰ, ਗੁਰੂਤਾ; ਪ੍ਰਚੰਡਤਾ, ਭਾਰਾਪਣ

heavy (ਹੈੱਵੀ) *a* ਭਾਰਾ, ਬੋਝਲ, ਵਜ਼ਨੀ; ਵੱਡਾ; ਭਰਪੂਰ, ਲੱਦਿਆ; ਸੋਕਮਈ, ਵਿਸ਼ਾਦਪੂਰਨ; ਨਿਰਸ

heed (ਹੀਡ) *n v* ਸਾਵਧਾਨੀ, ਚੌਕਸੀ, ਧਿਆਨ;

ਚੌਕਸੀ ਕਰਨੀ, ਪਰਵਾਹ ਕਰਨੀ, ਧਿਆਨ ਕਰਨਾ; ~**ful** ਸਚੇਤ, ਸਾਵਧਾਨ, ਚੌਕਸ; ~**less** ਅਚੇਤ, ਅਸਾਵਧਾਨ, ਲਾਪਰਵਾਹ

heel (ਹੀਲ) *n v* ਅੱਡੀ, ਪਸ਼ੂਆਂ ਦੇ ਖੁਰ, ਪਿਛਲੀਆਂ ਲੱਤਾਂ; ਅੱਡੀ ਲਾਉਣੀ; ਪਿੱਛੇ ਪਿੱਛੇ ਲੱਗੇ ਫਿਰਨਾ

hefty (ਹੈੱਫ਼ਟਿ) *a* ਰਿਸ਼ਟ-ਪੁਸ਼ਟ, ਹੱਟਾ-ਕੱਟਾ, ਮੋਟਾ ਤਾਜ਼ਾ

height (ਹਾਇਟ) *n* ਉਚਾਈ, ਬੁਲੰਦੀ; ਕੱਦ, ਲੰਬਾਈ; ਚੜ੍ਹਦੀ ਕਲਾ, ਚੋਟੀ; ਟਿੱਲਾ, ਸਿਖਰ; ~**en** ਉੱਚਾ ਕਰਨਾ, ਉਤਾਰਨਾ, ਡੂੰਘਾ ਕਰਨਾ, ਉਠਾਉਣਾ, ਚੜ੍ਹਾਉਣਾ

heinous (ਹੇਇਨਅਸ) *a* ਘਿਰਣਾਯੋਗ, ਘਿਰਣਤ

heir (ਏਅ*) *n* ਵਾਰਸ, ਉਤਰਾਧਿਕਾਰੀ, ਜਾਂਨਸ਼ੀਨ, ਵਾਲੀ ਵਾਰਸ; ~**less** ਲਾਵਾਰਸ

hell (ਹੈੱਲ) *n* ਪਾਤਾਲ, ਨਰਕ, ਦੋਜ਼ਖ, ਜਹੱਨਮ, ਯਮਲੋਕ, ਰਸਾਤਲ

helmet (ਹੈੱਲਮਿਟ) *n* ਲੋਹੇ ਦੀ ਟੋਪੀ; ਧੁੱਪ ਨੂੰ ਰੋਕਣ ਵਾਲੀ ਛੱਜੇਦਾਰ ਟੋਪੀ

help (ਹੈੱਲਪ) *n v* ਸਹਾਇਤਾ, ਮਦਦ, ਸਹਾਰਾ; ਉਪਾਉ; ਸਹਾਇਤਾ ਕਰਨਾ, ਸਹਾਇਕ ਹੋਣਾ, ਸਹਾਰਾ ਦੇਣਾ, ਹਿੰਮਤਿਆ ਕਰਨੀ, ਹੱਥ ਵਟਾਉਣਾ; ~**mate** ਹਮਦਮ, ਸਹਾਇਕ; ~**ful** ਸਹਾਇਕ, ਲਾਭਦਾਇਕ; ~**ing** ਸਹਾਇਤਾ ਕਰਨੀ, ਸਹਾਇਕ; ~**less** ਨਿਆਸਰਾ, ਨਿਤਾਣਾ, ਬੇਚਾਰਾ, ਬੇ-ਸਹਾਰਾ, ਮਜਬੂਰ

helter-skelter ('ਹੈੱਲਟਅ'ਸਕੈੱਲਟਅ*) *adv* ਖਲਬਲੀ

hemisphere ('ਹੈੱਮਿ'ਸਫ਼ਿਅ*) *n* ਅਰਧਗੋਲਾ, ਗੋਲਰਧ

hemlock ('ਹੈੱਮਲੌਕ) *n* ਧਤੂਰਾ

hemp (ਹੈੱਮਪ) *n* ਸਣ, ਪੱਟ, ਸੁਤਲੀ, ਭੰਗ, ਗਾਂਜਾ, ਸੁੱਖਾ

hen (ਹੈੱਨ) *n* ਕੁਕੜੀ, ਮੁਰਗੀ; ਡਰਪੋਕ ਬੰਦਾ; **~pecked** ਰੰਨ-ਸੁਰੀਦ, ਜੋਰੂ ਦਾ ਗ਼ੁਲਾਮ; **~nery** ਮੁਰਗ਼ੀਖ਼ਾਨਾ, ਪੋਲਟਰੀ ਫਾਰਮ

hence (ਹੈੱਸ) *adv* ਇਸ ਲਈ; ਏਥੋਂ, ਇਸ ਥਾਂ ਤੋਂ, ਹੁਣ ਤੋਂ; **~forth, ~forward** ਮੁੜ, ਹੁਣ ਤੋਂ, ਇਸ ਤੋਂ ਮਗਰੋਂ

henchman ('ਹੈਂਚਮਅਨ) *n* ਮੁੱਖ ਸੇਵਕ, ਦਾਸ; ਪਿਠੂ, ਚਮਚਾ

henna ('ਹੈੱਨਅ) *n* ਮਹਿੰਦੀ, ਹਿਨਾ

herald ('ਹੈਰੇ(ਅ)ਲਡ) *n v* ਦੂਤ, ਸੰਦੇਸ਼ਵਾਹਕ; ਨਕੀਬ; ਹਰਕਾਰਾ; ਮੁਨਾਦੀ; ਆਰੰਭ ਕਰਨਾ

herb (ਹਅ:ਬ) *n a* ਔਸ਼ਧੀ, ਜੜੀ ਬੂਟੀ, ਸਾਗ; **~al** ਜੜੀ ਬੂਟੀਆਂ ਦਾ ਬਣਿਆ

herd (ਹਅ:ਡ) *n v* ਦਲ, (ਪਸ਼ੂਆਂ ਦਾ) ਚੌਂਣਾ, ਵੱਗ, ਇੱਜੜ, ਝੁੰਡ, (ਜਨ-ਸਮੂਹ); ਗਵਾਲਾ, ਆਜੜੀ, ਪਸ਼ੂ-ਪਾਲਕ; ਪਸ਼ੂ ਚਾਰਨੇ; ਸਮੂਹ ਵਿਚ ਚੱਲਣਾ; **~sman** ਆਜੜੀ, ਚਰਵਾਹਾ, ਗਵਾਲਾ, ਪਾਲੀ

here (ਹਿਅ*) *n adv* ਇਸ ਥਾਂ, ਇਹ ਜਗ੍ਹਾ, ਇੱਧਰ; **~about** ਇੱਧਰ ਉੱਧਰ, ਨੇੜੇ ਹੀ; **~and there** ਥਾਂ, ਥਾਂ, ਇੱਥੇ ਉੱਥੇ, ਇੱਧਰ ਉੱਧਰ; **~by** ਇੰਜ ਕਰਕੇ; **~in** ਇਸ ਥਾਂ (ਇਸ ਪਸਤਕ ਵਿਚ); **~in after** ਇਸ ਤੋਂ ਮਗਰੋਂ, ਅੱਗੇ; **~to** ਇਸ ਵਾਸਤੇ, ਇਸ ਗੱਲ ਵਿਚ; **~to fore** ਇਸ ਤੋਂ ਪਹਿਲੋਂ; **~upon** ਇਸ ਤੋਂ ਮਗਰੋਂ, ਇਸ ਲਈ; **~with** ਇਸ ਦੇ ਨਾਲ, ਇਸ ਨਾਲ ਨੱਥੀ

hereditary (ਹਿਰੈਡਿਟ(ਅ)ਰਿ) *a* ਜੱਦੀ, ਪੁਸ਼ਤੀ; ਵੰਸ਼ ਦਾ, ਵੰਸ਼ਗਤ, ਕੁਲ ਦਾ; ਪੈਤਰਿਕ

heredity (ਹਿਰੈਡੋਅਟਿ) *n* ਵਿਰਾਸਤ, ਪੈਤਰਿਕ ਗੁਣ, ਵੰਸ਼ ਪਰੰਪਰਾ

heresy ('ਹੈਰਅਸਿ) *n* ਕੁਫ਼ਰ, ਪਖੰਡ

heretic ('ਹੈਰਿਟਿਕ) *n* ਕਾਫ਼ਰ, ਧਰਮ ਵਿਰੋਧੀ, ਪਖੰਡੀ, ਨਾਸਤਕ

heritage ('ਹੈਰਿਟਿਜ) *n* ਪਿਤਰੀ ਧਨ, ਪੈਤਰਿਕ ਪੂੰਜੀ, ਵਿਰਾਸਤ ਮੀਰਾਸ, ਉਤਰਾਧਿਕਾਰ

hermit ('ਹਅ:ਮਿਟ) *n* ਸੰਨਿਆਸੀ, ਬਨਵਾਸੀ, ਤਪਸਵੀ, ਬਾਨਪ੍ਰਸਥ, ਇਕਾਂਤਵਾਸੀ; **~age** ਆਸ਼ਰਮ, ਕੁਟੀਆ, ਮੱਠ, ਇਕਾਂਤਵਾਸ, ਗੋਸ਼ਾਨਸ਼ੀਨੀ

hero ('ਹਿਅਰਅਉ) *n* ਪਰਮ ਮਨੁੱਖ, ਦੇਵਤਿਆਂ ਵਰਗਾ ਮਨੁੱਖ, ਵੀਰ, ਜੋਧਾ, ਸੁਰਬੀਰ, ਬਹਾਦਰ, ਨਾਇਕ; ਸੂਰਮਾ; ਰਾਸ਼ਟਰ ਜੋਧਾ; **~ine** ਨਾਇਕਾ; **~ism** ਸੁਰਬੀਰਤਾ

heroic (ਹਿ'ਰੋਇਕ) *n a* ਵੀਰ-ਕਾਵਿ ਵਿਚ ਪ੍ਰਯੁਕਤ ਛੰਦ; ਵੀਰਤਾਪੁਰਨ; ਵੀਰਰਸ ਪ੍ਰਧਾਨ, ਤੇਜਸਵੀ, ਵੀਰ

hesitance, hesitancy ('ਹੈਜ਼ਿਟਅੱਸ, 'ਹੈਜ਼ਿਟਅੱਸਿ) *n* ਦੁਬਧਾ, ਸੰਕੋਚ, ਝੱਕ, ਸ਼ਸ਼ੋਪੰਜ, ਝਿਜਕ, ਹਿਚਕਚਾਹਟ

hesitant ('ਹੈਜ਼ਿਟ(ਅ)ਨਟ) *a* ਝਿਜਕਦਾ, ਦੁਚਿੱਤਾ

hesitate ('ਹੈਜ਼ਿਟੇਇਟ) *v* ਝਿਜਕਣਾ, ਹਿਚਕਚਾਉਣਾ, ਸ਼ਸ਼ੋਪੰਜ ਵਿਚ ਪੈਣਾ, ਦੁਬਧਾ ਵਿਚ ਪੈਣਾ, ਸੰਕੋਚ ਕਰਨਾ

hesitation ('ਹੈਜ਼ਿ'ਟੇਇਸ਼ਨ) *n* ਝਿਜਕ, ਦੁਬਧਾ, ਸੰਕੋਚ, ਦੁਚਿੱਤੀ

heterodox ('ਹੈਟ(ਅ)ਰਅ(ਉ)ਡੋਕਸ) *n a* ਭਿੰਨ-ਮੱਤ; ਭਿੰਨ-ਮਤੀਆ, ਮਨਮਤੀਆ

heterogeneous ('ਹੈਟਅਰਅ(ਉ)'ਜੀਨਯਅਸ) *a* ਵਿਖਮ, ਵਿਰੋਧੀ; ਭਿੰਨ, ਵਿਜਾਤੀ, ਭਿੰਨ ਜਾਤੀ

hexagon ('ਹੈਕਸਅਗਅਨ) *n* ਛੇ ਭੁਜ

hexameter (ਹੈੱਕ'ਸੈਮਿਟਅ*) *n* (ਕਾਵਿ) ਛੇ ਪਦੀ (ਛੰਦ)

hiccup ('ਹਿਕਅੱਪ) *n v* ਹਿੱਚਕੀ; ਹਿੱਚਕੀ ਲੱਗਣੀ; ਹਿੱਚਕੀ ਆਉਣੀ

hide (ਹਾਇਡ) *n v* ਪਸ਼ੂਆਂ ਦਾ ਚੰਮ, ਖੱਲ, ਚਮੜਾ, ਲੁਕਾਉਣਾ ਜਾਂ ਲੁਕਣਾ; **~out** (ਬੋਲ) ਲੁਕਣ ਦੀ ਥਾਂ

hideous ('ਹਿਡਿਅਸ) *a* ਭਿਆਨਕ, ਘਿਣਾਉਣਾ, ਘੋਰ

hierarch ('ਹਾਇਅਰਾਕ) *n* ਪਰੋਹਤ, ਇਮਾਮ, ਪ੍ਰਧਾਨ ਪਾਦਰੀ, ਮਹਾਆਚਾਰੀਆ; **~y** ਦੇਵ ਸ਼੍ਰੇਣੀ, ਮਹੰਤੀ, ਮਹੰਤਸ਼ਾਹੀ

high (ਹਾਇ) *a* ਉੱਚਾ, ਉਨਤ, ਬੁਲੰਦ, ਉਤੇ; ਉੱਤਮ, ਉਤਕ੍ਰਿਸ਼ਟ, ਅਤੀ ਅਧਿਕ; **~born** ਕੁਲੀਨ, ਸੁਜਾਤ; **~caste** ਉੱਚੀ ਜਾਤ; **~court** ਉੱਚ ਅਦਾਲਤ; **~handedness** ਧਾਂਦਲੀ, ਆਪਹੁਦਰਾਪਣ, ਉਦੰਡਤਾ; **~way** ਸ਼ਾਹ-ਰਾਹ; **~wayman** ਵੱਟ-ਮਾਰ; **~ten** ਉੱਨਤ ਕਰਨਾ, ਉੱਚਾ ਕਰਨਾ, ਤੀਬਰ ਕਰਨਾ, ਵਧਾਉਣਾ

hijacker ('ਹਾਇਜੈਕਅ*) *n* ਅਪਹਰਣਕਰਤਾ

hijacking ('ਹਾਇਜੈਕਿਙ) *n* ਠੱਗੀ; (ਜਹਾਜ਼ ਬੱਸ ਆਦਿ ਦਾ) ਅਪਹਰਣ

hike (ਹਾਇਕ) *n v* ਪੈਦਲ ਸੈਰ; ਲੰਮੀ ਪਦ ਯਾਤਰਾ; ਲੰਮੀ ਪਦ ਯਾਤਰਾ ਕਰਨਾ, ਤੇਜ਼ ਚੱਲਣਾ

hilarious (ਹਿ'ਲੇਅਰਿਅਸ) *a* ਪ੍ਰਫੁੱਲਤ, ਪ੍ਰਸੰਨ, ਉੱਲਾਸਮਈ, ਆਨੰਦਪੂਰਨ; **~ness** ਪ੍ਰਫੁੱਲਤਾ, ਪ੍ਰਸੰਨਤਾ, ਉੱਲਾਸ, ਆਨੰਦ, ਮਗਨਤਾ, ਖ਼ੁਸ਼ੀ

hill (ਹਿਲ) *n* ਡੂਗਰ, ਪਹਾੜੀ; ਟਿੱਲਾ; ਟਿੱਬਾ, ਢਿਗ; **~ock** ਛੋਟੀ ਪਹਾੜੀ; ਟਿੱਬਾ, ਟਿੱਲਾ, ਢੱਕੀ

hilly billy ('ਹਿਲਿਬਿਲਿ) *n* ਗਵਾਰੂ, ਉਜੱਡ; ਇਕ ਲੋਕ-ਗੀਤ

hind (ਹਾਇੰਡ) *n a* ਹਿਰਨੀ, ਮੂਨ, ਮੀਰਗਣੀ; ਗੰਵਾਰ, ਪੇਂਡੂ ਪਿਛਲੇ ਪਾਸੇ ਦਾ, ਪਿੱਠ-ਪਿਛਲਾ; **~er** ਰੋਕਣਾ, ਵਿਘਨ ਪਾਉਣਾ, ਅੜਚਨ ਪਾਉਣਾ, ਅਟਕਾਉਣਾ, ਪ੍ਰਤੀਬੰਧ ਲਾਉਣਾ; **~erance, ~rance** ਅੜਚਨ, ਰੁਕਾਵਟ, ਵਿਘਨ; ਨਿਸ਼ੇਧ, ਪ੍ਰਤੀਬੰਧ

hinge (ਹਿੰਜ) *n v* ਚੂਲ, ਕਬਜ਼ਾ, ਜੋੜ; ਕੋਰ; ਕੇਂਦਰ, ਮੂਲ, ਜੜ੍ਹ; ਸਿਧਾਂਤ

hint (ਹਿੰਟ) *n v* ਸੰਕੇਤ, ਸੂਚਨਾ, ਸੁਝਾਉ, ਭਿਣਕ, ਇਸ਼ਾਰਾ; ਸੰਕੇਤ ਜਾਂ ਸੂਚਨਾ ਦੇਣਾ, ਸੁਝਾਉ ਦੇਣਾ

hip (ਹਿਪ) *n v int* ਕੁੱਲਾ, ਚੂਲਾ, ਢਹਿੰਦੀ ਕਲਾ; ਸ਼ਾਬਾਸ਼ ਦੇਣਾ, ਹਿੱਪ ਹਿੱਪ ਹੁੱਰਾ ਕਰਨਾ, ਉਤਸ਼ਾਹ ਦੇਣਾ

hippocampus ('ਹਿਪਅ'ਕੈਂਪਅਸ) *n* ਸਮੁੰਦਰੀ ਘੋੜਾ, ਇਕ ਤਰ੍ਹਾਂ ਦੀ ਮੱਛੀ

hippopotamus ('ਹਿਪਅ'ਪੌਟਅਮਅਸ) *n* ਦਰਿਆਈ ਘੋੜਾ

hire ('ਹਾਇਅ*) *n v* ਭਾੜਾ, ਕਿਰਾਇਆ; ਮਿਹਨਤਾਨਾ, ਮਜ਼ਦੂਰੀ, ਕਿਰਾਏ ਤੇ ਲੈਣਾ, ਮਿਹਨਤਾਨਾ ਦੇ ਕੇ ਲਾਉਣਾ

hiss (ਹਿਸ) *n v* ਫੁੰਕਾਰਾ, ਛੁਣਕਾਰ, ਹਿੱਛ; ਫੁੰਕਾਰਾ ਮਾਰਨਾ, ਛਣਕਾਰ ਪੈਣੀ

historian (ਹਿ'ਸਟੋਰਿਅਨ) *n* ਇਤਿਹਾਸਕਾਰ, ਤਾਰੀਖ਼ਦਾਨ

historic (ਹਿ'ਸਟੌਰਿਕ) *a* ਇਤਿਹਾਸਕ, ਇਤਿਹਾਸ ਪ੍ਰਸਿੱਧ, ਇਤਿਹਾਸ ਅਨੁਸਾਰ, ਮਹੱਤਵਪੂਰਨ; **~al** ਇਤਿਹਾਸਕ, ਇਤਿਹਾਸ ਸਬੰਧੀ, ਤਾਰੀਖ਼ੀ

history ('ਹਿਸਟ(ਅ)ਰਿ) *n* ਇਤਿਹਾਸ, ਤਾਰੀਖ਼

hit (ਹਿਟ) *n v* ਚੋਟ, ਮਾਰ, ਵਾਰ, ਘਾਉ; ਚੋਟ ਲਾਉਣੀ, ਮਾਰਨਾ, ਵਾਰ ਕਰਨਾ, ਜ਼ਰਬ ਪਹੁੰਚਾਉਣਾ; **~below the belt** ਮਰਯਾਦਾ ਭੰਗ ਕਰਨੀ, ਕੋਝਾ ਵਾਰ ਕਰਨਾ; **~upon** ਸੁੱਝਣਾ

hither ('ਹਿਦਅ*) *adv* ਨੇੜੇ, ਹੋਰ ਨੇੜੇ; ਇੱਧਰ,

ਇਸ ਪਾਸੇ, ਇਸ ਥਾਂ; **~and thither** ਇੱਧਰ ਉੱਧਰ; **~to** ਹੁਣ ਤੋੜੀ, ਹੁਣ ਤੀਕ

hive ('ਹਾਇਵ) *n v* ਮਖਿਆਲ, ਸ਼ਹਿਦ ਦੀਆਂ ਮੱਖੀਆਂ ਦਾ ਛੱਤਾ; ਝੀੜ; ਸ਼ਹਿਦ ਦੀਆਂ ਮੱਖੀਆਂ ਪਾਲਣਾ

hives (ਹਾਇਵ੍ਜ਼) *n pl* ਛਪਾਕੀ

hoard (ਹੋਡ) *n v* ਖ਼ਜ਼ਾਨਾ, ਭੰਡਾਰ, ਜ਼ਖ਼ੀਰਾ; ਖ਼ਜ਼ਾਨਾ ਜੋੜਨਾ; **~ing** ਦੱਬੀ ਹੋਈ ਮਾਇਆ, ਗੁਪਤ ਸੰਗ੍ਰਹ

hoarse (ਹੋ'ਸ) *a* ਬੈਠਿਆ (ਗਲਾ), ਘੱਗੀ (ਅਵਾਜ਼), ਬੇਸੁਰੀ (ਅਵਾਜ਼); **~n** (ਗਲ ਜਾਂ ਅਵਾਜ਼ ਦਾ) ਬੈਠਣਾ, ਘਰਿਆਉਣਾ, ਭਰੜਾਉਣਾ, ਪਾਟਣਾ; **~ness** ਘਿੰਗਰੀ, ਭਰੜਾਹਟ, ਭਾਰਾਪਣ (ਬੋਲ ਜਾਂ ਅਵਾਜ਼ ਦਾ)

hoax (ਹਅਉਕਸ) *v n* ਝਾਂਸਾ ਦੇਣਾ, ਬੁੱਧੂ ਬਣਾਉਣਾ; ਝਾਂਸਾ

hob (ਹੋਬ) *n* ਪੇਂਡੂ, ਗੰਵਾਰ; **to play~** ਖਲਬਲੀ ਮਚਾਉਣਾ, ਗੜਬੜ ਪਾਉਣੀ

hobby (ਹੋਬਿ) *n* ਸ਼ੌਕੀਆ ਕੰਮ, ਸ਼ੁਗਲ; **~horse** ਬੱਚਿਆਂ ਦਾ ਲੱਕੜ ਦਾ ਘੋੜਾ

hobnob ('ਹੋਬਨੋਬ) *v* ਹਮ-ਪਿਆਲਾ ਹੋਣਾ, ਇਕੱਠੇ ਸ਼ਰਾਬ ਪੀਣੀ

hocus-pocus ('ਹਅਉਕਅਸ'ਪਅਉਕਅਸ) *n v* ਛਲ, ਧੋਖਾ, ਚਕਮਾ; ਇੰਦਰ-ਜਾਲ, ਛਲਣਾ, ਚਕਮਾ ਦੇਣਾ

hoist (ਹੋਇਸਟ) *n v* ਉਠਾਅ, ਚੜ੍ਹਾਅ; ਲਹਿਰਾਉਣਾ, ਖੜਾ ਕਰਨਾ, ਉਠਾਉਣਾ

hold (ਹਅਉਲਡ) *n v* ਬੰਨ੍ਹਣ, ਪਕੜ; ਕਬਜ਼ੀ, ਅਧਿਕਾਰ, ਪ੍ਰਭਾਵ; ਫੜਨਾ, ਫੜੀ ਰੱਖਣਾ; ਕਬਜ਼ਾ ਕਰਨਾ, ਰੋਕੀ ਰੱਖਣਾ; **~on** ਪ੍ਰਭਾਵ, ਅਸਰ; **~up** ਰੁਕਾਵਟ, ਅਟਕਾਅ; ਡਾਕੂਆਂ ਵੱਲੋਂ ਰਾਹ ਘੇਰਨਾ, ਰਾਹਮਾਰੀ; **~with** ਸਵੀਕਾਰ ਕਰਨਾ

hole (ਹਅਉਲ) *n v* ਛੇਕ, ਸੁਰਾਖ਼, ਛਿਦਰ, ਮੋਰੀ, ਟੋਆ ਪੁੱਟਣਾ, ਛੇਕ ਕਰਨਾ; ਖੁੱਤੀ ਜਾਂ ਖੁੱਤੀ ਵਿਚ ਗੋਂਦ ਜਾਂ ਗੋਲੀ ਪਾਉਣੀ; ਸੁਰੰਗ ਬਣਾਉਣਾ

holiday ('ਹੌਲਿਡੇਇ) *n* ਛੁੱਟੀ

holiness ('ਹਅਉਲਿਨਿਸ) *n* ਸੁੱਚਮ, ਪਵਿੱਤਰਤਾ, ਪਾਵਨਤਾ, ਪੁਨੀਤਤਾ

hollow ('ਹੌਲਅਉ) *n a adv* ਖੋਹ, ਖਾਲਾ; ਖੋਖਲਾ, ਪੋਲਾ; ਸੁੰਨ; ਭੁੱਖਾ; ਥੋਥਾ, ਕਪਟੀ; **~ness** ਖੋਖਪਣ, ਸੁੰਨਪਣ

holocaust ('ਹੌਲਅਕੋਸਟ) *n* ਕਤਲਾਮ, ਹੱਤਿਆ ਕਾਂਡ, ਘੱਲੂਘਾਰਾ, ਸਰਬਨਾਸ਼, ਤਬਾਹੀ

holy ('ਹਅਉਲਿ) *a* ਪਾਵਨ, ਪੱਵਿਤਰ, ਪੁਨੀਤ, ਪਾਕ; ਧਰਮਾਤਮਾ, ਮਹਾਤਮਾ

homage ('ਹੌਮਿਜ) *n* ਸਨਮਾਨ; ਸ਼ਰਧਾਂਜਲੀ

home (ਹਅਉਮ) *n a adv* ਘਰ, ਗ੍ਰਹਿ, ਰਿਹਾਇਸ਼, ਨਿਵਾਸ, ਸੁਦੇਸ਼, ਭਵਨ, ਮਕਾਨ, ਘਰ-ਬਾਰ; ਘਰੇਲੂ, ਸੁਦੇਸ਼ੀ; ਘਰ ਮੁੜਨਾ, ਘਰ ਭੇਜਣਾ; ਵਾਸ ਕਰਨਾ; ਘਰ ਬਣਾ ਦੇਣਾ; **~land** ਮਾਤ ਭੂਮੀ; **~spun** ਘਰ ਦਾ ਬੁਣਿਆ (ਕੱਪੜਾ); ਸਾਦਮੁਰਾਦਾ; **~less** ਬੇਘਰਾ, ਨਿਰਾਸਰਾ, ਗ੍ਰਹਿਹੀਣ, ਅਨਾਥ; **~like** ਘਰੇਲੂ, ਘਰ ਵਾਂਗ, ਜਾਣੀ ਪਛਾਣੀ, ਪਰਿਚਤ; **~ly** ਘਰੇਲੂ, ਸਧਾਰਨ, ਪੁਰਾਤਨ; ਸਿਧਾ-ਸਾਦਾ

homicide ('ਹੌਮਿਸਾਇਡ) *n* ਮਾਨਵ-ਹੱਤਿਆ; ਹੱਤਿਆਰਾ

homogeneous ('ਹੌਮਅ'ਜੀਨਿਯਅਸ) *a* ਸਜਾਤੀ, ਇਕਸਾਰ, ਸਮਰੂਪ, ਹਮਜਿਨਸ; ਸਮਾਨ, ਸਮ-ਅੰਗ, ਸਦ੍ਰਿਸ਼, ਇਕ ਰੂਪ; **~ness, homogenity** ਸਜਾਤੀਅਤ, ਸਮਰੂਪਤਾ, ਸਦ੍ਰਿਸ਼ਤਾ

homonym ('ਹੌਮਅਨਿਮ) *n* ਸਮ-ਰੂਪਕ, ਸ਼ਬਦ, ਇਕੋ ਜਿਹੇ ਰੂਪ ਪਰ ਭਿੰਨ ਭਿੰਨ ਅਰਥਾਂ ਵਾਲੇ ਸ਼ਬਦ

Homo sapiens ('ਹਅਉਮਅਿਓ, 'ਸੈਪਿਅੰਨਜ਼) *n* ਮਾਨਵਜਾਤੀ

homosexual ('ਹੋਮਅਉ'ਸੈਕਸਯੂਅਲ) *a n* ਸਮਲਿੰਗ, ਸਮਲਿੰਗੀ; ~**ity** ਸਮਲਿੰਗ ਕਾਮੁਕਤਾ

honest ('ਔਨਿਸਟ) *a* ਈਮਾਨਦਾਰ, ਖਰਾ, ਨੇਕਨੀਅਤ, ਦਿਆਨਤਦਾਰ; ਸ਼ੁੱਧਆਤਮਾ

honey ('ਹੌਨਿ) *n* ਮਾਖਿਉਂ, ਮਧੁ, ਸ਼ਹਿਦ; ਮਹਿਬੂਬਾ, ਪਿਆਰੀ; ~**moon** ਵਿਆਹ ਤੋਂ ਪਿੱਛੋਂ ਮਨਾਇਆ ਜਾਣ ਵਾਲਾ ਸੁਹਾਗ-ਸਮਾਂ

honorarium ('ਔਨਅ'ਰੇਅਰਿਅਮ) *n* ਮਾਨ-ਭੱਤਾ, ਕਾਰਜ-ਮੁਲਕ, ਮੇਵਾ-ਫਲ, ਕਿਰਤ-ਫਲ

honorary ('ਔਨ(ਅ)ਰਅਰਿ) *a* ਸਨਮਾਨ-ਸੂਚਕ, ਮਾਨ-ਅਰਥ, ਬਿਨਾ ਤਨਖ਼ਾਹ ਦੇ, ਮਾਨ-ਸੇਵੀ

honorific ('ਔਨਅ'ਰਿਫ਼ਿਕ) *a n* ਸਨਮਾਨ ਸੂਚਕ (ਉਪਾਧੀ)

honoris causa or gratia (ਹੋ'ਨੋਰਿਸ'ਕਾਉਜ਼ਾ) *(L) adv phr* ਸਨਮਾਨਕ

honour ('ਔਨਅ*) *n v* ਮਾਨ, ਆਦਰ; ਇੱਜ਼ਤ, ਸਤਿਕਾਰ, ਸ਼ਾਨ, ਵਡਿਆਈ, ਬਜ਼ੁਰਗੀ, ਕੀਰਤੀ, ਗੌਰਵ; ਇੱਜ਼ਤ ਕਰਨੀ, ਸਤਿਕਾਰ ਕਰਨਾ, ਇੱਜ਼ਤ ਬਖ਼ਸ਼ਣੀ, ਵਡਿਆਉਣਾ; ਹੁੰਡੀ ਸਵੀਕਾਰ ਕਰਨੀ; ਸਮੇਂ ਸਿਰ ਦੇਣਾ, ਕਰਜ਼ਾ ਯੁਕ'ਉਣਾ; ~**able** ਮਾਨਯੋਗ, ਪੂਜ, ਆਦਰਤੀਯ; ਦਿਆਨਤਦਾਰ, ਸਚਿਆਰ, ਸ਼ਾਖ਼ ਵਾਲਾ, ਪੂਜਨੀਕ

hooch (ਹੂਚ) *n* ਤਾੜੀ, ਸ਼ਰਾਬ, ਠੱਰਾ

hood (ਹੁਡ) *n v* ਕੰਟੋਪ; (ਸੱਪ ਦਾ, ਫੰਨ); (ਬਾਜ਼ ਲਈ) ਚਮੜੇ ਦੀ ਟੋਪੀ; (ਗੱਡੀ ਦਾ) ਟੱਪ; ਕੱਜਣਾ, ਲੁਕਾਉਣਾ; ਚੜ੍ਹਾਉਣੀ

hoodlum ('ਹੁਡਲਅਮ) *n* ਗੁੰਡਾ, ਲੜੰਗਾ, ਬਦਮਾਸ਼

hoof (ਹੁਫ਼) *n v* ਖੁਰ, ਟਾਪ, ਸੁੰਮ, ਪੌਂਡ, ਠੋਕਰ

hook (ਹੁਕ) *n v* ਕਾਂਟਾ, ਅੰਕੁਸ਼, ਕੁੰਡਾ; ਜਾਲ, ਘੁੰਡੀ; ਦਾਤੀ, ਦਾਤਰੀ; ਮੁੜਨਾ, ਝੁਕਣਾ; ਮੋੜਨਾ, ਝੁਕਾਉਣਾ, ਵਿੰਗਾ ਕਰਨਾ; ~**in**, ~**up** ਉਲਝਾਉਣਾ, ਫਾਹੁਣਾ; ~**on** ਸਹਾਰਾ ਦੇਣਾ; ~**worm** ਪੇਟ ਦਾ ਕੀੜਾ; **by**~ **or by crook** ਕਿਵੇਂ ਨਾ ਕਿਵੇਂ, ਕਿਸੇ ਨਾ ਕਿਸੇ ਤਰ੍ਹਾਂ; ~**ed** ਟੇਢਾ, ਹੁੱਕਦਾਰ ਹੋਣ ਦਾ ਗੁਣ

hooligan ('ਹੁਲਿਗਅਨ) *n* ਗੁੰਡਾ, ਬਦਮਾਸ਼; ~**ism** ਗੁੰਡਾਪਣ, ਗੁੰਡਪੁਣਾ, ਬਦਮਾਸ਼ੀ

hoop (ਹੂਪ) *n v* ਪਹੀਆਂ ਆਦਿ ਨੂੰ ਜਕੜਨ ਲਈ ਗੋਲ ਲੋਹੇ ਦਾ ਚੱਕਰ, ਕੜਾ; ਲਚਕੀਲੀ ਪੇਟੀ; ਮੁੰਦਰੀ, ਅੰਗੂਠੀ, (ਕਾਲੀ ਖਾਂਸੀ ਵਿਚ) ਖਊਂ-ਖਊਂ, ਠਊਂ-ਠਊਂ ਆਦਿ; ਲੋਹੇ ਦੀ ਪੱਤਰੀ ਨਾਲ ਜਕੜਨਾ, ਖਊਂ-ਖਊਂ ਕਰਨਾ; ~**ing cough** ਕਾਲੀ ਖੰਘ, ਕੁੱਤਾ-ਖੰਘ

hoot (ਹੂਟ) *n v* ਤਿਰਸਕਾਰ ਵਜੋਂ ਹੂ-ਹੂ, ਲੂ-ਲੂ, ਥੂ-ਥੂ, ਉਏ-ਉਏ, ਡੂੰ-ਡੂੰ; ਉੱਲੂ-ਬੋਲੀ ਉਏ-ਉਏ ਕਰਨਾ, ਡੂੰ-ਡੂੰ ਕਰਨਾ, ਛੀ-ਛੀ ਕਰਨਾ, ਧਿੱਕਾਰਨਾ; ਲੂ-ਲੂ ਕਰਕੇ ਭਜਾ ਦੇਣਾ; ਚਿਲਾਉਣਾ, ਸ਼ੋਰ ਪਾਉਣਾ

hope (ਹਅਉਪ) *n v* ਉਮੀਦ, ਭਰੋਸਾ, ਆਸ, ਆਸਰਾ; ਸੰਭਾਵਨਾ, ਵਿਸ਼ਵਾਸ, ਉਮੀਦ ਕਰਨੀ, ਆਸ ਕਰਨੀ ਜਾਂ ਲਾਉਣਾ, ਚਾਹੁਣਾ, ਭਰੋਸਾ ਕਰਨਾ; ~**fulness** ਆਸ਼ਾ, ਪੂਰਨਤਾ, ਆਸਵੰਦੀ; ~**less** ਨਿਰਾਸ, ਨਾਉਮੀਦ, ਮਾਯੂਸ, ਨਿਰਾਸ਼ਾਜਨਕ; ਨਿਕੰਮਾ

horizon (ਹਅ'ਰਾਇਜ਼ਨ) *n* ਦਿਸ-ਹੱਦਾ, ਦਿਗ-ਮੰਡਲ; ~**tal** ਦਿਸ-ਹੱਦੇ ਦਾ, ਦਿਗ-ਮੰਡਲੀ, ਸਮਤਲ ਪਈ ਰੇਖਾ, ਲੇਟਵੀਂ ਰੇਖਾ

horn (ਹੋ*ਨ) *v* ਸਿੰਗ; ਨਰਸਿੰਘਾ, ਸਿੰਗੀ, ਸਮਰਿਧੀ ਦਾ ਪ੍ਰਤੀਕ; ਉੱਲੂ ਦੀ ਕਲਗੀ; ਹਾਰਨ, ਭੋਂਪੂ; ਸਿੰਗ ਮਾਰਨਾ, ਸਿੰਗ ਚਲਾਉਣਾ; ਸਿੰਗੀ ਵਜਾਉਣੀ; ਦਖ਼ਲ ਦੇਣਾ; ਰੋਕਣਾ; ~**in** ਵਿਘਨ ਪਾਉਣਾ,

ਰੋਕਣਾ, ਦਖ਼ਲਅੰਦਾਜ਼ੀ ਕਰਨੀ; ~mad ਪੂਰਾ ਪਾਗਲ

hornet ('ਹੋਨਿਟ) *n* ਡੂੰਡ, ਭਰਿੰਡ, ਡਹਮੂ

horoscope (ਹੋ'ਰੌਸਕਅਉਪ) *n* ਨਖੱਤਰ ਨਿਰੀਖਣ; ਟੇਵਾ, ਜਨਮ-ਪਤਰੀ, ਜਨਮ-ਕੁੰਡਲੀ, ਕੁੰਡਲੀ

horoscopy (ਹੋ'ਰੌਸਕਅਪਿ) *n* ਜੋਤਸ਼, ਜੋਤਸ਼-ਵਿੱਦਿਆ

horrible ('ਹੌਰਅਬਲ) *a* ਘੋਰ, ਪ੍ਰਚੰਡ; ਭਿਆਨਕ, ਡਰਾਉਣਾ, ਵਿਕਰਾਲ, ਭਿਅੰਕਰ

horrid ('ਹੌਰਿਡ) *a* ਭਿਅੰਕਰ, ਵਿਕਰਾਲ, ਡਰਾਉਣਾ; ਕਠੋਰ; ~ness ਭਿਅੰਕਰਤਾ, ਵਿਕਰਾਲਤਾ; ਕਠੋਰਤਾ

horrific (ਹੋ'ਰਿਫ਼ਿਕ) *a* ਭਿਅੰਕਰ, ਭਿਆਨਕ

horrified ('ਹੌਰਿਫ਼ਾਇਡ) *a* ਭੈਭੀਤ, ਜੀ-ਭਿਆਨ

horrify ('ਹੌਰਿਫ਼ਾਇ) *v* ਡਰਾ ਦੇਣਾ, ਭੈਭੀਤ ਕਰਨਾ, ਦਿਲ ਦੁਖਾਉਣਾ, ਧੱਕਾ ਪਹੁੰਚਾਉਣਾ

horror ('ਹੌਰਅ*) *n* ਭੈ; ਖੋਫ਼, ਡਰ; ਘਿਰਣਾ, ਨਫ਼ਰਤ; ਭੈਦਾਇਕ ਚੀਜ਼

horse (ਹੋ'ਸ) *n v* ਘੋੜਾ; ਰਿਸਾਲਾ, ਘੋੜ- ਸਵਾਰ ਫ਼ੌਜ; ਘੋੜੇ ਤੇ ਚੜ੍ਹਨਾ; ~laugh ਉੱਚਾ ਹਾਸਾ, ਠਹਾਕਾ; ~power ਸ਼ਕਤੀ ਦਾ ਮਾਪ; ~shoe ਨਾਲ੍ਹ, ਘੋੜੇ ਦੀ ਨਾਲ੍ਹ; ~trading ਸੂਝ ਨਾਲ ਕੀਤੀ ਗਈ ਸੌਦੇਬਾਜ਼ੀ

horticulture ('ਹੌਟਿਕਅੱਲਚਅ*) *n* ਬਾਗ਼ਬਾਨੀ, ਬਾਗ਼ਬਾਨੀ-ਵਿਗਿਆਨ

horticulturist ('ਹੋਟਿ'ਕਅੱਲਚ(ਅ)ਰਿਸਟ) *n* ਬਾਗ਼ਬਾਨੀ ਦਾ ਮਾਹਰ, ਬਾਗ਼ਬਾਨੀ-ਵਿਗਿਆਨੀ

hosier ('ਹਅਉਜ਼ਿਅ*) *n* ਜੁਰਾਬਾਂ, ਬੁਨੈਣਾਂ ਆਦਿ ਵੇਚਣ ਵਾਲਾ, ਜੁਰਾਬਫ਼ਰੋਸ਼; ~y ਜੁਰਾਬਾਂ ਬੁਨੈਣਾਂ ਆਦਿ ਦੀ ਦੁਕਾਨ ਜਾਂ ਕਾਰਖ਼ਾਨਾ

hospitable (ਹੋ'ਸਪਿਟਅਬਲ) *a* ਮਹਿਮਾਨ ਨਿਵਾਜ਼, ਖ਼ਾਤਰਦਾਰ; ~ness ਮਹਿਮਾਨ ਨਿਵਾਜ਼ੀ, ਖ਼ਾਤਰਦਾਰੀ

hospital ('ਹੌਸਪਿਟਲ) *n* ਹਸਪਤਾਲ, ਸ਼ਫ਼ਾਖ਼ਾਨਾ; (ਇਤਿ) ਮਹਿਮਾਨਖ਼ਾਨਾ; ~ism ਚਿਕਿਤਸਾ-ਪ੍ਰਬੰਧ, ਹਸਪਤਾਲੀ, ਪ੍ਰਬੰਧ, ਹਸਪਤਾਲੀਪੁਣਾ; ~ization ਚਿਕਿਤਸਾ ਲਈ ਹਸਪਤਾਲ ਵਿਚ ਕੀਤੀ ਭਰਤੀ; ~ize ਚਿਕਿਤਸਾ ਲਈ ਹਸਪਤਾਲ ਵਿਚ ਭਰਤੀ ਕਰਨਾ, ਦਾਖ਼ਲ ਕਰਨਾ

hospitality ('ਹੌਸਪਿ'ਟੈਲਅਟਿ) *n* ਪਰਾਹੁਣਾਚਾਰੀ, ਮਹਿਮਾਨ ਨਿਵਾਜ਼ੀ, ਖ਼ਾਤਰਦਾਰੀ

host (ਹਅਉਸਟ) *n* ਜਜਮਾਨ; ~el ਛਾਤਰਾਵਾਸ ਸਰਾਂ, ਧਰਮਸ਼ਾਲਾ

hostage ('ਹੌਸਟਿਜਾ) *n* ਬੰਧਕ ਵਿਅਕਤੀ, ਯਰਗਮਾਲ

hostess ('ਹਅਉਸਟਿਸ) *n* ਮੇਜ਼ਬਾਨ ਔਰਤ; ਏਅਰ ਹੋਸਟੈੱਸ

hostile ('ਹੌਸਟਾਇਲ) *a* ਵਿਰੋਧੀ; ਪ੍ਰਤੀਕੂਲ, ਉਲਟ

hostility (ਹੌ'ਸਟਿਲਅਟਿ) *n* ਵਿਰੋਧ; ਵੈਰ, ਵੈਰ-ਭਾਵ, ਦੁਸ਼ਮਨੀ, ਲੜਾਈ-ਝਗੜਾ

hot (ਹੌਟ) *a* ਗਰਮ, ਤਪਿਆ ਹੋਇਆ, ਤੱਤਾ, ਕੌੜਾ, ਕਰਾਰਾ, ਚਟਪਟਾ; ਤੀਬਰ, ਗੁੱਸੈਲਾ; ਪ੍ਰਚੰਡ, ਜੋਸ਼ ਵਿਚ; ਉਤੇਜਤ; (ਖ਼ਬਰਾਂ ਆਦਿ) ਤਾਜ਼ਾ, ਗਰਮ-ਗਰਮ, ਨਵੀਆਂ; ~brained, ~headed ਗਰਮ ਮਿਜ਼ਾਜ, ਕਰੋਧੀ; ~line ਸੰਕਟਕਾਲੀ ਸੰਚਾਰ ਸਾਧਨ; ~water ਮੁਸੀਬਤ; ~ness ਗਰਮੀ, ਤਾਪ, ਤੀਖਣਤਾ, ਕਰੋਧ, ਪ੍ਰਚੰਡਤਾ

hotel (ਹਅ(ਉ)'ਟੈੱਲ) *n* ਤੋਜਨ ਖਾਣ ਦੀ ਥਾਂ, ਕਿਰਾਏ ਤੇ ਰਹਿਣ ਦੀ ਥਾਂ, ਵੱਡੀ ਸਰਾਂ ਜਾਂ ਮੁਸਾਫ਼ਰਖ਼ਾਨਾ

hound (ਹਾਉਂਡ) *n v* ਸ਼ਿਕਾਰੀ ਕੁੱਤਾ; ਨੀਚ ਆਦਮੀ, ਕਮੀਨਾ ਆਦਮੀ; ਕੁੱਤਿਆਂ ਨੂੰ ਲੈ ਕੇ ਸ਼ਿਕਾਰ ਖੇਡਣਾ, ਹੁਸਕਾਰਨਾ, (ਕੁੱਤੇ ਨੂੰ ਸ਼ਿਕਾਰ ਦੇ ਪਿੱਛੇ) ਛੱਡਣਾ

hour ('ਆਉਅ*) *n* ਘੰਟਾ; ਸੱਠ ਮਿੰਟ ਦੇ ਬਰਾਬਰ

house (ਹਾਉਸ) n v (1) ਮਕਾਨ, ਘਰ, ਨਿਵਾਸ-ਸਥਾਨ, ਧਾਮ; ਘਰਬਾਰ; (2) ਖ਼ਾਨਦਾਨ, ਘਰਾਣਾ, ਵੰਸ਼, ਕੁਲ, ਕੁਟੰਬ; ਥਾਂ ਦੇਣੀ, ਠਹਿਰਾਉਣਾ, ਸ਼ਰਨ ਦੇਣਾ, ਉਤਾਰਨਾ, ਗੁਦਾਮ ਵਿਚ ਰੱਖਣਾ; ~hold ਘਰਬਾਰ, ਕੁਟੰਬ, ਗ੍ਰਿਹਸਥ; ~holder ਘਰਬਾਰ ਵਾਲਾ, ਕੁਟੰਬ ਵਾਲਾ, ਗ੍ਰਿਹਸਥੀ (ਮਨੁੱਖ); ~keeper ਗ੍ਰਿਹਿਣੀ, ਸੁਆਣੀ, ਨਿਗਰਾਨ; maid ਨੌਕਰਾਣੀ, ~wife ਗ੍ਰਹਿਣੀ, ਸੁਆਣੀ

housing (ਹਾਉਜ਼ਿੰਡ) n ਸ਼ਰਨ, ਥਾਂ, ਘਰ, ਬਸੇਰਾ

hover (ਹੌਵੁਅ*) n v ਮੰਡਲਾਉਣ; ਦੁਬਧਾ, ਅਨਿਸ਼ਚਾ; ਮੰਡਲਾਉਣਾ, ਚੱਕਰ ਕੱਟਣਾ

how (ਹਾਉ) adv n ਕਿਸ ਤਰ੍ਹਾਂ, ਕਿਵੇਂ, ਕਿਸ ਕਾਰਨ, ਕੀਕਣ, ਕਿੰਦਾਂ, ਕਿਤਨਾ, ਕਿਹਾ, ਕਿੰਨਾ ਕੁ; ~ever ਪਰ ਕੁਝ ਵੀ ਹੋਵੇ, ਹਰ ਹਾਲਤ ਵਿਚ; ਫਿਰ ਵੀ; ਕਿੰਨਾ ਹੀ; ~soever ਜਿਵੇਂ ਕਿਵੇਂ, ਜਿਉਂ ਤਿਉਂ, ਜਿਹਾ-ਕਿਹਾ; ਕਿਵੇਂ ਨਾ ਕਿਵੇਂ, ਕਿਸੇ ਤਰ੍ਹਾਂ ਵੀ

howl (ਹਾਉਲ) n v ਅਰੁਕ, ਚੀਖ, ਆਵਾਜ਼; ਆਹ ਦਾ ਨਾਅਰਾ; ਹਾਸੇ ਠੱਠੇ ਦੀ ਆਵਾਜ਼; (ਗਾਲਵਾਂ ਦਾ) ਹਵਾਂਕਣਾ, ਅੜੁਕਣਾ, ਚਾਂਗਰਨਾ, ਭੌਂਕਣਾ; (ਆਦਮੀਆਂ ਦਾ) ਦਰਦ ਨਾਲ ਚੀਖਣਾ, ਚਿੱਲਾ ਕੇ ਰੋਣਾ; ~ing ਚੀਕ ਚਿਹਾੜਾ, ਹਾਲ ਪਾਹਰਿਆ; ~er ਚਿਲਾਉਣ ਵਾਲਾ; ਘੋਰ ਗ਼ਲਤੀ

howlet (ਹਾਉਲਿਟ) n ਉੱਲੂ, ਉੱਲੂ ਦਾ ਬੱਚਾ

hub (ਹੱਬ) n (ਪਹੀਏ ਦੀ) ਨਾਭ, ਨਾਭੀ, ਧੁਰਾ, ਵਿਚਕਾਰ ਦਾ ਹਿੱਸਾ; ਕੇਂਦਰ

hubble-bubble (ਹੱਬਲ-ਬੱਬਲ) n ਹੁੱਕਾ, ਗੁੜਗੁੜੀ; ਹੁੱਕੇ ਦੀ ਗੁੜਗੁੜ

huddle (ਹੱਡਲ) n v (ਲੋਕਾਂ ਦਾ) ਉੱਗੜ-ਦੁੱਗੜ ਇਕੱਠ; ਗੜਬੜ, ਖੜਮੱਸ, ਭੀੜ-ਭਾੜ, ਉੱਗੜ-ਦੁੱਗੜ; ਢੇਰ ਲਗਾ ਦੇਣਾ

hue (ਹਯੂ) n (1) ਰੰਗ, ਛਬ, ਆਭਾ, ਰੰਗਤ; (2) ਸ਼ੋਰ, ਹੱਲਾ-ਗੁੱਲਾ, ਚਿਲਾਹਟ; ~less ਰੰਗਹੀਨ

huff (ਹੱਫ) n v ਰੋਹ, ਗੁੱਸਾ, ਤਾਅ, ਕਾਵੜਾ; ਸ਼ੇਖ਼ੀ ਮਾਰਨੀ; ਤੈਸ਼ ਵਿਚ ਆਉਣਾ, ਗੁੱਸੇ ਵਿਚ ਹੋਣਾ; ਨਾਰਾਜ਼ ਕਰਨਾ

hug (ਹੱਗ) n v ਜੱਫੀ, ਗਲ ਲਾਉਣਾ, ਕਲਾਵੇ ਵਿਚ ਲੈਣਾ, ਜੱਫੀ ਪਾਉਣੀ; ਕਾਇਮ ਰਹਿਣਾ, ਆਪਣੇ ਮੂੰਹ ਮੀਆਂ-ਮਿੱਠੂ ਬਣਨਾ

huge (ਹਯੂਜ) a ਬਹੁਤ ਵੱਡਾ, ਵਿਸ਼ਾਲ, ਵਿਰਾਟ, ਭਾਰੀ; ~ly ਵਿਸ਼ਾਲ ਰੂਪ ਵਿਚ

hull (ਹੱਲ) n v ਛਿਲਕਾ, ਛਿਲੜ, ਫੋਕੜ, ਖੋਖਾ, ਖੋਲ; ਜਹਾਜ਼ ਦਾ ਢਾਂਚਾ, ਪੜ; ਛਿਲਕਾ, ਛਿਲਕਾ ਲਾਹੁਣਾ; ਪਰਦਾ ਲਾਹੁਣਾ, ਪਰੇ ਕਰਨਾ, ਹਟਾਉਣਾ

hum (ਹੱਮ) n v int ਭਿਣਕ, ਭਿਣ-ਭਿਣ, ਭੀਂ-ਭੀਂ, ਭਿਣਭਿਣਾਹਟ, ਘੂੰ-ਘੂੰ, ਹੈਰਾਨੀ ਦੀ ਅਵਾਜ਼; ~ming ਭਿਣ-ਭਿਣ ਕਰਨ ਵਾਲਾ, ਗੂੰਜਣ ਵਾਲਾ

human (ਹਯੂਮਅਨ) n a ਮਨੁੱਖ, ਮਾਨਵ, ਇਨਸਾਨ; ਮਨੁੱਖੀ, ਇਨਸਾਨੀ, ਮਾਨਵੀ; ~being ਮਾਨਵ, ਇਨਸਾਨ; ~kind ਮਾਨਵ ਜਾਤੀ; ~ism ਮਾਨਵਤਾ, ਮੈਤਰੀ-ਭਾਵ, ਇਨਸਾਨੀ ਦੋਸਤੀ; ਮਾਨਵਵਾਦ; ਮਾਨਵ-ਵਿੱਦਿਆ; ~itraian ਮਨੁੱਖਤਾਵਾਦੀ, ਖਲਕ-ਦੋਸਤ, ਜਨ-ਸੇਵੀ, ਲੋਕ-ਉਪਕਾਰੀ; ~itarianism ਮਾਨਵਹਿਤਵਾਦ, ਪਰਉਪਕਾਰਵਾਦ, ਜਨ-ਸੇਵਾਵਾਦ; ~ity ਮਨੁੱਖਤਾ, ਆਦਮਜਾਤ, ਮਾਨਵਤਾ, ਮਨੁੱਖਜਾਤੀ; ਹਮਦਰਦੀ, ਦਰਦਵੰਦੀ, ਦਿਆਲਤਾ; ~ize ਮਨੁੱਖੀ ਰੂਪ ਦੇਣਾ, ਆਦਮੀ ਬਣਾਉਣਾ, ਮਨੁੱਖਤਾ ਸਿਖਾਉਣਾ, ਇਨਸਾਨੀ ਸਿਫ਼ਤਾਂ ਵਾਲਾ ਬਣਾਉਣਾ; ~ness

ਇਨਸਾਨੀਅਤ, ਮਾਨਵਤਾ, ਮਨੁੱਖਤਾ

humane (ਹਯੂ'ਮੇਇਨ) *a* ਦਿਆਲੂ, ਮਾਨਵ ਹਿਤੈਸ਼ੀ; ਹਮਦਰਦ, ਮੈਤਰੀ ਭਾਵ ਵਾਲਾ, ਤਰਸਵਾਨ, ਨਰਮਦਿਲ; **~ness** ਦਇਆਲਤਾ, ਕਿਰਪਾਲਤਾ, ਮਾਨਵੀਯਤਾ, ਸੁੰਦਰਤਾ

humble ('ਹਅੱਮਬਲ) *a v* ਨਿਮਾਣਾ, ਮਸਕੀਨ, ਨਾਚੀਜ਼, ਘਮੰਡ ਰਹਿਤ, ਨਿਰਹੰਕਾਰ; ਤੁੱਛ; ਮਾਣ ਤੋੜਨਾ, ਹੀਣ ਕਰਨਾ, ਨੀਵਾਂ ਕਰਨਾ, ਨਿਵਾਉਣਾ; **~ness** ਤੁੱਛਤਾ, ਸਧਾਰਨਤਾ, ਮਾਮੂਲੀਪਣ; ਨਿਮਰਤਾ

humbug ('ਹਅੱਮਬਅੱਗ) *n a v* ਦੰਭ, ਪਖੰਡ, ਧੋਖਾ, ਠੱਗੀ; ਬਕਵਾਸ, ਊਟਪਟਾਂਗ, ਉਲ-ਜਲੂਲ ਧੋਖਾ ਦੇਣਾ, ਠੱਗਣਾ; ਛਲਣਾ; **~gery** ਛਲ, ਕਪਟ

humdrum ('ਹਅੱਮਡਰਅੱਮ) *n a* ਨੀਰਸਤਾ, ਫਿੱਕਾਪਣ; ਤੁੱਛ ਵਿਅਕਤੀ; ਨੀਰਸ, ਫਿੱਕਾ, ਬੇਸੁਆਦਾ, ਸਧਾਰਨ

humiliate (ਹਯੂ'ਮਿਲਿਏਇਟ) *v* ਮਾਣ ਤੋੜਨਾ, ਨੀਵਾਂ ਦਿਖਾਉਣਾ, ਬੇਇੱਜ਼ਤ ਕਰਨਾ, ਜਲੀਲ ਕਰਨਾ

humiliating (ਹਯੂ'ਮਿਲਿਏਇਟਿਙ) *a* ਬੇਇੱਜ਼ਤੀ ਭਰਿਆ, ਹੇਠਾ, ਤੁੱਛ, ਅਪਮਾਨਜਨਕ

humiliation (ਹਯੂ'ਮਿਲਿ'ਏਇਸ਼ਨ) *n* ਬੇਇੱਜ਼ਤੀ, ਅਪਮਾਨ, ਤਿਰਸਕਾਰ

humility (ਹਯੂ'ਮਿਲਅਟਿ) *n* ਨਿਮਰਤਾ, ਅਧੀਨਗੀ, ਨਿਰਮਾਣਤਾ; ਦੀਨਤਾ

humorous ('ਹਯੂਮਅਰਅਸ) *a* ਵਿਨੋਦਮਈ, ਹਾਸੇ ਭਰਿਆ, ਮਸਖਰਾ, ਮਜ਼ਾਕੀਆ

humour, humor ('ਹਯੂਮਅ*) *n* ਹਾਸ-ਰਸ; ਵਿਲਾਸ, ਵਿਨੋਦ, ਮੌਜ, ਲਹਿਰ, ਮਜ਼ਾਕ; ਸੁਭਾਅ, ਮਿਜਾਜ਼

hunger ('ਹਅੱਙਗਅ*) *n v* ਭੁੱਖ, ਭੋਖੜਾ, ਹਾਬੜੀ; ਤੀਬਰ ਇਛਿਆ, ਭੁੱਖਾ ਹੋਣਾ, ਭੁੱਖ ਲੱਗਣੀ, ਫਾਕੇ ਕਰਾਉਣੇ

hungriness ('ਹਅੱਙਗਰਿਨਿਸ) *n* ਭੁੱਖਾਪਣ

hungry ('ਹਅੱਙਗਰਿ) *a* ਭੁੱਖਾ, ਭੁੱਖਾ-ਭਾਣਾ; ਭੁੱਖੜ, ਲਾਲਸਾਵਾਨ

hunt (ਹਅੱਟ) *n v* ਸ਼ਿਕਾਰ, ਤਲਾਸ਼, ਖੋਜ, ਪਿੱਛਾ; **~er** ਸ਼ਿਕਾਰੀ, ਸ਼ਿਕਾਰੀ ਕੁੱਤਾ; **~ing** ਸ਼ਿਕਾਰ

hurdle ('ਹਅੱਡਲ) *n* ਰੋਕ, ਰੁਕਾਵਟ, ਅੜਿੱਕਾ, ਬਾਧਾ, ਅੜੀ, ਜੰਗਲਾ

hurl (ਹਅੱਲ) *n v* (ਪੱਥਰ ਆਦਿ) ਵਗਾਹ ਕੇ ਸੁੱਟਣਾ; ਧੱਕਣਾ, ਡੇਗ ਦੇਣਾ; ਸੋਟ, ਉਛਾਲ

hurrah, hurra (ਹੁ'ਰਾ) *int n* (ਪ੍ਰਸੰਸਾ ਤੇ ਖ਼ੁਸ਼ੀ ਦੇ ਪਰਗਟਾਉ ਵਜੋਂ) ਆਹਾ!, ਵਾਹ-ਵਾਹ!, ਵਾਹਵਾ; ਜੈਕਾਰਾ, ਹਰਸ-ਨਾਦ

hurricane ('ਹਅੱਰਿਕਅਨ) *n* ਤੂਫ਼ਾਨ, ਝੱਖੜ

hurried ('ਹਅੱਰਿਡ) *a* ਝਬਦੇ, ਤੁਰਤ; ਸ਼ੀਘਰ, ਉਤਾਵਲਾ; **~ness** ਸ਼ੀਘਰਤਾ, ਜਲਦਬਾਜ਼ੀ, ਫੁਰਤੀ, ਉਤਾਵਲਾਪਨ

hurry ('ਹਅੱਰਿ) *n* ਜਲਦੀ, ਛੇਤੀ, ਜਲਦਬਾਜ਼ੀ, ਕਾਹਲੀ, ਉਤਾਵਲ, ਬੇਚੈਨੀ

hurt (ਹਅੱਟ) *n v a* ਸੱਟ, ਜ਼ਰਬ, ਚੋਟ; ਘਾਉ, ਜ਼ਖ਼ਮ, ਸਦਮਾ, ਨੁਕਸਾਨ; ਜ਼ਖ਼ਮੀ ਕਰਨਾ; ਦੁੱਖ ਪਹੁੰਚਾਉਣਾ, ਦਰਦ ਹੋਣਾ

hurtle ('ਹਅੱਟਲ) *v* ਭਿੜਨਾ; ਰਿੜ੍ਹਨਾ, ਰੇੜ੍ਹਨਾ; ਪਰਬੰਮ ਕਰਕੇ ਡਿਗਣਾ

husband ('ਹਅੱਜ਼ਬਅੰਡ) *n v* ਪਤੀ, ਘਰ ਵਾਲਾ, ਖਾਵੰਦ, ਕੰਤ, ਸੁਆਮੀ; **~ry** ਕਿਸਾਨੀ, ਵਾਹੀ-ਖੇਤੀ, ਖੇਤੀ, ਕਾਸ਼ਤਕਾਰੀ, ਕਾਸ਼ਤਕਾਰੀ, ਕਾਸ਼ਤ, ਘਰੇਲੂ ਪ੍ਰਬੰਧ; **animal ~ry** ਪਸ਼ੂ-ਪਾਲਣ

hush (ਹਅੱਸ਼) *v int* ਚੁੱਪ-ਚਾਂ, ਸ਼ਾਂਤੀ, ਖ਼ਮੋਸ਼ੀ; ਚੁੱਪ ਕਰਾਉਣਾ ਜਾਂ ਹੋਣਾ, ਦੜ ਵੱਟਣੀ, ਸ਼ਾਂਤ ਕਰਨਾ

husk (ਹਅੱਸਕ) *n v* ਛਿਲਕਾ, ਭੂਸੀ, ਫੱਕ, ਸੂਹਤ

ਛਿਲੜ; ਛਿਲਕਾ ਲਾਹੁਣਾ, ਛੱਟਣਾ, ਛੜਨਾ, ਛਿਲਕਾ; **~ed** ਛਿਲਕੇਦਾਰ

hustle (ਹੱਸਲ) *n v* ਧਕੰਮ-ਧੱਕਾ, ਟੱਕਰ, ਜਲਦੀ, ਤੀਬਰਤਾ; ਜ਼ੋਰ ਨਾਲ ਧੱਕਾ ਮਾਰਨਾ, ਧੱਕਮ-ਧੱਕਾ ਕਰਨਾ

hut (ਹੱਟ) *n v* ਝੁੱਗੀ, ਝੌਂਪੜੀ, ਟੱਪਰੀ, ਛੱਪਰੀ, ਕੁੱਲੀ, (ਸੈਨਾ) ਪੜਾਉ, ਅਸਥਾਈ ਟਿਕਾਣਾ; ਝੁੱਗੀ ਵਿਚ ਰਹਿਣਾ ਜਾਂ ਰੱਖਣਾ; **~ment** ਫ਼ੌਜਾਂ ਲਈ ਲੱਕੜੀ ਦਾ ਮਕਾਨ, ਬੈਰਕ, ਡੇਰਾ

hyaena, hyena (ਹਾਇ'ਈਨਾ) *n* ਲੱਕੜਬੱਗਾ, ਬਘਿਆੜ ਵਰਗਾ ਇਕ ਮਾਸਖੋਰਾ ਜੰਗਲੀ ਪਸ਼ੂ; (ਅਲੰਕਾਰਕ) ਜ਼ਾਲਮ, ਬੇਰਹਿਮ, ਨਿਰਦਈ ਮਨੁੱਖ

hybrid ('ਹਾਇਬਰਿਡ) *n a* ਦੋਗਲਾਪਣ, ਦੋਗਲਾ, ਦੋ-ਨਸਲਾ; **~ism, ~ity** ਦੋਗਲਾਪਣ; **~ize** ਦੋ-ਨਸਲਾ ਜਾਂ ਦੋਗਲਾ ਬਣਾਉਣਾ

hygiene ('ਹਾਇਜੀਨ) *n* ਸਿਹਤ-ਵਿਗਿਆਨ, ਅਰੋਗ-ਵਿਗਿਆਨ; ਸਰੀਰ ਰੱਖਿਆ ਨਿਯਮ

hymn (ਹਿਮ) *n v* ਭਜਨ, ਪੂਜਾ ਦੇ ਗੀਤ, ਸ਼ਬਦ; ਭਜਨ ਕਰਨਾ; ਸ਼ਬਦ ਗਾਉਣਾ

hypocrisy (ਹਿ'ਪੌਕਰਅਸਿ) *n* ਪਖੰਡ, ਛਲ, ਦੰਭ, ਮੋਮੋਠਗਣੀ

hypocrite ('ਹਿਪਅਕਰਿਟ) *n* (ਵਿਅਕਤੀ) ਕਪਟੀ, ਪਖੰਡੀ, ਛਲੀਆ, ਦੰਭੀ, ਮੱਕਾਰ

hypothesis (ਹਾਇ'ਪੌਥਿਸਿਸ) *n* ਅਨੁਮਾਨ, ਕਲਪਨਾ; ਮਿਥੀ ਸਥਾਪਨਾ, ਫ਼ਰਜ਼ੀ ਮਨੌਤ, ਕਲਪਤ ਵਿਚਾਰ, ਪਰਿਕਲਪਨਾ

hysteria (ਹਿ'ਸਟਿਅਰਿਅ) *n* ਝੱਲ, ਪਾਗਲਪਣ, ਉਨਮਾਦ

I

I, i (ਆਇ) ਰੋਮਨ ਵਰਣਮਾਲਾ ਦਾ ਨੌਵਾਂ ਅੱਖਰ

I *pron n* ਮੈਂ, ਅਹੰ; ਹਉਂ, ਆਪਾ, ਅਹੰਵਾਦ

ibidem, ibid ('ਇਬਿਡੈੱਮ, 'ਇਬਿਡ) (L) *adv* ਉਹੀ, ਉਕਤ, ਉਸੇ (ਪੁਸਤਕ, ਅਧਿਆਇ ਜਾਂ ਪੈਰੇ) ਵਿਚ

ice (ਆਇਸ) *n v* ਬਰਫ਼, ਹਿਮ; (ਬ ਵ) ਕੁਲਫ਼ੀ, ਆਈਸ ਕ੍ਰੀਮ; ਬਰਫ਼ ਵਿਚ ਲਾ ਕੇ ਠੰਢਾ ਕਰਨਾ; **~berg** ਬਰਫ਼ ਦਾ ਤੋਦਾ, ਹਿਮ-ਪਰਬਤ; ਭਾਵਹੀਣ ਮਨੁੱਖ

icon ('ਆਇਕੌਨ) *n* ਬੁੱਤ, ਮੂਰਤੀ, ਚਿੱਤਰ; **~oclasm** ਬੁੱਤ-ਭੰਜਨ, ਮੂਰਤੀ-ਖੰਡਨ; **~ography** ਮੂਰਤੀ ਕਲਾ; **~olater** ਮੂਰਤੀ ਪੂਜਕ, ਬੁੱਤ ਪੂਜਾ ਕਰਨ ਵਾਲਾ; **~olatry** ਮੂਰਤੀ-ਪੂਜਾ-ਵਿਰੋਧ

idea (ਆਇ'ਡ੍ਰਿਅ) *n* ਵਿਚਾਰ, ਖ਼ਿਆਲ, ਆਸ਼ਾ, ਭਾਵ; ਮਾਨਸਕ ਰੂਪ-ਰੇਖਾ, ਢਾਂਚਾ, ਨਕਸ਼ਾ; ਯੋਜਨਾ, ਤਜਵੀਜ਼, ਯੁਕਤੀ

ideal (ਆਇ'ਡ੍ਰਿਅਲ) *a n* ਆਦਰਸ਼, ਨਮੂਨੇ ਦਾ, ਪ੍ਰਮਾਣਕ; ਖ਼ਿਆਲੀ, ਆਦਰਸ਼, ਵਿਚਾਰ-ਪਰਦਰਸ਼ਕ; **~ism** ਆਦਰਸ਼ਵਾਦ, ਕਲਪਨਾਵਾਦ; **~ist** ਆਦਰਸ਼ਵਾਦੀ, ਕਲਪਨਾਵਾਦੀ; **~ize** ਆਦਰਸ਼ਿਉਣਾ, ਆਦਰਸ਼ ਰੂਪ ਦੇਣਾ

identic (ਆਇ'ਡੈਂਟਿਕ) *a* ਠੀਕ ਉਹੋ ਜਿਹਾ, ਸਗਵਾਂ, ਸਮਾਨ, ਸਰਬਾਂਗ, ਸਮ

identification (ਆਇ'ਡੈਂਟਿਫ਼ਿ'ਕੇਇਸ਼ਨ) *n* ਪਛਾਣ, ਸ਼ਨਾਖ਼ਤ, ਅਭੇਦਤਾ, ਤਦਰੂਪਤਾ

identity (ਆਇ'ਡੈਂਟਅਟਿ) *n* ਪਛਾਣ; ਅਭੇਦਤਾ, ਇਕਾਤਮਕਤਾ, ਤਦਰੂਪਤਾ, ਇਕਰੂਪਤਾ, ਸਮਾਨਤਾ

ideologist ('ਆਇਡਿ'ਔਲਅਜਿਸਟ) *n* ਵਿਚਾਰ-ਵੇਤਾ, ਸਿੱਧਾਂਤਕਾਰ

ideology ('ਆਇਡਿ'ਔਲਅਜਿ) *n* ਭਾਵ-ਵਿਗਿਆਨ, ਵਿਚਾਰਧਾਰਾ, ਵਿਚਾਰ-ਪੱਧਤੀ, ਚਿੰਤਨ-ਸ਼ੈਲੀ, ਭਾਵ-ਪ੍ਰਣਾਲੀ; ਸਿਧਾਂਤ-ਸਮੂਹ

idiom ('ਇਡਿਅਮ) *n* ਮੁਹਾਵਰਾ; ਬੋਲ-ਚਾਲ, ਭਾਸ਼ਾ ਦੀ ਕੋਈ ਵਿਸ਼ੇਸ਼ਤਾ; **~atic** ਮੁਹਾਵਰੇਦਾਰ, ਠੇਠ; ਬੋਲ-ਚਾਲ ਸਬੰਧੀ

idiot ('ਇਡਿਅਟ) *n* ਮੂਰਖ, ਮੂੜ੍ਹ, ਅਹਿਮਕ, ਬੁੱਧੂ, ਬੁਝੜ; **~ic** ਮੂਰਖਤਾ ਭਰਿਆ, ਅਹਿਮਕਾਨਾ

idle ('ਆਇਡਲ) *a v* ਵਿਹਲਾ, ਬੇਕਾਰ, ਨਿਕੰਮਾ, ਨਕਾਰਾ, ਆਲਸੀ, ਸੁਸਤ; ਨਿਰਮੂਲ ਹੋਣਾ, ਨਿਰਥਕ ਹੋਣਾ; ਵਿਹਲੇ ਹੋਣਾ, ਬੇਕਾਰ ਹੋਣਾ, ਨਿਕੰਮੇ ਰਹਿਣਾ

idol ('ਆਇਡਲ) *n* ਬੁੱਤ, ਮੂਰਤੀ, ਪ੍ਰਤਿਮਾ; **~ater** ਬੁੱਤ-ਪੂਜ, ਮੂਰਤੀ-ਉਪਾਸ਼ਕ; **~atry** ਬੁੱਤ-ਪੂਜਾ, ਮੂਰਤੀ-ਪੂਜਾ

if (ਇਫ਼) *n conj* ਜੇਕਰ, ਅਗਰ; ਸ਼ਰਤ

ignite (ਇਗ'ਨਾਇਟ) *v* ਅੱਗ ਲਾਉਣੀ ਜਾਂ ਲੱਗਣੀ, ਬਾਲਣਾ ਜਾਂ ਬਲਣਾ; ਚੁਆਤੀ ਲਾਉਣੀ, ਬਲ ਉੱਠਣਾ, ਭਖਾਉਣਾ

ignition (ਇਗ'ਨਿਸ਼ਨ) *n* ਸੜਨ, ਬਲਣ, ਜਲਣ, ਭਖਣ

ignoble (ਇਗ'ਨਅਉਬਲ) *a* ਨੀਚ ਜਾਤ ਵਾਲਾ, ਹੀਣੀ ਜਾਤ ਦਾ, ਅਕੁਲੀਨ; ਕਮੀਨਾ, ਹੀਣਾ, ਨੀਚ, ਹੋਛਾ

ignorance ('ਇਗਨ(ਅ)ਰਅੰਸ) *n* ਅਗਿਆਨ, ਬੇਸਮਝੀ, ਨਾਦਾਨੀ

ignorant ('ਇਗਨ(ਅ)ਰਅੰਟ) *a* ਅਗਿਆਨੀ, ਅਲਪੱਗ, ਅਟਜਾਣ, ਬੇਸਮਝ, ਨਾਦਾਨ, ਅਬੋਧ, ਮੁਰਖ, ਮੁਟ੍

ill (ਇਲ) *a n adv* ਬੀਮਾਰ, ਰੋਗੀ, ਅਸੁਅਸਥ; ਬੁਰਾ, ਭੈੜਾ; ਨਾਮੁਆਫ਼ਕ, ਅਸ਼ੁਭ; ਦੁਖਦਾਈ; ਮੁਸ਼ਕਲ; ਕੋਝ; ਅਸੰਗਤ; ਅਨੁਚਿਤ; ਬੁਰਾਈ, ਭੈੜ, ਦੋਸ਼; ਵਿਕਾਰ, ਵਿਗਾੜ; ~**bred** ਕੁਚੱਜਾ, ਭੈੜਾ, ਬਦਤਮੀਜ਼; ~**favoured** ਕੋਝਾ, ਬਦਸ਼ਕਲ; ~**natured** ਭੈੜੇ ਸੁਭਾਅ ਵਾਲਾ, ਚਿੜਚੜਾ, ਅਵੈੜਾ, ਬਦਮਜਾਜ਼; ~**omened** ਕੁਲੱਗਣਾ, ਬਦਸ਼ਗਣਾ; ~**tempered** ਅਵੈੜ, ਅੜੁਭ, ਕਰੋਪੀ; ~**treat**, ~**use** ਬਦਸਲੂਕੀ ਕਰਨੀ; ~**treatment** ਬਦਸਲੂਕੀ, ਦੁਰਵਿਹਾਰ, ਦੁਰਵਰਤੋਂ; ~**ness** ਬੀਮਾਰੀ, ਰੋਗ, ਅਸੁਅਸਥਤਾ; ਬੁਰਾਈ, ਦੋਸ਼

illegal (ਇ'ਲੀਗਲ) *a* ਗ਼ੈਰਕਾਨੂੰਨੀ, ਅਵੈਧ, ਨਾਜਾਇਜ਼; ~**ity** ਅਵੈਧਤਾ

illegibillity (ਇ'ਲੈਜਿ'ਬਿਲਅਟਿ) *n* (ਪੜ੍ਹਨ ਵਿਚ) ਅਸਪਸ਼ਟਤਾ

illegible (ਇ'ਲੈਂਜਅਬਲ) *a* ਅਸਪਸ਼ਟ, ਜਿਹੜਾ ਚੰਗੀ ਤਰ੍ਹਾਂ ਪੜ੍ਹਿਆ ਨਾ ਜਾ ਸਕੇ

illegitimacy ('ਇਲਿ'ਜਿਟਅਮਅਸਿ) *n* ਅਯੋਗਤਾ, ਅਨੁਚਿਤਤਾ, ਹਰਾਮੀਪਨ

illegitimate (ਇਲਿ'ਜਿਟਿਮਅਟ) *a* ਅਯੋਗ, ਨਾਮੁਨਾਸਬ; ਗ਼ੈਰਕਾਨੂੰਨੀ, ਅਵੈਧ; ਹਰਾਮੀ

illicit (ਇ'ਲਿਸਿਟ) *a* ਵਰਜਤ, ਗ਼ੈਰਕਾਨੂੰਨੀ; ਅਨੁਚਿਤ, ਨਾਮੁਨਾਸਬ, ਨਾਜਾਇਜ਼

illiteracy (ਇ'ਲਿਟ(ਅ)ਰਅਸਿ) *n* ਅਨਪੜ੍ਹਤਾ, ਨਿਰੱਖਰਤਾ

illiterate (ਇ'ਲਿਟ(ਅ)ਰਅਟ) *a* ਅਨਪੜ੍ਹ, ਅਸਿੱਖਿਅਤ, ਉਜੱਡ

illogical (ਇ'ਲੌਜਿਕਲ) *a* ਤਰਕਹੀਨ, ਤਰਕ-ਵਿਰੁੱਧ, ਨਿਆਂਵਿਰੁੱਧ, ਅਸੰਗਤ, ਅਢੁੱਕਵਾਂ

illuminate (ਇ'ਲੂਮਿਨੇਇਟ) *v* ਚਾਨਣ ਕਰਨਾ, ਰੌਸ਼ਨ ਕਰਨਾ, ਪ੍ਰਕਾਸ਼ਮਾਨ ਕਰਨਾ, ਜ਼ਾਹਰ ਕਰਨੀ

illumination (ਇ'ਲ੍ਯੂਮਿ'ਨੇਇਸ਼ਨ) *n* ਚਾਨਣ, ਪ੍ਰਕਾਸ਼, ਰੌਸ਼ਨੀ

illumine (ਇ'ਲੂਮਿਨ) *v* ਗਿਆਨ ਦੇਣਾ, ਸੋਝੀ ਕਰਾਉਣੀ; ਚਾਨਣ ਕਰਨਾ, ਰੌਸ਼ਨੀ ਕਰਨੀ, ਪ੍ਰਕਾਸ਼ਮਾਨ ਕਰਨਾ

illusion (ਇ'ਲੂਯ਼ਨ) *n* ਭਰਮ, ਵਹਿਮ, ਭੁਲਾਵਾ; ਛਲ; ਮਾਇਆ, ਇੰਦਰ-ਜਾਲ, ਭੁਲੇਖਾ; ~**ism** ਮਾਇਆਵਾਦੀ, ਭਰਮਵਾਦ

illusive (ਇ'ਲੂਸਿਵ਼) *a* (ਸਿੱਖਿਆ) ਭਰਮਾਤਮਕ, ਭੁਲਾਵਾ, ਛਲਰੂਪ

illusory (ਇ'ਲੂਸਅਰਿ) *a* ਭਰਮ ਪਾਉਣ ਵਾਲਾ, ਭਰਮ ਉਪਜਾਊ; ਮਾਇਆਮਈ, ਛਲਰੂਪ

illustrate ('ਇਲਅਸਟਰੇਇਟ) *v* ਸਪਸ਼ਟ ਕਰਨਾ, ਉਦਾਹਰਨ ਦੇ ਕੇ ਸਮਝਾਉਣਾ, ਚਿੱਤਰਾਂ ਨਾਲ ਸਮਝਾਉਣਾ; ਵਿਆਖਿਆ ਕਰਨੀ, ਚਿੱਤਰਾਨੁਕਤ ਕਰਨਾ; ~**d** ਉਦਾਹਰਨਯੁਕਤ, ਸਚਿੱਤਰ

illustration ('ਇਲਅ'ਸਟਰੇਇਸ਼ਨ) *n* ਵਿਆਖਿਆ, ਸਪਸ਼ਟੀਕਰਨ, ਉਦਾਹਰਨ, ਮਿਸਾਲ, ਦ੍ਰਿਸ਼ਟਾਂਤ; ਚਿੱਤਰ, ਤਸਵੀਰ

illustrative ('ਇਲਅਸਟਰਅਟਿਵ਼) *a* ਚਿੱਤਰਮਈ; ਉਦਾਹਰਨਯੁਕਤ; ਦ੍ਰਿਸ਼ਟਾਂਤਯੁਕਤ; ਵਿਆਖਿਆ ਵਾਲਾ

illustrious (ਇ'ਲਅਸਟਰਿਅਸ) *n* ਪ੍ਰਸਿੱਧ, ਮਸ਼ਹੂਰ, ਨਾਮੀ, ਨੇਕਨਾਮ, ਕੀਰਤੀਵਾਨ, ਜਸਵੰਤ; ~**ness** ਕੀਰਤੀ, ਪ੍ਰਸਿੱਧੀ, ਜਸ, ਗੌਰਵ

image ('ਇਮਿਜ) *n v* ਸ਼ਕਲ, ਆਕਾਰ, ਰੂਪ, ਤਸਵੀਰ; ਮੂਰਤੀ, ਪ੍ਰਤਿਮਾ; ਪ੍ਰਤਿਬਿੰਬ, ਬਿੰਬ, ਹੂ-ਬਹੂ ਉਤਾਰਾ; ਚਿੱਤਰ ਬਣਾਉਣਾ, ਮੂਰਤੀ ਬਣਾਉਣੀ; ਮੂਰਤੀਮਾਨ ਕਰਨਾ, ਕੋਈ ਰੂਪ ਦੇਣਾ; ਕਲਪਨਾ ਕਰਨੀ, ਖ਼ਿਆਲ ਬੰਨ੍ਹਣਾ; ~**ry** ਅਲੰਕਾਰ, ਅਲੰਕਾਰਮਈ ਚਿੱਤਰਨ ਜਾਂ ਨਿਰੂਪਣ, ਬਿੰਬਾਵਲੀ, ਬਿੰਬ-ਵਿਧਾਨ, ਮੂਰਤੀ-ਨਿਰਮਾਣ

imaginary (ਇ'ਮੈਜਿਨ(ਅ)ਰਿ) *a* ਖ਼ਿਆਲੀ, ਕਲਪਤ, ਕਿਆਸੀ, ਕਾਲਪਨਕ, ਮਨਘੜੰਤ

imagination (ਇ'ਮੈਜਿ'ਨੇਇਸ਼ਨ) *n* ਕਲਪਨਾ, ਭਾਵਨਾ, ਸੰਕਲਪ, ਕਲਪਨਾ, ਸ਼ਕਤੀ, ਨਿਰੂਪਣ-ਸ਼ਕਤੀ, ਤਸੱਵਰ

imaginative (ਇ'ਮੈਜਿਨਅਟਿਵ) *a* ਕਲਪਨਾਮਈ, ਕਲਪਤ, ਭਾਵਨਾਪੂਰਨ, ਭਾਵਨਾਮਈ, ਉਸਾਰੂ ਖ਼ਿਆਲ

imagine (ਇ'ਮੈਜਿਨ) *v* ਕਲਪਨਾ ਕਰਨੀ, ਵਿਚਾਰ ਕਰਨਾ, ਖ਼ਿਆਲ ਬੰਨ੍ਹਣਾ, ਸੋਚਣਾ; ਅਨੁਮਾਨ ਲਾਉਣਾ, ਖ਼ਿਆਲ-ਉਡਾਰੀ ਲਾਉਣੀ;

imagism ('ਇਮਿਜਿਜ਼(ਅ)ਮ) *n* ਬਿੰਬਵਾਦ, ਚਿੱਤਰਨ-ਵਾਦ

imbibe (ਇਮ'ਬਾਇਬ) *v* ਗ੍ਰਹਿਣ ਕਰਨਾ, ਲੈ ਲੈਣਾ; ਮਨ ਵਿਚ ਧਾਰਨ ਕਰਨਾ, ਦਿਲ ਵਿਚ ਵਸਾਉਣਾ, ਆਪਣੇ ਅੰਦਰ ਰਚਾ ਲੈਣਾ; ਜਜ਼ਬ ਕਰ ਲੈਣਾ

imbroglio (ਇਮ'ਬਰਅਉਗਲਿਅਉ) *n* ਝਮੇਲਾ, ਝੰਜਟ, ਉਲਝਣ, ਔਕੜ, ਭੈੜੀ ਅਵਸਥਾ

imitate ('ਇਮਿਟੇਇਟ) *v* ਨਕਲ ਕਰਨੀ, ਸਾਂਗ ਲਾਉਣੀ, ਅਨੁਕਰਣ ਕਰਨਾ; ਅਨੁਸਰਣ ਕਰਨਾ, ਕਦਮਾਂ ਤੇ ਚੱਲਣਾ, ਰੀਸ ਕਰਨੀ; ਨਕਲ ਉਤਾਰਨੀ

imitation ('ਇਮਿ'ਟੇਇਸ਼ਨ) *n* ਨਕਲ, ਸਾਂਗ, ਅਨੁਕਰਣ; ਰੀਸ; ਨਕਲੀ, ਪ੍ਰਤੀਲਿਪੀ

imitative ('ਇਮਿਟਅਟਿਵ੍) *a* ਨਕਲੀ (ਜੋ ਮੌਲਕ ਨਹੀਂ), ਅਨੁਕਰਨੀ, ਅਨੁਕਰਣਾਤਮਕ, ਬਣਾਉਟੀ; ਨਕਲੀਆ

imitator ('ਇਮਿਟੇਇਟਅ*) *n* ਨਕਲੀਆ, ਅਨੁਗਾਮੀ, ਅਨੁਸਾਰੀ

immaculate (ਇ'ਮੈਕਯੁਲਅਟ) *a* ਪਵਿੱਤਰ, ਨਿਰਮਲ, ਸ਼ੁੱਧ, ਪੁਨੀਤ, ਬੇਦਾਗ਼, ਨਿਰਦੋਸ਼

immanence immanency ('ਇਮਅਨਅੰਸ, ਇਮਅਨਅੰਸਿ) *n* (ਪਰਮਾਤਮਾ ਦੀ) ਸਰਵ-ਵਿਆਪਕਤਾ, ਵਿਆਪਕਤਾ, ਅੰਤਰਭੂਤੀ

immanent ('ਇਮਅਨਅੰਟ) *a* ਸਰਵਵਿਆਪੀ, ਵਿਆਪਕ, ਸਰਵਅੰਤਰਜਾਮੀ

immaterial ('ਇਮਅ'ਟਿਅਰਿਅਲ) *a* ਅਸਰੀਰੀ, ਅਮੂਰਤ, ਨਿਗੁਣਾ; ਮਹੱਤਾਹੀਨ, ਮਾਮੂਲੀ

immature ('ਇਮਅ'ਟਯੂਅ*) *a* ਕੱਚਾ, ਅਣਪੱਕ, ਅਪੂਰਨ, ਅਧੂਰਾ, ਅਪ੍ਰੌੜ੍ਹ

immaturity ('ਇਮਅ'ਟਯੂਅਰਅਟਿ) *n* ਕਚਿਆਈ, ਅਪੂਰਤਾ, ਅਪ੍ਰੌੜ੍ਹਤਾ

immeasurable ('ਇ'ਮੈਯ਼(ਅ)ਰਅਬਲ) *a* ਅਮਿਤ, ਬੇਹੱਦ, ਬੇਅੰਤ, ਅਪਾਰ, ਅਨੰਤ, ਅਥਾਹ

immediate (ਇ'ਮੀਡਯਟ) *a* ਫ਼ੌਰੀ, ਤਤਕਾਲਕ, ਤੁਰਤ, ਨਜ਼ਦੀਕੀ, ਅਪਰੋਖ, ਸਿੱਧਾ; ~**ly** ਤਤਕਾਲ, ਤੁਰਤ ਹੀ, ਝੱਟ-ਪਟ; ਉਸੇ ਵੇਲੇ, ਫ਼ੌਰਨ

immemorial ('ਇਮਿ'ਮੋਰਿਅਲ) *a* ਸਮਰਤ-ਅਤੀਤ; ਬਹੁਤ ਪੁਰਾਣਾ, ਕਦੀਮੀ, ਅਤਿ ਪ੍ਰਾਚੀਨ

immense (ਇ'ਮੈਂਸ) *a* ਬੇਹੱਦ, ਅਪਾਰ, ਅਸੀਮ, ਅਮਿਤ; ਬਹੁਤ ਵੱਡਾ

immensity (ਇ'ਮੈਂਸਅਟਿ) ਅਸੀਮਤਾ, ਅਮਿੱਤਤਾ ਅਪਾਰਤਾ; ਵਿਸ਼ਾਲਤਾ, ਮਹਾਨਤਾ; ਉੱਤਮਤਾ

immensurability (ਇਮ'ਮੈਂਨਸੁਰਾ'ਬਿਲਿਅਟਿ) *n* ਅਸੀਮਤਾ, ਵਿਸ਼ਾਲਤਾ, ਉਤਕ੍ਰਿਸ਼ਟਤਾ

immerse (ਇ'ਮਅ:ਸ) *v* ਡੋਬਣਾ, ਡੋਬ ਦੇਣਾ; ਜਲ-ਪਰਵਾਹ ਕਰਨ, ਡੋਬਾ ਦੇਣਾ; ਲੀਨ ਕਰਨ (ਵਿਚਾਰ, ਫ਼ਿਕਰ ਆਦਿ ਵਿਚ) ਮਗਨ ਕਰਨ

immersion (ਇ'ਮਅ:ਸ਼ਨ) *n* ਜਲ-ਪਰਵਾਹ; ਡੋਬਾ, ਗੋਤਾ; ਮਗਨਤਾ, ਲੀਨਤਾ

immigrant ('ਇਮਿਗਰਅੰਟ) *a n* ਆਵਾਸੀ, ਪਰਵਾਸੀ

immigrate ('ਇਮਿਗਰੇਇਟ) *v* ਆ ਵੱਸਣਾ, ਆਵਾਸੀ ਬਣਨਾ

immigration ('ਇਮਿ'ਗਰੇਇਸ਼ਨ) *n* ਆਵਾਸ, ਪਰਵਾਸ

imminence, imminency ('ਇਮਿਨਅੰਸ 'ਇਮਿਨਅੰਸਿ) *n* ਨਿਕਟਤਾ, ਸਮੀਪਤਾ

imminent ('ਇਮਿਨੰਟ) *a* ਹੋਣ ਵਾਲਾ, ਅਟੱਲ, ਸਿਰ ਤੇ ਆਈ (ਬਿਪਤਾ, ਬਲਾ, ਔਕੜ ਆਦਿ), ਕੋਲ ਪੁੱਜਿਆ, ਲਾਗੇ ਹੀ, ਨਿਕਟਵਰਤੀ

immobile (ਇ'ਮਅਉਬਾਇਲ) *a* ਅਚੱਲ, ਸਥਿਰ, ਅਟੱਲ, ਨਿਸ਼ਚਲ

immobility ('ਇਮਅ(ਉ)'ਬਿਲਅਟਿ) *n* ਅਚੱਲਤਾ, ਸਥਿਰਤਾ, ਨਿਸ਼ਚੱਲਤਾ

immobilize (ਇ'ਮਅਉਬਿਲਾਇਜ਼) *v* ਅਚੱਲ ਕਰਨਾ, ਸਥਿਰ ਕਰਨਾ, ਬੇਹਰਕਤ ਕਰਨਾ

immolate ('ਇਮਅ(ਉ)ਲੇਇਟ) *v* ਬਲੀ ਦੇਣੀ; ਕੁਰਬਾਨੀ ਦੇਣੀ, ਆਹੂਤੀ ਦੇਣੀ

immolation ('ਇਮਅ(ਉ)'ਲੇਇਸ਼ਨ) *n* ਬਲੀ, ਕੁਰਬਾਨੀ, ਭੇਟਾ

immoral (ਇ'ਮੌਰ(ਅ)ਲ) *a* ਭ੍ਰਿਸ਼ਟਾਚਾਰੀ, ਦੁਰਵਿਹਾਰੀ, ਬਦ, ਬੁਰਾ, ਅਨੈਤਕ; ਕੁਕਰਮੀ, ਬਦਕਾਰ, ਦੁਰਾਚਾਰੀ, ਬਦਚਲਣ; **~ity** ਬਦਚਲਨੀ, ਬਦੀ, ਭ੍ਰਿਸ਼ਟਤਾ, ਦੁਰਾਚਾਰ, ਆਚਾਰਹੀਣਤਾ, ਅਨੈਤਕਤਾ

immortal (ਇ'ਮੋਟਲ) *a n* ਅਮਰ ਅਵਿਨਾਸ਼ੀ, ਅਕਾਲ; ਅਮਰ ਵਿਅਕਤੀ; **~ity** ਅਮਰਤਵ, ਅਵਿਨਾਸ਼ਤਾ; ਸਦੀਵਤਾ

immovable (ਇ'ਮੂਵਅਬਲ) *a* ਅਚੱਲ, (ਜਾਇਦਾਦ) ਗਤੀਹੀਨ, ਸਥਾਈ, ਅਟੱਲ

immovability (ਇ'ਮੂਵਅ'ਬਿਲਅਟਿ) *n* ਅਚੱਲਤਾ, ਅਹਿਲਤਾ, ਗਤੀਹੀਣਤਾ, ਸਥਿਰਤਾ, ਅਪਰਿਵਰਤਨਸ਼ੀਲਤਾ

immune (ਇ'ਮਯੂਨ) *a* ਮੁਕਤ, ਸੁਰੱਖਿਅਤ

immunity (ਇ'ਮਯੂਨਅਟਿ) *n* ਬਚਾਉ, ਸੁਰੱਖਿਆ; ਛੁਟਕਾਰਾ; ਮੁਕਤੀ

immunize ('ਇਮਯੂਨਾਇਜ਼) *v* (ਰੋਗ ਆਦਿ ਤੋਂ) ਸੁਰੱਖਿਅਤ ਕਰਨਾ, ਬਚਾਉ ਕਰ ਦੇਣਾ, ਛੁਟਕਾਰਾ ਕਰਾਉਣਾ

immutable (ਇ'ਮਯੂਟਅਬਲ) *a* ਅਟੱਲ, ਅਪਰਿਵਰਤਨਸ਼ੀਲ; ਸਥਿਰ, ਨਿਸ਼ਚੱਲ; ਨਿਰਵਿਕਾਰ

impact ('ਇਮਪੈਕਟ) *n v* ਟੱਕਰ, ਧੱਕਾ, ਸੱਟ, ਆਘਾਤ, ਅਸਰ, ਪ੍ਰਭਾਵ; ਟੱਕਰ ਮਾਰਨੀ ਜਾਂ ਮਰਵਾ ਦੇਣੀ

impair (ਇਮ'ਪੇਅ*) *v* ਵਿਗਾੜਨਾ, ਖ਼ਰਾਬ ਕਰਨਾ, ਵਿਕਾਰ ਪਾਉਣਾ, ਤੋੜ-ਮਰੋੜ ਦੇਣਾ; ਕਮਜ਼ੋਰ ਕਰਨਾ; **~ed** ਅਸਮਰਥ

impalpability (ਇਮ'ਪੈਲਪਅ'ਬਿਲਅਟਿ) *n* ਦੁਰਬੋਧਤਾ, ਅਸਪਸ਼ਟਤਾ

impalpable (ਇਮ'ਪੈਲਪਅਬਲ) *a* ਅਗੋਚਰ, ਦੁਰਬੋਧ, ਅਤੀ ਸੂਖਮ

impanel (ਇਮ'ਪੈਨਲ) *v* ਸੂਚੀ (ਲਿਸਟ) ਵਿਚ ਦਾਖ਼ਲ ਕਰਨਾ, ਸੂਚੀ ਵਿਚ ਲਿਖ ਲੈਣਾ

impart (ਇਮ'ਪਾ:ਟ) v ਦੇਣਾ, ਬਖ਼ਸ਼ਣਾ, ਪ੍ਰਦਾਨ ਕਰਨਾ ਦੇਣਾ, ਪ੍ਰਕਾਸ਼ਤ ਕਰਨਾ, ਪਹੁੰਚਾਉਣਾ

impartial (ਇਮ'ਪਾ'ਸ਼ਲ) a ਨਿਰਪੱਖ, ਬੇਲਾਗ; ਨਿਆਂਕਾਰੀ, ਇਨਸਾਫ਼ਪਸੰਦ; ਪੜੇਬਾਜ਼ੀ ਤੋਂ ਉਪਰ, ਸਮਦਰਸ਼ੀ; ~ity ਨਿਰਪੱਖਤਾ, ਸਮਦਰਸ਼ਤਾ; ਨਿਆਂਕਰਤਾ

impassability (ਇਮ'ਪਾਸਅ'ਬਿਲਅਟਿ) n ਦੁਰਗਮਤਾ, ਅਗਮਤਾ

impassable (ਇਮ'ਪਾਸਅਬਲ) a ਦੁਰਗਮ, ਅਗਮ, ਅਲੱਖ

impasse (ਐਮ'ਪਾਸ) n ਬੰਦ ਗਲੀ; ਉਲਝਣ, ਔਕੜ, ਘੋਰ ਸੰਕਟ, ਗਤੀਰੋਧ

impassibility (ਇਮ'ਪਾਸਅ'ਬਿਲਅਟਿ) n ਜੜਤਾ, ਅਚੇਤਨਤਾ, ਭਾਵਹੀਨਤਾ

impassible (ਇਮ'ਪਾਸਅਸਿਬਲ) a ਚੇਤਨਹੀਨ, ਜੜ੍ਹ; ਰਾਗਾਤੀਤ, ਸੁੱਖ-ਦੁੱਖਰਹਿਤ

impassionate (ਇਮ'ਪੈਸ਼ਨਅਟ) a ਆਤੁਰ, ਆਵੇਸ਼ਪੂਰਨ

impassioned (ਇਮ'ਪੈਸ਼ਿੰਡ) a ਜੋਸ਼ੀਲਾ, ਭੜਕਿਆ, ਆਵੇਗਪੂਰਨ, ਆਵੇਸ਼-ਪੂਰਨ

impassive (ਇਮ'ਪੈਸਿਵ) a ਭਾਵਹੀਨ, ਭਾਵਨਾਰਹਿਤ, ਨਿਰਵੇਗ, ਸਥਿਰ, ਅਡੋਲ, ਬੇਹਿਸ

impassivity ('ਇਮਪੈ'ਸਿਵੁਅਟਿ) n ਭਾਵਹੀਨਤਾ, ਨਿਰਵੇਗਤਾ; ਸਥਿਰਤਾ, ਅਡੋਲਤਾ

impatience (ਇਮ'ਪੇਇਸ਼ੰਸ) n ਬੇਸਬਰੀ, ਬੇਤਾਬੀ, ਬੇਚੈਨੀ, ਕਾਹਲ, ਉਤਾਵਲ, ਵਿਆਕੁਲਤਾ

impatient (ਇਮ'ਪੇਇਸ਼ੰਟ) a ਬੇਸਬਰ, ਕਾਹਲਾ, ਬੇਚੈਨ, ਉਤਾਵਲਾ, ਅਧੀਰ, ਵਿਆਕੁਲ

impawn (ਇਮ'ਪੋਨ) v ਗਹਿਣੇ ਪਾਉਣਾ, ਗਿਰਵੀ ਕਰਨਾ, ਰਹਿਨ ਰੱਖਣਾ; ਵਚਨ ਦੇਣਾ

impeach (ਇਮ'ਪੀਚ) v ਦੋਸ਼ ਲਾਉਣਾ, ਨੁਕਤਾਚੀਨੀ ਕਰਨੀ, ਅਪਰਾਧੀ ਸਿੱਧ ਕਰਨਾ, ਮਹਾਂਦੋਸ਼ ਲਾਉਣਾ; ~ment ਮਹਾਂਦੋਸ਼; ਕਿਸੇ ਅਦਾਲਤ ਦੇ ਸਾਮੁਣੇ ਜਾਂ ਸੰਸਦ ਵਿਚ ਵੱਡੇ ਅਧਿਕਾਰੀ ਦੇ ਆਚਰਨ ਬਾਰੇ ਵਾਦਵਿਵਾਦ

impeccability (ਇਮ'ਪੈੱਕਅ'ਬਿਲਅਟਿ) n ਪਾਪਹੀਨਤਾ, ਨਿਰਦੋਸ਼ਤਾ, ਮਾਸੂਮੀਅਤ

impeccable (ਇਮ'ਪੈੱਕਅਬਲ) a ਬੇ-ਐਬ, ਨਿਸ਼ਪਾਪ; ਨਿਰਦੋਸ਼ ਬੇਗੁਨਾਹ, ਮਾਸੂਮ

impecuniosity ('ਇਮਪਿ'ਕਯੁਨਿ'ਔਸਅਟਿ) n ਗ਼ਰੀਬੀ, ਕੰਗਾਲੀ, ਨਿਰਧਨਤਾ

impecunious ('ਇਮਪਿ'ਕਯੂਨਯਅਸ) a ਨਿਰਧਨ, ਕੰਗਾਲ; ਗ਼ਰੀਬ

impedance (ਇਮ'ਪੀਡਅੰਸ) n ਅੜਿੱਕਾ, ਰੁਕਾਵਟ, ਰੋਕ

impede (ਇਮ'ਪੀਡ) v ਰੁਕਾਵਟ ਪਾਉਣੀ, ਅੜਿੱਕਾ ਡਾਹੁਣਾ, ਵਿਘਨ ਪਾਉਣਾ, ਅੜਚਨ ਪਾਉਣੀ

impedient (ਇਮ'ਪੀਡਯਅੰਟ) a ਰੁਕਾਵਟੀ ਵਿਘਨਪਾਊ, ਅਟਕਾਊ

impediment (ਇਮ'ਪੈੱਡਿਮਅੰਟ) n ਵਿਘਨ ਰੁਕਾਵਟ

impel (ਇਮ'ਪੈੱਲ) v ਉਕਸਾਉਣਾ, ਜ਼ੋਰ ਪਾਉਣਾ ਮਜਬੂਰ ਕਰਨਾ; ਉਤੇਜਤ ਕਰਨਾ, ਉਤਸਾਹ ਕਰਨਾ; ਚਲਾਉਣਾ, ਰੇੜ੍ਹਨਾ

impenetrable (ਇਮ'ਪੈੱਨਿਟਰਅਬਲ) a ਅਛੇਦ ਅਟਿੱਛਿਦ, ਕਰੜਾ; ਠੋਸ; ਅਥਾਹ, ਅਸਗਾਹ ਅਪਾਰ; ਵਿਚਾਰਾਂ ਤੋਂ ਪਰੇ, ਬੁੱਧੀ ਦੀ ਪਹੁੰਚ ਬਾਹਰਾ, ਗੁੱਝ

impenetrate (ਇਮ'ਪੈੱਨਿਟਰੇਇਟ) v ਦਾਖ਼ਲ ਕਰਨਾ, ਪ੍ਰਵੇਸ਼ ਕਰਨਾ, ਧੁਰ ਤਾਈਂ ਜਾਣਾ, ਡੂੰ

ਧਸਣਾ, ਖ਼ੁਸ ਜਾਣਾ

imperative (ਇਮ'ਪੈੱਰਅਟਿਵ੍) *a n* (ਵਿਆ) ਆਗਿਆਵਾਚਕ, ਆਗਿਆਰਥ, ਆਦੇਸ਼ਾਤਮਕ, ਹੁਕਮੀ; ਅਤੀ ਅਵੱਸ਼ਕ

imperfect (ਇਮ'ਪਅ:ਫ਼ਿਕਟ) *a* ਅਧੂਰਾ, ਅਪੂਰਨ, ਅਸਮਾਪਤ, ਨਾਕਸ, ਦੋਸ਼ਪੂਰਨ; ~**ion** ਅਪੂਰਨਤਾ, ਅਸਮਾਪਤੀ; ਕਸਰ, ਨੁਕਸ, ਤਰੁਟੀ

imperial (ਇਮ'ਪਿਅਰਿਅਲ) *a n* ਸ਼ਾਹੀ, ਰਾਜਸੀ; ਸ਼ਹਿਨਸ਼ਾਹੀ; ਸਾਮਰਾਜੀ; ~**ism** ਸਾਮਰਾਜਵਾਦ, ਸ਼ਹਿਨਸ਼ਾਹੀਅਤ; ~**ist** ਸਾਮਰਾਜਵਾਦੀ

imperil (ਇਮ'ਪੈੱਰ(ਅ)ਲ) *v* ਖ਼ਤਰੇ ਵਿਚ ਪਾਉਣਾ, ਜੋਖੋਂ ਵਿਚ ਪਾਉਣਾ

imperishable (ਇਮ'ਪੈਰਿਸ਼ਅਬਲ) *a* ਅਮਰ, ਅਵਿਨਾਸ਼ੀ, ਅਮਿਟ

impersonal (ਇਮ'ਪਅ:ਸਨਲ) *a* ਅਵਿਅਕਤੀਗਤ, ਅਨਿੱਜੀ, ਗ਼ੈਰਸ਼ਖ਼ਸੀ; ~**verb** (ਵਿਆ) ਭਾਵਵਾਚੀ ਕਿਰਿਆ

impersonation (ਇਮ'ਪਅ:ਸਅ'ਨੇਇਸ਼ਨ) *n* ਮਾਨਵੀ-ਕਰਨ; ਰੂਪ ਧਾਰਨ, ਭੇਸ ਬਦਲਣਾ

impersonify ('ਇਮਪਅ'ਸੌਨਿਫ਼ਾਇ) *v* ਮਾਨਵੀਕਰਨ ਕਰਨਾ, ਮੂਰਤੀਕਰਨ ਕਰਨਾ

impertinence (ਇਮ'ਪਅ:ਟਿਨਅੰਸ) *n* ਬੇਅਦਬੀ, ਗੁਸਤਾਖ਼ੀ, ਅਸ਼ਿਸ਼ਟਤਾ, ਨਿਰਥਕਤਾ

impertinent (ਇਮ'ਪਅ:ਟਿਨਅੰਟ) *a* ਗੁਸਤਾਖ਼, ਬੇਅਦਬ

impetuous (ਇਮ'ਪੈੱਚੁਅਸ) *a* ਵੇਗਵਾਨ, ਜੋਸ਼ੀਲਾ, ਬੜਾ ਜੋਸ਼, ਪ੍ਰਚੰਡ

impetus ('ਇਮਪਿਟਅਸ) *n* ਜ਼ੋਰ, ਵੇਗ, ਗਤੀ-ਸ਼ਕਤੀ, ਚਾਲ ਦਾ ਜ਼ੋਰ, ਤੇਜ਼ੀ, ਪਰੇਰਨਾ

impious ('ਇਮਪਿਅਸ) *a* ਅਧਰਮੀ, ਸ਼ਰਧਾਹੀਨ, ਨਾਸਤਕ, ਅਪਵਿੱਤਰ, ਭ੍ਰਿਸ਼ਟ

implacability (ਇਮ'ਪਲੈਕਅ'ਬਿਲਅਟਿ) *n* ਕਰੜਾਈ, ਸਖ਼ਤੀ, ਨਿਰਦਇਤਾ

implacable (ਇਮ'ਪਲੈਕਅਬਲ) *a* ਸਖ਼ਤ, ਕਰੜਾ; ਸਖ਼ਤ ਦਿਲ, ਨਿਰਦਈ

implant (ਇਮ'ਪਲਾਂਟ) *v* ਗੱਡਣਾ; ਬੀਜਣਾ, (ਬੂਟਾ) ਲਾਉਣਾ; ਦਿਲ ਵਿਚ ਬਿਠਾਉਣਾ, ਧਾਰ ਲੈਣਾ, ਗ੍ਰਹਿਣ ਕਰ ਦੇਣਾ; ~**ation** (ਪੌਦੇ ਦੀ) ਗਡਾਈ; ਬਿਜਾਈ

implement ('ਇਮਪਲੀਮੈਂਟ, 'ਇਮਪਲਿਮੈਂਟ) *n v* ਸੰਦ, ਹਥਿਆਰ, ਜੰਤਰ; ਸਾਧਨ, ਵਸਤੂ, ਪੂਰਾ ਕਰਨਾ, ਨਿਭਾਉਣਾ, ਸਾਜ਼-ਸਾਮਾਨ, ਲਾਗੂ ਕਰਨਾ, ਪਾਲਣਾ ਕਰਨੀ; ਅਮਲ ਵਿਚ ਲਿਆਉਣਾ, (ਉੱਤੇ) ਅਮਲ ਕਰਨਾ; ~**ation** ਪਾਲਣ, ਅਮਲ, ਕਾਰਜ ਰੂਪ ਦੇਣ ਦੀ ਕਿਰਿਆ

implicate ('ਇਮਪਲਿਕੇਇਟ) *v* ਫਸਾਉਣਾ, ਉਲਝਾਉਣਾ, ਫਸਾ ਲੈਣਾ; ਭਾਵ-ਅਰਥ ਹੋਣੇ

implication ('ਇਮਪਲਿ'ਕੇਇਸ਼ਨ) *n* ਉਲਝਣ, ਅੜਿੱਕਾ, ਅੜਚਨ; ਭਾਵ-ਅਰਥ, ਅਰਥ-ਸੰਭਾਵਨਾ

implicit (ਇਮ'ਪਲਿਸਿਟ) *a* ਲੁਪਤ, ਨਿਹਿਤ; ਸੰਕੇਤਤ; ਨਿਸਚਤ

implied (ਇਮ'ਪਲਾਇਡ) *a* ਅਰਥਯੁਕਤ, ਸੰਕੇਤਤ, ਨਿਹਿਤ, ਅੰਤਰਨਿਹਿਤ; ਅਵਿਅਕਤ, ਅਸਪਸ਼ਟ

implore (ਇਮ'ਪਲੋ*) *v* ਬੇਨਤੀ ਕਰਨੀ, ਮਿੰਨਤ ਕਰਨੀ, ਤਰਲਾ ਕਰਨਾ; ਜਾਚਨਾ

implosion (ਇਮਪਲਅਉਯ਼ਨ) *n* ਅੰਤਰ ਵਿਸਫੋਟ

imply (ਇਮ'ਪਲਾਇ) *v* ਅਰਥ ਹੋਣਾ, ਭਾਵ ਹੋਣਾ, ਤਾਤਪਰਜ ਨਿਕਲਣਾ

impolite ('ਇਮਪਅ'ਲਾਇਟ) *a* ਅਸੱਭਿਅ, ਅਸ਼ਿਸ਼ਟ, ਬਦਤਮੀਜ਼; ਉਜੱਡ, ਗੰਵਾਰ; ~**ness**

ਅਸੰਡਿਅਤਾ, ਅਸ਼ਿਸ਼ਟਤਾ, ਉਜੱਡਪੁਣਾ

import (ਇਮਾ'ਪੋਟ, ਇਮਪੋਟ) *v n* ਦਰਾਮਦ ਕਰਨਾ, ਆਯਾਤ ਕਰਨਾ; ਅਰਥ ਦੇਣਾ, ਸੰਕੇਤ ਕਰਨਾ; ਬਾਹਰੋਂ ਆਉਂਦਾ ਮਾਲ, ਆਯਾਤ, ਦਰਾਮਦ; ਅਰਥ, ਭਾਵ; ~ed ਆਯਾਤ ਕੀਤਾ, ਦਰਾਮਦ ਕੀਤਾ

importance (ਇਮਪੋ:ਟੰਸ) *n* ਮਹੱਤਾ, ਮਹੱਤਵ, ਕਦਰ, ਗੌਰਵ, ਪ੍ਰਤਿਸ਼ਠਾ, ਦੰਭ; ਜ਼ਰੂਰਤ

important (ਇਮਪੋ:ਟੰਟ) *a* ਜ਼ਰੂਰੀ, ਮਹੱਤਵਪੂਰਨ, ਅਵੱਸ਼ਕ; ਸਨਮਾਨਤ

impose (ਇਮ'ਪਾਉਜ਼) *v* ਸਥਾਪਤ ਕਰਨਾ, ਉੱਪਰ ਰੱਖਣਾ; ਸਿਰ ਮੜ੍ਹਨਾ, ਠੋਸਣਾ

imposing (ਇਮ'ਪਾਉਜ਼ਿੰਡ) *a n* ਪ੍ਰਭਾਵਸ਼ਾਲੀ, ਪਰ੍ਹੂਲੇਦਾਰ, ਰੋਹਬਦਾਬ ਵਾਲਾ

imposition ('ਇਮਪਅ'ਜ਼ਿਸ਼ਨ) *n* ਭਾਰ; ਟੈਕਸ, ਕਰ, ਲਗਾਨ; ਦੰਡ; ਧੋਖਾ, ਕਪਟ ਆਰੋਪਣ

impossibility (ਇਮ'ਪੌਸਅ'ਬਿਲਅਟਿ) *n* ਅਸੰਭਵਤਾ, ਅਸੰਭਾਵਨਾ, ਅਨਹੋਣੀ, ਕਠਨਤਾ

impossible ('ਇਮ'ਪੌਸਅਬਲ) *a* ਅਸੰਭਵ, ਅਸਾਧ, ਅਨਹੋਣਾ, ਅਤੀ ਕਰੋਪੀ

impost ('ਇਮਪਅਉਸਟ) *n* ਕਰ, ਟੈਕਸ, ਲਗਾਨ, ਮਹਿਸੂਲ

impostor (ਇਮ'ਪੌਸਟਅ*) *n* ਪਖੰਡੀ, ਕਪਟੀ, ਠੱਗ, ਧੋਖੇਬਾਜ਼, ਛਲੀਆ; ਮਜ਼ਦੂਰੀ

impotence, impotency ('ਇਮਪਅਟਅੰਸ, 'ਇਮਪਅਟਅੰਸਿ) *n* ਨਾਮਰਦੀ, ਨਪੁੰਸਕਤਾ; ਕਮਜ਼ੋਰੀ; ਲਾਚਾਰੀ, ਮਜਬੂਰੀ

impotent ('ਇਮਪਅਟਅੰਟ) *a* ਨਾਮਰਦ, ਨਪੁੰਸਕ; ਕਮਜ਼ੋਰ, ਨਿਤਾਣਾ, ਹੀਣਾ, ਦੁਰਬਲ

impound (ਇਮ'ਪਾਉਂਡ) *v* ਰੋਕ ਲਾ ਲੈਣੀ, ਰੋਕ ਰੱਖਣਾ, ਪਾਬੰਦੀ ਲਾ ਦੇਣਾ; ਕਾਨੂੰਨੀ ਢੰਗ ਨਾਲ ਕਬਜ਼ੇ ਵਿਚ ਲੈ ਲੈਣਾ, ਖੋਹ ਲੈਣਾ; (ਪਸ਼ੂਆਂ ਨੂੰ) ਕਾਂਜੀ ਹਾਉਸ ਵਿਚ ਬੰਦ ਕਰ ਦੇਣਾ

impoverish (ਇਮ'ਪੌਵ(ਅ)ਰਿਸ਼) *v* ਕੰਗਾਲ ਕਰ ਦੇਣਾ, ਨਿਰਧਨ ਕਰ ਦੇਣਾ, ਸਾਧਨਹੀਨ ਕਰ ਦੇਣਾ; ~ment ਗ਼ਰੀਬੀ, ਕੰਗਾਲੀ; ਨਿਰਧਨਤਾ; ਬਲਹੀਨਤਾ, ਸ਼ਕਤੀਹੀਨਤਾ

impracticablity (ਇਮ'ਪਰੈਕਟਿਕਅ'ਬਿਲਟਿ) *n* ਅਵਿਹਾਰਕਤਾ; ਦੁਸ਼ਕਰਤਾ, ਦੁਰਗਮਤਾ

impracticable (ਇਮ'ਪਰੈਕਟਿਕਅਬਲ) *a* ਅਵਿਹਾਰਕ, ਗ਼ੈਰ-ਅਮਲੀ, ਲਾਇਲਾਜ, ਨਾਕਾਬਲੇ-ਅਮਲ; ਅਸਾਧ; ਔਖਾ, ਦੁਰਗਮ

imprecate ('ਇਮਪਰਿਕੇਇਟ) *v* ਬਦਅਸੀਸ ਦੇਣੀ, ਬਦਦੁਆ ਦੇਣੀ, ਸਰਾਪ ਦੇਣਾ; ਫਿਟਕਾਰਨਾ, ਲਾਨ੍ਹਤ ਪਾਉਣੀ, ਕੋਸਣਾ

imprecision ('ਇਮਪਰਿ'ਸਿਯ਼ਨ) *n* ਅਸਪੱਸ਼ਟਤਾ, ਅਨਿਸ਼ਚਤਤਾ

impregnability (ਇਮ'ਪਰੈਗਨਅ'ਬਿਲਅਟਿ) *n* ਮਜ਼ਬੂਤੀ, ਪਕਿਆਈ, ਅਜਿੱਤਤਾ, ਅਛੇਦਤਾ

impregnable (ਇਮ'ਪਰੈਗਨਅਬਲ) *a* ਅਜਿੱਤ, ਅਛੇਦ, ਪੱਕਾ, ਮਜ਼ਬੂਤ

impregnate ('ਇਮਪਰੈੱਗਨੇਇਟ) *v a* ਗਰਭ ਕਰਨਾ; ਭਰ ਦੇਣਾ, ਸੰਚਾਰ ਕਰਨਾ, (ਭਾਵ, ਗੁਣ ਆਦਿ) ਕੁੱਟ-ਕੁੱਟ ਕੇ ਭਰ ਦੇਣਾ, ਦਿਲ ਵਿਚ ਬਿਠਾ ਦੇਣਾ; ਗਰਭਵਤੀ

impress (ਇਮ'ਪਰੈੱਸ, 'ਇਮਪਰੈੱਸ) *v n* (1) ਮੋਹਰ ਲਾਉਣੀ, ਠੱਪਾ ਲਾਉਣਾ; ਅੰਕਤ ਕਰਨਾ, ਨਿਸ਼ਾਨ ਲਾਉਣਾ; ਪ੍ਰਭਾਵਤ ਕਰਨਾ; ਮਨ ਵਿਚ ਬਿਠਾ ਦੇਣਾ; (2) ਜ਼ਬਤ ਕਰਨਾ, ਜ਼ਬਰੀ ਭਰਤੀ ਕਰਨਾ; ਠੱਪਾ, ਛਾਪ, ਮੋਹਰ, ਸਿੱਕਾ, ਵਿਸ਼ੇਸ਼ਤਾ; ~ed ਅੰਕਤ, ਚਿੰਨ੍ਹਤ, ਮੁਦ੍ਰਿਤ, ਛਪਿਆ ਪ੍ਰਭਾਵਤ; ਆਰੋਪਤ; ~ible ਪ੍ਰਭਾਵਸ਼ੀਲ; ~ion ਠੱਪਾ, ਛਾਪ, ਮੋਹਰ, ਚਿੰਨ੍ਹ,

ਨਿਸ਼ਾਨ; ਪ੍ਰਭਾਵ, ਵਿਚਾਰ, ਰਾਏ; ~ionable ਸੰਵੇਦਨਸ਼ੀਲ, ਪ੍ਰਭਾਵਸ਼ੀਲ; ~ionist ਪ੍ਰਭਾਵਵਾਦੀ; ਭਾਵ-ਚਿੱਤਰ; ~ive ਪ੍ਰਭਾਵਸ਼ਾਲੀ, ਅਸਰ ਪਾਉਣ ਵਾਲਾ

imprest ('ਇਮਪਰੈੱਸਟ) *n* ਪੇਸ਼ਗੀ ਧਨ, ਪੇਸ਼ਗੀ ਤਨਖਾਹ

imprint (ਇਮ'ਪਰਿੰਟ) *v n* ਠੱਪਾ ਲਾਉਣਾ, ਮੋਹਰ ਲਾਉਣਾ, ਠੋਕਣਾ, ਨਿਸ਼ਾਨ ਲਾਉਣਾ; (ਪੁਸਤਕ ਉੱਤੇ) ਪ੍ਰਕਾਸ਼ਕ ਅਤੇ ਮੁਦ੍ਰਿਕ ਦਾ ਵੇਰਵਾ, ਠੱਪ, ਛਾਪਾ

imprison (ਇਮ'ਪਰਿਜ਼ਨ) *v n* ਕੈਦ ਕਰਨਾ, ਜੇਲ੍ਹ ਵਚ ਸੁੱਟਣਾ; ਘੇਰ ਲੈਣਾ, ਬੰਦ ਕਰਨਾ, ਡੱਕ ਲੈਣਾ; ~ **ment** ਕੈਦ, ਬੰਦੀ, ਜੇਲ੍ਹ-ਖਾਨਾ

improbability (ਇਮ'ਪਰੌਬਆ'ਬਿਲਿਟਿ) *n* ਅਸੰਭਾਵਤਾ, ਦੁਰਘਟਤਾ

improbable (ਇਮ'ਪਰੌਬਅਬਲ) *a* ਅਸੰਭਾਵੀ

improper (ਇਮ'ਪਰੌਪਅ*) *a* ਨਾਵਾਜਬ, ਅਯੋਗ, ਅਨੁਚਿਤ; ਗਲਤ, ਕੋਝਾ, ਕੁਵੇਲਾ

impropriety (ਇਮਪਰਅ'ਪਰਾਇਅਟਿ) *n* ਅਨੁਚਿਤਤਾ, ਅਯੋਗਤਾ; ਬੇਹੁਦਰੀ ਅਸ਼ਿਸ਼ਟਤਾ

improve (ਇਮ'ਪਰੁਵ) *v* ਸੁਧਾਰਨਾ, ਸਵਾਰਨਾ, ਉੱਨਤੀ ਕਰਾਉਣੀ, ਨੀਕ ਕਤਨਾ, ਵਧਾ-ਫੁੱਲਣਾ; ਅਵਸਰ ਦਾ ਠੀਕ ਲਾਭ ਉਠਾਉਣਾ; ਮੱਤ ਦੇਣੀ, ਉਚਿਤ ਸਿੱਖਿਆ ਦੇਣਾ; ~**d** ਸੰਸ਼ੋਧਤ, ਉੱਨਤ, ਉਤਕ੍ਰਿਸ਼ਟ, ਸੁਧਰਿਆ; ~**ment** ਸੁਧਾਰ, ਉੱਨਤੀ, ਬਿਹਤਰੀ

improvidence (ਇਮ'ਪਰੌਵਿਡਅੰਸ) *a* ਲਾਪਰਵਾਹ, ਅਸਾਵਧਾਨ; ਨਾ-ਦੂਰਦਰਸ਼ੀ, ਫਜ਼ੂਲ ਖਰਚ

improvident (ਇਮ'ਪਰੌਵਿਡਅੰਟ) *a* ਲਾਪਰਵਾਹ, ਅਸਾਵਧਾਨ; ਨਾ-ਦੂਰਦਰਸ਼ੀ, ਫਜ਼ੂਲ ਖਰਚ

improving (ਇਮ'ਪਰੂਵਿੰਡ) *a* ਵਿਕਾਸਮਾਨ, ਵਰਧਮਾਨ, ਅੱਛਾ ਹੋਣ ਜਾਂ ਹੋਣ ਵਾਲਾ

imprudence (ਇਮ'ਪਰੂਡਅੰਸ) *n* ਅਸਾਵਧਾਨੀ, ਅਵਿਵੇਕ, ਬੇਸਮਝ

imprudent (ਇਮਪਰੂਡਅੰਟ) *n* ਬੇਸਮਝੀ, ਅਸਾਵਧਾਨੀ, ਅਵਿਵੇਕੀ

impudence (ਇਮਪਯੂਡਅੰਸ) *n* ਬੇਅਦਬੀ, ਗੁਸਤਾਖੀ, ਬੇਹਯਾਈ, ਢੀਠਤਾ, ਨਿਲੱਜਤਾ

impudent (ਇਮਪਯੂਡਅੰਟ) *n* ਗੁਸਤਾਖ, ਬੇਅਦਬ, ਢੀਠ, ਨਿਲੱਜ, ਬੇਹਯਾ

impulse (ਇਮਪੌਲਸ) *n* ਮਨੋਵੇਗ, ਤਰੰਗ, ਅੰਤਰ ਪਰੇਰਨਾ; ਮਾਨਸਕ ਪਰੇਰਨਾ; ਗਤੀ, ਚਾਲ; ਆਵੇਗ

impulsion (ਇਮ'ਪੱਲਸ਼ਨ) *n* ਮਾਨਸਕ ਪਰੇਰਨਾ; ਉਕਸਾਹਟ

impulsive (ਇਮ'ਪੱਲਸਿਵ) *a* ਮਨੋਵੇਗੀ, ਵੇਗਵਾਨ, ਤਰੰਗੀ

impunity (ਇਮ'ਪਯੂਨਅਟਿ) *n* ਸਜ਼ਾ ਤੋਂ ਛੋਟ, ਦੰਡ ਮੁਕਤੀ, ਮਾਫੀ

impure (ਇਮ'ਪਯੂਅ*) *a* ਅਪਵਿੱਤਰ, ਮੈਲਾ, ਗੰਦਾ; ਭਿੱਟਿਆ, ਨਾਪਾਕ, ਨਿੰਦਾਯੋਗ

impurity (ਇਮ'ਪਯੂਅਰਅਟਿ) *n* ਅਪਵਿੱਤਰਤਾ; ਮੈਲਾਪਨ, ਗੰਦਗੀ; ਮਿਲਾਵਟ, ਖੋਟ, ਅਸ਼ੁੱਧਤਾ

imputation (ਇਮਪਯੂ'ਟੇਇਸ਼ਨ) *n* ਦੂਜ, ਆਰੋਪ, ਤੁਹਮਤ, ਇਲਜ਼ਾਮ

impute (ਇਮ'ਪਯੂਟ) *v* ਦੂੰਮੇ ਲਾਉਣਾ, ਸਿਰ ਮੜ੍ਹਨਾ, ਤੁਹਮਤ ਲਾਉਣੀ, ਆਰੋਪਣਾ

in (ਇਨ) *perp adv a n* ਵਿਚ, ਅੰਦਰ; ਉੱਤੇ; ਅੰਦਰ ਨੂੰ, ਅੰਦਰ ਵੱਲ, ਅੰਦਰਲਾ

inability (ਇਨਅ'ਬਿਲਅਟਿ) *n* ਅਸਮਰੱਥਾ, ਅਯੋਗਤਾ, ਨਾਲਾਇਕੀ; ਨਿਰਬਲਤਾ; ਬੇਵੱਸੀ

in absentia ('ਇਨਐਬ'ਸੈਂਟਿਆ) (L) *adv* ਗ਼ੈਰਹਾਜ਼ਰੀ ਵਿਚ

inaccessibility ('ਇਨਅਕ'ਸੈਸਅ'ਬਿਲਅਟਿ) *n* ਦੁਰਲੱਭਤਾ, ਦੁਰਗਮਤਾ

inaccessible ('ਇਨਅੈਕ'ਸੈਸਅਬਲ) *a* ਪਹੁੰਚ ਤੋਂ ਪਰੇ, ਅਪਹੁੰਚ; ਦੁਰਗਮ; ਅਗਮ, ਦੁਰਲੱਭ

inaccuracy (ਇਨ'ਐਕਯੁਰਅਸਿ) *n* ਅਸ਼ੁੱਧੀ, ਅਯਥਾਰਥ; ਦੋਸ਼

inaccurate (ਇਨ'ਐਕਯੁਰਅਟ) *a* ਅਸ਼ੁੱਧ, ਗ਼ਲਤ, ਅਯਥਾਰਥ; ਦੋਸ਼ਪੂਰਨ

inaction (ਇਨ'ਐਕਸ਼ਨ) *n* ਆਲਸ, ਸੁਸਤੀ; ਦਲਿੰਦਰ; ਨਿਸ਼ਕਿਰਿਆਤਾ

inactive (ਇਨ'ਐਕਟਿਵ਼) *a* ਸੁਸਤ, ਬੇਹਿੰਮਤ, ਆਲਸੀ, ਦਲਿੰਦਰੀ, ਨਿਕੰਮਾ, ਬੇਕਾਰ, ਨਿਸ਼ਕਿਰਿਆ

inactivity ('ਇਨਐਕ'ਟਿਵ਼ਅਟਿ) *n* ਆਲਸ, ਸੁਸਤੀ; ਬੇਕਾਰੀ, ਨਿਸ਼ਕਿਰਿਆਤਾ

inadequacy (ਇਨ'ਐਡਿਕਵਅਸਿ) *n* ਥੁੜ੍ਹ, ਘਾਟ, ਅਲਪਤਾ, ਅਪੂਰਨਤਾ

inadequate (ਇਨ'ਐਡਿਕਵਅਟ) *a* ਨਾ ਕਾਫ਼ੀ; ਥੋੜ੍ਹਾ, ਘੱਟ; ਅਪੂਰਨ; ਅਯੋਗ, ਅਸਮਰੱਥ

inadmissibility ('ਇਨਅਡ'ਮਿਸਅ'ਬਿਲਅਟਿ) *n* ਅਪ੍ਰਵਾਨਤਾ, ਨਾ ਮੰਨਣਯੋਗਤਾ, ਅਸਵੀਕਾਰਤਾ

inadmissible ('ਇਨਅਡ'ਮਿਸਅਬਲ) *a* ਨਾ ਮੰਨਣਯੋਗ, ਅਪ੍ਰਵੇਸ਼ੀ

in aeternum (ਇਨ'ਐਟਅਨਅਮ) (L) *adv* ਸਦਾ, ਸਦੈਵ

inanimate (ਇਨ'ਐਨਿਮਅਟ) *a* ਬੇਜਾਨ, ਨਿਰਜੀਵ, ਪ੍ਰਾਣਹੀਨ, ਅਚੇਤਨ, ਜੜ੍ਹ, ਮੁਰਦਾਦਿਲ

inanimation (ਇਨ'ਐਨ'ਮੇਇਸ਼ਨ) *n* ਪਰਾਹੀਨਤਾ, ਨਿਰਜੀਵਤਾ, ਜੜ੍ਹਤਾ, ਅਚੇਤਨਤਾ

inapplicable (ਇਨ'ਐਪਲਿਕਅਬਲਨ) *a* ਅਢੁੱਕਵਾਂ, ਲਾਗੂ ਨਾ ਹੋਣ ਯੋਗ, ਅਨੁਚਿਤ, ਨਾਵਾਜਬ

inappropriate ('ਇਨਅ'ਪਰਅਉਪਰਿਅਟ) *a* ਅਢੁੱਕਵਾਂ, ਅਨੁਚਿਤ, ਬੇਮੇਲ; ਅਸੰਗਤ, ਬੇਮੌਕਾ

inapt (ਇਨ'ਐਪਟ) *a* ਅਯੋਗ, ਨਲਾਇਕ, ਨਾਮੁਨਾਸਬ; **~itude** ਅਯੋਗਤਾ, ਨਲਾਇਕੀ

inasmuch (ਯ਼'ਇਨਅਜ਼'ਮਅੱਚ) *adv* ਜਿਥੋਂ ਤਕ ਕਿ

inattentive ('ਇਨਅਟੈਂਨਟਿਵ਼) *a* ਬੇਧਿਆਨਾ, ਘੇਸਲਾ, ਮਚਲਾ, ਲਾਪਰਵਾਹ

inaugural (ਇਨੈਗਯੁਰ(ਅ)ਲ) *v* ਉਦਘਾਟਨੀ, ਉਦਘਾਟਨਕਾਰੀ; **~function** ਉਦਘਾਟਨ-ਸਮਾਰੋਹ

inaugurate (ਇਨੈਗਯੁਰੇਇਟ) *v* ਉਦਘਾਟਨ ਕਰਨਾ, ਮੁਹੂਰਤ ਕਰਨਾ; ਚੋਣ ਕਰਨੀ

inauguration (ਇ'ਨੈਗਯੁ'ਰੇਇਸ਼ਨ) *n* ਉਦਘਾਟਨ, ਮੁਹੂਰਤ, ਚੋਣ; ਆਰੰਭ

inauspicious ('ਇਨਓ'ਸਪਿਸ਼ਅਸ) *a* ਅਸ਼ੁਭ, ਕੁਸ਼ਗਨਾ, ਦੁਰਭਾਗ ਸੂਚਕ

inborn, inbred (ਇਨ'ਬੋਨ, ਇਨ'ਬਰੈੱਡ) *a* ਜਮਾਂਦਰੂ, ਜਨਮ ਤੋਂ ਹੀ, ਸੁਭਾਵਕ, ਕੁਦਰਤੀ, ਜਨਮਜਾਤ, ਸਹਿਜ

incamera ('ਇਨ'ਕੈਮਅਰਅ) (L) *a* ਗੁਪਤ

incapability (ਇਨ'ਕੇਇਪਅ'ਬਿਲਅਟਿ) *n* ਅਸਮਰੱਥਾ, ਅਯੋਗਤਾ, ਨਲਾਇਕ, ਨਿਰਬਲਤਾ

incapable (ਇਨ'ਕੇਇਪਅਬਲ) *a* ਅਸਮਰੱਥ, ਅਯੋਗ, ਨਲਾਇਕ, ਨਾਕਾਬਲ; ਸ਼ਕਤੀਹੀਨ

incapacity (ਇਨਕਅ'ਪੈਸਅਟਿ) *n* ਅਸਮਰੱਥਾ, ਅਯੋਗਤਾ, ਨਲਾਇਕੀ; ਅਧਿਕਾਰਹੀਨਤਾ

incarnate ('ਇਨਕਾਨੇਇਟ, ਇਨ'ਕਾਨਅਟ) *v a*

incarnation | 539 | **incompatibility**

ਅਵਤਾਰ ਧਾਰਨਾ, ਜਨਮ ਲੈਣਾ; ਸਾਕਾਰ ਰੂਪ ਵਿਚ ਰੱਖਣਾ; ਸਾਕਾਰ, ਸਾਖਿਆਤ, ਸਰੂਪ, ਮੂਰਤੀਮਾਨ

incarnation ('ਇਨਕਾ'ਨੇਇਸ਼ਨ) *n* ਅਵਤਾਰ ਧਾਰਨ, ਅਵਤਾਰ; ਦੇਹਧਾਰੀ ਹੋਣ ਦੀ ਦਸ਼ਾ

incense (ਇਨ'ਸੈੱਸ) *v n* ਧੂਪ ਦੇਣਾ, ਧੂਣੀ ਦੇਣੀ, ਸੁਗੰਧੀ ਧੁਖਾਉਣੀ, ਮਹਿਕਾਉਣਾ; ਧੂਪ ਗੁੱਸਾ ਚੜ੍ਹਾਉਣਾ, ਕਰੋਧ ਚੜ੍ਹਾਉਣਾ; ਉਤੇਜਤ ਕਰਨਾ

incentive (ਇਨ'ਸੈੱਟਿਵ) *n a* ਉਤਸਾਹ, ਪਰੇਰਨਾ, ਉਤੇਜਨਾ, ਉਕਸਾਹਟ; ਪਰੇਰਕ, ਉਤੇਜਕ

incept (ਇਨ'ਸੈਪਟ) *v* ਗ੍ਰਹਿਣ ਕਰਨਾ, ਧੂਸ ਲੈਣਾ, ਸ਼ੁਕਾਉਣਾ; **~ion** ਮੁੱਢ, ਆਰੰਭ, ਸ਼ੁਰੂਆਤ, ਸ਼ੁਰੂ; **~ive** ਮੁੱਢਲਾ, ਆਰੰਭਕ, ਸ਼ੁਰੂ ਦਾ, ਆਰੰਭ ਸੂਚਕ

incertain (ਇਨ'ਸਅਃਟਨ) *a* ਅਨਿਸ਼ਚਤ, ਸੰਦੇਹਯੁਕਤ, ਸੰਦਿਗਧ

incessant (ਇਨ'ਸੈੱਸੰਟ) *a* ਅਟੁੱਟ, ਇਕਤਾਰ, ਲਗਾਤਾਰ, ਨਿਰੰਤਰ

inch (ਇੰਚ) *n* ਇੰਚ, ਗਜ਼ ਦਾ ਛੱਤੀਵਾਂ ਭਾਗ

incidence ('ਇਨਸਿਡੰਅੰਸ) *n* ਘਟਨਾ, ਸਥਿਤੀ, ਵਾਪਰਨ, ਮਾਜਰਾ, ਹਾਦਸਾ, ਵਾਕਿਆ

incident ('ਇਨਸਿਡੰਅੰਟ) *n a* ਘਟਨਾ, ਵਾਕਿਆ, ਬਿਰਤਾਂਤ, ਮਾਜਰਾ; ਪ੍ਰਸੰਗ; **~al** ਇਤਫ਼ਾਕੀਆ, ਆਰਜ਼ੀ

incipient (ਇਨ'ਸਿਪਿਅੰਟ) *a* ਮੁੱਢਲਾ, ਆਰੰਭਕ

incisive (ਇਨ'ਸਾਇਸਿਵ) *a* ਸਮਝਦਾਰ, ਬੁੱਧੀਵਾਨ, ਤੀਖਣ (ਬੁੱਧੀ), ਤਿੱਖਾ, ਬਾਰੀਕ

incite (ਇਨ'ਸਾਇਟ) *v* ਭੜਕਾਉਣਾ, ਉਕਸਾਉਣਾ, ਉਤਾਰਨਾ, ਉਤੇਜਤ ਕਰਨਾ, ਵਰਗਲਾਉਣਾ; **~ment, incitation** ਉਕਸਾਹਟ, ਉਭਾਰ, ਉਤੇਜਨਾ, ਭੜਕਾਹਟ

inclination ('ਇਨਕਲਿ'ਨੇਇਸ਼ਨ) *n* ਢਾਲ, ਝੁਕਾਉ, ਰੁਝਾਨ, ਪ੍ਰਵਿਰਤੀ, ਰੁਚੀ, ਇੱਛਾ

incline (ਇਨ'ਕਲਾਇਨ) *v n* ਰੌਂ ਹੋਣਾ, ਝੁਕਾਉਣਾ, ਝੁਕਣਾ; ਇੱਛਾ ਰੱਖਣੀ; ਮੁੜਨਾ, ਮੋੜਨਾ; **~d** ਝੁਕਿਆ, ਢਾਲਵਾਂ, ਪ੍ਰਵਿਰਤ

include (ਇਨ'ਕਲੂਡ) *v* ਸ਼ਾਮਲ ਕਰਨਾ, ਜੋੜਨਾ, ਸੰਮਿਲਤ ਕਰਨਾ, ਮਿਲਾਉਣਾ; ਦਾਖ਼ਲ ਕਰਨਾ; **~d** ਅੰਤਰਗਤ, ਅੰਤਰਭੂਤ, ਸੰਮਿਲਤ

inclusion (ਇਨ'ਕਲੂਯ਼ਨ) *n* ਸੰਮਿਲਨ, ਦਾਖ਼ਲਾ

inclusive (ਇਨ'ਕਲੂਸਿਵ) *a* ਸਹਿਤ, ਸੰਮਿਲਤ; **~ness** ਅੰਤਰ ਭਾਵ, ਸਮਾਵੇਸ਼ਨ

incognito ('ਇਨਕੋਗ'ਨੀਟਅਉ) *a n adv* ਬਹੁਰੂਪੀਆ; ਗੁਮਨਾਮ, ਅਗਿਆਤ

incongnizable (ਇਨ'ਕੋਗਨਿਜ਼ਅਬਲ) *a* ਅਬੋਧ, ਅਗੋਚਰ, ਅਗੰਮ

incoherence (ਇਨਕਅ(ਉ)'ਹਿਅਰਅੰਸ) *n* ਅਜੋੜਤਾ, ਅਸੰਗਤੀ, ਅਸਬੰਧਤਾ, ਅਜੋੜ

incoherent (ਇਨਕਅ(ਉ)'ਹਿਅਰਅੰਟ) *a* ਅਸੰਗਤ, ਅਜੋੜ, ਅਰਥਹੀਨ, ਉਘੜ-ਦੁਘੜ

incohesive (ਇਨਕਅ(ਉ)'ਹੀਸਿਵ) *a* ਅਸੰਗਤ, ਅਸੰਬੰਧ, ਘੋਮੇਲ

incomo ('ਇਨਕਅੰਮ) *n* ਆਮਦਨੀ, ਕਮਾਈ, ਆਮਦ, ਆਮਦ; ਲਾਭ

incoming ('ਇਨ'ਕੰਮਿਙ) *n* ਆਗਮਨ, ਆਮਦਨੀ, ਧਨ-ਆਗਮ; ਆਪੂਵਾਸੀ, ਆਗਾਮੀ

incommensurate ('ਇਨਕਅ'ਮੈੱਨਸ(ਅ)ਰਅਟ) *a* ਅਤੁੱਲ, ਅਸਮਾਨ; ਘੱਟ

incommunicable ('ਇਨਕਅ'ਮਯੂਨਿਕਅਬਲ) *a* ਅਕੱਥ, ਅਕਥਨੀ, ਅਵਰਤਨੀ

incompatibility ('ਇਨਕਅਮਪੈਟਅ'ਬਿਲਅਟਿ) *n* ਅਢੁੱਕਵਾਂਪਣ, ਅਸੰਗਤੀ

incompatible ('ਇਨਕਅਮ'ਪੈਟਅਬਲ) *a* ਵਿਰੁੱਧ, ਅਸੰਗਤ, ਅਢੁੱਕਵਾਂ, ਘੋਮੇਲ

incompetence, incompetency (ਇਨ'ਕੌਮਪਿਟਅੰਸ, ਇਨ'ਕੌਮਪਿਟਅੰਸਿ) *n* ਅਸਮਰਥਤਾ, ਅਜੋਗਤਾ, ਨਾਲਾਇਕੀ

incompetent (ਇਨ'ਕੌਮਪਿਟਅੰਟ) *a* ਅਸਮਰੱਥ, ਅਜੋਗ, ਨਾਲਾਇਕ, ਨਾਕਾਬਲ

incomplete ('ਇਨਕਅਮ'ਪਲੀਟ) *a* ਅਧੂਰਾ, ਅਪੂਰਨ, ਨਾਮੁਕੰਮਲ; **~ly** ਅਧੂਰੇ ਤੌਰ ਤੇ

incompliance ('ਇਨਕਅਮ'ਪਲਾਇਅੰਸ) *n* ਅਵੱਗਿਆ, ਅਸਵੀਕ੍ਰਿਤੀ

incomprehensibilty, incomprehensiveness (ਇਨ'ਕੌਮਪਰਿਹੈੱਨਸਅ'ਬਿਲਅਟਿ, ਇਨ'ਕੌਮਪਰਿਹੈੱਨਸਿਵਨਿਸ) *n* ਦੁਰਬੋਧਤਾ, ਗੁੜ੍ਹਤਾ; ਅਪਾਰਤਾ

incomprehensible (ਇਨ'ਕੌਂਪਰਿ'ਹੈਂਸਅਿਬਲ) *n* ਅਬੋਧ, ਦੁਰਬੋਧ, ਗੁੜ੍ਹ; ਅਨੰਤ, ਅਪਾਰ

incomprehension (ਇਨ'ਕੌਂਪਰਿ'ਹੈਂਨਸ਼ਨ) *n* ਅਬੋਧਤਾ, ਅਗਿਆਨ, ਨਾਸਮਝੀ, ਗੁੜ੍ਹਤਾ, ਅਸੀਮਤਾ

incomprehensive (ਇਨ'ਕੌਂਪਰਿਹੈਂਨਸਿਵ਼) *a* ਸੰਕੀਰਣ, ਸੀਮਤ, ਤੰਗ; ਦੁਰਬੋਧ, ਅਬੋਧ

inconclusive ('ਇਨਕਅਨ'ਕਲੂਸਿਵ਼) *a* ਅਨਿਸ਼ਚਤ, ਫ਼ੈਸਲਾਰਹਿਤ, ਅਸਪਸ਼ਟ; **~ness** ਅਨਿਸ਼ਚਤਤਾ, ਅਨਿਰਣਾ, ਅਨਿਸ਼ਚਾ, ਸੰਦੇਹਸ਼ੀਲਤਾ, ਸੰਦਿਗਧਤਾ

incongruity ('ਇਨਕੌਂਙ'ਗਰੂਅਟਿ) *n* ਅਸੰਗਤੀ, ਅਸੰਬੰਧਤਾ, ਵਿਰੋਧ, ਬੇਤੁਕਾਪਣ, ਬੇਢੰਗਾ

incongruous (ਇਨ'ਕੌਂਙਗਰੂਅਸ) *a* ਅਸਬੰਧਤ, ਅਸੰਗਤ, ਘੋਮੇਲ; ਵਿਰੋਧੀ, ਬੇਢੰਗਾ, ਬੇਡੌਲ, ਬੇਤੁਕਾ, ਘੋਮੌਕ, ਨਾਮੁਨਾਸਬ

inconsiderate ('ਇਨਕਅਨ'ਸਿਡ(ਅ)ਰਅਟ) *a* ਅਵਿਵੇਕੀ, ਬੁੱਧੀਹੀਨ, ਭਾਵਨਾਹੀਨ, ਬੇਪਰਵਾਹ, ਬੇ-ਲਿਹਾਜ਼ਾ ਕੋਰਾ; **~ness, inconsideration** ਅਵਿਵੇਕ, ਬੁੱਧੀ-ਹੀਣਤਾ, ਬੇਪਰਵਾਹੀ, ਬੇਲਿਹਾਜ਼ੀ

inconsistence, inconsistency ('ਇਨਕਅਨ'ਸਿਸਟਅੰਸ, ਇਕਅਨ'ਸਿਸਟਅੰਸਿ) *n* ਸਵੈ-ਵਿਰੋਧ; ਵਿਪਰੀਤਤਾ, ਅਸੰਗਤਾ, ਅਪ੍ਰਸੰਗਕਤਾ, ਬੇਅਸੂਲਪਣ

inconsistent ('ਇਨਕਅਨ'ਸਿਸਟਅੰਟ) *a* ਵਿਪਰੀਤ; ਘੋਮੇਲ; ਅਜੋੜ, ਅਸੰਗਤ, ਬੇਅਸੂਲ ਪ੍ਰਤੀਕੂਲ

inconsonance (ਇਨ'ਕੌਨਸਅਨਅੰਸ) *n* ਬੇਸੁਰਾਪਣ, ਅਸੰਗਤੀ

inconspicuous ('ਇਨਕਅਨ'ਸਪਿਕਯੁਅਸ) *a* ਅਪ੍ਰਤੱਖ, ਅਸਪਸ਼ਟ, ਅਪਰਗਟ; **~ness** ਅਪ੍ਰਤੱਖਤਾ, ਅਸਪਸ਼ਟਤਾ, ਅਪਰਗਟਾ, ਪੀਲਾਪਣ

inconvenience ('ਇਨਕਅਨ'ਵੀਨਯਅੰਸ) *n v* ਔਖਿਆਈ, ਤਕਲੀਫ਼, ਖੇਚਲ, ਦਿਕਤ; ਕਸ਼ਟ, ਜ਼ਹਿਮਤ, ਅਸੁਵਿਧਾ; ਦਿਕਤ ਦੇਦੀ, ਕਸ਼ਟ ਦੇਣਾ, ਹਰਜ ਕਰਨਾ

inconvenient ('ਇਨਕਅਨ'ਵੀਨਯਅੰਟ) *a* ਤਕਲੀਫ਼-ਦੇਹ, ਘੋਮੌਕਾ, ਬੇਜਾ, ਨਾਮੁਨਾਸਬ, ਨਾਮੁਆਫ਼ਕ, ਅਸੁਵਿਧਾਪੂਰਨ

incorporate ('ਇਨ'ਕੋਪਅਰਇਟ) *v* ਇਕੱਠਾ ਕਰਨਾ, ਇਕ ਜਾਨ ਕਰਨਾ, ਸੰਮਿਲਤ ਕਰਨਾ, ਸੰਯੁਕਤ ਹੋਣਾ, ਸੰਯੁਕਤ ਕਰਨਾ; **~d** ਸੰਮਿਲਤ, ਸੰਸਥਾਪਤ, ਨਿਗਮਤ

incorrect ('ਇਨਕਅ'ਰੈੱਕਟ) *a* ਗ਼ਲਤ, ਅਸ਼ੁੱਧ, ਝੂਠ, ਅਯੋਗ, ਤਰੁਟੀਪੂਰਨ, ਅਨੁਚਿਤ

incorrigibility (ਇਨ'ਕੌਰਿਜਿ'ਬਿਲਅਟਿ) *n*

ਅਸਾਮਥਤਾ

incorrigible (ਇਨ'ਕੌਰਿਜਅਬਲ) *a* ਅਸਾਧ

increase (ਇਨ'ਕਰੀਸ, 'ਇਨਕਰੀਸ) *v n* ਅਧਿਕ ਹੋਣਾ, ਵਧਣਾ, ਵਧਾਉਣਾ, ਉਨਤ ਹੋਣਾ; ਅਧਿਕਤਾ, ਵਾਧਾ, ਉਨਤ; ~d ਵਧਿਆ

increasing (ਇਨ'ਕਰੀਸਿਙ) *a* ਵਰਧਮਾਨ, ਵਧਣ ਵਾਲਾ

increment ('ਇਨਕਰਿਮੰਟ) *n* ਵਿਸਤਾਰ, ਵਾਧਾ, ਵ੍ਰਿਧੀ; ਲਾਭ, ਮੁਨਾਫ਼ਾ, ਤਰੱਕੀ

inculcate (ਇਨਕੱਲਕੇਇਟ) *v* ਗ੍ਰਹਿਣ ਕਰਾਉਣਾ, ਜ਼ਿਹਨ ਵਿਚ ਬਿਠਾਉਣਾ, ਮੁੜ-ਮੁੜ ਸਮਝਾਉਣਾ, ਤਾਕੀਦ ਕਰਨੀ

inculpable (ਇਨ'ਕੱਲਪਅਬਲ) *a* ਨਿਰਦੋਸ਼, ਅਕਲੰਕ, ਬੇਦੋਸ਼ਾ

incumbent (ਇਨ'ਕੱਮਬਅੰਟ) *a n* ਉਚਿਤ, ਅਤੀ ਅਵੱਸ਼ਕ, ਬਹੁਤ ਜ਼ਰੂਰੀ, ਨਿਰਤਰ; ਅਹੁਦੇਦਾਰ; ਪਦਧਾਰੀ, ਉਹ ਵਿਅਕਤੀ ਜਿਸਨੇ ਪਦ ਗ੍ਰਹਿਣ ਕੀਤਾ ਹੋਵੇ

incur (ਇਨ'ਕਅ:*) *v* ਗ੍ਰਸਤ ਹੋਣਾ, ਆਪਣੇ ਉੱਤੇ ਲੈਣਾ; ਉਠਾਉਣਾ

incurable (ਇਨ'ਕਯੂਅਰਅਬਲ) *a n* ਅਸਾਧ, ਲਾ-ਇਲਾਜ

indebted (ਇਨ'ਡੈਟਿਡ) *a* ਰਿਣੀ, ਦੇਣਦਾਰ; ਕਿਰਤੱਗ, ਇਹਸਾਨਮੰਦ, ਕਰਜ਼ਈ; ~ness ਰਿਣਗ੍ਰਸਤਤਾ, ਕਰਜ਼ਦਾਰੀ; ਕ੍ਰਿਤੱਗਤਾ, ਇਹਸਾਨਮੰਦੀ

indecency (ਇਨ'ਡੀਸੰਸੀ) *n* ਗੰਵਾਰਪੁਣ, ਅਸ਼ਿਸ਼ਟਤਾ; ਅਭੱਦਰਤਾ; ਅਸ਼ਲੀਲਤਾ; ਅਣਉਚਿਤਤਾ

indecent (ਇਨ'ਡੀਸੰਟ) *a* ਗੰਵਾਰ, ਅਸ਼ਿਸ਼ਟ, ਅਭੱਦਰ; ਬਦਤਮੀਜ਼, ਅਣਉਚਿਤ

indeed (ਇਨ'ਡੀਡ) *adv int* ਸਚੱਮੁਚ, ਯਕੀਨੀ ਤੌਰ ਤੇ, ਦਰਅਸਲ, ਨਿਰਸੰਦੇਹ, ਬੇਸ਼ੱਕ, ਠੀਕ

indefinite (ਇਨ'ਡੈੱਫ਼ਨਿਟ) *a* ਅਸਪਸ਼ਟਤਾ, ਅਨਿਸ਼ਚਤਤਾ, ਸੰਦੇਹਪੂਰਨ, ਬੇਹੱਦ; ~ly ਅਨਿਸ਼ਚਤ ਤੌਰ ਤੇ, ਅਣਮਿੱਥੇ ਤੌਰ ਤੇ; ~ness ਅਸਪਸ਼ਟਤਾ, ਸੰਦਿਗਧਤਾ, ਅਸੀਮਤਾ, ਗੋਲ-ਮਾਲ

indent ('ਇਨਡੈਂਟ, ਇਨ'ਡੈਂਟ) *n v* ਦੰਦੀਕਰਨ; ਟੱਕ; ~ure ਵਸਤੂ-ਸੂਚੀ; ਇਕਰਾਰਨਾਮਾ ਦੰਦਾ; ਮੰਗ-ਪੱਤਰ; ਦੰਦੇ ਕੱਢਣਾ, ਨਿਸ਼ਾਨ ਲਾਉਣੇ, ਠੱਪਾ ਲਾਉਣਾ, ਹਾਸ਼ੀਏ ਤੋਂ ਦੂਰ ਸ਼ੁਰੂ ਕਰਨਾ

independence ('ਇੰਡਿ'ਪੈਨਡਅੰਸ) *n* ਸੁਤੰਤਰਤਾ, ਸਵਾਧੀਨਤਾ, ਆਜ਼ਾਦੀ

independent (ਇੰਡਿਪੌਨਡਅੰਟ) *a n* ਸੁਤੰਤਰ, ਆਜ਼ਾਦ, ਸਵਾਧੀਨ; ਨਿਰਪੇਖ

index ('ਇਨਡੈੱਕਸ) *n v* ਸੂਚਕ ਨਿਸ਼ਾਨ, ਦਲੀਲ, ਚਿੰਨ੍ਹ; ~finger ਤਰਜਨੀ, ਅੰਗੂਠੇ ਦੇ ਨਾਲ ਦੀ ਉਂਗਲੀ

indian ('ਇਨਡੀਅਨ) *n* ਭਾਰਤੀ, ਹਿੰਦੁਸਤਾਨੀ

indicate ('ਇਨਡਿਕੇਇਟ) *v* ਸੁਝਾਉਣਾ, ਪ੍ਰਸਤਾਵਤ ਕਰਨਾ, ਪ੍ਰਤੀਕ ਹੋਣਾ, ਸੰਕੇਤ ਕਰਨਾ, ਇਸ਼ਾਰਾ ਕਰਨਾ, ਘੋਸ਼ਣਾ ਕਰਨੀ, ਦੱਸਣਾ, ਜਤਾਉਣਾ, ਪਰਗਟ ਕਰਨਾ; ~d ਸੂਚਤ, ਸੰਕੇਤਤ, ਨਿਰਦਿਸ਼ਟ

indication ('ਇਨਡਿ'ਕੇਇਸ਼ਨ) *n* ਚਿੰਨ੍ਹ, ਲੱਛਣ, ਪਰਦਰਸ਼ਕ ਸੰਕੇਤ, ਇਸ਼ਾਰਾ

indicative (ਇਨ'ਡਿਕਅਟਿਵ) *a n* (ਵਿਆ) ਨਿਸ਼ਚੇਵਾਚਕ; ਬੋਧਕ, ਸੁਝਾਉ, ਸੂਚਕ, ਸੰਦੇਤਕ ਸਵੀਕਾਰ ਸੂਚਕ; ਨਿਸ਼ਚੇ ਅਰਥ

indicator ('ਇਨਡਿਕੇਇਟ*) *n* ਸੂਚਕ, ਬੋਧਕ, ਨਿਰਦੇਸ਼ਕ, (ਜੰਤਰ ਦੀ) ਸੂਈ

indict (ਇਨ'ਡਿਕਟ) v ਦੋਸ਼ ਲਾਉਣਾ, ਅਪਰਾਧੀ ਠਹਿਰਾਉਣਾ; ~**able** ਦੋਸ਼ ਲਾਉਣ ਜੋਗ, ਅਪਰਾਧੀ ਠਹਿਰਾਉਣ ਜੋਗ; ~**ment** ਦੋਸ਼-ਆਰੋਪਣ, ਆਰੋਪਣ-ਵਿਧੀ, ਕਾਨੂੰਨੀ ਦਾਅਵਾ

indifference (ਇਨ'ਡਿਫ਼ਰਅੰਸ) n ਬੇਪਰਵਾਹੀ, ਬੇ-ਵਾਸਤਾ, ਉਦਸੀਨਤਾ, ਮਹੱਤਵਹੀਨਤਾ

indifferent (ਇਨ'ਡਿਫ਼ਰਅੰਟ) a ਉਦਸੀਨ, ਵਿਰਕਤ, ਬੇਲਾਗ, ਬੇਪਰਵਾਹ, ਅਲਗਰਜ਼

indigenous (ਇਨ'ਡਿਜਿਨਅਸ) a ਸੁਦੇਸ਼ੀ, ਦੇਸ਼ੀ

indigestion (ਇਨਡਿ'ਜੇਸ਼ਨ) n ਬਦਹਜ਼ਮੀ, ਅਜੀਰਣਤਾ, ਅਨਪਾਚ

indignity (ਇਨ'ਡਿਗਨਅਟਿ) n ਨਿਰਾਦਰ, ਅਨਾਦਰ, ਖੁਆਰੀ, ਅਵੱਗਿਆ, ਅਪਮਾਨ, ਹੱਤਕ, ਹੇਠੀ, ਤਿਰਸਕਾਰ, ਫਿਟਕਾਰ; ਅਸ਼ਿਸ਼ਟ ਆਚਰਨ

indigo (ਇਨਡਿਗਅਉ) n ਨੀਲ

indirect ('ਇਨਡਿ'ਰੈਕਟ) a ਟੇਢਾ, ਵਿੰਗਾ, ਅਸਿੱਧਾ, ਫੇਰਵਂ, ਵਕਰ, ਕੁਟਲ, ਚੱਕਰਦਾਰ, ਟੇਢਾ-ਮੇਢਾ; ਅਸਰਲ

indiscipline (ਇਨ'ਡਿ'ਸਿਪਲਿਨ) n ਬੇਜ਼ਬਤੀ, ਅਨੁਸ਼ਾਸਨਹੀਨਤਾ, ਅਸੰਜਮ

indiscretion ('ਇਨਡਿ'ਸਕਰੈੱਸ਼ਨ) n ਚਿੰਤਨਹੀਣਤਾ; ਨਾਦਾਨੀ, ਅਵਿਵੇਕ

indiscreet ('ਇਨਡਿ'ਸਕਰੀਟ) a ਅਸਾਵਧਾਨ, ਸੂਝ ਰਹਿਤ

indiscriminate ('ਇਨਡਿ'ਸਕਰਿਮਿਨਅਟ) a ਨਿਰਪੱਛਾਤ, ਵਿਵੇਕਹੀਨ, ਅੰਧਾਪੁੰਦ, ਰਲਿਆ-ਮਿਲਿਆ; ~**ness** ਨਿਰਪੱਛਾਤ, ਵਿਵੇਕਹੀਨਤਾ; ਗੱਡ-ਮੱਡ

indispensability ('ਇਨਡਿ'ਸਪੈੱਸਅ'ਬਿਲਅਟਿ) n ਅਵੱਸ਼ਕਤਾ

indispensable (ਇਨਡਿ'ਸਪੈੱਨਸਅਬਲ) a ਲਾਜ਼ਮੀ, ਜ਼ਰੂਰੀ, ਅਵੱਸ਼ਕ

indispose (ਇਨਡਿ'ਸਪਅਉਜ਼) v ਢਿੱਲਾ ਕਰਨਾ, ਅਸੁਅਸਥ ਕਰਨਾ, ਅਯੋਗ ਕਰਨਾ; ਘੇਮਖ ਕਰਨਾ, ਵਿਰਕਤ ਬਣਾਉਣਾ, ਅਰੁਚੀ ਪੈਦਾ ਕਰਨੀ, ਦਿਲ ਫੇਰ ਦੇਣਾ; ~**d** ਢਿੱਲਾ, ਅਸੁਅਸਥ, ਬੀਮਾਰ

indispostion ('ਇਨਡਿਸਪਅ'ਜ਼ਿਸ਼ਨ) n ਢਿੱਲ, ਕਸਰ, ਨਾਸਾਜ਼ਗੀ; ਬੇਦਿਲੀ, ਅਰੁਚੀ

indisputable ('ਇਨਡਿ'ਸਪਯੂਟਅਬਲ) a ਨਿਰਵਿਵਾਦ, ਨਿਸ਼ਚਤ

indistinct ('ਇਨਡਿ'ਸਟਿਙ੍ਕ(ਕ)ਟ) a ਅਸਪਸ਼ਟ, ਧੁੰਦਲਾ

individual ('ਇਨਡਿ'ਵਿਜੁਅਲ) n a ਵਿਅਕਤੀ, ਜਣਾ, ਜਨ, ਆਦਮੀ; ਜਾਤੀ, ਸ਼ਖ਼ਸੀ; ਇੱਕਲਾ, ਅੱਡੋ-ਅੱਡ; ਵਿਸ਼ੇਸ਼, ਵਿਅਕਤੀਗਤ; ~**ism** ਵਿਅਕਤੀਵਾਦ, ਅਹੰਵਾਦ, ਨਿਜਵਾਦ; ~**ist** ਵਿਅਕਤੀਵਾਦੀ, ਅਹੰਵਾਦੀ, ਨਿਜਵਾਦੀ, ਨਿਜਤਵਵਾਦੀ; ~**ity** ਆਪਾ, ਸ਼ਖ਼ਸੀਅਤ, ਜਾਤ

indivisibility ('ਇਨਡਿ'ਵਿਜ਼ਅ'ਬਿਲਅਟਿ) n ਅਵੰਡਤਾ, ਅਖੰਡਤਾ

indivisible ('ਇਨਡਿ'ਵਿਜ਼ਅਬਲ) a n ਅਵੰਡ, ਅੱਖੰਡ, ਅਭੇਦੀ

indolence ('ਇਨਡਅਲਅੰਸ) n ਆਲਸ, ਸੁਸਤੀ, ਵਿਮੁਖਤਾ

indolent ('ਇਨਡਅਲਅੰਟ) a ਆਲਸੀ, ਸੁਸਤ, ਪੀੜ-ਰਹਿਤ

indologist (ਇਨ'ਡੌਲਅਜਿਸਟ) n ਭਾਰਤ ਸਬੰਧੀ ਗਿਆਨ ਵੇਤਾ, ਭਾਰਤ-ਵਿਗਿਆਨੀ

indology (ਇਨ'ਡੌਲਅਜਿ) n ਭਾਰਤ-ਵਿਗਿਆਨ

indomitable (ਇਨ'ਡੌਮਿਟਅਬਲ) a ਅਜਿੱਤ, ਹਠੀ, ਜ਼ਿੱਦੀ, ਬੇਕਾਬੂ, ਹਠੀਲਾ

indoor ('ਇਨਡੋੰ*) *a* ਅੰਤਰਵਾਸੀ, ਅੰਦਰਲਾ, ਭੀਤਰੀ, ਨਿਵਾਸੀ (ਰੋਗੀ)

indubious (ਇਨ'ਡਯੂਬਯਅਸ) *a* ਨਿਸ਼ਚਤ, ਸੰਦੇਹਹੀਨ

induce (ਇਨ'ਡਯੂਸ) *v* ਪਰੇਰਨਾ, ਲੁਭਾ ਲੈਣਾ, ਫੁਸਲਾ ਦੇਣਾ, ਮੰਨਣਾ; ਲਿਆਉਣਾ, ਪੈਦਾ ਕਰਨਾ; ਕਾਰਨ ਬਣਨਾ; ~ment ਲੋੜ, ਉਤਸ਼ਾਹ

induct (ਇਨ'ਡਅੱਕਟ) *v* ਅਧਿਕਾਰ ਦੇਣਾ; ਕਬਜ਼ਾ ਦੇਣਾ; ਭਰਤੀ ਕਰਨਾ, ਪ੍ਰਵੇਸ਼ ਕਰਾਉਣਾ; ਪੂਰਵਤ ਕਰਨਾ; ~ion ਪ੍ਰਵੇਸ਼, ਭੂਮਕਾ, ਪ੍ਰਸਤਾਵਨਾ; (ਲਿਆਂ) ਆਗਮਨ; ~ive ਆਗਮਨਾਤਮਕ, ਅਨੁਮਾਨਾਤਮਕ

indulge (ਇਨ'ਡਅੱਲਜ) *v* ਤ੍ਰਿਪਤ ਕਰਨਾ ਜਾਂ ਹੋਣਾ, ਸਲਾਹ ਦੇਣਾ; ਭੋਗਣਾ; ਸ਼ੌਕ ਵਧਣਾ; ~nce ਮਜ਼ਾ, ਆਤਮਤ੍ਰਿਪਤੀ, ਆਤਮ-ਸੰਤੋਸ਼; ਅਤੀਭੋਗ; ~nt ਦਿਆਲੂ, ਕਿਰਪਾਲੂ, ਦਇਆਵਾਨ, ਮਿਹਰਬਾਨ; ਸ਼ੁਕੀਨ; ਆਸਕਤ, ਲਿਪਤ

industrial (ਇਨ'ਡਅੱਸਟਰਿਅਲ) *a* ਉਦੱਮੀ (ਆਦਮੀ) ਉਦੱਮ ਸਬੰਧੀ, ਉਦਯੋਗਕ; ~isation ਉਦਯੋਗੀਕਰਨ, ਸਨਅਤੀਕਰਨ; ~ism ਉਦਯੋਗਵਾਦ, ਸਨਅਤਵਾਦ, ~ist ਕਾਰਖ਼ਨੇਦਾਰ, ਉਦਯੋਗਪਤੀ, ਉਦਯੋਗਵਾਦੀ, ਉਦਯੋਗ ਵਿਸ਼ੇਸ਼ੱਗ; ~ize ਉਦਯੋਗੀਕਰਨ ਕਰਨਾ

industrious (ਇਨ'ਡਅੱਸਟਰਿਅਸ) *a* ਮਿਹਨਤੀ ਉਦਯੋਗੀ, ਉਦੱਮੀ

industry ('ਇਨਡਅਸਟਰਿ) *n* ਮਿਹਨਤ, ਉੱਦਮ, ਕਰਮ-ਨਿਸ਼ਠਾ; ਉਦਯੋਗ, ਸਨਅਤ, ਦਸਤਕਾਰੀ

indwell ('ਇਨ'ਡਵੈੱਲ) *v* ਰਹਿਣਾ, ਨਿਵਾਸ ਕਰਨਾ, ਘੁਸਣਾ, ਅਧਿਕਾਰ ਜਮਾਉਣਾ

ineffable (ਇਨ'ਐੱਫ਼ਅਬਲ) *a* ਅਕੱਥ, ਅਕਹੀ, ਪ੍ਰਸੰਸਾ ਤੋਂ ਬਾਹਰ

ineffaceable ('ਇਨਿ'ਫ਼ੇਇਸਅਬਲ) *a* ਅਮਿਟ, ਅਮੇਸ, ਪੱਕਾ

ineffective (ਇਨਿ'ਫ਼ੈੱਕਟਿਵ) *a* ਪ੍ਰਭਾਵਹੀਨ, ਬੇਅਸਰ, ਨਿਕੰਮਾ, ਵਿਅਰਥ; ~ness ਅਪ੍ਰਭਾਵਤਾ, ਨਿਸਫਲਤਾ; ਵਿਅਰਥਤਾ, ਅਯੋਗਤਾ

inefficient ('ਇਨਿ'ਫ਼ਿਸ਼ੰਟ) *a* ਅਕੁਸ਼ਲ, ਨਾਲਾਇਕ; ਨਿਸਫਲ, ਨਿਰਰਥਕ

inelastic ('ਇਨਿ'ਲੈਸਾਂਟਕ) *a* ਲਚਕਹੀਨ, ਬੇਲਚਕ, ਅੜੀਅਲ; ~ity ਲਚਕਹੀਨਤਾ, ਲੋਚਹੀਨਤਾ; ਮੁੱਲ-ਨਿਰਲੇਪਤਾ, ਹਠ

inept (ਇਨੈੱਪਟ) *a* ਅਢੁੱਕਵਾਂ, ਬੇਤੁਕਾ, ਕੁਢਾਂਗੀ; ਅਸੰਗਤ

inequality ('ਇਨਿ'ਕਵੈੱਲਅਟਿ) *n* ਨਾਬਰਾਬਰੀ, ਅਸਮਾਨਤਾ, ਅਸਮਤਾ, ਕਮੀ-ਬੇਸੀ, ਵਾਧਾ ਘਾਟਾ

inertia (ਇ'ਨਅਃਸ਼ਅ) *n* ਗਤੀਹੀਨਤਾ (ਭੌ) ਜੜ੍ਹਤਾ, ਸਥਿਰਤਾ, ਨਿਸ਼ਚਲਤਾ, ਸਿਥਲਤਾ

inesse (ਇਨ'ਐੱਸਿ) (L) *adv* ਅਸਲ ਵਿਚ, ਵਾਸਤਵ ਵਿਚ

inevitable (ਇਨ'ਐੱਵ਼ਿਟਅਬਲ) *a* ਅਟੱਲ, ਅਮਿਟ, ਲਾਜ਼ਮੀ

inexperience ('ਇਨਿਕ'ਸਪਿਅਰਿਅੰਸ) *n* ਨਾਤਜਰਬੇਕਾਰੀ, ਅਨਾੜੀਪਨ, ਅੱਲ੍ਹੜਪਨਾ, ਅਨੁਭਵਹੀਨਤਾ; ~d ਅਨਾੜੀ, ਅਨੁਭਵਹੀਨ

infancy ('ਇਨਫ਼ੰਸਿ) *n* ਵਿਕਾਸ ਦੀ ਆਰੰਭਕ ਅਵਸਥਾ; ਬਾਲਪਨ; ਬਚਪਨ; ਨਾਬਾਲਗ਼ਾ

infant ('ਇਨਫ਼ਅੰਟ) *n* ਬਾਲ, ਬਾਲਕ; ਬੱਚਾ, ਨਿਆਣਾ, ਮਾਸੂਮ, ਇਆਣਾ, ਅੰਵਾਣਾ, ਰੀਗਾ,

ਨਿਕੜਾ, ਨਾਬਾਲਗ਼	ਉਤੇਜਤ ਕਰਨਾ; ਭੜਕਾਉਣਾ, ਉਭਾਰਨਾ; ਤੇਜ਼ ਕਰਨਾ, ਅੰਗ ਉਠਣਾ

infantry ('ਇਨਫ਼ਅੰਟਰਿ) *n* ਪਿਆਦਾ ਫ਼ੌਜ, ਪੈਦਲ ਸੈਨਾ

infer (ਇਨ'ਫ਼ਅ:) *v* ਅਨੁਮਾਨ ਲਾਉਣਾ, ਦਲੀਲ ਦੇਣੀ, ਅਰਥ ਦੇਣਾ, ਸੂਚਤ ਕਰਨਾ, ਭਾਵ ਲੈਣਾ; ~**able** ਅਨੁਮਾਨ ਲਾਉਣ ਯੋਗ, ਅਰਥ ਦੇਣ ਯੋਗ, ਸੂਚਤ ਕਰਨ ਯੋਗ; ~**ence** ਅਨੁਮਾਨ, ਨਿਰਣਾ, ਪਰਿਣਾਮ; ਨਿਰਣੀਤ ਵਿਸ਼ਾ

inferior (ਇਨ'ਫ਼ਿਅਰਿਆ*) *n a* ਮਾਤਹਿਤ; ਤੁੱਛ, ਛੋਟਾ, ਨੀਵਾਂ, ਅਸ੍ਰੇਸ਼ਠ, ਘਟੀਆ; ~**ity** ਹੀਣਤਾ, ਤੁੱਛਤਾ, ਛੋਟਪਨ, ਨੀਵਾਂਪਨ, ਅਸ੍ਰੇਸ਼ਠਤਾ, ਘਟੀਆਪਣ; ~**ity complex** ਹੀਣਤਾ-ਭਾਵ, ਹੀਣ-ਭਾਵਨਾ, ਆਤਮ-ਹੀਣਤਾ

inferno (ਇਨ'ਫ਼ਅ:ਨਅਉ) *n* ਨਰਕ, ਦੋਜ਼ਖ

infidel ('ਇਨਫ਼ਿਡ(ਅ)ਲ) *n a* ਨਾਸਤਕ, ਕਾਫ਼ਰ, ਅਨੀਸ਼ਵਰਵਾਦੀ, ਧਰਮ-ਨਿੰਦਕ; ~**ity** ਵਿਸ਼ਵਾਸਘਾਤ, ਨਾਸਤਕਤਾ, ਧਰਮ-ਧਰੋਹ ਸ਼ਰਧਾਹੀਨਤਾ

infiltrate ('ਇਨਫ਼ਿਲਰੇਇਟ) *v* ਅੰਦਰ ਘੁਸਣਾ, ਘੁਸਪੈਠ ਕਰਨੀ, ਪ੍ਰਵੇਸ਼ ਕਰਨਾ, ਵਿਆਪਤ ਹੋਣਾ

infiltration ('ਇਨਫ਼ਿਲ'ਟਰੇਇਸ਼ਨ) *n* ਚੋਰੀ-ਛਿਪੇ ਘੁਸਣ ਦੀ ਕਿਰਿਆ, ਘੁਸਪੈਠ

infinite ('ਇਨਫ਼ਿਨਅਟ) *a* ਅਸੀਮ, ਅਨੰਤ, ਅਪਾਰ, ਬੇਹੱਦ; ਅਣਗਿਣਤ

infirm (ਇਨ'ਫ਼ਅ:ਮ) *a* ਨਿਰਬਲ, ਦੁਰਬਲ ਕਮਜ਼ੋਰ, ਨਿਤਾਣਾ, ਛੀਣ, ਸਿਥਲ; ~**ity** ਨਿਰਬਲਤਾ, ਦੁਰਬਲਤਾ, ਕਮਜ਼ੋਰੀ, ਨਿਤਾਣਾਪਨ ਖੀਣਤਾ

infix ('ਇਨਫ਼ਿਕਸ, ਇਨ'ਫ਼ਿਕਸ) *n v* (ਭਾਸ਼ਾ) ਪ੍ਰਤਯ; ਵਿਚ ਜੜਨਾ; ਟਿਕਾਉਣਾ

inflame (ਇਨ'ਫ਼ਲੇਇਮ) *v* ਅੱਗ ਲਾਉਣੀ;

inflammation ('ਇਨ'ਫ਼ਲਅ'ਮੇਇਸ਼ਨ) *n* ਦਾਹ, ਤਾਪ, ਜਲਣ, ਸੋਜ਼ਸ਼

inflammatory (ਇਨਫ਼ਲਅਟ(ਅ)ਰਿ) *a* ਅੱਗ-ਲਾਊ, ਭੜਕਾਊ; ਸੋਜ਼ਸ਼ਕਾਰੀ

inflate (ਇਨ'ਫ਼ਲੇਇਟ) *v* ਫੂਕ ਦੇਣੀ, ਫਲਾਉਣਾ, ਹਵਾ ਭਰਨੀ; ਅਭਿਮਾਨੀ ਬਣਾ ਦੇਣਾ

inflation (ਇਨ'ਫ਼ਲੇਇਸ਼ਨ) *n* ਫੈਲਾਉ, ਮੁਦਾ ਫੈਲਾਉ

inflect (ਇਨ'ਫ਼ਲੇਂਕਟ) *v* ਸ਼ਬਦ ਦਾ ਰੂਪ ਬਦਲਾਉਣਾ, ਰੂਪ ਸਾਧਨਾ ਕਰਨੀ; ~**ion**, **inflexion** (ਵਿਆ) ਵਿਭਕਤੀ; (ਸੰਗੀ) ਸੁਰ ਦਾ ਉਤਰ-ਚੜ੍ਹ

inflexible (ਇਨ'ਫ਼ਲੇਂਕਸਅਬਲ) *a* ਲਚਕਹੀਨ, ਬੇਲਚਕ, ਆਕੜਿਆ, ਤਰਿੰਗ, ਕਰੜਾ

inflexional (ਇਨ'ਫ਼ਲੇਂਕਸ਼ਨਲ) *a* (ਭਾਸ਼ਾ) ਵਿਕਾਰੀ

influence ('ਇਨਫ਼ਲੁਅੰਸ) *n v* ਪ੍ਰਭਾਵ, ਅਸਰ, ਰਸੂਖ, ਪ੍ਰਭਾਵਤ ਕਰਨਾ, ਅਸਰ ਪਾਉਣਾ

influential ('ਇਨਫ਼ਲੁ'ਐਂਸ਼ਲ) *a* ਪ੍ਰਭਾਵਸ਼ਾਲੀ, ਪ੍ਰਭਾਵ-ਪੂਰਨ, ਪ੍ਰਭਾਵੀ

influenza ('ਇਨਫ਼ਲੁ'ਐਂਜ਼ਾ) *n* ਨਜ਼ਲਾ, ਫਲੂ, ਸਰਦੀ-ਜ਼ੁਕਾਮ ਨਾਲ ਤਾਪ

influx ('ਇਨਫ਼ਲਅੱਕਸ) *n* ਅੰਦਰ ਨੂੰ ਵਹਿਣ; ਅੰਤਰ-ਪਰਵਾਹ, ਅੰਤਰ ਆਗਮ

inform (ਇਨ'ਫ਼ੋਮ) *v* ਪਤਾ ਦੇਣਾ, ਖ਼ਬਰ ਦੇਣੀ, ਸੂਹ ਦੇਣੀ, ਸੂਚਤ ਕਰਨਾ; ਇਲਜ਼ਾਮ ਲਾਉਣਾ; ਪਰੇਰਤ ਕਰਨਾ

informal (ਇਨ'ਫ਼ੋ'ਮਲ) *a* ਗ਼ੈਰ-ਰਸਮੀ, ਅਨੁਪਚਾਰਕ, ਸਾਦੀ, ਬੇਕਾਇਦਾ

informant (ਇਨ'ਫ਼ੋਮੈਂਟ) *n* ਮੁਖ਼ਬਰ; ਸੂਚਕ, ਸੰਦੇਸ਼ਵਾਹਕ

information ('ਇਨਫ਼ਅ'ਮੇਇਸ਼ਨ) *n* (ਕਾ) ਸ਼ਿਕਾਇਤ; ਸੂਚਨਾ, ਇਤਲਾਹ, ਸਮਾਚਾਰ, ਖ਼ਬਰ ਜਾਣਕਾਰੀ

infraction (ਇਨ'ਫ਼ਰੈਕਸ਼ਨ) *n* ਉਲੰਘਣਾ; ਭੰਗ ਕਰਨ (ਦਾ ਕਾਰਜ)

infuriate (ਇਨ'ਫ਼ਯੂਅਰਿਏਇਟ) *v* ਕਰੋਧ ਦੁਆਉਣਾ, ਗੁੱਸਾ ਚੜ੍ਹਾਉਣਾ

infuriation (ਇਨ'ਫ਼ਯੂਅਰਿ'ਏਇਸ਼ਨ) *n* ਕਰੋਧ, ਤੈਸ਼, ਝੁੰਜਲਾਹਟ

infuse (ਇਨ'ਫ਼ਯੂਜ਼) *v* ਉਲੰਡਣਾ, ਭਰਨਾ; ਜਾਨ ਪਾ ਦੇਣੀ, ਪਰੇਰਨਾ ਦੇਣੀ; ਭਿੱਜਣਾ, ਤਰ ਹੋਣਾ

infusion (ਇਨ'ਫ਼ਯੂਯ਼ਨ) *n* ਕਾੜ੍ਹਾ; ਸੰਚਾਰਨ; ਘੋਲ, ਨਚੋੜ

ingredient (ਇਨ'ਗਰੀਡਅਂਟ) *n* ਅੰਗ, ਅੰਸ਼; ਮੂਲ ਸਮਗਰੀ, ਸੰਘਟਕ ਅੰਸ਼

inhabit (ਇਨ'ਹੈਬਿਟ) *v* ਵੱਸਣਾ, ਰਹਿਣਾ, ਵਾਸ ਕਰਨਾ; ਅਧਿਕਾਰ ਕਰਨਾ

inhale (ਇਨ'ਹੇਇਲ) *v* ਸਾਹ ਅੰਦਰ ਖਿੱਚਣਾ, ਸਾਹ ਲੈਣਾ; ਕਸ਼ ਖਿੱਚਣਾ (ਸਿਗਰਟ ਜਾਂ ਹੁੱਕੇ ਦਾ), ਦਮ ਲਾਉਣਾ

inherit (ਇਨ'ਹੈਰਿਟ) *v* ਵਿਰਸੇ ਵਿਚ ਮਿਲਣਾ; ਉੱਤਰਾਧਿਕਾਰ ਵਿਚ ਪ੍ਰਾਪਤ ਕਰਨਾ; **~ance** ਉੱਤਰਾਧਿਕਾਰ; ਵਿਰਸਾ, ਵਿਰਾਸਤ

inhibit (ਇਨ'ਹਿਬਿਟ) *v* ਰੁਕਾਵਟ ਪਾਉਣਾ, ਵਿਘਨ ਪਾਉਣਾ, ਰੋਕਣਾ ਮਨ੍ਹਾਂ ਕਰਨਾ, ਵਰਜਣਾ; **~ion** ਨਿਰੋਧ, ਨਿਰੋਧਨ, (ਕਾ) ਨਿਰੋਧ-ਲੇਖ, ਰੋਕ, ਮਨਾਹੀ

inhuman (ਇਨ'ਹਯੂਮਅਨ) *a* ਅਮਾਨਵੀ, ਅਟਮਨੁੱਖੀ, ਗ਼ੈਰ-ਇਨਸਾਨੀ; ਵਹਿਸ਼ੀ

inhumane ('ਇਨਹਯੂ'ਮੇਇਨ) *a* ਨਿਰਦਈ, ਕਠੋਰ

initial (ਇ'ਨਿਸ਼ਲ) *n v a* (ਬ ਵ) ਨਾਉਂ-ਅੱਖਰ, ਨਾਉਂ ਦੇ ਪਹਿਲੇ ਅੱਖਰ; ਹਸਤਾਖ਼ਰ ਕਰਨੇ, ਛੋਟੇ ਦਸਤਖ਼ਤ ਕਰਨੇ, ਨਾਉਂ ਦੇ ਪਹਿਲੇ ਅੱਖਰ ਪਾਉਣੇ; ਮੁੱਢਲਾ, ਆਦਿ, ਪੁਰੰਤਕ

initiate (ਇ'ਨਿਸ਼ਿਅਟ, ਇ'ਨਿਸ਼ਿਏਇਟ) *v* ਆਰੰਭ ਕਰਨਾ, ਦੀਖਿਆ ਦੇਣੀ, ਚਾਲੂ ਕਰਨਾ; ਸਿਰਜਣ ਕਰਨਾ, ਦੀਖਿਅਤ

initiation (ਇ'ਨਿਸ਼ਿ'ਏਇਸ਼ਨ) *n* ਆਰੰਭ, ਸ਼ੁਰੂਗਟੇਸ਼, ਦੀਖਿਆ, ਪ੍ਰਵੇਸ਼

initiative (ਇ'ਨਿਸ਼ਿਅਟਿਵ) *n a* ਪਹਿਲ, ਆਰੰਭ, ਪਹਿਲਾ ਕਦਮ, ਆਰੰਭਕ, ਪੁਰੰਤਕ

initio (ਇ'ਨਿਸ਼ਿਅਉ) (*L*) *adv* ਸ਼ੁਰੂ ਵਿਚ

inject (ਇਨ'ਜੈੱਕਟ) *v* ਟੀਕਾ ਲਾਉਣਾ, ਸੂਆ ਲਾਉਣਾ, ਸੂਈ ਲਾਉਣੀ, ਇੰਜੈਕਸ਼ਨ ਦੇਣਾ; ਭਰਨਾ, ਪਾਉਣਾ

injunction (ਇਨ'ਜਅੰਙਕਸ਼ਨ) *n* ਹੁਕਮ, ਆਗਿਆ, ਆਦੇਸ਼, ਹਿਦਾਇਤ; (ਕਾ) ਮਨਾਹੀ ਦਾ ਹੁਕਮ

injure ('ਇਨਜਅ*) *v* ਘਾਇਲ ਕਰਨਾ, ਸੱਟ-ਫੇਟ ਮਾਰਨੀ, ਚੋਟ ਲਾਉਣੀ; ਹਰਜ ਪਹੁੰਚਾਉਣਾ, ਨੁਕਸਾਨ ਕਰਨਾ

injurious (ਇਨ'ਜੁਅਰਿਅਸ) *a* ਅੱਤਿਆਚਾਰ-ਪੂਰਨ, ਅਪਮਾਨਜਨਕ, ਘਾਤਕ, ਦੁੱਖਦਾਇਕ, ਹਿੰਸਕ

injustice (ਇਨ'ਜਅੱਸਟਿਸ) *n* ਅਨਿਆਂ, ਬੇਇਨਸਾਫ਼ੀ; ਅਧਰਮੀ ਕਾਰਜ

ink (ਇੰਙਕ) *n v* ਸਿਆਹੀ, ਮੱਸ, ਮਸੀ, ਰੋਸ਼ਨਾਈ; ਸਿਆਹੀ ਲਾਉਣੀ

inkling ('ਇੰਙਕਲਿਙ) *n* ਸੰਕੇਤ, ਝਲਕ, ਇਸ਼ਾਰਾ,

ਠਿਕਾ, ਆਭਾਸ

inland ('ਇਨਲੈਂਡ) *n a adv* ਦੇਸ਼ ਦਾ ਅੰਦਰਲਾ ਭਾਗ, ਦੇਸ-ਅਭਿਅੰਤਰ; ਅੰਤਰਦੇਸ਼ੀ, ਦੇਸ ਦੇ ਅੰਦਰਲਾ; ਅੰਦਰ

in-laws ('ਇਨਲੋਜ਼) *n pl* ਸਹੁਰੇ, ਸਹੁਰਾ ਘਰ, ਸੁਸਰਾਲ ਵਾਲੇ

inmate ('ਇਨਮੇਇਟ) *n* ਵਾਸੀ, ਵਸਨੀਕ, ਸਹਿਵਾਸੀ

in memoriam (ਇਨਮਿ'ਮੋਰਿਐਮ) (*L*) *adv* ਯਾਦ ਵਿਚ, ਸਿਮਰਤੀ

inn (ਇਨ) *n* ਸਰਾਂ, ਧਰਮਸ਼ਾਲਾ

innate (ਇ'ਨੇਇਟ) *a* ਅੰਤਰੀਵ; ਜਮਾਂਦਰੂ, ਅੰਦਰਲਾ, ਸਹਿਜ, ਜਨਮਜਾਤ, ਸੁਤਾਵਕ

inner ('ਇਨਅ*) *a* ਅੰਦਰਲਾ, ਅੰਦਰੂਨੀ, ਆਂਤਰਕ, ਭੀਤਰੀ

innings ('ਇਨਿਙਗਜ਼) *n* (ਕ੍ਰਿਕਟ ਆਦਿ ਵਿਚ) ਪਾਲ, ਸਿਤ, ਵਾਰੀ; ਇਨਿੰਗ

innocence ('ਇਨਅਸਅੰਸ) *n* ਸਰਲਤਾ, ਮਾਸੂਮੀਅਤ, ਨਿਰਦੋਸ਼ਤਾ, ਅਗਿਆਨ, ਭੋਲਾਪਨ

innocent ('ਇਨਅਸੰਟ) *a n* ਅਟਜਾਣ, ਅਜਾਣ, ਭੋਲਾ, ਸਰਲ ਚਿੱਤ, ਸਿੱਧਾ; ਮੁਤ੍ਰ, ਬੁੱਧੂ ਆਦਮੀ

innovate ('ਇਨਅ(ਉ)ਵੇਇਟ) *v* ਕਾਢ ਕੱਢਣੀ, ਨਵੀਂ ਰੀਤ ਚਲਾਉਣੀ, ਪਰਿਵਰਤਨ ਲਿਆਉਣਾ

innovation ('ਇਨਅ'ਵੇਇਸ਼ਨ) *n* ਕਾਢ, ਘਾੜਤ, ਨਵੀਂ ਰੀਤ

innovative ('ਇਨਅਵ੍ਅਟਿਵ੍) *a* ਨਵੀਨਤਾਕਾਰੀ

in nuce (ਇਨ'ਨਯੂਸੇਇ) (*L*) *adv* ਸੰਖੇਪ ਵਿਚ

innumerable (ਇ'ਨਯੂਮ(ਅ)ਰਅਬਲ) *a* ਅਟਗਿਣਤ, ਅਸੰਖ, ਬੇਹਿਸਾਬ, ਬੇਸ਼ੁਮਾਰ

inoculate (ਇ'ਨੋਕਯੁਲੇਇਟ) *v* ਟੀਕਾ ਲਾਉਣਾ, ਸੂਆ ਲਾਉਣਾ

inoculation (ਇ'ਨੋਕਯੁ'ਲੇਇਸ਼ਨ) *n* ਟੀਕਾ ਲੋਂਦਾ; ਕਲਮ

inordinate (ਇਨ'ਓਡਿਨਟ) *a* ਅਤੀ ਅਧਿਕ ਬੇਹੱਦ, ਹੋੱਦੋਂ ਵੱਧ, ਅਤੀਮਾਤਰ

input ('ਇਨਪੁਟ) *n* ਅੰਤਰਗਾਮੀ; ਨਿਵੇਸ਼, ਆਦਾਨ

inquire, enquire (ਇਨ'ਕਵਾਇਅ*) *v* ਖੋਜਣਾ ਖੋਜ ਕਰਨਾ, ਪੁੱਛ-ਗਿੱਛ ਕਰਨੀ; ਪ੍ਰਸ਼ਨ ਕਰਨਾ ਪੱਚਣਾ, ਜਾਂਚ ਕਰਨੀ; ਤਹਿਕੀਕਾਤ ਕਰਨੀ

inquiry (ਇਨ'ਕਵਾਇਅਰਿ) *n* ਖੋਜ, ਪੁੱਛ-ਗਿੱਛ ਪਤਾ, ਜਾਂਚ, ਤਹਿਕੀਕਾਤ

inquisition ('ਇਨਕਵਿ'ਜ਼ਿਸ਼ਨ) *n* ਖੋਜ; ਪੁੱਛ ਜਾਂਚ, ਤਹਿਕੀਕਾਤ

inquisitive (ਇਨ'ਕਵਿਜ਼ਿਅਟਿਵ੍) *a* ਜਿਗਿਆਸੂ ਜਾਨਣ ਲਈ ਉਤਸੁਕ; ਖੋਜੀ

insane (ਇਨ'ਸੇਇਨ) *a* ਪਾਗਲ, ਦੀਵਾਨਾ ਭਰਾਂਤੀਚਿੱਤ, ਮੂਤ੍ਰ

insanitation (ਇਨ'ਸੈਨਿ'ਟੇਇਸ਼ਨ) *ਾ* ਅਸੁਅੱਛਤਾ, ਗੰਦਗੀ

insanitary (ਇਨ'ਸੈਨਿਟ(ਅ)ਰਿ) *a* ਗੰਦਗੀ ਭਰਿਆ, ਅਸੁਅਸਥਕਾਰੀ

insanity (ਇਨ'ਸੈਨਟਿ) *n* ਮਨੋਰੋਗ, ਪਾਗਲਪਣ ਦੀਵਾਨਗੀ, ਭਰਾਂਤੀ-ਚਿੱਤਤਾ, ਬੁੱਧੀਹੀਣਤਾ

inscribe (ਇਨ'ਸਕਰਾਇਬ) *v* ਉਕਰਨਾ, ਲਿਖਣਾ ਅੰਕਤ ਕਰਨਾ, ਚਿੰਨ੍ਹਣਾ; ਕਰਜ਼ੇ ਦਾ ਕੁਝ ਹਿੱਸ ਚੁਕਾਉਣਾ

inscription (ਇਨ'ਸਕਰਿਪਸ਼ਨ) *n* ਸ਼ਿਲਾ-ਲੇਖ ਸਿੱਕਿਆਂ ਦੀ ਲਿਖਤ, ਮੁਦ੍ਰਾ-ਲੇਖ

insect ('ਇਨਸੈਕਟ) *n* ਕੀੜਾ, ਪਤੰਗਾ, ਮਕੌੜਾ ਕੀਟ; **~icide** ਕੀਟਨਾਸ਼ਕ ਦਵਾਈ ਕੀਟਨਾਸ਼ਕ; ਕੀੜੇ ਮਾਰ

insecure ('ਇਨਸਿ'ਕਯੂਅ*) *a* ਅਸੁਰੱਖਿਅਤ, ਅਦ੍ਰਿੜ, ਕੱਚਾ, ਪੋਲਾ

insecurity ('ਇਨਸਿ'ਕਯੂਅਰਅਟਿ) *n* ਅਸੁਰੱਖਿਅਤਾ, ਭੈ, ਸ਼ੰਕਾ

insensible (ਇਨ'ਸੈਂਸਅਬਲ) *a* ਅਤੀ ਸੂਖ਼ਮ; ਅਚੇਤਨ, ਚੇਤਨਾ ਰਹਿਤ; ਅਟੱਬਿੱਜ, ਅਸੰਵੇਦਨਸ਼ੀਲ

insensitive (ਇਨ'ਸੈਂਸਅਟਿਵ) *a* ਅਸੰਵੇਦਨਸ਼ੀਲ, ਸੰਵੇਦਨਾ ਰਹਿਤ, ਭਾਵਹੀਨ, ਅਨੁਭੂਤੀਹੀਨ

insensuous (ਇਨ'ਸੈਂਸਯੁਅਸ) *a* ਅਕਾਮੁਕ, ਅਵਿਲਾਸੀ

insert (ਇਨ'ਸਅ:ਟ) *v* ਸੰਮਿਲਤ ਕਰਨਾ, ਜੋੜਨਾ; ਦਰਜ ਕਰਨਾ, ਬਿਠਾ ਦੇਣਾ, ਜਮਾ ਦੇਣਾ, ਘੁਸੇੜਨਾ, ਫ਼ਿਟ ਕਰਨਾ

inside ('ਇਨ'ਸਾਇਡ) *adv n a* ਅੰਦਰ, ਅੰਦਰਲੀ, ਅੰਦਰੂਨੀ; ਅੰਤਰ; ਆਂਤਰਕ, ਭੀਤਰੀ

insight ('ਇਨਸਾਇਟ) *n* ਸੂਝ, ਨੀਝ, ਅੰਤਰਦ੍ਰਿਸ਼ਟੀ

insignia (ਇਨ'ਸਿਗਨਿਆ) *n* (ਬ ਵ) ਅਧਿਕਾਰ ਚਿੰਨ੍ਹ, ਨਿਸ਼ਾਨ, ਬਿੱਲਾ, ਤਮਗ਼ਾ

insignificant ('ਇਨਸਿਗਾ'ਨਿਫ਼ਿਕਅੰਟ) *a* ਤੁੱਛ, ਹੇਚ; ਛੋਟਾ, ਮਹੱਤਵਹੀਨ; ਵਿਅਰਥ, ਬੇਕਾਰ

insist (ਇਨ'ਸਿਸਟ) *v* ਹਠ ਕਰਨਾ, ਰਿਹਾੜ ਕਰਨੀ, ਜ਼ਿਦ ਕਰਨੀ, ਅੜ ਜਾਣਾ; ਜ਼ੋਰ ਪਾਉਣਾ; ~ence ਹਠ, ਜ਼ਿਦ, ਆਗ੍ਰਹ, ਅਨੁਰੋਧ; ਜ਼ੋਰ

inspect (ਇਨ'ਸਪੈੱਕਟ) *v* ਜਾਂਚਣਾ; ਛਾਣਬੀਨ ਕਰਨੀ; ਨਿਰੀਖਣ ਕਰਨਾ, ਮੁਆਇਨਾ ਕਰਨਾ, ਦੇਖ-ਭਾਲ ਕਰਨੀ; ~ion ਜਾਂਚ, ਛਾਣਬੀਨ, ਨਿਰੀਖਣ, ਮੁਆਇਨਾ; ~or ਨਿਰੀਖਕ

inspiration ('ਇਨਸਪਅ'ਰੇਇਸ਼ਨ) *n* ਪਰੇਰਨਾ, ਉਤੇਜਨਾ ਪ੍ਰੋਤਸਾਹਨ, ਆਵੇਸ਼; ਸਾਹ ਖਿੱਚਣਾ

inspire (ਇਨ'ਸਪਾਇਅ*) *v* ਸਾਹ (ਅੰਦਰ ਨੂੰ) ਲੈਣਾ; ਰੂਹ ਫੂਕ ਦੇਣੀ, ਉਤਸ਼ਾਹਤ ਕਰਨਾ, ਪਰੇਰਨਾ ਦੇਣੀ, ਜਮਾ ਦੇਣਾ

instability ('ਇਨਸਟਅ'ਬਿਲਅਟਿ) *n* ਅਸਥਿਰਤਾ, ਅਨਿੱਤਤਾ, ਛਿਣਭੰਗਰਤਾ, ਅਸਥਾਈਤਵ

install (ਇਨਸਟੇਲ) *v* ਸਥਾਪਨਾ, ਪ੍ਰਕਾਸ਼ ਕਰਨਾ, ਗੱਦੀ ਉੱਤੇ ਬਿਠਾਉਣਾ, ਜਮਾਉਣਾ, ਗੱਡਣਾ, (ਮਸ਼ੀਨ) ਲਾਉਣਾ; ~ation ਨਿਵੇਸ਼, ਅਭਿਸ਼ੇਕ, ਨਿਰੋਪਣ, ਸਥਾਪਨਾ, ਲਗਾਈ

instalment (ਇਨ'ਸਟੇਲਮਅੰਟ) *n* ਕਿਸ਼ਤ, ਕਿਸ਼ਤਬੰਦੀ

instance ('ਇਨਸਟਅੰਸ) *n v* ਮਿਸਾਲ, ਦ੍ਰਿਸ਼ਟਾਂਤ, ਪ੍ਰਮਾਣ ਦੇਣਾ, ਉੱਲੇਖ ਕਰਨਾ

instant ('ਇਨਸਟਅੰਟ) *a n* ਅਤੀ ਜ਼ਰੂਰੀ; ਤਤਕਾਲੀ, ਝਟਪਟੀ, ਇਸ ਖਿਣ, ਵਰਤਮਾਨ, ਤੁਰੰਤ, ਤਤਕਾਲਕ; ~aneous ਤਤਕਾਲੀ, ਝਟਪਟੀ; ~ly ਤਤਕਾਲ, ਉਸੇ ਵੇਲੇ, ਤੁਰੰਤ, ਝਟਪਟ

in status quo (ਇਨ'ਸਟੇਇਟਅਸ'ਕਵਅਉ) (*L*) *adv* ਪਹਿਲੀ ਜੇਹੀ ਅਵਸਥਾ ਵਿਚ

instead (ਇਨ'ਸਟੈੱਡ) *adv* ਬਜਾਏ, ਦੀ ਥਾਂ ਤੇ, ਇਸ ਦੇ ਬਦਲੇ, ਇਸ ਦੇ ਵੱਟੇ

instigate ('ਇਨਸਟਿਗੋਇਟ) *v* ਉਕਸਾਉਣਾ, ਉਤਾਰਨਾ, ਸ਼ਹਿ ਦੇਣੀ, ਚੁੰਕਣਾ; ਉਤੇਜਤ ਕਰਨਾ; (ਫ਼ਸਾਦ, ਬਗਾਵਤ ਆਦਿ) ਫੁਸਲਾ ਕੇ ਕਰਾਉਣਾ

instigation ('ਇਨਸਟਿ'ਗੋਇਸ਼ਨ) *n* ਉਕਸਾਹਟ, ਉਤਸ਼ਾਹਨ, ਚੁੱਕ, ਉਤਾਰ

instigator (ਇਨਸਟਿਗੋਇਟਅ*) *n* ਉਕਸਾਉਣ ਵਾਲਾ, ਭੜਕਾਊ

instil(l) (ਇਨ'ਸਟਿਲ) *v* ਟਪਕਾਉਣਾ, ਬੂੰਦ-ਬੂੰਦ ਕਰ ਕੇ ਪਾਉਣਾ, ਦਿਲ ਵਿਚ ਬਿਠਾਉਣਾ, ਦ੍ਰਿੜ੍ਹ ਕਰਾਉਣਾ, ਪੱਕਾ ਕਰਾਉਣਾ; ਚਿੱਤ ਵਿਚ ਸਮਾਉਣਾ

instinct ('ਇਨਸਟਿਙਕਟ, ਇਨ'ਸਟਿਙਕਟ) *n a* ਕੁਦਰਤੀ ਸੂਝ, ਮੂਲ ਪ੍ਰਵਿਰਤੀ, ਫਿਤਰਤ, ਅੰਤਰ ਪਰੇਰਨਾ, ਸਹਿਜ ਪਰੇਰਨਾ, ਸਹਿਜ ਗਿਆਨ, ਅਨੁਭਵਤਾ; ਪੂਰਨ; ~ive ਕੁਦਰਤੀ, ਮੂਲ, ਪ੍ਰਵਿਰਤਕ; ਸਹਿਜ, ਅੰਤਹ-ਪਰੇਰਨਾ ਸਬੰਧੀ

institute ('ਇਨਸਟਿਟਯੂਟ) *v n* ਸਥਾਪਨਾ, ਕਾਇਮ ਕਰਨਾ, (ਪੜਤਾਲ ਆਦਿ) ਸ਼ੁਰੂ ਕਰਾਉਣੀ, ਮੁਕੱਰਰ ਕਰਨਾ; ਵਿਦਿਆਲੇ ਦਾ ਭਵਨ ਜਾਂ ਦਫ਼ਤਰ, ਸਭਾ, ਸੰਸਥਾ; ਰੀਤੀ-ਸੰਗ੍ਰਹ, ਵਿਧੀ-ਸਾਰ

institution ('ਇਨਸਟਿ'ਟਯੂਸ਼ਨ) *n* ਸੰਸਥਾ, ਆਸ਼ਰਮ; (ਪਾਦਰੀ ਆਦਿ ਦੀ) ਨਿਯੁਕਤੀ, ਸਥਾਪਨ, ਦਸਤੂਰ, ਰਿਵਾਜ, ਸੰਸਥਾ-ਭਵਨ; ~al ਸੰਸਥਾਗਤ, ਸੰਸਥਾਨਕ, ਸੰਸਥਾਤਮਕ

instruct (ਇਨ'ਸਟਅੱਕਟ) *v* ਸਿਖਾਉਣਾ, ਪੜ੍ਹਾਉਣਾ; ਦੱਸਣਾ, ਜ਼ਰੂਰੀ ਗੱਲਾਂ ਸਮਝਾਉਣਾ; ਹਦਾਇਤ ਦੇਣੀ; ~ion ਸਿਖਿਆ, ਪੜ੍ਹਾਈ, ਵਿਦਿਆਦਾਨ; ਸੂਚਨਾ, ਇਤਲਾਹ, ਨਿਰਦੇਸ਼; ~ive ਸਿਖਿਆਦਾਇਕ; ~or ਸਿਖਿਅਕ, ਗੁਰੂ, ਅਧਿਆਪਕ, ਨਿਰਦੇਸ਼ਕ

instrument (ਇਨਸਟ੍ਰ'ਮਅੰਟ) *n* ਹਥਿਆਰ, ਔਜ਼ਾਰ; ਹੱਥਠੋਕਾ, ਸਾਜ਼; (ਵਿਗਿਆਨ ਵਿਚ ਵਰਤਿਆ ਜਾਣ ਵਾਲਾ) ਜੰਤਰ, (ਕਾ) ਲਿਖਤ ਜਾਂ ਕਾਗ਼ਜ਼, ਇਖ਼ਤਿਆਰ-ਪੱਤਰ, ਦਸਤਾਵੇਜ਼

instrumental (ਇਨਸਟਰੁ'ਮੈਂਟਲ) *a* ਸਹਾਇਕ, ਵਸੀਲਾ ਬਣਨ ਵਾਲਾ; (ਸੰਗੀ) ਸਾਜ਼ ਦਾ; ਸੰਗੀਤ ਦਾ; ਜੰਤਰ ਸਬੰਧੀ; ~**case** ਕਰਣ ਕਾਰਕ;

~**ist** ਸਾਜ਼-ਵਾਦਕ

insubordinate (ਇਨਸਅ'ਬੋਡਿਨਅਟ) *a* ਅਵੱਗਿਆਕਾਰੀ ਬਾਗ਼ੀ, ਨਾਬਰ

insubordination (ਇਨਸਅ'ਬੋਡਿ'ਨਿਏਸ਼ਨ) *n* ਨਾਬਰੀ, ਅੱਵਗਿਆ, ਆਗਿਆ-ਭੰਗ, ਆਕੀਪੁਣਾ, ਨਾ ਫ਼ਰਮਾਨੀ

insufficient (ਇਨਸਅ'ਫ਼ਿਸ਼ੰਟ) *a* ਥੋੜ੍ਹਾ, ਘੱਟ, ਕਸਰਵੰਦਾ, ਨਾਕਾਫ਼ੀ, ਅਲਪ

insulator (ਇਨਸਯੁਲੇਇਟਅ*) *n* ਤਾਪ ਰੋਕ, ਇਨਸੁਲੇਟਰ

insult (ਇਨਸਅੱਲਟ, ਇਨ'ਸਅੱਲਟ) *n v* ਹੇਠੀ, ਹੱਤਕ, ਨਿਰਾਦਰੀ, ਅਪਮਾਨ; ਹੇਠੀ ਕਰਨੀ; ਹੱਤਕ ਕਰਨੀ, ਤਿਰਸਕਾਰ ਕਰਨਾ, ਅਪਮਾਨ ਕਰਨਾ; ~ing ਅਪਮਾਨਜਨਕ, ਅਨਾਦਰਜਨਕ, ਬੇਇੱਜ਼ਤੀ ਵਾਲਾ

insurance (ਇਸ'ਸ਼ੋਰਅੰਸ) *n* ਬੀਮਾ; ਬੀਮੇ ਦੀ ਕਰਮ; ~**policy** ਬੀਮਾ-ਪਾਲਸੀ, ਬੀਮਾ-ਪੱਤਰ

insure (ਇਸ'ਸ਼ੋ*) *v* ਬੀਮਾ ਕਰਨਾ, ਬੀਮੇ ਰਾਹੀਂ ਜਾਇਦਾਦ ਆਦਿ ਸੁਰੱਖਿਅਤ ਕਰਾਉਣੀ

insurgent (ਇਨ'ਸਅਃਜਅੰਟ) *a n* ਆਕੀ, ਬਾਗ਼ੀ, ਵਿਦਰੋਹੀ; (ਸਮੁੰਦਰ ਆਦਿ) ਸੈਲਾਬੀ, ਅੱਗੇ ਵੱਧਦਾ, ਉਭਰਦਾ; ਬਾਗ਼ੀ ਆਦਮੀ, ਵਿਦਰੋਹੀ ਵਿਅਕਤੀ

insurrection (ਇਨਸਅ'ਰੈੱਕਸ਼ਨ) *n* ਬਗ਼ਾਵਤ, ਵਿਦਰੋਹ, ਸਾਜ਼ਸ਼, ਬਗ਼ਾਵਤ ਦੀ ਲਹਿਰ

intact (ਇਨ'ਟੈਕਟ) *n* ਜਿਸ ਨੂੰ ਹੱਥ ਨਾ ਲਾਇਆ ਹੋਵੇ, ਅਛੋਹ; ਸਾਲਮ, ਪੂਰਨ, ਠੀਕ

intake (ਇਨਟੇਇਕ) *n* ਹਵਾ ਪਚੁੰਚਾਉਣ ਦਾ ਰਸਤਾ; ਵਟਕ; ਅੰਦਰ ਆਉਣ ਵਾਲਾ ਵਿਅਕਤੀ, ਕਾਸ਼ਤ ਕਰਨਯੋਗ, ਭੂਮੀ; ਅੰਤਰ-ਗ੍ਰਹਿਤ

integral (ਇਨਟਿਗਰ(ਅ)ਲ) *a* ਅਖੰਡ ਵਸਤੂ ਦਾ; ਪੂਰਾ (ਹਿੱਸਾ); ਕੁਲ, ਸਮੁੱਚਾ

integrate (ਇਨਟਿਗਰੇਇਟ) *v a* ਪੂਰਾ ਕਰਨਾ, ਏਕੀਕਰਨ ਕਰਨਾ, ਸਮੁੱਚਾ

integration (ਇਨਟਿ'ਗਰੇਇਸ਼ਨ) *n* ਮਿਲਾਪ, ਏਕਤਾ, ਮੇਲ, ਏਕੀਕਰਨ, ਅਨੁਕੂਲਤ

integrity (ਇਨ'ਟੈਗਰਅਟਿ) *n* ਪੂਰਨਤਾ; ਅਖੰਡਤਾ; ਨੇਕ-ਨੀਤੀ, ਇਮਾਨਦਾਰੀ, ਦਿਆਨਤਦਾਰੀ

intellect (ਇਨਟਅਲੈੱਕਟ) *n* ਸਮਝ, ਸੂਝ, ਬੁੱਧੀ, ਬੁੱਧੀਮਾਨ, ਸਿਆਣਾ; ~ual ਸੋਗਰ, ਅਕਲੀ; ਬੁੱਧੀਮਾਨ, ਬੁੱਧੀਜੀਵੀ; ~ualist ਬੁੱਧੀਵਾਦੀ

intelligence (ਇਨ'ਟੈਲਿਜਅੰਸ) *n* ਅਕਲ, ਸਮਝ, ਬੁੱਧੀ, ਗਿਆਨ, ਸੁੱਖਤਾ, ਸੂਝ; ਗੁਪਤ ਸੂਚਨਾ

intelligent (ਇਨ'ਟੈਲਿਜਅੰਟ) *a* ਸੁੱਖਤ, ਸੂਝਵਾਨ, ਸਮਝਦਾਰ, ਅਕਲਮੰਦ; ~sia ਬੁੱਧੀਜੀਵੀ, ਪੜ੍ਹੇ-ਲਿਖੇ ਲੋਕ

intelligibility (ਇਨ'ਟੈਲਿਜਅ'ਬਿਲਅਟਿ) *n* ਸੁਗਮਤਾ, ਸੁਬੋਧਤਾ

intelligible (ਇਨ'ਟੈਲਿਜਬਲ) *a* ਸੁਗਮ, ਸੁਬੋਧ, ਸਪੱਸ਼ਟ, ਸਮਝ ਵਿਚ ਆਉਣ ਵਾਲਾ

intend (ਇਨ'ਟੈਂਡ) *v* ਚਾਹੁਣਾ, ਚਿਤਵਣਾ, ਮਨ ਬਣਾਉਣਾ, ਠਾਣ ਲੈਣਾ; ਸੰਕਲਪ ਕਰਨਾ, ਇਰਾਦਾ ਕਰਨਾ; ਨਿਯਤ ਹੋਣਾ; ਮਤਲਬ ਹੋਣਾ, ਅਰਥ ਲਾਉਣਾ, ਭਾਵ ਹੋਣਾ

intense (ਇਨ'ਟੈਂਸ) *a* ਡੂੰਘਾ, ਤੀਬਰ, ਬਹੁਤ ਜ਼ਿਆਦਾ, ਤੀਖਣ, ਜ਼ੋਰਦਾਰ, ਪ੍ਰਬਲ, ਭਾਵਮਈ

intensification (ਇਨ'ਟੈਂਸਿਫ਼ਿ'ਕੇਇਸ਼ਨ) *n* ਤੀਬਰੀਕਰਨ, ਡੂੰਘਾ ਕਰਨਾ, ਗੁੜ੍ਹਾ ਕਰਨਾ

intensify (ਇਨ'ਟੈਂਸਿਫ਼ਾਇ) *v* ਡੂੰਘਾ ਕਰਨਾ ਜਾਂ ਹੋਣਾ, ਵਧਾਉਣਾ, ਭਾਵੁਕ ਹੋਣਾ

intensity (ਇਨ'ਟੈਂਸਅਟਿ) *n* ਤੀਬਰਤਾ, ਗੰਭੀਰਤਾ, ਡੂੰਘਾਈ, ਪ੍ਰਚੰਡਤਾ, ਪ੍ਰਬਲਤਾ, ਭਾਵੁਕਤਾ

intensive (ਇਨ'ਟੈਂਸਿਵ) *a* ਤੀਬਰ, ਪ੍ਰਚੰਡ, ਡੂੰਘਾ; ਘਣੀ ਖੇਤੀ

intent (ਇਨ'ਟੈਂਟ) *n a* ਇਰਾਦਾ, ਉਦੇਸ਼, ਨੀਤ, ਆਸ਼ਾ, ਸੰਕਲਪ, ਮੁਰਾਦ, ਮਤਲਬ, ਮਨਸ਼ਾ, ਇੱਛਿਆ; ਜੁੱਟਿਆ, ਤਤਪਰ

inter ('ਇੰਟਅ*) *prep v* ਗੱਡਣਾ, ਦੱਬਣਾ; ਵਿਚ, ਦਰਮਿਆਨ, ਅੰਤਰ, ਪਰਸਪਰ; ~alla (*L*) ਹੋਰ ਗੱਲਾਂ ਨਾਲ; ~se ਆਪੇ ਵਿਚ; ~action ਪਰਸਪਰ ਪ੍ਰਭਾਵ; ~caste ਅੰਤਰਜਾਤੀ; ~cede ਵਿਚ ਪੈਣਾ, ਵਿਚੋਲਾ ਬਣਨਾ, ਝਗੜਾ ਨਿਪਟਾਉਣਾ; ਦਖ਼ਲ ਦੇਣਾ

intercept (ਇੰਟਅ'ਸੈਪਟ) *v* ਵਿਚਕਾਰ ਰੋਕਣਾ; ਰਾਹ ਵਿਚ ਰੋਕਣਾ, ਰਸਤੇ ਵਿਚ ਪਕੜਨਾ; ~ion ਰੋਕ

intercession (ਇਨਟਅ'ਸੈੱਸ਼ਨ) *n* ਵਿਚੋਲਗੀ, ਸਾਲਸੀ, ਵਕਾਲਤ

interchange (ਇਨਟਅ'ਚੇਇੰਜ) *v* ਅਦਲਾ-ਬਦਲੀ ਕਰਨੀ, ਅਦਲ-ਬਦਲ; ~able ਬਦਲਣਾ, ਬਦਲਣਯੋਗ

intercommunicate (ਇਨਟਅ'ਕਅਮਯੁਨਿ'ਕੇਇਟ) *v* ਆਪਸੀ ਆਵਾਜਾਈ ਕਰਨੀ, ਪਰਸਪਰ ਮੇਲ-ਜੋਲ ਰੱਖਣਾ

intercommunication (ਇਨਟਅ'ਕਅਮਯੁਨਿ'ਕੇਇਸ਼ਨ) *n* ਆਵਾਜਾਈ, ਅੰਤਰ ਸੰਚਾਰ, ਪਰਸਪਰ ਮੇਲ-ਜੋਲ

intercourse (ਇਨਟਅਕੋਸ) *n* ਮੇਲ-ਜੋਲ, ਵਰਤੋਂ-ਵਿਹਾਰ; ਬੋਲ-ਚਾਲ; ਸੰਭੋਗ, ਮੈਥੁਨ

interdepend (ਇਨਟਅਡਿ'ਪੈਂਡ) *v* ਅੰਤਰ-ਸਬਧਤ ਹੋਣਾ, ਪਰਸਪਰ ਨਿਰਭਰ ਹੋਣਾ, ਇਕ ਦੂਜੇ ਉੱਤੇ ਨਿਰਭਰ ਹੋਣਾ, ਇਕ ਦੂਜੇ ਨਾਲ ਬੱਝੇ ਹੋਣਾ; **~ence** ਅੰਤਰ-ਸਬੰਧ, ਪਰਸਪਰ ਨਿਰਭਰਤਾ, ਇਕ ਦੂਜੇ ਦਾ ਆਸਰਾ; **~ent** ਇਕ ਦੂਜੇ ਤੇ ਨਿਰਭਰ, ਪਰਸਪਰ, ਆਸਰਤ, ਅੰਤਰ-ਸਬੰਧਤ

interest (ਇਨਟਰੈੱਸਟ) *n v* (1) ਅਧਿਕਾਰ, ਸਬੰਧ, ਭਲਾਈ, ਲਾਭ, ਫ਼ਾਇਦਾ, ਹਿਤ; (2) ਸੁਆਰਥ, ਸਰੋਕਾਰ, ਦਿਲਚਸਪੀ, ਰੁਚੀ, ਸ਼ੌਕ; (3) ਸੂਦ, ਵਿਆਜ; ਦਿਲਚਸਪੀ ਪੈਦਾ ਕਰਨੀ, ਪਰੇਰਨਾ ਦੇਣੀ, ਉਤਸੁਕਤਾ ਪੈਦਾ ਕਰਨੀ; **~ing** ਦਿਲਚਸਪ, ਰੋਚਕ, ਮਨੋਰੰਜਕ, ਸੁਆਦੀ

interfere (ਇਨਟਅ'ਫ਼ਿਅ*) *v* ਦਖ਼ਲ ਦੇਣਾ; ਵਿਘਨ ਪਾਉਣਾ, ਰੁਕਾਵਟ ਪਾਉਣੀ; **~nce** ਦਖ਼ਲ; ਵਿਘਨ; ਰੋਕ-ਟੋਕ

interfuse (ਇਨਟਅ'ਫ਼ਯੂਜ਼) *v* ਇਕ ਦੂਜੇ ਵਿਚ ਮਿਲਣਾ

interim (ਇਨਟਅਰਿਮ) *n a adv* ਵਿਚਕਾਰਲਾ ਸਮਾਂ, ਆਰਜ਼ੀ ਸਮਾਂ; ਵਿਚਕਾਰਲਾ, ਅੰਤਰਮ, ਆਰਜ਼ੀ

interior (ਇਨ'ਟਿਅਰਿਅ*) *a n* ਅੰਦਰੂਨੀ, ਅੰਦਰਲਾ, ਘਰੇਲੂ; ਮਾਨਸਕ, ਆਂਤਰਕ; ਅੰਦਰਲਾ ਭਾਗ, ਹਿਰਦਾ, ਅੰਤਹਕਰਨ, ਹੀਆ, ਆਤਮਾ

interjacent (ਇਨਟਅ'ਜੇਇਸੰਟ) *a* ਵਿਚਕਾਰਲਾ; ਵਿਚਲਾ, ਦਰਮਿਆਨੀ

interject ('ਇਨਟਅ'ਜੈੱਕਟ) *v* ਟੋਕ ਦੇਣਾ, ਵਿਚੋਂ ਬੋਲ ਪੈਣਾ, ਗੱਲ ਟੁੱਕਣੀ; ਘੁਸੇੜ ਦੇਣਾ; **~ion** (ਵਿਆ) ਵਿਸਮਕ, ਹੈਰਾਨੀ, ਅਫ਼ਸੋਸ ਆਦਿ ਦਾ ਸੂਚਕ ਸ਼ਬਦ

interlock (ਇਨਟਅ'ਲੋਕ) *v* ਇਕ ਦੂਜੇ ਵਿਚ ਫਸਣਾ, ਅੜਾਉਣਾ, ਫਸਾ ਕੇ ਜੋੜਨਾ, ਗੰਠਣਾ

interlocution (ਇਨਟਅਲਅ(ਉ)'ਕਯੂਸ਼ਨ) *n* ਗੱਲਬਾਤ, ਵਾਰਤਾਲਾਪ

interlope (ਇਨਟਅ'ਲਅਉਪ) *v* ਟੰਗ ਅੜਾਉਣਾ, ਦਖ਼ਲ ਦੇਣਾ

intermarriage (ਇਨਟਅ'ਮੈਰਿਜ) *n* ਅੰਤਰਜਾਤੀ ਵਿਆਹ

intermediate (ਇਨਟਅ'ਮੀਡੀਅਟ) *a v* ਵਿਚਕਾਰਲਾ, ਵਿਚਲਾ; ਵਿਚ ਪੈਣਾ, ਵਿਚ-ਵਿਚਾਉ ਕਰਨਾ

intermediation (ਇਨਟਅ'ਮੀਡਿ'ਏਇਸ਼ਨ) *n* ਮਧਿਅਸਥਤਾ, ਵਿਚੋਲਗੀ, ਸਾਲਸੀ

intermingle (ਇਨਟਅ'ਮਿੰਗਲ) *v* ਰਲਾ-ਮਿਲਾ ਦੇਣਾ; ਰਲ-ਮਿਲ ਜਾਣਾ, ਗੱਡ-ਮੱਡ ਹੋ ਜਾਣਾ, ਆਪਸ ਵਿਚ ਮਿਲ ਜਾਣਾ

intermission (ਇਨਟਅ'ਮਿਸ਼ਨ) *n* ਵਕਫ਼ਾ, ਛੁੱਟੀ

intermix (ਇਨਟਅ'ਮਿਕਸ) *v* ਰਲਾ-ਮਿਲਾ ਦੇਣਾ, ਰਲ ਮਿਲ ਜਾਣਾ, ਆਪਸ ਵਿਚ ਮਿਲਣਾ, ਗੱਡ-ਮੱਡ ਹੋ ਜਾਣਾ

intern (ਇਨ'ਟਅ:ਨ,'ਇਨਟਅ:ਨ) *v n* ਨਜ਼ਰਬੰਦ ਕਰਨਾ, ਨਿਗਰਾਨੀ ਹੇਠ ਰੱਖਣਾ; ਸਿਖਲਾਈ ਅਧੀਨ ਡਾਕਟਰ; **~ment** ਨਜ਼ਰਬੰਦੀ

internal (ਇਨ'ਟਅ:ਨਲ) *a* ਅੰਦਰਲਾ, ਵਿਚਲਾ ਭੀਤਰੀ, ਆਂਤਰਕ; ਮੁਲਕੀ

international (ਇਨਟਅ'ਨੈਸ਼ਨਲ) *a n* ਅੰਤਰ-ਰਾਸ਼ਟਰੀ, ਕੌਮਾਂਤਰੀ

interpol (ਇਨਟਅ'ਪੋਲ) *n* ਅੰਤਰ-ਰਾਸ਼ਟਰੀ

interpolar (ਇਨਟਅ'ਪਅਉਲਅ*) *a* ਅੰਤਰ-ਧਰੁਵੀ

interpret (ਇਨ'ਟਅ:ਪਰਿਟ) *v* ਭਾਵ ਕੱਢਣਾ;

ਵਿਆਖਿਆ ਕਰਨੀ, ਅਰਥ ਕੱਢਣਾ; ਅਨੁਵਾਦ ਕਰਨਾ, ਤਰਜਮਾਨੀ ਕਰਨਾ; ~ation ਭਾਵ-ਅਰਥ; ਵਿਆਖਿਆ; ਅਨੁਵਾਦ; ~er ਟੀਕਾਕਾਰ; ਦੋ-ਭਾਸ਼ੀਆ

interprovincial (ਇਨਟਅਪਰਅ'ਵਿਨਸ਼ਲ) *a* ਅੰਤਰ-ਪ੍ਰਾਂਤੀ

interracial (ਇਨਟਅ'ਰੇਇਸ਼ਲ) *a* ਅੰਤਰ-ਜਾਤੀ

interrelated (ਇਨਟਅਰਿ'ਲੇਇਟਿਡ) *a* ਪਰਸਪਰ ਸਬੰਧਤ

interrogate (ਇਨ'ਟੈਰਅਉਗੇਇਟ) *v* ਸਵਾਲ ਕਰਨਾ, ਪੁੱਛਣਾ, ਪੁੱਛ-ਗਿੱਛ ਕਰਨੀ, ਫੜਬੀਸ਼ ਕਰਨੀ

interrogation (ਇਨਟੈਰੱਅ(ਉ)ਗੇਇਸ਼ਨ) *n* ਸਵਾਲ, ਪੁੱਛ, ਪੁੱਛ-ਗਿੱਛ, ਪੁੱਛ-ਪੜਤਾਲ

interrogative (ਇਨਟਅ'ਰੋਗਅਟਿਵ) *a n* ਸਵਾਲੀਆ, ਪ੍ਰਸ਼ਨਵਾਚੀ; ਕੀ, ਕੌਣ ਆਦਿ ਸਰਵਨਾਮ

interrogator (ਇਨਟੈਰੱਅਉਗੇਇਟਅ*) *n* ਸਵਾਲ ਕਰਨ ਵਾਲਾ, ਪੁੱਛ ਗਿੱਛ ਕਰਨ ਵਾਲਾ

interrupt (ਇਨਟਅ'ਰੱਪਟ) *v* ਰੋਕਣਾ; ਰੋੜਾ ਅਟਕਾਉਣਾ, ਵਿਘਨ ਪਾਉਣਾ, ਖਲਲ ਪਾਉਣਾ; ਗੱਲ ਟੁੱਕਣਾ; ~ion ਰੁਕਾਵਟ, ਵਿਘਨ, ਟੋਕ

intersect (ਇਨਟਅ'ਸੈਕਟ) *v* ਕੱਟਣਾ, ਕੱਟ ਕੇ ਲੰਘਣਾ, ਵਿਚੋਂ ਲੰਘਣਾ; ~ion ਲਾਂਘਾ; ਚੀਰ, ਕਾਟ (ਰੇਖਾ)

intertwine ('ਇਨਟਅ'ਟਵਾਇਨ) *v* ਗੁੰਦਣਾ, ਵੱਟਣਾ, ਵਲ੍ਹੇਟਣਾ, ਉਲਝਾਉਣਾ

interval (ਇਨਟਅ'ਵ਼ਲ) *n* ਵਕਫ਼ਾ; ਮਧਿਆਂਤਰ, ਵਿਚਲਾ ਸਮਾਂ, ਖ਼ਾਲੀ ਥਾਂ, (ਸੰਗੀ) ਧੁਨੀ-ਅੰਤਰ, ਫ਼ਰਕ

intervene (ਇਨਟਅ'ਵੀਨ) *v* ਵਿਚ ਪੈਣਾ;

(ਇਸ) ਸਮੇਂ ਵਿਚਕਾਰ ਹੋਣਾ; ਦਖ਼ਲ ਦੇਣਾ, ਵਿਘਨ ਪਾਉਣਾ

intervening (ਇਨਟਅ'ਵੀਨਿੰਡ) *a* ਮੱਧਵਰਤੀ, ਅੰਤਰਵਰਤੀ

intervention (ਇਨਟ'ਅਵੈਨੱਸ਼ਨ) *n v* ਦਖ਼ਲ, ਵਿਘਨ, ਰੁਕਾਵਟ

interview (ਇਨਟਅ'ਵ਼ਯੂ) *n v* ਮੁਲਾਕਾਤ, ਭੇਟ; ਮੁਲਾਕਾਤ ਕਰਨੀ, ਭੇਟ ਕਰਨੀ

intimacy (ਇੰਟਿਮਅਸਿ) *n* ਨੇੜ, ਨਿਕਟਤਾ, ਮਿੱਤਰਤਾਈ, ਅਪਣੱਤ, ਯਾਰਾਨਾ

intimate (ਇੰਟਿਮਇਟ) *a n v* ਗੂੜ੍ਹਾ (ਮਿੱਤਰ), ਜਿਗਰੀ, ਨਿਕਟ, ਦਿਲੀ; ਨਿਝੱਕ, ਯਾਰ, ਲੰਗੋਟੀਆ; ਪਤਾ ਦੇਣਾ, ਸੂਚਤ ਕਰਨਾ, ਖ਼ਬਰ ਦੇਣੀ, ਜਾਣੂ ਕਰਨਾ, ਗਿਆਤ ਕਰਨਾ, ਇਤਲਾਹ ਦੇਣੀ; ਹੁਸ਼ਿਆਰ ਕਰਨਾ, ਇਸ਼ਾਰਾ ਦੇਣਾ

intimation (ਇਨਟਿ'ਮੇਇਸ਼ਨ) *n* ਸੰਦੇਸ਼, ਪਤਾ, ਖ਼ਬਰ, ਇਤਲਾਹ, ਸੂਚਨਾ, ਇਸ਼ਾਰਾ

intimidate (ਇਨ'ਟਿਮਿਡੇਇਟ) *v* ਡਰਾਉਣਾ, ਧਮਕਾਉਣਾ, ਭੈਭੀਤ ਕਰਨਾ, ਦਬਕਾਉਣਾ

intimidation (ਇਨ'ਟਿਮਿ'ਡੇਇਸ਼ਨ) *n* ਡਰ, ਧਮਕੀ, ਭੈ, ਡਾਂਟ-ਡਪਟ

intolerable (ਇਨ'ਟੌਲਅਰ(ਅ)ਬਲ) *a* ਅਸਹਿ, ਬਰਦਾਸ਼ਤ ਤੋਂ ਬਾਹਰ, ਬੇਹੱਦ

intolerance (ਇਨ'ਟੌਲਅਰਅੰਸ) *n* ਤੰਗਦਿਲੀ, ਅਸਹਿਣਸ਼ੀਲਤਾ

intolerant (ਇਨ'ਟੌਲਅਰਅੰਟ) *a* ਅਸਹਿਣਸ਼ੀਲ, ਤੰਗ-ਦਿਲ, ਕੱਟੜ

intonation (ਇਨਟਅ(ਉ)'ਨੇਇਸ਼ਨ) *n* ਰਹਾ; ਅਲਾਪ, ਸੁਰ-ਲਹਿਰ

in toto (ਇਨ'ਟਅਉਟਅਉ) *(L) adv* ਪੂਰਨ ਰੂਪ ਵਿਚ

intoxicant (ਇਨ'ਟੌਕਸਿਕਅੰਟ) *a n* ਨਸ਼ੀਲਾ, ਨਸ਼ੀਲੀ; ਮਾਦਕ ਪਦਾਰਥ

intoxication (ਇਨ'ਟੌਕਸਿ'ਕੇਇਸ਼ਨ) *n* ਨਸ਼ਾ, ਮਸਤੀ, ਖੁਮਾਰ, ਖੁਮਾਰੀ; ਮਦਹੋਸ਼ੀ

intraouility (ਇਨਟਰੈਨ'ਕਵਿਲਅਟਿ) *n* ਬੇਚੈਨੀ, ਅਸ਼ਾਂਤੀ

intransitive (ਇਨ'ਟਰੈਂਸਅਟਿਵ੍) *a n* ਅਕਰਮਕ, (ਵਿਆ) ਅਕਰਮਕ ਕਿਰਿਆ

intra vires ('ਇਨਟਰਅ,ਵਾਇਰਜ਼) (L) *a* ਅਧਿਕਾਰਗਤ, ਅਧਿਕਾਰ ਅਨੁਕੂਲ, ਵਸੀਕਾਰ ਦੇ ਅੰਦਰ

intrepid (ਇਨ'ਟਰੈਪਿਡ) *a* ਨਿਡਰ, ਬਹਾਦਰ, ਦਲੇਰ, ਨਿਧੜਕ, ਨਿਰਭੈ, ਸਾਹਸੀ

intricacy (ਇਨਟਰਿਕਅਸਿ) *n* ਗੁੰਝਲ, ਪੇਚੀਦਗੀ, ਅਸਪਸ਼ਟਤਾ, ਜਟਿਲਤਾ, ਵਿਖਮਤਾ, ਦੁਰਬੋਧਤਾ, ਗੁੜ੍ਹਤਾ

intricate (ਇਨ'ਟਰਿਕਅਟ) *a* ਗੁੰਝਲਦਾਰ, ਵਲਾਵਾਂ, ਪੇਚੀਦਾ; ਅਸਪਸ਼ਟ

intrigue (ਇਨ'ਟਰੀਗ) *n v* ਆਸ਼ਨਾਈ, ਗੁਪਤ ਪਰੇਮ; ਸਾਜ਼ਸ਼; ਲੁਕਵਾਂ ਸਬੰਧ ਪੈਦਾ ਕਰਨਾ, ਵਿਤਕਾਰ ਕਰਨਾ, ਆਸ਼ਨਾਈ ਰੱਖਣੀ; ਗੰਢ-ਤੁੱਪ ਕਰਨਾ, ਸਾਜ਼ਸ਼ ਕਰਨੀ; ਭਰਮ ਪੈਦਾ ਕਰਨਾ

intrinsic (ਇੰ'ਟਰਿੰਸਿਕ) *a* ਅੰਤਰੀਵ, ਭੀਤਰੀ; ਸੁਭਾਵਕ, ਅਸਲੀ, ਵਾਸਤਵਿਕ, ਯਥਾਰਥਕ

introduce ('ਇੰਟਰਅ'ਡਯੂਸ) *v* ਜਾਣ ਪਛਾਣ ਦੇਣੀ, ਪਰਿਚਯ ਦੇਣਾ ਜਾਂ ਕਰਾਉਣਾ, ਉਪਸਥਿਤ ਕਰਨਾ, ਦਾਖ਼ਲ ਕਰਨਾ; ਪ੍ਰਸਤੁਤ ਕਰਨਾ, ਸ਼ੁਰੂ ਕਰਨਾ, ਪ੍ਰਚਲਤ ਕਰਨਾ, ਪੇਸ਼ ਕਰਨਾ (ਬਿਲ); ਭੂਮਕਾ ਬੰਨ੍ਹਣੀ, ਪ੍ਰਸਤਾਵਨਾ ਲਿਖਣੀ

introduction (ਇੰਟਰਅ'ਡਅੱਕਸ਼ਨ) *n* ਜਾਣ-ਪਛਾਣ; ਅਸਥਾਪਨ; ਆਰੰਭ; ਪ੍ਰਚਲਣ; ਭੂਮਕਾ, ਮੁੱਖ-ਬੰਧ

introductory (ਇੰਟਰਅ'ਡਅੱਕਟ(ਅ)ਰਿ) *a* ਜਾਣ-ਪਛਾਣ ਦੇ ਤੌਰ ਤੇ, ਪ੍ਰਵੇਸ਼ ਸਾਧਕ; ਪੁਰਤਕ; ਆਰੰਭਕ, ਭੂਮਕਾ ਸਵਰੂਪ

introgression (ਇੰਟਰਅ'ਗਰੈਸ਼ਨ) *n* ਅੰਦਰੂਨੀ ਗਤੀ, ਅੰਤਰਗਾਮਨ

introspect (ਇੰਟਰਅ(ਓ)'ਸਪੈਕਟ) *v* ਚਿਤੰਨ ਕਰਨਾ, ਅੰਦਰ ਧਿਆਨ ਕਰਨਾ, ਅੰਤਰ-ਧਿਆਨ ਕਰਨਾ, ਅੰਤਰ-ਧਿਆਨ ਹੋਣਾ, ਅੰਤਰ-ਦ੍ਰਿਸ਼ਟੀ ਕਰਨੀ; ~ion ਆਤਮ-ਚੀਨਣ, ਅੰਤਰ-ਧਿਆਨ, ਅੰਤਰ-ਦ੍ਰਿਸ਼ਟੀ; ~ive ਚਿੰਤਨਾਤਮਕ, ਅੰਤਰ-ਧਿਆਨਾਤਮਕ, ਅੰਤਰ-ਦ੍ਰਿਸ਼ਟੀ ਸਬੰਧੀ

introvert ('ਇੰਟਰਅ(ਓ)'ਵ੍ਅ:ਟ) *v n* ਮਨ ਨੂੰ ਅੰਦਰ ਮੋੜਨਾ, ਅੰਤਰ-ਮੁਖੀ ਹੋਣਾ, ਅੰਤਰ-ਮੁਖੀ ਵਿਅਕਤੀ

intrusion (ਇੰ'ਟਰੂਯ੍ਨ) *n* ਬਿਨਾ ਆਗਿਆ ਪ੍ਰਵੇਸ਼; ਅਯੋਗ ਦਖ਼ਲ, ਵਿਘਨ

intuition (ਇੰਟਯੂ'ਇਸ਼ਨ) *n* ਅਨੁਭਵ, ਅੰਤਰ-ਪਰੇਰਨਾ; ਅੰਤਰ-ਦ੍ਰਿਸ਼ਟੀ; ਸਹਿਜ-ਗਿਆਨ, ਸਹਿਜ-ਬੋਧ; ~al ਅਨੁਭਵੀ; ਅੰਤਰ-ਗਿਆਨਾਤਮਕ; ਸਹਿਜ ਬੋਧਾਤਮਕ

intuitive (ਇਨ'ਟਯੂਇਟਿਵ੍) *a* ਅਨੁਭਵੀ; ਅੰਤਰ-ਦ੍ਰਿਸ਼ਟੀਗਤ

invade (ਇਨ'ਵ੍ਏਇਡ) *v* ਹੱਲਾ ਕਰਨਾ, ਚੜ੍ਹਾਈ ਕਰਨੀ, ਚੜ੍ਹ ਆਉਣਾ, ਧਾਵਾ ਕਰਨਾ, ਘੁਸਣਾ; ~r ਹੱਲਾ ਕਰਨ ਵਾਲਾ, ਚੜ੍ਹਾਈ ਕਰਨ ਵਾਲਾ, ਹਮਲਾਵਰ

invalid (ਇਨ'ਵ੍ਅਲਿਡ, ਇਨਵ੍ਅਲਿਡ) *a n v* ਨਕਾਰ, ਅਪਾਹਜ, ਦੁਰਬਲ, ਅਸਮਰੱਥ, ਅਯੋਗ; ਰੋਗੀ, ਬਲਹੀਣ ਮਨੁੱਖ; ਨਕਾਰਾ ਕਰ ਦੇਣਾ

invaluable (ਇਨ'ਵੈਲਯੁਅਬਲ) *a* ਅਮੋਲਕ

ਬਹੁਮੁੱਲੀ, ਅਟਮੇਲ, ਅਮੋਲ

invariable (ਇਨ'ਵੇਅਰਿਅਬਲ) *a* ਅਡੋਲ, ਪੱਕਾ, ਸਥਿਰ, ਅਚੱਲ, ਇਕਸਾਰ; (ਗਣਿ) ਅਟੱਲ, ਸਥਿਰ, ਅਪਰਿਵਰਤਨੀ

invariant (ਇਨ'ਵੇਅਰਿਐਂਟ) *a* ਸਥਿਰ, ਅਡੋਲ, ਪੱਕਾ, ਇਕਸਾਰ; ਅਟੱਲ, ਅਚੱਲ

invasion (ਇਨ'ਵੇਇਯ਼ਨ) *n* ਹੱਲਾ, ਆਕਰਮਣ, ਚੜ੍ਹਾਈ, ਧਾਵਾ; ਵਿਘਨ

invent (ਇਨ'ਵੈਂਟ) *v* ਕਾਢ ਕੱਢਣੀ, ਵਿਉਂਤਣਾ, ਈਜਾਦ ਕਰਨੀ, ਆਵਿਸ਼ਕਾਰ ਕਰਨਾ; ਘੜ ਲੈਣੀ; ~ion ਈਜਾਦ, ਆਵਿਸ਼ਕਾਰ; ਕਾਢ, ਵਿਉਂਤ

invert (ਇਨ'ਵਅ:ਟ) *v* ਉਲਟਾਣਾ, ਪਲਟਣਾ, ਪੁੱਠਾ ਕਰ ਦੇਣਾ, ਸਿਲਸਿਲਾ ਤੋੜਨਾ; ਕ੍ਰਮ ਭੰਗ ਕਰਨਾ

invest (ਇਨ'ਵੈਸੱਟ) *v* ਰੁਪਿਆ ਲਾਉਣਾ, ਰਕਮ ਲਾਉਣੀ, ਧਨ ਲਾਉਣਾ; ਘੇਰਨਾ, ਘੇਰਾ ਘੱਤਣਾ; ~ment ਨਿਵੇਸ਼ ਲਾਗਤ, ਲਾਈ ਰਕਮ; ਲਿਬਾਸ; ਘੇਰਾ

investigate (ਇਨ'ਵੈੱਸਟਿਗੇਇਟ) *v* ਖੋਜ ਕਰਨੀ; ਛਾਣ-ਬੀਣ ਕਰਨੀ, ਪਤਾ ਲਾਉਣਾ, ਜਾਂਚ-ਪੜਤਾਲ ਕਰਨੀ, ਤਫ਼ਤੀਸ਼ ਕਰਨੀ

investigation (ਇਨ'ਵੈੱਸਟਿ'ਗੇਇਸ਼ਨ) *n* ਖੋਜ, ਛਾਣ-ਬੀਣ, ਜਾਂਚ-ਪੜਤਾਲ, ਪੁੱਛ-ਗਿੱਛ, ਤਹਿਕੀਕਾਤ, ਤਫ਼ਤੀਸ਼

investigator (ਇਨ'ਵੈੱਸਟਿਗੇਇਟਅ*) *n* ਖੋਜਕਾਰ, ਤਫ਼ਤੀਸ਼ਕਾਰ

inviable (ਇਨ'ਵਾਇਅਬਲ) *a* ਨਾ ਜਿਉਣ ਜੋਗ

invigilate (ਇਨ'ਵਿਜਿਲੇਇਟ) *v* (ਇਮਤਿਹਨ ਦੇਣ ਵਾਲਿਆਂ ਦੀ) ਨਿਗਰਾਨੀ ਕਰਨੀ

invigilation (ਇਨ'ਵਿਜਿ'ਲੇਇਸ਼ਨ) *n* ਨਿਗਰਾਨੀ, ਨਿਰਖਣ, ਦੇਖ-ਭਾਲ

invigilator (ਇਨ'ਵਿਜਿਲੇਇਟਅ*) *n* ਨਿਗਰਾਨ, ਨਿਰੀਖਕ

invisible (ਇਨ'ਵਿਜ਼ਿਬਲ) *a* ਅਦਿੱਖ, ਅਡਿੱਠ; ਅਦਿਸਵੀਂ, ਲੋਪ, ਨਿਰਾਕਾਰ

invitation (ਇਨਵਿ'ਟੇਇਸ਼ਨ) *n* ਸੱਦਾ, ਬੁਲਾਵਾ, ਨਿਉਤਾ, ਦਾਅਵਤ, ਨਿਮੰਤਰਣ

invite (ਇਨ'ਵਾਇਟ) *v* ਸੱਦਣਾ, ਦਾਅਵਤ ਦੇਣੀ, ਬੁਲਾਉਣਾ, ਨਿਉਤਾ ਦੇਣਾ, ਆਕਰਸ਼ਤ ਕਰਨਾ, ਖਿੱਚਣਾ; ~e ਨਿਮੰਤਰਤ ਵਿਅਕਤੀ

invocation (ਇਨਵਅ'ਕੇਇਸ਼ਨ) *n* ਅਰਦਾਸ, ਪੁਰਥਨਾ, ਮੰਗਲਾਚਰਨ, ਦੇਵ-ਉਸਤਤੀ

invoice (ਇਨਵੋਇਸ) *n v* ਬੀਚਕ, ਚਲਾਨ; (ਮਾਲ ਦਾ) ਬੀਚਕ ਬਣਾਉਣਾ, ਚਲਾਨ ਤਿਆਰ ਕਰਨਾ

invoke (ਇਨ'ਵਅਉਕ) *v* ਆਵਾਹਨ ਕਰਨਾ, ਵਾਸਤਾ ਪਾਉਣਾ, ਜਾਚਨਾ ਕਰਨੀ, ਅਰਦਾਸ ਕਰਨੀ, ਬੇਨਤੀ ਕਰਨੀ

involuntarily (ਇਨ'ਵੌਲਅਨਟ(ਅ)ਰਿਲਿ) *adv* ਆਪਣੇ ਆਪ, ਬਿਨਾ ਮਰਜ਼ੀ ਦੇ

involuntary (ਇਨ'ਵੌਲਅਨਟ(ਅ)ਰਿ) *a* ।ਗਾਪੂਰਨ, ਅਣਇੱਛਤ

involve (ਇਨ'ਵੌਲਵ) *v* ਉਲਝਾਉਣਾ, ਫਸਾਉਣਾ; ਲਪੇਟ ਵਿਚ ਲੈਣਾ, ਅੜੁੰਬਣਾ; ਅੰਦਰ ਵੱਲ ਚੱਕਰ ਦੇਣਾ; ਸੰਕੇਤ ਕਰਨਾ; ਸ਼ਾਮਲ ਕਰਨਾ, ਮਿਲਾਉਣਾ; ~ment ਲਪੇਟ, ਉਲਝਣ; ਸਮੱਸਿਆ

invulnerability (ਇਨ'ਵੁਅੱਲਨ(ਅ)ਰਅ'ਬਿਲਅਟਿ) *n* ਸੁਰੱਖਿਅਤਾ, ਅਖੰਡਤਾ, ਅਤੇਜਤਾ, ਅਜਿੱਤਤਾ

invulnerable (ਇਨ'ਵੁਅੱਲਨ(ਅ)ਰਅਬਲ) *a*

ਸੁਰੱਖਿਅਤ, ਅਖੰਡ, ਅਜਿੱਤ

inward (ਇਨਵ'ਅੱਡ) *a n* ਅੰਦਰਲਾ, ਆਂਤਰਕ, ਅੰਤਰੀਵ, ਆਗਾਮੀ, ਆਉਣ ਵਾਲਾ, (ਬ ਵ) ਆਂਦਰਾਂ; ~ly ਅੰਦਰੇ-ਅੰਦਰ, ਅੰਦਰੋਂ, ਦਿਲ ਵਿਚ

iota (ਆਈਅਉਟਾ) *n* ਯੂਨਾਨੀ ਲਿਪੀ ਦਾ ਇਕ ਅੱਖਰ; ਕਣ, ਭੋਰਾ, ਕਣ ਮਾਤਰ, ਬਹੁਤ ਥੋੜੀ ਮਿਕਦਾਰ

ipso facto (ਇਪਸਾਓ-ਫ਼ੈਕਟਾਓ) (*L*) *adv* ਆਪਣੇ-ਆਪ, ਤਦ ਅਨੁਸਾਰ

iron (ਆਇਅਨ) *n a v* ਲੋਹਾ; ਕੜਛਾਈ; ਲੋਹੇ ਦਾ ਜੰਤਰ ਇਸਤਰੀ (ਕੱਪੜੇ ਪ੍ਰੈੱਸ ਕਰਨ ਲਈ); (ਬ ਵ) ਹੱਥਕੜੀ, ਜ਼ੰਜੀਰ; ਪੱਕੇ ਇਰਾਦੇ ਵਾਲਾ; ਸਖ਼ਤ, ਮਜ਼ਬੂਤ; ਬੇਦਰਦ; ਲੋਹੇ ਨਾਲ ਮੜ੍ਹਨਾ; ਕੱਪੜੇ ਇਸਤਰੀ ਕਰਨਾ; ਹੱਥਕੜੀ

ironical (ਆਇਰੌਨਿਕਲ) *a* ਵਿਅੰਗਮਈ, ਕਾਟਵਾਂ

irony ('ਆਇ(ਅ)ਰਅਨਿ) *n a* ਵਿਅੰਗ, ਭਾਸ਼ਾ ਦੀ ਵਿਅੰਗਮਈ ਵਰਤੋਂ; ਦੁਰਘਟਨਾ; ਕਿਸਮਤ ਦਾ ਖੇਲ, ਵਿਡੰਬਣਾ; ਲੋਹੇ ਵਾਂਗੂ, ਲੋਹੇ ਵਰਗਾ

irrational (ਇ'ਰੈਸ਼ਨਲ) *a* ਅਨੁਚਿਤ, ਅਤਾਰਕਿਕ, ਬੇਰਵਾਜਬ, ਅਵਿਵੇਕੀ; ਤਰਕਹੀਣ; ~ity ਅਨੁਚਿੱਤਤਾ, ਨਾ-ਮਾਲੂਕੀਅਤ, ਤਰਕਹੀਣਤਾ; ਬੇਹੂਦਰਗੀ

irrefutable ('ਇਰਿ'ਫ਼ਯੂਟਾਬਲ) *a* ਅਖੰਡਨੀ, ਅਕੱਟ, ਜਿਸ ਨੂੰ ਝੁਠਲਾਇਆ ਨਾ ਜਾ ਸਕੇ

irregular (ਇ'ਰੈਗਯੂਲਅ*) *a n pl* ਅਸੰਗਤ, ਬੇਕਾਇਦਾ, ਬੇਨਿਯਮਾ, ਬੇਢੰਗਾ, ਕਸੂਤਾ; ਬੇਕਾਇਦਾ ਫ਼ੌਜੀ ਦਸਤੇ; ~ity ਬੇਕਾਇਦਗੀ

irrelevance (ਇ'ਰੈੱਲਅਵੰਅੱਸ) *n* ਅਸੰਗਤੀ, ਅਸੰਬੱਧਤਾ, ਅਪ੍ਰਸੰਗਕਤਾ

irrelevant (ਇ'ਰੈੱਲਅਵਅਨਟ) *a* ਅਸੰਬੱਧਤ, ਅਸੰਗਤ, ਗ਼ੈਰ-ਮੁਨਾਸਬ

irrepressible ('ਇਰਿ'ਪਰੈੱਸਅਬਲ) *a* ਨਾ ਦਬਣ ਵਾਲਾ, ਨਾ ਰੁਕਣ ਵਾਲਾ, ਮੂੰਹਜ਼ੋਰ, ਅੱਖੜ

irrespective ('ਇਰਿ'ਸਪੈੱਕਟਿਵ) *a* ਬਿਨਾ ਪਰਵਾਹ ਦੇ, ਬਿਨਾ ਲਿਹਾਜ਼

irresponsibility ('ਇਰਿ'ਸਪੌਂਸਿ'ਬਿਲਅਟਿ) *n* ਗ਼ੈਰ-ਜ਼ਿੰਮੇਵਾਰੀ

irresponsible ('ਇਰਿ'ਸਪੌਂਸਅਬਲ) *a* ਗ਼ੈਰ-ਜ਼ਿੰਮੇਵਾਰ, ਲਾਪਰਵਾਹ

irrigate ('ਇਰਿਗੇਇਟ) *v* ਸਿੰਚਣਾ, ਆਬਪਾਸ਼ੀਕਰਨੀ, ਪਾਣੀ ਦੇਣਾ

irrigation ('ਇਰਿ'ਗੇਇਸ਼ਨ) *n* ਸਿੰਚਾਈ, ਸੇਚਨ, ਆਬਪਾਸ਼ੀ

irritate ('ਇਰਿਟੇਇਟ) *v* ਗੁੱਸਾ ਦਿਵਾਉਣਾ, ਖਿਝਾਉਣਾ; ਚਿੜਾਉਣਾ, ਤੰਗ ਕਰਨਾ, ਉਤੇਜਤ ਕਰਨਾ; ਜਲਣ ਪੈਦਾ ਕਰਨੀ

irritation ('ਇਰਿ'ਟੇਇਸ਼ਨ) *n* ਉਤੇਜਨਾ, ਜਲਣ, ਚਿੜਚੜਾਹਟ, ਖਿਝ

island ('ਆਇਲਅੰਡ) *n* ਟਾਪੂ, ਦੀਪ, ਜਜ਼ੀਰਾ

isle (ਆਇਲ) *n* ਟਾਪੂ, ਦੀਪ; ~t ਛੋਟਾ ਟਾਪੂ

isogloss ('ਆਇਸਅਉਗਲੌਸ) *n* (ਭਾਸ਼ਾ) ਸਮਵਿਕਾਰ ਰੇਖਾ

isolate ('ਆਇਸਅਲੇਇਟ) *v* ਦੂਜਿਆਂ ਤੋਂ ਵੱਖ ਕਰਨਾ, ਵਿਤਰੇਕ ਕਰਨਾ; ਵੱਖਰਾ ਕਰਨਾ, ਨਵੇਕਲਾ ਰੱਖਣਾ, ਨਿਖੇੜਨਾ, ਅਲੱਗ ਕਰਨਾ

isolating ('ਆਇਸਅਲੇਇਟਿੰਙ) *a* ਅਯੋਗਾਤਮਕ

isolation ('ਆਇਸਅ'ਲੇਇਸ਼ਨ) *n* ਅੱਡਰਾਪਣ, ਵੱਖਰਤਾ, ਵਖਰੇਵਾਂ

issue ('ਇਸ਼ੂ) *n v* ਨਿਕਾਸ, ਨਤੀਜਾ, ਅੰਤ; ਸੰਤਾਨ, ਔਲਾਦ; ਅੰਕ ਪਰਚਾ (ਅਖ਼ਬਾਰ ਦਾ); (ਨਦੀ ਦਾ) ਮੂੰਹ; ਨਿਕਲਣਾ, ਪੈਦਾ ਹੋਣਾ, ਫੁੱਟਣਾ, ਨਤੀਜਾ ਨਿਕਲਣਾ; ਜਾਰੀ ਕਰਨਾ, ਕੱਢਣਾ,

ਪ੍ਰਕਾਸ਼ਤ ਕਰਨਾ; ~less ਨਿਰਸੰਤਨ

itch (ਇਚ) *n v* ਖਾਜ, ਖੁਜਲੀ, ਖ਼ਾਰਸ਼, ਜਲੂਟ; ਤੀਬਰ ਇੱਛਾ; ਖਾਜ ਹੋਣੀ, ਜਲਨ ਹੋਣੀ ਜਾਂ ਉਠਣੀ, ਖੁਰਕਣਾ

item ('ਆਇਟਮ) *n adv* ਮੱਦ, ਨਗ; (ਅਖਬਾਰ ਆਦਿ ਵਿਚ) ਸਮਾਚਾਰ, ਖ਼ਬਰ, ਮਜ਼ਮੂਨ

itineracy, itinerancy (ਇ'ਟਿਨ(ਅ)ਰਅਸਿ, ਇ'ਟਿਨ(ਅ)ਰਅੰਸਿ) *n* ਖ਼ਾਨਾਬਦੋਸ਼ੀ, ਭ੍ਰਮਣਸ਼ੀਲਤਾ, ਸੈਲਾਨੀਪਨ

itinerant (ਇ'ਟਿਨ(ਅ)ਰਅੰਟ) *a* ਫਿਰਤੂ, ਸਫ਼ਰੀ, (ਜੱਜ) ਦੌਰੇ ਤੇ

ivory ('ਆਇਵ੍(ਅ)ਰਿ) *n* ਹਾਥੀ-ਦੰਦ, ਦੰਦ-ਖੰਡ; (ਬ ਵ) ਥਿੜ੍ਹਿਅਰਡ-ਬਾਲ; ~tower ਖ਼ਿਆਲੀ ਮਹਿਲ

J

J, j (ਜੇਇ) *n* ਰੋਮਨ ਵਰਣਮਾਲਾ ਦਾ ਦਸਵਾਂ ਅੱਖਰ

jabber ('ਜੈਬਅ*) *v n* ਬੁੜਬੁੜਾਉਣਾ; ਕਾਹਲੀ ਕਾਹਲੀ ਬੋਲਣਾ, ਬਕ ਬਕ ਕਰਨਾ; ਚੀਕਾਂ-ਕੂਕਾਂ ਮਾਰਨੀਆਂ; ਬਕਵਾਸ, ਬਕਝਵਾਣ; ਅਸਪਸ਼ਟ ਗੱਲ; ~ing ਬਕਵਾਸ, ਬਕ-ਬਕ, ਗਿਟਮਿਟ, ਬੁੜਬੁੜ, ਚੂੰ ਚਾਂ, ਬਕਝਵਾਣ

jackal ('ਜੈਕੋਲ) *n v* ਗਿੱਦੜ; ਅਤਿਨੈ ਕਰਨਾ

jacket ('ਜੌਕਿਟ) *n* ਕੁੜਤੀ, ਫਤੂਹੀ, ਪੋਸਤੀਨ; ਗਿਲਾਫ਼

jade (ਜੇਇਡ) *n v* ਹੁੱਸਿਆ ਤੇ ਮਰੀਅਲ ਘੋੜਾ, ਮਾੜਾ ਟੱਟੂ; ਕੰਜਰੀ, ਵੇਸਵਾ, ਕਮਜ਼ਾਤ; ਹਰਾ, ਨੀਲਾ ਜਾਂ ਚਿੱਟਾ ਕੀਮਤੀ ਪੱਥਰ; ਥੱਕਣਾ, ਥੱਕਾਉਣ, ਘਸਣਾ, ਰਗੜਨਾ; ~d ਹੁੱਸਿਆ, ਥੱਕਿਆ, ਮੰਦਾ ਪਿਆ

jaggery ('ਜੈਗਅਰਿ) *n* ਗੁੜ

jaguar ('ਜੈਗਯੂਅ*) *n* ਚਿਤਕਬਰਾ ਜੰਗਲੀ ਬਿੱਲਾ, ਬਾਗੜਬਿੱਲਾ

jail, gaol (ਜੇਇਲ) *n v* ਜੇਲ੍ਹ, ਬੰਦੀਖ਼ਾਨਾ, ਕੈਦਖਾਨਾ; ਬੰਦੀ ਬਣਾਉਣਾ, ਜੇਲ੍ਹ ਵਿਚ ਦੇਣਾ, ਕੈਦ ਕਰਨਾ

jalousie ('ਯੈਲੂਜ਼ਿ) *n* ਖਿੜਕੀ ਦਾ ਪਰਦਾ, ਝਿਲਮਿਲ

jam (ਜੈਮ) *v n* (ਮਸ਼ੀਨ ਦੇ ਕਿਸੇ ਪੁਰਜ਼ੇ ਦਾ) ਜਾਮ ਹੋ ਜਾਣਾ; (ਰਸਤਾ) ਬੰਦ ਹੋ ਜਾਣਾ (ਭੀੜ ਆਦਿ ਦੇ ਕਾਰਨ); ਰਾਹ ਰੋਕਣਾ, ਰੁਕਾਵਟ ਪਾਉਣੀ, ਬੰਦ ਕਰਨਾ; ਜੰਮ ਕੇ ਬੈਠ ਜਾਣਾ; ਦੱਬ ਕੇ ਸਤ ਕੱਢਣਾ, ਨਚੋੜਨਾ; ਫੇਹ ਕੇ ਇਕ ਕਰਨਾ; ਪੀਹਣਾ; ਜੰਜਾਲ; ਦਬਾਅ, ਰੋਕ; ਭੀੜ; ਮੁਰੱਬਾ, ਜਾਮ; **~packed** ਖਚਾਖਚ ਭਰਿਆ

jangle ('ਜੈਙਗਲ) *n v* ਝੁਟਕਾਰ, ਠਟਕਾਰ, ਤਕਰਾਰ, ਝਗੜਾ, ਫ਼ਸਾਦ; ਬੇਸੁਰੀ ਅਵਾਜ਼ ਕੱਢਣੀ, ਘੰਟੀ ਦਾ ਟਣ-ਟਣ ਕਰਨਾ; ਝਗੜਨਾ, ਤਕਰਾਰ ਕਰਨੀ; **~r** ਹੁੱਜਤੀ, ਝਗੜਾਲੂ, ਲੜਾਕਾ, ਫ਼ਸਾਦੀ ਆਦਮੀ

jangling ('ਜੈਙਗਲਿਙ) *n* ਝੂਖ, ਝਗੜਾ, ਬਿਖੇੜਾ, ਲੜਾਈ, ਬਹਿਸ-ਮੁਬਾਹਸਾ

jar (ਜਾ*) *v n* ਝਗੜਾ ਕਰਨਾ, ਤਕਰਾਰ ਕਰਨਾ; ਸਹਿਮਤ ਨਾ ਹੋਣਾ, ਬਹਿਸ ਵਿਚ ਪੈਣਾ; (ਕਿਸੇ ਅੰਗ ਵਿਚ) ਕੰਬਣੀ ਆਉਣੀ; ਗੂੰਜ ਪੈਣੀ, ਝਟਕਾਰ ਪੈਣੀ, ਕਰਖ਼ਤ ਅਵਾਜ਼ ਕੱਢਣੀ, ਕੰਨ ਖਾਣੇ; (1) ਝਗੜਾ, ਤਕਰਾਰ; ਵਿਰੋਧ, ਕਰਖ਼ਤ ਅਵਾਜ਼; (2) ਮਰਤਬਾਨ, ਘੜਾ, ਮੱਘਾ, ਗੜਵਾ

jargon ('ਜਾ*ਗਅਨ) *n* ਸਮਝ ਵਿਚ ਨਾ ਆਉਣ ਵਾਲੀ ਬੋਲੀ, ਗਿਟਮਿਟ

jaundice ('ਜੋਨਡਿਸ) *n v* ਯਰਕਾਨ, ਪਰਨੇਹ, ਪੀਲੀਆ; ਸਾੜਾ; ਨਜ਼ਰ ਨੁਕਸ; ਯਰਕਾਨ ਦਾ ਰੋਗੀ ਹੋਣਾ; ਈਰਖਾ, ਭਰ ਦੇਈ

javelin ('ਜੈਵ੍ਲਿਨ) *n* ਬਰਛਾ, ਬੱਲਮ, ਨੇਜ਼ਾ

jaw (ਜੋ) *n v* ਹੜਬ, ਜਬਾੜਾ; ਤਕਰਾਰ, ਝਗੜਾ; ਝਗੜਨਾ, ਤਕਰਾਰ ਕਰਨੀ, ਵਾਪੂ ਗੱਲਾਂ ਮਾਰਨੀਆਂ; ਲਗਾਤਾਰ ਬੋਲਦੇ ਜਾਣਾ; ਵਿਆਖਿਆਨ ਦੇਣਾ

jay (ਜੇਇ) *n* (1) ਨੀਲਕੰਠ; (2) ਗਾਲੜੀ, ਗੱਪੀ ਖੱਪੀ; (3) ਮੂਰਖ, ਸਿੰਪੜ

jealous ('ਜੈੱਲਅਸ) *a* ਈਰਖਈ, ਦਵੈਖੀ, ਕੱਟੜ; **~y** ਈਰਖਾ, ਸਾੜਾ; ਦਵੈਖ

jeer (ਜਿਅ*) v n pl ਮਖੌਲ ਉਡਾਉਣਾ, ਮਸ਼ਕਰੀ ਕਰਨੀ; ਤਾਅਨਾ ਮਾਰਨਾ, ਬੋਲੀ ਮਾਰਨੀ; ਹਾਸਾ, ਮਸ਼ਕਰੀ, ਤਾਅਨਾ, ਬੋਲੀ

jejune (ਜਿ'ਜੂਨ) a ਬੰਜਰ, ਅਣ-ਉਪਜਾਉ; ਰਸਹੀਣ, ਖ਼ੁਸ਼ਕ, ਰੁੱਖਾ; ਬਹੁਤ ਥੋੜ੍ਹਾ, ਨਾਕਾਫ਼ੀ; **~ness** ਰਸਹੀਣਤਾ ਖ਼ੁਸ਼ਕੀ, ਰੁੱਖਾਪਣ, ਨੀਰਸਤਾ, ਫਿੱਕਾਪਣ

jelly ('ਜੈਲੀ) n ਇਕ ਲੇਸਵੀਂ ਮਿੱਠੀ ਚਟਨੀ, ਮੁਰੱਬਾ, ਜੈਲੀ

jeopard, jeopardize ('ਜੈੱਪਅਡ,'ਜੈੱਪਅ-ਡਾਇਜ਼) v ਖ਼ਤਰੇ ਵਿਚ ਪਾਉਣਾ, ਬਿਪਤਾ ਵਿਚ ਫਸਾਉਣਾ; **~ous** ਸੰਕਟ ਭਰਿਆ, ਸੰਕਟਮਈ, ਖ਼ਤਰਨਾਕ

jerk (ਜਅ:ਕ) n v ਧੱਕਾ, ਝਟਕਾ, ਮੋਚ, ਖਿੱਚ, ਤਣਾਉ; ਝਟਕਾ ਦੇਣਾ ਜਾਂ ਲੱਗਣਾ; ਝਟਕੇ ਨਾਲ ਖਿੱਚਣਾ; **~iness** ਝਟਕਾ, ਧੱਕਾ; ਸੰਕੋਚ

jest (ਜੈੱਸਟ) n v ਹਾਸਾ, ਠੱਠਾ, ਮਸ਼ਕਰੀ, ਮਖੌਲ, ਛੇੜ-ਛਾੜ, ਮਸ਼ਕਰੀ ਕਰਨੀ, ਹਾਸਾ-ਠੱਠਾ ਕਰਨਾ, ਛੇੜ-ਛਾੜ ਕਰਨੀ, ਦਿਲਲਗੀ ਕਰਨੀ; **~book** ਚੁਟਕਲਿਆਂ ਦੀ ਕਿਤਾਬ; **~er** ਮਖੌਲੀਆ, ਦਿਲਲਗੀਬਾਜ਼; ਭੰਡ, ਵਿਦੂਸ਼ਕ; **~ful** ਠੱਠੇ ਦਾ, ਮਜ਼ਾਕੀਆ, ਮਖੌਲੀਆ, ਹਸੰਦੜਾ

jetty (ਜੈੱਟੀ) n ਜਹਾਜ਼ ਤੋਂ ਮਾਲ ਲਾਹੁਣ ਵਾਲਾ ਘਾਟ, ਪੱਕਾ ਘਾਟ, ਜੈੱਟੀ; ਬੰਦਰਗਾਹ ਦੀ ਰੱਖਿਆ ਲਈ ਬਣਾਇਆ ਗਿਆ ਬੰਨ੍ਹ

jew (ਜੂ) n v ਯਹੂਦੀ; (ਬੋਲ) ਸੂਦ-ਖੋਰ

jewel ('ਜੂਅਲ) n v ਹੀਰਾ, ਨਗ, ਮਣੀ, ਰਤਨ, ਲਾਲ; ਬਹੁਮੁੱਲੀ ਵਸਤੂ, ਜੜਾਊ ਗਹਿਣਾ; ਰਤਨਾਂ ਨਾਲ ਅਲੰਕਰਤ ਕਰਨਾ, ਜੜਾਊ ਬਣਾਉਣਾ; **~ler, ~er** ਜੌਹਰੀ, ਸਰਾਫ਼ ਰਤਨਾਂ ਦਾ ਵਪਾਰੀ, ਲਾਲਾਂ ਦਾ ਵਟਣਜਾਰਾ; **~lery,ery** ਜ਼ੇਵਰ, ਗਹਿਣੇ, ਭੂਸ਼ਣ; ਜੜਾਊ ਹੀਰੇ, ਰਤਨਾਂ ਦਾ ਵਪਾਰ, ਜੌਹਰਾਂ ਦੀ ਸੌਦਾਗਰੀ

jiggle ('ਜਿਗਲ) n v (ਹੌਲੀ ਹੌਲੀ ਦਿੱਤਾ) ਧੱਕਾ, ਝਟਕਾ

jill (ਜਿਲ) n ਮੁਟਿਆਰ, ਕੁੜੀ, ਨੁਵਤੀ; **~flirt** ਛਿਨਾਲ, ਭੈੜੇ ਚਰਿੱਤਰ ਵਾਲੀ ਕੁੜੀ; **~et** ਛਿਨਾਲ ਔਰਤ; ਅਵਾਰਾ ਔਰਤ

jilit (ਜਿਲਟ) n v ਬੇਵਫ਼ਾਈ; ਬੇਵਫ਼ਾਈ ਕਰਨੀ

jimmy ('ਜਿਮਿ) n ਅਸ਼ਰਫ਼ੀ, ਪੌਂਡ

jingle ('ਜਿੰਙਗਲ) n v ਝਟਕਾਰ, ਟੁਣਕਾਰ, ਛਣਕਾਰ; ਅਨੁਪ੍ਰਾਸ, ਝਟ-ਪਟ ਕਰਨਾ

jingo ('ਜਿੰਙਗਅਉ) n a int ਜੰਗਬਾਜ਼, ਲੜਾਈ-ਝਗੜੇ ਦੀ ਨੀਤੀ ਨੂੰ ਅਪਣਾਉਣ ਵਾਲਾ; ਆਡੰਬਰੀ, ਦੰਤੀ; ਧੋਖੇਬਾਜ਼; (y~)

jink (ਜਿੰਙਕ) n v ਟਾਲ ਮਟੋਲ; ਟਲਣਾ, ਟਾਲਣਾ, ਖਿਸਕਣਾ, ਖਿਸਕਾਉਣਾ

jitter ('ਜਿਟਅ*) v ਘਬਰਾਉਣਾ

job (ਜੌਬ) n ਆਸਾਮੀ, ਨੌਕਰੀ; ਕੰਮ, ਰੁਜ਼ਗਾਰ, ਧੰਦਾ; ਪੇਸ਼ਾ; ਕਿਰਤ, ਮਜ਼ਦੂਰੀ; **~ber** ਦਲਾਲ; **~bery** ਦਲਾਲੀ, ਆੜ੍ਹਤ; ਬੇਈਮਾਨੀ ਵੱਢੀ-ਖੋਰੀ; ਸੁਆਰਥ

jocund ('ਜੌਕਅੰਡ) a ਹਸਮੁੱਖ, ਜ਼ਿੰਦਾਦਿਲ, ਪ੍ਰਸੰਨ-ਚਿੱਤ, ਮੌਜੀ, ਰੰਗੀਲਾ; **~ity** ਜ਼ਿੰਦਾਦਿਲੀ, ਰੰਗੀਲਾਪਣ, ਖੇੜਾ, ਪ੍ਰਸੰਨਤਾ, ਖ਼ੁਸ਼-ਮਿਜ਼ਾਜੀ

jog (ਜੌਗ) v n ਔਖਾ ਤੁਰਨਾ, ਡਿਗਦੇ-ਢਹਿੰਦੇ ਤੁਰਨਾ, ਦੁਲਕੀ ਚੱਲਣਾ; ਚੇਤਾ ਆਉਣਾ, ਠੁੰਗਾ ਮਾਰਨਾ, ਝੰਜੋੜਨਾ, ਹਲੂਣਨਾ; ਚਲੇ ਜਾਣਾ, ਤੁਰ ਪੈਣਾ; ਸੁਸਤ ਚਾਲ, ਮੱਠੀ ਚਾਲ

join (ਜੌਇਨ) v n ਜੋੜਨਾ ਜਾਂ ਜੁੜਨਾ, ਮਿਲਣਾ, ਇਕੱਠੇ ਹੋਣਾ, ਸਾਂਝ ਪਾਉਣੀ, ਭਿਆਲੀ ਕਰਨੀ, ਹਿੱਸਾ ਪਾਉਣਾ; ਮਿਲਣ ਵਾਲੀ ਥਾਂ, ਜੋੜ-ਰੇਖਾ;

ਸੰਗਮ, ਜੋੜ-ਬਿੰਦੂ; ~ing time ਕਾਰਜ ਗ੍ਰਹਿਣ-ਕਾਲ

joint ('ਜੌਇੰਟ) *n a v* ਜੋੜ, ਗੰਢ, ਟਾਂਕਾ, ਹੱਡੀਆਂ ਦਾ ਜੋੜ; ਜੋੜ-ਬਿੰਦੂ, ਚੂਲ; ਕਬਜ਼ਾ; ਸਾਂਝਾ; ਇਕੱਠਾ; ਮਿਲਵਾਂ; ਭਿਆਲੀ ਵਾਲਾ; ਜੋੜ ਬਿਠਾਉਣਾ, ਟਾਂਕਾ ਲਾਉਣਾ; ਚੂਲ ਲਾਉਣੀ; ~**family** ਸਾਂਝਾ ਪਰਿਵਾਰ; ~**secretary** ਸੰਯੁਕਤ-ਸਕੱਤਰ; ~**stock** ਸਾਂਝੀ ਪੂੰਜੀ, ਸਾਂਝਾ ਧਨ

joke (ਜਅਉਕ) *n v* ਮਖੌਲ, ਮਸ਼ਕਰੀ, ਹਾਸਾ-ਠੱਠਾ, ਚੁਟਕਲਾ, ਲਤੀਫ਼ਾ; ਹਸਾਉਣੀ ਗੱਲ, ਮਖੌਲ ਕਰਨਾ, ਦਿਲਲਗੀ ਕਰਨੀ, ਮਸ਼ਕਰੀ ਕਰਨੀ; ~**let** ਘਟੀਆ, ਮਸ਼ਕਰੀ; ~**r** ਮਖੌਲੀਆ, ਹਸਾਊ, ਦਿਲਲਗੀਬਾਜ਼; ਭੰਡ, ਵਿਦੂਸ਼ਕ

jollification ('ਜੌਲਿਫ਼ਿ'ਕੇਇਸ਼ਨ) *n* ਰੰਗ-ਰਲੀਆਂ, ਮੌਜ-ਮੇਲਾ

jolify ('ਜੌਲਿਫ਼ਾਇ) *v* ਖ਼ੁਸ਼ੀਆਂ ਮਨਾਉਣੀਆਂ, ਰੰਗ-ਰਲੀਆਂ ਮਨਾਉਣੀਆਂ, ਖ਼ੁਸ਼ ਹੋਣਾ ਜਾਂ ਕਰਨਾ, ਮਸਤ ਹੋਣਾ ਜਾਂ ਕਰਨਾ

jolly ('ਜੌਲਿ) *a n adv* ਰੰਗੀਲਾ, ਰੌਂਣਕੀ, ਮੌਜੀ, ਖ਼ੁਸ਼, ਆਨੰਦ ਵਿਚ; ਜ਼ਿੰਦਾਦਿਲ

jolt (ਜਅਉਲਟ) *v n* ਹੁੱਝਕਾ ਮਾਰਨਾ, ਹਲੂਣਾ, ਝੰਜੋੜਨਾ; ਹੁੱਝਕਾ, ਹਲੂਣਾ, ਧੱਕਾ

jostle ('ਜੌਸਲ) *v n* ਹੁਝਕਾ ਵੱਜਣਾ, ਧੱਕੋ-ਧੱਕੀ ਹੋਣਾ, ਝਟਕਾ ਮਾਰਨਾ; ਹੁਝਕਾ, ਹਲੂਣਾ, ਧੱਕਾ, ਝਟਕਾ

journal ('ਜਅਃਨਲ) *n* ਰਸਾਲਾ, ਪੱਤਰ, ਅਖ਼ਬਾਰ ਰੋਜ਼ਨਾਮਚਾ; ~**ism** ਪੱਤਰਕਾਰੀ, ਅਖ਼ਬਾਰ-ਨਵੀਸੀ, ਪੱਤਰਕਾਰਤਾ; ~**ist** ਪੱਤਰਕਾਰ, ਅਖ਼ਬਾਰ ਨਵੀਸ

journey ('ਜਅਃਨਿ) *n v* ਪੈਂਡਾ; ਸਫ਼ਰ, ਸਾਰ, ਯਾਤਰਾ; ਪੈਂਡਾ ਕਰਨਾ ਜਾਂ ਮਾਰਨਾ, ਸਫ਼ਰ ਕਰਨਾ, ਯਾਤਰਾ ਕਰਨੀ

jovial ('ਜਅਉਵਿਅਲ) *a* ਹਸਮੁੱਖ, ਖ਼ੁਸ਼ਦਿਲ, ਜ਼ਿੰਦਾਦਿਲ, ਮੌਜੀ, ਪ੍ਰਸੰਨ-ਚਿੱਤ; ਆਨੰਦਮਈ; ~**ity** ਹਸਮੁੱਖਤਾ, ਜ਼ਿੰਦਾਦਿਲੀ, ਖ਼ੁਸ਼ਦਿਲੀ, ਪ੍ਰਸੰਨਤਾ

joy (ਜੌਇ) *n v* ਖ਼ੁਸ਼ੀ, ਹੁਲਾਸ, ਪ੍ਰਸੰਨਤਾ; ਆਨੰਦਦਾਇਕ ਵਸਤੂ; ~**ful** ਖ਼ੁਸ਼, ਪ੍ਰਸੰਨ, ਆਨੰਦਤ; ~**fulness** ਪ੍ਰਸੰਨਤਾ, ਆਨੰਦ, ਖ਼ੁਸ਼ੀ, ਮੌਜ; ~**ous** ਆਨੰਦਮਈ, ਖ਼ੁਸ਼ੀ ਭਰਿਆ; ਖ਼ੁਸ਼, ਆਨੰਦ, ਪ੍ਰਸੰਨ

jubilance, jubilation ('ਜੁਬਿਲਅੰਸ, ਜੂਬਿ'ਲੇਇਸ਼ਨ) *n* ਖ਼ੁਸ਼ੀ, ਮੌਜ-ਮੇਲਾ, ਰੰਗ-ਰਲੀਆਂ

jubilant ('ਜੂਬਿਲਅੰਟ) *a* ਖ਼ੁਸ਼, ਪ੍ਰਸੰਨ; ਹਸੂੰ ਹਸੂੰ ਕਰਨਾ

jubilate ('ਜੂਬਿਲੇਇਟ) *v* ਖ਼ੁਸ਼ੀ ਮਨਾਉਣੀ, ਖਿੜੇ ਮੱਥੇ ਹੋਣਾ, ਆਨੰਦਤ ਹੋਣਾ

jubilee ('ਜੂਬਿਲੀ) *n* ਖ਼ੁਸ਼ੀ ਦਾ ਜਸ਼ਨ, ਆਨੰਦ-ਉਤਸਵ; ਜਯੰਤੀ

judaism ('ਜੂਡੇਇਇਜ਼ਮ) *n* ਯਹੂਦੀ ਮੱਤ, ਯਹੂਦੀਵਾਦ, ਯਹੂਦੀਅਤ, ਯਹੂਦੀ

judaist ('ਜੂਡੇਇਇਸਟ) *n* ਯਹੂਦੀ

judge (ਜਅੱਜ) *n v* ਜੱਜ, ਮੁਨਸਫ਼, ਨਿਆਂਅਧਿਕਾਰੀ; ਪਾਰਖੂ, ਪੰਚ, ਨਿਰਣਾਇਕ; ਫ਼ੈਸਲਾ ਕਰਨਾ, ਨਿਰਣੈ ਕਰਨਾ; (ਕਿਸੇ ਬਾਰੇ) ਅਨੁਮਾਨ ਲਾਉਣਾ, ਪਰਖ ਕਰਨੀ; ਮੁਕੱਦਮਾ ਸੁਣਨਾ; ~**ment, judgment** ਫ਼ੈਸਲਾ ਨਿਰਣੈ; ਰਾਇ; ਵਿਚਾਰ-ਸ਼ਕਤੀ, ਸੂਝ, ਸਮਝ ਵਿਵੇਕ; ~**ship** ਜੱਜੀ, ਜੱਜ ਦੀ ਪਦਵੀ

judicate ('ਜੂਡ੍ਰਿਕੇਇਟ) *v* ਇਨਸਾਫ਼ ਕਰਨਾ, ਨਿਆਂ

ਕਰਨਾ, ਵਿਵੇਚਨ ਕਰਨਾ, ਮੁਨਸਫ਼ੀ ਕਰਨਾ

judicial (ਜੁ'ਡਿਸ਼ਲ) *a* ਅਦਾਲਤੀ, ਕਚਹਿਰੀ ਬਾਰੇ, ਨਿਆਂ ਸਬੰਧੀ; ਨਿਰਪੱਖ, ਨਿਆਂਪੂਰਨ; ਮੁਨਸਫ਼ ਦਾ, ਜੱਜੀ; ਅਦਾਲਤ ਵੱਲੋਂ ਕੀਤਾ ਗਿਆ

judiciary (ਜੁ'ਡਿਸ਼ਅਰਿ) *n* ਨਿਆਂਪਾਲਕਾ, ਨਿਆਂਵਿਵੱਸਥਾ; ਨਿਆਂ-ਵਿਭਾਗ; ਅਦਾਲਤੀ ਅਮਲਾ

jug (ਜਅੱਗ) *n v* ਜੱਗ, ਗੰਗਾ ਸਾਗਰ; (ਅਪ) ਕੈਦਖ਼ਾਨਾ; ਚਹਿਕਣਾ, ਚੀਂ ਚੀਂ ਕਰਨਾ, ਚਹਿਚਾਉਣਾ

juggle ('ਜਅੱਗਲ) *v n* ਹੱਥ-ਫੇਰੀ ਕਰਨੀ, ਚਲਾਕੀ ਕਰਨੀ; ਧੋਖਾ ਕਰਨਾ, ਛਲ ਕਰਨਾ; ਹੱਥ ਫੇਰੀ, ਚਲਾਕੀ, ਬਾਜ਼ੀਗਰੀ, ਜਾਦੂਗਰੀ, ਮਦਾਰੀ ਦਾ ਖੇਲ; ~r ਮਦਾਰੀ, ਜਾਦੂਗਰ; ਧੋਖੇਬਾਜ਼

jugglery ('ਜਅੱਗਲਰਿ) *n* ਹੱਥ-ਫੇਰੀ, ਚਲਾਕੀ; ਜਾਦੂਗਰੀ; ~of words ਸ਼ਬਦ ਚਤੁਰਤਾ, ਸ਼ਬਦਜਾਲ, ਸ਼ਬਦਾਂ ਦਾ ਜਾਦੂ

juggling ('ਜਅੱਗਲਿਙ) *n* ਹੱਥ-ਫੇਰੀ, ਹੱਥ ਦੀ ਸਫ਼ਾਈ, ਜਾਦੂਗਰੀ; ਧੋਖਾ, ਮੱਕਾਰੀ, ਛਲਾਵਾ

juice (ਜੂਸ) *n* ਰਸ, ਨਚੋੜ, ਸਾਰ

juiciness ('ਜੂਸਿਨਿਸ) *n* ਰਸਿਕਤਾ, ਤਾਤਵਿਕਤਾ, ਰਸਦਾਇਕਤਾ, ਰੋਚਕਤਾ

juicy ('ਜੂਸਿ) *a* ਰਸਦਾਰ, ਰਸਦਾਇਕ; ਰੋਚਕ, ਮਨੋਰੰਜਕ; (ਗੱਲ) ਚੋਭੀ ਚੋਭੀ

jumbal ('ਜਅੱਮਬਲ) *n* ਖੰਡ ਦੀ ਟਿੱਕੀ; ਮਿੱਠੀ ਟਿੱਕੀ; ਨਾਨ-ਖਤਾਈ

jump (ਜਅੱਪ) *v n* ਛਾਲ ਮਾਰਨੀ, ਟੱਪਣਾ; ਛੜੱਪਾ ਮਾਰਨਾ, ਕੁੱਦਣਾ, ਭੁੜਕਣਾ; (ਮੁੱਲ) ਅਚਾਨਕ ਵਧ ਜਾਣਾ; ਅਨੁਕੂਲ ਹੋਣਾ; ਝਪਟਾ ਮਾਰਨਾ; ਝੱਟ ਕਬਜ਼ਾ ਕਰ ਲੈਣਾ; ਸਰਸਰੀ ਨਜ਼ਰ ਨਾਲ ਵੇਖਣਾ; ਉਲੰਘਣਾ; ਅਚਾਨਕ ਕਿਸੇ ਨਿਰਣੇ ਤੇ ਪੁੱਜਣਾ;

ਛਾਲ; ~in ਗੱਡੀ ਵਿਚ ਕਾਹਲੀ ਨਾਲ ਚੜ੍ਹਨਾ; ~upon ਧਾਮਕਾਉਣਾ, ਡਾਂਟਣਾ, ਧੌਂਸ ਦੇਣਾ; ਟੁੱਟ ਕੇ ਪੈਣਾ, ਚੜ੍ਹ ਜਾਣਾ; ~ing ਹੁਤਕੀ, ਟੱਪੂਸੀ, ਛਾਲ, ਹੰਡਲਾ

junction ('ਜਅੱਙਕਸ਼ਨ) *n* ਦੁਮੇਲ ਸੰਗਮ, ਜੰਕਸ਼ਨ; ਸੰਧੀ ਜੋੜ

juncture ('ਜਅੱਙਕਚਅ*) *n* ਅਵਸਰ, ਮੌਕਾ; ਜੋੜ

jungle ('ਜਅੱਙਗਲ) *n* ਜੰਗਲ; ਵਣ; ਘੜਮਸ

junior ('ਜੂਨਯਅ*) *n a* ਜੂਨੀਅਰ (ਕਰਮਚਾਰੀ), ਛੋਟਾ, ਨਿੱਕਾ, ਨੀਵੀਂ ਸ਼੍ਰੇਣੀ ਜਾਂ ਪਦਵੀ ਦਾ (ਵਿਅਕਤੀ)

junk (ਜਅੱਙਕ) *n v* ਪੁਰਾਣਾ ਮਾਲ, ਕਬਾੜ, ਟੋਟਾ, ਟੁਕੜਾ; ਟੁਕੜੇ ਟੁਕੜੇ ਕਰਨਾ

junto ('ਜਅੱਨਟਅਉ) *n* ਦਲ, ਟੋਲਾ, ਮੰਡਲੀ (ਰਾਜਨੀਤੀ), ਜੁੰਡੀ, ਜੁੰਡਲੀ

jupiter ('ਜੂਪਿਟਅ*) *n* (ਰੋਮਨ) ਦੇਵਰਾਜ; ਜੁਪੀਟਰ; ਬ੍ਰਿਹਸਪਤੀ ਨਖੱਤਰ, ਗੁਰੂ

jurisdiction ('ਜੁਅਰਿਸ'ਡਿਕਸ਼ਨ) *n* ਅਮਲਦਾਰੀ, ਅਧਿਕਾਰ-ਖੇਤਰ, ਨਿਆਂ-ਅਧਿਕਾਰ, ਨਿਆਂ-ਵਿਵੱਸਥਾ

jurisprudence ('ਜੁਅਰਿਸ'ਪਰੂਡਅੰਸ) *n* ਨਿਆਂ ਸ਼ਾਸਤਰ ਧਰਮ-ਸ਼ਾਸਤਰ; ਨਿਆਂ-ਪ੍ਰਵੀਣਤਾ, ਕਾਨੂੰਨ-ਦਾਨੀ

jurisprudent ('ਜੁਅਰਿਸ'ਪਰੂਡਅੰਟ) *n a* ਨਿਆਂ-ਸ਼ਾਸਤਰੀ, ਕਾਨੂੰਨ ਦਾ ਮਾਹਰ, ਕਾਨੂੰਨਦਾਨ; ~ial ਨਿਆਂ-ਸ਼ਾਸਤਰ ਬਾਰੇ

jurist ('ਜੁਅਰਿਸਟ) *n* ਕਾਨੂੰਨਦਾਨ; ਵਕੀਲ, ਐਡਵੋਕੇਟ, ਨਿਆਂ-ਨਿਪੁੰਨ, ਵਿਧਾਨਕਾਰ, ਨਿਆਇਕ, ਵਿਧੀ-ਵਿਦਿਆਰਥੀ

jury ('ਜੁਅਰਿ) *n* ਅਦਾਲਤੀ ਪੰਚਾਇਤ, ਜਿਊਰੀ; ~man ਪੰਚ, ਨਿਆਂ ਸਤਾ ਦਾ ਮੈਂਬਰ

just (ਜਅੱਸਟ) *a adv* ਠੀਕ, ਵਾਜਬ, ਮੁਨਾਸਬ, ਉਚਿਤ; ਨਿਆਂਪੂਰਨ, ਨਿਆਂਕਾਰੀ, ਅਦਲੀ, ਨਿਰਪੱਖ, ਸੱਚਾ, ਨਿਸ਼ਕਪਟ, ਈਮਾਨਦਾਰ; ਉਸੇ ਵੇਲੇ, ਠੀਕ ਓਦੋਂ, ਹੁਣੇ ਹੁਣੇ ਹੀ; ਜਿਉਂ ਹੀ; ਕੁਝ-ਕੁਝ; ਕੇਵਲ, ਮੁਸ਼ਕਲ ਨਾਲ; **~now** ਹੁਣੇ, ਤੁਰਤ

justice ('ਜਅੱਸਟਿਸ) *n* ਨਿਆਂ, ਇਨਸਾਫ਼, ਅਦਾਲਤੀ ਕਾਰਵਾਈ; ਨਿਆਂ-ਸੰਗਤੀ, ਨਿਰਪੱਖਤਾ

justifiability, justifiableness ('ਜਅੱਸਟਿ-ਫ਼ਾਇਬਲਅਟਿ' ਅੱਸਟਿਫ਼ਾਇਬਲਨਿਸ) *n* ਨਿਆਂ-ਸਿੱਧੀ, ਨਿਆਂ ਸਮਰਥਨ, ਨਿਆਂਖਮਤਾ, ਨਿਆਂ ਸੰਗਤੀ

justifiable ('ਜਅੱਸਟਿਫ਼ਾਇਬਲ) *a* ਉਚਿਤ, ਨਿਆਂ ਅਨੁਸਾਰ, ਠੀਕ

justification ('ਜਅੱਸਟਿਫ਼ਿ'ਕੇਇਸ਼ਨ) *n* ਉਚਿਤਤਾ, ਸਫ਼ਾਈ, ਸਮਰਥਨ, ਪ੍ਰਮਾਣਕਤਾ

justified ('ਜਅੱਸਟਿਫ਼ਾਇਡ) *a* ਉਚਿਤ, ਯੋਗ

justify ('ਜਅੱਸਟਿਫ਼ਾਇ) *v* ਠੀਕ ਸਿੱਧ ਕਰਨਾ, ਉਚਿਤ ਠਹਿਰਾਉਣਾ, ਹੱਕ ਵਿਚ ਦਲੀਲਾਂ ਦੇਣੀਆਂ; ਸਚਾਈ ਦਾ ਪ੍ਰਮਾਣ ਦੇਣਾ; ਸਮਰਥਨ ਕਰਨਾ; ਨਿਆਂ-ਸੰਗਤ ਸਿੱਧ ਕਰਨਾ

jute (ਜੂਟ) *n* ਪਟਸਨ, ਸਨ, ਸਨੁਕੜਾ

juvenescence ('ਜੂਵ਼ਅ'ਨੈੱਸੰਸ) *n* ਜਵਾਨੀ ਦਾ ਉਭਾਰ, ਚੜ੍ਹਦੀ ਜਵਾਨੀ

juvenescent ('ਜੂਵ਼ਅ'ਨੈੱਸੰਟ) *a* ਚੜ੍ਹਦੀ ਜਵਾਨੀ ਵਾਲਾ, ਮਸਫੁੱਟ (ਗੱਭਰੂ)

juvenile ('ਜੂਵ਼ਅਨਾਇਲ) *a n* ਨੌਜਵਾਨ, ਗਭਰੇਟ ਬਾਲਕ, ਅਲੂਆਂ ਮੁੰਡਾ, ਅੱਲੜ ਬੱਚਾ; **~ness, juvenility** ਅੱਲੜਪੁਣਾ; ਬਾਲਪਣ, ਚੜ੍ਹਦੀ ਜਵਾਨੀ

juxtapose ('ਜਅੱਕਸਟਅ'ਪਅਉਜ਼) *v* ਨਾਲ ਨਾਲ ਰੱਖਣਾ, ਕੋਲ ਕੋਲ ਰੱਖਣਾ

juxtaposition ('ਜਅੱਕਸਟਅਪਅ'ਜ਼ਿਸ਼ਨ) *n* ਨਿਕਟਤਾ, ਸਮੀਪਤਾ

K

K, k (ਕੇਇ) *n* ਰੋਮਨ ਵਰਨਮਾਲਾ ਦਾ ਗਿਆਰਵਾਂ ਅੱਖਰ

kago ('ਕਾਗਅਉ) *n* ਡੋਲੀ, ਪਾਲਕੀ

kar(r)oo (ਕਅ'ਰੂ) *n* ਪਠਾਰ

keck (ਕੈੱਕ) *v n* ਉਲਟੀ ਕਰਨੀ; ਕੈ ਕਰਨੀ; ਕੈ, ਉਲਟੀ

keen (ਕੀਨ) *a n* (1) ਚਾਹਵਾਨ, ਅਭਿਲਾਖੀ, ਇੱਛੁਕ; (2) ਭਾ'ਵੁਕ, ਤਿੱਖੀ ਖੁੱਧ ਵਾਲਾ; (3) ਸਖ਼ਤ, ਬਹੁਤ ਜ਼ਿਆਦਾ; (4) (ਇੱਛਾ) ਤੀਬਰ, ਭਾਰੀ; ਵਿਰਲਾਪ; ਵੈਣ; **~ness** ਉਤਸੁਕਤਾ, ਸ਼ੌਕ, ਉਤਕੰਠ, ਚਿੰਤਾ, ਬੇਚੈਨੀ; ਤੀਖਣਤਾ, ਤੀਬਰਤਾ, ਤੇਜ਼ੀ

keep (ਕੀਪ) *v n* ਰੱਖਣਾ, ਰਹਿਣਾ; ਧਿਆਨ ਰੱਖਣਾ, ਖ਼ਿਆਲ ਰੱਖਣਾ; ਪਾਲਣਾ ਕਰਨੀ, ਜ਼ਿੰਮੇ ਲੈਣਾ, ਹੱਥ ਵਿਚ ਲੈਂਣਾ; ਚਲਾਉਣਾ; ਹਿਸਾਬ-ਕਿਤਾਬ ਰੱਖਣਾ; ਰਖੇਲ ਰੱਖਣਾ; ਰੋਕਣਾ; ਗੁਪਤ ਰੱਖਣਾ, ਛੁਪਾਉਣਾ; ਡਟੇ ਰਹਿਣਾ; ਰਖੇਲ, ਘਰੇਲ; ਗੁਜ਼ਾਰਾ; **~away** ਨੇੜੇ ਨਾ ਢੁੱਕਣ ਦੇਣਾ; **~back** ਛੁਪਾਉਣਾ, ਗੁਪਤ ਰੱਖਣਾ, ਦੂਰ ਰਹਿਣਾ; **~body & soul together** ਜੀਊਂਦਾ ਰਹਿਣਾ; **~down** ਦਬਾਉਣਾ; **~from** (ਤੋਂ) ਦੂਰ ਰਹਿਣਾ; **~in** ਵੱਸ ਵਿਚ ਰੱਖਣਾ; **~on** ਚਲਦਾ ਰੱਖਣਾ; **~track** ਪਿੱਛਾ ਕਰਨਾ, ਪੈੜ ਦਬਾਣਾ

keg (ਕੈੱਗ) *n* ਪੀਪਾ (ਦਸ ਗੈਲਨ ਤੋਂ ਘੱਟ ਦਾ), ਛੋਟਾ ਢੋਲ

kell (ਕੈੱਲ) *n* ਮੱਕੜੀ ਦਾ ਜਾਲਾ

ken (ਕੈੱਨ) *v n* ਵੇਖ ਕੇ ਪਛਾਣਨਾ; ਬੁੱਝਣਾ, ਸਮਝਣਾ, ਜਾਣ ਲੈਣਾ; ਦ੍ਰਿਸ਼ਟੀ-ਸੀਮਾ, ਸੂਝ, ਗਿਆਨ-ਖੇਤਰ; **~ning** ਨਿਗਾਹ, ਦ੍ਰਿਸ਼ਟੀ; ਜਾਣਕਾਰੀ, ਗਿਆਨ, ਪਛਾਣ

kennel ('ਕੈੱਨਲ) *n* ਕੁੱਤੇਖਾਨਾ; ਘਟੀਆ ਮਕਾਨ; ਪਰਨਾਲਾ; ਪਾਣੀ ਦੀ ਮੋਰੀ

kernel ('ਕਅਃਨਲ) *n* ਗਿਰੀ, ਮਗਜ਼, ਗਿਟਕ; ਸਾਰ, ਮੂਲ, ਤੱਤ; ਕੇਦਰ-ਬਿੰਦੂ, ਅੰਦਰ

kerosene ('ਕੈੱਰੋਅਸੀਨ) *n* ਮਿੱਟੀ ਦਾ ਤੇਲ

kersey ('ਕਅਃਜ਼ਿ) *n* ਪਟੂ, ਮੱਟਾ ਉੱਨੀ ਕਪੜਾ

ketchup ('ਕੈੱਟਅਪ) *n* ਟਮਾਟਰਾਂ ਆਦਿ ਦੀ ਚਟਣੀ, ਸਾਸ, ਚਾਟ

kettle ('ਕੈੱਟਲ) *n* ਦੇਗਚੀ, ਪਤੀਲੀ, ਕੇਤਲੀ, ਚਾਹਦਾਨੀ

key (ਕੀ) *n a v* ਕੁੰਜੀ, ਚਾਬੀ; ਟੀਕਾ; ਹੱਲ; ਵਸੀਲਾ, ਰਾਹ, ਸਾਧਨ, ਪੇਪ ਦੇ ਅਧਿਕਾਰ; ਸਮੁੰਦਰੀ ਚੌਕੀ, (ਸੰਗੀ) ਸੁਰ; **~note** ਮੁੱਖ ਸੁਰ, ਮੂਲ ਸੁਰ, ਤਾਨ; ਮੂਲ ਭਾਵ; **~less** ਸਾਧਨਹੀਣ

kibble ('ਕਿਬਲ) *n v* ਡੋਲ, ਬਾਲਟੀ; ਪੀਹਣਾ, ਕੁਰਲਣਾ

kick (ਕਿਕ) *v n* ਲੱਤ ਮਾਰਨੀ, ਠੁੱਡਾ ਮਾਰਨਾ, ਦੁਲੱਤਾ (ਬੰਦੂਕ ਦਾ) ਧੱਕਾ ਮਾਰਨਾ; (ਫੁਟਬਾਲ ਨੂੰ) ਕਿੱਕ ਮਾਰਨੀ; ਧੱਕੇ ਮਾਰ ਕੇ ਕੱਢਣਾ, ਠੁੱਡਾ, ਦੁਲੱਤਾ, ਪਰਛੱਡਾ, (ਬੰਦੂਕ ਦਾ) ਧੱਕਾ, (ਫੁਟਬਾਲ ਵਿਚ) ਕਿੱਕ; **~back** (ਅਪ) ਵੱਢੀ; **~up** ਉਡਾ ਦੇਣਾ

kickshaw ('ਕਿਕਸ਼ੋ) *n* ਚੰਗਾ-ਚੋਖਾ (ਖਾਣਾ), ਸੁਆਦਲਾ ਖਾਣਾ; ਨਗੁਣੀ ਚੀਜ਼, ਤੁੱਛ ਵਸਤੁ, ਖਿਡੌਣਾ

kid (ਕਿਡ) *n* ਮੇਮਣਾ, ਬੱਕਰੀ ਦਾ ਬੱਚਾ, ਨਿਆਣਾ; ~dy ਨਿੱਕਾ ਨਿਆਣਾ, ਛੋਟਾ ਬੱਚਾ; ~ling ਪਠੋਰਾ, ਮੇਮਣਾ, ਬਕਰੋਟਾ

kidnap ('ਕਿਡਨੈਪ) *v* ਕੱਢ ਕੇ ਲੈ ਜਾਣਾ, (ਮਨੁੱਖ ਨੂੰ) ਜ਼ਬਰਦਸਤੀ ਚੁੱਕ ਲੈ ਜਾਣਾ; ਅਪਹਰਣ ਕਰਨਾ, ਅਗਵਾ ਕਰਨਾ; ~per ਬਾਲ-ਚੋਰ, ਅਪਹਰਣ-ਕਰਤਾ

kidney ('ਕਿਡਨਿ) *n* ਗੁਰਦਾ; ਸੁਭਾਅ, ਤਬੀਅਤ; ~bean ਲੋਬੀਆ

kill (ਕਿਲ) *v* ਮਾਰ ਸੁੱਟਣਾ, ਮਾਰ ਦੇਣਾ, ਕਤਲ ਕਰਨਾ; ਸ਼ਿਕਾਰ ਕਰਨਾ, ਝਟਕਾਉਣਾ, ਹਲਾਲ ਕਰਨਾ; ~er ਹਤਿਆਰਾ, ਖ਼ੂਨੀ, ਕਾਤਲ, ਘਾਤਕ

kiln (ਕਿਲਨ) *n* ਭੱਠਾ, ਆਵਾ

kilogram, kilogramme ('ਕਿਲਅ(ਉ)ਗਰੈਮ) *n* ਕਿਲੋਗਰਾਮ, ਇਕ ਹਜ਼ਾਰ ਗਰਾਮ

kilometre ('ਕਿਲਅਮੀਟਅ*) *n* ਕਿਲੋਮੀਟਰ, ਇਕ ਹਜ਼ਾਰ ਮੀਟਰ

kin (ਕਿਨ) *n a* ਸਾਕ-ਸਬੰਧੀ, ਗੋਤ-ਭਾਈ, ਸਮਾਜਾਤੀ; ਇਕੋ ਜਿਹੇ ਸੁਭਾਅ ਵਾਲੇ; ~sman ਰਿਸ਼ਤੇਦਾਰ, ਗੋਤੀ, ਨਿਕਟ ਸਬੰਧੀ, ਸਗੋਤਰ ਨਾਤੇਦਾਰ; ~ship ਖੂਨ ਦਾ ਰਿਸ਼ਤਾ, ਸਾਕ, ਸਾਕਾਦਾਰੀ, ਰਿਸ਼ਤੇਦਾਰੀ

kind (ਕਾਈਂਡ) *n a* ਕਿਸਮ, ਪ੍ਰਕਾਰ, ਵੰਨਗੀ, ਭਾਂਤ; ਨਸਲ, ਕਿਰਪਾਲੂ, ਦਿਆਲੂ; ਮਿਹਰਬਾਨ, ਰਹਿਮਦਿਲ; ਪਿਆਰਾ, ਪਰੇਮੀ; ਸ਼ੀਲਵਾਨ; ~hearted ਕੋਮਲ-ਚਿੱਤ, ਨਰਮ ਦਿਲ; ~liness ਉਦਾਰਤਾ, ਕਿਰਪਾਲਤਾ, ਦਿਆਲਤਾ, ਰਹਿਮਦਿਲੀ, ਕੋਮਲਚਿੱਤਤਾ; ~ness ਕਿਰਪਾਲਤਾ, ਦਇਆਲਤਾ, ਮਿਹਰਬਾਨੀ, ਮਿਹਰ, ਦਇਆ, ਹਮਦਰਦੀ

kindergarten ('ਕਿੰਡਅ'ਗਾਟਨ) *n* ਬਾਲਵਾੜੀ, ਕਿੰਡਰਗਾਰਟਨ

kindle ('ਕਿੰਡਲ) *v* ਬਾਲਣਾ, ਮਘਾਉਣਾ; ਪ੍ਰਜੂਲਤ ਕਰਨਾ, ਚਮਕਾਉਣਾ; ਉਤਸ਼ਾਹਤ ਕਰਨਾ, ਉਤੇਜਤ ਕਰਨਾ, ਭਖਾਉਣਾ, ਭੜਕ ਉੱਠਣਾ, ਬਲ ਉੱਠਣਾ

kinematic ('ਕਿਨਿ'ਮੈਟਿਕ) *a* ਗਤੀ-ਆਤਮਕ ਗਤੀ ਸਬੰਧੀ; ~s ਗਤੀ-ਵਿਗਿਆਨ, ਚਾਲ ਵਿਦਿਆ

kinetic (ਕਿ'ਨੈਟਿਕ) *a* ਗਤੀਆਤਮਕ

king (ਕਿੰਡ) *n v* ਬਾਦਸ਼ਾਹ, ਭੂਪ, ਨਰੇਸ਼, ਰਾਜਾ ~fisher ਬਿਰੂ ਜਾਂ ਬਹਿਰੀ, ਸ਼ਿਕਾਰੀ ਪੰਛੀ ~wood ਸਾਗਵਾਨ ਦੀ ਲੱਕੜ; ~dom ਬਾਦਸ਼ਾਹੀ, ਬਾਦਸ਼ਾਹਤ, ਸਲਤਨਤ, ਰਾਜ ਰਾਜਧਾਨੀ; ਰੱਬੀ; ~hood ਬਾਦਸ਼ਾਹੀ, ਰਾਜ-ਪਦ, ਰਾਜ; ~let, ~ling ਰਜਵਾੜਾ ~ship ਬਾਦਸ਼ਾਹੀ, ਰਾਜ; ਰਾਜ-ਪਦ, ਰਾਜ-ਅਧਿਕਾਰ

kiosk ('ਕੀਓਸਕ) *n* ਖੁੱਲ੍ਹਾ ਤੰਬੂ, ਛੋਟਾ ਸ਼ਾਮਿਆਨਾ ਖੋਖਾ

kip (ਕਿਪ) *n* (1) ਛੋਟੇ ਪਸ਼ੂ ਦੀ ਖਲੜੀ, ਮੇਮਣੇ ਦੀ ਖੱਲ, ਨਰਮ ਚਮੜਾ; (2) ਟਿਕਾਣਾ, ਆਸਰਾ

kiss (ਕਿਸ) *n v* ਚੁੰਮਣ, ਚੁੰਮੀ, ਬੁੱਕੀ; ਚੁੰਮਣਾ ਚੁੰਮੀ ਲੈਣੀ; ਪਿਆਰ ਕਰਨਾ; ~curl ਜੁਲਫ਼ ~ing ਚੁੰਮਣ, ਚੁੰਮੀ, ਚੁੰਮਾ-ਚੱਟੀ

kit (ਕਿਟ) *n v* (1) ਵਸਤ-ਵਲੇਵਾ, ਸਾਜ਼-ਸਾਮਾਨ ਫ਼ੌਜੀਆਂ ਦੇ ਹਥਿਆਰਾਂ ਦੀ ਕਿੱਟ; ਬਿਸਤਰਾ ਕਾਰੀਗਰ ਦੇ ਸੰਦ; ਸਫ਼ਰੀ ਸਾਮਾਨ (2) ਬਲੂੰਗੜਾ ਸਜਣਾ, ਸਜਾਉਣਾ; ਤਿਆਰ ਕਰਨੀ; ~bag ਸਿਪਾਹੀ ਦਾ ਜਾਂ ਯਾਤਰੀ ਦਾ ਸਾਮਾਨ ਵਾਲਾ ਝੋਲਾ

kit-cat ('ਕਿਟਕੈਟ) *n* ਗੁੱਲੀ-ਡੰਡਾ

kitchen ('ਕਿਚਨ) *n* ਰਸੋਈ, ਲੰਗਰ; ~garden ਘਰੋਗੀ ਬਗ਼ੀਚਾ; ~stuff ਰਸੋਈ ਦਾ ਸਾਮਾਨ

ਰਸਦ-ਪਾਣੀ

kite (ਕਾਇਟ) *n v* (1) ਇੱਲ੍ਹ; (2) ਲੋਭੀ ਮਨੁੱਖ; (3) ਪਤੰਗ, ਗੁੱਡੀ; ਹਵਾਈ ਜਹਾਜ਼; ~**flying** ਪਤੰਗਬਾਜ਼ੀ; ਛੁਰਲੀ

kith (ਕਿਥ) *n* ਸੰਕੇ-ਸਰਬੰਧੀ, ਸੱਜਣ-ਮਿੱਤਰ, ਰਿਸ਼ਤੇਦਾਰ, ਭਾਈਬੰਦੀ

kitten ('ਕਿਟਨ) *n v* ਬਲੂੰਗੜਾ, ਬਲੰਗਾ; ਚੰਚਲ ਕੁੜੀ, ਨਖਰੇਬਾਜ਼ ਕੁੜੀ;

klick (ਕ'ਲਿਕ) *v* ਟਿਕ-ਟਿਕ ਕਰਨਾ

knag (ਨੈਗ) *n* ਲੱਕੜੀ ਦੀ ਗੰਢ; ਟਾਹਣੀ ਦਾ ਮੁੱਢ

knave (ਨੈਇਵ) *n* ਲੁੱਚਾ, ਬਦਮਾਸ਼, ਲਫੰਗਾ, ਠੱਗ, ਬੇਈਮਾਨ; ~**ry, knavishness** ਲੁੱਚਪੁਣਾ, ਬਦਮਾਸ਼ੀ

knavish (ਨੈਇਵਿਸ਼) *a* ਬਦਮਾਸ਼, ਲੁੱਚਾ, ਠੱਗ, ਧੋਖੇਬਾਜ਼, ਫਰੇਬੀ

knee (ਨੀ) *n v* ਗੋਡਾ; ਗੋਡਾ ਛੁਹਾਉਣਾ

knickers ('ਨਿਕਅਜ਼) *n pl knickerbocker* ਦਾ ਛੋਟਾ ਰੂਪ, ਨਿੱਕਰ; ਤੀਵੀਆਂ ਦਾ ਕੱਛਾ

knife (ਨਾਇਫ) *n v* ਚਾਕੂ, ਕਰਦ, ਛੁਰੀ; ਚਾਕੂ ਮਾਰਨਾ, ਛੁਰਾ ਮਾਰਨਾ; ਛੁਰੀ ਨਾਲ ਵੱਢਣਾ; ~**grinder** ਸਾਣ, ਪੱਥਰੀ ਜਿਸ ਉੱਤੇ ਚਾਕੂ ਛੁਰੀਆਂ ਤਿੱਖੀਆਂ ਕਰਦੇ ਹਨ; **war to the~** ਘੋਰ ਯੁਧ, ਘਮਾਸਾਨ ਲੜਾਈ

knight (ਨਾਇਟ) *n v* ਨਾਇਕ, ਹਥਿਆਰਬੰਦ ਸੂਰਮਾ, ਬਹਾਦਰ ਸਿਪਾਹੀ, ਘੋੜ-ਸਿਪਾਹੀ; ਫੌਜੀ ਸਰਦਾਰ; ਨਾਈਟ; ਕੌਮੀ ਸੇਵਾ ਲਈ ਦਿੱਤਾ ਗਿਆ ਸਨਮਾਨ ਵਾਲਾ ਪਦ, ਨਾਈਟ ਜਾਂ ਸਰਦਾਰ ਬਣਾਉਣਾ, ਨਾਈਟ ਥਾਪਣਾ; ~**age** ਸਾਮੰਤ ਵਰਗ, ਨਾਈਟਾਂ ਦੀ ਸੂਚੀ, ਸ਼ਾਹੀ ਸਰਦਾਰਾਂ ਦਾ ਵੇਰਵਾ; ~**like, ~ly** ਬੀਰਤਾ ਪੂਰਨ, ਸਾਮੰਤ ਵਰਗ ਦਾ; ~**liness**
ਸਾਮੰਤਸ਼ਾਹੀ, ਸਰਦਾਰੀ; ਸੂਰਬੀਰਤਾ

knit (ਨਿਟ) *v* ਉਣਨਾ, ਬੁਣਨਾ; ~**wear** ਬੁਣੇ ਕੱਪੜੇ; ~**ting** ਬੁਣਤੀ, ਬੁਣਾਈ; ਜੋੜ ਮੇਲ

knob (ਨੌਬ) *n* ਲਾਟੂ, ਮੁੱਠਾ, ਡੂਡਣਾ; ਦਸਤਾ, ਹੱਥੀ; ਗੁੜ ਦੀ ਰੋੜੀ

knock (ਨੌਕ) *v* ਖੜਕਾਉਣਾ; ਖੜਾਕ ਕਰਨਾ, ਦਸਤਕ ਦੇਣੀ, ਕੁੰਡੀ ਖੜਕਾਉਣੀ, ਠੱਕ-ਠੱਕ ਕਰਨਾ; ਸੱਟ ਮਾਰਨੀ, ਹੱਥੋੜੇ ਆਦਿ ਨਾਲ ਠੋਕਣਾ; ਹੈਰਾਨ ਕਰ ਦੇਣਾ; ~**down** ਕਰਾਰੀ (ਸੱਟ), ਚਿਤ ਹੋਣ ਦਾ ਭਾਵ; ਨਿਲਾਮੀ ਵਿਚ ਰਾਖਵੀਂ ਕੀਮਤ; ~**about** ਅਵਾਰਾ ਫਿਰਨਾ; ~**off** ਕੰਮ ਛੱਡ ਬੈਠਣਾ; ~**out** ਪਛਾੜਨਾ; ~**ing** ਦਰਵਾਜ਼ੇ ਤੇ ਹੋਈ ਠੱਕ-ਠੱਕ; ਪੱਕਾ ਦੇਣ ਵਾਲਾ, ਪਛਾੜਨ ਵਾਲਾ

knot (ਨੌਟ) *n v* ਗੰਢ; (ਧਾਗੇ ਦੀ) ਹਰਦ, ਹਰੀਨ; ਜੂੜਾ, ਚੁੰਡਾ; ਘੁੰਡੀ, ਮਰੋੜੀ; ਸਮੁੰਦਰੀ ਮੀਲ (6080 ਫੁੱਟ); ਝਮੇਲਾ, ਕਠਨਾਈ, ਔਕੜ; ਗੰਢ ਦੇਣੀ, ਹਰਜ ਪਾਉਣੀ, ਜੂੜਾ ਕਰਨਾ, ਘੁੰਡੀ ਪਾਉਣੀ, ਮਰੋੜੀ ਦੇਣੀ; ~**ted** ਗੰਢਦਾਰ, ਗੁੰਝਲ, ਵਿਖਮ, ਪੇਚਕਾਰ, ਪੇਚੀਦਾ; ~**tiness** ਜਟਲਤਾ, ਗੁੰਝਲਪੁਰਨਤਾ; ~**ty** ਗੁੰਝਲਦਾਰ, ਔਖਾ, ਟੇਢਾ ਗੰਢਦਾਰ; ਗੰਢ ਵਾਲਾ

know (ਨਅਉ) *v* ਜਾਣਨਾ, ਪਛਾਣਨਾ, ਸਮਝਣਾ, ਵਾਕਫ਼ੀਅਤ ਹੋਣੀ, ਜਾਣੂ ਹੋਣਾ, ਗਿਆਨ ਹੋਣਾ; ~**ing** ਵਾਕਫ਼, ਜਾਣਕਾਰ; ਸਿਆਣਾ, ਸੁਝਵਾਨ, ਚੁਸਤ; ~**ingly** ਜਾਣ-ਬੁੱਝ ਕੇ ਵਿਸ਼ੇਸ਼ ਇਰਾਦੇ ਨਾਲ; ~**ingness** ਚੌਕਸੀ, ਚਤੁਰਾਈ, ਜਾਣਕਾਰੀ, ਸਮਝਦਾਰੀ, ਸਿਆਣਪ, ਹੁਸ਼ਿਆਰੀ; ~**n** ਮਸ਼ਹੂਰ, ਪ੍ਰਸਿੱਧ, ਉੱਘਾ; ਜਾਣਿਆ, ਪਛਾਣਿਆ; ਮਾਲੂਮ

knowledge ('ਨੌਲਿਜ) *n* ਗਿਆਨ, ਸੂਝ, ਸੋਝੀ,

knowledge	kyphotic
ਵਿੱਦਿਆ, ਜਾਣਕਾਰੀ, ਵਾਕਫ਼ੀ; ਪਛਾਣ, ਪਰਿਚਯ; ਆਮ ਸੂਝ-ਬੂਝ, ਅਨੁਭਵ; ਸਮਾਚਾਰ; *a little ~ is dangerous thing* ਨੀਮ ਹਕੀਮ ਖ਼ਤਰਾ ਜਾਨ; **~able** ਜਾਣਕਾਰ, ਸੂਝਵਾਨ, ਸੋਝੀ ਵਾਲਾ; ਬੁੱਧੀਮਾਨ; ਸਚੇਤ, ਚੇਤਨ	**kodak** ('ਕਅਉਡੈਕ) *n v* 'ਕੋਦਕ' ਨਾਮ ਦਾ ਕੈਮਰਾ; ਕੋਦਕ ਕੈਮਰੇ ਨਾਲ ਫੋਟੋ ਖਿੱਚਣੀ; ਝਟਪਟ ਫੜਨਾ, ਗ੍ਰਹਿਣ ਕਰਨਾ; ਸਪਸ਼ਟ ਵਰਣਨ ਕਰਨਾ **kulak** ('ਕੂਲੇਕ) *n* ਧਨੀ ਜਾਂ ਖ਼ੁਸ਼ਹਾਲ ਕਿਸਾਨ **kyphotic** (ਕਾਇ'ਫ਼ੌਟਿਕ) *a* ਕੁੱਬਾ, ਕੁੱਬ

L

L, l (ਔਲ) *n* ਰੋਮਨ ਵਰਣਮਾਲਾ ਦਾ ਬਾਰ੍ਹਵਾਂ ਅੱਖਰ; (ਰੋਮਨ) ਗਿਣਤੀ ਵਿਚ 50 ਦਾ ਅੰਕ

labarum ('ਲੈਬਅਰਅਮ) *n* ਝੰਡਾ, ਨਿਸ਼ਾਨ

label ('ਲੇਇਬਅਲ) *n v* ਲੇਬਲ, ਚਿਟ, ਚੇਪੀ, ਫੱਟੀ; ਲੇਬਲ ਚਿਪਕਾਉਣਾ, ਚੇਪੀ ਲਗਾਉਣੀ; ਨਾਂ ਦੇਣਾ; **~led** ਅੰਕਤ, ਚਿੰਨ੍ਹਤ, ਲੇਬਲ ਲੱਗਾ

laboratory (ਲਅ'ਬੌਰਅਟ(ਅ)ਰਿ) *n* ਪ੍ਰਯੋਗਸ਼ਾਲਾ

laborious (ਲਅ'ਬੋਰਿਅਸ) *a* ਮਿਹਨਤੀ; ਮੁਸ਼ਕਲ, ਕਠਨ; (ਸ਼ੈਲੀ) ਉਚੇਚ ਭਰੀ; **~ness** ਮਿਹਨਤ, ਮੁਸ਼ਕਲ ਭਰਪੂਰਤਾ, ਕਠਨਤਾ

labour ('ਲੇਇਬਅ*) *n v* (1) ਮਿਹਨਤ; ਮਜ਼ਦੂਰੀ, ਕਿਰਤ; ਮਜ਼ਦੂਰ, ਕੁਲੀ; ਮਜ਼ਦੂਰ-ਪੇਸ਼ਾ ਜਮਾਤ, (2) ਪ੍ਰਸੂਤ ਪੀੜਾਂ, ਮੁਸ਼ਕਲ ਕੰਮ; ਕਸ਼ਟ, ਕਲੇਸ਼; ਮਿਹਨਤ ਕਰਨਾ; ਮਜ਼ਦੂਰੀ ਕਰਨਾ; ਕਸ਼ਟ ਸਹਿਣਾ; **~of love** ਨਿਸ਼ਕਾਮ ਸੇਵਾ ਦਾ ਕੰਮ; **forced~** ਵਗਾਰ; **~er** ਮਜ਼ੂਰ, ਕਿਰਤੀ, ਮਜ਼ਦੂਰ, ਕਾਮਾ, ਕੁਲੀ, ਸ਼ਰਮਿਕ; **~ing** ਮਜ਼ਦੂਰ

labrum ('ਲੇਇਬਰਅਮ) *n* ਬੁੱਲ੍ਹ, ਹੋਂਠ

labyrinth ('ਲੈਬਅਰਿੰਥ) *n* ਭੁੱਲ-ਭੁਲੱਈਆ, ਚੱਕਰ, ਗੋਰਖਧੰਦਾ, ਪੇਚੀਦਗੀ, ਉਲਝਿਆ, ਮਾਮਲਾ, ਉਲਝਣ

lac, lakh (ਲੈਕ) *n* ਲੱਖ

lace (ਲੇਇਸ) *n v* ਫ਼ੀਤਾ, ਲੇਸ, ਝਾਲਰ, ਕਿੰਗਰੀ, ਕਿਨਾਰੀ; ਫ਼ੀਤਾ ਜਾਂ ਕਿਨਾਰੀ ਲਾਉਣੀ; ਤਸਮੇ ਨਾਲ ਕੱਸਣਾ (ਬੂਟ ਆਦਿ ਨੂੰ); ਕਮਰ ਨੂੰ ਕੱਸ ਕੇ ਬੰਨ੍ਹਣਾ

laches ('ਲੇਇਚਿਜ਼) *n* ਹੁਕਮ ਅਦੂਲੀ, ਗ਼ਫ਼ਲਤ; ਲਾਪਰਵਾਹੀ, ਢਿੱਲ

lack (ਲੈਕ) *n v* ਅਣਹੋਂਦ; ਘਾਟਾ, ਕਮੀ, ਬੁੜ, ਅਭਾਵ, ਤਰੁਟੀ, ਮੁਥਾਜੀ; ਘਾਟਾ ਹੋਣਾ, ਬੁੜ ਹੋਣੀ, ਮੁਥਾਜੀ ਹੋਣੀ; **~ing** ਰਹਿਤ, ਹੀਣ, ਘਾਟ ਵਾਲਾ, ਕਮੀ ਵਾਲਾ

lackadaisical (ਲੈਕਅ'ਡੇਇਜ਼ਿਕਲ) *a* ਨਿਸਤੇਜ, ਬੇਜਾਨ; ਨਿਰਉਤਸ਼ਾਹ

lackey, lacquey ('ਲੈਕਿ) *n v* ਝੋਲੀ ਚੁੱਕ, ਜੁੱਤੀ-ਚੱਟ, ਪਿਛਲੱਗ; ਝੋਲੀ-ਚੁੱਕਣੀ, ਚਾਪਲੂਸੀ ਕਰਨੀ

lactation (ਲੈਕ'ਟੇਇਸ਼ਨ) *n* ਦੁੱਧ ਪਿਲਾਉਣਾ, ਦੁੱਧ ਦੇਣਾ

lactic ('ਲੈਕ'ਟਿਕ) *a* ਦੁੱਧ ਦਾ, ਦੁਧੀਆ

lacuna (ਲਅ'ਕਯੂਨਅ) *n* (ਪੁਰਾਤਨ ਲਿਖਤਾਂ ਵਿਚ) ਪਾਠ-ਲੋਪ; ਵਿਰਲ, ਖ਼ਲਾਅ, ਛੋਟ, ਛਿਦਰ

lacy ('ਲੇਇਸਿ) *a* ਝਾਲਰਦਾਰ, ਲੇਸਦਾਰ, ਫ਼ੀਤੇਦਾਰ

lad (ਲੈਡ) *n* ਬਾਲਕ, ਲੜਕਾ, ਨੰਢਾ, ਛੋਕਰਾ, ਬਾਲ; ਜੱਟਾ, ਸ਼ਖ਼ਸ

ladder ('ਲੈਡਅ*) *n v* ਪੌੜੀ; ਜ਼ੀਨਾ, ਵਸੀਲਾ (ਤਰੱਕੀ ਦਾ); ਚਤੁਤ ਹੋਣੀ

laddie ('ਲੈਡਿ) *n* ਬੱਚੂ

lade (ਲੇਇਡ) *v* ਲੱਦਣਾ, ਮਾਲ ਭਰਨਾ; **~n** ਲੱਦਿਆ ਹੋਇਆ, ਲਦੂ

lading ('ਲੇਇਡਿਙ) *n* ਸਾਮਾਨ, ਮਾਲ-ਅਸਬਾਬ, ਬੋਝ, ਮਾਲ ਲੱਦ

ladle ('ਲੇਇਡਲ) *n v* ਕੜਛੀ, ਵੱਡਾ ਚਮਚਾ, ਕੜਛੀ ਨਾਲ ਕੱਢਣਾ

lady ('ਲੇਇਡਿ) *n* ਇਸਤਰੀ, ਮਹਿਲਾ; ਨਾਰੀ,

ਬੀਬੀ; ਬੇਗਮ; ਘਰ-ਵਾਲੀ, ਵਹੁਟੀ; ~finger ਤਿੰਡੀ

lag (ਲੈਗ) v n (1) ਮੱਠੀ ਚਾਲ ਚੱਲਣਾ, ਹੌਲੀ ਹੌਲੀ ਚੱਲਣਾ, ਪਿੱਛੇ ਰਹਿ ਜਾਣਾ, ਪਛੜਨਾ, ਢਿੱਲ, ਪੱਛੜੇਵਾਂ; (2) ਪਕੜਨਾ; ਗਰਿਫ਼ਤਾਰ ਕਰਨਾ; ਮੁਜਰਮ, ਦੋਸ਼ੀ; ~gard ਢਿੱਲਾ, ਮੱਠਾ, ਸੁਸਤ, ਢਿੱਲੜ; ~ging ਮੰਦਗਾਮੀ, ਪਛੜਿਆ

lake (ਲੇਇਕ) n ਝੀਲ, ਸਰੋਵਰ, ਸਰ, ਵੱਡਾ ਤਲਾਅ

laliation (ਲੈ'ਲੇਇਸ਼ਨ) n ਤੋਤਲਾ ਉਚਾਰਨ, ਥਥਲਾ ਉਚਾਰਨ

lama ('ਲਾਮਅ) n ਤਿੱਬਤੀ ਬੋਧੀ ਗੁਰੂ, ਲਾਮਾ

lamb (ਲੈਮ) n v ਮੇਮਣਾ; ਲੇਲਾ, ਭੱਡੂਰ, ਦੁੰਬਾ, ਗਾਊ ਆਦਮੀ

lambaste (ਲੈਮ'ਬੇਇਸਟ) v ਕਰੜੀ ਆਲੋਚਨਾ ਕਰਨੀ, ਖੱਲ ਲਾਹੁਣੀ

lame (ਲੇਇਮ) a v ਲੰਙਾ; ਅਸੰਤੋਸ਼ਜਨਕ; ਗ਼ੈਰਤਸੱਲੀ-ਬਖ਼ਸ਼; (ਛੰਦ) ਗਤੀਹੀਨ, ਰਵਾਨੀ ਤੋਂ ਬਿਨਾ; ਲੰਙਾ ਕਰ ਦੇਣਾ, ਨਕਾਰਾ ਕਰ ਦੇਣਾ, ਵਿਗਾੜ ਦੇਣਾ; ~ness ਲੰਗੜਾਹਟ, ਲੰਗੜਾਪਣ; ਅਸੰਤੁਸ਼ਟਤਾ

lament (ਲਅ'ਮੈਂਟ) n v ਵਿਰਲਾਪ, ਰੁਦਨ, ਰੋਣ-ਪੇਟ, ਕੀਰਨਾ, ਵੈਣ, ਰੋਣਾ, ਰੋਣਾ-ਧੋਣਾ, ਕੁਰਲਾਉਣਾ, ਕੀਰਨੇ ਪਾਉਣੇ, ਰੁਦਨ ਕਰਨਾ; ~able ਵਿਰਲਾਪ-ਯੋਗ; ~ation ਵਿਰਲਾਪ, ਕੀਰਨੇ, ਹਾਹਾਕਾਰ, ਵੈਣ, ਮਾਤਮ, ਰੋਣ-ਪਿੱਟਣ, ਕੁਰਲਾਹਟ, ਅਲਾਹੁਣੀ

lamp (ਲੈਂਪ) n ਲੈਂਪ, ਦੀਵਾ, ਦੀਪਕ, ਦੀਪ, ਪ੍ਰਕਾਸ਼, ਜੋਤੀ

lance (ਲਾਂਸ) n v ਨੇਜ਼ਾ, ਬਰਛਾ, ਭਾਲਾ; ਨੇਜ਼ੇਬਾਜ਼ ਸਿਪਾਹੀ; ਨੇਜ਼ਾ ਮਾਰਨਾ, ਚੀਰਨਾ

land (ਲੈਂਡ) n v ਧਰਤੀ, ਜ਼ਮੀਨ, ਭੋਂ, ਭੂਮੀ, ਖ਼ੁਸ਼ਕੀ, ਥਲ, ਦੇਸ਼, ਜਾਗੀਰ; ਇਲਾਕਾ; ਜਹਾਜ਼ ਆਦਿ ਤੋਂ ਉਤਰਨਾ ਜਾਂ ਉਤਾਰਨਾ; ~holder ਜ਼ਿਮੀਂਦਾਰ, ਪੱਟੇਦਾਰ; ~lady ਮਾਲਕਣ; ~slide ਢਾਰ, ਚਟਾਨਾਂ ਦਾ ਖਿਸਕਣਾ; ~ing ਧਰਤੀ ਉੱਤੇ ਉਤਰਾ (ਹਵਾਈ ਜਹਾਜ਼); ~less ਭੂਮੀਹੀਣ, ਬੇਜ਼ਮੀਨ

lane (ਲੇਇਨ) n ਗਲੀ, ਕੂਚਾ, ਤੰਗ ਰਸਤਾ

language ('ਲੈਂਡਗਵਜ) n ਜ਼ਬਾਨ, ਭਾਸ਼ਾ, ਬੋਲੀ, ਭਾਖਾ; national~ ਰਾਸ਼ਟਰ ਭਾਸ਼ਾ; regional~ ਪ੍ਰਦੇਸ਼ਕ ਭਾਸ਼ਾ

languish ('ਲੈਂਡਗਵਿਸ਼) v ਨਿਢਾਲ ਹੋਣਾ, ਮੁਰਝਾਉਣਾ, ਜ਼ੋਰ ਘਟਣਾ

languor ('ਲੈਂਡਗਅ*) n ਕਮਜ਼ੋਰੀ; ਨਿਰਬਲਤਾ, ਸੁਸਤੀ, ਢਿੱਲਾਪਣ, ਥਕੇਵਾਂ; ਬੇਦਿਲੀ

lantern ('ਲੈਨਟਅ:ਨ) n ਲਾਲਟੈਨ, ਬੱਤੀ, ਲੈਂਪ, ਫ਼ਾਨੂਸ

lap (ਲੈਪ) v n ਝੋਲੀ ਪਾਉਣਾ; ਪਲਟਨਾ, ਗੋਦੀ ਵਿਚ ਲੈਣਾ; ਝੋਲੀ, ਪੱਲਾ, ਗੋਦੀ; (ਕੱਪੜੇ ਦਾ) ਪੱਲੂ; ਦਾਮਨ

lapse (ਲੈਪਸ) n v ਉਕਾਈ ਭੁੱਲ, ਅਟਗਾਹਿਲੀ; ਉਤਰਨਾ, ਘਟਣਾ, ਸਮੇਂ ਦਾ ਲੰਘਣਾ; ~d ਪਤਿਤ, ਭ੍ਰਿਸ਼ਟ; ਸਮਾਪਤ, ਬੀਤਿਆ, ਪੂਰਗਾਮੀ

large (ਲਾ*ਜ) a adv ਵੱਡਾ, ਖੁੱਲ੍ਹਾ; ਮੋਕਲਾ; ਵਿਸਤਾਰ ਪੂਰਵਕ, ਵਿਆਪਕ; at~ ਸੁਤੰਤਰ, ਆਜ਼ਾਦ; (ਬਿਆਨ ਆਦਿ) ਵੇਰਵੇ ਸਹਿਤ; ~ly ਆਮ ਕਰਕੇ, ਜ਼ਿਆਦਾਤਰ; ~ness ਵਿਸਤਾਰ, ਬਹੁਲਤਾ, ਬਹੁਤਾਤ, ਵਿਆਪਕਤਾ

lark (ਲਾ:ਕ) n v (1) ਭੂਰੇ ਮਿਟਿਆਲੇ ਰੰਗ ਦੇ ਪੰਛੀਆਂ ਦੀਆਂ ਕਿਸਮਾਂ ਜਿਨ੍ਹਾਂ ਦੇ ਪੈਰਾਂ ਦੀਆਂ ਪਿਛਲੀਆਂ ਉਂਗਲਾਂ ਵੱਡੀਆਂ ਹੁੰਦੀਆਂ ਹਨ; (2)

larynx ਹਾਸਾ, ਦਿਲਲਗੀ, ਚੁਹਲ; ਮਜ਼ੇ ਦੀ ਗੱਲ, ਦਿਲਚਸਪ ਘਟਨਾ, ਚੁਹਲ ਕਰਨਾ, ਖੇਡਣਾ-ਕੁੱਦਣਾ

larynx ('ਲੈਰਿਙਕਸ) *n* ਗਲ, ਘੰਡੀ

lash (ਲੈਸ਼) *v n* ਚਾਬਕ ਜਾਂ ਕੋਰੜੇ ਮਾਰਨੇ; ਟੁੱਟ ਪੈਣਾ, ਝਪਟਣਾ; ਜ਼ੋਰ ਨਾਲ ਹਮਲਾ ਕਰਨਾ; ਉਬਲ ਪੈਣਾ; ~out ਊਧਮ ਮਚਾਉਣਾ; ~ing ਕੋਰੜੇ ਦੀ ਮਾਰ; ਬੰਧਨ, ਰੱਸੀਆਂ

lass, lassie (ਲੈਸ, 'ਲੈਸੀ) *n* ਮੁਟਿਆਰ, ਜਵਾਨ ਕੁੜੀ; ਪਰੇਮਕਾ, ਪਰੀਤਮਾ

lassitude ('ਲੈਸਿਟਯੂਡ) *n* ਸੁਸਤੀ, ਥਕਾਵਟ, ਸ਼ਕਤੀਹੀਣਤਾ, ਥਕੇਵਾਂ, ਬਾਂਦਲੀ

last (ਲ਼ਾਸਟ) *a adv n* ਅੰਤਮ, ਆਖ਼ਰੀ, ਅਖੀਰਲਾ, ਛੇਕੜਲਾ, ਘਟੀਆ, ਸਭ ਤੋਂ ਨੀਵੇਂ ਦਰਜੇ ਦਾ; ਅਢੁੱਕਵਾਂ; ਉੱਕਾ; ਸਭ ਤੋਂ ਪਿੱਛੇ, ਅਖੀਰ ਵਿਚ; ਆਖ਼ਰੀ ਵਾਰ, ਆਖਰ, ਛੇਕੜ; **at~** ਅਖੀਰ, ਆਖ਼ਰਕਾਰ; **~ly** ਅੰਤ ਵਿਚ, ਅੰਤ ਨੂੰ, ਅੰਤ ਤੇ, ਅਖੀਰ ਵਿਚ

late (ਲੇਇਟ) *a adv* ਪਛੜਿਆ, ਪਿੱਛੇਤਾ, ਚਿਰਾਕਾ, ਬੇਵਕਤ, ਕਵੇਲੜਾ, ਕਦੀਮ; ਸੁਰਗੀ, ਮਰਹੂਮ; ਦੇਰ ਕਰਕੇ, ਵਕਤ ਤੋਂ ਪਿੱਛੋਂ; ਬਹੁਤ ਦਿਨਾਂ ਪਿੱਛੋਂ, ਆਖ਼ਰੀ ਜ਼ਮਾਨੇ ਵਿਚ; ਬਹੁਤ ਦੇਰੀ ਨਾ਼; **of~ years** ਕੁਝ ਸਾਲਾਂ ਤੋਂ; **~ly** ਪਿੱਛੇ ਜਿਹੇ, ਹੁਣੇ ਹੁਣੇ, ਕੁਝ ਦਿਨ ਪਹਿਲਾਂ; **~st** ਨਵੀਨ, ਅਜੋਕਾ, ਆਧੁਨਿਕਤਮ; ਅੰਤਮ

latent ('ਲੇਇਟਅੰਟ) *a* ਛੁਪਿਆ, ਗੁਪਤ, ਨਿਹਿਤ; ਦੱਬਿਆ, ਭੀਤਰੀ

latex ('ਲੇਇਟੈੱਕਸ) *n* ਬਨਸਪਤੀ ਦੁੱਧ, ਬੂਟਿਆਂ ਦਾ ਦੁੱਧ, ਕੱਚੀ ਰਬੜ

lathe (ਲੇਇਦ) *n* ਖ਼ਰਾਦ

lather ('ਲਾਦਅ*) *n v* ਝੱਗ; ਫੇਗ ਆਉਣੀ, ਝੱਗ ਉੱਠਣੀ, ਛਲਕਣਾ; ਮੁਰੰਮਤ ਕਰਨਾ

lathy ('ਲਾਥਿ) *a* ਦੁਬਲਾ-ਪਤਲਾ, ਕਮਜ਼ੋਰ

latitude ('ਲੈਟਿਟਯੂਡ) *n* ਵਿਥ-ਕਾਰ, ਅਕਸ਼ਾਂਸ਼; ਚੌੜਾਈ, ਫੈਲਾਉ, ਵਿਸਤਾਰ ਖੇਤਰ; ਪੂਰਾ ਦਾਇਰਾ; ਆਜ਼ਾਦ, ਖ਼ਿਆਲੀ, ਵਿਚਾਰ ਸੁਤੰਤਰਤਾ

latrine ('ਲੈਟਰੀਨ) *n* ਟੱਟੀ, ਸ਼ੌਚਾਲਾ

latter ('ਲੈਟਅ*) *a* ਦੂਜਾ; ਪਿੱਛਲਾ, ਬਾਅਦ ਦਾ, ਪਿਛਲੇਰਾ, ਮਗਰਲਾ, ਆਧੁਨਿਕ

lattice ('ਲੈਟਿਸ) *n* ਜਾਲੀ; **~d** ਜਾਲੀਦਾਰ

laud (ਲੋਡ) *n v* ਸ਼ਲਾਘਾ, ਸਲਾਹੁਤਾ, ਪ੍ਰਸੰਸਾ, ਸ਼ਲਾਘਾ ਕਰਨੀ, ਪ੍ਰਸੰਸਾ ਕਰਨੀ, ਗੁਣ ਗਾਉਣੇ; **~able** ਸ਼ਲਾਘਾਯੋਗ; ਚੰਗਾ; ਠੀਕ

laugh (ਲਾਫ) *v n* ਹੱਸਣਾ; ਲਹਿਰਾਉਣਾ; ਹੱਸਣਾ, ਦਿਲਲਗੀ ਕਰਨੀ, (ਮਖ਼ੌਲ ਕਰ ਕੇ ਕਿਸੇ ਦੀ); **~at** ਮਜ਼ਾਕ ਉਡਾਉਣਾ; **~in one's sleeves** ਅੰਦਰੇ-ਅੰਦਰ ਖ਼ੁਸ਼ ਹੋਣਾ; **~off** ਹੱਸ ਕੇ ਟਾਲਣਾ; **~ing** ਹਾਸਾ; **~ing stock** ਹਾਸੇ ਦਾ ਨਿਸ਼ਾਨਾ, ਮੌਜੂ; **~ter** ਹਾਸਾ, ਖਿੱਲੀ, ਖਿੜਖਿੜ, ਮੁਸਕਾਣ

launch (ਲਾਂਚ) *v n* (ਜਹਾਜ਼) ਠੇਲ੍ਹਣਾ, ਵਹਾਉਣਾ, (ਮੁਹਿੰਮ ਤੇ) ਸ਼ੁਰੂ ਕਰਨਾ, ਸਖ਼ਤ-ਸੁਸਤ ਕਹਿਣਾ; ਸੈਲਾਨੀ ਕਿਸ਼ਤੀ, ਲਾਂਚ-ਬੋਟ, ਵੱਡੀ ਕਿਸ਼ਤੀ; ਠੇਲ੍ਹ, ਠੇਲ੍ਹਣ; (ਜਹਾਜ਼ ਦੀ) ਉਤਰਾਈ, ਜਲ-ਅਵਤਰਨ

launder (ਲਾਂਡਅ*) *v* ਕੱਪੜੇ ਧੋਣਾ, ਇਸਤਰੀ ਕਰਨਾ; **~er** ਧੋਬੀ

laundry (ਲਾਂਡਰਿ) *n* ਧੋਬੀ ਦੀ ਦੁਕਾਨ, ਧੋਬੀਖ਼ਾਨਾ, ਲਾਂਡਰੀ

laura (ਲੋਰਅ) *n* ਕੁਟੀਆ, ਝੁੱਗੀ, ਆਸ਼ਰਮ

laureate ('ਲੋਰਿਅਟ) *a n* ਲਾਰਲ ਦਾ, ਲਾਰਲ ਦੇ ਹਾਰ ਨਾਲ ਸਜਾਇਆ ਹੋਇਆ; ਸਨਮਾਨਤ; **poet~** ਰਾਜ-ਕਵੀ; ਮਹਾਂਕਵੀ; **~ship** ਰਾਜਕਵੀ ਦੀ ਪਦਵੀ

laurel ('ਲੋਰ(ਅ)ਲ) *n v* ਚਮਕੀਲੀਆਂ ਪੱਤੀਆਂ ਵਾਲੀ ਸਦਾਬਹਾਰ ਝਾੜੀ; ਪ੍ਰਸ਼ਪ-ਮੁਕਟ, ਜੈ-ਮਾਲਾ; ਲਾਰਲ ਦਾ ਮੁਕਟ ਕਿਸੇ ਦੇ ਸਿਰ ਤੇ ਰੱਖਣਾ

lava (ਲਾਵ਼ਾ) *n* ਲਾਵਾ, ਜੁਆਲਾਮੁਖੀ ਦਾ ਉਬਾਲ

lavation (ਲੈ'ਵ਼ੇਇਸ਼ਨ) *n* ਪੂਜ-ਇਸ਼ਨਾਂਨਾ, ਮੂੰਹ-ਹੱਥ ਧੋਣਾ, ਸਫ਼ਾਈ

lavatory (ਲੈਵ਼ਅਟ(ਅ)ਰਿ) *n* ਟੱਟੀ, ਗੁਸਲਖ਼ਾਨਾ

lavish (ਲੈਵ਼ਿਸ਼) *a v* ਸ਼ਾਹ-ਖ਼ਰਚ, ਫ਼ਜ਼ੂਲ-ਖ਼ਰਚ, ਵਾਫ਼ਰ, ਬੇ-ਅੰਦਾਜ਼ਾ, ਬਹੁਤਾ; ਪਾਣੀ ਵਾਂਗ ਰੋੜ੍ਹਨਾ, ਬਹੁਤ ਖ਼ਰਚ ਕਰਨਾ; **~ment, ~ness** ਫ਼ਜ਼ੂਲ-ਖ਼ਰਚੀ

law (ਲਾਅ) *n* ਕਾਨੂੰਨ, ਵਿਧਾਨ, ਵਿਧੀ; ਕਾਇਦਾ, ਜ਼ਾਬਤਾ; **~abiding** ਕਾਨੂੰਨ ਪਾਲਕ; **~and order** ਅਮਨ-ਕਾਨੂੰਨ; **~court** ਕਚਹਿਰੀ; **~suit** ਮੁਕੱਦਮਾ, ਦਾਵਾ; **to go to~** ਦਾਵਾ ਕਰਨਾ, ਮੁਕੱਦਮਾ ਕਰਨਾ; **~ful** ਕਾਨੂੰਨੀ, ਵਿਧੀਪੂਰਨ, ਵਿਧੀ ਅਨੁਸਾਰ; **~fulness** ਵਿਧੀਪੂਰਨਤਾ, ਵੈਧਤਾ; **~less** ਗ਼ੈਰ-ਕਾਨੂੰਨੀ, ਵਿਧੀਹੀਨ, ਅਵੈਧ, ਨਿਆਂ ਵਿਰੁੱਧ; **~yer** ਵਕੀਲ; ਕਾਨੂੰਨਦਾਨ

lax (ਲੈਕਸ) *a* ਢਿੱਲਾ, ਘੱਲੀ, ਕੋਮਲ, ਨਰਮ, ਲਚਕੀਲਾ; **~ation** ਢਿੱਲ, ਸਿਥਲਤਾ; **~ative** ਜੁਲਾਬੀ; ਜੁਲਾਬ; **~ity** ਢਿੱਲ, ਨਰਮੀ; ਅਸਪਸ਼ਟਤਾ; ਆਚਰਨਹੀਨਤਾ, ਲਾਪਰਵਾਹੀ

lay (ਲੇਇ) *v n a* ਰੱਖਣਾ, ਧਰਨਾ, ਲਿਟਾ ਦੇਣਾ; ਲੰਮਾ ਪਾ ਦੇਣਾ; ਗੀਤ, ਨਗ਼ਮਾ; ਸੰਸਾਰੀ, ਗ੍ਰਹਿਸਥੀ; **~down** ਨਿਰਧਾਰਤ ਕਰਨਾ; **~man** ਸਧਾਰਨ ਵਿਅਕਤੀ, ਗ਼ੈਰਮਾਹਰ; **~out** ਖ਼ਾਕਾ, ਰੂਪ-ਰੇਖਾ; **~waste** ਨਸ਼ਟ ਕਰਨਾ

layer (ਲੇਇਅ*) *n v* ਤਹਿ, ਪਰਤ, ਦਾਬ; ਫ਼ਸਲ ਦਾ ਢਹਿ ਜਾਣਾ; ਦਾਬ ਲਾਉਣੀ

laze (ਲੇਇਜ਼) *v n* ਆਲਸ ਕਰਨਾ, ਸੁਸਤ ਹੋਣਾ; ਸੁਸਤੀ, ਆਲਸ

laziness (ਲੇਇਜ਼ਿਨਿਸ) *n* ਆਲਸ, ਸੁਸਤੀ; ਦਲਿੱਦਰ, ਨੇਸਤੀ

lazy ('ਲੇਇਜ਼ਿ) *a v* ਸੁਸਤ, ਆਲਸੀ, ਢਿੱਲਾ ਕੰਮਚੋਰ; ਸੁਸਤੀ ਕਰਨੀ, ਆਲਸ ਵਿਚ ਸਮਾਂ ਬਿਤਾਉਣਾ

leach (ਲੀਚ) *v* ਟਪਕਾਉਣਾ, ਚੁਆਉਣਾ

lead (ਲੀਡ) *v n* ਸਿੱਕੇ ਦਾ ਚੌਖਟਾ ਜੜਨਾ ਅਗਵਾਈ ਕਰਨੀ, ਸਮਝਾਉਣਾ; (ਜ਼ਿੰਦਗੀ) ਬਿਤਾਉਣੀ, ਗੁਜ਼ਾਰਨੀ; ਆਰੰਭ ਕਰਨਾ, ਅੱਗੇ ਹੋਣਾ; ਦੌੜ ਵਿਚ ਅੱਗੇ ਹੋਣਾ, ਆਗੂ ਹੋਣਾ ਲੀਡਰ ਹੋਣਾ; ਸਿੱਕਾ; ਪਟਸਾਲ; ਸੰਧੁਰ; (ਛਾ ਦਾ) ਲੇਡ, ਸਿੱਕੇ ਦੀ ਪੱਤੀ; ਅਗਵਾਈ; ਮਿਸਾਲ **~en** ਸਿੱਕੇ ਵਰਗਾ, ਭਾਰੀ, ਬੋਝਲ; **~astray** ਬਹਿਕਾਉਣਾ, ਗੁਮਰਾਹ ਕਰਨਾ; **~the way** ਅਗਵਾਈ ਕਰਨਾ

leader (ਲੀਡਅ*) *n* ਆਗੂ, ਨੇਤਾ, ਮੁਖੀਆ ਸਰਦਾਰ, ਸਰਕਾਰੀ ਅਧਿਕਾਰੀ; **~of the opposition** ਵਿਰੋਧੀ ਦਲ ਦਾ ਨੇਤਾ; **~of the house** ਸਦਨ ਦਾ ਨੇਤਾ; **~ship** ਅਗਵਾਈ ਅਗਵਾਨੀ, ਲੀਡਰੀ

leading (ਲੀਡਿੰਡ) *a* ਵੱਡਾ, ਪ੍ਰਧਾਨ, ਮੁੱਖ, ਉੱਤਮ ਉੱਘਾ, ਅਗਲਾ; **~artical** ਸੰਪਾਦਕੀ ਲੇਖ

leaf (ਲੀਫ਼) *n* ਪੱਤਰਾ, ਪੱਤਾ, ਪੰਖੜੀ, ਪੱਤਰ (ਰੁੱ ਦਾ); (ਚਾਹ ਦੀ) ਪੱਤੀ; (ਕਿਤਾਬ ਦਾ) ਵਰਕਾ (ਚਾਂਦੀ, ਸੋਨੇ ਦਾ) ਵਰਕ; **~let** ਛੋਟਾ ਪੱਤ ਪੱਤੀ, ਕੋਂਪਲ, ਨਵੀਂ ਪੱਤੀ; ਦੁਪੱਤਰੀ

league (ਲੀਗ) *n v* ਮੇਲ; ਸੰਗਠਨ, ਏਕਤ ਸੰਘ, ਦਲ, ਲੀਗ; ਮਿਲਾਉਣਾ, ਮਿਲਣਾ, ਇਕ

leak   569   **leg**

ਹੋਣਾ, ਗਠਜੋੜ ਕਰਨਾ; L~ of Nations ਰਾਸ਼ਟਰਸੰਘ

leak (ਲੀਕ) *n v* ਛੇਕ, ਸੁਰਾਖ਼, ਦਰਾੜ, ਰਿਸਣਾ, ਟਪਕਣਾ, ਚੋਣਾ; (ਭੇਤ) ਪਤਾ ਲੱਗ ਜਾਣਾ, ਭੇਤ ਖੋਲ੍ਹਣਾ; ~age ਚੋਆ, ਖੋਰ, ਰਸਾ, ਟਪਕਾ; ਟੁੱਟ-ਭੱਜ

lean (ਲੀਨ) *a v n* ਦੁਬਲਾ, ਲਿੱਸਾ, ਸੁਕੜ, ਦੁਰਬਲ, ਕਮਜ਼ੋਰ; ਢੋਹ ਲਾਉਣੀ, ਟੇਕ ਲੱਈ, ਟਿਕਿਆ ਹੋਣਾ; ਭਰੋਸਾ ਕਰਨਾ; ਝੁਕਣਾ, ਝੁਕਾਉਣਾ; ਝੁਕਾਉ ਹੋਣਾ, ਹਾਮੀ ਹੋਣਾ; ਝੁਕਾਉ; ~ing ਝੁਕਾਉ, ਪ੍ਰਵਿਰਤੀ

leap (ਲੀਪ) *v n* ਕੁੱਦਣ, ਛਾਲ ਮਾਰਨੀ, ਉਛਲਣਾ, ਟੱਪਣਾ, ਟੱਪ ਜਾਣਾ, ਉਲੰਘਣਾ, ਛਲਾਂਗ, ਹੁੰਗ, ਚੌਕੜੀ; ~year ਲੰਘੂ ਵਰ੍ਹਾ, ਲੀਪ ਦਾ ਸਾਲ, 366 ਦਿਨਾਂ ਦਾ ਸਾਲ; by ~s and bounds ਅਤੀ ਸ਼ੀਘਰਤਾ ਨਾਲ, (ਤਰੱਕੀ) ਦਿਨ ਦੂਣੀ ਰਾਤ ਚੌਗੁਣੀ, ਝਟਪਟ

learn (ਲਅ:ਨ) *v* ਸਿੱਖਿਆ ਲੈਣੀ; ਗਿਆਨ ਪ੍ਰਾਪਤ ਕਰਨਾ, ਜਾਣਨਾ, ਪੜ੍ਹਨਾ; ਸੂਚਨਾ ਹੋਣੀ, ਪਤਾ ਲੱਗਣਾ; ~ed ਵਿਦਵਾਨ, ਆਲਮ, ਗਿਆਨੀ; ~er ਵਿਦਿਆਰਥੀ, ਸਿਖਾਂਦਰੂ, ਚੇਲਾ; ~ing ਗਿਆਨ, ਵਿੱਦਿਆ, ਇਲਮ, ਸਿੱਖਿਆ, ਪੜ੍ਹਾਈ

lease (ਲੀਸ) *n v* ਪੱਟਾ, ਠੇਕਾ; ਚਕੋਤਾ; ਪੱਟੇ ਤੇ ਦੇਣਾ, ਠੇਕੇ ਤੇ ਦੇਣਾ; ~hold ਪਟੇਦਾਰੀ, ਠੇਕਾ; ਪੱਟੇ ਤੇ ਲਈ ਜ਼ਮੀਨ; ~holder ਪਟੇਦਾਰ, ਠੇਕੇਦਾਰ

least (ਲੀਸਟ) *a adv n* ਘੱਟ ਤੋਂ ਘੱਟ, ਛੋਟੇ ਤੋਂ ਛੋਟਾ, ਸਭ ਤੋਂ ਛੋਟਾ; **at~** ਘੱਟੋ-ਘੱਟ, ਹੋਰ ਨਹੀਂ ਤਾਂ; **at the~** ਘੱਟ ਤੋਂ ਘੱਟ; **in the~** ਜ਼ਰਾ ਵੀ, ਥੋੜ੍ਹਾ ਵੀ, ਕੁਝ ਵੀ, ਉੱਕਾ

leather (ਲੈੱਦਅ*) *n v* ਚਮੜਾ, ਚੰਮ; ਧੋੜੀ; ਪੱਕਾ ਚਮੜਾ; ਚਮੜੇ ਦਾ ਸਾਮਾਨ; ਚਮੜਾ ਚੜ੍ਹਾਉਣਾ, ਤੰਦੁਤਾ ਦੀ ਮਾਰ ਦੇਣੀ

leave (ਲੀਵ) *n v* ਆਗਿਆ; ਅਨੁਮਤੀ; ਇਜਾਜ਼ਤ; ਛੁੱਟੀ; ਵਿਦਾ, ਵਿਦਾਈ; ਛੱਡ ਦੇਣਾ, ਰਹਿਤ ਦੇਣਾ, ਰਵਾਨਾ ਹੋਣਾ; ~taking ਵਿਦਾ, ਵਿਦਾਇਗੀ; ~out ਭੁੱਲ ਜਾਣਾ; ~to take ਵਿਦਾ ਹੋਣਾ

lecher (ਲੈੱਚਅ*) *n* ਲੱਚਰ, ਕਾਮੀ, ਭੋਗੀ, ਵਿਭਚਾਰੀ, ਲੁੱਚਾ; ~ous ਕਾਮੀ, ਲੰਪਟ, ਲੁੱਚਾ; ~ousness ਕਾਮੁਕਤਾ, ਕਾਮਵਾਸ਼ਨਾ, ਲੁੱਚਪੁਣਾ; ~y ਵਿਭਚਾਰ, ਲੁੱਚਪੁਣਾ

lection (ਲੈੱਕਸ਼ਨ) *n* ਪਾਠ, ਪੜ੍ਹਾਈ; ~ary ਪ੍ਰਾਰਥਨਾ-ਪੁਸਤਕ, ਭਜਨ-ਮਾਲਾ, ਉਸਤਤੀ-ਸੰਗ੍ਰਹਿ

lector (ਲੈੱਕਟਅ*) *n* ਪਾਦਰੀ

lecture (ਲੈੱਕਚਅ*) *n v* ਭਾਸ਼ਣ ਵਿਆਖਿਆਨ; ਤਕਰੀਰ ਕਰਨਾ; ਵਿੱਦਿਆ ਦੇਣੀ, ਜ਼ਬਾਨੀ ਸਬਕ ਦੇਣਾ; ਡਾਂਟਣਾ; ~r ਵਕਤਾ, ਵਿਆਖਿਆਨੀ

ledger (ਲੈੱਜਅ*) *n* ਵਹੀ-ਖਾਤਾ, ਖਾਤਾ

leech (ਲੀਚ) *n* (1) (ਪ੍ਰ) ਹਕੀਮ, ਤਬੀਬ; (2) ਜੋਕ; ਲਹੂ-ਚੂਸ, ਰੱਤ-ਪੀਣਾ; ਮੁਨਾਫ਼ੇਖੋਰ

leer (ਲਿਅ*) *n v* ਬੁਰੀ ਨਜ਼ਰ, ਭੁੱਖੀ ਨਜ਼ਰ; ~y ਚਲਾਕ, ਚੌਕਸ, ਚੁਕੰਨਾ

left (ਲੈੱਫਟ) *a adv n* ਖੱਬਾ; ਖੱਬੇ ਪਾਸੇ ਦਾ; ਉਲਟਾ ਹੱਥ; ਵਾਮ ਮਾਰਗੀ ਸੰਪਰਦਾਇ; ਖੱਬੇ-ਪੱਖੀ (ਰਾਜਨੀਤੀ); ~leave ਦਾ ਭੁਤਕਾਲ ਰੂਪ; ~handed ਖੱਬਰੂ, ਖੱਬੂ; ਘੇ-ਤੁਕਾ, ਦੁਬਾਜਰਾ, ਦੋ-ਰੁਖਾ

leg (ਲੈੱਗ) *n* ਲੱਤ, ਟੰਗ, ਜੰਘ; ਚਰਨ; (ਮੰਜੇ, ਕੁਰਸੀ ਆਦਿ ਦਾ) ਪਾਵਾ; **to pull one's~** ਲੱਤ ਖਿੱਚਣਾ

legacy (ਲੈੱਗਅਸਿ) *n* ਵਿਰਸਾ, ਸੰਪੱਤੀ

legal (ਲੀਗਲ) *a* ਕਾਨੂੰਨੀ; ਵਿਧੀ-ਮੂਲਕ; ਨਿਯਮਕ; ਉਚਿਤ, ਜਾਇਜ਼; **~ist** ਕਾਨੂੰਨਦਾਨ, ਕਾਨੂੰਨੀ ਪੰਡਤ; **~ity** ਕਾਨੂੰਨੀ ਹੈਸੀਅਤ, ਨਿਯਮਕਤਾ; **~ize** ਜਾਇਜ਼ ਠਹਿਰਾਉਣਾ, ਪ੍ਰਮਾਣਤ ਕਰਨਾ, ਕਾਨੂੰਨੀ ਰੂਪ ਦੇਣਾ; **~ly** ਵਿਧੀਪੂਰਬਕ ਕਾਨੂੰਨ ਦੀ ਦ੍ਰਿਸ਼ਟੀ ਵਿਚ

legend (ਲੈੱਜਅੰਡ) *n* ਲੋਕ-ਕਥਾ, ਦੰਦ-ਕਥਾ, ਪੁਰਾਤਕ ਕਥਾ, ਰਵਾਇਤ, ਕਿੱਸਾ- ਕਹਾਣੀ; ਦੇਵ-ਕਹਾਣੀ; **~ary** ਪੁਰਾਤਕ, ਪ੍ਰਸਿੱਧ; ਕਾਲਪਨਕ, ਸਿੱਖਿਆ, ਪੁਰਾਣ

legible (ਲੈੱਜਅਬਲ) *a* ਸਪਸ਼ਟ, ਪੜ੍ਹਿਆ ਜਾ ਸਕਣ ਵਾਲਾ; **~hand** ਖੁਸ਼ਖ਼ਤ, ਸੁਲੇਖ

legislate (ਲੈੱਜਿਸਲੇਇਟ) *v* ਕਾਨੂੰਨ ਬਣਾਉਣਾ, ਵਿਧਾਨ ਬਣਾਉਣਾ, ਨਿਯਮ ਬਣਾਉਣਾ

legislation (ਲੈੱਜਿਸ'ਲੇਇਸ਼ਨ) *n* ਵਿਧੀ-ਨਿਰਮਾਣ, ਵਿਧਾਨਕਾਰੀ, ਵਿਧੀ-ਵਿਵਸਥਾ, ਕਾਨੂੰਨ-ਨਿਰਮਾਣ, ਵਿਧਾਨ

legislative (ਲੈੱਜਿਸਲਅਟਿਵ) *a* ਵਿਧਾਨੀ, ਨਿਯਮ ਸਬੰਧੀ, ਵਿਧਾਨਕ

legislator (ਲੈੱਜਿਸਲੇਇਟਅ*) *n* ਵਿਧਾਇਕ ਵਿਧੀਕਰਤਾ, ਵਿਵਸਥਾਪਕ

legislature (ਲੈੱਜਿਸਲੇਇਚ*) *n* ਵਿਧਾਨ ਸਭਾ, ਵਿਧਾਨ-ਮੰਡਲ

legitimacy (ਲਿ'ਜਿਟਿਮਅਸਿ) *n* ਯੋਗਤਾ, ਉਚਿਤਤਾ; ਵਿਧੀ ਅਨੁਕੂਲਤਾ; ਸਚਾਈ, ਖਰਾਪਣ

legitimate (ਲਿ'ਜਿਟਿਮਅਟ, ਲਿ'ਜਿਟਿਮੇਇਟ) *a v* ਨਿਯਮਕ, ਵਿਧੀ ਅਨੁਕੂਲ, ਕਾਨੂੰਨੀ; ਜਾਇਜ਼ (ਔਲਾਦ); ਯਥਾਰਥ, ਸੱਚਾ, ਅਸਲੀ; ਵਿਧੀ ਅਨੁਕੂਲ ਸਿੱਧ ਕਰਨਾ

legitimise (ਲਿ'ਜਿਟਿਮਾਇਜ਼) *v* ਵਿਧੀ ਅਨੁਕੂਲ ਕਰਨਾ, ਪ੍ਰਮਾਣਕ-ਕਰਨਾ

leisure (ਲੈੱਜ਼ਅ*) *n* ਵਿਸ਼ਰਾਮ, ਫ਼ੁਰਸਤ, ਛੁੱਟੀ; ਖ਼ਾਲੀ ਸਮਾਂ; **~ly** ਹੌਲੀ, ਮੰਦ; ਫ਼ੁਰਸਤ ਦਾ; ਸੋਚਿਆ-ਸਮਝਿਆ; ਹੌਲੀ-ਹੌਲੀ, ਸਾਵਧਾਨੀ ਨਾਲ

lemon (ਲੈੱਮਅਨ) *n* ਨਿੰਬੂ; ਨਿੰਬੂ ਦਾ ਬੂਟਾ; ਹਲਕਾ ਪੀਲਾ (ਰੰਗ)

lend (ਲੈੱਡ) *v* ਉਧਾਰ ਦੇਣਾ; ਦੇਣਾ, ਕਿਰਾਏ ਦੇ ਦੇਣਾ; **~a hand** ਹੱਥ ਵਟਾਉਣਾ; **~an ear** ਸੁਣਨਾ, ਕੰਨ ਧਰਨੇ

length (ਲੈੱਙਥ) *n* ਲੰਬਾਈ, ਵਿਸਤਾਰ, ਫੈਲਾਉ, ਦੂਰੀ, ਅੰਤਮ ਸੀਮਾ, ਅੱਖਰਾਂ ਦੀ ਮਾਤਰਾ; **at an arm's~** ਪਰੇ, ਦੂਰ; **at~** ਵਿਸਤਾਰ ਪੂਰਬਕ; **~en** ਲੰਮਾ ਕਰਨਾ, ਵਧਾਉਣਾ, ਵਧਣਾ, ਫੈਲਾਉਣਾ; **~y** ਲੰਮਾ, ਦੀਰਘ

lenience, leniency (ਲੀਨਯਅੰਸ, ਲੀਨਯਅੰਸਿ) *n* ਨਰਮੀ, ਕੋਮਲਤਾ, ਹਲੀਮੀ, ਦਇਆਲਤਾ

lenient (ਲੀਨਯਅੰਟ) *a* ਨਰਮ, ਦਿਆਲੂ, ਉਦਾਰ

Leo (ਲੀਅਉ) *n* ਸਿੰਘ ਰਾਸ਼ੀ

leopard (ਲੈੱਪਅਡ) *n* ਚਿੱਤਰਾ, ਚੀਤਾ

leper (ਲੈੱਪਅ*) *n* ਕੋੜ੍ਹੀ, ਕੋੜ੍ਹ ਦਾ ਰੋਗੀ, ਕੁਸ਼ਟ-ਰੋਗੀ

lepra (ਲੈੱਪਰਅ) *n* ਕੋੜ੍ਹ, ਕੁਸ਼ਟ

leprosy (ਲੈੱਪਰਅਸਿ) *n* ਕੋੜ੍ਹ; ਇਖ਼ਲਾਕੀ ਗਿਰਾਵਟ

leprous (ਲੈੱਪਰਅਸ) *a* ਕੋੜ੍ਹੀ

less (ਲੈੱਸ) *a adv n prep* ਘੱਟ, ਥੋੜ੍ਹਾ, ਊਣਾ; ਘੱਟ ਗਿਣਤੀ; ਘਟਾ ਕੇ, ਕੱਢ ਕੇ, ਬਿਨਾ; **~en** ਘਟਣਾ, ਘਟਾਉਣਾ, ਹੌਲਾ ਹੋਣਾ, ਥੋੜ੍ਹਾ ਕਰਨਾ

lessee (ਲੈੱ'ਸੀ) *n* ਪੱਟੇਦਾਰ, ਕਿਰਾਏਦਾਰ

lesson (ਲੈੱਸਨ) *n v* ਪਾਠ, ਸਬਕ, ਪੜ੍ਹਾਈ, ਸਿੱਖਿਆ, ਉਪਦੇਸ਼, ਸਖ਼ਤ ਦੰਡ; ਸਿਖਾਉਣਾ

ਪੜ੍ਹਾਉਣਾ

lest (ਲੈੱਸਟ) *conj* ਮਤਾਂ, ਮਤੇ, ਇਉਂ ਨਾ ਹੋਵੇ ਕਿ

let (ਲੈੱਟ) *v n* ਰੁਕਾਵਟ ਪਾਉਣੀ, ਅੜਿੱਕਾ ਡਾਹੁਣਾ; ਨਿਕਲਣ ਦੇਣਾ, ਜਾਣ ਦੇਣਾ; ਹੋਣ ਦੇਣਾ; ਕਰਨ ਦੇਣਾ, ਛੱਡਣਾ; ਰੁਕਾਵਟ, ਰੋਕ-ਟੋਕ, ਕਿਰਾਏਦਾਰੀ; ~**alone** ਦਖਲ ਨਾ ਦੇਣਾ; ~**down** ਨੀਵਾਂ ਕਰਨਾ, ਨਿਰਾਸ ਕਰਨਾ; ~**into** ਟੁੱਟ ਕੇ ਪੈਣਾ; ~**on** ਰਿਹਾ ਕਰਨਾ, ਛੱਡਣਾ; ~**one know** ਮੁਖਬਰੀ ਕਰਨਾ, ਭੇਦ ਦੱਸਣਾ

lethal (ਲੀਥਲ) *a* ਘਾਤਕ, ਮਾਰੂ, ਮੁਹਲਕ, ਜਾਂ ਲੇਵਾ, (ਹਥਿਆਰ ਆਦਿ)

lethargic (ਲਅ'ਥਾਜਿਕ) *a* ਸੁਸਤ, ਆਲਸੀ, ਕੰਮਚੋਰ, ਮੱਠਾ, ਸਾਹ ਸਤ-ਹੀਨ

lethargy (ਲੈੱਥਅਜਿ) *n* ਆਲਸ, ਸੁਸਤੀ, ਕੰਮਚੋਰੀ; ਸਾਹ ਸਤ-ਹੀਨਤਾ

letter (ਲੈੱਟਅ) *n v* ਚਿੱਠੀ, ਪੱਤਰ, ਖ਼ਤ; ਅੱਖਰ, ਵਰਣ, ਹਰਫ਼; (ਛਾਪੇ ਵਿਚ) ਟਾਈਪ; ਵਿੱਦਿਆ, ਸਾਹਿਤ, ਗਿਆਨ; ਅੱਖਰ ਉੱਕਰਨੇ; ਠੱਪਾ ਲਾਉਣਾ; ~**ed** ਵਿਦਵਾਨ, ਗਿਆਨੀ, ਪੰਡਤ, ਪੜ੍ਹਿਆ-ਲਿਖਿਆ; ~**ing** ਅੱਖਰ-ਲੇਖਣ, ਨਾਮ ਅੰਕਣ, ਛਿਮਾਵਟ

level (ਲੈੱਵ਼ਲ) *n a v* ਪੱਧਰ, ਸਤਰ, ਦਰਜਾ, ਮਿਆਰ; ਸਮਤਾ; ਸੰਤੁਲਣ; ਫ਼ਰਕ ਮਿਟਾ ਕੇ ਬਰਾਬਰ ਕਰਨਾ; ਮਰਯਾਦਾ ਅਨੁਕੂਲ ਕਰਨਾ; ਮਿੱਟੀ ਵਿਚ ਮਿਲਾ ਦੇਣਾ, ਮਲੀਆਮੇਟ ਕਰ ਦੇਣਾ; ਸ਼ਿਸਤ ਬਨ੍ਹਣੀ; ਦੋਸ਼ ਲਾਉਣਾ; ~**crossing** ਪੱਧਰਾ ਲਾਂਘਾ, ਰੇਲਵੇ ਫਾਟਕ; **to do one's-best** ਪੂਰਾ ਕਰਨਾ, ਟਿੱਲ ਲਾਉਣਾ; ~**ling** ਪੱਧਰਾ ਕਰਨ ਦਾ ਕੰਮ, ਪੱਧਰ ਕਰਨ ਵਾਲਾ

lever (ਲੀਵ਼ਅ*) *n v* ਤੁਲ; ਲੀਵਰ; (ਬੰਦੂਕ ਆਦਿ ਦਾ) ਤੋੜਾ; ਤੁਲ ਦੇਣੀ, ਲੀਵਰ ਲਾਉਣਾ, ਤੋੜਾ ਦੱਬਣਾ

levy (ਲੈੱਵ਼ਿ) *n v* ਲਗਾਨ, ਮਹਿਸੂਲ, ਚੰਦਾ ਉਗਰਾਹੀ; ਲਗਾਨ ਦੀ ਮਾਤਰਾ ਜਾਂ ਦਰ; ਰੰਗਰੂਟਾਂ ਦੀ ਟੋਲੀ; ਵਸੂਲ ਕਰਨਾ, ਉਗਰਾਹੁਣਾ; (ਕਰ ਆਦਿ) ਲਾਉਣਾ; ਜੁੱਧ ਛੇੜਨਾ

lewd (ਲਯੂਡ) *a* ਹੋਛਾ; ਬਦਮਾਸ਼; ਵਿਸ਼ਈ, ਕਾਮੀ; ~**ness** ਲੁੱਚਪਣ, ਬਦਕਾਰੀ, ਕਾਮੁਕਤਾ

lexical (ਲੈੱਕਸਿਕਲ) *a* ਕੋਸੀ, ਕੋਸ਼ਗਤ

lexicographer (ਲੈੱਕਸਿ'ਕੌਗਰਅਫ਼ਅ*) *n* ਕੋਸ਼ਕਾਰ, ਕੋਸ਼ ਬਣਾਉਂਣ ਵਾਲਾ

lexicography (ਲੈੱਕਸਿ'ਕੌਗਰਅਫ਼ਿ) *n* ਕੋਸ਼ਕਾਰੀ

lexicon (ਲੈੱਕਸਿਕੌਨ) *n* ਕੋਸ਼, ਸ਼ਬਦ ਭੰਡਾਰ, ਸ਼ਬਦਾਵਲੀ

liability, liableness (ਲਾਇਅ'ਬਿਲਅਟਿ, ਲਾਇਬਲਨਿਸ) *n* ਜ਼ਿੰਮੇਵਾਰੀ, ਉਤਰਦਾਇਤਵ; ਦੇਣਦਾਰੀ, ਭਾਗ, ਕਰਜ਼, ਉਧਾਰ, ਸਿਰ ਪਈ ਰਕਮ

liable (ਲਾਇਬਲ) *a* ਦੇਣਦਾਰ, ਜ਼ਿੰਮੇਵਾਰ, ਕਰ ਵਾਲਾ, (ਕੋਈ ਕੰਮ ਕਰਨ ਲਈ) ਘੇਵੱਸ, ਯੋਗ, ਯੋਗਤਾ ਰਖੱਣ ਵਾਲਾ; ਜ਼ਰੂਰੀ, ਅਵੱਸ਼ਕ

liaise (ਲਿ'ਏਇਜ਼) *v* ਸੰਧੀ ਕਰਨਾ, ਅਧਿਦਨਾਮਾ' ਕਰਨਾ

liaison (ਲਿ'ਏਇਜ਼(ਅ)ਨ) *n* ਸੰਪਰਕ, ਤਾਲਮੇਲ, ਦੋਹਾਂ ਧਿਰਾਂ ਵਿਚਾਰਲੇ ਸਬੰਧ; ਨਾਜਾਇਜ਼ ਸਬੰਧ, ਯਾਰੀ; ~**officer** ਤਾਲਮੇਲ ਅਫ਼ਸਰ, ਸੰਪਰਕ ਅਧਿਕਾਰੀ

liar (ਲਾਇਅ*) *n* ਝੂਠਾ, ਝੂਠ ਬੋਲਣ ਵਾਲਾ

Lib (ਲਿਬ) *n* (*Women's Liberation* ਦਾ ਸੰਖੇਪ), ਨਾਰੀ ਮੁਕਤੀ

liberal (ਲਿਬ(ਅ)ਰ(ਅ)ਲ) *a n* ਖੁੱਲ੍ਹਦਿਲਾ, ਵੱਡੇ

ਦਿਲ ਵਾਲਾ, ਆਜ਼ਾਦ ਖ਼ਿਆਲ, ਉਦਾਰਚਿੱਤ, ਸਖੀ, ਦਾਨੀ; ਧਾਰਮਕ ਕੱਟੜਤਾ ਤੋਂ ਬਾਹਰ; ~ism ਖੁੱਲ੍ਹ-ਖ਼ਿਆਲੀ, ਨਰਮ ਵਿਚਾਰ, ਉਦਾਰਵਾਦ; ~ist ਉਦਾਰਵਾਦੀ; ~ity ਆਜ਼ਾਦ ਖ਼ਿਆਲੀ, ਉਦਾਰਤਾ; ਸਖ਼ਾਵਤ; ~ize ਨਰਮ ਕਰਨਾ, ਢਿੱਲਾ ਕਰਨਾ, ਉਦਾਰ ਬਣਾਉਣਾ

liberate ('ਲਿਬਅਰੇਇਟ) *v* ਆਜ਼ਾਦ ਕਰਨਾ, ਸੁਤੰਤਰ ਕਰਨਾ, ਮੁਕਤ ਕਰਨਾ; ਰਿਹਾ ਕਰਨਾ, ਛੁਟਕਾਰਾ ਦੇਣਾ; ~d ਰਿਹਾ, ਮੁਕਤ, ਆਜ਼ਾਦ

liberation (ਲਿਬਅ'ਰੇਇਸ਼ਨ) *n* ਆਜ਼ਾਦੀ, ਸੁਤੰਤਰਤਾ, ਛੁਟਕਾਰਾ, ਰਿਹਾਈ

liberator (ਲਿਬਅਰੇਇਟਅ*) *n* ਛੁਟਕਾਰਾ ਦੇਣ ਵਾਲਾ, ਮੁਕਤੀਦਾਤਾ, ਰਿਹਾ ਕਰਨ ਵਾਲਾ, ਸੁਤੰਤਰਤਾ ਦੇਣ ਵਾਲਾ

liberty (ਲਿਬਅਟਿ) *n* ਛੁਟਕਾਰਾ, ਮੁਕਤੀ, ਆਜ਼ਾਦੀ, ਸਵਾਧੀਨਤਾ, ਸੁਤੰਤਰਤਾ; **at~** ਰਿਹਾ, ਮੁਕਤ, ਸੁਤੰਤਰ

libido (ਲਿ'ਬਿਡਅਾਉ) *n* (ਮਨੋ) ਕਾਮ-ਸ਼ਕਤੀ, ਕਾਮ-ਤ੍ਰਿਪਤੀ, ਕਾਮ-ਵਾਸ਼ਨਾ, ਕਾਮ-ਉਤੇਜਨਾ

Libra (ਲਾਇਬਅਰ) *n* ਤੁਲਾ ਰਾਸ਼ੀ

librarian (ਲਾਇ'ਬਰੇਅਰਿਅਨ) *n* ਪੁਸਤਕ-ਪਾਲ

library (ਲਾਇਬਰਅਰਿ) *n* ਪੁਸਤਕਾਲਾ, ਕਿਤਾਬ-ਘਰ, ਗ੍ਰੰਥ-ਘਰ, ਲਾਇਬਰੇਰੀ

licence, license (ਲਾਇਸਅੰਸ) *n v* ਲਾਇਸੈਂਸ, ਆਗਿਆ, ਅਨੁਮਤੀ, ਆਗਿਆ-ਪੱਤਰ, ਸਨਦ; ਛੋਟ; ਲਾਈਸੈਂਸ ਦੇਣਾ, ਆਗਿਆ ਦੇਣੀ, ਖੁੱਲ੍ਹ ਦੇਣੀ

licensee (ਲਾਇਸਅੰ'ਸੀ) *n* ਲਾਈਸੈਂਸਦਾਰ

lick (ਲਿਕ) *v n* ਜੀਭ ਨਾਲ ਚੱਟਣਾ, ਕੁੱਟਣਾ, ਠੇਕਣਾ; ਚੱਟਣਾ; **~one's shoes** ਝੋਲੀ ਚੁੱਕਣਾ, ਚਾਪਲੂਸੀ ਕਰਨੀ, ਜੁੱਤੀ ਚੱਟਣਾ; **~ing** ਮਾਰ-ਕੁਟਾਈ, ਹਾਰ; ਦੰਡ

lid (ਲਿਡ) *n* ਢੱਕਣ, ਢੱਕਣਾ, ਚੱਪਣੀ; ਛੱਪਰ, (ਅੱਖਾਂ ਦੀ) ਪਲਕ, ਪਪੋਟਾ; **~ded** ਢੱਕਣਦਾਰ

lie (ਲਾਇ) *n v* ਝੂਠ, ਮਿਥਿਆ-ਕਥਨ, ਝੂਠੀ ਗੱਲ, ਛਲ, ਅਸਤ; ਝੂਠ ਬੋਲਣਾ, ਲੇਟਣਾ, ਪੈਣਾ, ਪਏ ਹੋਣਾ; ਹਮਬਿਸਤਰ ਹੋਣਾ; **white~** ਮਾਮੂਲੀ ਝੂਠ

lien (ਲਿਅਨ) *n* ਹੱਕ-ਰਖਾਈ, ਅਧਿਕਾਰ ਗ੍ਰਹਿਤ ਅਧਿਕਾਰ, ਕਾਨੂੰਨੀ ਅਧਿਕਾਰ, ਪੁਨਰ ਗ੍ਰਹਿਤ ਅਧਿਕਾਰ, ਪੀਲੀਆ, ਤਿਲੀ, ਤਾਪਤਿਲੀ

lieu, in~ of (ਲਯੂ) *n* ਦੀ ਥਾਂ, ਦੀ ਜਗ੍ਹਾ, ਬਦਲੇ ਵਿਚ

lieutenant (ਲੈਫ਼'ਟੈਨਅੰਟ) *n* ਲੈਫ਼ਟੀਨੈਂਟ ਨਾਇਬ, ਲਫਟੈਨ; ਪ੍ਰਤੀਨਿਧੀ; ਉਪ; **~governor** ਉਪ-ਰਾਜਪਾਲ

life (ਲਾਇਫ਼) *n* ਜਿੰਦ, ਜਾਨ, ਪ੍ਰਾਣ; ਆਯੂ, ਜੀਵਨਕਾਲ, ਜੀਵਨ; ਦਮ, ਸਜੀਵਤਾ, ਜ਼ਿੰਦਾ-ਦਿਲੀ; ਜੀਵ, ਪਰਾਣ ਸ਼ਕਤੀ, ਜ਼ਿੰਦਗੀ; **~long** ਜੀਵਨ ਭਰ (ਦਾ); **~sentence** ਉਮਰ ਕੈਦ; **come to~** ਜਿਉਂਦਾ ਹੋਣਾ; **~ful** ਜੀਉਂਦਾ ਜਾਗਦਾ, ਬਲਵਾਨ, ਬਲਸ਼ਾਲੀ, ਸਜੀਵ; **~less** ਨਿਰਜਿੰਦ, ਨਿਸ਼ਪ੍ਰਾਣ, ਨਿਰਜੀਵ, ਮੁਰਦਾ

lift (ਲਿਫ਼ਟ) *n v* ਉਠਾਉ, ਉਂਥਾਪਨ; ਚੜ੍ਹਾਉ, ਚੁੱਕ, ਉਠਾਣ, ਉਠਾਉਣਾ, ਉਂਥਾਪਨ ਕਰਨਾ, ਉਤਾਰਨਾ, ਉੱਚਾ ਕਰਨਾ; ਉਤਰ ਦੇਣਾ, ਲਾਹ ਦੇਣਾ, ਚੁੱਕ ਦੇਣਾ (ਪਰਦਾ ਆਦਿ); ਉਘੇੜਨਾ

light (ਲਾਇਟ) *n v a* ਲੋਅ, ਚਾਨਣ, ਪ੍ਰਕਾਸ਼, ਜੋਤ, ਰੋਸ਼ਨੀ; ਉਜਾਲਾ; ਦੀਵਾ; ਚਿਰਾਗ; ਚਾਨਣ ਦਾ ਖੰਡਾ; ਰੋਸ਼ਨੀ ਕਰਨੀ; ਹਲਕਾ, ਹੌਲਾ, ਬਰੀਕ; **bring to~** ਪ੍ਰਕਾਸ਼ਤ ਕਰਨਾ, ਪਰਗਟ ਕਰਨਾ; **come to~** ਪ੍ਰਕਾਸ਼ਤ ਹੋਣਾ, ਪਰਗਟ ਹੋਣਾ;

~en ਚਾਨਣ ਹੋਣਾ, ਪ੍ਰਕਾਸ਼ਤ ਹੋਣਾ; ਰੌਸ਼ਨੀ ਪਾਉਣੀ, ਚਾਨਣ ਪਾਉਣਾ; ਚਮਕਾਉਣਾ; ਹੌਲਾ ਕਰਨਾ ਜਾਂ ਹੋਣਾ, ਪੀਰਜ ਦੇਣਾ, ਜੀ ਹੌਲਾ ਕਰਨਾ; ~er ਦੀਵਾ; ਹੌਲੀ ਕਿਸ਼ਤੀ, ਮਾਲਬੋਟ; ~ning ਬਿਜਲੀ ਦੀ ਲਿਸ਼ਕ, ਲਿਸ਼ਕੋਰ; ਚਮਕ; ਅਸਮਾਨੀ ਬਿਜਲੀ; ~some ਗੁੰਦਰ, ਹੌਲਾ, ਮੌਜੀ, ਖ਼ੁਸ਼ਦਿਲ, ਪ੍ਰਸੰਨ; ਫੁਰਤੀਲਾ, ਚਮਕੀਲਾ

like (ਲਾਇਕ) *n v a adv conj* ਰੁਚੀ, ਪਸੰਦ, ਚਾਹ; ਚੰਗਾ ਲੱਗਣਾ, ਚਾਹੁਣਾ, ਅਨੁਕੂਲ ਹੋਣਾ; ਸਮਾਨ, ਤੁੱਲ, ਅਨੁਸਾਰ, ਬਰਾਬਰ, ਵਰਗਾ; ਸੰਭਵ ਤੌਰ ਤੇ, ਉਸੇ ਢੰਗ ਨਾਲ; ਜਿਵੇਂ, ਜਿਹੋ ਜਿਹਾ; ~lihood ਸੰਭਾਵਨਾ, ਸੰਭਵਤਾ; ~ly ਸੰਭਵ, ਯੋਗ, ਉਪਯੋਗੀ; ~n ਉਪਮਾ ਦੇਣੀ, ਤੁਲਨਾ ਦੇਣੀ, ਮੇਲ ਕਰਨਾ, ਮਿਲਾਉਣਾ; ~ness ਸਮਾਨਤਾ, ਇਕਰੂਪਤਾ, ਸਮਰੂਪਤਾ, ਉਪਮਾ, ਪ੍ਰਤੀਰੂਪ, ਅਨੁਰੂਪਤਾ

liking (ਲਾਇਕਿਙ) *n* ਪਸੰਦ ਦੀ ਵਸਤੂ; ਰੁਚੀ, ਪਸੰਦ; ਇੱਛਾ; ਪਰੀਤ, ਤੁਸ਼ਟੀ

Lilliputian (ਲਿਲਿ'ਪਯੂਸ਼ਨ) *a n* ਬੌਣਾ, ਨਾਟਾ, ਠਿਗਣਾ, (ਕਲਪਤ ਪ੍ਰਦੇਸ਼) ਲਿਲੀਪੁਟ ਦਾ ਵਸਨੀਕ, ਵਾਮਨ-ਦੇਸ਼

lily (ਲਿਲਿ) *n* ਦੁੱਧ ਵਰਗੀ ਚਿੱਟੀ ਜੀਹ; ਲਿੱਲੀ, ਕੁਮਦਿਨੀ, ਨਲਿਨੀ; ਬਹੁਤ ਚਿੱਟੀ ਵਸਤੂ; ਅਤੀ ਸ਼ੁੱਧ ਵਿਅਕਤੀ; ਸਫ਼ੈਦ, ਦੁਧੀਆ ਪਦਾਰਥ

limb (ਲਿਮ) *n v* ਅੰਗ-ਉਪਾਂਗ, ਹੱਥ-ਪੈਰ; ਸ਼ਰਾਰਤੀ ਮੁੰਡਾ, ਸ਼ੈਤਾਨ ਲੜਕਾ; ਹੱਥ-ਪੈਰ ਕੱਟਣੇ, ਅੰਗ ਭੰਗ ਕਰਨੇ, ਅੰਗ ਛੇਦਨ ਕਰਨਾ; ~less ਅਪਾਹਜ, ਅੰਗਹੀਨ, ਲੂਲ੍ਹਾ

limbo (ਲਿੰਬਅਓ) *n* ਨਰਕ, ਕੈਦ; ਭੁੱਲਣ ਦੀ ਦਸ਼ਾ; ਕਬਾੜਖ਼ਾਨਾ

lime (ਲਾਇਮ) *n v* ਚੂਨਾ, ਸਫ਼ੈਦੀ, ਚੂਨੇ ਦਾ ਪੱਥਰ; ਲਾਸਾ; ਕਲੀ ਕਰਨੀ; (ਖੱਲਾ ਨੂੰ) ਚੂਨੇ ਦੇ ਪਾਣੀ ਵਿਚ ਡਿਊਣਾ; ਜੋਤਨਾ, ਚਿਪਕਾਉਣਾ; ~juice ਨਿੰਬੂ ਦਾ ਰਸ; ~light ਪ੍ਰਸਿੱਧੀ, ਮਸ਼ਹੂਰੀ; ਤੇਜ ਰੌਸ਼ਨੀ; ~stone ਚੂਨੇ ਦਾ ਪੱਥਰ

limit (ਲਿਮਿਟ) *n v* ਹੱਦ; ਸੀਮਾ, ਅਵਧੀ; ਸੀਮਾਹੇਪ, ਸੀਮਤ ਕਰਨਾ, ਹੱਦਬੰਦੀ ਕਰਨੀ; ਸੀਮਾਬੱਧ ਕਰਨਾ; ਪ੍ਰਤੀਬੰਧ ਲਾਉਣਾ, ਰੋਕਣਾ; ~ed ਸੀਮਿਤ, ਤੰਗ, ਪਾਬੰਦ; ਸੰਕੀਰਣ; ~ing ਸੀਮਾਕਾਰੀ, ਸੀਮਾਂਤ; ਚਰਮ; ~less ਬੇਹੱਦ, ਅਮਿਤ, ਅਨੰਤ, ਅਟੱਲ, ਅਸੀਮ

limp (ਲਿੰਪ) *n v* ਲਗੜਾਹਟ, ਲੰਗ; ਲੰਗੜਾਉਣਾ; ~er ਲੰਗਾ, ਲੰਗੜਾ ਕੇ ਟੁਰਨ ਵਾਲਾ; ~ing ਲੰਗੜਾਹਟ; ਲੰਗੜਾ; ~ness ਲੰਗੜਾਹਟ, ਲੰਗੜਾਪਣ

line (ਲਾਇਨ) *n v* ਪੰਗਤ, ਪੰਗਤੀ, ਕਤਾਰ; ਸਿਲਸਲਾ; ਦਿਸ਼ਾ; ਪਾਸਾ; ਅਸਤਰ ਲਗਾਉਣਾ, ਲੀਕ ਖਿਚਣਾ; dividing~ ਸਰਹੱਦ; hard ~s ਕਰੜੀ ਨੀਤੀ ਅਪਨਾਉਣ ਵਾਲਾ; to come into~ ਅਨੁਕੂਲ ਹੋਣਾ; toe the~ (ਕਿਸੇ ਦੀ) ਨੀਤੀ ਅਪਣਾਉਣਾ, ਪਿੱਠ ਬਟਨਾ; ~age, lineage ਪੰਗਤੀ-ਬੰਧਨ, ਪੰਗਤੀ-ਕਰਨ; ਵੰਸ਼, ਵੰਸ਼-ਪਰੰਪਰਾ, ਕੁਲ, ਨਸਲ; ਜੰਦ

lineal (ਲਿਨਿਅਲ) *a* ਪਿੱਤਰੀ, ਵੰਸ਼ ਦਾ, ਪੰਰਪਰਾਗਤ, ਕੁਲ ਦਾ, ਨਸਲ ਦਾ, ਖ਼ਾਨਦਾਨੀ, ਜੱਦੀ; ~ity ਕੁਲ, ਜਾਤ, ਗੋਤ, ਪਿੱਤਰ, ਵੰਸ਼, ਪਰੰਪਰਾ

linger (ਲਿੰਗਰਾਅ*) *v* ਲਟਕਾਉਣਾ, ਲਮਕਣਾ, ਪਛੜਾਉਣਾ, ਢਿਲ ਕਰਨੀ, ਠਹਿਰਨਾ; ~ing ਦੀਰਘਕਾਲ, ਚਿਰ, ਦੇਰ; ਦੀਰਘਕਾਲੀਨ, ਚਿਰਕਾਲੀਨ

linguafranca (ਲਿੰਗਵਅ'ਫਰੈਂਕਅ) *n* ਸੰਪਰਕ

ਭਾਸ਼ਾ; ਭਾਸ਼ਾ ਮਿਸ਼ਰਨ, ਸਾਂਝੀ ਭਾਸ਼ਾ

linguist ('ਲਿੰਡਗਵਿਸਟ) *a* ਭਾਸ਼ਾ-ਵਿਗਿਆਨੀ; ~ics ਭਾਸ਼ਾ-ਵਿਗਿਆਨ

link (ਲਿੰਡਕ) *n v* ਲੜੀ; ਕੜੀ, ਜੋੜ; ਸੰਜੋਗੀ ਭਾਗ, ਸੰਬੰਧ ਜੋੜਨ ਵਾਲਾ, ਜੋੜਨਾ, ਸ੍ਰੇਣੀ-ਬੱਧ ਕਰਨਾ, ਗੁੰਦਣਾ, ਤਰੁੰਪਣਾ; ਸੰਯੁਕਤ ਕਰਨਾ, ਸੰਬੰਧ ਕਰਨਾ; ~boy ਮਸ਼ਾਲਚੀ ਮੁੰਡਾ; ~age ਕੜੀ, ਸ਼ਰਿੰਖਲਾ; ~ed ਜੁੜਿਆ, ਸੰਯੁਕਤ, ਸੰਬੰਧ

lion ('ਲਾਇਅਨ) *n* ਸ਼ੇਰ, ਬੱਬਰ ਸ਼ੇਰ, ਸ਼ੀਂਹ, ਕੇਸਰ ਸਿੰਘ, ਸਾਰਦੂਲ; ~ess ਸ਼ੇਰਨੀ, ਸ਼ੀਹਣੀ

lip (ਲਿਪ) *n v* ਬੁੱਲ੍ਹ; ਹੋਠ, ਕੰਢ, ਕੁੰਢ; ਬੇਅਦਬੀ; ਬੁੱਲ੍ਹਾਂ ਨਾਲ ਲਾਉਣਾ; ਚੁੰਮਣ ਲੈਣਾ, ਚੁੰਮਣਾ, ਪਿਆਰ ਕਰਨਾ, ਘੁਸਰ-ਮੁਸਰ ਕਰਨਾ; ਮਿਨਮਿਨਾਉਣਾ; ~service ਮੂੰਹ ਰੱਖਣੀ

liquid ('ਲਿਕਵਿਡ) *n a* ਦ੍ਰਵ, ਤਰਲ, ਦ੍ਰਵ ਰੂਪ, ਪਾਣੀ ਵਰਗਾ, ਪਤਲਾ; ਪਾਰਦਰਸ਼ੀ, ਚਮਕੀਲਾ; ~ity, ~ness ਤਰਲਤਾ; ਬੈਂਕ ਨਕਦੀ; ~ize ਪਿਘਲਾਉਣਾ, ਤਰਲ ਬਣਾਉਣਾ

liquidate ('ਲਿਕਵਿਡੇਇਟ) *n* ਰਿਣ ਚੁਕਾਉਣਾ, ਕਰਜ਼ਾ ਲਾਹੁਣਾ; ਹਿਸਾਬ ਸਾਫ਼ ਕਰਨਾ; ਦਿਵਾਲਾ ਨਿਕਲਣਾ; ~d ਸਮਾਪਤ, ਨਿਰਧਾਰਤ, ਨਿਰਣੀਤ, ਮੁਕਤ

liquidation ('ਲਿਕਵਿ'ਡੇਇਸ਼ਨ) *n* ਭੁਗਤਾਨ, ਚੁਕਤਾ; ਕਾਰੋਬਾਰ ਬੰਦ ਕਰਨ ਦਾ ਕਾਰਜ; ਦੀਵਾਲਾ, ਸਫ਼ਾਇਆ

liquor ('ਲਿਕਅ*) *n v* ਸ਼ਰਾਬ, ਮਦਰਾ, ਸੁਰਾ, ਮਦਪਾਨ ਕਰਨਾ

lisp (ਲਿਸਪ) *n v* ਤੋਤਲਪਣ, ਤੁਤਲਾਹਟ; ਤੁਤਲਾਉਣਾ, ਤੁਤਲਾ ਕੇ ਬੋਲਣਾ, ਲੱਲ੍ਹਾ ਮਾਰਨਾ

list (ਲਿਸਟ) *n v* ਪੰਗਤੀ, ਸੂਚੀ-ਪੱਤਰ, ਸੂਚੀ, ਕੰਨੀ ਲਾਉਣੀ, ਕਿਨਾਰੀ ਬਣਾਉਣੀ; ਸੂਚੀ ਬਣਾਉਣੀ; ~ed ਸੂਚੀਬੱਧ; ~ing ਸੂਚੀਕਰਨ; ~er ਸਰੋਤਾ, ਸੁਨਣ ਵਾਲਾ

literacy ('ਲਿਟ(ਅ)ਰਅਸਿ) *n* ਸਾਖਰਤਾ, ਅੱਖਰ-ਗਿਆਨ

literal ('ਲਿਟ(ਅ)ਰ(ਅ)ਲ) *a* ਸ਼ਾਬਦਕ, ਅੱਖਰੀ, ਅੱਖਰਬੱਧ; ਮੂਲ ਅਰਥਕ, ਤੱਥਵਾਦੀ

literary ('ਲਿਟ(ਅ)ਰਅਰਿ) *a* ਸਾਹਿਤਕ; ਲੇਖਕਾਂ ਦੁਆਰਾ ਪ੍ਰਯੁਕਤ, ਸਾਹਿਤਕ ਭਾਸ਼ਾ, ਸ਼ਾਸਤਰੀ

literature ('ਲਿਟ(ਅ)ਰਅਚਅ*) *n* ਸਾਹਿਤ, ਅਦਬ; ਸਾਹਿਤ-ਖੇਤਰ

litigate ('ਲਿਟਿਗੇਇਟ) *v* ਮੁਕੱਦਮਾ ਲੜਨਾ, ਵਾਦਵਿਵਾਦ ਕਰਨਾ, ਦਾਅਵਾ ਕਰਨਾ, ਨਾਲਸ਼ ਕਰਨੀ

litigation ('ਲਿਟਿ'ਗੇਇਸ਼ਨ) *v* ਮੁਕੱਦਮਾ, ਦਾਅਵਾ, ਮੁਕੱਦਮੇਬਾਜ਼ੀ

litre ('ਲੀਟਅ*) *n* ਲਿਟਰ, ਮੀਟਰ ਪੱਧਤੀ ਵਿਚ ਧਾਰਤਾ ਜਾਂ ਸਮਾਈ ਦੀ ਇਕ ਇਕਾਈ

litter ('ਲਿਟਅ*) *v n* ਪਰਾਲੀ ਵਿਛਾਉਣੀ, ਘਾਹ ਵਿਛਾਉਣਾ; ਉਘੜ-ਦੁਘੜ ਸੁੱਟ ਦੇਣਾ; ਕੂੜਾ ਗੋਹਾ; ਉਤਸ਼ਾਹੀਣਤਾ; ਗੜਬੜ; ਝੋਲੀ

litterateur ('ਲਿਟਅਰਾ*ਟਅ*) (F) *n* ਸਾਹਿਤਕਾਰ, ਅਦੀਬ, ਲੇਖਕ, ਸਾਹਿਤਕਾਰ

little ('ਲਿਟਲ) *a* ਛੋਟਾ, ਨਿੱਕਾ, ਨੰਨ੍ਹਾ, ਲਘੂ ਅਲਪ, ਥੋੜ੍ਹਾ, ਕੁਝ, ਕੁਛ, ਘੱਟ, ਕਮ; ਅਲਪ ਕਾਲਕ, ਠਿੰਗਣਾ, ਬੌਣਾ, ਨਾਟਾ; ~worth ਬੇਕਾਰ, ਨਿਕੰਮਾ, ਵਿਅਰਥ; ~ness ਛੁਟਿਆਈ, ਛੋਟਾਪਣ, ਨਿੱਕਪਣ, ਕਮੀ, ਲਘੁਤਾ; ਦੀਨਤਾ, ਤੁੱਛਤਾ, ਸੁਆਰਥ

live (ਲਿਵ, ਲਾਇਵ) *v a* ਜੀਉਂਦੇ ਹੋਣਾ, ਜੀਉਣਾ, (ਕਿਸੇ ਚੀਜ਼ ਉੱਤੇ) ਨਿਰਬਾਹ ਕਰਨਾ; ਕਾਇਮ ਰਹਿਣਾ; ਵਿਹਾਰ ਕਰਨਾ; ਨਿਵਾਸ ਕਰਨਾ, ਵੱਸਣਾ

ਰਹਿਣਾ; ਸਜੀਵ, ਜੀਵਤ, ਜ਼ਿੰਦਾ; ~and let ~ ਜਿਓ ਤੇ ਜੀਣ ਦਿਓ; ~ stock ਪਸ਼ੂ ਧਨ; ~d ਜੀਵਤ, ਜੀਵਨਯੁਕਤ; ~lihood ਰੋਜ਼ੀ, ਰੋਟੀ, ਰੁਜ਼ਗਾਰ, ਨਿਰਬਾਹ, ਰਿਜ਼ਕ, ਜੀਵਨਾ, ਉਪਜੀਵਕਾ, ਜੀਵਨ-ਸਾਧਨ; ~long (ਕਾਵਿ) ਸਾਰਾ ਦਿਨ; ~ly ਜਿਊਂਦਾ-ਜਾਗਦਾ, ਹੂਬਹੂ, ਵਾਸਤਵਿਕ, ਯਥਾਰਥਕ; ਸਜੀਵ, ਪਰਾਣਮਈ; ਫੁਰਤੀਲਾ, ਪ੍ਰਸੰਨਚਿੱਤ, ਪ੍ਰਫੁੱਲਤ, ਆਨੰਦਮਈ; ~n (ਬੋ) ਮਘਟਾ, ਮਘਾਉਣਾ

liver ('ਲਿਵ੍ਅ*) n ਜਿਗਰ, ਕਲੇਜਾ, ਕਲੇਜੀ; ~y (ਨੋਂਤਾਂ ਜਾਂ ਛੋਟੇ ਜਗਾਹਾਰੀ ਦੀ) ਦਰਦੀ ਤੇ ਖ਼ੁਰਾਕ, ਜਿਗਰ ਦਾ, ਜਿਗਰੀ; ਚੀਕਣਾ, ਸੁਸਤ, ਚਿੜਚਿੜਾ

living ('ਲਿਵ੍ਇੰਡ) n a ਵਾਸ, ਰੋਜ਼ੀ, ਨਿਰਬਾਹ, ਰੁਜ਼ਗਾਰ, ਰੋਟੀ; ਸਮਕਾਲੀ, ਸਮਕਾਲਕ, ਵਿੰਦਮਾਨ; ਯਥਾ-ਤੱਥ; ਪਰਾਣਮਈ, ਪਰਾਣਧਾਰੀ, ਸਜੀਵ, ਜੀਵਤ, ਜਿਊਂਦਾ; ~ness ਸਜੀਵਤਾ; ਸਮਕਾਲੀਨਤਾ

lizard ('ਲਿਜ਼੍ਅਡ) n ਛਿਪਕਲੀ, ਕਿਰਲੀ

load (ਲਅਉਡ) n v ਦਬਾਉ, ਦਾਬਾ, ਭਾਰ, ਬੋਝ, ਮਾਲ-ਅਸਬਾਬ, ਲੱਦ, ਖੇਪ; ਰੁਕਾਵਟ; ਬਿਜਲੀ ਦੀ ਮਾਤਰਾ; (ਜ਼ੁੰਮੇਵਾਰੀ ਜਾਂ ਚਿੰਤਾ ਦਾ) ਭਾਰ; ਅਧਿਕਤਾ, ਬਹੁਤਾਤ; ~stone ਚੁੰਬਕ, ਲੋਹਮਣੀ, ਲੋਹਕਾਂਤ; ~ed ਭਾਰਾ, ਤਰਿਆ, ਲੱਦਿਆ; ~ing ਲੱਦਣ ਵਾਲਾ, ਭਰਨ ਵਾਲਾ; ਭਾਰ, ਬੋਝ; ਲਦਾਈ, ਤਰਾਈ

loaf (ਲਅਉਫ) n v ਨਾਨ, ਰੋਟੀ, ਡਬਲਰੋਟੀ; ਅਵਾਰਾਗਰਦੀ, ਮਟਰਗਸ਼ਤ; ਅਵਾਰਾਗਰਦੀ ਕਰਨੀ; ~er ਅਵਾਰਾਗਰਦ, ਬਦਮਾਸ਼

loan (ਲਅਉਨ) n v ਰਿਣ, ਉਧਾਰ, ਤਕਾਵੀ, ਕਰਜ਼; ਰਿਣ ਦੇਣਾ, ਉਧਾਰ ਦੇਣਾ

loath, loth (ਲਅਉਥ) a ਵਿਮੁਖ, ਵਿਰਕਤ, ਅਣਇਛੁਕ

loathe (ਲਅਉਦ) v ਘਿਰਨਾ ਕਰਨੀ, ਨਫਰਤ ਕਰਨੀ, ਪਸੰਦ ਨਾ ਕਰਨਾ

lobby ('ਲੌਬਿ) n v ਦਲਾਨ, ਡਿਉੜੀ; ਸਭਾ-ਮੰਡਲ, ਸਦੱਸ-ਗੈਲਰੀ, ਲਾਂਬੀ; ਪ੍ਰਭਾਵ ਮੰਡਲ; ਮੁਲਾਕਾਤੀ ਕਮਰਾ

local ('ਲਅਉਕਲ) a n ਸਥਾਨਕ; ਅਲਪ ਵਿਸਤਰਤ, ਦੇਸੀ; ~e ਘਟਨਾ-ਸਥਲ, ਸਥਾਨ, ਮੌਕਾ; ~ity ਸਥਾਨ, ਸਥਿਤੀ, ਪ੍ਰਦੇਸ, ਇਲਾਕਾ; ~ize ਸਥਾਨਕ ਬਣਾਉਂਣਾ, ਇਕ ਦੇਸ਼ ਦਾ ਬਣਾਉਣਾ, ਕੇਂਦਰਤ ਕਰਨਾ

locate (ਲਅ(ਉ)'ਕੇਇਟ) v ਪਤਾ ਕੱਢਣਾ, ਸੂਹ ਲਾਉਣੀ, ਸਥਾਨ ਦੱਸਣਾ, ਬਿਠਾਉਣਾ, ਰੱਖਣਾ

locative ('ਲੌਕਅਟਿਵ੍) n a (ਵਿਆ) ਅਧਿਕਰਣ ਕਾਰਕ, ਸੱਤਵੀਂ ਵਿਭਕਤੀ, ਸਥਾਨ ਨਿਰਦੇਸ਼ਕ

lock (ਲੌਕ) n v ਜਿੰਦ, ਲਟ, ਕੇਸਾਂ ਦਾ ਗੁੱਛਾ, ਅਲਕਾ, ਸ਼ਿਖਾ, ਜੁਲਫ, ਜੰਦਰਾ; ਬੰਦੂਕ ਦਾ ਘੋੜ, ਨਹਿਰ ਦਾ ਬੰਨ੍ਹ; ਆਲਿੰਗਨ; ਤਾਲਾ ਲਾਉਣਾ, ਜੰਦਰਾ ਮਾਰਨਾ; ਬੰਦ ਕਰਨਾ, ਜਕੜ ਲੈਣਾ; ਗੁੰਨ੍ਹਣਾ, ਫਾਹੁਣਾ, ਉਲਝਾਉਣਾ, ਵਲੇਟਣਾ; under ~and key ਜਿੰਦੇ ਅੰਦਰ, ਤਾਲਾ ਲਾ ਕੇ; ~er ਤਾਲੇਦਾਰ ਅਲਮਾਰੀ, (ਬੈਂਕ ਦਾ) ਲਾਕਰ; ਕੋਠਾ; ~out ਤਾਲਾਬੰਦੀ ਕਰਨਾ; ~up ਹਵਾਲਾਤ

locket ('ਲੌਕਿਟ) n ਲੋਹੇ ਦੀ ਪੱਟੀ; ਸੋਨੇ ਜਾਂ ਚਾਂਦੀ ਦਾ ਕੁੰਡਾ, ਢੋਲਣ; ਲਾਕਟ, ਇਕ ਪ੍ਰਕਾਰ ਦਾ ਹਾਰ

locomotion ('ਲਅਉਕਅ'ਮਅਉਸ਼ਨ) n ਗਮਨ, ਚਲਨ, ਗਤੀਸ਼ੀਲਤਾ, ਹਰਕਤ; ਯਾਤਰਾ ਪੱਧਤੀ

locomotive ('ਲਅਉਕਅ'ਮਅਉਟਿਵ੍) n a ਰੇਲ-ਇੰਜਣ, ਚੱਲਣਸ਼ੀਲ, ਗਤੀਸ਼ੀਲ, ਗਤੀ

ਉਤਪਾਦਕ

locus ('ਲਾਉਕਸ) *n* ਮੌਕਾ; ਵਕੂਅ; ਠੀਕ ਥਾਂ, ਸਥਾਨ, ਸੰਸਥਿਤੀ; ਬਿੰਦੂ-ਪੱਖ; ~**standi** (*L*) ਦਖ਼ਲ-ਅੰਦਾਜ਼ੀ ਜਾਂ ਪੱਖ ਪੇਸ਼ ਕਰਨ ਦਾ ਅਧਿਕਾਰ

locust ('ਲਅਉਕਅਸਟ) *n* ਟਿੱਡੀ, ਟਿੱਡੀ-ਦਲ

locution (ਲਅ(ਉ)'ਕਯੂਸ਼ਨ) *n* ਭਾਸ਼ਣ-ਸ਼ੈਲੀ, ਮੁਹਾਵਰਾ, ਅੰਦਾਜ਼ੇ ਤਕਰੀਰ, ਤਰਜ਼ੇ ਗੁਫ਼ਤਗੂ; ਵਾਕ, ਉਕਤੀ, ਪਦ, ਸ਼ਬਦ

lodge (ਲੌਜ) *n v* ਰਿਹਾਇਸ਼, ਵਾਸ, ਛੋਟਾ ਮਕਾਨ; ਤੰਬੂ, ਖ਼ੇਮਾ; ਰਿਹਾਇਸ਼ ਦੇਣੀ, ਰੱਖਣਾ, ਵਸਾਉਣਾ, ਨਿਵਾਸ ਦੇਣਾ, ਧਾਰਨ, ਰੱਖਣਾ, ਟਿਕਾਉਣਾ, ਠਹਿਰਾਉਣਾ; ਵੱਸਣਾ, ਬਸੇਰਾ ਕਰਨਾ, ਰਾਤ ਕੱਟਣਾ

lodging ('ਲੌਜਿਙ) *n* ਰਿਹਾਇਸ਼, ਵਾਸ-ਗ੍ਰਹਿ, ਆਵਾਸ

loft (ਲੌਫ਼ਟ) *n v* ਮੰਮਟੀ, ਅਟਾਰੀ, ਛੱਤਰੀ, ਕਬੂਤਰਖ਼ਾਨਾ; ਗੇਂਦ ਨੂੰ ਉੱਚਾ ਸੁੱਟਣਾ; ~**y** ਉੱਚਾ, ਉੱਚ, ਉਤੰਗ, ਉੱਨਤ

log (ਲੌਗ) *n v* ਲੱਕੜ ਦਾ ਕੁੰਦਾ, ਖੁੰਢ, ਗੋਲੀ, ਗੱਟਾ; ਮੰਜ਼ਲ ਤੈ ਕਰਨਾ, ਜੁਰਮਾਨਾ ਕਰਨਾ, ਦੰਡ ਦੇਣਾ; ~**book** ਰੋਜ਼ਨਾਮਚਾ, ਯਾਤਰੂ ਦੀ ਡਾਇਰੀ

logarithm ('ਲੌਗਅਰਿਦ(ਅ)ਮ) *n* (ਸੰਖੇਪ log) (ਹਿਸਾਬ) ਲਾਗਾ, ਲਾਗਾਰਿਥਮ, ਲਘੂਗਣਕ, ਛੇਦ; ਘਾਤ (ਜਿਸ ਤਕ ਸੰਖਿਆ ਨੂੰ ਵਧਾਉਣਾ ਚਾਹੀਦੇ ਜਿਵੇਂ ਦੋ ਦੀ ਤਿੰਨ ਘਾਤ=2^3)

logger ('ਲੌਗਅ*) *n* ਲੱਕੜਹਾਰਾ; ~**head** ਮੂਰ੍ਹ, ਵਿਅਕਤੀ; ਉੱਲੂ; ਲੋਹੇ ਦਾ ਜੰਤਰ

logic ('ਲੌਜਿਕ) *n* ਤਰਕ-ਸ਼ਾਸਤਰ, ਨਿਆਇ-ਸ਼ਾਸਤਰ, ਤਰਕ, ਮੰਤਕ; ~**al** ਤਾਰਕਿਕ, ਤਰਕ-ਸ਼ਾਸਤਰ ਸਬੰਧੀ; ਤਰਕ-ਪੂਰਨ, ਯੁਕਤੀ-ਯੁਕਤ; ਤਰਕਸਿੱਧ

logos ('ਲੌਗੌਸ) *n* ਸ਼ਬਦ; (cap) ਸ਼ਬਦ-ਬ੍ਰਹਮ

loin (ਲੌਇਨ) *n* ਕੁੱਲ੍ਹਾ, ਕਮਰ, ਪੁੱਠਾ, ਪੁੱਠ; ~**cloth** ਧੋਤੀ, ਲੰਗੋਟ, ਜਾਂਘੀਆ

loiter ('ਲੌਇਟਅ*) *v* ਮਟਰ-ਗਸ਼ਤ ਕਰਨਾ, ਟਹਿਲਣਾ, ਵਿਅਰਥ ਸਮਾਂ ਨਸ਼ਟ ਕਰਨਾ, ਮਾਰੇ-ਮਾਰੇ ਫਿਰਨਾ; ~**over one's work** ਜੀ ਚੁਰਾਉਣਾ, ਕੰਮ-ਚੋਰ ਹੋਣਾ

lollipop ('ਲੌਲਿਪੌਪ) *n* (ਬ ਵ) ਮਿਠਿਆਈਆਂ, ਖੰਡ ਦਾ ਚੂਪਾ, ਲਾਲੀਪਾਪ

lone, lonely (ਲਅਉਨ, 'ਲਅਉਨਲਿ) *a n* ਇਕੱਲਾ, ਨਿਆਸਰਾ, ਬੇਆਸਰਾ; ਸੁੰਵਾਂ, ਉਜਾੜ; ਉਦਾਸ; ~**liness** ਇਕੱਲ, ਸੁੰਨਪਟ, ਵੀਰਾਨਾ, ਉਜਾੜ; ਤਨਹਾਈ; ਇਕਲਾਪਾ

long (ਲੌਙ) *n v adv* ਲੰਬਾ; ਦੀਰਘ ਕਾਲ, ਲੰਮੀ ਅਵਧੀ; ਵਿਸਤਾਰ, ਵੇਰਵਾ; ਬਹੁਤ ਚਾਹੁਣਾ, ਲਾਲਸਾ ਹੋਣੀ; ਤਾਂਘਣਾ, ਰੀਝਣਾ, ਲੰਮਾ, ਦੂਰ ਦਾ, ਅਤੀਤ ਕਾਲੀਨ; ਚਿਰਕਾਲੀ, ਲੰਮੇ ਸਮੇਂ ਤੋਂ, ਚਿਰ ਤੋਂ; ~**cloth** ਲੱਠਾ; ~**eared** ਮੂਰਖ, ਗਾਂਡ, ਲਮਕੰਨਾ; ~**standing** ਚਿਰਕਾਲੀ, ਚਿਰੋਕਣਾ, ਪੁਰਾਣਾ; **in the ~run** ਅਖ਼ੀਰ ਨੂੰ, ਆਖ਼ਰਕਾਰ; ~**evity** ਚਿਰਜੀਵਤਾ, ਦੀਰਘ ਆਯੂ; ~**ing** ਤਾਂਘ, ਅਕਾਂਖਿਆ; ਉਤਸੁਕ, ਅਤਿਲਾਸ਼ੀ

longitude (ਲੌਙੀਟਯੂਡ) *n* ਲੰਮਾਈ; ਤੂਲ, (ਭੂਗੋ.) ਰੇਖਾਂਸ਼, (ਗਣਿ, ਜੋ) ਖਰੌਲੀ ਰੇਖਾਂਸ਼

longitudinal (ਲੌਙੀਟਯੂਡਨਅਲ) *a* ਲੰਮਾ, ਲੰਮਾਈ ਸਬੰਧੀ, ਦੇਸ਼ਾਂਤਰੀ; ਭੋਗ ਸਬੰਧੀ

loof (ਲੂਫ਼) *n* ਹਥੇਲੀ

look (ਲੁਕ) *v n* ਤੱਕਣਾ, ਦਰਸ਼ਨ ਕਰਨਾ, ਤਾੜਨਾ, ਵੇਖਣਾ; ਨਿਰੀਖਣ ਕਰਨਾ, ਪਰੀਖਿਆ ਕਰਨੀ; ਸੁੱਝਣਾ, ਦਿਸਣਾ; ਰਾਹ ਵੇਖਣਾ; ਆਭਾ, ਛੱਬ, ਰੂਪ, ਸੂਰਤ, ਅੰਦਾਜ਼, ਚਿਹਰਾ-ਮੁਹਰਾ, ਨੈਣ-ਨਕਸ਼, ਦਿੱਖ; ਦਰਸ਼ਨ; ~**about** ਖ਼ਬਰਦਾਰ ਹੋਣਾ; ~**after** ਦੇਖ

ਭਾਲ ਕਰਨਾ; ~**down (up) on** ਨਫ਼ਰਤ ਕਰਨੀ; ~**into** ਨਿਰੀਖਣ ਕਰਨਾ; ~**on** ਤਮਾਸ਼ਾ ਵੇਖਣਾ; ~**to** ਵੱਲ ਧਿਆਨ ਦੇਣਾ; ~**through** ਘੋਖਣਾ, ਚੰਗੀ ਤਰ੍ਹਾਂ ਪੜਤਾਲਣਾ; ~**ing** ਦ੍ਰਿਸ਼ਟੀ, ਦਰਸ਼ਨ

loom (ਲੂਮ) *n* ਕਰਘਾ, ਖੱਡੀ, ਕੱਪੜਾ ਬੁਣਨ ਦੀ ਮਸ਼ੀਨ

loop (ਲੂਪ) *n v* (ਰੱਸੇ, ਡੋਰੀ ਆਦਿ ਦਾ) ਵਲ; ਘੁੰਡੀ; (ਮੁੱਠੀ ਦਾ ਕੰਮ ਦੇਣ ਵਾਲਾ) ਚੱਕਰ, ਧਾਤ ਦੀ ਅੰਗੂਠੀ; ਨਿਰੋਧਕ ਛੱਲਾ; ਫੰਧਾ ਪਾਉਣਾ; ਚੱਕਰ ਵਿਚ ਫਸਾਣਾ; ~**hole** ਝਰੋਖਾ, ਛਿਦਰ, ਨੌਗ; ਮਾਘਰ, ਚੋਰ ਗਹਾਟ, ਧਹਾਉ ਦਾ ਹਾਣ

loose (ਲੂਸ) *v a* ਸੁੰਤਤਰ ਕਰਨਾ, ਛੱਡਣਾ, ਖੋਲ੍ਹਣਾ; ਢਿੱਲਾ ਕਰਨਾ, ਉਤਾਰਨਾ; ਦਾਗਣਾ; ਬੰਧਨ-ਮੁਕਤ, ਖੁੱਲ੍ਹਾ ਹੋਇਆ; ਸੁਤੰਤਰ, ਮੁਕਤ, ਬੇਰੋਕ; ਅਸਥਿਰ, ਅਦਿੜ੍ਹ, ਢਿੱਲਾ; ਅਸਪਸ਼ਟ; (ਅਨੁਵਾਦ) ਅਸ਼ਲੀਲ, ਅਵਾਰਾ; ~**n** ਸੁਤੰਤਰ ਕਰਨਾ, ਮੁਕਤ ਕਰਨਾ, ਢਿੱਲਾ ਕਰਨਾ, ਛੱਡਣਾ; ਦਸਤ ਲੱਗਣੇ; ਜ਼ਾਬਤਾ ਢਿੱਲਾ ਕਰ ਦੇਣਾ; ~**ness** ਢਿੱਲ, ਸਿਥਲਤਾ, ਢਿੱਲਾਪਣ; ਵਿਭਚਾਰ, ਦੁਰਾਚਾਰ; ਮਰੋੜ, ਦਸਤ, ਪੇਚਸ਼

loot (ਲੂਟ) *n v* ਲੁੱਟ, ਲੁੱਟ ਦਾ ਮਾਲ; ਲੁੱਟਣਾ

lord (ਲੌਡ) *n v* (L~) ਇਸ਼ਵਰ, ਪ੍ਰਭੁ; ਸੁਆਮੀ, ਮਾਲਕ, ਸਾਹਿਬ, ਸਰਦਾਰ; ਸਾਮੰਤ, ਨਵਾਬ, ਜਾਗੀਰਦਾਰ, ਲਾਟ; ਰਈਸ; ਨੇਤਾ; ਪਤੀ, ਨਾਥ; ਸ਼ਾਸਨ ਕਰਨਾ, ਹੁਕਮ ਚਲਾਉਣਾ; ਲਾਰਡ ਦੀ ਉਪਾਧੀ ਦੇਣੀ, ਲਾਰਡ ਬਣਾਉਣਾ; ~**ship** ਪ੍ਰਭਾਵਤ, ਸਰਦਾਰੀ, ਸਾਹਿਬਪੁਣਾ, ਸੁਆਮੀਤੁਣਵ; ਰਾਜ, ਜਾਗੀਰ

lorn (ਲੌਨ) *n* ਉਜਾੜ, ਵੀਰਾਨ, ਇਕੱਲਾ, ਅਨਾਥ, ਲਾਚਾਰ, ਵਿਚਾਰਾ, ਬੇਕਸ

lorry ('ਲੌਰਿ) *n* ਠੇਲ੍ਹਾ, ਟਰੱਕ; ਮੋਟਰ ਲਾਰੀ, ਛਕੜਾ, ਲਾਰੀ

lose (ਲੂਜ਼) *v* ਗੁਆਉਣਾ, ਗੁਆਚਣਾ, ਵਾਂਝਿਆਂ ਹੋਣਾ; ਲੁਪਤ ਹੋਣਾ, ਮਰ ਜਾਣਾ; ~**one's temper** ਕਰੋਧ ਵਿਚ ਆਉਣਾ; ਗੁੱਸੇ ਹੋਣਾ

loss (ਲੌਸ) *n* ਘਾਟਾ, ਟੋਟਾ, ਨੁਕਸਾਨ, ਹਾਨੀ

lot (ਲੌਟ) *n* ਤਕਦੀਰ, ਨਸੀਬ, ਲੇਖ, ਭਾਗ, ਕਿਸਮਤ; ਹਾਲਤ; ਬੋਕ ਮਾਲ, ਢੇਰ, ਨੀਲਾਮੀ ਲਈ ਢੇਰੀ, ਟੁਕੜੀ; ~**tery** ਲਾਟਰੀ; ਕਿਸਮਤ ਦੀ ਗੱਲ, ਭਾਗਾਂ ਦੀ ਖੇਡ, ਜੂਆ

lotus ('ਲਅਉਟਅਸ) *n* ਕੰਵਲ, ਕਮਲ, ਪਦਮ, ਪੰਕਜ, ਕੁਮੁਦਿਨੀ, ਨਲਿਨੀ

luud (ਲਅਉਡ) *a adv* ਉੱਚ, ਉੱਚਾ, ਭਾਰਾ; ਜ਼ੋਰਦਾਰ; ਭੜਕੀਲਾ; ~**ness** ਉੱਚੀ ਅਵਾਜ਼, ਜ਼ੋਰ-ਸ਼ੋਰ

lounge (ਲਾਉਨਜ) *v n* ਮਟਕ ਮਟਕ ਕੇ ਟੁਰਨਾ, ਟਹਿਲਣਾ, ਅਵਾਰਾਗਰਦੀ ਕਰਨੀ; ਆਲਸ ਵਿਚ ਸਮਾਂ ਗੁਆਉਣਾ, ਸੁਸਤਾਉਣਾ; ਮਟਰਗਸ਼ਤ; ਸੋਫ਼ਾ, ਸੈਰਗਾਹ; ਡਿਉੜੀ, ਬੈਠਕ, ਲਾਊਂਜ

louse (ਲਾਉਸ) *n* ਜੂੰ

lout (ਲਾਉਟ) *n v* ਪੇਂਡੂ; ਗੰਵਾਰ, ਉਜੱਡ, ਅਨਾੜੀ ਬੰਦਾ; ਆਦਰ ਨਾਲ ਝੁਕਣਾ, ਸਲਾਮ ਕਰਨਾ

love (ਲਅੱਵ) *n v* ਪਿਆਰ, ਪਰੇਮ, ਮੁਹੱਬਤ, ਇਸ਼ਕ, ਪਰੀਤ, ਸਨੇਹ, ਚਾਹ; ਕਾਮਵਾਸ਼ਨਾ; ਪਿਆਰ ਕਰਨਾ, ਗੁੱਠਬਣ ਕਰਨਾ; ~**d** ਪਿਆਰਾ, ਪ੍ਰਿਯ; ~**ly** ਪਿਆਰਾ, ਲਲਿਤ, ਰਮਣੀਕ, ਹੁਸੀਨ, ਦਿਲਕਸ਼; ~**r** ਪਰੇਮੀ, ਅਨੁਰਾਗੀ, ਆਸ਼ਕ, ਆਸ਼ਨਾ

loving ('ਲਅੱਵਿੰਡ) *a* ਪਿਆਰਾ, ਨਿੱਘਾ, ਪ੍ਰਿਯ, ਸਨੇਹੀ

low (ਲਅਉ) *n v a adv* ਨੀਵਾਂ, ਹੇਠਲਾ, ਛੋਟਾ; ਨੀਚ, ਹੋਛਾ; ਨਿਸਤੇਜ, ਦਲਿਤ; (ਸਵਰ) ਕੋਮਲ, ਮੰਧਮ, ਹੇਠਾਂ; ਥੱਲੇ, ਧੀਰੇ ਧੀਰੇ, ਹੌਲੀ ਹੌਲੀ; ~**lying** ਨੀਵਾਂ; ~**er** ਉਤਾਰਨਾ, ਝੁਕਾਉਣਾ, ਨੀਵਾਂ ਕਰਨਾ; ਲੰਬਾਈ ਘਟਾਉਣੀ, ਉਚਾਈ ਘਟਾਉਣੀ; (ਮੁੱਲ ਆਦਿ ਦਾ) ਘਟਾਣਾ, ਡਿਗਣਾ,

ਹੇਠਾਂ ਆਉਣਾ; ਹੇਠਲਾ, ਹੋਰ ਹੇਠਾਂ ਦਾ

loyal ('ਲੋਇ(ਅ)ਲ) *a* ਵਫ਼ਾਦਾਰ, ਬਾਵਫ਼ਾ; ਸਾਦਿਕ, ਨਮਕਹਲਾਲ

lubricant ('ਲੂਬਰਿਕਐਂਟ) *n* ਸਨੇਹਕ, ਚੋਪੜ, ਗਰੀਸ, ਚਿਕਨਾਈ

lubricate ('ਲੂਬਰਿਕੇਇਟ) *v* ਤੇਲ ਦੇਣਾ, ਚੋਪੜਨਾ, ਵਾਂਗਣਾ; ਮੁਸ਼ਕਲਾਂ ਨੂੰ ਸੌਖਿਆਂ ਪਾਰ ਕਰ ਲੈਣਾ

lucid ('ਲੂਸਿਡ) *a* ਪ੍ਰਕਾਸ਼ਮਈ, ਉੱਜਲ, ਸੁਅੱਛ, ਨਿਰਮਲ, ਨਿੱਖਰਿਆ, ਸਾਫ਼, ਚਮਕੀਲਾ; ~**ity** ਸੁਅੱਛਤਾ, ਉੱਜਲਤਾ, ਸਪਸ਼ਟਤਾ, ਸਫ਼ਾਈ, ਚਮਕ; ~**ly** ਸਪਸ਼ਟ ਰੂਪ ਵਿਚ

luck (ਲਅੱਕ) *n* ਭਾਗ, ਲੇਖ, ਕਿਸਮਤ, ਤਕਦੀਰ, ਨਸੀਬ, ਸੁਭਾਗ; ~**y** ਭਾਗਸ਼ਾਲੀ, ਸੁਭਾਗਵਾਨ, ਖ਼ੁਸ਼ਕਿਸਮਤ, ਧੰਨ

luggage ('ਲਅੱਗਿਜ) *n* ਸਫ਼ਰੀ ਸਾਮਾਨ, ਅਸਬਾਬ, ਬੋਰੀਆ-ਬਿਸਤਰਾ, ਗੰਢੜੀ, ਪੋਟਲੀ

lukewarm ('ਲੂਕ'ਵੋਮ) *a* ਕੋਸਾ, ਨਿੱਘਾ; ਨੀਮ ਗਰਮ; ਉਦਾਸੀਨ (ਆਦਮੀ); ~**ness** ਕੋਸਾਪਣ, ਨਿੱਘ, ਨੀਮ-ਗਰਮੀ; ਨਿਰਉਤਸ਼ਾਹ

luminous ('ਲੂਮਿਨਅਸ) *a* ਨੂਰਾਨੀ, ਤੇਜਮਈ, ਚਮਕੀਲਾ, ਚਮਕਦਾਰ, ਪ੍ਰਕਾਸ਼ਵਾਨ; ~**ness** ਤੇਜ, ਚਮਕ, ਪ੍ਰਕਾਸ਼

lump (ਲਅੱਪ) *n v* ਇਕ ਕੰਡੇਦਾਰ ਸੁਰਮਈ ਮੱਛੀ; ਘਾਟ, ਡਲਾ, ਠੇਲੀ, ਪਿੰਡ, ਢੇਲਾ; ਪੇੜਾ (ਆਟਾ), ਪਿੰਨਾ (ਮੱਖਣ), ਪਿੰਨੀ, ਢੇਰ, ਅਧਿਕਤਾ; ਮਿੱਟੀ ਦਾ ਮਾਧੋ, ਗੋਬਰ-ਗਟੇਸ਼; ਇੱਕਤਰ ਕਰਨਾ, ਢੇਰ ਲਾਉਣਾ, ਢੇਰ ਹੋਣਾ; ਬਰਾਬਰ ਸਮਝਣਾ; ਸਾਰਾ ਧਨ ਲਾ ਦੇਣਾ, ਬੇਢੰਗੀ ਤੋਰ ਟੁਰਨਾ; ~**sum** ਇਕ ਮੁਸ਼ਤ ਰਾਸ਼ੀ

lunacy ('ਲੂਨਅਸਿ) *n* ਪਾਗਲਪਣ, ਉਨਮਾਦ; ਸੁਦਾਅ, ਸੁਦਾਈਪਣ, ਝੱਲ, ਝੱਲਪਣ

lunar ('ਲੂਨਅ*) *a* ਚੰਦ ਦੀ ਦੂਰੀ; ਫਿੱਕਾ ਹਲਕਾ, ਮੱਧਮ

lunatic ('ਲੂਨਅਟਿਕ) *a* ਪਾਗਲ, ਦੀਵਾਨਾ, ਬਾਵਲਾ, ਖ਼ਬਤੀ; ~**asylum** ਪਾਗਲਖ਼ਾਨਾ

lunch, luncheon (ਲਅੰਚ, 'ਲਅੰਚ(ਅ)ਨ) *n v* ਲੰਚ ਦੁਪਹਿਰ ਦਾ ਖਾਣਾ; ਭੋਜਨ ਦੇਣਾ, ਲੰਚ ਦੇਣਾ

lung (ਲਅੰਡ) *n* ਫੇਫੜਾ, ਫਿੱਫੜਾ

lurch (ਲਅ:ਚ) *n* ਬਿਪਤਾ, ਸੰਕਟ, ਮੁਸੀਬਤ, ਆਪਤਕਾਲ; ਝਟਕਾ; ਜ਼ਖ਼ਮ; **leave in the~** ਮੁਸੀਬਤ ਵਿਚ ਛੱਡ ਜਾਣਾ

lure (ਲੁਅ*) *n v* ਆਕਰਸ਼ਣ, ਲੁਭਾਉਣਾ, ਝਾਂਸਾ, ਫੁਸਲਾਹਟ; ਲੋੜ ਵਿਚ ਪਾਉਣਾ, ਫੁਸਲਾਉਣਾ, ਝਾਂਸਾ ਦੇਣਾ, ਚਕਮਾ ਦੇਣਾ

lust (ਲਅੱਸਟ) *n v* ਕਾਮ-ਵਾਸ਼ਨਾ; ਹਵਸ; ਆਵੇਗਪੂਰਨ ਕਾਮਨਾ ਕਰਨੀ, ਹਾਬੜਨਾ, ਹਵਸ ਕਰਨੀ; ~**ful** ਲਾਲਸੀ, ਹਾਬੜਿਆ; ~**fulness** ਕਾਮੁਕਤਾ, ਕਾਮ ਆਤੁਰਤਾ, ਲਾਲਸਾ; ~**y** ਰਿਸ਼ਟ-ਪੁਸ਼ਟ, ਤਗੜਾ

lustre ('ਲਅੱਸਟਅ*) *n v* ਚਮਕ; ਆਭਾ, ਆਬ; ਤੇਜ, ਸ਼ੋਭਾ, ਮਹਿਮਾ; ਚਮਕਣਾ

luxurious (ਲਅੱਗ'ਯੂਅਰਿਅਸ) *a* ਵਿਲਾਸੀ, ਸੁਖਭੋਗੀ, ਸੁਖਰਾਇਤ; ਵਿਲਾਸਮਈ, ਅਤੀ ਸੁਖਾਵਾਂ, ਅਨੰਦਪੂਰਨ; ~**ness** ਵਿਲਾਸ, ਸੁਖ, ਭੋਗ; ਆਨੰਦਪੂਰਨਤਾ, ਭਰਪੂਰਤਾ

luxury ('ਲਅੱਕਸ਼(ਅ)ਰਿ) *n* ਅੱਯਾਸ਼ੀ, ਰੰਗ-ਰਸ; ਵਿਲਾਸ, ਸੁਆਦ, ਸੁਖ

lyric ('ਲਿਰਿਕ*) *n a* ਗੀਤ, ਗੀਤ ਕਾਵਿ; ਵੀਣਾ ਦਾ, ਵੈਣਿਕ, ਵੀਣਾ ਸਬੰਧੀ, ਗੀਤਾਤਮਕ, ਗੀਤਮਈ; ~**al** ਸਰੋਦੀ;~**ism** ਗੀਤਾਤਮਕਤਾ, ਸਰੋਦੀਪੁਣਾ; ~**ist** ਗੀਤਕਾਰ

lyrist ('ਲਿਰਿਸਟ) *n* ਵੀਣਾਵਾਦਕ, ਗੀਤਕਾਰ

M

M, m (ਐੱਮ) *n* ਰੋਮਨ ਵਰਣਮਾਲਾ ਦਾ ਤੇਰ੍ਹਵਾਂ ਅੱਖਰ; ਰੋਮਨ ਗਿਣਤੀ ਦਾ ਇਕ ਹਜ਼ਾਰ ਦਾ ਅੰਕ

M. A. ('ਐੱਮ 'ਏਇ) Master of Arts, ਐੱਮ. ਏ. ਦੀ ਡਿਗਰੀ

ma (ਮਾ) *n* ਅੰਮੀ, ਮੰਮੀ, ਮਾਂ

machine (ਮਅ'ਸ਼ੀਨ) *n v* ਮਸ਼ੀਨ, ਕਲ, ਜੰਤਰ, ਪੁਰਜ਼ਾ; ਸਾਧਨ; ਮਸ਼ੀਨ ਚਲਾਉਣਾ; **~ry** ਮਸ਼ੀਨਾਂ, ਕਲਾਂ ਜੰਤਰਾਂ ਦਾ ਸਮੂਹ; ਜੰਤਰਾਂ ਦਾ ਕਾਰਜ, ਕਲ ਦੀ ਬਣਾਵਟ; ਕਲ-ਪੁਰਜ਼ੇ, ਮਸ਼ੀਨਰੀ

machinist (ਮਅ'ਸ਼ੀਨਿਸਟ) *n* ਮਿਸਤਰੀ, ਮਸ਼ੀਨ-ਸਾਜ਼; ਮਸ਼ੀਨ ਚਾਲਕ

mad (ਮੈਡ) *a v* ਪਾਗਲ, ਝੱਲਾ, ਸੁਦਾਈ, ਦੀਵਾਨਾ, ਕਮਲਾ, ਬਾਉਲਾ, ਖ਼ਬਤੀ; ਪਾਗਲ ਬਣਾਉਣਾ ਜਾਂ ਹੋਣਾ, ਮੂਰਖ ਹੋਣਾ ਜਾਂ ਕਰਨਾ; **~cap** ਮਸਤਾਨਾ, ਸਿਰ ਫਿਰਿਆ, ਭਾਵੁਕ; **~house** ਪਾਗਲਖ਼ਾਨਾ; **~den** ਝੱਲਾ ਕਰ ਦੇਣਾ, ਸੁਦਾਈ ਬਣਾ ਦੇਣਾ; **~ly** ਪਾਗਲਾਂ ਵਾਂਗੂ, ਸੁਦਾਈਆਂ ਵਰਗਾ ; **~ness** ਪਾਗਲਪਣ, ਝੱਲ, ਮੂਰਖਤਾ

madam ('ਮੈਡਅਮ) *n* ਸ੍ਰੀਮਤੀ, ਬੇਗਮ, ਮੇਮ ਸਾਹਿਬ

mafia ('ਮੌਫ਼ਿਅ) *n* ਮਾਫ਼ੀਆ, ਨਾਜਾਇਜ਼ ਧੰਦਾ ਕਰਨ ਵਾਲਿਆਂ ਦਾ ਗਰੋਹ

mag (ਮੈਗ) *n v* ਬਕਵਾਸ; ਬਕਵਾਸ ਕਰਨਾ, ਗੱਪ ਮਾਰਨਾ, ਬੁੜ੍ਹਬੁੜ੍ਹ ਕਰਨਾ

magazine ('ਮੈਗਅ'ਜ਼ੀਨ) *n* (1) ਰਸਾਲਾ, ਪਰਚਾ, ਪਤੱਰਕਾ; (2) ਸਟੋਰ, ਭੰਡਾਰ, ਖ਼ਜ਼ਾਨਾ, ਗੁਦਾਮ; (3) ਅਸਲਾਖ਼ਾਨਾ, ਸ਼ਸਤਰ-ਘਰ, ਬਾਰੂਦਖ਼ਾਨਾ

magic ('ਮੈਜਿਕ) *n* ਜਾਦੂ; ਜਾਦੂਗਰੀ, ਟੂਣਾ; **~al** ਜਾਦੂ ਦਾ; **~ian** ਜਾਦੂਗਰ, ਟੂਣੇਹਾਰ, ਬਾਜ਼ੀਗਰ

magisterial ('ਮੈਜਿ'ਸਟਿਅਰਿਅਲ) *a* ਮੈਜਿਸਟਰੇਟੀ, ਮੈਜਿਸਟਰੇਟ ਦਾ, ਹਾਕਮਾਨਾ, ਅਫ਼ਸਰਾਨਾ

magistrate ('ਮੈਜਿਸਟਰੇਇਟ) *n* ਮੈਜਿਸਟਰੇਟ, ਦੰਡ ਅਧਿਕਾਰੀ

magmatic (ਮੈਗ'ਮੈਟਿਕ) *a* ਚਿਪਚਪਾ, ਲੇਸਦਾਰ

magna C(h)arta ('ਮੈਗਨਅ'ਕਾਟਅ) *n* (ਸੰਨ 1512 ਈ. ਵਿਚ ਇੰਗਲੈਂਡ ਦੇ ਬਾਦਸ਼ਾਹ ਰਾਹੀਂ ਪ੍ਰਦਾਨ ਕੀਤਾ) ਮਹਾਂ ਅਧਿਕਾਰ ਪੱਤਰ

magnanimity ('ਮੈਗਨਅ'ਨਿਮਅਟਿ) *n* ਉਦਾਰਤਾ, ਖ਼ੁਸ਼ਦਿਲੀ

magnanimous (ਮੈਗ'ਨੈਨਿਮਅਸ) *a* ਉਦਾਰ-ਚਿੱਤ, ਸਖੀ, ਖੁੱਲ੍ਹਦਿਲਾ, ਜਿਗਰੇ ਵਾਲਾ, ਉਦਾਰ-ਆਤਮਾ

magnate ('ਮੈਗਨੇਇਟ) *n* ਧਨਾਢ, ਰਈਸ, ਧਨੀ

magnet ('ਮੈਗਨਿਟ) *n* ਚੁੰਬਕ, ਮਿਕਨਾਤੀਸ ਕੁਤਬਨੁਮਾਂ; (ਅਲੰਕਾਰਕ) ਆਕਰਸ਼ਕ ਵਸਤੂ; **~ic** ਚੁੰਬਕੀ, ਮਿਕਨਾਤੀਸ, ਖਿਚਵਾਂ, ਆਕਰਸ਼ਣਸ਼ੀਲ; **~ize** ਚੁੰਬਕ-ਸ਼ਕਤੀ ਦੇਣਾ, ਆਕਰਸ਼ਣ ਸ਼ਕਤੀ ਦੇਣਾ, ਚੁੰਬਕ ਸ਼ਕਤੀ ਵਾਲਾ ਹੋਣਾ; **~ized** ਚੁੰਬਕ ਯੁਕਤ

magneto (ਮੈਗ'ਨੀਟਅਉ) *n* ਚੁੰਬਕੀ-ਸ਼ਕਤੀ ਦੇਣ ਵਾਲਾ ਜੰਤਰ

magnified ('ਮੈਗ'ਨਿਫ਼ਾਇਡ) *n* ਵਿਸਤਰਤ, ਵਿਸ਼ਾਲ

magnify ('ਮੈਗਨਿਫ਼ਾਇ) v ਵਡਿਆਉਣਾ, ਵਧਾਉਣਾ, ਵੱਡਾ ਕਰਨਾ; ਵਧਾ ਕੇ ਦਸੱਣਾ; ਮਹਿਮਾ ਕਰਨੀ; ~ing ਆਵਰਧਕ, ਆਵਰਧਨ

magnitude ('ਮੈਗਨਿਟਯੁਡ) n ਆਕਾਰ, ਕੱਦ, ਮਾਤਰ, ਵਡੱਪਣ, ਮਹੱਤਾ, ਮਹੱਤਵ

magnum ('ਮੈਗਨਅਮ) n ਅੱਧੇ ਗੈਲੱਨ ਦੀ ਬੋਤਲ, ਵੱਡੀ ਬੋਤਲ

magus ('ਮੇਇਗਅਸ) n ਜਾਦੂਗਰ, ਸਿਆਣਾ

maid (ਮੇਇਡ) n ਕੰਨਿਆ, ਕੁਆਰੀ ਲੜਕੀ, ਮੁਟਿਆਰ; ਨੌਕਰਾਣੀ, ਦਾਸੀ, ਗੋਲੀ; ~en ਕੰਨਿਆ, ਕੁਆਰੀ ਲੜਕੀ; (ਕ੍ਰਿਕਟ) ਖ਼ਾਲੀ ਓਵਰ, ਨਵੀਂ; ਅਛੂਤੀ, ਕੋਰੀ; ਪਲੇਠਾ, ਪਹਿਲਾ; ~en speech ਪਹਿਲੀ ਤਕਰੀਰ, ਪ੍ਰਥਮ ਭਾਸ਼ਣ; ~enhood ਕੁਆਰਪੁਣਾ, ਅਛੂਤਪਨ

mail (ਮੇਇਲ) n v ਡਾਕ, ਡਾਕ ਦਾ ਥੈਲਾ; ਡਾਕ ਵਿਚ ਪਾਉਣਾ (ਖ਼ਤ)

maim (ਮੇਇਮ) v ਅੰਗ-ਭੰਗ ਕਰਨਾ, ਕੱਟਣਾ, ਲੂਲ੍ਹਾ ਜਾਂ ਟੁੰਡਾ ਕਰ ਦੇਣਾ; ਨਿਕੰਮਾ ਕਰਨਾ, ਬੇਕਾਰ ਕਰਨਾ

main ('ਮੇਇਨ) a ਪਰਮ, ਉੱਤਮ, ਪ੍ਰਮੁੱਖ, ਮੁੱਖ, ਅਸਲੀ, ਪ੍ਰਧਾਨ, ਵੱਡਾ; ~land ਮਹਾਂਦੀਪ; ~yard ਚਹੁਤਰਾ (ਮੁੱਖ ਮਸਤੂਲ ਦੇ ਹੇਠਾਂ ਦਾ); ~ly ਮੁੱਖ ਤੌਰ ਤੇ, ਬਹੁਤ ਕਰਕੇ, ਪ੍ਰਮੁੱਖ ਰੂਪ ਵਿਚ

maintain (ਮੇਇਨ'ਟੇਇਨ) v ਕਾਇਮ ਰੱਖਣਾ, ਕਰਦੇ ਰਹਿਣਾ; ਸੰਭਾਲੀ ਰੱਖਣਾ, ਕਬਜ਼ੇ ਵਿਚ ਰੱਖਣਾ, ਨਿਰਬਾਹ ਕਰਨਾ, ਪਾਲਾ ਕਰਨੀ; ~ed ਪੋਸ਼ਤ; ਰੱਖਿਆ ਹੋਇਆ, ਪੁਸ਼ਟ

maintenance ('ਮੇਇਨਟਅਨਅੰਸ) n ਦੇਖ-ਭਾਲ, ਰੱਖਿਆ; ਪਾਲਣ-ਪੋਸ਼ਣ, ਸਹਾਰਾ, ਨਿਰਬਾਹ

maize (ਮੇਇਜ਼) n ਮੱਕੀ

majestic (ਮਅ'ਜੈਸਟਿਕ) a ਸ਼ਾਹੀ, ਸ਼ਾਹਾਨਾ, ਗੌਰਵਸ਼ਾਲੀ, ਸ਼ਾਨਦਾਰ, ਆਲੀਸ਼ਾਨ, ਤੇਜਸਵੀ

majesty ('ਮੈਜਅਸਟਿ) n ਸ਼ਾਨ, ਸ਼ੋਭ ਦਬਦਬਾ, ਵਕਾਰ; ਰਾਜ-ਪ੍ਰਤਾਪ; ਮਹਾਂਬਲੀ

major ('ਮੇਇਜਆ*) n a ਪ੍ਰਧਾਨ, ਮੁੱ (ਵਿਅਕਤੀ) ਸ੍ਰੇਸ਼ਠ, ਵੱਡਾ (ਆਦਮੀ), ਬਾਲਗ਼ ਮੇਜਰ (ਫ਼ੌਜੀ ਅਫ਼ਸਰ); ਗੰਭੀਰ; ~ship ਮੇਜ ਦੀ ਪਦਵੀ; ਪ੍ਰਮੁੱਖਤਾ, ਵਡੱਪਣ

majority (ਮਅ'ਜੌਰਅਟਿ) n ਬਹੁ-ਸੰਮਤੀ, ਬਹੁ-ਮੱਤ ਪ੍ਰੋਢ਼ਤਾ

make (ਮੇਇਕ) v n ਬਣਾਉਣਾ; ਪੈਦਾ ਕਰਨ ਰਚਨਾ; ਤਿਆਰ ਕਰਨਾ (ਚਾਹ ਆਦਿ); ਵਿਛਾਉਣ (ਬਿਸਤਰਾ ਆਦਿ); ਕਰਨਾ, ਅਮਲ ਵਿ ਲਿਆਉਣਾ; ਕਾਇਮ ਕਰਨਾ; ਆਕਾਰ, ਰੁ ਆਕ੍ਰਿਤੀ, ਰਚਨਾ, ਨਿਤੀ; ~good ਘਾਟਾ ਪੁ ਕਰਨਾ; ~up ਕਸਰ ਪੂਰੀ ਕਰਨੀ; ਭੇਸ ਬਦਲਣ ਸ਼ਿੰਗਾਰ ਸਮਗਰੀ; ਮਨਘੜਤ (ਕਿੱਸਾ); ਇਕੱਤ ਕਰਨਾ (ਪੈਸੇ ਆਦਿ); ~r ਕਰਤਾ; ਪਾਲ ਨਿਰਮਾਤਾ

making ('ਮੇਇਕਿਙ) n ਰਚਨਾ, ਬਣਾਵ ਆਮਦਨੀ

maladjustment ('ਮੈਲਅ'ਜਅੱਸ(ਟ)ਮਅੰਟ) ਅਟੱਜੋੜ, ਬੇਤਰਤੀਬੀ, ਕੁਵਿਵਸਥਾ, ਭੈੜਾ ਪ੍ਰਬ

maladministration ('ਮੈਲਅਡ'ਮਿ ਨਿ'ਸਟਰੇਇਸ਼ਨ) n ਬਦਅਮਨੀ, ਬਦਇੰਤਜ਼ਾਮ ਭੈੜਾ ਰਾਜ-ਪ੍ਰਬੰਧ, ਕੁਸ਼ਾਸਨ

maladroit ('ਮੈਲਅ'ਡਰੋਇਟ) a ਬਦਤਮੀ ਭੱਦਾ, ਅਨਾੜੀ; ~ness ਭੱਦਾਪਣ, ਅਨਾੜੀਪਨ ਬੇਢੰਗਾਪਣ

malady ('ਮੈਲਅਡਿ) n ਵਿਕਾਰ, ਰੋਗ, ਬੀਮਾਰ

mala fide ('ਮੇਇਲਆ'ਫ਼ਾਇਡਿ) a ac ਬਦਨੀਤੀ ਵਾਲੀ, ਖੋਟੀ ਭਾਵਨਾ ਨਾਲ

malaise (ਮੈਂ'ਲੇਇਜ਼) *n* ਬੇਚੈਨੀ, ਸਰੀਰਕ ਕਸ਼ਟ (ਬਿਨਾ ਕਿਸੇ ਵਿਸ਼ੇਸ਼ ਬੀਮਾਰੀ ਦੇ, ਖ਼ਰਾਬੀ, ਵਿਗਾੜ

malaria (ਮਾ'ਲੇਅਰਿਆ) *n* ਮਲੇਰਿਆ, ਮੌਸਮੀ ਬੁਖ਼ਾਰ, ਕਾਂਬੇ ਦਾ ਤਾਪ

malconduct (ਮੈਲ'ਕੌਂਡਅਕਟ) *n* ਦੁਰਵਿਹਾਰ, ਬੁਰੀ ਵਰਤੋਂ

maldistribution (ਮੈਲ'ਡਿਸਟਰਿ'ਬਯੂਸ਼ਨ) *n* ਕਾਣੀ ਵੰਡ

male (ਮੇਇਲ) *n a* ਨਰ, ਪੁਰਸ਼; ਪੁਲਿੰਗ, ਨਰ-ਜਾਤੀ, ਮਰਦਾਵਾਂ

maledict (ਮੈਲਿ'ਡਿਕਟ) *v a* ਸਰਾਪ ਦੇਣਾ, ਸਰਾਪਣਾ; ਸਰਾਪਿਆ; **~ion** ਸਰਾਪ, ਬਦ-ਦੁਆ, ਬਦ-ਅਸੀਸ

malevolence (ਮਾ'ਲੈੱਵ੍ਅਲਅੰਸ) *n* ਮੰਦਭਾਵਨਾ, ਦੁਰਇੱਛਾ, ਵੈਰ, ਧਰੋਹ, ਦੋਖ

malevolent (ਮਾ'ਲੈੱਵ੍ਅਲਅੰਟ) *a* ਮੰਦਇੱਛਿਤ, ਦੁਰਭਾਵਨਾ-ਪੂਰਨ; ਦੁਰਆਤਮਾ, ਵੈਰੀ

malice ('ਮੈਲਿਸ) *n* ਵੈਰ, ਈਰਖਾ, ਦੋਖ, ਖਾਰ, ਖੁਣਸ, ਬਦਨੀਤੀ

malicious (ਮਾ'ਲਿਸ਼ਅਸ) *a* ਵੈਰੀ, ਦੋਖੀ, ਖੁਣਸੀ; ਬਦਨੀਤੀ ਦਾ; ਪਾਪ-ਆਤਮਾ ਵਾਲਾ; **~ness** ਖੁਣਸ, ਦੋਖ, ਵੈਰ

malign (ਮਾ'ਲਾਇਨ) *v a* ਨਿੰਦਾ ਕਰਨੀ, ਬੁਰਾਈ ਕਰਨੀ, ਬਦਨਾਮ ਕਰਨਾ, ਅਸ਼ੁੱਭ, ਘਾਤਕ; **~ance, ~ancy** (ਰੋਗ ਦੀ) ਘਾਤਕਤਾ, ਪ੍ਰਚੰਡਤਾ; ਈਰਖਾ; ਕਪਟ

mall (ਮੈਲ) *n* ਠੰਢੀ ਸੜਕ, ਜਨਪਥ, ਛਾਂ-ਦਾਰ ਮਾਰਗ

malnutrition (ਮੈਲਨਯੂ'ਟਰਿਸ਼ਨ) *n* ਅਪੂਰਨ ਖ਼ੁਰਾਕ, ਅਸੰਤੁਲਤ ਭੋਜਨ

malodour (ਮੈਲ'ਅਉਡਅ*) *n* ਬਦਬੂ, ਦੁਰਗੰਧ

malpractice (ਮੈਲ'ਪਰੈਕਟਿਸ) *n* ਬਦਚਲਨ, ਭ੍ਰਿਸ਼ਟਾਚਾਰ, ਦੁਰਾਚਾਰ; ਬੇ-ਪਰਵਾਹੀ, ਗੜਬੜਤ; ਖਿਆਨਤ

malpractitioner (ਮੈਲ'ਪਰੈਕਟਿਸ਼ਨਾ*) *n* ਬਦਚਲਨ, ਭ੍ਰਿਸ਼ਟਾਚਾਰੀ, ਕੁਕਰਮੀ, ਬੇਈਮਾਨ, ਦੁਰਾਚਾਰੀ; ਬੇਪਰਵਾਹ, ਗਾਫ਼ਿਲ

maltreat ('ਮੈਲ'ਟਰੀਟ) *v* ਬੁਰਾ ਸਲੂਕ ਕਰਨਾ, ਬੁਰਾ ਵਰਤਾਓ ਕਰਨਾ, ਦੁਰਵਿਹਾਰ ਕਰਨਾ, ਬਦਸਲੂਕੀ ਕਰਨੀ; **~ment** ਦੁਰਾਚਾਰ, ਦੁਰਿਹਾਰ, ਬਦਾਸੂਬੀ

mamma (ਮਅ'ਮਾ) *n* ਅੰਮੀ, ਅੰਬੜੀ, ਮਾਂ ਜੀ, ਬੀ ਜੀ; ਬੀਬੀ ਜੀ; **~l** ਥਣਧਾਰੀ ਪ੍ਰਾਣੀ, ਦੁੱਧ ਪਿਲਾਉਣ ਵਾਲੇ ਜੀਵ

mammon ('ਮੈਮਅਨ) *n* ਧਨ-ਦੇਵਤਾ, ਕੁਬੇਰ; ਮਾਇਆ, ਦੌਲਤ

mammoth ('ਮੈਮਅਥ) *a n* ਵਿਸ਼ਾਲ, ਬਹੁਤ ਵੱਡਾ, ਮਹਾਨ

mammy ('ਮੈਮਿ) *n* ਮਾਂ, ਮੰਮੀ, ਅੰਬੜੀ; ਆਯਾ

man (ਮੈਨ) *n v* ਪੁਰਸ਼, ਆਦਮੀ, ਨਰ, ਇਨਸਾਨ, ਮਾਨਵ; ਮਨੁੱਖ ਜਾਤੀ; ਦਾਸ, ਸੇਵਕ, ਸੈਨਕ ਜਵਾਨ; ਪਤੀ, ਖਾਵੰਦ; ਸੁਰੱਖਿਆ ਲੱਸੀ ਆਦਮੀ ਹੋਣਾ; ਹੌਸਲਾ ਵਧਾਉਣਾ, ਦਿਲ ਮਜ਼ਬੂਤ ਕਰਨਾ; **~at-arms** ਸਿਪਾਹੀ, ਸੈਨਕ; ਯੋਧਾ, ਸੈਨਕ; **~ful** ਬਹਾਦਰ, ਸੂਰਬੀਰ, ਦਲੇਰ, ਸਾਹਸੀ; **~fulness** ਮਰਦਾਨਗੀ, ਸੂਰਬੀਰਤਾ, ਬਹਾਦਰੀ, ਦਲੇਰੀ; ਦ੍ਰਿੜ੍ਹਤਾ; **~kind** ਮਾਨਵ-ਜਾਤੀ; ਪੁਰਸ਼, ਮਨੁੱਖ, ਮਾਨਵ; **~less** ਉਜਾੜ, ਸੁੰਞਾ, ਨਿਰਜਨ; **~like** ਮਾਨਵ ਰੂਪ; ਇਨਸਾਨੀ ਮਰਦਾਨਗੀ ਭਰਿਆ, ਨਰ-ਰੂਪ; **~power** ਮਨੁੱਖੀ ਸ਼ਕਤੀ

manacle ('ਮੈਨਅਕਲ) *n v* ਹਥਕੜੀ, ਬੇੜੀ, ਜ਼ੰਜ਼ੀਰ, ਸੰਗਲ; ਰੁਕਾਵਟ; ਹੱਥਕੜੀ ਪਹਿਨਾਉਣੀ, ਜ਼ੰਜ਼ੀਰ ਨਾਲ ਕੱਸਣਾ

manage ('ਮੈਨਿਜ) *n v* ਸਿਖਲਾਈ; ਪ੍ਰਬੰਧ ਕਰਨਾ, ਬੰਦੋਬਸਤ ਕਰਨਾ, ਇੰਤਜ਼ਾਮ ਕਰਨਾ; ਦੇਖ-ਭਾਲ ਕਰਨੀ, ਸੰਭਾਲਣਾ; ਚਲਾਉਣਾ; **~able** ਅਧੀਨ, ਵੱਸ (ਪ੍ਰਬੰਧ ਵਿਚ); **~ment** ਪ੍ਰਬੰਧ, ਇੰਤਜ਼ਾਮ, ਬੰਦੋਬਸਤ; ਉਪਾਉ, ਛਲ, ਜੁਗਤੀ; ਸ਼ਾਸਨ, ਪ੍ਰਬੰਧਨ; **~r** ਪ੍ਰਬੰਧਕ, ਸੰਚਾਲਕ, ਮੈਨੇਜਰ; **~rial** ਪ੍ਰਬੰਧਕੀ, ਪ੍ਰਬੰਧ-ਸਬੰਧੀ

managing ('ਮੈਨਿਜਿਙ) *n a* ਪ੍ਰਬੰਧ ਕਰਨ, ਪ੍ਰਬੰਧ; ਪ੍ਰਬੰਧਕ, ਚਾਲਕ; **~body** ਪ੍ਰਬੰਧਕੀ ਸੰਸਥਾ; **~committee** ਪ੍ਰਬੰਧਕੀ ਕਮੇਟੀ; **~director** ਪ੍ਰਬੰਧ ਨਿਰਦੇਸ਼ਕ

mandate ('ਮੈਨਡੇਇਟ) *n v* ਫ਼ਰਮਾਨ, ਸਰਕਾਰੀ ਆਦੇਸ਼, ਅਧਿਆਦੇਸ਼, ਅਗਿਆ-ਪੱਤਰ; ਸੌਂਪਣਾ, ਸਮਰਪਣ ਕਰਨਾ

mandatory ('ਮੈਨਡਅਟ(ਅ)ਰਿ) *a* ਅਧਿਦੇਸ਼ਾਤਮਕ, ਅਧਿਦੇਸ਼ੀ; ਅਨਿਵਾਰਯ, ਲਾਜ਼ਮੀ, ਅਵੱਸ਼ਕ

mandrill ('ਮੈਨਡਰਿਲ) *n* ਬਣ-ਮਾਣਸ, ਵੱਡਾ ਲੰਗੂਰ

mango ('ਮੈਙਗਅਓ) *n* ਅੰਬ

manhandle ('ਮੈਨ'ਹੈਂਡਲ) *v* ਹੱਥੋਪਾਈ ਕਰਨੀ

mania ('ਮੇਇਨਯਅ) *n* ਖ਼ਬਤ, ਸਨਕ; **~c** ਖ਼ਬਤੀ, ਸ਼ੁਦਾਈ, ਸਨਕੀ, ਦੀਵਾਨਾ, ਸਿਰੜੀ, ਪਾਗਲ (ਆਦਮੀ)

manifest ('ਮੈਨਿਫ਼ੈਸਟ) *n v a* ਪਾਲਸੂਚੀ; ਪਰਗਟਾਉਣਾ, ਪ੍ਰਤੱਖ ਕਰਨਾ, ਉਘਾੜਨਾ; ਸਿੱਧ ਕਰਨਾ, ਸਾਖਿਆਤ ਕਰਨਾ, ਅਭਿਵਿਕਤ ਕਰਨਾ; ਪਰਕਟ, ਸਪਸ਼ਟ; **~ation** ਅਭਿਵਿਅੰਜਨ, ਪ੍ਰਕਾਸ਼, ਜ਼ਹੂਰ; **~ed** ਸਪਸ਼ਟ, ਪਰਗਟ; **~o** ਮਨੋਰਥ-ਪੱਤਰ, ਘੋਸ਼ਣਾ-ਪੱਤਰ, ਨੀਤੀ-ਘੋਸ਼ ਮੈਨੀਫੈਸਟੋ; ਪ੍ਰਵਿਅੰਜਨਾ

manifold ('ਮੈਨਿਫ਼ਅਉਲਡ) *v a* ਬਹੁ-ਗੁਣ ਕਰਨਾ, ਬਹੁ-ਵਿਧੀ ਬਣਾਉਣਾ; ਬਹੁ-ਭਾਂਤੀ, ਬਹੁ ਵਿਧ, ਨਾਨਾ-ਵਿਧ, ਵੰਨ-ਸੁਵੰਨਾ

manipulate (ਮਅ'ਨਿਪਯੁਲੇਇਟ) *v* ਹੱਥਾਂ ਨਾਲ ਚਲਾਉਣਾ, ਕੰਮ ਵਿਚ ਲਿਆਉਣਾ; ਆਪਣੇ ਹਿਤ ਵਿਚ ਵਰਤਣਾ; ਜੋੜ-ਤੋੜ ਕਰਨਾ

manipulation (ਮਅ'ਨਿਪਯੁ'ਲੇਇਸ਼ਨ) *n* ਹੱਥ ਫੇਰੀ, ਜੁਗਤ; ਜੋੜ-ਤੋੜ; ਪੱਤੇਬਾਜ਼ੀ, ਹੁਸ਼ਿਆਰੀ

manipulative (ਮਅ'ਨਿਪਯੁਲਅਟਿਵ਼) *a* ਛਲ ਭਰਿਆ

manipulator (ਮਅ'ਨਿਪਯੁਲੇਇਟਅ*) *n* ਪੱਤੇਬਾਜ਼, ਛਲੀਆ, ਸਾਜ਼-ਬਾਜ਼ ਕਰਨ ਵਾਲਾ

manner ('ਮੈਨਅ*) *n* ਵਿਧੀ, ਢੱਬ, ਤਰਜ਼, ਤੌਰ ਤਰੀਕਾ, ਆਚਾਰ, ਸ਼ਿਸ਼ਟਾਚਾਰ, ਵਿਹਾਰ (ਬ ਵ) ਚੱਜ, ਰੀਤ, ਢੰਗ, ਰੀਤੀ, ਦਸਤੂਰ; **~ed** ਸੁਸ਼ੀਲ, ਭੱਦਰ, ਸ਼ਿਸ਼ਟ, ਵਿਨੀਤ; **~ism** ਸ਼ਿਸ਼ਟਤਾ, ਆਚਾਰ, ਆਚਰਨ, ਵਿਹਾਰ; **~less** ਕੁਚੱਜਾ, ਅਸ਼ਿਸ਼ਟ, ਦੁਰਾਚਾਰੀ

manoeuvrability (ਮਅ'ਨੂਵ਼ਰਅ'ਬਿਲਅਟਿ) *n* ਜੁੱਧ-ਅਭਿਆਸ ਵਿਚ ਨਿਪੁੰਨਤਾ

manoeuvre (ਮਅ'ਨੂਵ਼ਅ*) *n* ਪੈਂਤੜੇ-ਬਾਜ਼ੀ, ਚਲਾਕੀ, ਜੁਗਤੀ, ਦਾਅ, ਚਾਲ, ਉਪਾਉ, ਤੋੜ-ਜੋੜ; ਜੁੱਧ ਅਭਿਆਸ ਕਰਨਾ; ਦਾਅ ਲਾਉਣਾ

manor ('ਮੈਨਅ*) *n* ਜਾਗੀਰ, ਮਿਲਖ, ਤਅੱਲੁਕਾ, ਜ਼ਿਮੀਂਦਾਰੀ

mansion ('ਮੈਨਸ਼ਨ) *n* ਹਵੇਲੀ, ਮਹਲ, ਕੋਠੀ, ਭਵਨ

mantle ('ਮੈਨਟਲ) *n v* ਚੋਗਾ, ਲਬਾਦਾ; ਦੁਪੱਟਾ,

ਨਕਾਬ; ਜਾਲੀ, ਕੱਜਣ; ਚੋਗਾ ਜਾਂ ਲਬਾਦਾ ਪਾਉਣਾ, ਚੋਗੇ ਨਾਲ ਢੱਕ ਲੈਣਾ, ਢੱਕ ਲੈਣਾ, ਛੁਪਾ ਲੈਣਾ, ਪਰਦਾ ਪਾਉਣਾ

manual ('ਮੈਨੂਅਲ) *n a* ਕਿਤਾਬੜੀ, ਪੁਸਤਕਾ, ਗੁਟਕਾ, ਨੇਮਾਵਲੀ, ਮੈਨੂਅਲ; ਦਸਤੀ, ਹੱਥਾਂ-ਸਬੰਧੀ, ਹੱਥ ਦਾ, ਸਰੀਰਕ; ~**art** ਹਸਤ-ਕਲਾ; ~**excercise** ਸਰੀਰਕ ਕਸਰਤ; ~**labour** ਸਰੀਰਕ ਕਿਰਤ; ~**work** ਹੱਥ ਦਾ ਕੰਮ

manufactory ('ਮੈਨਯੂ'ਫ਼ੈਕਟ(ਅ)ਰਿ) *n* ਕਾਰਖ਼ਾਨਾ, ਸ਼ਿਲਪਗ੍ਰਹਿ, ਸ਼ਿਲਪਸ਼ਾਲਾ, ਨਿਮਾਣਸ਼ਾਲਾ

manufacture ('ਮੈਨਯੂ'ਫ਼ੈਕਚਰ*) *n v* ਕਾਰੀਗਰੀ, ਸ਼ਿਲਪਕਾਰੀ, ਨਿਰਮਾਣ, ਨਿਰਮਾਣ ਕਰਨਾ, ਰਚਨਾ, ਬਣਾਉਣਾ; ~d ਰਚਿਆ ਗਿਆ, ਬਣਾਇਆ ਗਿਆ, ਨਿਰਮਤ; ~r ਉਤਪਾਦਕ, ਨਿਰਮਾਤਾ, ਕਾਰਖ਼ਾਨੇਦਾਰ; ਕਾਰੀਗਰ

manure (ਮਅ'ਨਯੂਅ*) *n v* ਰੂੜੀ, ਖਾਦ; ਰੂੜੀ ਪਾਉਣੀ, ਖਾਦ ਪਾਉਣੀ

manuscript ('ਮੈਨਯੂਸਕਰਿਪਟ) *n a* ਹੱਥ-ਲਿਖਤ ਮਸੌਦਾ, ਦਸਤਾਵੇਜ਼; ਹੱਥ-ਲਿਖਤ, ਲਿਖਤੀ, ਕਲਮੀ, ਦਸਤੀ

Many ('ਮੈਨਿ) *a n* ਬਹੁਤ, ਬਹੁਤੇ, ਅਨੇਕ, ਕਈ; ਅਧਿਕ; ~ **sided** ਬਹੁ-ਪੱਖੀ; **as** ~ ਜਿੰਨੇ, ਉਨੇ, ਜਿਤਨੇ, ਉਤਨੇ; **how**~ ਕਿੰਨੇ, ਕਿਤਨੇ

map (ਮੈਪ) *n v* ਨਕਸ਼ਾ ਮਨ-ਚਿਤਰ; ਨਕਸ਼ਾ ਵਾਹੁਣਾ, ਚਿਤਰ ਖਿਚਣਾ; ~**out** ਉਲੀਕਣਾ, ਵਿਉਂਤਣਾ, ਯੋਜਨਾ ਬਣਾਉਣੀ; **off the** ~ ਮਹੱਤਵਹੀਣ **on the** ~ ਮਹੱਤਵਪੂਰਨ

mar (ਮਾ*) *v* ਵਿਗਾੜਨਾ, ਖ਼ਰਾਬ ਕਰਨਾ, ਉਜਾੜਨਾ, ਨੁਕਸਾਨ ਪੁਚਾਉਣਾ

marathon ('ਮੈਰਅਥਨ) *n* (ਕਈ ਮੀਲ ਦੀ) ਲੰਮੀ ਦੌੜ; ਲੰਮੇ ਦਮ ਵਾਲਾ ਕੰਮ

maraud (ਮਅ'ਰੋਡ) *v* ਲੁੱਟ-ਮਾਰ ਕਰਨੀ, ਠੱਗੀ ਕਰਨੀ, ਚੋਰੀ ਕਰਨੀ, ਲੁੱਟਣਾ, ਡਾਕਾ ਮਾਰਨਾ

marble ('ਮਾਬਲ) *n v* ਸੰਗਮਰਮਰ; ਅਬਰੀ ਬਣਾਉਣਾ; ~**d** ਸੰਗਮਰਮਰ ਦੀ ਤਰ੍ਹਾਂ, ਅਬਰੀਕਾਰ

March (ਮਾ'ਚ) *n v* (1) ਅੰਗਰੇਜ਼ੀ ਸਾਲ ਦਾ ਤੀਜਾ ਮਹੀਨਾ; (2) ਕੂਚ, ਰਵਾਨਗੀ, (3) (ਇਤਿ) ਸੀਮਾ, ਸਰਹੱਦ; ਕੂਚ ਕਰਨਾ, ਮਾਰਚ ਕਰਨਾ, ਚਲਾਉਂਦੇ ਜਾਣਾ, ਵਧਾਉਂਦੇ ਜਾਣਾ; ~**past** ਸਲਾਮੀ ਦੇਂਦੇ ਲੰਘਣਾ

mare (ਮੇਅ*) *n* ਘੋੜੀ

margin ('ਮਾਜਿਨ) *n v* ਹਾਸ਼ੀਆ ਕਿਨਾਰੀ, ਕੰਨੀ, ਕੋਰ; ਕੰਢਾ, ਕਿਨਾਰਾ; ਗੁੰਜਾਇਸ਼; ਹਾਸ਼ੀਆ ਰੱਖਣਾ, ਹਾਸ਼ੀਆ ਮਾਰਨਾ; ~**al** ਕੰਨੀ ਦਾ; ਹਾਸ਼ੀਏ ਦਾ; ਮਾਮੂਲੀ

marigold ('ਮੈਰਿਗਅਉਲੜ) *n* (ਪੌਦਾ ਜਾਂ ਫੁੱਲ) ਗੋਂਦਾ, ਗੁੱਟਾ

marine (ਮਅ'ਰੀਨ) *n a* ਵਪਾਰੀ ਜਹਾਜ਼; ਜਹਾਜ਼ੀ ਬੇੜਾ; ਜਹਾਜ਼ੀ; ਸਮੁੰਦਰੀ; ~**r** ਮੱਲਾਹ, ਜਹਾਜ਼ੀ, ਜਹਾਜ਼ਰਾਨ

marish ('ਮੈਰਿਸ਼) *n a* ਦਲਦਲ, ਚਿੱਕੜ; ਦਲਦਲੀ

marital ('ਮੈਰਿਟਲ) *a* ਵਿਵਾਹਕ, ਵਿਆਹ-ਸਬੰਧੀ, ਦੰਪਤੀ-ਸਬੰਧੀ

maritime ('ਮੈਰਿਟਾਇਮ) *a* ਸਮੁੰਦਰੀ, ਸਾਗਰੀ, ਸਾਗਰ-ਸਬੰਧੀ

mark (ਮਾਕ) *n v* ਨਿਸ਼ਾਨ; ਅੰਕ, ਚਿੰਨ੍ਹ, ਮੁਹਰ, ਤਮਗ਼ਾ, ਪੱਟਾ; ਬਿੰਦੂ, ਕਲੰਕ, ਦਾਗ਼, ਧੱਬਾ; ਨਿਸ਼ਾਨ ਲਾਉਣਾ; ਨਾਂ ਲਿਖਣਾ; ਮੁਹਰ ਲਾਉਣੀ, ਚਿੰਨ੍ਹ ਲਾਉਣਾ; ਵੇਖਣਾ, ਧਿਆਨ ਕਰਨਾ; (ਫੁਟਬਾਲ); ~**ed** ਵਿਸ਼ਿਸ਼ਟ, ਅੰਕਤ; ਸਪਸ਼ਟ;

market 584 **masque**

~edly ਉਘੇ ਤੌਰ ਤੇ; ~er ਨਿਸ਼ਾਨ ਲਗਾਉਣ ਵਾਲਾ, ਅੰਕਕ; ਮੁਨੀਮ; ~ing ਨਿਸ਼ਾਨ; ਅੰਕਣ; ਰੰਗਣ; ~s manship ਨਿਸ਼ਾਨੇਬਾਜ਼ੀ

market ('ਮਾਕਿਟ) *n v* ਬਜ਼ਾਰ, ਮੰਡੀ, ਮਾਰਕੀਟ; ਖ਼ਰੀਦੋ-ਫ਼ਰੋਖ਼ਤ ਕਰਨਾ, ਬਜ਼ਾਰ ਵਿਚ ਚੀਜ਼ਾਂ ਵੇਚਣਾ-ਖ਼ਰੀਦਣਾ; ~ing ਲੈਣ-ਦੇਣ, ਖ਼ਰੀਦੋ-ਫ਼ਰੋਖ਼ਤ, ਵਪਾਰ

maroon (ਮਅ'ਰੂਨ) *n a v* ਪਟਾਕਾ, ਆਤਸ਼ਬਾਜ਼ੀ; ਉਨਾਬੀ (ਰੰਗ), ਗੁੜ੍ਹਾ ਲਾਲ (ਰੰਗ), ਮੈਰੂਨ (ਰੰਗ); ਅਵਾਰਾਗਰਦੀ ਕਰਨੀ, ਲੋਫਰਾਂ ਵਾਂਗ ਫਿਰਨਾ

marriage ('ਮੈਰਿਜ) *n* ਵਿਵਾਹ, ਸ਼ਾਦੀ, ਨਿਕਾਹ; ਲਾਵਾਂ-ਫੇਰੇ; (ਅਲੰਕਾਰਕ) ਏਕਤਾ, ਸੰਯੋਗ, ਇਤਫ਼ਾਕ; ~procession ਬਰਾਤ, ਜੰਝ, ਜਨੇਤ; civil ~ ਅਦਾਲਤੀ ਸ਼ਾਦੀ

married ('ਮੈਰਿਡ) *a* ਸ਼ਾਦੀ-ਸ਼ੁਦਾ, ਵਿਆਹੁਤਾ, ਵਿਆਹਿਆ; ~ couple ਜੋੜੀ, ਦੰਪਤੀ

marry ('ਮੈਰਿ) *v* ਵਿਆਹੁਣਾ; ਵਿਆਹ ਕਰਨਾ, ਸ਼ਾਦੀ ਕਰਨੀ, ਹੱਥ ਪੀਲੇ ਕਰਨੇ, ਵਰਨਾ; (ਅਲੰਕਾਰਕ) ਅਧਿਕ ਪਿਆਰ ਕਰਨਾ, ਡੂੰਘੇ ਸਬੰਧ ਜੋੜਨੇ

Mars (ਮਾਜ਼) *n* ਮੰਗਲ (ਤਾਰਾ) ਯੁੱਧ ਦਾ ਦੇਵਤਾ

marsh (ਮਾਸ਼) *n* ਖੋਭਾ, ਖੁਭਣ, ਦਲਦਲ, ਦਲਦਲੀ ਜ਼ਮੀਨ; ~iness ਦਲਦਲੀ ਸਥਿਤੀ; ~y ਦਲਦਲੀ, ਖੋਭੇਵਾਲਾ, ਜਿਲਣ ਭਰਿਆ

marshal ('ਮਾਸ਼ਲ) *n v* ਸੈਨਾਪਤੀ, ਮਾਰਸ਼ਲ; ਇਕੱਤਰ ਕਰਨਾ, ਇਕੱਠਾ ਕਰਨਾ; ਕ੍ਰਮਵਾਰ ਰੱਖਣਾ, ਅੱਗੇ ਚੱਲਣਾ; ~ship ਮਾਰਸ਼ਲ ਦਾ ਅਹੁਦਾ, ਸੈਨਾਪਤੀ ਦੀ ਪਦਵੀ

mart (ਮਾਃਟ) *n* ਮੰਡੀ, ਬਜ਼ਾਰ, ਵਪਾਰ ਕੇਂਦਰ; ਨੀਲਾਮੀ ਦਾ ਕੇਂਦਰ

martial (ਮਾ'ਸ਼ਲ) *a* ਜੰਗੀ, ਫ਼ੌਜੀ, ਸੈਨਕ, ਲੜਾਕੂ; ~law ਫ਼ੌਜੀ ਕਾਨੂੰਨ, ਮਾਰਸ਼ਲ ਲਾਅ

martyr ('ਮਾਟਅ*) *n* ਸ਼ਹੀਦ, ਆਤਮ-ਬਲੀਦਾਨੀ ਧਰਮ ਲਈ ਪ੍ਰਾਣ ਦੇਣਾ, ਸ਼ਹੀਦ ਕਰਨਾ, ਆਤਮ-ਬਲੀਦਾਨ ਦੇਣਾ; ~dom ਸ਼ਹੀਦੀ, ਸ਼ਹਾਦਤ, ਆਤਮ-ਬਲੀਦਾਨ

marvel ('ਮਾਵ਼ਲ) *n v* ਕਮਾਲ, ਅਜੂਬਾ, ਅਦਭੁਤ, ਅਸਚਰਜ, ਅਚੰਭਾ, ਹੈਰਾਨ ਹੋਣਾ, ਅਚੰਭੇ ਵਿਚ ਪੈਣਾ; ~lous ਅਜੀਬ, ਅਸਚਰਜ, ਅਦਭੁਤ, ਅਨੋਖਾ, ਅਨੂਠਾ; ~lousness ਅਦਭੁਤੱਤਾ, ਅਸਚਰਜਤਾ ਵਚਿੱਤਰਤਾ, ਅਨੋਖਾਪਣ; ਅਲੌਕਕਤਾ

marxism (ਮਾਕਸਿਜ਼(ਅ)ਮ) *n* ਮਾਰਕਸਵਾਦ

masculine (ਮੈਸਕਯੁਲਿਨ) *a n* ਮਰਦਾਵਾਂ, ਨਰ, ਆਦਮੀ ਜਿਹਾ, ਤਕੜਾ, ਬਲਵਾਨ; ~gender ਪੁਲਿੰਗ

masculinity (ਮੈਸਕਯੁ'ਲਿਨਅਟਿ) *n* ਮਰਦਊਪਨਾ, ਮਰਦਾਨਗੀ, ਪੁਰਸ਼ਤਾ

mash (ਮੈਸ਼)*n v a* ਕਚੂਮਰ, ਭਡਥਾ; ਜੌਂ ਅਤੇ ਗਰਮ ਪਾਣੀ ਦਾ ਘੋਲ, ਘੋੜੇ ਦਾ ਦਾਣਾ ਜਾਂ ਉਬਲਿਆ ਦਲੀਆ; ਫੇਹਣਾ, ਕਚੂਮਰ ਕੱਢਣਾ; ਮੋਹ ਲੈਣਾ; ਜਾਨੀ, ਮਨਮੋਹਕ; ~er ਰੰਗੀਲਾ, ਰਸੀਆ, ਫ਼ੈਲ-ਫ਼ਬੀਲਾ; ਫ਼ੈਲਾ

mask (ਮਾਸਕ) *n v* ਪਰਦਾ, ਨਕਾਬ, ਬੁਰਕਾ, ਕੱਜਣ; (ਅਲੰਕਾਰਕ) ਸਾਂਗ, ਮਖੋਟਾ, ਬਹੁਰੂਪੀਆ; ਨਕਾਬਪੋਸ਼; ਪਰਦਾ ਪਾਉਣਾ, ਕੱਜਣਾ; ਲੁਕਾਉਣਾ; ~ed ਗੁਪਤ, ਭੇਖੀ; ~er masquer ਬਹੁਰੂਪੀਆ, ਨਕਾਬਪੋਸ਼

mason ('ਮੇਇਸਨ) *n* ਰਾਜ, ਚਿਣਾਈਗਰ, ਸੰਗਤਰਾਸ਼

masque (ਮਾਸਕ) *n* ਮੂਕ ਰਾਸਲੀਲਾ; ~rade

ਮਝੌਟੀ ਨਾਚ; ਦਿਖਾਵਾ, ਭੇਖ

mass (ਮੈਸ) *n v* ਪੂਜਾ-ਸਮਾਰੋਹ; ਢੇਰ, ਪੁੰਜ, ਸਮੂਹ; ਇਕੱਠ, ਇਕੱਠੇ ਹੋਣਾ; ਢੇਰ ਲਾਉਣਾ

massacre (ਮੈਸਅਕਅ*) *n v* ਖ਼ੂਨ-ਖ਼ਰਾਬਾ, ਕਤਲਾਮ, ਹੱਤਿਆ, ਤਬਾਹੀ, ਕਤਲ; ਖ਼ੂਨ-ਖ਼ਰਾਬਾ ਕਰਨਾ, ਕਤਲਾਮ ਕਰਨਾ, ਹੱਤਿਆ ਕਰਨੀ

massage (ਮੈਸਾਯ਼) *n v* ਮਾਲਸ਼ (ਸਰੀਰ ਦੀ); ਮਾਲਸ਼ ਕਰਨੀ, ਹੱਥ-ਪੈਰ ਦਬਾਉਣਾ

masseur, masseuse (ਮੈ'ਸਅ:, ਮੈ'ਸਅ:ਜ਼) *n* ਮਾਲਸ਼ੀ, ਮਾਲਸ਼ੀਆ

massive (ਮੈਸਿਵ਼) *a* ਭਾਰੀ, ਵੱਡਾ, ਭਾਰਾ, ਵਜ਼ਨੀ, ਠੋਸ, ਸਥੂਲ; ਸ਼ਾਨਦਾਰ; ਵਿਸ਼ਾਲ (ਗ੍ਰੰਥ); **~ness** ਸਥੂਲਤਾ, ਵਿਸ਼ਾਲਤਾ

mast (ਮਾਸਟ) *n* ਬੱਲੀ, ਸ਼ਤੀਰ, ਮਸਤੂਲ

master (ਮਾਸਟਅ*) *n v* ਮਾਲਕ, ਆਕਾ, ਵਪਾਰਕ ਜਹਾਜ਼ ਦਾ ਕਪਤਾਨ, ਹਾਕਮ, ਉਸਤਾਦ, ਸਿਖਿਅਕ, ਮਾਸਟਰ; ਜਿੱਤ ਲੈਣਾ, ਅਧੀਨ ਕਰਨਾ, ਹੁਕਮ ਚਲਾਉਣਾ, ਵਿਸ਼ੇਸ਼ਗਤਾ ਬਟਣਾ, ਮੁਹਾਰਤ ਪ੍ਰਾਪਤ ਕਰਨੀ, ਚੰਗੀ ਤਰ੍ਹਾਂ ਸਿੱਖ ਲੈਣਾ; **~piece** ਸ਼ਾਹਕਾਰ; **~ly** ਨਿਪੁੰਨ, ਪ੍ਰਵੀਨ, ਕਮਾਲ ਦੀ; ਅਦੁੱਤੀ, ਅਤਿ ਉੱਤਮ; **~y** ਮੁਹਾਰਤ; ਹਕੂਮਤ, ਕਾਰੀਗੀਰੀ; ਕਾਬੂ; ਪ੍ਰਭੂਤਾ, ਅਧਿਕਾਰ, ਕਾਬੂ

masturbate (ਮੈਸਟਅਬੇਇਟ) *v* ਮੁੱਠ ਮਾਰਨੀ, ਹੱਥਰਸੀ ਕਰਨੀ, ਹਸਤ-ਮੈਥਨ ਕਰਨਾ

masturbation (ਮੈਸਟਅ'ਬੇਇਸ਼ਨ) *n* ਮੁੱਠਬਾਜ਼ੀ, ਹੱਥਰਸੀ, ਹਸਤ-ਮੈਥਨ

mat, matt (ਮੈਟ) *a v n* ਮੱਧਮ, ਮੈਲਾ; ਮੈਲਾ ਕਰਨਾ, ਚਮਕ ਮਾਰਨਾ; ਸੜ ਵਿਛਾਉਣੀ, ਫ਼ਰਸ਼ੀ ਪਾਉਣੀ; ਚਟਾਈ, ਟਾਟ, ਸੜ; **~ting** ਚਟਾਈ ਬਣਾਉਣ ਦਾ ਕੰਮ; **~tress** ਫ਼ਰਸ਼ੀ, ਗੱਦਾ

matador (ਮੈਟਅਡੋ*) *n* ਸਾਨ੍ਹਮੱਲ, ਸਾਨ੍ਹ ਨਾਲ ਲੜਨ ਵਾਲਾ ਪਹਿਲਵਾਨ; ਤਾਸ਼ ਦਾ ਵੱਡਾ ਪੱਤਾ

match (ਮੈਚ) *n v* (1) ਮਾਚਸ, ਅੱਗ ਬਾਲਣ ਵਾਲੀ ਤੀਲੀ; ਪਲੀਤਾ; (2) ਮੈਚ, ਖੇਡ, ਟਾਕਰਾ; ਜੋੜ, ਮੁਕਾਬਲੇ ਦਾ; (3) ਨਾਤਾ, ਵਿਆਹ-ਸਬੰਧ; ਵਰ (ਲਾੜਾ ਜਾਂ ਲਾੜੀ), ਜੋੜਾ; ਵਾਰੇ ਆਉਣਾ, ਬਰਾਬਰ ਹੋਣਾ, ਜੋੜ ਦਾ ਹੋਣਾ, ਮੇਲ ਮਿਲਾਉਣਾ; ਟੱਕਰਨਾ, ਭਿੜਨਾ, ਮਿਲਣਾ; ਵਿਆਹ ਕਰਾਉਣਾ; **~box** ਤੀਲੀਆਂ ਦੀ ਡੱਬੀ; **~ed** ਵਿਆਹਤ, ਅਨੁਰੂਪ, ਸੁਮੇਲ, ਮੇਲ ਖਾਂਦਾ ਹੋਇਆ; **~ing** ਸੁਮੇਲ, ਤੁੱਲ, ਢੁੱਕਵਾਂ; **~less** ਅਨੁਪਮ, ਅਤੁੱਲ, ਅਦੁੱਤੀ, ਅਨੋਖਾ; **~lessness** ਅਨੁਪਮਤਾ, ਅਨ-ਅਨੁਰੂਪਤਾ, ਅਤੁਲਨੀਅਤ

mate (ਮੇਇਟ) *n v* ਮਿੱਤਰ, ਸਖਾ, ਸਖੀ, ਯਾਰ, ਦੋਸਤ, ਸਹੇਲੀ, ਹਮਜੋਲੀ, ਸੰਗੀ, ਸਾਥੀ, ਜੀਵਨ ਸਾਥੀ; ਮੁਖੀਆ, ਜਹਾਜ਼ ਦਾ ਮੇਟ; ਜੋੜੇ ਦਾ ਮਿਲਣਾ, ਜੋੜੇ ਦਾ ਮਿਲਾਉਣਾ, ਸਾਥੀ ਬਣਾਉਣਾ, ਸੰਗ ਕਰਨਾ; ਵਿਆਹ ਹੋਣਾ

mater (ਮੇਇਟਅ*) *n* ਅੰਮਾ, ਮਾਂ, ਮਾਤਾ

material (ਮਅ'ਟਿਅਰਿਅਲ) *n a* ਸਾਮਾਨ, ਸਮਗਰੀ, ਮਾਲ, ਵਸਤੂ, ਭੌਤਕ ਦ੍ਰਵ; ਸਥੂਲ, ਪਟਾਧਕ, ਭੌਤਕ, ਸੰਸਾਰਕ, ਦੁਨੀਆਵੀ, ਮਾਇਕ; **~ism** ਪਦਾਰਥਵਾਦ, ਮਾਦਾ-ਪਰਸਤੀ; ਜੜ੍ਹਵਾਦ, ਅਨਾਤਮਵਾਦ; ਭੌਤਕਵਾਦੀ; **~ist** ਭੌਤਕਵਾਦੀ, ਪਦਾਰਥਵਾਦੀ, ਮਾਦਾਵਾਦੀ, ਜੜ੍ਹਵਾਦੀ; **~istic** ਭੌਤਕਵਾਦੀ, ਪਦਾਰਥਵਾਦੀ; **~ize** ਸਾਕਾਰ ਕਰਨਾ, ਭੌਤਕ ਰੂਪ ਪ੍ਰਦਾਨ ਕਰਨਾ

maternal (ਮਅ'ਟਅ:ਨਲ) *a* ਮਾਤਰੀ, ਨਾਨਕੀ, ਮਾਂ ਦੇ ਰਿਸ਼ਤੇ ਦਾ; **~grand father** ਨਾਨਾ; **~uncle** ਮਾਮਾ, ਮਾਸੜ

maternity (ਮਅ'ਟਅ:ਨਅਟਿ) *n* ਜਣੇਪਾ; ਪ੍ਰਸੂਤ;

~home ਵਿਆਮਸ਼ਾਲਾ, ਪ੍ਰਸੂਤ-ਘਰ; ~nurse ਦਾਈ, ਨਰਸ

mathematical (ਮੈਥਅ'ਮੈਟਿਕਲ) *a* ਗਣਿਤਕ, ਗਣਿਤ-ਸ਼ਾਸਤਰੀ, ਹਿਸਾਬੀ, ਗਣਿਤੀ, ਸਖਿਰ, ਨਿਸ਼ਚਤ; ~ly ਗਣਿਤ ਅਨੁਸਾਰ, ਹਿਸਾਬ ਦੇ ਨੁਕਤੇ ਤੋਂ

mathematician (ਮੈਥ(ਅ)ਮਅ'ਟਿਸ਼ਨ) *n* ਗਣਿਤਸਾਸ਼ਤਰੀ, ਹਿਸਾਬਦਾਨ

mathematics (ਮੈਥ(ਅ)'ਮੈਟਿਕਸ) *n* ਹਿਸਾਬ, ਗਣਿਤ-ਸ਼ਾਸਤਰ, ਗਣਿਤ, ਗਣਨਾ

matin ('ਮੈਟਿਨ) *n pl a* ਪ੍ਰਾਤਕਾਲ, ਅੰਮ੍ਰਿਤ-ਵੇਲਾ

matinee (ਮੈਟਿਨੇਇ) *n* ਲੌਢੇ ਵੇਲੇ ਦਾ ਤਮਾਸ਼ਾ (ਸਿਨਮੇ ਜਾਂ ਥੀਏਟਰ ਦਾ)

matins (ਮੈਟਿਨਜ਼) *n* ਪ੍ਰਾਤਕਾਲ ਦੀ ਪ੍ਰਾਰਥਨਾ

matriarch (ਮੇਇਟਰਿਆਕ) *n* ਰਾਜ ਮਾਤਾ, ਪ੍ਰਧਾਨ ਇਸਤਰੀ; ~al ਮਾਤਾ ਪ੍ਰਧਾਨ (ਸਮਾਜ); ~y ਮਾਤਰੀ-ਰਾਜ, ਇਸਤਰੀ-ਪ੍ਰਧਾਨ ਸਮਾਜ

matricide (ਮੈਟਰਿ'ਸਾਇਡ) *n* ਮਾਤ-ਹੱਤਿਆ, ਮਾਤਰ ਘਾਤੀ, ਮਾਤਰ-ਘਾਤਕ, ਮਾਂ ਦਾ ਕਤਲ

matriculate (ਮਅ'ਟਰਿਕਯੁਲੇਇਟ) *n a* ਮੈਟਰਿਕ ਪਾਸ ਵਿਦਿਆਰਥੀ; ਦਸਵੀਂ ਦਰਜਾ ਪਾਸ

matrimonial (ਮੈਟਰਿ'ਮਅਉਨਯਅਲ) *n a* ਵਿਵਾਹਕ, ਵਿਆਹ-ਸਬੰਧੀ

matrimony (ਮੈਟਰਿਮ(ਅ)ਨਿ) *n* ਵਿਆਹ, ਸ਼ਾਦੀ

matrix ('ਮੇਇਟਰਿਕਸ) *n* ਕੁੱਖ, ਬੱਚੇਦਾਨੀ, (ਛਾਪੇ ਦਾ) ਸੰਚਾ, ਕਾਲਬ

matron (ਮੇਇਟਰ(ਅ)ਨ) *n* ਵਿਆਹੁਤਾ ਨਾਰੀ, ਮਾਈ; ਮਾਤਾ, ਪ੍ਰਧਾਨ ਪ੍ਰਚਾਰਕਾ, ਦਾਈ; ਦਵਾਈਖਾਨੇ ਦੀ ਨਿਗਰਾਨ; ਸਕੂਲ ਦੀ ਪ੍ਰਬੰਧਕ ਮੈਟਰਨ; ~age ਗ੍ਰਹਿਣੀ-ਪਦ, ਦਾਈਪੁਣਾ

matter (ਮੈਟਅ*) *n v* ਪਦਾਰਥ, ਵਿਸ਼ੈ-ਵਸਤੂ, ਵਿਚਾਰ-ਸਮਗਰੀ; ਸਾਰ, ਪੁਸਤਕ-ਸਾਰ; ਪ੍ਰਕਰਨ, ਮਾਮਲਾ

maturation (ਮੈਟਯੁ'ਰੇਇਸ਼ਨ) *n* ਪਕਿਆਈ, ਪਰਿਪੱਕਤਾ; ਪ੍ਰੌੜ੍ਹਤਾ, ਸਿਆਣਪ

mature (ਮਅ'ਟਯੁਅ*) *a n v* ਪੱਕਾ, ਭਰਵਾਂ, ਪੱਕਿਆ; ਗੱਭਰੂ, ਬਾਲਗ, ਪੂਰੀ ਹੋਈ, ਗੱਭਰੂ ਹੋਣਾ, ਬਾਲਗ ਜਾਂ ਮੁਟਿਆਰ ਹੋਣਾ; ~ness, maturity ਪਕਿਆਈ, ਪ੍ਰੌੜ੍ਹਤਾ, ਪੱਕੀ ਉਮਰ, ਸਿਆਣੀ ਉਮਰ, ਪਰਿਪੱਕਤਾ

mausoleum (ਮੋਸਅ'ਲਿਅਮ) *n* ਦੇਹਰਾ, ਸਮਾਧ, ਮਕਬਰਾ, ਰੋਜ਼ਾ

maxim (ਮੈਕਸਿਮ) *n* (ਪ੍ਰਸਿੱਧ) ਲੋਕੋਕਤੀ, ਕਹਾਵਤ, ਅਖੌਤ, ਨੀਤੀ-ਵਚਨ, ਤੱਤ, ਸੂਤਰ, ਸਿਧਾਂਤ; ~al ਅਧਿਕਤਮ

maximum (ਮੈਕਸਿਮਮ) *n* ਵੱਧ ਤੋਂ ਵੱਧ, ਅਧਿਕਤਮ

May (ਮੇਇ) *v aux n* ਸੰਭਵ ਹੋਣਾ, ਕਰ ਸਕਣਾ; (1) ਮਈ, ਅੰਗਰੇਜ਼ੀ ਸਾਲ ਦਾ ਪੰਜਵਾਂ ਮਹੀਨਾ; (2) ਬਹਾਰ, ਨਵ-ਜੋਬਨ, ਭਰ-ਜਵਾਨੀ; ਕੁਮਾਰੀ, ਕੁਆਰੀ, ਬਾਲਾ; ~day ਪਹਿਲੀ ਮਈ ਦਾ ਦਿਨ, ਮਈ ਦਿਵਸ, ਕਿਰਤੀ ਦਿਵਸ

mayor (ਮੇਅ*) *n* ਮੇਅਰ, ਨਗਰ-ਨਾਇਕ, ਨਗਰਪਤੀ

maze (ਮੇਇਜ਼) *n v* ਭੁੱਲ-ਭੁੱਲਈਆ, ਭੰਵਰਜਾਲ, ਜੰਜਾਲ, ਉਲਝਨ, ਗੁੰਝਲ, ਗੋਰਖ-ਧੰਦਾ; ਵਿਆਕੁਲ

mazy (ਮੇਇਜ਼ੀ) *a* ਗੁੰਝਲਦਾਰ, ਵਲੇਵੇਂਦਾਰ, ਕੁਟਲ, ਜਟਿਲ

meadow (ਮੈਡਅਉ) *n* ਚਰਾਗਾਹ, ਸਬਜ਼ਾਜ਼ਾਰ, ਤਰਾਈ, ਉਪਜਾਊ ਜ਼ਮੀਨ

meagre ('ਮੀਗਅ*) a ਥੋੜ੍ਹਾ, ਘੱਟ, ਪਤਲਾ, ਲਿੱਸਾ; ਅਧੂਰਾ, ਅਪੂਰਨ; ~**ness** ਥੁੜ੍ਹ, ਘਾਟ, ਪਤਲਾਪਨ, ਅਪੂਰਨਤਾ, ਊਣਾ

meal (ਮੀਲ) n v ਖਾਣਾ, ਭੋਜਨ, ਆਹਾਰ; ਮੈਦਾ, ਆਟਾ, ਸੱਤੂ; ਰੋਟੀ ਖਾਣੀ, ਭੋਜਨ ਕਰਨਾ

mean (ਮੀਨ) n v (ਗਣਿ) ਮੱਧਮਾਨ, ਔਸਤ, ਮੱਧਵਰਤੀ; ਸਾਧਨ, ਉਪਾਉ; ਉਦੇਸ਼ ਰੱਖਣਾ, ਅਰਥ ਹੋਣਾ, ਭਾਵ ਹੋਣਾ; ਚਾਹੁਣਾ, ਅਰਥ ਕਰਨਾ, ਸੂਚਤ ਕਰਨਾ, ਪਰਗਟ ਕਰਨਾ; **by all ~s** ਅਵੱਸ਼ ਹੀ, ਹਰ ਤਰ੍ਹਾਂ ਨਾਲ; **by no ~s** ਕਿਸੇ ਤਰ੍ਹਾਂ ਵੀ ਨਹੀਂ; ~**time** ਏਧਰ, ਇੰਨੇ ਵਿਚ; ~**while** ਇਸ ਸਮੇਂ ਵਿਚ, ਇੰਨੇ ਨੂੰ; ~**ness** ਨੀਚਤਾ, ਹੋਛਾਪਣ, ਕਮੀਨਪਣ; ~**ing** ਅਰਥ, ਭਾਵ, ਮਤਲਬ, ਪ੍ਰਯੋਜਨ, ਤਾਤਪਰਜ; ~**ingful** ਅਰਥਪੂਰਣ; ~**ingless** ਨਿਰਰਥਕ, ਅਰਥਹੀਨ

meander (ਮਿ'ਐਂਡਅ*) n v (ਬ ਵ) ਚੱਕਰ, ਭੁੱਲ-ਭੁਲਈਆਂ; ਵਿੰਗਵਲਾਵੇਂ ਵਾਲਾ ਰਾਹ; ਚੱਕਰਦਾਰ ਯਾਤਰਾ; ਪੇਚ, ਮੋੜ, ਕੁਟਲਤਾ; ਚੱਕਰ ਖਾਣਾ, ਅਵਾਰਾਗਰਦੀ ਕਰਨੀ, ਫਿਰਦੇ ਰਹਿਣਾ; ~**ed** ਭੁੱਲ-ਭੁਲੇਈਆਂ ਵਾਲਾ, ਮੋੜਦਾਰ, ਵਿੰਗ-ਤੜਿੰਗਾ

measles (ਮੀਜ਼ਲਜ਼) n pl ਖਸਰਾ, ਧੱਸਲ; ਛੋਟੀ ਚੇਚਕ, ਦੇਵੀ, ਛੋਟੀ ਸੀਤਲਾ; ਫਫੋਲੇ

measurable (ਮੈਂਹ੍ਅਰਅਬਲ) a ਮਾਪਣ ਯੋਗ, ਨਾਪਣ ਯੋਗ; ਅਨੁਮਾਨ ਯੋਗ

measure (ਮੈਂਯਅ*) n v ਮਾਪ, ਨਾਪ, ਪੈਮਾਨਾ, ਤੋਲ, ਮਾਤਰਾ; ਮਾਪਕ, ਫ਼ੀਤਾ; ਉਪਾਉ, ਕੰਮ; ਮਾਪਣ ਦਾ ਢੰਗ, ਅਨੁਮਾਨ, ਅੰਦਾਜ਼ਾ; ਨਾਪਣਾ, ਪੈਮਾਇਸ਼ ਕਰਨੀ, ਤੋਲਣਾ, (ਕੱਪੜਿਆਂ ਲਈ) ਨਾਪ ਲੈਣਾ, ਮੇਚ ਲੈਣਾ; ਅਜ਼ਮਾਉਣਾ; ਕੱਛਣਾ; ~**d** ਮਾਪਿਆ ਤੋਲਿਆ; ਸੰਤੁਲਤ, ਧਿਆਨ; ~**ment** ਪੈਮਾਇਸ਼, ਨਾਪ, ਮਾਪ, ਅਨੁਮਾਨ

meat (ਮੀਟ) n ਮਾਸ, ਗੋਸ਼ਤ; ~**less** ਨਿਰਮਾਸ, ਮਾਸ ਰਹਿਤ

mechanic (ਮਿ'ਕੈਨਿਕ) n ਕਾਰੀਗਰ, ਮਿਸਤਰੀ, ਮਸ਼ੀਨਸਾਜ਼; ਮਕੈਨਿਕ; ~**al** ਮਕਾਨਕੀ, ਮਸ਼ੀਨੀ, ਜੰਤਰਕ ਵਿਗਿਆਨ ਸਬੰਧੀ; ~**ally** ਜੰਤਰਵਤ, ਮਸ਼ੀਨ ਵਾਂਗ; ~**s** ਜੰਤਰ-ਵਿਗਿਆਨ, ਮਸ਼ੀਨ ਬਣਾਉਣ, ਜੰਤਰ-ਸ਼ਾਸਤਰ

mechanism ('ਮੈਕਅਨਿਜ਼(ਅ)ਮ) n ਜੰਤਰ-ਵਿਧੀ, ਬਣਤਰ, ਪੁਰਜ਼ੇ; ਰਚਨਾ

mechanist ('ਮੈਕਅਨਿਸਟ) n ਕਾਰੀਗਰ, ਮਸ਼ੀਨ ਬਣਾਉਣ ਵਾਲਾ; ਜੰਤਰ-ਵਿਗਿਆਨੀ

mechanization (ਮੈਂ'ਕਅਨਾਇ'ਜ਼ੇਇਸ਼ਨ) n ਮਸ਼ੀਨੀਕਰਨ, ਜੰਤਰੀਕਰਨ

mechanize (ਮੈਂ'ਕਅਨਾਇਜ਼) v ਮਸ਼ੀਨ ਵਾਂਗ ਬਣਾਉਣਾ, ਜੰਤਰ-ਪ੍ਰਯੋਗ ਕਰਨਾ; ~**d** ਜੰਤਰ-ਛਿਤ, ਜੰਤਰ-ਚਾਲਤ

medal (ਮੈਂਡਲ) n ਮੈਡਲ, ਤਮਗਾ, ਤਕਮਾ

meddle (ਮੈਂਡਲ) v ਦਖ਼ਲ ਦੇਣਾ, ਟੰਗ ਅੜਾਉਣੀ

meddling (ਮੈਂਡਲਿਙ) a ਵਿਘਨਕਾਰਕ

media (ਮੀਡਿਅ) n ਸੰਚਾਰ ਸਾਧਨ; ~**n** ਮੱਧ, ਮੱਧਵਰਤੀ, ਦਰਮਿਆਨੀ; ਮੱਧਮ, ਮਾਧਿਅਕ; ~**te** ਮੱਧ-ਵਰਤੀ, ਮਧਿਅਸਥ, ਮੱਧ-ਸਥਿਤ; ਵਿਚ ਪੈਣਾ, ਸਮਝੌਤਾ ਕਰਾਉਣਾ, ਵਸੀਲਾ ਬਣਨਾ, ਮਧਿਅਸਥ ਬਣਨਾ; ~**tion** ਮਧਿਅਸਥਤਾ, ਸਾਲਸੀ; ~**tor** ਮਧਿਅਸਥ, ਵਿਚੋਲਾ, ਸਾਲਸ

medieval, mediaeval (ਮੈਂਡਿ'ਈਵ਼ਲ) a ਮੱਧਕਾਲੀਨ, ਮੱਧ-ਯੁਗੀ, ਮੱਧ-ਕਾਲ ਦਾ; ~**ism**

medical | 588 | **melt**

ਮੱਧਕਾਲੀਨਤਾ, ਮੱਧਯੁਗੀਨਤਾ, ਮੱਧਕਾਲੀਨ ਰੀਤਾਂ

medical (ਮੈਡਿਕਲ) *a n* ਚਿਕਿਤਸਕੀ, ਡਾਕਟਰੀ; ਔਸ਼ਧੀ; ਚਿਕਿਤਸਾ ਸਬੰਧੀ

medicate (ਮੈਡਿਕੇਟ) *v* ਦਵਾ ਦੇਣਾ, ਦਵਾ-ਦਾਰੂ ਕਰਨਾ, ਦਵਾਈ ਕਰਨੀ, ਇਲਾਜ ਕਰਨਾ; ਦਵਾਈ ਮਿਲਾਉਣੀ

mediocre (ਮੀਡਿ'ਅਉਕਅ*) *a* (ਵਿਅਕਤੀ) ਸਧਾਰਨ, ਵਿਚਕਾਰਲਾ, ਮਾਮੂਲੀ, ਔਸਤ ਦਰਜੇ

meditate (ਮੈਡਿਟੇਇਟ) *v* ਲਿਵਲੀਨ ਹੋਣਾ, ਧਿਆਨ ਲਾਉਣਾ, ਮਗਨ ਹੋਣਾ, ਵਿਚਾਰਨਾ, ਇਕਾਗਰ ਚਿੱਤ ਹੋਣਾ, ਸਮਾਧੀ ਲਾਉਣੀ; **~d** ਚਿੰਤਤ, ਨਿਰਧਾਰਤ

meditation (ਮੈਡਿਟੇਇਸ਼ਨ) *n* ਧਿਆਨ, ਮਨਨ, ਚਿੰਤਨ, ਮਗਨਤਾ, ਇਕਾਗਰਤਾ, ਸਮਾਧੀ, ਅਰਾਧਨਾ; **~ness** ਮਗਨਸ਼ੀਲਤਾ, ਚਿਤੰਨਸ਼ੀਲਤਾ, ਧਿਆਨਸ਼ੀਲਤਾ, ਵਿਚਾਰ ਮਗਨਤਾ, ਲਿਵਲੀਨਤਾ

meditator (ਮੈਡਿਟੇਇਟਅ*) *n* ਧਿਆਨੀ, ਮਨਨ ਕਰਤਾ, ਚਿੰਤਕ

medium (ਮੀਡ੍ਯਅਮ) *n a* ਮਾਧਿਅਮ; ਵਿਚਲਾ ਗੁਣ, ਵਿਚਲਾ-ਮੇਲ, ਵਿਚਲਾ ਦਰਜਾ, ਵਿਚਲੀ ਚੀਜ਼; ਸਾਧਨ, ਵਸੀਲਾ, ਮਾਰਗ

meek (ਮੀਕ) *a* ਨਿਰਮਾਣ, ਮਸਕੀਨ, ਨਿਮਾਣਾ, ਦੀਨ, ਸ਼ਾਂਤ, ਬੇਜ਼ਬਾਨ; **~ly** ਨਿਮਰਤਾ ਪੂਰਬਕ, ਚੁਪਚਾਪ

meet (ਮੀਟ) *n a v* ਇਕੱਤਰਤਾ, ਜੋੜ-ਮੇਲ, ਇਕੱਠ; ਮੀਟਿੰਗ; ਉਚਿਤ, ਯੋਗ, ਠੀਕ, ਉਪਯੁਕਤ; ਮਿਲਣਾ, ਮੇਲ ਹੋਣਾ, ਜਾਣ-ਪਛਾਣ ਕਰਨੀ; ਗ੍ਰਹਿਣ ਕਰਨਾ, ਪ੍ਰਾਪਤ ਕਰਨਾ; **~ing** ਸਮਾਗਮ, ਜਲਸਾ, ਸਭਾ, ਸੰਮੇਲਨ, ਗੋਸ਼ਠੀ, ਇਕੱਠ; ਮਿਲਾਵਾ, ਸੰਗਮ

mega (ਮੈਗਅ) *a* ਮਹਾਂ, ਵਿਸ਼ਾਲ, ਵੱਡਾ

melancholic (ਮੈੱਲਅਨ'ਕੌਲਿਕ) *a* ਉਦਾਸ, ਵਿਸ਼ਾਦੀ, ਦਿਲਗੀਰ

melancholy (ਮੈੱਲਅਨਕਅਲਿ) *n a* ਵਿਸ਼ਾਦ, ਚਿੰਤਾ, ਉਦਾਸੀ, ਦਿਲਗੀਰੀ

melee (ਮੈੱਲੇਇ) (F) *n* ਮੁੱਠ-ਭੇੜ, ਝਪਟ, ਲੜਾਈ, ਸੰਗਰਾਮ, ਝਗੜਾ, ਦੰਗਾ

mellorate (ਮੀਲਿਅਰੇਇਟ) *v* ਸੁਧਾਰਨਾ, ਸੰਵਾਰਨਾ, ਚੰਗਾ ਬਣਾਉਣਾ, ਬਿਹਤਰ ਬਣਾਉਣਾ; ਸੁਧਰਨਾ

melioration (ਮੀਲਿਅ'ਰੇਇਸ਼ਨ) *n* ਸੁਧਾਰ, ਉੱਨਤੀ, ਚੰਗਿਆਈ

mellow (ਮੈੱਲਅਉ) *a* ਰਸੀਲਾ, ਨਰਮ, ਰਸਿਆ (ਫ਼ਲ), ਮਿੱਠਾ, ਪੱਕਿਆ ਹੋਇਆ; ਕੁਸ਼ੀ, ਮੱਧਮ, ਮਿਲਾਪੜਾ, ਖ਼ੁਸ਼ ਮਿਜਾਜ; ਕੋਮਲ ਬਣਾਉਣਾ, ਪ੍ਰਸੰਨ ਕਰਨਾ; ਪੱਕਣਾ; ਰਸਣਾ; **~ness** ਕੋਮਲਤਾ, ਰਸੀਲਾਪਨ, ਮਤਵਾਲਾਪਨ; **~y** ਕੋਮਲ, ਰਸੀਲਾ, ਮਧੁਰ; ਪੱਕਿਆ

melodic (ਮਿ'ਲੌਡਿਕ) *a* ਮਧੁਰ, ਮਿੱਠਾ, ਸੁਰੀਲਾ

melodious (ਮਿ'ਲਅਉਡਿਅਸ) *a* ਸੁਰੀਲਾ, ਮਧੁਰ, ਸੰਗੀਤਮਈ, ਰਸੀਲਾ, ਮਿੱਠਾ

melodrama ('ਮੈੱਲਅ(ਉ)ਡਰਾਮਅ) *n* ਅਤੀ ਭਾਵੁਕਤਾ ਭਰਪੂਰ ਨਾਟਕ, ਸਨਸਨੀ ਭਰਿਆ ਨਾਟਕ; ਸੰਗੀਤਮਈ ਨਾਟਕ

melody (ਮੈੱਲਅਡਿ) *n* ਧੁਨ; ਸੁਰੀਲਾ ਗੀਤ ਤਰਾਨਾ

melon (ਮੈੱਲਅਨ) *n* ਖੱਖੜੀ, ਫੁੱਟ, ਖਰਬੂਜਾ

melt (ਮੈੱਲਟ) *n v* ਪਿਘਲੀ ਧਾਤ; ਪਿਘਲਣਾ, ਪੰਘਰਨਾ; ਘੁਲਣਾ; ਪਸੀਜਣਾ, ਢਲਣਾ; ਰੋਣ ਲਗਣਾ; (ਧੁਨੀ ਦਾ) ਕੋਮਲ ਹੋਣਾ; **~away** ਘੁਲਣਾ, ਪਿਘਲ ਜਾਣਾ; **~into tears** ਫਿਸ

| melting | merchandise |

ਪੈਣਾ, ਰੋ ਪੈਣਾ

melting (ਮੈਲਟਿਙ) *n a* ਦ੍ਰਵਣ, ਗਲਣ, ਪਿਘਲਣ, ਪਿਘਲਾਉਣ, ਦ੍ਰਵਣਸ਼ੀਲ, ਗਲਦਾ; ~**point** ਦ੍ਰਵ ਅੰਕ, ਪਿਘਲਣ ਅੰਕ; ~**pot** ਕੁਠਾਲੀ

member ('ਮੈਮਬਅ*) *n* ਸਦੱਸ, ਸਭਾ-ਸਦੱਸ; ਭਾਗ, ਅੰਸ਼, ਅੰਗ (ਖ਼ਾਸ ਕਰਕੇ ਹੱਥ ਪੈਰ); ~**ship** ਸਦੱਸਤਾ

membrane (ਮੈੱਮਬਰੇਇਨ) *n* ਝਿੱਲੀ, ਪਰਦਾ

membranous (ਮੈੱਮ'ਬਰੇਇਨਅਸ) *a* ਝਿੱਲੀਦਾਰ

memo (ਮੈੱਮਅਉ) *n* ਯਾਦ-ਪੱਤਰ, ਸਿਮਰਤੀ-ਪੱਤਰ, ਯਾਦਗਾਰ, ਸਮਾਰਕ

memoir (ਮੈੱਮਵਾ:) *n* ਬਿਰਤਾਂਤ, ਵਿਵਰਣ; ਯਾਦਦਾਸ਼ਤ, ਸੰਸਮਰਣ, ਨਿਜੀ ਗਿਆਨ

memorable (ਮੈੱਮ(ਅ)ਰਅਬਲ) *a* ਯਾਦਗਾਰੀ, ਨਾਮਵਰ, ਪ੍ਰਸਿੱਧ, ਮਸ਼ਹੂਰ

memorandum (ਮੈੱਮਅ'ਰੈਂਡਅਮ) *n* ਯਾਦਦਾਸ਼ਤ, ਸਿਮਰਤੀ-ਪੱਤਰ; (ਕਾ) ਦਸਤਾਵੇਜ਼; ਪੱਤਰ, ਯਾਦ-ਪੱਤਰ

memorial (ਮਅ'ਮੋਰਿਅਲ) *n a* ਯਾਦਗਾਰ, ਸਿਮਰਤੀ ਚਿੰਨ੍ਹ, ਸਮਾਰਕ; ਯਾਦਗਾਰੀ ਲੇਖ

memorize (ਮੈੱਮਅਰਾਇਜ਼) *v* ਯਾਦ ਕਰਨਾ, ਚੇਤੇ ਕਰਨਾ

memory (ਮੈੱਮਅਰਿ) *n* ਚੇਤਾ, ਯਾਦ, ਯਾਦਦਾਸ਼ਤ, ਸਿਮਰਤੀ

menace (ਮੈੱਨਅਸ) *n v* ਧਮਕੀ, ਡਰਾਵਾ, ਖ਼ਤਰਾ; ਧਮਕਾਉਣਾ, ਡਰਾਉਣਾ, ਖ਼ਤਰੇ ਵਿਚ ਪਾਉਣਾ

mend (ਮੈੰਡ) *v n* ਸੁਧਾਰਨਾ ਜਾਂ ਸੁਧਰਨਾ, ਠੀਕ ਕਰਨਾ ਜਾਂ ਹੋਣਾ, ਸੋਧ ਕਰਨੀ, ਸੰਵਾਰਨਾ, ਮੁਰੰਮਤ ਕਰਨਾ; ਗੰਢਣਾ-ਤਰੁਪਣਾ; ~**able** ਸੌਂਪਣ ਯੋਗ, ਮੁਰੰਮਤ ਲਾਇਕ; ~**ing** ਸੁਧਾਰ,

ਉਧਾਰ, ਮੁਰੰਮਤ

mendicant (ਮੈੰਡਿਕਅੰਟ) *n* ਫ਼ਕੀਰ, ਜਾਚਕ, ਮੰਗਤਾ,

menial (ਮੀਨਯਅਲ) *n a* ਕੰਮੀ, ਕਮੀਨ, ਘਰੇਲੂ ਨੌਕਰ, ਸੇਵਕ, ਦਾਸ; ਨੌਕਰ-ਚਾਕਰ; ਹੀਣਾ, ਨੀਵਾਂ, ਨੀਚ

meningitis (ਮੈਨਿਨ'ਜਾਇਟਿਸ) *n* ਗਰਦਨ-ਤੋੜ ਬੁਖ਼ਾਰ; ਦਿਮਾਗ਼ ਦੇ. ਨੇੜੇ ਸੋਜ ਹੋ ਜਾਣ ਦਾ ਰੋਗ

menses (ਮੈੱਨਸੀਜ਼) *n pl* ਮਾਹਵਾਰੀ, ਮਾਸਕ ਧਰਮ

menstruate (ਮੈੱਨਸਟਰੁ'ਏਇਟ) *n* ਮਾਹਵਾਰੀ ਆਉਣੀ

menstruation (ਮੈੱਨਸਟਰੁ'ਏਇਸ਼ਨ) *n* ਮਾਹਵਾਰੀ, ਮਾਸਕ ਧਰਮ

mensuration (ਮੈੱਨਸ੍ਯੁਅ'ਰੇਇਸ਼ਨ) *n* ਜ਼ਮੀਨ ਦੀ ਪੈਮਾਇਸ਼, ਮਾਪ

mental (ਮੈੱਨਟਲ) *a* ਦਿਮਾਗ਼ੀ, ਮਾਨਸਕ; ~**ity** ਸੁਭਾਅ, ਖ਼ਸਲਤ, ਮਿਜ਼ਾਜ; ਮਾਨਸਕ ਅਵਸਥਾ, ਮਨੋਬਿਰਤੀ

menthol (ਮੈੱਥੋਲ) *n* ਪੁਦੀਨੇ ਦਾ ਸਤ, ਮੈੱਥੋਲ

mention (ਮੈਨਸ਼ਨ) *v n* ਜ਼ਿਕਰ ਕਰਨਾ, ਉੱਲੇਖ ਕਰਨਾ, ਨਾਂ ਲੈਣਾ, ਕਹਿਣਾ; ਜ਼ਿਕਰ, ਉੱਲੇਖ, ਕਥਨ, ਵਰਣਨ; ~**able** ਉਲੇਖਨੀਯ, ਜ਼ਿਕਰ ਲਾਇਕ, ਹਵਾਲੇ ਯੋਗ; ~**ed** ਕਥਿਤ, ਨਿਰਦਿਸ਼ਟ, ਨਿਰਦੇਸ਼ਤ, ਉਲਿਖਤ, ਵਰਤਤ

menu (ਮੈੱਨਯੂ) *n* ਭੋਜਨ-ਸੂਚੀ, ਮੀਨੂ

mercantile (ਮਅ:ਕਅੰਟਾਇਲ) *a* ਵਪਾਰਕ, ਤਜਾਰਤੀ, ਵਣਜੀ

mercenary (ਮਅ:ਸਿਨ(ਅ)ਰਿ) *a n* ਸੁਆਰਥੀ; ਭਾੜੇ ਦਾ ਟੱਟੂ

merchandise ('ਮਅ:ਚਅੰਡਾਇਜ਼) *n* ਵਪਾਰਕ

ਮਾਲ, ਤਜਾਰਤੀ ਸਾਮਾਨ

merchant ('ਮਅ:ਚਅੰਟ) *n* ਵਪਾਰੀ, ਸੌਦਾਗਰ

merciful ('ਮਅ:ਸਿਫ਼ੁਲ) *a* ਦਿਆਲੂ, ਦਿਆਵਾਨ, ਕਿਰਪਾਲੂ, ਮਿਹਰਬਾਨ

merciless ('ਮਅ:ਸਿਲਿਸ) *a* ਬੇਰਹਿਮ, ਨਿਰਦਈ, ਨਿਸ਼ਠੁਰ, ਬੇਦਰਦ, ਪੱਥਰਦਿਲ

mercury ('ਮਅ:ਕਯੁਰਿ) *n* ਪਾਰਾ, ਚੰਚਲਤਾ, ਚੁਸਤੀ, ਫੁਰਤੀ; (ਗ੍ਰਹਿ) ਬੁੱਧ

mercy ('ਮਅ:ਸਿ) *n* ਦਇਆ, ਮਿਹਰ, ਰਹਿਮ, ਕਿਰਪਾ, ਦਇਆਲਤਾ, ਤਰਸ, ਕਰੁਣਾ

mere (ਮਿਅ*) *n v a* (ਕਾਵਿਕ, ਪ੍ਰ) ਤਲਾ, ਝੀਲ, ਛੰਭ; ਹੱਦ, ਸੀਮਾ; ਹੱਦਬੰਦੀ ਕਰਨਾ; ਸਿਰਫ਼, ਕੇਵਲ, ਨਿਰਾ, ਨਿਰਾਪੁਰਾ, ਉੱਕਾ; **~ly** ਸਿਰਫ਼, ਕੇਵਲ, ਨਿਰਾ

merge (ਮਅ:ਜ) *v* ਵਿਲੀਨ ਹੋਣਾ, ਅਭੇਦ ਕਰਨਾ ਜਾਂ ਹੋਣਾ, ਸ਼ਾਮਲ ਹੋਣਾ ਜਾਂ ਕਰਨਾ, ਸਮਾ ਜਾਣਾ; **~d** ਵਿਲੀਨ, ਸਮਾਵਿਸ਼ਟ

merit ('ਮੈਰਿਟ) *n* ਯੋਗਤਾ, ਕਾਬਲੀਅਤ, ਪ੍ਰਵੀਨਤਾ, ਚੰਗਿਆਈ, ਖ਼ੂਬੀ, ਸਿੱਧਤਾ; ਉੱਤਮਤਾ; **~orious** ਗੁਣਵਾਨ, ਗੁਣੀ, ਕਾਬਲ, ਪ੍ਰਸੰਸਾਯੋਗ, ਨੇਕ, ਭਲਾ; **~oriousness** ਯੋਗਤਾ, ਭਲਾਈ, ਨੇਕੀ

merriment ('ਮੈਰਿਮਅੰਟ) *n* ਹਾਸ-ਵਿਲਾਸ, ਖੇਡ-ਤਮਾਸ਼ਾ, ਹਾਸਾ-ਮਸ਼ਕਰੀ, ਖ਼ੁਸ਼ੀ, ਆਨੰਦ, ਮੌਜਮੇਲਾ

merry ('ਮੈਰਿ) *a* ਖ਼ੁਸ਼, ਪ੍ਰਸੰਨ, ਖਿੜਿਆ-ਫੁੱਲਿਆ; ਰੰਗੀਲਾ, ਹੱਸਮੁੱਖ, ਮੌਜੀ, ਰੌਂਕੀ; **~making** ਰੰਗ-ਰਲੀਆਂ, ਮੌਜ-ਮੇਲਾ

mesmerism ('ਮੈੱਜ਼ਮਅਰਿਜ਼(ਅ)ਮ) *n* ਵਸ਼ੀਕਰਨ, ਵਸ਼ੀਕਰਨ-ਵਿੱਦਿਆ, ਸੰਮੋਹਨ

mesmerize ('ਮੈੱਜ਼ਮਅਰਾਇਜ਼) *v* ਬੇਹੋਸ਼ ਕਰਨ, ਬੇਸੁਧ ਕਰਨ, ਮੂਰਛਤ ਕਰਨ, ਮੈਸਮਰਿਜ਼ਮ ਨਾਲ ਪ੍ਰਭਾਵਤ ਕਰਨ

mess (ਮੈੱਸ) *n v* ਮਿਲਗੋਭਾ, ਮਿਸ਼ਰਨ, ਰਲਾਮਿਲਾ; ਰੋਲਘਚੋਲਾ; ਪੁਆੜਾ, ਝੰਜਟ, ਬਖੇੜਾ; (ਫੌਜੀ) ਲੰਗਰ; ਸਾਂਝਾ ਲੰਗਰ; ਰਲਾ-ਮਿਲਾ ਦੇਣਾ; ਗੜਬੜ ਪਾ ਦੇਣੀ; ਲੰਗਰ ਵਿਚ ਖਾਣਾ, ਇੱਕਠੇ ਖਾਣਾ

message ('ਮੈੱਸਿਜ) *n* ਸੁਨੇਹਾ, ਸੰਦੇਸ਼ਾ, ਬਿਰਤਾਂਤ, ਖ਼ਬਰ

messenger ('ਮੈੱਸਿੰਜਅ*) *n* ਕਾਸਦ, ਹਰਕਾਰਾ, ਦੂਤ, ਸੰਦੇਸ਼ਵਾਚਕ

Messiah (ਮਿ'ਸਾਇਆ) *n* ਹਜ਼ਰਤ ਈਸਾ; ਈਸਾ ਮਸੀਹ, ਮਸੀਹਾ, ਮੁਕਤੀ ਦਾਤਾ

Messianic ('ਮੈੱਸਿ'ਐਨਿਕ) *a* ਮਸੀਹੀ, ਈਸਾ-ਸਬੰਧੀ

Messrs (ਮੈੱਸਅਜ਼) *n* mister (Mr) ਦਾ ਬਹੁਵਚਨ, ਸਰਵਸੀ

metal ('ਮੈਟਲ) *n v* ਧਾਤ; ਸੜਕ ਬਣਾਉਣ ਵਾਲੀ ਬਜਰੀ ਜਾਂ ਰੋੜੀ; ਧਾਤ ਲਾਉਣੀ, ਧਾਤ ਨਾਲ ਮੜ੍ਹਨਾ; ਪੱਕੀ ਸੜਕ ਬਣਾਉਣੀ; ਸੜਕ ਤੇ ਰੋੜੀ ਪਾਉਣੀ; **~lic** ਧਾਤਵੀ, ਧਾਤ ਦਾ, ਧਾਤ ਨਾਲ ਬਣਿਆ, (ਸੜਕ) ਪੱਕੀ; ਧਾਤ ਵਰਗਾ; **~lurgy** ਧਾਤ-ਵਿੱਦਿਆ, ਧਾਤ ਨੂੰ ਸਾਫ਼ ਜਾਂ ਸ਼ੁੱਧ ਕਰਨ ਦੀ ਵਿੱਦਿਆ; ਧਾਤ ਦਾ ਕੰਮ; ਧਾਤ-ਕਰਮ

metaphor ('ਮੈਟਅਫ਼ਅ*) *n* ਰੂਪਕ, ਰੂਪਕ ਅਲੰਕਾਰ; **~ical** ਰੂਪਕ ਦਾ, ਅਲੰਕਾਰ

metaphrase ('ਮੈਟਅ'ਫ਼ਰੇਇਜ਼) *n v* ਸ਼ਬਦ-ਅਨੁਵਾਦ; ਲਫ਼ਜ਼ੀ ਤਰਜਮਾ ਕਰਨਾ

metaphysical ('ਮੈਟਅ'ਫ਼ਿਜ਼ਿਕਲ) *a* ਅਧਿਆਤਮਕ, ਪਰਾਭੌਤਕ, ਅਮੂਰਤ, ਸੂਖਮ,

ਤਾਤਵਿਕ, ਪਾਰਲੌਕਕ

metaphysics ('ਸੌਟਅ'ਫ਼ਿਜ਼ਿਕਿਸ) *n pl* ਅਧਿਆਤਮਵਾਦ; ਪਰਾਭੌਤਕ ਗਿਆਨ, ਗੁੜ੍ਹ ਵਿਚਾਰ

meterology ('ਮੀਟਯਅ'ਗੌਲਿਅਜਿ) *n* ਜਲ ਵਾਯੂ-ਵਿਗਿਆਨ, ਮੌਸਮ-ਵਿਗਿਆਨ

meter ('ਮੀਟਅ*) *n* ਨਾਪਕ, ਮਾਪਕ, ਨਾਪਣ ਵਾਲਾ; ਮੀਟਰ, ਇਕ ਮਾਪ

method ('ਮੈੱਥਅਡ) *n* ਤਰੀਕਾ, ਢੰਗ, ਵਿਧੀ, ਜਾਚ, ਪ੍ਰਣਾਲੀ, ਕ੍ਰਮ, ਤਰਤੀਬ; ਵਿਵਸਥਾ, ਯੋਜਨਾਬੰਦੀ; ~ical ਵਿਧੀ-ਅਨੁਸਾਰ, ਵਿਧੀਬੱਧ, ਵਿਵਸਥਿਤ, ਕ੍ਰਮ-ਅਨੁਸਾਰ, ਢੁੱਕਵਾਂ; ~ist ਦ੍ਰਿੜ੍ਹ ਧਾਰਮਕ, ਵਿਚਾਰਾਂ ਵਾਲਾ ਵਿਅਕਤੀ, ਕੱਟੜ; ਇਸਾਈਆਂ ਦੀ ਵਿਸ਼ੇਸ਼ ਸੰਪਰਦਾਇ ਦਾ ਸਦੱਸ; ~ology ਵਿਧੀ-ਵਿਗਿਆਨ, ਕਾਰਜ-ਵਿਧੀ, ਵਿਧੀ-ਸ਼ਾਸਤਰ

meticulous (ਮਿ'ਟਿਕਯੁਲਅਸ) *a* ਅਤੀ ਸਾਵਧਾਨ, ਸੌਂਘਾ, ਬਾਰੀਕਬੀਨ; ~ness ਅਤੀ ਸਾਵਧਾਨਤਾ

metre ('ਮੀਟਅ*) *n* ਲੰਬਾਈ ਦਾ ਨਾਪ, ਮੀਟਰ; ਕਵਿਤਾ ਦੀ ਬਹਿਰ, ਛੰਦ

metric ('ਮੈੱਟਰਿਕ) *a* ਮੀਟਰ ਸਬੰਧੀ; ਦਸ ਔਂਸੀ, ਦਾਸ਼ਮਿਕ; ~al ਛੰਦ ਸਬੰਧੀ

metropolis (ਮਿ'ਟਰੌਪੁਲਿਸ) *n* ਮਹਾਂਨਗਰ; ਮੁੱਖ ਸ਼ਹਿਰ, ਰਾਜਧਾਨੀ, ਕਾਰਜ-ਕੇਂਦਰ

metropolitan ('ਮੈਟਰਅ'ਪੌਲਿਟ(ਅ)ਨ) *a* ਮੁੱਖ ਨਗਰ ਦਾ, ਰਾਜਧਾਨੀ ਦਾ

mettle ('ਮੈੱਟਲ) *n* ਹਿੰਮਤ, ਜੋਰ, ਜਿਗਰਾ; ਸੁਭਾਅ, ਤਬੀਅਤ; ~d, ~some ਹਿੰਮਤੀ, ਹੌਂਸਲੇ ਵਾਲਾ, ਸਾਹਸੀ, ਵੱਡੇ ਜਿਗਰੇ ਵਾਲਾ

mica (ਮਾਇਕਅ) *n* ਅਬਰਕ

miche (ਮਿਚ) *v n* ਗੁਪਤ ਰੱਖਣਾ, ਛੁਪਾਉਣਾ, ਲੁਕਾਉਣਾ; ਸ਼ਰਮਿੰਦਾ ਹੋਣਾ; ਅਵਾਰਾਗਰਦੀ ਕਰਨਾ; ~r ਗੁਪਤ ਰੱਖਣ ਵਾਲਾ, ਅਵਾਰਾ

micro ('ਮਾਇਕਰਅਉ) *a* ਸੂਖਮ, ਦਸ ਲੱਖਵਾਂ ਭਾਗ

microbiological ('ਮਾਇਕਰਅ'ਬਾਇਅ-ਲੌਜਿਕਲ) *a* ਸੂਖਮ-ਜੀਵ-ਵਿਗਿਆਨ ਸਬੰਧੀ

microbiology ('ਮਾਇਕਰਅਬਾਇ'ਔਲਅਜਿ) *n* ਅਣੂ-ਵਿਗਿਆਨ, ਸੂਖਮ ਜੀਵ-ਵਿਗਿਆਨ

microfilm ('ਮਾਇਕਰਅ(ਉ)ਫ਼ਿਲਮ) *n* ਛੋਟੀ ਫ਼ਿਲਮ

microscope ('ਮਾਇਕਰੋਸਕਅਉਪ) *n* ਖ਼ੁਰਦਬੀਨ, ਸੂਖਮ ਦਰਸ਼ਕ ਜੰਤਰ, ਅਣੂਦਰਸ਼ਕ ਜੰਤਰ

microscopic ('ਮਾਇਕਰਅ'ਸਕੌਪਿਕ) *a* ਖ਼ੁਰਦਬੀਨ ਦਾ, ਖ਼ੁਰਦਬੀਨੀ, ਸੂਖਮ, ਸੂਖਮ-ਦਰਸ਼ੀ; ~al ਖ਼ੁਰਦਬੀਨੀ, ਸੂਖਮ ਦਰਸ਼ਕ ਜੰਤਰ ਸਬੰਧੀ; ਅਤੀ ਸੂਖਮ

microwave ('ਮਾਇਕਰਅਵੇਇਵ) *n* ਸੂਖਮ ਲਹਿਰ, (ਹਵਾ ਦੀ) ਸੂਖਮ ਤਰੰਗ

mid (ਮਿਡ) *a prep* ਦਰਮਿਆਨ, ਮੰਝਲਾ, ਗਾਂਧਵਰਤੀ, ਮੰਧ ਸਹਿਤ, ਵਿਚਕਾਰ ਦਾ; ~day ਦੁਪਹਿਰ; ~night ਅੱਧੀ ਰਾਤ, ਘੁੱਪ ਹਨੇਰਾ; ~way ਮੱਧ ਮਾਰਗ, ਵਿਚਕਾਰਲਾ ਰਸਤਾ

middle ('ਮਿਡਲ) *n a* ਮੱਧ ਦੇਸ਼, ਮੱਧ-ਵਰਤੀ, ਅੰਤਰ, ਵਿਚਕਾਰ, ਦਰਮਿਆਨੀ, ਮਰਕਜ਼ੀ, ਔਸਤ ਦਰਜੇ ਦਾ; ~man ਦਲਾਲ, ਵਿਚੋਲਾ, ਆੜ੍ਹਤੀ

middling ('ਮਿਡਲਿੰਡ) *adv a* ਸਧਾਰਨ ਤੌਰ ਤੇ; ਕੁਝ ਕੁਝ; ਮੱਧ ਦਾ; ਮੱਧ ਸ਼੍ਰੇਣੀ ਦਾ, ਦੂਜੇ ਦਰਜੇ ਦਾ

midst (ਮਿਡਸਟ) *a* ਮੱਧ (ਵਿਚ); ਵਿਚਕਾਰ; ਦਰਮਿਆਨ

midwife ('ਮਿਡਵਾਇਫ਼) *n* ਦਾਈ

might (ਮਾਇਟ) *n v aux* ਬਲ ਸ਼ਕਤੀ; ਜ਼ੋਰ, ਤਾਣ, ਤਾਕਤ; may ਦਾ ਭੂਤ ਕਾਲ; ~**y** ਜ਼ੋਰਾਵਰ, ਜ਼ਬਰਦਸਤ, ਪ੍ਰਬਲ, ਬਲਵਾਨ, ਸ਼ਕਤੀਮਾਨ, ਬਲੀ, ਸਮਰੱਥ, ਮਹਾਨ; ਅਤੀਅੰਤ, ਬਹੁਤ

migraine ('ਮੀਗਰੇਇਨ) *n* ਅੱਧੇ ਸਿਰ ਦੀ ਪੀੜ

migrant ('ਮਾਇਗਰਅੰਟ) *n* ਦੇਸੋਸਮੀ ਪੰਛੀ

migrate (ਮਾਇ'ਗਰੇਇਟ) *v* ਪਰਵਾਸ ਕਰਨਾ, ਥਾਂ ਬਦਲਣਾ; ਹਿਜਰਤ ਕਰਨਾ

migration (ਮਾਇ'ਗਰੇਇਸ਼ਨ) *n* ਪਰਵਾਸ, ਹਿਜਰਤ

milch (ਮਿਲਚ) *a* ਦੁੱਧ ਦੇਣ ਵਾਲੀ, ਦੁੱਧੈਲ; ਲਾਭ-ਸਰੋਤ; ਲਾਭ ਦਾ ਸਾਧਨ

mild (ਮਾਇਲਡ) *a* ਸ਼ਾਂਤ, ਦਿਆਲੂ, ਹਲੀਮ, ਹਲਕਾ, ਨਰਮ; ਸੋਮਦਿਲ; ਦੁਰਬਲ, ਕਮਜ਼ੋਰ; ~**ness** ਸ਼ਾਂਤੀ, ਦਇਆਲਤਾ, ਕਿਰਪਾਲਤਾ, ਕੋਮਲਤਾ, ਨਰਮੀ, ਮਜ਼ਰਤਾ, ਦੁਰਬਲਤਾ, ਕਮਜ਼ੋਰੀ

mile (ਮਾਇਲ) *n* ਮੀਲ, 1760 ਗਜ ਦੀ ਵਿੱਥ; ~**stone** ਮੀਲ-ਪੱਥਰ, ਮਾਰਗ-ਸ਼ਿਲਾ, ਮਹੱਤਵਪੂਰਨ ਘਟਨਾ

milk (ਮਿਲਕ) *n v* ਦੁੱਧ, ਸ਼ੀਰ; ਦੁੱਧ ਚੋਣਾ, ਦੋਹਣਾ; ~**y** ਦੁੱਧੀਆ

mill (ਮਿਲ) *n v* ਚੱਕੀ, ਕਾਰਖ਼ਾਨਾ, ਮਿਲ; ਪੀਹਣਾ, ਪੀਸਣਾ

millet ('ਮਿਲਿਟ) *n* ਬਾਜਰਾ, ਮੋਟਾ ਅਨਾਜ

milleu ('ਮੀਲਯਆ:) *n* ਸਮਾਜਕ ਵਾਤਾਵਰਨ, ਮਾਹੌਲ

milli ('ਮਿਲਿ) *n* ਹਜ਼ਾਰਵਾਂ ਭਾਗ, ਜਿਵੇਂ ਕਿ ਮੀਟਰਕ; ~**gram** ਗਰਾਮ ਦਾ ਹਜ਼ਾਰਵਾਂ ਭਾਗ; ~**litre** ਲਿਟਰ ਦਾ ਹਜ਼ਾਰਵਾਂ ਭਾਗ

million ('ਮਿਲਯਅਨ) *n a* ਦਸ ਲੱਖ; ~**aire** ਲੱਖਪਤੀ, ਕਰੋੜਪਤੀ; ਧਨਵਾਨ

militant ('ਮਿਲਿਟਅੰਟ) *a* ਲੜਾਕਾ, ਜੰਗੀ, ਜੋਧਾ, ਖਾੜਕੂ, ਜੁਝਾਰ, ਮੁਜਾਹਦ, ਜੰਗਜੂ

military ('ਮਿਲਿਟ(ਅ)ਰਿ) *n* ਸੈਨਾ, ਫ਼ੌਜ, ਲਸ਼ਕਰ, ਜੰਗੀ, ਫ਼ੌਜੀ, ਸਿਪਾਹੀਆਨਾ, ਸੈਨਕ

militate ('ਮਿਲਿਟੇਇਟ) *v* ਯੁੱਧ ਕਰਨਾ, ਜੰਗ ਕਰਨਾ; ਲੜਨਾ, ਵਿਰੋਧ ਕਰਨਾ; ਪ੍ਰਭਾਵ ਪਾਉਣਾ

militia (ਮਿ'ਲਿਸ਼ਅ) *n* ਦੇਸ਼-ਰੱਖਿਅਕ ਸੈਨਾ, ਰਾਸ਼ਟਰੀ ਸੈਨਾ, ਰਜ਼ਾਕਾਰ ਫ਼ੌਜ

mimic ('ਮਿਮਿਕ) *n a v* ਬਹੁਰੂਪੀਆ, ਨਕਲੀਆ, ਭੰਡ, ਸਾਂਗੀ; ਨਕਲੀ, ਮਜ਼ਾਕੀਆ; ਨਕਲ ਉਤਾਰਨਾ; ~**ry** ਸਾਂਗ, ਨਕਲ, ਅਨੁਕਰਨ, ਭੰਡੌਤੀ

minar (ਮਿਨਾ*) *n* ਮੀਨਾਰ, ਲਾਠ, ਬੁਰਜ, ਚਾਨਣ-ਮੁਨਾਰਾ; ~**et** ਛੋਟਾ ਮੀਨਾਰ, ਬੁਰਜ, ਚਾਨਣ-ਮੁਨਾਰਾ

mince (ਮਿੰਸ) *v* ਕੀਮਾ; ਕੀਮਾ ਬਣਾਉਣਾ, ਟੁਕੜੇ ਕਰਨਾ

mind (ਮਾਇਨਡ) *n v* ਮਨ, ਚਿੱਤ, ਮਨਸ਼ਾ; ਮੱਤ, ਬੁੱਧ, ਸਮਝ, ਬੁੱਧੀ, ਚੇਤਾ, ਯਾਦਦਾਸ਼ਤ; ਖ਼ਿਆਲ, ਰੁਚੀ; ਵਿਚਾਰਧਾਰਾ, ਹਿਰਦਾ, ਜੀਆ, ਦਿਲ; ਅੰਤਹਕਰਨ; ਵਿਚ ਦਿਲ ਲਗਾਉਣਾ; *to make up one's* ~ ਫ਼ੈਸਲਾ ਕਰਨਾ, ਦ੍ਰਿੜ੍ਹਤਾ ਧਾਰਨ ਕਰਨੀ, ਨਿਸ਼ਚਾ ਕਰਨਾ, ਪੱਕਾ ਇਰਾਦਾ ਬਣਾਉਣਾ; ~**ful** ਹੁਸ਼ਿਆਰ, ਸਾਵਧਾਨ, ਖ਼ਬਰਦਾਰ, ਚੌਕੰਨਾ; ~**less** ਸੁਤ੍ਰ, ਮੂਰਖ, ਬੇਵਕੂਫ਼, ਬੁੱਧੀਹੀਨ

mine (ਮਾਇਨ) *pron n v* ਮੇਰਾ; ਮੇਰਾ ਭਾਗ, ਮੇਰਾ ਹਿੱਸਾ; ਖਾਨ; ਸੁਰੰਗ; ਖ਼ਜ਼ਾਨਾ, ਭੰਡਾਰ; ਖਾਨ ਪੁੱਟਣਾ; ~**ral** ਖਾਨਾਂ ਦੀ (ਧਾਤ), ਧਾਤ ਸਬੰਧੀ

ਬਣਾਉਟੀ ਖਣਿਜ-ਜਲ; **~ralogy** ਖਣਿਜ-ਵਿਗਿਆਨ, ਧਾਤ-ਵਿੱਦਿਆ; ਧਾਤੂ-ਪਰੀਖਿਅਣ-ਸ਼ਾਸਤਰ

Minerva (ਮਿ'ਨਅ:ਵ੍ਹਅ) *n* ਰੋਮ ਦੀ ਵਿੱਦਿਆ ਦੇਵੀ, ਸਰਸਵਤੀ

mingle (ਮਿੰਗਲ) *v* ਘੁਲਮਿਲ ਜਾਣਾ, ਮਿਲਾਉਣਾ, ਮੇਲ ਕਰਨਾ, ਮਿਲਣਾ, ਮਿਸ਼ਰਤ ਕਰਨਾ; **~d** ਮਿਸ਼ਰਤ, ਮਿਲਿਆ ਹੋਇਆ

miniature ('ਮਿਨਅਚਅ*) *n a* ਲਘੂ-ਚਿਤਰ, ਲਘੂਕ੍ਰਿਤ ਚਿਤਰ; ਬੌਣਾ, ਵਾਮਨ; ਛੋਟਾ

minimal (ਮਿਨਿਮਲ) *a* ਅਲਪਤਮ, ਨਿਊਨਤਮ, ਘੱਟ ਤੋਂ ਘੱਟ

minimize (ਮਿਨਿਮਾਇਜ਼) *v* ਘਟਾਉਣਾ, ਅਲਪੀਕਰਨ ਕਰਨਾ, ਮਾਤਰਾ ਘੱਟ ਕਰਨੀ, ਛੋਟਾ ਕਰਨਾ, ਘੱਟ ਕਰਨਾ

mining ('ਮਾਇਨਿੰਙ) *n* ਖਾਣ ਦੀ ਖੁਦਾਈ, ਸੁਰੰਗ ਦੀ ਪੁਟਾਈ

minister ('ਮਿਨਿਸਟਅ*) *n v* ਮੰਤਰੀ, ਵਜ਼ੀਰ, ਦੀਵਾਨ; ਪਰੋਹਤ, ਪਾਦਰੀ; ਆਚਾਰੀਆ; ਸੇਵਾ ਕਰਨੀ, ਸਹਾਇਤਾ ਕਰਨੀ, ਪ੍ਰਬੰਧ ਕਰਨਾ

ministerial ('ਮਿਨਿ'ਸਟਿਅਰਿਅਲ) *a* ਵਜ਼ਾਰਤੀ, ਮੰਤਰੀ ਦਾ; ਤਾਜ਼ਨੀ, ਸਰਕਾਰੀ ਪੱਖ ਦਾ; ਪਾਦਰੀ ਸਬੰਧੀ

ministration ('ਮਿਨਿ'ਸਟਰੇਇਸ਼ਨ) *n* ਦੇਖ-ਭਾਲ, ਖਿਦਮਤ; ਸੇਵਾ

ministry ('ਮਿਨਿਸਟਰਿ) *n* ਮੰਤਰੀ ਸਭਾ, ਵਜ਼ਾਰਤ, ਮੰਤਰਾਲਿਆ; ਮੰਤਰੀ-ਮੰਡਲ, ਮੰਤਰੀ-ਪਰਿਸ਼ਦ, ਮੰਤਰੀਗਣ; ਪਰੋਹਤਪਣ

minor ('ਮਾਇਨਅ*) *n a* ਬਾਲ, ਨਾਬਾਲਗ ਸੈਂਟ; ਫ਼ਰਾਂਸਿਸ ਦੇ ਸਮੇਂ ਅਤੇ ਸੰਪਰਦਾਇ ਦਾ ਇਕ ਸੰਨਿਆਸੀ; ਸਧਾਰਣ; **~ity** ਅਲਪ ਸੰਖਿਆ, ਅਲਪ ਸੰਖਿਅਕ; ਲੜਕਪਣ, ਨਾਬਾਲਗੀ, ਬਾਲਪਣ, ਬਾਲ-ਅਵਸਥਾ; ਘੱਟ ਗਿਣਤੀ ਦੀ ਜਮਾਤ, ਅਲਪ ਸੰਖਿਅਕ

minster ('ਮਿਨਸਟਅ*) *n* ਮੱਠ, ਆਸ਼ਰਮ, ਵੱਡਾ ਗਿਰਜਾ

minstrel ('ਮਿਨਸਟਰ(ਅ)ਲ) *n* ਭੱਟ, ਗਵੱਈਆ, ਕੀਰਤਨੀਆ, ਗਾਇਕ

mint (ਮਿੰਟ) *n v* ਟਕਸਾਲ; ਕੋਸ਼ ਖ਼ਜ਼ਾਨਾ; ਖਾਣ; ਪੁਦੀਨਾ; ਟਕਸਾਲਣਾ, ਢਾਲਣਾ, ਸਿੱਕੇ ਬਣਾਉਣਾ, ਸ਼ਬਦਾਂ ਆਦਿ ਦੀ ਕਾਢ ਕੱਢਣਾ; **~age** ਸਿੱਕਾ ਢਲਾਈ, ਠੱਪਾ ਲੁਆਈ; ਢਲਾਈ (ਦਰ), ਢਲਿਆ ਹੋਇਆ ਸਿੱਕਾ

minus ('ਮਾਇਨਅਸ) *prep a n* ਬਿਨਾ, ਬਾਕੀ, ਨਫ਼ੀ, ਨਫ਼ੀ ਦਾ ਨਿਸ਼ਾਨ, ਰਿਣ-ਚਿੰਨ੍ਹ, ਰਿਣ ਘੱਟ

minute ('ਮਿਨਿਟ) *n v a* (1) ਮਿੰਟ, ਘੰਟੇ ਦਾ ਸੱਠਵਾਂ ਹਿੱਸਾ; ਛਿਣ, ਪਲ; (2) ਸਧਾਰਨ ਲੇਖ, ਕਾਰਵਾਈ, (ਬ ਵ) ਕਾਰਜ-ਵੇਰਵਾ (ਕਿਸੇ ਸਭਾ ਆਦਿ ਦਾ); ਸੰਖੇਪ ਵੇਰਵਾ ਲਿਖਣਾ; ਮਸੌਦਾ ਤਿਆਰ ਕਰਨਾ; ਸਬੂਤ ਤਿਆਰ ਕਰਨਾ, ਠੀਕ ਸਮੇਂ ਦਾ ਪਤਾ ਲਾਉਣਾ; ਅਤੀ ਅਲਪ; ਸੁਖਮ, ਅਤੀ ਲਘੂ, ਮਹੀਨ, ਬਾਰੀਕ; **~ly** ਛਿਣ ਦਾ, ਮਿੰਟ ਮਿੰਟ ਦਾ, ਸੂਖਮ ਰੂਪ

minx (ਮਿੰਙਕਸ) *n* ਸ਼ੋਖ਼ ਅੱਖਾਂ ਵਾਲੀ ਕੁੜੀ, ਚੰਚਲ ਕੁੜੀ

miracle (ਮਿਰਅਕਲ) *n* ਕਰਾਮਾਤ, ਕ੍ਰਿਸ਼ਮਾ, ਕਮਾਲ, ਚਮਤਕਾਰ

miraculous (ਮਿ'ਰੈਕਯੁਅਲਸ) *a* ਦਿੱਬ, ਦੈਵੀ, ਕਰਾਮਾਤੀ, ਚਮਤਕਾਰੀ; ਅਲੌਕਿਕ, ਅਦਭੁਤ

mirador ('ਮਿਰਾ'ਡੋ*) *n* ਘੰਟਾਘਰ, ਬੁਰਜ, ਚਬੂਤਰਾ

mirage ('ਮਿਰਾਯ਼) *n* ਮ੍ਰਿਗ-ਤ੍ਰਿਸ਼ਨਾ, ਮਰੀਚਕਾ,

ਮਿਗਰਾ-ਜਾਲ, ਨਜ਼ਰ ਦਾ ਧੋਖਾ

mire ('ਮਾਇਅ*) *n v* ਚਿਕੜ, ਦਲਦਲ, ਖੋਭਾ; ਚਿਕੜ ਵਿਚ ਫਸਣਾ, ਮੈਲਾ ਕਰਨਾ

mirror ('ਮਿਰਅ*) *n v* ਸ਼ੀਸ਼ਾ, ਆਰਸੀ, ਆਈਨਾ; ਦਰਪਣ, ਹੂ-ਬਹੂ ਅਕਸ ਜਾਂ ਨਕਸ਼ਾ, ਪ੍ਰਤੀਬਿੰਬਤ ਕਰਨਾ, ਅਕਸ ਦਿਖਾਉਣਾ

mirth (ਮਅਃਥ)· *n* ਖ਼ੁਸ਼ੀ, ਦਿਲਲਗੀ, ਹਾਸਾ, ਆਨੰਦ, ਹੁਲਾਸ; ~**ful** ਪ੍ਰਸੰਨ, ਖ਼ੁਸ਼, ਰੰਗੀਲਾ, ਮੌਜੀ; ~**less** ਉਦਾਸ, ਅਪ੍ਰਸੰਨ

miry ('ਮਾਇਰਿ) *a* ਚਿਕੜ ਭਰਿਆ; ਲਿਥੜਿਆ, ਜ਼ਲੀਲ, ਨੀਚ,· ਗੰਦਾ

misapply ('ਮਿਸਅ'ਪਲਾਇ) *v* ਦੁਰਉਪਯੋਗ ਕਰਨਾ, ਮਿਥਿਆ ਪ੍ਰਯੋਗ ਕਰਨਾ, ਅਯੋਗ ਵਰਤੋਂ ਕਰਨੀ

misapprehend ('ਮਿਸ'ਐਪਰਿ'ਹੈਂਡ) *v* ਉਲਟਾ ਜਾਂ ਗ਼ਲਤ ਸਮਝਣਾ

misapprehension ('ਮਿਸ'ਐਪਰਿ'ਹੈਂਨਸ਼ਨ) *n* ਮਿਥਿਆ-ਬੋਧ, ਭਰਮ, ਭੁੱਲ, ਗ਼ਲਤ-ਫਹਿਮੀ

misappropriate ('ਮਿਸਅ'ਪਰਅਉਪਰਿਏਇਟ) *v* (ਪਰਏ ਧਨ ਦਾ) ਗ਼ਬਨ ਕਰਨਾ, ਖੁਰਦ-ਬੁਰਦ ਕਰਨਾ, ਨਜਾਇਜ਼ ਖ਼ਰਚ ਕਰਨਾ, ਗ਼ਲਤ ਕੰਮ ਵਿਚ ਖ਼ਰਚ ਕਰਨਾ

misappropriation ('ਮਿਸਅ'ਪਰਅਉਪਰਿ-'ਏਇਸ਼ਨ) *n* ਕੁਵਰਤੋਂ, ਘਾਲਾਮਾਲਾ, ਦੁਰਉਪਯੋਗ, (ਰੁਪਏ ਦਾ) ਗ਼ਬਨ

misarrange ('ਮਸਅ'ਰੇਂਜਿ) *v* ਬੇਤਰਤੀਬੀ ਨਾਲ ਰੱਖਣਾ, ਬਿਨਾ ਕ੍ਰਮ ਦੇ ਰੱਖਣਾ, ਬਿਨਾ ਸਿਲਸਲੇ ਦੇ ਰੱਖਣਾ

misbecome ('ਮਿਸਬਿ'ਕੱਮ) *v* ਅਯੋਗ ਹੋਣਾ, ਅਟਉਪਯੋਗੀ ਹੋਣਾ, ਸ਼ੋਭਾ ਨਾ ਦੇਣਾ, ਸ਼ਾਨ ਦੇ ਖਿਲਾਫ਼ ਹੋਣਾ

misbecoming ('ਮਿਸਬਿ'ਕੱਮਿਂਗ) *a* ਅਸ਼ੋਭਨੀਕ, ਅਯੋਗ, ਅਟਉਪਯੋਗੀ

misbehave ('ਮਿਸਬਿ'ਹੇਇਵ) *v* ਦੁਰਵਿਹਾਰ ਕਰਨਾ, ਬੁਰਾ ਵਰਤਾਉ ਕਰਨਾ; ~**d** ਅਸੱਭਿਅ, ਬਦਚਲਨ, ਬਦਤਮੀਜ਼

misbehaviour ('ਮਿਸਬਿ'ਹੇਇਵਯਅ*) *n* ਦੁਰਵਿਹਾਰ, ਦੁਰਾਚਾਰ, ਬਦਤਮੀਜ਼ੀ, ਕੁਚਾਲ

misbelief ('ਮਿਸਬਿ'ਲੀਫ਼) *v* ਗ਼ਲਤ ਧਾਰਣਾ ਦੁਰ-ਵਿਸ਼ਵਾਸ; ਗ਼ਲਤ-ਰਾਇ

miscalculate ('ਮਿਸ'ਕੈਲਕਯੁਲੇਇਟ) *v* ਗ਼ਲਤ ਹਿਸਾਬ ਲਾਉਣਾ, ਝੂਠਾ ਅਨੁਮਾਨ ਲਾਉਣਾ

miscalculation ('ਮਿਸ'ਕੈਲਕਯ'ਲੇਇਸ਼ਨ) *n* ਗ਼ਲਤ ਹਿਸਾਬ, ਝੂਠਾ ਅਨੁਮਾਨ, ਭੁੱਲ-ਚੁੱਕ

miscarriage ('ਮਿਸ'ਕੈਰਿਜ) *n* ਪਤੇ ਤੇ ਨ ਪਹੁੰਚਣਾ, ਅਸਫਲਤਾ; ਗਰਭਪਾਤ

miscarry ('ਮਿਸ'ਕੈਰਿ) *v* ਗਰਭ ਡਿੱਗਣਾ; ਤੁਟ ਨਿਸਫਲ ਹੋਣਾ, ਭਟਕ ਜਾਣਾ

miscellaneous ('ਮਿਸਅ'ਲੇਇਨਯਅਸ) *a* ਫੁਟਕਲ, ਅਨੇਕ, ਵਿਭਿੰਨ, ਵਿਵਿਧ (ਵਿਅਕਤੀ) ਭਿੰਨ ਭਿੰਨ ਪ੍ਰਕਾਰ ਦੇ

mischief ('ਮਿਸਚਿਫ਼) *n* ਸ਼ਰਾਰਤ; ਉਪੱਦਰ ਖ਼ਰਾਬੀ, ਛੇੜਖ਼ਾਨੀ, ਇਲਤ

mischievous ('ਮਿਸਚਿਵ੍ਅਸ) *a* ਉਪੱਦਰੀ ਖ਼ਰਾਬ, ਇਲੱਤੀ, ਸ਼ਰਾਰਤੀ

misconceive ('ਮਿਸਕਅੰ'ਸੀਵ੍) *v* ਗ਼ਲਤ ਸਮਝਣਾ, ਉਲਟ ਸਮਝਣਾ, ਮਿਥਿਆ ਧਾਰ ਕਰਨਾ, ਗ਼ਲਤ ਮਤਲਬ ਲੈਣਾ; ਗ਼ਲਤ ਰਾਇ ਕਾਇਮ ਕਰਨਾ

misconception ('ਮਿਸਕਅੰ'ਸੈਂਪਸ਼ਨ) *n* ਗ਼ਲ ਧਾਰਣਾ, ਗ਼ਲਤ-ਫਹਿਮੀ, ਭਰਾਂਤੀ

misconduct ('ਮਿਸ'ਕੌਂਡਅੱਕਟ, ਮਿਸਕਅ

'ਡਅੰਕਟ) *n v* ਕੁਕਰਮ; ਦੁਰਾਚਾਰ; ਬਦਸਲੂਕੀ; ਕੁਚਾਲ, ਬਦਇੰਤਜ਼ਾਮੀ; ਭੈੜਾ ਪ੍ਰਬੰਧ ਕਰਨਾ

miconstrue ('ਮਿਸਕਆਂ'ਸਟਰੂ) *v* ਅਰਥ ਦਾ ਅਨਰਥ ਕਰਨਾ, ਅਰਥ ਠੀਕ ਨਾ ਲਾਉਣਾ; (ਵਿਅਕਤੀ ਨੂੰ) ਗ਼ਲਤ ਸਮਝਣਾ

miscreant ('ਮਿਸਕਰਿਅੰਟ) *n* ਸ਼ਰਾਰਤੀ, ਬਦਮਾਸ਼, ਗੁੰਡਾ, ਬਦਜ਼ਾਤ

misdeed ('ਮਿਸ'ਡੀਡ) *n* ਕੁਕਰਮ, ਕਰਤੂਤ, ਦੁਰਾਚਾਰ, ਬੁਰਾ ਕੰਮ, ਬਦਕਾਰੀ

misdirect ('ਮਿਲਡ੍ਰਿ'ਰੈੱਕਟ) *v* ਗ਼ਲਤ ਰਾਹ ਦੱਸਣਾ; ਕੁਰਾਹੇ ਪਾਉਣਾ, ਹੁੱਝਣਾ, ਬਹਿਕਾਉਣਾ

misdo ('ਮਿਸ'ਡੂ) *v* ਬੁਰਾ ਕੰਮ ਕਰਨਾ, ਕੁਕਰਮ ਕਰਨਾ, ਅਪਰਾਧ ਕਰਨਾ, ਕਰਤੂਤ ਘੋਲਣੀ; **~er** ਦੋਸ਼ੀ, ਕੁਕਰਮੀ; **~ing** ਕਰਤੂਤ, ਕਾਰਾ, ਦੁਰਾਚਾਰ, ਕੁਚਾਲ

miser ('ਮਾਇਜ਼ਅ*) *n* ਸੂਮ, ਕੰਜੂਸ, ਚੀਪੜ, ਮੱਖੀਚੂਸ; **~liness** ਕੰਜੂਸੀ, ਸੂਮਪੁਣਾ, ਲੋਭ

miserable ('ਮਿਜ਼(ਅ)ਰਅਬਲ) *a* ਦੁਖੀ, ਪੀੜਤ, ਦਰਦਵੰਦ; ਮੰਦਭਾਗਾ, ਅਭਾਗਾ, ਨਿਰਧਨ, ਕਮੀਨਾ, ਜ਼ਲੀਲ, ਹਕੀਰ

misery ('ਮਿਜ਼(ਅ)ਰਿ) *n* ਸੰਤਾਪ, ਵੇਦਨਾ, ਦੁੱਖ, ਦੀਨਤਾ, ਦੁਰਦਸ਼ਾ, ਪਰੇਸ਼ਾਨੀ, ਦੁਰਗਤੀ; ਕਲੇਸ਼, ਕਸ਼ਟ, ਮੁਸੀਬਤ, ਆਫ਼ਤ, ਬਦਕਿਸਮਤੀ

misfit ('ਮਿਸਫ਼ਿਟ) *n* ਅਣਮਿਚਵਾਂ ਕੱਪੜਾ, ਕਸੂਤਾ ਆਦਮੀ

misgive ('ਮਿਸ'ਗਿਵ਼) *v* ਸੰਦੇਹ ਕਰਨਾ, ਮੱਥਾ ਠਣਕਣਾ; (ਦਿਲ ਵਿਚ) ਖ਼ਤਰਾ ਪੈਦਾ ਹੋਣਾ

misgiving ('ਮਿਸ'ਗਿਵ਼ਿੰਡ) *n* ਸੰਦੇਹ, ਸ਼ੰਕਾ, ਤੌਖਲਾ, ਪੁੜਕੂ, ਡਰ

misgovern ('ਮਿਸ'ਗਅੱਵ਼ਅਨ) *v* ਬੁਰਾ ਪ੍ਰਬੰਧ ਕਰਨਾ, ਕੁਸ਼ਾਸਨ ਕਰਨਾ, ਚੰਗੀ ਤਰ੍ਹਾਂ ਰਾਜ ਨਾ ਕਰਨਾ; **~ment** ਕੁਸ਼ਾਸਨ, ਅਨਿਆਈ ਰਾਜ

misguide ('ਮਿਸ'ਗਾਇਡ) *v* ਬਹਿਕਾਉਣਾ, ਕੁਰਾਹੇ ਪਾਉਣਾ; ਗੁਮਰਾਹ ਕਰਨਾ

mishandle ('ਮਿਸ'ਹੈਂਡਲ) *v* ਦੁਰਉਪਯੋਗ ਕਰਨਾ, ਗ਼ਲਤ ਢੰਗ ਨਾਲ ਵਰਤਣਾ; (ਕੰਮ) ਬੁਰੀ ਤਰ੍ਹਾਂ ਕਰਨਾ, ਬੁਰਾ ਸਲੂਕ ਕਰਨਾ

mishap ('ਮਿਸਹੈਪ) *n* ਹਾਦਸਾ, ਦੁਰਘਟਨਾ; ਬਿਪਤਾ, ਆਪੱਤੀ, ਮੁਸੀਬਤ, ਉਪੱਦਰ, ਆਫ਼ਤ

misinform ('ਮਿਸਇਨ'ਫ਼ੋਮ) *v* ਗ਼ਲਤ ਖ਼ਬਰ ਹੋਣੀ, ਝੂਠਾ ਸਮਾਚਾਰ ਦੱਸਣਾ; ਧੋਖਾ ਦੇਣਾ, ਧਮਕਿਾਉਣਾ, ਗ਼ਲਤਫ਼ਹਿਮੀ ਵਿਚ ਪਾਉਣਾ

misinterpret ('ਮਿਸਇਨ'ਟਅ:ਪਰੈੱਟ) *v* ਝੂਠਾ ਅਰਥ ਲਾਉਣਾ, ਗ਼ਲਤ ਅਰਥ ਕੱਢਣਾ, ਗ਼ਲਤ ਸਿੱਟਾ ਕੱਢਣਾ; **~ation** ਮਿਥਿਆ ਅਰਥ, ਅਨਰਥ, ਗ਼ਲਤ ਨਤੀਜਾ, ਗ਼ਲਤ ਵਿਆਖਿਆ

misjudge ('ਮਿਸ'ਜਅੱਜ) *v* ਗ਼ਲਤ ਨਿਰਣੈ ਦੇਣਾ, ਗ਼ਲਤ ਧਾਰਨਾ ਬਣਾਉਣੀ, ਗ਼ਲਤ ਅੰਦਾਜ਼ਾ ਲਾਉਣਾ; **~ment** ਗ਼ਲਤ ਫ਼ੈਸਲਾ, ਦੁਰ-ਨਿਰਣਾ

mislead ('ਮਿਸ'ਲੀਡ) *v* ਧੋਖਾ ਦੇਣਾ, ਗੁਮਰਾਹ ਕਰਨਾ, ਕੁਰਾਹੇ ਪਾਉਣਾ, ਟਪਲਾ ਲਾਉਣਾ; ਗ਼ਲਤਫ਼ਹਿਮੀ ਵਿਚ ਪਾਉਣਾ; **~ing** ਤਰਾਂਜੀਗਾਲ਼, ਟਪਲਾ ਲਾਉ

mismanage ('ਮਿਸ'ਸੈਨਿਜ) *v* ਬਦਇੰਤਜ਼ਾਮੀ ਕਰਨੀ, ਵਿਗਾੜਨਾ; **~ment** ਭੈੜਾ ਪ੍ਰਬੰਧ, ਬਦਇੰਤਜ਼ਾਮੀ

misplace ('ਮਿਸ'ਪਲੇਇਸ) *v* ਗ਼ਲਤ ਥਾਂ ਤੇ ਰੱਖਣਾ, ਕੁਥਾਵੇਂ ਰੱਖਣਾ, ਗ਼ਲਤ ਹੱਥਾਂ ਵਿਚ ਦੇਣਾ; **~d** ਖੋਹਿਆ ਹੋਇਆ, ਬੇਠਿਕਾਨੇ, ਭ੍ਰਿਸ਼ਟ

misprint ('ਮਿਸਪਰਿੰਟ, ਮਿਸ'ਪਰਿੰਟ) *n v* ਛਪਾਈ ਦੀ ਭੁੱਲ; ਅਸ਼ੁੱਧ ਛਾਪਣਾ, ਗ਼ਲਤ ਛਾਪਣਾ, ਛਪਾਏ ਵਿਚ ਗ਼ਲਤੀ ਕਰਨੀ

misquote ('ਮਿਸ'ਕਅਉਟ) v ਅਸ਼ੁੱਧ ਹਵਾਲਾ ਦੇਣਾ

misreport ('ਮਿਸਰਿ'ਪੋਟ) v n ਗ਼ਲਤ ਖ਼ਬਰ ਦੇਣੀ; ਗ਼ਲਤ ਬਿਆਨੀ ਕਰਨੀ; ਗ਼ਲਤ ਬਿਆਨੀ

misrepresent ('ਮਿਸਰਿ'ਪੌਰਿ'ਜ਼ੈਂਟ) v ਗ਼ਲਤ ਪੇਸ਼ ਕਰਨਾ, ਗ਼ਲਤ ਬਿਆਨੀ ਕਰਨੀ, ਤੋੜ-ਮਰੋੜ ਕੇ ਦੱਸਣਾ; ਉਲਟਾ ਅਰਥ ਕੱਢਣਾ; ~ation ਗ਼ਲਤ ਬਿਆਨੀ, ਮਿਥਿਆਵਾਦ, ਅਪਕਥਨ, ਝੂਠ

misrule ('ਮਿਸ'ਰੂਲ) n ਹਕੂਮਤ ਜਾਂ ਸ਼ਾਸਨ ਦੀ ਖ਼ਰਾਬੀ, ਕੁਸ਼ਾਸਨ, ਅੰਧੇਰਗਰਦੀ, ਬਦਅਮਨੀ, ਬਦਇੰਤਜ਼ਾਮੀ

miss (ਮਿਸ) v n ਅਸਫਲ ਹੋਣਾ, ਪ੍ਰਾਪਤ ਨਾ ਕਰਨਾ; ਨਿਸ਼ਾਨ ਚੁੱਕ ਜਾਣਾ; ਛੱਡ ਜਾਣਾ; (ਗੱਡੀ) ਨਿਕਲ ਜਾਣੀ, ਨਾ ਮਿਲਣੀ; ਅਵਸਰ ਹੱਥ ਨਾ ਆਉਣਾ; ਗ਼ਲਤੀ; ਕੁਆਰੀ, ਅਵਿਵਾਹਤ ਕੁੜੀ ਜਾਂ ਬੀਬੀ; ~ing ਲੁਕਿਆ, ਲੁਪਤ, ਗੁੰਮ, ਗੁਆਚਿਆ, ਗ਼ਾਇਬ

missile ('ਮਿਸਾਇਲ) n a ਮਿਸਾਈਲ, ਗੋਲਾ, ਹਥਿਆਰ, ਅਸਤਰ

mission ('ਮਿਸ਼ਨ) n ਦੂਤ ਮੰਡਲ, ਪ੍ਰਚਾਰਕ ਮੰਡਲ, ਧਰਮ-ਪ੍ਰਚਾਰਕ, ਸੰਸਥਾ, ਮਿਸ਼ਨ; ਧਰਮ-ਪ੍ਰਚਾਰ, ਧਾਰਮਕ-ਸੇਵਾ; ~ary ਮਿਸ਼ਨ ਦਾ, ਮਿਸ਼ਨਰੀ; ਪਾਦਰੀ, ਧਰਮ-ਪ੍ਰਚਾਰਕ

mist (ਮਿਸਟ) n v ਧੁੰਦ, ਕੁਹਰਾ; ਧੁੰਦ ਪੈਣੀ, ਧੁੰਦਲਾ ਕਰਨਾ

mistake (ਮਿ'ਸਟੇਇਕ) n v ਭੁੱਲ, ਗ਼ਲਤੀ; ਭਰਾਂਤੀ, ਅਸ਼ੁੱਧੀ; ਤਰੁਟੀ, ਦੋਸ਼, ਭੁਲੇਖਾ, ਟਪਲਾ, ਉਕਾਈ, ਖ਼ਤਾ; ਗ਼ਲਤੀ ਲੱਗਣੀ, ਉਂਕਤਾ, ਖ਼ਤਾ ਕਰਨੀ; ~n ਭਰਾਂਤ, ਭਰਮਪੂਰਨ, ਅਸ਼ੁੱਧ

mister ('ਮਿਸਟਅ*) n ਜਨਾਬ, ਸ੍ਰੀਮਾਨ

mistreat ('ਮਿਸ'ਟਰੀਟ) v ਬੁਰਾ ਵਰਤਾਉ ਕਰਨਾ, ਦੁਰਵਿਹਾਰ ਕਰਨਾ, ਬਦਸਲੂਕੀ ਕਰਨਾ

mistress ('ਮਿਸਟਰਿਸ) n ਸ੍ਰੀਮਤੀ; ਬੀਬੀ, ਉਸਤਾਨੀ; ਗ੍ਰਹਿਣੀ, ਗ੍ਰਹਿਸਥਣ, ਬੇਗਮ, ਘਰ ਵਾਲੀ, ਮਾਲਕਣ

misturst ('ਮਿਸ'ਟਰਅੱਸਟ) v n ਅਵਿਸ਼ਵਾਸ ਕਰਨਾ, ਇਤਬਾਰ ਨਾ ਕਰਨਾ, ਭਰੋਸਾ ਨਾ ਕਰਨਾ, ਬਦਜ਼ਨ ਹੋਣਾ

misty ('ਮਿਸਟਿ) a ਮਿਟਿਆਲਾ, ਅੰਧਕਾਰਮਈ, ਧੁੰਦਲਾ; ਅਸਪਸ਼ਟ, ਅਨਿਸ਼ਚਤ

misunderstand ('ਮਿਸਅੰਡਅ'ਸਟੈਂਡ) v ਉਲਟਾ ਜਾਂ ਗ਼ਲਤ ਸਮਝਣਾ; ਅਨਰਥ ਕਰਨਾ, ਉਲਟਾ ਅਰਥ ਸਮਝਣਾ, ਕੁਝ ਦਾ ਕੁਝ ਸਮਝਣਾ; ~ing ਗ਼ਲਤਫ਼ਹਿਮੀ, ਗ਼ਲਤ ਸੋਚ, ਭੁਲੇਖਾ, ਭਰਮ

misuse ('ਮਿਸ'ਯੂਜ਼) v n ਅਸ਼ੁੱਧ ਪ੍ਰਯੋਗ ਕਰਨਾ; ਦੁਰਵਰਤੋਂ ਕਰਨੀ; ਇਸਤੇਮਾਲ ਕਰਨਾ;

mix (ਮਿਕਸ) v ਮਿਲਾਉਣਾ, ਮਿਲਣਾ, ਘੋਲਣਾ, ਰਲਾਉਣਾ, ਰਲਣਾ, ਮਿਸ਼ਰਨ ਕਰਨਾ; ਸੰਯੁਕਤ ਕਰਨਾ; ~ed ਮਿਲਿਆ, ਘੁਲਿਆ, ਮਿਸ਼ਰਤ, ਸੰਯੁਕਤ, ਮਿਲਿਆ ਜੁਲਿਆ; ~ture ਰਲਾਵਟ, ਮਿਲਾਵਟ, ਮਿਸ਼ਰਨ, ਘੋਲ; ~up ਘਾਲਾ ਮਾਲਾ

mizzle ('ਮਿਜ਼ਲ) n v (ਪਾਣੀ ਦੀ) ਫੁਹਾਰ, ਨਿੱਕੀ ਨਿੱਕੀ ਕਣੀ; ਦੌੜ ਜਾਣਾ, ਨੱਸ ਜਾਣਾ, ਫਰਾਰ ਹੋ ਜਾਣਾ

moan (ਮਅਉਨ) n v ਸਿਸਕੀ, ਸਿਸਕਣ ਵਿਰਲਾਪ; ਮਾਤਮ; ਮਾਤਮ ਕਰਨਾ; ਵਿਰਲਾਪ ਕਰਨਾ, ਅਫ਼ਸੋਸ ਕਰਨਾ; ਕਰਾਹੁਣਾ; ਆਹ ਭਰਨੀ; ~ful ਵਿਰਲਾਪਮਈ, ਸ਼ੋਕਯੁਕਤ, ਸਿਸਕੀਆਂ ਭਰਿਆ

mob (ਮੌਬ) n v ਜਨ-ਸਮੂਹ, ਜਮਘਟਾ, ਭੀੜ, ਮਜਮਾ, ਭੀੜ-ਭਾੜ; ਅਵਾਮ, ਜਨਤਾ; ਭੀੜ

ਹੋਣੀ ਜਾਂ ਕਰਨੀ, ਮਜਮਾ ਲੱਗਣਾ ਜਾਂ ਲਾਉਣਾ

mobile ('ਮਅਉਬਾਇਲ) *a n* ਗਤੀਸ਼ੀਲ, ਚਲੰਤਸ਼ੀਲ, ਚਲੰਤ, ਚੰਚਲ, ਚਲਦਾ-ਫਿਰਦਾ; ਗਤੀਸ਼ੀਲ ਦਸਤਾ

mobility (ਮਅ(ਉ)'ਬਿਲਅਟਿ) *n* ਗਤੀਸ਼ੀਲਤਾ, ਚੱਲਣਸ਼ੀਲਤਾ; ਚਪਲਤਾ

mock (ਮੌਕ) *n v a* ਮਖ਼ਕਰੀ, ਠੱਠਾ, ਹਾਸਾ, ਨਕਲ, ਠੱਠਾ-ਮਸ਼ਕਰੀ ਕਰਨਾ, ਮਖ਼ੋਲ ਉਡਾਉਣਾ, ਖਿੱਲੀ ਉਡਾਉਣੀ; ਨਕਲ ਉਤਾਰਨੀ; ਝੂਠਾ, ਨਕਲੀ; **~ery** ਹਾਸਾ, ਮਜ਼ਾਕ; ਝੂਠਾ ਦਿਖਾਵਾ; ਨਕਲ

modal ('ਮਅਉਡਲ) *a* ਦਿਖਾਵੇ ਦਾ; ਰੀਤੀ ਦਾ, ਰੀਤੀਆਤਮਕ; ਵਿਧੀਗਤ

mode (ਮਅਉਡ) *n* ਵਿਧੀ, ਪੱਧਤੀ, ਪ੍ਰਣਾਲੀ; ਤਰੀਕਾ, ਢੰਗ, ਤਰਜ਼, ਅੰਦਾਜ਼, ਤੌਰ; ਦਸਤੂਰ

moderate ('ਮੌਡ(ਅ)ਰਅਟ, ਮੌਡਅਰੇਇਟ) *a v* ਉਦਾਰ ਵਿਚਾਰਾਂ ਵਾਲਾ; ਨਰਮ ਖ਼ਿਆਲੀਆ; ਸੰਜਮੀ, ਸੰਤੁਲਤ; ਔਸਤ ਦਰਜੇ ਦਾ; ਮੱਧਮ ਪੈਣਾ ਜਾਂ ਪਾਉਣਾ; **~ness** ਨਰਮ ਖ਼ਿਆਲੀ, ਸੰਜਮਤਾ

moderation ('ਮੌਡਅ'ਰੇਇਸ਼ਨ) *n* ਸੰਤੁਲਨ; ਨਿਯੰਤਰਣ; ਨਰਮੀ, ਸੰਜਮ, ਹਲਕਾਪਣ

moderator ('ਮੌਡਅਰੇਇਟਅ*) *n* ਵਿਚੋਲਾ, ਮਧਿਅਸਥ, ਪੰਚ

modern ('ਮੌਡ(ਅ)ਨ) *a* ਆਧੁਨਿਕ, ਅਜੋਕਾ, ਵਰਤਮਾਨ, ਨਵੀਨ, ਨਵਾਂ; **~ism** ਆਧੁਨਿਕਤਾ, ਨਵੀਨਤਾ, ਆਧੁਨਿਕ ਵਿਚਾਰ; **~ist** ਆਧੁਨਿਕਤਾ ਵਾਦੀ, ਨਵੀਨਤਾਵਾਦੀ; **~ity** ਆਧੁਨਿਕਤਾ, ਨਵੀਨਤਾ; **~ization** ਆਧੁਨਿਕੀਕਰਨ, ਨਵੀਨੀਕਰਨ; **~ize** ਆਧੁਨਿਕ ਕਾਲ ਦੀਆਂ ਲੋੜਾਂ ਦੇ ਅਨੁਸਾਰ ਬਣਾਉਣਾ

modest ('ਮੌਡਿਸਟ) *a* ਸ਼ਰਮਾਕਲ, ਸੰਗਾਊ, ਸੰਕੋਚਵਾਨ, ਲੱਜਾਵਾਨ; ਸਰਲ, ਸਾਦਾ; ਨਮਰ; **~y** ਲੱਜਾਸ਼ੀਲਤਾ, ਲੱਜਾ, ਸ਼ਰਮੀਲਾਪਣ, ਨਿਮਰਸ਼ੀਲਤਾ, ਕਾਜ

modification ('ਮੌਡਿਫ਼ਿ'ਕੇਇਸ਼ਨ) *n* ਪਰਿਵਰਤਨ, ਸੁਧਾਈ, ਤਰਮੀਮ, ਸੰਸ਼ੋਧਨ

modify ('ਮੌਡਿਫ਼ਾਇ) *v* ਬਦਲਣਾ, (ਸਵਰ) ਪਰਿਵਰਤਨ ਕਰਨਾ; ਸੁਧਾਰਨਾ, ਸੁਧਾਈ ਕਰਨੀ, ਠੀਕ ਕਰਨਾ; ਤਰਮੀਮ ਕਰਨੀ

modulate ('ਮੌਡਯੁਲੇਇਟ) *v* (ਸੰਗੀ) ਸੁਰ ਨੂੰ ਉੱਚਾ ਨੀਵਾਂ ਕਰਨਾ; ਸੁਰ ਨੂੰ ਠੀਕ ਠੀਕ ਕਰਨਾ, ਸਾਧਣਾ; ਲੋੜ ਅਨੁਸਾਰ ਬਦਲਣਾ, ਘਟਾਉਣਾ ਜਾਂ ਵਧਾਉਣਾ

modulation ('ਮੌਡਯੁ'ਲੇਇਸ਼ਨ*) *n* ਸੁਰ ਦਾ ਲਹਿਰਾਉ, ਅਵਾਜ਼ ਦਾ ਉਤਰਾ-ਚੜ੍ਹਾ, ਅਲਾਪ

module ('ਮੌਡਯੂਲ) *n* ਛੋਟੀ ਮਾਤਰਾ, ਲੰਮਾਈ ਦੇ ਅਨੁਪਾਤ ਨੂੰ ਪਰਗਟ ਕਰਨ ਵਾਲੀ ਇਕਾਈ, ਨਾਪਣ ਦੀ ਇਕਾਈ

modulus ('ਮੌਡਯੂਲਅ) *n* ਗੁਣਾਂਕ, ਮਾਪਾਂਕ, ਗੁਟਕ

modus operandi ('ਮਅਉਡਅਸ' ਔਪਅ'ਰੈਨਡੀ) (L) ਕਾਰਜ ਵਿਧੀ

moist (ਮੌਇਸਟ) *a* ਭਿੱਜਿਆ ਹੋਇਆ, ਸਿੱਲ੍ਹਾ, ਨਮ, ਗਿੱਲਾ, ਤਰ; **~en** ਭਿਊਣਾ, ਸਿੱਲ੍ਹਾ ਕਰਨਾ, ਨਮ ਦੇਣੀ, ਗਿੱਲਾ ਕਰਨਾ, ਤਰ ਕਰਨਾ; ਭਿੱਜਣਾ, ਗਿੱਲਾ ਹੋਣਾ; **~ure** ਨਮੀ, ਸਿੱਲ੍ਹ, ਤਰੀ, ਗਿੱਲਾਪਣ

moke (ਮਅਉਕ) *n* (ਅਪ) ਗਧਾ, ਖੋਤਾ, ਖ਼ਰ; ਟੱਟੂ

moiasses (ਮਅ(ਉ)'ਲੈਸਿਜ਼) *n* ਸ਼ੀਰਾ

molecular (ਮਅ(ਉ)'ਲੈਕਯੁਅਲ*) *a* ਆਣਵਿਕ, ਆਣਵੀ

molecule ('ਮੌਲਿਕਯੂਲ) *n* (ਭੌ ਅਤੇ ਰਸਾ) ਅਣੂ,

ਕਟ, ਕਿਟਕਾ, ਰੇਜ਼ਾ, ਕਿਰਚ

molest (ਮਅ(ਉ)ਲੈੱਸਟ) *v* ਛੇੜਨਾ, ਛੇੜ-ਛਾੜ ਕਰਨੀ, ਔਖਾ ਕਰਨਾ, ਸਤਾਉਣਾ, ਦਿਕ ਕਰਨਾ, ਦਖ਼ਲ ਦੇਣਾ; ~ation ਔਖਿਆਈ, ਪਰੇਸ਼ਾਨੀ, ਛੇੜ-ਛਾੜ

molification ('ਮੌਲਿਫ਼ਿ'ਕੇਇਸ਼ਨ) *n* ਸ਼ਾਂਤੀ, ਕੋਮਲਤਾ, ਨਰਮੀ, ਮੁਲਾਇਮਤਾ

mollify ('ਮੌਲਿਫ਼ਾਇ) *v* ਸ਼ਾਂਤ ਕਰਨਾ, ਪ੍ਰਸੰਨ ਕਰਨਾ; ਠੰਡਾ ਕਰਨਾ; ਕੋਮਲ ਕਰਨਾ, ਮੁਲਾਇਮ ਕਰਨਾ; ਸ਼ਿੱਦਤ ਘਟਾ ਦੇਣੀ

moment ('ਮਅਉਮਅੰਟ) *n* ਛਿਣ, ਖਿਣ, ਝਟ, ਨਿਮਖ, ਪਲ, ਦਮ, ਲਮ੍ਹਾ; ~ary ਅਸਥਾਈ, ਛਿਣ-ਭੰਗੁਰ, ਛਿਣ-ਸਥਾਈ; ~ous ਮਹੱਤਵਪੂਰਨਤਾ, ਅਵੱਸ਼ਕ; ~ousness ਮਹੱਤਵਪੂਰਨਤਾ, ਅਵੱਸ਼ਕਤਾ

momentum (ਮਅ(ਉ)'ਮੈਂਨਟਅਮ) *n* (ਭੋ) ਗਤੀ-ਮਾਤਰਾ, ਸੰਵੇਗ

monarch ('ਮੌਨਅਃਕ) *n* ਸਮਰਾਟ, ਰਾਜਾ, ਰਾਜ, ਅਧਿਰਾਜ, ਸੁਲਤਾਨ, ਬਾਦਸ਼ਾਹ; ~y ਰਾਜ, ਬਾਦਸ਼ਾਹੀ, ਰਾਜ-ਤੰਤਰ

monastery ('ਮੌਨਅਸਟ(ਅ)ਰਿ) *n* ਈਸਾਈ ਮੱਠ, ਖ਼ਾਨਕਾਹ, ਆਸ਼ਰਮ; ਵਿਹਾਰ

monastic (ਮਅ'ਨੈਸਟਿਕ) *a* ਮੱਠ-ਸਬੰਧੀ, ਆਸ਼ਰਮ-ਸਬੰਧੀ, ਸੰਨਿਆਸੀਆਂ ਦਾ; ~ism ਵਿਰਕਤ ਜੀਵਨ, ਤਿਆਗੀ ਜੀਵਨ, ਮੱਠਵਾਸ, ਵਾਨਪ੍ਰਸਥ, ਸੰਨਿਆਸ, ਵਿਰਾਗ

Monday ('ਮਅੰਡਿ) *n* ਸੋਮਵਾਰ

monetary ('ਮਅੰਨਿਟ(ਅ)ਰਿ) *a* ਮੁਦਰਾ ਸਬੰਧੀ, ਵਿੱਤੀ; ਆਰਥਕ, ਧਨ ਸਬੰਧੀ, ਮਾਲੀ

monetization ('ਮਅੰਨਿਟਾਇ'ਜ਼ੇਇਸ਼ਨ) *n* ਮੁਦਰੀਕਰਨ, ਧਾਤ ਦਾ ਸਿੱਕਾ ਬਣਾਉਣ ਦੀ ਕਿਰਿਆ

money ('ਮਅੰਨਿ) *n* ਧਨ, ਰੁਪਏ, ਪੈਸੇ, ਮੁਦਰਾ; ਵਿੱਤ, ਸਿੱਕਾ, ਧਨ-ਰਾਸ਼ੀ, ਦੌਲਤ, ਪੂੰਜੀ, ਨਕਦੀ; ~lending ਸ਼ਾਹੂਕਾਰਾ, ਮਹਾਜਨੀ

monger ('ਮਅੱਙਗਅ*) *n* ਦੁਕਾਨਦਾਰ, ਵਪਾਰੀ

mongoose ('ਮੌਙਗੂਸ) *n* ਨਿਉਲਾ

monitor ('ਮੌਨਿਟਅ*) *n v* ਮਾਨੀਟਰ, ਉਪਦੇਸ਼ਕ, ਨਿਰੀਖਕ, ਬੋਧਕ, ਖ਼ਤਰੇ ਦੀ ਖ਼ਬਰ ਦੇਣ ਵਾਲਾ ਵਿਅਕਤੀ; ਜੰਗੀ ਜਹਾਜ਼; ਨਿਰੀਖਣ ਕਰਨਾ; ~y ਪਾਦਰੀ ਦਾ ਉਪਦੇਸ਼ਾਤਮਕ ਪੱਤਰ

monk (ਮਅੱਙਕ) *n* ਜੋਗੀ, ਸਾਧੂ, ਸੰਨਿਆਸੀ, ਮੱਠਵਾਸੀ, ਉਦਾਸੀ, ਫ਼ਕੀਰ, ਦਰਵੇਸ਼, ਵਿਰਾਗੀ, ਤਿਆਗੀ

monkey ('ਮਅੱਙਕਿ) *n v* ਬਾਂਦਰ, ਵਾਨਰ; ਸੁਰਾ-ਪਾਤਰ, ਸ਼ਰਾਬ ਵਾਲਾ ਭਾਂਡਾ; ਹਾਸਾ ਉਡਾਉਣਾ, ਨਕਲ ਲਾਉਣੀ

monocracy (ਮਅ'ਨੌਕਰਅਸਿ) *n* ਤਾਨਾਸ਼ਾਹੀ, ਇਕਪੁਰਖੀ ਰਾਜ

monocrat ('ਮੌਨਅਕਰੈਟ) *n* ਤਾਨਾਸ਼ਾਹ

monogamy (ਮੋ'ਨੌਗਅਮਿ) *n* ਇਕ ਪਤਨੀਤਵ; ਇਕ ਵਿਆਹ ਕਰਨ ਦੀ ਪ੍ਰਥਾ

monolatry (ਮੋ'ਨੌਲਅਟਰਿ) *n* ਇਕ ਇਸ਼ਟ-ਪੂਜਾ

monologue ('ਮੌਨਅਲੌਗ) *n* ਮਨ-ਬਚਨੀ, ਸਵੈਗਤ ਕਥਨ

monopolist (ਮਅ'ਨੌਪਅਲਿਸਟ) *n* ਇਜਾਰਾਦਾਰ, ਏਕਾਧਿਕਾਰ ਦਾ ਪੱਖੀ, ਏਕਾਧਿਕਾਰੀ

monopolize (ਮਅ'ਨੌਪਲਾਇਜ਼) *v* ਇਜਾਰਾਦਾਰੀ ਚਲਾਉਣੀ

monopoly (ਮਅ'ਨੌਪਅਲਿ) *n* ਇਜਾਰਾਕਾਰੀ ਏਕਾਧਿਕਾਰ

monotonous (ਮਅ'ਨੌਟਅਨਅਸ) *a* ਇਕ ਲੈਅ

ਇਕ ਸੁਰ; ਇਕ ਰਸ, ਨੀਰਸ; ਅਕਾਊ; ~ness, monotony ਇਕਸਾਰਤਾ, ਇਕਸੁਰਤਾ, ਅਕੇਵਾਂ, ਉਕਤਾਹਟ, ਨੀਰਸਤਾ

monsieur (ਮਅਾਂਸਯਅ:) *(F) n* ਸ੍ਰੀ, ਸ੍ਰੀਮਾਨ

monsoon ('ਮੌਨ'ਸੂਨ) *n* ਮੌਨਸੂਨ, ਮੌਸਮੀ ਹਵਾ; ਵਰਖਾ, ਵਰਖਾ, ਰੁੱਤ

monster ('ਮੌਂਸਟਅ*) *a n* ਰਾਖਸ਼, ਦਾਨਵ, ਦੁਰਾਤਮਾ; ਅਤੀ ਵਿਸ਼ਾਲ

monstrous ('ਮੌਂਸਟਰਅਸ) *a adv* ਰਾਖਸ਼ੀ, ਬਹੁਤ ਵੱਡਾ, ਦਿਉ ਵਰਗਾ; ਅਜੀਬ, ਵੀਤਤਰਸ, ਡਰਾਉਣਾ; ਘੋਰ; ਹਰ ਤਰ੍ਹਾਂ ਅਯੋਗ, ਸਰਾਸਰ ਗ਼ਲਤ; ਬਹੁਤ ਜ਼ਿਆਦਾ

month (ਮਅੰਥ) *n* ਮਹੀਨਾ, ਮਾਹ, ਮਾਸ; ਮਹੀਨੇ ਦੇ

monument ('ਮੌਨਯੁਮਅੰਟ) *n* ਪੁਰਾਤਨ ਇਮਾਰਤ, ਸਮਾਰਕ, ਸਮਾਰਕ ਚਿੰਨ੍ਹ; ~al ਯਾਦਗਾਰੀ; ਸ਼ਾਨਦਾਰ; ਮਹਾਨ; ਸਮਾਰਕੀ

mooch (ਮੂਚ) *v* (ਉਪ) ਮੁੱਛਣਾ, ਚੁੱਕ ਲੈਣਾ, ਚੁਰਾ ਲੈਣਾ, ਉਡਾ ਲੈਣਾ; ਇੱਧਰ ਉੱਧਰ ਐਵੇਂ ਫਿਰਨਾ, ਮਟਰ-ਗਸ਼ਤ ਕਰਨੀ, ਵਿਹਲਾ ਫਿਰਨਾ

mood (ਮੂਡ) *n* ਮਿਜ਼ਾਜ, ਬਿਰਤੀ, ਮਨੋਦਸ਼ਾ, ਚਿੱਤ, ਜੀਅ, ਭਾਵ, ਭਾਵੁਕ ਦਸ਼ਾ, ਕਿਰਿਆ ਦੇ ਰੂਪ; ~y ਦਿਲਗੀਰ, ਉਦਾਸ; ਮਨਮੌਜੀ, ਮਨਚਲਾ; ਗੁਸੈਲਾ, ਚਿੜਚਿੜਾ

moon (ਮੂਨ) *n* ਚੰਨ, ਚੰਦ, ਚੰਦਰਮਾ, ਸਸਿ, ਸ਼ਸ਼ੀ, ਮਹਿਤਾਬ; ~calf ਜਮਾਂਦਰੂ ਮੂਰਖ; ~face ਚੰਦਰ ਮੁਖ; ~light ਚੰਦ ਦੀ ਚਾਨਣੀ, ਚੰਦਰਕਾ, ਚੰਦ ਪ੍ਰਭਾ, ਜਯੋਤਸਨਾ; full ~ ਪੂਰਨਮਾਸ਼ੀ ਦਾ ਚੰਨ, ਪੂਰਾ ਚੰਨ

mop (ਮੌਪ) *n v* ਪੂੰਝਣਟ, ਪੂੰਝਣਾ, ਸਾਫ਼ ਕਰਨਾ, ਬੁਹਾਰਨਾ, ਮੂੰਹ ਚੜ੍ਹਾਉਣਾ

mope (ਮਅਉਪ) *n v* ਉਦਾਸ ਆਦਮੀ, ਦਿਲਗੀਰ ਹੋਣਾ, ਉਦਾਸ ਰਹਿਣਾ, ਗੁਆਚਿਆ ਗੁਆਚਿਆ ਰਹਿਣਾ

moped (ਮਅਉਪੈੱਡ) *n* ਇੰਜਣਦਾਰ ਸਾਈਕਲ, ਪੈਡਲ ਵਾਲਾ ਮੋਟਰ ਸਾਈਕਲ, ਮੋਪੈਡ

moral (ਮੌਰ(ਅ)ਲ) *n a* ਨੀਤੀ ਬਚਨ, ਉਪਦੇਸ਼; ਅਖ਼ਲਾਕੀ, ਨੈਤਕ; ~ity ਆਚਾਰ, ਨੀਤੀ, ਨੈਤਕਤਾ, ਸਦਾਚਾਰ

morale (ਮੌ'ਰਾਲ) *n* (ਸੈਨਕ ਆਦਿ ਦਾ) ਹੌਸਲਾ, ਮਨੋਬਲ, ਧੀਰਜ

moratorium (ਮੌਰਅ'ਟੌਰਿਅਮ) *n* ਰਿਣ ਜਾਂ ਕਰਜ਼ਾ ਚੁਕਾਉਣ ਦੀ ਕਾਨੂੰਨੀ ਮੁਹਲਤ; ਰੋਕ, ਬੰਦਸ਼, ਬੰਦੀ

morbid ('ਮੌਬਿਡ) *a* (ਚਿਕਿ) ਰੋਗੀ, ਰੋਗ-ਗ੍ਰਸਤ; ਸੰਬੰਧੀ; ਵਿਕ੍ਰਿਤ, ਦੂਸ਼ਤ, ਬੀਮਾਰ; ~ity, ~ness ਅਸੁਅਸਥਤਾ, ਵਿਗਾੜ, ਵਿਕ੍ਰਿਤੀ, ਰੋਗਗ੍ਰਸਤਤਾ

morbus (ਮੌਬਅਸ) *n* ਰੋਗ, ਬੀਮਾਰੀ, ਵਿਕਾਰ

more (ਮੌ*) *n a adv* ਅਧਿਕਤਾ; ਅਧਿਕ, ਬਹੁਤ ਜ਼ਿਆਦਾ; ਹੋਰ ਜ਼ਿਆਦਾ; ਅਧਿਕ ਮਾਤਰਾ ਵਿਚ; ~over ਇਸ ਤੋਂ ਛੁਟ, ਇਸ ਦੇ ਅਤਿਰਿਕਤ, ਇਮ ਦੇ ਸਿਵਾਇ; ਪਰ, ਬਲਕਿ

morgue (ਮੋਗਾ) *n* ਹੰਕਾਰ, ਅਭਿਮਾਨ, ਘਮੰਡ

moribund (ਮੌਰਿਬੰਡ) *a* ਅੰਤਲੇ ਦਮਾਂ ਤੇ, ਅਖੀਰਲੇ ਸੁਆਸਾਂ ਤੇ, ਮਰਨ ਕਿਨਾਰੇ, ਮੌਤ ਦੇ ਕੰਢੇ ਤੇ

morning ('ਮੌਨਿਙ) *n* ਸਵੇਰਾ, ਪ੍ਰਭਾਤ, ਵੱਡਾ ਵੇਲਾ, ਅੰਮ੍ਰਿਤ ਵੇਲਾ, ਪਹੁ-ਫੁਟਾਲਾ, ਤੜਕਾ, ਭੋਰ; ਉਸ਼ਾ ਕਾਲ; ~good ਸੁਪ੍ਰਭਾਤ ਸਵੇਰ, ਨਮਸਕਾਰ

morsel (ਮੌਸਅਲ) *n* ਗਰਾਹੀ, ਟੁੱਕ, ਟੁੱਕਰ, ਬੁਰਕੀ, ਲੁਕਮਾ, ਨਿਵਾਲਾ; ਟੁਕੜਾ

mortal (ਮੋ'ਟਲ) *n a* ਮਰਨਹਾਰ ਜੀਵ, ਮਨੁੱਖ, ਜਨ, ਨਾਸਵਾਨ, ਵਿਨਾਸ਼ੀ, ਮਰਨਹਾਰ, ਮਰਨਧਰਮੀ; (ਦੁਸ਼ਮਣ) ਜਾਨੀ, ਜਾਨ ਲੇਵਾ

mortar (ਮੋਟਾਅ*) *n v* ਉੱਖਲੀ, ਖਰਲ, ਕੁੰਡਾ; ਛੋਟੀ ਮਾਰਟਰ ਬੰਦੂਕ; ਗਾਰਾ, ਚੂਨਾ, ਮਸਾਲਾ; ਤੋਪਾਂ ਨਾਲ ਹਮਲਾ ਕਰਨਾ, ਗੋਲਾਬਾਰੀ ਕਰਨੀ, ਗਾਰੇ ਨਾਲ ਜੋੜਨਾ

mortgage (ਮੋਗਿਜ) *n v* ਗਿਰਵੀ, ਰਹਿਣ; ਗਿਰਵੀ ਰੱਖਣਾ ਗਹਿਣੇ ਰੱਖਣਾ

mortification (ਮੋਟਿਫ਼ਿ'ਕੇਇਸ਼ਨ) *n* ਆਤਮ-ਦਮਨ; ਸੰਜਮ, ਤਪੱਸਿਆ; ਅਪਮਾਨ

mortify (ਮੋਟਿਫ਼ਾਇ) *v* (ਸਰੀਰ ਜਾਂ ਭਾਵਾਂ ਨੂੰ) ਵੱਸ ਵਿਚ ਕਰਨਾ, ਇੰਦਰੀਆਂ ਦਾ ਦਮਨ ਕਰਨਾ, ਮਨ ਮਾਰਨਾ; ਹੰਕਾਰ ਤੋੜਨਾ, ਅਪਮਾਨ ਕਰਨਾ, ਭਾਵਾਂ ਨੂੰ ਠੇਸ ਪਹੁੰਚਾਉਣਾ

mortuary (ਮੋਚੁਅਰਿ) *n a* ਮੁਰਦਾਘਾਟ, ਲਾਸ਼-ਘਰ, ਮੁਰਦਾਖਾਨਾ

mortum (ਮੋ'ਟਅਮ) *n* ਮਿਰਤੁ, ਮੌਤ, ਮਰਨ

mosque (ਮੌਸਕ) *n* ਮਸੀਤ, ਮਸਜਦ

mosquito (ਮਅ'ਸਕੀਟਅਉ) *n* ਮੱਛਰ; **~net** ਮੱਛਰਦਾਨੀ, ਮਛਹਿਰੀ

moss (ਮੌਸ) *n v* ਚਿੱਕੜ, ਦਲਦਲ, ਚਲ੍ਹਾ; ਗਿੱਲੀ ਧਰਤੀ; ਕਾਈ; ਕਾਈ ਉਗਣੀ

most (ਮਅਉਸਟ) *a adv* ਸਭ ਤੋਂ ਜ਼ਿਆਦਾ, ਸਭ ਤੋਂ ਵੱਧ, ਵੱਧ ਤੋਂ ਵੱਧ, ਅਧਿਕਤਮ, ਸਭ ਤੋਂ ਵਧ ਕੇ

mot (ਮਅਉ) *n* ਚੁਟਕਲਾ, ਲਤੀਫ਼ਾ

mote (ਮਅਉਟ) *n* ਧੂੜ, ਧੂੜ-ਕਣ, ਅਣੂ, ਕਣ, ਰਵਾ, ਮਿੱਟੀ ਦਾ ਜ਼ੱਰਾ

motel (ਮਅਉ'ਟੈੱਲ) *n* ਮਾਟਲ, ਹੋਟਲ ਜਿਥੇ ਮੋਟਰਾਂ ਵਾਲੇ ਰਾਤ ਠਹਿਰ ਸਕਦੇ ਹਨ

moth (ਮੌਥ) *n* ਭੰਬਟ, ਪਤੰਗਾ, ਪਰਵਾਨਾ; ਲੋੜੀ ਆਦਮੀ

mother (ਮਅੱਦਅ*) *n v* ਮਾਤਾ, ਅੰਮਾ, ਮਾਈ, ਜਣਨੀ; ਧਾਰਮਕ ਸੰਘ ਦੀ ਪ੍ਰਧਾਨ ਇਸਤਰੀ; ਮਾਂ ਵਾਂਗ ਰੱਖਿਆ ਕਰਨੀ, ਗੋਦੀ ਲੈਣਾ, ਪਾਲਣਾ ਪੋਸਣਾ; ਜਨਮ ਦੇਣਾ; **~in law** ਸੱਸ; **~land** ਮਾਤ-ਭੂਮੀ; **~of peare** ਸਿੱਪੀ; **~tongue** ਮਾਤ-ਭਾਸ਼ਾ, ਮਾਦਰੀ ਜ਼ਬਾਨ; **~less** ਮਾਤਹੀਣ ਅਨਾਥ

motif (ਮਅਉ'ਟੀਫ਼) *n* ਆਧਾਰੀ ਗੁਣ ਜਾਂ ਵਿਚਾਰ, ਬੂਟੀ

motion (ਮਅਉਸ਼ਨ) *v* (1) ਚਾਲ, ਗਤੀ ਕਿਰਿਆ, ਚੱਲਣ, ਹਰਕਤ; ਪ੍ਰਸਤਾਵ, (2) ਅੰਤੜੀਆਂ ਦਾ ਮਰੋੜ, ਢਿੱਡ ਪੀੜ, ਵੱਟ ਮੱਲ-ਤਿਆਗ; **~less** ਗਤੀਹੀਨ, ਸਥਿਰ ਨਿਸ਼ਚਲ, ਅਚਲ

motivation (ਮਅਉਟਿ'ਵੇਇਸ਼ਨ) *n* ਪਰੇਰਨਾ ਪ੍ਰੋਤਸਾਹਨ, ਕਾਰਨ, ਪ੍ਰਯੋਜਨ

motive (ਮਅਉਟਿਵ) *n a v* ਪਰੇਰਨਾ; ਕਾਰਜ ਨਿਮਿੱਤ, ਪ੍ਰਯੋਜਨ, ਮਨੋਰਥ, ਅਰਥ, ਮਨਸ਼ਾ ਗਰਜ਼, ਮਕਸਦ; ਪਰੇਰਕ, ਪ੍ਰਵਰਤਕ; ਪਰੇਰਣ ਕਰਨਾ; ਕਾਰਨ ਹੋਣਾ

motivity (ਮਅਉ'ਟਿਵ਼ਅਟਿ) *n* ਪਰੇਰਨਾ ਚਾਲਕਤਾ, ਚਾਲਕ ਸ਼ਕਤੀ

motor (ਮਅਉਟਅ*) *n v a* ਗੱਡੀ, ਮੋਟਰ ਪਰੇਰਕ, ਸੰਚਾਲਕ, ਗਾਮੀ, ਚਾਲਕ; ਚਾਲਕ ਨਾੜੀ; **~cade** ਮੋਟਰਾਂ ਦਾ ਕਾਫ਼ਲਾ

motto (ਮੋਟਅਉ) *n* ਆਦਰਸ਼ ਵਾਕ, ਲੋਕੋਕਤੀ ਮੁਦਰਾਲੇਖ; ਨੀਤੀ ਵਾਕ; ਟੇਕ, ਵਾਕ-ਖੰਡ

mould (ਮਅਉਲਡ) *n v* ਕਾਲਬ (ਉਸਾਰੀ) ਨਮੂਨਾ, ਤਰਾਸ਼; ਉੱਲੀ; ਢਾਲਣਾ, ਸਾਂਚੇ ਵਿੱਚ

ਢਾਲਣਾ, ਨਮੂਨਾ ਬਣਾਉਣਾ, ਗੁੰਨ੍ਹਣਾ, ਮਿਲਾਉਣਾ; ਸੁਆਰਨਾ, ਮਾਡਲ ਬਣਾਉਣਾ

mound (ਮਾਉਂਡ) *n v* ਮੋਰਚਾ; ਟਿੱਲਾ; ਮਿੱਟੀ ਦਾ ਢੇਲਾ; ਪਹਾੜੀ; ਟਿੱਲਿਆਂ ਨਾਲ ਘੇਰਨਾ, ਢੇਰ ਲਾਉਣਾ; ਮੋਰਚਾ ਬੰਦੀ ਕਰਨਾ

mount (ਮਾਉਂਟ) *v n* ਚੜ੍ਹਨਾ; (ਘੋੜੇ ਤੇ) ਸਵਾਰ ਹੋਣਾ; ਵਧਣਾ; ~ed ਚੜ੍ਹਿਆ ਹੋਇਆ, ਸਵਾਰ

mountain (ਮਾਉਨਟਿਨ) *n* ਪਰਬਤ, ਪਹਾੜ, ਕੋਹ

mourn (ਮੋ:ਨ) *v* ਸੋਗ ਮਨਾਉਣਾ; ਸੰਤਾਪ ਕਰਨਾ; ਮਾਤਮ ਕਰਨਾ, ਵਿਰਲਾਪ ਕਰਨਾ; ਦੁਖੀ ਹੋਣਾ; ~er ਸੋਗ ਮਨਾਉਣ ਵਾਲਾ, ਮਾਤਮ ਕਰਨ ਵਾਲਾ; ~ful ਮਾਤਮੀ, ਸੋਗੀ, ਸੋਗਵਾਨ; ~ing ਸੋਕ, ਸੋਗ, ਖੇਦ, ਦੁੱਖ, ਰੰਜ, ਗਮ, ਮਾਤਮ, ਵਿਰਲਾਪ, ਰੁਦਨ

mouse (ਮਾਉਸ) *n* ਚੂਹਾ, ਮੂਸਾ, ਮੂਸ; ਸ਼ਰਮਾਕਲ ਆਦਮੀ

moustache ('ਮਅ'ਸਟਾਸ਼) *n* ਮੁੱਛ

mouth (ਮਾਉਥ) *n v* ਮੁੱਖ, ਚਿਹਰਾ, ਮੂੰਹ

move (ਮੂਵ) *v* ਚੱਲਣਾ, ਟੁਰਨਾ, ਹਰਕਤ ਕਰਨੀ, ਹਿੱਲਣਾ, ਕਾਰਵਾਈ ਕਰਨੀ; ਅਰਜ਼ੀ ਦੇਣਾ, (ਸਰੀਰ ਦੇ ਅੰਗ ਨੂੰ) ਹਿਲਾਉਣਾ, ਉੱਨਤੀ ਕਰਨਾ, ਅੱਗੇ ਵਧਣਾ; ਟੱਟੀ ਜਰਨੀ; ~ability ਗਾਮਸ਼ੀਲਤਾ, ਹਿੱਲਣ ਜਾਂ ਚੱਲਣ ਦੀ ਸਮਰੱਥਾ ਚੱਲਤਾ; ~able ਚੱਲ-ਸੰਪਤੀ; ਸਾਮਾਨ; ਚੱਲਣਸ਼ੀਲ, ਚਲਾਇਮਾਨ; ~d ਪ੍ਰੇਰਤ, ਚਲਤ; ਪ੍ਰਸਤੁਤ, ਪ੍ਰਸਤਾਵਤ, ਪ੍ਰਤਾਵਤ; ~ment ਚਾਲ, ਟੋਰ, ਹਰਕਤ; ਗਤੀ; ਕਾਰਵਾਈ; ਅੰਦੋਲਨ; ਹਲਚਲ; ਹਿਲਜੁਲ, ਭਾਵਨਾ; ਗਤੀ-ਵਿਧੀ

movie (ਮੂਵਿ) *a* ਚਲਚਿੱਤਰ ਸਬੰਧੀ, ਫ਼ਿਲਮ ਸਬੰਧੀ; ~s ਚਲਚਿੱਤਰ, ਸਿਨੇਮਾ

moving (ਮੂਵਿੰਗ) *a* ਚੱਲਦਾ-ਫਿਰਦਾ, ਚੱਲਤ,

ਗਤੀਮਾਨ, ਗਤੀਸ਼ੀਲ; ਕਰੁਣਾਮਈ, ਪ੍ਰਭਾਵਸ਼ਾਲੀ

much (ਮਅੱਚ) *a adv* ਚੋਖਾ, ਢੇਰ, ਬਹੁਤਾ, ਬਾਹਲਾ; ਅਤੀਅੰਤ, ਅਧਿਕ ਮਾਤਰਾ ਵਿਚ

mucous (ਮਯੂਕਅਸ) *a* ਚਿਪਚਿਪਾ, ਲੇਸਦਾਰ, ਕੱਫਦਾਰ

mucus (ਮਯੂਕਅਸ) *n* ਚੀਪ, ਕੱਫ, ਬਲਗਮ, ਚਿਪਚਿਪਾ, ਪੇਚਸ

mud (ਮਅੱਡ) *n* ਚਿੱਕੜ, ਦਲਦਲ, ਭੱਦੀ ਗੱਲ, ਗੰਦਗੀ; ~dy ਗੰਧਲਾ, ਚਿੱਕੜ ਭਰਿਆ, ਪੁੰਦਲਾ, ਮੈਲਾ, ਅਸਪਸ਼ਟ; ਗੰਧਲਾ ਕਰਨਾ, ਲਬੇੜਨਾ, ਪੁੰਦਲਾ ਕਰਨਾ

muddle (ਮਅੱਡਲ) *v n* ਕੰਮ ਨੂੰ ਵਿਗਾੜ ਦੇਣਾ, ਖ਼ਰਾਬ ਕਰ ਦੇਣਾ, ਰਲਗੱਡ ਕਰ ਦੇਣਾ; ਨਸ਼ੇ ਨਾਲ ਚੂਰ ਕਰਨਾ; ~some ਕੰਮ-ਵਿਗਾੜੂ, ਗੜਬੜ ਕਰਨ ਵਾਲਾ

muffle ('ਮਅੱਫਲ) *n v* ਉਂਗਲਾਂ ਤੋਂ ਬਿਨਾ ਦਸਤਾਨਾ; ਭੱਠੀ ਦਾ ਖ਼ਾਨਾ; ਗਲ ਢਕਣਾ (ਗਰਮ ਰੱਖਣ ਲਈ), ਗਲੂ-ਬੰਦ ਪਾਉਣਾ; ਅਵਾਜ਼ ਦਬਾਉਣਾ; ~r ਗਲੂਬੰਦ, ਮਫ਼ਲਰ; ਮੋਟਾ ਦਸਤਾਨਾ

mug (ਮਅੱਗ) *n v* ਗਲ ਪਾਤਰ, ਲੋਟਾ, ਗੜਵਾ, ਮੱਗ; ਠੰਢਾ ਸ਼ਰਬਤ; ਮੂਰ੍ਹ, ਆਦਮੀ, ਮੂਰਖ-ਬੰਦਾ; ਕਿਸੇ ਵਿਸ਼ੇ ਦਾ ਡੂੰਘਾ ਅਧਿਐਨ ਕਰਨਾ, ਬਹੁਤ ਪੜ੍ਹਨਾ, ਰਟ ਲੈਣਾ

muggy (ਮਅੱਗਿ) *n a* ਘੁਟਣ; ਗਲਾ ਘੋਟਣ ਵਾਲਾ, ਸਾਹ-ਘੋਟੂ, ਹੁਸੜ ਵਾਲਾ

mule (ਮਯੂਲ) *n* ਖੱਚਰ, ਦੋਗਲਾ ਜਾਨਵਰ, ਅੜੀਅਲ ਟੱਟੂ; ਮੂਰਖ ਆਦਮੀ; ~teer ਖੱਚਰ ਵਾਲਾ

multi (ਮਅੱਲਟਿ) *a* ਅਨੇਕ, ਬਹੁਤ

multicellular (ਮਅ'ਲਟਿ'ਸੈੱਲਯੁਲਅ*) *a* ਬਹੁਕੋਸ਼ਕੀ, ਬਹੁਕੋਸ਼ੀ

multicolour (ਮਅਲਟਿ'ਕਅੱਲਅ*) *n* ਬਹੁਰੰਗ, ਕਈ ਰੰਗ, ਅਨੇਕ ਵਰਨ

multifarious (ਮਅਲਟਿ'ਫੇਅਰਿਅਸ) *a* ਰੰਗ-ਬਰੰਗਾ, ਬਹੁਮੁਖੀ, ਬਹੁਰੂਪ

multifold (ਮਅਲਟਿਫਅਉਲਡ) *a* ਬਹੁਗੁਣ

multimillionaire (ਮਅਲਟਿਮਿਲਯਅ'ਨੇਅ*) *n* ਕਰੋੜਪਤੀ, ਬਹੁਤ ਧਨਵਾਨ (ਬਹੁਲੱਖਪਤੀ)

multinational (ਮਅੱਲਟਿ'ਨੈਸ਼ਨਲ) *n a* ਬਹੁਰਾਸ਼ਟਰੀ (ਕੰਪਨੀ)

multiple (ਮਅਲਟਿ'ਪਲ) *n a* ਗੁਣਜ; ਅਨੇਕ ਤੱਤੀ, ਬਹੁ ਭਾਗੀ, ਕਿਸਮ ਕਿਸਮ ਦਾ

multiplicity (ਮਅਲਟਿ'ਪਲਿਸਅਟਿ) *n* ਬਹੁਲਤਾ, ਵਿਵਿਧਤਾ

multiply (ਮਅੱਲਟਿਪਲਾਇ) *v* (ਗਣਿ) ਗੁਣਾ ਕਰਨਾ, ਜ਼ਰਬ ਦੇਣੀ

multipurpose (ਮਅਲਟਿ'ਪਅ:ਪਅਜ਼) *n a* ਬਹੁ-ਪੱਖੀ, ਬਹੁ-ਪ੍ਰਯੋਜਨ, ਬਹੁ-ਮਨੋਰਥੀ

multitude (ਮਅਲਟਿਟਯੂਡ) *n* ਅਧਿਕ ਗਿਣਤੀ, ਬਹੁ ਸੰਖਿਆ, ਬਹੁਲਤਾ, ਵਿਵਿਧਤਾ, ਬਹੁਰੂਪਤਾ

mum (ਮਅੱਮ) *n int a v* ਖ਼ਾਮੋਸ਼, ਚੁੱਪ, ਸ਼ਾਂਤ; ਚੁੱਪ ਰਹਿਣਾ, ਚੁੱਪ ਕਰਨ (ਮੂਕ) ਐਕਟਿੰਗ ਕਰਨੀ

mumble (ਮਅੰਬਲ) *n v* ਬੁੜਬੁੜਾਹਟ, ਗੁਟਗੁਟਾਹਟ, ਅਸਪਸ਼ਟ ਵਚਨ, ਅਵਿਅਕਤ ਬਾਨੀ; ਅਸਪਸ਼ਟ ਬੋਲਣਾ, ਮੂੰਹ ਵਿਚ ਗੱਲਾਂ ਕਰਨੀਆਂ, ਗੁਟਗੁਟਾਉਣਾ, ਬੁੜਬੁੜਾਉਣਾ

mummy (ਮਅੱਮਿ) *n* ਲਾਸ਼ ਜੋ ਮਸਾਲੇ ਲਾ ਕੇ ਸੁਰੱਖਿਅਤ ਰੱਖੀ ਜਾਵੇ, ਪੁਰਾਤਨ ਲਾਸ਼, ਸੁਰੱਖਿਅਤ

mump (ਮਅੰਪ) *v* ਸ਼ਾਂਤ ਰੂਪ ਧਾਰਨਾ, ਚੁੱਪ ਕਰਨਾ, ਚੁੱਪਚਾਪ ਬੈਠਣਾ; ਮਨ ਵਿਚ ਕੁੜ੍ਹਨਾ, ਬੁੜਬੁੜਾਉਣਾ; ~s ਕਨੇਡੂ, ਕੰਨ ਪੇੜੇ; ਰੁਸੇਵਾਂ, ਮੂੰਹ-ਮੁਟਾਪਾ, ਰੋਸਾ

mumpish ('ਮਅੰਪਿਸ਼) *a* ਤੁਨਕਮਿਜ਼ਾਜ

munch (ਮਅੰਚ) *v* ਚੱਬਣਾ (ਦਾਣੇ); ਕਰਚ ਕਰਚ ਕਰਕੇ ਖਾਣਾ, ਮੁਰਤ ਮੁਰਤ ਚੱਬਣਾ; ਚਿੱਥਣਾ

mundane (ਮਅੰ'ਡੇਇਨ) *a* ਦੁਨਿਆਵੀ, ਲੌਕਿਕ, ਸੰਸਾਰਕ; ਵਿਸ਼ਵ ਸਬੰਧੀ, ਸ੍ਰਿਸ਼ਟੀ ਸਬੰਧੀ; **~ness** ਲੌਕਿਕਤਾ, ਸੰਸਾਰਕਤਾ

municipal (ਮਯੂ'ਨਿਸਿਪਲ) *a* ਨਗਰਪਾਲਕਾ, ਨਗਰਪਾਲਕਾ ਨਾਲ ਸਬੰਧਤ; ਸ਼ਹਿਰੀ; **~ity** ਨਗਰਪਾਲਕਾ, ਨਗਰ ਸਤਾ

munificence (ਮਯੂ'ਨਿਫ਼ਿਸੰਸ) *n* ਦਇਆਲਤਾ, ਉਦਾਰਤਾ, ਸਖਾਵਤ, ਖੁੱਲ੍ਹਦਿਲੀ

munificent (ਮਯੂ'ਨਿਫ਼ਿਸੰਟ) *n* ਦਿਆਲੂ, ਸਖ਼ੀ, ਦਾਤਾ, ਦਾਨੀ

munify (ਮਯੂਨਿਫ਼ਾਇ) *v* ਸੁਰੱਖਿਅਤ ਕਰਨਾ, ਮਜ਼ਬੂਤ ਕਰਨਾ, ਕਿਲ੍ਹਾਬੰਦੀ ਕਰਨਾ

munition (ਮਯੂ'ਨਿਸ਼ਨ) *n v* ਅਸਲਾ, ਗੋਲਾਬਾਰੂਦ; ਜੁੱਧ-ਸਮਗਰੀ, ਲੜਾਈ ਦਾ ਸਮਾਨ; ਜੁੱਧ ਸਮਗਰੀ ਇਕੱਠੀ ਕਰਨੀ, ਗੋਲਾਬਾਰੂਦ ਜਮ੍ਹਾਂ ਕਰਨਾ

murder (ਮਅ:ਡਅ*) *n v* ਖ਼ੂਨ, ਹੱਤਿਆ, ਘਾਤ, ਹਿੰਸਾ, ਕਤਲ; ਖ਼ੂਨ ਕਰਨਾ, ਹੱਤਿਆ ਕਰਨੀ, ਘਾਤ ਕਰਨਾ, ਕਤਲ ਕਰਨਾ, ਮਾਰ ਸੁੱਟਣਾ; **~er** ਕਾਤਲ, ਖ਼ੂਨੀ, ਹੱਤਿਆਰਾ

murmur (ਮਅ:ਮਅ*) *n v* ਕਾਨਾਫੂਸੀ; ਮਰਮਰ ਧੁਨੀ, ਕਲਕਲ, ਭਿਣਭਿਣ, ਸਰਸਰਾਉਣਾ

muscle (ਮਅੱਸਲ) *n* ਪੱਠਾ; ਜ਼ੋਰ, ਬਾਹੂਬਲ

muscular (ਮਅੱਸਕਯੁਲਅ*) *a* ਪੱਠੇਦਾਰ;

ਗਠੀਲਾ, ਗੁੰਦਿਆ, ਪ੍ਰਸ਼ਟ

muse (ਮਯੂਜ਼) *n v* (ਕਾਵਿ) ਕਵੀ, ਸ਼ਾਇਰ; ਸਰਸਵਤੀ; ਕਾਵਿ-ਪ੍ਰਤਿਭਾ, ਧਿਆਨ; ਗੰਭੀਰ ਵਿਚਾਰ ਵਿਚ ਪੈਣਾ, ਮਨਨ ਕਰਨਾ, ਚਿੰਤਨ ਕਰਨਾ; ~**ful** ਧਿਆਨ ਮਗਨ, ਚਿੰਤਤ; ~**less** ਵਿਚਾਰਹੀਨ, ਅਭਾਵਕ

museum (ਮਯੂਜ਼ਿਅਮ) *n* ਅਜਾਇਬ ਘਰ, ਅਜਾਇਬਘਰਾਨਾ

mushroom (ਮਅੱਸ਼ਰੂਮ) *n v* ਖੁੰਭ; ਕੁਕਰਮੁੱਤਾ; ਨਵਾਂ ਨਵਾਬ, ਕੱਲ ਦਾ ਰਈਸ; ਖੁੰਭਾਂ ਤੋੜਨਾ

music (ਮਯੂਜ਼ਿਕ) *n* ਸੰਗੀਤ; ਸੰਗੀਤਸ਼ਾਸਤਰ, ਸੁਰ, ਰਾਗ; ~**ian** ਸੰਗੀਤ-ਸ਼ਾਸਤਰੀ, ਸੰਗੀਤੱਗ, ਵਾਦਕ; ਗਾਇਕ; ~**ologist** ਸੰਗੀਤ-ਸ਼ਾਸਤਰੀ; ~**ology** ਸੰਗੀਤ-ਸ਼ਾਸਤਰ, ਸੰਗੀਤ-ਵਿਗਿਆਨ

musk (ਮਅੱਸਕ) *n* ਕਸਤੂਰੀ, ਮੁਸ਼ਕ; ~**y** ਕਸਤੂਰੀ ਦੀ ਵਾਸ਼ਨਾ ਵਾਲਾ, ਕਸਤੂਰੀ ਯੁਕਤ, ਸੁਗੰਧਤ; ਖ਼ੁਸ਼ਬੂਦਾਰ

musket (ਮਅੱਸਕਿਟ) *n* ਪੁਰਾਣੇ ਵੇਲੇ ਦੀ ਬੰਦੂਕ; ~**eer** ਬੰਦੂਕ ਲੈ ਕੇ ਚੱਲਣ ਵਾਲਾ ਸਿਪਾਹੀ, ਬੰਦੂਕਚੀ

muslin (ਮਅੱਜ਼ਲਿਨ) *n a* ਮਲਮਲ, ਪਤਲਾ ਕੱਪੜਾ

musquash (ਮਅੱਸਕਵੈੱਸ਼) *n* ਛਛੂੰਦਰ

must (ਮਅੱਸਟ) *n v aux a* ਕੱਚੀ ਸ਼ਰਾਬ; ਉੱਲੀ, ਫ਼ਫ਼ੂੰਦੀ, ਭਕਜੀ; ਉੱਲੀ ਲੱਗਣੀ, ਚਾਹੀਦਾ ਹੈ; ਅਵੱਸ਼, ਲਾਜ਼ਮੀ

mustard (ਮਅੱਸਟਅਡ) *n* ਰਾਈ, ਸਰ੍ਹੋਂ; ਸੁਆਦੀ ਚੀਜ਼, ਦਿਲਚਸਪ ਆਦਮੀ

muster ('ਮਅੱਸਟਅ*) *n v* ਗਿਣਤੀ, ਹਾਜ਼ਰੀ, ਜੋੜ; ਸਮਾਗਮ, ਸਮੂਹ, ਜਮਘਟ; ਗਿਣਤੀ ਕਰਨੀ, ਹਾਜ਼ਰੀ ਲੈਣੀ, ਇਕੱਠ ਕਰਨਾ ਜਾਂ ਹੋਣਾ;

ਸ਼ਕਤੀ ਇਕੱਠੀ ਕਰਨੀ, ਸਾਹਸ ਕਰਨਾ

mutability (ਮਯੂਟਅ'ਬਿਲਅਟਿ) *n* ਚੰਚਲਤਾ, ਅਸਥਿਰਤਾ; ਪਰਿਵਰਤਨਸ਼ੀਲਤਾ

mutation (ਮਯੂ'ਟੇਇਸ਼ਨ) *n* ਅਦਲ-ਬਦਲ, ਤਬਦੀਲੀ, ਪਰਿਵਰਤਨ

mute (ਮਯੂਟ) *a n v* ਖਾਮੋਸ਼ ਜਾਂ ਗੂੰਗਾ; ਅਵਾਕ, ਮੂਕ, ਚੁੱਪ; ਮੌਨ, ਖਾਮੋਸ਼; ਸਪਰਸ਼ ਵਿਅੰਜਨ; ਮੂਕ ਐਕਟਰ; ਧੀਮਾ ਕਰਨਾ, ਦਬਾਉਣਾ; ~**ness** ਧੁਨੀਹੀਨਤਾ, ਮੂਕ ਭਾਵ, ਖ਼ਮੋਸ਼ੀ, ਗੂੰਗਾਪਨ

mutilate ('ਮਯੂਟਿਲੇਇਟ) *v* ਕੋਈ ਅੰਗ ਕੱਟ ਦੇਣਾ, ਹੱਥ-ਪੈਰ ਕੱਟ ਦੇਣਾ, ਅੰਗ ਭੰਗ ਕਰਨਾ, ਪੁਸਤਕ ਦਾ ਕੋਈ ਹਿੱਸਾ ਕੱਟ ਦੇਣਾ, ਖੰਡਤ ਕਰਨਾ; ~**d** ਵਿਕ੍ਰਿਤ, ਭਿੰਨ ਭਿੰਨ, ਖੰਡਤ, ਲੰਗੜਾ-ਲੂਲ੍ਹਾ, ਕੌਟਿਆ-ਵੱਢਿਆ

mutilation ('ਮਯੂਟਿ'ਲੇਇਸ਼ਨ) *n* ਅੰਗ-ਭੰਗ, ਖੰਡਨ, ਕਾਂਟ-ਛਾਂਟ

mutineer (ਮਯੂਟਿ'ਨਿਅ*) *n* ਗ਼ਦਰੀ, ਵਿਦਰੋਹੀ, ਬਾਗ਼ੀ

mutiny (ਮਯੂਟਿਨਿ) *n v* (ਫ਼ੌਜੀ) ਗ਼ਦਰ, ਬਗ਼ਾਵਤ, ਕਰਾਂਤੀ, ਵਿਦਰੋਹ, ਗ਼ਦਰ ਕਰਨਾ, ਬਗ਼ਾਵਤ ਕਰਨੀ, ਵਿਦਰੋਹ ਕਰਨਾ

mutt (ਮਅੱਟ) *n* ਗਧਾ, ਬੇਵਕੂਫ਼, ਬੁੱਧੂ, ਬੇਅਕਲ

mutter (ਮਅੱਟਅ*) *n v* ਅਸਪਸ਼ਟ ਉਚਾਰਨ, ਗੁਣਗੁਣਾਹਟ, ਬੁੜਬੁੜਾਉਣਾ; ਮੂੰਹ ਵਿਚ ਬੋਲਣਾ, ਕਾਨਾਫੂਸੀ ਕਰਨੀ, ਘੁਸਰ-ਫੁਸਰ ਕਰਨਾ; ~**ing** ਅਸਪਸ਼ਟ ਭਾਸ਼ਣ, ਅਵਿਅਕਤ ਉਚਾਰਨ, ਬੁੜਬੁੜ

mutton (ਮਅੱਟਨ) *n* ਭੇਡ ਜਾਂ ਬੱਕਰੀ ਦਾ ਮਾਸ

mutual ('ਮਯੂਚੁਅਲ) *a* ਪਰਸਪਰ, ਆਪਸੀ, ਬਾਹਮੀ, ਸਾਂਝਾ, ਸੰਮਿਲਤ; ~**ity** ਪਰਸਪਰਤਾ; ~**ly** ਆਪਸ ਵਿਚ, ਪਰਸਪਰ

muzziness (ਮਅੱਜ਼ਿਨਿਸ) *n* ਸੁਸਤੀ, ਆਲਸ, ਉਤਸ਼ਾਹੀਣਤਾ

muzzle (ਮਅੱਜ਼ਲ) *n v* ਬੁਥਨੀ; ਘੁੱਸੀ, ਬੰਦੂਕ ਦੀ ਨਾਲੀ ਦਾ ਮੂੰਹ, ਮੋਰੀ; ਦਹਾਨਾ; ਜ਼ਬਾਨਬੰਦੀ ਕਰਨੀ, ਬੋਲਣ ਦੇ ਲਿਖਣ ਦੀ ਮਨਾਹੀ ਕਰਨੀ

my (ਮਾਇ) *pron* ਮੇਰਾ, ਮੇਰੀ, ਮੇਰੇ; **~self** ਆਪਣੇ ਆਪ, ਖ਼ੁਦ, ਆਪਣੇ ਆਪ ਨੂੰ, ਮੈਂ ਖ਼ੁਦ

myopia, myopy (ਮਾਇ'ਅਉਪਯਅ, ਮਾਇਅਉਪਿ) *n* ਨਿਕਟ ਦ੍ਰਿਸ਼ਟੀ, ਅਲਪ ਦ੍ਰਿਸ਼ਟੀ

myriad (ਮਿਰਿਅਡ) *n a* ਬਹੁਤ ਵੱਡੀ ਸੰਖਿਆ; ਅਣਗਿਣਤ, ਅਸੰਖ, ਬੇਸ਼ੁਮਾਰ

mysterious (ਮਿ'ਸਟਿਅਰਿਅਸ) *a* ਭੇਦ-ਭਰਿਆ, ਭੇਦ-ਯੁਕਤ, ਰਹੱਸਪੂਰਨ, ਰਹੱਸਮਈ; **~ness** ਅਸਪਸ਼ਟਤਾ, ਰਹੱਸਪੂਰਨਤਾ, ਗੁੜੂਤਾ ਦੁਰਬੋਧਤਾ

mystery (ਮਿਸਟ(ਅ)ਰਿ) *n* ਰਹੱਸ, ਭੇਦ, ਰਾਜ਼, ਦੁਰਬੋਧਤਾ, ਅਸਪਸ਼ਟਤਾ, ਗੁੜੂਤਾ

mystic (ਮਿਸਟਿਕ) *a n* ਰਹੱਸਮਈ, ਸੂਫ਼ੀਆਨਾ, ਰਹੱਸਾਤਮਕ; ਅਲੌਕਕ, ਜੋਗੀ; **~ism** ਰਹੱਸਵਾਦ, ਅਧਿਆਤਮ-ਵਿੱਦਿਆ

mystify ('ਮਿਸਟੀਫ਼ਾਇ) *v* ਰਹੱਸਮਈ ਬਣਾ ਦੇਣਾ, ਗੁੜੂ ਕਰ ਦੇਣਾ; ਭੇਦਪੂਰਨ ਬਣਾਉਣਾ; ਵਿਸਮਿਤ ਕਰਨਾ

mystique (ਮਿ'ਸਟੀਕ) *n* ਰਹੱਸ

myth (ਮਿਥ) *n* ਮਿੱਥ, ਮਿਥਿਆ, ਪੁਰਾਣ ਕਥਾ; **~ical** ਮਿਥਕ, ਪੁਰਾਣਕ; ਕਾਲਪਨਕ; **~ological** ਮਿਥਹਾਸਕ, ਪੁਰਾਣਕ, ਪੁਰਾਣ ਸਬੰਧੀ, ਪੁਰਾਣ ਉਕਤ; **~ology** ਮਿਥਹਾਸ, ਪੁਰਾਣ; ਪੁਰਾਣ, ਵਿੱਦਿਆ, ਪੁਰਾਣ ਕਥਾ-ਸ਼ਾਸਤਰ; **~onomy** ਪੁਰਾਣ-ਸ਼ਾਸਤਰ

N

N, n (ਐੱਨ) *n* ਰੋਮਨ ਵਰਣਮਾਲਾ ਦਾ ਚੌਦੂਵਾਂ ਅੱਖਰ; ਮਾਪ ਦੀ ਇਕਾਈ; (ਗਣਿ) ਅਨਿਸ਼ਚਤ ਸੰਖਿਆ

nab (ਨੈਬ) *v n* ਫੜਨਾ, ਫੜ ਲੈਣਾ; ਗਰਿਫ਼ਤਾਰ ਕਰਨਾ, ਰੰਗੇ ਹੱਥੀਂ ਫੜ ਲੈਣਾ; ਪਹਾੜ ਦੀ ਸਿਖਰ, ਚੋਟੀ

nacarat (ਨੈਕਅਰੈਟ) *n* ਸੰਤਰੀ ਰੰਗ, ਜੋਗੀਆ, ਰੰਗ, ਭਗਵਾ ਰੰਗ

nag (ਨੈਗ) *n* ਟੱਟੂ, ਛੋਟਾ ਘੋੜਾ; ~**gy** ਲੜਾਕੂ, ਝਗੜਾਲੂ

naiad ('ਨਾਇਐਡ) *n* ਜਲ-ਦੇਵੀ, ਜਲ-ਪਰੀ

nail (ਨੇਇਲ) *n v* ਨਹੁੰ; ਨਹੁੰਦਰ; (ਪਸ਼ੂਆਂ ਦਾ) ਪੰਜਾ, ਕਿੱਲ, ਮੇਖ, ਕੋਕਾ; ਥਿਰੰਜੀ; ਲੰਮਾਈ ਦਾ ਇਕ ਮਾਪ; ਕਿੱਲ ਠੋਕਣਾ, ਕੱਸਣਾ, ਫੜ ਲੈਣਾ

naive (ਨਾਈ'ਈਵ਼) *a* ਭੋਲਾ-ਭਾਲਾ, ਸਿੱਧਾ-ਸਾਦਾ, ਸਿੱਧੜ

naivety (ਨਾਇ'ਈਵ਼ਿਟੀ) *n* ਭੋਲਾਪਨ, ਨਿਰਛਲਤਾ, ਸਰਲਤਾ, ਸਾਦਗੀ

naked ('ਨੇਇਕਿਡ) *a* ਨੰਗਾ, ਅਣਕੱਜਿਆ, ਨਗਨ; ਬੇਪਰਦਾ; ਸਪਸ਼ਟ, ਗਾਡ਼੍ਹ ਗਾਡ਼੍ਹ; ਗਾਡ਼ਾ; **~ness** ਨੰਗਾਪਨ, ਨਗਨਤਾ, ਨੰਗੇਜ, ਬੇਪਰਦਗੀ

name (ਨੇਇਮ) *n v* ਨਾਂ, ਨਾਮ; ਯਾਦਗਾਰ; ਪ੍ਰਤਿਸ਼ਠਤ ਵਿਅਕਤੀ; ਪ੍ਰਸਿੱਧੀ, ਸ਼ੁਹਰਤ, ਨਾਮਣਾ; ਕੁਲ, ਵੰਸ਼; ਨਾਂ ਰੱਖਣਾ; ਨਾਂ ਲੈਣਾ; ਜ਼ਿਕਰ ਕਰਨਾ, ਚਰਚਾ ਕਰਨੀ; **to call ~s** ਗਾਲ੍ਹਾਂ ਕੱਢਣਾ; ~**d** ਪ੍ਰਸਿੱਧ, ਨਾਮੀ; ~**less** ਅਪ੍ਰਸਿੱਧ, ਨਾਮਹੀਨ, ਗੁਮਨਾਮ, ਅਗਿਆਤ; ~**ly** ਅਰਥਾਤ, ਭਾਵ ਇਹ ਕਿ; ~**sake** ਹਮਨਾਮ, ਇਕੋ ਨਾਂ ਵਾਲਾ

naming ('ਨੇਇਮਿਙ) *n* ਨਾਮਕਰਨ

nancy ('ਨੈਂਸਿ) *a* ਜਨਾਨੜਾ, ਜਨਾਨੇ ਸੁਭਾਅ ਵਾਲਾ (ਆਦਮੀ)

naos ('ਨੇਇਔਸ) *n* ਮੰਦਰ ਦਾ ਅੰਦਰਲਾ ਹਿੱਸਾ, ਗਰਭ-ਗ੍ਰਹਿ

nap (ਨੈਪ) *v n* ਪਲ ਭਰ ਅੱਖ ਲਾਉਣੀ; ਠੋਕਾ ਲਾਉਣਾ; ਠੋਕਾ; ਬਾਜ਼ੀ, ਚਾਲ; ਤਾਸ਼ ਦੀ ਇਕ ਖ਼ਾਸ ਖੇਡ; ਮੰਜ, ਕੱਪੜੇ ਦੀ ਖੁਰ ਜਾਂ ਲੂਈਂ

nape (ਨੇਇਪ) *n* ਧੌਣ ਦਾ ਪਿਛਲਾ ਪਾਸਾ, ਗਿੱਚੀ

napkin (ਨੈਪਕਿਨ) *n* ਤੌਲੀਆ, ਰੁਮਾਲ, ਅੰਗੋਛਾ

narcotic (ਨਾ'ਕੌਟਿਕ) *a n* ਨਸ਼ੀਲੀ, ਮੁਰਛਾਕਾਰ; ਨੀਂਦ ਲਿਆਉਣ ਵਾਲੀ ਦਵਾਈ, ਨਸ਼ੀਲੀ ਚੀਜ਼

narcotization ('ਨਾ'ਕਅਟਾਇ'ਜ਼ੇਇਸ਼ਨ) *n* ਬੇਹੋਸ਼ੀ, ਬੇਸੁੱਧੀ, ਨਸ਼ੇ ਦੀ ਹਾਲਤ, ਸੁੰਨਤਾ

narcotize ('ਨਾ'ਕਅਟਾਇਜ਼) *v* ਬੇਹੋਸ਼ ਕਰਨਾ, ਨਸ਼ਾ ਚੜ੍ਹਾ ਦੇਣਾ, ਸੁੰਨ ਕਰਨਾ, ਬੇਹਿੱਸ ਕਰਨਾ

narrate (ਨਅ'ਰੇਇਟ) *v* ਵਰਣਨ ਕਰਨਾ, ਬਿਆਨ ਕਰਨਾ, ਸੁਣਾਉਣਾ

narration (ਨਅ'ਰੇਇਸ਼ਨ) *n* ਵਰਣਨ, ਬਿਆਨ, ਕਥਨ, ਕਥਾ, ਕਿੱਸਾ, ਵਿਆਖਿਆ

narrative ('ਨੈਰਅਟਿਵ਼) *n a* ਬਿਰਤਾਂਤ, ਵਰਣਨ, ਕਥਾ, ਕਿੱਸਾ; ਵਰਣਨਾਤਮਕ

narrator (ਨਅ'ਰੇਇਟਅ*) *n* ਬਿਆਨ ਕਰਨ ਵਾਲਾ, ਦੱਸਣ ਵਾਲਾ, ਕਥਾਵਾਚਕ

narrow ('ਨੈਰਅਉ) *a n v* ਤੰਗ, ਭੀੜ, ਸੌੜਾ, ਸੀਮਤ, ਸੰਕੁਚਤ; ਛੋਟਾ; ਤੰਗਦਿਲ, ਤੁਅੱਸਬੀ; ਸੁਆਰਥੀ; ਤੰਗ ਨਜ਼ਰੀਆ; ਸੰਖੇਪ ਕਰਨਾ; ਸੁਕੜਨਾ; ~**escape** ਬਾਲ ਬਾਲ ਬਚਣਾ; ~**ly**

ਮਸਾਂ ਹੀ, ਮਸਾਂ; ਮੁਸ਼ਕਲ ਨਾਲ, ਬਾਰੀਕੀ ਨਾਲ; ~minded ਤੰਗਦਿਲ, ਤੁਅੱਸਬੀ, ਸੁਆਰਥੀ, ਹੋਛਾ; ~ness ਸੌੜ, ਸੰਕੀਰਣਤਾ, ਤੰਗੀ, ਸੰਕੋਚ

nasal ('ਨੇਇਜ਼ਲ) *a* ਨਾਸਕੀ, ਅਨੁਨਾਸਕ; ਨੱਕ ਦਾ, ਨੱਕ ਜਾਂ ਨਾਸ ਸਬੰਧੀ

nascent ('ਨੈਸੰਟ) *a* ਨਵ-ਜਨਮਿਆ, ਉਸਰਦਾ; ਵਿਕਾਸਸ਼ੀਲ

nasty ('ਨਾਸਟਿ) *a* ਗੰਦਾ, ਭੈੜਾ, ਕੋਝਾ, ਘਿਰਣਾਯੋਗ; ਅਸ਼ੁੱਧ, ਅਸ਼ਲੀਲ; ਲੱਚਰ; ਹੋਛਾ

natal ('ਨੇਇਟਲ) *a* ਪ੍ਰਸੂਤ ਸਬੰਧੀ; ਜਨਮ ਸਬੰਧੀ; ~ty ਜਨਮ, ਪੈਦਾਇਸ਼, ਉਤਪਤੀ

nation ('ਨੇਇਸ਼ਨ) *n* ਕੌਮ, ਜਾਤੀ, ਰਾਸ਼ਟਰ; ਪਰਜਾ; ~al ਰਾਸ਼ਟਰੀ, ਕੌਮੀ; ਕੌਮ ਦਾ ਬੰਦਾ; ਵਸਨੀਕ; ~alism ਰਾਸ਼ਟਰਵਾਦ, ਕੌਮਪਰਸਤੀ, ਵਤਨਪਰਸਤੀ; ~alist ਰਾਸ਼ਟਰਵਾਦੀ, ਕੌਮਪਰਸਤ, ਦੇਸ਼ ਭਗਤ; ~ality ਕੌਮੀਅਤ, ਰਾਸ਼ਟਰੀਅਤਾ; ਰਾਸ਼ਟਰੀ ਭਾਵਨਾ, ਕੌਮੀ ਜਜ਼ਬਾ; ~alization ਰਾਸ਼ਟਰੀਕਰਣ; ~alize ਰਾਸ਼ਟਰੀਕਰਣ ਕਰਨਾ, ਰਾਸ਼ਟਰੀ ਜਾਂ ਕੌਮੀ ਬਣਾਉਣਾ; ~alized ਰਾਸ਼ਟਰੀਕ੍ਰਿਤ

native ('ਨੇਇਟਿਵ) *n a* ਵਾਸੀ, ਵਸਨੀਕ; ਦੇਸ਼-ਵਾਸੀ; ਦੇਸੀ ਮਨੁੱਖ

nativity (ਨਅ'ਟਿਵ੍ਅਟਿ) *n* ਜਨਮ, ਪੈਦਾਇਸ਼, ਉਤਪਤੀ; n~ ਹਜ਼ਰਤ ਈਸਾ, ਮਾਤਾ ਮਰੀਅਮ ਜਾਂ ਯੂਹਨਾ ਦਾ ਜਨਮ; ਜਨਮ-ਉਤਸਵ; ਜਨਮ-ਪੱਤਰੀ, ਕੁੰਡਲੀ

natural ('ਨੈਚਰ(ਅ)ਲ) *a n* ਕੁਦਰਤੀ, ਸੁਭਾਵਕ; ਪ੍ਰਕਿਰਤਕ; ਅਸਲੀ; ਮੂਲ, ਭੌਤਕ; ~ism ਪ੍ਰਕਿਰਤੀਵਾਦ, ਕੁਦਰਤੀ ਧਰਮ, ਨਾਸਤਕਤਾ; ਪ੍ਰਕਿਰਤਕ ਜੀਵਨ ਦੇ ਸਿਧਾਂਤ; ਯਥਾਰਥਵਾਦੀ ਪੱਧਤੀ; ਆਜ਼ਾਦ ਖ਼ਿਆਲੀ; ~istic ਪ੍ਰਕਿਰਤਕ

ਇਤਿਹਾਸ ਬਾਰੇ; ਪਸ਼ੂ-ਜੀਵਨ-ਸ਼ਾਸਤਰ ਬਾਰੇ; ਪ੍ਰਕਿਰਤੀਵਾਦੀ; ~ization ਦੇਸੀਕਰਣ, ਰਾਸ਼ਟਰੀਕਰਣ, ਨਾਗਰੀਕਰਣ; ~ize ਕੁਦਰਤੀ ਬਣਾਉਣਾ; ਰਸਮ-ਰੀਤੀ ਤੋਂ ਮੁਕਤ ਕਰਨਾ; (ਕਿਸੇ ਵਿਦੇਸ਼ੀ ਨੂੰ) ਨਾਗਰਿਕਤਾ ਦੇ ਅਧਿਕਾਰ ਦੇਣੇ; (ਬੇਗਾਨੀ) ਰਸਮ-ਰੀਤੀ ਆਦਿ ਨੂੰ ਅਪਣਾਉਣਾ; ~ly ਕੁਦਰਤੀ ਤੌਰ ਤੇ, ਸੁਭਾਵਕ ਤੌਰ ਤੇ; ਹਾਂ, ਠੀਕ; ~ness ਸੁਭਾਵਕਤਾ, ਸਹਿਜਤਾ, ਵਾਸਤਵਿਕਤਾ

nature ('ਨੇਇਚਅ*) *n* ਕੁਦਰਤ, ਪ੍ਰਕਿਰਤੀ, ਸ੍ਰਿਸ਼ਟੀ; ਸੁਭਾਅ, ਤਬੀਅਤ; ਖ਼ਸਲਤ; ਜਾਤੀ, ਵਰਗ, ਕਿਸਮ, ਪ੍ਰਕਾਰ; by ~ ਸੁਭਾਅ ਵੱਲੋਂ; in a state of ~ ਨੰਗਾ

naturing ('ਨੇਇਚਅਰਿੰਡ੍) *a* ਰਚਨਾਤਮਕ, ਸਿਰਜਣਾਤਮਕ, ਉਤਪਾਦਕ

naturopathy (ਨੇਇਚਅਰ'ਓਪਅਥਿ) *n* ਕੁਦਰਤੀ ਇਲਾਜ, ਪ੍ਰਕਿਰਤਕ ਚਿਕਿਤਸਾ

naught (ਨੈਟ) *n a* ਕੁਝ ਨਹੀਂ; (ਅੰਕ) ਸਿਫ਼ਰ, ਸੂਨ, ਜ਼ੀਰੋ; ਨਗੂਣਾ, ਹੀਣਾ; to come to ~ ਅਸਫ਼ਲ ਹੋਣਾ; ~iness ਢੀਠਾਈ, ਦੁਸ਼ਟਤਾ, ਉਪੱਦਰਸ਼ੀਲਤਾ; ਸ਼ਰਾਰਤ; ~y ਸ਼ਰਾਰਤੀ, ਨਟਖਟ (ਬੱਚਾ), ਜ਼ਿੱਦੀ, ਹਠੀ; ਬਦਮਾਸ਼

nausea ('ਨੋਸਯਅ) *n* ਮਤਲੀ; ਕਚਿਆਣ, ਘਿਰਣਾ, ਅਰੁਚੀ

nautical ('ਨੋਟਿਕਲ) *a* ਸਮੁੰਦਰੀ; ਜਹਾਜ਼ੀ, ਜਹਾਜ਼ ਸਬੰਧੀ, ਜਹਾਜ਼ਰਾਨੀ ਬਾਰੇ

naval ('ਨੇਇਵ੍ਲ) *a* ਜਲ-ਸੈਨਾ ਸਬੰਧੀ, ਸਮੁੰਦਰੀ ਫ਼ੌਜ ਲਈ; ਜਹਾਜ਼ੀ; ~force ਜਲ-ਸੈਨਾ, ਨੌ-ਸੈਨਾ, ਸਮੁੰਦਰੀ ਬੇੜਾ

nave (ਨੇਇਵ੍) *n* ਨਾਭੀ; ਪਹੀਏ ਦੀ ਪੁਰੀ; ਗਿਰਜੇ ਦਾ ਵਿਚਕਾਰਲਾ ਭਾਗ; ~l ਨਾਭੀ, ਨਾਭ; ਧੁੰਨੀ,

ਧਰਨ; ਕੇਂਦਰ-ਬਿੰਦੂ

navigate (ਨੈਵਿਗੇਇਟ) *v* ਜਹਾਜ਼ ਚਲਾਉਣਾ, ਜਹਾਜ਼ ਵਿਚ ਸਫ਼ਰ ਕਰਨਾ

navigator (ਨੈਵਿਗੇਇਟਅ*) *n* ਜਹਾਜ਼ ਚਲਾਉਣ ਵਾਲਾ; ਮਾਰਗ-ਨਿਰਦੇਸ਼ਕ

navy (ਨੇਇਵਿ) *n* ਜੰਗੀ ਜਹਾਜ਼ਾਂ ਦਾ ਬੇੜਾ, ਜਲ-ਸੈਨਾ, ਨੌ-ਸੈਨਾ; (ਕਵਿਤਾ) ਬੇੜਾ

nay (ਨੇਇ) *n adv* ਨਹੀਂ, ਨਾ; ਇੰਜ ਨਹੀਂ, ਕਿਉਂ ਨਹੀਂ, ਨਾ ਨਾ

near (ਨਿਅ*) *adv prep a v* ਨੇੜੇ, ਲਾਗੇ, ਕੋਲ; ਲਗਭਗ, ਕਰੀਬ-ਕਰੀਬ; ਲਾਗਲਾ, ਨੇੜੇ ਦਾ, ਨਜ਼ਦੀਕੀ; ਨੇੜੇ ਆਉਣਾ, ਲਾਗੇ ਪੁੱਜਣਾ, ਕੋਲ ਪਹੁੰਚਣਾ; **~ly** ਲਗਭਗ, ਕਰੀਬ-ਕਰੀਬ, ਨੇੜੇ-ਨੇੜੇ; **~ness** ਨੇੜ, ਨੇੜਤਾ, ਨਿਕਟਤਾ, ਸਮੀਪਤਾ

neat (ਨੀਟ) *a n* ਸਾਫ਼, ਸੁਅੱਛ, ਸੁਥਰਾ; ਉੱਜਲ; ਸੁੱਧ, ਖ਼ਾਲਸ; ਗੋਕਾ ਪਸ਼ੂ; ਗਾਂ ਜਾਂ ਬਲਦ; **~ness** ਸੁਅੱਛਤਾ, ਨਿਰਮਲਤਾ, ਸੁੱਘੜਤਾ

neath (ਨੀਥ) *prep* ਥੱਲੇ, ਹੇਠਾਂ

necessary (ਨੈੱਸਅਸ(ਅ)ਰਿ) *a n* ਜ਼ਰੂਰੀ, ਲੋੜੀਂਦਾ, ਅਵੱਸ਼ਕ

necessitate (ਨਿੱਸੈੱਸਿਟੇਇਟ) *v* ਅਵੱਸ਼ਕ ਬਣਾ ਦੇਣਾ; ਜ਼ਰੂਰੀ ਨਤੀਜਾ ਹੋਣਾ; ਮਜਬੂਰ ਕਰ ਦੇਣਾ, ਬੇਵਸ ਕਰ ਦੇਣਾ

necessity (ਨਿੱਸੈੱਸਅਟਿ) *n* ਲੋੜ, ਜ਼ਰੂਰਤ, ਅਵੱਸ਼ਕਤਾ; ਲੋੜੀਂਦੀ ਵਸਤੂ; ਕਾਰਨ, ਸਬੱਬ; ਰੁਕਾਵਟ; ਬੇਵਸੀ, ਲਾਚਾਰੀ, ਮਜਬੂਰੀ

neck (ਨੈੱਕ) *n v* ਧੌਣ, ਗਲਾ, ਗਰਦਨ; ਗਲ ਘੁੱਟਣਾ, ਗਲ ਲਾਉਣਾ; **~cloth** ਗਲੂਬੰਦ; **~lace** ਹਾਰ, ਗਲ ਪਾਉਣ ਵਾਲੀ ਗਾਨੀ, ਕੰਠਾ, ਕੰਠੀ; **~tie** ਟਾਈ, ਨਕਟਾਈ

nector (ਨੈੱਕਟਅ*) *n* ਅੰਮ੍ਰਿਤ; ਆਬੇ-ਹਯਾਤ

Neddy (ਨੈੱਡਿ) *n* (ਬੋਲ) ਖੱਚਰ, ਖੋਤਾ

nee (ਨੇਇ) *a* ਪੇਕਿਆਂ ਦਾ (ਗੋਤ ਜਾਂ ਨਾਂ); ਕੁਆਰੀ ਹੁੰਦੀ ਦਾ ਨਾਂ; ਕੁਆਰਾ ਨਾਂ

need (ਨੀਡ) *n* ਲੋੜ, ਜ਼ਰੂਰਤ; ਥੁੜ੍ਹ, ਤੰਗੀ, ਸੰਕਟ, ਕਸ਼ਟ, ਮੁਥਾਜੀ, ਦੁੱਖ; ਕੰਗਾਲੀ, ਗ਼ਰੀਬੀ; ਇੱਛਾ, ਆਕਾਂਖਿਆ; **~ful** ਜ਼ਰੂਰੀ, ਅਵੱਸ਼ਕ, ਲੋੜੀਂਦੀ ਯੋਗ, ਉਚਿਤ, ਮੁਨਾਸਬ (ਕਾਰਵਾਈ); **~iness** ਲੋੜ, ਜ਼ਰੂਰਤ, ਤੰਗੀ; **~y** ਲੋੜਵੰਦ, ਥੁੜ੍ਹਿਆ ਹੋਇਆ, ਗ਼ਰੀਬ, ਮੁਥਾਜ

needle (ਨੀਡਲ) *n v* ਸੂਈ, ਸੂਆ, ਸਲਾਈ, ਨੋਕਦਾਰ ਪੱਥਰ; ਸਿਊਣਾ; ਚੋਭਣਾ; ਨੋਕਦਾਰ ਪੱਥਰ ਬਣਾਉਣਾ; ਅੰਦਰ ਵੜ ਜਾਣਾ; ਚੀਰ-ਫਾੜ ਕਰਨੀ; ਛੇਕ ਕਰਨਾ; **~work** ਸੀਣਾ ਪਰੋਣਾ, ਸਿਲਾਈ-ਕਢਾਈ ਦਾ ਕੰਮ; ਕਸੀਦਾ

nefarious (ਨਿੱਫ਼ੇਅਰਿਅਸ) *n a* ਬਦ, ਭੈੜਾ, ਬੁਰਾ; **~ness** ਦੁਸ਼ਟਤਾ

negate (ਨਿੱਗੇਇਟ) *v* ਰੱਦਣਾ, ਮਿਟਾਉਣਾ, ਮੇਸਣਾ, ਨਿਸਫਲ ਕਰਨਾ, ਅਸਵੀਕਾਰ ਕਰਨਾ; ਖੰਡਨ ਕਰਨਾ

negation (ਨਿੱਗੇਇਸ਼ਨ) *n* ਨਿਖੇਧ, ਨਾਬਰਾਤਮਾਨ, ਖੰਡਨ, ਇਨਕਾਰ; ਅਸਤੀਕਰਨ; ਤਰਦੀਦ

negative (ਨੈੱਗਅਟਿਵ਼) *a n v* ਨਿਖੇਪੀਪੂਰਨ; ਇਨਕਾਰੀ; (ਗਣਿ) ਨਫ਼ੀ; ਅਸਵੀਕਾਰ ਕਰਨਾ, ਨਾਮਨਜ਼ੂਰ ਕਰਨਾ; ਰੱਦ ਕਰਨਾ, ਖੰਡਨ ਕਰਨਾ

neglect (ਨਿੱਗਲੈੱਕਟ) *n v* ਅਣਗਹਿਲੀ, ਉਪੇਖਿਆ, ਲਾਪਰਵਾਹੀ, ਭੁੱਲ, ਉਕਾਈ; ਅਣਗਹਿਲੀ ਕਰਨੀ, ਉਕਾਈ ਕਰਨੀ, ਅਸਾਵਧਾਨੀ ਵਰਤਣੀ, ਧਿਆਨ ਨਾ ਦੇਣਾ; **~able** ਛੱਡਣਯੋਗ, ਭੁੱਲਣ ਯੋਗ,

ਵਿਸਾਰਨਯੋਗ; ~ed ਭੁੱਲਿਆ ਹੋਇਆ, ਵਿਸਰਿਆ, ਉਪੇਖਿਅਤ, ਅਣਗੌਲਿਆ

negligence (ਨੈਗਲਿਜਅੰਸ) *n* ਲਾਪਰਵਾਹੀ, ਅਣਗਹਿਲੀ, ਕੁਤਾਹੀ, ਅਸਾਵਧਾਨੀ, ਉਕਾਈ; ਭੁੱਲ; ਉਪੇਖਿਆ, ਗਫ਼ਲਤ

negligent (ਨੈਗਲਿਜਅੰਟ) *a* ਲਾਪਰਵਾਹ, ਅਸਾਵਧਾਨ, ਆਲਸੀ, ਅਵੇਸਲਾ, ਗਫ਼ਲਤ ਭਰਿਆ, ਉਪੇਖਿਆਕਾਰੀ

negligible (ਨੈਗਲਿਜਅਬਲ) *a* ਨਗੂਣਾ, ਤੁੱਛ, ਨਾਂ-ਮਾਤਰ; ਬਹੁਤ ਥੋੜ੍ਹਾ, ਜ਼ਰਾ ਕੁ

negotiable (ਨਿ'ਗਅਉਸ਼ਅਬਲ) *a* ਸਮਝੌਤੇ ਯੋਗ, (ਹੁੰਡੀ) ਸਕਾਰਨ ਯੋਗ

negotiate (ਨਿ'ਗਅਉਸ਼ਿਏਇਟ) *v* (ਸਮਝੌਤੇ ਲਈ) ਗੱਲਬਾਤ ਕਰਨੀ; (ਮੁਆਮਲਾ) ਨਜਿੱਠਣਾ; (ਕਾਰ-ਵਿਹਾਰ ਦਾ) ਪ੍ਰਬੰਧ ਕਰਨਾ; ਵੇਚਣਾ, ਵਪਾਰ ਕਰਨਾ

Negro ('ਨੀਗਰਅਉ) *n a* ਹਬਸ਼ੀ; ਹਬਸ਼ੀ ਜਾਤੀ ਦਾ; ਕਾਲਾ-ਸਿਆਹ

neigh (ਨੇਇ) *v n* ਹਿਣਕਣਾ; ਹਿਣਕ (ਘੋੜੇ ਦੀ); ~ing ਹਿਣਹਿਣਾਹਟ

neighbour, neighbor ('ਨੇਇਬਅ*) *n v* ਗੁਆਂਢੀ, ਪੜੋਸੀ, ਹਮਸਾਇਆ; ਗੁਆਂਢ ਵਿਚ ਹੋਣਾ, ਕੋਲ ਹੋਣਾ; ~hood ਗੁਆਂਢ; ਆਂਢ-ਗੁਆਂਢ, ਚੁਫੇਰਾ, ਚੁਗਿਰਦਾ; ~ing ਗੁਆਂਢ ਦਾ; ਨਾਲ ਲੱਗਦਾ; ਸਾਂਝੀ ਬੰਨੀ ਵਾਲਾ; ~liness ਨੇੜਤਾ, ਨਿਕਟਤਾ, ਗੁਆਂਢ

neither ('ਨਾਇਦਅ*) *conj adv a pron* ਨਾ, ਨਾ ਹੀ; ਬਿਲਕੁਲ ਨਹੀਂ, ਕੋਈ ਵੀ ਨਹੀਂ

neo ('ਨੀਅਉ) (ਸੰਯੁਕਤ ਰੂਪ) ਨਵ, ਨਵਾਂ, ਨਵੀਂ

neologist (ਨੀ'ਔਲਅਜਿਸਟ) *n* ਨਵੀਨਤਾਵਾਦੀ; ਬੁੱਧੀਵਾਦੀ; ਨਵੇਂ ਸ਼ਬਦ ਘੜਨ ਵਾਲਾ

nephew ('ਨੈਂਫ੍ਯੂ) *n* ਭਤੀਜਾ; ਭਾਣਜਾ

nepotism ('ਨੈਪਅਟਿਜ਼(ਅ)ਮ) *n* ਭਾਈ-ਭਤੀਜਾਵਾਦ, ਕੁੰਬਾਪਰਸਤੀ

Neptune ('ਨੈਪਟਯੂਨ) *n* ਸਾਗਰ-ਦੇਵ, ਵਰੁਣ

nerve (ਨਅ:ਵ) *n v* ਤੰਤੂ, ਨਸ, ਰਗ ਬੇਚੈਨੀ; ਸਾਹਸ ਵਧਾਉਣਾ; ~less ਮੱਠਾ, ਢਿੱਲਾ, ਨਿਢਰਿਆ, ਸਿਥਲ

nervous ('ਨਅ:ਵ੍ਅਸ) *a* ਬੇਚੈਨ, ਭਾਵੁਕ, ਘਬਰਾਇਆ ਹੋਇਆ, ਪਰੇਸ਼ਾਨ; ~system ਨਸ-ਪ੍ਰਬੰਧ; ~ness ਬੇਚੈਨੀ, ਘਬਰਾਹਟ, ਪਰੇਸ਼ਾਨੀ

nest (ਨੈਸਟ) *n v* ਆਲ੍ਹਣਾ, ਆਸ਼ਿਆਨਾ, ਘੁਰਨਾ, ਖੁੱਡਾ; ਰੈਣ ਬਸੇਰਾ; ਡੇਰਾ; ਘਰ ਬਣਾਉਣਾ ਆਲ੍ਹਣਾ ਪਾਉਣਾ ~le ਰਹਿਣਾ, ਵਸਣਾ, ਟਿਕਾਣਾ ਬਣਾਉਣਾ; ਸ਼ਰਨ ਲੈਣੀ; ਪਾਲਣਾ

net (ਨੈੱਟ) *n a* ਜਾਲ, ਜਾਲੀ, ਫਾਹੀ, ਫੰਧਾ; ਧੋਖਾ; ਭਰਮ; ਮੂਲ, ਅਸਲ, ਉੱਕਾ, ਨਿਰੋਲ, ਖ਼ਾਲਸ, ਉੱਕਾ-ਪੁੱਕਾ, ਨਿਰਾ; ਜਾਲ ਵਿਚ ਫਸਾਉਣਾ; ~work ਜਾਲੀ ਦਾ ਕੰਮ; ਜਾਲੀ; ਜਾਲੀਦਾਰ ਲਕੀਰਾਂ, (ਰੇਲਾਂ, ਸੜਕਾਂ, ਪ੍ਰਸਾਰਨ ਆਦਿ ਦਾ) ਜਾਲ; ~ting ਜਾਲ, ਜਾਲੀ ਦਾ ਕੰਮ; ਜਾਲ ਲਾਉਣਾ

neurology ('ਨਯੁਅ'ਰੌਲਅਜਿ) *n* ਤੰਤਰ-ਵਿਗਿਆਨ, ਚੇਤਾ ਵਿਗਿਆਨ

neuropathy ('ਨਯੁਅ'ਰੌਪਅਥਿ) *n* ਤੰਤੂ-ਰੋਗ

neurosis ('ਨਯੁਅਰਉਸਿਸ) *n* ਤੰਤੂ ਵਿਕਾਰ, ਨਾੜਾਂ ਵਿਚ ਕੋਈ ਵਿਗਾੜ; ਪਾਗਲਪਨ; ਮਾਨਸਕ ਬੇਚੈਨੀ

neutral ('ਨਯੂਟਰ(ਅ)ਲ) *a* ਨਿਰਪੱਖ, ਬੇਲਾਗ, ਅਨਿਸ਼ਚਤ, ਵੱਖਰਾ, ਅਲਿੰਗ; ~ity ਨਿਰਪੱਖਤਾ, ਉਦਾਸੀਨਤਾ; ਨਪੁੰਸਕਤਾ; ~ization

ਨਿਰਾਕਰਨ, ਪ੍ਰਭਾਵਹੀਨਤਾ; ~ize ਬਰਾਬਰ ਕਰਨਾ, ਪ੍ਰਭਾਵਹੀਨ ਕਰਨਾ, ਉਦਾਸੀਨ ਕਰਨਾ; ਨਿਰਪੱਖ ਬਣਾਉਣਾ

never ('ਨੈੱਵ਼ਅ*) *adv* ਕਦੇ ਨਹੀਂ, ਉੱਕਾ ਹੀ ਨਹੀਂ; ~**more** ਫੇਰ ਕਦੇ ਨਹੀਂ, ਮੁੜ ਕੇ ਨਹੀਂ, ਬੱਸ ਫੇਰ ਨਹੀਂ; ~**theless** ਤਾਂ ਵੀ, ਫੇਰ ਵੀ; ਪਰੇ

new (ਨਯੂ) *a adv* ਨਵਾਂ, ਨਵੀਨ, ਆਧੁਨਿਕ, ਅਜੋਕਾ, ਨਵੇਂ ਸਿਰੇ ਤੋਂ, ਨਵੇਂ ਢੰਗ ਨਾਲ; ~**comer** ਨੌਂਵਰਦ; ~**ly** ਨਵਾਂ ਨਵਾਂ, ਹੁਣੇ ਹੁਣੇ, ਥੋੜ੍ਹੇ ਚਿਰ ਤੋਂ

news (ਨਯੂਜ਼) *n* ਖ਼ਬਰ, ਗਾਹਾਜ, ਹਾਲਚਾਲ, ਬਿਰਤਾਂਤ; ~**paper** ਅਖ਼ਬਾਰ, ਸਮਾਚਾਰ-ਪੱਤਰ

next (ਨੈੱਕਸਟ) *a adv prep n* ਅਗਲਾ, ਦੂਜਾ; ਆਗਾਮੀ; ਉਪਰੰਤ; ਕੋਲ, ਲਾਗੇ, ਨੇੜੇ, ਠੀਕ ਅੱਗੇ, ਠੀਕ ਪਿੱਛੇ

nexus (ਨੈੱਕਸਅੱਸ) *n* ਸਬੰਧ, ਮੇਲ; ਗੰਠਜੋੜ

nib (ਨਿਬ) *n* ਨੋਕ; ਹੁੰਝ, ਜੀਭ, ਨੋਕ ਜਾਂ ਜੀਭ

nice (ਨਾਇਸ) *a adv* ਸੁਹੱਜਾ, ਸੁਖੜ, ਚੰਗਾ, ਸੋਹਣਾ; ਪਿਆਰਾ; ~**ty** ਖ਼ੂਬੀ, ਚੰਗਿਆਈ; ਸੁਖਮਤਾ, ਬਾਰੀਕੀ; ਕੋਮਲਤਾ

niche (ਨਿਚ) *n v* ਆਲਾ, ਤਾਕ; ਟਿਕਾਣਾ, ਸਥਾਨ; ਆਲੇ ਵਿਚ ਰੱਖਣਾ; ਸਾਂਚਾ

nick (ਨਿਕ) *n v* ਵੱਢਾ; ਦੰਦਾ; ਸ਼ੁਭ ਸਮਾਂ; ਦੰਦੇਦਾਰ ਬਣਾਉਣਾ; ਦੰਦੇ ਕੱਢਣੇ; ਨਿਸ਼ਾਨ ਜਾਂ ਚਿੰਨ੍ਹ ਲਾਉਣਾ; ~**er** ਗੰਢ ਕੱਪ, ਜੇਬ ਕੁਤਰਾ; ਉਚਕਾ; ਹਿਟਕਣਾ, ਹਿਲਹਿਲਾਉਣਾ

nickle ('ਨਿਕਲ) *n v a* ਰੁਪਾ, ਗਿਲਟ, ਨਿਕਲ, ਕਲਈ, ਮੁਲੰਮਾ; ਨਿਕਲ ਚੜ੍ਹਾਉਣਾ

nickname ('ਨਿਕਨੇਇਮ) *n v* ਉਪ-ਨਾਂ; ਅੱਲ ਪਾਉਣੀ, ਨਾਂ ਪਾਉਣਾ

nid nod (ਨਿਡ'ਨੌਡ) *v* ਸਿਰ ਹਿਲਣਾ ਜਾਂ ਹਿਲਾਉਣਾ

niece (ਨੀਸ) *n* ਭਤੀਜੀ, ਭਾਣਜੀ

niffy ('ਨਿਫ਼ਿ) *a* (ਅਪ) ਬਦਬੂਦਾਰ

nifty ('ਨਿਫ਼ਟਿ) *a* ਚੁਸਤ, ਫੁਰਤੀਲਾ, ਫ਼ੈਸ਼ਨਦਾਰ

niggard ('ਨਿਗਅਃਡ) *n a* ਸੂਮ, ਕੰਜੂਸ; ~**liness** ਕੰਜੂਸੀ; ~**ly** ਸੂਮ, ਕੰਜੂਸ

niggling ('ਨਿਗਲਿਙ) *a* ਘਟੀਆ, ਨਗੂਣਾ, ਤੁੱਛ, ਨੀਚ

nigh (ਨਾਇ) *adv a prep* ਨੇੜੇ, ਲਾਗੇ, ਕੋਲ, ਨੇੜੇ ਦਾ

night (ਨਾਇਟ) *n* ਰਾਤ, ਹਨੇਰਾ; ~**and day** ਰਾਤ ਦਿਨੇ, ਨਿਸਦਿਨ; ~**blindness** ਅੰਧਰਾਤਾ

nightingale ('ਨਾਇਟਿਙਗੇਇਲ) *n* ਬੁਲਬੁਲ

nil (ਨਿਲ) *n* ਸਿਫ਼ਰ, ਕੁਝ ਨਹੀਂ

nimble ('ਨਿੰਬਲ) *a* ਫੁਰਤੀਲਾ, ਚੁਸਤ; ਹੁਸ਼ਿਆਰ; ~**ness** ਫੁਰਤੀ; ਚੁਸਤੀ; ਨਿਪੁੰਨਤਾ

nine (ਨਾਇਨ) *a n* ਨੌਂ; (ਤਾਸ਼ ਦਾ) ਨਹਿਲਾ; ~**day's wonder** ਚਹੁੰ ਦਿਨਾਂ ਦੀ ਚਾਨਣੀ; ~**teen** ਉੱਨੀ; ~**ty** ਨੱਬੇ

nip (ਨਿਪ) *v n* ਰੁੰਡੀ ਵੱਢਣੀ; ਖੋਹਣਾ, ਕਤਰਨਾ, ਛਾਂਟਣਾ; ਨਾਸ ਕਰਨਾ; ਤਾਅਨੇ ਮਾਰਨੇ; ਜਿੱਚ ਕਰਨਾ; ਦਬਾਉ; ਹੁਸਜੀ; *to ~ in the bud* ਜੰਮਦਿਆਂ ਹੀ ਕੁਚਲ ਦੇਣਾ

nipple ('ਨਿਪਲ) *n* ਥਣ ਦੀ ਚੂਚੀ, ਡੋਡੀ, ਨਿਪਲ

nit (ਨਿਟ) *n* ਲੀਖ, ਜੂੰ

no (ਨਅਉ) *a adv n* ਨਹੀਂ, ਨਾ; ਕੋਈ ਨਹੀਂ, ਕੁਝ ਨਹੀਂ; ~**where** ਕਿਸੇ ਥਾਂ ਵੀ ਨਹੀਂ, ਕਿਧਰੇ ਵੀ ਨਹੀਂ; *by ~means* ਕਿਸੇ ਤਰ੍ਹਾਂ ਵੀ ਨਹੀਂ

nobility (ਨਅ(ਉ)'ਥਿਲਅਟਿ) *n* ਕੁਲੀਨਤਾ, ਸਾਊਪੁਣਾ, ਵਡੱਤਣ

noble ('ਨਅਉਬਲ) *a n* ਕੁਲੀਨ, ਸ੍ਰੇਸ਼ਟ;

ਖ਼ਾਨਦਾਨੀ, ਉਦਾਰ, ਸੁਖੀ, ਸ਼ਰੀਫ਼; ਪ੍ਰਭਾਵਸ਼ਾਲੀ; ਅਮੀਰ; ~man ਅਮੀਰ, ਸਰਦਾਰ; ਦਰਬਾਰੀ; ~ness ਖ਼ਾਨਦਾਨੀ, ਕੁਲੀਨਤਾ, ਸ੍ਰੇਸ਼ਠਤਾ

nod (ਨੌਡ) v ਸਿਰ ਹਿਲਾਉਣਾ, ਸਵੀਕਾਰ ਕਰਨਾ; ਉਘਲਾਉਣਾ; ਸਿਰ ਦਾ ਇਸ਼ਾਰਾ, ਸਿਰ, ਨੀਂਦ ਦੀ ਝੋਕ; ~ding ਸਿਰ ਹਿਲਾਉਣ, ਨਮਸਕਾਰ ਕਰਨ, ਸਿਰ ਨਿਵਾਉਣ; ~dle (ਬੋਲ) ਸਿਰ, ਖੋਪਰੀ, ਮੁੰਡੀ; ਸਿਰ ਹਿਲਾਉਣਾ, ਸਿਰ ਮਾਰਨਾ ਜਾਂ ਝੁਕਾਉਣਾ

node (ਨਅਉਡ) n ਗੰਢ; ਘੁੰਡੀ; ਕਟਾਨ-ਬਿੰਦੂ; ਕੇਂਦਰੀ-ਬਿੰਦੂ

nodus ('ਨੌਅਉਡਅਸ) n ਗੁੰਝਲ, ਔਕੜ, ਕਠਨਾਈ

noise (ਨੌਇਜ਼) n ਰੌਲਾ, ਸ਼ੋਰ, ਰੌਲਾਗੌਲਾ, ਸ਼ੋਰ ਸ਼ਰਾਬਾ; ਧੁੰਮ

noisy ('ਨੌਇਜ਼ਿ) v ਹੁਲੜਬਾਜ਼, ਖਰੂਦੀ; ਰੌਲੇ-ਗੌਲੇ ਵਾਲਾ; ਸ਼ੋਰ-ਸ਼ਰਾਬੇ ਵਾਲਾ

nomenclator ('ਨਅਉਮਅਨਕਲੇਇਟਅ*) n ਨਾਮਦਾਤਾ, ਨਾਂ ਰੱਖਣ ਵਾਲਾ, ਨਾਮਦਾਤਾ, ਮੁਅਕਿਲ

nomenclature ('ਨਅਉ'ਮੈਨਕਲਚਅ*) n ਨਾਮ, ਪਾਰਿਭਾਸ਼ਕ ਸ਼ਬਦਾਵਲੀ; ਨਾਮਾਵਲੀ; ਨਾਮ-ਸੂਚੀ

nominal ('ਨੌਮਿਨਲ) n ਨਾਂ ਬਾਰੇ, ਨਾਮ ਦਾ; ਨਾਂ ਵਰਗਾ, ਫ਼ਰਜ਼ੀ; ਸ਼ਾਬਦਕ

nominate ('ਨੌਮਿਨੇਇਟ) v ਨਾਮਜ਼ਦ ਕਰਨਾ, ਮਨੋਨੀਤ ਕਰਨਾ; ~d ਨਾਮਜ਼ਦ ਨਿਯੁਕਤ

nomination ('ਨੌਮਿ'ਨੇਇਸ਼ਨ) n ਨਾਮਜ਼ਦਗੀ; ਨਿਯੁਕਤੀ

nominee ('ਨੌਮਿ'ਨੀ) n ਨਾਮਜ਼ਦ, ਆਦਮੀ, ਮਨੋਨੀਤ ਵਿਅਕਤੀ

non (ਨੌਨ) pref ਸ਼ਬਦਾਂ ਨਾਲ ਲਾਇਆ ਜਾਣ ਵਾਲਾ ਅਗੇਤਰ ਜੋ ਨਾ, ਅਣ-, ਅਨ-, ਅ-, ਨਿਰ-, ਬੇ-, ਗ਼ੈਰ ਆਦਿ ਦੇ ਅਰਥਾਂ ਵਿਚ ਆਉਂਦਾ ਹੈ

non-aligned ('ਨੌਨ-ਅ'ਲਾਇੰਡ) a ਗੁਟ ਨਿਰਖੇਪ, ਗ਼ੈਰ-ਜਾਨਬਦਾਰ

non-aggression ('ਨੌਨ-ਅ'ਗਰੈਸ਼ਨ) n ਅਨ-ਆਕਰਮਣ

non-attendance ('ਨੌਨ-ਅ'ਟੈਂਡਅੰਸ) n ਗ਼ੈਰ-ਹਾਜ਼ਰੀ

non-being ('ਨੌਨ'ਬੀਇਡ) n ਅਹੋਂਦ, ਅਭਾਵ

non-committal ('ਨੌਨ-ਕਅ'ਮਿਟਲ) a ਬੰਧਨ ਮੁਕਤ; ਪ੍ਰਤਿਬੱਧਤਾ ਰਹਿਤ

non-compliance ('ਨੌਨ-ਕਅਮ'ਪਲਾਇਅੰਸ) n ਅਪਾਲਟਾ

non-conservative ('ਨੌਨ-ਕਅਂ'ਸਅ:-ਵ੍ਵਅਟਿਵ) a ਰੂੜ੍ਹੀ ਵਿਰੋਧੀ

non-cooperation ('ਨੌਨ-ਕਅਉ'ਔਪਅ-ਰੇਇਸ਼ਨ) a ਨਾ-ਮਿਲਵਰਤਨ

none (ਨੱਨ) pron a adv ਕੋਈ ਨਹੀਂ, ਕੋਈ ਵੀ ਨਾ; ਨਹੀਂ, ਜ਼ਰਾ ਵੀ ਨਹੀਂ

nonentity (ਨੌਨੇ'ਨਟਅਟਿ) n ਅਣਅਸਤਿਤਵ, ਅਭਾਵ; ਅਸਤਿਤਵਹੀਨਤਾ; ਨਾਚੀਜ਼, ਤੁੱਛ ਵਿਅਕਤੀ

non-essential ('ਨੌਨਇ'ਸੈਂਸ਼ਲ) a ਗ਼ੈਰ-ਜ਼ਰੂਰੀ, ਅਨਾਵੱਸ਼ਕ

non-existent ('ਨੌਨਿਗ'ਜ਼ਿਸਟਅੰਟ) a ਹੋਂਦ ਰਹਿਤ, ਅਸਤਿਤਵਹੀਨ

non-official ('ਨੌਨਅ'ਫ਼ਿਸ਼ਲ) a ਗ਼ੈਰ-ਸਰਕਾਰੀ

non-recurring ('ਨੌਨਰਿ'ਕਅ:ਰਿੰਡ) a ਮੁੜ ਨਾ ਹੋਣ ਵਾਲਾ

non-resident ('ਨੌਨ'ਰੈਜ਼ਿਡਅੰਟ) *n a* ਅਸਥਾਈ ਵਸਨੀਕ

nonsense ('ਨੌਨਸਅੰਸ) *n a* ਅਰਥਹੀਨ (ਵਾਕ), ਬੇਸੁਰੀ (ਗੱਲ), ਬੇਮੌਕਾ (ਕਥਨ), ਉਲ-ਜਲੂਲ; ਬਕਵਾਸ, ਫਜ਼ੂਲ (ਗੱਲ), ਵਾਹਯਾਤ

nonsensical (ਨੌਨ'ਸੈਂਸਿਕਲ) *a* ਅਰਥਹੀਨ, ਬੇਸੁਰਾ, ਬੇਤੁਕਾ, ਫਜ਼ੂਲ

nonstop ('ਨੌਨ'ਸਟੌਪ) *a* ਲਗਾਤਾਰ, ਨਿਰੰਤਰ

non-vegetarian ('ਨੌਨ'ਵੈੱਜਿ'ਟੇਅਰਿਅਨ) *a* ਮਾਸਾਹਾਰੀ

non-violence ('ਨੌਨ'ਵਾਇਅਲਅੰਸ) *a* ਅਹਿੰਸਾ

non-violent ('ਨੌਨ'ਵਾਇਲੰਟ) *a* ਅਹਿੰਸਕ, ਅਹਿੰਸਾਤਮਕ

noodle (ਨੂਡਲ) *n* (1) ਇਕ ਪ੍ਰਕਾਰ ਦੀਆਂ ਸੇਂਵੀਆਂ, ਨੂਡਲ; (2) ਮੂਰਖ, ਲੋੱਲ੍ਹੂ, ਬੁੱਧੂ, ਉੱਲੂਘਾਟਾ, ਗੰਵਾਰ; ਅਨਾੜੀ; **~dom** ਮੂਰਖਤਾ, ਲੋੱਲ੍ਹੂਪਨ, ਬੁੱਧੂਹੀਨਤਾ; ਅਬੋਧਤਾ

nook (ਨੁਕ) *n* ਨੁੱਕਰ, ਗੁੱਠ; ਆਲ਼ਾ; ਵੱਖਰੀ ਥਾਂ

noon (ਨੂਨ) *n a* ਦੁਪਹਿਰ; **~day** ਦੁਪਹਿਰ, ਅੱਧਾ ਦਿਨ

nor (ਨੋ*) *adv conj* ਅਤੇ ਨਾ.ਹੀ, ਦੋਹਾਂ ਵਿਚੋਂ ਇਕ ਵੀ ਨਾ

norm (ਨੋਮ) *n* ਮਾਪ, ਪ੍ਰਤੀਮਾਨ, ਕਸਵੱਟੀ; ਆਦਰਸ਼, ਨਮੂਨਾ

normal ('ਨੋਮਲ) *a* ਸਧਾਰਨ, ਆਮ; ਸੁਭਾਵਕ, ਕੁਦਰਤੀ; ਨਿਯਮਤ, ਸੰਗਤ; **~cy** ਸਧਾਰਨਤਾ, ਸੁਭਾਵਕਤਾ; **~ize** ਇਕ ਸਾਰ ਕਰਨਾ; ਨਮੂਨੇ ਦਾ ਬਣਾਉਣਾ; ਸਧਾਰਨ ਹਾਲਤ ਵਿਚ ਲਿਆਉਣਾ; **~ly** ਸਧਾਰਨ ਤੌਰ ਤੇ, ਆਮ ਤੌਰ ਤੇ, ਆਮੁਮਨ

north (ਨੋਥ) *n a adv* ਉੱਤਰ, ਸ਼ਮਾਲ, (ਕਿਸੇ ਦੇਸ਼ ਦਾ) ਉੱਤਰੀ ਭਾਗ; ਉੱਤਰ ਵੱਲ; **~ern** ਉੱਤਰੀ

nose (ਨਅਉਜ਼) *n v* ਨੱਕ; ਨਾਸ; ਸੁੰਘਣ ਦੀ ਸ਼ਕਤੀ; ਸੁੰਘਣਾ; ਸੁੰਘ ਕੇ ਜਾਂਚਣਾ; ਨੱਕ ਨਾਲ ਰਗੜਨਾ; ਜ਼ੋਰ ਨਾਲ ਸਾਹ ਲੈਣਾ; ਖੋਜ ਕਰਨੀ, ਪਤਾ ਕਰਨਾ; **~gay** ਗੁਲਦਸਤਾ, ਫੁੱਲਾਂ ਦਾ ਗੁੱਛਾ; **to turn one's ~ at** ਨੱਕ ਚੜ੍ਹਾਉਣਾ; **~less** ਨਕਟਾ, ਨੱਕਹੀਨ

not (ਨੌਟ) *adv* ਨਹੀਂ, ਨਾ

notable ('ਨਅਉਟਅਬਲ) *a n* ਪ੍ਰਸਿੱਧ, ਵਰਨਣਯੋਗ, ਦੱਸਣਯੋਗ, ਸ੍ਰੇਸ਼ਠ, ਵਿਸ਼ੇਸ਼; ਉੱਘਾ, ਪਤਵੰਤਾ, ਅਸਧਾਰਨ

notably ('ਨਅਉਟਅਬਲਿ) *adv* ਖ਼ਾਸ ਤੌਰ ਤੇ

notch (ਨੌਚ) *n v* ਦੰਦਾ; ਖੱਪਾ; ਤੰਗ ਰਸਤਾ; ਛੇਕ; ਟੱਕ, ਕਾਟ, ਕਤਰ; ਛੇਕ ਕਰਨਾ, ਦਰਾੜ ਪਾਉਣੀ

note (ਨਅਉਟ) *n v* ਟਿੱਪਣੀ, ਨੋਟ, ਸੂਚਨਾ, ਚੇਤਾਵਨੀ; ਐਲਾਨ; ਟੀਕਾ, ਵਿਆਖਿਆ, ਕੁੰਜੀ; ਟੀਕਾ ਕਰਨਾ; **~worthy** ਧਿਆਨਯੋਗ, ਵਿਚਾਰਨਯੋਗ; **~d** ਪ੍ਰਸਿੱਧ, ਮਸ਼ਹੂਰ, ਉੱਘਾ, ਨਾਮੀ, ਨਾਮਵਰ

nothing ('ਨੱਥਿਙ) *n adv* ਕੁਝ ਨਾ, ਕੱਖ ਨਹੀਂ; ਬਿਲਕੁਲ ਮਾਮੂਲੀ ਚੀਜ਼, ਮੂਲ਼ ਨਹੀਂ, ਕਿਸੇ ਤਰ੍ਹਾਂ ਵੀ ਨਹੀਂ, ਕਦੇ ਵੀ ਨਹੀਂ; **~ness** ਅਣਹੋਂਦ, ਅਭਾਵ, ਸੁੰਨਤਾ; ਅਸਾਰਤਾ, ਗੌਰਵਹੀਨਤਾ; ਨਿਰਥਕਤਾ

notice ('ਨਅਉਟਿਸ) *n v* ਚੇਤਾਵਨੀ; ਸੂਚਨਾ; ਸੂਚਨਾ-ਪੱਤਰ, ਖ਼ਬਰ, ਇਤਲਾਹ; ਐਲਾਨ; ਤਵੱਜੋ; ਧਿਆਨ ਦੇਣਾ, ਵਿਚਾਰਨਾ; ਸੂਚਨਾ ਦੇਣੀ; ਨੋਟਿਸ ਦੇਣਾ, ਟੀਕਾ-ਟਿੱਪਣੀ ਕਰਨੀ; **to bring to ~** ਧਿਆਨ ਵਿਚ ਲਿਆਉਣਾ

notification ('ਨਅਉਟਿਫ਼ਿ'ਕੇਇਸ਼ਨ) *n*

ਅਧਿਸੂਚਨਾ, ਐਲਾਨ, ਘੋਸ਼ਣਾ; ਐਲਾਨਨਾਮਾ, ਘੋਸ਼ਣਾ-ਪੱਤਰ

notify ('ਨਾਉਟਿਫ਼ਾਇ) v ਸੂਚਤ ਕਰਨਾ, ਖ਼ਬਰ ਦੇਣੀ; ਐਲਾਨ ਕਰਨਾ

noting ('ਨਾਉਟਿਙ) n ਟਿੱਪਣ, ਟਿੱਪਣੀ, ਨੋਟ

notion ('ਨਾਉਸ਼ਨ) n ਖ਼ਿਆਲ, ਧਾਰਨਾ, ਸੰਕਲਪ; ਭਾਵ; ਭਾਵਨਾ, ਮਨੋਭਾਵ; ਮੱਤ, ਵਿਚਾਰ, ਰਾਇ; ~al ਕਲਪਤ, ਸਿਧਾਂਤਕ; ਅਨੁਮਾਨਤ; ਖ਼ਿਆਲੀ

notoriety ('ਨਾਉਟਅ'ਰਾਇਅਟਿ) n ਬਦਨਾਸੀ

notorious (ਨਅ(ਉ)'ਟੋਰਿਅਸ) a ਬਦਨਾਮ, ਨਾਮੀ (ਭੈੜੇ ਅਰਥਾਂ ਵਿਚ)

notwithstanding ('ਨੌਟਵਿਥ'ਸਟੈਂਡਿਙ) prep adv conj ਦੇ ਬਾਵਜੂਦ, ਭਾਵੇਂ, ਤਾਂ ਵੀ, ਹੁੰਦਿਆਂ ਹੋਇਆਂ, ਹੁੰਦਿਆਂ-ਸੁੰਦਿਆਂ

noun (ਨਾਉਨ) n ਨਾਂ, ਨਾਮ, ਸੰਗਿਆ

nourish ('ਨਅ:ਰਿਸ਼) v ਪਾਲਣਾ, ਪਾਲਣਾ-ਪੋਸਣਾ; ਪਾਲਣਾ ਕਰਨੀ; ਖ਼ੁਰਾਕ ਦੇਣੀ

novel ('ਨੌਵਲ) a n ਨਵਾਂ, ਨਵੀਨ; ਨਿਰਾਲਾ, ਅਨੋਖਾ; ਉਪਨਿਆਸ ਨਾਵਲ, ਨਾਵਲ ਸਾਹਿਤ; ~ist ਨਾਵਲਕਾਰ, ਉਪਨਿਆਸਕਾਰ; ~ty ਅਨੋਖੀ, ਵਸਤੂ, ਨਵੀਨਤਾ, ਨਵਾਂਪਣ

novice ('ਨੌਵਿਸ) n ਸਿਖਾਂਦਰੂ; ਨਵਾਂ ਚੇਲਾ; ਪਾਦਰੀ ਪਦ ਦਾ ਉਮੀਦਵਾਰ

now (ਨਾਉ) a conj adv n ਹੁਣੇ ਹੁਣੇ, ਅੱਜਕਲ, ਹੁਣ ਤਕ; ਤਤਕਾਲ, ਫ਼ੌਰਨ, ਝਟ-ਪਟ ਤੁਰਤ; ~a-days ਅੱਜਕਲ, ਇਸ ਸਮੇਂ ਵਿਚ, ਇਨ੍ਹੀਂ ਦਿਨੀਂ

nowhere ('ਨਾਉਵੇਅ*) a ਕਿਧਰੇ ਨਹੀਂ, ਕਿਤੇ ਨਹੀਂ,

nozzle ('ਨੌਜ਼ਲ) n ਟੂਟੀ; ਮੂੰਹ, ਨੋਕ;

nuance ('ਨਯੂਆਂਸ) n ਸੂਖਮ ਅੰਤਰ, ਬਾਰੀਕ ਫ਼ਰਕ

nuclear ('ਨਯੂਕਲਿਅ*) a ਕੇਂਦਰੀ; ਨਿਊਕਲੀ

nucleus ('ਨਯੂਕਲਿਅਸ) n ਨਾਭ, ਕੇਂਦਰ-ਬਿੰਦੂ ਮੂਲ ਕੇਂਦਰ; ਬੀਜ-ਕੇਂਦਰ, ਅੰਦਰਲਾ ਹਿੱਸਾ ਮਗਜ਼; (ਬ) ਅੱਖਰ ਮੁੱਖ

nude (ਨਯੂਡ) a n ਨੰਗਾ, ਨਗਨ, ਨੰਗ-ਮੁਨੰਗਾ ਨੰਗੀ ਤਸਵੀਰ; ~ness, **nudity** ਨੰਗੇਜ ਨਗਨਤਾ

nuisance ('ਨਯੂਸੰਸ) n ਪੁਆੜਾ, ਖੱਜ; ਦੁੱਖਦਾਈ ਵਸਤੂ

null (ਨੱਲ) a n v ਮਨਸੂਖ, ਰੱਦ; ਨਾਜਾਇਜ਼ ਝੂਠਾ, ਬੇਕਾਨੂੰਨੀ; ~ify ਨਿਸਫਲ ਕਰਨਾ, ਰੱਦ ਕਰਨਾ, ਮਨਸੂਖ ਕਰਨਾ, ਮਿਟਾ ਦੇਣਾ

nullah ('ਨੱਲਅ) n ਛੋਟੀ ਨਦੀ, ਨਾਲਾ

numb (ਨੱਮ) a v ਸਿਥਲ, ਸੁੰਨ, ਅਚੇਤਨ ਬੇਹੋਸ਼ ਜੜ੍ਹ; ਸੁੰਨ ਕਰਨਾ, ਚੇਤਨਾਹੀਨ ਕਰਨਾ; ~ness ਸਿਥਲਤਾ, ਸੁੰਨ; ਅਚੇਤਨਾ, ਬੇਹੋਸ਼ੀ, ਜੜ੍ਹਤਾ

number ('ਨੱਮਬਅ*) n v ਸੰਖਿਆ, ਗਿਣਤੀ ਅੰਕ, ਹਿੰਦਸਾ; ਨੰਬਰ; ਜੋੜ; ਰਕਮ, ਰਾਸ਼ ਗਿਣਨਾ, ਗਿਣਤੀ ਕਰਨੀ, ਗਿਣਤੀ ਦਾ ਨਿਸਚਾ ਕਰਨਾ; ਗਿਣਤੀ ਵਿਚ ਆਉਣਾ; ਨੰਬਰ ਲਾਉਣੇ ਸ਼ਾਮਲ ਕਰਨਾ; ~ing ਗਾਨ, ਗਾਨਾ, ਅੰਕ ਕ੍ਰਮਅੰਕ; ~less ਅਣਗਿਣਤ, ਬੇਸ਼ੁਮਾਰ ਅਸੰਖ, ਬਿਨਾ ਨੰਬਰ ਤੋਂ

numerable ('ਨਯੂਮ(ਅ)ਰਅਬਲ) a ਗਿਣਨਯੋਗ

numeral ('ਨਯੂਮ(ਅ)ਰ(ਅ)ਲ) a n ਸੰਖਿਆਸੂਚਕ; ਸੰਖਿਆ, ਹਿੰਦਸਾ, ਅੰਕ; ਗਿਣਤੀ-ਬੋਧਕ ਸ਼ਬਦ

numerate ('ਨਯੂਮਅਰੇਇਟ) v ਗਿਣਨਾ, ਗਿਣਤੀ ਕਰਨਾ

numerical (ਨਯੂ'ਮੈਰਿਕਲ) *a* ਸੰਖਿਆਵਾਚੀ; ਗਿਣਤੀ ਵਾਲਾ, ਸੰਖਿਆਤਮਕ, ਅੰਕੀ

numerosity ('ਨਯੂਮਅ'ਰੌਸਅਟਿ) *n* ਬਹੁਲਤਾ, ਅਧਿਕਤਾ, ਬਹੁਤਾਤ, ਅਕਸਰੀਅਤ

numerous ('ਨਯੂਮਅਰਅਸ) *a* ਅਨੇਕ, ਅਣਗਿਣਤ, ਵਿਸ਼ਾਲ, ਭਾਰੀ ਗਿਣਤੀ ਵਾਲਾ; ~ness ਬਹੁਲਤਾ, ਬਹੁਤਾਤ

nummet ('ਨਅੱਮਿਟ) *n* (ਉਪ) ਦੁਪਹਿਰ ਦਾ ਭੋਜਨ, ਲੰਚ

numskull ('ਨਅੱਮਸਕਅੱਲ) *n* ਮੂਰਖ, ਬੁੱਧੂ, ਲੋਲ੍ਹੂ, ਭੌਂਦੂ, ਗਿਵਾਰ, ਉਜੱਡ

nun (ਨਅੱਨ) *n* (ਇਸਾਈ) ਸੰਤਣੀ, ਯੋਗਣ, ਸਾਧਣੀ, ਨਨ; ~clo ਪੋਪ ਦਾ ਦੂਤ; ~nery ਆਸ਼ਰਮ, ਮੱਠ, ਵਿਹਾਰ

nuptial ('ਨਅੱਪਸ਼ਲ) *a n* ਵਿਆਹ ਸਬੰਧੀ, ਵਿਆਹ, ਵਿਆਹ ਦੀ ਰਸਮ, ਵਿਆਹ-ਉਤਸਵ

nurse (ਨਅਃਸ) *n v* ਦਾਈ, ਪਾਲਕਾ, ਰੋਗੀ ਸੇਵਕਾ, ਨਰਸ; ਪਾਲਣਾ-ਪੋਸਣਾ, ਦੁੱਧ ਚੁੰਘਾਉਣਾ; ਖਿਡਾਵੀ ਦਾ ਕੰਮ ਕਰਨਾ; ਰੋਗੀ ਦੀ ਸੇਵਾ ਕਰਨੀ; ~ry ਬਾਲਵਾੜੀ, ਪਨੀਰੀ, ਖੇਤ; ਜ਼ਖੀਰਾ

nursing ('ਨਅਃਸਿਙ) *n* ਪਾਲਣ ਪੋਸਣ; ਸੇਵਾ

nurture ('ਨਅਃਚਅ*) *n v* ਪਾਲਣ-ਪੋਸਣ; ਪਾਲਣਾ ਕਰਨੀ, ਖੁਆਉਣਾ-ਪਿਆਉਣਾ, ਉਤਸ਼ਾਹਤ ਕਰਨਾ; ਪੜ੍ਹਾਉਣਾ-ਲਿਖਾਉਣਾ

nut (ਨਅੱਟ) *n v* ਗਿਰੀ ਮੇਵਾ; ਸਨਕੀ, ਪਾਗਲ; ਛਿਬਰੀ; ਮਾੜੂਆ ਵਿਅਕਤੀ; ਗਿਰੀਦਾਰ ਫਲ ਇਕੱਠੇ ਕਰਨੇ; ਲੱਭਣਾ; ~oil ਗਿਰੀ ਦਾ ਤੇਲ; *hard ~ to crack* ਔਖਾ ਸੁਆਲ; ਅਣੁਭ ਬੰਦਾ

nutrition (ਨਯੂ'ਟਰਿਸ਼ਨ) *a* ਪਾਲਣ-ਪੋਸਣ; ਪੁਸ਼ਟ ਭੋਜਨ; ਆਹਾਰ ਪੁਸ਼ਟੀ

nutritious (ਨਯੂ'ਟਰਿਸ਼ਅਸ) *a* ਪੁਸ਼ਟੀਕਰ, ਬਲਵਰਧਕ, ਨਰੋਆ

nutritive ('ਨਯੂਟਰਅਟਿਵ਼) *a n* ਪੁਸ਼ਟ, ਪੁਸ਼ਟੀਕਰ; ਆਹਾਰ, ਭੋਜਨ, ਖੁਰਾਕ, ਗਿਜ਼ਾ

nutshell ('ਨਅੱਟਸ਼ੈੱਲ) *n* ਅਖਰੋਟ ਆਦਿ ਦਾ ਛਿਲਕਾ; ਸੰਖੇਪ, ਖੁਲਾਸਾ

nymph (ਨਿੰਫ) *n* ਪਰੀ; ਅਪੱਛਰਾਂ, ਹੂਰ; (ਕਾਵਿ) ਸੁੰਦਰ ਮੁਟਿਆਰ, ਸੁੰਦਰ ਕੰਨਿਆ

O

O, o (ਅਉ) *n* ਰੋਮਨ ਲਿਪੀ ਦਾ ਪੰਦਰੂਵਾਂ ਅੱਖਰ; o ਰੂਪੀ ਚਿੰਨ੍ਹ; ਚੱਕਰ, ਦਾਇਰਾ; ਸਿਫ਼ਰ, ਜ਼ੀਰੋ

O, oh (ਅਉ) *int* ਹੈ! ਉਹ! ਉਫ਼!

oar (ਓ*) *n v* ਚੱਪੂ, ਪਤਵਾਰ; ਮੁਹਾਣਾ; ਚੱਪੂ ਚਲਾਉਣਾ, ਬੇੜੀ ਚਲਾਉਣਾ; **~sman** ਮੱਲਾਹ

oasis (ਅਉ'ਏਇਸਿਸ) *n* ਨਖ਼ਲਿਸਤਾਨ

oast ('ਅਉਸਟ) *n* ਭੱਠੀ

oat (ਅਉਟ) *n* ਜਵੀ; **~cake** ਜਵੀ ਦੀ ਰੋਟੀ

oath (ਅਉਥ) *n* ਸੌਂਹ, ਕਸਮ, ਸੌਗੰਧ, ਸ਼ਪਥ, ਹਲਫ਼

obdurate ('ਔਬਡੁਅਰਅਟ) *a* ਹਠੀ, ਅੜੀਅਲ, ਜ਼ਿੱਦੀ, ਢੀਠ

obedience (ਅ'ਬੀਡਯਅੰਸ) *n* ਆਗਿਆ-ਪਾਲਨ, ਆਗਿਆਕਰਤਾ, ਤਾਬੇਦਾਰੀ

obedient (ਅ'ਬੀਡਯਅੰਟ) *a* ਆਗਿਆਕਾਰ, ਆਗਿਆਕਾਰੀ, ਤਾਬੇਦਾਰ; **~ly** ਆਗਿਆ ਅਨੁਸਾਰ

obeisance (ਅ(ਉ)'ਬੇਇਸਅੰਸ) *n* ਨਮਸਕਾਰ, ਪ੍ਰਣਾਮ; ਸ਼ਰਧਾਂਜਲੀ, ਸਨਮਾਨ

obese (ਅ(ਉ)'ਬੀਸ) *a* ਮੋਟਾ, ਵੱਡੇ ਸਰੀਰ ਵਾਲਾ, ਢਿੱਡਲ

obesity (ਅ(ਉ)'ਬਿਸਅਟਿ) *n* ਮੋਟਾਪਾ, ਸਰੀਰ ਦਾ ਭਾਰਾਪਨ

obey (ਅ'ਬੋਇ) *v* ਅਖੇ ਲੱਗਣਾ, ਕਿਹਾ ਮੰਨਣਾ, ਆਗਿਆ ਦਾ ਪਾਲਣ ਕਰਨਾ, ਹੁਕਮ ਮੰਨਣਾ; ਮੰਨ ਲੈਣਾ; ਤਾਬੇਦਾਰੀ ਕਰਨੀ

object ('ਔਬਜਿਕਟ, ਅਬ'ਜੈੱਕਟ) *n v* ਵਸਤੂ, ਪਦਾਰਥ, ਚੀਜ਼; (ਮੂਖੇਲ ਦਾ) ਪਾਤਰ, ਮੌਜੂ; ਮੰਤਵ, ਮਨੋਰਥ, ਉਦੇਸ਼ ਪ੍ਰਯੋਜਨ (ਛਿਲਾਸਫੀ) ਵਿਸ਼ਾ; ਇਤਰਾਜ਼ ਕਰਨਾ, ਸ਼ੰਕਾ ਕਰਨਾ, ਉਜ਼ਰ ਕਰਨਾ, ਵਿਰੋਧ ਕਰਨਾ; **~ion** ਇਤਰਾਜ਼, ਸ਼ੰਕ, ਉਜ਼ਰ ਵਿਰੋਧ, ਹੁੱਜਤ, ਆਪੱਤੀ; **~ionable** ਇਤਰਾਜ਼ਯੋਗ, ਆਪੱਤੀਜਨਕ; ਅਨੁਚਿਤ, ਨਾਮੁਨਾਸਬ; **~ive** *a n* ਬਾਹਰਮੁਖੀ, ਬਾਹਰਲਾ, ਵਾਸਤਵਿਕ, ਵਸਤੁਪਰਕ, ਯਥਾਰਥਕ, ਕਰਮ ਕਾਰਕ; ਕਰਮ ਬਾਰੇ; (ਸੈਨਾ) ਟੀਚਾ (ਜਿਥੇ ਪੁੱਜਣਾ ਹੋਵੇ), ਉਦੇਸ਼, ਮੰਤਵ, ਮਨੋਰਥ; **~ivity** ਵਾਤਵਿਕਤਾ; ਯਥਾਰਥਕਤਾ, ਬਾਹਰਮੁਖਤਾ

objurgate ('ਔਬਜਅਗੋਇਟ) *v* ਫਿਟਕਾਰਨਾ, ਝਿੜਕਣਾ, ਫਿਟਲਾਨੁਤਾ ਕਰਨੀ, ਬੁਰਾ-ਭਲਾ ਕਹਿਣਾ, ਤਾੜਨਾ, ਡਾਂਟਣਾ

objurgation ('ਔਬਜਅ'ਗੋਇਸ਼ਨ) *n* ਫਿਟਕਾਰ, ਝਿੜਕ, ਡਾਂਟ-ਡਪਟ, ਝਾੜ-ਝੰਬ, ਧਿੱਕਾਰ, ਲਾਨੁਤ-ਮੁਲਾਮਤ

obligate ('ਔਬਲਿਗੋਇਟ) *v* ਇਹਸਾਨ ਕਰਨਾ, (ਕਾਨੂੰਨੀ ਜਾਂ ਅਖ਼ਲਾਕੀ) ਬੰਦਸ਼ ਲਾ ਦੇਣੀ

obligation ('ਔਬਲਿ'ਗੋਇਸ਼ਨ) *n* ਜ਼ਿੰਮੇਵਾਰੀ, ਭਾਰ, ਫ਼ਰਜ਼, ਕਾਨੂੰਨੀ ਜਾਂ ਅਖ਼ਲਾਕੀ ਬੰਦਸ਼, ਇਕਰਾਰਨਾਮਾ, ਪ੍ਰਤਿਗਿਆ-ਪੱਤਰ, ਇਹਸਾਨ, ਉਪਕਾਰ

obligatory (ਅ'ਬਲਿਗਾਟ(ਅ)ਰਿ) *a* ਜ਼ਰੂਰੀ, ਅੱਵਸ਼ਕ, (ਕਾ) ਲਾਗੂ, ਪੱਕਾ

oblige (ਅ'ਬਲਾਇਜ) *v* ਉਪਕਾਰ ਕਰਨਾ, ਇਹਸਾਨ ਕਰਨਾ, ਮਜਬੂਰ ਕਰਨਾ, (ਕੋਈ ਕੰਮ) ਬਦੋਬਦੀ ਕਰਾਉਣਾ; ਬੰਦਸ਼ ਲਾਉਣੀ; (ਬੋਲ) ਦਿਲਪਰਚਾਵ ਕਰਨਾ; **~d** ਮਜਬੂਰ, ਕਰਤਗ, ਆਤਾਰੀ

obliging (ਅ'ਬਲਾਇਜਿਙ) *a* ਮਿਲਾਪੜਾ, ਮਿੱਠੇ ਸੁਭਾਅ ਵਾਲਾ, ਉਪਕਾਰੀ, ਨਿਮਰਤਾ ਵਾਲਾ, ਆਤਾਰੀ, ਇਹਸਾਨ ਕਰਨ ਵਾਲਾ

oblique (ਅ'ਬਲੀਕ) *a v* ਟੇਢਾ, ਤਿਰਛਾ, ਆੜਾ; ਟੇਢੀ ਚਾਲ ਨਾਲ ਵਧਣਾ, ਕੁਟਿਲ ਨੀਤੀ ਨਾਲ ਅੱਗੇ ਵਧਣਾ

oblivion (ਅ'ਬਲਿਵਿਅਨ) *n* ਭੁਲਾਵਾਂ ਗੁਮਨਾਮੀ; ਉਪੇਖਿਆ

oblong ('ਔਬਲੌਙ) *a* ਚੌਰਸ, ਚੌਕੋਰ, ਲੰਬੂਤਰਾ; ਆਇਤ

obnoxious (ਅਯ'ਨੌਕਸ਼ਅਸ) *a* ਘਿਣਾਉਯੋਗ, ਨਿੰਦਣਯੋਗ, ਵਰਜਤ, ਇਤਰਾਜ਼ਯੋਗ, ਬੇਹੂਦਾ, ਕੋਝਾ

obscene (ਅਬ'ਸੀਨ) *a* ਅਸ਼ਲੀਲੀ, ਲੱਚਰ, ਫ਼ਾਹਸ਼

obsenity (ਅਬ'ਸੈਨਅਟਿ) *n* ਅਸ਼ਲੀਲਤਾ

obscure (ਅਬ'ਸਕਯੂਅ*) *a n v* ਧੁੰਦਲਾ, ਘਸਮੈਲਾ; ਹਨੇਰਾ; ਅਸਪਸ਼ਟ, ਤੇਜਹੀਣ; ਗੁੱਝੂ, ਦੁਰਬੋਧ, ਕਠਨ, ਗੁਪਤ, ਅਗਿਆਤ, ਗੁਮਨਾਮ; ਧੁੰਦਲਾਪਣ; ਅਸਪਸ਼ਟਤਾ

obscurity (ਅਬ'ਸਕਯੂਅਰਅਟਿ) *n* ਧੁੰਦਲਾਪਣ, ਹਨੇਰਾ; ਗੁੱਝਤਾ, ਦੁਰਬੋਧਤਾ, ਗ੍ਹਾਂਲਾਗੀ, ਅਪ੍ਰਸਿੱਧੀ; ਤੇਜਹੀਣਤਾ

obsecrate ('ਔਬਸਿਕਰੇਇਟ) *n* ਬੇਨਤੀ ਕਰਨੀ, ਪ੍ਰਾਰਥਨਾ ਕਰਨੀ, ਹਾੜ੍ਹੇ ਕੱਢਣੇ, ਮਿੰਨਤ ਕਰਨੀ

obsecration ('ਔਬਸਿ'ਕਰੇਇਸ਼ਨ) *n* ਬੇਨਤੀ, ਪ੍ਰਾਰਥਨਾ, ਅਰਦਾਸ, ਮਿੰਨਤ-ਤਰਲਾ

obsequies ('ਔਬਸਿਕਵਿਜ਼) *n* ਅੰਤਮ ਸੰਸਕਾਰ, ਦਾਹ-ਸੰਸਕਾਰ, ਕਿਰਿਆ-ਕਰਮ

observance (ਅਬ'ਜ਼ਅ:ਵੰਸ) *n* ਪਾਬੰਦੀ, ਪਾਲਣ (ਰੀਤੀ-ਰਿਵਾਜ, ਕਾਨੂੰਨ ਆਦਿ ਦੀ); ਮਨੌਤ; (ਪ੍ਰ) ਕਰਮ-ਕਾਂਡ, ਧਾਰਮਕ ਰੀਤੀ

observation ('ਔਬਜ਼ਅ'ਵ਼ੇਇਸ਼ਨ) *n* ਦੇਖ-ਭਾਲ; ਨਿਰੀਖਣ, ਪੜਚੋਲ, ਟਿੱਪਣੀ, ਆਲੋਚਨਾ; ਵਿਚਾਰ, ਸੋਚ; ਰਾਇ, ਕਥਨ, ਉਕਤੀ

observatory (ਅਬ'ਜ਼ਅਵ਼ਟਅਰਿ) *n* ਜੰਤਰ-ਮੰਤਰ, ਨੀਝਸ਼ਾਲਾ, ਨਿਰੀਖਣਸ਼ਾਲਾ

observe (ਅਬ'ਜ਼ਅ:ਵ਼) *v* ਪਾਲਟਾ ਕਰਨੀ (ਨਿਯਮ, ਰੀਤੀ ਆਦਿ ਦੀ); ਮਨਾਉਣਾ; ਵੇਖਣਾ, ਨਿਰੀਖਣ ਕਰਨਾ, ਪੜਚੋਲ ਕਰਨੀ; ਧਿਆਨ ਦੇਣਾ, ਅਨੁਭਵ ਕਰਨਾ; ਸਤਰਕ ਹੋਣਾ, ਸਾਵਧਾਨ ਹੋਣਾ; ~d ਨਿਰੀਖਤ, ਦੇਖਿਆ, ਦ੍ਰਿਸ਼ਟ, ਅਵਲੋਕਿਤ; ~r ਨਿਰੀਖਕ; ਵੇਖਣ ਵਾਲਾ, ਦਰਸ਼ਕ; ਆਲੋਚਕ

obsolesce ('ਔਬਸਅ'ਲੈੱਸ) *v* ਪੁਰਾਣਾ ਪੈ ਜਾਣਾ, ਬੇਕਾਰ ਹੋ ਜਾਣਾ, ਅਪ੍ਰਚਲਤ ਹੋਣਾ; ~nce ਅਪ੍ਰਚਲਨ

obsolete ('ਔਬਸਅਲੀਟ) *a* ਅਪ੍ਰਚਲਤ, ਅਵਿਹਾਰੀ, ਪੁਰਾਣਾ, ਲੁਪਤ

obstacle ('ਔਬਸਟਅਕਲ) *n* ਰੁਕਾਵਟ, ਅੜਿੱਕਾ, ਵਿਘਨ, ਰੋਕ, ਅੜਚਨ

obstinacy ('ਔਬਸਟਿਨਅਸਿ) *n* ਢੀਠਤਾ; ਸਿਰੜ, ਹ਼ਿਟ, ਹਠ, ਹੀਂਜ਼ੁਪਟ, ਅੜੀ

obstinate ('ਔਬਸਟਿਨਅਟ) *a* ਜ਼ਿੱਦੀ, ਢੀਠ, ਸਿਰੜੀ, ਹਠੀ, ਚੀੜ੍ਹਾ; ਕਰੜਾ, ਦਿੜ੍ਹ; ਹਠਵਾਦੀ

obstruct (ਅਬ'ਸਟਰਅੱਕਟ) *v* ਰੋਕ ਪਾਉਣੀ, ਅੜਿੱਕਾ ਡਾਹੁਣਾ, ਰਾਹ ਰੋਕਣਾ; ਗਤੀਰੋਧ ਕਰਨਾ, ਵਿਘਨ ਪਾਉਣਾ, ਗੜਬੜ ਕਰਨੀ; ~ed ਅਵਰੁੱਧ, ਰੋਕਿਆ ਹੋਇਆ; ~ion ਰੋਕ, ਰੁਕਾਵਟ, ਗਤੀਰੋਧ, ਅੜਿੱਕਾ, ਅੜਿੱਚਣ, ਵਿਘਨ, ਅਟਕਾਉ; ~ive ਵਿਘਨਕਾਰੀ, ਗਤੀਰੋਧਕ; ~ing ਪ੍ਰਚਲਤ, ਪ੍ਰਵਰਤ, ਪ੍ਰਪਤ

obtrude (ਅਬ'ਟਰੂਡ) v ਦਖ਼ਲ ਦੇਣਾ, ਘੁਸਣਾ, ਦਖ਼ਲ-ਅੰਦਾਜ਼ੀ ਕਰਨਾ; ਗੱਲ ਮੜ੍ਹਨ, ਥੋਪਣਾ

obtrusion (ਅਬ'ਟਅੁਰੂਯ਼ਨ) n ਨਜਾਇਜ਼ ਦਖ਼ਲ, ਠੋਸਣ

obtuse (ਅਬ'ਟਯੂਸ) a ਮੰਦ, ਖੁੰਢਾ, ਮੁਰ੍ਹ; (ਪੱਤਾ) ਗੋਲ, (ਰੇਖਾ) ਸਮਕੋਣ ਤੋਂ ਵੱਡਾ ਕੋਣ, ਅਧਿਕਕੋਣ

obvert (ਔਬ'ਵ੍ਅ:ਟ) v ਉਲਟਾ ਦੇਣਾ, ਉਲਟਾ ਕਰਨਾ, ਮੁਧਾ ਕਰਨਾ; ਫੇਰ ਦੇਣਾ

obviate ('ਔਬਵਿਏਇਟ) v (ਲੋੜ ਆਦਿ) ਦੂਰ ਕਰਨੀ, ਨਿਵਾਰਨ, ਛੁਟਕਾਰਾ ਦਿਵਾਉਣਾ, ਖਹਿੜਾ ਛੁਡਾਉਣਾ

obvious ('ਔਬਵਿਅਸ) a ਸਪਸ਼ਟ, ਜ਼ਾਹਰ, ਪ੍ਰਤੱਖ, ਪਰਗਟ

occasion ('ਅ'ਕੇਇਯ਼ਨ) n ਅਵਸਰ, ਮੌਕਾ, ਢੋਅ; ਸਮਾਂ, ਵੇਲਾ; ਕਾਰਨ, ਸਬੱਬ, ਪ੍ਰਯੋਜਨ, ਲੋੜ; ~al ਖ਼ਾਸ ਮੌਕੇ ਦਾ; ਵਿਸ਼ੇਸ਼ ਅਵਸਰ ਦਾ; ਅਨਿਯਮਤ; ~ally ਕਦੇ-ਕਦੇ, ਕਦੇ-ਕਦਾਈਂ; ਮੌਕੇ-ਮੌਕੇ ਤੇ, ਗਾਹੇਬਗਾਹੇ, ਖ਼ਾਸ ਖ਼ਾਸ ਮੌਕਿਆਂ ਤੇ; ਪ੍ਰਸੰਗਵਸ

occupancy ('ਔਕਯੁਪਅੰਸਿ) a ਕਬਜ਼ਾ, ਅਧਿਕਾਰ, ਦਖ਼ਲ, ਕਿਰਾਏਦਾਰੀ, ਪਟਾਕਾਰੀ; ਰਿਹਾਇਸ਼

occupant ('ਔਕਯੁਪਅੰਟ) n ਕਾਬਜ਼, ਕਬਜ਼ਾਦਾਰ, ਨਿਵਾਸੀ, ਰਿਹਾਇਸ਼ ਕਰਨ ਵਾਲਾ; ਕਿਰਾਏਦਾਰ, ਪਟਾਦਾਰ

occupation ('ਔਕਯੁ'ਪੇਇਸ਼ਨ) n ਪੇਸ਼ਾ, ਧੰਦਾ, ਕਾਰ-ਵਿਹਾਰ; ਕਬਜ਼ਾਦਾਰੀ, ਅਧਿਕਾਰ, ਕਬਜ਼ਾ; ~al ਵਿਵਸਾਇਕ

occupy ('ਔਕਯੁਪਾਇ) v ਕਬਜ਼ਾ ਕਰਨਾ, ਅਧਿਕਾਰ ਵਿਚ ਲੈ ਲੈਣਾ, ਮੱਲਣਾ; ਸਾਂਭ ਲੈਣਾ; ਪਟਾਕਾਰ ਹੋਣਾ, ਕਿਰਾਏਦਾਰ ਹੋਣਾ; ਰਿਹਾਇਸ਼ ਰੱਖਣੀ, ਰਹਿਣਾ; ਥਾਂ ਮੱਲਣੀ

occur (ਅ'ਕਅ:*) v ਵਾਪਰਨਾ, ਹੋਣਾ; ਪੇਸ਼ ਆਉਣਾ; ਸੁੱਝਣਾ, ਔੜਨਾ, ਫੁਰਨਾ, ਚੇਤੇ ਆਉਣਾ; ~rence ਘਟਨਾ, ਵਾਰਦਾਤ; ਉਤਪਤੀ, ਸੰਯੋਗ

ocean ('ਅਉਸ਼ਨ) n ਸਮੁੰਦਰ, ਮਹਾਂਸਾਗਰ; ~ography ਸਾਗਰ-ਵਿਗਿਆਨ

octagon ('ਔਕਟਅਗਅਨ) n ਅੱਠਕੋਨੀ, ਅੱਠਬਾਹੀ

octave ('ਔਕਟਿਵ) n ਅਸ਼ਟਪਦੀ, ਅੱਠਾਂ ਵਸਤੂਆਂ ਦਾ ਸਮੂਹ, ਅਸ਼ਟਮੀ

octogenarian ('ਔਕਟਅਉਜਿ'ਨੇਅਰਿਅਨ) a n ਅੱਸੀ ਸਾਲ ਦੀ ਉਮਰ ਵਾਲਾ

octopod ('ਔਕਟਅਪੌਡ) n ਅੱਠ ਪੈਰਾਂ ਵਾਲਾ, ਅੱਠ-ਪਦ-ਜੰਤੂ, ਅੱਠਪਾਦ

octroi ('ਔਕਟਰਵਾ) n ਚੁੰਗੀ, ਮਹਿਸੂਲ, ਮਸੂਲ; ਚੁੰਗੀ-ਘਰ

ocular ('ਔਕਯੁਲਅ*) a ਅੱਖਾਂ ਦਾ; ਅੱਖੀਂ ਡਿੱਠਾ

oculist ('ਔਕਯੁਲਿਸਟ) n ਅੱਖਾਂ ਦਾ ਡਾਕਟਰ; ਅੱਖਾਂ ਦੇ ਰੋਗਾਂ ਦਾ ਮਾਹਰ

odd (ਔਡ) a n ਵਿੱਲਖਣ, ਅਨੋਖਾ, ਵਚਿੱਤਰ, ਅਸਧਾਰਨ; ਬੇਜੋੜ, ਬਿਖਮ; ਟੁਟਕਲ, ਬਾਕੀ; ~ity ਵਿਲੱਖਣਤਾ, ਅਨੋਖਾਪਨ, ਅਸਧਾਰਨਤਾ; ~s ਅਣਮੇਲ, ਫ਼ਰਕ, ਵਿਰੋਧ, ਅਸਮਾਨਤਾ; ਵੈਰ, ਵਿਰੋਧ; ਮੁਖ਼ਾਲਫ਼ਤ

ode (ਅਉਡ) n ਗੀਤ-ਕਾਵਿ

odorous ('ਅਉਡਅਰਅਸ) a ਖ਼ੁਸ਼ਬੂਦਾਰ, ਸੁਗੰਧਮਈ

odour ('ਅਉਡਅ*) n ਖ਼ੁਸ਼ਬੂ, ਮਹਿਕ, ਸੁਗੰਧ; ਮਸ਼ਹੂਰੀ; ਰੰਗ; ~less ਗੰਧਹੀਨ, ਨਿਰਗੰਧ, ਬੇਮਹਿਕ

off (ਔਫ) *adv prep a n* ਦੂਰ, ਪਰ੍ਹਾਂ, ਵੱਖਰਾ, ਲਾਂਭੇ, ਅਸਬੰਧਤ; ਲੋਪ, ਅਪ੍ਰਾਪਤ, ਪਰਲਾ, ਦੂਰ ਦਾ; (ਕ੍ਰਿਕਟ ਵਿਚ) ਖੇਡਣ ਵਾਲੇ ਦਾ ਸੱਜਾ ਪਾਸਾ; ਮੁਕਰਨਾ, ਬੇਮੁਖ ਹੋਣਾ; ~**hand** ਬਿਨਾ ਤਿਆਰੀ, ਵੇਲੇ ਦੇ ਵੇਲੇ

offence (ਅਫ਼ੈਂਸ) *n* ਦੋਸ਼, ਅਪਰਾਧ, ਕਸੂਰ

offend (ਅਫ਼ੈਂਡ) *v* ਨਾਰਾਜ਼ ਕਰਨਾ, ਗੁੱਸੇ ਕਰਨਾ; ਅਪਰਾਧ ਕਰਨਾ, ਉਲੰਘਣਾ ਕਰਨੀ; ~**er** ਅਪਰਾਧੀ, ਕਸੂਰਵਾਰ, ਦੋਸ਼ੀ; ~**ing** ਅੱਤਿਆਚਾਰੀ, ਅਪਰਾਧੀ

offensive (ਆਫ਼ੈਂਸਿਵ਼) *a n* ਘਿਰਣਾਜਨਕ, ਦੁਰਗੰਧਕ; ਦੁੱਖਦਾਈ, ਅਪਮਾਨਜਨਕ; ਵਧੀਕੀ ਭਰਿਆ; ਹਮਲਾਵਰ, ਹਮਲਾ; ਆਕ੍ਰਮਣ

offer (ਔਫ਼ਅ*) *v n* ਪੇਸ਼ ਕਰਨਾ, ਦੇਣਾ, ਅੱਗੇ ਰੱਖਣਾ; ਭੇਟ ਕਰਨਾ, ਚੜ੍ਹਾਉਣਾ; ਅਰਪਣਾ, ਸੌਂਪ ਦੇਣਾ; ਜ਼ਾਹਰ ਹੋਣਾ; ਰਾਇ, ਪ੍ਰਸਤਾਵ, ਪੇਸ਼ਕਸ਼, ਭੇਟ

office (ਔਫ਼ਿਸ) *n* ਦਫ਼ਤਰ, ਪਦਵੀ, ਅਹੁਦਾ; ਫ਼ਰਜ਼, ਉਪਕਾਰ, ਸਰਕਾਰੀ ਮਹਿਕਮਾ ਜਾਂ ਵਿਭਾਗ; ~**bearer** ਅਹੁਦੇਦਾਰ, ਪਦ-ਅਧਿਕਾਰੀ; ~**r** ਅਫ਼ਸਰ, ਪਦ-ਅਧਿਕਾਰੀ, ਕਰਮਚਾਰੀ

official (ਅ'ਫ਼ਿਸ਼ਲ) *a n* ਸਰਕਾਰੀ, ਦਫ਼ਤਰੀ, ਕਾਨੂੰਨੀ, ਅਹੁਦੇ ਨਾਲ ਸਬੰਧਤ, ਪਦ ਸਬੰਧੀ; ਸਰਕਾਰੀ ਮੁਲਾਜ਼ਮ, ਕਿਸੇ ਦਫ਼ਤਰ ਦਾ ਅਧਿਕਾਰੀ; ~**dom** ਅਫ਼ਸਰੀ; ਅਧਿਕਾਰੀ ਵਰਗ, ਅਫ਼ਸਰ ਲੋਕ; ~**ism** ਅਫ਼ਸਰੀ ਸ਼ਾਨ, ਅਫ਼ਸਰਸ਼ਾਹੀ

officiate (ਅ'ਫ਼ਿਸ਼ਿਏਇਟ) *v* ਕਾਇਮ-ਮੁਕਾਮ ਹੋਣਾ, ਕਿਸੇ ਦੀ ਥਾਂ ਕੰਮ ਕਰਨਾ, ਕਾਰਜਕਾਰੀ ਬਣਨਾ

offing (ਔਫ਼ਿਙ) *n* ਦ੍ਰਿਸ਼ਟਮਾਨ ਦੁਮੇਲ; ਸਾਗਰ-ਖੰਡ; **in the ~** ਸੰਭਾਵਤ ਘਟਨਾ

offset ('ਔਫ਼ਸੈੱਟ) *n v* ਆਫ਼ਸੈੱਟ ਛਪਾਈ; ਰਵਾਨਗੀ, ਪ੍ਰਸਥਾਨ, ਅਰੰਭ; ਹਰਜਾਨਾ; ਹਰਜਾਨਾ ਭਰਨਾ, ਬਰਾਬਰ ਕਰਨਾ

offshoot ('ਔਫ਼ਸ਼ੂਟ) *n* ਟਾਹਣੀ, ਅੱਖ (ਟਾਹਣੀ ਵਿਚੋਂ ਫੁੱਟੀ), ਗੌਣ ਵਸਤੂ, ਵਿਉਤਪੱਤ ਵਸਤੂ

offspring ('ਔਫ਼ਸਪਰਿਙ) *n* ਸੰਤਾਨ, ਬਾਲ-ਬੱਚੇ, ਵੰਸ਼

oft (ਔਫ਼ਟ) *adv* ਕਈ ਵਾਰ, ਬਹੁਤ ਵੇਰਾਂ, ਬਹੁਤ ਕਰਕੇ, ਬਹੁਤਾ; ~**en** ਬਹੁਤਾ, ਬਹੁਤ ਕਰਕੇ, ਕਈ ਵਾਰ, ਥੋੜੀ ਥੋੜੀ ਦੇਰ ਨਾਲ, ਅਕਸਰ

ogle ('ਅਉਗਲ) *v n* ਅੱਖ ਮਾਰਨੀ, ਅੱਖ ਮਟੱਕਾ ਕਰਨਾ; ਲਲਚਾਈ ਨਜ਼ਰ

oil (ਔਇਲ) *n v* ਤੇਲ, ਰੋਗਨ; ਤੇਲ ਦੇਣਾ, ਤੇਲ ਪਾਉਣਾ; ~**cake** ਖਲ; ~**painting** ਤੇਲ-ਚਿੱਤਰ; **burn the midnight ~** ਬਹੁਤ ਰਾਤ ਤਕ ਪੜ੍ਹਨਾ ਲਿਖਣਾ; **pour ~ on the waters** ਮਾਮਲੇ ਨੂੰ ਠੰਢਾ ਜਾਂ ਸ਼ਾਂਤ ਕਰਨਾ; ~**y** ਚਿਕਣਾ, ਤੇਲ ਯੁਕਤ, ਤੇਲ ਪੂਰਨ; ਅਸ਼ਬਿਰ, ਖ਼ੁਸ਼ਾਮਦੀ

ointment ('ਔਇੰਟਮਅੰਟ) *n* ਮੱਲ੍ਹਮ, ਲੇਪ

O.K., okay ('ਅਉ'ਕੇਇ) *adv a* ਸਭ ਠੀਕ ਹੈ, ਸੁਖ ਸਾਂਦ ਹੈ, ਸਭ-ਅੱਛਾ, ਪ੍ਰਵਾਨ

old (ਅਉਲਡ) *a n* ਬੁੱਢਾ, ਬਿਰਧ, ਸਿਆਣਾ, ਬਜ਼ੁਰਗ; ਪੁਰਾਣਾ, ਹੰਢਿਆ, ਮੁੰਡਲਾ, ਆਰੰਭਕ; ਅਪ੍ਰਚਲਤ; ~**fashioned** ਅਪ੍ਰਚਲਤ, ਪੁਰਾਣੀ ਸ਼ੈਲੀ ਦਾ, ਪੁਰਾਣਪੰਥੀ, ਦਕਿਆਨੂਸੀ; ~**en** ਪੁਰਾਣੇ ਸਮੇਂ ਦਾ, ਪੁਰਾਤਨ, ਪ੍ਰਾਚੀਨ ਕਾਲ ਦਾ; ਪੁਰਾਣਾ, ਪ੍ਰਾਚੀਨ; ~**ness** ਬੁਢਾਪਾ, ਪ੍ਰਾਚੀਨਤਾ, ਪੁਰਾਤਨਤਾ, ਜਰਜਰਤਾ

ombudsman ('ਔਮਬੁਡੑਜ਼ਮਅਨ) *n* ਲੋਕਪਾਲ

omelet, omelette ('ਔਮਲਿਟ) *n* ਅੰਡਿਆਂ ਦਾ ਪੂੜਾ, ਆਮਲੇਟ

omen ('ਔਉਮੈਨ) *n* ਸ਼ਗਨ (ਚੰਗਾ ਜਾਂ ਬੁਰਾ)

omission (ਅ'ਮਿਸ਼ਨ) *n* ਭੁੱਲ, ਭੁੱਲ-ਚੁੱਕ, ਗ਼ਲਤੀ, ਉਕਾਈ, ਤਰੁਟੀ

omit (ਅ'ਮਿਟ) *v* ਛੱਡ ਜਾਣਾ, ਖੁੰਝਾ ਦੇਣਾ, ਸ਼ਾਮਲ ਨਾ ਕਰਨਾ, ਭੁੱਲ ਜਾਣਾ

omniform ('ਔਮਨਿਫ਼ੋਮ) *a* ਸਰਬ ਰੂਪੀ

omnipotent (ਔਮ'ਨਿਪਅਟਅੰਟ) *a* ਸਰਬ-ਸ਼ਕਤੀਮਾਨ

omnipresent ('ਔਮਨਿ'ਪਰੈਜ਼ੰਟ) *a* ਸਰਬਵਿਆਪਕ, ਸਰਬਵਿਆਪੀ

omniscient (ਔਮ'ਨਿਸਿਅੰਟ) *a* ਸਰਬੱਗ, ਸਰਬਗਿਆਤਾ, ਸਰਬਦਰਸ਼ੀ, ਤ੍ਰੈਕਾਲ-ਦਰਸ਼ੀ

on (ਔਨ) *prep a adv* ਉੱਤੇ, ਉੱਪਰ, ਵਿਚ, ਨੂੰ; ਉਦੇਸ਼, ਪ੍ਰਯੋਜਨ, ਮੰਤਵ, ਅਭਿਪ੍ਰਾਯ; ਆਧਾਰ, ਕੇਂਦਰ, ਧੁਰਾ; ਨੇੜੇ, ਕੋਲ, ਲਾਗੇ, ਪਾਸ, ਸਾਮ੍ਹਣੇ, ਅੱਗੇ ਵੱਲ, ਠੀਕ ਪਿੱਛੇ, ਠੀਕ ਉੱਤੇ ਜਾਂ ਉੱਪਰ, ਪ੍ਰਭਾਵ ਪਾਉਂਦੇ ਹੋਏ; ਨਿਰੰਤਰ, ਲਗਾਤਾਰ, ਅਵਿਰਾਮ, ਪਰੇ

once (ਵਅੰਸ) *adv conj n* ਇਕ ਵਾਰ, ਇਕ ਵਾਰੀ, ਇਕ ਮੌਕਾ

one (ਵਅੰਨ) *a n pron* ਇਕ, ਇਕੋ, ਬਰਾਬਰ, ਸਮਾਨ, ਕੇਵਲ ਇਕ, ਕੋਈ ਇਕ; **~eyed** ਕਾਣਾ; **~ness** ਏਕਤਾ, ਇਕਰੂਪਤਾ, ਇਕਜੁੱਟਤਾ, ਅਭਿੰਨਤਾ

onerous ('ਔਨਅਰਅਸ) *a* ਔਖਾ, ਕਠਨ, ਦੁੱਭਰ; ਭਾਰਾ

ongoings ('ਔਨਗਅਉਇਙਜ਼) *n pl* ਕਾਰਵਾਈਆਂ

onion ('ਅਨਯਅਨ) *a* ਗੰਢਾ, ਗੱਠਾ, ਪਿਆਜ਼

onlooker ('ਔਨਲੁਕਅ*) *n* ਦਰਸ਼ਕ

only ('ਅਉਨਲਿ) *a adv conj* ਕੇਵਲ, ਸਿਰਫ਼, ਨਿਰਾ

onomatopoeia ('ਔਨਅ(ਉ)ਮੈਟਅ(ਉ)'ਪੀਅ) *n* ਨਾਦ-ਅਲੰਕਾਰ, ਧੁਨੀ-ਅਨੁਕਰਨ

onset ('ਔਨਸੈਟ) *n* ਸਖ਼ਤ ਹਮਲਾ, ਜੋਸ਼ੀਲਾ ਧਾਵਾ, ਚੜ੍ਹਾਈ

onsalught ('ਔਨਸਲੋਟ) *n* ਢਾਢਾ ਹਮਲਾ, ਪ੍ਰਚੰਡ ਆਕਰਮਣ; ਕਰਾਰਾ ਵਾਰ

onus ('ਅਉਨਅਸ) *n* ਜ਼ੁੰਮੇਵਾਰੀ, ਫ਼ਰਜ਼, ਕਰਤੱਵ

onward ('ਔਨਵਅਡ) *a* ਅਗਲਾ, ਅੱਗੇ ਵਧਣ ਵਾਲਾ; **~s** ਅੱਗੇ, ਅਗਾਂਹ, ਅਗੇਰੇ

oof (ਊਫ਼) *n* (ਬੋਲ) ਰੁਪਿਆ-ਪੈਸਾ, ਦੌਲਤ; ਨਕਦ

opacity (ਅਉ'ਪੈਸਅਟਿ) *n* ਧੁੰਦਲਾਪਣ; ਅਪਾਰਦਰਸ਼ਕਤਾ; ਮੰਦ-ਬੁੱਧੀ, ਮੋਟੀ ਅਕਲ; ਅਰਥ ਦੀ ਅਸਪਸ਼ਟਤਾ

opaque (ਅ(ਉ)'ਪੇਇਕ) *a n* ਧੁੰਦਲਾ, ਅਸਪਸ਼ਟ; ਅਪਾਰਦਰਸ਼ੀ, ਅੰਨ੍ਹਾ ਸ਼ੀਸ਼ਾ

open ('ਅਉਪਨ) *a n v* ਖੁੱਲ੍ਹਾ, ਮੋਕਲਾ, ਚੌੜਾ, ਜ਼ਾਹਰ, ਪਰਗਟ, ਅਟਕੌਜਿਆ, ਖੁੱਲ੍ਹਮ-ਖੁੱਲ੍ਹਾ, ਆਮ (ਖ਼ਾਸ ਦੇ ਵਿਰੋਧ ਵਿਚ); ਖਿਲਰਿਆ ਹੋਇਆ, ਫੈਲਿਆ ਹੋਇਆ; ਖਿਝਿਆ ਹੋਇਆ, ਆਂਰਭ ਕਰਨਾ, ਉਦਘਾਟਨ ਕਰਨਾ; **~eyed** ਸਚੇਤ, ਹੁਸ਼ਿਆਰ; ਸਾਵਧਾਨ; **~ended** (ਭਾਸ਼ਾ) ਖੁੱਲ੍ਹਾ; ਚੱਲਦੀ, ਜਾਰੀ (ਗੱਲਬਾਤ); **~faced** ਸਾਫ਼ ਦਿਲ; **~handed** ਸਖੀ, ਦਾਨੀ, ਉਦਾਰ; **~hearted** ਸਾਫ਼ ਦਿਲ, ਮਿਲਣਸਾਰ; **~minded** ਨਿਰਪੱਖ, ਖੁੱਲ੍ਹ-ਦਿਲਾ, ਖੇਤਅੱਸਭ; **~ing** ਵਿਰਲ, ਛੇਕ, ਮੂੰਹ, ਗਲੀ; ਉਦਘਾਟਨ; **~ly** ਖੁੱਲ੍ਹਮ-ਖੁੱਲ੍ਹ; ਖੁੱਲ੍ਹੇ ਤੌਰ ਤੇ, ਸਪਸ਼ਟ ਰੂਪ

ਵਿਚ, ਸਰੇ-ਆਮ

opera ('ਔਪ(ਅ)ਰਅ) *n* ਗੀਤ-ਨਾਟ, ਓਪੇਰਾ

operate ('ਔਪਅਰੇਇਟ) *v* ਅਮਲ ਕਰਨਾ, ਅਮਲ ਵਿਚ ਲਿਆਉਣਾ; ਕਿਰਿਆਸ਼ੀਲ ਕਰਨਾ, ਚਲਾਉਣਾ

operation ('ਔਪਅ'ਰੇਇਸ਼ਨ) *n* ਉਪਰੇਸ਼ਨ, ਚੀਰ-ਫਾੜ; ਕਾਰਵਾਈ, ਕਿਰਿਆ-ਪ੍ਰਣਾਲੀ ਕਾਰੋਬਾਰ, ਕੰਮ-ਕਾਜ; ਕਾਰਜ-ਖੇਤਰ, ਪ੍ਰਭਾਵ-ਖੇਤਰ; ਉੱਦਮ; ਸੈਨਕ ਕਾਰਵਾਈ

operative ('ਔਪ(ਅ)ਰਅਟਿਵ) *a n* ਕਾਰਜਸ਼ੀਲ, ਕਾਰਗਰ, ਅਸਰਦਾਇਕ, ਫਲਦਾਇਕ, ਲਾਗੂ, ਮਜ਼ਦੂਰ

operator ('ਔਪਅਰੇਇਟਅ*) *n* ਚਾਲਕ; ਕਰਮਕਾਰੀ; ਓਪਰੇਸ਼ਨ (ਚੀਰ-ਫਾੜ) ਕਰਨ ਵਾਲਾ

ophthalmology ('ਔਫਥੈਲ'ਮੌਲਅਜਿ) *n* ਅੱਖ ਰੋਗ ਵਿਗਿਆਨ, ਨੇਤਰ-ਚਿਕਿਤਸਾ

opine (ਅ(ਉ)ਪਾਇਨ) *v* ਰਾਇ ਹੋਣੀ, ਰਾਇ ਦੇਣੀ; ਵਿਚਾਰ ਹੋਣਾ

opinion (ਅ'ਪਿਨਯਅਨ) *n* ਰਾਇ, ਮੱਤ, ਸੰਮਤੀ, ਖ਼ਿਆਲ

opium ('ਅਉਪਯਅਮ) *n* ਅਫ਼ੀਮ, ਢੀਆ

opponent (ਅ'ਪਅਉਨਅੰਟ) *n a* ਵਿਰੋਧੀ, ਵੈਰੀ, ਦੁਸ਼ਮਣ

opportune ('ਔਪਅਟਯੂਨ) *a* ਠੀਕ, ਉਚਿਤ, ਅਨੁਕੂਲ, ਯੋਗ; ਢੁੱਕਵਾਂ

opportunism ('ਔਪਅਟਯੂਨਿਜ਼(ਅ)ਮ) *n* ਮੌਕਾ-ਪਰਸਤੀ, ਅਵਸਰਵਾਦ, ਜ਼ਮਾਨਾਸਾਜ਼ੀ

opportunist ('ਔਪਅਟਯੂਨਿਸਟ) *a* ਮੌਕਾਪਰਸਤ, ਜ਼ਮਾਨਾਸਾਜ਼, ਅਵਸਰਵਾਦੀ

opportunity ('ਔਪਅ'ਟਯੂਨਅਟਿ) *n* ਮੌਕਾ, ਅਵਸਰ; ਢੋਅ, ਸੰਜੋਗ, ਦਾਅ

oppose (ਅ'ਪਅਉਜ਼) *v* ਵਿਰੋਧ ਕਰਨਾ, ਮੁਖ਼ਾਲਫ਼ਤ ਕਰਨੀ; ਟਾਕਰੇ ਤੇ ਲਿਆਉਣਾ; ਵਿਰੋਧੀ ਪੱਖ ਲੈਣਾ

opposite ('ਔਪਅਜ਼ਿਟ) *a n prep* ਵਿਰੋਧੀ, ਉਲਟਾ; ਵਿਪਰੀਤ, ਪ੍ਰਤੀਕੂਲ

opposition ('ਔਪਅ'ਜ਼ਿਸ਼ਨ) *n* ਵਿਰੋਧ, ਮੁਖ਼ਾਲਫ਼ਤ, ਟਾਕਰਾ; ਦੁਸ਼ਮਨੀ; ਵਿਰੋਧੀ ਧੜਾ, ਵਿਰੋਧੀ ਪੱਖ; ਤੁਲਨਾ, ਪ੍ਰਤੀਕੂਲਤਾ

oppress (ਅ'ਪਰੈਸ) *v* ਸਤਾਉਣਾ, ਦੁੱਖ ਦੇਣਾ, ਜਿਚ ਕਰਨਾ, ਦਬਾਉਣਾ, ਜ਼ੁਲਮ ਕਰਨਾ, ਦਮਨ ਕਰਨਾ; ~ion ਸਖ਼ਤੀ, ਜਬਰ, ਅੱਤਿਆਚਾਰ, ਜ਼ੁਲਮ, ਵਧੀਕੀ, ਜ਼ੋਰਾਵਰੀ; ~ive ਅੱਤਿਆਚਾਰੀ, ਜਾਬਰ

opt (ਔਪਟ) *v* ਆਪਣੀ ਪਸੰਦ ਦੱਸਣੀ, ਆਪਣੀ ਇੱਛਾ ਪਰਗਟ ਕਰਨਾ, ਆਪਣੀ ਮਰਜ਼ੀ ਦੱਸਣੀ; ~ative (ਵਿਆ) ਇੱਛਾਸੂਚਕ; ~ion ਚੁਨਣ ਦਾ ਅਧਿਕਾਰ, ਚੋਣ, ਇੱਛਾ, ਸਵੈਇੱਛਾ, ਇਖ਼ਤਿਆਰ, ਮਰਜ਼ੀ; ~ional ਇੱਛਕ, ਵਿਕਲਪਕ, ਇਖ਼ਤਿਆਰੀ

optimism ('ਔਪਟਿਮਿਜ਼(ਅ)ਮ) *n* ਆਸ਼ਾਵਾਦ, ਚੜ੍ਹਦੀ ਕਲਾ, ਖ਼ੁਸ਼ ਉਮੀਦੀ

optimist ('ਔਪਟਿਮਿਸਟ) *n* ਆਸ਼ਾਵਾਦੀ, ਖ਼ੁਸ਼ ਉਮੀਦ; ~ic ਆਸ਼ਾਵਾਦੀ

optimum ('ਔਪਟਿਮਅਮ) *a* ਸਰਵੋਤਮ, ਆਦਰਸ਼ਕ, ਅਨੁਕੂਲਤਮ

opulence ('ਔਪਯੁਲਅੰਸ) *n* ਦੌਲਤ, ਧਨ-ਮਾਲ; ਅਮੀਰੀ, ਰੁਪਇਆ-ਪੈਸਾ

opulent ('ਔਪਯੁਲਅੰਟ) *a* ਧਨਵਾਨ, ਮਾਲਦਾਰ, ਅਮੀਰ, ਦੌਲਤਮੰਦ, ਗੱਜਿਆ-ਪੁੱਜਿਆ

opus ('ਅਉਪਅਸ) *n* ਉੱਤਮ ਸਾਹਿਤਕ ਰਚਨਾ; ਸ਼ਾਹਕਾਰ

oracle ('ਔਰਅਕਲ) *n* ਦੇਵ-ਬਾਨੀ, ਇਲਹਾਮ, ਅਗੰਮੀ ਸੂਝ; ਭਵਿੱਖ-ਵਕਤਾ; ਮਾਰਗ-ਦਰਸ਼ਕ; ਲਾਲ-ਬੁਝੱਕੜ

oracular (ਔ'ਰੈਕਯੁਲਅ*) *a* ਅਗੰਮੀ, ਇਲਹਾਮੀ; ਭੇਦ-ਭਰਿਆ; ਗੁਹਜ

oral ('ਓਰ(ਅ)ਲ) *a* ਜ਼ਬਾਨੀ, ਮੂੰਹ-ਜ਼ਬਾਨੀ, ਸ਼ੈਖਕ

orange ('ਔਰਿੰਜ) *n a* ਸੰਤਰਾ, ਸੰਤਰੇ ਰੰਗਾ, ਭਗਵਾਂ; **~ry** ਸੰਤਰਿਆਂ ਦਾ ਬਾਗ਼

orate (ਓ'ਰੇਇਟ) *v* ਭਾਸ਼ਣ ਦੇਣਾ, ਤਕਰੀਰ ਕਰਨੀ

oration (ਓ'ਰੇਇਸ਼ਨ) *n* ਪ੍ਰਵਚਨ, ਭਾਸ਼ਣ, ਸੁਭਾਸ਼ਣ, ਵਿਆਖਿਆਨ, ਤਕਰੀਰ; ਲੈਕਚਰ

orator ('ਔਰਅਟਅ*) *n* ਵਕਤਾ, ਵਿਆਖਿਆਤਾ

oratory ('ਔਰਅਟ(ਅ)ਰਿ) *n* ਉਪਾਸਨਾ-ਗ੍ਰਹਿ, ਛੋਟਾ ਗਿਰਜਾ; ਭਾਸ਼ਣ-ਕਲਾ

orb (ਓਬ) *n v* ਨੇਤਰ, ਅੱਖ ਦੀ ਪੁਤਲੀ ਪ੍ਰਿਥਵੀ-ਮੰਡਲ, ਗੋਲਾ; (ਜੋਤਸ਼) ਪਿੰਡ; ਚੰਦਰ-ਮੰਡਲ; ਚੱਕਰ, ਘੇਰਾ, ਵ੍ਰਿਤ; ਘੇਰਨਾ, ਪਰਕਰਮਾ ਕਰਨਾ; **~it** ਗ੍ਰਹਿ-ਪਥ, ਕਾਰਜ-ਮੰਡਲ, ਚੱਕਰ; ਅੱਖ ਦੀ ਕਟੋਰੀ

orchard ('ਓਚਅਡ) *n* ਵਾੜੀ, ਬਗ਼ੀਚੀ, ਚਮਨ, ਬਗ਼ੀਚਾ; **~man** ਮਾਲੀ

orchestra ('ਓਕਿਸਟਰਆ) *n* ਰਕਸ ਗਾਹ, ਸਰੋਦ ਗਾਹ, ਵਾਦਕ ਦਲ, ਗਾਉਣ ਵਜਾਉਣ ਵਾਲੀ ਮੰਡਲੀ; ਬਾਂਸਰੀ, ਸਾਰੰਗੀ; ਸਾਰੰਗੀ ਤੇ ਹੋਰ ਵਾਜਿਆਂ ਦਾ ਸੰਜੋਗ, ਆਰਕੈਸਟਰਾ

ordeal (ਓ'ਡੀਲ) *n* ਕਰੜੀ ਅਜ਼ਮਾਇਸ਼, ਅਗਨੀ-ਪਰੀਖਿਆ; ਦੈਵੀ ਕਰੋਪੀ

order ('ਓਡਅ*) *n v* ਹੁਕਮ, ਆਗਿਆ, ਆਦੇਸ਼; ਜੁਗਤ, ਕਰੀਨਾ, ਕ੍ਰਮ, ਸਿਲਸਿਲਾ; ਸ਼੍ਰੇਣੀ, ਵਰਗ, ਦਰਜਾ, ਪਦ, ਪੰਗਤੀ; ਤਰਕੀਬ; ਕਿਸਮ; ਤਬਕਾ; ਧਰਮ-ਸੰਘ; ਬਿੱਲਾ ਜਾਂ ਤਮਗਾ; ਰੀਤੀ, ਰਿਵਾਜ; ਆਦੇਸ਼ ਦੇਣਾ; ਮਾਲ ਮੰਗਵਾਉਣ ਵਾਸਤੇ ਹੁਕਮ ਭੇਜਣਾ; ਤਰਤੀਬ ਨਾਲ ਰੱਖਣਾ, ਅਧਿਕਾਰ ਜਤਾਉਣਾ; **~ly** ਸੈਨਾ-ਆਦੇਸ਼-ਪਾਲ, ਅਰਦਲੀ; ਸੁਡੌਲ, ਅਨੁਸ਼ਾਸਨਪਾਲਕ; ਸਲੀਕਾ ਪਸੰਦ

ordinance ('ਓਡਿਨਅੰਸ) *n* ਫ਼ਰਮਾਨ, ਅਧਿਆਦੇਸ਼; ਧਰਮ-ਵਿਧੀ

ordinary ('ਓਡਨਰਿ) *a* ਸਧਾਰਨ, ਰਿਵਾਜੀ, ਮਾਮੂਲੀ, ਰੀਤੀਗਤ, ਪ੍ਰਥਾਗਤ

ordnance ('ਓਡਨਅੰਸ) *n* ਸਰਕਾਰੀ ਜੁੱਧ-ਵਿਭਾਗ; ਗੋਲਾ-ਬਾਰੂਦ; ਤੋਪਖ਼ਾਨਾ

ordure ('ਓਡਯੁਅ*) *n* ਗੋਹਾ, ਲਿੱਦ, ਵਿੱਠ, ਮਲ; ਭੈੜੇ ਸ਼ਬਦ

ore (ਓ*) *n* ਕੱਚੀ ਧਾਤ

organ ('ਓਗਅਨ) *v* ਅੰਗ, ਇੰਦਰੀ, ਅੰਸ਼ (ਪਾਰਟੀ ਆਦਿ ਦੇ) ਸੰਚਾਰ ਸਾਧਨ; **~ic** ਅੰਗ-ਸਬੰਧੀ, ਕਾਇਕ, ਸਰੀਰ ਤੇ ਪ੍ਰਭਾਵ ਪਾਉਣ ਵਾਲਾ; ਸਜੀਵੀ, ਬਨਸਪਤੀ ਜਗਤ ਜਾਂ ਜੀਵ ਸਬੰਧੀ; ਸੰਗਠਤ; ਕਾਰਬਨ ਯੁਕਤ, ਕਾਰਬਨਿਕ

organization ('ਓਗਅਨਾਇਸ਼ਨ) *v* ਜਥੇਬੰਦੀ, ਸੰਗਠਨ, ਰਚਨਾ

organize ('ਓਗਅਨਾਇਜ਼) *v* ਜਥੇਬੰਦ ਕਰਨਾ, ਪ੍ਰਬੰਧ ਕਰਨਾ; ਸੰਗਠਤ ਕਰਨਾ; **~d** ਸੰਗਠਤ, ਵਿਵਸਥਿਤ; **~r** ਸੰਗਠਕ, ਜਥੇਦਾਰ, ਪ੍ਰਬੰਧਕ ਵਿਵਸਥਾਪਕ, ਆਯੋਜਕ

orient (ਓਰਿਐਂਟ) *n a* ਮੋਤੀ ਦੀ ਝਲਕ, ਪੂਰਬ ਦੇਸ਼, ਚੜ੍ਹਦਾ ਸੂਰਜ, ਆਬ, ਚਮਕ (ਸ਼ੀਸ਼ੇ ਜਾਂ ਜ਼ੇਵਰ ਆਦਿ ਦੀ), ਉਜਲ, ਨਿਰਮਲ, ਆਬਦਾਰ, ਚਮਕਦਾਰ, ਚਮਕੀਲਾ, ਪੂਰਬੀ; **~al** ਪੂਰਬ-ਵਾਸੀ, ਪੂਰਬ ਦੇਸ਼ਾਂ ਦੀ ਸੰਸਕ੍ਰਿਤੀ ਸਬੰਧੀ, ਪੂਰਬੀ (ਭਾਸ਼ਾ)

origin ('ਔਰਿਜਨ) *n* ਮੂਲ, ਉਤਪੱਤੀ, ਉਦਭਵ, ਬੀਜ, ਆਰੰਭ, ਜਨਮ, ਆਦਿ, ਬੁਨਿਆਦ, ਸਰੋਤ;

~al ਮੂਲ, ਮੌਲਕ; ਨਵੀਨ; ~ality ਮੌਲਕਤਾ; ਰਚਨਾਤਮਕਤਾ; ~ate ਉਤਪੰਨ ਹੋਣਾ ਜਾਂ ਕਰਨਾ, ਵਿਉਤਪੰਨ ਹੋਣਾ ਜਾਂ ਕਰਨਾ, ਪੈਦਾ ਕਰਨਾ ਜਾਂ ਹੋਣਾ; ਆਰੰਭ ਕਰਨਾ; ਜਨਮ ਦੇਣਾ; ~ating ਆਰੰਭਕ, ਉਦਭਾਵਕ; ~ator ਉਤਪਾਦਕ, ਜਨਮਦਾਤਾ

ornament ('ਓਨਅਮਅੰਟ) *n v* ਗਹਿਣਾ, ਜ਼ੇਵਰ, ਭੂਸ਼ਣ, ਅੰਲਕਾਰ; ਸ਼ੋਭਾ; ਸ਼ਿੰਗਾਰ, ਸਜਾਵਟ; ~al ਸਜਾਵਟੀ, ਅਲੰਕਾਰਕ

ornithology ('ਓਨਿਥਅਲੋਜਿ) *n* ਪੰਛੀ-ਵਿਗਿਆਨ, ਖਗ-ਵਿਗਿਆਨ, ਵਿਹਗ-ਸ਼ਾਸਤਰ

orphan ('ਓ:ਫ਼ਨ) *a n v* ਯਤੀਮ, ਅਨਾਥ; ਅਨਾਥ ਬਣਾਉਣਾ; ~age ਯਤੀਮਖ਼ਾਨਾ, ਅਨਾਥ-ਆਸ਼ਰਮ, ਅਨਾਥਾਲਿਆ

orthodox ('ਓਥਅਡੋਕਸ) *a* ਕੱਟੜ, ਰੂੜ੍ਹੀਬੱਧ, ਪਰੰਪਰਾਗਤ, ਸਨਾਤਨੀ ਮੱਤ

orthography (ਓ'ਥੋਗਰਅਫ਼ਿ) *n* ਸ਼ੁੱਧ ਲੇਖਣ, ਸ਼ੁੱਧ ਅੱਖਰਜੋੜ

oscillate ('ਔਸਿਲੇਇਟ) *v* ਅਸਥਿਰ ਹੋਣਾ, ਕੰਬਣਾ, ਡਾਵਾਂ-ਡੋਲ ਹੋਣਾ, ਝੂਲਣਾ, ਝੁਲਾਉਣਾ, ਹਲਾਉਣਾ, ਡੋਲਣਾ

oscillation ('ਔਸਿ'ਲੇਇਸ਼ਨ) *n* ਅਸਥਿਰਤਾ, ਕੰਬਣ, ਝੂਲਣ, ਡੋਲਣ, ਘੁਮਾਉ

ostensible (ਔ'ਸਟੈਂਸਅਬਲ) *a* ਆਡੰਬਰਪੂਰਨ, ਪਖੰਡਪੂਰਨ, ਦੰਭਪੂਰਨ, ਬਣਾਉਟੀ

ostentation ('ਔਸਟੈਂਟ'ਇਸ਼ਨ) *n* ਦਿਖਾਵਾ, ਠਾਠ-ਬਾਠ, ਦੰਭ, ਆਤਮ-ਸ਼ਲਾਘਾ, ਆਤਮ-ਪਰਦਰਸ਼ਨ; ਆਡੰਬਰਪੂਰਨ, ਤੜਕ-ਭੜਕ

ostrich ('ਔਸਟਰਿਚ) *n* ਸ਼ੁਤਰ ਮੁਰਗ

other ('ਅੱਦਅ*) *n* ਹੋਰ, ਦੂਜਾ, ਅਗਲਾ, ਕੋਈ ਹੋਰ; ਭਿੰਨ; ~wise ਨਹੀਂ ਤਾਂ, ਵਰਨਾ, ਜਾਂ

otto ('ਔਟਅਉ) *n* ਇਤਰ, ਅਤਰ

ouch (ਆਉਚ) *n int* (ਪ੍ਰ) ਜੜਾਊ, ਬਕਸੂਆ, ਨਗੀਨਾ ਛੇਕ; ਉਹ!, ਹਾਇ!

oust (ਆਉਸਟ) *v* ਕੱਢ ਦੇਣਾ; ਬੇਦਖ਼ਲ ਕਰਨਾ, ਹਟਾਉਣਾ, ਵੰਚਤ ਕਰਨਾ

out (ਆਉਟ) *n v a adv int* ਖੁੱਲ੍ਹਾ ਮੈਦਾਨ; ਬੇਦਖ਼ਲ ਕਰਨਾ; ਬਾਹਰ ਕਰਨਾ; ਬਾਹਰ ਦਾ; ਬਾਹਰ, ਪਰੇ; ਦੂਰ ਹੋ; ~**break** ਯੁੱਧ ਦਾ ਆਰੰਭ; ਵਿਦਰੋਹ, ਫ਼ਸਾਦ; ~**burst** ਉਬਾਲ; ਭੜਕਾਹ; ~**cast** ਅਧਰਮੀ, ਭ੍ਰਿਸ਼ਟ, ਨਿਕੰਮਾ; ~**caste** (ਬਰਾਦਰੀ ਵਿਚੋਂ) ਛੇਕਣਾ, ਨਿਠਾਵਾਂ ਬਰਾਦਰੀ ਵਿਚੋਂ ਕੱਢ ਦੇਣਾ; ~**come** ਨਤੀਜਾ, ਫ਼ਲ, ਪਰਿਣਾਮ, ਨਿਸ਼ਕਰਸ; ~**cry** ਹਾਹਾਕਾਰ, ਚੀਕ-ਚਿਹਾੜਾ, ਦੁਹਾਈ, ਰੌਲਾ-ਰੱਪਾ; ~**date** ਪੁਰਾਣਾ ਕਰ ਦੇਣਾ; ~**dated** ਅਪ੍ਰਚਲਤ, ਪੁਰਾਣਾ; ~**door** ਬਾਹਰਲਾ, ਬਾਹਰੀ, ਮੈਦਾਨੀ, ਖੁੱਲ੍ਹਾ; ~**doors** ਅਸਮਾਨ ਥੱਲੇ, ਖੁੱਲ੍ਹੀ ਹਵਾ ਵਿਚ; ~**fall** ਮੁਹਾਣਾ, ਦਹਾਣਾ; ~**goings** ਖ਼ਰਚ, ਲਾਗਤ; ~**lay** ਲਾਗਤ, ਖ਼ਰਚ; ਖ਼ਾਕਾ; ~**let** ਨਿਕਾਸ, ਮੋਰੀ, ਲਾਂਘਾ; ~**line** ਰੂਪ-ਰੇਖਾ, ਖ਼ਾਕਾ, ਰੇਖਾ-ਚਿਤਰ; ਸੰਖੇਪ ਸਾਰ-ਅੰਸ਼; ~**look** ਨਜ਼ਰੀਆ, ਦ੍ਰਿਸ਼ਟੀਕੋਣ; ਰੰਗ-ਢੰਗ; ~**lying** ਦੂਰ-ਦੁਰਾਡਾ, ਬਾਹਰਵਰਤੀ, ਸੀਮਾਵਰਤੀ; ~**moded** ਅਪ੍ਰਚਲਤ; ~**number** ਗਿਣਤੀ ਵਿਚ ਵੱਧ ਹੋਣਾ; ~**patient** ਬਾਹਰੀ ਰੋਗੀ; ~**post** ਸਰਹੱਦੀ ਚੌਕੀ; ਸੈਨਾ-ਦਲ; ਸੀਮਾ-ਸਥਾਨ; ~**put** ਉਪਜ, ਉਤਪਾਦਨ; (ਕੰਪਿਊਟਰ) ਆਉਟਪੁਟ; ~**rage** ਉਪੱਦਰ, ਅਤਿਆਚਾਰ; ਘੋਰ ਅਪਮਾਨ, ਹੱਤਕ; ~**rageous** (ਅਤੀ) ਨਿਰਦਈ, ਉਪੱਦਰੀ, ਭ੍ਰਿਸ਼ਟਾਚਾਰੀ; ~**right** ਕਤਈ, ਸਰਾਸਰ, ਪੱਕਾ; ~**run** ਹੱਦ ਲੰਘ ਜਾਣਾ,

ਸੀਮਾ ਪਾਰ ਕਰ ਜਾਣਾ, ਹੋਰ ਤੇਜ਼ ਦੌੜਨਾ; ~side ਬਾਹਰਲਾ ਤਲ, ਬਾਹਰੀ ਭਾਗ, ਅਸੰਮਿਲਤ, ਅਸੰਯੁਕਤ; ~sider ਪਰਦੇਸੀ, ਅਪਰਿਚਿਤ ਆਦਮੀ; ~spoken ਮੂੰਹਫਟ, ਖ਼ਰਾ, ਸਾਫ਼ਗੋ, ਬੇਬਾਕ; ~standing ਬਕਾਇਆ, ਬਾਕੀ, ਪ੍ਰਮੁੱਖ, ਸਿਰਮੌਰ; ~ing ਛੋਟੀ ਸੈਰ, ਤਫ਼ਰੀਹੀ ਸਫ਼ਰ, ਹਵਾਖੋਰੀ; ~ward ਬਾਹਰ, ਬਾਹਰ ਦਾ, ਬੈਰੂਨੀ; ਬਾਹਰਮੁਖੀ; ~wardly ਬਾਹਰ, ਬਾਹਰ ਤੋਂ, ਬਾਹਰੋਂ; ~wards ਬਾਹਰੀ ਰੂਪ ਵਿਚ, ਬਾਹਰ ਬਾਹਰ ਵੱਲ

oval ('ਅਉਵਲ) *a n* ਅੰਡਾਕਾਰ; ਅੰਡਾਕਾਰ ਵਸਤੁ

ovary ('ਅਉਵਅਰਿ) *n* ਅੰਡਕੋਸ਼, ਬੀਜ-ਕੋਸ਼

oven ('ਅੋਵਨ) *n* ਤੰਦੂਰ, ਚੁੱਲ੍ਹਾ, ਭੱਠੀ

over ('ਅਉਵਅ*) *n adv a prep* ਅਧਿਕਤਾ; ਵਾਧਾ; ਮੁੜ ਮੁੜ, ਵਾਰ ਵਾਰ, ਇਕ ਵੇਰ ਫੇਰ; ਬਾਹਰ ਵੱਲ, ਉੱਪਰ, ਅੱਗੇ, ਅਗਲੇ ਪਾਰ; (ਕ੍ਰਿਕਟ) ਓਵਰ; ~act ਅਤਿ ਅਭਿਨੈ ਕਰਨਾ; ~age ਨਿਰਧਾਰਤ ਉਮਰ ਤੋਂ ਵੱਧ; ~all ਸਮੁੱਚੇ ਤੌਰ ਤੇ, ਕੁੱਲ ਮਿਲਾ ਕੇ; ~bridge ਉੱਪਰਲਾ ਪੁਲ; ~burden ਹੋਰ ਲੱਦ ਦੇਣਾ, ਦੱਬ ਦੇਣਾ; ~cast ਬਦਲਵਾਈ, ਛਾਇਆ ਹੋਇਆ, ਅੰਧਕਾਰ ਕਰ ਦੇਣਾ, ਢਕਣਾ, ਛਾ ਜਾਣਾ; ~charge ਵਧੇਰੇ ਭਾਰ; ਵਧੇਰੇ ਪੈਸੇ ਲੈਣੇ; ~coat ਫ਼ਰਗਲ, ਵੱਡਾ ਕੋਟ, ਓਵਰ ਕੋਟ; ~come ਜਿੱਤਣਾ, ਕਾਬੂ ਪਾਉਣਾ, ਛਾ ਜਾਣਾ, ਸਰ ਕਰਨਾ; ~date ਪਿੱਛਲੀ ਤਾਰੀਖ਼ ਪਾਉਣਾ; ~do ਅੰਤ ਕਰਨਾ, ਬਹੁਤ ਦੂਰ ਤਕ ਚਲੇ ਜਾਣਾ; ~dose (ਦਵਾਈ ਦੀ) ਅਧਿਕ ਮਾਤਰਾ, ਅਜਿਹੀ ਖ਼ੁਰਾਕ ਦੇਣੀ; ~draft ਵਾਧੂ ਵਸੂਲੀ; ~draw ਵਧਾ ਚੜ੍ਹਾ ਕੇ ਦੱਸਣਾ, ਵਧੇਰੇ ਲੈਣਾ; ~due ਮਿਆਦ ਪੁਗਿਆ; ~estimate ਅਤੀ ਅਨੁਮਾਨ, ਬਹੁਤ ਅਧਿਕ ਅਨੁਮਾਨ ਕਰਨਾ, ਅਧਿਕ ਅੰਕਣਾ; ~flow ਛਲਕਾਉ, ਛਲਕ; ~haul ਨਵਾਂ ਕਰਨਾ, ਕਾਇਆ-ਕਲਪ ਕਰਨੀ; ~head ਉਤਲਾ, ਉੱਪਰਲਾ, ਉੱਚਾ, ਉੱਪਰਲਾ (ਖ਼ਰਚ); ~hear ਚੋਰੀ ਛਿਪੇ ਸੁਣ ਲੈਣਾ; ~lapping ਪਰਸਪਰ ਵਿਆਪੀ, ਉੱਪਰ ਚੜ੍ਹੀ ਹੋਈ; ~load ਅਤੀ ਬੋਝ, ਅਤਿ ਭਾਰ; ਭਾਰੀ ਕਰਨਾ, ਵੱਧ ਭਾਰ ਲੱਦਣਾ; ~look ਅਣਦੇਖੀ ਕਰ ਜਾਣਾ; ਨਜ਼ਰ-ਅੰਦਾਜ਼ ਕਰਨਾ; ਨਿਗਰਾਨੀ ਕਰਨੀ; ~night ਪਿਛਲੀ ਰਾਤ ਦਾ; ਰਾਤੋ-ਰਾਤ ਭਰ ਦਾ; ~payment ਅਧਿਕ ਭੁਗਤਾਨ; ~rule (ਫ਼ੈਸਲੇ ਜਾਂ ਤਜਵੀਜ਼ ਨੂੰ) ਰੱਦਣਾ, ਰੱਦ ਕਰਨਾ, ਮਨਸੂਖ਼ ਕਰਨਾ; ~sea(s) ਸਮੁੰਦਰੋਂ ਪਾਰ ਦੇਸ਼; ਵਿਦੇਸ਼ੀ, ਸਮੁੰਦਰ ਪਾਰਲਾ; ~see (ਕਰਮਚਾਰੀਆਂ ਦੇ ਕੰਮ ਦੀ) ਦੇਖ-ਭਾਲ ਕਰਨੀ, ਨਿਗਰਾਨੀ ਕਰਨੀ; ~seer ਨਿਗਰਾਨ, ਨਿਗਾਹਬਾਨ, ਦਰੋਗ਼ਾ, ਓਵਰਸੀਅਰ, ਸਰਵੇਖਕ; ~set ਉਲਟਾਣਾ, ਮੂਧਾ ਕਰਨਾ, ਪਲਟਾਣਾ, ਹੇਠਾਂ ਡਿੱਗਣਾ; ~shadow ਛਾਂ ਕਰਨੀ, ਧੁੱਪ ਤੋਂ ਬਚਾਉਣਾ, ਢਕ ਦੇਣਾ; ~sight ਨਿਰੀਖਣ, ਦੇਖ-ਭਾਲ, ਨਿਗਰਾਨੀ; ਅਣਗਹਿਲੀ; ~take ਜਾ ਕੇ ਫੜ ਲੈਣਾ, ਬਰਾਬਰ ਆ ਜਾਣਾ; (ਮੁਸੀਬਤ ਦਾ) ਅਚਾਨਕ ਆ ਪੈਣਾ; ~time ਅਧਿ-ਸਮਾਂ, ਵਾਧੂ ਸਮੇਂ ਲਈ ਕੀਤੀ ਅਦਾਇਗੀ; ~weight ਅਤੀ ਭਾਰ, ਜ਼ਿਆਦਾ ਬੋਝ; *throw* ~ ਛੱਡਣਾ, ਤਿਆਗਣਾ, ਤਿਰਸਕਾਰਨਾ

overt ('ਅਉਵਅ:ਟ) *a* ਸਪਸ਼ਟ, ਖੁੱਲ੍ਹਾ, ਪਰਗਟ, ਪ੍ਰਤੱਖ, ਖੁੱਲ੍ਹ-ਖੁੱਲ੍ਹਾ ਕੀਤਾ; ~ness ਸਪਸ਼ਟਤਾ, ਖੁੱਲ੍ਹਾਪਣ

owe (ਅਓ) *n* ਰਿਣੀ ਹੋਣਾ, ਦੇਣਦਾਰ ਹੋਣਾ

owing ('ਅਉਇਙ) *pred a* ਬਾਕੀ, ਰਿਣਬੱਧ, ਫਲਸਰੂਪ, ਕਾਰਨ ਕਰਕੇ, ਦੇ ਕਾਰਨ

owl (ਆਉਲ) *n* ਉੱਲੂ, ਘੁੰਗੂ, ਆਡੰਬਰਪੂਰਨ ਵਿਅਕਤੀ

own (ਅਉਨ) *v a* ਅਧਿਕਾਰ ਰੱਖਣਾ, ਹੱਕਦਾਰ ਹੋਣਾ, ਇਕਬਾਲ ਕਰਨਾ, ਮੰਨਣਾ; ਨਿੱਜੀ, ਵਿਅਕਤੀਗਤ; ~**er** ਮਾਲਕ, ਸੁਆਮੀ; ~**ership** ਮਲਕੀਅਤ, ਮਾਲਕੀ, ਪ੍ਰਭੁਤਾ

ox (ਔਕਸ) *n* ਬਲਦ, ਬੈਲ

oxygen ('ਔਕਸਿਜ(ਅ)ਨ) *n* ਆਕਸੀਜਨ ਗੈਸ, ਪ੍ਰਾਣਵਾਯੂ

oyster ('ਔਇਸਟਅ*) *n* ਇਕ ਤਰ੍ਹਾਂ ਦੀ ਝੀਂਗਾ ਮੱਛੀ, ਘੋਗਾ

ozone ('ਅਉਜ਼ਅਉਨ) *n* ਆਕਸੀਜਨ ਵਰਗੀ ਇਕ ਗੈਸ, ਆਨੰਦਦਾਇਕ ਪ੍ਰਭਾਵ

P

P, p (ਪੀ) *n* ਰੋਮਨ ਵਰਨਮਾਲਾ ਦਾ ਸੋਲ੍ਹਵਾਂ ਅੱਖਰ

pace (ਪੇਇਸ) *n v* ਕਦਮ, ਪਗ, ਡਗ, ਪਦ, ਚਾਲ, ਗਤੀ, ਰਫਤਾਰ (ਚਲੱਣ ਜਾਂ ਦੌੜਨ ਦੀ); ਪ੍ਰਗਤੀ, ਟੁਰਨਾ, ਘੁੰਮਣਾ; ~**maker** ਗਤੀ ਨਿਰਧਾਰਕ; (ਦਿਲ ਦੀ ਗਤੀ ਦਾ) ਨਿਰਧਾਰਕ ਜੰਤਰ; ~**setter** ਗਤੀ-ਨਿਰਧਾਰਕ; **keep ~** ਸਮਾਨ ਗਤੀ ਨਾਲ ਟੁਰਨਾ; ਕਦਮ ਮਿਲਾ ਕੇ ਚੱਲਣਾ

pacific (ਪਅ'ਸਿਫ਼ਿਕ) *a* ਸ਼ਾਂਤ, ਪ੍ਰਸ਼ਾਂਤ, ਸ਼ਾਂਤਮਈ

pacification ('ਪੈਸਿਫ਼ਿ'ਕੇਇਸ਼ਨ) *n* ਸੁਲ੍ਹਾਨਾਮਾ, ਸੰਧੀਨਾਮਾ; ਸ਼ਾਂਤੀ ਸਥਾਪਨ

pacificist (ਪੈਸਿਫ਼ਾਇਸਿਸਟ) *n* ਅਮਨਪਸੰਦ, ਸ਼ਾਂਤੀਵਾਦੀ

pacify ('ਪੈਸਿਫ਼ਾਇ) *v* ਸ਼ਾਂਤ ਕਰਨਾ, ਦਾਰਸ ਦੇਣੀ, ਮਨਾਉਣਾ

pack (ਪੈਕ) *n v* ਪੋਟਲੀ, ਬੁਗਚਾ, ਗੰਢੜੀ, ਗੰਢ, ਸਮੂਹ, ਗੁੱਟ, ਡੱਬਿਆਂ ਵਿਚ ਬੰਦ ਕਰਨਾ, ਠੋਸ ਦੇਣਾ, ਖਰਖਚ ਭਰ ਦੇਣਾ, ਤੁਨਣਾ, ਬੋਰੀਆ ਬਿਸਤਰ ਬੰਨ੍ਹ ਕੇ ਤਿਆਰ ਹੋਣਾ, ਗਠੜੀ ਜਾਂ ਪੰਡ ਸਟੇ ਭੱਜ ਪੈਣਾ; ~**age** ਗੰਢ, ਗਠੜੀ, ਬੰਡਲ, ਪੁਲੰਦਾ; ਗੰਢ ਬੰਨ੍ਹਤੀ, ਪੁਲੰਦਾ ਬਣਾਉਣਾ, ਪਾਰਸਲ ਕਰਨਾ, ਵਲੇਟਣਾ; ~**et** ਪੁਲੰਦਾ, ਛੋਟਾ ਬੰਡਲ, ਪੁੜਾ, ਪੁੜੀ, ਮੁੱਠ, ਪੈਕਟ; ~**ing** ਪੈਕਿੰਗ; ਪੁਲੰਦਾ ਬੰਨ੍ਹਣ ਦਾ ਕੰਮ; ਬੰਨ੍ਹਾਈ, ਭਰਾਈ

pact (ਪੈਕਟ) *n v* ਸੰਧੀ, ਅਹਿਦਨਾਮਾ, ਸੁਲ੍ਹਾਨਾਮਾ; ਸੰਧੀ (ਕਰਨੀ), ਸਮਝੌਤਾ (ਕਰਨਾ)

pad (ਪੈਡ) *n v* ਜੀਨ, ਨਰਮ ਕਾਠੀ, ਗੱਦਾ, ਗੱਦੀ; ~**ding** ਭਰਾਈ

paddle ('ਪੈਡਲ) *n v* ਚੱਪੂ, ਕਿਸ਼ਤੀ ਦਾ ਡੰਡਾ, ਛੋਟਾ ਬੇਹਲਾ, ਹੌਲੀ-ਹੌਲੀ ਕਿਸ਼ਤੀ ਚਲਾਉਂਦੀ, ਖੰਭਾਂ ਨਾਲ ਪਾਣੀ ਵਿਚ ਤਰਨਾ, ਜਲ-ਕ੍ਰੀੜਾ ਕਰਨਾ, ਠੁਮਕ-ਠੁਮਕ ਟੁਰਨਾ, ਚੱਲਣਾ; ~**r** ਚਲਾਉਣ ਵਾਲਾ, ਚਾਲਕ, ਖੇਵਈਆ, ਮੱਲਾਹ

paddy ('ਪੈਡਿ) *n v* ਧਾਨ; (ਉਪ) ਰੋਸਾ, ਖਿਝ

padlock ('ਪੈਡਲੌਕ) *n v* ਜੰਦਰਾ, ਤਾਲਾ, ਕੁਫ਼ਲ; ਤਾਲਾ ਲਾਉਣਾ, ਕੁਫ਼ਲਬੰਦ ਕਰਨਾ

paean ('ਪੀਅਨ) *n* ਵਿਜੈ-ਗੀਤ, ਜੈ-ਧੁਨੀ, ਉਸਤਤ ਗਾਨ; ਸ਼ੁਕਰਾਨੇ ਦਾ ਗੀਤ, ਸੋਹਲਾ

paederast ('ਪੈਡਅਰੈਸਟ) *n* ਮੁੰਡੇਬਾਜ਼, ਲੋਂਡੇਬਾਜ਼

paediatric ('ਪੀਡਿ'ਐਟਰਿਕ) *a* ਬਾਲ ਚਿਕਿਤਸਾ-ਸਬੰਧੀ, ਬਾਲ ਰੋਗ-ਸਬੰਧੀ

pagan ('ਪੇਇਗਅਨ) *n a* ਕਾਫ਼ਰ, ਨਾਸਤਕ; ਅੰਧਵਿਸ਼ਵਾਸੀ, ਮੂਰਤ

page (ਪੇਇਜ) *n v* ਪੰਨਾ, ਸਫ਼ਾ; ਚਾਕਰ; ਸਾਕਾ; ਸਫ਼ੇ ਲਾਉਣਾ, ਬੁਲਾਵਾ ਘੱਲਣਾ

pagination ('ਪੈਜਿ'ਨੇਇਸ਼ਨ) *n* ਪੰਨਾ-ਸੰਖਿਆ, ਪੰਨਿਆਂ ਦੀ ਕੁੱਲ ਗਿਣਤੀ

pagoda (ਪਅ'ਗਅਉਡਅ) *n* ਸ਼ਿਵਾਲਾ, ਦੇਵਾਲਾ, (ਦੱਖਣੀ ਭਾਰਤ ਦਾ ਪ੍ਰਾਚੀਨ) ਸੋਨੇ ਦਾ ਸਿੱਕਾ

paid (ਪੇਇਡ) *a* ਭੁਗਤਾਨ ਕੀਤਾ, ਚੁਕਾ ਦਿੱਤਾ

pail (ਪੇਇਲ) *n* ਤੋੜਾ, ਬਾਲਟੀ, ਡੋਲ

pain (ਪੇਇਨ) *n v* ਦਰਦ, ਦੁੱਖ, ਪੀੜ, ਸੰਤਾਪ, ਵੇਦਨਾ, ਤਕਲੀਫ਼, ਪ੍ਰਸਵ-ਵੇਦਨਾ; ਸਤਾਉਣਾ, ਦੁੱਖ ਦੇਣਾ, ਪੀੜਾ ਦੇਣੀ, ਬੇਚੈਨ ਕਰਨਾ; ~**killer** ਪੀੜ-ਨਾਸਕ; ~**ed** ਪੀੜਤ, ਦੁਖੀ; ~**ful** ਦੁਖੀ, ਕਸ਼ਟਦਾਇਕ, ਦੁਖਦਾਈ; ਕਠਨ; ~**less**

ਪੀੜਹੀਨ, ਕਸ਼ਟ-ਰਹਿਤ, ਦੁੱਖਹੀਨ

paint (ਪੇਂਟ) *n v* ਰੰਗ, ਲੇਪ; ਰੋਗਨ; ਰੰਗਣਾ, ਰੰਗ ਲਾਉਣਾ ਜਾਂ ਭਰਨਾ; ~**er** ਚਿਤਰਕਾਰ, ਰੰਗ-ਲੇਪਕ, ਰੰਗਸਾਜ਼, ਨੱਕਾਸ਼, ਮੁਸੱਵਰ; ਰੰਜ਼ਕ; ~**ing** ਚਿਤਰਕਾਰੀ, ਨੱਕਾਸ਼ੀ, ਰੰਗਾਈ; ਚਿਤਰ

pair (ਪੇਅ*) *n* ਜੋੜ, ਜੁੱਟ, ਜੋੜਾ, ਜੋੜੀ, ਜੋਟਾ; ਦੰਪਤੀ, ਪਤੀ-ਪਤਨੀ, ਜੋੜੀਦਾਰ, ਜੋੜ ਜੋੜਨਾ, ਜੋੜੀ ਬਣਾਉਣਾ

pal (ਪੈਲ) *n v* ਸੰਗੀ, ਸਾਥੀ, ਮਿੱਤਰ; ਦੋਸਤ ਬਣਨ; ਮਿਲਣਾ-ਜੁਲਣਾ

palace ('ਪੈਲਿਸ) *n* ਰਾਜ ਭਵਨ, ਸ਼ਾਹੀ ਮਹੱਲ, ਹਵੇਲੀ, ਸ਼ਾਨਦਾਰ ਇਮਾਰਤ

palaeography ('ਪੈਲਿ'ਔਗਰਅਫ਼ਿ) *n* ਪੁਰਾ-ਲੇਖ-ਸ਼ਾਸਤਰ

palaestra (ਪੈ'ਲੀਸਟਰਅ) *n* ਅਖਾੜਾ, ਕਸਰਤ ਘਰ

palanquin ('ਪੈਲਅਨ'ਕੀਨ) *n* ਡੋਲੀ, ਪਾਲਕੀ

palatable ('ਪੈਲਅਟਅਬਲ) *a* ਸੁਆਦੀ, ਜ਼ਾਇਕੇਦਾਰ, ਮਜ਼ੇਦਾਰ, ਸੁਆਦਿਸ਼ਟ

palate ('ਪੈਲਅਟ) *n* ਤਾਲੂ; ਸੁਆਦ, ਜ਼ਾਇਕਾ

palatial ('ਪਅ'ਲੇਇਸ਼ਲ) *a* ਮਹੱਲ ਵਰਗਾ; ਆਲੀਸ਼ਾਨ, ਸ਼ਾਨਦਾਰ, ਵਿਸ਼ਾਲ, ਸ਼ਾਹੀ

pall (ਪੈਲ) *n v* ਖੱਫਣ, ਮੁਰਦੇ ਨੂੰ ਢਕਣ ਵਾਲਾ ਕੱਪੜਾ; ਪਰਦਾ; ਚੋਗਾ; ਘੋਮਜ਼ਾ ਹੋ ਜਾਣਾ; ਹਿੰਮਤ ਹਾਰਨਾ, ਜੀ ਚੁਰਾਉਣਾ; ~**bearer** (ਅਰਥੀ ਨੂੰ) ਮੋਢਾ ਦੇਣ ਵਾਲਾ

palm (ਪਾਮ) *n v* (1) ਤਾੜ, (ਵਿਜੈ-ਚਿੰਨ੍ਹ ਵਜੋਂ) ਤਾੜ ਦਾ ਪੱਤਾ, ਸਰਬਸ਼੍ਰੇਸ਼ਠਤਾ, ਸਰਬਉੱਚਤਾ; (2) ਤਲੀ, ਹਥੇਲੀ; ਫੜਨਾ; ਰਿਸ਼ਵਤ ਦੇਣੀ, ਮੁੱਠੀ ਗਰਮ ਕਰਨੀ; ~**ist** ਹੱਥ ਵੇਖਣ ਵਾਲਾ, ਪਾਂਡਾ

palpitate ('ਪੈਲਪਿਟੇਇਟ) *v* (ਦਿਲ ਦਾ) ਧੜਕਣਾ, ਧਕ ਧਕ ਕਰਨਾ; (ਨਬਜ਼ ਜਾਂ ਨਾੜ ਦਾ) ਫੜਕਣਾ; ਖਟਖਟਾਉਣਾ, ਫੜਕ ਉਠਣਾ

palpitation ('ਪੈਲਪਿ'ਟੇਇਸ਼ਨ) *n* ਧੜਕਣ, ਧਕ ਧਕ, ਕਾਂਬਾ, ਥਰਥਰਾਹਟ

paltry ('ਪੋਲਟਰਿ) *a* ਤੁੱਛ, ਘਟੀਆ, ਮਾਮੂਲੀ

pamper ('ਪੈਂਪਅ*) *v* ਪੁਚ ਪੁਚ ਕਰਨਾ, ਆਦਤ ਵਿਗਾੜ ਦੇਣੀ; ~**ed** ਵਿਗੜਿਆ, ਚਾਂਭਲਿਆ

pamphlet ('ਪੈਂਫ਼ਲਿਟ) *n* ਛੋਟਾ ਰਸਾਲਾ, ਪੱਤਰਕਾ, ਪੁਸਤਕਾ, ਕਿਤਾਬਚਾ, ਪੈਂਫਲਿਟ, ਚੋਪੰਨਾ

pan (ਪੈਨ) *n v* *pl* ਕੜਾਹੀ; ਤਮਾਂ; ਤੱਕੜੀ ਦਾ ਪਲੜਾ; ਥੇਪੜੀ

panacea (ਪੈਨਅ'ਸਿਅ) *n* ਸਰਬਰੋਗ ਔਸ਼ਧ, ਅਕਸੀਰ, ਹਰ ਮਰਜ਼ ਦੀ ਦਵਾ

pandemonium ('ਪੈਂਡਿ'ਮਅਉਨਯਅਮ) *n* ਭੂਤ-ਘਰ; ਪਰੇਤਵਾਸ; ਅਸ਼ਾਂਤੀਪੁਰਨ ਥਾਂ, ਧਮਚੱਕੜ, ਸ਼ੋਰ-ਸ਼ਰਾਬਾ, ਕਾਵਾਂ-ਰੋਲੀ, ਮੱਛੀ-ਬਜ਼ਾਰ; ਉਪੱਦਰ, ਗੜਬੜ

pander ('ਪੈਂਡਅ*) *n v* ਭੜੂਆ, ਦਲਾਲ, ਬੁਰੇ ਕੰਮ ਵਿਚ ਸਹਾਇਤਾ ਦੇਣੀ

panel ('ਪੈਨਲ) *n v* ਵਿਅੱਕਤੀਆਂ ਦੇ ਨਾਵਾਂ ਦੀ ਸੂਚੀ; ਪੰਚ ਜਿਊਰੀ; ਡਾਕਟਰਾਂ ਦੀ ਟੋਲੀ; ਸੂਚੀ, ਕ੍ਰਮਟਿਕਾ; ਦਲ; ਕਾਠੀ ਕੱਸਣੀ; ਚੌਖਟਾ ਬਣਾਉਣਾ

pang (ਪੈਂਡ) *n* ਵੇਦਨਾ; ਪੀੜਾ, ਦਰਦ, ਚੀਸ

panic (ਪੈਨਿਕ) *n v* ਅਤੀਅੰਤ ਭੈ, ਦਹਿਸ਼ਤ, ਤ੍ਰਾਸ, ਸੰਤ੍ਰਾਸ, ਆਂਤਕ; ਦਹਿਲਣਾ, ਦਹਿਸ਼ਤ ਵਿਚ ਪੈਣਾ, ਤ੍ਰਾਸ ਵਿਚ ਹੋਣਾ; ~**stricken** ਭੈਭੀਤ; ~**ky** ਭੈਭੀਤ, ਤ੍ਰਾਸਤ

panorama ('ਪੈਨਅ'ਰਾਮਅ) *n* ਵਿਸ਼ਾਲ-ਦ੍ਰਿਸ਼, ਚਿਤਰਾਵਲੀ; ਫਿਰਨ ਵਾਲੀ ਤਸਵੀਰ

pant (ਪੈਂਟ) *n v* ਧੜਕਣ, ਹੌਂਕਣੀ ਹਫਣੀ; ਧੜਕਣਾ, ਸਾਹ ਫੁੱਲਣਾ, ਕਾਮਨਾ ਰੱਖਣੀ

pantaloon (ਪੈਂਟਅ'ਲੂਨ) *n* ਪਤਲੂਨ, ਪੈਂਟ

panther (ਪੈਂਥਅ*) *n* ਚੀਤਾ, ਬਾਘ

pantomime (ਪੈਂਟਅਮਾਇਮ) *n v* ਮੂਕ ਅਭਿਨੈ, ਮੂਕ ਨਾਚ; ਮੂਕ ਅਭਿਨੇਤਾ; ਮੂਕ ਅਭਿਨੈ ਕਰਨਾ; ਮੂਕ ਨਾਚ ਨੱਚਣਾ

pantomimist (ਪੈਂਟਅਮਿਮਿਸਟ) *n* ਮੂਕ ਅਭਿਨੇਤਾ

pantomorphic (ਪੈਂਟਅ'ਮੋਰਫ਼ਿਕ) *a* ਬਹੁਰੂਪੀਆ

pantry (ਪੈਂਟਰਿ) *n* ਪੈਂਟਰੀ, ਭੰਡਾਰ, ਰਸਦਖ਼ਾਨਾ

papa ('ਪਅ'ਪਾ) *n* ਪਾਪਾ, ਭਾਪਾ, ਬਾਪੂ

papacy (ਪੇਇਪਅਸਿ) *n* ਪੋਪ-ਪਦ, ਪੋਪ-ਤੰਤਰ, ਪੋਪ-ਪ੍ਰਣਾਲੀ

paper (ਪੇਇਪਅ*) *n* ਪੱਤਰ; ਕਾਗ਼ਜ਼ੀ, ਧਨ, ਹੁੰਡੀ, ਨੋਟ, ਪ੍ਰਮਾਣ-ਪੱਤਰ, ਪ੍ਰਸ਼ਨ ਪੱਤਰ, ਸਮਾਚਾਰ-ਪੱਤਰ; ਨਿਬੰਧ, ਲੇਖ; ~back ਕਾਗ਼ਜ਼ੀ ਜਿਲਦ ਵਾਲੀ ਪੁਸਤਕ; ~ing (ਪੁਸਤਕਾ ਆਦਿ ਉੱਤੇ) ਕਾਗ਼ਜ਼ੀ ਮੜ੍ਹਾਈ, ਕਾਗ਼ਜ਼ੀ ਸਜਾਵਟ

pappy ('ਪੈਪਿ) *a* ਨਰਮ, ਪਿਲਪਿਲਾ, ਪਿਲ-ਪਿਲ ਕਰਦਾ; ਅਤੀਅੰਤ ਸਿੱਧਾ

par (ਪਾ*) *n* ਸਮਾਨਤਾ, ਬਰਾਬਰੀ, ਸਮਤਾ, ਤੁਲਨਾ; ਬਰਾਬਰ ਮਾਤਰਾ, ਔਸਤ ਪਰਿਣਾਮ ਜਾਂ ਰਾਸ਼ੀ

para (ਪੈਰਅ) *n* ਪੈਰਾ, ਪੈਰਾਗ੍ਰਾਫ਼

parachute (ਪੈਰਅਸ਼ੂਟ) *n v* ਹਵਾਈ ਛਤਰੀ, ਪੈਰਾਸ਼ੂਟ; ਪੈਰਾਸ਼ੂਟ ਨਾਲ ਉਤਰਨਾ

parade (ਪਅ'ਰੇਇਡ) *n v* ਦਿਖਾਵਾ, ਪਰਦਰਸ਼ਨ; ਕਵਾਇਦ, ਪਰੇਡ; ਸੈਨਾ ਪਰਦਰਸ਼ਨ ਕਰਨਾ, ਆਡੰਬਰ ਦਿਖਾਉਣਾ

paradigm (ਪੈਰਅਡਾਇਮ) *n* ਮਿਸਾਲ; ਨਕਸ਼ਾ, ਨਮੂਨਾ, ਸ਼ਬਦ ਰੂਪਾਵਲੀ

paradise (ਪੈਰਅਡਾਇਸ) *n* ਜੰਨਤ, ਬਹਿਸ਼ਤ, ਸੁਰਗ

paradox (ਪੈਰਅਡੌਕਸ) *n* ਵਿਰੋਧਾਭਾਸ, ਅਸੰਗਤ ਕਥਨ, ਉੱਲਟੀ ਗੱਲ; ~ical ਵਿਰੋਧਾਭਾਸੀ

paragraph (ਪੈਰਅਗਰਾਫ਼) *n v* ਖੰਡ, ਪੈਰਾ, ਪੈਰਾਗ੍ਰਾਫ਼; ਪੈਰਾ ਲਿਖਣਾ, ਲੇਖ ਨੂੰ ਪੈਰਿਆਂ ਵਿਚ ਵੰਡਣਾ

parallel (ਪੈਰਅਲੈੱਲ) *n v a* ਅਖਸ਼ਾਂਸ ਰੇਖਾ; ਸਮਾਂਤਰ; ਤੁਲਨਾਂ; ਸਦ੍ਰਿਸ਼ ਵਿਅਕਤੀ ਜਾਂ ਵਸਤੁ; ਸਮਾਂਤਰ ਅਵਸਥਾ, ਸਮਾਂਤਰ ਰੇਖਾ ਜਾਂ ਸਥਿਤੀ; ਤੁਲਨਾ ਸਮਾਨਤਾ; ਸਮਾਨ ਦਿਖਾਉਣਾ, ਤੁਲਨਾ ਕਰਨੀ; ਸਮਾਂਤਰ ਕਰਨਾ; ਬਰਾਬਰ ਕਰਨਾ, ਮਿਲਾਉਣਾ; ਸਦ੍ਰਿਸ਼, ਸਮਾਨ; ~ism ਸਮਾਂਤਰਤਵ, ਸਮਾਂਤਰਤਾ, ਸਮਾਂਤਰਵਾਦ; ਸਮਾਨਤਾ, ਤੁਲਨਾ, ਬਰਾਬਰੀ

paralyse (ਪੈਰਅਲਾਇਜ਼) *v* ਲਕਵਾ ਮਾਰਨਾ, ਅਧਰੰਗ ਹੋਣਾ; ਗਤੀਹੀਨ ਕਰਨਾ, ਸ਼ਕਤੀਹੀਨ ਕਰਨਾ, ਲੂਲ੍ਹਾ ਲੰਗੜਾ ਬਣਾ ਦੇਣਾ

paralysis (ਪਅ'ਰੈਲਿਸਿਸ) *n* ਲਕਵਾ, ਅਧਰੰਗ; ਅਤੀ ਸ਼ਕਤੀ-ਹੀਨਤਾ

parameter (ਪਅ'ਰੈਮਿਟਅ*) *n* (ਗਣਿ) ਪੈਰਾਮੀਟਰ; ਮਾਪਦੰਡ

paramilitary (ਪੈਰਅ'ਮਿਲਿਟਰਿ) *a* ਅਰਧ-ਸੈਨਕ, ਨੀਮ ਫ਼ੌਜੀ

paramount (ਪੈਰਅਮਾਉਂਟ) *a* ਪਰਮ, ਸਰਬਸ੍ਰੇਸ਼ਠ, ਸਰਬੋਤਮ, ਸਰਬਉੱਚ, ਪ੍ਰਮੁਖ

paramour (ਪੈਰਅ'ਮੁਅ*) *n* ਯਾਰ, ਧਗੜਾ, ਯਾਰਨੀ, ਆਸ਼ਨਾ

paraphernalia (ਪੈਰਅਫ਼ਅ'ਨੇਇਲਯਅ) *n pl* ਨਿਕਸੁਕ, ਟਿੰਡ-ਫ਼ਹੁੜੀ, ਨਿੱਜੀ ਸਾਮਾਨ, ਲੀੜੇ-ਲੱਤੇ; ਸਾਜੋ-ਸਾਮਾਨ; ਮਸ਼ੀਨ ਦੇ ਕਲ-ਪੁਰਜ਼ੇ

paraphrase (ਪੈਰਅਫਰੇਇਜ਼) *n v* ਸ਼ਬਦਾਰਥ, ਭਾਵ ਅਨੁਵਾਦ; ਟੀਕਾ, ਵਿਆਖਿਆ, ਅਰਥ-ਪ੍ਰਕਾਸ਼; ਭਾਸ਼, ਤਸ਼ਰੀਹ, ਭਾਸ਼ ਲਿਖਣਾ, ਟੀਕਾ ਵਿਆਖਿਆ ਕਰਨਾ, ਭਾਵ ਪ੍ਰਕਾਸ਼ਤ ਕਰਨਾ; **~r** ਵਿਆਖਿਆਕਾਰ, ਅਨੁਵਾਦਕ

parasite (ਪੈਰਅਸਾਇਟ) *n* ਪਰਜੀਵੀ; ਸੁਆਰਥੀ; ਪਿਛਲੱਗ; ਚਾਪਲੂਸ

parathesis (ਪਅਰੈਥਿਸਿਸ) *n* ਸੰਯੋਜਤ, ਏਕਤਾ, ਸਮਾਨਤਾ

parcel (ਪਾਸਲ) *n v adv* ਪੁਲੰਦਾ, ਪੋਟਲੀ, ਅੰਗ, ਖੰਡ, ਤਾਗ, ਪੁਹਾਰਾ, ਪਾਰਸਲ; (ਵ੍ਯ•ਰ) ਮਾਲ ਦਾ ਚਾਲਾਨ, ਮਾਲ ਦੀ ਇਕ ਖੇਪ; ਖੰਡਤ ਕਰਨਾ, ਵੰਡਣਾ; ਪੁਲੰਦਾ ਜਾਂ ਪਾਰਸਲ ਬੰਨ੍ਹਣਾ

pardon (ਪਾਡਨ) *n v* ਖਿਮਾ, ਛੁਟਕਾਰਾ, ਮਾਫ਼ੀ, ਦੋਸ਼-ਮੁਕਤੀ; ਖਿਮਾ ਕਰਨਾ, ਦੋਸ਼-ਮੁਕਤ ਕਰਨਾ

pare (ਪੇਅ*) *v* ਛਾਂਗਣਾ, ਛਾਂਟਣਾ, ਸੁਡੌਲ ਬਣਾਉਣਾ, ਤਰਾਸ਼ਣਾ; ਛਿੱਲਣਾ, ਛਿੱਲ ਲਾਹੁਣੀ, ਕੱਟਣਾ, ਕਤਰਨਾ, ਮੁੰਡਣਾ

parent (ਪੇਅਰਅੰਟ) *n* ਮਾਂ-ਪਿਉ, ਮਾਂ-ਬਾਪ, ਮਾਤਾ-ਪਿਤਾ, ਪਿਤਰ; ਬਜ਼ੁਰਗ, ਵੱਡ-ਵਡੇਰੇ, ਪੁਰਖੇ; (ਬਨ); **~al** ਪਿਤਰੀ, ਪੈਤ੍ਰਿਕ

parenthesis (ਪਅ'ਰੈਂਨਸਿਸ) *n* ਉਪਵਾਕ, ਅਪ੍ਰਧਾਨ ਵਾਕ; ਬ੍ਰੈਕਟਾਂ ਦੁਆਰਾ ਚਿੰਨ੍ਹਿਆ ਸ਼ਬਦ-ਸਮੂਹ; ਛੋਟੀ ਬ੍ਰੈਕਟ (); ਮੱਧਵਰਤੀ ਘਟਨਾ, ਵਕਫ਼ਾ, ਵਿਰਾਮ

par excellence ('ਪਾਰ'ਐੱਕਸਅ'ਲਾਂਸ) (*F*) *adv* ਸ੍ਰੇਸ਼ਠ, ਸਭ ਤੋਂ ਵਧੀਆ, ਪਰਮ ਉਤਕ੍ਰਿਸ਼ਟ

parity (ਪੈਰਅਟਿ) *n* ਬਰਾਬਰੀ, ਤੁਲਨਾ, ਸਮਾਨਤਾ; ਅਨੁਪਾਤ, ਸਮਾਨਾਂਤਰਤਾ

park (ਪਾਕ) *n v* ਪਾਰਕ, ਉਪਵਨ, ਉਦਿਆਨ; ਵਾੜਾ; ਮੈਦਾਨ; ਪੜਾਉ, ਕੈਂਪ; ਪਾਰਕ ਬਣਾਉਣੀ; ਮੋਟਰ ਖੜ੍ਹੀ ਕਰਨੀ (ਚੌਕ ਆਦਿ ਵਿਚ); **~ing** ਗੱਡੀਆਂ ਖੜਾਉਣ ਦਾ ਥਾਂ, ਪਾਰਕਿੰਗ

parlance ('ਪਾਲਅੰਸ) *n* ਸੰਵਾਦ, ਸਮਭਾਸ਼ਣ, ਭਾਸ਼ਾ, ਸ਼ਬਦਾਵਲੀ, ਬੋਲ-ਚਾਲ, ਮੁਹਾਵਰਾ

parley ('ਪਾਲਿ) *n* (ਵਿਵਾਦੀ ਮਾਮਲਿਆਂ ਨੂੰ ਹਲ ਕਰਨ ਲਈ ਬੁਲਾਇਆ) ਸੰਮੇਲਨ; ਵਾਰਤਾ, ਵਾਰਤਾਲਾਪ, ਬਹਿਸ, ਵਿਵਾਦ

parliament ('ਪਾਲਅਮਅੰਟ) *n* ਪਾਰਲੀਮੈਂਟ, ਸੰਸਦ, ਵਿਚਾਰ ਸਭਾ; **~arian** ਸੰਸਦੀ ਮੈਂਬਰਵਾਦੀ; **~ary** ਸੰਸਦੀ; ਅਧਿਨਿਯਮਤ ਜਾਂ ਸਥਾਪਤ; ਸੋਭਿਆ, ਸ਼ਿਸ਼ਟ

parlour ('ਪਾ*ਲਅ*) *n* ਦੀਵਾਨਖ਼ਾਨਾ, ਬੈਠਕ, ਖਿਲਵਤਖ਼ਾਨਾ; ਸਥਾਨ

parlous ('ਪਾ*ਲਅਸ) *a adv* ਸੰਕਟਪੂਰਨ, ਭਿਅੰਕਰ, ਖ਼ਤਰਨਾਕ; ਕਠਨ, ਕਰੜਾ; ਹੁਸ਼ਿਆਰ

parody (ਪੈਰਅਡਿ) *n v* ਪੈਰੋਡੀ, ਵਿਅੰਗ ਕਾਵਿ, ਨਕਲ, ਸੁਆਂਗ

parrot (ਪੈਰਅਟ) *n v* ਤੋਤਾ, ਸੂਕ

parson ('ਪਾ*ਸਨ) *n* ਪਾਦਰੀ, ਪਰੋਹਤ; ਸਿੱਖਿਅਕ, ਮੁੱਖ ਸਿੱਖਿਅਕ

part (ਪਾ*ਟ) *n v* ਹਿੱਸਾ, ਅੰਗ, ਅੰਸ਼, ਖੰਡ, ਟੁਕੜਾ; (ਅਤਿਨੇ) ਰੋਲ; ਇਲਾਕਾ, ਪ੍ਰਦੇਸ, ਦਲ, ਪੱਖ; ਕਾਂਡ; ਹਿੱਸੇ ਕਰਨਾ; ਵੰਡਣਾ, ਟੁੱਟਣਾ, ਅੱਡ ਕਰਨਾ ਜਾਂ ਹੋਣਾ; **~of speech** ਸ਼ਬਦ-ਸ੍ਰੇਣੀ; **~ly** ਅੰਸ਼ ਰੂਪ ਵਿਚ, ਕੁਝ ਕੁਝ, ਕਿਸੇ ਕਦਰ; ਕੁਝ ਹੱਦ ਤਕ

partake (ਪਾ*ਟੇਇਕ) *v* ਸ਼ਾਮਲ ਹੋਣਾ, ਹਿੱਸਾ ਲੈਣਾ, ਸ਼ਰੀਕ ਹੋਣਾ, ਗ੍ਰਹਿਣ ਕਰਨਾ, ਲੈ ਲੈਣਾ

partial ('ਪਾ*ਸ਼ਲ) *n a* (ਸੰਗੀ) ਅੰਸ਼ਕ ਸੁਰ; ਤਰਫ਼ਦਾਰ, ਪੱਖਪਾਤੀ; ਅਪੂਰਾ, ਅਪੂਰਨ; **~ity**

ਪੱਖ-ਪਾਤ, ਤਰਫ਼ਦਾਰੀ; ਅਨੁਚਿਤ ਲਗਾਉ

participant (ਪਾ*ਟਿਸਿਪਅੰਟ) *n* ਭਾਈਵਾਲ, ਸਾਂਝੀਦਾਰ, ਹਿੱਸੇਦਾਰ, ਭਾਗੀ, ਸਹਿਤਾਗੀ

participate (ਪਾ*ਟਿਸਿਪੇਇਟ) *v* ਸ਼ਾਮਲ ਹੋਣਾ, ਭਾਗ ਲੈਣਾ, ਸੰਮਿਲਤ ਹੋਣਾ

participation (ਪਾ*ਟਿਸਿ'ਪੇਇਸ਼ਨ) *n* ਸਾਂਝਾਦਾਰੀ, ਸਹਿਤਾਗਤਾ, ਸ਼ਮੂਲੀਅਤ, ਸ਼ਿਰਕਤ, ਭਾਗ

particle ('ਪਾ*ਟਿਕਲ) *n* ਕਣ, ਅਣੂ; ਅਲਪਤਮ ਅੰਸ਼, (ਵਿਆ) ਅੰਸ਼ਕ

particular (ਪਅ*ਟਿਕਯੁਲਅ*) *n a* ਥਿਓਰਾ; ਵਿਸ਼ੇਸ਼, ਖ਼ਾਸ, ਵਿਲੱਖਣ, ਅਸਧਾਰਨ; ~ity ਵਿਸ਼ੇਸ਼ਤਾ; ਵਿਸ਼ੇਸ਼ ਕਥਨ, ਵਿਸ਼ੇਸ਼ ਨਿਰਦੇਸ਼; ਅਸਧਾਰਨਤਾ; ਨਿਰਾਲਾਪਨ

partisan ('ਪਾ*ਟਿਜ਼ੈਨ) *n* ਪੱਖਪਾਤੀ, ਤਰਫ਼ਦਾਰੀ; ~ship ਪੱਖਪਾਤ, ਹਿਮਾਇਤ, ਤਰਫ਼ਦਾਰੀ

partition (ਪਾ*ਟਿਸ਼ਨ) *n v* ਬਟਵਾਰਾ, ਵਿਭਾਜਨ, ਵੰਡ, ਭਾਗ, ਖੰਡ; ਵਿਭਾਗ, ਵਿਭਾਗੀਕਰਨ; ਬਟਵਾਰਾ ਕਰਨਾ, ਵਿਭਾਜਨ ਕਰਨਾ, ਵੰਡਣਾ; ~ed ਵਟਜਤ, ਵਿਭਕਤ, ਵੰਡਿਆ

partner ('ਪਾ*ਟਨਅ*) *n* ਸਾਂਝੀਦਾਰ, ਸਾਥੀ, ਭਾਈਵਾਲ, ਹਿੱਸੇਦਾਰ, ਭਾਗੀ, ਪੱਤੀਦਾਰ; ਜੀਵਨ ਸਾਥੀ; ਜੋੜਾ; ਸੰਗੀ ਬਣਨਾ, ਸਾਥੀ ਹੋਣਾ, ਸਹਿਤਾਗੀ ਬਣਨੀ, ਹੱਥ ਵਟਾਉਣਾ; ~ship ਸਾਂਝ, ਸਹਿਤਾਗਤਾ, ਪੱਤੀਦਾਰੀ, ਸਾਂਝਾਦਾਰੀ

partridge ('ਪਾ*ਟਰਿਜ) *n* ਤਿੱਤਰ

party ('ਪਾ*ਟਿ) *n a* ਗੁੱਟ, ਪੱਖ, ਦਲ, ਸੰਘ, ਜੱਥਾ, ਜੁੱਟ, ਮੰਡਲੀ, ਟੋਲੀ, ਪ੍ਰੀਤੀ-ਭੋਜ, ਪਰਵਾਰਕ ਸਮਾਰੋਹ; ਵਾਦੀ, ਪ੍ਰਤੀਵਾਦੀ, ਸਹਾਇਕ, ਅਪਰਾਧ ਸਹਿਕਾਰੀ; ~ism ਦਲਵਾਦ, ਪਾਰਟੀਬਾਜ਼ੀ

pass (ਪਾਸ) *n v* ਸਫਲਤਾ; ਨਾਜ਼ਕ ਹਾਲਤ, ਸੰਕਟਮਈ ਦਸ਼ਾ; ਆਗਿਆ-ਪੱਤਰ, ਪਾਸ, ਵਾਰ, ਚੋਟ, ਸੱਟ; ਅੱਗੇ ਵਧਣਾ, ਟੁਰਨਾ; ਪ੍ਰਚਲਤ ਹੋਣਾ; ਭੇਜਿਆ ਜਾਣਾ; ਪਾਰ ਹੋਣਾ, ਕੱਟੇ ਜਾਣਾ, ਚਲੇ ਜਾਣਾ; ਮਨਜ਼ੂਰ ਹੋਣਾ, ਪਾਸ ਹੋਣਾ; ਨਿਰਣਾ ਕਰਨਾ; ~able ਲੰਘਣਯੋਗ, ਕੰਮ ਚਲਾਊ; ~ed ਬੀਤ ਚੁੱਕਿਆ, ਗੁਜ਼ਰਿਆ, ਲੰਘ ਚੁੱਕਿਆ

passage (ਪੈਸਿਜ) *n* ਲਾਂਘਾ, ਮਾਰਗ, ਰਾਹਦਾਰੀ; ਗੁਜ਼ਰ, ਗਮਨ; ਜਲ-ਯਾਤਰਾ ਦਾ ਭਾੜਾ; (ਬਿਲ ਦੀ) ਸਵੀਕ੍ਰਿਤੀ; ਬਰਾਮਦਾ, ਵਰਾਂਡਾ; ਗੁਜ਼ਰਗਾਹ

passenger ('ਪੈਸਿੰਜਅ*) *n* ਪਾਂਧੀ, ਯਾਤਰੀ, ਰਾਹਗੀਰ, ਮੁਸਾਫ਼ਰ

passing ('ਪਾਸਿਙ) *n a adv* ਸਵੀਕਰਨ, ਪਾਸ; ਗਮਨ, ਚਲਣ; ਮੌਤ, ਮਿਰਤੂ; ਅਸਥਾਈ, ਛਿਣ-ਭੰਗਰ; ਬਾਹਰੀ; ਇਤਫ਼ਾਕੀਆ, ਸਰਸਰੀ

passion ('ਪੈਸ਼ਨ) *n v* ਆਵੇਗ, ਮਨੋਵੇਗ, ਗੁੱਸਾ, ਜੋਸ਼, ਰੋਸਾ, ਸੰਤਾਪ; ਤੀਬਰ ਲਾਲਸਾ; ਆਵੇਸ਼, ਕਾਮ-ਉਨਮਾਦ; ਕਾਮ

passive ('ਪੈਸਿਵ) *a n* ਉਦਾਸੀਨ, ਨਿਸ਼ਕਿਰਿਆ; (ਵਿਆ) ਅਕਰਮਕ; ਸਿਥਲ, ਸੁਸਤ

passport ('ਪਾਸਪੋ*ਟ) *n* ਪਾਸਪੋਰਟ, ਪਰਵਾਨਾ, ਰਾਹਦਾਰੀ

past (ਪਾਸਟ) *a prep adv* ਭੂਤ ਕਾਲਕ, ਪੂਰਵ ਕਾਲਕ, ਅਤੀਤ ਕਾਲੀਨ, ਅਤੀਤ, ਵਿਗਤ, ਗਤ, ਪਹਿਲਾ; ਭੂਤ ਕਾਲ, ਪੂਰਵਕਾਲ, ਅਤੀਤ ਕਾਲ; ~**master** ਉਸਤਾਦ

paste ('ਪੇਇਸਟ) *n v* ਲੇਵੀ, ਲੇਪੀ, ਘੁਲੀ ਹੋਈ ਗੁੰਦ, ਗਾਰਾ; ਲੇਵੀ ਨਾਲ ਚੇਪਣਾ, ਮਢੂਨਾ, ਢਕਣਾ, (ਅਪ) ਕੁੱਟਣਾ

pasture ('ਪਾਸਚਅ*) *n v* ਚਰਾਗਾਹ, ਚਰਾਂਦ, ਗੋਚਰ, ਚਰਾ, ਘਾਹ, ਪੱਠਾ; ਚਾਰਨਾ, ਚਾਰਨ ਲਈ ਲੈ ਜਾਣਾ

patch (ਪੈਚ) *n v* ਟੁਕੜਾ, ਖੰਡ, ਭੂ-ਖੰਡ; ਫਹਿਆ, ਪੱਟੀ, ਪਿਉਂਦ, ਜੋੜ; (ਸਤ੍ਹਾ ਦੇ) ਵੱਡੇ ਦਾਗ਼; ਤਰੁੱਪਣਾ, ਟਾਂਕਾ ਲਾਉਣਾ; ਟਾਂਕਣਾ, ਪਿਉਂਦ ਲਾਉਣੀ; ਜੋੜ ਲਾਉਣਾ; (ਸਤ੍ਹਾ ਉੱਤੇ) ਵੱਡੇ ਵੱਡੇ ਦਾਗ ਦਿਸਣੇ; ਮੁਰੰਮਤ ਕਰਨਾ; ਨਿਪਟਾਉਣਾ, ਨਿਬੇੜਨਾ, (ਝਗੜਾ ਆਦਿ)

path (ਪਾਥ) *n* ਪਾਥ, ਪੰਧ, ਮਾਰਗ, ਰਾਹ, ਰਸਤਾ, ਵਾਟ, ਪਗਡੰਡੀ; ਪੱਧਤੀ

pathetic (ਪਅ'ਥੈਟਿਕ) *n a* ਦਰਦ ਭਰਿਆ, ਕਰੁਣਾਮਈ, ਭਾਵਨਾਪੂਰਨ, ਮਾਰਮਕ, ਹਿਰਦੇ-ਵੇਧਕ, ਅਫ਼ਸੋਸਨਾਕ

patience (ਪੇਇਸ਼ੰਸ) *n* ਸਬਰ, ਧੀਰਜ, ਸ਼ਾਂਤੀ ਤਹਮਲ, ਸਹਿਣਸ਼ੀਲਤਾ, ਸਹਿਣ-ਸ਼ਕਤੀ

patois (ਪੈਟਵਾ) *n* ਲੋਕ-ਬੋਲੀ, ਸਥਾਨਕ ਬੋਲੀ

patriarch ('ਪੇਇਟਰਿਆਕ) *n* ਪਿਤਾਮਾ, ਨਾਇਕ ਪਿਤਾ, ਕੁਲਪਤੀ; ਮੁਖੀਆ, ਸਰਦਾਰ; **~y** ਪਿਤਰਤੰਤਰ, ਪੈਤ੍ਰਿਕ ਵਿਵਸਥਾ; ਪਿਤਾ-ਪ੍ਰਧਾਨ-ਤੰਤਰ, ਪੈਤ੍ਰਿਕ ਸਮਾਜ

patrimony ('ਪੈਟਰਿਮਅਨਿ) *n* ਵਿਰਾਸਤ, ਵਿਰਸਾ; ਪੈਤ੍ਰਿਕ ਸੰਪੱਤੀ; ਪਿਤਰੀ ਧਨ

patriot ('ਪੈਟਰਿਅਟ) *n v* ਦੇਸ਼-ਭਗਤ, ਦੇਸ਼-ਬੰਧੂ, ਵਤਨਪ੍ਰਸਤ; **~ic** ਦੇਸ਼-ਭਗਤੀਪੂਰਨ; **~ism** ਦੇਸ਼-ਪ੍ਰੇਮ, ਦੇਸ਼-ਭਗਤੀ

patrol (ਪਅ'ਟਰਅਉਲ) *n* ਪੈਟਰੋਲ, ਗਸ਼ਤ; ਪੁਲੀਸ ਦਾ ਪਹਿਰੇਦਾਰ ਸਿਪਾਹੀ; ਪਹਿਰਾ ਦੇਣਾ, ਗਸ਼ਤ ਕਰਨੀ, ਨਿਗਰਾਨੀ ਕਰਨੀ, ਚੌਕਸ ਰਹਿਣਾ

patron ('ਪੇਇਟਰ(ਅ)ਨ) *n* ਸਰਪਰਸਤ, ਵਲੀ, ਰੱਖਿਅਕ; ਪਾਲਣਹਾਰ, ਪਾਲਕ; **~age** ਸਰਪਰਸਤੀ, ਹਿਮਾਇਤ, ਰੱਖਿਆ, ਪਾਲਣ; **~ize** ਆਸਰਾ ਦੇਣਾ, ਸਹਾਇਤਾ ਦੇਣੀ, ਪਾਲਣਾ ਕਰਨਾ, ਸਰਪਰਸਤੀ ਕਰਨਾ, ਉਤਸਾਹਤ ਕਰਨਾ

pattern ('ਪੈਟਅ*ਨ) *n* ਨਮੂਨਾ, ਵੰਨਗੀ, ਆਦਰਸ਼; ਆਦਰਸ਼ ਮਨੁੱਖ; ਸ਼ੈਲੀ

paucity (ਪੋਸਅਟਿ) *n* ਥੁੜ, ਕਮੀ, ਘਾਟ, ਕਿੱਲਤ

pauper ('ਪੋਪਅ*) *n* ਮੁਥਾਜ, ਕੰਗਾਲ, ਅਨਾਥ, ਭਿਖਮੰਗਾ

pause (ਪੋਜ਼) *n v* ਰੁਕਾਵਟ, ਰੋਕ, ਅਟਕ, ਵਕਫ਼ਾ, ਠਹਿਰਾਉ, ਵਿਰਾਮ; ਅੰਤਰ, ਅੰਤਰਕਾਲ, ਵਿਸ਼ਰਾਮ; ਰੁਕਣਾ, ਠਹਿਰਨਾ, ਅਟਕਣਾ, ਵਕਫ਼ਾ ਦੇਣਾ

pave (ਪੇਇਵ) *v* ਫ਼ਰਸ਼ਬੰਦੀ ਕਰਨੀ, ਫ਼ਰਸ਼ ਬੰਨ੍ਹਣਾ ਜਾਂ ਲਾਉਣਾ, ਫ਼ਰਸ਼ ਤੇ ਪੱਥਰ ਜਾਂ ਇੱਟਾਂ ਜੜਨੀਆਂ, ਖੜੰਜਾ ਲਾਉਣਾ, ਪਥ-ਬੰਧ ਕਰਨਾ; **~ment** ਪਟੜੀ, ਪੱਕਾ ਰਾਹ, ਪਗਡੰਡੀ

pavilion (ਪਅ'ਵਿਲਯਅਨ) *n v* ਮੰਡਪ; ਤੰਬੂ, ਖੇਮਾ, ਡੇਰਾ; ਮੰਡਪ ਉਸਾਰਨਾ; ਇਮਾਰਤ ਦੇ ਬਾਹਰ ਸਜਾਵਟ ਕਰਨੀ

paw (ਪੋ) *n v* (ਪਸ਼ੂ ਦਾ) ਪੰਜਾ, ਚੰਗਾਲ, ਨਹੁੰਦਰਾਂ ਵਾਲਾ ਪੈਰ, ਚਪੇੜ, ਹੱਥ; ਪੰਜਾ ਮਾਰਨਾ

pawn (ਪੋਨ) *n v* ਸ਼ਤਰੰਜ ਦਾ ਪਿਆਦਾ; ਮੁਹਰਾ, ਕੱਠਪੁਤਲੀ; ਅਮਾਨਤ; ਗਹਿਣਾ, ਗਿਰਵੀ, ਧਰੋਹਰ; ਅਮਾਨਤ ਰੱਖਣੀ, ਗਿਰਵੀ ਰੱਖਣਾ; **~broker** ਸ਼ਾਹੂਕਾਰ

pay (ਪੇਇ) *v n* ਵੇਤਨ, ਤਨਖ਼ਾਹ ਜਾਂ ਮਜ਼ਦੂਰੀ ਦੇਣੀ; ਅਦਾ ਕਰਨਾ, ਭੁਗਤਾਉਣਾ, ਚੁਕਾਉਣਾ; **~able** ਭੁਗਤਾਨਯੋਗ, ਅਦਾਇਗੀ; **~ee** ਲੈਣ ਵਾਲਾ, ਭੁਗਤਾਨ ਕਰਤਾ; **~er** ਦੇਣ ਵਾਲਾ, ਪ੍ਰਾਪਤ ਕਰਨਾ; **~ing** ਲਾਭਦਾਇਕ, ਫ਼ਾਇਦੇਮੰਦ; **~ment** ਭੁਗਤਾਨ, ਅਦਾਇਗੀ

pea (ਪੀ) *n* ਮਟਰ

peace (ਪੀਸ) *n* ਅਮਨ, ਸ਼ਾਂਤੀ, ਮੇਲ-ਮਿਲਾਪ, ਜੁੱਧਬੰਦੀ; ਮਿੱਤਰਤਾ, ਸੁਲ੍ਹਾ; ਸਕੂਨ; **~ful** ਸ਼ਾਂਤੀ-

ਪਰੇਸੀ, ਸ਼ਾਂਤ, ਸ਼ਾਂਤੀ-ਪੂਰਨ

peach (ਪੀਚ) *n v* ਆੜੂ; ਅਤੀ ਸੁੰਦਰ ਕੁੜੀ; ਜਾਸੂਸ ਬਣਨਾ, ਮੁਖ਼ਬਰ ਹੋਣਾ; **~er** ਜਾਸੂਸ, ਮੁਖ਼ਬਰ

peacock (ਪੀਕੌਕ) *n* ਮੋਰ, ਤਾਊਸ

peahen (ਪੀਹੈੱਨ) *n* ਮੋਰਨੀ

peak (ਪੀਕ) *n* ਚੋਟੀ, ਸਿਖਰ, ਸਿਰਾ, ਕੂਟ, ਪਰਬਤ ਦੀ ਟੀਸੀ, ਨੋਕ

peanut (ਪੀਨਅਟ) *n* ਮੂੰਗਫਲੀ

pear (ਪੇਅ*) *n* ਨਾਸ਼ਪਾਤੀ

pearl (ਪਅːਲ) *n* ਮੋਤੀ, ਮਣੀ, ਰਤਨ, ਬਹੁਮੁੱਲਾ ਪਦਾਰਥ

peasant (ਪੈਜ਼ੰਟ) *n* ਕਿਸਾਨ, ਹਲਵਾਹਕ; ਪੇਂਡੂ; **~ry** ਕਿਸਾਨੀ, ਕਿਸਾਨ-ਵਰਗਾ

pebble (ਪੈੱਬਲ) *n* ਠੀਕਰੀ, ਰੋੜਾ, ਕੰਕਰ, ਕੰਕਰੀ, ਛੋਟਾ ਟੁਕੜਾ

peccable (ਪੈੱਕਅਬਲ) *a* ਪਾਪੀ, ਅਪਰਾਧੀ ਪਾਪ-ਅਧੀਨ, ਪਾਪ-ਵੱਸ

peculiar (ਪਿ'ਕਯੂਲਿਅ*) *n a* ਵਿਸ਼ੇਸ਼, ਨਿੱਜੀ, ਵਿਸ਼ੇਸ਼ ਅਧਿਕਾਰੀ; ਵਿਸ਼ੇਸ਼ ਸੁਵਿਧਾ, ਨਿਜੀ ਜਾਇਦਾਦ; **~ity** ਵਿਸ਼ੇਸ਼ਤਾ, ਵਿਲੱਖਣਤਾ, ਅਸਧਾਰਨਤਾ, ਅਨੋਖਾਪਨ

pecuniary (ਪਿ'ਕਯੂਨਯਅਰਿ) *a* ਆਰਥਕ, ਮਾਲੀ, ਰੁਪਏ ਪੈਸੇ ਦਾ, ਧਨ-ਸਬੰਧੀ, ਆਰਥਕ ਦੰਡ ਸਬੰਧੀ; ਤਾਵਾਲੀ

pedal (ਪੈਡਲ) *n v a* ਪਦ-ਜੰਤਰ; ਪਾਇਦਾਨ; ਸਾਈਕਲ ਆਦਿ ਦਾ ਪੈਡਲ; ਵਾਜੇ ਨੂੰ ਵਜਾਉਣਾ, ਪੈਡਲ ਨੂੰ ਚਲਾਉਣਾ; ਪੈਰ ਦਾ

peddle (ਪੈੱਡਲ) *v* ਘਟੀਆ ਕੰਮਾਂ ਵਿਚ ਰੁੱਝੇ ਰਹਿਣਾ; ਫੁਟਕਲ ਵੇਚਣਾ, ਫੇਰੀ ਲਾਉਣੀ; ਹੌਲੀ-ਹੌਲੀ ਵਿਚਾਰ ਪਰਗਟ ਕਰਨਾ

pedestal (ਪੈੱਡਿਸਟਲ) *n v* ਚੌਂਕੀ ਆਧਾਰ, ਨੀਂਹ, ਬੁਨਿਆਦ; ਆਧਾਰਤ ਕਰਨਾ, ਪਾਵੇ ਦੇ ਸਹਾਰੇ ਟਿਕਾਉਣਾ ਜਾਂ ਸਥਿਰ ਕਰਨਾ, ਬੈਠਣਾ; ਸਹਾਰਾ ਦੇਣਾ

pedestrian (ਪਿ'ਡੈਸਟਰਿਅਨ) *n a* ਪੈਦਲ (ਯਾਤਰੀ), ਪਿਆਦਾ (ਵਿਅਕਤੀ)

peel (ਪੀਲ) *n v* ਸਰਹੱਦੀ ਮੀਨਾਰ, ਸੀਮਾ-ਬੰਮ੍ਹ, ਨਾਨਬਾਈ ਦੀ ਕੜਛੀ, ਰੋਟੀ ਵਾਲੇ ਦੀ ਹੱਸੀ; ਛਿਲਕਾ; ਫਲ ਦਾ ਛਿੱਲੜ ਲਾਹੁਣਾ; ਛਿੱਲਣਾ, ਉੱਧੇੜਨਾ; ਉੱਧੜਨਾ

peep (ਪੀਪ) *n* ਲੁਕਵੀਂ ਨਜ਼ਰ, ਝਾਤੀ, ਚੋਰ-ਅੱਖ; 'ਚੀ'-'ਚੀ' ਕਰਨਾ, ਚੀਕਣਾ; ਚੋਰ-ਅੱਖ ਨਾਲ ਵੇਖਣਾ, ਲੁਕ ਕੇ ਵੇਖਣਾ, ਝਾਕਣਾ

peer (ਪਿਅ*) *n v* (ਪਦ, ਸ਼੍ਰੇਣੀ ਆਦਿ ਦੇ ਪੱਖੋਂ) ਬਰਾਬਰ ਦਾ ਆਦਮੀ; ਕੁਲੀਨ, ਰਈਸ, ਬਰਾਬਰ ਕਰਨਾ ਜਾਂ ਹੋਣਾ; ਕਿਸੇ ਆਦਮੀ ਨੂੰ ਸੱਭਿਆ ਸਮਾਜ ਵਿਚ ਸ਼ਾਮਲ ਕਰਨਾ; ਤੱਕਣਾ, ਝਾਕਣਾ, ਧਿਆਨ ਨਾਲ ਵੇਖਣਾ

peeve (ਪੀਵ) *v* ਦੁਖੀ ਹੋਣਾ, ਉਤੇਜਤ ਕਰਨਾ, ਸੜਨਾ ਜਾਂ ਸਾੜਨਾ, ਕੁੜ੍ਹਨਾ

peevish (ਪੀਵਿਸ਼) *a* ਖਿਝੂ, ਰੁੱਖਾ, ਚਿੜਚੜਾ;

peg (ਪੈੱਗ) *n v* ਮੇਖ, ਕਿੱਲ, ਕਿੱਲੀ, ਖੁੰਟੀ, ਖੁੰਟਾ ਸ਼ਰਾਬ ਦਾ ਪਿਆਲਾ, ਪੈਗ; ਕਿੱਲ ਨਾਲ ਜੜਨਾ ਮੇਖ ਨਾਲ ਜੜਨਾ

pejorate ('ਪਿਜੋਰੇਇਟ) *v* ਕਿਸੇ ਨੂੰ ਘਟੀਆ ਸਿੱਧ ਕਰਨਾ, ਗੁਣ ਘਟਾਉਣਾ, ਦੋਸ਼ਪੂਰਨ ਬਣਾਉਣਾ

pelican ('ਪੈੱਲਿਕਨ) *n* ਪੈਲੀਕਨ, ਇਕ ਜਲ-ਪੰਛੀ

pen (ਪੈੱਨ) *n v* ਕਿਲਕ, ਕਲਮ, ਹੋਲਡਰ, ਲੇਖਣੀ ਖੰਭ ਦੀ ਕਲਮ, ਪੈੱਨ; ਨਿਬੰਧ, ਲੇਖ, ਰਚਨਾ ਰਚਨਸ਼ੈਲੀ

penal ('ਪੀਨਲ) *a n* ਦੰਡਾਤਮਕ, ਤਾਜ਼ੀਰੀ, ਸਜ਼ਾ

ਪਾਉਣਯੋਗ, ਦੰਡਯੋਗ; ~code ਦੰਡ-ਸੰਹਿਤਾ; ~ize ਦੰਡ ਦੇਣਾ, ਸਜ਼ਾ ਦੇਣੀ; ~ty ਜੁਰਮਾਨਾ, ਦੰਡ, ਹਰਜਾਨਾ, ਤਾਵਾਨ

penance ('ਪੈਨੇਂਸ) *n v* ਪ੍ਰਾਸ਼ਚਿਤ, ਪਛਤਾਵਾ, ਪਸ਼ਚਾਤਾਪ; ਆਤਮ-ਨਿਗ੍ਰਹਿ; ਤਪੱਸਿਆ; ਪ੍ਰਾਸ਼ਚਿਤ ਕਰਨਾ, ਤਪ ਕਰਨਾ

pencil ('ਪੈਂਸਲ) *n v* ਕੂਚੀ, ਬੁਰਸ਼, ਨੱਕਾਸ਼ੀ, ਚਿੱਤਰਕਾਰੀ ਦੀ ਸ਼ੈਲੀ, ਚਿੱਤਰਕਾਰਤਾ, ਪੈਨਸਿਲ, ਰੇਖਾ-ਸੂਚੀ; ਪੈਨਸਿਲ ਨਾਲ ਚਿੰਨ੍ਹਣਾ, ਨਿਸ਼ਾਨ ਲਾਉਣਾ, ਲਿਖ ਰੱਖਣਾ, ਦਰਜ ਕਰਨਾ

pendant ('ਪੈਂਡਅੰਟ) *n a* ਲਮਕਣ ਵਾਲਾ ਗਹਿਣਾ, ਝੁਮਕੇ, ਕੰਟੇ; ਜਹਾਜ਼ ਦਾ ਤਿਕੋਨਾ ਝੰਡਾ

pendent ('ਪੈਂਡਅੰਟ) *a* ਲਟਕਦਾ, ਅਗਾਂਹ ਨੂੰ ਵਧਿਆ, ਅਨਿਸ਼ਚਤ, ਵਿਚਾਰ-ਅਧੀਨ

pending ('ਪੈਂਨਡਿੰਙ) *a prep* ਲੰਬਿਤ, ਸਥਗਤ, ਵਿਚਾਰ-ਅਧੀਨ; ਅਨਿਸ਼ਚਤ, ਅਪੂਰਨ

pendulous ('ਪੈਂਡਯੁਲਅਸ) *a* ਝੂਲਦਾ, ਲਟਕਦਾ, ਅਸਥਿਰ

pendulum ('ਪੈਂਡਯੁਲਅਮ) *n* (ਘੜੀ ਜਾਂ ਕਲਾਕ ਆਦਿ ਦਾ) ਪੈਂਡੂਲਮ, ਲਟਕਣ, ਲੰਗਰ; ਲਟਕਣ ਵਾਲੀ ਚੀਜ਼

penelope (ਪਅ'ਨੈੱਲਪਿ) *n* ਪਤਿਬਰਤਾ ਇਸਤਰੀ, ਸਤੀ ਸਵਿਤਰੀ; ਸਤਵੰਤੀ; ਇਕ ਪੰਛੀ

penetrate ('ਪੈਨਿਟਰੇਇਟ) *v* ਆਰ-ਪਾਰ ਲੰਘਣਾ, ਛੇਕਣਾ, ਮੋਰੀ ਕਰਨੀ, ਦਾਖ਼ਲ ਹੋਣਾ, ਪ੍ਰਵੇਸ਼ ਕਰਨਾ, ਵਿੰਨ੍ਹਣਾ, ਘੁੰਮਣਾ, ਚੁੱਭਣਾ

penetrating ('ਪੈਨਿ'ਟਰੇਇਟਿਙ) *a* ਭੇਦਕਾਰੀ, ਭੇਦਕ, ਅੰਤਰਪ੍ਰਵੇਸ਼ੀ, ਤੀਖਣ

penetration ('ਪੈਨਿ'ਟਰੇਇਸ਼ਨ) *v* ਪ੍ਰਵੇਸ਼, ਘੁਮਣ, ਭੇਦਕਰਨ; ਬੁੱਧੀ ਦੀ ਤੀਖਣਤਾ

penguin ('ਪੈਂਙਗਵਿਨ) *n* ਪੈਂਗੁਇਨ, ਇਕ ਸਮੁੰਦਰੀ ਪੰਛੀ

peninsula (ਪਅ'ਨਿਨਸੁਲਅ) *n* ਟਾਪੂਨਮਾ, ਪ੍ਰਾਇਦੀਪ, ਦੀਪ ਕਲਪ

penitence ('ਪੈਨਿਟਅੰਸ) *n* ਪਛਤਾਵਾ, ਪ੍ਰਾਸ਼ਚਿਤ, ਪਸ਼ਚਾਤਾਪ

penitent ('ਪੈਨਿਟਅੰਟ) *n a* ਪ੍ਰਾਸ਼ਚਿਤਮਾਨ, ਪਸ਼ਚਾਤਾਪੀ, ਤੋਬਾ ਕਰਨ ਵਾਲਾ, ਪਛਤਾਉਣ ਵਾਲਾ

penniless ('ਪੈਨਿਲਿਸ) *a* ਮੁਥਾਜ, ਨਦਾਰ, ਨਿਰਧਨ, ਗ਼ਰੀਬ

pension ('ਪੈਨਸ਼ਨ) *n v* ਪੈਨਸ਼ਨ, ਵਜ਼ੀਫ਼ਾ, ਰੀਟਾਇਰ ਹੋਣ ਪਿੱਛੋਂ ਮਿਲਦੀ ਰਹਿਣ ਵਾਲੀ ਤਨਖ਼ਾਹ; ਪੈਨਸ਼ਨ ਦੇਣੀ

pensive ('ਪੈਂਸਿਵ਼) *n* ਸੋਚੀ-ਡੁੱਬਾ, ਧਿਆਨ-ਮਗਨ, ਉਦਾਸ, ਗ਼ਮਗੀਨ; ~ness ਧਿਆਨ-ਮਗਨਤਾ, ਉਦਾਸੀ

pentagon ('ਪੈਂਟਅਗਅਨ) *n* ਪੰਚਕੋਣ, ਪੰਚਭੁਜ, ਪੰਚਕੋਨਾ

penury ('ਪੈਨਯੁਰਿ) *n* ਨਿਰਧਨਤਾ, ਕੰਗਾਲੀ, ਤੰਗਦਸਤੀ, ਗ਼ਰੀਬੀ, ਘਾਟਾ, ਕਮੀ, ਥੁੜ

peon (ਪਯੂਨ) *n* ਚਪੜਾਸੀ, ਹਰਕਾਰਾ, ਸਿਪਾਹੀ, ਸੇਵਾਦਾਰ, ਸੇਵਕ, ਅਰਦਲੀ

people ('ਪੀਪਲ) *n v* ਲੋਕ, ਲੋਕੀ, ਜਨ, ਜਨਤਾ, ਜਨ-ਸਧਾਰਨ, (in *pl*) ਪਰਜਾ; ਆਬਾਦ ਕਰਨਾ; ਵੱਸਣਾ

pepper ('ਪੈੱਪਅ*) *n* ਕਾਲੀ ਮਿਰਚ, ਗੋਲ ਮਿਰਚ, ਕੌੜੀ ਚੀਜ਼; ਮਿਰਚਾਂ ਛਿੜਕਣਾ, ਮਿਰਚਾਂ ਪਾਉਣਾ; ~mint ਪੇਪਰਮਿੰਟ; ਪੁਦੀਨਾ

per (ਪਅ:*) *perp* ਤੋਂ, ਦੁਆਰ, ਦੀ ਸਹਾਇਤਾ ਨਾਲ, ਦੇ ਸਾਧਨ ਦੁਆਰਾ; ਪ੍ਰਤੀ, ਛੀ, ਹਰ ਇਕ

perambulate (ਪਅ'ਰੈਂਬਯੁਲੇਇਟ) *v* ਗਸ਼ਤ

ਕਰਨੀ, ਚੱਕਰ ਲਾਉਣਾ, ਗਸ਼ਤ ਲਾਉਣੀ; ਸਫ਼ਰ ਕਰਨਾ, ਘੁੰਮਣਾ, ਫਿਰਨਾ ਚੱਲਣਾ, ਪ੍ਰਦੱਖਣਾ ਕਰਨੀ, ਪਰਿਕਰਮਾ ਕਰਨੀ

perambulation (ਪਅਰੈਂਬਯੁ'ਲੇਇਸ਼ਨ) *n* ਗਸ਼ਤ, ਪ੍ਰਦੱਖਣਾ, ਪਰਿਕਰਮਾ, ਵਿਚਰਤ; ਸਫ਼ਰ

per annum (L) (ਪਅਰ'ਐਨਅਮ) *adv* ਪ੍ਰਤੀ ਵਰ੍ਹਾ, ਵਾਰਸ਼ਕ

per bearer (ਪਅ'ਬੇਰਿਅ*) *adv* ਦਸਤੀ, ਕਿਸੇ ਦੇ ਹੱਥੀਂ

perceive (ਪਅ'ਸੀਵ਼) *v* ਧਿਆਨ ਦੇਣਾ; ਸਮਝਣਾ; ਅਨੁਭਵ ਕਰਨਾ, ਪ੍ਰਤੱਖ ਗਿਆਨ ਪ੍ਰਾਪਤ ਕਰਨਾ, ਪ੍ਰਤੀਤ ਕਰਨਾ, ਪਛਾਣਨਾ, ਵਿਚਾਰਨਾ; **~d** ਗਿਆਤ, ਵਿਦਿਤ, ਅਨੁਭੂਤ, ਦੇਖਿਆ ਹੋਇਆ

per cent, per centum (ਪਅ'ਸੈਂਟ, ਪਅ-'ਸੈਂਟਅਮ) (L) *adv* ਪ੍ਰਤੀ ਸੈਂਕੜਾ, ਫ਼ੀ ਸਦੀ, ਪ੍ਰਤੀਸ਼ਤ; **~age** ਫ਼ੀ ਸਦੀ, ਫ਼ੀ ਸੈਂਕੜਾ, ਪ੍ਰਤੀ ਸੈਂਕੜਾ, ਪ੍ਰਤੀਸ਼ਤਤਾ

percept ('ਪਅ:ਸੈਂਪਟ) *n* ਪ੍ਰਤੱਖ ਗਿਆਨ, ਪ੍ਰਤੀਤੀ-ਬੋਧ; ਅਨੁਭੂਤੀ, ਅਨੁਭਵ; **~ible** ਅਨੁਭਵਯੋਗ, ਗ੍ਰਹਿਣ ਕਰਨ ਯੋਗ, ਸਪਸ਼ਟ, ਵਿਅਕਤ; ਗੋਚਰ; **~ion** ਪ੍ਰਤੱਖ ਗਿਆਨ, ਅਨੁਭੂਤੀ, ਅਨੁਭਵ, ਸੋਝੀ, ਬੋਧ, ਗ੍ਰਹਿਣ-ਸ਼ਕਤੀ, ਸਹਿਜ-ਅਨੁਭੂਤੀ, ਪ੍ਰਤੀਤੀ

perchance (ਪਅ'ਚਾਂਸ) *adv* (ਪ੍ਰ) ਸੰਯੋਗ ਨਾਲ, ਸਬੱਬੀ, ਇਤਫ਼ਾਕਨ, ਸੰਯੋਗਵੱਸ

peripicient (ਪਅ'ਸਿਪਿਐਂਟ) *n a* ਪ੍ਰਤੱਖ, ਪ੍ਰਤੱਖ ਬੋਧ (ਰੱਖਣ ਵਾਲਾ), ਪ੍ਰਤੱਖ-ਦਰਸ਼ੀ (ਵਿਅਕਤੀ), ਪ੍ਰਤੱਖ ਗਿਆਨੀ, ਅਨੁਭਵੀ (ਪੁਰਸ਼), ਸੁਝਵਾਨ, ਅਨੁਭੂਤੀਸ਼ੀਲ

percolate ('ਪਅ:ਕਅਲੇਇਟ) *v* ਨਿਤਰਨਾ; ਝਰਨਾ, ਨੁੱਚੜਨਾ, ਰਿਸਣਾ, ਚੋਣਾ, ਨੁਚੜਾਉਣਾ, ਰਿਸਾਉਣਾ; ਚੁਆਉਣਾ, ਛਾਣਨਾ

perennial (ਪਅ'ਰੈਨਅਲ) *n a* ਨਿਰੰਤਰ, ਲਗਾਤਾਰ ਰਹਿਣ ਵਾਲਾ, ਚਿਰਜੀਵੀ, ਬਾਂਹਾਂ ਮਾਸੀ, ਨਿੱਤ

perfect (ਪਅ:ਫ਼ਿਕਟ, ਪਅ:ਫ਼ੈੱਕਟ) *n v* ਪੂਰਨ ਕਾਲ, ਪੂਰਨ, ਸੰਪੂਰਨ, ਸੰਪੰਨ, ਪੂਰਾ, ਭਰਪੂਰ, ਨਿਪੁੰਨ, ਸਿੱਧ, ਵਾਸਤਵਿਕ, ਸੱਚਾ; ਉੱਤਮ, ਪੂਰਾ ਕਰਨਾ, ਸੰਪੂਰਨ ਕਰਨਾ; **~ion** ਪੂਰਨਤਾ, ਸਿੱਧੀ, ਸਮਾਪਤੀ, ਸੰਪੰਨਤਾ, ਪੂਰਤੀ, ਪ੍ਰਵੀਣਤਾ, ਕੌਸ਼ਲਤਾ, ਪਰਿਪੱਕਤਾ; ਪੂਰਨੀਕਰਨ, ਨਿਰਦੇਸ਼ੀਕਰਨ; **~ly** ਪੂਰੇ ਤੌਰ ਤੇ, ਮੁਕੰਮਲ ਤੌਰ ਤੇ

perfidy ('ਪਅ:ਫ਼ਿੱਡਿ) *n* ਕਪਟ, ਛਲ, ਧੋਖਾ, ਬੇਈਮਾਨੀ, ਵਿਸਾਹਘਾਤ; ਗੱਦਾਰੀ, ਬੇਵਫ਼ਾਈ

perforate ('ਪਅ:ਫ਼ਅਰੇਇਟ) *v* ਛੇਕਣਾ, ਵਿੰਨ੍ਹਣਾ, ਵਰਮੇ ਨਾਲ ਛੇਕ ਕਰਨਾ, ਮੋਰੀ ਕਰਨੀ, ਥੱਪਰ ਬਣਾਉਣਾ; ਪਾੜਨਾ, ਘਰ ਬਣਾਉਣਾ, ਰਾਹ ਬਣਾਉਣਾ; **~d** ਛਿਦਰੀ, ਛੇਕਾਂ ਵਾਲਾ, ਛਿਦਕਦਾਰ, ਛੇਕਦਾਰ

perforation ('ਪਅ:ਫ਼ਅ'ਰੇਇਸ਼ਨ) *n* ਸੁਰਾਖ਼, ਸੁਰਾਖ਼, ਛਿਦਰ, ਛੇਦ, ਛੇਦਨ

perforator ('ਪਅ:ਫ਼ਅਰੇਇਟਅ*) *n* ਵੇਧਕ, ਛੇਦਕ, ਵਰਮਾ, ਮੋਰੀ ਕਰਨ ਵਾਲਾ ਔਜ਼ਾਰ

perforce (ਪਅ'ਫ਼ੋਸ) *adv* ਬਲ ਪੂਰਵਕ, ਜਬਰਨ, ਜਬਰਦਸਤੀ; ਮਜਬੂਤੀ ਨਾਲ, ਬੇਵੱਸੀ ਨਾਲ, ਲਾਚਾਰੀ ਨਾਲ

perform (ਪਅ'ਫ਼ੋਮ) *v* ਪੂਰਨ ਕਰਨਾ, ਪਾਲਣਾ ਕਰਨੀ, ਤਾਮੀਲ ਕਰਨੀ, ਪੂਰਾ ਕਰਨਾ, ਨਿਭਾਉਣਾ, ਨਿਰਬਾਹ ਕਰਨਾ; ਅਭਿਨੈ ਕਰਨਾ, ਕੌਤਕ ਦਿਖਾਉਣਾ, ਕਰਤਬ ਦਿਖਾਉਣਾ; **~ance** ਪੂਰਤੀ, ਪਾਲਣ, ਤਾਮੀਲ; ਨਿਭਾਉ, ਤਕਮੀਲ,

ਕਾਰਜ, ਕਰਤਬ, ਹੁਨਰ; ਕੌਤਕ, ਤਮਾਸ਼ਾ; ਪਰਦਰਸ਼ਨ, ਅਭਿਨੈ, ਅਦਾਕਾਰੀ; ~er ਪੂਰਕ, ਪਾਲਕ; ਕਰਤਾ, ਕੰਮ ਕਰਨ ਵਾਲਾ, ਅਭਿਨੇਤਾ, ਪਰਦਰਸ਼ਕ, ਕਰਤਬੀ

perfume ('ਪਅ:ਫ਼ਯੂਮ, ਪਅ'ਫ਼ਯੂਮ) *n v* ਖ਼ੁਸ਼ਬੂ, ਮਹਿਕ, ਅਤਰ, ਸੁਗੰਧੀ; ਸੁਗੰਧਤ ਕਰਨਾ, ਮਹਿਕਾਉਣਾ; ~d ਸੁਗੰਧਤ, ਖ਼ੁਸ਼ਬੂਦਾਰ

perfuse (ਪਅ'ਫ਼ਯੂਜ਼) *v* ਛਿੜਕਣਾ, ਤਰੌਂਕਣਾ; ਫੈਲਾਉਣਾ; ਭਰਨਾ

perhaps (ਪਅ'ਹੈਪਸ) *adv* ਖ਼ਬਰੇ, ਸ਼ਾਇਦ; ਸੰਭਵ ਤੌਰ ਤੇ

peril ('ਪੈਰੱਅਲ) *n* ਸੰਕਟ, ਖ਼ਤਰਾ, ਜੋਖਮ, ਵਿਪੱਤੀ, ਆਸ਼ੰਕਾ; ਜੋਖੋਂ ਵਿਚ ਪਾਉਣਾ, ਸੰਕਟ ਵਿਚ ਪਾਉਣਾ; ~ous ਸੰਕਟਪੂਰਨ, ਸੰਕਟਮਈ, ਜੋਖਮਮਈ, ਖ਼ਤਰਨਾਕ

period ('ਪਿਅਰਿਅਡ) *n* ਸਮਾਂ, ਅਵਧੀ, ਮੁੰਦਤ, ਦੌਰ, ਜ਼ਮਾਨਾ, ਅਯੁਧ, ਅਯੁਧੀ, ਮਿਆਦ; (*in pl*) ਮਾਸਕ ਧਰਮ, ਮਾਹਵਾਰੀ; ਯੁਗ, ਕਾਲ

periphery (ਪਅ'ਰਿਫ਼ਅਰਿ) *n* ਘੇਰ, ਘੇਰਾ, ਪਰਿਧੀ; ਦਾਇਰਾ

perish ('ਪੈਰਿਸ਼) *v n* ਫ਼ਨਾ ਹੋਣਾ, ਨਸ਼ਟ ਕਰਨਾ, ਮਿਟਨਾ, ਮਿਟਾਉਣਾ; ਬਰਬਾਦ ਹੋਣਾ; ਵਿਨਾਸ਼ ਹੋਣਾ; ~able ਨਾਸਵਾਨ (ਵਸਤੂ), ਵਿਕਾਰੀ, ਵਿਗੜਨ ਵਾਲਾ, ਪਤਨਸ਼ੀਲ (ਪਦਾਰਥ ਆਦਿ)

perjure ('ਪਅ:ਜਅ*) *v refl* ਝੂਠੀ ਸੁਗੰਧ ਖਾਣੀ, ਝੂਠੀ ਗਵਾਹੀ ਦੇਣੀ, ਹਲਫ਼ ਚੁੱਕਣਾ

perk (ਪਅ:ਕ) *n v a* ਉੱਪਰਲੀ ਆਮਦਨੀ, ਤਨਖ਼ਾਹ ਤੋਂ ਇਲਾਵਾ ਸਹੂਲਤ, ਭੱਤਾ, ਦਸਤੂਰੀ; ਆਕੜ ਕੇ ਟੁਰਨਾ; ~iness ਆਕੜ; ਜ਼ਿੰਦਾਦਿਲੀ; ~y ਢੀਠ, ਬੇਅਦਬ; ਅਹੰਕਾਰੀ, ਅਭਿਮਾਨੀ

permanence ('ਪਅ:ਮ(ਅ)ਨਅੰਸ) *n* ਨਿੱਤਤਾ, ਸਥਾਈਪੁਣਾ, ਸਥਿਰਤਾ; ਟਿਕਾਉਪੁਣਾ, ਪਾਇਦਾਰੀ

permanent ('ਪਅ:ਮ(ਅ)ਨਅੰਟ) *a* ਸਥਾਈ, ਸਥਿਰ, ਨਿੱਤ, ਅਟੱਲ, ਚਿਰਸਥਾਈ, ਟਿਕਾਉ, ਪੱਕਾ

permeate ('ਪਅ:ਮਿਏਇਟ) *v* ਪ੍ਰਵੇਸ਼ ਕਰਨਾ, ਰਮ ਜਾਣਾ; ਸਮਾਉਣਾ, ਭਰ ਦੇਣਾ

permeation ('ਪਅ:ਮਿ'ਏਇਸ਼ਨ) *n* ਫੈਲਾਉ, ਪ੍ਰਸਾਰ, ਵਿਆਪਤੀ; ਰਚਣ

per mensum (ਪਅ:ਮੈਂਨਸਅਮ) (*L*) *adv* ਮਾਸਕ, ਪ੍ਰਤੀ ਮਾਸ

permissible (ਪਅ:ਮਿਸਅਬਲ) *a* ਉਚਿਤ, ਯੁਕਤ, ਜਾਇਜ਼, ਯੋਗ, ਰਵਾ, ਮੁਨਾਸਬ

permission (ਪਅ'ਮਿਸ਼ਨ) *n* ਆਗਿਆ, ਅਨੁਮਤੀ, ਸਵੀਕ੍ਰਿਤੀ, ਇਜਾਜ਼ਤ, ਰਜਾਮੰਦੀ

permit (ਪਅ:ਮਿਟ, ਪਅ'ਮਿਟ) *n v* ਇਜਾਜ਼ਤ, ਆਗਿਆ, ਅਨੁਮਤੀ; ਆਗਿਆ-ਪੱਤਰ, ਇਜਾਜ਼ਤਨਾਮਾ, ਪਰਚੀ, ਪਰਮਟ; ਪਰਵਾਨਾ; ਇਜਾਜ਼ਤ ਦੇਣੀ

permutation ('ਪਅ:ਮਿਯੂ'ਟੇਇਸ਼ਨ) *n* ਕ੍ਰਮ-ਪਰਿਵਰਤਨ, ਪਹਿਵਟਨ; (ਪ੍ਰ) ਵਸਤੂ ਵਟਾਂਦਰਾ

pernicious (ਪਅ'ਨਿਸ਼ਅਸ) *a* ਘਾਤਕ, ਵਿਨਾਸ਼ੀ, ਨਾਸਕ; ~ness ਵਿਨਾਸ਼ਕਤਾ, ਘਾਤਕਤਾ, ਦੁਸ਼ਟਤਾ

perpendicular ('ਪਅ:ਪੈਂ'ਡਿਕਯੂਲ*) *a* ਲੰਬ ਰੂਪ, ਖੜਾ, ਸਰਲ, ਬਿਲਕੁਲ ਸਿੱਧਾ; ਲੰਬ ਮਾਪਕ; ਸਮਕੋਣਕ, ਰੇਖਾ, ਖੜ੍ਹੀ ਰੇਖਾ, ਲੰਬ; ~ity ਲੰਬਰੂਪਤਾ, ਸਮਕੋਣਤਾ, ਖੜ੍ਹਾਪਨ

perpetual (ਪਅ:ਪੈਂਚੁਅਲ) *a* ਨਿੱਤ, ਨਿਰੰਤਰ,

ਸਥਾਈ, ਚਿਰਸਥਾਈ, ਚਿਰੋਕਣਾ, ਸਨਾਤਨ, ਸਰਵਕਾਲਕ, ਕ੍ਰਮਬੱਧ

perpetuate (ਪਅ'ਪੈਂਚੁਏਇਟ) v ਸਥਾਈ ਬਣਾਉਣਾ, ਚਿਰਸਥਾਈ ਕਰਨਾ, ਕਾਇਮ ਰੱਖਣਾ, ਬਣਾਈ ਰੱਖਣਾ, ਅਮਰ ਕਰਨਾ

perplex (ਪਅ'ਪਲੇੱਕਸ) v ਵਿਆਕੁਲ ਕਰਨਾ, ਭਟਕਾਉਣਾ, ਉਲਝਾਉਣਾ, ਹੈਰਾਨ ਕਰਨਾ, (ਵਿਸ਼ੇ ਨੂੰ) ਸੰਦਿਗਧ ਕਰਨਾ, ਔਖਾ ਕਰਨਾ, ਪੇਚੀਦਾ ਬਣਾਉਣਾ; **~ity** ਹੈਰਾਨੀ, ਅਸਚਰਜਤਾ, ਉਲਝਣ, ਅੜਾਉਣੀ, ਭਟਕਣ; ਕਠਿਨਾਈ, ਪੇਚੀਦਾਪਣ; ਵਿਆਕੁਲਤਾ

perquisite ('ਪਅ:ਕਵਿਜ਼ਿਟ) n ਉੱਪਰਲੀ ਆਮਦਨੀ, ਭੱਤਾ, ਦਸਤੂਰੀ, ਬਾਲਾਈ ਆਮਦਨੀ; ਬਖ਼ਸ਼ੀਸ਼, ਇਨਾਮ

perquisition ('ਪਅ:ਕਵਿੱਜ਼ਿਸ਼ਨ) n ਪੁੱਛ-ਪੜਤਾਲ, ਗੰਭੀਰ ਪੁੱਛ-ਗਿੱਛ, ਤਫ਼ਤੀਸ਼

persecute ('ਪਅ:ਸਿਕਯੂਚਟ) v (ਵਿਸ਼ੇਸ਼ ਕਰਕੇ ਵਿਰੋਧੀ ਵਿਚਾਰ ਵਾਲ਼ਿਆਂ ਨੂੰ) ਕਸ਼ਟ ਦੇਣਾ, ਪੀੜਤ ਕਰਨਾ, ਸਿਤਮ ਕਰਨਾ, ਅਤਿਆਚਾਰ ਕਰਨਾ, ਸਤਾਉਣਾ, ਜ਼ੁਲਮ ਕਰਨਾ; ਤਸੀਹੇ ਦੇਣਾ

persecution ('ਪਅ:ਸਿ'ਕਯੂਸ਼ਨ) n ਅਤਿਆਚਾਰ, ਜ਼ੁਲਮ, ਤੰਗੀ, ਸਖ਼ਤੀ, ਤਸੀਹਾ

perseverance ('ਪਅ:ਸਿ'ਵ਼ਿਅਰਅੰਸ) n ਉੱਦਮ, ਅਥੱਕ ਪ੍ਰਜਤਨ, ਮਿਹਨਤ; ਦ੍ਰਿੜ੍ਹਤਾ, ਸਾਬਤ ਕਦਮੀ

persevere ('ਪਅ:ਸਿ'ਵ਼ਿਅ*) v ਸਾਬਤ ਕਦਮ ਰਹਿਣਾ, ਧੀਰਜ ਕਰਨਾ, ਦ੍ਰਿੜ੍ਹ ਰਹਿਣਾ, ਉੱਦਮਸ਼ੀਲ ਰਹਿਣਾ, ਪੱਕੀ ਲਗਨ ਨਾਲ ਕੰਮ ਕਰਨਾ, ਡਟੇ ਰਹਿਣਾ

persevering ('ਪਅ:ਸਿ'ਵ਼ਿਅਰਿਙ) a ਦ੍ਰਿੜ੍ਹ, ਉੱਦਮੀ, ਧੀਰਜਵਾਨ, ਧੁਨ ਦਾ ਪੱਕਾ

persist (ਪਅ'ਸਿਸਟ) v ਅਟੱਲ ਰਹਿਣਾ, ਅਚੱਲ ਹੋਣਾ, ਸਥਿਰ ਰਹਿਣਾ, ਪੱਕੇ ਰਹਿਣਾ, ਜੰਮ ਕੇ ਰਹਿਣਾ, ਡਟੇ ਰਹਿਣਾ, ਬਟੇ ਰਹਿਣਾ; **~ence** ਅਟੱਲਤਾ, ਸਥਿਰਤਾ, ਪਕਿਆਈ, ਹਠ, ਜ਼ਿਦ; **~ent** ਅਟੱਲ, ਸਥਿਰ, ਪੱਕਾ, ਹਠੀ, ਜ਼ਿੱਦੀ, ਸਥਾਈ, ਪ੍ਰਜਤਨਸ਼ੀਲ, ਚਿਰਜੀਵੀ

person ('ਪਅ:ਸਨ) n ਪੁਰਸ਼, ਪੁਰਖ, ਮਨੁੱਖ, ਆਦਮੀ, ਵਿਅਕਤੀ; **~al** ਵਿਅਕਤੀਗਤ ਸਮਾਚਾਰ; ਨਿੱਜੀ; ਆਪਣਾ, ਦੇਹੀ; **~ality** ਸ਼ਖ਼ਸੀਅਤ, ਵਿਅਕਤਿੱਤਵ; ਮਨੁੱਖਤਵ, ਨਿੱਜੀ ਅਸਤਿੱਤਵ; ਨਿੱਜੀਪਣ, ਆਪਟਾਪਣ; **~ally** ਖ਼ੁਦ, ਆਪ, ਨਿੱਜੀ ਰੂਪ ਵਿਚ, ਜਾਤੀ ਤੌਰ ਤੇ, ਵਿਅਕਤੀਗਤ ਰੂਪ ਵਿਚ; ਬਜਾਤੇ ਖ਼ੁਦ; **~ification** ਮਾਨਵੀਕਰਨ, ਪ੍ਰਤੀਬਿੰਬ; **~ify** ਮਾਨਵੀਕਰਨ ਕਰਨਾ, ਮੂਰਤੀਕਰਨ ਕਰਨਾ; (ਗੁਣ ਆਦਿ ਦਾ) ਰੂਪਮਾਨ ਹੋਣਾ; **~nel** ਕਰਮਚਾਰੀ-ਵਰਗ, ਕਾਰਜ-ਕਰਤਾ ਵਰਗ, ਸੇਵਾ-ਦਲ, ਅਮਲਾ

perspective (ਪਅ'ਸਪੈੱਕਟਿਵ਼) n a ਪਰਿਪੇਖ, ਚਿੱਤਰ; ਦ੍ਰਿਸ਼ਟੀਕੋਣ; ਅਵਲੋਕਨ; ਦ੍ਰਿਸ਼ਟੀ-ਸੀਮਾ

perspiration ('ਪਅ:ਸਪਿ'ਰੇਇਸ਼ਨ) n ਪਸੀਨਾ, ਮੁੜ੍ਹਕਾ

perspire (ਪਅ*ਸਪਾਇਅ*) v ਮੁੜ੍ਹਕਾ ਆਉਣਾ, ਪਸੀਨਾ ਆਉਣਾ, ਪਸਿੰਜਣਾ

persuade (ਪਅ*ਸਵੇਇਡ) v ਪਰੇਰਨਾ, ਮਨਾਉਣਾ, ਰਾਜ਼ੀ ਕਰਨਾ, ਪਰੇਰਤ ਕਰਨਾ; ਉਤੇਜਤ ਕਰਨਾ, ਉਕਸਾਰਨਾ

persuasion (ਪਅ*ਸਵੇਇਸ਼ਨ) n ਪਰੇਰਨਾ, ਪ੍ਰੋਤਸਾਹਨ; ਸੰਪਰਦਾਈ, ਫ਼ਿਰਕਾ, ਵਿਸ਼ਵਾਸ

pertain (ਪਅ*ਟੇਇਨ) v ਵਾਹ ਪੈਣਾ, ਸਬੰਧ

ਰੱਖਣਾ, ਮੇਲ ਹੋਣਾ; ਮਿਲਣਾ, ਉਪਯੁਕਤ ਹੋਣਾ

pertinacious ('ਪਅ:ਟਿ'ਨੇਇਸ਼ਅਸ) *a* ਹੱਠੀ, ਜ਼ਿੱਦੀ, ਜ਼ਿੱਦਲ, ਦ੍ਰਿੜ੍ਹ, ਅੜੀਅਲ, ਪੱਕਾ; **~ness** ਹਠ, ਜ਼ਿੱਦ, ਦ੍ਰਿੜ੍ਹਤਾ, ਅੜੀ, ਪਕਿਆਈ

pertinence ('ਪਅ:ਟਿਨਅੰਸ) *n* ਪ੍ਰਸੰਗਕਤਾ, ਢੁਕਵਾਂਪਣ; ਉਚਿਤਤਾ

pertinent ('ਪਅ:ਟਿਨਅੰਟ) *n a* ਸੁਲੱਗ, ਸੰਗਤ, ਸਬੰਧਤ; ਯੋਗ, ਠੀਕ, ਉਚਿਤ, ਢੁਕਵਾਂ

perturb (ਪਅ*ਟਅ:ਬ) *v* ਪਰੇਸ਼ਾਨ ਹੋਣਾ; ਗੜ੍ਹ-ਮੱਡ ਕਰਨਾ, ਤਰਤੀਬ ਭੰਨਣੀ, ਉਲਟ ਫੇਰ ਕਰਨਾ, ਤਿੱਤਰ-ਬਿੱਤਰ ਕਰਨਾ; ਉਪੱਦਰ ਕਰਨਾ, ਅਰਾਜਕਤਾ ਉਤਪੰਨ ਕਰਨੀ, ਹੁੱਲੜ ਮਚਾਉਣਾ; ਪਰੇਸ਼ਾਨ ਕਰਨਾ, ਬੇਚੈਨ ਕਰਨਾ; **~ed** ਵਿਆਕੁਲ, ਬੇਚੈਨ, ਘਬਰਾਇਆ

pertussis (ਪਅ*ਟਅੱਸਿਸ) *n* ਕਾਲੀ ਖਾਂਸੀ, ਕੁੱਤੇ-ਖੰਘ

perusal (ਪਅ'ਰੂਜ਼ਲ) *n* ਮੁਤਾਲਿਆ, ਪਠਨ, ਪੜ੍ਹਾਈ, ਅਧਿਐਨ; ਨਿਰੀਖਣ, ਪਰਖ, ਪੜਚੋਲ

pervade (ਪਅ'ਵੇਇਡ) *v* ਸਮਾਉਣਾ, ਵਿਆਪਣਾ, ਸੰਚਰਨਾ, ਰਸਣਾ, ਪ੍ਰਸਾਰ ਕਰਨਾ, ਪੱਸਰਨਾ

perverse (ਪਅ'ਵਅ:ਸ) *a* ਪਤਿਤ; ਪੁੱਠਾ, ਅਵੱਲਾ, ਅੜੀਅਲ, ਅਹੋੜ, ਜ਼ਿੱਦੀ, ਉਲਟਾ

perversion (ਪਅ'ਵਅ:ਸ਼ਨ) *n* ਉਲਟ-ਫੇਰ; ਵਿਗਾੜ, ਆਚਾਰ-ਭ੍ਰਿਸ਼ਟਤਾ, ਪਥ-ਭ੍ਰਿਸ਼ਟਤਾ

pervert (ਪਅ'ਵਅ:ਟ, ਪਅ:ਵਅ:ਟ) *v n* ਵਿਗਾੜਨਾ, ਪੁੱਠੇ ਰਾਹ ਪਾਉਣਾ; ਵਿਗੜਿਆ ਆਦਮੀ, ਪੁੱਠਾ ਆਦਮੀ, ਪਤਿਤ ਪੁਰਸ਼, ਪਥ-ਭ੍ਰਿਸ਼ਟ ਆਦਮੀ, ਆਚਾਰ-ਭ੍ਰਿਸ਼ਟ ਬੰਦਾ

pessimism ('ਪੈਸਿਮਿਜ਼(ਅ)ਮ) *n* ਨਿਰਾਸ਼ਾਵਾਦ, ਦਹਿੰਦੀ ਕਲਾ, ਨਿਰਸਤਾ

pessimist ('ਪੈਸਿਮਿਸਟ) *a* ਨਿਰਾਸ਼ਾਵਾਦੀ, ਨਿਰਾਸ਼; **~ic** ਨਿਰਾਸ਼ਾਵਾਦੀ, ਦੁਖੀ, ਦੁੱਖਵਾਦੀ

pest (ਪੈਸਟ) *n* ਬਲਾ, ਜ਼ਹਿਮਤ; ਵਿਨਾਸ਼ਕਾਰੀ ਕੀੜਾ ਜਾਂ ਕਿਰਮ; **~icide** ਕੀੜੇ ਮਾਰ ਦਵਾਈ; **~iferous** ਦੁਸ਼ਟਕਾਰੀ; ਹਾਨੀਕਾਰਕ; ਘਾਤਕ, ਵਿਨਾਸ਼ਕ, ਦੁਰਾਚਾਰੀ

pet (ਪੈਟ) *n a v* ਪਾਲਤੂ ਪਸ਼ੂ, ਪਾਲਿਆ ਜਾਨਵਰ; ਚਿੜਚੜਾਪਣ; ਲਾਡਲਾ, ਲਾਡਲੀ; ਲਾਡ ਲੜਾਉਣਾ, ਲਾਡ ਪਿਆਰ ਕਰਨਾ; **~name** ਲਾਡਲਾ ਨਾਂ

petal ('ਪੈਟਲ) *n* ਫੁੱਲ-ਪੱਤੀ, ਪੰਖੜੀ

petition (ਪਅ'ਟਿਸ਼ਨ) *n v* ਅਰਜ਼ੀ, ਪ੍ਰਾਰਥਨਾ-ਪੱਤਰ; ਯਾਚਨਾ, ਆਵੇਦਨ; ਉਜ਼ਰਦਾਰੀ; ਪ੍ਰਾਰਥਨਾ ਕਰਨੀ, ਦਰਖ਼ਾਸਤ ਦੇਣੀ; **~er** ਪ੍ਰਾਰਥਕ, ਯਾਚਕ, ਉਜ਼ਰਦਾਰ

petrify ('ਪੈਟਰਿਫ਼ਾਇ) *v* ਪਥਰਾਉਣਾ, ਕਰੜਾ ਕਰਨਾ, ਕਠੋਰ ਕਰਨਾ; ਸੁੰਨ ਹੋ ਜਾਣਾ; (ਅੱਖਾਂ) ਪਥਰਾ ਜਾਣੀਆਂ, ਨਿਰਜੀਵ ਕਰਨਾ, ਅਚੇਤਨ ਹੋਣਾ

petrol ('ਪੈਟਰੌਲ) *n* ਪੈਟਰੋਲ, (ਮੋਟਰਾਂ, ਕਾਰਾਂ ਆਦਿ ਵਿਚ ਪਾਉਣ ਵਾਲਾ) ਤੇਲ; **~eum** ਕੱਚਾ ਪੈਟਰੋਲ, ਖਣਿਜ ਤੇਲ, ਮਿੱਟੀ ਦਾ ਤੇਲ

petticoat ('ਪੈਟਿਕਅਉਟ) *n* ਪੈਟੀਕੋਟ (ਸਾੜ੍ਹੀ ਹੇਠਲਾ) ਲਹਿੰਗਾ, ਘੱਗਰੀ; (ਬੋਲ) ਔਰਤ, ਜ਼ਨਾਨੀ; **~Government** ਜ਼ਨਾਨਾ ਸਰਕਾਰ, ਰੰਨਾਂ ਦੀ ਹਕੂਮਤ, ਚੋਲੀ ਸ਼ਾਸਨ, ਤ੍ਰਿਆ ਰਾਜ

pettines ('ਪੈਟਿਨਿਸ) *n* ਤੁੱਛਤਾ, ਅਲਪਤਾ, ਸੰਕੀਰਣਤਾ, ਛੋਟਾਪਨ

pettish ('ਪੈਟਿਸ਼) *a* ਚਿੜਚੜਾ, ਖਿਝਿਆ, ਖਿਝੂ, ਤੁਨਕ ਮਿਜ਼ਾਜ; ਹਠੀਲਾ, ਜ਼ਿੱਦੀ

petty ('ਪੈਟਿ) *a* ਨਿੱਕਾ, ਛੋਟਾ, ਮਾਮੂਲੀ; ਤੁੱਛ, ਤੰਗਦਿਲ

phallic ('ਫ਼ੈਲਿਕ) *a* ਲਿੰਗਰੂਪ, ਲਿੰਗ-ਪੂਜਾ ਸਬੰਧੀ; ~ism ਲਿੰਗ-ਪੂਜਾ

phantasm ('ਫ਼ੈਂਟੈਜ਼(ਅ)ਮ) *n* ਛਲਾਵਾ, ਤਰਾਂਟੀ; ਛਲੇਡਾ, ਮਿਥਿਆਤਮ, ਮਾਇਆ

phantom ('ਫ਼ੈਂਟਮ) *n* ਬੇਤਾਲ, ਪਿਸ਼ਾਚ; ਪਰੇਤ, ਛਾਂ, ਛਾਇਆ, ਭੂਤ-ਪਰੇਤ; ਕਲਪਨਾ; ਮਨੋਲੀਲਾ, ਮਾਇਆ

pharmacology ('ਫ਼ਾਮਅ'ਕੌਲਅਜਿ) *n* ਔਸ਼ਧੀ-ਵਿਗਿਆਨ

pharmacist ('ਫ਼ਾਮਅਸਿਸਟ) *n* ਦਵਾ-ਫ਼ਰੋਸ਼

pharmacy ('ਫ਼ਾਮਅਸਿ) *n* ਦਵਾਈ-ਘਰ, ਦਵਾਖ਼ਾਨਾ, ਔਸ਼ਧਾਲਿਆ

phase (ਫ਼ੇਇਜ਼) *n* ਚਰਨ, ਪੱਖ, ਪਹਿਲੂ, ਅਵਸਥਾ

phenomenal (ਫ਼ਅ'ਨੌਮਿਨਲ) *a* ਦ੍ਰਿਸ਼ਟਮਾਨ, ਪ੍ਰਤੱਖ, ਨਜ਼ਰ ਬਾਰੇ; ਜ਼ਾਹਰ ਕੁਦਰਤ ਬਾਰੇ, ਅਨੋਖਾ, ਅਸਚਰਜ, ਅਲੌਕਕ, ਸ਼ਾਨਦਾਰ; ~ist ਦ੍ਰਿਸ਼ਟੀ-ਗਿਆਨ, ਪ੍ਰਤੱਖ ਗਿਆਨਵਾਦੀ, ਵਾਦੀ

phenomenology (ਫ਼ਅ'ਨੌਮਿ'ਨੌਲਅਜਿ) *n* (ਸਿੰਥਿਆ) ਘਟਨਾ-ਕਿਰਿਆ-ਵਿਗਿਆਨ

phenomenon (ਫ਼ਅ'ਨੌਮਿਨਅਨ) *n* ਗੋਚਰ ਪਦਾਰਥ, ਪ੍ਰਤੱਖ ਵਸਤੂ; ਘਟਨਾ, ਤੱਥ; ਕ੍ਰਿਸ਼ਮਾ

philanthropist (ਫ਼ਿ'ਲੈਨਥਰਅਪਿਸਟ) *n* ਜਨ-ਹਿਤੈਸ਼ੀ, ਸਮਾਜ-ਸੇਵਕ, ਲੋਕ-ਪ੍ਰੇਮੀ, ਪਰਉਪਕਾਰੀ, ਮਾਨਵਪ੍ਰੇਮੀ ਵਿਅਕਤੀ

philanthropy (ਫ਼ਿ'ਲੈਨਥਰਅਪਿ) *n* ਲੋਕ-ਹਿੱਤ, ਪਰਉਪਕਾਰ, ਲੋਕ-ਭਲਾਈ; ਮਨੁੱਖ ਜਾਤੀ ਪ੍ਰਤੀ ਭਰਾਤਰੀ ਭਾਵ; ਉਦਾਰਤਾ, ਹਮਦਰਦੀ

philatelic ('ਫ਼ਿਲਅ'ਟੈਲਿਕ) *a* ਟਿਕਟ-ਸੰਗ੍ਰਹਣ ਬਾਰੇ, ਟਿਕਟਾਂ ਇਕੱਠੀਆਂ ਕਰਨ ਸਬੰਧੀ

philologist (ਫ਼ਿ'ਲੌਲਅਜਿਸਟ) *n* ਭਾਸ਼ਾ-ਵਿਗਿਆਨੀ; ਭਾਸ਼ਾ ਸਾਹਿਤ-ਪ੍ਰੇਮੀ

philology (ਫ਼ਿ'ਲੌਲਅਜਿ) *n* ਭਾਸ਼ਾ-ਵਿਗਿਆਨ, ਭਾਸ਼ਾ-ਸ਼ਾਸਤਰ, ਭਾਸ਼ਾ-ਤੱਤ; ਵਿੱਦਿਆ ਪ੍ਰੇਮ

philosopher (ਫ਼ਿ'ਲੌਸਅਫ਼ਅ*) *n* ਦਾਰਸ਼ਨਕ, ਫ਼ਿਲਸਫ਼ਰ; ਗਿਆਨੀ, ਪੰਡਤ

philosophy (ਫ਼ਿ'ਲੌਸਅਫ਼ਿ) *n* ਫ਼ਲਸਫ਼ਾ, ਦਰਸ਼ਨ, ਫ਼ਿਲਸਫ਼ੀ, ਤੱਤ-ਗਿਆਨ

phlegm (ਫ਼ਲੈੱਮ) *n* ਬਲਗਮ, ਖੰਗਾਰ, ਕਫ਼, ਢਿੱਲੜਪੁਣਾ

phobia ('ਫ਼ਅਉਬਯਅ) *n* ਤ੍ਰਾਸ, ਭੈ

phoneme ('ਫ਼ਅਉਨੀਮ) *n* ਧੁਨੀ-ਗ੍ਰਾਮ

phonetic (ਫ਼ਅ'ਨੈਟਿਕ) *a* ਧੁਨੀ ਸਬੰਧੀ, ਸ਼ਰੁਤੀ, ਧੁਨੀਆਤਮਕ; ~s ਧੁਨੀ-ਵਿੱਦਿਆ, ਧੁਨੀ-ਵਿਗਿਆਨ, ਸਵਰ-ਵਿਗਿਆਨ

phonic ('ਫ਼ਅਉਨਿਕ) *a* ਧੁਨੀ ਦਾ; ਧੁਨੀਯੁਕਤ, ਸੁਰ ਸਬੰਧੀ; ਸ਼ਬਦੀ, ਸ਼ਾਬਦਕ

phonogram ('ਫ਼ਅਉਨਅਗਰਾਮ) *n* ਫ਼ੋਨੋਗ੍ਰਾਫ਼ ਨਾਲ ਰਿਕਾਰਡ ਕੀਤੀ ਹੋਈ ਅਵਾਜ਼; ਧੁਨੀ ਅੰਕਣ, ਧੁਨੀ-ਸੰਕੇਤ; ਧੁਨੀ-ਲੇਖ; ਸੰਖਿਪਤ ਰੂਪ ਵਿਚ ਧੁਨੀ-ਚਿੰਨ੍ਹ; ਫ਼ੋਨੋਗ੍ਰਾਮ

photo ('ਫ਼ਅਉਟਅਉ) *n v* ਫੋਟੋ, ਫ਼ੋਟੋਗ੍ਰਾਫ਼, ਪ੍ਰਕਾਸ਼-ਚਿੱਤਰ, ਆਲੇਖ-ਚਿੱਤਰ, ਅਕਸੀ ਤਸਵੀਰ; ਫੋਟੋ ਖਿੱਚਣੀ; ~stat ਕਿਸੇ ਲਿਖਤ ਦੀ ਫ਼ੋਟੋ ਕਾਪੀ; ~graph ਅਕਸੀ ਤਸਵੀਰ, ਫੋਟੋਗ੍ਰਾਫ਼

phrase (ਫ਼ਰੇਇਜ਼) *n v* ਵਾਕੰਸ਼, ਉਕਤੀ, ਕਥਨ; ਬਿਆਨ ਕਰਨਾ, ਵਰਨਣ ਕਰਨਾ, ਕਹਿਣਾ, ਸ਼ਬਦਾਂ ਵਿਚ ਬੀੜਨਾ; ~less ਉਕਤੀ-ਰਹਿਤ, ਵਰਨਣ-ਅਤੀਤ; ਅਵਰਨਣੀ

physic ('ਫ਼ਿਜ਼ਿਕ) *n v* ਹਿਕਮਤ, ਡਾਕਟਰੀ, ਵੈਦਗੀ; ਚਿਕਿਤਸਾ ਸ਼ਾਸਤਰ; ਦਵਾਈ, ਔਸ਼ਧੀ ਦਵਾਈ ਦੇਣੀ; ਇਲਾਜ ਕਰਨਾ; ~ian ਡਾਕਟਰ,

ਹਕੀਮ, ਵੈਦ; ਚਿਕਿਤਸਕ

physical ('ਫ਼ਿਜ਼ਿਕਲ) *a* ਪਦਾਰਥਕ, ਭੌਤਕ, ਸਥੂਲ, ਜੜ੍ਹ, ਸਾਕਾਰ; ਸੰਸਾਰਕ; ਸਰੀਰ-ਸਬੰਧੀ; ਸਰੀਰਕ; ਕੁਦਰਤੀ; ਪ੍ਰਕਿਰਤਕ; ਭੌਤਕ-ਵਿਗਿਆਨ ਸਬੰਧੀ

physicist ('ਫ਼ਿਜ਼ਿਸਿਸਟ) *n* ਭੌਤਕ-ਵਿਗਿਆਨੀ, ਭੌਤਕ-ਵਿਗਿਆਨ-ਸ਼ਾਸਤਰੀ; ਪਦਾਰਥਵਾਦੀ

physics ('ਫ਼ਿਜ਼ਿਕਸ) *n pl* ਭੌਤਕ-ਵਿਗਿਆਨ, ਭੌਤਕੀ-ਪਦਾਰਥ-ਵਿਗਿਆਨ

physiologist (ਫ਼ਿਜ਼ਿ'ਔਲਅਜਿਸਟ) *n* ਸਰੀਰ-ਵਿਗਿਆਨੀ

physiology (ਫ਼ਿਜ਼ਿ'ਔਲਅਜਿ) *n* ਸਰੀਰ-ਵਿਗਿਆਨ, ਸਰੀਰ-ਕਿਰਿਆ-ਵਿਗਿਆਨ

physique (ਫ਼ਿ'ਜ਼ੀਕ) *n* ਸਰੀਰਕ ਬਣਤਰ, ਕਾਇਆ, ਦੇਹ, ਜੁੱਸਾ

piano, pianoforte (ਪਿ'ਐਨਅਉ, ਪਿ'ਐਨਅ(ਉ)-'ਫ਼ੋਟਿ) *n* ਪਿਆਨੋ, ਇਕ ਸੰਗੀਤਕ ਸਾਜ਼, ਵਾਜਾ

pice (ਪਾਇਸ) *v* ਪੈਸਾ

pick (ਪਿਕ) *v* ਚੁਣਨਾ, ਛਾਂਟਣਾ, ਇਕੱਠਾ ਕਰਨਾ; ਸਾਫ਼ ਕਰਨਾ; ਪੁੱਟਣਾ, ਟੋਆ ਕੱਢਣਾ; ~**pocket** ਜੇਬ-ਕਤਰਾ

piokot (ਪਿਪਿਟ) *n v* ਪਿਕਟ, ਕੁਮਕ, ਹੱਥਿਆ ਦਲ; ਕੰਮ ਤੇ ਜਾਣ ਤੋਂ ਰੋਕਣ ਵਾਲੇ ਵਿਅਕਤੀ; ਧਰਨਾ ਮਾਰਨਾ, ਰੁਕਾਵਟ ਪਾਉਣੀ; ~**eer** ਪਿਕਟਿੰਗ ਕਰਨ ਵਾਲਾ ਵਿਅਕਤੀ, ਧਰਨਾ ਮਾਰਨ ਵਾਲਾ; ~**ing** ਧਰਨਾ

pickle (ਪਿਕਲ) *n v* (1) ਅਚਾਰ, ਸਿਰਕਾ; (2) ਸ਼ਰਾਰਤੀ ਮੁੰਡਾ; ਅਚਾਰ ਪਾਉਣਾ

picnic (ਪਿਕਨਿਕ) *n v* ਪਿਕਨਿਕ, ਸੈਰ-ਸਪਾਟਾ; ਪਿਕਨਿਕ ਕਰਨੀ

pictorial (ਪਿਕ'ਟੋਰਿਅਲ) *a n* ਸਚਿੱਤਰ, ਚਿਤਰਮਈ; ਤਸਵੀਰਾਂ ਵਾਲਾ, ਮੂਰਤਾਂ ਵਾਲਾ

picture ('ਪਿਕਚਅ*) *n v* ਤਸਵੀਰ, ਮੂਰਤ, ਚਿੱਤਰ; ਤਸਵੀਰ ਖਿਚਣੀ, ਚਿਤਰ ਕਰਨਾ; ~**gallery** ਚਿਤਰਸ਼ਾਲਾ, ਤਸਵੀਰ-ਘਰ; ~**sque** ਚਿਤਰਮਈ, ਚਿਤਰਵਤ, ਤਸਵੀਰ ਵਾਂਗ, ਸਜੀਵ, ਕੁਦਰਤੀ ਰੂਪ ਵਾਲਾ

pidgin, pigeon ('ਪਿਜੀਨ) *n* (ਬੋਲ) ਕਾਰੋਬਾਰ, ਵਾਸਤਾ; ਦੋ ਭਾਸ਼ਾਵਾਂ ਦਾ ਮਿਸ਼ਰਿਤ ਰੂਪ; ~**English** ਵਿਹਾਰਕ ਅੰਗਰੇਜ਼ੀ, ਕਾਰੋਬਾਰੀ ਅੰਗਰੇਜ਼ੀ, ਮਿਸ਼ਰਤ ਅੰਗਰੇਜ਼ੀ, ਖਿਚੜੀ ਅੰਗਰੇਜ਼ੀ

piece (ਪੀਸ) *n v* ਟੁਕੜਾ, ਟੋਟਾ, (ਕਾਗ਼ਜ਼ ਦਾ) ਫ਼ਜ਼ਕਾ, ਕਤਰ, ਭੋਂ ਦਾ ਟੋਟਾ, ਅੰਸ਼, ਅੰਗ; ਜੋੜ ਲਾਉਣਾ; ~**meal** ਥੋੜ੍ਹਾ ਥੋੜ੍ਹਾ ਕਰਕੇ, ਥੋੜ-ਥੋੜ ਕਰਕੇ, ਟੋਟਿਆਂ ਵਿਚ, ਟੁਕੜਿਆਂ ਵਿਚ; ~**work** ਠੇਕੇ ਦਾ ਕੰਮ, ਉਜਰਤੀ ਕੰਮ

pierce ('ਪਿਅਃਸ) *n a* ਵਿੰਨ੍ਹਣਾ, ਖੋਭਣਾ ਜਾਂ ਖੁਭਣਾ, ਚੋਭਣਾ ਜਾਂ ਚੁੱਭਣਾ

piercing ('ਪਿਅਃਸਿਙ) *n a* ਵੇਧਨ, ਭੇਦਨ; ਤੀਖਣ, ਵੇਧਕ, ਵੇਧਨਸ਼ੀਲ; ਚੀਕਵੀਂ (ਅਵਾਜ਼); ਘੋਖਵੀਂ (ਨਜ਼ਰ)

pig (ਪਿਗ) *n v* ਸੂਰ, ਸੂਰ ਦਾ ਮਾਸ; ਮੈਲਾ, ਗੰਦਾ (ਮਨੁੱਖ); ਲਾਲਚੀ ਆਦਮੀ, ਲੋਭੀ ਵਿਅਕਤੀ; ਗੰਦੇ ਰਹਿਣਾ, ਸੂਰ ਵਾਂਗ ਰਹਿਣਾ; ~**iron** ਕੱਚਾ ਲੋਹਾ, ਲੋਹੇ ਦਾ ਡਲਾ; ~**jump** (ਘੋੜੇ ਦੀ) ਛਲਾਂਗ, ਚੋਕੜੀ; ~**gery** ਸੂਰਖ਼ਾਨਾ, ਸੂਰਾਂ ਦਾ ਵਾੜਾ; ਗੰਦੀ ਥਾਂ, ਕੂੜੇ ਵਾਲੀ ਥਾਂ; ਹੋਛਾਪਣ, ਕਮੀਨਾਪਣ

pigeon ('ਪਿਜੀਨ) *n v* ਕਬੂਤਰ; ਬੁੱਧੂ, ਭੋਂਦੂ, ਲੋਲ੍ਹਾ; ਠੱਗਣਾ, ਧੋਖਾ ਦੇਣਾ; ~**hole** ਕੰਧ ਦੀ ਮੋਰੀ ਜਾਂ ਆਲਾ ਜਿਸ ਵਿਚ ਕਬੂਤਰ ਬੈਠ ਜਾਂਦੇ ਹਨ; ਕਾਗ਼ਜ਼ ਆਦਿ ਰੱਖਣ ਲਈ ਬਣਾਏ ਖ਼ਾਨੇ;

~ry ਕਬੂਤਰਖ਼ਾਨਾ, ਕਬੂਤਰਾਂ ਦਾ ਆਲ੍ਹਣਾ

pigmy ('ਪਿਗਮਿ) *n a* ਬੌਣਾ, ਬਹੁਤ ਛੋਟੇ ਕੱਦ ਦਾ; ਥੋੜ੍ਹੀ ਅਕਲ ਵਾਲਾ

pike (ਪਾਇਕ) *n* ਬਰਛੀ, ਭਾਲਾ, ਨੇਜਾ; (ਪਹਾੜ ਦੀ) ਨੋਕਦਾਰ ਟੀਸੀ; ਚੁੰਗੀ ਘਰ, ਚੁੰਗੀ, ਮਹਿਸੂਲ

pile (ਪਾਇਲ) *n v* (1) ਢੇਰ, ਥਹੀ, ਧਾਕ; (ਬੋਲ) ਬਹੁਤ ਜ਼ਿਆਦਾ ਧਨ; (2) ਕਿੱਲੀ, ਕਿੱਲ, ਕਿੱਲਾ; (3) ਬਵਾਸੀਰ; (4) (ਭੇਡ ਦੀ) ਲੂੰਈ, ਲੂੰ; ਢੇਰ ਲਾਉਣਾ, ਇਕੱਠਾ ਕਰਨਾ; ਤਰਨਾ, ਤੁੜਨਾ, ਮੂੰਹੋਂ ਮੂੰਹ ਭਰਨਾ

pilfer ('ਪਿਲਫ਼ਅ*) *v* ਨਿੱਕੀ-ਮੋਟੀ ਚੋਰੀ ਕਰਨੀ, ਹੇਰਾ ਫੇਰੀ ਕਰਨੀ, ਹੱਥ ਮਾਰਨਾ, ਠੂੰਗ ਲੈਣਾ; ~age ਨਿੱਕੀ-ਮੋਟੀ ਚੋਰੀ

pilgarlic (ਪਿਲ'ਗਾਰਲਿਕ) *n* ਰੰਜਾ ਸਿਰ, ਰੋੜਾ ਸਿਰ; ਰੰਜਾ ਵਿਅਕਤੀ; ਨਿਰਧਨ ਵਿਅਕਤੀ

pilgrim ('ਪਿਲਗਰਿਮ) *n* ਯਾਤਰੀ, ਤੀਰਥ-ਯਾਤਰੀ, ਹਾਜੀ, ਜ਼ਿਆਰਤੀ; ਤੀਰਥ-ਯਾਤਰਾ ਕਰਨਾ, ਹੱਜ ਕਰਨਾ; ~age ਤੀਰਥ-ਯਾਤਰਾ; ਜ਼ਿਆਰਤ; ਹੱਜ, ਤੀਰਥ-ਕਰਨ

pill (ਪਿਲ) *n v* (ਦਵਾਈ ਦੀ) ਗੋਲੀ; ਕੌੜੀ ਤੇ ਅਸਹਿ ਗੱਲ; ਪੱਤਾ ਕਟਣਾ; ਲੁੱਟਣਾ

pillar ('ਪਿਲਅ*) *n* ਥੰਮ੍ਹ, ਥਮੂਲਾ, ਥੰਮ੍ਹੀ, ਮਦਦਗਾਰ, ਸਹਾਇਕ

pillion ('ਪਿਲਯਅਨ) *n* ਸਾਈਕਲ ਜਾਂ ਮੋਟਰ ਸਾਈਕਲ ਦੀ ਪਿਛਲੀ ਕਾਠੀ

pillow ('ਪਿਲਅਉ) *n v* ਸਿਰ੍ਹਾਣਾ; ਸਹਾਰਾ, ਟੇਕ, ਢੋਹ; ਸਹਾਰਾ ਲੈਣਾ, ਢੋਹ ਲਾਉਣੀ

pilot ('ਪਾਇਲਅਟ) *n v* ਹਵਾਈ ਜਹਾਜ਼ ਦਾ ਚਾਲਕ, ਪਾਇਲਟ; ਜਹਾਜ਼ਰਾਨ

pimp (ਪਿੰਪ) *n v* ਦੱਲਾ, ਦਲਾਲ, ਭੜੂਆ; ਦੱਲਪੁਣਾ ਕਰਨਾ

pimple ('ਪਿੰਪਲ) *n* ਫਿਨਸੀ, ਫੋੜਾ; ਕਿੱਲ, ਮੁਹਾਂਸਾ; ~d ਫੋੜਿਆਂ ਵਾਲਾ, ਮੁਹਾਂਸਿਆਂ ਵਾਲਾ

pin (ਪਿਨ) *n v* ਪਿੰਨ (ਕਾਗ਼ਜ਼ ਨੱਥੀ ਕਰਨ ਵਾਲਾ), ਸੂਈ, ਕੰਢਾ; ਮੇਖ, ਕਿੱਲ; ~money ਘਰ ਵਾਲੀ ਦਾ ਨਿੱਜੀ ਖ਼ਰਚ, ਜੇਬ-ਖ਼ਰਚ; ~point ਸੁਨਿਸ਼ਚਤ (ਕਰਨਾ), ਠੀਕ ਨਿਸ਼ਾਨਾ (ਲਾਉਣਾ); ~prick ਚੁਭਵੀਂ ਗੱਲ ਜਾਂ ਕਾਰਵਾਈ

pinch (ਪਿੰਚ) *v n* ਚੁੰਢੀ ਵੱਢਣੀ; (ਭੁੱਖ, ਠੰਢ ਆਦਿ ਦਾ) ਕਸ਼ਟ ਹੋਣਾ; ਦੁੱਖ ਹੋਣਾ, ਔਖਿਆਂ ਕਰਨਾ; (ਜੁੱਤੀ) ਲੱਗਣੀ

pine (ਪਾਇਨ) *v n* ਵਿਆਕੁਲ ਹੋਣਾ, ਝੂਰਨਾ, ਦੁਖੀ ਹੋਣਾ; ਵਿਆਕੁਲਤਾ, ਕਲੇਸ਼, ਦੁੱਖ; ਚੀੜ੍ਹ, ਦਿਆਰ; ~apple ਅਨਾਨਾਸ

pink (ਪਿੰਕ) *n a v* ਗੁਲਾਬੀ ਰੰਗ, ਪਿਆਜ਼ੀ ਰੰਗ; ਗੁਲਾਬੀ, ਪਿਆਜ਼ੀ; ਵਾਰ ਕਰਨਾ, ਸਜਾਉਣਾ, ਅਲੰਕਰਤ ਕਰਨਾ; (ਇੰਜਣ ਦਾ) ਪਟਾਕੇ ਮਾਰਨਾ; ~ing ਖੜਕਝਾਹਟ; ~y ਗੁਲਾਬੀ, ਪਿਆਜ਼ੀ

pinnacle ('ਪਿਨਅਕਲ) *n v* ਬੁਰਜ, ਗੁੰਬਦ; ਸਿਖਰ, ਚੋਟੀ, ਟਿੱਲਾ, ਸਿਰਾ, ਕਲਸ

pioneer ('ਪਾਇਅ'ਨਿਅ*) *n v* ਆਗੂ, ਮੋਢੀ, ਨੇਤਾ, ਸੰਸਥਾਪਕ, ਪ੍ਰਵਰਤਕਾਰ; ਅਗਵਾਈ ਕਰਨੀ, ਰਾਹ ਵਿਖਾਉਣਾ; ਅੱਗੇ ਚਲਣਾ, ਪਹਿਲ ਕਰਨੀ; ਰਾਹ ਸਾਫ਼ ਕਰਨਾ

pious ('ਪਾਇਅਸ) *a* ਧਰਮੀ, ਸਦਾਚਾਰੀ, ਪਵਿੱਤਰ, ਧਰਮਾਤਮਾ, ਨੇਕ; ~ness ਪਵਿੱਤਰਤਾ, ਪੁੰਨਸ਼ੀਲਤਾ, ਭਗਤੀ, ਸਦਾਚਾਰਤਾ

pipe (ਪਾਇਪ) *n v* ਨਾਲ, ਨਲਕੀ, ਨਲਕਾ, ਪਾਈਪ, ਵੰਝਲੀ, ਬੰਸਰੀ; ਹੁੱਕਾ, ਨੜੀ; ~line ਨਲ ਪ੍ਰਬੰਧ, ਪਾਈਪ ਲਾਈਨ

piquancy ('ਪੀਕਅੰਸਿ) *n* ਤੀਖਣਤਾ,

ਚਟਪਟਾਪਨ, ਕਰਾਰਾਪਨ, ਰੋਚਕਤਾ, ਤੇਜ਼ੀ

piquant ('ਪੀਕਅੰਟ) *a* ਰੁਚੀਕਰ, ਸੁਆਦੀ; ਕਰਾਰਾ, ਮਜ਼ੇਦਾਰ, ਮਸਾਲੇਦਾਰ, ਚਟਪਟਾ

pique (ਪੀਕ) *v n* ਖਿਝਾਉਣਾ, ਚਿੜਾਉਣਾ, ਗੁੱਸਾ ਚੜ੍ਹਾਉਣਾ, ਸਤਾਉਣਾ; ਚਿੜ, ਖਿਝ

piracy ('ਪਾਇ(ਅ)ਰਅਸਿ) *n* ਸਮੁੰਦਰੀ ਡਾਕਾ; ਸਾਹਿਤਕ ਚੋਰੀ

pirate ('ਪਾਇ(ਅ)ਰਅਟ) *n v* ਸਮੁੰਦਰੀ ਡਾਕੂ, ਲੁਟੇਰਾ; ਸਾਹਿਤਕ ਚੋਰ; ਚੋਰੀ (ਕਿਤਾਬ) ਛਾਪਣੀ, ਡਾਕਾ ਮਾਰਨਾ, ਲੁੱਟ-ਮਾਰ ਕਰਨੀ

pisciculture ('ਪਿਸਿਕਅਲਚਅ*) *n* ਮੱਛੀ-ਪਾਲਣ

pish (ਪਿਸ਼) *v int* ਫਿਟਕਾਰਨਾ, ਦੁਰਕਾਰਨਾ, ਛੀ ਛੀ ਕਰਨਾ; ਹੂ ਹੂ, ਛੀ ਛੀ

piss (ਪਿਸ) *n v* (ਉਪ) ਮੂਤਰ, ਪਿਸ਼ਾਬ, ਮੂਤ; ਪਿਸ਼ਾਬ ਕਰਨਾ, ਮੂਤਰਨਾ

pistol ('ਪਿਸਟਲ) *n v* ਪਿਸਤੌਲ; ਪਿਸਤੌਲ ਚਲਾਉਣਾ

pit (ਪਿਟ) *n v* ਟੋਆ, ਖਤਾਨ, ਖੱਡ, ਖਾਈ, ਖੁੰਧੀ; ਛੇਕ, ਮੋਰੀ; ਟੋਆ ਪੁੱਟਣਾ, ਛੇਕ ਕਰਨਾ, ਮੋਰੀ ਕਰਨੀ; ਦਾਗ਼ ਪੈਣਾ; **~fall** ਜੰਗਲੀ ਜਾਨਵਰਾਂ ਨੂੰ ਫੜਨ ਲਈ ਚੋਰ-ਟੋਆ; ਲੁਕਿਆ ਖ਼ਤਰਾ

pitch (ਪਿਚ) *n v* (1) ਲੁਨ੍ਹ; (2) (ਕ੍ਰਿਕਟ) ਗੇਂਦ ਸੁੱਟਣ ਦਾ ਢੰਗ; ਕ੍ਰਿਕਟ ਦੀਆਂ ਵਿਕਟਾਂ ਦੇ ਵਿਚਕਾਰਲੀ ਥਾਂ; ਤਘੁੰ ਲਾਉਣਾ; ਕੈਂਪ ਲਾਉਣਾ, ਪੜਾਉ ਕਰਨਾ; ਸਥਾਪਤ ਕਰਨਾ, ਕਾਇਮ ਕਰਨਾ, ਨੁਮਾਇਸ਼ ਲਈ ਰੱਖਣਾ; ਲੁੱਕ ਲਾਉਣੀ; ਮੂੰਹ ਭਾਰ ਡਿਗਣਾ; ਭਿਆਨਕ ਹਮਲਾ ਕਰਨਾ; **~ed** ਸਥਿਰ, ਜੰਮਿਆ, ਪੱਕਾ; **~ed battle** ਘਮਸਾਨ ਦਾ ਜੁੱਧ, ਘੋਰ ਜੁੱਧ; **~ed roof** ਢਲਵੀਂ ਛੱਤ

pitcher ('ਪਿਚਅ*) *n* ਘੜਾ, ਮਟਕਾ, ਝੱਜਰ; ਕਲਸ ਪੱਤਰ

piteous ('ਪਿਟਿਅਸ) *a* ਤਰਸਯੋਗ, ਦੁੱਖ ਭਰੀ, ਦਰਦਨਾਕ, ਅਫ਼ਸੋਸਨਾਕ, ਕਰੁਣਾਜਨਕ

pith (ਪਿਥ) *n* ਗੁੱਦਾ; ਤੱਤ, ਸਾਰ, ਨਿਚੋੜ; ਗਿਰੀ; ਬਲ, ਤਾਕਤ, ਹਿੰਮਤ, ਉਤਸ਼ਾਹ

pitiable ('ਪਿਟਿਅਬਲ) *a* ਤਰਸਯੋਗ, ਕਰੁਣਾਜਨਕ, ਦਇਆਯੋਗ; ਦੁੱਖ ਭਰਿਆ

pitiful ('ਪਿਟਿਫ਼ੁਲ) *a* ਦਿਆਲੂ, ਦਇਆਵਾਨ, ਕਿਰਪਾਲੂ, ਰਹਿਮ-ਦਿਲ, ਦਰਦਮੰਦ; ਤਰਸਵਾਨ

pitiless ('ਪਿਟਿਲਿਸ) *a* ਬੇਤਰਸ, ਨਿਰਦਈ, ਬੇਰਹਿਮ, ਕਠੋਰ-ਚਿੱਤ, ਕਰੜਾ

pity ('ਪਿਟਿ) *n v* ਤਰਸ, ਰਹਿਮ, ਦਇਆ, ਕਿਰਪਾ, ਹਮਦਰਦੀ; ਹਮਦਰਦੀ ਵਿਖਾਉਣਾ, ਰਹਿਮ ਕਰਨਾ, ਦਇਆ ਕਰਨੀ; ਅਫ਼ਸੋਸ ਕਰਨਾ

pivot (ਪਿਵ੍ਅਟ) *n v* ਚੂਲ, ਚੂਬੀ, ਧੁਰਾ; ਕਿੱਲੀ (ਜਿਵੇਂ ਚੱਕੀ ਦੀ); ਕੇਂਦਰ-ਬਿੰਦੂ, ਮੂਲ-ਆਧਾਰ, ਮੂਲ ਸਮੱਸਿਆ; **~al** ਕੇਂਦਰੀ; ਧੁਰੇ ਦਾ; ਮੂਲ ਸਮੱਸਿਆ ਵਾਲਾ

placard ('ਪਲੈਕਾਡ) *n v* ਫੱਟਾ, ਬੋਰਡ, ਪਲੈਕਾਰਡ; ਇਸ਼ਤਿਹਾਰ, ਐਲਾਨ, ਵਿਗਿਆਪਨ-ਪੱਤਰ; ਇਸ਼ਤਿਹਾਰ ਲਗਾਉਣਾ, ਪਰਚੀ ਵੰਡਣਾ

placate (ਪਲਅ'ਕੇਇਟ) *v* ਤਸੱਲੀ ਕਰਾਉਣੀ, ਸੰਤੁਸ਼ਟ ਕਰਨਾ, ਮਨਾ ਲੈਣਾ, ਸ਼ਾਂਤ ਕਰਨਾ

place (ਪਲੇਇਸ) *n v* ਥਾਂ, ਜਗ੍ਹਾ, ਠਾਹਰ, ਟਿਕਾਣਾ, ਪਿੰਡ, ਸਥਾਨ; ਹੈਸੀਅਤ, ਪਦਵੀ; ਲਾਉਣਾ, ਸਥਾਪਨ ਕਰਨਾ; ਥਾਂ ਦੇਣੀ, ਟਿਕਾਉਣਾ, ਰੱਖਣਾ, ਧਰਨਾ; ਨਿਯੁਕਤ ਕਰਨਾ, ਤਾਇਨਾਤ ਕਰਨਾ; **~man** ਸਰਕਾਰੀ ਨੌਕਰ; **~ment** ਸਥਾਪਨਾ; (ਰਾਜ) ਆਸਣ-ਅਵਸਥਾ; ਰੁਜ਼ਗਾਰ ਦਿਵਾਉਣ ਦਾ ਅਮਲ

placid ('ਪਲੈਸਿਡ) *a* ਸ਼ਾਂਤ, ਗੰਭੀਰ; **~ity** ਸ਼ਾਂਤੀ,

ਨਿਮਰਤਾ, ਠਰ੍ਹੰਮਾ, ਧੀਰਜ, ਗੰਭੀਰਤਾ

plagiarism ('ਪਲੇਇਜਯਅਰਿਜ਼(ਅ)ਮ) *n* ਸਾਹਿਤ-ਚੋਰੀ, ਵਿਚਾਰ-ਚੋਰੀ

plagiarist ('ਪਲੇਇਜਯਅਰਿਸਟ) *n* ਸਾਹਿਤ-ਚੋਰ; ਵਿਚਾਰ-ਚੋਰ

plagiarize ('ਪਲੇਇਜਯਰਾਇਜ਼) *v* ਕਿਸੇ ਦੀ ਰਚਨਾ ਜਾਂ ਵਿਚਾਰ ਚੁਰਾ ਲੈਣਾ, ਸਾਹਿਤ-ਚੋਰੀ ਕਰਨੀ

plague (ਪਲੇਇਗ) *n* ਪਲੇਗ, ਤਾਊਨ; ਬਿਪਤਾ, ਦੁੱਖ, ਰੱਬੀ ਮਾਰ, ਆਫ਼ਤ

plain (ਪਲੇਇਨ) *a adv n* ਸਾਦਾ, ਸਰਲ, ਆਸਾਨ, ਸਿੱਧਾ-ਸਾਦਾ, ਬੇਰੰਗ, ਬਿਨਾ ਸਜਾਵਟ ਖਰਾ; ਮਾਮੂਲੀ, ਘਰੇਲੂ; ਮੈਦਾਨੀ ਇਲਾਕਾ, ਮੈਦਾਨ, ਪੱਧਰ; **~spoken** ਖਰੀ ਖਰੀ ਸੁਣਾਉਣ ਵਾਲਾ; **~ness** ਸਾਦਗੀ, ਸਰਲਤਾ, ਸਪਸ਼ਟਤਾ

plaint (ਪਲੇਇੰਟ) *n* ਅਰਜ਼ੀ-ਦਾਅਵਾ, ਨਾਲਿਸ਼; ਸ਼ਿਕਾਇਤ, ਸ਼ਿਕਵਾ, ਫ਼ਰਿਆਦ; **~iff** ਮੁੱਦਈ, ਦਾਅਵੇਦਾਰ, ਵਾਦੀ

plaintive ('ਪਲੇਇਨਟਿਵ਼) *a* ਸੋਗ ਵਾਲਾ, ਸੋਗਵਾਨ, ਸੋਗਸੂਚਕ, ਮਾਤਮੀ, ਦੁੱਖ ਭਰਿਆ

plan (ਪਲੈਨ) *n v* ਯੋਜਨਾ, ਤਜਵੀਜ਼, ਮਨਸੂਬਾ; ਤਰਤੀਬ, ਵਿਵਸਥਾ, ਨਕਸ਼ਾ; ਖ਼ਾਕਾ, ਢਾਂਚਾ, ਯੋਜਨਾ ਬਣਾਉਣੀ; ਨਕਸ਼ਾ ਬਣਾਉਣਾ; ਢਾਂਚਾ ਤਿਆਰ ਕਰਨਾ; **~ned** ਵਿਉਂਤਬੱਧ, ਯੋਜਨਾਬੱਧ, ਆਯੋਜਤ; **~ner** ਵਿਉਂਤਕਰ, ਯੋਜਕ, ਆਯੋਜਕ; **~ning** ਆਯੋਜਨ, ਵਿਉਂਤਬੰਦੀ, ਯੋਜਨਾਬੰਦੀ; ਉਪਾਉ, ਪਰਿਕਲਪਨਾ

plane (ਪਲੇਇਨ) *n v* (1) ਰੰਦਾ; ਤਲ, ਸਤ੍ਹਾ, ਪਟੜੀ; (2) ਫੱਟਾ; (3) ਪੱਧਰ, ਮੈਦਾਨ, ਪੱਧਰਾ ਇਲਾਕਾ; (4) ਹਵਾਈ ਜਹਾਜ਼; ਰੰਦਾ ਫੇਰਨਾ, ਰੰਦੇ ਨਾਲ ਛਿੱਲਣਾ

planet ('ਪਲੈਨਿਟ) *n* ਗ੍ਰਹਿ

plank (ਪਲੈਂਕ) *n v* ਤਖ਼ਤਾ, ਫੱਟਾ, ਪਟੜਾ, ਪਟੜੀ, ਚੌਂਕੀ; ਰਾਜਨੀਤਕ ਯੋਜਨਾ; ਤਖ਼ਤੇ ਲਾਉਣੇ

plant (ਪਲਾਂਟ) *n v* (1) ਬੂਟਾ, ਪੌਦਾ; (2) ਮਸ਼ੀਨ; (3) ਕਾਰਖ਼ਾਨਾ; (4) ਫ਼ਰੇਬ; ਸਾਜ਼ਿਸ਼; ਬੂਟਾ ਲਾਉਣਾ, ਬੀਜਣਾ; **~ation** ਫ਼ਾਰਮ; ਖੇਤੀ; ਬਸਤੀ, ਚੱਕ, ਆਬਾਦੀ; **~er** ਹਲਵਾਹ, ਕਿਰਸਾਨ, ਕਾਸ਼ਤਕਾਰ; ਮਾਲੀ; **~ing** ਪੌਦਾ ਲਾਉਣ ਦਾ ਕਾਰਜ, ਬਿਜਾਈ; ਬਗ਼ੀਚਾ, ਬਾਗ਼, ਖੇਤੀ

plaster ('ਪਲਾਸਟਅ*) *n v* ਲੇਪ, ਪਲਸਤਰ, ਲੇਅ, ਪੋਚਾ; ਗੋਹਾ-ਮਿੱਟੀ; ਲੇਪ ਕਰਨਾ, ਪਲਸਤਰ ਲਾਉਣਾ

plate (ਪਲੇਇਟ) *n v* ਤਖ਼ਤੀ, ਤਖ਼ਤਾ; (ਧਾਤ ਦੀ) ਪੱਤਰੀ, ਚਾਦਰ, ਧਾਤ ਦੇ ਭਾਂਡੇ; ਤਸ਼ਤਰੀ, ਥਾਲੀ, ਰਕਾਬੀ, ਪਲੇਟ; ਛੱਤ ਜਾਂ ਸਤੀਰ; ਪੱਤਰਾ ਚਾੜ੍ਹਨਾ, ਸੋਨੇ ਚਾਂਦੀ ਦਾ ਪਾਣੀ ਫੇਰਨਾ

plateau ('ਪਲੈਟਅਉ) *n* ਪੱਥੀ, ਪਠਾਰ

platform ('ਪਲੈਟਫ਼ੋ:ਮ) *n* (ਰੇਲ ਦਾ) ਪਲੇਟ-ਫ਼ਾਰਮ; ਥੜ੍ਹਾ, ਚਬੂਤਰਾ, ਚੌਂਤਰਾ, ਰੰਗਮੰਚ, ਸਭਾ-ਮੰਚ, ਮੰਚ; ਆਸਣ

platoon ('ਪਅਲ'ਟੂਨ) *n* (ਇਤਿ) ਪੈਦਲ ਫ਼ੌਜ ਦੀ ਛੋਟੀ ਟੁਕੜੀ, ਪਲਟਨ

platter ('ਪਲੈਟਅ*) *n* ਥਾਲੀ, ਤਸ਼ਤਰੀ, ਪਲੇਟ; ਕਠੌਤੀ, ਕਠਰੀ, ਪ੍ਰਤ

plausible ('ਪਲੋਜ਼ਿਬਲ) *a* ਨਿਆਇਸੰਗਤ, ਯੁਕਤੀਸੰਗਤ, ਤਰਕਸ਼ੀਲ; ਸਪਸ਼ਟਵਾਦੀ, ਸਤਿਵਾਦੀ

play (ਪਲੇਇ) *n* ਖੇਡ, ਤਮਾਸ਼ਾ, ਸ਼ੁਗਲ, ਮਜ਼ਾਕ, ਦਿਲਗੀਰ; ਨਾਟਕ, ਡਰਾਮਾ, ਖੇਡ-ਤਮਾਸ਼ਾ; ਖੇਡਣਾ; ਉਛਲਣਾ, ਫੁਦਕਣਾ; ਕਲੋਲ ਕਰਨਾ;

(ਕਿਸੇ ਨਾਲ) ਚਾਲ ਚੱਲਣਾ; ਰੰਗ ਰਲੀਆਂ ਮਨਾਉਣਾ, ਆਨੰਦ ਮਨਾਉਣਾ; ਨਾਟਕ ਵਿਚ ਭਾਗ ਲੈਣਾ, ਅਭਿਨੈ ਕਰਨਾ; ~boy ਅੱਯਾਸ਼ੀ ਬੰਦਾ (ਵਿਸ਼ੇਸ਼ ਕਰਕੇ ਨੌਜਵਾਨ), ਐਸ਼ੀ-ਪੱਠਾ; ~ful ਖਿੜਾਰੂ, ਚੰਚਲ, ਸੁਗਲੀ, ਹਸਮੁੱਖ, ਜ਼ਿੰਦਾਦਿਲ; ਰੌਂਣਕੀ; ~ground ਖੇਡ ਦਾ ਮੈਦਾਨ; ~house ਰੰਗਸ਼ਾਲਾ, ਤਮਾਸ਼ਘਰ; ~mate ਸਾਥੀ, ਜੋੜੀਦਾਰ, ਆੜੀ; ਲੰਗੋਟੀਆ ਯਾਰ; ~wright ਨਾਟਕਕਾਰ; ~fullness ਖਿੜਾਰੂਪਣ; ਚੰਚਲਤਾ, ਮੌਜ-ਮੇਲਾ, ਦਿਲਲਗੀ, ਮਖੌਲ

player (ਪਲੇਇਅ*) *n* ਖਿੜਾਰੀ; ਜੁਆਰੀਆ; ਗਾਇਕ; ਅਭਿਨੇਤਾ

plaza (ਪਲਾਜ਼ਅ) *n* ਬਜ਼ਾਰ ਦਾ ਚੌਕ, ਜਨ-ਸਭਾਨ

plea (ਪਲੀ) *n* ਦਲੀਲ, ਤਰਕ; ਜਵਾਬ-ਦੇਹੀ, ਪ੍ਰਤੀਵਾਦ, ਪ੍ਰਤੀਕਥਨ

plead (ਪਲੀਡ) *v* ਦਲੀਲ ਪੇਸ਼ ਕਰਨੀ, ਤਰਕ ਕਰਨਾ; ਵਕਾਲਤ ਕਰਨੀ; ~er ਵਕੀਲ, ਪਲੀਡਰ; ~ing ਸਫ਼ਾਈ, ਬਚਾਉ ਲਈ ਬਿਆਨ, ਪੱਖ ਦਾ ਸਮਰਥਨ

pleasant ('ਪਲੈਜ਼ਅੰਟ) *a* ਸੁਹਾਵਣਾ, ਰਮਣੀਕ, ਮਨੋਹਰ, ਸੁਖਦਾਈ, ਮਜ਼ੇਦਾਰ; ~ry ਹਾਸਵਿਨੋਦ, ਵਿਨੋਦਸ਼ੀਲਤਾ; ਠੱਠਾ, ਦਿਲਲਗੀ; ਹਾਸਾ, ਮਖੌਲ; ਵਿਅੰਗ

please (ਪਲੀਜ਼) *v adv* ਸੰਤੁਸ਼ਟ ਕਰਨਾ, ਤ੍ਰਿਪਤ ਕਰਨਾ; ਖ਼ੁਸ਼ ਕਰਨਾ, ਪ੍ਰਸੰਨ ਕਰਨਾ ਜਾਂ ਹੋਣਾ; ਕਿਰਪਾ ਕਰਕੇ, ਕਿਰਪਾਪੂਰਵਕ; ~d ਖ਼ੁਸ਼, ਪ੍ਰਸੰਨ, ਤ੍ਰਿਪਤ, ਸੰਤੁਸ਼ਟ, ਆਨੰਦਤ

pleasing ('ਪਲੀਜ਼ਿੰਡ) *a* ਸੁਹਾਵਣਾ, ਸੁਖਦਾਈ, ਮਨੋਹਰ, ਆਨੰਦਦਾਇਕ

pleasurable ('ਪਲੈਣ੍ਹ(ਅ)ਰਅਬਲ) *a* ਸੁਖਦਾਈ, ਆਨੰਦਦਾਇਕ, ਸੁਖਾਵਾਂ

pleasure ('ਪਲੈਣ੍ਹਅ*) *n* ਖ਼ੁਸ਼ੀ, ਆਨੰਦ, ਪ੍ਰਸੰਨਤਾ, ਤ੍ਰਿਪਤੀ; ਸੁਖ, ਮਜ਼ਾ; ਮੌਜ-ਮੇਲਾ

plebiscite ('ਪਲੈਬਿਸਿਟ) *n* ਲੋਕ-ਮੱਤ, ਜਨ-ਮੱਤ, ਜਨਤਾ ਦੀ ਰਾਇ, ਜਨ-ਮੱਤ-ਸੰਗ੍ਰਹ

pledge (ਪਲੈੱਜ) *n v* ਪ੍ਰਤਿੱਗਿਆ, ਪ੍ਰਣ, ਸਹੁੰ, ਵਾਅਦਾ, ਇਕਰਾਰ, ਵਚਨ; ਪ੍ਰਤਿੱਗਿਆ ਕਰਨੀ, ਪ੍ਰਣ ਕਰਨਾ; ~d ਵਚਨਬੱਧ

plenary ('ਪਲੀਨਅਰਿ) *a* ਪੂਰਾ, ਸਮੁੱਚਾ, ਕੁੱਲ, ਸਾਰਾ, ਸਗਲਾ, ਅਖਿਲ

plenty ('ਪਲੈੱਟਿ) *n adv* ਬਹੁਤਾਤ, ਬਹੁਲਤਾ, ਅਧਿਕਤਾ, ਤਗਾਣ, ਪ੍ਰਫੁੱਲਤਾ, ਬਿਲਕੁਲ, ਕਾਫ਼ੀ

pliable, pliant (ਪਲਾਇਬਲ, ਪਲਾਇਅੰਟ) *a* ਨਰਮ, ਲਚਕਦਾਰ, ਲਿਫਵਾਂ

plight (ਪਲਾਇਟ) *n v* ਦੁਰਦਸ਼ਾ, ਦੁਰਗਤੀ, ਦਸ਼ਾ, ਅਵਸਥਾ, ਸਥਿਤੀ; ਵਚਨ, ਪ੍ਰਣ; ਪ੍ਰਤਿੱਗਿਆ ਕਰਨੀ, ਵਚਨ ਦੇਣਾ; ਕਿਸੇ ਨਾਲ ਸਾਕ ਕਰਨਾ

plot (ਪਲੋਟ) *n v* (1) ਜ਼ਮੀਨ ਜਾ ਟੁਕੜਾ, ਕਿਆਰਾ, ਪਲਾਟ; (2) (ਨਾਟਕ ਆਦਿ ਦਾ) ਕਥਾਨਕ; (3) ਛਲ, ਸਾਜ਼ਸ਼, ਗੁਪਤ ਯੋਜਨਾ; ਸਾਜ਼ਸ਼ ਕਰਨੀ, ਸਾਜ਼-ਬਾਜ਼ ਕਰਨੀ; ਖ਼ਾਕਾ ਖਿੱਚਣਾ, ਰੂਪ-ਰੇਖਾ ਬਣਾਉਣੀ

plough (ਪਲਾਉ) *n v* ਹਲ; ਵਾਹਣ, ਵਾਹੀ ਹੋਈ ਭੋਂ; ਹਲ ਵਾਹੁਣਾ; ~man ਹਾਲ਼ੀ, ਹਲਵਾਹ

ploy (ਪਲੋਇ) *n* (ਬੋਲ) ਕੰਮ, ਕਾਰਜ, ਪੰਦਾ; ਪੇਸ਼ਾ, ਕਿਰਤ; ਮੁਹਿੰਮ

pluck (ਪਲੱਕ) *v n* ਤੋੜਨਾ (ਫੁੱਲ ਆਦਿ), ਮਰੋੜਨਾ, ਖੋਹਣਾ, ਨੋਚਣਾ, ਝਪਟਣਾ, ਖਿੱਚਣਾ; ਜਿਗਰਾ, ਹੌਂਸਲਾ, ਕਲੇਜੀ

plug (ਪਲੱਗ) *n v* ਡੱਟਾ, ਗੱਟਾ, ਡਾਟ, ਬੂੰਜ, ਕਾਗ; ਮਸ਼ੀਨ ਦਾ ਪਲੱਗ; ਡੱਟਾ ਦੇਣਾ, ਡਾਟ ਲਾਉਣੀ

plumber ('ਪਲਅੱਮਅ*) *n* ਨਲਸਾਜ਼; ਨਲਕੇ ਲਾਉਣ ਵਾਲਾ; ~y ਨਲਕੇ ਨਾਲਾਂ ਆਦਿ ਫਿਟ ਕਰਨ ਦਾ ਕੰਮ

plump (ਪਲੱਅਪ) *n a adv v* ਦਸਤਾ, ਜੱਥਾ; ਸਮੂਹ, ਦਲ; ਮੋਟਾ-ਤਾਜ਼ਾ, ਗੁਦਗੁਦਾ, ਰਿਸ਼ਟ-ਪੁਸ਼ਟ; ਸਪਸ਼ਟਤਾ ਨਾਲ, ਖਰੇ ਢੰਗ ਨਾਲ; ਧੜੰਮ ਡਿਗਣਾ, ਕੁੱਟਣਾ, ਗੋਤਾ ਲਾਉਣਾ; ਫੁਲਾਉਣਾ, ਤਕੜਾ ਕਰਨਾ

plunder ('ਪਲਅੰਡਅ*) *n* ਲੁੱਟ ਦਾ ਮਾਲ, ਲੁੱਟਮਾਰ ਕਰਨੀ; ~er ਡਾਕੂ, ਲੁਟੇਰਾ, ਅਪਹਰਣ-ਕਰਤਾ

plunge (ਪਲਅੰਜ) *v n* ਡੁਬਕੀ ਮਾਰਨੀ, ਡੋਬਣਾ, ਗੋਤਾ ਦੇਣਾ; ਛਾਲ; ਔਖਾ ਕੰਮ

plural (ਪਲੁਅਰ(ਅ)ਲ) *a n* ਬਹੁਵਚਨ, ਅਨੇਕ; ~ity ਬਹੁਲਤਾ, ਅਧਿਕਤਾ, ਅਨੇਕਤਾ; ਬਹੁਤ ਜ਼ਿਆਦਾ ਗਿਣਤੀ

plus (ਪਲੱਅਸ) *prep n a* ਜਮ੍ਹਾਂ, ਜੋੜ ਕੇ, ਅਤੇ, ਨਾਲੇ, ਹੋਰ; ਵਾਧੂ; ਜੋੜ ਦਾ ਨਿਸ਼ਾਨ (+)

pluto (ਪਲੂਟਅਉ) *n* ਕੁਬੇਰ, ਯਮ, ਪਲੂਟੋ, ਨਰਕ ਦਾ ਦੇਵਤਾ; ~cracy ਪੂੰਜੀਪਤੀ ਰਾਜ; ਸਾਮੰਤ-ਵਰਗ, ਸ਼ਾਸਕ-ਵਰਗ, ਅਮੀਰਾਂ ਦਾ ਰਾਜ, ਧਨਾਢ ਤੰਤਰ; ~crat ਕੁਬੇਰ, ਸਾਮੰਤ, ਮਹਾਜਨ; ਧਨਾਢ, ਪਠਾਢ ਸ਼ਾਸਕ

ply (ਪਲਾਇ) *n v* (ਕੱਪੜੇ ਦੀ) ਤਹਿ, ਪਰਤ, ਮੁਟਾਈ; ਝੁਕਾਉ; ਚਲਾਉਣਾ (ਹਥਿਆਰ ਆਦਿ) ਲਗਾਤਾਰ ਵਰਤਣਾ, ਵਰਤੋਂ ਵਿਚ ਲਿਆਉਣਾ, ਕਾਰਜ ਕਰਨਾ

pocket ('ਪਅਕਿਟ) *n v* ਜੇਬ, ਖੀਸਾ, ਬੋੜਾ; ਥੈਲੀ, ਗੁਥਲੀ, ਝੋਲਾ; ਆਮਦਨੀ, ਆਰਥਕ ਸਾਧਨ; ਹੜੱਪ ਕਰਨਾ, ਹਜ਼ਮ ਕਰ ਜਾਣਾ; (ਵਿਅੰਗਾ) ਬੇਇੱਜ਼ਤੀ ਆਦਿ) ਸਹਾਰ ਜਾਣਾ; ~book ਜੇਬੀ ਕਿਤਾਬ, ਛੋਟੇ ਆਕਾਰ ਦੀ ਕਿਤਾਬ, ਗੁਟਕਾ; ~money ਜੇਬ ਖ਼ਰਚ

podex ('ਪਅਉਡਿਕਸ) *n* (ਸਰੀਰ ਦਾ) ਪਿੱਛਲਾ, ਹਿੱਸਾ; ਚੂਤੜ, ਡੁੱਲੀ; ਗੁਦਾ

podium ('ਪਅਉਡਿਅਮ) *n* ਮੰਚ, ਚਬੂਤਰਾ

poem (ਪਅਉਇਮ) *n* ਕਵਿਤਾ, ਕਾਵਿ-ਰਚਨਾ, ਪਦ, ਛੰਦ-ਬਧ ਰਚਨਾ

poesy ('ਪਅਉਇਜ਼ਿ) *n* (ਪ੍ਰ) ਕਾਵਿ-ਕਲਾ, ਕਾਵਿ-ਰਚਨਾ, ਛੰਦ-ਰਚਨਾ; ਕਾਵਿ-ਸੰਗ੍ਰਹਿ

poet ('ਪਅਉਇਟ) *n* ਕਵੀ, ਸ਼ਾਇਰ; ਛੰਦਕਾਰ, ਗੀਤਕਾਰ; ~aster ਤੁਕਬੰਦ, ਕਵੀਸ਼ਰ, ਘਟੀਆ ਸ਼ਾਇਰ; ~ess ਕਵਿੱਤਰੀ; ~ic, ~ical ਕਾਵਿਕ, ਕਾਵਿਮਈ, ਕਾਵਿ-ਆਤਮਕ; ~ics ਕਾਵਿ-ਸ਼ਾਸਤਰ, ਛੰਦ-ਸ਼ਾਸਤਰ, ਅਲੰਕਾਰ-ਸ਼ਾਸਤਰ, ਅਲੰਕਾਰ-ਸ਼ਾਸਤਰ, ਕਾਵਿ-ਵਿੰਨਿਆ, ਰੀਤੀ-ਸ਼ਾਸਤਰ; ~ry ਕਾਵਿ, ਕਾਵਿ-ਰਚਨਾ

poignancy ('ਪੋਇਨਯਅੰਸਿ) *n* (ਸੁਆਦ, ਗੰਧ ਦੀ) ਤੁਰਸ਼ੀ; ਚੋਭ, ਤੀਖਣਤਾ

poignant ('ਪੋਇਨਯਅੰਟ) *a* ਤੀਖਣ, ਤੀਬਰ, ਤੇਜ਼, ਚਟਪਟੀ, ਤਿੱਖੀ; ਚੁਭਵਾਂ

point ('ਪੋਇੰਟ) *n v* ਬਿੰਦੀ, ਨੁਕਤਾ, ਨੋਕ, ਦਸ਼ਮਲਵ-ਚਿੰਨ੍ਹ, ਥਾਂ, ਟਿਕਾਣਾ; ਵਿਸ਼ੈ; ਗੱਲ, ਦਰਜਾ, ਨੰਬਰ; ਇਸ਼ਾਰਾ ਕਰਨਾ, ਸੰਕੇਤ ਕਰਨਾ; ਨਿਸ਼ਾਨ ਲਾਉਣਾ; ~ed ਨੋਕਦਾਰ, ਨੋਕ ਵਾਲਾ, ਤਿੱਖੀ ਨੋਕ ਵਾਲਾ, ਚੁਭਵੀਂ, ਸਾਫ਼ ਸਾਫ਼, ਖਰੀ ਖਰੀ; ~edly ਵਿਸ਼ੇਸ਼ ਜ਼ੋਰ ਦੇ ਕੇ, ਸਾਫ਼ ਸਾਫ਼ ਦੱਸ ਕੇ, ਸਪਸ਼ਟ ਸੰਕੇਤ ਕਰ ਕੇ; ~less ਨਿਰਥਕ, ਸਾਰਹੀਣ

poison ('ਪੋਇਜ਼ਨ) *n v* ਜ਼ਹਿਰ, ਵਿਸ਼, ਵਿਸ਼ ਵਿਗਾੜਨਾ; ਵਿਸ਼ਘਣ ਪਾਉਣਾ, ਬਾਧਾ ਪਾਉਣਾ ~ous ਜ਼ਹਿਰੀਲਾ, ਜ਼ਹਿਰੀ, ਵਿਸ਼ੈਲਾ, ਵਿਹੁਲਾ

poke (ਪਊਕ) v ਹੁੱਝ ਮਾਰਨੀ, ਖੋਭਣਾ, ਚੋਭਣਾ; ਧੱਕਾ ਦੇਣਾ; ਅਰਕ ਮਾਰਨੀ

polar ('ਪਲਊਲਅ*) a ਧਰੁਵੀ, ਧਰੁਵਾਂ ਦਾ; ਕੁਤਬੀ; **~bear** ਧਰੁਵੀ ਰਿੱਛ; **~ity** ਧਰੁਵੀ ਉਲਾਰ, ਧਰੁਵੀਪਨ

pole (ਪਅਊਲ) n v (ਉੱਤਰੀ ਜਾਂ ਦੱਖਣੀ) ਧਰੁਵ; ਥੰਮ੍ਹ, ਖੰਭਾ; ਵੰਝ, ਬਾਂਸ; ਪੋਲੈਂਡ ਦਾ ਵਸਨੀਕ; ਖੰਭਾ ਗੱਡਣਾ, ਬੱਲੀ ਲਾਉਣਾ

police (ਪਅ'ਊਲੀਸ) n v ਪੁਲੀਸ; ਪੁਲੀਸ-ਵਿਭਾਗ; ਪੁਲੀਸ ਕਰਮਚਾਰੀ, ਪੁਲਸੀਏ; ਪੁਲੀਸ ਨਿਯੁਕਤ ਕਰਨੀ, ਪੁਲੀਸ ਲਾਉਣੀ; ਪ੍ਰਬੰਧ ਕਰਨਾ; **~man** ਪੁਲੀਸ ਦਾ ਸਿਪਾਹੀ, ਪੁਲੀਸ ਕਰਮਚਾਰੀ

policy ('ਪੌਲਅਸਿ) n ਨੀਤੀ, ਜੁਗਤ, ਢੰਗ, ਰੀਤ, ਵਿਧੀ; ਬੀਮਾ-ਪੱਤਰ, ਪਾਲਿਸੀ

polio (ਪਅਊਲਿਅਉ) n ਪੋਲਿਓ ਦੀ ਬੀਮਾਰੀ

polish ('ਪੌਲਿਸ਼) v n ਪਾਲਸ਼ ਕਰਨੀ, ਰੋਗਨ ਕਰਨਾ; ਚਮਕਾਉਣਾ, ਲਿਸ਼ਕਾਉਣਾ; ਪਾਲਸ਼, ਰੋਗਨ, ਚਮਕ, ਲਿਸ਼ਕ; ਸ਼ਿਸ਼ਟਤਾ; **~ed** ਪਰਿਸ਼ਕ੍ਰਿਤ, ਸ਼ਿਸ਼ਟ, ਪਾਲਸ਼ਦਾਰ

polite (ਪਅ'ਲਾਇਟ) a ਨਿਮਰਤਾ ਵਾਲਾ, ਸ਼ਿਸ਼ਟ, ਸੱਭਿਅ, ਸੁਸ਼ੀਲ; **~ness** ਨਿਮਰਤਾ, ਸ਼ਿਸ਼ਟਤਾ, ਸੁਸ਼ੀਲਤਾ

politic ('ਪੌਲਅਟਿਕ) a ਸਿਆਣਾ, ਬੁੱਧੀਮਾਨ; ਦੰਕਾਸ਼ਨਾਸ; ਨੀਤੀਵਾਨ, ਨੀਤੀਕੁਸ਼ਲ; ਅਨੁਭਵੀ, ਤਜਰਬਾਕਾਰ

political (ਪਅ'ਲਿਟਿਕਲ) a n ਰਾਜਨਤਿਕ, ਸਿਆਸੀ; ਰਾਜਸੀ, ਸ਼ਾਸਕੀ, ਰਾਜ ਪ੍ਰਬੰਧ ਸਬੰਧੀ

politician ('ਪੌਲਿ'ਟਿਸ਼ਨ) n ਸਿਆਸਤਦਾਨ; ਰਾਜਨੀਤੀਵਾਨ; ਪੇਸ਼ਾਵਰ ਰਾਜਨੀਤੀਵੇਤਾ

politicking ('ਪੌਲਿਟਿਕਿੰਡ਼) n ਸਿਆਸਤ ਬਾਜ਼ੀ

politics ('ਪੌਲਿਟਿਕਸ) n ਰਾਜਨੀਤੀ-ਸ਼ਾਸਤਰ, ਰਾਜਨੀਤੀ-ਵਿਗਿਆਨ; ਸਿਆਸਤ

polity ('ਪੌਲਅਟਿ) n ਰਾਜ-ਪ੍ਰਬੰਧ, ਰਾਜ-ਵਿਵਸਥਾ, ਸ਼ਾਸਨ-ਪ੍ਰਣਾਲੀ

poll (ਪਅਊਲ) n v ਵੋਟ ਗਿਨਣ, ਵੋਟ ਪਾਉਣ, ਵੋਟਾਂ ਦੀ ਗਿਣਤੀ; ਵੋਟ ਸਵੀਕਾਰ ਹੋਣਾ; **~ing** ਮੱਤਦਾਨ; **~ing station** ਮੱਤਦਾਨ ਕੇਂਦਰ

pollute (ਪਅ'ਲੂਟ) v ਵਿਗਾੜਨਾ, ਖ਼ਰਾਬ ਕਰਨਾ, ਗੰਦਾ ਕਰਨਾ, ਅਪਵਿੱਤਰ ਕਰਨਾ, ਪਲੀਤ ਕਰਨਾ, ਮੈਲਾ ਕਰਨਾ; **~d** ਦੂਸ਼ਿਤ, ਅਪਵਿੱਤਰ, ਗੰਧਲਾ, ਗੰਦਾ

pollution (ਪਅ'ਲੂਸ਼ਨ) n ਗੰਦਾਪਣ, ਦੂਸ਼ਣ, ਭ੍ਰਿਸ਼ਟਤਾ

polo ('ਪਅਊਲਅਉ) n ਚੁਗਾਨ, ਪੋਲੋ

polyandry ('ਪੌਲਿਐਂਡਰਿ) n ਬਹੁ-ਕੰਤੀ, ਬਹੁ-ਪਤੀਤਵ, ਇਕ ਤੀਵੀਂ ਦੇ ਇਕ ਤੋਂ ਵਧੇਰੇ ਪਤੀ ਹੋਣ ਦੀ ਪ੍ਰਥਾ

polygamy (ਪਅ'ਲਿਗਾਮਿ) n ਬਹੁ-ਵਿਆਹ, ਬਹੁ-ਪਤਨੀਤਵ

polyglot ('ਪੌਲਿਗਲੌਟ) a n ਬਹੁ-ਭਾਸ਼ਾਈ; ਬਹੁ-ਭਾਸ਼ੀ ਮਨੁੱਖ

polysemy ('ਪਅ'ਲਿਸਅਮਿ) n ਬਹੁਅਰਥਕ, ਅਨੇਕ ਅਰਥਕਤਾ

pomegranate ('ਪੌਮਿ'ਗਰੈਨਿਟ) n ਅਨਾਰ

pomp (ਪੌਂਪ) n ਠਾਠ-ਬਾਠ, ਸਜ-ਧਜ, ਧੂਮ-ਧਾਮ, ਸ਼ਾਨ, ਸ਼ੋਭਾ, ਚਮਕ-ਦਮਕ, ਆਡੰਬਰ

pomposity (ਪੌਮ'ਪੌਸਅਟਿ) n ਸ਼ਾਨ, ਠਾਠ, ਚਮਕ-ਦਮਕ; ਅਲੰਕਾਰਕਤਾ

pompous ('ਪੌਮਪਅਸ) a ਸ਼ਾਨਦਾਰ, ਭੜਕੀਲਾ, ਲਿਸ਼ਕਦਾਰ, ਸ਼ੋਭਾ ਵਾਲਾ

pond (ਪੌਂਡ) n ਟੋਭਾ, ਤਲਾਅ, ਸਰੋਵਰ; ਛੱਪੜ

ponder ('ਪੌਂਡਅ*) *v* ਵਿਚਾਰਨਾ, ਸੋਚਣਾ, ਗੌਲਣਾ; ਧਿਆਨ ਦੇਣਾ, ਗਹੁ ਕਰਨਾ, ਜਾਚਣਾ; **~able** ਭਾਰਾ, ਬੋਝਲ; ਵਜ਼ਨੀ; **~ous** ਔਖਾ, ਕਠਨ, ਬੇਢੱਬਾ, (ਸ਼ੈਲੀ) ਨੀਰਸ, ਖੁਸ਼ਕ, ਰੁੱਖੀ, ਸ਼ਬਦ-ਆਡੰਬਰ ਵਾਲੀ

pony ('ਪਅਉਨਿ) *n* ਟੱਟੂ, ਛੋਟੇ ਕੱਦ ਦਾ ਘੋੜਾ

pooh-pooh ('ਪੂ-'ਪੂ) *v* ਤਿਰਸਕਾਰਨਾ; ਦੁਰਕਾਰਨਾ, ਥੂਹ-ਥੂਹ ਕਰਨਾ

pool (ਪੂਲ) *n v* ਤਲਾਅ, ਕੁੰਡ, ਛੱਪੜ, ਟੋਭਾ, ਸਰ; ਸਾਂਝੀ ਪੂੰਜੀ, ਸਾਂਝਾ ਧਨ; ਵਿਹਾਰਕ ਸਾਧਨ ਸਾਂਝੇ ਕਰ ਲੈਣੇ; **~ed** ਇਕੱਤਰਤ, ਸੰਗ੍ਰਹਤ, ਸੰਚਤ

poor (ਪੁਅ*) *a* ਗ਼ਰੀਬ, ਕੰਗਾਲ, ਨਿਰਧਨ; ਮਾੜਾ, ਹੀਣਾ, ਨਿਮਾਣਾ, ਮੰਦੀ ਹਾਲਤ ਵਿਚ, ਬਲਹੀਣ, ਕਮਜ਼ੋਰ; **~ly** ਥੁੜ੍ਹ ਨਾਲ; ਘਟੀਆ ਤਰੀਕੇ ਨਾਲ

pop (ਪੌਪ) *n v* ਠਾਹ ਦੀ ਅਵਾਜ਼, ਟੱਕ ਦੀ ਅਵਾਜ਼, ਅਚਾਨਕ ਫਟਣ ਜਾਂ ਧਮਾਕੇ ਨਾਲ ਖੁੱਲ੍ਹਣ ਦੀ ਅਵਾਜ਼; ਟੱਕ ਕਰਕੇ ਖੋਲ੍ਹਣਾ; ਪਿਸਤੌਲ, ਬੰਦੂਕ ਆਦਿ ਚਲਾਉਣੀ; ਠਾਹ ਦੀ ਅਵਾਜ਼ ਹੋਣਾ; ਅਚਾਨਕ ਕੋਈ ਸਵਾਲ ਕਰ ਦੇਣਾ; ਟੁੱਟ ਕੇ ਪੈਣਾ; ਮੱਕੀ ਦੀਆਂ ਖਿੱਲਾਂ ਕਰਨੀਆਂ, (ਬੋਲ) ਪੌਪ, ਇਕ ਲੋਕ ਸੰਗੀਤ; **~corn** ਮੱਕੀ ਦੀਆਂ ਖਿੱਲਾਂ

pope (ਪਅਉਪ) *n* ਰੋਮਨ ਕੈਥੋਲਿਕ ਇਸਾਈਆਂ ਦਾ ਸਭ ਤੋਂ ਵੱਡਾ ਪਾਦਰੀ, ਧਰਮ-ਅਧਿਅਕਸ਼, ਪੋਪ; ਮਹਾਤਮਾ, ਧਰਮਾਤਮਾ, ਦੇਵਤਾ

poppy ('ਪੌਪਿ) *n* ਪੋਸਤ ਦਾ ਬੂਟਾ, ਖਸਖਸ

populace ('ਪੌਪਯੁਅਲਸ) *n* ਆਮ ਲੋਕ, ਜਨਤਾ, ਭੀੜ

popular ('ਪੌਪਯੁਲਅ*) *a* ਲੋਕ-ਪ੍ਰਿਯ, ਪ੍ਰਸਿੱਧ, ਮਸ਼ਹੂਰ, ਸਰਬਪ੍ਰਿਯ; ਪ੍ਰਚਲਤ; **~ity** ਲੋਕ-ਪ੍ਰਿਯਤਾ; ਪ੍ਰਸਿੱਧੀ; ਮਸ਼ਹੂਰੀ, ਸਰਬਮਾਨਤਾ

populate ('ਪੌਪਯੁਲੇਇਟ) *v* ਵੱਸਣਾ, (ਕਿਸੇ ਥਾਂ ਨੂੰ) ਵਸਾਉਣਾ, ਆਬਾਦ ਕਰਨਾ, ਆਬਾਦ ਹੋਣਾ

population ('ਪੌਪਯੁ'ਲੇਇਸ਼ਨ) *n* ਵੱਸੋਂ, ਆਬਾਦੀ; ਜਨ-ਸੰਖਿਆ, ਜਨਤਾ

populism ('ਪੌਪਯੁਲਿਜ਼(ਅ)ਮ) *n a* ਸੋਸ਼ੇਬਾਜ਼ੀ, ਸਸਤੀ ਸ਼ੋਹਰਤ

populous ('ਪੌਪਯੁਲਅਸ) *a* ਵੱਸਦਾ, ਘੁੱਗ ਵੱਸਦਾ, ਸੰਘਣੀ ਵੱਸੋਂ ਵਾਲਾ, ਘਣੀ ਆਬਾਦੀ ਵਾਲਾ, ਜਨਪੂਰਨ

porcelain ('ਪੋਸ(ਅ)ਲਿਨ) *n* ਚੀਨੀ, ਮਿੱਟੀ, ਚੀਨੀ ਦੇ ਭਾਂਡੇ; ਕੋਮਲ, ਨਾਜ਼ਕ, ਟੁੱਟਣਹਾਰ

porch (ਪੋ'ਚ) *n* ਡਿਓਡੀ; ਮਕਾਨ ਦੇ ਸਾਹਵੇਂ ਪਾਇਆ ਛੱਜਾ

pornography (ਪੋ'ਨੌਗਰਅਫ਼ਿ) *n* ਫਾਅਸ਼ ਲਿਖਤ, ਅਸ਼ਲੀਲ ਸਾਹਿਤ, ਕਾਮ ਉਕਸਾਊ ਰਚਨਾ

port (ਪੋ'ਟ) *n* (1) ਬੰਦਰਗਾਹ; (2) ਫ਼ਾਟਕ, ਮੁੱਖ ਦੁਆਰ, ਸਦਰ ਦਰਵਾਜ਼ਾ; (3) ਮਿੱਠੀ, ਲਾਲ ਰੰਗ ਦੀ ਅਤੇ ਤੇਜ਼-ਨਸ਼ੇ ਵਾਲੀ ਇਕ ਸ਼ਰਾਬ; ਜਹਾਜ਼ ਦੇ ਖੱਬੇ ਪਾਸੇ ਵੱਲ ਲੈ ਜਾਣਾ

portable ('ਪੋਟਅਬਲ) *a* ਚੁੱਕਵਾਂ, ਸਫ਼ਰੀ

portage ('ਪੋਟਿਜ) *n v* ਢੁਆਈ, ਢੋਆ-ਢੁਆਈ; ਢੋਣਾ, ਲੈ ਜਾਣਾ

porter ('ਪੋਟਅ*) *n* ਕੁਲੀ, ਭਾਰ ਮਜ਼ਦੂਰ, ਪਾਂਡੀ; ਦਰਬਾਨ, ਡਿਉਢੀਦਾਰ; **~house** ਸ਼ਰਾਬਖ਼ਾਨਾ, ਮੈਖਾਨਾ, ਸ਼ਰਾਬ ਦੀ ਦੁਕਾਨ, ਠੇਕਾ

portfolio ('ਪੋਟ'ਫੁਅਉਲਿਅਉ) *n* ਬਸਤਾ ਵਜ਼ਾਰਤ ਦਾ ਅਹੁਦਾ, ਵਜ਼ਾਰਤ ਦਾ ਵਿਭਾਗ ਮੰਤਰੀ-ਪਦ

portion ('ਪੋਸ਼ਨ) *n v* ਹਿੱਸਾ, ਵੰਡ, ਪੱਤੀ, ਦਾਜ ਵੰਡਣਾ, ਵੰਡ ਪਾਉਣੀ, ਹਿੱਸਾ ਦੇਣਾ, ਦਾਜ ਦੇਣ

portmanteau ('ਪੋਟ'ਮੈਨਟਅਉ) *n* ਚਮੜੇ ਦ

ਬਕਸਾ, ਚਮੜੇ ਦਾ ਥੈਲਾ, ਸੰਯੁਕਤ ਸ਼ਬਦ, ਸਮਾਸ

portrait ('ਪੋਟਰੇਇਟ) *n* ਤਸਵੀਰ, ਚਿੱਤਰ, ਮੂਰਤ; ਹੂ-ਬ-ਹੂ ਸ਼ਕਲ; ~**ure** ਚਿੱਤਰਕਾਰੀ, ਤਸਵੀਰ-ਸਾਜ਼ੀ, ਚਿੱਤਰਣ, ਸ਼ਬਦ-ਚਿੱਤਰ

portray (ਪੋ'ਟਰੇਇ) *v* ਚਿੱਤਰ ਬਣਾਉਣਾ, ਤਸਵੀਰ ਖਿਚਣੀ; ਉਲੀਕਣਾ, ਸ਼ਬਦ-ਚਿੱਤਰ ਉਲੀਕਣਾ

pose (ਪਾਉਜ਼) *v n* (ਸਵਾਲ) ਪੇਸ਼ ਕਰਨਾ, ਸਾਮ੍ਹਣੇ ਰੱਖਣਾ; ਦਿਖਾਵਾ ਕਰਨਾ, ਦੰਭ ਕਰਨਾ; ਢੌਂਗ ਰਚਣਾ; ਅੰਦਾਜ਼, ਢੰਗ, ਰੂਪ, ਸਥਿਤੀ, ਰੌਂ, ਢੌਂਗ; ਦਿਖਾਵਾ

position (ਪਅ'ਜ਼ਿਸ਼ਨ) *n v* ਹਾਲਤ, ਅਵਸਥਾ, ਦਸ਼ਾ, ਥਾਂ, ਟਿਕਾਣਾ, ਮੌਕਾ, ਸਥਿਤੀ; ਸਿਧਾਂਤ; ਦ੍ਰਿਸ਼ਟੀਕੋਣ; ਬਿਠਾਉਣਾ, ਟਿਕਾਉਣਾ, ਥਾਂ ਸਿਰ ਰੱਖਣਾ, ਮੋਰਚੇ ਤੇ ਡਟਣਾ; ਪਦ ਸੰਭਾਲਣਾ

positive ('ਪੌਜ਼ਅਟਿਵ) *n a* (ਗਣਿਤ) ਧਨ, (ਰਿਣ ਦੇ ਵਿਰੋਧ ਵਿਚ) ਸਕਾਰਾਤਮਕ, (ਵਿਆ) ਸਧਾਰਨ ਵਿਸ਼ੇਸ਼ਣ, ਅਵੱਸ਼ਕ, ਸਪਸ਼ਟ, ਨਿਰਸੰਦੇਹ, ਸੱਚਾ, ਨਿਸ਼ਚੇਆਤਮਕ, ਅਸਲੀ, ਭੌਤਕ

positivism ('ਪੌਜ਼ਅਟਿਵਜ਼(ਅ)ਮ) *n* ਪ੍ਰਤੱਖਵਾਦ, ਪ੍ਰਮਾਣਵਾਦ

possess (ਪਅ'ਜ਼ੈਸ) *v* ਮਾਲਕ ਹੋਣਾ, ਮੁਆਮੀ ਹੋਣਾ, ਅਧਿਕਾਰ ਰੱਖਣਾ, ਕਬਜ਼ਾ ਕਰਨਾ, ਯੁਕਤ ਹੋਣਾ, (ਭੂਤ ਪਰੇਤ ਦਾ) ਚੰਬੜੇ ਹੋਣਾ; ~**ion** ਅਧਿਕਾਰ, ਮਾਲਕੀ, (ਕਾ) ਦਖ਼ਲ, ਕਾਨੂੰਨੀ ਕਬਜ਼ਾ, ਮਲਕੀਅਤ, ਮਿਲਖ, ਜਾਇਦਾਦ, ਧਨ-ਮਾਲ ਦੌਲਤ; ~**ive** (ਵਿਆ) ਸੰਬੰਧ-ਵਾਚੀ, ਸੰਬੰਧ (ਕਾਰਕ), ਅਧਿਕਾਰਾਤਮਕ, ਕਬਜ਼ੇ ਦਾ

possibility ('ਪੌਸਅ'ਬਿਲਅਟਿ) *n* ਸੰਭਾਵਤਾ, ਸੰਭਾਵਨਾ, ਹੋਣਹਾਰੀ, ਸੰਭਵ ਘਟਨਾ, ਸੰਭਵ ਅਵਸਥਾ

possible ('ਪੌਸਅਬਲ) *a n* ਸੰਭਵ, ਮੁਮਕਨ, ਹੋ ਸਕਣ ਵਾਲਾ, ਹੋਣਹਾਰ, ਮਾਕੂਲ

possibly ('ਪੌਸਅਬਲਿ) *a n* ਸ਼ਾਇਦ, ਸੰਭਾਵਨਾ ਦੇ ਰੂਪ ਵਿਚ

post (ਪਾਉਸਟ) *n v adv* (1) ਥੰਮ੍ਹਾ, ਥਮੂਲਾ, ਖੰਭਾ, ਕੌਲਾ, ਮੁੰਨਾ, ਕਿਲਾ; (2) ਡਾਕ ਰਾਹੀਂ ਚਿੱਠੀਆਂ ਪਹੁੰਚਾਉਣਾ; ਮੁਕੱਰਰ ਕੀਤੀਆਂ ਚੌਂਕੀਆਂ; ਮੋਰਚਾ, ਕਿਲ੍ਹਾ, ਗਾਰਡ, ਕੋਟ, ਵਪਾਰਕ ਕੇਂਦਰ, ਡਿਊਟੀ ਦੀ ਥਾਂ, ਆਸਾਮੀ, ਪਦ, ਨੌਕਰੀ, ਅਹੁਦਾ, ਕਾਗ਼ਜ਼ ਦਾ ਆਕਾਰ; (3) ਮਗਰਲਾ, ਉੱਤਰ-ਕਾਲੀਨ, ਪਿੱਛੋਂ, ਮਗਰੋਂ ਪਿਛਲਾ; ਚਿੱਠੀਆਂ ਆਦਿ ਡਾਕ ਵਿਚ ਪਾਉਂਦੀਆਂ, ਡਾਕ ਰਾਹੀਂ ਭੇਜਣਾ, ਚਿਪਕਾਉਣਾ, ਪ੍ਰਚਾਰ ਕਰਨਾ; ਕਾਹਲ ਕਰਨੀ (ਪਦਵੀ ਉੱਤੇ) ਨਿਯੁਕਤ ਕਰਨਾ, (ਹਿਸਾਬ ਵਾਲੀ ਵਹੀ ਉੱਤੇ) ਚੜ੍ਹਾ ਦੇਣਾ, ਸੂਚਨਾ ਦੇਣੀ; ਕਾਹਲ ਵਿਚ; ਤੇਜ਼ੀ ਨਾਲ; ~**card** ਪੱਤਰ, ਡਾਕ ਦਾ ਕਾਰਡ; ~**man** ਡਾਕੀਆ, ਹਰਕਾਰਾ; ~**office** ਡਾਕਖ਼ਾਨਾ, ਡਾਕਘਰ, ਟੱਪਾਘਰ; **by return of~** ਵਾਪਸੀ ਡਾਕ; ~**age** ਡਾਕ ਦਾ ਮਹਿਸੂਲ, ਡਾਕ-ਭਾੜਾ; ~**ing** ਡਾਕ ਵਿਚ ਭੇਜਣਾ, ਸਥਾਪਨਾ, ਨਿਯੁਕਤੀ; ਤੈਨਾਤੀ, ਰਜਿਸਟਰ ਵਿਚ ਚੜ੍ਹਾਉਣਾ; ~**al** ਡਾਕ ਸਬੰਧੀ, ਡਾਕਖ਼ਾਨੇ ਸਬੰਧੀ; ~**date** ਆਗਾਮੀ ਮਿਤੀ ਪਾਉਣੀ; ~**war** ਜੁੱਧ-ਉਪਰੰਤ

poster ('ਪਾਉਸਟਅ*) *n* ਇਸ਼ਤਿਹਾਰ, ਵਿਗਿਆਪਨ-ਪੱਤਰ

posterior (ਪੌਸ'ਟਿਅਰਿਅ*) *a n* ਪਿੱਛੇ ਦਾ, ਮਗਰਲਾ, ਚਿੱਤੜ, ਪਿੱਛਾ, ਉੱਤਰ-ਵਰਤੀ

posterity (ਪੌ'ਸਟੈਰਅਟਿ) *n* (ਦਰਸ਼) ਵੰਸ਼, ਸੰਤਾਨ, ਔਲਾਦ, ਆਉਣ ਵਾਲੀਆਂ ਨਸਲਾਂ

post-facto ('ਪਅਉਸਟ'ਫੈਕਟਅਉ) *n* ਘਟਨਾ ਤੋਂ

ਪਿੱਛੋਂ, ਕੰਮ ਹੋਣ ਦੇ ਬਾਦ

posthumous ('ਪੌਸਟਯੁਮਅਸ) *a* ਮਰਨ ਉਪਰੰਤ

postmeridiem ('ਪਅਉਸਟਮਅ'ਰਿਡਅਮ) *adv* ਛੋਟਾ ਰੂਪ P.M., ਦੁਪਹਿਰ ਮਗਰੋਂ

post-mortem ('ਪਅਉਸਟ'ਮੋਟਅਮ) *n* ਲਾਸ਼ ਦਾ ਮੁਆਇਨਾ, ਸ਼ਵ-ਪਰੀਖਿਆ

post-nuptial ('ਪਅਉਸਟ'ਨਅੱਪਸ਼ਨਅਲ) *n* ਵਿਵਾਹ-ਉਪਰੰਤ

postpone ('ਪਅਉਸ(ਟ)'ਪਅਉਨ) *v* ਸਥਗਤ ਕਰਨਾ, ਮੁਲਤਵੀ ਕਨਰਾ, ਟਾਲਣਾ; ~**d** ਸਥਗਤ, ਅੱਗੇ ਪਾਇਆ; ~**ment** ਟਾਲ-ਮਟੋਲ, ਸਥਗਨ

postposition ('ਪਅਉਸਟਪਅ'ਜ਼ਿਸ਼ਨ) *n* ਪਰਸਰਗ

postulate ('ਪੌਸਟਯੁਲਅਟ, 'ਪੌਸਟਯੁਲੇਇਟ) *n v* ਬੁਨਿਆਦੀ ਅਸੂਲ, ਆਧਾਰ-ਤੰਤ, ਪੂਰਵ-ਅਨੁਮਾਨ, ਪੂਰਵ-ਧਾਰਨਾ; ਮੰਨ ਲੈਣਾ, ਸ਼ਰਤ ਲਾ ਦੇਣਾ, ਪ੍ਰਤੀਬੰਧ ਲਾਉਣਾ, ਜ਼ਰੂਰੀ ਸ਼ਰਤ ਸਵੀਕਾਰ ਕਰਨੀ, ਦਾਅਵਾ ਕਰਨਾ

postulation ('ਪੌਸਟਯੁ'ਲੇਇਸ਼ਨ) *n* ਮੂਲ ਸ਼ਰਤ; ਆਧਾਰ ਤੱਤ

posture ('ਪੌਸਚਅ*) *n v* ਪੈਂਤੜਾ, ਅਦਾ, ਅੰਦਾਜ਼, ਸਥਿਤੀ, ਆਸਣ (ਯੋਗ ਦਾ), ਮੁਦਰਾ; ਬੈਠਕ; ਬੈਠਣ ਦਾ ਢੰਗ; ਢੰਗ ਬਣਨਾ

pot (ਪੌਟ) *n v* ਭਾਂਡਾ, ਬਰਤਨ, ਪਤੀਲਾ; ਗਮਲਾ; ਚਾਦਨੀ; ~**belly** ਰੋਗੜ; ਗੋਗੜੀਆ

potato (ਪਅ'ਟੇਇਟਅਉ) *n* ਆਲੂ; ~**chips** ਤਲੇ ਹੋਏ ਆਲੂਆਂ ਦੇ ਪਤਲੇ ਪਤਲੇ ਟੁਕੜੇ

potency ('ਪਅਉਟਅੰਸਿ) *n* ਬਲ, ਸ਼ਕਤੀ, ਸਮਰੱਥਾ, ਪ੍ਰਭਾਵਸ਼ੀਲਤਾ

potent ('ਪਅਉਟਅੰਟ) *a* ਬਲਵਾਨ, ਸ਼ਕਤੀਵਾਨ, ਤਕੜਾ, ਜ਼ੋਰਦਾਰ; ~**ial** ਹੋ ਸਕਣ ਵਾਲਾ, ਹੋਣ ਵਾਲਾ; ਸੰਭਾਵੀ; ~**iality** ਸ਼ਕਤੀ ਬਲ, ਸਮਰੱਥਾ, ਯੋਗਤਾ; ਸੰਭਾਵਨਾ, ਸੰਭਵਤਾ, ਸੰਭਵ ਸ਼ਕਤੀ, ਸਿਖਰੀ ਬਲ

potter (ਪੌਟਅ*) *n v* ਕੁਮ੍ਹਾਰ, ਘੁਮਿਆਰ, ਕੁੰਭਕਾਰ; ਨਿਕੰਮੇ ਰਹਿਣਾ, ਝੱਖ ਮਾਰਨੀ, ਟੱਕਰਾਂ ਮਾਰਨੀਆਂ; ~**y** ਕੁੰਭਕਾਰੀ, ਕੁਮ੍ਹਾਰ ਦੀ ਦੁਕਾਨ, ਕਰਕਰੀ ਦਾ ਕਾਰਖ਼ਾਨਾ

pouch ('ਪਾਉਚ) *n v* ਥੈਲੀ, ਜੇਬ, ਖੀਸਾ, ਗੁਥਲੀ; (ਪ੍ਰ) ਕਬਜ਼ੇ ਵਿਚ ਲੈਣਾ; ਹੱਥ ਵਿਚ ਲੈਣਾ; (ਬੋਲ) ਇਨਾਮ ਦੇਣਾ, ਭੇਟਾ ਕਰਨਾ, ਗੁਥਲੀ ਵਾਂਗੂੰ ਲਮਕਾਉਣਾ; ਹੜੱਪ ਕਰ ਜਾਣਾ, ਮਾਰ ਲੈਣਾ

pounce (ਪਾਉਂਸ) *v* ਝਪਟਣਾ, ਝਪਟ ਮਾਰਨੀ; ਤਾੜ ਲੈਣਾ, ਜਾਣ ਜਾਣਾ; ਪੰਜਾ, ਨਹੁੰਦਰ, ਝਪਟ

pound (ਪਾਉਂਡ) *v n* ਫੇਹਣਾ, ਚਿੱਥਣਾ, ਘੋਟਣਾ, ਕੁੱਟਣਾ, ਪੀਹਣਾ; (1) ਬਰਤਾਨੀਆ ਦਾ ਸੋਨੇ ਦਾ ਸਿੱਕਾ, ਪੌਂਡ; (2) ਤੋਲ ਦਾ ਇਕ ਵੱਟਾ, 16 ਔਂਸ; (3) ਕਾਂਜੀ ਹਾਊਸ, ਫਾਟਕ, ਕੈਦਖ਼ਾਨਾ; ਵਾੜਾ ਅਹਾਤਾ; ਔਖੀ ਘਾਟੀ

pour (ਪੋ*) *v* ਵਹਾਉ, ਡੋਲ੍ਹਣਾ, ਉਲੱਦਣਾ, ਪਲਟਨਾ, ਧਾਰ ਵਗਾਉਣੀ; ਵਗਾ ਦੇਣਾ, ਵਹਾ ਦੇਣਾ; ਪਰਵਾਹਤ ਕਰਨਾ; ਡੁਲ੍ਹਣਾ, ਵਗਣਾ, ਵਹਿਣਾ; ਪਾਉਣਾ, ਕਰਨਾ; (ਸੰਗੀਤ ਨਾਲ) ਸੁਰਾਂ ਕੱਢਦੀਆਂ; ਬਹੁਤ ਮਾਤਰਾ ਵਿਚ ਆਉਣਾ

poverty ('ਪੌਵਅਟਿ) *n* ਗ਼ਰੀਬੀ, ਕੰਗਾਲੀ, ਨਿਰਧਨਤਾ; (ਗੁਣ ਆਦਿ) ਅਣਹੋਂਦ, ਅਭਾਵ

powder ('ਪਾਉਡਅ*) *n v* ਪਾਊਡਰ, ਵਟਣਾ, ਧੂੜਾ; ਬੂਰਾ, ਚੂਰਾ, ਧੂੜ; ਚੂਰਨ, ਫੱਕੀ; ਬਾਰੂਦ; ਤਾਕਤ, ਸ਼ਕਤੀ; ਪਾਊਡਰ ਮਲਣਾ; ਪਾਊਡਰ ਜਾਂ ਧੂੜਾ ਛਿੜਕਣਾ, ਪੀਹਣਾ

power ('ਪਾਉਅ*) *n* ਸ਼ਕਤੀ, ਬਲ; ਤਾਕਤ, ਜ਼ੋਰ, ਪ੍ਰਤਿਭਾ; ਤੇਜ, ਓਜ, ਰੋਅਬ; ਸੱਤਾ, ਰਾਜ, ਹਕੂਮਤ, ਸ਼ਾਸਨ; ਅਧਿਕਾਰ; **~house, ~station** ਬਿਜਲੀ ਘਰ; **~ful** ਸ਼ਕਤੀਮਾਨ, ਬਲਵਾਨ, ਜ਼ੋਰਾਵਰ, ਤਾਕਤਵਰ; ਸਮਰੱਥ; **~less** ਨਿਰਬਲ, ਦੁਰਬਲ, ਮਾੜਾ, ਨਿਤਾਣਾ, ਹੀਣਾ, ਅਸਮਰੱਥ

practicability ('ਪਰੈਕਟਿਕ'ਬਿਲਅਟਿ) *n* ਵਿਹਾਰਕਤਾ, ਉਪਯੋਗਤਾ; ਸੰਭਵਤਾ, ਸੰਭਾਵਨਾ

practicable ('ਪਰੈਕਟਿਕਅਬਲ) *a* ਹੋਣ ਯੋਗ, ਵਿਹਾਰਕ, ਵਰਤ ਵਿਚ ਲਿਆਂਦਾ ਜਾ ਸਕਣ ਵਾਲਾ, ਸੰਭਵ

practical ('ਪਰੈਕਟੀਕਲ) *a n* ਅਮਲੀ, ਵਿਹਾਰਕ, ਕਿਰਿਆਤਮਕ, ਅਭਿਆਸ-ਸਿੱਧ; **~ity** ਵਿਹਾਰਕਤਾ; ਕਿਰਿਆਤਮਕਤਾ; **~ly** ਅਮਲੀ ਤੌਰ ਤੇ, ਵਾਸਤਵ ਵਿਚ, ਅਮਲ ਵਿਚ

practice ('ਪਰੈਕਟਿਸ) *n* ਅਭਿਆਸ, ਮਸ਼ਕ; ਵਿਹਾਰ, ਆਚਾਰ, ਘਾਸ, ਵਰਤੋਂ, ਰੀਤ, ਦਸਤੂਰ, ਪ੍ਰਥਾ, ਪੱਧਤੀ, ਰਿਵਾਜ; ਕਾਰਜ-ਪ੍ਰਣਾਲੀ, ਚਲਨ

practise ('ਪਰੈਕਟਿਸ) *v* ਅਭਿਆਸ ਕਰਨਾ, ਮਸ਼ਕ ਕਰਨੀ; ਵਿਹਾਰਕ ਰੂਪ ਦੇਣਾ; ਕੰਮ ਵਿਚ ਲਿਆਉਣਾ; ਅਮਲ ਕਰਨਾ, ਵਰਤੋਂ ਕਰਨੀ; **~d** ਅਭਿਆਸਤ, ਅਨੁਭਵੀ, ਗਿਆਨ-ਵਿਦ

practising ('ਪਰੈਕਟਿਸਿਙ) *a* ਕਿਰਿਆਸ਼ੀਲ, ਅਭਿਆਸੀ

practitioner ('ਪਰੈਕਟਿਸ਼ਨਅ*) *n* ਅਭਿਆਸੀ, ਪੇਸ਼ਾਵਰ; ਪੰਦਾ ਕਰਨ ਵਾਲਾ

pragmatic, ~al (ਪਰੈਗ'ਮੈਟਿਕ, ਪਰੈਗ'ਮੈਟਿਕਲ) *a n* ਯਥਾਰਥੀ, ਅਮਲੀ, ਕਿਰਿਆਤਮਕ, ਵਿਹਾਰਕ; ਅਸਲੀ; ਕੱਟੜ, ਪਰਿਣਾਮਵਾਦੀ, ਹਠਵਾਦੀ

pragmatist ('ਪਰੈਗਮਅਟਿਸਟ) *n* ਯਥਾਰਥਵਾਦੀ, ਵਸਤੂਵਾਦੀ, ਪ੍ਰਯੋਗਵਾਦੀ

praise (ਪਰੇਇਜ਼) *n v* ਵਡਿਆਈ, ਸਿਫ਼ਤ, ਗੁਣ, ਪ੍ਰਸੰਸਾ, ਉਸਤਤੀ, ਕੀਰਤੀ, ਮਹਿਮਾ, ਸਲਾਘਾ, ਸਲਾਹੁਣੀ; ਵਡਿਆਈ ਕਰਨੀ, ਸਿਫ਼ਤ ਦੱਸਣੀ, ਗੁਣ ਗਾਉਣੇ, ਪ੍ਰਸੰਸਾ ਕਰਨੀ, ਉਸਤਤੀ ਗਾਉਣੀ, ਕੀਰਤੀ ਕਰਨੀ; **~worthy** ਪ੍ਰਸੰਸਾਯੋਗ, ਵਡਿਆਉਣਯੋਗ

pray (ਪਰੇਇ) *v* ਬੇਨਤੀ ਕਰਨੀ, ਅਰਜ਼ ਕਰਨੀ, ਅਰਦਾਸ ਕਰਨੀ, ਪੂਜਾ ਕਰਨੀ, ਉਪਾਸਨਾ ਕਰਨੀ; **~er** ਪ੍ਰਾਰਥਨਾ, ਬੇਨਤੀ, ਅਰਜ਼, ਅਰਦਾਸ; ਜਾਚਨਾ, ਅਰਾਧਨਾ, ਉਪਾਸਨਾ, ਅਰਾਧਕ, ਪੁਜਾਰੀ, ਉਪਾਸਕ

preach (ਪਰੀਚ) *n v* ਉਪਦੇਸ਼, ਸਿੱਖਿਆ, ਪ੍ਰਵਚਨ; ਉਪਦੇਸ਼ ਦੇਣਾ; ਸਿੱਖਿਆ ਦੇਣੀ, ਦੀਖਿਆ ਦੇਣੀ; ਸਿਖਾਉਣਾ, ਪਾਠ ਪੜ੍ਹਾਉਣਾ, ਧਾਰਮਕ ਵਿਆਖਿਆ ਕਰਨੀ; **~er** ਉਪਦੇਸ਼ਕ, ਪ੍ਰਚਾਰਕ

preamble (ਪਰੀ'ਐਮਬਲ) *n* ਪ੍ਰਾਕਥਨ, ਉਥਾਨਕਾ, ਪ੍ਰਸਤਾਵਨਾ, ਭੂਮਕਾ; ਮੁੱਖਬੰਧ ਲਿਖਣਾ

precarious (ਪਰਿ'ਕੇਅਰਿਅਸ) *a* (ਪ੍ਰ) ਸੰਕਟਪੂਰਨ, ਅਨਿਸ਼ਚਤ, ਖ਼ਤਰਨਾਕ

precaution (ਪਰਿ'ਕੋਸ਼ਨ) *n* ਸਾਵਧਾਨੀ, ਸਤਰਕਤਾ, ਖ਼ਬਰਦਾਰੀ; **~ary** ਸਤਰਕਤਾਪੂਰਨ, ਖ਼ਬਰਦਾਰੀ ਵਾਲਾ

precautious (ਪਰਿ'ਕੋਸ਼ਅਸ) *a* ਸਾਵਧਾਨ, ਚੌਕਸ, ਖ਼ਬਰਦਾਰ, ਜਾਗਰੂਕ

precede (ਪਰੀ'ਸੀਡ) *v* ਪਹਿਲਾਂ ਹੋਣਾ ਜਾਂ ਵਾਪਰਨਾ, ਅੱਗੋਂ ਲਾਉਣਾ; ਪਹਿਲ ਕਰਨੀ; ਰਾਹ ਵਿਖਾਉਣਾ; ਪੂਰਵਵਰਤੀ ਹੋਣਾ; **~nce** ਪਹਿਲ, ਪ੍ਰਮੁੱਖਤਾ, ਤਰਜੀਹ, ਪ੍ਰਥਮਕਤਾ; **~nt** ਪੂਰਵ-

ਪ੍ਰਮਾਣ, ਦ੍ਰਿਸ਼ਟਾਂਤ, ਮਿਸਾਲ

preceding (ਪਰੀ'ਸੀਡਿੰਙ) *a* ਪੂਰਬਲਾ, ਪਹਿਲਾ, ਪੂਰਵ-ਵਰਤੀ, ਪੂਰਵਗਾਮੀ

precept ('ਪਰੀਸੈਪਟ) *n* ਉਪਦੇਸ਼, ਸਿੱਖਿਆ, ਨਸੀਹਤ

precinct ('ਪਰਿਸਿਡ(ਕ)ਟ) *n* ਅਹਾਤਾ, ਵਲਗਣ, ਚੁਫੇਰਾ, ਚੁਗਿਰਦਾ; ਸਰਹੱਦ

precious ('ਪਰੈੱਸ਼ਅਸ) *a* ਬਹੁਮੁੱਲਾ, ਕੀਮਤੀ, ਅਮੁੱਲਾ; ਅਤੀ ਉੱਤਮ, ਸ੍ਰੇਸ਼ਠ

precipitance, precipitancy (ਪਰਿ'ਸਿਪਿਟਅੰਸ, ਪਰਿ'ਸਿਪਿਟਅੰਸਿ) *n* ਕਾਹਲੀ, ਹਫੜਾ-ਦਫੜੀ, ਉਤਾਵਲ, ਘਾਬਰ; ਅੰਨ੍ਹੇ-ਵਾਹੀ; ਬੇਤਹਾਸ਼ਾਪਣ

precipitate (ਪਰਿ'ਸਿਪਿਟੇਇਟ) *v a* ਸੁੱਟਣਾ, ਡੇਗਣਾ; ਨਾਜ਼ਕ ਸਿਰੇ ਤਕ ਪਹੁੰਚਾਉਣਾ; ਮੂੰਹ ਭਾਰ, ਸਿਰ ਭਾਰ

precipitation (ਪਰਿ'ਸਿਪਿ'ਟੇਇਸ਼ਨ) *n* ਉਤਾਵਲਪਨ, ਕਾਹਲ, ਹਫੜਾ-ਦਫੜੀ; ਬੇਸਮਝੀ

precis ('ਪਰੇਇਸੀ) *n* ਸਾਰ, ਸਾਰਾਂਸ਼, ਤੱਤ, ਨਿਚੋੜ

precise (ਪਰਿ'ਸਾਇਸ) *a* ਅਸਲੀ, ਯਥਾਰਥ, ਵਾਸਤਵਿਕ; ਠੀਕ-ਠੀਕ, ਪੂਰਾ-ਪੂਰਾ, ਸ਼ੁੱਧ, ਸਹੀ; **~ly** ਹੂ-ਬਹੂ, ਯਥਾਰਥ ਤੌਰ ਤੇ, ਅਸਲ ਵਿਚ; **~ness** ਸੁਨਿਸ਼ਚਤਾ, ਸ਼ੁੱਧਪਤਾ

precision (ਪਰਿ'ਸਿਯ਼ਨ) *n* ਸੁਨਿਸ਼ਚਤਤਾ, ਵਿਸ਼ੁੱਧਤਾ, ਸ਼ੁੱਧਤਾ, ਠੀਕ ਦਰੁਸਤ

preclude (ਪਰਿ'ਕਲੂਡ) *v* ਰੋਕਣਾ, ਬੰਦ ਕਰਨਾ; ਪਰੇ ਰੱਖਣਾ, ਬਾਹਰ ਰੱਖਣਾ, ਵੱਖਰਾ ਕਰਨਾ

preconceive ('ਪਰੀ'ਕਅੰਨਸੀਵ) *n* ਪੂਰਵ ਸੰਕਲਪ ਬਣਾਉਣਾ, ਪੂਰਵ ਕਲਪਨਾ ਕਰਨੀ, ਪੂਰਵ ਨਿਰਣੈ ਕਰਨਾ, ਪੂਰਵ ਧਾਰਣਾ ਬਣਾਉਣਾ; **~d** ਪੂਰਵ-ਚਿੰਤਤ, ਪੂਰਵ ਅਨੁਮਾਨਤ, ਪੂਰਵ ਨਿਰਣੀਤ

preconception ('ਪਰੀਕਅੰ'ਸੈਪਸ਼ਨ) *n* ਮਨ ਦੀ ਗੰਢ, ਭਰਮ, ਬਦਗੁਮਾਨੀ, ਤਰਫਦਾਰੀ; ਪੂਰਵ-ਬੋਧ, ਪੂਰਵ-ਚਿੰਤਨ, ਪੂਰਵ-ਕਲਪਨਾ, ਪੂਰਵ-ਧਾਰਨਾ

precursive (ਪਰੀ'ਕਅ:ਸਿਵ) *a* ਪੂਰਵ-ਵਰਤੀ, ਪਹਿਲਾ, ਮੁੱਢਲਾ

precursor (ਪਰੀ'ਕਅ:ਸਅ*) *n* ਮੋਹਰੀ, ਪੂਰਵਗਾਮੀ, ਅਗਰਦੂਤ

predesignate ('ਪਰੀ'ਡੈਜ਼ਿਗਨੇਇਟ) *a v* ਪੂਰਵ-ਨਿਯਤ, ਪੂਰਵ-ਨਿਰਦਿਸ਼ਟ, ਪੂਰਵ-ਨਿਯੁਕਤ; ਪਹਿਲਾਂ ਨਿਯਤ ਕਰਨਾ

predetermine (ਪਰੀਡਿ'ਟਅ:ਮਿਨ) *v* ਅਗਾਊਂ ਮਿਥਣਾ, ਪਹਿਲਾਂ ਹੀ ਨਿਰਣੈ ਕਰ ਲੈਣਾ, ਪੂਰਵ-ਨਿਸ਼ਚੈ ਕਰਨਾ, ਪੂਰਵ-ਨਿਰਧਾਰਨ ਕਰਨਾ

predicate ('ਪਰੈਡਿਕੇਇਟ, 'ਪਰੈਂਡਿਕਅਟ) *v n* ਦਾਅਵੇ ਨਾਲ ਕਹਿਣਾ; ਵਿਧੇਯ

predication (ਪਰਿ'ਡਿਕਸ਼ਨ) *n* ਨਿਰੂਪਨ, ਪੁਸ਼ਟੀ, ਪੂਰਕ ਕਥਨ

predict (ਪਰਿ'ਡਿਕਟ) *v* ਪੂਰਵ-ਸੂਚਤ ਕਰਨਾ, ਭਵਿੱਖ-ਵਾਕ ਕਹਿਣਾ; **~ability** ਹੋਣੀ, ਭਵਿੱਖ-ਬਾਣੀ, ਭਵਿੱਖ-ਵਾਕ; **~ion** ਭਵਿੱਖ-ਵਾਕ, ਅਗੇਤੀ ਖ਼ਬਰ, ਭਾਵੀ ਕਥਨ, ਪੂਰਵ-ਸੂਚਨਾ

predominance (ਪਰਿ'ਡੌਮਿਨਅੰਸ) *n* ਜ਼ੋਰ, ਦਬਾਉ, ਦਬਦਬਾ, ਪ੍ਰਭੁਤਾ; ਅਧਿਕਤਾ; ਬੋਲਬਾਲਾ

predominant (ਪਰਿ'ਡੌਮਿਨਅੰਟ) *a* ਭਾਰੂ, ਪ੍ਰਬਲ, ਹਾਵੀ, ਪ੍ਰਮੁਖ, ਪ੍ਰਧਾਨ

predominate (ਪਰਿ'ਡੌਮਿਨੇਇਟ) *v* (ਕਿਸੇ ਉੱਤੇ) ਅਧਿਕਾਰ ਜਮਾਉਣਾ, ਭਾਰੂ ਹੋਣਾ, ਜ਼ੋਰ ਪਕੜਨਾ, ਪ੍ਰਬਲ ਹੋਣਾ, ਦਬਾਉਣਾ, ਪ੍ਰਭੁਤਾ ਜਮਾਉਣੀ, ਹਾਵੀ ਹੋਣਾ

predomination ('ਪਰਿ'ਡੋਮਿ'ਨੇਇਸ਼ਨ) *n* ਅਧਿਕਾਰ, ਪ੍ਰਭੁਤਾ, ਦਬਦਬਾ, ਪ੍ਰਬਲਤਾ, ਪ੍ਰਧਾਨਤਾ

preface ('ਪਰੈਫ਼ਿਸ) *n v* ਭੂਮਿਕਾ, ਉੱਥਾਨਕਾ, ਪ੍ਰਸਤਾਵਨਾ, ਮੁੱਖ-ਬੰਧ; ਮੁੱਖ-ਬੰਧ ਲਿਖਣਾ; ਪ੍ਰਾਰੰਭ ਕਰਨਾ

prefer (ਪਰਿਫ਼ਅ*) *n v* ਤਰੱਕੀ ਦੇਣੀ; ਵਾਧਾ ਦੇਣਾ, ਵਧਾਉਣਾ; ਬਹੁਤਾ ਪਸੰਦ ਕਰਨਾ, ਪਹਿਲ ਦੇਣੀ, ਤਰਜੀਹ ਦੇਣੀ; ~**able** ਚੰਗੇਰਾ, ਉੱਤਮ, ਅਧਿਕ ਅੱਛਾ; ~**ably** ਚੰਗੇਰਾ ਸਮਝ ਕੇ, ਤਰਜੀਹ ਦੇ ਕੇ; ~**ence** ਤਰਜੀਹ, ਲਿਹਾਜ਼, ਵਿਸ਼ੇਸ਼ਤਾ; ਪਸੰਦ; ਆਦਰ, ਸਤਿਕਾਰ; ~**ential** ਤਰਜੀਹੀ, ਲਿਹਾਜ਼ੀ, ਰਿਆਇਤੀ, ਵਿਸ਼ੇਸ਼

prefigure ('ਪਰੀ'ਫ਼ਿਗਅ*) *v* ਪੂਰਬ-ਚਿਤਰਨ ਕਰਨਾ, ਝਲਕ ਪਾਉਣਾ, ਪੂਰਬ ਆਭਾਸ ਦੇਣਾ

prefix (ਪਰੀ'ਫ਼ਿਕਸ) *v n* ਅਗੇਤਰ ਲਾਉਣਾ, ਉਪਸਰਗ ਲਾਉਣਾ, ਅੱਗੇ ਜੋੜਨਾ; ਉਪਸਰਗ, ਅਗੇਤਰ

preform (ਪਰੀ'ਫ਼ੋਮ) *v n* ਪਹਿਲਾਂ ਤੋਂ ਰਚਨਾ ਕਰਨੀ, ਪੂਰਬ-ਰਚਨਾ ਕਰਨਾ, ਪੂਰਬ-ਨਿਰਮਾਣ ਕਰਨਾ; ~**ation** ਪੂਰਬ-ਨਿਰਮਾਣ, ਪੂਰਬ-ਰਚਨਾ

pregnancy ('ਪਰੈੱਗਨਅੰਸਿ) *n* ਗਰਭ, ਪਸ

pregnant ('ਪਰੈੱਗਨਅੰਟ) *a* ਹਾਮਲਾ, ਗਰਭਵਤੀ; ਗੱਭਣ, ਆਸ ਲੱਗੀ, ਭਾਵਪੂਰਨ, ਕਲਪਨਾਸ਼ੀਲ; ਗੁਰੂ, ਅਰਥ-ਪੂਰਵ

prejudge ('ਪਰੀ'ਜਅੱਜ) *v* (ਬਿਨਾ ਪੁੱਛ-ਪੜਤਾਲ ਤੋਂ) ਫ਼ੈਸਲਾ ਕਰਨਾ, ਪੂਰਵ-ਨਿਰਣੈ ਕਰਨਾ, ਪੂਰਵ-ਨਿਸ਼ਕਰਸ਼ ਕੱਢਣਾ, ਪਹਿਲਾਂ ਤੋਂ ਹੀ ਮਨ ਬਣਾ ਲੈਣਾ

prejudice ('ਪਰੈੱਜੁਡਿਸ) *n v* ਪੱਖਪਾਤ, ਤਰਫ਼ਦਾਰੀ, ਵਿਗਾੜ; ਹਰਜ; ਪੱਖਪਾਤ ਕਰਨਾ, ਤਰਫ਼ਦਾਰੀ ਕਰਨੀ; ਵਿਗਾੜ ਦੇਣਾ; ~**d** ਪੱਖਪਾਤ ਵਾਲਾ

prejudicial ('ਪਰੈੱਜੋ'ਡਿਸ਼ਲ) *a* ਪੱਖਪਾਤੀ; ਹਾਨੀਕਾਰਕ, ਵਿਰੋਧ

preliminary (ਪਰਿ'ਲਿਮਿਨਅਰਿ) *a n* ਪ੍ਰਾਰੰਭਕ, ਮੁੱਢਲੀ, ਪ੍ਰਾਰੰਭਕ ਵਿਵਸਥਾ; ਤਿਆਰੀ

prelude ('ਪਰੈੱਲਯੂਡ) *n v* ਉੱਥਾਨਕਾ, ਪ੍ਰਸਤਾਵਨਾ, ਆਮੁਖ, ਮੁੰਡ, ਆਰੰਭ, ਭੂਮਿਕਾ; ਭੂਮਿਕਾ ਬੰਨ੍ਹਣੀ; ਮੰਗਲਾਚਰਨ ਦੇ ਤੌਰ ਤੇ ਵਰਤਣਾ

prelusive (ਪਰਿ'ਲਯੂਸਿਵ) *a* ਆਰੰਭਕ, ਮੁੱਢਲਾ, ਭੂਮਿਕਾ ਸਰੂਪ, ਪੂਰਵ-ਸੂਚਨਾਤਮਕ

premature ('ਪਰੈੱਮਅਟਯੂਅ*) *a* ਅਗੇਤਰਾ ਅਧੂਰਾ, ਕੱਚਾ, ਅਕਾਲ-ਪੱਠੂ, ਕਚਰੋਈ; ~**ly** ਅਗੇਤਰੇ ਹੀ, ਵਕਤ ਤੋਂ ਪਹਿਲਾਂ, ਕਾਹਲੀ ਕਾਹਲੀ

premeditate (ਪਰੀ'ਮੈੱਡੀਟੇਇਟ) *v a* ਪੂਰਵ-ਵਿਚਾਰ ਕਰਨਾ, ਪੂਰਵ-ਚਿੰਤਨ ਕਰਨਾ, (ਮਨ ਵਿਚ) ਨੀਂਹ ਬੰਨ੍ਹਣੀ, ਮਨਸੂਬਾ ਬੰਨ੍ਹਣਾ; ~**d** ਪੂਰਵ-ਚਿੰਤਤ, ਜਾਣ-ਬੁੱਝੀ, ਪੂਰਵ-ਕਲਪਤ

premeditation (ਪਰੀ'ਮੈੱਡਿ'ਟੇਇਸ਼ਨ) *n* ਪੂਰਵ-ਸੰਕਲਪ, ਅਗਾਊਂ ਚਿਤਵਣ

premier ('ਪਰੈੱਮਯਅ*) *n a* ਪ੍ਰਧਾਨ-ਮੰਤਰੀ, ਪ੍ਰਮੁੱਖ, ਮੁਖੀਆ, ਆਗੂ; ਪ੍ਰਧਾਨ, ਸ੍ਰੇਸ਼ਠ, ਸਰਵ-ਸ੍ਰੇਸ਼ਠ; ~**ship** ਪ੍ਰਧਾਨ-ਮੰਤਰੀ ਪਦ, ਪ੍ਰਧਾਨ-ਮੰਤਰੀ ਕਾਲ

premise ('ਪਰੈੱਮਿਸ) *n v* ਆਧਾਰ-ਵਾਕ, ਪੂਰਵ-ਵਾਕ, ਪੂਰਵ-ਕਥਿਤ ਤੱਥ; ਚਾਰ ਦੀਵਾਰੀ, ਅਹਾਤਾ

premium ('ਪਰੀਮਯਅਮ) *n* ਪ੍ਰਤਿਫਲ, ਇਵਜ਼ਾਨਾ; ਬੋਨਸ, ਲਾਭ-ਅੰਸ਼; ਬੀਮੇ ਦੀ ਕਿਸ਼ਤ, ਸਿਖਲਾਈ, ਪਟੁਵਾਈ, ਕਿਸੇ ਕਿੱਤੇ ਨੂੰ

ਸਿੱਖਣ ਦੀ ਫ਼ੀਸ; ਬਦਲਵਾਈ

promonition ('ਪਰੌਮੌਅਨਿਸ਼ਅਨ) *n* ਪੂਰਵ-ਸੂਚਨਾ, ਅਗੇਤੀ ਚੇਤਾਵਨੀ, ਅਗਾਊਂ ਸੂਹ, ਖੁੜਕ, ਪ੍ਰਬੋਧ, ਪੂਰਵ-ਬੋਧ

prenatal ('ਪਰੀਨੇਇਟਲ) *a* ਗਰਭ ਅਵਸਥਾ ਸਬੰਧੀ, ਜਨਮ ਤੋਂ ਪਹਿਲੇ, ਜਨਮ-ਪੂਰਵ

prentice ('ਪਰੈਂਨਟਿਸ) *a* ਅਨੁਭਵਹੀਣ, ਅਨਾੜੀ, ਅਲੂਣਾ, ਅਟਜਾਣ, ਮੂੜ੍ਹ

preoccupation (ਪਰੀ'ਔਕਯੁ'ਪੇਇਸ਼ਨ) *n* ਪੂਰਵ-ਧਾਰਣਾ, ਪੂਰਵ-ਨਿਰਣੈ; ਅਗੇਤਾ ਕਬਜ਼ਾ, ਪੂਰਵ ਰੁਝੇਵਾਂ, ਧਿਆਨ-ਮਗਨਤਾ

preoccupy ('ਪਰੀਔਕਯੁਪਾਇ) *v* ਕਬਜ਼ੇ ਵਿਚ ਕਰ ਲੈਣਾ, ਪੂਰਵ-ਅਧਿਕਾਰ ਕਰਨਾ, ਅਗਾਊਂ ਕਬਜ਼ਾ ਕਰਨਾ, ਸੋਚਾਂ ਵਿਚ ਡੋਬ ਰੱਖਣਾ, ਰੁੱਝਿਆ ਰੱਖਣਾ, ਪੂਰਵ-ਅਧਿਕਾਰ ਕਰਨਾ, ਵਿਚਾਰ-ਮਗਨ ਹੋਣਾ

prepaid ('ਪਰੀਪੇਇਡ) *a* ਪਹਿਲਾਂ ਦਿੱਤਾ ਗਿਆ, ਪਹਿਲੋਂ ਅਦਾ ਕੀਤਾ

preparation ('ਪਰੈੱਪਅਰੇਇਸ਼ਨ) *n* ਤਿਆਰੀ, ਪੂਰਵ-ਵਿਵਸਥਾ ਇੰਤਜ਼ਾਮ, ਬੰਦੋਬਸਤ, ਸਾਜ਼-ਸਾਮਾਨ, ਸਬਕ ਪੜਨ ਦੀ ਤਿਆਰੀ

preparatory (ਪਰਿ'ਪੈਰਅਟ(ਅ)ਰਿ) *a* ਆਯੋਜਨਾਤਮਕ, ਤਿਆਰੀ; ਆਰੰਭਕ; ਪੂਰੰਭਕ

prepare (ਪਰਿ'ਪੇਆ*) *v* ਤਿਆਰ ਕਰਨਾ; ਤੱਤਪਰ ਕਰਨਾ; ਪ੍ਰਸਤੁਤ ਕਰਨਾ; ਸਿੱਧ ਕਰਨਾ; ~d ਤਿਆਰ, ਤੱਤਪਰ; ਉਤਪੰਨ; ਪ੍ਰਾਪਤ, ਸੁਸੱਜਤ; ~dness ਤਿਆਰੀ, ਤੱਤਪਰਤਾ

preponderance (ਪਰਿ'ਪੌਨਡ੍ਰ(ਅ)ਰਅੰਸ) *n* ਪ੍ਰਬਲਤਾ, ਪ੍ਰਧਾਨਤਾ, ਅਧਿਕਤਾ, ਬਹੁਲਤਾ

preposition ('ਪਰੈੱਪਅ'ਜ਼ਿਸ਼ਨ) *n* ਪੂਰਵ-ਸਰਗ, ਸੰਬਧ ਸੂਚਕ ਸ਼ਬਦ; ~al ਸਬੰਧਕੀ, ਪੂਰਵ-ਸਰਗੀ

prerequisite ('ਪਰੀ'ਰੈਕਵਿਜ਼ਿਟ) *a n* ਬਹੁਤ ਜ਼ਰੂਰੀ, ਅਤੀ ਲੋੜੀਂਦਾ, ਪਰਤ, ਪਹਿਲੀ ਲੋੜ, ਪੂਰਵ-ਆਕਾਂਖਿਆ, ਪ੍ਰਮੁੱਖ ਅਵੱਸ਼ਕਤਾ

prerogative (ਪਰਿ'ਰੌਗਅਟਿਵ) *n* ਸ਼ਾਹੀ ਇਖ਼ਤਿਆਰ, ਪਰਮ-ਅਧਿਕਾਰ, ਜਨਮ-ਸਿੱਧ ਅਧਿਕਾਰ, ਪ੍ਰਭੁਸੱਤਾ, ਸਹਿਜ-ਸ਼ਕਤੀ; ਵਿਸ਼ੇਸ਼ ਅਧਿਕਾਰ ਵਾਲਾ

prescribe (ਪਰਿ'ਸਕਰਾਇਬ) *v* ਨਿਰਦੇਸ਼ ਕਰਨਾ, ਤਜਵੀਜ਼ ਕਰਨੀ; ਹੁਕਮ ਦੇਣਾ; ਆਗਿਆ ਕਰਨੀ; ਨੁਸਖਾ ਲਿਖਣਾ, ਨਿਯਤ ਕਰਨਾ; ~d ਨਿਯਤ, ਨਿਸ਼ਚਤ, ਨਿਰਦਿਸ਼ਟ; ਪ੍ਰਕਲਪਤ

prescription (ਪਰੀ'ਸਕਰਿਪਸ਼ਨ) *n* ਨੁਸਖਾ, ਤਜਵੀਜ਼; ਨਿਰਧਾਰਨ, ਨਿਰਦੇਸ਼ਨ, ਵਿਧੀ; ਪਰਿਪਾਟੀ

prescriptive (ਪਰੀ'ਸਕਰਿਪਟਵ) *a* ਨਿਰਧਾਰਨਾਤਮਕ, ਆਗਿਆ ਅਨੁਸਾਰ, ਵਿਧੀਪੂਰਵਕ

presence ('ਪਰੈੱਜ਼ੰਸ) *n* ਹਾਜ਼ਰੀ, ਮੌਜੂਦਗੀ, ਉਪਸਥਿਤੀ

present ('ਪਰੈੱਜ਼ੰਟ) *a n v* (1) ਹਾਜ਼ਰ, ਮੌਜੂਦ, ਅਜੋਕਾ, ਵਰਤਮਾਨ; (2) ਭੇਟਾ, ਬਖ਼ਸ਼ੀਸ਼, ਤੋਹਫ਼ਾ, ਦਛਣਾ, ਪੁਰਸਕਾਰ, ਉਪਹਾਰ, ਮਿਲਾਉਣਾ, ਭੇਟ ਕਰਾਉਣਾ, ਅੱਗੇ ਰੱਖਣਾ, ਸਾਖਿਆਤ ਕਰਨਾ, ਹਾਜ਼ਰ ਹੋਣਾ, ਉਪਸਥਿਤ ਹੋਣਾ; ~able ਸੁਡੌਲ, ਵੇਖਣਯੋਗ, ਪੇਸ਼ ਕਰਨਯੋਗ; ~ation ਭੇਟਾ, ਦਾਨ, ਉਪਹਾਰ, ਦੱਖਣਾ, ਅਰਪਣ

presently ('ਪਰੈੱਜ਼ੰਟਲਿ) *adv* ਹੁਣੇ ਹੀ, ਹੁਣ; ਥੋੜੀ ਦੇਰ ਨੂੰ, ਛੇਤੀ ਹੀ, ਤਤਕਾਲ, ਤੁਰੰਤ

preservation ('ਪਰੈੱਜ਼ਅ'ਵੇਇਸ਼ਨ) *n* ਸੰਭਾਲ,

ਸੁਰੱਖਿਆ, ਬਚਾਉ, ਰੱਖਿਆ, ਕਾਇਮੀ

preserve (ਪਰਿ'ਜ਼ਅਵ) *v n* (ਖ਼ਰਾਬ ਜਾਂ ਨੁਕਸਾਨ ਤੋਂ) ਬਚਾਉ ਰੱਖਣਾ, ਰੱਖਿਆ ਕਰਨੀ, ਸਹੀ ਸਲਾਮਤ ਰੱਖਣਾ, ਬਰਕਰਾਰ ਰੱਖਣਾ, ਕਾਇਮ ਰੱਖਣਾ; **~d** ਸੁਰੱਖਿਅਤ, ਮਹਿਫ਼ੂਜ਼

preside (ਪਰਿ'ਜ਼ਾਇਡ) *v* ਸਭਾਪਤੀ ਬਣਨਾ, ਪ੍ਰਧਾਨਗੀ ਕਰਨੀ; ਪ੍ਰਮੁੱਖ ਹੋਣਾ; **~ncy** ਪ੍ਰਧਾਨਗੀ, ਪ੍ਰਧਾਨਤਾ, ਰਾਜ, ਮਹਾਂ ਪ੍ਰਾਂਤ; **~nt** ਪ੍ਰਧਾਨ, ਰਾਸ਼ਟਰਪਤੀ, ਸਭਾਪਤੀ, ਅਧਿਅਕਸ਼; **~ntial** ਪ੍ਰਧਾਨਗੀ, ਰਾਸ਼ਟਰਪਤੀ ਸਬੰਧੀ

presiding (ਪਰਿ'ਜ਼ਾਇਡਿੰਡ) *a* ਪ੍ਰਧਾਨਗੀ ਕਰਨ ਵਾਲਾ; **-officer** ਨਿਰਵਾਚਨ ਅਫ਼ਸਰ

presidium (ਪਰਿ'ਸਿਡਿਅਮ) *n* ਸਭਾਪਤੀ-ਮੰਡਲ, ਪ੍ਰਧਾਨਗੀ-ਮੰਡਲ, (ਸਾਮਵਾਦੀ ਦੇਸ਼ਾਂ ਦੀ) ਸਥਾਈ ਸੰਮਤੀ

press (ਪਰੈੱਸ) *n v* (1) ਛਾਪਖ਼ਾਨਾ, ਛਾਪਾ, ਮਸ਼ੀਨ; (2) ਕੱਪੜੇ ਇਸਤਰੀ ਕਰਨ ਵਾਲਾ ਲੋਹਾ; (3) ਪੱਤਰਕਾਰੀ; (4) ਸ਼ਿਕੰਜਾ, ਦਬਾਉਣਾ, ਦੱਬਣਾ, ਦਬਾਉਣਾ, ਨੱਪਣਾ, ਜ਼ੋਰ ਪਾਉਣਾ, ਸ਼ਿਕੰਜੇ ਵਿਚ ਰੱਖਣਾ; **~conference** ਪੱਤਰਕਾਰੀ-ਸੰਮੇਲਨ; **~man** ਪੱਤਰਕਾਰ; ਛਪਾਈ ਕਰਮਚਾਰੀ; **~ing** ਅਤੀ ਜ਼ਰੂਰੀ; ਪ੍ਰਬਲ; ਜ਼ੋਰਦਾਰ; ਭਾਰੀ; **~ure** ਦਬਾਉ; ਦਾਬ; ਜ਼ੋਰ, ਤੰਗੀ, ਮੁਸੀਬਤ; ਸਖ਼ਤੀ; ਤਕਲੀਫ਼, ਜ਼ਬਰ, ਜ਼ਬਰਦਸਤੀ; ਨਪੀੜ; **~urize** ਦਬਾਉ ਪਾਉਣਾ; ਜ਼ੋਰ ਪਾਉਣਾ

prestige (ਪਰੈਸੰਟੀਜ) *n* ਪ੍ਰਤਿਸ਼ਠਾ; ਚਤੁਤਲ; ਇੱਜ਼ਤ, ਮਾਨ, ਸਾਖ਼, ਪ੍ਰਤਾਪ, ਗੌਰਵ

presumably (ਪਰਿ'ਜ਼ਯੂਮਅਬਲਿ) *adv* ਸੰਭਵ ਤੌਰ ਤੇ, ਮਿਥਤ ਰੂਪ ਵਿਚ

presume (ਪਰਿ'ਜ਼ਯੂਮ) *v* ਪਰਿਕਲਪਨਾ ਕਰਨੀ, ਫ਼ਰਜ਼ ਕਰਨਾ, ਕਿਆਸ ਕਰਨਾ, ਮੰਨਣਾ

presumption (ਪਰਿ'ਜ਼ਅੰ(ਪ)ਸ਼ਨ) *n* ਕਿਆਸ, ਗੁਮਾਨ, ਪਰਿਕਲਪਨਾ, ਖ਼ਿਆਲ, ਸੰਭਾਵਨਾ; ਗੁਸਤਾਖ਼ੀ

presumptive (ਪਰਿ'ਜ਼ਅੰ(ਪ)ਟਿਵ) *a* ਕਿਆਸੀ; ਫ਼ਰਜ਼ੀ, ਅਨੁਮਾਨੀ

presumptuous (ਪਰਿ'ਜ਼ਅੰ(ਪ)ਚੁਅਸ) *a* ਗੁਸਤਾਖ਼, ਸ਼ੋਖ, ਜ਼ਿੱਦੀ, ਹਠੀ, ਢੀਠ ਅਤਿ ਅਭਿਮਾਨੀ

presuppose (ਪਰੀ'ਸਅੱਪਅਊਜ਼) *v* ਪੂਰਵ ਧਾਰਨਾ ਬਣਾਉਣੀ, ਪੂਰਵ ਅਨੁਮਾਨ ਲਾਉਣਾ

presupposition (ਪਰੀ'ਸਅੱਪਅ'ਜ਼ਿਸ਼ਨ) *n* ਪੂਰਵ-ਅਨੁਮਾਨ, ਪੂਰਵ-ਧਾਰਨਾ

pretence (ਪਰਿ'ਟੈੱਸ) *n* ਬਹਾਨਾ, ਛਲ, ਕਪਟ; ਅਡੰਬਰ

pretend (ਪਰਿ'ਟੈਂਡ) *v* ਬਹਾਨਾ ਕਰਨਾ, ਮਕਰ ਕਰਨਾ, ਢੌਂਗ ਕਰਨਾ, ਦਿਖਾਵਾ ਕਰਨਾ

pretension (ਪਰਿ'ਟੈਨਸ਼ਨ) *n* ਦਾਅਵਾ; ਬਹਾਨਾ; ਡੀਂਗ, ਫੜ੍ਹ, ਆਡੰਬਰ; ਦੰਭ

pretext ('ਪਰੀਟੈਕਸਟ) *n v* ਛਲ, ਕਪਟ, ਬਹਾਨਾ, ਚੁੱਚਰ, ਹੀਲ-ਹੁੱਜਤ, ਕਪਟ ਕਰਨਾ, ਹੀਲ-ਹੁੱਜਤ ਕਰਨੀ

pretty ('ਪਰਿਟਿ) *a adv* (ਬੱਚੇ ਜਾਂ ਤੀਵੀਂ ਲਈ) ਸੁੰਦਰ, ਮਲੂਕ, ਬਾਂਕਾ, ਅਲਬੇਲਾ; (ਗੀਤ) ਉੱਤਮ;

prevail (ਪਰਿ'ਵੇਇਲ) *v* ਹਾਵੀ ਹੋਣਾ, ਛਾ ਜਾਣਾ, ਗ਼ਾਲਬ ਹੋਣਾ, ਪ੍ਰਬਲ ਹੋਣਾ, ਭਾਰੂ ਹੋਣਾ, ਜ਼ੋਰ ਫੜਨਾ; **~ing** ਪ੍ਰਚਲਤ; ਪ੍ਰਧਾਨ, ਪ੍ਰਬਲ, ਸਰਬ ਸਧਾਰਨ

prevalence ('ਪਰੈੱਵਅਲਅੰਸ) *a* ਪ੍ਰਚਲਨ; ਬੋਲ-ਬਾਲਾ, ਹੋਂਦ

prevalent (ਪਰੈੱਵ੍ਯਅਲਅੰਟ) *a* ਪ੍ਰਚਲਤ, ਵਿਆਪਕ

prevent (ਪਰਿਵੈੱਂਟ) *v* ਰੋਕਣਾ, ਹੋੜਨਾ, ਵਰਜਣਾ, ਨਿਸ਼ੇਧ ਕਰਨਾ, ਮਨ੍ਹਾ ਕਰਨਾ; ~ion ਰੋਕ, ਵਿਘਨ, ਰੁਕਾਵਟ, ਨਿਰੋਧ, ਠਾਕ, ਅਟਕਾ; ~ive ਨਿਵਾਰਕ, ਨਿਰੋਧਕ, ਨਿਸ਼ੇਧਕ

previous ('ਪਰੀਵ੍ਯਅਸ) *a* ਪਿਛਲਾ, ਪੂਰਵ, ਬੀਤਿਆ; ~ly ਪਹਿਲਾਂ, ਪੂਰਵ

prey (ਪਰੇਇ) *n v* ਸ਼ਿਕਾਰ; ਬਲੀ; ਸ਼ਿਕਾਰ ਮਾਰਨਾ ਜਾਂ ਕਰਨਾ

price (ਪਰਾਇਸ) *n v* ਮੁੱਲ, ਕੀਮਤ, ਦਰ; ਭਾਅ; ਮੁੱਲ ਲਾਉਣਾ; ~less ਅਮੋਲ, ਅਣਮੋਲ

prick (ਪਰਿਕ) *v n* ਚੋਭਣਾ ਜਾਂ ਚੁੱਭਣਾ, ਵਿੰਨ੍ਹਣਾ, ਗੱਡਣਾ; ਚਿੰਦਣਾ, ਚੋਭ, ਸੁਰਾਖ, ਛਿਦਰ, ਛੇਕ; ~le ਨੋਕਦਾਰ ਕੰਡਾ; ਕੰਡਾ ਚੁਭਣਾ ਜਾਂ ਚੁਭਾਉਣਾ; ਸੱਲਣਾ; ਵਿੰਨ੍ਹਣਾ; ~ly ਕੰਡਿਆਲੀ (ਝਾੜੀ); ਕੰਡੇਦਾਰ; ਖਿਝੂ, ਚਿੜਚੜਾ (ਵਿਅਕਤੀ); ~ly heat ਪਿੱਤ

pride (ਪਰਾਇਡ) *n v* ਅਭਿਮਾਨ, ਘਮੰਡ; ਗੁਮਾਨ; ਅਹੰਕਾਰ; ਘਮੰਡ ਕਰਨਾ; ਅਭਿਮਾਨ ਕਰਨਾ

priest (ਪਰੀਸਟ) *n* ਪਾਦਰੀ; ਪੁਜਾਰੀ, ਪਰੋਹਤ, ਇਮਾਮ; ~craft ਪਰੋਹਤਾਈ; ~hood ਪਰੋਹਤਪਣ, ਪਾਦਰੀਗਿਰੀ

prima ('ਪਰੀਮਅ) *a* ਪ੍ਰਮੁੱਖ, ਪ੍ਰਧਾਨ, ਪ੍ਰਥਮ; ~cy ਪ੍ਰਧਾਨਤਾ, ਪ੍ਰਮੁੱਖਤਾ, ਲਾਟ ਪਾਦਰੀ ਦਾ ਪਦ

prima facie ('ਪਰਾਇਮਅ'ਫੇਇਸੀ) (L) *adv a* ਪਹਿਲੀ ਦ੍ਰਿਸ਼ਟੀ ਨਾਲ, ਪ੍ਰਤੱਖ, ਪਰਗਟ ਤੌਰ ਤੇ

primarily ('ਪਰਾਇਮ(ਅ)ਰਅਲਿ) *adv* ਮੂਲ ਰੂਪ ਵਿਚ, ਮੁੱਖ ਰੂਪ ਵਿਚ, ਪ੍ਰਧਾਨ, ਵੱਡਾ

primary ('ਪਰਾਇਮਅਰਿ) *a* ਪੁਰੱਤਕ, ਮੁੱਢਲਾ, ਪ੍ਰਥਮ; ਬੁਨਿਆਦੀ, ਮੂਲਕ, ਮੂਲ

prime ('ਪਰਾਇਮ) *a n v* ਪ੍ਰਧਾਨ, ਪ੍ਰਮੁੱਖ, ਮਹੱਤਵਪੂਰਨ; ਉੱਤਮ, ਸਰਵਸ਼੍ਰੇਸ਼ਠ, ਪ੍ਰਥਮ, ਮੌਲਕ, ਪ੍ਰਾਥਮਕ; ~cost ਮੂਲ ਲਾਗਤ; ~minister ਪ੍ਰਧਾਨ ਮੰਤਰੀ

primer ('ਪਰਾਇਮਅ*) *n* ਬਾਲ-ਬੋਧ, ਕਾਇਦਾ, ਪ੍ਰਾਇਮਰ

primitive ('ਪਰਿਮਿਟਿਵ਼) *a n* ਪ੍ਰਾਚੀਨ, ਪੁਰੱਤਕ, ਆਦਿ ਕਾਲੀਨ; ਆਦਿ ਵਾਸੀ; ਬੁਨਿਆਦੀ ਮੂਲ; ~ness ਪ੍ਰਾਚੀਨਤਾ, ਪੁਰਾਤਨਤਾ, ਸਾਦਾਪਣ, ਮੌਲਕਤਾ

primitivism ('ਪਰਿਮਿਟਿਵ਼ਿਜ਼(ਅ)ਮ) *n* ਪ੍ਰਾਚੀਨਤਾਵਾਦ, ਆਦਿਮਤਾਵਾਦ

prince (ਪਰਿੰਸ) *n* ਸ਼ਹਿਜ਼ਾਦਾ, ਰਾਜ-ਕੁਮਾਰ, ਯੁਵਰਾਜ, ਅਧਿਰਾਜ, ਟਿੱਕਾ; ~ly ਸ਼ਾਹੀ, ਅਮੀਰੀ, ਰਈਸੀ, ਸ਼ਾਨਦਾਰ; ~ss (ਪ੍ਰ) ਸ਼ਹਿਜ਼ਾਦੀ, ਰਾਜਕੁਮਾਰੀ, ਰਾਜ-ਦੁਲਾਰੀ, ਰਾਣੀ, ਮਲਕਾ; ਯੁਵਰਾਣੀ

principal ('ਪਰਿੰਸਅਪਲ) *a n* (1) ਪ੍ਰਧਾਨ, ਮੁੱਖ, ਮੁਖੀ, ਸਰਦਾਰ, ਹੁਕਮਰਾਨ, ਅਧਿਕਰਤਾ, ਪ੍ਰਿੰਸੀਪਲ; (2) ਮੂਲ ਰਾਸ਼ੀ, ਮੂਲ, ਅਸਲ

principle ('ਪਰਿੰਸਅਪਲ) *n* ਨਿਯਮ, ਸਿਧਾਂਤ, ਅਸੂਲ, ਵਿਧੀ, ਵਿਸ਼ਵਸਥਾ

print (ਪਰਿੰਟ) *n v* ਛਾਪ, ਨਿਸ਼ਾਨ, ਠੱਪਾ, ਮੋਹਰ, ਚਿੰਨ੍ਹ; ਛਾਪਣਾ; ਛਪਵਾਉਣਾ; ਛਪਵਾ ਕੇ ਪ੍ਰਕਾਸ਼ਤ ਕਰਨਾ; ਛਿੰਬਣਾ; ਠੇਕਣਾ; ~ed matter ਛਪੀ ਹੋਈ ਸਮੱਗਰੀ; ~er ਛਾਪਕ, ਛਾਪਕਾਰ, ਮੁਦਰਕ; ਛਾਪੀ ਮਸ਼ੀਨ; ~ing ਛਪਾਈ, ਛਾਪਣ ਕਲਾ, ਮੁਦਰਣ

prior ('ਪਰਾਇਅ*) *a adv n* ਪਹਿਲਾ, ਪਹਿਲੋਂ ਦਾ, ਅਗੇਤਰਾ, ਪੂਰਵ-ਵਰਤੀ, ਪ੍ਰਥਮ; ਪਹਿਲੋਂ; ~ity ਪਹਿਲ, ਅਗੇਤ, ਪ੍ਰਥਮਤਾ, ਪੂਰਵਵਰਤਤਾ

prism ('ਪਰਿਜ਼(ਅ)ਮ) *n* ਰੰਗਾਵਲੀ ਸ਼ੀਸ਼ਾ,

(ਬ ਵ) ਇੰਦਰ-ਧਨੁਸ਼ ਦਾ ਰੰਗ, ਸਪਤ-ਵਰਣ

prison (ਪਰਿਜ਼ਨ) *n v* ਜੇਲ੍ਹਖਾਨਾ, ਬੰਦੀਖਾਨਾ, ਕੈਦਖਾਨਾ, ਹਵਾਲਾਤ, ਕਾਰਾਵਾਸ, ਬੰਦੀ-ਗ੍ਰਹਿ; ਕੈਦ ਕਰਨਾ, ਬੰਦੀ ਬਣਾਉਣਾ, ਡੱਕਣਾ; ~**er** ਕੈਦੀ, ਬੰਦੀਵਾਨ

prittle-prattle (ਪ੍ਰਿਟਲ-ਪ੍ਰੈਟਲ) *n* ਚੀਕ ਚਿਹਾੜਾ, ਬਕ-ਬਕ, ਝੱਖ

privacy (ਪਰਿਵਅਸਿ) *n* ਇਕਾਂਤ; ਪਰਦਾ, ਰਹੱਸ, ਇਕਾਂਤ ਥਾਂ

private (ਪਰਾਇਵਿਟ) *n a* ਇਕਾਂਤ, ਸੁੰਨਸਾਨ; ਗੁਪਤ ਅੰਗ, ਗੁਪਤ, ਲੁਕਵੀਂ, ਇਕਾਂਤਵਾਸੀ; ~**ly** ਗੁਪਤ ਤੌਰ ਤੇ, ਨਿਜੀ ਤੌਰ ਤੇ, ਲੁਕਵੇਂ ਢੰਗ ਨਾਲ

privation (ਪਰਾਇ'ਵੁਇਸ਼ਨ) *n* ਥੁੜ੍ਹ, ਕਮੀ, ਤੰਗੀ, ਅਭਾਵ, ਕੰਗਾਲੀ

privilege (ਪਰਿਵਿਲਿਜ਼) *n v* ਵਿਸ਼ੇਸ਼ ਅਧਿਕਾਰ; ਉਚੇਚਾ ਹੱਕ, ਰਿਆਇਤ; ਅਧਿਕਾਰ ਦੇਣਾ; ~**ed** ਵਿਸ਼ੇਸ਼ਾਧਿਕ੍ਰਿਤ

privy (ਪਰਿਵਿ) *a n* ਲੁਕਵੀਂ, ਗੁਪਤ, ਆਪਟੀ; ਟੱਟੀ-ਖ਼ਾਨਾ; ~**purse** ਰਾਜ-ਭੱਤਾ, ਨਿਜੀ ਖ਼ਰਚ; ~**seal** ਸਰਕਾਰੀ ਮੋਹਰ

prize (ਪਰਾਇਜ਼) *n* (1) ਇਨਾਮ, ਪੁਰਸਕਾਰ; (2) ਲੁੱਟ ਦਾ ਮਾਲ; ਲਛਤ

pro (ਪਰਉ) *prep* ਲਈ, ਵਾਸਤੇ, ਵਜੋਂ, ਪਤੀ; ~**s and cons** ਹੱਕ ਵਿਚ ਅਤੇ ਵਿਰੋਧੀ (ਦਲੀਲਾਂ); ਪੱਖ-ਵਿਪੱਖ ਤਰਕ

probability (ਪਰੌਬਅ'ਬਿਲਅਟਿ) *n* ਸੰਭਾਵਨਾ, ਸੰਭਵ ਗੱਲ; ਸੰਭਾਵਤ

probable (ਪਰੌਬਅਬਲ) *a* ਸੰਭਵ, ਸੰਭਾਵੀ, ਅਨੁਮਾਨਕ

probably (ਪਰੌਬਅਬਲਿ) *adv* ਸ਼ਾਇਦ, ਸੰਭਾਵਨਾ ਹੈ ਕਿ, ਆਸ ਹੈ ਕਿ, ਗ਼ਾਲਬਨ

probation (ਪਰਅ'ਬੇਇਸ਼ਨ) *n* ਪਰਤਾਵਾ, ਪਰਖ; ਪਰੀਖਿਆ, ਅਜ਼ਮਾਇਸ਼; **on**~ ਪਰਤਾਵੇ ਦੇ ਤੌਰ ਤੇ, ਪਰਖ ਅਧੀਨ, ਪਰਖ ਤੇ; ~**ary** ਅਜ਼ਮਾਇਸ਼ੀ (ਸਮਾ); ~**er** ਸਿਖਾਂਦਰੂ, ਪਰੀਖਿਆ-ਅਧੀਨ

probe ('ਪਰਅਉਬ) *n v* ਜਾਂਚ, ਛਾਣਬੀਣ; ਟਟੋਲਣਾ; ਛਾਣਬੀਣ ਕਰਨੀ; ਜਾਂਚ ਕਰਨੀ; ਪੜਤਾਲ ਕਰਨੀ, ਫਰੋਲਣਾ, ਖਰੋਚਨਾ

problem ('ਪਰੌਬਲਅਮ) *n* ਸਮੱਸਿਆ, ਪ੍ਰਸ਼ਨ, ਉਲਝਣ, ਧਰਮ-ਸੰਕਟ, ਗੁੰਝਲ; ~**atic (al)** ਸਮੱਸਿਆਤਮਕ, ਸ਼ੱਕੀ, ਅਨਿਸ਼ਚਤ, ਸੰਦੇਹੀ

procedure (ਪਰਅ'ਸੀਜਅ*) *n* ਕਾਰਜ-ਪ੍ਰਣਾਲੀ, ਪ੍ਰਕਿਰਿਆ; ਕਾਰਵਾਈ, ਅਮਲ.

proceed (ਪਰਅ'ਸੀਡ) *v* ਅੱਗੇ ਵਧਣਾ, ਨਿਕਲਣਾ (ਮਕਾਨ ਤੋਂ), ਅੱਗੇ ਚੱਲਣਾ, ਵਧਣਾ (ਕਿਸੇ ਕੰਮ ਜਾਂ ਲੇਖ ਆਦਿ ਵਿਚ) ਸ਼ੁਰੂ ਕਰਨਾ, ਕਾਰਵਾਈ ਕਰਨੀ, ਜਾਰੀ ਰੱਖਣਾ; ~**ing** ਕਾਰਵਾਈ, ਆਚਰਨ, ਵਿਹਾਰ

proceeds ('ਪਰਅਉਸੀਡਜ਼) *n* (*pl*) ਵੱਟਕ, ਪ੍ਰਾਪਤੀ, ਪੈਦਾਵਾਰ, ਆਮਦਨੀ, ਮੁਨਾਫ਼ਾ, ਵਾਧਾ, ਬਚਤ

process ('ਪਰਅਉਸੈੱਸ) *n v* ਪ੍ਰਕਿਰਿਆ, ਆਮਲ, ਤਰੀਕਾ, ਕਾਨੂੰਨੀ ਕਾਰਵਾਈ, ਇਤਲਾਹਨਾਮਾ, ਅਦਾਲਤੀ ਹੁਕਮਨਾਮਾ; ਮੁਕੱਦਮਾ ਚਲਾਉਣਾ; ਅਮਲ ਕਰਨਾ

procession (ਪਰਅ'ਸੈੱਸ਼ਨ) *n v* ਜਲੂਸ, ਸਵਾਰੀ; ਜਲੂਸ ਕੱਢਣਾ; ~**al** ਜਲੂਸੀ

proclaim (ਪਰਅ'ਕਲੇਇਮ) *v* ਐਲਾਨ ਕਰਨਾ, ਘੋਸ਼ਣਾ ਕਰਨੀ, ਢੰਡੋ ਪਿਟਣੀ, ਇਸ਼ਤਿਹਾਰ ਦੇਣਾ; ਜੰਗ ਦਾ ਐਲਾਨ ਕਰਨਾ; ~**ed** ਘੋਸ਼ਤ, ਐਲਾਨ ਕੀਤਾ, ਪ੍ਰਚਾਰਤ

proclamation ('ਪਰੌਕਲਅ'ਮੇਇਸ਼ਨ) *n* ਐਲਾਨ, ਫ਼ਰਮਾਨ; ਢੰਡੋਰਾ; ਹੋਕਾ; ਐਲਾਨ, ਘੋਸ਼ਣਾ, ਮੁਨਾਦੀ, ਡੌਂਡੀ; ਸ਼ਾਹੀ ਐਲਾਨ

procuration ('ਪਰੌਕਯੁ'ਰੇਇਸ਼ਨ) *n* ਪ੍ਰਾਪਤੀ, ਵਸੂਲੀ, ਉਪਲਬਧੀ, ਅਧਿਕਾਰ-ਪੱਤਰ, ਮੁਖ਼ਤਾਰਨਾਮਾ

procurator ('ਪਰੌਕਯੁਰੇਇਟਅ*) *n* ਖ਼ਜ਼ਾਨਾ ਅਫ਼ਸਰ, ਕਾਰਿੰਦਾ, ਗੁਮਾਸ਼ਤਾ, ਪ੍ਰਤੀਨਿਧੀ, ਮੁਖ਼ਤਾਰ

procure (ਪਰਅ'ਕਯੁਅ*) *a* ਪ੍ਰਾਪਤ ਕਰਨਾ, ਪਾਉਣਾ, ਉਪਲਬਧ ਕਰਨਾ, ਹਾਸਲ ਕਰਨਾ; ~ment ਪ੍ਰਾਪਤੀ, ਵਸੂਲੀ, ਉਪਲਬਧੀ

prodigal ('ਪਰੌਡਿਗਲ) *a* ਸ਼ਾਹ-ਖ਼ਰਚ, ਉਡਾਊ, ਉਜਾੜੂ, ਫ਼ਜ਼ੂਲ ਖ਼ਰਚ; ਮੁਕਤ-ਹੱਥ; ~ity ਸ਼ਾਹ-ਖ਼ਰਚੀ, ਫ਼ਜ਼ੂਲ ਖ਼ਰਚੀ; ਖੁੱਲ੍ਹ-ਖ਼ਰਚੀ

prodigious (ਪਰਅ'ਡਿਜਅਸ) *a* ਅਦਭੁਤ, ਅਲੋਕਕ, ਵਚਿਤੱਰ, ਅਜੀਬ, ਬਹੁਤ ਸਾਰਾ; ਵਿਰਾਟ, ਮਹਾਨ, ਜ਼ਬਰਦਸਤ; ਤੀਬਰ, ਅਸਾਧਾਰਨ

produce (ਪਰਅ'ਡਯੂਸ, 'ਪਰੌਡਯੂਸ) *v n* ਪੇਸ਼ ਕਰਨਾ, ਹਾਜ਼ਰ ਕਰਨਾ; ਪ੍ਰਕਾਸ਼ਤ ਕਰਨਾ; (ਰੇਖਾ) ਲਕੀਰ ਵਧਾਉਣੀ; ਪੈਦਾ ਕਰਨਾ, ਉਪਜਾਉਣਾ; (ਨਾਟਕ, ਤਮਾਸ਼ਾ) ਖੇਡਣਾ; ਪੈਦਾਵਾਰ, ਉਪਜ, ਉਤਪਤੀ; ਪ੍ਰਾਪਤੀ, ਆਮਦਨੀ; ~d ਉਤਪੰਨ, ਉਤਪਾਦਤ; ~r ਪੈਦਾ ਕਰਨ ਵਾਲਾ, ਪੇਸ਼ ਕਰਨ ਵਾਲਾ, ਉਤਪਾਦਕ, (ਵਸਤੂਆਂ) ਬਣਾਉਣ ਵਾਲਾ; (ਨਾਟਕ, ਤਮਾਸ਼ੇ) ਨਿਰਮਾਤਾ

producibility (ਪਰਅ'ਡਯੂਸਅ'ਬਿਲਅਟਿ) *n* ਉਤਪਾਦਨ-ਸ਼ਕਤੀ

product ('ਪਰੌਡੱਅਕਟ) *n* ਪੈਦਾਵਾਰ, ਉਪਜ, ਉਤਪਤੀ; ਫਲ, ਲਾਭ; (ਹਿਸਾਬ) ਗੁਣਨ-ਫਲ; ~ion ਪੈਦਾਵਾਰ, ਉਤਪਤੀ; ਉਪਜ; ਨਿਰਮਾਣ, ਕਲਾਕ੍ਰਿਤੀ; ~ive ਉਪਜਾਊ, ਉਤਪਾਦੀ; ~ivity ਉਤਪਾਦਤਾ; ਉਪਜਾਊਪਨ

profess (ਪਰਅ'ਫ਼ੈੱਸ) *v* ਦਾਅਵਾ ਕਰਨਾ, ਪਰਗਟ ਕਰਨਾ; ਪ੍ਰਚਾਰ ਕਰਨਾ, ਖੁੱਲ੍ਹੇ ਆਮ ਕਹਿਣਾ, ਘੋਸ਼ਣਾ ਕਰਨੀ; ਸਵੀਕਾਰ ਕਰਨਾ, ਅੰਗੀਕਾਰ ਕਰਨਾ, ਮੰਨਣਾ; ~ion ਧੰਦਾ, ਪੇਸ਼ਾ, ਰੁਜ਼ਗਾਰ, ਉਪਜੀਵਕਾ, ਕਿਰਤ-ਵਿਰਤ; ~ional ਪੇਸ਼ੇਵਰ, ਪੇਸ਼ੇ ਦਾ; ~or ਆਚਾਰੀਆ, ਪ੍ਰਾਧਿਆਪਕ, ਪ੍ਰੋਫ਼ੈਸਰ; ਨਿਸ਼ਚੇਧਾਰੀ

proficiency (ਪਰਅ'ਫ਼ਿਸ਼ੰਸਿ) *n* ਨਿਪੁੰਨਤਾ, ਪਰਿਪੱਕਤਾ, ਪ੍ਰਵੀਨਤਾ, ਮੁਹਾਰਤ

proficient (ਪਰਅ'ਫ਼ਿਸ਼ੰਟ) *a n* ਨਿਪੁੰਨ; ਮਾਹਰ, ਲਾਇਕ, ਪ੍ਰਵੀਨ

profile ('ਪਰਅਉਫ਼ਾਇਲ) *n v* ਇਕ-ਰੁਖੀ ਤਸਵੀਰ; ਇਕ-ਪਾਸੀ ਤਸਵੀਰ, ਇਕ-ਰੁਖ ਖ਼ਾਕਾ; ਸਿੰਟੀ ਦਾ ਬੰਨ੍ਹ; ਕਿਲੇ ਦਾ ਵਿੰਗਾ ਖੜ੍ਹ ਭਾਗ; ਇਕ-ਪਾਸੀ ਤਸਵੀਰ ਬਣਾਉਣਾ; ਰੇਖਾ-ਚਿੱਤਰ ਲਿਖਣਾ

profit ('ਪਰੌਫ਼ਿਟ) *n v* ਲਾਭ; ਨਫ਼ਾ; ਵਾਧਾ; ਲਾਭ ਲੈਣਾ, ਫ਼ਾਇਦਾ ਉਠਾਉਣਾ; ~able ਲਾਭਦਾਇਕ, ਲਾਹੇਵੰਦਾ, ਲਾਭਵੰਦ, ਉਪਯੋਗੀ; ~eer ਮੁਨਾਫ਼ਾਖ਼ੋਰੀ, ਨਾਜਾਇਜ਼ ਲਾਭ ਲੈਣਾ, ਨਫ਼ਾਖ਼ੋਰੀ ਕਰਨੀ; ~eering ਮੁਨਾਫ਼ਾਖ਼ੋਰੀ, ਨਫ਼ਾਖ਼ੋਰੀ, ਸੂਦਖ਼ੋਰੀ; ~less ਲਾਭਰਹਿਤ, ਨਿਰਾਰਥਕ, ਬੇਫ਼ਾਇਦਾ, ਬੇਕਾਰ

profound (ਪਰਅ'ਫ਼ਾਉਂਡ) *a n* ਡੂੰਘਾ, ਗੁੜ੍ਹਾ, (ਭਾਵ) ਘੁਕ, (ਨੀਂਦ), ਘੁੱਪ (ਹਨੇਰਾ); ਭਰਵਾਂ, ਅਤੀਅੰਤ, ਅਤੀਅਧਿਕ, ਤੀਬਰ; ਹਾਰਦਿਕ; ਗੰਭੀਰਤਾ, ਡੂੰਘਾਈ, ਤੀਬਰਤਾ; ~ness, ~ity ਗੁੜ੍ਹਤਾ, ਅਗਾਧਪਤਾ, ਘਟਾਪਟ; ਤੀਬਰਤਾ

profuse (ਪਰਅ'ਫ਼ਯੂਜ਼) *a* ਸਖ਼ੀ, ਉਦਾਰ, ਲੁਟਾਊ; ਭਰਪੂਰ, ਬਹੁਤ ਅਧਿਕ

progeny ('ਪਰੋਜਅਨਿ) *n* ਸੰਤਾਨ; ਨਸਲ, ਨਤੀਜਾ; ਫਲ

programme (ਪਰਅਉਗਰੈਮ) *n v* ਕਾਰਜਕ੍ਰਮ, ਯੋਜਨਾ, ਕਾਰਜ-ਸੂਚੀ; ਪ੍ਰੋਗਰਾਮ ਬਣਾਉਣਾ, ਯੋਜਨਾ ਬਣਾਉਣੀ; **~d** ਯੋਜਨਾਬੱਧ, ਕਾਰਜ-ਕ੍ਰਮਬੱਧ, ਪੂਰਵ-ਯੋਜਤ

progress ('ਪਰਅਉਗਰੈਸ, ਪਰਅ(ਉ)'ਗਰੈਸ) *n v* ਤਰੱਕੀ, ਉੱਨਤੀ, ਵਾਧਾ, ਪ੍ਰਗਤੀ, ਵਿਕਾਸ-ਅਵਸਥਾ; ਜਾਰੀ ਰਹਿਣਾ, ਚੱਲ ਰਿਹਾ, ਗੇੜਾ; ਪ੍ਰਗਤੀ ਕਰਨੀ, ਅੱਗੇ ਵਧਣਾ; **~ion** ਵਿਕਾਸ, ਉੱਨਤੀ, ਪ੍ਰਗਤੀ ਸਿਲਸਲਾ; **~ive** ਪ੍ਰਗਤੀਵਾਦੀ, ਅਗਾਂਹ-ਵਧੂ, ਤਰੱਕੀ-ਪਸੰਦ, ਅਗਾਂਹਗਾਮੀ, ਵਿਕਾਸਵਾਦੀ, ਸਿਲਸਲੇਵਾਰ, ਪ੍ਰਗਤੀਸ਼ੀਲ

prohibit (ਪਰਅ'ਹਿਬਿਟ) *v* ਵਰਜਤ ਕਰਨਾ, ਰੋਕਣਾ, ਹਟਕਣਾ, ਮਨ੍ਹਾ ਕਰਨਾ, ਵਰਜਣਾ, ਪ੍ਰਤੀਬੰਧ ਲਾਉਣਾ; **~ed** ਵਰਜਤ; ਮਨ੍ਹਾ; **~ion** ਵਰਜਣ, ਬੰਦੇਜ਼, ਮਨਾਹੀ, ਨਸ਼ੇਬੰਦੀ, ਸ਼ਰਾਬਬੰਦੀ; **~ory** ਨਿਸ਼ੇਧਾਤਮਕ, ਨਿਸ਼ੇਧੀ, ਨਿਸ਼ੇਧਵਾਦੀ

project (ਪਰਅ'ਜੈਕਟ, 'ਪਰੋਜੈਕਟ) *v n* ਸੁੱਟਣਾ, ਤਜਵੀਜ਼ ਕਰਨੀ, ਵਿਉਂਤ ਬਣਾਉਣੀ, ਯੋਜਨਾ ਤਿਆਰ ਕਰਨਾ; ਤਜਵੀਜ਼, ਖ਼ਾਕਾ, ਯੋਜਨਾ; **~or** ਚਲਚਿੱਤਰ ਜੰਤਰ, ਪ੍ਰੋਜੈਕਟਰ, ਯੋਜਨਾਕਾਰ, ਨਿਰੂਪਕ

proliferate (ਪਰਅ(ਉ)'ਲਿਫ਼ਅਰੇਇਟ) *v* ਪਸਰਨਾ, ਵਾਧਾ ਹੋਣਾ

proliferation (ਪਰਅ(ਉ)'ਲਿਫ਼ਅ'ਰੇਇਸ਼ਨ) *n* ਵਾਧਾ, ਪਸਾਰ, ਪਲਰਣ

prolific (ਪਰਅ(ਉ)'ਲਿਫ਼ਿਕ) *a* ਉਪਜਾਊ, ਫਲਦਾਇਕ; ਬਹੁ-ਉਪਜਾਊ; ਭਰਿਆ, ਭਰਵਾਂ; **~ation** ਕ੍ਰਮਕ ਵਿਕਾਸ; ਕ੍ਰਮਬੱਧ ਵਾਧਾ; ਸਿਲਸਲੇਵਾਰ ਤਰੱਕੀ

prologue ('ਪਰਅਉਲੋਂਗ) *n* ਮੁੱਖ-ਬੰਧ, ਪ੍ਰਸਤਾਵਨਾ, ਮੰਗਲਾਚਰਨ, ਭੂਮਕਾ

prolong (ਪਰਅ(ਉ)'ਲੋਂਡ) *v* ਲਮਕਾਉਣਾ, ਵਿਸਤਾਰ ਦੇਣਾ, ਦੀਰਘ ਕਰਨਾ, ਵਧਾ ਦੇਣਾ, ਪ੍ਰਸਾਰਤ ਕਰਨਾ; **~ation** ਲਮਕਾਉ, ਵਧਣ, ਵਿਸਤਾਰ, ਫੈਲਾਉ

prominence, prominency ('ਪਰੋਮਿਨਅੰਸ, 'ਪਰੋਮਿਨਅੰਸਿ) *n* ਮਹੱਤਾ, ਮਸ਼ਹੂਰੀ, ਪ੍ਰਸਿੱਧੀ, ਉਭਾਰ; ਦਬਾਣ; ਪ੍ਰਧਾਨਤਾ, ਪ੍ਰਮੁੱਖਤਾ, ਵਿਸ਼ਿਸ਼ਟਤਾ

prominent ('ਪਰੋਮਿਨਅੰਟ) *a* ਉੱਭਰਿਆ; ਅੱਗੇ ਵਧਿਆ; ਉੱਨਤ, ਪ੍ਰਸਿੱਧ, ਉੱਘਾ, ਮਸ਼ਹੂਰ, ਸ਼੍ਰੇਸ਼ਠ, ਵਿਸ਼ਿਸ਼ਟ

promise ('ਪਰੋਮਿਸ) *n v* ਵਚਨ, ਇਕਰਾਰ, ਕੌਲ, ਪ੍ਰਣ; ਪ੍ਰਤਿਗਿਆ; ਇਕਰਾਰ ਕਰਨਾ; **~d** ਸੰਭਾਵਤ, ਕਲਪਤ

promising ('ਪਰੋਮਿਸਿਙ) *a* ਹੋਣਹਾਰ, ਸੰਭਾਵਨਾ ਪੂਰਨ, ਆਸ਼ਾਜਨਕ

promissory ('ਪਰੋਮਿਸਅਰਿ) *a* ਆਸ਼ਾਪੂਰਨ, ਸੰਭਾਵਨਾ-ਪੂਰਨ; **~note** ਪਰਨੋਟ, ਵਚਨ-ਪੱਤਰ

promote (ਪਰਅ'ਮਅਉਟ) *v* ਵਧਾਉਣਾ, ਤਰੱਕੀ ਦੇਣੀ, ਦਰਜਾ ਵਧਾਉਣਾ, ਪਦ-ਉੱਨਤੀ ਕਰਨਾ, ਅਨੁਪ੍ਰਾਣਤ ਕਰਨਾ; **~r** ਸਮਰਥਕ, ਉਤੇਜਤ ਕਰਨ ਵਾਲਾ; ਉਤਸਾਹਕ

prompt (ਪਰੋਂ(ਪ)ਟ) *a v* ਤਿਆਰ, ਤਤਪਰ, ਤਿਆਰ-ਬਰ-ਤਿਆਰ, ਝਟਪਟ, ਤੁਰੰਤ; ਉਕਸਾਉਣਾ, ਚੁੱਕਣਾ; **~er** ਉਤੇਜਕ, ਪਰੇਰਕ, ਪ੍ਰਾਮਪਟਰ; **~ing** ਪਰੇਰਨਾ, ਟੁੰਬਣ, ਉਤੇਜਨਾ, ਅਨੁਬੋਧਨ, ਪ੍ਰਾਪਟਿੰਗ

promulgate ('ਪਰੌਮਲਗੇਇਟ) v ਐਲਾਨ ਕਰਨਾ, ਘੋਸ਼ਤ ਕਰਨਾ; (ਕਾ) ਲਾਗੂ ਕਰਨਾ, ਜਾਰੀ ਕਰਨਾ

promulgation ('ਪਰੌਮਲਗੇਇਸ਼ਨ) n ਪ੍ਰਕਾਸ਼ਨ, ਘੋਸ਼ਣਾ, ਡੌਂਡੀ, ਮੁਨਾਦੀ, ਐਲਾਨ

prone (ਪ੍ਰਅਉਨ) a ਮੂਧਾ, ਉਂਧੀ, ਮੂੰਹ-ਭਾਰ; ਚੁਫ਼ਾਲ, ਚਿੱਤ

pronoun (ਪ੍ਰਅਉਨਾਉਨ) n (ਵਿਆ) ਸਰਵਨਾਮ, ਪੜਨਾਂਵ

pronounce (ਪ੍ਰਅ'ਨਾਉਂਸ) v ਉਚਾਰਨਾ, ਬੋਲਣਾ, ਕਹਿਣਾ, ਪੜ੍ਹਨਾ; ਐਲਾਨ ਕਰਨਾ; ਨਿਰਣਾ ਦੇਣਾ; ~d ਉਚਾਰਨ, ਸਪਸ਼ਟ, ਨਿਸਚਤ, ਘੋਸ਼ਤ

pronunciation (ਪ੍ਰਅ'ਨੱਨਸਿ'ਏਇਸ਼ਨ) n ਉਚਾਰਨ, ਉਚਾਰਨ-ਵਿਧੀ

proof (ਪਰੂਫ਼) n v ਸਬੂਤ, ਪ੍ਰਮਾਣ, ਗਵਾਹੀ, ਸਾਖੀ, ਸਿੱਧੀ; ਸੋਧ ਕਰਨੀ, ਸਿੱਧ ਬਣਾਉਣਾ, ਨਿਸ਼ਪ੍ਰਭਾਵੀ ਬਣਾਉਣਾ; **~reader** ਪਰੂਫ਼-ਰੀਡਰ, ਸੋਧਨ-ਕਰਤਾ

prop (ਪ੍ਰੌਪ) n v ਥੰਮ੍ਹੀ, ਟੇਕ, ਆਸਰਾ, ਢੋਹ, ਸਹਾਰਾ, ਅਸਰਾ; ਥੰਮ੍ਹੀ ਦੇਣੀ, ਢੋਹ ਲਾਉਣੀ, ਟੇਕ ਦੇਣੀ, ਆਸਰਾ ਦੇਣਾ, ਸੰਭਾਲਣਾ

propaganda ('ਪਰੌਪਅ'ਗੈਂਡਅ) n ਪ੍ਰਚਾਰ, ਪ੍ਰਸਾਰ

propagandist (ਪਰੌਪਅ'ਗੈਂਡਿਸਟ) n ਪ੍ਰਚਾਰਕ, ਪ੍ਰਸਾਰਕ

propagate ('ਪਰੌਪਅਗੇਇਟ) v ਪ੍ਰਚਾਰ ਕਰਨਾ, ਪ੍ਰਕਾਸ਼ਤ ਕਰਨਾ; ਅੱਗੇ ਵਧਾਉਣਾ; ਵਧਾਉਣਾ, ਫੈਲਾਉਣਾ

propagation ('ਪਰੌਪਅ'ਗੇਇਸ਼ਨ) n ਵਾਧ-ਫੁਲਾਟ, ਵਰਧਨ, ਖਿਲਾਰ

propagator ('ਪਰੌਪਅਗੇਇਟਅ*) n ਉਤਪਾਦਕ, ਪ੍ਰਚਾਰਕ, ਪ੍ਰਸਾਰਕ

propel (ਪਰਅ'ਪੈੱਲ) v ਪਰੇਰਤ ਕਰਨਾ, ਅੱਗੇ ਧੱਕਣਾ, ਠੇਲ੍ਹਣਾ, ਰੇੜ੍ਹਨਾ; **~ler** ਪਰੇਰਕ, ਪ੍ਰਵਰਤਕ

proper (ਪਰੌਪਅ*) a ਵਾਸਤਵਿਕ, ਯੋਗ, ਸਹੀ, ਉਚਿਤ, (ਪ੍ਰ) ਨਿੱਜੀ, ਸੰਗਤ, ਯਥਾਰਥ, ਠੀਕ-ਠਾਕ; **~ly** ਉਚਿਤ ਰੀਤੀ ਨਾਲ, ਠੀਕ ਤਰ੍ਹਾਂ, ਸਾਊ ਢੰਗ ਨਾਲ

property ('ਪਰੌਪਅਟਿ) n ਜਾਇਦਾਦ; ਸੰਪੱਤੀ, ਮਾਲ-ਧਨ, ਮਲਕੀਅਤ

prophecy ('ਪਰੌਫ਼ਿਸਿ) n ਭਵਿੱਖਬਾਣੀ; ਇਲਹਾਮ

prophesy ('ਪਰੌਫ਼ਿਸਾਇ) v ਭਵਿੱਖ ਬਾਰੇ ਦੱਸਣਾ, ਭਵਿੱਖਬਾਣੀ ਕਰਨੀ, ਪੂਰਵ-ਸੂਚਨਾ ਦੇਣੀ

prophet ('ਪਰੌਫ਼ਿਟ) n ਈਸ਼ਵਰ-ਦੂਤ, ਭਵਿੱਖ-ਵਕਤਾ, ਪੈਗ਼ੰਬਰ; **~ic, ~ical** ਅਗੰਮੀ; ਇਲਹਾਮੀ, ਪੈਗ਼ੰਬਰੀ

propitious (ਪਰਅ'ਪਿਸ਼ਅਸ) a ਸੁਲੱਖਣਾ, ਅਨੁਕੂਲ, ਸੁਤ (ਲਗਨ), ਕਿਰਪਾਲੂ, ਕਲਿਆਣਕਾਰੀ

proportion (ਪਰਅ'ਪੋਸ਼ਨ) n ਅਨੁਪਾਤ; ਨਿਸਬਤ; **~able** ਤੁਲ, ਸਮ-ਤੋਲ, ਤੁਲਵਾਂ; **~al** ਅਨੁਰੂਪ, ਤੁਲ ਨਿਸਬਤੀ, ਸਮ-ਤੁਲ; **~ate** ਸਮ-ਤੋਲ, ਤੁਲਵਾਂ, ਅਨੁਰੂਪ

proposal (ਪਰਅ'ਪਅਉਜ਼ਲ) n ਪ੍ਰਸਤਾਵ, ਸੁਝਾਉ, ਪ੍ਰਸਥਾਪਨਾ, ਤਜਵੀਜ਼, ਵਿਆਹ-ਪ੍ਰਸਤਾਵ

propose (ਪਰਅ'ਪਅਉਜ਼) v ਤਜਵੀਜ਼ ਕਰਨਾ, ਪ੍ਰਸਤਾਵ ਰੱਖਣਾ, ਇਰਾਦਾ ਰੱਖਣਾ, ਸੁਝਾਉ ਦੇਣਾ, ਮਤਾ ਪੇਸ਼ ਕਰਨਾ; **~d** ਪ੍ਰਸਤਾਵਤ; ਪ੍ਰਸਥਾਪਤ; **~r** ਪ੍ਰਸਤਾਵਕ, ਇੱਛਾ ਪਰਗਟ ਕਰਨ ਵਾਲਾ

propound (ਪਰਅ'ਪਾਉਂਡ) v ਪੇਸ਼ ਕਰਨਾ,

ਵਿਚਾਰ-ਗੋਚਰੇ ਕਰਨੀ

proprietor (ਪਰਅ'ਪਰਾਇਟਅ*) n ਸੁਆਮੀ, ਮਾਲਕ

propriety (ਪਰਅ'ਪਰਾਇਟਿ) n ਉਚਿਤਤਾ, ਮਰਯਾਦਾ

propulsion (ਪਰਅ'ਪਅਲਸ਼ਨ) n ਧੱਕਾ, ਠੇਲ੍ਹਾ, ਦਬਾਉ, ਉਤਸਾਹ, ਉਤੇਜਨਾ

prorogate ('ਪਰਅਉਅਰੋਇਟ) v ਉਠਾ ਦੇਣਾ; ਸਥਗਤ ਕਰਨਾ

prorogation ('ਪਰਅਉਰਅ'ਗੋਇਸ਼ਨ) n ਸਥਗਨ

prorogue (ਪਰਅ'ਰਗਉ) v ਸਭਾ ਨੂੰ ਅਨੀਸ਼ਮਿਥ ਸਮੇਂ ਲਈ ਸਥਗਤ ਕਰਨਾ, ਵਿਸਰਜਨਾ

prosaic (ਪਰਅ(ਉ)ਜ਼ੇਇਕ) a ਗੱਦ ਰੂਪ; ਨੀਰਸ, ਬੇਸੁਆਦੀ, ਰੁੱਖਾ

proscribe (ਪਰਅ(ਉ)'ਸਕਰਾਇਬ) v ਨਾਜਾਇਜ਼ ਕਰਾਰ ਦੇਣਾ, ਮਨਾਹੀ ਕਰਨੀ, ਜ਼ਬਤ ਕਰਨਾ, ਦੇਸ਼ ਨਿਕਾਲਾ ਦੇਣਾ

proscription (ਪਰਅ(ਉ)'ਸਕਰਿਪਸ਼ਨ) n ਮਨਾਹੀ, ਰੁਕਾਵਟ, ਜ਼ਬਤੀ, ਦੇਸ਼ ਨਿਕਾਲਾ

prose (ਪਰਅਉਜ਼) n v ਗੱਦ, ਵਾਰਤਕ, ਖ਼ੁਸ਼ਕ ਭਾਸ਼ਨ, ਗੱਦ ਰੂਪ ਦੇਣਾ

prosecute ('ਪਰੌਸਿਕਯੂਟ) v ਪਿੱਛਾ ਕਰਨਾ; ਪੈਰਵੀ ਕਰਨਾ ਮੁਕੱਦਮਾ ਚਲਾਉਣਾ

prosecution ('ਪਰੌਸਿ'ਕਯੂਸ਼ਨ) n ਪੈਰਵੀ ਮੁਕੱਦਮਾ

prosodic (ਪਰਅ'ਸੌਡਿਕ) a ਛੰਦ-ਸ਼ਾਸਤਰ ਸੰਬਧੀ

prosody ('ਪਰੌਸਅਡਿ) n ਛੰਦ-ਸ਼ਾਸਤਰ, ਪਿੰਗਲ

prospect ('ਪਰੌਸਪੈੱਕਟ, ਪਰਅ'ਸਪੈੱਕਟ) n v ਦ੍ਰਿਸ; ਭਵਿੱਖ, ਸੰਭਾਵਨਾ; ~ive ਹੋਣ ਵਾਲਾ, ਸੰਭਾਵੀ; ~us ਵਿਵਰਣ-ਪੱਤਰਕਾ, ਬਿਉਰਾ ਪੁਸਤਕ, ਪ੍ਰਾਸਪੈਕਟਸ

prosper ('ਪਰੌਸਪਅ*) v ਉੱਨਤੀ ਕਰਨੀ, ਵਧਣਾ-ਫੁੱਲਣਾ, ਸਫਲ ਹੋਣਾ, ਖ਼ੁਸ਼ਹਾਲ ਹੋਣਾ; ~ity ਪ੍ਰਫੁੱਲਤਾ, ਉੱਨਤੀ, ਖ਼ੁਸ਼ਹਾਲੀ

prostitute ('ਪਰੌਸਟਿਟਯੂਟ) n v ਵੇਸਵਾ, ਕੰਜਰੀ, ਰੰਡੀ; ਬੁਰੇ ਪਾਸੇ ਵਰਤਣਾ, ਭ੍ਰਿਸ਼ਟ ਕਰਨਾ

prostitution ('ਪਰੌਸਟਿ'ਟਯੂਸ਼ਨ) n ਵੇਸਵਾ-ਜੀਵਨ, ਕੰਜਰਪੁਣਾ, ਪੇਸ਼ਾ; ਬਦਕਾਰੀ

prostrate ('ਪਰੌਸਟਰੇਇਟ) a v ਮੂਧਾ, ਚੁਫਾਲ, ਲੰਮਾ ਪਿਆ, ਮੂੰਹ ਭਾਰ ਪਿਆ; ਡੱਠਾ, ਹਾਰਿਆ; ਮੂਧਾ ਪਾਉਣਾ, ਲੰਮਾ ਪਾਉਣਾ; ਢਾਹ ਦੇਣਾ; ਡੰਡੌਤ ਕਰਨੀ

prostration (ਪਰੋ'ਸਟਰੇਇਸ਼ਨ) n (1) ਡੰਡੌਤ, ਪ੍ਰਣਾਮ; (2) ਬੇਚਾਰਗੀ

protagonist (ਪਰਅ(ਉ)'ਟੈਗਅਨਿਸਟ) n ਨੇਤਾ, ਸਮਰਥਕ, ਪੱਖ-ਪੂਰਕ, ਹਿਮਾਇਤੀ

protect (ਪਰਅ'ਟੈੱਕਟ) v ਸੁਰੱਖਿਆ ਕਰਨੀ, ਬਚਾਉਣਾ, ਰੱਖਿਆ ਕਰਨੀ, ਸ਼ਰਨ ਦੇਣੀ; ~ed ਸੁਰੱਖਿਅਤ; ~ion (ਪਾਲਟ-ਪੋਸਟ) ਰੱਖਿਆ, ਰਖਵਾਲੀ, ਬਚਾਉ, ਆਸਰਾ, ਓਹਲਾ; ~ive ਰੱਖਿਅਕ; ਸ਼ਰਨ ਦੇਣ ਵਾਲਾ

protege ('ਪਰੌਟਿਝੇਇ) n ਪਿੱਛ ਲੱਗ, ਚਮਚਾ

protest (ਪਰਅ'ਟੈੱਸਟ, 'ਪਰਅਉਟੈੱਸਟ) v n ਵਿਰੋਧ ਕਰਨਾ, ਰੋਸ ਪਰਗਟ ਕਰਨਾ; ਉਜ਼ਰ ਕਰਨਾ; ਉਜ਼ਰ, ਅਸਵੀਕਾਰ; ਰੋਸ; ਵਿਰੋਧ ਵਾਕ

protestant ('ਪਰੌਟਿਸਟਅਨਟ) n ਇਸਾਈਆਂ ਦੇ ਉਸ ਪੰਥ ਦਾ ਮੈਂਬਰ ਜੋ ਪੋਪ ਦੇ ਸਾਰੇ ਅਧਿਕਾਰਾਂ ਨੂੰ ਨਹੀਂ ਮੰਨਦਾ, ਪ੍ਰੋਟੈਸਟੈਂਟ

prototype ('ਪਰਅਉਟਅ(ਉ)ਟਾਇਪ) n ਮੂਲ ਰੂਪ, ਆਦਿ ਤੇ ਨਮੂਨਾ, ਮੂਲ, ਆਦਿ ਰੂਪ, ਮੂਲ ਵਸਤੂ, ਆਦਰਸ਼ ਰੂਪ

protrude (ਪਰਅ'ਟਰੂਡ) v ਲਮਕਾਉਣਾ,

ਵਧਾਉਣਾ, ਬਾਹਰ ਕੱਢਣਾ ਜਾਂ ਨਿਕਲਣਾ; ਜ਼ਬਰਦਸਤੀ ਘੁਸਣਾ, ਦਖ਼ਲ ਦੇਣਾ

proud (ਪਰਾਉਡ) *a* ਅਭਿਮਾਨੀ, ਘਮੰਡੀ, ਹੰਕਾਰੀ, ਮਾਣ ਕਰਨਯੋਗ, ਕਾਬਲੇ ਫ਼ਖ਼ਰ

prove (ਪਰੂਵ੍) *v* ਸਿੱਧ ਕਰਨਾ ਜਾਂ ਹੋਣਾ, ਸਾਬਤ ਕਰਨਾ ਜਾਂ ਹੋਣਾ; ਸਬੂਤ ਦੇਣਾ; ਨਿਸ਼ਚਤ ਕਰਨਾ; ਸਹੀ ਕਰਨਾ ਜਾਂ ਹੋਣਾ; ਤਸਦੀਕ ਕਰਨੀ; ~**d** ਸਿੱਧ, ਸਾਬਤ, ਪ੍ਰਮਾਣਤ

proverb ('ਪਰੌਵਅ:ਬ) *n* ਕਹਾਵਤ, ਅਖਾਣ, ਅਖਾਉਤ, ਲੋਕੋਕਤੀ

provide (ਪਰਅ'ਵਾਇਡ) *v* ਪ੍ਰਬੰਧ ਕਰਨਾ, ਤਿਆਰੀ ਕਰਨੀ, ਗੁੰਜਾਇਸ਼ ਰੱਖਣੀ, ਨਿਯੁਕਤ ਕਰਨਾ; ~**d** ਸ਼ਰਤ ਇਹ ਕਿ, ਜੇ ਕਰ, ਅਜਿਹਾ ਹੋਣ ਤੇ, ਨਿਰਦਿਸ਼ਟ ਦਿੱਤਾ

providence ('ਪਰੌਵਿਡਅੰਸ) *n* ਪੂਰਵ ਪ੍ਰਬੰਧ, ਦੂਰ-ਦ੍ਰਿਸ਼ਟੀ; ਰੱਬ, ਪਰਮੇਸ਼ਵਰ

provident ('ਪਰੌਵਿਡਅੰਟ) *a* ਵਿਵੇਕੀ, ਦਾਨਾਬੀਨਾ, ਦੂਰ-ਦਰਸ਼ੀ, ਸੰਜਮੀ; ~**ial** ਦੈਵੀ, ਭਾਗਸ਼ਾਲੀ, ਦੈਵਨੇਤੀ

providing (ਪਰਅ'ਵਾਇਡਿੰਡ) *conj* ਬਸ਼ਰਤੇ, ਜੇ, ਸ਼ਰਤ ਇਹ ਹੈ ਕਿ

province (ਪਰੌਵਿੰਸ) *n* ਪ੍ਰਦੇਸ਼, ਸੂਬਾ, ਪ੍ਰਾਂਤ, ਅਧਿਕਾਰ-ਖੇਤਰ, ਕਾਰਜ-ਖੇਤਰ

provincial (ਪਰਅ'ਵਿਨਸ਼ਲ) *n a* ਪ੍ਰਾਂਤ ਵਾਸੀ, ਪ੍ਰਾਂਤਕ, ਸੂਬਾਈ, ਗ੍ਰਾਮੀਨ

provision (ਪਰਅ'ਵਿਯ਼ਨ) *n v* ਰਸਦ, ਰਸਦ-ਪਾਣੀ, ਸਮਗਰੀ, ਸਾਮਾਨ; ਰਸਦ ਪਹੁੰਚਾਉਣਾ ਜਾਂ ਇਕੱਠਾ ਕਰਨਾ; ~**al** ਆਰਜ਼ੀ, ਅੰਤਰਕਾਲੀ, ਵਕਤੀ, ਸਾਮੇਕ, ਅਸਥਾਈ, ਅਲਪ-ਕਾਲੀਨ

proviso (ਪਰਅ'ਵਾਇਜ਼ਅਉ) *n* ਸ਼ਰਤ, ਸ਼ਰਤੀ ਵਾਕ, ਉਪਬੰਧ

provocation ('ਪਰੌਵਅ'ਕੇਇਸ਼ਨ) *n* ਉਕਸਾਹਟ, ਭੜਕਾਹਟ; ਚੁੱਕ-ਚੁਕਾ

provocative (ਪਰਅ'ਵੌਕਅਟਿਵ) *a* ਉਤੇਜਕ, ਉਕਸਾਊ, ਭੜਕਾਊ, ਭੜਕਾਵਾਂ

provoke (ਪਰਅ'ਵ੍ਅਉਕ) *v* ਉਤੇਜਤ ਕਰਨਾ, ਉਕਸਾਉਣਾ, ਚਿੜ੍ਹਾਉਣਾ, ਭੜਕਾਉਣਾ

provoking (ਪਰਅ'ਵ੍ਅਉਕਿੰਡ) *a* ਉਤੇਜਕ, ਉਕਸਾਉਣ ਵਾਲਾ, ਛੇੜਨ ਵਾਲਾ

provost ('ਪਰੌਵਅਸਟ) *n* ਕਾਲਜ ਦਾ ਮੁਖੀ, ਅਧਿਅਕਸ਼, ਧਰਮਾਚਾਰੀਆ

proximate (ਪਰੌਕਸਿਮਅਟ) *a* ਸਮੀਪ, ਨੇੜੇ ਦਾ, ਨਿਕਟਵਰਤੀ

proximity (ਪਰੌਕ'ਸਿਮਅਟਿ) *n* ਨਿਕਟਤਾ, ਸਮੀਪਤਾ, ਨੇੜ

proxy ('ਪਰੌਕਸਿ) *n* ਪ੍ਰਤਿਨਿਧਤਾ, ਦੂਜੇ ਦੀ ਥਾਂ ਤੇ ਕੰਮ ਕਰਨ ਦਾ ਅਧਿਕਾਰੀ, ਮੁਖ਼ਤਾਰਨਾਮਾ, ਪ੍ਰਤੀਨਿਧੀ ਪੱਤਰ

prude (ਪਰੂਡ) *n* ਮੀਸਣੀ; ਨਖ਼ਰੇਲੋ; ~**nce** ਸੂਝ, ਸਿਆਣਪ, ਵਿਵੇਕ, ਬੁੱਧੀ, ਦੁਨੀਆਦਾਰੀ; ~**nt** ਚੌਕਸ, ਵਿਵੇਕੀ; ਦੂਰਦਰਸ਼ੀ, ਸਿਆਣਾ, ਦੁਨੀਆਦਾਰ; ~**ntial** ਸਿਆਣਪ ਭਰਿਆ, ਵਿਵੇਕਸ਼ੀਲ, ਸਮਝਦਾਰ; ~**ry** ਨਖ਼ਰੇਬਾਜ਼ੀ

prune (ਪਰੂਨ) *v* ਕਾਂਟ-ਛਾਂਟ ਕਰਨੀ; ਕਤਰਨਾ, ਤਰਾਸ਼ਣਾ

pseudo ('ਸਯੂਡਅਉ) *pref* ਨਕਲੀ 'ਫਰਜ਼ੀ' 'ਬਣਾਉਟੀ' 'ਜਾਅਲੀ'; ~**nym** (ਲੇਖਕ ਦਾ) ਬਣਾਉਟੀ ਨਾਂ, ਉਪਨਾਮ, ਫਰਜ਼ੀ ਨਾਂ; ਕਲਪਤ ਨਾਂ

psyche ('ਸਾਇਕੀ) *n* ਮਨ; ਆਤਮਾ, ਅੰਤਹਕਰਨ

psychiatrist (ਸਾਇ'ਕਾਇਟਰਿਸਟ) *n* ਮਨੋ ਚਿਕਿਤਸਕ

psychiatry (ਸਾਇ'ਕਾਇਅਟਰਿ) *n* ਚਿਕਿਤਸਾ

psychic, -al ('ਸਾਇਕਿਕ, 'ਸਾਇਕਿਕਲ) *a* ਮਾਨਸਕ; ਆਤਮਕ; ਮਨੋ-ਵਿਗਿਆਨਕ

psycho ('ਸਾਇਕਅਉ) *pref* 'ਆਤਮਕ', 'ਮਨੋ', 'ਮਾਨਸਕ'; **~analysis** ਮਨੋ-ਵਿਸ਼ਲੇਸ਼ਣ; **~therapy** ਮਨੋਰੋਗ-ਚਿਕਿਤਸਾ; **~logical** ਮਨੋਵਿਗਿਆਨਕ, ਮਾਨਸਕ **~logist** ਮਨੋਵਿਗਿਆਨੀ; **~logy** ਮਨੋਵਿਗਿਆਨ

puberty ('ਪਯੂਬਅ'ਟਿ) *n* ਗਭਰੇਟ ਅਵਸਥਾ; ਮੁਟਿਆਰਪਣ; ਚੜ੍ਹਦੀ ਜਵਾਨੀ; ਜਵਾਨੀ ਦਾ ਆਲਮ

public ('ਪਅੱਬਲਿਕ) *n a* ਲੋਕ, ਜਨ, ਜਨ-ਸਧਾਰਨ, ਜਨਤਾ, ਆਮ ਲੋਕ; ਲੋਕਕ, ਕੌਮੀ, ਲੋਕਾਂ-ਸਬੰਧੀ; ਸਰਵਪ੍ਰਚਲਤ; **~house** ਸ਼ਰਾਬਖ਼ਾਨਾ; **~ation** ਪ੍ਰਕਾਸ਼ਤ ਪੁਸਤਕ; **~ity** ਲੋਕ-ਪ੍ਰਸਿੱਧੀ, ਪ੍ਰਕਾਸ਼ਨ, ਵਿਗਿਆਪਨ; ਪ੍ਰਚਾਰ; **~ly** ਖੁੱਲ੍ਹੇ ਤੌਰ ਤੇ, ਪਬਲਿਕ ਤੌਰ ਤੇ; ਪਰਗਟ ਰੂਪ ਵਿਚ

publication ('ਪਅੱਬਲਿਕੇਸ਼ਨ) *n* ਪ੍ਰਕਾਸ਼ਤ ਪੁਸਤਕ, ਪ੍ਰਕਾਸ਼ਨ

publish ('ਪਅੱਬਲਿਸ਼) *v* ਪ੍ਰਕਾਸ਼ਤ ਕਰਨਾ, ਛਾਪਣਾ; **~ed** ਪ੍ਰਕਾਸ਼ਤ; **~er** ਪ੍ਰਕਾਸ਼ਕ; ਪ੍ਰਚਾਰਕ, ਵਿਗਿਆਪਕ

pudency ('ਪਯੂਡਅੰਸਿ) *n* ਲੱਜਾ, ਸ਼ਰਮ; ਹਯਾ

puff (ਪਅੱਫ਼) *n v* ਫਰਾਟਾ, ਸਾਹ, ਫੂਕ, (ਹੁੱਕੇ ਦਾ) ਸੂਟਾ; ਫੂਕ ਦੇਣੀ; ਫੁਲਾਹੁਟੀ ਦੇਣਾ; ਫੁਲਾਉਣਾ; **~ing** ਅਤੀ ਪ੍ਰਸੰਸਾ, ਫੂਕ

pull (ਪੁਲ) *v n* ਆਪਣੇ ਵੱਲ ਖਿੱਚਣਾ, ਜ਼ੋਰ ਲਾਉਣਾ, ਚੁੰਬਣਾ, ਪੁੱਟ ਸੁੱਟਣਾ, ਤੋੜਨਾ; ਖਿੱਚ, ਪੂਹ-ਖਸੀਟ; ਤੜਾਉ; ਸੂਟਾ; **~down** ਇਮਾਰਤ ਢਾਹੁਣੀ; (ਹਿੰਮਤ) ਡੇਗਣੀ, ਢਾਹੁਣੀ

pulley ('ਪੁਲਿ) *n v* ਚਰਖੀ, ਗਰਾਰੀ, ਘਿਰਨੀ, ਭੌਣੀ; ਚਰਖੀ ਲਾਉਣਾ, ਘਿਰਨੀ ਲਾਉਣਾ

pullover ('ਪੁਲ'ਅਉਵਅ*) *n* ਵੱਡਾ ਸਵੈਟਰ, ਜਰਸੀ, ਕੋਟੀ

pulmonary ('ਪਅੱਲਮਅਨਅਰਿ) *a* ਫੇਫੜੇ ਬਾਰੇ; ਫੇਫੜਿਆਂ ਦਾ, ਫੇਫੜਿਆਂ ਦੇ ਰੋਗ ਨਾਲ ਪੀੜਤ

pulp (ਪਅੱਲਪ) *n v* ਗੁੱਦਾ, ਮਗ਼ਜ਼, ਮਾਵਾ (ਕਾਗ਼ਜ਼ ਬਣਾਉਣ ਲਈ); ਸਾਰ; ਗੁੱਦਾ ਕੱਢਣਾ; ਪਿਲਪਿਲਾ ਕਰਨਾ; ਫੁੱਲ ਜਾਣਾ; **~y** ਗੁੱਦੇਦਾਰ

pulse (ਪਅੱਲਸ) *n* (1) ਨਬਜ਼, ਨਾੜੀ, ਉਮੰਗ, ਜੋਸ਼, ਤਰੰਗ, ਲਹਿਰ; (2) ਦਾਲ

pulverize ('ਪਅੱਲਵ੍ਅਰਾਇਜ਼) *v* ਮਹੀਨ ਕਰਨਾ, ਪੀਹਣਾ, ਦਲਣਾ, ਬਾਰੀਕ ਕਰਨਾ, ਚੂਰ-ਚੂਰ ਕਰਨਾ

pump (ਪਅੱਮਪ) *n v* (1) ਨਲ, ਨਲਕਾ, ਪੰਪ; ਪਿਚਕਾਰੀ; (2) ਪੰਪ ਜੁਤਾ, ਗੁਰਗਾਬੀ; ਪੰਪ ਚਲਾਉਣਾ; ਪਿਚਕਾਰੀ ਚਲਾਉਣੀ

pumpkin ('ਪਅੱਮ(ਪ)ਕਿਨ) *n* ਪੇਠਾ, ਮਿੱਠਾ ਕੱਦੂ, ਹਲਵਾ ਕੱਦੂ

punch (ਪਅੱਨਚ) *n v* ਛੇਕ ਕੱਢਣ ਵਾਲੀ ਮਸ਼ੀਨ, ਛੇਦਕ ਸੰਦ, ਪੰਚ, ਛਾਪਾ; ਪੇਚਕਸ; ਮੁੱਕਾ, ਘਸੁੰਨ; ਠੂੰਗਾ, ਪੰਚ ਨਾਲ ਛੇਕ ਕਰਨਾ, ਮਰੀ ਕਰਨੀ, ਬੁਥਾੜ ਭੰਨਣਾ; ਮੁੱਕਾ ਮਾਰਨਾ

punctual ('ਪਅੰਕਚੁਅਲ) *a* ਨਿਯਮਤ, ਸਮੇਂ ਤੇ, ਵੇਲੇ ਸਮੇਂ ਦਾ ਪਾਬੰਦ, ਠੀਕ ਸਮੇਂ ਦਾ; **~ity** ਸਮੇਂ ਦਾ ਪਾਲਣ, ਸਮੇਂ ਦੀ ਪਾਬੰਦੀ, ਸਮਾਂ-ਨਿਸ਼ਠਤਾ; **~ly** ਠੀਕ ਸਮੇਂ ਤੇ, ਸਮੇਂ ਸਿਰ

punctuate ('ਪਅੰਕਚੁਏਇਟ) *v* ਵਿਸ਼ਰਾਮ-ਚਿੰਨ੍ਹ ਲਾਉਣੇ, ਟੋਕਣਾ, ਜ਼ੋਰ ਦੇਣਾ

punctuation ('ਪਅੰਕਚੁ'ਏਇਸ਼ਨ) *n* ਵਿਸ਼ਰਾਮ-ਚਿੰਨ੍ਹ, ਵਿਸ਼ਰਾਮ

puncture ('ਪਅੱਡਕਚਅ*) n v ਮੋਰੀ, ਛੇਕ, ਚੋਭਾ, ਚੋਭਤ, ਪੰਕਚਰ; ਪੰਚਰ, (ਸਾਈਕਲ); ਪੰਕਚਰ ਕਰ ਦੇਣਾ

pungency ('ਪਅੱਨਜਅੱਸਿ) n ਚੋਭ; ਤੀਖਣਤਾ; ਤੀਬਰਤਾ

pungent ('ਪਅੱਨਜਅੰਟ) a ਚੁੱਭਵਾਂ, ਕਾਟਵਾਂ, ਤਿੱਖਾ, ਕਰਾਰਾ

punish ('ਪਅੱਨਿਸ਼) v ਸਜ਼ਾ ਦੇਣੀ, ਦੰਡ ਦੇਣਾ, ਜੁਰਮਾਨਾ ਕਰਨਾ, ਜ਼ੋਰ ਨਾਲ ਮੁੱਕੇ ਮਾਰਨੇ; **~ment** ਦੰਡ, ਸਜ਼ਾ, ਚੱਟੀ, ਜੁਰਮਾਨਾ

punition (ਪਯੂ'ਨਿਸ਼ਨ) n ਦੰਡ, ਸਜ਼ਾ

punitive ('ਪਯੂਨਿਟਿਵ੍) a ਦੰਡਾਤਮ; ਦੰਡ ਰੂਪ

puny ('ਪਯੂਨਿ) a ਕਮਜ਼ੋਰ, ਮਾੜੂਆ, ਸ਼ਕਤੀਹੀਣ; ਨਿਤਾਣਾ; ਗਿੱਠਾ

pup (ਪਅੱਪ) n ਕੁੱਤੇ ਦਾ ਬੱਚਾ; ਕਤੂਰਾ

pupil ('ਪਯੂਪਲ) n ਵਿਦਿਆਰਥੀ; ਸ਼ਾਗਿਰਦ; ਸ਼ਿਸ਼; ਚੇਲਾ

puppet ('ਪਅੱਪਿਟ) n ਕੱਠਪੁਤਲੀ; ਗੁੱਡਾ; ਚਮਚਾ; **~play** ਪੁਤਲੀਆਂ ਦਾ ਤਮਾਸ਼ਾ; **~ry** ਕੱਠਪੁਤਲੀ ਕਲਾ

puppy ('ਪੱਅਪਿ) n ਕਤੂਰਾ; ਕੁੱਤੇ ਦਾ ਬੱਚਾ; ਹੋਛਾ; ਮੂਰਖ; ਛੈਲਾ; ਛਬੀਲਾ

purchase ('ਪਅ:ਚਅਸ) v n ਖਰੀਦਣਾ; ਵਿਹਾਜਣਾ, ਪ੍ਰਾਪਤ ਕਰਨਾ; ਹਾਸਲ ਕਰਨਾ; ਖ਼ਰੀਦ, ਖ਼ਰੀਦਦਾਰੀ; ਸੌਦਾ, ਮਾਲ

purchasing ('ਪਅ:ਚਅਸਿਙ) n ਖ਼ਰੀਦ; ਵਿਨਿਮਯ

pure (ਪਯੂਅ*) a ਨਿਰਮਲ, ਪਵਿੱਤਰ, ਸੁੱਚਾ, ਪਾਕ; **~ly** ਸ਼ੁਧੱਤਾ ਨਾਲ, ਨਿਰਮਲਤਾ ਨਾਲ, ਸਰਾਸਰ, ਬਿਲਕੁਲ; ਸਾਰੇ ਦਾ ਸਾਰਾ

purgation (ਪਅ:'ਗੇਇਸ਼ਨ) n ਸ਼ੋਧਣ; ਸਫ਼ਾਈ; ਰੇਚਨ, ਵਿਰੇਚਨ, ਜੁਲਾਬ; ਆਤਮ-ਸ਼ੁੱਧੀ

purgative (ਪਅ:ਗਅਟਿਵ੍) a n ਵਿਰੇਚਕ, ਰੇਚਕ; ਜੁਲਾਬੀ; ਜੁਲਾਬ; ਦਸਤਾਂ ਦੀ ਦਵਾਈ

purge (ਪਅ:ਜ) n v ਸਾਫ਼ ਕਰਨਾ, ਜੁਲਾਬ ਦੇਣਾ, ਸ਼ੁੱਧ ਕਰਨਾ, ਵਿਰੇਚਨ, ਦਸਤ

purification ('ਪਯੁਅਰਿਫ਼ਿ'ਕੇਇਸ਼ਨ) n ਸੋਧ, ਸੁਧਾਈ, ਸ਼ੁੱਧੀ, ਸ਼ੋਧਨ

purifier ('ਪਯੁਅਰਿਫ਼ਾਇਅ*) n ਸ਼ੋਧਕ, ਨਿਰਮਲਕਾਰ

purify ('ਪਯੁਅਰਿਫ਼ਾਇ) v ਸ਼ੁੱਧ ਕਰਨਾ, ਸਾਫ਼ ਕਰਨਾ, ਨਿਤਾਰਨਾ, ਸੂਤਕ ਦੂਰ ਕਰਨਾ

puritan ('ਪਯੁਅਰਿਟ(ਅ)ਨ) n ਸ਼ੁੱਧਤਾਵਾਦੀ, ਕੱਟੜਵਾਦੀ

purity ('ਪਯੁਅਰਅਟਿ) n ਪਵਿੱਤਰਤਾ, ਪਾਵਨਤਾ, ਸੁਧੱਤਾ, ਸ਼ੁੱਧੀ, ਸੁੱਚਮ, ਨਿਰਮਲਤਾ

purport (ਪਅ'ਪੋਟ,'ਪਅ:ਪੋਟ) v n ਭਾਵ ਦੇਣਾ, ਅਰਥ ਹੋਣਾ, ਮਤਲਬ ਹੋਣਾ, ਉਦੇਸ਼ ਹੋਣਾ, ਪ੍ਰਤੀਤ ਕਰਨਾ, ਤਾਤਪਰਜ, ਮਤਲਬ, ਅਰਥ, ਸਾਰਾਂਸ਼

purpose ('ਪਅ:ਪਅਸ) n v ਮੰਤਵ; ਉਦੇਸ਼, ਇਰਾਦਾ; ਨੀਅਤ, ਇਰਾਦਾ ਰੱਖਣਾ; **~ful** ਉਦੇਸ਼ਪੂਰਨ, ਅਰਥ-ਪੂਰਨ; **~less** ਵਿਅਰਥ, ਪ੍ਰਯੋਜਨਹੀਨ, ਅਰਥਹੀਨ, ਬੇਮਤਲਬ

purse (ਪਅ:ਸ) n v ਥੈਲੀ, ਬਟੂਆ, ਧਨ, ਕੋਸ਼; ਖੀਸੇ ਪਾਉਣਾ

pursuance (ਪਅ'ਸਯਅੱਸ) n ਪੈਰਵੀ, ਪਿੱਛਾ, ਪਾਲਨਾ, ਅਨੁਸਰਣ

pursue (ਪਅ'ਸਯੂ) v ਪਿੱਛਾ ਕਰਨਾ, ਖਹਿੜੇ ਪੈਣਾ, ਦੁਆਲੇ ਹੋਣਾ; ਪਾਲਣਾ ਕਰਨੀ, ਅਨੁਵਰਤਨ ਕਰਨਾ, ਮਗਰ ਪੈਣਾ, ਲੱਗੇ ਰਹਿਣਾ, ਅਨੁਸਰਣ ਕਰਨਾ

pursuit (ਪਅ'ਸਯੂਟ) n ਪੈਰਵੀ, ਪਿੱਛਾ, ਖਹਿੜਾ,

ਕੰਮ-ਕਾਜ

purview ('ਪਅ:ਵਯੂ) *n* (ਕਾ) ਅਧਿਕਾਰ ਖੇਤਰ; ਵਿਸਤਾਰ; ਪਰਯੋਜਨ

pus (ਪਅੱਸ) *n* ਪੀਪ, ਮੁਆਦ

push (ਪੁਸ਼) *v n* ਧੱਕਾ ਦੇਣਾ, ਠੇਲ੍ਹਣਾ, ਸਰਕਾਉਣਾ ਝਪਟਣਾ, ਉਛਲਣਾ, ਖਿਸਕਣਾ, ਸਰਕਣਾ, ਸਿੰਗ ਮਾਰਨਾ, ਬਾਹਰ ਕਢੱਣਾ; ਧੱਕਾ, ਠੇਲ੍ਹਾ; ਹੁੱਝ, ਹੁਝਕਾ; **~over** ਆਸਾਨੀ ਨਾਲ ਜਿੱਤਿਆ ਜਾਣ ਵਾਲਾ ਮੁਕਾਬਲਾ; **~ing** ਹੋਣਹਾਰ ਹਿੰਮਤੀ

put (ਪੁਟ) *v* ਰੱਖਣਾ, ਪਾਉਣਾ; ਧੋਣਾ; ਘੱਪਣਾ; ਚਲਾਉਣਾ ਪੱਕਣਾ, ਰਵਾਨਾ ਹੋਣਾ; **down~** ਦਬਾ ਦੇਣਾ

putrid ('ਪਯੂਟਰਿਡ) *a* ਗੰਦਾ, ਬਦਬੂ ਵਾਲਾ, ਦੁਰਗੰਧਤ, ਅਪਵਿੱਤਰ, ਹਾਨੀਕਾਰਕ; **~ity** ਦੁਰਗੰਧ, ਮਤੁੰਦ, ਬਦਬੂ

puzzle (ਪਅੱਜ਼ਲ) *n v* ਬੁਝਾਰਤ, ਉਲਝਣ, ਸਮੱਸਿਆ, ਗੁੱਝ ਪ੍ਰਸ਼ਨ; ਉਲਝਾਉਣਾ, ਭਚਲਾਉਣਾ, ਪਰੇਸ਼ਾਨ ਕਰਨਾ

pygmy ('ਪਿਗਮਿ) *n* ਬੌਣਾ, ਗਿਠਮੁਠੀਆ

pyramid ('ਪਿਰਅਮਿਡ) *n* ਮੀਨਾਰ (ਮਿਸਰੀ), ਮੀਨਾਰਾਕਾਰ, ਖੇਤਰ

pyre ('ਪਾਇਅ*) *n* ਚਿਤਾ, ਚਿਖਾ, ਅੰਗੀਠਾ

python ('ਪਾਇਥਨ) *n* ਅਜਗਰ, ਸ਼ੇਸ਼ਨਾਗ; ਪਰੇਤ

pyxis ('ਪਿਕਸਿਸ) *n* ਪਟਾਰੀ

Q

Q, q (ਕਯੂ) ਕਿਊ, ਰੋਮਨ ਵਰਣਮਾਲਾ ਦਾ ਸਤਾਰਵੂਵਾਂ ਅੱਖਰ

quack (ਕਵੈਕ) *n v* ਅਨਾੜੀ ਵੈਦ, ਵੈਦੜਾ, ਨੀਮ ਹਕੀਮ; ਨੀਮ ਹਕੀਮ ਹੋਣਾ; ਸ਼ੇਖ਼ੀ ਮਾਰਨੀ; ~ery ਝੂਠੀ ਵੈਦਗਰੀ, ਨੀਮ ਹਕੀਮੀ; ਝੂਠਾ ਅਹੰਕਾਰ

quadrangle ('ਕਵੱਡਰੈਂਡ਼ਗਲ) *n* ਚਤੁਰਭੁਜ, ਚੌਖਟਾ, ਵਿਹੜਾ, ਚੌਕੋਰ, ਚੌਖੰਡੀ; ਚੌਕ

quadrangular ('ਕਵੱਡਰੈਂਡ਼ਯੂਲ*) *n* ਆਇਤਕਾਰ, ਚੌਕੋਣ

quadrate ('ਕਵੱਡ਼ਰਅਟ, ਕਵੱਡ਼ਰੇਇਟ) *n a v* ਚਤੁਰਭੁਜ; ਆਇਤਕਾਰ; ਚਤੁਰਭੁਜੀ; ਆਇਤਕਾਰ ਬਣਾਉਣਾ

quadruped ('ਕਵੱਡ਼ਰੁਪੈਂਡ਼) *n a* ਚੌਪਾਇਆ, ਚਾਰ ਪੈਰਾਂ ਵਾਲਾ (ਜਾਨਵਰ)

quag (ਕਵੈਗ) *n* ਖੋਭਾ, ਦਲਦਲ, ਖੁੱਭਣ, ਖੋਭ; ~mire ਦਲਦਲ, ਚਿੱਕੜ ਵਾਲੀ ਧਰਤੀ, ਖੁੱਭਣ, ਖੋਭਾ, ਜਿੱਲ੍ਹਣ; ਕਛਾਰ; ~gy ਦਲਦਲੀ

quail (ਕਵੇਇਲ) *n v* ਬਟੇਰਾ, ਬਟੇਰ; ਕੰਬਣਾ; ਤ੍ਰਾਸਤ ਹੋਣਾ, ਹੌਸਲਾ ਛੱਡਣਾ

quaint (ਕਵੇਇੰਟ) *a* ਅਨੋਖਾ, ਅਨੂਠਾ, ਅਜੀਬ, ਵਿਲੱਖਣ, ਵਿਚਿੱਤਰ; ਅਸੰਗਤ; ~ness ਵਿਲੱਖਣਤਾ, ਅਨੋਖਾਪਣ, ਅਨੂਠਾਪਣ, ਅਲੋਕਕਤਾ

quake (ਕਵੇਇਕ) *n v* ਕਾਂਬਾ, ਕੰਬਣਾ, ਥਰਥਰ, ਥਰਥਰਾਹਟ; ਭੁਚਾਲ, ਭੂ-ਕੰਪ, (ਭੁਚਾਲ ਕਾਰਨ) ਕੰਬਣਾ, ਥਰ-ਥਰ ਕਰਨਾ

quakiness (ਕਵੇਇਕਿਨਿਸ) *n* ਕਾਂਬਾ, ਕੰਬਟੀ, ਥਰਕਣ, ਥਰਥਰਾਹਟ

quaky ('ਕਵੇਇਕਿ) *a* ਕੰਬਦਾ, ਕੰਬਣ ਵਾਲਾ

qualification ('ਕਵੱਲਿਫ਼ਿ'ਕੇਇਸ਼ਨ) *n* ਯੋਗਤਾ, ਕਾਬਲੀਅਤ, ਪਾਤਰਤਾ; ਸਮਰੱਥਾ

qualified ('ਕਵੱਲਿਫ਼ਾਇਡ) *a* ਯੋਗ, ਯੋਗਤਾ-ਪ੍ਰਾਪਤ, ਲਾਇਕ

qualify ('ਕਵੱਲਿਫ਼ਾਇ) *v* ਯੋਗ ਹੋਣਾ ਜਾਂ ਕਰਨਾ, ਕਾਬਲ ਹੋਣਾ; ਸਮਰੱਥ ਹੋਣਾ; ਮਸ਼ਰੂਤ ਬਿਆਨ ਕਰਨਾ

qualitative ('ਕਵੱਲਿਟਅਟਿਵ) *a* ਗੁਣਵਾਚਕ, ਗੁਣਾਤਮਕ

quality ('ਕਵੱਲੇਅਟਿ) *n* ਗੁਣ, ਲੱਛਣ; ਪ੍ਰਕਿਰਤੀ, ਰੰਗ-ਢੰਗ, ਪ੍ਰਕਾਰ; ਸਰੂਪ, ਖ਼ੂਬੀ

qualm (ਕਵਾਮ) *n* ਚਿੰਤਾ, ਖਟਕਾ, ਪੜ੍ਹਕਾ, ਅੰਦੇਸ਼ਾ; ~ish ਚਿੰਤਾਸ਼ੀਲ, ਜੀ ਮਤਲਾਉਣ ਵਾਲਾ

quandary ('ਕਵੈਂਡ(ਅ)ਰਿ) *n* ਦੁਬਧਾ, ਸੰਕਟ, ਪਰੇਸ਼ਾਨੀ, ਉਲਝਣ

quantification ('ਕਵੈਂਟਿਫ਼ਿ'ਕੇਇਸ਼ਨ) *n* ਪ੍ਰਮਾਣ-ਨਿਰਧਾਰਨ, ਮਾਤਰਾ-ਨਿਰਧਾਰਨ

quantify ('ਕਵੈਂਟਿਫ਼ਾਇ) *v* (ਪਦ ਦੇ) ਪ੍ਰਯੋਗ ਦਾ ਲੱਛਣ ਦੱਸਣਾ; (ਕਿਸੇ ਵਸਤੂ ਦਾ) ਪਰਿਮਾਣ ਸਾਬਿਤ ਕਰਨਾ; ਮਾਤਰਾ ਨਿਰਧਾਰਤ ਕਰਨਾ

quantitative ('ਕੱਵੈਂਟਿਟਅਟਿਵ) *a* ਪਰਿਮਾਣਾਤਮਕ, ਗਿਣਨਾਤਮਕ

quantity ('ਕਵੱਟਿਟਅਟਿ) *n* ਵਿਸਤਾਰ; ਮਾਪ, ਮਾਤਰਾ, ਪਰਿਮਾਣ; ਸੰਖਿਆ; ਭਾਰ ਤੋਲ, ਯੋਗ, ਜੋੜ; ਬਹੁਲਤਾ

quantum ('ਕਵੈਂਟਅਮ) *n* ਮਾਤਰਾ, ਪਰਿਮਾਣ, ਰਾਸ਼ੀ, ਮਿਕਦਾਰ, ਭਾਗ

quarantine ('ਕਵੌਰ(ਅ)ਨਟੀਨ) *n v* ਚਾਲ਼ੀ ਦਿਨ, ਕੁਰਾਟੀਨ, ਪੱਤਣ-ਰੋਕ

quarrel ('ਕਵੌਰ(ਅ)ਲ) *n v* ਝਗੜਾ, ਕਲਹ, ਟੰਟਾ, ਤਕਰਾਰ, ਵਿਵਾਦ, ਲੜਾਈ; ਝਗੜਾ ਕਰਨਾ, ਲੜਾਈ ਕਰਨੀ, ਹੱਥੋ-ਪਾਈ ਕਰਨੀ, ਝਗੜਨਾ; **to pick a–** ਲੜਾਈ ਮੁੱਲ ਲੈਣਾ; **~some** ਲੜਾਕਾ, ਵਿਵਾਦੀ, ਝਗੜਾਲੂ

quarter (ਕਵੋਟਅ*) *n v* (1) ਚੌਥਾ ਭਾਗ, ਚੌਥਾਈ ਹਿੱਸਾ; (2) ਤਿਮਾਹੀ, (3) ਪ'ਮਾ, ਦਿਸ਼ਾ; (4) ਪ੍ਰਾਂਤ, ਬਸਤੀ, ਛਾਉਣੀ; ਚਾਰ ਟੁਕੜੇ ਕਰ ਦੇਣਾ; ਟਿਕਾਉਣਾ; **at close ~s** ਨਾਲ਼-ਨਾਲ਼; **~ly** ਤ੍ਰੈ ਮਾਸਕ (ਪੱਤਰ, ਪੱਤਰਕਾ); ਤਿਮਾਹੀ; **~master** (ਸੈਨਾ) ਰਸਦ ਪ੍ਰਬੰਧਕ; ਇਕ ਜਹਾਜ਼ੀ ਅਫ਼ਸਰ; **~s** ਟਿਕਾਣਾ, ਰਹਿਣ ਦੀ ਥਾਂ

quartz (ਕਵੋਟਸ) *n* ਕੱਚਮਣੀ, ਸਫਟਿਕ, ਬਿਲੌਰੀ ਪੱਥਰ

quasi ('ਕਵੇਇਜ਼ਾਇ) *con a prep* ਅਰਥਾਤ, ਗੋਇਆ ਕਿ, ਜਿਵੇਂ ਕਿ; ਅੱਧਾ, ਨੀਮ, ਅਧੂਰਾ

quay (ਕੀ) *n* ਘਾਟ, ਗੋਦੀ

queen (ਕਵੀਨ) *n* ਰਾਣੀ, ਬੇਗਮ, ਮਹਾਰਾਣੀ, ਮਲਕਾ, ਸੁਲਤਾਨਾ

queer (ਕਵਿਅ*) *v a* ਵਿਗਾੜ ਦੇਣਾ, ਚਕਰਾ ਦੇਣਾ; ਅਜੀਬ, ਨਿਰਾਲਾ, ਅਨੋਖਾ; **~ness** ਅਨੋਖਾਪਣ ਵਿਲੱਖਣਤਾ, ਵਚਿੱਤਰਤਾ; ਖ਼ਬਤ, ਸਨਕ

quell (ਕਵੈੱਲ) *v* ਦਮਨ ਕਰਨਾ, ਕੁਚਲਣਾ, ਦਬਾਉਣਾ, ਸ਼ਾਂਤ ਕਰਨਾ

quench (ਕਵੈਂਚ) *v* ਬੁਝਾਉਣਾ, ਗੁਲ ਕਰਨਾ (ਉਪਜ) ਘਟਾਉਣੀ, ਠੰਡੀ ਕਰਨੀ; ਬੁਝਾਉਣੀ; **~less** ਅਬੁੱਝ, ਅਤ੍ਰਿਪਤ

querimonious ('ਕਵੈੱਰਿ'ਮਅਉਨਿਅਸ) *a* ਚੁਗਲਖੋਰ, ਸ਼ਿਕਾਇਤੀ, ਝਗੜਾਲੂ; **~ness** ਚੁਗਲਖੋਰੀ; ਸ਼ਿਕਾਇਤਬਾਜ਼ੀ, ਲੜਾਕਾਪਣ

quern (ਕਵਅਃਨ) *n* ਚੱਕੀ

querulous (ਕਵੈਰੁਲਅਸ) *a* ਬਦਮਿਜਾਜ, ਚਿੜਚਿੜਾ

query ('ਕਵਿਅਰਿ) *n v* ਪੁੱਛ-ਗਿੱਛ, ਪ੍ਰਸ਼ਨ, ਸਵਾਲ; ਪੁੱਛਣਾ-ਗਿੱਛਣਾ, ਪ੍ਰਸ਼ਨ ਕਰਨਾ, ਸਵਾਲ ਕਰਨਾ, ਸ਼ੱਕ ਪਰਗਟ ਕਰਨਾ

quest (ਕਵੈੱਸਟ) *n v* ਦੇਖ-ਭਾਲ, ਜਾਂਚ, ਪੜਤਾਲ, ਨਿਰੂਪਣ, ਖੋਜ; ਜਾਂਚ ਕਰਨੀ, ਖੋਜ ਕੱਢਣੀ, ਭਾਲ ਕਰਨੀ

question ('ਕਵੈੱਸਚ(ਅ)ਨ) *n v* ਸਵਾਲ, ਪ੍ਰਸ਼ਨ, ਜਿਗਿਆਸਾ, ਸ਼ੰਕਾ; ਸੰਦੇਹ, ਸਮੱਸਿਆ, ਮਾਮਲਾ; ਵਿਚਾਰ ਕਰਨਾ, ਦਰਿਆਫ਼ਤ ਕਰਨਾ; ਸੰਦੇਹ ਕਰਨਾ; ਪੁੱਛ-ਪੜਤਾਲ ਕਰਨੀ; **~naire** ਪ੍ਰਸ਼ਨਾਵਲੀ, ਪ੍ਰਸ਼ਨਮਾਲਾ, ਸਵਾਲਨਾਮਾ

queue (ਕਯੂ) *n v* ਪੰਗਤੀ, ਕਤਾਰ, ਲਾਈਨ; ਗੁੱਤ ਗੁੰਦਣੀ; ਪੰਗਤ ਲਾਉਣੀ, ਕਤਾਰ ਵਿਚ ਖਲੋਣਾ

quey (ਕਵੇਇ) *n* (ਉਪ) ਵੱਛੀ, ਵਹਿੜਕੀ

quibbling (ਕਵਿਬਲਿਙ) *n* ਵਾਕ-ਛਲ, ਬਕਵਾਸ; ਟਾਲ-ਮਟੋਲ, ਬਹਾਨਾ, ਹੁੱਜਤ

quick (ਕਵਿਕ) *a adv* ਜਾਨਦਾਰ; ਚੌਕੰਨਾ, ਚੰਚਲ; ਹੁਸ਼ਿਆਰ; ਸ਼ੀਘਰ, ਛੇਤੀ, ਜਲਦੀ, ਤੁਰੰਤ, ਝਟਪਟ; **~sliver** ਪਾਰਾ; **~witted** ਹਾਜ਼ਰ ਜਵਾਬ; **~en** ਜਾਨ ਪਾਉਣਾ, ਸਜੀਵ ਕਰਨਾ; ਸਚੇਤ ਕਰਨਾ, ਛੇਤੀ ਹੋਣੀ, ਹੋਰ; **~ly** ਛੇਤੀ, ਜਲਦੀ, ਫ਼ੌਰਨ; ਝਟਪਟ, ਤੁਰੰਤ; **~ness** ਛੇਤੀ, ਫ਼ੌਰਨ, ਝਟਪਟ, ਤੁਰੰਤ

quiescence, quiescency (ਕਵਾਇ'ਐੱਸੰਸ, ਕਵਾਇ'ਐੱਸੰਸਿ) *n* ਸਥਿਰਤਾ, ਨਿਸ਼ਚਲਤਾ,

ਅੱਚਲਤਾ, ਗਤੀਹੀਨਤਾ, ਸ਼ਾਂਤੀ, ਸੁਖ, ਚੈਨ; ਚੁੱਪ, ਖ਼ਮੋਸ਼ੀ

quiescent (ਕਵਾਇ'ਐਸੰਟ) *a* ਸਥਿਰ, ਨਿਸ਼ਚਲ, ਅੱਚਲ, ਸ਼ਾਂਤ, ਖ਼ਮੋਸ਼, ਮੌਨ

quiet ('ਕਵਾਇਅਟ) *n v a* ਸ਼ਾਂਤੀ, ਚੁੱਪ, ਮੌਨ, ਵਿਸ਼ਰਾਮ, ਸੁੱਖ; ਚੈਨ; ਸ਼ਾਂਤ ਕਰਨਾ, ਸਥਿਰ ਕਰਨਾ, ਚਿੰਤਾਹੀਨ ਕਰਨਾ; ਸ਼ਾਂਤ, ਨਿਸ਼ਚਲ, ਅਪਰਗਟ, ਸਥਿਰ; ~ness, ~ude ਅਮਨ, ਚੈਨ; ਆਰਾਮ; ਆਨੰਦ, ਸ਼ਾਂਤੀ

quilt (ਕਵਿਲਟ) *n v* ਰਜਾਈ, ਲੇਫ਼, ਤੁਲਾਈ, (ਉੱਤੇ) ਰਜਾਈ ਸੈਣਾ, ਰਜਾਈ ਨਾਲ ਢਕਣਾ

quinine (ਕਵੀਨ'ਨੀਨ) *n* ਕੁਨੀਨ, ਕੁਨੈਣ

quintal, kintal ('ਕਵਿੰਟਲ) *n* ਸੌ ਕਿਲੋਗਰਾਮ, ਕੁਵਿੰਟਲ

quintessence (ਕਵਿੰ'ਟੈਸੰਅੰਸ) *n* (ਪ੍ਰਾਚੀਨ ਦਰਸ਼ਨ) ਪੰਜਵਾਂ ਤੱਤ; ਸਾਰ; ਸਾਰਾਂਸ਼, ਸਤ

quip (ਕਵਿਪ) *n v* ਮਸ਼ਕਰੀ, ਤਾਅਨਾ; ਮਿਹਣਾ, ਵਾਕ-ਛਲ, ਗੋਲ-ਮੋਲ ਗੱਲ; ਵਿਅੰਗ ਵਚਨ ਬੋਲਣਾ, ਤਾਅਨਾ ਮਾਰਨਾ, ਬੋਲੀ ਮਾਰਨੀ

quire (ਕਵਾਇਅ*) *n v* ਦਸਤਾ, ਚੌਵੀ ਕਾਗ਼ਜ਼

quirk (ਕਵਅਃਕ) *n* ਸੰਜੋਗ, ਢੋ; ਆਦਤ

quisling ('ਕਵਿਜ਼ਲਿਙ) *n* ਗ਼ਦਾਰ, ਦੇਸ਼ ਧਰੋਹੀ, ਵਿਸਾਹਘਾਤੀ, ਵਿਸ਼ਵਾਸਘਾਤੀ; ~ite ਗ਼ਦਾਰ, (ਸ਼ਖ਼ਸ), ਦੇਸ਼ ਧਰੋਹੀ (ਆਦਮੀ), ਵਿਸਾਹਘਾਤੀ (ਮਨੁੱਖ)

quit (ਕਵਿਟ) *v pred a* (ਕੰਮ) ਛੱਡਣਾ, ਛੁਟਕਾਰਾ ਪਾਉਣਾ, ਬੰਦ ਕਰਨਾ, ਰੋਕ ਦੇਣਾ, ਚੱਲ ਪੈਣਾ, ਵਿਦਾ ਹੋਣਾ; ~tance ਨਿਸਤਾਰਾ, ਛੁਟਕਾਰਾ; ਬੇਬਾਕ-ਪੱਤਰ, ਰਸੀਦ

quite (ਕਵਾਇਟ) *adv* ਅਤੀਅੰਤ, ਨਿਰਾ, ਸਰਾਸਰ, ਬਿਲਕੁਲ, ਪੂਰਨ ਤੌਰ ਤੇ

quiver (ਕਵਿਵ਼ਅ*) *n v* ਤਰਕਸ਼, ਕਾਂਬਾ ਥਰਥਰਾਹਟ; ਕੰਬਣਾ, ਥਰਾਉਣਾ, ਲਰਜ਼ਣਾ

qui vive ('ਕੋਇ ਵੀਵ਼) (F) *n* ਚੌਕਸ, ਹੁਸ਼ਿਆਰ ਖ਼ਬਰਦਾਰ

quiz (ਕਵਿਜ਼) *n v* ਪ੍ਰਸ਼ਨ-ਉੱਤਰ, ਪ੍ਰਸ਼ਨਾਵਲੀ ਸਮੱਸਿਆ, ਬੁਝਾਰਤ, ਪਰੀਖਿਆ; ਜਾਂਚ; ਹਾਸਾ ਮਜ਼ਾਕ, ਦਿਲਲਗੀ; ਨਿਰਾਲਾ ਆਦਮੀ, ਨਮੂਨਾ ਮਸਖ਼ਰਾ, ਦਿਲਲਗੀ ਕਰਨ ਵਾਲਾ; ਮਜ਼ਾਕ ਉਡਾਉਣਾ, ਹਸੇ ਵਿਚ ਉਡਾਉਣਾ

quorum ('ਕਵੋਰਅਮ) *n* ਗਣਪੂਰਤੀ, ਗਣਪੂਰਣ ਸੰਖਿਆ; ਕੋਰਮ

quota ('ਕਵਅਉਟਅ) *n* ਨਿਰਧਾਰਤ ਮਾਤਰਾ ਹਿੱਸਾ, ਨਿਯਤ ਪਰਿਮਾਣ, ਕੋਟਾ

quotable ('ਕਵਅਉਟਅਬਲ) *a* ਪ੍ਰਮਾਣਯੋਗ ਉਦਾਹਰਣ ਯੋਗ, ਹਵਾਲੇ ਯੋਗ

quotation (ਕਵਅਉ'ਟੇਇਸ਼ਨ) *n* ਪਰਉਕਤੀ ਉਤਕਥਨ, ਉਦਾਹਰਣ; ਬਜ਼ਾਰੀ ਭਾਉ, ਮੁੱਲ ਕੀਮਤਾਂ ਦੀ ਦਰ

quote (ਕਵਅਉਟ) *n v* ਹਵਾਲਾ, ਪਰਉਕਤੀ ਉਦਾਹਰਣ; ਉਦਾਹਰਣ ਦੇਣਾ, ਹਵਾਲਾ ਦੇਣ ਭਾਅ ਦੱਸਣਾ; ~d ਉੱਧਰਤ, ਕਥਿਤੀ

quotient ('ਕਵਅਉਸ਼ੰਟ) *n* ਵੰਡ-ਫਲ, ਭਾਗ-ਫਲ ਭਜਨ-ਫਲ

quotum ('ਕਵਅਉਟਅਮ) *n* ਨਿਯਤ ਮਾਤਰ ਨਿਸ਼ਚਤ ਸੰਖਿਆ ਜਾਂ ਭਾਗ

R

R, r (ਆ*) *n* ਰੋਮਨ ਵਰਟਮਾਲਾ ਦਾ ਅਠਾਰਵਾਂ ਅੱਖਰ

the three R's reading, (w)riting and (a)rithmatic ਪੜ੍ਹਨਾ, ਲਿਖਣਾ ਤੇ ਗਣਿਤ

rabbit (ਰੈਬਿਟ) *n* ਖ਼ਰਗੋਸ਼, ਸਹਿਆ; ਅਨਾੜੀ

rabble (ਰੈਬਲ) *n* ਭੀੜ, ਹਜੂਮ, ਜਮਘਟਾ; ~**rouser** ਮਜਮੇਬਾਜ਼

rabies (ਰੇਇਬੀਜ਼) *n* ਹਲਕ; ਕੁੱਤੇ ਦਾ ਹਲਕ, ਜਲਤ੍ਰਾਸ-ਰੋਗ

race (ਰੇਇਸ) *n v* (1) ਪਰਵਾਹ; ਪ੍ਰਬਲ ਧਾਰਾ; ਚੰਦਰ-ਪਥ; ਜੀਵਨ ਯਾਤਰਾ; (2) ਦੌੜ; ਦੌੜਾਂ ਦਾ ਮੁਕਾਬਲਾ; (3) ਵੰਸ਼, ਜਾਤੀ; ਨਸਲ; ਸ਼੍ਰੇਣੀ; ਦੌੜ ਲਗਾਣਾ; ਦੌੜਨਾ ~**course** ਘੋੜ-ਦੌੜ ਦਾ ਮੈਦਾਨ

racial (ਰੇਇਸ਼ਲ) *a* ਨਸਲੀ, ਜਾਤੀਗਤ, ਜਾਤੀਮੂਲਕ; ਵੰਸ਼ਗਤ; ਨਸਲੀ; ~**ism** ਨਸਲਵਾਦ, ਨਸਲਪਰਸਤੀ, ਜਾਤੀਵਾਦ

racing (ਰੇਇਸਿਙ) *n* ਘੋੜ-ਦੌੜ; ਘੋੜ-ਦੌੜ ਪ੍ਰਤੀਯੋਗਤਾ

rack (ਰੈਕ) *n* ਲੱਕੜ ਜਾਂ ਧਾਤ ਦਾ ਡੱਗਾ, ਰੈੱਕ, ਚਾਰਦਾਨ; ਸ਼ਿਕੰਜਾ; ਸਤ, ਅਰਕ; ਸਾੜਨ; ਮਰੋੜਨਾ; ਰੁੱਸਣਾ; ਧਰਤੀ ਦਾ ਸਤ ਖਿੱਚਣਾ

racket, racquet (ਰੈਕਿਟ) *n v* (ਟੈਨਿਸ ਆਦਿ ਦਾ) ਬੱਲਾ; ਡੰਡਾ; ਰੈਕਿਟ; ਹੰਗਾਮਾ; ਖ਼ਲਬਲੀ; ਰੌਣਕ, ਚਹਿਲ-ਪਹਿਲ; ਤਿਗੜਮ ਨੀਤੀ; ਗ਼ੈਰ-ਕਾਨੂੰਨੀ ਧੰਦਾ; ਹੱਲਾ ਮਚਾਉਣਾ, ਗੁਲਛੱਰੇ ਉਡਾਉਣਾ; ~**eer** (ਅਪਮਾਨਜਨਕ) ਨਾਜਾਇਜ਼ ਧੰਦਾ ਕਰਨ ਵਾਲਾ

radar (ਰੇਇਡਾ*) *n* ਰਾਡਾਰ, ਸਰਵਦਰਸ਼ੀ ਜੰਤਰ

radial (ਰੇਇਡਯਅਲ) *n a* ਕੂਹਣੀ ਦੀ ਨਾੜ; ਕਿਰਨਗਤ, ਰਿਸ਼ਮਯੁਕਤ

radiance (ਰੇਇਡਯਅੰਸ) *n* ਤੇਜ, ਪ੍ਰਕਾਸ਼, ਜੋਤੀ, ਚਮਕ, ਵਿਕੀਰਨਤਾ

radiant (ਰੇਇਡਯਅੰਟ) *n a* ਜੋਤੀ-ਕੇਂਦਰ, ਪ੍ਰਕਾਸ਼-ਕੇਂਦਰ, ਜੋਤਸ਼ਮਈ, ਚਮਤਕਾਰ, ਉੱਜਲ, (ਅੱਖਾਂ) ਪ੍ਰਕਾਸ਼ਮਈ; ਅਲੌਕਕ, ਚਮਤਕਾਰੀ, ਦਗਦਗਾਉਂਦੀ ਆਭਾਪੂਰਨ

radiate (ਰੇਇਡਿਏਇਟ) *v* ਕਿਰਨਾਂ ਖਿਲਾਰਨਾ, ਵਿਕੀਰਨ ਕਰਨਾ, ਪ੍ਰਕਾਸ਼ ਸੁੱਟਣਾ

radical (ਰੇਇਡਕਲ) *n a* ਮੂਲਭੂਤ ਸਿਧਾਂਤ, ਮੂਲ, ਮੂਲ ਸ਼ਬਦ; ਮੌਲਕ; ਆਧਾਰੀ, ਮਹੱਤਾਪੂਰਨ, ਬੁਨਿਆਦੀ

radish (ਰੇਡਿਸ਼) *n* ਮੂਲੀ

radius (ਰੇਇਡਿਅਸ) *n* ਅਰਧ-ਵਿਆਸ; ਘੇਰਾ, ਖੇਤਰ, ਕੂਹਣੀ ਦੀ ਹੱਡੀ

raffish (ਰੈਫ਼ਿਸ਼) *a* ਨੀਚ, ਲੰਪਟ, ਹੋਛਾ, ਕਮੀਨਾ, ਬਦਮਾਸ਼

raffle (ਰੈਫ਼ਲ) *n v* ਕੂੜਾ-ਕਰਕਟ, ਗੰਦ-ਮੰਦ, ਕੰਕਰ, ਕਬਾੜ, ਲਾਟਰੀ; ਲਾਟਰੀ ਪਾਉਣੀ

rag (ਰੈਗ) *n v* ਚੀਥੜਾ, ਲੱਤਾ, ਧੱਜੀ, ਪਾਟੇ-ਪੁਰਾਣੇ ਕੱਪੜੇ, ਗੁੱਦੜ, ਟਾਕੀ; ਚੀਥੜੇ ਬਣਾ ਦੇਣਾ, ਡਾਂਟਣਾ; ~**man** ਕਬਾੜੀਆ; ~**ged** ਪਾਟਿਆ-ਝਰੀਆ, ਚੀਥੜਾ ਬਣਿਆ, ਜੀਰਣ, ਭੱਦਾ, ਖੁਰਦਰਾ, ਫਟੇ ਹਾਲ; ~**gedness** ਚੀਥੜਾਪਨ, ਭੱਦਾਪਨ, ਖ਼ਰਾਬੀ, ਅਸੰਗਤੀ

raid (ਰੇਇਡ) *n v* ਚੜ੍ਹਾਈ, ਅਚਾਨਕ ਆਕਰਮਣ, ਛਾਪਾ, ਧਾਵਾ, ਹਮਲਾ, ਹੱਲਾ ਬੋਲਣਾ, ਹਮਲਾ

ਕਰਨਾ, ਛਾਪਾ ਮਾਰਨਾ

rail ('ਰੇਇਲ) *n v* (1) ਰੋਕ, ਜੰਗਲਾ, ਕਟਿਹਰਾ; (2) ਸਲਾਖ, ਛੜ; (3) ਲੋਹੇ ਦੀ (ਰੇਲ ਦੀ) ਪਟੜੀ, ਰੇਲ; ਰੋਕ ਜਾਂ ਘੇਰਾ ਬਣਾਉਣਾ, ਵਾੜ ਲਾਉਣੀ, (ਰੇਲ ਦੀ) ਪਟੜੀ ਵਿਛਾਉਣੀ; ~way ਰੇਲ; ਰੇਲਵੇ; ਰੇਲਵੇ ਲਾਈਨ; ਰੇਲ ਮਾਰਗ; ਰੇਲ ਪਥ; ਰੇਲ ਵਿਭਾਗ; ~ing ਜੰਗਲਾ; ਫਿਟਕਾਰ; ਦੁਰਵਚਨ; ਕਟਿਹਰਾ

rain (ਰੇਇਨ) *n v* ਵਰਖਾ, ਮੀਂਹ, ਬਰਸਾਤ, ਵਾਛੜ, ਛਿੱਟੇ; ਮੀਂਹ ਪੈਣਾ, ਵਰਖਾ ਹੋਣੀ; ~bow ਇੰਦਰਧਨੁਸ਼; ਬਹੁਰੰਗੀ, ਸਤਰੰਗੀ, ਪੀਂਘ; ~y ਬਰਸਾਤੀ, ਵਰਖਾਕਾਰੀ; ~y day ਵਰਖਾ ਦਾ ਦਿਨ, ਸੰਕਟ-ਕਾਲ, ਔਖਾ-ਵੇਲਾ; ਆਪੱਤੀ ਕਾਲ

raise (ਰੇਇਜ਼) *v n* ਉੱਚਾ ਚੁੱਕਣਾ ਜਾਂ ਹੋਣਾ, ਜੋਸ਼ ਦੁਆਉਣਾ, ਘਣਨਾ; ਉੱਨਤ ਕਰਨਾ ਜਾਂ ਹੋਣਾ; ਤਨਖਾਹ ਦਾ ਵਾਧਾ; ਪੂਜ ਦੀ ਖੇਡ ਦਾ ਦਾਉ; ~d ਉਤਪੰਨ, ਸਿਖਿਅਤ, ਪਾਲਿਆ ਪੋਸਿਆ, ਪੋਸਤ; ਉਤਰਿਆ, ਉਠਾਇਆ

raison d'etre ('ਰੇਇਜ਼ੋਨ 'ਡੇਇਟਰ(ਅ)) (F) ਮੂਲ ਮਨੋਰਥ

rake ('ਰੇਇਕ) *n v* ਵਿਲਾਸੀ; ਗੁੰਡਾ; ਤੰਗਲੀ, ਫਹੁੜਾ; ਸਮੇਟਣਾ, ਬੁਹਾਰਨਾ, ਕੁਰੇਦਣਾ; ~hell ਲੁੱਚਾ, ਸ਼ੁਹਦਾ

rally ('ਰੈਲਿ) *v n* ਜਮ੍ਹਾ ਹੋਣਾ, ਇਕੱਠਾ ਹੋਣਾ; ਦੁਬਾਰਾ ਲੜਾਈ ਆਰੰਭ ਕਰਨੀ, ਹਮਲਾ ਕਰਨਾ; ਇਕੱਠ, ਇਕੱਤਰਤਾ; (ਟੈਨਿਸ) ਤੇਜ਼ ਮੁਕਾਬਲਾ

ram (ਰੈਮ) *n v* ਮੇਢਾ, ਛੱਤਰਾ, ਭੇੜਾ, ਦੁੰਬਾ; ਮੇਖਰਾਸ਼ੀ; ਦੁਰਮਟ, ਠੋਕਣਾ, ਕੁੱਟਣਾ; ਕੁੱਟ ਕੁੱਟ ਕੇ ਭਰਨਾ, ਤੁੰਨਣਾ, ਤੁਸਣਾ, ਤੁੰਨਣਾ, ਠੋਸਣਾ, (ਸਿਰ) ਖੱਪਣਾ, ਬਿਠਾਉਣਾ, ਦਬਾਉਣਾ

ramble ('ਰੈਂਬਲ) *v n* ਟੁਰਨਾ-ਫਿਰਨਾ, ਘੁੰਮਣਾ, ਫਿਰਨਾ, ਗਸ਼ਤ ਲਾਉਣੀ, ਬਹਿਕਣਾ; ਮਟਰ-ਗਸ਼ਤ, ਸੈਰ-ਸਪਾਟਾ

rambling ('ਰੈਂਬਲਿਙ) *a* ਬੁਮਣਸ਼ੀਲ; ਅਸੰਗਤ, ਉਲ-ਜਲੂਲ, ਬੇਢੰਗਾ, ਘੇਰਤਬੀਆ

ramification ('ਰੈਮਿਫ਼ਿ'ਕੇਇਸ਼ਨ) *n* ਸ਼ਾਖਾ ਵਿਚ ਖਿਲਾਰ, ਸ਼ਾਖਾ-ਵਿਸਤਾਰ, ਸ਼ਾਖਾ-ਵੰਡ

ramify ('ਰੈਮਿਫ਼ਾਇ) *v* ਖਿਲਾਰਨਾ, ਫੈਲਣਾ, ਟਾਹਣੇ-ਟਾਹਣੀਆਂ ਦਾ ਫੁੱਟਣਾ, ਵੰਡੇ ਜਾਣਾ

ramming ('ਰੈਮਿਙ) *n* ਕੁਟਾਈ

ramp (ਰੈਂਪ) *n v* ਝੁਕਾਉ, ਢਾਲ, ਢਲਾਉ; ਕੰਧਾਂ ਵਿਚ ਢਲਵਾਨ ਪਾਉਣਾ, ਗੁੱਸੇ ਮਚਾਉਣਾ, ਝੱਲ ਖਿਲਾਰਨਾ; ~ancy ਪ੍ਰਚੰਡਤਾ, ਪ੍ਰਬਲਤਾ; ~ant ਜ਼ਬਰਦਸਤ, ਵਿਆਪਕ, ਫੈਲਿਆ, ਬੇਰੋਕਟੋਕ

rampart ('ਰੈਂਪਾਟ) *n v* ਮੋਰਚਾਬੰਦੀ, ਚਾਰ ਦੀਵਾਰੀ, ਫ਼ਸੀਲ, ਦਮਦਮਾ; ਰੱਖਿਆ ਕਰਨਾ, ਬਚਾਉਣਾ

rancour ('ਰੈਙਕਅ*) *n* ਲਾਗਤਬਾਜ਼ੀ; ਸਾੜਾ, ਕੀਨਾ; ਵੈਰ-ਭਾਵ

random ('ਰੈਨਡਅਮ) *n a* ਬੇਤਰਤੀਬੀ, ਅੰਨ੍ਹੇਵਾਹ; (ਗੱਲ ਜਾਂ ਕੰਮ) ਅਟਕਲ-ਪੱਚੂ, ਬੇਤੁਕੀ; ਉਟਪਟਾਂਗ

range (ਰੇਇੰਜ) *v n* ਬੀਜਣਾ; ਬੀਜ ਕੇ ਰੱਖਣਾ; ਤਰਤੀਬ ਦੇਣੀ; ਸਜਾਉਣਾ; ਫੈਲੇ ਹੋਣਾ; ਹੱਦ; ਦਾਇਰਾ; ਹਲਕਾ; ਦੌਰ; ਹਦਬੰਦੀ, ਦਰਜਾ; ~r ਪ੍ਰਬੰਧਕ, ਦਰੋਗਾ (ਵਣ-ਵਿਭਾਗ)

rank (ਰੈਙਕ) *n* ਪਾਲ, ਕਤਾਰ; ਸੱਫ; ਸਿਲਸਲਾ; ਰੁਤਬਾ, ਮਰਤਬਾ; ਤਬਕਾ; ਸ਼੍ਰੇਣੀ; ਦਰਜਾ, ਸਥਾਨ, ਪਦਵੀ

ransack ('ਰੈਨਸੈਕ) *v* ਲੁੱਟਣਾ, ਲੁੱਟਪੁੱਟ ਲੈਣਾ; ਚੰਗੀ ਤਰ੍ਹਾਂ ਟਟੋਲਣਾ, ਭਾਲਣਾ, ਛਾਣ ਮਾਰਨਾ

ransom ('ਰੈਨਸਅਮ) *n v* ਫਰੌਤੀ (ਦੇਣਾ),

ਰਿਹਾਈ ਲਈ ਮੁਆਵਜ਼ਾ (ਦੇਣਾ); ਦੰਡ ਭਰਨਾ

rape (ਰੇਇਪ) *v n* ਬਲਾਤਕਾਰ ਕਰਨਾ, ਅਸਮਤ ਲੁੱਟਣੀ, ਜ਼ਬਰ ਜ਼ਨਾ ਕਰਨਾ; ਸਤ ਭੰਗ, ਜ਼ਬਰ ਜ਼ਨਾ, ਬਲਾਤਕਾਰ; ਤੋਰੀਆ, ਤਾਰਾ ਮੀਰਾ, ਸਰ੍ਹੋਂ ਆਦਿ ਤੇਲ ਕਢੱਣ ਵਾਲੇ ਬੀਜ

rapid ('ਰੇਪਿਡ) *a n* ਤੇਜ਼, ਗਤੀਸ਼ੀਲ, ਤਿਲਕਵਾਂ, ਚਾਲੂ, ਰੋਤੂ, ਢਾਲ

rapport (ਰਾ'ਪੋ*) *n* ਰਾਬਤਾ, ਸੰਪਰਕ

rapprochement (ਰੈ'ਪਰੋਸ਼ਮਾਂਡ) *n* ਸੁਲ੍ਹਾ-ਸਫ਼ਾਈ, ਪੁਨਰ ਮੇਲ, ਰਾਜ਼ੀਨਾਮਾ

rapscallion (ਰੈਪ'ਸਕੈਲਯਅਨ) *n* (ਪੁ) ਪਾਜੀ, ਕਮੀਨਾ

rapture (ਰੈਪਚਰ) *n* ਬੇਖ਼ੁਦੀ, ਮਸਤੀ, ਮਗਨਤਾ, ਲੀਨਤਾ

rare (ਰੇਅ*) *a* ਦੁਰਲੱਭ, ਅਨੂਪਮ, ਅਨੂਠਾ, ਨਾਦਰ, ਨਾਯਾਬ, ਵਿਰਲਾ, ਟਾਵਾਂ; ~ly ਕਦੇ ਕਦੇ, ਕਦੇ ਕਦਾਈਂ, ਬਹੁਤ ਘੱਟ

rarity ('ਰੇਅਰਅਟਿ) *n* ਥੁੜ, ਦੁਰਲੱਭਤਾ

rascal ('ਰਾਸਕ(ਅ)ਲ) *n* ਬਦਮਾਸ਼, ਬਦਜ਼ਾਤ, ਲੁੱਚਾ, ਸ਼ਰੀਰ, ਪਾਜੀ

rash (ਰੈਸ਼) *n a* ਛਪਾਕੀ, ਰਕਤ-ਪਿੱਤੀ, ਚਟਾਕ; ਜ਼ਲਦਬਾਜ਼; ਕਾਹਲਾ; ਨਿਡੱਰਕ; ~ly ਧਿਆ ਵਿਚਾਰੇ; ਕਾਹਲੇਪਨ ਨਾਲ, ਦਲੇਰੀ ਨਾਲ; ਉਤਾਵਲ ਨਾਲ; ~ness ਉਜੰਡਪੁਣਾ; ਨਿਧੱੜਕਤਾ, ਖੇਤਹਾਸ਼ਾਪਣ

rasp (ਰਾਸਪ) *n v* ਰੇਤੀ; ਰੇਤਨਾ; ਰੇਤੀ ਨਾਲ ਰਗੜਨਾ, ਰਗੜਨਾ, ਘਸਾਉਣਾ ਜਾਂ ਘਸਨਾ

raspberry ('ਰਾਜ਼ਬ(ਅ)ਰਿ) *n* ਰਸਭਰੀ; ਨਾਪਸੰਦਗੀ

rat (ਰੈਟ) *n v* ਚੂਹਾ; ਮੂਸਾ; ਗੱਦਾਰ; ਬੇਵਫ਼ਾ, ਚੂਹਾ ਮਾਰਨਾ, ਚੂਹਾ ਫੜਨਾ, ਧੋਖਾ ਦੇਣਾ (ਰਾਜਨੀਤਿ ਵਿਚ)

rate (ਰੇਇਟ) *n v* ਦਰ, ਭਾਅ, ਨਿਰਖ, ਚਾਲ, ਰਫ਼ਤਾਰ; ਸਥਾਨਕ ਮਸੂਲ; ਦਰਜਾ; ਕਦਰ ਕਰਨੀ; ਅੰਦਾਜ਼ਾ ਲਾਉਣਾ

rather ('ਰਾਦਅ*) *adv* ਅਸਲ ਵਿਚ, ਵਧੇਰੇ ਕਰਕੇ, ਅਧਿਕਤਰ, ਕਿਸੇ ਤਰ੍ਹਾਂ, ਸਗੋਂ, ਬਲਕਿ

ratify ('ਰੈਟਿਫ਼ਾਇ) *v* ਤਸਦੀਕ ਕਰਨਾ, ਪ੍ਰਸ਼ਟੀ ਕਰਨੀ, ਜਾਇਜ਼ ਦੱਸਣਾ, ਪ੍ਰਮਾਣਤ ਕਰਨਾ

rating ('ਰੇਇਟਿੰਙ) *n* ਮੁੱਲ-ਅੰਕਣ, ਮੁੱਲਾਂਕਣ, ਨਿਸ਼ਚਤ ਮੁੱਲ; ਪਦ, ਦਰਜਾ; ਝਿੜਕ, ਘੁਰਕ, ਡਾਂਟ

ratio ('ਰੇਇਸ਼ਿਅਉ) *n* ਅਨੁਪਾਤ, ਪ੍ਰਮਾਣ, ਪ੍ਰਮਾਣਕ ਰਿਸ਼ਤਾ, ਮੂਲ ਅਨੁਪਾਤ, ਨਿਸਬਤ

ration ('ਰੈਸ਼ਨ) *n* ਅੰਨ, ਰਸਦ, ਅਨਾਜ

rational ('ਰੈਸ਼ਨਲ) *a* ਵਿਚਾਰਵਾਨ, ਵਿਚਾਰਸ਼ੀਲ, ਸਮਝਦਾਰ, ਤਰਕਸ਼ੀਲ, ਵਿਵੇਕੀ, ਯੁਕਤੀਪੂਰਨ ਨਿਆਂ-ਪੂਰਨ; ~e ਯੁਕਤੀ-ਯੁਕਤ ਵੇਰਵਾ, ਤਰਕ ਜਾਂ ਦਲੀਲ ਦਾ ਆਧਾਰ, ਨਿਆਂ-ਆਧਾਰ; ~ism ਯੁਕਤੀਵਾਦ, ਬੁੱਧੀਵਾਦ; ~ity ਤਰਕ, ਵਿਵੇਕ, ਤਰਕ-ਸਕਤੀ; ~ize ਸਿੱਧ ਕਰਨਾ, ਪ੍ਰਮਾਣਤ ਕਰਨਾ, ਯੁਕਤੀ-ਯੁਕਤ ਕਰਨਾ

ravage ('ਰੈਵਿਜ) *n v* ਨਾਸ, ਲੁੱਟ ਪਾਂਟ, ਤਬਾਹੀ; ਨਾਸ ਕਰਨਾ, ਉਪੱਦਰ ਕਰਨਾ

ravine (ਰਅ'ਵੀਨ) *n* ਖੱਡ, ਡੂੰਘੀ ਘਾਟੀ

ravish ('ਰੈਵਿਸ਼) *v* ਅਪਹਰਣ ਕਰਨਾ, ਹਰ ਕੇ ਲੈ ਜਾਣਾ, ਹਰਨਾ; ਖੋਹਣਾ

raw (ਰੋ) *n v a* ਕੱਚਾ ਜ਼ਖ਼ਮ; ਰਗੜ ਕੇ ਸਾਫ਼ ਕਰਨਾ; ਫ਼ੁੱਢ, ਕੱਚਾ, ਅਪ੍ਰਿੰਤੂ; ਅਣਘੜ, ਕਚਘਰੜ, ਨਵਾਂ ਸਿੱਖਿਆ; ~material ਕੱਚਾ ਮਾਲ

ray (ਰੇਇ) *n v* ਕਿਰਨ, ਰਿਸ਼ਮ, ਸ਼ੁਆ; ਰੌਸ਼ਨੀ, ਫੈਲਾਉਣਾ, ਪਰਗਟ ਹੋਣਾ, ਝਲਕਣਾ,

ਚਮਕਾਉਣਾ

rayon ('ਰੇਇਔਨ) *n* ਨਕਲੀ ਰੇਸ਼ਮ, ਰੇਅਨ

raze, rase (ਰੇਇਜ਼) *v* ਘਸਾ ਕੇ ਸਾਫ਼ ਕਰਨਾ, ਖੁਰਚਣਾ, ਛਿੱਲਣਾ, ਰਗੜਨਾ, ਮਲੀਆਮੇਟ ਕਰਨਾ

razor ('ਰੇਇਜ਼ਅ*) *v* ਉਸਤਰਾ; ਉਸਤਰਾ ਚਲਾਉਣਾ; ~**edge** ਤਿੱਖੀ ਧਾਰ; ਤਲਵਾਰ ਦੀ ਧਾਰ; ਨਾਜ਼ੁਕ ਮੌਕਾ

reach (ਰੀਚ) *n v* ਪਹੁੰਚ, ਪ੍ਰਭਾਵ-ਖੇਤਰ, ਘੇਰਾ, ਦਾਇਰਾ, ਫੈਲਾਉ; ਪਹੁੰਚਣਾ, ਹੱਥ ਆਉਣਾ, ਕਾਬੂ ਕਰਨਾ, ਫੜਨਾ

react (ਰਿ'ਐਕਟ) *v* ਪ੍ਰਤੀਕਿਰਿਆ ਕਰਨੀ, ਜਵਾਬੀ ਹਮਲਾ ਕਰਨਾ; ਬਦਲ ਜਾਣਾ; ਅਸਰ ਪੈਣਾ, ਗਤੀ ਪਰਗਟ ਕਰਨਾ, ਪ੍ਰਤੱਖ ਕਰਨਾ; ~**ion** ਪ੍ਰਤੀਕਿਰਿਆ, ਉਲਟੀ ਗਤੀ ਜਾਂ ਕਿਰਿਆ, ਜਵਾਬੀ ਹਮਲਾ, ਪ੍ਰਤੀਆਕਰਮਣ; ~**ionary** ਪ੍ਰਤੀਗਾਮੀ, ਪਿਛਾਖੜ, ਪ੍ਰਤੀਕਿਰਿਆਵਾਦੀ

read (ਰੀਡ) *v* ਵਾਚਣਾ, ਪੜਨਾ, ਅਧਿਐਨ ਕਰਨਾ; ~**er** ਪਾਠਕ, ਵਾਚਕ, ਵਿਸ਼ਵ-ਵਿਦਿਆਲੇ ਦਾ ਰੀਡਰ, ਪ੍ਰਧਿਆਪਕ, ਪਾਠ-ਪੁਸਤਕ; ~**ing** ਵਾਚਣ, ਪੜ੍ਹਾਈ, ਪਠਨ; ਪੜ੍ਹਤ, ਸਵੈਅਧਿਐਨ

readily ('ਰੈਡਿਲਿ) *adv* ਸੌਖਿਆਂ, ਛੇਤੀ, ਇਕਦਮ; ਖ਼ੁਸ਼ੀ ਨਾਲ, ਖ਼ੁਸ਼ੀ ਖ਼ੁਸ਼ੀ

readiness ('ਰੈਡਿਨਿਸ) *n* ਤਤਪਰਤਾ, ਤਿਆਰੀ; ਰਜ਼ਾਮੰਦੀ

ready ('ਰੈਡਿ) *v a* ਤਿਆਰ ਕਰਨਾ; ਤਿਆਰ ਬਰ ਤਿਆਰ; ਬਣਿਆ-ਠਣਿਆ; ਠੀਕ, ਚੁਸਤ; ਸੌਖਾ, ਸੀਘਰ, ਤੁਰੰਤ, ਝੱਟ; ~**made** ਤਿਆਰਸ਼ੁਦਾ, ਬਣਿਆ ਬਣਾਇਆ; ਮਾਮੂਲੀ

real (ਰਿਅਲ) *a* ਅਸਲੀ; ਸੱਚਾ; ਵਾਸਤਵਿਕ; ਯਥਾਰਥਕ, ਹਕੀਕੀ; ~**estate** ਅਚੱਲ ਸੰਪੱਤੀ; ~**ism** ਯਥਾਰਥਵਾਦ; ਵਾਸਤਵਵਾਦ, ਅਸਲਵਾਦ; ~**ity** ਯਥਾਰਥਤਾ, ਵਾਸਤਵਿਕਤਾ, ਤਾਤਵਿਕਤਾ; ਮੂਲਰੂਪਤਾ; ਅਸਲੀਅਤ, ਹਕੀਕਤ; ~**ize** ਸਿੱਧ ਕਰਨਾ, ਕਰ ਕੇ ਦਿਖਾਉਣਾ; ਪ੍ਰਤੱਖ ਕਰਨਾ, ਅਨੁਭਵ ਕਰਨਾ, ਸਮਝ ਲੈਣਾ, ਠੀਕ ਅੰਦਾਜ਼ਾ ਲਾਉਣਾ; ~**ly** ਯਥਾਰਥ ਤੌਰ ਤੇ, ਨਿਸ਼ਚਤ ਰੂਪ ਵਿਚ, ਵਾਸਤਵ ਵਿਚ, ਸੱਚਮੁੱਚ, ਦਰਅਸਲ

realign ('ਰੀਅ'ਲਾਇਨ) *v* ਮੁੜ, ਗੱਠਜੋੜ ਕਰਨਾ; ~**ment** ਮੁੜ-ਕਤਾਰਬੰਦੀ, ਮੁੜ-ਗੱਠਜੋੜ

realm ('ਰੈਲਮ) *n* ਸਲਤਨਤ, ਰਾਜ ਬਾਦਸ਼ਾਹਤ, ਖੇਤਰ

ream (ਰੀਮ) *n v* (ਕਾਗ਼ਜ਼) 20 ਦਸਤੇ=1 ਰਿਮ; ਕਾਗ਼ਜ਼ ਦਾ ਢੇਰ; ਸਿਰਾਂ; ਜੋੜ; ਮਲਾਈ; ਝੱਗ ਵਧਾਉਣਾ

reap (ਰੀਪ) *v* ਕੱਟਣਾ, (ਫ਼ਸਲ) ਇਕੱਠੀ ਕਰਨਾ, ਸੰਗ੍ਰਹ ਕਰਨਾ, ਫਲ ਭੋਗਣਾ

rear (ਰਿਅ*) *n v* ਪਿੱਛਤੀ, ਪਿਛਵਾੜਾ, ਪਿਛਲਾ ਇਲਾਕਾ, ਦੁੰਗ; ਉੱਚਾ ਚੁੱਕਣਾ

reason ('ਰੀਜ਼ਨ) *n v* ਦਲੀਲ, ਯੁਕਤੀ, ਤਰਕ, ਪ੍ਰਯੋਜਨ ਕਾਰਨ, ਅਨੁਮਾਨ ਲਾਉਣਾ, ਸਮਝ ਲੈਣਾ, ਮਨਾਉਣਾ; ~**able** ਵਾਜਬ, ਮੁਨਾਸਬ, ਜਾਇਜ਼; ਸੁਝਵਾਨ; ~**ing** ਤਰਕ, ਵਿਵੇਚਨ, ਯੁਕਤੀ, ਵਿਚਾਰ; ਦਲੀਲ

rebate ('ਰੀਬੇਇਟ) *n v* ਕੱਟੋਤੀ, ਛੋਟ, ਵੱਟਾ, ਮੁਜਰਾਈ, ਕਮੀ; ਛੋਟ ਦੇਣੀ; ਘਟਾਉਣਾ

rebel ('ਰੈਬੱਲ, ਰਿਬੈੱਲ) *n v* ਵਿਦਰੋਹ, ਬਾਗ਼ੀ, ਰਾਜ-ਧਰੋਹੀ; ਵਿਦਰੋਹ ਕਰਨਾ, ਬਾਗ਼ੀ ਹੋਣਾ; ~**lious** ਬਾਗ਼ੀ, ਦੇਸ਼-ਧਰੋਹੀ, ਅਵੱਗਿਆਕਾਰੀ

rebirth (ਰੀ'ਬਅ:ਥ) *n* ਪੁਨਰ-ਜਨਮ

rebound ('ਰੀਬਾਉਂਡ, ਰਿ'ਬਊਂਡ) *n v* ਟੱਪ ਖਾਣਾ, ਟਕਰਾ ਦੇ ਮੁੜਨਾ, ਬੁਝਕਣਾ, ਪਲਟਨਾ

rebuff (ਰਿ'ਬਆੱਫ) *n v* ਦੋ ਟੁੱਕ ਜਵਾਬ, ਝਿੜਕ, ਧਿੱਕਾਰ; ਝਿੜਕਣਾ, ਧਿੱਕਾਰਨਾ

rebuke (ਰਿ'ਬਯੂਕ) *n v* ਝਿੜਕ, ਘੁਰਕ, ਡਾਂਟ, ਫਿਟਕਾਰ, ਝਿੜਕਣਾ, ਡਾਂਟਣਾ

recall (ਰਿ'ਕੋਲ) *v n* ਮੋੜਨਾ, ਵਾਪਸ ਸੱਦਣਾ, ਵਾਪਸ ਬੁਲਾਉਣਾ, ਪਲਟਾਉਣਾ; ਪੁਨਰ ਸੱਦਾ

recapitulate ('ਰੀਕਅ'ਪਿਯੂਲੇਇਟ) *v* ਸੰਖੇਪ ਵਿਚ ਦੁਹਰਾਉਣਾ

recapture ('ਰੀ'ਕੈਪਚਅ*) *v n* ਪੁਨਰ-ਬੰਦੀਕਰਨ; ਫਿਰ ਜਿੱਤ ਲੈਣਾ; ਫਿਰ ਬੰਦੀ ਬਣਾਉਣਾ

recast ('ਰੀ'ਹਾਸਟ) *n v* ਨਵਾਂ ਸਾਂਚਾ, ਨਵਾਂ ਰੂਪ, ਨਵੀਂ ਸ਼ਕਲ; ਦੁਬਾਰਾ ਢਾਲਣਾ, ਨਵਾਂ ਰੂਪ ਦੇਣਾ

recede (ਰਿ'ਸੀਡ) *v* ਪਿੱਛੇ ਹਟਣਾ, ਵਾਪਸ ਹੋਣਾ, ਮੁੜਨਾ, ਬਦਲ ਜਾਣਾ

receipt (ਰੀ'ਸੀਟ) *n* ਵਸੂਲੀ, ਵਸੂਲ ਹੋਈ ਰਕਮ; ਰਸੀਦ, ਪ੍ਰਾਪਤੀ-ਪੱਤਰ

receive (ਰਿ'ਸੀਵ) *v* ਲੈਣਾ, ਪ੍ਰਾਪਤ ਕਰਨਾ, ਸਵੀਕਾਰ ਕਰਨਾ, ਅਧਿਕਾਰ ਵਿਚ ਲੈਣਾ, ਕਾਬੂ ਕਰਨਾ, ਫੜਨਾ; ~r ਸੁਆਗਤ ਕਰਨ ਵਾਲਾ; ਅਤਿਥੀ-ਪਾਲਨ ਕਰਨ ਵਾਲਾ, ਗ੍ਰਹੀ

recent ('ਰੀਸੰਟ) *a* ਹੁਣ ਦਾ, ਮੌਜੂਦਾ, ਨਵਾਂ ਨਵੀਨ, ਨੂਤਨ, ਆਧੁਨਿਕ; ~ly ਹੁਣੇ ਹੁਣੇ, ਹਾਲ ਹੀ

receptacle (ਰਿ'ਸੈਂਪਟਅਕਲ) *a* ਥਾਂ, ਭਾਂਡਾ, ਪਾਤਰ, (ਬਨ) ਬੀਜਦਾਨੀ

reception (ਰਿ'ਸੈਂਪਸ਼ਨ) *n* ਸੁਆਗਤ, ਆਉ-ਭਗਤ, ਮਿਲਣੀ, ਸਤਿਕਾਰ

receptive (ਰਿ'ਸੈਂਪਟਿਵ) *a* ਤੇਜ਼ (ਦਿਮਾਗ਼), ਸੁਗ੍ਰਹਿਕ, ਗ੍ਰਹਿਣਸ਼ੀਲ

recess (ਰਿ'ਸੈਸ) *n v* ਵਿਸ਼ਰਾਮ, ਛੁੱਟੀ, ਵਾਪਸੀ, ਗੁਪਤ ਥਾਂ, ਗੁਫ਼ਾ, ਖੋਹ; ਟੋਆ ਪਾਉਣਾ, ਪਿੱਛੇ ਹਟਣਾ; ~ion ਸੰਕੋਚ, ਸਿਮਟਣ, ਸੁੰਗੜਨ, ਮੰਦਵਾੜਾ; ਵਿਰਾਮ

recipe ('ਰੈਸਿਪਿ) *n* ਨੁਸਖ਼ਾ; ਤਰੀਕਾ; ਜੁਗਤ

recipiency (ਰਅ'ਸਿਪਿਅੰਸਿ) *n* ਪ੍ਰਾਪਤੀ; ਗ੍ਰਹਿਣ-ਸ਼ੀਲ; ਆਦਾਨ

recipient (ਰਅ'ਸਿਪਿਅੰਟ) *n* ਪ੍ਰਾਪਤ ਕਰਤਾ

reciprocal (ਰਿ'ਸਿਪ੍ਰਅਕਲ) *a* ਦੋਤਰਫ਼ਾ; ਪਰਸਪਰ; ਸਮਾਨ, ਮਿਲਦਾ-ਜੁਲਦਾ, ਹੂਬਹੂ

reciprocate (ਰਿ'ਸਿਪ੍ਰਅਕੇਇਟ) *v* ਅਦਲਾ-ਬਦਲੀ ਕਰਨੀ; ਪ੍ਰਤਿਫਲ, ਬਦਲਾ ਦੇਣਾ

reciprocation (ਰਿ'ਸਿਪ੍ਰਅ'ਕੇਇਸ਼ਨ) *n* ਆਦਾਨ-ਪ੍ਰਦਾਨ; ਲੈਣ-ਦੇਣ; ਅਦਲ-ਬਦਲ

recision (ਰਿ'ਸਿਯ਼ਨ) *n* ਰੱਦਣ, ਨਿਰਾਕਰਨ

recital (ਰਿ'ਸਾਇਟਲ) *n* ਬਿਰਤਾਂਤ; ਪਾਠ; (ਸੰਗੀ) ਗਾਇਨ

recitation ('ਰੈਸਿ'ਟੇਇਸ਼ਨ) *n* ਪਾਠ ਉਚਾਰਨ; ਗਾਇਨ; ਗਾਣਾ

recite (ਰਿ'ਸਾਇਟ) ਅਲਾਪਣਾ, ਪਾਠ ਕਰਨਾ; ਪੜ੍ਹਨਾ, ਕ੍ਰਮ ਅਨੁਸਾਰ ਗਿਣਨਾ; ਯਾਦ-ਸ਼ਕਤੀ ਨਾਲ ਕਵਿਤਾ ਪੜ੍ਹਨੀ

reckon ('ਰੈਕ(ਅ)ਨ) *v* ਨਿਸ਼ਚਤ ਕਰਨਾ, ਤੈ ਕਰਨਾ; ਗਿਣਤੀ ਕਰਨੀ; ਹਿਸਾਬ-ਕਿਤਾਬ ਕਰਨਾ; ਵਿਸ਼ੇਸ਼ਤਾਵਾਂ ਗਿਣਲੀਆਂ, ਵਿਚਾਰਨਾ, ਸਮਝਾਉਣਾ, ਮੰਨਣਾ; ਨਤੀਜਾ ਕੱਢਣਾ; ~er ਗਣਕ, ਗਿਣਤੀਕਾਰ, ਹਿਸਾਬ ਲਗਾਉਣ ਵਾਲਾ; ~ing ਗਣਨਾ, ਗਿਣਤੀ, ਲੇਖਾ (ਹਿਸਾਬ)

reclaim (ਰਿ'ਕਲੇਇਮ) *n v* ਪੁਨਰ-ਪ੍ਰਾਪਤੀ, ਸੁਧਾਰ; ਕੱਢਣਾ, ਮੁਕਤ ਕਰਨਾ, ਸੱਭਿਅ ਬਣਾਉਣਾ, ਸੁਧਾਰਨਾ

reclamation ('ਰੈਕਲਅ'ਮੇਇਸ਼ਨ) *n* ਉਧਾਰ, ਭੋ ਸੁਧਾਰ, ਮੁੜ-ਪ੍ਰਾਪਤੀ

reclame ('ਰੇਇਕਲਾਮ) (F) n ਇਸ਼ਤਿਹਾਰਬਾਜ਼ੀ, ਸਵੈ-ਪ੍ਰਸਿੱਧੀ, ਸ਼ੁਹਰਤਬਾਜ਼ੀ

recline (ਰਿ'ਕਲਾਇਨ) v ਟਿਕਾਉਣਾ, ਝੁਕਾਉਣਾ, ਲਿਟਾਉਣਾ; ਆਸਰਾ ਲੈਣਾ; ਸਹਾਰਾ ਲੈਣਾ

recluse (ਰਿ'ਕਲੂਸ) a n ਇਕਾਂਤ; ਸੰਨਿਆਸੀ, ਵੈਰਾਗੀ, ਤਪੱਸਵੀ, ਇਕਾਂਤਵਾਸੀ

recognition ('ਰੈੱਕਅਗ'ਨਿਸ਼ਨ) n ਪਛਾਣ, ਸ਼ਨਾਖ਼ਤ; ਸਵੀਕਾਰ, ਮਾਨਤਾ

recongnizable ('ਰੈੱਕਅਗਨਾਇਜ਼ਅਬਲ) a ਮੰਨਿਆ, ਮਾਨਯੋਗ, ਸਵੀਕਾਰ ਕਰਨ ਯੋਗ

recongizance (ਰਿ'ਕੌਗਨਿਜ਼ਅੰਸ) n ਮੁਚੱਲਕਾ, ਜ਼ਮਾਨਤ; ਪਛਾਣ

recognize ('ਰੈੱਕਅਗਨਾਇਜ਼) v ਵਿਅਕਤ ਕਰਨਾ, ਪਰਗਟ ਕਰਨਾ; ਜਾਣਨਾ, ਪਛਾਣਨਾ, ਸਵੀਕਾਰ ਕਰਨਾ, ਮਾਨਤਾ ਦੇਣੀ; **~d** ਮਾਨਤਾ-ਪ੍ਰਾਪਤ, ਪਰਿਚਿਤ

recollect ('ਰੈੱਕਅ'ਲੈੱਕਟ) v ਯਾਦ ਕਰ ਲੈਣਾ; ਯਾਦ ਵਿਚ ਲੈ ਆਉਣਾ; **~ion** ਯਾਦ, ਸਿਮਰਤੀ, ਯਾਦਗਾਰ, ਯਾਦਦਾਸ਼ਤ

recommend ('ਰੈੱਕਅ'ਮੈਂਡ) v ਸਿਫ਼ਾਰਸ਼ ਕਰਨੀ; ਪ੍ਰਸੰਸਾ ਕਰਨੀ, ਸਲਾਹੁਣਾ; **~ation** ਸਿਫ਼ਾਰਸ਼, ਪ੍ਰਸੰਸਾ, ਸ਼ਲਾਘਾ

recompensation ('ਰੈੱਕਅਪੈੱਨ'ਸੇਇਸ਼ਨ) n ਮੁਆਵਜ਼ਾ, ਪੁਨਰ-ਪੂਰਤੀ, ਹਾਨੀ-ਪੂਰਤੀ

recompense ('ਰੈੱਕਅਮਪੈੱਸ) n v ਮੁਆਵਜ਼ਾ, ਹਰਜਾਨਾ; ਇਨਾਮ, ਪੁਰਸਕਾਰ; ਪ੍ਰਤੀਫਲ; ਹਰਜਾਨਾ ਦੇਣਾ, ਮੁਆਵਜ਼ਾ ਦੇਣਾ

reconnaissance (ਰਿ'ਕੌਨਿਸਅੰਸ) n ਜਾਸੂਸੀ, ਦੇਖ-ਭਾਲ; ਜਾਸੂਸੀ ਦਸਤਾ

reconsider ('ਰੀਕਅੰ'ਸੀਡ਼*) v ਪੁਨਰ-ਵਿਚਾਰ ਕਰਨਾ, ਫਿਰ ਤੋਂ ਸੋਚਣਾ

reconstitute ('ਰੀ'ਕੌੱਨਸਟਿਟਯੂਟ) v ਪੁਨਰ-ਸਿਰਜਨਾ ਕਰਨੀ, ਮੁੜ ਬਣਾਉਣਾ, ਮੁੜ ਉਸਾਰਨਾ

reconstitution ('ਰੀ'ਕੌੱਨਸਟਿ'ਟਯੂਸ਼ਨ) n ਪੁਨਰ-ਸਥਾਪਨਾ, ਪੁਨਰ-ਨਿਰਮਾਣ; ਪੁਨਰ-ਗਠਨ

reconstruct ('ਰੀਕਅੰ'ਸਟਰਅੱਕਟ) v ਪੁਨਰ-ਰਚਨਾ ਕਰਨੀ, ਪੁਨਰ-ਨਿਰਮਾਣ ਕਰਨਾ

record ('ਰੈੱਕੌਡ, ਰਿਕੋਡ) n v ਦਸਤਾਵੇਜ਼; ਤਹਰੀਰ, ਨਕਲ, ਪਰਤ, ਫ਼ਰਦ, ਪ੍ਰਤੀਲਿਪੀ; ਲਿਖਤੀ ਪ੍ਰਮਾਣ, ਸੁਰੱਖਿਅਤ ਵੇਰਵਾ; ਲਿਪੀਬੱਧ ਕਰਨਾ; ਕਿਸੇ ਪੱਕੇ ਰੂਪ ਵਿਚ ਰੱਖਣਾ

recoup (ਰਿ'ਕੂਪ) v ਰੁੱਖ ਛੱਡਣਾ; ਮੁਆਵਜ਼ਾ ਜਾਂ ਪ੍ਰਤੀਫਲ ਦੇਣਾ, ਹਾਨੀ ਪੂਰੀ ਕਰਨੀ

recourse (ਰਿ'ਕੋਸ) n ਆਸਰਾ, ਉਪਾਉ, ਚਾਰਾਜੋਈ; *have ~ to* ਸਹਾਰਾ ਲੈਣਾ

recover (ਰਿ'ਕਅੱਵ਼*) n ਪੁਨਰ-ਪ੍ਰਾਪਤ ਕਰਨਾ, ਪਹਿਲਾਂ ਵਾਲੀ ਹਾਲਤ ਵਿਚ ਫਿਰ ਆਉਣਾ; ਭਾਲ ਲੈਣਾ; ਪਹੁੰਚਣਾ, ਪੂਰਾ ਕਰਨਾ; ਪਲਟਣਾ; ਪਰਤਣਾ; **~y** ਪੁਨਰ-ਪ੍ਰਾਪਤੀ, ਰੋਗ-ਮੁਕਤੀ, ਅਰੋਗਤਾ; ਵਸੂਲੀ

recreation ('ਰੈੱਕਰਿ'ਏਇਸ਼ਨ) n ਦਿਲ-ਪਰਚਾਵਾ, ਦਿਲ-ਪਰਚਾਵਾ, ਦਿਲ-ਬਹਿਲਾਵਾ, ਮਨੋਰੰਜਨ

recruit (ਰਿ'ਕਰੂਟ) n v ਰੰਗਰੂਟ, ਨਵੀਂ ਭਰਤੀ, ਸਿਖਾਂਦਰੂ; ਭਰਤੀ ਕਰਨਾ, ਦਾਖ਼ਲ ਕਰਨਾ; **~ment** ਭਰਤੀ, ਪ੍ਰਵੇਸ਼, ਦਾਖ਼ਲਾ

rectangle ('ਰੈੱਕ'ਟੈਂਗਗਲ) a ਆਇਤ, ਸਮਚਤੁਰਭੁਜ, ਸਮਕੋਣ

rectify ('ਰੈੱਕਟਿਫਾਇ) v ਸੋਧਣਾ, ਠੀਕ ਕਰਨਾ, ਸਵਾਰਨਾ, ਦਰੁਸਤ ਕਰਨਾ

rector ('ਰੈੱਕਟਅ*) n ਸ਼ਾਸਕ, ਪ੍ਰਬੰਧਕ, ਮੁਖ-ਪਾਦਰੀ, (ਵਿਸ਼ਵ ਵਿਦਿਆਲੇ) ਦਾ ਮੁਖੀ, ਰੈਕਟਰ

recur (ਰਿ'ਕਮ:*) *v* ਦੁਹਰਾਉਣਾ, ਪੁਨਰ-ਉਕਤੀ ਕਰਨੀ, ਸੁਧ-ਪਤਾ ਲੱਗਣਾ, ਮੁੜ ਕੇ ਵਾਪਰਨਾ; **~ring** ਆਵਰਤੀ, ਆਵਰਤਕ

red (ਰੈਡ) *a n* ਲਾਲ, ਸੁਰਖ਼; ਖ਼ੂਨੀ, ਸਾਮਵਾਦੀ; **~carpet** ਸ਼ਾਹੀ ਸਵਾਗਤ; **~letter** ਯਾਦਗਾਰੀ; **~tape** ਦਫ਼ਤਰੀ ਢਿੱਲ

redeem (ਰਿ'ਡੀਮ) *v* ਛੁਡਾਉਣਾ, ਵਿਮੁਕਤ ਕਰਾਉਣਾ; ਵਾਪਸ ਲੈਣਾ

redemption (ਰਿ'ਡੈਂਪਸ਼ਨ) *n* ਬਚਾਉ, ਛੁਟਕਾਰਾ, ਖ਼ਲਾਸੀ, ਮੁਕਤੀ

redress (ਰਿ'ਡਰੈੱਸ) *v/n* ਇਲਾਜ ਕਰਨਾ, ਸੁਧਾਰਨਾ, ਦਰੁਸਤ ਕਰਨਾ, ਠੀਕ ਕਰਨਾ; ਸੁਧਾਰ, ਹਰਜਾਨਾ

reduce (ਰਿ'ਡਯੂਸ) *v* ਘਟਣਾ, ਘਟਾਉਣਾ, ਘੱਟ ਕਰਨਾ, ਖੀਣ ਕਰਨਾ, ਦੁਰਬਲ ਕਰਨਾ, ਕਮਜ਼ੋਰ ਕਰਨਾ; ਸੰਕੁਚਤ ਕਰਨਾ

reduction (ਰਿ'ਡਾਕਸ਼ਨ) *n* ਕਮੀ, ਘਾਟਾ, ਛਾਂਟ

redunant (ਰਿ'ਡਾਨਡਅੰਟ) *a* ਫ਼ਾਲਤੂ, ਅਤੀ-ਅਧਿਕ; ਵਿਅਰਥ, ਫ਼ਜ਼ੂਲ; ਭਰਪੂਰ

reduplicate (ਰਿ'ਡਯੂਪਲਿਕੇਇਟ) *v* ਦੂਣਾ ਕਰਨਾ, ਦੁਗਣਾ ਕਰਨਾ, ਵਧਾਉਣਾ; ਦੁਹਰਾਉਣਾ

reel (ਰੀਲ) *n v* ਵੇਲਣ, ਘਿਰਨੀ, ਚਰਖੀ, ਗਿੱਟੀ, ਜਤਖਜੀ, ਜੋਲਾ, ਜੀਲ; ਸੂਤ ਅਟੇਰਨ, ਉਤਾਰਨ, (ਅੱਖਾਂ ਜਾਂ ਸਿਰ) ਕੰਬਣਾ, ਡਗਮਗਾਉਣਾ

refer (ਰਿ'ਫ਼ਅ*) *n* ਸਪੁਰਦ ਕਰਨਾ, ਭੇਜਣਾ, ਹਵਾਲਾ ਦੇਣਾ, ਸੰਕੇਤ ਕਰਨਾ

referee ('ਰੈੱਫ਼ਅ'ਰੀ ਪੰਚ) *n* ਨਿਰਣਾਇਕ, ਵਿਚਾਰਕ, ਰੈਫ਼ਰੀ

reference ('ਰੈੱਫ਼ਅਰੰਸ) *n v* ਪ੍ਰਸੰਗ, ਸੰਦਰਭ, ਉਲੇਖ, ਹਵਾਲਾ, ਸੰਕੇਤ-ਚਿੰਨ੍ਹ, ਪੁਸਤਕਾਂ ਵਿਚੋਂ ਪ੍ਰਮਾਣ ਦੇਣਾ

referendum ('ਰੈੱਫ਼ਅ'ਰੈੱਨਡਅਮ) *n* ਲੋਕ-ਮੰਤ, ਜਨਮੰਤ, ਲੋਕ-ਨਿਰਣੈ

refine (ਰਿ'ਫ਼ਾਇਨ) *v* ਸੋਧਣਾ, ਸ਼ੁੱਧ ਕਰਨਾ, ਸਾਫ਼ ਕਰਨਾ ਜਾਂ ਹੋਣਾ, ਨਿਖਾਰਨਾ; **~d** ਸ਼ੁੱਧ, ਵਿਸ਼ੁੱਧ, ਨਿਰਮਲ, ਪਰਿਸ਼ਕ੍ਰਿਤ, ਸਾਫ਼

reflect (ਰਿ'ਫ਼ਲੈੱਕਟ) *v* ਪ੍ਰਤੀਬਿੰਬਤ ਕਰਨਾ, ਅਕਸ ਪਾਉਣਾ, ਉਛਲਣਾ, ਉਲਟਾ ਫਲ ਹੋਣਾ, ਪਲਟਾ ਖਾਣਾ; **~ion** ਪ੍ਰਤਿਬਿੰਬ, ਅਕਸ, ਪਰਛਾਵਾਂ; ਛਾਇਆ, ਤੁਹਮਤ, ਇਲਜ਼ਾਮ

reflex ('ਰੀਫ਼ਲੈੱਕਸ) *n a* ਪਰਤੇ, ਜੋਤ, ਝਲਕ; ਤੇਜ, ਜਲਵਾ, ਪ੍ਰਤੀਬਿੰਬਤ ਕੀਰਤੀ; ਪ੍ਰਭਾਵਤ ਭਾਗ; ਅਕਸ, ਛੋਭ, ਪਰਛਾਈਂ; ਪ੍ਰਤੀਕਿਰਿਆ, ਮੁੜਿਆ ਹੋਇਆ; (ਵਿਚਾਰ) ਅੰਤਰਮੁਖ, ਆਤਮ-ਚਿੰਤਨਮਈ

reform ('ਰੀਫ਼ੋਮ) *v n* ਪੁਨਰ-ਗਠਨ ਕਰਨਾ; ਸੋਧਣਾ; ਸੁਧਾਰਨਾ; ਸੁਧਾਰਨਾ; ਠੀਕ ਕਰਨਾ ਜਾਂ ਹੋਣਾ; **~ation** ਪੁਨਰ-ਨਿਰਮਾਣ, ਨਵ-ਨਿਰਮਾਣ, ਪੁਨਰ-ਗਠਨ, ਸੁਧਾਰ, **~er** ਸੁਧਾਰਕ ਸੰਸਕਾਰਕ; ਸੰਸ਼ੋਧਕ, ਧਰਮ-ਪਰਵਰਤਕ

refractory (ਰਿਫ਼ਰੈਕਟ(ਅ)ਰਿ) *a* ਜ਼ਿੱਦੀ, ਅੜੀਅਲ; ਅਮੋੜ, ਅਸਾਧ, ਹਠੀਲਾ, ਢੀਠ

refrain (ਰਿ'ਫ਼ਰੇਇਨ) *n v* (ਗੀਤ ਆਦਿ ਵਿਚ) ਟੇਕ; ਅੰਤਰਾ; ਰੋਕਣਾ; ਰੁਕਣਾ; ਟਲਣਾ; ਬਾਜ਼ ਆਉਣਾ, ਹਟਣਾ, ਨਾ ਕਰਨਾ; ਦਮਨ ਕਰਨਾ

refresh (ਰਿਫ਼ਰੈੱਸ਼) *v* ਮੁੜ ਜਾਨ ਪਾਉਣੀ, ਤਕੜਾ ਕਰਨਾ, ਨਵਾਂ ਕਰਨਾ; (ਅੱਗ ਨੂੰ) ਮੁੜ ਕੇ ਸੁਲਗਾਉਣਾ; ਜਗਾਉਣਾ; ਸੁਰਜੀਤ ਕਰਨਾ; ਜਲਪਾਨ ਕਰਨਾ; **~ment** ਜਲਪਾਨ; ਉਪ-ਆਹਾਰ, ਤਾਜ਼ਗੀ

refrigerate (ਰਿ'ਫ਼ਰਿਜਰੇਇਟ) *v* ਠੰਢਾ ਕਰਨਾ, ਸੀਤਲ ਕਰਨਾ; ਜਮਾਉਣਾ

refrigeration (ਰਿ'ਫ਼ਰਿਜਅਰੇਇਸ਼ਨ) *n* ਸੀਤਲੀਕਰਨ, ਠੰਢਾ ਕਰਕੇ ਜਮਾਉਣ ਦੀ ਕਿਰਿਆ

refrigerator (ਰਿਫ਼ਰਿਜਅਰੇਇਟਅ*) *n* ਰੈਫ਼ਿਜਰੇਟਰ; ਫ਼ਰਿੱਜ; ਪ੍ਰਸ਼ੀਤਕ; ਸ਼ੀਤਣ-ਜੰਤਰ

refuge ('ਰੈਫ਼ਯੂਜ) *n v* ਸ਼ਰਨ; ਓਟ; ਆੜ; ਠਿਕਾਣਾ; ਪਨਾਹ; ਆਸਰਾ ਦੇਣਾ, ਸ਼ਰਨ ਦੇਣੀ, ਪਨਾਹ ਦੇਣੀ; **~e** ਸ਼ਰਨਾਰਥੀ; ਸ਼ਰਨਾਗਤ, ਪਨਾਹਗੀਰ

refund (ਰਿਫ਼ੰਡ) *v n* ਰੁਪਿਆ ਵਾਪਸ ਕਰਨਾ; ਰਕਮ ਮੁੜ ਜਮ੍ਹਾਂ ਕਰਨੀ; ਮੋੜ ਦੇਣਾ, ਪਰਤਾ-ਉਣਾ; ਵਾਪਸ ਦੇ ਦੇਣਾ; ਵਾਪਸੀ, ਦੁਬਾਰਾ ਅਦਾਇਗੀ

refusal (ਰਿ'ਫ਼ਯੂਜ਼ਲ) *n* ਇਨਕਾਰ; ਅਪ੍ਰਵਾਨਗੀ; ਅਸਵੀਕ੍ਰਿਤੀ, ਨਾਮਨਜ਼ੂਰੀ

refuse (ਰਿਫ਼ਯੂਜ਼, 'ਰੈਫ਼ਯੂਸ) *v n a* ਨਾਂਹ ਕਰਨੀ, ਇਨਕਾਰ ਕਰਨਾ, ਨਾਬਰ ਹੋਣਾ; ਨਾਮਨਜ਼ੂਰ ਕਰਨਾ, ਅਸਵੀਕਾਰ ਕਰਨਾ; ਕੂੜਾ, ਮੈਲ; ਜੂਠ; ਰਹਿੰਦ-ਖੂੰਹਦ, ਰੱਦੀ, ਫੋਗ

refutation ('ਰੈਫ਼ਯੂਟੇਇਸ਼ਨ) *n* ਖੰਡਨ, ਨਿਸ਼ੇਧ, ਨਿਰਾਕਰਨ

refute (ਰਿ'ਫ਼ਯੂਟ) *v* ਖੰਡਨ ਕਰਨਾ, ਰੱਦ ਕਰਨਾ, ਝੁਠਲਾਉਣਾ, ਅਸਿੱਧ ਕਰਨਾ, ਤਰਦੀਦ ਕਰਨੀ

regal (ਰੀਗਲ) *a* ਰਾਜਕੀ, ਸ਼ਾਹੀ, ਸ਼ਹਾਨਾ, ਸ਼ਾਨਦਾਰ; **~ity** ਪ੍ਰਭੁਤਵ, ਰਾਜਤਵ, ਰਾਜ-ਕਾਜ, ਰਈਸੀ, ਰਾਜਕੀ ਠਾਠ

regale (ਰਿ'ਗੇਇਲ) *n v* ਦਾਅਵਤ; ਤ੍ਰਿਪਤ ਕਰਨਾ, ਪ੍ਰਸੰਨ ਕਰਨਾ, ਪ੍ਰਫੁੱਲਤ ਹੋਣਾ; **~ment** ਜ਼ਿਆਫ਼ਤ; ਜਸ਼ਨ, ਮਨੋਰੰਜਨ

regard (ਰਿ'ਗਾਰਡ) *v n* ਆਦਰ ਕਰਨਾ, ਸਤਿਕਾਰ ਕਰਨਾ; ਸਮਝਣਾ; ਸਨਮਾਨ, ਆਦਰ, ਸਤਿਕਾਰ; **~ful** ਸਾਵਧਾਨ; ਖ਼ਬਰਦਾਰ, ਸਚੇਤ, ਸਨਮਾਨ ਕਰਨ ਵਾਲਾ; ਆਦਰ ਕਰਨ ਵਾਲਾ; **~less** ਬੇਪਰਵਾਹ, ਧੋਖਿਕਰ, ਅਣ-ਉਤਸੁਕ

regency ('ਰੀਜਅੰਸਿ) *n* ਨਵਾਬ-ਸ਼ਾਹੀ, ਰਾਜ-ਪ੍ਰਤੀਨਿਧਤਾ, ਰਾਜ-ਪ੍ਰਤੀਨਿਧ ਪਦ

regent ('ਰੀਜਅੰਟ) *n* ਸ਼ਾਹੀ-ਪ੍ਰਤੀਨਿਧ, ਸ਼ਾਸਨ-ਪਾਲ

regime (ਰੇਇ'ਯ਼ੀਮ) *n* ਸ਼ਾਸਨ, ਸ਼ਾਸਨ-ਪੱਧਤੀ, ਰਾਜ-ਸ਼ਾਸਨ-ਪ੍ਰਣਾਲੀ; ਰਾਜ-ਪ੍ਰਬੰਧ, ਸ਼ਾਸਨ-ਕਾਲ, ਰਾਜ-ਕਾਲ

regiment ('ਰੈਜਿਮਅੰਟ, 'ਰੈਜਿਮੈਂਟ) *n v* ਰਜਮੰਟ, ਪਲਟਨ, ਨਿਯਮ, ਵਿਧਾਨ, ਸ਼ਾਸਨ; ਰਜਮੰਟ ਬਣਾਉਣਾ, ਜਥੇਬੰਦ ਕਰਨਾ, ਸੰਗਠਤ ਕਰਨਾ; **~ation** ਜਥੇਬੰਦੀ, ਸੰਗਠਨ; ਕਠੋਰ ਨਿਯੰਤਰਨ

region ('ਰੀਜ(ਅ)ਨ) *n* ਖੇਤਰ, ਪ੍ਰਦੇਸ਼, ਇਲਾਕਾ, ਖੰਡ, ਅਧਿਕਾਰ-ਖੇਤਰ; **~al** ਖੇਤਰੀ, ਪ੍ਰਾਦੇਸ਼ਕ; ਇਲਾਕਾਈ; ਸਥਾਨਕ

register ('ਰੈਜਿਸਟਅ*) *n v* ਰਜਿਸਟਰ, ਵਹੀ, ਸੂਚੀ; (ਭਾਸ਼ਾ) ਪਰਯੁਕਤੀ; ਇੰਦਰਾਜ ਕਰਨਾ, ਲੇਖਬੱਧ ਕਰਨਾ; (ਅਲੰਕਾਰ) ਯਾਦ ਕਰ ਲੈਣਾ

registrar ('ਰੈਜਿ'ਸਟਰਾ*) *n* (ਯੂਨੀਵਰਸਿਟੀ ਦਾ) ਰਜਿਸਟਰਾਰ, ਆਲੇਖਕ, ਪੰਜੀਕਾਰ

registration ('ਰੈਜਿ'ਸਟਰੇਇਸ਼ਨ) *n* ਦਾਖ਼ਲਾ, ਇੰਦਰਾਜ, ਅੰਕਣ

registry ('ਰੈਜਿਸਟਰਿ) *n* ਇੰਦਰਾਜ, ਆਲੇਖਨ, ਦਫ਼ਤਰ ਰਜਿਸਟਰੀ

regress ('ਰੀਗਰੈਸ, ਰਿ'ਗਰੈਸ) *n v* ਵਾਪਸੀ, ਪਿਛਾੜ, ਉਤਰਾਈ, ਅਵਨਤੀ, ਪ੍ਰਤੀਗਮਨ; ਪਿੱਛੇ ਹਟਣਾ, ਵਾਪਸ ਜਾਣਾ; **~ion** ਉਲਟੀ ਚਾਲ, ਵਾਪਸੀ, ਪ੍ਰੀਵਰਤਨ; **~ive** ਮੁੜਵੀਂ, ਪਿਛਾਖੜੀ, ਪਛੜਵੀਂ, ਪ੍ਰਤੀਗਾਮੀ, ਪ੍ਰੀਵਰਤਨਸ਼ੀਲ

regret (ਰਿ'ਗਰੈੱਟ) *v n* ਅਫ਼ਸੋਸ ਕਰਨ, ਖੇਦ ਪਰਗਟ ਕਰਨਾ, ਦੁੱਖੀ ਹੋਣਾ, ਪਛਤਾਉਣਾ, ਸ਼ਰਮਸਾਰ ਹੋਣਾ; ਖੇਦ, ਅਫ਼ਸੋਸ, ਦੁੱਖ

regular ('ਰੈਗਯੁਲਅ*) *a* ਨਿਯਮਕ, ਬਾਕਾਇਦਾ, ਬਰਾਬਰ, ਨਿਯਮਬੱਧ, ਨਿਯਮ-ਪੁਰਵਕ; **~ity** ਨਿਯਮੱਤਤਾ, ਬਾਕਾਇਦਗੀ, ਸੰਜਮ, ਪਾਬੰਦੀ, ਨਿਰੰਤਰਤਾ; **~ize** ਨਿਯਮਬੱਧ ਕਰਨਾ, ਸੁਵਿਵਸਥਿਤ ਕਰਨਾ; ਵਿਧੀ ਰੂਪ ਦੇਣਾ; ਪੱਕਾ ਕਰਨਾ; **~ization** ਨਿਯਮਿਤਾ, ਬਾਕਾਇਦਗੀ, ਨਿਯਮਬੰਧਨ, ਵਿਧੀ ਅਨੁਸਰਣ

regulato ('ਰੈਗਯੁਲੇਇਟ) *v* ਨਿਯਮਤ ਕਰਨਾ, ਵਿਧਾਨ ਬਣਾਉਣਾ, ਸ਼ਾਸਨ ਕਰਨਾ, ਕ੍ਰਮਬੱਧ ਕਰਨਾ, ਦਰੁਸਤ ਕਰਨਾ, ਠੀਕ ਕਰਨਾ

rehabillate ('ਰੀਅ'ਬਿਲਿਟੇਇਟ) *v* ਮੁੜ ਵਸਾਉਣਾ, ਪੁਨਰਵਾਸ ਦੇਣਾ, ਬਹਾਲ ਕਰਨਾ

rehabilitation ('ਰੀਅ'ਬਿਲਿ'ਟੇਇਸ਼ਨ) *n* ਮੁੜ-ਵਸੇਬਾ, ਪੁਨਰਵਾਸ; ਬਹਾਲੀ, ਪੁਨਰ-ਸਥਾਪਨ

rehearsal (ਰਿ'ਹਅ:ਸਲ) *n* ਦੁਹਰਾਉ, ਅਭਿਆਸ, ਤਿਆਰੀ

reign (ਰੇਇਨ) *n v* ਪ੍ਰਭੁਤਾ, ਰਾਜ, ਬਾਦਸ਼ਾਹੀ; ਸ਼ਾਸਨ-ਕਾਲ; ਰਾਜ ਕਰਨਾ, ਸ਼ਾਸਨ ਕਰਨਾ

reimburse ('ਰੀਇਮ'ਬਅ:ਸ) *v* ਅਦਾ ਕਰਨਾ, ਚੁਕਾਉਣਾ, ਵਾਪਸ ਕਰਨਾ, ਭਰਨਾ; **~ment** ਵਾਪਸੀ, ਅਦਾਇਗੀ

rein (ਰੇਇਨ) *n v* ਵਾਗ, ਵਾਗਾ-ਡੋਰ, ਰਾਸ; ਕਾਬੂ ਕਰਨਾ, ਵਾਗਾਂ ਕੱਸਣੀਆਂ

reinforce ('ਰੀਇਨ'ਫ਼ੋਸ) *v* ਸਹਾਰਾ ਦੇਣਾ, ਬਲਵਾਨ ਬਣਾਉਣਾ, ਤਕੜਾ ਕਰਨਾ; ਵਾਪਾ ਕਰਨਾ, ਸਮਰਥਨ ਕਰਨਾ, ਪੁਸ਼ਟੀ ਕਰਨੀ; **~ment** ਪੁਨਰ ਬਲ-ਸੰਗਠਨ, ਪੁਸ਼ਟੀਕਰਨ

reinstate ('ਰੀਇਨ'ਸਟੇਇਟ) *v* ਮੁੜ ਕੇ ਸਥਾਪਤ ਕਰਨਾ, ਬਹਾਲ ਕਰਨਾ; **~ment** ਬਹਾਲੀ, ਪੁਨਰ-ਸਥਾਪਨਾ

reiterate (ਰੀ'ਇਟਅਰੇਇਟ) *v* ਦੁਹਰਾਉਣਾ, ਬਾਰ ਬਾਰ ਕਹਿਣਾ; ਪੁਨਰਾਵ੍ਰਿਤੀ ਕਰਨੀ

reject (ਰਿ'ਜੈੱਕਟ) *v* ਰੱਦ ਕਰਨਾ, ਇਨਕਾਰ ਕਰਨਾ, ਅਸਵੀਕਾਰ ਕਰਨਾ, ਪਰਿਤਿਆਗਾ ਕਰਨਾ; **~ion** ਅਸਵੀਨਿਤੀ, ਅਸਵੀਕਰਨ, ਤਿਆਗ

rejoice (ਰਿ'ਜੋਇਸ) *v* ਖ਼ੁਸ਼ ਕਰਨਾ ਜਾਂ ਹੋਣਾ, ਪ੍ਰਸੰਨ ਕਰਨਾ ਜਾਂ ਹੋਣਾ, ਪ੍ਰਫੁੱਲਤ ਕਰਨਾ, ਆਨੰਦਤ ਕਰਨਾ

rejoicings (ਰਿ'ਜੋਇਸਿਙਜ਼) *n* ਖ਼ੁਸ਼ੀਆਂ, ਆਨੰਦ-ਉਤਸਵ, ਰੰਗ-ਰਲੀਆਂ, ਰਾਗਾ-ਰੰਗ

rejoin ('ਰੀ'ਜੋਇਨ) *v* ਮੁੜ ਸ਼ਾਮਲ ਹੋਣਾ, ਮੁੜ ਮਿਲਾਉਣਾ; ਦੁਬਾਰਾ ਜੋੜਨਾ; ਪੁਨਰ-ਸੰਮਿਲਤ ਹੋਣਾ; **~der** ਮੋੜਵਾਂ ਉੱਤਰ, ਜਵਾਬ, ਪ੍ਰਤੀ-ਉੱਤਰ

rejuvenate (ਰਿ'ਜੂਵ਼ਅਨੇਇਟ) *v* ਮੁੜ ਕੇ ਜਵਾਨ ਹੋਣਾ, ਕਾਇਆ-ਕਲਪ ਹੋਣੀ

rejuvenation (ਰਿ'ਜੂਵ਼ਅ'ਨੇਇਸ਼ਨ) *n* ਕਾਇਆ ਕਲਪ, ਪੁਨਰ-ਜੋਬਨ

relate (ਰਿ'ਲੇਇਟ) *v* ਕਹਿਣਾ, ਧਿਆਨ ਕਰਨਾ; ਵਰਣਨ ਕਰਨਾ; ਦੁਹਰਾਉਣਾ; ਪੁਨਰਾਵ੍ਰਿਤੀ ਕਰਨੀ

relation (ਰਿ'ਲੇਇਸ਼ਨ) *n* ਸਬੰਧ ਮੇਲ; ਜੋੜ; ਰਾਬਤਾ, ਵਾਸਤਾ; ਸੰਪਰਕ; **~ship** ਸਬੰਧ; ਨਾਤਾ, ਰਿਸ਼ਤਾ, ਰਿਸ਼ਤੇਦਾਰੀ, ਸ਼ਰੀਕਾ, ਭਾਈਬੰਦੀ

relative ('ਰੈੱਲਅਟਿਵ਼) *a n* (ਵਿਆ) ਸੰਯੋਜਕ, ਸਬੰਧ-ਸੂਚਕ; ਸਾਪੇਖ, ਪਰਸਪਰ ਸਬੰਧ, ਪ੍ਰਾਸੰਗਕ, ਰਿਸ਼ਤੇਦਾਰ, ਸ਼ਰੀਕ

relativism ('ਰੈੱਲਅਟਿਵ਼ਿਜ਼(ਅ)ਮ) *n* ਸਾਪੇਖਵਾਦ

relativity (ਰੈਲਅ'ਟਿਵ੍ਅਟਿ) *n* ਸਾਪੇਖਤਾ

relax (ਰਿ'ਲੈਕਸ) *v* ਸਿਥਲ ਕਰਨਾ ਜਾਂ ਪੈਣਾ; ਢਿੱਲਾ ਕਰਨਾ ਜਾਂ ਪੈਣਾ, ਰਿਆਇਤ ਕਰਨੀ, ਠੰਢਾ ਪੈ ਜਾਣਾ, ਹਲਕਾ ਕਰਨਾ, ਨਰਮ ਕਰਨਾ; ~ation ਢਿੱਲ, ਅਲਸਾਹਟ, ਨਰਮੀ, ਰਿਆਇਤ; ਸਿਥਲੀਕਰਨ, ਵਿਸ਼ਰਾਮ

relay ('ਰੀਲੇਇ, ਰੀ'ਲੇਇ) *n v* ਨਵੇਂ ਘੋੜਿਆਂ ਦਾ ਸਮੂਹ; ਰਿਲੇ ਦੌੜ; ਨਵੀਂ ਸਮਗਰੀ ਰਿਲੇ; ਅਲੰਕਰਤ ਕਰਨਾ; ਕ੍ਰਮਵਾਰ ਰੱਖਣਾ, ਮੁੜ ਰੱਖਣਾ; (ਰੇਡਿਓ ਤੋਂ) ਅੱਗੇ ਪ੍ਰਸਾਰਤ ਕਰਨਾ

release (ਰਿ'ਲੀਜ਼) *v n* ਮੁਕਤ ਕਰਨਾ, ਛੱਡ ਦੇਣਾ; ਸੁਤੰਤਰ ਕਰਨਾ, ਆਜ਼ਾਦ ਕਰਨਾ

relegate ('ਰੈਲਿਗੇਇਟ) *n* ਦੇਸ਼-ਨਿਕਾਲਾ ਦੇਣਾ; ਪਿੱਛੇ ਸੁੱਟਣਾ, ਦਰਜਾ ਘਟਾਉਣਾ

relegation ('ਰੈਲਿ'ਗੇਇਸ਼ਨ) *n* ਦੇਸ਼-ਨਿਕਾਲਾ, ਸਪੁਰਦਗੀ

relent (ਰਿ'ਲੈਂਟ) *v* ਪਸੀਜਣਾ, ਪਿਘਲਣਾ, ਨਰਮ ਪੈਣਾ, ਤਰਸ ਖਾਣਾ

relevance, relevancy ('ਰੈਲਅਵ੍ਅੰਸ, 'ਰੈਲਅਵ੍ਅੰਸਿ) *n* ਪ੍ਰਸੰਗ ਅਨੁਕੂਲਤਾ, ਸੰਬੰਧਤਾ; ਪ੍ਰਾਸੰਗਕਤਾ

relevant ('ਰੈਲਅਵ੍ਅੰਟ) *a* ਸਬੰਧਿਤ, ਪ੍ਰਾਸੰਗਕ, ਸੰਗਤ, ਸੰਬਧ

reliability (ਰਿਲਾਇਅ'ਬਿਲਅਟਿ) *n* ਵਿਸ਼ਵਾਸ ਯੋਗਤਾ; ਪਕਿਆਈ

reliable (ਰਿ'ਲਾਇਅਬਲ) *a* ਭਰੋਸੇਯੋਗ, ਵਿਸ਼ਵਾਸਯੋਗ

reliance (ਰਿ'ਲਾਇਅੰਸ) *n* ਆਸਰਾ; ਨਿਰਭਰਤਾ, ਵਿਸ਼ਵਾਸ, ਭਰੋਸਾ

relic ('ਰੈਲਿਕ) *n* ਨਿਸ਼ਾਨੀ, ਯਾਦਗਾਰ, ਸਮਾਰਕ; ਸਿਮਰਤੀ-ਚਿੰਨ੍ਹ, ਲਾਸ਼ ਜਾਂ ਅਸਥੀਆਂ, ਪਵਿੱਤਰ ਨਿਸ਼ਾਨੀਆਂ

relieve (ਰਿ'ਲੀਵ) *v* ਆਰਾਮ ਦੇਣਾ, ਸ਼ਾਂਤੀ ਦੇਣੀ, ਸਹਾਰਾ ਦੇਣਾ; ਭਾਰਮੁਕਤ ਕਰਨਾ, ਛਾਰਗ ਕਰਨਾ, ਪਦ-ਮੁਕਤ ਕਰਨਾ

religion (ਰਿ'ਲਿਜ(ਅ)ਨ) *n* ਧਰਮ; ਪੰਥ, ਮੱਤ, ਮਜ਼ੂਬ, ਦੀਨ; ਕਰੱਤਵ

religious (ਰਿ'ਲਿਜਅਸ) *n a* ਧਾਰਮਕ, ਭਗਤ, ਦੀਨਦਾਰ, ਧਰਮਾਤਮਾ; ਧਰਮ-ਸੰਘੀ

relinquish (ਰਿ'ਲਿੰਕਵਿਸ਼) *v* ਤਿਆਗਣਾ, ਛੱਡਣਾ, ਮੁਕਤ ਹੋਣਾ, ਤੰਜਣਾ, ਸਬੰਧ ਵਿੱਛੇਦ ਕਰਨੇ, ਸਬੰਧ ਤੋੜਨੇ; ~ment ਤਿਆਗ, ਛੱਡ-ਛੜਾ, ਦਸਤਬਰਦਾਰਗੀ

relish ('ਰੈਲਿਸ਼) *n v* ਸੁਆਦ, ਰਸ, ਮਜ਼ਾ, ਚਾਟ, ਮਸਾਲਾ, ਚਟਣੀ, ਸੁਆਦ ਆਉਣਾ, ਮਜ਼ਾ ਲੈਣਾ, ਰਸ ਲੈਣਾ

reluctance (ਰਿ'ਲਅਕਟਇੰਸ) *n* ਅਸੰਤੁਸ਼ਟਤਾ; ਅਰੁਚੀ, ਝਿਜਕ, ਸੰਕੋਚ, ਵਿਮੁਖਤਾ, ਵਿਰਕਤਾ

reluctant (ਰਿ'ਲਅਕਟਅੰਟ) *a* ਅਸੰਤੁਸ਼ਟ, ਵਿਮੁਖ, ਝਿਜਕਦਾ, ਬੇਦਿਲਾ

rely (ਰਿ'ਲਾਇ) *v* ਨਿਰਭਰ ਹੋਣਾ, ਆਸਰਤ ਹੋਣਾ, ਆਸਰਾ ਤੱਕਣਾ ਜਾਂ ਲੈਣਾ; ਭਰੋਸਾ ਕਰਨਾ ਜਾਂ ਰੱਖਣਾ, ਵਿਸਾਹ ਕਰਨਾ

remain (ਰਿ'ਮੇਇਨ) *v* ਬਾਕੀ ਬਚਣਾ, ਟਿਕਣਾ, ਕਾਇਮ ਰਹਿਣਾ, ਵਿਦਮਾਨ ਹੋਣਾ; ~s ਦੇਹ, ਲੋਥ, ਹੱਡੀਆਂ, ਫੁੱਲ, ਅਸਥੀਆਂ; ਬਚਿਆ-ਖੁਚਿਆ; ਨਿਸ਼ਾਨ, ਯਾਦਗਾਰ

remand (ਰਿ'ਮਾਂਡ) *n v* ਪੁਨਰ-ਅਰਪਣ, ਸਪੁਰਦਗੀ, ਰੀਮਾਂਡ; ਵਾਪਸੀ, ਹੁਕਮ ਦੇਣਾ, ਵਾਪਸ ਕਰਨਾ, ਸਪੁਰਦ ਕਰਨਾ

remark (ਰਿ'ਮਾਕ) *v* ਆਲੋਚਨਾ ਕਰਨੀ, ਵਿਚਾਰ ਦੇਣਾ, ਟੀਕਾ-ਟਿੱਪਣੀ ਕਰਨੀ; ~able ਵਚਿੱਤਰ,

ਅਨੂਠਾ; ਉਘੜਵਾਂ, ਅਸਧਾਰਨ; ਮਾਅਰਕੇ ਦਾ; ~ed ਪ੍ਰਮੁੱਖ, ਸਪਸ਼ਟ, ਸਾਫ਼

remedial (ਰਿ'ਮੀਡਯਅਲ) *a* ਉਪਾਉ ਵਾਲਾ, ਸਾਧਕ

remedy ('ਰਿੱਮਅਡਿ) *n v* ਇਲਾਜ, ਉਪਾਉ, ਉਪਚਾਰ; ਇਲਾਜ ਕਰਨਾ, ਉਪਚਾਰ ਕਰਨਾ

remember (ਰਿ'ਮੈੱਮਬ*) *v* ਯਾਦ ਰੱਖਣਾ; ਯਾਦ ਆਉਣਾ; ਖ਼ਿਆਲ ਵਿਚ ਰੱਖਣਾ; ਕੰਠਸਥ ਕਰਨਾ

remembrance (ਰਿ'ਸੈਂਮਬਰਅੰਸ) *n* ਯਾਦ, ਸਿਮਰਤੀ, ਯਾਦਗਾਰ, ਨਿਸ਼ਾਨੀ

remind (ਰਿ'ਮਾਇੰਡ*) *v* ਯਾਦ ਦਿਆਉਣਾ, ਹੇਤੇ ਕਰਾਉਣਾ, ਜਤਾਉਣਾ; ~er ਤਾਕੀਦ, ਚੇਤਾਵਨੀ; ਸਮਰਥ-ਪੱਤਰ

reminiscence ('ਰਿਮਿ'ਨਿਸੰਸ) *n* ਯਾਦ, ਸਮਰਥ, ਯਾਦਾਂ, ਆਪ-ਬੀਤੀਆਂ; ਨਿਸ਼ਾਨੀ, ਝਲਕ

reminiscent ('ਰਿਮਿ'ਨਿਸੰਟ) *a* ਸਮਾਰਕ; ਮੇਲ-ਖਾਂਦਾ, ਮਿਲਦਾ

remit (ਰਿ'ਮਿਟ) *v* ਬਖ਼ਸ਼ਣਾ; ਮਾਫ਼ ਕਰਨਾ ਜਾਂ ਹੋਣਾ; ਖਿਮਾ ਕਰਨੀ, ਤਿਆਗ ਕਰਨਾ; ~tence ਭੇਜੀ ਹੋਈ ਰਕਮ, ਘਲਵਾਈ, ਭਿਜਵਾਈ

remnant ('ਰੈੱਮਨਅੰਟ) *n* ਬਚਿਆ-ਖੁਚਿਆ, ਰਹਿੰਦ-ਖੂੰਹਦ

remonstrate ('ਰੈੱਮਅਨਸਟਰੇਇਟ) *v* ਰੋਸ ਪਰਗਟ ਕਰਨਾ, ਵਿਰੋਧ ਕਰਨਾ, ਹੁੱਜਤ ਕਰਨਾ, ਸਮਝਾਉਣਾ-ਬੁਝਾਉਣਾ

remorse (ਰਿ'ਮੋ:ਸ) *n* ਪਛਤਾਵਾ, ਪਸ਼ੇਮਾਨੀ, ਪਸ਼ਚਾਤਾਪ; ~ful ਪਸ਼ਚਾਤਾਪ-ਪੂਰਨ

remote (ਰਿ'ਮਅਉਟ) *a* ਦੂਰ, ਅਲੱਗ, ਦੂਰਾਡਾ; ਬੇਗਾਨਾ; ਦੂਰਵਰਤੀ; ਨਿਵੇਕਲਾ, ਇਕਾਂਤ

remove (ਰਿ'ਮੂਵ) *v n* ਹਟਾਉਣਾ, ਹਟਾ ਦੇਣਾ, ਮੌਕੂਫ਼ ਕਰ ਦੇਣਾ, ਉਠਾ ਲੈਣਾ

remunerate (ਰਿ'ਮਯੂਨਅਰੇਇਟ) *v* ਮੁਆਵਜ਼ਾ ਦੇਣਾ, ਸੇਵਾ-ਫਲ ਦੇਣਾ, ਪ੍ਰਤੀਫਲ ਦੇਣਾ, ਉਜਰਤ ਦੇਣੀ, ਭਾੜਾ ਦੇਣਾ, ਮਜ਼ਦੂਰੀ ਦੇਣੀ; ਪੁਰਸਕਾਰ ਦੇਣਾ

remuneration (ਰਿ'ਮਯੂਨਅ:ਰੇਇਸ਼ਨ) *n* ਸੇਵਾ-ਫਲ, ਬਦਲਾ, ਭੇਟ, ਮਿਹਨਤਾਨਾ, ਪ੍ਰਤੀਫਲ

renal ('ਰੀਨਲ) *a* ਗੁਰਦੇ ਸਬੰਧੀ

renascence (ਰਿ'ਨਿਸੰਸ) *a* ਪੁਨਰ-ਜਨਮ; ਨਵਾਂ ਜਨਮ, ਪੁਨਰ-ਉਤਪਤੀ, ਨਵਾਂ ਯੁੱਗ

rend (ਰੈਂਡ) *v* ਫਾੜ ਦੇਣਾ, ਫੱਟ ਜਾਣਾ, ਚੀਰਨਾ, ਫਾੜਨਾ, ਖੰਡ ਖੰਡ ਕਰਨਾ, ਛਿੰਨ-ਭਿੰਨ ਕਰ ਦੇਣਾ

render (ਰੈਂਡਅ*) *v* (ਲੇਖਾ) ਦੇਣਾ, ਚੁਕਾਉਣਾ; ਅਦਾ ਕਰਨਾ; ਪੂਰਾ ਕਰਨਾ, ਸਾਫ਼ ਕਰਨਾ; ਨਵਾਂ ਪਲਸਤਰ ਕਰਨਾ; ~ing ਅਨੁਵਾਦ, ਉਲਥਾ, ਤਰਜਮਾਨੀ; ਸਮਰਪਣ

renew (ਰਿ'ਨਯੂ) *v* ਨਵਾਂ ਕਰਨਾ, ਜਾਨ ਪਾਉਣੀ, ਤਾਜ਼ਾ ਕਰਨਾ, ਸੋਲਖ ਰੂਪ ਦੇਣਾ, ਪੁਨਰ-ਉੱਥਾਨ ਕਰਨਾ, ਦਰੁਸਤ ਕਰਨਾ, ਬਦਲ ਦੇਣਾ; ~al ਨਵਿਆਉਣ, ਬਹਾਲੀ, ਪੁਨਰ-ਆਰੰਭ

renounce (ਰਿ'ਨਾਉਂਸ) *v* (ਹੱਕ ਜਾਂ ਕਬਜ਼ਾ) ਤਿਆਗਣਾ, ਤਜਣਾ, ਛੱਡ ਦੇਣਾ, ਸਬੰਧ ਤੋੜ ਲੈਣਾ

renovate ('ਰੈੱਨਅ(ਉ)ਵੇਇਟ) *v* ਨਵਾਂ ਕਰਨਾ, ਬਹਾਲ ਕਰਨਾ, ਦਰੁਸਤ ਕਰਨਾ; ਠੀਕ-ਠਾਕ ਕਰਨਾ; ਮੁਰੰਮਤ ਕਰਨੀ

renovation ('ਰੈੱਨਅ(ਉ)'ਵੇਇਸ਼ਨ) *n* ਨਵਿਆਉਣ; ਸੁਰਜੀਤੀ

renown (ਰਿ'ਨਾਉਨ) *n* ਪ੍ਰਸਿੱਧੀ, ਨਾਮਣਾ, ਸ਼ੁਹਰਤ, ਮਸ਼ਹੂਰੀ; ~ed ਮਸ਼ਹੂਰ, ਪ੍ਰਸਿੱਧ, ਨਾਮਵਰ

rent (ਰੈਂਟ) *n* (1) ਭਾੜਾ, ਕਿਰਾਇਆ, ਕਿਰਾਇਆ ਤੇ ਕਰਨ; (2) ਦਰਾੜ, ਛੇਕ; **~al** ਕਿਰਾਇਆ, ਮਾਲਗੁਜ਼ਾਰੀ ਲਗਾਨ

renunciation (ਰਿ'ਨਅੰਨਸਿ'ਏਇਸ਼ਨ) *n* ਤਿਆਗ; ਵਿਰਾਗ, ਵਿਰਕਤੀ, ਆਤਮ-ਤਿਆਗ, ਸੰਨਿਆਸ

reorient ('ਰੀ'ਓਰਿਐਂਟ) *v a* ਨਵੀਂ ਦਿਸ਼ਾ ਦੇਣਾ, ਮੁੜ ਅਨੁਕੂਲ ਬਣਾਉਣਾ; **~ation** ਪੁਨਰ-ਸ਼ੋਧ; ਪੁਨਰ-ਅਨੁਕੂਲਣ

repair (ਰਿ'ਪੇਅ*) *v* ਮੁਰੰਮਤ ਕਰਨੀ, ਸੁਧਾਰ ਕਰਨਾ, ਸੰਵਾਰਨਾ, ਇਲਾਜ ਕਰਨਾ, ਗੰਢਣਾ

reparation ('ਰੈਪਅ'ਰੇਇਸ਼ਨ) *n* ਮੁਰੰਮਤ, ਦਰੁਸਤੀ, ਸੁਧਾਰ, ਨਵ-ਸੰਸਕਾਰ; ਹਾਨਪੂਰਤੀ

rapartee (ਰੈ'ਪਾਟੀ) *n v* ਪਰਤਾਵਾਂ ਜਵਾਬ, ਵਿਅੰਗਮਈ ਉੱਤਰ, ਹਾਜ਼ਰ-ਜਵਾਬੀ; ਪਰਤਾਵਾਂ ਜਵਾਬ ਦੇਣਾ, ਹਾਜ਼ਰ-ਜਵਾਬ ਹੋਣਾ

repatriate (ਰੀ'ਪੈਟਰਿ'ਏਇਟ) *v* ਵਤਨ ਨੂੰ ਮੋੜਨਾ ਜਾਂ ਮੁੜਨਾ

repartriation ('ਰੀਪੈਟਰਿ'ਏਇਸ਼ਨ) *n* ਵਤਨ-ਮੋੜ, ਦੇਸ਼ ਵਾਪਸੀ

repay ('ਰੀ'ਪੇਇ) *v* ਚੁਕਾ ਦੇਣਾ, ਅਦਾ ਕਰਨਾ, ਵਾਪਸ ਕਰ ਦੇਣਾ; ਬਦਲਾ ਲੈਣਾ, ਜਵਾਬ ਦੇਣਾ, ਪ੍ਰਤੀਰੋਧ ਕਰਨਾ, ਪ੍ਰਤੀਕਰਮ ਕਰਨਾ; **~ment** ਅਦਾਇਗੀ, ਚੁਕੌਤੀ

repeal (ਰਿ'ਪੀਲ) *v n* ਖੰਡਤ ਕਰਨਾ, ਕੱਟਣਾ, ਤੋੜਨਾ, ਹਟਾਉਣਾ, ਰੱਦ ਕਰਨਾ, ਬਦਲ ਦੇਣਾ; ਵਾਪਸ ਕਰਨਾ, ਮਨਸੂਖ ਕਰਨਾ; ਖੰਡਨ; ਮਨਸੂਖੀ

repeat (ਰੀ'ਪੀਟ) *v* ਦੁਹਰਾਉਣਾ; (ਨਾਮ) ਜਪਣਾ; ਵਰਤਨ ਕਰਨਾ; ਚਿਤਰਣ ਕਰਨਾ, ਸੂਚਨਾ ਦੇਣੀ; **~edly** ਵਾਰ ਵਾਰ, ਮੁੜ ਮੁੜ, ਘੜੀ-ਮੁੜੀ

repel (ਰਿ'ਪੈੱਲ) *v* ਪਿਛਾਂਹ, ਪਿੱਛੇ ਧੱਕਣਾ ਹਟਾਉਣਾ; ਨਿਵਿਰਤ ਕਰਨਾ, ਪ੍ਰਤੀਰੋਧ ਕਰਨਾ ਦੁਰਕਾਰਨਾ, ਪਰਾਂ ਸੁੱਟਣਾ; ਅਸਵੀਕਰਨ ਕਰਨਾ

repent (ਰਿ'ਪੈਂਟ) *v* ਪਛਤਾਪ ਕਰਨਾ ਪਛਤਾਉਣਾ, ਸ਼ਰਮਿੰਦਾ ਹੋਣਾ, ਪਸ਼ੇਮਾਨ ਹੋਣਾ ਹੱਥ ਮਲਣੇ, ਤੋਬਾ ਕਰਨੀ; **~ance** ਪਛਤਾਵਾ ਤੋਬਾ, ਪਸ਼ੇਮਾਨੀ, ਪਛਤਾਪ; **~ant** ਪਛਤਾਵੇ ਨਾਲ ਭਰਿਆ, ਪਸ਼ੇਮਾਨ

repercussion ('ਰੀਪਅ'ਕਅੱਸ਼ਨ) *n* ਧਮਕ, ਗੂੰਜ; ਪ੍ਰਤੀਕਿਰਿਆ, ਮੋੜਵਾਂ ਅਸਰ

repertoire, repertory ('ਰੈੱਪਅਟਵਾ, 'ਰੈੱਪਅਟ(ਅ)ਰਿ) *n* ਖ਼ਜ਼ਾਨਾ; ਕੋਸ਼-ਭਵਨ, ਗੁਦਾਮ

repetition ('ਰੈਪਿ'ਟਿਸ਼ਨ) *n* ਦੁਹਰਾਉ, ਨਕਲ, ਪ੍ਰਤੀਲਿਪੀ, ਪ੍ਰਤਿਰੂਪ; (ਵਿਆ) ਪੁਨਰ-ਉਕਤੀ

replace (ਰਿ'ਪਲੇਇਸ) *v* ਬਦਲਾਉਣਾ, (ਕਿਸੇ ਦੀ) ਥਾਂ ਮੱਲਣੀ; ਪੁਨਰ-ਸਥਾਪਤ ਕਰਨਾ, ਅਸਲੀ ਥਾਂ ਤੇ ਕਾਇਮ ਰੱਖਣਾ; **~ment** ਥਾਂ ਬਦਲੀ; ਸਥਾਨਾਂਤਰਣ, ਪਦ ਤੋਂ ਅਲਹਿਦਗੀ;

replenish (ਰਿ'ਪਲੈੱਨਿਸ਼) *v* ਫਿਰ ਤੋਂ ਭਰਨਾ, ਭਰਪੂਰ ਕਰਨਾ, ਪਰਿਪੂਰਨ ਕਰਨਾ; **~ed** ਪੂਰਨ, ਪਰਿਪੂਰਨ, ਲਬਾਲਬ ਭਰਿਆ

replete (ਰਿ'ਪਲੀਟ) *a* ਭਰਪੂਰ, ਭਰਿਆ, ਪਰਿਪੂਰਨ; ਤ੍ਰਿਪਤ

repletion (ਰਿ'ਪਲੀਸ਼ਨ) *n* ਭਰਪੂਰਨ, ਪਰਿਪੂਰਨਤਾ; ਬਹੁਤਾਤ; ਤ੍ਰਿਪਤੀ, ਸੰਤੁਸ਼ਟਤਾ

replica ('ਰੈੱਪਲਿਕਅ) *n* ਪ੍ਰਤੀਰੂਪ, ਪ੍ਰਤੀਲਿਪੀ, ਨਕਲ, ਹੂਬਹੂ ਨਕਲ, ਜੋੜ

reply (ਰਿ'ਪਲਾਇ) *v n* ਉੱਤਰ ਦੇਣਾ, ਜਵਾਬ ਦੇਣਾ; ਉੱਤਰ, ਜਵਾਬ

report (ਰਿ'ਪੋਟ) *v n* ਸੂਚਨਾ ਦੇਣੀ, ਖ਼ਬਰ ਦੇਣੀ,

epose ਆਗਾਹ ਕਰਨਾ, ਸਮਾਚਾਰ ਦੇਣਾ, ਸੁਣਾਉਣਾ; **~er** ਸੰਵਾਦਦਾਤਾ, ਸੰਵਾਦ ਲੇਖਕ, ਰਿਪੋਰਟਰ, ਨਾਮਨਿਗਾਰ, ਮੁਖ਼ਬਰ

epose (ਰਿ'ਪਅਉਜ਼) *v n* ਵਿਸ਼ਰਾਮ ਕਰਨਾ, ਆਰਾਮ ਪਹੁੰਚਾਉਣਾ; ਦਮ ਲੈਣਾ, ਕਿਸੇ ਦੇ ਸਹਾਰੇ ਟਿਕਿਆ ਹੋਣਾ; (ਕਿਸੇ ਉੱਤੇ) ਭਰੋਸਾ ਰੱਖਣਾ; **~ful** ਸ਼ਾਂਤੀਪੂਰਨ, ਟਿਕਾਉ ਵਿਚ, ਆਰਾਮ ਵਾਲੀ

eposit (ਰਿ'ਪੌਜ਼ਿਟ) *v* ਨਿਯੁਕਤ ਕਰਨਾ, ਜਮ੍ਹਾਂ ਕਰਨਾ, ਧਰਨਾ, ਰੱਖਣਾ; **~or** ਨਿਯੋਜਕ, ਜਮ੍ਹਾਂ-ਕਰਤਾ; **~ory** ਭਾਂਡਾ, ਖ਼ਾਨਾ; ਭੰਡਾਰ, ਗੁਦਾਮ, ਮਾਲਖ਼ਾਨਾ, ਖ਼ਜ਼ਾਨਾ; ਅਜਾਇਬ-ਘਰ

reprehend ('ਰੈਪਰਿ'ਹੈਂਡ) *v* ਡਾਂਟਣਾ, ਝਾੜਣਾ, ਫਿਟਕਾਰਨਾ; ਝਿੜਕਣਾ

reprehensible ('ਰੈਪਰਿ'ਹੈਂਸਅਬਲ) *a* ਨਿੰਦਣੀ, ਨਿੰਦਣਯੋਗ, ਧਿਕਾਰਨਯੋਗ

reprehension ('ਰੈਪਰਿ'ਹੈਂਨਸ਼ਨ) *n* ਤਾੜਣਾ, ਨਿੰਦਾ, ਡਾਂਟ, ਫਿਟਕਾਰ, ਧਿਕਾਰ

represent ('ਰੈਪਰਿ'ਜ਼ੈਂਟ) *v* ਵਰਣਨ ਕਰਨਾ; ਪ੍ਰਸਤੁਤ ਕਰਨਾ, ਚਿਤਰਨ ਕਰਨਾ, ਨਿਰੂਪਣ ਕਰਨਾ, ਪ੍ਰਤਿਨਿਧ ਹੋਣਾ; **~ation** ਪ੍ਰਤੀਨਿਧਤਾ; ਪ੍ਰਤੀਰੂਪ, ਮੂਰਤ, ਖ਼ਾਕਾ; ਪ੍ਰਸਤੁਤੀਕਰਨ, ਆਵੇਦਨ-ਪੱਤਰ; ਵਰਣਨ, ਨਿਰੂਪਣ, ਚਿਤਰਨ; **~ative** ਪ੍ਰਤੀਨਿਧੀ; ਉਦਾਹਰਣ, ਆਦਰਸ਼

repress (ਰਿ'ਪਰੈਸ) *v* ਦਮਨ ਕਰਨਾ, ਦਬਾਉਣਾ, ਰੋਕ ਰੱਖਣਾ, ਘੁੱਟ ਰੱਖਣਾ, ਕਾਬੂ ਰੱਖਣਾ; **~ion** ਦਬਾਉ, ਦਮਨ, ਜਬਰ; **~or** ਅੱਤਿਆਚਾਰੀ

reprieve (ਰਿ'ਪਰੀਵ੍) *n* (ਫਾਂਸੀ) ਮੁਹਲਤ ਦੇਣੀ, ਮੁਲਤਵੀ ਕਰਨਾ, ਮੁਹਲਤ, ਪ੍ਰਾਣ-ਦੰਡ ਦੀ ਅਸਥਾਈ ਸਮੇਂ ਲਈ ਰੁਕਾਵਟ, ਵਿਸ਼ਰਾਮ, ਛੁੱਟੀ

reprimand ('ਰੈਪੁਰਿਮਾਂਡ) *n v* ਝਾੜ, ਡਾਂਟ-ਡਪਟ, ਤਾੜਨਾ, ਡਾਂਟ, ਫਿਟਕਾਰ; ਝਾੜਨਾ

reprint ('ਰਿ'ਪਰਿੰਟ, 'ਰੀਪਰਿੰਟ) *v n* ਦੁਬਾਰਾ ਛਾਪਣਾ, ਮੁੜ ਛਾਪ, ਦੂਜੀ ਛਾਪ

reprisal (ਰਿ'ਪਰਾਇਜ਼ਅਲ) *n* ਬਦਲਾ, ਜੋਤਵੀਂ ਕਾਰਵਾਈ, ਹਰਜਾਨਾ, ਪ੍ਰਤਿਹਿੰਸਾ

reproach (ਰਿ'ਪਰਅਉਚ) *v* ਧਿਕਾਰਨਾ, ਬੁਰਾ-ਭਲਾ ਕਹਿਣਾ, ਨਿੰਦਾ ਕਰਨੀ; **~ful** ਨੀਚ, ਨਿੰਦਾਮਈ, ਲੱਜਾਜਨਕ

reprobation ('ਰੈਪਰਅ(ਉ)'ਬੇਇਸ਼ਨ) *n* ਫਿਟਕਾਰ, ਮਲਾਮਤ

reproduce ('ਰੀਪਰ'ਡਯੂਸ) *v* ਦੁਬਾਰਾ ਉਤਪੰਨ ਕਰਨਾ; ਯਾਦ ਤੋਂ ਲਿਖਣਾ, ਬੋਲਣਾ ਜਾਂ ਸੁਣਾਉਣਾ

reproof (ਰਿ'ਪਰੂਫ਼) *v* ਨਿੰਦਾ, ਧਿਕਾਰ, ਝਿੜਕ, ਝਾੜ, ਫਿਟਕਾਰ

reprove (ਰਿ'ਪਰੂਵ) *v* ਝਿੜਕਣਾ, ਡਾਂਟਣਾ, ਨਿੰਦਣਾ, ਫਿਟਕਾਰਨਾ

republic (ਰਿ'ਪਅੱਬਲਿਕ) *n* ਗਣਰਾਜ, ਗਣਤੰਤਰ, ਲੋਕਤੰਤਰ, ਲੋਕ-ਰਾਜ; **~an** ਗਣਤੰਤਰਵਾਦੀ, ਲੋਕ-ਤੰਤਰ ਸਮਰਥਕ

repudiate (ਰਿ'ਪਯੂਡ੍ਰਿਏਇਟ) *v* ਤਲਾਕ ਦੇਣਾ, ਇਸਤਰੀ ਦਾ ਪਰਿਤਿਆਗ ਕਰਨਾ, ਖੰਡਨ ਕਰਨਾ; **~d** ਅਸਵੀਕ੍ਰਿਤ

repudiation (ਰਿ'ਪਯੂਡਿ'ਏਇਸ਼ਨ) *n* ਤਲਾਕ; ਤਿਆਗ, ਨਕਾਰਨ, ਰੱਦਣ, ਇਨਕਾਰ

repugn (ਰਿ'ਪਯੂਨ) *v* ਵਿਰੋਧ ਹੋਣਾ, ਵਿਰੋਧ ਕਰਨਾ; ਵਿਪਰੀਤ ਹੋਣਾ, ਪ੍ਰਤੀਕੂਲ ਹੋਣਾ; **~ance** (ਭਾਵਾਂ, ਮਨੁੱਖਾਂ ਵਿਚ) ਵਿਰੋਧ, ਅਸੰਗਤੀ, ਪ੍ਰਤੀਕੂਲਤਾ, ਵਿਪਰੀਤਤਾ; **~ant** ਵਿਪਰੀਤ, ਵਿਰੁਧ, ਵਿਮੁੱਖ, ਵਿਦਰੋਹੀ, ਪਰਸਪਰ ਵਿਰੋਧੀ, ਅਸੰਗਤ ਅਣਮੇਲ

repulse (ਰਿ'ਪਅੱਲਸ) *v n* ਹਟਾ ਦੇਣਾ, ਪਿਛਾੜ ਦੇਣਾ, ਪਿੱਛੇ ਹਟਾਉਣਾ, ਹਰਾਉਣਾ, ਖਦੇੜਨਾ, ਅਸਵੀਕਾਰ ਕਰਨਾ

repulsion (ਰਿ'ਪਅੱਲਸ਼ਨ) *n* ਵਿਕਰਸ਼ਣ, ਹਾਰ, ਅਸਵੀਕਾਰ, ਵਿਰਾਗ, ਵਿਰਕਤੀ

repulsive (ਰਿ'ਪਅੱਲਸਿਵ੍) *a* ਨਿਖੇਧਕ, ਵਿਰੋਧਕ; ਨਿਰਉਤਸ਼ਾਹ, ਘਿਰਣਤ

reputable ('ਰੈਪ੍ਯੁਟਅਬਲ) *a* ਪ੍ਰਤਿਸ਼ਠਤ, ਪ੍ਰਸਿੱਧ, ਨਾਮੀ, ਨਾਮਵਰ, ਵਿਖਿਆਤ

reputation ('ਰੈਪ੍ਯੁ'ਟੇਇਸ਼ਨ) *n* ਕੀਰਤੀ, ਜਸ, ਪ੍ਰਸਿੱਧੀ, ਮਸ਼ਹੂਰੀ, ਸ਼ੁਹਰਤ; ਪ੍ਰਤਿਸ਼ਠਾ;

repute (ਰਿ'ਪਯੂਟ) *v n* ਮਸ਼ਹੂਰ ਹੋਣਾ, ਗਿਣਿਆ ਜਾਣਾ, ਮਸ਼ਹੂਰੀ, ਸ਼ੁਹਰਤ, ਮਾਨਤਾ, ਪ੍ਰਸਿੱਧੀ; **~d** ਪ੍ਰਸਿੱਧ, ਨਾਮੀ, ਮਸ਼ਹੂਰ, ਨਾਮਵਰ, ਪ੍ਰਤਿਸ਼ਠਤ, ਵਿਖਿਆਤ

request (ਰਿ'ਕਵੈੱਸਟ) *n v* ਬੇਨਤੀ, ਪ੍ਰਾਰਥਨਾ, ਅਰਜੋਈ; ਬੇਨਤੀ ਕਰਨੀ, ਪ੍ਰਾਰਥਨਾ ਕਰਨੀ, ਮਿੰਨਤ ਕਰਨੀ, ਨਿਵੇਦਨ ਕਰਨਾ

requiem ('ਰੈੱਕਵਿਅਮ) *n* (ਮਰ ਚੁਕੇ ਲੋਕਾਂ ਲਈ ਈਸ਼ਵਰ ਅੱਗੇ) ਅਰਦਾਸ, ਫ਼ਾਤਿਹਾ; ਸੋਗ ਸੰਗੀਤ; ਵੈਣ, ਕੀਰਨੇ, ਮਰਸੀਆ

require (ਰਿ'ਕਵਾਇਅ) *v* ਲੋੜ ਸਮਝਣੀ, ਜ਼ਰੂਰਤ ਅਨੁਭਵ ਕਰਨੀ, ਮੰਗਣਾ, ਚਾਹੁਣਾ, ਲੋੜ ਹੋਣੀ; **~ment** ਮੰਗ, ਲੋੜ, ਅਵੱਸ਼ਕਤਾ, ਜ਼ਰੂਰਤ, ਪ੍ਰਾਰਥਨਾ

requisite ('ਰੈੱਕਵਿਜ਼ਿਟ) *a n* ਜ਼ਰੂਰੀ, ਲੋੜੀਂਦੀ, ਅਵੱਸ਼ਕ

requisition (ਰੈੱਕਵਿ'ਜ਼ਿਸ਼ਨ) *n v* ਪ੍ਰਾਰਥਨਾ, ਲਿਖਤੀ, ਪ੍ਰਾਰਥਨਾ, ਜਾਚਨਾ, ਮੰਗ; ਫ਼ਰਮਾਇਸ਼; ਕਿਸੇ ਕੰਮ ਲਈ ਸੱਦਣਾ, ਮੰਗਣਾ

rescind (ਰਿ'ਸਿੰਡ) *v* ਮਨਸੂਖ ਕਰਨਾ, ਖੰਡਣ ਕਰਨਾ, ਰੱਦ ਕਰਨਾ

rescission ('ਰਿਸਿਯ਼ਨ) *n* ਮਨਸੂਖ਼ੀ, ਖੰਡਨ, ਨਿਰਾਕਰਨ, ਰੱਦਣ

rescript ('ਰੀਸਕਰਿਪਟ) *n* ਸ਼ਾਹੀ ਫ਼ਰਮਾਨ, ਪੋਪ ਦਾ ਹੁਕਮਨਾਮਾ; ਨਿਰਦੇਸ਼

rescue ('ਰੈੱਸਕਯੂ) *n v* ਪਰਿਤ੍ਰਾਣ, ਬਚਾਉ, ਮੁਕਤੀ; ਨਿਸਤਾਰਾ, ਛੁਟਕਾਰਾ; ਖ਼ਲਾਸੀ, ਬਚਾਉਣਾ, ਉਧਾਰ ਕਰਨਾ, ਛੁਟਕਾਰਾ ਕਰਨਾ

research (ਰਿ'ਸਅਃਚ) *n v* ਸੋਧ; ਖੋਜ, ਤੱਤ-ਨਿਰੀਖਣ, ਛਾਣਬੀਣ, ਖੋਜ ਕਰਨੀ, ਛਾਣਬੀਣ ਕਰਨੀ, ਅਨੁਸ਼ੀਲਨ ਕਰਨਾ; ਅਨੁਸੰਧਾਨ ਕਰਨਾ

resect (ਰਿ'ਸੈੱਕਟ) *v* ਦੁਬਾਰਾ ਟੁਕੜੇ ਕਰਨਾ, ਕੱਟ ਦੇਣਾ, ਕਤਰਨਾ

resemble (ਰਿ'ਜ਼ੈੱਮਬਲ) *v* ਮੇਲ ਖਾਣਾ; ਸ਼ਕਲ ਮਿਲਣੀ, ਸਦ੍ਰਿਸ਼ ਹੋਣਾ; ਸਮਰੂਪ ਹੋਣਾ; ਮਿਲਦਾ ਹੋਣਾ

resembling (ਰਿ'ਜ਼ੈੱਮਬਲਿਙ) *a* ਸਮਰੂਪ ਮਿਲਦਾ-ਜੁਲਦਾ; ਸਮਾਨ; ਸਦ੍ਰਿਸ਼

resent (ਰਿ'ਜ਼ੈਂਟ) *v* ਬੁਰਾ ਮਨਾਉਣਾ; ਕਰੋਧ ਕਰਨਾ; ਨਾਰਾਜ਼ ਹੋਣਾ; ਰੋਸ ਪਰਗਟ ਕਰਨਾ; **~ment** ਕਰੋਪੀ, ਨਾਰਾਜ਼ਗੀ, ਗੁੱਸਾ

reservation ('ਰੈੱਜ਼ਅ'ਵੇਇਸ਼ਨ) *n* ਰਾਖਵਾਂ ਕਰਨ, ਰਾਖਵਾਂ ਹੱਕ; ਸੰਜਮ; ਸੰਕੋਚ, ਪ੍ਰਤਿਬੰਧ

reservoir ('ਰੈੱਜ਼ਅਵ਼ਵ਼*) *n v* ਹੌਜ਼; ਸਰੋਵਰ, ਕੁੰਡ; ਸੰਗ੍ਰਹ, ਖ਼ਜ਼ਾਨਾ; ਭੰਡਾਰ; ਇਕੱਠਾ ਕਰਨਾ, ਸੰਚਤ ਕਰਨਾ

reside (ਰਿ'ਜ਼ਾਇਡ) *v* ਵੱਸਣਾ; ਟਿਕਣਾ, ਰਹਿਣਾ, ਵਾਸ ਕਰਨਾ; **~nce** ਘਰ, ਨਿਵਾਸ-ਸਥਾਨ ਰਿਹਾਇਸ਼, ਟਿਕਾਣਾ, ਡੇਰਾ; **~nt** ਵਾਸੀ, ਵਸਨੀਕ, ਰੈਜ਼ੀਡੈਂਟ, ਰਾਜ ਪ੍ਰਤੀਨਿਧੀ; **~ntial** ਨਿਵਾਸ ਸਬੰਧੀ, ਰਿਹਾਇਸ਼ੀ

residual (ਰਿ'ਜ਼ਿਡਯੂਅਲ) *a* ਬਾਕੀ (ਗਤਿ); ਰਹਿੰਦ-ਖੂੰਹਦ

residuary (ਰਿ'ਜ਼ਿਡਯੂਅਰਿ) *a* ਪਿੱਛੇ ਰਿਹਾ, ਅਟਵਰਤਿਆ, ਅਟਵੰਡਿਆ, ਬਾਕੀ ਬਚਿਆ

residue (ਰੈਜ਼ਿਡਯੂ) *n* ਬਕਾਇਆ; ਬਚਿਆ-ਖੁਚਿਆ, ਰਹਿੰਦ-ਖੂੰਹਦ, ਫੋਗ

resign (ਰਿ'ਜ਼ਾਇਨ) *v* ਅਸਤੀਫ਼ਾ ਦੇਣਾ; ਤਿਆਗ-ਪੱਤਰ ਦੇਣਾ, ਅਹੁਦਾ ਤਿਆਗਣਾ, ਛੱਡ ਦੇਣਾ; ~ation ਅਸਤੀਫ਼ਾ, ਤਿਆਗ-ਪੱਤਰ, ਪਦ-ਤਿਆਗ; ਵੈਰਾਗ; ~ed ਸੰਤੋਖੀ; ਸਹਿਨਸ਼ੀਲ, ਗੰਭੀਰ, ਵਿਰਕਤ, ਸਮਰਪਤ

resilience, resiliency (ਰਿ'ਜ਼ਿਲਿਅੰਸ, ਰਿ'ਜ਼ਿਲਿਅੰਸਿ) *n* ਲਚਕ, ਲੋਚ

resilient (ਰਿ'ਜ਼ਿਲਿਅੰਟ) *a* ਲਚਕਦਾਰ, ਲਚਕੀਲਾ

resist (ਰਿ'ਜ਼ਿਸਟ) *v* ਵਿਰੋਧ ਕਰਨਾ; ਰੋਕਣਾ; ਖ਼ਿਲਾਫ਼ ਹੋਣਾ, ਦੂਰ ਰੱਖਣਾ; ~ance ਰੋਕ, ਰੁਕਾਵਟ, ਟਾਕਰਾ, ਵਿਰੋਧ, ਅੜਿੰਗਾ

resolute ('ਰੈਜ਼ਿਅਲੂਟ) *a* ਦ੍ਰਿੜ੍ਹ, ਸਥਿਰ, ਪੱਕਾ, ਹਠੀ, ਅਟੱਲ, ਦ੍ਰਿੜ੍ਹ ਸੰਕਲਪ, ਹਿੰਮਤੀ, ਸਾਹਸੀ

resolution ('ਰੈਜ਼ਅਲੂਸ਼ਨ) *n* ਪ੍ਰਸਤਾਵ, ਸੰਕਲਪ; ਰੂਪਾਂਤਰ, ਮਤਾ, ਸਥਿਰ ਚਿਤ, ਦ੍ਰਿੜ੍ਹਤਾ; ਵਿਸ਼ਲੇਸ਼ਣ

resolve (ਰਿ'ਜ਼ੋਲਵ) *n v* ਸੰਕਲਪ ਸ਼ਕਤੀ, ਦ੍ਰਿੜ੍ਹਤਾ, ਪ੍ਰਤਿਗਿਆ; ਪੱਕਾ ਇਰਾਦਾ ਕਰਨਾ, ਦ੍ਰਿੜ੍ਹ ਹੋਣਾ, ਸੰਕਲਪ ਕਰਨਾ; ਠਾਨਣਾ, ਹੱਲ ਕਰਨਾ

resonance ('ਰੈਜ਼ਅਨਅੰਸ) *n* ਗੂੰਜ, ਪ੍ਰਤੀਧੁਨੀ

resonant (ਰੈਜ਼ਅਨਅੰਟ) *a* ਗੂੰਜਵਾਂ, ਪ੍ਰਤੀਧੁਨਿਤ

resort (ਰਿ'ਜ਼ੋਟ) *v n* (ਦਾ) ਆਸਰਾ ਲੈਣਾ, ਸਹਾਰਾ ਲੈਣਾ; ਆਸਰਾ, ਤਫ਼ਰੀਹਗਾਹ

resource (ਰਿ'ਸੋਸ) *n* ਸਾਧਨ, ਸਰੋਤ, ਵਸੀਲਾ, ਜੁਗਤੀ, ਚਾਰਾ; ~ful ਸਾਧਨ-ਸੰਪੰਨ, ਉਦਯੋਗਸ਼ੀਲ, ਜੁਗਤੀਪੂਰਨ, ਹਾਜ਼ਰ ਦਿਮਾਗ਼, ਚੁਸਤ

respect (ਰਿ'ਸਪੈਕਟ) *n v* ਸਤਿਕਾਰ, ਮਾਣ, ਆਦਰ, ਇੱਜ਼ਤ, ਲਿਹਾਜ਼; ਸਤਿਕਾਰ ਕਰਨਾ, ਮਾਨਤਾ ਦੇਣੀ, ਸਨਮਾਨ ਕਰਨਾ; ~able ਪੂਜਣਯੋਗ, ਮਾਨਯੋਗ, ਕੁਲੀਨ, ਸਾਊ, ਆਦਰਯੋਗ, ਮਹੱਤਵਪੂਰਨ; ~ful ਸਤਿਕਾਰ ਸੂਚਕ, ਆਦਰਯੋਗ; ਆਦਰ ਸੂਚਕ, ਸਨਮਾਨ-ਪੂਰਨ, ਸ਼ਰਧਾਪੂਰਵਕ

respective (ਰਿ'ਸਪੈਕਟਿਵ) *a* ਆਪੋ-ਆਪਣਾ, ਅਲੱਗ ਅਲੱਗ, ਪਰਸਪਰ ਸਬੰਧੀ; ~ly ਤਰਤੀਬਵਾਰ, ਕ੍ਰਮਵਾਰ, ਇਕ ਇਕ ਕਰਕੇ, ਆਪੋ ਆਪਣੇ ਢੰਗ ਨਾਲ

respiration ('ਰੈਸਪਅ'ਰੇਇਸ਼ਨ) *n* ਸੁਆਸ-ਕਿਰਿਆ, ਸੁਆਸ-ਗਤੀ, ਪ੍ਰਾਣ, ਸੁਆਸ, ਸਾਹ

respirator (ਰਿੱਸਪਅਰੇਇਟਅ*) *n* ਸਵਾਸ-ਜੰਤਰ

respire (ਰਿ'ਸਪਾਇਅ*) *v* ਸੁਆਸ ਲੈਣਾ, ਸਾਹ ਲੈਣਾ, ਆਰਾਮ ਕਰਨਾ, ਦਮ ਲੈਣਾ

respite ('ਰੈਸਪਾਇਟ) *n v* ਮੁਹਲਤ, ਦੇਰ, ਵਿਰਾਮ, ਫ਼ੁਰਸਤ, ਢਿੱਲ, ਵਿਸ਼ਰਾਮ, ਨਾਗ਼ਾ; ਮੁਹਲਤ ਦੇਣੀ

respond (ਰਿ'ਸਪੌਂਡ) *n v* ਉੱਤਰ ਦੇਣਾ, ਸਵਾਲ-ਜਵਾਬ ਕਰਨਾ, ਪ੍ਰਸ਼ਨ-ਉੱਤਰ ਕਰਨਾ, ਪ੍ਰਭਾਵਤ ਹੋਣਾ, ਪ੍ਰਤੀਕਿਰਿਆ ਵਿਖਾਉਣੀ, ਅਨੁਕੂਲ ਹੋਣਾ

response (ਰਿ'ਸਪੌਂਸ) *n* ਉੱਤਰ, ਜਵਾਬ, ਪ੍ਰਤੀਕਿਰਿਆ

responsibility (ਰਿ'ਸਪੌਂਸਅ'ਬਿਲਅਟਿ) *n* ਜ਼ਿੰਮੇਵਾਰੀ, ਉੱਤਰਦਾਇਤਾ, ਜਵਾਬਦੇਹੀ; ਬੀੜਾ

responsible (ਰਿ'ਸਪੌਂਸਅਬਲ) *a* ਜ਼ਿੰਮੇਵਾਰ, ਉੱਤਰਦਾਈ, ਜਵਾਬਦੇਹ

rest (ਰੈਸਟ) *v n* ਆਰਾਮ ਕਰਨਾ, ਸੁਸਤਾਉਣਾ, ਸ਼ਾਂਤ ਹੋਣਾ, ਟਿਕਣਾ, ਸਹਾਰਾ ਦੇਣਾ; ਬਾਕੀ ਰਹਿਣਾ, ਬਚਣਾ, ਆਰਾਮ, ਸੁਖ, ਚੈਨ, ਵਿਰਾਮ; ਬਾਕੀ ਹਿੱਸਾ, ਅਵਸ਼ੇਸ਼; ~**house** ਡਾਕ-ਬੰਗਲਾ, ਵਿਸ਼ਰਾਮ ਘਰ; ~**ful** ਸ਼ਾਂਤ; ਨਿਚਲਾ, ਸ਼ਾਂਤੀ ਵਾਲਾ, ਸੁਖਦਾਈ

restaurant (ਰੈਸਟਅਰੌਂਡ) *n* ਰੈਸਟਰਾਂ, ਆਰਾਮ-ਘਰ, ਭੋਜਨਸ਼ਾਲਾ

restitution ('ਰੈਸਟਿਹਿਊਸ਼ਨ) *n* ਵਾਪਸੀ, ਬਹਾਲੀ, ਪੁਨਰ-ਸਥਾਪਨ, ਸ਼ਕਤੀ ਪੂਰਤੀ

restive ('ਰੈਸਟਿਵ) *a* ਬੇਕਾਬੂ, ਅਸ਼ਾਂਤ, ਅੜੀਅਲ, ਹਠੀ; ਮੂੰਹਜ਼ੋਰ (ਘੋੜਾ); ਚੱਲਣਸ਼ੀਲ; ~**ness** ਅਸ਼ਾਂਤੀ, ਵਿਆਕੁਲਤਾ; ਅੜੀਅਲਪਣ, ਹਠ, ਜ਼ਿਦ

restoration ('ਰੈਸਟਅ'ਰੇਇਸ਼ਨ) *n* ਵਾਪਸੀ, ਪ੍ਰਾਵਰਤਨ, ਬਹਾਲੀ, ਪੁਨਰ-ਸਥਾਪਨ, ਪੁਨਰ-ਉਧਾਰ

restore (ਰਿ'ਸਟੋ*) *v* ਮੋੜ ਦੇਣਾ, ਵਾਪਸ ਕਰਨਾ, ਪੁਨਰ-ਸਥਾਪਤ ਕਰਨਾ, ਬਹਾਲ ਕਰਨਾ, ਸੰਵਾਰਨਾ

restrain (ਰਿ'ਸਟਰੇਇਨ) *v* ਰੋਕਣਾ, ਬੰਦਸ਼ ਲਾਉਣਾ, ਜ਼ਬਤ ਵਿਚ ਰੱਖਣਾ, ਕਾਬੂ ਵਿਚ ਰੱਖਣਾ; ~**t** ਦਮਨ, ਸੰਜਮ, ਪ੍ਰਤੀਬੰਧ, ਬੰਦਸ਼, ਪਾਬੰਦੀ, ਅਟਕਾ, ਮਨਾਹੀ, ਕੈਦ

restrict (ਰਿ'ਸਟਰਿਕਟ) *v* ਸੀਮਤ ਕਰਨਾ, ਸੀਮਾਬੱਧ ਕਰਨਾ, ਰੋਕ ਪਾਉਣੀ, ਰੋਕਣਾ, ਪਾਬੰਦੀ ਲਾਉਣਾ; ਪ੍ਰਤੀਬੰਧ ਲਾਉਣਾ; ~**ion** ਪਾਬੰਦੀ; ਬੰਧੇਜ; ਬੰਦਸ਼; ਰੁਕਾਵਟ, ਪ੍ਰਤੀਬੰਧਨ; ~**ive** ਪ੍ਰਤੀਬੰਧਕ, ਬੰਦਸ਼ੀ; ਬੰਨ੍ਹਵਾਂ, ਅਵਰੋਧਕ

result (ਰਿ'ਜ਼ਅਲਟ) *v n* ਨਤੀਜਾ ਨਿਕਲਣਾ; ਸਿੱਟਾ ਨਿਕਲਣਾ; ਪਰਿਣਾਮ; ~**ant** ਸਹਿ-ਉਤਪੰਨ; ਪਰਿਣਾਮੀ, ਪਰਿਣਾਮ

resume (ਰਿ'ਜ਼ਯੂਮ) *v n* ਪੁਨਰ-ਗ੍ਰਹਿਣ ਕਰਨਾ; ਪੁਨਰਧਾਰਨ ਕਰਨਾ, ਮੁੜ ਪ੍ਰਾਪਤ ਕਰਨਾ; ਪੁਨਰ-ਆਰੰਭ ਕਰਨਾ; ਜਾਰੀ ਰੱਖਣਾ; ਸੰਖਿਪਤ ਕਰਨਾ; ਸਾਰ-ਅੰਸ਼

resumption (ਰਿ'ਜ਼ਅੰਮਪਸ਼ਨ) *n* ਪੁਨਰ-ਗ੍ਰਹਿਣ; ਪੁਨਰ-ਅਧਿਕਾਰ, ਦੁਬਾਰਾ ਦਖ਼ਲ, ਪੁਨਰ-ਆਰੰਭ

resurge (ਰਿ'ਸਅਃਜ) *v* ਫਿਰ ਉਠਣਾ; ਦੁਬਾਰਾ ਤਾਕਤ ਫੜਨਾ; ~**nce** ਪੁਨਰ-ਉਦਗਮ, ਪੁਨਰ-ਉੱਥਾਨ, ਪੁਨਰ-ਉੱਥਾਨਸ਼ੀਲਤਾ, ਪੁਨਰ-ਜੀਵਨ

resurrect ('ਰੈਜ਼ਅ'ਰੈਕਟ) *v* ਪੁਨਰ-ਜੀਵਨ ਕਰਨਾ; ਮੁੜ ਚਾਲੂ ਕਰਨਾ; ~**ion** (ਹਜ਼ਰਤ ਈਸਾ ਦੇ ਕਬਰ 'ਚੋਂ ਉਠਣ ਦੀ ਯਾਦ ਵਿਚ) ਇਕ ਇਸਾਈ ਪੁਰਬ, ਪੁਨਰ-ਉੱਥਾਨ; ਕਿਆਮਤ; ਪੁਨਰ-ਜੀਵਨ, ਪੁਨਰ-ਉਧਾਰ

retail ('ਰੀਟੇਇਲ, ਰੀ'ਟੇਇਲ) *n v* ਪ੍ਰਚੂਨ; ਪ੍ਰਚੂਨ ਵੇਚਣਾ, ਵੇਰਵਾ ਦੇਣਾ; ~**er** ਪ੍ਰਚੂਨ ਮਾਲ ਵੇਚਣ ਵਾਲਾ, ਫੁਟਕਲ ਵਿਕਰੇਤਾ

retain (ਰਿ'ਟੇਇਨ) *v* ਰੱਖਣਾ, ਫੜਨਾ, ਧਾਰਨ ਕਰਨਾ, ਰੋਕਣਾ, ਅਟਕਾਉਣਾ; ਕਬਜ਼ਾ ਰੱਖਣਾ, ਨਾ ਛੱਡਣਾ, ਅਧਿਕਾਰ ਵਿਚ ਰੱਖਣਾ

retaliate (ਰਿ'ਟੈਲਿਏਇਟ) *v* ਜਵਾਬ ਦੇਣਾ, ਉਲਟਾ ਦੋਸ਼ ਥੱਪਣਾ, ਕਸਰ ਕੱਢਣੀ

retaliation (ਰਿ'ਟੈਲਿ'ਏਇਸ਼ਨ) *n* ਬਦਲਾ, ਜਵਾਬੀ ਇਲਜ਼ਾਮ; ਜਵਾਬੀ ਮਹਿਸੂਲ

retard (ਰਿ'ਟਾਡ) *n v* ਗਤੀਰੋਧ; ਢਿੱਲਾ ਛੱਡਣਾ, ਢਿੱਲਾ ਕਰਨਾ, ਧੀਮਾ ਕਰਨਾ, ਮੱਠਾ ਕਰਨਾ, ਅਟਕਾਉਣਾ, ਗਤੀ ਰੋਕਣੀ; ~**ation**, ~**ment** ਢਿੱਲ, ਦੇਰੀ; ਅਟਕਾ, ਰੋਕ, ਰੁਕਾਵਟ

retention (ਰਿ'ਟੈਨਸ਼ਨ) *n* ਰੁਕਾਵਟ; ਚੇਤਾ, ਯਾਦ-ਸ਼ਕਤੀ, ਧਾਰਨਾ; ਕੈਦ, ਪਕੜ

retina ('ਰੈਟਿਨਅ) *n* ਅੱਖ ਦਾ ਪਰਦਾ, ਦ੍ਰਿਸ਼ਟੀਪਟ

ਰੈਟਿਨਾ

retinue ('ਰੈਟਿਨਯੂ) *n* ਨੌਕਰ-ਚਾਕਰ, ਅਮਲਾ-ਫੈਲਾ, ਅਰਦਲੀ ਲੋਕ

retire (ਰਿ'ਟਾਇਅ*) *n* ਪਿੱਛੇ ਹਟਣਾ, ਵਾਪਸ ਹੋਣਾ; ਇਕਾਂਤ ਵਿਚ ਜਾਣਾ, ਪੈਨਸ਼ਨ ਲੈ ਲੈਣੀ, ਸੇਵਾਨਿਵਿਰਤ ਹੋਣਾ; ~ment ਕਾਰਜ-ਤਿਆਗ, ਪਦ-ਤਿਆਗ, ਸੇਵਾ-ਨਿਵਿਰਤੀ, ਸੰਨਿਆਸ, ਇਕਾਂਤ

retiring (ਰਿ'ਟਾਇਰਿਙ) *a* ਸ਼ਰਮੀਲਾ, ਖ਼ਮੋਸ਼, ਲੱਜਾਸ਼ੀਲ, ਇਕਾਂਤ-ਪਰੇਮੀ, ਸੰਗਾਊ; ਵੈਰਾਗੀ, ਤਿਆਗੀ; ~room ਵਿਸ਼ਰਾਮ-ਕਮਰਾ, ਆਰਾਮ-ਕਮਰਾ

retort (ਰਿ'ਟੋਟ) *v n* ਤੁਰਤ ਉੱਤਰ ਦੇਣਾ, ਮੂੰਹ ਤੋੜ ਜਵਾਬ ਦੇਣਾ, ਬਦਲਾ ਚੁਕਾਉਣਾ, ਪਲਟਾਉਣਾ; ਤੁਰਤ ਉੱਤਰ, ਮੂੰਹ-ਤੋੜ ਜਵਾਬ, ਪ੍ਰਤੀਸ਼ੋਧ, ਪ੍ਰਤੀਵਿਧਾਨ

retrace (ਰਿ'ਟਰੇਇਸ) *v* ਆਰੰਭ ਦਾ ਪਤਾ ਲਾਉਣਾ, ਮੂਲ-ਸਰੋਤ ਖੋਜਣਾ; ਢੂੰਡਣਾ, ਤਲਾਸ਼ ਕਰਨੀ, ਸੁਰਾਗ ਲਾਉਣਾ, ਪਰਤਣਾ; ਪਾਢੀ ਫੇਰਨਾ, ਆਪਣੀ ਕਾਰਵਾਈ ਰੱਦ ਕਰਨੀ

retread ('ਰੀਟਰੈੱਡ) *v* ਟਾਇਰ ਉੱਤੇ ਮੁੜ ਰਬੜ ਚੜ੍ਹਾਉਣਾ; ਫਿਰ ਚੱਲਣਾ

retreat (ਰਿ'ਟਰੀਟ) *v n* ਪਿੱਛੇ ਹਟਣਾ, ਮੋਰਚਾ ਛੱਡਣਾ, ਪਲਾਇਨ ਕਰਨਾ, ਪਿੱਛੇ ਹਟਾਉਣਾ; ਇਕਾਂਤ ਵਾਸ, ਪਲਾਇਨ

retrench (ਰਿ'ਟਰੈਂਚ) *v* (ਅਮਲਾ) ਛਾਂਟਣਾ, ਛਾਂਟੀ ਕਰਨੀ, ਕਟੌਤੀ ਕਰਨੀ; ~ment ਛਾਂਟੀ, ਕਮੀ, ਕਟੌਤੀ; ਘੱਟ ਖ਼ਰਚ, ਮੋਰਚਾਬੰਦੀ

retribute ('ਰੈਟਿਰਬਯੂਟ) *v* ਪ੍ਰਤੀਦਾਨ ਕਰਨਾ, ਵਾਪਸ ਪਲਟਾ ਦੇਣਾ

retribution ('ਰੈਟਰਿ'ਬਯੂਸ਼ਨ) *n* ਬਦਲਾ, ਪਲਟਾ, ਬੁਰਾਈ ਦਾ ਬਦਲਾ, ਪ੍ਰਤੀਫਲ

retrieval (ਰਿ'ਟਰੀਵਲ) *n* ਮੁੜ-ਪ੍ਰਾਪਤੀ, ਦੁਬਾਰਾ ਪ੍ਰਾਪਤੀ, ਪੁਨਰ-ਸਥਾਪਨਾ, ਦੁਬਾਰਾ ਯਾਦ

retrieve (ਰਿ'ਟਰੀਵ) *v* ਲੱਭ ਲੈਣਾ; ਕਢਾ ਲੈਣਾ, ਦੁਬਾਰਾ ਪ੍ਰਾਪਤ ਕਰ ਲੈਣਾ; ਯਾਦ ਹੋ ਜਾਣਾ, ਦਿਮਾਗ਼ ਵਿਚ ਬੈਠ ਜਾਣਾ; ਸੁਪਰਦ ਹੋਣਾ

retrograde ('ਰੈਟਰਅ(ਉ)ਗਰੇਇਡ) *a v* ਪ੍ਰਤੀਗਾਮੀ, ਪਿਛਾਂਹ-ਖਿਚੂ, ਡ੍ਰਿੰਗਦਾ; ਉਲਟਾ, ਵਿਪਰੀਤ; ਪ੍ਰਤੀਕੂਲ; ਉਲਟਾ ਚੱਲਣਾ, ਪਿੱਛੇ ਹੋਣਾ

retrospect ('ਰੈਟਰਅ(ਉ)ਸਪੈੱਕਟ) *n* ਪਰਤਵੀਂ ਨਜ਼ਰ, ਪੂਰਵ, ਦ੍ਰਿਸ਼ਟੀ, ਪੁਰਾਣਾ ਵਿਚਾਰ, ਪ੍ਰਤੀਗਾਮੀ ਦ੍ਰਿਸ਼ਟੀਕੋਣ; ~ion ਪਿੱਛਲ-ਝਾਤ; ~ive ਪਿੱਛਲੀ, ਅਤੀਤ-ਪ੍ਰਭਾਵੀ, ਅਤੀਤ-ਦਰਸੀ; (ਕਾ) ਪੂਰਵ-ਵਿਆਪੀ

return (ਰਿ'ਟਅ:ਨ) *v n* ਵਾਪਸ ਆਉਣਾ ਜਾਂ ਹੋਣਾ, ਪਰਤਣਾ ਜਾਂ ਪਰਤਾਉਣਾ, ਮੁੜਨਾ ਮੋੜਨਾ, ਮੋੜ ਦੇਣਾ, ਵਾਪਸ ਕਰਨਾ, ਦੇ ਦੇਣਾ, ਚੁਕਾਉਣਾ, ਵਾਪਸੀ, ਆਮਦਨ, ਲਾਭ; ਰਿਪੋਰਟ, ਲੇਖਾ

reveal (ਰਿ'ਵੀਲ) *v* ਵਿਅਕਤ ਕਰਨਾ, ਪਰਗਟ ਕਰਨਾ, ਪ੍ਰਕਾਸ਼ਤ ਕਰਨਾ, ਖੋਲ੍ਹਣਾ, ਦੱਸਣਾ; ਉਘਾੜਨਾ, ਪੋਲ ਖੋਲ੍ਹਣਾ

revenge (ਰਿ'ਵੈਂਜ) *v n* ਬਦਲਾ ਲੈਣਾ, ਪ੍ਰਤਿਸ਼ੋਧ ਕਰਨਾ; ਪ੍ਰਤਿਸ਼ੋਧ, ਬਦਲਾ

revenue ('ਰੈੱਵਅਨਯੂ) *n* ਲਗਾਨ, ਮਾਲ-ਗੁਜ਼ਾਰੀ, ਲਾਭ, ਕਰ, ਸਰਕਾਰੀ ਆਮਦਨ

reverberation (ਰਿ'ਵ੍ਹਅਃਬਅ'ਰੇਇਸ਼ਨ) *n* ਗੂੰਜ, ਪ੍ਰਤੀਧੁਨੀ, ਪ੍ਰਤੀਕਿਰਿਆ, ਪ੍ਰਾਵਰਤਨ

revere ('ਰਿਵ੍ਹਿਅ*) *v* ਸਤਿਕਾਰਨਾ, ਸਨਮਾਨਣਾ, ਆਦਰ ਕਰਨਾ, ਇੱਜ਼ਤ ਕਰਨੀ, ਅਦਬ ਕਰਨਾ;

~d ਪੂਜਨਯੋਗ, ਸਤਿਕਾਰਯੋਗ, ਆਦਰਯੋਗ, ਸਨਮਾਨ-ਯੋਗ; ~nce ਸਨਮਾਨ, ਸਤਿਕਾਰ, ਆਦਰ, ਇੱਜ਼ਤ, ਅਦਬ, ਪੂਜਾ-ਭਾਵ, ਸ਼ਰਧਾ; ਆਦਰ ਕਰਨ, ਸਨਮਾਨ ਕਰਨ; ~nd ਪਾਦਰੀ; ਸਨਮਾਨਯੋਗ, ਸਤਿਕਾਰਯੋਗ, ਪੂਜਨੀਕ, ਆਦਰਯੋਗ; ~nt ਸਨਮਾਨਕਾਰੀ, ਆਦਰਭਾਵੀ, ਸ਼ਰਧਾਲੂ, ਸ਼ਰਧਾਪੂਰਨ

reversal (ਰਿ'ਵ੍ਅਃਸਲ) *n* ਉਲਟ-ਪੁਲਟ; ਮਨਸੁਖ਼ੀ; ਪਰਾਵਰਤਨ, ਵਿਪਰੀਤਤਾ

reverse (ਰਿ'ਵ੍ਅਃਸ) *a v n* (ਲਹਿਰਾਂ) ਪ੍ਰਤੀਵਰਤੀ, ਉਲਟੀ, ਪੁੱਠੀ, ਮੂਧੀ; ਵਿਪਰੀਤ, ਪ੍ਰਤੀਕੂਲ; ਉਲਟਾਉਣਾ ਜਾਂ ਉਲਟਣਾ; ਪ੍ਰਤੀਕੂਲਤਾ, ਵਿਪਰੀਤਤਾ, ਵਿਪੱਖ, ਪ੍ਰਤੀਪੱਖ

reversible (ਰਿ'ਵ੍ਅਃਸਅਬਲ) *a* ਉਲਟਣਯੋਗਾ, ਉਲਟਵਾਂ, ਮੁੜਵਾਂ, ਪਰਿਵਰਤਨੀ

reversion (ਰਿ'ਵ੍ਅਃਸ਼ਨ) *n* ਵਾਪਸੀ, ਪਰਤਾਉ, ਉਤਰਾਧਿਕਾਰ (ਜਾਇਦਾਦ ਦਾ)

revert (ਰਿ'ਵ੍ਅਃਟ) *v* ਪਰਤਣਾ, ਪਿੱਛੇ ਕਰਨਾ ਜਾਂ ਹੋਣਾ, ਵਾਪਸ ਲਿਆਉਣਾ. ਪਹਿਲੀ ਹਾਲਤ ਵਿਚ ਪਹੁੰਚਣਾ

review (ਰਿ'ਵਯੂ) *n v* ਆਲੋਚਨਾ, ਸਮੀਖਿਆ, ਪੁਸਤਕ ਪੜਚੋਲ, ਪੁਨਰ-ਨਿਰੀਖਣ, ਪੁਨਰ-ਅਵਲੋਕਨ; ਆਲੋਚਨਾ ਕਰਨੀ; ~er ਸਮੀਖਿਅਕ, ਸਮਾਲੋਚਕ, ਆਲੋਚਕ

revile (ਰਿ'ਵਾਇਲ) *v* ਬੁਰਾ-ਭਲਾ ਕਹਿਣਾ, ਨਿੰਦਾ ਕਰਨੀ, ਸਖ਼ਤ ਸ਼ਬਦ ਬੋਲਣਾ

revise (ਰਿ'ਵਾਇਜ਼) *v n* ਦੁਹਰਾਉਣਾ, ਸੁਧਾਰਨਾ; ਦੁਬਾਰਾ ਜਾਂਚਣਾ, (ਕਾ) ਨਿਗਰਾਨੀ ਕਰਨੀ

revision (ਰਿ'ਵਿਯ਼ਨ) *n* ਦੁਬਾਰਾ ਪਰੀਖਿਆ, ਸੰਸ਼ੋਧਨ, ਪੁਨਰ-ਨਿਰੀਖਣ

revival (ਰਿ'ਵਾਇਵਲ) *n* ਪੁਨਰ-ਉੱਥਾਨ, ਪੁਨਰ-ਜੀਵਨ, ਪੁਨਰ-ਉੱਧਾਰ, ਪੁਨਰ-ਪ੍ਰਚਲਨ; ਜਾਗਾ-ਰਤੀ, ਜਾਗਰਣ; ~ism ਧਾਰਮਕ, ਪੁਨਰ-ਜਾਗਰਣਵਾਦ

revive (ਰਿ'ਵਾਇਵ) *v* ਜਿਵਾਉਣਾ, ਜੀ ਉੱਠਣਾ; ਫਿਰ ਹੋਸ਼ ਵਿਚ ਲਿਆਉਣਾ, ਮੁੜ ਚਾਲੂ ਕਰਨਾ, ਪ੍ਰਚਲਤ ਹੋਣਾ, ਰਿਵਾਜ ਵਿਚ ਆਉਣਾ

revocation ('ਰੈਵ੍ਅ'ਕੇਇਸ਼ਨ) *n* ਖੰਡਨ, ਪ੍ਰਤਾਈ, ਮਨਸੂਖ਼ੀ

revoke (ਰਿ'ਵ੍ਅਉਕ) *v* ਖੰਡਨ ਕਰਨਾ, ਰੱਦ ਕਰਨਾ, ਮਨਸੂਖ਼ ਕਰਨਾ, ਹਟਾਉਣਾ

revolt (ਰਿ'ਵ੍ਅਉਲਟ) *v n* ਰਾਜ-ਧਰੋਹ ਕਰਨਾ, ਬਗ਼ਾਵਤ ਕਰਨੀ, ਬਾਗ਼ੀ ਹੋਣਾ, ਗ਼ਦਰ ਮਚਾਉਣਾ, ਵਿਦਰੋਹ ਕਰਨਾ, ਆਕੀ ਹੋ ਜਾਣਾ; ਗ਼ਦਰ, ਬਗ਼ਾਵਤ, ਰਾਜ-ਧਰੋਹ

revolution ('ਰੈਵ੍ਅ'ਲੂਸ਼ਨ) *n* ਇਨਕਲਾਬ, ਅੰਦੋਲਨ, ਕਰਾਂਤੀ; ਰਾਜ-ਰੋਲਾ, ਰਾਜ-ਗ਼ਾਰਦੀ; ~ary ਕਰਾਂਤੀਕਾਰੀ, ਇਨਕਲਾਬੀ, ਰਾਜ-ਪਰਿਵਰਤਨ ਸਬੰਧੀ

revolve (ਰਿ'ਵੌਲਵ) *v* ਚੱਕਰ ਖਾਣਾ, ਘੁੰਮਣਾ ਜਾਂ ਘੁਮਾਉਣਾ, ਫੇਰਨਾ ਜਾਂ ਫਿਰਨਾ, ਗੋਡਣਾ ਜਾਂ ਗਿੜਨਾ

reward (ਰਿ'ਵੋਡ) *n v* ਇਨਾਮ, ਪੁਰਸਕਾਰ; ਫਲ ਦੇਣਾ, ਇਨਾਮ ਦੇਣਾ

rhetoric ('ਰੀਟਅ*ਇਕ) *n* ਅਲੰਕਾਰ-ਵਿੱਦਿਆ, ਪ੍ਰਭਾਵਸ਼ਾਲੀ ਲਿਖਤ ਜਾਂ ਬੋਲ, ਆਕਰਸ਼ਕ ਭਾਸ਼ਨ, ਪ੍ਰਭਾਵਸ਼ਾਲੀ ਭਾਸ਼ਨ, ਅਲੰਕਾਰ-ਸ਼ਾਸਤਰ; ~ical ਅਲੰਕ੍ਰਿਤ, ਪ੍ਰਭਾਵਸ਼ਾਲੀ; ~ician ਅਲੰਕਾਰ-ਸ਼ਾਸਤਰੀ, ਭਾਸ਼ਨਕਾਰ

rheumatic (ਰੁਮੈਟਿਕ) *n* ਸਰੀਰ ਤੋਂ ਤਰਲ ਪਦਾਰਥਾਂ ਦਾ ਨਿਕਾਸ, ਹੰਝੂ, ਥੁੱਕ, ਕਫ਼, ਨਜ਼ਲਾ; ਜੋੜਾਂ ਜਾਂ ਗੰਠੀਏ ਦਾ ਦਰਦ; ਗੰਠੀਆ, ਵਾਈ,

rhinoceros 683 **ring**

ਜੋੜਾਂ ਦੇ ਦਰਦ ਦਾ ਰੋਗ

rhinoceros (ਰਾਇ'ਨੌਸ(ਅ)ਰਅਸ) *n* ਗੈਂਡਾ

rhyme, rime (ਰਾਇਮ) *n v* ਕਾਫ਼ੀਆ, ਅੰਤ ਅਨੁਪ੍ਰਾਸ, ਤੁਕਬੰਦੀ; ਤੁਕਾਂਤ ਮਿਲਾਉਣਾ, ਕਵਿਤਾ ਲਿਖਣੀ

rhythm ('ਰਿਦ(ਅ)ਮ) *n* (ਕਵਿਤਾ ਵਿਚ) ਪਰਵਾਹ, ਰਵਾਨੀ, ਲੈਅ; ਸੁਰਾਂ ਦੀ ਇਕਸਾਰਤਾ

rib (ਰਿਬ) *n v* (1) ਪਸਲੀ; (2) ਪਤਨੀ, ਘਰ ਵਾਲੀ, (3) ਖੰਡ ਦੀ ਡੰਡੀ; (4) (ਸਿਆੜ ਜਾਂ ਨਾਲੀ ਦੀ) ਵੱਟ; (5) (ਖਾਣ ਵਿਚ) ਧਾਤ ਦੀ ਤਹਿ; (6) (ਪਹਾੜ ਦਾ) ਅਗਾਂਹ ਵਧਿਆ ਹਿੱਸਾ; (7) ਰੇਤ ਉੱਤੇ ਲਹਿਰਾਂ ਦੇ ਚਿੰਨ੍ਹ; (8) (ਗੁੰਬਦ ਦੀ) ਡਾਟ; (9) ਪੁਲ ਦੇ ਗਾਰਡਰ, ਛਤਰੀ ਦੀ ਕਮਾਨੀ; ਪਸਲੀ ਚੜ੍ਹਾਉਣਾ, ਪਸਲੀਆਂ ਜੋੜਨਾ; ਡਾਟ ਲਗਾਉਣਾ, ਉਭਰੀਆਂ ਰੇਖਾਵਾਂ ਉੱਤੇ ਨਿਸ਼ਾਨ ਲਾਉਣੇ

ribbon, riband ('ਰਿਬਅਨ, 'ਰਿਬਅਨਡ) *n* ਰਿਬਨ, ਫ਼ੀਤਾ; ਕੌਰ

rice (ਰਾਇਸ) *n* ਚੌਲ, ਜੀਰੀ, ਧਾਨ; **~paper** ਬਹੁਤ ਪਤਲਾ ਕਾਗ਼ਜ਼

rich (ਰਿਚ) *a* ਧਨਵਾਨ, ਧਨਾਡ, ਅਮੀਰ, ਦੌਲਤਮੰਦ, ਰੰਜਿਆ-ਪੁੰਜਿਆ; **~ly** ਪੂਰੀ ਤਰ੍ਹਾਂ, ਚੰਗੀ ਤਰ੍ਹਾਂ, ਭਰਪੂਰ, ਅਮੀਰੀ ਨਾਲ

rid (ਰਿਡ) *v* ਛੁਟਕਾਰਾ ਦੇਣਾ, ਮੁਕਤ ਕਰਨਾ, ਖ਼ਲਾਸੀ ਕਰਨੀ, (ਕਿਸੇ ਥਾਂ ਨੂੰ) ਛੱਡ ਦੇਣਾ, ਨਸ਼ਟ ਕਰਨਾ, ਨਾਸ ਕਰਨਾ, ਦੂਰ ਕਰਨਾ; **~dance** ਛੁਟਕਾਰਾ, ਖ਼ਲਾਸੀ, ਮੁਕਤੀ, ਰਿਹਾਈ, ਨਜਾਤ

riddle ('ਰਿਡਲ) *n v* ਮੋਟੀ ਛਾਨਣੀ, ਛਾਨਣੇ; ਬੁਝਾਰਤ, ਗੁੰਝਲ, ਗੁੰਝਲਦਾਰ ਗੱਲ; ਬੁਝਾਰਤਾਂ ਪਾਉਣੀਆਂ, ਬੁਝਾਰਤ ਬੁੱਝਣੀ

ride (ਰਾਇਡ) *v n* ਸਵਾਰੀ ਕਰਨੀ; **~r** ਸਵਾਰ; ਘੋੜ-ਚੜ੍ਹਿਆ

ridge (ਰਿਜ) *n v* ਪਹਾੜੀ; ਛੱਤ; ਉਤਰੀ ਰੇਖਾ; ਚੋਟੀ

ridicule ('ਰਿਡਿਕਯੂਲ) *v* ਟਿਚਕਰ ਕਰਨੀ, ਖਿੱਲੀ ਉਡਾਉਣੀ, ਮਜ਼ਾਕ ਬਣਾਉਣਾ

riding ('ਰਾਇਡਿੰਡ) *n* ਸਵਾਰੀ; ਘੋੜੇ ਦੀ ਸਵਾਰੀ

rifle ('ਰਾਇਫ਼ਲ) *n v* ਬੰਦੂਕ ਦੀ ਨਾਲੀ; ਬੰਦੂਕ ਚਲਾਉਣਾ

rift (ਰਿਫ਼ਟ) *n* ਦਰਾੜ, ਕਾਟ; ਫੁੱਟ, ਅਟਬਣ

rig (ਰਿਗ) *n v* ਛਲ, ਧੋਖਾ, ਕਪਟ; ਛਲ ਕਰਨਾ, ਹੇਰਾ ਫੇਰੀ ਕਰਨਾ; ਸਜਾਉਣਾ; ਪੁਸ਼ਾਕ ਪਵਾਉਣੀ; ਕੰਮ ਚਲਾਊ ਪ੍ਰਬੰਧ ਕਰਨਾ

right (ਰਾਇਟ) *a n v adv* ਠੀਕ, ਸੱਚ; ਸਹੀ; ਸਿੱਧਾ; ਸਮਕੋਣੀ, ਮੁਨਾਸਬ; ਯੋਗ, ਉਚਿਤ; **~angle** ਖੜ੍ਹਾ ਕੋਣ, 90 ਡਿਗਰੀ ਦਾ ਕੋਣ; **~minded** ਸਾਫ਼-ਦਿਲ, ਸੱਚਾ, ਨੇਕ, ਚੰਗਾ; **~eous** ਨੇਕ, ਨਿਆਂਕਾਰੀ, ਨਿਆਂਈਂ, ਸੱਚਾ, ਭੱਦਰ, ਈਮਾਨਦਾਰ, ਧਰਮਾਤਮਾ, ਸਤਵਾਦੀ; **~ful** ਜਾਇਜ਼, ਠੀਕ, ਉਚਿਤ, ਨਿਆਂ-ਪੁਰਵਕ, ਨਿਆਂਯੁਕਤ, ਅਧਿਕਾਰੀ, ਅਧਿਕਾਰ-ਪੁਰਨ, ਵਿਸ਼ਿਸ਼ਟ; **~ist** ਸੱਜੇ ਪੱਖੀ, ਸੱਜੂ; **~ly** ਮੁਨਾਸਬ ਢੰਗ ਨਾਲ, ਜਾਇਜ਼ ਤਰੀਕੇ ਨਾਲ, ਠੀਕ ਤਰ੍ਹਾਂ

rigid ('ਰਿਜਿਡ) *a* ਕਰੜਾ, ਸਖ਼ਤ, ਦ੍ਰਿੜ੍ਹ, ਕੱਟੜ; **~ity** ਕਠੋਰਤਾ, ਦ੍ਰਿੜ੍ਹਤਾ, ਕਰੜਪਣ, ਕੱਟੜਤਾ

rigorous ('ਰਿਗਅਰਅਸ) *a* ਕਰੜਾ, ਸਖ਼ਤ, ਕਠੋਰ, ਨਿਰਦਈ, ਦੁਖਦਾਈ, ਬੇਰਹਿਮ

rigour ('ਰਿਗਅ*) *n* ਸਖ਼ਤੀ, ਕਰੜਾਈ, ਕਠੋਰਤਾ, ਨਿਰਦਇਤਾ

ring (ਰਿੰਡ) *n v* (1) ਛੱਲਾ, ਮੁੰਦਰੀ; ਵਾਲੀ; (2) ਚੱਕਰ, ਘੇਰਾ, ਫਿਰਨੀ; ਗੋਲ; (3) ਅਖਾੜਾ, ਛਣਕ, ਟਣਕਾਰ, ਗੂੰਜਾਰ; ਵੱਜਣਾ, ਵਜਾਉਣਾ,

ਛਟਕਾਣਾ, ਛਟਕਾਉਣਾ, ਟਟਕਾਉਣਾ; ਟੱਲੀ ਵਜਾਇਣੀ; ਟੈਲੀਫੋਨ ਰਾਹੀਂ ਬੁਲਾਉਣਾ; ~leader ਵਿਦਰੋਹੀਆਂ ਦਾ ਸਰਦਾਰ; ਦਾਦਾ, ਸਰਗਨਾ; ~worm ਦੱਦ, ਚੱਦਰ ਦੀ ਬੀਮਾਰੀ

rinse (ਰਿੰਸ) v ਹੰਘਾਲਣਾ, ਨਚੋੜਨਾ; ਕੁਰਲੀ ਕਰਨੀ, ਚੁਲੀ ਕਰਨੀ

riot ('ਰਾਇਅਟ) n v ਦੰਗਾ, ਫ਼ਸਾਦ, ਬਲਵਾ; ਹੁਲੜ; ਦੰਗਾ-ਫ਼ਸਾਦ ਕਰਨਾ

rip (ਰਿਪ) v n ਪਾੜਨਾ ਜਾਂ ਪਾਟਣਾ, ਚੀਰਨਾ ਜਾਂ ਚਿਰਨਾ, ਉਧੇੜਨਾ ਜਾਂ ਉੱਧੜਨਾ; ਚੀਰਨ, ਪਾੜਨ, ਚੀਰ, ਵੱਢ; ਨਿਕੰਮਾ ਟੱਟੂ, ਕਾਮੀ, ਆਦਮੀ, ਬਦਚਲਨ ਬੰਦਾ; ~per ਇਕ ਆਰਾ, ਚੀਰਨ ਵਾਲਾ, ਪਾੜਨ ਵਾਲਾ

ripe (ਰਾਇਪ) a ਪੱਕ, ਤਿਆਰ, ਰਸਿਆ, ਹੰਢਿਆ; ~n ਪੱਕਣਾ, ਰਸਣਾ; ਸੁਝਵਾਨ ਬਣਨਾ, ਅਨੁਭਵ ਵਧਣਾ

ripple ('ਰਿਪਲ) n v ਛੋਟੀ ਲਹਿਰ, ਲਹਿਰਦਾਰ ਅਵਾਜ਼; ਲਹਿਰਨਾ, ਲਹਿਰਾਂ ਉਠਣੀਆਂ, ਛਲਕਣਾ

rise (ਰਾਇਜ਼) v n ਉੱਠਣਾ, ਉੱਠ ਬੈਠਣਾ, ਉੱਠ ਖਲੋਣਾ, ਜਾਗਣਾ; (ਸੂਰਜ, ਚੰਦ ਦਾ) ਚੜ੍ਹਨ, ਨਿਕਲਣਾ; ਜਿਊ ਉੱਠਣਾ, ਜੀ ਪੈਣਾ; ਵਿਦਰੋਹ ਕਰਨਾ; ਉਦੈ; ਚੜ੍ਹਾਈ; ਉਭਾਰ; ਪਹਾੜੀ, ਟਿੱਲਾ; ਉੱਨਤੀ, ਵਾਧਾ, ਮੂਲ ਸਰੋਤ

rising ('ਰਾਇਜ਼ਿੰਡ) n ਵਿਦਰੋਹ, ਉੱਨਤੀ, ਵਿਕਾਸ; ਉਦੈ, ਨਿਕਾਸ

risk (ਰਿਸਕ) n ਖ਼ਤਰਾ, ਸੰਕਟ, ਬਿਪਤਾ, ਆਫ਼ਤ; ~y ਖ਼ਤਰੇ ਵਾਲਾ, ਸੰਕਟਮਈ, ਇਤਰਾਜ਼ਯੋਗ

rite (ਰਾਇਟ) n ਰਸਮ, ਰੀਤ, ਸੰਸਕਾਰ, ਧਾਰਮਕ ਮਰਯਾਦਾ, ਕਰਮ ਕਾਂਡ

ritual ('ਰਿਚੁਅਲ) a n ਰਸਮੀ, ਰਿਵਾਜੀ, ਸੰਸਕਾਰਕ; ਧਾਰਮਕ ਰੀਤਾਂ

rival ('ਰਾਇਵਲ) n v ਸ਼ਰੀਕ; ਵਿਰੋਧੀ, ਰਕੀਬ, ਪ੍ਰਤੀਪੰਖੀ; ਵਿਰੋਧ ਕਰਨਾ, ਟਾਕਰਾ ਕਰਨਾ, ਲਾਗ-ਡਾਟ ਕਰਨੀ; ਬਰਾਬਰੀ ਕਰਨੀ; ~ry ਸ਼ਰੀਕਾ, ਵਿਰੋਧ, ਬਰਾਬਰੀ, ਰੀਸ, ਟਾਕਰਾ

rive ('ਰਾਇਵ) v ਚੀਰਨਾ ਜਾਂ ਚਿਰਨਾ, ਪਾੜਨਾ ਜਾਂ ਪਾਟਣਾ

river ('ਰਿਵ੍ਹਅ*) n ਦਰਿਆ, ਨਦੀ; ~ain, ~ine ਦਰਿਆ ਦਾ, ਦਰਿਆਈ

rivulet ('ਰਿਵ੍ਹਯੁਲਿਟ) n ਛੋਟਾ ਦਰਿਆ, ਨਦੀ, ਨਾਲਾ

road ('ਰਅਉਡ) n ਸੜਕ, ਮਾਰਗ, ਰਾਹ, ਰਸਤਾ

roam (ਰਅਉਮ) v ਟੁਰਨਾ-ਫਿਰਨਾ, ਸੈਰ-ਸਪਾਟਾ ਕਰਨਾ, ਘੁਮੱਣਾ-ਘੁਮਾਉਣਾ, ਅਵਾਰਾ ਫਿਰਨਾ, ਬਿਨਾ ਕੰਮ ਘੁੰਮਣਾ

roar (ਰੋ*) n v ਭਬਕ (ਸ਼ੇਰ ਦੀ); ਚਿੰਘਾੜ, ਦਹਾੜ; ਗੱਜਣਾ, ਬੜ੍ਹਕਣਾ

roast (ਰਅਉਸਟ) v n ਭੁੰਨਣਾ ਜਾਂ ਭੁੱਜਣਾ, ਸੇਕਣਾ ਜਾਂ ਸਿਕਣਾ, ਰਤੂਨਾ ਜਾਂ ਰਤੂਨਾ; (ਧਾਤ ਨੂੰ) ਤਪਾਉਣਾ; ਭੁੰਨਵਾਂ ਮਾਸ, ਕਬਾਬ

rob (ਰੌਬ) v ਲੁੱਟਣਾ, ਡਾਕਾ ਮਾਰਨਾ, ਖੋਹ ਲੈਣਾ; ~ber ਲੁਟੇਰਾ, ਡਾਕੂ, ਡਕੈਤ, ਰਾਹਜ਼ਨ; ~bery ਡਾਕਾ, ਧਾੜ, ਲੁੱਟ-ਮਾਰ

robe (ਰਅਉਬ) n v ਪੁਸ਼ਾਕ, ਚੋਗਾ, ਵਸਤਰ, ਉਪਰਲਾ ਕੋਟ, ਵੱਡਾ ਕੋਟ; ਪੁਸ਼ਾਕ ਪਹਿਨਣਾ

robust (ਰਅ(ਉ)'ਬਅੱਸਟ) a ਤਕੜਾ, ਮਜ਼ਬੂਤ, ਹੱਟਾ-ਕੱਟਾ, ਰਿਸ਼ਟਪੁਸ਼ਟ

rock (ਰੌਕ) n v ਚਟਾਨ; ਪਹਾੜੀ, ਪੱਥਰ, ਸ਼ਕਤੀ, ਬਲ; ਆਸਰਾ; ਝੂਲਣਾ, ਝੂਮਣਾ, ਹਲੂਣਾ, ਝੂਟਾ ਦੇਣਾ; ~er ਪੰਘੂੜਾ; ਝੂਲਟ ਜਾਂ ਝੁਲਾਉਣ ਵਾਲਾ

rod (ਰੌਡ) n ਸੀਖ, ਡੰਡਾ, ਛੜੀ, ਬੈਂਤ, ਸੋਟਾ

rodent (ਰਅਉਡਅੰਟ) *a n* ਕੁਤਰਨ ਵਾਲਾ ਜੀਵ (ਜਿਵੇਂ ਚੂਹਾ ਆਦਿ)

rogue (ਰਅਉਗ) *n* (ਪ੍ਰ) ਬਦਮਾਸ਼, ਗੁੰਡਾ, ਲੁੱਚਾ, ਮਸਤ (ਹਾਥੀ)

role (ਰਅਉਲ) *n* ਫ਼ਰਜ਼, ਜ਼ੁੰਮੇਵਾਰੀ, (ਐਕਟਰ ਦਾ) ਪਾਰਟ, ਭੂਮਕਾ

roll (ਰਅਉਲ) *n v* ਸੂਚੀ, ਫ਼ਹਿਰਿਸਤ, ਨਾਮਾਵਲੀ, ਹਾਜ਼ਰੀ ਦਾ ਰਜਿਸਟਰ; ਰੇਤੂਨ; ਵਲੑੇਟਣਾ ਜਾਂ ਵਲੑੇਟੇ ਜਾਣਾ; ਘੁਮਾਉਣਾ ਜਾਂ ਘੁੰਮਣਾ, ਫੇਰਨ ਜਾਂ ਫਿਰਨ; ਲੇਟਣਾ; ਝਮਣਾ, ਝਲਣਾ, ਸੁਲਾਉਣਾ; **~call** ਹਾਜ਼ਰੀ; **~er** (ਲੱਕੜੀ ਜਾਂ ਧਾਤ ਦਾ) ਵੇਲਣ, ਵੇਲਣਾ, ਰੋਲਰ; ਰਿੜ੍ਹਨ ਜਾਂ ਰੇੜ੍ਹਨ ਵਾਲਾ

Roman ('ਰਅਉਮਅਨ) *a n* ਰੋਮ ਦਾ, ਰੋਮ-ਸਬੰਧੀ, ਰੋਮ ਬਾਰੇ; ਰੋਮ-ਨਿਵਾਸੀ

romance, Romance (ਰਅ(ਉ)'ਮੈਂਸ) *n v* ਰੋਮਾਂਚਕ ਕਹਾਣੀ, ਪਿਆਰ, ਇਸ਼ਕ; ਮੱਧ-ਕਾਲ ਦੀ ਵੀਰ ਕਥਾ, ਸਰਲ ਗੀਤ, ਛੋਟਾ ਗੀਤ; ਰੋਮਾਂਸ

romantic (ਰਅ(ਉ)'ਮੈਂਟਿਕ) *a* ਰੋਮਾਂਚਕ; ਰੋਮਾਂਸ ਵਾਲਾ, ਕਲਪਤ, ਭਾਵੁਕ, ਕਲਪਨਾ ਪ੍ਰਧਾਨ; ਚਿੱਤਰਮਈ, ਰੋਮਾਂਸਵਾਦੀ; **~ism** ਰੋਮਾਂਸਵਾਦ; ਰੋਮਾਂਸਕਤਾ, ਭਾਵਪ੍ਰਧਾਨਤਾ

roof (ਰੂਫ਼) *n v* ਛੱਤ, ਛੱਪਰ, ਅਸਮਾਨ; ਘਰ, ਟਿਕਾਣਾ

room (ਰੂਮ) *n* ਕਮਰਾ, ਕੋਠਾ, ਥਾਂ, ਜਗ੍ਹਾ, ਸਥਾਨ, ਸਮਾਈ, ਗੁੰਜਾਇਸ਼, ਮੌਕਾ

root (ਰੂਟ) *n v* ਜੜ੍ਹ, ਧਾਤੁ, ਮੂਲ, ਨੀਂਹ, ਆਧਾਰ, ਬੁਨਿਆਦ; ਦ੍ਰਿੜ੍ਹ ਕਰਨਾ, ਪੱਕਾ ਕਰਨਾ, ਜੜ੍ਹ ਲਾਉਂਟੀ; (ਕਿਸੇ ਨੂੰ) ਹੱਲਾਸ਼ੇਰੀ ਦੇਂਦੀ, ਵਾਹਵਾ ਕਰਨੀ, ਸ਼ਾਬਾਸ਼ ਕਹਿਣੀ

rope (ਰਅਉਪ) *n v* ਰੱਸੀ, ਕਮੰਦ; ਲੜੀ; ਰੱਸਾ ਵੱਟਣਾ; (ਪਹਾੜਾਂ ਦੀ ਚੜ੍ਹਾਈ ਵਿਚ) ਰੱਸੀ ਨਾਲ ਬੰਨ੍ਹਣਾ; **~dancer** ਰੱਸੇ ਤੇ ਨੱਚਣ ਵਾਲਾ, ਨਟ

rosary ('ਰਅਉਜ਼ਅਰਿ) *n* ਮਾਲਾ, ਤਸਬੀ, ਸਿਮਰਨੀ, ਗੁਲਾਬ ਦਾ ਬਗ਼ੀਚਾ

rose (ਰਅਉਜ਼) *n* ਗੁਲਾਬ; ਗੁਲਾਲ, ਗੁਲਾਬੀ ਰੰਗ; **~bud** ਗੁਲਾਬ ਦੀ ਕਲੀ; ਸੁੰਦਰ ਮੁਟਿਆਰ; **~colour** ਗੁਲਾਬੀ ਰੰਗ; **~water** ਗੁਲਾਬ ਦਾ ਅਰਕ

roset ('ਰਅਉਜ਼ੈੱਟ) *n* ਲਾਲ ਰੰਗ

rosette (ਰਅ(ਉ)'ਜ਼ੈੱਟ) *n* ਬਣਾਉਟੀ ਫੁੱਲ

roster ('ਰੌਸਟਅ*) *n* ਕਾਰਜ-ਸੂਚੀ, ਸਮਾਂ-ਸਾਰਨੀ

rostrum ('ਰੌਸਟਰਅਮ) *n* ਸਭਾ-ਮੰਚ; ਡਾਇਸ; (ਪੰਛੀਆਂ ਦੀ) ਚੁੰਝ

rosy ('ਰਅਉਜ਼ਿ) *a* ਗੁਲਾਬੀ, ਗੁਲਾਬੀ ਰੰਗ ਦਾ, ਆਸ਼ਾਜਨਕ

rot (ਰੌਟ) *v n* ਗਲਣਾ ਜਾਂ ਗਾਲਣਾ, ਗਲ-ਸੜ ਜਾਣਾ, ਬੁੱਸਣਾ, ਸੜਾਂਦ ਮਾਰਨੀ, (ਕੈਦ ਵਿਚ) ਸੜਨਾ; ਨਿਰਥਕ ਗੱਲ, ਫ਼ਜ਼ੂਲ ਬਕਵਾਸ; ਖੱਖੜ

rotate (ਰਅ(ਉ)'ਟੇਇਟ) *v* ਆਪਣੇ ਧੁਰੇ ਦੇ ਦੁਆਲੇ ਘੁੰਮਣਾ; ਘਿਰਨਾ ਜਾਂ ਗੇੜਨਾ; ਵਾਰੀ ਬੰਨ੍ਹਣੀ, ਵਾਰੀ ਅਨੁਸਾਰ ਹੋਣਾ

rotation (ਰਅ(ਉ)'ਟੇਇਸ਼ਨ) *n* ਗੇੜਾ, ਗੇੜ, ਚੱਕਰ, ਵਾਰੀ

rote (ਰਅਉਟ) *n* ਰੱਟਾ, ਘੋਟਾ

rotten ('ਰੌਟਨ) *a* ਬੁੱਸਿਆ, ਸੜਾਂਦ ਮਾਰਦਾ, ਗਲਿਆ-ਸੜਿਆ, ਨਿਕੰਮਾ, ਰੱਦੀ, (ਹਾਲਤ) ਵਿਗੜੀ ਹੋਈ, ਭੈੜੀ; ਨਾਕਸ, ਖ਼ਰਾਬ; ਗੰਦਾ

rough (ਰੱਫ਼) *a n v* ਖੁਰਵਾਂ; ਅਣਪੱਧਰਾ; ਉੱਚਾ-ਨੀਵਾਂ; ਕੋਝਾ; ਅਟਪਟਤ; ਕਰਖਤ; ਮੋਟਾ;

ਅਟਸਵਾਰਿਆ; ਕੱਚਾ-ਪੱਕਾ; ਖਿਚਣਾ; ਮੋਟੀ ਰੂਪ-ਰੇਖਾ ਬਣਾਉਣੀ

round (ਰਾਉਂਡ) *a n prep v* ਗੋਲ, ਗੋਲ ਆਕਾਰ, ਚੱਕਰ ਵਾਲੀ ਵਸਤੁ, ਗੋਲ ਪਦਾਰਥ; ਮੂੰਹਫਟ, ਬਏਖੋਲਾ, ਤਕਰੀਬਨ, ਲਗਾਤਰ; ਚੱਕਰ, ਦਾਇਰਾ, ਘੇਰਾ; ਘੇਰਨਾ, ਵਲਗਣਾ; ~**about** ਕਰੀਬ-ਕਰੀਬ, ਨੇੜੇ-ਨੇੜੇ, ਲਾਗੇ-ਚਾਗੇ; ~**ly** ਪੂਰੀ ਤਰ੍ਹਾਂ, ਚੰਗੀ ਤਰ੍ਹਾਂ, ਸਾਫ਼ ਸ਼ਬਦਾਂ ਵਿਚ, ਗੋਲਾਈ ਵਿਚ; ਘੇਰਾ ਬਣਾ ਕੇ

rousing ('ਰਾਉਜ਼ਿਡ) *a* ਤੇਜ਼, ਤਿੱਖਾ; ਗਰਮ; ਸ਼ਾਨਦਾਰ; ਉਤੇਜਕ

roust (ਰਾਉਸਟ) *v n* ਹਟਾਉਣਾ, ਕੱਢਣਾ

rout (ਰਾਉਟ) *n v* ਪੂਰੀ ਹਾਰ; (ਕ) ਫ਼ਸਾਦ; ਦੰਗਾ; ਜਤੂ, ਮੂਲ; ਬੁਰੀ ਤਰ੍ਹਾਂ ਹਰਾਉਣਾ, ਖਦੇੜਨਾ; ਜਤੂ ਲਾਉਣੀ; ਜਤੂ ਫਟਣਾ

route (ਰੂਟ) *n* ਰਸਤਾ; ਕੂਚ ਕਰਨ ਦਾ ਲਿਖਤੀ ਹੁਕਮ

routine (ਰਾ'ਟੀਨ) *n a* ਨਿੱਤ ਦਾ ਕੰਮ; ਰੋਜ਼ ਦੀ ਕਾਰਵਾਈ, ਨਿੱਤ-ਨੇਮ, ਨਿਯਮਬੱਧ, ਨੇਮੀ

row (ਰਅਉ) *n v* ਪਾਲ, ਪੰਗਤ, ਕਤਾਰ; ਫ਼ਸਾਦ, ਝਗੜਾ, ਰੌਲਾ-ਰੱਪਾ, ਮਾਰ-ਕੁਟਾਈ; ਬੇੜੀ ਚਲਾਉਣਾ, ਚੱਪੂ ਚਲਾਉਣਾ; ਝਿੜਕਣਾ, ਡਾਂਟਣਾ; ਫਿਟਕਾਰਨਾ; ~**er** ਮਾਂਝੀ, ਖੇਵਟ, ਖਵੈਯਾ, ਮਲਾਹ; ~**ing** ਝਿੜਕ-ਝੰਭ, ਝਾੜ-ਫਿਟਕਾਰ

rowdiness ('ਰਾਉਡਿਨਿਸ) *n* ਹੁੱਲੜਬਾਜ਼ੀ; ਝਗੜਾ-ਲੁਪਟ, ਉਧਮ

rowdy ('ਰਾਉਡਿ) *n adv* ਕੁਪੱਤਾ, ਝਗੜਾਲੂ, ਫ਼ਸਾਦੀ, ਹੁੱਲੜਬਾਜ਼, ਦੰਗਾਈ; ~**ism** ਹੁੱਲੜਬਾਜ਼ੀ

royal ('ਰੋਇਅਲ) *a n* ਬਾਦਸ਼ਾਹੀ, ਰਾਜਸੀ, ਰਾਜਨੀਤਕ, ਸ਼ਾਨਦਾਰ; ਰਾਯਲ (ਕਾਗ਼ਜ਼) ~**standard** ਸ਼ਾਹੀ ਝੰਡਾ; ~**ty** ਬਾਦਸ਼ਾਹੀ, ਸ਼ਾਹੀ, ਸ਼ਾਹੀ ਪਦ, ਸ਼ਾਹੀ ਖ਼ਾਨਦਾਨ, ਰਾਜਵੰਸ਼, ਰਾਜ ਹੱਕ, ਹੱਕ-ਮਾਲਕੀ; ਪ੍ਰਕਾਸ਼ਕ ਵੱਲੋਂ ਪੁਸਤਕ ਦੇ ਲੇਖਕ ਨੂੰ ਦਿੱਤੇ ਜਾਣ ਵਾਲੇ ਫ਼ਿਤਫਲ ਦੇ ਦਰ

rub (ਰੱਬ) *v n* ਰਗੜਨਾ, ਮਲਣਾ, ਘਸਾਉਣਾ, ਮਾਂਜਣਾ, ਖਰੋਚਣਾ, ਮਾਲਸ਼ ਕਰਨੀ, ਰਗੜ ਖਾਣੀ ਰਗੜ, ਘਸਾਈ; ਰੋੜਾ; ~**ber** ਰਬੜ, ਮਲਣ ਵਾਲਾ, ਘਸਾਉਣ ਵਾਲਾ, ਮਾਲਸ਼ ਕਰਨ ਵਾਲਾ

rubbish ('ਰਅਬਿਸ਼) *n* ਕੂੜਾ, ਰੱਦੀ, ਗੰਦ-ਮੰਦ; ਨਿਕੰਮੀ ਚੀਜ਼; ਬਹੁਤ ਘਟੀਆ ਮਾਲ, ਫ਼ਜ਼ੂਲ ਬਕਵਾਸ; ~**y** ਨਿਕੰਮਾ; ਅਣ-ਉਪਯੋਗੀ; ਨਿਰਰਥਕ; ਘੇਕਾਰ; ਫ਼ਜ਼ੂਲ

rubble ('ਰਅੱਬਲ) *n* ਮਲਬਾ, ਇੱਟਾਂ-ਰੋੜੇ, ਅਣਘੜੇ ਪੱਥਰ

rubric ('ਰੂਬਰਿਕ) *n* ਸਿਰਲੇਖ, ਹੈਡਿੰਗ, ਸੁਰਖ਼ੀ

rude (ਰੂਡ) *a* ਉੱਜਡ, ਅਸੱਭਿਆ, ਗੁਸਤਾਖ਼, ਅਸ਼ਿਸ਼ਟ, ਬਦਤਮੀਜ਼; (ਘਰ-ਘਾਟ) ਅਣਘੜਤ

rudiment ('ਰੂਡਿਮਅੰਟ) *n* ਅਰੰਭਕ ਸਿਧਾਂਤ, ਬੁਨਿਆਦ, ਅਸੂਲ; ਅਰੰਭ, ਪ੍ਰਾਰੰਭ; ~**ary** ਅਰੰਭਕ, ਬੁਨਿਆਦੀ, ਅਪੂਰਨ, ਅਧੂਰਾ

ruffian ('ਰਅੱਫ਼ਿਅਨ) *n* ਗੁੰਡਾ, ਬਦਮਾਸ਼, ਖ਼ੂਨੀ, ਹਤਿਆਰਾ; ~**ism** ਗੁੰਡਪੁਣਾ; ਬਦਮਾਸ਼ੀ, ਗੁੰਡਾਗਰਦੀ

ruffle ('ਰਅੱਫ਼ਲ) *v n* ਖਿਲਾਰ ਦੇਣਾ; ਬੇਤਰਤੀਬ ਕਰ ਦੇਣਾ, ਪਰੇਸ਼ਾਨ ਕਰ ਦੇਣਾ ਹੋਣਾ, ਸ਼ਾਂਤੀ ਭੰਗ ਕਰ ਦੇਣੀ; ਗੜਬੜ ਪਾ ਦੇਣੀ; ਅਸ਼ਾਂਤੀ, ਘਬਰਾਹਟ, ਗੜਬੜ

rugged ('ਰਅੱਗਿਡ) *a* ਅਣ-ਪੱਧਰਾ, ਉੱਚਾ-ਨੀਵਾਂ, ਪਥਰੀਲਾ, ਅਣਘੜਤ, ਬੇਡੌਲ

ruin (ਰੂਇਨ) *n v* ਤਬਾਹੀ, ਬਰਬਾਦੀ, ਨਾਸ, ਵੀਰਾਨੀ; ਉਜਾੜ, ਪਤਨ, ਗਿਰਾਵਟ, ਮਲੀਆਮੇਟ; ਉਜਾੜਨਾ, ਬਰਬਾਦ ਕਰਨਾ, ਗਾਰਕ

ਕਰਨਾ, ਮਲੀਆਮੇਟ ਕਰਨਾ; ~ation ਤਬਾਹੀ, ਉਜਾੜਾ, ਬਰਬਾਦੀ

rule (ਰੂਲ) *n v* (1) ਨਿਯਮ, ਅਸੂਲ; (2) ਸਿਧਾਂਤ, ਰੀਤ, ਰਿਵਾਜ; ਤਰੀਕਾ, ਢੰਗ; (3) ਹਕੂਮਤ, ਰਾਜ, ਸ਼ਾਸਨ; ਫੁੱਟਾ, ਪੈਮਾਨਾ; ਹਕੂਮਤ ਕਰਨੀ, ਰਾਜ ਕਰਨਾ, ਹੁਕਮ ਦੇਣਾ; ਨਿਰਣੈ ਕਰਨਾ; ~r ਰਾਜਾ, ਬਾਦਸ਼ਾਹ, ਸ਼ਾਸਕ, ਪੈਮਾਨਾ

ruling ('ਰੂਲਿਙ) *n* ਫ਼ੈਸਲਾ; ਹੁਕਮ

rumble ('ਰਅੰਬਲ) *v n* ਗੁੜਗੁੜਾਉਣਾ, (ਪੇਟ ਦਾ) ਗੁੜਗੁੜ ਕਰਨਾ; ਗੜ-ਗੜ, ਕੜ-ਕੜ, ਗੜਬੜ੍ਹਾਟ

ruminate ('ਰੂਮਿਨੇਇਟ) *v* ਉਗਾਲੀ ਕਰਨੀ, ਸੋਚਣਾ, ਸੋਚੀਂ ਪੈਣਾ, ਗੰਭੀਰ ਵਿਚਾਰ ਕਰਨਾ

rumination ('ਰੂਮਿ'ਨੇਇਸ਼ਨ) *n* ਉਗਾਲੀ; ਸੋਚ-ਵਿਚਾਰ, ਧਿਆਨ, ਚਿੰਤਨ

rumour ('ਰੂਮਅ*) *n v* ਅਫ਼ਵਾਹ, ਡਿਟਕ, ਉਡਦੀ ਉਡਦੀ ਖ਼ਬਰ, ਅਪ੍ਰਮਾਣਤ ਕਥਨ, ਨਿਰਧਾਰ ਖ਼ਬਰ; ਅਫ਼ਵਾਹ ਉਡਾਉਣੀ

run (ਰਅੱਨ) *v n* ਦੌੜਨਾ, ਭੱਜਣਾ, ਨੱਸਣਾ; ਚਲਾਉਣਾ; ਫ਼ਰਾਰ ਹੋ ਜਾਣਾ; ਦੌੜ; ਸੂਟ, ਭਾਜੜ; (ਕ੍ਰਿਕਟ ਦੀ) ਰਨ; ~away ਭਗੌੜਾ, ਅੱਥਰਾ; ~over ਭਾਰ ਮਾਨਣਾ; ਲਿਤਾੜਨਾ; ·way ਹਵਾਈ ਅੱਡੇ ਦੀ ਪਟੜੀ; ~ning ਦੌੜ-ਭੱਜ, ਦੌੜ; ਵਗਦਾ ਹੋਇਆ; ਲਗਾਤਾਰ

rupee (ਰੂ'ਪੀ) *n* ਰੁਪਇਆ

rupture ('ਰਅੱਪਚਅ*) *n v* ਵਿਗਾੜ, ਅਟਬਨ, ਆਂਦਰ ਦਾ ਵਧਾ, 'ਹਰਨੀਆ'; ਤੇੜਨਾ, ਫਟਣਾ; ਆਂਦਰ ਵਧਣੀ, ਹਰਨਿਆ ਹੋਣਾ

rural ('ਰੂਅਰ(ਅ)ਲ) *a* ਪੇਂਡੂ, ਗ੍ਰਾਮੀਣ, ਦਿਹਾਤੀ; ਖੇਤੀ ਸਬੰਧੀ

rush (ਰਅੱਸ਼) *n v* ਦੌੜ, ਕਾਹਲ ਨਾਲ ਪੁੱਜਣਾ; ਧਾਵਾ; ਭੀੜ, ਗਾਹੜ, ਘੜਮੱਸ; ਤੇਜ਼ੀ ਨਾਲ ਵਧਣਾ; ਕਾਹਲ ਨਾਲ ਵਰਗਣਾ, ਧੁੱਸ ਦੇਣਾ

rust (ਰਅੱਸਟ) *n v* ਜੰਗਾਲ, ਜੰਗ, ਬੁਰੀ ਹਾਲਤ, ਸੜੀ-ਗਲੀ ਹਾਲਤ; ਜੰਗਾਲ ਲੱਗਣਾ

rustic ('ਰਅੱਸਟਿਕ) *a n* ਪੇਂਡੂ, ਗ੍ਰਾਮੀਣ, ਦਿਹਾਤੀ; ਗੰਵਾਰ, ਉਂਜੜ, ਸਿੰਧੜ

rustle ('ਰਅੱਸਲ) *n v* ਸਰਸਰਾਹਟ, ਖੜਖੜਾਹਟ; ਸਰਵਰ ਕਰਨਾ, ਖੜਖੜ ਕਰਨਾ

ruth (ਰੂਥ) *n* ਤਰਸ, ਦਇਆ, ਰਹਿਮ; ~ful ਤਰਸਵਾਨ, ਦਇਆਵਾਨ, ਰਹਿਮ-ਦਿਲ; ~less ਬੇਤਰਸ, ਨਿਰਦਈ, ਪੱਥਰ-ਦਿਲ, ਬੇਰਹਿਮ

rux (ਰਅੱਕਸ) *n* ਵਾਸਨਾ, ਲਾਲਸਾ, ਕਾਮਨਾ

ryot ('ਹਾਇਅਟ) *n* ਕਿਸਾਨ, ਕ੍ਰਿਸ਼ਕ, ਹਲਵਾਹਕ

S

S, s (ਐੱਸ) *n* ਐੱਸ, ਰੋਮਨ ਵਰਣਮਾਲਾ ਦਾ ਉਨੀਵਾਂ ਅੱਖਰ; ਲਹਿਰੀਆ ਮੋੜ

sabotage ('ਸੈਬਅਟਾਯ਼) *n v* ਤੋੜ-ਫੋੜ, ਗੁਪਤ ਤੋੜ-ਫੋੜ, ਨੁਕਸਾਨ; ਤੋੜ-ਫੋੜ ਕਰਨਾ, ਨੁਕਸਾਨ ਪਹੁੰਚਾਉਣਾ, ਵਿਗਾੜ ਦੇਣਾ

sack (ਸੈਕ) *n v* ਬੋਰੀ, ਥੈਲੀ, ਢਿੱਲਾ ਪਹਿਰਾਵਾ; ਇਸਤਰੀਆਂ ਦਾ ਚੋਗਾ, ਲੁੱਟ-ਮਾਰ; ਬੋਰਾ ਭਰਨਾ, ਥੈਲੀ ਵਿਚ ਪਾਉਣਾ; ਨੌਕਰੀ ਵਿਚੋਂ ਕੱਢਣਾ, ਬਰਖ਼ਾਸਤ ਕਰਨਾ; ਲੁੱਟਣਾ

sacrament ('ਸੈਕਰਅਮਅੰਟ) *n v* ਇਸਾਈਆਂ ਦਾ ਧਾਰਮਕ ਸੰਸਕਾਰ; ਪਵਿੱਤਰ ਭਾਵ; ਪ੍ਰਤਿੱਗਿਆ; ਵਚਨਬੱਧ ਕਰਨਾ

sacred ('ਸੇਇਕਰਿਡ) *a* ਪਾਕ, ਮੁਤੱਬਰਕ; ਮੁੱਕਦਸ, ਸੁੱਚਾ, ਸ਼ੁੱਧ, ਪਵਿੱਤਰ, ਪੁਨੀਤ

sacrifice ('ਸੈਕਰਿਫ਼ਾਇਸ) *n v* ਬਲੀਦਾਨ, ਕੁਰਬਾਨੀ, ਤਿਆਗ, ਸਮਰਪਣ; ਯੱਗ; ਭੇਟ; ਬਲੀ ਦੇਣੀ, ਕੁਰਬਾਨ ਕਰਨਾ; ਅਰਪਣ ਕਰਨਾ

sacrilege ('ਸੈਕਰਿਲਿਜ) *n* ਬੇਅਦਬੀ, ਪਵਿੱਤਰ ਥਾਂ ਦਾ ਅਪਵਿੱਤਰੀਕਰਨ, ਬੇ-ਹੁਰਮਤੀ, ਮਰਯਾਦਾ-ਭੰਗ, ਧਰਮ-ਉਲੰਘਣ

sacrosanct ('ਸੈਕਰਅ(ਉ)ਸੈਂਕ(ਕ)ਟ) *a* ਪਾਕ, ਮੁਕੱਦਸ, ਮੁਤੱਬਰਕ, ਪੁਨੀਤ, ਅਤੀ ਪਵਿੱਤਰ, ਪਾਵਨ

sad (ਸੈਡ) *a* ਦਿਲਗੀਰ, ਰੰਜੀਦਾ, ਉਦਾਸ, ਗ਼ਮਗੀਨ, ਦੁਖੀ; **~ness** ਦੁੱਖ, ਚਿੰਤਾ, ਉਦਾਸੀ, ਅਫ਼ਸੋਸ, ਮਲਾਲ, ਗ਼ਮ, ਰੰਜ

saddle ('ਸੈਡਲ) *n v* ਪਾਲਣਾ, ਕਾਠੀ, ਜ਼ੀਨ; ਭਾਰ ਲੱਦਣਾ

safari (ਸਅ'ਫ਼ਾਰਿ) *n* ਸ਼ਿਕਾਰ ਦਾ ਸਫ਼ਰ, ਯਾਤਰੀਆਂ ਦਾ ਦਲ, ਬੰਦ ਗੱਡੀ; **~park** ਜੰਗਲੀ ਜਾਨਵਰਾਂ ਦੀ ਰੱਖ

safe (ਸੇਇਫ਼) *n a* ਸੁਰੱਖਿਆ, ਸਹੀ-ਸਲਾਮਤ; ਯਕੀਨੀ; **~guard** ਆੜ, ਬਚਾਉ; **~ty** ਸੁਰੱਖਿਆ, ਕੁਸ਼ਲ ਰੱਖਿਆ, ਖੈਰੀਅਤ, ਨਿਰਭੈਤਾ, ਬਚਾਉ, ਸਲਾਮਤੀ

saffron ('ਸੈਫ਼ਰ(ਅ)ਨ) *n a* ਕੇਸਰ, ਜ਼ਾਅਫ਼ਰਾਨ; ਕੇਸਰੀ ਰੰਗ

saga ('ਸਾਗਅ) *n* ਵੀਰਗਾਥਾ, ਸ਼ਾਹਨਾਮਾ; (ਮੱਧ ਯੁੱਗ ਦੇ ਨਾਰਵੇ ਦਾ) ਗੱਦ-ਸਾਹਿਤ; ਸਾਕਾ

sagacious (ਸਅ'ਗੇਇਸ਼ਅਸ) *a* ਸੁਝਵਾਨ, ਸਿਆਣਾ, ਹੁਸ਼ਿਆਰ; ਅਕਲਮੰਦ; ਦੂਰਦਰਸ਼ੀ

sagacity (ਸਅ'ਗੈਸਅਟਿ) *n* ਤੀਖਣ ਬੁੱਧੀ, ਤੇਜ਼ ਸੂਝ, ਸਮਝਦਾਰੀ, ਹੁਸ਼ਿਆਰੀ

sage (ਸੇਇਜ) *n a* ਦਾਰਸ਼ਨਕ; ਰਿਸ਼ੀ, ਮੁਨੀ; ਵਿਵੇਕੀ, ਦਾਨਾ

sail (ਸੇਇਲ) *n v* ਜਹਾਜ਼; ਜਹਾਜ਼ੀ ਬੇੜਾ; ਬਾਦਬਾਨ; ਜਲ-ਯਾਤਰਾ; ਜਹਾਜ਼ ਵਿਚ ਸਮੁੰਦਰੀ ਸਫ਼ਰ ਕਰਨਾ; ਜਹਾਜ਼ ਚਲਾਉਣਾ; ਆਕਾਸ਼ ਵਿਚ ਉੱਡਣਾ; **~or** ਮੱਲਾਹ, ਜਹਾਜ਼ਰਾਨ, ਕਿਸ਼ਤੀਵਾਨ

saint (ਸੇਇੰਟ) *n v a* ਸੰਤ, ਸਾਧੂ, ਮੁਨੀ, ਸਿੱਧ, ਮਹਾਤਮਾ, ਦਰਵੇਸ਼; ਸੰਤ ਮੰਨਣਾ; ਧਾਰਮਕ, ਅਤਿ ਪਵਿੱਤਰ

sake (ਸੇਇਕ) *n* ਨਿਮਿੱਤ, ਹਿਤ, ਕਾਰਨ, ਖ਼ਾਤਰ

salad (ਸੈਲਅਡ) *n* ਕੱਚਾ ਸਾਗ, ਸਲਾਦ

salaried ('ਸੈਲਅਰਿਡ) *a* ਤਰਖ਼ਾਹਦਾਰ

salary ('ਸੈਲਅਰਿ) *n v* ਤਨਖ਼ਾਹ, ਵੇਤਨ; ਵੇਤਨ

ਦੇਣਾ, ਤਨਖ਼ਾਹ ਦੇਣੀ

sale (ਸੇਇਲ) *n* ਵੇਚ, ਵਿਕਰੀ; ਵੱਟਕ; ਬੋਲੀ; ~sman ਵੇਚਣ ਵਾਲਾ

salient ('ਸੇਇਲਯੰਟ) *n a* ਪ੍ਰਪਤ, ਮੁੱਖ; ਉਂਘੜਵਾਂ, ਮਹੱਤਵਪੂਰਨ

saline ('ਸੇਇਲਾਇਨ) *a n* ਖਾਰਾ, ਲੂਣਾ, ਨਮਕੀਨ

saliva (ਸਅ'ਲਾਇਵਅ) *n* ਲਾਰ, ਥੁੱਕ, ਲੁਆਬ

saloon (ਸਅ'ਲੂਨ) *n* ਹਾਲ, ਬੈਠਕ, ਸਭਾ; ਸੈਲੂਨ; ਰੇਲ ਦਾ ਪਹਿਲੇ ਦਰਜੇ ਦਾ ਡੱਬਾ

salt (ਸੋਲਟ) *n a v* ਲੂਣ, ਨਮਕ, ਕੱਟੂਤਾ, ਉਤੇਜਕਤਾ, **ਤੀਬਰਤਾ**; ਲੂਣ-ਮਿਰਚ ਲਾਉਂਣਾ, ਨਮਕ ਛਿੜਕਣਾ

salutary ('ਸੈਲਯੁਟ(ਅ)ਰਿ) *a* ਸਿਹਤਮੰਦ ਕਲਿਆਣਕਾਰੀ, ਹਿਤਕਾਰੀ ਉਪਯੋਗੀ,

salutation ('ਸੈਲਯਅ'ਟੇਇਸ਼ਨ) *n* ਨਮਸਕਾਰ, ਪ੍ਰਣਾਮ, ਸਲਾਮ, ਅਭਿਵਾਦਨ, ਬੰਦਗੀ

salute (ਸਅ'ਲੂਟ) *n v* ਸਲਾਮ, ਅਭਿਨੰਦਨ, ਨਮਸਕਾਰ, ਪ੍ਰਣਾਮ; (ਸੈਨਾ) ਤੋਪਾਂ ਦੀ ਸਲਾਮੀ, ਫ਼ੌਜੀ ਸਨਮਾਨ; ਸਲਾਮ ਕਰਨਾ, ਨਮਸਕਾਰ ਕਰਨੀ, ਸੁਆਗਤ ਕਰਨਾ

salvage ('ਸੈਲਵਿਜ) *n v* ਬਚਾਉ, ਨਿਸਤਾਰਾ; ਸਮਗਰੀ, ਸਾਮਾਨ; ਰਿਹਾਨੁਹਾਣਾ; ਨਸ਼ਟ ਹੋਣ ਤੋਂ ਬਚਾਉਣਾ

salvation (ਸੈਲ'ਵੇਇਸ਼ਨ) *n* ਰੱਖਿਆ, ਨਿਸਤਾਰਾ, ਮੋਖ, ਮੁਕਤੀ, ਨਿਰਵਾਣ, ਨਜਾਤ

same (ਸੇਇਮ) *a pron adv* ਸਮਾਨ, ਉਹ, ਉਸੇ ਵਰਗਾ, ਉਸੇ ਤਰ੍ਹਾਂ ਨਾਲ, ਉਹੀ ਗੱਲ, ਉਹੀ ਚੀਜ਼; ਸਮਾਨ ਰੂਪ ਵਿਚ, ਉਸੇ ਤਰ੍ਹਾਂ, ਉਸੇ ਢੰਗ ਨਾਲ

sample ('ਸਾਂਪਲ) *n v* ਵੰਨਗੀ, ਉਦਾਹਰਨ, ਨਮੂਨਾ, ਨਮੂਨਾ ਲੈਣਾ

Samson ('ਸੈਮਸਅਨ) *n* ਸ਼ਕਤੀਸ਼ਾਲੀ ਆਦਮੀ, ਬਲਵਾਨ ਪੁਰਸ਼

sanatorium ('ਸੈਨਅ'ਟੋਰਿਅਮ) *n* ਅਰੋਗਤਾ-ਸਥਾਨ, ਸੈਨੇਟੇਰੀਅਮ

sanctify ('ਸੈਙ(ਕ)ਟਿਫ਼ਾਇ) *v* ਪਵਿੱਤਰ ਕਰਨ, ਪਾਵਨ ਕਰਨ, ਪਵਿੱਤਰਤਾ ਵਧਾਉਣੀ, ਸ਼ੁੱਧ ਕਰਨਾ, ਪਾਕੀਜ਼ਾ ਕਰਨਾ

sanctimony ('ਸੈਙ(ਕ)ਟਿਮਅਨਿ) *n* ਦੰਭ; ਕਪਟ, ਪਖੰਡ, ਢੋਂਗ

sanction ('ਸੈਙ(ਕ)ਸ਼ਨ) *n v* (1) ਸਵੀਕ੍ਰਿਤੀ, ਮਨਜ਼ੂਰੀ; (2) ਪ੍ਰਤੀਬੰਧ, ਪਾਬੰਦੀ; ਦੰਡ, ਸਜ਼ਾ, ਦੰਡ ਦੀ ਕਾਨੂੰਨੀ ਧਾਰਾ; ਅਧਿਕਾਰ ਦੇਣਾ, ਮਨਜ਼ੂਰੀ ਦੇਣੀ; ~ed ਮਨਜ਼ੂਰ, ਸਵੀਕ੍ਰਿਤ

sanctity ('ਸੈਙ(ਕ)ਟਅਟਿ) *n* ਪਵਿੱਤਰਤਾ, ਧਾਰਮਕਤਾ, ਪਾਵਨਤਾ

sanctuary ('ਸੈਙ(ਕ)ਚੁਅਰਿ) *n* ਧਰਮ-ਸਥਾਨ, ਮੰਦਰ, ਦਰਗਾਹ; ਪਨਾਹਗਾਹ

sanctum ('ਸੈਙ(ਕ)ਟਅਮ) *n* ਉਪਾਸਨਾ-ਗ੍ਰਹਿ, ਇਕਾਂਤ ਕਮਰਾ; ਤੀਰਥ; ਪਵਿੱਤਰ ਆਸਨ

sand (ਸੈਂਡ) *n v* ਰੇਤ, ਧੂੜ, ਰੇਤ ਦੇ ਕਿਣਕੇ; ਰੇਤਲੀ ਧਰਤੀ, ਰੇਗਿਸਤਾਨ, ਰੇਤੇ ਵਿਚ ਗੱਡਣਾ ਰੇਗਮਾਰ ਮਾਰਨਾ, ਘਸਾਉਣਾ; ~y ਰੇਤਲਾ; ਰੇਗਿਸਤਾਨੀ; ਕੱਚਾ, ਬੂਰਾ, ਭੂਰਾ

sandal ('ਸੈਂਡਲ) *n* ਸੰਦਲ, ਚੰਦਨ; ਸੈਂਡਲ; ~wood ਚੰਦਨ ਦੀ ਲੱਕੜੀ, ਚਿੱਟਾ ਚੰਦਨ

sandwich ('ਸੈਨਵਿਜ) *n v* ਸੈਂਡਵਿਚ, ਘੁਸੇੜਨਾ, ਠੋਸਣਾ; ਨਪੀੜਨਾ

sane (ਸੇਇਨ) *a* ਸਮਝਦਾਰ, ਸਿਆਣਾ; ਉਦਾਰ

sanitary ('ਸੈਨਿਟ(ਅ)ਰਿ) *a* ਸਫ਼ਾਈ ਬਾਰੇ; ਨਿਰੋਗਤਾ ਸਬੰਧੀ, ਅਰੋਗ ਰੱਖਿਅਕ; ਸੁਆਸਥ-ਵਰਧਕ

sanitation ('ਸੈਨਿ'ਟੇਇਸ਼ਨ) *n* ਸਫ਼ਾਈ, ਅਰੋਗ-ਪ੍ਰਬੰਧ

sanity ('ਸੈਨਅਟਿ) *n* ਸਿਹਤ, ਸੁਅਸਥ, ਦਿਮਾਗ਼ੀ ਸਿਹਤ

sans (ਸੈਂਜ਼) *prep* ਬਿਨਾਂ, ਬਗ਼ੈਰ, ਹੀਣ, ਰਹਿਤ, ਬਿਲਾ, ਵਿਹੀਣ

sap (ਸੈਪ) *n* ਰਸ; ਸਤ, ਸਾਰ, ਤੱਤ, (ਪੌਦਿਆਂ ਦਾ) ਦੁੱਧ, ਦ੍ਰਵ; ਰਸ ਸੁੱਕਣਾ, ਰਸ ਨਚੋੜਨਾ, ਸਤ ਕੱਢਣਾ, ਸਾਰ ਜਾਂ ਤੱਤ ਕੱਢ ਲੈਣਾ, ਸਾਹ-ਸਤ ਕੱਢਣਾ

sapling ('ਸੈਪਲਿਙ) *n* ਬਰੂਟਾ, ਨਵਾਂ ਪੌਦਾ; ਬਿਰਵਾ, ਨੌਨਿਹਾਲ, ਯੁਵਕ

sapphire ('ਸੈਫ਼ਾਇਅ*) *n a* ਨੀਲਮ, ਨੀਲ-ਕਾਂਤਮਣੀ, ਨੀਲਮਣੀ

sarcasm ('ਸਾਕੈਜ਼(ਅ)ਮ) *n* ਚੁਭਣ ਵਾਲੀ ਗੱਲ, ਕਟਾਕਸ਼, ਵਿਅੰਗ-ਵਾਕ, ਵਿਅੰਗ

sarcastic (ਸਾ'ਕੈਸਟਿਕ) *a* ਵਿਅੰਗਪੂਰਨ, ਵਿਅੰਗਮਈ; ਤੀਖਣ

Satan ('ਸੇਇਟ(ਅ)ਨ) *n* ਸ਼ੈਤਾਨ, ਇਬਲੀਸ

satellite ('ਸੈਟਅਲਾਇਟ) *n* ਉਪਗ੍ਰਹਿ; ਪਿਛਲੱਗ, ਅਨਗਾਮੀ, ਅਨੁਯਾਈ, ਸਹਾਇਕ

satire ('ਸੈਟਾਇਅ*) *n* ਵਿਅੰਗ, ਵਿਅੰਗ-ਲੇਖ, ਵਿਅੰਗ ਉਕਤੀ, ਵਿਅੰਗ-ਕਾਵਿ

satiric (ਸਅ'ਟਿਰਿਕ) *a* ਵਿਅੰਗਪੂਰਨ, ਵਿਅੰਗ-ਸਾਹਿਤ, ਨਿੰਦਾਤਮਕ

satirist ('ਸੈਟਅਰਿਸਟ) *n* ਵਿਅੰਗਕਾਰ, ਨਿੰਦਕ

satisfaction ('ਸੈਟਿਸ'ਫ਼ੈਕਸ਼ਨ) *n* ਸੰਤੋਖ, ਸੰਤੁਸ਼ਟੀ, ਤ੍ਰਿਪਤੀ, ਤੁਸ਼ਟੀ, ਇੱਛਾ-ਪੂਰਤੀ

satisfactory ('ਸੈਟਿਸ'ਫ਼ੈਕਟ(ਅ)ਰਿ) *a* ਸੰਤੋਖਜਨਕ, ਤਸੱਲੀਬਖ਼ਸ਼

satisfied ('ਸੈਟਿਸਫ਼ਾਇਡ) *a* ਸੰਤੁਸ਼ਟ, ਤ੍ਰਿਪਤ

satisfy ('ਸੈਟਿਸਫ਼ਾਇ) *v* ਸੰਤੁਸ਼ਟ ਕਰਨਾ, ਸੰਤੋਖ ਦੇਣਾ, ਤ੍ਰਿਪਤਾਉਣਾ, ਤ੍ਰਿਪਤ ਕਰਨਾ; ਮੰਨਣਾ, ਖ਼ੁਸ਼ ਹੋਣਾ, ਰਾਜ਼ੀ ਹੋਣਾ

saturation ('ਸੈਚਅ'ਰੇਇਸ਼ਨ) *n* ਸੰਤ੍ਰਿਪਤੀ, ਸੰਪੂਰਤੀ, ਤਵਾਰਤ, ਰਜਾਓ

Saturday ('ਸੈਟਅਡਿ) *n* ਸਨਿੱਚਰਵਾਰ, ਸ਼ਨੀਵਾਰ

sauce (ਸੋਸ) *n v* ਚਟਣੀ; ਲੂਣ ਘੋਲ; ਸੁਆਦ, ਰਸ ਮਜ਼ਾ, ਗੁਸਤਾਖ਼ੀ, ਸ਼ੇਖ਼ੀ; ਮਸਾਲੇਦਾਰ ਬਣਾਉਣਾ, ਚਟਪਟਾ ਬਣਾਉਣਾ

saucer ('ਸੋਸਅ*) *n* (ਚਾਹ ਦੀ) ਪਲੇਟ; ਤਸ਼ਤਰੀ; ਰਕਾਬੀ

saucy ('ਸੋਸਿ) *a* ਚੰਚਲ, ਮੂੰਹ ਫਟ, ਗੁਸਤਾਖ਼, ਸ਼ੋਖ਼; ਚੁਸਤ, ਜ਼ਿੰਦਾਦਿਲ

savage (ਸੈਵਿਜ) *a n v* ਜੰਗਲੀ, ਦਰਿੰਦਾ ਖੂੰਖਾਰ, ਅਸੱਭਿਅ, ਰਾਖਸ਼ੀ, ਅੱਖੜ; ਰਾਖਸ਼, ਅੱਖੜ ਬੰਦਾ; ਜੰਗਲੀ ਬਣਾਉਣਾ; **~ness** ਅਸਿੱਭਅਤਾ, ਜੰਗਲੀਪਣ; ਬਰਬਰਤਾ, ਬੇਰਹਿਮੀ, ਵਹਿਸ਼ੀਪਣ; **~ry** ਬਰਬਰਤਾ, ਨਿਸ਼ਠੁਰਤਾ, ਵਹਿਸ਼ੀਪਣ, ਦਰਿੰਦਗੀ

savant ('ਸੈਵਅੰਟ) *n* ਬੁੱਧੀਵਾਨ ਲੋਕ, ਵਿਦਵਾਨ ਪੁਰਸ਼, ਮਹਾਂ ਪੰਡਤ, ਗਿਆਨੀ

save (ਸੇਇਵ੍) *v n prep* ਬਚਾਉਣਾ, ਬੱਚਤ ਕਰਨੀ; ਰੱਖ ਲੈਣਾ, ਜੋੜਨਾ, ਜਮ੍ਹਾਂ ਕਰਨਾ; ਨਾ ਦੇਣਾ, ਗ੍ਰਹਿਣ ਕਰਨਾ; (ਫੁਟਬਾਲ) ਗੋਲ ਦਾ ਬਚਾਉ; ਧਨ ਬਚਾਉਣਾ; ਪਰ, ਲੇਕਿਨ, ਕਿੰਤੂ, ਬਿਨਾ

saving ('ਸੇਇਵ੍ਙ) ਬਚਤ, ਜੋੜਿਆ ਧਨ; ਬਚਾਉ ਕਿਫ਼ਾਇਤ

saviour ('ਸੇਇਵ੍ਯਅ*) *n* ਰਾਜ-ਰੱਖਿਅਕ ਮੁਕਤੀਦਾਤਾ

savour ('ਸੇਇਵ੍ਅ*) *n v* ਗੰਧ, ਮਹਿਕ; ਬਾਸ

savvy ਸੁਆਦ, ਮਜ਼ਾ; ਜ਼ਾਇਕਾ; ਸੁਆਦੀ ਬਣਾਉਣਾ, ਸੁਗੰਧਤ ਕਰਨਾ; ~y ਸੁਆਦੀ; ਮਸਾਲੇਦਾਰ, ਚਟਪਟਾ

savvy ('ਸੈਵਿ) *n* (ਅਪ) ਚਤਰਾਈ, ਹੁਸ਼ਿਆਰੀ, ਸਮਝ

saw (ਸੋ) *n* ਆਰਾ, ਆਰੀ, ਕਲਵੱਤਰ; ਆਰਾ ਚਲਾਉਣਾ, ਚੀਰਨਾ; (ਜਿਲਦਸਾਜ਼ੀ) ਚੀਰਾ ਦੇਣਾ; ~ing ਚਿਰਾਈ

say (ਸੇਇ) *n v* ਕਥਨ, ਮੱਤ, ਕਹਿਣੀ, ਗੱਲ-ਬਾਤ; ਉਚਾਰਨਾ, ਆਖਣਾ; ਬੋਲਣਾ, ਟਿੱਪਣੀ ਦੇਣੀ; ਵਚਨ ਦੇਣਾ; ਵਰਣਨ ਕਰਨਾ; ~ing ਉਕਤੀ, ਕਥਨ, ਬਾਣੀ, ਮੱਤ, ਅਖਾਣ, ਬਚਨ; ਕਹਾਵਤ, ਮੁਹਾਵਰਾ, ਲੋਕੋਕਤੀ; ਮਿਸਾਲ

scale (ਸਕੇਇਲ) *n v* ਤਰਾਜ਼ੂ ਦਾ ਪਲੜਾ, ਤੁਲਾ; ਸਧਾਰਨ ਤੱਕੜੀ; ਪੰਗਤੀ, ਦਰਜਾ; ਅੰਕਾਂ ਦਾ ਪੈਮਾਨਾ, ਅੰਕਣ ਚਿੰਨ੍ਹ; ਮਾਪ-ਦੰਡ; ਪ੍ਰਤੀਮਾਨ; ਜਾਂਚਣਾ, ਤੱਕੜੀ ਵਿਚ ਤੋਲਣਾ, ਜੋਖਣਾ, ਪੈਮਾਇਸ਼ ਕਰਨੀ; ਮਾਪਣਾ

scalp (ਸਕੈਲਪ) *n v* ਖੋਪੜੀ, ਸਿਰ ਦਾ ਉਤਲਾ ਭਾਗ; ਖੋਪਰੀ ਲਾਹੁਣੀ, ਸਿਰ ਕਲਮ ਕਰਨਾ

scam (ਸਕੈਮ) *n* (ਅਪ) ਘੋਟਾਲਾ

scamble ('ਸਕੈਂਬਲ) *v* ਸੰਘਰਸ਼ ਕਰਨਾ, ਧੱਕਾ-ਧੱਕੀ ਕਰਨਾ, ਗੋਡਿਆਂ ਆਸਰੇ ਚੜ੍ਹਨਾ

scamp (ਸਕੈਂਪ) *n v* ਲੁੱਚਾ, ਬਦਮਾਸ਼, ਕੰਮਚੋਰ; ਵਗਾਰ ਟਾਲਣੀ

scan (ਸਕੈਨ) *v* ਤਕਤੀਹ ਕਰਨੀ; ਛੰਦ ਦੀਆਂ ਮਾਤਰਾਂ ਗਿਣਨਾ; ਪਰਖਣਾ, ਜਾਂਚਣਾ; ~ning ਬਾਰੀਕ ਜਾਂਚ, ਪਰੀਖਣ

scandal ('ਸਕੈਂਡਲ) *n* ਘੋਟਾਲਾ, ਕੁਕਰਮ, ਬੁਰਾਈ, ਲੋਕ-ਨਿੰਦਿਆ, ਨਿੰਦਾ

scant (ਸਕੈਂਟ) *v a* ਸੀਮਤ ਕਰਨਾ, ਘੱਟ ਘੱਟ ਦੇਣਾ; ਬਹੁਤ ਘੱਟ, ਬਹੁਤ ਥੋੜ੍ਹਾ, ਨਾਕਾਫ਼ੀ, ਬਰਾਏ ਨਾਮ; ~y ਵਿਰਲਾ, ਘੱਟ, ਨਾਕਾਫ਼ੀ, ਦੁਰਲੱਭ

scapegoat ('ਸਕੇਇਪਗਅਉਟ) *a* ਕੁਰਬਾਨੀ ਦਾ ਬੱਕਰਾ, ਬਲੀ

scar (ਸਕਾ*) *n* ਦਾਗ, ਬੀਜ-ਨਾਭੀ; ਨਿਸ਼ਾਨ, ਖਰੀਂਢ, ਝਰੀਟ, ਧੱਬਾ; ਦਾਗ; ਰਾਜ਼ੀ ਹੋਣਾ; ਜ਼ਖ਼ਮ ਤੇ ਖਰੀਂਢ ਆਉਣਾ, ਦਾਗ ਲੱਗਣਾ

scarce (ਸਕੇਅ:ਸ) *a* ਮਸਾਂ, ਮੁਸ਼ਕਲ ਨਾਲ, ਅਲਪ, ਬਹੁਤ ਘੱਟ; ਥੋੜ੍ਹਾ; ~ly ਮੁਸ਼ਕਲ ਨਾਲ; ਬਿਲਕੁਲ ਨਹੀਂ, ਨਾਂਹ ਦੇ ਬਰਾਬਰ; ਸ਼ਾਇਦ, ਹੁਣੇ ਹੁਣੇ

scarcity ('ਸਕੇਅ:ਸਅਟਿ) *n* ਥੁੜ੍ਹ, ਤੰਗੀ, ਟੋਟ, ਦੁਰਲੱਭਤਾ, ਅਭਾਵ

scare (ਸਕੇਅ*) *n v* ਸਹਿਮ, ਡਰ, ਦਹਿਲ, ਧੁੜਕੂ, ਅਚਾਨਕ ਭੈਭੀਤ ਕਰਨਾ, ਡਰਾਉਣਾ

scarf (ਸਕਾ:ਫ) *n v* ਦੁਪੱਟਾ, ਪਟਕਾ, ਰੁਮਾਲ, ਗਲੂਬੰਦ, ਸਕਾਰਫ਼; ਰਲ ਬੈਠਾਉਣਾ, ਮੇਲ ਮਿਲਾਉਣਾ

scarlet ('ਸਕਾ:ਲਅਟ) *n a* ਲਾਲ ਰੰਗ ਦਾ ਕੱਪੜਾ; ਸੰਧੂਰੀ, ਗੁਲਨਾਰੀ, ਕਿਰਮਚੀ

scatter ('ਸਕੈਟਅ*) *v* ਖਿੰਡਾਉਣਾ, ਖਿੰਡਣਾ; ਖਿਲਾਰਨਾ, ਖਿਖੇਰਨਾ, ਤਿੱਤਰ-ਬਿੱਤਰ ਕਰਨਾ; ਫੈਲਾਉਣਾ, ਭਗਦੜ ਮਚਾਉਣੀ; ~ed ਖਿਖਰਿਆ, ਤਿੱਤਰ-ਬਿੱਤਰ

scavenge ('ਸਕੈਵਿੰਜ) *v* ਕੂੜਾ-ਕਰਕਟ ਉਠਾਉਣਾ, ਸਫ਼ਾਈ ਕਰਨਾ; ~r ਮਿਹਤਰ, ਜਮਾਂਦਾਰ, ਸੜਕਾਂ ਸਾਫ਼ ਕਰਨ ਵਾਲਾ; ਅਸ਼ਲੀਲ ਲੇਖਕ, ਲੱਚਰ ਲੇਖਕ

scene (ਸੀਨ) *n* ਦ੍ਰਿਸ਼, ਘਟਨਾ ਸਥਾਨ; ਰੰਗ-ਮੰਚ, ਰੰਗ-ਭੂਮੀ, ਰੰਗਸ਼ਾਲਾ, ਪਰਦਰਸ਼ਨ-ਭੂਮੀ;

scenic ਨਾਟਕ ਦੇ ਅੰਕ ਦਾ ਭਾਗ; ਝੜਪ; ~ry ਦਿਸ਼ ਦ੍ਰਿਸ਼ਾਵਲੀ, ਕੁਦਰਤੀ ਦ੍ਰਿਸ਼

scenic ('ਸੀਨਿਕ) *a* ਰਮਟੀਕ, ਸਜੀਵ, ਰੰਗਮੰਚੀ

scent (ਸੈਂਟ) *n v* ਸੁਗੰਧੀ, ਮਹਿਕ, ਖ਼ੁਸ਼ਬੂ; ਅਤਰ, ਫੁਲੇਲ; ਅਤਰ ਲਾਉਣਾ, ਸੁਗੰਧਿਤ ਕਰਨਾ

schedule ('ਸੈੱਡਯੂਲ) *n v* ਸੂਚੀ, ਸਾਰਨੀ, ਫ਼ਰਦ, ਪੱਟੀ, ਸਮਾਂ-ਸੂਚੀ, ਕਾਰਜ-ਕ੍ਰਮ, ਨਾਮਾਵਲੀ; ਚਿੱਠਾ, ਯੋਜਨਾਲੇਖ; ਸੂਚੀ ਬਣਾਉਣੀ, ਅਨੁਸੂਚਤ ਕਰਨਾ; ~d ਅਨੁਸੂਚਤ, ਨਿਯਤ

schema ('ਸਕੀਮਅ) *n* ਯੋਜਨਾ, ਖ਼ਾਕਾ, ਨਕਸ਼ਾ, ਆਕਾਰ

scheme (ਸਕੀਮ) *n v* ਯੋਜਨਾ, ਪ੍ਰਬੰਧ, ਜੁਗਤ, ਉਪਾਉ, ਮਨਸੂਬਾ, ਚਾਲ, ਸਾਜ਼ਸ਼; ਸੂਚੀ, ਵੇਰਵਾ, ਰੂਪ-ਰੇਖਾ, ਨਕਸ਼ਾ; ਯੋਜਨਾ ਬਣਾਉਣੀ; ਰੂਪ-ਰੇਖਾ ਬਣਾਉਣਾ

schism (ਸਕਿਜ਼(ਅਮ) *n* ਧੜੇਬੰਦੀ, ਫੁੱਟ, ਮੱਤ-ਭੇਦ; ਸੰਪਰਦਾਇਕ ਵਖਰੇਵਾਂ; ਫ਼ਿਰਕੇਬੰਦੀ

scholar ('ਸਕੌਲਅ*) *n* ਵਿਦਵਾਨ, ਪੰਡਤ, ਗਿਆਨੀ; ਵਿਦਿਆਰਥੀ, ਸ਼ਾਗਿਰਦ; ~ly ਵਿਦਵਾਨ-ਵਰਗਾ; ਵਿਦਵਤਾਪੂਰਨ; ~ship ਵਜ਼ੀਫ਼ਾ; ਵਿਦਵਤਾ ਗਿਆਨ

school (ਸਕੂਲ) *n* (1) ਵਿਦਿਆਲਾ, ਮਦਰਸਾ, ਪਾਠਸ਼ਾਲਾ; (2) ਸੰਪਰਦਾਇ, ਫ਼ਿਰਕਾ; (3) ਮੱਤ, ਵਾਦ, ਪੰਥ, ਮਾਰਗ, ਵਰਗ

schwa (ਸ਼ਵਾ) *n* (ਵਿਆ) ਲਘੁ ਸਵਰ ਧੁਨੀ

science ('ਸਾਇੰਸ) *n* ਵਿਗਿਆਨ, ਗਿਆਨ, ਵਿੱਦਿਆ ਸ਼ਾਸਤਰੀ

scientific ('ਸਾਇਅੰਟਿਫ਼ਿਕ) *a* ਵਿਗਿਆਨਕ, ਸ਼ਾਸਤਰ-ਅਨੁਕੂਲ; ਵਿਵਸਥਿਤ, ਕ੍ਰਮਬੱਧ

scientist ('ਸਾਇਅੰਟਿਸਟ) *n* ਵਿਗਿਆਨੀ, ਸਾਇੰਸਦਾਨ

sciolism ('ਸਾਇਅ(ਉ)ਲਿਜ਼(ਅ)ਮ) *n* ਸਧਾਰਨ ਗਿਆਨ, ਗਿਆਨ ਦਾ ਝੂਠਾ ਅਹੰਕਾਰ, ਪਖੰਡ

scissor ('ਸਿੱਜ਼ਅ*) *v* ਕੱਟਣਾ, ਕਤਰਨਾ, ਛਾਂਟਣਾ, ਕੈਂਚੀ ਨਾਲ ਕਤਰਨਾ; ~s ਕੈਂਚੀ, ਕਾਤੀ, ਕਤਰਨੀ

scissure ('ਸਿਸ਼ਅ*) *n* ਚੀਰਾ, ਚੀਰ, ਘਾਉ

scoff (ਸਕੌਫ਼) *n v* ਖਿੱਲੀ, ਟਿਚਕਰ, ਮਸ਼ਖਰੀ, ਮਖੌਲ; ਗੁੱਡਾ; ਉਪਹਾਸ; ਮਜ਼ਾਕ, ਠੱਠਾ; ਹਾਸਾ-ਠੱਠਾ ਕਰਨਾ, ਮਜ਼ਾਕ ਉਡਾਉਣਾ, ਤਿਰਸਕਾਰ ਕਰਨਾ

scold (ਸਕਅਉਲਡ) *n v* ਤਾੜਨਾ, ਝਿੜਕਣਾ, ਡਾਂਟਣਾ, ਧਮਕਾਉਣਾ; ਬੁਰਾ-ਭਲਾ ਆਖਣਾ, ਖ਼ਬਰ ਲੈਣੀ, ਲਿਤਾੜਨਾ; ~ing ਨਿੰਦਾ, ਧਿੱਕਾਰ, ਝਿੜਕ, ਡਾਂਟ-ਡਪਟ, ਡਾਂਟ-ਫਿਟਕਾਰ

scoop (ਸਕੂਪ) *n v* ਕੜਛੀ; ਕੋਲੇ ਪਾਉਣ ਵਾਲਾ ਬੇਲਚਾ, ਤਕੜਾ ਲਾਭ; ਤਾਜ਼ਾ ਖ਼ਬਰ, ਚਪੇੜ, ਮਾਰ-ਕੁੱਟ; (ਡੋਈ ਨਾਲ) ਕੱਢਣਾ, ਖੋਖਲਾ ਕਰਨਾ; ਅਫ਼ਵਾਹ ਫੈਲਾਉਣਾ

scoot (ਸਕੂਟ) *v* ਭੱਜ ਜਾਣਾ, ਰਫ਼ੂਚੱਕਰ ਹੋਣਾ, ਭੱਜ ਨਿਕਲਣਾ; ਝਪਟਣਾ; ~er ਗੱਡੀ, ਯਾਨ, ਸਕੂਟਰ, ਮੋਟਰ ਬੋਟ

scope (ਸਕਅਉਪ) *n* (rare) ਮੰਤਵ, ਗੁੰਜਾਇਸ਼; ਕਾਰਜ-ਖੇਤਰ, ਪਹੁੰਚ

score (ਸਕੋ*) *n v* ਵੀਹ ਦੀ ਗਿਣਤੀ, ਕੋੜੀ, ਬੀਸੀ; ਅੰਕ ਬਣਾਉਣੇ, ਪੁਆਇੰਟ ਜਿੱਤਣੇ; ਗੋਲ ਕਰਨਾ, ਰਨ ਬਣਾਉਣਾ

scorn (ਸਕੌਨ) *a v* ਘਿਰਣਾ, ਨਫ਼ਰਤ, ਹਿਕਾਰਤ; ਨਫ਼ਰਤ ਕਰਨੀ; ~ful ਤਿਰਸਕਾਰਪੂਰਨ, ਅਪਮਾਨਜਨਕ, ਘਿਣਾਉਣਾ

scorpio ('ਸਕੋਪਿਅਉ) *n* ਬਿਰਖ ਰਾਸ਼ੀ; ~n ਬਿੱਛੂ, ਠੂਹਾਂ, ਅਠੂਹਾਂ; ਬ੍ਰਿਸ਼ਚਕ ਰਾਸ਼ੀ

scoundrel ('ਸਕਾਉਨਡਰ(ਅ)ਲ) *n* ਲੁੱਚਾ, ਗੁੰਡਾ,

ਪਾਜੀ, ਬਦਮਾਸ਼, ਸ਼ੋਹਦਾ

scour ('ਸਕਾਉਅ*) *n v* ਸਫ਼ਾਈ, ਧੁਆਈ; ਮਾਂਜਣਾ, ਰਗੜਨਾ, ਮਲਣਾ, ਸਾਫ਼ ਕਰਨਾ, ਚਮਕਾਉਣਾ; ਧੋਣਾ

scourge (ਸਕਅਃਜ) *n v* ਝਾਂਬਾ, ਕੋਰੜਾ, ਚਾਬੁਕ; ਅੱਤਿਆਚਾਰ ਕਰਨਾ, ਕਸ਼ਟ ਦੇਣਾ, ਝੰਬਣਾ, ਝੰਮਣਾ, ਬੈਂਤਾਂ ਲਾਉਣੀਆਂ

scout (ਸਕਾਊਟ) *n v* ਸਕਾਊਟ; ਮੁਖ਼ਬਰ ਗੁਪਤਚਰ; ਪਹਿਰੇਦਾਰ; ਜਾਸੂਸੀ ਕਰਨੀ, ਭੇਤ ਲਾਉਣਾ, ਦੇਖਣਾ; ਤਿਰਸਕਾਰ ਕਰਨਾ; ਹਾਸਾ ਉਡਾਉਣਾ, ਨਾਨੁੱਕਰ ਕਰਨਾ

scrab (ਸਕਰੈਬ) *v* ਖੁਰਚਣਾ, ਖਾਜ ਕਰਨੀ, ਖੁਜਲਾਉਣਾ, ਰਗੜਨਾ

scrabble ('ਸਕਰੈਬਲ) *n v* ਚੀਂਢੜ-ਮੀਂਢੜ ਲਿਖਤ; ਹਨੇਰੇ ਵਿਚ ਭਾਲਣਾ, ਟੋਲਣਾ, ਧੱਕਮ-ਧੱਕੀ ਹੋਣਾ; ਅਸਪਸ਼ਟ ਲਿਖਣਾ

scramble ('ਸਕਰੈਂਬਲ) *n v* ਧੱਕਾ-ਮੁੱਕੀ, ਹਫ਼ੜਾ-ਦਫ਼ੜੀ, ਦੌੜ-ਭੱਜ; ਧੱਕਮ-ਧੱਕਾ ਕਰਨਾ

scrape (ਸਕਰੇਇਪ) *n v* ਰਗੜਨ ਦੀ ਅਵਾਜ਼, ਘਸਣ ਦੀ ਅਵਾਜ਼; ਰਗੜ; ਰਗੜਨਾ, ਘਸਾਉਣਾ; ਇਕਸਾਰ ਪੱਧਰਾ ਕਰਨਾ

scratch (ਸਕਰੈਚ) *n v n* ਫਲੂੰਗਰ, ਆਗੂੰਛ, ਖਰੁੰਢ, ਝਰੀਟ, ਰਗੜ, ਖੁਰਚਣ; ਖੁਰਕਣ, ਖਰੋਚਣਾ, ਖੁਰਕਣਾ; ਘਿੱਚਮਿੱਚ ਲਿਖਣਾ

scream (ਸਕਰੀਮ) *v* ਚੀਕਣਾ, ਕੂਕਣਾ, ਡਡਿਆਉਣਾ, ਕਿਲਕਾਰੀਆਂ ਮਾਰਨੀਆਂ, ਲੇਰਾਂ ਮਾਰਨੀਆਂ; ਕਰਾਹੁਣਾ, ਢਾਹਾਂ ਮਾਰਨੀਆਂ

screen (ਸਕਰੀਨ) *n v* ਪਰਦਾ, ਓਟ, ਆੜ, ਖਸ ਦੀ ਟੱਟੀ; ਪਰਦਾ, ਕਨਾਤ, ਚਿਕ, ਚਿਲਮਨ; ਸੂਚਨਾ-ਪਟ; ਚਿੱਤਰਪਟ; ਸਿਨੇਮਾ ਦਾ ਚਿੱਟਾ ਪਰਦਾ; ਲੁਕਾਉਣਾ, ਬਚਾਉਣਾ, ਪਰਦਾ ਪਾਉਣਾ, ਅੱਖਾਂ ਤੋਂ ਓਝਲ ਕਰਨਾ; ~ing ਐਕਸ-ਰੇ ਪ੍ਰੇਖਣ, ਛਾਣ-ਬੀਣ

screw (ਸਕਰੂ) *n v* ਪੇਚ ਦੀ ਮਰੋੜੀ; ਤਮਾਕੂ ਆਦਿ ਦਾ ਛੋਟਾ ਮਰੋੜਿਆ ਹੋਇਆ ਕਾਗ਼ਜ਼; ਤਨਖ਼ਾਹ ਦੀ ਰਕਮ, ਸੂਮ; ਪੇਚਾਂ ਨਾਲ ਪੀਚਣਾ, ਕੱਸਣਾ; **~driver** ਪੇਚਕੱਸ

scribble ('ਸਕਰਿਬਲ) *v n* ਚੀਂਢੜ-ਮੀਂਢੜ ਲਿਖਤ ਲਿਖਣਾ, ਅਸਪਸ਼ਟ ਤੇ ਭੱਦਾ ਲਿਖਣਾ, ਊਟ-ਪਟਾਂਗ ਲਿਖਣਾ, ਕੁਲੇਖ ਲਿਖਣਾ; ਕਲਮ ਘਸਾਉਣਾ : ਘਸੀਟ

scribe (ਸਕਰਾਇਬ) *n v* ਲਿਖਾਰੀ, ਮੁਨਸ਼ੀ, ਮੁਹੱਰਰ, ਕਾਤਿਬ, ਕਲਰਕ, ਲੇਖਕ, ਲਿਪੀਕਾਰ, ਨਕਲਨਵੀਸ; ਲਕੀਰਨਾ, ਨਿਸ਼ਾਨ ਲਾਉਣੇ, ਅੰਕਤ ਕਰਨਾ, ਲਿਖਣਾ

scrimmage ('ਸਕਰਿਮਿਜ) *n v* ਹੱਥੋ-ਪਾਈ, ਗੁੱਥਮ-ਗੁੱਥਾ, ਖਿੱਚੋਤਾਣ; ਖਿੱਚੋਤਾਣ ਕਰਨੀ, ਗੁੱਥਮ-ਗੁੱਥਾ ਹੋਣਾ, ਤੇੜਾ-ਖੋਹੀ ਕਰਨੀ, ਸੰਘਰਸ਼ ਕਰਨਾ

script (ਸਕਰਿਪਟ) *n* ਲਿਪੀ, ਵਰਣਮਾਲਾ

scripture ('ਸਕਰਿਪਚਅ*) *n* ਧਰਮ-ਗ੍ਰੰਥ, ਪਵਿੱਤਰ ਗ੍ਰੰਥ

scroll (ਸਕਰਾਉਲ) *n v* (ਪ੍ਰ) ਫਹਿਰਿਸਤ, ਸੂਚੀ, ਤਾਲਕਾ; ਗੋਲ ਵਲ੍ਹੇਟਣਾ, ਵੇਲ-ਬੂਟੇ ਕੱਢਣੇ, ਵੇਲ-ਬੂਟਿਆਂ ਨਾਲ ਸਜਾਉਣਾ

scrub (ਸਕਰਅੱਬ) *n v* ਝਾੜ-ਬਰੋਟਾ; ਖੜ੍ਹੀਆਂ ਮੁੱਛਾਂ, ਅਜਿਹਾ ਬੁਰਸ਼; ਤੁੱਛ ਵਿਅਕਤੀ, ਕੁਹੀ ਮਾਂਜਣਾ, ਝੜਨਾ, ਪੂੰਝਣਾ, ਮਲਣਾ, ਘਸਾਉਣਾ, ਰਗੜਨਾ; ਝਾੜੂ ਦੇਣਾ, ਬੁਰਸ਼ ਕਰਨਾ

scrutinize ('ਸਕਰੂਟਿਨਾਇਜ਼) *v* ਸੂਖਮ ਪਰੀਖਿਆ ਕਰਨਾ, ਪੜਤਾਲਣਾ, ਜਾਚਣਾ, ਛਾਣ-ਬੀਣ ਕਰਨੀ

scrutiny ('ਸਕਰੂਟਿਨਿ) *n* ਦੇਖ-ਭਾਲ, ਪਰਖ, ਪੜਤਾਲ, ਪਰੀਖਿਆ, ਨਿਰੀਖਣ, ਖੋਜ

scuffle ('ਸਕਅੱਫ਼ਲ) *n v* ਹੱਥੋ-ਪਾਈ, ਗੁੱਥਮ-ਗੁੱਥਾ, ਧੱਕਮ-ਧੱਕਾ, ਧੀਂਗਾ-ਮੁਸ਼ਤੀ, ਹੱਥੋ-ਪਾਈ ਹੋਈ; ਗੁੱਥਮ-ਗੁੱਥਾ ਹੋਣਾ, ਭਿੜਨਾ

sculp (ਸਕਅੱਲਪ) *v* ਨੱਕਾਸ਼ੀ ਕਰਨਾ, ਸੰਗਤਰਾਸ਼ੀ ਕਰਨਾ; **~ture** ਬੁੱਤ-ਤਰਾਸ਼ੀ, ਸੰਗ-ਤਰਾਸ਼ੀ; ਮੂਰਤੀ ਕਲਾ; ਮੂਰਤੀ ਪ੍ਰਤਿਮਾ; **~tor** ਸੰਗ-ਤਰਾਸ਼; ਮੂਰਤੀਕਾਰ

scum (ਸਕਅੱਮ) *n v* ਝੱਗ, ਮੈਲ, ਰਹਿੰਦ-ਖੂੰਹਦ; ਝੱਗ ਉਠਣਾ

scuttle ('ਸਕਅੱਟਲ) *n v* ਨੱਠ-ਭੱਜ; ਝੱਗ ਆਉਣੀ; ਨਾਕਾਮ ਬਣਾਉਣਾ; ਖਿਸਕਣਾ, ਭੱਜ ਜਾਣਾ, ਹਵਾ ਹੋਣਾ, ਚੱਲਦੇ ਬਣਨਾ

sea (ਸੀ) *n* ਸਮੁੰਦਰ, ਸਾਗਰ, ਤਰੰਗ, ਵਿਸ਼ਾਲਤਾ, ਫੈਲਾਉ, ਵਿਸਤਾਰ; **~man** ਜਹਾਜ਼ੀ; **~shore** ਸਾਗਰ-ਤੱਟ; **~sickness** ਕਚਿਆਣ

seal (ਸੀਲ) *n v* ਛਾਪ, ਮੁਹਰ, ਠੱਪਾ, ਮੁਦਰਾ, ਸੀਲ; ਸਬੂਤ; ਸੀਲ ਮੱਛੀ; ਸ਼ਿਕਾਰ ਕਰਨਾ, ਮੁਹਰ ਲਾਉਣਾ, ਠੱਪਾ ਲਾਉਣਾ, ਪੱਕਾ ਕਰਨਾ; ਸੱਚਾ ਪਰੇਮ ਜਤਲਾਉਣਾ; **~ed** ਮੁਹਰਬੰਦ, ਮੁਹਰ ਲੱਗਿਆ; ਬੰਦ ਕੀਤ

search (ਸਅ:ਚ) *n v* ਖੋਜ, ਢੂੰਡ, ਜਾਂਚ, ਤਲਾਸ਼, ਦੇਖ-ਭਾਲ; ਭਾਲਣਾ, ਖੋਜਣਾ, ਢੂੰਡਣਾ, ਜਾਂਚਣਾ, ਤਲਾਸ਼ ਕਰਨੀ, ਦੇਖ-ਭਾਲ ਕਰਨੀ

season ('ਸੀਜ਼ਨ) *n v* ਰੁੱਤ, ਮੌਸਮ, ਅਨੁਕੂਲ ਅਵਸਰ; ਛੌਂਕਣਾ; **~al** ਮੌਸਮੀ

seat (ਸੀਟ) *n* ਆਸਣ, ਗੱਦੀ, ਕੁਰਸੀ; ਆਧਾਰ ਪੈਂਦਾ; ਟਿਕਾਣਾ, ਕੇਂਦਰ; ਕਾਠੀ

secession (ਸਿ'ਸੈੱਸ਼ਨ) *n* ਸਮਾਜ-ਤਿਆਗ; ਸਬੰਧ-ਤਿਆਗ; ਅਲਹਿਦਗੀ, ਵਖਰੇਵਾਂ

seclude (ਸਿ'ਕਲੂਡ) *v* ਇਕਾਂਤ ਵਿਚ ਰੱਖਣਾ, ਲੋਕ-ਸੰਪਰਕ ਤੋਂ ਦੂਰ ਰੱਖਣਾ, ਸੁਤੰਤਰ ਰੱਖਣਾ; **~d** ਦੂਰਸਥਾਪਤ, ਨਿਰਜਨ, ਇਕਾਂਤ

seclusion (ਸਿ'ਕਲੂਯ਼ਨ) *n* ਇਕਾਂਤਵਾਸ, ਨਿਰਜਨ ਥਾਂ, ਸੁੰਨੀ ਥਾਂ, ਇਕਾਂਤਤਾ; **~ist** ਇਕਾਂਤਵਾਦੀ, ਨਿਰਜਨਤਾ-ਪ੍ਰਿਯ

second ('ਸੈਕੰਡ) *n a v* ਪਿੱਛੇ ਆਇਆ ਆਦਮੀ, ਦੂਜਾ ਆਦਮੀ ਜਾਂ ਦਰਜਾ; ਛਿਣ, ਮਿੰਟ ਦਾ 1/60 ਭਾਗ, ਸੈਕੰਡ; ਤਾਈਦ ਕਰਨੀ; **~ary** ਗੌਣ, ਅਪ੍ਰਧਾਨ, ਅਮੁੱਖ, ਘੱਟ ਮਹੱਤਵ ਵਾਲਾ; ਮਗਰੋਂ ਵਾਲਾ; **~er** ਅਨੁਮੋਦਕ, ਪ੍ਰਸਤਾਵ-ਸਮਰਥਕ; **~ly** ਦੂਜੇ ਨੰਬਰ ਤੇ, ਦੂਜੀ ਥਾਂ ਤੇ, ਦੂਜੇ

secrecy ('ਸੀਕਰਅਸਿ) *n* ਗੁੱਝਾਪਣ, ਗੁਪਤਤਾ; ਰਹੱਸ, ਰਹੱਸਪੂਰਨਤਾ, ਲੁਕਾਉ-ਛਿਪਾਉ, ਭੇਤ, ਰਾਜ਼

secret ('ਸੀਕਰਿਟ) *n a* ਭੇਤ; ਰਾਜ਼, ਗੁਪਤ, ਗੁੱਝੂ, ਅਦਿੱਸਟ, ਖ਼ੁਫ਼ੀਆ; ਨਿੱਜੀ

secretarial ('ਸੈਕਰਿ'ਟੇਅਰਿਅਲ) *a* ਸੱਕਤਰੇਤ ਦਾ, ਸੱਕਤਰੇਤ ਸਬੰਧੀ; ਸਕੱਤਰ ਸਬੰਧੀ

secretariat(e) ('ਸੈਕਰਿ'ਟੇਰਿਅਟ) *a* ਸਕੱਤਰੇਤ, ਸਰਕਾਰ ਦਾ ਵੱਡਾ ਦਫ਼ਤਰ

secretion (ਸਿ'ਕਰੀਸ਼ਨ) *n* ਰਹੱਸ, ਲੁਕਾਉ, ਛਿਪਾਉ

secretive (ਸੀਕਰਅਟਿਵ) *a* ਰਹੱਸਪੂਰਨ, ਲੁਕਵਾਂ; ਛਿਪਵਾਂ, ਚੁੱਪ-ਚੁਪੀਤਾ, ਖ਼ਮੋਸ਼

sect (ਸੈਕਟ) *n* (1) ਪੰਥ, ਫ਼ਿਰਕਾ, ਮਾਰਗ, ਮੱਤ; ਧਾਰਮਕ ਸੰਪਰਦਾਇ; (2) ਛੇਦਨ, ਵਿਨ੍ਹਣ; **~arian** ਸੰਪਰਦਾਇਕ, ਫ਼ਿਰਕਾਪਰਸਤ, ਸੰਕੀਰਣ, ਫ਼ਿਰਕੁ; **~or** ਖੇਤਰ, ਖੰਡ; ਸ਼ਹਿਰ ਦਾ ਇਕ ਹਿੱਸਾ

section (ਸੈਕਸ਼ਨ) *n v* ਵਿਭਾਜਨ, ਕਾਟ; ਭਾਗ,

ਖੰਡ, ਹਿੱਸਾ; ਅਨੁਭਾਗ, ਮੰਡਲ, ਸੈਕਸ਼ਨ; ~al ਵਿਤਾਗੀ, ਅੰਸ਼ਕ, ਅਨੁਤਾਗੀ, ਵਰਗੀ

secular ('ਸੈੱਕਯੁਲਅ*) *n a* ਅਸੰਪਰਦਾਇਕ; ਧਰਮ-ਨਿਰਪੇਖ; ~ism ਧਰਮ-ਨਿਰਪੇਖਤਾ, ਧਰਮ-ਨਿਰਪੇਖਵਾਦ, ਅਧਾਰਮਕਤਾ

secure (ਸਿ'ਕਯੁਅ*) *v a* ਸੁਰੱਖਿਅਤ ਰੱਖਣਾ; ਪੱਕਾ ਕਰਨਾ, ਪੁਖਤਾ ਕਰਨਾ; ਪ੍ਰਾਪਤ ਕਰਨਾ, ਬੇਫ਼ਿਕਰ, ਬੇਪਰਵਾਹ; ਦੁਬਧਾਹੀਨ; ~d ਸੁਰੱਖਿਅਤ

security (ਸਿ'ਕਯੁਅਰਅਟਿ) *n* ਸੁਰੱਖਿਆ, ਸਲਾਮਤੀ, ਬਚਾਉ; ਤੱਖਿਅਕ; ਜ਼ਾਮਨੀ; ਜ਼ਮਾਨਤਨਾਮਾ, ਜ਼ਮਾਨਤ, ਸਾਖ-ਪੱਤਰ; ਰਿਣ-ਪੱਤਰ

sedation (ਸਿ'ਡੇਇਸ਼ਨ) *n* ਸ਼ਾਂਤੀਕਰਨ, ਸੀਤਲੀਕਰਨ

sediment ('ਸੈਡ਼ਿਮਅੰਟ) *n* ਫੋਗ, ਤਲਛਟ; ~ary ਗਾਦ-ਭਰਿਆ, ਮੈਲ ਵਾਲਾ, ਤਲਛਟੀ

sedition (ਸਿ'ਡ਼ਿਸ਼ਨ) *n* ਬਗਾਵਤ; ਵਿਦਰੋਹ; ਰਾਜ-ਸੰਤਾ, ਵਿਦਰੋਹ, ਅੰਦੋਲਨ

seduce (ਸਿ'ਡਯੂਸ) *v* ਇਸਤਰੀ ਨੂੰ ਫੁਸਲਾਣਾ, ਬਹਿਕਾਉਣਾ; ਸਤ ਭੰਗ ਕਰਨਾ; ਗੁਮਰਾਹ ਕਰਨਾ, ਦੂਸ਼ਤ ਕਰਨਾ, ਪਤਿਤ ਕਰਨਾ

seduction (ਸਿ'ਡਯਅੱਕਸ਼ਨ) *n* ਝਾਂਸਾ, ਵਰਗਲਾਹਟ

see (ਸੀ) *v* ਤੱਕਣਾ, ਵੇਖਣਾ, ਦਿਸਣਾ, ਦਰਸ਼ਨ ਕਰਨਾ, ਦ੍ਰਿਸ਼ਟੀਗਤ ਕਰਨਾ; ਧਿਆਨ ਕਰਨਾ, ਗੌਰ ਕਰਨਾ, ਪਰਖਣਾ, ਨਿਰੀਖਣ ਕਰਨਾ; ਮਹਿਸੂਸ ਕਰਨਾ, ਮੁਲਾਕਾਤ ਕਰਨੀ

seed (ਸੀਡ) *n v* ਤੁਖਮ, ਨਸਲ, ਬੀਜ, ਦਾਣਾ; ਬੀਜਾਊ, ਮਤੀ, ਵੀਰਜ; ਮੁੱਢ, ਸ਼ੁਰੂਆਤ, ਬੀ ਬੀਜਣਾ, ਛਿੜਕਣਾ

seek (ਸੀਕ) *v* ਭਾਲਣਾ, ਖੋਜਣਾ, ਪਤਾ ਲਾਉਣਾ, ਢੂੰਡਣਾ; ਯਾਚਨਾ ਕਰਨੀ, ਪ੍ਰਾਰਥਨਾ ਕਰਨੀ

seem (ਸੀਮ) *v* ਪ੍ਰਤੀਤ ਹੋਣਾ, ਗਿਆਤ ਹੋਣਾ, ਲੱਗਣਾ, ਅਨੁਭਵ ਹੋਣਾ; ਦਿਸਣਾ, ਨਜ਼ਰ ਆਉਣਾ, ਜ਼ਾਹਰ ਹੋਣਾ; ~ly ਭੱਦਰ, ਉੱਤਮ; ਉਚਿਤ, ਸ਼ਿਸ਼ਟ, ਉਪਯੁਕਤ, ਸੁਸੰਗਤ, ਸੁੰਦਰ

seep (ਸੀਪ) *v* ਰਿਸਣਾ, ਟਪਕਣਾ, ਸਿੰਮਣਾ

seer ('ਸੀਅ*) *n* ਭਵਿੱਖ-ਦ੍ਰਸ਼ਟਾ; ਰਿਸ਼ੀ; ਸਿੱਧ ਪੁਰਸ਼; ਪੈਗਾਂਬਰ, ਨੱਬੀ

seesaw ('ਸੀਸੋ) *n v* ਪੀਲ-ਪਲੰਘਾ; ਝੂਲਾ; ਬਰਾਬਰ ਦਾ ਗੁਥਮਗੁਥਾ; ਝੂਮਾ ਝੂਮਾ ਪੇਲਣਾ

seethe (ਸੀਦ) *v* ਤਾਉ ਦੇਣਾ, ਜੋਸ਼ ਦੁਆਉਣਾ; ਕਰੋਧ ਵਿਚ ਆਉਣਾ; ਉਤੇਜਤ ਕਰਨਾ

segment ('ਸੈੱਗਮਅੰਟ, ਸੈਗਾਂ'ਮੈਂਟ) *n v* ਭਾਗ; ਖੰਡ, ਟੁਕੜਾ; ਫਾਂਕ; ਵਿਭਾਜਤ ਕਰਨਾ; ~ation ਵਿਤਾਜਨ, ਵਿਛੇਦ

segregate ('ਸੈੱਗਰਿਗੇਇਟ) *v* ਅੱਡ ਕਰਨਾ, ਅੱਲਗ ਕਰਨਾ; ਕੱਟਣਾ, ਹਟਾਉਣਾ

segregation ('ਸੈੱਗਰਿ'ਗੇਇਸ਼ਨ) *n* ਵਿਯੋਗ, ਅਲਹਿਦਾਪਣ; ਵਿਤਕਰਾ, ਭੇਦਭਾਵ

seize (ਸੀਜ਼) *v* (ਕਾ) ਅਧਿਕਾਰ ਵਿਚ ਲੈਣਾ, ਕਾਬੂ ਕਰਨਾ, ਕਬਜ਼ਾ ਕਰਨਾ

seizure ('ਸੀਯ਼ਅ*) *n* ਕਬਜ਼ਾ; ਪਕੜ; ਧਾਰਣ; ਹਮਲਾ, ਆਵੇਸ਼

seldom ('ਸੈੱਲਡਅਮ) *adv* ਵਿਰਲਾ ਹੀ; ਕਦੀ-ਕਦਾਈਂ, ਬਹੁਤ ਘੱਟ; ਕਦਚਿਤ; ਕਦੇ ਕਦੇ

select (ਸਿ'ਲੈੱਕਟ) *v a* ਚੁਨਣਾ, ਛਾਂਟਣਾ, ਪਸੰਦ ਕਰਨਾ; ਮਨੋਨੀਤ ਕਰਨਾ; ਚੋਣਵਾਂ; ~ed ਵਧੀਆ, ਚੁਣਿਆ, ਪਵਿੱਤਰ; ~ion ਚੋਣ; ਮਨੋਨੀਤ, ਚੁਣਾਉ; ਛਾਂਟ; ~ive ਚੁਨਣਯੋਗ, ਚੋਣਸ਼ੀਲ; ਵਰਣਾਤਮਕ

self (ਸੈੱਲਫ਼) *n* ਆਪਾ, ਖ਼ੁਦੀ, ਅਹੰ, ਆਤਮ ਭਾਵ, ਨਿਜੀ ਹੋਂਦ; ਨਿਜ; **~abandoned** ਵਿਲਾਸੀ, ਭੋਗੀ, ਵਿਸ਼ਈ; **~acquired** ਸਵੈ-ਪ੍ਰਾਪਤ; **~centred** ਸਵੈ-ਕੇਂਦਰਤ, ਸੁਆਰਥੀ, ਮਤਲਬੀ; **~confidence** ਆਤਮ-ਵਿਸ਼ਵਾਸ; **~ish** ਸੁਆਰਥੀ, ਮਤਲਬੀ, ਖ਼ੁਦਗ਼ਰਜ਼; **~ishness** ਸੁਆਰਥ, ਖ਼ੁਦਗ਼ਰਜ਼ੀ; **~less** ਸੁਆਰਥਹੀਣ, ਬੇਗ਼ਰਜ਼, ਤਿਆਗੀ; **~sufficiency** ਆਤਮ-ਨਿਰਭਰਤਾ;

sell (ਸੈੱਲ) *v* ਵੇਚਣਾ, ਵਿਕਰੀ ਕਰਨੀ, ਫ਼ਰੋਖ਼ਤ ਕਰਨਾ; ਵਿਕਣਾ; ਠੱਗਣਾ, ਧੋਖਾ ਦੇਣਾ, ਝਾਂਸਾ ਦੇਣਾ; **~er** ਵਿਕ੍ਰੇਤਾ, ਵੇਚਣ ਵਾਲਾ

semantics (ਸਿ'ਮੈਂਟਿਕਸ) *n* ਅਰਥ-ਵਿਗਿਆਨ, ਅਰਥਕੀ

semblance ('ਸੈੱਬਲਅੰਸ) *n* ਬਾਹਰੀ ਰੂਪ, ਸਮਾਨਤਾ, ਝਲਕ, ਆਭਾਸ

semen ('ਸੀਮੈੱਨ) *n* ਵੀਰਜ, ਬੀਜ, ਮਣੀ; ਧਾਤ

semester (ਸਿ'ਮੈੱਸਟਅ*) *n* ਛਿਮਾਹੀ ਪਾਠ-ਕ੍ਰਮ; ਛਿਮਾਹੀ

semi ('ਸੈੱਮੀ) *pref* ਅੱਧ, ਅਰਧ (ਅਗੇਤਰ ਰੂਪ); ਨੀਮ; ਅਪੂਰਣ; **~colon** ਅਰਧਵਿਰਾਮ

seminar ('ਸੈੱਮਿਨਾ*) *n* ਗੋਸ਼ਟੀ, ਵਿਚਾਰ-ਗੋਸ਼ਟੀ

seminary ('ਸੈੱਮਿਨਅਰਿ) *n* ਸਿੱਖਿਆਲਾ, ਸਕੂਲ, ਪਾਠਸ਼ਾਲਾ, ਵਿਦਿਆਲਾ,

semiotics ('ਸੈੱਮਿ'ਔਟਿਕਸ) *n* ਚਿੰਨ੍ਹ ਵਿਗਿਆਨ

semolina ('ਸੈੱਮਅ'ਲੀਨਅ) *n* ਸੂਜੀ

senate ('ਸੈੱਨਿਟ) *n* ਉੱਚ-ਸਦਨ; ਵਿਧਾਨ-ਸਭਾ, ਵੱਡੀ ਸਭਾ; ਵਿਸ਼ਵ-ਵਿਦਿਆਲਾ ਦੀ ਪ੍ਰਬੰਧ-ਸੰਮਤੀ, ਪ੍ਰਸ਼ਾਸਨ ਸੰਮਤੀ

send (ਸੈੱਡ) *v* ਘੱਲਣਾ, ਭੇਜਣਾ, ਪਹੁੰਚਾਉਣਾ, ਵਿਦਾ ਕਰਨਾ, ਟੋਰਨਾ, ਰਵਾਨਾ ਕਰਨਾ; ਚਲਾਉਣਾ, ਭਜਾਉਣਾ, ਧੱਕਣਾ, ਠੇਲ੍ਹਣਾ; **~off** ਵਿਦਾਇਗੀ

senility (ਸਿ'ਨਿਲਅਟਿ) *n* ਬਿਰਧ ਅਵਸਥਾ, ਬੁਢਾਪਾ; ਕਮਜ਼ੋਰੀ

senior ('ਸੀਨਯਅ*) *n a* ਜਠੇਰਾ, ਬਿਰਧਜਨ, ਵੱਡਾ; ਪ੍ਰਧਾਨ, ਉੱਚ, ਸ੍ਰੇਸ਼ਠ; **~ity** ਉੱਚਤਾ, ਵੱਡਪਣ, ਬਜ਼ੁਰਗੀ, ਸਿਆਣਾਪਣ, ਜੇਠਾਪਣ

sensation (ਸੈੱਨ'ਸੇਇਸ਼ਨ) *n* ਸੰਵੇਦਨਾ, ਉਦਵੇਗ, ਤੀਬਰ ਅਨੁਭਵ, ਸਨਸਨੀ, ਚੇਤਨਤਾ, ਅੰਤਰ-ਅਨੁਭਵ; ਸਮਝ, ਇਹਸਾਸ, ਝਰਨਾਹਟ, ਲਹਿਰ; **~al** ਸਨਸਨੀਖੇਜ਼, ਉਤੇਜਨਾਪੂਰਨ, ਸੰਵੇਦਨਾਤਮਕ

sense (ਸੈੱਸ) *n* ਵਿਵੇਕ, ਸਹਿਜ ਬੁਧੀ, ਹੋਸ਼; ਗਿਆਨ ਇੰਦਰੀ, ਚੇਤਨਤਾ, ਸੰਵੇਦਨਾ; ਸਧਾਰਨ ਗਿਆਨ, ਵਿਹਾਰਕਤਾ, ਵਿਹਾਰਕ ਗਿਆਨ, ਸਮਝਦਾਰੀ; ਭਾਵਨਾ, ਵਿਚਾਰ, ਭਾਵੁਕਤਾ; ਤਾਤਪਰਜ, ਅਰਥ, ਭਾਵ, ਮਤਲਬ; ਤੱਤ; **~less** ਚੇਤਨਾਹੀਣ, ਬੇਹੋਸ਼; ਬੁੱਧੀਹੀਣ, ਨਾਸਮਝ, ਨਾਦਾਨ, ਮੂਰਖ

sensible ('ਸੈੱਸਅਬਲ) *a* ਸੰਵੇਦਨਸ਼ੀਲ; ਵਿਹਾਰਕ; ਗਿਆਨਵਾਨ, ਵਿਵੇਕੀ, ਸਮਝਦਾਰ

sensitive ('ਸੈੱਸਿਟਿਵ਼) *n a* ਸੰਵੇਦੀ, ਸੰਵੇਦਨਸ਼ੀਲ, ਸਚੇਤ, ਚੇਤਨਾਸ਼ੀਲ, ਸੂਖਮਗ੍ਰਾਹੀ, ਭਾਵੁਕ, ਨਾਜ਼ੁਕ ਮਿਜ਼ਾਜ, ਛੁਈਮੁਈ; **~ness** ਸੰਵੇਦਨਸ਼ੀਲਤਾ, ਭਾਵੁਕਤਾ, ਭਾਵਗ੍ਰਾਹਿਕਤਾ, ਨਾਜ਼ੁਕ-ਮਿਜ਼ਾਜੀ

sensory ('ਸੈੱਸਅਰਿ) *a* ਸੰਵੇਦੀ, ਸੰਵੇਦਕ, ਸੰਵੇਦਨਾਤਮਕ, ਅਨੁਭੂਤੀ ਸਬੰਧੀ

sensual ('ਸੈੱਸਯੁਅਲ) *a* ਪ੍ਰਤੱਖਵਾਦੀ, ਸੰਵੇਦਨਾਵਾਦੀ; ਕਾਮੁਕ; ਵਾਸਨਾਤਮਕ

sensuos ('ਸੈੱਸਯੁਅਸ) *a* ਇੰਦਰੀ-ਭੋਗ ਸਬੰਧੀ,

ਇੰਦਰੀ-ਗਤ

sentence ('ਸੈੱਟਅੰਸ) *n v* ਵਾਕ; ਸੂਤਰ, (ਪ੍ਰ) ਕਹਾਵਤ; ਨਿਰਣੈ; ਜਿਊਰੀ ਦਾ ਫ਼ੈਸਲਾ; ਸਜ਼ਾ ਦਾ ਹੁਕਮ; ਫ਼ੈਸਲਾ ਦੱਸਣਾ, ਨਿਰਣੈ ਦੇਣਾ, ਹੁਕਮ ਸੁਣਾਉਣਾ

sentiment ('ਸੈਂਟਿਮਅੰਟ) *n* ਭਾਵਨਾ, ਮਨੋਭਾਵ, ਭਾਵਾਤਮਕ ਵਿਚਾਰ, ਜਜ਼ਬਾ; ~**al** ਭਾਵੁਕ, ਜਜ਼ਬਾਤੀ

sentinel, sentry ('ਸੈਂਟਿਨਲ, 'ਸੈਂਟਰਿ) *n v* ਸੰਤਰੀ, ਰੱਖਿਅਕ, ਪਹਿਰੇਦਾਰ; ਪਹਿਰਾ ਦੇਣਾ, ਤੱਖਿਆ ਕਰਨੀ

separable ('ਸੈਪ(ਅ)ਰਅਬਲ) *a* ਨਿੱਖੜਵਾਂ, ਅੱਡ ਹੋਣ ਯੋਗ, ਅਲੱਗ ਕਰਨ ਯੋਗ

separate ('ਸੈੱਪਅਰਅਟ, 'ਸੈੱਪਅਰੇਇਟ) *n a v* ਵੱਖ; ਸੁਤੰਤਰ, ਨਿਜੀ, ਆਪਣਾ; ਵਖਰਾਉਣਾ, ਅੱਡ ਕਰਨਾ, ਵਿਯੁਕਤ ਕਰਨਾ, ਵਿਭਕਤ ਕਰਨਾ, ਭੇਦ ਕਰਨਾ, ਅੱਲਗ ਕਰਨਾ, ਜੁਦਾ ਕਰਨਾ, ਵਿਛੜਨਾ

separation ('ਸੈੱਪਅ'ਰੇਇਸ਼ਨ) *n* ਜੁਦਾਈ; ਵਿਯੁਕਤੀ, ਵਿਯੋਗ, ਬਿਰਹ, ਵਿਭੇਦ

sepoy ('ਸੀਪੋਇ) *n* ਸੈਨਕ, ਸਿਪਾਹੀ

sequel ('ਸੀਕਵ(ਅ)ਲ) *n* ਸਮਾਪਤੀ, ਅੰਤਮ ਰੂਪ, ਉੱਤਰ, ਬਾਕੀ, ਬਚਿਆ ਹਿੱਸਾ, ਪਰਿਣਾਮ

sequence ('ਸੀਕਵਅੰਸ) *n* ਕੜੀ, ਸਿਲਸਲਾ, ਤਰਤੀਬ

seraglio (ਸੈਰਾਗਲਾਓੁ) *n* ਹਰਮ, ਰਣਵਾਸ

serape (ਸੈਂਰਾਪਿ) *n* ਸ਼ਾਲ, ਦੁਸ਼ਾਲਾ, ਚੱਦਰਾ

serene (ਸਿ'ਰੀਨ) *n v a* ਸ਼ਾਂਤ ਵਿਸਥਾਰ; ਸ਼ਾਂਤ ਕਰਨਾ; ਸਥਿਰ; ਨਿਰਮਲ, ਸ਼ੁੱਧ, ਪ੍ਰਸੰਨ; ਨਿਖਰਿਆ, ਉੱਜਲ

serf (ਸਅਃਫ਼) *n* ਪੀੜਤ ਵਿਅਕਤੀ; ਗ਼ੁਲਾਮ, ਵਗਾਰੀ; ~**dom** ਦਾਸ ਪ੍ਰਥਾ, ਦਾਸਤਾ

serial ('ਸਿਅਰਿਅਲ) *n a* ਪ੍ਰਕਾਸ਼ਨ ਲੜੀ; ਲੜੀਦਾਰ, ਧਾਰਾਵਾਹਕ, ਸਿਲਸਲੇਵਾਰ; ~**number** ਲੜੀ ਨੰਬਰ, ਕ੍ਰਮ ਸੰਖਿਆ; ~**ly** ਕ੍ਰਮ ਅਨੁਸਾਰ, ਕ੍ਰਮ ਪੂਰਵਕ, ਸਿਲਸਲੇਵਾਰ

sericulture ('ਸੈਰਿ'ਕਅੱਲਚਅ*) *n* ਰੇਸ਼ਮ-ਉਤਪਾਦਨ

series ('ਸਿਅਰੀਜ਼) *n* ਲੜੀ, ਕੜੀ, ਮਾਲਾ, ਸਿਲਸਲਾ; ਸ਼੍ਰੇਣੀ; ਅੰਕਮਾਲਾ, ਲੇਖਮਾਲਾ, ਪੁਸਤਕਮਾਲਾ

serious ('ਸਿਅਰਿਅਸ) *a* ਗੰਭੀਰ, ਪੀਰ, ਸੰਜੀਦਾ, ਚਿੰਤਨਸ਼ੀਲ, ਵਿਚਾਰਸ਼ੀਲ, ਧਿਆਨ, ਮਗਨ; ~**ness** ਗੰਭੀਰਤਾ, ਸੰਜੀਦਗੀ, ਵਿਚਾਰਸ਼ੀਲਤਾ, ਉਤਸੁਕਤਾ

sermon ('ਸਅਃਮਅਨ) *n v* ਪ੍ਰਵਚਨ, ਉਪਦੇਸ਼, ਧਰਮ-ਉਪਦੇਸ਼, ਧਰਮ-ਵਿਆਖਿਆਨ; ਵਿਆਖਿਆਨ ਦੇਣਾ, ਸਿੱਖਿਆ ਦੇਣੀ

serpent ('ਸਅਃਪਅੰਟ) *n* ਸੱਪ, ਨਾਗ, ਭੁਜੰਗ; ਵਿਸ਼ਵਾਸਘਾਤੀ ਆਦਮੀ, ਧੋਖੇਬਾਜ਼ ਆਦਮੀ

servant ('ਸਅਃਵਅੰਟ) *n* ਕਰਮਚਾਰੀ, ਨੌਕਰ, ਮੁਲਾਜ਼ਮ, ਸੇਵਕ, ਦਾਸ

serve (ਸਅਃਵ਼) *v* ਗੋਵਾ ਕਰਨੀ, ਨੌਕਰੀ ਕਰਨੀ, ਕੰਮ ਕਰਨਾ, ਖ਼ਿਦਮਤ ਕਰਨੀ; ਲਾਭਦਾਇਕ ਹੋਣਾ, ਉਪਯੋਗੀ ਹੋਣਾ, ਕੰਮ ਆਉਣਾ; ਮਤਲਬ ਪੂਰਾ ਕਰਨਾ, ਸੰਤੁਸ਼ਟ ਕਰਨਾ; ਤਹਿਲ ਕਰਨੀ

service ('ਸਅਃਵ਼ਿਸ) *n v* ਸੇਵਾ, ਨੌਕਰੀ, ਖ਼ਾਤਰ, ਖ਼ਿਦਮਤ, ਮੁਲਾਜ਼ਮਤ; ਉਪਕਾਰ, ਪਰੋਪਕਾਰ, ਸੇਵਾ-ਭਾਵ; ਸਹਾਇਤਾ; ਪੂਜਾ-ਪਾਠ; ਮੁਰੰਮਤ ਕਰਨੀ, ਸਫ਼ਾਈ ਕਰਨੀ; ~**able** ਉਪਕਾਰੀ ਹਿੱਤਕਾਰੀ, ਸੇਵਾ ਯੋਗ, ਟਿਕਾਊ, ਮਜ਼ਬੂਤ

serviette ('ਸਅਃਵ਼ਿ'ਅੱਟ) *n* ਰੁਮਾਲ, ਤੌਲੀਆ

servile ('ਸਅ:ਵਾਇਲ) *a* ਨੀਚ, ਤੁੱਛ; ਹੀਣ; ਖ਼ੁਸ਼ਾਮਦੀ; ਕਮੀਨਾ; ਜੀ ਹਜ਼ੂਰੀਆ, ਚਾਪਲੂਸ

servitude ('ਸਅ:ਵਿਟਯੂੜ) *n* ਦਾਸਤਾ; ਗ਼ੁਲਾਮੀ, ਸੇਵਾ ਭਾਵ

sesame ('ਸੈੱਸਅਮਿ) *n* ਤਿਲ

session ('ਸੈੱਸ਼ਨ) *n* ਵਿਧਾਨ ਸਭਾ ਦੀ ਬੈਠਕ, ਸਭਾ, ਵਿਸ਼ਵਵਿਦਿਆਲੇ ਦਾ ਸਿੱਖਿਆ-ਕਾਲ, ਅਧਿਆਪਨ ਵਰ੍ਹਾ; ਅਜਲਾਸ

set (ਸੈੱਟ) *n v* ਜੁੱਟ; ਸੂਰਜ ਦਾ ਢਲਣਾ; ਢਾਂਚਾ, ਬਣਾਵਟ, ਧਾਰਾ, ਵਹਾਉ; ਬੈਠਾਉਣ, ਜੜਨਾ; ਸਥਾਪਤ ਕਰਨਾ; ਨਿਰਣੇ ਕਰਨਾ, ਨਿਸ਼ਚਤ ਕਰਨਾ, ਨਿਯਤ ਕਰਨਾ; ਪੱਕਾ ਕਰਨਾ, ਠਾਣ ਲੈਣਾ; ਠੀਕ ਕਰਨਾ; ~**ting** ਯੋਜਨਾ; ਸਥਾਪਨ, ਜੜਾਉ, ਬੈਠਾਉ; ਦ੍ਰਿਸ਼ਪਟ, ਚੁਗਿਰਦਾ, ਵਾਤਾਵਰਨ

settle ('ਸੈੱਟਲ) *v* ਸਥਾਪਨ ਕਰਨਾ, ਲਾਉਣਾ, ਜਮਾਉਣਾ; ਸ਼ਾਂਤ ਕਰਨਾ, ਸੁਲਝਣਾ, ਸੁਲਝਾਉਣਾ; ਫ਼ੈਸਲਾ ਕਰਨਾ; ਨਿਸ਼ਚੈ ਕਰਨਾ, ਠਾਨਣਾ, ਨਿਯੁਕਤ ਕਰਨਾ; ਸਹਿਮਤ ਕਰਨਾ; ਰਾਜ਼ੀ ਹੋਣਾ; ~**d** ਨਿਸ਼ਚਤ, ਨਿਯਤ, ਸਥਾਪਤ, ਚੁਕਤਾ ਕੀਤਾ, ਚੁਕਾਇਆ; ~**ment** ਨਿਰਣਾ, ਨਿਸ਼ਚਾ; ਨਿਪਟਾਰਾ; ਸਥਾਪਨ; ਸਮਾਧਾਨ, ਸਮਝੌਤਾ; ਉਪਨਿਵੇਸ਼; ਬਸਤੀ

seven ('ਸੈੱਵ੍ਨ) *a n* ਸੱਤਵਾਂ; ਸੱਤ ਦੀ ਗਿਣਤੀ, ਸੱਤਾਂ ਦਾ ਇੱਕਠ; ~**fold** ਸੱਤ-ਗੁਣਾ; ~**teen** ਸਤਾਰਾਂ; **sweet** ~**teen** ਨਵਯੁਵਤੀ ਦਾ ਸੁੰਦਰਤਾ-ਕਾਲ, ਸਤਾਰਾਂ ਸਾਲਾ ਸੁੰਦਰੀ; ~**th** ਸੱਤਵਾਂ ਭਾਗ; ਸੱਤਵਾਂ; ~**ty** ਸੱਤਰ ਦੀ ਸੰਖਿਆ ਜਾਂ ਅੰਕ; ਸੱਤਰਵਾਂ

several (ਸੈੱਵ੍ਰ*ਲ) *a pron* ਤੋੜਨਾ (ਸਬੰਧ) ਅੱਡ ਕਰਨਾ, ਵੱਖ ਕਰਨਾ, ਅੱਲਗ ਕਰਨਾ; ਅਲਹਿਦਾ, ਨਿਆਰਾ, ਭਿੰਨ, ਸੁਤੰਤਰ, ਵਿਭਿੰਨ, ਵਿਸ਼ੇਸ਼, ਅਨੇਕ, ਨਾਨਾ ਪ੍ਰਕਾਰ

severe (ਸਿਵ੍ਇਅ*) *a* ਘੋਰ, ਅਤੀਅੰਤ, ਬੇਹੱਦ, ਪ੍ਰਚੰਡ, ਉਗਰ, ਤੀਬਰ, ਤੀਖਣ, ਅਸਹਿ, ਭਾਰੀ, ਸਖ਼ਤ; ਦੰਡਸ਼ੀਲ; ਤਿੱਖਾ, ਕੌੜਾ

severity (ਸਿ'ਵੈੱਅਟਿ) *n* ਤੀਖਣਤਾ, ਤੀਬਰਤਾ, ਗਰਮੀ, ਤੇਜ਼ੀ, ਨਿਰਦਇਤਾ, ਕਠੋਰਤਾ, ਨਿਸ਼ਠੁਰਤਾ

sew (ਸਅਉ) *v* ਸਿਉਣਾ, ਸੀਣਾ, ਸਿਲਾਈ ਕਰਨਾ; ~**er** ਦਰਜ਼ੀ; ~**ing** ਸਿਲਾਈ, ਸਿਉਣ

sewage ('ਸੂਇਜ) *n* ਗੰਦੀ ਨਾਲੀ ਦਾ ਪਾਣੀ, ਮਲ-ਪਰਵਾਹ

sewer (ਸੂਅ*) *n* (ਇਤਿ) ਖਾਨਸਾਮਾ; ਗੰਦਾ ਨਾਲਾ

sex (ਸੈੱਕਸ) *n* ਲਿੰਗ, ਲਿੰਗ ਭੇਦ, ਯੋਨੀ, ਕਾਮ; ~**ology** ਲਿੰਗ-ਵਿਗਿਆਨ, ਕਾਮ-ਵਿਗਿਆਨ; ~**ual** ਲਿੰਗੀ, ਮੈਥਨੀ, ਲਿੰਗ ਮੂਲਕ, ਯੋਨੀ ਸਬੰਧੀ, ਇਸਤਰੀ-ਪੁਰਸ਼ ਸਬੰਧੀ; ~**uality** ਕਾਮਵਾਸਨਾ, ਕਾਮੁਕਤਾ; ~**y** ਅਤੀ ਕਾਮੀ, ਅਤੀ ਵਿਲਾਸੀ, ਕਾਮੁਕ

shabby ('ਸ਼ੈਬੀ) *a* ਘੁੱਥੜ; ਪਾਟਿਆ, ਪੁਰਾਣਾ, ਲੀਚੜ, ਨੀਚ, ਕੰਜੂਸ; ਹੋਛਾ

shack (ਸ਼ੈਕ) *n* ਝੁੱਗੀ, ਟਪਰੀ

shackle ('ਸ਼ੈਕਲ) *n v* ਹੱਥਕੜੀ; (in *pl* s) ਰੁਕਾਵਟ; ਬੰਧਨ, ਕੁੰਡਾ; ਜੋੜਨਾ, ਮਿਲਾਉਣਾ; ਸੰਗਲ ਪਾਉਣਾ; ਰੋੜਾ ਅਟਕਾਉਣਾ

shade (ਸ਼ੇਇਡ) *n v* ਪਰਛਾਈਂ, ਛਾਂ, ਛਾਂ-ਦਾਰ ਥਾਂ; ਘੁਸਮੁਸਾ; ਭਰਾਂਤੀ; ਹਨੇਰਾ ਕਰਨਾ, ਧੁੰਦਲਾ ਕਰਨਾ; ਛਾਂ ਕਰਨੀ, ਧੁੱਪ ਤੋਂ ਬਚਾਉਣਾ; ਪਰਦਾ ਪਾਉਣਾ, ਲੁਕਾਉਣਾ; ~**d** ਛਾਇਆ ਕ੍ਰਿਤ, ਥੋੜ੍ਹਾ ਘਟਾਇਆ

shadow ('ਸ਼ੈਡਅਉ) *n v* ਛਾਂ; ਪ੍ਰਤੀਬਿੰਬ,

ਸਹਿਚਰ, ਸਹਿਗਾਮੀ, ਸੰਗੀ, ਪ੍ਰਤੀਰੂਪ, ਛਾਇਆ; ਝਲਕ, ਹਲਕਾ ਖ਼ਾਕਾ; ਛਾਉਣਾ, ਛਾ ਜਾਣਾ, ਲੁਕਾ ਲੈਣਾ; ਧੁੰਦਲਾ ਖ਼ਾਕਾ ਚਿੱਤਣਾ; ਛਾਂ ਪਾਉਣੀ, ਛਾਂ ਕਰਨੀ

shady ('ਸ਼ੇਇਡਿ) *a* ਛਾਂਦਾਰ, ਛਾਇਆਮਈ; ਘਣਾ; ਅਪਰਗਟ, ਗੁਪਤ, ਨਿਖਿੱਧ

shake (ਸ਼ੇਇਕ) *n v* ਹਲੂਣਾ, ਹੁਝਕਾ, ਥਰਕਣ, ਝਟਕਾ, ਧੱਕਾ, ਹਿਚਕੋਲਾ; ਕੰਬਣ, ਥਰਕਣਾ, ਡੋਲਣਾ; ਕੰਬਾਉਣਾ, ਘੁਮਾਉਣਾ

shaky ('ਸ਼ੇਇਕਿ) *a* ਅਸਥਿਰ, ਨਿਰਬਲ, ਕਾਵਾਂਡੋਲ, ਸੰਦੇਹ-ਪੂਰਨ, ਕੰਬਣ ਵਾਲਾ, ਝਿੰਜਕਦਾ; ਹਿੱਲਦਾ ਅਟਿਕਵਾਂ, ਢਿੱਲਾ

shallow ('ਸ਼ੈਲਅਉ) *n v a* ਕਛਾਰ, ਘੱਟ ਪਾਣੀ ਦੀ ਥਾਂ; ਹੋਛਾ ਹੋਣਾ; ਤੁੱਛ, ਸਾਰਹੀਣ, ਹੋਛਾ; ~ness ਹੋਛਾਪਨ, ਥੋਥਾਪਨ, ਹਲਕਾਪਨ

shamble ('ਸ਼ੈਂਬਲ) *n v* ਭੱਦੀ ਚਾਲ, ਵਿਰੂਪ ਗਤੀ, ਬੇਢੰਗੀ ਦੌੜ, ਡਿਗਦੇ ਢਹਿੰਦੇ ਤੁਰਨਾ, ਲੜਖੜਾਂਦੇ ਹੋਏ ਚੱਲਣਾ

shambles ('ਸ਼ੈਂਬਲਜ਼) *n* ਬੁੱਚੜਖ਼ਾਨਾ; ਰੋਲ ਘਚੋਲਾ; ਦੁਰਦਸ਼ਾ, ਤਬਾਹੀ

shame (ਸ਼ੇਇਮ) *n v* ਲੱਜਾ, ਲਾਜ, ਸ਼ਰਮ, ਝਿਜਕ, ਝੇਂਪ, ਹਿਆ, ਸ਼ੌਰਤ; ਸਰਮਿੰਦਗੀ, ਲਾਨ੍ਹਤ; ਸ਼ਰਮਿੰਦਾ ਕਰਨਾ, ਨੀਵਾਂ ਦਿਖਾਉਣਾ, ਅਪਮਾਨਤ ਕਰਨਾ; ~**full** ਸ਼ਰਮਨਾਕ, ਲੱਜਜਨਕ; ਅਸ਼ਲੀਲ, ਖ਼ਰਾਬ; ~**less** ਬੇਸ਼ਰਮ, ਬੇਹਯਾ, ਲੱਜਾਹੀਣ, ਨਿਰਲੱਜ, ਢੀਠ

shanty ('ਸ਼ੈਨਟਿ) *n* ਛੱਪਰੀ, ਟੱਪਰੀ, ਕੁਟੀਆ, ਕੁਟੀਰ, ਝੋਂਪੜੀ

shape (ਸ਼ੇਇਪ) *n v* ਰਚਨਾ, ਰੂਪ, ਡੀਲ-ਡੋਲ, ਬਣਤਰ, ਆਕਾਰ, ਆਕ੍ਰਿਤੀ, ਸੂਰਤ, ਸ਼ਕਲ; ਰੰਗ-ਰੂਪ, ਪ੍ਰਕਾਰ; ਸਿਰਜਣਾ, ਰੂਪ ਦੇਣਾ, ਸ਼ਕਲ ਦੇਣੀ; ਸ਼ਕਲ ਇਖ਼ਤਿਆਰ ਕਰਨ; ਨਿਰਮਾਣ ਕਰਨਾ, ਸਾਂਚੇ ਵਿਚ ਢਾਲਣਾ; ~**d** ਸਾਕਾਰ, ਸਰੂਪ, ਰੂਪਯੁਕਤ; ਆਕਾਰਯੁਕਤ

share (ਸ਼ੇਅ*) *n v* ਵੰਡਾਈ, ਬਟਾਈ, ਹਿੱਸਾ; ਵੰਡ, ਅੰਸ਼; ਹਿੱਸਾ ਲੈਣਾ, ਸ਼ਾਮਲ ਹੋਣਾ, ਸਹਿਤਾਗੀ ਹੋਣਾ

shark (ਸ਼ਾਕ) *n v* ਸਮੁੰਦਰੀ ਮੱਛੀ, ਵੱਡਾ ਮੱਛ; ਧੋਖੇਬਾਜ਼ ਸ਼ਖ਼ਸ; ਠਰਾਂਟਾ, ਚਾਰ ਸੌ ਵੀਹ ਕਰਨੀ

sharp (ਸ਼ਾਪ) *a v* ਤਿੱਖਾ, ਤੇਜ਼, ਧਾਰਦਾਰ, ਬਾਰੀਕ, ਨੋਕੀਲਾ, ਨੋਕਦਾਰ, ਅਣਿਆਲਾ, ਤਤਪਰ; ਹੁਸ਼ਿਆਰ, ਹੌਸ਼ਾਸ, ਸੰਵੇਦਨਸ਼ੀਲ, ਚਲਾਕ, **ਝੁਰਤ-ਫੁਰਤ ਕਰਨ ਵਾਲਾ**; ਤਿੱਖ ਕਰਨਾ, ਤੇਜ਼ ਕਰਨਾ, ਧਾਰ ਬਣਾਉਣਾ; ~**en** ਤੇਜ਼ ਕਰਨਾ ਜਾਂ ਹੋਣਾ, ਧਾਰ ਲਗਾਉਣਾ, ਸਾਣ ਉੱਤੇ ਚੜ੍ਹਾਉਣਾ; ਸਪਸ਼ਟ ਕਰਨਾ; ਉਤਸੁਕ ਕਰਨਾ; ਕਾਇਆਂ ਹੋਣਾ; ~**ness** ਤੀਖਣਤਾ, ਤੇਜ਼ੀ, ਤੀਬਰਤਾ, ਨੁਕੀਲਾਪਨ, ਪ੍ਰਚੰਡਤਾ; ਕਠੋਰਤਾ, ਤੀਬਰ ਦ੍ਰਿਸ਼ਟੀ, ਸਤਰਕਤਾ; ਸੰਵੇਦਨਸ਼ੀਲਤਾ

shatter ('ਸ਼ੈਟਅ*) *v* ਛਿੰਨ-ਭਿੰਨ ਕਰਨਾ, ਉਲਟਣਾ-ਪੁਲਟਣਾ, ਬਰਬਾਦ ਕਰਨਾ, ਧੱਜੀਆਂ ਉਡਾਉਣਾ, ਖਿਲਾਰਨਾ

shave (ਸ਼ੇਇਵ) *n v* ਹਜਾਮਤ; ਹਜਾਮਤ ਕਰਨੀ, ਮੁੰਨਣਾ; ਵਾਲ ਬਣਾਉਣਾ, ਵਾਲ ਕੱਟਣਾ; ~**r** ਨਾਈ, ਹੱਜਾਮ; ਮੁੰਡਾ; ਛੋਕਰਾ, ਲੁਟੇਰਾ

shaving ('ਸ਼ੇਇਵਿਙ) *n* ਕਤਰਨਾਂ; ਛਿਲਤਰਾਂ

shawl (ਸ਼ੋਲ) *n* ਫਰਦ, ਗਰਮ ਲੋਈ ਜਾਂ ਬੂਰੀ, ਸ਼ਾਲ, ਦੁਸ਼ਾਲਾ

sheaf (ਸ਼ੀਫ਼) *n v* ਦੱਥਾ, ਭਰੀ, ਪੂਲਾ, ਪੂਲੰਦਾ, ਮੁੱਠ; ਪੂਲਾ ਬੰਨ੍ਹਣਾ

sheath (ਸ਼ੀਥ) *n* ਮਿਆਨ, ਗਿਲਾਫ਼, ਕੋਸ਼, ਖੋਲ; ~**e** ਮਿਆਨ ਵਿਚ ਪਾਉਣਾ, ਗਿਲਾਫ਼ ਚੜ੍ਹਾਉਣਾ,

ਖੇਲ ਚਤੁਰਾਉਣਾ; ਮੜ੍ਹਨਾ; ਸੁਰੱਖਿਅਤ ਕਰਨਾ; ਬਕਸੇ ਵਿਚ ਬੰਦ ਕਰਨਾ

shed (ਸ਼ੈੱਡ) *n v* ਛੰਨ, ਛੱਪਰ, ਢਾਰਾ, ਉਤਾਰਨਾ, ਲਾਹੁਣਾ

sheep (ਸ਼ੀਪ) *n* ਭੇਡ; ਮੀਢਾ; ਮੇਖ (ਰਾਸ਼ੀ); ਸੰਕੋਚੀ, ਸ਼ਰਮਾਕਲ ਮਨੁੱਖ; ~ish ਦੱਬੂ

sheer (ਸ਼ਿਅ*) *a adv* (ਢਲਾਨ) ਸਿੱਧੀ ਖੜਵੀਂ; ਨਿਰਾ, ਨਿਪਟ, ਸਰਾਸਰ; ਸਿਰਫ਼, ਖੜ੍ਹਵੇਂ ਢੰਗ ਨਾਲ; ਪ੍ਰਤੱਖ ਤੌਰ ਤੇ

sheet (ਸ਼ੀਟ) *n v* ਚਾਦਰ, ਪਲੰਘ-ਪੋਸ਼; ਝਾਲਰ; ਅਖ਼ਬਾਰ, ਪਰਚਾ, ਕਾਗ਼ਜ਼; ਚਾਦਰ ਲੈਣੀ, ਚਾਦਰ ਵਿਛਾਉਣੀ

shelf (ਸ਼ੈੱਲਫ਼) *n* ਕਿਤਾਬਖ਼ਾਨਾ, ਅਲਮਾਰੀ ਦਾ ਖ਼ਾਨਾ; ਰਖਣਾ

shell (ਸ਼ੈੱਲ) *n v* (1) ਖੋਲ, ਖੋਪਰੀ; (2) ਸੰਖ, ਸਿੱਪੀ, ਘੋਗਾ; (3) ਛਿਲੜ, ਪਰਤ, ਤਹਿ; (4) ਰੂਪ-ਰੇਖਾ, ਖ਼ਾਕਾ; (5) ਫ਼ੌਜੀ ਸਿਪਾਹੀ ਦੀ ਜਾਕਟ ਜਾਂ ਝੱਗੀ; ਛਿਲਣਾ, ਹੌਲੇ ਸੁੱਟਣਾ

shelter ('ਸ਼ੈੱਲਟਅ*) *n v* ਆਸਰਾ, ਸ਼ਰਨ, ਬਚਾਉ, ਓਟ, ਆੜ; ਝੌਂਪੜੀ, ਛੈਡ, ਛਤਰ, ਪਨਾਹ; ਆਸਰਾ ਲੈਣਾ, ਸ਼ਰਨ ਵਿਚ ਆਉਣਾ; ~less ਬੇਆਸਰਾ, ਬੇਸਹਾਰਾ, ਨਿਰਾਧਾਰ, ਸ਼ਰਨਹੀਨ, ਅਨਾਥ

shelve (ਸ਼ੈੱਲਵ਼) *v* ਪੁਸਤਕ ਆਦਿ ਨੂੰ ਅਲਮਾਰੀ ਵਿਚ ਰੱਖਣਾ, ਤਾਕ ਕੇ ਰੱਖਣਾ; ਮੁਲਤਵੀ ਕਰਨਾ, ਛੱਡ ਦੇਣਾ; (ਕਿਸੇ ਆਦਮੀ ਨੂੰ) ਕੱਢ ਦੇਣਾ, ਕੰਮ ਤੋਂ ਹਟਾਉਣਾ; ਅਲਮਾਰੀ ਦੇ ਤਖ਼ਤੇ ਜਾਂ ਦਰਾਜ਼ ਬਣਵਾਉਣਾ

shield (ਸ਼ੀਲਡ) *n v* ਢਾਲ, ਆਸਰਾ, ਸ਼ਰਨ; ਰੱਖਿਆ ਕਰਨੀ, ਲੁਕਾਉਣਾ, ਬਚਾਉ ਕਰਨਾ

shift (ਸ਼ਿਫ਼ਟ) *v n* ਬਦਲਣਾ; ਬਦਲੀ ਕਰਨੀ; ਪਲਟਾਉਣਾ; ਤਬਦੀਲੀ, ਬਦਲੀ, ਜੋੜ-ਤੋੜ; ~ing ਪਰਿਵਰਤਨ; ਸਥਾਨਾਂਤਰਨ

shimmer ('ਸ਼ਿਮਅ*) *n v* ਝਿਲਮਿਲ, ਟਿਮਟਿਮਾਹਟ, ਝਿਲਮਿਲਾਹਟ; ਟਿਮਟਿਮਾਣਾ, ਝਿਲਮਿਲ ਕਰਨਾ; ਝਲਕਣਾ

shine (ਸ਼ਾਇਨ) *v n* ਚਮਕਣਾ, ਲਿਸ਼ਕਣਾ; ਡਲ੍ਹਕਣਾ, ਜਗਮਗਾਉਣਾ, ਪ੍ਰਕਾਸ਼ਤ ਹੋਣਾ; ਚਮਕਾਉਣਾ; ਚਮਕ, ਡਲ੍ਹਕ, ਲਿਸ਼ਕ; ਸਾਫ਼ ਮੌਸਮ

shining ('ਸ਼ਾਇਨਿਙ) *a* ਪ੍ਰਕਾਸ਼ਮਾਨ, ਚਮਕੀਲਾ, ਚਮਕਦਾਰ, ਤੇਜਸਵੀ

shiny ('ਸ਼ਾਇਨਿ) *a* ਚਮਕਦਾ, ਲਿਸ਼ਕਦਾਰ

ship (ਸ਼ਿਪ) *n v* ਜਹਾਜ਼, ਸਮੁੰਦਰੀ ਜਹਾਜ਼; ਜਹਾਜ਼ ਤੋਂ ਭੇਜ ਦੇਣਾ; ~wright ਜਹਾਜ਼ ਸਾਜ਼; ~ping ਜਹਾਜ਼ਰਾਨੀ, ਜਹਾਜ਼ ਦੀ ਲਦਾਈ ਜਾਂ ਭਰਾਈ

shirk (ਸ਼ਅ:ਕ) *v* ਘੁਮਾਈ ਮਾਰਨੀ, ਜੀ ਚੁਰਾਉਣਾ, ਕੰਮ-ਚੋਰੀ ਕਰਨੀ

shirt (ਸ਼ਅ:ਟ) *n* ਕਮੀਜ਼, ਕੁੜਤਾ, ਝੱਗਾ

shit (ਸ਼ਿਟ) *n v* ਗੂੰਹ, ਗੰਦ, ਵਿਸ਼ਟਾ; ਹੱਗਣਾ, ਜੰਗਲ ਜਾਣਾ, ਟੱਟੀ ਕਰਨੀ

shiver ('ਸ਼ਿਵ਼ਅ*) *v n* (1) ਕੰਬਣਾ, ਕਾਂਬਾ ਪੈਣਾ, ਥਰਥਰਾਉਣਾ; ਕਾਂਬਾ, ਕੰਬਣੀ; ਝੁਣਝੁਣੀ; (2) ਟੁਕੜੇ ਕਰਨੇ, ਭੰਨ ਸੁੱਟਣਾ, ਚੂਰਾ ਕਰ ਦੇਣਾ; ਟੁਕੜਾ, ਟੋਟਾ, ਚੂਰ

shock (ਸ਼ੌਕ) *n v* ਝਟਕਾ; ਮਾਨਸਕ ਸੱਟ, ਸਦਮਾ, ਅਚਾਨਕ ਪਿਆ ਦੁੱਖ; ਧੱਕਾ; ਝਟਕਾ ਵੱਜਣਾ

shoe (ਸ਼ੂ) *n v* ਜੁੱਤੀ; ਘੋੜੇ ਦੀ ਖੁਰੀ; ਖੁਰੀਆਂ ਲਾਉਣੀਆਂ; ਸ਼ੂਮ ਚਤੁਰਾਉਣਾ; ~maker ਮੋਚੀ

shoot (ਸ਼ੂਟ) *v* ਜ਼ੋਰ ਨਾਲ ਨਿਕਲਣਾ, ਅਚਾਨਕ ਨਿਕਲਣਾ; ਬੰਦੂਕ ਚਲਾਉਣੀ; ਜ਼ੋਰ ਨਾਲ ਸੁੱਟਣਾ; ਸਿਨਮਾ ਦੀ ਤਸਵੀਰ ਲੈਣੀ; ~er ਬੰਦੂਕਚੀ, ਨਿਸ਼ਾਨੇਬਾਜ਼; ~ing ਨਿਸ਼ਾਨੇਬਾਜ਼ੀ,

ਤੀਰਅੰਦਾਜ਼ੀ, ਸ਼ਿਕਾਰੀ; ਸਿਨੇਮੇ ਦੀ ਤਸਵੀਰ ਲੈਣ ਦਾ ਅਮਲ; ~out (ਬੋਲ) ਗੋਲੀਬਾਰੀ

shop (ਸ਼ੌਪ) *n v* ਦੁਕਾਨ, ਹੱਟੀ, ਸ਼ਾਲਾ, ਮਹਿਕਮਾ, ਵਿਭਾਗ; ਸੌਦਾ-ਸੁਲੱਫ ਲੈਣਾ, ਹੱਟੀ ਤੇ ਜਾਣਾ, (ਕੁਝ) ਖ਼ਰੀਦਣਾ; ~ping ਖ਼ਰੀਦਦਾਰੀ, ਬਜ਼ਾਰ ਜਾਣਾ, ਸੌਦਾ-ਸੁਲੱਫ ਲੈਣ (ਦਾ ਕਾਰਜ)

shore (ਸ਼ੋ*) *n* (ਸਮੁੰਦਰ ਦਾ) ਕੰਢਾ, ਕਿਨਾਰਾ, ਤਟ, ਸਾਹਿਲ; ਥੂਹਣੀ, ਸਹਾਰਾ; ਥੰਮੀ ਲਾਉਣੀ

short (ਸ਼ੌਟ) *a adv n* ਨਿੱਕਾ, ਛੋਟਾ, ਸੰਖਿਪਤ, ਮਧਰਾ; ਥੋੜ੍ਹਾ, ਘੱਟ; ਨਿਗੁਣਾ, ਮਾਮੂਲੀ; ਨਾਕਾਫ਼ੀ, ਅਪੂਰਨ, ਹ੍ਰਸਵ; ਨਿੱਕਰ, ਕੱਛਾ; ~coming ਘਾਟ, ਕਮਜ਼ੋਰੀ, ਉਣਤਾਈ; ~hand ਸੰਕੇਤ, ਲਿਪੀ, ਸ਼ਾਰਟਹੈਂਡ; ~lived ਅਲਪਕਾਲਕ; ਅਸਥਿਰ, ਅਨਿੱਤ; ~sighted ਤੰਗ-ਨਜ਼ਰ, ਤੰਗ ਸੂਝ ਵਾਲਾ; ~sightedness ਤੰਗ-ਨਜ਼ਰੀਆ, ਅਲਪਦ੍ਰਿਸ਼ਟੀ, ਤੰਗ-ਸੂਝ; ~tempered ਚਿੜਚਿੜਾ, ਖਿਝੂ, ਤਲਖ਼ ਸੁਭਾਅ ਵਾਲਾ; ~age ਘਾਟਾ, ਘਾਟ, ਥੁੜ੍ਹ, ਕਮੀ, ਅਭਾਵ, ਤੋੜਾ; ~en ਘੱਟ ਹੋਣਾ; ਸੰਖਿਪਤ ਕਰਨਾ; ~ly ਛੇਤੀ ਹੀ, ਹੁਣੇ ਹੀ; ਥੋੜ੍ਹਾ ਚਿਰ ਪਹਿਲਾਂ ਜਾਂ ਮਗਰੋਂ; ਸੰਖੇਪ ਵਿਚ, ਥੋੜ੍ਹੇ ਸ਼ਬਦਾਂ ਵਿਚ, ਮੁੱਕਦੀ ਗੱਲ

shot (ਸ਼ੌਟ) *n v* ਬੰਦੂਕ ਦੀ ਗੋਲੀ, ਤੋਪ ਦਾ ਗੋਲਾ, ਛੱਰਾ; ਬੰਦੂਕ ਤੋਪ ਆਦਿ ਦਾ ਫ਼ਾਇਰ; ਨਿਸ਼ਾਨਾ; ਨਿਸ਼ਾਨੇਬਾਜ਼, ਨਿਸ਼ਾਨੇਮਾਰ; (ਅਲੰਕਾਰਕ) ਅੰਦਾਜ਼ਾ; ਗੋਲੀ ਦਾਗਣੀ, ਗੋਲਾ ਦਾਗਣਾ, ਛੱਰੇ ਦਾਗਣੇ

shoulder ('ਸ਼ਾਉਲਡਾ*) *n v* ਮੋਢਾ, ਕੰਧਾ, ਮੋਢੇ, ਮੋਢੇ ਨਾਲ ਧੱਕਣਾ; ਜ਼ਿੰਮੇਵਾਰੀ ਲੈਣੀ; ਮੋਢੇ ਤੇ ਭਾਰ ਸੰਭਾਲਣਾ

shout (ਸ਼ਾਉਟ) *n v* ਚੀਕਣਾ, ਕੂਕਣਾ, ਜ਼ੋਰ ਦੀ ਅਵਾਜ਼ ਮਾਰਨੀ; ਰੌਲਾ ਪਾਉਣਾ; ਚੀਕ, ਕੂਕ, ਜ਼ੋਰ ਦੀ ਅਵਾਜ਼, ਰੌਲਾ

shove (ਸ਼ਅੱਵ) *v n* ਧੱਕਣਾ, ਧੱਕਾ ਦੇਣਾ, ਰੇੜ੍ਹਨਾ; ਧੱਕੇ ਮਾਰ ਕੇ ਹਟਾਉਣਾ; ਅੱਗੇ ਖਿਸਕਾਉਣਾ ਜਾਂ ਖਿਸਕਣਾ; ਪਾਉਣਾ; ਧੱਕਣ; ਧੱਕਾ

shovel ('ਸ਼ਅੱਵਲ) *n v* ਬੇਲਚਾ

show (ਸ਼ਅਉ) *v n* ਵਿਖਾਉਣਾ; ਪੇਸ਼ ਕਰਨਾ, ਪਰਗਟ ਕਰਨਾ, ਪ੍ਰਕਾਸ਼ਤ ਕਰਨਾ, ਜ਼ਾਹਰ ਕਰਨਾ; ਸਾਖਿਆਤ ਹੋਣਾ; ਵਿਖਾਵਾ, ਪਰਦਰਸ਼ਨ, ਨੁਮਾਇਸ਼, ਪਰਦਰਸ਼ਨੀ, ਦ੍ਰਿਸ਼, ਪਰਗਟਾਉ; ਆਡੰਬਰ, ਠਾਠ-ਬਾਠ; ਬਾਹਰੀ ਰੂਪ; ~y ਭੜਕੀਲਾ, ਚਮਕੀਲਾ, ਦਿਖਾਵਟੀ, ਆਡੰਬਰਪੂਰਨ

shower ('ਸ਼ਾਉਅ*) *n* ਵਾਛੜ; ਫੁਹਾਰ; ਝੜੀ

shrewd (ਸ਼ਰੂਡ) *a* ਸੂਝਵਾਨ, ਸਿਆਣਾ, ਚਤਰ, ਸੁਲਝੇ ਵਿਚਾਰਾਂ ਵਾਲਾ

shriek (ਸ਼ਰੀਕ) *v n* ਚੀਕਣਾ, ਲੇਰ ਕੱਢਣੀ, ਚਾਂਗਰ ਮਾਰਨੀ, ਡਾਡ ਮਾਰਨੀ; ਚੀਕ, ਕੂਕ

shrine (ਸ਼ਰਾਇਨ) *n* ਮੰਦਰ, ਮੱਠ; ਦਰਗਾਹ, ਖ਼ਾਨਗਾਹ, ਸਮਾਧ; ਬਲੀਦਾਨ ਸਥਾਨ; ਪਵਿੱਤਰ ਸਮਾਰਕ, ਯਾਦਗਾਰ; ਅਸਥੀ-ਪਾਤਰ

shrink (ਸ਼ਰਿੰਕ) *v n* ਸੰਕੁਚਨ, ਸਿਮਟਨ; ਸੁੰਗੜਨ; ਝਿਜਕ; ਸਿਮਟਣਾ, ਸੰਕੁਚਤ ਹੋਣਾ, ਛੋਟਾ ਹੋ ਜਾਣਾ; ਝੁਰੀਆਂ ਪੈਣੀਆਂ, ਸੁਕੜਾ ਦੇਣਾ, ਸੰਕੋਚ ਕਰਨਾ

shrive (ਸ਼ਰਾਇਵ) *v* (ਕਿਸੇ ਇਸਾਈ ਪਾਦਰੀ ਦੇ ਸਾਮ੍ਹਣੇ) ਗੁਨਾਹ ਸਵੀਕਾਰ ਕਰਨਾ, ਤੋਬਾ ਕਰਨੀ; ਗੁਨਾਹ ਬਖ਼ਸ਼ਵਾਉਣਾ

shrub (ਸ਼ਰਅੱਬ) *n* ਝਾੜੀ; ~by ਝਾੜੀਦਾਰ

shudder ('ਸ਼ਅੱਡਾ*) *v n* ਕੰਬਣੀ ਛਿੜਨੀ, ਕੰਬ ਉੱਠਣਾ, ਸਹਿਮ ਜਾਣਾ; ਕੰਬਣੀ, ਥਰਥਰਾਹਟ

shuffle ('ਸ਼ਅੱਫ਼ਲ) *v n* ਘਿਸਰ ਕੇ ਚਲਣਾ, ਪੈਰ ਘਸੀਟਣੇ, ਵਿਆਕੁਲ ਹੋਣਾ; ਇਕ ਗੱਲ ਤੇ ਨਾ ਟਿਕਣਾ; ਖਿਡਕਣਾ, ਡੋਲਣਾ; ਟਾਲ-ਮਟੋਲ ਕਰਨਾ; ਡਾਵਾਂ-ਡੋਲ ਹੋਣਾ; ਘਸੀਟ, ਰਗੜ, ਖਿਸਕਣ, ਸਰਕਣ; ਅਦਲਾ-ਬਦਲੀ

shun (ਸ਼ਅੱਨ) *v* ਦੂਰ ਰਹਿਣਾ, ਪਰ੍ਹਾਂ ਰਹਿਣਾ; ਬਚਣਾ; ਕਤਰਾਉਣਾ; ਪਰਹੇਜ਼ ਕਰਨਾ

shunt (ਸ਼ਅੱਟ) *v n* ਲਾਂਭੇ ਹੋ ਜਾਣਾ; ਰਾਹ ਛੱਡਣਾ; ਬਦਲਣਾ; ਪਟੜੀ ਬਦਲਣ, ਲਾਂਭੇ ਹੋਣ (ਦਾ ਕਾਰਜ); ਬਿਜਲੀ ਦੀ ਲਾਈਨ ਬਦਲਣ ਵਾਲਾ ਜੰਤਰ; **~er** ਪਟੜੀ ਬਦਲਣ ਵਾਲਾ, ਲਾਈਨ ਬਦਲਣ ਵਾਲਾ

shut (ਸ਼ਅੱਟ) *v* ਬੰਦ ਕਰਨਾ (ਮੂੰਹ); ਬੰਦ ਹੋਣਾ; ਨਿਰਾਸ ਕਰਨਾ; ਵਾਂਝਿਆਂ ਕਰਨਾ; ਬੰਦ ਅਵਸਥਾ ਵਿਚ ਡਿਗਣਾ ਜਾਂ ਸੁੰਗੜਨਾ; ਮੀਟਿਆ

shuttle ('ਸ਼ਅੱਟਲ) *n* ਨਲੀ, ਫਿਰਕੀ, ਜੁਲਾਹੇ ਦੀ ਨਾਲ, ਸ਼ਟਿਲ; ਛੋਟੇ ਰੂਟ ਦੀ ਬੱਸ; **~cock** ਬੈਡਮਿੰਟਨ ਦੀ ਚਿੜੀ; **~train** ਸਥਾਨਕ ਰੇਲ ਗੱਡੀ

shy (ਸ਼ਾਇ) *a v n* ਸੰਗਾਊ, ਸ਼ਰਮੀਲਾ; ਕਤਰਾਉਣ ਵਾਲਾ; ਤੜਕ ਉੱਠਣਾ, ਚੌਂਕ ਉੱਠਣਾ; ਨਿਸ਼ਾਨਾ, ਸੁੱਟਣ ਦੀ ਕੋਸ਼ਿਸ਼

sibling ('ਸਿਬਲਿੰਡ) *n* ਇੱਕੇ ਮਾਂ ਬਾਪ ਦੇ ਬੱਚੇ, ਸਹੋਦਰ, ਭਰਾ-ਭੈਣ

sick (ਸਿਕ) *a* ਰੋਗੀ, ਬੀਮਾਰ; ਖਿਝਿਆ, ਅੱਕਿਆ; ਉਚਾਟ; **~en** ਸ਼ਰੀਰ ਕੁਝ ਢਿੱਲਾ ਹੋਣਾ, ਬੀਮਾਰ ਹੁੰਦੇ ਜਾਪਣਾ; **~ly** ਰੋਗੀ ਜਿਹਾ, ਬੀਮਾਰਾਂ ਵਰਗਾ

sickle ('ਸਿਕਲ) *n* ਦਾਤਰੀ, ਦਾਤੀ

side (ਸਾਇਡ) *n v* ਪਾਸਾ, ਬੰਨਾ, ਦਿਸ਼ਾ; ਰੁਖ਼, ਪੱਖ; ਪੜਾ; ਬਾਹੀ, ਭੁਜਾ; ਕੰਢਾ, ਕਿਨਾਰਾ; ਪੱਖ ਲੈਣਾ, ਸਾਥ ਦੇਣਾ, ਨਾਲ ਹੋਣਾ; **~effect** ਗੌਣ ਪ੍ਰਭਾਵ (ਆਮ ਕਰਕੇ ਮਾੜਾ); **~track** ਮੁੱਖ ਸੜਕ ਦੇ ਨਾਲ ਰਸਤਾ ਜਾਂ ਛੋਟੀ ਸੜਕ; ਰੇਲ ਦੀ ਲਾਂਭੇ ਵਾਲੀ ਪਟੜੀ; ਟਾਲ ਦੇਣਾ; ਲਾਂਭੇ ਲੈ ਜਾਣਾ

siege (ਸੀਜ) *n v* ਘੇਰਾ, ਕਿਲ੍ਹਾਬੰਦੀ, ਨਾਕਾਬੰਦੀ; ਪਿੱਛੇ ਪੈ ਜਾਣਾ; ਘੇਰਾ ਪਾਉਣਾ

sigh (ਸਾਇ) *v* ਹਉਕਾ ਲੈਣਾ, ਠੰਢਾ ਸਾਹ ਲੈਣਾ, ਸਿਸਕਣਾ

sight (ਸਾਇਟ) *n v* ਨਜ਼ਰ ਨਿਗਾਹ, ਦ੍ਰਿਸ਼ਟੀ ਟੱਕਣੀ; ਨਜ਼ਾਰਾ, ਦ੍ਰਿਸ਼, ਦਰਸ਼ਨ; ਦ੍ਰਿਸ਼ਟੀ-ਸੀਮਾ; ਵੇਖਣਾ, ਵੇਖ ਲੈਣਾ; **~seer** ਸੈਲਾਨੀ, ਦਰਸ਼ਕ

sign (ਸਾਇਨ) *n v* ਨਿਸ਼ਾਨ, ਚਿੰਨ੍ਹ, ਪ੍ਰਤੀਕ, ਪ੍ਰਮਾਣ, ਲੱਛਣ; ਝੰਡਾ; ਇਸ਼ਾਰਾ, ਸੰਕੇਤ; ਦਸਤਖ਼ਤ ਕਰਨੇ; **~ed** ਹਸਤਾਖ਼ਰਤ

signature ('ਸਿਗਨਅਚਅ*) *n* ਦਸਤਖ਼ਤ, ਹਸਤਾਖ਼ਰ, ਸਹੀ

significant (ਸਿਗ'ਨਿਫ਼ਿਕਅੰਟ) *a* ਵਿਸ਼ੇਸ਼; ਜ਼ਰੂਰੀ, ਪ੍ਰਭਾਵਸ਼ਾਲੀ, ਅਰਥਪੂਰਨ, ਭਾਵਪੂਰਨ

signification ('ਸਿਗਨਿਫ਼ਿ'ਕੇਇਸ਼ਨ) *n* ਭਾਵ, ਤਾਤਪਰਜ, ਅਰਥ, ਭਾਵਾਰਥ; ਸਾਰਥਕਤਾ; ਸ਼ਬਦ-ਸ਼ਕਤੀ

signify ('ਸਿਗਨਿਫ਼ਾਇ) *v* ਪਰਗਟ ਕਰਨਾ, ਜ਼ਾਹਰ ਕਰਨਾ; ਅਰਥ ਦੇਣਾ, ਭਾਵ ਦੇਣਾ

silence ('ਸਾਇਲਅੰਸ) *n v* ਸ਼ਾਂਤੀ, ਚੁੱਪ-ਚਾਪ, ਮੌਨ, ਖ਼ਮੋਸ਼ੀ, ਸੰਨਾਟਾ; ਚੁੱਪ ਕਰਾ ਦੇਣਾ, ਸ਼ਾਂਤ ਕਰ ਦੇਣਾ

silent ('ਸਾਇਲਅੰਟ) *a* ਚੁੱਪ, ਸ਼ਾਂਤ, ਖ਼ਮੋਸ਼, ਮੌਨ; ਚੁਪ-ਚਾਪ

silk (ਸਿਲਕ) *n* ਰੇਸ਼ਮ, ਰੇਸ਼ਮੀ ਕੱਪੜਾ; **~worm** ਰੇਸ਼ਮ ਦਾ ਕੀੜਾ; **~y** ਰੇਸ਼ਮ ਵਰਗਾ ਕੋਮਲ ਤੇ ਨਰਮ; ਚਮਕਦਾਰ

silly ('ਸਿਲਿ) *a* ਮੂਰਖ, ਬੇਵਕੂਫ਼, ਬੁੱਧੂ, ਬੇਅਕਲ, ਸਿੰਧੜ, ਭੋਲਾ-ਭਾਲਾ

silt (ਸਿਲਟ) *n v* ਗੋਲ, ਵਗਦੇ ਪਾਣੀ ਦੇ ਹੇਠਾਂ ਬੈਠੀ ਮਿੱਟੀ, ਗਾਰ, ਤਲਛਟ, ਰੇਤ ਆਦਿ; ਗੋਲ ਪੈਂਦੀ

silver ('ਸਿਲਵ੍ਅ*) *n a v* ਚਾਂਦੀ, ਚਾਂਦੀ ਦਾ ਸਿੱਕਾ; ਚਾਂਦੀ ਦਾ; ਚਾਂਦੀ ਚੜ੍ਹਾਉਣਾ; ~paper ਵਰਕ; ~tongued ਮਿੱਠਬੋਲਾ, ਪ੍ਰਭਾਵਸ਼ਾਲੀ ਲੈਕਚਰ ਕਰਨ ਵਾਲਾ

similar ('ਸਿਮਿਲਅ*) *a* ਵਰਗਾ, ਜਿਹਾ, ਮਿਲਦਾ ਜੁਲਦਾ, ਸਮਾਨ; ~ity ਸਮਰੂਪਤਾ, ਸਾਰੂਪਤਾ, ਸਮਾਨਤਾ, ਸਮਤਾ; ~ly ਉਂਝੇ ਤਰ੍ਹਾਂ ਸਮਾਨ ਰੂਪ ਵਿਚ

simile ('ਸਿਮਿਲਿ) *n* ਉਪਮਾ, ਤਸ਼ਬੀਹ, ਉਪਮਾ-ਅਲੰਕਾਰ

simple ('ਸਿੰਪਲ) *a n* ਸਾਦਾ, ਸਿੱਧਾ, ਸਰਲ ਸਿੱਧਾ-ਸਾਦਾ, ਸਧਾਰਨ; ਭੋਲਾ-ਭਾਲਾ; ਖ਼ਾਲਸ

simpleton ('ਸਿੰਪਲਟ(ਅ)ਨ) *n* ਸਿੰਧੜ, ਸਿੱਧਾ-ਸਾਦਾ, ਲੋੱਲ੍ਹੂ, ਮੂਰਖ, ਬੁੱਧੂ

simplicity (ਸਿੰ'ਪਲਿਸਿਅਟਿ) *n* ਸਾਦਗੀ, ਸਰਲਤਾ; ਸੁੰਢਤਾ; ਅਸੰਯੁਕਤਤਾ; ਨਿਸ਼ਕਪਟਤਾ, ਭੋਲਾਪਣ

simplification ('ਸਿਮ'ਪਲਿਫ਼ਿ'ਕੇਇਸ਼ਨ) *n* ਸਰਲੀਕਰਨ

simplify ('ਸਿੰਪਲਿਫ਼ਾਇ) *v* ਸੌਖਾ ਕਰਨਾ, ਸਰਲ ਬਣਾਉਣਾ; ਸਾਦਾ ਕਰਨਾ; ਗੁੰਝਲ ਦੂਰ ਕਰਨੀ; ਸੁਬੋਧ ਬਣਾਉਣਾ

simulate ('ਸਿਮਯੁਲੇਇਟ) *v* ਸਾਂਗ ਕਰਨਾ, ਢੋੰਗ ਰਚਣਾ, ਝੂਠਾ ਰੂਪ ਬਣਾਉਣਾ; ਨਕਲ ਕਰਨਾ; ਭੇਸ ਬਦਲਣਾ, ਰੂਪ ਧਾਰਨਾ

simulation ('ਸਿਮਯੁ'ਲੇਇਸ਼ਨ) *n* ਬਹਾਨਾ, ਢੌਂਗ; ਨਕਲ, ਰੀਸ, ਸਾਂਗ; ਪਖੰਡ

simultaneity ('ਸਿਮ(ਅ)ਲਟ(ਅ)'ਨਿਅਟਿ) *n* ਸਮਕਾਲੀਪਣ, ਸਮਕਾਲੀਨਤਾ

simultaneous ('ਸਿਮ(ਅ)ਲ'ਟੇਇਨਯਅਸ) *a* ਸਮਕਾਲੀ, ਸਮਕਾਲਕ; ~ly ਨਾਲ ਨਾਲ, ਇਕੋ ਸਮੇਂ ਵਿਚ

sin (ਸਿਨ) *n v* ਪਾਪ, ਗੁਨਾਹ; ਕੁਕਰਮ, ਅਧਰਮ, ਪਾਪ ਕਰਨਾ, ਗੁਨਾਹ ਕਰਨਾ, ਦੁਰਾਚਾਰ ਕਰਨਾ; ~ner ਗੁਨਾਹਗਾਰ, ਪਾਪੀ, ਅਪਰਾਧੀ

since ('ਸਿੰਸ) *prep conj adv* ਤੋਂ, ਤੋਂ ਲੈ ਕੇ, ਤੋਂ ਹੁਣ ਤਕ; ਕਿਉਂਕਿ, ਇਸ ਲਈ ਕਿ; ਇਹ ਵੱਖਦਾ ਹੋਏ

sincere ('ਸਿੰਸਿਅ*) *a* ਸੱਚਾ, ਖਰਾ; ਨਿਰਛਲ, ਨਿਸ਼ਕਪਟ; ਈਮਾਨਦਾਰ

sincerity (ਸਿੰ'ਸੈਰਿਅਟਿ) *n* ਨਿਸ਼ਕਪਟਤਾ, ਨਿਰਛਲਤਾ, ਸਾਫ਼-ਦਿਲੀ, ਸਚਾਈ, ਈਮਾਨਦਾਰੀ

sine (ਸਾਇਨ) *prep* ਬਿਨਾ, ਬਗ਼ੈਰ, ਬਾਝ; ~die (L) ਅਨਿਸ਼ਚਿਤ ਸਮੇਂ ਲਈ, ਦਿਨ ਨਿਸ਼ਚਤ ਕੀਤੇ ਬਿਨਾ; ~qua non (L) ਜ਼ਰੂਰੀ ਸ਼ਰਤ

sinew ('ਸਿਨਯੂ) *n v* ਜਾਨ; ਸਰੀਰਕ ਬਲ, ਸਾਧਨ, ਵਸੀਲੇ; ਜੋੜੀ ਰੱਖਣਾ, ਸੰਗਠਤ ਰੱਖਣਾ; ਧਾਰਨਾ, ਗੰਢਣਾ; ~y ਤਕੜਾ; ਮਜ਼ਬੂਤ; ਬਲਵਾਨ

sing (ਸਿਙ) *v n* ਗਾਉਣਾ, ਰਾਗ ਅਲਾਪਣਾ; ਗੂੰਜਣਾ; ~er ਗਾਇਕ, ਗਾੳਂਵਈਆ, ਰਾਗੀ; ~ing ਗਾਣਾ, ਗੀਤ, ਗਾਇਨ

single ('ਸਿੰਗਲ) *a n v* ਇੱਕਲਾ, ਕੱਲਮ-ਕੱਲਾ; ਇਕਹਿਰਾ, ਇਕਵੱਲੀ ਦਾ; ਬੇਸਹਾਰਾ, ਕੰਵਾਰਾ, ਅਟਵਿਆਹਿਆ; ਨਿਤਾਰਨਾ, ਵੱਖ ਕਰਨਾ; ~handed ਬਿਨਾ ਕਿਸੇ ਸਹਾਇਤਾ ਦੇ ਇੱਕ-ਹੱਥਾ; ~hearted ਬਿਨਾ ਦੁਭਾਵਨਾ; ਖਰਾ, ਭੋਲਾਗ; ~minded ਇਕਾਗਰ ਚਿੱਤ, ਇੱਕ ਮਨ, ਦ੍ਰਿੜ੍ਹ

ਇਰਾਦੇ ਵਾਲਾ

singlet ('ਸਿਙਗਲਿਟ) *n* ਬੁਨੈਣ, ਫ਼ਤੂਹੀ

singular ('ਸਿਙਗਯੁਲਅ*) *n a* (ਵਿਆ) ਇਕਵਚਨ; ਨਿਰਾਲਾ, ਅਨੋਖਾ, ਅਦੁੱਤੀ, ਅਸਧਾਰਨ, ਬੇਤੁਕਾ; ~**ity** ਇਕਮਾਤਰਤਾ, ਇਕੱਲਪਣ; ਵਿਸ਼ਿਸ਼ਟਤਾ, ਵਿਲੱਖਣਤਾ

sink (ਸਿਙਕ) *n v* ਡੁੱਬਣਾ ਜਾਂ ਡੋਬਣਾ; (ਭੌਂ ਦਾ) ਹੇਠਾਂ ਬੈਠ ਜਾਣਾ, ਦਿਲ ਘਟਣਾ, ਹੌਸਲਾ ਡਿਗਣਾ; ਖ਼ਤਮ ਹੋਣਾ; ਹੌਲੀ ਹੌਲੀ ਮੁੱਕਣਾ; ਗੰਦਗੀ ਜਾਂ ਗੰਦਾ ਪਾਣੀ ਸੁੱਟਣ ਵਾਲਾ ਟੋਆ ਜਾਂ ਚੁਬੱਚਾ; ~**ing** ਦਿਲ ਘਟਣ ਦੀ ਅਵਸਥਾ

sip (ਸਿਪ) *v n* ਘੁੱਟ ਭਰਨਾ, ਘੁੱਟੋ-ਵੱਟੀ ਪੀਣਾ

sir (ਸਅ:*) *n* ਸ੍ਰੀਮਾਨ, ਜਨਾਬ, ਹਜ਼ੂਰ, ਮਹਾਰਾਜ

sire ('ਸਾਇਅ*) *n* ਪਿਤਾ ਜਾਂ ਵਡੇਰਾ, ਖ਼ਾਨਦਾਨ ਦਾ ਬਜ਼ੁਰਗ; ਸ੍ਰੀਮਾਨ, ਜਨਾਬ

sissy ('ਸਿਸਿ) *n* ਜ਼ਨਾਨੜਾ, ਕੁੜੀਆਂ ਵਰਗਾ ਮੁੰਡਾ

sister ('ਸਿਸਟਅ*) *n* ਭੈਣ; ਸਹੇਲੀ, ਸਖੀ; ਸਤ-ਸੰਗਣ, ਧਰਮ-ਭੈਣ; ~**in law** ਸਾਲੀ; ਨਨਾਣ; ਭਰਜਾਈ; ਸਾਲੇਹਾਰ, ਦਰਾਣੀ, ਜਿਠਾਣੀ

sit (ਸਿਟ) *v* ਬੈਠਣਾ, ਬਹਿਣਾ; ਬਿਠਾਉਣਾ; ਟਿਕਾਉਣਾ; ~**ting** ਸਭਾ, ਬੈਠਕ, ਲਗਾਤਾਰ ਬੈਠਣ ਜਾ ਸਮਾਂ, ਇਜਲਾਸ; ~**ting member** ਚੱਲਦਾ ਆ ਰਿਹਾ ਮੈਂਬਰ; ~**ting room** ਬੈਠਕ, ਦੀਵਾਨਖ਼ਾਨਾ

site (ਸਾਇਟ) *n* ਥਾਂ, ਮੌਕਾ

situate(d) ('ਸਿਟਯੁਏਇਟਿਡ) *a* ਸਥਿਤ; ਸਥਾਪਤ

situation ('ਸਿਟਯੁ'ਏਇਸ਼ਨ) *n* ਥਾਂ, ਮੌਕਾ, ਜਗ੍ਹਾ; ਸਥਿਤੀ; ਹਾਲ, ਹਾਲਤ, ਦਸ਼ਾ

six (ਸਿਕਸ) *n* ਛੇ, ਛੇ ਦਾ ਅੰਕ, ਛੀਕਾ; ~**fold** ਛੇ ਗੁਣਾ; ~**er** ਛੱਕਾ; ~**teen** ਸੋਲਾਂ ਸੋਲਾਂ ਦੀ ਸੰਖਿਆ; ~**teenth** ਸੋਲ੍ਹਵਾਂ; ~**th** ਛੇਵਾਂ ਭਾਗ, ਛੇਵਾਂ; ~**ty** ਸੱਠ

sizable ('ਸਾਇਜ਼ਅਬਲ) *a* ਉਪਯੁਕਤ ਆਕਾਰ ਦਾ, ਲੰਮਾ-ਚੌੜਾ, ਬੜਾ, ਕਾਫ਼ੀ

size (ਸਾਇਜ਼) *n* (1) ਆਕਾਰ; ਕੱਦ; ਨਾਪ, ਪਰਿਮਾਣ, ਲੰਮਾਈ-ਚੌੜਾਈ; (2) ਮਾਵਾ, ਕਲਫ਼

sizy ('ਸਾਇਜ਼ਿ) *a* ਚਿਪਚਿਪਾ, ਲੇਸਦਾਰ

skeleton ('ਸਕੈਲਿਟਨ) *n* ਹੱਡੀਆਂ ਦਾ ਪਿੰਜਰ; ਢਾਂਚਾ, ਖ਼ਾਕਾ, ਸੰਖੇਪ, ਸੰਖਿਪਤ ਰੂਪ, ਸਾਰ

skelter ('ਸਕੈਲਟਅ*) *n* ਹਫ਼ੜਾ-ਦਫ਼ੜੀ, ਹੜਬੜੀ, ਹਫ਼ੜਾ-ਦਫ਼ੜੀ ਮਚਾਉਣਾ

sketch (ਸਕੈੱਚ) *n v* ਖ਼ਾਕਾ, ਢਾਂਚਾ, ਰੇਖਾ-ਚਿੱਤਰ, ਰੂਪ ਰੇਖਾ; ਸੰਖੇਪ ਬਿਆਨ; ਖ਼ਾਕਾ ਤਿਆਰ ਕਰਨਾ, ਰੂਪ-ਰੇਖਾ ਬਣਾਉਣੀ, ਸੰਖੇਪ ਵਿਚ ਬਿਆਨ ਕਰਨਾ; ~**y** ਖ਼ਾਕਾ ਜਿਹਾ, ਢਾਂਚਾ ਮਾਤਰ, ਸਧਾਰਨ ਰੂਪ-ਰੇਖਾ ਵਿਚ

skill (ਸਕਿਲ) *n* ਮੁਹਾਰਤ, ਨਿਪੁੰਨਤਾ, ਸੁੱਚਜ, ਕੌਸ਼ਲ; ~**ed** ਜਾਂਚ ਵਾਲਾ, ਚੱਜ ਵਾਲਾ, ਕੁਸ਼ਲ, ਮਾਹਰ, ਨਿਪੁੰਨ, ਪ੍ਰਵੀਣ

skim (ਸਕਿਮ) *n v* ਝੱਗ, ਮਲਾਈ, ਪੇਪੜੀ; (ਦੁੱਧ ਉੱਤੋਂ) ਮਲਾਈ ਲਾਹੁਣੀ, ਝੱਗ ਲਾਹੁਣੀ, ਪੇਪੜੀ ਲਾਹੁਣੀ; ਸਰਸਰੀ ਨਜ਼ਰ ਮਾਰਨੀ; ~**med milk** ਸਪਰੇਟਾ, ਕਰੀਮ ਕੱਢਿਆ ਦੁੱਧ

skin (ਸਕਿਨ) *n v* ਖੱਲ, ਖੱਲੜੀ, ਚਮੜੀ, ਛਿੱਲ, ਛਿੱਲੜ; ਖੱਲ ਲਾਹੁਣੀ; ਛਿੱਲਣਾ; ~**deep** ਉਤਲਾ-ਉਤਲਾ, ਮਾਮੂਲੀ; ~**flint** ਕੰਜੂਸ, ਸੂਮ; ~**ny** ਪਤਲਾ, ਲਿੱਸਾ, ਮਾੜੂਆ

skip (ਸਕਿਪ) *n* ਟੱਪਣਾ, ਕੁੱਦਣਾ, ਛੜੱਪੇ ਮਾਰਨੇ; ਰੱਸੀ ਟੱਪਣਾ; (ਬੋਲ) ਨੱਸ ਜਾਣਾ, ਭੱਜ ਨਿਕਲਣਾ; (ਕੋਈ ਕੰਮ) ਵਿਚੋਂ ਛੱਡ ਛੱਡ ਕੇ ਕਰਨਾ

skirt (ਸਕਅ:ਟ) *n v* ਲਹਿੰਗਾ, ਘਗੱਰਾ; ਤੀਵੀਂ; ਕਿਨਾਰਾ, ਸੀਮਾ

skull (ਸਕੱਅਲ) *n* ਖੋਪਰੀ, ਕਪਾਲ

sky (ਸਕਾਇ) *n v* ਆਕਾਸ਼, ਅਸਮਾਨ; ਉੱਚਾ ਟੰਗਣਾ; **~blue** ਅਸਮਾਨੀ (ਰੰਗ)

slab (ਸਲੈਬ) *n a* ਸਿਲ, ਫੱਟੀ, ਲੇਸਦਾਰ, ਚਿਪਚਿਪਾ

slack (ਸਲੈਕ) *a n v* ਸੁਸਤ, ਢਿੱਲਾ, ਢਿੱਲੜ, ਆਲਸੀ; ਮੰਦਵਾੜਾ, ਵਪਾਰ ਦੀ ਮੰਦਗੀ; (ਬ ਵ) ਪਾਜਾਮਾ ਜਾਂ ਪਤਲੂਨ; ਮੱਧਮ ਕਰਨਾ, ਸੁਸਕਾਉਣਾ, ਮਠੇ ਗੈਣਾ, ਆਲਸ ਕਰਨਾ; **on** ਢਿੱਲਾ ਕਰਨਾ, ਢਿੱਲਾ ਛੱਡ ਦੇਣਾ; ਸੁਸਤ ਹੋ ਜਾਣਾ; **~ness** ਆਲਸ, ਸੁਸਤੀ, ਢਿੱਲ

slang (ਸਲੈਙ) *n v* ਵਰਗ ਭਾਸ਼ਾ, ਬਜ਼ਾਰੀ ਬੋਲੀ, ਬੋਲ-ਕੁਬੋਲ, ਅਪਭਾਸ਼ਾ; ਗਾਲ੍ਹ ਕਢਣੀ

slant ('ਸਲਾਂਟ) *v n* ਤਿਰਛਾ ਹੋਣਾ, ਢਾਲਵਾਂ ਬਣਾਉਣਾ; ਢਾਲ, ਢਲਾਨ, ਤਿਰਛਾਪਨ

slap (ਸਲੈਪ) *n v* ਚਪੇੜ, ਧੱਫਾ, ਲੱਫੜ, ਥੱਪੜ; ਚਪੇੜ ਮਾਰਨੀ

slash (ਸਲੈਸ਼) *v n* (ਤਲਵਾਰ, ਚਾਬੁਕ ਆਦਿ ਨਾਲ) ਅੰਨ੍ਹੇਵਾਹ ਵਾਰ ਕਰਨਾ, ਵਾਢੀ ਲਾਉਣਾ, ਵੱਢਣਾ, ਪਛੜੇ ਲਾਹੁਣੇ, ਚੀਰਨਾ; ਚੀਰਾ

slaughter ('ਸਲੋਟਅ*) *v n* ਵੱਢਣਾ, ਝਟਕਾਉਣਾ; ਕਤਲ-ਏ-ਆਮ ਕਰਨਾ, ਵੱਢ-ਟੁੱਕ ਕਰਨੀ; ਕਤਲ ਕਰਨਾ, ਖ਼ੂਨ ਕਰਨਾ; ਵੱਢਣ, ਝਟਕਾਉਣ (ਦੀ ਕਿਰਿਆ); ਕਤਲ-ਏ-ਆਮ, ਕਤਲ, ਹੱਤਿਆ

slave (ਸਲੇਇਵ) *n v* ਗ਼ੁਲਾਮ, ਗੋਲਾ, ਬਰਦਾ, ਦਾਸ, ਨੀਚ ਕੰਮ ਕਰਨਾ **~ry** ਗ਼ੁਲਾਮੀ, ਦਾਸਤਾ; ਦਾਸ-ਪ੍ਰਥਾ

slaver (ਸਲੇਵਅ*) *n v* (1) ਲਾਲ੍ਹਾਂ, ਥੁੱਕ; (2) ਹੋਛੀ ਖੁਸ਼ਾਮਦ, ਤੁੱਛ ਚਾਪਲੂਸੀ; ਲਾਲ੍ਹਾਂ ਵਗਣੀਆਂ; ਚਾਪਲੂਸੀ ਕਰਨੀ

slavish ('ਸਲੇਇਵੀਸ਼) *a* ਹੋਛਾ, ਨੀਚ, ਤੁੱਛ; ਗ਼ੁਲਾਮਾਂ ਵਰਗਾ

slay (ਸਲੇਇ) *v* ਕਤਲ ਕਰਨਾ, ਮਾਰ ਸੁੱਟਣਾ, ਵੱਢ ਦੇਣਾ

sleek ('ਸਲੀਕ) *a v* ਕੂਲਾ, ਕੋਮਲ, ਨਰਮ, ਮੁਲਾਇਮ, ਚਿਕਣਾ; ਗੁਦਗੁਦ; ਮੁਲਾਇਮ ਕਰਨਾ; ਗੁਦਗੁਦਾ ਬਣਾਉਣਾ

sleep (ਸਲੀਪ) *n v* ਨੀਂਦਰ; ਸੌਂਣ; ਖ਼ਮੋਸ਼ੀ; ਆਰਾਮ; ਗੋਟਾ, ਸੌਂ ਜਾਣਾ, ਅੱਖ ਲੱਗਣੀ, **ਠੰਢੇ** ਪੈਣਾ; **~er** ਸੁੱਤਾ ਵਿਅਕਤੀ; ਲੱਕੜੀ ਦੇ ਗੱਟੂ ਜਿਨ੍ਹਾਂ ਉੱਤੇ ਰੇਲ ਪਟੜੀ ਵਿਛਾਈ ਜਾਂਦੀ ਹੈ, ਸਲੀਪਰ

sleeve (ਸਲੀਵ) *n* ਆਸਤੀਨ

slender ('ਸਲੈਂਡਅ*) *a* ਪਤਲਾ; ਮਾੜਾ; ਥੋੜ੍ਹਾ, ਸੂਖਮ, ਨਾਜ਼ੁਕ, ਕਮਜ਼ੋਰ

slice (ਸਲਾਇਸ) *n v* ਡਬਲ ਰੋਟੀ ਜਾਂ ਪਤਲਾ ਟੁਕੜਾ, ਟੋਟਾ, ਫਾੜੀ, ਗਰਾਹੀ, ਡੱਕਰਾ, ਹਿੱਸਾ, ਭਾਗ, ਅਸ਼ੰ; ਟੁਕੜੇ ਕੱਟਣੇ, ਫਾੜੀਆਂ ਕਰਨੀਆਂ

slick (ਸਲਿਕ) *adv a* ਪੂਰੀ ਤਰ੍ਹਾਂ ਠੀਕ-ਠਾਕ, ਸਿੱਧਾ; ਸਫ਼ਾਈ ਵਾਲਾ, ਫੁਰਤੀਲਾ; ਚੰਟ, ਚਤਰ

slide (ਸਲਾਇਡ) *v n* ਤਿਲਕਣਾ, ਖਿਸਕਣਾ; ਸਰਕਣਾ; ਸਰਕਾਉਣਾ, ਰੇੜ੍ਹਨਾ; ਬਰਫ਼ ਉੱਤੇ ਰਿੜ੍ਹਨ ਕਰਕੇ ਬਣਿਆ ਰਾਹ; ਤਿਲਕਵੀਂ ਢਲਾਨ; ਖਿਸਕਣ; ਰਿੜ੍ਹਨ

slight (ਸਲਾਇਟ) *a v n* ਥੋੜ੍ਹਾ ਜਿਹਾ, ਮਾੜਾ ਜਿਹਾ, ਮਾਮੂਲੀ, ਕਮਜ਼ੋਰ; ਹੇਠੀ ਕਰਨੀ; ਤੁੱਛ ਸਮਝਣਾ; ਲਾਪਰਵਾਹੀ ਕਰਨੀ; ਹੇਠੀ, ਅਵੱਗਿਆ

slip (ਸਲਿਪ) *n v* ਕਾਗ਼ਜ਼ ਦੀ ਚਿਟ; ਲੱਕੜੀ ਦੀ ਫੱਟੀ; ਪੱਤਰੀ; ਕਾਗ਼ਜ਼ ਦੀ ਲੰਮੀ ਕਤਰ; ਭੁੱਲ,

ਭੁੱਲ-ਚੁਕ, ਉਕਾਈ, ਤਰੁਟੀ; ਤਿਲਕਣਾ, ਖਿਸਕਣਾ, ਛਿਲਕਣਾ, ਸਰਕਣਾ; ਅੱਖ ਬਚਾ ਕੇ ਨਿਕਲ ਜਾਣਾ, ਚੁੱਪ-ਚਾਪ ਸਰਕ ਜਾਣਾ; ਖਿੜਕਣਾ, ਭੁੱਲ ਕਰਨੀ; ~per ਸਲਿਪਰ (ਪੈਰੀਂ ਪਾਉਣ ਵਾਲਾ); ~pery ਤਿਲਕਵਾਂ; ਅਸਥਿਰ, ਚਲਾਕ, ਬੇਇਤਬਾਰਾ

slit (ਸਲਿਟ) *v n* ਚੀਰਨਾ, ਚੀਰ ਪਾਉਣਾ, ਪਾੜਨਾ; ਚੀਰ, ਰਗੜ

slogan ('ਸਲਅਉਗਅਨ) *n* ਨਾਅਰਾ; ਸੰਕੇਤਕ ਸ਼ਬਦ, ਨੀਤੀਵਾਕ; ਇਸ਼ਤਿਹਾਰਬਾਜ਼ੀ ਵਿੱਚ ਵਰਤੇ ਜਾਣ ਵਾਲੇ ਚੁਸਤ ਵਾਕ

slope (ਸਲਅਉਪ) *n v* ਢਾਲ, ਢਲਵਾਨ; ਢਲਵੀਂ ਜ਼ਮੀਨ; ਟਹਿਲਣਾ, ਘੁੰਮਣਾ-ਫਿਰਨਾ, ਨੱਸ ਜਾਣਾ; ਤਿਰਛਾ ਕਰਨਾ, ਢਾਲਵਾਂ ਕਰਨਾ

sloppy ('ਸਲੌਪਿ) *a* ਚੂਹੜ, ਖੁੱਬੜ, ਵੱਲਲਾ

slow (ਸਲਅਉ) *a adv v* ਮੱਠਾ, ਢਿੱਲਾ, ਸੁਸਤ, ਮੰਦਮ, ਆਲਸੀ; ਹੌਲੀ ਹੌਲੀ; ਸੁਸਤ ਹੋ ਜਾਣਾ; ਢਿੱਲੇ ਪੈ ਜਾਣਾ

slum (ਸਲਅੱਮ) *n* ਝੁੱਗੀ-ਝੌਂਪੜੀ; ਗੰਦਾ ਮਹੱਲਾ

slumber ('ਸਲਅੱਬਅ*) *n v* ਨੀਂਦ, ਸੌਣ ਦੀ ਦਸ਼ਾ; ਸੌਂ ਜਾਣਾ; ~ous ਸੁੱਤਾ, ਆਲਸੀ ਆਦਮੀ, ਸੁਸਤ-ਮਨੁੱਖ

slur (ਸਲਅਃ*) *v n* ਕਲੰਕ ਲਾਉਣਾ, ਦਾਗ਼ ਲਾਉਣਾ; ਦੂਸ਼ਤ ਕਰਨਾ; ਤੁਹਮਤ ਲਾਉਣੀ; ਇਲਜ਼ਾਮ ਲਾਉਣਾ; ਕਲੰਕ; ਬਦਨਾਮੀ, ਦੋਸ਼, ਇਲਜ਼ਾਮ

sly (ਸਲਾਇ) *a* ਛਰੇਬੀ, ਦਗ਼ੇਬਾਜ਼, ਪੱਤੇਬਾਜ਼, ਖਰਾ; ਗੁੱਝਾ, ਵਿਅੰਗ ਭਰਿਆ

small (ਸਮੋਲ) *a* ਨਿੱਕ, ਛੋਟਾ, ਮਧਰਾ; ਥੋੜ੍ਹਾ, ਮਾੜਾ, ਬਾਰੀਕ, ਪਤਲਾ; ~hours ਰਾਤ ਦਾ ਤੀਜਾ ਜਾਂ ਚੌਥਾ ਪਹਿਰ; ~pox ਚੀਚਕ, ਮਾਤਾ, ਸੀਤਲਾ

smart (ਸਮਾਟ) *a v n* ਚੁਸਤ, ਫੁਰਤੀਲਾ; ਜ਼ੋਰਦਾਰ; ~ness ਚਤੁਰਤਾ, ਹੁਸ਼ਿਆਰੀ, ਸਜੀਵਤਾ, ਤੀਖਣਤਾ, ਫੁਰਤੀ, ਤੇਜ਼ੀ, ਚੁਸਤੀ

smash (ਸਮੈਸ਼) *v n* ਭੰਨ ਦੇਣਾ, ਤੋੜ ਦੇਣਾ, ਟੋਟੇ ਟੋਟੇ ਕਰ ਦੇਣਾ; ਸਖ਼ਤ ਸੱਟ ਮਾਰਨੀ; ਟੱਕਰ (ਟੈਨਿਸ ਵਿਚ); ਬਰਬਾਦੀ (ਵੈਪਾਰ ਆਦਿ ਦੀ)

smear (ਸਮਿਅ*) *v n* ਲਿਬੇੜਨਾ; ਮਲਣਾ, ਧੁੰਦਲਾ ਕਰਨਾ, ਅਸਪਸ਼ਟ ਬਣਾ ਦੇਣਾ; ਦਾਗ਼ੀ ਕਰਨਾ; ਵਿਗਾੜਨਾ; ਬਦਨਾਮ ਕਰਨਾ; ਦਾਗ਼, ਧੱਬਾ, ਕਲੰਕ; ਲੇਪ

smell (ਸਮੈੱਲ) *n v* ਸੁਗੰਧ, ਗੰਧ, ਬੂ, ਮੁਸ਼ਕ; ਸੁੰਘਣਾ; ਖ਼ੁਸ਼ਬੂ ਦੇਣੀ, ਗੰਧਯੁਕਤ ਹੋਣਾ; ਸੜ ਜਾਣਾ, ਸੜ੍ਹਾਂਦ ਮਾਰਨੀ; ਸੂਹ ਕੱਢ ਲੈਣੀ, ਖੋਜ ਕੱਢਣਾ; ~ing ਗੰਧ, ਬਾਸ; ਗੰਧਯੁਕਤ, ਖ਼ੁਸ਼ਬੂਦਾਰ

smelt *v* ਕੱਚੀ ਧਾਤ ਨੂੰ ਗਾਲਣਾ (ਪਿਘਲਾਉਣਾ)

smicker ('ਸਮਿਕਅ*) *n v* ਬਣਾਉਟੀ ਹਾਸਾ; ਹੱਸਣਾ; ਮੂਰਖਾਂ ਵਾਂਗ ਹੱਸਣਾ, ਦੰਦ ਕੱਢਣਾ

smile (ਸਮਾਇਲ) *n v* ਮੁਸਕਾਨ, ਮੁਸਕਰਾਹਟ; ਮੁਸਕਾਉਣਾ, ਖ਼ੁਸ਼ ਹੋਣਾ, ਪ੍ਰਸੰਨਤਾ ਵਿਚ ਹੋਣਾ

smog (ਸਮੌਗ) ਧੁਆਂਖੀ ਧੁੰਦ

smoke (ਸਮਅਉਕ) *n v* ਧੂੰਆਂ, ਸਿਗਰਟ ਪੀਣ ਦੀ ਕਿਰਿਆ; (ਬੋਲ) ਸਿਗਰਟ; ਦਮ, ਹੁੱਕੇ ਦੇ ਸੂਟੇ; (ਚਿਮਨੀ ਦਾ) ਧੂੰ ਕੱਢਣਾ; ਧੁਖਣਾ; ਤਾੜ ਜਾਣਾ, ਸਮਝ ਜਾਣਾ; ~y ਧੁਆਂਖਿਆ, ਧੂੰ ਨਾਲ ਭਰਿਆ

smooth (ਸਮੂਦ) *a v* ਸਮਤਲ; ਚਿਕਨਾ, ਮੁਲਾਇਮ, ਕੁਲਾ; (ਪਾਣੀ ਦਾ ਤਲ) ਸ਼ਾਂਤ; ਰਵਾਂ; ਸੁਹਾਵਣਾ, (ਸਫ਼ਰ) ਨਿਰਵਿਘਨ; ਮਿਲਣਸਾਰ (ਸੁਭਾਅ, ਵਿਹਾਰ); ਸਮਤਲ ਕਰਨਾ, ਚਿਕਨਾ ਬਣਾਉਣਾ, ਹਮਵਾਰ ਕਰਨਾ; ~spoken,

~tongued ਮਿਠਬੋਲਾ; ਖ਼ੁਸ਼ਾਮਦੀ

smother ('ਸਮਅੱਦਅ*) *v* ਗਲ ਘੁੱਟਣਾ; ਸਾਹ ਘੁੱਟ ਕੇ ਮਾਰ ਦੇਣਾ; (ਮੁਆਮਲੇ ਨੂੰ) ਦਬਾਈ ਰੱਖਣਾ; ਜ਼ਾਹਰ ਨਾ ਹੋਣ ਦੇਣਾ

smuggle ('ਸਮਅੱਗਲ) *v* (ਕਾਨੂੰਨ ਵਿਰੁਧ) ਮਾਲ ਦੇਸ਼ ਤੋਂ ਬਾਹਰ ਭੇਜਣਾ ਜਾਂ ਅੰਦਰ ਲਿਆਉਣਾ, ਛੁਪਾ ਦੇਣਾ; ਚੁੰਗੀ ਚੋਰੀ ਕਰਨੀ; ਤਸਕਰੀ ਕਰਨੀ

smuggling ('ਸਮਅੱਗਲਿਙ) *n* ਚੁੰਗੀ ਚੋਰੀ, ਚੋਰੀ ਛਿਪਾ ਵਪਾਰ, ਕਾਨੂੰਨ ਵਿਰੁੱਧ ਮਾਲ ਅਯਾਤ ਨਿਰਯਾਤ

snack (ਸਨੈਕ) *n* ਹਿੱਸਾ, ਅੰਸ਼; ਹਲਕਾ ਭੋਜਨ

snag (ਸਨੈਗ) *n* ਖੁੰਢ, ਕੱਟਿਆ ਨੋਕਦਾਰ ਮੁੱਢ; ਗੰਢ

snake (ਸਨੇਇਕ) *n v* ਸੱਪ; ਦਗ਼ੇਬਾਜ਼ ਮਨੁੱਖ

snap (ਸਨੈਪ) *v n* ਅਚਨਚੇਤ ਵੱਢ ਲੈਣਾ, ਕਿਸੇ ਦੀ ਗੱਲ ਟੁੱਕਣੀ; ਅਚਾਨਕ ਖਿਝ ਕੇ ਬੋਲਣਾ; ਝੱਟ ਫੋਟੋ ਲੈ ਲੈਣੀ; ਕੜਾਕਾ, ਖੜਾਕ; ਫੁਰਤੀ, ਜੋਸ਼; ਸਧਾਰਨ ਫੋਟੋ

snare (ਸਨੇਅ*) *n v* ਫਾਹੀ, ਕੁੜੱਕੀ, ਜਾਲ, ਫੰਧਾ; ਧੋਖੇ ਨਾਲ ਅੜਾ ਦੇਣਾ, ਫਸਾ ਦੇਣਾ

snatch (ਸਨੈਚ) *v n* ਖੋਹਣਾ, ਖੋਹ ਲੈਣਾ, ਝਪਟ ਮਾਰਨੀ; ਲੈ ਕੇ ਭੱਜ ਜਾਣਾ; ਅਚਨਚੇਤ ਫੜਨਾ, ਥੋੜੇ ਸਮੇਂ ਦਾ ਆਵੇਸ਼

sneer (ਸਨਿਅ*) *v* ਮਖੌਲ ਉਡਾਉਣਾ, ਹਾਸਾ ਉਡਾਉਣਾ; ਨੀਚ ਸਮਝਣਾ, ਤੁੱਛ ਸਮਝਣਾ; ਤਾਅਨਾ ਮਾਰਨਾ

sneeze (ਸਨੀਜ਼) *n v* ਛਿੱਕ, ਨਿੱਛ; ਛਿੱਕਣਾ, ਨਿੱਛ ਮਾਰਨੀ

sniff (ਸਨਿਫ਼) *v n* ਨਕ ਵਿਚ ਚੜ੍ਹਾਉਣਾ, ਸਾਹ ਨਾਲ ਨੱਕ ਵਿਚ ਅੰਦਰ ਨੂੰ ਖਿੱਚਣਾ; ਸੁਰੜ-ਸੁਰੜ ਕਰਨਾ; ਨੱਕ ਵਿਚ ਅੰਦਰ ਨੂੰ ਖਿੱਚਿਆ ਸਾਹ; ~y ਹਕਾਰਤ ਭਰਿਆ; ਬਦਬੂ ਵਾਲਾ

snivel ('ਸਨਿਵ੍ਲ) *v n* ਨੱਕ ਵਗਣਾ, ਸੂੰ-ਸੂੰ ਕਰਨਾ, ਨੱਕ ਨਾਲ ਸੁਰੜ-ਸੁਰੜ ਕਰਨਾ; ਡੁਸਕਣਾ, ਬੁਸਕਣਾ; ਨੱਕ ਦੀ ਸੁਰੜ-ਸੁਰੜ

snob (ਸਨੌਬ) *n* ਬੜੀ ਫੂੰ-ਫਾਂ ਵਾਲਾ, ਆਕੜਖ਼ਾਨ, ਪਾਟੇਖ਼ਾਂ, ਹੋਛਾ, ਨੀਵੇਂ ਵਿਚਾਰਾਂ ਵਾਲਾ; ~bery ਘਮੰਡ, ਫੂੰ-ਫਾਂ, ਫੋਕੀ ਆਕੜ

snoop (ਸਨੂਪ) *v* ਲੁਕੇ-ਛਿਪੇ ਆਉਣਾ ਜਾਣਾ, ਮੁਖ਼ਬਰੀ ਕਰਨਾ, ਨਾਜਾਇਜ਼ ਦਖ਼ਲ ਦੇਣਾ

snooze (ਸਨੂਜ਼) *v n* ਥੋੜ੍ਹੇ ਚਿਰ ਲਈ ਸੌਣਾ; ਉਂਘਲਾਉਣਾ; ਉਂਘ

snore (ਸਨੋ*) *n v* ਘੁਰਾੜੇ; ਘੁਰਾੜੇ ਮਾਰਨੇ

snout (ਸਨਾਉਟ) *n* ਥੁਥਨੀ, ਥੁੰਨੀ; ਬੂਥੀ

snow (ਸਨਅਉ) *n v* ਬਦਲਾਂ ਵਿਚੋਂ ਡਿਗਣ ਵਾਲੀ ਬਰਫ਼; ਬਰਫ਼ ਪੈਣੀ, ਬਰਫ਼ ਡਿੱਗਣੀ; ~fall ਬਰਫ਼ਬਾਰੀ

snub (ਸਨਅੱਬ) *v n* ਝਿੜਕ ਦੇਣਾ, ਝਾੜ ਦੇਣਾ, ਡਾਂਟਣਾ; ਝਿੜਕ, ਝਾੜ, ਡਾਂਟ

snuff *v n* ਨਸਵਾਰ ਲੈਣੀ; ਨਸਵਾਰ

so (ਸਅਉ) *adv conj int pron* ਏਨਾ, ਇੰਨਾ; ਇੰਝ, ਇਸ ਤਰ੍ਹਾਂ; ਇਸ ਲਈ, ਇਸ ਕਰਕੇ, ਸੱਚ-ਮੁਚ ਹੀ, ਅਸਲ ਵਿਚ; ਇਹੋ ਗੱਲ; ~and so ਫਲਾਣਾ ਆਦਮੀ, ਫਲਾਣੀ ਚੀਜ਼; ਫਲਾਣਾ-ਢਿਮਕਾ; ~called ਕਥਿਤ, ਨਾਮ ਨਿਹਾਦ; ~far as ਜਿਥੋਂ ਤਕ ਕਿ; ~so (ਬੋਲ) ਠੀਕ-ਠਾਕ, ਨਾ ਚੰਗਾ ਨਾ ਮਾੜਾ, ਗੁਜ਼ਾਰੇ ਮੁਆਫ਼ਕ

soak (ਸਅਉਕ) *v n* ਭਿਓਂਣਾ, ਪਾਣੀ ਵਿਚ ਡੋਬਣਾ; ਪੂਰੀ ਤਰ੍ਹਾਂ ਭਿੱਜ ਜਾਣਾ; ਰੱਜ ਕੇ ਪੀਣਾ; ਡੁਬਾਉ; ਜ਼ੋਰ ਦੀ ਬਰਸਾਤ

soap (ਸਅਉਪ) *n v* ਸਾਬਣ; ਸਾਬਣ ਨਾਲ ਧੋਣਾ; ਚਾਪਲੂਸੀ ਕਰਨੀ

soar (ਸੋ*) *v* ਹਵਾ ਵਿਚ ਤਰਨਾ; ਉੱਚੀ ਸੋਚ-

ਉਡਾਰੀ ਲਾਉਂਣੀ; ਉਚਾਈ ਤੇ ਚੜ੍ਹਨ

sob (ਸੋਬ) *n v* ਡੁਸਕੀ, ਸਿਸਕੀ; ਡੁਸਕਣਾ; ਹੁਬਕਣਾ, ਸਿਸਕੀਆਂ ਲੈਣੀਆਂ, ਹੌਕੇ ਭਰਨੇ

sober (ਸਅਉਬਅ*) *a v* ਗੰਭੀਰ, ਸੁਝਵਾਨ, ਸੰਜਮੀ; ਸ਼ਾਂਤ ਕਰਨਾ, ਹੋਸ਼ ਵਿਚ ਹੋਣਾ; **~ness** ਸਥਿਰ ਬੁੱਧੀ, ਗੰਭੀਰਤਾ, ਸਥਿਰਤਾ, ਵਿਚਾਰਸ਼ੀਲਤਾ

sociable ('ਸਅਉਸ਼ਅਬਲ) *a n* ਮਿਲਣਸਾਰ, ਮਿਲਾਪੜਾ, ਸਨੇਹੀ, ਆਪਸੀ, ਦੋਸਤਾਨਾ; ਵਾਧੂ ਸ਼ਿਸ਼ਟਾਚਾਰ ਤੋਂ ਬਿਨਾ

social ('ਸਅਉਸ਼ਲ) *a n* ਸਮਾਜਕ, ਸਮਾਜੀ ਮਿਲਾਪੜਾ, ਆਪਸੀ; **~security** ਸਮਾਜਕ ਸੁਰੱਖਿਆ; **~ism** ਸਮਾਜਵਾਦ, ਸਾਂਝੀਵਾਲਤਾ **~ist** ਸਮਾਜਵਾਦੀ **~ize** ਸਮਾਜੀਕਰਨ ਕਰਨਾ

society (ਸਅ'ਸਾਇਅਟਿ) *n* ਸਮਾਜ, ਭਾਈਚਾਰਾ; ਬਿਰਾਦਰੀ; ਉਚ ਵਰਗ; ਵੱਡੇ ਲੋਕ; ਸਭਾ, ਪਰਿਸ਼ਦ, ਸਮਿਤੀ, ਸੰਘ; ਸੰਗਤ

sociology ('ਸਅਉਸਿ'ਔਲਅਜਿ) *n* ਸਮਾਜ-ਵਿਗਿਆਨ, ਸਮਾਜ-ਸ਼ਾਸਤਰ

sock (ਸੌਕ) *n v* ਜੁਰਾਬ, ਪਟਾਵਾ; ਡੀਮ ਮਾਰਨੀ, ਕੋਈ ਚੀਜ਼ ਵਗਾਹ ਕੇ ਮਾਰਨੀ

sodomite ('ਸੌਡਅਮਾਇਟ) *n* ਲੋਂਡੇਬਾਜ਼, ਮੁੰਡੇਬਾਜ਼; ਪਸ਼ੂ-ਸੰਭੋਗੀ

sodomy ('ਸੌਡਅਮਿ) *n* ਮੁੰਡੇਬਾਜ਼ੀ, ਲੋਂਡੇਬਾਜ਼ੀ

soft (ਸੌਫਟ) *a adv* ਕੂਲਾ, ਨਰਮ, ਮੁਲਾਇਮ, ਚਿਕਨਾ; ਲਚਕਦਾਰ, ਢਿਲਵਾਂ, ਸੁਹਾਵਣਾ, ਨਿਰਬਲ, ਪੋਲਾ, ਜ਼ਨਾਨਾ; (ਰਾਗ) ਮੱਧਮ, ਧੀਮੀ ਸੁਰ ਵਿਚ; **~currency** ਨਾ-ਬਦਲਣਯੋਗ ਮੁਦਰਾ; **~en** ਨਰਮ ਹੋਣਾ, ਢਲਣਾ; ਮੋਮ ਹੋਣਾ ਵਾਲਾ; ਮੱਧਮ ਕਰਨਾ, ਧੀਮਾ ਕਰਨਾ; **~ness** ਕੋਮਲਤਾ, ਨਰਮੀ, ਨਿਮਰਤਾ; **~ware**

ਕੰਪਿਊਟਰ ਦਾ ਪ੍ਰੋਗਰਾਮ **~y** ਸਿੱਧੜ, ਸਿੱਧਾ-ਸਾਦਾ (ਆਦਮੀ), ਭੋਲਾ-ਭਾਲਾ (ਮਨੁੱਖ); ਮੂਰਖ; ਕਮਜ਼ੋਰ (ਵਿਅਕਤੀ); ਛਿੱਲੀ ਕੁਲਫ਼ੀ

soil (ਸੌਇਲ) *v n* ਮੈਲਾ ਕਰਨਾ, ਲਿਬੇੜਨਾ; ਦਾਗ਼ ਪੈ ਜਾਣਾ; ਧੱਬਾ; ਮਿੱਟੀ, ਜ਼ਮੀਨ, ਦੇਸ਼, ਵਤਨ

sojourn ('ਸੌਜਅ:ਨ) *n v* ਥੋੜ੍ਹੇ ਸਮੇਂ ਦਾ ਡੇਰਾ; ਠਹਿਰਨਾ, ਰੁਕਣਾ, ਡੇਰਾ ਕਰਨਾ; ਟਿਕਣਾ

solace ('ਸੌਲਅਸ) *n v* ਦਿਲਾਸਾ, ਢਾਰਸ, ਧੀਰਜ, ਤੱਸਲੀ, ਹੌਸਲਾ; ਦਿਲਾਸਾ ਦੇਣਾ, ਤੱਸਲੀ ਦੇਣੀ; **~ment** ਢਾਰਸ, ਤੱਸਲੀ; ਦਿਲਾਸਾ

solar ('ਸਅਉਲ੍ਹ*) *a* ਸੂਰਜ ਦਾ, ਸੂਰਜੀ; **~system** ਸੌਰ-ਮੰਡਲ

solder ('ਸੌਲਡਅ*) *n v* ਧਾਤ ਦਾ ਟਾਂਕਾ; ਜੋੜ; ਟਾਂਕਾ ਲਾਉਣਾ; ਜੋੜ ਲਾਉਣਾ

soldier ('ਸਅਉਲਜਆ*) *n* ਫ਼ੌਜੀ ਸੈਨਕ; ਫ਼ੌਜ ਦਾ ਸਿਪਾਹੀ

sole (ਸਅਉਲ) *n a v* ਜੁੱਤੀ ਦਾ ਤਲਾ, (ਕਿਸੇ ਚੀਜ਼ ਦਾ) ਥੱਲਾ, ਪੇਂਦਾ, ਆਧਾਰ; ਇੱਕਲਾ, ਇੱਕੋ-ਇਕ, ਸਿਰਫ਼; (ਕਾ) ਕੰਵਾਰਾ, ਛੜਾ; ਜੁੱਤੀ ਦਾ ਤਲਾ ਲਾਉਣਾ

solemn ('ਸੌਲਅਮ) *a* ਗੰਭੀਰ, ਸੰਜੀਦਾ; ਵਿਧੀ-ਅਨੁਕੂਲ; ਮਰਯਾਦਾਪੂਰਵਕ, ਰਸਮ; **~ity** ਗੰਭੀਰਤਾ, ਸੰਜੀਦਗੀ; ਮਹਾਨਤਾ, ਠਾਠ; ਧਾਰਮਕ ਰਸਮ, ਧਾਰਮਕ ਸੰਸਕਾਰ; ਪਵਿੱਤਰਤਾ; **~ize** ਮਨਾਉਣਾ (ਤਿਉਹਾਰ, ਉਤਸਵ ਆਦਿ); (ਰੀਤੀ, ਰਸਮ) ਵਿਧੀ ਅਨੁਸਾਰ ਨਿਭਾਉਣੀ

solicit (ਸਅ'ਲਿਸਿਟ) *v* ਬੇਨਤੀ ਕਰਨੀ, ਯਾਚਨਾ ਕਰਨੀ, ਅਰਜ਼ ਕਰਨੀ; **~ation** ਬੇਨਤੀ, ਮਿੰਨਤ, ਯਾਚਨਾ; **~or** ਯਾਚਕ; ਉਪਵਕੀਲ; ਮੁਕਦਮਾ ਚਲਾਣ ਦੀ ਰਾਇ ਦੇਣ ਵਾਲਾ

solid ('ਸੌਲਿਡ) *a* ਠੋਸ, ਨਿੱਗਰ; ਪੱਕਾ, ਦ੍ਰਿੜ੍ਹ,

ਮਜ਼ਬੂਤ; ਸੁਖ; ਤਰਕਸੰਗਤ, ਪ੍ਰਮਾਣਤ; ਸੱਚਾ, ਵਾਸਤਵਿਕ, ਅਸਲੀ; **~arity** ਏਕਤਾ, ਸੰਗਠਨ, ਇਕਜੁੱਟਤਾ

solitary ('ਸੌਲਿਟ(ਅ)ਰਿ) *a n* ਇੱਕਲਾ, ਇਕੋ-ਇਕ, ਕੱਲਮ-ਕੱਲਾ; ਲੁੱਗਾ, ਸੁੰਨਸਾਨ; ਇਕਾਂਤ, ਇਕਾਂਤਵਾਸੀ; ਵੈਰਾਗੀ

solitude ('ਸੌਲਿਟਯੂਡ) *n* ਇਕਾਂਤ, ਸੁੰਵ, ਸੁੰਨਸਾਨ; ਇੱਕਲਾਪਨ

soluble ('ਸੌਲਯੁਬਲ) *a* ਘੁਲਣਹਾਰ; ਹੱਲ ਕਰਨ ਯੋਗ, ਸੁਲਝਾਉਣ ਯੋਗ

solution (ਸਅ'ਲੂਸ਼ਨ) *n* ਘੋਲ, ਘੁਲਣ, ਘੁਲਾਈ, (ਸਮੱਸਿਆ ਦਾ) ਉਪਾਉ; ਸੁਲਝਾਉ; (ਗੁੰਝ) ਹੱਲ; ਮੁਕਤੀ

solve (ਸੌਲਵ) *v* (ਗੁੰਝ) ਸਵਾਲ ਹੱਲ ਕਰਨਾ; ਬੁੱਝਣਾ, ਹੱਲ ਕੱਢਣਾ; (ਸਮੱਸਿਆ) ਸੁਲਝਾਉਣੀ, ਖੋਲ੍ਹਣੀ

sombre ('ਸੌਮਬਅ*) *a* ਹਨੇਰਾ, ਧੁੰਦਲਾ, ਕਾਲਾ; ਉਦਾਸ, ਮੁਰਝਾਇਆ

some (ਸਅੱਮ) *a pron adv* ਕੋਈ; ਕੁਝ, ਕਈ, ਕਿੰਨੇ ਹੀ; **~how** ਕਿਸੇ ਨਾ ਕਿਸੇ ਤਰ੍ਹਾਂ, ਕਿਸੇ ਤਰ੍ਹਾਂ, ਕਿਵੇਂ ਨਾ ਕਿਵੇਂ; **~one** ਕੋਈ, ਕੋਈ ਆਦਮੀ; **~thing** ਕੁਝ, ਕੋਈ, ਕੁਝ ਨਾ ਕੁਝ, ਕੁਝ ਕੁ; **~time** ਕੁਝ ਚਿਰ, ਥੋੜ੍ਹਾ ਸਮਾਂ; ਕਿਸੇ ਵੇਲੇ; **~what** ਕੁਝ ਕੁ, ਥੋੜ੍ਹਾ ਜਿਹਾ, ਕੋਈ ਚੀਜ਼; **~where** ਕਿਤੇ, ਕਿੱਧਰੇ, ਕਿਸੇ ਪਾਸੇ

somersault ('ਸਅਮਅਸੋਲਟ) *n* ਪੁੱਠੀ ਛਾਲ, ਉਲਟ-ਚੱਕਰ, ਬਾਜ਼ੀ (ਪਾਉਣੀ), ਬਾਜ਼ੀਆਂ (ਪਾਉਣੀਆਂ), ਕਲਾਬਾਜ਼ੀ

son (ਸਅੱਨ) *n* ਪੁੱਤਰ, ਬੇਟਾ, ਸੰਤਾਨ; **~in law** ਜਵਾਈ, ਦਾਮਾਦ

sonant ('ਸਅਉਨਅੰਟ) *a n* ਧੁਨੀਪੂਰਨ, ਨਾਦੀ, ਸੁਰੀਲਾ

song (ਸੌਙ) *n* ਗੀਤ; ਪਦ; ਗਾਉਣ

soon (ਸੂਨ) *adv* ਛੇਤੀ, ਤੁਰੰਤ, ਸ਼ੀਘਰ, ਹੁਣੇ ਹੀ, ਥੋੜ੍ਹੇ ਚਿਰ ਨੂੰ

soot (ਸੁਟ) *n v* ਧੁਆਂਖ, ਕਾਲਖ; ਧੁਆਂਖਣਾ, ਕਾਲਾ ਕਰਨਾ, ਕਾਲਖ ਲਾਉਣੀ

soothe (ਸੂਦ) *v* (ਗੁੱਸਾ) ਠੰਡਾ ਕਰਨਾ; ਸ਼ਾਂਤ ਕਰਨਾ, (ਪੀੜ) ਘਟ ਕਰਨੀ, ਖ਼ੁਸ਼ਾਮਦ ਕਰਨੀ

sophistic, ~al (ਸਅਫ਼ਿਸਟਿਕ, ਸਅਫ਼ਿਸਟਿਕਲ) *a* ਝੂਠੀ ਦਲੀਲ ਵਾਲਾ; ਕੁਤਰਕੀ, ਧੋਖੇ ਵਾਲਾ; **~ated** ਦੁਨੀਆਦਾਰ; ਸਿਆਣਪ, ਭਰਪੂਰ, ਵਿਵੇਕਪੂਰਨ; ਨਫ਼ੀਸ; **~ation** ਦੁਨੀਆਦਾਰੀ, ਸਿਆਣਪ, ਸੂਝ, ਨਫ਼ਾਸਤ

sordid ('ਸੋਡਿਡ) *a* ਸ਼ੋਹਦਾ, ਸੂਮ; ਹੋਛਾ, ਨੀਚ ਘਿਣਾਉਣਾ, ਭੈੜਾ

sore (ਸੌ*) *a n adv* ਦੁਖਦਾ; ਖਿਝਿਆ, ਅੱਕਿਆ, ਦੁੱਖੀ; (ਗੱਲ) ਚੁੱਭਵੀਂ; ਜ਼ਖ਼ਮ; ਡਾਢਾ

sorrow ('ਸੌਰਅਉ) *n* ਉਦਾਸੀ, ਸੋਗ, ਗ਼ਮ, ਅਫ਼ਸੋਸ, ਕਲੇਸ਼, ਚਿੰਤਾ, ਦੁੱਖ; ਬਿਪਤਾ, ਸੰਕਟ; **~ful** ਉਦਾਸ, ਗ਼ਮਗੀਨ, ਸੋਗੀ

sorry ('ਸੌਰਿ) *a* ਦੁੱਖੀ, ਉਦਾਸ, ਗ਼ਮਗੀਨ; ਪਛਤਾਉਂਦਾ, ਦਿਲਗੀਰ; ਹੀਣਾ

sort (ਸੌਟ) *n v* ਪ੍ਰਕਾਰ, ਕਿਸਮ, ਵੰਨਗੀ; ਵੱਖ ਵੱਖ ਕਰਨਾ, ਛਾਂਟਣਾ; **~ing** ਛੰਟਾਈ, ਛਾਂਟ, ਪ੍ਰਿਥਕਕਰਨ, ਵਰਗੀਕਰਨ

soul (ਸਅਉਲ) *n* ਆਤਮਾ, ਰੂਹ; ਅੰਤਹਕਰਨ, ਆਪਾ, ਮਨ, ਚਿੱਤ, ਦਿਲ; ਜੀਵ; **~less** ਨਿਰਜੀਵ, ਪ੍ਰਾਣਹੀਣ; ਉਤਸ਼ਾਹਹੀਣ; ਬੇਜ਼ਮੀਰਾ

sound (ਸਾਉਂਡ) *a adv* ਅਵਾਜ਼, ਧੁਨੀ, ਖੜਾਕ; ਉਚਾਰਨ; ਅਵਾਜ਼ ਨਿਕਲਣੀ, ਧੁਨੀ ਉਤਪੰਨ

ਹੋਣੀ; ਰਾਜ਼ੀ-ਬਾਜ਼ੀ, ਤੰਦਰੁਸਤ, ਚੰਗਾ-ਭਲਾ; ਠੀਕ ਹਾਲਤ ਵਿਚ

soup (ਸੂਪ) *n* ਤਰੀ, ਸ਼ੋਰਬਾ, ਸੂਪ

sour ('ਸਾਉਅ*) *a v* ਖੱਟਾ (ਸੁਆਦ); (ਰੋਟੀ) ਬੁਸੀ ਹੋਈ, ਖ਼ਮੀਰੀ; (ਵਾਸ਼ਨਾ) ਖ਼ਮੀਰ ਵਰਗੀ

source (ਸੋਸ) *n* ਸਰੋਤ, ਨਿਕਾਸ, ਪੈਦਾ ਹੋਣ ਵਾਲੀ ਥਾਂ; ਮੂਲ, ਮੁੱਢ

south (ਸਾਉਥ) *n a adv* ਦੱਖਣ, ਦੱਖਣ ਦਿਸ਼ਾ; ਦੱਖਣੀ

souvenir ('ਸੂਵ਼(ਅ)'ਨਿਅ*) *n* ਯਾਦਗਾਰ, ਨਿਸ਼ਾਨੀ, ਸਮਾਰਕ

sovereign ('ਸੌਵ਼੍ਰਿਨ) *a n* ਉੱਤਮ, ਉੱਚਤਮ, ਸਿਰਮੌਰ, ਸਿਰਤਾਜ; ਸਰਬ-ਸੱਤਾਧਾਰੀ; ~**ty** ਰਾਜਗੀਰੀ, ਹਕੂਮਤ; ਸਰਬ ਸਮਰੱਥਾ, ਪ੍ਰਭੁਤਾ

sow (ਸੌਅਉ) *v* ਬੀਜਣਾ, ਬੀ ਪਾਉਣਾ; ਪ੍ਰਚਾਰ ਕਰਨਾ

space (ਸਪੇਇਸ) *n v* ਖ਼ਾਲੀ ਥਾਂ, ਵਿੱਥ; ਪੁਲਾੜ, ਆਕਾਸ਼, ਖ਼ਲਾਅ; ਵਿਸਤਾਰ; ਵਿਚਾਲੇ ਦਾ ਸਮਾਂ; ਸਮੇਂ ਦਾ ਅੰਤਰ; ਵਿੱਥ ਤੇ ਰੱਖਣਾ, ਵਿੱਥ ਦੇਣੀ; ~**craft** ਪੁਲਾੜੀ ਜਹਾਜ਼; ~**man** ਪੁਲਾੜੀ ਯਾਤਰੀ

spacious (ਸਪੇਇਸ਼ਅਸ) *a* ਖੁੱਲ੍ਹਾ, ਮੋਕਲਾ, ਵਿਸ਼ਾਲ, ਲੰਮਾ-ਚੌੜਾ; ~**ness** ਵਿਸਤਾਰ, ਫੈਲਾਉ, ਲੰਮਾਈ-ਚੌੜਾਈ, ਗੁੰਜਾਇਸ਼

spade (ਸਪੇਇਡ) *n* ਬੇਲਚਾ, ਫਾਉੜਾ, ਕਹੀ; ~**work** ਮੁੱਢਲਾ ਸਖ਼ਤ ਕੰਮ, ਕਰੜੀ ਮਿਹਨਤ ਵਾਲਾ ਆਰੰਭਕ ਕੰਮ, ਮੋਟਾ ਮੋਟਾ ਕੰਮ

spado ('ਸਪੇਇਡਅਉ) *a* ਕਮਜ਼ੋਰ ਆਦਮੀ, ਨਪੁੰਸਕ ਵਿਅਕਤੀ; ਹੀਜੜਾ

span (ਸਪੈਨ) *n v* ਗਿੱਠ, ਅਵਧੀ, ਕਾਲ; ਥੋੜ੍ਹਾ ਸਮਾਂ ਜਾਂ ਥੋੜ੍ਹੀ ਦੂਰੀ; ਪੂਰਾ ਵਿਸਤਾਰ ਜਾਂ ਖਿਲਾਰ; 9 ਇੰਚ; ਗਿੱਠਾਂ ਨਾਲ ਮਿਣਨਾ; ਦਰਿਆ ਆਦਿ ਉੱਤੇ ਪੁਲ ਬਣਾਉਣਾ; ਆਰਪਾਰ ਫੈਲਣਾ

spare (ਸਪੇਅ*) *a v* ਵਾਧੂ, ਫ਼ਾਲਤੂ; ਵਿਹਲਾ, ਖ਼ਾਲੀ (ਸਮਾਂ); ਲੋੜ ਨਾ ਸਮਝਣੀ, ਛੱਡਣਾ, ਵਿਹਲਾ ਕਰਨਾ, ਛੋਟ ਕਰਨੀ, ਵਰਤੋਂ ਵਿਚ ਨਾ ਲਿਆਉਣਾ, ਲਾਂਭੇ ਰੱਖਣਾ; ਬਚਾ ਰੱਖਣਾ; ~**part** ਫ਼ਾਲਤੂ ਪੁਰਜ਼ੇ

spark (ਸਪਾ:ਕ) *n v* ਚਿਣਗਾ; ਬਿਜਲੀ ਦੀ ਚੰਗਿਆੜੀ; (ਗੁਣ ਦੀ) ਝਲਕ; ਚੰਗਿਆੜੀਆਂ ਨਿਕਲਣੀਆਂ; ~**ie** ਲਿਸ਼ਕਣਾ, ਚਮਕਣਾ, ਝਲਕ ਮਾਰਨੀ; ਚੰਗਿਆੜੇ ਛੱਡਣੇ; ਲਿਸ਼ਕ, ਚਮਕ, ਝਲਕ, ਲਿਸ਼ਕਾਰਾ

sparrow ('ਸਪੈਰਅਉ) *n* ਚਿੜੀ

spawl (ਸਪੋਲ) *n v* ਥੁੱਕ, ਲਾਰ, ਥੁੱਕਣਾ, ਲਾਰਾਂ ਛੱਡਣੀਆਂ

speak (ਸਪੀਕ) *v* ਬੋਲਣਾ, ਕਹਿਣਾ, ਦੱਸਣਾ; ਗੱਲਬਾਤ ਕਰਨੀ; ~**er** ਵਕਤਾ, ਬੋਲਣ ਵਾਲਾ

spear (ਸਪਿਅ*) *v* ਬਰਛਾ, ਬੱਲਮ, ਨੇਜਾ, ਬਰਛਾ ਮਾਰਨਾ; ~**head** ਅੱਗੇ ਵਧਾਉਣਾ, ਆਗੂ, ਹਰਾਵਲ; ~**mint** ਪੁਦਨਾ

special (ਸਪੈੱਸ਼ੱਲ) *a* ਖ਼ਾਸ, ਵਿਸ਼ੇਸ਼, ਵਿਸ਼ਿਸ਼ਟ; ਅਸਾਧਾਰਨ; ~**ist** ਵਿਸ਼ੇਸ਼ੱਗ; ~**ity** ਵਿਸ਼ੇਸ਼ ਗੁਣ; ਵਿਸ਼ੇਸ਼ਤਾ; ~**ization** ਵਿਸ਼ੇਸ਼ੱਗਤਾ, ਮੁਹਾਰਤ; ~**ize** ਵਿਸ਼ੇਸ਼ਤਾ ਦੇਣੀ; ~**ized** ਵਿਸ਼ਿਸ਼ਟ, ਵਿਸ਼ੇਸ਼ੀਕ੍ਰਿਤ

species ('ਸਪੀਸ਼ੀਜ਼) *n* ਜਾਤੀ, ਉਪ-ਜਾਤੀ, ਨਸਲ; ਸ਼੍ਰੇਣੀ, ਕੋਟੀ, ਵਰਗ

specific (ਸਪਅ'ਸਿਫ਼ਿਕ) *a* ਵਿਸ਼ੇਸ਼, ਖ਼ਾਸ; ਉਚੇਚਾ; ਨਿਸ਼ਚਤ; ਜਿਨਸੀ, ਜਾਤੀਗਤ; ~**ation** ਸਪਸ਼ਟਤਾ; ਵਿਸ਼ੇਸ਼ ਵਿਵਰਨ

specified ('ਸਪੈੱਸਿਫ਼ਾਇਡ) *a* ਨਿਸ਼ਚਤ ਉੱਲਿਖਤ

specify ('ਸਪੈਸਿਫ਼ਾਇ) v ਸਪਸ਼ਟ ਕਰਨਾ, ਨਿਸ਼ਚਤ ਕਰਨਾ; ਵਿਸ਼ੇਸ਼ ਢੰਗ ਨਾਲ ਕਹਿਣਾ

specimen ('ਸਪੈਸਿਮਅਨ) n ਨਮੂਨਾ, ਵੰਨਗੀ, ਉਦਾਹਰਨ

spectacle ('ਸਪੈੱਕਟਅਲ) n ਨਜ਼ਾਰਾ, ਝਾਕੀ, (ਬਵ) ਐਨਕ; ~d ਐਨਕ ਵਾਲਾ, ਚਸ਼ਮਾਧਾਰੀ

spectator (ਸਪੈੱਕ'ਟੇਇਟਅ*) n ਦਰਸ਼ਕ, ਤਮਾਸ਼ਬੀਨ, ਦ੍ਰਸ਼ਟਾ

spectrum ('ਸਪੈੱਕਟਰਅਮ) n ਕਿਰਨ-ਪਰਛਾਈਂ, ਵਰਣ-ਕ੍ਰਮ; ਰੰਗ-ਦ੍ਰਿਸ਼; ਸਿਲਸਲਾ

speculate ('ਸਪੈੱਕਯੁਲੇਇਟ) v ਅਨੁਮਾਨ ਲਾਉਣਾ, ਅੰਦਾਜ਼ਾ ਲਾਉਣਾ, ਖ਼ਿਆਲੀ ਘੋੜੇ ਦੁੜਾਉਣੇ

speculation ('ਸਪੈੱਕਯੁ'ਲੇਇਸ਼ਨ) n ਅਨੁਮਾਨ, ਅੰਦਾਜ਼ਾ, ਕਿਆਸ, ਸੱਟਾਬਾਜ਼ੀ; ਚਿੰਤਨ

speculative ('ਸਪੈੱਕਯੁਲਅਟਿਵ਼) a ਕਾਲਪਨਕ, ਖ਼ਿਆਲੀ, ਕਿਆਸੀ, ਵਿਚਾਰਸ਼ੀਲ; ਸੱਟੇ ਵਿਚ ਲੱਗਿਆ

speech (ਸਪੀਚ) n ਭਾਸ਼ਣ, ਤਕਰੀਰ, ਕਥਨ-ਸ਼ਕਤੀ; ਬੋਲ, ਬੋਲੀ; ~less ਬੇਜ਼ਬਾਨ, ਗੁੰਗਾ, ਚੁੱਪ, ਮੋਨ, ਖ਼ਮੋਸ਼; ਅਵਾਕ

speed (ਸਪੀਡ) n v ਗਤੀ, ਚਾਲ; ਛੁਹਤੀ, ਤੇਜ਼ੀ, ਤੀਬਰਤਾ; ਫੁਰਤੀ ਵਖਾਉਣੀ; ਛੇਤੀ ਘੱਲਣਾ; ਉਨੱਤੀ ਕਰਨੀ; ~y ਵੇਗਵਾਨ, ਵੇਗਪੂਰਨ, ਤੀਬਰ

spell (ਸਪੈੱਲ) n v ਮੰਤਰ, ਟੂਣਾ, ਆਕਰਸ਼ਣ; ਕੁਝ ਚਿਰ; ਸ਼ਬਦ-ਜੋੜ ਕਰਨਾ, ਹਿੱਜੇ ਕਰਨਾ; ~bound ਕੀਲਿਆ, ਮੋਹਤ, ਮੰਤਰ-ਮੁਗਧ; ~ing ਹਿੱਜੇ, ਸ਼ਬਦ-ਜੋੜ, ਵਰਣ-ਵਿਨਿਆਸ

spend (ਸਪੈਂਡ) v ਖ਼ਰਚਣਾ, ਖ਼ਰਚ ਕਰਨਾ, ਖ਼ਰਚ ਹੋ ਜਾਣਾ; ~thrift ਫ਼ਜ਼ੂਲ ਖ਼ਰਚ

sperm (ਸਪਅਃਮ) n ਨਰ ਦਾ ਵੀਰਜ; ਮਣੀ, ਸ਼ੁਕਰਾਣੂ

sphere ('ਸਫ਼ਿਅ*) n ਖੇਤਰ, ਦਾਇਰਾ; ਗੋਲਾ, ਆਕਾਸ਼ੀ ਪਿੰਡ

sphinx (ਸਫ਼ਿੰਕਸ) n ਨਰਸਿੰਘ, ਗੁੰਝਾ ਮਨੁੱਖ

spice (ਸਪਾਇਸ) n v ਮਸਾਲਾ, ਮਿਰਚ-ਮਸਾਲਾ; ਮਸਾਲੇਦਾਰ ਬਣਾਉਣਾ

spick and span ('ਸਪਿਕ ਅਨ'ਸਪੈਨ) a ਨਵਾਂ, ਕੋਰਾ, ਤਾਜ਼ਾ; ਨਵਾਂ-ਨਿਕੋਰ, ਚੁਸਤ

spicy ('ਸਪਾਇਸਿ) a ਮਸਾਲੇਦਾਰ; ਕਰਾਰਾ; ਚਟਕੀਲਾ, ਲੱਛੇਦਾਰ

spider ('ਸਪਾਇਡਅ*) n ਮੱਕੜੀ

spike (ਸਪਾਇਕ) n v ਤਿੱਖੀ ਨੋਕ; ਲੰਮਾ ਕਿੱਲ, ਨੋਕਦਾਰ ਸੀਖ; ਜੁੱਤੀ ਦੇ ਥੱਲੇ ਲੱਗੀ ਮੇਖ; ਸੁੰਥਾ; ਮੇਖਾਂ ਲਾਉਣੀਆਂ

spile (ਸਪਾਇਲ) n v ਕਿੱਲ, ਤਿੱਖੀ ਮੇਖ; ਕਿੱਲ ਲਾਉਣਾ, ਮੇਖ ਗੱਡਨੀ

spill (ਸਪਿਲ) v n ਡੋਲ੍ਹਣਾ, ਰੋੜ੍ਹਨਾ; ਡੁੱਲ੍ਹਣਾ; ਰੁੜ੍ਹਨਾ; ਵਗਾਣਾ; ਕਾਗਜ਼ ਜਾਂ ਲਕੜੀ ਦੀ ਘੱਤੀ

spin (ਸਪਿਨ) v n ਕੱਤਣਾ, ਪੂਣੀਆਂ ਕੱਤਣੀਆਂ, ਚਰਖਾ ਕੱਤਣਾ, ਤੱਕਲੀ ਨਾਲ ਵੱਟਣਾ; ਚੱਕਰੀ; ~ning ਕਤਾਈ, ਕੰਤਣ, ਘੁਣਨ, ਘੁਮਾਈ, ਚੱਕਰ; ~dle ਤੱਕਲਾ (ਚਰਖੇ ਦਾ); ਤੱਕਲੀ (ਵਾਟ; ਸੂਤ ਆਦਿ ਵੱਟਣ ਵਾਲੀ), ਫੇਰਨੀ; ਜੁਲਾਹੇ ਦੀ ਨੀਲ; ਧੁਰਾ, ਧੁਰੀ, ਲੱਠ (ਚਰਖੇ ਦੀ)

spinal ('ਸਪਾਇਨਲ) a ਰੀੜ੍ਹ ਦੀ ਹੱਡੀ ਦਾ; ~cord ਰੀੜ੍ਹ ਦੀ ਹੱਡੀ

spine (ਸਪਾਇਨ) n ਕੰਗਰੋੜ, ਸੂਲ; ਉੱਭਰਵਾਂ ਹਿੱਸਾ; ~less a ਬਿਨਾ ਕਮਰੋੜ, ਰੀੜ੍ਹ ਦੀ ਹੱਡੀ ਬਿਨਾ; ਨਿਤਾਣਾ, ਡਰਪੋਕ, ਕਮਜ਼ੋਰ

spinster ('ਸਪਿੰਸਟਅ*) n ਅਣਵਿਆਹੀ ਤੀਵੀਂ,

ਛੜੀ, ਬੁੱਢ-ਕੁਆਰੀ

spiral ('ਸਪਾਇਰਲ) *a n* ਚੱਕਰਦਾਰ, ਕੁੰਡਲਦਾਰ, ਚੂੜੀਦਾਰ; ਚੱਕਰਦਾਰ ਕਮਾਨੀ

spirit ('ਸਪਿਰਿਟ) *n v* ਆਤਮਾ, ਰੂਹ, ਜੀਵ-ਆਤਮਾ, ਪ੍ਰਾਣ, ਬ੍ਰਹਮ, ਪਰਮਾਤਮਾ; ਭੂਤ, ਪਰੇਤ; ਹਿੰਮਤ, ਹੌਸਲਾ, ਜੋਸ਼, ਖ਼ੁਸ਼ਦਿਲੀ, ਜ਼ਿੰਦਾਦਿਲੀ, ਚੜ੍ਹਦੀ ਕਲਾ ਵਾਲੀ ਦਸ਼ਾ, ਸਤ, ਸ਼ਰਾਬ; ਸਪਿਰਿਟ, (ਕਿਸੇ ਨੂੰ) ਪ੍ਰਸੰਨ ਕਰਨਾ, ਉਤਸ਼ਾਹਤ ਕਰਨਾ; ~**less** ਮੁਰਦਦਿਲ, ਬੇਹੌਸਲਾ, ਢਿੱਲੜ, ਫੋਸੜ; ਉਦਾਸ; ~**ual** ਆਤਮਕ, ਰੂਹਾਨੀ, ਆਤਮਾ ਸਬੰਧੀ, ਅਧਿਆਤਮਕ, ਮਜ਼ਹਬੀ, ਪਰਮਾਰਥਕ, ਅਸਰੀਰੀ, ਅਮੂਰਤ; ~**ualism** ਆਤਮਵਾਦ, ਅਧਿਆਤਮਵਾਦ, ਅਧਿਆਤਮਕਤਾ; ~**ualist** ਅਧਿਆਤਮਵਾਦੀ, ਬ੍ਰਹਮਵਾਦੀ; ~**uality** ਅਧਿਆਤਮਕਤਾ, ਅਧਿਆਤਮ, ਰੂਹਾਨੀਅਤ

spit (ਸਪਿਟ) *v n* ਥੁੱਕਣਾ, ਥੁੱਕ ਸੁੱਟਣਾ; ਗੁੱਸੇ ਵਿਚ ਮੂੰਹੋਂ ਕੱਢਣਾ; ਸੀਖ ਨਾਲ ਕਬਾਬ ਚੰਭੇੜਨਾ; ਫੁੰਕਾਰ, ਥੁੱਕ; ~**tie** ਥੁੱਕ, ਉਗਾਲ; ~**toon** ਪੀਕਦਾਨ, ਥੁੱਕਦਾਨ, ਉਗਾਲਦਾਨ

spite (ਸਪਾਇਟ) *n v* ਲਾਗਤਬਾਜ਼ੀ, ਲਾਗ-ਡਾਟ; ਦਵੈਸ਼; ਖੁਨਸ, ਈਰਖਾ, ਸਾੜਾ; ਵੈਰ; ਲਾਗਤਬਾਜ਼ੀ ਕਰਨੀ

splash (ਸਪਲੈਸ਼) *v n* ਪਾਣੀ ਦੇ ਛਿੱਟੇ ਉਡਣੇ, (ਕਿਸੇ ਉੱਤੇ) ਛਿੱਟੇ ਪਾਉਣੇ; ਛਿੱਟ, ਛਿੱਟਾ, ਧੱਬਾ

spleen (ਸਪਲੀਨ) *n* ਤਿੱਲੀ, ਕੌੜਾ ਸੁਭਾਅ, ਅੜ੍ਹਬਪੁਣਾ, ਖਿਝ; ਗੁੱਸਾ

splendid ('ਸਪਲੈਂਡਿਡ) *n* ਸ਼ਾਨਦਾਰ, ਪ੍ਰਭਾਵਸ਼ਾਲੀ, ਪ੍ਰਸਿਸ਼ਯੋਗ, ਗੌਰਵਮਈ, ਸ਼ਾਹਾਨਾ, ਆਲੀਸ਼ਾਨ; ~**ness** ਪ੍ਰਭਾਵਸ਼ੀਲਤਾ, ਗੌਰਵ

splendour ('ਸਪਲੈਂਡਅ*) *n* ਸ਼ਾਨ, ਠਾਠ, ਠਾਠ-ਬਾਠ, ਸਜਧਜ; ਗੌਰਵ

split (ਸਪਲਿਟ) *v n* ਵੱਖਰਾ ਹੋਣਾ; ਪਾੜਨਾ; ਵੰਡਣਾ, ਫਟਣਾ; ਫਟ ਕੇ ਟੁਕੜੇ ਉਡ ਜਾਣੇ; ਦਰਾੜ, ਮੋਰੀ, ਧਾਤ ਦੀ ਇਕ ਛੜ

spoil (ਸਪੌਇਲ) *n v* ਲੁਟ, ਨਫ਼ਾ, ਖ਼ਰਾਬ ਕਰਨਾ, ਵਿਗਾੜਨਾ; ਲੁੱਟਣਾ, ਲੁੱਟ ਲੈਣਾ; ~**ed** ਵਿਗਾੜਿਆ, ਦੂਸ਼ਤ, ਵਿਕ੍ਰਿਤ

spoke (ਸਪਅਉਕ) *n v* (ਪਹੀਏ ਦੀ) ਅਰ, ਤਾਰ, ਰੁਕਾਵਟ ਪਾਉਣੀ

spokesman ('ਸਪਅਉਕਸਮਅਨ) *n* ਪ੍ਰਵਕਤਾ; ਬੁਲਾਰਾ, ਪ੍ਰਤੀਨਿਧ, ਨੁਮਾਇੰਦਾ

sponge ('ਸਪਅੰਜ) *n v* ਸਪੰਜ; ਅਸਪੰਜ; ਸਪੰਜ ਨਾਲ ਸਫ਼ਾਈ ਕਰਨਾ; ਖ਼ੁਸ਼ਾਮਦ ਨਾਲ ਕੰਮ ਕੱਢਣਾ; ~**r** ਮੁਫ਼ਤਖੋਰ, ਸਪੰਜ ਨਾਲ ਸਾਫ਼ ਕਰਨ ਵਾਲਾ

spongy ('ਸਪਅੰਜਿ) *a* ਸਪੰਜ ਵਰਗਾ, ਗੁਦਗੁਦਾ

sponsor ('ਸਪੌਂਸਅ*) *n* ਸਰਪਰਸਤ; ਜ਼ਾਮਨ ਪੇਸ਼ਕਾਰ, ਨਾਂ ਪੇਸ਼ ਕਰਨਾ; ~**ship** ਸਰਪਰਸਤੀ, ਜ਼ਾਮਨੀ

spontaneity (ਸਪੌਂਅ'ਨੇਇਅਟਿ) *n* ਸਵੈ-ਇੱਛਾ, ਆਪਮੁਹਾਰਤਾ, ਸੁਭਾਵਕਤਾ, ਕੁਦਰਤੀਪਨ

spontaneous (ਸਪੌਂ'ਟੇਇਨਅਸ) *a* ਕੁਦਰਤੀ, ਸੁਭਾਵਕ, ਸਵੈਚਾਲਕ, ਬਿਨਾ ਇਰਾਦੇ, ਸਵੈ-ਪਰੇਰਤ

spoon (ਸਪੂਨ) *n v* ਚਮਚਾ, ਕੜਛੀ, ਡੋਈ; ਚਮਚੇ ਨਾਲ ਕੱਢਣਾ; ~**feed** ਮੂੰਹ ਵਿੱਚ ਪਾਉਣਾ, ਚਮਚੇ ਨਾਲ ਖੁਆਉਣਾ; ~**y** ਆਸ਼ਕ; ਭੌਂਦੂ, ਵਲੱਲਾ

sporadic (ਸਪਅ'ਰੈਡਿਕ) *a* ਕਦੇ ਕਦੇ, ਕਦੇ ਕਦਾਈਂ, ਇਕਾਦੁਕਾ; ਇਤਫ਼ਾਕੀਆ, ਖਿਲਰਿਆ, ਵੱਖਰਾ ਵੱਖਰਾ; ~**al** ਕਿਤੇ ਕਿਤੇ ਮਿਲਣ ਵਾਲਾ

sport (ਸਪੋਟ) *n v* ਖੇਡ, ਮਨੋਰੰਜਨ, ਹਾਸਾ-ਠੱਠਾ, ਦਿਲਲਗੀ; ਖੇਡਣਾ; ਦਿਲ-ਪਰਚਾਵਾ ਕਰਨਾ, ਹਾਸਾ-ਮਖੌਲ ਕਰਨਾ; ~ing ਖਿਡਾਰੀ, ਖੇਡਾਂ ਦਾ ਸ਼ੁਕੀਨ ~ive ਖੇਡਣ ਦਾ ਸ਼ੁਕੀਨ, ਵਿਨੋਦੀ; ~sman ਖਿਡਾਰੀ; ~smanship ਖੇਡ, ਖਿਡਾਰੀ ਰੁਚੀ, ਨਿਆਂਕਾਰੀ ਸੁਭਾਅ

spot (ਸਪੌਟ) *n v* ਦਾਗ਼, ਡੱਬ, ਨਿਸ਼ਾਨ, ਧੱਬਾ, ਤਿਲ, ਟਿਮਕਣਾ; ਜਗ੍ਹਾ; ਮੌਕਾ, ਨਿਸ਼ਚਤ ਸਥਾਨ, ਸਥਿਤੀ; ਐਬ, ਕਲੰਕ, ਮੱਛੀ ਤੇ ਪਾਲਵੇਂ ਕਬੂਤਰਾਂ ਦੀ ਕਿਸਮ; (ਕਿਸੇ ਚੀਜ਼ ਦੀ) ਬੋਦੀ ਜਿਹੀ ਮਾਤਰਾ, ਥੋਰਾ ਕੁ; ਦਾਗ਼ ਲਾਉਣਾ, ਧੱਬਾ ਪਾਉਣਾ, ਲੱਭ ਲੈਣਾ, ਪਛਾਣ ਲੈਣਾ; ~less ਨਿਰਮਲ, ਬੇਦਾਗ਼, ਕਲੰਕਰਹਿਤ; ਨਿਸ਼ਕਲੰਕ

spouse (ਸਪਾਉਜ਼) *n* ਪਤੀ ਜਾਂ ਪਤਨੀ

spout (ਸਪਾਊਟ) *n v* (ਭਾਂਡੇ ਦੀ) ਟੂਟੀ; ਘੁੱਲ੍ਹ, ਧਾਰ, ਤਤੀਰੀ; ਫੁਹਾਰਾ; ਤਤੀਰੀ ਛੁੱਟਣੀ, ਜ਼ੋਰ ਦੀ ਧਾਰ ਪੈਣੀ

sprain (ਸਪਰੇਇਨ) *v n* ਮਰਕੋੜਨ, ਮਰੋੜਾ ਚਾੜ੍ਹ ਦੇਣਾ, ਵਲ ਪੈ ਜਾਣਾ; ਸੋਚ

spray (ਸਪਰੇਇ) *n v* ਫੁਹਾਰ, ਛਿੜਕਾ; ਛਿੜਕਣਾ

spread (ਸਪਰੈੱਡ) *v n* ਖਿਲਾਰਨਾ; ਵਿਛਾਉਣਾ; ਖਿੱਲਰਨਾ, ਵਿਛਣਾ; ਹੂਟਾਣਾ ਪਸਾਰਨਾ, ਪਿਲਾਰ, ਵਿਸਤਾਰ, ਪਸਾਰਾ; ਪ੍ਰਸਾਰ

sprightly ('ਸਪਰਾਇਟਲਿ) *a* ਛੋਹਲਾ, ਚੁਸਤ, ਉਤਸ਼ਾਹੀ, ਸਜੀਵ; ਖ਼ੁਸ਼, ਖਿੜਿਆ

spring (ਸਪਰਿੰਗ) *v n* ਬੁਤੂਕਣਾ, ਟੱਪਣਾ, ਭੁੜਕਣਾ; ਸਰੋਤ, ਚਸ਼ਮਾ; ਲਚਕ, ਕਮਾਨੀ, ਸਪ੍ਰਿੰਗ; ਬਸੰਤ ਰੁੱਤ

sprinkle ('ਸਪਰਿੰਙਕਲ) *v n* ਛਿੜਕਣਾ, ਤਰੌਂਕਾ ਦੇਣਾ, ਤਰੌਂਕਣਾ; ਤਰੌਂਕਾ

spur (ਸਪਅ:*) *v* ਅੱਡੀ ਮਾਰਨੀ; ਜੋਸ਼ ਦਿਵਾਉਣਾ, ਉਤਸ਼ਾਹ ਵਧਾਉਣਾ

spurious ('ਸਪਯੁਅਰਿਅਸ) *a* ਖੋਟਾ, ਝੂਠਾ, ਬਣਾਉਟੀ, ਨਕਲੀ (ਸਿੱਕਾ ਆਦਿ)

spurt, spirt (ਸਪਅ:ਟ) *v n* ਬੜੀ ਤੇਜ਼ੀ ਨਾਲ ਵਧਣਾ, ਫਰਾਟਾ ਭਰ ਕੇ ਨਿਕਲ ਜਾਣਾ; ਫਰਾਟਾ, ਸਰਨਾਟਾ, ਉਬਾਲ

sputum ('ਸਪਯੂਟਅਮ) *n* ਥੁੱਕ, ਖੰਘਾਰ

spy (ਸਪਾਇ) *n v* ਜਾਸੂਸ, ਸੁਹੀਆ; ਜਾਸੂਸੀ ਕਰਨੀ, ਭੇਦ ਲੈਣਾ

squab (ਸਕਵੌਬ) *n a* ਗੋਲ-ਮਟੋਲ, ਗੀਢਾ, ਮਠੂਨ; ਮੱਟਾ ਤੇ ਮਧਰਾ

squabble ('ਸਕਵੌਬਲ) *n v* ਝਗੜਾ, ਲੜਾਈ; ਤੂ-ਤੂ ਮੈਂ-ਮੈਂ; SISs G[s Ej`s

squad (ਸਕਵੌਡ) *n* ਜੱਥਾ, ਦਸਤਾ, ਫ਼ੌਜੀਆਂ ਦੀ ਨਿੱਕੀ ਟੋਲੀ

squall (ਸਕਵੋਲ) *v n* ਚੀਕਣਾ; ਚੀਕ-ਚਿਹਾੜਾ, ਚੀਕਣ ਦੀ ਅਵਾਜ਼; ਹਨੇਰੀ, ਝੱਖੜ; ~y ਮੀਂਹ-ਹਨੇਰੀ ਵਾਲਾ (ਮੌਸਮ)

squander ('ਸਕਵੌਂਡਅ*) *v* ਉਡਾਉਣਾ, ਗੁਆਉਣਾ, ਫ਼ਜ਼ੂਲ-ਖ਼ਰਚੀ ਕਰਨੀ, ਅਣਿਵਾਹ ਖ਼ਰਚਣਾ; ~ing ਫ਼ਜ਼ੂਲ-ਖ਼ਰਚੀ

square (ਸਕਵੇਅ*) *a adv n v* ਵਰਗਾਕਾਰ, ਬਰਾਬਰ ਲੰਮਾਈ-ਚੌੜਾਈ ਤੇ ਸਮਕੋਣਾਂ ਵਾਲਾ; ਟਿਕਾਣੇ ਸਿਰ, ਉਚਿਤ ਵਿਧੀ ਨਾਲ; ਵਰਗ, ਮੁਰੱਬਾ (ਸ਼ਕਲ), ਬਰਾਬਰ ਬਾਹੀਆਂ ਤੇ ਦੋਨਾਂ ਪਾਸੀ ਚੌਕੋਰ, ਚੌਕ; ਠੀਕ ਕਰਨਾ, ਸੰਵਾਰਨਾ, ਅਨੁਕੂਲ ਹੋਣਾ; ~root ਵਰਗ ਮੂਲ

squash (ਸਕਵੌਸ਼) *v n* ਮਿੱਚਣਾ, ਫੇਹਣਾ, ਚਿੱਥਣਾ; ਦਰੜਨਾ; ਨਚੋੜਨਾ; ਮੂੰਹ ਤੋੜ ਜਵਾਬ ਦੇਣਾ; ਦੱਬੇ ਜਾਣਾ, ਫਸ ਜਾਣਾ; ਭੀੜ-ਭਾੜ, ਭੁਰਤਾ, ਸ਼ਰਬਤ

squeeze (ਸਕਵੀਜ਼) *v n* ਨਚੋੜਨਾ, ਫੇਹਣਾ, ਘੁੱਟਣਾ; ਮਲਣਾ; ਦਬਾਉਣਾ; ਜ਼ਬਰਦਸਤੀ ਵਸੂਲੀ ਕਰਨੀ; ਮਜਬੂਰ ਕਰਨਾ, ਦਬਾਅ ਪਾਉਣਾ; ਦਬਾਉ, ਨਚੋੜ

squint (ਸਕਵਿੰਟ) *n v* ਭੈਂਗਾ, ਟੀਰਾ; ਭੈਂਗਾਪਣ, ਟੱਕਣੀ, ਝਾਤ; ਟੀਰ ਕੱਢਣਾ, ਟੀਰਾ ਤੱਕਣਾ

squirrel ('ਸਕਵਿਰ(ਅ)ਲ) *n* ਗਾਲੜੂ, ਕਾਟੋ, ਗਾਲ੍ਹਿਰੀ

stability (ਸਟਅ'ਬਿਲਅਟਿ) *n* ਮਜ਼ਬੂਤੀ, ਸਥਿਰਤਾ, ਪਕਿਆਈ, ਸੰਤੁਲਨ

stabilization ('ਸਟੇਇਬਅਲਾਇ'ਜ਼ੇਇਸ਼ਨ) *n* ਸਥਿਤੀ-ਕਰਨ, ਸਥਾਈਕਰਨ, ਦ੍ਰਿੜ੍ਹੀਕਰਨ

stabilize ('ਸਟੇਇਬਅਲਾਇਜ਼) *v* ਮਜ਼ਬੂਤ ਕਰਨਾ, ਪੱਕਾ ਕਰਨਾ, ਸਥਿਰਤਾ ਦੇਣੀ

stable ('ਸਟੇਇਬਲ) *a n* ਪੱਕਾ, ਮਜ਼ਬੂਤ; ਟਿਕਾਉ; ਤਬੇਲਾ, ਅਸਤਬਲ

stadium ('ਸਟੇਇਡ੍ਯਅਮ) *n* ਦੌੜ ਦਾ ਮੈਦਾਨ, ਖੇਡ ਦਾ ਮੈਦਾਨ

staff (ਸਟਾਫ਼) *n v* ਸਰਕਾਰੀ ਅਧਿਕਾਰੀ ਜਾਂ ਕਰਮਚਾਰੀ; ਸੋਟਾ, ਡੰਡਾ, ਸੋਟੀ; ਸਹਾਰਾ; ਕਰਮਚਾਰੀ ਰਖਣ

stag (ਸਟੈਗ) *n* ਬਾਰਾਂ-ਸਿੰਗਾ

stage (ਸਟੇਇਜ) *n v* ਥੜ੍ਹਾ, ਚਬੁਤਰਾ, ਡਾਇਸ; ਰੰਗ-ਮੰਚ; ਨਾਟ-ਕਲਾ; ਅਖਾੜਾ

stagger ('ਸਟੈਗਅ*) *v n* ਡਗਮਗਾਉਣਾ; ਲੜਖੜਾਉਣਾ; ਹਿਚਕਾਉਣਾ, ਸ਼ਸ਼ੋਪੰਜ ਵਿਚ ਪੈਣਾ; ਚਕਰਾਉਣਾ; ਡਗਮਗਾਹਟ, ਲੜਖੜਾਹਟ

stagnant ('ਸਟੈਗਨਅੰਟ) *a* ਗਤੀਹੀਣ, ਰੁਕਿਆ, ਖਲੋਤਾ, ਸਥਿਰ, ਪਰਵਾਹਹੀਣ

stagnate ('ਸਟੈਗਨੇਇਟ) *v* (ਪਾਣੀ ਆਦਿ ਦਾ) ਖੜ੍ਹਾ ਰਹਿਣਾ, ਗਤੀਹੀਣ ਹੋਣਾ, ਖਲੋਤਾ ਰਹਿਣਾ

stagnation (ਸਟੈਗ'ਨੇਇਸ਼ਨ) *n* ਗਤੀਹੀਣਤਾ, ਸਥਿਰਤਾ; ਪਰਵਾਹਹੀਣਤਾ; ਖੜੋਤ, ਨਿਸਚਲਤਾ

stain (ਸਟੇਇਨ) *v n* ਧੱਬਾ ਲਾਉਣਾ, ਡੱਬ ਪਾ ਦੇਣੇ, ਮੈਲਾ ਹੋਣਾ; ਕਲੰਕ ਲਾਉਣਾ; ਵੱਟਾ, ਕਲੰਕ; **~less** ਬੇਦਾਗ਼, ਬੇਐਬ, ਨਿਰਮਲ;

stair (ਸਟੇਅ*) *n* ਪੌੜੀ, ਸੀੜ੍ਹੀ; **~case** ਪੌੜੀਆਂ, ਜ਼ੀਨਾ

stake (ਸਟੇਇਕ) *n v* ਕਿੱਲ, ਮੇਖ, ਖੁੰਟਾ, ਚੋੜ, ਖੰਡਾ; ਸਹਾਰਾ ਦੇਣਾ; ਦਾਅ ਤੇ ਲਾਉਣਾ

stale (ਸਟੇਇਲ) *a n v* ਘਿਸਿਆ ਪਿਟਿਆ, ਬਾਸੀ, ਨੀਰਸ; ਪਸ਼ੂਆਂ ਦਾ ਪਿਸ਼ਾਬ; ਮੂਤਣਾ (ਪਸ਼ੂਆਂ ਦਾ)

stalemate ('ਸਟੇਇਲਮੇਇਟ) *n v* ਗਤੀਰੋਧ, ਅਟਕਾਉ; ਅਟਕਾਉ ਪੈਦਾ ਕਰਨਾ, ਜਮੂਦ ਪੈਦਾ ਕਰਨਾ

stall (ਸਟੱਲ) *n v* ਸਾਮਾਨ ਵੇਚਣ ਦੀ ਦੁਕਾਨ, ਖੋਖਾ, ਹੱਟ; ਠੱਪ ਹੋ ਜਾਣਾ; ਰੁਕਾਵਟ ਪਾਉਣਾ, ਦੇਰ ਕਰਨਾ, ਰੋੜਾ ਅਟਕਾਉਣਾ

stamina (ਸਟੈਮਿਨਅ) *n* ਬਲ, ਤੇਜ, ਸਰੀਰਕ ਸ਼ਕਤੀ, ਦਮ

stammer ('ਸਟੈਮਅ*) *v n* ਥਥਲਾਉਣਾ, ਤੋਤਲਾ ਹੋਣਾ; ਹਕਲਾਉਣਾ; ਥਥਲਾਹਟ, ਤੁਤਲਾਹਟ, ਹਕਲਾਹਟ

stamp (ਸਟੈਂਪ) *v n* ਮੁਹਰ ਲਗਾਉਣਾ, ਠੱਪਾ ਲਗਾਉਣਾ, ਛਾਪਣਾ; ਸਿੱਕਾ ਬਣਾਉਣਾ; ਠੋਕਣਾ, ਠੱਪਾ, ਛਾਪਾ; ਸਰਕਾਰੀ ਮੁਹਰ ਦਾ ਠੱਪਾ; ਟਿਕਟ, ਰਸੀਦੀ ਟਿਕਟ; ਅਸ਼ਟਾਮ

stampede (ਸਟੈਂ'ਪੀਡ) *n* ਭਾਜੜ, ਖਲਬਲੀ, ਹਫੜਾ-ਦਫੜੀ

stand (ਸਟੈਂਡ) *v n* ਖੜ੍ਹਾ ਹੋਣਾ, ਖਲੋਣਾ; ਰੋਕ ਦੇਣਾ; ਕਾਇਮ ਹੋਣਾ; ਸਹਾਰਨਾ; (ਖਰਚ) ਬਰਦਾਸ਼ਤ ਕਰਨਾ, ਆਪਣੇ ਸਿਰ ਲੈਣਾ, ਭਰ

ਦੇਣਾ; ਘਰਵੰਜੀ, ਬਣ੍ਹ; ਅੰਡਾ; ਚਬੂਤਰਾ; ~ by ਸਾਥ ਦੇਣਾ ਜਾਂ ਨਿਭਾਉਣਾ; ਕਾਇਮ ਰਹਿਣਾ, ਨੇੜੇ ਰਹਿਣਾ; ~point ਵਿਚਾਰ, ਨਜ਼ਰੀਆ, ਦ੍ਰਿਸ਼ਟੀਕੋਟ; ~still ਸਥਿਰ, ਅਹਿਲ, ਠਹਿਰਾਉ

standard ('ਸਟੈਂਡਅਂਡ) *n* ਪੱਧਰ, ਸਤਰ, ਦਰਜਾ, ਕੋਟੀ, ਮਿਆਰ; ਆਦਰਸ਼; ~ization ਪ੍ਰਮਾਣੀਕਰਨ, ਮਿਆਰੀਕਰਨ; ~ize ਮਿਆਰ ਕਾਇਮ ਕਰਨਾ, ਟਕਸਾਲਣਾ

standing ('ਸਟੈਂਡਿੰਡ) *a n* ਸਥਾਈ, ਪੱਕੀ; ਖੜ੍ਹੀ (ਫ਼ਸਲ); ਕੋਟੀ, ਸਤਰ; ~orders ਸਥਾਈ ਆਦੇਸ਼

stanza ('ਸਟੈਂਜ਼ਆ) *n* ਬੰਦ, ਸ਼ਲੋਕ, ਛੰਦ

staple ('ਸਟੇਇਪਲ) *n v* (ਕਾਗ਼ਜ਼ ਨੱਥੀ ਕਰਨ ਵਾਲਾ) ਕੁੰਡੀ, ਛੱਲਾ, ਸਟੇਪਲ; ਕੱਚਾ ਮਾਲ; ਮੁੱਖ ਸਮਗਰੀ; ਤਾਰ ਨਾਲ ਨੱਥੀ ਕਰਨਾ; ਵਰਗੀਕਰਨ ਕਰਨਾ, ਅਲੱਗ ਅਲੱਗ ਛਾਂਟਣਾ

star (ਸਟਾ*) *n* ਤਾਰਾ; ਸਿਤਾਰਾ; (ਨਾਟਕ ਜਾਂ ਫ਼ਿਲਮ ਦਾ) ਵਧੀਆ ਐਕਟਰ; ਉੱਘਾ ਆਦਮੀ; ਤਾਰਿਆਂ ਨਾਲ ਸਜਾਉਣਾ, ਤਾਰੇ ਜੜਨਾ

starch (ਸਟਾਚ) *n v* ਨਸ਼ਾਸਤਾ, ਕਲਫ਼, ਸਟਾਰਚ; ਮਾਇਆ, ਪਾਣ, ਪਾਹ; ਆਕੜ; ਕਲਫ਼ ਲਗਾਣਾ

stare (ਸਟੇਅ*) *v n* ਅੱਖਾਂ ਫਾੜ ਫਾੜ ਕੇ ਤੱਕਣਾ, ਘੂਰਨਾ, ਝਾਕਣਾ; ਤਾੜ, ਸਥਿਰ ਦ੍ਰਿਸ਼ਟੀ, ਟਿਕਟਿਕੀ

stark (ਸਟਾਕ) *a adv* ਸਖ਼ਤ ਆਕੜਿਆ; ਅਟੱਲ, ਕਠੋਰ; ਘੋਰ; ਨਿਰਾ

start (ਸਟਾਟ) *n v* ਪ੍ਰਸਥਾਨ, ਆਰੰਭ; ਸ੍ਰੀ ਗਣੇਸ਼, ਸ਼ੁਰੂਆਤ; ਕੂਚ ਕਰਨਾ, ਚੱਲਣਾ, ਨਿਕਲਣਾ

startle ('ਸਟਾ'ਟਲ) *v n* ਡਰਾ ਦੇਣਾ, ਘਬਰਾ ਦੇਣਾ; ਚੌਂਕ

stravation (ਸਟਾ'ਵੇਇਸ਼ਨ) *n* ਭੁੱਖਮਰੀ, ਕੰਗਾਲੀ, ਭੋਖੜਾ, ਫ਼ਾਕਾ, ਨਾਗਾ

starve (ਸਟਾਵ*) *v* ਭੁੱਖਿਆਂ ਮਾਰਨਾ ਜਾਂ ਫ਼ਾਕੇ ਕੱਟਣੇ; ਅਤੀ ਗ਼ਰੀਬ ਜਾਂ ਮੁਹਤਾਜ ਹੋਣਾ; (ਬੋਲ) ਭੁੱਖ ਲੱਗਣੀ

state (ਸਟੇਇਟ) *n a v* (1) ਹਾਲ, ਹਾਲਤ, ਅਵਸਥਾ; (2) ਰਿਆਸਤ, ਸਲਤਨਤ, ਰਾਜ, ਸਰਕਾਰ; (3) ਪ੍ਰਦੇਸ਼; (4) ਰੁਤਬਾ; ਠਾਠ-ਬਾਠ, ਸਰਕਾਰੀ; ਰਸਮੀ ਕਥਨ ਕਰਨਾ, ਮੁਕਰਰ ਕਰਨਾ; ~ly ਸ਼ਾਨਦਾਰ; ~ment ਬਿਆਨ, ਕਥਨ; ~sman ਨੀਤੀਵਾਨ, ਸਿਆਸਤਦਾਨ, ਰਾਜਨੀਤੀਵੇਤਾ; ~smanship ਰਾਜਨੀਤਗਤਾ, ਸਿਆਸਤ, ਸਿਆਸਤਦਾਨੀ

static ('ਸਟੈਟਿਕ) *a* ਗਤੀਹੀਨ, ਸਥਿਰ, ਨਿਸ਼ਚਲ; ~al ਗਤੀਹੀਨ, ਸਥਿਰ, ਅਹਿਲ

station ('ਸਟੇਇਸ਼ਨ) *n v* ਸਟੇਸ਼ਨ, ਰੇਲ-ਘਰ; ਅੱਡਾ, ਟਿਕਾਣਾ, ਥਾਂ ਦੇਣੀ, ਰੱਖਣਾ; ~ary ਟਿਕਿਆ, ਸਥਿਰ, ਸਥਿਤ, ਅਹਿੱਲ, ਟਿਕਾਉ

stationer ('ਸਟੇਇਸ਼ਨਅ*) *n* ਲਿਖਣ ਸਮਗਰੀ ਵੇਚਣ ਵਾਲਾ, ਸਟੇਸ਼ਨਰ; ~y ਲਿਖਣ-ਸਮਗਰੀ (ਕਾਗ਼ਜ਼, ਕਲਮ, ਦਵਾਤ ਆਦਿ)

statistics (ਸਟਟਿਸਟਿਕਸ) *n* ਸਾਖਿਅਕੀ

statistician (ਸਟੈਟਿ'ਸਟਿਸ਼ਨ) *n* ਅੰਕੜਾ-ਵਿਗਿਆਨੀ; ~ical ਅੰਕੜਿਆਂ ਸਬੰਧੀ, ਸਾਂਖਿਅਕੀ; ~ics ਅੰਕੜਾ-ਵਿਗਿਆਨ

statue ('ਸਟੈਚੂ) *n* ਮੂਰਤੀ, ਬੁੱਤ; ~tte ਛੋਟੀ ਮੂਰਤੀ, ਛੋਟਾ ਬੁੱਤ

stature ('ਸਟੈਚਅ*) *n* ਕੱਦ, ਡੀਲ, ਕੱਦ-ਕਾਠ; ਰੁਤਬਾ

status ('ਸਟੇਇਟਅਸ) *n* ਪਦ, ਪਦਵੀ, ਅਹੁਦਾ, ਦਰਜਾ, ਰੁਤਬਾ, ਹੈਸੀਅਤ; ਅਵਸਥਾ, ਦਸ਼ਾ, ਹਾਲਤ; ~quo, ~quo ante (*L*) ਜਿਉਂ ਦੀ

ਤਿਉਂ ਹਾਲਤ, ਯਥਾ-ਸਥਿਤੀ

statute ('ਸਟੈਟਯੂਟ) *n* ਵਿਧਾਨ-ਸਭਾ ਦਾ ਲਿਖਤੀ ਕਾਨੂੰਨ, ਅਧਿਨਿਯਮ; ਰੱਬੀ ਕਾਨੂੰਨ, ਦੈਵੀ ਵਿਧਾਨ

statutory ('ਸਟੈਟਯੂਟ(ਅ)ਰਿ) *a* ਕਾਨੂੰਨੀ, ਕਾਨੂੰਨ-ਅਨੁਸਾਰੀ

staunch (ਸਟੰਚ) *a* ਪੱਕਾ, ਨਿਸ਼ਚੇਵਾਨ, ਸਿਦਕਵਾਨ, ਵਫ਼ਾਦਾਰ

stay (ਸਟੇਇ) *n v* ਡੇਰਾ, ਬਸੇਰਾ, ਅਟਕਾਉ, ਰੋਕ, ਬੰਧਨ, ਸੰਜਮ; ਆਸਰਾ, ਸਹਾਰਾ; ਅਟਕਾਉਣਾ, ਠਹਿਰਾਉਣਾ; ਰੁਕ ਜਾਣਾ, ਸਹਿਣਾ, ਬਰਦਾਸ਼ਤ ਕਰਨਾ; ਉਡੀਕਣਾ; **~ing** ਨਿਵਾਸ ਠਹਿਰਾਉ

stead (ਸਟੈੱਡ) *n* ਭੂਮੀ; ਸਥਾਨ, ਦਸ਼ਾ; ਪਲੰਘ

steadfast ('ਸਟੈੱਡਫ਼ਾਸਟ) *a* ਦ੍ਰਿੜ੍ਹ, ਅਟੱਲ, ਸਥਿਰ, ਪੱਕਾ, ਸਾਬਤ-ਕਦਮ

steady (ਸਟੈਡਿ) *a v* ਅਚੱਲ, ਅਟੱਲ, ਇਕਸਾਰ, ਸਥਿਰ, ਟਿਕਵਾਂ, ਦ੍ਰਿੜ੍ਹ, ਟਿਕਿਆ, ਠਹਿਰਿਆ; ਸੰਭਲ ਜਾਣਾ; ਟਿਕਾਉਣਾ

steal (ਸਟੀਲ) *v* ਚੁਰਾਉਣਾ, ਚੋਰੀ ਲੈਣਾ, ਚੁਪ ਚੁਪ ਕੇ ਲੈ ਜਾਣਾ, ਮੋਹ ਲੈਣਾ, ਲੁੜ ਲੈਣਾ; **~th** ਚੋਰੀ; ਛਲ; **~thy** ਗੁਪਤ, ਲੁਕਵੀਂ, ਗੁੱਝੀ, ਚੁੱਪ-ਚਾਪ, ਖੁਫ਼ੀਆ ਤੌਰ ਤੇ

steam (ਸਟੀਮ) *n v* ਭਾਫ਼, ਹਵਾੜ; ਭਾਫ਼ ਦੇਣੀ, ਭਾਫ਼ ਛੱਡਣੀ

steel (ਸਟੀਲ) *n v* ਫ਼ੌਲਾਦ, ਇਸਪਾਤ; ਤਕੜਾ ਕਰਨਾ; **~y** ਫ਼ੌਲਾਦੀ, ਕਰੜਾ, ਬੰਜਰ, ਸਖ਼ਤ, ਬੇਦਰਦ

steep (ਸਟੀਪ) *v n a* ਤਿੱਖਣ, ਤਰ ਕਰਨਾ, ਡੋਬਾ ਦੇਣਾ; ਡੋਬਾ, ਢਲਾਣ (ਖੜ੍ਹਵੀਂ); ਦੰਦੀ; ਢਲਵਾਂ; **~ness** ਢਲਾਣ, ਢਲਵਾਂਪਣ, ਦੁਰਗਮਤਾ

steer (ਸਟਿਅ*) *n* ਕਿਸੇ ਖ਼ਾਸ ਦਸ਼ਾ ਵਿਚ ਚੱਲਣਾ, (ਜਹਾਜ਼ ਨੂੰ) ਖੇਉਣਾ, ਚਲਾਉਣਾ ਵੱਛਾ, ਵਛੜਾ; **~sman** ਵਾਹਕ, ਨਾਵਕ

stem (ਸਟੈਮ) *n v* ਤਣਾ, ਡੰਡੀ, ਸ਼ਬਦ-ਮੂਲ, ਧਾਤੁ; ਗਤੀ ਰੋਕਣਾ

stench (ਸਟੈਂਚ) *n* ਦੁਰਗੰਧ, ਸੜਾਂਦ, ਬਦਬੂ, ਹੁਮਕ

step ('ਸਟੈੱਪ) *v n pref* ਕਦਮ ਚੁੱਕਣਾ, ਹਿੱਲਣਾ; ਕਦਮ; (ਪੈਰ ਦਾ) ਖੜਾਕ ਪੈਰ-ਚਿੰਨ੍ਹ; ਚਾਲ ਦਾ ਢੰਗ; (ਦੂਜਿਆਂ ਨਾਲ) ਕਦਮ ਮਿਲਾ ਕੇ ਚੱਲਣਾ; ਤਦਬੀਰ, ਕਾਰਵਾਈ; ਇਕ ਅਗੇਤਰ, ਮਤਰੇਈ, ਮਤਰੇਆ ਦੇ ਅਰਥਾਂ ਵਿਚ; **~ping-stone** ਪੱੜੁਲ, ਅੱਡਾ; ਲਾਂਘੇ ਦਾ ਪੱਥਰ; ਸਾਧਨ, ਵਸੀਲਾ; **~up** ਅੱਗੇ ਆਉਣਾ, ਤੇਜ਼ ਕਰਨਾ, ਵਧਾਉਣਾ; **~child** ਮਤਰੇਆ ਬੱਚਾ; **~daughter** ਮਤਰੇਈ ਧੀ; **~son** ਮਤਰੇਆ ਪੁੱਤਰ

stepney ('ਸਟੈੱਪਨਿ) *n* ਵਾਧੂ ਟਾਇਰ ਅਤੇ ਟਿਊਬ, ਵਾਧੂ ਪਹੀਆ

sterile ('ਸਟੈਰਾਇਲ) *a* ਬੰਜਰ, (ਜ਼ਮੀਨ); ਬਾਂਝ (ਜੀਵ)

sterility (ਸਟਅ'ਰਿਲਅਟਿ) *n* ਬਾਂਝਪਨ; ਅਫ਼ਲਤਾ

sterilize ('ਸਟੈਰਿਲਾਇਜ਼) *v* ਬਾਂਝ ਕਰਨਾ, ਜਰਮ ਰਹਿਤ ਕਰਨਾ

stern (ਸਟਅ:ਨ) *a* ਕਰੜੀ, ਸਖ਼ਤ, ਤੁਰਸ਼, ਬੇਦਰਦ, ਕਠੋਰ, ਨਿਰਦਈ; **~ness** ਨਿਰਦਇਤਾ, ਨਿਸ਼ਠੁਰਤਾ, ਕਠੋਰਤਾ, ਕਰੜਾਈ

steward ('ਸਟਯੁਅ:ਡ) *n* ਮੁਖ਼ਤਾਰ ਜਾਇਦਾਦ; ਠੇਕੇਦਾਰ, ਭੰਡਾਰੀ, ਸੇਵਾਦਾਰ,

stick (ਸਟਿਕ) *v* ਚੋਭਣਾ; ਲੱਗਣਾ, ਲਗਾਉਣਾ (ਬੋਲ) ਰੱਖਣਾ, ਜੰਮਣਾ, ਜਮਾਉਣਾ; ਡੱਟ ਜਾਣਾ; ਚਿਪਕਣਾ, ਚਿਪਕਾਉਣਾ, ਲੱਗੇ ਰਹਿਣਾ; ਅਟਕ ਜਾਣਾ, ਅੜ ਜਾਣਾ; ਸੋਟੀ, ਡਾਂਗ, ਬੈਂਤ, ਡੰਡਾ,

(ਲਾਖ ਦੀ) ਬੱਤੀ; (ਡੋਬੀ ਦੀ) ਤੀਲੀ; ਫੋਸੜ; ਭੌਂਦੂ; ~y ਲੇਸਲਾ, ਚਿਪਚਿਪਾ, ਪਿਚ-ਪਿਚ ਕਰਨਾ, ਚਿਕਨਾ

stiff (ਸਟਿਫ) *a* ਸਖ਼ਤ, ਕਰੜਾ, ਅੜੀਅਲ, ਅੱਖੜ, ਗਾੜ੍ਹਾ, ਸੰਘਣਾ; ~**necked** ਘਮੰਡੀ, ਆਕੜਖਾਨ, ਹੰਕਤਾਬਾਜ਼; ~**en** ਆਕੜ ਜਾਣਾ; ਕਠੋਰ ਬਣਾਉਣਾ, ਅੱਖੜ ਜਾਂ ਜ਼ਿੱਦੀ ਹੋਣਾ; ਗਾੜ੍ਹਾ ਕਰਨਾ

stifile ('ਸਟਾਇਫਲ) *v n* ਕੁਚਲਣਾ, ਗਲਾ ਘੁੱਟਣਾ; ਪੱਠਾ

stigma ('ਸਟਿਗਮਅ) *n* ਦਾਗ਼, ਕਲੰਕ; tizo ਦਾਗ਼ ਲਾਉਣਾ, ਕਲੰਕਤ ਕਰਨਾ, ਬਦਨਾਮ ਕਰਨਾ

still *a n v adv* ਸ਼ਾਂਤ, ਅਹਿੱਲ, ਠਹਿਰਿਆ, ਬੰਦ; ਖੜ੍ਹਾ (ਪਾਣੀ); ਚੁੱਪ-ਚੁਪੀਤਾ, ਬੇਜਾਨ; ਖੜੀ ਫ਼ਿਲਮ ਜਾਂ ਤਸਵੀਰ; ਠੰਢਾ ਕਰਨਾ; ਉਸ ਵਕਤ ਤੀਕ, ਫਿਰ ਵੀ, ਬਾਵਜੂਦ ਇਸ ਦੇ; ~**born** ਮੁਰਦਾ ਬੱਚਾ; ~**room** ਸ਼ਰਾਬ ਕੱਢਣ ਦੀ ਥਾਂ

stimulate ('ਸਟਿਮਯੁਲੇਇਟ) *v* ਉਤੇਜਕ ਕਰਨਾ, ਜੋਸ਼ ਦਿਵਾਉਣਾ, ਨਸ਼ਾ ਚਾੜ੍ਹਨਾ ਜਾਂ ਲਿਆਉਣਾ; ਉਤਾਰਨਾ, ਉਕਸਾਉਣਾ

stimulation ('ਸਟਿਮਯੁ'ਲੇਇਸ਼ਨ) *n* ਉਤੇਜਨਾ, ਨਸ਼ਾ, ਉਕਸਾਹਟ, ਟੁੰਬ

stimulus ('ਸਟਿਮਯੁਲਅਸ) *n* ਉਤਸ਼ਾਹ, ਉਕਸਾਹਟ, ਟੁੰਬ

sting ('ਸਟਿਙ) *n v* ਡੰਗ; ਕੰਡਾ; ਕਸੀਰ; ਡੰਗ ਮਾਰਨਾ (ਬਿਛੂ ਜਾਂ ਸੱਪ ਦਾ); ਚੁੜਕਣਾ (ਸੂਲ ਦਾ); ਜਲਣ ਹੋਣੀ, ਦਰਦ ਕਰਨਾ, ਚੀਸ ਉਠਣੀ

stingy ('ਸਟਿੰਜੀ) *a* ਕੰਜੂਸ, ਲੀਚੜ

stink (ਸਟਿਙਕ) *v n* ਬੂ ਮਾਰਨਾ, ਤੁਕਣਾ, ਦੁਰਗੰਧ ਛੱਡਣਾ, ਸੜਿਆਂਧ ਮਾਰਨੀ; ਬਦਬੂ, ਦੁਰਗੰਧ, ਸੜਿਆਂਧ

stint (ਸਟਿੰਟ) *v n* ਥੋੜ੍ਹਾ ਦੇਣਾ, ਕਸਰ ਰੱਖਣੀ, ਭੁੱਖਾ ਰੱਖਣਾ, ਹੱਥ ਘੁੱਟਣਾ, ਸੰਕੋਚ ਕਰਨਾ; ਕਸਰ, ਸੰਕੋਚ, ਕੰਜੂਸੀ

stipend ('ਸਟਾਇਪੈਂਡ) *n* ਵਜ਼ੀਫ਼ਾ, ਭੱਤਾ

stipulate ('ਸਟਿਪਯੁਲੇਇਟ) *v* ਸਮਝੌਤਾ ਕਰਨਾ ਜਾਂ ਸੌਦਾ ਕਰਨਾ, ਬੰਧੇਜ ਕਰਨਾ, ਸ਼ਰਤ ਕਰ ਲੈਣੀ, ਬਿਦਣਾ

stipulation ('ਸਟਿਪਯੁ'ਲੇਇਸ਼ਨ) *n* ਸ਼ਰਤ, ਇਕਰਾਰ-ਨਾਮਾ, ਬੰਧ, ਬੰਧਾਨ

otir (ਗਟਾਃ*) *v n* ਚਲਾਉਣਾ, ਹਿਲਾਉਣਾ, ਸਰਕਣਾ, ਹਰਕਤ ਕਰਨੀ, ਹਰਕਤ ਦੇਣੀ; ਅੰਦੋਲਨ ਕਰਨਾ; ਜਾਗਰਤੀ ਪੈਦਾ ਕਰਨੀ, ਪਰੇਰਨਾ ਦੇਣੀ, ਉਠਾਉਣਾ; ਉਕਸਾਉਣਾ, ਭੜਕਾਉਣਾ; ਉਤਸ਼ਾ-ਹਤ ਕਰਨਾ, ਹਲਚਲ, ਗੜਬੜੀ, ਖਲਬਲੀ, ਹੰਗਾਮਾ; ਗਤੀ, ਹਰਕਤ

stitch (ਸਟਿਚ) *n* ਚੋਭ, ਹੋਕ, ਟਾਂਕਾ (ਫੱਟ ਦਾ); ਤੋਪਾ, ਤਰੋਪਾ, ਨਗੰਦਾ, ਬਖ਼ੀਆ, ਸਿਲਾਈ; ਟਾਂਕਾ ਲਗਾਉਣਾ, ਟਾਂਕਣਾ; ਤੋਪਾ ਮਾਰਨਾ; ~**ing** ਸਿਲਾਈ; ਸਿਉਣ

stock (ਸਟੌਕ) *n* ਜ਼ਖੀਰਾ; ਮਾਲ ਸਾਮਾਨ; ਕੱਚਾ ਮਾਲ; (ਸੱਜ ਦਾ) ਦਸਤਾ, ਮੁੱਠੀ, ਕੁੰਦਾ, ਸਟਾਫ, ਹੁੰਡੀ; (ਕੰਪਨੀ ਦੀ) ਸਾਂਝੀ ਪੂੰਜੀ, ਭੰਡਾਰ; ਮੂਲ ਧਨ; ~**broker** ਸਟਾਕ ਦਲਾਲ; ~**exchange** ਸਰਾਫ਼ਾ ਬਜ਼ਾਰ, ਸਟਾਕ ਐਕਸਚੇਂਜ

stocking ('ਸਟੌਕਿਙ) *n* ਵੱਡੀ ਜੁਰਾਬ; ਮਾਲ ਇਕੱਤਰ ਕਰਨ (ਦੀ ਕਿਰਿਆ)

stoke (ਸਟਅਉਇਕ) *v* (ਭੱਠੀ) ਝੋਕਣਾ; ਕੋਲੇ ਪਾਉਣੇ; (ਬੋਲ) ਜਲਦੀ ਜਲਦੀ ਖਾਣਾ ਨਿਗਲਣਾ

stomach ('ਸਟਅੱਮਅਕ) *n* ਪੇਟ, ਉਦਰ, ਢਿੱਡ; ਮਿਹਦਾ, ਓਝਰੀ, ਪੋਟਾ (ਪੰਛੀਆ ਦਾ); ਭੁੱਖ,

ਉਤਸ਼ਾਹ

stone (ਸਟਅਉਨ) *n a v* ਪੱਥਰ; ਹੀਰਾ; ਗੁਠਲੀ, ਗਿਟਕ; (ਅੰਗੂਰਾਂ ਦਾ) ਬੀਜ; ਗੜਾ; ਪੱਥਰ ਦਾ; ਪਥਰਾਉਣ; ਪੱਥਰਾਂ ਨਾਲ ਮਾਰਨਾ; ਗਿਟਕਾਂ ਕੱਢਦੀਆ; ਪੱਥਰ ਲਗਾਉਣੇ

stony ('ਸਟਅਉਨਿ) *a* ਪਥਰੀਲਾ, ਗਿਟਕ ਵਾਲਾ; ਕਰੜਾ

stool (ਸਟੂਲ) *n* (1) ਚੌਕੀ, ਸਟੂਲ, ਤਿਪਾਈ, ਪੀੜ੍ਹੀ; (2) ਖੁੱਡੀ; (3) ਟੱਟੀ, ਪਖਾਨਾ

stoop (ਸਟੂਪ) *v n* ਝੁਕਣਾ ਜਾਂ ਝੁਕਾਉਣਾ, ਕੋਡਾ ਹੋਣਾ ਜਾਂ ਕਰਨਾ, ਕੁੱਬਾ ਹੋਣਾ, ਝਪਟਣਾ, ਝਪਟਾ ਮਾਰਨਾ, ਟੁੱਟ ਪੈਣਾ; (1) ਝੁਕਾਉ; ਕੁੱਬ; (ਪ੍ਰ) ਬਾਜ ਦਾ ਝਪਟਾ (2) ਘਰ ਦੇ ਸਾਹਮਣੇ ਦਾ ਖੁੱਲ੍ਹਾ ਚਬੂਤਰਾ

stop (ਸਟੈਪ) *n v* ਪ੍ਰਤੀਬੰਧ, ਵਿਰਾਮ, ਠਹਿਰਾਉ, ਅਟਕਾਉ, ਰੁਕਾਵਟ, ਅਟਕਣਾ, ਅਟਕਾਉਣਾ, ਠਹਿਰਨਾ, ਠਹਿਰਾਉਣਾ, ਟਿਕਣਾ, ਟਿਕਾਉਣਾ, ਬੱਸ ਕਰਨੀ, ਡੇਰਾ ਕਰਨਾ; ~**cock** ਟੂਟੀ; ~**gap** ਵੇਲਾ ਟਪਾਉ, ਕੰਮ ਟਪਾਉ; ~**press** ਤਾਜ਼ੀ ਖ਼ਬਰ, ਛਾਪਦਿਆਂ ਛਾਪਦਿਆਂ ਆਈ ਖ਼ਬਰ; ~**page** ਅਟਕਾਉ, ਠਹਿਰਾਉ, ਰੋਕ, ਅਟਕ; ਮੁਕਾਮ; ~**per** ਡੱਕਾ, ਡਾਟ, ਡੱਟ, ਗੱਟ, ਬੁੱਜਾ, ਰੋਕੂ, ਰੋਕ, ਅੜਾ

storage ('ਸਟੋਰਿਜ) *n* ਭੰਡਾਰ, ਗੁਦਾਮ; ਮਾਲ ਭਰਾਈ ਦਾ ਮਹਿਸੂਲ

store (ਸਟੋ*) *n v* ਜ਼ਖੀਰਾ, ਗੁਦਾਮ, ਭੰਡਾਰ; ਸੰਚਤ ਕਰਨਾ, ਜੋੜਨਾ, ਜਖ਼ਮੀਹ ਕਰਨਾ; ~**house** ਖ਼ਾਤਾ, ਕੋਠੀ, ਗੁਦਾਮ; ਖ਼ਜ਼ਾਨਾ; ~**keeper** ਮੋਦੀ, ਭੰਡਾਰੀ, ਦੁਕਾਨਦਾਰ

storey (ਸਟੋਰਿ) *n* ਮੰਜ਼ਲ, ਛੱਤ

stork (ਸਟੋਕ) *n* ਸਾਰਸ, ਲਕਲਕ, ਕਰੌਂਚ

storm (ਸਟੋਮ) *n v* ਝੱਖੜ, ਤੇਜ਼ ਹਨੇਰੀ, ਤੁਫ਼ਾਨ; ਧਮੱਚੜ, ਘੜੰਮਸ, ਹੁੱਲੜ; ਹਨੇਰੀ ਵਾਂਗ ਗਰਜਣਾ, ਡਾਂਟਣਾ; ਕਿਲ੍ਹੇ ਤੇ ਸਿੱਧਾ ਧਾਵਾ ਬੋਲ ਕੇ ਕਬਜ਼ੇ ਵਿਚ ਕਰ ਲੈਣਾ; ~**y** ਤੁਫ਼ਾਨੀ, ਝੱਖੜ ਵਾਲੀ (ਰੁੱਤ); ਕਰੋਪਪੂਰਨ, ਕਰੋਪੀ, ਤੇਜ਼, ਹੁੱਲੜੀ

story ('ਸਟੋਰਿ) *n* ਕਿੱਸਾ ਵਾਰਤਾ; ਕਹਾਣੀ; ਬਣਾਈ ਹੋਈ ਗੱਲ, ਗੱਪ; ~**teller** ਕਥਾਕਾਰ, ਕਹਾਣੀ-ਕਾਰ, ਕਹਾਣੀ-ਲੇਖਕ, ਵਾਰਤਾਕਾਰ

stout (ਸਟਾਉਟ) *a n* ਪੱਕਾ; ਵਫ਼ਾਦਾਰ ਮਜ਼ਬੂਤ, ਤਾਕਤਵਰ, ਮੁਸ਼ਟੰਡਾ; ਹੱਟ-ਕੱਟਾ

stove *n* ਚੁੱਲ੍ਹਾ, ਅੰਗੀਠੀ, ਗਰਮ-ਘਰ

straight ('ਸਟਰੇਇਟ) *a n adv* ਸਿੱਧਾ, ਟਿੱਕਵਾਂ (ਨਿਸ਼ਾਨਾ, ਵਾਰ, ਨਜ਼ਰ, ਤਰੀਕਾ ਆਦਿ); ਖਰਾ, ਘੇਲਗਾ (ਵਿਹਾਰ, ਹਿਸਾਬ); ਠੀਕ, ਹਮਵਾਰ, ਦਰੁਸਤ; ਠੀਕ ਤਰ੍ਹਾਂ; ~**forward** ਖਰਾ, ਸਪਸ਼ਟ, ਸੁਖਾਲਾ, ਸਿੱਧਾ; ~**way** ਅਚਾਨਕ ਹੀ, ਉਸੇ ਵੇਲੇ, ਉਸੇ ਵਕਤ, ਫ਼ੌਰਨ; ~**en** ਠੀਕ ਕਰਨਾ, ਦਰੁਸਤ ਕਰਨਾ, ਸੁਲਝਾਉਣਾ, ਸੁਲਝਣਾ, ਸਿੱਧਾ ਹੋਣਾ; ~**ness** ਸਿੱਧਾਪਣ, ਸਰਲਤਾ; ਸਚਾਈ, ਨਿਸ਼ਕਪਟਤਾ

strain (ਸਟਰੇਇਨ) *n* ਤਣਾਉ, ਖਿੱਚ; ਜ਼ੋਰ, ਦਬਾਅ, ਕੱਸਣਾ, ਤਣਨਾ, ਦੱਬਣਾ; ਖਿੱਚਣਾ; ਜ਼ੋਰ ਪਾਉਣਾ, ਜ਼ੋਰ ਖਾ ਜਾਣਾ, ਥਕਾ ਦੇਣਾ

strange (ਸਟਰੇਇੰਜ) *a* ਅਜੀਬ, ਅਦਭੁਤ, ਅਸਧਾਰਨ, ਨਿਰਾਲਾ, ਪਰਦੇਸੀ, ਉਪਰਾ, ਪਰਾਇਆ; ~**ness** ਅਨੋਖਾਪਣ, ਵਚਿੱਤਰਤਾ, ਨਿਰਾਲਾਪਣ, ਨਵਾਂਪਣ; ~**r** ਅਜਨਬੀ, ਪਰਦੇਸੀ, ਉਪਰਾ, ਪਰਾਇਆ, ਨਵਾਂ ਵਿਅਕਤੀ; ਅਨੁਭਵ-ਹੀਣ, ਅਣਜਾਣ, ਅਨਾੜੀ ਵਿਅਕਤੀ

strangle ('ਸਟਰੈਙਗਲ) *v* ਸੰਘੀ, ਘੁੱਟਣੀ, ਗਲਾ ਘੁੱਟ ਕੇ ਮਾਰ ਦੇਣਾ, ਗਲਾ ਘੋਟਣਾ

strangulate ('ਸਟਰੈਂਗਯੁਲੇਇਟ) *v* ਸੰਘੀ ਘੁੱਟਣਾ, ਗਲਾ ਘੁੱਟਣਾ; ਦਬਾ ਕੇ ਲਹੂ ਦਾ ਗੇੜ ਰੋਕਣਾ

strap (ਸਟਰੈਪ) *n v* ਚਮੜੇ ਦੀ ਪੇਟੀ, ਫ਼ੀਤਾ, ਪੱਟਾ; ਕੱਸਣਾ, ਬੰਨ੍ਹਣਾ; **~ping** ਰਿਸ਼ਟ-ਪੁਸ਼ਟ, ਹੱਟਾ-ਕੱਟਾ, ਮੁਸ਼ਟੰਡਾ

strategic, ~al (ਸਟਰਾ'ਟੀਜ਼ਿਕ, ਸਟਰਾ'ਟੀਜ਼ਿਕੱਲ) *a* ਜੁੱਧ-ਕਲਾ ਸਬੰਧੀ, ਫ਼ੌਜੀ ਨੁਕਤਾ, ਜੁੱਧਨੀਤਕ

strategy ('ਸਟਰੈਟਿਜਿ) *n* ਕਾਰਜਨੀਤੀ, ਜੁੱਧ-ਨੀਤੀ

stratify ('ਸਟਰੈਟਿਫ਼ਾਇ) *v* ਪਰਤ ਤੇ ਪਰਤ ਜਮਾਉਣੀ, ਤਹਿ ਤੇ ਤਹਿ ਜਮਾਉਣੀ; ਦਰਜਾਬੰਦੀ ਕਰਨਾ

stratum ('ਸਟਰਾਟਅਮ) *n* ਤਹਿ, ਪਰਤ, ਤਬਕਾ; ਸਤਰ, ਵਰਗ, ਸ਼੍ਰੇਣੀ

straw (ਸਟਰੋ) *n* ਤੂੜੀ, ਭੋਹ; ਕੱਖ, ਤੀਲਾ; ਪਰਾਲੀ, ਨੀਰਾ

stray (ਸਟਰੇਇ) *v a n* ਭਟਕਦੇ ਫਿਰਨਾ, ਅਵਾਰਾ ਫਿਰਨਾ, ਟੱਕਰਾਂ ਮਾਰਨੀਆਂ; ਭੁੱਲਿਆ-ਭਟਕਿਆ, ਅਵਾਰਾ (ਪਸ਼ੂ); ਲਾਵਾਰਸ ਵਸਤੂ; ਅਵਾਰਾ ਆਦਮੀ

streak (ਸਟਰੀਕ) *n v* ਧਾਰੀ, ਸੀਕ, (ਖ਼ਾਸ ਕਰ ਰੰਗਦਾਰ); ਝਲਕਾਰਾ (ਬਿਜਲੀ ਦਾ); ਧਾਰੀਆਂ ਪਾਉਣੀਆਂ; **~y** ਧਾਰੀਦਾਰ; ਘਰਾਲੀ

stream (ਸਟਰੀਮ) *n v* ਨਦੀ, ਛੋਟੀ ਨਹਿਰ, ਨਾਲਾ, ਧਾਰਾ, ਸਰੋਤ, ਪਰਵਾਹ, ਲੋਕਾਂ ਦੀ ਵਧਦੀ ਭੀੜ; ਵਹਿਣਾ ਜਾਂ ਵਗਣਾ

street (ਸਟਰੀਟ) *n* ਸਰਵਜਨਕ ਰਸਤਾ; ਗਲੀ, ਸੜਕ, ਨਗਰ-ਮਾਰਗਾ

strength ('ਸਟਰੈਂਙ੍ਥ) *n* ਤਾਕਤ, ਜ਼ੋਰ, ਬਲ ਮਜ਼ਬੂਤੀ, ਤਕੜਾਈ, ਪਕਿਆਈ; **~en** ਤਕੜਾ ਕਰਨਾ ਜਾਂ ਹੋਣਾ; **~ening** ਮਜ਼ਬੂਤ ਬਣਾਉਣ ਵਾਲਾ, ਬਲਕਾਰੀ, ਸ਼ਕਤੀਦਾਇਕ

strenuous ('ਸਟਰੈਨਯੁਅਸ) *a* ਕਠਨ, ਕਰੜਾ, (ਜਤਨ), ਜਾਨਮਾਰ

stress (ਸਟਰੈੱਸ) *n v* ਭਾਰ, ਦਬਾਉ, ਤਣਾਉ, ਖਿੱਚਾਉ; ਜ਼ੋਰ ਦੇਣਾ, ਮੱਹਤਵ ਪ੍ਰਦਾਨ ਕਰਨਾ

stretch (ਸਟਰੈੱਚ) *v n* ਖਿੱਚ ਕੇ ਸਿੱਧਾ ਕਰਨਾ, ਤਾਣਨਾ, ਪਸਾਰਨਾ, ਫੈਲਾਉਣਾ, ਫੈਲਣਾ, ਖਿੱਚਣਾ; ਖਿਲਾਰ, ਲਮਕਾਅ; **~er** ਵਿਸਤਾਰਕ, ਫੈਲਾਉਣ ਵਾਲਾ, ਕੱਸਣ ਵਾਲਾ, ਸਟਰੈੱਚਰ

strew (ਸਟਰੂ) *v* ਛਿੜਕਣਾ (ਖੇਡ ਆਦਿ); ਖਿਲਾਰਨਾ

stricken ('ਸਟਰਿਕਨ) *a* ਮਾਰਿਆ, ਘਾਇਲ ਪੀੜਤ

strict (ਸਟਰਿਕਟ) *a* ਕੜੀ, ਬਾਬਾਬਤਾ, ਸਖ਼ਤ, ਕਠੋਰ (ਨਿਗਰਾਨੀ); ਕਰੜਾ, ਝਬਤੀ; **~ly** ਬਿਲਕੁਲ, ਠੀਕ ਠੀਕ; **~ly speaking** ਠੀਕ ਠੀਕ ਅਰਥਾਂ ਵਿਚ, ਸੱਚ ਪੁੱਛੋ ਤਾਂ, ਵਾਸਤਵ ਵਿਚ, ਅਸਲ ਵਿਚ, ਪੱਕੇ ਤੌਰ ਤੇ; **~ness** ਨਿਸ਼ਚਤਤਾ, ਸਖ਼ਿਰਤਾ, ਦ੍ਰਿੜ੍ਹਤਾ, ਕਠੋਰਤਾ, ਕਰੜਾਈ, ਸਖ਼ਤੀ

stricture ('ਸਟਰਿਕਚਅ*) *n* ਕਰੜੀ ਨੁਕਤਾਚੀਨੀ, ਟੀਨਾ-ਟਿੱਪਣੀ; ਨਾੜੀ ਦਾ ਗੁੰਗੜਾਉ

stride (ਸਟਰਾਇਡ) *v n* ਲੰਮੇ ਕਦਮ ਰੱਖਣਾ, ਉਲੰਘਣ, ਉਲੰਘ ਭਰਨੀ, ਡਗ ਭਰਨਾ; ਟੱਪ ਜਾਣਾ, ਉਲੰਘ; ਕਦਮ

strident ('ਸਟਰਾਇਡੰਟ) *a* ਕਰਖਸ਼, ਕੜਕਵੀਂ

strife ('ਸਟਰਾਇਫ਼) *n* ਲੜਾਈ-ਭਿੜਾਈ, ਝੇੜਾ, ਘਖੇੜਾ, ਝੰਜਟ, ਵਿਵਾਦ, ਕਲਹ

strike ('ਸਟਰਾਇਕ) *v n* ਮਾਰਨਾ, ਵਾਰ ਕਰਨਾ, ਧਿਆਨ ਖਿੱਚਣਾ; ਖ਼ਿਆਲ ਆਉਣਾ; ਸੁੱਝਣਾ; ਪੁੱਟਣਾ; ਹਾਰ ਮੰਨਣਾ, ਹਥਿਆਰ ਸੁੱਟਣਾ;

striking

(ਮਜ਼ਦੂਰਾਂ ਦਾ) ਹੜਤਾਲ ਕਰਨ; ਕੰਮ ਛੱਡ ਦੇਣਾ; (ਘੰਟਾ) ਵਜਾਉਣਾ; (ਚਾਕੂ ਆਦਿ) ਖੋਭਣਾ; ਹੜਤਾਲ; ਹਮਲਾ, ਹਵਾਈ ਹਮਲਾ

striking ('ਸਟਰਾਇਕਿੰਡ) *a* ਚਮਤਕਾਰੀ, ਉਘੜਵਾਂ

string ('ਸਟਰਿੰਡ) *n v* ਡੋਰੀ, ਸੂਤਲੀ, ਧਾਗਾ, ਤੰਦ, ਤਣੀ; ਤਾਰ, ਤੰਦੀ, ਲੜੀ ਪਰੋਣਾ; ਛਿੱਲਣਾ, ਧਾਗੇ ਕੱਢਣੇ

stringency ('ਸਟਰਿਨਜਅੰਸਿ) *n* ਸਖ਼ਤੀ, ਕਠੋਰਤਾ, ਕਰੜਪਨ; ਦਰਿਦਤਾ

stringent ('ਸਟਰਿਨਜਅੰਟ) *a* ਸਖ਼ਤ, ਕਰੜਾ (ਨੇਮ, ਪਾਬੰਦੀ), ਤੰਗ ਹਾਲ

strip (ਸਟਰਿਪ) *v* ਨੰਗਾ ਕਰਨਾ, ਕੱਪੜੇ ਉਛਾੜ ਆਦਿ ਲਾਹੁਣੇ; (ਦਰਖ਼ਤ ਦੀ) ਛਾਲ ਲਾਹੁਣੀ; ਸੰਖਣਾ ਕਰਨਾ, ਵਾਂਝਿਆਂ ਕਰਨਾ; ਲੈ ਲੈਣਾ

stripe (ਸਟਰਾਇਪ) *n* ਚੌੜੀ ਧਾਰੀ, ਫ਼ਾਂਟ, ਪੱਟੀ; (ਪ੍ਰ) ਚਾਬੁਕ ਦੀ ਮਾਰ; (ਬ ਵ) ਬੈਂਤ ਦੀ ਸਜ਼ਾ; **~d** ਧਾਰੀਦਾਰ, ਪੱਟੀਦਾਰ, ਲਹਿਰੀਏ ਵਾਲਾ

strive (ਸਟਰਾਇਵ਼) *v* ਜਤਨ ਕਰਨਾ, ਘਾਲਣਾ; ਜ਼ੋਰ ਲਾਉਣਾ ਜਾਂ ਮਾਰਨਾ, ਵਾਹ ਲਾਉਣੀ; ਸੰਘਰਸ਼ ਕਰਨਾ, ਟਾਕਰਾ ਕਰਨਾ, ਭਿੜਨਾ

stroke (ਸਟਰਅਉਕ) *n v* ਥਪਕੀ, ਥਾਪੜੀ, ਟਹੋਕਾ; ਵਾਰ, ਚੋਟ, ਮਾਰ, ਹੱਲਾ; ਥਾਪੜੀ ਦੇਣੀ, ਥਪਕੀ ਮਾਰਨੀ, ਥਾਪੜਨਾ

stroll (ਸਟਰੋਲ) *v n* ਸੈਰ ਕਰਨਾ, ਟਹਿਲਣਾ, ਇੱਧਰ-ਉੱਧਰ ਘੁੰਮਣਾ, ਮਟਰ-ਗਸ਼ਤ ਕਰਨੀ; ਚਹਿਲ-ਕਦਮੀ, ਸੈਰ, ਹਵਾਖੋਰੀ; **~er** ਘੁੰਮਕੜ, ਟਹਿਲਣ ਵਾਲਾ, ਮਟਰ-ਗਸ਼ਤ ਕਰਨ ਵਾਲਾ

strong (ਸਟਰੌਂਡ) *a* ਰਿਸ਼ਟ-ਪੁਸ਼ਟ, ਤਾਕਤਵਰ, ਬਲਵਾਨ, ਤਕੜਾ; ਮਜ਼ਬੂਤ, ਪੱਕਾ; **~box**, **room** ਤਿਜੋਰੀ, ਤਹਿਖ਼ਾਨਾ; **~hold** ਗੜ੍ਹ, ਕੋਟ, ਕਿਲ੍ਹਾ

structure ('ਸਟਰਅੱਕਚਆ*) *n* ਬਣਾਵਟ, ਬਣਤਰ, ਬਣਤ, ਰਚਨਾ

struggle ('ਸਟਰਅੰਗਲ) *v n* (ਛੁੱਟਣ ਲਈ) ਸਖ਼ਤ ਕੋਸ਼ਸ਼ ਕਰਨਾ, ਹੱਥ-ਪੈਰ ਮਾਰਨੇ; ਵਾਹ ਲਾਉਣੀ, ਜ਼ੋਰ ਮਾਰਨਾ, ਜਾਂ ਲਾਉਣਾ; (ਵਿਰੋਧੀ ਨਾਲ) ਸੰਘਰਸ਼ ਕਰਨਾ, ਕਸ਼ਮਕਸ਼ ਕਰਨਾ; ਟਿੱਲ, ਜ਼ੋਰ, ਸੰਘਰਸ਼, ਦੌੜ-ਭੱਜ, ਜਦੋਜਹਿਦ

strumpet ('ਸਟਰਅੰਪਿਟ) *n* ਵੇਸਵਾ, ਰੰਡੀ, ਕਸਬਣ

stubborn ('ਸਟਅੱਬਅਨ) *a* ਹਠੀ, ਜ਼ਿੱਦੀ, ਹਠੀਲਾ, ਅੜੀਅਲ, ਕਰੜਾ, ਸਖ਼ਤ; ਸਿਰੜੀ; **~ness** ਹਠ, ਦ੍ਰਿੜ੍ਹਤਾ, ਕੱਟੜਤਾ, ਕਠੋਰਤਾ, ਜ਼ਿੱਦ, ਅੜੀ

stud (ਸਟਅੱਡ) *n v* ਕੋਕਾ, ਕਿੱਲ, (ਸਜਾਵਟ ਲਈ) ਫੁੱਲਦਾਰ ਕਿੱਲ; ਬੁਧੀਆਂ ਜੜਨੀਆਂ; ਸਟੱਡ ਲਗਾਉਣਾ

student ('ਸਟਯੂਡਅੰਟ) *n* ਵਿਦਿਆਰਥੀ, ਛਾਤਰ, ਸਿਖਿਆਰਥੀ, ਚੇਲਾ, ਸ਼ਾਗਿਰਦ

studio ('ਸਟਯੂਡਿਅਉ) *n* ਕਲਾ-ਮੰਦਰ, ਚਿੰਤਰਸ਼ਾਲਾ, ਸਟੂਡੀਓ; ਸਿਨੇਮਾ ਸਟੂਡਿਓ

studious ('ਸਟਯੂਡਅਸ) *a* ਮਿਹਨਤੀ, ਪੜ੍ਹਾਕੂ, ਉਤਸ਼ਾਹੀ, ਤਤਪਰ, ਉਤਸ਼ਾਹ-ਪੂਰਨ

study ('ਸਟਅੱਡਿ) ਪੜ੍ਹਾਈ, ਪਾਠ; ਅਭਿਆਸ, ਪੜ੍ਹਾਈ ਕਰਨੀ; ਸਬਕ ਯਾਦ ਕਰਨਾ; ਘੋਖਣਾ, ਤਾੜ ਵਿਚ ਰਹਿਣਾ; ਚਿੰਤਨ ਕਰਨਾ

stuff (ਸਟਅੱਫ਼) *n v* ਪਦਾਰਥ, ਵਸਤੂ, ਮੂਲ, ਧਾਤੂ ਤੱਤ, ਜਿਨਸ, ਕੱਚਾ ਮਾਲ; ਫ਼ਜ਼ੂਲ ਗੱਲ; ਹਾਬੜ ਕੇ ਖਾਣਾ; ਝੂਠ ਬੋਲ ਕੇ ਧੋਖਾ ਦੇਣਾ, ਛਲਣਾ; **~y** ਵੱਟ ਵਾਲਾ, ਹੁੰਮਸੀ, ਸਾਹ-ਘੋਟੂ, ਨਾਰਾਜ਼, ਰੁੱਸਿਆ

stumble ('ਸਟਅੰਬਲ) *v n* ਠੋਕਰ ਖਾਣਾ, ਠੇਡਾ ਖਾਣਾ; ਚੁੱਕ ਜਾਣਾ; ਦੁਬਧਾ ਵਿਚ ਪੈਣਾ; ਠੋਕਰ,

ਠੰਡਾ, ਭਾਰੀ ਭੁਲ

stump (ਸਟੰਪ) *n v* ਕ੍ਰਿਕਟ ਦੀਆਂ ਤਿੰਨ ਡੰਡੀਆਂ ਵਿਚੋਂ ਇਕ; ਮੁੱਢ, ਖੁੰਢ; ਟੁੱਟੇ ਹੋਏ ਦੰਦ ਦੀ ਜੜ੍ਹ; ਹੱਥ ਜਾਂ ਪੈਰ ਦਾ ਟੁੰਡ, ਡੁੰਡ; ਸਿਗਾਰ ਦਾ ਟੋਟਾ; (ਕ੍ਰਿਕਟ) ਵਿਕਟ ਆਊਟ ਕਰਨਾ; ਵਿਕਟ-ਕੀਪਰ (ਬੋਲ); ਮੁਤਾਲਬਾ ਪੂਰਾ ਕਰਨਾ, ਮੰਗ ਪੂਰੀ ਕਰਨੀ

stun (ਸਟੱਨ) *v* ਬੇਹੋਸ਼ ਕਰ ਦੇਣਾ, ਹੋਸ਼ ਗੁਆਉਣੇ, ਚਕਰਾ ਦੇਣਾ, ਸੁਰਤ ਭੁਲਾ ਦੇਣੀ; ~ning ਹੋਸ਼-ਗੁਆਊ; ਸ਼ਾਨਦਾਰ, ਚਮਤਕਾਰੀ

stunt (ਸਟੰਟ) *v n* ਵਿਕਾਸ ਰੋਕਣਾ; ਉੱਨਤੀ ਰੋਕ ਦੇਣੀ; ਇਸ਼ਤਿਹਾਰਬਾਜ਼ੀ, ਉਸਟੰਡ, ਸ਼ੋਸ਼ਾ

stupendous (ਸਟਯੂਪੈਂਡਅਸ) *a* ਅਸਚਰਜਮਈ, ਬਹੁਤ ਵੱਡਾ, ਬਹੁਤ ਭਾਰੀ, ਸ਼ਾਨਦਾਰ; ਜ਼ਬਰਦਸਤ (ਕੰਮ, ਭੁਲ)

stupid ('ਸਟਯੂਪਿਡ) *a* ਬੇਵਕੂਫ਼ (ਆਦਮੀ), ਮੂਰਖ (ਵਿਅਕਤੀ), ਮੂੜ੍ਹ (ਮਨੁੱਖ); ਬੁੱਧ, ਨਿਰਬੁੱਧ, ਪਗਲਾ, ਖ਼ਰ-ਦਿਮਾਗ਼, ਉੱਜਡ਼;~ity ਮੂਰਖਤਾ, ਬੇਵਕੂਫ਼ੀ, ਉਜਪੁਣਾ, ਉੱਜਡ਼ਪੁਣਾ

sturdy ('ਸਟਅਃਡਿ) *a* ਮਜ਼ਬੂਤ, ਤਕੜਾ, ਕਾਠਾ, ਹੱਟਾ-ਕੱਟਾ

stutter (ਸਟਅੱਟਅ*) *v n* ਥਥਲਾਉਣਾ, ਥਥਿਆਉਣਾ, ਥਥਲਾ ਕੇ ਬੋਲਣਾ, ਅਟਕ ਅਟਕ ਕੇ ਬੋਲਣਾ; ਥਥਲਾਹਟ, ਥੱਥ

style (ਸਟਾਇਲ) *n* ਸ਼ੈਲੀ, ਢੰਗ, ਪੱਧਤੀ, ਰੀਤੀ, ਤਰਜ਼; ਵਿਸ਼ੇਸ਼ਤਾਵਾਂ, ਰੰਗਿਆਈਆਂ; ਠਾਠ

stylish ('ਸਟਾਇਲਿਸ਼) *a* ਛਬੀਲਾ, ਲੱਛੇਦਾਰ, ਫ਼ੈਸ਼ਨਦਾਰ

suave ('ਸਵਾਵ) *a* ਮਧੁਰ, ਸੁਹਾਵਾ, ਨਰਮ, ਮਿੱਠਾ, ਸੁਆਦੀ, ਮਿੱਠਬੋਲੜਾ

sub (ਸਅੱਬ) *prep pref* ਹੇਠਾਂ, ਥੱਲੇ, ਅਧੀਨ; ਨਿਚਲਾ, ਉਪ, ਲਘੂ, ਛੋਟਾ; ~**class** ਉਪਵਰਗ; ~**conscious** ਅਵਚੇਤਨ

subdue (ਸਅਬ'ਡਯੂ) *v* ਵੱਸ ਕਰਨਾ, ਕਾਬੂ ਕਰਨਾ, ਅਧੀਨ ਕਰਨਾ, ਦਬਾ ਲੈਣਾ; ਜਿੱਤ ਲੈਣਾ, ਹਲਕਾ ਕਰਨਾ, ਘੱਟ ਕਰਨਾ

subject ('ਸਅੱਬਜੈਕਟ) *a n v* ਅਧੀਨ; ਪਰਜਾ; ਰਈਅਤ; ਮਜ਼ਮੂਨ, ਵਿਸ਼ਾ, ਪ੍ਰਕਰਣ; (ਵਿਆ) ਕਰਤਾ; ਅਧੀਨ ਕਰਨਾ, ਹੇਠ ਕਰਨਾ, ਵਸੀਕਾਰ ਕਰਨਾ, (ਠੰਠੇ, ਮਖੌਲ ਦਾ) ਵਿਸ਼ਾ ਬਣਾਉਣਾ, ਨਿਸ਼ਾਨਾ ਬਣਾਉਣਾ; ~**ion** ਅਧੀਨਤਾ, ਦਾਸਤਾ, ਵਸੀਕਰਨ; ~**ive** (ਦਰਸ਼) ਅੰਤਰਮੁਖੀ; ਕਾਲਪਨਕ, ਖ਼ਿਆਲੀ; ਕਰਤਾ; ~**ive case** ਕਰਤਾ ਕਾਰਕ; ~**ivity** ਆਤਮਨਿਸ਼ਠਤਾ, ਅੰਤਰਮੁੱਖਤਾ

sub-judice ('ਸਅੱਬ'ਜੂਡਿਸ) (L) *a* ਪੇਸ਼ ਅਦਾਲਤ, ਵਿਚਾਰ ਅਧੀਨ, ਨਿਆਂਇ ਅਧੀਨ

subjugate (ਸਅੱਬਜੂਗੇਇਟ) *v* ਵੱਸ ਵਿਚ ਕਰਨਾ, ਅਧੀਨ ਕਰਨਾ, ਜਿੱਤ ਲੈਣਾ, ਕਾਬੂ ਵਿਚ ਕਰਨਾ, ਦਬਾ ਲੈਣਾ, ਦਮਨ ਕਰਨਾ

subjugation ('ਸਅੱਬਜੂ'ਗੇਇਸ਼ਨ) *a* ਵਸੀਕਰਨ, ਅਧੀਨਤਾ, ਦਮਨ, ਦਬਾਉ, ਤਾਬੇਦਾਰੀ

sublimation ('ਸਅੱਬਲਿ'ਮੇਇਸ਼ਨ) *n* ਜੋਹਰ-ਉਡਾਈ; ਸੁੱਧਤਾਈ; ਉਚਿਆਉਣ

sublime (ਸਅ'ਬਲਾਇਮ) *a v* ਉਦਾਤ, ਸਿਰੋਮਣੀ, ਗੌਰਵਮਈ, ਸ਼ਾਨਦਾਰ, ਜੋਹਰ ਉਡਾਉਣਾ, ਉੱਪਰ ਚੁੱਕਣਾ; ਮਹਾਨ ਜਾਂ ਪ੍ਰਭਾਵਸ਼ਾਲੀ ਬਣਾਉਣਾ

sublimity (ਸਅ'ਬਲਿਮਅਟਿ) *n* ਮਹਾਨਤਾ, ਪ੍ਰਭਾਵਸ਼ੀਲਤਾ, ਗੌਰਵਤਾ, ਉਚਤਾ; ਉਦਾਤਤਾ

submarine (ਸਅੱਬਮੈਰਿਨ) *n* ਜਲਵਰਤੀ, ਡੁਬਕਨੀ, ਪਣ ਡੁਬਕੀ

submerge (ਸਅਬ'ਮਅːਜ) v ਪਾਣੀ ਵਿਚ ਡੋਬਣਾ ਜਾਂ ਡੁੱਬਣਾ, ਗਰਕ ਕਰਨਾ ਜਾਂ ਹੋਣਾ; ~nce ਡੋਬ, ਡੋਬਾ, ਡੁਬਕੀ, ਜਲ-ਪਰਵਾਹ; ਗੋਤਾ

submission (ਸਅਬ'ਮਿਸ਼ਨ) n ਅਧੀਨਗੀ, ਤਾਬੇਦਾਰੀ; (ਕਾ) ਬੇਨਤੀ

submissive (ਸਅਬ'ਮਿਸਿਵ੍) a ਆਗਿਆਪਾਲ, ਆਗਿਆਕਾਰ, ਤਾਬੇਦਾਰ, ਦੀਨ, ਸੁਸ਼ੀਲ; ਨਿਮਰ, ਹੁਕਮਬਰਦਾਰ

submit (ਸਅਬ'ਮਿਟ) v ਹਵਾਲੇ ਕਰਨਾ, ਸ਼ਰਨ ਲੈਣਾ, ਅਧੀਨ ਹੋਣਾ, ਪੇਸ਼ ਕਰਨਾ; ਅੱਗੇ ਰੱਖਣਾ ਬੇਨਤੀ ਕਰਨਾ; ਝੁਕ ਜਾਣਾ, ਮੰਨ ਲੈਣਾ

subordinate (ਸਅੱਬਾ*ਡਿਨੇਟ) a n v ਅਧੀਨ, ਸਹਾਇਕ, ਮਾਤਹਿਤ; ਹੇਠਲਾ, ਅਧੀਨ ਵਿਅਕਤੀ; ਮਾਤਹਿਤ ਬਣਾਉਣਾ

subordination (ਸਅੱਬਾ*ਡਿਨੇਸ਼ਨ) n ਅਧੀਨਗੀ, ਮਾਤਹਿਤੀ

subscribe (ਸਅਬ'ਸਕਰਾਇਬ) v ਹਾਮੀ ਭਰਨੀ, ਤਾਈਦ ਕਰਨੀ, ਚੰਦਾ ਦੇਣਾ, ਗਾਹਕ ਬਣਨਾ; ~r ਸਹੀਕਾਰ, ਗਾਹਕ, ਚੰਦਾ ਦੇਣ ਵਾਲਾ

subscript ('ਸਅੱਬਸਕਰਿਪਟ) a ਹੇਠ ਲਿਖਿਆ, ਨਿਮਨਲਿਖਤ; ~ion ਚੰਦਾ, ਦਾਨ; ਮੁੱਲ, ਕੀਮਤ, ਨਾਮ ਲੇਖਨ

subsequence ('ਸਅੱਬਸਿਕਵਅੱਸ) n ਉੱਤਰਵਰਤਤਾ, ਪਰਿਣਾਮ

subsequent ('ਸਅੱਬਸਿਕਵਅੱਟ) a ਉੱਤਰਵਰਤੀ, ਉੱਤਰਕਾਲੀਨ, ਆਗਾਮੀ, ਅਗਲਾ, ਪਿੱਛੋਂ ਦਾ; ~ly ਬਾਅਦ, ਵਿਚ, ਪਿੱਛੋਂ

subservient (ਸਅਬ'ਸਅːਵ੍ਯਅੱਟ) a ਉਪਯੋਗੀ, ਕਾਰਕ ਸਹਾਇਕ, ਹੱਥ-ਠੋਕਾ

subside (ਸਅਬ'ਸਾਇਡ) v (ਪਾਣੀ) ਉੱਤਰ ਜਾਣਾ, ਥੱਲੇ ਆ ਜਾਣਾ, ਘਟ ਜਾਣਾ, ਗਾਇਬ ਹੋ ਜਾਣਾ

subsidiary (ਸਅਬ'ਸਿਡਯਅਰਿ) a n ਸਹਾਇਕ, ਅਧੀਨ, ਉਪਸੰਗੀ; ਮਾਤਹਿਤ

subsidize ('ਸਅੱਬਸਿਡਾਇਜ਼) v ਮਾਲੀ ਸਹਾਇਤਾ ਕਰਨੀ, ਅਰਥ-ਸਹਾਇਤਾ ਦੇਣੀ

subsidy ('ਸਅੱਬਸਿਡਿ) n ਆਰਥਕ ਸਹਾਇਤਾ, ਇਮਦਾਦੀ ਰਕਮ; ਅਨੁਦਾਨ

subsist (ਸਅਬ'ਸਿਸਟ) v ਜੀਉਂਦੇ ਰਹਿਣਾ, ਰਹਿਣਾ, ਟਿਕਣਾ, ਖੁਆਉਣਾ-ਪਿਆਉਣਾ, ਜੀਵਨ-ਨਿਰਬਾਹ ਕਰਨਾ, ਜਿੰਦਾ ਰਹਿਣਾ, ਜੀਉਣਾ; ~ence ਉਪਜੀਵਕਾ, ਜੀਵਨ-ਨਿਰਬਾਹ, ਰੋਜੀ, ਗੁਜ਼ਾਰਾ

substance ('ਸਅੱਬਸਟਅੱਸ) n ਸਾਰ, ਸਾਰਾਂਸ਼, ਭਾਵ, ਨਚੋੜ; ਅਸਲੀ ਮਤਲਬ; ਵਿਸ਼ਾ-ਵਸਤੂ, ਵਾਸਤਵਿਕਤਾ

substandard ('ਸਅੱਬ'ਸਟੈਂਡਅːਡ) a ਮਿਆਰ ਤੋਂ ਡਿੱਗਿਆ, ਘਟਿਆ

substantial (ਸਅਬ'ਲਟੈਨਸ਼ਲ) a n ਮਹੱਤਪੁਰਨ, ਠੋਸ, ਨਿੱਗਰ, ਵਾਸਤਵਿਕ, ਧਨਵਾਨ, (ਬ ਵ) ਮਹੱਤਵਪੂਰਨ ਅੰਗ; ~ity ਵਾਸਤਵਿਕਤਾ, ਯਥਾਰਥਕਤਾ, ਸਾਰ, ਸਚਾਈ; ਮਹੱਤਵਪੂਰਨਤਾ; ~ly ਉਚਿਤ ਰੂਪ ਵਿਚ

substantiate (ਸਅਬ'ਸਟੈਂਸ਼ਿਏਟ) v ਸਚਾਈ ਸਿੱਧ ਕਰਨਾ, ਸਾਬਤ ਕਰਨਾ, ਸਬੂਤ ਦੇਣਾ, ਪ੍ਰਮਾਣ ਦੇਣਾ

substantive ('ਸਅੱਬਸਟਅੰਟਿਵ) a n ਸੁਤੰਤਰ, ਵਾਸਤਵਿਕ, ਮੌਲਕ, ਅਸਲੀ

substitute ('ਸਅੱਬਸਟਿਟਯੂਟ) n v ਇਵਜ਼, ਬਦਲ, ਪ੍ਰਤੀਸ਼ਾਪਨ; ਬਦਲ ਕੇ ਰੱਖਣਾ, ਵਟਾ ਕੇ ਰੱਖਣਾ; ਅਦਲਾ-ਬਦਲੀ ਕਰਨੀ

substiution ('ਸਅੱਬਸਟਿ'ਟਯੂਸ਼ਨ) n ਅਦਲਾ-ਬਦਲੀ, ਬਦਲੀ, ਪ੍ਰਤੀਸ਼ਾਪਨ

substratum ('ਸਅੱਬ'ਸਟਰਾਟਅਮ) *n* ਆਧਾਰ, ਨੀਂਹ; ਨਿਮਨ ਵਰਗ

subterranean ('ਸਅੱਬਟਆ'ਰੇਇਨਯਅਨ) *a* ਥੱਲੇ ਦਾ, ਜ਼ਮੀਨ ਦੇ ਹੇਠਾਂ ਦਾ, ਭੂਮੀਗਤ

subtle ('ਸਅੱਟਲ) *a* ਸੂਖਮ; ਪਤਲਾ, ਵਿਰਲਾ, ਲਤੀਫ਼, ਰਹੱਸਮਈ; ਬਾਰੀਕ; ਤੀਬਰ; ਮੱਕਾਰ; ~**ty** ਵਿਰਲਤਾ; ਸੂਖਮਤਾ; ਤੀਖਣਤਾ

subtract (ਸਅੱਬ'ਟਰੈਕਟ) *v* ਘਟਾਉਣਾ, ਤਫ਼ਰੀਕ ਕਰਨਾ, ਮਨਫ਼ੀ ਕਰਨਾ, ਕੱਢਣਾ; ~**ion** ਘਟਾਉ, ਤਫ਼ਰੀਕ, ਮਨਫ਼ੀ; ~**or** ਘਟਾਉਣ ਵਾਲਾ, ਤਫ਼ਰੀਕ ਕਰਨ ਵਾਲਾ, ਕੱਢਣ ਵਾਲਾ

suburb ('ਸਅੱਬਅ:ਬ) *n* ਸ਼ਹਿਰ ਦੇ ਆਸ-ਪਾਸ ਦਾ ਇਲਾਕਾ, ਸ਼ਹਿਰ ਦਾ ਚੁਗਿਰਦਾ, ਉਪ-ਨਗਰ; ~**an** ਆਲੇ-ਦੁਆਲੇ ਸਬੰਧੀ; ਉਪ-ਨਗਰ ਸਬੰਧੀ

subvent (ਸਅੱਬ'ਵੈਂਟ) *v* ਸਹਾਇਤਾ ਕਰਨਾ, ਮਾਲੀ ਸਹਾਇਤਾ ਕਰਨਾ, ਧਰਮਾਰਥ ਸਹਾਇਤਾ ਦੇਣੀ

subversion (ਸਅਬ'ਵ੍ਯਅ:ਸ਼ਨ) *n* ਉਲਟ-ਪੁਲਟ, ਭੰਨ-ਤੋੜ, ਵਿਨਾਸ਼, ਉਲਟ-ਫੇਰ

subvert (ਸਅਬ'ਵ੍ਯਅ:ਟ) *v* ਉਲਟ-ਪੁਲਟ ਦੇਣਾ, ਨਸ਼ਟ ਕਰਨਾ, ਸਤਿਆਨਾਸ ਕਰਨਾ; ਵਿਗਾੜਨਾ ਖ਼ਰਾਬ ਕਰਨਾ

subway ('ਸਅੱਬਵੇਇ) *n* ਭੂਮੀ ਥੱਲੇ ਦਾ ਮਾਰਗ

succeed (ਸਅਕ'ਸੀਡ) *v* ਸਫ਼ਲ ਹੋਣਾ, ਮਨੋਰਥ ਪੂਰਾ ਹੋਣਾ; (ਕਿਸੇ ਦੀ) ਥਾਂ ਲੈਣੀ; ਉੱਤਰਾਧਿਕਾਰੀ ਹੋਣਾ, ਗੱਦੀ ਤੇ ਬਹਿਣਾ, ਜਾਨਸ਼ੀਨ ਹੋਣਾ; ~**ing** ਆਗਾਮੀ; ਉੱਤਰਵਰਤੀ

success (ਸਅਕ'ਸੈਸ) *n* (1) ਸਫ਼ਲਤਾ, ਕਾਮਯਾਬੀ, (2) ਰੱਟੂ ਤੋਤਾ; ~**ful** ਸਫ਼ਲ, ਕਾਮਯਾਬ; ~**ion** ਉੱਤਰ-ਅਧਿਕਾਰ, ਜਾਨਸ਼ੀਨੀ; ਵਿਰਾਸਾ, ਸਿਲਸਿਲਾ; ~**ive** ਕ੍ਰਮ-ਅਨੁਸਾਰ, ਸਿਲਸਲੇਵਾਰ, ਲਗਾਤਾਰ; ~**or** ਉੱਤਰਾਧਿਕਾਰੀ; ਜਾਨਸ਼ੀਨ, ਵਾਰਸ; **nothing succeeds like~** ਚਲਦੀ ਦਾ ਨਾਂ ਗੱਡੀ

succinct (ਸਅਕ'ਸਿੰਡ(ਕ)ਟ) *a* ਸੰਖੇਪ, ਥੋੜ੍ਹੇ ਸ਼ਬਦਾਂ ਦਾ, ਸੰਖਿਪਤ

succour ('ਸਅੱਕਅ*) *v n* (ਮੁਸ਼ਕਲ ਸਮੇਂ) ਸਹਾਇਤਾ ਦੇਣਾ, ਮਦਦ ਕਰਨਾ, ਆਸਰਾ ਦੇਣਾ; ਸਹਾਇਤਾ, ਮਦਦ, ਆਸਰਾ, ਬਹੁੜੀ

succumb (ਸਅ'ਕਅੱਮ) *v* ਹਾਰ ਜਾਣਾ, ਹਥਿਆਰ ਸੁੱਟ ਦੇਣਾ, ਸ਼ਿਕਸਤ ਖਾਣਾ, ਮਰ ਜਾਣਾ; ਸ਼ਿਕਾਰ ਹੋਣਾ (ਰੋਗ, ਲਾਲਚ, ਦਬਾਉ ਦਾ)

such (ਸੱਚ) *a pron* ਇਸ ਤਰ੍ਹਾਂ ਦਾ, ਅਜਿਹਾ, ਇਤਨਾ, ਇਸ ਢੰਗ ਦਾ; (ਕ) ਪਹਿਲਾਂ ਕਿਹਾ; ਫ਼ਲਾਂ-ਫ਼ਲਾਂ; ਉਹ ਲੋਕ, ਇਹ; ਅਜਿਹੀਆਂ ਚੀਜ਼ਾਂ; ~**and such** ਫ਼ਲਾਂ-ਫ਼ਲਾਂ, ਫ਼ਲਾਨਾ, ਢਿਮਕਾ

suck (ਸੱਕ) *v n* ਚੁੰਘਣਾ; ਚੁਸਕੀ ਲਾਉਣੀ; ਚੂਪਣਾ; ਜੀਭ ਫੇਰਨਾ, ਸੁੜਕਣਾ; ਚੁਸਕੀ, ਸੁੜਕਾ; ~**in** (ਭੰਵਰ ਆਦਿ ਦਾ) ਹੜੱਪ ਜਾਣਾ, ਗਰਕ ਕਰ ਦੇਣਾ

suckle ('ਸਅੱਕਲ) *v* ਦੁੱਧ ਪਿਆਉਣਾ, ਚੁੰਘਾਉਣਾ; ਦੁੱਧ ਪੀਣਾ, ਚੁੰਘਣਾ

suction ('ਸਅੱਕਸ਼ਨ) *n* ਚੂਸ਼, ਚੁੰਘਾਈ

sudden ('ਸਅੱਡਨ) *a n* ਅਚਾਨਕ, ਅਚਨਚੇਤੀ, ਬਹੁਤ ਤੇਜ਼; ~**ly** ਅਚਾਨਕ, ਅਕਸਮਾਤ, ਛੇਤੀ ਨਾਲ, ਤੇਜ਼ੀ ਨਾਲ

sue (ਸੂ) *v* ਮੁੱਕਦਮਾ ਚਲਾਉਣਾ, ਦਾਅਵਾ ਕਰਨਾ, ਦਰਖ਼ਾਸਤ ਕਰਨਾ,

suffer ('ਸਅੱਫ਼ਅ*) *v* ਨੁਕਸਾਨ ਸਹਿਣਾ, ਸਹਾਰਨਾ; ਝੱਲਣਾ, ਭੋਗਣਾ, ਭੁਗਤਣਾ, ਦੁੱਖ ਪਾਉਣਾ; ~**ing** ਦੁਖੜਾ, ਵੇਦਨਾ, ਪੀੜਾ, ਸੰਤਾਪ, ਕਸ਼ਟ ਕਲੇਸ਼, ਜਫ਼ਰ

suffice (ਸਅ'ਫ਼ਾਇਸ) *v* ਪੂਰਾ ਹੋਣਾ, ਕਾਫ਼ੀ ਹੋਣਾ,

ਬਹੁਤ ਹੋਣਾ, ਸਰਨਾ, ਕੰਮ ਚਲਾਉਣਾ

sufficiency (ਸਅ'ਫ਼ਿਸ਼ੰਿਸਿ) *n* ਰੱਜ-ਪੁੱਜ, ਬਹੁਤਾਤ, ਖ਼ੁਸ਼ਹਾਲੀ, ਯੋਗਤਾ

sufficient (ਸਅ'ਫ਼ਿਸ਼ੰਟ) *a* ਕਾਫ਼ੀ, ਰੱਜਵਾਂ, ਪੂਰਾ, ਚੋਖਾ, ਸਮਰੱਥ; ਯੋਗ

suffix ('ਸਅੱਫ਼ਿਕਸ) *n v* ਪਿਛੇਤਰ, ਪ੍ਰਤਯ; ਪਿਛੇਤਰ ਲਾਉਣਾ

suffocate ('ਸਅੱਫ਼ਅਕੇਇਟ) *v* ਸਾਹ ਰੋਕਣਾ, ਸਾਹ ਰੁਕਣਾ, ਸਾਹ ਘੁੱਟਣਾ, ਗਲਾ ਦਬਾਉਣਾ, ਦਮ ਘੁੱਟਣਾ, ਦਮ ਘੁੱਟਣਾ

suffocation ('ਸਅੱਫ਼ਅ'ਕੇਇਸ਼ਨ) *n* ਸਾਹ-ਰੋਧ, ਦਮਘੁਟੀ

sugar ('ਸ਼ੁਗਾਅ*) *n v* ਸ਼ੱਕਰ, ਖੰਡ, ਚੀਨੀ; ਚਾਪਲੂਸੀ; ਖੰਡ ਪਾਉਣੀ; ਖੰਡ ਚਾਤੂਨੀ, ਗਲੇਫਣਾ; ~**cane** ਗੰਨਾ; ~**plum** ਪਤਾਸਾ, ਮਿੱਠੀ ਗੋਲੀ

suggest (ਸਅ'ਜੈੱਸਟ) *v* ਸੁਝਾਉ ਦੇਣਾ, ਸੁਝਾਉਣਾ, ਸੰਕੇਤ ਕਰਨਾ; ਰਾਇ ਦੇਣੀ, ਤਜਵੀਜ਼ ਕਰਨਾ, ਪ੍ਰਸਤਾਵ ਕਰਨਾ; ~**ion** ਸੁਝਾਉ, ਤਜਵੀਜ਼; ਉਪਦੇਸ਼, ਰਾਇ, ਸਲਾਹ; ਆਤਮ-ਪਰੇਰਨਾ; ~**ive** ਸੁਝਾਉਣ ਵਾਲਾ, ਸੰਕੇਤਕ, ਸੂਚਕ; ਸੰਕੇਤ-ਪੂਰਨ

suicidal (ਸੁਇ'ਸਾਇਡਲ) *a* ਆਤਮਘਾਤੀ, ਆਤਮਨਾਸੀ, ਆਤਮ-ਹੱਤਿਆ ਸਬੰਧੀ

suicide ('ਸੁਇਸਾਇਡ) *n* ਆਤਮ-ਹੱਤਿਆ, ਖ਼ੁਦਕਸ਼ੀ

suit (ਸੂਟ) *n v* (1) ਮੁਕੱਦਮਾ, ਦਾਅਵਾ, ਕਾਨੂੰਨੀ ਜਾਂ ਅਦਾਲਤੀ; (2) ਕੱਪੜਿਆਂ ਦਾ ਜੋੜਾ, ਸੂਟ (ਜਿਸ ਵਿਚ ਕੋਟ, ਪਤਲੂਨ ਆਦਿ ਇਕੋ ਹੀ ਕੱਪੜੇ ਦੇ ਹੋਣ); ਜਾਚਨਾ, ਪ੍ਰਾਰਥਨਾ; ਸ਼ਾਦੀ ਦੀ ਗੱਲਬਾਤ; ਮੇਲ ਖਾਣਾ, ਫਬਣਾ, ਸਜਣਾ,

ਅਨੁਕੂਲ ਬਣਾਉਣਾ; ਅਨੁਸਾਰ ਬਣਾਉਣਾ, ਰਾਸ ਆਉਣਾ; ~**case** ਸੂਟ ਕੇਸ, ਛੋਟਾ ਬਕਸਾ; ~**ability** ਠੁੱਕ, ਅਨੁਕੂਲਤਾ, ਯੋਗਤਾ, ਢੁਕਾਉ; ~**able** ਉਚਿਤ, ਅਨੁਕੂਲ, ਮਿਲਦਾ-ਜੁਲਦਾ, ਮੁਆਫ਼ਕ, ਜਚਦਾ, ਢੁੱਕਵਾਂ, ਫੱਬਵਾਂ

suite (ਸਵੀਟ) *n* (1) (ਕਮਰਿਆਂ, ਫ਼ਰਨੀਚਰ ਆਦਿ ਦਾ) ਇਕ ਸਿਲਸਲਾ, ਨੌਕਰ-ਚਾਕਰ, ਲਾਮ-ਡੋਰੀ; (2) (ਸੰਗੀ) ਵਾਦਕ ਸੰਗੀਤ ਸਬੰਧੀ ਕ੍ਰਿਤੀ

sullen ('ਸਅੱਲਅਨ) *a* ਉਦਾਸ, ਚਿੰਤਤ, ਚਿੜਚੜਾ, ਮੂੰਹ ਵੱਟਿਆ

sully ('ਸੂਅੱਲਿ) *v* (ਕਾਵਿਕ) ਬਦਨਾਮ ਕਰਨਾ, ਧੱਬਾ ਲਾਉਣਾ; ਭ੍ਰਸ਼ਟ ਕਰਨਾ, ਮੈਲਾ ਕਰਨਾ

sultry ('ਸਅੱਲਟਰਿ) *a* (ਹਵਾ ਜਾਂ ਰੁੱਤ) ਹੁੰਮਸੀ, ਗਰਮ; (ਸੁਭਾਅ) ਤੇਜ਼, ਤੀਖਣ, ਉਤੇਜਨਾਸ਼ੀਲ

sum ('ਸਅੱਮ) *n v* ਕੁੱਲ, ਜੋੜ, ਮਿਜ਼ਾਨ, ਯੋਗਫਲ; ਜੋੜ ਕਰਨਾ, ਜੋੜਨਾ; ~**total** ਕੁੱਲ ਜੋੜ

summarize ('ਸਅੱਮਅਰਾਇਜ਼) *v* ਸਾਰ ਦੇਣਾ, ਸੰਖੇਪ ਕਰਨਾ, ਖ਼ੁਲਾਸਾ ਕਰਨਾ, ਸਾਰਾਂਸ਼ ਕੱਢਣਾ

summary ('ਸਅੱਮਅਰਿ) *a n* ਸੰਖੇਪ; ਸਾਰ, ਸਾਰਾਂਸ਼, ਖ਼ੁਲਾਸਾ, ਨਚੋੜ, ਤਾਤਪਰਜ

summer ('ਸਅੱਮਅ*) *n v* ਗਰਮੀਆਂ, ਗਰਮੀ ਦੀ ਰੁੱਤ, ਹੁਨਾਲਾ; ਗਰਮੀ ਕੱਟਣੀ

summit ('ਸਅੱਮਿਟ) *n* ਚੋਟੀ, ਸਿਖਰ, ਸਿਖਰ ਸੰਮੇਲਨ

summon ('ਸਅੱਮਅਨ) *v* ਸੱਦਣਾ, ਬੁਲਾ ਭੇਜਣਾ, ਤਲਬ ਕਰਨਾ, ਪੁਕਾਰਨਾ, ਯਾਦ ਕਰਨਾ; (ਕਾ) ਸੰਮਨ ਭੇਜ ਕੇ ਤਲਬ ਕਰਨਾ; ~**s** ਅਦਾਲਤੀ ਸੱਦਾ, ਤਲਬੀ, ਹੁਕਮਨਾਮਾ, ਸੰਮਨ, ਬੁਲਾਵਾ

sumptuous ('ਸਅੱਮਪਚੂਅਸ) *a* ਖੁੱਲ੍ਹਾ-ਡੁੱਲ੍ਹਾ, ਸ਼ਾਹਨਾ, ਅਮੀਰਾਨਾ, ਕੀਮਤੀ, ਸ਼ਾਹ ਖ਼ਰਚ ਵਾਲਾ

sun (ਸਅੱਨ) *n v* ਸੂਰਜ, ਰਵੀ, ਆਫ਼ਤਾਬ; ਦਿਨ;

ਧੁੱਪ; ਧੁੱਪ ਸੇਕਣੀ, ਧੁੱਪੇ ਬਹਿਣਾ, ਧੁੱਪ ਲੁਆਈ; ~bath ਧੁੱਪ ਇਸ਼ਨਾਨ; ~beam ਸੂਰਜ ਦੀ ਕਿਰਨ; ~down ਸੂਰਜ-ਡੁੱਬੇ, ਦਿਨ-ਲੱਥੇ; ~flower ਸੂਰਜਮੁਖੀ; ~rise ਪਹੁ-ਫੁਟਾਲਾ; ~set ਅਸਤ, ਆਥਣ; ~shine ਧੁੱਪ; ਖੇੜਾ; ~stroke ਗਰਮੀ ਦਾ ਧੱਕਾ, ਲੂ, ਲੂਹਾ

Sunday ('ਸਅੰਡਿ) *n* ਐਤਵਾਰ

sunder ('ਸਅੰਡਅ*) *v* ਅਲੱਗ ਕਰਨਾ ਜਾਂ ਹੋਣਾ, ਵੱਖ ਕਰਨਾ ਜਾਂ ਹੋਣਾ, ਨਿਖੇੜਨਾ ਜਾਂ ਨਿੱਖੜਨਾ; ਤੋੜਨਾ, ਅਲੱਗ ਰੱਖਣਾ

sundry ('ਸਅੰਡਰਿ) *a* ॥ (ਪ੍ਰ) ਕਈ, ਅਨੇਕ, ਕਈ ਇਕ; ਨਿੱਕ-ਸੁੱਕ, ਉਰਲੀਆਂ-ਪਰਲੀਆਂ ਚੀਜ਼ਾਂ

sup (ਸਅੱਪ) *v n* ਘੁੱਟ ਘੁੱਟ ਪੀਣਾ, ਸੁੜਕਣਾ, ਘੋੜ੍ਹੂ ਘੋੜ੍ਹੂ ਪੀਣਾ; ਘੁੱਟ; ਚੁਸਕੀ

super ('ਸੂਪਅ*) *n a pref* ਵਾਧੂ ਆਦਮੀ; ਵਧੀਆ ਕਿਸਮ ਦਾ ਕੱਪੜਾ ਜਾਂ ਵਸਤੂ; ਵਾਧੂ, ਐਰਾ-ਗੈਰਾ; ਬਹੁਤ ਵਧੀਆ; ਅੰਗੇਤਰ, ਉਤਲਾ, ਪਾਰਲਾ, ਪਰਾ; ~fine ਅਤੀ ਉੱਤਮ, ਬਹੁਤ ਹੀ ਵਧੀਆ; ਮਹੀਨ, ਬਾਰੀਕ (ਕੱਪੜਾ); ~human ਦੈਵੀ, ਅਲੌਕਕ; ~man ਮਹਾਂ-ਮਾਨਵ; ਪਰਮ ਪੁਰਸ਼, ਬ੍ਰਹਮ-ਗਿਆਨੀ; ~natural ਦੈਵੀ, ਅਲੌਕਕ, ਪ੍ਰਾਸਰੀਰਕ, ਅਸਰਜਤਾਮਈ; ~structure ਉੱਤਲੀ ਉਸਾਰੀ, ਉੱਪਰਲਾ ਢਾਂਚਾ; ~tax ਵਾਧੂ ਕਰ, ਅਧਿ-ਕਰ

superannuate ('ਸੂਪਅ'ਰੈਨਯੁਏਇਟ) *v* ਬੁਢਾਪੇ ਕਾਰਨ ਨੌਕਰੀ ਤੋਂ ਮੁਕਤ ਕਰਨਾ, ਪੈਨਸ਼ਨ ਦੇ ਕੇ ਮੁਕਤ ਕਰਨਾ

superannuation ('ਸੂਪਅ'ਰੈਨਯੁ'ਏਇਸ਼ਨ) *n* ਬੁਢਾਪੇ ਕਾਰਨ ਕੰਮ ਯੋਗ ਨਾ ਰਹਿਣਾ, ਬੁਢਾਪੇ ਦੀ ਪੈਨਸ਼ਨ

superb (ਸ'ਪਅ:ਬ) *a* ਸ਼ਾਨਦਾਰ; ਅਤੀ ਚੰਗਾ, ਵਧੀਆ; ਗ਼ਜ਼ਬ ਦਾ

superficial ('ਸੂਪਅ'ਫ਼ਿਸ਼ਲ) *a* ਬਾਹਰ-ਬਾਹਰ ਦਾ, ਉੱਪਰਲਾ-ਉੱਪਰਲਾ, ਦਿਖਾਵੇ ਦਾ, ਮੋਟਾ-ਮੋਟਾ, ਥੋਥਾ, ਹਲਕਾ

superficiality ('ਸੂਪਅ'ਫ਼ਿਸ਼ਿ'ਐਲਅਟਿ) *n* ਉੱਪਰ-ਲਾਪਟ, ਦਿਖਾਵਾ, ਥੋਥਾਪਣ, ਕਚਿਆਈ, ਹਲਕਾਪਣ

superfluous (ਸੂ'ਪਅ:ਫ਼ਲੁਸ) *a* ਨਿਰਥਕ, ਬੋਲੇੜਾ, ਫ਼ਾਲਤੂ

superintend ('ਸੂਪ(ਅ)ਰਿਨ'ਟੈਂਡ) *v* ਪ੍ਰਬੰਧ ਕਰਨਾ, ਦੇਖ-ਭਾਲ ਕਰਨੀ; ~ence ਪ੍ਰਬੰਧ, ਨਿਗਰਾਨੀ, ਦੇਖ-ਭਾਲ; ~ent ਪ੍ਰਬੰਧਕ, ਸੰਚਾਲਕ, ਸੁਪਰਿਟੈਂਡੈਂਟ

superior (ਸੂ'ਪਿਅਰਿਅ*) *a n* ਵੱਡਾ ਉੱਤਮ, ਵੱਡਾ; ਵਧੀਆ, ਬਿਹਤਰ; ਸ੍ਰੇਸ਼ਠ, ਬਹੁਰਗ; ਅਸਧਾਰਨ ਪ੍ਰਮੁੱਖ; ~ity ਉੱਤਮਤਾ, ਪ੍ਰਮੁੱਖਤਾ, ਵਿਸ਼ੇਸ਼ ਯੋਗਤਾ, ਵਡਿਆਈ; ਉੱਚਤਾ; ਗੁਮਾਨ

supersede ('ਸੂਪਅ'ਸੀਡ) *v* ਮਨਸੂਖ ਕਰਨਾ, ਛੱਡ ਦੇਣਾ, ਉਲੰਘਣਾ, ਬਦਲਣਾ, ਥਾਂ ਮੱਲਣਾ

supersession ('ਸੂਪਅ'ਸੈਸ਼ਨ) *n* ਪ੍ਰਤੀਸਥਾਪਨ, ਇਕ ਦੀ ਉਲੰਘਣਾ ਕਰਕੇ ਕਿਸੇ ਦੂਜੇ ਦੀ ਨਿਯੁਕਤੀ

supersitition ('ਸੂਪਅ'ਸਟਿਸ਼ਨ) *n* ਵਹਿਮ, ਭਰਮਜਾਲ, ਅੰਧ-ਸ਼ਰਧਾ, ਅੰਧ-ਵਿਸ਼ਵਾਸ

supervise (ਸੂਪਅਵਾਇਜ਼) *v* ਦੇਖ-ਰੇਖ ਕਰਨਾ, ਦੇਖ-ਭਾਲ ਕਰਨੀ, ਤਾਕ ਰੱਖਣੀ, ਨਿਗਰਾਨੀ ਕਰਨੀ

supervision ('ਸੂਪਅ'ਵ਼ਿਯ਼ਨ) *n* ਦੇਖ-ਰੇਖ, ਦੇਖ-ਭਾਲ, ਨਿਗਰਾਨੀ, ਧਿਆਨ

supervisor ('ਸੂਪਅ'ਵਾਇਜ਼ਅ*) *n* ਨਿਗਰਾਨ,

ਨਿਰੀਖਕ

supper ('ਸਅੱਪਅ*) *n* ਰਾਤ ਦਾ ਖਾਣਾ

supplement ('ਸਅੱਪਲਿਮਅੰਟ, 'ਸਅੱਪਲਿਮੈਂਟ) *n* (ਹਿਸਾਬ) ਸਮਪੂਰਕ, (ਅਖ਼ਬਾਰ ਦਾ) ਪੂਰਕ-ਪੱਤਰ, ਅਤੀਰਿਕਤ ਅੰਸ਼; ਸੰਪੂਰਨ ਕਰਨਾ, ਵਧਾਉਣਾ, ਲਗਾਉਣਾ, ਵਾਧਾ ਕਰਨਾ; **~al, ~ary** ਪੂਰਕ, ਸਮਪੂਰਕ; ਪਿੱਛੋਂ ਜੁੜਿਆ, ਜ਼ਮੀਨੀ

supplicate ('ਸਅੱਪਲਿਕੇਇਟ) *v* ਬੇਨਤੀ ਕਰਨੀ, ਅਰਜ਼ ਕਰਨੀ, ਤਰਲੇ ਕੱਢਣੇ, ਮਿੰਨਤ ਕਰਨੀ, ਹਾੜ੍ਹੇ ਕੱਢਣੇ

supplication ('ਸਅੱਪਲਿ'ਕੇਇਸ਼ਨ) *n* ਬੇਨਤੀ, ਅਰਜ਼, ਤਰਲਾ, ਮਿੰਨਤ, ਵਾਸਤਾ, ਜਾਚਨਾ

supplier (ਸਅੱ'ਪਲਾਇਅ*) *n* ਭੰਡਾਰੀ, ਪੂਰਤੀਕਰਤਾ, ਮੁੱਹਈਆ ਕਰਨ ਵਾਲਾ,

supply (ਸਅ'ਪਲਾਇ) *v n* ਰਸਦ ਪਹੁੰਚਾਉਣੀ, ਲੋੜ ਪੂਰੀ ਕਰਨੀ; ਪੂਰਾ ਕਰਨਾ; ਭਰਤੀ ਕਰਨਾ; ਭੰਡਾਰ, ਰਸਦ; ਪੂਰਤੀ; ਰਸਦ-ਪਾਣੀ

support (ਸਅ'ਪੋਟ) *v n* ਸਮਰਥਨ ਕਰਨਾ, ਸਹਾਰਾ ਦੇਣਾ; ਥੰਮ੍ਹਣਾ, ਹਿਮਾਇਤ ਕਰਨੀ; ਸੰਭਾਲਣਾ, ਭਾਰ ਉਠਾਉਣਾ; (ਮਤੇ ਦੀ) ਪੁਸ਼ਟੀ ਕਰਨੀ; ਪਿੱਠ ਠੋਕਣੀ, ਪਾਲਣ-ਪੋਸਣ ਕਰਨਾ; ਹਾਮੀ, ਪੁਸ਼ਟੀ, ਹਿਮਾਇਤ; ਆਸਰਾ; **~ed** ਸਮਰਥਤ; **~er** ਪੁਸ਼ਟੀਕਾਰ; ਸਹਾਇਕ, ਸਹਾਈ, ਅੰਗਪਾਲ; ਹਿਮਾਇਤੀ, ਮਦਦਗਾਰ; **~ing** ਸਮਰਥਕ, ਸਹਾਇਕ, ਸਹਾਈ

suppose ('ਸਅ'ਪਅਉਜ਼) *v* ਮੰਨ ਲੈਣਾ, ਸਮਝਣਾ, ਕਲਪਤ ਕਰਨਾ, ਅਨੁਮਾਨ ਕਰਨਾ, ਸੋਚ ਲੈਣਾ; **~d** ਅਨੁਮਾਨਤ, ਕਲਪਤ, ਮੰਨਿਆ

supposition ('ਸਅਪਅ'ਜ਼ਿਸ਼ਨ) *n* ਅਨੁਮਾਨ, ਮਨੌਤ, ਧਾਰਨਾ, ਅੰਦਾਜ਼ਾ; ਸਮਝ

suppress (ਸਅ:ਪਰੈੱਸ) *v* ਦਬਾਉਣਾ, ਬੰਦ ਕਰਨਾ, ਰੋਕ ਦੇਣਾ; ਕੁਚਲ ਦੇਣਾ; ਪ੍ਰਕਾਸ਼ਤ ਨਾ ਹੋਣ ਦੇਣਾ; **~ion, ~or** ਦਬਾਈ, ਦਮਨ; ਜਬਤੀ, ਬੰਦਸ਼, ਲੁਕਾਅ

supremacy (ਸ'ਪਰੈੱਮਅਸਿ) *n* ਸਰਦਾਰੀ, ਸ੍ਰੇਸ਼ਟਤਾ, ਪ੍ਰਮੁੱਖਤਾ, ਬੋਲਬਾਲਾ

supreme (ਸੁ'ਪਰੀਮ) *a* ਸਰਵ-ਉੱਚ, ਸਰਵ-ਸ੍ਰੇਸ਼ਟ, ਸਰਵ-ਪ੍ਰਧਾਨ; ਸ਼ਰੋਮਣੀ, ਸਰਬੋਤਮ, ਸਰਵ-ਉੱਚ, ਉਚਤਮ (ਅਦਾਲਤ); ਮਹੱਤਵਪੂਰਨ

surcharge ('ਸਅ:ਚਾਜ, ਸਅ:'ਚਾਜ) *n v* ਅਧਿਕ ਕਿਰਾਇਆ, ਭਾੜਾ ਜਾਂ ਮਹਿਸੂਲ; ਵਾਧੂ ਤਾਰ ਪਾਉਣਾ, ਚੱਟੀ ਲਾਉਣੀ

sure (ਸ਼ੋ*) *a adv* ਅਚੁਕ; ਨਿਸ਼ਚਤ, ਦ੍ਰਿੜ੍ਹ, ਪੱਕਾ; ਵਿਸ਼ਵਾਸੀ, ਭਰੋਸੇ ਯੋਗ, ਬਿਨਾ ਸ਼ੱਕ, ਬਿਲਕੁਲ ਸੱਚ; **~ly** ਯਕੀਨੀ ਤੌਰ ਤੇ, ਪੱਕੀ ਤਰ੍ਹਾਂ, ਜ਼ਰੂਰ; **~ty** ਜ਼ਾਮਨ, ਜ਼ਮਾਨਤ ਦੇਣ ਵਾਲਾ; ਮੁਚੱਲਕਾ, ਜ਼ਮਾਨਤ, ਯਕੀਨ, ਨਿਸ਼ਚਾ

surface ('ਸਅ:ਫ਼ਿਸ) *n a* ਤਲ, ਭੂ-ਤਲ, ਸਤ੍ਹਾ; ਉਪਰਲਾ-ਉਪਰਲਾ

surge (ਸਅ:ਜ) *v n* ਠਾਠਾਂ ਮਾਰਦਾ, ਲਹਿਰ ਉਠਣੀ, ਲਹਿਲਾਉਣਾ; ਚੜ੍ਹਨਾ, ਉਤਰਨਾ; ਲਹਿਰ, ਤਰੰਗ, ਮੌਜ

surname ('ਸਅ:ਨੇਇਮ) *n* ਉਪ-ਨਾਂ, ਕੁਲ ਨਾਂ, ਖ਼ਾਨਦਾਨੀ ਨਾਂ; ਉਪਾਧੀ

surpass (ਸਅ'ਪਾਸ) *v* ਅੱਗੇ ਵਧ ਜਾਣਾ, ਪਿੱਛੇ ਛੱਡ ਜਾਣਾ

surplus ('ਸਅ:ਪਲਅਸ) *n a* ਬਚਤ, ਰੋਕੜ, ਵਾਧੂ ਮਿਕਦਾਰ, ਵਾਧਾ, ਫ਼ਾਲਤੂ, ਅਤਿਰਿਕਤ

surprise (ਸਅ'ਪਰਾਇਜ਼) *n v* ਹੈਰਾਨੀ, ਅਸਚਰਜਤਾ, ਅਸਚਰਜ, ਅਚੰਭਾ; ਪਰੇਸ਼ਾਨ ਕਰਨਾ; ਹੈਰਾਨ ਕਰਨਾ, ਅਚਿੰਤਤ ਕਰਨਾ

surprising (ਸਅ'ਪਰਾਇਜ਼ਿੰਡ) *a* ਅਨੋਖਾ, ਵਚਿੱਤਰ

surrender (ਸਅ'ਰੈਂਡਅ*) v n (ਤਾਕਤ ਜਾਂ ਕਬਜ਼ਾ) ਸੌਂਪ ਦੇਣਾ, ਹਵਾਲੇ ਕਰਨਾ, ਛੱਡਣਾ, ਤਿਆਗਣਾ, ਹਥਿਆਰ ਸੁੱਟਣੇ, ਹਾਰ ਮਨੰਣੀ; ਹਾਰ, ਸਮਰਪਣ, ਆਤਮ-ਸਮਰਪਣ

surround (ਸਅ'ਰਾਉਂਡ) v ਘੇਰਨਾ, ਦੁਆਲੇ ਹੋਣਾ, ਘੇਰਿਆ ਹੋਣਾ; ਚੌਤਰਫੀ ਹੋਣਾ; ~ings ਆਸ-ਪਾਸ ਦਾ ਵਾਤਾਵਰਣ, ਚੁਗਿਰਦਾ, ਅੜੋਸ-ਪੜੋਸ

surveillance (ਸਅ:'ਵ੍ਹੇਇਲਅੰਸ) n ਰਖਵਾਲੀ, ਨਿਗਰਾਨੀ, ਦੇਖ-ਭਾਲ

survey (ਸਅ'ਵ੍ਹੇਇ, 'ਸਅ:ਵ੍ਹੇਇ) v n ਪੜਤਾਲ ਕਰਨੀ, ਨਿਰੀਖਣ ਕਰਨਾ; ਦੇਖਣਾ, ਗਾਂਚ ਕਹਿਣੀ; ਪੈਮਾਇਸ਼ ਕਰਨੀ, ਕੱਛਣਾ; ਸਰਵੇ, ਪੈਮਾਇਸ਼, ਕੱਛ; ਜਾਂਚ, ਪੜਤਾਲ; ~or ਸਰਵੇ ਕਰਨ ਵਾਲਾ, ਪੈਮਾਇਸ਼ ਕਰਨ ਵਾਲਾ ਅਫ਼ਸਰ

survival (ਸਅ'ਵਾਇਵ੍ਹਲ) n ਯਾਦਗਾਰ, ਉੱਤਰਜੀਵਤਾ, ਬਚਾਉ; ~of the fittest ਯੋਗਤਮ ਦੀ ਜੈ

survive (ਸਅਵ੍ਹਾਇਵ੍ਹ) v ਬਚਿਆ ਰਹਿਣਾ, ਟਿਕਿਆ ਰਹਿਣਾ, ਜੀਉਂਦੇ ਰਹਿਣਾ

survivor (ਸਅ'ਵ੍ਹਾਇਵਅ*) n ਬਚਿਆ ਰਹਿਣ ਵਾਲਾ; (ਬ ਵ) ਪਿਛਲੇ ਰਹਿੰਦੇ, ਉੱਤਰਜੀਵੀ

susceptibillty (ਸਅ:ਸੈਪਟਅ'ਬਿਲਅਟਿ) n ਗੁੰਜਾਇਸ਼, ਸੰਭਾਵਨਾ, ਗ੍ਰਹਿਣਸ਼ੀਲਤਾ

susceptible (ਸਅ'ਸੈਂਪਟਅਬਲ) a ਭਾਵਗ੍ਰਹੀ, ਗ੍ਰਹਿਣਸ਼ੀਲ, ਗੁੰਜਾਇਸ਼ ਵਾਲਾ; ਭਾਵੁਕ, ਪ੍ਰਭਾਵਕ, ਸੰਵੇਦਨਸ਼ੀਲ

suspect ('ਸਅਸਪੈੱਕਟ) v a n ਸ਼ੱਕ ਕਰਨਾ, (ਕਿਸੇ ਗੱਲ ਦਾ) ਅੰਦੇਸ਼ਾ ਹੋਣਾ, ਸ਼ੱਕ ਹੋਣਾ; ਸੁਭਾ ਹੋਣਾ, ਗੁਮਾਨ ਹੋਣਾ; ਸੰਦੇਹਪੂਰਨ; ਸ਼ੱਕ, ਸੰਦੇਹ

suspend (ਸਅ'ਸਪੈਂਡ) v ਮੁਅੱਤਲ ਕਰਨਾ; ਰੋਕ ਰੱਖਣਾ, ਟੰਗਣਾ; ਲਮਕਾਉਣਾ, ਲਟਕਾਉਣਾ

suspense (ਸਅ'ਸਪੈਂਸ) n ਦੋ-ਚਿੰਤੀ, ਦੋ-ਦਿਲੀ, ਦੁਬਧਾ, ਜੱਕੋਤਕੀ, ਸਸ਼ੋਪੰਜ

suspension (ਸਅ'ਸਪੈਨਸ਼ਨ) n ਲਮਕਾਅ, ਲਟਕਾਉ; ਮੁਅੱਤਲੀ, ਰੁਕਾਅ

suspicion (ਸਅ'ਸਪਿਸ਼ਨ) n ਸੰਦੇਹ, ਸ਼ੰਕਾ, ਖਟਕਾ

suspicious (ਸਅ'ਸਪਿਸ਼ਅਸ) a ਸ਼ੱਕੀ, ਸੰਦੇਹੀ, ਸ਼ੰਕਾਵਾਦੀ

sustain (ਸਅ'ਸਟੇਇਨ) v ਸਹਾਰਾ ਦੇਣਾ, ਭਾਰ ਉਠਾਉਣਾ; ਜੀਉਂਦਾ ਰੱਖਣਾ, ਹਿੰਮਤ ਕਾਇਮ ਹੱਪਣਾ, ਮੁਕਾਬਲਾ ਕਰਨਾ, **ਤਸਦੀਕ ਕਰਨਾ**, ਪੁਸ਼ਟੀ ਕਰਨੀ, ਪ੍ਰੋੜ੍ਹਤਾ ਕਰਨੀ; ਜਾਰੀ ਰੱਖਣਾ; ~d ਪ੍ਰਮਾਣਤ, ਦੀਰਘਕਾਲਕ; ਲਗਾਤਾਰ

sustenance ('ਸਅੱਸਟਿਨਅੰਸ) n ਜੀਵਕਾ, ਗੁਜ਼ਾਰਾ; ਆਹਾਰ, ਪਾਲਣ-ਪੋਸਣ, ਖ਼ੁਰਾਕ

swag (ਸਵੈਗ) n (ਅਪ) ਚੋਰੀ ਦਾ ਮਾਲ, ਲੁੱਟ ਦਾ ਧਨ

swagger ('ਸਵੈਗਅ*) v a ਫੜ ਮਾਰਨੀ; ਆਕੜ ਕੇ ਚੱਲਣਾ, ਠਾਠ ਨਾਲ ਚੱਲਣਾ; ਧੌਂਸ ਜਮਾਉਂਟੀ, ਡੀਂਗ ਮਾਰਨੀ; ਫੁਰਤੀਲਾ, ਤੇਜ਼, ਰੋਹਬ ਵਾਲਾ

swallow ('ਸਵੈਲਆਉ) v ਹੜੱਪ ਕਰਨਾ; ਨਿਗਲਣਾ, ਮਾ ਲੈਣਾ, ਹੋੜ੍ਹਨਾ, ਨਿਘਾਰਨਾ, ਹੜਪਣਾ; ਨਸ਼ਟ ਕਰਨਾ, ਸਹਿਣਾ, ਪੀ ਜਾਣਾ

swan (ਸਵੈਨ) n ਹੰਸ; ਰਾਜਹੰਸ

swap (ਸਵੈਪ) n v ਅਦਲਾ-ਬਦਲੀ, ਅਦਲਾ-ਬਦਲੀ ਕਰਨਾ

sway (ਸਵੇਇ) v n ਉੱਲਰਨਾ; ਡੁਲਾਉਂਟਾ; ਲਚਕਾ ਖਾਣਾ; ਝੂਮਣਾ, ਝੂਟਣਾ, ਝੂਲਰਨਾ; ਅਸਰ ਪਾਉਂਟਾ; ਜਿੱਕਾ ਬਿਠਾਉਂਟਾ; ਰਾਜ ਕਰਨਾ; ਉਲਾਰ; ਝਟਕਾ; ਅਸਰ

swear (ਸਵੇਰ*) v n ਸੰਹੁ ਖਾਣੀ ਜਾਂ ਚੁੱਕਣੀ,

ਕਸਮ ਖਾਣੀ, ਸੌਗੰਦ ਖਾਣੀ, ਸਹੁੰ ਖੁਆਣੀ; ਸਹੁੰ, ਸੌਗੰਦ, ਕਸਮ; ~ing ਹਲਫ਼ ਉਠਾਉਣ, ਸਹੁੰ, ਸੌਗੰਦ, ਕਸਮ

sweat (ਸਵੈੱਟ) *n v* ਪਸੀਨਾ, ਮੁੜ੍ਹਕਾ, ਪਰਸੇਉ; ਪਸੀਨਾ ਆਉਣਾ; ਤੇਲ ਕੱਢਣਾ, ਕਰੜੀ ਮਿਹਨਤ ਕਰਨੀ; ~er ਕਰੜੀ ਮਿਹਨਤ ਕਰਨ ਵਾਲਾ; ਸਵੈਟਰ

sweep (ਸਵੀਪ) *v n* ਝਾੜੂ ਦੇਣਾ, ਸੁੰਬਰਨਾ, ਝਾੜਨਾ, ਬੁਹਾਰਨਾ, ਹੁੰਝਣਾ, ਝਪਟਣਾ; ਸਫ਼ਾਈ; ~er ਮਿਹਤਰ, ਸਫ਼ਾਈ ਕਰਨ ਵਾਲਾ; ~ing ਦੂਰਗਾਮੀ; ਵਿਆਪਕ; ਮਹੱਤਵਪੂਰਨ

sweet (ਸਵੀਟ) *a n* ਮਿੱਠਾ; ਸੁਆਦੀ, ਸੁਰੀਲਾ; ਪਰੀਤਮ; ~heart ਪਰੇਮੀ ਪਰੇਮ ਕਾ, ਜਾਨੀ ਛੋਲਾ, ਦਿਲਦਾਰ; ~potato ਸ਼ਕਰਕੰਦੀ

swell (ਸਵੈੱਲ) *v a n* ਸੁੱਜਣਾ, ਸੁਜਾਉਣਾ, ਸੁੱਜ ਜਾਣਾ, ਫੈਲਣਾ, ਉਭਾਰ ਦੇਣਾ; ਫੁਲਣਾ ਜਾਂ ਫੁਲਾਉਣਾ, ਸੋਜ, ਉਭਾਰ, ਉਫਾਰ, ਉਮੜ ਉਛਾਲਾ; ਹੁਲਾਰਾ; ~ing ਸੋਜ, ਫੁਲਾਉ, ਉਭਾਰ; ਉਠਾਅ, ਧੱਫੜ

swift (ਸਵਿਫ਼ਟ) *a adv* ਤੀਬਰ, ਤੇਜ਼, ਫੁਰਤੀਲਾ, ਵੇਗਵਾਨ; ਤੀਬਰਤਾ ਨਾਲ, ਤੇਜ਼ੀ ਨਾਲ; ਜਲਦੀ ਨਾਲ; ~ness ਤੀਬਰਤਾ, ਤੇਜ਼ੀ, ਸਫੁਰਤੀ, ਤਤਪਰਤਾ

swim (ਸਵਿਮ) *v n* ਤਰਨਾ, ਤਾਰੀ ਲਾਉਣੀ, ਪਾਰ ਕਰਨਾ; ਤੈਰਾਕੀ; ~mer ਤਾਰੂ, ਤੈਰਾਕ;

swindle (ਸਵਿੰਡਲ) *v n* ਛਲ ਕਰਨਾ, ਠੱਗਣਾ, ਲੁੱਟ ਲੈਣਾ, ਮੁੱਠਣਾ, ਮੁੰਛਣਾ, ਛਲ ਲੈਣਾ; ਕਪਟ, ਛਲ, ਧੋਖਾ, ਠੱਗੀ, ਫ਼ਰੇਬ

swine (ਸਵਾਇਨ) *n* ਸੂਰ; ਲਾਲਚੀ ਆਦਮੀ, ਲੋਭੀ ਵਿਅਕਤੀ, ਨੀਚ ਆਦਮੀ

swing (ਸਵਿੰਙ) *v n* ਝੂਲਣਾ, ਝੁਲਾਉਣਾ; ਹੁਲਰਨਾ, ਹੁਲਾਰੇ ਖਾਣਾ, ਪੀਂਘ ਝੂਟਣਾ; ਫੇਰਨਾ, ਝੁਲਾਰਨਾ (ਬਾਂਹ); ਘੁਮਾਉਣਾ, ਝੂਮਦੇ ਹੋਏ ਚੱਲਣਾ; ਝੂਮਣਾ; ਫਾਂਸੀ ਤੇ ਲਟਕਣਾ, ਝੂਲਾ ਝੂਟਾ, ਹੂਟਾ; ਹੁਲਾਰਾ, ਝਲ

sword (ਸੋਡ) *n* ਤਲਵਾਰ, ਤੇਗ, ਸ਼ਮਸ਼ੀਰ, ਖੜਗ, ਕਿਰਪਾਨ

sycophancy ('ਸਿਕਅਫ਼ਅੰਸਿ) *n* ਖ਼ੁਸ਼ਾਮਦ, ਚਾਪਲੂਸੀ, ਜੀ-ਹਜ਼ੂਰੀ

sycophant ('ਸਿਕਅਫ਼ਅੰਟ) *n* ਚਾਪਲੂਸ, ਖ਼ੁਸ਼ਾਮਦੀ ਟੱਟੂ, ਜੀ ਹਜ਼ੂਰੀਆ

syllable ('ਸਿਲਅਬਲ) *n v* ਉਚਾਰਖੰਡ; ਸਾਫ਼ ਸਾਫ਼ ਬੋਲਣਾ, ਇਕ ਇਕ ਸ਼ਬਦਾਂਸ਼ ਬੋਲਣਾ

syllabus ('ਸਿਲਅਬਅਸ) *n* ਵਿਸ਼ੇ-ਪ੍ਰਣਾਲੀ, ਸਾਰਾਂਸ਼, ਸਾਰ-ਸੰਗ੍ਰਹ, ਖ਼ਾਕਾ

symbol (ਸਿੰਬਲ) *n* ਸੰਕੇਤ, ਨਿਸ਼ਾਨ, ਪ੍ਰਤੀਕ; ਚਿੰਨ੍ਹ; ~ic, ~ical ਸੰਕੇਤਕ; ਚਿੰਨ੍ਹ ਮਾਤਰ; ਲਿਪੀ ਚਿੰਨ੍ਹ ਪ੍ਰਤੀਕਾਤਮਕ; ~ism ਚਿੰਨ੍ਹਵਾਦ, ਸੰਕੇਤਕਤਾ, ਸੰਕੇਤ-ਪੱਧਤੀ, ਪ੍ਰਤੀਕਵਾਦ

symmetric, -al (ਸਿ'ਮੈਟਰਿਕ, ਸਿ'ਮੈਟਰਿਕਲ) *a* ਸਡੌਲ, ਮੇਲ ਖਾਂਦਾ, ਸਮ-ਮਾਪੀ, ਸਮਰੂਪੀ

symmetry ('ਸਿਮਅਟਰਿ) *n* ਸੁਡੌਲਤਾ, ਸਮਤਾ, ਮੇਲ, ਸਮ-ਤੁਲਨਾ, ਸਮਰੂਪ

sympathetic ('ਸਿੰਪਅ'ਥੈਟਿਕ) *a* ਹਮਦਰਦ, ਦਰਦਵੰਦ, ਹਮਦਮ, ਦਿਆਲੂ; ਹਿਮਾਇਤੀ

sympathize ('ਸਿੰਪਥਾਇਜ਼) *v* ਹਮਦਰਦੀ ਰੱਖਣੀ, ਹਮਦਰਦੀ ਪਰਗਟ ਕਰਨੀ; ਦਰਦ ਵੰਡਾਉਣਾ; ਦਇਆ ਕਰਨਾ

sympathy ('ਸਿੰਪਅਥਿ) *n* ਹਮਦਰਦੀ, ਦਰਦਵੰਦੀ, ਸੰਮਤੀ, ਤਾਈਦ, ਹਿਮਾਇਤ

symptom ('ਸਿਮ(ਪ)ਟਅਮ) *n* (ਰੋਗ ਦੀ) ਨਿਸ਼ਾਨੀ; ਲੱਛਣ, ਸੰਕੇਤ; ~atic ਲਾਖਣਿਕ,

ਚਿੰਨ੍-ਮਾਤਰ, ਬੋਧਕ

synchronize ('ਸਿੰਙਕਰਅਨਾਇਜ਼) *v* ਸਮਕਾਲਵਰਤੀ ਹੋਣਾ

synopsis (ਸਿ'ਨੌਪਸਿਸ) *n* ਖ਼ੁਲਾਸਾ, ਸੰਖੇਪ, ਸਾਰਾਂਸ਼, ਰੂਪ-ਰੇਖਾ, ਵਸਤੁਸਾਰ

syntax ('ਸਿੰਟੈਕਸ) *n* ਵਾਕ-ਰਚਨਾ, ਵਾਕ-ਵਿਊਂਤ

syrup, sirup ('ਸਿਰਅਪ) *n* ਸੀਰਾ, ਚਾਸ਼ਨੀ; ਸ਼ਰਬਤ

system ('ਸਿਸਟਅਮ) *n* ਪ੍ਰਣਾਲੀ, ਪਧੱਤੀ, ਤਰੀਕਾ, ਚਾਲ; ਜਗਤ, ਸੰਸਾਰ; ਕ੍ਰਮ; ਸਿਲਸਲਾ, ਵਿਵਸਥਾ, ਯੋਜਨਾ, ਤੰਤਰ, ਸਮੁਦਾਇ; **~atic** ਕ੍ਰਮਬੱਧ, ਵਿਵਸਥਿਤ, ਨਿਯਮਤ, ਵਿਧੀਪੂਰਵਕ, ਰੀਤੀਬੱਧ, ਸਿਲਸਿਲੇਵਾਰ, ਬਾਕਾਇਦਾ

T

T, t (ਟੀ) *n* ਰੋਮਨ ਵਰਨਮਾਲਾ ਦਾ ਵੀਹਵਾਂ ਅੱਖਰ; *cross the ~ 's* ਪੂਰੀ ਤਰ੍ਹਾਂ ਠੀਕ ਕਰ ਦੇਣਾ

tab (ਟੈਬ) *n* ਤਸਮਾ; ਟੋਪੀ ਦਾ ਕੰਨ-ਪਟਾ; ਤਸਮੇ ਦਾ ਛੱਲਾ; (ਬੋਲ) ਜਾਂਚ, ਹਿਸਾਬ-ਕਿਤਾਬ, ਨਿਰੀਖਣ; *keep ~s on* ਹਿਸਾਬ-ਕਿਤਾਬ, ਨਿਰੀਖਣ

table ('ਟੇਇਬਲ) *n v* ਮੇਜ਼, ਖਾਣੇ ਦੀ ਮੇਜ਼, ਚੌਕੀ; ਪਟੜਾ, ਪਟੜੀ; ਸਾਰਨੀ ਸੂਚੀ; ਮੇਜ਼ ਉੱਤੇ ਰੱਖਣਾ, ਪਰੋਸਣਾ; ~land ਪਠਾਰ, ਪੱਥੀ

tableau ('ਟੈਬਲਅਉ) *n* ਦ੍ਰਿਸ਼, ਝਾਕੀ, ਸਚਿੱਤਰ ਪੇਸ਼ਕਾਰੀ; ~curtains ਕਣਤੀ ਪਰਦੇ

tabloid ('ਟੈਬਲੋਇਡ) *n* ਸਮਾਚਾਰ-ਪੱਤਰ; ਪੱਤਰਕਾ, ਛੋਟੇ ਆਕਾਰ ਦੀ ਅਖ਼ਬਾਰ

taboo, tabu (ਟਅ'ਬੂ) *n a v* ਮਨਾਹੀ; ਵਿਵਰਜਤ; ਮਨਾਹੀ ਕਰਨੀ, ਵਿਵਰਜਤ ਠਹਿਰਾਉਣਾ; ਪਰੇ ਰੱਖਣਾ

tabor ('ਟੈਇਬਅ*) *n v* (ਇਤਿਹਾਸਕ) ਢੋਲਕੀ; ਤਬਲਾ; ਤਬਲਾ ਵਜਾਉਣਾ

tabulate ('ਟੈਬਯੁਲਅ) *v a* ਸੂਚੀ ਬਣਾਉਣਾ, ਸਾਰਨੀਬੱਧ ਕਰਨਾ, ਖ਼ਾਨੇ ਵਾਹੁਣਾ; ਸਾਰਨੀਬੱਧ, ਤਾਲਿਕਾਬੱਧ

tabulation ('ਟੈਬਯੁ'ਲੇਇਸ਼ਨ) *n* ਸਾਰਨੀਕਰਨ

tacit ('ਟੈਸਿਟ) *a* ਗੁਪਤ, ਅਣਕਿਹਾ, ਗੁੰਝਾ, ਬਿਨਬੋਲਿਆ; ਖ਼ਮੋਸ਼

tack (ਟੈਕ) *n v* ਕਿੱਲ, ਕੋਕਾ, ਥਿਰੰਜੀ; (ਬ ਵ) ਕੱਚੀ ਸਿਲਾਈ, ਠੋਪੇ, ਨਗੰਦੇ; ਟਾਂਕਣਾ, ਨੱਥੀ ਕਰਨਾ; (ਜਹਾਜ਼ ਦਾ) ਰਾਹ ਬਦਲਣਾ, ਰੁਖ਼ ਫੇਰਨਾ; ~ing ਕਿੱਲ ਠੋਕਣਾ; ਬਖ਼ੀਆ ਕਰਨਾ, ਠੋਪੇ ਲਾਉਣਾ; ਕ੍ਰਮਬੱਧ ਕਰਨਾ, ਇਕੰਤਰਤ ਕਰਨਾ

tackle ('ਟੈਕਲ) *v* ਬਹਿਸ ਕਰਨਾ, ਤਕਰਾਰ ਕਰਨਾ; ਟਿਪਟਾਉਣ ਦਾ ਜਤਨ ਕਰਨਾ, ਨਿਜਿੱਠਣਾ, ਸਿੱਝਣਾ; ਮੁਕਾਬਲਾ ਕਰਨਾ

tact (ਟੈਕਟ) *n* ਸੁੱਚਜ, ਜੁਗਤ, ਢੰਗ, ਵਿਧੀ, ਸਿਆਣਪ; ~ful ਸੁੱਚਜਾ, ਸਿਆਣਾ, ਵਿਓਤੀਆ, ਜੁਗਤੀ, ਚਤਰ; ~ical ਯੁਕਤੀਪੂਰਣ; ~ics ਜੁੱਧ-ਕਲਾ, ਜੰਗੀ ਚਾਲਾਂ, ਦਾਅ-ਪੇਚ, ਨਿਪੁੰਨਤਾ, ਚਾਤਰੀ, ਪ੍ਰਪੰਚ, ਚਾਲਬਾਜ਼ੀ, ਤਰਕੀਬ

tag (ਟੈਗ) *n v* ਨੱਥੀ, ਜੋੜ, ਫ਼ੀਤਾ, ਤਸਮਾ, ਨੱਥੀ ਕਰਨਾ, ਟਾਂਕਣਾ, ਜੋੜ ਦੇਣਾ; ਜੋੜ ਲਾਉਣਾ; ਤੁਕ ਜੋੜਨੀ

tail (ਟੇਇਲ) *n v* ਪੂਛ, ਪੂਛਲ, ਦੁਮ; ਅੰਤ, ਪਿੱਛਾ, ਪਿਛਾੜੀ; ਹੇਠਲਾ ਭਾਗ, ਸਿਰਾ; ਦੋ ਸਿਰੇ ਤਰਾਸ਼ ਦੇਣਾ; ਜੋੜਨਾ; ਜੁੜਨਾ, ਲੱਗਣਾ

tailor ('ਟੇਇਲਅ*) *n v* ਦਰਜ਼ੀ, ਸਿਲਾਈ ਕਰਨ ਵਾਲਾ; ਕਪੜੇ ਸੀਉਣੇ; ~ing ਦਰਜ਼ੀਗੀਰੀ, ਸਿਲਾਈ ਦਾ ਕੰਮ

taint ('ਟੇਇੰਟ) *n* ਕਲੰਕ; ਦੋਸ਼, ਖਰਾਬੀ, ਧੱਬਾ, ਦਾਗ਼, ਨਿਸ਼ਾਨ, ਬਦਮਾਸ਼ੀ ਦਾ ਟਿੱਕਾ; ਛੂਤ; ~ed ਦੂਸ਼ਤ, ਬਦਨਾਮ, ਕਲੰਕਤ, ਭ੍ਰਿਸ਼ਟ, ਗੰਦਾ; ~less ਨਿਰਦੋਸ਼, ਨਿਸ਼ਕਲੰਕ, ਬੇਦਾਗ਼, ਸਾਫ਼

take (ਟੇਇਕ) *n v* ਸ਼ਿਕਾਰ; ਆਮਦਨੀ, ਰੋਕੜ; ਲੈਣਾ, ਫੜਨਾ, ਕਬਜ਼ਾ ਕਰ ਲੈਣਾ, ਅਧਿਕਾਰ ਵਿਚ ਲੈ ਆਉਣਾ; ਲੈ ਜਾਣਾ, ਪ੍ਰਾਪਤ ਕਰ ਲੈਣਾ; ~action ਕਾਰਵਾਈ ਕਰਨਾ; ~after ਕਿਸੇ ਵਰਗਾ ਹੋਣਾ; ~arms ਹਥਿਆਰ ਚੁੱਕਣਾ; ~in

taking / **tarnish**

hand ਆਰੰਭ ਕਰਨਾ, ਸ਼ੁਰੂ ਕਰਨਾ; ~off ਨਕਲ, ਵਿਅੰਗ-ਚਿੱਤਰ, ਲਾਹ ਲੈਣਾ, ਘਟਾ ਦੇਣਾ; ਹਵਾਈ ਜਹਾਜ਼ ਦੀ ਚੜ੍ਹਾਈ; ਛਾਲ ਮਾਰਨ ਦਾ ਅੱਡਾ; ~out ਵੱਖਰਾ ਕਰਨਾ, ਬਾਹਰ ਲੈ ਜਾਣਾ; ਕੱਢਣਾ; ~to task ਡਾਂਟਣਾ, ਝਾੜ-ਝੰਬ ਕਰਨਾ, ਝਾੜਨਾ; ~up with ਨਾਲ ਰਹਿਣਾ

taking ('ਟੇਇਕਿਙ) *n a* ਲੈਣ, ਲੈ ਜਾਣ; ਪਕੜ, ਗਿਰਫ਼ਤਾਰੀ; ਬੇਚੈਨੀ; ਦਿਲ-ਖਿੱਚਵਾਂ

tale (ਟੇਇਲ) *n* ਕਹਾਣੀ, ਅਫ਼ਸਾਨਾ; ਕਿੱਸਾ; ~bearer ਚੁਗ਼ਲ ਖ਼ੋਰ

talent ('ਟੈਲਅੰਟ) *n* ਯੋਗਤਾ, ਪ੍ਰਤਿਭਾ, ਬੁਧੀ; ~ed ਪ੍ਰਤਿਭਾਸ਼ੀਲ, ਗੁਣਵਾਨ, ਬੁੱਧੀਵਾਨ

tailsman ('ਟੈਲਿਜ਼ਮਅਨ) *n* ਤਾਵੀਜ਼, ਜੰਤਰ, ਰੱਖ; ਤਲਿਸਮ, ਜਾਦੂ

talk (ਟੋਕ) *n v* ਵਾਰਤਾ; ਬੋਲ; ਗੱਲ-ਕੱਥ; ਬੋਲਣਾ, ਗੱਲ ਕਰਨੀ, ਵਾਰਤਾਲਾਪ ਕਰਨੀ; ਗੱਪ ਮਾਰਨੀ; ~ative ਬੜਬੋਲਾ ਗਾਲੜੀ, ਗੱਲਹਦਰ; ~er ਵਾਰਤਾਕਾਰ, ਵਕਤਾ, ਗੱਪੀ, ਸ਼ੇਖ਼ੀਬਾਜ਼; ~ing ਬੋਲਣ ਵਾਲਾ

tall (ਟੋਲ) *a adv* ਲੰਮਾ, ਉੱਚਾ, ਵੱਡਾ; ਹੱਦ ਤੋਂ ਵਧ; ~ness ਲੰਬਾਈ, ਉਚਾਈ, ਬੁਲੰਦੀ, ਚੋਟ

tally ('ਟੈਲਿ) *n v* (ਇਤਿ) ਲੇਖਾ-ਪੱਟੀ, ਹਿਸਾਬ, ਲੇਖ; ਹੋਣਾ, (ਲੇਖ) ਮੇਲ ਖਾਣਾ, ਬਰਾਬਰ ਹੋਣਾ, ਠੀਕ ਨਿਕਲਣਾ, ਮਿਲਣਾ

tame (ਟੇਇਮ) *a v* ਘਰੇਲੂ, ਪਾਲਿਆ, ਪਾਲਤੂ; ਪ੍ਰਭਾਹੀਣ; ਫਿੱਕਾ, ਬੇਅਸਰ, ਸਿਧਾਉਣਾ, ਪਾਲਤੂ ਬਣਾ ਲੈਣਾ; ਵੱਸ ਕਰਨਾ, ਕਾਬੂ ਕਰਨਾ

tamper ('ਟੈਮਪਅ*) *v* ਦਖ਼ਲ ਦੇਣਾ, ਤੋੜ-ਮਰੋੜ ਕਰਨਾ; ਪ੍ਰਭਾਵ ਪਾਉਣਾ

tangible ('ਟੈਂਜਅਬਲ) *a* ਸਪਰਸ਼ੀ; ਸਥੂਲ, ਨਿੱਗਰ, ਯਥਾਰਥ, ਸਪੱਸ਼ਟ; ਵਾਸਤਵਿਕ, ਭੌਤਕ, ਸਰੀਰਕ, ਨਿਸ਼ਚਤ; ~ness ਸਪਰਸ਼ਤਾ, ਸਥੂਲਤਾ, ਵਾਸਤਵਿਕਤਾ, ਭੌਤਕਤਾ; ~d ਜਟਿਲ, ਪੇਚੀਦਾ, ਗੁੱਝਲਦਾਰ, ਉਲਝਿਆ ਹੋਇਆ

tank (ਟੈਙਕ) *n* ਟੈਂਕੀ, ਹੌਜ਼, ਟੈਂਕ, ਸਰੋਵਰ, ਤਲਾਬ, ਜੰਗੀ ਮੋਟਰ ਗੱਡੀ; ~er ਤੇਲ ਦਾ ਜਹਾਜ਼, ਟੈਂਕੀ ਵਾਲਾ ਜਹਾਜ਼

tantalize ('ਟੈਂਟਅਲਾਇਜ਼) *v* ਤਰਸਾਉਣਾ, ਕਲਪਾਉਣਾ, ਝੂਠੀਆਂ ਆਸਾਂ ਦੇਣੀਆਂ, ਮਾਨਸਕ ਕਸ਼ਟ ਦੇਣਾ; ਖਿਝਾਉਣਾ

tantamount ('ਟੈਂਟਆਮਾਉਂਟ) *a* ਤੁੱਲ, ਸਮਾਨ, ਬਰਾਬਰ, ਤੁਲਾਰਥ

tap (ਟੈਪ) *n v* (1) ਨਲ, ਬੰਬਾ; ਡਾਟ, ਡੱਟਾ; ਖੜਕਾਰ, (2) ਖਟ-ਖਟ, ਟਕੋਰ, ਟੂਟੀ ਲਾਉਣੀ, ਖੜਕਾਉਣਾ

tape (ਟੇਇਪ) *n v* ਫ਼ੀਤਾ, ਨਵਾਰ, ਟੇਪ; ਫ਼ੀਤੇ ਲਗਾਉਣਾ

tar (ਟਾ*) *n v* ਲੁੱਕ, ਤਾਰਕੋਲ, ਕੋਲਤਾਰ; ਲੁੱਕ ਮਲਣੀ, ਲੁੱਕ ਵਿਛਾਉਣੀ (ਸੜਕ ਉੱਤੇ); ਕਾਲਾ ਕਰਨਾ

tardiness ('ਟਾਡਿਨਿਸ) *n* ਸੁਸਤੀ, ਆਲਸ, ਮੰਦਤਾ, ਢਿੱਲ, ਹਿਚਕਚਾਹਟ, ਟਾਲ-ਮਟੋਲ

tardo ('ਟਾਡਅਉ) *a* ਹੌਲੀ-ਹੌਲੀ, ਆਹਿਸਤਾ-ਆਹਿਸਤਾ, ਮੰਦ-ਮੰਦ

tardy ('ਟਾਡਿ) *a* ਆਲਸੀ, ਸੁਸਤ, ਢਿੱਲਾ, ਮੱਠਾ, ਮੰਦ

target ('ਟਾਗਿਟ) *n* ਨਿਸ਼ਾਨਾ, ਟੀਚਾ

tariff ('ਟੈਰਿਫ਼) *n v* ਮਹਿਸੂਲ, ਚੁੰਗੀ, ਕਰ, ਨਿਰਖਨਾਮਾ; ਮੁੱਲ ਲਿਖਣਾ

tarnish ('ਟਾਨਿਸ਼) *n v* ਦਾਗ਼, ਬੱਜ; ਬਦਰੰਗ

ਕਰਨਾ ਜਾਂ ਹੋਣਾ, ਸ਼ਕਲ ਵਿਗਾੜਨੀ ਜਾਂ ਵਿਗਾੜਨੀ; ~ed ਕਲੰਕਤ, ਦਾਗ਼ੀ, ਬੇਆਬਰੂ

taro ('ਟਾਰਅਉ) *n* ਕਚਾਲੂ

tarpaulin (ਟਾ'ਪੌਲਿਨ) *n* ਤਿਰਪਾਲ; ਮੱਲਾਹ

task (ਟਾਸਕ) *n v* ਕੰਮ; ਸੌਂਪਿਆ ਕੰਮ; ਧੰਦਾ, ਘਾਲ; ਬੋਝ ਪਾਉਣਾ, ਕੰਮ ਉੱਤੇ ਲਾਉਣਾ, ਕੰਮ ਲੈਣਾ, ਮਿਹਨਤ ਕਰਾਉਣੀ; ~**master** ਕੰਮ ਲੈਣ ਵਾਲਾ, ਮਾਲਕ, ਸੁਆਮੀ

taste (ਟੇਇਸਟ) *n v* ਸੁਆਦ, ਰਸ, ਜ਼ਾਇਕਾ; ਰੁਚੀ, ਸ਼ੌਕ, ਸੁਆਦ ਲੈਣਾ, ਚੱਖਣਾ, ਮਜ਼ਾ ਚੱਖਣਾ; ਆਨੰਦ ਲੈਣਾ, ਲੁਤਫ਼ ਲੈਣਾ; ~**ful** *a* ਮਿੱਠਾ, ਮਜ਼ੇਦਾਰ, ਸੁਆਦੀ (ਵਸਤੂ); ਰੋਚਕ, ਰਸਿਕ (ਵਿਅਕਤੀ); ~**less** ਫਿੱਕਾ, ਅਲੂਣਾ, ਬੇਸੁਆਦਾ

tasty ('ਟੇਇਸਟਿ) *a* ਸੁਆਦੀ, ਸੁਆਦਲਾ, ਮਜ਼ੇਦਾਰ, ਰਸੀਲਾ

taunt (ਟੌਂਟ) *n v a* ਮਿਹਣਾ, ਮਲਾਮਤ, ਉਲਾਂਭਾ; ਮਿਹਣਾ ਮਾਰਨਾ, ਬੋਲੀ ਮਾਰਨੀ, ਨਿੰਦਾ ਕਰਨੀ; ਉੱਚਾ, ਲੰਮਾ ਉੱਚਾ, ਬੁਲੰਦ

tautologize (ਟੋ'ਟੌਲਅਜਾਇਜ਼) *v* ਦੁਹਰਾਉਣਾ, ਪੁਨਰ-ਉਕਤੀ ਕਰਨਾ

tautology (ਟੋ'ਟੌਲਅਜਿ) *n* ਦੁਹਰਾਉ, ਪੁਨਰ-ਉਕਤੀ

tavern ('ਟੈਵ੍(ਅ)ਨ) *n* ਸ਼ਰਾਬਖ਼ਾਨਾ, ਕਲਾਲ ਖ਼ਾਨਾ, ਠੇਕਾ

tax (ਟੈਕਸ) *n v* ਕਰ, ਮਹਿਸੂਲ, ਟੈਕਸ, ਲਗਾਨ; ਕਰ ਲਾਉਣਾ; ਭਾਰ ਪਾਉਣਾ; ~**payer** ਕਰ-ਦਾਤਾ; ~**ation** ਕਰਧਾਨ, ਲਗਾਨਬੰਦੀ, ਮਹਿਸੂਲਬੰਦੀ

taxi ('ਟੈਕਸਿ) *n v* ਟੈਕਸੀ, ਕਿਰਾਏ ਦੀ ਮੋਟਰ; ਟੈਕਸੀ ਵਿਚ ਜਾਣਾ

tea (ਟੀ) *n* ਚਾਹ, ਚਾਹ ਦੀ ਪੱਤੀ, ਚਾਹ ਦਾ ਪੌਦਾ

teach (ਟੀਚ) *v* ਪੜ੍ਹਾਉਣਾ, ਪੜ੍ਹਾਈ ਕਰਾਉਣੀ, ਅਧਿਆਪਨ ਕਰਨਾ, ਸਿਖਾਉਣਾ, ਦਿਮਾਗ਼ ਵਿਚ ਬਿਠਾਉਣਾ; ~**er** ਅਧਿਆਪਕ, ਸਿਖਿਅਕ, ਗੁਰੂ, ਉਸਤਾਦ, ਪ੍ਰਚਾਰਕ; ~**ing** ਅਧਿਆਪਨ, ਸਿਖਿਅਣ, ਸਿਖਲਾਈ; ਸਿੱਖਿਆ, ਉਪਦੇਸ਼

teak (ਟੀਕ) *n* ਸਾਗਵਾਨ ਦੀ ਲਕੜੀ, ਸਾਲ

team (ਟੀਮ) *n* (ਖਿਡਾਰੀਆਂ ਦੀ) ਟੀਮ; ਜੁੱਟ, ਜੋਟੀ, ਝੁੰਡ, ਸਮੂਹ, ਗਰੋਹ, ਟੋਲੀ

tear (ਟੇਅ*) *v n* ਪਾੜਨਾ, ਟੋਟੇ ਕਰਨਾ, ਫਾੜਨਾ ਜਾਂ ਫਟਣਾ, ਚੀਰਨਾ, ਅੱਲਗ ਅੱਲਗ ਕਰਨਾ, ਚਾਕ ਕਰਨਾ, ਚੀਰਾ ਲਾਉਣਾ; ਚੀਰ; ਅੱਥਰੂ, ਹੰਝੂ, ਕਤਰਾ; ~**gas** ਅੱਥਰੂ ਗੈਸ; ~**ful** ਹੰਝੂਆਂ ਨਾਲ ਭਰਿਆ, ਸੱਜਲ; ਰੋਣਹਾਕਾ; ~**ing** ਚੀਰਨ ਵਾਲਾ, ਫਾੜਨ ਵਾਲਾ

tease (ਟੀਜ਼) *v* ਛੇੜਨਾ, ਸਤਾਉਣਾ, ਤੰਗ ਕਰਨਾ, ਹੈਰਾਨ ਕਰਨਾ; ਚਿੜਾਉਣਾ, ਧਪਾਉਣਾ ਖਿਝਾਉਣਾ, ਪਿੱਛੇ ਪੈ ਜਾਣਾ; ਝਕਾਉਣਾ

teat (ਟੀਟ) *n* ਪਸ਼ੂਆਂ ਦਾ ਥਣ, ਖੀਰੀ; ਚੂਚੀ ਚੁੰਘਣੀ, ਨਿਪਲ

technical ('ਟੈਕਨਿਕਲ) *a* ਤਕਨੀਕੀ; ਜੰਤਰਕ ਪਰਿਭਾਸ਼ਕ; ~**ity** ਤਕਨੀਕੀਪੁਣਾ, ਪਰਿਭਾਸ਼ਕਤਾ, ਸ਼ਾਸਤਰੀਅਤਾ

technician (ਟੈੱਕ'ਨਿਸ਼ਨ) *a* ਤਕਨੀਕੀ ਮਾਹਰ ਮਿਸਤਰੀ

technicolor ('ਟੈੱਕਨਿ'ਕਅੱਲਅ*) *n* ਚਲਚਿੱਤਰ ਰੰਗੀਨ ਬਣਾਉਣ ਦੀ ਵਿਧੀ

technique (ਟੈੱਕ'ਨੀਕ) *n* ਤਕਨੀਕ, ਪੱਧਤੀ ਰੀਤੀ, ਵੱਲ, ਕਾਰੀਗਰੀ; ਚਾਤਰਤਾ

technology (ਟੈਕ'ਨੌਲਅਜਿ) *n* ਸ਼ਿਲਪ ਵਿਗਿਆਨ, ਉਦਯੋਗ-ਵਿਗਿਆਨ

tedious ('ਟੀਡਯਸ) *a* ਹੰਢਾਊ, ਅਕਾਊ, ਅੱਚਵਕ, ਉਕਤਾਉਣ ਵਾਲਾ; **~ness** ਥਕਾਵਟ, ਥਕੇਵਾਂ, ਅਕੇਵਾਂ, ਉਕਤਾਹਟ

teen (ਟੀਨ) *n* (ਅਪ) ਦੁੱਖ, ਕਸ਼ਟ, ਕਲੇਸ਼

teens (ਟੀਨਜ਼) *n* ਕਿਸ਼ੋਰ ਅਵਸਥਾ; ਲੜਕਪਣ

teetotal (ਟੀ'ਟਉਟਲ) *n* ਨਸ਼ੇ-ਵਿਰੋਧੀ, ਨਸ਼ੇ-ਵਿਰੋਧ ਸਬੰਧੀ; **~ism** ਨਸ਼ਾ-ਵਿਰੋਧ, ਨਸ਼ਾ-ਤਿਆਗ, ਸੁਧੀਪੁਣਾ; **~ler** ਨਸ਼ਿਆਂ ਦਾ ਕੱਟੜ ਵਿਰੋਧੀ; ਸੁਧੀ

telecommunication(s) ('ਟੈਲਿਕਅਮਯੂਨਿ'ਕੇਇਸ਼ਨ(ਜ਼)) *n pl* ਦੂਰ ਸੰਚਾਰ

telegram ('ਟੈਲਿਗਰਾਮ) *n* ਤਾਰ (ਸੁਨੇਹਾ), ਦੂਰ ਸੰਵਾਦ, ਦੂਰ ਲੇਖ

telegraph ('ਟੈਲਿਗਰਾਫ਼) *v* ਤਾਰ-ਪ੍ਰਬੰਧ, ਤਾਰ-ਜੰਤਰ; **~y** ਤਾਰ ਪ੍ਰਣਾਲੀ

telepathy (ਟਿ'ਲੈਪੱਅਥਿ) *n* ਦੂਰ-ਸੰਵੇਦਨ, ਟੈਲੀਪੰਥੀ

telephone ('ਟੈਲਿਫ਼ਅਉਨ) *n v* ਦੂਰਭਾਸ਼, ਟੈਲੀਫ਼ੋਨ; ਫ਼ੋਨ ਕਰਨਾ

teleprint ('ਟੈਲਿਪਰਿੰਟ) *v* ਦੂਰ ਲੇਖੀ ਦੁਆਰਾ ਲਿਖਣਾ, ਟੈਲੀਪ੍ਰਿੰਟਰ ਦੁਆਰਾ ਛਾਪਣਾ; **~er** ਤਾਰ ਲੇਪੀ, ਦੂਰ ਮੁਦ੍ਰਕ

telescope ('ਟੈਲਿਸਕਅਉਪ) *n v* ਦੂਰਦਰਸ਼ਕ ਜੰਤਰ, ਦੂਰਦਰਸ਼ੀ, ਦੂਰਬੀਨ; ਘੁੱਸ ਜਾਣਾ, ਟਿਕ ਜਾਣਾ

television ('ਟੈਲਿ'ਵਿਯ਼ਨ) *n* ਦੂਰਦਰਸ਼ਨ, ਪਰੋਖ ਦਿਸ਼

tell (ਟੈੱਲ) *v* ਕਹਿਣਾ, ਵਰਨਣ ਕਰਨਾ, ਸੁਣਾਉਣਾ, ਬਿਆਨ ਕਰਨਾ; ਪਰਗਟ ਕਰਨਾ, ਸਮਝਾਉਣਾ, ਦੱਸਣਾ; **~tale** ਚੁਗ਼ਲ, ਭੇਤ-ਪਰਗਟਾਊ

temblor ('ਟੈਂਬਲਅ*) *n* ਭੁਚਾਲ, ਭੁਕੰਪ

temper ('ਟੈੱਪਅ*) *n v* ਸੁਭਾਅ, ਮਿਜ਼ਾਜ; ਕਰੋਧ, ਚਿੜਚੜਾਪਣ; ਨਰਮ ਕਰਨਾ; ਜ਼ੋਰ ਘਟਾਉਣਾ; **~ament** ਸੁਭਾਅ, ਪ੍ਰਕਿਰਤੀ, ਮਿਜ਼ਾਜ, ਤਬੀਅਤ; **~ature** ਤਾਪਮਾਨ, ਤਾਪ, ਬੁਖ਼ਾਰ, ਗਰਮੀ

tempest ('ਟੈੰਪਿਸਟ) *n* ਝੱਖੜ, ਤੁਫ਼ਾਨ, (ਬੋਲ) ਉਪਦਰ, ਹਲਚਲ, ਹੰਗਾਮਾ, ਹੁੱਲੜ, ਸ਼ੋਰ-ਸ਼ਰਾਬਾ

temple ('ਟੈੰਪਲ) *n* (1) ਮੰਦਰ, ਸ਼ਿਵਾਲਾ, ਦੇਵ ਮੰਦਰ ਗਿਰਜਾ-ਘਰ, ਪੂਜਾ-ਸਥਾਨ, ਠਾਕਰ-ਦੁਆਰਾ; (2) ਪੁੱਛਪੁੜੀ, ਕਨਪਟੀ

tempo ('ਟੈੰਪਅਉ) *n* ਤਾਲ; ਗਤੀ, ਚਾਲ; ਜੋਸ਼

temporal ('ਟੈੰਪ(ਅ)ਰ(ਅ)ਲ) *a* ਕਨਪਟੀ ਸਬੰਧੀ; ਸੰਸਾਰੀ, ਸੰਸਾਰਕ, ਦੁਨਿਆਵੀ, ਕਾਲ-ਸੂਚਕ; ਲੌਕਿਕ, ਭੌਤਕ

temporary ('ਟੈੰਪ(ਅ)ਰਅਰਿ) *a* ਕੱਚੀ, ਆਰਜ਼ੀ, ਵਕਤੀ, ਕੰਮ-ਚਲਾਊ, ਵੇਲਾ-ਟਪਾਊ

temporize ('ਟੈੰਪਅਰਾਇਜ਼) *v* ਵੇਲਾ ਟਪਾਉਣਾ, ਢੰਗ ਟਪਾਈ, ਵਕਤ ਟਾਲਣਾ, ਟਾਲਮਟੋਲ ਕਰਨਾ; ਦੁਨੀਆਸਾਜ਼ੀ ਕਰਨਾ

tempt (ਟੈੰ(ਪ)ਟ) *v* ਵਰਗਲਾਉਣਾ, ਭਰਮਾਉਣਾ, ਲੁਭਾਉਣਾ; ਕੋਸ਼ਿਸ਼ ਕਰਨੀ; **~ation** ਲਾਲਚ, ਲੋਭ, ਚਕਮਾ, ਭਰਮਾਉਣਾ, ਭੁਲਾਵਾ

ten (ਟੈਨ) *a n* ਦਸ; ਦਹਾਕਾ, ਦਹਾਈ, ਦਹਾ

tenable ('ਟੈੱਨਅਬਲ) *a* ਚਾਲੂ, ਟਿਕਾਊ, ਤਰਕ-ਸੰਗਤ

tenacious ('ਟਿ'ਨੇਇਸ਼ਅਸ) *a* ਮਜ਼ਬੂਤ, ਪੱਕਾ, ਕੱਟੜ, ਦ੍ਰਿੜ੍ਹ-ਸਿਧਾਂਤਵਾਦੀ; ਕੰਜੂਸ, ਸੂਮ, ਹਠੀ, ਚੀੜ੍ਹਾ; ਤਕੜਾ; **~ness, tenacity** ਮਜ਼ਬੂਤੀ, ਪਕਿਆਈ, ਦ੍ਰਿੜ੍ਹਤਾ, ਹਠ

tenancy ('ਟੈੱਨਅੰਸਿ) *n* ਕਿਰਾਏਦਾਰੀ; ਭਾੜੇਦਾਰੀ; ਲਗਨਦਾਰੀ, ਕਾਸ਼ਤਕਾਰੀ

tenant ('ਟੈੱਨਅੰਟ) *n v* ਕਿਰਾਏਦਾਰ, ਪੱਟੇਦਾਰ, ਮੁਜ਼ਾਰਾ; ਲਗਾਨਦਾਰ; ਵੱਸਣਾ, ਕਬਜ਼ਾ ਕਰਨਾ; ਕਿਰਾਏ ਤੇ ਲੈਣਾ

tend (ਟੈਂਡ) *v* (ਬੀਮਾਰੀ ਦੀ) ਸੇਵਾ ਕਰਨੀ, ਟਹਿਲ ਕਰਨੀ, ਨਾਲ ਰਹਿਣਾ, ਖ਼ਬਰਗੀਰੀ ਕਰਨੀ, ਨਿਗਰਾਨੀ ਕਰਨੀ, ਤੀਮਾਰਦਾਰੀ ਕਰਨਾ; ਦੇਖਭਾਲ ਕਰਨੀ

tendency (ਟੈਂਡੇਂਸੀ) *n* ਝੁਕਾਉ; ਰੁਖ, ਰੁਝਾਨ, ਪ੍ਰਵਿਰਤੀ

tender ('ਟੈਂਡੁਅ*) *n v a* ਠੇਕਾ, ਟੈਂਡਰ; ਪੇਸ਼ ਕਰਨਾ, ਭੇਟਾ ਦੇਣਾ; ਤਖ਼ਮੀਨਾ ਪੇਸ਼ ਕਰਨਾ, ਅਨੁਮਾਨ ਪੇਸ਼ ਕਰਨਾ (ਠੇਕੇਦਾਰ ਵੱਲੋਂ); ਨਰਮ, ਮੁਲਾਇਮ, ਨਾਜ਼ੁਕ, ਕੂਲਾ; **~foot** ਕੋਮਲ; ਨਵਾਂ ਆਦਮੀ, ਸਿਖਾਂਦਰੂ

tenement ('ਟੈਨਅਮਅੰਟ) *n* ਮਕਾਨ ਨਿਵਾਸ ਸਥਾਨ, ਹਵੇਲੀ; ਜਾਇਦਾਦ

tenor ('ਟੈੱਨਅ*) *n* ਚਾਲ, ਵਿਧੀ, ਤਰੀਕਾ; ਤਰਜ਼

tense ('ਟੈਂਸ) *a v n* ਤਣਿਆ, ਖਿੱਚਿਆ, ਆਕੜਿਆ, ਕੱਸਿਆ; ਬੇਚੈਨ, ਉਤੇਜਤ; ਤਾਣਨਾ, ਖਿੱਚਣਾ, ਕੱਸਣਾ; (ਵਿਆ) ਕਾਲ

tension ('ਟੈੱਨਸ਼ਨ) *n* ਤਣਾਉ, ਕੱਸ, ਖਿੱਚ, ਖਿਚਾਉ, ਕਸਾਉ, ਫੈਲਾਉ; ਤਣਾਤਣੀ, ਖਿੰਚੋਤਾਣ

tent (ਟੈਂਟ) *n* ਤੰਬੂ, ਖ਼ੇਮਾ, ਛੋਲਦਾਰੀ; ਡੇਰਾ ਲਾਉਣਾ; **~ed** ਤੰਬੂਦਾਰ, ਖ਼ੇਮੇ ਵਾਲਾ

tenuous ('ਟੈੱਨਯੁਅਸ) *a* ਮਹੀਨ, ਬਾਰੀਕ, ਪਤਲਾ, ਸੁਖਮ, ਅਲਪ

tenure ('ਟੈੱਨਯੁਅ*) *a* ਮਿਆਦ ਅਧਿਕਾਰ-ਕਾਲ, ਕਾਰਜ-ਕਾਲ ਮਲਕੀਅਤ, ਕਬਜ਼ਾ, ਦਖ਼ਲ

term (ਟਅ:ਮ) *n v* ਮਿਆਦ, ਮੁੱਦਤ, ਅਵਧੀ; ਸਿੱਖਿਆ-ਕਾਲ; ਹੱਦ, ਸੀਮਾ; ਨਿਸ਼ਚਤ ਦਿਵਸ, ਨਿਸ਼ਚਤ ਤਿਥੀ; (ਕਾ) ਮਿਆਦੀ ਕਬਜ਼ਾ (ਭਾਸ਼ਾ) ਸ਼ਬਦ, ਪਦ; ਬੰਧਨ; ਸ਼ਰਤ; ਕਹਿਣਾ, ਨਾਮਜ਼ਦ ਕਰਨਾ

terminal ('ਟਅ:ਮਿਨਲ) *a n* ਅੰਤਲਾ, ਮਿਆਦੀ; ਅਖੀਰੀ; ਮਾਤਰਕ (ਖ਼ਰਚ); ਛੇਕੜਲਾ; ਹੱਦ, ਧੁਰ, ਅੰਤ, ਸਿਰਾ

terminate ('ਟਅ:ਮਿਨੇਇਟ) *v a* ਅੰਤ ਕਰਨਾ ਜਾਂ ਖ਼ਤਮ ਕਰਨਾ ਜਾਂ ਹੋਣਾ; ਸੀਮਤ ਕਰਨਾ, ਹੱਦ ਬੰਨ੍ਹਣਾ; ਖ਼ਤਮ ਹੋਣ ਵਾਲਾ; ਸੀਮਿਤ

termination ('ਟਅ:ਮਿ'ਨੇਇਸ਼ਨ) *n* ਅੰਤ, ਖ਼ਾਤਮਾ, ਸੀਮਾ, ਹੱਦਬੰਦੀ

terminology ('ਟਅ:ਮਿ'ਨੌਲਅਜਿ) *n* ਪਰਿਭਾਸ਼ਾ-ਵਿਗਿਆਨ, ਪਰਿਭਾਸ਼ੀ, ਪਰਿਭਾਸ਼ਕ ਸ਼ਬਦਾਵਲੀ

terminus ('ਟਅ:ਮਿਨਅਸ) *n* ਅੰਤਲਾ ਸਟੇਸ਼ਨ

termite ('ਟਅ:ਮਾਇਟ) *n* ਦੀਮਕ, ਸਿਉਂਕ

terrace ('ਟੈੱਰਅਸ) *n* ਚਬੂਤਰਾ, ਚੌਂਤਰਾ; ਖੁੱਲ੍ਹੀ ਛੱਤ

terrain ('ਟੈ'ਰੇਇਨ) *n* ਜ਼ਮੀਨ ਦਾ ਭਾਗ, ਖੇਤਰ ਧਰਾਤਲ

terrible ('ਟੈੱਰਅਬਲ) *a* ਭਿਆਨਕ, ਵਿਕਰਾਲ ਭਿਅੰਕਰ, ਡਰਾਉਣਾ; ਤੀਬਰ, ਅਤੀ ਪ੍ਰਚੰਡ ਬਹੁਤ ਤੇਜ਼, ਬੜਾ ਭਾਰੀ, ਡਾਢਾ

terrific (ਟਅ'ਰਿਫ਼ਿਕ) *a* ਭਿਅੰਕਰ, ਵਿਕਰਾਲ ਡਰਾਉਣਾ, ਭਿਆਨਕ, ਘੋਰ, ਡਾਢਾ

terrify ('ਟੈੱਰਿਫ਼ਾਇ) *v* ਭੈਭੀਤ ਕਰਨਾ, ਡਰਾਉਣਾ ਭੈ ਦੇਣਾ

territorial ('ਟੈੱਰਅ'ਟੋਰਿਅਲ) *n* ਪ੍ਰਦੇਸ਼ਕ, ਰਾ ਖੇਤਰੀ

territory ('ਟੈੱਰਅਟ(ਅ)ਰਿ) *n* ਪ੍ਰਦੇਸ਼, ਰਾ ਰਾਜਖੇਤਰ, ਇਲਾਕਾ, ਖੰਡ

terror ('ਟੈੱਰਅ*) *n* ਡਰ, ਖੌਫ਼, ਤਰਾਸ, ਹੈ **~stricken** ਭੈਭੀਤ, ਡਰ ਮਾਰਿਆ; **~is**

ਆਤੰਕਵਾਦ; ~ist ਆਤੰਕਵਾਦੀ, ਦਹਿਸ਼ਤ ਪਸੰਦ; ~ize ਭੈਭੀਤ ਕਰਨਾ, ਡਰਾਉਣਾ

terse (ਟਾ:ਸ) *a* ਸਪਸ਼ਟ, ਸਾਫ਼-ਸੁਥਰਾ, ਸੰਖਿਪਤ

tertiary (ਟਾ:ਸ਼ਅਰਿ) *a n* ਤੀਜੇ ਦਰਜੇ ਦਾ; ਤੀਜਾ; (ਭੂ) ਤੀਜਾ ਯੁੱਗ

test (ਟੈਸਟ) *n v* ਪਰਖ, ਪਰੀਖਿਆ, ਜਾਂਚ, ਇਮਤਿਹਾਨ; ਕਸੌਟੀ; ਆਧਾਰ; ਕੁਠਾਲੀ; ਪਰੀਖਿਆ ਕਰਨਾ, ਪਰਖਣਾ, ਅਜ਼ਮਾਉਣਾ, ਇਮਤਿਹਾਨ ਲੈਣਾ

Testament (ਟੈਸਟਅਮੈਂਟ) *n* ਪੁਰਾਣਾ ਧਰਮ ਨੇਮ, ਨੇਮ-ਪੱਤਰ; ਵਸੀਅਤ, ਇੱਛਾ-ਪੱਤਰ

testicle ('ਟੈਸਟਿਕਲ) *n* ਅੰਡਕੋਸ਼, ਅੰਡ, ਟੱਟਾ, ਨਲ, (ਬੱਕਰੇ ਦਾ) ਕਪੂਰਾ

testify ('ਟੈਸਟਿਫ਼ਾਇ) *v* ਪ੍ਰਮਾਣ ਦੇਣਾ, ਗਵਾਹੀ ਦੇਣੀ, ਸਬੂਤ ਦੇਣਾ, ਸਾਬਤ ਕਰਨਾ, ਸਿੱਧ ਕਰਨਾ

testimonial ('ਟੈਸਟਿ'ਮਅਉਨਯਅਲ) *n* ਸਨਦ, ਪ੍ਰਮਾਣ-ਪੱਤਰ; ਪ੍ਰਸੰਸਾ-ਪੱਤਰ, ਚਰਿੱਤਰ ਪੱਤਰ; ਉਪਹਾਰ

testimony ('ਟੈਸਟਿਮਅਨਿ) *n* (ਕਾ) ਸ਼ਹਾਦਤ, ਹਲਫ਼ੀਆ ਬਿਆਨ, ਸਬੂਤ, ਪ੍ਰਮਾਣ

testy ('ਟੈਸਟਿ) *a* ਕਰੋਧੀ, ਚਿੜਚਿੜਾ, ਖਿਝੂ

tete-a-tete ('ਟੇਇਟ'ਟੇਇਟ) *n a adv* ਗੁਪਤ ਵਾਰਤਾਲਾਪ, ਖੁਸਰ-ਮੁਸਰ, ਘੋਰ-ਮਸ਼ੌਰਾ; ਗੁਪਤ, ਇਕਾਂਤ, ਆਮੁਣੇ-ਸਾਮੁਣੇ; ਨਿੱਜੀ ਤੌਰ ਤੇ, ਅੰਦਰਖਾਨੇ

tetter ('ਟੈਟਅ) *n v* ਖੁਜਲੀ, ਦੱਦ, ਧੱਦਰ, ਚੰਬਲ (ਬੀਮਾਰੀਆਂ); ਖਾਜ ਕਰਨਾ, ਖੁਜਲੀ ਕਰਨਾ

text (ਟੈਕਸਟ) *n* ਮੂਲ ਪਾਠ, ਵਿਸ਼ਾ-ਵਸਤੂ, ਪਾਠ-ਪੁਸਤਕ, ਸੂਤਰ, ਵਚਨ, ਗ੍ਰੰਥ ਦਾ ਸਾਰ; ~book ਪਾਠ-ਪੁਸਤਕ; ~ual ਪਾਠ-ਸਬੰਧੀ, ਪਾਠਗਤ

textile ('ਟੈਕਸਟਾਇਲ) *a n* ਬੁਣਾਈ ਸਬੰਧੀ, ਬੁਣਿਆ; ਕੱਪੜਾ, ਬੁਣੀ ਸਮਗਰੀ

texture ('ਟੈਕਸਚਅ*) *n* ਰਚਨਾ, ਬੁਣਤ, ਬੁਣਾਈ, ਜੜਤ, ਗਠਨ

than (ਦੈਨ) *conj prep* ਕੋਲੋਂ, ਨਾਲੋਂ, ਪਾਸੋਂ, ਬਨਿਸਬਤ, ਤੁਲਨਾ ਵਜੋਂ

thank (ਥੈਂਕ) *n v* ਧੰਨਵਾਦ, ਸ਼ੁਕਰੀਆ; ਧੰਨਵਾਦ ਕਰਨਾ; ~ful ਧੰਨਵਾਦੀ, ਕ੍ਰਿਤੱਗ, ਮਸ਼ਕੂਰ, ਇਹਸਾਨਮੰਦ; ~less ਨਾਸ਼ੁਕਰਾ, ਅਕ੍ਰਿਤਘਣ; ਨਮਕ ਹਰਾਮ

thatch (ਥੈਚ) *n v* ਛੱਪਰ; ਘਾਹ, ਫੂਸ; ਛੱਪਰ ਪਾਉਣਾ; ਛੱਪਰ ਨਾਲ ਢਕਣਾ

theatre (ਥਿਅੱਟਅ*) *n* ਰੰਗਭੂਮੀ, ਨਾਟਕ-ਗ੍ਰਿਹ, ਥੀਏਟਰ, ਨਾਟਘਰ, ਲੈਕਚਰ ਹਾਲ

theft (ਥੈਫ਼ਟ) *n* ਚੋਰੀ, ਲੁੱਟ

theism ('ਥੀਇਜ਼(ਅ)ਮ) *n* ਆਸਤਕਤਾ, ਈਸ਼ਵਰਵਾਦ, ਆਸਤਕਵਾਦ, ਖ਼ੁਦਾਪਰਸਤੀ

theist ('ਥੀਇਸਟ) *n* ਆਸਤਕ, ਇਸ਼ਵਰਵਾਦ-ਸਬੰਧੀ, ਖ਼ੁਦਾਪਰਸਤੀ ਦਾ

thematic (ਥੀ'ਮੈਟਿਕ) *a* ਵਿਸ਼ੇਗਤ, ਆਤਮਕ ਵਿਸ਼ੇ ਸਬੰਧੀ, ਵਿਕਰਨ-ਯੁਕਤ

theme (ਥੀਮ) *n* ਵਿਸ਼ਾ-ਵਸਤੂ, ਪ੍ਰਕਰਣ, ਕਥਾ-ਪ੍ਰਸੰਗ; ਰਚਨਾ, ਨਿਬੰਧ

thence (ਦੈੱਸ) *adv* (ਪ੍ਰ) ਉਸ ਥਾਂ ਤੋਂ, ਉੱਥੋਂ, ਉਸ ਸਮੇਂ ਤੋਂ, ਤਦ ਤੋਂ, ਉਧਰੋਂ; ~forth ਉਦੋਂ ਅੱਗੇ, ਤਦ ਤੋਂ; ~forward ਉਦੋਂ ਅੱਗੇ, ਤਦ ਤੋਂ

theocracy (ਥਿਅੱਕਰਅਸਿ) *n* ਦੀਨੀ ਹਕੂਮਤ, ਧਰਮ-ਤੰਤਰ, ਇਸ਼ਵਰਤੰਤਰ

theology (ਥਿ'ਔਲਅਜਿ) *n* ਧਰਮ-ਸ਼ਾਸਤਰ

theorem ('ਥਿਅਰਅਮ) *n* (ਗਣਿ) ਮਸਲਾ; ਪ੍ਰਮੇਯ, ਸੂਤਰ

theoretic-al (ਥਿਅ'ਰੈਟਿਕ, ਥਿਅ'ਰੈਟਿਕਲ) *a* ਸਿਧਾਂਤਕ; ਇਲਮੀ; ਵਿਚਾਰਾਤਮਕ, ਦਿਮਾਗ਼ੀ

theorist ('ਥਿਅਰਿਸਟ) *n* ਸਿਧਾਂਤੀ, ਸਿਧਾਂਤਕਾਰ; ਗ਼ੈਰ-ਅਮਲੀ ਆਦਮੀ

theorize ('ਥਿਅਰਾਇਜ਼) *v* ਸਿਧਾਂਤ ਘੜਨੇ, ਨਿਯਮ ਬਣਾਉਣਾ, ਮੱਤ ਸਥਾਪਤ ਕਰਨਾ, ਅਨੁਮਾਨ ਲਾਉਣਾ

theory ('ਥਿਅਰਿ) *n* ਸਿਧਾਂਤ; ਮੱਤ; ਅਸੂਲ, ਨੇਮ; ਵਿਚਾਰ, ਕਲਪਨਾ; ਸ਼ਾਸਤਰ, ਵਿੱਦਿਆ

theosophy (ਥਿ'ਔਸਅਫ਼ਿ) *n* ਬ੍ਰਹਮ-ਵਿਗਿਆਨ, ਬ੍ਰਹਮ-ਵਿੱਦਿਆ, ਬ੍ਰਹਮਵਾਦ, ਇਸ਼ਵਰਵਾਦ

therapy (ਥਰੈਅਪਿ) *n* ਇਲਾਜ, ਚਿਕਿਤਸਾ

there (ਦੇਅ*) *adv n int* ਉਥੇ; ਉਹ ਥਾਂ; ਹੱਛਾ ਹੱਛਾ! ~**about(s)** ਉਥੇ, ਕਿਥੇ, ਨੇੜੇ, ਤੇੜੇ, ਉਸ ਦੇ ਆਸ ਪਾਸ; ਉੱਨਾ ਕੁ; ~**after** ਉਸ ਤੋਂ ਪਿਛੋਂ; ~**at** ਇਸ ਤੇ; ~**by** ਇੰਜ ਕਰਕੇ; ~**fore** ਤਾਹੀਂਓ, ਇਸ ਲਈ, ਤਦੇ ਹੀ; ~**in** ਉਸ ਵਿਚ; ~**of** ਉਸ ਦਾ; ~**upon** ਉਸ ਤੇ; ਫਲਸਰੂਪ; ਫ਼ੌਰਨ, ਤਤਕਾਲ; ~**with** (ਪ੍ਰ) ਉਸ ਦੇ ਨਾਲ, ਨਾਲੇ, ਨਾਲ ਹੀ

thermal (ਥਅ:ਮ) *n a* ਤਾਪ; ਗਰਮੀ ਦਾ, ਤਾਪਕ, ਤਾਪੀ, ਥਰਮ ਸਬੰਧੀ

thermometer (ਥਅ:ਮੌਮਿਟਅ*) *n* ਤਾਪਮਾਪੀ, ਤਾਪਮਾਨ ਜੰਤਰ, ਥਰਮਾਮੀਟਰ

thesis ('ਥੀਸਿਸ) *n* ਪ੍ਰਤਿਗਿਆ, ਵਾਦ; ਖੋਜ-ਪ੍ਰਬੰਧ

thick (ਥਿਕ) *a adv* ਮੋਟਾ, ਸਥੂਲ, ਘਚਪੀਚ, ਗੁੰਨ੍ਹਿਆ, ਗੁੰਦਿਆ, ਲੱਦਿਆ; ਠੋਸ, ਗਾੜ੍ਹਾ; ਅਸਪਸ਼ਟ, ਧੁੰਦਲਾ; ਮੂਰਖ; ਮੋਟੇ ਤੋਰ ਤੇ, ਲਗਾਤਾਰ; ~**skinned** ਮੋਟੀ ਚਮੜੀ ਵਾਲਾ; ~**ness** ਸਥੂਲਤਾ, ਮੁਟਾਪਾ, ਮੁਟਾਈ, ਘਣਤਾ, ਗਾੜ੍ਹਾਪਣ; ਮੂੜ੍ਹਤਾ; ਬੁੱਧੂਪਣ

thicket ('ਥਿਕਿਟ) *n* ਝਾੜੀ, ਝੁੰਡ, ਝੁਰਮਟ

thief (ਥੀਫ਼) *n* ਚੋਰ, ਉਚੱਕਾ, ਲੁਟੇਰਾ, ਸੰਨ੍ਹਮਾਰ

thieve (ਥੀਵ) *v* ਚੋਰੀ ਕਰਨਾ, ਚੁਰਾਉਣਾ

thigh (ਥਾਇ) *n* ਪੱਟ, ਜੰਘ

thin (ਥਿਨ) *a v* ਮਹੀਨ, ਬਾਰੀਕ, ਸੂਖਮ, ਪਤਲਾ; ਦੁਬਲਾ; ਵਿਰਲਾ, ਝਿਰਝਿਰਾ, ਪਾਰਦਰਸੀ; ਘਟਾਉਣਾ, ਘੱਟ ਕਰਨਾ, ਪਤਲਾ ਕਰਨਾ ਜਾਂ ਪੈਣਾ

thing (ਥਿਙ) *n* ਸੈ, ਵਸਤੁ, ਚੀਜ਼, ਜਿਨਸ, ਸਮਗਰੀ, ਪਰਸਥਿਤਿ; ਵਿਸ਼ਾ, ਗੱਲ, ਮਾਮਲਾ

think (ਥਿਙਕ) *v* ਵਿਚਾਰ ਕਰਨਾ, ਖ਼ਿਆਲ ਕਰਨਾ, ਗਿਆਨ ਹੋਣਾ, ਖ਼ਬਰ ਹੋਣੀ, ਸਮਝਣਾ ਸੋਚਣਾ ਵਿਚਾਰਨਾ; ~**highly of** ਬਹੁਤ ਜ਼ਿਆਦਾ ਸਨਮਾਨ ਦੇਣਾ; ~**of** ਕਲਪਨਾ ਕਰਨਾ, ਵਿਚਾਰਨਾ, ਸੋਚਣਾ; ~**out** ਸੋਚ ਵਿਚਾਰ ਕਰਕੇ ਫ਼ੈਸਲਾ ਕਰਨਾ; ~**er** ਚਿੰਤਕ, ਵਿਚਾਰਕ, ਦਾਰਸ਼ਨਕ; ~**ing** ਚਿੰਤਨ, ਸੋਚ-ਵਿਚਾਰ, ਵਿਚਾਰ-ਕਿਰਿਆ

third (ਥਅ:ਡ) *a n* ਤੀਜਾ; ਤਿਹਾਈ

thirst (ਥਅ:ਸਟ) *n v* ਤ੍ਰਿਖਾ, ਤਰੇਹ, ਚਾਹ; ਤੇਹ ਲੱਗਣੀ, ਪਿਆਸ ਲੱਗਣੀ

thirteen ('ਥਅ:ਟੀਨ) *n* ਤੇਰ੍ਹਾਂ

thirty ('ਥਅ:ਟਿ) *n* ਤੀਹ

thorax ('ਥੋਰੈਕਸ) *n* ਛਾਤੀ, ਸੀਨਾ

thorn (ਥੋਨ) *n* ਸੂਲ; ਖਾਰ, ਕੰਡਾ

thorough ('ਥਅ‌ਰਅ) *n a* ਅੱਤਵਾਦੀ ਨੀਤੀ; ਸੰਪੂਰਨ, ਪੂਰਨ, ਪੂਰਾ ਤਮਾਮ; ਸੁੱਧ (ਆਦਮੀ); ~**fare** ਸਰੇ ਆਮ, ਆਮ, ਲਾਂਘਾ

though (ਦਅਉ) *adv* ਭਾਵੇਂ, ਚਾਹੇ, ਹਾਲਾਂ ਕਿ ਖ਼ੈਰ

thought (ਥੋਟ) *n* ਚਿੰਤਨ, ਵਿਚਾਰ, ਧਿਆਨ

ਮਨਨ, ਸੋਚ, ਇਰਾਦਾ, ਧਾਰਨਾ ਸਮਝ, ਵਿਵੇਕ; ~ful ਵਿਚਾਰਸ਼ੀਲ, ਮਨਨਸ਼ੀਲ, ਧਿਆਨਮਗਨ, ਗੰਭੀਰ; ਸੁਹਿਰਦ, ਹਮਦਰਦ; ~less ਵਿਚਾਰਹੀਨ, ਮਨਹੀਨ, ਬੇਖ਼ਬਰ

thousand ('ਥਾਊਜ਼ਅੰਡ) *a n* ਹਜ਼ਾਰ; ਸਹੰਸਰ, ਬੇਸ਼ੁਮਾਰ

thrash (ਥਰੈਸ਼) *v* ਝੰਬਣਾ, ਫੰਡਣਾ, ਠੋਕਣਾ; ਕੁੱਟਣਾ, ਪਿੱਟਣਾ; ਫਾਂਟੀ ਚਾੜ੍ਹਨਾ, ਹਰਾਉਣਾ

thread (ਥਰੈੱਡ) *n v* ਧਾਗਾ, ਡੋਰੀ, ਸੂਤ, ਸੂਤਰ, ਤੰਦ, ਤਾਰ; ਕਢਾਈ ਕਰਨੀ

threat (ਥਰੈੱਟ) *n* ਧਮਕੀ, ਨਤੀ, ਦਾਬਾ, ਦੌਂਸ, ਘੁਰਕੀ, ਖਟਕਾ; ~en ਧਮਕਾਉਣਾ, ਡਰਾਉਣਾ; (ਦੀ) ਧਮਕੀ ਦੇਣਾ

threshold ('ਥਰੈਸ਼(ਹ)ਅਉਲਡ) *n* ਚੌਖਟ, ਦੇਹਰੀ; ਸਰਦਲ, ਮੁਹਾਠ, ਪ੍ਰਵੇਸ਼, ਸ਼ੁਰੂਆਤ

thrice (ਥਰਾਇਸ) *adv* ਤਿੰਨ ਵਾਰੀ, ਤਿਗੁਣਾ, ਤਿੰਨ ਗੁਣਾ

thrift (ਥਰਿਫਟ) *n* ਕਿਰਸ, ਸੰਜਮ, ਕਿਫ਼ਾਇਤਸ਼ਾਰੀ; (ਪ੍ਰ) ਖ਼ੁਸ਼ਹਾਲੀ

thrill (ਥਰਿਲ) *n v* ਰੋਮਾਂਚ; ਧੜਕਣ; ਝਰਨਾਹਟ; ਕੰਬਣੀ; ਝਰਨਾਹਟ ਛਿੜਨੀ; ਰੋਮਾਂਚ ਹੋਣਾ

thrive (ਥਰਾਇਵ੍) *v* ਪ੍ਰਫੁਲਤ ਹੋਣਾ, ਵਾਧਾ ਹੋਣਾ, ਉੱਨਤੀ ਕਰਨੀ, ਫਲਣਾ, ਹਰਿਆ ਭਰਿਆ ਹੋਣਾ

throat (ਥਰਅਉਟ) *n* ਸੰਘ, ਗਲ, ਕੰਠ

throb (ਥਰੋਬ) *v n* ਡਹਿਕਣਾ, ਟੀਸਣਾ, ਚਸਕਣਾ, ਟੀਸ ਪੈਣੀ; ਫੜਕਣਾ, ਪੜਕਣਾ; ਜਜ਼ਬਾਤੀ ਹੋਣਾ; ਪੜਕਣ, ਟੀਸ, ਚੀਸ; ਫੜਕਣ

throe (ਥਰਅਉ) *n v* ਜੰਮਣ ਪੀੜਾ, ਦਰਦਾਂ, ਪ੍ਰਸੂਤ ਵੇਦਨਾ, ਸੰਤਾਪ, ਕਸ਼ਟ, ਪੀੜਾ; ਕਸ਼ਟ ਪਾਉਣਾ, ਪੀੜ ਹੋਣੀ

throne (ਥਰਅਉਨ) *n v* ਤਖ਼ਤ, ਰਾਜ-ਗੱਦੀ, ਸਿੰਘਾਸਨ; ਪ੍ਰਭੂ-ਸੱਤਾ, ਰਾਜ-ਸੱਤਾ, ਹਕੂਮਤ; ਤਖ਼ਤ ਉੱਤੇ ਬਿਠਾਉਣਾ

throng (ਥਰੌਂਗ) *n v* ਭੀੜ, ਜਮਘਟਾ, ਇੱਕਠ; ਭੀੜ ਹੋਣੀ ਜਾਂ ਕਰਨੀ, ਜਮਘਟਾ ਜੰਮਣਾ

throttle ('ਥਰੌਟਲ) *n v* ਸੰਘ, ਗਲਾ, ਸਾਹ-ਨਾਲੀ; ਗਲ ਘੁੱਟਣਾ

through (ਥਰੂ) *prep adv a* ਵਿਚੋਂ ਦੀ, ਆਰ-ਪਾਰ, ਦੇ ਰਾਹੀਂ, ਦੇ ਦੁਆਰਾ, ਦੇ ਕਾਰਨ, ਮਾਰਫ਼ਤ; ਬਿਲਕੁਲ; ~out ਪੂਰੀ ਤਰ੍ਹਾਂ, ਸਾਰੇ ਦਾ ਸਾਰਾ, ਮੁੱਢੋਂ ਅਖੀਰ ਤਕ

throw (ਥਰਅਉ) *n v* ਟੱਪਾ, ਉਛਾਲ; ਫੈਂਕ, ਸੁੱਟਣਾ, ਡੇਗਣਾ, ਟੱਪਣਾ, ਦੇਣਾ ਜਾਂ ਦਿਵਾਉਣਾ; ਪੱਕਾਂ, ਡੁੰਜੇ ਸੁੱਟਣਾ; ~away ਵਰਤ ਕੇ ਸੁੱਟਣਯੋਗ

thrust (ਥਰਅੱਸਟ) *n v* ਘੁਸੇੜ, ਚੋਭ, ਖੋਭ; ਤੇਜ਼ ਹੁੱਝ; ਘੁਸੇੜਨ, ਖੋਭਣਾ, ਖੁਭਣਾ, ਵਿਨ੍ਹੁਣਾ, ਪੱਕਾ ਦੇਣਾ, ਹਟਾਉਣਾ

thud (ਥਅੱਡ) *n v* ਧੜੰਮ, ਧੜੰਮ ਦੀ ਅਵਾਜ਼, ਖੜਾਕ; ਧਮਾਕਾ (ਹੋਣਾ), ਧੜੰਮ ਕਰਕੇ ਡਿਗਣਾ

thug (ਥਅੱਗ) *n* ਗੁੰਡਾ, ਠਗ, ਖ਼ੂਨੀ; ਹਤਿਆਰਾ

thumb (ਥਅੱਮ) *n v* ਅਗੂੰਠਾ; ਠੂੰਠ; ਅੰਗੂਠੇ ਨਾਲ ਘਸਾਉਣਾ, ਦਬਾਉਣਾ

thump (ਥਅੱਪ) *n v* ਮੁੱਕਾ (ਮਾਰਨਾ), ਥੱਪੜ; ਲੱਫੜ (ਲਾਉਣਾ); ਡੰਡਾ (ਮਾਰਨਾ); ਕੁੱਟਣਾ

thunder ('ਥਅੱਡਅਅ*) *n v* ਗੜਗੜਾਹਟ, ਕੜਕ, ਗੜਗੱਜ, ਬੜੁਕ, ਥਬਕ; ਗੜਗੜਾਉਣਾ, ਗੱਜਣਾ, ਗਰਜਣਾ, ਬੜੁਕਣਾ, ਕੜਕਣਾ; ~bolt (ਬਿਜ) ਅਸਮਾਨੀ ਗੋਲਾ

tick (ਟਿਕ) *n v* (ਘੜੀ ਦੀ) ਟਿਕ-ਟਿਕ, ਖਟਕਟ; ਛਿਣ, ਪਲ; ਟਿੱਕਟ ਚਿੰਨ੍ਹ (✓), ਟਿਕ ਮਾਰਕ; ਚੰਮ ਜੂੰ, ਚਿੱਚੜ, (ਘੜੀ ਦਾ) ਟਿਕ-ਟਿਕ ਕਰਨਾ;

ਸਹੀ ਲਾਉਣੀ

ticket ('ਟਿਕਿਟ) *n v* ਟਿਕਟ, ਪ੍ਰਵੇਸ਼-ਪੱਤਰ; ਟਿਕਟ ਦੇਣਾ; (ਵੇਚਣ ਲਈ) ਲੇਬਲ ਲਾਉਣਾ

tickle ('ਟਿਕਲ) *n v* ਕੁਤਕੁਤਾੜੀ, ਕੁਤਕੁਤੀ, ਕੁਤਕੁਤਾਹਟ; ਪਲੋਸਣਾ, ਕੁਤਕੁਤਾਉਣਾ

tickling ('ਟਿਕਲਿਙ) *n* ਕੁਤਕੁਤਾਹਟ

tide (ਟਾਇਡ) *n* ਜਵਾਰਭਾਟਾ; ਅਵਸਰ; ਮੌਸਮ; (ਵਕਤ ਦੀ) ਚਾਲ, ਗੇੜ, ਕਾਲ-ਚੱਕਰ

tidy ('ਟਾਇਡਿ) *n a v* ਸਮੇਂ ਅਨੁਕੂਲ; ਸੁਅੱਛ, ਸੁਥਰਾ, ਸਾਫ; ਠੀਕ-ਠਾਕ, ਅਤੀ-ਅਧਿਕ, ਕਾਫੀ; ਚੰਗਾ-ਭਲਾ, ਤੰਦਰੁਸਤ; ਸੱਜਿਆ, ਸਲੀਕੇਦਾਰ; ਸਜਾਉਣਾ, ਠੀਕ-ਠਾਕ ਕਰਨਾ, ਸਾਫ-ਸੁਥਰਾ ਰੱਖਣਾ

tie (ਟਾਇ) *n v* ਗੰਢ, ਜੋੜ; ਬੰਨ੍ਹਣ, ਰੱਸੀ, ਸੂਤਲੀ, ਡੋਰੀ; ਯੋਗ; (ਸੰਗੀ) ਮੇਲ-ਚਿੰਨ੍ਹ; ਡੰਡਾ; ਰੇਲ ਦਾ ਸਲੀਪਰ; ਨੈਕਟਾਈ; ਗੰਢਣਾ, ਮਿਲਾਉਣਾ, ਪੱਕਾ ਕਰਨਾ, ਵਿਚੁ ਬਣਾਉਣਾ, ਜਕੜਨਾ, ਦੱਸਣਾ

tiffin (ਟਿਫਿਨ) *v* ਖਾਣਾ, ਟਿਫਿਨ; ਲੰਚ ਕਰਨਾ, ਰੋਟੀ ਖਾਣੀ, ਖਾਣਾ ਖਾਣਾ

tiger ('ਟਾਇਗਰਅ*) *n* ਸ਼ੇਰ, ਸ਼ੀਹ, ਬਾਘ, ਚੀਤਾ

tight (ਟਾਇਟ) *n a* ਘੁੱਟਵੇਂ; ਦ੍ਰਿੜ, ਠੋਸ, ਗੋਠਿਆ; ਅਭੇਦ; ਸੁਰੱਖਿਅਤ, ਕੱਸਿਆ; ਤੰਗ; ਸੱਡੋਲ; ਤਣਿਆ; ~**fisted** ਮੁੱਠੀ ਘੁੱਟ ਕੇ ਰੱਖਣ ਵਾਲਾ, ਕੰਜੂਸ; ~**lipped** ਚੁੱਪ ਸਾਧ

tile ('ਟਾਇਲ) *n v* ਘਰਚੈਲ, ਪਟੜੀ, ਚੌਕੀ; ਟਾਇਲਾਂ ਲਾਉਣੀਆਂ, ਪਟੜੀਬੰਦ ਬਣਾਉਣਾ

till (ਟਿਲ) *n v prep conj* ਦੁਕਾਨ ਦੀ ਗੋਲਕ, ਗੱਲਾ; ਤਦ, ਜਦ ਤਕ; ਜਦ ਤਕ ਕਿ, ਜਦ ਕਿ, ਇਥੋਂ ਤਕ ਕਿ; ਖੇਤੀ ਕਰਨਾ, ਹਲ ਚਲਾਉਣਾ, ਵਾਹੁਣਾ, ਜੋਤਣਾ, ਕਾਸ਼ਤ ਕਰਨਾ; ~**er** ਕਿਸਾਨ, ਕਾਸ਼ਤਕਾਰ

tilt (ਟਿਲਟ) *n v* ਢਾਲ, ਉਲਾਰ, (ਵੈਰੀ ਉੱਤੇ) ਵਾਰ, ਹਮਲਾ, ਮੁਠਭੇੜ, ਨੇਜ਼ੇਬਾਜ਼ੀ, ਹਚੋੜਾ, ਚੰਦੇਆ ਲਾਉਣਾ, ਟੇਢਾ ਕਰਨਾ

timber ('ਟਿੰਬਅ*) *n* ਕਾਠ, ਲੱਕੜ, ਇਮਾਰਤੀ ਲੱਕੜ; ਜੰਗਲ, ਵਨ; ਕੜੀ, ਸ਼ਹਿਤੀਰ

time (ਟਾਇਮ) *n* ਸਮਾਂ, ਵਕਤ; ਯੁੱਗ, ਕਾਲ, ਅਵਧੀ, ਫੁਰਸਤ, ਮਿਰਤੂ ਕਾਲ; ਮੌਕਾ; ਜ਼ਮਾਨਾ; ਜੀਵਨ-ਦਸ਼ਾ; ਦਫਾ; ਮਿਆਦ, ਜੀਵਨ-ਦਸ਼ਾ, ਮੁਹਲਤ; ~**table** ਸਮਾਂ ਸਾਰਣੀ, ਟਾਇਮ ਟੇਬਲ; ~**server** ਮੌਕਾਪਰਸਤ, ਜਮਾਨਾਸਾਜ਼; ~**ly** ਸਮੇਂ ਅਨੁਸਾਰ, ਵੇਲੇ ਸਿਰ

timid ('ਟਿਮਿਡ) *a* ਡਰਾਕਲ, ਡਰਪੋਕ, ਬੁਜ਼ਦਿਲ, ਝੇਂਪੂ, ਦੀਨ; ~**ity**, ~**ness** ਸਾਹਸ-ਹੀਣਤਾ, ਕਾਇਰਤਾ, ਬੁਜ਼ਦਿਲੀ; ਦੀਨਤਾ

timing ('ਟਾਇਮਿਙ) *n* ਸਮਾਂ, ਵਕਤ, ਸਮਾਂ-ਮਾਨ, ਸਮਾਂ-ਨਿਰਧਾਰਨ, ਸਮੇਂ ਦਾ ਹਿਸਾਬ

tin (ਟਿਨ) *n v* ਕਲੀ, ਕਲੀ ਵਾਲੀ ਲੋਹੇ ਦੀ ਚਾਦਰ, (ਬੋਲ) ਟੀਨ; ਪੀਪੀ, ਪੀਪਾ; ਕਲੀ ਕਰਨਾ

ting (ਟਿਙ) *n v* ਟਿਣਟਿਣਾਹਟ, ਖਿਣਖਿਣਾਹਟ; ਟਿਣਟਿਣਾਉਣਾ, ਖਿਣਖਿਣਾਉਣਾ

tinge (ਟਿੰਜ) *n v* ਰੰਗਤ, ਬਾਹ, ਆਭਾ, ਝਲਕ, ਹਲਕਾ ਰੰਗ; ਰੰਗਤ ਦੇਣੀ, ਪੁੱਠ ਹੋਣੀ, ਝਲਕ ਮਾਰਨੀ

tingle ('ਟਿਙਗਲ) *n v* ਖੁਤਖੁਤੀ, ਦੁਖਦੁਖੀ, ਝੁਣਝੁਣੀ; ਛੋਟਾ ਕਿੱਲ, ਸਿੱਕੇ ਦਾ ਕਲਿੱਪ; ਟਣ-ਟਣ, ਛਣ-ਛਣ; ਦੁਖਦੁਖੀ ਲੱਗਣੀ; ਵੱਜਣਾ; ਸਨਸਨੀ ਪੈਦਾ ਕਰਨਾ

tinsel ('ਟੀਨਸਲ) *n v* ਗੋਟਾ, ਕਿਨਾਰੀ, ਸਲਮਾ, ਪੰਨਾ; ਚਮਕ-ਦਮਕ, ਤੜਕ-ਭੜਕ, ਟੀਪ-ਟਾਪ; ਗੋਟਾ ਲਾਉਣਾ, ਸਲਮਾ ਸਿਤਾਰਾ ਜੜਨਾ

tip (ਟਿਪ) *n v a adv* ਸਿਰਾ, ਨੋਕ, ਮੂੰਹ; ਕੂਚੀ,

ਬੁਰਸ਼; ਇਨਾਮ, ਬਖ਼ਸ਼ੀਸ਼, ਟਿਪ; ਗੁਰ; ਬਾਪੀ; ਧੱਕਾ; ਝੁਕਾਉ, ਝੁਕਾਉਣਾ; ਟੇਢਾ ਕਰਨਾ; ਉਲਟਣਾ, ਉਲਟਾਉਣਾ; ~top ਬਹੁਤ ਵਧੀਆ, ਟਿਚਨ

tire ('ਟਾਇਅ*) v n (1) ਸ਼ਿੰਗਾਰ ਕਰਨਾ, ਸਜਾਉਣਾ; (2) ਥਕਾਉਣਾ, ਥੱਕਣਾ, (3) ਉਕਤਾ ਜਾਣਾ; ਵੇਸ, ਪੁਸ਼ਾਕ, ਕਪੜੇ; ~some ਥਕਾਊ

tit (ਟਿਟ) n ਮਰੀਅਲ ਘੋੜਾ, ਟੱਟੂ; ਪਿੰਡਾ

Titan ('ਟਾਇਟਨ) n (ਯੂਨਾਨ ਦਾ) ਸੂਰਜ ਦੇਵਤਾ, ਮਹਾਂ ਮਾਨਵ, ਦੈਂਤ

titbit ('ਟਿਟਬਿਟ) n ਮੁਆਦਲਾ ਭੋਜਨ; ਚਟਕਲਾ; ਚਟਪਟੀ ਖ਼ਬਰ

title ('ਟਾਇਟਲ) n ਸ਼ੀਰਸ਼ਕ; ਪਦਵੀ, ਖ਼ਿਤਾਬ; ਹੱਕ-ਮਾਲਕੀ, ਸਿਰਲੇਖ; ਅਧਿਕਾਰ-ਪੱਤਰ, ਦਸਤਾਵੇਜ਼

tittle-tattle ('ਟਿਟਲ-ਟੈਟਲ) n v ਬਕਵਾਸ (ਕਰਨਾ), ਗੱਪ (ਮਾਰਨਾ), ਬੜਬੜ ਕਰਨਾ

toad (ਟਅਉਡ) n ਡੱਡੂ ਵਰਗਾ ਜੀਵ; ਘਿਰਣਤ ਵਿਅਕਤੀ; ~stool ਕੁਕਰ ਮੁੱਤਾ; ~y ਚਾਪਲੂਸੀ, ਟੁਕੜਖੋਰੀ; ਖ਼ੁਸ਼ਾਮਦ ਕਰਨਾ

toast (ਟਅਉਸਟ) v n ਸਿਹਤ ਦਾ ਜਾਮ ਪੀਣਾ; ਡਬਲ ਰੋਟੀ ਦਾ ਟੁਕੜਾ ਭੁੰਨਣਾ, ਸੇਕਣਾ; ਸੇਕਿਆ ਡਬਲ ਰੋਟੀ ਦਾ ਟੁਕੜਾ, ਟੋਸਟ

toddle ('ਟੌਡਲ) n v ਨਮਕ-ਨਮਕ ਚਾਲ, ਝੁਮਕੀ ਟੋਰ, ਡਿੰਕ-ਡੋਲਾ, ਡਗਮਗਾਉਂਦੀ ਟੋਰ; ਚੁਹਲ-ਕਦਮੀ, ਮਟਰਗਸ਼ਤੀ; ਠੁਮਠੁਮ ਕਰਕੇ ਟੁਰਨਾ, ਚੁਹਲ ਕਦਮੀ ਕਰਨਾ, ਮਟਰਗਸ਼ਤੀ ਕਰਨਾ

toe (ਟਅਉ) n v ਪੈਰ ਦੀ ਉਂਗਲ; ਪੰਜੇ ਲਾਉਣਾ, ਖੁਰਾਂ ਵਿਚ ਖੁਰੀਆਂ

together (ਟਅ'ਗੇਂਦਅ*) adv ਇੱਕਠੇ; ਲਗਾਤਾਰ

toil (ਟੋਇਲ) n ਸਖ਼ਤ ਮਿਹਨਤ (ਕਰਨੀ), ਫੰਦਾ, ਜਾਲ

toilet ('ਟੋਇਲਿਟ) n ਇਸ਼ਨਾਨ ਗ੍ਰਹਿ; ਮੂੰਹ-ਹੱਥ ਧੋਣਾ, ਟੱਟੀ, ਗੁਸਲਖ਼ਾਨਾ; ਬਣਾਉ-ਸ਼ਿੰਗਾਰ, ਕੰਘੀ-ਪੱਟੀ; ਕੱਪੜਾ-ਲੱਤਾ

token ('ਟਅਉਕ(ਅ)ਨ) n ਨਿਸ਼ਾਨੀ, ਯਾਦ-ਚਿੰਨ੍ਹ, ਪ੍ਰਤੀਕ, ਲੱਛਣ, ਪ੍ਰਮਾਣ; ਸਿੱਕਾ

tolerable ('ਟੌਲਅਰਬਲ) a ਸਹਿਨਸ਼ੀਲ, ਸਹਿਣਯੋਗ, ਚੰਗਾ, ਤਸੱਲੀਬਖ਼ਸ਼, ਸੰਤੋਖਜਨਕ, ਸਧਾਰਨ

tolerance ('ਟੌਲਅਰਅੰਸ) n ਧੀਰਜ, ਸਹਿਣਸ਼ੀਲਤਾ, ਉਦਾਰਤਾ, ਬਰਦਾਸ਼ਤ

tolerant ('ਟੌਲਅਰਅੰਟ) a ਖਿਮਾਸ਼ੀਲ, ਸਹਿਣਸ਼ੀਲ, ਉਦਾਰ

tolerate ('ਟੌਲਅਰੇਇਟ) v ਬਰਦਾਸ਼ਤ ਕਰਨਾ, ਸਹਿਣਾ, ਝੱਲਣਾ, ਸਹਾਰਨਾ

toleration ('ਟੌਲਅ'ਰੇਇਸ਼ਨ) n ਉਦਾਰਤਾ, ਸਹਿਣ-ਸ਼ੀਲਤਾ, ਬਰਦਾਸ਼ਤ

toll (ਟਅਉਲ) n v ਪੰਥ-ਕਰ; ਟੱਲੀ ਜਾਂ ਘੰਟੀ ਦੀ ਅਵਾਜ਼, ਚੁੰਗੀ ਲੈਣਾ, ਮਹਿਸੂਲ ਲੈਣਾ

tomato (ਟਅ'ਮਾਟਅਉ) n ਟਮਾਟਰ

tomb (ਟੂਮ) n v ਸਮਾਧ; ਕਬਰ, ਮਕਬਰਾ; ਮਜ਼ਾਰ, ਦਰਗਾਹ; ਦਫ਼ਨਾਉਣਾ, ਲੁਕਾਉਣਾ

tomfool ('ਟੌਮਫੂਲ) ਮਹਾਮੁਰਖ

tomorrow (ਟਅ'ਮੌਰਅਉ) n ਕੱਲ੍ਹ, ਆਉਣ ਵਾਲਾ ਦਿਨ, ਆਗਾਮੀ ਦਿਵਸ

ton (ਟਅੱਨ) n ਟਨ, 2240 ਪੌਂਡ ਜਾਂ 1000 ਕਿਲੋਗ੍ਰਾਮ ਦਾ ਭਾਰ

tone (ਟਅਉਨ) n v ਤਰਜ਼, ਅੰਦਾਜ਼, ਲਹਿਜਾ; ਟੋਨ, ਸਵਰਾਘਾਤ; (ਸੰਗੀ) ਧੁਨ, ਨਾਦ; ਧੁਨੀ ਉਤਪੰਨ ਕਰਨਾ, ਤਾਨ ਭਰਨਾ, ਉਚਿਤ ਰੰਗ ਭਰਨਾ, ਸੁਰ ਮਿਲਾਉਣਾ; ਸਾਜ਼ ਸੁਰ ਕਰਨਾ

tonga ('ਟੌਂਗਗਅ) *n* ਟਾਂਗਾ, ਯੱਕਾ

tongs (ਟੌਂਡਜ਼) *n pl* ਚਿਮਟਾ, ਸੰਨ੍ਹੀ, ਚਿਮਟੀ

tongue (ਟਅੰਡ) *n v* ਜੀਭ, ਰਸਨਾ, ਜ਼ਬਾਨ; ਭਾਸ਼ਾ, ਬੋਲੀ, ਬਾਣੀ, ਜ਼ਬਾਨ ਖੇਲ੍ਹਣਾ, ਗੱਲ ਕਰਨੀ

tonight (ਟਅ'ਨਾਇਟ) *adv* ਅੱਜ ਦੀ ਰਾਤ, ਅੱਜ ਰਾਤ ਨੂੰ

tonsil ('ਟੈਂਸਲ) *n* ਗਲਾ, ਗਲ ਦੇ ਕੰਡੇ; ਟਾਨਸਿਲ

tony ('ਟਅਉਨਿ) *a* ਸੁਰੀਲਾ, ਮੂਰਖ, ਬੇਵਕੂਫ਼

too (ਟੂ) *adv* ਬਹੁਤ ਵਧੇਰੇ, ਅਤੀਅੰਤ, ਅਤੀ ਅਧਿਕ

tool (ਟੂਲ) *n v* ਸੰਦ, ਕਲ, ਜੰਤਰ, ਜੁੱਧ-ਸਮਗਰੀ, ਗੋਲੀ-ਸਿੱਕਾ, ਗੋਲਾ-ਬਾਰੂਦ; ਸਾਧਨ, ਹੱਕਣਾ, ਚਲਾਉਣਾ, ਸਵਾਰੀ ਕਰਨੀ

tooth (ਟੂਥ) *n v* ਦੰਦ, ਦੰਦਾ (ਆਰੀ ਜਾਂ ਕੰਘੀ ਦਾ); ਚਰਖੀ, ਆਰੀ; ਦੰਦੇ ਕੱਢਣੇ

top (ਟੌਪ) *n v a* ਟੀਸੀ, ਸਿਖਰ, ਚੋਟੀ, ਸਿਰਾ; ਸਿਖਰ ਤੇ ਅਪੜਨਾ; ਕੋਂਦ ਵਿਚ ਲੰਮਾ ਹੋਣਾ; ਵਧ ਜਾਣਾ, ਬਾਜ਼ੀ ਲੈ ਜਾਣੀ; ਮੁਖੀਆ, ਸ੍ਰੇਸ਼ਠ, ਸਰਵ-ਉੱਚ

topaz (ਟਅਉਪੈਜ਼) *n* ਪੁਖਰਾਜ

topple ('ਟੌਪਲ) *v* ਡਗਮਗਾ ਕੇ ਡਿਗਣਾ; ਡੇਗਣਾ, ਗਿਰਾਉਣਾ

topsyturvy ('ਟੌਪਸਿ'ਟਅ:ਵਿ) *n v a adv* ਉਲਟ-ਪੁਲਟ; ਉਲਟਣਾ, ਪੁਲਟਣਾ, ਥੱਲੇ-ਉੱਤੇ ਕਰਨਾ, ਗੜਬੜ ਕਰਨਾ; ਉਲਟਾ-ਪੁਲਟਾ

torch (ਟੋਚ) *n* ਟਾਰਚ, ਬੱਤੀ, ਮਸ਼ਾਲ, ਜੋਤ; ਚਾਨਣ

torment ('ਟੋਮੈਂਟ, ਟ'ਮੈਂਟ) *n v* ਤਸੀਹਾ, ਦੁੱਖ; ਕਸ਼ਟ; ਘੋਰ ਸੰਤਾਪ ਦੇਣਾ, ਬਹੁਤ ਦੁੱਖ ਦੇਣਾ, ਕਸ਼ਟ ਦੇਣਾ

tornado (ਟੋ'ਨੇਇਡਅਉ) *n* ਝੱਖੜ, ਤੇਜ਼ ਤੁਫ਼ਾਨ, ਵਾਛੜ

torpedo (ਟੋ'ਪੀਡਅਉ) *n v* ਡੁਬਕਣੀ ਕਿਸ਼ਤੀ, ਟਾਰਪੀਡੋ; ਵਿਸਫੋਟਕ, ਸੁਰੰਗ, ਟਾਰਪੀਡੋ ਨਾਲ ਮਾਰਨਾ; ਅਸਫਲ ਕਰਨਾ, ਵਿਅਰਥ ਕਰਨਾ

tortoise ('ਟੋਟਅਸ) *n* ਕੱਛੂ ਕੁੰਮਾ, ਕੱਛੂ

tortuous ('ਟੋਚੁਅਸ) *a* ਵਲੇਵੇਂਦਾਰ; ਟੇਢਾ-ਮੇਢਾ, ਪੇਚੀਦਾ

torture (ਟੋਚਅ*) *n v* ਤਸੀਹਾ, ਅਜ਼ਾਬ, ਮਾਨਸਕ ਪੀੜਾ, ਕਸ਼ਟ; ਤਸੀਹਾ ਦੇਣਾ; ਸਤਾਉਣਾ; ਤੋੜਨਾ-ਮਰੋੜਨਾ

toss (ਟੌਸ) *n v* ਸਿੱਕੇ ਦਾ ਉਛਾਲ, ਸਿੱਕਾ ਸੁੱਟਣ ਦੀ ਕਿਰਿਆ, ਟਾਸ; (ਹਵਾ ਦਾ) ਬੁੱਲਾ; ਉਥਲ-ਪੁਥਲ; ਉਛਾਲ; ਸਿੱਕਾ ਸੁੱਟਣਾ; ਹਿੱਲਣਾ-ਜੁਲਣਾ; ਡਾਵਾਂ-ਡੋਲ ਹੋਣਾ

total ('ਟਅਉਟਲ) *n a v* ਜੋੜ, ਜੋੜ-ਫਲ, ਜਮਾਂ; ਕੁੱਲ; ਸਾਰਾ, ਸਮੁੱਚਾ; ਉੱਕਾ; ਜੋੜ ਕਰਨਾ, ਜੋੜ ਹੋਣਾ; ~**itarian** ਸਰਵ ਅਧਿਕਾਰਵਾਦੀ, ਸਰਵ ਸੱਤਾਵਾਦੀ, ਇਕ ਦਲਵਾਦੀ, ਤਾਨਾਸ਼ਾਹੀ; ~**ity** ਪੂਰਨਤਾ, ਸਮਗਰਤਾ, ਕੁੱਲ ਜੋੜ; ਕੁੱਲ ਸੰਖਿਆ

totty ('ਟੌਟਿ) *a* ਹੱਕਾ-ਬੱਕਾ, ਚੁੰਧਿਆਇਆ, ਲੜਖੜਾਉਂਦਾ, ਨਸ਼ੇ ਵਿਚ ਚੂਰ

touch (ਟਅੱਚ) *n v* ਛੋਹ, ਸਪਰਸ਼, ਸੰਪਰਕ, ਲਗਾਉ; ਹੱਥ ਲਾਉਣਾ, ਛੋਹਣਾ; ਹੌਲੀ-ਹੌਲੀ ਦੱਬਣਾ, ਤੀਰ ਵਾਂਗ ਲੱਗਣਾ, ਸੁੱਤਾ ਕਰੋਧ ਜਗਾਉਣਾ; (ਤਕ) ਪਹੁੰਚਣਾ; (ਨਾਲ) ਲੱਗਣਾ; ~**ing** ਦਰਦਨਾਕ, ਦਿਲ ਟੁੰਬਵਾਂ; ~**y** ਚਿੜਚੜਾ, ਸੜੀਅਲ ਮਿਜ਼ਾਜ

tough (ਟਅੱਫ) *a n* ਸਖਤ, ਕਰੜਾ, ਮਜ਼ਬੂਤ, ਔਖਾ; ਰੁੰਡਾ, ਬਦਮਾਸ਼

tour (ਟੂਅ*) *n v* ਦੌਰਾ (ਕਰਨਾ), ਯਾਤਰਾ (ਕਰਨੀ),

ਭ੍ਰਮਣ (ਕਰਨਾ)

tournament ('ਟੋਨਅਮਅੰਟ) *n* ਖੇਡਾਂ ਦਾ ਮੁਕਾਬਲਾ, ਖੇਡ ਪ੍ਰਤੀਯੋਗਤਾ; ਫ਼ੌਜੀ ਨੁਮਾਇਸ਼; ਮੁਕਾਬਲਾ

tout (ਟਾਉਟ) *n v* ਦਲਾਲ; ਦਲਾਲੀ ਕਰਨਾ

toward, towards ('ਟਅਉਅਡ, ਟਅ'ਵੋਡਜ਼) *a prep* ਵੱਲ, ਪਾਸੇ, ਦੀ ਦਿਸ਼ਾ ਵਿਚ, ਦੇ ਪ੍ਰਤੀ, ਦੇ ਵਿਸ਼ੇ ਵਿਚ

towel ('ਟਾਉਅਲ) *n v* ਤੌਲੀਆ, ਪਰਨਾ; ਸਰੀਰ ਪੂੰਝਣਾ; ਠੋਕਣਾ, ਰਗੜਨਾ

tower (ਟਾਉਅ*) *n v* ਬੁਰਜ, ਮੁਨਾਰਾ; ਉੱਚਾ ਉਠਣਾ ਜਾਂ ਚੜ੍ਹਨਾ, ਹਵਾ ਵਿਚ ਖੜ੍ਹਾ ਹੋਣਾ

town (ਟਾਉਨ) *n* ਕਸਬਾ, ਸ਼ਹਿਰ, ਨਗਰ; **~ship** ਨਗਰ ਖੇਤਰ, ਨਵੀਂ ਬਸਤੀ

toxic ('ਟੈਕਸਿਕ) *a* ਜ਼ਹਿਰੀਲਾ; ਜ਼ਹਿਰ-ਸਬੰਧੀ; **~ant** ਜ਼ਹਿਰ, ਵਿਸ਼ੈਲਾ ਜ਼ਹਿਰੀਲਾ

toy (ਟੌਇ) *n v* ਖਿਡੌਣਾ; ਘੁੱਗੂ-ਘੋੜਾ, ਖੇਡ; ਮਨੋਰੰਜਨ ਕਰਨਾ, ਦਿਲ ਬਹਿਲਾਉਣਾ

trace (ਟਰੇਇਸ) *n v* ਖੁਰਾ-ਖੋਜ, ਚਿੰਨ੍ਹ, ਨਿਸ਼ਾਨ, ਪਦ-ਚਿੰਨ੍ਹ, ਸੁਰਾਗ; ਰੂਪ-ਰੇਖਾ ਉਲੀਕਣੀ, ਖ਼ਾਕਾ ਖਿੱਚਣਾ; ਟ੍ਰੇਸ ਕਰਨਾ, ਨਕਲ ਕਰਨੀ, ਭਾਲਣਾ, ਲੱਭਣਾ; ਸੁਰਾਗ ਲਾਉਣਾ

trachoma (ਟਰਅ'ਕਅਉਮਅ) *n* ਕੁੱਕਰੇ

track (ਟਰੈਕ) *n* ਮਾਰਗ, ਪਥ; ਪਟੜੀ, ਰੇਲ ਦੀ ਪਟੜੀ; ਪੈੜ ਪਗਡੰਡੀ, ਖੁਰਾਂ ਦੇ ਨਿਸ਼ਾਨ, ਚਿੰਨ੍ਹ; ਪੈੜ ਕਢਣੀ

tract (ਟਰੈਕਟ) *n* ਭੂ-ਖੰਡ ਖੇਤਰ, ਅਰਸਾ; ਛੋਟਾ ਗ੍ਰੰਥ, ਛੋਟਾ ਪੱਤਰ, ਟਰੈਕਟ; **~ion** ਖਿਚਾਉ, ਖਿੱਚ, ਆਕਰਸ਼ਣ; **~or** ਟਰੈਕਟਰ, ਹਲਵਾਹਕ ਇੰਜਣ

trade (ਟਰੇਇਡ) *n* ਧੰਦਾ, ਕਾਰੋਬਾਰ, ਪੇਸ਼ਾ; ਵਣਜ, ਵਪਾਰ, ਤਿਜਾਰਤ, ਸੌਦਾਗਰੀ; ਵਪਾਰ ਕਰਨਾ, ਕਾਰੋਬਾਰ ਕਰਨਾ, ਤਿਜਾਰਤ ਕਰਨੀ; **~mark** ਮਾਰਕਾ; ਵਿੱਲਖਣਤਾ

tradition (ਟਰਅ'ਡਿਸ਼ਨ) *n* ਰਿਵਾਜ, ਪਰੰਪਰਾ, ਰੀਤ, ਰਵਾਇਤ, ਦਸਤੂਰ, ਦੈਵੀ ਸਿਧਾਂਤ

traffic ('ਟਰੈਫ਼ਿਕ) *n* ਆਵਾਜਾਈ, ਆਉਣ-ਜਾਣਾ, ਆਮਦੋ-ਰਫ਼ਤ; ਧੰਦਾ, ਵਣਜ, ਲੈਣ-ਦੇਣ; ਸੌਦਾ ਕਰਨਾ, ਲੈਣ-ਦੇਣ ਕਰਨਾ

tragedy (ਟਰੈਜਅਡਿ) *n* ਬੜੀ ਸ਼ੋਕਮਈ ਦੁਰਘਟਨਾ, ਦੁਖਾਂਤ ਨਾਟਕ; ਦੁਖਾਂਤਕ ਰਚਨਾ; ਵੱਡੀ ਆਫ਼ਤ, ਭਾਰੀ ਮੁਸੀਬਤ

tragic, -al ('ਟਰੈਜਿਕ 'ਟਰੈਜਿਕਲ) *a* ਸ਼ੋਕਮਈ, ਸੋਗ ਭਰਿਆ, ਦੁਖਦਾਈ; ਦਰਦਨਾਕ; ਦੁਖਾਂਤ ਨਾਟਕ ਦਾ

trail (ਟਰੇਇਲ) *n v* ਪਗਡੰਡੀ, ਪੈੜ, ਲੀਹ, ਪੇਹਾ; ਤੋਪ ਨੂੰ ਖਿੱਚਣ ਵਾਲੀ ਮੋਟਰ ਗੱਡੀ ਦਾ ਹੇਠਲਾ ਹਿੱਸਾ; ਖੋਜ ਕੱਢਣਾ; (ਘਾਹ ਆਦਿ ਨੂੰ) ਪੈਰਾਂ ਨਾਲ ਲਿਤਾੜਨਾ; ਪਿੱਛੇ ਘਸੀਟੇ ਜਾਣਾ

train (ਟਰੇਇਨ) *v n* ਸਿਖਾਉਣਾ, ਸਿਖਲਾਈ ਦੇਣੀ; ਅਭਿਆਸ ਕਰਾਉਣਾ; ਲਾਮ-ਡੋਰੀ; ਪਿਛਲੱਗ; ਰੇਲ-ਗੱਡੀ; **~down** (ਕਸਰਤ ਰਾਹੀਂ) ਭਾਰ ਘਟਾਉਣਾ; **~with** ਸਾਥੀ ਬਣਨਾ; **~ee** ਸਿਖਿਆਰਥੀ; **~ing** ਸਿਖਲਾਈ

trait (ਟਰੇਇਟਅ) *n* ਗੁਣ, ਲੱਛਣ, ਵਿਸ਼ੇਸ਼ਤਾ

traitor ('ਟਰੇਇਟਅ*) *n* ਦਰੋਹੀ, ਦੇਸ਼-ਧਰੋਹੀ

trample ('ਟਰੈਂਪਲ) *v n* ਮਿੱਧਣਾ, ਲਿਤਾੜਨਾ; ਲਿਤਾੜ ਦੇਣਾ; ਪਦ-ਦਲਨ; **~d** ਲਿਤਾੜਿਆ, ਕੁਚਲਿਆ; ਦਬਾਇਆ, ਅਪਮਾਨਤ

trance (ਟਰਾਂਸ) *n v* ਸਮਾਧੀ, ਅੰਤਰਲੀਨਤਾ, ਵਜਦ, ਪਰਮ-ਆਨੰਦ ਦੀ ਅਵਸਥਾ, ਵਿਚ ਲੈ ਆਉਣਾ

tranquil ('ਟਰੈਂਕਵਿਲ) *a* ਸ਼ਾਂਤ, ਚੁੱਪ-ਚਾਪ, ਟਿਕਿਆ; **~ity** ਟਿਕਾਉ, ਸ਼ਾਂਤੀ, ਅਮਨ-ਚੈਨ, ਸਕੂਨ; **~lize** ਸ਼ਾਂਤ ਕਰਨਾ, ਟਿਕਾਉ ਵਿਚ ਲਿਆਉਣਾ, ਸ਼ਾਂਤੀ ਸਥਾਪਤ ਕਰਨੀ; ਧੀਰਜ ਦੇਣਾ

transact (ਟਰੈਂ'ਜ਼ੈਕਟ) *v* ਅਮਲ ਕਰਨਾ, ਨੇਪਰੇ ਚਾੜ੍ਹਨਾ, ਨਿਭਾਹੁਣਾ, ਪੂਰਾ ਕਰਨਾ; ਪ੍ਰਬੰਧ ਕਰਨਾ; **~ion** ਸੌਦਾ, ਮੁਆਮਲਾ, ਕਾਰਵਾਈ; ਸਮਝੌਤਾ, ਸੁਲ੍ਹਾ-ਸਫ਼ਾਈ; ਨਿਰਵਾਹ; ਕਾਰਜ-ਪ੍ਰਬੰਧ; ਵਿਧਾਨਕ ਕਾਰਵਾਈ

transcend (ਟਰੈਂ'ਸੈਂਡ) *v* ਮਨੁੱਖੀ ਅਨੁਭਵ ਤੋਂ ਪਰ੍ਹੇ ਹੋਣਾ; ਕਮਾਲ ਤੇ ਪਹੁੰਚਣਾ; ਪਾਰਗਾਮੀ ਹੋਣਾ; **~ence, ~ency** (ਇੰਦਰੀਆਂ ਦੀ ਪਹੁੰਚ ਤੋਂ ਪਾਰ ਦੀ ਦਸ਼ਾ; ਪਾਰਗਮਨ; **~ent** ਅਤੀ ਉੱਚਾ, ਪਾਰਗਾਮੀ, ਅਨੁਭਵ-ਅਤੀਤ-ਤੱਤਵ, ਸੂਝ ਤੇ ਅਨੁਭਵ ਤੋਂ ਪਰ੍ਹਾਂ ਦਾ

transcribe (ਟਰੈਂ'ਸਕਰਾਇਬ) *v* ਪ੍ਰਤੀਲਿਪੀ ਬਣਾਉਣੀ; (ਲਿਖਤ ਨੂੰ) ਨਕਲ ਕਰਨਾ, ਉਤਾਰਾ ਲੈਣਾ

transcript ('ਟਰੈਂਸਕਰਿਪਟ) *n* ਪ੍ਰਤੀਲਿਪੀ; ਨਕਲ (ਲਿਖਤ ਦੀ), ਉਤਾਰਾ; **~ion** ਲਿਪੀ-ਅੰਤਰਨ ਪ੍ਰਤੀਲਿਪੀ, ਨਕਲ

transect (ਟਰੈਂ'ਸੈਕਟ) *v* ਨਿਖੇੜਨਾ, ਪਾੜਨਾ, ਵੱਖ ਕਰਨਾ, ਭਿੰਨ-ਭਿੰਨ ਕਰਨਾ, ਵਿਭਾਜਤ ਕਰਨਾ; **~ion** ਨਿਖੇੜਾ, ਵਿਭਾਜਤ, ਵੰਡ

transfer (ਟਰੈਂਸ'ਫ਼ਅ*, 'ਟਰੈਨਸਫ਼ਅ*) *v n* ਬਦਲਣਾ, ਤਬਦੀਲ ਕਰਨਾ, ਸਥਾਨ-ਅੰਤਰਣ ਕਰਨਾ; ਸੌਂਪ ਦੇਣਾ, ਹਵਾਲੇ ਕਰਨਾ; ਤਬਦੀਲੀ, ਸਥਾਨ-ਅੰਤਰਣ; ਇੰਤਕਾਲ; ਨਕਸ਼ੇ ਆਦਿ ਦਾ ਉਤਾਰਾ; **~ence** ਤਬਦੀਲੀ, ਬਦਲੀ; ਇੰਤਕਾਲ; ਨਕਲ

transform (ਟਰੈਂਸ'ਫ਼ੋਮ) *v* ਰੂਪ ਬਦਲ ਦੇਣਾ, ਕਾਇਆ ਪਲਟ ਦੇਣੀ, (ਵਿਆ) ਰੂਪਾਂਤਰ ਕਰਨਾ; **~er** (ਬਿਜਲੀ) ਪਰਿਵਰਤਨ ਜੰਤਰ, ਪਰਿਮਾਣਕ ਜੰਤਰ; ਪਰਿਵਰਤਨ ਕਰਤਾ

transgress (ਟਰੈਂਸ'ਗਰੈੱਸ) *v* ਉਲੰਘਣਾ ਕਰਨੀ, ਅਵੱਗਿਆ ਕਰਨੀ; ਭੁੱਲ ਕਰਨੀ, ਪਾਪ ਕਰਨਾ; **~ion** ਉਲੰਘਣਾ, ਅਵੱਗਿਆ, ਜੁਰਮ, ਅਪਰਾਧ

transit ('ਟਰੈਂਸਿਟ) *n v* ਗੁਜ਼ਰ, ਲਾਂਘਾ, ਆਉਣ-ਜਾਣ, ਪਾਰਗਮਨ; **~ion** ਪਰਿਵਰਤਨ, ਬਦਲੀ; **~ional** ਅਸਥਾਈ, ਥੋੜ੍ਹੇ ਚਿਰ ਲਈ, ਆਰਜ਼ੀ; **~ory** ਅਸਥਿਰ, ਛਿਣ-ਭੰਗੁਰ; ਅਲਪਕਾਲੀ, ਅਸਥਾਈ

translate (ਟਰੈਂਸ'ਲੇਇਟ) *v* ਅਨੁਵਾਦ ਕਰਨਾ, ਉਲਥਾ ਕਰਨਾ; ਤਾਤਪਰਜ ਕੱਢਣਾ, ਵਿਆਖਿਆ ਕਰਨੀ

translation (ਟਰੈਂਸ'ਲੇਇਸ਼ਨ) *n* ਅਨੁਵਾਦ, ਉਲਥਾ; ਤਰਜਮਾ

translator (ਟਰੈਂਸ'ਲੇਇਟਅ*) *n* ਅਨੁਵਾਦਕ, ਉਲਥਾਕਾਰ

transliterate (ਟਰੈਂਜ਼'ਲਿਟਅਰੇਇਟ) *v* ਲਿਪੀ-ਅੰਤਰਨ, ਵਰਨਾਂਤਰ

transmission (ਟਰੈਂਜ਼'ਮਿਸ਼ਨ) *n* ਲਾਂਘਾ, ਸੰਚਾਰਨ; ਪਾਰਗਮਨ

transmit (ਟਰੈਂਜ਼'ਮਿਟ) *v* ਭੇਜਣਾ, ਘੱਲਣਾ, ਪਹੁੰਚਾਣਾ; ਖ਼ਬਰ ਭੇਜਣੀ ਜਾਂ ਪਹੁੰਚਾਉਣੀ

transmutation ('ਟਰੈਂਜ਼ਮਯੂ'ਟੇਇਸ਼ਨ) *n* ਕਾਇਆ-ਕਲਪ, ਰੂਪ-ਬਦਲੀ, ਰੂਪਾਂਤਰਣ; ਗੁਣ-ਪਰਿਵਰਤਨ

transparence (ਟਰੈਂਜ਼'ਪੈਰਅੰਸ) *n* ਪਾਰਦਰਸ਼ਤਾ; ਨਿਰਮਲਤਾ, ਸੁਅੱਛਤਾ

transparency (ਟਰੈਂਜ਼'ਪੈਰਅੰਸਿ) *n* ਪਾਰਦਰਸ਼ੀ

ਚਿੱਤਰ

transparent (ਟਰੈਂਜ਼'ਪੈਰਅੰਟ) *a* ਪਾਰਦਰਸ਼ੀ ਨਿਰਮਲ; ਖਰਾ, ਸਪੱਸ਼ਟ

transpire (ਟਰੱਸ'ਪਾਇਆ*) *v* ਅਵਾਈ ਉਡਣੀ, ਪਤਾ ਲੱਗਣਾ; ਵਾਪਰਨਾ, ਹੋਣਾ

transplant (ਟਰੱਸ'ਪਲਾਂਟ) *v* ਇਕ ਥਾਂ ਤੋਂ ਪੁਟ ਕੇ ਦੂਜੀ ਥਾਂ ਬੀਜਣਾ; (ਸਰੀਰ ਦੇ ਅੰਗ ਦਾ) ਦੂਜੇ ਥਾਂ ਜਾਂ ਦੂਜੇ ਸਰੀਰ ਵਿਚ ਲਾਉਣਾ; ~ation ਅੰਗ ਦੀ ਪਿਉਂਦ; ~ing ਪਿਉਂਦ ਲਾਉਣੀ, ਪਨੀਰੀ ਲਾਉਣੀ

transport (ਟਰੱਂਸ'ਪੋਟ) *v n* ਢੋਣਾ; ਦੇਸ਼ ਨਿਕਾਲਾ ਦੇਣਾ; ਢੁਆਈ; ਆਵਾਜਾਈ; ਵਾਹਨ; ਦੇਸ਼-ਨਿਕਾਲਾ; ਵਜਦ; ਢੁਆਈ ਦਾ ਸਾਧਨ, ਆਵਾਜਾਈ ਲਈ ਵਰਤੀਆਂ ਜਾਣ ਵਾਲੀਆਂ ਗੱਡੀਆਂ ਆਦਿ; ~ation ਢੋਆ-ਢੁਆਈ; ਦੇਸ਼-ਨਿਕਾਲਾ; ਸਫ਼ਰ

transverbate (ਟਰੱਂਜ਼'ਵਅਃਬੇਇਟ) *v* ਸ਼ਬਦ-ਅਨੁਵਾਦ ਕਰਨਾ; ਅਨੁਵਾਦ ਕਰਨਾ

transverse ('ਟਰੱਨਜ਼ਵਅਃਸ) *a* ਤਿਰਛਾ, ਆੜੇ ਰੁਖ, ਟੇਢੇ ਰੁਖ

trap (ਟਰੈਪ) *n v* (1) ਛਲ, ਕਪਟ; (2) ਕੁੜਿੱਕੀ, ਫਾਹੀ, ਫੰਦਾ; (3) ਖਿਡਕੀਦਾਰ ਪਿੰਜਰਾ; (4) ਸਾਜ਼-ਸਾਮਾਨ; ਧੋਖੇ ਨਾਲ ਕਾਬੂ ਕਰਨਾ; ~s ਸਾਮਾਨ, ਸਮਗਰੀ, ਉਪਕਰਣ, ਅਸਬਾਬ

travail ('ਟਰੈਵੇਇਲ) *n v* ਪ੍ਰਸੂਤ ਪੀੜਾਂ, ਵਿਆਂਮ ਦੀ ਪੀੜ; ਕਸ਼ਟ; ਸਖ਼ਤ ਮਿਹਨਤ; ਦੁੱਖ ਝੱਲਣਾ, ਕਸ਼ਟ ਸਹਿਣਾ

travel ('ਟਰੈਵਲ) *v n* ਸਫ਼ਰ ਕਰਨਾ, ਯਾਤਰਾ ਕਰਨੀ, ਘੁਮਾਉਣਾ-ਫਿਰਾਉਣਾ; ਸਫ਼ਰ, ਯਾਤਰਾ, ਘੁੰਮਣ-ਘੁਮਾਉਣ; ਚਾਲ, ਗਤੀ; ~ler ਯਾਤਰੀ, ਪਾਂਧੀ, ਮੁਸਾਫ਼ਰ, ਰਾਹਗੀਰ; ~ling ਸਫ਼ਰ, ਯਾਤਰਾ, ਭੁਮਣ; ਸਫ਼ਰ ਦਾ ਸਾਮਾਨ, ਸਫ਼ਰੀ, ਚੱਲਦਾ-ਫਿਰਦਾ; ~ogue ਸਫ਼ਰਨਾਮਾ

traverse ('ਟਰੈਵ੍ਅਸ) *v n* ਆਰ-ਪਾਰ ਕਰਨਾ; (ਵਿਸ਼ੇ ਦੇ) ਹਰ ਪੱਖ ਤੇ ਨਜ਼ਰ ਮਾਰਨੀ; (ਕਚਹਿਰੀ ਵਿਚ) ਕਿਸੇ ਮੁਆਮਲੇ ਨੂੰ ਰੱਦ ਕਰਨਾ; ਵਿਰੋਧ ਕਰਨਾ; ਖੰਡਨ, ਇਨਕਾਰ

travesty ('ਟਰੱਵਅਸਟਿ) *n v* ਪ੍ਰਹਸਨ, ਹਾਸੋਹੀਣੀ ਨਕਲ, ਘਟੀਆ ਨਕਲ; ਮੁਖੌਟਾ; ਨਕਲ ਲਾਹੁਣੀ, ਮਜ਼ਾਕ ਉਡਾਉਣਾ

tray (ਟਰੇਇ) *n* ਥਾਲੀ, ਤਸ਼ਤਰੀ, ਦੇ

treacher (ਟਰੈਚਅ*) *n* ਵਿਸਾਹਘਾਤੀ, ਧਰੋਹੀ, ਗ਼ੱਦਾਰ, ਕਿਰਤਘਣ; ~y ਧੋਖਾ, ਛਰੋਹ, ਧਰੋਹ, ਵਿਸਾਹਘਾਤ, ਗ਼ੱਦਾਰੀ, ਕਪਟ

tread (ਟਰੈਡ) *v n* ਟੁਰਨਾ, ਚੱਲਣਾ, ਪੈਰ ਰੱਖਣਾ; ਲਿਤਾੜਣਾ, ਮਿੱਧਣਾ; ਸਮਾਪਤ ਕਰਨਾ, ਸੰਪੁਰਨ ਕਰਨਾ; ਚਾਲ, ਗਤੀ; ਕਦਮ

treason ('ਟਰੀਜ਼ਨ) *n* ਵਿਦਰੋਹ, ਬਗਾਵਤ, ਗ਼ੱਦਰ, ਰਾਜ-ਧਰੋਹ, ਗ਼ੱਦਾਰੀ; ਵਿਸਾਹਘਾਤ

treasure ('ਟਰੈਯ਼ਅ*) *n v* ਖ਼ਜ਼ਾਨਾ, ਕੋਸ਼; ਦੌਲਤ, ਮਾਲ, ਕਦਰ ਕਰਨੀ, ਸਾਂਭ ਕੇ ਰੱਖਣਾ; ਯਾਦ-ਦਾਸ਼ਤ ਵਿਚ ਰੱਖਣਾ; ~r ਖ਼ਜ਼ਾਨਚੀ, ਕੋਸ਼-ਅਧਿਕਾਰੀ, ਕੋਸ਼ਪਾਲ

treasury ('ਟਰੈਯ਼ਅਰਿ) *n* ਕੋਸ਼, ਕੋਸ਼ਗ੍ਰਹਿ, ਖ਼ਜ਼ਾਨਾ, ਮਹਿਕਮਾ ਮਾਲ; ਗਿਆਨ ਭੰਡਾਰ

treat (ਟਰੀਟ) *v n* ਵਰਤਾਅ ਕਰਨਾ, ਸਲੂਕ ਕਰਨਾ, ਵਿਹਾਰ ਕਰਨਾ; ਉਪਚਾਰ ਕਰਨਾ, ਨਿਬਾਹੁ ਕਰਨਾ; ਦਾਅਵਤ ਦੇਣੀ, ਦਾਅਵਤ; ਮੌਜ-ਮੇਲਾ, ਮਨੋਰੰਜਨ, ਆਨੰਦ; ~ment ਵਰਤਾਉ, ਸਲੂਕ, ਵਤੀਰਾ, ਭੋਜ, ਬੰਦੋਬਸਤ, ਪ੍ਰਬੰਧ, ਨਿਰੂਪਣ

treble ('ਟਰੈਬੱਲ) *a v n* ਤਿਹਰਾ; ਤਿਗੁਣਾ;

ਤਿਗੁਣਾ ਕਰਨਾ

treddle ('ਟਰੈੱਡਲ) *n v* ਪਾਇਦਾਨ, ਪੈਡਲ; ਪੈਡਲ ਮਾਰਨਾ, ਪੈਰ ਨਾਲ ਚਲਾਉਣਾ

tree (ਟਰੀ) *n* ਰੁੱਖ, ਬਿਰਛ, ਦਰਖ਼ਤ; ਵੰਸਾਵਲੀ

trek (ਟਰੈੱਕ) *n v* ਸਫ਼ਰ, ਪੈਂਡਾ, ਯਾਤਰਾ; ਬੈਲ-ਗੱਡੀ ਉੱਤੇ ਸਫ਼ਰ; ਲੰਮੀ ਯਾਤਰਾ, ਪੈਂਡੇ ਪੈਣਾ, ਪੰਥ ਮਾਰਨਾ, ਸਫ਼ਾਟਾ ਕਰਨਾ; ~ker ਪਾਂਧੀ, ਮੁਸਾਫ਼ਰ, ਘੁਮੱਕੜ, ਯਾਤਰੀ

tremble ('ਟਰੈੱਬਲ) *v n* ਕਬਣਾ, ਕੰਬਣੀ ਆਉਣੀ, ਥਰਥਰਾਉਣਾ; ਡਗਮਗਾਉਣਾ; ਭੈਭੀਤ ਹੋ ਜਾਣਾ; ਕੰਬਣੀ, ਕੰਬਾ, ਥਰਥਰਾਹਟ, ਥਰਥਰੀ

tremendous (ਟਰਿਮੈੱਨਡਅਸ) *a* ਡਰਾਉਣਾ, ਭਿਆਨਕ; ਡਾਢਾ, ਪ੍ਰਬਲ, ਬਹੁਤ ਜ਼ਿਆਦਾ; ਬੜਾ ਵੱਡਾ

tremor ('ਟਰੈੱਮਅ*) *n* ਕੰਬਣੀ, ਕੰਬਾ, ਥਰਥਰਾਹਟ; ਹਲਕਾ ਭੁਚਾਲੀ ਝਟਕਾ

trench (ਟਰੈੱਚ) *n v* ਖਾਈ; ਮੋਰਚਾ, ਖੰਦਕ; ਖਾਈ ਪੁੱਟਣੀ; ਮੋਰਚਾ ਪੁੱਟਣਾ, ਖੰਦਕ ਬਣਾਉਣੀ

trend (ਟਰੈੱਡ) *n v* ਰੁਝਾਨ, ਪ੍ਰਵਿਰਤੀ, ਰੌਂ, ਰੁਖ਼; ਖਾਸ ਰੁਝਾਨ ਰਖਣਾ

trespass ('ਟਰੈੱਸਪਅਸ) *v n* ਨਾਜਾਇਜ਼ ਜਾ ਵੜਨਾ, ਨਾਜਾਇਜ਼ ਦਖ਼ਲ ਦੇਣਾ, ਮਰਯਾਦਾ ਦਾ ਉਲੰਘਣ ਕਰਨਾ, ਅਵੱਗਿਆ ਕਰਨੀ; ਉਲੰਘਣ, ਅਵੱਗਿਆ

trial ('ਟਰਾਇ(ਅ)ਲ) *n* ਪਰਖ, ਅਜ਼ਮਾਇਸ਼, ਪਰੀਖਿਆ; ਅਜ਼ਮਾਇਸ਼ੀ ਮੁਕਾਬਲਾ

triangle ('ਟਰਾਇਐਂਗਲ) *n* ਤਿਕੋਣ, ਤ੍ਰਿਭੁਜ, ਤਿਕੋਣ ਜੰਤਰ

triangular (ਟਰਾਇ'ਐਂਗਗੁਲਅ*) *a* ਤਿਕੋਣਾ

tribal ('ਟਰਾਇਬਲ) *a* ਕਬੀਲੇ ਦਾ, ਕਬਾਇਲੀ; ਗੋਤ

tribe ('ਟਰਾਇਬ) *a* ਜਾਤੀ, ਕਬੀਲਾ; ਟੱਬਰ, ਉਪਵੰਸ਼, ਉਪਕੁਲ

tribulation ('ਟਰਿਬਯੁ'ਲੇਇਸ਼ਨ) *n* ਕਸ਼ਟ, ਦੁੱਖ, ਸੰਤਾਪ, ਤਸੀਹਾ, ਮੁਸੀਬਤ

tribunal (ਟਰਾਇ'ਬਯੂਨਲ) *n* ਕਚਹਿਰੀ, ਅਦਾਲਤ, ਨਿਆਂ-ਸਭਾ, ਵਿਸ਼ੇਸ਼ ਅਦਾਲਤ

tribune ('ਟਰਿਬਯੂਨ) *n* (1) ਲੋਕ-ਨੇਤਾ, ਲੋਕਪਿਯ ਆਗੂ, ਮੰਚ; ਅਦਾਲਤ ਵਿਚ ਜੱਜ ਦੇ ਬੈਠਣ ਦੀ ਕੁਰਸੀ ਜਾਂ ਥਾਂ

tributary ('ਟਰਿਬਯੁਟ(ਅ)ਰਿ) *n a* ਸਹਾਇਕ ਨਦੀ; ਅਧੀਨ ਰਾਜਾ, ਸ਼ਾਖ਼ਾ; ਅਪ੍ਰਧਾਨ, ਸਹਾਇਕ

tribute ('ਟਰਿਬਯੂਟ) *n* ਸ਼ਰਧਾਂਜਲੀ; ਨਜ਼ਰਾਨਾ, ਖਿਰਾਜ

trick (ਟਰਿਕ) *n v* ਦਾਅ, ਚਾਲ, ਚਲਾਕੀ, ਫ਼ਰੇਬ, ਧੋਖਾ, ਛਲ, ਕਪਟ; ਚਤੁਰਾਈ, ਹੱਥ-ਫੇਰੀ; ਧੋਖਾ ਕਰਨਾ, ਕਪਟ ਕਰਨਾ, ਹੱਥ-ਫੇਰੀ ਕਰਨੀ; ~y ਧੋਖੇਬਾਜ਼, ਛਲੀ, ਕਪਟੀ, ਚਾਲਬਾਜ਼

trickle ('ਟਰਿਕਲ) *n v* ਹੌਲੀ-ਹੌਲੀ ਵਹਿਣ ਵਾਲੀ ਧਾਰਾ; ਮੰਦ ਪਰਵਾਹ; ਪਤਲੀ ਧਾਰ; ਤੁਪਕੇ ਡਿਗਣੇ, ਤੁਪਕਾ ਤੁਪਕਾ ਕਰਕੇ ਚੋਣਾ

tricolour ('ਟਰਾਇਕਲੇ*) *a n* ਤਿਰੰਗਾ, ਤਿੰਨ ਰੰਗਾਂ ਵਾਲਾ; ਭਾਰਤ ਦਾ ਰਾਸ਼ਟਰੀ ਝੰਡਾ

trident ('ਟਰਾਇਡੰਟ) *n* ਤਿੰਨ ਸਾਂਗਾ, ਹਥਿਆਰ, ਤ੍ਰਿਸ਼ੂਲ

triennial (ਟਰਾਇ'ਐਨਯਅਲ) *a n* ਤਿੰਨ-ਵਰਸੀ, ਤ੍ਰੈ-ਵਾਰਸ਼ਕ

trifle ('ਟਰਾਇਫ਼ਲ) *n v* ਨਿਗੁਣੀ ਚੀਜ਼, ਤੁੱਛ ਵਸਤੂ; ਮਾਮੂਲੀ ਰਕਮ; ਛੋਟਾ ਖਿਡਾਉਣਾ; ਹੋਛੀਆਂ ਗੱਲਾਂ ਕਰਨੀਆਂ, ਘਟੀਆ ਕੰਮ ਕਰਨਾ

trigger ('ਟਰਿਗਅ*) *n* (ਬੰਦੂਕ, ਪਿਸਤੌਲ ਆਦਿ ਦਾ) ਘੋੜਾ

trigonometry ('ਟਰਿਗਆ'ਨੋਮਅਟਰਿ) *n* ਤਿਕੋਣ-ਮਿਤੀ

trilingual (ਟਰਾਇ'ਲਿਙਗਵ(ਅ)ਲ) *a* ਤ੍ਰੈਭਾਸ਼ੀ, ਤਿੰਨ ਭਾਸ਼ਾਵਾਂ ਦਾ

trim (ਟਰਿਮ) *a v* ਸਾਫ਼ ਸੁਥਰਾ, ਸੱਜਿਆ ਸੰਵਰਿਆ, ਬਣਿਆ-ਠਣਿਆ, ਸੁਅੱਛ, ਲਤਰਨਾ-ਲਾਪਰਨਾ, ਸਾਫ਼-ਸੁਥਰਾ ਕਰਨਾ, (ਪੁਸ਼ਾਕ) ਸੰਵਾਰਨੀ; (ਦਾੜ੍ਹੀ) ਕਤਰਨੀ; ਖ਼ਤ ਕੱਢਣਾ

trio (ਟਰੀਅਉ) *n pl* ਤਿਗੜੀ, ਤਿੰਨਾਂ ਜਣਿਆਂ ਦੀ ਮੰਡਲੀ, ਤਿੰਨ ਗਾਇਕਾਂ ਦੀ ਟੋਲੀ, ਵਿਸ਼ੇਸ਼ ਭਾਂਤ ਦਾ ਨਾਚ

trip (ਟਰਿਪ) *v n* ਕਾਹਲੇ-ਕਾਹਲੇ ਤੁਰਨਾ, ਸੈਰ-ਸਪਾਟਾ ਕਰਨਾ, ਕਿਸੇ ਥਾਂ ਨੂੰ ਵੇਖਣ ਲਈ ਜਾਣਾ, ਥਿੜਕਣਾ; ਚੱਕਰ, ਠੋਕਰ, ਥਿੜਕ, ਉਕਾਈ

triple ('ਟਰਿਪਲ) *a v* ਤਿਹਰਾ, ਤੀਣਾ, ਤਿੰਨ ਗੁਣਾ; ਤਿਹਰਾ ਹੋਣਾ ਜਾਂ ਕਰਨਾ

triplicate ('ਟਰਿਪਲਿਕੇਇਟ) *v a* ਤਿਹਰਾ ਕਰਨਾ, ਤਿੰਨ ਕਾਪੀਆਂ ਬਣਾਉਣੀਆਂ; ਤਿਗੁਣਾ; ਤੀਜੀ ਨਕਲ

triumph ('ਟਰਾਇਅੰਫ਼) *n v* ਜਿੱਤ, ਵਿਜੈ, ਫ਼ਤਿਹ, ਜਿੱਤ ਪ੍ਰਾਪਤ ਕਰਨੀ, ਫ਼ਤਿਹ ਪਾਉਣੀ; **~ant** ਵਿਜੇਤਾ, ਜਿੱਤਿਆ, ਕਾਮਯਾਬ

trivial ('ਟਰਿਵ੍ਇਅਲ) *a* ਤੁੱਛ, ਨਿਗੁਣਾ, ਬੋਥਾ, ਬਹੁਤ ਮਾਮੂਲੀ; ਨਿਕੰਮਾ; **~ity** ਤੁੱਛ ਚੀਜ਼, ਨਿਗੁਣੀ ਵਸਤੂ; ਤੁੱਛਤਾ, ਨਿਗੁਣਾਪਨ

Trojan ('ਟਰਅਉਜ(ਅ)ਨ) *a* ਸੂਰਮਾ, ਵੀਰ, ਸਾਹਸੀ

trolley ('ਟੌਲਿ) *n* ਠੇਲ੍ਹਾ, ਸਟੇਸ਼ਨ ਤੇ ਸਾਮਾਨ ਢੋਣ ਵਾਲੀ ਰੇੜ੍ਹੀ; ਰੇਲ ਦੀ ਪਟੜੀ ਤੇ ਚਲਾਇਆ ਜਾਣ ਵਾਲਾ ਠੇਲ੍ਹਾ; ਟਰਾਲੀ

troop (ਟਰੂਪ) *n v* ਟੋਲੀ, ਮੰਡਲੀ, ਜੁੰਡਲੀ; ਫ਼ੌਜ, ਸੈਨਾ; ਇਕੱਠਾ ਹੋਣਾ, ਇਕੱਤਰ ਕਰਨਾ, ਜੱਥਾ ਬਣਾਉਣਾ; ਫ਼ੌਜ ਨੂੰ ਟੁਕੜੀਆਂ ਵਿਚ ਵੰਡਣਾ

trophy ('ਟਰਅਉਫ਼ਿ) *n* ਫ਼ਤਿਹ ਦੀ ਨਿਸ਼ਾਨੀ; ਜਿੱਤ ਦਾ ਇਨਾਮ, ਵਿਜੇ ਪੁਰਸਕਾਰ

trouble ('ਟਰਅੰਬਲ) *n v* ਦੁੱਖ, ਕਸ਼ਟ ਤਕਲੀਫ਼, ਬਿਪਤਾ, ਸੰਕਟ; ਰੋਗ, ਬੀਮਾਰੀ; ਔਕੜ, ਅਸੁਵਿਧਾ; ਤਕਲੀਫ਼ ਦੇਣੀ, ਕਸ਼ਟ ਦੇਣਾ

trounce (ਟਰਾਉਂਸ) *v* ਛੱਕੇ ਛੁਡਾ ਦੇਣਾ, ਸਜ਼ਾ ਦੇਣੀ, ਭੁਗਤ ਸੁਆਰਨੀ; ਬੁਰੀ ਤਰ੍ਹਾਂ ਹਰਾਉਣਾ, ਖੂਬ ਠੋਕਣੀ

troupe (ਟਰੂਪ) *n* ਅਭਿਨੇਤਾ-ਦਲ, ਨਾਟ-ਮੰਡਲੀ, ਐਕਟਰਾਂ ਦੀ ਮੰਡਲੀ

trousers ('ਟਰਾਉਜ਼ਅਜ਼) *n pl* ਪਤਲੂਨ

truancy ('ਟਰੂਅੰਸਿ) *n* ਅਵਾਰਾਪਨ, ਕੰਮ-ਚੋਰੀ, ਘੁਸਾਈ

truant ('ਟਰੂਅੰਟ) *a n* ਸਕੂਲ ਤੋਂ ਭੱਜਿਆ (ਬੱਚਾ); ਕੰਮ ਚੋਰ (ਬੱਚਾ); ਨਿਕੰਮਾ; ਭਰੀਂਡਾ (ਬੱਚਾ), ਅਵਾਰਾ

truck (ਟਰਅੱਕ) *v n* ਵੱਟਾ-ਸੱਟਾ ਕਰਨਾ; ਅਦਲਾ-ਬਦਲੀ ਕਰਨੀ, ਸੌਦਾ ਕਰਨਾ, ਵਪਾਰ ਕਰਨਾ; (ਮਾਲ) ਵੇਚਦੇ ਫਿਰਨਾ; ਲੈਣ-ਦੇਣ; ਮਾਲ ਢੋਣ ਵਾਲੀ ਮੋਟਰ ਗੱਡੀ, ਟਰੱਕ

true (ਟਰੂ) *a n* ਸੱਚਾ, ਖਰਾ, ਸ਼ੁੱਧ; ਸੱਚ, ਸਤਿਵਾਦੀ, ਅਸਲੀ, ਵਾਸਤਵਿਕ; ਠੀਕ; ਵਫ਼ਾਦਾਰ, ਈਮਾਨਦਾਰ, ਵਿਸ਼ਵਾਸਯੋਗ

truly (ਟਰੂਅੱਲੀ) *adv* ਅਸਲ ਵਿਚ; ਵਾਸਤਵ ਵਿਚ, ਸੱਚ-ਮੁੱਚ, ਈਮਾਨਦਾਰੀ ਨਾਲ, ਸੱਚੇ ਦਿਲੋਂ

trump (ਟਰਅੰਪ) *n v* (ਤਾਸ਼ ਵਿਚ) ਰੰਗ ਦਾ ਪੱਤਾ, ਤੁਰਪ ਦਾ ਪੱਤਾ; (ਬੋਲ) ਬੜਾ ਸੂਰਮਾ, ਉੱਤਮ ਮਨੁੱਖ, ਅੰਤਮ ਸਾਧਨ, ਆਖ਼ਰੀ ਚਾਲ, ਤੁਰਪ

ਲਾਉਣਾ, ਚਾਲ ਚੱਲਣੀ

trumpet ('ਟਰਅੰਪਿਟ) *n v* ਬਿਗਲ, ਤੁਰ੍ਹੀ, ਤੁਰਮ, ਨਰਸਿੰਘਾ; ਬਿਗਲ ਵਜਾਉਣਾ, ਡੌਂਡੀ ਪਿੱਟਣੀ; (ਹਾਥੀ ਦਾ) ਚਿੰਘਾੜਨਾ

truncate ('ਟਰਅੰਨਕੇਇਟ) *v a* ਛਾਂਗਣਾ (ਰੁੱਖ ਆਦਿ ਨੂੰ); ਹੱਥ-ਪੈਰ ਵੱਢਣੇ (ਮਨੁੱਖ ਦੇ)

truncation (ਟਰਅੰਨ'ਕੇਇਸ਼ਨ) *n* ਛੰਗਾਈ, ਕਟਾਈ, ਮੁਛਾਈ, ਕਾਂਟ-ਛਾਂਟ

trunk (ਟਰਅੰਙਕ) *n* ਰੁੱਖ ਦਾ ਤਣਾ; (ਮਨੁੱਖ ਦਾ) ਧੜ, ਮੁੱਖ ਰੇਲ ਲਾਈਨ, ਸੜਕ; ਬਕਸਾ, ਸੰਦੂਕ, ਟਰੰਕ; ਹਾਥੀ ਦੀ ਸੁੰਡ; ~call ਟੈਲੀਫ਼ੋਨ ਤੇ ਦੂਸਰੇ ਸ਼ਹਿਰ ਨੂੰ ਸੰਦੇਸ਼; ~line, ~road ਮੁੱਖ ਸੜਕ, ਜਰਨੈਲੀ ਸੜਕ, ਸ਼ਾਹ ਰਾਹ

trust (ਟਰਅੱਸਟ) *n v* ਵਿਸ਼ਵਾਸ, ਭਰੋਸਾ, ਯਕੀਨ, ਪ੍ਰਤੀਤੀ; ਪੱਕੀ ਆਸ; ਅਮਾਨਤ; ਨਿਆਸ; (ਵਪਾਰ) ਵਪਾਰੀ ਸੰਘ, ਟਰਸਟ; ਵਿਸ਼ਵਾਸ ਕਰਨਾ, ਯਕੀਨ ਕਰਨਾ, ਭਰੋਸਾ ਰੱਖਣਾ; ~deed ਸਾਖ਼-ਪਟਾ, ਵਸੀਕਾਨਾਮਾ, ਅਮਾਨਤਨਾਮਾ; ~worthy ਇਤਬਾਰਯੋਗ, ਵਿਸ਼ਵਾਸਯੋਗ, ਭਰੋਸੇਯੋਗ; ~ee ਨਿਆਸੀ, ਨਿਆਸਧਾਰੀ, ਟਰਸਟੀ, ਸਰਕਾਰੀ ਅਮੀਨ, ਅਮਾਨਤਦਾਰ; ~ful ਸੱਚਾ, ਸਤਿਵਾਦੀ, ਈਮਾਨਦਾਰ, ਵਿਸ਼ਵਾਸਯੋਗ; ਅਸਲੀ, ਵਾਸਤਵਿਕ; ~y ਵਿਸ਼ਵਾਸਯੋਗ, ਇਤਬਾਰੀ, ਈਮਾਨਦਾਰ

truth (ਟਰੂਥ) *n* ਸੱਚ, ਸਚਾਈ, ਅਸਲੀਅਤ ਵਾਸਤ-ਵਿਕਤਾ, ਹਕੀਕਤ, ਯਥਾਰਥਕਤਾ, ਈਮਾਨਦਾਰੀ; ~ful ਸੱਚਾ, ਸਤਿਵਾਦੀ, ਈਮਾਨਦਾਰ, ਵਿਸ਼ਵਾਸ-ਯੋਗ; ਅਸਲੀ, ਵਾਸਤਵਿਕ

try (ਟਰਾਇ) *v n* ਕੋਸ਼ਿਸ਼ ਕਰਨੀ, ਜਤਨ ਕਰਨਾ; ਅਜ਼ਮਾਉਣਾ, ਪਰਤਾਵਾ ਲੈਣਾ, ਪਰਖਣਾ, ਜਾਂਚਣਾ; ਮੁੱਕਦਮਾ ਚਲਾਉਣਾ; ਕੋਸ਼ਿਸ਼, ਉਪਰਾਲਾ; ~out

ਪਰਖਣਾ, ਅਜ਼ਮਾ ਕੇ ਵੇਖਣਾ; ਆਜ਼ਮਾਇਸ਼; ~ing ਔਖਾ, ਕਰੜਾ, ਕਠਨ, ਮੁਸ਼ਕਲ, ਦੁੱਖਦਾਈ, ਕਸ਼ਟਕਾਰੀ

tub (ਟਅੱਬ) *n v* ਟੱਬ ਵਿਚ ਕੀਤਾ ਇਸ਼ਨਾਨ; ਟੱਬ ਵਿਚ ਨਹਾਉਣਾ

tube (ਟਯੂਬ) *n* ਨਕਲੀ, ਨਾਲ; ਨਲੀ; ਸੁਰੰਗ; ਨਾੜ

tuberculosis (ਟਯੂ'ਬਅ:ਕਯੁ'ਲਅਉਸਿਸ) *n* ਤਪਦਿਕ, ਖਈ ਰੋਗ, ਖੰਘ-ਤਾਪ, ਟੀ ਬੀ

tuck (ਟਅੱਕ) *n v* (ਕਪੜੇ ਦਾ) ਪਲੇਟ; (ਅਪ) ਮਿਠਿਆਈ, ਛੋਟੇ ਕੇਕ ਆਦਿ; ~in ਰੱਜ ਕੇ ਖਾਣਾ, ਸੰਖ ਤਕ ਭਰ ਲੈਣਾ; ~shop ਮਿਠਿਆਈ ਆਦਿ ਦੀ ਦੁਕਾਨ

Tuesday ('ਟਯੂਜ਼ਡਿ) *n* ਮੰਗਲਵਾਰ

tug (ਟਅੱਗ) *v n* ਧੂਹਣਾ, ਘਸੀਟਣਾ, ਝਟਕਾ ਦੇ ਕੇ ਖਿੱਚਣਾ; (ਦਿਲ ਨੂੰ) ਧੂਹ ਪਾਉਣੀ; (ਕਿਸੇ ਵਿਸ਼ੇ ਨੂੰ) ਖਿੱਚ, ਧਹੁ, ਘਸੀਟ; ਝਟਕਾ, ਕਠੋਰ ਜਤਨ; ~of war ਰੱਸਾ ਖਿੱਚਣ ਦਾ ਮੁਕਾਬਲਾ

tuition (ਟਯੂ'ਇਸ਼ਨ) *n* ਪੜ੍ਹਾਈ, ਟਿਊਸ਼ਨ, ਨਿਜੀ ਪੜ੍ਹਾਈ ਦੀ ਫ਼ੀਸ

tumour ('ਟਯੂਮਅ*) *n* ਗਰੋੜੀ, ਰਸੌਲੀ, ਗੰਢ, ਗਿਲਟੀ

tumult ('ਟਯੂਮਅੱਲਟ) *n* ਸ਼ੋਰ-ਸ਼ਰਾਬਾ, ਰੌਲਾ-ਗੌਲਾ, ਦੰਗਾ-ਫ਼ਸਾਦ, ਹੰਗਾਮਾ, ਅਸ਼ਾਂਤੀ; ਉਤੇਜਨਾ; ~uous ਖਰੂਦੀ, ਫ਼ਸਾਦੀ, ਦੰਗੇਬਾਜ, ਵੈਰ, ਕੱਥਾ

tune (ਟਯੂਨ) *n v* ਸੁਰ, ਲੈਅ, ਤਰਜ਼, ਧੁਨ, ਤਾਲ; ਰਾਗ; ਤਰੰਨਮ, ਸੁਰ-ਸੰਗੀਤ; ਅਨੁਕੂਲਤਾ, ਉਪ-ਯੁਕਤਤਾ; ਅਨੁਕੂਲ ਬਣਾਉਣਾ; (ਕਾਵਿ) ਗਾਉਣਾ; ਰਾਗ ਛੋਹਣਾ

tunnel ('ਟਅੱਨਲ) *n v* ਸੁਰੰਗ, ਸੁਰੰਗ ਕੱਢਣੀ; ਸੁਰੰਗ ਵਿਚੋਂ ਲੰਘਣਾ

urban ('ਟਅ:ਬਅਨ) *n* ਪੱਗ, ਪਗੜੀ, ਦਸਤਾਰ

urbulence ('ਟਅ:ਬਯੁਲਅੰਸ) *n* ਖਲਬਲੀ, ਗੜਬੜ, ਖਰੂਦ, ਫ਼ਸਾਦ, ਦੰਗਾ, ਹੰਗਾਮਾ

urbulent ('ਟਅ:ਬਯੁਲਅੰਟ) *a* ਖਰੂਦੀ, ਉਪੱਦਰੀ, ਫ਼ਸਾਦੀ; ਅਸ਼ਾਂਤ, ਵਿਆਕੁਲ, ਬੇਚੈਨ

urmeric ('ਟਅ:ਮਅਰਿਕ) *n* ਹਲਦੀ

urmoil ('ਟਅ:ਮੌਇਲ) *n v* ਗੜਬੜ, ਰੋਲਾ-ਗੌਲਾ, ਹਫੜਾ-ਦਫੜੀ; ਅਸ਼ਾਂਤੀ, ਬੇਚੈਨੀ, ਹਲਚਲ, ਖਲਬਲੀ; ਹਲਚਲ ਮਚਾਉਣਾ

urn (ਟਅ:ਨ) *v n* ਮੋੜਨਾ, ਮੁੜਨਾ, ਘੁਮਾਉਣਾ, ਘੁੰਮਣਾ, ਫੇਰਨਾ ਜਾਂ ਫਿਰਨਾ, ਗੇੜਨਾ ਜਾਂ ਗਿੜਨਾ; ਭੁਆਉਣਾ ਜਾਂ ਭੌਣਾ, ਪਰਤਣਾ ਜਾਂ ਪਰਤ ਜਾਣਾ, ਪਾਸਾ ਬਦਲਣਾ; ਉਲਟਣਾ; ਮੋੜ, ਚੱਕਰ, ਮੋੜਾ; ਰੁਚੀ, ਰੁਝਾਨ, ਰੱਸੇ ਦਾ ਵਲਾਵਾਂ; ~**coat** ਦਲ-ਬਦਲੂ, ਚੱਕਵਾਂ-ਚੁਲ੍ਹਾ, ਆਇਆ-ਰਾਮ ਗਿਆ-ਰਾਮ; ~**down** ਨਾਮਨਜ਼ੂਰ ਕਰਨਾ, ਰੱਦ ਕਰ ਦੇਣਾ; ~**out** ਕੱਢ ਦੇਣਾ; ਬਾਹਰ ਵੱਲ ਮੋੜਨਾ; ਕੰਮ ਤੇ ਪੁੱਜਣਾ; ਪੈਦਾਵਾਰ, ਉਪਜ, ਹਾਜ਼ਰੀ, ਇਕੱਠ; ~**over** ਉਲੱਟਣਾ, ਉਲਟਾਉਣਾ, ਪਲਟਾਉਣਾ; ਉਲਟ ਜਾਣਾ, ਮੂਧੇ ਹੋ ਜਾਣਾ; ~**round** ਪਿੱਛੇ ਨੂੰ ਮੁੜਨਾ, ਆਪਣੀ ਨੀਤੀ ਬਦਲ ਦੇਣੀ; ~**turtle** ਗੁਪਾ ਹੋ ਜਾਣਾ, ਉਲਟ ਜਾਣਾ, ~**ing-point** ਮੋੜ

urnip ('ਟਅ:ਨਿਪ) ਗੋਂਗਲੂ

rtle ('ਟਅ:ਟਲ) *n* ਘੁੱਗੀ; ~**dove** ਘੁੱਗੀ

sk (ਟਅਸਕ) *n v* ਹਾਥੀ-ਦੰਦ, ਹਾਥੀ ਦਾ ਲੰਮਾ ਦੰਦ, ਦੰਦ ਚੁਭਾਉਣਾ

ssle ('ਟਅਸਲ) *n v* ਖਿੱਚ-ਧੂਹ, ਝੜਪ, ਲੜਾਈ-ਝਗੜਾ, ਸੰਘਰਸ਼; ਝਗੜਾ ਕਰਨਾ, ਲੜਾਈ ਕਰਨੀ

tor ('ਟਯੂਟਅ*) *n v* ਨਿਜੀ ਤੌਰ ਤੇ ਪੜ੍ਹਾਉਣ ਵਾਲਾ; ਉਸਤਾਦ; ਨਾਬਾਲਗ ਬੱਚੇ ਦਾ ਸਰ-ਪਰਸਤ; ਬੱਚੇ ਦੀ ਵਿੱਦਿਆ ਲਈ ਜ਼ਿੰਮੇਵਾਰ ਹੋਣਾ, ਟਿਊਟਰ ਹੋਣਾ; ~**ship** ਕਿਸੇ ਬੱਚੇ ਦੀ ਪੜ੍ਹਾਈ ਲਈ ਜ਼ਿੰਮੇਵਾਰੀ, ਨਿਗਰਾਨੀ

twelfth ('ਟਵੈੱਲਫ਼ਥ) *a n* ਬਾਰ੍ਹਵਾਂ; ਬਾਰ੍ਹਵਾਂ ਹਿੱਸਾ

twelve ('ਟਵੈੱਲਵ) *a n* ਬਾਰਾਂ, ਬਾਰਾਂ ਦੀ ਸੰਖਿਆ

twentieth ('ਟਵੈੱਨਟਿਅਥ) *a* ਵੀਹਵਾਂ

twenty ('ਟਵੈੱਨਟਿ) *a n* ਵੀਹ, ਵੀਹ ਦੀ ਗਿਣਤੀ; ~**fold** ਵੀਹ ਗੁਣਾ

twice (ਟਵਾਇਸ) *adv* ਦੋ ਵਾਰੀ, ਦੋ ਗੁਣਾ

twilight ('ਟਵਾਇਲਾਇਟ) *n v* ਸੰਝ, ਸ਼ਾਮ, ਸਵੇਰ ਜਾਂ ਤ੍ਰਿਕਾਲਾਂ ਦਾ ਘੁਸਮੁਸਾ, ਝਟਪਟਾ, ਮੱਧਮ ਰੌਸ਼ਨੀ ਕਰਨਾ, ਧੁੰਦਲੇ ਪ੍ਰਕਾਸ਼ ਨਾਲ ਪ੍ਰਕਾਸ਼ਤ ਕਰਨਾ

twin (ਟਵਿਨ) *n a* ਜੋੜੇ, ਜੋੜੇ ਜੰਮੇ ਹੋਏ ਬੱਚੇ ਜਾਂ ਵਿਅਕਤੀ; ਜੌੜਾ ਜੰਮਿਆ

twine (ਟਵਾਇਨ) *n v* ਰੱਸੀ, ਡੋਰੀ, ਧਾਗਾ, ਵਾਟਵੀਂ ਰੱਸੀ; ਵਲ, ਪੇਚ, ਮਰੋੜੀ; ਧਾਗਾ ਜਾਂ ਰੱਸੀ ਵੱਟਮੀ, ਵੱਟ ਚੜ੍ਹਾਉਣਾ, ਵਲ੍ਹੇਟਣਾ

twink (ਟਵਿੰਕ) *n v* ਘੜੀ, ਪਲ, ਪਲਕ ਮਾਤਰ, ਅੱਖ ਦਾ ਫੋਰ; ਝਮਕਾਟ, ਪਲਕ ਮਾਰਨਾ; ਟਿਮ-ਟਿਮਾਉਣਾ, ਮਗਮਗਾਉਣਾ; ~**le** ਚਮਕਣਾ, ਲਿਸ਼ਕਣਾ, ਟਿਮਟਿਮਾਉਣਾ, ਮਟਕਾਉਣਾ; ਚਮਕ, ਲਿਸ਼ਕ, ਲਿਸ਼ਕਾਰ

twirl (ਟਵਅ:ਲ) *v n* ਘੁਮਾਉਣਾ, ਭੁਆਉਣਾ, ਭੁਆਟਣੀ ਦੇਣੀ, ਕਾਹਲੀ-ਕਾਹਲੀ ਚੱਕਰ ਦੇਣਾ; ਮੁੱਛਾਂ ਨੂੰ ਤਾਅ ਦੇਣਾ; ਭੁਆਂਟਣੀ, ਚੱਕਰ, ਘੁਮਾਉ

twist (ਟਵਿਸਟ) *v n* ਮਰੋੜਨਾ, ਮਰੋੜੀ ਦੇਣਾ, ਮੋਲਣਾ, ਵੱਟ ਚਾੜ੍ਹਨਾ, ਵੱਟਣਾ; ਟਵਿਸਟ ਨਾਚ ਨੱਚਣਾ; ਗੁੰਦਣਾ; ਮਰੋੜ; ਵੱਟਿਆ ਧਾਗਾ

twitter ('ਟਵਿਟਅ*) *n* ਚਹਿਕਣਾ; ਫੜਕਣਾ; ਹੌਲੀ

ਅਵਾਜ਼ ਵਿਚ ਬੋਲਣਾ; ਚਹਿਚਹਾਟ, ਫੜਫੜਾਹਟ

type (ਟਾਇਪ) *n v* ਪ੍ਰਕਾਰ, ਕਿਸਮ, ਵੰਨਗੀ, ਮਿਸਾਲ, ਨਮੂਨਾ; ਕਿਸੇ ਵੰਨਗੀ ਦਾ ਨਮੂਨਾ ਹੋਣਾ, ਟਾਈਪ ਕਰਨਾ

typhoid ('ਟਾਇਫ਼ੌਇਡ) *a* ਮੁਹਰਕਾ ਤਾਪ, ਮਿਆਦੀ ਬੁਖ਼ਾਰ, ਟਾਈਫਾਈਡ

typhoon (ਟਾਇ'ਫ਼ੂਨ) *n* ਜ਼ੋਰਦਾਰ ਹਨੇਰੀ, ਸਖ਼ਤ ਝੱਖੜ; ਸਮੁੰਦਰੀ ਝੱਖੜ; ਪ੍ਰਚੰਡ ਤੂਫ਼ਾਨ

typify ('ਟਿਪਿਫ਼ਾਇ) *v* ਉਦਾਹਰਣ ਦੇ ਕੇ ਸਪਸ਼ਟ ਕਰਨਾ, ਨਮੂਨਾ ਪੇਸ਼ ਕਰਨਾ; ਨਮੂਨੇ ਵਜੋਂ ਹੋਣਾ

typist ('ਟਾਇਪਿਸਟ) *n* ਟਾਈਪ ਕਰਨ ਵਾਲਾ, ਟਾਈਪਿਸਟ

tyrannical (ਟਿ'ਰੈਨਿਕਲ) *a* ਅਤਿਆਚਾਰੀ, ਜਾਬਰ ਸਿਤਮਗਰ, ਨਿਰਦਈ, ਕਹਿਰਵਾਨ, ਡਾਢ ਤਾਨਾਸ਼ਾਹ

tyrannize ('ਟਿਰਅਨਾਇਜ਼) *v* ਜਬਰ ਕਰਨ ਜ਼ੁਲਮ ਕਰਨਾ, ਧੱਕਾ ਕਰਨਾ

tyranny ('ਟਿਰਅਨਿ) *n* ਜ਼ੁਲਮ, ਅਤਿਆਚਾ ਜਬਰ, ਧੱਕੇਸ਼ਾਹੀ

tyrant ('ਟਾਇ(ਅ)ਰਅੰਟ) *n* ਜ਼ਾਲਮ, ਜਾਬ ਅਤਿਆਚਾਰੀ; ਜ਼ਾਲਮ ਰਾਜਾ

tyre, tyro (ਟਾਇ'ਅ, 'ਟਾਇ(ਅ)ਰਅਉ) (1) ਸਿਖਾਂਦਰੂ, ਨਵਾਂ ਸਿਖਿਆ, (2) ਟਾਇ (ਮੋਟਰ, ਸਾਈਕਲ ਆਦਿ ਦਾ)

U

, u (ਯੂ) *n* ਰੋਮਨ ਵਰਨਮਾਲਾ ਦਾ ਇਕੀਵਾਂ ਅੱਖਰ

biquitous (ਯੂ'ਬਿਕਵਿਟਅਸ) *a* ਸਰਵਵਿਆਪਕ, ਸਰਵਵਿਆਪੀ

gh (ਅੱਖ਼) *int* ਉਹ! ਉਫ਼! ਤੋਬਾ

gliness ('ਅੱਗਲਿਨਿਸ) *n* ਕਰੂਪਤਾ, ਕੋਝ, ਕੁੱਢਬ

gly ('ਅੱਗਲਿ) *a* ਕਰੂਪ, ਬਦਸ਼ਕਲ, ਬਦਸੂਰਤ, ਕੋਝਾ, ਅੱਸਭਿਅ, ਆਸ਼ਿਸ਼ਟ, ਭੰਡਾ, ਬੁਰਾ

lcer ('ਅਲਸਅ*) *n* ਫੋੜਾ, ਨਾਸੂਰ, ਅਲਸਰ; ਵਿਭਚਾਰ, ਦੁਰਾਚਾਰ; ਗੰਦਗੀ

lterior ('ਅੱਲਟਿਅਰਿਅ*) *a* ਦੁਰੇਡਾ, ਪਰਲਾ, ਪਰੇ ਸਥਿਤ, ਦੂਰਵਰਤੀ; (ਮਨੋਰਥ ਆਦਿ) ਗੁਪਤ, ਅਪ੍ਰਤੱਖ, ਗੁੱਝਾ

ltimate ('ਅੱਲਟਿਮਅਟ) *a* ਮੁੱਢਲਾ, ਮੂਲ; ਕੱਟੜੀ; ਅੰਤਲਾ, ਆਖ਼ਰੀ; ~**ly** ਆਖ਼ਰ ਨੂੰ, ਸਿੱਟੇ ਵਜੋਂ

ltimatum ('ਅੱਲਟਿ'ਮੇਇਟਅਮ) *n* ਮੌਲਕ ਸਿਧਾਂਤ; ਅੰਤਮ ਚੇਤਾਵਨੀ, ਅੰਤਮ ਗੱਲ

ltra ('ਅੱਲਟਰਅ) *n* ਅੱਤ-ਪੰਥੀ, ਅੱਤਵਾਦੀ, ਉਗਰਪੰਥੀ ਪ੍ਰਗਤੀਵਾਦੀ

ltra-sonics ('ਅੱਲਟਰਅ'ਸੌਨਿਕਸ) *n* ਪਰਾ-ਧੁਨਿਕ ਵਿਗਿਆਨ

ltra-rays ('ਅੱਲਟਰਅ'ਰੇਇਜ਼) *n* ਪਰਾਕਿਰਨਾਂ

mbrage ('ਅੱਮਬਰਿਜ) *n* (ਕਾਵਿ) ਦਰਖ਼ਤ ਦੀ ਛਾਂ, ਛਾਇਆ; ਨਾਰਾਜ਼ਗੀ, ਗੁੱਸਾ; ~**ous** ਛਾਇਆਮਈ, ਛਾਂ-ਦਾਰ; ਨਾਰਾਜ਼, ਖ਼ਫ਼ਾ

mbrella (ਅੱਮਬਰੈੱਲਅ) *n* ਛਤਰੀ, ਛਾਤਾ; ਛਤਰ

mlaut ('ਉਮਲਾਉਟ) *n v* (ਵਿਆ) ਸਵਰ-ਪਰਿਵਰਤਨ

umpire ('ਅੱਮਪਾਇਅ*) *n* ਨਿਰਣਾਯਕ; ਪੰਚ, ਅਮਪਾਇਰ, ਰੈਫ਼ਰੀ, (ਕਾ) ਸਰਪੰਚ, ਸਾਲਸ; ਅਮਪਾਇਰੀ ਜਾਂ ਸਾਲਸੀ ਕਰਨੀ

umpteen ('ਅੱਮ(ਪ)ਟੀਨ) *a* (ਅਪ) ਅਨੇਕ, ਬੇਹਿਸਾਬ

un (ਅੱਨ) *pref* 'ਨਾ' ਦੇ ਅਰਥਾਂ ਵਿਚ ਅਗੇਤਰ

unabashed (ਅੱਨਬੈਸ਼ਡ) *a* ਨਿਰਲੱਜ, ਬੇਸ਼ਰਮ

unabated (ਅਨਬੈਟਿਡ) *a* ਲਗਾਤਾਰ, ਬੇਰੋਕ

unable (ਅਨੇਬਲ) *a* ਅਸਮੱਰਥ, ਅਯੋਗ, ਨਾਕਾਬਲ

unacceptable (ਅਨ'ਅਕਸੇਪੱਟਬਲ) *a* ਅਸਵੀਕ੍ਰਿਤ, ਨਾਪਸੰਦ

unaccustomed (ਅੱਨ'ਅਕਸਟਮਡ) *a* ਅਣਜਾਣ, ਅਪਰਿਚਿਤ; ਅਸਧਾਰਨ

unaffected (ਅੱਨ'ਅਫ਼ੇਕਟਿਡ) *a* ਅਪ੍ਰਭਾਵਤ, ਅਟੱਬਿੱਜ; ਨਿਸ਼ਕਪਟ, ਸਹਿਜ, ਸੁਭਾਵਕ

unanimity, unanimousness ('ਯੂਨਅ'ਨਿਮਆਟ, ਯੂ'ਨੈਨਿਮਅਸਨਿਸ) *a* ਇਕ ਰਾਇ, ਇਕ ਮੱਤ, ਸਰਵ-ਸੰਮਤੀ

unanimous (ਯੂ'ਨੈਨਿਮਅਸ) *a* ਇਕ ਰਾਇ, ਮੁਤਫ਼ਿਕ, ਇਕ ਵਿਚਾਰ

unanswerable (ਅਨ-ਆਨਸਰੇਬੱਲ) *a* ਲਾਜਵਾਬ; ਨਿਰੁੱਤਰ, ਅਖੰਡਨੀ

unarmed (ਅਨ-ਆ*ਮਡ) *a* ਨਿਹੱਥਾ, ਖ਼ਾਲੀ ਹੱਥ, ਨਿਸ਼ਸਤਰ

unashamed (ਅਨ(ਅ)ਸ਼ੇਮਡ) *a* ਨਿਰਲੱਜ, ਬੇਹਯਾ

unassuming (ਅਨ(ਅ)ਸਯੂਮਇਙ) *a* ਸਰਲ, ਸਾਦਾ

unauthorised (ਅਨ-ਆਥਰਾਇਜ਼ਡ) *a* ਨਾਜਾਇਜ਼, ਅਣ-ਅਧਿਕ੍ਰਿਤ

unavoidable (ਅਨ(ਅ)ਵ੍ਾਡੇਬਲ) *a* ਅਵੱਸ਼ਕ, ਅਨਿਵਾਰੀ, ਲਾਜ਼ਮੀ

unaware (ਅਨ(ਅ)ਵੇ*) *a* ਅਚੇਤ, ਅਚਿੰਤ, ਬੇਖ਼ਬਰ, ਅਟਜਾਣ, ਗਾਫ਼ਿਲ

unbalanced (ਅਨਬੈਲੈਂਸਡ) *a* ਬਿਡਕਿਆ, ਉਖੜਿਆ-ਪੁਖੜਿਆ; ਅਸੰਤੁਲਤ

unbearable (ਅਨਬੇਅਰੱਬਲ) *a* ਦੁੱਭਰ, ਅਸਹਿ

unbecoming (ਅਨ-ਬਿਕਮ-ਇਙ) *a* ਅਨੁਚਿਤ, ਬੁਰਾ, ਅਯੋਗ, ਅੱਛੁਕਵਾਂ

unbelieving (ਅਨ-ਬਿਲੀਵਿੰਙ) *a* ਅਧਰਮੀ, ਨਾਸਤਕ, ਅਵਿਸ਼ਵਾਸੀ

unbias(s)ed (ਅਨਬਾਇਅਸਡ) *a* ਨਿਰਪੱਖ, ਪੱਖਪਾਤਹੀਨ

unblemished (ਅਨ-ਬਲੇਮਇਸ਼ਡ) *a* ਨਿਹਕਲੰਕ, ਬੇਦਾਗ਼, ਨਿਰਦੋਸ਼

unbounded (ਅਨ-ਬਾਉਂਡਿਡ) *a* ਅਨੰਤ, ਅਪਾਰ, ਬੇਹੱਦ, ਅਸੀਮਿਤ, ਬੇਅੰਤ

uncertain (ਅਨਸਃਟੱਨ) *a* ਡਾਵਾਂ-ਡੋਲ, ਦੁੱਚਿਤਾ, ਗ਼ੈਰ-ਯਕੀਨੀ; **~ty** ਅਨਿਸ਼ਚਤਤਾ, ਸੰਦੇਹ

uncle ('ਅੰਙਕਲ) *n* ਚਾਚਾ, ਤਾਇਆ, ਮਾਮਾ, ਮਾਸੜ, ਫੁੱਫੜ

Uncle Sam ('ਅੰਙਕਲ'ਸੈਮ) *n* ਅਮਰੀਕੀ ਸਰਕਾਰ

uncomfortable (ਅਨਕਮੱਫਟੇਬਲ) *a* ਬੇਆਰਾਮ, ਕਸ਼ਟਦਾਇਕ, ਅਸੁਵਿਧਾਜਨਕ

uncommon (ਅਨਕਾਮਨ) *a* ਅਸਧਾਰਨ, ਵਿਸ਼ੇਸ਼, ਨਿਰਾਲਾ, ਅਨੋਖਾ

uncompromising (ਅਨਕਾਂਪ੍ਰਮਾਇਜ਼ਿੰਙ) ਹਠਧਰਮੀ, ਅੱਟਲ, ਕਰੜਾ

unconcern (ਅਨਕੰਸੱਨ) *n* ਉਦਾਸੀਨਤਾ, ਨਿਸ਼ਚਿੰਤਤਾ, ਬੇਪਰਵਾਹੀ

unconcerned (ਅਨਕੰਸਨੱਡ) *a* ਉਦਾਸੀਨ, ਅਸਬੰਧਤ, ਬੇਪਰਵਾਹ, ਬੇਫ਼ਿਕਰ

unconditional (ਅਨਕੰਡਿਸ਼ਨਲ) *a* ਉੱਕ ਸੁਤੰਤਰ, ਨਿਰਪੇਖ, ਬਿਨਾ, ਸ਼ਰਤ

unconfirmed (ਅਨਕਫ਼ੱਮਡ) *a* ਅਪੁਸ਼ਟ ਅਪ੍ਰਮਾਣਤ

unconscious (ਅਨਕਾਂਸ਼ਸ) *a* ਅਚੇਤ, ਬੇਸੁਧ ਬੇਖ਼ਬਰ, ਬੇਹੋਸ਼

unconstitutional (ਅੱਨ-ਕਾਂਸਟਿ-ਟਯੂ-ਸ਼ਨਲ) ਸੰਵਿਧਾਨ ਵਿਰੁੱਧ, ਅਵਿਧਾਨਕ

unconstrained (ਅਨਕਨਸਟਰੋੱਡ) *a* ਆਜ਼ਾਦ ਬਿਨਾ ਰੋਕ, ਪਾਬੰਦੀਰਹਿਤ

unconventional (ਅਨਕਨਵੇਂਸ਼ਨਲ) ਰੂੜੀਮੁਕਤ, ਗ਼ੈਰ-ਰਵਾਇਤੀ

uncover (ਅਨਕਵ*) *v* ਪਰਗਟ ਕਰਨਾ, ਪਰ ਹਟਾਉਣਾ, ਨੰਗਾ ਕਰਨਾ, ਢੱਕਣ ਉਤਾਰਨਾ

undefined (ਅਨ-ਡਿਫ਼ਾਇੰਡ) *a* ਅਨਿਸ਼ਚ ਅਸਪਸ਼ਟ; ਅਪਰਿਭਾਸ਼ਤ, ਪਰਿਭਾਸ਼ਾਰਹਿਤ

under ('ਅੰਡਅ*) *a prep* ਹੇਠਲਾ; ਘੱਟ, ਥੋੜ੍ਹ ਦੇ ਅਧੀਨ, (ਨਿਯਮ ਆਦਿ ਦੇ) ਅਨੁਸਾਰ, ਵਿਚ, ਅੰਦਰ, ਮਾਤਹਿਤ

underconsideration (ਅਡੰਅ*ਕੰਸੀਡ਼ਰੇਸ਼ਨ) ਵਿਚਾਰ ਅਧੀਨ

undercurrent (ਅੰਡਅ*ਕਰੰਟ) *a* ਅੰਤਰ-ਧਾ ਅੰਤਰ-ਪਰਵਾਹ; ਅਦ੍ਰਿਸ਼ਟ ਪ੍ਰਭਾਵ; ਗੁਪਤ

underdeveloped (ਅੰਡਅ*ਡਿਵੈਲਪਡ) *a* ਪਿ ਰਿਹਾ, ਪਛੜਿਆ, ਘੱਟ ਵਿਕਸਤ, ਅਰ

ਵਿਕਸਤ, ਘੱਟ ਉੱਨਤ

underemployment (ਅੰਡਅ*ਇਮ'ਪਲੋਇਮੈਂਟ) *n* ਅਪੂਰਨ ਰੁਜ਼ਗਾਰ, ਯੋਗਤਾ ਨਾਲੋਂ ਛੋਟੇ ਕੰਮ ਤੇ ਲਗਾ

underestimate (ਅੰਡਅ*ਐਸਟਿਮੇਟ) *v* ਗਲਤ ਅੰਦਾਜ਼ਾ ਕਰਨਾ; ਅਸਲ ਨਾਲੋਂ ਘੱਟ ਸਮਝਣਾ, ਅਲਪ ਅਨੁਮਾਨ ਕਰਨਾ

undergo (ਅੰਡਅ*ਗੋ) *v* ਬਰਦਾਸ਼ਤ ਕਰਨਾ, ਸਹਿਣਾ, ਝੱਲਣਾ, ਭੋਗਣਾ

undergraduate (ਅੰਡਅ*ਗਰੇਡਯੂਇਟ) ਡਿਗਰੀ ਅਪ੍ਰਾਪਤ ਵਿਦਿਆਰਥੀ, ਪੂਰਵਸਨਾਤਕ

underground (ਅੰਡਅਗਰਾਉਂਡ) *a* ਪਧਰੀ ਦੇ ਤਲ ਦੇ ਹੇਠਾਂ, ਜ਼ਮੀਨਦੋਜ਼, (ਨਹਿਰ, ਰੇਲ); (ਬੋਲ) ਗੁਪਤ, ਛੁਪਿਆ

underline (ਅੰਡਅਲਾਇਨ) *a* ਪੁਸਤਕ ਜਾਂ ਚਿੱਠੀ ਦੇ ਜ਼ਰੂਰੀ ਵਾਕਾਂ ਨੂੰ ਲਕੀਰਨਾ; ਰੇਖਾ ਅੰਕਤ ਕਰਨਾ, ਮਹੱਤਵ ਦੇਣਾ

underlying (ਅੰਡਅਲਾਇੰਗ) *a* ਬੁਨਿਆਦੀ; ਅੰਤਰੀਵ, ਅੰਦਰਲਾ

undermentioned (ਅੰਡਅਮੇਨਸ਼ੰਡ) *a* ਨਿਮਨ ਲਿਖਤ

undermine (ਅੰਡਅ*ਮਾਇਨ) *v* ਨਸ਼ਟ ਕਰਨਾ, ਕਮਜ਼ੋਰ ਬਣਾਉਣਾ, ਨੀਂਹ ਖੋਖਲੀ ਕਰ ਦੇਣੀ, ਅੰਦਰੋਂ-ਅੰਦਰ ਸੁਰੰਗ ਪੁੱਟਣੀ (ਦਰਿਆ ਆਦਿ ਦੀ)

underneath (ਅੰਡਅ:ਨੀਥ) *n a* ਹੇਠਲਾ ਤਲ, ਨੀਵੀਂ ਸਤ੍ਹਾ; ਨੀਵੇਂ ਥਾਂ ਉੱਤੇ; ਥੱਲੇ; ਹੇਠਲਾ

underproduction (ਅੰਡਅ:ਪਰਡਕਸ਼ਨ) *n* ਨਾਕਾਫੀ ਉਪਜ, ਘੱਟ ਪੈਦਾਵਾਰ, ਅਲਪ ਉਤਪਾਦਨ

underquote (ਅੰਡਅ:ਕਵੋਟ) *v* (ਦੂਜੇ ਦੇ ਮੁਕਾਬਲੇ ਦੇ) ਘੱਟ ਕੀਮਤ ਲਗਾਉਣੀ (ਮਾਲ ਆਦਿ ਦੀ)

underrate (ਅੰਡਅ:ਰੇਟ) *v* ਘੱਟ ਮੁੱਲ ਲਗਾਉਣਾ

under ripe (ਅੰਡਅ:ਰਾਇਪ) *a* ਕੱਚਾ, ਅੱਧ-ਪੱਕਾ

under secretary (ਅੰਡਅ:ਸੇਕਰਿਟਰਿ) *a* ਉਪ-ਸੱਕਤਰ

undersigned (ਅੰਡਅ:ਸਾਇੰਡ) *n* ਨਿਮਨ-ਹਸਤਾਖ਼ਰੀ, ਹੇਠਾਂ ਦਸਤਖ਼ਤ ਕਰਨ ਵਾਲਾ

undersized (ਅੰਡਅ:ਸਾਇਜ਼ਡ) *a* ਛੋਟਾ, ਠਿਗਣਾ, ਗਿਠ-ਮੁੰਠਾ, ਬੌਣਾ

understamped (ਅੰਡਅ:ਸਟੈਂਪਡ) *a* ਥੋੜੀਆਂ ਟਿਕਟਾਂ ਵਾਲਾ, ਅਲਪਮੁਦਰਾ ਅੰਕਤ (ਲਿਫ਼ਾਫ਼ਾ ਜਾਂ ਕਾਰਡ)

understate (ਅੰਡਅ:ਸਟੇਟ) *v* ਘੱਟ ਦੱਸਣਾ; ~ment ਘੱਟ ਬਿਆਨ

understock (ਅੰਡਅ:ਸਟਾਕ) *v* (ਦੁਕਾਨ ਜਾਂ ਕਾਰਖ਼ਾਨੇ ਵਿਚ) ਘੱਟ ਸਮਾਨ ਰੱਖਣਾ

undertake (ਅੰਡਅ:ਟੇਕ) *v* (ਕਿਸੇ ਕੰਮ ਨੂੰ ਕਰਨ ਦਾ) ਵਚਨ ਦੇਣਾ, ਹਾਮੀ ਭਰਨੀ; ਕਿਸੇ ਨੂੰ ਵਿਚ ਲੈਣਾ, ਕਬੂਲ ਕਰਨਾ, ਬੀੜਾ ਚੁੱਕਣਾ, ਆਪਣੇ ਜ਼ਿੰਮੇ ਲੈਣਾ; ~**taking** ਕਾਰੋਬਾਰ; ਅੰਗੀਕਾਰ (ਕੰਮ ਦੇ ਭਾਰ ਨੂੰ), ਵਚਨ, ਪ੍ਰਤਿਗਿਆ; ਜ਼ੁੰਮੇਵਾਰੀ; ਅੰਤਮ-ਸੰਸਕਾਰ-ਪ੍ਰਬੰਧ

undertone (ਅੰਡਅ:ਟੋਨ) *n* ਧੀਮਾ ਸੁਰ; ਪਤਲਾ ਜਾਂ ਹਲਕਾ ਰੰਗ

undertrial (ਅੰਡਅ:ਟਰਾਇਲ) *a* ਪਰੀਖਿਆ-ਅਧੀਨ

underwear (ਅੰਡਅ:ਵੇਅ*) *n* ਕੱਛੀ, ਲੰਗੋਟੀ

underweight (ਅੰਡਅ:ਵੇਟ) *n* (ਔਸਤ ਤੋਂ) ਘੱਟ ਭਾਰ, ਘਟ ਵਜ਼ਨ

underwork (ਅੰਡਅ:ਵ'ਕ) *n* ਇਮਦਾਦੀ ਕੰਮ, ਸਹਾਇਤਾ ਕਾਰਜ; ਹੌਲਾ ਕੰਮ, ਹੌਲਾ ਕੰਮ ਕਰਨਾ

underworld (ਅੰਡਅ:ਵ'ਲਡ) *n* ਨਰਕ, ਰਸਾਤਲ; ਪਾਤਾਲ-ਲੋਕ, ਤਹਿ, ਗੁਪਤਸਤਾਨ ਅਪਰਾਪੀ-ਜਗਤ

understand ('ਅੰਡਅ'ਸਟੈਂਡ) *v* ਅਰਥ ਕੱਢਣਾ; ਬੁੱਝਣਾ, ਗੱਲ ਸਮਝਣਾ; ਅਨੁਮਾਨ ਕਰ ਲੈਣਾ; ਜਾਣਨਾ; ~ing ਸਮਝ, ਗਿਆਨ, ਬੋਧਸ਼ਕਤੀ; ਰਜ਼ਾਮੰਦੀ, ਸਹਿਮਤੀ, ਇਕਮੱਤਤਾ

undeserving (ਅਨ-ਡਿਜ਼ਰਵਿਙ) *a* ਅਣਧਿਕਾਰੀ, ਅਪਾਤਰ

undesirable (ਅਨ-ਡਿਜ਼ਾਇਅਰੇਬਲ) *a* ਅਣਚਾਹਿਆ (ਵਿਅਕਤੀ); ਅਣਇਛੱਤ

undivided (ਅਨ-ਡਿਵ੍ਹਾਇਡਇਡ) *a* ਅੰਵਡ, ਅਣਵੰਡਿਆ, ਅਭਿੰਨ, ਇਕਾਗਰ, ਸਮੁੱਚਾ, ਸਾਰਾ, ਸਬੂਤਾ, ਸਾਲਮ

undo (ਅੱਨਡੂ) *v* ਬਰਬਾਦ ਕਰਨਾ, ਨਸ਼ਟ ਕਰਨਾ, ਤਬਾਹ ਕਰਨਾ, ਵਿਗਾੜਨਾ; ਮਿਟਾਉਣਾ

undone (ਅਨਡਨ) *a* ਬਰਬਾਦ, ਤਬਾਹ, ਨਸ਼ਟ

undoubtedly (ਅਨਡਾਉਟਇਡਲਿ) *a* ਨਿਰੰਸੰਦੇਹ, ਬੇਸ਼ਕ, ਯਕੀਨੀ

undressed (ਅਨਡਰੈਸਡ) *a* ਨੰਗਾ, ਨੰਗਾ-ਧੜੰਗਾ, ਵਸਤਰਹੀਣ

undue (ਅਨ'ਡਯੂ) *a* ਨਾਜਾਇਜ਼, ਨਾ-ਮੁਨਾਸਬ; ਅਸੰਤੁਲਤ

unduly (ਅਨਡਯੂਲਿ) *adv* ਅਸਧਾਰਨ, ਰੂਪ ਵਿਚ; ਅਵ-ਅਵਸ਼ਕ ਰੂਪ ਵਿਚ

unearned (ਅਨਅੱ*ਡ) *a* ਅਣਕਮਾਇਆ; ਨਾਜਾਇਜ਼; ਹਰਾਮ ਦਾ, ਮੁਫ਼ਤ ਦਾ

unearth (ਅਨਅੱ*ਥ) *v* ਪਤਾ ਕੱਢਣਾ, ਸੂਹ ਕੱਢਣੀ; ਜ਼ਮੀਨ ਤੋਂ ਬਾਹਰ ਕੱਢਣਾ

uneasy (ਅਨ-ਇਜ਼ਾਇ) *a* ਬੇਚੈਨ, ਬੇਆਰਾਮ, ਵਿਆਕੁਲ, ਪਰੇਸ਼ਾਨ

uneconomic (ਅਨਇਕਨਾਮਇਕ) *a* ਲਾਭਰਹਿਤ, ਬੇਫ਼ਾਇਦਾ

unempolyed (ਅਨਇਮਪਲਾਇਡ) *a* ਬੇਕਾਰ, ਬੇਰੁਜ਼ਗਾਰ

unempolyment (ਅਨਾਇੰਪਲਾਇਮੇਂਟ) *n* ਬੇਕਾਰੀ, ਬੇਰੁਜ਼ਗਾਰੀ

unending (ਅਨਏਂਡਿਗ) *a* ਅਨੰਤ; ਅਮੁੱਕ, ਨਿਰੰਤਰ, ਅਖੰਡ, ਬੇਅੰਤ

unequal (ਅਨ'ਇਕਯੂਲ) *a* ਬੇਮੇਲ, ਅਸਮਾਨ, ਨਾਬਰਾਬਰ

unequivocal (ਅਨ'ਇਕਵ੍ਵਿਵੌਕਲ) *a* ਸਪਸ਼ਟ, ਸਾਫ਼, ਸੰਦੇਹ ਰਹਿਤ, ਖ਼ਰਾ ਖ਼ਰਾ

unerring (ਅਨ'ਅਰਇੰਗ) *a* ਅਭੁੱਲ, ਅਚੁੱਕ

uneven (ਅਨ'ਈਵ੍ਨ) *a* ਉਚਾ-ਨੀਵਾਂ; ਅਪਧੱਰਾ, ਉਘੜ-ਦੁੱਘੜ, ਅਸਮਾਨ

unexampled (ਅਨਿਗਜ਼ਾਂਪਲਡ) *a* ਅਦੁੱਤੀ ਅਨੂਪ; ਲਾਸਾਨੀ, ਬੇਨਜ਼ੀਰ

unexceptionable (ਅਨਿਕਸੇਪਸ਼ਨੇਬਲ) *a* ਤੱਸਲੀਬਖ਼ਸ਼

unexceptional (ਅਨਿਕਸੇਪਸ਼ਨਲ) *a* ਮਾਮੂਲੀ ਸਾਧਾਰਨ

unexpected (ਅਨਿਕਸੇਪਕਟਿਡ) *a* ਅਚਾਨਕ ਅਕਾਸਮਕ

unexperienced (ਅਨਿਕਸੇਪਿਅਰਇੰਸਡ) ਅਨੁਭਵਹੀਣ, ਨਾਤਜਰਬੇਕਾਰ

unfair (ਅਨੱਫੇਅ*) *a* ਬੇਜਾ, ਖੋਟਾ, ਨਾਵਾਜ ਅਨੁਚਿਤ

unfaithful (ਅੱਨਫ਼ੇਥਫ਼ੁਲ) *a* ਬੇਵਫ਼ਾ, ਨਮ ਹਰਾਮ, ਕਿਰਤਘਣ, ਝੂਠਾ

unfasten (ਅਨਫ਼ੱਾਸਨ) *v* ਖੋਲ੍ਹਣਾ, ਢਿੱਲਾ ਕਰ

unfavourable (ਅਨਫ਼ੇਵਰਬਲ) *a* ਵਿਰੋ ਪ੍ਰਤੀਕੂਲ, ਵਿਖਮ

unfit (ਅਨਫ਼ਿਟ) *a v* ਅਯੋਗ, ਅਢੁੱਕਵਾਂ, ਅਨੁਚਿ ਨਿਕੰਮਾ, ਨਕਾਰਾ; ਨਕਾਰਾ ਬਣਾ ਦੇਣਾ; ~ti

ਅਢੁੱਕਵਾਂ, ਕਸੂਤਾ

unfortunate (ਅਨਫ਼ਾ:ਚਨਿਟ) *a* ਅਭਾਗਾ ਵਿਅਕਤੀ; ਭਾਰਹੀਣ, ਅਭਾਗਾ, ਬਦਨਸੀਬ, ਬਦਕਿਸਮਤ, ਮੰਦਭਾਗਾ, ਨਾਮੁਰਾਦ

unfounded (ਅਨਫ਼ਾਉਂਡਿਡ) *a* ਨਿਰਮੂਲ, ਮਿਥਿਆ, ਬੇਬੁਨਿਆਦ, ਸਰਾਸਰ ਗ਼ਲਤ

unfurl (ਅਨਫ਼ਃਲ) *v* ਖੋਲ੍ਹਣਾ, ਸੁੱਟਣਾ ਜਾਂ ਖੁੱਲ੍ਹਣਾ; ਪਸਾਰਨਾ, ਲਹਿਰਾਉਣਾ, ਫੈਲਾਉਣਾ, ਫੈਲਣਾ

unfurnished (ਅਨਫ਼ਃਰਨਿਸ਼ਡ) *a* ਖ਼ਾਲੀ, ਅਸਜਿਤ, ਬਿਨਾ ਸਜਾਵਟ ਤੋਂ

ungracious (ਅਨਗਰੇਸ਼ਅਸ) *a* ਨੀਚ, ਦੁਸ਼ਟ, ਕਠੋਰ

ungrammatical (ਅਨਗਰਾਮੈਟਿਕਲ) *a* ਵਿਆਕਰਣ-ਵਿਰੁੱਧ, ਵਿਆਕਰਣ-ਵਿਪਰੀਤ

ungrounded (ਅਨਗਰਾਉਂਡਿਡ) *a* ਨਿਰਮੂਲ, ਬੇ-ਬੁਨਿਆਦੀ, ਫ਼ਜ਼ੂਲ, ਨਿਰਾਆਧਾਰ

unguarded (ਅਨਗਾ*ਡਿਡ) *a* ਵਿਚਾਰ-ਰਹਿਤ, ਅਚੇਤ, ਬੇਧਿਆਨ (ਪਰਗਟਾਉ), ਅਰੱਖਿਅਤ

unhappy (ਅਨਹੈਪਿ) *a* ਨਾਮੁਰਾਦ; ਦੁਖੀ; ਅਪ੍ਰਸੰਨ, ਨਾਖ਼ੁਸ਼, ਉਦਾਸ

unhealthy (ਅਨਹੈਲਥਿ) *a* ਅਸੁਅਸਥ, ਰੋਗੀ, ਬੀਮਾਰ; ਹਾਨੀਕਾਰਕ

unheard (ਅਨਹਃਡ) *a* ਅਣਸੁਣਿਆ, ਅਣਜਾਣਿਆ, ਅਗਿਆਤ

unholy (ਅਨਹੋਲਿ) *a* ਅਪਵਿੱਤਰ, ਨਾਪਾਕ, ਅਸ਼ੁੱਧ, ਭ੍ਰਿਸ਼ਟ, ਮਲੀਨ

unhuman (ਅਨਹਯੂਮਨ) *a* ਅਮਨੁੱਖੀ, ਨਿਰਦਈ, ਅਮਾਨਵੀ

unicameral ('ਯੂਨਿ'ਕੈਮਅਰਲ) *a* ਇਕ-ਘਰਾ, ਇਕ-ਕਕਸ਼ੀ, ਇਕ ਸਦਨੀ (ਪਾਰਲੀਮੈਂਟ)

unification ('ਯੂਨਿਫ਼ਿ'ਕੇਇਸ਼ਨ) *n* ਮੇਲ, ਇਤਿਹਾਦ, ਮਿਲਾਉਣੀ, ਏਕੀਕਰਨ

uniform ('ਯੂਨਿਫ਼ੋਮ) *a* ਇਕਸਾਰ, ਬਰਾਬਰ, ਇਕ ਸਮਾਨ; ਨਿਰੰਤਰ; ਵੇਸ, ਭੇਸ, ਵਰਦੀ; ~ity ਸਮਤਾ, ਸਮਰੂਪਤਾ, ਇਕਸਾਰਤਾ, ਇਕਰੂਪਤਾ, ਮੇਲ

unify ('ਯੂਨਿਫ਼ਾਇ) *v* ਇਕਰੂਪ ਕਰਨਾ, ਇਕ ਰੰਗ ਕਰਨਾ, ਇਕ ਕਰ ਦੇਣਾ

unilateral ('ਯੂਨਿ'ਲੈਟ(ਅ)ਰ(ਅ)ਲ) *a* ਇਕ ਪੱਖੀ, ਇਕ ਤਰਫ਼ਾ

unimpeachable (ਅਨਇੰਪੀਚਬਲ) *a* ਨਿਰਦੋਸ਼, ਬੇਕਸੂਰ, ਨਿਰਅਪਰਾਧ, ਸੱਚਾ

unimportant (ਅਨਿਪਾ*ਟੰਟ) *a* ਗ਼ੈਰ-ਜ਼ਰੂਰੀ, ਅਟਵੱਸ਼ਕ, ਮਹੱਤਵਹੀਣ

uninformed (ਅਨਇਨਫ਼*ਮਡ) *a* ਅਸੂਚਤ, ਅਣਜਾਣ, ਨਾਦਾਨ, ਬੇ-ਖ਼ਬਰ

uninhabited (ਅਨਇਨਹੈਬਿਟਿਡ) *a* ਨਿਰਜਨ, ਗ਼ੈਰ-ਆਬਾਦ, ਵੀਰਾਨ, ਉਜੜਿਆ-ਪੁੱਜੜਿਆ

unintelligibillity (ਅਨਇੰਟੇਲਇਜਿਲਿਟੀ) *n* ਅਸਪਸ਼ਟਤਾ, ਅਬੋਧਤਾ, ਅਬੁੱਝਤਾ

unintelligible (ਅਨਇੰਟੇਲਇਜਿਬਲ) *a* ਅਸਪਸ਼ਟ, ਅਬੋਧ

uninterrupted (ਅਨਇੰਟਰਪਟਿਡ) *a* ਨਿਰਵਿਘਨ, ਅਖੰਡ, ਨਿਰੰਤਰ, ਲਗਾਤਾਰ

union ('ਯੂਨਯਅਨ) *n* ਸੰਘ, ਸਭਾ-ਭਵਨ, ਸਭਾ, ਸਮਾਗਮ, ਜਥੇਬੰਦੀ, ਜੋੜ; ਮੇਲ; ਵਿਆਹ, ਏਕਾ

unique (ਯੂ'ਨੀਕ) *a* ਅਨੋਖਾ, ਅਨੂਠਾ, ਨਿਰਾਲਾ, ਬੇਜੋੜ, ਲਾਜਵਾਬ; ~ness ਅਨੋਖਾਪਨ, ਅਨੂਠਾਪਨ, ਨਿਰਾਲਾਪਨ, ਅਨੂਪਤਾ

unisexual ('ਯੂਨਿ'ਸੈੱਕਸੁਅਲ) *a* ਇਕ-ਲਿੰਗੀ

unison ('ਯੂਨਿਸ਼ਨ) *n* ਧੁਨੀਆਂ ਜਾਂ ਸੁਰਾਂ ਵਿਚ ਤਾਲ ਦੀ ਏਕਤਾ; ਸੁਰ-ਮੇਲ, ਏਕਤਾ, ਮੇਲ-ਮਿਲਾਪ

unit ('ਯੂਨਿਟ) *n* ਇਕ, ਇਕਾਈ; ਮਾਤਰਕ, ਇਕਾਈ ਦਾ ਪਰਿਮਾਣ (ਬਿਜਲੀ); ਦਲ, ਟੁਕੜੀ, ਯੂਨਿਟ (ਫ਼ੌਜ), ਸ਼ਾਖ਼ਾ

unitary ('ਯੂਨਿਟ(ਅ)ਰਿ) *a* ਏਕਤਮਕ, ਇਕਾਈ ਦਾ

unite ('ਯੂਨਾਇਟ) *v* ਮਿਲ ਕੇ ਕੰਮ ਕਰਨਾ, ਜੁੜਨਾ, ਪਰਸਪਰ ਮਿਲਾਉਣਾ ਜਾਂ ਮਿਲਣਾ, ਜੋੜਨਾ, ਇਕ ਕਰਨਾ ਜਾਂ ਹੋਣਾ; ਵਿਆਹ ਬੰਧਨ ਵਿਚ ਬੰਨ੍ਹਣਾ; ~d ਸੰਯੁਕਤ, ਯੁਕਤ, ਸਾਂਝਾ

unity ('ਯੂਨਅਟਿ) *n* ਮੇਲ, ਸਮਰੂਪਤਾ; ਸਮਾਨਤਾ, ਸੰਗਤੀ; ਏਕਤਾ, ਏਕਾ (ਗਣਿ) ਇਕਾਈ

universal ('ਯੂਨਿ'ਵ੍ਯਅਃਸਲ) *a* ਵਿਆਪਕ, ਸਾਮਾਨਯ, ਸਰਵਵਿਆਪਕ, ਸੰਪੂਰਨ, ਕੁੱਲ; ~ity ਵਿਆਪਕਤਾ, ਸਰਵ-ਵਿਆਪਕਤਾ; ~ize ਵਿਸ਼ਵ-ਵਿਆਪੀ ਬਣਾਉਣਾ; ਸਰਵ-ਦੇਸ਼ੀ ਬਣਾਉਣਾ

universe ('ਯੂਨਿਵ੍ਯਅਃਸ) *n* ਬ੍ਰਹਿਮੰਡ, ਵਿਸ਼ਵ, ਸ੍ਰਿਸ਼ਟੀ, ਜਗਤ

university ('ਯੂਨਿ'ਵ੍ਯਅਃਸਅਟਿ) *n* ਵਿਸ਼ਵਵਿਦਿਆਲਾ

unjust (ਅਨਜਸਟ) *a* ਨਿਆਂਹੀਣ, ਅਨੁਚਿਤ, ਅਨਿਆਂਪੂਰਨ; ~ified ਨਾਵਾਜਬ, ਅਯੋਗ, ਅਨੁਚਿਤ, ਨਿਆਂਰਹਿਤ

unkind (ਅਨਕਾਇੰਡ) *a* ਬੇਰਹਿਮ, ਬੇਦਰਦ, ਨਿਰਦਈ, ਕਠੋਰ, ਨਿਸ਼ਠੁਰ

unknown (ਅਨਨੋਨ) *a* ਅਣਜਾਣ, ਨਾਮਲੂਮ; ਬੇਗਾਨਾ, ਅਜਨਬੀ, ਉਪਰਾ

unlawful (ਅਨਲਾਫ਼ੁਲ) *a* ਗ਼ੈਰ-ਕਾਨੂੰਨੀ, ਅਵੈਧ, ਹਰਾਮੀ

unlearned (ਅਨਲੰੑਡ) *a* ਅਣਜਾਣ; ਮੂਰੁ, ਅਗਿਆਨ

unless (ਅਨ'ਲੈਸ) *conj* ਜਦ ਤੀਕ ਨਾ, ਨਹੀਂ ਤਾਂ, ਜੇ ਕਰ ਨਾ; ਇਸ ਨੂੰ ਛੱਡ ਕੇ, ਸਿਵਾਏ ਇਸ ਦੇ

unlettered (ਅਨਲੇਟੱਡ) *a* ਨਿਰੱਖਰ, ਅਨਪੜ੍ਹ, ਬੇਇਲਮ

unlike (ਅਨਲਾਇਕ) *a* ਭਿੰਨ, ਅਣਮਿਲਦਾ, ਪ੍ਰਤੀਕੂਲ; ~ly ਅਸੰਭਾਵੀ

unlimited (ਅਨਲਿਮਿਟਿਡ) *a* ਅਪਾਰ, ਅਸੀਮਤ, ਬੇਹੱਦ, ਬੇਅੰਤ, ਅਤੀ ਅਧਿਕ

unload (ਅਨਲੋਡ) *v* ਭਾਰ ਲਾਹੁਣਾ, ਭਾਰਮੁਕਤ ਕਰਨਾ, ਖ਼ਾਲੀ ਕਰ ਦੇਣਾ, ਮਾਲ ਲਾਹੁਣਾ

unlock (ਅਨਲੌਕ) *v* ਜੰਦਾ ਖੋਲ੍ਹਣਾ; (ਬੋਲ) ਦਿਲ ਦੀ ਗੱਲ ਖੋਲ੍ਹਣੀ, ਫੁੱਟ ਪੈਣਾ

unlucky (ਅਨੱਲਕੀ) *a* ਭਾਗਹੀਨ, ਅਭਾਗਾ, ਅਸ਼ੁਭ, ਅਸਫਲ, ਨਾਮੁਰਾਦ, ਬਦਕਿਸਮਤ

unmanageable (ਅਨਮੈਨਿਜਬਲ) *a* ਕਾਬੂ ਤੋਂ ਬਾਹਰ, ਬੇਕਾਬੂ, ਪ੍ਰਬੰਧ ਰਹਿਤ

unmanly (ਅਨਮੈਨਲਿ) *a* ਜਨਾਨੜਾ; ਬੁਜ਼ਦਿਲ, ਬੋਥਾ

unmannerly (ਅਨਮੈਨਃਲਿ) *adv* ਕੁਚੱਜਾ, ਬਦਤਮੀਜ਼, ਬੇਹੁਦਾ, ਅਸ਼ਿਸ਼ਟ, ਗੰਵਾਰ

unmarried (ਅਨਮੈਰਿਡ) *a* ਕੁਆਰਾ, ਕੁਆਰੀ, ਅਵਿਵਾਹਤ

unmatched (ਅਨਮੈਚਡ) *a* ਅਛੂਹਕਵਾਂ, ਬੇਢੰਬਾ

unmentioned (ਅਨਮੇਨਸ਼ੰਡ) *a* ਅੱਕਥ ਨਾ-ਕਥਨ ਯੋਗ, ਅਨੁਲਿਖਤ

unnatural (ਅਨਨੈਚਰਲ) *a* ਗ਼ੈਰ-ਕੁਦਰਤੀ, ਅਸੁਭਾਵਕ, ਬਣਾਉਟੀ, ਨਾਜਾਇਜ਼, ਹਰਾਮੀ

unnecessary (ਅਨਨੇਸਿਸਰਿ) *a* ਬੇਲੋੜਾ, ਅਣਅਵੱਸ਼ਕ

unnumbered (ਅਨੱਨਬਃਡ) *a* ਅਣਗਿਣਤ,

ਬੇਹੱਦ, ਬੇਸ਼ੁਮਾਰ

unofficial (ਅਨਅਫਿਸ਼ਲ) *a* ਗ਼ੈਰ-ਸਰਕਾਰੀ, ਗ਼ੈਰਰਸਮੀ

unopposed (ਅਨਪੋਸਡ) *a* ਬਿਨਾ ਮੁਕਾਬਲੇ ਤੋਂ, ਬਿਨਾ ਮੁਕਾਬਲਾ, ਨਿਰਵਿਰੋਧ

unpaid (ਅਨਪੇਡ) *a* ਅਦਾ ਨਾ ਕੀਤਾ

unparalleled (ਅਨਪੈਰਲਲਡ) *a* ਅਨੂਠਾ, ਬੇਨਜ਼ੀਰ, ਲਾਸਾਨੀ, ਨਿਰਾਲਾ

unparliamentary (ਅਨਪਾਃਲਮੈਂਟਰਿ) *a* ਸਭਾ ਦੇ ਨੇਮ-ਵਿਰੁੱਧ, ਅਸੰਸਦੀ; ਅਸ਼ਲੀਲ, ਅਸ਼ਿਸ਼ਟ

unpleasant (ਅਨਪਲੇਜ਼ੈਂਟ) *a* ਘੋਮਜ਼ਾ, ਬੁਰਾ, ਨਾਗਵਾਰ

unpopular (ਅਨਪਾਪੂਯੂਲ*) *a* ਬਦਨਾਮ, ਅਪ੍ਰਸਿੱਧ

unprecedented (ਅਨਪਰੇਸਿਡੈਂਟਿਡ) *a* ਅਨੋਖਾ; ਨਵੇਕਲਾ, ਬੇਮਿਸਾਲ

unprejudiced (ਅਨਪਰਿਜੁਡਿਸਡ) *a* ਬੇਲਾਗ, ਪੱਖਪਾਤ-ਰਹਿਤ, ਨਿਰਪੱਖ

unprepared (ਅਨਪਰਿਪੇਅਃਡ) *a* ਬਿਨਾ ਤਿਆਰੀ ਕੀਤੇ, ਅਚਿੰਤ; ਪਹਿਲਾਂ ਨਾ ਸੋਚਿਆ

unpresentable (ਅਨਪਰਿਜ਼ੈਂਟਬਲ) *a* ਭੱਦਾ, ਅਪਰਦਰਸ਼ਾਨੀ

unpresumptuous (ਅਨਪਰਿਜ਼ਟਯੂਅਸ) *a* ਸਰਲ, ਸਾਦਾ; ਨਿਮਰਤਾ ਭਰਪੂਰ

unprincipled (ਅਨਪਰਿਸਪਲਡ) *a* ਬੇਅਸੂਲਾ, ਸਦਾਚਾਰਹੀਨ, ਚਰਿੱਤਰਹੀਨ, ਸਿਧਾਂਤਹੀਨ

unproductive (ਅਨਪਰਡਕਟਿਵ) *a* ਬਾਂਝ, ਬੰਜਰ, ਬੇਕਾਰ, ਅਣਉਪਜਾਊ

unprofitable (ਅਨਪਰਾਫ਼ਿਟਬਲ) *a* ਵਿਅਰਥਤਾ, ਲਾਭਹੀਣਤਾ

unpublished (ਅਨਪਬਲਿਸ਼ਡ) *a* ਅਣਛਪਿਆ, ਅਪ੍ਰਕਾਸ਼ਤ, ਗੁਪਤ

unquestionable (ਅਨਕਵੇਸਚਨਬਲ) *a* ਨਿਰਸੰਦੇਹ, ਨਿਰਵਿਵਾਦ; ~questioned ਨਿਰਵਿਵਾਦ, ਨਿਸ਼ਚਤ

unreal (ਅਨਰਿਅਲ) *a* ਝੂਠਾ, ਅਵਾਸਤਵਿਕ, ਨਕਲੀ

unregistered (ਅਨਰੇਜਿਸਟ'ਡ) *a* ਗ਼ੈਰ-ਰਜਿਸਟਰੀ-ਸ਼ੁਦਾ, ਸਧਾਰਨ (ਪੱਤਰ ਆਦਿ)

unrest (ਅਨਰੇਸਟ) *n* ਬੇਚੈਨੀ, ਗੜਬੜ, ਅਸ਼ਾਂਤੀ, ਫ਼ਸਾਦ

unriddle (ਅਨਰਿਡਲ) *a* (ਅੜਾਉਣੀ, ਗੁੰਝਲ, ਬੁਝਾਰਤ, ਸੰਮਸਿਆ ਆਦਿ) ਖੋਲ੍ਹਣੀ, ਹੱਲ ਕਰਨੀ

unrighteous (ਅਨਰਾਇਚਸ) *a* ਅਧਰਮੀ, ਪਾਪੀ, ਬੇਈਮਾਨ; ~ness ਅਧਰਮ, ਬੁਰਾਈ, ਦੁਸ਼ਟਤਾ, ਬੇਈਮਾਨੀ

unripe (ਅਨਰਾਇਪ) *a* ਕੱਚਾ, ਹਰਾ, ਅਣਪੱਕਿਆ, ਅਵਿਕਸਤ; ਨਾਬਾਲਗ਼

unruly (ਅਨਰੂਲਿ) *a* ਨੇਮ ਰਹਿਤ, ਮੂੰਹਜ਼ੋਰ, ਤੁਫ਼ਾਨੀ

unsatisfied (ਅਨਸੈਟਿਸਫਾਇਡ) *a* ਅਸੰਤੁਸ਼ਟ, ਅਤ੍ਰਿਪਤ

unscientific (ਅਨਸਾਇੰਟਫ਼ਿਕ) *a* ਅਵਿਗਿਆਨਕ, ਨਿਯਮ-ਵਿਰੁੱਧ, ਸਿਧਾਂਤਹੀਨ

unscrupulous (ਅਨਸਕਰੁਪਯੂਲਸ) *a* ਚਰਿੱਤਰਹੀਨ; ਬੇਅਸੂਲਾ; ਬੇਸ਼ਰਮ

unseasonable (ਅਨਸੀਜ਼ਨਬਲ) *a* ਬੇਮੌਸਮ (ਬਾਰਸ਼ ਆਦਿ), ਬੇਮੌਕਾ

unseat (ਅਨਸੀਟ) *v* ਥਾਂ ਤੋਂ ਹਟਾਉਣਾ; ਸੱਥਰੀ ਤੋਂ ਹਟਾਉਣਾ

unseen (ਅਨਸੀਨ) *a* ਅਣਵੇਖਿਆ, ਅਡਿੱਠ, ਨਾ ਪੜ੍ਹਿਆ ਹੋਇਆ ਪਾਠ

unsophisticated (ਅਨਸਫ਼ਿਸਟਿਕੇਟਿਡ) *a* ਨਿਰਛਲ; ਸਿੱਧਾ-ਸਾਦਾ, ਭੋਲਾ, ਸਰਲ	ਪਰਮਾਰਥੀ
unspent (ਅਨਸਪੈਂਟ) *a* ਅਣਖਰਚਿਆ, ਅਣਵਰਤਿਆ, ਅਣਬੀਤਿਆ	**unworthy** (ਅਨਵ:ਇ) *a* ਅਯੋਗ, ਨਿਖਿੱਧ, ਨਾਲਾਇਕ, ਨਿਗੁਣਾ
unstable (ਅਨਸਟੇਬਲ) *a* ਅਸਥਾਈ, ਅਸਥਿਰ	**unwritten** (ਅਨਰਿਟਨ) *a* ਅਣਲਿਖਿਆ, ਅਲਿਖਤ, ਜ਼ੋਖਕ, ਜ਼ਬਾਨੀ
unstitch (ਅਨਸਟਿਚ) *v* ਟਾਂਕਾ ਖੋਲ੍ਹਣਾ, ਬਖ਼ੀਆ ਉਧੇੜਨਾ	**unyielding** (ਅਨਯੀਲਡਿੰਗ) *a* ਅੜੀਅਲ, ਜ਼ਿੱਦੀ, ਪੱਕਾ, ਬੇਲੋਚ
until (ਅਨ'ਟਿਲ) *prep conj* ਜਦ ਤੀਕ, ਤੀਕ, ਇਸ ਹੱਦ ਤੀਕ, ਜਦ ਤੀਕ ਨਾ	**up** (ਅੱਪ) *n v a adv prep* ਉੱਨਤੀ, ਉਚਾਈ; ਉੱਪਰ ਉੱਠ ਕੇ ਖਲੋਣਾ; ਸਮਾਪਤ; ਉੱਪਰਲਾ, ਉੱਚਾ; ਉੱਤੇ, ਉੱਪਰ ਨੂੰ, ਉੱ ਪਰ ਤਕ; ਤਰਤੀਬ ਵਿਚ
unto ('ਅੰਨਟੂ) *prep* ਤੀਕ ਨੂੰ; ਵੇਖੋ *to*	
untimely (ਅਨਟਾਇਮਲਿ) *a* ਅਕਾਲਕ, ਸਮੇਂ ਤੋਂ ਪਹਿਲਾਂ; ਘੇਸੋਕਾ, ਕੁਵੇਲੇ	**upbringing** (ਅਪਬਰਿੰਗਿੰਗ) *n* ਪ੍ਰਾਰੰਭਿਕ ਸਿੱਖਿਆ, ਪਾਲਣਾ, ਪਾਲਣ-ਪੋਸਣ
untold (ਅਨਟੋਲਡ) *a* ਅੱਕਥ; ਅਣਵਰਤਣ; ਬੇਹੱਦ	**update** (ਅਪਡੇਟ) *v* ਆਧੁਨਿਕ ਬਣਾਉਣਾ
untouchability (ਅਨਟੱਚਬਿਲਇਟਿ) *n* ਛੂਆ-ਛੂਤ, ਛੂਤ-ਛਾਤ; ~**touchable** ਅਛੂਤ; ਹਰਿਜਨ	**upgrade** (ਅਪਗਰੇਡ) *n v* ਪਦ-ਉੱਨਤੀ, ਪਦ ਉੱਨਤ, ਉੱਨਤ ਕਰਨਾ, ਕਰਜਾ ਵਧਾਉਣਾ
untoward (ਅਨਟੋਅ'ਡ) *a* ਭੈੜਾ, ਕਸੂਤਾ; ਅਵੱਲਾ, ਅਵੈੜਾ	**uphill** (ਅਪਹਿਲ) *adv a* ਪਹਾੜ ਦੇ ਉੱਪਰ ਵੱਲ; ਕਠਨ, ਕਰੜਾ
untrained (ਅਨਟਰੇਂਡ) *a* ਅਣਸਿੰਖਿਆ, ਨਾ ਸਿਖਲਾਇਆ	**uphold** (ਅਪਹੋਲਡ) *v* ਪੁਸ਼ਟੀ ਕਰਨਾ; ਸਿੱਧਾ ਖੜਾ ਰੱਖਣਾ, ਉੱਪਰ ਚੁੱਕੀ ਰੱਖਣਾ; ਕਾਇਮ ਰੱਖਣਾ, (ਫ਼ੈਸਲਾ ਆਦਿ) ਬਹਾਲ ਰੱਖਣਾ, ਜਥਾਪੂਰਵ ਰੱਖਣਾ
unusual (ਅਨਯੂਯੂਅਲ) *a* ਅਤਰਿੱਠ, ਅਸਧਾਰਨ, ਅਨੋਖਾ, ਅਲੋਕਕ	
unwanted (ਅਨਵਾਂਟਿਡ) *a* ਅਣਚਾਹਿਆ, ਬੇਲੋੜਾ, ਵਾਧੂ, ਅਣਅਵੱਸ਼ਕ	**upkeep** (ਅਪਕੀਪ) *n* ਪਾਲਣ-ਪੋਸ਼ਣ, ਨਿਗਰਾਨੀ, ਸੰਭਾਲ
unwell (ਅਨਵੇਲ) *a* ਅਸੁਅਸਥ, ਬੀਮਾਰ	**uplift** (ਅੱਪਲਿਫ਼ਟ) *v n* ਉੱਚਾ ਕਰਨਾ, ਉੱਪਰ ਨੂੰ ਚੁੱਕਣਾ, ਸੁਧਾਰਨਾ; ਸੁਧਾਰ, ਉੱਨਤੀ
unwilling (ਅਨਵਿਲਇੰਗ) *a* ਅਣਇਛੁਕ, ਬੇਦਿਲ; ਅਸਹਿਮਤ; ~**ness** ਨਾਰਾਜ਼ਮੰਦੀ, ਅਸਹਿਮਤੀ	**upper** (ਅਪਅ*) *n a* ਉਤਲਾ, ਉਤੇਰਾ; ਵੱਡਾ (ਪਦਵੀ ਵਿਚ)
unwise (ਅਨਵਾਇਜ਼) *a* ਅਗਿਆਨੀ, ਬੇਸਮਝ, ਕੁਵੱਲਾ (ਕੰਮ)	**uppermost** (ਅਪ*ਮੋਸਟ) *a* ਸਾਰਿਆਂ ਤੋਂ ਇਹਰ ਦਾ; ਸਭ ਤੋਂ ਉੱਤੇ
unworldly (ਅਨਵ:ਲਡਲਿ) *a* ਅਸੰਸਾਰਕ;	**upright** (ਅਪਰਾਇਟ) *a* ਸਿੱਧਾ; ਖੜਾ, ਸਰਲ

ਸਾਦਾ; ਈਮਾਨਦਾਰ

uprising (ਅਪਰਾਇਜ਼ਿੰਗ) *n* ਉਭਾਰ; ਝਗੜਾ, ਬਲਵਾ, ਬਗਾਵਤ, ਕਰਾਂਤੀ

uproar (ਅਪਰੋਅ*) *n* ਰੌਲਾ, ਰੌਲਾ-ਰੱਪਾ, ਹੁੱਲੜ, ਹੱਲਾ-ਗੁੱਲਾ

uproot (ਅਪਰੂਟ) *v* ਜੜ੍ਹੋਂ ਉਖਾੜਨਾ, ਬਰਬਾਦ ਕਰਨਾ

upset (ਅਪਸੇਟ) *v n* ਉਲਟਣਾ; ਉਲਟ-ਪੁਲਟ ਕਰਨਾ, ਪਰੇਸ਼ਾਨ ਕਰਨਾ; ਗੜਬੜ; (ਨੀਲਾਮੀ ਵਿਚ) ਸਰਕਾਰੀ ਕੀਮਤ

upshot (ਅਪਸ਼ਾਟ) *n* ਸਿੱਟਾ, ਨਤੀਜਾ, ਅਤ

upside (ਅਪਸਾਇਡ) *n* ਉਪਰਲਾ ਹਿੱਸਾ, ਉਪਰੀ ਸਤ੍ਹਾ; ~down ਉਲਟਾ, ਉਲਟਾ-ਪੁਲਟਾ, ਪਰਤਿਆ, ਪੁੱਠਾ, ਮੂਧਾ; ~to (ਅਪ-ਟੂ-ਡੇਟ) (ਅਪ-ਟੂ) ਠੀਕ, ਤਾਈਂ, ਤੀਕਰ, ਤਕ; ~to date ਆਧੁਨਿਕ, ਸਮੇਂ ਦਾ ਹਾਣੀ

upward(s) (ਅਪਵਅ:ਡ(ਜ਼)) *adv a* ਉੱਪਰ ਦਾ, ਉੱਪਰ ਵੱਲ; ਵਧਣ ਦਾ, ਤਰੱਕੀ ਦਾ; ਬਹੁਤਾ

upon (ਅ'ਪੌਨ) *prep* ਉੱਤੇ, ਉੱਪਰ, ਉੱਪਰ ਵੱਲ; ਪਿੱਛੇ; ਪਾਸ; ਬਾਬਤ

Uranus (ਯੁਅਰਅਨਅਸ) *n* ਮੰਗਲ-ਗ੍ਰਹਿ

urban ('ਅ:ਬਅਨ) *a* ਸ਼ਹਿਰਿ, ਨਾਗਰਿਕ, ਸੁਖੜ; ~e ਸੁਘੜ, ਸਾਊ; ਸ਼ੀਲਵਾਨ, ਸੁਸ਼ੀਲ, ਸ਼ਿਸ਼ਟ; ~ity ਸੁਘੜਤਾ, ਸਾਊਪੁਣਾ, ਸ਼ਿਸ਼ਟਤਾ, ਨਾਗਰਿਕ ਜੀਵਨ

urchin ('ਅ:ਚਿਨ) *n* ਮੁੰਡਾ, ਲੜਕਾ, ਛੋਹਰ; ਸ਼ਰਾਰਤੀ ਲੜਕਾ; ਜੰਗਲੀ ਚੂਹਾ

urea (ਯੁ(ਅ)'ਰਿਅ) *n* (ਰਸਾ) ਘੁਲਣਸ਼ੀਲ, ਰੰਗਹੀਨ ਅਤੇ ਰਵੇਦਾਰ ਯੋਗਕ

urge (ਅ:ਜ) *v n* ਪਰੇਰਨਾ, ਉਤੇਜਤ ਕਰਨਾ, ਤਾਕੀਦ ਕਰਨਾ, ਵਾਹ; ~ncy ਅਤੀ ਅਵਸ਼ੰਕਤਾ, ਲੋੜਵੰਦੀ, ਤਾਂਗ, ਤੀਬਰ, ਮਹੱਤਵ; (ਟੱਟੀ-ਪਿਸ਼ਾਬ ਦੀ) ਹਾਜਤ; ~nt ਜ਼ਰੂਰੀ, ਅਵਸ਼ੰਕ, ਬਹੁਤ ਲੋੜੀਂਦਾ

urinal ('ਯੁਅਰਿਨਲ) *a n* ਮੂਤਰਾਲਾ; ਪਿਸ਼ਾਬ-ਘਰ

urine ('ਯੁਅਰੀਨ) *n* ਪਿਸ਼ਾਬ, ਮੂਤਰ, ਮੂਤ

urn (ਅ:ਨ) *n v* ਕਲਸ਼; ਅਸਥੀ-ਪਾਤਰ; ਵੱਡੀ ਚਾਦਾਨੀ

usage ('ਯੂਸਿਜ) *n* ਰੀਤੀ, ਪਰਿਪਾਟੀ, ਰਿਵਾਜ, ਰਸਮ, ਦਸਤੂਰ

use ('ਯੂਸ) *n v* ਵਰਤੋਂ ਦੀ ਸ਼ਕਤੀ; ਲਾਭ; ਵਰਤੋਂ ਕਰਨਾ; ਕੰਮ ਵਿੱਚ ਲਿਆਉਣਾ; ਖ਼ਰਚ ਕਰਨਾ ਜਾਂ ਹੋਣਾ; ~ful ਉਪਯੋਗੀ; ਉਪਕਾਰੀ, ਹਿਤਕਾਰੀ, ਲਾਭਦਾਇਕ; ~less ਨਿਰਥਕ, ਵਿਅਰਥ, ਨਿਸਫਲ; ਘਟੀਆ

usher ('ਅੱਸ਼ਅ*) *n v* (ਕਿਸੇ ਮਹਿਮਾਨ ਨੂੰ) ਅੰਦਰ ਲਿਆਉਣਾ

ususal ('ਯੂਯੁਲ) *a* ਪ੍ਰਚਲਤ, ਰਿਵਾਜੀ, ਆਮ; ~ly ਆਮ ਤੌਰ ਤੇ, ਸਧਾਰਨ ਤੌਰ ਤੇ

usurer ('ਯੂਯ(ਅ)ਰਅ*) *n* ਸੂਦਖੋਰ

utensil (ਯੂ'ਟੈਂਨਸਲ) ਬਰਤਨ, ਭਾਂਡਾ

uterus ('ਯੂਟਅਰਅਸ) *n* ਗਰਭ-ਕੋਸ਼, ਗਰਭਾਸ਼ਯ, ਬੱਚੇਦਾਨੀ, ਗਰਭ

utilitraian ('ਯੂਟਿਲਿ'ਟੇਅਰਿਅਨ) *n a* ਉਪਯੋਗਤਾ-ਵਾਦੀ; ਉਪਯੋਗੀ, ਸੁਆਰਥੀ; ~ism ਉਪਯੋਗਤਾਵਾਦ, ਸੁਆਰਥਵਾਦ

utility (ਯੂ'ਟਿਲਅਟਿ) *n* ਉਪਯੋਗ, ਲਾਭ, ਉਪਯੋਗਤਾ

utilization ('ਯੂਟਿਅਲਾਇ'ਜ਼ੇਸ਼ਨ) *n* ਉਪਯੋਗਤਾ

utilize ('ਯੂਟਿਅਲਾਇਜ਼) *v* ਕੰਮ ਵਿੱਚ ਲਿਆਉਣਾ, ਉਪਯੋਗ ਕਰਨਾ

utmost ('ਅੰਟਮਅਉਸਟ) *a* ਅਤੀਅੰਤ, ਅਧਿਕ,

ਬੇਹੱਦ, ਅਤੀ

Utopia (ਯੂ'ਟਅਉਪਯਅ) *n* ਯੂਟੋਪੀਆ ਆਦਰਸ਼-ਚਿੱਤਰ, ਕਾਲਪਨਕ, ਸੁਖ-ਚਿੱਤਰ, ਸ਼ੇਖ਼-ਚਿੱਲੀ ਦਾ ਸੁਪਨਾ; ~n ਕਾਲਪਨਕ, ਮਾਨਸਕ, ਖ਼ਿਆਲੀ, ਅਵਿਹਾਰਕ; ~ly ਸਰਾਸਰ, ਨਿਪਟ, ਨਿਰਾ, ਉੱਕਾ, ਬਿਲਕੁਲ

utter (ਅੱਟਅ*) *v* ਕਹਿਣਾ, ਉਚਾਰਨ, ਕਰਨਾ; ਜਾਰੀ ਕਰਨਾ; ~ance ਉਚਾਰਨ, ਬੋਲ; ਵਾਕ-ਸ਼ਕਤੀ, ਬੋਲੀ

uvula ('ਯੂਵ੍ਯੁਲਅ) *n* ਗਲੇ ਦੀ ਘੰਡੀ, ਕਾਂ, ਕਾਂਉ

uxorious (ਅੱਕ'ਸੋਰਿਅਸ) *a* ਜਨ-ਮੁਰੀਦ, ਜੋਰੂ ਦਾ ਗ਼ੁਲਾਮ

V

V, v (ਵੀ) *n* ਰੋਮਨ ਵਰਨਮਾਲਾ ਦਾ ਬਾਈਵਾਂ ਅੱਖਰ; ਰੋਮਨ ਅੰਕਾਂ ਵਿਚੋਂ ਪੰਜ ਦਾ ਅੰਕ; ਆਕਾਰ; ਵਿਜੇ ਦਾ ਨਿਸ਼ਾਨ

vacancy ('ਵੇਇਕਅੰਸਿ) *n* ਖ਼ਾਲੀ ਥਾਂ; ਖ਼ਾਲੀ ਅਸਾਮੀ; ਖ਼ਲਾਅ, ਫ਼ੁਰਸਤ

vacant ('ਵੇਇਕੰਟ) *a* ਖ਼ਾਲੀ; ਸੁੰਞਾ; ਵਿਹਲਾ

vacate (ਵਅ'ਕੇਇਟ) *v* ਖ਼ਾਲੀ ਕਰਨਾ, ਵਿਹਲਾ ਕਰਨਾ, ਰੱਦ ਕਰਨਾ, ਬੇਕਾਰ ਕਰਨਾ; ਛੱਡਣ ਕਰਨਾ; ~d ਖ਼ਾਲੀ ਕੀਤਾ, ਖ਼ਾਲੀ

vacation (ਵਅ'ਕੇਇਸ਼ਨ) *n* ਵਿਹਲ, ਫ਼ੁਰਸਤ; ਲੰਮੀਆਂ ਛੁੱਟੀਆਂ; ਵਕਫ਼ਾ

vaccary ('ਵੈਕਅਰਿ) *n* ਗਊਸ਼ਾਲਾ

vaccinate ('ਵੈਕਸਿਨੇਇਟ) *v* ਲੋਦਾ ਲਾਉਣਾ, ਟੀਕਾ ਲਾਉਣਾ (ਚੀਚਕ ਦਾ)

vaccine ('ਵੈਕਸੀਨ) *n* ਚੀਚਕ ਦੇ ਟੀਕੇ ਦੀ ਦਵਾਈ, ਵੈਕਸੀਨ

vacillate ('ਵੈਸਇਲੇਇਟ) *v* ਡੋਲਣਾ, ਦੁਚਿੱਤੀ ਵਿਚ ਪੈਣਾ, ਜੱਕੋ-ਤੱਕੀ ਕਰਨਾ

vacillation ('ਵੈਸਅਿ'ਲੇਇਸ਼ਨ) *n* ਜੱਕੋ ਤੱਕੀ, ਦੁਚਿੱਤੀ, ਅਸਥਿਰਤਾ

vacuum ('ਵੈਕਯੁਅਮ) *n* ਖ਼ਲਾਅ, ਸੁੰਨ-ਸਥਾਨ

vagabond ('ਵੈਗਅਬੌਂਡ) *a n v* ਅਵਾਰਾ, ਲੋਫ਼ਰ; ਅਵਾਰਾਗਰਦ, ਲੁੱਚਾ; ਅਵਾਰਾ ਫਿਰਨਾ, ਬਦਮਾਸ਼ੀ ਕਰਨਾ

vagarious (ਵਅ'ਗੇਇਰਿਅਸ) *a* ਵਹਿਮੀ, ਸਨਕੀ, ਮੌਜੀ, ਖ਼ਬਤੀ

vagary ('ਵੇਇਗਅਰਿ) *n* ਤਰੰਗ, ਮੌਜ, ਲਹਿਰ, ਖ਼ਿਆਲ, ਵਹਿਮ

vagina (ਵ਼ਅ'ਜਾਇਨਅ) *n* ਭਗ, ਯੋਨੀ; (ਇਸਤਰੀ ਦਾ) ਗੁਪਤ ਅੰਗ; ਖੋਲ

vagrancy ('ਵੇਇਗਰਅੰਸਿ) *n* ਅਵਾਰਾਗਰਦੀ, ਲਟੌਰਪੁਣਾ

vagrant ('ਵੇਇਗਰਅੰਟ) *a n* ਅਵਾਰਾ, ਭੌਂਦੂ; ਲਟੌਰ, ਖ਼ਾਨਾ-ਬਦੋਸ਼, ਸੈਲਾਨੀ, ਹਰਜਾਈ

vague (ਵੇਇਗ) *a* ਅਸਪਸ਼ਟ, ਧੁੰਦਲਾ ਜਿਹਾ, ਝੰਕੀ; ~ness ਸੰਦੇਹ, ਅਸਪਸ਼ਟਤਾ, ਧੁੰਦਲਾਪਣ

vail (ਵੇਇਲ) *n* (ਪੁ) ਲਾਭ, ਇਨਾਮ, ਬਖ਼ਸ਼ੀਸ਼; ਸਿਰ ਝੁਕਾਉਣਾ; ਲਾਭ ਉਠਾਉਣਾ, ਸਹਾਈ ਹੋਣਾ

vain (ਵੇਇਨ) *a* ਅਭਿਮਾਨੀ, ਘਮੰਡੀ, ਬਿਰਥਾ, ਵਿਅਰਥ, ਨਿਸਫਲ, ਥੋਥਾ; in~ ਬੇਫ਼ਾਇਦਾ, ਫ਼ਜ਼ੂਲ, ਨਿਸਫਲ, ਅਜਾਈਂ

vale (ਵੇਇਲ) *n* (ਕਾਵਿਕ) ਘਾਟੀ, ਵਾਦੀ

valediction ('ਵੈਲਿ'ਡਿਕਸ਼ਨ) *n* ਵਿਦਾ, ਅਲਵਿਦਾ, ਵਿਦਾਇਗੀ, ਰੁਖ਼ਸਤ

valedictory ('ਵੈਲਿ'ਡਿਕਟ(ਅ)ਰਿ) *a n* ਅਲਵਿਦਾਈ; ਵਿਦਾਇਗੀ ਭਾਸ਼ਨ

valiance ('ਵੈਲਯਅੰਸ) *n* ਗੁਰਵੀਰਤਾ, ਪਹਾਦਰੀ, ਦਲੇਰੀ, ਜਵਾਂਮਰਦੀ

valiant ('ਵੈਲਯਅੰਟ) *a* ਸੂਰਵੀਰ, ਜੋਧਾ, ਦਲੇਰ, ਬਹਾਦਰ, ਜਵਾਂਮਰਦ, ਸੂਰਮਾ

valid ('ਵੈਲਿਡ) *a* ਯੋਗ, ਉਚਿਤ, ਜਾਇਜ਼, ਦਰੁਸਤ, ਠੀਕ, ਵਾਜਬ; ~ate ਪੱਕਾ ਕਰਨਾ, ਪ੍ਰਮਾਣਤ ਕਰਨਾ; ~ity ਪ੍ਰਮਾਣਕਤਾ, ਉਚਿਤਤਾ, ਵੈਧਤਾ

valley ('ਵੈਲਿ) *n* ਵਾਦੀ, ਘਾਟੀ, ਦੂਨ

valorous ('ਵੈਲਅਰਅਸ) *a* ਬਹਾਦਰ, ਜਵਾਂਮਰਦ,

ਦਲੇਰ, ਵੀਰ, ਸੂਰਮਾ

valour ('ਵੈਲਅ*) *n* ਬਹਾਦਰੀ, ਜਵਾਂਮਰਦੀ, ਦਲੇਰੀ, ਵੀਰਤਾ, ਵੀਰ-ਰਸ

valuable ('ਵੈਲਯੂਅਬਲ) *a n* ਬਹੁ-ਮੁੱਲਾ, ਕੀਮਤੀ, ਮਾਨਯੋਗ; ਕੀਮਤੀ ਸਾਮਾਨ

valuate ('ਵੈਲਯੂਏਇਟ) *v* ਮੁੱਲਾਂਕਣ ਕਰਨਾ, ਮੁੱਲ ਨਿਸਚਤ ਕਰਨਾ, ਮੁੱਲ ਨਿਰਧਾਰਤ ਕਰਨਾ

valuation ('ਵੈਲਯੂਏਇਸ਼ਨ) *n* ਮੁੱਲ-ਨਿਰਧਾਰਨ, ਮੁੱਲਾਂਕਣ

value ('ਵੈਲਯੂ) *n v* ਲਾਭ, ਗੁਣ, ਮਹੱਤਵ; ਮੁੱਲ, ਕੀਮਤ; ਮਾਲੀਅਤ; ਭਾਵ

vamp (ਵੈਂਪ) *n v* ਜੋੜ, ਗੰਢ-ਤੁੱਪ (ਜੁੜੀ); ਪੰਜਾ ਲਾਉਣਾ; ਗੰਢ-ਤੁੱਪ ਕਰਨਾ; ਤਤਕਾਲੀ ਸੰਗੀਤ ਦੇਣਾ; ~er ਮੋਚੀ; ਗੰਢਣ ਵਾਲਾ; ਫਸਾਉਣ; ਫੁਸਲਾਉਣਾ, ਲੁਭਾਉਣਾ; ~ire ਅਤਿਆਚਾਰੀ, ਲੁਟੇਰਾ, ਠੱਗ

van (ਵੈਨ) *n* (1) ਬੰਦ ਛਕੜਾ, (ਰੇਲ ਵਿਚ) ਮਾਲ ਡੱਬਾ; (2) (ਫੌਜ ਦਾ) ਅਗਲਾ ਹਿੱਸਾ, ਹਰਾਵਲ ਦਸਤਾ, ਆਗੂ; (3) (ਪ੍ਰ) ਖੰਭ, ਪੱਖ; ਬਾਂਹ

vanish ('ਵੈਨਿਸ਼) *n v* ਲੋਪ ਹੋ ਜਾਣਾ, ਓਹਲੇ ਹੋ ਜਾਣਾ, ਲੁਕਣਾ, ਗਾਇਬ ਹੋ ਜਾਣਾ, ਨਸ਼ਟ ਹੋ ਜਾਣਾ

vanity ('ਵੈਨਅਟਿ) *n* ਸਾਰਹੀਨਤਾ, ਵਿਅਰਥਤਾ, ਨਿਰਥਕਤਾ ਦਿਖਾਵਾ, ਫੂੰ ਫਾਂ, ਅਡੰਬਰ; ~case ਸ਼ਿੰਗਾਰਦਾਨੀ

vanquish ('ਵੈਙਕਵਿਸ਼) *v* ਹਰਾਉਣਾ, ਜਿੱਤਣਾ, ਕਾਬੂ ਪਾਉਣਾ

vaporization ('ਵ੍ਹੇਇਪਅਰਾਇ'ਜ਼ੇਇਸ਼ਨ) *n* ਵਾਸ਼ਪੀ-ਕਰਨ, ਭਾਫ਼ ਬਣਨ

vaporize ('ਵ੍ਹੇਇਪਅਰਾਇਜ਼) *v* ਵਾਸ਼ਪ ਵਿਚ ਬਦਲਣਾ, ਭਾਫ਼ ਬਣਨਾ ਜਾਂ ਬਣਾਉਣਾ, ਉਡ ਜਾਣਾ, ਹਵਾਈਪੁਣਾ

vapour ('ਵ੍ਹੇਇਪਅ*) *n* (ਹਵਾ ਵਿਚ) ਵਾਸ਼ਪ, ਭਾਫ਼, ਕੁਹਰਾ, ਧੁੰਆਂ; ਕਾਲਪਨਕ ਵਸਤੂ, ਮਿਥਿਆ ਅਭਿਮਾਨ, ਹੰਕਾਰ; ~y ਵਾਸ਼ਪੀ, ਭਾਫ਼ਦਾਰ, ਕੁਹਰੇਦਾਰ; ਧੁੰਦਲਾ

variability ('ਵ੍ਹੇਅਰਿਅ'ਬਿਲਅਟਿ) *n* ਅਨਿੱਤਤਾ ਅਸਥਿਰਤਾ; ਪਰਿਵਰਤਤਾ, ਹੇਰ-ਫੇਰ

variable ('ਵ੍ਹੇਅਰਿਅਬਲ) *a n* ਪਰਿਵਰਤਨਸ਼ੀਲ, ਅਸਥਿਰ, ਚੰਚਲ, ਬਦਲਣਹਾਰ, ਅਸਥਾਈ; (ਬਨ) ਭਿੰਨ-ਭਿੰਨ

variance ('ਵ੍ਹੇਅਰਿਅੰਸ) *n* ਭੇਦ, ਵਖੇਵਾਂ, ਵਿਭਿੰਨਤਾ, ਅੰਤਰ; ਮੱਤ-ਭੇਦ, ਅਸੰਮਤੀ; ਫੁੱਟ ਭਿੰਨਤਾ

variant ('ਵ੍ਹੇਅਰਿਅੰਟ) *a n* ਵੱਖਰਾ, ਭਿੰਨ, ਪਰਿਵਰਤਨਸ਼ੀਲ

variation ('ਵ੍ਹੇਅਰਿ'ਏਇਸ਼ਨ) *n* ਭੇਦ, ਅੰਤਰ, ਤਬਦੀਲੀ, ਉਤਾਰ-ਚੜ੍ਹਾਉ; (ਵਿਆ) ਰੁਪਾਂਤਰ

varied ('ਵ੍ਹੇਅਰਿਡ) *a* ਵਿਭਿੰਨ, ਵਿਵਿਧ, ਪਰਿਵਰਤਤ

variegated ('ਵ੍ਹੇਅਰਿਗੇਇਟਿਡ) *a* ਰੰਗ-ਬਰੰਗਾ, ਵੰਨ-ਸੁਵੰਨਾ, ਬਹੁਰੰਗਾ, ਚਿਤਕਬਰਾ

variety ('ਵ੍ਹਅ'ਰਾਇਅਟਿ) *n* ਰੰਗਾ-ਰੰਗ, ਬਹੁਰੰਗੀ, ਕਿਸਮ; ਵਚਿੱਤਰ; ਅਨੇਕਤਾ

various ('ਵ੍ਹੇਅਰਿਅਸ) *a* ਅਨੇਕ, ਤਰ੍ਹਾਂ-ਤਰ੍ਹਾਂ ਦਾ, ਨਾਨਾ

varnish ('ਵਾ*ਨਿਸ਼) *n v* ਰੋਗਨ, ਵਾਰਨਿਸ਼, ਬਣਾਉਟੀ ਚਮਕ-ਦਮਕ, ਟੀਪ-ਟਾਪ, ਰੋਗਨ ਕਰਨਾ, ਵਾਰਨਿਸ਼ ਕਰਨੀ

varsity ('ਵਾਸਅਟਿ) *n* (ਬੋਲ) ਵਿਸ਼ਵਵਿਦਿਆਲਾ

vary ('ਵ੍ਹੇਅਰਿ) *v* ਬਦਲਣਾ, ਪਲਟਣਾ, ਘਟਣਾ, ਵਧਣਾ, ਘਟਾਉਣਾ-ਵਧਾਉਣਾ, ਤਬਦੀਲ ਕਰਨਾ;

vascular

ਨਾਨਾ ਰੂਪ ਕਰਨਾ ਜਾਂ ਹੋਣਾ, ਭਿੰਨ-ਭਿੰਨ ਕਰਨਾ ਜਾਂ ਹੋਣਾ, ਰੂਪ ਬਦਲਣਾ

vascular ('ਵੂਸਕਯੂਲਅ*) *a* ਖ਼ੂਨ ਵਗਣ ਵਾਲੀ (ਨਾਲੀ), ਵਾਹਿਕਾ ਸਬੰਧੀ, ਨਾੜੀ ਸਬੰਧੀ

vase (ਵਾਜ਼) *n* ਫੁੱਲਦਾਨ, ਗੁਲਦਾਨ, ਸਜਾਵਟੀ ਗਲਾਸ

vasectomy (ਵਅ'ਸੈਂਕਟਅਮਿ) *n* (ਮਰਦਾਂ ਸਬੰਧੀ) ਨਲਬੰਦੀ

vast (ਵਾਸਟ) *a n* ਵਿਸ਼ਾਲ, ਅਪਾਰ, ਬਹੁਤ ਵੱਡਾ, ਭਾਰੀ; ਖੁੱਲ੍ਹੀ ਥਾਂ; **~ness** ਵਿਸ਼ਾਲਤਾ, ਅਪਾਰਤਾ, ਲਬਾਈ-ਚੜ੍ਹਾਈ

vault (ਵੋਲਟ) *n v* (1) ਕਮਾਨੀਦਾਰ ਛੱਤ; ਗੁੰਬਜ਼; ਤਹਿਖਾਨਾ, ਗੁਦਾਮ (ਸ਼ਰਾਬ ਆਦਿ ਲਈ), ਡਾਟਦਾਰ ਬਣਾਉਣਾ; ਤਹਿਖਾਨਾ ਬਣਾਉਣਾ; (2) ਛਾਲ, ਪਲਾਂਘਣਾ, ਉਛਾਲ, ਉੱਛਲ-ਕੁੰਦ; ਛਾਲ ਮਾਰਨਾ, ਉਛਲਣਾ ਜਾਂ ਉਛਾਲਣਾ

vaunt (ਵੋਂਟ) *v n* ਘਮੰਡ ਕਰਨਾ; ਡੀਂਗ, ਸ਼ੇਖੀ, ਹੰਕਾਰ, ਫੜ

veer (ਵਿਅ*) *v* ਦਿਸ਼ਾ ਬਦਲਣਾ, ਘੁੰਮਣਾ, ਘੁਮਾਉਣਾ, ਮੁੜਨਾ, ਰੁਖ ਫੇਰਨਾ, ਪਾਸਾ ਪਰਤਾਉਣਾ; ਦਿਮਾਗ਼ ਫਿਰਨਾ ਜਾਂ ਫੇਰਨਾ; (ਨੇਵੀ) ਢਿੱਲਾ ਕਰਨਾ, ਛੱਡਣਾ

vegetable ('ਵੈਜੱਟਅਬਲ) *n a* ਸਾਗ-ਭਾਜੀ, ਸਬਜ਼ੀ ਤਰਕਾਰੀ; ਸਾਗ-ਭਾਜੀ ਦਾ, ਤਰਕਾਰੀ ਦਾ

vegetarian ('ਵੈਜਿ'ਟੇਅਰਿਅਨ) *n* ਵੈਸ਼ਨੂ, ਸ਼ਾਕਾਹਾਰੀ

vegetate ('ਵੈਜਿਟੇਇਟ) *v* (ਪੌਦਿਆਂ ਦਾ) ਉੱਗਣਾ, ਲੱਗਣਾ, ਵਧਣਾ; (ਬੋਲ) ਪਏ-ਪਏ ਜੀਵਨ ਬਿਤਾਉਣਾ

vehemence ('ਵੀਅਮੰਸ) *n* ਜੋਸ਼, ਜ਼ੋਰ, ਵੇਗ, ਤੀਬਰਤਾ, ਪ੍ਰਚੰਡਤਾ

vehement ('ਵੀਅਮੰਟ) *a* (ਭਾਵਨਾ, ਵਿਚਾਰ) ਜੋਸ਼ੀਲੀ, ਧੜੱਲੇਦਾਰ, ਜ਼ੋਰਦਾਰ, ਉਤਸ਼ਾਹੀ; ਤੀਬਰ, ਤੇਜ਼, ਪ੍ਰਬਲ (ਹਵਾ ਆਦਿ)

vehicle ('ਵਿਅਕਲ) *n* ਸਵਾਰੀ, ਵਾਹਨ, ਰੱਥ, ਗੱਡੀ; ਮਾਧਿਅਮ

vehicular (ਵਿ'ਹਿਕਯੂਲਅ*) *a* ਸਵਾਰੀ ਦਾ; ਮਾਧਿਅਮ ਰੂਪ

veil (ਵੇਇਲ) *n v* ਘੁੰਡ, ਪੱਲਾ, ਪਰਦਾ, ਬੁਰਕਾ, ਨਕਾਬ, ਦੁਪੱਟਾ; ਗ਼ਿਲਾਫ਼; ਓਟ, ਆੜ, ਉਹਲਾ, ਬਹਾਨਾ; ਘੁੰਡ ਕੱਢਣਾ, ਕੱਜਣਾ, ਲੁਕਾਉਣਾ

vein (ਵੇਇਨ) *n* ਸ਼ਿਰਾ; (ਆਮ ਵਰਤੋਂ ਵਿਚ) ਨਾੜੀ, ਰਗ, ਲਹਿਰ, ਮੌਜ

velocity (ਵਿ'ਲੋਸਅਟਿ) *n* ਵੇਗ, ਰਫ਼ਤਾਰ, ਜ਼ੋਰ ਦੀ ਚਾਲ

velvet ('ਵੈੱਲਵਿਟ) *n a* ਮਖਮਲ, ਪੱਲਛ; ਮਖ਼ਮਲੀ, ਕੋਮਲ, ਗੁਦਗੁਦਾ

vend (ਵੈੱਡ) *v* ਵੇਚਣਾ, ਵਿਕਰੀ ਕਰਨਾ; **~ee** ਖ਼ਰੀਦਾਰ; **~or** ਵੇਚਣ ਵਾਲਾ, ਫੇਰੀ ਵਾਲਾ, ਛਾਬੜੀ ਵਾਲਾ

vendetta (ਵੈੱਨ'ਡੈੱਟਅ) *n* ਜੱਦੀ ਵੈਰ, ਵੈਰ

venerability ('ਵੈੱਨ(ਅ)ਰਅ'ਬਿਲਅਟਿ) *n* ਸ਼ਰਧਾ, ਆਦਾਰ, ਸਤਿਕਾਰਯੋਗਤਾ

venerable ('ਵੈੱਨ(ਅ)ਰਅਬਲ) *a* ਆਦਰਯੋਗ, ਸਤਿਕਾਰਯੋਗ, ਪੂਜਨੀਕ; **~ness** ਸਤਿਕਾਰਯੋਗਤਾ

venerate ('ਵੈੱਨਅਰੇਇਟ) *v* ਸਤਿਕਾਰਨਾ, ਮਾਨਤਾ ਕਰਨੀ, ਪੂਜਾ ਕਰਨੀ, ਆਦਰ ਕਰਨਾ, ਸਨਮਾਨ ਕਰਨਾ, ਪੂਜਣਾ

veneration ('ਵੈੱਨਅਰੇਇਸ਼ਨ) *n* ਆਦਰ, ਮਾਨ, ਪੂਜਾ, ਭਗਤੀ

venereal (ਵੁਅ'ਨਿਅਰਿਅਲ) *a* ਜਿਨਸੀ; ਲਿੰਗ-

ਰੋਗ ਸਬੰਧੀ, ਗੁਪਤ ਰੋਗ ਸਬੰਧੀ

venery ('ਵੈਨੰਅਰਿ) *n* (ਪ੍ਰ) ਸ਼ਿਕਾਰ; ਵਿਸ਼ੇ-ਭੋਗ, ਕਾਮ-ਭੋਗ

vengeance ('ਵੈਨੰਜਅੰਸ) *n* ਬਦਲਾ, ਵੈਰ

venom ('ਵੈਨੰਅਮ) *n* ਜ਼ਹਿਰ, ਵਿਹੁ, ਵਿਸ; (ਬੋਲ) ਵੈਰ, ਈਰਖਾ; ~**ous** ਜ਼ਹਿਰੀ, ਵਿਹੁਲਾ, ਵਿਸ਼ੈਲਾ, ਜ਼ਹਿਰੀਲਾ

vent (ਵੈਂਟ) *n v* ਵਿਰਲ, ਮੋਰੀ, ਸੁਰਾਖ਼, ਸੇਘਾ; (ਬੋਲ) ਨਿਕਾਸ; ਮੋਰੀ ਕਰਨੀ; ~**age** ਸੁਰਾਖ਼, ਮੋਰੀ, ਗਾਲੀ, ਝੋਕ, ਛਿਦਰ

ventilate ('ਵੈਂਟਿਲੇਇਟ) *v* ਹਵਾ ਨਾਲ ਸ਼ੁੱਧ ਕਰਨਾ, ਹਵਾਦਾਰ ਕਰਨਾ, ਪਰਗਟ ਕਰਨਾ, ਹਵਾਤੁ ਕੱਢਣਾ

ventilation ('ਵੈਂਟਿ'ਲੇਇਸ਼ਨ) *n* ਹਵਾ ਦੀ ਆਵਾਜਾਈ, ਹਵਾਦਾਰੀ

ventilator ('ਵੈਂਨਟਿਲੇਇਟਅ*) *n* ਰੋਸ਼ਨਦਾਨ, ਵਾਯੂਮਾਰਗ, ਪੱਖਾ

venture ('ਵੈਨੰਚਅ*) *n v* ਖ਼ਤਰੇ ਵਾਲਾ ਕੰਮ, ਔਖਾ ਕੰਮ, ਖ਼ਤਰਾ, ਸੰਕਟ; ਹਿੰਮਤ ਕਰਨਾ, ਖ਼ਤਰੇ ਵਿਚ ਪੈਣਾ; ਬਾਜ਼ੀ ਲਾਉਣੀ

venue ('ਵੈਨੰਯੂ) *n* (ਕਾ) ਸੋਕਾ, ਘਟਨਾ ਸਥਾਨ, ਸੰਮੇਲਨ ਸਥਾਨ

Venus ('ਵੀਨਅਸ) *n* ਹੁਸਨ-ਇਸ਼ਕ ਦੀ ਦੇਵੀ; ਸੁੰਦਰੀ, ਰੂਪਵਤੀ, ਹੁਸੀਨਾ; ਸ਼ੁਕੱਰ (ਤਾਰਾ)

veracious (ਵ੍ਅ'ਰੇਇਸ਼ਅਸ) *a* ਸੱਚਾ, ਈਮਾਨਦਾਰ, ਸਤਿਵਾਦੀ

veracity (ਵ੍ਅ'ਰੈਸਅਟਿ) *n* ਸਚਾਈ, ਯਥਾਰਥਕਤਾ

veranda(h) (ਵ੍ਅ'ਰੈਂਡਅ) *n* ਵਰਾਂਡਾ, ਪਸਾਰ

verb (ਵ੍ਅ:ਬ) *n* ਕਿਰਿਆ (ਵਿਆ); ~**al** ਕਿਰਿਆਵੀ, ਅੱਖਰੀ, ਸ਼ਾਬਦਕ ਜ਼ਬਾਨੀ (ਸਨੇਹਾ); ਸ਼ਾਬਦਕ; ~**ally** ਲਫ਼ਜ਼-ਬਲਫ਼ਜ਼ ਸ਼ਬਦ-ਸ਼ਬਦ; ਜ਼ਬਾਨੀ; ~**atim** ਅੱਖਰ-ਅੱਖਰ, ਸ਼ਾਬਦਕ; ~**ose** ਸ਼ਬਦ-ਬਹੁਤਲਤਾ, ਸ਼ਬਦ-ਅਧਿਕਤਾ; ~**osity** ਸ਼ਬਦ-ਅਡੰਬਰ

verdict ('ਵ੍ਅ:ਡਿਕਟ) *n* ਅਦਾਲਤੀ ਫ਼ੈਸਲਾ, ਫ਼ਤਵਾ, ਅੰਤਮ ਨਿਰਣਾ

verecund ('ਵੈਰਿਕਅੰਡ) *a* ਸ਼ਰਮਾਕਲ, ਸ਼ਰਮੀਲਾ ਲੱਜਾਵਾਨ

verge (ਵ੍ਅ:ਜ) *n v* ਕੰਢਾ; ਸਿਰਾ ਝੁਕਣਾ, ਢਲਣਾ (ਕਿਸੇ ਸਿਰੇ ਵੱਲ)

verification ('ਵੈਰਿਫ਼ਿ'ਕੇਇਸ਼ਨ) *n* ਜਾਂਚ, ਪੜਤਾਲ, ਤਸਦੀਕ

verify ('ਵੈਰਿਫ਼ਾਇ) *v* ਨਿਤਾਰਾ ਕਰਨਾ, ਪੜਤਾਲ ਕਰਨੀ, ਸਚਾਈ ਦੀ ਛਾਣਬੀਨ ਕਰਨੀ; ਯਥਾਰਥ ਖੋਜਣਾ; ਮਿਲਾਉਣਾ, ਤਸਦੀਕ ਕਰਨਾ, ਸਹੀ ਕਰਨਾ

verily ('ਵੈਰਅਲਿ) *a* ਦਰਅਸਲ, ਸੱਚਮੁੱਚ, ਅਸਲ ਵਿਚ, ਵਾਸਤਵ ਵਿਚ, ਨਿਸਚੇ ਹੀ, ਅਵੱਸ਼

vermilion (ਵ੍ਅ'ਮਿਲਯਅਨ) *n a v* ਸੰਧੂਰ, ਲਾਲ ਰੰਗ; ਸ਼ਿੰਗਰਫ਼ੀ, ਸੰਧੂਰੀ; ਸੰਧੂਰ ਲਾਉਣਾ

versatile ('ਵ੍ਅ:ਸਅਟਾਇਲ) *a* (ਲੇਖਕ) ਬਹੁਮੁਖੀ, ਬਹੁਪੱਖੀ ਪ੍ਰਤਿਭਾਸ਼ਾਲੀ, ਛੇਤੀ ਹੀ ਪਰਿਵਰਤਨਸ਼ੀਲ; ~**ness, versatility** ਬਹੁਮੁਖੀ, ਪ੍ਰਤਿਭਾ, ਚਪਲਤਾ, ਅਸਥਿਰਤਾ

verse (ਵ੍ਅ:ਸ) *n* ਸਲੋਕ ਕਵਿਤਾ; ਕਵਿਤਾਉਣਾ, ਪਦਬੱਧ ਕਰਨਾ, ਕਵਿਤਾ ਕਰਨਾ

versification ('ਵ੍ਅ:ਸਿਫ਼ਿ'ਕੇਇਸ਼ਨ) *n* ਕਾਵਿ-ਰਚਨਾ, ਕਾਵਿ-ਸਿਰਜਨਾ

versifier ('ਵ੍ਅ:ਸਿਫ਼ਾਇਅ*) *n* ਕਵੀ, ਸ਼ਾਇਰ

versify ('ਵ੍ਅ:ਸਿਫ਼ਾਇ) *v* ਨਜ਼ਮਾਉਣਾ, ਛੰਦਬੱਧ ਕਰਨਾ, ਕਵਿਤਾ ਰਚਣੀ, ਤੁਕਬੰਦੀ ਕਰਨੀ

version ('ਵ੍ਯਅ:ਸ਼ਨ) *n* ਪਾਠਾਂਤਰ, ਤਰਜਮਾ, ਭਾਸ਼ਾਂਤਰ, ਅਨੁਵਾਦ, ਉਲਥਾ; ਸੰਸਕਰਨ

versus ('ਵ੍ਯਅ:ਸਾਸ) *prep* ਟਾਕਰੇ ਉੱਤੇ, ਪ੍ਰਤੀ, ਬਨਾਮ

vertex ('ਵ੍ਯਅ:ਟੈੱਕਸ) *n* ਟੀਸੀ, ਸਿਰ, ਸਿਖਰ, ਚੋਟੀ

vertical ('ਵ੍ਯਅ:ਟਿਕਲ) *n a* ਸਿੱਧੀ (ਰੇਖਾ) ਸਿਖਰਲਾ, ਚੋਟੀ ਦਾ, ਖੜ੍ਹਾ; **~ly** ਖੜ੍ਹਵੇਂ ਪਾਸੇ, ਖੜ੍ਹੋਤੇ ਢੰਗ ਨਾਲ

vertigo ('ਵ੍ਯਅ:ਟਿਗਅਉ) *n* ਘੇਰਨੀ, ਘੁਮਾਟੀ, ਭੁਆਂਟਨੀ, ਭੌਂ, ਚੱਕਰ

very ('ਵੇਰਿ) *a adv* ਅਤੀਅੰਤ, ਅਧਿਕ, ਬਹੁਤ, ਬਹੁਤ ਹੀ, ਅਸਲੀ, ਖ਼ਰਾ, ਠੀਕ, ਸਹੀ, ਸੱਚਾ, ਵਾਸਤਵਿਕ; ਸੰਪੂਰਨ ਰੂਪ ਵਿਚ

vesicotomy ('ਵੈੱਸਿ'ਕੌਟਅਮਿ) *n* ਨਸਬੰਦੀ, ਮਸਾਨੇ ਦਾ ਉਪਰੇਸ਼ਨ

vessel ('ਵੈੱਸਲ) *n* ਭਾਂਡਾ, ਪਾਤਰ, ਬਰਤਨ; ਬੇੜੀ; ਕਿਸ਼ਤੀ, ਜਹਾਜ਼; ਨਾੜ, ਵਾਹਿਨੀ; *weaker~* ਅਬਲਾ ਔਰਤ, ਨਾਰੀ

vest (ਵੈੱਸਟ) *n v* ਅੰਗੀ, ਚੋਲੀ, ਬੰਡੀ, ਬੁਨੈਨ; ਸੁਪਰਦ ਕਰਨਾ, ਹਵਾਲੇ ਕਰਨਾ; ਕੱਪੜੇ ਪਾਉਣੇ ਜਾਂ ਪੁਆਉਣੇ; **~in** ਅਧਿਕਾਰ ਵਿਚ ਦੇਣਾ, ਕਬਜ਼ੇ ਵਿਚ ਦੇਣਾ, ਸੌਂਪਣਾ; **~ed** ਸਹਿਤ, ਨਿਹਿਤ; **~ing** ਬੁਨੈਨ, ਕਮੀਜ਼ ਤੋਂ ਹੇਠਾਂ ਪਹਿਨਣ ਵਾਲਾ ਵਸਤਰ

veteran ('ਵੈੱਟ(ਅ)ਰ(ਅ)ਨ) *v a* ਅਨੁਭਵੀ, ਨਿਪੁੰਨ ਤੇ ਕੁਸ਼ਲ ਮਨੁੱਖ; ਸਾਬਕਾ ਫ਼ੌਜੀ, ਪੁਰਾਣਾ ਖੁੰਢ; ਤਜਰਬਾਕਾਰ, ਨਿਪੁੰਨ, ਕੁਸ਼ਲ

veterinary ('ਵੈੱਟ(ਅ)ਰਿਨ(ਅ)ਰਿ) *a n* ਪਸ਼ੂ ਚਿਕਿਤਸਕ

veto ('ਵੀਟਅਉ) *n v* ਰੱਦ ਕਰਨ ਦੀ ਕਿਰਿਆ, ਅਸਵੀਕ੍ਰਿਤੀ ਨਿਖੇਪੀ, ਰੋਕ, ਵੀਟੋ; ਨਿਖੇਪੀ-ਪੱਤਰ; ਨਿਖੇਪੀ ਕਰਨੀ, ਨਾਮਨਜ਼ੂਰ ਕਰਨੀ

vex (ਵੈੱਕਸ) *v* ਛੇੜਨਾ, ਤੰਗ ਕਰਨਾ, ਜਿੱਚ ਕਰਨਾ, ਔਖਾ ਕਰਨਾ; **~ation** ਪਰੇਸ਼ਾਨੀ, ਚਿੜ੍ਹ, ਤੰਗੀ, ਖਿਝ, ਕਲੇਸ਼

via ('ਵਾਇਅ) *a prep* ਰਾਹੀਂ, ਦੁਆਰਾ, ਬਰਸਤਾ

viable ('ਵਾਇਅਬਲ) *a* ਜੀਊਣਯੋਗ; ਵਿਹਾਰਕ

viability ('ਵਾਇਅ'ਬਿਲਅਟਿ) *n* ਜੀਊਣਯੋਗਤਾ, ਜੀਵਨ-ਸਮਰੱਥਾ, ਵਿਹਾਰਕਤਾ

via media ('ਵਾਇਅ'ਮੀਡਿਅ) *n* ਵਿਚਕਾਰਲਾ ਰਾਹ, ਮਧ ਮਾਰਗ

viaticum (ਵਾਇ'ਐਟਿਕਅਮ) *n* ਸਫ਼ਰ-ਖਰਚ, ਭੱਤਾ, ਸਫ਼ਰ-ਭੱਤਾ

vibrate (ਵਾਇ'ਬਰੇਇਟ) *v* ਕੰਬਣਾ, ਥੱਰਾਉਣਾ, ਥਰਕਣਾ; ਹਿੱਲਣਾ, ਡੋਲਣਾ, ਲਹਿਰਾਉਣਾ, ਪੈਂਡੂਲਮ ਦਾ ਹਿੱਲਣਾ, ਟਿਕ-ਟਿਕ ਕਰਨਾ

vibration (ਵਾਇ'ਬਰੇਇਸ਼ਨ) *n* ਕਾਂਬਾ, ਥੱਰਾਹਟ, ਥਰਕ, ਲਰਜ਼

vice (ਵਾਇਸ) *n v perp* ਦੁਰਾਚਾਰ, ਭ੍ਰਿਸ਼ਟਤਾ; ਕਲੰਕ, ਦਾਗ਼, ਔਗੁਣ; ਬਦੀ, ਐਬ, ਖ਼ਰਾਬੀ; ਵਿਕਾਰ; ਸ਼ਿਕੰਜੇ ਵਿਚ ਕੱਸਣਾ; ਬਦਲੇ ਵਿਚ; ਉਪ (ਜਿਵੇਂ vice chairman, vice principle ਆਦਿ)

vice versa ('ਵਾਇਸਿ'ਵ੍ਯਅ:ਸਅ) *adv* ਦੂਜੇ ਪਾਸੇ, ਦੂਜੀ ਤਰ੍ਹਾਂ, ਵਿਪਰੀਤ ਤੌਰ ਤੇ, ਇਸ ਦੇ ਉਲਟ

vicinity (ਵਿ'ਸਿਨਅਟਿ) *n* ਨੇੜਤਾ, ਨਜ਼ਦੀਕੀ, ਗੁਆਂਢ, ਪੜੋਸ, ਇਰਦ-ਗਿਰਦ ਦਾ ਇਲਾਕਾ

viciosity, viciousness ('ਵਿਸਿ'ਔਸਅਟਿ, 'ਵਿਸ਼ਿਸਨਿਸ) *n* ਪਾਪ, ਨੀਚਤਾ, ਦੁਸ਼ਟਤਾ, ਬੁਰਾਈ, ਕੁਕਰਮ, ਬਦਕਾਰੀ

vicious ('ਵਿਸ਼ਅਸ) *a* ਪਾਪੀ, ਨੀਚ, ਦੁਸ਼ਟ, ਬੁਰਾ, ਦੁਰਆਤਮਾ, ਦੁਰਾਚਾਰੀ, ਬਦਕਾਰ, ਐਬੀ, ਖੋਟਾ; ਥੋਥੀ; ਚਿੜਚਿੜਾ, ਦਵੈਸ਼ ਭਰਿਆ

victim ('ਵਿਕਟਿਮ) *n* ਬਲੀ, ਭੇਟ, ਸ਼ਿਕਾਰ, ਬਲੀ ਦਾ ਬੱਕਰਾ; **~ization** ਬਲੀਦਾਨ ਅਤਿਆਚਾਰ, ਦੰਡ; **~ize** ਸ਼ਿਕਾਰ ਬਣਾਉਣਾ, ਬਲੀ ਦਾ ਬੱਕਰਾ ਬਣਾਉਣਾ

victor ('ਵਿਕਟਅ*) *n* ਜੇਤੂ, ਵਿਜਈ; **~ious** ਵਿਜੇਤਾ, ਫ਼ਤਿਹ ਕਰਨ ਵਾਲਾ; **~y** ਜਿੱਤ, ਵਿਜੇ, ਫ਼ਤਿਹ

vide ('ਵਾਇਡੀ) *v imp* ਹਵਾਲਾ ਦੇਣ ਲਈ ਆਖਣਾ ਜਾਂ ਲਿਖਣਾ, ਸੰਕੇਤ ਵਜੋਂ (ਵੇਖੋ)

viduity (ਵਿ'ਡਯੂਅਟਿ) *n* ਵਿਧਵਾਪਨ, ਰੰਡੇਪਾ

vie (ਵਾਇ) *v* ਬੁਰਦ ਲਾਉਣੀ, ਵਾਰੀ ਲੈਣੀ, ਬਿਦਣਾ, ਮੁਕਾਬਲਾ ਕਰਨਾ, ਬਰਾਬਰੀ ਕਰਨੀ, ਰੀਸ ਕਰਨੀ

view (ਵ੍ਯੂ) *n v* ਨਿਰੀਖਣ, ਅਵਲੋਕਣ; (ਕਾ) ਮੁਆਇਨਾ; ਦ੍ਰਿਸ਼ਟਿ-ਦਿੱਖ, ਸਮੀਖਿਆ ਕਰਨੀ, ਪਰਖਣਾ; **~point** ਦ੍ਰਿਸ਼ਟੀ ਬਿੰਦੂ, ਨੁਕਤਾ-ਨਿਗਾਹ, ਦ੍ਰਿਸ਼ਟੀਕੋਣ; *in ~ of* ਇਹ ਦੇਖਦੇ ਹੋਏ, ਇਸ ਖ਼ਿਆਲ ਨਾਲ

vigil ('ਵਿਜਿਲ) *n* ਜਾਗਰਤੀ, ਚੌਕਸੀ; ਸਜਗਤਾ; **~ance** ਸਾਵਧਾਨੀ, ਚੌਕਸੀ, ਹੁਸ਼ਿਆਰੀ, ਖ਼ਬਰਦਾਰੀ; **~ant** ਸਾਵਧਾਨ, ਹੁਸ਼ਿਆਰ, ਚੌਕਸ

vigorous ('ਵਿਗਅਰਅਸ) *a* ਜ਼ੋਰਦਾਰ, ਪਰਫੁੱਲੇਦਾਰ, ਪ੍ਰਬਲ, ਸ਼ਕਤੀਵਾਨ, ਤੀਖਣ; **~ness** ਸ਼ਕਤੀ, ਬਲ, ਜ਼ੋਰ-ਪਰਫੁੱਲੇਦਾਰੀ, ਪ੍ਰਬਲਤਾ

vigour, vigor ('ਵਿਗਅ*) *n* ਬਲ, ਸ਼ਕਤੀ, ਜ਼ੋਰ; ਸਜੀਵਤਾ, ਜੀਵਨ ਸ਼ਕਤੀ; ਮਾਨਸਕ ਸ਼ਕਤੀ

vile (ਵਾਇਲ) *a* (ਪ੍ਰ) ਬੇਕਾਰ, ਨਿਕੰਮਾ; ਨੀਚ, ਕਮੀਨਾ, ਘਟੀਆ; ਦੁਸ਼ਟ, ਪਾਜੀ

vilification ('ਵਿਲਿਫ਼ਿ'ਕੇਇਸ਼ਨ) *n* ਭੰਡੀ, ਨਿੰਦਾ ਬਦਨਾਮੀ, ਬੁਰਾਈ

vilify ('ਵਿਲਿਫ਼ਾਇ) *v* ਭੰਡਣਾ, ਬਦਨਾਮੀ ਕਰਨੀ, ਨਿੰਦਣਾ, ਬੁਰਾ ਭਲਾ ਆਖਣਾ

villa ('ਵਿਲਅ) *n* ਪਿੰਡ ਦਾ ਬੰਗਲਾ ਜਾਂ ਹਵੇਲੀ, ਗ੍ਰਾਮ-ਨਿਵਾਸ

village ('ਵਿਲੀਜ) *n* ਪਿੰਡ, ਗਿਰਾਂ, ਦੇਹਾਤ; **~r** ਪੇਂਡੂ ਗਿਰਾਈਂ, ਦੇਹਾਤੀ

villain ('ਵਿਲਅਨ) *n a* ਦੁਸ਼ਟ, ਦੁਰਜਨ; ਸ਼ੈਤਾਨ, ਲੁੱਚਾ; ਗੰਵਾਰ

vim (ਵਿਮ) *n* ਜਾਨ, ਸ਼ਕਤੀ, ਬਲ, ਉਤਸਾਹ

vincible ('ਵਿੰਸਅਬਲ) *a* ਜਿੱਤਣਯੋਗ, ਸਰ ਕਰਨਯੋਗ

vindicate ('ਵਿੰਡਿਕੇਇਟ) *v* ਖੋਰੀ, ਖੁਨਸੀ; ਬਦਲੇ ਭਰਿਆ

vindictive ('ਵਿੰ'ਡਿਕਟਿਵ) *a* ਖੋਰੀ, ਖੁਨਸੀ; ਬਦਲੇ ਭਰਿਆ

vine (ਵਾਇਨ) *n* ਅੰਗੂਰ ਦੀ ਵੇਲ; **~yard** ਅੰਗੂਰਾਂ ਦਾ ਬਾਗ਼; **~ry** ਅੰਗੂਰ-ਖੇਤਰ ਅੰਗੂਰਸਤਾਨ

vinegar ('ਵਿਨਿਗਾਅ*) *n* ਸਿਰਕਾ; ਖਟਾਸ; ਸਿਰਕਾ ਮਿਲਾਉਣਾ

vintage ('ਵਿੰਟਿਜ) *n* ਦਾਖ, ਅੰਗੂਰ; ਅੰਗੂਰਾਂ ਦਾ ਝਾੜ; ਵਧੀਆ, ਉੱਤਮ

violate ('ਵਾਇਅਲੇਇਟ) *v* ਉਲੰਘਣਾ ਕਰਨੀ; ਭ੍ਰਿਸ਼ਟ ਕਰਨਾ, ਦੁਰਵਿਹਾਰ ਕਰਨਾ; ਵਿਘਨ ਪਾਉਣਾ; ਜ਼ਬਰਦਸਤੀ ਕਰਨੀ, ਸਤੀਤਵ ਭੰਗ ਕਰਨਾ

violation ('ਵਾਇਅ'ਲੇਇਸ਼ਨ) *n* ਉਲੰਘਣਾ, ਖੰਡਨ; ਦੂਸ਼ਨ; ਜ਼ਬਰਦਸਤੀ; ਸਤ ਭੰਗ

violence ('ਵਾਇਅਲਅੰਸ) *n* ਹਿੰਸਾ, ਤਸ਼ੱਦਦ,

ਉਪੰਦਰ, ਢਾਢਾਪਣ, ਪ੍ਰਚੰਡਤਾ; ਜ਼ਬਰਦਸਤੀ

violent ('ਵਾਇਅਲਅੰਟ) *a* ਹਿੰਸਕ ਹਿੰਸਾਤਮਕ, ਹਿੰਸਾਪੂਰਨ ਜ਼ਬਰਦਸਤੀ ਵਾਲਾ; ਪ੍ਰਚੰਡ

violet ('ਵਾਇਅਲਅਟ) *n a* ਬਨਫ਼ਸ਼ਾ, ਜਾਮਨੀ ਰੰਗ, ਵੈਂਗਣੀ ਰੰਗ; •ਵੈਂਗਣੀ, ਜਾਮਨੀ

violin ('ਵਾਇਅ'ਲਿਨ) *n* ਸਾਰੰਗੀ, ਵੀਨਾ, ਛੇਤਾਰਾ

virago (ਵਿ'ਰਾਗਊ) *n* ਚੰਡੀ, ਵੀਰਾਂਗਣਾਂ, ਮਰਦਾਵੀਂ ਔਰਤ

viral ('ਵਾਇਅਰ(ਅ)ਲ) *a* ਵਿਹੁਲਾ, ਜ਼ਹਿਰੀਲਾ, ਵਿਸ਼ੈਲਾ

virgin ('ਵ:ਜਿਨ) *n a* ਕੰਨਿਆ, ਕੰਜਕ ਕੁਆਰੀ, ਕੁਮਾਰੀ, ਪਵਿੱਤਰ, ਬੇਦਾਗ਼; **~hood, ~ity** ਸ਼ੁਧੱਤਾ, ਪਵਿੱਤਰਤਾ, ਕੁਆਰਾਪਣ

Virgo ('ਵ:ਗਾਊ) *n* ਕੰਨਿਆ ਰਾਸ਼ੀ

virile ('ਵਿਰਾਇਲ) *a* ਮਰਦਾਵਾਂ, ਨਰ, ਰਿਸ਼ਟ-ਪੁਸ਼ਟ, ਤਕੜਾ, ਬਲਵਾਨ

virility (ਵਿ'ਰਿਲਅਟਿ) *n* ਵੀਰਜ, ਮਰਦਾਊਪੁਣਾ, ਮਰਦਾਨਗੀ; ਨਰਤਵ, ਪਰਸ਼ਾਰਥ

virose ('ਵਾਇਰਅਊਸ) *a* ਵਿਹੁਲਾ, ਵਿਸ਼ੈਲਾ, ਜ਼ਹਿਰੀਲੀ; ਬਦਬੂਦਾਰ

virous ('ਵਾਇਰਅਸ) *a* ਵਿਹੁਲਾ, ਵਿਸ਼ੈਲਾ, ਜ਼ਹਿਰੀਲਾ

virtual ('ਵ:ਚੁਅਲ) *a* ਅਮਲੀ, ਅਸਲੀ, ਸੱਚੀ-ਮੁੱਚੀ

virtue ('ਵ:ਚੁ) *n* ਸਦਾਚਾਰ, ਨੈਤਿਕਤਾ, ਉੱਤਮਤਾ, ਨੇਕੀ, ਭਲਾਈ; *by (in) ~ of* ਨਾਲ, ਦੇ ਜ਼ੋਰ ਨਾਲ; ਦੇ ਸਦਕੇ, ਦੀ ਬਦੌਲਤ, ਦੇ ਕਾਰਨ

virtuous ('ਵ:ਚੁਅਸ) *a* ਸਦਾਚਾਰੀ, ਧਰਮਾਤਮਾ, ਨੇਕ ਪਵਿੱਤਰ; **~ness** ਸਦਾਚਾਰ, ਸੰਜਤਾ, ਧਾਰਮਕਤਾ, ਨੇਕੀ ਭਲਾਈ, ਚੰਗਿਆਈ

virus ('ਵਾਇਅਰਸ) *n* ਜ਼ਹਿਰੀਲਾ ਮਾਦਾ, ਵਿਹੁ, ਵਾਇਰਸ; ਮਲੀਨਤਾ; ਕੁਰੱਤਣ, ਕੜਵਾਹਟ

vis (ਵਿਸ) *n* ਤਾਣ, ਬਲ, ਜ਼ੋਰ, ਸ਼ਕਤੀ

visa ('ਵੀਜ਼ਅ) *n* ਰਾਹਦਾਰੀ, ਵੀਜ਼ਾ

vis-a-vis ('ਵੀਜ਼ਾ'ਵੀ) *n a adv* ਆਮੂਣੇ-ਸਾਮੂਣੇ ਬੈਠੇ ਵਿਅਕਤੀ, ਸਨਮੁਖ, ਆਮੂਣੇ-ਸਾਮੂਣੇ; ਵਿਸ਼ੇ ਵਿਚ, ਸਬੰਧ ਵਿਚ, ਮੁਕਾਬਲੇ

viscid ('ਵਿਸਿਡ) *a* ਲੇਸਦਾਰ, ਚਿਪਚਿਪਾ, ਲਿਸਲਿਸਾ, ਲੁਆਬਦਾਰ; **~ity** ਚਿਪਚਿਪਾਹਟ

viscose ('ਵਿਸਕਅਊਸ) *n a* ਮਾਵਾ, ਕਲਫ਼, ਮਾਇਆ; ਲੇਸਦਾਰ, ਚਿਪਚਿਪਾ

viscosity (ਵਿ'ਸਕੌਸਅਟਿ) *n* ਲੇਸ, ਲੁਆਬ, ਚਿਪਚਿਪਾਪਣ

visibility ('ਵਿਜ਼ਅ'ਬਿਲਅਟਿ) *n* ਦ੍ਰਿਸ਼ਟਵਾ, ਦ੍ਰਿਸ਼ਮਾਨਤਾ, ਸਪਸ਼ਟਤਾ, ਪ੍ਰਤੱਖਤਾ

visible ('ਵਿਜ਼ਅਬਲ) *a* ਦਿਸਦਾ, ਦ੍ਰਿਸ਼ਟੀਗੋਚਰ, ਦ੍ਰਿਸ਼ਮਾਨ, ਜ਼ਾਹਰ, ਪ੍ਰਤੱਖ, ਪਰਗਟ, ਵਿਅਕਤ

vision ('ਵਿਯ਼ਨ) *n v* ਦ੍ਰਿਸ਼ਟੀ, ਨਜ਼ਰ, ਨਿਗਾਹ; ਝਲਕ, ਝਾਕੀ, ਆਭਾਸ; ਸੁਪਨਾ, ਮ੍ਰਿਗਾ-ਤ੍ਰਿਸ਼ਨਾ, ਮਾਇਆ; ਸੁਪਨਾ ਦੇਖਣਾ, ਕਲਪਨਾ ਕਰਨਾ; **~ary** ਮਾਇਆਗ੍ਰਸਤ ਝੌਰ-ਅਮਲੀ, ਕਾਲਪਨਕ, ਖ਼ਿਆਲੀ; **~less** ਦ੍ਰਿਸ਼ਟੀਹੀਨ, ਅੰਨ੍ਹਾ, ਜੋਤਹੀਣ

visit ('ਵਿਜ਼ਿਟ) *n v* ਮੁਲਾਕਾਤ, ਦਰਸ਼ਨ, ਭੇਟ, ਮੇਲ; ਦੌਰਾ, ਫੇਰੀ; ਨਿਰੀਖਣ, ਮੁਆਇਨਾ; ਮੁਲਾਕਾਤ ਕਰਨੀ, ਦਰਸ਼ਨ ਕਰਨਾ; ਮਿਲਣਾ; **~ation** ਦੌਰਾ, ਮੁਆਇਨਾ; ਰੱਬੀ ਮਾਰ, ਅਜ਼ਾਬ; **~ing** ਮੁਲਾਕਾਤ, ਦਰਸ਼ਨ, ਨਿਰੀਖਣ, ਮੁਆਇਨਾ; **~ing card** ਮੁਲਾਕਾਤੀ-ਪੱਤਰ; **~ing hours** ਮੁਲਾਕਾਤੀ ਸਮਾਂ; **~ing professor** ਮਹਿਮਾਨ ਪ੍ਰੋਫ਼ੈਸਰ; **~or** ਮੁਲਾਕਾਤੀ, ਦਰਸ਼ਕ, ਮਹਿਮਾਨ; **~ors gallery** ਦਰਸ਼ਕ-ਗੈਲਰੀ

vista ('ਵਿਸਟਾ) *n* ਦ੍ਰਿਸ਼, ਪਹਿਲਾਂ ਵਾਪਰ ਚੁੱਕੀਆਂ ਘਟਨਾਵਾਂ ਦੀ ਝਾਕੀ, ਦੂਰ-ਬ੍ਹਾਤ

visual ('ਵਿਜ਼ੂਅਲ) *a* ਦ੍ਰਿਸ਼ਟੀਗਤ, ਦ੍ਰਿਸ਼ਟੀ ਸਬੰਧੀ, ਦਰਸ਼ਨੀ; **~ity** ਨਜ਼ਰ, ਦ੍ਰਿਸ਼ਟੀ; **~ization** ਸਪਸ਼ਟੀਕਰਨ, ਸਪਸ਼ਟ ਦਰਸ਼ਨ; ਦ੍ਰਿਸ਼ਟੀਗਤ ਚਿਤਰਣ; **~ize** ਦ੍ਰਿਸ਼ਟੀਗੋਚਰ ਕਰਨ; ਬਾਹਰਲਾ ਰੂਪ ਦੇਖਣ, ਵਿਅਕਤ ਕਰਨ

vital ('ਵਾਇਟਲ) *a* (in *pl*) ਜਾਨਦਾਰ, ਜੀਵਨਮਈ, ਮਹੱਤਵਪੂਰਨ, ਅਤਿ ਲੋੜੀਂਦਾ, ਨਾਜ਼ੁਕ ਮਾਰਮਕ; **~ity** ਸਜੀਵਤਾ, ਜੀਵਨ ਤੱਤ, ਪ੍ਰਾਣ-ਸ਼ਕਤੀ, ਜਾਨ ਜੀਵਨ ਸ਼ਕਤੀ

vitiate ('ਵਿਸ਼ਿਏਇਟ) *v* ਬਿੱਟਣਾ, ਦੁਸ਼ਟ ਕਰਨਾ, ਭ੍ਰਿਸ਼ਟ ਕਰਨਾ, ਵਿਗਾੜਨਾ, ਖ਼ਰਾਬ ਕਰਨਾ

viva ('ਵੀਵਾ) ਜ਼ਿੰਦਾਬਾਦ, ਜੁਗ ਜੁਗ ਜੀਵੇ!

vivacious (ਵਿ'ਵੇਇਸ਼ਅਸ) *a* ਰਹਿਣਾ, ਮੌਜੀ, ਸਜੀਵ, ਪ੍ਰਫੁੱਲਤ, ਉੱਲਾਸਪੂਰਨ, ਉਤਸ਼ਾਹਪੂਰਨ, ਜੋਸ਼ੀਲਾ, ਜ਼ਿੰਦਾਦਿਲ; **~ness** ਉਤਸਾਹ, ਜ਼ਿੰਦਾਦਿਲੀ

vivacity (ਵਿ'ਵੈਸਅਟਿ) *n* ਜ਼ਿੰਦਾਦਿਲੀ, ਸਜੀਵਤਾ, ਉਤਸਾਹ, ਪ੍ਰਫੁੱਲਤਾ, ਜੋਸ਼

viva voce ('ਵਾਇਵਅ'ਵਅਉਸਿ) *n a adv* ਜ਼ਬਾਨੀ ਪਰੀਖਿਆ, ਮੌਖਕ ਪਰੀਖਿਆ; ਜ਼ਬਾਨੀ, ਮੌਖਕ; ਮੌਖਕ ਤੌਰ ਤੇ

vive, viva (ਵੀਵ਼) *(F) int* ਜ਼ਿੰਦਾਬਾਦ! ਅਮਰ ਰਹੇ!

vivid ('ਵਿਵਿੜ) *a* ਜੀਉਂਦੀ, ਸਜੀਵ; ਸਪਸ਼ਟ; ਭੜਕੀਲਾ, ਚਟਕੀਲਾ, ਚਮਕਦਾਰ; ਬਲਸ਼ਾਲੀ, ਸ਼ਕਤੀਸ਼ਾਲੀ; **~ity, ~ness** ਜ਼ਿੰਦਾਦਿਲੀ, ਸਜੀਵਤਾ; ਸਪਸ਼ਟਤਾ, ਚਟਕ-ਮਟਕ, ਭੜਕ

vivify ('ਵਿਵ਼ਿਫ਼ਾਈ) *v* ਜੀਵਨ ਦੇਣਾ, ਜੀਵਤ ਕਰਨਾ, ਸਜੀਵ ਕਰਨਾ, ਜਾਨ ਪਾਉਣੀ, ਪ੍ਰਾਣ ਪਾਉਣੇ

vocable ('ਵ਼ਅਉਕਅਬਲ) *n* ਨਾਉਂ; ਪਦ, ਸ਼ਬਦ, ਬੋਲ

vocabulary (ਵ਼ਅ(ਉ)'ਕੈਬਯੁਲਅਰਿ) *n* ਸ਼ਬਦਾਵਲੀ, ਸ਼ਬਦ-ਸੰਗ੍ਰਹ; ਸ਼ਬਦ-ਕੋਸ਼

vocal ('ਵ਼ਅਉਕਲ) *a n* ਉਚਰਤ, ਵਾਚਕ; ਸਵਰ, ਉਚਾਰਨ; **~cord** ਸਵਰ-ਤੰਤੂ

vocation (ਵ਼ਅ(ਉ)'ਕੇਇਸ਼ਨ) *n* ਪੁਕਾਰ, ਮੁਨਾਦੀ, ਬੁਲਾਵਾ; ਪੇਸ਼ਾ, ਜੀਵਨ ਨਿਰਬਾਹ; **~al** ਪੇਸ਼ੇ ਜਾਂ ਰੁਜ਼ਗਾਰ ਸਬੰਧੀ, ਵਿਵਸਾਇਕ

vociferate (ਵ਼ਅ(ਉ)'ਸਿਫ਼ਅਰੇਇਟ) *v* ਚਿਚਿਆਉਣਾ, ਕੂਕਣਾ, ਕਿਲਕਾਰੀਆਂ ਮਾਰਨੀਆਂ, ਚੀਕਣਾ, ਚਿਲਾਉਣਾ, ਰੌਲਾ ਪਾਉਣਾ

vogue (ਵ਼ਅਉਗ) *n* ਚਾਲ, ਦਸਤੂਰ, ਰਿਵਾਜ; *in~* ਪ੍ਰਚਲਤ ਫ਼ੈਸ਼ਨ ਵਿਚ, ਵਰਤੋਂ ਵਿਚ

voice (ਵੌਇਸ) *n v* ਬਾਣੀ, ਧੁਨੀ, ਸ਼ਬਦ, ਬੋਲ, ਅਵਾਜ਼; ਆਖਤਾ, ਬੋਲਣਾ, ਕਹਿਣਾ; ਰਾਇ ਦੇਣੀ, ਵਿਚਾਰ ਜ਼ਾਹਰ ਕਰਨਾ; *active~* ਕਰਤਰੀ ਵਾਚ; *with one~* ਸਰਬ ਸੰਮਤੀ ਨਾਲ, ਇਕ ਮੱਤ ਹੋ ਕੇ

void (ਵੌਇਡ) *a n v* ਖ਼ਾਲੀ, ਸੁੰਨ, ਵੀਰਾਨ, ਸੁੰਨ, ਨਾਜਾਇਜ਼; ਨਿਸਫਲ, ਨਿਰਥਕ; *null and~* ਰੱਦ, ਮਨਸੂਖ

volcano (ਵੌਲ'ਕੇਇਨਅਉ) *n* ਜੁਆਲਾਮੁਖੀ ਪਹਾੜ

volition (ਵ਼ਅ(ਉ)'ਲਿਸ਼ਨ) *n* ਸੰਕਲਪ; ਇੱਛਾ-ਸ਼ਕਤੀ, ਕਾਮਨਾ-ਸ਼ਕਤੀ; ਮਰਜ਼ੀ, ਪਸੰਦ

volte ('ਵੌਲਟਿ) *n* ਪੈਂਤੜਾ, ਪੈਂਤੜੇਬਾਜ਼ੀ; **~face** ਪਾਸਾ ਬਦਲੀ, ਪਲਟ; (ਸਿਆਸਤ ਵਿਚ) ਪਾਸਾ ਬਦਲਣਾ, ਉਲਟਾ, ਪੈਂਤੜਾ

volume ('ਵੌਲਯੁਮ) *n* ਬੀੜ, ਗ੍ਰੰਥ, ਸੈਂਚੀ; ਭਾਗ, ਖੰਡ, ਗ੍ਰੰਥ-ਖੰਡ, ਜਿਲਦ, ਪੁਸਤਕਾਂ ਦਾ ਪ੍ਰਾਚੀਨ

ਰੂਪ; ਘਟਫਲ, ਆਇਤਨ, ਜਸਾਮਤ, ਸਮਾਈ, ਘਟਤਾ; ਮਾਤਰਾ, ਰਾਸ਼ੀ

voluminous (ਵ੍ਯਲੂਮਿਨਸ) *a* ਕੁੰਡਲਦਾਰ, ਪੇਚਦਾਰ, ਚੱਕਰਦਾਰ; ਕਈ ਖੰਡਾਂ ਦਾ, ਅਨੇਕ ਹਿੱਸਿਆਂ ਦਾ; ਵਿਸਤਾਰਮਈ, ਲੰਮਾ-ਚੌੜਾ

voluntarily ('ਵੌਲਅੰਟ(ਅ)ਰਿਲਿ) *adv* ਮਰਜ਼ੀ ਨਾਲ, ਆਪਣੇ, ਆਪ, ਮਨ ਤੋਂ, ਸਵੈਇੱਛਾ ਪੂਰਵਕ

voluntary ('ਵੌਲਅੰਟ(ਅ)ਰਿ) *n a* ਸਵੈਇੱਛਤ, ਮਨ-ਮਰਜ਼ੀ ਦਾ

volunteer ('ਵੌਲਅੰ'ਟਿਅਾ*) *n v* ਗਦੈਸੇਵਕ; ਸਵੈਇੱਛਿਕ ਸੈਨਾ, ਵਲੰਟੀਅਰ; ਬਿਨਾ ਮੰਗਿਆਂ ਦੇਣਾ, ਅਰਪਣ ਕਰਨਾ

voluptuary (ਵ੍ਯ'ਲਅੱਪਟਯੁਅਰਿ) *n a* ਵਿਸ਼ਈ, ਵਿਲਾਸੀ, ਭੋਗੀ, ਕਾਮੀ, ਵਿਭਚਾਰੀ, ਅੱਯਾਸ਼

voluptuous (ਵ੍ਯ'ਲਅੱਪਚੁਅਸ) *a* ਐਸ਼ ਭਰਿਆ, ਕਾਮੁਕ, ਵਾਸ਼ਨਾਮਈ

volution (ਵ੍ਯ'ਲੂਸ਼ਨ) *n* ਵਲ, ਵਲੇਵਾਂ, ਵਲਾਵਾਂ, ਕੁੰਡਲੀ, ਚੱਕਰ, ਲਪੇਟ

vomit ('ਵੌਮਿਟ) *n v* ਕੈ, ਉਲਟੀ, ਉਪਰਛੱਲ (ਆਉਣੀ)

voracious (ਵ੍ਯ'ਰੇਿਸ਼ਅਾਗ) *a* ਨਾਭੜਜ਼ਿਆ, ਭੁੱਖਾ, ਭੁੱਖੜ, ਖਾਊ ਪੇਟੂ

vote (ਵਅਉਟ) *n v* ਮੱਤ; ਵੋਟ; ਰਾਇ, ਸੰਮਤੀ, ਵੋਟ ਪਾਉਣੀ, ਰਾਇ ਦੇਣੀ ਮੱਤ ਦੇਣਾ; ਵਿਧਾਨ ਬਣਾਉਣਾ; **~of censure** ਨਿੰਦਾ ਪ੍ਰਸਤਾਵ; *casting~* ਨਿਰਣਾਇਕ ਵੋਟ; *~r* ਵੋਟਰ, ਮੱਤਦਾਤਾ

voting ('ਵਅਉਟ) ਮੱਤਦਾਨ

vouch (ਵਾਉਚ) *v* ਪੁਸ਼ਟੀ ਕਰਨੀ, ਸਾਖੀ ਭਰਨੀ, ਗਵਾਹੀ ਦੇਣੀ; ਜ਼ਮਾਨਤ ਦੇਣੀ, ਜ਼ਾਮਨ ਹੋਣਾ; **~er** ਪ੍ਰਮਾਣ-ਪੱਤਰ, ਆਧਾਰ-ਪੱਤਰ, ਬੀਚਕ, ਖ਼ਰਚ ਦਾ ਕਾਗ਼ਜ਼, ਵਾਉਚਰ

vouchsafe (ਵਾਉਚ'ਸੇਇਫ਼) *n v* ਕਿਰਪਾ ਕਰਨੀ, ਦਇਆ ਕਰਨੀ; ਮਨਜ਼ੂਰ ਕਰਨਾ, ਮੰਨ ਲੈਣਾ, ਕਿਰਪਾ ਪੂਰਵਕ ਦੇ ਦੇਣਾ

vow (ਵਾਉ) *n v* ਮਨੌਤ, ਸੁੱਖਣਾ, ਸੰਕਲਪ; ਵਾਅਦਾ, ਪ੍ਰਤਿੱਗਿਆ, ਪ੍ਰਣ, ਇਕਰਾਰ, ਵਚਨ; ਸੰਕਲਪ ਕਰਨਾ, ਪ੍ਰਤੀਗਿਆ ਕਰਨੀ, ਪ੍ਰਣ ਕਰਨਾ

vowel ('ਵਾਉ(ਅ)ਲ) *n* ਸਵਰ, ਅ, ਇ, ਅਰਥਾਤ a, e, i, o, u

vox populi ('ਵੌਕਸ'ਪੌਪਯੂਲਿ) (L) *n* ਲੋਕਾਂ ਦੀ ਆਵਾਜ਼, ਜਨਤਾ ਦੀ ਰਾਇ

voyage ('ਵੌਇਇਜ) *n v* ਜਲ-ਯਾਤਰਾ; ਸਮੁੰਦਰ ਦੀ ਯਾਤਰਾ; ਜਲ-ਯਾਤਰਾ ਕਰਨੀ, ਲੰਮਾ ਸਫ਼ਰ ਕਰਨਾ

vulgar ('ਵਅੱਲਗਾਅ*) *a* ਅਸ਼ਲੀਲ, ਗੰਵਾਰ, ਪੇਂਡੂ ਅਸ਼ਿਸ਼ਟ, ਦੇਹਾਤੀ

vulnerability, vulnerableness ('ਵਅੱਲਨ(ਅ)ਰਅ'ਬਿਲਅਟਿ, 'ਵਅੱਲਨ(ਅ)ਰ ਅਬਲਨਿਸ) *n* ਨਿਰਬਲਤਾ, ਦੁਰਬਲਤਾ

vulnerable ('ਵਅੱਲਨਅਰਅਬਲ) *a* ਕਮਜ਼ੋਰ, ਆਲੋਚਨਾਯੋਗ, ਸਮੀਖਿਆਯੋਗ

vulture ('ਵਅੱਲਚਅ*) *n* ਗਿਰਝ, ਗਿੱਧ; ਲੋਭੀ ਆਦਮੀ

vulva ('ਵਅੱਲਵਅ) *n* ਭਗ-ਦੁਆਰ, ਯੋਨੀ, ਜਟਨ-ਅੰਗ

W

W, w ('ਡਅੱਬਲਯੂ) *n* ਰੋਮਨ ਵਰਨਮਾਲਾ ਦਾ ਤੇਈਵਾਂ ਅੱਖਰ

wacky ('ਵੈਕਿ) *a n* (ਅਪ) ਸਨਕੀ, ਖ਼ਬਤੀ (ਬੰਦਾ)

wafer ('ਵੇਇਫ਼ਅ*) *n v* ਪੇਪੜੀ, ਪਾਪੜ, ਪਤਲਾ ਬਿਸਕੁਟ

wage ('ਵੇਇਜ) *n v* ਦਿਹਾੜੀ, ਉਜਰਤ, ਮਿਹਨਤਾਨਾ, ਮਜ਼ਦੂਰੀ; ਪੁਰਸਕਾਰ; ਬਾਜ਼ੀ ਲਾਉਣਾ, ਦਾਉ ਲਾਉਣਾ

waggery ('ਵੈਗਅਰਿ) *n* ਖਿੱਲੀ, ਠੱਠਾ, ਹਾਸਾ-ਮਜ਼ਾਕ, ਵਿਦੂਸ਼ਕਤਾ

wag(g)on ('ਵੈਗਅਨ) *n* ਮਾਲ ਗੱਡੀ ਦਾ ਡੱਬਾ; ਛਕੜਾ, ਗੱਡਾ

wail (ਵੇਇਲ) *n v* ਵਿਰਲਾਪ, ਕੁਰਲਾਹਟ, ਵੈਣ, ਰੁਦਨ; ਵਿਰਲਾਪ ਕਰਨਾ, ਰੁਦਨ ਕਰਨਾ, ਚੀਕਣਾ, ਰੋਣਾ ਪਿੱਟਣਾ, ਮਾਤਮ ਕਰਨਾ

waist (ਵੇਇਸਟ) *n* ਲੱਕ, ਕਮਰ, ਵਿਚਾਲਾ; ਕਮਰਬੰਦ, ਮੇਖਲਾ; ਚੋਲੀ, ਅੰਗੀ; **~cloth** ਧੋਤੀ, ਲੂੰਗੀ, ਲੰਗੋਟੀ; **~coat** ਕੁੜਤੀ, ਵਾਸਕਟ

wait (ਵੇਇਟ) *v n* ਤੱਕਣਾ, ਰਾਹ ਦੇਖਣਾ, ਵਾਟ ਜੋਹਣਾ; ਠਹਿਰਨਾ, ਰੁਕਣਾ; ਆਸ ਕਰਨੀ, ਆਸਰਾ ਤਕਣਾ; ਚਿਰ ਲਾਉਣਾ, ਉਡੀਕ, ਨਿਗਰਾਨੀ, ਗੁਪਤ ਥਾਂ; ਦੇਰੀ, ਚਿਰ; **~er** ਬੈਰਾ, ਖਿਦਮਤਗਾਰ, ਸੇਵਾ ਕਰਨ ਵਾਲਾ ਆਦਮੀ, ਉਡੀਕਣ ਵਾਲਾ ਆਦਮੀ

wake (ਵੇਇਕ) *n v* (1) ਜਾਗਰਤੀ; ਜਗਰਾਤਾ; ਪਦ-ਚਿੰਨ੍ਹ; ਜਾਗਣਾ; ਜਗਾਉਣਾ, ਉਠਾਉਣਾ, ਸਚੇਤ ਰਹਿਣਾ

walk (ਵੌਕ) *n v* ਟੋਰ, ਚਾਲ, ਗਮਨ; ਚੁਹਲ ਕਦਮੀ, ਘੁੰਮਣ-ਫਿਰਨ, ਹਵਾ ਖੋਰੀ; ਸੈਰਗਾਹ; ਟਹਿਲਣਾ, ਚੱਲਣਾ, ਭ੍ਰਮਣ ਕਰਨਾ, ਘੁੰਮਣਾ, ਗਸ਼ਤ ਕਰਨੀ, ਸੈਰ ਕਰਨੀ; ਵਿਹਾਰ ਕਰਨਾ; **~out** ਸਭਾ-ਤਿਆਗ; **~way** ਰਾਹ, ਮਾਰਗ, ਰਸਤਾ, ਪਰਾਡੰਡੀ; **~ing** ਟੁਰਨ ਸਬੰਧੀ, ਟਹਿਲਣ ਬਾਰੇ

wall (ਵੌਲ) *n v* ਕੰਧ, ਦੀਵਾਰ, ਭਿੱਤੀ; ਕਿਲ੍ਹਾ, ਮੋਰਚਾਬੰਦੀ, ਕਿਲ੍ਹਾਬੰਦੀ; ਕੰਧ ਖੜੀ ਕਰਨੀ ਜਾਂ ਖਿੱਚਣੀ

wallet ('ਵੌਲਿਟ) *n* (ਚਮੜੀ) ਝੋਲਾ, ਥੈਲਾ, ਥੈਲੀ; ਚਮੜੇ ਦੀ ਪੇਟੀ ਜਾਂ ਬਟੂਆ

walnut ('ਵੋਲਨਅੱਟ) *n* ਅਖਰੋਟ

wamble ('ਵੌਂਬਲ) *n v* ਕੰਬਣ, ਥਰਥਰਾਹਟ, ਕੰਬਣਾ, ਥਰਥਰਾਉਣਾ; ਚਿੱਤ ਕੱਚਾ ਹੋਣਾ

wand (ਵੌਂਡ) *n* ਡੰਡਾ, ਸੋਟਾ; ਜਾਦੂ ਦਾ ਡੰਡਾ, ਝੁਰਲੂ

wander ('ਵੌਂਡਅ*) *v* ਵਿਚਰਨਾ, ਭ੍ਰਮਣ ਕਰਨ, ਘੁੰਮਣਾ, ਭੌਂਦੇ ਫਿਰਨਾ, ਭਟਕਨਾ, ਮਾਰੇ-ਮਾਰੇ ਫਿਰਨਾ; ਡੋਲਣਾ; ਬੇ-ਸਿਰ ਪੈਰ ਬੋਲਣਾ; **~lust** ਅਵਾਰਗੀ ਦਾ ਚਸਕਾ

wane (ਵੇਇਨ) *n v* ਕਮੀ, ਘਾਟਾ, ਉਤਰ, ਹ੍ਰਾਸ; ਖੀਣ ਹੋਣਾ, ਥੋਂ ਹੋਣਾ, ਢਲ ਜਾਣਾ

want (ਵੌਂਟ) *n v* ਮੰਗ, ਇੱਛਾ; ਭੁੱਖ, ਮੁਥਾਜੀ, ਅਣਹੋਂਦ, ਅਭਾਵ, ਘਾਟਾ, ਕਮੀ, ਅਵਸ਼ਕੰਤਾ; ਦਲਿੱਦਰ, ਗ਼ਰੀਬੀ; ਜ਼ਰੂਰੀ ਲੋੜ; ਲੋੜੀਂਦੀ ਚੀਜ਼; ਚਾਹੁਣਾ, ਮੰਗਣਾ, ਕਾਮਨਾ ਕਰਨੀ ਅਭਾਵ ਹੋਣਾ; ਘਟਣਾ; ਲੋੜ ਹੋਣੀ

wanton ('ਵੌਂਟਅਨ) *n a v* ਬਹੁਤ ਕਾਮੀ, ਅਵਾਰਾ; ਲੁੱਚਾ; ਸਨਕੀ, ਬੇਲਗਾਮ, ਸ਼ੋਖ਼, ਚੰਚਲ, ਚਪਲ, ਕ੍ਰੀੜਾ-ਪ੍ਰਿਯ; ਕਲੋਲ ਕਰਨਾ, ਕ੍ਰੀੜਾ ਕਰਨਾ, ਵਿਹਾਰ ਕਰਨਾ, ਅਵਾਰਾ ਫਿਰਨਾ; ਛੇੜਨਾ

war (ਵੋ*) *n v* ਸੰਗ੍ਰਾਮ, ਰਣ, ਜੁੱਧ, ਜੰਗ, ਲੜਾਈ; ਜੰਗ ਲੜਨਾ, ਲੜਾਈ ਕਰਨੀ; **~fare** ਜੁੱਧ, ਸੰਗ੍ਰਾਮ, ਲੜਾਈ; **~ship** ਜੰਗੀ ਜਹਾਜ਼; **civil~** ਖ਼ਾਨਾਜੰਗੀ, ਘਰੇਲੂ ਜੁੱਧ, ਗ੍ਰਹਿ ਜੁੱਧ; **cold~** ਸੀਤ ਜੁੱਧ, ਠੰਢੀ ਜੰਗ

ward (ਵੋਡ) *n v* ਰੱਖਿਆ, ਨਿਗਰਾਨੀ, ਜ਼ਿੰਮਾ, ਚੌਕੀਦਾਰ, ਇਹਾਤਾ, ਹਲਕਾ; ਨਿਗਰਾਨੀ ਰੱਖਣੀ; ਪਹਿਰਾ ਦੇਣਾ, ਚੌਕੀਦਾਰੀ ਕਰਨੀ; **~off** ਬਚਾਉ ਕਰਨਾ, ਰੋਕਥਾਮ ਕਰਨਾ; **~robe** ਕੱਪੜੇ ਰੱਖਣ ਵਾਲੀ ਅਲਮਾਰੀ; ਵਸਤਰ, ਲਿਬਾਸ; **~room** ਜੰਗੀ ਜਹਾਜ਼ ਵਿਚ ਅਫ਼ਸਰ ਦਾ ਕਮਰਾ; **~en** ਰਖਵਾਲਾ ਜਾਂ ਨਿਗੂਬਾਨ; ਛਾਤਰਾਵਾਸ ਦਾ ਅਧਿਕਕਸ਼, ਪ੍ਰਬੰਧਕ, ਨਿਗਰਾਨ

ware (ਵੇਅ*) *n a v* ਭਾਂਡੇ, ਬਰਤਨ; ਪਦਾਰਥ; ਸੌਦਾ, ਸੌਦਾ-ਪੱਤਾ, ਸਾਮਾਨ; **~house** ਮਾਲ ਗੁਦਾਮ, ਮਾਲਖ਼ਾਨਾ, ਭੰਡਾਰ

warm (ਵੋਮ) *a v n* ਨਿੱਘਾ, ਗਰਮ, ਕੋਸਾ; ਉਤਸਾਹੀ, ਸਰਗਰਮ, ਜੋਸ਼ੀਲਾ; ਸਜੀਵ, ਭੜਕਾਉਣਾ, ਭੜਕਣਾ; ਉਕਸਾਉਣਾ; ਤੱਤਾ ਹੋਣਾ, ਧੁੱਪ ਲੁਆਉਣੀ; ਸੰਵੇਦਨਸ਼ੀਲ ਹੋਣਾ ਜਾਂ ਕਰਨਾ; ਗਰਮੀ, ਤਾਪ, ਤਪਸ਼

warn (ਵੋਨ) *v* ਸਾਵਧਾਨ ਕਰਨਾ, ਸਚੇਤ ਕਰਨਾ, ਚੇਤਵਨੀ ਦੇਣਾ, ਸੂਚਨਾ ਦੇਣਾ; **~ing** ਚੇਤਾਵਨੀ, ਤਾੜਨਾ, ਇਤਲਾਹ, ਆਗਾਹੀ

warrant ('ਵੋਰਅੰਟ) *n v* ਅਧਿਕਾਰ-ਪੱਤਰ, ਆਦੇਸ਼-ਪੱਤਰ, ਫ਼ਰਮਾਨ, ਹੁਕਮਨਾਮਾ; ਸਨਦ; ਜ਼ਮਾਨਤ; ਨਿਸਚਾ ਕਰਨਾ; ਵਿਸ਼ਵਾਸ ਦੁਆਉਣਾ; ਸੰਭਾਲਣਾ, ਸਹਾਰਾ ਦੇਣਾ, ਥੰਮ੍ਹਣਾ; **~y** ਇਕ ਤਰ੍ਹਾਂ ਦੀ ਗਰੰਟੀ; ਅਧਿਕਾਰ

warrior ('ਵੋਰਿਅ*) *n* ਸੂਰਬੀਰ; ਲੜਾਕੀ ਕੌਮ, ਜੁੱਧਪ੍ਰਿਯ

wary ('ਵੇਅਰਿ) *a* ਚਤੁਰ, ਸਾਵਧਾਨ, ਖ਼ਬਰਦਾਰ, ਚੌਕਸ, ਹੁਸ਼ਿਆਰ, ਚੁਕੰਨਾ

wash (ਵੌਸ਼) *n v* ਧੋਣ, ਧੁਆਈ; ਧੋਣਾ, ਨਹਾਉਣਾ, ਧੋ ਕੇ ਸਾਫ਼ ਕਰਨਾ, ਹੰਗਾਲਣਾ; **~basin** ਚਿਲਮਚੀ; **~erman** ਧੋਬੀ; **~erwoman** ਧੋਬਣ

wasp (ਵੌਸਪ) *n* ਭਰਿੰਡ, ਧਮੂੜੀ, ਬੱਰ

wastage ('ਵੇਇਸਟਿਜ) *n* ਫ਼ਜ਼ੂਲਖ਼ਰਚੀ, ਨੁਕਸਾਨ, ਹਾਨੀ, ਨਾਸ, ਉਜਾੜਾ, ਬਰਬਾਦੀ

waste (ਵੇਇਸਟ) *a v n* ਵੀਰਾਨ, ਉਜਾੜ; ਨਿਕੰਮੀ; ਬਰਬਾਦ, ਨਸ਼ਟ, ਰਹਿੰਦ-ਖੂੰਹਦ; ਉਡਾ ਦੇਣਾ, ਫ਼ਜ਼ੂਲ ਖ਼ਰਚੀ ਕਰਨੀ; ਦੁਰਬਲ ਹੋਣਾ; ਕੂੜਾ-ਕਰਕਟ, ਲੀਰਾਂ; ਫ਼ਜ਼ੂਲ-ਖ਼ਰਚੀ; **~land** ਬੰਜਰ ਧਰਤੀ, ਵੀਰਾਨ ਧਰਤੀ; **~paper basket** ਰੱਦੀ ਦੀ ਟੋਕਰੀ

watch (ਵੌਚ) *n v* ਘੜੀ; ਜਗਰਾਤਾ; ਸਾਵਧਾਨੀ, ਰੱਖਿਆ, ਨਿਗਰਾਨੀ, ਪਹਿਰਾ, ਚੌਕੀ; ਪਹਿਰਾ ਦੇਣਾ, ਜਾਗਦੇ ਰਹਿਣਾ, ਚੌਕਸ ਹੋਣਾ; ਰਾਤ ਜਾਗਣਾ, ਜਗਰਾਤਾ ਕਰਨਾ; **~and ward** ਪਹਿਰਾ ਚੌਕੀ; **~dog** ਰਾਖਾ ਕੁੱਤਾ; ਨਿਗਰਾਨ, ਰਖਵਾਲ; **~man** ਰਾਖਾ, ਪਹਿਰੇਦਾਰ ਚੌਕੀਦਾਰ; **~tower** ਅਟਾਰੀ; **~word** (ਸੈਨਕ ਪਹਿਰੇ ਲਈ) ਸੰਕੇਤ ਸ਼ਬਦ; ਨਾਰਾ; **on the~** ਖ਼ਬਰਦਾਰ; **~ful** ਖ਼ਬਰਦਾਰ, ਚੌਕਸ; **~fulness** ਚੌਕਸੀ, ਖ਼ਬਰਦਾਰੀ, ਸਾਵਧਾਨੀ

water (ਵੌਟਅ*) *n v* ਪਾਣੀ, ਜਲ, ਨੀਰ; ਪਿਸ਼ਾਬ; ਹੰਝੂ; ਰਾਲ, ਚਮਕ, ਆਭਾ, ਆਬ; ਸਿੰਜਣਾ,

ਸਿੰਚਾਈ ਕਰਨੀ, ਪਾਣੀ ਦੇਣਾ, ਆਬਪਾਸ਼ੀ ਕਰਨੀ, ਛਿੜਕਾ ਕਰਨਾ; ਤਰ ਕਰਨਾ, ਭਿਉਂਣਾ, ਗਿੱਲਾ ਕਰਨਾ, ਪਿਆਉਣਾ; ਪਾਣੀ ਆ ਜਾਣਾ; ਮੂਤਣਾ, ਪਿਸ਼ਾਬ ਕਰਨਾ; ਵਧਾਉਣਾ, ਵਾਧਾ ਕਰਨਾ; **~bearer** ਕਹਾਰ, ਪਨਹਾਰ, ਝਿਊਰ; **~course** ਜਲਮਾਰਗਾ; **~craft** ਬੇੜੀ, ਨਈਆ ਜਾਂ ਜਹਾਜ਼; **~fall** ਝਰਨਾ, ਆਬਸ਼ਾਰ; **~fowl** ਮੁਰਗਾਬੀ, ਜਲ-ਪੰਛੀ; **~lily** ਕੰਵਲ, ਕਮਲ, ਕੁਮਦਨੀ; **~melon** ਮਤੀਰਾ, ਤਰਬੂਜ਼, ਹਦਵਾਣਾ; **~nymph** ਜਲਪਰੀ; **~proof** ਬਰਸਾਤੀ; ਅਭਿੱਜ; **~tight** ਜਲ ਰੋਕ; (ਸੂਬਾ-ਨਾਮਾ) ਸ਼ੰਕਾ ਰਹਿਤ; *in hot~* ਔਖ ਵਿਚ, ਔਕੜ ਵਿਚ; *make ~ pass* ਮੂਤਣਾ, ਪਿਸ਼ਾਬ ਕਰਨਾ; *rose~* ਅਰਕ ਗੁਲਾਬ; *throw cold ~ on* ਪਾਣੀ ਫੇਰਨਾ, ਦਬਾਉਣਾ; **~y** ਪਣਿਆਲਾ; ਸਜਲ

wave (ਵੇਇਵ) *n v* ਛੱਲ, ਲਹਿਰ, ਤਰੰਗ, ਹਿਚਕੋਲਾ; ਹਿੱਲਣਾ, ਹਿਲੋਰੇ ਖਾਣੇ; ਹੱਥ ਹਿਲਾਉਣਾ; ਲਹਿਰਾਂ ਉਠਈਆਂ

wavy ('ਵੇਇਵਿ) *n a* ਲਹਿਰੀਆਦਾਰ, ਲਹਿਰਦਾਰ; ਤਰੰਗਤ, ਤਰੰਗਮਈ, ਕਲੋਲਮਈ; ਘੁੰਗਰਾਲਾ

wax ('ਵੈਕਸ) *n v* ਮੋਮ; ਕੰਨਾਂ ਦੀ ਮੈਲ; ਮੋਮੀ ਬਣਾਉਣਾ, ਮੋਮ ਲਾਉਣੀ, ਮੋਮ ਦੀ ਤਹਿ ਦੇ ਦੇਣੀ; ਲਾਖ ਨਾਲ ਜੋੜਨਾ; ਚੰਦ ਦਾ ਆਕਾਰ ਵਧਣਾ; ਉੱਨਤੀ ਕਰਨਾ; **~y** ਮੋਮੀ, ਮੋਮਦਾਰ; ਚਿਪਚਿਪਾ, ਨਰਮ, ਕੂਲਾ; ਛੇਤੀ ਨਾਰਾਜ਼ ਹੋਣ ਵਾਲਾ

way (ਵੇਇ) *n* ਰਾਹ, ਰਸਤਾ, ਮਾਰਗ, ਪੰਥ, ਡਗਰ; ਵੀਹੀ; ਗਲੀ, ਸੜਕ; ਜੁਗਤ, ਉਪਾਓ, ਰੀਤ, ਵਿਧੀ, ਤਰਕੀਬ, ਢੰਗ, ਢਬ, ਕਾਇਦਾ; **~farer** ਪੈਦਲ ਯਾਤਰਾ ਕਰਨ ਵਾਲਾ, ਪਾਂਧੀ; *by ~ of* ਤੌਰ ਤੇ; *by the~* ਐਵੇਂ

weak (ਵੀਕ) *a* ਕਮਜ਼ੋਰ, ਨਿਰਬਲ, ਢਿੱਲਾ, ਨਿਤਾਣਾ, ਨਿਸੱਤਾ, ਖੀਣ; ਮੱਧਮ, ਹਲਕਾ; **~character** ਕਮਜ਼ੋਰ ਆਚਰਨ ਵਾਲਾ; *the ~er sex* ਨਾਰੀ, ਔਰਤ ਜਾਤ, ਅਬਲਾ; **~ness** ਕਮਜ਼ੋਰੀ, ਦੁਰਬਲਤਾ, ਸ਼ਕਤੀਹੀਣਤਾ, ਸੁਸਤੀ; ਤਰੁੱਟੀ, ਐਬ, ਬੁਰਾਈ

weal (ਵੀਲ) *n* ਖ਼ੁਸ਼ਹਾਲੀ, ਵਾਧਾ, ਸਮਰਿਧੀ; ਭਲਾਈ, ਕਲਿਆਣ; ਆਨੰਦ, ਪ੍ਰਸੰਨਤਾ; ਚੰਗੀ, ਕਿਸਮਤ; ਚੰਗਿਆਈ, ਅੱਛਾਈ

wealth (ਵੈੱਲਥ) *n* ਧਨ, ਧਨ-ਸੰਪੱਤੀ, ਅਮੀਰੀ, ਦੌਲਤਮੰਦੀ; ਆਨੰਦ; ਸੁਭਾਗ, ਬਹੁਤਾਤ; **~y** ਧਨਵਾਨ, ਅਮੀਰ, ਦੌਲਤਮੰਦ, ਮਾਲਦਾਰ

weapon ('ਵੈੱਪਅਨ) *n* ਹਥਿਆਰ, ਸ਼ਸਤਰ, ਅਸਤਰ-ਸ਼ਸਤਰ

wear (ਵੇਅ*) *n v* ਪੁਸ਼ਾਕ, ਲਿਬਾਸ, ਵੇਸ, ਪਹਿਰਾਵਾ; ਘਟਾਉਣਾ, ਨੁਕਸਾਨ ਕਰਨਾ; ਘਸਣਾ, ਰਗੜ ਖਾਣੀ, ਘਸਾਉਣਾ, ਰਗੜਨਾ, ਥੱਕਣਾ, ਫੇਰਨਾ, ਘੁਕਣਾ, ਘੁਕਾਉਣਾ; ਘੁਮਾਉਣਾ; ਘੰਮਣਾ, ਮੁੜ ਜਾਣਾ; **~and tear** ਟੁੱਟ ਭੱਜ; **~down** ਰਗੜ ਦੇਣਾ, ਕਮਜ਼ੋਰ ਕਰਨਾ; **~off** ਘਸ ਦੇਣਾ; **~iness** ਥਕਾਵਟ; **~y** ਥਕਿਆ, ਅੱਕਿਆ, ਉਚਾਟ; ਨਿਰਾਸ, ਉਦਾਸੀਨ

weather ('ਵੈੱਦਅ*) *n a* ਰੁੱਤ, ਮੌਸਮ; ਹਵਾ ਵਾਲੇ ਪਾਸੇ ਸਥਿਤ, ਹਵਾ ਦੀ ਦਿਸ਼ਾ ਦਾ; **~cock** ਪੌਣ-ਕੁੱਕੜ; ਫਸਲੀ ਬਟੇਰਾ

weave (ਵੀਵ) *n v* ਬੁਣਤੀ, ਬੁਣਨਾ; ਕੱਪੜਾ ਬਣਾਉਣਾ, ਤਾਣੀ ਬੁਣਨਾ; ਗੁੰਦਣਾ; ਘੜਨਾ, ਗੁੰਦਣਾ; **~r** ਜੁਲਾਹਾ; ਬਈਆ

web (ਵੈੱਬ) *n* ਜਾਲ; ਜਾਲਾ (ਮੱਕੜੀ ਦਾ); ਕੱਪੜਾ, ਤਾਣਾ, ਰੇਜ਼ਾ

webster ('ਵੈਬਸਟਅ*) *n* ਜੁਲਾਹਾ

wed (ਵੈਡ) *v* ਵਰ ਲੈਣਾ, ਵਿਆਹ ਕਰਨਾ, ਵਿਆਹੁਣਾ, ਨਿਕਾਹ ਕਰਨਾ, ਪਰਨਾਉਣਾ, ਪਰਨਾਏ ਜਾਣਾ, ਜੋੜਨਾ, ਮਿਲਾਉਣਾ; ~ding ਵਿਆਹ, ਨਿਕਾਹ, ਸ਼ਾਦੀ, ਪਰਨੇਵਾਂ

wedlock ('ਵੈਡਲੌਕ) *n* ਵਿਆਹ, ਬੰਨ੍ਹਣ, ਗਠਜੋੜ

Wednesday ('ਵੈੱਨਜ਼ਡਿ) *n* ਬੁੱਧਵਾਰ

wee (ਵੀ) *n* ਨਿੱਕ, ਨੰਨ੍ਹਾ, ਛੋਟਾ

weed (ਵੀਡ) *n v* ਘਾਹ-ਪੱਤਾ, ਨਦੀਨ ਮਰੀਅਲ ਘੋੜਾ, ਗੁੱਡਣਾ, ਗੋਡੀ ਕਰਨੀ, ਛਾਂਟਣਾ, ਛਾਂਟੀ ਕਰਨੀ, ਕੱਢਣਾ, ਪੁੱਟਣਾ

week (ਵੀਕ) *n* ਹਫ਼ਤਾ, ਸਪਤਾਹ; ~ly ਹਫ਼ਤਾਵਾਰ, ਸਪਤਾਹਕ

weep (ਵੀਪ) *v* ਰੋਣਾ, ਵਿਰਲਾਪ ਕਰਨਾ, ਅੱਖਾਂ ਭਰਨੀਆਂ; ਸੋਗ ਮਨਾਉਣਾ, ਅਫ਼ਸੋਸ ਕਰਨਾ; ਚੋਣਾ, ਰਿਸਣਾ; ~ing ਰੋਣ-ਪੋਟ, ਰੁਦਨ, ਵਿਰਲਾਪ; ਅੰਥਰੂਪੂਰਨ

weigh (ਵੇਇ) *v* ਭਾਰ ਤੋਲਣਾ, ਤੁੱਲ ਹੋਣਾ, ਬਰਾਬਰ ਹੋਣਾ; ਅੰਕਣਾ, ਜਾਚਣਾ, ਮੁੱਲਾਂਕਣ ਕਰਨਾ, ਅਨੁਮਾਨ ਲਾਉਣਾ, ਮਹਤਵ ਹੋਣਾ; ~t ਵਜ਼ਨ, ਭਾਰ, ਬੋਝ, ਤੋਲ, ਵੱਟਾ; ਭਾਰੀ ਚੀਜ਼। ਮਹੱਤਵ, ਪ੍ਰਭਾਵ, ਪ੍ਰਧਾਨਤਾ; ਮਹੱਤਾ

welcome ('ਵੈੱਲਕਅਮ) *n v a int* ਸੁਆਗਤ, ਸਤਿਕਾਰ, ਆਓਭਗਤ; ਸੁਆਗਤ ਕਰਨਾ, ਸਤਿਕਾਰ ਕਰਨਾ; ਸੁਖਾਵਾਂ; ਜੀ ਆਇਆਂ ਨੂੰ; ~address ਅਭਿਨੰਦਨ-ਪੱਤਰ, ਸੁਆਗਤੀ ਭਾਸ਼ਨ

weld (ਵੈੱਲਡ) *v* ਢਾਲ ਕੇ ਜੋੜਨਾ, ਸੰਯੁਕਤ ਕਰਨਾ; ਸਰੂਪ ਬਣਾਉਣਾ; ~ing ਗਰਮ ਕਰਕੇ ਜੋੜਨਾ, ਵੈਲਡਿੰਗ

welfare ('ਵੈੱਲਫੇਅ*) *n* ਕਲਿਆਣ, ਭਲਾਈ; ਸੁੱਖ; ਉੱਨਤੀ

welkin ('ਵੈੱਲਕਿਨ) *n* (ਕਾਵਿ) ਅੰਬਰ, ਗਗਨ, ਆਕਾਸ਼, ਨਭ

well (ਵੈੱਲ) *n v adv int* ਖੂਹ, ਬਾਉਲੀ; ਸੋਤਾ, ਚਸ਼ਮਾ; ਉੱਠਣਾ, ਉਮੜਨਾ, ਉੱਛਰਨਾ, ਫ਼ਹਾਰਾ ਚੱਲਣਾ; ਤਦੰਰੁਸਤ; ਚੰਗਾ ਭਲਾ, ਠੀਕ-ਠਾਕ; ਤਸਲੀਬਖ਼ਸ਼ ਰੂਪ ਵਿਚ; ਭਲੀ-ਭਾਂਤੀ, ਚੰਗੀ ਤਰ੍ਹਾਂ; ਬਖ਼ੂਬੀ, ਨਿਰਾ; ਨਿਪਟ, ਬਿਲਕੁਲ; ~behaved ਆਚਰਨਸ਼ੀਲ, ਸੁਘੜ, ਸੁਸ਼ੀਲ; ~being ਭਲਾਈ, ਖੈਰ, ਸਲਾਮਤੀ

welt (ਵੈੱਲਟ) *n v* ਕਿਨਾਰੀ, ਗੋਟਾ; ਮਗਜ਼ੀ; ਗੋਟਾ ਲਾਉਣਾ; ਛਾਂਟੇ ਮਾਰਨੇ, ਲਾਸਾਂ ਪਾ ਦੇਣੀਆਂ, ਨੀਲ ਪਾ ਦੇਣੇ; ~ing ਗੋਟਾ ਲਾਉਣਾ; ਕੋਰੜਿਆਂ ਦੀ ਮਾਰ, ਕੁਟਾਈ

wench (ਵੈੱਚ) *n v* ਛੋਕਰੀ, ਪੱਠੀ; ਵੇਸਵਾ, ਰੰਡੀ, ਵੇਸਵਾ ਗਾਮਨ ਕਰਨਾ, ਰੰਡੀਬਾਜ਼ੀ ਕਰਨਾ

wend (ਵੈੱਡ) *v* ਬਦਲਣਾ, ਚਲੇ ਜਾਣਾ, ਗੁਜ਼ਰਨਾ; ਰਾਹ ਪੈਣਾ

west (ਵੈੱਸਟ) *n a adv* ਪੱਛਮ; ਪੱਛਮੀ ਦੇਸ਼; ਪੱਛਮੀ; ਪੱਛਮ ਵਾਲੇ ਪਾਸੇ; ~ern ਪੱਛਮੀ, ਪੱਛਮ ਦਾ ਨਿਵਾਸੀ

wet (ਵੈੱਟ) *n a v* ਗਿੱਲਾ, ਨਮੀ, ਤਰੀ, ਸੇਜਲ, ਸਿਲ੍ਹ; ਗਿੱਲਾ ਕਰਨਾ, ਤਰ ਕਰਨਾ, ਨਮ ਦੇਣਾ; ~lands ਛੰਭ; ~weather ਵਰਖਾ ਰੁੱਤ

wharf (ਵੋਢ) *n v* ਜਹਾਜ਼ ਦਾ ਘਾਟ; ਘਾਟ ਤੇ ਮਾਲ ਲਾਹੁਣਾ

what (ਵੌਟ) *a pron* ਕਿਹੜਾ, ਕਿਹੋ ਜਿਹਾ, ਕਿੱਡਾ, ਕੌਣ; ਕਿੰਨਾ; ਕੀ; ~ever ਕਿਹੋ ਜਿਹਾ, ਕੈਸਾ, ਕੁਝ ਵੀ, ਜੋ ਵੀ, ਕੁਝ; ਕਿਸੇ ਤਰ੍ਹਾਂ ਦਾ

wheat (ਵੀਟ) *n* ਕਣਕ, ਗੰਦਮ, ਗੇਹੂੰ; ~en ਕਣਵੰਨਾ, ਗੰਦਮੀ, ਗੇਹੂੰ ਦੇ ਰੰਗ ਦਾ

wheel (ਵੀਲ) *n v* ਚੱਕਾ, ਪਹੀਆ; ਚੱਕਰ; ਚਰਖਾ, ਚਰਖੀ; ਫਿਰਕੀ; ਬੈੜ, ਘਿਰਨੀ; ਟੇਢੇ ਵਿੰਗੇ ਟੁਰਨਾ; ਸਾਈਕਲ ਚਲਾਉਣਾ

whelm (ਵੈੱਲਮ) *v* ਮਗਨ ਕਰਨਾ, ਘੇਰਨਾ; ਪ੍ਰਭਾਵਤ ਕਰਨਾ; ਲਪੇਟ ਵਿਚ ਲੈਣਾ

whelp (ਵੈੱਲਪ) *n v* ਕਤੂਰਾ, ਕੁੱਤੇ ਦਾ ਬੱਚਾ, ਪਿੱਲਾ; ਜਣਨਾ, ਵਿਆਉਣਾ; (ਮਨਸੂਬਾ) ਘੜਨਾ

when (ਵੈੱਨ) *adv pron n* ਕਦ, ਕਿਸੇ ਵੇਲੇ, ਕਦੋਂ; ਜਦ; ਜਿਸ ਵੇਲੇ, ਜਿਉਂ ਹੀ, ਜਦ ਕਿ; ਕਿੰਨੇ ਵਜੇ, ਕਿਸ ਸਮੇਂ; ਅਵਸਰ, ਵੇਲਾ; **~ever** ਜਦ ਕਦੇ, ਜਿਸ ਮੌਕੇ ਤੇ, ਜਿਉਂ ਹੀ

whence (ਵੈੱਸ) *n pron adv* ਕਿਥੋਂ; ਜਿੱਥੋਂ; ਕਿਸ ਮਾਧਿਅਮ ਦੁਆਰਾ, ਕਿਸ ਤਰ੍ਹਾਂ ਕਿੱਧਰੋਂ, ਕਿਵੇਂ; ਜਿਵੇਂ

where (ਵੇਅ*) *n pron adv* ਕਿੱਥੇ, ਕਿਹੜੀ ਥਾਂ; ਜਿੱਥੇ, ਜਿਹੜੀ ਥਾਂ, ਕਿਸ ਸਥਿਤੀ ਵਿਚ; ਕਿਸ ਥਾਂ; ਜਿਸ ਥਾਂ; ਜਿਧਰ ਨੂੰ, ਜਿੰਧਰ; **~abouts** ਪੱਤਾ, ਥਾਂ-ਟਿਕਾਣਾ; **~as** ਜਦ ਕਿ, ਜਦੋਂ; ਪਰੰਤੂ, ਚੁਨਾਂਚਿ, ਇਸ ਦੇ ਉਲਟ

whether ('ਵੈੱਦਅ*) *pron conj a* ਦੋਹਾਂ ਵਿਚੋਂ ਕਿਹੜਾ; ਭਾਵੇਂ, ਚਾਹੇ

whey (ਵੇਇ) *n a* ਫਿਟਾਏ ਦੁੱਧ ਦਾ ਪਾਣੀ, ਦਹੀਂ ਵਿਚਲਾ ਪਾਣੀ; ਲੱਸੀ ਵਰਗਾ

which (ਵਿਚ) *a pron* ਕੌਣ, ਜਿਹੜਾ, ਜੋ, ਜਿਹੜੀ ਚੀਜ਼; ਕਿਹੜੀ ਚੀਜ਼; ਜਿਸ ਨੂੰ; **~ever, soever** ਜਿਹੜਾ ਵੀ, ਜੋ ਵੀ, ਜੋ ਕੋਈ ਵੀ

while (ਵਾਇਲ) *n v conj* ਸਮਾਂ, ਵੇਲਾ, ਵਕਤ; ਵੇਲਾ ਗਵਾਉਣਾ, ਵੇਲਾ ਟਪਾਉਣਾ; ਜਦ, ਜਦ ਤਕ, ਜਿਸ ਸਮੇਂ ਵਿਚ, ਤਦ ਤਕ

whim (ਵਿਮ) *n* ਮਨ-ਮੌਜ, ਤਰੰਗ, ਖ਼ਬਤ, ਸਨਕ, ਖ਼ਿਆਲ, ਵਹਿਮ; **~sical** ਮਨ-ਮੌਜੀ, ਤਰੰਗੀ, ਵਹਿਮੀ, ਖ਼ਬਤੀ; **~sy** ਮੌਜ, ਤਰੰਗ, ਵਹਿਮ, ਖ਼ਬਤ

whinny (ਵਿਨਿ) *v n* ਹਿਣਹਿਣਾਹਟ; ਹਿਣਕਣਾ

whip (ਵਿਪ) *n v* ਕੋਰੜਾ, ਚਾਬੁਕ, ਹੰਟਰ, ਛਾਂਟਾ; ਕੋਚਵਾਨ; ਪ੍ਰਬੰਧਕ, ਰਾਜਸੀ ਦਲ ਦਾ ਸਚੇਤਕ; ਖ਼ਬਰਦਾਰ ਕਰਨ ਵਾਲਾ; ਕੋਰੜਾ ਮਾਰਨਾ, ਚਾਬੁਕ ਨਾਲ ਮਾਰਨਾ; ਭੱਜ ਕੇ ਨਿਕਲ ਜਾਣਾ

whirl (ਵਅ:ਲ) *v n* ਭਵਾਉਣਾ ਜਾਂ ਭੌਣਾ, ਚੱਕਰ ਦੇਣੇ ਜਾਂ ਚੱਕਰ ਖਾਣਾ, ਘੁਕਾਉਣਾ ਜਾਂ ਘੁਰਨਾ, ਘੁਮਾ ਕੇ ਸੁੱਟਣਾ, ਘੁਮਾ ਕੇ ਵਗਾ ਮਾਰਨਾ; ਤੇਜ਼ ਚੱਕਰ, ਘੁਮਾਈ

whisper ('ਵਿਸਪਅ*) *v* ਕਾਨਾਫੂਸੀ ਕਰਨੀ, ਖ਼ੁਸਰਮੁਸਰ ਕਰਨੀ, ਕੰਨ ਵਿਚ ਕਹਿਣਾ

whistle ('ਵਿਸਲ) *n v* ਸੀਟੀ, ਸੀਟੀ ਦੀ ਅਵਾਜ਼; ਸਾਂ ਦੀ ਅਵਾਜ਼; ਸੀਟੀ ਵਜਾਉਣੀ, ਸਾਂ-ਸਾਂ ਦੀ ਅਵਾਜ਼ ਨਿਕਲਣੀ ਜਾਂ ਕੱਢਣੀ

white (ਵਾਇਟ) *a n v* ਚਿੱਟਾ, ਧੌਲਾ, ਬੱਗਾ; ਸਫ਼ੈਦ; ਅੰਡੇ ਦੀ ਸਫ਼ੈਦੀ; ਗੋਰੇ ਰੰਗ ਵਾਲੀ ਜਾਤੀ; ਚਿੱਟਾ ਕਰਨਾ, ਸਾਫ਼ ਕਰਨਾ, ਸਫ਼ੈਦੀ ਕਰਨੀ; **~alloy** ਨਕਲੀ ਚਾਂਦੀ; **~ant** ਸਿਉਂਕ, ਦੀਮਕ; **~lie** ਮਾਮੂਲੀ ਝੂਠ; **~livered** ਕਾਇਰ, ਬੁਜ਼ਦਿਲ; **~man** ਗੋਰਾ, ਫ਼ਰੰਗੀ; **~Paper** ਲੋਕਾਂ ਦੀ ਜਾਣਕਾਰੀ ਲਈ ਛਾਪੀ ਸਰਕਾਰੀ ਰਿਪੋਰਟ; **~smith** ਕਲੀਗਰ; **~wash** ਸਫ਼ੈਦੀ (ਕਰਨਾ), ਲਿੰਬਾਈ, ਸਫ਼ਾਈ (ਕਰਨੀ); **~n** ਚਿੱਟਾ ਕਰਨਾ, ਚਿੱਟਾ ਹੋ ਜਾਣਾ; **~ning** ਚਿਟਿਆਉਣ, ਕਲੀ, ਸਫ਼ੈਦੀ, ਚਿੱਟੀ ਮਿੱਟੀ

whither ('ਵਿਦਅ*) *adv n* ਕਿੱਧਰ, ਕਿੱਧਰ ਨੂੰ, ਕਿੱਥੇ, ਕਿਹੜੇ ਪਾਸੇ; ਜਿਧਰ, ਜਿੱਥੇ; ਲਕਸ਼

who (ਹੂ) *pron* ਕੌਣ, ਕਿਹੜਾ; ਕਿਹੜੇ; ਕਿਨ,

whole / **wilful**

ਕਿਨ੍ਹਾਂ, ਜਿਨ, ਜਿਨ੍ਹਾਂ; **~ever** ਜੋ ਕੋਈ ਵੀ, ਜੋ ਵੀ; **~soever** ਜਿੰਨੇ ਵੀ, ਜਿਨੇ ਕਿਨੇ, ਜਿਸ ਕਿਸੇ, ਜੋ ਕੋਈ ਵੀ, ਜਿਹੜਾ ਕੋਈ ਵੀ

whole (ਹਉਲ) *a n* ਸਾਰਾ, ਪੂਰਾ, ਸਮੁੱਚਾ, ਪੂਰੇ ਦਾ ਪੂਰਾ; ਸਬੂਤਾ; **~hearted** ਪੂਰੇ ਦਿਲ ਨਾਲ, ਸੱਚੇ ਦਿਲੋਂ; **~sale** ਥੋਕ ਵਿਕਰੀ, ਥੋਕ; **~some** ਨਿਰੋਆ, ਪੌਸ਼ਟਿਕ, ਲਾਭਕਾਰੀ, ਗੁਣਕਾਰੀ, ਹਿਤਕਾਰੀ

wholly ('ਹਉਲਿ) *adv* ਪੂਰੇ ਦਾ ਪੂਰਾ, ਸਾਰੇ ਦਾ ਸਾਰਾ, ਸਮੁੱਚਾ, ਸਮੁੱਚੇ ਰੂਪ ਵਿਚ; ਪੂਰੀ ਤਰ੍ਹਾਂ; ਬਿਲਕੁਲ; ਮੂਲੋਂ ਹੀ ਮੂੱਢੋਂ

whom (ਹੂਮ) *pron* ਵੇਖੋ who, ਕਿਸ ਨੂੰ; ਜਿਸ ਨੂੰ; **~soever** ਜਿਸ ਨੂੰ, ਜਿਸ ਨੇ ਵੀ, ਜਿਨ੍ਹਾਂ ਨੂੰ ਵੀ

whoop (ਹੂਪ) *n* ਖਯੂੰ-ਖਯੂੰ ਕਰਨ ਦੀ ਕਿਰਿਆ, ਖੰਘ ਦਾ ਗੋਤਾ; ਚਾਂਗਰ; **~ing**, **~ping cough** ਕਾਲੀ ਖਾਂਸੀ, ਕੁੱਤਾ ਖਾਂਸੀ

whore (ਹੋ*) *pron* ਵੇਸਵਾ, ਕੰਜਰੀ; ਲੁੱਚਪੁਣਾ ਕਰਨਾ, ਬਦਮਾਸ਼ੀ ਕਰਨਾ; **~dom** ਰੰਡੀਬਾਜ਼ੀ, ਵੇਸਵਾਪੁਣਾ

whose (ਹੂਜ਼) *pron* ਕੀਹਦਾ, ਕਿਸ ਦਾ, ਕਿਨ੍ਹਾਂ ਦਾ; ਜੇਹਦਾ, ਜਿਸ ਦਾ, ਜਿਨ੍ਹਾਂ ਦਾ

why (ਵਾਇ) *adv int n* ਕਿਉਂ, ਕਿਸ ਲਈ, ਕਿਸ ਕਾਰਨ, ਕਿਸ ਕਰਕੇ; ਜਿਸ ਲਈ, ਜਿਸ ਕਰਕੇ; ਕੀ ਇਹ ਵੀ ਹੋ ਸਕਦਾ ਹੈ; ਕਾਰਨ; ਵਿਆਖਿਆ

wicked ('ਵਿਕਿਡ) *a* ਬਦਮਾਸ਼, ਬਦਚਲਨ, ਬਦ, ਬੁਰਾ, ਦੁਸ਼ਟ, ਪਾਪੀ, ਦੁਰਾਚਾਰੀ; **~ness** ਬਦਮਾਸ਼ੀ, ਬਦਚਲਨੀ, ਬਦੀ, ਬੁਰਾਈ, ਦੁਸ਼ਟਤਾ

wicket ('ਵਿਕਿਟ) *n* ਫਾਟਕ, ਖਿੜਕ; ਕ੍ਰਿਕਟ ਵਿਕਟ; **~gate** ਛੋਟਾ ਦਰਵਾਜ਼ਾ, ਉਪ-ਦੁਆਰ

wide (ਵਾਇਡ) *adv a* ਖੁੱਲ੍ਹਾ; ਚੌੜਾ, ਮੋਕਲਾ, ਦੂਰ ਤਕ ਪਸਰਿਆ; ਕਾਫ਼ੀ, ਚੋਖਾ; **~awake** ਪੂਰੀ ਤਰ੍ਹਾਂ ਸਚੇਤ; **~eyed** ਹੈਰਾਨ, ਹੱਕਾ-ਬੱਕਾ; **~spread** ਦੂਰ ਤਕ ਪਸਰਿਆ; ਵਿਸਤਰਤ, ਵਿਸ਼ਾਲ; **~n** ਖੁੱਲ੍ਹਾ ਕਰਨਾ, ਮੋਕਲਾ ਹੋਣਾ, ਵਿਸਤਾਰ ਦੇਣਾ

widow ('ਵਿਡਅਉ) *n v* ਵਿਧਵਾ; ਰੰਡੀ ਕਰ ਦੇਣਾ; **~er** ਰੰਡੂ; **~hood** ਰੰਡੇਪਾ, ਵਿਧਵਾਪਣ

width ('ਵਿਡਥ) *n* ਚੌੜਾਈ; ਘਰ (ਕੱਪੜੇ ਦਾ), ਅਰਜ; ਵਿਸਤਾਰ, ਵਿਆਪਕਤਾ; ਉਦਾਰਤਾ; ਉੱਚਤਾ

wife (ਵਾਇਫ) *n* ਵਹੁਟੀ, ਪਤਨੀ, ਘਰ ਵਾਲੀ, ਤੀਵੀਂ, ਜ਼ਨਾਨੀ

wig (ਵਿਗ) *n v* ਵਿਗ, ਸਿਰ ਦੇ ਨਕਲੀ ਵਾਲ; ਜੱਜਾਂ ਅਤੇ ਵਕੀਲਾਂ ਦੇ ਪਦ ਦਾ ਚਿੰਨ੍ਹ; ਡਾਂਟਣਾ, ਤਾੜਨਾ, ਝਾੜਝੰਬ ਕਰਨੀ; **~ging** ਡਾਟ, ਝਾੜ-ਝੰਬ, ਫਿੱਟ-ਲਾਨ੍ਹਤ

wiggle ('ਵਿਗਲ) *v* ਇੱਧਰ ਉੱਧਰ ਘੁਮਾਉਣਾ, ਫੇਰਨਾ

wild (ਵਾਇਲਡ) *a adv n* ਜੰਗਲੀ, ਜਾਂਗਲੀ; ਵਹਿਸ਼ੀ, ਝੱਲਾ; ਬੇਕਾਬੂ, ਬੇ-ਲਗਾਮ; ਬੇ-ਤਰਤੀਬ, ਅਵਿਵਸਥਿਤ; ਉਜਾੜ, ਬੀਆਬਾਨ; **~cat** ਸ਼ੇਰ, ਚੀਤਾ ਆਦਿ; **~goose** ਜੰਗਲੀ ਹੰਸ; ਮੂਰਖ ਆਦਮੀ; **~goose chase** ਫ਼ਜ਼ੂਲ ਕੋਸ਼ਿਸ਼, ਅਸੰਭਵ ਕੰਮ ਲਈ ਜਤਨ; **~life** ਜੰਗਲੀ ਜਾਨਵਰ

wile (ਵਾਇਲ) *n v* (in pl) ਫ਼ਰੇਬ, ਮਕਰ, ਛਲਿੱਤਰ, ਕਪਟ; ਫ਼ਰੇਬ ਕਰਨਾ, ਮਕਰ ਕਰਨਾ, ਛਲ ਕਰਨਾ

wilful ('ਵਿਲਫ਼ੁਲ) *a* ਮਨਮਰਜ਼ੀ ਦਾ, ਜਾਣ ਬੁੱਝ ਕੇ, ਜਾਣਦਿਆਂ ਹੋਇਆਂ; ਜ਼ਿੱਦੀ

will (ਵਿਲ) *v aux n* ਭਵਿੱਖਵਾਚੀ ਸਹਾਇਕ ਕਿਰਿਆ, (ਗਾ, ਗੇ, ਗੀ, ਗੀਆਂ ਆਦਿ); ਇੱਛਾ ਕਰਨਾ, ਇਰਾਦਾ ਹੋਣਾ, ਮਰਜੀ ਹੋਣਾ; ਚਾਹੁਣ; ਇੱਛਾ; ~**power** ਇੱਛਾ-ਸ਼ਕਤੀ; *at*~ ਮਰਜੀ ਨਾਲ; **good**~ ਸੁਭਭਾਵਨਾ, ਸਦਭਾਵਨਾ; **ill**~ ਦੁਰਭਾਵਨਾ; ~**ing** ਰਾਜੀ, ਰਜ਼ਾਮੰਦ, ਸਹਿਮਤ; ~**ness** ਰਜ਼ਾਮੰਦੀ, ਸਹਿਮਤੀ; ਇੱਛਾ; ਸ਼ੌਕ

willy ('ਵਾਇਲਿ) *a* ਚਾਲਬਾਜ਼, ਚਲਾਕ

willy-nilly ('ਵਿਲ਼ਿ'ਨਿਲ਼ਿ) *adv* ਚਾਹੇ-ਅਣਚਾਹੇ, ਔਖੇ-ਸੌਖੇ; ਰੋਂਦੇ-ਧੋਂਦੇ

wimp (ਵਿੰਪ) *n* (ਅਪ) ਲੱਲੂ

win (ਵਿਨ) *v n* ਜਿੱਤਣਾ, ਫ਼ਤਿਹ ਪਾਉਣੀ; ਸਫਲ ਹੋਣਾ; ਜਿੱਤ, ਵਿਜੈ; ~**prize** ਇਨਾਮ ਹਾਸਲ ਕਰਨਾ; ~**out** ਸਫਲ ਹੋਣਾ, ਕਾਮਯਾਬ ਹੋਣਾ; ~**ner** ਜੇਤੂ, ਵਿਜਈ; ~**ning** ਜਿੱਤ, ਵਿਜੈ, ਫ਼ਤਿਹ, ਸਫਲਤਾ; ਵਿਜਈ

wind (ਵਿੰਡ) *n v* ਹਵਾ, ਵਾਯੂ, ਝੱਖੜ, ਵਾਈ, ਬਾਈ ਜਾਂ ਵਾ ਦਾ ਰੋਗ, ਵਾਤ-ਰੋਗ; ਗੰਧ, ਵਾਸਨਾ, ਸਾਹ ਚੜ੍ਹਨਾ; ਸਾਹ ਕੱਢਣਾ; ~**fall** ਹਵਾ ਨਾਲ ਡਿੱਗਾ ਫਲ, ਟਪਕਾ; ~**mill** ਪੌਣ-ਚੱਕੀ; ~**pipe** ਸਾਹ-ਨਾਲੀ; *take, get*~ ਪ੍ਰਸਿੱਧ ਹੋਣਾ, ਉੱਘਾ ਹੋਣਾ

wind (ਵਾਇੰਡ) *v n* ਚੱਕਰ ਖਾਣਾ, ਵਲ ਖਾਣੇ, ਚੱਕਰ ਖਾਂਦਿਆਂ ਵਧਣਾ, ਵਲ੍ਹੇਟਣਾ, ਲੱਛਾ ਬਣਾਉਣਾ; ~-**up** ਪੂਰਾ-ਪੂਰਾ ਵਲੇਟ ਦੇਣਾ, ਸਾਰਾ ਇੱਕਠਾ ਕਰ ਲੈਣਾ; ਸਮੇਟ ਦੇਣਾ; ਸਮਾਪਤ ਕਰਨਾ; ਤੜਕਾਉਣਾ; ~**ing up** ਸਮਾਪਤਕਾਰੀ

window ('ਵਿੰਡਅਉ) *n* ਬਾਰੀ, ਖਿੜਕੀ, ਤਾਕੀ, ਝਰੋਖਾ; ~**shopping** ਦੁਕਾਨਾਂ ਦੀ ਸੈਰ

wine (ਵਾਇਨ) *n v* ਸ਼ਰਾਬ; ~**bowl** ਜਾਮ, ਪਿਆਲਾ; ~**cup** ਜਾਮ

wing (ਵਿੰਡ) *n v* (ਪੰਛੀ ਦਾ) ਖੰਭ; ਕਿਸੇ ਚੀਜ਼ ਦੇ ਬਾਹਰ ਨੂੰ ਵਧਿਆ ਇਕ ਪਾਸਾ, ਬਾਹੀ, ਖੰਡ ਲਾਉਣੇ; (ਤੀਰ) ਚਲਾਉਣਾ; ਉਡ ਕੇ ਜਾਣਾ; *on the* ~ ਉੱਡਦਾ ਹੋਇਆ

wink (ਵਿੰਕ) *v n* ਅੱਖ ਝਮਕਣੀ, ਪਲਕ ਫਰਕਣੀ; ਅੱਖ ਨਾਲ ਇਸ਼ਾਰਾ ਕਰਨਾ; (ਤਾਰੇ ਦਾ) ਟਿਮਟਿਮਾਉਣਾ; ਝਪਕਾ, ਇਸ਼ਾਰਾ

winter ('ਵਿੰਟਅ*) *n* ਸਿਆਲ, ਸਰਦੀ ਦੀ ਰੁੱਤ

wipe (ਵਾਇਪ) *v* ਪੂੰਝਣਾ, ਮਾਂਜਣਾ, ਰਗੜ ਕੇ ਸਾਫ਼ ਕਰਨਾ ਜਾਂ ਮਿਟਾਉਣਾ; ਪੋ ਦੇਣਾ; ~**out** ਮਿਟਾਉਣਾ, ਸਫਾਇਆ ਕਰਨਾ

wire ('ਵਾਇਅ*) *n v* ਤਾਰ; ਤਾਰ ਲਾਉਣੀ; ਤਾਰ ਭੇਜਣੀ; ~**less** ਬੇਤਾਰ, ਆਕਾਸ਼ਬਾਣੀ

wisdom ('ਵਿਜ਼ਡਅਮ) *n* ਬੁੱਧੀਮਾਨੀ, ਅਕਲ, ਮੱਤ, ਸਿਆਣਪ, ਦਾਨਾਈ, ਅਕਲਮੰਦੀ; ਗਿਆਨ, ਵਿਵੇਕ; ~**tooth** ਅਕਲ-ਦਾੜ੍ਹ; *god of*~ ਗਣੇਸ਼

wise (ਵਾਇਜ਼) *a* ਬੁੱਧੀਮਾਨ, ਅਕਲਮੰਦ, ਸਿਆਣਾ, ਗਿਆਨਵਾਨ, ਵਿਵੇਕੀ, ਦੂਰਦਰਸ਼ੀ, ਸੂਝਵਾਨ

wish (ਵਿਸ਼) *v n* ਚਾਹੁਣਾ, ਇੱਛਾ ਕਰਨੀ, ਇਰਾਦਾ ਕਰਨਾ

wit (ਵਿਟ) *n v* ਸੂਝ, ਸਮਝ; ਹਾਜ਼ਰ-ਜਵਾਬੀ ਸਿਆਣਾ, ਬੁੱਧੀਵਾਨ, ਸੂਝਵਾਨ ਵਿਅਕਤੀ ਮਖੌਲੀਆ, ਹਾਜ਼ਰ ਜਵਾਬ

witch (ਵਿਚ) *n v* (1) ਜਾਦੂਗਰਨੀ, ਟੂਣੇਹਾਰੀ ਡੈਣ; (2) ਸੁੰਦਰ ਮੁਟਿਆਰ; ਮੁਗਧ ਕਰਨਾ ਮੋਹਤ ਕਰਨਾ, ਜਾਦੂ ਕਰਨਾ; ~**craft** ਜਾਦੂ ਟੂਣਾ, ਜਾਦੂਗਰੀ; ~**ery** ਜਾਦੂ, ਟੂਣਾ; ~**hun** ਵਿਰੋਧੀਆਂ ਦਾ ਸ਼ਿਕਾਰ

with (ਵਿਦ) *prep* ਨਾਲ; ਸਟੇ, ਸਮੇਤ; ਕੋਲ ਕਾਰਨ, ਕਰਕੇ; ਹੁੰਦਿਆਂ ਵੀ

withdraw (ਵਿਦ'ਡਰੋ) v ਹਟਾ ਲੈਣਾ ਜਾਂ ਹਟ ਜਾਣਾ, ਮੋੜ ਲੈਣਾ ਜਾਂ ਮੁੜ ਜਾਣਾ, ਕੱਢ ਲੈਣਾ ਜਾਂ ਨਿਕਲ ਜਾਣਾ; ਲਾਂਭੇ ਹੋਣਾ, ਇਕ ਪਾਸੇ ਹੋ ਜਾਣਾ; ~al ਵਾਪਸੀ; ਪਰਤਾਉ, (ਪੈਸਾ) ਕੱਢਣ

wither ('ਵਿਦਾ*) v ਕੁਮਲਾ ਜਾਣਾ, ਮੁਰਝਾ ਜਾਣਾ, ਸੁੱਕ ਜਾਣਾ; ~ed ਨੀਰਸ, ਖ਼ੁਸ਼ਕ, ਕੁਮਲਾਇਆ, ਮੁਰਝਾਇਆ

withheld (ਵਿਦ'ਹੈਲਡ) a ਰੋਕਿਆ, ਦਬਾਇਆ

withhold (ਵਿਦ'ਹਾਉਲਡ) v ਰੋਕ ਲੈਣਾ, ਅਟਕਾ ਲੈਣਾ, ਰੋਕੀ ਰੱਖਣਾ, ਦਬਾਈ ਰੱਖਣਾ

within (ਇ'ਦਿਨ) adv prep ਅੰਦਰ, ਅੰਦਰਵਾਰ; ਅੰਦਰੋਂ, ਅੰਦਰਲੇ ਤੌਰ ਤੇ; ਵਿਚ, ਅੰਦਰ; ਸੀਮਾ ਵਿਚ, ਸਮੇਂ ਦੇ ਅੰਦਰ

without (ਵਿਦ'ਾਉਟ) adv prep ਬਿਨਾ, ਬਗ਼ੈਰ, ਰਹਿਤ, ਸਿਵਾ; ਬਾਹਰ, ਬਾਹਰੀ, ਬਾਹਰੀ ਤੌਰ ਤੇ

withstand (ਵਿਦ'ਸਟੈਂਡ) v ਟਾਕਰਾ ਕਰਨਾ, ਸਾਮੂਲਾ ਕਰਨਾ

witness ('ਵਿਟਨਿਸ) n v ਗਵਾਹੀ, ਸ਼ਹਾਦਤ; ਸਬੂਤ, ਪ੍ਰਮਾਣ; ਗਵਾਹ, ਸਾਖੀ; ਗਵਾਹੀ ਦੇਣੀ, ਸ਼ਹਾਦਤ ਦੇਣੀ; ਪ੍ਰਮਾਣ ਜਾਂ ਸਬੂਤ ਦੇਣਾ; **eye~** ਚਸ਼ਮਦੀਦ ਗਵਾਹ, ਮੌਕੇ ਦਾ ਗਵਾਹ

witticism ('ਵਿਟਿਸਿਜ਼(ਅ)ਮ) n ਹਾਸੇ ਵਾਲੀ ਗੱਲ, ਮਿੱਠਾ-ਮਖੌਲ, ਰਸਮਈ ਵਾਕ, ਬੁੱਧੀ-ਵਿਲਾਸ

wittingly ('ਵਿਟਿਙਲਿ) adv ਜਾਣ ਬੁੱਝ ਕੇ, ਜਾਣਦਿਆਂ, ਸਮਝਦਿਆਂ

witty ('ਵਿਟਿ) a ਮਖੌਲੀਆ, ਮਸਕਰਾ, ਹਾਸੇ-ਮਖੌਲ ਭਰਿਆ, ਰਸਿਕ

wizard ('ਵਿਜ਼ਅਃਡ) n a ਜਾਦੂਗਰ, ਪੂਰਾ ਨਿਪੁੰਨ, ਮਾਹਰ

woe (ਵਅਉ) n (ਕਾਵਿਕ) ਕਸ਼ਟ, ਦੁੱਖ, ਮੁਸੀਬਤ, ਗ਼ਮ; ~ful ਦੁੱਖ ਭਰਿਆ, ਸੋਗ ਵਾਲਾ, ਸੋਕਮਈ; ਗ਼ਮਗੀਨ; ਦੁਖੀ, ਅਭਾਗਾ; ਅਨੁਚਿਤ; ~fulness ਦੁੱਖ ਭਰਪੂਰਤਾ, ਗ਼ਮਗੀਨੀ

wolf (ਵੁਲਫ) n v ਬਘਿਆੜ; ਲੋਭੀ ਮਨੁੱਖ

woman ('ਵੂਮਅਨ) n ਤੀਵੀਂ, ਜਨਨੀ, ਇਸਤਰੀ, ਨਾਰੀ, ਔਰਤ; ~hood ਜਨਨਾਪਨ, ਨਾਰੀਤਵ; ਕੋਮਲਤਾ, ਇਸਤਰੀ ਜਾਤੀ, ਨਾਰੀ ਵਰਗ, ਤੀਵੀਆਂ, ਜਨਨੀਆਂ; ~ish (ਘਿਰਨਾ ਵਿਚ, ਮਰਦ ਲਈ) ਜਨਾਨਾ, ਤੀਵੀਆਂ ਜਿਹਾ; ਤੀਵੀਆਂ ਵਰਗਾ; ~ly ਜਨਾਨਾ, ਇਸਤਰੀਆਂ ਵਾਲਾ, ਕੋਮਲ, ਸਨੇਹਮਈ; ਨਿੰਘਾ

womb (ਵੂਮ) n ਕੁੱਖ, ਬੱਚੇਦਾਨੀ; ਢਿੱਡ; **fruit of the~** ਔਲਾਦ

wonder ('ਵਅੰਡਅ*) v n ਹੈਰਾਨ ਹੋਣਾ, ਚਕਿਤ ਹੋਣਾ, ਅਚੰਭਾ ਹੋਣਾ; ਹੈਰਾਨੀ, ਅਚੰਭਾ, ਅਸਚਰਜਤਾ; ਕਰਾਮਾਤ, ਕੌਤਕ, ਚਮਤਕਾਰ; ਅਸਧਾਰਨ ਘਟਨਾ; ~land ਪਰੀਲੋਕ; ~ful ਅਜੀਬ, ਅਸਚਰਜ, ਨਿਰਾਲਾ, ਅਨੋਖਾ, ਅਦਭੁਤ, ਉੱਤਮ, ਪ੍ਰਸੰਸਾਯੋਗ, ਬਹੁਤ ਵਧੀਆ

wondrous ('ਵਅੰਡਰਅਸ) a ਅਦਭੁਤ, ਅਜੀਬ, ਨਿਰਾਲਾ, ਵਚਿੱਤਰ; ਬਹੁਤ ਹੀ ਚੰਗਾ, ਬੜਾ ਹੀ ਵਧੀਆ

woo (ਵੂ) v ਪਿਆਰ ਜਤਾਉਣਾ, ਪਰੇਮ ਕਰਨਾ, ਇਸ਼ਕਬਾਜ਼ੀ ਕਰਨੀ; ਪਿੱਛੇ ਪੈਣਾ

wood (ਵੁਡ) n (pl) ਜੰਗਲ, ਬੀੜ, ਵਣ; ਲੱਕੜ; ਲੱਕੜੀ, ਰੁੱਖ; ~craft ਲੱਕੜੀ ਦਾ ਕੰਮ; ~land ਜੰਗਲੀ ਇਲਾਕਾ; ~man ਜੰਗਲ ਦਾ ਦਰੋਗਾ; ਲੱਕੜਹਾਰਾ, ਜੰਗਲੀ; ~en ਲਕੜੀ ਦਾ, ਲੱਕੜੀ ਤੋਂ ਬਣਾਇਆ; ਸਖ਼ਤ, ਕਾਠਾ; ਪ੍ਰਾਣਹੀਨ, ਬੇਰੌਣਕ, ਬੇਲੋਚ

wool (ਵੁਲ) n ਊਨ, ਪਸ਼ਮ; ਊਨੀ ਧਾਗਾ; pull

the ~ over one's eyes ਝਾਂਸਾ ਦੇਣਾ; ~len ਊਨੀ, ਊੱਨ ਦਾ, ਪਸ਼ਮ ਦਾ; ਊਨੀ ਕੱਪੜਾ, ਗਰਮ ਕੱਪੜਾ; ~ly ਊਨਦਾਰ, ਰੁੰਈ ਵਾਲਾ, ਅਸਪਸ਼ਟ, ਧੁੰਦਲਾ; ਢਿੱਕਾ; ਊਨੀ ਕੱਪੜੇ

word (ਵਅ:ਡ) *n* ਸ਼ਬਦ, ਲਫ਼ਜ਼, ਪਦ; ਗੱਲ, ਕਥਨ; ਸਮਾਚਾਰ, ਆਗਿਆ, ਆਦੇਸ਼; ਵਾਅਦਾ, ਬਚਨ; **a ~ to the wise** ਅਕਲਮੰਦ ਨੂੰ ਇਸ਼ਾਰਾ ਕਾਫ਼ੀ ਹੈ; **keep one's~** ਵਚਨ ਪਾਲਣਾ; ~iness ਸ਼ਬਦ-ਜਾਲ, ਵਾਕ-ਜਾਲ, ਸ਼ਬਦ-ਅਡੰਬਰ; ~ing ਸ਼ਬਦ-ਚੋਣ, ਸ਼ੈਲੀ, ਵਾਕ ਰਚਨਾ, ਵਰਤਨ-ਸ਼ੈਲੀ; ਸ਼ਬਦ, ਸ਼ਬਦਾਵਲੀ

work (ਵਅ:ਕ) *n v* ਕੰਮ, ਕਾਰ; ਧੰਦਾ, ਪੇਸ਼ਾ; ਕਾਰੀਗਰੀ, ਕੁਸ਼ਲਤਾ; ਰਚਨਾ, ਕਿਰਤ, ਲਿਖੀ ਹੋਈ ਕਿਤਾਬ; ਕਾਰਖ਼ਾਨਾ; ਵਿਭਾਗ, ਮਹਿਕਮਾ; ਕੰਮ ਕਰਨਾ; ਘਾੜਤ ਕਰਨੀ, ਕਿਸੇ ਚੀਜ਼ ਦਾ ਕਾਰੀਗਰ ਹੋਣਾ; ਮਸ਼ੀਨ ਦਾ ਚਾਲੂ ਹੋਣਾ; ਪਾਉਣਾ, ਅਸਰ ਕਰਨਾ; ਪ੍ਰਭਾਵ ਪਾਉਣਾ, ਅਸਰ ਕਰਨਾ; ~**house** ਅਨਾਥ ਘਰ; ~**load** ਕੰਮ ਦਾ ਭਾਰ; ~**man** ਮਜ਼ਦੂਰ; ਮਿਸਤਰੀ, ਕਾਰੀਗਰ; ~**manship** ਕਾਰੀਗਰੀ; ਕੁਸ਼ਲਤਾ, ਨਿਪੁੰਨਤਾ; ਰਚਨਾ, ਘਾੜਤ; ~**out** ਹਿਸਾਬ ਲਾਉਣਾ; ਹੱਲ ਕਰਨਾ, ਕੱਢਣਾ (ਸਵਾਲ ਆਦਿ); ~**shop** ਕਾਰਖ਼ਾਨਾ, ਕਰਮਸ਼ਾਲਾ, ਦੁਕਾਨ; **set to ~** ਕੰਮ ਵਿਚ ਜੁੱਟ ਜਾਣਾ, ਕੰਮ ਅਰੰਭਣਾ; ~**er** ਕਿਰਤੀ, ਕਾਮਾ, ਮਜ਼ਦੂਰ, ਸੇਵਕ; ~**ing** ਪ੍ਰਬੰਧ, ਕਾਰਜ-ਸੰਚਾਲਨ; ਕਾਰਜ ਪ੍ਰਣਾਲੀ; ਕੰਮ-ਚਲਾਊ, ਚਲੰਤ, ਉਦਯੋਗੀ, ਚਾਲੂ, ਕਿਰਿਆ-ਸ਼ੀਲ, ਕਾਰਜਕਾਰੀ; ਕੰਮ ਦਾ

workaholic ('ਵਅ:ਕਅ'ਹੌਲਿਕ) *n* ਕੰਮ ਦਾ ਕੀੜਾ

world (ਵਅ:ਲਡ) *n* ਸੰਸਾਰ, ਦੁਨੀਆ, ਜਗਤ, ਜਹਾਨ; ਦੁਨੀਆਵੀ ਧੰਦੇ; ਜੀਵਨ ਦੇ ਕਾਰ-ਵਿਹਾਰ; ਬ੍ਰਹਿਮੰਡ, ਬਾਹਰੀ ਦੁਨੀਆ; **lower-**ਪਾਤਾਲ, ਨਰਕ; ~**liness** ਸੰਸਾਰਕਤਾ, ਲੋਕਕਤਾ, ਦੁਨੀਆਦਾਰੀ, ਲੋਕਚਾਰੀ, ਪ੍ਰਪੰਚ, ਪਾਰਥਿਵਤਾ; ~**ly** ਸੰਸਾਰੀ, ਲੋਕਕ, ਦੁਨੀਆਵੀ, ਸੰਸਾਰਕ, ਐਸ਼ਪਰਸਤੀ ਵਾਲਾ, ਵਿਹਾਰਕ

worm (ਵਅ:ਮ) *n* ਕੀੜਾ, ਕਿਰਮ; ਨਿਗੁਣਾ ਜਾਂ ਘਟੀਆ ਆਦਮੀ

worried ('ਵਅੌਰਿਡ) *a* ਚਿੰਤਾਤੁਰ, ਪਰੇਸ਼ਾਨ, ਵਿਆਕੁਲ

worry ('ਵਅੌਰਿ) *v n* ਚਿੰਤਾ ਕਰਨੀ, ਫ਼ਿਕਰ ਕਰਨੀ; ਪਰੇਸ਼ਾਨ ਕਰਨਾ, ਦਿੱਕ ਕਰਨਾ; ਚਿੰਤਾ, ਫ਼ਿਕਰ, ਪਰੇਸ਼ਾਨੀ, ਬਿਪਤਾ

worse (ਵਅ:ਸ) *a adv n* (ਕਿਸੇ ਹੋਰ ਨਾਲੋਂ) ਭੈੜਾ, ਬੁਰਾ, ਘਟੀਆ, ਨਿਕੰਮਾ, ਮਾੜਾ; ~**n** ਹੋਰ ਭੈੜੀ ਹਾਲਤ ਕਰ ਦੇਣੀ ਜਾਂ ਹੋ ਜਾਣੀ, ਹੋਰ ਵਿਗਾੜ ਦੇਣਾ ਜਾਂ ਵਿਗੜ ਜਾਣਾ, ਹੋਰ ਖ਼ਰਾਬ ਕਰ ਦੇਣਾ ਜਾਂ ਹੋ ਜਾਣਾ

worship ('ਵਅ:ਸ਼ਿਪ) *v* ਪੂਜਾ, ਅਰਾਧਨਾ, ਉਪਾਸਨਾ; ਭਜਨ; ਪੂਜਾ ਕਰਨੀ, ਉਪਾਸਨ ਕਰਨੀ, ਅਰਾਧਨਾ ਕਰਨੀ

worst (ਵਅ:ਸਟ) *a adv n* ਸਭ ਤੋਂ ਬੁਰਾ ਨਿਕੰਮਾ, ਖ਼ਰਾਬ; ਨੀਚਤਮ; ਬਹੁਤ ਬੁਰਾ, ਭੈੜੇ ਤੋਂ ਭੈੜਾ; ਬਹੁਤ ਬੁਰੀ ਤਰ੍ਹਾਂ; ਮੰਦੀ ਤੋਂ ਮੰਦੀ ਹਾਲਤ

worsted (ਵੁਸਟਿਡ) *n* ਊਨੀ ਧਾਗਾ; ਊਨੀ ਧਾਗੇ ਨਾਲ ਉਣਿਆ ਕੱਪੜਾ

worth (ਵਅ:ਥ) *a n* ਦੇ ਮੁੱਲ ਦਾ, ਕੀਮਤ ਦਾ ਯੋਗ, ਜੋਗਾ, ਲਾਇਕ, ਉਚਿਤ; ਦੇ ਬਰਾਬਰ ਹੈਸੀਅਤ ਵਾਲਾ, ਸੰਪੱਤੀ ਵਾਲਾ; ਮੁੱਲ; ਮਹੱਤਾ ਕਦਰ; ~**while** ਉਚਿਤ; ~**less** ਨਿਕੰਮਾ ਫ਼ਜ਼ੂਲ, ਬੇਕਾਰ, ਖ਼ਰਾਬ; ਨਿਗੁਣਾ, ਤੁੱਛ ਘਟੀਆ ~**y** ਯੋਗ, ਕਾਬਲ, ਲਾਇਕ, ਉਚਿਤ; ਪੂਜਨੀਕ

ਸਤਿਕਾਰਯੋਗ, ਸ੍ਰੇਸ਼ਠ ਮਨੁੱਖ

would-be ('ਵੁਡਬੀ) *a adv* ਹੋਣ ਵਾਲਾ, ਆਗਾਮੀ, ਭਾਵੀ

wound (ਵੂੰਡ) *n v* ਜ਼ਖਮ, ਘਾਉ, ਸੱਟ, ਫੱਟ; ਠੇਸ; ਜ਼ਖ਼ਮ ਕਰਨਾ, ਸੱਟ ਲਾਉਣੀ; ਮਾਨਸਕ ਕਸ਼ਟ ਦੇਣਾ; **~ed** ਘਾਇਲ; ਜ਼ਖ਼ਮੀ; ਜਰਜਰ

wrack (ਰੈਕ) *n* ਵਿਨਾਸ਼, ਤਬਾਹੀ, ਬਰਬਾਦੀ; ਜਹਾਜ਼ ਦੇ ਗਰਕਣ ਦੀ ਕਿਰਿਆ; **~ful** ਟੁਟਿਆ-ਭੰਜਿਆ

wrangle ('ਰੈਙਗਲ) *n* ਝਗੜਾ, ਤੂੰ-ਤੂੰ ਮੈਂ-ਮੈਂ, ਬਖੇੜਾ, ਵਿਵਾਦ, ਤਕਰਾਰ; ਝਗੜਨਾ, ਤਕਰਾਰ ਕਰਨੀ

wrap (ਰੈਪ) *v* ਵਲ੍ਹੇਟਣਾ, ਢਕਣਾ (ਕੱਪੜੇ ਆਦਿ ਵਿਚ); ਬੰਨ੍ਹਣਾ, ਪੈਕ ਕਰਨਾ, ਬੰਡਲ ਬਣਾਉਣਾ; ਢਕ ਲੈਣਾ, ਕੱਜ ਦੇਣਾ; **~per** ਵਲ੍ਹੇਟਣ ਵਾਲਾ; ਸਿਰ ਦਾ ਲੀੜਾ; ਵਲ੍ਹੇਟਣ ਵਾਲਾ ਕੱਪੜਾ; (ਕਿਤਾਬ ਦੀ) ਜਿਲਦ ਉੱਤੇ ਚਾੜ੍ਹਿਆ ਕਾਗ਼ਜ਼

wrath (ਰੋਥ) *n* ਗੁੱਸਾ, ਕਰੋਧ, ਨਾਰਾਜ਼ਗੀ; **~ful** ਗੁੱਸੇਖੋਰ, ਕਰੋਪੀ, ਗੁਸੈਲਾ

wreath (ਰੀਥ) *n* ਹਾਰ, ਫੁੱਲਮਾਲਾ, ਮੁਕਟ

wreathe (ਰੀਦ) *v* ਗੁੰਦਣਾ, ਹਾਰ ਬਣਾਉਣਾ; ਹਾਰ ਪਾਉਣਾ

wreck (ਰੈੱਕ) *n v* ਤਬਾਹੀ, ਬਰਬਾਦੀ, ਵਿਨਾਸ਼; ਜਹਾਜ਼ ਦੇ ਗਰਕ ਹੋਣਾ; ਟੁੱਟਾ ਤੇ ਬਰਬਾਦ ਹੋਇਆ ਜਹਾਜ਼; ਢੱਠਾ ਘਰ; ਬਰਬਾਦ ਕਰਨਾ, ਤਬਾਹੀ ਕਰਨੀ; **~age** ਮਲਬਾ; **~ing** ਤਬਾਹ ਕਰਨਾ, ਬਰਬਾਦੀ, ਵਿਨਾਸ਼

wrench (ਰੈਂਚ) *n v* ਜ਼ੋਰ ਦਾ ਝਟਕਾ, ਮਰੋੜਾ; ਪੇਚਕਸ, ਸੰਨ੍ਹੀ, ਰੈਂਚ; ਝਟਕਾ ਦੇਣਾ, ਮਰੋੜ ਦੇਣਾ

wrest (ਰੈੱਸਟ) *v* ਤੋੜ-ਮਰੋੜ ਕਰਨੀ, ਕਾਂਟ-ਛਾਂਟ ਕਰਨੀ; ਵਿਗਾੜਨੀ; ਖੋਹਾ-ਖਾਹੀ ਕਰਨੀ

wrestle ('ਰੈੱਸਲ) *n v* ਘੋਲ, ਕੁਸ਼ਤੀ, ਦੰਗਲ; ਸਖ਼ਤ ਮੁਕਾਬਲਾ; ਘੁਲਣਾ, ਕੁਸ਼ਤੀ ਕਰਨੀ; **~r** ਬਲਵਾਨ, ਪਹਿਲਵਾਨ, ਘੁਲਣ ਵਾਲਾ

wrestling ('ਰੈੱਸਲਿਙ) *n* ਘੋਲ, ਕੁਸ਼ਤੀ

wretch (ਰੈੱਚ) *n* ਬੇਨਸੀਬ, ਕਰਮਾਂ ਮਾਰਿਆ, ਅਭਾਗਾ ਆਦਮੀ; ਵਿਚਾਰਾ; ਹੀਣ ਆਦਮੀ; **~ed** ਬੇਨਸੀਬ, ਕਿਸਮਤ ਦਾ ਮਾਰਿਆ, ਕਰਮਾਂ ਮਾਰਿਆ; ਪੀੜਤ, ਅਭਾਗਾ, ਦਲਿੱਦਰੀ; **~edness** ਬਦਨਸੀਬੀ, ਬੇਨਸੀਬੀ, ਬਦਕਿਸਮਤੀ

wriggle ('ਰਿਗਲ) *v n* ਪਲਸੇਟੇ ਮਾਰਨੇ, ਪਾਸੇ ਮਰੋੜਨੇ, ਵਲ ਪਾਉਂਦੇ ਜਾਣਾ, ਵਲ-ਵਲੇਵੇਂ ਖਾਂਦੇ ਜਾਣਾ, ਸੱਪ ਵਾਂਗ ਘਸੀਟਦੇ ਚੱਲਣਾ; ਵੱਟ, ਪਲਸੇਟਾ

wright (ਰਾਇਟ) *n* ਕਾਰੀਗਰ, ਮਿਸਤਰੀ, ਸ਼ਿਲਪੀ

wring (ਰਿਙ) *v n* ਮਰੋੜਨਾ, ਮਰੋੜ ਦੇਣਾ; ਦੇ ਤੋੜ ਦੇਣਾ; ਮਲਣਾ; ਨਚੋੜਨਾ (ਕੱਪੜਾ); ਮਰੁੰਡਣਾ; (ਪੈਸਾ) ਨਚੋੜਨਾ, ਮਰੋੜਾ

wrinkle ('ਰਿਙਕਲ) *n v* ਝੁਰੜੀ; ਝੁਰੜੀਆਂ ਪੈ ਜਾਣੀਆਂ

wrist (ਰਿਸਟ) *n* ਵੀਣੀ, ਗੁੱਟ; **~let** ਕੜਾ, ਕੰਗਣ; ਹੱਥਕੜੀ

writ (ਰਿਟ) *n* (ਅਦਾਲਤੀ) ਪਰਵਾਨਾ, ਹੁਕਮਨਾਮਾ; ਲਿਖਤ, ਲਿਖਿਆ

write (ਰਾਇਟ) *v* ਲਿਖਣਾ; ਦਰਜ ਕਰਨਾ; ਰਜਿਸਟਰ, ਵਹੀ ਆਦਿ ਤੇ ਚੜ੍ਹਾਉਣਾ, ਰਚਨਾ ਕਰਨੀ; **~off** ਵੱਟੇ ਖਾਤੇ ਪਾਉਣਾ, ਕਲਮ ਫੇਰ ਦੇਣਾ; **~r** ਲੇਖਕ, ਲਿਖਾਰੀ; (ਕਿਤਾਬ ਦਾ) ਕਰਤਾ, ਗ੍ਰੰਥਕਾਰ, ਮੁਨਸ਼ੀ, ਕਲਰਕ

writhe (ਰਾਇਦ) *v n* ਤੜਫਣਾ, ਸਰੀਰ ਨੂੰ ਮਰੋੜਨਾ; ਬੜਾ ਕਸ਼ਟ ਹੋਣਾ, ਅਤੀ ਦੁਖੀ ਹੋਣਾ; ਤਿਲਮਲਾਹਟ

writing ('ਰਾਇਟਿਙ) *n* ਲਿਖਾਈ, ਲੇਖ; ਦਸਤਾਵੇਜ਼, ਸਨਦ; ਕ੍ਰਿਤੀ, ਰਚਨਾ, ਪੁਸਤਕ

wrong (ਰੌਙ) *a adv n* ਗ਼ਲਤ, ਅਸ਼ੁੱਧ; ਖਰਾਬ, ਨਾਜਾਇਜ਼, ਅਨੁਚਿਤ, ਨਾਵਾਜਬ; ਉਲਟਾ; ਗ਼ਲਤੀ; ~**ful** ਅਯੋਗ, ਅਨੁਚਿਤ, ਨਾਜਾਇਜ਼, ਬੇਜਾ, ਦੋਸ਼ਪੂਰਨ

wrought (ਰੋਟ) *n v* ਉਤੇਜਤ, ਪ੍ਰਭਾਵਤ, ਹਾਵੀ; ਘੜਿਆ, ਕੁੱਟ ਕੇ ਬਣਾਇਆ; ਕੱਢਿਆ, ਸਜਾਇਆ; ~**on** ਪ੍ਰਭਾਵਤ, ਹਾਵੀ; ~**up** ਉਤੇਜਤ, ਭੜਕਿਆ

wry (ਰਾਇ) *a* (ਮੂੰਹ) ਵਿੰਗਾ, ਟੇਢਾ, ਝੰਵਿਆ, ਵਿਗੜਿਆ

X

X, x (ਐਕੱਸ) *n* ਰੋਮਨ ਵਰਣਮਾਲਾ ਦਾ ਚੌਵੀਵਾਂ ਅੱਖਰ, (ਰੋਮਨ ਅੱਕਾਂ ਵਿਚ) ਦਸ; ਅਗਿਆਤ ਵਿਅਕਤੀ, ਪਹਿਲੀ ਰਾਸ਼ੀ ਜਾਂ ਵਸਤੂ

xanthic ('ਜ਼ੈਨਥਿਕ) *a* ਬਸੰਤੀ, ਪੀਲਾ, ਖੱਟਾ

xanthichromia ('ਜ਼ੈਨਥਕ(ਉ)'ਕਰਅਉਮਿਅ) *n* ਪੀਲਿਆ, ਚਮੜੀ ਦਾ ਪੀਲਾਪਣ, ਪਿਲਤਣ

Xantippe (ਜ਼ੈਨ'ਟਿਪਿ) *n* ਲੜਾਕੀ ਔਰਤ, ਕਲਾਹਣੀ ਤੀਵੀਂ

xenium ('ਜ਼ੀਨਿਅਮ) *n* (ਰਾਜਦੂਤਾਂ ਜਾਂ ਪਰਾਹੁਣੇ ਨੂੰ ਦਿੱਤਾ ਜਾਣ ਵਾਲਾ) ਨਜ਼ਰਾਨਾ, ਭੇਟਾ

xenodochy (ਜ਼ਿ'ਨੌਡ਼ਅਕਿ) *n* ਮਹਿਮਾਨ-ਨਿਵਾਜ਼ੀ, ਅਤਿਥੀ-ਸਤਿਕਾਰ

Xmas ('ਕਰਿਸਮਅਸ) *n* ਕ੍ਰਿਸਮਿਸ, ਵੱਡਾ ਦਿਨ

X-ray ('ਐਕੱਸਰੇਇ) *v* ਐਕਸ-ਰੇ ਲੈਣਾ, ਐਕਸ-ਰੇ ਦਾ ਚਿੱਤਰ ਲੈਣਾ; **~s** ਐਕਸ-ਰੇਜ਼, ਕ੍ਰਾਸ-ਕਿਰਨਾਂ, ਰੁੰਟਜਨ ਕਿਰਨਾਂ

xylophagous (ਜ਼ਾਇ'ਲੌਫ਼ਅਗਅਸ) *a* ਕਾਠ-ਭੰਖੀ, ਲੱਕੜ ਖਾਣ ਵਾਲਾ

xyster ('ਜ਼ਿਸਟਅ*) *n* (ਹੱਡੀਆਂ ਖੁਰਚਣ ਲਈ) ਖੁਰਚਣੀ

Y

Y, y (ਵਾਇ) *n* ਰੋਮਨ ਵਰਨਮਾਲਾ ਦਾ ਪੰਝੀਵਾਂ ਅੱਖਰ, ਦੂਜੀ ਅਗਿਆਤ ਰਾਸ਼ੀ ਜਾਂ ਵਸਤੁ

yacht (ਯੌਟ) *n v* ਸੈਰ-ਸਪਾਟੇ ਲਈ ਜਾਂ ਦੌੜਾਂ ਲਈ ਪੱਲਾਂ ਵਾਲੀ ਬੇੜੀ, ਡੋਂਗੀ; ਬੇੜੀਆਂ ਦੀ ਦੌੜ ਵਿੱਚ ਸ਼ਾਮਲ ਹੋਣਾ; **~er** ਬੇੜੀ ਜਾਂ ਡੋਂਗੀ ਦਾ ਮਲਾਹ, ਪਾਤਰੀ, ਖੇਵਟ; **~ing** ਡੋਂਗੀ ਜਾਂ ਬੇੜੀ ਦੀ ਯਾਤਰਾ; ਡੋਂਗੀ ਜਾਂ ਬੇੜੀ ਬਾਰੇ

yackety-yack ('ਯੈਕਟਿ'ਯੈਕ) *n* (ਅਪ) ਚਪੜ ਚਪੜ, ਬਕਵਾਸ

yam (ਯੈਮ) *n* ਰਤਾਲੂ, ਕਚਾਲੂ; ਅਰਬੀ

yap (ਯੈਪ) *v n* ਘਬਰਾਹਟ ਵਿਚ ਜਾਂ ਚਿੜ ਕੇ ਭੌਂਕਣਾ; ਬਕਣਾ, ਬਕਵਾਸ ਕਰਨਾ; ਭੌਂਕਣ ਦੀ ਉੱਚੀ ਅਵਾਜ਼

yard (ਯਾਡ) *n* ਗਜ਼, ਤਿੰਨ ਫੁੱਟ ਦੀ ਲੰਬਾਈ; ਵਿਹੜਾ; ਅਹਾਤਾ; ਵਾੜਾ, ਵਲਗਣ; **~stick** ਗਜ਼, ਕਸਵੱਟੀ, ਪੈਮਾਨਾ

yarn (ਯਾਨ) *n v* ਸੂਤ, ਤੰਦ, ਤਾਰ, ਧਾਗਾ; ਉੱਨੀ ਧਾਗਾ, ਕਿੱਸਾ ਘੜਨਾ

yawn (ਯੌਨ) *v n* ਉਬਾਸੀ ਲੈਣੀ, ਉਬਾਸੀ ਆਉਣੀ; ਉਬਾਸੀ; **~ing** ਉਬਾਸੀ, ਉਬਾਸੀ ਲੈਂਦਾ ਹੋਇਆ

yea (ਯੇਇ) *partical* (ਪ੍ਰ) ਹਾਂ; ਅਵੱਸ਼, ਜ਼ਰੂਰ; ਠੀਕ; ਸੱਚਮੁਚ; ਸਗੋਂ

yeah (ਯੇਅ) *adv* (ਬੋਲ) ਹਾਂ

year (ਯਿਅ*) *n* ਵਰ੍ਹਾ, ਸਾਲ; ਲੰਮੀ ਮੁਦੱਤ; ਸੰਨ, ਸੰਮਤ; **~book** ਸਾਲਨਾਮਾ, ਵਰ੍ਹਾ-ਕੋਸ਼, ਵਰ੍ਹਾ-ਪੁਸਤਕ; **~ly** ਵਾਰਸ਼ਕ, ਸਾਲਾਨਾ; ਸਾਲ ਭਰ ਦਾ, ਹਰ ਸਾਲ, ਪ੍ਰਤੀ ਵਰਸ਼, ਵਰ੍ਹੇ ਤੇ ਵਰ੍ਹੇ

yearn (ਯਅ:ਨ) *v* ਤਾਂਘ ਹੋਣੀ, ਤੀਬਰ ਇੱਛਾ ਹੋਣੀ, ਉਤਸੁਕ ਹੋਣਾ, ਵਿਆਕੁਲ ਹੋਣਾ; **~ful** ਦੁੱਖਦਾਈ, ਸੋਗੀ, ਅਫ਼ਸੋਸਨਾਕ; **~ing** ਤ੍ਰਿਸ਼ਨਾ, ਉਤਸੁਕਤਾ, ਲਾਲਸਾ, ਇੱਛਾ; ਪਿਆਰ, ਤ੍ਰਿਸ਼ਨਾਪੂਰਨ, ਇੱਛਾਪੂਰਨ

yeast (ਯੀਸਟ) *n* ਖ਼ਮੀਰ, ਖ਼ਮੀਰ ਉਠਣ ਨਾਲ ਆਈ ਝੱਗ

yell (ਯੈੱਲ) *v n* ਚੀਕਣਾ, ਚਾਂਗਰ ਮਾਰਨੀ, ਚੰਘਾੜ ਮਾਰਨੀ; ਚੀਕ; ਚਾਂਗਰ; ਰੌਲਾ

yellow ('ਯੈੱਲਅਉ) *a* ਪੀਲਾ; ਖੱਟਾ, (ਪ੍ਰ) ਈਰਖਾਲੂ

yelp (ਯੈੱਲਪ) *v n* ਕੁਤੇ ਦੇ ਭੌਂਕਣ ਦੀ ਅਵਾਜ਼, ਚਿਚਲਾਉਣਾ, ਚੁਕਣਾ; ਉੱਚੀ ਅਵਾਜ਼ ਵਿਚ ਗੱਲ ਕਰਨੀ, ਚੀਕਣਾ

yeoman ('ਯਅਉਮਅਨ) *n* (ਇਤਿ) ਸ਼ਾਹੀ ਘਰਾਣੇ ਦਾ ਨੌਕਰ; ਕਿਸਾਨ, ਛੋਟਾ ਜ਼ਿਮੀਂਦਾਰ; ਆਮ ਮਨੁੱਖ; **~ly** ਕੱਟੜ, ਪੱਕਾ; ਬਹਾਦਰਾਂ ਵਾਂਗ

yes (ਯੇਸ) *particle n* ਹਾਂ, ਚੰਗਾ, ਹੱਛਾ; ਹੂੰ, ਹਾਂਰੇ, ਹਾਂ ਜੀ; **~man** ਜੀ-ਹਜ਼ੂਰੀਆ

yesterday ('ਯੈੱਸਟਅਡਿ) *n adv* ਕੱਲ (ਬੀਤ ਚੁੱਕਾ), ਕੱਲ ਦਾ ਦਿਨ; ਕੱਲ ਨੂੰ, ਕੱਲ ਦਿਨੇ

yesteryear ('ਯੈੱਸਟਅ'ਯਿਅ*) *n* ਪਿਛਲਾ ਸਾਲ, ਪਿਛਲੇ ਸਾਲ, ਬੀਤੇ ਸਾਲ

yet (ਯੈੱਟ) *adv conj* ਅਜੇ, ਅਜੇ ਤਕ, ਹੁਣ ਤਕ, ਹਾਲਾਂ, ਹਾਲੇ; ਅਜੇ ਵੀ, ਹੋਰ ਵੀ; ਪਰ ਇਸ ਦੇ ਨਾਲ

yex (ਯੈੱਕਸ) *n v* ਹਿਚਕੀ (ਲੈਣਾ)

yield (ਯੀਲਡ) *v n* (ਫ਼ਸਲ ਆਦਿ) ਉਪਜਾਉਣਾ,

ਪੈਦਾ ਕਰਨਾ; ਝਾੜ ਹੋਣਾ; ਹਾਰ ਮੰਨ ਲੈਣੀ, ਹੀਣਾ ਹੋਣਾ; ਪੈਦਾਵਾਰ, ਉਪਜ, ਫ਼ਸਲ; ਮੁਨਾਫ਼ਾ; ~ing ਉਪਜ, ਉਤਪਾਦਨ, ਲਾਭ; ਆਤਮ-ਸਮਰਪਣ; ਨਰਮ; ਅਨੁਕੂਲ

yoghurt ('ਯੋਗਅਃਟ) *n* ਦਹੀਂ

yoke (ਯਅਉਕ) *n v* ਜੂਲਾ, ਪੰਜਾਲੀ; ਨਰੜ; ਜੋੜਨਾ; ਜਕੜਨਾ, ਅਧੀਨ ਬਣਾਉਣਾ, ਦਾਸ ਬਣਾਉਣਾ

yolk, yelk (ਯਅਉਕ, ਯੈੱਲਕ) *n* ਅੰਡੇ ਦਾ ਪੀਲਾ ਅੰਸ਼, ਜ਼ਰਦੀ

younder ('ਯੌਂਡਅ*) *adv a* ਪਹੁੰ, ਦੂਹ, ਉਧੇ, ਉਧਰ; ਸਾਹਵੇਂ, ਸਾਮ੍ਹਣੇ; ਪਰਲਾ; ਸਾਮ੍ਹਣਾ, ਸਾਮ੍ਹਣੇ ਵਾਲਾ

yore (ਯੋ*) *n* ਪ੍ਰਾਚੀਨ ਕਾਲ, ਪੁਰਾਣਾ ਜ਼ਮਾਨਾ

young (ਯਅੱਙ) *a n* ਗੱਭਰੂ, ਗਭਰੇਟ, ਨਿੱਕਾ, ਚੜ੍ਹਦੀ ਜਵਾਨੀ ਵਾਲਾ; ਅੱਲ੍ਹੜ ਜਵਾਨ; ~man ਗੱਭਰੂ, ਨੌਜਵਾਨ; ~woman ਮੁਟਿਆਰ, ਜਵਾਨ ਤੀਵੀਂ; ~er ਛੋਟਾ (ਬੱਚਾ), ਨੰਢਾ; ~ster ਬੱਚਾ, ਮੁੰਡਾ

your (ਯੋ*) *pro* ਤੁਹਾਡਾ; ਤੇਰਾ; ਆਪ ਜੀ ਦਾ; ~self ਤੁਸੀਂ ਆਪ, ਤੁਸੀਂ ਖ਼ੁਦ, ਆਪਣੇ ਆਪ ਨੂੰ

youth (ਯੂਥ) *n* ਜਵਾਨੀ; ਜੋਬਨ ਕਾਲ, ਚੜ੍ਹਦੀ ਜਵਾਨੀ; ਜਵਾਨ, ਗਭਰੂ, ਯੁਵਕ; ਨੌਜਵਾਨ ਮੁੰਡੇ-ਕੁੜੀਆਂ; ~ful ਨੌਜਵਾਨ, ਚੜ੍ਹਦੀ ਜਵਾਨੀ ਵਾਲਾ; ਜਵਾਨੀ ਦਾ; ~fulness ਜਵਾਨੀ, ਜੋਬਨ, ਜਵਾਨੀ ਦਾ ਸਮਾਂ, ਗੱਭਰੇਟਪਣ, ਨੌਜਵਾਨੀ

yule (ਯੂਲ) *n* ਕ੍ਰਿਸਮਿਸ ਦਾ ਦਿਨ, ਵੱਡਾ ਦਿਨ, ਕ੍ਰਿਸਮਿਸ ਦਾ ਪੁਰਬ

yummy ('ਯਅੱਮਿ) *a* (ਬਾਲ ਬੋਲੀ) ਮਿੱਠੀ, ਸੁਆਦੀ

Z

Z, z (ਜ਼ੈੱਡ) *n* ਰੋਮਨ ਵਰਣਮਾਲਾ ਦਾ ਛੱਬੀਵਾਂ ਤੇ ਅੰਤਲਾ ਅੱਖਰ, ਤੀਜੀ ਅਗਿਆਤ ਰਾਸ਼ੀ

zany ('ਜ਼ੇਇਨਿ) *n* ਭੰਡ, ਮਖੌਲੀਆ, ਵਿਦੂਸ਼ਕ; ਮੂਰਖ, ਲੋੜ੍ਹੂ ਆਦਮੀ; ~ism ਭੰਡੀ, ਵਿਦੂਸ਼ਕਤਾ, ਭੰਡਪੁਣਾ, ਮਸ਼ਕਰਾਪਣ

zeal (ਜ਼ੀਲ) *n* ਉਤਸ਼ਾਹ, ਜੋਸ਼, ਸ਼ੋਕ, ਸਰਗਰਮੀ, ਲਗਨ; ~ful ਉਤਸ਼ਾਹਪੂਰਨ, ਉਤਸੁਕ, ਜੋਸ਼ੀਲਾ, ਸਰਗਰਮ, ਧੁਨ ਦਾ ਪੱਕਾ; ~less ਉਤਸ਼ਾਹੀਨ, ਸੁਸਤ; ~ous ਤੇਜ਼, ਤਿੱਖਾ, ਤੀਬਰ; ਉਤਸ਼ਾਹਪੂਰਨ, ਜੋਸ਼ੀਲਾ, ਉੱਦਮੀ, ਸ਼ੁਕੀਨ, ਸਰਗਰਮ; ~ousness ਤਿੱਖਾਪਣ, ਉਤਸ਼ਾਹਪੂਰਨਤਾ, ਜੋਸ਼ੀਲਾਪਣ, ਸਰਗਰਮੀ, ਲਗਨਪੂਰਨਤਾ

zebra ('ਜ਼ੇਬ੍ਰਅ) *n* ਜ਼ੈਬਰਾ, ਘੋੜੇ ਵਰਗਾ ਧਾਰੀਆਂ ਵਾਲਾ ਜਾਨਵਰ; ~crossing ਪੈਦਲ ਚੱਲਣ ਵਾਲਿਆਂ ਲਈ ਬਣਾਇਆ ਧਾਰੀਦਾਰ ਰਸਤਾ

zenith ('ਜ਼ੈਨਿਥ) *n* ਆਕਾਸ਼ ਵਿਚ ਉਹ ਬਿੰਦੂ ਜਿਹੜਾ ਵੇਖਣ ਵਾਲੇ ਦੇ ਸਿਰ ਦੇ ਉੱਪਰ ਹੋਵੇ; ਸਿਖਰ-ਬਿੰਦੂ, ਉੱਚ-ਸੀਮਾ; ਕਮਾਲ, ਵੱਧ ਤੋਂ ਵੱਧ ਉੱਨਤੀ, ਉੱਥਾਨ

zephyr ('ਜ਼ੈਫ਼ਅ*) *n* ਬਸੰਤ ਰੁੱਤ ਦੀ ਵਾਯੂ, ਸਮੀਰ, ਝਿੰਨੀ-ਝਿੰਨੀ ਹਵਾ, ਪੱਛਮ ਦੀ ਹਵਾ; ਜਾਲੀਦਾਰ ਕੱਪੜਾ; ਪਵਨ ਦੇਵ Also **Zephyrus**

zero ('ਜ਼ਿਅਰਅਉ) *n* ਸਿਫ਼ਰ, ਸੂਨ; 0 ਦਾ ਅੰਕ; ਮਾਪਦੰਡ ਦਾ ਅਰੰਭਲਾ ਬਿੰਦੂ, ਨੀਵੇਂ ਤੋਂ ਨੀਵਾਂ ਬਿੰਦੂ; ਅਣਹੋਇਆ, ਨਾ ਹੋਇਆ ਮਨੁੱਖ; ~hour ਅਰੰਭ-ਬਿੰਦੂ; ਅਰੰਭ-ਕਾਲ, ਸ਼ੂਨ ਕਾਲ

zest (ਜ਼ੈਸੱਟ) *n v* ਚਾਅ, ਰੀਝ, ਦਿਲਚਸਪੀ, ਸੁਆਦ, ਚਸਕਾ; ਮਜ਼ਾ ਦੇਣਾ, ਸੁਆਦ ਦੇਣਾ

zigzag ('ਜ਼ਿਗਜ਼ੈਗ) *a n adv v* ਵਲਾਵੇਂਦਾਰ, ਵਿੰਗਾ-ਟੇਢਾ, ਵਿੰਗ-ਤੜਿੰਗਾ; ਵਿੰਗੀ ਟੇਢੀ ਲਕੀਰ; ਵਲਾਵੇਂ ਖਾਂਦਾ; ਟੇਢਾ ਚੱਲਣਾ, ਤੇੜ-ਮੇੜ ਦੇਣਾ

zinc ('ਜ਼ਿੰਕ) *n v* ਜਿਸਤ, ਜ਼ਿੰਕ; ਜਿਸਤ ਦੀ ਪਾਲਸ਼ ਕਰਨਾ

Zingaro ('ਜ਼ਿੰਡਗਅਰਅਉ) *n* ਖ਼ਾਨਾਬਦੋਸ਼ ਫਿਰਤੂ ਲੋਕ, ਜਿਪਸੀ

zingiber ('ਜ਼ਿੰਜਿਬਅ*) ਸੁੰਢ, ਅਦਰਕ

zippy ('ਜ਼ਿਪਿ) *n* ਜਾਨਦਾਰ, ਜੀਵਤ, ਫੁਰਤੀਲਾ, ਸਜੀਵ

zodiac ('ਜ਼ਅਉਡਿਐਕ) *n* (ਆਕਾਸ਼ ਦਾ) ਰਾਸ਼ੀ-ਮੰਡਲ, ਰਾਸ਼ੀ

zonal ('ਜ਼ਅਉਨਲ) *n a* ਖੇਤਰੀ, ਮੰਡਲੀ, ਇਲਾਕਾਈ, ਪ੍ਰਦੇਸ਼ਕ

zone (ਜ਼ਅਉਨ) *n* ਮੰਡਲ, ਘੇਰਾ, ਚੱਕਰ, ਪੱਟੀ, ਧਾਰੀ; ਖੇਤਰ, ਇਲਾਕਾ, ਖੰਡ, ਪ੍ਰਦੇਸ਼, ਭੂ-ਮੰਡਲ; ਕਮਰਬੰਦ, ਕਮਰ ਪੇਟੀ

zoo (ਜ਼ੂ) *n* ਚਿੜੀਆਘਰ; ~logical garden ਚਿੜੀਆਘਰ; ~logist ਜੰਤੂ ਵਿਗਿਆਨੀ; ~logy ਜੰਤੂ ਵਿਗਿਆਨ

zoom (ਜ਼ੂਮ) *v n* ਹਵਾਈ ਜਹਾਜ਼ ਦਾ ਤਿੱਖੀ ਗਤੀ ਨਾਲ ਉੱਡਣਾ; ਕੀਮਤਾਂ ਚੜ੍ਹਨਾ; ਸ਼ੋਰ ਕਰਨਾ

zymosis (ਜ਼ਾਇ'ਮਅਉਸਿਸ) *n* ਖ਼ਮੀਰ; ਖਲੜੀ ਦੀ ਇਕ ਛੂਤ ਦੀ ਬੀਮਾਰੀ

Other Asian Language Titles from Hippocrene ...

English-Bengali Dictionary
38,000 entries • 1,354 pages • 5½ x 8½ • $28.95 hardcover • ISBN 0-7818-0373-X • W except India • (166)

Bengali-English Dictionary
30,000 entries • 1,074 pages • 5½ x 8½ • $28.95 hardcover • ISBN 0-7818-0372-1 • W except India • (177)

Learn Bengali
160 pages • 5 x 7 • $7.95 paperback
• ISBN 0-7818-0224-5 • NA • (190)

Bogutu-English/English-Bogutu Concise Dictionary
4,700 entries • 98 pages • 5½ x 9 • $9.95 paperback • ISBN 0-7818-0660-7 • W • (747)

Cambodian-English/English-Cambodian Standard Dictionary
15,000 entries • 355 pages • 5½ x 8¼ • $16.95 paperback • ISBN 0-87052-818-1 • W • (143)

Cantonese Basic Course
416 pages • 5½ x 8¼ • $19.95 paperback
• ISBN 0-7818-0289-X • W • (117)

Dictionary of 1,000 Chinese Proverbs
200 pages • 5½ x 8½ • $11.95 paperback
• ISBN 0-7818-0682-8 • W • (773)

Chinese Handy Dictionary
2,000 entries • 120 pages • 5 x 7¾ • $8.95 paperback
• ISBN 0-87052-050-4 • USA • (347)

English-Chinese Pinyin Dictionary
10,000 entries • 500 pages • 4 x 6 • $19.95 paperback
• ISBN 0-7818-0427-2 • USA • (509)

Beginner's Chinese
150 pages • 5½ x 8 • $14.95 paperback
• ISBN 0-7818-0566-X • W • (690)

English-Gujarati Standard Dictionary
20,000 entries • 640 pages • 5 x 8½ • $29.95 hardcover
• ISBN 0-7818-0680-1 • NA • (743)

Hindi-English/English-Hindi Standard Dictionary
30,000 entries • 800 pages • 6 x 9 • $37.50 hardcover
• ISBN 0-7818-0387-X • W except India • (280)
30,000 entries • 800 pages • 6 x 9 • $27.50 paperback
• ISBN 0-7818-0470-1 • W except India • (559)

Hindi-English/English-Hindi Practical Dictionary
25,000 entries • 745 pages • 4 3/8 x 7 • $19.95 paperback
• ISBN 0-7818-0064-6 • W • (442)

English-Hindi Practical Dictionary
15,000 entries • 399 pages • 4 3/8 x 7 • $11.95 paperback
• ISBN 0-87052-978-1 • NA • (362)

Teach Yourself Hindi
207 pages • 4 3/8 x 7 • $8.95 paperback
• ISBN 0-87052-831-9 • NA • (170)

Indonesian-English/English-Indonesian Practical Dictionary
17,000 entries • 289 pages • 4¼ x 7 • $11.95 paperback
• ISBN 0-87052-810-6 • NA • (127)

Japanese-English/English-Japanese Concise Dictionary, Romanized
8,000 entries • 235 pages • 4 x 6 • $11.95 paperback
• ISBN 0-7818-0162-1 • W • (474)

Mastering Japanese
368 pages • 5½ x 8½ • $14.95 paperback
• ISBN 0-87052-983 • USA • (523)

2 cassettes: • ISBN 0-87052-983-8 • $12.95 • USA • (524)

Korean-English/English-Korean Practical Dictionary
8,500 entires • 365 pages • 4 x 7¼ • $14.95 paperback
• ISBN 0-87052-092-X • Asia and NA • (399)

Malay-English/English-Malay Standard Dictionary
21,000 entires • 631 pages • 7¼ x 5 • $16.95 paperback
• ISBN 0-7818-0103-6 • NA • (428)

Nepali-English/English-Nepali Concise Dictionary
6,000 entires • 286 pages • 4 x 6 • $8.95 paperback
• ISBN 0-87052-106-3 • W except India and Nepal • (398)

Concise Sanskrit-English Dictionary
18,000 entires • 366 pages • 5 x 7 • $14.95 paperback
• ISBN 0-7818-0203-2 • NA • (605)

Sinhalese-English Dictionary
20,000 entires • 276 pages • 5¾ x 8¾ • $24.95 paperback
• ISBN 0-7818-0219-9 • NA • (319)

English-Telugu Pocket Dictionary
12,000 entires • 386 pages • 5 x 7 1/3 • $17.50 hardcover
• ISBN 0-7818-0747-6 • W • (952)

Beginner's Vietnamese
517 pages ● 7 x 10 ●$19.95 paperback
●ISBN 0-7818-0411-6 ●W ●(253)

Vietnamese-English/English-Vietnamese Standard Dictionary
12,000 entires ● 501 pages ● 5½ x 7 paperback ● $19.95 ● paperback● ISBN 0-87052-924-2 ●W ●(529)

All prices are subject to change without prior notice. To order Hippocrene Books, contact your local bookstore, call (718) 454-2366, or write to: Hippocrene Books, 171 Madison Ave. New York, NY 10016. Please enclose check or money order adding $5.00 shipping (UPS) for the first book and $.50 for each additional title.